TEACHER EDITION with Solutions Key

Houghton
Mifflin
Harcourt

Algebra 1

TIMOTHY D. KANOLD

EDWARD B. BURGER

JULI K. DIXON

MATTHEW R. LARSON

STEVEN J. LEINWAND

Authors

Timothy D. Kanold, Ph.D., is an award-winning international educator, author, and consultant. He is a former superintendent and director of mathematics and science at Adlai E. Stevenson High School District 125 in Lincolnshire, Illinois. He is a past president of the National Council of Supervisors of Mathematics (NCSM) and the Council for the Presidential Awardees of Mathematics (CPAM). He  has served on several writing and leadership commissions for NCTM during the past decade. He presents motivational professional development seminars with a focus on developing professional learning communities (PLC's) to improve the teaching, assessing, and learning of students. He has recently authored nationally recognized articles, books, and textbooks for mathematics education and school leadership, including *What Every Principal Needs to Know about the Teaching and Learning of Mathematics.*

Edward B. Burger, Ph.D., is the President of Southwestern University, a former Francis Christopher Oakley Third Century Professor of Mathematics at Williams College, and a former vice provost at Baylor University. He has authored or coauthored more than sixty-five articles, books, and video series; delivered over five hundred addresses and workshops throughout the world;  and made more than fifty radio and television appearances. He is a Fellow of the American Mathematical Society as well as having earned many national honors, including the Robert Foster Cherry Award for Great Teaching in 2010. In 2012, Microsoft Education named him a "Global Hero in Education."

Juli K. Dixon, Ph.D., is a Professor of Mathematics Education at the University of Central Florida. She has taught mathematics in urban schools at the elementary, middle, secondary, and post-secondary levels. She is an active researcher and speaker with numerous publications and conference presentations. Key areas of focus are deepening teachers' content knowledge and communicating and justifying  mathematical ideas. She is a past chair of the NCTM Student Explorations in Mathematics Editorial Panel and member of the Board of Directors for the Association of Mathematics Teacher Educators.

Matthew R. Larson, Ph.D., is the K–12 mathematics curriculum specialist for the Lincoln Public Schools and served on the Board of Directors for the National Council of Teachers of Mathematics from 2010 to 2013. He is a past chair of NCTM's Research Committee and was a member of NCTM's Task Force on Linking Research and Practice. He is the author of several books on implementing the Common Core Standards for Mathematics. He has taught mathematics at the secondary and college levels and held an appointment as an honorary visiting associate professor at Teachers College, Columbia University.

Steven J. Leinwand is a Principal Research Analyst at the American Institutes for Research (AIR) in Washington, D.C., and has over 30 years in leadership positions in mathematics education. He is past president of the National Council of Supervisors of Mathematics and served on the NCTM Board of Directors. He is the author of numerous articles, books, and textbooks and has made countless presentations with topics including student achievement, reasoning, effective assessment, and successful implementation of standards.

Performance Task Consultant

STEM Consultants
Science, Technology, Engineering, and Mathematics

Reviewers

Quantities and Modeling

MODULE 1

Quantitative Reasoning

MODULE 2

Algebraic Models

UNIT 2

Volume 1

Understanding Functions

MODULE 3 — Functions and Models

MODULE 4 — Patterns and Sequences

Linear Functions, Equations, and Inequalities

 **5** ## Linear Functions

 **6** ## Forms of Linear Equations

UNIT 3

Volume 1

MODULE 7 — Linear Equations and Inequalities

COMMON CORE

© Houghton Mifflin Harcourt Publishing Company • Image Credits: ©Image Source/Getty Images

Statistical Models

MODULE 8

Multi-Variable Categorical Data

MODULE 9

One-Variable Data Distributions

Linear Modeling and Regression

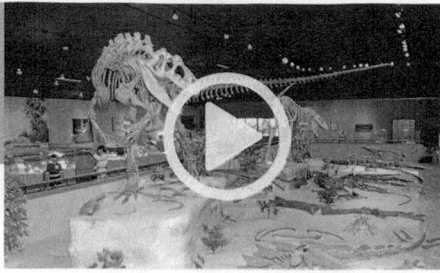

COMMON CORE

© Houghton Mifflin Harcourt Publishing Company • Image Credits: ©John Elk III/Alamy

Linear Systems and Piecewise-Defined Functions

UNIT **5**

COMMON CORE

Volume 1

MODULE **11**

Solving Systems of Linear Equations

MODULE **12**

Modeling with Linear Systems

MODULE 13

Piecewise-Defined Functions

COMMON CORE

Exponential Relationships

MODULE 14 — Rational Exponents and Radicals

MODULE 15 — Geometric Sequences and Exponential Functions

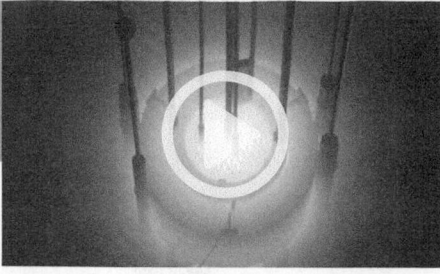

COMMON CORE

Polynomial Operations

MODULE 17 Adding and Subtracting Polynomials

COMMON CORE

MODULE 18

Multiplying Polynomials

COMMON
CORE

Quadratic Functions

UNIT 8

COMMON CORE

Volume 2

MODULE 19

Graphing Quadratic Functions

MODULE 20

Connecting Intercepts, Zeros, and Factors

MODULE 21 Using Factors to Solve Quadratic Equations

MODULE 22 Using Square Roots to Solve Quadratic Equations

© Houghton Mifflin Harcourt Publishing Company • Image Credits: (t)©Sergio Pitamitz/Robert Harding World Imagery/Getty Images; (b) ©Getty Images/PhotoDisc

MODULE **23**

Linear, Exponential, and Quadratic Models

MODULE 24

Functions and Inverses

COMMON CORE

HMH Algebra 1
Online State Resources

Scan the QR code or visit:
my.hrw.com/nsmedia/osp/2015/ma/hs/te_1/tempaga
for correlations and other state-specific resources.

Common Core State Standards

CORRELATION FOR HMH ALGEBRA 1

Standard	Description	Citations
N-RN The Real Number System		
Extend the properties of exponents to rational exponents.		
N-RN.A.1[1]	Explain how the definition of the meaning of rational exponents follows from extending the properties of integer exponents to those values, allowing for a notation for radicals in terms of rational exponents.	**SE:** 637–646
N-RN.A.2[1]	Rewrite expressions involving radicals and rational exponents using the properties of exponents.	**SE:** 637–646, 647–660
Use properties of rational and irrational numbers.		
N-RN.B.3[1]	Explain why the sum or product of two rational numbers is rational; that the sum of a rational number and an irrational number is irrational; and that the product of a nonzero rational number and an irrational number is irrational.	**SE:** 647–660
N-Q Quantities		
Reason quantitatively and use units to solve problems.		
N-Q.A.1	Use units as a way to understand problems and to guide the solution of multi-step problems; choose and interpret units consistently in formulas; choose and interpret the scale and the origin in graphs and data displays. ★	**SE:** 15–26, 27–38, 301–308, 389–400, 401–416, 417–428
N-Q.A.2	Define appropriate quantities for the purpose of descriptive modeling. ★	**SE:** 5–14, 15–26, 45–54, 301–308
N-Q.A.3	Choose a level of accuracy appropriate to limitations on measurement when reporting quantities. ★	**SE:** 27–38
Algebra		
A-SSE Seeing Structure in Expressions		
Interpret the structure of expressions.		
A-SSE.A.1	Interpret expressions that represent a quantity in terms of its context. ★	**SE:** 45–54, 647–660, 805–816, 817–828, 829–840, 847–854, 855–866, 867–876

★ Indicates a modeling standard linking mathematics to everyday life, work, and decision-making.
(+) Indicates additional mathematics to prepare students for advanced courses.

Scan the QR code or visit my.hrw.com/nsmedia/osp/2015/ma/hs/te_1/tempaga for additional correlations and state specific resources.

Standard	Description	Citations
A-SSE.A.1a[1]	Interpret parts of an expression, such as terms, factors, and coefficients. ★	**SE:** 45–54, 805–816
A-SSE.A.1b[1]	Interpret complicated expressions by viewing one or more of their parts as a single entlty. ★	**SE:** 45–54, 647–660, 805–816
A-SSE.A.2	Use the structure of an expression to identify ways to rewrite it.	**SE:** 805–816, 951–960, 961–972, 985–996, 997–1008, 1009–1026, 1045–1058
Write expressions in equivalent forms to solve problems.		
A-SSE.B.3	Choose and produce an equivalent form of an expression to reveal and explain properties of the quantity represented by the expression. ★	**SE:** 739–750, 961–972, 997–1008, 1009–1026, 1045–1058
A-SSE.B.3a	Factor a quadratic expression to reveal the zeros of the function it defines. ★	**SE:** 961–972, 985–996, 997–1008, 1009–1026, 1045–1058
A-SSE.B.3b	Complete the square in a quadratic expression to reveal the maximum or minimum value of the function it defines. ★	**SE:** 1045–1058
A-SSE.B.3c	Use the properties of exponents to transform expressions for exponential functions. ★	**SE:** 739–750
A-APR Arithmetic with Polynomials and Rational Expressions		
Perform arithmetic operations on polynomials.		
A-APR.A.1	Understand that polynomials form a system analogous to the integers, namely, they are closed under the operations of addition, subtraction, and multiplication; add, subtract, and multiply polynomials.	**SE:** 805–816, 817–828, 829–840, 847–854, 855–866, 867–876, 951–960
Understand the relationship between zeros and factors of polynomials		
A-APR.B.3	Identify zeros of polynomials when suitable factorizations are available, and use the zeros to construct a rough graph of the function defined by the polynomial.	**SE:** 938–950, 989–996, 1000–1008

[1] These standards are not included in the PARCC Model Content Framework for Algebra 1.

Common Core State Standards (continued)

Standard	Description	Citations
A-CED Creating Equations		
Create equations that describe numbers or relationships.		
A-CED.A.1	Create equations and inequalities in one variable and use them to solve problems.	**SE:** 55–66, 73–80, 81–92, 601–610, 611–624, 739–750, 783–798, 805–816, 817–828, 829–840, 847–854, 855–866, 867–876
A-CED.A.2	Create equations in two or more variables to represent relationships between quantities; graph equations on coordinate axes with labels and scales. ★	**SE:** 127–136, 239–248, 249–260, 261–268, 765–778, 1107–1122
A-CED.A.3	Represent constraints by equations or inequalities, and by systems of equations and/or inequalities, and interpret solutions as viable or non-viable options in a modeling context. ★	**SE:** 55–66, 73–80, 301–308, 323–334, 533–546, 547–556, 557–570
A-CED.A.4	Rearrange formulas to highlight a quantity of interest, using the same reasoning as in solving equations. ★	**SE:** 57–72, 1167–1178
A-REI Reasoning with Equations and Inequalities		
Understand solving equations as a process of reasoning and explain the reasoning.		
A-REI.A.1	Explain each step in solving a simple equation as following from the equality of numbers asserted at the previous step, starting from the assumption that the original equation has a solution. Construct a viable argument to justify a solution method.	**SE:** 5–14
Solve equations and inequalities in one variable.		
A-REI.B.3	Solve linear equations and inequalities in one variable, including equations with coefficients represented by letters.	**SE:** 55–66, 57–72, 73–80, 81–92, 601–610, 611–624, 667–680, 681–696, 997–1008, 1009–1026, 1033–1044, 1045–1058, 1059–1072, 1073–1088
A-REI.B.4	Solve quadratic equations in one variable.	**SE:** 937–950, 961–972
A-REI.B.4a	Use the method of completing the square to transform any quadratic equation in x into an equation of the form $(x - p)^2 = q$ that has the same solutions. Derive the quadratic formula from this form.	**SE:** 1045–1058, 1059–1072

★ Indicates a modeling standard linking mathematics to everyday life, work, and decision-making.
(+) Indicates additional mathematics to prepare students for advanced courses.

Standard	Description	Citations
A-REI.B.4b	Solve quadratic equations by inspection (e.g., for $x^2 = 49$), taking square roots, completing the square, the quadratic formula, and factoring, as appropriate to the initial form of the equation. Recognize when the quadratic formula gives complex solutions and write them as $a \pm bi$ for real numbers a and b.	**SE:** 961–972, 997–1008, 1009–1026, 1033–1044, 1045–1058, 1059–1072, 1073–1088

Solve systems of equations.

Standard	Description	Citations
A-REI.C.5	Prove that, given a system of two equations in two variables, replacing one equation by the sum of that equation and a multiple of the other produces a system with the same solutions.	**SE:** 515–526
A-REI.C.6	Solve systems of linear equations exactly and approximately (e.g., with graphs), focusing on pairs of linear equations in two variables.	**SE:** 479–490, 491–502, 503–514, 515–526
A-REI.C.7[1]	Solve a simple system consisting of a linear equation and a quadratic equation in two variables algebraically and graphically.	**SE:** 1089–1100

Represent and solve equations and inequalities graphically.

Standard	Description	Citations
A-REI.D.10	Understand that the graph of an equation in two variables is the set of all its solutions plotted in the coordinate plane, often forming a curve (which could be a line).	**SE:** 199–210, 239–248, 249–260, 261–268
A-REI.D.11	Explain why the x-coordinates of the points where the graphs of the equations $y = f(x)$ and $y = g(x)$ intersect are the solutions of the equation $f(x) = g(x)$; find the solutions approximately, e.g., using technology to graph the functions, make tables of values, or find successive approximations. Include cases where $f(x)$ and/or $g(x)$ are linear, polynomial, rational, absolute value, exponential, and logarithmic functions. ★	**SE:** 309–322, 739–750, 765–778, 937–950
A-REI.D.12	Graph the solutions to a linear inequality in two variables as a half-plane (excluding the boundary in the case of a strict inequality), and graph the solution set to a system of linear inequalities in two variables as the intersection of the corresponding half-planes.	**SE:** 323–334, 547–556

[1] These standards are not included in the PARCC Model Content Framework for Algebra 1.

Common Core State Standards (continued)

Standard	Description	Citations
Functions		
F-IF Interpreting Functions		
Understand the concept of a function and use function notation.		
F-IF.A.1	Understand that a function from one set (called the domain) to another set (called the range) assigns to each element of the domain exactly one element of the range. If f is a function and x is an element of its domain, then $f(x)$ denotes the output of f corresponding to the input x. The graph of f is the graph of the equation $y = f(x)$.	**SE:** 115–126, 127–136, 137–148
F-IF.A.2	Use function notation, evaluate functions for inputs in their domains, and interpret statements that use function notation in terms of a context.	**SE:** 127–136, 137–148, 693–706, 889–902, 903–916, 917–930
F-IF.A.3	Recognize that sequences are functions, sometimes defined recursively, whose domain is a subset of the integers.	**SE:** 155–164, 165–174, 175–186
Interpret functions that arise in applications in terms of the context.		
F-IF.B.4	For a function that models a relationship between two quantities, interpret key features of graphs and tables in terms of the quantities, and sketch graphs showing key features given a verbal description of the relationship.	**SE:** 105–114, 211–220, 889–902, 903–916, 917–930, 1107–1122
F-IF.B.5	Relate the domain of a function to its graph and, where applicable, to the quantitative relationship it describes. ★	**SE:** 751–764, 1107–1122, 1167–1178
F-IF.B.6	Calculate and interpret the average rate of change of a function (presented symbolically or as a table) over a specified interval. Estimate the rate of change from a graph. ★	**SE:** 221–232, 1123–1142
Analyze functions using different representations.		
F-IF.C.7	Graph functions expressed symbolically and show key features of the graph, by hand in simple cases and using technology for more complicated cases. ★	**SE:** 199–210, 211–220, 239–248, 577–588, 589–600, 693–706, 707–720, 751–764, 889–902, 937–950, 1123–1142, 1179–1190, 1191–1202
F-IF.C.7a	Graph linear and quadratic functions and show intercepts, maxima, and minima. ★	**SE:** 199–210, 211–220, 239–248, 889–902, 937–950

★ Indicates a modeling standard linking mathematics to everyday life, work, and decision-making.
(+) Indicates additional mathematics to prepare students for advanced courses.

Standard	Description	Citations
F-IF.C.7b	Graph square root, cube root, and piecewise-defined functions, including step functions and absolute value functions. ★	**SE:** 577–588, 589–600, 1123–1142, 1179–1190, 1191–1202
F-IF.C.7e[1]	Graph exponential and logarithmic functions, showing intercepts and end behavior, and trigonometric functions, showing period, midline, and amplitude. ★	**SE:** 693–706, 707–720, 751–764
F-IF.C.8	Write a function defined by an expression in different but equivalent forms to reveal and explain different properties of the function.	**SE:** 707–720, 917–930, 1059–1072
F-IF.C.8a	Use the process of factoring and completing the square in a quadratic function to show zeros, extreme values, and symmetry of the graph, and interpret these in terms of a context.	**SE:** 1045–1058
F-IF.C.8b[1]	Use the properties of exponents to interpret expressions for exponential functions.	**SE:** 707–720
F-IF.C.9	Compare properties of two functions each represented in a different way (algebraically, graphically, numerically in tables, or by verbal descriptions).	**SE:** 281–294, 721–732

F-BF Building Functions

Build a function that models a relationship between two quantities.

Standard	Description	Citations
F-BF.A.1	Write a function that describes a relationship between two quantities. ★	**SE:** 165–174, 175–186, 577–588, 679–692, 721–732, 739–750, 751–764, 903–916, 917–930
F-BF.A.1a	Determine an explicit expression, a recursive process, or steps for calculation from a context. ★	**SE:** 165–174, 175–186, 679–692, 751–764
F-BF.A.1b[1]	Combine standard function types using arithmetic operations. ★	**SE:** 577–588, 721–732
F-BF.A.2[1]	Write arithmetic and geometric sequences both recursively and with an explicit formula, use them to model situations, and translate between the two forms. ★	**SE:** 156–164, 165–174, 679–692

[1] These standards are not included in the PARCC Model Content Framework for Algebra 1.

Common Core State Standards (continued)

Standard	Description	Citations
Build new functions from existing functions.		
F-BF.B.3	Identify the effect on the graph of replacing $f(x)$ by $f(x) + k$, $kf(x)$, $f(kx)$, and $f(x + k)$ for specific values of k (both positive and negative); find the value of k given the graphs. Experiment with cases and illustrate an explanation of the effects on the graph using technology.	**SE:** 269–280, 589–600, 721–732, 889–902, 903–916, 1155–1166, 1179–1190, 1191–1202
F-BF.B.4	Find inverse functions.	**SE:** 903–916, 1167–1178, 1179–1190, 1191–1202
F-BF.B.4a	Solve an equation of the form $f(x) = c$ for a simple function f that has an inverse and write an expression for the inverse.	**SE:** 1167–1178, 1179–1190, 1191–1202
F-LE Linear, Quadratic, and Exponential Models		
Construct and compare linear, quadratic, and exponential models and solve problems.		
F-LE.A.1	Distinguish between situations that can be modeled with linear functions and with exponential functions. ★	**SE:** 199–210, 751–764, 765–778, 779–792, 1123–1142
F-LE.A.1a[1]	Prove that linear functions grow by equal differences over equal intervals, and that exponential functions grow by equal factors over equal intervals. ★	**SE:** 199–210, 779–792
F-LE.A.1b[1]	Recognize situations in which one quantity changes at a constant rate per unit interval relative to another. ★	**SE:** 199–210, 779–792, 1123–1142
F-LE.A.1c[1]	Recognize situations in which a quantity grows or decays by a constant percent rate per unit interval relative to another. ★	**SE:** 751–764, 765–778, 779–792
F-LE.A.2	Construct linear and exponential functions, including arithmetic and geometric sequences, given a graph, a description of a relationship, or two input-output pairs (include reading these from a table). ★	**SE:** 156–164, 165–174, 175–186, 199–210, 667–678, 679–692, 693–706, 739–750, 751–764
F-LE.A.3	Observe using graphs and tables that a quantity increasing exponentially eventually exceeds a quantity increasing linearly, quadratically, or (more generally) as a polynomial function. ★	**SE:** 667–678, 779–792, 1123–1142

★ Indicates a modeling standard linking mathematics to everyday life, work, and decision-making.
(+) Indicates additional mathematics to prepare students for advanced courses.

Standard	Description	Citations
Interpret expressions for functions in terms of the situation they model.		
F-LE.B.5	Interpret the parameters in a linear or exponential function in terms of a context. ★ [Linear and exponential of form $f(x) = b^x + k$.]	**SE:** 211–220, 221–232, 269–280, 435–450, 451–466, 533–546
Statistics and Probability		
S-ID Interpreting Categorical and Quantitative Data		
Summarize, represent, and interpret data on a single count or measurement variable.		
S-ID.A.1	Represent data with plots on the real number line (dot plots, histograms, and box plots). ★	**SE:** 389–400, 401–416, 417–428
S-ID.A.2	Use statistics appropriate to the shape of the data distribution to compare center (median, mean) and spread (interquartile range, standard deviation) of two or more different data sets. ★	**SE:** 377–388, 389–400, 401–416, 417–428
S-ID.A.3	Interpret differences in shape, center, and spread in the context of the data sets, accounting for possible effects of extreme data points (outliers). ★	**SE:** 389–400
Summarize, represent, and interpret data on two categorical and quantitative variables.		
S-ID.B.5	Summarize categorical data for two categories in two-way frequency tables. Interpret relative frequencies in the context of the data (including joint, marginal, and conditional relative frequencies). Recognize possible associations and trends in the data. ★	**SE:** 347–358, 359–370
S-ID.B.6	Represent data on two quantitative variables on a scatter plot, and describe how the variables are related. ★	**SE:** 435–450, 451–466, 765–778
S-ID.B.6a	Fit a function to the data; use functions fitted to data to solve problems in the context of the data. ★	**SE:** 435–450, 765–778
S-ID.B.6b	Informally assess the fit of a function by plotting and analyzing residuals. ★	**SE:** 451–466, 765–778
S-ID.B.6c	Fit a linear function for a scatter plot that suggests a linear association. ★	**SE:** 435–450, 451–466

[1] These standards are not included in the PARCC Model Content Framework for Algebra 1.

Standard	Description	Citations
Interpret linear models.		
S-ID.C.7	Interpret the slope (rate of change) and the intercept (constant term) of a linear model in the context of the data. ★	**SE:** 301–308, 435–450
S-ID.C.8	Compute (using technology) and interpret the correlation coefficient of a linear fit. ★	**SE:** 451–466
S-ID.C.9	Distinguish between correlation and causation. ★	**SE:** 435–450

★ Indicates a modeling standard linking mathematics to everyday life, work, and decision-making.
(+) Indicates additional mathematics to prepare students for advanced courses.

STANDARDS FOR MATHEMATICAL PRACTICE

Standard	Description	Citations
MP.1	Make sense of problems and persevere in solving them.	*Integrated throughout the book. Examples:* **SE:** 15, 16, 40, 42, 53, 60–61, 66, 97–99
MP.2	Reason abstractly and quantitatively.	*Integrated throughout the book. Examples:* **SE:** 5, 7–8, 13–14, 27–38, 52, 65, 67, 70, 98–99
MP.3	Construct viable arguments and critique the reasoning of others.	*Integrated throughout the book. Examples:* **SE:** 31, 35, 52, 65, 125, 147, 156, 167, 201, 279
MP.4	Model with mathematics.	*Integrated throughout the book. Examples:* **SE:** 45–54, 55–66, 127–136, 175–186, 301–308, 451–466
MP.5	Use appropriate tools strategically.	*Integrated throughout the book. Examples:* **SE:** 27–29, 140, 269, 309, 456–457, 707, 767
MP.6	Attend to precision.	*Integrated throughout the book. Examples:* **SE:** 17–18, 27–38, 68, 179–180, 615–616
MP.7	Look for and make use of structure.	*Integrated throughout the book. Examples:* **SE:** 45–46, 53, 138–139, 175–186, 188, 199–200
MP.8	Look for and express regularity in repeated reasoning.	*Integrated throughout the book. Examples:* **SE:** 138–139, 156–160, 221–226, 637–638, 1059–1060

Common Core Cluster Progressions

HMH Algebra 1 carefully develops the instructional progression of each cluster from the Common Core Standards. The table below shows where key topics from each cluster are taught in HMH Algebra 1.

HMH ALGEBRA 1

Common Core Clusters		Unit 1	Unit 2	Unit 3
N-RN.A	Extend the properties of exponents to rational exponents.			
N-Q.A	Reason quantitatively and use units to solve problems.	covered in full		
A-SSE.A	Interpret the structure of expressions.	linear		
A-SSE.B	Write expressions in equivalent forms to solve problems.			
A-APR.A	Perform arithmetic operations on polynomials.			
A-APR.B	Understand the relationship between zeros and factors of polynomials.			
A-CED.A	Create equations that describe numbers or relationships.	linear one-variable, including formulas		two-variable linear
A-REI.A	Understand solving equations as a process of reasoning and explain the reasoning.	covered in full		
A-REI.B	Solve equations and inequalities in one variable.	linear		
A-REI.C	Solve systems of equations.			
A-REI.D	Represent and solve equations and inequalities graphically.			linear equations and inequalities

	Unit 4	Unit 5	Unit 6	Unit 7	Unit 8	Unit 9	Unit 10
			covered in full				
			exponential		polynomial, quadratic		
			exponential		factoring quadratics	completing the square	
				covered in full			
		linear systems	exponential		quadratics		
						quadratic	
					quadratic	quadratic	
		linear systems				linear/ quadratic systems	
		linear systems, absolute-value	exponential			quadratic	

Common Core Cluster Progressions (continued)

HMH ALGEBRA 1

Common Core Clusters		Unit 1	Unit 2	Unit 3
F-IF.A	Understand the concept of a function and use function notation.		definition and notation, arithemetic sequences	
F-IF.B	Interpret functions that arise in applications in terms of a context.		introduction	linear
F-IF.C	Analyze functions using different representations.			linear
F-BF.A	Build a function that models a relationship between two quantities.		arithmetic sequences	linear
F-BF.B	Build new functions from existing functions.		arithmetic sequences	linear
F-LE.A	Construct and compare linear, quadratic, and exponential models and solve problems.			linear
F-LE.B	Interpret expressions for functions in terms of the situation they model.			linear
S-ID.A	Summarize, represent, and interpret data on a single count or measurement variable.			
S-ID.B	Summarize, represent, and interpret data on two categorical and quantitative variables.			
S-ID.C	Interpret linear models.			

Unit 4	Unit 5	Unit 6	Unit 7	Unit 8	Unit 9	Unit 10
		geometric sequences				
	linear systems	exponential		quadratics	quadratics	polynomial, radical
	linear systems, absolute-value, piecewise	exponential		quadratics	quadratics, comparing models	polynomial, square root, cube root
		exponential, geometric sequences		quadratics	quadratics	polynomial
		exponential	covered in full		quadratics	inverse
		exponential, comparing linear/ exponential			quadratics, comparing models	
		exponential				
covered in full						
linear		exponential				
covered in full						

Succeeding with HMH Algebra 1

HMH Algebra 1 is built on the 5E instructional model--Engage, Explore, Explain, Elaborate, Evaluate--to develop strong conceptual understanding and mastery of key mathematics standards.

💡 ENGAGE

Preview the Lesson Performance Task in the Interactive Student Edition.

Lesson 19.2 Precision and Accuracy

Engage
Essential Question

How do you use significant digits when reporting the results of calculations involving measurement?

Preview
Lesson Performance Task

The sun is an excellent source of electrical energy. Suppose a company owns a field of solar panels. How much electricity is produced by the field? The answer depends on the amount of power the field yields per square foot, as well as the size of the field.

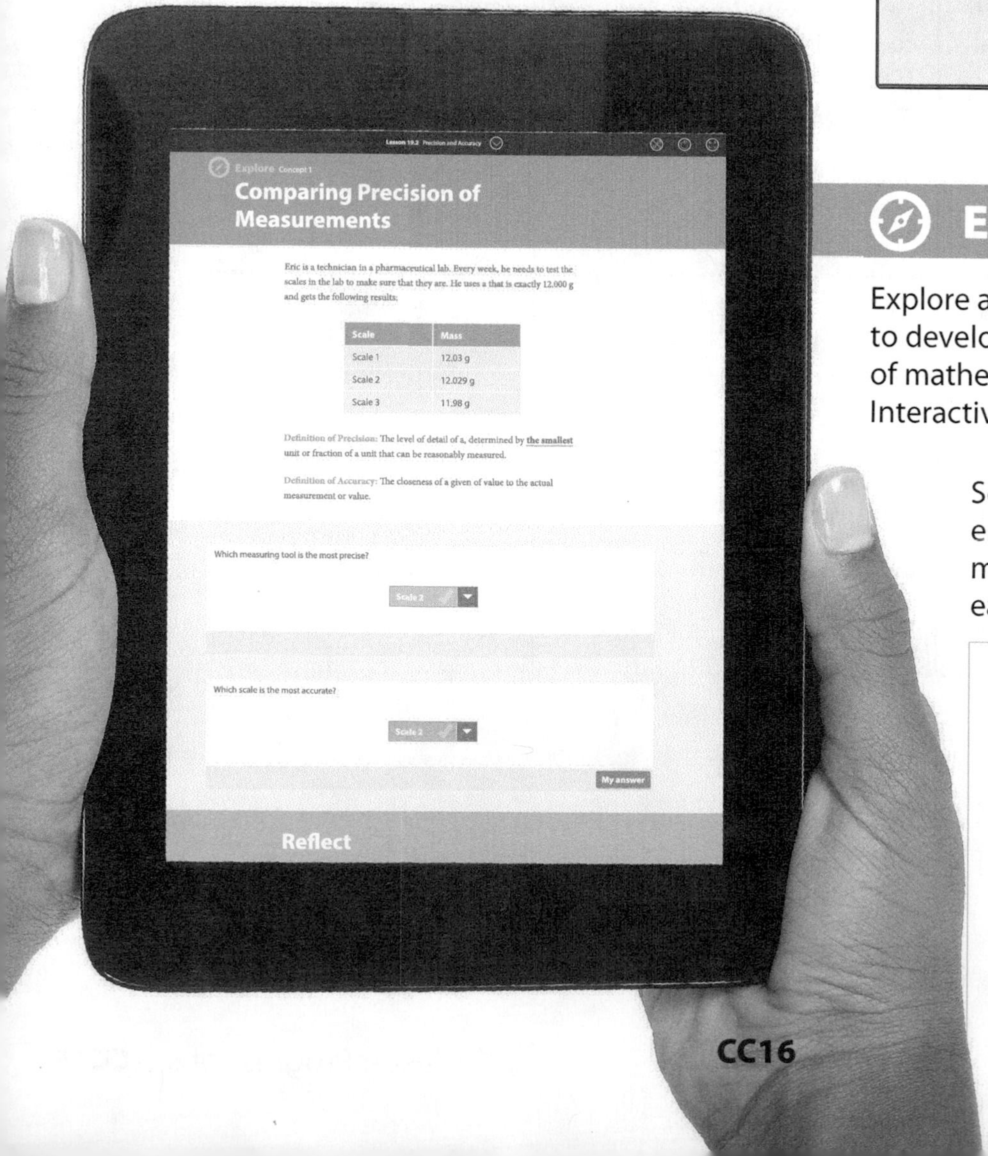

Lesson 19.2 Precision and Accuracy

Explore Concept 1
Comparing Precision of Measurements

Eric is a technician in a pharmaceutical lab. Every week, he needs to test the scales in the lab to make sure that they are. He uses a that is exactly 12.000 g and gets the following results:

Scale	Mass
Scale 1	12.03 g
Scale 2	12.029 g
Scale 3	11.98 g

Definition of Precision: The level of detail of a, determined by the smallest unit or fraction of a unit that can be reasonably measured.

Definition of Accuracy: The closeness of a given of value to the actual measurement or value.

Which measuring tool is the most precise?

Which scale is the most accurate?

My answer

Reflect

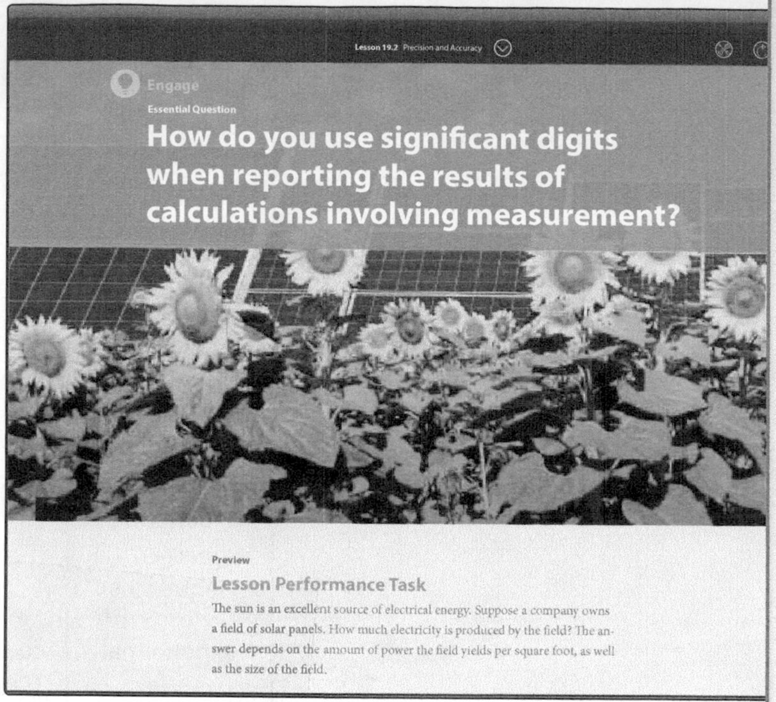

🧭 EXPLORE

Explore and interact with new concepts to develop a deeper understanding of mathematics in your book and the Interactive Student Edition.

Scan the QR code to access engaging videos, activities, and more in the Resource Locker for each lesson.

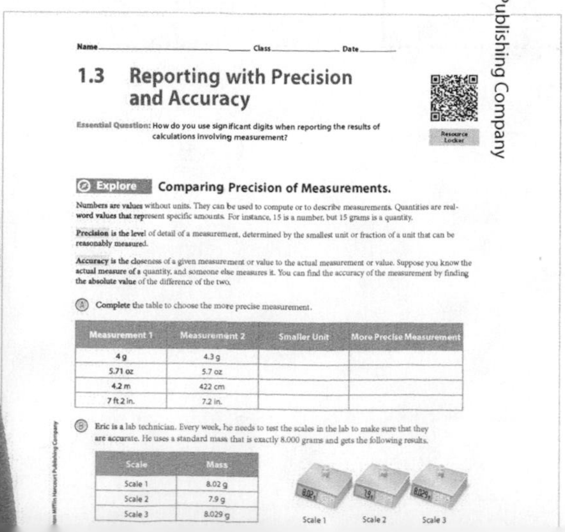

Name_____ Class_____ Date_____

1.3 Reporting with Precision and Accuracy

Essential Question: How do you use significant digits when reporting the results of calculations involving measurement?

Explore Comparing Precision of Measurements.

Numbers are values without units. They can be used to compute or to describe measurements. Quantities are real-word values that represent specific amounts. For instance, 15 is a number, but 15 grams is a quantity.

Precision is the level of detail of a measurement, determined by the smallest unit or fraction of a unit that can be reasonably measured.

Accuracy is the closeness of a given measurement or value to the actual measurement or value. Suppose you know the actual measure of a quantity, and someone else measures it. You can find the accuracy of the measurement by finding the absolute value of the difference of the two.

Complete the table to choose the more precise measurement.

Measurement 1	Measurement 2	Smaller Unit	More Precise Measurement
4 g	4.3 g		
5.71 oz	5.7 oz		
4.2 m	422 cm		
7 ft,2 in.	7.2 in.		

Eric is a lab technician. Every week, he needs to test the scales in the lab to make sure that they are accurate. He uses a standard mass that is exactly 8.000 grams and gets the following results:

Scale	Mass
Scale 1	8.02 g
Scale 2	7.9 g
Scale 3	8.029 g

Scale 1   Scale 2   Scale 3

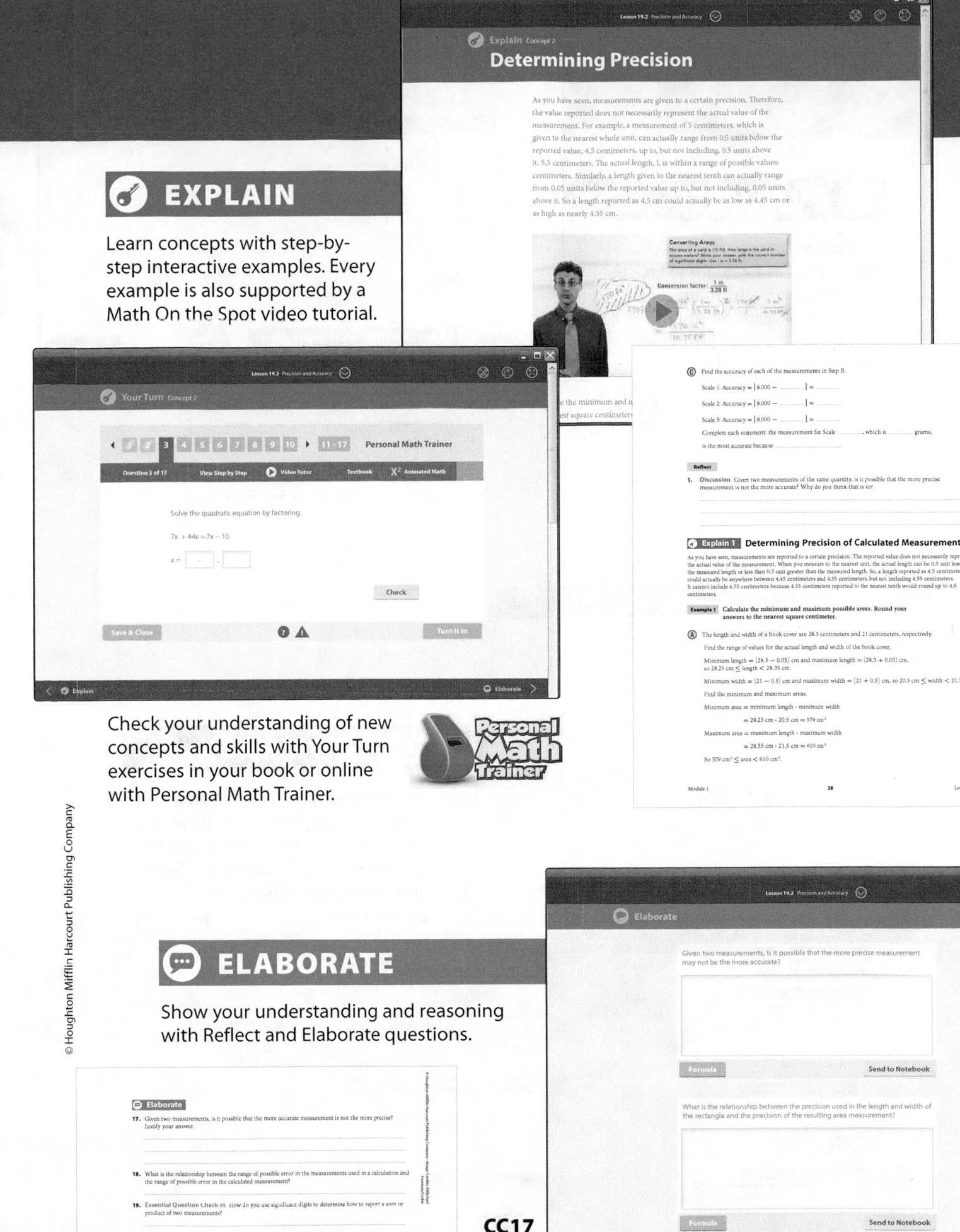

🔑 EXPLAIN

Learn concepts with step-by-step interactive examples. Every example is also supported by a Math On the Spot video tutorial.

Check your understanding of new concepts and skills with Your Turn exercises in your book or online with Personal Math Trainer.

💬 ELABORATE

Show your understanding and reasoning with Reflect and Elaborate questions.

CC17

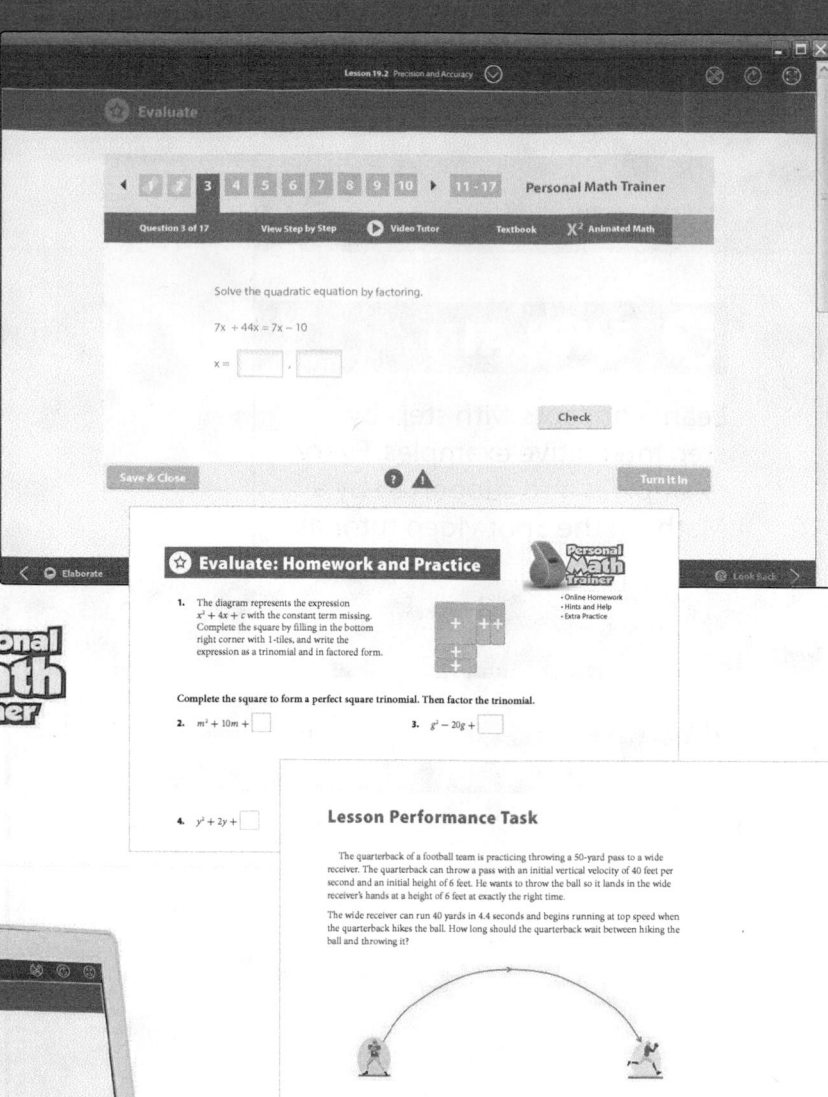

⭐ EVALUATE

Practice and apply skills and concepts with Evaluate exercises and a Lesson Performance Task in your book with plenty of workspace, or complete these exercises online with Personal Math Trainer.

Personal Math Trainer

Solve the quadratic equation by factoring.

$7x + 44x = 7x - 10$

$x = \boxed{} \cdot \boxed{}$

Check

Save & Close   Turn it In

⭐ Evaluate: Homework and Practice

- Online Homework
- Hints and Help
- Extra Practice

1. The diagram represents the expression $x^2 + 4x + c$ with the constant term missing. Complete the square by filling in the bottom right corner with 1-tiles, and write the expression as a trinomial and in factored form.

Complete the square to form a perfect square trinomial. Then factor the trinomial.

2. $m^2 + 10m + \boxed{}$ 3. $g^2 - 20g + \boxed{}$

4. $y^2 + 2y + \boxed{}$

Lesson Performance Task

The quarterback of a football team is practicing throwing a 50-yard pass to a wide receiver. The quarterback can throw a pass with an initial vertical velocity of 40 feet per second and an initial height of 6 feet. He wants to throw the ball so it lands in the wide receiver's hands at a height of 6 feet at exactly the right time.

The wide receiver can run 40 yards in 4.4 seconds and begins running at top speed when the quarterback hikes the ball. How long should the quarterback wait between hiking the ball and throwing it?

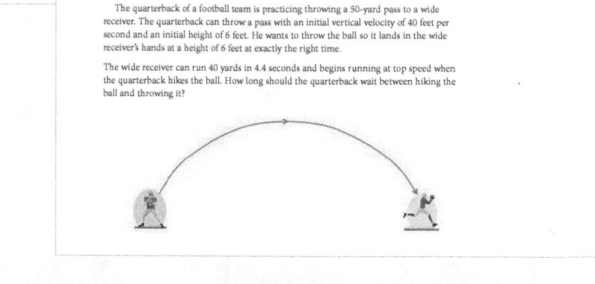

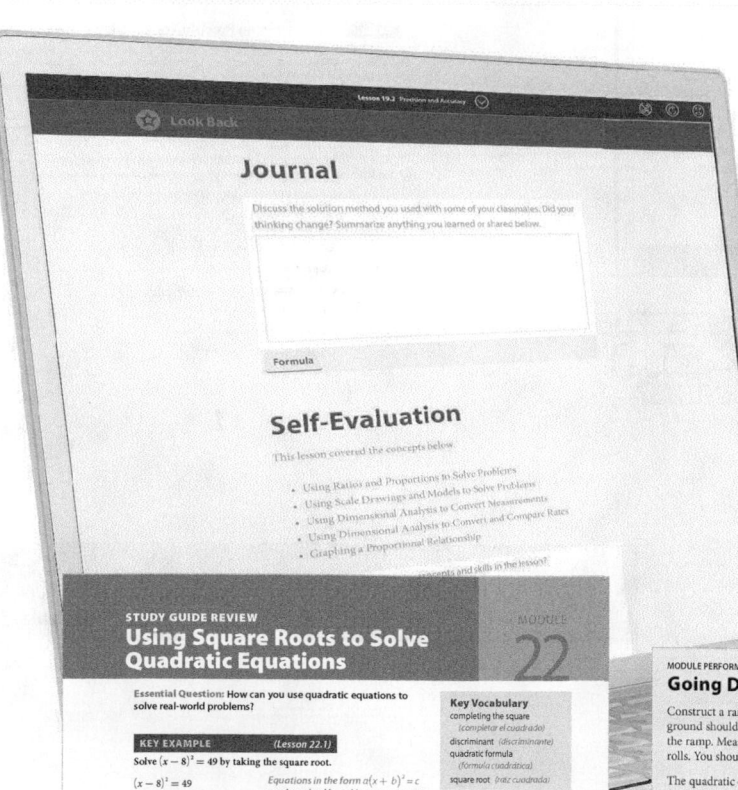

Journal

Discuss the solution method you used with some of your classmates. Did your thinking change? Summarize anything you learned or shared below.

Formula

Self-Evaluation

This lesson covered the concepts below.

- Using Ratios and Proportions to Solve Problems
- Using Scale Drawings and Models to Solve Problems
- Using Dimensional Analysis to Convert Measurements
- Using Dimensional Analysis to Convert and Compare Rates
- Graphing a Proportional Relationship

STUDY GUIDE REVIEW
Using Square Roots to Solve Quadratic Equations

MODULE **22**

Essential Question: How can you use quadratic equations to solve real-world problems?

Key Vocabulary
completing the square (completar el cuadrado)
discriminant (discriminante)
quadratic formula (fórmula cuadrática)
square root (raíz cuadrada)

KEY EXAMPLE *(Lesson 22.1)*

Solve $(x - 8)^2 = 49$ by taking the square root.

$(x - 8)^2 = 49$ Equations in the form $a(x + b)^2 = c$ can be solved by taking square roots.
$x - 8 = \pm 7$ Take the square root of both sides.
$x = \pm 7 + 8$
$x = 7 + 8$ and $x = -7 + 8$ Solve both cases.
$x = 15$ and $x = 1$

KEY EXAMPLE *(Lesson 22.2)*

Solve $9x^2 - 6x = 20$ by completing the square.

$\dfrac{(-6)^2}{4(9)} = 1$ Find $\dfrac{b^2}{4a}$.

$9x^2 - 6x + 1 = 20 + 1$ Complete the square.
$(3x - 1)^2 = 21$
$x = \dfrac{\sqrt{21} + 1}{3}$ and $x = \dfrac{-\sqrt{21} + 1}{3}$

KEY EXAMPLE *(Lesson 22.3)*

Solve $8x^2 - 8x + 2 = 0$ using the quadratic equation.

$a = 8, b = -8, c = 2$ Identify a, b, and c.
$x = \dfrac{-b \pm \sqrt{b^2 - 4ac}}{2a}$ Use the quadratic formula.
$x = \dfrac{8 \pm \sqrt{(-8)^2 - (4)(8)(2)}}{2(8)}$
$x = \dfrac{8 \pm \sqrt{0}}{16}$ Since $b^2 - 4ac = 0$, the equation has one real solution.
$x = \dfrac{1}{2}$

⭐ LOOK BACK

Review what you have learned and prepare for high-stakes tests with a variety of resources, including Study Guide Reviews, Performance Tasks, and Assessment Readiness test preparation.

MODULE PERFORMANCE TASK
Going Down?

Construct a ramp that is at least 4 feet long. The angle the ramp makes with the ground should be 30°. Working with a partner, release a ball from various points on the ramp. Measure the distance the ball rolls and the time (using a stopwatch) that it rolls. You should perform several trials for various distances.

The quadratic equation $d = \frac{1}{4}gt^2$ models the distance d (in feet) that the ball rolls in t seconds. Use your data and the equation to estimate the value of g. Create a report that explains your approach, organizes all of the collected data in tables, and shows your calculations. You can use a graphing calculator to fit your data to a quadratic regression line.

Use the space below to write down any questions you have or important information from your teacher.

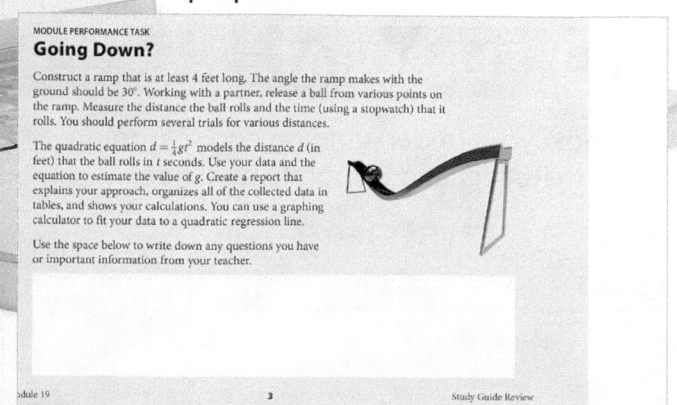

Module 19   3   Study Guide Review

CC18

Synergy Through Collaboration

Tim Kanold
Program Author

Great teaching materials do not provide great education in and of themselves. Educators who collaborate in Professional Learning Communities can have a profound impact on their students. As a mathematics teacher, your grade-level or course-based collaborative team is the engine that can drive your professional learning and the professional learning community (PLC) process.

You and your colleagues hold a critical key to helping *all* students successfully learn the Common Core Mathematics Standards in your school. Through your hard work and the work of your collaborative team, effective instruction, assessment, and intervention practices become more coherent and focused.

The National Board for Professional Teaching Standards states the following:

> Seeing themselves as partners with other teachers, [faculty members] are dedicated to improving the profession. They care about the quality of teaching in their schools, and, to this end, their collaboration with colleagues is continuous and explicit. They recognize that collaborating in a professional learning community contributes to their own professional growth, as well as to the growth of their peers, for the benefit of student learning. Teachers promote the ideal that working collaboratively increases knowledge, reflection, and quality of practice and benefits the instructional program. (*Mathematics Standards for Teachers of Students Ages 11–18+*, ©2010, p. 75)

As a highly accomplished mathematics teacher you understand the value in the practice of effective collaboration with your colleagues. Teacher collaboration is not the icing on top of the proverbial cake of your work. Instead, it is the egg in the batter, holding the cake together.

As your school becomes a learning institution for the adults, it also becomes a learning institution dedicated to preparing all students for the future. The process of your collaboration in a PLC culture capitalizes on the fact that you and your colleagues come together with diverse experiences and knowledge to create a whole that is larger than the sum of the parts. Teacher collaboration is the solution to your sustained professional learning—the ongoing and never-ending process of growth necessary to meet the classroom demands of the CCSS expectations and the unit-by-unit mathematics content described in our series.

Quantities and Modeling

CONTENTS

Unit Pacing Guide

45-Minute Classes

Module 1

DAY 1	DAY 2	DAY 3	DAY 4	
Lesson 1.1	Lesson 1.2	Lesson 1.3	Module Review and Assessment Readiness	

Module 2

DAY 1	DAY 2	DAY 3	DAY 4	DAY 5
Lesson 2.1	Lesson 2.1	Lesson 2.2	Lesson 2.2	Lesson 2.3

DAY 6	DAY 7	DAY 8	DAY 9	DAY 10
Lesson 2.3	Lesson 2.4	Lesson 2.4	Lesson 2.5	Lesson 2.5

DAY 11	DAY 12			
Module Review and Assessment Readiness	Unit Review and Assessment Readiness			

90-Minute Classes

Module 1

DAY 1	DAY 2			
Lesson 1.1 Lesson 1.2	Lesson 1.3 Module Review and Assessment Readiness			

Module 2

DAY 1	DAY 2	DAY 3	DAY 4	DAY 5
Lesson 2.1	Lesson 2.2	Lesson 2.3	Lesson 2.4	Lesson 2.5

DAY 6				
Module Review and Assessment Readines Unit Review and Assessment Readiness				

Program Resources

PLAN

HMH Teacher App

Access a full suite of teacher resources online and offline on a variety of devices. Plan present, and manage classes, assignments, and activities.

ePlanner Easily plan your classes, create and view assignments, and access all program resources with your online, customizable planning tool.

Professional Development Videos

Authors Juli Dixon and Matt Larson model successful teaching practices and strategies in actual classroom settings.

QR Codes Scan with your smart phone to jump directly from your print book to online videos and other resources.

Teacher's Edition

Support students with point-of-use Questioning Strategies, teaching tips, resources for differentiated instruction, additional activities, and more.

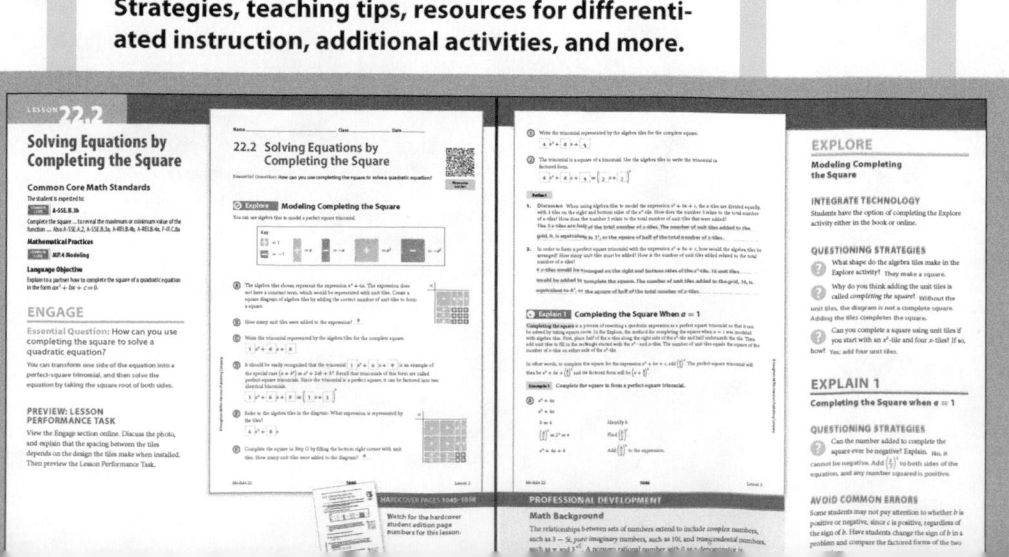

ENGAGE AND EXPLORE

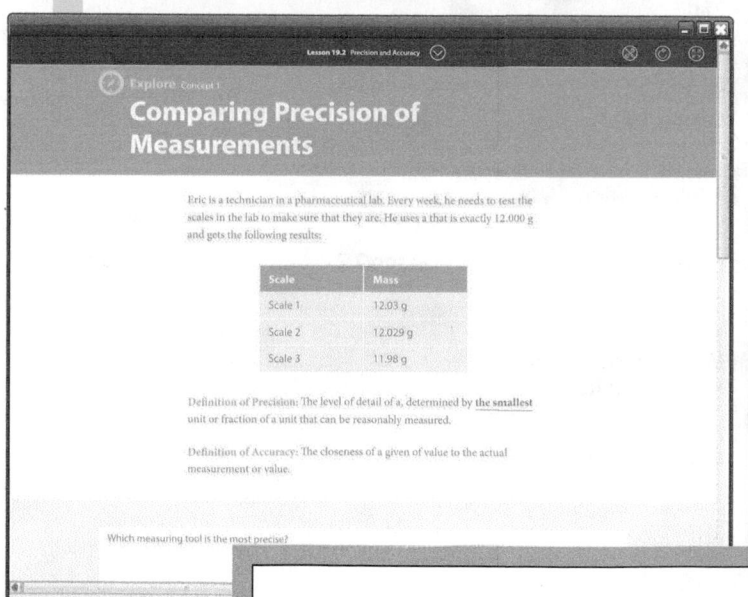

Real-World Videos Engage students with interesting and relevant applications of the mathematical content of each module.

Explore Activities

Students interactively explore new concepts using a variety of tools and approaches.

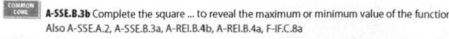

Comparing Precision of Measurements

Eric is a technician in a pharmaceutical lab. Every week, he needs to test the scales in the lab to make sure that they are. He uses a that is exactly 12.000 g and gets the following results:

Scale	Mass
Scale 1	12.03 g
Scale 2	12.029 g
Scale 3	11.98 g

Definition of Precision: The level of detail of a, determined by the smallest unit or fraction of a unit that can be reasonably measured.

Definition of Accuracy: The closeness of a given of value to the actual measurement or value.

Which measuring tool is the most precise?

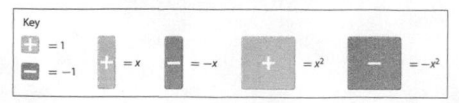

Name _____ Class _____ Date _____

22.2 Solving Equations by Completing the Square

Essential Question: How can you use completing the square to solve a quadratic equation?

COMMON CORE A-SSE.B.3b Complete the square ... to reveal the maximum or minimum value of the function ... Also A-SSE.A.2, A-SSE.B.3a, A-REI.B.4b, A-REI.B.4a, F-IFC.8a

Resource Locker

Explore Modeling Completing the Square

You can use algebra tiles to model a perfect square trinomial.

Key

$+ = 1$ $+ = x$ $- = -x$ $+ = x^2$ $- = -x^2$

$- = -1$

(A) The algebra tiles shown represent the expression $x^2 + 6x$. The expression does not have a constant term, which would be represented with unit tiles. Create a square diagram of algebra tiles by adding the correct number of unit tiles to form a square.

(B) How many unit tiles were added to the expression? _____

(C) Write the trinomial represented by the algebra tiles for the complete square.

□$x^2 +$ □$x +$ □

(D) It should be easily recognized that the trinomial □$x^2 +$ □$x +$ □ is an example of the special case $(a + b)^2 = a^2 + 2ab + b^2$. Recall that trinomials of this form are called perfect-square trinomials. Since the trinomial is a perfect square, it can be factored into two

TEACH

Math On the Spot video tutorials, featuring program author Dr. Edward Burger, accompany every example in the textbook and give students step-by-step instructions and explanations of key math concepts.

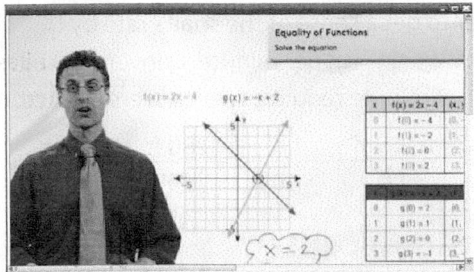

Interactive Teacher Edition

Customize and present course materials with collaborative activities and integrated formative assessment.

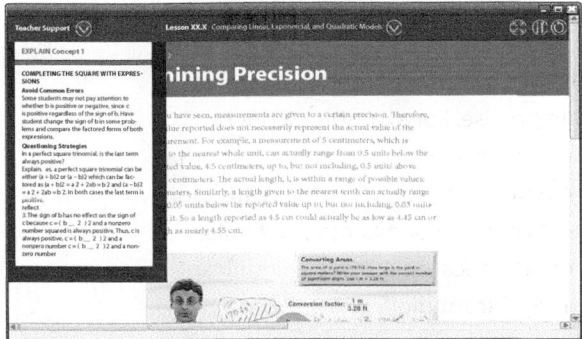

Differentiated Instruction Resources

Support all learners with Differentiated Instruction Resources, including

- **Leveled Practice and Problem Solving**
- **Reading Strategies**
- **Success for English Learners**
- **Challenge**

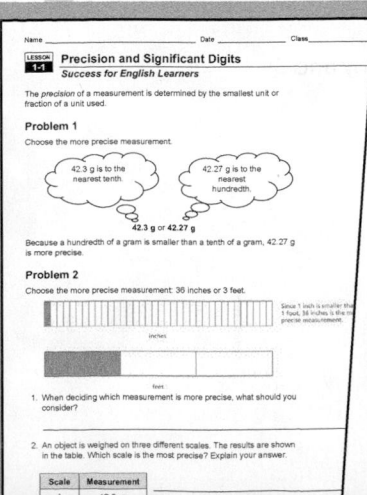
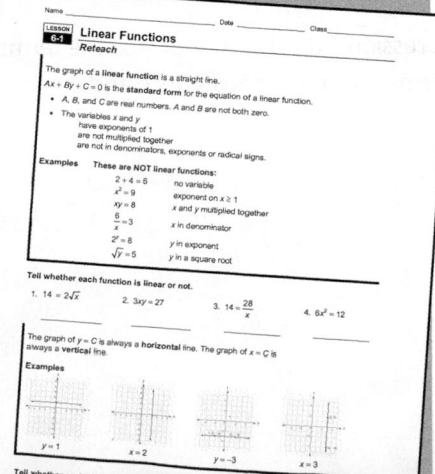

ASSESSMENT AND INTERVENTION

The Personal Math Trainer provides online practice, homework, assessments, and intervention. Monitor student progress through reports and alerts. Create and customize assignments aligned to specific lessons or Common Core standards.

- **Practice** – With dynamic items and assignments, students get unlimited practice on key concepts supported by guided examples, step-by-step solutions, and video tutorials.

- **Assessments** – Choose from course assignments or customize your own based on course content, Common Core standards, difficulty levels, and more.

- **Homework** – Students can complete online homework with a wide variety of problem types, including the ability to enter expressions, equations, and graphs. Let the system automatically grade homework, so you can focus where your students need help the most!

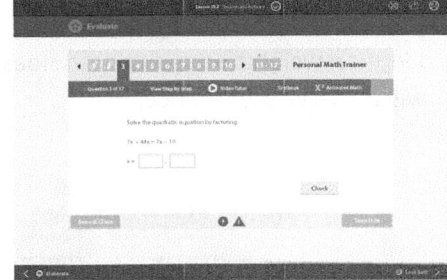

- **Intervention** – Let the Personal Math Trainer automatically prescribe a targeted, personalized intervention path for your students.

Focus on Higher Order Thinking

Raise the bar with homework and practice that incorporates higher-order thinking and mathematical practices in every lesson.

Assessment Readiness

Prepare students for success on high stakes tests for Algebra 1 with practice at every module and unit

Assessment Resources

Tailor assessments and response to intervention to meet the needs of all your classes and students, including

- Leveled Module Quizzes
- Leveled Unit Tests
- Unit Performance Tasks
- Placement, Diagnostic, and Quarterly Benchmark Tests
- Tier 1, Tier 2, and Tier 3 Resources

Math Background

Solving Equations 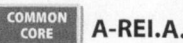 A-REI.A.1

LESSON 1.1

Solving equations is one of the most important skills in K–12 mathematics. It is sometimes possible to find a solution by testing values of the variable, but this is not generally the most efficient solution method. Students learn to solve an equation by transforming it into equivalent equations. *Equivalent equations* are equations that have the same solution set. During the solution process, each transformation of an equation should be backed up by a general mathematical principle. As such, a proper justification for a step in the solution of an equation is not simply a description of what was done to the equation ("I added 3 to both sides"), but rather a general principle, such as the Addition Property of Equality ("equals added to equals are equal"). The figure shows how this general principle may be understood in terms of a balanced scale: identical weights added to both sides of a balanced scale will preserve the balance.

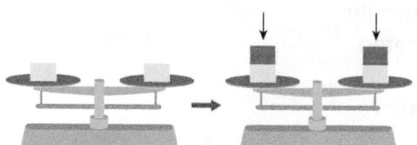

In the same way, identical quantities added to both sides of an equation will preserve the equality. A similar analogy can be made for the Subtraction Property of Equality.

Dimensional Analysis N-Q.A.1

LESSON 1.2

When students are asked to convert 24 feet to inches, they sometimes have difficulty deciding whether to multiply by 12 or divide by 12. Using conversion factors makes it easier to decide what to do. A conversion factor is simply a fraction that is equal to 1. Since 1 foot = 12 inches, you can write two conversion factors: $\frac{1\ foot}{12\ inches}$ and $\frac{12\ inches}{1\ foot}$. To convert 24 feet to inches, multiply by the conversion factor that has feet in the denominator so that these units "cancel."

$$24\ ft = 24\ \cancel{ft} \cdot \frac{12\ in.}{1\ \cancel{ft}} = 288\ in.$$

Dimensional analysis is especially effective with compound units, such as miles per hour or gallons per minute. As such, it is a valuable tool for checking the reasonableness of answers in problems that deal with ratios or rates. For example, the answer to a problem about the rate of a garden snail's movement may be 0.03 mi/h. However, it would be easier to get a sense of the snail's rate by expressing the answer in feet per minute. Converting miles per hour to feet per minute requires two conversion factors.

$$\frac{0.03\ mi}{1\ h} = \frac{0.03\ \cancel{mi}}{1\ \cancel{h}} \cdot \frac{1\ \cancel{h}}{60\ min} \cdot \frac{5280\ ft}{1\ \cancel{mi}} = \frac{2.64\ ft}{1\ min}$$

Precision and Accuracy  N-Q.A.3

LESSON 1.3

In the real world, no measurement can be exact. The accuracy of a measurement is how close it is to the actual measurement. The significant digits of a number are those digits that carry meaning contributing to its precision. The more precise a measurement is, the more significant digits the measurement will have. When different units are used, the smaller unit is more precise. For example, 35 inches is more precise than 3 feet since an inch is a smaller unit than a foot. When the same unit is used, the measure with more significant digits is more precise. For example, 4.2 miles is more precise than 4 miles because 4.2 has 2 significant digits and 4 has only 1 significant digit.

Expressions A-SSE.A.1a

LESSON 2.1

The terms of an expression are the parts that are added or subtracted. Like terms are terms that contain the same variables raised to the same power. Constants are like terms because all of the variables in a constant term are, in effect, raised to the zero power.

In the expression $6y + 4 + 3y + x + 2$, the terms $6y$ and $3y$ are like terms, as are the constants 4 and 2.

A coefficient is a number multiplied by a variable in a term. In the term $6y$, the coefficient is 6. A variable without a coefficient, such as the x in the above expression, has a coefficient of 1. Students learn to simplify expressions by combining like terms. To simplify an algebraic expression, you can use properties to combine like terms and eliminate grouping symbols. The Commutative, Associative, and Distributive Properties make this possible, since they give the justification for rearranging and regrouping terms in an algebraic expression. In particular, combining like terms uses the Distributive Property. Students may quickly write $4x + 5x = 9x$, but the intermediate step shown below illustrates that the Distributive Property is at work.

$$4x + 5x = (4 + 5)x = 9x$$

Solutions to Equations A-REI.B.3
LESSON 2.2

Before they solve equations, students need to understand what is meant by a solution. A solution of an equation in one variable is a value of the variable that makes the equation true. The equation $5(x + 2) - 3x = 18$, for example, is neither true nor false until a specific value replaces x. It is worthwhile to have students test various values of x in the left-hand side of the equation.

x	$5(x + 2) - 3x$
1	12
2	14
3	16
4	18

The table shows that $x = 1$, $x = 2$, and $x = 3$ are not solutions of the equation and that $x = 4$ is a solution.

Literal Equations  A-CED.A.4
LESSON 2.3

A literal equation is an equation with two or more variables. A formula is a type of literal equation that describes a relationship among two or more different quantities. You can solve for a variable in the formula and rearrange the formula as needed. Formulas occur throughout algebra, especially in application problems.

Inequalities A-REI.B.3
LESSON 2.4

Solving an inequality in one variable is similar to solving an equation in one variable. The goal is to isolate the variable on one side of the inequality by writing a series of equivalent inequalities—that is, a series of inequalities with the same solution set.

The Addition and Subtraction Properties of Inequality are analogous to their counterparts for equations: the same quantity may be added to or subtracted from both sides of an inequality. For multiplication and division there is an important caveat.

Consider the inequality $a > b$. By the Subtraction Property of Inequality, $a - a > b - a$ or, equivalently, $0 > b - a$. Applying the Subtraction Property of Inequality again shows that $0 - b > b - a - b$ or $-b > -a$, which is the same as $-a < -b$. In other words, when both sides of the original inequality are multiplied by -1, the direction of the inequality is reversed. More generally, the direction of the inequality is reversed when both sides of an inequality are multiplied or divided by any negative number.

Quantities and Modeling

MATH IN CAREERS
Unit Activity Preview

After completing this unit, students will complete a Math in Careers task by interpreting a table of data and writing and using an algebraic expression based on an individual's exercise patterns. Critical skills include modeling real-world situations and interpreting algebraic expressions.

For more information about careers in mathematics as well as various mathematics appreciation topics, visit The American Mathematical Society at http://www.ams.org.

UNIT 1

Quantities and Modeling

MODULE **1**
Quantitative Reasoning

MODULE **2**
Algebraic Models

MATH IN CAREERS

Personal Trainer A personal trainer works with clients to help them achieve their personal fitness goals. A personal trainer needs math to calculate a client's heart rate, body fat percentage, lean muscle mass, and calorie requirements. Personal trainers are often self-employed, so they need to understand the mathematics of managing a business.

If you are interested in a career as a personal trainer, you should study these mathematical subjects:
- Algebra
- Business Math

Research other careers that require knowledge of the mathematics of business management. Check out the career activity at the end of the unit to find out how **personal trainers** use math.

Unit 1   1

TRACKING YOUR LEARNING PROGRESSION

Before	In this Unit	After
Students understand: • evaluating expressions • simplifying expressions • writing expressions • solving one-step equations • order of operations • the Commutative, Associative, and Distributive properties	Students will learn about: • creating and solving equations • solving proportions • using dimensional analysis • determining precision of measurements • using significant digits • algebraic expressions • solving for a variable • creating and solving inequalities	Students will study: • linear functions • sequences • modeling linear relationships • polynomials

Reading Start-Up

Visualize Vocabulary

Use the ✔ words to complete the graphic. Put one term in each section of the square.

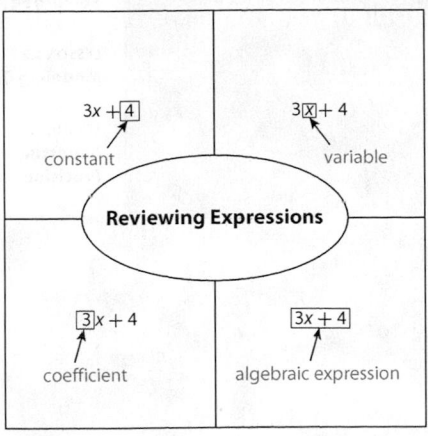

constant — $3x + \boxed{4}$

variable — $3\boxed{x} + 4$

coefficient — $\boxed{3}x + 4$

algebraic expression — $\boxed{3x + 4}$

Reviewing Expressions

© Houghton Mifflin Harcourt Publishing Company

Vocabulary

Review Words

✔ absolute value *(función de valor absoluto)*
✔ algebraic expression *(expresión algebraica)*
✔ coefficient *(coeficiente)*
✔ constant *(constante)*
✔ numeric expression *(expresión numérica)*
✔ simplify *(simplificar)*
✔ solution *(solución)*
✔ term *(término)*
✔ variable *(variable)*

Preview Words

accuracy *(exactitud)*
literal equation *(ecuación literal)*
precision *(precisión)*
proportion *(proporción)*
ratio *(razón)*
scale model *(modelo a escala)*

Understand Vocabulary

To become familiar with some of the vocabulary terms in this unit, consider the following. You may refer to the module, the glossary, or a dictionary.

1. The level of detail of a measurement, determined by the unit of measure, is _____**precision**_____ .

2. A statement that two ratios are equal is called a _____**proportion**_____ .

3. A _____**ratio**_____ is a comparison of two quantities by division.

Active Reading

Two-Panel Flip Book Before beginning the lessons, create a two-panel flip chart to help you compare concepts in this unit. Label the flaps "Creating and Solving Equations" and "Creating and Solving Inequalities." As you study each lesson, write important ideas under the appropriate flap. Include any examples that will help you remember the concepts later when you look back at your notes.

Reading Start Up

Have students complete the activities on this page by working alone or with others.

VISUALIZE VOCABULARY

The four-square graphic helps students review vocabulary associated with expressions. If time allows, ask students to provide examples for the remaining vocabulary words.

UNDERSTAND VOCABULARY

Use the following explanations to help students learn the preview words.

> The **precision** of a measurement is the level of detail of a measurement determined by the unit of measure. **Accuracy** is the closeness of a given measurement or value to the actual measurement or value. A **scale model** uses a scale to represent an object as smaller or larger than the actual object. The scale is a **ratio,** which is a comparison of two quantities by division. A **proportion** is a statement that two ratios are equal.

ACTIVE READING

Students can use these reading and note-taking strategies to help them organize and understand the new concepts and vocabulary. Encourage them to ask for help when they encounter new vocabulary that seems unclear. Work together to connect new concepts with familiar terms. Suggest that students highlight examples that help them understand the vocabulary.

ADDITIONAL RESOURCES

Differentiated Instruction

- Reading Strategies **EL**

Quantitative Reasoning

ESSENTIAL QUESTION:

Answer: When the units are the same, you can use the rules of significant digits to calculate. When the units are different, you can convert them using dimensional analysis.

PROFESSIONAL DEVELOPMENT VIDEO

Professional Development Video

Learn effective ways of integrating technology into your classroom to meet a variety of different needs.

Professional
Development
my.hrw.com

MODULE 1

Quantitative Reasoning

Essential Question: How do you use quantitative reasoning to solve real-world problems?

LESSON 1.1
Solving Equations

LESSON 1.2
Modeling Quantities

LESSON 1.3
Reporting with Precision and Accuracy

© Houghton Mifflin Harcourt Publishing Company • Image Credits: Photodisc/Getty Images

REAL WORLD VIDEO
In order to function properly and safely, electronics must be manufactured to a high degree of precision. Material tolerances and component alignment must be precisely matched in order to not interfere with each other.

MODULE PERFORMANCE TASK PREVIEW

What an Impossible Score!

Darts is a game of skill in which small pointed darts are thrown at a circular target mounted on a wall. The target is divided into regions with different point values, and scoring depends on which segment the dart hits. Is there some score that is impossible to achieve no matter how many darts are thrown in a simple game of darts? Keep your eye on the target and let's figure it out!

Module 1   3

DIGITAL TEACHER EDITION

Access a full suite of teaching resources when and where you need them:

- Access content online or offline
- Customize lessons to share with your class
- Communicate with your students in real-time
- View student grades and data instantly to target your instruction where it is needed most

PERSONAL MATH TRAINER
Assessment and Intervention

Assign automatically graded homework, quizzes, tests, and intervention activities. Prepare your students with updated, Common Core-aligned practice tests.

Are YOU Ready?

Complete these exercises to review skills you will need for this module.

One-Step Equations

Example 1	Solve.

$$y - 11 = 7$$
$$y - 11 + 11 = 7 + 11$$

Isolate the variable by adding 11 to both sides of the equation.

$$y = 18$$

- Online Homework
- Hints and Help
- Extra Practice

Solve each equation.

1. $4x = 32$

$x = 8$

2. $9 + a = 23$

$a = 14$

3. $\frac{n}{3} = 16$

$n = 48$

Scale Factor and Scale Drawings

Example 2	Length of car: 132 in. Length of model of car: 11 in.

$$\frac{\text{model length}}{\text{actual length}} = \frac{11}{132}$$

Write a ratio using the given dimensions comparing the model length to the actual length.

$$= \frac{1}{12}$$

Simplify.

The scale factor is $\frac{1}{12}$.

Identify the scale factor.

4. Length of room: 144 in.
Length of room on scale drawing: 18 in.

$\frac{1}{8}$

5. Wingspan of airplane: 90 ft
Wingspan of model of airplane: 6 ft

$\frac{1}{15}$

Significant Digits

Example 3	Determine the number of significant digits in 37.05.

The significant digits in 37.05 are 3, 7, 0, and 5.

37.05 has 4 significant digits.

Significant digits are nonzero digits, zeros at the end of a number and to the right of a decimal point, and zeros between significant digits.

Determine the number of significant digits.

6. 0.0028

2

7. 970.0

4

8. 50,000

1

9. 4000.01

6

Are You Ready?

ASSESS READINESS

Use the assessment on this page to determine if students need strategic or intensive intervention for the module's prerequisite skills.

ASSESSMENT AND INTERVENTION

RtI Response to Intervention — TIER 1, TIER 2, TIER 3 SKILLS

Personal Math Trainer will automatically create a standards-based, personalized intervention assignment for your students, targeting each student's individual needs!

ADDITIONAL RESOURCES

See the table below for a full list of intervention resources available for this module.

Response to Intervention Resources also includes:

- Tier 2 Skill Pre-Tests for each Module
- Tier 2 Skill Post-Tests for each skill

Response to Intervention			Differentiated Instruction
Tier 1 Lesson Intervention Worksheets	**Tier 2** Strategic Intervention Skills Intervention Worksheets	**Tier 3** Intensive Intervention Worksheets available online	
Reteach 1.1 Reteach 1.2 Reteach 1.3	13 One-Step Equations 17 Scale Factor and Scale Drawings 19 Significant Digits 24 Writing Linear Equations	Building Block Skills 13, 19, 22, 23, 27, 52, 57, 77, 78, 79, 81, 92, 93, 95, 111	Challenge worksheets Extend the Math Lesson Activities in TE

Solving Equations

Common Core Math Standards

The student is expected to:

COMMON CORE **A-REI.A.1**

Explain each step in solving a simple equation... Construct a viable argument to justify a solution method. Also N-Q.A.2

Mathematical Practices

COMMON CORE **MP.7 Using Structure**

Language Objective

Explain to a partner the meaning of each Property of Equality.

ENGAGE

Essential Question: How do you solve an equation in one variable?

Apply the same inverse operation to each side of the equation to isolate the variable.

PREVIEW: LESSON PERFORMANCE TASK

View the Engage section online. Discuss what a company needs to consider when setting prices for the products they sell. Then preview the Lesson Performance Task.

1.1 Solving Equations

Essential Question: How do you solve an equation in one variable?

Resource Locker

Explore — Solving Equations by Guess-and-Check or by Working Backward

An **equation** is a mathematical sentence that uses the equal sign = to show two expressions are equivalent. The expressions can be numbers, variables, constants, or combinations thereof.

There are many ways to solve an equation. One way is by using a method called *guess-and-check*. A guess-and-check method involves guessing a value for the variable in an equation and checking to see if it is the solution by substituting the value in the equation. If the resulting equation is a true statement, then the value you guessed is the solution of the equation. If the equation is not a true statement, then you adjust the value of your guess and try again, continuing until you find the solution.

Another way to solve an equation is by *working backward*. In this method, you begin at the end and work backward toward the beginning.

Solve the equation $x - 6 = 4$ using both methods.

Use the *guess-and-check* method to find the solution of the equation $x - 6 = 4$.

(A) Guess 11 for x.

$$x - 6 = 4$$

$\boxed{11} - 6 \overset{?}{=} 4$

$\boxed{5} \overset{?}{=} 4$

Is 11 the solution

of $x - 6 = 4$? _____no_____

(B) The value 11 is too high.

Guess 10 for x.

$$x - 6 = 4$$

$\boxed{10} - 6 \overset{?}{=} 4$

$\boxed{4} \overset{?}{=} 4$

Is 10 the solution

of $x - 6 = 4$? _____yes_____

(C) Use the *working backward* method to find the solution of the equation $x - 6 = 4$.

$4 + 6 = \boxed{10}$ Is this the value of x before taking away 6?

$\boxed{10} - 6 \overset{?}{=} 4$ _____yes_____

Reflect

1. **Discussion** Which method of solving do you think is more efficient? Explain your answer.
   Using a guess-and-check method could take many guesses to find the solution. Working backward seems more efficient because it uses reasoning about the values.

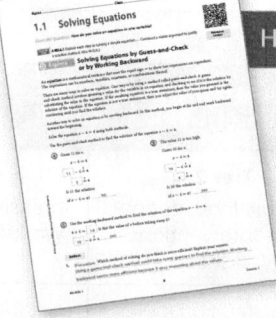

HARDCOVER PAGES 5–10

Turn to these pages to find this lesson in the hardcover student edition.

A **solution of an equation** is a value for the variable that makes the equation true. To determine the solution of an equation, you will use the Properties of Equality.

Properties of Equality		
Words	**Numbers**	**Algebra**
Addition Property of Equality You can add the same number to both sides of an equation, and the statement will still be true.	$3 = 3$ $3 + 2 = 3 + 2$ $5 = 5$	$a = b$ $a + c = b + c$
Subtraction Property of Equality You can subtract the same number from both sides of an equation, and the statement will still be true.	$7 = 7$ $7 - 5 = 7 - 5$ $2 = 2$	$a = b$ $a - c = b - c$
Multiplication Property of Equality You can multiply both sides of an equation by the same number, and the statement will still be true.	$3 = 3$ $3 \cdot 4 = 3 \cdot 4$ $12 = 12$	$a = b$ $a \cdot c = b \cdot c$
Division Property of Equality You can divide both sides of an equation by the same nonzero number, and the statement will still be true.	$15 = 15$ $\dfrac{15}{3} = \dfrac{15}{3}$ $5 = 5$	$a = b$ $\dfrac{a}{c} = \dfrac{b}{c}$, where $c \neq 0$

Example 1 Solve the equation by using Properties of Equality.

Ⓐ $3x - 2 = 6$

Use the Addition Property of Equality.	$3x - 2 + 2 = 6 + 2$
Combine like terms.	$3x = 8$
Now use the Division Property of Equality.	$\dfrac{3x}{3} = \dfrac{8}{3}$
Simplify.	$x = \dfrac{8}{3}$

Ⓑ $\frac{1}{2}z + 4 = 10$

Use the Subtraction Property of Equality.	$\frac{1}{2}z + 4 - \boxed{4} = 10 - \boxed{4}$
Combine like terms.	$\frac{1}{2}z = \boxed{6}$
Now use the Multiplication Property of Equality to multiply each side by 2.	$2 \cdot \frac{1}{2}z = 2 \cdot \boxed{6}$
Simplify.	$z = \boxed{12}$

PROFESSIONAL DEVELOPMENT

 Integrate Mathematical Practices

This lesson provides an opportunity to address Mathematical Practice **MP.7**, which calls for students to "look for structure" to connect and communicate mathematical ideas. Students must understand the relationships between inverse operations in order to solve equations. For example, to solve an equation involving addition, such as $x + 3 = 7$, students must recognize that they need to apply the Subtraction Property of Equality, because subtraction is the inverse of addition. Similarly, if an equation involves division, they must use multiplication, which is the inverse of division.

EXPLORE

Solving Equations by Guess-and-Check or by Working Backward

INTEGRATE MATHEMATICAL PRACTICES
Focus on Modeling

MP.4 Some students may benefit from using algebra tiles to model the equations in the Explore exercise and to verify their solutions.

QUESTIONING STRATEGIES

 When using the guess-and-check method to solve an equation, how do you adjust your guesses when your first guess is not correct? If your first guess is too great, pick a lesser number for the second guess. If your second guess is too small, pick a greater number for the third guess. Continue in this manner until you find the solution. Reverse the process if your first guess is too small.

EXPLAIN 1

Solving One-Variable Two-Step Equations

QUESTIONING STRATEGIES

What determines whether you use the Addition or Subtraction Property of Equality to solve an equation? If a number is added to the variable, you use the Subtraction Property. If a number is subtracted from the variable, you use the Addition Property.

AVOID COMMON ERRORS

When applying the Properties of Equality, students sometimes may use the operation in the equation instead of using the inverse operation. Have students practice first identifying the operation in the equation and then naming the inverse operation.

INTEGRATE MATHEMATICAL PRACTICES

Focus on Modeling

MP.4 Model the concept of solving an equation by showing students a two-pan balance with equal weight on both sides. Ask students what will happen if you add or subtract weight on one side only. Demonstrate that adding or removing weights on one side of the scale makes it unbalanced. Then ask students what will happen if you add or subtract the same amount of weight on *both* sides of the scale. Demonstrate this. Explain that equations are like balances. The two sides must be kept equal, so the same operation must be performed on both sides of the equation.

EXPLAIN 2

Solving Equations to Define a Unit

QUESTIONING STRATEGIES

? When writing an equation to solve a real-world problem, how do you decide what the variable will represent? **The variable represents the quantity you are trying to find.**

CONNECT VOCABULARY **EL**

Point out that the words *equation*, *equal*, *equality*, and *equivalent* all share the same root (*equ*) and they all have to do with being equal, or the same.

Reflect

2. **Discussion** What is the goal when solving a one-variable equation?
The goal is to obtain the value of the variable that makes the equation true.

Your Turn

Solve the equation by using Properties of Equality.

3. $5x - 10 = 20$

$$5x - 10 = 20$$
$$5x - 10 + 10 = 20 + 10$$
$$5x = 30$$
$$\frac{5x}{5} = \frac{30}{5}$$
$$x = 6$$

4. $\frac{1}{3}x + 9 = 21$

$$\frac{1}{3}x + 9 = 21$$
$$\frac{1}{3}x + 9 - 9 = 21 - 9$$
$$\frac{1}{3}x = 12$$
$$3 \cdot \left(\frac{1}{3}x\right) = 12 \cdot 3$$
$$x = 36$$

✪ Explain 2 Solving Equations to Define a Unit

One useful application of algebra is to use an equation to determine what a unit of measure represents. For instance, if a person uses the unit of time "score" in a speech and there is enough information given, you can solve an equation to find the quantity that a "score" represents.

Example 2 Solve an equation to determine the unknown quantity.

(A) In 1963, Dr. Martin Luther King, Jr., began his famous "I have a dream" speech with the words "Five score years ago, a great American, in whose symbolic shadow we stand, signed the Emancipation Proclamation." The proclamation was signed by President Abraham Lincoln in 1863. But how long is a score? We can use algebra to find the answer.

Let s represent the quantity (in years) represented by a score.

s = number of years in a score

Calculate the quantity in years after President Lincoln signed the Emancipation Proclamation.

$$1963 - 1863 = 100$$

Dr. Martin Luther King, Jr. used "five score" to describe this length of time. Write the equation that shows this relationship.

$$5s = 100$$

Use the Division Property of Equality to solve the equation.

$$\frac{5s}{5} = \frac{100}{5}$$
$$s = 20$$

A score equals 20 years.

COLLABORATIVE LEARNING

Peer-to-Peer Activity

Have students work in pairs to solve $4b - 6 = -10$. One student should add/subtract first, and the other student should multiply/divide first. They should discuss whether their solutions match.

Student 1: I added 6 first and then divided by 4. I found that $b = -1$.

Student 2: I divided by 4 first and then added 1.5 to each side. I also found that $b = -1$.

Ⓑ An airplane descends in altitude from 20,000 feet to 10,000 feet. A gauge at Radar Traffic Control reads that the airplane's altitude drops 1.8939 miles. How many feet are in a mile?

Let m represent the quantity (in feet) represented by a mile.

m = number of feet in a mile

Calculate the quantity in feet of the descent. $\qquad$ 20,000 − $\boxed{10,000}$ = $\boxed{10,000}$

A gauge described this quantity as 1.8939 miles. Write the equation that shows this relationship.

$$1.8939m = \boxed{10,000}$$

Use the Division Property of Equality to solve the equation. $\qquad \dfrac{1.8939m}{\boxed{1.8939}} = \dfrac{\boxed{10,000}}{\boxed{1.8939}}$

Round to the nearest foot. $\qquad m \approx \boxed{5280}$

There are 5280 feet in a mile.

Your Turn

Solve an equation to determine the unknown quantity.

5. An ostrich that is 108 inches tall is 20 inches taller than 4 times the height of a kiwi. What is the height of a kiwi in inches?

Let k = the height of a kiwi.

$108 = 20 + 4k$

$88 = 4k$

$22 = k$

The kiwi is 22 inches tall.

6. An emu that measures 60 inches in height is 70 inches less than 5 times the height of a kakapo. What is the height of a kakapo in inches?

Let k = the height of a kakapo.

$5k - 70 = 60$

$5k = 130$

$k = 26$

The kakapo is 26 inches tall.

Elaborate

7. How do you know which operation to perform first when solving an equation?
In general, you want to "undo" the operations in reverse order of the order of operations.

8. How can you create an equivalent equation by using the Properties of Equality?
Every time you apply the Properties of Equality, you are creating an equivalent equation.

9. When a problem involves more than one unit for a characteristic (such as length), how can you tell which unit is more appropriate to report the answer in?
Report the answer with a unit that is an appropriate size for the situation. For example, use kilometers instead of millimeters for the length of a road.

10. **Essential Question Check-In** Describe each step in a solution process for solving an equation in one variable.
1) Eliminate parentheses if necessary. 2) Combine like terms. 3) Apply the Properties of Equality to isolate the variable on one side of the equation.

ELABORATE

QUESTIONING STRATEGIES

❓ Do you usually add/subtract first or multiply/divide first when isolating a variable? Explain why this might be helpful. You usually add/subtract first, because these are simpler operations. When you multiply or divide, you have to distribute the factor or divisor over the whole equation. Division can also make later calculations more difficult when it creates fractions.

SUMMARIZE THE LESSON

❓ How do the Properties of Equality help you solve equations? The Properties of Equality say that performing any operation on one side of the equation, then performing the same operation on the other side, will always give you an equivalent equation. By doing this repeatedly, you can isolate the variable and find the solution.

DIFFERENTIATE INSTRUCTION

Critical Thinking

Have students create their own two-step equations by writing a simple equation and performing operations, one at a time, on both sides. For example:

$x = 3$

$x + 2 = 5$ Add 2.

$4(x + 2) = 20$ Multiply by 4.

Then have students solve their own two-step equations. They should work back to their original equations.

EVALUATE

ASSIGNMENT GUIDE

Concepts and Skills	Practice
Explore Solving Equations by Guess-and-Check or by Working Backward	Exercises 1–2
Example 1 Solving One-Variable Two-Step Equations	Exercises 3–17, 26
Example 2 Solving Equations to Define a Unit	Exercises 18–25, 27

9 Lesson 1.1

 Evaluate: Homework and Practice

• Online Homework
• Hints and Help
• Extra Practice

Student work will vary.

Use the *guess-and-check* method to find the solution of the equation. Show your work.

1. $2x + 5 = 19$

Guess 8 for x.	Guess 6 for x.	Guess 7 for x.
$2x + 5 = 19$	$2x + 5 = 19$	$2x + 5 = 19$
$2(8) + 5 \stackrel{?}{=} 19$	$2(6) + 5 \stackrel{?}{=} 19$	$2(7) + 5 \stackrel{?}{=} 19$
$21 \neq 19$	$17 \neq 19$	$19 = 19$
The value 8 is too high.	The value 6 is too low.	The value 7 is a solution.

Use the *working backward* method to find the solution of the equation. Show your work.   Student work will vary.

2. $4y - 1 = 7$

If you get 7 *after* taking away 1 from something, then it is $7 + 1 = 8$ *before* taking away 1. So $4y = 8$.

If multiplying 4 times a number is 8, then it is $\frac{1}{4}$ of 8, or $\frac{1}{4} \cdot 8 = 2$, before the multiplication. So $y = 2$. The value 2 is the solution of $4y - 1 = 7$.

Solve each equation using the Properties of Equality. Check your solutions.

3. $4a + 3 = 11$

$4a + 3 - 3 = 11 - 3$

$4a = 8$

$\dfrac{4a}{4} = \dfrac{8}{4}$

$a = 2$

4. $8 = 3r - 1$

$8 + 1 = 3r - 1 + 1$

$9 = 3r$

$\dfrac{9}{3} = \dfrac{3r}{3}$

$3 = r$

5. $42 = -2d + 6$

$42 - 6 = -2d + 6 - 6$

$36 = -2d$

$\dfrac{36}{-2} = \dfrac{-2d}{-2}$

$-18 = d$

6. $3x + 0.3 = 3.3$

$3x + 0.3 - 0.3 = 3.3 - 0.3$

$3x = 3$

$x = 1$

7. $15y + 31 = 61$

$15y + 31 - 31 = 61 - 31$

$15y = 30$

$\dfrac{15y}{15} = \dfrac{30}{15}$

$y = 2$

8. $9 - c = -13$

$9 - 9 - c = -13 - 9$

$-c = -22$

$\dfrac{-c}{-1} = \dfrac{-22}{-1}$

$c = 22$

LANGUAGE SUPPORT **EL**

Connect Context

Students may struggle with translating verbal descriptions into equations. Discuss some word problems, showing how each word or phrase corresponds to a term or symbol in the equation. For example, in the description "Angela's weight is 5 pounds more than 4 times the weight of her baby brother Hector," Angela's weight may be represented by the variable a, the word "is" may be represented by an equal sign, "5 pounds more than" can be written as "5 +," and "4 times the weight of … Hector" can be written as $4h$, to produce the equation $a = 5 + 4h$.

9. $\frac{x}{6} + 4 = 15$

$\frac{x}{6} + 4 - 4 = 15 - 4$

$\frac{x}{6} = 11$

$6\left(\frac{x}{6}\right) = 6(11)$

$x = 66$

10. $\frac{1}{3}y + \frac{1}{4} = \frac{5}{12}$

$\frac{1}{3}y + \frac{1}{4} - \frac{1}{4} = \frac{5}{12} - \frac{1}{4}$

$\frac{1}{3}y = \frac{5}{12} - \frac{3}{12}$

$\frac{1}{3}y = \frac{2}{12}$

$3\left(\frac{1}{3}y\right) = 3\left(\frac{2}{12}\right)$

$y = \frac{6}{12}$ or $\frac{1}{2}$

11. $\frac{2}{7}m - \frac{1}{7} = \frac{3}{14}$

$\frac{2}{7}m - \frac{1}{7} + \frac{1}{7} = \frac{3}{14} + \frac{1}{7}$

$\frac{2}{7}m = \frac{3}{14} + \frac{2}{14}$

$\frac{7}{2} \cdot \left(\frac{2}{7}m\right) = \frac{7}{2} \cdot \frac{5}{14}$

$m = \frac{35}{28}$ or $\frac{5}{4}$

12. $15 = \frac{a}{3} - 2$

$15 + 2 = \frac{a}{3} - 2 + 2$

$17 = \frac{a}{3}$

$3 \cdot 17 = 3 \cdot \frac{a}{3}$

$51 = a$

13. $4 - \frac{m}{2} = 10$

$4 - 4 - \frac{m}{2} = 10 - 4$

$-\frac{m}{2} = 6$

$-2 \cdot \left(-\frac{m}{2}\right) = (-2) \cdot 6$

$m = -12$

14. $\frac{x}{8} - \frac{1}{2} = 6$

$\frac{x}{8} - \frac{1}{2} + \frac{1}{2} = 6 + \frac{1}{2}$

$\frac{x}{8} = \frac{13}{2}$

$8 \cdot \frac{x}{8} = 8 \cdot \frac{13}{2}$

$x = 52$

Justify each step.

15. $2x - 5 = -20$

$2x = -15$ Addition Property of Equality

$x = -\frac{15}{2}$ Division Property of Equality

16. $\frac{x}{3} - 7 = 11$

$\frac{x}{3} = 18$ Addition Property of Equality

$x = 6$ Multiplication Property of Equality

17. $\frac{9x}{4} = -9$

$9x = -36$ Multiplication Property of Equality

$x = -4$ Division Property of Equality

INTEGRATE MATHEMATICAL PRACTICES

Focus on Modeling

MP.4 Choose one of the equations in the exercises and challenge students to come up with a real-world scenario that can be modeled by it.

Exercise	Depth of Knowledge (D.O.K.)	COMMON CORE Mathematical Practices	
1–2	**1** Recall of Information		**MP.5** Using Tools
3–14	**1** Recall of Information		**MP.3** Logic
15–17	**2** Skills/Concepts		**MP.3** Logic
18–24	**1** Recall of Information		**MP.4** Modeling
25–26	**2** Skills/Concepts	H.O.T.	**MP.2** Reasoning
27	**3** Strategic Thinking	H.O.T.	**MP.3** Logic

VISUAL CUES

Have students create a chart they can use as a reference for class work or homework.

When Solving Equations	
I see ...	I use ...
Addition	Subtraction
Subtraction	Addition
Multiplication	Division
Division	Multiplication

18. In 2003, the population of Zimbabwe was about 12.6 million people, which is 1 million more than 4 times the population in 1950. Write and solve an equation to find the approximate population p of Zimbabwe in 1950.

$$12.6 = 4p + 1$$

$$11.6 = 4p$$

$$\frac{11.6}{4} = p$$

$$2.9 = p$$

The population of Zimbabwe in 1950 was about 2.9 million people.

19. Julio is paid 1.4 times his normal hourly rate for each hour he works over 30 hours in a week. Last week he worked 35 hours and earned $436.60. Write and solve an equation to find Julio's normal hourly rate, r. Explain how you know that your answer is reasonable.

$$30r + 5(1.4r) = 436.6$$

$$30r + 7r = 436.6$$

$$37r = 436.6$$

$$r = 11.8$$

Julio's normal hourly rate is $11.80 per hour.

Working 35 hours at $12 per hour is 35 · 12 = 420, and $420 is close to $436.60.

20. The average weight of the top 5 fish caught at a fishing tournament was 12.3 pounds. Some of the weights of the fish are shown in the table.

Top 5 Fish	
Caught by	Weight (lb)
Wayne S.	14.6
Carla P.	12.8
Deb N.	12.6
Vincente R.	11.8
Armin G.	9.7

What was the weight of the heaviest fish?

$$\frac{x + 12.8 + 12.6 + 11.8 + 9.7}{5} = 12.3$$

$$x + 12.8 + 12.6 + 11.8 + 9.7 = 5 \cdot 12.3$$

$$x + 46.9 = 61.5$$

$$x = 14.6$$

The weight of the heaviest fish was 14.6 pounds.

© Houghton Mifflin Harcourt Publishing Company

21. Paul bought a student discount card for the bus. The card allows him to buy daily bus passes for $1.50. After one month, Paul bought 15 passes and spent a total of $29.50. How much did he spend on the student discount card?

Total Cost $= c +$ number of passes $\cdot$ price per pass, where c is the cost of the discount card

$$29.50 = c + 15 \cdot 1.50$$

$$29.5 = c + 22.5$$

$$7 = c$$

Paul spent $7 on the discount card.

22. Jennifer is saving money to buy a bike. The bike costs $245. She has $125 saved, and each week she adds $15 to her savings. How long will it take her to save enough money to buy the bike?

cost of bike $=$ amount saved $+$ weekly savings

$$245 = 125 + 15w$$

$$120 = 15w$$

$$8 = w$$

It will take her 8 weeks to save for the bike.

23. Astronomy The radius of Earth is 6378.1 km, which is 2981.1 km greater than the radius of Mars. Find the radius of Mars.

$$6378.1 = 2981.1 + r$$

$$6378.1 - 2981.1 = 2981.1 + r - 2981.1$$

$$3397 = r$$

So the radius of Mars is 3397 km.

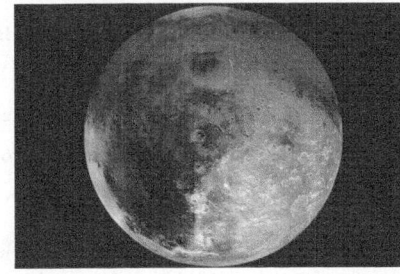

24. Maggie's brother is 3 years younger than twice her age. The sum of their ages is 24. How old is Maggie?

Let Maggie's age be x.

$$(2x - 3) + x = 24$$

$$3x - 3 = 24$$

$$3x = 27$$

$$x = 9$$

Maggie is 9 years old.

AVOID COMMON ERRORS

When checking their solutions, students should be sure to substitute the variable into the original equation, not into a version of the equation they manipulated while finding the solution.

JOURNAL

Have students explain how to solve a two-step equation. Students should write and solve a word problem as part of the explanation.

25. Analyze Relationships One angle of a triangle measures 120°. The other two angles are congruent. Write and solve an equation to find the measure of the congruent angles.

$$120 + x + x = 180$$
$$120 + 2x = 180$$
$$2x = 60$$
$$x = 30$$

The congruent angles each measure 30°.

26. Explain the Error Find the error in the solution, and then solve correctly.

$$9x + 18 + 3x = 1$$
$$9x + 18 = -2$$
$$9x = -20$$
$$x = -\frac{20}{9}$$

3x was subtracted from the left side, but 3 was subtracted from the right side. The Subtraction Property of Equality states that you can subtract the *same number* from each side and the equation will remain true. But 3x and 3 are not the same number (unless x is 1). The correct solution is shown.

$9x + 18 + 3x = 1$

$12x + 18 = 1$	Combine like terms.
$12x = -17$	Subtraction Property of Equality
$x = -\frac{17}{12}$	Division Property of Equality

27. Check for Reasonableness Marietta was given a raise of $0.75 per hour, which gave her a new wage of $12.25 per hour. Write and solve an equation to determine Marietta's hourly wage before her raise. Show that your answer is reasonable.

Student answers will vary.

$$x + 0.75 = 12.25$$
$$x + 0.75 - 0.75 = 12.25 - 0.75$$
$$x = 11.5$$

Marietta's hourly wage before the raise was $11.50.

Marietta received a raise that was less than $1.00 per hour, so her new hourly wage should be less than $11.50 + $1 = $12.50. Her new hourly wage of $12.25 is less than $12.50, so the answer is reasonable.

Lesson Performance Task

The formula $p = 8n - 30$ gives the profit p when a number of items n are each sold at $8 and expenses totaling $30 are subtracted.

a. If the profit is $170.00, how many items were bought?

b. If the same number of items were bought but the expenses changed to $40, would the profit increase or decrease, and by how much? Explain.

a. Solve the formula for n.

$$p = 8n - 30$$
$$170 = 8n - 30$$
$$170 + 30 = 8n - 30 + 30$$
$$200 = 8n$$
$$\frac{200}{8} = \frac{8n}{8}$$
$$25 = n$$

Therefore, 25 items were bought.

b. Use the number of items from part a along with the original formula, but change 30 to 40.

$$p = 8n - 40$$
$$p = 8(25) - 40$$
$$p = 200 - 40$$
$$p = 160$$

The profit would decrease by $10 to $160. Since the amount of the expenses is being increased, this takes money away from the profit.

Some students may not be familiar with the terms in the Lesson Performace Task. Have a student volunteer describe *profit* and *expenses*.

INTEGRATE MATHEMATICAL PRACTICES
Focus on Reasoning

MP.2 Some students may think that a business always makes a profit. Explain that p could equal 0 (no profit) or even a negative value (a loss) depending on the value of n. Ask: What values of n in the given formula would cause a loss? $n = 0, 1, 2,$ and 3, given that n must be a whole number. What values of n in the formula $p = 8n - 40$ would cause either no profit or a loss? When $n = 5$, there would be no profit. When $n = 0, 1, 2, 3,$ or 4, there would be a loss, given that n must be a whole number.

EXTENSION ACTIVITY

Have students create and analyze a two-column table of values for each of the following formulas: $p = 8n - 30$ and $p = 9n - 35$. In the left column of each table, list the values 0–10 for n. In the right column, write the corresponding values for p. Students will find that when $n = 5$ the value of p is the same for both formulas, $p = 10$. When $n < 5$, the value of p is greater for the first equation. But when $n > 5$, the value of p is greater for the second equation. Discuss what this means, namely that increasing both price per item and total expenses may result in lower profits (or greater losses) when few items are sold, but greater profits when more items are sold.

Scoring Rubric
2 points: Student correctly solves the problem and explains his/her reasoning.
1 point: Student shows good understanding of the problem but does not fully solve or explain his/her reasoning.
0 points: Student does not demonstrate understanding of the problem.

Solving Equations   **14**

Modeling Quantities

Common Core Math Standards

The student is expected to:

COMMON CORE N-Q.A.2

Define appropriate quantities for the purpose of descriptive modeling.
Also N-Q.A.1

Mathematical Practices

COMMON CORE MP.2 Reasoning

Language Objective

Demonstrate to a partner how to use dimensional analysis to convert a rate.

ENGAGE

Essential Question: How can you use rates, ratios, and proportions to solve real-world problems?

Rates, ratios, and proportions can be used to create scale drawings and models, convert measurements, determine lengths, etc.

PREVIEW: LESSON PERFORMANCE TASK

View the Engage section online. Discuss how a scale model of the Wright Flyer was designed by using proportions to determine the length and wingspan of the model, given the dimensions of the actual plane. Then preview the Lesson Performance Task.

Name _____ Class _____ Date _____

1.2 Modeling Quantities

Essential Question: How can you use rates, ratios, and proportions to solve real-world problems?

Resource Locker

🧭 Explore — Using Ratios and Proportions to Solve Problems

Ratios and *proportions* are very useful when solving real-world problems. A **ratio** is a comparison of two numbers by division. An equation that states that two ratios are equal is called a **proportion**.

A totem pole that is 90 feet tall casts a shadow that is 45 feet long. At the same time, a 6-foot-tall man casts a shadow that is x feet long.

The man and the totem pole are both perpendicular to the ground, so they form right angles with the ground. The sun shines at the same angle on both, so similar triangles are formed.

90 ft · 6 ft · 45 ft · x ft

(A) Write a ratio of the man's height to the totem pole's height. $\dfrac{6}{90}$

(B) Write a ratio of the man's shadow to the totem pole's shadow. $\dfrac{x}{45}$

(C) Write a proportion.

$$\frac{\text{man's height}}{\text{pole's height}} = \frac{\text{man's shadow}}{\text{pole's shadow}} \qquad \frac{6}{90} = \frac{x}{45}$$

(D) Solve the proportion by ___multiplying___ both sides by 45.

(E) Solve the proportion to find the length of the man's shadow in feet. $x = \boxed{3}$

Reflect

1. **Discussion** What is another ratio that could be written for this problem? Use it to write and solve a different proportion to find the length of the man's shadow in feet. **Answers may vary. Sample answer:**

$$\frac{\text{man's shadow}}{\text{man's height}} = \frac{\text{pole's shadow}}{\text{pole's height}} \qquad \frac{x}{6} = \frac{45}{90} \qquad x = 3$$

2. **Discussion** Explain why your new proportion and solution are valid.
The proportion and solution are valid because the corresponding side lengths are in the same position in both ratios, and the units are the same.

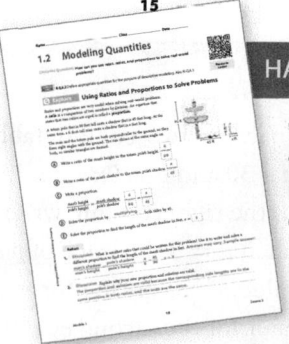

HARDCOVER PAGES 11–20

Turn to these pages to find this lesson in the hardcover student edition.

⚙ Explain 1　Using Scale Drawings and Models to Solve Problems

A **scale** is the ratio of any length in a *scale drawing* or *scale model* to the corresponding actual length. A drawing that uses a scale to represent an object as smaller or larger than the original object is a **scale drawing**. A three-dimensional model that uses a scale to represent an object as smaller or larger than the actual object is called a **scale model**.

Example 1　Use the map to answer the following questions.

(A)　The actual distance from Chicago to Evanston is 11.25 mi. What is the distance on the map?

Write the scale as a fraction.
$$\frac{\text{map} \to}{\text{actual} \to} \frac{1 \text{ in.}}{18 \text{ mi}}$$

Let d be the distance on the map.
$$\frac{1}{18} = \frac{d}{11.25}$$

Multiply both sides by 11.25.
$$\frac{11.25}{18} = d$$

$$0.625 = d$$

The distance on the map is about 0.625 in.

(B)　The actual distance between North Chicago and Waukegan is 4 mi. What is this distance on the map? Round to the nearest tenth.

Write the scale as a fraction.　　Let d be the distance on the map.　　Multiply both sides by 4.

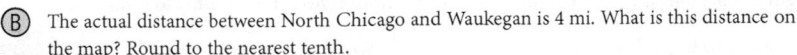

$$\frac{\text{map} \to}{\text{actual} \to} \quad \frac{1 \text{ in.}}{18 \text{ mi}} \qquad \frac{1}{18} = \frac{d}{4} \qquad \frac{4}{18} = d$$

$$0.2 \approx d$$

The distance on the map is about ___0.2___ in.

Your Turn

3.　A scale model of a human heart is 196 inches long. The scale is 32 to 1. How many inches long is the actual heart? Round your answer to the nearest whole number.

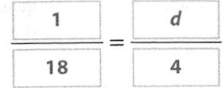

$$\frac{\text{actual} \to}{\text{model} \to} \frac{1}{32} \qquad \frac{1}{32} = \frac{\ell}{196} \qquad \frac{196}{32} = \ell \qquad 6 \approx \ell$$

The actual heart is about 6 inches long.

PROFESSIONAL DEVELOPMENT

Math Background

Dimensional analysis works because of the Multiplicative Identity Property. This property states that any number can be multiplied by 1 and maintain its value. In dimensional analysis, you are multiplying by a fraction whose numerator and denominator are equivalent amounts, such as 16 ounces and 1 pound. Whenever the numerator and denominator are equivalent, the fraction is equal to 1.

EXPLORE

Using Ratios and Proportions to Solve Problems

INTEGRATE TECHNOLOGY

Students have the option of completing the Explore Activity either in the book or online.

QUESTIONING STRATEGIES

?　When writing a proportion, how do you know which numbers should be the numerators of the ratios and which should be the denominators? The quantity or variable that is the numerator of one ratio must also be the numerator of the other. The quantity that is the denominator of one ratio must also be the denominator of the other. As long as both ratios are set up the same way, the proportion will be valid.

EXPLAIN 1

Using Scale Drawings and Models to Solve Problems

QUESTIONING STRATEGIES

?　When you solve a proportion, why is the equation still true even after multiplication is used on it? Both sides of the equation are multiplied by the same number, so the resulting equation is true by the Multiplication Property of Equality.

?　If the scale of a drawing is represented by a ratio greater than 1, what do you know about the actual object? The actual object is smaller than the drawing.

EXPLAIN 2

Using Dimensional Analysis to Convert Measurements

QUESTIONING STRATEGIES

? When setting up a conversion factor, do you put the given units in the numerator or in the denominator? Why? **The given units must be in the denominator so that when you multiply the measurement by the conversion factor, they cancel out.**

? How do you ensure that the result of your calculation is in the desired unit? **The desired unit must be in the numerator of the conversion factor, so that it remains when the given units cancel out.**

INTEGRATE MATHEMATICAL PRACTICES
Focus on Reasoning

MP.2 Tell students that the length of an American football field, including the end zones, is exactly 360 feet, and the width is 160 feet. Have students convert the measurements to meters. Ask them why customary units may be more appropriate to describe the dimensions of a football field. **The exact dimensions are whole numbers in customary units but decimals in metric units.**

⚙ Explain 2 **Using Dimensional Analysis to Convert Measurements**

Dimensional analysis is a method of manipulating unit measures algebraically to determine the proper units for a quantity computed algebraically. The comparison of two quantities with different units is called a **rate**. The ratio of two equal quantities, each measured in different units, is called a **conversion factor**.

Example 2 Use dimensional analysis to convert the measurements.

Ⓐ A large adult male human has about 12 pints of blood. Use dimensional analysis to convert this quantity to gallons.

Step 1 Convert pints to quarts.

Multiply by a conversion factor whose first quantity is quarts and whose second quantity is pints.

$$12 \text{ pt} \cdot \frac{1 \text{ qt}}{2 \text{ pt}} = 6 \text{ qt}$$

12 pints is 6 quarts.

Step 2 Convert quarts to gallons.

Multiply by a conversion factor whose first quantity is gallons and whose second quantity is quarts.

$$6 \text{ qt} \cdot \frac{1 \text{ gal}}{4 \text{ qt}} = \frac{6}{4} \text{ gal} = 1\frac{1}{2} \text{ gal}$$

A large adult male human has about $1\frac{1}{2}$ gallons of blood.

Ⓑ The length of a building is 720 in. Use dimensional analysis to convert this quantity to yards.

Step 1 Convert inches to feet.

Multiply by a conversion factor whose first quantity is feet and whose second quantity is inches.

$$720 \text{ in.} \cdot \frac{\boxed{1} \text{ ft}}{\boxed{12} \text{ in.}} = \boxed{60} \text{ ft}$$

720 inches is $\boxed{60}$ feet.

Step 2 Convert feet to yards.

Multiply by a conversion factor whose first quantity is yards and whose second quantity is feet.

$$\boxed{60} \text{ ft} \cdot \frac{\boxed{1} \text{ yd}}{\boxed{3} \text{ ft}} = \boxed{20} \text{ yd}$$

$\boxed{60}$ feet is $\boxed{20}$ yards.

Therefore, 720 inches is ___20___ yards.

Your Turn

Use dimensional analysis to convert the measurements. Round answers to the nearest tenth.

4. 7500 seconds ≈ ___2.1___ hours

$$7500 \text{ sec} \cdot \frac{1 \text{ min}}{60 \text{ sec}} = 125 \text{ min} \qquad 125 \text{ min} \cdot \frac{1 \text{ h}}{60 \text{ min}} \approx 2.1 \text{ h}$$

5. 3 feet ≈ ___0.9___ meters

$$3 \text{ ft} \cdot \frac{1 \text{ m}}{3.28 \text{ ft}} \approx 0.9 \text{ m}$$

6. 4 inches ≈ ___0.1___ yards

$$4 \text{ in.} \cdot \frac{1 \text{ ft}}{12 \text{ in.}} = \frac{1}{3} \text{ ft} \qquad \frac{1}{3} \text{ ft} \cdot \frac{1 \text{ yd}}{3 \text{ ft}} \approx 0.1 \text{ yd}$$

COLLABORATIVE LEARNING

Peer-to-Peer Activity

Have students work in pairs to find the solution for a rate conversion exercise by different methods. One student should arrive at the answer by converting the numerator first, and the other should convert the denominator first.

Use dimensional analysis to determine which rate is greater.

Example 3 During a cycling event for charity, Amanda traveled 105 kilometers in 4.2 hours and Brenda traveled at a rate of 0.2 mile per minute. Which girl traveled at a greater rate? Use 1 mi = 1.61 km.

Ⓐ Convert Amanda's rate to the same units as Brenda's rate. Set up conversion factors so that both kilometers and hours cancel.

$$\frac{x \text{ miles}}{\text{minute}} \approx \frac{105 \text{ km}}{4.2 \text{ h}} \cdot \frac{1 \text{ mi}}{1.61 \text{ km}} \cdot \frac{1 \text{ h}}{60 \text{ min}}$$

$$\approx \frac{105 \text{ mi}}{4.2 \cdot 1.61 \cdot 60 \text{ min}}$$

$$\approx 0.2588 \text{ mi/min}$$

Amanda traveled approximately 0.26 mi/min.

Amanda traveled faster than Brenda.

Ⓑ A box of books has a mass of 4.10 kilograms for every meter of its height. A box of magazines has a mass of 3 pounds for every foot of its height. Which box has a greater mass per unit of height? Use 1 lb = 0.45 kg and 1 m = 3.28 ft. Round your answer to the nearest tenth.

Convert the mass of the box of books to the same units as the mass of the box of magazines. Set up conversion factors so that both kilograms and pounds cancel.

$$\frac{x \text{ lb}}{\text{ft}} \approx \frac{4.10 \text{ kg}}{1 \text{ m}} \cdot \frac{\boxed{1} \text{ lb}}{\boxed{0.45} \text{ kg}} \cdot \frac{\boxed{1} \text{ m}}{\boxed{3.28} \text{ ft}} \approx \frac{\boxed{4.10} \text{ lb}}{\boxed{0.45 \cdot 3.28} \text{ ft}} \approx \boxed{2.8} \text{ lb/ft}$$

The box of ___magazines___ has a greater mass per unit of height.

Reflect

7. Why is it important to convert rates to the same units before comparing them?
When comparing rates that are in the same units, the numbers can easily be compared to see which number is greater. If the rates being compared are not in the same units, then an incorrect comparison may be made.

Your Turn

Use dimensional analysis to determine which rate is greater.

8. Alan's go-kart travels 1750 feet per minute, and Barry's go-kart travels 21 miles per hour. Whose go-kart travels faster? Round your answer to the nearest tenth.

$$\frac{x \text{ miles}}{\text{hour}} \approx \frac{1750 \text{ ft}}{\text{min}} \cdot \frac{1 \text{ mi}}{5280 \text{ ft}} \cdot \frac{1 \text{ min}}{0.017 \text{ h}} \approx \frac{1750 \text{ mi}}{5280 \cdot 0.017 \text{ h}} \approx 19.5 \text{ mi/h}$$

Alan's go-kart travels approximately 19.5 mi/h. Barry's go-kart travels faster than Alan's go-kart.

EXPLAIN 3

Using Dimensional Analysis to Convert and Compare Rates

QUESTIONING STRATEGIES

? Compare converting rates to converting single measurements. How are the processes similar? How are they different? **They are similar because you need conversion factors for both. They are different because in converting rates, you often have to convert units in both the numerator and denominator, so you must multiply by more than one conversion factor.**

INTEGRATE TECHNOLOGY

Have students use the conversion tools available in graphing calculators or online to verify their solutions.

DIFFERENTIATE INSTRUCTION

Modeling

Have students work in groups of two or three. Assign each group a ruler and a task of finding certain measurements, such as dimensions of the room, desks, tables, shelves, doors, and so on. Collect and present all measurements. Have students determine a scale that would let them draw a diagram of their classroom on a sheet of paper. Then have them use that scale to draw the diagram.

EXPLAIN 4

Graphing a Proportional Relationship

QUESTIONING STRATEGIES

? Why is it important to consider the situation in a real-world problem before choosing the scale for a graph? You need to know the range and magnitude of the numbers you are working with in order to produce a graph that will display all of the information you need.

AVOID COMMON ERRORS

Students sometimes label the scales in their graphs inaccurately, using increments that are not consistent. To avoid this error, they should check that the difference between each pair of equally-spaced numbers along an axis is the same. Note that the same scale does not need to be used for both axes.

⚙ Explain 4 **Graphing a Proportional Relationship**

To graph a proportional relationship, first find the unit rate, then create scales on the x- and y-axes and graph points.

Example 4 Simon sold candles to raise money for the school dance. He raised a total of $25.00 for selling 10 candles. Find the unit rate (amount earned per candle). Then graph the relationship.

Ⓐ Find the unit rate. $\dfrac{\text{Amount earned}}{\text{Candles sold}}$: $\dfrac{25}{10} = \dfrac{x}{1}$

$$2.5 = x$$

Simon's Earnings

The unit rate is $2.50 per candle.

Using this information, create scales on the x- and y-axes.

The x-axis will represent the candles sold, since this is the independent variable.

The y-axis will represent the amount earned, since this is the dependent variable.

The origin represents what happens when Simon sells 0 candles. The school gets $0.

Simon sold a total of 10 candles, so the x-axis will need to go from 0 to 10.

Since the school gets a total of $25 from Simon, the y-axis will need to go from 0 to 25.

Plot points on the graph to represent the amount of money the school earns for the different numbers of candles sold.

A local store sells 8 corn muffins for a total of $6.00. Find the unit rate. Then graph the points.

Ⓑ Find the unit rate. $\dfrac{\text{Amount earned}}{\text{Muffins sold}}$: $\dfrac{6}{8} = \dfrac{x}{1}$

$$\boxed{0.75} = x$$

The unit rate is $\underline{\$0.75}$ per muffin.

Using this information, create scales on the x- and y-axes.

The x-axis will represent the ___muffins being sold___, since this is the independent variable.

The y-axis will represent the ___earnings (in dollars)___, since this is the dependent variable.

The origin in this graph represents what happens when ___zero muffins are sold___

The x-axis will need to go from ___0___ to ___8___.

The y-axis will need to go from ___0___ to ___6___.

Plot points on the graph to represent the earnings from the different numbers of muffins sold.

Reflect

9. In Example 4A, Simon raised a total of $25.00 for selling 10 candles. If Simon raised $30.00 for selling 10 candles, would the unit rate be higher or lower? Explain.

   The unit rate would be $3.00 per candle instead of $2.50 per candle, so it would be higher.

LANGUAGE SUPPORT **EL**

Connect Vocabulary

Explain to students that dimensional analysis is a method of manipulating measurements, or dimensions, to find the desired units. Point out the word *analysis*. Note that analysis means carefully paying attention to everything in order to draw conclusions. In dimensional analysis, you are paying attention to all the units in order to draw a conclusion about how to convert the units.

Your Turn

Find the unit rate, create scales on the *x*- and *y*-axes, and then graph the function.

10. Alex drove 135 miles in 3 hours at a constant speed.

$$\frac{135}{3} = \frac{x}{1}$$

$$45 = x$$

Alex drove 45 mi/h.

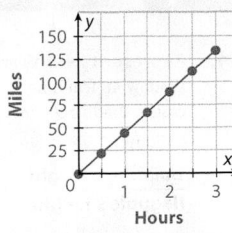

11. Max wrote 10 pages of his lab report in 4 hours.

Find the unit rate. $\quad \frac{10}{4} = \frac{x}{1}$

$$2.5 = x$$

Max wrote an average of 2.5 pages per hour.

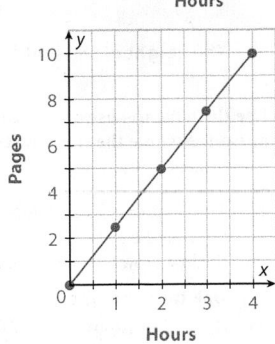

💬 Elaborate

12. Give three examples of proportions. How do you know they are proportions? Then give three nonexamples of proportions. How do you know they are not proportions?

$\frac{1}{2} = \frac{3}{6}; \frac{1}{4} = \frac{5}{20}; \frac{3}{7} = \frac{6}{14}$ In each case the ratio on the right side of the equal sign can be simplified to equal the ratio on the left side of the equal sign.

$\frac{1}{2} \neq \frac{5}{6}; \frac{1}{4} \neq \frac{6}{7}; \frac{3}{4} \neq \frac{2}{3}$ In each case the ratio on the right side of the equal sign can not be simplified to equal the ratio on the left side of the equal sign.

13. If a scale is represented by a ratio less than 1, what do we know about the actual object? If a scale is represented by a ratio greater than 1, what do we know about the actual object?

If a scale is represented by a ratio less than 1, then the actual object is larger than the model or drawing. If a scale is represented by a ratio greater than 1, then the actual object is smaller than the model or drawing.

14. How is dimensional analysis useful in calculations that involve measurements?

Dimensional analysis can be used to convert between different units and different measurement systems. This allows you to work with measurements in different units.

15. **Essential Question Check In** How is finding the unit rate helpful before graphing a proportional relationship?

Because the relationship is proportional, the unit rate makes is easy to find more points that will be on the graph.

© Houghton Mifflin Harcourt Publishing Company

ELABORATE

QUESTIONING STRATEGIES

? When using dimensional analysis, how do you know that the final answer is equal to the original measurement? You multiply by conversion factors whose numerator and denominator are equal, so that multiplying by the conversion factor is equivalent to multiplying by 1.

SUMMARIZE THE LESSON

? How can you use proportions to interpret a distance on a map? Set up a proportion that sets the scale of the map equal to the ratio of the map distance to the actual distance, then solve to find the actual distance.

? How do you choose and set up conversion factors correctly? Find equivalent units in a reference table or from memory. For each conversion factor, write equivalent quantities as the numerator and denominator of a fraction. Set up the conversion factors so that when you multiply them by the given measurement or rate, the given units will cancel out, leaving the desired units.

EVALUATE

Personal
Math
Trainer

ASSIGNMENT GUIDE

Concepts and Skills	Practice
Explore Using Ratios and Proportions to Solve Problems	Exercises 1–5
Example 1 Using Scale Drawings and Models to Solve Problems	Exercises 6–8
Example 2 Using Dimensional Analysis to Convert Measurements	Exercises 9–16, 24–25
Example 3 Using Dimensional Analysis to Convert and Compare Rates	Exercises 17–20
Example 4 Graphing a Proportional Relationship	Exercises 21–23, 26

QUESTIONING STRATEGIES

? How would you interpret a scale without any units, such as 18:1? **18 units of any measure on the actual object correspond to 1 unit of that same measure on the scale drawing or model.**

⭐ Evaluate: Homework and Practice

1. **Represent Real-World Problems** A building casts a shadow 48 feet long. At the same time, a 40-foot-tall flagpole casts a shadow 9.6 feet long. What is the height of the building?

   $\dfrac{\text{building's height}}{\text{flagpole's height}}$ $\dfrac{h}{40} = \dfrac{48}{9.6}$

   $h = 200$

   The height of the building is 200 ft.

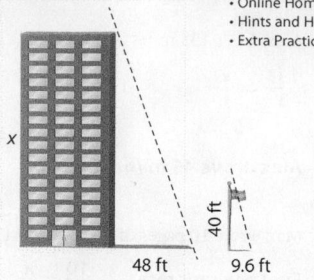

Use the table to answer questions 2–4. Select the best answer. Assume the shadow lengths were measured at the same time of day.

2. The flagpole casts an 8-foot shadow, as shown in the table. At the same time, the oak tree casts a 12-foot shadow. How tall is the oak tree?

   $\dfrac{\text{oak tree's height}}{\text{flagpole's height}}$ $\dfrac{t}{20} = \dfrac{12}{8}$

   $t = 30$

   The oak tree is 30 feet tall.

Object	Length of Shadow (ft)	Height (ft)
Flagpole	8	20
Oak tree	12	30
Goal post	18	45
Fence	2.6	6.5

3. How tall is the goal post?

   $\dfrac{\text{goal post's height}}{\text{flagpole's height}}$ $\dfrac{g}{20} = \dfrac{18}{8}$

   $g = 45$

   The goal post is 45 feet tall.

4. What is the length of the fence's shadow?

   $\dfrac{\text{fence's height}}{\text{flagpole's height}}$ $\dfrac{6.5}{20} = \dfrac{f}{8}$

   $f = 2.6$

   The fence's shadow is 2.6 feet long.

5. **Decorating** A particular shade of paint is made by mixing 5 parts red paint with 7 parts blue paint. To make this shade, Shannon mixed 12 quarts of blue paint with 8 quarts of red paint. Did Shannon mix the correct shade? Explain.

   No; $\dfrac{5}{7}$ is not proportional to $\dfrac{8}{12}$.

6. **Geography** The scale on a map of Virginia shows that 1 inch represents 30 miles. The actual distance from Richmond, VA, to Washington, D.C., is 110 miles. On the map, how many inches are between the two cities?

   $\dfrac{\text{map}}{\text{actual}}$ $\dfrac{1}{30} = \dfrac{d}{110}$ $3\dfrac{2}{3} = d$

   The distance on the map is $3\dfrac{2}{3}$ in.

7. Sam is building a model of an antique car. The scale of his model to the actual car is 1:10. His model is $18\dfrac{1}{2}$ inches long. How long is the actual car?

   $\dfrac{\text{model}}{\text{actual}}$ $\dfrac{18.5}{\ell} = \dfrac{1}{10}$ $\ell = 185$

   The length of the actual car is 185 inches.

Exercise	Depth of Knowledge (D.O.K.)	COMMON CORE Mathematical Practices
1–8	**1** Recall of Information	**MP.4** Modeling
9–12	**1** Recall of Information	**MP.2** Reasoning
13–16	**1** Recall of Information	**MP.4** Modeling
17–19	**1** Recall of Information	**MP.2** Reasoning
20	**1** Recall of Information	**MP.4** Modeling
21–23	**1** Recall of Information	**MP.4** Modeling

8. Archaeology Stonehenge II in Hunt, Texas, is a scale model of the ancient construction in Wiltshire, England. The scale of the model to the original is 3 to 5. The Altar Stone of the original construction is 4.9 meters tall. Write and solve a proportion to find the height of the model of the Altar Stone.

$$\frac{model}{actual}: \frac{3}{5} = \frac{h}{4.9} \quad 2.94 = h$$

The model is 2.94 meters high.

For 9–11, tell whether each scale *reduces*, *enlarges*, or *preserves* the size of an actual object.

9. 1 m to 25 cm

Reduces; 100 cm > 25 cm.

10. 8 in. to 1 ft

Enlarges; 8 in. < 12 in.

11. 12 in. to 1 ft

Preserves; 12 in. = 1 ft

12. Analyze Relationships When a measurement in inches is converted to centimeters, will the number of centimeters be greater or less than the number of inches? Explain.

greater than; Because centimeters are smaller than inches, it takes more centimeters to make the same length.

Use dimensional analysis to convert the measurements.

13. Convert 8 milliliters to fluid ounces. Use 1 mL ≈ 0.034 fl oz.

$$\frac{8\ mL}{1} \cdot \frac{0.034\ fl\ oz}{1\ mL} \approx 0.272\ fl\ oz$$

14. Convert 12 kilograms to pounds. Use 1 kg ≈ 2.2 lb.

$$\frac{12\ kg}{1} \cdot \frac{2.2\ lb}{1\ kg} \approx 26.4\ lb$$

15. Convert 950 US dollars to British pound sterling. Use 1 US dollar = 0.62 British pound sterling.

$$\frac{950\ dollars}{1} \cdot \frac{0.62\ pounds}{1\ dollar} = 589\ pounds$$

16. The dwarf sea horse *Hippocampus zosterae* swims at a rate of 52.68 feet per hour. Convert this speed to inches per minute.

The speed is 10.536 inches per minute.

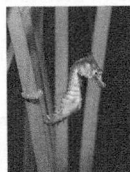

Use dimensional analysis to determine which rate is greater.

17. Tortoise A walks 52.0 feet per hour and tortoise B walks 12 inches per minute. Which tortoise travels faster? Explain.

$$\frac{x\ inches}{minute} = \frac{52\ ft}{1\ h} \cdot \frac{12\ in.}{1\ ft} \cdot \frac{1\ h}{60\ min} = \frac{52 \cdot 12\ in.}{60\ min} = 10.4\ in./min$$

Tortoise A travels at 10.4 in./min. Tortoise B travels faster than tortoise A.

18. The pitcher for the Robins throws a baseball at 90.0 miles per hour. The pitcher on the Bluebirds throws a baseball 121 feet per second. Which pitcher throws a baseball faster? Explain.

$$\frac{x\ miles}{hour} = \frac{121\ ft}{1\ sec} \cdot \frac{1\ mi}{5280\ ft} \cdot \frac{3600\ sec}{1\ h} = \frac{121 \cdot 3600\ mi}{5280\ h} = 82.5\ mi/h$$

The pitcher on the Robins throws a baseball faster.

© Houghton Mifflin Harcourt Publishing Company • Image Credits: (t) ©Stephen Saks Photography/Alamy; (b) ©Gregory G. Dimijian/Photo Researchers/Getty Images

Exercise	Depth of Knowledge (D.O.K.)	COMMON CORE Mathematical Practices
24	2 Skills/Concepts **H.O.T.**	**MP.2** Reasoning
25	3 Strategic Thinking **H.O.T.**	**MP.4** Modeling
26	3 Strategic Thinking **H.O.T.**	**MP.4** Modeling

MODELING

Have students form small groups and work together to create bar diagrams to help visualize the conversions between metric units and customary units. Have them make bar diagrams comparing meters to feet, kilometers to miles, and kilograms to pounds.

AVOID COMMON ERRORS

Some students might write conversion factors "upside down," reversing the numerator and denominator. Make sure students understand that conversion factors must be set up so that the units you are given cancel when you multiply, and you are left with the needed units.

19. For a science experiment Marcia dissolved 1.0 kilogram of salt in 3.0 liters of water. For a different experiment, Bobby dissolved 2.0 pounds of salt in 7.0 pints of water. Which person made a more concentrated salt solution? Explain. Use 1 L = 2.11 pints. Round your answer to the nearest hundredth.

Marcia's rate: $\frac{1}{3}$ kg/L = 0.33 kg/L

Bobby's rate: $\frac{x \text{ kg}}{\text{L}} = \frac{2 \text{ lb}}{7 \text{ pt}} \cdot \frac{2.11 \text{ pt}}{1 \text{ L}} \cdot \frac{1 \text{ kg}}{2.2 \text{ lb}} = \frac{2 \cdot 2.11 \text{ kg}}{7 \cdot 2.2 \text{ L}} \approx 0.27$ kg/L

Marcia made a more concentrated salt solution.

20. Will a stand that can hold up to 40 pounds support a 21-kilogram television? Explain. Use 2.2 lb = 1 kg.

$\frac{21 \text{ kg}}{1} \cdot \frac{2.2 \text{ lb}}{1 \text{ kg}} = 21 \cdot 2.2 \text{ lb} = 46.2 \text{ lb}$

No, the TV weighs more than 40 pounds.

Find the unit rate, create scales on the *x*- and *y*-axes, and then graph the function.

21. Brianna bought a total of 8 notebooks and got 16 free pens.

$\frac{\text{pens}}{\text{notebooks}}: \frac{16}{8} = \frac{x}{1}$

$2 = x$

The unit rate is 2 pens per noteboook.

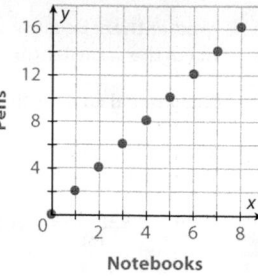

22. Mason sold 10 wristbands and made a total of 5 dollars.

$\frac{\text{dollars}}{\text{wristbands}}: \frac{5}{10} = \frac{x}{1}$

$0.5 = x$

The unit rate is $0.50 per wristband.

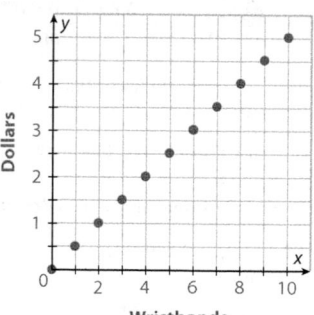

23. Match each graph to the data it goes with. Explain your reasoning.

A.

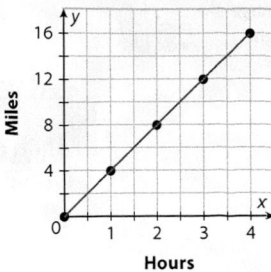

B.

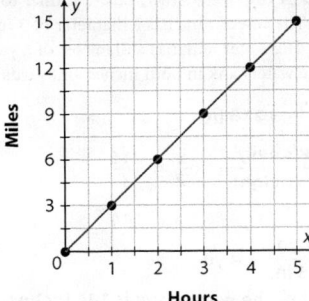

C.

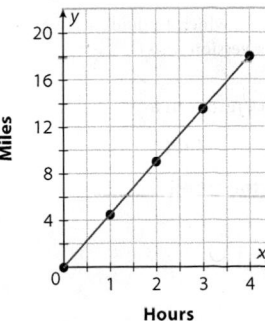

D.

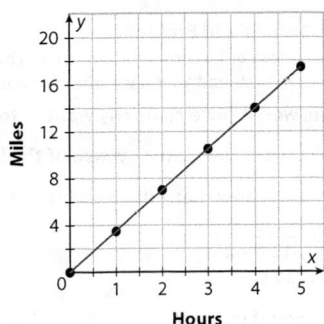

Mike walks 3 miles per hour for 5 hours.

Graph B because the *x*-axis goes to 5 and the unit rate is 3.

Brad walks 3.5 miles per hour for 5 hours.

Graph D because the *x*-axis goes to 5 and the unit rate is 3.5.

Jesse walks 4 miles per hour for 4 hours.

Graph A because the *x*-axis goes to 4 and the unit rate is 4.

Josh walks 4.5 miles per hour for 4 hours.

Graph C because the *x*-axis goes to 4 and the unit rate is 4.5.

Have students create conversion tables for measures of length, volume, weight, and mass, including both customary and metric units. Suggest that they copy these tables into their journals as reference.

24. Multi-Step A can of tuna has a shape similar to the shape of a large water tank. The can of tuna has a diameter of 3 inches and a height of 2 inches. The water tank has a diameter of 6 yards. What is the height of the water tank in both inches and yards?

$$6 \text{ yd} \cdot \frac{36 \text{ in.}}{1 \text{ yd}} = 216 \text{ in.}$$

$$\frac{\text{water tank's height}}{\text{tuna can's height}} \qquad \frac{x}{2} = \frac{216}{3}$$

$$x = 144$$

$$144 \text{ in.} \cdot \frac{1 \text{ yd}}{36 \text{ in.}} = 4 \text{ yd}$$

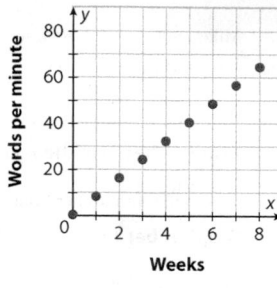

The height of the water tank is 144 inches, or 4 yards.

25. Represent Real-World Problems Write a real-world scenario in which 12 fluid ounces would need to be converted into liters. Then make the conversion. Use 1 fl oz = 0.0296 L. Round your answer to the nearest tenth.

Sample answer: A juice company wanted to sell one of its juices in a country that uses the metric system. If the bottle contains 12 fluid ounces of juice, how many liters should be indicated on the label?

$$\frac{0.0296 \text{ L}}{1 \text{ fl oz}} = \frac{x}{12 \text{ fl oz}}$$

$$0.3552 \text{ L} = x$$

The label should indicate 0.4 L.

26. Find the Error The graph shown was given to represent this problem. Find the error(s) in the graph and then create a correct graph to represent the problem.

Jamie took an 8-week keyboarding class. At the end of each week, she took a test to find the number of words she could type per minute and found out she improved the same amount each week. Before Jamie started the class, she could type 25 words per minute, and by the end of week 8, she could type 65 words per minute.

The first error is that there should not be a point at the origin. Before Jamie started the class, she could type 25 words per minute. Therefore, the first point should be at (0, 25). The second error is the unit rate. The unit rate shown on the graph is about 8 words per week. The correct unit rate should be 5 words per week.

$$\frac{65 - 25}{8} = \frac{x}{1}$$

$$5 = x$$

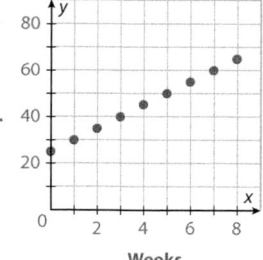

Lesson Performance Task

The Wright Flyer was the first successful powered aircraft. A model was made to display in a museum with the length of 35 cm and a wingspan of about 66.9 cm. The length of the actual plane was 21 ft 1 in., and the height was 2.74 m. Compare the length, height, and wingspan of the model to the actual plane and explain why any errors may occur. (Round any calculations to the nearest whole number.)

$$\frac{21 \text{ ft}}{1} \cdot \frac{12 \text{ in.}}{1 \text{ ft}} = 252 \text{ in.}$$

$$252 \text{ in.} + 1 \text{ in.} = 253 \text{ in.}$$

$$\frac{253 \text{ in.}}{1} \cdot \frac{2.54 \text{ cm}}{1 \text{ in.}} \approx 643 \text{ cm}$$

So, the length of the actual plane is about 643 cm.

$$\frac{2.74 \text{ m}}{1} \cdot \frac{100 \text{ cm}}{1 \text{ m}} = 274 \text{ cm}$$

So, the height of the actual plane is 274 cm.

$$\frac{\text{model's length}}{\text{plane's length}} = \frac{\text{model's height}}{\text{plane's height}}$$

$$\frac{35}{643} = \frac{h}{274}$$

$$274 \cdot \frac{35}{643} = h$$

$$15 \approx h$$

So, the height of the model is about 15 cm.

$$\frac{\text{plane's length}}{\text{model's length}} = \frac{\text{plane's wingspan}}{\text{model's wingspan}}$$

$$\frac{643}{35} = \frac{w}{66.9}$$

$$66.9 \cdot \frac{643}{35} = w$$

$$1229 \approx w$$

The wingspan of the actual plane is about 1229 cm.

$$\frac{\text{model's height}}{\text{plane's height}} = \frac{\text{model's length}}{\text{plane's length}} = \frac{\text{model's wingspan}}{\text{plane's wingspan}}$$

$$\frac{15}{274} = \frac{35}{643} = \frac{66.9}{1229}$$

When you do the calculations of each fraction, you get about 0.05. The slight error that occurs in any position after the hundredths place is most likely due to rounding issues.

© Houghton Mifflin Harcourt Publishing Company

LANGUAGE SUPPORT EL

The word *model* has multiple meanings in English. Ask students to suggest different ways that it can be used. Explain that in a mathematical context, *model* can be used either as a noun or as a verb (to construct a model), and it can refer both to physical copies, such as a model airplane, and to conceptual representations, such as equations. Students may also point out that a model can be a person who displays clothes in the fashion industry, or a verb describing what a fashion model does.

INTEGRATE MATHEMATICAL PRACTICES
Focus on Modeling

MP.4 The symbol $\approx$ stands for "is approximately equal to." This symbol is often used in expressing irrational numbers or in giving a rounded result of a computation. It should not be confused with, or used interchangeably with, the symbols $\sim$ (is similar to) and $\cong$ (is congruent to), which are used in discussing geometric figures. Point out that a statement such as "$h \approx 15$ cm" must be read as "the height is *about* fifteen centimeters" or "the height is *approximately* fifteen centimeters," not "the height is equal to fifteen centimeters."

EXTENSION ACTIVITY

Have students research the dimensions of a large object that interests them, such as a modern airplane, a skyscraper, or a dinosaur. Then have them calculate the dimensions of a model of the object on the same scale as the Wright Flyer model. Compile class results to compare the sizes of all the models, and discuss whether it would be practical to display them in the classroom. If time permits, have students work together to determine a new scale that would enable them to make scale drawings of all the objects on poster board. Have them make posters with drawings at that scale.

Reporting with Precision and Accuracy

Common Core Standards

The student is expected to:

COMMON CORE N-Q.A.3

Choose a level of accuracy appropriate to limitations on measurement when reporting quantities. Also N-Q.A.1

Mathematical Practices

COMMON CORE MP.5 Using Tools

Language Objective

Show how to determine how many significant digits to report in the results of measurement calculations, such as finding perimeter and area.

ENGAGE

Essential Question: How do you use significant digits when reporting the results of calculations involving measurement?

You use the place value of the last significant digit in the least precise measurement to report a sum or difference. You use the number of significant digits in the least precise measurement to report a product or quotient.

PREVIEW: LESSON PERFORMANCE TASK

View the Engage section online. Discuss how you can find the amount of electricity produced by a field of solar panels if you know how much is produced by one square foot of solar panel. Then preview the Lesson Performance Task.

Name_____ Class_____ Date_____

1.3 Reporting with Precision and Accuracy

Resource Locker

Essential Question: How do you use significant digits when reporting the results of calculations involving measurement?

🧭 Explore   Comparing Precision of Measurements

Numbers are values without units. They can be used to compute or to describe measurements. Quantities are real-word values that represent specific amounts. For instance, 15 is a number, but 15 grams is a quantity.

Precision is the level of detail of a measurement, determined by the smallest unit or fraction of a unit that can be reasonably measured.

Accuracy is the closeness of a given measurement or value to the actual measurement or value. Suppose you know the actual measure of a quantity, and someone else measures it. You can find the accuracy of the measurement by finding the absolute value of the difference of the two.

(A) Complete the table to choose the more precise measurement.

Measurement 1	Measurement 2	Smaller Unit	More Precise Measurement
4 g	4.3 g	0.1 g	4.3 g
5.71 oz	5.7 oz	0.01 oz	5.71 oz
4.2 m	422 cm	1 cm	422 cm
7 ft 2 in.	7.2 in.	0.1 in.	7.2 in.

(B) Eric is a lab technician. Every week, he needs to test the scales in the lab to make sure that they are accurate. He uses a standard mass that is exactly 8.000 grams and gets the following results.

Scale	Mass
Scale 1	8.02 g
Scale 2	7.9 g
Scale 3	8.029 g

Scale 1   Scale 2   Scale 3

Complete each statement:

The measurement for Scale ___3___ is the most precise

because it measures to the nearest ___0.001 g___, which is smaller than the smallest unit measured on the other two scales.

HARDCOVER PAGES 21–30

Turn to these pages to find this lesson in the hardcover student edition.

Ⓒ Find the accuracy of each of the measurements in Step B.

Scale 1: Accuracy = $\left| 8.000 - \underline{8.02} \right| = \underline{0.02}$

Scale 2: Accuracy = $\left| 8.000 - \underline{7.9} \right| = \underline{0.1}$

Scale 3: Accuracy = $\left| 8.000 - \underline{8.029} \right| = \underline{0.029}$

Complete each statement: the measurement for Scale __1__, which is __8.02__ grams, is the most accurate because __$0.02 < 0.029 < 0.1$__.

Reflect

1. **Discussion** Given two measurements of the same quantity, is it possible that the more precise measurement is not the more accurate? Why do you think that is so?
   Yes. Possible answer: An electronic measuring device may not be functioning properly, or a device such as a ruler may not have been produced carefully. The person making the measurement may have made a mistake.

⊘ Explain 1 Determining Precision of Calculated Measurements

As you have seen, measurements are reported to a certain precision. The reported value does not necessarily represent the actual value of the measurement. When you measure to the nearest unit, the actual length can be 0.5 unit less than the measured length or less than 0.5 unit greater than the measured length. So, a length reported as 4.5 centimeters could actually be anywhere between 4.45 centimeters and 4.55 centimeters, but not including 4.55 centimeters. It cannot include 4.55 centimeters because 4.55 centimeters reported to the nearest tenth would round *up* to 4.6 centimeters.

Example 1 Calculate the minimum and maximum possible areas. Round your answers to the nearest square centimeter.

Ⓐ The length and width of a book cover are 28.3 centimeters and 21 centimeters, respectively.

Find the range of values for the actual length and width of the book cover.

Minimum length = $(28.3 - 0.05)$ cm and maximum length = $(28.3 + 0.05)$ cm, so 28.25 cm $\leq$ length < 28.35 cm.

Minimum width = $(21 - 0.5)$ cm and maximum width = $(21 + 0.5)$ cm, so 20.5 cm $\leq$ width < 21.5 cm.

Find the minimum and maximum areas.

Minimum area = minimum length · minimum width

$\qquad$ = 28.25 cm · 20.5 cm ≈ 579 cm^2

Maximum area = maximum length · maximum width

$\qquad$ = 28.35 cm · 21.5 cm ≈ 610 cm^2

So 579 cm^2 $\leq$ area < 610 cm^2.

© Houghton Mifflin Harcourt Publishing Company

PROFESSIONAL DEVELOPMENT

 Integrate Mathematical Practices

This lesson provides an opportunity to address Mathematical Practice **MP.5**, which calls for students to "use tools." By understanding that the measuring tools which measure to the smallest increment are the most precise, while those that provide measurements closest to the actual value are the most accurate, students learn how to select the most precise or most accurate measuring tools for an application.

Comparing Precision of Measurements

AVOID COMMON ERRORS

Students may expect a measurement written with a smaller unit to be more precise than one written with a larger unit, but this is not necessarily true. For example, 0.025 m is more precise than 3 cm because 0.025 m is a measurement to the nearest 0.001 m and 3 cm is a measurement to the nearest 0.01 m.

QUESTIONING STRATEGIES

? Is a more precise measurement always a more accurate measurement? Explain. No; a measurement could be very precise (specified to a very small unit) but still be inaccurate (not close to the actual value of the quantity being measured).

EXPLAIN 1

Determining Precision of Calculated Measurements

QUESTIONING STRATEGIES

? How do you find the minimum and maximum possible values for the actual length of an object, given a measurement to the nearest unit? Add and subtract half of the measured unit.

? Would you get a more precise value for the area of a painting if you measured its dimensions in inches or in centimeters? Explain. Centimeters; a centimeter is smaller than an inch, so the range of possible values for the length and width measurements would be smaller, and as a result the range of possible values for the area would be smaller.

Ⓑ The length and width of a rectangle are 15.5 centimeters and 10 centimeters, respectively.

Find the range of values for the actual length and width of the rectangle.

Minimum length $= (15.5 - \underline{0.05})$ cm and maximum length $= (15.5 + \underline{0.05})$ cm,

so $\underline{15.45} \leq$ length $< \underline{15.55}$.

Minimum width $= (10 - \underline{0.5})$ cm and maximum width $= (10 + \underline{0.5})$ cm,

so $\underline{9.5} \leq$ width $< \underline{10.5}$.

Find the minimum and maximum areas.

Minimum area = minimum length · minimum width

$$= \underline{15.45} \text{ cm} \cdot \underline{9.5} \text{ cm} \approx \underline{147} \text{ cm}^2$$

Maximum area = maximum length · maximum width

$$= \underline{15.55} \text{ cm} \cdot \underline{10.5} \text{ cm} \approx \underline{163} \text{ cm}^2$$

So $\underline{147}$ cm$^2 \leq$ area $< \underline{163}$ cm^2.

Reflect

2. How do the ranges of the lengths and widths of the books compare to the range of the areas? What does that mean in terms of the uncertainty of the dimensions?

The range of the areas is much greater than the range of both the length and the width.

The uncertainty in the length and width results in much greater uncertainty in the area.

Your Turn

Calculate the minimum and maximum possible areas. Round your answers to the nearest whole square unit.

3. Sara wants to paint a wall. The length and width of the wall are 2 meters and 1.4 meters, respectively.

   1.5 m $\leq$ length $<$ 2.5 m

   1.35 m $\leq$ width $<$ 1.45 m

   Minimum area $= 1.35$ m $\cdot 1.5$ m ≈ 2 m^2

   Maximum area $= 1.45$ m $\cdot 2.5$ m ≈ 4 m^2

   So 2 m$^2 \leq$ area $<$ 4 m^2.

4. A rectangular garden plot measures 15 feet by 22.7 feet.

   22.65 ft $\leq$ length $<$ 22.75 ft

   14.5 ft $\leq$ width $<$ 15.5 ft

   Minimum area $= 14.5$ ft $\cdot 22.65$ ft ≈ 328 ft^2

   Maximum area $= 15.5$ ft $\cdot 22.75$ ft ≈ 353 ft^2

   So 328 ft$^2 \leq$ area $<$ 353 ft^2.

COLLABORATIVE LEARNING

Peer-to-Peer Activity

Have students work in pairs to find the number of significant digits in 0.0070. One student should find the number of significant digits directly and the other should find the number of non-significant digits and subtract them from the total digits.

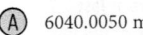

Significant digits are the digits in measurements that carry meaning about the precision of the measurement.

Identifying Significant Digits	
Rule	**Examples**
All nonzero digits are significant.	55.98 has 4 significant digits.
	115 has 3 significant digits.
Zeros between two other significant digits are significant.	102 has 3 significant digits.
	0.4000008 has 7 significant digits.
Zeros at the end of a number to the right of a decimal point are significant.	3.900 has 4 significant digits.
	0.1230 has 4 significant digits.
Zeros to the left of the first nonzero digit in a decimal are *not* significant.	0.00035 has 2 significant digits.
	0.0806 has 3 significant digits.
Zeros at the end of a number without a decimal point are assumed to be *not* significant.	60,600 has 3 significant digits.
	77,000,000 has 2 significant digits.

Example 2   Determine the number of significant digits in a given measurement.

Ⓐ 6040.0050 m

Significant Digits Rule	Digits	Count
Nonzero digits:	⑥0④0.00⑤0	3
Zeros between two significant digits:	6⓪4⓪.0⓪50	4
End zeros to the right of a decimal:	6040.005⓪	1
	Total	8

So, 6040.0050 m has 8 significant digits.

Ⓑ 710.080 cm

Significant Digits Rule	Digits	Count
Nonzero digits:	⑦①0.0⑧0	3
Zeros between two significant digits:	71⓪.⓪80	2
End zeros to the right of a decimal:	710.08⓪	1
	Total	6

710.080 cm has _____6_____ significant digit(s).

EXPLAIN 2

Identifying Significant Digits

INTEGRATE MATHEMATICAL PRACTICES
Focus on Math Connections

MP.1 Point out that significant digits relate to precision. If two measurements of the same quantity are in the same units, the more precise measurement will have more significant digits. For example, 800.258 m, with six significant digits, is more precise than 800.3 m, with four significant digits.

QUESTIONING STRATEGIES

? Why is the first step in identifying significant digits to identify the nonzero digits? **All nonzero digits are significant. To determine whether a zero is significant, you look at its position relative to the nonzero digits.**

EXPLAIN 3

Using Significant Digits in Calculated Measurements

QUESTIONING STRATEGIES

? If you want to calculate the area of a figure to three significant digits, what must be true about the measurements of the figure's dimensions? Why? **Each measurement must be precise enough to have at least three significant digits. Calculating the area involves multiplying the dimensions, and the product may not have more significant digits than the factors.**

5. Critique Reasoning A student claimed that 0.045 and 0.0045 m have the same number of significant digits. Do you agree or disagree?
Agree. Zeros to the right of the decimal point only count as significant digits if they are either to the right of the last nonzero digit or between other significant digits.

Your Turn

Determine the number of significant digits in each measurement.

6. 0.052 kg **two**   **7.** 10,000 ft **one**   **8.** 10.000 ft **five**

⚙ Explain 3 Using Significant Digits in Calculated Measurements

When performing calculations with measurements of different precision, the number of significant digits in the solution may differ from the number of significant digits in the original measurements. Use the rules from the following table to determine how many significant digits to include in the result of a calculation.

Rules for Significant Digits in Calculated Measurements	
Operation	**Rule**
Addition or Subtraction	The sum or difference must be rounded to the same place value as last significant digit of the least precise measurement.
Multiplication or Division	The product or quotient must have no more significant digits than the least precise measurement.

Example 3 Find the perimeter and area of the given object. Make sure your answers have the correct number of significant digits.

Ⓐ A rectangular swimming pool measures 22.3 feet by 75 feet.

Find the perimeter of the swimming pool using the correct number of significant digits.

$$\text{Perimeter} = \text{sum of side lengths}$$
$$= 22.3 \text{ ft} + 75 \text{ ft} + 22.3 \text{ ft} + 75 \text{ ft}$$
$$= 194.6 \text{ ft}$$

The least precise measurement is 75 feet. Its last significant digit is in the ones place. So round the sum to the ones place. The perimeter is 195 ft.

Find the area of the swimming pool using the correct number of significant digits.

$$\text{Area} = \text{length} \cdot \text{width}$$
$$= 22.3 \text{ ft} \cdot 75 \text{ ft} = 1672.5 \text{ ft}^2$$

The least precise measurement, 75 feet, has two significant digits, so round the product to a number with two significant digits. The area is 1700 ft².

Ⓑ A rectangular garden plot measures 21 feet by 25.2 feet.

Find the perimeter of the garden using the correct number of significant digits.

Perimeter = sum of side lengths

= | 21 ft | + | 25.2 ft | + | 21 ft | + | 25.2 ft | = | 92.4 ft |

The least precise measurement is ___21 ft___. Its last significant digit is in the ones place. So round the sum

to the ___ones___ place. The perimeter is ___92 ft___.

Find the area of the garden using the correct number of significant digits.

Area = length · width

= | 21 ft | · | 25.2 ft | = | 529.2 ft² |

The least precise measurement, ___21 ft,___ has ___2___ significant digit(s), so round to a number with

___2___ significant digit(s). The area is ___530 ft²___.

Reflect

9. In the example, why did the area of the garden and the swimming pool each have two significant digits?
In each example, the least precise dimension had two significant digits.

10. Is it possible for the perimeter of a rectangular garden to have more significant digits than its length or width does?
Yes. For example, if the width were 13 ft and the length were 501 ft, the perimeter would

be 1028 ft, and 1028 has 4 significant digits.

Your Turn

Find the perimeter and area of the given object. Make sure your answers have the correct number of significant digits.

11. A children's sandbox measures 7.6 feet by 8.25 feet.
Perimeter = 7.6 ft + 8.25 ft + 7.6 ft + 8.25 ft = 31.7 ft. The perimeter is 31.7 ft.

Area = 7.6 ft · 8.25 ft = 62.7 ft². The area is 63 ft².

12. A rectangular door measures 91 centimeters by 203.2 centimeters.
Perimeter = 91 cm + 203.2 cm + 91 cm + 203.2 cm = 588.4 cm. The perimeter is 588 cm.

Area = 91 cm · 203.2 ft = 18,491.2 cm². The area is 18,000 cm².

AVOID COMMON ERRORS

Students often confuse the rules for significant digits in calculations involving addition or subtraction with those for multiplication or division. The *number* of significant digits only matters when multiplying or dividing. One way to recognize that sums must instead be rounded by place value is to vertically align the numbers to be added. The rounded result should not have any nonzero digits in places to the right of the last significant digit of an addend. The same rule applies for subtraction.

DIFFERENTIATE INSTRUCTION

Critical Thinking

Explain that it is sometimes useful to describe the precision of a measurement by finding the possible error as a percentage. For example, a measurement of 4 cm could represent an actual length ranging from 3.5 cm to 4.5 cm. Since 0.5 cm is 12.5% of 4 cm, the measurement has a possible error of ±12.5%. On the other hand, a measurement of 1004 cm has a possible error of only ±0.05%, since 0.5 cm is only 0.05% of 1004 cm. This difference in percent error reflects the fact that the same absolute error (0.5 cm) matters more when measuring a small object than when measuring a large object.

Reporting with Precision and Accuracy   **32**

EXPLAIN 4

Using Significant Digits in Estimation

AVOID COMMON ERRORS

When estimating, students may apply the rules for significant digits in calculated measurements to the original numbers instead of the rounded numbers. The rules should be applied to whichever numbers are actually used in the calculation.

QUESTIONING STRATEGIES

? If you are given several numbers to add, some of which are rounded to the nearest thousand, does it make sense to give an answer to the nearest whole number? Explain. **No, that would be too much precision. Since some of the addends have already been rounded, the final answer should also be rounded.**

 **Explain 4** **Using Significant Digits in Estimation**

Real-world situations often involve estimation. Significant digits play an important role in making reasonable estimates.

> A city is planning a classic car show. A section of road 820 feet long will be closed to provide a space to display the cars in a row. In past shows, the longest car was 18.36 feet long and the shortest car was 15.1 feet long. Based on that information, about how many cars can be displayed in this year's show?

Analyze Information

- Available space: **820 feet**
- Length of the longest car: **18.36 feet**
- Length of the shortest car: **15.1 feet**

Formulate a Plan

The word *about* indicates that your answer will be a(n) **estimate**.

$$\text{Available Space} = \text{Number of Cars} \cdot \underline{\text{Length of Car}}$$

Find the number of longest cars and the number of shortest cars, and then use the average.

Solve

Longest:

$$820 = L \cdot \boxed{18.36}$$

$$L = \frac{820}{\boxed{18.36}} \approx \boxed{45}$$

Shortest:

$$820 = S \cdot \boxed{15.1}$$

$$S = \frac{820}{\boxed{15.1}} \approx \boxed{54}$$

To find a numerical estimate for the number of cars, average the two estimates.

$$\text{Number of cars} = \frac{L + S}{2} = \frac{\boxed{45} + \boxed{54}}{2} \approx \boxed{50}$$

So, on average, **50** cars can be displayed.

Justify and Evaluate

Because the cars will probably have many different lengths, a reasonable estimate is a whole number between **estimates of S and L**.

13. In the example, why wouldn't it be wise to use the length of a shorter car?

Using the length of a shorter car creates

a risk of overestimating the number of

cars that will fit.

14. Critical Thinking How else might the number of cars be estimated? Would you expect the estimate to be the same? Explain.

Sample answer: The average length of the

shortest and longest cars could be used.

It is unlikely any two methods would

produce exactly the same estimate.

Your Turn

Estimate the quantity needed in the following situations. Use the correct number of significant digits.

15. Claire and Juan are decorating a rectangular wall of 433 square feet with two types of rectangular pieces of fabric. One type has an area of 9.4 square feet and the other has an area of 17.2 square feet. About how many decorative pieces can Claire and Juan fit in the given area?

Larger: $\frac{433}{17.2} = 25.174$, or about 25

Smaller: $\frac{433}{9.4} = 46.064$, or about 46

Estimate: $\frac{25 + 46}{2} = 35.5$, or about 36

16. An artist is making a mosaic and has pieces of smooth glass ranging in area from 0.25 square inch to 3.75 square inches. Suppose the mosaic is 34.1 inches wide and 50.0 inches long. About how many pieces of glass will the artist need?

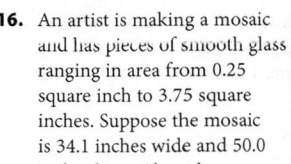

The area of the mosaic is 34.1 · 50.0, or 1705 in².

Larger: $\frac{1705}{3.75} = 454.667$, or about 450

Smaller: $\frac{1705}{0.25} = 6820$, or about 6800

Estimate: $\frac{450 + 6{,}800}{2} = 3625$, or about 3600

💬 Elaborate

17. Given two measurements, is it possible that the more accurate measurement is not the more precise? Justify your answer.

Yes. Sample answer: Suppose two friends measure a bench. One says the bench is

1.25 meters long, and the other says it is 1.5 meters long. If the bench is actually

1.48 meters long, the less precise measurement is more accurate.

18. What is the relationship between the range of possible error in the measurements used in a calculation and the range of possible error in the calculated measurement?

The range of possible error in the calculated values is greater.

19. Essential Question Check-In How do you use significant digits to determine how to report a sum or product of two measurements?

A sum should be rounded to the same place value as the last significant digit of the least

precise measurement. A product should have the same number of significant digits as the

least precise measurement.

ELABORATE

INTEGRATE MATHEMATICAL PRACTICES
Focus on Math Connections

MP.1 Many of the measurements in this lesson are in metric units. Explain that the metric system is used by scientists because all the units are related by factors of ten, which simplifies calculations.

SUMMARIZE THE LESSON

? How can you determine the number of significant digits to use when reporting the results of calculations based on measurements? The result of adding or subtracting measurements should be rounded to the same place value as the least precise measurement. The result of multiplying or dividing measurements should have the same number of significant digits as the least precise measurement.

LANGUAGE SUPPORT EL

Connect Vocabulary

Remind students that significant digits are the digits that carry meaning in measurements. Have students notice the word *significant*. Things that are significant are important. Have students discuss laws or rules that are significant or not significant in their lives. Significant examples may include school rules or household rules. Non-significant rules might include rules or laws that affect people in a different age group.

EVALUATE

ASSIGNMENT GUIDE

Concepts and Skills	Practice
Explore Comparing Precision of Measurements	Exercises 1–8
Example 1 Determining Precision of Calculated Measurements	Exercises 9–12
Example 2 Identifying Significant Digits	Exercises 13–17
Example 3 Using Significant Digits in Calculated Measurements	Exercises 18–19, 22–24
Example 4 Using Significant Digits in Estimation	Exercises 20–21

⭐ Evaluate: Homework and Practice

• Online Homework
• Hints and Help
• Extra Practice

1. Choose the more precise measurement from the pair 54.1 cm and 54.16 cm. Justify your answer.

   54.16 cm is more precise because 0.01 is smaller than 0.1 cm.

   Choose the more precise measurement in each pair.

2. 1 ft; (12 in.)   3. 5 kg; (5212 g)   4. 7 m; (7.7 m)   5. 123 cm; (1291 mm)

6. True or False? A scale that measures the mass of an object in grams to two decimal places is more precise than a scale that measures the mass of an object in milligrams to two decimal places. Justify your answer.

   False. Both scales measure to the hundredths place, and 1 mg is smaller than 1 g. So, the scale that measures in milligrams is more precise.

7. Every week, a technician in a lab needs to test the scales in the lab to make sure that they are accurate. She uses a standard mass that is exactly 4 g and gets the following results.

   Scale 1   Scale 2   Scale 3

   a. Which scale gives the most precise measurement?

   Scales 1 and 2 measure to the nearest 0.01 gram, and Scale 3 measures to the nearest 0.001 gram. Scale 3 is the most precise.

   b. Which scale gives the most accurate measurement?

   Scale 1: |4.000 − 4.05| = 0.05, Scale 2: |4.000 − 3.98| = 0.02, Scale 3: |4.000 − 4.021| = 0.021 Scale 2 is the most accurate.

8. A manufacturing company uses three measuring tools to measure lengths. The tools are tested using a standard unit exactly 7 cm long. The results are as follows.

Measuring Tool	Length
Tool 1	7.033 cm
Tool 2	6.91 cm
Tool 3	7.1 cm

   a. Which tool gives the most precise measurement?

   Tool 1 measures to the nearest 0.001 cm, Tool 2 to the nearest 0.01 cm, and Tool 3 to the nearest 0.1 cm. Tool 1 is the most precise.

   b. Which tool gives the most accurate measurement?

   Tool 1: |7.000 − 7.033| = 0.033, Tool 2: |7.000 − 6.91| = 0.09, Tool 3: |7.000 − 7.1| = 0.1. Tool 1 is the most accurate.

© Houghton Mifflin Harcourt Publishing Company

Exercise	Depth of Knowledge (D.O.K.)	COMMON CORE Mathematical Practices
1	**2** Skills/Concepts	**MP.5** Using Tools
2–5	**1** Recall of Information	**MP.5** Using Tools
6–19	**2** Skills/Concepts	**MP.5** Using Tools
20–21	**2** Skills/Concepts	**MP.4** Modeling
22–24	**3** Strategic Thinking H.O.T.	**MP.3** Logic

Given the following measurements, calculate the minimum and maximum possible areas of each object. Round your answer to the nearest square whole square unit.

9. The length and width of a book cover are 22.2 centimeters and 12 centimeters, respectively.

22.15 cm ≤ length < 22.25 cm; 11.5 cm ≤ width < 12.5 cm

22.15 cm · 11.5 cm ≤ area < 22.25 cm 12.5 cm

So 255 cm² ≤ area < 278 cm².

10. The length and width of a rectangle are 19.5 centimeters and 14 centimeters, respectively.

19.45 cm ≤ length < 19.55 cm; 13.5 cm ≤ width < 14.5 cm

19.45 cm · 13.5 cm ≤ area < 19.55 cm · 14.5 cm

So 263 cm² ≤ area < 283 cm².

11. Chris is painting a wall with a length of 3 meters and a width of 1.6 meters.

2.5 m ≤ length < 3.5 m; 1.55 m ≤ width < 1.65 m

2.5 m · 1.55 m ≤ area < 3.5 m · 1.65 m

So 4 m² ≤ area < 6 m².

12. A rectangular garden measures 15 feet by 24.1 feet.

24.05 ft ≤ length < 24.15 ft; 14.5 ft < width < 15.5 ft

24.05 ft · 14.5 ft ≤ area < 24.15 ft · 15.5 ft

So 349 ft² ≤ area < 374 ft².

Show the steps to determine the number of significant digits in the measurement.

13. 123.040 m

4 nonzero digits, 1 digit between two nonzero digits, 1 end zero right of the decimal
Altogether, 123.040 has 6 significant digits.

14. 0.00609 cm

2 nonzero digits, 1 digit between two nonzero digits, 0 end zero right of the decimal
Altogether, 0.00609 has 3 significant digits.

Determine the number of significant digits in each measurement.

15. 0.0070 ft
Two significant digits

16. 3333.33 g
Six significant digits

17. 20,300.011 lb
Eight significant digits

QUESTIONING STRATEGIES

Is it possible for one measurement to be more precise than a second measurement even though the second measurement is closer to the actual length? Yes, it is possible for a measurement to be more precise than another that is more accurate.

VISUAL CUES

As students are finding how many significant digits a number has, have them color the significant digits blue and the non-significant digits green. This will make it easier to count the significant digits.

AVOID COMMON ERRORS

Make sure students understand that zeros at the end of a whole number are not usually considered significant digits. For example, 4550 has 3 significant digits, not 4.

JOURNAL

Have students describe one situation in which both accuracy and precision are important, and one in which other priorities might outweigh the expense or effort of obtaining a high degree of accuracy and/or precision.

Find the perimeter and area of each garden. Report your answers with the correct number of significant digits.

18. A rectangular garden plot measures 13 feet by 26.6 feet.

Perimeter = 13 ft + 26.6 ft + 13 ft + 26.6 ft = 79.2 ft. The perimeter is 79 ft.

Area = 26.6 ft · 13 ft = 345.8 ft². The area is 350 ft².

19. A rectangular garden plot measures 24 feet by 25.3 feet.

Perimeter = 24 ft + 25.3 ft + 24 ft + 25.3 ft = 98.6 ft. The perimeter is 99 ft.

Area = 24 ft · 25.3 ft = 607.2 ft². The area is 610 ft².

20. Samantha is putting a layer of topsoil on a garden plot. She measures the plot and finds that the dimensions of the plot are 5 meters by 21 meters. Samantha has a bag of topsoil that covers an area of 106 square meters. Should she buy another bag of topsoil to ensure that she can cover her entire plot? Explain.

Yes. The actual dimensions of the plot could be greater than 5 m and 21 m given the precision of Samantha's measurements. The maximum dimensions of the garden plot could be slightly less than 5.5 m by 21.5 m, resulting in a maximum possible area of 118.25 m². In this case, she would need a second bag of topsoil to ensure uniform coverage.

21. Tom wants to tile the floor in his kitchen, which has an area of 320 square feet. In the store, the smallest tile he likes has an area of 1.1 square feet and the largest tile he likes has an area of 1.815 square feet. About how many tiles can be fitted in the given area?

Available Space = Number of Tiles · Area of One Tile

L = number of large tiles; S = number of small tiles

$320 = L \cdot 1.815; L = \dfrac{320}{1.815} \approx 180$ large tiles

$320 = S \cdot 1.1; S = \dfrac{320}{1.1} = 290$ small tiles

The average of L and S is $\dfrac{180 + 290}{2} = 240$.

So, on average, about 240 tiles will be needed.

© Houghton Mifflin Harcourt Publishing Company · Image Credits: ©Andrzej Kubik/Shutterstock

22. Communicate Mathematical Ideas Consider the calculation 5.6 mi ÷ 9s = 0.62222 mi/s. Why is it important to use significant digits to round the answer?

Without rounding, it would imply that the answer is accurate to the hundred-thousandths place.

23. Find the Error A student found that the dimensions of a rectangle were 1.20 centimeters and 1.40 centimeters. He was asked to report the area using the correct number of significant digits. He reported the area as 1.7 cm^2. Explain the error the student made.

The 0 in each dimension, 1.20 cm and 1.40 cm, is significant, so the answer should be given with three significant digits as 1.68 cm^2 and not as 1.7 cm^2.

24. Make a Conjecture Given two values with the same number of decimal places and significant digits, is it possible for the sum or product of the two values to have a different number of decimal places or significant digits than the original values?

Yes, it is possible. For addition, the number of significant digits is determined by the smallest place value of the least precise number. If the sum results in an additional place value added to the left of the decimal point, the sum will have more significant digits than the addends. In multiplication, the number of significant digits is determined by the factor with the smallest number of significant digits. For instance, if you were to multiply 0.3 and 0.6, you would get 0.18. Each factor has 1 significant digit and 1 decimal place, but the product has 2 significant digits and 2 decimal places.

Lesson Performance Task

The sun is an excellent source of electrical energy. A field of solar panels yields 16.22 Watts per square feet. Determine the amount of electricity produced by a field of solar panels that is 305 feet by 620 feet.

Area: 305 ft · 620 ft = 189,100 ft²

$189,100 \text{ ft}^2 \cdot \dfrac{16.22 \text{ W}}{\text{ft}^2} = 3,067,202 \text{ W}$

The factors are 305, 620, and 16.22, so the product should be rounded to 2 significant digits.

So, the field yields 3,100,000 watts, or 3.1 megawatts.

EXTENSION ACTIVITY

Have students calculate the minimum and maximum possible area of the field of solar panels, then discuss how the uncertainty in the linear measurements affects the precision of the calculated area.

Students should find that because the length is between 615 ft and 625 ft and the width is between 304.5 ft and 305.5 ft, the area is between 187,267.5 ft² and 190,937.5 ft². Although this is a range of more than 3000 square feet, students should recognize that rounding either of these numbers to the correct number of significant digits (two) results in an appropriate estimate of the area (190,000 ft²).

LANGUAGE SUPPORT 〔EL〕

Some students may not be familiar with the units in the Lesson Performance Task. W stands for watt, which is a unit of power. To represent large quantities of power, units of megawatts (MW) may be used. One megawatt is equal to one million watts. The unit ft² is read "square feet."

QUESTIONING STRATEGIES

? What operation do you use when finding area? multiplication

? What rule for significant digits should you use when writing the product of the area and the yield? The product must have the same number of significant digits as the least precise measurement.

INTEGRATE MATHEMATICAL PRACTICES

Focus on Math Connections

MP.1 Show how dimensional analysis can help you verify that the result of a calculation is in the correct units. When multiplying length • width • yield, the units are ft • ft • W/ft² = W, so the result is in watts.

INTEGRATE MATHEMATICAL PRACTICES

Focus on Technology

MP.5 Students may use online calculators or graphing calculators when completing the Lesson Performance Task. Discuss how precision and significant digits are used or ignored by the tools that are available.

Scoring Rubric
2 points: Student correctly solves the problem and explains his/her reasoning.
1 point: Student shows good understanding of the problem but does not fully solve or explain his/her reasoning.
0 points: Student does not demonstrate understanding of the problem.

Study Guide Review

ASSESSMENT AND INTERVENTION

Assign or customize module reviews.

MODULE PERFORMANCE TASK

COMMON CORE

Mathematical Practices: MP.1, MP.2, MP.4, MP.7, MP.8
N-Q.A.2

SUPPORTING STUDENT REASONING

Students should begin this problem by thinking about how to determine possible scores on this dartboard. Students might believe that an infinite number of scores are impossible—reassure them that only a few scores are not possible.

SCAFFOLDING SUPPORT

- Students should start by thinking about what scores are possible using the two numbers 5 and 7. They should immediately recognize that multiples of 5 and multiples of 7 are all possible.

- Encourage students to make a list of possible scores, using x as the number of 5-point throws, and y as the number of 7-point throws, so that all possible scores are of the form $5x + 7y$.

Essential Question: How do you use quantitative reasoning to solve real-world problems?

KEY EXAMPLE   (Lesson 1.1)

Two fortnights have passed from January 3rd to January 31st. How many days long is a fortnight?

$31 - 3 = 28$	*Calculate the number of days that have passed.*
$2f = 28$	*Write an equation.*
$\dfrac{2f}{2} = \dfrac{28}{2}$	*Use the division property of equality.*
$f = 14$	

A fortnight equals 14 days.

KEY EXAMPLE   (Lesson 1.2)

The scale on a map is 1 in: 8 mi. The distance from Cedar Park, TX to Austin, TX on the map is 2.5 in. How long is the actual distance?

$\dfrac{\text{actual}}{\text{map}} \rightarrow \dfrac{8 \text{ mi}}{1 \text{ in.}}$	*Write the scale as a fraction.*
$\dfrac{8}{1} = \dfrac{d}{2.5}$	*Let d be the actual distance.*
$2.5 \times 8 = 2.5 \times \dfrac{d}{2.5}$	*Multiply both sides by 2.5.*
$20 = d$	

The actual distance is 20 mi.

KEY EXAMPLE   (Lesson 1.3)

Find the sum and product of the following measurements using the correct number of significant digits: 15 ft and 9.25 ft.

$15 \text{ ft} + 9.25 \text{ ft} = 24.25 \text{ ft}$	*Round to the place value of the last significant digit of the least precise measurement.*
24 ft	*The last significant digit of 15 is in the ones place.*
$15 \text{ ft} \times 9.25 \text{ ft} = 138.75 \text{ ft}^2$	*Round so it has the number of significant digits of the least precise measurement.*
140 ft^2	*15 has 2 significant digits.*

Key Vocabulary

accuracy *(exactitud)*
conversion factor
   (factor de conversión)
dimensional analysis
   (análisis dimensional)
equation *(ecuación)*
precision *(precisión)*
proportion *(proporción)*
rate *(tasa)*
ratio *(razón)*
scale *(escala)*
significant digits
   (dígitos significativos)
solution of an equation
   (solución de una ecuación)

©Houghton Mifflin Harcourt Publishing Company

SCAFFOLDING SUPPORT (CONTINUED)

- Students must use reasoning to narrow the list of possible scores. By rewriting the possible scores as multiples of 5 with remainders from 0 to 4, they will likely recognize that all scores greater than or equal to a certain value, 28, are possible. Encourage students to write scores in the form $5(x + a) + b$, where a and b are whole numbers from 0 to 4.

EXERCISES

Solve. Check your solutions. *(Lesson 1.1)*

1. $z - 12 = 30$

$$z = 42$$

2. $-\dfrac{y}{7} = 8$

$$y = -56$$

3. $5x + 13 = 48$

$$x = 7$$

4. $25 - 3p = -11$

$$p = 12$$

5. The height of a scale model building is 15 in. The scale is 5 in. to 32 in. Find the height of the actual building in inches and in feet. *(Lesson 1.2)*

96 in.; 8 ft

6. Which of the following measurements is least precise, and how many significant digits does it have? *(Lesson 1.3)*

50.25 cm, 12.5 cm, 101 cm

101 cm; 3

7. A square countertop has a side length of 28 inches. Find the perimeter and area of the countertop using the correct number of significant digits. *(Lesson 1.3)*

110 in.; 780 in²

MODULE PERFORMANCE TASK
What an Impossible Score!

The simple dartboard shown has two sections, a 5-point outer ring and a 7-point inner circle. What is the largest integer score that is impossible to achieve for this simple dartboard, even if you are allowed to throw as many darts as you want?

Start by listing in the space below how you plan to tackle the problem. Then use your own paper to complete the task. Be sure to write down all your data and assumptions. Then use graphs, numbers, words, or algebra to explain how you reached your conclusion.

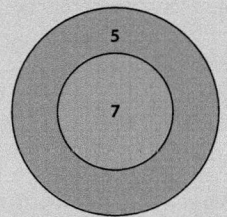

DISCUSSION OPPORTUNITIES

- Why was it important to eliminate scores greater than a certain value for this task? Is it possible to test every possible score?

- Research the scoring for a tournament dart board. Are there any impossible scores in a regular game of darts?

SAMPLE SOLUTION

All possible scores can be of the form $5x + 7y$, with x and y whole numbers.

All possible scores, starting at $y = 0$, are:

$$5x + 7 \cdot 0 = 5x$$

$$5x + 7 \cdot 1 = 5x + 7$$

$$5x + 7 \cdot 2 = 5x + 14$$

$$5x + 7 \cdot 3 = 5x + 21$$

$$5x + 7 \cdot 4 = 5x + 28$$

These are multiples of 5 with remainders:

$5x$ (remainder 0)

$5x + 7 = 5(x + 1) + 2$ (remainder 2)

$5x + 14 = 5(x + 2) + 4$ (remainder 4)

$5x + 21 = 5(x + 4) + 1$ (remainder 1)

$5x + 28 = 5(x + 5) + 3$ (remainder 3)

Note that a remainder of 5 is also a remainder of 0, a remainder of 6 is also a remainder of 1, etc. So any score greater than or equal to $5(0 + 5) + 3 = 28$ is a possible score.

To find the greatest impossible score, start by working your way down from 28, first excluding multiples of 5 and 7. See if each remaining number can be written in the form $5x + 7$.

$$27 = 5 \cdot 4 + 7 \cdot 1$$

$$26 = 5 \cdot 1 + 7 \cdot 3$$

$$24 = 5 \cdot 2 + 7 \cdot 2$$

23 cannot be written in the form $5x + 7y$.

The greatest impossible score is 23.

Ready to Go On?

ASSESS MASTERY

Use the assessment on this page to determine if students have mastered the concepts and standards covered in this module.

ASSESSMENT AND INTERVENTION

Access Ready to Go On? assessment online, and receive instant scoring, feedback, and customized intervention or enrichment.

ADDITIONAL RESOURCES

Response to Intervention Resources

- Reteach Worksheets

Differentiated Instruction Resources

- Reading Strategies **EL**
- Success for English Learners **EL**
- Challenge Worksheets

Assessment Resources

- Leveled Module Quizzes

(Ready) to Go On?

1.1–1.3 Quantitative Reasoning

- Online Homework
- Hints and Help
- Extra Practice

Solve. *(Lesson 1.1)*

1. $7 = 4s + 19$

$s = -3$

2. $\frac{x}{4} + 8 = 16$

$x = 32$

3. A student's pay of $23 an hour at a new job is $6 more than twice the amount the student earned per hour at an internship. Write and solve an equation to find the hourly pay of the internship. *(Lesson 1.1)*

$23 = 2x + 6$; The internship pays $8.50 per hour.

4. Susan enlarged to scale a rectangle with a height of 4 cm and length of 11 cm on her computer. The length of the new rectangle is 16.5 cm. Find the height of the new rectangle. *(Lesson 1.2)*

6 cm

5. An instructional video is 5.4 minutes long. How long is the video in seconds? How long is it in hours? *(Lesson 1.2)*

324 seconds; 0.09 hour

Solve using the correct number of significant digits. *(Lesson 1.3)*

6. $70.8 \text{ m} \times 11 \text{ m}$

780 m²

7. $16.5 \text{ ft} + 2.25 \text{ ft} + 12.5 \text{ ft}$

31.3 ft

ESSENTIAL QUESTION

8. How do you calculate correctly with real-world measurements?

Possible Answer: Use the rules of significant digits to calculate. This ensures that calculations based on measurements are not reported as more accurate than the measurements themselves.

COMMON CORE Common Core Standards

Lesson	Items	Content Standards	Mathematical Practices
1.1	1	**A-REI.A.1**	**MP.2**
1.1	2	**A-REI.A.1**	**MP.2**
1.2	3	**N-Q.A.1, N-Q.A.2**	**MP.4**
1.2	4	**N-Q.A.1, N-Q.A.2**	**MP.4**
1.2	5	**N-Q.A.1, N-Q.A.2**	**MP.4**
1.3	6	**N-Q.A.3**	**MP.6**
1.3	7	**N-Q.A.3**	**MP.6**

Assessment Readiness

1. Look at each equation and possible solution. Is the solution correct? Select Yes or No for each equation.

   A. $-3x = -30; x = -10$ ○ Yes   ● No

   B. $25 - 2y = 13; y = 6$ ● Yes   ○ No

   C. $\frac{z}{3} + 2 = 6; z = 16$ ○ Yes   ● No

2. During a 5-kilometer run to raise money for the school band, Tabitha ran 0.08 kilometer per minute. Use 1 mi ≈ 1.61 km. Choose True or False for each statement.

   A. Tabitha ran 4.8 miles per hour.   ○ True   ● False

   B. Tabitha ran about 0.05 mile per minute.   ● True   ○ False

   C. Tabitha ran faster than 4 kilometers per hour.   ● True   ○ False

3. A carpenter took the following measurements: 3.4 m, 10.25 m, 20.2 m, and 19 m. Choose True or False for each statement.

   A. The most precise measurement has 4 significant digits.   ● True   ○ False

   B. The least precise measurement has 2 significant digits.   ● True   ○ False

   C. Written using the correct number of significant digits, the sum of the measurements should be rounded to the tenths place.   ○ True   ● False

4. Stanley is putting wallpaper strips on his bathroom walls that have a total area of 450 square feet. Each strip of wall paper covers between 20 and 24 square feet. Estimate how many strips of wallpaper Stanley will need. Explain how you solved this problem.

   Possible answer: Stanley will need about 21 strips of wallpaper. First I divided 450 by 20 and got 22.5, and I divided 450 by 24 and got 18.75. Then, I found the average of 22.5 and 18.75 which is 20.625. Since the number with the fewest significant digits has 2 significant digits, I rounded 20.625 to 21.

MIXED REVIEW
Assessment Readiness

ASSESSMENT AND INTERVENTION

Assign ready-made or customized practice tests to prepare students for high-stakes tests.

ADDITIONAL RESOURCES

Assessment Resources

- Leveled Module Quizzes: Modified, B

AVOID COMMON ERRORS

Item 1 Some students have a hard time with substituting negative numbers. Remind students that the opposite of a negative number is positive, and encourage them to use a calculator to check their answers.

Algebraic Models

ESSENTIAL QUESTION:

Answer: You can write an equation or inequality to model the real-world problem. Then solve the equation or inequality by using inverse operations on each side to isolate the variable.

PROFESSIONAL DEVELOPMENT VIDEO

Professional Development Video

Author Juli Dixon models successful teaching practices in an actual high-school classroom.

Professional
Development
my.hrw.com

MODULE 2

Algebraic Models

★

Essential Question: How can you use algebraic models to solve real-world problems?

© Houghton Mifflin Harcourt Publishing Company • Image Credits: ©Monkey Business Images/Shutterstock

LESSON 2.1
Modeling with Expressions

LESSON 2.2
Creating and Solving Equations

LESSON 2.3
Solving for a Variable

LESSON 2.4
Creating and Solving Inequalities

LESSON 2.5
Creating and Solving Compound Inequalities

REAL WORLD VIDEO
In a grocery store receipt, some items are taxed and some items are not taxed. You can write an expression that shows a simplified method for calculating the total grocery bill.

MODULE PERFORMANCE TASK PREVIEW
Menu Math

What if you opened a menu in a restaurant and saw this: "Special Today!!! All G's just $2.95 a piece! M's reduced 20%!" You might decide to try another restaurant. On the other hand, you might decide that you wanted to decipher the code. Deciphering codes is one way of describing what you do when you solve equations. In this module, you'll decipher a lot of codes and then use what you've learned to discover the mathematics of menus!

DIGITAL TEACHER EDITION

Access a full suite of teaching resources when and where you need them:

- Access content online or offline
- Customize lessons to share with your class
- Communicate with your students in real-time
- View student grades and data instantly to target your instruction where it is needed most

PERSONAL MATH TRAINER
Assessment and Intervention

Assign automatically graded homework, quizzes, tests, and intervention activities. Prepare your students with updated, Common Core-aligned practice tests.

Are YOU Ready?

Complete these exercises to review skills you will need for this module.

• Online Homework
• Hints and Help
• Extra Practice

One-Step Inequalities

Example 1   Solve.

$$x + 8 < 15$$
$$x + 8 - 8 < 15 - 8 \qquad \text{Isolate the variable by subtracting 8}$$
$$\qquad\qquad\qquad\qquad \text{from both sides of the inequality.}$$
$$x < 7$$

Solve each inequality.

1. $n - 23 \geq 17$ $\quad n \geq 40$

2. $p + 14 \leq 9$ $\quad p \leq -5$

3. $\frac{n}{5} > -13$ $\quad n > -65$

Two-Step Equations

Example 2   Solve.

$$6k - 12 = 18$$
$$6k - 12 + 12 = 18 + 12 \qquad \text{Add 12 to both sides of the equation.}$$
$$6k = 30$$
$$\frac{6k}{6} = \frac{30}{6} \qquad\qquad\quad \text{Divide both sides of the equation by 6.}$$
$$k = 5$$

Solve each equation.

4. $3n + 19 = 28$ $\quad n = 3$

5. $34 - 4b = 18$ $\quad b = 4$

6. $\frac{2}{3}y + 7 = 15$ $\quad y = 12$

Two-Step Inequalities

Example 3   Solve.

$$15 - 3f > 75$$
$$15 - 15 - 3f > 75 - 15 \qquad \text{Subtract 15 from both sides of the inequality.}$$
$$-3f > 60$$
$$\frac{-3f}{-3} < \frac{60}{-3} \qquad\qquad \text{Divide both sides of the inequality by } -3.$$
$$\qquad\qquad\qquad\qquad \text{Reverse the inequality symbol.}$$
$$f < -20$$

Solve each inequality.

7. $8c - 21 < 35$ $\quad c < 7$

8. $-6h + 17 > 41$ $\quad h < -4$

9. $\frac{r}{5} - 2 \leq 9$ $\quad r \leq 55$

Are You Ready?

ASSESS READINESS

Use the assessment on this page to determine if students need strategic or intensive intervention for the module's prerequisite skills.

ASSESSMENT AND INTERVENTION

RtI Response to Intervention **TIER 1, TIER 2, TIER 3 SKILLS**

Personal Math Trainer will automatically create a standards-based, personalized intervention assignment for your students, targeting each student's individual needs!

ADDITIONAL RESOURCES

See the table below for a full list of intervention resources available for this module.

Response to Intervention Resources also includes:

• Tier 2 Skill Pre-Tests for each Module
• Tier 2 Skill Post-Tests for each skill

Response to Intervention			Differentiated Instruction
Tier 1	**Tier 2**	**Tier 3**	
Lesson Intervention Worksheets	Strategic Intervention Skills Intervention Worksheets	Intensive Intervention Worksheets available online	
Reteach 2.1	2 Algebraic Expressions	Building Block Skills	Challenge worksheets
Reteach 2.2	13 One-Step Equations	19, 22, 23, 24, 27, 40,	
Reteach 2.3	14 One-Step Inequalities	52, 54, 59, 81, 88, 92,	Extend the Math
Reteach 2.4	21 Two-Step Equations	93, 98, 110	Lesson Activities
Reteach 2.5	22 Two-Step Inequalities		in TE

Modeling with Expressions

Common Core Math Standards

The student is expected to:

COMMON CORE A-SSE.A.1a

Interpret parts of an expression, such as terms, factors, and coefficients.
Also A-SSE.A.1b, N-Q.A.2

Mathematical Practices

COMMON CORE MP.6 Precision

Language Objective

Explain the meaning of each term of an algebraic expression that models a real-world situation.

ENGAGE

Essential Question: How do you interpret algebraic expressions in terms of their context?

Identify the meaning of the individual parts of the expression and their relationships to each other.

PREVIEW: LESSON PERFORMANCE TASK

View the Engage section online. Discuss what makes a "good deal" when purchasing a car. Then preview the Lesson Performance Task.

2.1 Modeling with Expressions

Essential Question: How do you interpret algebraic expressions in terms of their context?

Resource Locker

⊘ Explore   Interpreting Parts of an Expression

An **expression** is a mathematical phrase that contains operations, numbers, and/or variables. The **terms** of an expression are the parts that are being added. A **coefficient** is the numerical factor of a variable term. There are both *numerical expressions* and *algebraic expressions*. A **numerical expression** contains only numbers while an **algebraic expression** contains at least one variable.

(A) Identify the terms and the coefficients of the expression $8p + 2q + 7r$.

terms: __8p, 2q, 7r__ ; coefficients: __8, 2, 7__

(B) Identify the terms and coefficients of the expression $18 - 2x - 4y$. Since the expression involves __subtraction__ rather than addition, rewrite the expression as the __sum__ of the terms: $18 - 2x - 4y =$ __$18 + (-2x) + (-4y)$__ . So, the terms of the expression are __$18, -2x, -4y$__ and the coefficients are __$-2, -4$__ .

(C) Identify the terms and coefficients in the expression $2x + 3y - 4z + 10$. Since the expression involves both __subtraction__ and addition, rewrite the expression as the __sum__ of the terms: $2x + 3y - 4z + 10 =$ __$2x + 3y + (-4z) + 10$__. So, the terms of the expression are __$2x, 3y, -4z, 10$__ and the coefficients are __$2, 3, -4$__ .

Tickets to an amusement park are $60 for adults and $30 for children. If a is the number of adults and c is the number of children, then the cost for a adults and c children is $60a + 30c$.

(D) What are the terms of the expression? __$60a, 30c$__

(E) What are the factors of $60a$? __$60, a$__

(F) What are the factors of $30c$? __$30, c$__

(G) What are the coefficients of the expression? __$60, 30$__

(H) Interpret the meaning of the two terms of the expression. __$60a$ is the cost for a adults. $30c$ is the cost for c children.__

The price of a case of juice is $15.00. Fred has a coupon for 20 cents off each bottle in the case. The expression to find the final cost of the case of juice is $15 - 0.2b$, wherein b is the number of bottles.

(I) What are the terms of the expression? __$15, -0.2b$__

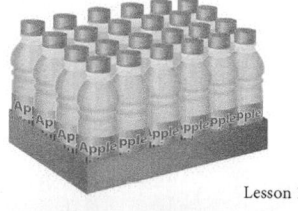

© Houghton Mifflin Harcourt Publishing Company

HARDCOVER PAGES 37–44

Turn to these pages to find this lesson in the hardcover student edition.

Ⓙ What are the factors of each term? __15__ is the only factor of the __first__ term and __−0.2__ and __b__ are the factors of the __second__ term.

Ⓚ Do both terms have coefficients? Explain. **No, the term 15 has no variable part, so 15 is not a coefficient.** What are the coefficients? __−0.2__

Ⓛ What does the expression $15 − 0.2b$ mean in the given situation?
If Fred has a coupon, 20 cents is subtracted from the price of every bottle in the case. If Fred does not have a coupon, then the case costs $15.

Reflect

1. Sally identified the terms of the expression $9a + 4b − 18$ as $9a$, $4b$, and 18. Explain her error. **$9a + 4b + (−18)$, so the terms are $9a$, $4b$, and $−18$.**

2. What is the coefficient of b in the expression $b + 10$? Explain. **$1; b = 1(b)$, so the coefficient of b is 1.**

✏️ Explain 1   Interpreting Algebraic Expressions in Context

In many cases, real-world situations and algebraic expressions can be related. The coefficients, variables, and operations represent the given real-world context.

Interpret the algebraic expression corresponding to the given context.

Example 1

Ⓐ Curtis is buying supplies for his school. He buys p packages of crayons at $1.49 per package and q packages of markers at $3.49 per package. What does the expression $1.49p + 3.49q$ represent?

Interpret the meaning of the term $1.49p$. What does the coefficient 1.49 represent?

The term $1.49p$ represents the cost of p packages of crayons. The coefficient represents the cost of one package of crayons, $1.49.

Interpret the meaning of the term $3.49q$. What does the coefficient 3.49 represent?

The term $3.49q$ represents the cost of q packages of markers. The coefficient represents the cost of one package of markers, $3.49.

Interpret the meaning of the entire expression.

The expression $1.49p + 3.49q$ represents the total cost of p packages of crayons and q packages of markers.

Ⓑ Jill is buying ink jet paper and laser jet paper for her business. She buys 8 more packages of ink jet paper than p packages of laser jet paper. Ink jet paper costs $6.95 per package and laser jet paper costs $8 per package. What does the expression $8p + 6.95(p + 8)$ represent?

Interpret the meaning of the first term, $8p$. What does the coefficient 8 represent?

The term $8p$ represents the cost of __p packages of laser jet paper__. The coefficient represents the cost of one package of laser jet paper __, $8.

Interpret the meaning of the second expression, $6.95(p + 8)$. What do the factors 6.95 and $(p + 8)$ represent?

PROFESSIONAL DEVELOPMENT

Integrate Mathematical Practices

This lesson provides an opportunity to address Mathematical Practice **MP.6**, which calls for students to "communicate with precision." Students learn to interpret the meaning of a mathematical expression in reference to a real-world context rather than seeing the expression as numbers alone. This encourages students to think about how variables represent real-world quantities as well as how various words and phrases can represent mathematical operations.

EXPLORE

Interpreting Parts of an Expression

INTEGRATE TECHNOLOGY

Students may complete the Explore activity either online or in the book.

CONNECT VOCABULARY 🔲

Distinguish the terms *expression*, *term*, and *coefficient* from one another. Point out that an expression is composed of one or more terms. A term can be a variable, a constant, or a variable that is multiplied by a constant, which is called a coefficient.

AVOID COMMON ERRORS

Note that in middle school, students may have seen terms of an expression defined as parts of an expression that are added or subtracted. Point out that in this course, terms are defined as "parts of an expression that are added."

EXPLAIN 1

Interpreting Algebraic Expressions in Context

INTEGRATE MATHEMATICAL PRACTICES
Focus on Communication

MP.3 Stress that to understand the meaning of a mathematical expression, students must consider the meaning of every term and operation. Have students make a list of the words that represent each mathematical operation.

QUESTIONING STRATEGIES

? When you multiply the price of an item by the number of those items purchased, what does the product represent? **the cost of buying the given number of items**

? If each term of an expression represents the cost of an item purchased, what does the whole expression represent? **the total cost of all items purchased**

EXPLAIN 2

Comparing Algebraic Expressions

QUESTIONING STRATEGIES

? The real-world meaning of a variable may limit the numerical values it can have. What do you know about the possible value of a variable that represents the population of a city? **It must be a positive integer.**

? What do you know about the possible value of a variable that represents a tax rate? **It must be a positive number less than one.**

INTEGRATE MATHEMATICAL PRACTICES

Focus on Critical Thinking

MP.3 When comparing two algebraic expressions to determine which is greater, students can check their answers by choosing numbers to substitute for the variables, then evaluating each expression and comparing the results.

The term $6.95(p + 8)$ represents **the cost of the ink jet paper**. 6.95 represents the cost of **one package of ink jet paper**. $(p + 8)$ represents **the number of ink jet paper packages** that Jill bought.

Interpret the expression $8p + 6.95(p + 8)$.

The expression represents **the total cost of packages of ink jet and laser jet paper** that Jill bought.

Your Turn

Interpret the algebraic expression corresponding to the given context.

3. George is buying watermelons and pineapples to make fruit salad. He buys w watermelons at \$4.49 each and p pineapples at \$5 each. What does the expression $4.49w + 5p$ represent?
   The expression $4.49w + 5p$ represents the total cost of w watermelons and p pineapples

4. Sandi buys 5 fewer packages of pencils than p packages of pens. Pencils costs \$2.25 per package and pens costs \$3 per package. What does the expression $3p + 2.25(p - 5)$ represent?
   The expression $3p + 2.25(p - 5)$ represents the total cost of pens and pencils.

⊘ Explain 2 **Comparing Algebraic Expressions**

Given two algebraic expressions involving two variables, we can compare whether one is greater or less than the other. We can denote the inequality between the expressions by using $<$ or $>$ symbols. If the expressions are the same, or **equivalent expressions**, we denote this equality by using $=$.

Suppose x and y give the populations of two different cities where $x > y$. Compare the expressions and tell which of the given pair is greater.

Example 1

(A) $x + y$ and $2x$

The expression $2x$ is greater.

- Putting the lesser population, y, together with the greater population, x, gives a population that is less than double the greater population.

(B) $\frac{x}{y}$ and $\frac{y}{x}$

Since $x > y$, $\frac{x}{y}$ will be **greater** than 1 and $\frac{y}{x}$ will be **less** than 1.

So $\frac{x}{y}$ **>** $\frac{y}{x}$.

Your Turn

Suppose x and y give the populations of two different cities where $x > y$ and $y > 0$. Compare the expressions and tell which of the given pair is greater.

5. $\frac{x}{x + y}$ and $\frac{x + y}{x}$

Since $x < x + y$, the first ratio must be less than 1. Since $x < x + y$, the second ratio must be greater than 1.

So $\frac{x + y}{x} > \frac{x}{x + y}$.

6. $2(x + y)$ and $(x + y)^2$

- $2(x + y)$ represents doubling $(x + y)$
- $(x + y)^2$ represents squaring $(x + y)$

Since x and y are the populations of two cities, their sum is much greater than 2. Thus, squaring the sum produces a greater number. So, $(x + y)^2 > 2(x + y)$.

COLLABORATIVE LEARNING

Peer-to-Peer Activity

Have students work in pairs, taking turns writing situations and trying to translate each other's situation into an algebraic expression. Have students compare their expressions and discuss why they wrote them in the way that they did.

Explain 3 Modeling Expressions in Context

The table shows some words and phrases associated with the four basic arithmetic operations. These words and phrases can help you translate a real-world situation into an algebraic expression.

Operation	Words	Examples
Addition	the sum of, added to, plus, more than, increased by, total, altogether, and	1. A number increased by 2 2. The sum of n and 2 3. $n + 2$
Subtraction	less than, minus, subtracted from, the difference of, take away, taken from, reduced by	1. The difference of a number and 2 2. 2 less than a number 3. $n - 2$
Multiplication	times, multiplied by, the product of, percent of	1. The product of 0.6 and a number 2. 60% of a number 3. $0.6n$
Division	divided by, division of, quotient of, divided into, ratio of,	1. The quotient of a number and 5 2. A number divided by 5 3. $n \div 5$ or $\frac{n}{5}$

Example 3 Write an algebraic expression to model the given context. Give your answer in simplest form.

Ⓐ the price of an item plus 6% sales tax

Price of an item	+	6% sales tax
p	+	$0.06p$

The algebraic expression is $p + 0.06p$, or $1.06p$.

Ⓑ the price of a car plus 8.5% sales tax

The price of a car	+	8.5% sales tax
p	+	$0.085p$

The algebraic expression is $p + 0.085p$,
or $p + 0.085p = 1.085p$.

Reflect

7. Use the Distributive Property to show why $p + 0.06p = 1.06p$.
$p + 0.06p = 1p + 0.06p = p(1 + 0.06) = 1.06p$

8. What could the expression $3(p + 0.06p)$ represent? Explain.
Sample Answer: $3(p + 0.06p)$ is 3 times the expression $p + 0.06p$. It could represent the cost of 3 identical items with a 6% sales tax.

Your Turn

Write an algebraic expression to model the given context. Give your answer in simplest form.

9. the number of gallons of water in a tank, that already has 300 gallons in it, after being filled at 35 gallons per minute for m minutes
$300 + 35m$

10. the original price p of an item less a discount of 15%
$p - 0.15p = 0.85p$

DIFFERENTIATE INSTRUCTION

Multiple Representations

Students with conceptual processing difficulties may struggle with the many different verbal descriptions and symbolic notations for expressing the same operation. For example, "k divided by 2" or "the quotient of k and 2" can both be written as $k \div 2$ or $\frac{k}{2}$. Resource sheets listing a variety of possible descriptions and notations for each standard operation may be helpful to such students.

EXPLAIN 3

Modeling Expressions in Context

QUESTIONING STRATEGIES

? How is "3 *less* a number" translated into an algebraic expression? How is "3 *less than* a number" translated? Are they equivalent expressions? $3 - n$ and $n - 3$; no, the order matters in subtraction.

INTEGRATE MATHEMATICAL PRACTICES
Focus on Modeling

MP.4 Encourage students to follow the pattern "Quantity—Operation—Quantity" when modeling a real-world situation. Once students identify the quantities and choose an operation, the writing of an algebraic expression becomes a straightforward process.

Quantity	$+ - \times \div$	Quantity

ELABORATE

QUESTIONING STRATEGIES

? What is the difference between a variable and a constant? A variable represents a value that can change. A constant is a numerical value that does not change.

? What are "like terms" in an expression? Like terms are terms that contain the same variables raised to the same power.

AVOID COMMON ERRORS

When modeling situations that involve subtraction or division, some students may write the terms in the incorrect order. Tell students to double-check that the order makes sense within the context of the verbal expression when they write a subtraction or division expression.

SUMMARIZE THE LESSON

? How can you translate a real-world situation into an algebraic expression? First look for key words that indicate which operation or operations are involved. Identify the quantities that you are dealing with, and choose a variable to represent the unknown. Write each quantity and operation in algebraic notation. Simplify, if necessary.

Elaborate

11. When given an algebraic expression involving subtraction, why is it best to rewrite the expression using addition before identifying the terms?
Subtraction is defined as adding a negative term. Rewriting all subtraction as addition keeps the negative sign with the term and helps avoid errors.

12. How do you interpret algebraic expressions in terms of their context?
In order to interpret algebraic expressions in terms of their context, identify the meaning of the individual parts of the expression and their relationships to each other.

13. How do you simplify algebraic expressions?
You can simplify algebraic expressions by using the properties of real numbers and combining like terms.

14. Essential Question Check In How do you write algebraic expressions to model quantities?
First identify the descriptive words that indicate which basic arithmetic operations are involved. Then create a verbal model relating the quantities. Finally, choose a variable to represent the unknown quantity and write the expression.

⭐ Evaluate: Homework and Practice

- Online Homework
- Hints and Help
- Extra Practice

Identify the terms and the coefficients of the expression.

1. $-20 + 5p - 7z$
$-20 + 5p - 7z = (-20) + 5p + (-7z)$
terms: -20, $5p$, and $-7z$; coefficients: 5 and -7

2. $8x - 20y - 10$
$8x - 20y - 10 = 8x + (-20y) + (-10)$
terms: $8x$, $-20y$, and -10; coefficients: 8 and -20

Identify the factors of the terms of the expression.

3. $5 + 6a + 11b$
5; 6 and a; 11 and b

4. $13m - 2n$
13 and m; -2 and n

5. Erin is buying produce at a store. She buys c cucumbers at \$0.99 each and a apples at \$0.79 each. What does the expression $0.99c + 0.79a$ represent?
The expression represents the total cost of c cucumbers and a apples.

6. The number of bees that visit a plant is 500 times the number of years the plant is alive, where t represents the number of years the plant is alive. What does the expression $500t$ represent?
The expression represents the total number of bees that will visit the plant in its lifetime.

LANGUAGE SUPPORT **EL**

Visual Cues

Have students copy and complete the graphic organizer. Next to each operation, write a word phrase in the left box and its corresponding algebraic symbol or expression in the right box.

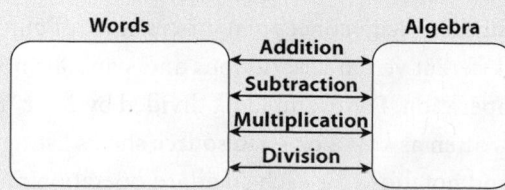

7. Lorenzo buys 3 shirts at s dollars apiece and 2 pairs of pants at p dollars a pair. What does the expression $3s + 2p$ represent?

The expression represents the total cost of 3 shirts and 2 pairs of pants.

8. If a car travels at a speed of 25 mi/h for t hours, then travels 45 mi/h for m hours, what does the expression $25t + 45m$ represent?

The expression represents the total distance traveled by the car.

9. The price of a sandwich is $1.50 more than the price of a smoothie, which is d dollars. What does the expression $d + 1.5$ represent?

The expression represents the price of a sandwich.

10. A bicyclist travels 1 mile in 5 minutes. If m represents minutes, what does the expression $\frac{m}{5}$ represent?

The expression represents the number of miles the bicyclist travels in m minutes.

11. What are the factors of the expression $(y - 2)(x + 3)$?

The factors of the expression are $(y - 2)$ and $(x + 3)$.

12. Explain the Error A student wrote that there are two terms in the expression $3p - (7 - 4q)$. Explain the student's error.

There are three terms, $3p$, -7, and $4q$ in the expression:
$3p - (7 - 4q) = 3p - 7 + 4q = 3p + (-7) + 4q$

13. Yolanda is buying supplies for school. She buys n packages of pencils at $1.40 per package and m pads of paper at $1.20 each. What does each term in the expression $1.4n + 1.2m$ represent? What does the entire expression represent?

The term 1.4n represents the cost of n packages of pencils at $1.40 per package.

The term 1.2m represents the cost of m pads of paper at $1.20 per pad.

The expression represents the total cost of n packages of pencils and m pads of paper.

14. Chris buys p pairs of pants and 4 more shirts than pairs of pants. Shirts cost $18 each and pair of pants cost $25 each. What does each term in the expression $25p + 18(p + 4)$ represent? What does the entire expression represent?

The term 25p represents the cost p pairs of pants at $25 each.

The term 18($p + 4$) represents the cost of the shirts at $18 per shirt.

The entire expression represents the total cost of the shirts and pants that Chris bought.

Exercise	Depth of Knowledge (D.O.K.)	COMMON CORE Mathematical Practices
1–14	**1** Recall of Information	**MP.4** Modeling
15–19	**2** Skills/Concepts	**MP.2** Reasoning
20–24	**2** Skills/Concepts	**MP.4** Modeling
25–27	**3** Strategic Thinking **H.O.T.**	**MP.3** Logic

EVALUATE

ASSIGNMENT GUIDE

Concepts and Skills	Practice
Explore Interpreting Parts of an Expression	Exercises 1–4, 11–12
Example 1 Interpreting Algebraic Expressions in Context	Exercises 5–10, 13–14
Example 2 Comparing Algebraic Expressions	Exercises 15–19, 25
Example 3 Modeling Expressions in Context	Exercises 20–24, 26–27

VISUAL CUES

English language learners may have difficulty with the word *term* because it has so many different meanings. Explain that in mathematics a *term* is a part of an expression that is added. You may wish to have students highlight each term in a different color, then circle the addition signs between the terms.

INTEGRATE MATHEMATICAL PRACTICES
Focus on Communication

MP.3 In the algebraic expression $2x^2 - 9x$, $-9x$ is listed as a term rather than $9x$. By definition, a term is added, so the subtraction is rewritten as addition of the inverse: $2x^2 - 9x = 2x^2 + (-9x)$.

GRAPHIC ORGANIZERS

Present a table like the one below to help students organize information for writing expressions. In the first column, they can write words or phrases. They can use the second column for the corresponding variables and operation symbols.

	Words	Symbols
Quantity 1		
Quantity 2		
Quantity 3		
Operation		
Operation		

Point out that students should customize their tables for each problem. For example, this organizer is used for a problem that has three different quantities and two operations. Other problems will have different numbers of quantities and operations.

Suppose a and b give the populations of two states where $a > b$. Compare the expressions and tell which of the given pair is greater or if the expressions are equal.

15. $\frac{b}{a+b}$ and 0.5

Since $a > b$, $\frac{b}{a+b} < \frac{b}{b+b} = \frac{1}{2}$. So $0.5 > \frac{b}{a+b}$.

16. $a + 13c$ and $b + 13c$, where c is the population of a third state

In both the expressions, the same value, $13c$, is being added to the population. Since $a > b$, adding $13c$ to a results in a greater value than adding $13c$ to b.

$a + 13c > b + 13c$

17. $\frac{a-b}{2}$ and $a - \frac{b}{2}$

$\frac{a-b}{2} = \frac{a}{2} - \frac{b}{2}$. Since $\frac{a}{2} < a$, the expression $\frac{a}{2} - \frac{b}{2} < a - \frac{b}{2}$.

Therefore, $\frac{a-b}{2} < a - \frac{b}{2}$.

18. $a + b$ and $2b$

$2b = b + b$; This is less than $a + b$ because $a > b$, which implies that adding b to b is less than adding a to b. So, $a + b > 2b$.

19. $5(a + b)$ and $(a + b)5$

The expression $5(a + b) = (a + b) + (a + b) + (a + b) + (a + b) + (a + b)$, which is adding the total populations 5 times.

The expression $(a + b)5 = (a + b) + (a + b) + (a + b) + (a + b) + (a + b)$, which also is adding the total populations 5 times.

Therefore, $5(a + b) = (a + b)5$.

Write an algebraic expression to model the given context. Give your answer in simplest form.

20. the price s of a pair of shoes plus 5% sales tax.

$s + 0.05s = 1.05s$

21. the original price p of an item less a discount of 20%

$p - 0.20p = 0.80p$

22. the price h of a recently bought house plus 10% property tax

$h + 0.1h = 1.1h$

23. the principal amount P originally deposited in a bank account plus 0.3% interest

$P + 0.003P = 1.003P$

24. Match each statement with the algebraic expression that models it.

A. the price of a winter coat and a 20% discount   __B__ $x + 0.02x = 1.02x$

B. the base salary of an employee and a 2% salary increase   __A__ $x - 0.20x = 0.80x$

C. the cost of groceries and a 2% discount with coupons   __D__ $x + 0.20x = 1.20x$

D. the number of students attending school last year and a 20% increase from last year   __C__ $x - 0.02x = 0.98x$

H.O.T. Focus on Higher Order Thinking

25. Critique Reasoning A student is given the rectangle and the square shown. The student states that the two figures have the same perimeter. Is the student correct? Explain your reasoning.

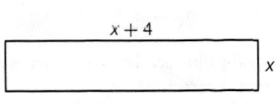

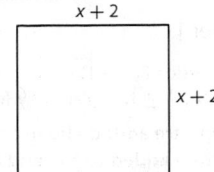

Yes, the student is correct.

For the rectangle, the perimeter is: $(x + 4) + x + (x + 4) + x = 4x + 8$

For the square, the perimeter is: $(x + 2) + (x + 2) + (x + 2) + (x + 2) = 4x + 8$

Because $(x + 4) + x + (x + 4) + x = 4x + 8 = (x + 2) + (x + 2) + (x + 2) + (x + 2)$, the perimeters are equal.

26. Multi-Step Yon buys tickets to a concert for himself and a friend. There is a tax of 6% on the price of the tickets and an additional booking fee of $20 for the transaction. Write an algebraic expression to represent the price per person. Simplify the expression if possible.

Price of 2 tickets in dollars: t
Tax on the 2 tickets: $0.06t$
Additional fee: 20

Total price for both Yon and his friend: $t + 0.06t + 20$

Since there are two people, divide the total price by 2 to get the price per person: $\dfrac{t + 0.06t + 20}{2}$

The price per person is $\dfrac{t + 0.06t + 20}{2}$, where the variable t represents the price of the two tickets in dollars.

After simplifying the expression, it becomes $\dfrac{1.06t + 20}{2}$, or $0.53t + 10$.

AVOID COMMON ERRORS

Some students may write division expressions in the wrong order. Explain that they need to pay attention to the order of the numbers and variables in the verbal description. For example, the quotient of 3 and a number p is $3 \div p$, not $p \div 3$.

INTEGRATE MATHEMATICAL PRACTICES
Focus on Communication

MP.3 Stress that students should strive to be precise with language and should look for key words and phrases that determine how to translate words into mathematical expressions. When students hear the phrase "the quotient of 5 and 3 more than a number n," they should immediately break it down into component quantities "5" and "3 more than a number n." Quotient indicates division of the first quantity, 5, by the second quantity, 3 more than a number n. Three *more* than a number n indicates that the second quantity is the sum of 3 and the variable n.

VISUAL CUES

Encourage students to circle or underline the key words that represent mathematical operations in a verbal description before translating it to an algebraic expression.

Have students describe quantities they encounter in their own lives, and then write algebraic expressions that model them.

27. Persevere in Problem Solving Jerry is planting white daisies and red tulips in his garden and he wants to choose a pattern in which the tulips surround the daisies. He uses tiles to generate patterns starting with two rows of three daisies. He surrounds these daisies with a border of tulips. The design continues as shown.

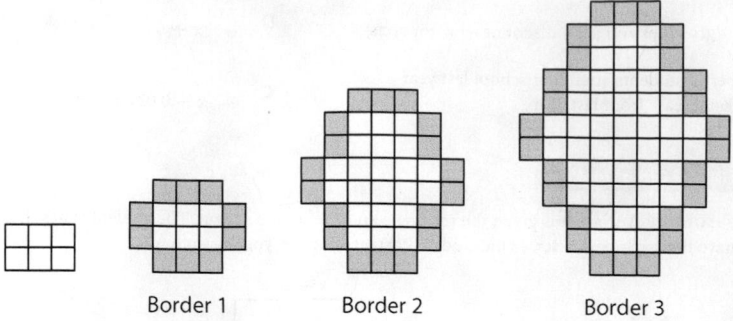

Border 1   Border 2   Border 3

a. Jerry writes the expression $8(b-1)+10$ for the number of tulips in each border, wherein b is the border number and $b \geq 1$. Explain why Jerry's expression is correct.

For Border 1, tulips are added above and below the daisies, which gives a total of six tulips. A tulip is then added to the end of each row of daisies, which gives four tulips. So, there is a total of ten tulips in Border 1.

For Border 2, there are eight additional tulips added to the garden plus the ten original tulips from Border 1. $8 + 10$

For Border 3, there are eight additional tulips added to the garden plus the ten original tulips from Border 1. $8(2) + 10$

So, the expression for the number of tulips in the garden with Border b is $8(b-1)+10$.

So, Jerry's expression is correct.

b. Elaine wants to start with two rows of four daisies. Her reasoning is that Jerry started with two rows of three daisies and his expression was $8(b-1)+10$, so if she starts with two rows of four daisies, her expression will be $10(b-1)+10$. Is Elaine's statement correct? Explain.

In part a, the number 10 comes from the top and bottom rows of 3 tulips in Border 1 and the 4 tulips on the ends of the two original rows of daisies. If Elaine starts with two rows of four tulips, then the number of tulips in Border 1 would change to 12 since a daisy in each row is being added. So, Elaine's expression is not correct. The correct expression for starting with two rows of four daisies would be $8(b-1)+12$.

Lesson Performance Task

Becky and Michele are both shopping for a new car at two different dealerships. Dealership A is offering $500 cash back on any purchase, while Dealership B is offering $1000 cash back. The tax rate is 5% at Dealership A but 8% at Dealership B. Becky wants to buy a car that is $15,000, and Michele is planning to buy a car that costs $20,000. Use algebraic expressions to help you answer the following questions.

a. At which dealership will Becky get the better deal? How much does she save?

b. At which dealership will Michele get the better deal? How much does she save?

c. What generalization can you make that would help any shopper know which dealership has the better deal? [Hint: At what price point would the two deals be equal?]

a. **First write an algebraic expression to represent each dealership's special.**

   Dealership A
   $$p + 0.05p - 500 = 1.05p - 500$$

   Dealership B
   $$p + 0.08p - 1000 = 1.08p - 1000$$

   Now substitute the price that Becky plans to pay to see which deal is better for her.

   Dealership A: $1.05(15,000) - 500 = 15,750 - 500 = 15,250$

   Dealership B: $1.08(15,000) - 1000 = 16,200 - 1000 = 15,200$

   Dealership A $>$ Dealership B

   So, Becky will get a better deal with Dealership B, since it is $50 cheaper.

b. **Substitute the price that Michele plans to pay into each expression.**

   Dealership A: $1.05(20,000) - 500 = 21,000 - 500 = 20,500$

   Dealership B: $1.08(20,000) - 1000 = 21,600 - 1000 = 20,600$

   Dealership A $<$ Dealership B

   So, Michele will get a better deal with Dealership A, since it is $100 cheaper.

c. **The two deals are equivalent when the additional 3% tax equals $500 ($0.03p = 500$), which occurs when the purchase price is $16,667. Students' generalizations may suggest that any shopper planning to buy a car with a price less than $16,667 will get the better deal at Dealership B, while anyone planning to buy a car at a price higher than $16,667 will get a better deal at Dealership A.**

EXTENSION ACTIVITY

Have students research the various incentives offered by car dealers, such as cash rebates, financing offers, down payments, leasing deals, special warranties, and tune-up packages. Then have students write a few paragraphs describing how comparison shopping and understanding dealers' offers could save them thousands of dollars when buying a new car. They should include one numerical example that shows how the same car could cost them different amounts with two different sets of incentives.

QUESTIONING STRATEGIES

? Why is the dealership that is offering the greatest amount of cash back not necessarily the best deal? The dealership that gives the greatest amount of cash back has a higher tax rate. The greater the cost of the car, the more the buyer must pay in tax.

INTEGRATE MATHEMATICAL PRACTICES
Focus on Modeling

MP.4 Before students can model the situation in the Lesson Performance Task, they need to understand how tax is calculated. Review with students their experience with sales tax when purchasing an item at a store. The rate of the tax, written as a decimal, is multiplied by the price, p, of the item to find the amount of tax owed. The cost of the item is then added to the tax amount to find the total cost. For a tax rate of 5% this can be written as $p + 0.05p$ or as $1.05p$.

Scoring Rubric

2 points: Student correctly solves the problem and explains his/her reasoning.

1 point: Student shows good understanding of the problem but does not fully solve or explain his/her reasoning.

0 points: Student does not demonstrate understanding of the problem.

Creating and Solving Equations

Common Core Math Standards

The student is expected to:

 A-CED.A.1

Create equations… in one variable and use them to solve problems. Also A-CED.A.3, A-REI.B.3

Mathematical Practices

 MP.5 Using Tools

Language Objective

Explain to a partner how to solve an equation with the variable on both sides.

ENGAGE

Essential Question: How do you use an equation to model and solve a real-world problem?

Use a verbal description or a table to write an equation, solve the equation, then check that your answer makes sense.

PREVIEW: LESSON PERFORMANCE TASK

View the Engage section online. Discuss the various ways savings can be invested to make more money. Then preview the Lesson Performance Task.

2.2 Creating and Solving Equations

Essential Question: How do you use an equation to model and solve a real-world problem?

Resource Locker

⊙ Explore   Creating Equations from Verbal Descriptions

You can use what you know about writing algebraic expressions to write an equation that represents a real-world situation.

Suppose Cory and his friend Walter go to a movie. Each of their tickets costs the same amount, and they share a frozen yogurt that costs $5.50. The total amount they spend is $19.90. How can you write an equation that describes the situation?

Ⓐ **Identify the important information.**

The word _____ **is** _____ tells you that the relationship describes an equation.

The word *total* tells you that the operation involved in the relationship is _____ **addition** _____.

What numerical information do you have? **The frozen yogurt costs $5.50, and the total amount spent is $19.90.**

What is the unknown quantity? _____ **the cost of each ticket** _____

Ⓑ **Write a verbal description.**

Choose a name for the variable. In this case, use *c* for _____ **cost** _____.

The verbal description is: Twice the cost of _____ **a ticket** _____ plus the cost

of _____ **the frozen yogurt** _____ equals _____ **the total amount** _____

Ⓒ To write an equation, write a numerical or _____ **algebraic** _____ expression for each quantity

and insert an equal sign in the appropriate place. An equation is: _____ **$2c + 5.50 = 19.90$** _____

Reflect

1. How can you use a verbal model to write an equation for the situation described?

Use the information to write the model

| Twice the cost of a ticket (dollars) | + | Cost of frozen yogurt (dollars) | = | Total cost (dollars) |

© Houghton Mifflin Harcourt Publishing Company

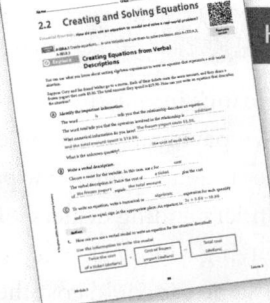

2. Could you write a different equation to describe the situation? Explain your reasoning.

Yes; you could write a different but equivalent equation, such as 19.90 − 2c = 5.50, or

c + c + 5.50 = 19.90.

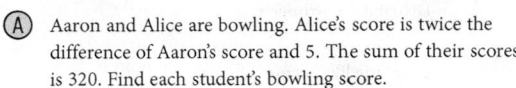 **Creating and Solving Equations Involving the Distributive Property**

When you create an equation to model a real-world problem, your equation may involve the Distributive Property. When you solve a real-world problem, you should always check that your answer makes sense.

Example 1 Write and solve an equation to solve each problem.

Ⓐ Aaron and Alice are bowling. Alice's score is twice the difference of Aaron's score and 5. The sum of their scores is 320. Find each student's bowling score.

Write a verbal description of the basic situation.

The sum of Aaron's score and Alice's score is 320.

Choose a variable for the unknown quantity and write an equation to model the detailed situation.

Let a represent Aaron's score. Then $2(a - 5)$ represents Alice's score.

$$a + 2(a - 5) = 320$$

Solve the equation for a.

$$a + 2(a - 5) = 320$$

$a + 2a - 10 = 320$	Distributive Property
$3a - 10 = 320$	
$3a - 10 + 10 = 320 + 10$	Addition Property of Equality
$3a = 330$	
$\dfrac{3a}{3} = \dfrac{330}{3}$	Division Property of Equality
$a = 110$	

So, Aaron's score is 110 and Alice's score is $2(a - 5) = 2(110 - 5) = 2(105) = 210$.

Check that the answer makes sense.

$110 + 210 = 320$, so the answer makes sense.

Ⓑ Mari, Carlos, and Amanda collect stamps. Carlos has five more stamps than Mari, and Amanda has three times as many stamps as Carlos. Altogether, they have 100 stamps. Find the number of stamps each person has.

Write a verbal description of the basic situation.

The total of the numbers of stamps Mari, Carlos, and Amanda have is 100.

© Houghton Mifflin Harcourt Publishing Company • Image Credits: Digital Vision/Getty Images

PROFESSIONAL DEVELOPMENT

Math Background

In this lesson, students will use the Distributive Property along with the properties of equality (addition, subtraction, multiplication, and division) to solve equations. Solving equations involves using inverse operations to get the variable alone on one side of the equation and the solution on the other side of the equation. At each step of the solving process, students use properties to derive equivalent equations, or equations with the same solution set.

Creating Equations from Verbal Descriptions

INTEGRATE TECHNOLOGY

Students may complete the Explore activity either in the book or online.

CONNECT VOCABULARY EL

The word *equation* begins with the root *equa-*. Have students think of some other words that begin with equa-. Discuss what all these words have in common.

QUESTIONING STRATEGIES

? What words in a verbal description could be represented by the equal sign in an equation? **equals, is, is equal to, is the same as**

EXPLAIN 1

Creating and Solving Equations Involving the Distributive Property

QUESTIONING STRATEGIES

? What is the first step in solving an equation that contains parentheses? **Remove the parentheses by distributing any factor in front of the parentheses to all terms within the parentheses.**

AVOID COMMON ERRORS

Students may try to multiply a coefficient in front of parentheses by only one of the enclosed terms. Remind students to multiply the coefficient by *every* term within the parentheses.

Choose a variable for the unknown quantity and write an equation to model the detailed situation.

Let s represent the number of stamps Mari has. Then Carlos has ___$s + 5$___ stamps, and Amanda has ___$3(s + 5)$___ stamps.

$$s + \boxed{s + 5} + 3\left(\boxed{s + 5}\right) = \boxed{100}$$

Solve the equation for s.

$$s + \boxed{s + 5} + 3\left(\boxed{s + 5}\right) = \boxed{100}$$

$s + s + 5 + 3s + \boxed{15} = \boxed{100}$	Distributive Property
$\boxed{5s} + \boxed{20} = \boxed{100}$	Combine like terms
$\boxed{5}\,s = \boxed{80}$	Subtraction Property of Equality
$s = \boxed{16}$	Division Property of Equality

So, Mari has ___16___ stamps, Carlos has ___21___ stamps, and Amanda has ___63___ stamps.

Check that the answer makes sense.

$$\boxed{16} + \boxed{21} + \boxed{63} = \boxed{100}$$
; the answer makes sense.
$$\boxed{100} = \boxed{100}$$

Reflect

3. Would a fractional answer make sense in this situation?
   No; a fractional number of stamps does not make sense.

4. **Discussion** What might it mean if a check revealed that the answer to a real-world problem did not make sense?
   Possible answers: The equation may have been written incorrectly; the equation may have been correct, but been solved incorrectly; there may not be any solution to the problem.

COLLABORATIVE LEARNING

Whole Class Activity

Give each student a card with an expression such as $2x + 4$ or $3x - 7$ written on it. Have students pair up and solve the equation that is formed by setting their expressions equal to each other. Students should pair up with as many students as time allows.

Peer-to-Peer Activity

Have students work in pairs. Give each pair an equation to solve. Have each student solve the equation and write an explanation next to each step of the solution, then have students compare their steps.

Your Turn

Write and solve an equation to solve the problem.

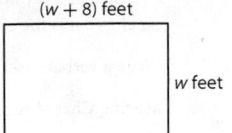

5. A rectangular garden is fenced on all sides with 256 feet of fencing. The garden is 8 feet longer than it is wide. Find the length and width of the garden.

$2w + 2(w + 8) = 256$

$2w + 2w + 16 = 256$	**Distributive Property**
$4w + 16 = 256$	**Combining like terms**
$4w = 240$	**Subtraction Property of Equality**
$w = 60$	**Division property of Equality**

Width = 60 ft, length = 60 + 8 = 68 ft

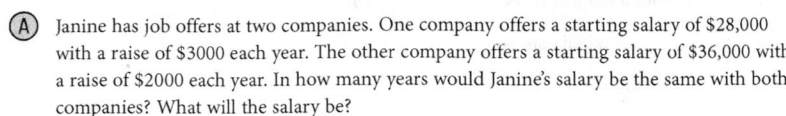

In some equations, variables appear on both sides. You can use the properties of equality to collect the variable terms so that they all appear on one side of the equation.

Example 2 Write and solve an equation to solve each problem.

Ⓐ Janine has job offers at two companies. One company offers a starting salary of $28,000 with a raise of $3000 each year. The other company offers a starting salary of $36,000 with a raise of $2000 each year. In how many years would Janine's salary be the same with both companies? What will the salary be?

Write a verbal description of the basic situation.

Let n represent the number of years it takes for the salaries to be equal.

Base Salary A plus $3000 per year raise = Base Salary B + $2000 per year raise

$$28,000 + 3000n = 36,000 + 2,000n$$

$28,000 + 3000n - 2000n = 36,000 + 2,000n - 2000n$	Subtraction Property of Equality
$28,000 + 1000n = 36,000$	Combine like terms.
$28,000 + 1000n - 28,000 = 36,000 - 28,000$	Subtraction Property of Equality
$1000n = 8000$	
$\dfrac{1000n}{1000} = \dfrac{8000}{1000}$	Division Property of Equality
$n = 8$	

$$28,000 + 3,000(8) = 36,000 + 2,000(8)$$

$$52,000 = 52,000$$

In 8 years, the salaries offered by both companies will be $52,000.

DIFFERENTIATE INSTRUCTION

Manipulatives

Put 7 pencils in a closed container. Have one student hold the container in one hand and 5 pencils in the other hand. Have another student hold 12 pencils. Tell the class that both students have the same number of pencils. Ask how they can figure out the number of pencils in the container without opening it. Give or take pencils away from each student as suggestions are made. When the class has arrived at an answer, check by counting the number of pencils in the container. Relate this activity to solving the equation $x + 5 = 12$.

EXPLAIN 2

Creating and Solving Equations with Variables on Both Sides

QUESTIONING STRATEGIES

? What words or phrases in a word problem tell you what the variable in your equation should represent? **how many, what number of**

? Why should you use the original form of the equation to check your solution? **It is possible that you made a mistake while transforming the equation. If you use the original equation, you won't repeat the same error.**

AVOID COMMON ERRORS

When students have a variable on both sides of an equation, they often forget to pay attention to the sign of the coefficient of the variable. To avoid this error, encourage students to add and subtract variable terms so that the result is a positive coefficient. Often this means to subtract the variable term with the lesser coefficient on both sides. For example, for the first step in solving $3x + 2 = x + 10$, subtracting x, rather than $3x$, from both sides will result in an equation with a positive coefficient for x.

INTEGRATE TECHNOLOGY

A graphing calculator can be used to check the solution to an equation with variables on both sides. For example, to solve $3x + 2 = x + 10$, enter Y1 as $3x + 2$ and Y2 as $x + 10$. Graph both lines, adjusting the window if necessary. Then select the intersect feature to determine the intersection point of the two lines. Point out that the x-coordinate of the intersection point, which is 4, is the solution.

Ⓑ One moving company charges $800 plus $16 per hour. Another moving company charges $720 plus $21 per hour. At what number of hours will the charge by both companies be the same? What is the charge?

Write a verbal description of the basic situation. Let t represent the number of hours that the move takes.

Moving Charge A plus $16 per hour = Moving Charge B plus $21 per hour

$$800 + \boxed{16}\, t = 720 + \boxed{21}\, t$$

$$800 + \boxed{16}\, t - \boxed{16}\, t = 720 + \boxed{21}\, t - \boxed{16}\, t \qquad \text{Subtraction Property of Equality}$$

$$800 = 720 + \boxed{5}\, t$$

$$800 - 720 = 720 + \boxed{5}\, t - 720 \qquad \text{Subtraction Property of Equality}$$

$$\boxed{80} = \boxed{5}\, t$$

$$\frac{\boxed{80}}{\boxed{5}} = \frac{\boxed{5}}{\boxed{5}}\, t \qquad \text{Division Property of Equality}$$

$$t = \boxed{16}$$

The charges are the same for a job that takes ____16____ hours.

Substitute the value 16 in the original equation.

$$800 + 16t = 720 + 21t$$

$$800 + 16\left(\boxed{16} \right) = 720 + 21\left(\boxed{16} \right)$$

$$800 + \boxed{256} = 720 + \boxed{336}$$

$$\boxed{1056} = \boxed{1056}$$

After ____16____ hours, the moving charge for both companies will be ____$1056____.

Reflect

6. Suppose you collected the variable terms on the other side of the equal sign to solve the equation. Would that affect the solution?
   No; the solution of the equation is the value that makes it true. The solution method does not change the solution.

© Houghton Mifflin Harcourt Publishing Company

LANGUAGE SUPPORT **EL**

Visual Cues

Encourage students to break down a written description of a real-world problem by identifying and highlighting key parts of the description. For example, they might highlight the unknown quantity in one color and highlight each of the given quantities in a different color. Then they can look for a phrase meaning *is equal to* and identify the two quantities that are equal to one another.

Write and solve an equation to solve each problem.

7. Claire bought just enough fencing to enclose either a rectangular garden or a triangular garden, as shown. The two gardens have the same perimeter. How many feet of fencing did she buy?

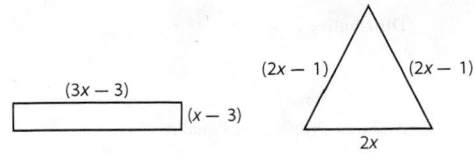

$(3x - 3)$
$(x - 3)$

$(2x - 1)$ $(2x - 1)$
$2x$

$2(3x - 3) + 2(x - 3) = (2x - 1) + (2x - 1) + 2x$

$6x - 6 + 2x - 6 = 2x - 1 + 2x - 1 + 2x$

$8x - 12 = 6x - 2$

$2x = 10$

$x = 5$

Substitute the value 5 in the original equation.

$2\big(3(5) - 3\big) + 2(5 - 3) = \big(2(5) - 1\big) + \big(2(5) - 1\big) + 2(5)$

$28 - 28$

Claire bought 28 feet of fencing.

8. A veterinarian is changing the diets of two animals, Simba and Cuddles. Simba currently consumes 1200 Calories per day. That number will increase by 100 Calories each day. Cuddles currently consumes 3230 Calories a day. That number will decrease by 190 Calories each day. The patterns will continue until both animals are consuming the same number of Calories each day. In how many days will that be? How many Calories will each animal be consuming each day then?

$1200 + 100n = 3230 - 190n$

$n = 7$

$1200 + 100(7) = 3230 - 190(7)$

$1900 = 1900$

In 7 days, each animal will be consuming 1900 Calories per day.

Explain 3   Constructing Equations from an Organized Table

You can use a table to organize information and see relationships.

Example 3   Construct and solve an equation to solve the problem.

Kim works 4 hours more each day than Jill does, and Jack works 2 hours less each day than Jill does. Over 2 days, the number of hours Kim works is equal to the difference of 4 times the number of hours Jack works and the number of hours Jill works. How many hours does each person work each day?

Analyze Information

Identify the important information.

- Kim works 4 hours more per day than Jill does.

- Jack works 2 hours less per day than Jill does.

Formulate a Plan

Make a table using the information given. Let x be the number of hours Jill works in one day.

	Hours Worked Per Day	Hours Worked Over 2 Days
Kim	$x + 4$	$2(x + 4)$
Jill	x	$2x$
Jack	$x - 2$	$2(x - 2)$

Over 2 days, the number of hours Kim works is equal to the difference of 4 times the number of hours Jack works and the number of hours Jill works.

$2(x + 4) = 4 \cdot 2(x - 2) - 2x$

EXPLAIN 3

Constructing Equations from an Organized Table

QUESTIONING STRATEGIES

? When you create a table to represent the information in a real-world problem, what do the rows and columns represent? **Possible answer:** Each row might represent a different person in the problem, and each column represents the situation at different times.

AVOID COMMON ERRORS

When a problem asks for several related quantities, such as the ages of three people, students may become confused and forget which quantity the variable represents. Constructing a table is especially helpful in solving this type of problem, because it forces students to write out how each quantity is related to the variable.

ELABORATE

INTEGRATE MATHEMATICAL PRACTICES

Focus on Patterns

MP.8 Discuss with students how to use inverse operations to solve an equation.

AVOID COMMON ERRORS

Make sure students understand that they must keep an equation balanced by adding/subtracting or multiplying/dividing on both sides of the equation, not just one side.

QUESTIONING STRATEGIES

? How is the process of solving an equation with a leading coefficient of 1 different from solving an equation with a leading coefficient not equal to 1? After the variable term is isolated, you must divide by the leading coefficient if it is not 1.

SUMMARIZE THE LESSON

? How do you know if a solution to a real-world problem is correct? You verify that the original equation was written correctly by re-reading the problem, and then substitute your answer for the variable in the original equation.

🧩 Solve

$$2(x + 4) = 4 \cdot 2(x - 2) - 2x$$

$2(x + 4) = \boxed{8} \,(x - 2) - 2x$ Simplify.

$2x + \boxed{8} = 8x - \boxed{16} - 2x$ Distributive Property

$2x + 8 = \boxed{6}\, x - 16$

$2x + 8 + \boxed{16} = 6x - 16 + \boxed{16}$ Addition Property of Equality

$2x + \boxed{24} = 6x$

$2x + 24 - \boxed{2}\, x = 6x - \boxed{2}\, x$ Subtraction Property of Equality

$24 = \boxed{4}\, x$

$\dfrac{24}{\boxed{4}} = \dfrac{\boxed{4}\, x}{\boxed{4}}$ Division Property of Equality

$\boxed{6} = x$

Jill works $\boxed{6}$ hours per day, Kim works $\boxed{10}$ hours per day, and Jack works $\boxed{4}$ hours per day.

🧩 Justify and Evaluate

Substitute $x = 6$ into the original equation.

$$2(6 + 4) = 4 \cdot 2(6 - 2) - 2x$$

$2\left(\boxed{10}\right) = 8\left(\boxed{4}\right) - 2\left(\boxed{6}\right)$

$\boxed{20} = \boxed{20}$

Your Turn

Write and solve an equation to solve the problem.

9. Lisa is 10 centimeters taller than her friend Ian. Ian is 14 centimeters taller than Jim. Every month, their heights increase by 2 centimeters. In 7 months, the sum of Ian's and Jim's heights will be 170 centimeters more than Lisa's height. How tall is Ian now?

	Height now	Height after 7 months
Lisa	$h + 10$	$(h + 10) + 14$
Ian	h	$h + 14$
Jim	$h - 14$	$(h - 14) + 14$

$(h + 14) + (h - 14) + 14 = (h + 10) + 14 + 170; h = 180;$ Ian is 180 cm tall now.

Elaborate

10. How can you use properties to solve equations with variables on both sides?
Use the Properties of Equality and the Distributive Property to isolate the variable on one

side of the equation using inverse operations.

11. How is a table helpful when constructing equations?
A table can help organize the information and let you recognize relationships and, possibly,

how they change over time, which makes writing an equation easier.

12. When solving a real-world problem to find a person's age, would a negative solution make sense? Explain.
No, because a person cannot have a negative age.

13. **Essential Question Check-In** How do you write an equation to represent a real-world situation?
Read the information carefully so that you can write a verbal description, build a verbal model,

or use a table to represent the situation. Use the numerical information you have along with

appropriate algebraic expressions for the unknown quantities to write an equation.

Evaluate: Homework and Practice

- Online Homework
- Hints and Help
- Extra Practice

Write an equation for each description.   Possible answers given.

1. The sum of 14 and a number is equal to 17.

$$14 + x = 17$$

2. A number increased by 10 is 114.

$$n + 10 = 114$$

3. The difference between a number and 12 is 20.

$$n - 12 = 20$$

4. Ten times the sum of half a number and 6 is 8.

$$10\left(\tfrac{1}{2}x + 6\right) = 8$$

5. Two-thirds a number plus 4 is 7.

$$\tfrac{2}{3}x + 4 = 7$$

6. Tanmayi wants to raise $175 for a school fundraiser. She has raised $120 so far. How much more does she need to reach her goal?

$$m + 120 = 175$$

7. Hector is visiting a cousin who lives 350 miles away. He has driven 90 miles. How many more miles does he need to drive to reach his cousin's home?

$$d + 90 = 350$$

8. The length of a rectangle is twice its width. The perimeter of the rectangle is 126 feet.

$$2(2w) + 2w = 126$$

Exercise	Depth of Knowledge (D.O.K.)	COMMON CORE Mathematical Practices
1–5	**1** Recall of Information	**MP.2** Reasoning
6–9	**2** Skills/Concepts	**MP.4** Modeling
10	**2** Skills/Concepts	**MP.2** Reasoning
11–16	**2** Skills/Concepts	**MP.4** Modeling
17–19	**3** Strategic Thinking	**MP.1** Problem Solving
20	**3** Strategic Thinking	**MP.4** Modeling

EVALUATE

ASSIGNMENT GUIDE

Concepts and Skills	Practice
Explore Creating Equations from Verbal Descriptions	Exercises 1–8
Example 1 Creating and Solving Equations Involving the Distributive Property	Exercises 9–12, 21, 23
Example 2 Creating and Solving Equations with Variables on Both Sides	Exercises 13–16, 22, 24
Example 3 Constructing Equations from an Organized Table	Exercises 17–20, 25

INTEGRATE MATHEMATICAL PRACTICES
Focus on Reasoning

MP.2 Students can check their solutions for correctness by substituting the value into the original equation and verifying that the solution makes the equation true.

COGNITIVE STRATEGIES

Remind students that an equation is like a balanced scale. To keep the balance, whatever you do on one side of the equation, you must also do on the other side. Tell students that in order to solve the equation, they have to undo the operations on each side of the scale. Have students name each operation in an equation and then identify the operation that undoes it.

AVOID COMMON ERRORS

When solving problems using division, some students may automatically divide the larger number by the smaller number every time. For example, a student may try to solve $6x = 3$ by dividing both sides by 3. Remind students that they must isolate the variable, and that the variable is being multiplied by 6, not by 3.

Write and solve an equation for each situation.

9. In one baseball season, Peter hit twice the difference of the number of home runs Alice hit and 6. Altogether, they hit 18 home runs. How many home runs did each player hit that season?

$h + 2(h - 6) = 18; h = 10$

So, Alice hit 10 home runs and Peter hit
$2(10 - 6) = 8$ **home runs.**

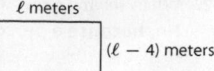

10. The perimeter of a parallelogram is 72 meters. The width of the parallelogram is 4 meters less than its length. Find the length and the width of the parallelogram.

$2\ell + 2(\ell - 4) = 72; \ell = 20$

The length of the parallelogram is 20 meters and the width is
$20 - 4 = 16$ **meters.**

ℓ meters

$(\ell - 4)$ meters

11. One month, Ruby worked 6 hours more than Isaac, and Svetlana worked 4 times as many hours as Ruby. Together they worked 126 hours. Find the number of hours each person worked.

$h + (h + 6) + 4(h + 6) = 126; h = 16$

Isaac worked 16 hours, Ruby worked 22 hours, and Svetlana worked 88 hours.

12. In one day, Annie traveled 5 times the sum of the number of hours Brian traveled and 2. Together they traveled 20 hours. Find the number of hours each person traveled.

$h + 5(h + 2) = 20; h = 1\frac{2}{3}$

Brian traveled for $1\frac{2}{3}$ hours and Annie traveled for $5\left(1\frac{2}{3} + 2\right) = 18\frac{1}{3}$ hours.

13. Xian and his cousin Kai both collect stamps. Xian has 56 stamps, and Kai has 80 stamps. The boys recently joined different stamp-collecting clubs. Xian's club will send him 12 new stamps per month. Kai's club will send him 8 new stamps per month. After how many months will Xian and Kai have the same number of stamps? How many stamps will each have?

$56 + 12m = 80 + 8m; m = 6$

$56 + 12(6) = 128$ **and** $80 + 8(6) = 128$

After 6 months, they will each have 128 stamps.

14. Kenya plans to make a down payment plus monthly payments in order to buy a motorcycle. At one dealer she would pay $2,500 down and $150 each month. At another dealer, she would pay $3,000 down and $125 each month. After how many months would the total amount paid be the same for both dealers? What would that amount be?

$2500 + 150m = 3000 + 125m; m = 20$

$2500 + 150(20) = 5500$ **and** $3000 + 125(20) = 5500$

After 20 months, the total amount paid to both dealers will be $5500.

Exercise	Depth of Knowledge (D.O.K.)		COMMON CORE Mathematical Practices
21	**2** Skills/Concepts		**MP.4** Modeling
22	**3** Strategic Thinking	H.O.T.	**MP.2** Reasoning
23	**2** Skills/Concepts	H.O.T.	**MP.4** Modeling
24	**3** Strategic Thinking	H.O.T.	**MP.2** Reasoning
25	**3** Strategic Thinking	H.O.T.	**MP.3** Logic

15. Community Gym charges a $50 membership fee and a $55 monthly fee. Workout Gym charges a $200 membership fee and a $45 monthly fee. After how many months will the total amount of money paid to both gyms be the same? What will the amount be?

$50 + 55m = 200 + 45m; m = 15$

$50 + 55(15) = 875$ and $200 + 45(15) = 875$

After 15 months, the total amount paid to both gyms is $875.

16. Tina is saving to buy a notebook computer. She has two options. The first option is to put $200 away initially and save $10 every month. The second option is to put $100 away initially and save $30 every month. After how many months would Tina save the same amount using either option? How much would she save with either option?

$200 + 10n = 100 + 30n; n = 5$ $200 + 10(5) = 250$ and $100 + 30(5) = 250$

After 5 months Tina will save $250 using either option.

Use the table to answer each question.

	Starting Salary	Yearly Salary Increase
Company A	$24,000	$3000
Company B	$30,000	$2400
Company C	$36,000	$2000

17. After how many years are the salaries offered by Company A and Company B the same?

$24,000 + 3,000n = 30,000 + 2,400n; n = 10$ **years**

18. After how many years are the salaries offered by Company B and Company C the same?

$30,000 + 2,400n = 36,000 + 2,000n; n = 15$ **years**

19. Paul started work at Company B ten years ago at the salary shown in the table. At the same time, Sharla started at Company C at the salary shown in the table. Who earned more during the last year? How much more?

In the last year, Sharla earned $2000 more than Paul. Paul earned $30,000 + 10($2400) = $54,000. Sharla earned $36,000 + 10($2000) = $56,000.

20. George's page contains twice as many typed words as Bill's page and Bill's page contains 50 fewer words than Charlie's page. If each person can type 60 words per minute, after one minute, the difference between twice the number of words on Bill's page and the number of words on Charlie's page is 210. How many words did Bill's page contain initially? Use a table to organize the information.

	Initial number of words	Total number of words after one minute
George	$2x$	$2x + 60$
Charlie	$x + 50$	$(x + 50) + 60$
Bill	x	$x + 60$

$2(x + 60) - ((x + 50) + 60) = 210; x = 200$

Bill's page contained 200 words initially.

INTEGRATE MATHEMATICAL PRACTICES
Focus on Patterns

MP.8 Before students solve problems involving perimeter, it may be helpful to review that the *perimeter* of a figure is the total distance around its edges. Ask students how they can calculate the perimeter of a rectangle. **The perimeter of a rectangle is $2\ell + 2w$, where ℓ is the length and w is the width.**

COGNITIVE STRATEGIES

Point out that a good pattern to use when solving equations is to clear parentheses, if there are any, by using the Distributive Property, and then finish solving by using the properties of equality.

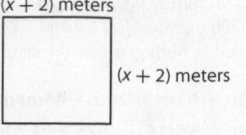

Have students use the equation-solving tools available in graphing calculators or online. Students should consider how technology can be used to verify solutions.

JOURNAL

Have students write a journal entry in which they describe how to find the solution of an equation that contains parentheses and has the variable on both sides.

---

21. Geometry Sammie bought just enough fencing to border either a rectangular plot or a square plot, as shown. The perimeters of the plots are the same. How many meters of fencing did she buy?

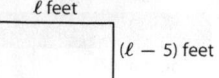

$(x + 2)$ meters

$(x + 2)$ meters

$2(3x + 2) + 2(x - 1) = 4(x + 2); x = 1.5$

$2(3(1.5) + 2) + 2(1.5 - 1) = 14$ and $4(1.5 + 2) = 14$.
Sammie bought 14 meters of fencing.

$(3x + 2)$ meters

$(x - 1)$ meters

H.O.T. Focus on Higher Order Thinking

22. Justify Reasoning Suppose you want to solve the equation $2a + b = 2a$, where a and b are nonzero real numbers. Describe the solution to this equation. Justify your description.

There is no solution; Sample answer: If you subtract $2a$ from each side, you get the statement $b = 0$. Since a and b are nonzero real numbers, this statement is false. Therefore, there is no solution.

23. Multi-Step A patio in the shape of a rectangle, is fenced on all sides with 134 feet of fencing. The patio is 5 feet less wide than it is long.

ℓ feet

$(\ell - 5)$ feet

a. What information can be used to solve the problem? How can you find the information?

Possible answer: You need the length and width of the patio. You can write algebraic expressions for the length and width. Use the expressions in the formula for the perimeter of a rectangle, and then solve to find the length and the width.

b. Describe how to find the area of the patio. What is the area of the patio?

Find the length and width using the formula for the perimeter of a rectangle. Let ℓ be the length and let $\ell - 5$ be the width. $2\ell + 2(\ell - 5) = 134; \ell = 36$. The length of the patio is 36 ft and the width is $36 - 5 = 31$ ft. The area is $36 \times 31 = 1{,}116$ ft^2.

24. Explain the Error Kevin and Brittany write an equation to represent the following relationship, and both students solve their equation. Who found the correct equation and solution? Why is the other person incorrect?

5 times the difference of a number and 20 is the same as half the sum of 4 more than 4 times a number.

Kevin:

$$5(x - 20) = \frac{1}{2}(4x + 4)$$

$$5x - 100 = 2x + 2$$

$$3x - 100 = 2$$

$$3x = 102$$

$$x = 34$$

Brittany:

$$5(20 - x) = \frac{1}{2}(4x + 4)$$

$$100 - 5x = 2x + 2$$

$$100 - 7x = 2$$

$$-7x = -98$$

$$x = 14$$

Kevin is correct. Brittany expressed the difference of a number and 20 incorrectly. Kevin's expression $x - 20$ was correct.

25. What If? Alexa and Zack are solving the following problem.

The number of miles on Car A is 50 miles more than the number of miles on Car B, and the number of miles on Car B is 30 miles more than the number of miles on Car C. All the cars travel 50 miles in 1 hour. After 1 hour, twice the number of miles on Car A is 70 miles less than 3 times the number of miles on Car C. How many miles were there on Car B initially?

Alexa assumes there are m miles on Car B. Zack assumes there are m miles on Car C. Will Zack's answer be the same as Alexa's answer? Explain.

Alexa's Table	Initial Miles	Miles after One Hour
Car A	$m + 50$	$(m + 50) + 50$
Car B	m	$m + 50$
Car C	$m - 30$	$(m - 30) + 50$

Zack's Table	Initial Miles	Miles after One Hour
Car A	$m + 80$	$(m + 80) + 50$
Car B	$m + 30$	$(m + 30) + 50$
Car C	m	$m + 50$

$2((m + 50) + 50) = 3((m - 30) + 50) - 70$

$m = 210$ miles

$2((m + 80) + 50) = 3(m + 50) - 70; m = 180$

Initially: A: 260 mi, B: 210 mi, C: 180 mi; Zack's answer is the same as Alexa's.

Lesson Performance Task

Stacy, Oliver, and Jivesh each plan to put a certain amount of money into their savings accounts that earn simple interest of 6% per year. Stacy puts $550 more than Jivesh, and Oliver puts in 2 times as much as Jivesh. After a year, the amount in Stacy's account is 2 times the sum of $212 and the amount in Oliver's account. How much does each person initially put into his or her account? Who had the most money in his or her account after a year? Who had the least? Explain.

	Amount in Account Initially	Amount in Account after One Year
Stacy	$a + 550$	$1.06(a + 550)$
Oliver	$2a$	$1.06(2a)$
Jivesh	a	$1.06a$

$1.06(a + 550) = 2(212 + 1.06\,(2a))$

$1.06a + 583 = 424 + 4.24a$

$583 = 424 + 3.18a$

$159 = 3.18a$

$50 = a$

Initially: Jivesh $50, Stacy $600, Oliver $100

Stacy: $1.06(50 + 550) = 1.06(600) = 636$

Oliver: $1.06(2 \cdot 50) = 1.06(100) = 106$

Jivesh: $1.06 \cdot 50 = 53$

So Stacy had the most in her account after one year and Jivesh had the least.

© Houghton Mifflin Harcourt Publishing Company

AVOID COMMON ERRORS

Because of the need to use parentheses within parentheses, some students may write the equation incorrectly. Suggest that students use brackets in place of the outer parentheses, making the equation.

$1.06(a + 550) = 2[212 + 1.06(2a)]$.

INTEGRATE MATHEMATICAL PRACTICES
Focus on Math Connections

MP.1 Simple interest is interest paid on the original principal only. Simple interest can be calculated using the formula $I = Prt$, where I is the interest, P is the principal, r is the interest rate per year, and t is the time in years. Note that interest at a bank is more likely to be calculated using compound interest, which is earned not only on the original principal, but also on all interest earned previously. Accounts earning compound interest make more money than accounts earning simple interest. The formula for compound interest involves an exponential function, which students will learn later in this course.

EXTENSION ACTIVITY

Have students research the Rule of 72 and use it to estimate how long it will take to double an investment of $100 in an account earning 8% interest compounded once a year. Then ask them how this compares to the value of $100 invested in an account earning 8% simple interest for the same amount of time. Students should find that the time needed for an investment to double can be estimated by dividing 72 by the compound interest rate, so $100 earning 8% compound interest will double to $200 in 9 years. However, $100 earning 8% simple interest for 9 years is worth only $100 + 100(0.08)(9) = \$172$.

Scoring Rubric
2 points: Student correctly solves the problem and explains his/her reasoning.
1 point: Student shows good understanding of the problem but does not fully solve or explain his/her reasoning.
0 points: Student does not demonstrate understanding of the problem.

Creating and Solving Equations   **66**

Solving for a Variable

Common Core Math Standards

The student is expected to:

 A-CED.A.4

Rearrange formulas to highlight a quantity of interest, using the same reasoning as in solving an equation. Also A-REI.B.3

Mathematical Practices

 MP.8 Patterns

Language Objective

Explain to a partner how to solve an equation for a specified variable.

ENGAGE

Essential Question: How do you rewrite formulas and literal equations?

Use the properties of equality to undo operations to isolate a variable.

PREVIEW: LESSON PERFORMANCE TASK

View the Engage section online. Discuss various familiar benchmark temperatures, such as the freezing point of water at 32°F or 0°C and the boiling point of water at 212°F or 100°C. Then preview the Lesson Performance Task.

2.3   Solving for a Variable

Essential Question: How do you rewrite formulas and literal equations?

Resource Locker

⊘ Explore   Rearranging Mathematical Formulas

Literal Equations are equations that contain two or more variables. There are many literal equations in the form of math, science, and engineering formulas. These formulas may seem like they can only be solved for the variable that is isolated on one side of the formula. By using inverse operations and the properties of equality, a formula can be rearranged so any variable in the formula can be isolated. It is no different than how equations are solved by using inverse operations and the properties of equality.

How can you solve the equation $42 = 6x$?

Ⓐ $\dfrac{42}{6} = \dfrac{6x}{6}$ What is the reason for dividing? **Multiplication must be undone to solve for x.**
The inverse of multiplication is division.

Why divide by $\boxed{6}$? **To undo multiplying by 6, divide by 6.**

$7 = x$ By rearranging the equation x was isolated and the solution was found.

The mathematical formula for the volume of a rectangular prism, $B = Vh$ or $V = \ell wh$, is a literal equation. V represents volume, ℓ represents length, w represents width, and h represents height. Using inverse operations, the formula can be rearranged to solve for any one of the variables that might be unknown. Like solving for x, a formula can be rearranged to isolate a variable.

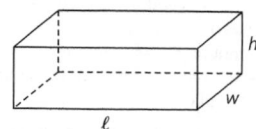

Ⓑ   In the formula $V = \ell wh$, the variable h needs to be isolated.

The operation of ___**multiplication**___ is used in the formula. The inverse operation, ___**division**___, should be used to isolate $\boxed{h}$.

Ⓒ $\dfrac{V}{\ell w} = \dfrac{\ell wh}{\ell w}$

$\dfrac{V}{\ell w} = \boxed{h}$

The formula rearranged in this way can easily produce the height of the rectangular prism, when the volume, length, and width are known.

Reflect

1. Using the formula for a rectangular prism, rewrite the formula to solve for ℓ.

$$V = \ell wh$$
$$\frac{V}{wh} = \frac{\ell wh}{wh}$$
$$\frac{V}{wh} = \ell, \text{ or}$$
$$\ell = \frac{V}{wh}$$

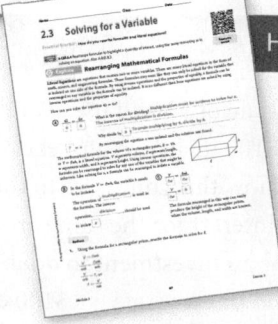

HARDCOVER PAGES 55–60

Turn to these pages to find this lesson in the hardcover student edition.

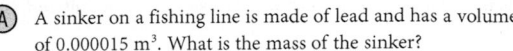

Explain 1 Rearranging Scientific Formulas

Use inverse operations to isolate the unknown variable in a scientific formula.

The formula for density is $D = \frac{m}{V}$. Lead has a very high density of 11,340 kg/m³. Plastic foam has a very low density of 75 kg/m³. The formula for density can be rearranged to solve for V, volume or m, mass.

Example 1

(A) A sinker on a fishing line is made of lead and has a volume of 0.000015 m³. What is the mass of the sinker?

The density formula can be rearranged to isolate m, the mass. The values for volume and density can then be substituted into the formula to find the mass.

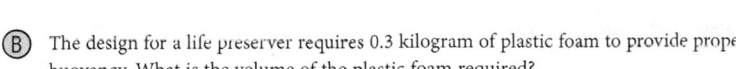

$$D = \frac{m}{V}$$
$$DV = \left(\frac{m}{V}\right)V$$
$$DV = m$$
$$\left(11{,}340 \text{ kg/m}^3\right)\left(0.000015 \text{ m}^3\right) = m$$
$$0.17 \text{ kg} \approx m$$

(B) The design for a life preserver requires 0.3 kilogram of plastic foam to provide proper buoyancy. What is the volume of the plastic foam required?

Rearrange the density formula to isolate V.

$$D = \frac{m}{V}$$
$$(D)V = \frac{m}{V}\ \boxed{V}$$
$$DV = \boxed{m}$$
$$\frac{DV}{\boxed{D}} = \frac{m}{\boxed{D}}$$
$$V = \boxed{\frac{m}{D}}$$

Now substitute the given values.

$$V = \frac{\boxed{0.3 \text{ kg}}}{\boxed{75 \text{ kg/m}^3}}$$
$$V = \boxed{0.004}\ \text{m}^3$$

Your Turn

2. For altitudes up to 36,000 feet, the relationship between ground temperature and atmospheric temperature can be described by the formula $t = -0.0035a + g$, in which t is the atmospheric temperature in degrees Fahrenheit, a is the altitude, in feet, at which the atmospheric temperature is measured, and g is the ground temperature in degrees Fahrenheit. Determine the altitude in feet when t is $-27.5\,°$F and g is $60\,°$F.

$t = -0.0035a + g$

$a = \dfrac{t-g}{-0.0035} = \dfrac{-27.5 - 60}{-0.0035} = 25{,}000$ **The altitude will be 25,000 feet.**

© Houghton Mifflin Harcourt Publishing Company · Image Credits: Beck Photography/Aurora Photos/Corbis

---

PROFESSIONAL DEVELOPMENT

Math Background

Some literal equations are general forms of equations that students frequently encounter. For instance, the equation $3x = 12$ has the general form $ax = b$. The solution of such an equation represents the solutions of all members of that class of equations. For instance, $x = \frac{b}{a}$ gives the solution of all equations of the form $ax = b$. Restrictions may apply to the letters in a literal equation. One common restriction is that the coefficient of a variable cannot be 0; otherwise, the variable term drops out of the equation.

EXPLORE

Rearranging Mathematical Formulas

INTEGRATE TECHNOLOGY

Have students use a calculator to evaluate a common formula to find a value, such as the volume of a three-dimensional figure with given dimensions, or the Celsius temperature equivalent to a given Fahrenheit temperature.

QUESTIONING STRATEGIES

How is the process of rearranging a literal equation similar to solving an equation in one variable? In both cases, you use inverse operations to isolate a variable.

EXPLAIN 1

Rearranging Scientific Formulas

INTEGRATE MATHEMATICAL PRACTICES
Focus on Math Connections

MP.1 Ask students to list some scientific formulas they have used.

AVOID COMMON ERRORS

Encourage students to read the questions carefully. Some students may not pay attention to which variable they are solving for.

QUESTIONING STRATEGIES

How can you tell whether a rewritten formula is correct? Choose values for the variables that make the original formula a true statement. Then substitute those values in the rewritten formula to see if it is a true statement.

Solving for a Variable   **68**

EXPLAIN 2

Rearranging Literal Equations

CONNECT VOCABULARY 🔲

The term *literal* means expressed by letters. A *literal equation* contains two or more variables that are represented by letters. Contrast this meaning to the more common use of the word *literal* to mean "according to the strict meaning of a word; not figurative."

QUESTIONING STRATEGIES

? How does the solution of a literal equation differ from the solution of a specific equation of the same form? Unlike a specific equation, the literal equation's solution is not a number; it is an expression that involves the letters representing the coefficients and constants in the literal equation.

ELABORATE

INTEGRATE MATHEMATICAL PRACTICES
Focus on Patterns

MP.8 Point out that a literal equation can be used to provide a rule for calculating the solution of any specific equation having the same form. For example, when the literal equation $ax + b = c$ (where $a \neq 0$) is solved for x, the result is $x = \frac{c - b}{a}$. You can substitute values for a, b, and c into this rule to solve any equation of the form $ax + b = c$ without going through the steps of solving the specific equation.

SUMMARIZE THE LESSON

? How do you solve a formula for a variable? You isolate the variable by using properties of equality. Make sure to do the same thing to both sides of the equation to maintain balance.

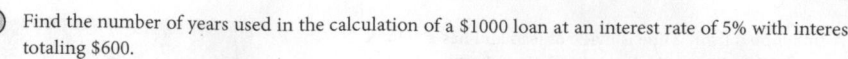

Using inverse operations to rearrange literal equations can be applied to any formula. The interest formula, $I = prt$, is another example of a literal equation. In the formula, I represents interest, p the principal or the initial amount to which interest will be applied, r the rate at which interest will be paid, and t is the time in years.

Example 2

Ⓐ Find the number of years used in the calculation of a $1000 loan at an interest rate of 5% with interest totaling $600.

Solve the formula for t.

$$I = prt$$
$$\frac{I}{pr} = \frac{prt}{pr}$$
$$\frac{I}{pr} = t$$

Substitute the given values. Since the interest rate is 5%, $r = 0.05$.

$$\frac{\$600}{\$1000 \cdot 0.05} = t$$
$$12 = t$$

So the length of time for the loan is 12 years.

Ⓑ Determine the interest rate for a $2000 loan that will be paid off in 4 years with interest totaling $640. In order to find the interest rate, solve the formula for r.

$$I = prt$$
$$\frac{I}{\boxed{pt}} = \frac{prt}{\boxed{pt}}$$
$$\frac{I}{\boxed{pt}} = r$$

Now substitute the values and simplify.

$$\frac{\boxed{\$640}}{\left(\boxed{\$2000}\right)\left(\boxed{4}\right)} = r$$
$$0.08 = r$$

So the interest rate is $\underline{\quad 8 \quad}$% per year.

Your Turn

3. The formula $y = mx + b$ is the slope-intercept form of the equation of a line. Solve the equation for m.

$$y = mx + b$$
$$y - b = mx$$
$$\frac{y - b}{x} = m$$

COLLABORATIVE LEARNING

Peer-to-Peer Activity

Have students work in pairs. Have each pair work with the equation $v = v_0 + at$, or have them select a literal equation from a list that you provide. Both students should solve the equation for each of the variables it contains (v_0, a, and t). Then have the students compare their solutions to make sure they are the same. If not, they should check each other's work to see where a mistake was made.

4. **Discussion** What could be a reason for isolating a variable in a literal equation?
Possible answer: A reason could be to rewrite an equation to make it easier to evaluate an unknown variable.

5. Describe a situation in which a formula could be used more easily if it were rearranged. Include the formula in your description.
Possible answer: The formula $d = rt$ is more useful in the form $\frac{d}{r} = t$ when you need to determine the time it takes to travel a certain distance at a certain speed.

6. **Essential Question Check-In** How do you isolate a variable?
Possible answer: Isolate a variable by using the properties of equality and inverse operations.

⭐ **Evaluate: Homework and Practice**

- Online Homework
- Hints and Help
- Extra Practice

Solve for the indicated variable in each mathematical formula.

1. $C = 2\pi r$ for r
$$\frac{C}{2\pi} = \frac{2\pi r}{2\pi}$$
$$\frac{C}{2\pi} = r$$

2. $A = \frac{1}{2}bh$ for b
$$\frac{2}{h}(A) = \frac{2}{h}\left(\frac{1}{2}bh\right)$$
$$\frac{2A}{h} = b$$

3. $y = mx + b$ for x
$$y = mx + b$$
$$y - b = mx$$
$$\frac{y - b}{m} = x$$

4. $A = \frac{1}{2}(a + b)h$ for h
$$A = \frac{1}{2}(a + b)h$$
$$2A = (a + b)h$$
$$\frac{2A}{(a + b)} = h$$

5. $V = \pi r^2 h$ for h
$$V = \pi r^2 h$$
$$\frac{V}{\pi r^2} = h$$

6. $SA = 2\pi r^2 + 2\pi rh$ for h
$$SA = 2\pi r^2 + 2\pi rh$$
$$SA - 2\pi r^2 = 2\pi rh$$
$$\frac{SA - 2\pi r^2}{2\pi r} = h$$

Solve for the indicated variable in each scientific formula.

7. $d = rt$ for t
$$\frac{d}{r} = t$$

8. $PV = nRT$ for T
$$\frac{PV}{nR} = T$$

9. $A = \frac{FV - OV}{T}$ for OV
$$A = \frac{FV - OV}{T}$$
$$AT = FV - OV$$
$$AT - FV = -OV$$
$$FV - AT = OV$$

10. $C = \frac{Wtc}{1000}$ for W
$$C = \frac{Wtc}{1000}$$
$$1000C = Wtc$$
$$\frac{1000C}{tc} = W$$

Exercise	Depth of Knowledge (D.O.K.)	COMMON CORE Mathematical Practices	
1–20	**1** Recall of Information		**MP.2** Reasoning
21–22	**3** Strategic Thinking		**MP.4** Modeling
23	**3** Strategic Thinking	H.O.T.	**MP.2** Reasoning
24	**3** Strategic Thinking	H.O.T.	**MP.4** Modeling
25	**3** Strategic Thinking	H.O.T.	**MP.2** Reasoning

EVALUATE

ASSIGNMENT GUIDE

Concepts and Skills	Practice
Explore Rearranging Mathematical Formulas	Exercises 1–6, 23, 25
Example 1 Rearranging Scientific Formulas	Exercises 7–10, 22
Example 2 Rearranging Literal Equations	Exercises 11–21, 24

CURRICULUM INTEGRATION

Have students complete the table below by writing a formula that is used in each subject. Then ask the students to solve each formula for each of its variables.

Common Formulas	
Subject	**Formula**
Geometry	
Personal finance	
Physical science	

AVOID COMMON ERRORS

Make sure students check that they solved for the correct variable. After finding a solution, have students go back to the original question to make sure they answered the question fully.

QUESTIONING STRATEGIES

? How are the properties of equality used when solving for a specified variable? The properties are used to move numbers from one side of the equation to another by adding, subtracting, multiplying, or dividing the same number on both sides of the equation.

? Of the four properties of equality, which two properties of equality have restrictions? Explain. The Multiplication and Division Properties of Equality have restrictions; the numbers that you multiply or divide by may not equal zero.

INTEGRATE TECHNOLOGY

Have students choose values for the variables they are *not* solving for in a literal equation. Using these values, have students use a calculator to find the value of the variable they are solving for. Then have them substitute all the values in the original literal equation to check their answers.

JOURNAL

In their journals, have students describe a problem that can be solved more easily if they first solve a literal equation for a specified variable. Then have them summarize the steps for solving the literal equation.

Solve for the indicated variable in each literal equation.

11. $2p + 5r = q$ for p

$2p = q - 5r$

$p = \dfrac{q - 5r}{2}$

12. $-10 = xy + z$ for x

$-10 - z = xy$

$\dfrac{-10 - z}{y} = x$

13. $\dfrac{a}{b} = c$ for b

$a = cb$

$\dfrac{a}{c} = b$

14. $\dfrac{h - 4}{j} = k$ for j

$h - 4 = kj$

$\dfrac{h - 4}{k} = j$

15. $\dfrac{x}{5} - g = a$ for x

$\dfrac{x}{5} = a + g$

$x = 5(a + g)$

16. $5p + 9c = p$ for c

$9c = p - 5p$

$9c = -4p$

$c = -\dfrac{4}{9}p$

17. $\dfrac{2}{5}(z + 1) = y$ for z

$z + 1 = \dfrac{5}{2}y$

$z = \dfrac{5}{2}y - 1$

18. $g\left(h + \dfrac{2}{3}\right) = 1$ for h

$h + \dfrac{2}{3} = \dfrac{1}{g}$

$h = \dfrac{1}{g} - \dfrac{2}{3}$

19. $a(n - 3) + 8 = bn$ for n

$an - 3a + 8 = bn$

$-3a + 8 = bn - an$

$-3a + 8 = n(b - a)$

$\dfrac{-3a + 8}{b - a} = n$

$\dfrac{8 - 3a}{b - a} = n$

20. Which is a possible way to rewrite the equation $y = 3x + 3b$ to solve for b?

A. $b = \dfrac{y - 3x}{3}$ **C.** $b = \dfrac{y - 3}{3x}$

B. $b = 3(y - 3x)$ **D.** $b = x(y - 3)$

Choice A, $b = \dfrac{y - 3x}{3}$, is the correct answer.

21. Sports To find a baseball pitcher's earned run average (ERA), you can use the formula $Ei = 9r$, in which E represents ERA, i represents the number of innings pitched, and r represents the number of earned runs allowed. Solve the equation for E. What is a pitcher's ERA if he allows 5 earned runs in 18 innings pitched?

$Ei = 9r$

$E = \dfrac{9r}{i}$

$E = \dfrac{9 \cdot 5}{18} = 2.5$

22. Meteorology For altitudes up to 36,000 feet, the relationship between ground temperature and atmospheric temperature can be described by the formula $t = -0.0035a + g$, in which t is the atmospheric temperature in degrees Fahrenheit, a is the altitude, in feet, at which the atmospheric temperature is measured, and g is the ground temperature in degrees Fahrenheit. Solve the equation for a. If the atmospheric temperature is $-65.5\,°F$ and the ground temperature is $57\,°F$, what is the altitude?

$t - g = -0.0035a$

$\dfrac{t - g}{-0.0035} = a$

If the atmospheric temperature is $-65.5\,°F$ and the ground temperature is $57\,°F$, then

$a = \dfrac{-65.5 - 57}{-0.0035} = 35{,}000 \text{ ft}$

23. Explain the Error A student was asked to use the formula for the perimeter of a rectangle, $P = 2\ell + 2w$, to solve for ℓ. The student came up with an answer, $P - 2w = 2\ell$. What error did the student make? Explain. Then solve for ℓ.

The student only rearranged the formula so the variable was on a side by itself but did not simplify further to remove the coefficient. The formula for ℓ is $\ell = \frac{P - 2w}{2}$.

24. Multi-Step The formula $c = 5p + 215$ relates c, the total cost in dollars of hosting a birthday party at a skating rink, to p, the number of people attending. If Allie's parents are willing to spend $300 for a party, how many people can attend?

$$c = 5p + 215$$

$$c - 215 = 5p$$

$$\frac{c - 215}{5} = p$$

$$p = \frac{300 - 215}{5} = \frac{85}{5} = 17$$

The number of people that can attend the party is 17.

25. Multi-Step The formula for the area of a triangle is $A = \frac{1}{2}bh$, in which b represents the length of the base and h represents the height. If a triangle has an area of 192 mm² and the height is 12 mm, what is the measure of the base?

$$A = \frac{1}{2}bh \qquad \frac{2(192)}{12} = b$$

$$2A = bh \qquad 32 = b$$

$$\frac{2A}{h} = b \qquad \text{Therefore, the measure of the base is 32 mm.}$$

Lesson Performance Task

The following table shows the average low temperatures in Fahrenheit for the city of Boston for several months during the year. The formula $F = \frac{9}{5}C + 32$ allows you to determine the temperature in Fahrenheit when given the temperature in Celsius.

Month	Temperature in Fahrenheit	Temperature in Celsius
January	22°	−5.6°
April	41°	5.0°
July	65°	18.3°
October	47°	8.3°
December	28°	−2.2°

a. Use the information given to determine the average low temperatures in Celsius. $C = \frac{5}{9}(F - 32)$

b. Would it ever be possible for the temperature in Celsius to have a greater value than the temperature in Fahrenheit? Explain why or why not. **Yes, for any Fahrenheit temperature less than −40°, the Celsius temperature will have a value greater than the temperature in Fahrenheit. For example, −49 °F = −45 °C.**

EXTENSION ACTIVITY

Ask students whether "double a Celsius value and then add 30" is a good shortcut for estimating a temperature in Fahrenheit. Then have students find a similar method for estimating a temperature in Celsius given the temperature in Fahrenheit.

Students should find that the given shortcut is fairly accurate for temperatures between about −15°C and 35°C, and less accurate for more extreme temperatures. A similar method for estimating a temperature in Celsius given the temperature in Fahrenheit is "subtract 30 from the Fahrenheit value and then halve the result."

CONNECT VOCABULARY EL

Note that the words for *Celsius* and *Fahrenheit* in Spanish are the cognates *Celsio* and *Fahrenheit*.

QUESTIONING STRATEGIES

? If you rewrite the fraction $\frac{9}{5}$ as a decimal, the formula for converting Celsius temperatures to Fahrenheit becomes $F = 1.8C + 32$. Solve this equation to isolate C. Is the result equivalent to the result you got when you used a fraction?

$C = \frac{F - 32}{1.8}$; yes, because $\frac{1}{1.8} = \frac{10}{18} = \frac{5}{9}$

INTEGRATE MATHEMATICAL PRACTICES
Focus on Math Connections

MP.1 Explain that a *kelvin* is a unit of temperature that is used in many scientific calculations. The unit is called a *kelvin*, not a *degree kelvin*. The temperature 0 K is absolute zero, the coldest temperature possible, so there are no negative values on the kelvin temperature scale. The formula $K = C + 273$ is used to convert degrees Celsius to kelvins.

Scoring Rubric
2 points: Student correctly solves the problem and explains his/her reasoning.
1 point: Student shows good understanding of the problem but does not fully solve or explain his/her reasoning.
0 points: Student does not demonstrate understanding of the problem.

Creating and Solving Inequalities

Common Core Math Standards

The student is expected to:

COMMON CORE A-CED.A.3

Represent constraints by... Inequalities... and interpret solutions as viable or nonviable options in a modeling context. Also A-CED.A.1, A-REI.B.3

Mathematical Practices

COMMON CORE MP.4 Modeling

Language Objective

Describe a real-world situation that can be modeled by an inequality, and write the inequality.

ENGAGE

Essential Question: How do you write and solve an inequality that represents a real-world situation?

Use a verbal or tabular model to write an inequality, solve the inequality, and then check for reasonableness.

PREVIEW: LESSON PERFORMANCE TASK

View the Engage section online. Discuss the fact that a plane this size uses more than 5 gallons of fuel per mile flown but can hold about 500 people, so it gets about 100 miles per gallon per person. Then preview the Lesson Performance Task.

Name _____ Class _____ Date _____

2.4 Creating and Solving Inequalities

Resource Locker

Essential Question: How do you write and solve an inequality that represents a real-world situation?

 Explore **Creating Inequalities from Verbal Descriptions**

An **inequality** is a statement that compares two expressions that are not strictly equal by using one of the following inequality signs.

Symbol	Meaning
$<$	is less than
$\leq$	is less than or equal to
$>$	is greater than
$\geq$	is greater than or equal to
$\neq$	is not equal to

You have probably seen a sign at an amusement park saying something like, "You must be at least 48 inches tall to ride this ride." This statement could be written as $h \geq 48$ in., where h represents the height of a person allowed to ride.

Nora is planning a birthday party for her little sister, Colleen. Nora's budget will allow her to spend no more than $50 for party supplies. Eight children, including Colleen, will attend the party, and Nora wants to determine how much she could spend on party favors for each child. She will also purchase a cake for $10. Write an inequality that represents the situation, and find possible solutions.

(A) First, let c represent the cost of a party favor for each child. Write an expression for the total cost of the party as a function of c.

$$\boxed{8}\; c + \boxed{10}$$

(B) Which inequality symbol should be used to represent the phrase "no more than"? _____ $\leq$

(C) Write the inequality that represents Nora's budget goal.

$$8c + 10 \leq \boxed{50}$$

(D) Suppose Nora finds party favors that cost $4 each. Use a value of 4 for c and check to see if this inequality is true.

$$8 \cdot 4 + 10 \overset{?}{\leq} 50$$

$$\boxed{42} \overset{?}{\leq} 50$$

© Houghton Mifflin Harcourt Publishing Company • Image credits: ©Patrick Lane/Somos Images/Corbis

HARDCOVER PAGES 61–66

Turn to these pages to find this lesson in the hardcover student edition.

(E) Is the inequality true? __Yes, $42 \leq 50$.__

(F) Could Nora buy $6 party favors for all of her guests without going over budget?

$8 \cdot 6 + 10 = 58$

No, because $58 \nleq 50$.

Reflect

1. Why does an inequality represent Nora's budget calculation better than an equation?
   Nora does not need to spend exactly $50 to meet her budget goal. If she can find
   inexpensive party favors that allow her to spend less than $50 total, that's acceptable.

2. The solution set of an inequality consists of all values that make the statement true. Describe the whole dollar amounts that are in the solution set for this situation.
   $1, $2, $3, $4, $5

⊘ Explain 1 Creating and Solving Inequalities Involving the Distributive Property

You may need to use the Distributive Property before you can solve an inequality.

Distributive Property	If a, b, and c are real numbers, then $a(b + c) = ab + ac$.

The inequality sign must be reversed when multiplying or dividing both sides of an inequality by a negative number.

Example 1

(A) Trina is buying 12 shirts for the drama club. She will choose a style for the blank shirts and then pay an additional charge of $2.75 for each shirt to have the club logo. If Trina cannot spend more than $99, how much can she spend on each blank shirt? Write and solve an inequality to find the possible cost of each blank shirt.

Let s represent the cost of each blank shirt.

Write an inequality to represent the situation.	$12(s + 2.75) \leq 99$
Use the Distributive Property.	$12s + 33 \leq 99$
Subtraction Property of Inequality	$12s + 33 - 33 \leq 99 - 33$
Simplify.	$12s \leq 66$
Division Property of Inequality	$\frac{12s}{12} \leq \frac{66}{12}$
Simplify.	$s \leq 5.5$

PROFESSIONAL DEVELOPMENT

Math Background

To demonstrate why the direction of an inequality is reversed when both sides are multiplied or divided by a negative number, consider the inequality $a > b$. By the Subtraction Property of Inequality, $a - a > b - a$ or, equivalently, $0 > b - a$. Applying the Subtraction Property of Inequality again shows that $0 - b > b - a - b$ or $-b > -a$, which is the same as $-a < -b$. In other words, when both sides of the inequality are multiplied by -1, the direction of the inequality is reversed. Multiplying or dividing by any negative number involves a factor of -1.

EXPLORE

Creating Inequalities from Verbal Descriptions

INTEGRATE TECHNOLOGY

Students may complete the Explore activity either in the book or online.

CONNECT VOCABULARY EL

Remind students that an *inequality* is a statement that compares two expressions that are *not strictly equal*. Compare this to an unbalanced scale.

QUESTIONING STRATEGIES

❓ What phrases in a problem can be represented by the $\geq$ symbol? greater than or equal to, at least, no less than

❓ What phrases in a problem can be represented by the $\leq$ symbol? less than or equal to, at most, no more than

EXPLAIN 1

Creating and Solving Inequalities Involving the Distributive Property

AVOID COMMON ERRORS

When using the Distributive Property, students who use mental math sometimes fail to distribute the factor to all the numbers inside the parentheses. Encourage students to get into the habit of checking for this error.

QUESTIONING STRATEGIES

? Compare solving inequalities with solving equations. Which steps are the same, and which are different? **In both cases, you first apply the Distributive Property, if needed, then use inverse operations to isolate the variable. Most operations are the same for solving equations and inequalities, but when you multiply or divide both sides of an inequality by a negative number, you must reverse the inequality sign.**

Check your answer.

Since $s \le 5.5$, check a smaller number. $12(5 + 2.75) \overset{?}{\le} 99$

Trina can order blank shirts that cost $5.50 or less. $93 \le 99$ true

Ⓑ Sergio needs to buy gifts for 8 friends. He wants to give the same gift to all his friends and he plans to have the gifts wrapped for an additional charge of $1.50 each. If Sergio spends at least $70, he will receive free shipping on his order. Write and solve an inequality to determine how much Sergio needs to spend on each gift in order to receive free shipping.

Let g be the cost of one gift.

Write an inequality to represent the situation. $8 \left(g + \boxed{1.50} \right) \ge 70$

Use the Distributive Property. $8 \, g + \boxed{12} \ge 70$

Subtraction Property of Inequality $8 \, g + 12 - \boxed{12} \ge 70 - \boxed{12}$

Simplify. $8g \ge \boxed{58}$

Division Property of Inequality $\dfrac{8g}{\boxed{8}} \ge \dfrac{58}{\boxed{8}}$

Simplify. $g \ge \boxed{7.25}$

Check your answer.

Since $g \ge 7.25$, check a larger number. $8(8 + 1.50) \overset{?}{\ge} 70$

Sergio must spend at least $\boxed{\$7.25}$ on each gift. $\boxed{76} \overset{?}{\ge} 70$

Reflect

3. Discussion Why is the first step in solving the inequality to use the Distributive Property instead of working inside the parentheses?
The terms inside the parentheses cannot be combined, so you have to distribute 8 to each term in parentheses in order to remove the parentheses.

Your Turn

4. Zachary is planning to send a video game to each of his two brothers. If he buys the same game for both brothers and pays $4.75 to ship each game, how much can he spend on each game without spending more than $100? Write and solve an inequality for this situation.

$2(v + 4.75) \le 100$ **Zachary can spend no more than $45.25 on each video game.**
$2v + 9.5 \le 100$
$2v \le 90.5$
$v \le 45.25$

Solve each inequality.

5. $\frac{4}{3}(6x + 9) < 4$ $8x + 12 < 4$
$8x < -8$
$x < -1$

6. $-2\left(\frac{1}{4}x + 2\right) \ge 5$ $-\frac{1}{2}x - 4 \ge 5$
$-\frac{1}{2}x \ge 9$
$x \le -18$

COLLABORATIVE LEARNING

Small Group Activity

Divide students into groups of four, then tell each group to split into two pairs. Each pair should make two sets of index cards. On one set, have them write inequalities that involve the Distributive Property or have variables on both sides. On the second set, have them write the corresponding solutions. Have each pair trade cards with the other pair in their group, who will solve the inequalities and find the matching solution cards. If the solutions do not match, have the students work together to find the error.

Some inequalities have variable terms on both sides of the inequality symbol. You can solve these inequalities the same way you solved equations with variables on both sides. Use the properties of inequality to collect all the variable terms on one side and all the constant terms on the other side.

Example 2

(A) The *Daily Info* charges a fee of $650 plus $80 per week to run an ad. The *People's Paper* charges $145 per week. For how many weeks must an ad run for the total cost at the *Daily Info* to be less expensive than the cost at the *People's Paper*? Let w be the number of weeks the ad runs in the paper.

Write an inequality to represent the situation.	$650 + 80w < 145w$
Subtraction Property of Inequality	$650 + 80w - 80w < 145w - 80w$
Simplify.	$650 < 65w$
Division Property of Inequality	$\dfrac{650}{65} < \dfrac{65w}{65}$
Simplify.	$10 < w$

The total cost at the *Daily Info* is less than the cost at the *People's Paper* if the ad runs for more than 10 weeks.

(B) The Home Cleaning Company charges $312 to power-wash the siding of a house plus $12 for each window. Power Clean charges $36 per window, and the price includes power-washing the siding. How many windows must a house have to make the total cost from The Home Cleaning Company less expensive than Power Clean? Let w be the number of windows.

Write an inequality to represent the situation.	$\boxed{312} + 12w < 36w$
Subtraction Property of Inequality	$312 + 12w - \boxed{12w} < 36w - \boxed{12w}$
Simplify.	$312 < \boxed{24w}$
Division Property of Inequality	$\dfrac{312}{\boxed{24}} < \dfrac{24w}{\boxed{24}}$
Simplify.	$\boxed{13} < w$

A house must have more than 13 windows for The Home Cleaning Company to be less expensive than Power Clean.

Reflect

7. How would the final inequality change if you divided by –24 in the next to last step?
The inequality sign would be reversed so the answer would be $w < 13$.

Your Turn

8. The school band will sell pizzas to raise money for new uniforms. The supplier charges $100 plus $4 per pizza. The band members sell the pizzas for $7 each. Write and solve an inequality to find how many pizzas the band members will have to sell to make a profit?
$100 + 4p < 7p$; $100 < 3p$; $33\frac{1}{3} < p$ The band members will need to sell at least 34 pizzas.

DIFFERENTIATE INSTRUCTION

Cognitive Strategies

Have students consider different ways of remembering which sign is "greater than" and which sign is "less than." A classic device is to remember that the "alligator mouth always bites toward the larger amount."

EXPLAIN 2

Creating and Solving Inequalities with Variables on Both Sides

QUESTIONING STRATEGIES

? Consider how you would solve the inequality $3x + 1 < 4x - 5$. Does it matter whether you collect the variable terms on the right or left side of the inequality? Would one method be easier than the other? Explain. **No; the solution is the same either way, but it might be easier to collect the variable terms on the right, so that the variable has a positive coefficient.**

? How can you use properties to justify solutions to inequalities? **For each step, cite the property you use, or state that you are simplifying or combining like terms.**

AVOID COMMON ERRORS

When the variable is on the right side of the inequality, some students may have difficulty rewriting it with the variable on the left. For example, a student might rewrite $2 > c$ as $c > 2$. To check whether they are writing it correctly, suggest that they choose a number for c that makes the inequality true. If $2 > 1$, then $1 < 2$, so if $2 > c$, then $c < 2$.

INTEGRATE MATHEMATICAL PRACTICES
Focus on Modeling

MP.4 Have students suggest examples of real-world situations that can be modeled by inequalities. List the examples on the board. Some possible answers are staying within budgets, using limited resources, staying below a speed limit, fitting something into a container, and making a profit.

ELABORATE

INTEGRATE MATHEMATICAL PRACTICES

Focus on Critical Thinking

MP.3 Have students refer to the properties of equality and use them as a starting point for writing out the properties of inequality. The addition and subtraction properties of inequality should be nearly the same as the corresponding properties of equality. The multiplication and division properties each need to be divided into two parts to create different rules depending on whether you are multiplying/dividing by a positive or negative number.

AVOID COMMON ERRORS

Students may reverse the inequality whenever there is multiplication or division in the problem or whenever there is a negative sign involved in the problem. Remind students that they should reverse the inequality symbol only when they have to multiply or divide by a negative number.

SUMMARIZE THE LESSON

How do you know if a solution to an inequality is correct? Check the value that the variable is less than or greater than by substituting it in the equation related to the original inequality. Then choose another number from your solution set and substitute its value in the original inequality. If both statements are true, your solution is correct. For real-world contexts, consider whether every value in the solution set makes sense.

💬 Elaborate

9. Which inequality symbol would you use to represent the following words or phrases? Can you come up with more examples?

   a. at most $\leq$ **b.** farther than $>$ **c.** younger than $<$ **d.** up to $\leq$

   Sample answers: at least ($\geq$), larger than ($>$), smaller than ($<$), heavier than ($>$)

10. **Discussion** How are the steps to solving an inequality similar to those for solving an equation? How are they different?
    Many processes are the same: working backwards, simplifying, and using the same operation on both expressions. An important difference is the need to reverse direction of the inequality when both sides are multiplied or divided by a negative number.

11. **Essential Question Check-In** How can you write an inequality that represents a real-world situation?
    Write a description of the expressions using mathematical operations, and select an inequality symbol that matches the relationship described between the expressions.

⭐ Evaluate: Homework and Practice

- Online Homework
- Hints and Help
- Extra Practice

Write an inequality that represents the description, and then solve.

1. Max has more than 5 carrots (number of carrots Max has $= c$).

   $c > 5$

2. Brigitte is shorter than 5 feet (Brigitte's height $= h$).

   $h < 5$

3. Twice a number (x) is less than 10.

   $2x < 10$
   $x < 5$

4. Six more than five times a number (x) is at least twenty-one.

   $6 + 5x \geq 21$
   $5x \geq 15$
   $x \geq 3$

5. Dave has \$15 to spend on an \$8 book and two birthday cards (c) for his friends. How much can he spend on each card if he buys the same card for each friend?

   $2c + 8.00 \leq 15.00$
   $2c \leq 7.00$
   $c \leq 3.50$

6. Toni can carry up to 18 lb in her backpack. Her lunch weighs 1 lb, her gym clothes weigh 2 lb, and her books (b) weigh 3 lb each. How many books can she carry in her backpack?

   $3b + 1 + 2 \leq 18$
   $3b + 3 \leq 18$
   $3b \leq 15$
   $b \leq 5$

LANGUAGE SUPPORT 🟦 EL

Connect Vocabulary

Point out to English learners that reading and writing in English have many conventions or rules that govern the language. In math there are also rules and conventions that dictate the order of operations and how we proceed through our work. Remind students how to read an inequality containing a variable. $-2 > y$ is read, "negative two is greater than y." The equivalent statement $y < -2$ is read, "y is less than -2."

Solve each inequality.

7. $3(x - 2) > -3$

$3x - 6 > -3$

$3x > 3$

$x > 1$

8. $5 + 5(x + 4) \leq 20$

$5 + 5x + 20 \leq 20$

$5x + 25 \leq 20$

$5x \leq -5$

$x \leq -1$

9. $3 + \frac{1}{2}(3 - x) < -7$

$3 + \frac{1}{2}(3 - x) < -7$

$3 + \frac{3}{2} - \frac{1}{2}x < -7$

$\frac{9}{2} - \frac{1}{2}x < -7$

$-\frac{1}{2}x < -\frac{23}{2}$

$x > 23$

10. $3(x + 6) - 2(x + 2) \geq 10$

$3x + 18 - 2x - 4 \geq 10$

$x + 14 \geq 10$

$x \geq -4$

11. $5(3 - x) - 4(2 - 3x) > 2$

$15 - 5x - 8 + 12x > 2$

$7x + 7 > 2$

$7x > -5$

$x > -\frac{5}{7}$

12. $\frac{1}{2}(4x - 2) - \frac{2}{3}(6x + 9) \leq 4$

$2x - 1 - 4x - 6 \leq 4$

$-2x - 7 \leq 4$

$-2x \leq 11$

$x \geq -\frac{11}{2}$

13. $x + 1 > -5(7 - 2x)$

$x + 1 > -35 + 10x$

$-9x + 1 > -35$

$-9x > -36$

$x < 4$

14. $\frac{5}{3}(6x + 3) \leq 2x - 7$

$10x + 5 \leq 2x - 7$

$8x + 5 \leq -7$

$8x \leq -12$

$x \leq -\frac{3}{2}$

15. $2x \leq -\frac{2}{3}(4x + 4)$

$2x \leq -\frac{8}{3}x - \frac{8}{3}$

$\frac{14}{3}x \leq -\frac{8}{3}$

$x \leq -\frac{4}{7}$

16. $\frac{1}{2}(-2x - 10) > 3(4 - 6x)$

$-x - 5 > 12 - 18x$

$17x - 5 > 12$

$17x > 17$

$x > 1$

17. $-5 - 3x \geq 2(10 + 2x) + 3$

$-5 - 3x \geq 20 + 4x + 3$

$-5 - 3x \geq 23 + 4x$

$-5 - 7x \geq 23$

$-7x \geq 28$

$x \leq -4$

18. $-3(9x + 20) \geq 15x - 20$

$-27x - 60 \geq 15x - 20$

$-42x - 60 \geq -20$

$-42x \geq 40$

$x \leq -\frac{20}{21}$

19. $8\left(\frac{1}{4}x - 3\right) + 24 < 4(x + 5)$

$2x - 24 + 24 < 4x + 20$

$2x < 4x + 20$

$-2x < 20$

$x > -10$

20. $6x - 2(x + 2) > 2 - 3(x + 3)$

$6x - 2x - 4 > 2 - 3x - 9$

$4x - 4 > -3x - 7$

$7x - 4 > -7$

$7x > -3$

$x > -\frac{3}{7}$

EVALUATE

Personal Math Trainer

ASSIGNMENT GUIDE

Concepts and Skills	Practice
Explore Creating Inequalities from Verbal Descriptions	Exercises 1–6, 21, 23
Example 1 Creating and Solving Inequalities Involving the Distributive Property	Exercises 7–12, 22, 24–25
Example 2 Creating and Solving Inequalities with Variables on Both Sides	Exercises 13–20

INTEGRATE MATHEMATICAL PRACTICES

Focus on Modeling

MP.4 Have students discuss how to model an inequality using algebra tiles. At each step, they should ask themselves how many of each tile should be used and what inequality symbol should be placed between the sides of the inequality.

Exercise	Depth of Knowledge (D.O.K.)	COMMON CORE Mathematical Practices
1–2	**1** Recall of Information	**MP.4** Modeling
3–4	**1** Recall of Information	**MP.2** Reasoning
5–6	**1** Recall of Information	**MP.4** Modeling
7–12	**1** Recall of Information	**MP.2** Reasoning
13–20	**2** Skills/Concepts	**MP.2** Reasoning

Creating and Solving Inequalities   **78**

INTEGRATE MATHEMATICAL PRACTICES

Focus on Communication

MP.3 Instruct students to write a real-world problem that can be modeled by an inequality requiring at least three steps to solve. Ask students to solve the inequality, explaining each step. Students should explain the meaning of the solution in the context of the problem.

COMMUNICATING MATH

Students should read problems carefully in order to determine which inequality symbol to use. Remind them to look for key words and phrases such as "no more than," "up to," "maximum," and "at least." Some problems may include key phrases specific to the problem context, such as "shorter than" or "older than."

AVOID COMMON ERRORS

Some students may think they need to change the inequality symbol when distributing a negative factor to a quantity in parentheses. Remind them that the inequality symbol is changed only when *both* sides of the inequality are multiplied or divided by a negative number.

JOURNAL

Have students write step-by-step methods for solving inequalities with variables on both sides and for solving inequalities that involve the Distributive Property.

21. **Physics** A crane cable can support a maximum load of 15,000 kg. If a bucket has a mass of 2,000 kg and gravel has a mass of 1,500 kg for every cubic meter, how many cubic meters of gravel (g) can be safely lifted by the crane?

$$1,500g + 2,000 \leq 15,000$$

$$1,500g \leq 13,000$$

$$g \leq \frac{13,000}{1,500}$$

$$g \leq \frac{26}{3}; g \leq \frac{26}{3} \text{ cubic meters, or } 8\frac{2}{3} \text{ cubic meters}$$

22. Find the solution set of each inequality below, and then determine which inequalities have the same solution set as $\frac{1}{3}(-5x - 3) < 14$.

$$\frac{1}{3}(-5x - 3) < 14$$
$$-\frac{5}{3}x - 1 < 14$$
$$-\frac{5}{3}x < 15$$
$$x > -9$$

a. $\frac{1}{3}(5x + 3) > -14$

$$\frac{5}{3}x + 1 > -14$$
$$\frac{5}{3}x > -15$$
$$x > -9 \quad \text{same}$$

b. $\frac{2}{5}(10x + 20) > 44$

$$4x + 8 > 44$$
$$4x > 36$$
$$x > 9 \quad \text{not the same}$$

c. $-\frac{2}{5}(10x + 20) < -44$

$$-4x - 8 < -44$$
$$-4x < -36$$
$$x > 9 \quad \text{not the same}$$

d. $-\frac{1}{3}(5x + 3) < 14$

$$-\frac{5}{3}x - 1 < 14$$
$$-\frac{5}{3}x < 15$$
$$x > -9 \quad \text{same}$$

e. $\frac{2}{5}(10x - 20) > -44$

$$4x - 8 > -44$$
$$4x > -36$$
$$x > -9 \quad \text{same}$$

f. $\frac{1}{3}(5x + 3) < -14$

$$\frac{5}{3}x + 1 < -14$$
$$\frac{5}{3}x < -15$$
$$x < -9 \quad \text{not the same}$$

H.O.T. Focus on Higher Order Thinking

23. **Explain the Error** Sven is trying to find the maximum amount of time he can spend practicing the five scales of piano music he is supposed to be working on. He has 60 minutes to practice piano and would like to spend at least 35 minutes playing songs instead of practicing scales. So, Sven sets up the following inequality, where t is the number of minutes he spends on each scale, and solves it.

$$60 - 5t \leq 35$$
$$-5t \leq -25$$
$$t \geq 5$$

Sven has concluded that he should spend 5 minutes or more on each scale. Is this correct? If not, what mistake did he make? Then solve for the correct answer.

Sven's original inequality is backwards. He should have started with $60 - 5t \geq 35$.

$$60 - 5t \geq 35$$
$$-5t \geq -25$$
$$t \leq 5$$

So, Sven should spend 5 minutes or less on each scale.

© Houghton Mifflin Harcourt Publishing Company

Exercise	Depth of Knowledge (D.O.K.)		COMMON CORE Mathematical Practices
21	**2** Skills/Concepts		**MP.4** Modeling
22	**2** Skills/Concepts		**MP.2** Reasoning
23	**3** Strategic Thinking	H.O.T.	**MP.3** Logic
24–25	**3** Strategic Thinking	H.O.T.	**MP.1** Problem Solving

24. Critical Thinking Anika wants to determine the maximum number of tulip bulbs (t) she can purchase if each bulb costs $1.50. She will also need to purchase separate pots for each bulb at $1.25 each and a bag of potting soil for $10.00. Set up an inequality to determine how many tulip bulbs Anika can purchase without spending more than $20.00, and solve it. Can Anika buy exactly enough bulbs and pots to spend the full $20.00? Explain. Can you think of a better inequality to describe the answer?

$t(1.50 + 1.25) + 10.00 \leq 20.00$

$2.75t + 10.00 \leq 20.00$

$2.75t \leq 10.00$

$t \leq 3.6363...$

You cannot buy partial bulbs and pots, so Anika cannot spend the full $20.00. A better answer is $t \leq 3$, where t is a whole number.

25. Geometry The area of the triangle shown is no more than 10 square inches.

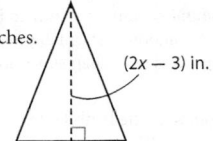

(2x − 3) in.

4 in.

a. Write an inequality that can be used to find x.

$A = \frac{1}{2}bh; \quad b = 4$ and $h = (2x - 3)$

$10 > \frac{1}{2} \cdot 4(2x - 3)$

b. Solve the inequality from part **a.**

$10 \geq \frac{1}{2} \cdot 4(2x - 3)$

$10 \geq 4x - 6$

$16 \geq 4x$

$4 \geq x$

c. What is the maximum height of the triangle?

$h = (2x - 3); \quad x \leq 4$

$h \leq 2(4) - 3$

$h \leq 5$

The maximum height is 5 inches.

Lesson Performance Task

When planning an airplane route, the trip planner must be careful to consider the range the aircraft can travel and the availability of airports to stop and refuel.

A large commercial jet airplane burns approximately 5 gallons of fuel per mile flown, plus about 8500 gallons of fuel per trip to reach cruising altitude. With a useable fuel capacity of 50,000 gallons (there is additional fuel reserved for emergencies), describe the acceptable distance for which an airline could establish a non-stop flight.

For flights originating from Chicago, determine which cities could be safely reached by a non-stop flight.

City	Distance from Chicago (miles)	
Bangalore, India	8530	no
Jakarta, Indonesia	9810	no
Johannesburg, South Africa	8680	no
Moscow, Russia	4970	yes
Paris, France	4130	yes
Perth, Australia	10,970	no
Tokyo, Japan	6300	yes

$5d + 8500 \leq 50,000$

$5d \leq 41,500$

$d \leq 8300$

LANGUAGE SUPPORT EL

Some students may not be familiar with the cities mentioned in the Lesson Peformance Task. Post a world map with each of these cities connected to Chicago using colored string, or use an online mapping program to create a map with each city labeled. Review the pronunciation of each city name. Point out that some city names are different in their native languages from the English names. For example, Moscow is pronounced "Moskva" in Russian, and Paris is pronounced "Paree" in French.

AVOID COMMON ERRORS

Students might conclude, before performing any calculations in the Lesson Peformance Task, that Paris is a safe distance to fly and that Perth is not, simply because these two cities represent the shortest and greatest distances. Caution students to not make such assumptions. Although they would be correct in this case, similar assumptions might be wrong in other real-world situations.

QUESTIONING STRATEGIES

? Could there be other cities that this plane could fly to non-stop? Explain. **Yes, the plane could fly to any city that is less than or equal to 8300 miles from Chicago.**

EXTENSION ACTIVITY

Have students find a flight route that a commercial jet could fly either non-stop or with one or more layovers along the route. Then, using the data in the Lesson Performance Task, have students calculate the approximate number of gallons of fuel used for the non-stop route vs. the routes with layovers.

Students should find that the routes with layovers require more fuel. Ask students to surmise why, then, not all trips are non-stop and why taking a non-stop flight usually costs more than a flight with layovers.

Scoring Rubric

2 points: Student correctly solves the problem and explains his/her reasoning.

1 point: Student shows good understanding of the problem but does not fully solve or explain his/her reasoning.

0 points: Student does not demonstrate understanding of the problem.

Creating and Solving Compound Inequalities

Common Core Math Standards

The student is expected to:

 A-CED.A.1

Create equations and inequalities in one variable and use them to solve problems. Also A-REI.B.3

Mathematical Practices

COMMON CORE **MP.2 Reasoning**

Language Objective

Describe the difference between the graph of a compound inequality involving AND and the graph of a compound inequality involving OR.

ENGAGE

Essential Question: How can you solve a compound inequality and graph the solution set?

First, write the compound inequality as two simple inequalities involving AND or OR. Solve each simple inequality to find the solution set. Graph each solution. The graph of a compound inequality with AND is the intersection of the solutions. The graph of a compound inequality with OR is the union of the solutions.

PREVIEW: LESSON PERFORMANCE TASK

View the Engage section online. Discuss the temperature at which ice melts, changing from solid to liquid water (0°C or 32°F), and the temperature at which water boils, changing to a gas (100°C or 212°F). Then preview the Lesson Performance Task.

2.5 Creating and Solving Compound Inequalities

Essential Question: How can you solve a compound inequality and graph the solution set?

⊘ Explore   Truth Tables and Compound Statements

A **compound statement** is formed by combining two or more simple statements. A compound statement can be true or false. A compound statement involving **AND** is true when *both* simple statements are true. A compound statement involving **OR** is true when *either* one simple statement *or both* are true.

Ⓐ Complete the truth table.

P	Q	P True or False?	Q True or False?	P AND Q True or False?
A dog is a mammal.	Red is a color.	True	True	True
A dog is a mammal.	Red is not a color.	True	False	False
A dog is a fish.	Red is a color.	False	True	False
A dog is a fish.	Red is not a color.	False	False	False

Ⓑ P **AND** Q is true when ___both P and Q are true___

Ⓒ Complete the truth table.

P	Q	P True or False?	Q True or False?	P OR Q True or False?
1 is an odd number.	2 is an even number.	True	True	True
1 is an odd number.	2 is an odd number.	True	False	True
1 is an even number.	2 is an even number.	False	True	True
1 is an even number.	2 is an odd number.	False	False	False

Ⓓ P **OR** Q is true when ___either P is true or Q is true or both are true___

Reflect

1. Give two simple statements P and Q for which P **AND** Q is false and P **OR** Q is true.
   Possible answer: Let P be "A fish is a cow." Let Q be "Fish swim." Then P AND Q is false and P OR Q is true.

© Houghton Mifflin Harcourt Publishing Company

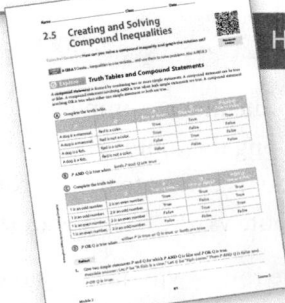

HARDCOVER PAGES 67–74

Turn to these pages to find this lesson in the hardcover student edition.

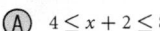 **Explain 1**   **Solving Compound Inequalities Involving AND**

Combining two or more simple inequalities forms a **compound inequality**. The graph of a compound inequality involving **AND** is the **intersection**, or the overlapping region, of the simple inequality graphs.

Compound Inequalities: AND		
Words	**Algebra**	**Graph**
All real numbers greater than 2 **AND** less than 6	$x > 2$ **AND** $x < 6$ $2 < x < 6$	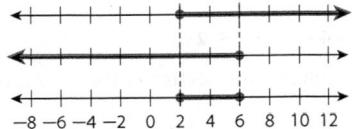
All real numbers greater than or equal to 2 **AND** less than or equal to 6	$x \geq 2$ **AND** $x \leq 6$ $2 \leq x \leq 6$	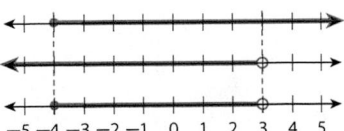

Example 1   Solve each compound inequality and graph the solutions.

(A) $4 \leq x + 2 \leq 8$

$4 \leq x + 2$ **AND** $x + 2 \leq 8$ Write the compound inequality using AND.

$4 - 2 \leq x + 2 - 2$ $x + 2 - 2 \leq 8 - 2$ Subtract 2 from both sides of each simple inequality.

$2 \leq x$ $x \leq 6$ Simplify.

Graph $2 \leq x$.

Graph $x \leq 6$.

Graph the intersection by finding where the two graphs overlap.

(B) $-5 \leq 2x + 3 < 9$

$-5 - \boxed{3} \leq 2x + 3 - \boxed{3} < 9 - \boxed{3}$ Subtract $\boxed{3}$ from each part of the inequality.

$\boxed{-8} \leq 2x < \boxed{6}$ Simplify.

$\dfrac{\boxed{-8}}{\boxed{2}} \leq \dfrac{2x}{\boxed{2}} < \dfrac{\boxed{6}}{\boxed{2}}$ Divide each part of the inequality by $\boxed{2}$.

$\boxed{-4} \leq x < \boxed{3}$ Simplify.

Graph $-4 \leq x$.

Graph $x < 3$.

Graph the intersection by finding where the two graphs overlap.

© Houghton Mifflin Harcourt Publishing Company

PROFESSIONAL DEVELOPMENT

 Integrate Mathematical Practices

This lesson provides an opportunity to address Mathematical Practice **MP.2**, which calls for students to "reason abstractly and quantitatively." Students will solve compound inequalities and graph the solutions. Students will also write compound inequalities using AND or OR for given graphs. As they translate between graphical and algebraic representations of inequalities, students must keep in mind the meanings of the symbols as well as the logical relationships between statements.

EXPLORE

Truth Tables and Compound Statements

INTEGRATE TECHNOLOGY

Students may complete the Explore activity either online or in the book.

QUESTIONING STRATEGIES

? For any two statements P and Q, when will both P AND Q and P OR Q have the same truth value? Explain. Both compound statements will have the same truth value when both P and Q have the same truth value. When P and Q are both true, then P AND Q is true and P OR Q is true. When P and Q are both false, then P AND Q is false and P OR Q is false.

EXPLAIN 1

Solving Compound Inequalities Involving AND

INTEGRATE MATHEMATICAL PRACTICES
Focus on Modeling

MP.4 Discuss with students how some compound inequalities involving AND can be written as a connected chain of inequalities, while others cannot. Discuss what the graph of a compound inequality involving AND looks like when the graphs of both simple inequalities point in the same direction.

QUESTIONING STRATEGIES

? Will every compound inequality involving AND have a solution? If not, provide a counterexample. No; the compound inequality $x > 10$ AND $x < 8$ has no solution, because the graphs of $x > 10$ and $x < 8$ do not overlap.

EXPLAIN 2

Solving Compound Inequalities Involving OR

INTEGRATE MATHEMATICAL PRACTICES

Focus on Technology

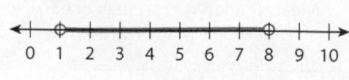 **MP.5** Using a graphing calculator to model an absolute value inequality can be a good way to introduce students to the most common shapes of graphs of compound inequalities. For example, $|x| < 3$ is equivalent to $x > -3$ AND $x < 3$, while $|x| \geq 4$ is equivalent to $x \geq 4$ OR $x \leq -4$.

AVOID COMMON ERRORS

When solving compound inequalities involving OR, students may want to write the statements as a connected chain of inequalities. Remind students that only compound inequalities involving AND can be written this way.

QUESTIONING STRATEGIES

? What must be true in order for the union of a compound inequality involving OR to be the set of all real numbers? The graphs of the two simple inequalities must either overlap or meet at a point (as do, for example, the graphs of $x < 5$ and $x \geq 5$), and the graphs must point in opposite directions.

Reflect

2. **Discussion** Explain why $2 \leq x \leq 6$ can be considered the *short method* for writing the **AND** compound inequality $x \geq 2$ **AND** $x \leq 6$.
   The two simple inequalities can be connected at x to form one compound inequality.

YourTurn

Solve each compound inequality and graph the solutions.

3. $-2 < x - 3 < 5$

   $-2 < x - 3$ **AND** $x - 3 < 5$

   $1 < x$ $x < 8$

   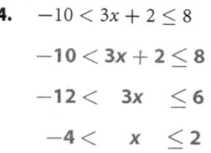

   Graph the intersection of the graphs of $1 < x$ and $x < 8$.

4. $-10 < 3x + 2 \leq 8$

   $-10 < 3x + 2 \leq 8$

   $-12 < \quad 3x \quad \leq 6$

   $-4 < \quad x \quad \leq 2$

   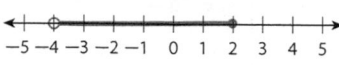

   Graph the intersection of the graphs of $-4 < x$ and $x \leq 2$.

Explain 2   **Solving Compound Inequalities Involving OR**

The graph of a compound inequality involving **OR** is the **union**, or the combined region, of the simple inequality graphs.

Compound Inequalities: OR		
Words	**Algebra**	**Graph**
All real numbers less than 2 **OR** greater than 6	$x < 2$ **OR** $x > 6$	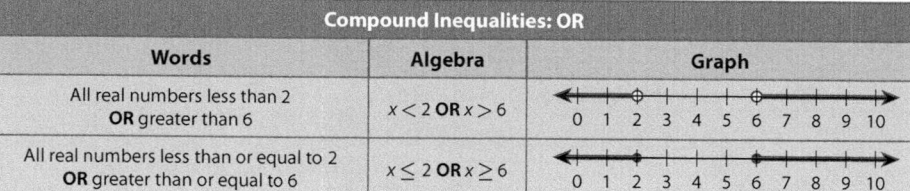
All real numbers less than or equal to 2 **OR** greater than or equal to 6	$x \leq 2$ **OR** $x \geq 6$	

COLLABORATIVE LEARNING

Whole Class Activity

Assign each student a different number. Then read aloud a series of statements describing compound inequalities, and have students stand when you read a statement that describes their numbers. Here are several examples of such statements:

- greater than 15 OR less than 2
- less than 12 AND greater than or equal to 8
- greater than or equal to 3 AND less than or equal to 3
- greater than 2 OR less than 3

Example 2 Solve each compound inequality and graph the solutions.

(A) $-4 + x > 1$ OR $-4 + x < -3$

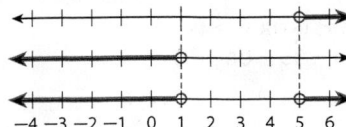

    $-4 + x > 1$ **OR** $-4 + x < -3$ Write the compound inequality using OR.

  $-4 + 4 + x > 1 + 4$ $-4 + 4 + x < -3 + 4$ Add 4 to both sides of each simple inequality.

      $x > 5$ $x < 1$ Simplify.

Graph $x > 5$.

Graph $x < 1$.

Graph the union by combining the graphs.

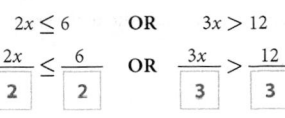

(B) $2x \leq 6$ OR $3x > 12$

    $2x \leq 6$ **OR** $3x > 12$ Write the compound inequality using OR.

  $\dfrac{2x}{\boxed{2}} \leq \dfrac{6}{\boxed{2}}$ **OR** $\dfrac{3x}{\boxed{3}} > \dfrac{12}{\boxed{3}}$ Divide the first simple inequality by $\boxed{2}$.

                             Divide the second simple inequality by $\boxed{3}$.

  $x \leq \boxed{3}$ **OR** $x > \boxed{4}$.   Simplify.

Graph $x \leq 3$.

Graph $x > 4$.

Graph the union by combining the graphs.

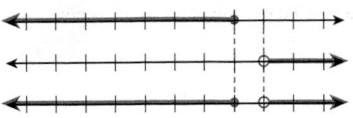

Reflect

5. **Critical Thinking** What kind of compound inequality has no solution?
   A compound inequality that involves OR has no solution if both simple inequalities have

   no solution. A compound inequality that involves AND has no solution if either simple

   inequality has no solution, or if the graphs of the two simple inequalities do not overlap.

DIFFERENTIATE INSTRUCTION

Modeling

When working with with compound inequalities that use AND, students should be familiar with different ways of reading the inequalities. When reading the expression $a < x < b$, students may say, "x is greater than a AND x is less than b" or "a is less than x AND x is less than b." Students should understand that both statements represent the same compound inequality.

EXPLAIN 3

Creating Compound Inequalities From Graphs

INTEGRATE MATHEMATICAL PRACTICES
Focus on Math Connections

MP.1 Discuss with students whether more than one compound inequality can be represented by the same graph. Students should understand that once they have created one compound inequality that represents a graph, they can perform the same operation to both sides of either simple inequality to create another compound inequality that represents the graph. They may also recognize that a graph of all real numbers can represent many different compound inequalities.

QUESTIONING STRATEGIES

? Describe a graph that must be represented by a compound inequality involving AND. The graph would show a line segment connecting two values on the graph, with either an open circle or a closed circle at each end.

? Describe a graph that must be represented by a compound inequality involving OR. The graph would show two non-overlapping arrows pointing in opposite directions. Each would have either an open circle or a closed circle on one end.

Your Turn

Solve each compound inequality and graph the solutions.

6. $x - 5 \geq -2$ OR $x - 5 \leq -6$

$\quad x - 5 \geq -2 \quad$ OR $\quad x - 5 \leq -6$

$\quad\quad x \geq 3 \quad\quad\quad\quad x \leq -1$

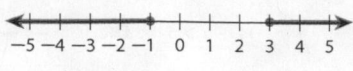

7. $4x - 1 < 15$ OR $8x \geq 48$

$\quad 4x - 1 < 15 \quad$ OR $\quad 8x \geq 48$

$\quad\quad 4x < 16 \quad\quad\quad x \geq 6$

$\quad\quad x < 4$

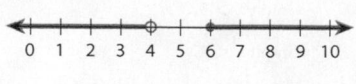

🖉 Explain 3   Creating Compound Inequalities From Graphs

Given a number line graph with a solution set graphed, you can create a compound inequality to fit the graph.

Example 3   Write the compound inequality shown by each graph.

(A)
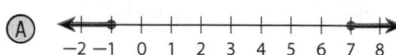

The shaded portion of the graph is not between two values, so the compound inequality involves OR.

On the left, the graph shows an arrow pointing left from −1 and a solid circle, so use $\leq$.

The inequality is $x \leq -1$.

On the right, the graph shows an arrow pointing right from 7 and a solid circle, so use $\geq$.

The inequality is $x \geq 7$.

The compound inequality is $x \leq -1$ OR $x \geq 7$.

(B)
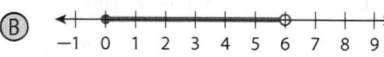

The graph is shaded between the values $\boxed{0}$ and $\boxed{6}$, so the compound inequality involves **AND**.

The graph is shaded to the (right)/left of $\boxed{0}$ and the circle is open/(solid), so use the inequality symbol $\underline{\geq}$.

The inequality is $\underline{x \geq 0}$.

The graph is shaded to the right/(left) of $\boxed{6}$ and the circle is (open)/solid, so use the inequality symbol $\underline{<}$.

The inequality is $\underline{x < 6}$.

The compound inequality is $\underline{x \geq 0 \text{ AND } x < 6}$.

LANGUAGE SUPPORT **EL**

Connect Vocabulary

Discuss the everyday meanings of the terms *intersection* and *union*, and how they relate to the meanings of the words in a mathematical context. For example, the intersection of two streets is the place where they cross each other, and a labor union is an organization of workers who join together.

8. What is a *short method* to write the compound inequality $x \geq 0$ AND $x < 6$?

$0 \leq x < 6$

Write the compound inequality shown by each graph.

9.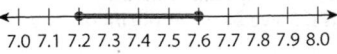

$$-10\,-9\,-8\,-7\,-6\,-5\,-4\,-3\,-2\,-1\quad 0$$

The graph is shaded to the right of an open circle at −8, so $x > -8$.

The graph is shaded to the left of an open circle at −3, so $x < -3$.

The graph is shaded between two values, so the compound inequality involves AND.

$x > -8$ AND $x < -3$ or $-8 < x < -3$

10.

$$-5\,-4\,-3\,-2\,-1\quad 0\quad 1\quad 2\quad 3\quad 4\quad 5$$

The graph is shaded to the left of an open circle at −4, so $x < -4$.

The graph is shaded to the right of a closed circle at 2, so $x \geq 2$.

The graph is shaded in two different directions, so the compound inequality involves OR.

$x < -4$ OR $x \geq 2$

Explain 4 — Expressing Acceptable Levels with Compound Inequalities

You can express quality-controls levels in real-world problems using compound inequalities.

Example 4 Write a compound inequality to represent the indicated quality-control level, and graph the solutions.

(A) The recommended pH level for swimming pool water is between 7.2 and 7.6, inclusive.

Let p be the pH level of swimming pool water.

7.2	is less than or equal to	pH level	is less than or equal to	7.6
7.2	$\leq$	p	$\leq$	7.6

The compound inequality is $7.2 \leq p \leq 7.6$.

Graph the solutions.

$$7.0\ 7.1\ 7.2\ 7.3\ 7.4\ 7.5\ 7.6\ 7.7\ 7.8\ 7.9\ 8.0$$

© Houghton Mifflin Harcourt Publishing Company

EXPLAIN 4

Expressing Acceptable Levels with Compound Inequalities

AVOID COMMON ERRORS

Make sure students understand the meanings of the words *inclusive* and *exclusive* as used in compound inequalities. The word *inclusive* means including endpoints, while *exclusive* means excluding endpoints.

QUESTIONING STRATEGIES

? Can a range of acceptable levels be represented by a compound inequality involving OR? Explain. No; a range of levels is the set of values between two given values, which is represented by a compound inequality involving AND. A compound inequality involving OR describes the union of two separate sets of values.

ELABORATE

INTEGRATE MATHEMATICAL PRACTICES
Focus on Math Connections

MP.1 Review how to solve multi-step inequalities. Students should understand that when solving a compound inequality with AND or OR, the operations performed to solve one simple inequality may not be the same operations performed to solve the other simple inequality.

SUMMARIZE THE LESSON

? How do you differentiate between a compound inequality involving AND and a compound inequality involving OR? **A compound inequality involving AND represents an intersection, and the solutions are those values that make both simple inequalities true. A compound inequality involving OR represents a union of two sets of numbers, which may or may not overlap; their solutions are values that make either simple inequality true.**

Ⓑ The recommended free chlorine level for swimming pool water is between 1.0 and 3.0 parts per million, inclusive.

Let c be the free chlorine level in the pool.

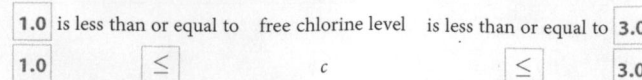

| 1.0 | is less than or equal to | free chlorine level | is less than or equal to | 3.0 |
| 1.0 | $\leq$ | c | $\leq$ | 3.0 |

The compound inequality is $\boxed{1.0} \leq c \leq \boxed{3.0}$.

Graph the solutions.

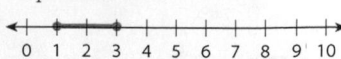

0 1 2 3 4 5 6 7 8 9 10

Reflect

11. **Discussion** What does the phrase "between 7.2 and 7.6, inclusive" mean?
The boundary numbers of the solution, 7.2 and 7.6, are included in the solution. The graph will have solid circles at those numbers.

Your Turn

Write a compound inequality to represent the indicated quality-control level, and graph the solutions.

12. The recommended alkalinity level for swimming pool water is between 80 and 120 parts per million, inclusive.

$80 \leq a \leq 120$

0   40   80   120   160   200

💬 Elaborate

13. Explain the difference between graphing a compound inequality involving **AND** and graphing a compound inequality involving **OR**.
When graphing a compound inequality involving AND, find the intersection of the graphs of the two simple inequalities. When graphing a compound inequality involving OR, find the union of the graphs of the two simple inequalities.

14. How can you tell whether a compound inequality involves **AND** or **OR** from looking at its graph?
If the graph is made up of a single graph between two endpoints, then the compound inequality involves AND. If the graph is made up of two separate graphs, then the compound inequality involves OR.

15. **Essential Question Check-In** Explain how to find the solutions of a compound inequality.
Split the compound inequality into two simple inequalities. Solve each simple inequality separately. The solution of the compound inequality is either the union or the intersection of the solutions of the simple inequalities.

• Online Homework
• Hints and Help
• Extra Practice

Complete the truth tables.

1.

P	Q	P True or False?	Q True or False?	P AND Q True or False?
An apple is a fruit.	A carrot is a vegetable.	True	True	True
An apple is a fruit.	A carrot is a fruit.	True	False	False
An apple is a vegetable.	A carrot is a vegetable.	False	True	False
An apple is a vegetable.	A carrot is a fruit.	False	False	False

2.

P	Q	P True or False?	Q True or False?	P OR Q True or False?
Blue is a color.	Five is a number.	True	True	True
Blue is a color.	Five is a color.	True	False	True
Blue is a number.	Five is a number.	False	True	True
Blue is a number.	Five is a color.	False	False	False

Solve each compound inequality and graph the solutions.

3. $-3 < 3x \leq 9$
$-1 < x \leq 3$

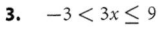
$-5\ -4\ -3\ -2\ -1\ \ 0\ \ 1\ \ 2\ \ 3\ \ 4\ \ 5$

4. $0 \leq 2x - 10 \leq 20$
$10 \leq 2x \leq 30$
$5 \leq x \leq 15$

$-20\quad -10\quad\ 0\quad\ 10\quad\ 20$

5. $x - 5 < 3$ OR $x - 5 \geq 8$
$x < 8 \qquad x \geq 13$

$5\ \ 6\ \ 7\ \ 8\ \ 9\ \ 10\ 11\ 12\ 13\ 14\ 15$

6. $1 \leq x + 7 < 7$
$-6 \leq x < 0$

$-8\ -7\ -6\ -5\ -4\ -3\ -2\ -1\ \ 0\ \ 1\ \ 2$

7. $4x + 3 < -5$ OR $4x + 3 > 23$
$4x < -8 \qquad 4x > 20$
$x < -2 \qquad x > 5$

$-3\ -2\ -1\ \ 0\ \ 1\ \ 2\ \ 3\ \ 4\ \ 5\ \ 6\ \ 7$

8. $\frac{x}{5} - 2 \leq -6$ OR $8x + 1 \geq 41$
$\frac{x}{5} \leq -4 \qquad 8x \geq 40$
$x \leq -20 \qquad x \geq 5$

$-30\quad -20\quad -10\quad\ 0\quad\ 10\quad\ 20$

9. $-6 < \frac{x - 12}{4} < -2$
$-24 < x - 12 < -8$
$-12 < \quad x \quad < 4$

$-12\quad -8\quad -4\quad\ 0\quad\ 4$

10. $x + 7 \leq 7$ OR $5 + 2x > 7$
$x \leq 0 \qquad 2x > 2$
$\qquad\qquad x > 1$

$-5\ -4\ -3\ -2\ -1\ \ 0\ \ 1\ \ 2\ \ 3\ \ 4\ \ 5$

Exercise	Depth of Knowledge (D.O.K.)	COMMON CORE Mathematical Practices
1–2	**1** Recall	**MP.2** Reasoning
3–10	**1** Recall	**MP.5** Using Tools
11–16	**1** Recall	**MP.6** Precision
17–22	**2** Skills/Concepts	**MP.4** Modeling
23	**2** Skills/Concepts	**MP.5** Using Tools
24	**3** Strategic Thinking **H.O.T.**	**MP.4** Modeling
25–26	**3** Strategic Thinking **H.O.T.**	**MP.3** Logic

EVALUATE

ASSIGNMENT GUIDE

Concepts and Skills	Practice
Explore Truth Tables and Compound Statements	Exercises 1–2
Example 1 Solving Compound Inequalities Involving AND	Exercises 3–4, 6, 9, 25
Example 2 Solving Compound Inequalities Involving OR	Exercises 5, 7–8, 10, 23, 26
Example 3 Creating Compound Inequalities From Graphs	Exercises 11–16
Example 4 Expressing Acceptable Levels with Compound Inequalities	Exercises 17–22, 24

INTEGRATE MATHEMATICAL PRACTICES
Focus on Math Connections

MP.1 Discuss with students the connection between absolute value functions and compound inequalities. The difference between AND statements and OR statements is better visualized when students learn that "the absolute value of an expression is less than a number" is an AND statement, and "the absolute value of an expression is greater than a number" is an OR statement.

Write the compound inequality shown by each graph.

11.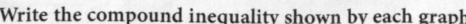

$$-2\ -1\ \ 0\ \ 1\ \ 2\ \ 3\ \ 4\ \ 5\ \ 6\ \ 7\ \ 8$$

The graph is shaded to the left of a solid circle at -2, so $x \leq -2$.

The graph is shaded to the right of a solid circle at 7, so $x \geq 7$.

The graph is shaded in two different directions, so the compound inequality involves OR.

The compound inequality is $x \leq -2$ OR $x \geq 7$.

12.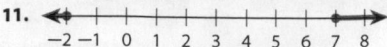

$$-10\ -9\ -8\ -7\ -6\ -5\ -4\ -3\ -2\ -1\ \ \ 0$$

The graph is shaded to the right of an open circle at -8, so $x > -8$.

The graph is shaded to the left of a closed circle at -1, so $x \leq -1$.

The graph is shaded between two values, so the compound inequality involves AND.

The compound inequality is $x > -8$ AND $x \leq -1$, or $-8 < x \leq -1$.

13.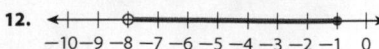

$$5\ \ 6\ \ 7\ \ 8\ \ 9\ \ 10\ \ 11\ \ 12\ \ 13\ \ 14\ \ 15$$

The graph is shaded to the left of an open circle at 9, so $x < 9$.

The graph is shaded to the right of an open circle at 11, so $x > 11$.

The graph is shaded in two different directions, so the compound inequality involves OR.

The compound inequality is $x < 9$ OR $x > 11$.

14.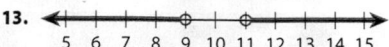

$$-4\ -3\ -2\ -1\ \ 0\ \ 1\ \ 2\ \ 3\ \ 4\ \ 5\ \ 6$$

The graph is shaded to the right of a closed circle at -3, so $x \geq -3$.

The graph is shaded to the left of an open circle at 6, so $x < 6$.

The graph is shaded between two values, so the compound inequality involves AND.

The compound inequality is $x \geq -3$ AND $x < 6$, or $-3 \leq x < 6$.

15.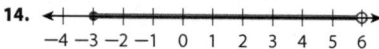

$$0\ \ 1\ \ 2\ \ 3\ \ 4\ \ 5\ \ 6\ \ 7\ \ 8\ \ 9\ \ 10$$

The graph is shaded to the right of an open circle at 2, so $x > 2$.

The graph is shaded to the left of an open circle at 10, so $x < 10$.

The graph is shaded between two values, so the compound inequality involves AND.

The compound inequality is $x > 2$ AND $x < 10$, or $2 < x < 10$.

16.

$$-5\ -4\ -3\ -2\ -1\ \ 0\ \ 1\ \ 2\ \ 3\ \ 4\ \ 5$$

The graph is shaded to the left of a closed circle at 0, so $x \leq 0$.

The graph is shaded to the right of a closed circle at 2, so $x \geq 2$.

The graph is shaded in two different directions, so the compound inequality involves OR.

The compound inequality is $x \leq 0$ OR $x \geq 2$.

Write a compound inequality to show the levels that are within each range. Then graph the solutions.

17. Biology An iguana needs to live in a warm environment. The temperature in a pet iguana's cage should be between 70 °F and 95 °F, inclusive.

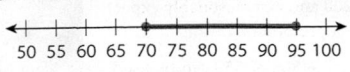

50 55 60 65 70 75 80 85 90 95 100

$70 \leq t \leq 95$

18. Meteorology One layer of Earth's atmosphere is called the stratosphere. At one point above Earth's surface, the stratosphere extends from an altitude of 16 kilometers to an altitude of 50 kilometers.

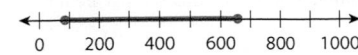

0 5 10 15 20 25 30 35 40 45 50

$16 \leq k \leq 50$

19. Music A typical acoustic guitar has a range of three octaves. When the guitar is tuned to "concert pitch," the range of frequencies for those three octaves is between 82.4 Hertz and 659.2 Hertz inclusive.

0 200 400 600 800 1000

$82.4 \leq f \leq 659.2$

20. Transportation The cruise-control function on Georgina's car should keep the speed of the car within 3 miles per hour of the set speed. The set speed is 55 miles per hour.

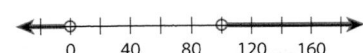

50 51 52 53 54 55 56 57 58 59 60

$52 \leq s \leq 58$

21. Chemistry Water is not a liquid if its temperature is above 100 °C or below 0 °C.

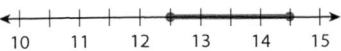

0 40 80 120 160

$0 < t \text{ OR } t > 100$

22. Sports The ball used in a soccer game may not weigh more than 16 ounces or less than 14 ounces at the start of the match. After 1.5 ounces of air were added to a ball, the ball was approved for use in a game.

10 11 12 13 14 15

$12.5 \leq w \leq 14.5$

23. Match the compound inequalities with the graphs of their solutions.

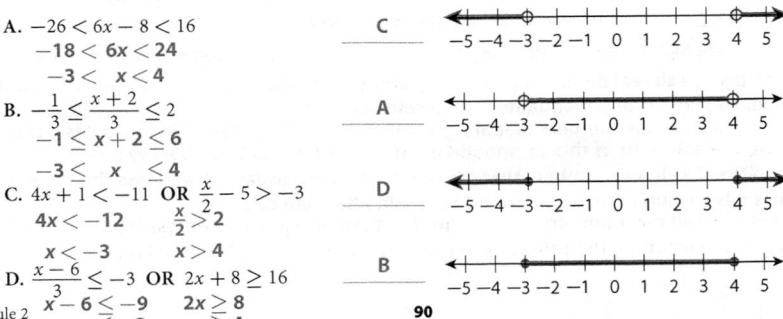

A. $-26 < 6x - 8 < 16$
   $-18 < 6x < 24$
   $-3 < \ x < 4$

B. $-\frac{1}{3} \leq \frac{x+2}{3} \leq 2$
   $-1 \leq x + 2 \leq 6$
   $-3 \leq \ x \ \leq 4$

C. $4x + 1 < -11 \text{ OR } \frac{x}{2} - 5 > -3$
   $4x < -12 \qquad \frac{x}{2} > 2$
   $x < -3 \qquad x > 4$

D. $\frac{x-6}{3} \leq -3 \text{ OR } 2x + 8 \geq 16$
   $x - 6 \leq -9 \qquad 2x \geq 8$
   $x \leq -3 \qquad x \geq 4$

C
−5 −4 −3 −2 −1 0 1 2 3 4 5

A
−5 −4 −3 −2 −1 0 1 2 3 4 5

D
−5 −4 −3 −2 −1 0 1 2 3 4 5

B
−5 −4 −3 −2 −1 0 1 2 3 4 5

QUESTIONING STRATEGIES

? How can you rewrite a connected chain of inequalities as a compound inequality involving AND? Rewrite the chain of inequalities as two simple inequalities connected by the word AND.

VISUAL CUES

Use color to help students compare AND and OR statements. On a transparency, graph the solutions of $x < 3$ with a yellow marker and the solutions of $x < 7$ with a blue marker. Show that the solution set for $x < 3$ AND $x < 7$ is the green area described by $x < 3$. Then discuss the solution set for $x < 3$ OR $x < 7$. The solution is everywhere the graph is shaded, as described by $x < 7$.

AVOID COMMON ERRORS

Remind students that only compound inequalities involving AND can be written as a connected chain of inequalities. In solving compound inequalities involving OR, there is no way to write the compound inequality without using the word OR.

MULTIPLE REPRESENTATIONS

Interval notation is another way of representing compound inequalities and is used more often in higher-level math. In this notation, a parenthesis, like an empty circle on a graph, indicates that an end value is not included, and a square bracket, like a solid circle on a graph, indicates that an end value is included. For example, the set of values described by $a < x \leq b$ can be written as $(a, b]$. These symbols may also be used on a graph.

JOURNAL

Have students explain the difference between compound inequalities using AND and compound inequalities using OR. Students should include differences between the inequalities as well as differences between the graphs.

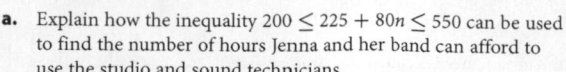

24. Multi-Step Jenna's band is going to record a CD at a recording studio. They will pay $225 to use the studio for one day and $80 per hour for sound technicians. Jenna has $200 and can reasonably expect to raise up to an additional $350 by taking pre-orders for the CDs.

a. Explain how the inequality $200 \leq 225 + 80n \leq 550$ can be used to find the number of hours Jenna and her band can afford to use the studio and sound technicians.

The total cost is equal to the cost of the studio for one day plus the cost of the technicians.

Let n be the number of hours in the studio.

The cost of the studio for one day is $225. The cost of the technicians is $80 per hour, or $80n for n hours. So, the total cost of the studio for one day is $225 + 80n$.

Jenna's band is willing to spend between $200 and $550. So, the total cost $225 + 80n$ must be in this range. The inequality that models this is $200 \leq 225 + 80n \leq 550$.

b. Solve the inequality. Are there any numbers in the solution set that are not reasonable in this situation?

$$200 \leq 225 + 80n \leq 550$$
$$-25 \leq 80n \leq 325$$
$$-0.3125 \leq n \leq 4.0625$$

n cannot be negative, so the solution set is $0 \leq n \leq 4.0625$.

c. Suppose Jenna raises $350 in pre-orders. How much more money would she need to raise if she wanted to use the studio and sound technicians for 6 hours?
$225 + 80(6) = 705$

Jenna has $200 and she raises $350 in pre-orders.

$705 - 200 - 350 = 155$

Jenna needs to raise $155 more.

25. Explain the Error A student solves the compound inequality $15 \leq 2x + 5 \leq 17$ and finds the solutions of the compound inequality to be all real numbers. Explain and correct the student's mistake. Graph the actual solutions to back up your answer.

$$15 \leq 2x + 5 \leq 17$$
$$10 \leq 2x \leq 12$$
$$5 \leq x \leq 6$$

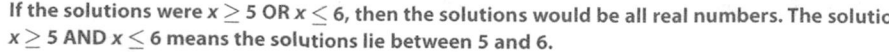

The solutions are $x \geq 5$ AND $x \leq 6$.

If the solutions were $x \geq 5$ OR $x \leq 6$, then the solutions would be all real numbers. The solution $x \geq 5$ AND $x \leq 6$ means the solutions lie between 5 and 6.

26. Communicate Mathematical Thinking Describe the solutions of the compound inequalities.

$x > 9$ AND $x < 9$ all real numbers that are greater than 9 and less than 9. Because 9 is not a solution, this compound inequality has no solution.

$x < 9$ OR $x > 9$ all real numbers that are greater than 9 or less than 9. Because 9 is not a solution, the solutions of this compound inequality are all real numbers except 9.

$x \geq 9$ AND $x \leq 9$ all real numbers that are greater than or equal to 9 and less than or equal to 9. Because 9 is a solution, this compound inequality has one solution, 9.

$x \leq 9$ OR $x \geq 9$ all real numbers that are greater than or equal to 9 or less than or equal to 9. Because 9 is a solution, the solutions of this compound inequality are all real numbers.

Lesson Performance Task

The table gives the melting point and boiling point of various elements. Write a compound inequality for each element to show the temperature range of the element in its liquid state. Graph the solutions of each. Suppose you were to set the temperature of each element to its melting point and increase the temperature of each element at the same rate. Which element will remain liquid for the longest amount of time? Which element will reach its boiling point first? Explain.

Element	Melting Point (°C)	Boiling Point (°C)
Gold	1064	2856
Copper	1085	2562
Iron	1538	2861
Lead	327	1749
Aluminum	660	2519

Gold
Let g be the temperature of gold in its liquid state.
g is greater than 1064 AND g is less than 2856.
$$g > 1064 \text{ AND } g < 2856$$
$$1064 < g < 2856$$

Copper
Let c be the temperature of copper in its liquid state.
c is greater than 1085 AND c is less than 2562.
$$c > 1085 \text{ AND } c < 2562$$
$$1085 < c < 2562$$

Iron
Let i be the temperature of iron in its liquid state.
i is greater than 1538 AND i is less than 2861.
$$i > 1538 \text{ AND } i < 2861$$
$$1538 < i < 2861$$

Lead
Let ℓ be the temperature of lead in its liquid state.
ℓ is greater than 327 AND ℓ Is less than 1749.
$$\ell > 327 \text{ AND } \ell < 1749$$
$$327 < \ell < 1749$$

Aluminum
Let a be the temperature of aluminum in its liquid state. a is greater than 660 AND a is less than 2519.
$$a > 660 \text{ AND } a < 2519$$
$$660 < a < 2519$$

Aluminum will remain liquid for the longest time, because it is a liquid over the greatest range of temperatures. Iron will reach its boiling point first, because it is a liquid over the smallest range of temperatures.

INTEGRATE MATHEMATICAL PRACTICES
Focus on Math Connections

MP.1 Some students may be unsure how the melting point and boiling point of an element relate to whether it is a solid, liquid, or gas at a given temperature. Remind students that most materials change from solid to liquid and then to gas as their temperatures increase. Explain that the melting point is the temperature at which a material changes from solid to liquid, and the boiling point is the temperature at which it changes from liquid to gas.

INTEGRATE MATHEMATICAL PRACTICES
Focus on Communication

MP.3 Have students share their reasons for determining which element remains a liquid for the longest time and which reaches its boiling point first. Then have students explain why subtracting the melting point from the boiling point for each element could also help them answer the questions in the Lesson Performance Task.

EXTENSION ACTIVITY

Have students research the temperature range for a situation that interests them, such as human body temperatures, the weather in a particular city, or candy-making temperatures. Have each student first write a verbal description of the temperature range and cite a reference for the data. Then have students write a compound inequality for the range and graph the inequality. Remind students to specify whether their inequalities show temperatures in degrees Fahrenheit or degrees Celsius. You may wish to have all students graph their inequalities on the same scale, then create a class poster comparing the temperature ranges.

Scoring Rubric
2 points: Student correctly solves the problem and explains his/her reasoning.
1 point: Student shows good understanding of the problem but does not fully solve or explain his/her reasoning.
0 points: Student does not demonstrate understanding of the problem.

Study Guide Review

ASSESSMENT AND INTERVENTION

Assign or customize module reviews.

MODULE PERFORMANCE TASK

COMMON CORE

Mathematical Practices: MP.1, MP.2, MP.4, MP.7
A-CED.A.1, A-CED.A.3, A-REI.B.3

SUPPORTING STUDENT REASONING

Students should begin the task by looking at the variety of equations in this module. Here is some information they may ask for.

- **How many variables should I use?** Urge students to be creative, favoring an equation such as $3(v + f) = \$10.20$ over long but unchallenging equations such as $h + c + v + f + x + t + s + l = 15.00$.

- **Can the order be for more than one person?** Suggest that students consider what up to three or four people might normally order from the menu.

- **How can I use the Distributive Property to write my equation?** Suggest that two or more people order one or more of the same items on the menu.

- Have students trade equations with a classmate to solve.

Algebraic Models

Essential Question: How can you use algebraic models to solve real-world problems?

Key Vocabulary

algebraic expression
  (expresión algebraica)
coefficient *(coeficiente)*
expression *(expresión)*
inequality *(desigualdad)*
literal equation
  (ecuación literal)
numerical expression
  (expresión numérica)
term *(término)*

KEY EXAMPLE   (Lesson 2.1)

Write an expression for each situation.

The total cost of two notebooks that cost x dollars each and a pen that costs $3.50

$2x + 3.5$

The price of three identical items that are each 25% off

$3(p - 0.25p) = 2.25p$

KEY EXAMPLE   (Lesson 2.2)

Solve the equation $3(2y - 5) = 9$ for y.

$$3(2y - 5) = 9$$
$$6y - 15 = 9 \qquad \text{Distributive Property}$$
$$6y = 24 \qquad \text{Addition Property of Equality}$$
$$y = 4 \qquad \text{Division Property of Equality}$$

KEY EXAMPLE   (Lesson 2.3)

The formula for the area of a triangle is $A = \frac{1}{2}bh$. The base b of a triangle is 8 cm, and the area A is 40. Solve the formula for h, and then find the height of the triangle.

$$A = \frac{1}{2}bh$$
$$\frac{2A}{b} = h \qquad \text{Solve for h.}$$
$$\frac{2(40)}{8} = h \qquad \text{Substitute 40 for A and 8 for b.}$$
$$10 = h \qquad \text{Simplify.}$$

KEY EXAMPLE   (Lesson 2.4)

Solve the inequality for a.

$$-2a - 13 \leq 9a + 20$$
$$-11a - 13 \leq 20 \qquad \text{Subtract 9a from both sides.}$$
$$-11a \leq 33 \qquad \text{Add 13 to both sides.}$$
$$a \geq -3 \qquad \text{Divide by} -11. \text{ Reverse the inequality sign.}$$

SCAFFOLDING SUPPORT

- For students who need more support writing the equation, provide a format such as $2(_ + _) + _ = $ total amount. Suggest they choose three different variables from the menu items to fill in the blanks and compute the total amount. Then they can replace one variable with an x.

- If students want to increase the complexity of their problems, suggest that they try to create an equation based on the menu items that cannot be solved.

Write an expression for each situation. *(Lesson 2.1)*

1. The original price of an item plus a sales tax of 8.5%

$x + 0.085x = 1.085x$

2. The total cost of 6 pens and 3 folders. A folder costs $1.15 more than a pen.

$6p + 3(p + 1.15) = 9p + 3.45$

3. The sum of Andre and Brandon's scores on a math quiz is 180. Andre's score is 2 times as much as 30 less than Brandon's score. Find each student's quiz score. *(Lesson 2.2)*

$2(x - 30) + x = 180$; Andre 100; Brandon 80

4. The formula for finding the area of a trapezoid is $A = \frac{1}{2}(b_1 + b_2)h$ where A represents the area of the trapezoid, b_1 and b_2 are bases, and h represents the height. Solve the formula for h.
(Lesson 2.3)

$h = \dfrac{2A}{b_1 + b_2}$

5. Solve $7(3 - x) \leq 5x - 15$ for x. *(Lesson 2.4)*

$x \geq 3$

MODULE PERFORMANCE TASK

Menu Math

You and some friends have ordered from this restaurant menu. When the checks come, you find that your server has written all the orders as equations such as "$c + f + 2s = 6.70$," using the first letter of each menu item as the variable. Use the menu to write an equation to challenge a classmate, letting x represent the price of an unknown item. ($x + t = 3.45$. What's x?) You can use coefficients, fractions, decimals, percents, the distributive property, verbal descriptions, and all of the elements of writing and solving equations that you've learned.

Start by listing some of your ideas in the space below. Then use your own paper to complete the task.

Menu	
Hamburger	$1.95
Cheeseburger	$2.45
Veggie burger	$2.15
Fries	$1.25
Green salad	$1.65
Tomato soup	$1.80
Juice	
Small	$1.50
Large	$2.25

DISCUSSION OPPORTUNITIES

- Have students discuss any difficulties they had while writing the equation.

- Ask students to share how they solved their equations. If any equations could not be solved, have students analyze why not.

SAMPLE SOLUTION

$c + 2(x + s) = 7.95$

c represents a cheeseburger at $2.45.

s represents a small juice at $1.50.

$2.45 + 2(x + 1.5) = 7.95$	Substitute.
$2.45 + 2x + 3 = 7.95$	Multiply.
$2x + 5.45 = 7.95$	Add like terms.
$2x = 2.50$	Subtract.
$x = 1.25$	Divide.

The item on the menu that is $1.25 is fries.

So, x represents fries.

Assessment Rubric

2 points: Student correctly solves the problem and explains his/her reasoning.
1 point: Student shows good understanding of the problem but does not fully solve or explain his/her reasoning.
0 points: Student does not demonstrate understanding of the problem.

Ready to Go On?

ASSESS MASTERY

Use the assessment on this page to determine if students have mastered the concepts and standards covered in this module.

ASSESSMENT AND INTERVENTION

Access Ready to Go On? assessment online, and receive instant scoring, feedback, and customized intervention or enrichment.

ADDITIONAL RESOURCES

Response to Intervention Resources

- Reteach Worksheets

Differentiated Instruction Resources

- Reading Strategies **EL**
- Success for English Learners **EL**
- Challenge Worksheets

Assessment Resources

- Leveled Module Quizzes

95   Module 2

(Ready) to Go On?

2.1–2.5 Algebraic Models

- Online Homework
- Hints and Help
- Extra Practice

Write an expression in simplest form for each verbal description. *(Lesson 2.1)*

1. The sum of the cost of dinner d and a $12 tip divided equally between 3 people

$$(d + 12) \div 3 = \frac{1}{3}d + 4$$

2. The total pay for 12 hours of work at a base rate of p per hour plus a temporary raise of $2.50 per hour

$$12(p + 2.5) = 12p + 30$$

3. Given $x < y$, compare the following expressions and determine which is greater: $2x - y$; $2y - x$. Explain your answer. *(Lesson 2.1)*

$2y - x$; Since $y > x$, $2y > 2x$ and $-y < -x$ (or $-x > -y$). Adding these: $2y - x > 2x - y$

4. The formula $y - y_1 = m(x - x_1)$ is the point-slope form of the equation of a line where m is the slope of the line and (x, y) and (x_1, y_1) are points of the line. Solve the equation for m, and find the slope of a line that includes the points $(4, -2)$ and $(5, 0)$. *(Lesson 2.3)*

$$m = \frac{y - y_1}{x - x_1}; 2$$

Solve. *(Lessons 2.2, 2.4, 2.5)*

5. $-17 - 5(x + 3) = 3x$

$x = -4$

6. $100x - 200 > 50x - 75$

$x > 2.5$

7. $12 < 2x + 2 \leq 22$

$5 < x \leq 10$

8. $-13 < -x + 5 < 8$

$-3 < x < 18$

ESSENTIAL QUESTION

9. What is the general process for solving an equation with one variable?

Possible Answer: Apply the properties of equality with the aim of isolating the variable on one side of the equation.

COMMON CORE Common Core Standards

Lesson	Items	Content Standards	Mathematical Practices
2.1	1–2	A-CED.A.1, A-REI.B.3	MP.4
2.1	3	A-SSE.A.1a	MP.3
2.3	4	A-CED.A.4	MP.7
2.2,	5	A-REI.B.3	MP.2
2.2, 2.4	6	A-REI.B.3	MP.2
2.2, 2.5	7	A-REI.B.3	MP.2
2.2, 2.5	8	A-REI.B.3	MP.2

Assessment Readiness

1. Consider the new expression that is obtained by simplifying $8(x - 1) + 15$. Select True or False for each statement.

   A. The new expression has 3 terms. ○ True ● False

   B. The coefficient of x in the new expression is 8. ● True ○ False

   C. The constant in the new expression is 14. ○ True ● False

2. Look at each equation and possible solution. Is the solution correct? Select Yes or No for each equation.

   A. $3 - m = -2(m + 6); m = -15$ ● Yes ○ No

   B. $5(p + 3) = -35; p = -4$ ○ Yes ● No

   C. $8q = 3(10 + q); q = 6$ ● Yes ○ No

3. The formula for finding the volume of a triangular prism $V = \frac{1}{2}(bh)\ell$ where b represents the base length, h represents the base height, and ℓ represents the length of the prism. Select True or False for each statement.

   A. The formula solved for h is $h = \frac{2V\ell}{b}$. ○ True ● False

   B. The formula solved for ℓ is $\ell = \frac{2V}{bh}$. ● True ○ False

   C. The formula solved for b is $b = \frac{2V}{bh}$. ○ True ● False

4. Sherman hopes to get at least a 90 average on his science tests. He has one more test before the end of the school year. His past test scores are 79, 94, 91, and 92. Write and solve an inequality that represents this situation. What is the lowest score Sherman can get on his final test and reach his goal? Show your work.

$$\frac{79 + 94 + 91 + 92 + x}{5} \geq 90$$

$$356 + x \geq 450$$

$$x \geq 94$$

The lowest score he can get is 94.

ASSESSMENT AND INTERVENTION

Assign ready-made or customized practice tests to prepare students for high-stakes tests.

ADDITIONAL RESOURCES

Assessment Resources

- Leveled Module Quizzes: Modified, B

AVOID COMMON ERRORS

Item 1 Some students forget to distribute a number to all terms within parentheses and will only distribute to the first term. Remind students that the number outside the parentheses must be multiplied by every term inside the parentheses.

COMMON CORE **Common Core Standards**

Lesson	Items	Content Standards	Mathematical Practices
2.1	1	**A-SSE.A.1a**	**MP.2**
1.1, 2.2	2*	**A-REI.B.3**	**MP.2**
2.3	3	**A-CED.A.4**	**MP.2**
1.1, 2.4	4*	**A-CED.A.1**	**MP.4**

* Item integrates mixed review concepts from previous modules or a previous course.

MIXED REVIEW
Assessment Readiness

ASSESSMENT AND INTERVENTION

Assign ready-made or customized practice tests to prepare students for high-stakes tests.

ADDITIONAL RESOURCES

Assessment Resources

- Leveled Unit Tests: Modified, A, B, C
- Performance Assessment

AVOID COMMON ERRORS

Item 6 Some students have difficulty converting between the customary and metric systems. Remind students that they can eliminate unwanted units much the same way as eliminating unwanted coefficients. Divide by unwanted units in the numerator, and multiply by unwanted units in the denominator. The units will cancel.

• Online Homework
• Hints and Help
• Extra Practice

1. Consider each equation and solution. Is each solution correct? Select Yes or No.

   A. $6 = -\frac{r}{3}; r = -2$ ○ Yes ● No

   B. $1 - 2s = 3; s = 5$ ○ Yes ● No

   C. $4 + 6t = -20; t = -4$ ● Yes ○ No

2. The distance from Town A to Town B on a map is 6 inches. The actual distance from Town B to Town C is 12 miles. The scale on the map is 1 in: 4 mi. Determine if each statement is True or False.

   A. The actual distance from A to B is 24 mi. ● True ○ False

   B. The distance from B to C on the map is 36 in. ○ True ● False

   C. The actual distance from A to C is 4.5 mi. ○ True ● False

3. The dimensions of a storage container in the shape of a rectangular prism are 54 in. × 32.25 in. × 24.5 in. Choose True or False for each statement.

   A. The most precise dimension has 4 significant digits. ● True ○ False

   B. Written using the correct number of significant digits, the volume of the container has 3 significant digits. ○ True ● False

   C. Written using the correct number of significant digits, the surface area of the container is rounded to the ones place. ○ True ● False

4. Hank bought 3 more boxes of cereal than gallons of milk. He bought x boxes of cereal at $2.79 each. Each gallon of milk costs $4.49. Consider the expression $2.79x + 4.49(x - 3)$. Determine if each statement is True or False.

   A. The term $x - 3$ represents the number of gallons of milk. ● True ○ False

   B. The coefficient 2.79 represents the cost of one box of cereal. ● True ○ False

   C. The expression represents the total number of boxes of cereal and gallons of milk. ○ True ● False

---

COMMON CORE ## Common Core Standards

Items	Content Standards	Mathematical Practices
1	A-REI.A.1	MP.2
2	N-Q.A.1	MP.4
3	N-Q.A.3	MP.1
4	A-SSE.A.1	MP.4
5	A-CED.A.4	MP.2
6	N-Q.A.1	MP.6

5. The formula $y = mx + b$ is the slope-intercept form of the equation of a line where m is the slope of the line, b is the y-intercept, and (x, y) is a solution of the equation.

   A. The equation solved for b is $b = y - mx$.   ● True   ○ False

   B. The equation solved for x is $x = \dfrac{y - b}{m}$.   ● True   ○ False

   C. The equation solved for m is $m = x(y - b)$.   ○ True   ● False

6. Carla and Ross competed in the long-jump at a track meet. Carla jumped 3.5 meters. Ross jumped 99 inches. Who jumped farther and by approximately how many feet? Use 1 m ≈ 3.27 ft. Explain how you solved this problem.

   Carla jumped about 3.2 feet farther. I found the distance Carla and Ross jumped in feet. Carla jumped about 11.45 feet, and Ross jumped 8.25 feet. Then, I subtracted 8.25 from 11.45 to find how much farther Carla jumped.

7. Solve the following equation for x: $\frac{1}{2}(5x + 12) = 2x - 3$. Show your work.

   $$\frac{1}{2}(5x + 12) = 2x - 3$$
   $$2.5x + 6 = 2x - 3$$
   $$0.5x = -9$$
   $$x = -18$$

8. A factory produces 5-packs of pencils. To be within the weight specifications, a pack of 5 pencils should weigh between 60 grams and 95 grams. The cardboard for each package has a mass of 15 grams. Write a compound inequality to represent the mass of a single pencil in a pack. Can each pencil have a mass of 10.5 grams? Explain.

   $60 \leq 5x + 15 \leq 95$, or $9 \leq x \leq 16$; Yes, each pencil has a mass between 9 and 16 g, inclusive, so a pencil can have a mass of 10.5 g.

Performance Tasks

★ 9. Fernando is starting a new sales job and needs to decide which of two salary plans to choose from. For plan A, he will earn $100/week plus 15% commission on all sales. For plan B, he will earn $150/week plus 10% commission on all sales.

   A. Write an expression for each salary plan if Fernando's total weekly sales are s.

   B. For what amount of weekly sales is plan B better than plan A?

   A. $100 + 0.15s$

       $150 + 0.1s$

   B. $s < 1000$

PERFORMANCE TASKS

There are three different levels of performance tasks:

* **Novice:** These are short word problems that require students to apply the math they have learned in straightforward, real-world situations.

** **Apprentice:** These are more involved problems that guide students step-by-step through more complex tasks. These exercises include more complicated reasoning, writing, and open ended elements.

*****Expert:** These are open-ended, nonroutine problems that, instead of stepping the students through, ask them to choose their own methods for solving and justify their answers and reasoning.

SCORING GUIDES

Item 9 (2 points)

A. 1 point for correct expressions

B. 1 point for correct answer

Common Core Standards

Items	Content Standards	Mathematical Practices
7	A-REI.B.3	MP.2
8	A-CED. A.1	MP.4

SCORING GUIDES

Item 10 (6 points)

A. 1 point for correct inequality
   1 point for work

B. 1 point for correctly calculating new cost
   1 point for correct number of devices (must be a whole number)

C. 1 point for correct price
   1 point for explanation

Item 11 (6 points)

A. 1 point for correct expression
   1 point for explanation

B. 1 point for correct expression
   1 point for explanation

C. 1 point for writing correct inequality
   1 point for solving inequality

★★10. An electronics company has developed a new hand-held device. The company predicts that the start-up cost to manufacture the new product will be $125,000, and the cost to make one device will be $6.50.

A. If the company plans on selling the device at a wholesale price of $9, write and solve an inequality to determine how many must be sold for the company to make a profit. Show your work.

B. The cost of making one device is 10% more than the company predicted. What is the new cost of making one device? How many devices must it now sell at the same wholesale price to make a profit?

C. Suppose the company wants to start making a profit after selling the same number of devices you found in part **A**. What should the new wholesale price be? Explain how you found this price.

A. $9x > 125,000 + 6.5x, x > 50,000$

B. $7.15, x > 67,568$

C. If y is the new wholesale price, the revenue from selling 50,000 devices is 50,000y. The new cost of making 50,000 devices is $125,000 + (7.15)(50,000)$, or $482,500. Solve $50,000y > \$482,500$ to get $y > 9.65$. The new wholesale price should be greater than $9.65.

★★★11. A company that sells computers and other electronic equipment wants to hire some new sales staff. The company offers salary packages that combine a base salary and commissions from sales. It is willing to pay a base salary of between $20,000 and $30,000 per year and a commission rate between 2.5% and 6.5% of total sales per year. The company has a rule that if someone makes the maximum base salary, he or she cannot earn the highest commission rate, and vice versa.

A. Javier is very confident in his ability to generate large sales. What salary package would appeal to him? Explain your reasoning, and write an algebraic expression for Javier's salary package.

B. Catherine prefers to have a more stable income that is less affected by sales. What salary package would appeal to her? Explain your reasoning, and write an algebraic expression for her salary package.

C. For what amounts of sales will Catherine make more than Javier? Use your expressions from parts **A** and **B** to write and solve an inequality to find the answer.

A. Javier would like to have the maximum commission rate. His salary would be $29,999 + 1.065s$, where s is the amount of sales he had that year.

B. Catherine would prefer to have a maximum base salary: $30,000 + 1.064s$, where s is the amount of sales she had that year.

C. $30,000 + 1.064s > 29,999 + 1.065s, s < 1000$; Catherine will make more than Javier when each one makes less than $2000 in sales.

Personal Trainer Kayla is a personal trainer and is working with Jed to devise a plan to help him lose weight. Kayla explained to Jed that each pound of body fat is equal to 3500 Calories. So, if Jed eliminates 500 Calories per day through diet and exercise, he will lose one pound per week. The table shows how many Calories are burned per hour of exercise for people of different weights who are walking or running at various speeds.

Calories Burned per Hour of Exercise by Body Weight				
	Body Weight			
Exercise (1 Hour)	**130 lb**	**155 lb**	**180 lb**	**205 lb**
Walking 2.0 mph	148	176	204	233
Walking 3.0 mph	195	232	270	307
Walking 4.0 mph	295	352	409	465
Running 5.0 mph	472	563	654	745
Running 6.0 mph	590	704	817	931
Running 7.0 mph	649	774	899	1024

Jed currently weighs 205 pounds. He walks on a treadmill at a speed of 3 miles per hour and runs at a speed of 5 miles per hour, and he exercises for 30 minutes each day.

a. Use the information in the table to find an expression for the number of Calories Jed burns while walking for t minutes.

b. If Jed exercises for 30 minutes, then $30 - t$ is the number of minutes Jed runs at 5.0 miles per hour. Write an expression for the number of Calories Jed burns while running for t minutes.

c. Write an equation relating the total number of Calories Jed burns to the number of minutes he walks each day.

d. What is the domain of the equation you found in part c?

e. Is it possible for Jed to burn 500 Calories per day from exercising for 30 minutes? Explain how you determined your answer.

---

a. $5.12t$

b. $12.42(30 - t)$

c. $C = 5.12t + 12.42(30 - t)$ or $C = -7.3t + 372.6$

d. $\{t \mid 0 \leq t \leq 30\}$

e. Set $C = 500$, and solve for t.

$-7.3t + 372.6 = 500$

$-7.3t + 127.4$

$t = -17.5$

Since t represents time spent walking, t must be nonnegative; the value of t is negative, so it is not possible for Jed to burn 500 Calories in 30 minutes.

MATH IN CAREERS

Personal Trainer In this Unit Performance Task, students can see how a personal trainer uses mathematics on the job.

For more information about careers in mathematics as well as various mathematics appreciation topics, visit the American Mathematical Society http://www.ams.org

SCORING GUIDES

Task (6 points)

a. 1 point for correct expression

b. 1 point for correct expression

c. 1 point for correct equation

d. 1 point for correct domain

e. 1 point for correct answer
   1 point for correct explanation

Understanding Functions

CONTENTS

Unit Pacing Guide

45-Minute Classes

Module 3

DAY 1	DAY 2	DAY 3	DAY 4	DAY 5
Lesson 3.1	**Lesson 3.1**	**Lesson 3.2**	**Lesson 3.3**	**Lesson 3.3**

DAY 6	DAY 7	DAY 8		
Lesson 3.4	**Lesson 3.4**	**Module Review and Assessment Readiness**		

Module 4

DAY 1	DAY 2	DAY 3	DAY 4	DAY 5
Lesson 4.1	**Lesson 4.1**	**Lesson 4.2**	**Lesson 4.2**	**Lesson 4.3**

DAY 6	DAY 7	DAY 8		
Lesson 4.3	**Module Review and Assessment Readiness**	**Unit Review and Assessment Readiness**		

90-Minute Classes

Module 3

DAY 1	DAY 2	DAY 3	DAY 4
Lesson 3.1	**Lesson 3.2** **Lesson 3.3**	**Lesson 3.3** **Lesson 3.4**	**Lesson 3.4** **Module Review and Assessment Readiness**

Module 4

DAY 1	DAY 2	DAY 3	DAY 4
Lesson 4.1	**Lesson 4.2**	**Lesson 4.3**	**Module Review and Assessment Readiness** **Unit Review and Assessment Readiness**

Program Resources

PLAN

HMH Teacher App

Access a full suite of teacher resources online and offline on a variety of devices. Plan present, and manage classes, assignments, and activities.

ePlanner Easily plan your classes, create and view assignments, and access all program resources with your online, customizable planning tool.

Professional Development Videos

Authors Juli Dixon and Matt Larson model successful teaching practices and strategies in actual classroom settings.

QR Codes Scan with your smart phone to jump directly from your print book to online videos and other resources.

Teacher's Edition

Support students with point-of-use Questioning Strategies, teaching tips, resources for differentiated instruction, additional activities, and more.

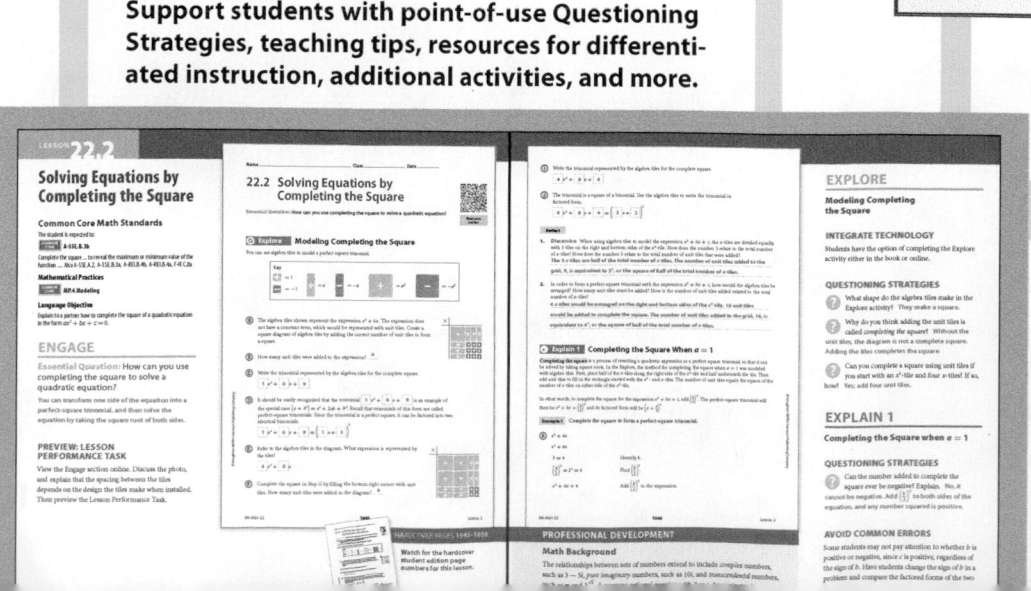

ENGAGE AND EXPLORE

Real-World Videos Engage students with interesting and relevant applications of the mathematical content of each module.

Explore Activities

Students interactively explore new concepts using a variety of tools and approaches.

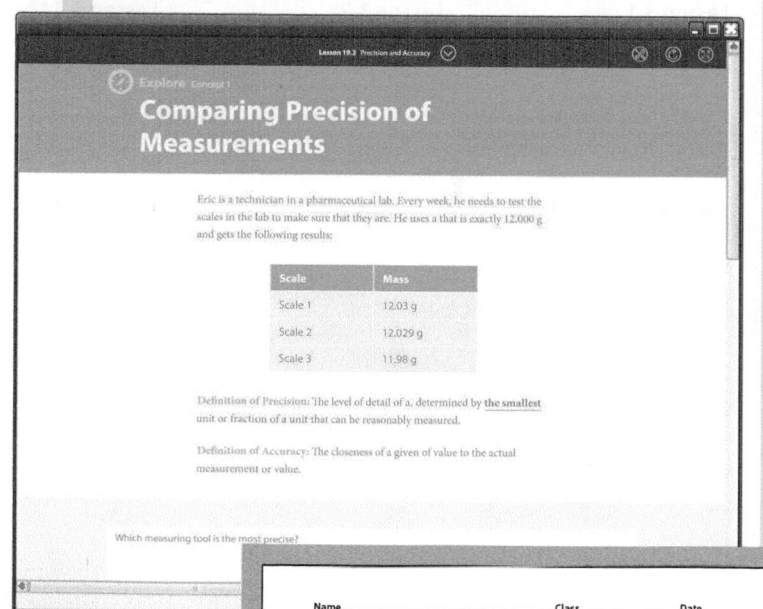

Comparing Precision of Measurements

Eric is a technician in a pharmaceutical lab. Every week, he needs to test the scales in the lab to make sure that they are. He uses a that is exactly 12.000 g and gets the following results:

Scale	Mass
Scale 1	12.03 g
Scale 2	12.029 g
Scale 3	11.98 g

Definition of Precision: The level of detail of a, determined by the smallest unit or fraction of a unit that can be reasonably measured.

Definition of Accuracy: The closeness of a given of value to the actual measurement or value.

Which measuring tool is the most precise?

Name_____ Class_____ Date_____

22.2 Solving Equations by Completing the Square

Essential Question: How can you use completing the square to solve a quadratic equation?

A-SSE.B.3b Complete the square ... to reveal the maximum or minimum value of the function ... Also A-SSE.A.2, A-SSE.B.3a, A-REI.B.4b, A-REI.B.4a, F-IF.C.8a

Explore Modeling Completing the Square

You can use algebra tiles to model a perfect square trinomial.

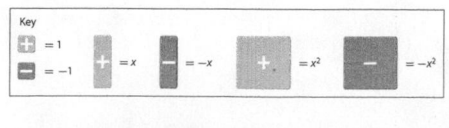

(A) The algebra tiles shown represent the expression $x^2 + 6x$. The expression does not have a constant term, which would be represented with unit tiles. Create a square diagram of algebra tiles by adding the correct number of unit tiles to form a square.

(B) How many unit tiles were added to the expression? _____

(C) Write the trinomial represented by the algebra tiles for the complete square.

$\boxed{} x^2 + \boxed{} x + \boxed{}$

(D) It should be easily recognized that the trinomial $\boxed{} x^2 + \boxed{} x + \boxed{}$ is an example of the special case $(a + b)^2 = a^2 + 2ab + b^2$. Recall that trinomials of this form are called

TEACH

Math On the Spot video tutorials, featuring program author Dr. Edward Burger, accompany every example in the textbook and give students step-by-step instructions and explanations of key math concepts.

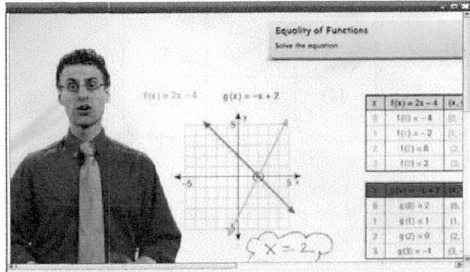

Interactive Teacher Edition

Customize and present course materials with collaborative activities and integrated formative assessment.

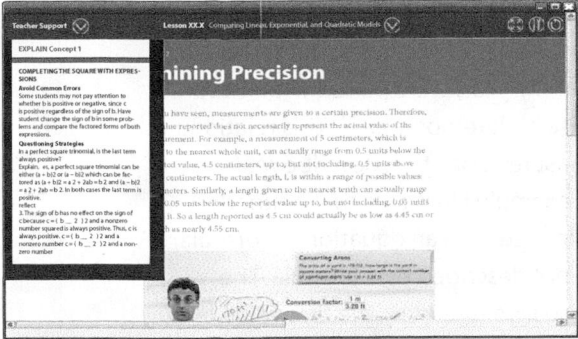

Differentiated Instruction Resources

Support all learners with Differentiated Instruction Resources, including

- **Leveled Practice and Problem Solving**
- **Reading Strategies**
- **Success for English Learners**
- **Challenge**

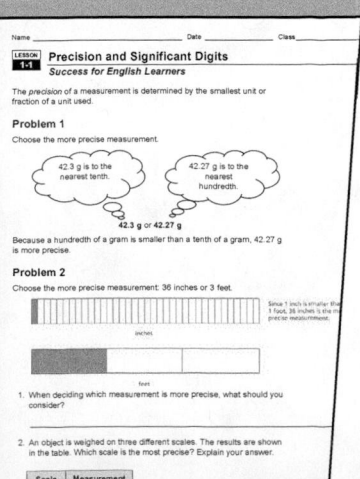

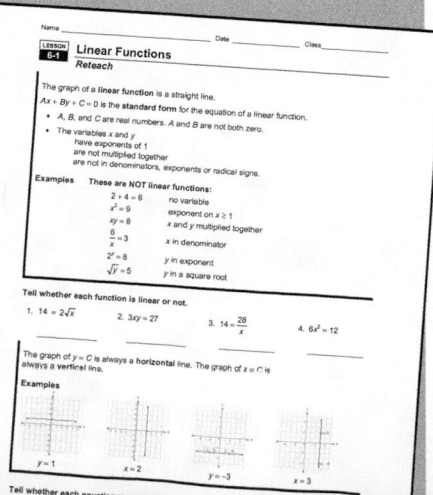

ASSESSMENT AND INTERVENTION

 The **Personal Math Trainer** provides online practice, homework, assessments, and intervention. Monitor student progress through reports and alerts. Create and customize assignments aligned to specific lessons or Common Core standards.

- **Practice** – With dynamic items and assignments, students get unlimited practice on key concepts supported by guided examples, step-by-step solutions, and video tutorials.

- **Assessments** – Choose from course assignments or customize your own based on course content, Common Core standards, difficulty levels, and more.

- **Homework** – Students can complete online homework with a wide variety of problem types, including the ability to enter expressions, equations, and graphs. Let the system automatically grade homework, so you can focus where your students need help the most!

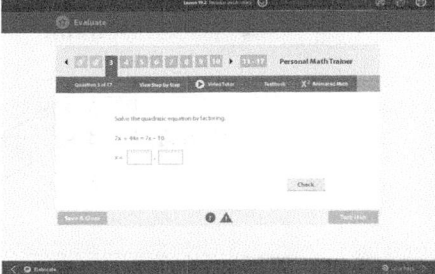

- **Intervention** – Let the Personal Math Trainer automatically prescribe a targeted, personalized intervention path for your students.

Focus on Higher Order Thinking

Raise the bar with homework and practice that incorporates higher-order thinking and mathematical practices in every lesson.

Assessment Readiness

Prepare students for success on high stakes tests for Algebra 1 with practice at every module and unit

Assessment Resources

Tailor assessments and response to intervention to meet the needs of all your classes and students, including

- Leveled Module Quizzes
- Leveled Unit Tests
- Unit Performance Tasks
- Placement, Diagnostic, and Quarterly Benchmark Tests
- Tier 1, Tier 2, and Tier 3 Resources

Math Background

Understanding Relations  F-IF.A.1

LESSON 3.2

Many students have the mistaken belief that relations and functions must be described by equations. Presenting relations and functions as sets of ordered pairs right from the start helps avoid this misconception.

A *relation* is any set of ordered pairs. The *domain* of a relation is the set of all first coordinates or (*x*-values) of the ordered pairs. The *range* of a relation is the set of all second coordinates (or *y*-values) of the ordered pairs.

There are several ways to represent a relation. The relation represented by the set $\{(-1, 2), (4, 0), (4, 3), (7, -5)\}$ can also be represented by a table, a graph, and a mapping diagram. The mapping diagram below represents a relation.

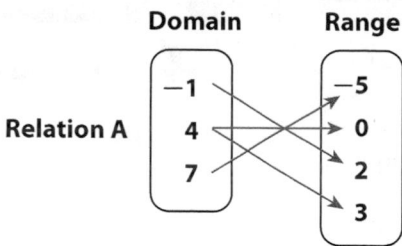

A relation can be described by the way it matches domain and range values. Relation A is *one-to-many*. This means there is at least one domain value (in this case, 4) that is paired with more than one range value (0 and 3).

A relation is *many-to-one* if more than one domain value is paired with a single range value. Relation B, shown below, is many-to-one because the domain values 0 and 9 are both paired with the range value 8.

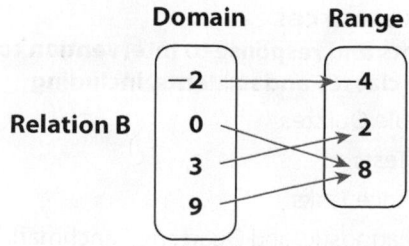

A relation is *one-to-one* if each domain value is paired with a unique range value and each range value is paired with a unique domain value. Relation C is one-to-one.

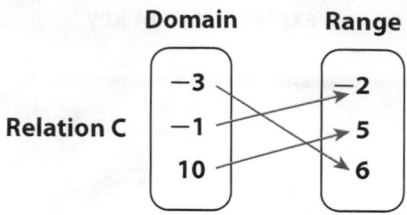

Functions  F-IF.B.5

LESSON 3.3

The definition of *function* may seem somewhat arbitrary to students. It is helpful to explicitly point out the important role that functions play in real-world situations. For example, a meteorologist might study the relation in which each day of the year is paired with the daily high temperature in Los Angeles. It would not make sense if one domain value (a day of the year) were paired with more than one range value (a high temperature). This relation is a function, as are most relations that describe real-world situations. This example illustrates that a function does not have to be defined with an equation or formula; the function above is not described by a formula. The real-world example also illustrates why the first value of a function is the *independent variable* and the second value is the *dependent variable*. The second value (for example, temperature) depends on the first value (for example, day of the year). Functions may be one-to-one or many-to-one. The function that gives the daily high temperature in Los Angeles is likely to be many-to-one, as there may be several days that are paired with the same temperature. However, by definition, a function cannot be one-to-many.

Recursive and Explicit Rules  F-IF.A.3

LESSON 4.1

A *sequence* is a list of numbers in a specific order. A sequence can be represented by a function whose domain is a set of consecutive whole numbers greater than 0. For example, the domain might be $\{1, 2, 3, 4, 5\}$ or $\{1, 2, 3, ...\}$. Each whole number is paired with a term of the sequence; hence the range is the terms of the sequence. The figure shows how the natural numbers are paired with the terms of the sequence formed by adding 1 to the positive multiples of 3.

1	2	3	4...
4	7	10	13...
$f(1)$	$f(2)$	$f(3)$	$f(4)$...

A recursive rule for a sequence is a rule that specifies the first term of the sequence and specifies what the nth term is using one or more terms that precede it. For example, the following is a recursive rule for the sequence above: $f(1) = 4$ and for each whole number $n \geq 2$, $f(n) = f(n - 1) + 3$.

An explicit rule for a sequence is the rule that defines how each term is derived from its position number in the sequence. An explicit rule for the sequence above is $f(n) = 4 + 3(n - 1)$.

Arithmetic Sequences  F-LE.A.2

LESSON 4.2

In an *arithmetic sequence*, all pairs of successive terms differ by the same nonzero constant, called the *common difference*. Equivalently, each term after the first term is equal to the previous term plus the common difference. For example, in the sequence 2, 6, 10, 14…, the common difference is 2.

The general form of an explicit rule for an arithmetic sequence is $f(n) = f(1) + d(n - 1)$. Students are sometimes puzzled by the use of $n - 1$. Exploring simple cases can help students see why $n - 1$ makes sense. For example, to find the 2nd term of the sequence, start with the first term and add the common difference once. To find the 3rd term, start with the first term and add the common difference twice. Generally, to find the nth term, start with the first term and add the common difference $n - 1$ times, as stated in the formula.

Understanding Functions

MATH IN CAREERS
Unit Activity Preview

After completing this unit, students will complete a Math in Careers task by writing and interpreting a function based on floor area. Critical skills include understanding domain and interpreting function values.

For more information about careers in mathematics as well as various mathematics appreciation topics, visit The American Mathematical Society at http://www.ams.org.

UNIT 2

Understanding Functions

MODULE 3
Functions and Models

MODULE 4
Patterns and Sequences

© Houghton Mifflin Harcourt Publishing Company • Image Credits: ©Design Pics Inc./Alamy

MATH IN CAREERS

Interior Designer Interior designers create and improve interior spaces in homes and buildings, making them safe, functional, and visually pleasing. Interior designers must understand the geometry of spaces and how to interpret measurements on blueprints. They also need to be able to calculate the amount and cost of materials needed for a project.

If you are interested in a career as an interior designer, you should study these mathematical subjects:
- Algebra
- Geometry
- Trigonometry
- Business Math

Research other careers that require determining costs and amounts of materials for a project. Check out the career activity at the end of the unit to find out how **interior designers** use math.

Unit 2   101

TRACKING YOUR LEARNING PROGRESSION

Before	In this Unit	After
Students understand: • solving an equation for a variable • patterns and sequences • graphing ordered pairs	Students will learn about: • graphing relationships • understanding relations and functions • modeling functions • graphing functions • identifying and graphing sequences • constructing and modeling arithmetic sequences	Students will study: • parallel lines and perpendicular lines • equations of a line • geometric sequences

Reading Start-Up

Visualize Vocabulary

Use the ✔ words to identify a–e in the graphic. Put one term on each line and one term in the circle.

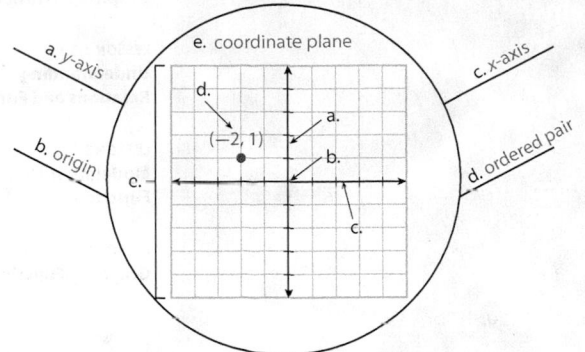

a. y-axis
b. origin
c. x-axis
d. ordered pair
e. coordinate plane

d. (−2, 1)

Vocabulary

Review Words
✔ coordinate plane (plano cartesiano)
✔ input (entrada)
✔ ordered pair (par ordenado)
✔ origin (origen)
✔ output (salida)
✔ x-axis (eje x)
✔ y-axis (eje y)

Preview Words
continuous graph (gráfica continua)
discrete graph (gráfica discreta)
domain (dominio)
function (función)
function rule (regla de función)
range (rango)
relation (relación)
sequence (sucesión)

Understand Vocabulary

Match the term on the left to the correct expression on the right.

1. __B__ discrete graph   A. a graph made up of connected lines or curves
2. __D__ function rule   B. a graph made up of unconnected points
3. __A__ continuous graph   C. a set of ordered pairs
4. __C__ relation   D. an algebraic expression that describes how the output comes from the input

Active Reading

Booklet Before beginning the unit, create a booklet for taking notes as you learn the concepts in this unit. Write the main idea of each module on the appropriate pages to create an outline of the unit. As you study each lesson, write the important details that support the main idea, such as vocabulary and formulas. Refer to your finished booklet as you work on assignments and study for tests.

Reading Start Up

Have students complete the activities on this page by working alone or with others.

VISUALIZE VOCABULARY

The information wheel graphic helps students review vocabulary associated with the coordinate plane. If time allows, discuss how input and output might correspond to the coordinates in an ordered pair.

UNDERSTAND VOCABULARY

Use the following explanations to help students learn the preview words.

A **relation** is a set of ordered pairs. The set of all first coordinates of a relation or function is its **domain**. The set of all second coordinates of a relation or function is its **range**. A **function rule** is an algebraic expression that defines a function. A **function** is a relation in which every domain value is paired with exactly one range value. A relation or a function can be graphed in the coordinate plane. A **discrete graph** is made up of unconnected points. A **continuous graph** is made up of connected lines or curves.

ACTIVE READING

Students can use these reading and note-taking strategies to help them organize and understand the new concepts and vocabulary. Encourage them to ask for additional explanation as needed when new academic vocabulary is introduced. Suggest they include as much detail in their booklets as they need to clarify vocabulary, because they will use these words throughout the year.

ADDITIONAL RESOURCES

Differentiated Instruction

- Reading Strategies

MODULE 3

Functions and Models

ESSENTIAL QUESTION:

Answer: A real-world functional relationship can be modeled using a two-variable equation or rule, a graph, a table, or a word description.

PROFESSIONAL DEVELOPMENT VIDEO

Professional Development Video

Author Juli Dixon models successful teaching practices in an actual high-school classroom.

Professional Development
my.hrw.com

Functions and Models

Essential Question: How can you use functions to solve real-world problems?

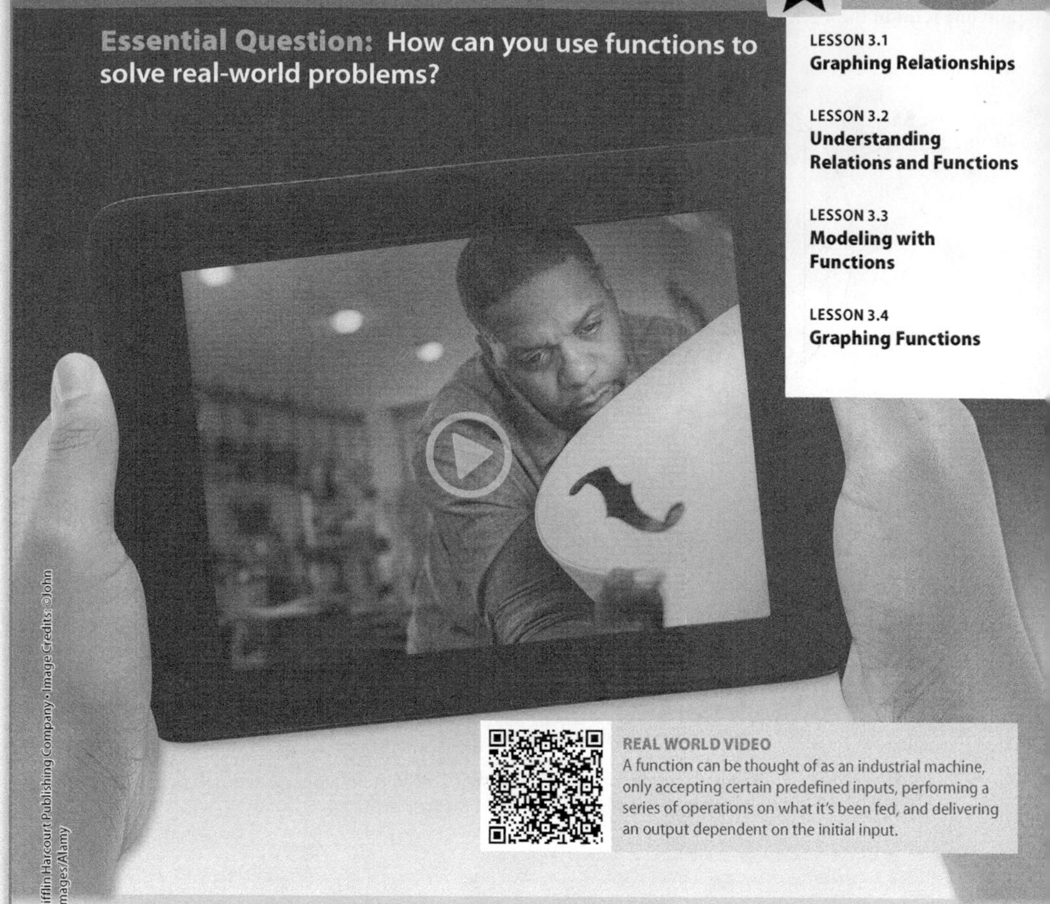

© Houghton Mifflin Harcourt Publishing Company • Image Credits: ©John Fedele/Blend Images/Alamy

REAL WORLD VIDEO
A function can be thought of as an industrial machine, only accepting certain predefined inputs, performing a series of operations on what it's been fed, and delivering an output dependent on the initial input.

MODULE PERFORMANCE TASK PREVIEW
Season Passes

Decisions, decisions! Wild Planet Theme Park has just opened, and you've decided to buy a season pass but aren't sure which payment option is the least expensive. How can you decide? Looks like the theme of this theme park is mathematics!

DIGITAL TEACHER EDITION

Access a full suite of teaching resources when and where you need them:

- Access content online or offline
- Customize lessons to share with your class
- Communicate with your students in real-time
- View student grades and data instantly to target your instruction where it is needed most

PERSONAL MATH TRAINER
Assessment and Intervention

Assign automatically graded homework, quizzes, tests, and intervention activities. Prepare your students with updated, Common Core-aligned practice tests.

Are YOU Ready?

Complete these exercises to review skills you will need for this module.

Graphing Linear Relationships

Example 1

Tell whether the graph represents a linear nonproportional or proportional relationship.

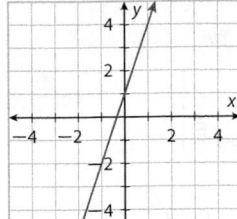

The graph of a linear nonproportional relationship is a straight line that does not pass through the origin.

The graph of a linear proportional relationship is a straight line that passes through the origin.

The graph represents a linear nonproportional relationship because it is a straight line that does not pass through the origin.

Tell whether the graph represents a linear nonproportional or proportional relationship.

1.

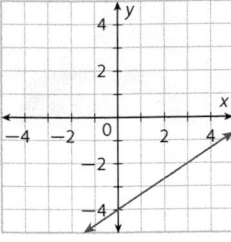

nonproportional

2.

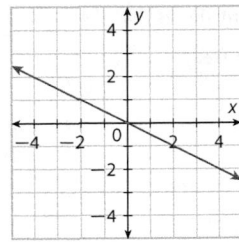

proportional

Linear Functions

Example 2

Tell whether $y = x^2 + 5$ represents a linear function.

$y = x^2 + 5$ does not represent a linear function because x has an exponent of 2.

When a linear equation is written in standard form, the following are true.

- x and y both have exponents of 1.
- x and y are not multiplied together.
- x and y do not appear in denominators, exponents, or radicands.

Tell whether the equation represents a linear function.

3. $0.3x + y = 7$

yes

4. $xy - 2 = 9$

no

5. $y = 2^x + 5$

no

Are You Ready?

ASSESS READINESS

Use the assessment on this page to determine if students need strategic or intensive intervention for the module's prerequisite skills.

ASSESSMENT AND INTERVENTION

RtI Response to Intervention **TIER 1, TIER 2, TIER 3 SKILLS**

Personal Math Trainer will automatically create a standards-based, personalized intervention assignment for your students, targeting each student's individual needs!

ADDITIONAL RESOURCES

See the table below for a full list of intervention resources available for this module.

Response to Intervention Resources also includes:

- Tier 2 Skill Pre-Tests for each Module
- Tier 2 Skill Post-Tests for each skill

Response to Intervention			*Differentiated Instruction*
Tier 1	**Tier 2**	**Tier 3**	
Lesson Intervention Worksheets	Strategic Intervention Skills Intervention Worksheets	Intensive Intervention Worksheets available online	
Reteach 3.1 Reteach 3.2 Reteach 3.3 Reteach 3.4	6 Graphing Linear Nonproportional Relationships 7 Graphing Linear Proportional Relationships 10 Linear Functions	Building Block Skills 22, 23, 27, 40, 46, 70	Challenge worksheets Extend the Math Lesson Activities in TE

Graphing Relationships

Common Core Math Standards

The student is expected to:

 F-IF.B.4

For a function that models a relationship between two quantities, interpret key features of graphs...

Mathematical Practices

COMMON CORE **MP.4 Modeling**

Language Objective

Explain to a partner the difference between discrete and continuous graphs and the difference between domain and range.

ENGAGE

Essential Question: How can you describe a relationship given a graph and sketch a graph given a description?

You can describe a situation represented by a graph by using key words to denote where the graph increases, decreases, or stays the same, and you can use key words in a description to sketch a graph.

PREVIEW: LESSON PERFORMANCE TASK

View the Engage section online. Discuss how a rain gauge works and how the amount of rain in the gauge can be represented with a graph. Then preview the Lesson Performance Task.

Name_____ Class_____ Date_____

3.1   Graphing Relationships

Essential Question: How can you describe a relationship given a graph and sketch a graph given a description?

Resource Locker

⊘ Explore   Interpreting Graphs

The distance a delivery van is from the warehouse varies throughout the day. The graph shows the distance from the warehouse for a day from 8:00 am to 5:00 pm.

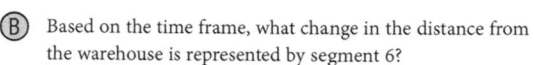

Time (hours)

(A) Segment 1 shows that the delivery van moved away from the warehouse. What does segment 2 show?

 Segment 2 shows that the truck moved away from the warehouse at a slower speed than segment 1.

(B) Based on the time frame, what change in the distance from the warehouse is represented by segment 6?

 The segment shows that the truck begins to return to the warehouse.

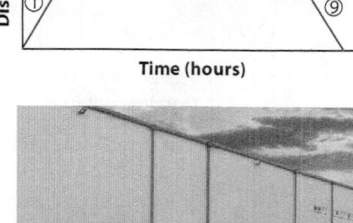

(C) Which line segments show intervals where the distance did not change?

 Segments 3, 5, and 7.

(D) What is a possible explanation for these segments?

 The truck was not moving, so it could have been delivering packages.

Reflect

1. **Discussion** Explain how the slope of each segment of the graph is related to whether the delivery truck is not moving, is moving away from, or is moving toward the warehouse.
 When the slope is positive (segment rises from left to right), the truck is moving away from the warehouse. When the slope is negative (segment falls from left to right), the truck is moving toward the warehouse. And when the slope is 0 (segment is horizontal), the truck is not moving.

Module 3   **105**   Lesson 1

HARDCOVER PAGES 87–96

Turn to these pages to find this lesson in the hardcover student edition.

⊘ Explain 1 Relating Graphs to Situations

Graphs can often be drawn to represent real life situations. These graphs are not always easily derived from equations, but rather represent certain situations. For example, these graphs may include the amount of rain over a certain period of time, or the height of a bouncing ball over a certain period of time.

Example 1   Three hoses fill three different water barrels. A green hose fills a water barrel at a constant rate. A black hose is slowly opened when filling the barrel. A blue hose is completely open at the beginning and then slowly closed. The three graphs of the situations are shown.

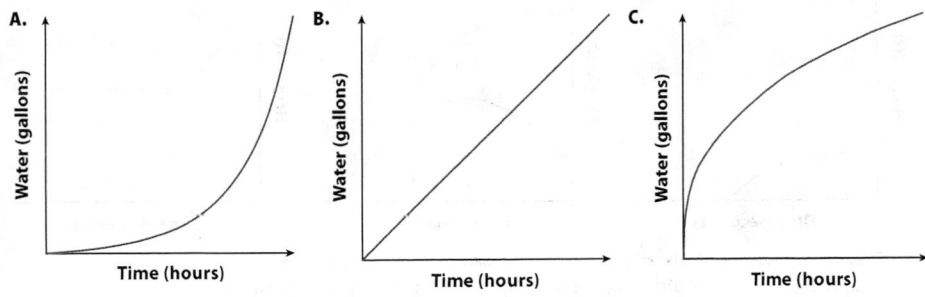

(A) Which graph best represents the amount of water in the barrel filled by the green hose?

Since the flow of the water is constant, the amount of water in the barrel should be a steady increase. Thus, graph B best represents the situation.

(B) Describe the water level represented by each graph. Then determine which graph represents each situation.

Describe the water level for graph A.

The water level for graph A begins slowly and then increases rapidly over time.

Describe the water level for graph C.

The water level for graph C increases rapidly and then slows down over time.

Graph A represents the _____black_____ hose and graph C represents the _____blue_____ hose.

Reflect

2. Could a graph of the amount of water in a water barrel slant downward from left to right? Explain.
Yes, if the barrel had water in it to begin with and was being drained at a constant rate.

PROFESSIONAL DEVELOPMENT

Integrate Mathematical Practices

This lesson provides an opportunity to address Mathematical Practice **MP.4**, which calls for students to use "modeling." Students learn to interpret graphs, relate graphs to real-world situations, and sketch graphs to represent real-world situations. Students learn when to use a discrete graph or a continuous graph to represent a real-world situation.

EXPLORE

Interpreting Graphs

INTEGRATE TECHNOLOGY

Students have the option of completing the graph interpretation activity either in the book or online.

QUESTIONING STRATEGIES

? How can you tell whether a graph segment represents an increase or a decrease in the dependent variable as the independent variable increases? **If the graph slopes upward from left to right, it represents an increase; if it slopes downward, it represents a decrease.**

? What does a horizontal section on a graph represent? **A horizontal section represents a situation in which the dependent variable remains constant as the independent variable changes.**

EXPLAIN 1

Relating Graphs to Situations

QUESTIONING STRATEGIES

? What does the steepness of a graph segment tell you about the situation it models? **It indicates how quickly a quantity is increasing or decreasing. A steeper slope indicates a faster increase or decrease.**

AVOID COMMON ERRORS

Some students may interpret a horizontal line to mean that the *x*-value is constant. Label some points on the line to show that it is the *y*-value that is constant.

EXPLAIN 2

Sketching Graphs for Situations

AVOID COMMON ERRORS

Some students may have trouble identifying the domain and range in this situation. Remind them that the domain consists of the possible values of the independent variable, which is shown on the *x*-axis, and the range consists of the possible values of the dependent variable, which is shown on the *y*-axis.

CONNECT VOCABULARY EL

Distinguish the term *discrete* from the similar word *discreet*. *Discrete* means *consisting of separate and distinct parts,* while *discreet* means *cautious or unlikely to be noticed.* A *discrete graph* is made up of distinct, unconnected points.

QUESTIONING STRATEGIES

? How do you know when to use discrete points instead of connected segments or curves? Use discrete points when the values between certain numbers are unknown or have no meaning within the situation.

Your Turn

You and a friend are playing catch. You throw three different balls to your friend. You throw the first ball in an arc and your friend catches it. You throw the second ball in an arc, but this time the ball gets stuck in a tree. You throw the third ball directly at your friend, but it lands in front of your friend, and rolls the rest of the way on the ground. The three graphs of these situations are shown.

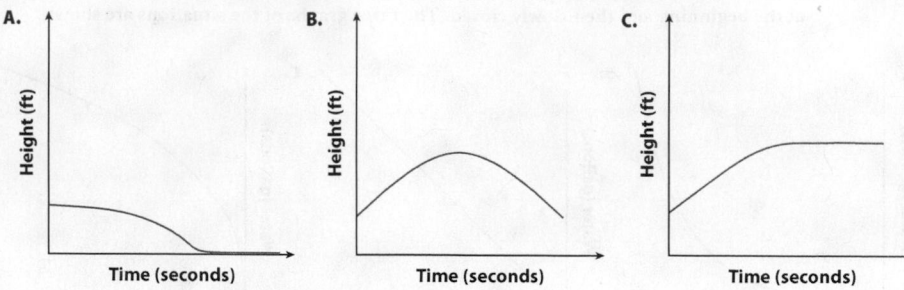

3. Which graph represents the situation where the ball gets stuck in the tree?
Graph C. The ball should increase in height and then stay at a certain height.

4. Describe the height of the ball represented by the other two graphs.
Graph A shows the ball thrown from a certain height with the height decreasing until the

ball hits the ground and then rolls. Graph B shows the ball thrown from a certain height with

the height increasing then decreasing in an arc until the ball is caught at a certain height.

✐ Explain 2 Sketching Graphs for Situations

Some graphs that represent real-world situations are drawn without any interruptions. In other words, they are *continuous graphs*. A **continuous graph** is a graph that is made up of connected lines or curves. Other types of graphs are not continuous. They are made up of distinct, unconnected points. These graphs are called **discrete graphs**.

Example 2 Sketch a graph of the situation, tell whether the graph is continuous or discrete, and determine the domain and range.

 A A student is taking a test. There are 10 problems on the test. For each problem the student answers correctly, the student received 10 points.

The graph is made up of multiple unconnected points, so the graph is discrete.

The student can get anywhere from 0 to 10 questions right, so the domain is the whole numbers from 0 to 10.

If the student gets 0 problems correct, the student gets 0 points. If the student gets 10 problems correct, the student gets 100 points. So the range is whole number multiples of 10 from 0 to 100.

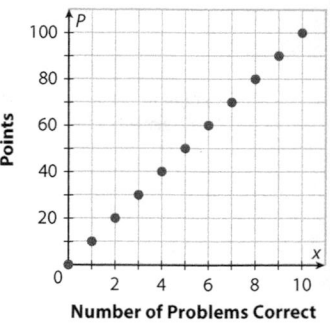

COLLABORATIVE LEARNING

Small Group Activity

Group students in threes or fours. Instruct each group to write a situation on one piece of paper and draw a corresponding graph on a separate piece. Collect and shuffle all graphs, then all situation papers. Randomly label graphs *A, B, C, . . . ,* and situations *1, 2, 3, ...* Display graphs and situations on the wall. Have groups match each graph with the correct description.

Ⓑ A bathtub is being filled with water. After 10 minutes, there are 75 quarts of water in the tub. Then someone accidentally pulls the drain plug while the water is still running, and the tub begins to empty. The tub loses 15 quarts in 5 minutes, and then someone plugs the drain and the tub fills for 6 more minutes, gaining another 45 quarts of water. After a 15-minute bath, the person gets out and pulls the drain plug. It takes 11 minutes for the tub to drain.

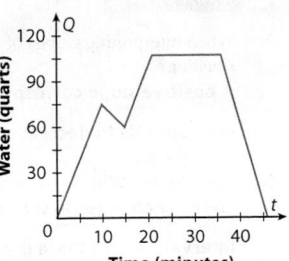

The graph is a ___continuous___ graph.

The domain is ___$0 \leq t \leq 47$___ .

The range is ___$0 \leq Q \leq 105$___ .

Your Turn

Sketch a graph of the situation, tell whether the graph is continuous or discrete, and determine the domain and range.

5. At the start of a snowstorm, it snowed two inches an hour for two hours, then slowed to one inch an hour for an additional hour before stopping. Three hours after the snow stopped, it began to melt at one-half an inch an hour for two hours.

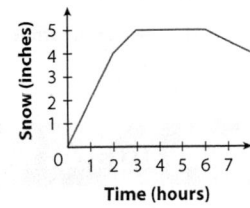

The graph is a continuous graph.

The domain is $0 \leq t \leq 8$.

The range is $0 \leq S \leq 5$.

6. A local salesman is going door to door trying to sell vacuums. For every vacuum he sells, he makes $20. He can sell a maximum of 10 vacuums a day.

The graph is a discrete graph.

The domain is whole numbers from 0 to 10.

The range is whole number multiples of 20 from 0 to 200.

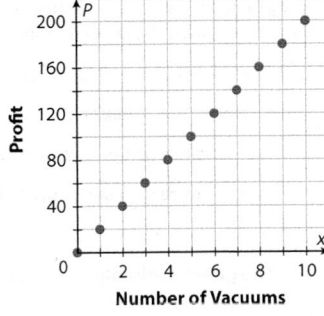

DIFFERENTIATE INSTRUCTION

Curriculum Integration

Have students write a real-world situation with an independent and dependent variable from another discipline, such as physics or biology, and sketch a graph to represent the situation.

ELABORATE

INTEGRATE MATHEMATICAL PRACTICES
Focus on Reasoning

MP.2 Help students identify which label to put on which axis by suggesting they ask themselves which variable depends on the other variable. For instance, "Does time depend on distance, or does distance depend on time?" The dependent variable (distance) goes on the y-axis. Note that the independent variable in one situation may be the dependent variable in another one, so it is important to think through each situation separately.

SUMMARIZE THE LESSON

? What can a graph tell you about the independent variable in a real-world situation? whether it is increasing, decreasing, or staying the same as the dependent variable increases; whether it is changing quickly or slowly; what its range is; and whether it is discrete or continuous

---

💬 Elaborate

7. When interpreting graphs of real world situations, what can the slope of each part tell you about the situation?

A positive slope corresponds to increases in amounts, whereas a negative slope corresponds to decreases in amounts.

8. **Discussion** What is the best way to sketch the graph of a situation?

Look for changes in the situation, like increases or decreases in a value, or certain intervals where there is no change in the value.

9. **Essential Question Check-In** How can you tell when to use a discrete graph as opposed to using a continuous graph? Give an example of each.

When the data describes discrete values that correspond to other discrete values, the graph should be a discrete graph. An example is the total cost of buying x items at a specific price per item. When a problem involves data that change continually through all values over an interval, the graph should be a continuous graph. An example is the change in the temperature in an oven for a given time.

⭐ Evaluate: Homework and Practice

- Online Homework
- Hints and Help
- Extra Practice

The graph shows the attendance at a hockey game, and the rate at which the fans enter and exit the arena.

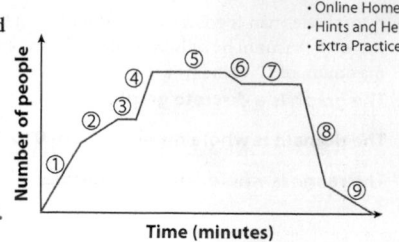

1. Compare segments 1 and 2. What do they represent?

Segment 1 is steeper than segment 2. This means more people were entering the arena at a faster rate in segment 1 than in segment 2.

2. What does segment 8 represent in terms of the game?

The game probably just ended, since many fans are leaving in a short amount of time.

3. What is the significance of segments 5 and 7?

Segments 5 and 7 are horizontal, which means no fans are entering or leaving the game.

4. What does segment 6 mean?

Some fans started to leave before the end of the game.

LANGUAGE SUPPORT **EL**

Graphic Organizers

English learners may have trouble keeping track of the many different ways of expressing a similar change. Encourage them to make a chart listing key words and phrases for each type of graph segment.

Horizontal	Slanting upward	Slanting downward
stays the same	increases	decreases
does not change	goes up	goes down
remains constant	climbs	descends
does not move		

Use Graphs A–D for Exercises 5–8. Janelle alternates between running and walking. She begins by walking for a short period, and then runs for the same amount of time. She takes a break before beginning to walk again. Consider the graphs shown.

A.

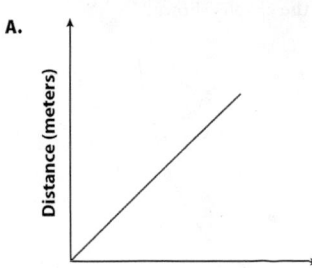

B.

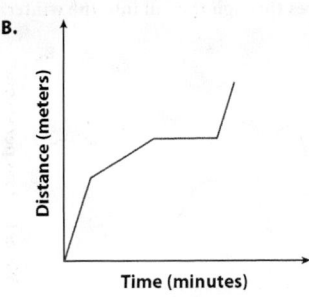

C.

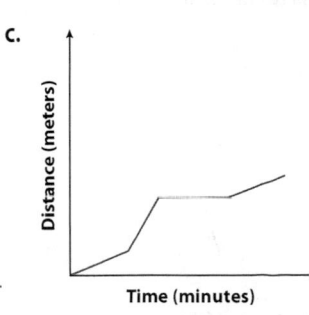

D.

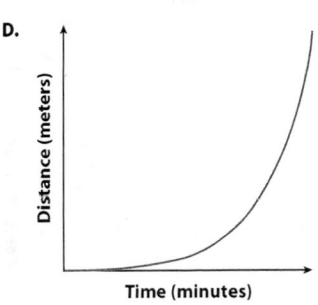

5. Which graph best represents the given situation?

    Graph C

6. Describe the other three graphs.

    In graph A, Janelle moves at a constant rate. In graph B, she begins at a high speed,

    then slows down, stops for a period, and then begins at a high speed again.

    In graph D, she starts at a slow rate, then she speeds up at a consistent rate.

7. What if Janelle began by running, then slowed to a walk, stopped, and then began running again. Which graph would represent this situation?

    Graph B

8. What are possible situations for graphs A and D?

    Graph A could represent when Janelle only walks or only runs. Graph D could

    represent when Janelle begins at a slow walk and then speeds up to a run.

Exercise	Depth of Knowledge (D.O.K.)	COMMON CORE Mathematical Practices
1–5	**1** Recall of Information	**MP.2** Reasoning
6–8	**2** Skills/Concepts	**MP.4** Modeling
9	**1** Recall of Information	**MP.4** Modeling
10–11	**2** Skills/Concepts	**MP.4** Modeling
12	**1** Recall	**MP.4** Modeling

ASSIGNMENT GUIDE

Concepts and Skills	Practice
Explore Interpreting Graphs	Exercises 1–4
Example 1 Relating Graphs to Situations	Exercises 5–14, 23
Example 2 Sketching Graphs for Situations	Exercises 15–22, 24–25

INTEGRATE MATHEMATICAL PRACTICES
Focus on Reasoning

MP.2 Explain that when the *x*-axis of a graph represents time, the graph should be read from left to right to interpret a sequence of events. Encourage students to write down key phrases from a situation in the order they appear to help match situations to graphs.

INTEGRATE MATHEMATICAL PRACTICES
Focus on Communication

MP.3 Point out to students that some graphs start at (0, 0) while others start higher on the vertical axis. Have students describe an example of each type of graph and explain what the *y*-intercept represents.

AVOID COMMON ERRORS

Some students may think that forward or upward motion is always represented by an upward-slanting graph. Remind them to pay attention to what the axes represent. For example, if a person runs uphill at a constant speed, then a distance or height vs. time graph will slant upward, but a speed vs. time graph will be horizontal.

QUESTIONING STRATEGIES

? On a graph of speed vs. time, how would you represent someone running downhill with an increasing speed? **upward slant**

? On the same graph, how would you represent someone running on a flat path at a decreasing speed? **downward slant**

Use Graphs A–D for Exercises 9–11. During the winter, the amount of water that flows down a river remains at a low constant. In the spring, when the snow melts, the flow of water increases drastically, until it decreases to a steady rate in the summer. The flow then slowly decreases through the fall into the winter. Consider the graphs shown.

A.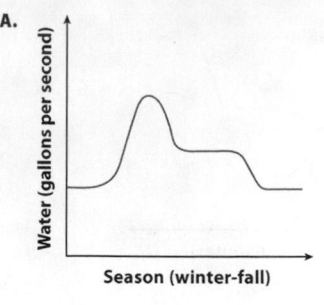

B.

C.

D.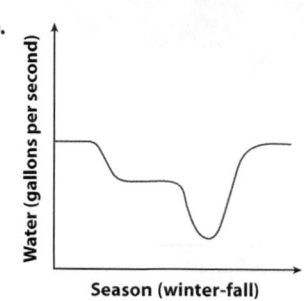

9. Which graph best represents the given situation?

Graph A

10. Describe the other three graphs.

Graph B increases quickly throughout the seasons. Graph C increases at a constant rate. Graph D starts out with a steady rate, decreases slightly, becomes steady again, then decreases drastically before returning rapidly back to the beginning rate.

11. What are possible situations for graphs B, C, and D?

Graph B could represent a rapidly increasing release of water over a dam during a year; graph C could represent a constant release of water over a dam during a year; and graph D could represent a river in a dry climate that almost dries up in the summer and then returns to its original rate due to heavy fall rains.

© Houghton Mifflin Harcourt Publishing Company

Exercise	Depth of Knowledge (D.O.K.)	COMMON CORE Mathematical Practices
13	**2** Skills/Concepts	**MP.4** Modeling
14–22	**1** Recall of Information	**MP.4** Modeling
23	**3** Strategic Thinking **H.O.T.**	**MP.2** Reasoning
24	**2** Skills/Concepts **H.O.T.**	**MP.4** Modeling
25	**3** Strategic Thinking **H.O.T.**	**MP.3** Logic

Two children are selling lemonade. They are charging $1 for a cup.
They only sell 10 cups. Consider the graphs shown.

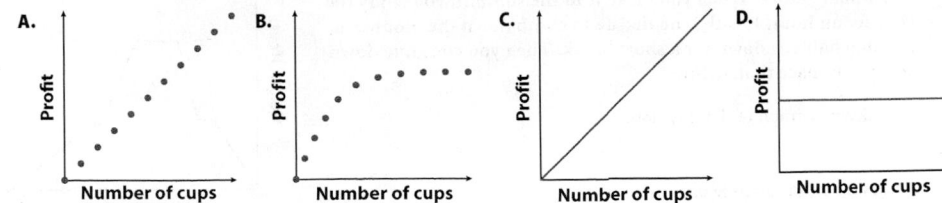

A. Profit / Number of cups
B. Profit / Number of cups
C. Profit / Number of cups
D. Profit / Number of cups

12. Which graph best represents the given situation?
Graph A

13. What situations could the other graphs represent?

Graph B represents that after a certain number of cups are sold, the profit will reach a limit. Graph C represents when partial cups are being sold, and the profit increases as long as there are cups to sell. Graph D represents that the profit will always stay constant no matter how many cups are sold.

14. Is the graph that represents the given situation discrete or continuous?
Discrete

A plane takes off and climbs steadily for 15 minutes until it reaches 30,000 feet. It travels at that altitude for 2 hours until it begins to descend to land, which it takes 15 minutes at a constant rate.

15. Sketch a graph of the situation.

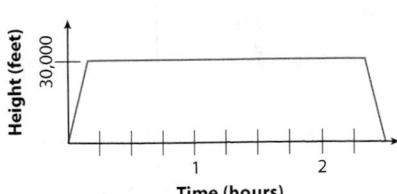

Height (feet) 30,000 / Time (hours)   1   2

16. Is the graph discrete or continuous?
Continuous

17. Determine the domain and range.
The domain is $0 \leq t \leq 2.5$ and the range is $0 \leq H \leq 30,000$.

A contestant on a game show is given $100 and is asked five questions. The contestant loses $20 for every wrong answer.

18. Sketch a graph of the situation.

19. Is the graph discrete or continuous?
Discrete

20. Determine the domain and range.
The domain is whole numbers from 0 to 5.

The range is multiples of 20 from 0 to 100.

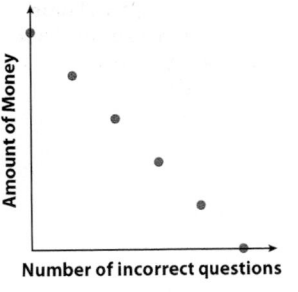

Amount of Money / Number of incorrect questions

KINESTHETIC EXPERIENCE

You may want to have students act out the events happening in the situations to more easily match the situations to the graphs.

QUESTIONING STRATEGIES

? Can a graph that represents a real-world situation include a vertical line segment? If so, what could a vertical section represent? Yes; a vertical section indicates that the dependent variable increases or decreases while the independent variable is constant. For example, a vertical line in a graph of speed vs. time could represent an object stopping suddenly.

INTEGRATE MATHEMATICAL PRACTICES
Focus on Math Connections

MP.1 To help students understand the difference between discrete and continuous graphs, ask them to think about what the variables represent. Discrete graphs usually represent situations where one or both of the variables can have only an integer value. Examples are the number of objects sold or the number of people in a class. A continuous graph represents a situation where both variables can have a continuous range of values. Continuous variables include time, distance, and speed.

Have students write a journal entry in which they briefly describe an everyday situation that involves a changing relationship. Have them sketch a graph representing the situation and write an explanation of how each part of the graph matches the situation.

You decide to hike up a mountain. You climb steadily for 2 hours, then take a 30 minute break for lunch. Then you continue to climb, faster than before. When you make it to the summit, you enjoy the view for an hour. Finally, you decide to climb down the mountain, but stop halfway down for a short break. Then you continue down at a slower pace than before.

21. Sketch a graph of the situation.

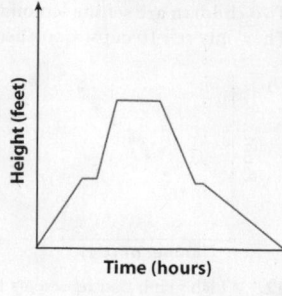

22. Is the graph discrete or continuous?

Continuous

H.O.T. **Focus on Higher Order Thinking**

23. Analyze Relationships Write a possible situation for the graph shown.

Sample answer: The graph is the distance a person driving a car is from a destination. The person is driving on a highway and then exits, where the car slows down and then stops at a red light. The car continues at a slower pace until it stops at another red light. Then the car continues to its destination.

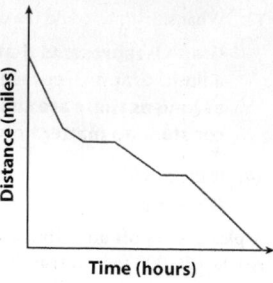

24. Represent Real-World Problems Scientists are conducting an experiment on a bacteria colony that causes its population to fluctuate. The population of a bacteria colony is shown in the graph.

a. What happened to the bacteria colony before time *t*?

The population decreased until it hit a minimum and then increased quickly.

b. Suppose at time *t*, a second colony of bacteria is added to the first. Draw a new graph to show how this action might affect the population after time *t*.

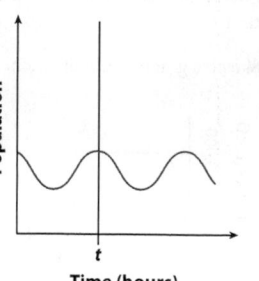

c. Suppose at some point after time *t*, scientists add a substance to the colony that destroys some of the bacteria. Describe how your graph from part b might change.

The graph will drop sharply at that time. It might have the same basic shape afterward, but the whole curve will be lower.

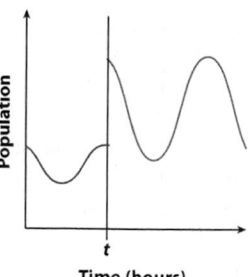

25. Explain the Error A student is told to draw a graph of the situation which represents the height of a skydiver with respect to time. He drew the following graph. Explain the student's error and draw the correct graph.

The student drew a discrete graph instead of a continuous graph. The height of the skydiver continuously changes so a discrete graph cannot be used. The correct graph is as shown.

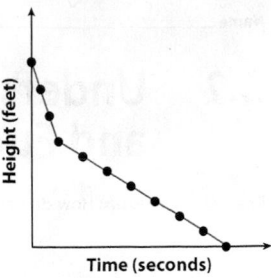

Lesson Performance Task

A digital rain gauge has an outdoor sensor that collects rainfall and transmits data to an indoor display. Assume you produced a graph of all the data collected by the rain gauge over a 24-hour period.

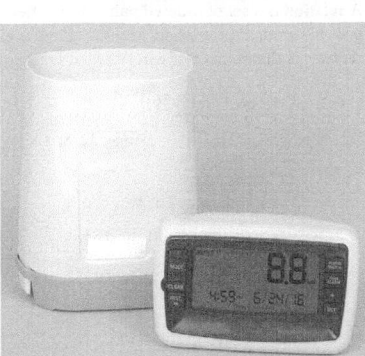

a. Would that graph be a discrete graph or a continuous graph? Explain your reasoning.

b. Describe the general shape of the graph assuming it rained at a rate of 0.1 inch per hour for the entire 24-hour period.

c. Describe the general shape of the graph assuming it rained 0.1 inch per hour for 6 hours, stopped raining for 6 hours, and then rained 0.2 inch for 12 hours.

a. continuous; the measure of rain includes rational numbers.

b. The graph would be a line slanting upward.

c. The graph would be a line segment slanting upward for the first 6 hours, a horizontal segment for the second 6 hours, and a segment slanting upward for the last 12 hours. The last segment would be twice as steep (twice the slope) as the first segment.

© Houghton Mifflin Harcourt Publishing Company

INTEGRATE MATHEMATICAL PRACTICES
Focus on Reasoning

MP.2 Discuss with students what the x- and y-axis on the graph of rainfall should represent. They should recognize that the two variables involved are time (in hours) and amount of rain (in inches). By asking themselves, "Does time depend on amount of rain, or does amount of rain depend on time?" they should conclude that amount of rain is the dependent variable and should be shown on the y-axis.

QUESTIONING STRATEGIES

? Suppose that a total of 3 inches of rain fell. Would all values from 0 to 3 inches of rain be included on the graph? Explain. **Yes; the rain gauge fills one drop at a time, even when it is raining very fast, so all fractions of an inch would be included.**

? How would the shape of the graph be related to the amount of rain collected in the rain gauge? **Before it begins to rain, there would be no rain in the gauge and the graph would show a beginning value at $(0, 0)$. As rain falls, the amount of water in the gauge would increase and the graph would slope upward. When the rain stops, the amount of rain in the gauge would remain the same and the graph would be a horizontal line.**

? Could the graph of a rainfall ever slant downward as you read the graph from left to right? Explain. **No; the rate at which the rain falls can increase and decrease, but the amount of rain in the gauge can only stay the same or increase.**

EXTENSION ACTIVITY

Have small groups of students design and construct a simple rain gauge. Give each group the same amount of water and have groups simulate rain falling as they video record the rain gauge. Then have them play back the video, stopping it at intervals to record the amount of rain in a graph. Discuss why they should connect their data points to make a continuous graph. Have groups compare their results. Students should notice how their graphs are affected by the precision of their gauges and the frequency of their intervals, as well as by the rate of the simulated rainfall.

Scoring Rubric
2 points: Student correctly solves the problem and explains his/her reasoning.
1 point: Student shows good understanding of the problem but does not fully solve or explain his/her reasoning.
0 points: Student does not demonstrate understanding of the problem.

Graphing Relationships   **114**

Understanding Relations and Functions

Common Core Math Standards

The student is expected to:

 F-IF.A.1

Understand that a function from one set (called the domain) to another set (called the range) assigns to each element of the domain exactly one element of the range. If f is a function and x is an element of its domain, then f(x) denotes the output of f corresponding to the input x. The graph of f is the graph of the equation $y = f(x)$.

Mathematical Practices

 MP.6 Precision

Language Objective

Use examples from the lesson to explain the meaning of the terms *relation, function, domain,* and *range*.

ENGAGE

Essential Question: How do you represent relations and functions?

Relations and functions can be represented in many ways, including as ordered pairs, in a table, as a graph, and in a mapping diagram.

PREVIEW: LESSON PERFORMANCE TASK

View the Engage section online. Discuss how the cost of spending the day at an amusement park would depend on the number of rides you go on, and consider different ways of representing that relationship. Then preview the Lesson Performance Task.

Name_____ Class_____ Date_____

3.2 Understanding Relations and Functions

Essential Question: How do you represent relations and functions?

Resource Locker

⊘ Explore **Understanding Relations**

A **relation** is a set of ordered pairs (x, y) where x is the input value and y is the output value. The **domain** is all possible inputs of a relation, and the **range** is all possible outputs of a relation. For example, the given relation represents the number of whole-wheat cracker boxes sold and the money earned.

$\{(1, 4), (2, 8), (3, 12), (4, 16)\}$.

Domain: $\{1, 2, 3, 4\}$ Range: $\{2, 8, 12, 16\}$

Ⓐ For the following relation, the input, x, is the ages of boys and the output, y, is their corresponding height, in inches.

$\{(7, 41), (8, 45), (9, 49), (10, 52), (10, 53), (11, 55), (12, 59)\}$

Ⓑ Fill the values in the table.

x	y
7	41
8	45
9	49
10	52
10	53
11	55
12	59

Ⓒ Plot the points on the graph.

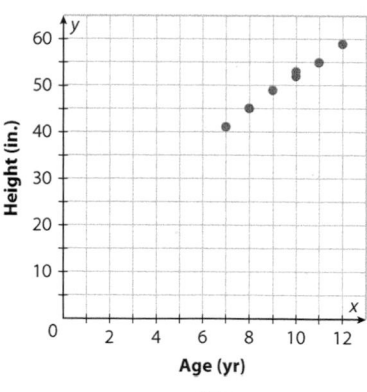

Module 3   **115**   Lesson 2

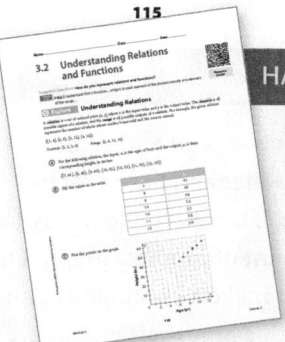

HARDCOVER PAGES 97–106

Turn to these pages to find this lesson in the hardcover student edition.

Ⓓ Complete the mapping diagram.

Ⓔ State the domain of the relation.
{7, 8, 9, 10, 11, 12}

Ⓕ State the range of the relation.
{41, 45, 49, 52, 53, 55, 59}

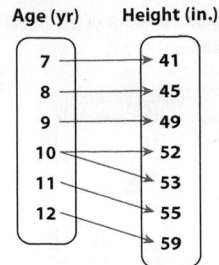

Age (yr)	Height (in.)
7	41
8	45
9	49
10	52
11	53
12	55
	59

Reflect

1. **Discussion** The number 10 appears twice in the *x* column of the table. How many times is it written in the domain? Explain.
The number 10 is written only once in the domain. The domain is a list of the input values and a

number should only be listed once no matter how many times it actually appears in the relation.

🖋 Explain 1 Recognizing Functions

A **function** is a type of relation in which there is only one output value for each input value.

For every input value, there is a unique output value.

Example: $y = x^2$. When $x = 3$, y will always be equal to 9.

Example 1 Give the domain and range of each relation. State the corresponding outputs for the given inputs in context and explain whether the relation is a function.

Ⓐ The given relation represents the number of students and the number of classrooms the school has to have for the corresponding number of students.

Students *x*	Classrooms *y*
40	2
45	3
50	4

Domain: {40, 45 50}

The domain represents the number of students.

Range: {2, 3, 4}

The range represents the number of classrooms.

For an input of 40 students, there is an output of 2 classrooms.

For an input of 45 students, there is an output of 3 classrooms.

For an input of 50 students, there is an output of 4 classrooms.

This relation is a function. Each domain value is paired with exactly one range value.

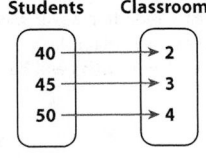

Students	Classrooms
40	2
45	3
50	4

© Houghton Mifflin Harcourt Publishing Company

EXPLORE

Understanding Relations

INTEGRATE TECHNOLOGY

Students have the option of completing the Explore activity either in the book or online.

AVOID COMMON ERRORS

Students may forget which value in an ordered pair is the *x*-value and which is the *y*-value. Remembering that *x* comes before *y* in the alphabet may help them remember that the *x*-value is always listed first.

QUESTIONING STRATEGIES

❓ In a mapping diagram, where do the arrows start, and where do they point? **They start at the inputs, or *x*-values, and point to the outputs, or *y*-values.**

EXPLAIN 1

Recognizing Functions

AVOID COMMON ERRORS

Students may have difficulty remembering the rule for determining whether a relation is a function. Suggest that they think of *x* as a person and *y* as a place. Just as a person cannot be in more than one place at a time, an *x*-value in a function cannot correspond to more than one *y*-value.

PROFESSIONAL DEVELOPMENT

Learning Progressions

In this lesson, students build on semiformal notions of functions from previous courses. Key concepts are that a *function* is a set of ordered pairs in which each input value is paired with exactly one output value, and that functions can be represented by ordered pairs, tables, graphs, and mapping diagrams. Students begin to use formal notation and language for functions. Now, the input-output relationship evident in a mapping diagram is a correspondence between two sets, the domain and the range. In later math courses, students will work with more complicated functions and more sophisticated applications.

? What would be true about a relation that is *not* a function? Give an example of a relation that is not a function. **In a relation that is not a function, an input value would be paired with more than one output value. Possible example: the relation whose domain is the number of bookshelves per classroom and whose range is the number of books per classroom**

(B) The given relation represents the amount of gas in gallons and the distance traveled in miles from that amount of gas.

Gas (gal)	Distance (mi)
10	150
16	240
17	240
20	300

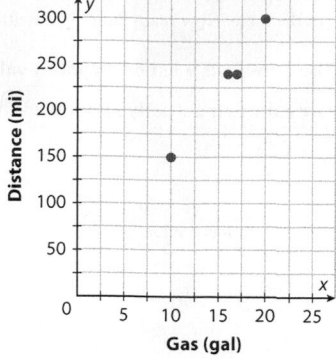

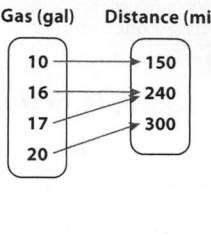

Domain: $\{10, 16, 17, 20\}$

The domain represents **the different amounts of gas.**

Range: $\{150, 240, 300\}$

The range represents **the distance traveled.**

For an input of **10 gallons of gas**, there is an output of **150 miles**.

For an input of **16 gallons of gas**, there is an output of **240 miles**.

For an input of **17 gallons of gas**, there is an output of **240 miles**.

For an input of **20 gallons of gas**, there is an output of **300 miles**.

This relation **is** a function. Each domain value is paired with **exactly one** range value.

Reflect

2. If each month in a year was paired with all the possible numbers of days in the month, will the result be a function? Explain.
   Yes; the months will be the domain, and no month is repeated in one year.

COLLABORATIVE LEARNING

Peer-to-Peer Activity

Have students work in pairs. Have each student write a list of six ordered pairs and then write the same relation as a table, a graph, and a mapping diagram. Next, partners swap papers, find the domain and range of each other's relations, and explain whether each relation is a function.

Your Turn

Give the domain and range of each relation and interpret them in context. State the corresponding outputs for the given inputs in context and explain whether the relation is a function.

3. The relation represents the number of books sold and the price for the corresponding number of books.

Number of books sold	Price ($)
2	4
3	6
4	7
5	9

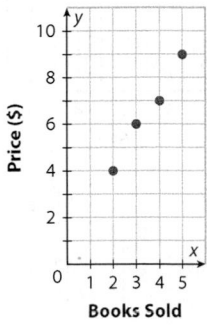

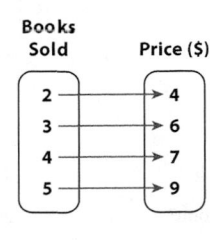

Domain: $\{2, 3, 4, 5\}$; Books sold.

Range: $\{4, 6, 7, 9\}$; Price amounts.

input of 2 books sold, output of $4.00.

input of 3 books sold, output of $6.00.

input of 4 books sold, output of $7.00.

input of 5 books sold, output of $9.00.

This relation is a function. Each domain value is paired with exactly one range value.

4. The relation represents the time spent exercising and the number of calories burned during that time.

Time (min)	Calories burned
20	50
30	85
35	85
60	100

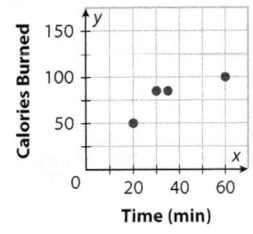

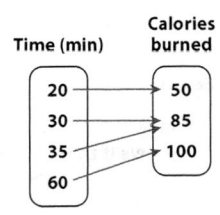

Domain: $\{20, 30, 35, 60\}$ times spent exercising.

Range: $\{50, 85, 100\}$ number of calories;

input of 20 minutes output of 50 calories burned; input of 30 minutes output of 85 calories burned input of 35 minutes output of 85 calories burned; input of 60 minutes output of 100 calories burned This relation is a function. Each domain value is paired with exactly one range value.

© Houghton Mifflin Harcourt Publishing Company • Image Credits: ©Martin Child/Getty Images

DIFFERENTIATE INSTRUCTION

Graphic Organizers

Have students complete a graphic organizer to summarize how x– and y–values appear in various representations of relations.

	x-value (input)	y-value (output)
In an ordered pair	first value	second value
In a mapping diagram	start of arrow	end of arrow
In a graph	horizontal axis	vertical axis
Set of all values	domain	range

EXPLAIN 2

Understanding the Vertical Line Test

INTEGRATE MATHEMATICAL PRACTICES

Focus on Math Connections

MP.1 Relate the vertical line test to the definition of a function. A vertical line has many y-values for the same x-value, while a function has exactly one y-value (output) for each x-value (input).

QUESTIONING STRATEGIES

? Can a relation be a function if a horizontal line passes through more than one point on its graph? Explain. Yes; if a horizontal line passes through more than one point, it means that the same y-value corresponds to more than one x-value. Each x-value could still have only one y-value, so the relation could be a function.

INTEGRATE TECHNOLOGY

To perform the vertical line test with a graphing calculator, press **GRAPH**, then **2nd**, then **DRAW**, choose **4:Vertical**, and use arrow keys to move the vertical line across the graph.

INTEGRATE MATHEMATICAL PRACTICES

Focus on Communication

MP.3 Show students that one way to write a domain or range for a continuous function is by using set-builder notation. For example, the domain $\{x | 1 \le x \le 3\}$ is read, "all x such that x is greater than or equal to 1 and x is less than or equal to 3."

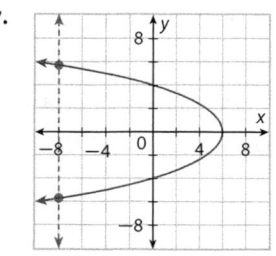
© Houghton Mifflin Harcourt Publishing Company

Explain 2 **Understanding the Vertical Line Test**

A test, called the *vertical line test*, can be used to determine if a relation is a function. The **vertical line test** states that a relation is a function if and only if a vertical line does not pass through more than one point on the graph of the relation.

Example 2 Use the vertical line test to determine if each relation is a function. Explain.

(A) Draw a vertical line through each point of the graph.

Does any vertical line touch more than one point? Yes

Since a vertical line does pass through more than one point, the graph fails the vertical line test. So, the relation is not a function.

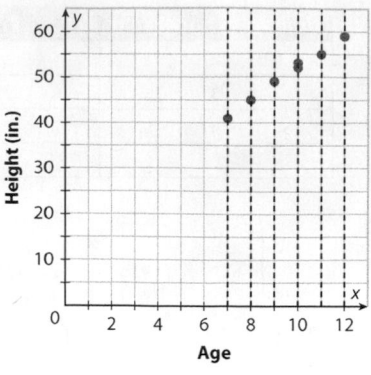

(B) Draw a vertical line through each point of the graph.

Does any vertical line touch more than one point? ___No___

Since a vertical line ___does not___ pass through more than one point, the graph ___passes___ the vertical line test. So, the relation ___is___ a function.

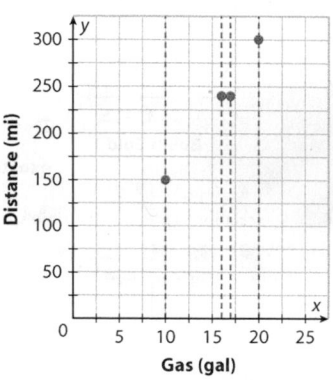

Reflect

5. Why does the vertical line test work?
It shows if there is more than one y-value for any x-value.

Your Turn

Use the vertical line test to determine if each relation is a function.

6.

The relation is a function.

7.

The relation is not a function.

LANGUAGE SUPPORT **EL**

Communicate Math

To help students formulate explanations about functions and relations, provide them with sentence frames such as the following:

In this problem, the domain represents _____ and the range represents _____.

{ *Each domain value is paired with exactly one range value.* OR
  The domain value _____ is paired with the range values _____.

Therefore, the relation _____ (is/is not) a function.

8. How can you use a mapping diagram to determine the domain and the range of a relation?
The domain is the set of all input values (starting points of the arrows), and the range is

the set of all output values (arrows pointing toward the values).

9. Discussion For a discrete function, can the number of elements in the range be greater than the number of elements in the domain? Explain.
No; if the number of range values is greater than the number of domain values, then there

must be a domain value that is paired with more than one range value.

10. Is a relation a function if its graph intersects the y-axis twice?
No; the y-axis is a vertical line, and according to the vertical line test, the y-axis should not

pass through more than one point of the graph of a function.

11. Essential Question Check-In You are asked to determine if the relation $y = x^2 - 8x + 4$ is a function. What would be the best way to represent this relation in order to determine if it is a function or not? Explain.
The domain of the relation $y = x^2 - 8x + 4$ is all real numbers, which means there are an

infinite number of values. You cannot represent this with a table, a mapping diagram, or

a set of ordered pairs. The best way to represent this relation would be with a graph. This

method allows you to use the vertical line test to determine if this relation is a function.

⭐ Evaluate: Homework and Practice

• Online Homework
• Hints and Help
• Extra Practice

Express each relation as a table, as a graph, and as a mapping diagram.

1. The relation represents ages of students and the number of words they can write per minute.
$$\{(5, 10), (6, 20), (6, 23), (7, 35)\}$$

x	y
5	10
6	20
6	23
7	35

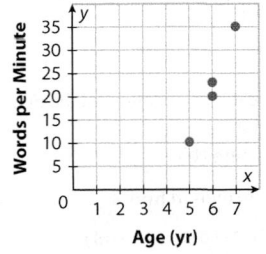

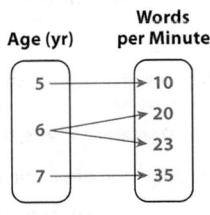

ELABORATE

QUESTIONING STRATEGIES

❓ Which representation (mapping diagram, table, or graph) do you think makes it easiest to determine if a relation is a function? Why? **Possible answer: A graph is easiest, because I can apply the vertical line test to a graph.**

❓ How do you determine if a set of ordered pairs is a function? **Check whether there are two or more ordered pairs with the same x-value and different y-values. If there are not, the relation is a function.**

SUMMARIZE THE LESSON

❓ When is a relation a function? When is a relation not a function? **A relation is a function if there is exactly one range element for each domain element. A relation is not a function if there is more than one range element for a domain element.**

EVALUATE

ASSIGNMENT GUIDE

Concepts and Skills	Practice
Explore Understanding Relations	Exercises 1–5
Example 1 Recognizing Functions	Exercises 6–14, 23–24
Example 2 Understanding the Vertical Line Test	Exercises 15–22, 25

Exercise	Depth of Knowledge (D.O.K.)	COMMON CORE Mathematical Practices
1–2	**1** Recall of Information	**MP.6** Precision
3–5	**1** Recall of Information	**MP.2** Reasoning
6–12	**1** Recall of Information	**MP.4** Modeling
13–14	**1** Recall of Information	**MP.4** Modeling
15–22	**1** Recall of Information	**MP.5** Using Tools
23	**2** Skills/Concept **H.O.T.**	**MP.2** Reasoning

VISUAL CUES

Remind students that an ordered pair consists of (x, y). When students are given a relation in the form of a mapping diagram, encourage them to list the ordered pairs by following one arrow at a time.

COGNITIVE STRATEGIES

Show students the following to help them remember which values are in the domain and which are in the range.

- x and y are in alphabetical order.
- Input and output are in alphabetical order.
- Domain and range are in alphabetical order.

So the x-values, or inputs, make up the domain, and the y-values, or outputs, make up the range.

Express each relation as a table, as a graph, and as a mapping diagram.

2. The relation represents the place won in a track meet and the number of points that place finish is worth.

$$\{(1, 5), (2, 3), (3, 2), (4, 1), (5, 0)\}$$

x	y
1	5
2	3
3	2
4	1
5	0

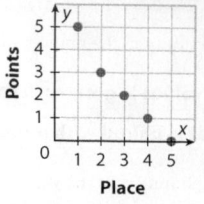

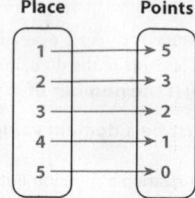

State the domain and range of each relation.

3.

x	y
2	5
7	8
8	15
11	12
15	19

Domain: {2, 7, 8, 11, 15}

Range: {5, 8, 15, 12, 19}

4.

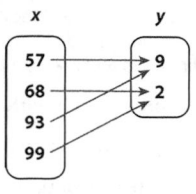

Domain: {57, 68, 93, 99}

Range: {9, 2}

5.

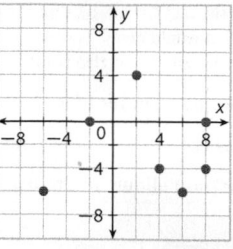

Domain: {−6, −2, 2, 4, 6, 8}

Range: {−6, −4, 0, 4}

State the domain and range of each relation, interpret in context, and explain if it is a function or not.

6. The relation represents the age of each student and the number of pets the student has.

Domain: {6, 8, 9, 11}; student ages

Range: {0, 1, 2, 3}; number of pets

This relation is not a function. The domain value 11 is paired with both 1 and 2.

Age	Number of Pets
6	3
8	2
9	0
11	1
11	2

7. The relation represents time driven in hours and the number of miles traveled at the end of each hour.

Domain: {1, 2, 3, 4, 5}; time (h)

The domain is the time driven in hours.

Range: {50, 100, 150, 200}; distance (mi)

This relation is a function. Each domain value is paired with exactly one range value.

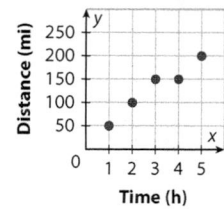

© Houghton Mifflin Harcourt Publishing Company

Exercise	Depth of Knowledge (D.O.K.)	COMMON CORE	Mathematical Practices
24	**3** Strategic Thinking **H.O.T.**		**MP.3** Logic
25	**3** Strategic Thinking **H.O.T.**		**MP.3** Logic

State the domain and range of each relation, interpret in context, and explain if it is a function or not.

8. The relation represents the number of hours a person is able to rent a canoe and the cost of renting the canoe for that many hours.

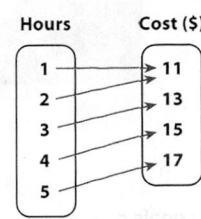

Hours   **Cost ($)**

1 → 11
2 → 13
3 → 15
4 → 17
5

Domain: {1, 2, 3, 4, 5}; hours. **Range:** {11, 13, 15, 17}; cost

This relation is a function. Each domain value is paired with exactly one range value.

9. A person can burn about 6 calories per minute bicycling. Let x represent the number of minutes bicycled, and let y represent the number of calories burned. Create a mapping diagram to show the number of calories burned by bicycling for 60, 120, 180, or 240 minutes.

Minutes   **Calories**

60 → 360
120 → 720
180 → 1080
240 → 1440

Domain: {60, 120, 180, 240}; minutes bicycling

Range: {360, 720, 1080, 1440}; calories burned

This relation is a function. Each domain value is paired with exactly one range value.

10. The table represents a sample of ages of people and their shoe size.

Domain: {11, 12, 13, 15, 16}; ages

Range: {7, 8, 10, 10.5, 11}; shoe sizes

This relation is not a function. The age 15

corresponds to two different shoe sizes, 10 and 10.5.

Age	Shoe Size
x	y
11	7
12	8
13	10
15	10
15	10.5
16	11

11. An electrician charges a base fee of $75 plus $50 for each hour of work. The minimum the electrician charges is $175. Create a table that shows the amount the electrician charges for 1, 2, 3, and 4 hours of work.

Domain: {1, 2, 3, 4}; hours of work

Range: {175, 225, 275}; amount charged

This relation is a function. Each domain value is paired with exactly one range value.

x	y
1	175
2	175
3	225
4	275

To help students remember that the range is all possible y-values, show students that the letter g in range goes below the reading line like the letter y. Domain and x do not have any letters below the reading line.

Understanding Relations and Functions   **122**

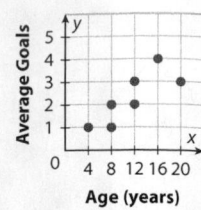

When a relation is represented as a mapping diagram, how can you tell whether it is a function? If there is only one arrow starting at each *x*-value, the relation is a function. If more than one arrow starts at the same *x*-value, it is not a function.

12. The graph represents the average soccer goals scored for players of different ages. Determine the domain and range of the relation in context and explain whether or not this represents a function.

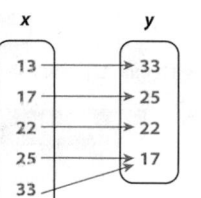

Domain: {4, 8, 12, 16, 20}; ages   Range: {1, 2, 3, 4}; goals scored

This relation is not a function. The age 8 is paired with two different range values, 1 and 2, and the age 12 is paired with two different range values, 2 and 3.

Express each relation as a mapping diagram and explain whether or not the relation represents a function.

13. $\{(13, 33), (17, 25), (22, 22), (25, 17), (33, 17)\}$ **14.** $\{(1, 2), (5, 2), (5, 4), (7, 6), (11, 6) (11, 8)\}$

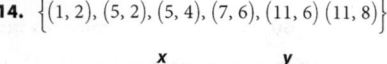

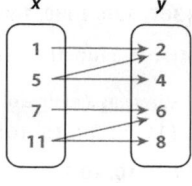

The relation is a function. Each domain value is paired with exactly one range value.

The relation is not a function. The domain value 5 is paired with both 2 and 4. The domain value 11 is paired with both 6 and 8.

Use the vertical line test to determine if each relation is a function.

15.

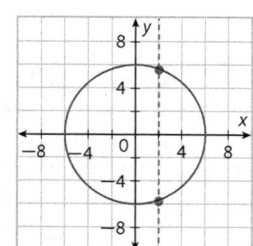

The relation is not a function.

16.

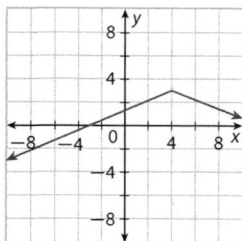

The relation is a function.

Use the vertical line test to determine if each relation is a function.

17.

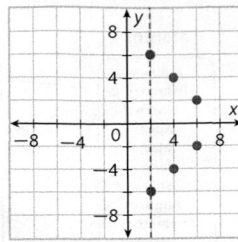

The relation is not a function.

18.

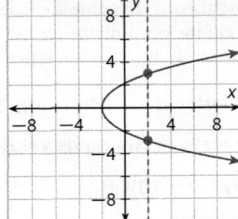

The relation is not a function.

19.

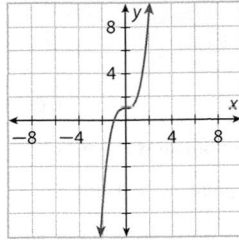

The relation is a function.

20.

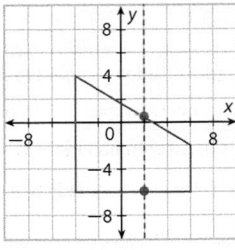

The relation is not a function.

21.

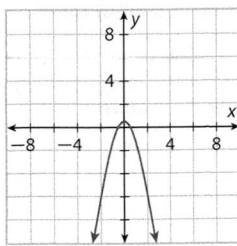

The relation is a function.

22.

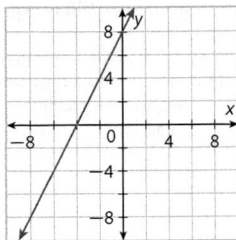

The relation is a function.

Some students may use a horizontal line instead of a vertical line to check whether a graph represents a function. Emphasize that a vertical line must be used because if there is more than one y-value for any x-value, the points representing those values will be lined up vertically on the graph.

JOURNAL

Have students explain how to determine whether a relation is a function from a graph, from a mapping diagram, and from a set of ordered pairs.

23. Draw Conclusions Examine the mapping diagram. The first set is the months of the year, and the second set is the possible number of days per month. Is the relation a function? Explain.

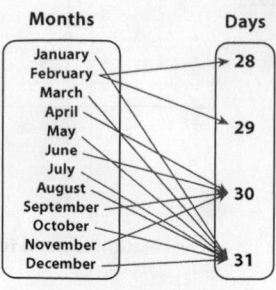

No; the relation is not a function. The domain value

February maps to two range values, 28 and 29. February

has 28 days in a regular year and 29 days in a leap year.

24. Justify Reasoning Tell whether each situation represents a function. Explain your reasoning. If the situation represents a function, give the domain and range.

a. Each U.S. coin is mapped to its monetary value.

Function; no coin has more than one monetary value. The domain is the set of

all U.S. coins. The range is the set of monetary values assigned to each coin.

b. A $1, $5, $10, $20, $50, or $100 bill is mapped to all the sets of coins that are the same as the total value of the bill.

Not a function; each bill is equivalent to many different combinations of coins.

25. Explain the Error A student was given a graph and asked to use the vertical line test to determine if the relation was a function or not. The student said that the relation failed the vertical line test and the graph was not a function. What error did the student make? Explain the error and give the correct answer.

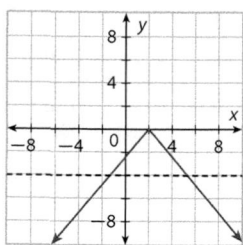

The student used a horizontal line, rather than a vertical line. A function

is allowed to have more than one *x*-value paired to the same *y*-value, so

there is no horizontal line test. The relation passes the vertical line test

and is a function.

Lesson Performance Task

At an amusement park, a person spends $30 on admission and food, and then goes on r number of rides that cost $2 each.

a. Write an equation to represent the total amount A spent at the amusement park if a person goes on anywhere from 0 to 5 rides.

b. Represent the relation as a table, as a graph, and as a mapping diagram.

c. Find the domain and range, and then determine whether the relation is a function or not.

a. $A = 2r + 30$

b.

Rides	Total Amount
0	30
1	32
2	34
3	36
4	38
5	40

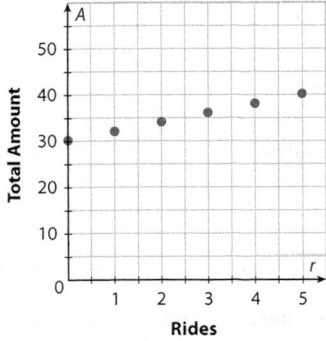

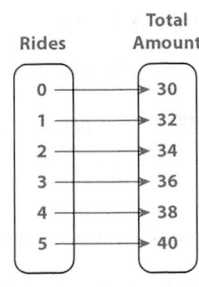

c. Domain: $\{0, 1, 2, 3, 4, 5\}$

Range: $\{30, 32, 34, 36, 38, 40\}$

This relation is a function. The total amount is different for each number of rides a person goes on. Therefore, no domain value will have two different range values.

EXTENSION ACTIVITY

Suppose that instead of charging $2 per ride, the amusement park sells a $5 pass that allows you to go on up to 3 rides. Have students create a table, graph, and mapping diagram for this situation and determine whether the relation between number of rides and total amount spent is a function. Discuss which pricing system they prefer. Students should find that the relation is a function, but that the graph shows a stepped pattern, and more than one x-value corresponds to each y-value. Per-ride pricing is better if you go on only one or two rides, but the 3-ride pass is a better choice for going on many rides.

AVOID COMMON ERRORS

Students may start the values for number of rides in their tables with 1 instead of 0. Remind students that it is possible to attend the amusement park without riding any of the rides.

INTEGRATE MATHEMATICAL PRACTICES
Focus on Patterns

MP.8 Discuss with students any patterns they see in their tables, graphs, and mappings. In the table, students should note that as the number of rides increases by 1, the total amount spent increases by 2. In the graph, students should see that the points lie along an upward-sloping line. In the mapping diagram, students should see that there is a one-to-one correspondence between the values in the domain and range.

INTEGRATE MATHEMATICAL PRACTICES
Focus on Technology

MP.5 Students can find the values of the range using the table function of a graphing calculator. Input the equation into the **Y=** function of the calculator. Press **2nd**, then **TBLSET**, and enter 0 after **TblStart** and 1 after **ΔTbl**. Then press **2nd**, then **TABLE**. The resulting table will display the domain in the column labeled **X** and the range in the column labeled **Y₁**.

Scoring Rubric

2 points: Student correctly solves the problem and explains his/her reasoning.

1 point: Student shows good understanding of the problem but does not fully solve or explain his/her reasoning.

0 points: Student does not demonstrate understanding of the problem.

Understanding Relations and Functions   **126**

Modeling with Functions

Common Core Math Standards

The student is expected to:

 F-IF.A.2

Use function notation, evaluate functions for inputs in their domains, and interpret statements that use function notation in terms of a context. Also F-IF.A.1, A-CED.A.2

Mathematical Practices

 MP.4 Modeling

Language Objective

Explain to a partner how to determine a reasonable domain and range for a real-world function.

ENGAGE

Essential Question: What is function notation and how can you use functions to model real-world situations?

Function notation uses $f(x)$ to represent the dependent value. You can write equations to model real-world situations using $f(x)$ for the dependent variable y.

PREVIEW: LESSON PERFORMANCE TASK

View the Engage section online. Discuss how a loan can be paid off with monthly payments. Then preview the Lesson Performance Task.

Name_____ Class_____ Date_____

3.3 Modeling with Functions

Essential Question: What is function notation and how can you use functions to model real-world situations?

Resource Locker

⊘ Explore 1 Identifying Independent and Dependent Variables

The input of a function is the **independent variable**. The output of the function is the **dependent variable**. The value of the dependent variable depends on, or is a function of, the value of the independent variable.

Identify dependent and independent variables in each situation.

In the winter, more electricity is used when the outside temperature goes down, and less is used when the outside temperature rises.

Ⓐ The __amount of electricity__ depends on the __temperature__

Ⓑ Dependent: __amount of electricity__

Independent: __temperature__

Ⓒ The cost of shipping a package is based on its weight.

The __cost__ depends on the __weight__

Ⓓ Dependent: __cost__ Independent: __weight__

Ⓔ The faster Tom walks, the quicker he gets home.

The __time__ depends on the __speed__

Ⓕ Dependent: __time__ Independent: __speed__

Reflect

1. **Discussion** Give a situation where "time" is the dependent variable and "distance" is the independent variable.
    Answers may vary. Sample answer: The time spent driving is dependent upon the distance driven.

2. In Explore 1, explain how you know that the amount of electricity used is not the independent variable.
    The outside temperature does not depend on the amount of electricity used.

© Houghton Mifflin Harcourt Publishing Company

HARDCOVER PAGES 107–112

Turn to these pages to find this lesson in the hardcover student edition.

⊘ Explore 2   Applying Function Notation

If x is the independent variable and y is the dependent variable, then you can use **function notation** to write $y = f(x)$, which is read "y equals f of x," where f names the function. When an equation in two variables describes a function, you always can use function notation to write it.

The dependent variable	is	a function of	the independent variable.
y	is	a function of	x.
y	=	f	(x)

Write an equation in function notation.

Amanda babysits and charges $5 per hour.

Time Worked in Hours (x)	1	2	3	4
Amount Earned in Dollars (y)	5	10	15	20

Ⓐ   The <u>amount of money earned</u> is $5 times the <u>number of hours worked</u>.

Ⓑ   An algebraic expression that defines a function is a **function rule**. Write an equation using two variables to show this relationship.

Amount earned	is	$5	times		the number of hours worked.
↓	↓	↓	↓		↓
<u> y </u>	=	5	•		<u> x </u>

Ⓒ   The dependent variable is a function of the independent variable. Write the equation in function notation.

Amount earned	is	$5	times	the number of hours worked.
↓	↓	↓	↓	↓
y	=	5	•	x
<u>$f(x)$</u>	=	5	•	x

Reflect

3.   **Discussion**   Can y be used instead of $f(x)$ in function notation? If so, tell why. If not, give an example of a function not written in function notation and the same function written in function notation.
No; function notation requires that you use $f(x)$ instead of y. Sample answer: $y = 3x + 7$ is not in function notation; $f(x) = 3x + 7$ is in function notation.

PROFESSIONAL DEVELOPMENT

Math Background

The input of a function is also called the *argument* of the function. The output of a function is also called the *value* of the function. For example, in $f(2) = 10$, the argument of the function is 2 and the value of the function is 10.

EXPLORE 1

Identifying Independent and Dependent Variables

CONNECT VOCABULARY   🔲EL

Have students describe the meaning of the following phrases:

- independently wealthy   doesn't need a job
- Independence Day   day celebrating freedom
- works independently   works without needing help
- dependent child   needs a parent
- insulin dependent   needs insulin
- dependent on friends   needs friends

EXPLORE 2

Applying Function Notation

AVOID COMMON ERRORS

Students might mistakenly interpret the notation $f(x)$ as meaning f times x. Remind them that $f(x)$ is a special notation for functions and represents the output of a function.

QUESTIONING STRATEGIES

?   How would you change an equation written using function notation to an equation without function notation?   Replace $f(x)$ with y.

EXPLAIN 1

Modeling Using Function Notation

QUESTIONING STRATEGIES

In the function rule $f(x) = 5x + 2$, what is the independent variable and what is the dependent variable? **The independent variable is x and the dependent variable is $f(x)$.**

INTEGRATE MATHEMATICAL PRACTICES
Focus on Reasoning

MP.2 Make sure students understand that once you have written a function rule, you can evaluate it for any value of the independent variable by substituting that value into the function rule and simplifying.

© Houghton Mifflin Harcourt Publishing Company • Image Credits: ©Photodisc/Getty Images

⊘ Explain 1 Modeling Using Function Notation

The value of the dependent variable depends on, or is a function of, the value of the independent variable. If x is the independent variable and y is the dependent variable, then the function notation for y will read "f of x," where f names the function. When an equation in two variables describes a function, you can use function notation to write it.

Example 1 For each example identify the independent and dependent variables. Write an equation in function notation for each situation, and then use the equation to solve the problem.

Ⓐ A lawyer's fee is $180 per hour for his services. How much does the lawyer charge for 5 hours?

The fee for the lawyer depends on how many hours he works.

Dependent: fee; Independent: hours

Let h represent the number of hours the lawyer works.

The function for the lawyer's fee is $f(h) = 180h$.

$$f(h) = 180h$$
$$f(5) = 180(5) \quad \text{Substitute 5 for } h.$$
$$= 900 \quad \text{Simplify.}$$

The lawyer charges $900 for 5 hours of work.

Ⓑ The admission fee at a carnival is $9. Each ride costs $1.75. How much does it cost to go to the carnival and then go on 12 rides?

The __total cost__ depends on the __number of rides__, plus $9.

Dependent: __total cost__ Independent: __the number of rides__

Let r represent the __number of rides__. The function for the total cost of the carnival is $f(r)=$ __$1.75r + 9$__.

Substitute 12 for r into the function for the total cost of the carnival, and find the total cost.

$$f\left(\boxed{12}\right) = \boxed{1.75(12) + 9}$$
$$f\left(\boxed{12}\right) = \boxed{30}$$

It costs __$30__ to go to the carnival and go on __12__ rides.

Your Turn

For each example identify the independent and dependent variables. Write an equation in function notation for each situation. Then use the equation to solve the problem.

4. Kate earns $7.50 per hour. How much money will she earn after working 8 hours?
    Dependent: total earnings Independent: the number of hours h
    $f(h) = 7.50h.\ f(8) = 7.50(8) = 60.$ **Kate earns $60 for working 8 hours.**

Module 3   **129**   Lesson 3

COLLABORATIVE LEARNING

Peer-to-Peer Activity

Group students in pairs. Designate one student in each pair as the "function machine." This student must create a secret function rule. The second student gives input values to the "function machine," who must state the corresponding output values. The second student then guesses the secret function rule and explains how he or she deduced it. Then have students switch roles and repeat.

⊘ Explain 2 · Choosing a Reasonable Domain and Range

When a function describes a real-world situation, every real number is not always a reasonable choice for the domain and range. For example, a number representing the length of an object cannot be negative, and only whole numbers can represent a number of people.

Example 2 Write a function in function notation for each situation. Find a reasonable domain and range for each function.

(A) Manuel has already sold $20 worth of tickets to the school play. He has 4 tickets left to sell at $2.50 per ticket. Write a function for the total amount collected from ticket sales.

Let *t* represent the number of tickets to sell.

Total amount collected from ticket sales	is	$2.50	per	ticket	plus	tickets already sold
f(t)	=	$2.50	·	t	+	20

Manuel has only 4 tickets left to sell, so a reasonable domain is {0, 1, 2, 3, 4}.

Substitute these values into the function rule 2.50*t* + 20 to find the range values.

The range is {$20, $22.50, $25, $27.50, $30}.

(B) A telephone company charges $0.25 per minute for the first 5 minutes of a call plus a $0.45 connection fee per call. Write a function for the total cost in dollars of making a call.

Let *m* represent the number of minutes used.

Total cost for one call	is	$0.25	per	minute	plus	$0.45 fee.
f(m)	=	$0.25	·	m	+	$0.45

The charges only occur if a call is made, so a reasonable domain is { 1, 2, 3, 4, 5 }.

Substitute these values into the function rule 0.25*m* + 0.45 to find the range values.

The range is {$0.70, $0.95, $1.20, $1.45, $1.70} .

Your Turn

Write a function in function notation for each situation. Find a reasonable domain and range for each function.

5. The temperature early in the morning is 17 °C. The temperature increases by 2 °C for every hour for the next 5 hours. Write a function for the temperature in degrees Celsius.
   Let *h* represent the number of hours. f(h) = 17 + 2h
   Reasonable domain: {0, 1, 2, 3, 4, 5} Range: {17 °C, 19 °C, 21 °C, 23 °C, 25 °C, 27 °C}

6. Takumi earns $8.50 per hour proofreading advertisements at a local newspaper. He works no more than 5 hours a day. Write a function for his earnings.
   Let *h* represent the number of hours. f(h) = 8.5h
   Reasonable domain: {1, 2, 3, 4, 5} Range: {$8.50, $17, $25.50, $34, $42.50}

© Houghton Mifflin Harcourt Publishing Company

DIFFERENTIATE INSTRUCTION

Cognitive Strategies

If students have a hard time finding the relationship between the independent and dependent variables when writing a function, have them consider each of the four basic operations in the context of the problem. ("Is the same value added to the dependent variable, or multiplied by the dependent variable?") Students should remember that the situation may call for a combination of operations.

EXPLAIN 2

Choosing a Reasonable Domain and Range

QUESTIONING STRATEGIES

? What do you look for when finding the reasonable domain? **Look for numbers that make sense as the independent variable in the real-world situation.**

? What are some limitations that might apply to the domain? **Possible answer: The domain values may have to be nonnegative numbers, may have to be integers, and may have to be within a specified range.**

? How do you find the reasonable range once you have determined the reasonable domain? **Substitute the domain values into the function rule and evaluate to find all possible values of the range.**

AVOID COMMON ERRORS

Students might forget to include 0 in the domain of a function. Encourage them to consider whether it makes sense for the independent variable to have a value of a 0 in the context of each problem.

Modeling with Functions   **130**

ELABORATE

INTEGRATE MATHEMATICAL PRACTICES

Focus on Math Connections

MP.1 Explain that a function can be thought of as a machine that processes inputs in a particular way and always produces the same output for a given input. For example, when you input water into an ice machine, the output is ice cubes. Have students suggest some other real-world objects that have an output and an input.

SUMMARIZE THE LESSON

Complete the graphic organizer with students to summarize the relationship between the domain and range of a function.

Domain	Range
input values	output values
independent variable	dependent variable
x	$f(x)$

© Houghton Mifflin Harcourt Publishing Company

💬 Elaborate

7. How can you identify the independent variable and the dependent variable given a situation?
Sample answer: If one set of data depends on the other, the first set represents the dependent variable and the second set represents the independent variable.

8. Describe how to write $3x + 2y = 12$ in function notation. Assume that y represents the dependent variable.
$3x + 2y = 12$

$$2y = -3x + 12$$

$$y = -\frac{3}{2}x + 6$$

$$f(x) = -\frac{3}{2}x + 6$$

9. **Discussion** What is the advantage of using function notation instead of using y?
Function notation allows you to see how the independent and dependent variables of a function are related.

10. **Essential Question Check-In** Explain how to find reasonable domain values for a function.
Find what makes sense for the real-world situation represented by the function. Time, for example, cannot be negative or you cannot buy a fraction of a shirt.

⭐ Evaluate: Homework and Practice

Identify the dependent and independent variables in each situation.

- Online Homework
- Hints and Help
- Extra Practice

1. Identify the dependent and independent variables in each situation.

 A. The total cost of running a business is based on its expenses.
 Independent: expenses;
 Dependent: total cost

 B. The price of a house depends on its area.
 Independent: area;
 Dependent: price

 C. The time it takes you to run a certain distance depends on the distance.
 Independent: distance;
 Dependent: time

 D. The number of items in a carton depends on the size of the carton.
 Independent: size of carton;
 Dependent: number of items

2. Charles will babysit for up to 4 hours and charges $7 per hour.

Write a function in function notation for this situation.

Amount charged	is	$7	times	the number of hours.
$f(x)$	=	7	•	x

LANGUAGE SUPPORT 🔵EL

Graphic Organizers

Divide students into groups and have them write examples of various ways of expressing dependent relationships. Then have them identify the independent and dependent variable in each situation. For example:

- I get cranky when I don't eat.
- If I don't work, then I don't get paid.

Independent	Dependent
• when I don't eat	• I get cranky
• if i don't work	• then I don't get paid

For each situation, identify the independent and dependent variables. Write a function in function notation. Then use the function to solve the problem.

3. Almira earns $50 an hour. How much does she earn in 6 hours?

Dependent: amount of money Independent: number of hours

Let h represent the number of hours Almira works. $f(h) = 50h$.

$f(6) = 50(6) = 300$ Almira earns $300 in 6 hours.

4. Stan, a local delivery driver, is paid $3.50 per mile driven plus a daily amount of $75. On Monday, he is assigned a route that is 30 miles long. How much is he being paid for that day?

Dependent: amount of money Independent: number of miles driven

Let m represent miles Stan drives. $f(m) = 3.5m + 75$.

$f(30) = 3.5(30) + 75 = 180$ Stan earns $180 for Monday.

5. Bruce owns a small grocery store and charges $4.75 per pound of produce. If a customer orders 5 pounds of produce, how much does Bruce charge the customer?

Dependent: amount of money Independent: pounds of produce

Let p represent the number of pounds of produce ordered. $f(p) = 4.75p$.

$f(5) = 4.75(5) = 23.75$ Bruce charges the cutomer $23.75.

6. Georgia, a florist, charges $10.95 per flower bundle plus a $15 delivery charge per order. If Charlie orders 8 bundles of flowers and has them delivered, how much does Georgia charge Charlie?

Dependent: total charge

Independent: number of bundles b

$f(b) = 10.95b + 15$.

$f(8) = 10.95(8) + 15 = 102.6$ Georgia charges Charlie $102.60.

7. Allison owns a music store and sells DVDs at $17.75 per DVD. If Craig orders 5 DVDs, how much does it cost?

Dependent: total cost Independent: number of DVDs

Let d represent the number of DVDs ordered. $f(d) = 17.75d$.

$f(5) = 17.75(5) = 88.75$ Craig owes Allison $88.75 for 5 DVDs.

8. Anne buys used cars at auction for $2000 per car. There is a $150 fee to take part in the auction. If Anne buys 13 used cars, how much does she pay in total?

Dependent: amount of money Independent: number of cars purchased

Let c represent the number of cars purchased. $f(c) = 2000c + 150$.

$f(13) = 2000(13) + 150 = 26,150$ Anne pays $26,150.

9. Harold, a real estate developer, sells houses at $250,000 per house. If he sells 9 houses, how much does he earn?

Dependent: amount of money Independent: number of houses sold

Let h represent the number of houses sold. $f(h) = 250,000h$.

$f(9) = 250,000(9) = 2,250,000$ Harold earns $2,250,000 for selling 9 houses.

© Houghton Mifflin Harcourt Publishing Company • Image Credits: ©Tetra Images/Corbis

Personal Math Trainer

ASSIGNMENT GUIDE

Concepts and Skills	Practice
Explore 1 Identifying Independent and Dependent Variables	Exercise 1
Explore 2 Applying Function Notation	Exercises 2
Example 1 Modeling Using Function Notation	Exercises 3–12
Example 2 Choosing a Reasonable Domain and Range	Exercises 13–23

AUDITORY CUES

Point out to students that the *in*put is the *in*dependent variable.

Exercise	Depth of Knowledge (D.O.K.)	COMMON CORE Mathematical Practices
1	**1** Recall of Information	**MP.2** Reasoning
2	**1** Recall of Information	**MP.4** Modeling
3–12	**2** Skills/Concepts	**MP.4** Modeling
13–20	**2** Skills/Concepts	**MP.2** Reasoning
21–23	**2** Skills/Concepts **H.O.T.**	**MP.3** Logic

AVOID COMMON ERRORS

If students have trouble identifying the independent and dependent variables in a situation, encourage them to use the words *depends on*, instead of *is a function of*. For example, if someone's pay depends on the number of hours worked, the total pay, $f(h)$, is a function of the number of hours, h. Emphasize that the output values "depend on" the input values.

10. Gordon buys 3 HD TVs for $1200 each. There is a shipping charge of $90 to have the TVs delivered to his house. How much does Gordon pay in total?

Dependent: amount of money Independent: number of HD TVs

Let *t* represent the number of TVs bought. $f(t) = 1200t + 90$

$f(3) = 1200(3) + 90 = 3690$ **Gordon pays $3690 total.**

11. Cindy is buying jackets for her local community charity's auction. Each jacket costs $50. If Cindy bought 23 jackets, what is the total cost?

Dependent: amount of money Independent: number of jackets

Let *j* represent the number of jackets purchased. $f(j) = 50j$.

$f(23) = 50(23) = 1150$ **Cindy's total cost for 23 jackets is $1150.**

12. Autumn sells laptop computers for $600 each. If she sells 68 computers, how much money does she earn?

Dependent: amount of money Independent: number of computers sold

Let *c* represent the number of computers sold. $f(c) = 600c$.

$f(68) = 600(68) = 40{,}800$ **Autumn earns $40,800.**

Write a function using function notation to describe each situation. Find a reasonable domain and range for each function.

13. Elijah has already sold $40 worth of tickets for a local raffle. He has 5 tickets left to sell at $5 per ticket.

$$f(t) \quad = \quad \$5.00 \quad \cdot \quad t \quad + \quad 40$$

A reasonable domain is {0, 1, 2, 3, 4, 5}. The range is {$40, $45, $50, $55, $60, $65}.

14. Mary has already sold $55 worth of tickets to the benefit concert. She has 3 tickets left to sell at $7 per ticket.

$$f(t) \quad = \quad \$7.00 \quad \cdot \quad t \quad + \quad 55$$

A reasonable domain is {0, 1, 2, 3}. The range is {$55, $62, $69, $76}.

15. A law firm charges $100 per hour for the first 3 hours plus a $300 origination fee for its services.

$$f(t) \quad = \quad \$100 \quad \cdot \quad h \quad + \quad 300$$

A reasonable domain is {1, 2, 3}. The range is {$400, $500, $600}.

16. A pay-for-service Internet company charges $5 per hour for the first 3 hours of service plus a $10 connection fee.

$$f(h) \quad = \quad \$5 \quad \cdot \quad h \quad + \quad 10$$

A reasonable domain is {1, 2, 3}. The range is {$15, $20, $25}.

© Houghton Mifflin Harcourt Publishing Company

17. A high definition radio station charges $200 per year in addition to $50 per month for the first 3 months to receive its broadcast.

$$f(m) = \$50 \cdot m + 200$$

A reasonable domain is {1, 2, 3}. The range is {$250, $300, $350}.

18. A newspaper charges $3 per line for the first 4 lines plus a $20 fee to advertise.

$$f(l) = \$3 \cdot l + 20$$

A reasonable domain is {1, 2, 3, 4}. The range is {$23, $26, $29, $32}.

19. Matt has already sold $72 worth of tickets to the benefit concert. He has 6 tickets left to sell at $9 per ticket.

$$f(t) = \$9.00 \cdot t + 72$$

A reasonable domain is {0, 1, 2, 3, 4, 5, 6}. The range is {$72, $81, $90, $99, $108, $117, $126}.

20. Sarah has sold $33 worth of tickets to the comedy show. She has 4 tickets left to sell at $11 per ticket.

$$f(t) = \$11.00 \cdot t + 33$$

A reasonable domain is {0, 1, 2, 3, 4}. The range is {$33, $44, $55, $66, $77}.

INTEGRATE MATHEMATICAL PRACTICES

Focus on Patterns

MP.8 Have students think about the relationship between the independent and dependent variable before writing functions. Have them consider how the dependent variable changes as the independent variable changes. For example, do the output values increase or decrease as the input values increase? Do they change by the same amount as the input values, or by a multiple of the input values?

QUESTIONING STRATEGIES

? What does the phrase *a reasonable domain* mean? the set of numbers that makes sense for a given situation

JOURNAL

Have students explain the meaning of $f(3) = 12$, create a function such that $f(3) = 12$, and describe a real-world situation that the function could represent.

21. **Justify Reasoning** The function $f(x) = -6x + 11$ has a range given by $\{-37, -25, -13, -1\}$. Select the domain values of the function from the list 1, 2, 3, 4, 5, 6, 7, 8. Explain how you arrived at your answer.

    The domain values are 2, 4, 6, and 8. Sample answer: I substituted each range value for $f(x)$ and solved for x. $f(2) = -1$, $f(4) = -13$, $f(6) = -25$, $f(8) = -37$

22a. **Represent Real-World Problems** Victor needs to find the volume of 6 cube-shaped boxes with sides lengths of between 2 feet and 7 feet. The side lengths of the boxes can only be whole numbers. The volume of a cube-shaped box with a side length of s is given by the function $V(s) = s^3$.

    What is a reasonable domain for this situation? Explain.

    A reasonable domain is $\{2, 3, 4, 5, 6, 7\}$. The least side length is 2 feet and the greatest is 7 feet, so all whole numbers from 2 to 7.

   b. What is a reasonable range for this situation? Explain.

    A reasonable range is cubes between 2^3 and 7^3, or $\{8, 27, 64, 125, 216, 343\}$.

23a. **Represent Real-World Problems** Tanya is printing a report. There are 100 sheets of paper in the printer, and the number of sheets of paper p left after t minutes of printing is given by the function $p(t) = -8t + 100$.

    How many minutes would it take the printer to use all 100 sheets of paper? Show your work.

    $$0 = -8t + 100$$
    $$-100 = -8t$$
    $$t = 12.5 \text{ It would take the printer 12.5 minutes.}$$

   b. What is a reasonable domain for this situation? Explain.

    Since time is continuous, a reasonable domain would be $0 \leq t \leq 12.5$. The printer starts printing at 0 minutes and finishes printing at 12.5 minutes.

   c. What is a reasonable range for this situation? Explain.

    Since there are 100 sheets of paper in the printer and the printer can use them all, a reasonable range would be all whole numbers from 0 to 100.

Lesson Performance Task

Jenna's parents have given her an interest-free loan of $100 to buy a new pair of running shoes. She plans to pay back the loan with monthly payments of $20 each.

a. Write a function rule for the balance function $B(p)$, where p represents the number of payments that Jenna has made.

b. After how many payments will Jenna have paid back more than half the loan? Explain your reasoning.

c. Suppose the loan amount were $120 and the monthly payments were $15. Write a rule for the new balance function and use it to determine how long it would take Jenna to pay off the loan.

a. $B(p) = 100 - 20p$

b. After 3 payments. Students may reason that $B(p)$ will never equal exactly half of the loan ($50), but after 3 payments the balance will be less than $50.

c. $B(p) = 120 - 15p$; set $B(p)$ equal to zero and solve for p:

$$B(p) = 120 - 15p$$
$$0 = 120 - 15p$$
$$-120 = -15p$$
$$8 = p$$

Thus, it would take Jenna 8 months to pay off the loan.

© Houghton Mifflin Harcourt Publishing Company • Image Credits: ©OSOMEDIA/age fotostock

---

EXTENSION ACTIVITY

Have students research their graphing calculator manuals to learn how to enter selected x values in the **TABLE** feature of their calculators. Then have students explain how to use their graphing calculators to find the balance after each payment, using the function rules they determined for the Lesson Performance Task.

Students should find that they can enter any domain value x and generate a table that shows the corresponding range value $f(x)$ in the second column.

LANGUAGE SUPPORT EL

Act out a situation that involves loaning money and paying it back to help students understand the meaning of the terms *interest-free*, *loan*, *balance*, and *payment*.

INTEGRATE TECHNOLOGY

Have students work in pairs to use a computer spreadsheet program to construct a schedule showing Jenna's repayment of the loan.

INTEGRATE MATHEMATICAL PRACTICES
Focus on Reasoning

MP.2 Half of $100 is $50. Since $50 is not evenly divisible by $20, the balance of a $100 loan will never be exactly $50. Half of $120 is $60. Since $15 goes into $60 exactly 4 times, the balance of a $120 loan will be exactly $60 after 4 payments. Have students find other examples and counterexamples to justify the conclusion that for the balance to equal exactly half the interest-free original loan, the value of half the loan must be evenly divisible by the monthly payment.

Scoring Rubric
2 points: Student correctly solves the problem and explains his/her reasoning.
1 point: Student shows good understanding of the problem but does not fully solve or explain his/her reasoning.
0 points: Student does not demonstrate understanding of the problem.

Graphing Functions

Common Core Math Standards

The student is expected to:

 F-IF.A.1

Understand that... if *f* is a function and *x* is an element of its domain, then *f(x)* denotes the output of f corresponding to the input *x*... the graph of *f* is the graph of... $y = f(x)$. Also F-IF.A.2

Mathematical Practices

COMMON CORE **MP.6 Precision**

Language Objective

Explain to a partner how to graph a real-world function.

ENGAGE

Essential Question: How do you graph functions?

You can use a table of values to generate ordered pairs. If the graph is discrete, plot only the points; if the graph is continuous, connect the points with a line or curve.

PREVIEW: LESSON PERFORMANCE TASK

View the Engage section online. Discuss how the bullet train differs from typical commuter trains found in most cities. Then preview the Lesson Performance Task.

3.4 Graphing Functions

Essential Question: How do you graph functions?

Resource Locker

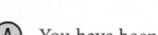 Explore Graphing Functions Using a Given Domain

Recall that the domain of a function is the set of input values, or *x*-values, of the function and that the range is the set of corresponding output values, or *y*-values, of the function. One way to understand a function and its features is to graph it. You can graph a function by finding ordered pairs that satisfy the function.

Graph the function for the given domain.

$x + 3y = 15$ D: {0, 3, 6, 9}

(A) You have been given the input values, *x*, of the domain. You need to solve the function for *y*.

$$x + 3y = 15$$

$$\underline{\quad -x \qquad -x \quad}$$ Subtract *x* from both sides.

$$3y = \boxed{-x + 15}$$

$$\frac{3y}{3} = \frac{\boxed{-x + 15}}{3}$$ Since *y* is multiplied by 3, divide both sides by 3.

$$y = \boxed{-\frac{x}{3}} + \boxed{\frac{15}{3}}$$ Rewrite the right side as two separate fractions.

$$y = \boxed{-\frac{1}{3}x} + \boxed{5}$$ Simplify.

(B) Substitute the given values of the domain for *x* to find the values of *y*.

(C) Graph the ordered pairs.

x	$y = -\frac{1}{3}x + 5$	(x, y)
0	$y = -\frac{1}{3}(0) + 5 = \boxed{5}$	$\left(0, \boxed{5}\right)$
3	$y = -\frac{1}{3}\left(\boxed{3}\right) + 5 = 4$	$\left(\boxed{3}, 4\right)$
6	$y = -\frac{1}{3}(6) + 5 = \boxed{3}$	$\left(6, \boxed{3}\right)$
9	$y = -\frac{1}{3}\left(\boxed{9}\right) + 5 = 2$	$\left(\boxed{9}, \boxed{2}\right)$

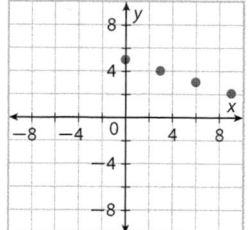

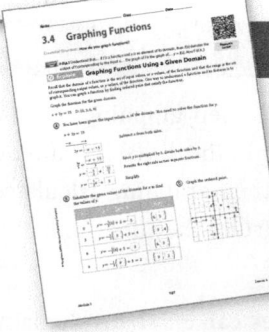

HARDCOVER PAGES 113–120

Turn to these pages to find this lesson in the hardcover student edition.

Reflect

1. **Discussion** Why do you not connect the points of the graph?
   The domain is {0, 3, 6, 9}. This results in a range of {2, 3, 4, 5}. Since there are no other numbers in the domain, there are no other numbers in the range and the function consists of only four points.

2. **Discussion** How would the graph be different if the domain was $0 \leq x \leq 9$?
   The range would consist of all numbers from 2 to 5 ($2 \leq y \leq 5$). The graph would be a line segment going from (0, 5) to (9, 2).

⊘ Explain 1 **Graphing Functions Using a Domain of All Real Numbers**

If the domain of a function is all real numbers, any number can be used as an input value producing an infinite number of ordered pairs that satisfy the function. Arrowheads are drawn at both ends of a smooth line or curve to represent the infinite number of ordered pairs. If a domain is not provided, it should be assumed that the domain is all real numbers.

Graphing Functions Using a Domain of All Real Numbers	
Step 1	Use the function to generate ordered pairs by choosing several values of x.
Step 2	Plot enough points to see a pattern for the graph.
Step 3	Connect the points with a line or smooth curve.

Example 1 Graph each function.

Ⓐ $y = x^2$

Use several values of x to generate ordered pairs. Plot the points from the table, and draw a smooth curve through the points. Include an arrowhead at each end.

x	$y = x^2$	(x, y)
−3	$y = (-3)^2 = 9$	(−3, 9)
−2	$y = (-2)^2 = 4$	(−2, 4)
−1	$y = (-1)^2 = 1$	(−1, 1)
0	$y = (0)^2 = 0$	(0, 0)
1	$y = (1)^2 = 1$	(1, 1)
2	$y = (2)^2 = 4$	(2, 4)
3	$y = (3)^2 = 9$	(3, 9)

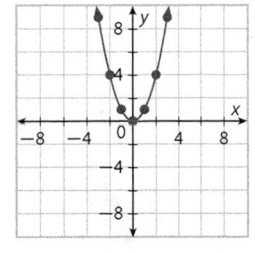

PROFESSIONAL DEVELOPMENT

 Integrate Mathematical Practices

This lesson provides an opportunity to address Mathematical Practice **MP.6**, which calls for students to "communicate with precision." Students learn to graph functions with discrete domains and with domains of all real numbers. They create tables and graphs from function rules and from verbal descriptions of real-world functions, and they find the value of a function from its graph.

EXPLORE

Graphing Functions Using a Given Domain

INTEGRATE TECHNOLOGY

Students have the option of completing the graphing activity either in the book or online.

AVOID COMMON ERRORS

Students sometimes reverse the x- and y-coordinates of a point when they plot it. Remind them that the domain values of a function are the x-coordinates of the points. Point out that they can quickly compare the given domain values to the labels of the vertical grid lines to make sure they have plotted points with the correct x-values.

EXPLAIN 1

Graphing Functions Using a Domain of All Real Numbers

QUESTIONING STRATEGIES

? How is the graph of a function whose domain is all real numbers different from the graph of a function whose domain is a specified set of distinct numbers? If the domain is all real numbers, the graph is a continuous graph (a smooth line or curve); if the domain is a specified set of numbers, the graph is a discrete graph (one consisting of distinct points).

AVOID COMMON ERRORS

Students may think that $-x^2$ is the same as $(-x)^2$. Show students that $-x^2$ will be negative for any value of x, and $(-x)^2$ will be positive for any value of x. For example, $-3^2 = -9$ and $(-3)^2 = 9$.

Ⓑ $f(x) = 3x - 5$

Use several values of x to generate ordered pairs.

x	$f(x) = 3x - 5$	$(x, f(x))$
-1	$f(-1) = 3(-1) - 5 = \boxed{-8}$	$\left(-1, \boxed{-8}\right)$
0	$f\left(\boxed{0}\right) = 3\left(\boxed{0}\right) - 5 = -5$	$\left(\boxed{0}, -5\right)$
1	$f(1) = 3(1) - 5 = \boxed{-2}$	$\left(1, \boxed{-2}\right)$
2	$f\left(\boxed{2}\right) = 3\left(\boxed{2}\right) - 5 = 1$	$\left(\boxed{2}, 1\right)$
3	$f(3) = 3(3) - 5 = \boxed{4}$	$\left(3, \boxed{4}\right)$
4	$f\left(\boxed{4}\right) = 3\left(\boxed{4}\right) - 5 = 7$	$\left(\boxed{4}, 7\right)$

Plot the points from the table to see a pattern.

The points appear to form a ____line____. Draw a ____line____ through all the points to show the ordered pairs that satisfy the function. Draw ____arrowheads____ on both ends of the graph.

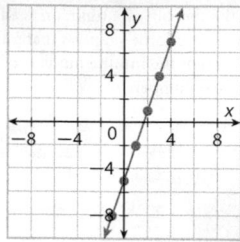

Reflect

3. When graphing a function, does it matter if the function is written in function notation? Explain.

   No; it does not matter it is written using $f(x) =$ or $y =$. In either case, you use the function

   rule to find output values.

Your Turn

Graph each function.

4. $y = -x^2$

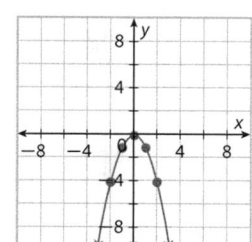

5. $y = -4x + 2$

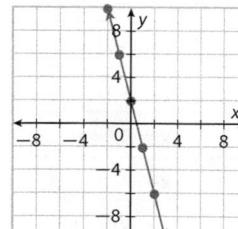

© Houghton Mifflin Harcourt Publishing Company

COLLABORATIVE LEARNING

Whole Class Activity

Give students the function $y = 2.5x$. Explain that it describes the mass in grams of a stack of x pennies minted after 1982. Have each student create a table of values and graph the function. Obtain a balance (displaying grams) and several pennies (post-1982). Ask students to use their graphs to predict the mass of a given number of pennies. Measure the mass of the pennies to check the answers. Repeat with a different number of pennies.

Explain 2   Using a Graph to Find Values

To find the value of a function for a given value of x using a graph, locate the value of x on the x-axis, move up or down to the graph of the function, and then move left or right to the y-axis to find the corresponding value of y.

Example 2   Use a graph to find the value of $f(x)$ when $x = -2$ for each function.

(A) $f(x) = -\frac{1}{2}x + 3$

Use a graphing calculator to graph $y = -\frac{1}{2}x + 3$, and use TRACE to find the function value when $x = -2$.

Therefore, the value of y is 4 when x is -2.

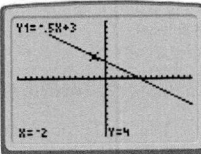

(B) $f(x) = \frac{3}{2}x - 4$

First graph the line. Locate ____**-2**____ on the x-axis. Draw a vertical line segment

from ____**-2**____ on the x-axis to the graph of the function and a horizontal line segment from the graph of the function to the y-axis.

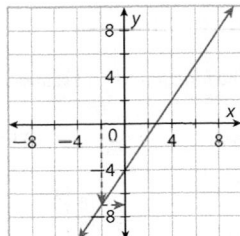

The value of y on the y-axis is the value of the function. Therefore,

the value of $f(x)$ is ____**-7**____ when x is -2.

Your Turn

6.   Use a graph to find the value of $f(x)$ when $x = 3$ for the function $f(x) = -x + 7$.

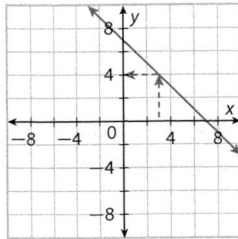

The value of $f(x)$ is 4 when x is 3.

© Houghton Mifflin Harcourt Publishing Company

EXPLAIN 2

Using a Graph to Find Values

AVOID COMMON ERRORS

Students may read $f(x)$ as f times x. To reinforce understanding of function notation, have them first write the function rule, then replace the variable x by the given value. For example, if a problem says to find the value of $f(x)$ when $x = 2$ for the function $f(x) = 3x - 5$, students would write:

$$f(x) = 3x - 5$$

$$f(2) = 3 \cdot 2 - 5$$

QUESTIONING STRATEGIES

?   How could you use a graph to find the value of x for which $f(x)$ equals a given value? **Locate the given value of $f(x)$ on the y-axis. Draw a horizontal line segment from there to the graph of the function, and then draw a vertical line segment to the x-axis to find the corresponding x-value.**

DIFFERENTIATE INSTRUCTION

Modeling

Some students may find it counterintuitive to think of x-values increasing to the right and y-values increasing upward. Due to this, they may have difficulty constructing graphs on a coordinate plane. Have these students draw coordinate planes by first drawing the x- and y-axes with the arrows properly indicating the increasing direction of the x- and y-values.

EXPLAIN 3

Modeling Using a Function Graph

QUESTIONING STRATEGIES

 When you use a graph to find the value of a function for a fractional value of x, why is the result an estimate? The grid lines of the graph are usually shown at whole number intervals, and it is impossible to determine the exact coordinates of a point that does not lie on a grid line.

AVOID COMMON ERRORS

Students may prefer to simply evaluate the function for $x = n$ rather than using the graph. Tell students that learning to read values from a graph is important because some real-world situations are represented by complicated functions that are not easy to evaluate.

INTEGRATE MATHEMATICAL PRACTICES
Focus on Critical Thinking

MP.3 Discuss with students what negative values of x could represent. For example, if x represents time in years, lead them to see that an x-value of -2 could represent 2 years ago. However, if a function describes a process that started at time $x = 0$, then it does not make sense to extend the graph to negative values of x.

⊘ Explain 3   Modeling Using a Function Graph

The domain of a real-world situation may have to be limited in order to have reasonable answers. Only nonnegative numbers can be used to represent quantities such as time, distance, and the number of people. When both the domain and the range of a function are limited to nonnegative values, the function is graphed only in Quadrant I.

The Mid-Atlantic Ridge separates the North and South American Plates from the Eurasian and African Plates. The function $y = 2.5x$ relates the number of centimeters y the Mid-Atlantic Ridge spreads after x years. Graph the function and use the graph to estimate how many centimeters the Mid-Atlantic Ridge spreads in 4.5 years.

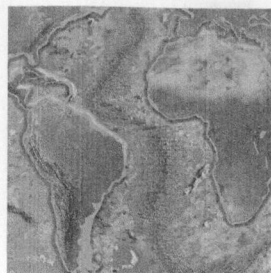

⊞ Analyze Information

Identify the important information:
- The function __$y = 2.5x$__ describes how many centimeters the Mid-Atlantic Ridge spreads after __x__ years.

⊞ Formulate a Plan

Only use __nonnegative__ values of x and y. Use a graph to find the value of __y__ when x is __4.5__.

⊞ Solve

Choose several values of x that are in the domain of the function to find values of y.

x	y = 2.5x	(x, y)
0	$y = 2.5\big(\,0\,\big) = 10$	$\big(\,0\,,0\big)$
2	$y = 2.5(2) = \boxed{5}$	$\big(2,\,\boxed{5}\,\big)$
4	$y = 2.5\big(\,4\,\big) = 10$	$\big(\,4\,,10\big)$
5	$y = 2.5(5) = \boxed{12.5}$	$\big(5,\,\boxed{12.5}\,\big)$

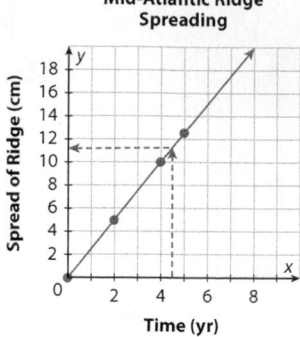

Mid-Atlantic Ridge Spreading
(Spread of Ridge (cm) vs Time (yr))

Plot the points that represent the ordered pairs on the graph. Draw a __line__ through all of the points because the points appear to form a __line__.

Use the graph to estimate the y-value when x is 4.5.
The Mid-Atlantic Ridge spreads about __11.25__ centimeters after 4.5 years.

⊞ Justify and Evaluate

The distance of the Mid-Atlantic Ridge spread __increases__ as the number of years increases, so the graph is reasonable. When x is between 4 and 5, y is between __10__ and __12.5__. Since 4.5 is between 4 and 5, it is reasonable to estimate y to be __11.25__ when x is 4.5.

LANGUAGE SUPPORT EL

Connect Vocabulary

As you work with English learners in this lesson, preview the words and topics of the word problems. Previewing the lesson for words and topics that students may struggle with can help eliminate extra distractions, making it easier for students to focus on the math.

7. A cruise ship is currently 5 kilometers away from its port and is traveling away from the port at 15 kilometers per hour. The function $y = 15x + 5$ relates the number of kilometers y the ship will be from its port x hours from now. How far will the cruise ship be from its port 2.5 hours from now?

x	y = 15x + 5	(x, y)
0	$y = 15(0) + 5 = 5$	(0, 5)
1	$y = 15(1) + 5 = 20$	(1, 20)
2	$y = 15(2) + 5 = 35$	(2, 35)
3	$y = 15(3) + 5 = 50$	(3, 50)

Distance from Port

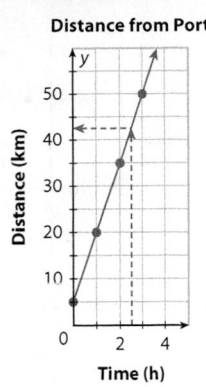

Use the graph to estimate the y-value when $x = 2.5$. The cruise ship will be about 42.5 kilometers from port 2.5 hours from now.

When x is between 2 and 3, y is between 35 and 50, so 42.5 km is reasonable.

Elaborate

8. Is it enough to plot two points to see a pattern for a graph? Explain.
No; two points will not allow you to see whether the pattern is a line or a smooth curve. It is best to plot at least four or five points to see the pattern.

9. **Discussion** When you use a graph to find the value of a function for a specific value of x, do you always get an exact answer? Explain.
No; if the graph involves very large or very small numbers, the scales on the graph may not be accurate enough to give an exact answer. Using a graphing calculator will most likely give a more exact answer than drawing vertical and horizontal lines on a graph on paper.

10. **Essential Question Check-In** How do you graph a function that has a domain of all real numbers?
Use the function to find several ordered pairs by choosing values of x, plot enough points to find a pattern for the graph, and connect the points with a line or smooth curve.

ELABORATE

AVOID COMMON ERRORS

When graphing a function, students may try to draw a curve without plotting enough points to show its shape correctly. Encourage them to plot at least five points and to include both positive and negative values of x.

SUMMARIZE THE LESSON

? How is graphing a function that describes a real-world situation similar to graphing a function that is not a real-world situation? How is it different? In both cases, you choose some values for x, substitute them in the function to find corresponding values for y, and plot the points. If the function describes a real-world situation, use the given context to choose an appropriate domain and to decide whether the points should be distinct or connected. If it is not a real-world situation, use a domain of all real numbers and connect the points with a smooth line or curve.

ASSIGNMENT GUIDE

Concepts and Skills	Practice
Explore Activity Graphing Functions Using a Given Domain	Exercises 1–4
Example 1 Graphing Functions Using a Domain of All Real Numbers	Exercises 5–8, 24
Example 2 Using a Graph to Find Values	Exercises 9–16, 23
Example 3 Modeling Using a Function Graph	Exercises 17–22

QUESTIONING STRATEGIES

? What is the benefit of solving for y before graphing a function? It is easier to substitute values for x and solve for the corresponding y values when the equation has been solved for y.

⭐ Evaluate: Homework and Practice

• Online Homework
• Hints and Help
• Extra Practice

Graph each function for the given domain.

1. $y = 2x$ D:$\{-2, 0, 2, 4\}$

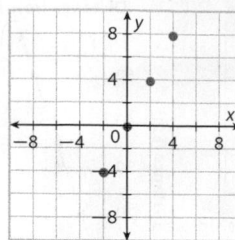

2. $y = \frac{1}{4}x + 5$ D:$\{-8, -4, 0, 4\}$

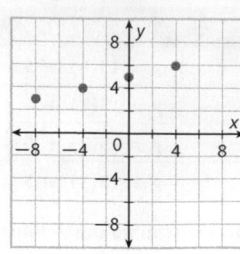

3. $-3x - 5y = 20$ D:$\{-10, -5, 0, 5\}$

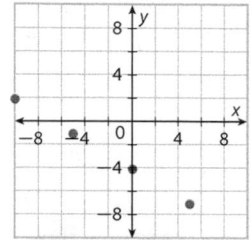

4. $y = x^2 - 3$ D:$\{-2, -1, 0, 1, 2\}$

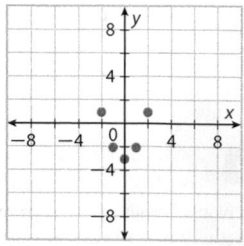

Graph each function.

5. $y = -x^2 + 5$

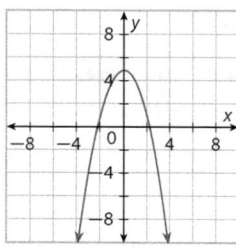

6. $y = \frac{2}{3}x - 1$

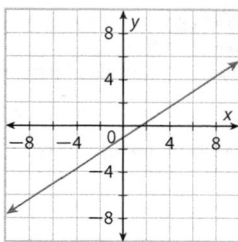

Exercise	Depth of Knowledge (D.O.K.)	COMMON CORE Mathematical Practices
1–8	**1** Recall of Information	**MP.4** Modeling
9–13	**1** Recall of Information	**MP.5** Using Tools
14–16	**1** Recall of Information	**MP.2** Reasoning
17–22	**2** Skills/Concepts	**MP.4** Modeling
23	**3** Skills/Concepts H.O.T.	**MP.3** Logic
24	**3** Strategic Thinking H.O.T.	**MP.3** Logic

7. $x + y = 0$

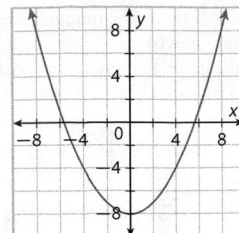

8. $y = \frac{1}{4}x^2 - 8$

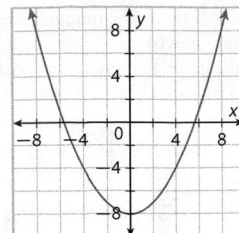

Use a graphing calculator to find the value of $f(x)$ when $x = 3$ for each function.

9. $f(x) = \frac{1}{3}x - 2$

$f(3) = -1$

10. $f(x) = -x^2 - 4$

$f(3) = -13$

Use a graphing calculator to find the value of $f(x)$ when $x = -4$ for each function.

11. $fx = x^2 - 3$

$f(-4) = 13$

12. $f(x) = -4x - \frac{3}{2}$

$f(-4) = 14.5$

13. $f(x) = -\frac{9}{2}x^2 - 5$

$f(-4) = -77$

14. Graph $f(x) = 8 + 2x$. Then find the value of $f(x)$ when $x = \frac{1}{2}$.

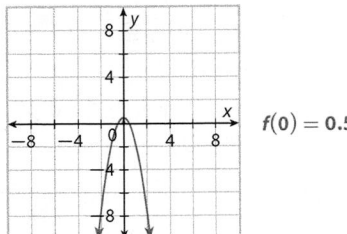

$f\left(\frac{1}{2}\right) = 9$

15. Graph $f(x) = 0.5 - 2x^2$. Then find the value of $f(x)$ when $x = 0$.

$f(0) = 0.5$

16. Graph $f(x) = \frac{1}{4}x^2$. Then find the value of $f(x)$ when $x = -6$.

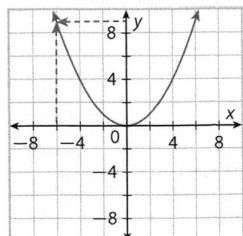

$f(-6) = 9$

AVOID COMMON ERRORS

After creating a table of values to graph a function, students may forget to connect the points that they plot. Remind students that if the domain of a function is all real numbers, they need to connect the points to create a smooth line or curve. Arrows should be drawn at the ends of the curve to show that it continues in both directions.

INTEGRATE TECHNOLOGY

It may be difficult for students to see whether points they have plotted lie along a curve or a line. To verify the shape of the curve, have students graph the function on a graphing calculator using a large window.

When graphing a function, suggest that students choose simple values for *x*, such as 0, 1, and 2. They should also be sure to choose negative values when the domain is all real numbers.

17. The fastest recorded Hawaiian lava flow moved at an average speed of 6 miles per hour. The function $y = 6x$ describes the distance *y* the lava moved on average in *x* hours. Graph the function. Use the graph to estimate how many miles the lava moved after 4.5 hours.

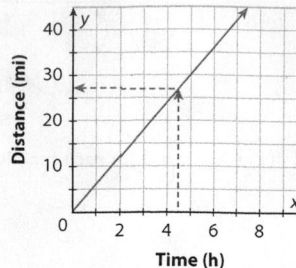

The lava flowed about 27 miles after 4.5 hours.

18. The total cost of a cab ride can be represented by the function $f(x) = 3x + 2.5$, where *x* is the number of miles driven. Graph the function. Use the graph to estimate how much the cab will cost if the cab ride is 8 miles.

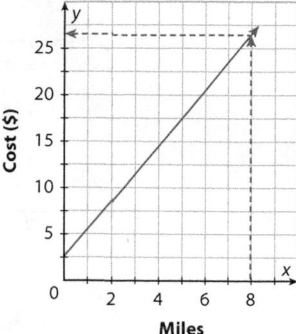

The cab ride will cost about $26.50.

19. Joshua is driving to the store. The average distance *d* in miles he travels over *t* minutes is given by the function $d(t) = 0.5t$. Graph the function. Use the graph to estimate how many miles he drove after 5 minutes.

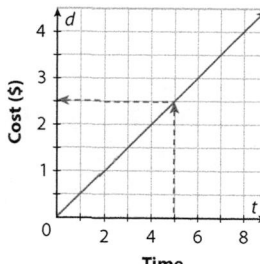

Joshua drove 2.5 miles in 5 minutes.

20. The production cost for g graphing calculators is $C(g) = 15g$. Graph the function and then evaluate it when $g = 15$. What does the value of the function at $g = 15$ represent?

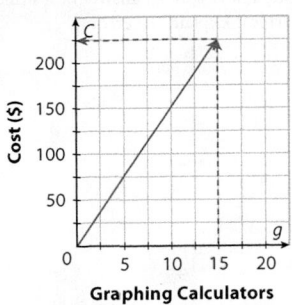

The function is about 225 when $g = 15$.

This means that the production cost for

15 graphing calculators is about $225.

21. The temperature, in degrees Fahrenheit, of a liquid that is increasing can be represented by the equation $f(t) = 64 + 4t$, where t is the time in hours. Graph the function to show the temperatures over the first 10 hours. Use the graph to find the temperature after 7 hours.

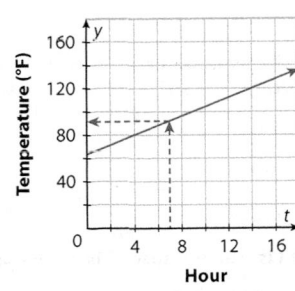

The temperature after 7 hours is about

92 °F.

22. A snowboarder's elevation, in feet, can be represented by the function $E(t) = 3000 - 70t$, where t is in seconds. Graph the function and find the elevation of the snowboarder after 30 seconds.

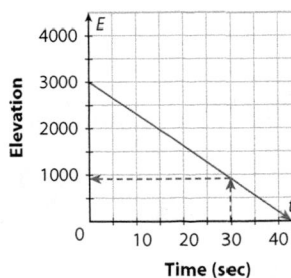

After 30 seconds, the snowboarder is at

about 900 feet.

INTEGRATE TECHNOLOGY

To use a graphing calculator to find a value of a continuous function, press **Y =** and enter the function rule. Press **TRACE**, enter the given value of x, and the display will show the corresponding value of y.

QUESTIONING STRATEGIES

What are the steps for graphing a function? Solve for y, choose values for x, generate ordered pairs, and graph.

Have students explain how to choose points when graphing a function, using the function $y = x^2 + 1$ to illustrate the process.

23. Explain the Error Student A and student B were given the following graph and asked to find the value of $f(x)$ when $x = 1$. Student A gave an answer of 0 while student B gave an answer of -2. Who is incorrect? Explain the error.

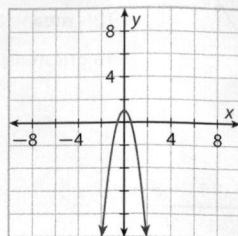

Student A is incorrect. Student A found the value of x when $f(x)$ is 1. The student moved vertically upward first to get to the graph. The student should have moved horizontally first and then vertically downward to get to the graph.

24. Justify Reasoning Without graphing, tell which statement(s) are true for the graph of the function $y = x^2 + 1$. Explain your choices.

  I. All points on the graph are above the origin.

  II. All points on the graph have positive x-values.

  III. All points on the graph have positive y-values.

Statements I and III are true. Statement I is true because x^2 is nonnegative for all values of x, so the minimum value of x^2 is 0. Thus, the minimum y-value for the function is 1 and the lowest point on the graph is (0, 1), which is above the origin. Statement III is true because the lowest point on the graph is (0, 1) so all other points have a y-value that is greater than 1 and must be positive.

Lesson Performance Task

The Japanese Shinkansen, or bullet train, can accelerate rapidly to reach its maximum traveling speed of about 170 miles per hour. The table gives the speed of the train in feet per second at several different times.

Time (seconds)	Speed (feet per second)
0	0
1	2.5
4	10
6	15
10	25

a. Convert the data from the table to a set of ordered pairs and graph them on a coordinate grid. Connect the points with a line. What does the line represent?

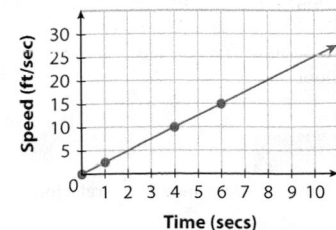

b. What is the slope of the line? What does the slope represent?

c. If the acceleration remains constant, how long will it take the train to reach its maximum speed of 170 miles per hour (mph)? [1 mph equals about 1.5 feet per second]

a. The line represents the speed of the train over time.

b. The slope of the line is 2.5; the slope represents the acceleration of the train (2.5 ft/sec/sec).

c. At a constant acceleration, it will take the train 102 seconds to reach its maximum speed.

© Houghton Mifflin Harcourt Publishing Company

EXTENSION ACTIVITY

Have students locate two cities found along the same interstate highway. Have them calculate the time it would take to travel by car from the exit for one of the cities to the exit for the other, following the posted speed limits. Discuss how the travel time would change if the interstate were replaced by a bullet train going 170 miles per hour. Students should find that the bullet train takes less than half as long as a car to travel a given distance, but they might note that additional time would be needed at the station to wait for a train.

CONNECT VOCABULARY EL

Clarify that to *accelerate* is to change speed or velocity. In everyday use, it refers to increasing speed, but in formal scientific language, *accelerate* can refer to any change in speed or direction. Have students suggest other contexts in which they have heard these words, such as the *accelerator pedal* on a car, or an *accelerated program*, which allows students to complete a course more quickly.

INTEGRATE MATHEMATICAL PRACTICES

Focus on Critical Thinking

MP.3 Discuss what a reasonable domain is for the situation in the Lesson Performance Task. Since x represents time (in seconds), students should see that an x-value of -1 represents 1 second before the train started moving, so negative values for x would not make sense. Since all positive values of x could be acceptable, students should conclude that x is a continuous variable and not a discrete variable.

Study Guide Review

ASSESSMENT AND INTERVENTION

Assign or customize module reviews.

MODULE PERFORMANCE TASK

COMMON CORE

Mathematical Practices: MP.1, MP.2, MP.4, MP.6
F-IF.B.4, A-CED.A.2

SUPPORTING STUDENT REASONING

Students should begin this problem by writing an equation for each Plan. Here are some questions they might have.

- **What is the maximum number of months?** Tell students that a season pass is for no more than one year.

- **Can I just pick a number of months and decide which Plan is best for it?** Encourage students to compare the Plans for a full year.

- **For Plans B and C, is the first monthly payment in the first or second month?** Have students assume that the first bi-monthly payment for Plan B is in month 2 and the first monthly payment for Plan C is in month 1.

Essential Question: How can you use functions to solve real-world problems?

© Houghton Mifflin Harcourt Publishing Company

Key Vocabulary

continuous graph
(gráfica continua)
dependent variable
(variable dependiente)
discrete graph
(gráfica discreta)
domain *(dominio)*
function *(función)*
function notation
(notación de función)
independent variable
(variable independiente)
range *(rango)*
relation *(relación)*

KEY EXAMPLE *(Lesson 3.1)*

The graph below represents Robert's total distance traveled during his walk to school. Write a possible situation for the graph.

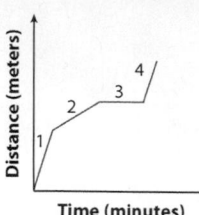

Sections 1 and 4 are steeper than section 2, so Robert was walking faster during these times.

Section 3 is horizontal, so Robert was not moving during this time.

Possible Situation: Robert walked quickly at the beginning of his walk, then he walked at a slower pace. He stopped for a while to talk to some friends. Then, he walked quickly the rest of the way to school.

KEY EXAMPLE *(Lesson 3.2)*

Give the domain and range of the relation. Explain whether the relation is a function.

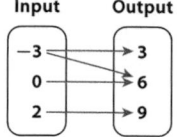

The domain is all inputs, or $\{-3, 0, 2\}$.

The range is all outputs, or $\{3, 6, 9\}$.

A function has at most one output value for each input. The relation is not a function, because the input value -3 has more than one output.

KEY EXAMPLE *(Lessons 3.3, 3.4)*

Write an equation in function notation for the following example, and graph the function.

A study skills tutor charges $8 an hour for sessions lasting 1, 2, 3, or 4 hours.

The independent variable x is the number of hours.

The dependent variable $f(x)$ is the total cost.

The function for the total cost is $f(x) = 8x$.

The ordered pairs for the function $f(x) = 8x$ for the domain $\{1, 2, 3, 4\}$ are $(1, 8)$, $(2, 16)$, $(3, 24)$, and $(4, 32)$.

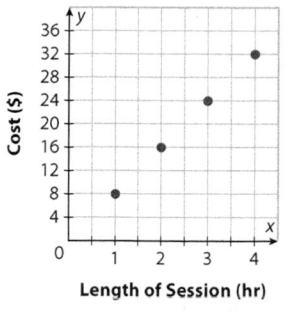

Length of Session (hr)

SCAFFOLDING SUPPORT

- For students who need more structure, suggest they compare only Plans A and C.

- Watch for students who want to represent each of these functions as a linear model. Ask them how they might represent plans to reflect the total cost after a fractional part of a month.

EXERCISES

1. Sketch a graph that represents the following situation. A person gets on a ride at an amusement park. The ride rises slowly and then quickly to its highest point. Then, to build anticipation, the ride stops for a period of time before quickly falling. Then, the ride descends more slowly before coming to a stop. *(Lesson 3.1)*

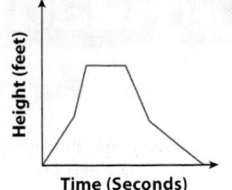

Height (feet)

Time (Seconds)

2. Identify the independent and dependent variables of the following relation. Give the domain and range, and explain whether the relation is a function.

   A farmer has up to 3 pigs at a time on his farm. The given relation represents the average number of pounds of feed needed for *x* pigs daily. *(Lesson 3.2)*

Number of Pigs, x	Pounds of Feed, y
1	55
2	110
3	165

independent variable: number of pigs; dependent variable: pounds of feed; Domain: {1, 2, 3}; Range: {55, 110, 165}; The relation is a function, because each input has a unique output.

3. A store sells roasted peanuts in 1, 2, 2.5, and 4 pound bags. The peanuts cost $4 per pound. Write an equation in function notation that represents the cost of the peanuts in terms of the number of pounds, and graph the function. *(Lessons 3.3, 3.4)*

$f(x) = 4x$

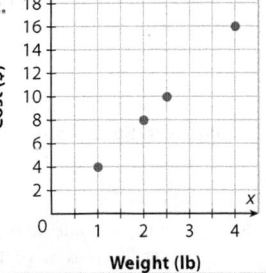

Cost ($) / Weight (lb)

MODULE PERFORMANCE TASK

Season Passes

Wild Planet Theme Park offers three season-pass purchase options.

Plan A	Plan B	Plan C
One payment of $500	$80 down payment 6 payments of $75 every other month	$60 down payment 11 monthly payments of $45

Which payment option is the least expensive?

Use your own paper to complete the task. Be sure to write down all your data. Then use graphs, numbers, words, or algebra to explain how you reached your conclusion.

DISCUSSION OPPORTUNITIES

- Ask if there might be good reasons for choosing Plan B or Plan C, even though they cost more than Plan A in the long run.

- Ask students to interpret the *y*-intercepts of their graphs.

- Have students write an equation that will give *y*, the total amount for Plan C, for all whole number values of *x* from 0 to 11.

$y = 60 + 45n$

Points to plot (month, total paid):

Plan A	Plan B	Plan C
The total amount is $500 for all values of x.	(0, 80)	(0, 60)
	(1, 80)	(1, 105)
	(2, 155)	(2, 150)
	(3, 155)	(3, 195)
	(4, 230)	(4, 240)
	(5, 230)	(5, 285)
	(6, 305)	(6, 330)
	(7, 305)	(7, 375)
	(8, 380)	(8, 420)
	(9, 380)	(9, 465)
	(10, 455)	(10, 510)
	(11, 455)	(11, 555)
	(12, 530)	(12, 555)

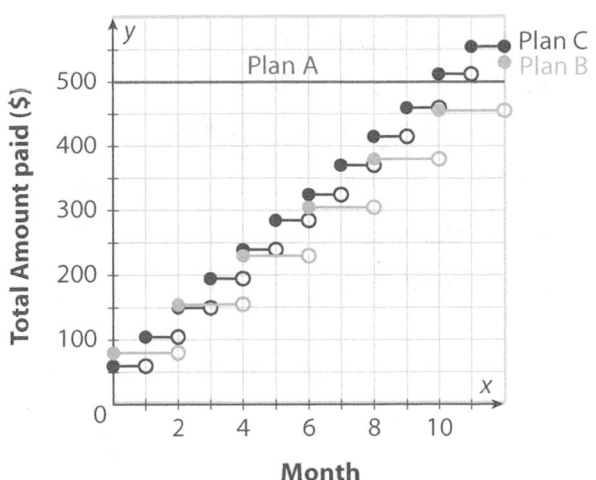

Plan A is most expensive in months 0 through 9. It becomes least expensive in month 12.

Assessment Rubric

2 points: Student correctly solves the problem and explains his/her reasoning.

1 point: Student shows good understanding of the problem but does not fully solve or explain.

0 points: Student does not demonstrate understanding of the problem.

Ready to Go On?

ASSESS MASTERY

Use the assessment on this page to determine if students have mastered the concepts and standards covered in this module.

ASSESSMENT AND INTERVENTION

Access Ready to Go On? assessment online, and receive instant scoring, feedback, and customized intervention or enrichment.

ADDITIONAL RESOURCES

Response to Intervention Resources

- Reteach Worksheets

Differentiated Instruction Resources

- Reading Strategies **EL**
- Success for English Learners **EL**
- Challenge Worksheets

Assessment Resources

- Leveled Module Quizzes

(Ready) to Go On?

3.1–3.4 Functions and Models

1. The graph shown represents the altitude of a hiker during a period of time. Write a possible situation represented by the graph. *(Lesson 3.1)*

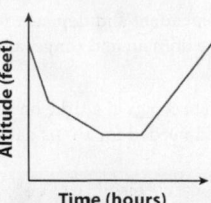

Possible Situation: The hiker walked downhill quickly and then slowly. The hiker rested at the lowest point of the hike. Then, the hiker hiked back uphill at a steady pace.

2. Use the vertical line test to determine if the relation represented on the graph from **Exercise 1** is a function. Explain. *(Lesson 3.2)*

Since no vertical line will pass through more than one point, the graph passes the vertical line test. So, the relation is a function.

3. A math test is made up of 7 problems, each worth 10 points. There is no partial credit. Every test taker receives 30 points for taking the test. Write a function to describe the test score determined by the number of correct answers. Graph the function using a reasonable domain and range. *(Lessons 3.3, 3.4)*

$f(x) = 10x + 30$

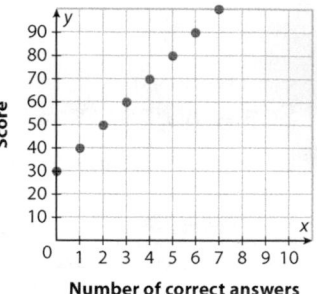

ESSENTIAL QUESTION

4. What is a function?

Possible Answer: A function is a set of ordered pairs in which each term in the domain is paired with exactly one term in the range.

© Houghton Mifflin Harcourt Publishing Company

COMMON CORE Common Core Standards

Lesson	Items	Content Standards	Mathematical Practices
3.1	1	**A-REI.A.1**	**8.1.A**
3.2	2	**8.2.A**	**8.1.F**
3.3, 3.4	3	**8.2.A**	**8.1.F**

MODULE 3
MIXED REVIEW

Assessment Readiness

1. Kyle is installing new baseboards and carpet in his rectangular living room. He measured the length as 24.25 feet and the width as 16.4 feet. Select Yes or No for each statement.

   A. The length is a more precise measurement.   ● Yes   ○ No

   B. The area of the room should be given with 3 significant digits.   ● Yes   ○ No

   C. The perimeter of the room should be given with 4 significant digits   ○ Yes   ● No

2. The graph represents the function $f(x) = -x^2 + 2$. Select True or False for each statement.

   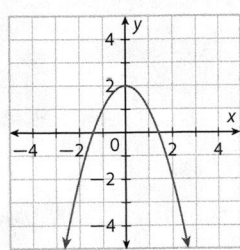

   A. When $x = 1$, $f(x) = 1$.   ● True   ○ False

   B. When $f(x) = 2$, $x = -2$.   ○ True   ● False

   C. When $x = -1$, $f(x) = 1$.   ● True   ○ False

3. The mapping diagram represents the age, in years, and height, rounded to the nearest inch, of a group of friends. Does the diagram represent a function? Explain your answer.

   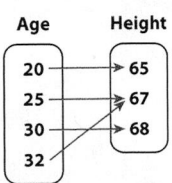

   Yes, the diagram represents a function, because each input value is assigned to exactly one output value.

4. An amusement park charges an entrance fee of $25 plus $3.50 per ride. Write a function to represent this situation. How much would it cost to go to the park and ride 8 rides?

   $f(x) = 3.5x + 25$; **it would cost $53.**

MIXED REVIEW
Assessment Readiness

ASSESSMENT AND INTERVENTION

Assign ready-made or customized practice tests to prepare students for high-stakes tests.

ADDITIONAL RESOURCES

Assessment Resources

- Leveled Module Quizzes: Modified, B

AVOID COMMON ERRORS

Item 2   Some students have difficulty associating $f(x)$ and y. Encourage students to label the y-axis with $f(x)$ to remind them that the notations represent the same thing.

COMMON CORE | Common Core Standards

Lesson	Items	Content Standards	Mathematical Practices
1.1	1*	8.2.B	8.1.A
8.1	2	8.2.A	8.1.F
12.2	3	8.2.A	8.1.F
18.2	4*	8.2.A	8.1.A

* Item integrates mixed review concepts from previous modules or a previous course.

Patterns and Sequences

ESSENTIAL QUESTION:

Answer: You can find an explicit rule for a real-world sequence. You can then use that explicit rule to find any specific term in a sequence without finding any of the previous terms.

PROFESSIONAL DEVELOPMENT VIDEO

Professional Development Video

Learn effective ways of integrating technology into your classroom to meet a variety of different needs.

Professional
Development
my.hrw.com

MODULE **4**

Patterns and Sequences

Essential Question: How are patterns and sequences used to solve real-world problems?

LESSON 4.1
Identifying and Graphing Sequences

LESSON 4.2
Constructing Arithmetic Sequences

LESSON 4.3
Modeling with Arithmetic Sequences

© Houghton Mifflin Harcourt Publishing Company · Image Credits: ©Dusit/Shutterstock

REAL WORLD VIDEO
Today's calculators, apps, and computer software can perform even the most complex calculations almost instantly. Programming based on patterns and sequences makes these modern marvels possible.

MODULE PERFORMANCE TASK PREVIEW
There Has to Be an Easier Way

Carl Friedrich Gauss, one of the greatest mathematicians of all time, showed his genius at a very early age. When he was just ten, his teacher presented a math problem that the teacher thought would keep the class occupied for a long time. Surprise! Gauss solved the problem almost before the teacher had finished stating it. In this module, you'll get a chance to tackle the same problem Gauss solved. Use a creative method to find the answer and you'll be famous too!

DIGITAL TEACHER EDITION

Access a full suite of teaching resources when and where you need them:

- Access content online or offline
- Customize lessons to share with your class
- Communicate with your students in real-time
- View student grades and data instantly to target your instruction where it is needed most

PERSONAL MATH TRAINER
Assessment and Intervention

Assign automatically graded homework, quizzes, tests, and intervention activities. Prepare your students with updated, Common Core-aligned practice tests.

Are (YOU) Ready?

Complete these exercises to review skills you will need for this module.

- Online Homework
- Hints and Help
- Extra Practice

Number Patterns

Example 1   Find the next three numbers in the pattern 2, 5, 8, 11, …

$$2 \quad 5 \quad 8 \quad 11$$

$$\underbrace{\qquad}_{+3} \underbrace{\qquad}_{+3} \underbrace{\qquad}_{+3}$$

Study the pattern in the sequence.

Each number is 3 more than the number before it.

$11 + 3 = 14$

$14 + 3 = 17$

$17 + 3 = 20$

The next 3 numbers will be 14, 17, and 20.

Find the next three numbers in each pattern.

1. 2, 4, 8, 16, …

32, 64, 128

2. 5, 11, 17, 23, …

29, 35, 41

3. 50, 43, 36, 29, …

22, 15, 8

4. 1, 4, 9, 16, …

25, 36, 49

Algebraic Expressions

Example 2   Evaluate $2x + 3y$ for $x = 4$ and $y = -5$.

$2x + 3y$

$2(4) + 3(-5)$ Substitute 4 for *x* and −5 for *y*.

$8 + (-15)$ Multiply.

-7 Add.

Evaluate each expression for the given values of the variables.

5. $4p - 7p$ for $p = 8$ and $q = 5$

−3

6. $(n - 1)^2$ for $n = -4$

25

7. $8d + 5e - 11$ for $d = 6$ and $e = -9$

−8

8. $a^2 - b$ for $a = 7$ and $b = 12$

37

Are You Ready?

ASSESS READINESS

Use the assessment on this page to determine if students need strategic or intensive intervention for the module's prerequisite skills.

ASSESSMENT AND INTERVENTION

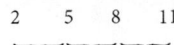

RtI Response to Intervention   **TIER 1, TIER 2, TIER 3 SKILLS**

Personal Math Trainer will automatically create a standards-based, personalized intervention assignment for your students, targeting each student's individual needs!

ADDITIONAL RESOURCES

See the table below for a full list of intervention resources available for this module.

Response to Intervention Resources also includes:
- Tier 2 Skill Pre-Tests for each Module
- Tier 2 Skill Post-Tests for each skill

Response to Intervention			*Differentiated Instruction*
Tier 1	**Tier 2**	**Tier 3**	
Lesson Intervention Worksheets	Strategic Intervention Skills Intervention Worksheets	Intensive Intervention Worksheets available online	
Reteach 4.1 Reteach 4.2 Reteach 4.3	1 Add and Subtract Integers 2 Algebraic Expressions 12 Multiply and Divide Integers	Building Block Skills 19, 22, 23, 24, 26, 27, 40, 58, 59, 81, 105, 107	Challenge worksheets Extend the Math Lesson Activities in TE

Identifying and Graphing Sequences

Common Core Math Standards

The student is expected to:

 **F-IF.A.3**

Recognize that sequences are functions, sometimes defined recursively, whose domain is a subset of the integers. Also F-BF.A.2, F-LE.A.2

Mathematical Practices

 MP.7 Using Structure

Language Objective

Describe rules for sequences using words and symbols.

ENGAGE

Essential Question: What is a sequence and how are sequences and functions related?

Possible answer: A sequence is a list of numbers in a specific order. Because each position number is associated with exactly one term, you can create a function whose domain is the set of the position numbers and whose range is the set of the terms.

PREVIEW: LESSON PERFORMANCE TASK

View the Engage section online. Discuss the photo and the exhibits someone might see at one of the museums in your area. Then preview the Lesson Performance Task.

4.1 Identifying and Graphing Sequences

Essential Question: What is a sequence and how are sequences and functions related?

Resource Locker

⊘ Explore Understanding Sequences

A go-kart racing track charges $5 for a go-kart license and $2 for each lap. If you list the charges for 1 lap, 2 laps, 3 laps, and so on, in order, the list forms a sequence of numbers:

$$7, 9, 11, 13,\ldots$$

A **sequence** is a list of numbers in a specific order. Each element in a sequence is called a **term**. In a sequence, each term has a position number. In the sequence $7, 9, 11, 13,\ldots$, the second term is 9, so its position number is 2.

(A) The total cost (term) of riding a go-kart for different numbers of laps (position) is shown below. Complete the table.

Position number, n	1	2	3	4	5	6	Domain
Term of the sequence, $f(n)$	7	9	11	13	15	17	Range

(B) You can use the term and position number of a sequence to write a function. Using function notation, $f(2) = 9$ indicates that the second term is 9. Use the table to complete the following statements.

$f(1) = \boxed{7}$ $f(3) = \boxed{11}$ $f(6) = \boxed{17}$ $f\left(\boxed{4}\right) = 13$ $f\left(\boxed{5}\right) = 15$

(C) Identify the domain of the function $f(n)$. ___ $\{1,2,3,4,5,6,\ldots\}$

(D) Identify the range of the function $f(n)$. ___ $\{7,9,11,13,15,17,\ldots\}$

Reflect

1. **Discussion** What does $f(4) = 13$ mean in the context of the go-kart problem?
   $f(4) = 13$ **means that the charge for 4 laps will be $13.**

2. **Discussion** Explain how to find the missing values in the table.
   The position number increases by 1; each term in the sequence increases by 2.

3. **Communicate Mathematical Ideas** Explain why the relationship between the position numbers and the corresponding terms of a sequence can be considered a function.
   Each position number corresponds to exactly one term of the sequence.

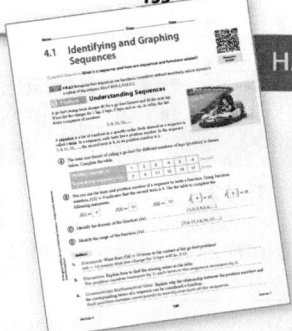

HARDCOVER PAGES 127–134

Turn to these pages to find this lesson in the hardcover student edition.

An **explicit rule** for a sequence defines the nth term as a function of n for any whole number n greater than 0. Explicit rules can be used to find any specific term in a sequence without finding any of the previous terms.

Example 1 Write the first 4 terms of the sequence defined by the **explicit rule**.

Ⓐ $f(n) = n^2 + 2$

Make a table and substitute values for $n = 1, 2, 3, 4$ to find the first 4 terms.

The first 4 terms of the sequence defined by the explicit rule $f(n) = n^2 + 2$ are 3, 6, 11, and 18.

n	$f(n) = n^2 + 2$	$f(n)$
1	$f(1) = 1^2 + 2 = 3$	3
2	$f(2) = 2^2 + 2 = 6$	6
3	$f(3) = 3^2 + 2 = 11$	11
4	$f(4) = 4^2 + 2 = 18$	18

Ⓑ $f(n) = 3n^2 + 1$

Make a table and substitute values for $n = $ **1, 2, 3, 4** .

The first 4 terms are **4, 13, 28, and 49** .

n	$f(n) = 3n^2 + 1$	$f(n)$
1	$f\left(\boxed{1}\right) = 3\left(\boxed{1}\right)^2 + 1 = \boxed{4}$	4
2	$f\left(\boxed{2}\right) = 3\left(\boxed{2}\right)^2 + 1 = \boxed{13}$	13
3	$f\left(\boxed{3}\right) = 3\left(\boxed{3}\right)^2 + 1 = \boxed{28}$	28
4	$f\left(\boxed{4}\right) = 3\left(\boxed{4}\right)^2 + 1 = \boxed{49}$	49

Reflect

4. **Communicate Mathematical Ideas** Explain how to find the 20th term of the sequence defined by the explicit rule $f(n) = n^2 + 2$.

   $f(20) = 20^2 + 2 = 402$ So, the 20ᵗʰ term is 402.

5. **Justify Reasoning** The number 125 is a term of the sequence defined by the explicit rule $f(n) = 3n + 2$. Which term in the sequence is 125? Justify your answer.

   $125 = 3n + 2$

   $123 = 3n$

   $n = 41$ The number 125 is the 41ˢᵗ term.

PROFESSIONAL DEVELOPMENT

COMMON CORE **Integrate Mathematical Practices**

This lesson provides an opportunity to address Mathematical Practice **MP.7**, which calls for students to "look for structure." Students learn to recognize the relationship between sequences and functions. Students learn the precise terms used to describe sequences.

EXPLORE

Understanding Sequences

INTEGRATE TECHNOLOGY

Students have the option of completing the activity either in the book or online.

CONNECT VOCABULARY **EL**

Help students make connections between the ordinary meaning of *sequence* and the mathematical meaning of the term. In ordinary language, a *sequence* is the order in which things occur or are arranged, such as a sequence of events. Point out that a sequence of numbers is a particular type of sequence.

EXPLAIN 1

Generating Sequences Using an Explicit Rule

AVOID COMMON ERRORS

Be sure students pay attention to the domain of the function that defines a sequence. While 1 is often the first number in the domain, some other number (typically 0) can be used instead. A change in the function's inputs will result in a change in the function's outputs, thereby creating a different sequence. For instance, if the domain of

$f(n) = n^2 + 1$ is $\left\{0, 1, 2, 3, \dots\right\}$ rather than $\left\{1, 2, 3, 4, \dots\right\}$, then the function generates the sequence 1, 2, 5, 10, … rather than the sequence 2, 5, 10, 17, ….

QUESTIONING STRATEGIES

? What sequence is generated by the rule $f(n) = 3n$ when the domain is the set of whole numbers greater than 0? Explain your reasoning. **The sequence generated is 3, 6, 9, 12, …; each term is three times the corresponding position number.**

Identifying and Graphing Sequences **156**

EXPLAIN 2

Generating Sequences Using a Recursive Rule

INTEGRATE MATHEMATICAL PRACTICES

Focus on Patterns

MP.8 Have students describe the patterns in the table in the example. Some students may focus on the pattern in the successive terms in the last column of the table. Other students may focus on the rule that associates each number in the domain with a number in the range of the function associated with the sequence.

QUESTIONING STRATEGIES

? How is the sequence $f(n) = 3n$ with the domain the set of whole numbers greater than 0 related to the sequence given by $f(1) = 3$ and $f(n) = f(n-1) + 3$ for each whole number n greater than 1? **Both rules generate the same sequence: 3, 6, 9, 12, ...**

? If you know only that the rule for a sequence is $f(n) = f(n-1) + 2$ and that $f(4) = 9$, is it possible to determine $f(1)$? Explain. **Yes, if you know that $f(4) = 9$, the recursive rule tells you that adding 2 to $f(3)$ gives $f(4)$, so $f(3)$ is 7. Again, the recursive rule tells you that adding 2 to $f(2)$ gives $f(3)$, so $f(2)$ is 5. Finally, the recursive rule tells you that adding 2 to $f(1)$ gives $f(2)$, so $f(1) = 3$.**

AVOID COMMON ERRORS

Some students may confuse explicit and recursive rules. Remind students that an explicit rule for a sequence defines the nth term as a function of n. For example, $f(n) = 4n + 1$, where the domain is the set of whole numbers greater than 0. A recursive rule for a sequence defines the nth term in terms of one or more previous terms. For example, $f(1) = 5$ and $f(n) = f(n-1) + 4$ for each whole number greater than 1; for each whole number greater than 1, the term $f(n)$ is defined in terms of the previous term $f(n-1)$.

157 Lesson 4.1

---

6. Write the first 4 terms of the sequence defined by the explicit rule. $f(n) = n^2 - 5$

n	$f(n) = n^2 - 5$	$f(n)$
1	$f(1) = 1^2 - 5 = -4$	-4
2	$f(2) = 2^2 - 5 = -1$	-1
3	$f(3) = 3^2 - 5 = 4$	4
4	$f(4) = 4^2 - 5 = 11$	11

The first 4 terms are -4, -1, 4, and 11.

7. Find the 15th term of the sequence defined by the explicit rule. $f(n) = 4n - 3$.

Substitute 15 for n in the function $f(n) = 4n - 3$.

$f(15) = 4(15) - 3 = 57$

So, the 15th term is 57.

🔧 Explain 2 Generating Sequences Using a Recursive Rule

A **recursive rule** for a sequence defines the nth term by relating it to one or more previous terms.

The following is an example of a recursive rule:

$f(1) = 4, f(n) = f(n-1) + 10$ for each whole number n greater than 1

This rule means that after the first term of the sequence, every term $f(n)$ is the sum of the pervious term $f(n-1)$ and 10.

Example 2 Write the first 4 terms of the sequence defined by the recursive rule.

(A) $f(1) = 2, f(n) = f(n-1) + 3$ for each whole number n greater than 1

For the first 4 terms, the domain of the function is 1, 2, 3, and 4.

The first term of the sequence is 2.

n	$f(n) = f(n-1) + 3$	$f(n)$
1	$f(1) = 2$	2
2	$f(2) = f(1) + 3 = 2 + 3 = 5$	5
3	$f(3) = f(2) + 3 = 5 + 3 = 8$	8
4	$f(4) = f(3) + 3 = 8 + 3 = 11$	11

The first 4 terms are 2, 5, 8, and 11.

(B) $f(1) = 4, f(n) = f(n-1) + 5$ for each whole number n greater than 1

For the first 4 terms, the domain of the function is <u>1, 2, 3, and 4.</u>

The first term of the sequence is 4 .

n	$f(n) = f(n-1) + 5$	$f(n)$
1	$f(1) = $ 4	4
2	$f(2) = f($ 1 $) + 5 = $ 4 $ + 5 = $ 9	9
3	$f(3) = f($ 2 $) + 5 = $ 9 $ + 5 = $ 14	14
4	$f(4) = f($ 3 $) + 5 = $ 14 $ + 5 = $ 19	19

The first 4 terms are <u>4, 9, 14, and 19</u>.

© Houghton Mifflin Harcourt Publishing Company

COLLABORATIVE LEARNING

Peer-to-Peer Activity

Have students work in pairs. Instruct one student in each pair to generate an explicit rule and specify a domain. Have the second student identify the first four terms in the sequence. Then have the second student generate a recursive rule that will generate the sequence. Have students switch roles and repeat the exercise with a different explicit rule.

Explain 3 **Constructing and Graphing Sequences**

You can graph a sequence on a coordinate plane by plotting the points $(n, f(n))$ indicated in a table that you use to generate the terms.

Example 3 Construct and graph the sequence described.

(A) The go-kart racing charges are $5 for a go-kart license and $2 for each lap. Use the explicit rule $f(n) = 2n + 5$.

Complete the table to represent the cost for the first 4 laps.

n	$f(n) = 2n + 5$	$f(n)$
1	$f(1) = 2(1) + 5 = 2 + 5 = 7$	7
2	$f(2) = 2(2) + 5 = 4 + 5 = 9$	9
3	$f(3) = 2(3) + 5 = 6 + 5 = 11$	11
4	$f(4) = 2(4) + 5 = 8 + 5 = 13$	13

The ordered pairs are (1, 7), (2, 9), (3, 11), (4, 13).

Graph the sequence using the ordered pairs.

Notice that the graph is a set of points that are not connected.

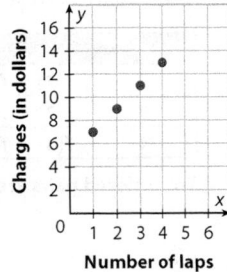

© Houghton Mifflin Harcourt Publishing Company

EXPLAIN 3

Constructing and Graphing Sequences

QUESTIONING STRATEGIES

? How can you graph data from a table representing a sequence? Convert each position number and its related term in the table to an ordered pair, and then plot the pairs on a coordinate plane.

? Should the points on a sequence graph be connected? Explain. No; because a sequence is a set of separate values with no other values between them

INTEGRATE TECHNOLOGY

You may wish to show students how to use a graphing calculator in sequence mode to generate and graph a sequence. Remind students that they must specify a starting value for the sequence, nMin; a pattern or rule for the sequence, $u(n)$; and the first term in the sequence, $u(n$Min$)$.

(B) A movie rental club charges $20 a month plus a $5 membership fee. Use the explicit rule $f(n) = 20n + 5$.

Complete the table to represent the charges paid for 6 months.

n	$f(n) = \boxed{20}\, n + \boxed{5}$							$f(n)$
1	f	$\boxed{1}$	$=$	20	$\boxed{1}$	$+$	5 $=$ $\boxed{25}$	25
2	f	$\boxed{2}$	$=$	20	$\boxed{2}$	$+$	5 $=$ $\boxed{45}$	45
3	f	$\boxed{3}$	$=$	20	$\boxed{3}$	$+$	5 $=$ $\boxed{65}$	65
4	f	$\boxed{4}$	$=$	20	$\boxed{4}$	$+$	5 $=$ $\boxed{85}$	85
5	f	$\boxed{5}$	$=$	20	$\boxed{5}$	$+$	5 $=$ 105	105
6	f	$\boxed{6}$	$=$	20	$\boxed{6}$	$+$	5 $=$ 125	125

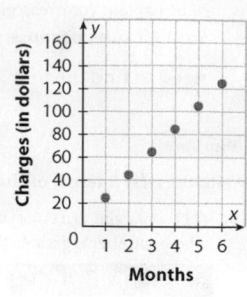

The ordered pairs are <u>(1, 25), (2, 45), (3, 65), (4, 85), (5, 105), and (6, 125)</u>

Graph the sequence using the ordered pairs.

Notice that the graph is a set of points that are not connected.

Reflect

12. Explain why the points in the graphs in Example 3 are not connected.
The domains of these functions only include whole numbers.

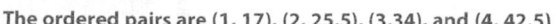

Your Turn

Construct and graph the sequence described.

13. A pizza place is having a special. If you order a large pizza for a regular price $17, you can order any number of additional pizzas for $8.50 each. Use the recursive rule $f(1) = 17$ and $f(n) = f(n - 1) + 8.5$ for each whole number n greater than 1.

n	$f(n) = f(n - 1) + 8.5$	$f(n)$
2	$f(2) = f(1) + 8.5 = 17 + 8.5 = 25.5$	25.5
3	$f(3) = f(2) + 8.5 = 25.5 + 8.5 = 34$	34
4	$f(4) = f(3) + 8.5 = 34 + 8.5 = 42.5$	42.5

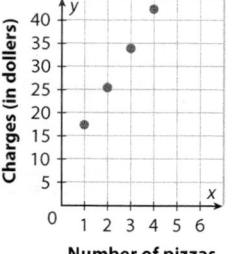

The ordered pairs are (1, 17), (2, 25.5), (3,34), and (4, 42.5).

LANGUAGE SUPPORT **EL**

Communicate Math

Bring English Learners together in a small group to review notes and questions they may have had throughout the unit. Discussing the individual questions in a group setting can strengthen all students' understanding of critical concepts. Have each group member make up a question related to the content. Students can exchange questions, solve them, and then discuss any problems they had.

14. A gym charges $100 as the membership fee and $20 monthly fee. Use the explicit rule $f(n) = 20n + 100$ to construct and graph the sequence.

n	$f(n) = 20n + 100$	$f(n)$
1	$f(1) = 20(1) + 100 = 120$	120
2	$f(2) = 20(2) + 100 = 140$	140
3	$f(3) = 20(3) + 100 = 160$	160
4	$f(4) = 20(4) + 100 = 180$	180
5	$f(5) = 20(5) + 100 = 200$	200
6	$f(6) = 20(6) + 100 = 220$	220

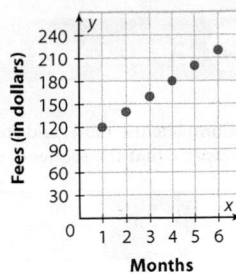

The ordered pairs are (1, 120), (2, 140), (3,160), (4, 180), (5, 200), and (6, 220).

💬 **Elaborate**

15. What is the difference between an explicit rule and a recursive rule?
An explicit rule for a sequence defines the nth term as a function of n and can be used directly to find any specific term in a sequence. A recursive rule defines the nth term relative to a previous term and cannot be used directly to find a specific term.

16. Describe how to use an explicit rule to find the position number of a given term in a sequence.
Substitute the given term for $f(n)$ in the explicit rule, and solve for n.

17. Explain why the graph of a sequence is a set of points that are not connected.
The domain of a sequence is the collection of position numbers, so the domain includes only whole numbers.

18. Essential Question Check-In Why can the rule for a sequence be considered a function?
Each domain value (position number) corresponds to exactly one range value (term of the sequence).

ELABORATE

QUESTIONING STRATEGIES

? Must the difference between successive terms in a sequence always be the same? Explain.
No. There is not a constant difference in the sequence 1, 4, 9, 16,....

? Predict the next term in the sequence $\frac{1}{8}, \frac{1}{4}, \frac{3}{8}, \frac{1}{2}, \frac{5}{8}$.... Explain your reasoning. The next value is $\frac{3}{4}$ because each term is $\frac{1}{8}$ more than the previous term. $\frac{3}{4}$ is $\frac{1}{8}$ more than $\frac{5}{8}$.

SUMMARIZE THE LESSON

? How do you generate a sequence if you are given an explicit rule? A recursive rule? If you are given an explicit rule, you substitute the first few elements of the domain into the rule for the function. If you are given a recursive rule, the first number in the sequence is given by $f(1)$. You use that value to find $f(2)$, $f(3)$, $f(4)$, and so on.

EVALUATE

ASSIGNMENT GUIDE

Concepts and Skills	Practice
Explore Understanding Sequences	Exercises 1–2
Example 1 Generating Sequences Using an Explicit Rule	Exercises 4, 6, 8, 10, 12, 13–15
Example 2 Generating Sequences Using a Recursive Rule	Exercises 3, 5, 7, 9, 11, 16–18, 21–24
Example 3 Constructing and Graphing Sequences	Exercises 19, 20

INTEGRATE MATHEMATICAL PRACTICES

Focus on Communication

MP.3 Encourage students to explain each step of the process they used to solve several of the problems.

Complete the table, and state the domain and range for the sequence it represents. Assume that the sequence continues without end.

1.

n	1	2	3	4	5	6
$f(n)$	15	30	45	60	75	90

Domain: $\{1, 2, 3, 4, 5, 6, \ldots\}$

Range: $\{15, 30, 45, 60, 75, 90, \ldots\}$

2.

n	1	2	3	4	5	6
$f(n)$	6	8	10	12	14	16

Domain: $\{1, 2, 3, 4, 5, 6, \ldots\}$

Range: $\{6, 8, 10, 12, 14, 16, \ldots\}$

Write the first 4 terms of the sequence defined by the given rule.

3. $f(1) = 65{,}536, f(n) = \sqrt{f(n-1)}$

$f(1) = 65{,}536$

$f(2) = \sqrt{65{,}536} = 256$

$f(3) = \sqrt{256} = 16$

$f(4) = \sqrt{16} = 4$

4. $f(n) = n^3 - 1$

$f(1) = 1^3 - 1 = 0$

$f(2) = 2^3 - 1 = 7$

$f(3) = 3^3 - 1 = 26$

$f(4) = 4^3 - 1 = 63$

5. $f(1) = 7, f(n) = -4 \cdot f(n-1) + 15$

$f(1) = 7$

$f(2) = -4 \cdot 7 + 15 = -13$

$f(3) = -4 \cdot (-13) + 15 = 67$

$f(4) = -4 \cdot 67 + 15 = -253$

6. $f(n) = 2n^2 + 4$

$f(1) = 2(1)^2 + 4 = 6$

$f(2) = 2(2)^2 + 4 = 12$

$f(3) = 2(3)^2 + 4 = 22$

$f(4) = 2(4)^2 + 4 = 36$

7. $f(1) = 3, f(n) = [f(n-1)]^2$

$f(1) = 3$

$f(2) = 3^2 = 9$

$f(3) = 9^2 = 81$

$f(4) = 81^2 = 6561$

8. $f(n) = (2n-1)^2$

$f(1) = (2 \cdot 1 - 1)^2 = 1$

$f(2) = (2 \cdot 2 - 1)^2 = 9$

$f(3) = (2 \cdot 3 - 1)^2 = 25$

$f(4) = (2 \cdot 4 - 1)^2 = 49$

© Houghton Mifflin Harcourt Publishing Company

Exercise	Depth of Knowledge (D.O.K.)		COMMON CORE Mathematical Practices
1–18	**2** Skills/Concepts		**MP.2** Reasoning
19–20	**2** Skills/Concepts		**MP.4** Modeling
21–22	**3** Strategic Thinking	H.O.T.	**MP.2** Reasoning
23	**3** Strategic Thinking	H.O.T.	**MP.6** Precision
24	**3** Strategic Thinking	H.O.T.	**MP.2** Reasoning

Find the 10th term of the sequence defined by the given rule.

9. $f(1) = 2, f(n) = f(n-1) + 7$

$f(1) = 2$ $f(2) = 2 + 7 = 9$

$f(3) = 9 + 7 = 16$ $f(4) = 16 + 7 = 23$

$f(5) = 23 + 7 = 30$ $f(6) = 30 + 7 = 37$

$f(7) = 37 + 7 = 44$ $f(8) = 44 + 7 = 51$

$f(9) = 51 + 7 = 58$ $f(10) = 58 + 7 = 65$

The 10th term is 65.

10. $f(n) = \sqrt{n+2}$

$f(10) = \sqrt{10 + 2} = \sqrt{12}$, or $2\sqrt{3}$

11. $f(1) = 30, f(n) = 2 \cdot f(n-1) - 50$

$f(1) = 30$

$f(2) = 2 \cdot 30 - 50 = 10$

$-30, -110, -270, -590, -1230,$
$-2510, -5070, -10,190$

The 10th term is $-10,190$.

12. $f(n) = \frac{1}{2}(n-1) + 3$

$f(10) = \frac{1}{2}(10 - 1) + 3 = \frac{15}{2}$, or $7\frac{1}{2}$, or 7.5

The explicit rule for a sequence and one of the specific terms is given. Find the position of the given term.

13. $f(n) = 1.25n + 6.25; 25$

$25 = 1.25n + 6.25$

$15 = n$

So, 25 is the 15th term.

14. $f(n) = -3(n-1); -51$

$-51 = -3(n-1)$

$18 = n$

So, -51 is the 18th term.

15. $f(n) = (2n - 2) + 2; 52$

$52 = (2n - 2) + 2$

$26 = n$

So, 52 is the 26th term.

The recursive rule for a sequence and one of the specific terms is given. Find the position of the given term.

16. $f(1) = 8\frac{1}{2}; f(n) = f(n-1) - \frac{1}{2}; 5\frac{1}{2}$

$f(1) = 8\frac{1}{2}$ $f(2) = 8\frac{1}{2} - \frac{1}{2} = 8$

$f(3) = 7\frac{1}{2}$ $f(4) = 7$ $f(5) = 6\frac{1}{2}$

$f(6) = 6$ $f(7) = 5\frac{1}{2}$

So, $5\frac{1}{2}$ is the 7th term.

17. $f(1) = 99, f(n) = f(n-1) + 4; 119$

$f(1) = 99$ $f(2) = 99 + 4 = 103$

$f(3) = 107$ $f(4) = 111$ $f(5) = 115$

$f(6) = 119$

So, 119 is the 6th term.

18. $f(1) = 33.3, f(n) = f(n-1) + 0.2; 34.9$

$f(1) = 33.3$ $f(2) = 33.3 + 0.2 = 33.5$

$f(3) = 33.7$ $f(4) = 33.9$ $f(5) = 34.1$ $f(6) = 34.3$ $f(7) = 34.5$

$f(8) = 34.7$ $f(9) = 34.9$ **So, 34.9 is the 9th term.**

VISUAL CUES

Students may benefit from drawing diagrams that illustrate how the nth term of a sequence with a recursive rule is generated by the terms that come before it. Students can use arrows to show how previous terms become the inputs to generate the terms that follow.

INTEGRATE MATHEMATICAL PRACTICES

Focus on Math Connections

MP.1 Reinforce the concept that a sequence can be represented by a function by emphasizing the domain and range of a sequence. Write the positive integers 1, 2, 3, and so on across the top of the board in front of the class. Explain that, for a sequence, the positive integers correspond to the positions of the terms in the sequence. Then, have students write the terms of the sequence 1, 3, 5, 7, 9, … directly below the position numbers and draw arrows between each position number and its corresponding term. Identify the set of position numbers as the domain and the set of terms as the range. Then, ask students to use what they know about relations to explain why this particular relation is a function.

AVOID COMMON ERRORS

Some students may connect the dots in the graph of a sequence. For example, suppose the explicit rule is $f(n) = 2n - 1$ and the domain is the set of whole numbers greater than 0. The ordered pairs include $(1, 1)$, $(2, 3)$, and $(3, 5)$. Help students understand why the points representing those ordered pairs should not be graphed. For example, since 1.5 is not in the domain of the function, $(1.5, 2)$ should not be graphed. If the points $(1, 1)$ and $(2, 3)$ are connected, then $(1.5, 2)$ should be graphed.

COLLABORATIVE LEARNING

In small groups, have students discuss how they would go about solving an everyday problem involving sequences. For example, a salesperson in a computer store gets a weekly base salary of $100, plus an additional $10 for every computer she sells. Have students identify an explicit rule for the sequence and discuss how they can use it to determine the salesperson's salary if she sells 7 computers in a week. Then have students identify a recursive rule for the sequence.

JOURNAL

Have students compare and contrast the methods they have learned for representing a sequence of numbers. Students should explain the difference between explicit and recursive rules for sequences and give examples of both.

© Houghton Mifflin Harcourt Publishing Company • Image Credits: (t) ©Comstock/Getty Images; (b) PhotoDisc/Getty Images

---

Graph the sequence that represents the situation on a coordinate plane.

19. Jessica had $150 in her savings account after her first week of work. She then started adding $35 each week to her account for the next 5 weeks. The savings account balance can be represented by a sequence.

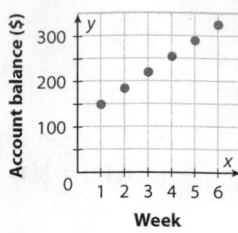

20. Carrie borrowed $840 from a friend to pay for a car repair. Carrie promises to repay her friend in 8 equal monthly payments. The remaining amount Carrie has to repay can be represented by a sequence.

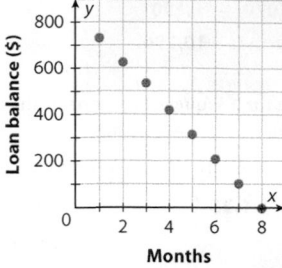

H.O.T. Focus on Higher Order Thinking

21. A park charges $12 for one round of miniature golf and a reduced fee for each additional round played. If Tom paid $47 for 6 rounds of miniature golf, what is the reduced fee for each additional round played?

$f(1) = 12$

$f(2) = 12 + x$

$f(3) = 12 + 2x$

$f(4) = 12 + 3x$

$f(5) = 12 + 4x$

$f(6) = 12 + 5x = 47$

$\qquad 12 + 5x = 47; \qquad x = 7$

The reduced fee for each additional round played is $7.

22. **Analyze Relationships** Construct a recursive rule to describe the sequence: 2, 4, 6, 8,…

$f(1) = 2, f(n) = f(n - 1) + 2$ **for each whole number greater than 1**

23. Explain the Error To find the 5th term of a sequence where $f(1) = 4$ and $f(n) = 2 \cdot f(n-1) + 1$ for each whole number greater than 1, Shane calculates $(4 \cdot 2 \cdot 2 \cdot 2 \cdot 2) + 1 = 65$. Is this correct? Justify your answer.

No, it is not correct. Shane multiplied each term by 2 to find the next term, and only added 1 at the end instead of adding 1 to each doubled term. The correct calculation would be:

$$f(1) = 4$$
$$f(2) = 4 \cdot 2 + 1 = 9$$
$$f(3) = (4 \cdot 2 + 1) \cdot 2 + 1 = 19$$
$$f(4) = \left((4 \cdot 2 + 1) \cdot 2 + 1\right) \cdot 2 + 1 = 39$$
$$f(5) = \left(\left((4 \cdot 2 + 1) \cdot 2 + 1\right) \cdot 2 + 1\right) \cdot 2 + 1 = 79$$

24. Critical Thinking Write a recursive rule for a sequence where every term is the same.

Sample answer: $f(1) = 5$, $f(n) = f(n-1)$ for each whole number greater than 1.

Lesson Performance Task

A museum charges $10 per person for admission and $2 for each of 8 special exhibits.

a. Use function notation to write an equation to represent the cost for attending n events.

b. Make a table to represent the total cost of admission plus 1, 2, and 3 special exhibits.

c. What would $f(0) = 10$ represent?

d. What would the total cost be for going to all 8 special exhibits?

e. Determine an explicit rule for the total cost if the first special exhibit were free.

a. $f(n) = 2n + 10$

b.

n	$f(n) = 2n + 10$
1	12
2	14
3	16

c. $f(0) = 10$ would represent the cost , $10, for admission and no special exhibits

d. $26.00

e. $f(n) = 2(n-1) + 10$

EXTENSION ACTIVITY

Tell students that at another museum, the cost of admission for a person who wants to go to n special event exhibits is determined by a function with a domain that is the set of whole numbers n greater than 0 and $f(n) = 15 + 4n$. Have students make a table for the function and make a graph of the sequence represented by the function.

CONNECT VOCABULARY [EL]

Make sure that students understand the terms, such as *special event exhibit*, in the Lesson Performance Task. Have students give examples of special event exhibits that might be seen at a museum.

INTEGRATE MATHEMATICAL PRACTICES
Focus on Math Connections

MP.1 Help students make connections between the problem situation in the Lesson Performance Task and the function representing the situation. For example, ask students which value of the function corresponds to the cost for a person to go to one special event exhibit.

Scoring Rubric

2 points: Student correctly solves the problem and explains his/her reasoning.

1 point: Student shows good understanding of the problem but does not fully solve or explain his/her reasoning.

0 points: Student does not demonstrate understanding of the problem.

Identifying and Graphing Sequences   **164**

Constructing Arithmetic Sequences

Common Core Math Standards

The student is expected to:

 F-LE.A.2

Construct... arithmetic... sequences, given a graph, a description of a relationship, or two input-output pairs... Also F-BF.A.1a, F-BF.A.2, F-IF.A.3

Mathematical Practices

 MP.4 Modeling

Language Objective

Define and give examples of *arithmetic sequence* and *common difference*.

ENGAGE

Essential Question: What is an arithmetic sequence?

An arithmetic sequence is a sequence in which the difference between any pair of consecutive terms is constant.

PREVIEW: LESSON PERFORMANCE TASK

View the online Engage. Discuss the photo and what the common difference will be each time Carl uses his gift card to pay for admission to a movie. Then preview the Lesson Performance Task.

Name_____ Class_____ Date_____

4.2 Constructing Arithmetic Sequences

Essential Question: What is an arithmetic sequence?

Resource Locker

Explore   Exploring Arithmetic Sequences

You can order tickets for the local theater online. There is a fee of \$2 per order. Matinee tickets cost \$10 each. The total cost, in dollars, of ordering n matinee tickets online can be found by using $C(n) = 10n + 2$. The table shows the cost of 1, 2, 3, and 4 tickets.

Ⓐ Complete the table of values for $C(n) = 10n + 2$.

Tickets	1	2	3	4
Total Cost (\$)	12	22	32	42

What is the domain of the sequence? ___1, 2, 3, 4___

Ⓑ What is the range of the sequence? _12, 22, 32, 42_

Ⓒ What is the first term of the sequence? ___12___

Ⓓ Find the difference between each two consecutive terms in the sequence:

$22 - 12 =$ ___10___ $32 - 22 =$ ___10___ $42 - 32 =$ ___10___

Reflect

1. **Discussion** Suppose you extended the table for up to 15 tickets. Would you expect the difference between consecutive terms to be the same? Explain your reasoning.
   Yes; for any whole number n, the nth term is $10n + 2$, and the

   next term is $10(n + 1) + 2 = 10n + 10 + 2$. The difference is

   $10n + 10 + 2 - (10n + 2) = 10n + 10 + 2 - 10n - 2 = 10.$

2. **Communicate Mathematical Ideas** Explain how the domain is limited in this situation.
   The domain values must be nonzero whole numbers.

_____

_____

© Houghton Mifflin Harcourt Publishing Company

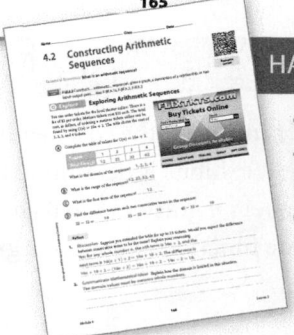

HARDCOVER PAGES 135–142

Turn to these pages to find this lesson in the hardcover student edition.

Explain 1 **Constructing Rules for Arithmetic Sequences**

In an **arithmetic sequence**, the difference between consecutive terms is always equal. This difference, written as d, is called the **common difference**.

An arithmetic sequence can be described in two ways, explicitly and recursively. As you saw earlier, in an **explicit** rule for a sequence, the nth term of the arithmetic sequence is defined as a function of n. In a **recursive** rule for a sequence, the first term of the sequence is given and the nth term is defined by relating it to the previous term. An arithmetic sequence can be defined using either a recursive rule or an explicit rule.

Example 1 Write a recursive rule and an explicit rule for the sequence described by each table.

(A) The table shows the monthly balance in a savings account with regular monthly deposits. The savings account begins with $2000, and $500 is deposited each month.

Time (months)	n	1	2	3	4	5
Balance	$f(n)$	2000	2500	3000	3500	4000

Write a recursive rule.

$f(1) = 2000$, and the common difference d is 500.

The recursive rule is $f(1) = 2000$, $f(n) = f(n - 1) + 500$ for $n \geq 2$.

Write an explicit rule.

n	$f(n)$	$f(1) + d \cdot x = f(n)$
1	2000	$2000 + 500(0) = 2000$
2	2500	$2000 + 500(1) = 2500$
3	3000	$2000 + 500(2) = 3000$

Since d is always multiplied by a number equal to $(n - 1)$, you can generalize the result from the table. The explicit rule is $f(n) = 2000 + 500(n - 1)$.

(B) The table shows the monthly balance in a savings account with regular monthly deposits.

Time (months)	n	1	2	3	4	5
Balance	$f(n)$	5000	6000	7000	8000	9000

Write a recursive rule.

$f(1) = $ __5000__ and the common difference d is __1000__.

The recursive rule is $f(1) = $ __5000__, $f(n) = f(n - 1) + $ __1000__ for $n \geq 2$.

Write an explicit rule.

n	$f(n)$	$f(1) + d \cdot x = f(n)$
1	5000	$5000 + 1000(0) = 5000$
2	6000	$5000 + 1000(1) = 6000$
3	7000	$5000 + 1000(2) = 7000$

Since d is always multiplied by a number equal to __$(n - 1)$__, you can generalize the result from

the table. $f(n) = $ __5000__ $+$ __$1000(n - 1)$__.

PROFESSIONAL DEVELOPMENT

 Integrate Mathematical Practices

This lesson provides an opportunity to address Mathematical Practice **MP.4**, which calls for students to use "modeling." Students define explicit and recursive functions to represent sequences.

Exploring Arithmetic Sequences

INTEGRATE TECHNOLOGY

Students have the option of completing the activity either in the book or online.

CONNECT VOCABULARY **EL**

Make sure that students understand the expressions *consecutive terms* and *difference of two consecutive terms*. You can explain that two consecutive terms are two terms that are next to each other. Have students give examples of pairs of consecutive terms.

EXPLAIN 1

Constructing Rules for Arithmetic Sequences

INTEGRATE MATHEMATICAL PRACTICES
Focus on Patterns

MP.8 Explain that students should be looking for a pattern in the sequence numbers. Is the difference between each pair of consecutive terms always the same? If so, the sequence is an arithmetic sequence.

QUESTIONING STRATEGIES

? In the Example, you are told that each sequence is arithmetic. How would you verify that this is true? **Find the difference between each pair of consecutive terms and make sure that the differences are all the same.**

EXPLAIN 2

Using a General Form to Construct Rules for Arithmetic Sequences

INTEGRATE TECHNOLOGY

Display the Example. Have one student circle the term representing $f(1)$. Then have another student or students determine and write the differences between consecutive terms to verify that the sequence is arithmetic.

QUESTIONING STRATEGIES

? What kinds of rules can you use to describe an arithmetic sequence? You can describe an arithmetic sequence with an explicit rule and with a recursive rule.

AVOID COMMON ERRORS

Some students may confuse explicit rules and recursive rules. In an explicit rule, the value of $f(n)$ is defined in terms of n. In a recursive rule, the first term of the sequence is given and the nth term is defined in terms of one or more previous terms. Have students compare and contrast the two types of rules defined in the Example.

---

3. **Critique Reasoning** Jerome says that the sequence 1, 8, 27, 64, 125,... is not an arithmetic sequence. Is that correct? Explain.

Yes; the sequence is not arithmetic because the difference between consecutive terms is not always the same.

4. An arithmetic sequence has a common difference of 3. If you know that the third term of the sequence is 15, how can you find the fourth term? **Add 3 to the third term to get 18.**

YourTurn

5. The table shows the number of plates left at a buffet after n hours. Write a recursive rule and an explicit rule for the arithmetic sequence represented by the table.

Time (hours)	n	1	2	3	4	5
Number of plates	$f(n)$	155	141	127	113	99

$f(1) = 155$, and the common difference is -14.

The recursive rule is $f(1) = 155$, $f(n) = f(n-1) - 14$.

The explicit rule is $f(n) = 155 - 14(n-1)$.

🔊 Explain 2 Using a General Form to Construct Rules for Arithmetic Sequences

Arithmetic sequences can be described by a set of general rules. Values can be substituted into these rules to find a recursive and explicit rule for a given sequence.

General Recursive Rule	General Explicit Rule
Given $f(1)$, $f(n) = f(n-1) + d$ for $n \geq 2$	$f(n) = f(1) + d(n-1)$

Example 2 Write a general recursive and general explicit rule for each arithmetic sequence.

Ⓐ 100, 88, 76, 64, ...

$f(1) = 100$, common difference $= 88 - 100 = -12$

The recursive rule is $f(1) = 100$, $f(n) = f(n-1) - 12$ for $n \geq 2$.

The explicit rule is $f(n) = 100 - 12(n-1)$.

Ⓑ 0, 8, 16, 24, 32, ...

$f(1) = \underline{0}$, common difference $= \underline{8} - \underline{0} = \underline{8}$.

The recursive rule is $f(1) = \underline{0}$, $f(n) = f(n-1) + \underline{8}$ for $n \geq 2$.

The explicit rule is $f(n) = \underline{0} + \underline{8} (n-1)$.

COLLABORATIVE LEARNING

Small Group Activity

Have students work in groups of three. Instruct one student in each group to write down an arithmetic sequence with four values. The second student writes an explicit and recursive rule for the sequence. The third student generates a table and ordered pairs for the first five values and then graphs the data. Have students switch roles and repeat the exercise using a different arithmetic sequence.

Reflect

6. What is the recursive rule for the sequence $f(n) = 2 + (-3)(n-1)$? How do you know?
$f(1) = 2, f(n) = f(n-1) - 3$ for $n \geq 2$; you know from the explicit formula that $f(1) = 2$

and $d = -3$. You can substitute those values in the general recursive rule.

YourTurn

7. Write a recursive rule and an explicit rule for the arithmetic sequence 6, 16, 26, 36,...
$f(1) = 6$, and the common difference is 10.

Recursive rule: $f(1) = 6, f(n) = f(n-1) + 10$ for $n \geq 2$

Explicit rule: $f(n) = 10(n-1) + 6$

⚙ Explain 3 Relating Arithmetic Sequences and Functions

The explicit rule for an arithmetic sequence can be expressed as a function. You can use the graph of the function to write an explicit rule.

Example 3 Write an explicit rule in function notation for each arithmetic sequence.

Ⓐ The cost of a whitewater rafting trip depends on the number of passengers. The base fee is $50, and the cost per passenger is $25. The graph shows the sequence.

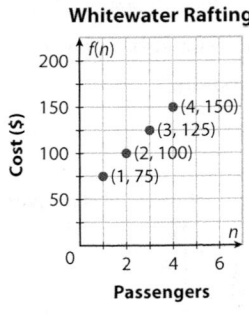

Whitewater Rafting

Step 1 Represent the sequence in a table.

Number of passengers n	1	2	3	4
Cost ($) $f(n)$	75	100	125	150

Step 2 Find the common difference.

$f(2) - f(1) = 100 - 75 = 25$

$f(3) - f(2) = 125 - 100 = 25$

$f(4) - f(3) = 150 - 125 = 25$

The common difference d is 25.

Step 3 Write an explicit rule for the sequence.

Substitute 75 for $f(1)$ and 25 for d.

$f(n) = f(1) + d(n-1)$

$f(n) = 75 + 25(n-1)$

EXPLAIN 3

Relating Arithmetic Sequences and Functions

QUESTIONING STRATEGIES

? What can you say about the domain of a function if the function is a rule for an arithmetic sequence? The domain is the set of whole numbers or a subset of that set.

? How can you tell from the graph that this is an arithmetic sequence? The points of the graph are in a straight line, indicating that there is a constant difference between consecutive terms.

DIFFERENTIATE INSTRUCTION

Multiple Representations

To develop a recursive rule for an arithmetic sequence, suggest that students follow a general plan. First, write the sequence as a horizontal list. Under each term, write $f(1), f(2), f(3)$ .... Find the common difference, d, between any pair of consecutive terms. Then, have students write $f(2)$ in terms of $f(1)$, $f(3)$ in terms of $f(2)$, and so on. Finally, have them write the general equation $f(n) = f(n-1) + d$.

ELABORATE

QUESTIONING STRATEGIES

? What is the value of $f(1)$ in the sequence 5, 9, 13, 17, ...? How can you use $f(1)$ to generate $f(2)$? How can you use these values to create a recursive rule? $f(1) = 5$. You can use $f(1)$ to generate $f(2)$ as follows: $f(2) = f(1) + 4$. Each $f(n)$ is equal to the previous number plus 4, so the recursive rule is $f(1) = 5$, $f(n) = f(n-1) + 4$ for $n \geq 2$.

SUMMARIZE THE LESSON

? How would you summarize the steps involved in writing an explicit rule for an arithmetic sequence? Compute the common difference, d. Write $f(n) = f(1) + d(n-1)$. Simplify the expression on the right.

(B) The number of seats per row in an auditorium depends on which row it is. The first row has 6 seats, the second row has 9 seats, the third row has 12 seats, and so on. The graph shows the sequence.

Auditorium Seats

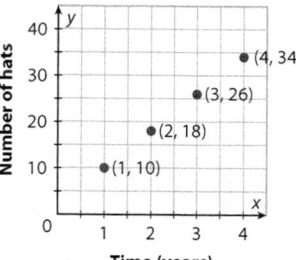

Step 1 Represent the sequence in a table.

Row number n	1	2	3	4
Number of seats $f(n)$	6	9	12	15

Step 2 Find the common difference.

$f(2) - f(1) = \boxed{9} - \boxed{6} = \boxed{3}$

$f(3) - f(2) = \boxed{12} - \boxed{9} = \boxed{3}$

$f(4) - f(3) = \boxed{15} - \boxed{12} = \boxed{3}$

The common difference is $d = \underline{\quad 3 \quad}$.

Step 3 Write an explicit rule for the sequence.

$f(n) = f(1) + d(n-1)$

Substitute $\underline{\quad 6 \quad}$ for $f(1)$ and $\underline{\quad 3 \quad}$ for d.

$f(n) = \boxed{6} + \boxed{3}(n-1)$

Reflect

8. **Analyze Relationships** Compare the graph of the function $f(x) = 3 + 5(x - 1)$ and the graph of the sequence $f(n) = 3 + 5(n - 1)$.

The domain and range of the function $f(x) = 3 + 5(x - 1)$ include all real numbers, and the graph of the function is a line. The graph of the sequence is a discrete set of points. Every point on the graph of the sequence is on the graph of the function.

YourTurn

9. Jerry collects hats. The total number of hats in Jerry's collection depends on how many years he has been collecting hats. After the first year, Jerry had 10 hats. Each year he has added the same number of hats to his collection. The graph shows the sequence. Write an explicit rule in function notation for the arithmetic sequence.

Number of Hats over Time

Time (years) n	1	2	3	4
Number of hats $f(n)$	10	18	26	34

The common difference is 8.

$f(n) = f(1) + d(n-1)$

$f(n) = 10 + 8(n-1)$

LANGUAGE SUPPORT **EL**

Connect Vocabulary

Explain that the word *common* comes from the Latin word *communis* meaning *shared by all or many*. Point out that the word *common* has other meanings in everyday language, such as *ordinary*, or *unoriginal*. The term *common difference* refers to a difference shared by all members of an arithmetic sequence.

💬 Elaborate

10. What information do you need to write a recursive rule for an arithmetic sequence that you do not need to write an explicit rule?

You need the first term to write a recursive rule, but you do not need it to write an

explicit rule.

11. Suppose you want to be able to determine the ninetieth term in an arithmetic sequence and you have both an explicit and a recursive rule. Which rule would you use? Explain.

The explicit rule; you can just substitute 90 for *n* in the explicit rule. If you have only the

recursive rule, you would have to determine how many times to add the common difference

to the first term, and then do the calculation. More calculation involves more risk of error.

12. Essential Question Check-In The explicit equation for an arithmetic sequence and a linear equation have a similar form. How is the value of m in the linear equation $y = mx + b$ similar to the value of d in the explicit equation $f(n) = f(1) + d(n-1)$?

***m* represents a constant change in *y*—coordinates; *d* represents a constant change in**

consecutive terms of the sequence.

☆ Evaluate: Homework and Practice

• Online Homework
• Hints and Help
• Extra Practice

1. Farah pays a \$25 signup fee to join a car sharing service and a \$7 monthly charge. The total cost of using the car sharing service for n months can be found using $C(n) = 25 + 7n$. The table shows the cost of the service for 1, 2, 3, and 4 months.

a. Complete the table for $C(n) = 25 + 7n$

Months	n	1	2	3	4
Cost (\$)	$f(n)$	32	39	46	53

b. What are the domain and range of the sequence?
Domain: {1, 2, 3, 4} Range: {32, 39, 46, 53}

c. What is the common difference d?
$d = 39 - 32 = 7$

Tell whether each sequence is an arithmetic sequence.

2.

a. 6, 7, 8, 9, 10,… **Yes**

b. 5, 10, 20, 35, 55,… **No**

c. 0, −1, 1, −2, 2,… **No**

d. 1, 16, 81, 625, 1296 **No**

e. −2, −4, −6, −8, −10, … **Yes**

3. Chemistry A chemist heats up several unknown substances to determine their boiling point. Use the table to determine whether the sequence is arithmetic. If it is arithmetic, write an explicit rule and a recursive rule for the sequence. If not, explain why it is not arithmetic.

Substance	1	2	3	4	5
Boiling Point (°F)	100	135	149	165	188

The sequence is not arithmetic. There is no common difference.

Exercise	Depth of Knowledge (D.O.K.)	COMMON CORE Mathematical Practices
1	**2** Skills/Concepts	**MP.6** Precision
2–3	**1** Recall of Information	**MP.6** Precision
4–9	**2** Skills/Concepts	**MP.4** Modeling
10–15	**2** Skills/Concepts	**MP.2** Reasoning
16–19	**2** Skills/Concepts	**MP.4** Modeling
20–21	**2** Skills/Concepts	**MP.4** Modeling

EVALUATE

ASSIGNMENT GUIDE

Concepts and Skills	Practice
Explore Exploring Arithmetic Sequences	Exercises 1–3
Example 1 Constructing Rules for Arithmetic Sequences	Exercises 4–9, 21
Example 2 Using a General Form to Construct Rules for Arithmetic Sequences	Exercises 10–15, 20, 22–24
Example 3 Relating Arithmetic Sequences and Functions	Exercises 16–19

INTEGRATE MATHEMATICAL PRACTICES

Focus on Technology

MP.5 Encourage students to use their graphing calculators to check answers to complicated problems.

Students may use the wrong sign in rules for arithmetic sequences when the common difference is a negative number. Remind students that the common difference is the difference between a term and the one *before* it, and this difference will be negative if a term is less than the one before it.

QUESTIONING STRATEGIES

? Why does the explicit rule for the sequence 1, 3, 5, 7, 9, … involve multiplying the common difference by $n-1$ and not n? The explicit rule is $f(n) = f(1) + d(n-1)$. If you used the rule $f(n) = f(1) + d(n)$, the sequence would be 3, 5, 7, 9, 11….

Write a recursive rule and an explicit rule for the arithmetic sequence described by each table.

4.

Month	n	1	2	3	4	5
Account balance ($)	$f(n)$	35	32	29	26	23

$f(1) = 35$, common difference $= -3$

Recursive rule: $f(1) = 35$, $f(n) = f(n-1) - 3$ for $n \geq 2$

Explicit rule: $f(n) = f(1) + d(n-1)$, so $f(n) = 35 - 3(n-1)$

5.

Tickets	n	1	2	3	4	5
Total cost (S)	$f(n)$	58	65	72	79	86

$f(1) = 58$, common difference $= 7$

Recursive rule: $f(1) = 58$, $f(n) = f(n-1) + 7$ for $n \geq 2$

Explicit rule: $f(n) = f(1) + d(n-1)$, so $f(n) = 58 + 7(n-1)$

6.

Month	n	1	2	3	4	5
Total deposits ($)	$f(n)$	84	100	116	132	148

$f(1) = 84$, common difference $= 16$

Recursive rule: $f(1) = 84$, $f(n) = f(n-1) + 16$ for $n \geq 2$

Explicit rule: $f(n) = f(1) + d(n-1)$, so $f(n) = 84 + 16(n-1)$

7.

Delivery number	n	1	2	3	4	5
Weight of truck (lb)	$f(n)$	4567	3456	2345	1234	123

$f(1) = 4567$, common difference $= -1111$

Recursive rule: $f(1) = 4567$, $f(n) = f(n-1) - 1111$ for $n \geq 2$

Explicit rule: $f(n) = f(1) + d(n-1)$, so $f(n) = 4567 - 1111(n-1)$

8.

Week	n	1	2	3	4	5
Account owed ($)	$f(n)$	125	100	75	50	25

$f(1) = 125$, common difference $= -25$

Recursive rule: $f(1) = 125$, $f(n) = f(n-1) - 25$ for $n \geq 2$

Explicit rule: $f(n) = f(1) + d(n-1)$, so $f(n) = 125 - 25(n-1)$

9.

Skaters	n	1	2	3	4	5
Charge for lesson ($)	$f(n)$	60	80	100	120	140

$f(1) = 60$, common difference $= 20$

Recursive rule: $f(1) = 60$, $f(n) = f(n-1) + 20$ for $n \geq 2$

Explicit rule: $f(n) = f(1) + d(n-1)$, so $f(n) = 60 + 20(n-1)$

Exercise	Depth of Knowledge (D.O.K.)	COMMON CORE Mathematical Practices
22	**2** Skills/Concepts **H.O.T.**	**MP.2** Reasoning
23	**3** Strategic Thinking **H.O.T.**	**MP.4** Modeling
24	**3** Strategic Thinking **H.O.T.**	**MP.6** Precision

Write a recursive rule and an explicit rule for each arithmetic sequence.

10. 95, 90, 85, 80, 75, . . .

$f(1) = 95$, and common difference $= -5$

$f(1) = 95, f(n) = f(n-1) - 5$ for $n \geq 2$

$f(n) = 95 - 5(n-1)$

11. 63, 70, 77, 84, 91, . . .

$f(1) = 63$, and common difference $= 7$

$f(1) = 63, f(n) = f(n-1) + 7$ for $n \geq 2$

$f(n) = 63 + 7(n-1)$

12. 86, 101, 116, 131, 146, . . .

$f(1) = 86$, and common difference $= 15$

$f(1) = 86, f(n) = f(n-1) + 15$ for $n \geq 2$.

$f(n) = 86 + 15(n-1)$

13. 112, 110, 108, 106, 104, . . .

$f(1) = 112$, and common difference $= -2$

$f(1) = 112, f(n) = f(n-1) - 2$ for $n \geq 2$

$f(n) = 112 - 2(n-1)$

14. 5, 9, 13, 17, 21, . . .

$f(1) = 5$, and common difference $= 4$

$f(1) = 5, f(n) = f(n-1) + 4$ for $n \geq 2$

$f(n) = 5 + 4(n-1)$

15. 67, 37, 7, −23, −53, . . .

$f(1) = 67$, and common difference $= -30$

$f(1) = 67, f(n) = f(n-1) - 30$ for $n > 2$

$f(n) = 67 - 30(n-1)$

Write an explicit rule in function notation for each arithmetic sequence.

16. A student loan needs to be paid off beginning the first year after graduation. Beginning at Year 1, there is $52,000 remaining to be paid. The graduate makes regular payments of $8,000 each year. The graph shows the sequence.

Time (years) n	1	2	3	4
Remaining amount ($1000s) $f(n)$	52	44	36	28

$f(1) = 52$, common difference $= -8$

Explicit rule: $f(n) = 52 - 8(n-1)$

Paying off Debt

17. A grocery cart is 38 inches long. When the grocery carts are put away in a nested row, the length of the row depends on how many carts are nested together. Each cart added to the row adds 12 inches to the row length. The graph shows the sequence.

Number of grocery carts n	1	2	3	4	5
Row length (in.) $f(n)$	38	50	62	74	86

$f(1) = 38$, common difference $= 12$

Explicit rule: $f(n) = 38 + 12(n-1)$

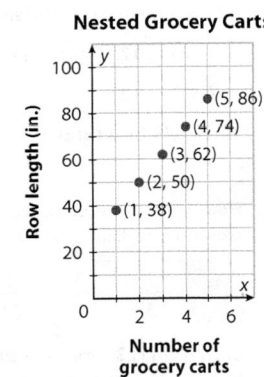

Nested Grocery Carts

INTEGRATE MATHEMATICAL PRACTICES

Focus on Modeling

MP.4 If the points plotted on a graph are $(1, 25)$, $(2, 75)$, $(3, 125)$, and $(4, 175)$, what explicit rule would you write for the sequence? $f(n) = 25 + 50(n-1)$

SMALL GROUP ACTIVITY

In groups of three, have each student write the first five values in an arithmetic sequence. Each sequence should have the same first term but a different common difference. Then have students discuss and write a prediction about how the graphs of their sequences will be alike and/or different. Students then graph their sequences. Students compare graphs and explain whether their predictions were correct or incorrect.

Focus on Reasoning

MP.2 Write the following sequence on the board:
$-1, -5, -9, -13, ...$ Challenge students to generate a
table and find the explicit rule for the function $f(n)$.
$f(1) = -1$ and $d = -4$. Therefore,
$f(n) = -1 + (-4)(n-1)$.

Then have students determine the sixth term in the
sequence in two different ways. Encourage students
to explain their reasoning as they solve the problem.

$f(6) = -1 + (-4)(6-1)$
$\quad = -1 + (-20)$
$\quad = -21$

$f(5) = f(4) + (-4)$
$\quad = -13 + (-4) = -17$
$f(6) = f(5) + (-4)$
$\quad = -17 + (-4) = -21$

JOURNAL

Have students summarize the steps they can
take to write explicit and recursive rules for an
arithmetic sequence and then extend the sequence
using the rules.

---

18. A dog food for overweight dogs claims that a dog weighing
85 pounds will lose about 2 pounds per week for the first 4 weeks
when following the recommended feeding guidelines. The graph
shows the sequence.

n	1	2	3	4
f(n)	83	81	79	77

$f(1) = 83$, common difference $= -2$

Explicit rule: $f(n) = 83 - 2(n-1)$

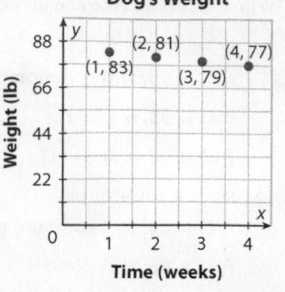

Dog's Weight

19. A savings account is opened with $6300. Monthly deposits of
$1100 are made. The graph shows the sequence.

Time (months) n	1	2	3	4
Balance ($100s) f(n)	74	85	96	107

$f(1) = 74$, common difference $= 11$

Explicit rule: $f(n) = 74 + 11(n-1)$

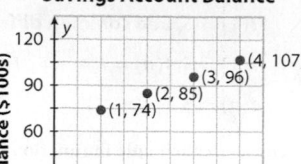

Savings Account Balance

20. **Biology** The wolf population in a local wildlife area is
currently 12. Due to a new conservation effort, conservationists
hope the wolf population will increase by 2 animals each year for
the next 50 years. Assume that the plan will be successful. Write an
explicit rule for the population sequence. Use the rule to predict the
number of animals in the wildlife area in the fiftieth year.

Time (years) n	1	2	3	4
Wolf population f(n)	12	14	16	18

$f(1) = 12$, common difference $= 2$

$\quad f(n) = 12 + 2(n-1)$

$\quad f(50) = 12 + 2(50-1) = 110$

There will be a total of 110 animals in 50 years.

21. How are the terms in the sequence in the table related? Is the sequence an arithmetic
sequence? Explain.

n	1	2	3	4	5
f(n)	3	9	27	81	243

**Each term is 3 times the previous term. The sequence is not arithmetic
because the difference between consecutive terms is not always the same.**

© Houghton Mifflin Harcourt Publishing Company • Image Credits: ©Comstock Images/Getty Images

22. **Explain the Error** The cost of a hamburger is $2.50. Each additional hamburger costs $2.00. Sully wrote this explicit rule to explain the sequence of costs: $f(n) = 2 + 2.5(n − 1)$. Using this rule, he found the cost of 12 hamburgers to be $29.50. Is this number correct? If not, identify Sully's error.

    No; Sully's explicit rule was incorrect. He confused the first term and the common difference. The correct rule is $f(n) = 2.5 + 2(n − 1)$. The actual cost of 12 hamburgers is $24.50.

23. **Critical Thinking** Lucia knows the fourth term in a sequence is 55 and the ninth term in the same sequence is 90. Explain how she can find the common difference for the sequence. Then use the common difference to find the second term of the sequence.

    The difference between the fourth term and the ninth term in the sequence will be 5 times the common difference. Find the difference between the ninth term and the fourth term and divide the result by 5.

    90 − 55 = 35, and 35 ÷ 5 = 7.

    The common difference is 7. By subtracting 7 from the fourth term twice, you can find the second term.

    55 − 7 − 7 = 41

    The second term in the arithmetic sequence is 41.

24. **Represent Real-World Problems** Write and solve a real-world problem involving a situation that can be represented by the sequence $f(n) = 15 + 2(n − 1)$.

    Possible answer: A worker's hourly pay during his first year of work is $15. Every year after that, the worker's hourly pay increases by $2 per hour. What will the worker's pay be during the fifth year? $23

Lesson Performance Task

For Carl's birthday, his grandparents gave him a $50 gift card to a local movie theater. The theater charges $6 admission for each movie. How can Carl use an arithmetic sequence to determine the value left on his card after each movie he sees?

a. Write an explicit rule for the arithmetic sequence and use it to determine how much value is left on the card after Carl has seen 4 movies.

   a. $f(n) = 50 − 6n$

   $f(4) = 50 − 6(4)$

   $f(4) = 50 − 24 = 26$

   There is $26 on the card.

b. How much is left on the card after Carl has seen the maximum number of movies?

   b. **Now let $n = 8$ and solve.**

   $f(8) = 50 − 6(8)$

   $f(8) = 50 − 48$

   $f(8) = 2$

   There will be $2 left on the card.

EXTENSION ACTIVITY

Some gift cards lose a part of their value each month. Have students assume that Carl's gift card loses $2 each month. Have students determine whether Carl can still use the same arithmetic sequence he used for the Lesson Performance Task to determine the value left on his card.

QUESTIONING STRATEGIES

? What is a sequence that represents the situation in the Lesson Performance Task?
50, 44, 38, 32, 26, …, 2

? What is the common difference between consecutive terms? 6

INTEGRATE MATHEMATICAL PRACTICES

Focus on Critical Thinking

MP.3 Some students may not understand how to determine the maximum number of movies Carl can see in order to answer Part B in the Lesson Performance Task. Suggest that students use reasoning to determine the maximum number. As long as there are $6 or more left on the card, Carl can see another movie. At $6 a movie, 9 movies will cost $54, so the maximum number is less than 9.

Scoring Rubric
2 points: Student correctly solves the problem and explains his/her reasoning.
1 point: Student shows good understanding of the problem but does not fully solve or explain his/her reasoning.
0 points: Student does not demonstrate understanding of the problem.

Constructing Arithmetic Sequences   **174**

Modeling with Arithmetic Sequences

Common Core Math Standards

The student is expected to:

 F-BF.A.1a

...Determine an explicit expression, a recursive process, or steps for calculation from a context. Also F-LE.A.2, F-IF.A.3

Mathematical Practices

 MP.4 Modeling

Language Objective

Interpret the meaning of questions about real-world situations.

ENGAGE

Essential Question: How can you solve real-world problems using arithmetic sequences?

If a real-world situation can be modeled using an arithmetic sequence, you can write a rule for the sequence and use the rule to solve the problem.

PREVIEW: LESSON PERFORMANCE TASK

View the online Engage. Discuss the photo and that an ant colony consists of an egg-laying queen, a large number of male ants, and female worker ants, who gather food and build, maintain, and guard the nest. Then preview the Lesson Performance Task.

Name_____ Class_____ Date_____

4.3 Modeling with Arithmetic Sequences

Essential Question: How can you solve real-world problems using arithmetic sequences?

Explore Interpreting Models of Arithmetic Sequences

You can model real-world situations and solve problems using models of arithmetic sequences. For example, suppose watermelons cost $6.50 each at the local market. The total cost, in dollars, of n watermelons can be found using $c(n) = 6.5n$.

(A) Complete the table of values for 1, 2, 3, and 4 watermelons.

Watermelons n	1	2	3	4
Total cost ($) $c(n)$	6.5	13	19.5	26

(B) What is the common difference?

6.5

(C) What does n represent in this context?

The variable n represents the number of watermelons.

(D) What are the dependent and independent variables in this context?

The variable n is the independent variable and $c(n)$ is the dependent variable.

(E) Find $c(7)$. What does this value represent?

$c(7) = 6.5 \cdot 7 = 45.5$

This value represents the cost of 7 watermelons: $45.50.

Reflect

1. Discussion What domain values make sense for $c(n) = 6.5n$ in this situation?
Only nonnegative integers make sense for the domain of $c(n) = 6.5n$ in this situation.

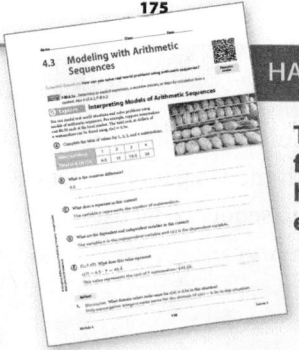

HARDCOVER PAGES 143–152

Turn to these pages to find this lesson in the hardcover student edition.

Given a table of data values from a real-world situation involving an arithmetic sequence, you can construct a function model and use it to solve problems.

Example 1 Construct an explicit rule in function notation for the arithmetic sequence represented in the table. Then interpret the meaning of a specific term of the sequence in the given context.

(A) Suppose the table shows the cost, in dollars, of postage per ounce of a letter.

Number of ounces	n	1	2	3	4
Cost ($) of postage	$f(n)$	0.35	0.55	0.75	0.95

Determine the value of $f(9)$, and tell what it represents in this situation.

Find the common difference, d. $d = 0.55 - 0.35 = 0.20$

Substitute 0.35 for $f(1)$ and 0.20 for d.

$f(n) = f(1) + d(n - 1)$

$f(n) = 0.35 + 0.20(n - 1)$

$f(9) = 0.35 + 0.20(8) = 1.95$

So, the cost of postage for a 9-ounce letter is $1.95.

(B) The table shows the cumulative total interest paid, in dollars, on a loan after each month.

Number of months	n	1	2	3	4
Cumulative total ($)	$f(n)$	160	230	300	370

Determine the value of $f(20)$ and tell what it represents in this situation.

Find the common difference, d. $d = \boxed{230} - 160 = \boxed{70}$

Substitute $\boxed{160}$ for $f(1)$ and $\boxed{70}$ for d.

$f(n) = f(1) + d(n - 1)$

$f(n) = \boxed{160} + \boxed{70}\,(n - 1)$

Find $f(20)$ and interpret the value in context.

$f(n) = f(1) + d(n - 1)$

$f\left(\boxed{20}\right) = \boxed{160} + \boxed{70}\left(\boxed{19}\right) = \boxed{1490}$

So, the cumulative total $\underset{\text{interest}}{\underline{}}$ paid after $\underset{20}{\underline{}}$ months is $\underset{\$1490}{\underline{}}$.

Your Turn

Construct an explicit rule in function notation for the arithmetic sequence represented in the table. Then interpret the meaning of a specific term of the sequence in the given context.

2. The table shows $f(n)$, the distance, in miles, from the store after Mila has traveled for n hours.

Time (h)	n	1	2	3	4
Distance (mi)	$f(n)$	20	32	44	56

Determine the value of $f(10)$ and tell what it represents in this situation.

$d = 12$, so $f(n) = 20 + 12(n - 1)$

$f(10) = 20 + 12(9) = 128$ So, Mila is 128 miles from the store after 10 hours.

Interpreting Models of Arithmetic Sequences

INTEGRATE TECHNOLOGY

Students have the option of completing the activity either in the book or online.

CONNECT VOCABULARY EL

Remind students that a *variable* is a quantity that can change or take on different values. An *independent variable* is a value that does not depend on any other variable. A *dependent variable* depends on the independent variable.

EXPLAIN 1

Modeling Arithmetic Sequences From a Table

INTEGRATE MATHEMATICAL PRACTICES
Focus on Math Connections

MP.1 Review the connections among an arithmetic sequence, the table representing the sequence, and an explicit rule for the sequence.

PROFESSIONAL DEVELOPMENT

COMMON CORE **Integrate Mathematical Practices**

This lesson provides an opportunity to address Mathematical Practice **MP.4**, which calls for students to use "modeling." In this lesson, students interpret models of arithmetic sequences in everyday situations, represented in tables, graphs, and word descriptions.

EXPLAIN 2

Modeling Arithmetic Sequences from a Graph

INTEGRATE TECHNOLOGY

Display the Example. Provide students with a domain value and have a student circle that point on the graph. Then ask the student to explain what the point means in the context of the problem. Ask another student to locate and plot the next value that would appear on the graph.

QUESTIONING STRATEGIES

? How would a graph for the sequence 52, 48, 44, 40, ... be similar to and different from the graph in this exercise? The points of the graph would still be in a straight line, but the points would go from upper left to lower right to indicate a sequence with a constant decrease rather than a constant increase.

---

3. The table below shows the total cost, in dollars, of purchasing n battery packs.

Number of battery packs	n	1	2	3	4
Total cost ($)	$f(n)$	4.90	8.90	12.90	16.90

Determine the value of $f(18)$ and tell what it represents in this situation.

$d = 4$ $f(n) = 4.9 + 4(n-1)$

$f(18) = 4.9 + 4(17) = 72.9$

So, the total cost of 18 battery packs is $72.90.

 Explain 2 **Modeling Arithmetic Sequences From a Graph**

Given a graph of a real-world situation involving an arithmetic sequence, you can construct a function model and use it to solve problems.

Example 2 Construct an explicit rule in function notation for the arithmetic sequence represented in the graph, and use it to solve the problem.

(A) D'Andre collects feather pens. The graph shows the number of feather pens D'Andre has collected over time, in weeks. According to this pattern, how many feather pens will D'Andre have collected in 12 weeks?

Represent the sequence in a table.

n	1	2	3	4
$f(n)$	18	37	56	75

Find the common difference.

$d = 37 - 8 = 19$

Use the general explicit rule for an arithmetic sequence to write the rule in function notation. Substitute 18 for $f(1)$ and 19 for d.

$f(n) = f(1) + d(n-1)$

$f(n) = 18 + 19(n-1)$

To determine the number of feather pens D'Andre will have collected after 12 weeks, find $f(12)$.

$f(n) = 18 + 19(n-1)$

$f(12) = 18 + 19(11)$

$f(12) = 18 + 209$

$f(12) = 227$

So, if this pattern continues, D'Andre will have collected 227 feather pens in 12 weeks.

© Houghton Mifflin Harcourt Publishing Company

COLLABORATIVE LEARNING

Small Group Activity

Have students work in groups of three. Have each student write a problem involving an arithmetic sequence in a different real-world context, such as the savings or cost of one or more items of the same price. Each student solves the problem on a separate sheet of paper. Students pass the problems to students on their right, then solve the new problems using separate sheets of paper. When all students are finished, they pass the problems to the right once more. When all students have solved the problems, have them compare answers and discuss any differences.

Ⓑ Eric collects stamps. The graph shows the number of stamps that Eric has collected over time, in months. According to this pattern, how many stamps will Eric have collected in 10 months?

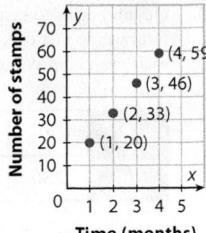

Represent the sequence in a table.

n	1	2	3	4
f(n)	20	33	46	59

Find the common difference.

$d =$ | 33 | $- 20 =$ | 13 |

Use the general explicit rule for an arithmetic sequence to write the rule in function notation.

Substitute | 20 | for $f(1)$ and | 13 | for d.

$f(n) = f(1) + d(n - 1)$

$f(n) =$ | 20 | $+$ | 13 | $(n - 1)$

To determine the number of stamps Eric will have collected in 10 months, find $f($ | 10 | $)$.

$f(n) = f(1) + d(n - 1)$

$f($ | 10 | $) =$ | 20 | $+$ | 13 | $($ | 9 | $) =$ | 137 |

So, if this pattern continues, Eric will have collected ___137 stamps___ in ___10___ months.

Reflect

4. How do you know which variable is the independent variable and which variable is the dependent variable in a real-world situation involving an arithmetic sequence?
The independent variable indicates the term of the sequence so it will usually increase by

1 unit. The other variables have a constant difference between consecutive terms.

Your Turn

Construct an explicit rule in function notation for the arithmetic sequence represented in the graph, and use it to solve the problem.

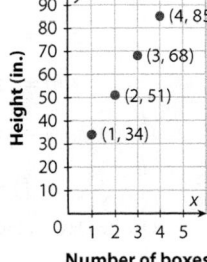

5. The graph shows the height, in inches, of a stack of boxes on a table as the number of boxes in the stack increases. Find the height of the stack with 7 boxes.

n	1	2	3	4
f(n)	34	51	68	85

$d = 51 - 34 = 17$ $f(n) = 34 + 17(n-1)$

$f(7) = 34 + 17(6) = 136$

So, the height of the stack with 7 boxes is 136 inches.

DIFFERENTIATE INSTRUCTION

Critical Thinking

Have students think about the following question: Is it possible for two real-world problems to generate the same graph? Explain. Invite students to give their answers and explain their reasoning. Challenge them to come up with real-world situations to support their answers. **Yes, if both the domain and common difference are the same for both situations.**

EXPLAIN 3

Modeling Arithmetic Sequences from a Description

QUESTIONING STRATEGIES

? A student is getting better at math. On his first test, he scores 60 points, then he scores 65, 70, 74, and 80 on his next 4 tests. Can you calculate how many points he will score on his eighth test? Explain. **No, because this is not an arithmetic sequence. There is no common difference.**

---

6. Quynh begins to save the same amount each month to save for a future shopping trip. The graph shows total amount she has saved after each month, n. What will be the total amount Quynh has saved after 12 months?

f	1	2	3	4
$f(n)$	250	300	350	400

$d = 300 - 250 = 50$ $f(n) = 250 + 50(n-1)$

$f(12) = 250 + 50(11) = 800$

So, Quynh will have saved a total of $800 after 12 months.

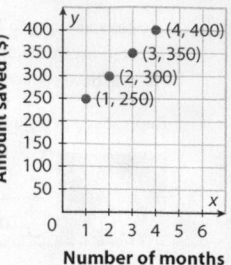
Amount saved ($)
• (4, 400)
• (3, 350)
• (2, 300)
• (1, 250)
Number of months

🔧 Explain 3   Modeling Arithmetic Sequences From a Description

Given a description of a real-world situation involving an arithmetic sequence, you can construct a function model and use it to solve problems.

Example 3 Construct an explicit rule in function notation for the arithmetic sequence represented, and use it to solve the problem. Justify and evaluate your answer.

The odometer on a car reads 34,240 on Day 1. Every day the car is driven 57 miles. If this pattern continues, what will the odometer read on Day 15?

🧩 Analyze Information

- The odometer on the car reads __34,240__ miles on Day 1.
- Every day the car is driven __57__ miles.

$f(1) = $ __34,240__ and
$d = $ __57__

🧩 Formulate a Plan

Write an explicit rule in function notation for the arithmetic sequence, and use it to find __$f(15)$__, the odometer reading on Day 15.

🧩 Solve

$$f(n) = f(1) + d(n - 1)$$

$$f(n) = \boxed{34{,}240} + \boxed{57}(n - 1)$$

$$f\left(\boxed{15}\right) = \boxed{34{,}240} + \boxed{57}\left(\boxed{14}\right)$$

$$f\left(\boxed{15}\right) = \boxed{35{,}038}$$

On the Day 15, the odometer will show __35,038__ miles.

© Houghton Mifflin Harcourt Publishing Company

Module 4   **179**   Lesson 3

LANGUAGE SUPPORT EL

Connect Context

As students work through this lesson, have them explain the new concepts in their own words. Suggest that they work together to provide explanations that are as complete as possible. Ask students to suggest connections to concepts they have already learned and tell how those concepts are extended by the new material.

Using an arithmetic sequence model ___is___ reasonable because the number of miles on the odometer increases by the same amount each day.

By rounding and estimation:

$34{,}200 + 60(14) =$ | 34,200 | $+$ | 840 | $=$ | 35,040 | miles

So ___35,038___ miles is a reasonable answer.

Your Turn

Construct an explicit rule in function notation for the arithmetic sequence represented, and use it to solve the problem. Justify and evaluate your answer.

7. Ruby signed up for a frequent-flier program. She receives 3400 frequent-flier miles for the first round-trip she takes and 1200 frequent-flier miles for all additional round-trips. How many frequent-flier miles will Ruby have after 5 round-trips?

   $f(1) = 3400$ and $d = 1200$ $f(n) = 3400 + 1200(n - 1)$

   $f(5) = 3400 + 1200(4) = 8200$

   After 5 round-trips, Ruby will have 8200 frequent-flier miles.

8. A gym charges each member $100 for the first month, which includes a membership fee, and $50 per month for each month after that. How much money will a person spend on their gym membership for 6 months?

   $f(1) = 100$ and $d = 50$ $f(n) = 100 + 50(n - 1)$

   $f(6) = 100 + 50(5) = 350$

   After 6 months, a person will have spent $350 on their gym membership.

💬 Elaborate

9. What domain values usually make sense for an arithmetic sequence model that represents a real-world situation?
   The domain is the set of term numbers or positions, so the domain values that make sense

   are usually positive integers.

10. When given a graph of an arithmetic sequence that represents a real-world situation, how can you determine the first term and the common difference in order to write a model for the sequence?
   The first term is the y-coordinate of the point that has an x-coordinate of 1. To find the

   common difference when you know the difference between consecutive terms is constant,

   find the difference between any two consecutive terms.

11. What are some ways to justify your answer when creating an arithmetic sequence model for a real-world situation and using it to solve a problem?
   You can make sure that the situation is accurately represented by the growth pattern of an

   arithmetic sequence (repeated addition), and you can use estimation to make sure that the

   answer is reasonable.

12. **Essential Question Check-In** How can you construct a model for a real-world situation that involves an arithmetic sequence?
   Construct an explicit rule for the sequence in function notation, and specify reasonable

   domain values.

© Houghton Mifflin Harcourt Publishing Company

ELABORATE

INTEGRATE MATHEMATICAL PRACTICES
Focus on Math Connections

MP.1 Draw an arrow diagram representing a sequence. In a set representing the domain, show the first few position numbers of the sequence. In a set representing the range, show the first few terms of the sequence. Connect each position number with an arrow to its corresponding term. Have students identify the domain and the range of the function representing the sequence.

SUMMARIZE THE LESSON

? What must be true about a real-world problem in order to use arithmetic sequences to solve it? The problem must describe a situation that can be represented by a sequence that is increasing or decreasing at a constant rate.

EVALUATE

ASSIGNMENT GUIDE

Concepts and Skills	Practice
Explore Interpreting Models of Arithmetic Sequences	Exercises 1–3
Example 1 Modeling Arithmetic Sequences from a Table	Exercises 4–5, 15, 17
Example 2 Modeling Arithmetic Sequences from a Graph	Exercises 6–9, 16, 19
Example 3 Modeling Arithmetic Sequences from a Description	Exercises 10–14, 18

INTEGRATE MATHEMATICAL PRACTICES

Focus on Communication

MP.3 Write or project the following problem. James is given 75 vocabulary words the first week in English class. He learns 10 words the first day and five more each day after that. How many days will it take James to learn all 75 vocabulary words? Invite volunteers to take turns explaining how they would solve this problem.

⭐ Evaluate: Homework and Practice

1. A T-shirt at a department store costs $7.50. The total cost, in dollars, of a T-shirts is given by the function $C(a) = 7.5a$.

   a. Complete the table of values for 4 T-shirts.

T-shirts	1	2	3	4
Cost ($)	$7.50	$15.00	$22.50	$30.00

   b. Determine the common difference.

     Each shirt costs $7.50, so the common difference is 7.5.

   c. What does the variable a represent? What are the reasonable domain values for a?
     The variable a represents the number of T-shirts. Only nonnegative integers make sense for a in this situation.

2. A car dealership sells 5 cars per day. The total number of cars C sold over time in days is given by the function $C(t) = 5t$.

   a. Complete the table of values for the first 4 days of sales.

Time (days)	1	2	3	4
Number of Cars	5	10	15	20

   b. Determine the common difference.

     Each day 5 cars are sold, so the common difference is 5.

   c. What do the variables represent? What are the reasonable domain and range values for this situation?
     The variable C represents the total number of cars sold. The variable t represents time, in days. The reasonable domain and range values are positive integers.

3. A telemarketer makes 82 calls per day. The total number of calls made over time, in days, is given by the function $C(t) = 82t$.

   a. Complete the table of values for 4 days of calls.

Time (days)	1	2	3	4
Number of Calls	82	164	246	328

   b. Determine the common difference.

     Each day 82 calls are made, so the common difference is 82.

   c. What do the variables represent? What are the reasonable domain and range values for this situation?
     The variable C represents the total number of calls over time, in days. The variable t represents time in days. The reasonable values for both domain and range values is positive integers.

Exercise	Depth of Knowledge (D.O.K.)	COMMON CORE Mathematical Practices
1–3	**2** Skills/Concepts	**MP.4** Modeling
4–5	**2** Skills/Concepts	**MP.4** Modeling
6–9	**2** Skills/Concepts	**MP.4** Modeling
10–14	**2** Skills/Concepts	**MP.4** Modeling
15	**2** Skills/Concepts H.O.T.	**MP.4** Modeling
16	**3** Strategic Thinking H.O.T.	**MP.4** Modeling

Construct an explicit rule in function notation for the arithmetic sequence represented in the table. Then determine the value of the given term, and explain what it means.

4. Darnell starts saving the same amount from each week's paycheck. The table shows the total balance $f(n)$ of his savings account over time in weeks.

Time (weeks) n	1	2	3	4
Savings Account Balance($) $f(n)$	$250	$380	$510	$640

Determine the value of $f(9)$, and explain what it represents in this situation.

$d = 130$ $f(n) = 250 + 130(n-1)$

$f(9) = 250 + 130(8) = 1290$

After 9 weeks, Darnell's savings account will have a total of $1290.

5. Juan is traveling to visit universities. He notices mile markers along the road. He records the mile markers every 10 minutes. His father is driving at a constant speed. Complete the table.

a.

Time Interval	Mile Marker
1	520
2	509
3	498
4	487
5	476
6	465

b. Find $f(10)$, and tell what it represents in this situation.

$d = -11$

$f(n) = 520 - 11(n - 1)$

$f(10) = 520 - 11(9)$

$f(10) = 421$

The mile marker at time interval 10 is 421.

Construct an explicit rule in function notation for the arithmetic sequence represented in the graph. Then determine the value of the given term, and explain what it means.

6. The graph shows total cost of a whitewater rafting trip and the corresponding number of passengers on the trip. Find $f(8)$, and explain what it represents.

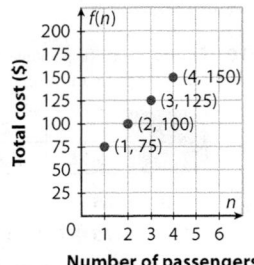

Number of Passengers n	1	2	3	4
Total Cost ($) $f(n)$	75	100	125	150

$d = 25$ $f(n) = 75 + 25(n - 1)$

$f(8) = 75 + 25(7) = 250$

It will cost $250 for 8 passengers on the whitewater rafting trip.

7. Ed collects autographs. The graph shows the total number of autographs that Ed has collected over time, in weeks. Find $f(12)$, and explain what it represents.

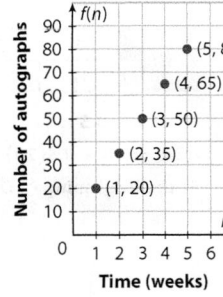

n	1	2	3	4	5
$f(n)$	20	35	50	65	80

$d = 15$ $f(n) = 20 + 15(n - 1)$

$f(12) = 20 + 15(11) = 185$

At 12 weeks, Ed will have collected 185 autographs.

Exercise	Depth of Knowledge (D.O.K.)	COMMON CORE Mathematical Practices
17	2 Skills/Concepts **H.O.T.**	MP.4 Modeling
18	2 Skills/Concepts **H.O.T.**	MP.4 Modeling
19	3 Strategic Thinking **H.O.T.**	MP.4 Modeling

8. Finance Bob purchased a bus pass card with 320 points. Each week costs 20 points for unlimited bus rides. The graph shows the points remaining on the card over time in weeks. Determine the value of $f(10)$, and explain what it represents.

n	1	2	3	4	5
f(n)	300	280	260	240	220

$d = -20$ $f(n) = 300 - 20(n - 1)$

$f(10) = 300 - 20(9) = 120$

At 10 weeks, Bob will have 120 points remaining.

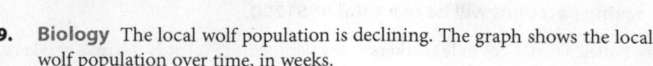

9. Biology The local wolf population is declining. The graph shows the local wolf population over time, in weeks.

Find $f(9)$, and explain what it represents.

n	1	2	3	4	5
f(n)	100	94	88	82	76

$d = -6$ $f(n) = 100 - 6(n - 1)$

$f(9) = 100 - 6(8) = 52$

There will be 52 wolves in 9 weeks.

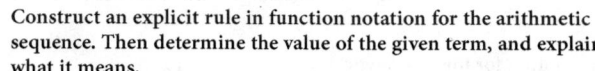

Construct an explicit rule in function notation for the arithmetic sequence. Then determine the value of the given term, and explain what it means.

10. Economics To package and ship an item, it costs $5.75 for the first pound and $0.75 for each additional pound. Find the 12th term, and explain what it represents.

n	1	2	3	4
f(n)	5.75	6.50	7.25	8.00

$d = 0.75$ $f(n) = 5.75 + 0.75(n - 1)$

$f(12) = 5.75 + 0.75(11) = 14$

The total shipping cost of a 12-pound package is $14.00.

11. A new bag of cat food weighs 18 pounds. At the end of each day, 0.5 pound of food is removed to feed the cats. Find the 30th term, and explain what it represents.

n	1	2	3	4
f(n)	18	17.5	17	16.5

$d = -0.5$ $f(n) = 18 - 0.5(n - 1)$

$f(30) = 18 - 0.5(29) = 3.5$

At the beginning of Day 30, the weight of the bag is 3.5 pounds.

12. Carrie borrows $960 interest-free to pay for a car repair. She will repay $120 monthly until the loan is paid off. How many months will it take Carrie to pay off the loan? Explain.

n	1	2	3	4	5
$f(n)$	840	720	600	480	360

$d = -120$ $f(n) = 840 - 120(n - 1)$

Find the value of n for when $f(n) = 0$.

$0 = 840 - 120(n - 1)$

$0 = 840 - 120n + 120$

$120n = 960$

$n = 8$

Therefore, it will take 8 months to pay off the loan.

13. The rates for a go-kart course are shown.

Number of Laps n	1	2	3	4
Total cost ($) $f(n)$	7	9	11	13

a. What is the total cost for 15 laps?

$f(n) = 7 + 2(n - 1)$

$f(15) = 7 + 2(14)$

$f(15) = 35$

The total cost of 15 laps is $35.00.

b. Suppose that after paying for 9 laps, the 10th lap is free. Will the sequence still be arithmetic? Explain.

No, it would not be an arithmetic sequence after the 9th term because the difference between $f(10)$ and $f(9)$ would not be 2.

14. Multi-Part Seats in a concert hall are arranged in the pattern shown.

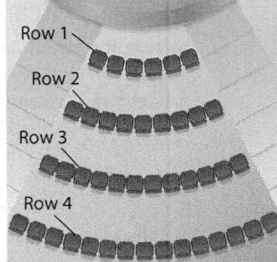

Row 1
Row 2
Row 3
Row 4

a. The numbers of seats in the rows form an arithmetic sequence. Write a rule for the arithmetic sequence.

Row 1 has 6 seats, Row 2 has 9 seats, Row 3 has 12 seats, and so on.

$d = 3$ $f(n) = 6 + 3(n - 1)$

b. How many seats are in Row 15?

$f(15) = 6 + 3(14) = 48$

There are 48 seats in Row 15.

c. Each ticket costs $40. If every seat in the first 10 rows is filled, what is the total revenue from those seats?

$f(1) + f(2) + f(3) + f(4) + f(5) + f(6) + f(7) + f(8) + f(9) + f(10)$

$= 6 + 9 + 12 + 15 + 18 + 21 + 24 + 27 + 30 + 33 = 195$

$195 \cdot 40 = 7800$ **The total revenue will be $7800.**

d. An extra chair is added to each row. Write the new rule for the arithmetic sequence and find the new total revenue from the first 10 rows.

$f(n) = 7 + 3(n - 1)$ **There will be 10 additional chairs: $195 + 10 = 205$.**

$205 \cdot 40 = 8200$ **The total revenue for the first 10 rows will be $8200.**

Have students compare and contrast the way they solve problems by modeling arithmetic sequences from tables, graphs, and descriptions.

15. Explain the Error The table shows the number of people who attend an amusement park over time, in days.

Time (days) n	1	2	3	4
Number of people $f(n)$	75	100	125	150

Sam writes an explicit rule for this arithmetic sequence: $f(n) = 25 + 75(n - 1)$

He then claims that according to this pattern, 325 people will attend the amusement park on Day 5. Explain the error that Sam made.

Sam did not write the explicit form of the sequence correctly. The formula should be $f(n) = 75 + 25(n - 1)$. Therefore, 175 people will attend the park on the Day 5 because $f(5) = 75 + 25(4) = 175$.

16. Communicate Mathematical Ideas Explain why it may be harder to find the nth value of an arithmetic sequence from a graph if the points are not labeled.

Without points labeled, it will be difficult to determine the exact values of the variables.

17. Make a prediction Verona is training for a marathon. The first part of her training schedule is given in the table.

Session n	1	2	3	4	5	6
Distance (mi) $f(n)$	3.5	5	6.5	8	9.5	11

a. Is this training schedule an arithmetic sequence? Explain. If it is, write an explicit rule for the sequence.

The training schedule is an arithmetic sequence because the common difference between each pair of consecutive sessions is 1.5 miles.
$f(n) = 3.5 + 1.5(n - 1)$

b. If Verona continues this pattern, during which training session will she run 26 miles?

Find the session n for which $f(n)$ is 26.

$26 = 3.5 + 1.5(n - 1)$

$26 = 3.5 + 1.5n - 1.5$

$16 = n$

Verona will run 26 miles on the sixteenth session.

18. If Verona's training schedule starts on a Monday and she runs every third day, on which day will she run 26 miles?

Monday, Thursday, Sunday, Wednesday, Saturday, Tuesday, Friday, Monday, Thursday, Sunday, Wednesday, Saturday, Tuesday, Friday, Monday, Thursday

If she trains every third day and begins on a Monday, then she will run 26 miles on a Thursday.

19. Multiple Representations Determine whether the following graph, table, and verbal description all represent the same arithmetic sequence.

Time (months) n	1	2	3	4
Amount of money ($) $f(n)$	250	300	350	400

A person deposits $250 dollars into a bank account. Each month, he adds $25 dollars to the account, and no other transactions occur in the account.

No, the verbal description does not represent the same sequence. The graph and table have a common difference of $50, but the verbal description has a common difference of $25.

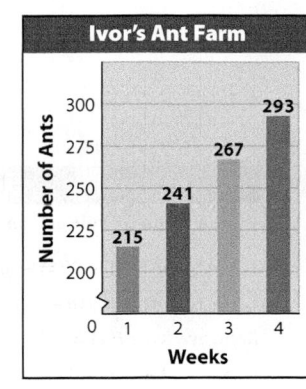

Amount of money ($)

f(n) • (4, 400)
• (3, 350)
• (2, 300)
• (1, 250)

Time (months)

Lesson Performance Task

The graph shows the population of Ivor's ant colony over the first four weeks. Assume the ant population will continue to grow at the same rate.

a. Write an explicit rule in function notation.

The common difference for each week is 26 ants. Therefore, the explicit rule for this situation can be written as $a(n) = 215 + 26(n - 1)$.

b. If Ivor's ants have a mass of 1.5 grams each, what will be the total mass of all of his ants in 13 weeks?

$a(n) = 215 + 26(n - 1)$
$a(13) = 215 + 26(13 - 1)$
$a(13) = 215 + 312$
$a(13) = 527$
$527 \cdot 1.5\,g = 790.5\,g$

Therefore, in 13 weeks, the colony will have a mass of about 790 grams.

c. When the colony reaches 1385 ants, Ivor's ant farm will not be big enough for all of them. In how many weeks will the ant population be too large?

$a(n) = 215 + 26(n - 1)$
$1385 = 215 + 26(n - 1)$
$1170 = 26(n - 1)$
$46 = n$

Therefore, in 46 weeks the ant farm will not be big enough.

Ivor's Ant Farm

Number of Ants

300 | | | | 293
275 | | | 267 |
250 | | 241 | |
225 | 215 | | |
200 | | | |

0   1   2   3   4

Weeks

QUESTIONING STRATEGIES

? What do the bars in the graph represent? The first four terms in the sequence, 215, 241, 267, and 293.

? What does the difference in the heights of the bars tell you? The difference in their heights discloses the common difference of the sequence. In this situation, it is 26.

INTEGRATED MATHEMATICAL PRACTICES
Focus on Communication

MP.3 Have students formulate an explanation of why the explicit rule could also be $a(n) = 189 + 26n$. Students should explain that $a(n) = 189 + 26n$ is a simplified version of $a(n) = 215 + 26(n - 1)$.

Scoring Rubric

2 points: Student correctly solves the problem and explains his/her reasoning.

1 point: Student shows good understanding of the problem but does not fully solve or explain his/her reasoning.

0 points: Student does not demonstrate understanding of the problem.

EXTENSION ACTIVITY

Have students create a bar graph of an arithmetic sequence for the number of seats in each of the first 4 rows of a theater. The first term should be the number of seats in the longest row of seats. Students should trade bar graphs and determine how many rows of seats there are in all, given a row must have at least 4 seats in it.

Students should note that the explicit rule involves subtraction of $(n - 1)d$ value from the value of the first term since the number of seats is declining by a constant difference.

Modeling with Arithmetic Sequences   **186**

Study Guide Review

ASSESSMENT AND INTERVENTION

Assign or customize module reviews.

MODULE PERFORMANCE TASK

 COMMON CORE

Mathematical Practices: MP.1, MP.2, MP.5, MP.7, MP.8
F-BF.A.1a, F-IF.A.3

SUPPORTING STUDENT REASONING

Students may be completely baffled by the challenge before them. Here are some questions they might have.

- **Can I just write the numbers in a very long column and then add them normally?** Of course you can. How quickly do you think you can do that?

- **Can I add the numbers in groups of 10, and then find the sum of all of the groups?** Yes, this is a more efficient method than adding a list of 100 numbers.

Patterns and Sequences

Essential Question: How are patterns and sequences used to solve real-world problems?

KEY EXAMPLE (Lesson 4.1)

A software subscription is $4 a month plus a start-up fee of $8. Use the explicit rule $f(n) = 4n + 8$. Construct and graph the first 4 terms of the sequence described.

n	1	2	3	4
$f(n)$	12	16	20	24

Represent the sequence in a table.

$(1, 12), (2, 16), (3, 20), (4, 24)$ *Generate ordered pairs.*

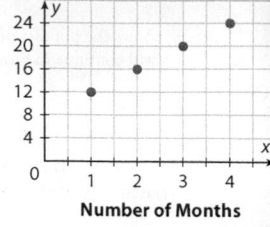

KEY EXAMPLE (Lesson 4.2)

Write a recursive rule and an explicit rule for the sequence 20, 14, 8, 2 ….

$f(1) = 20, d = 14 - 20 = -6$ *Find the first term and common difference.*

Given $f(1)$, $f(n) = f(n-1) + d$ for $n \geq 2$.   *Use the general form of the recursive rule.*

Recursive Rule: $f(1) = 20, f(n) = f(n-1) - 6$

$f(n) = f(1) + d(n-1)$ *Use the general form of the explicit rule.*

Explicit Rule: $f(n) = 20 - 6(n-1)$

KEY EXAMPLE (Lesson 4.3)

Construct an explicit rule in function notation for the arithmetic sequence represented in the graph, and use it to solve the problem.

The graph shows the total predicted sales $f(n)$ for the next n days at a clothing store. What are the total predicted sales on day 10?

15, 20, 25, 30…   *Write a sequence to represent the information.*

$d = 20 - 15 = 5$ *Find the common difference.*

$f(n) = f(1) + d(n-1)$ *Use the general explicit rule.*

$f(n) = 15 + 5(n-1)$

$f(10) = 15 + 5(10-1)$ *Find $f(10)$.*

$f(10) = 60$

The total predicted sales on day 10 are $60,000.

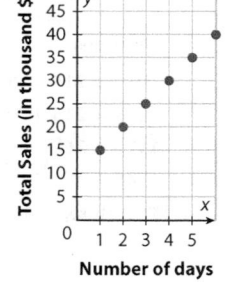

Key Vocabulary

arithmetic sequence
(sucesión aritmética)
common difference
(diferencia común)
explicit rule *(fórmula explícita)*
recursive rule
(fórmula recurrente)
sequence *(sucesión)*
term *(término)*

© Houghton Mifflin Harcourt Publishing Company

SCAFFOLDING SUPPORT

- For students needing more structure, show them the expression Gauss used to solve this problem: $\dfrac{n(n+1)}{2}$. Ask students to explain why it works.

- Challenge students who finish early to write an expression that can be used to find the sum of consecutive numbers from 1 to n for any value of n.

Write the first 4 terms of each sequence following the given rule. *(Lesson 4.1)*

1. $f(n) = n^2 - 4$

$-3, 0, 5, 12$

2. $f(1) = -12, f(n) = 2f(n-1)$

$-12, -24, -48, -96$

Determine if each of the following sequences is arithmetic. If so, write a recursive rule and an explicit rule for the sequence. If not, explain why. *(Lesson 4.2)*

3. $-8, -1, 6, 13...$
$f(1) = -8, f(n) = f(n-1) + 7; f(n) = -8 + 7(n-1)$

4. $1, 8, 27, 81...$
Not an arithmetic sequence, because there is no common difference.

5. The table below shows the balance of a savings account each month after being opened. The balance can be represented with an arithmetic sequence. Write an explicit rule and a recursive rule for the sequence. What will the account balance be after 10 months? *(Lesson 4.3)*

Time (months)	1	2	3	4
Balance ($)	750	715	680	645

$f(n) = 750 - 35(n-1); f(1) = 750; f(n) = f(n-1) - 35;$ **The balance will**

be $435 after 10 months.

MODULE PERFORMANCE TASK

There Has to Be an Easier Way

Quick, now, what's the sum: $1 + 2$?

Okay, you got that one. How about this: $1 + 2 + 3$?

You're really sailing along! Okay, how about this one: $1 + 2 + 3 + ... + 98 + 99 + 100$?

Whoops. That's the problem that mathematician Carl Friedrich Gauss solved quickly when he was 10 years old. And that's the problem you're being asked to solve now. Getting the right answer isn't as important as coming up with some interesting observations about the problem or some ideas that might lead you in the direction of the right answer.

Gauss was 10 years old in 1787, so he didn't have a calculator! No calculator for you either—just use your own paper to work on the task. Then use numbers, words, pictures, or algebra to explain how you reached your conclusion.

SAMPLE SOLUTION

$$1 + \quad 2 + \quad 3 + ... + \quad 98 + \quad 99 + 100$$
$$100 + \quad 99 + \quad 98 + ... + \quad 3 + \quad 2 + \quad 1$$
$$\overline{101 + 101 + 101 + ... + 101 + 101 + 101}$$

If you add the whole numbers from 1 to 100 *twice*, the sum is $100 \times 101 = 10,100$. So the sum of the whole numbers from 1 to 100 *once* is $10,100 \div 2 = 5,050$.

DISCUSSION OPPORTUNITIES

- Ask students to share other ways they could have grouped numbers to add them more efficiently than adding a list of 100 numbers. Compare different methods.

- Have students share how they overcame their "roadblocks" in solving this problem.

Assessment Rubric

2 points: Student correctly solves the problem and explains his/her reasoning.

1 point: Student shows good understanding of the problem but does not fully solve or explain.

0 points: Student does not demonstrate understanding of the problem.

Ready to Go On?

ASSESS MASTERY

Use the assessment on this page to determine if students have mastered the concepts and standards covered in this module.

ASSESSMENT AND INTERVENTION

Access Ready to Go On? assessment online, and receive instant scoring, feedback, and customized intervention or enrichment.

ADDITIONAL RESOURCES

Response to Intervention Resources

- Reteach Worksheets

Differentiated Instruction Resources

- Reading Strategies **EL**
- Success for English Learners **EL**
- Challenge Worksheets

Assessment Resources

- Leveled Module Quizzes

189 Module 4

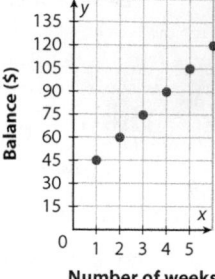

4.1–4.3 Patterns and Sequences

- Online Homework
- Hints and Help
- Extra Practice

Write the first 4 terms of each sequence defined by the rule given. *(Lesson 4.1)*

1. $f(1) = 8, f(n) = f(n-1) - 4$

8, 4, 0, −4

2. $f(n) = \frac{n^2}{2}$

0.5, 2, 4.5, 8

Write a recursive rule and an explicit rule for each arithmetic sequence. Then, find the 20th term of each sequence. *(Lessons 4.2, 4.3)*

3. $2, 0, -2, -4\ldots$

$f(1) = 2, f(n) = f(n-1) - 2; f(n) = 2 - 2(n-1); f(20) = -36$

4. $45, 55, 65, 75\ldots$

$f(1) = 45, f(n) = f(n-1) + 10; f(n) = 45 + 10(n-1); f(20) = 235$

5. Each Saturday, Tina mows lawns to earn extra money which she puts into a savings account. The graph shows the balance of Tina's savings account over the first six weeks of mowing lawns. Write an explicit function to describe this sequence. According to this pattern, how much will Tina have in her account after 15 weeks of mowing lawns? *(Lesson 4.3)*

$f(n) = 45 + 15(n-1);$ **She will have \$255 after 15 weeks.**

ESSENTIAL QUESTION

6. What are two ways of representing an arithmetic sequence?

Possible Answer: An arithmetic sequence can be represented by a recursive rule which gives the first term and defines the nth term by relating it to the previous term, or by an explicit rule which defines the nth term as a function of n.

© Houghton Mifflin Harcourt Publishing Company

COMMON CORE | Common Core Standards

Lesson	Items	Content Standards	Mathematical Practices
4.1	1	F-IF.A.3	MP.2
4.1	2	F-IF.A.3	MP.2
4.2	3	F-BF.A.2, F-LE.A.2, F-IF.A.3	MP.7
4.2	4	F-BF.A.2, F-LE.A.2, F-IF.A.3	MP.7
4.3	5	F-BF.A.1a, F-LE.A.2, F-IF.A.3	MP.4

Assessment Readiness

1. Consider a sequence defined by the recursive rule $f(1) = 15$; $f(n) = f(n-1) - 6$ for $n \geq 2$. Choose True or False for each statement.
   A. The second term of the sequence is 8. ○ True ● False
   B. The third term of the sequence is 3. ● True ○ False
   C. The fourth term of the sequence is −3. ● True ○ False

2. The cost of renting a moped for 1, 2, 3, or 4 hours and can be represented by an arithmetic sequence. The base fee is $30, and the cost per hour is $15. The graph shows the sequence. Choose True or False for each statement.

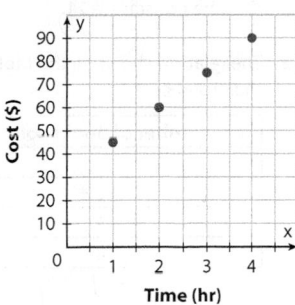

   A. The domain of the sequence is {1, 2, 3, 4}. ● True ○ False
   B. The range of the sequence is the set of all real numbers. ○ True ● False
   C. An explicit rule for the sequence is $f(n) = 15 + 30n$. ○ True ● False

3. Look at each possible solution of the inequality $-12 < 2x + 8 < -6$ below. Is the value of x actually a solution of the inequality? Select Yes or No for each value of x.
   A. $x = -10$ ○ True ● False
   B. $x = -8$ ● True ○ False
   C. $x = -14$ ○ True ● False

4. On Monday, Mr. Sanchez started reading a 225-page biography. He plans to read 15 pages each day until he finishes the book. Write an explicit function to represent the number of pages he has left to read depending on the day number; Monday is day number 1, Tuesday is day number 2, and so on. Find f(5) and interpret its meaning in this situation.

   $f(n) = 225 - 15(n - 1); f(5) = 165$

   On Friday, he'll have 165 pages left to read.

ASSESSMENT AND INTERVENTION

Assign ready-made or customized practice tests to prepare students for high-stakes tests.

ADDITIONAL RESOURCES

Assessment Resources

- Leveled Module Quizzes: Modified, B

AVOID COMMON ERRORS

Item 1 Some students get recursive and explicit rules confused, and they will use the position number n to substitute for $f(n-1)$ in a recursive rule rather than use the previous term of the sequence. Emphasize that since the notation $f(n-1)$ is for the *output* of a function, they cannot substitute the position number.

 Common Core Standards

Lesson	Items	Content Standards	Mathematical Practices
4.1	1	F-IF.A.3	MP.2
4.2	2	F-IF.A.1, F-BF.A.2	MP.4
2.5	3*	A-REI.B.3	MP.2
4.3	4	F-BF.A.1a	MP.4

* Item integrates mixed review concepts from previous modules or a previous course.

MIXED REVIEW
Assessment Readiness

ASSESSMENT AND INTERVENTION

Assign ready-made or customized practice tests to prepare students for high-stakes tests.

ADDITIONAL RESOURCES

Assessment Resources

- Leveled Unit Tests: Modified, A, B, C
- Performance Assessment

AVOID COMMON ERRORS

Item 4 Some students have difficulty remembering that n represents position in a sequence. Sequences can also be confusing when students don't know whether the first term is numbered 0 or 1. Remind students that any time they see $(n-1)$ in the rule, the first term will always be represented with $n = 1$ rather than $n = 0$.

• Online Homework
• Hints and Help
• Extra Practice

1. Write $18z - 7(-3 + 2z)$ in simplest form. Select True or False for each statement.
   A. The expression has 2 terms. ● True ○ False
   B. The coefficient of z is 13. ○ True ● False
   C. The constant is 21. ● True ○ False

2. The relation shown in the table represents the number of various books sold and their total cost.

Number of books sold, x	Cost ($), y
1	5
2	6
2	8
4	12

   Is each statement True?
   A. The domain is all real numbers. ○ Yes ● No
   B. The range is {5, 6, 8, 12}. ● Yes ○ No
   C. The relation is a function. ○ Yes ● No

3. A dog walker charges a flat rate of $6 per walk plus an hourly rate of $30. How much does the dog walker charge for a 45 minute walk? Write an equation in function notation for the situation, and then use it to solve the problem. Determine if the given statement is True or False.
   A. The dependent variable is the number of hours. ○ True ● False
   B. The function for the walker's fee is $f(h) = 30h + 6$. ● True ○ False
   C. The dog walker charges $22.50 for a 45 minute walk. ○ True ● False

4. Consider a sequence defined by the explicit rule $f(n) = -8 + 3(n - 1)$. Choose True or False for each statement.
   A. $f(1) = -8$ ● True ○ False
   B. The common difference is 3. ● True ○ False
   C. The fifth term of the sequence is 7. ○ True ● False

COMMON CORE | **Common Core Standards**

Items	Content Standards	Mathematical Practices
1*	A-SSE.A.1a	MP.7
2	F-IF.A.1	MP.7
3*	N-Q.A.1, A-CED.A.2	MP.4
4	F-LE.A.2	MP.2
5	F-IF.A.2	MP.1
6	F-IF.A.3	MP.2

* Item integrates mixed review concepts from previous modules or a previous course.

5. Graph $f(x) = -2x + 4$. What is x when $f(x) = -8$?
Explain how you found x.

**6; Possible answer: I graphed the function
by plotting the points (0, 4) and (2, 0) and
connecting them with a line. Then, I found
the point where $y = -8$, which is (6, –8). The
x-coordinate is 6.**

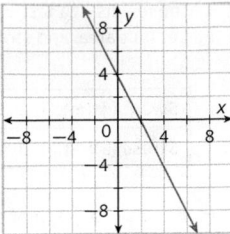

6. Find the first 4 terms of the sequence defined by the explicit rule
$f(n) = 7(n - 1) - 10$. Is it an arithmetic sequence? Explain your answer.

−10, −3, 4, 11…

**Yes, it is an arithmetic sequence. Each term is increasing by a common
difference of 7.**

Performance Tasks

★ **7.** A construction company's cost to build a new home is $35,000 plus $95 for each
square foot of floor space.

   A. Find a function for the cost c to build a house with f square feet of floor space.

   B. Use your function to determine how much it will cost to build a house that
   contains 1600 square feet.

   A. $c = 35,000 + 95f$

   B. $187,000

★★ **8.** The weight in pounds that can be supported by a diving board is given by the
function $w(x) = \frac{5000}{x}$, where x is the distance in feet from the base to a point along
the length of the diving board.

   A. What is the domain of the function? Can the domain include zero? Explain.

   B. Make a table of values and generate five ordered pairs to represent the function.

   C. Plot the ordered pairs, and draw a smooth curve connecting the points.

   **A. The domain is $\{x|\ 0<x\le l\}$, where l is the length of the board. The domain does
   not include 0 as division by 0 is undefined.**

B.

x	$w(x)$
$0.2l$	$25,000/l$
$0.4l$	$12,500/l$
$0.6l$	$8333.3/l$
$0.8l$	$6250/l$
l	$5000/l$

C.

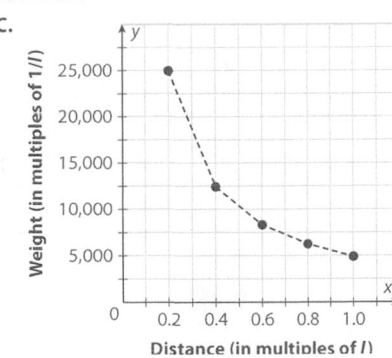

PERFORMANCE TASKS

There are three different levels of performance tasks:

* **Novice:** These are short word problems that
require students to apply the math they have learned
in straightforward, real-world situations.

** **Apprentice:** These are more involved problems
that guide students step-by-step through more
complex tasks. These exercises include more
complicated reasoning, writing, and open ended
elements.

*****Expert:** These are open-ended, nonroutine
problems that, instead of stepping the students
through, ask them to choose their own methods for
solving and justify their answers and reasoning.

SCORING GUIDES

Item 7 (2 points)

A. 1 point for correct function

B. 1 point for correctly evaluating function

Item 8 (6 points)

A. 1 point for correct domain
   1 point for explanation

B. 2 points for a correct table with at least five points

C. 2 points for a correct graph

SCORING GUIDES

Item 9 (6 points)

A. 2 points for a correct graph

B. 1 point for correct domain
   1 point for explanation

C. 1 point for correct function

D. 1 point for correct stress and strain values

★★★ **9.** The results of a test of an alloy are shown in the table. Stress is the tension force per unit area, and strain is deformation of the alloy.

Strain (m/m)	0.01	0.02	0.03	0.04	0.05	0.06	0.07	0.08	0.09
Stress (MPa)	100	200	300	400	500	540	560	550	525

A. Make a graph of the data using strain on the horizontal axis.

B. Hooke's law states that stress is directly proportional to strain. For what domain does the material obey Hooke's law? How did you determine your answer?

C. Write a function to represent Hooke's law for this material.

D. The ultimate tensile strength is the maximum stress value on the stress-strain curve. What are the stress and strain values for this material's ultimate tensile strength?

A.

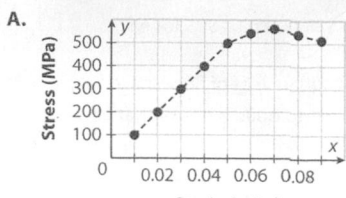

B. For the domain {0.01, 0.02, 0.03, 0.04, 0.05}, the material obeys Hooke's Law. Notice that that there is a constant change in y for the constant change in the first few values of x. This means the function can be modeled by a line $y = ax + b$. Including the point (0, 0) you get $b = 0$. Stress is directly proportional to strain on this domain.

C. $y = 10,000x$ for the domain in part B.

D. $\left(0.07 \text{ m/m}, 560 \text{ MPa}\right)$

Interior Designer Ben is an interior designer and plans to have part of a floor tiled with 36 square tiles. The tiles come in whole-number side lengths from 2 to 6 inches.

a. Write a function for the area, $A(s)$, where s is the side length of the tile.

b. Identify the domain of this function.

c. Make a table of values for this domain. Write the results as ordered pairs in the form (independent variable, dependent variable).

d. Graph the function by plotting the ordered pairs.

e. What does the function evaluated at $s = 3$ mean in this context?

---

a. $A(s) = 36s^2$

b. domain: $\{2, 3, 4, 5, 6\}$

c.

Independent variable, s	Dependent variable, $A(s)$	$(s, A(s))$
2	144	(2, 144)
3	324	(3, 324)
4	576	(4, 576)
5	900	(5, 900)
6	1296	(6, 1296)

d.

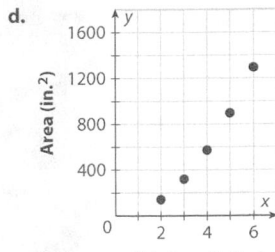

e. $A(3) = 324$; This means the area covered by 36 three-inch square tiles is 324 in².

MATH IN CAREERS

Interior Designer In this Unit Performance Task, students can see how an interior designer uses mathematics on the job.

For more information about careers in mathematics as well as various mathematics appreciation topics, visit the American Mathematical Society http://www.ams.org

SCORING GUIDE

Task (6 points)

a. 1 point for correct function

b. 1 point for correct domain

c. 1 point for correct table
   1 point for correct points

d. 1 point for correct graph

e. 1 point for correct interpretation

Linear Functions, Equations, and Inequalities

CONTENTS

Unit Pacing Guide

45-Minute Classes

Module 5

DAY 1	DAY 2	DAY 3	DAY 4	
Lesson 5.1	Lesson 5.2	Lesson 5.3	Module Review and Assessment Readiness	

Module 6

DAY 1	DAY 2	DAY 3	DAY 4	DAY 5
Lesson 6.1	Lesson 6.2	Lesson 6.3	Lesson 6.4	Lesson 6.5

DAY 6				
Module Review and Assessment Readiness				

Module 7

DAY 1	DAY 2	DAY 3	DAY 4	DAY 5
Lesson 7.1	Lesson 7.1	Lesson 7.2	Lesson 7.2	Lesson 7.3

DAY 6	DAY 7	DAY 8		
Lesson 7.3	Module Review and Assessment Readiness	Unit Review and Assessment Readiness		

90-Minute Classes

Module 5

DAY 1	DAY 2		
Lesson 5.1 Lesson 5.2	Lesson 5.3 Module Review and Assessment Readiness		

Module 6

DAY 1	DAY 2	DAY 3	
Lesson 6.1 Lesson 6.2	Lesson 6.3 Lesson 6.4	Lesson 6.5 Module Review and Assessment Readiness	

Module 7

DAY 1	DAY 2	DAY 3	DAY 4
Lesson 7.1	Lesson 7.2	Lesson 7.3	Module Review and Assessment Readiness Unit Review and Assessment Readiness

Program Resources

PLAN

HMH Teacher App

Access a full suite of teacher resources online and offline on a variety of devices. Plan present, and manage classes, assignments, and activities.

ePlanner
Easily plan your classes, create and view assignments, and access all program resources with your online, customizable planning tool.

Professional Development Videos
Authors Juli Dixon and Matt Larson model successful teaching practices and strategies in actual classroom settings.

QR Codes
Scan with your smart phone to jump directly from your print book to online videos and other resources.

Teacher's Edition

Support students with point-of-use Questioning Strategies, teaching tips, resources for differentiated instruction, additional activities, and more.

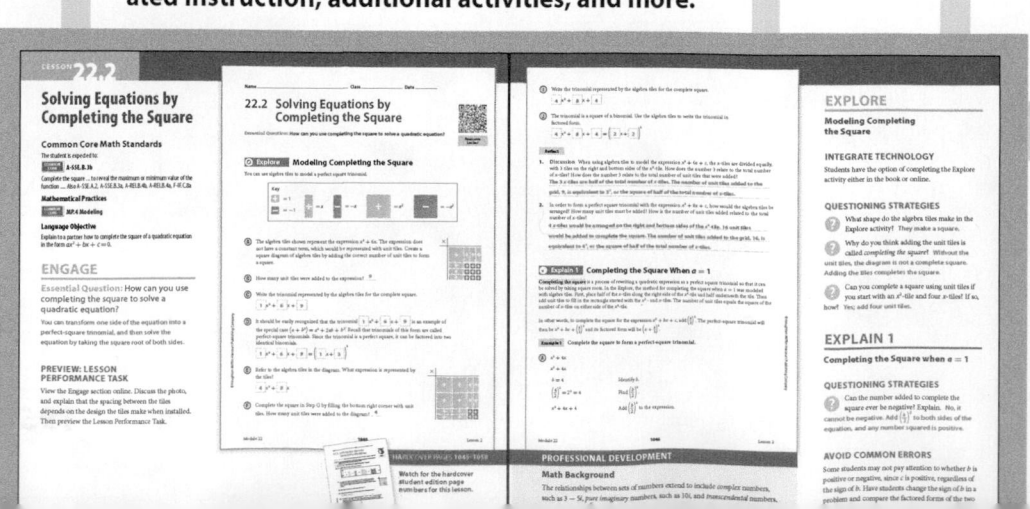

ENGAGE AND EXPLORE

Real-World Videos
Engage students with interesting and relevant applications of the mathematical content of each module.

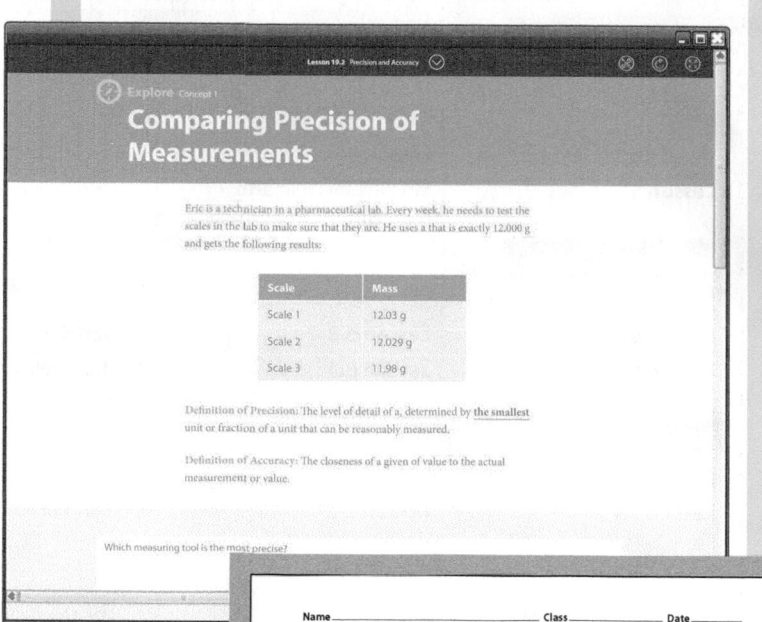

Explore Activities

Students interactively explore new concepts using a variety of tools and approaches.

Name _____ Class _____ Date _____

22.2 Solving Equations by Completing the Square

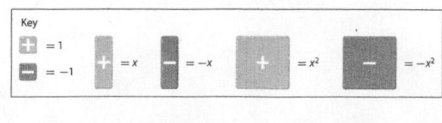

Essential Question: How can you use completing the square to solve a quadratic equation?

A-SSE.B.3b Complete the square ... to reveal the maximum or minimum value of the function ... Also A-SSE.A.2, A-SSE.B.3a, A-REI.B.4b, A-REI.B.4a, F-IFC.8a

Resource Locker

Explore   Modeling Completing the Square

You can use algebra tiles to model a perfect square trinomial.

(A) The algebra tiles shown represent the expression $x^2 + 6x$. The expression does not have a constant term, which would be represented with unit tiles. Create a square diagram of algebra tiles by adding the correct number of unit tiles to form a square.

(B) How many unit tiles were added to the expression? _____

(C) Write the trinomial represented by the algebra tiles for the complete square.

$\boxed{~}x^2 + \boxed{~}x + \boxed{~}$

(D) It should be easily recognized that the trinomial $\boxed{~}x^2 + \boxed{~}x + \boxed{~}$ is an example of the special case $(a + b)^2 = a^2 + 2ab + b^2$. Recall that trinomials of this form are called

TEACH

Math On the Spot video tutorials, featuring program author Dr. Edward Burger, accompany every example in the textbook and give students step-by-step instructions and explanations of key math concepts.

Interactive Teacher Edition

Customize and present course materials with collaborative activities and integrated formative assessment.

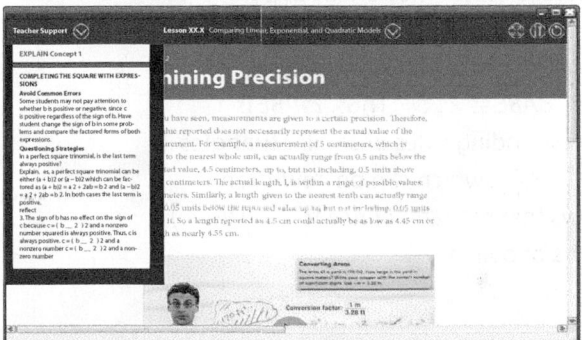

Differentiated Instruction Resources

Support all learners with Differentiated Instruction Resources, including

- **Leveled Practice and Problem Solving**
- **Reading Strategies**
- **Success for English Learners**
- **Challenge**

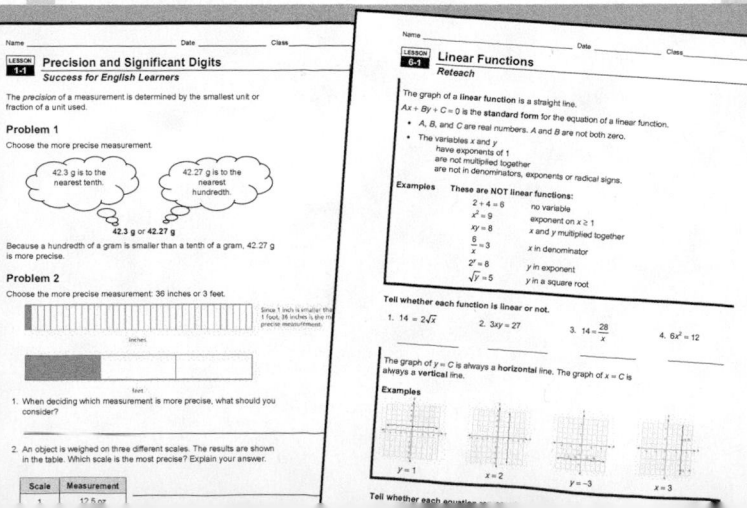

ASSESSMENT AND INTERVENTION

 The **Personal Math Trainer** provides online practice, homework, assessments, and intervention. Monitor student progress through reports and alerts. **Create and customize assignments aligned to specific lessons or Common Core standards.**

- **Practice** – With dynamic items and assignments, students get unlimited practice on key concepts supported by guided examples, step-by-step solutions, and video tutorials.

- **Assessments** – Choose from course assignments or customize your own based on course content, Common Core standards, difficulty levels, and more.

- **Homework** – Students can complete online homework with a wide variety of problem types, including the ability to enter expressions, equations, and graphs. Let the system automatically grade homework, so you can focus where your students need help the most!

- **Intervention** – Let the Personal Math Trainer automatically prescribe a targeted, personalized intervention path for your students.

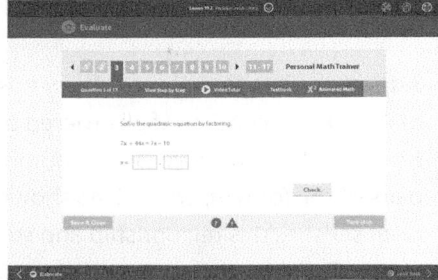

Focus on Higher Order Thinking

Raise the bar with homework and practice that incorporates higher-order thinking and mathematical practices in every lesson.

Assessment Readiness

Prepare students for success on high stakes tests for Algebra 1 with practice at every module and unit

Assessment Resources

Tailor assessments and response to intervention to meet the needs of all your classes and students, including

- Leveled Module Quizzes
- Leveled Unit Tests
- Unit Performance Tasks
- Placement, Diagnostic, and Quarterly Benchmark Tests
- Tier 1, Tier 2, and Tier 3 Resources

Math Background

Understanding Linear Functions COMMON CORE F-LE.A.1b

LESSON 5.1

A solution of a linear equation in two variables, x and y, is an ordered pair, (a, b), such that when a is substituted for x and b is substituted for y, the resulting equation is true. Thus, the ordered pair $(2, 5)$ is a solution of $y = 3x - 1$ because $5 = 3(2) - 1$ is a true statement. The ordered pair $(5, 4)$ is not a solution of the equation because $4 \neq 3(5) - 1$.

In contrast to linear equations in one variable, linear equations in two variables usually have infinitely many solutions. It is important for students to understand the connection between the solutions of a linear equation and the graph of the equation—the graph of an equation is precisely the set of ordered pairs that are solutions of the equation.

A specific example helps to clarify this last point. The graph of $y = 3x - 1$ consists of all ordered pairs (a, b) such that $b = 3a - 1$. In other words, the graph consists of all ordered pairs of the form $(a, 3a - 1)$. As shown above, the point $(2, 5)$ satisfies this relationship and so it must lie on the graph. Conversely, the point $(1, 2)$ lies on the graph, so it must be a solution of the equation, and indeed $2 = 3(1) - 1$. It was also shown above that $(5, 4)$ is *not* a solution of the equation; therefore this point does *not* lie on the graph.

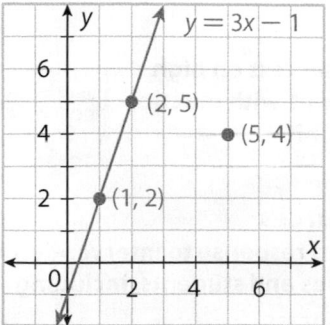

Slope COMMON CORE F-LE.A.1b

LESSON 5.3

The slope of a line is defined as the ratio of rise to run for *any pair* of points on the line.

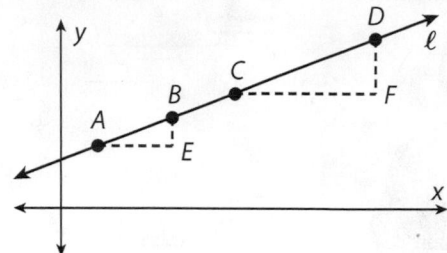

To see why the slope of line ℓ is the same whether points A and B are used or points C and D are used, draw $\overline{AE}$ and $\overline{CF}$ parallel to the x-axis, and $\overline{BE}$ and $\overline{DF}$ parallel to the y-axis. Then $\overline{AE}$ and $\overline{CF}$ are parallel (since they are both parallel to the x-axis) and $\angle BAE \cong \angle DCF$, since they are corresponding angles formed by parallel lines cut by a transversal. By a similar argument, $\angle ABE \cong \angle CDF$. Thus, $\triangle ABE$ is similar to $\triangle CDF$. Corresponding sides of similar triangles are proportional so $\frac{BE}{DF} = \frac{AE}{CF}$, which can be rewritten as $\frac{BE}{AE} = \frac{DF}{CF}$. This shows that the ratio of rise to run (slope) is the same for both pairs of points.

Transforming Linear Functions **F-BF,B.3**

LESSON 6.4

Any linear function may be written in slope-intercept form, $y = mx + b$, where m is the slope of the line and b is the y-intercept. It is useful to understand how m and b affect the appearance of the line. The graph of $y = mx$ is a stretch or compression of the graph of $y = x$. For nonnegative values of m, the greater the value of m, the steeper the resulting line. The figure shows how $y = 2x$ represents a vertical stretch of $y = x$. When m is negative, the line is reflected across the x-axis, as seen in the graph of $y = -2x$.

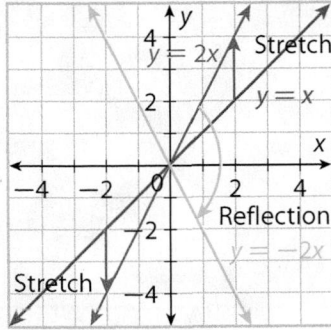

In general, the graph of $y = mx + b$ is a *vertical translation* of the graph of $y = mx$. If b is positive, the translation is upward by b units. If b is negative, the translation is downward by $|b|$ units. Comparing the graphs of $y = x$, $y = x + 3$, $y = x - 2$, and $y = x - 4$ illustrates this.

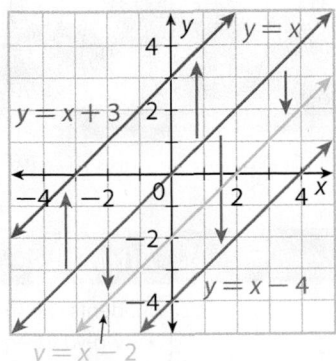

Putting all of these ideas together shows that the graph of every linear function is the result of one or more transformations of the graph of the *parent function* $y = x$. For example, to get the graph of $y = -5x + 3$, the graph of $y = x$ is first stretched vertically, then reflected across the x-axis, and then translated upward by 3 units.

Modeling Linear Relationships **A-CED.A.3**

LESSON 7.1

A graph is frequently used when analyzing raw data from an experiment. Fitting data to a function can be complicated. However, if the data can be fitted to a linear model, it is a straightforward task to evaluate any constants.

Many nonlinear functions can be modeled using a linear relationship. Consider the distance an object in free fall travels in time t, given by $d = \frac{1}{2}gt^2$, where g is the gravitational constant.

A typical experiment to measure g, which varies slightly depending on the location on Earth, is dropping an object from a height and measuring the time it takes for the object to travel a certain distance.

If the time is then squared, the relationship takes on the form $y = mx + b$, where $x = t^2$, $y = d$, $b = 0$, and $m = \frac{1}{2}g$.

Once the data are plotted, the slope of the line of best fit can be set equal to $\frac{1}{2}g$, and the experimental value of g can be easily calculated.

Linear Functions, Equations, and Inequalities

MATH IN CAREERS
Unit Activity Preview

After completing this unit, students will complete a Math in Careers task by writing and solving equations and inequalities related to facts about black bears. Critical skills include reading information from graphs and relating distance, speed, and time.

For more information about careers in mathematics as well as various mathematics appreciation topics, visit The American Mathematical Society at http://www.ams.org.

UNIT 3

Linear Functions, Equations, and Inequalities

MODULE 5
Linear Functions

MODULE 6
Forms of Linear Equations

MODULE 7
Linear Equations and Inequalities

MATH IN CAREERS

Wildlife Field Researcher Wildlife field researchers observe wildlife and their habitats. Wildlife field researchers utilize geometry and trigonometry when surveying habitats. They use statistics, exponential functions, and differential equations to study population changes.

If you are interested in a career as a wildlife field researcher, you should study these mathematical subjects:
- Algebra
- Geometry
- Trigonometry
- Calculus
- Differential Equations

Research other careers that require using exponential equations to understand populations. Check out the career activity at the end of the unit to find out how **wildlife field researchers** use math.

Unit 3   195

TRACKING YOUR LEARNING PROGRESSION

Before	In this Unit	After
Students understand: • graphing ordered pairs • graphing inequalities with one variable • using equations in one and two variables • solving inequalities in one variable • solving for a variable	Students will learn about: • linear functions • rate of change and slope • slope-intercept form and point-slope form • modeling linear relationships • using functions to solve one-variable equations • linear inequalities in two variables	Students will study: • two-way frequency tables • measures of center and spread • histograms and box plots • normal distributions • scatter plots and trend lines

Reading Start-Up

Visualize Vocabulary

Use the ✔ words to complete the graphic. You will put one word in each oval.

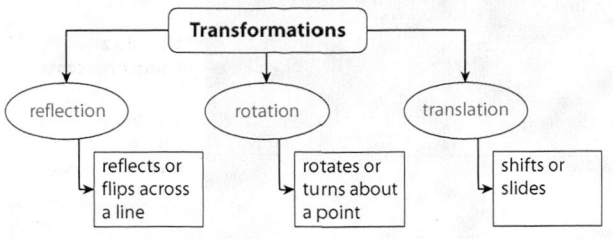

| Transformations |
| reflection | rotation | translation |
| reflects or flips across a line | rotates or turns about a point | shifts or slides |

Understand Vocabulary

Complete the sentences using the preview words.

1. The _____**y-intercept**_____ of a graph is the *y*-coordinate of the point where the graph intersects the *y*-axis.

2. The _____**x-intercept**_____ of a graph is the *x*-coordinate of the point where the graph intersects the *x*-axis.

3. A _____**boundary line**_____ is a line that divides a coordinate plane into two halves.

Active Reading

Layered Book Before beginning the unit, create a layered book to help you learn the concepts in this unit. Label the flaps "Linear Functions," "Forms of Linear Equations," and "Linear Equations and Inequalities." As you study the lessons in each module, write important ideas, such as vocabulary, and sample problems under the appropriate flap.

Reading Start Up

Have students complete the activities on this page by working alone or with others.

VISUALIZE VOCABULARY

The case diagram graphic helps students review vocabulary associated with transformations. If time allows, review how coordinates change for translations, reflections, and rotations in the coordinate plane.

UNDERSTAND VOCABULARY

Use the following explanations to help students learn the preview words.

> **Slope** is a measure of the steepness of a line. **Perpendicular lines** intersect to form right angles. **Parallel lines** in the same plane never intersect. Some transformations preserve slope and parallel and perpendicular relationships. The simplest function with the defining characteristics of a family is the **parent function**. Functions in the same family are transformations of their parent function.

ACTIVE READING

Students can use these reading and note-taking strategies to help them organize and understand the new concepts and vocabulary. Encourage them to ask for help if needed. Suggest that they write detailed verbal descriptions to affirm their understanding.

ADDITIONAL RESOURCES

Differentiated Instruction

• Reading Strategies **EL**

Linear Functions

ESSENTIAL QUESTION:

Answer: You can find the rate of change which is represented by the slope of the linear relationship. The y-intercept b in the slope-intercept form of the linear equation represents the initial value.

PROFESSIONAL DEVELOPMENT VIDEO

Professional Development Video

Author Juli Dixon models successful teaching practices in an actual high-school classroom.

Professional
Development
my.hrw.com

MODULE **5**

Linear Functions

Essential Question: How can you use a linear function to solve real-world problems?

© Houghton Mifflin Harcourt Publishing Company •Image Credit: ©George Doyle/Getty Images

REAL WORLD VIDEO
Cyclists adjust their gears to climb up a steep grade or through rocky terrain. Check out how gear ratios, rates of speed, and slope ratios can be used to solve problems involving speed, distance, and time when mountain biking.

MODULE PERFORMANCE TASK PREVIEW

How Many Cups Do You Need?

Paper or foam cups are convenient for drinking out of, but they can also be used to explore mathematical concepts. They can be used to build a structure by stacking individual cups. Just how many cups would you need to build a structure the same height as your math teacher? Get ready to discover the mathematics of cup-stacking!

Module 5   197

DIGITAL TEACHER EDITION

Access a full suite of teaching resources when and where you need them:

- Access content online or offline
- Customize lessons to share with your class
- Communicate with your students in real-time
- View student grades and data instantly to target your instruction where it is needed most

PERSONAL MATH TRAINER

Assessment and Intervention

Assign automatically graded homework, quizzes, tests, and intervention activities. Prepare your students with updated, Common Core-aligned practice tests.

Are YOU Ready?

Complete these exercises to review skills you will need for this module.

• Online Homework
• Hints and Help
• Extra Practice

Slope

Example 1 Describe the slope of the line that joins the points.

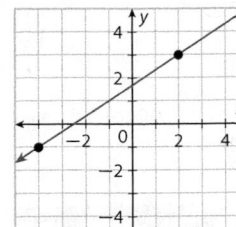

The slope is positive if the line slants up.

The slope is negative if the line slants down.

The slope is 0 if the line is horizontal.

The slope is undefined if the line is vertical.

The line slants up, so the slope is positive.

Describe the slope of the line that joins the points.

1.

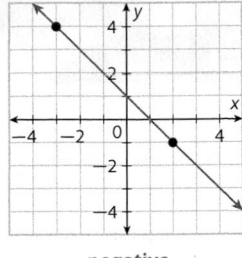

negative

2.

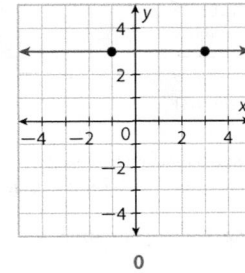

0

Multi-Step Equations

Example 2 Solve.

$$3x + 5 + 4x - 9 = 24$$

$$7x - 4 = 24$$ Combine like terms.

$$7x - 4 + 4 = 24 + 4$$ Add 4 to both sides of the equation.

$$7x = 28$$

$$\frac{7x}{7} = \frac{28}{7}$$ Divide both sides of the equation by 7.

$$x = 4$$

Solve each equation.

3. $3(2n - 7) + 12 = 39$ ___ $n = 8$

4. $4a + 23 - 9a - 17 = 21$ ___ $a = -3$

Are You Ready?

ASSESS READINESS

Use the assessment on this page to determine if students need strategic or intensive intervention for the module's prerequisite skills.

ASSESSMENT AND INTERVENTION

RtI Response to Intervention **TIER 1, TIER 2, TIER 3 SKILLS**

Personal Math Trainer will automatically create a standards-based, personalized intervention assignment for your students, targeting each student's individual needs!

ADDITIONAL RESOURCES

See the table below for a full list of intervention resources available for this module.

Response to Intervention Resources also includes:

• Tier 2 Skill Pre-Tests for each Module
• Tier 2 Skill Post-Tests for each skill

Response to Intervention			Differentiated Instruction
Tier 1	**Tier 2**	**Tier 3**	
Lesson Intervention Worksheets	Strategic Intervention Skills Intervention Worksheets	Intensive Intervention Worksheets available online	
Reteach 5.1 Reteach 5.2 Reteach 5.3	4 Constant Rate of... 7 Graphing Linear... 8 Interpreting the... 11 Multi-Step Equations 20 Slope 23 Unit Rates	Building Block Skills 5, 46, 51, 59, 63, 65, 68, 70, 95, 98, 111	Challenge worksheets Extend the Math Lesson Activities in TE

Understanding Linear Functions

Common Core Math Standards

The student is expected to:

 COMMON CORE F-LE.A.1b

...Reccognize situations in which one quantity changes at a constant rate per unit interval relative to another. Also F-LE.A.1a, F-LE.A.2, A-REI.D.10, F-IF.C.7a

Mathematical Practices

 COMMON CORE MP.2 Reasoning

Language Objective

Describe a situation that can be represented by a linear function, and write an equation for the function.

ENGAGE

Essential Question: What is a linear function?

A linear function is a function whose graph is a straight nonvertical line. It can be represented by an equation written in the standard form $Ax + By = C$.

PREVIEW: LESSON PERFORMANCE TASK

View the Engage section online. Discuss how Jordan could use his known weekly earnings from dog walking to help him project the future profits of his company. Then preview the Lesson Performance Task.

Resource Locker

5.1 Understanding Linear Functions

Essential Question: What is a linear function?

⊘ Explore 1 Recognizing Linear Functions

A race car can travel up to 210 mph. If the car could travel continuously at this speed, $y = 210x$ gives the number of miles y that the car would travel in x hours. Solutions are shown in the graph below.

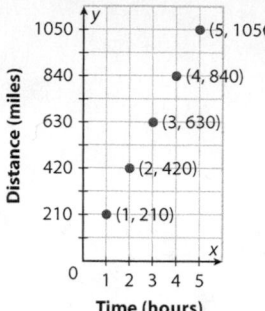

The graph of the car's speed is a function because every x-value is paired with exactly one y-value. Because the graph is a non-vertical straight line, it is also a **linear function**.

(A) Fill in the table using the data points from the graph above.

x	y
1	210
2	420
3	630
4	840
5	1050

(B) Using the table, check that x has a constant change between consecutive terms.

$2 - 1 = 1$
$3 - 2 = 1$
$4 - 3 = 1$
$5 - 4 = 1$

Because x changes by 1 hour between consecutive terms, it has constant change.

© Houghton Mifflin Harcourt Publishing Company • Image Credits: ©Corbis

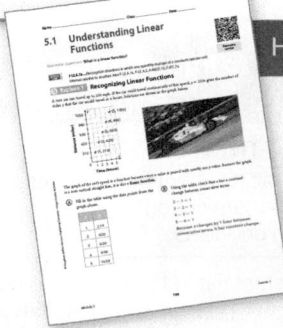

HARDCOVER PAGES 165–172

Turn to these pages to find this lesson in the hardcover student edition.

Ⓒ Now check that y has a constant change between consecutive terms.

$$420 - 210 = 210$$
$$630 - 420 = 210$$
$$840 - 630 = 210$$
$$1050 - 840 = 210$$

Because y changes by 210 miles between consecutive terms, it has constant change.

Ⓓ Using the answers from before, what change in x corresponds to a change in y?

A change in x of 1 corresponds to a change in y of 210.

Ⓔ All linear functions behave similarly to the one in this example. Based on this information, a generalization can be made that a ___**constant**___ change in x will correspond to a ___**constant**___ change in y.

Reflect

1. **Discussion** Will a non-linear function have a constant change in x that corresponds to a constant change in y?
   No; in a non-linear function, a constant change in x will not correspond to a constant
   change in y.

2. $y = x^2$ represents a typical non-linear function. Using the table of values, check whether a constant change in x corresponds to a constant change in y.
   A constant change in x does not correspond to a constant change in y.

   For example, from $x = 1$ to $x = 2$, $y = x^2$ changes by $4 - 1 = 3$ units.

   However, from $x = 2$ to $x = 3$, $y = x^2$ changes by $9 - 4 = 5$ units.

x	$y = x^2$
1	1
2	4
3	9
4	16
5	25

EXPLORE 1

Recognizing Linear Functions

CONNECT VOCABULARY 🔲EL🔲

Point out that the word *linear* includes the word *line*. The graph of a linear function forms a straight line.

QUESTIONING STRATEGIES

? How do you calculate the difference between consecutive values of x or y? **Subtract the lesser value from the greater value.**

PROFESSIONAL DEVELOPMENT

 Integrate Mathematical Practices

This lesson provides an opportunity to address Mathematical Practice **MP.2**, which calls for students to "reason abstractly and quantitatively." By calculating the differences between pairs of x-values and y-values for a function, students demonstrate that linear functions grow by equal differences over equal intervals.

EXPLORE 2

Proving Linear Functions Grow by Equal Differences Over Equal Intervals

INTEGRATE MATHEMATICAL PRACTICES

Focus on Reasoning

MP.2 Some students may not understand the use of the Distributive Property in rewriting $-mx - b$. Remind them that subtracting a number is the same as adding "−1 times the number," so $-mx - b = (-1)(mx) + (-1)(b)$. The Distributive Property can be applied to this expression to get $(-1)(mx + b)$. Adding this term is the same as subtracting $(mx + b)$.

QUESTIONING STRATEGIES

? Does adding $b - b$ to both sides of the equation change either side? Explain. No; it is the same as adding zero to both sides.

CONNECT VOCABULARY EL

Point out that the word *interval* is used in many real-world contexts. Such meanings of *interval* include the difference in pitch between musical notes; a period of time between events; or, in athletic training, fast-paced exercises interspersed with slower ones.

Linear functions change by a constant amount (change by equal differences) over equal intervals. Now you will explore the proofs of these statements. $x_2 - x_1$ and $x_4 - x_3$ represent two intervals in the x-values of a linear function.

It is also important to know that any linear function can be written in the form $f(x) = mx + b$, where m and b are constants.

Complete the proof that linear functions grow by equal differences over equal intervals.

Given: $x_2 - x_1 = x_4 - x_3$

f is a linear function of the form $f(x) = mx + b$.

Prove: $f(x_2) - f(x_1) = f(x_4) - f(x_3)$

Proof:
1. $x_2 - x_1 = x_4 - x_3$ Given.

2. $m(x_2 - x_1) = \boxed{m}(x_4 - x_3)$ Mult. Property of Equality

3. $mx_2 - \boxed{mx_1} = mx_4 - \boxed{mx_3}$ Distributive Property

4. $mx_2 + b - mx_1 - b = mx_4 + \boxed{b} - mx_3 - \boxed{b}$ Add. & Sub. Prop of Equality

5. $mx_2 + b - (mx_1 + b) = mx_4 + b - \boxed{(mx_3 + b)}$ Distributive Property

6. $f(x_2) - f(x_1) = \boxed{f(x_4) - f(x_3)}$ Definition of $f(x)$

Reflect

3. **Discussion** Consider the function $y = x^3$. Use two equal intervals to determine if the function is linear. The table for $y = x^3$ is shown.

x	$y = x^3$
1	1
2	8
3	27
4	64
5	125

From $x = 1$ to $x = 2$ the difference in $y = x^3$ is 7. On the other hand, from $x = 4$ to $x = 5$, the difference in $y = x^3$ is 61. The function is not linear because over equal intervals the function does not grow by an equal amount.

4. In the given of the proof it states that: f is a linear function of the form $f(x) = mx + b$. What is the name of the form for this linear function?
The form is the slope-intercept form of a linear equation.

COLLABORATIVE LEARNING

Whole Class Activity

Set up a list of five ordered pairs in which the change between the x-values is constant and the y-values are left blank. Have half the class select y-values so that the change between consecutive y-values is also constant. Have the other half choose y-values so that the change is not constant. Graph some examples of each type on the board. Show that the points lie on a straight line only when the change between the y-values is constant.

Any linear function can be represented by a linear equation. A **linear equation** is any equation that can be written in the **standard form** expressed below.

Standard Form of a Linear Equation

$Ax + By = C$ where A, B, and C are real numbers and A and B are not both 0.

Any ordered pair that makes the linear equation true is a **solution of a linear equation in two variables**. The graph of a linear equation represents all the solutions of the equation.

Example 1 Determine whether the equation is linear. If so, graph the function.

 5x + y = 10

The equation is linear because it is in the standard form of a linear equation:
$A = 5$, $B = 1$, and $C = 10$.

To graph the function, first solve the equation for y.

Make a table and plot the points. Then connect the points.

x	−1	0	1	2	3
y	15	10	5	0	−5

Note that because the domain and range of functions of a non-horizontal line are all real numbers, the graph is continuous.

$$5x + y = 10$$
$$y = 10 - 5x$$

Ⓑ $-4x + y = 11$

The equation is linear because it is in the <u>standard</u> form of a linear equation:

$A = \underline{-4}$, $B = \underline{1}$, and $C = \underline{11}$.

To graph the function, first solve the equation for <u>y</u>.

Make a table and plot the points. Then connect the points.

x	−4	−2	0	2	4
y	−5	3	11	19	27

$$-4x + y = 11$$
$$y = 11 + \underline{4}x$$

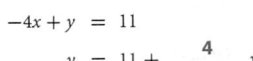

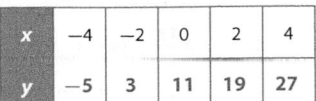

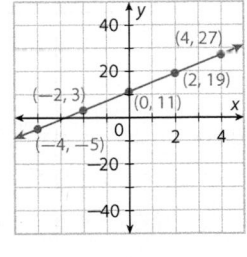

© Houghton Mifflin Harcourt Publishing Company

DIFFERENTIATE INSTRUCTION

Critical Thinking

Students should be aware that there is more than one way (in fact, infinitely many ways) to write a linear equation in standard form. This is because for any linear equation $Ax + By = C$, you can multiply or divide both sides of the equation by any nonzero constant and the resulting equation will be equivalent; it will have exactly the same solution set.

EXPLAIN 1

Graphing Linear Functions Given in Standard Form

QUESTIONING STRATEGIES

? If an equation is in standard form, what are the exponents of x and y? Explain. **Since the exponents are not visible, they must be 1.**

? Is $\pi xy = 4$ a linear equation? Why or why not? **No; in a linear equation, the x and y terms may not be multiplied together; they must be added together.**

? Is π an acceptable value for any of the coefficients in a linear equation? Explain. **Yes; π is a real number, so it can be a coefficient in a linear equation.**

? How can you determine whether an ordered pair is a solution to a linear equation? **Substitute the coordinates for x and y in the equation, and simplify. If the result is a true statement, the ordered pair is a solution.**

AVOID COMMON ERRORS

Students might think that any equation with x and y on the left side is in standard form. Remind them of the other conditions: the exponents of x and y are 1; x and y are not multiplied together; and x and y are not in denominators, exponents, or radical signs.

INTEGRATE TECHNOLOGY

To quickly verify whether an equation is linear, students can solve the equation for y and graph it using a graphing calculator. Remind students that the graph of a linear function forms a nonvertical straight line.

EXPLAIN 2

Modeling With Linear Functions

QUESTIONING STRATEGIES

(?) What must be true about the domain and range of a function for its graph to be continuous? There must not be any gaps in the domain or range.

(?) Is it possible for a continuous linear function and a discrete linear function to share the same linear equation? If so, give an example. Yes; the equation $y = 20x$ could represent the distance traveled after driving 20 miles per hour for x hours (a continuous function) or the total cost of buying x shirts priced at $20 each (a discrete function).

INTEGRATE MATHEMATICAL PRACTICES
Focus on Reasoning

MP.2 Encourage students to determine the domain or the range of a function before graphing it. Discuss how that will help them decide what numbers to use when making a table of values. For example, if values less than 0 do not make sense in the context of the problem, the table should not include negative values. Upper limits may also apply to the domain or range.

5. Write an equation that is linear but is not in standard form.
Sample answer: $x = 64y$.

6. If $A = 0$ in an equation written in standard form, how does the graph look?
If $A = 0$ in standard form, the graph would be a horizontal line at $y = \dfrac{C}{B}$.

Your Turn

7. Determine whether $6x + y = 12$ is linear. If so, graph the function.

The equation is linear because it is in the standard form of a linear equation:
$A = 6, B = 1,$ and $C = 12.$
$$6x + y = 12$$
$$y = 12 - 6x$$

x	−2	−1	0	1	2
y	24	18	12	6	0

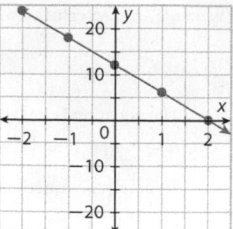

Explain 2 Modeling with Linear Functions

A **discrete function** is a function whose graph has unconnected points, while a **continuous function** is a function whose graph is an unbroken line or curve with no gaps or breaks. For example, a function representing the sale of individual apples is a discrete function because no fractional part of an apple will be represented in a table or a graph. A function representing the sale of apples by the pound is a continuous function because any fractional part of a pound of apples will be represented in a table or graph.

Example 2 Graph each function and give its domain and range.

(A) Sal opens a new video store and pays the film studios $2.00 for each DVD he buys from them. The amount Sal pays is given by $f(x) = 2x$, where x is the number of DVDs purchased.

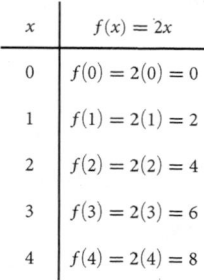

x	$f(x) = 2x$
0	$f(0) = 2(0) = 0$
1	$f(1) = 2(1) = 2$
2	$f(2) = 2(2) = 4$
3	$f(3) = 2(3) = 6$
4	$f(4) = 2(4) = 8$

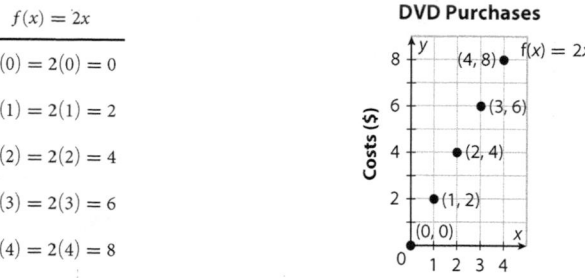

DVD Purchases

This is a discrete function. Since the number of DVDs must be a whole number, the domain is $\{0, 1, 2, 3, \ldots\}$ and the range is $\{0, 2, 4, 6, 8 \ldots\}$.

© Houghton Mifflin Harcourt Publishing Company

LANGUAGE SUPPORT **EL**

Connect Vocabulary

Caution English language learners that the graph of a linear equation on the coordinate plane is a *graph of a line* and should not be confused with a *line graph*. A *line graph* is a graph that uses line segments to connect data points. A *graph of a line* is the graph of a linear equation.

(B) Elsa rents a booth in her grandfather's mall to open an ice cream stand. She pays $1 to her grandfather for each hour of operation. The amount Elsa pays each hour is given by $f(x) = x$, where x is the number of hours her booth is open.

x	$f(x) = x$
0	$f(0) = $ **0**
1	$f(1) = $ **1**
2	$f(2) = $ **2**
3	$f(3) = $ **3**
4	$f(4) = $ **4**

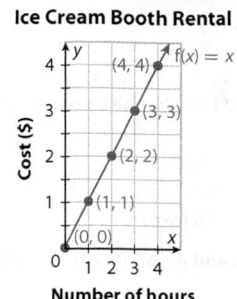

Ice Cream Booth Rental

This is a ___continuous___ function. The domain is ___all real numbers greater than 0___ and the range is ___all real numbers greater than 0___ .

Reflect

8. Why are the points on the graph in Example 2B connected?

The points on the graph are connected because fractional parts of hours are possible, so the function is continuous.

9. **Discussion** How is the graph of the function in Example 2A related to the graph of an arithmetic sequence?

Possible answer: Both graphs consist of discrete points, and for consecutive points on each graph, the difference of second coordinates is constant.

Your Turn

10. Kristoff rents a kiosk in the mall to open an umbrella stand. He pays $6 to the mall owner for each umbrella he sells. The amount Kristoff pays is given by $f(x) = 6x$, where x is the number of umbrellas sold. Graph the function and give its domain and range.

Since the number of umbrellas must be a whole number, the domain is $\{0, 1, 2, 3, 4, \ldots\}$ and the range is $\{0, 6, 12, 18, 24, \ldots\}$.

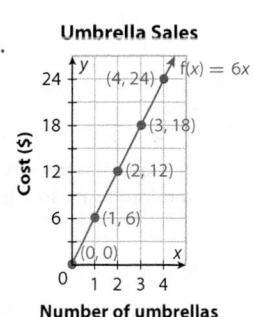

Umbrella Sales

x	$f(x) = x$
0	$f(0) = (0) = 0$
1	$f(1) = 6(1) = 6$
2	$f(2) = 6(2) = 12$
3	$f(3) = 6(3) = 18$
4	$f(4) = 6(4) = 24$

ELABORATE

INTEGRATE MATHEMATICAL PRACTICES
Focus on Critical Thinking

MP.3 Remind students that the y-value of a linear function changes by equal amounts for equal changes in the x-value. If the intervals between consecutive x-values given in a table of values are not equal, you cannot determine whether the function is linear from the table alone. Instead, you can graph the points to see if they form a line.

QUESTIONING STRATEGIES

? Suppose you are given five ordered pairs that satisfy a function. When you graph them, four lie on a straight line, but the fifth does not. Is the function linear? Why or why not? **No; all the points of the function must form a line in order for it to be a linear function.**

SUMMARIZE THE LESSON

? How are discrete and continuous linear functions alike, and how are they different? **Discrete and continuous linear functions are alike in having the points on their graphs lie on a line. They differ in that the graph of a discrete function consists of isolated points, while the graph of a continuous function is an unbroken line or part of a line.**

💬 Elaborate

11. What is a solution of a linear equation in two variables?
A solution of a linear equation in two variables is any ordered pair that makes the equation true.

12. What type of function has a graph with a series of unconnected points?
A discrete function has a graph with a series of unconnected points.

13. **Essential Question Check-In** What is the standard form for a linear equation?
The standard form for a linear equation is: $Ax + By = C$, where A, B, and C are real numbers and A and B cannot both be 0.

⭐ Evaluate: Homework and Practice

- Online Homework
- Hints and Help
- Extra Practice

Determine if the equation is linear. If so, graph the function.

1. $2x + y = 4$

The equation is linear because it is in the standard form of a linear equation:
$A = 2$, $B = 1$, and $C = 4$. $y = 4 - 2x$

x	−2	−1	0	1	2
y	8	6	4	2	0

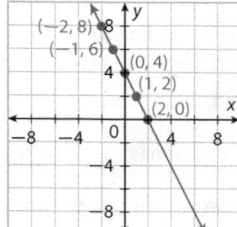

2. $2x^2 + y = 6$

The equation has a variable with an exponent other than one, so it is not linear.

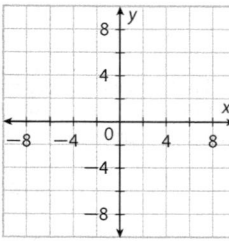

3. $\frac{2}{x} + \frac{y}{4} = \frac{3}{2}$

The equation can not be written in standard form, so it is not linear.

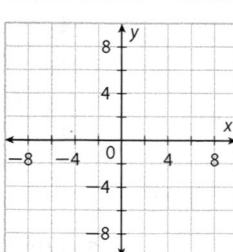

4. $3x + 4y = 8$

The equation is linear because it is in the standard form of a linear equation:

$A = 3$, $B = 4$, and $C = 8$.

$y = 2 - \dfrac{3}{4}x$

x	−8	−4	0	4	8
y	8	5	2	−1	−4

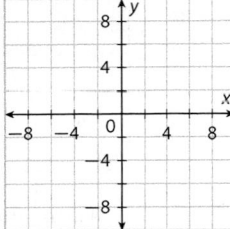

5. $x + y^2 = 1$

The equation has a variable with an exponent other than one so it is not linear.

6. $x + y = 1$

The equation is linear because it is in the standard form of a linear equation.

$A = 1$, $B = 1$, and $C = 1$.

$y = 1 - x$

x	−6	−3	0	3	6
y	7	4	1	−2	−5

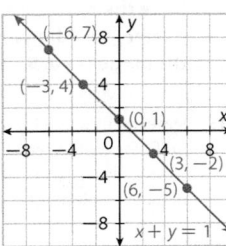

State whether each function is discrete or continuous.

7. The number of basketballs manufactured per day

Discrete

8. $x = \dfrac{y}{4}$, where x is the number of hours and y is the miles walked

Continuous

9. The number of bulls eyes scored for each hour of practice

Discrete

10. $y = 4^4 x$, where x is the time and y is gallons of water

Continuous

11. $y = 35x^1$, where x is distance and y is height

Continuous

12. The amount of boxes shipped per shift

Discrete

ASSIGNMENT GUIDE

Concepts and Skills	Practice
Explore 1 Recognizing Linear Functions	Exercises 1–6, 18
Explore 2 Proving Linear Functions Grow by Equal Differences Over Equal Intervals	Exercises 17, 23
Example 1 Graphing Linear Functions Given in Standard Form	Exercises 13–16, 24
Example 2 Modeling with Linear Functions	Exercises 7–12, 19–22

Exercise	Depth of Knowledge (D.O.K.)	COMMON CORE Mathematical Practices
1–6	**1** Recall of Information	**MP.2** Reasoning
7–12	**2** Skills/Concepts	**MP.2** Reasoning
13–16	**2** Skills/Concepts	**MP.4** Modeling
17	**2** Skills/Concepts	**MP.2** Reasoning
18	**1** Recall of Information	**MP.2** Reasoning

VISUAL CUES

Suggest that students highlight the x in a linear equation in one color and the y in a contrasting color. When checking whether a given ordered pair is a solution to the equation, they can use the same colors to highlight the x and y coordinates. Then they can match the color of each coordinate to the correct variable when they substitute it in the equation.

AVOID COMMON ERRORS

Some students may think that any linear equation written in the standard form $Ax + By = C$ represents a linear function. However, if $B = 0$, then the equation simplifies to $Ax = C$, or $x = \frac{C}{A}$. This is a vertical line and not a function.

PEER-TO-PEER ACTIVITY

Have students work in pairs. Have each student write ten functions, some of which are linear and some of which are not. Have students exchange papers and identify which functions are linear and which are not. For the functions that are not linear, have students explain their reasoning and discuss their answers with their partners.

Graph each function and give its domain and range.

13. Hans opens a new video game store and pays the gaming companies $5.00 for each video game he buys from them. The amount Hans pays is given by $f(x) = 5x$, where x is the number of video games purchased.

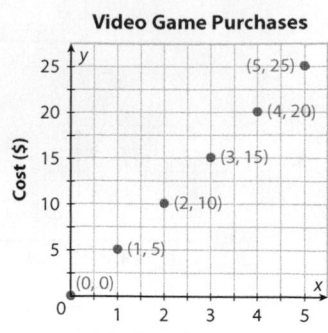

Video Game Purchases

Since the number of games must be a whole number, the domain is $\{0, 1, 2, 3, 4, ...\}$ and the range is $\{0, 5, 10, 15, 20, ...\}$.

14. Peter opens a new bookstore and pays the book publisher $3.00 for each book he buys from them. The amount Peter pays is given by $f(x) = 3x$, where x is the number of books purchased.

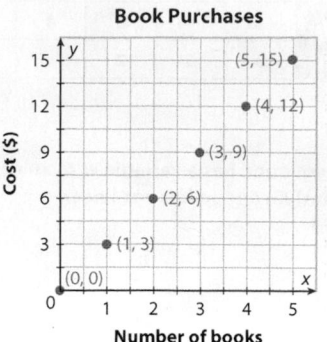

Book Purchases

Since the number of books must be a whole number, the domain is $\{0, 1, 2, 3, 4, ...\}$ and the range is $\{0, 3, 6, 9, 12, ...\}$.

15. Steve opens a jewelry shop and makes $15.00 profit for each piece of jewelry sold. The amount Steve makes is given by $f(x) = 15x$, where x is the number of pieces of jewelry sold.

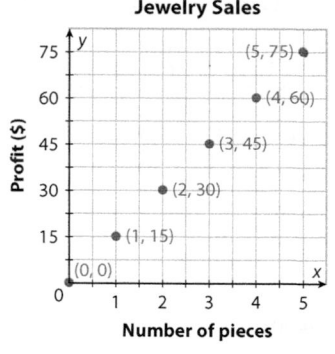

Jewelry Sales

Since the number of pieces of jewelry must be a whole number, the domain is $\{0, 1, 2, 3, 4, ...\}$ and the range is $\{0, 15, 30, 45, 60, ...\}$.

16. Anna owns an airline and pays the airport $35.00 for each ticket sold. The amount Anna pays is given by $f(x) = 35x$, where x is the number of tickets sold.

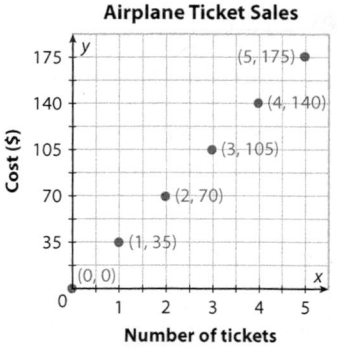

Airplane Ticket Sales

Since the number of tickets must be a whole number, the domain is $\{0, 1, 2, 3, 4, ...\}$ and the range is $\{0, 35, 70, 105, 140, ...\}$.

Exercise	Depth of Knowledge (D.O.K.)	COMMON CORE Mathematical Practices
19–21	**2** Skills/Concepts	**MP.2** Reasoning
22	**2** Skills/Concepts H.O.T.	**MP.4** Modeling
23	**2** Skills/Concepts H.O.T.	**MP.3** Logic
24	**1** Strategic Thinking H.O.T.	**MP.4** Modeling

17. A hot air balloon can travel up to 85 mph. If the balloon travels continuously at this speed, $y = 85x$ gives the number of miles y that the hot air balloon would travel in x hours.

Fill in the table using the data points from the graph. Determine whether x and y have constant change between consecutive terms and whether they are in a linear function.

x	1	3	5	7	9
y	85	255	425	595	765

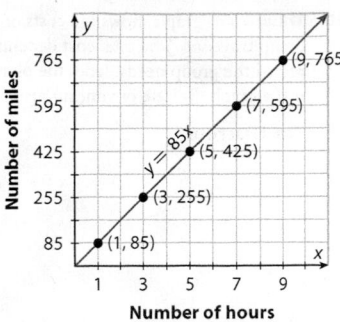

Number of miles (y-axis), *Number of hours* (x-axis)

Points: (1, 85), (3, 255), (5, 425), (7, 595), (9, 765), line labeled $y = 85x$

$3 - 1 = 2 \qquad 5 - 3 = 2 \qquad 7 - 5 = 2$

Because x changes by 2 hours between consecutive terms, it has constant change.

$255 - 85 = 170 \qquad 425 - 255 = 170 \qquad 595 - 425 = 170$

Because y changes by 170 mph between consecutive terms, it has a constant change.

x and y are described by a linear function.

18. State whether each function is in standard form.

a. $3x + y = 8$ **b.** $x - y = 15z$

c. $x^2 + y = 11$ **d.** $3xy + y^2 = 4$

e. $x + 4y = 12$ **f.** $5x + 24y = 544$

a. Yes

b. No

c. No

d. No

e. Yes

f. Yes

19. Physics A physicist working in a large laboratory has found that light particles traveling in a particle accelerator increase velocity in a manner that can be described by the linear function $-4x + 3y = 15$, where x is time and y is velocity in kilometers per hour. Use this function to determine when a certain particle will reach 30 km/hr.

$-4x + 3y = 15$

$$y = 5 + \frac{4}{3}x$$

$$30 = 5 + \frac{4}{3}x$$

$$25 = \frac{4}{3}x$$

$$(3)25 = 4x$$

$$\frac{75}{4} = \frac{4}{4}x$$

$$18.75 = x$$

It will reach 30 km/hr in 18.75 hours.

© Houghton Mifflin Harcourt Publishing Company · Image Credits: ©Cultura Creative/Alamy

QUESTIONING STRATEGIES

? Why is the graph of $y = b$ a horizontal line for any value of b? All the y-coordinates are the same for every value of x, so a line connecting points on the graph is horizontal.

AVOID COMMON ERRORS

Some students may think that any real-world function that involves one continuous variable is a continuous function. Remind them that both the domain and the range must be continuous for the function to be continuous. For example, a function describing the amount of water that flows under a bridge in x hours is continuous, but a function describing the number of cars that drive under a bridge in x hours is discrete.

Have students explain how to identify a linear function from its graph and from its equation.

20. Travel The graph shows the costs of a hotel for one night for a group traveling. The total cost depends on the number of hotel rooms the group needs. Does the plot follow a linear function? Is the graph discrete or continuous?

Yes, Discrete

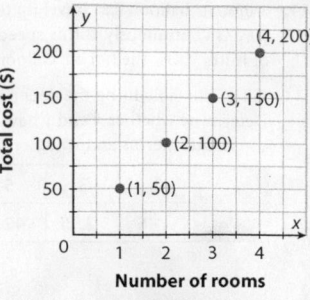

21. Biology The migration pattern of a species of tree frog to different swamp areas over the course of a year can be described using the graph below. Fill in the table and express whether this pattern follows a linear function. If the migration pattern is a linear function, express what constant change in y corresponds to a constant change in x.

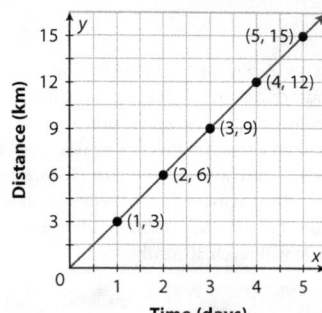

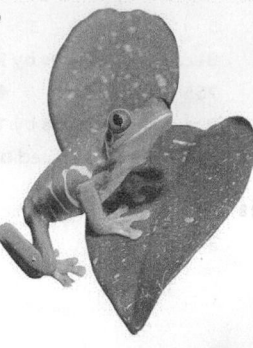

x	y
1	3
2	6
3	9
4	12
5	15

This pattern follows a linear function and the constant change of 3 for y corresponds to a constant change of 1 for x.

H.O.T. Focus on Higher Order Thinking

22. Representing Real-World Problems Write a real-world problem that is a discrete non-linear function.

Sample Answer: The Browns have a $200,000 bank loan. According to the terms of their loan, they must pay back $500 for the first month and 120% of that amount for each following month.

Month 1: $500

Month 2: 500(1.2) = 600

Month 3: 600(1.2) = 720

23. Explain the Error A student used the following table of values and stated that the function described by the table was a linear function. Explain the student's error.

x	−1	0	2	3	4
y	−5	0	5	10	15

The student did not check if *x* had a constant change with respect to *y*. Since *x* from 0 to 2 corresponds to a change in *y* of 5 and *x* from 2 to 3 corresponds to a change in *y* of 5, this cannot be a linear equation.

24. Communicate Mathematical Ideas Explain how graphs of the same function can look different.

If the scales of the graphs are different, the graphs will look different even though they are for the same function.

Lesson Performance Task

Jordan has started a new dog-walking service. His total profits over the first 4 weeks are expressed in this table.

Time (weeks)	Profits($)
1	150
2	300
3	450
4	600

a. Show that his business results can be described by a linear function.

$2 - 1 = 1$ $300 - 150 = 150$
$3 - 2 = 1$ $450 - 300 = 150$
$4 - 3 = 1$ $600 - 450 = 150$

Time and profits have a constant change between terms.

b. Graph this function and use the graph to predict his business profit 9 weeks after he opens.

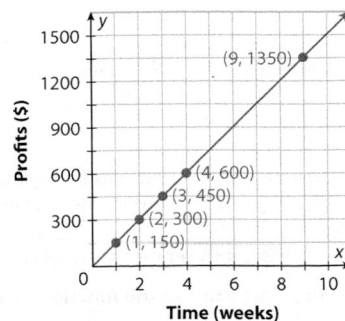

The predicted profit after 9 weeks equals $1350.

c. Explain why it is or is not a good idea to project his profits so far into the future. Give examples to support your answer.

It is not a good idea to project his profits so far into the future because of the number of unknown variables that could affect his business that are not included in the graph. For example, if a competitor starts a new dog-walking service and charges a lower rate, Jordan may lose customers.

EXTENSION ACTIVITY

Have students research the costs of using a dog-walking service. Then have them create a table of values for Time (minutes) and Cost ($) and determine whether the cost of the service is a linear function. Ask students to explain the advantages or disadvantages of a non-linear rate structure. Students will likely find that cost per minute for a dog-walking service is not linear, as customers may receive a discount for dogs that are walked for a longer time.

QUESTIONING STRATEGIES

? Why is it important to show that both time and profits have a constant change between consecutive terms? A linear function grows by equal differences over equal intervals, so if both sets of values have constant change, this situation can be represented by a linear function.

? Why is it helpful for Jordan to graph his data? A graph gives Jordan a visual depiction of his company's profits over time. He can use the graph to estimate his expected future profits.

INTEGRATE MATHEMATICAL PRACTICES
Focus on Math Connections

MP.1 Students can use the table of values to write a linear function, $y = 150x$, that represents the data. Students can use this equation to verify their answers for the predicted profit at 9 weeks.

Scoring Rubric
2 points: Student correctly solves the problem and explains his/her reasoning.
1 point: Student shows good understanding of the problem but does not fully solve or explain his/her reasoning.
0 points: Student does not demonstrate understanding of the problem.

Understanding Linear Functions   **210**

Using Intercepts

Common Core Math Standards

The student is expected to:

 F-IF.C.7a

Graph linear... functions and show intercepts... Also F-IF.B.4, F-LE.B.5

Mathematical Practices

COMMON CORE **MP.4 Modeling**

Language Objective

Explain to a partner how to find the *x*-and *y*-intercepts for an equation.

ENGAGE

Essential Question: How can you identify and use intercepts in linear relationships?

An intercept describes a point where a graph crosses one of the axes, so one of the coordinates of the point is 0. You can use intercepts to graph functions and to find initial and terminal points in real-world applications.

PREVIEW: LESSON PERFORMANCE TASK

View the Engage section online. Discuss the photo and consider what the shape of a sail must be if one side of it is called the hypotenuse. Then preview the Lesson Performance Task.

Name_____ Class_____ Date_____

5.2 Using Intercepts

Essential Question: How can you identify and use intercepts in linear relationships?

Resource Locker

⊘ Explore   Identifying Intercepts

Miners are exploring 90 feet underground. The miners ascend in an elevator at a constant rate over a period of 3 minutes until they reach the surface. In the coordinate grid, the horizontal axis represents the time in minutes from when the miners start ascending, and the vertical axis represents the miners' elevation relative to the surface in feet.

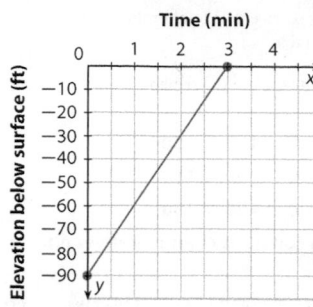

Ⓐ What point represents the miners' elevation at the beginning of the ascent?

$(0, -90)$ Plot this point.

Ⓑ What point represents the miners' elevation at the end of the ascent?

$(3, 0)$ Plot this point.

Ⓒ Connect the points with a line segment.

Ⓓ What is the point where the graph crosses the *y*-axis? $(0, -90)$ the *x*-axis? $(3, 0)$

Reflect

1. **Discussion** The point where the graph intersects the *y*-axis represents the beginning of the miners' ascent. Will the point where a graph intersects the *y*-axis always be the lowest point on a linear graph? Explain.

No; the point where the graph intersects the *y*-axis represents the value of the function

when *x* = 0, which may or may not be the least value of the function. The point may or may

not be the lowest point of the graph.

© Houghton Mifflin Harcourt Publishing Company · Image Credits: ©Lowell Georgia/Corbis

HARDCOVER PAGES 173–178

Turn to these pages to find this lesson in the hardcover student edition.

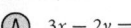

The graph in the Explore intersected the axes at (0, −90) and (3, 0).

The **y-intercept** of a graph is the *y*-coordinate of the point where the graph intersects the *y*-axis. The *x*-coordinate of this point is always 0. The *y*-intercept of the graph in the Explore is −90.

The **x-intercept** of a graph is the *x*-coordinate of the point where the graph intersects the *x*-axis. The *y*-coordinate of this point is always 0. The *x*-intercept of the graph in the Explore is 3.

Example 1 Find the *x*- and *y*-intercepts.

(A) $3x - 2y = 6$

To find the *x*-intercept, replace *y* with 0 and solve for *x*.

$3x - 2(0) = 6$

$3x = 6$

$x = 2$

The *x*-intercept is 2.

To find the *y*-intercept, replace *x* with 0 and solve for *y*.

$3(0) - 2y = 6$

$-2y = 6$

$y = -3$

The *y*-intercept is −3.

(B) $-5x + 6y = 60$

To find the *x*-intercept, replace *y* with ___0___ and solve for *x*.

$-5x + 6(\boxed{0}) = 60$

$-5x = 60$

$x = \boxed{-12}$

The *x*-intercept is ___−12___.

To find the *y*-intercept, replace ___*x*___ with 0 and solve for ___*y*___.

$-5(\boxed{0}) + 6y = 60$

$6y = 60$

$y = \boxed{10}$

The *y*-intercept is ___10___.

Reflect

2. If the point (5, 0) is on a graph, is (5, 0) the *y*-intercept of the graph? Explain.
   No, (5, 0) is the *x*-intercept.

Your Turn

Find the *x*- and *y*-intercepts.

3. $8x + 7y = 28$

$8x + 7(0) = 28$

$8x = 28$

$x = \dfrac{7}{2}$

The *x*-intercept is $\dfrac{7}{2}$.

$8(0) + 7y = 28$

$7y = 28$

$y = 4$

The *y*-intercept is 4.

4. $-6x - 8y = 24$

$-6x - 8(0) = 24$

$-6x = 24$

$x = -4$

The *x*-intercept is −4.

$-6(0) - 8y = 24$

$-8y = 24$

$y = -3$

The *y*-intercept is −3.

PROFESSIONAL DEVELOPMENT

Learning Progressions

In this lesson, students continue to build their understanding of linear functions and their real-world applications. They learn how to find the intercepts of the graph of a function and how to interpret the intercepts of a function that models a real-world situation. Work with linear functions will continue as students learn the meaning of the slope of a line and use linear equations in other forms, such as Slope-Intercept Form and Point-Slope Form.

EXPLORE

Identifying Intercepts

INTEGRATE TECHNOLOGY

Students have the option of completing the Explore activity either in the book or online.

QUESTIONING STRATEGIES

? What other situations could be represented by a graph that goes from a negative *y*-value when $x = 0$ to a *y*-value of 0 at a positive value of *x*? Possible answer: The graph could represent the temperature in degrees Celsius of an ice cube as it warms to the melting point (0°C) or the amount of money owed as you pay off a loan.

EXPLAIN 1

Determining Intercepts of Linear Equations

CONNECT VOCABULARY **EL**

Ask students where else they have heard the word *intercept*. They may be familiar with the term in sports: to *intercept* the ball means *to take the ball away from the other team*. To do so, a player must cross the path of the ball as it is thrown through the air. Help students connect this situation to the *x*- and *y*-intercepts, which are coordinates of the points where a graph crosses the *x*- and *y*-axes.

QUESTIONING STRATEGIES

? Why do you replace *y* with 0 when finding the *x*-intercept of a graph? You are trying to locate the point where the graph crosses the *x*-axis, and the *y*-coordinate of any point on the *x*-axis is 0.

? What intercept do you find by substituting 0 for *x*? the *y*-intercept

EXPLAIN 2

Interpreting Intercepts of Linear Equations

QUESTIONING STRATEGIES

? Describe the significance of the y-intercept in real-world problems where x represents time. The y-intercept represents the initial condition or starting value in the situation.

? In real-world linear models, does the graph always end at the point described by the x-intercept? Explain or give an example. No; possible answer: a function representing temperatures that start below zero and keep rising to above zero would not end at the x-axis.

INTEGRATE TECHNOLOGY

A graphing calculator can be used to find the linear equation containing any two points. Press **STAT**, select **EDIT**, and enter the x-coordinates of the points in list **L1** and the y-coordinates in list **L2**. Then press the **STAT** key, select **CALC**, and then scroll down to **4:LinReg**. Show the students how to use the answer to write an equation in $y =$ format. Once they have an equation, they can enter it using the **Y =** button and view its graph or check the table for the intercepts.

⊘ **Explain 2** **Interpreting Intercepts of Linear Equations**

You can use intercepts to interpret a situation that is modeled by a linear function.

Example 2 Find and interpret the x- and y-intercepts for each situation.

Ⓐ The Sandia Peak Tramway in Albuquerque, New Mexico, travels a distance of about 4500 meters to the top of Sandia Peak. Its speed is 300 meters per minute. The function $f(x) = 4500 - 300x$ gives the tram's distance in meters from the top of the peak after x minutes.

To find the x-intercept, replace $f(x)$ with 0 and solve for x.

$$f(x) = 4500 - 300x$$
$$0 = 4500 - 300x$$
$$x = 15$$

It takes 15 minutes to reach the peak.

To find the y-intercept, replace x with 0 and find $f(0)$.

$$f(x) = 4500 - 300x$$
$$f(0) = 4500 - 300(0) = 4500$$

The distance from the peak when it starts is 4500 m.

Sandia Peak Tramway

Ⓑ A hot air balloon is 750 meters above the ground and begins to descend at a constant rate of 25 meters per minute. The function $f(x) = 750 - 25x$ represents the height of the hot air balloon after x minutes.

To find the x-intercept, replace $f(x)$ with 0 and solve x.

$$f(x) = 750 - 25x$$
$$\boxed{0} = 750 - 25x$$
$$x = \boxed{30}$$

It takes $\underline{30\ \text{minutes}}$ to reach the ground.

To find the y-intercept, replace x with 0 and find $f(0)$.

$$f(x) = 750 - 25x$$
$$f(0) = 750 - 25\left(\boxed{0}\right) = 750$$

The height above ground when it starts is $\underline{750\ \text{meters}}$.

Height of Hot Air Balloon

Reflect

5. **Critique Reasoning** A classmate says that the graph shows the path of the tram. Do you agree? **No; the graph represents the distance between the tram and the peak over time.**

Your Turn

6. The temperature in an experiment is increased at a constant rate over a period of time until the temperature reaches $0\,°C$. The equation $y = \frac{5}{2}x - 70$ gives the temperature y in degrees Celsius x hours after the experiment begins. Find and interpret the x- and y-intercepts.

$$0 = \frac{5}{2}x - 70; \qquad 28 = x \qquad\qquad y = \frac{5}{2}(0) - 70 = -70$$

So it takes 28 hours to reach $0\,°C$. **So the temperature begins at $-70\,°C$.**

COLLABORATIVE LEARNING

Small Group Activity

Have students work in groups of three or four. Give each group a graph that can be used to model a real-world situation. Include functions with both positive and negative slopes. Have each group use the graph to make a poster, giving the graph a title, labeling the axes, and describing a real-world situation that fits the relationship it models. Then students should identify the intercepts of the graph and interpret their meaning in context.

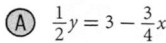 **Explain 3** **Graphing Linear Equations Using Intercepts**

You can use the x- and y-intercepts to graph a linear equation.

Example 3 Use intercepts to graph the line described by each equation.

(A) $\frac{1}{2}y = 3 - \frac{3}{4}x$

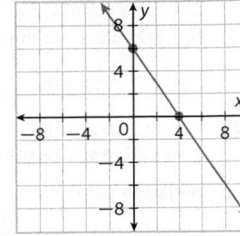

Write the equation in standard form. $\frac{3}{4}x + \frac{1}{2}y = 3$

Find the intercepts.

x-intercept: y-intercept:

$\frac{3}{4}x + \frac{1}{2}(0) = 3$ $\frac{3}{4}(0) + \frac{1}{2}y = 3$

$\frac{3}{4}x - 3$ $\frac{1}{2}y = 3$

$x = 4$ $y = 6$

Graph the line by plotting the points (4, 0) and (0, 6) and drawing a line through them.

(B) $18y = 12x + 108$

Write the equation in standard form. $\boxed{-12x + 18y} = 108$

Find the intercepts.

x-intercept: y-intercept:

$-12x + 18\left(\boxed{0}\right) = 108$ $-12\boxed{0} + 18y = 108$

$-12x = 108$ $18y = 108$

$x = \boxed{-9}$ $y = \boxed{6}$

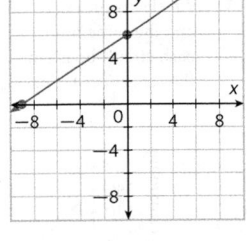

Graph the line by plotting the points $\underline{(-9, 0)}$ and $\underline{(0, 6)}$
and drawing $\underline{\text{line}}$ through them.

Your Turn

7. Use intercepts to graph $3y = -5x - 30$.

The equation in standard form is $5x + 3y = -30$.
When $y = 0$, $x = -6$, so the x-intercept is -6.
When $x = 0$, $y = -10$, so the y-intercept is -10.

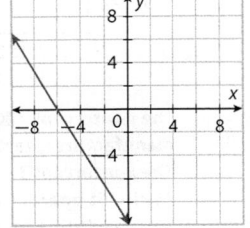

© Houghton Mifflin Harcourt Publishing Company

EXPLAIN 3

Graphing Linear Equations Using Intercepts

QUESTIONING STRATEGIES

? Is it necessary to write equations in standard form to graph them? Explain. No, it is not necessary. Substituting 0 for one variable and solving for the other can be done regardless of the form in which the equation is written.

? Which is easier, graphing a line by using intercepts or graphing a line by generating a table of ordered pairs? Explain. It is easier to use intercepts because you need to find only two points and because you can substitute 0 for x and then y.

AVOID COMMON ERRORS

Students may try to combine the x- and y- intercepts to form an ordered pair. Remind students that an intercept is a number that represents *either* the x-coordinate or the y-coordinate of an ordered pair. To graph a line using intercepts, they need to plot the points (0, y-intercept) and (x-intercept, 0).

DIFFERENTIATE INSTRUCTION

Communicating Math

Show students the "cover-up" method of finding intercepts from an equation. To use this method, make sure the equation is in standard form. First, cover the term containing x with your finger and solve the equation you can still see. The result is the y-intercept. Then move your finger to cover the term containing y, and solve again. The result is the x-intercept. Have students explain why this method works. They should see that covering a term is the same as substituting 0 for the variable.

ELABORATE

INTEGRATE MATHEMATICAL PRACTICES

Focus on Critical Thinking

MP.3 Encourage students to think about the number and type of intercepts that a linear equation may have. For example, an equation of the form $y = C$ has only a y-intercept because its graph is a horizontal line. An equation of the form $x = C$ has only an x-intercept because its graph is a vertical line. (The graphs of $y = 0$ and $x = 0$ are exceptions, because they lie along the axes.) The graph of $y = x$ intersects both axes at the origin, so both the x- and y-intercept are 0.

SUMMARIZE THE LESSON

? How do you use intercepts to graph an equation? Find the x- and y-intercepts by substituting 0 for y in the equation and solving for x, then substituting 0 for x and solving for y. Plot the points that correspond to the intercepts, and then connect the points by drawing a line or line segment through them.

💬 Elaborate

8. A line intersects the y-axis at the point (a, b). Is $a = 0$? Is $b = 0$? Explain.
The x-coordinate of the point, a, is 0 because the x-coordinate of every point on the y-axis is 0. It is possible that the y-coordinate, b, is also 0. (a, b) may be the origin.

9. What does a negative y-intercept mean for a real-world application?
A negative y-intercept means that the situation represented by the line begins with a negative value.

10. **Essential Question Check-in** How can you find the x-intercept of the graph of a linear equation using the equation? How is using the graph of a linear equation to find the intercepts like using the equation?
To use the graph, you identify the point where the graph crosses the x-axis and the x-coordinate of that point. To use the equation, you substitute 0 for y in the equation and solve for x. In both cases, you find the value of x for which $y = 0$.

☆ Evaluate: Homework and Practice

- Online Homework
- Hints and Help
- Extra Practice

Identify and interpret the intercepts for each situation, plot the points on the graph, and connect the points with a line segment.

1. An electronics manufacturer has 140 capacitors, and the same number of capacitors is needed for each circuit board made. The manufacturer uses the capacitors to make 35 circuit boards.

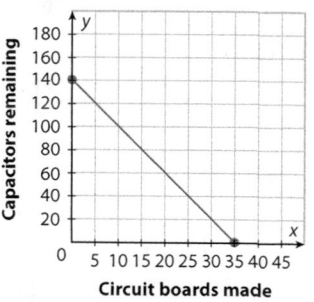

The y-intercept 140 means that the manufacturer started with 140 capacitors. The x-intercept 35 means that when 35 circuit boards have been made, there are no capacitors remaining.

2. A dolphin is 42 feet underwater and ascends at a constant rate for 14 seconds until it reaches the surface.

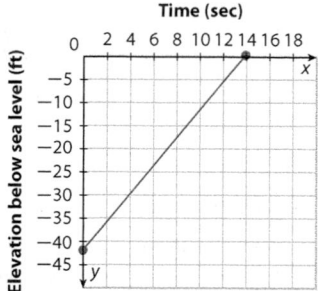

The y-intercept −42 means that the dolphin's starting elevation is −42 feet. The x-intercept 14 means that it takes 14 seconds to reach the surface.

LANGUAGE SUPPORT 🔲EL

Connect Vocabulary

Explain that the prefix *inter-* means *between, among,* or *together.* Help English learners create a list of words they have encountered that contain this prefix, such as the following:

intersection – the place where two roads come together
interact – to act on each other
intermission – the time between two parts of a performance
interview – a face-to-face meeting between two or more people

Find the *x*- and *y*-intercepts.

3. $2x - 3y = -6$

   x-intercept: *y*-intercept:

   $2x - 3(0) = -6$ $2(0) - 3y = -6$

         $x = -3$ $y = 2$

4. $-4x - 5y = 40$

   x-intercept: *y*-intercept:

   $-4x - 5(0) = 40$ $-4(0) - 5y = 40$

         $x = -10$ $y = -8$

5. $8x + 4y = -56$

   x-intercept: *y*-intercept:

   $8x + 4(0) = -56$ $8(0) + 4y = -56$

         $x = -7$ $y = -14$

6. $-9x + 6y = 72$

   x-intercept: *y*-intercept:

   $-9x + 6(0) = 72$ $-9(0) + 6y = 72$

         $x = -8$ $y = 12$

7. $\frac{3}{5}x + \frac{1}{2}y = 30$

   x-intercept: *y*-intercept:

   $\frac{3}{5}x + \frac{1}{2}(0) = 30$ $\frac{3}{5}(0) + \frac{1}{2}y = 30$

         $x = 50$ $y = 60$

8. $-\frac{3}{4}x + \frac{5}{6}y = 15$

   x-intercept: *y*-intercept:

   $-\frac{3}{4}x + \frac{5}{6}(0) = 15$ $-\frac{3}{4}(0) + \frac{5}{6}y = 15$

         $x = -20$ $y = 18$

Interpret the intercepts for each situation. Use the intercepts to graph the function.

9. **Biology** A lake was stocked with 350 trout. Each year, the population decreases by 14. The population of trout in the lake after *x* years is represented by the function $f(x) = 350 - 14x$.

   x-intercept: 25; *y*-intercept: 350

   The *x*-intercept means that it takes 25 years for there to be no trout in the lake. The *y*-intercept represents the number of trout, 350, that were in the lake at the beginning of the population decrease.

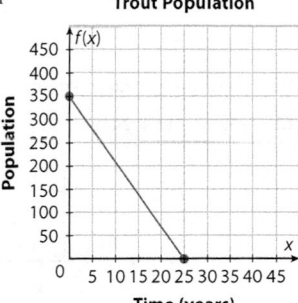

Trout Population

10. The air temperature is −6 °C at sunrise and rises 3 °C every hour for several hours. The air temperature after *x* hours is represented by the function $f(x) = 3x - 6$.

   x-intercept: 2; *y*-intercept: −6

   The *x*-intercept means that it takes 2 hours for the temperature to reach 0 °C. The *y*-intercept represents the temperature at sunrise, −6 °C.

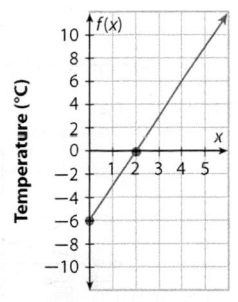

Time (hours)

Exercise	Depth of Knowledge (D.O.K.)	COMMON CORE Mathematical Practices
1–2	**2** Skills/Concepts	**MP.4** Modeling
3–8	**1** Recall of Information	**MP.2** Reasoning
9–12	**2** Skills/Concepts	**MP.4** Modeling
13–18	**1** Recall of Information	**MP.2** Reasoning
19	**2** Skills/Concepts	**MP.4** Modeling
20	**2** Skills/Concepts	**MP.3** Logic

EVALUATE

Personal Math Trainer

ASSIGNMENT GUIDE

Concepts and Skills	Practice
Explore Identifying Intercepts	Exercises 1–2
Example 1 Determining Intercepts of Linear Equations	Exercises 3–8, 20–21
Example 2 Interpreting Intercepts of Linear Equations	Exercises 9–12, 19, 22–24, 26
Example 3 Graphing Linear Equations Using Intercepts	Exercises 13–18, 25

AVOID COMMON ERRORS

Students may plot points on the wrong axes when using intercepts to graph an equation. Remind students that the *x*-intercept is the *x*-coordinate of a point on the *x*-axis, and the *y*-intercept is the *y*-coordinate of a point on the *y*-axis. Suggest that they write the ordered pairs that correspond to the intercepts before plotting the points.

? If an equation has fractional coefficients, how can it be rewritten as an equivalent equation that does not have the fractions? Multiply both sides of the equation by the least common denominator to eliminate of the fractions.

COGNITIVE STRATEGIES

Have students write step-by-step instructions for graphing the line described by an equation of the form $Ax + By = C$. Provide the following sentence starters to help students organize their thinking:
1. Find the x-intercept by …
2. Find the y-intercept by …
3. Graph the line by …

11. The number of brake pads needed for a car is 4, and a manufacturing plant has 480 brake pads. The number of brake pads remaining after brake pads have been installed on x cars is $f(x) = 480 - 4x$.

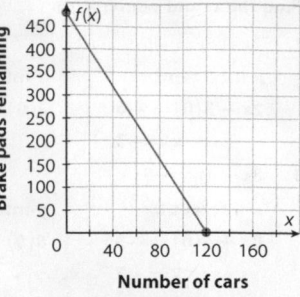

x-intercept: 120; y-intercept: 480

The x-intercept means that it would take 120 cars to run out of brake pads. The y-intercept represents the number of brake pads before any are installed.

12. Connor is running a 10-kilometer cross country race. He runs 1 kilometer every 4 minutes. Connor's distance from the finish line after x minutes is represented by the function $f(x) = 10 - \frac{1}{4}x$.

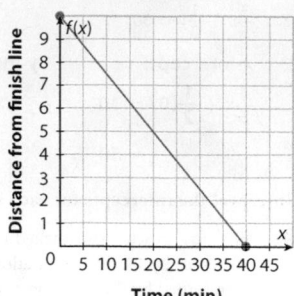

x-intercept: 40; y-intercept: 10

The x-intercept means that it takes Connor 40 minutes to reach the finish line. The y-intercept represents Connor's distance from the finish line, 10 km, at the beginning of the race.

Use intercepts to graph the line described by each equation.

13. $-6y = -4x + 24$

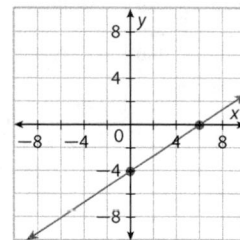

x-intercept: 6; y-intercept: –4

14. $9y = 3x + 18$

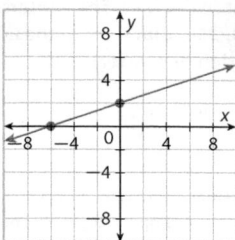

x-intercept: —6; y-intercept: 2

15. $y = \frac{1}{5}x + 2$

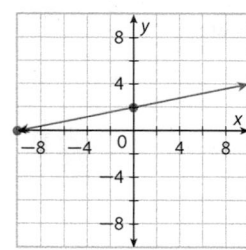

x-intercept: —10; y-intercept: 2

16. $-3y = 7x - 21$

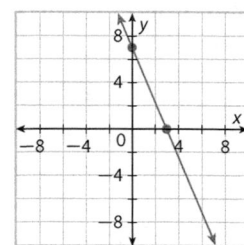

x-intercept: 3; y-intercept: 7

Exercise	Depth of Knowledge (D.O.K.)	COMMON CORE Mathematical Practices
21	**1** Recall of Information	**MP.2** Reasoning
22–23	**2** Skills/Concepts	**MP.4** Modeling
24	**3** Strategic Thinking H.O.T.	**MP.4** Modeling
25	**2** Skills/Concepts H.O.T.	**MP.2** Reasoning
26	**3** Strategic Thinking H.O.T.	**MP.4** Modeling

17. $\frac{3}{2}x = -4y - 12$

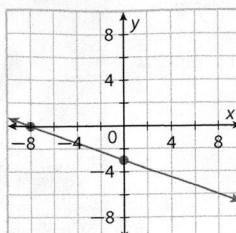

18. $\frac{2}{3}y = 2 - \frac{1}{2}x$

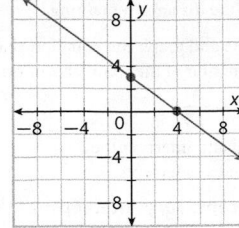

x-intercept: 4; y-intercept: 3

19. Kim owes her friend $245 and plans to pay $35 per week. Write an equation of the function that shows the amount Kim owes after x weeks. Then find and interpret the intercepts of the function.

The equation of the function is $f(x) = 35x - 245$.

x-intercept: 7; y-intercept: −245

The x-intercept means that it takes Kim 7 weeks to repay the amount completely. The y-intercept represents the amount Kim owes her friend, $245, before she starts making payments.

20. Explain the Error Arlo incorrectly found the x-intercept of $9x + 12y = 144$. His work is shown.

$9x + 12y = 144$

$9(0) + 12y = 144$

$12y = 144$

$y = 12$ The x-intercept is 12.

Arlo substituted 0 for x and solved for y, so he found the y-intercept. He should have substituted 0 for y and solved for x.

Explain Arlo's error.

21. Determine whether each point could represent an x-intercept, y-intercept, both, or neither.

A. $(0, 5)$ **y-intercept**   **B.** $(0, 0)$ **both**   **C.** $(-7, 0)$ **x-intercept**

D. $(3, -4)$ **neither**   **E.** $(19, 0)$ **x-intercept**

22. A bank employee notices an abandoned checking account with a balance of $360. The bank charges an $8 monthly fee for the account.

a. Write and graph the equation that gives the balance $f(x)$ in dollars as a function of the number of months, x.

$f(x) = 360 - 8x$

b. Find and interpret the x- and y-intercepts.

x-intercept: 45; y-intercept: 360

It takes 45 months for the balance to be $0. The initial balance is $360.

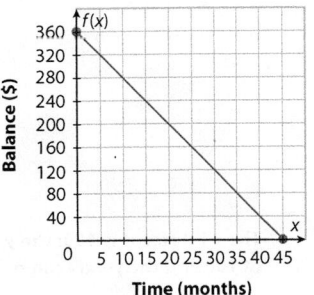

INTEGRATE MATHEMATICAL PRACTICES

Focus on Communication

MP.3 In many real-world contexts, negative values for intercepts do not make sense. Discuss situations where they do make sense, such as a submarine rising from below the sea's surface, or a company that may have either a profit or a loss.

INTEGRATE MATHEMATICAL PRACTICES

Focus on Modeling

MP.4 Remind students that the scales for the x- and y-axis are not necessarily the same. Discuss how they can use the x- and y-intercepts to determine appropriate scales for their graphs.

Focus on Critical Thinking

MP.3 Have students find the x- and y-intercepts of the equation $y = 4x$, and discuss whether they can graph the equation based on the intercepts. Students should find that because both the x- and y-intercepts are 0, they produce the same point, $(0, 0)$. One point is not enough to graph a line, so another graphing method is needed.

JOURNAL

Pose the following problem: School T-shirts cost $9 and sweatshirts cost $12. How many of each could you buy with $144? Have students write an equation to model the situation, find and interpret the intercepts, and graph the equation.

23. Kathryn is walking on a treadmill at a constant pace for 30 minutes. She has programmed the treadmill for a 2-mile walk. The display counts backward to show the distance remaining.

a. Write and graph the equation that gives the distance $f(x)$ left in miles as a function of the number x of minutes she has been walking.

$$f(x) = 2 - \frac{1}{15}x$$

b. Find and interpret the x- and y-intercepts.

x-intercept: 30; y-intercept: 2

The x-intercept means that it takes Kathryn 30 minutes to complete her walk. The y-intercept represents the distance remaining when Kathryn begins, 2 mi.

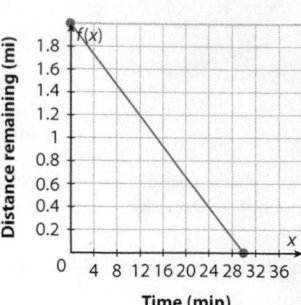

H.O.T. Focus on Higher Order Thinking

24. **Represent Real-World Problems** Write a real-world problem that could be modeled by a linear function whose x-intercept is 6 and whose y-intercept is 60.

Sample answer: Courtney sprints across a field that is 60 meters wide. It takes her 6 seconds to reach the other side of the field. Her distance from the other side of the field after x seconds is represented by y.

25. **Draw Conclusions** For any linear equation $Ax + By = C$, what are the intercepts in terms of A, B, and C?

If A is not zero, the x-intercept is $\frac{C}{A}$, and if B is not zero, the y-intercept is $\frac{C}{B}$.

26. **Multiple Representations** Find the intercepts of $3x + 40y = 1200$. Explain how to use the intercepts to determine appropriate scales for the graph and then create a graph.

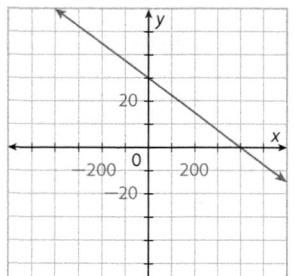

The x-intercept is 400; the y-intercept is 30. So the x-axis can go from -500 to 500 in steps of 100 and the y-axis can go from -50 to 50 in steps of 10.

Lesson Performance Task

A sail on a boat is in the shape of a right triangle. If the sail is superimposed on a coordinate plane, the point where the horizontal and vertical sides meet is $(0, 0)$ and the sail is above and to the right of $(0, 0)$. The equation of the line that represents the sail's hypotenuse in feet is $10x + 4y = 240$.

a. Find and interpret the intercepts of the line and use them to graph the line. Then use the triangle formed by the x-axis, y-axis, and the line described by the above equation to find the area of the sail.

b. Now find the area of a sail whose hypotenuse is described by the equation $Ax + By = C$, where A, B, and C are all positive.

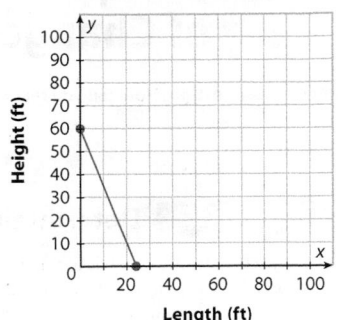

Length (ft)

a. x-intercept:

$$10x + 4y = 240$$
$$10x + 4(0) = 240$$
$$10x - 240$$
$$\frac{10x}{10} = \frac{240}{10}$$
$$x = 24$$

y-intercept:

$$10x + 4y = 240$$
$$10(0) + 4y = 240$$
$$4y = 240$$
$$\frac{4y}{4} = \frac{240}{4}$$
$$y = 60$$

The x-intercept is $(24, 0)$ and that means the sail is 24 feet wide. The y-intercept is $(0, 60)$ and that means the sail is 60 feet tall.

The area of a triangle is $A = \frac{1}{2}bh$.

$$A = \frac{1}{2}(24)(60)$$
$$= \frac{1}{2}(1440)$$
$$= 720$$

The area of the sail is 720 ft².

b. The x-intercept is $\left(\frac{C}{A}, 0\right)$ so the sail is $\frac{C}{A}$ feet wide. The y-intercept is $\left(\frac{C}{B}, 0\right)$ so the sail is $\frac{C}{A}$ feet tall. The area of the sail is $\frac{1}{2}\left(\frac{C}{A}\right)\left(\frac{C}{B}\right) = \frac{1}{2}\left(\frac{C^2}{AB}\right)$ ft².

EXTENSION ACTIVITY

Have students determine the x- and y- intercepts of some other right triangles that would have the same area as the sail in the Lesson Performance Task. Discuss which triangles would make the most effective sails.

There are many possible solutions, including the pairs of intercepts 2 and 720, 15 and 96, and 36 and 40. Students may reason that a sail that is too long or too narrow would not catch the wind well, so a sail whose base and height are not too different in length would work best.

AVOID COMMON ERRORS

Some students may substitute 0 for the wrong variable when finding intercepts. Remind them that any point on the x-axis has a y-coordinate of 0, so they must let $y = 0$ to find the x-intercept. Similarly, any point on the y-axis has an x-coordinate of 0, so they must let $x = 0$ to find the y-intercept.

INTEGRATE MATHEMATICAL PRACTICES

Focus on Patterns

MP.8 Have students use the formulas they find for the x- and y-intercepts of the equation $Ax + By = C$ to explore patterns relating the values of intercepts to the coefficients in a linear equation. For example, after finding that because A is not 0, the x-intercept for $Ax + By = C$ is given by $\frac{C}{A}$, have them verify that the x-intercept for the given equation can be found by dividing 240 by 10.

Scoring Rubric

2 points: Student correctly solves the problem and explains his/her reasoning.

1 point: Student shows good understanding of the problem but does not fully solve or explain his/her reasoning.

0 points: Student does not demonstrate understanding of the problem.

Interpreting Rate of Change and Slope

Common Core Math Standards

The student is expected to:

 **F-IF.B.6**

Calculate and interpret the average rate of change of a function… Estimate the rate of change from a graph. Also F-LE.B.5

Mathematical Practices

 MP.2 Reasoning

Language Objective

Describe the rate of change in a real-world situation by using the words *for every, each,* or *per* to relate two quantities.

ENGAGE

Essential Question: How can you relate rate of change and slope in linear relationships?

The rate of change for a function can be expressed as a ratio of the change in *y*-values over the change in *x*-values for a specified part of the domain of the function. For a linear function, the rate of change is the slope of the line.

PREVIEW: LESSON PERFORMANCE TASK

View the Engage section online. Discuss how you could analyze different Internet service providers' charges for various amounts of data to decide which one has the best plan. Then preview the Lesson Performance Task.

Name_____ Class_____ Date_____

5.3 Interpreting Rate of Change and Slope

Essential question: How can you relate rate of change and slope in linear relationships?

⊘ Explore   Determining Rates of Change

For a function defined in terms of *x* and *y*, the **rate of change** over a part of the domain of the function is a ratio that compares the change in *y* to the change in *x* in that part of the domain.

$$\text{rate of change} = \frac{\text{change in } y}{\text{change in } x}$$

The table shows the year and the cost of sending 1-ounce letter in cents.

Years after 2000 (x)	3	4	6	8	13
Cost (cents)	37	37	39	42	46

Find the rate of change, $\dfrac{\text{change in postage}}{\text{change in year}}$, for each time period using the table.

(A) From 2003 to 2004: $\dfrac{\boxed{37} - \boxed{37}}{4 - 3} = \boxed{0}$ cent(s) per year

(B) From 2004 to 2006: $\dfrac{\boxed{39} - \boxed{37}}{6 - 4} = \boxed{\frac{2}{2}} = \boxed{1}$ cent(s) per year

(C) From 2006 to 2008: $\dfrac{\boxed{42} - \boxed{39}}{8 - 6} = \boxed{\frac{3}{2}} = \boxed{1.5}$ cent(s) per year

(D) From 2008 to 2013: $\dfrac{\boxed{46} - \boxed{42}}{13 - 8} = \boxed{\frac{4}{5}} = \boxed{0.8}$ cent(s) per year

© Houghton Mifflin Harcourt Publishing Company • Image Credits: ©David R. Frazier Photolibrary, Inc./Alamy

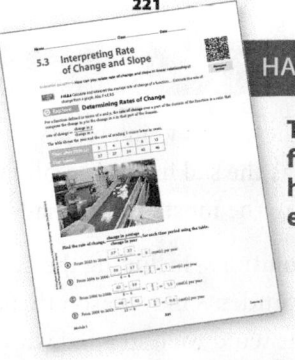

HARDCOVER PAGES 179–188

Turn to these pages to find this lesson in the hardcover student edition.

(E) Plot the points represented in the table. Connect the points with line segments to make a statistical line graph.

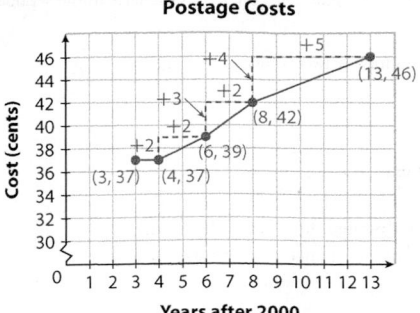

Postage Costs

Find the rate of change for each time period using the graph.

(F) Label the vertical increase (*rise*) and the horizontal increase (*run*) between points (4, 37) and (6, 39). Then find the rate of change, $\frac{rise}{run}$.

$$\frac{rise}{run} = \frac{\boxed{2}}{\boxed{2}} = \boxed{1} \text{ cent(s) per year}$$

(G) Label the vertical increase (*rise*) and the horizontal increase (*run*) between points (6, 39) and (8, 42). Then find the rate of change, $\frac{rise}{run}$.

$$\frac{rise}{run} = \frac{\boxed{3}}{\boxed{2}} = \boxed{1.5} \text{ cent(s) per year}$$

(H) Label the vertical increase (*rise*) and the horizontal increase (*run*) between points (8, 42) and (13, 46). Then find the rate of change, $\frac{rise}{run}$.

$$\frac{rise}{run} = \frac{\boxed{4}}{\boxed{5}} = \boxed{0.8} \text{ cent(s) per year}$$

Reflect

1. **Discussion** Between which two years is the rate of change $\frac{\text{change in postage}}{\text{change in years}}$ the greatest?

   The greatest rate of change, 1.5 cents per year, occurred from 2006 to 2008.

2. **Discussion** Compare the line segment between 2006 and 2008 with the line segment between 2008 and 2013. Which is steeper? Which represents a greater rate of change?

   The line segment between 2006 and 2008 is steeper and it represents a greater rate of

   change.

3. **Discuss** How do you think the steepness of the line segment between two points is related to the rate of change it represents?

   The greater the rate of change, the steeper the line segment between the two points.

Determining Rates of Change

INTEGRATE TECHNOLOGY

Students have the option of completing the Explore activity either in the book or online.

QUESTIONING STRATEGIES

 A rate of change is a ratio of the changes in two variables. Which change goes in the numerator? Which goes in the denominator? The change in the dependent variable, *y*, goes in the numerator, and the change in the independent variable, *x*, goes in the denominator.

PROFESSIONAL DEVELOPMENT

Integrate Mathematical Practices

This lesson provides an opportunity to address Mathematical Practice **MP.2**, which calls for students to "reason abstractly and quantitatively." Students learn to find the rate of change of a function and use the slope formula to calculate the slope of a line. By connecting these two concepts, they learn to analyze and explain how the slope of a graph is related to the rate of change in real-world situations.

EXPLAIN 1

Determining the Slope of a Line

AVOID COMMON ERRORS

Students may write 0 for the slope of a vertical line, thinking that 0 and *undefined* are the same. Remind students that 0 is a real number; it is not undefined.

QUESTIONING STRATEGIES

? When you determine the slope of a line from two points, does it matter which one you use as the first point and which one as the second? Explain. No; you can subtract the coordinates of either point from the coordinates of the other point, as long as you subtract both *x*- and *y*-values in the same order.

CONNECT VOCABULARY EL

Explain to students that the words *rise* and *run* are also used to describe how steep steps are. The *rise* of a step is the difference in height between two consecutive steps, and the *run* is the depth from the front of a step to where the next step begins.

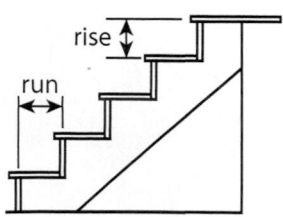

⚙ Explain 1 **Determining the Slope of a Line**

The rate of change for a linear function can be calculated using the rise and run of the graph of the function. The **rise** is the difference in the *y*-values of two points on a line. The **run** is the difference in the *x*-values of two points on a line.

The **slope** of a line is the ratio of rise to run for any two points on the line.

$$\text{Slope} = \frac{\text{rise}}{\text{run}} = \frac{\text{difference in } y\text{-values}}{\text{difference in } x\text{-values}}$$

Example 1   Determine the slope of each line.

Ⓐ Use $(3, 4)$ as the first point. Subtract *y*-values to find the change in *y*, or rise. Then subtract *x*-values to find the change in *x*, or run.

$\text{slope} = \dfrac{4 - 1}{3 - 2} = \dfrac{3}{1} = 3.$

Slope of the line is 3.

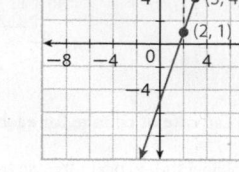

Ⓑ Use $\left(-2, \boxed{3}\right)$ as the first point. Subtract *y*-values to find the change in *y*, or rise. Then subtract *x*-values to find the change in *x*, or run.

$\text{slope} = \dfrac{\boxed{3} - \boxed{0}}{\boxed{-2} - \boxed{1}} = \dfrac{\boxed{3}}{\boxed{-3}} = \boxed{-1}.$

The slope of the line is $\boxed{-1}$.

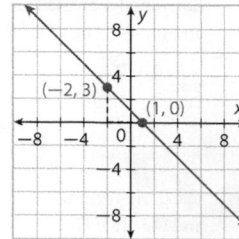

Reflect

4. Find the rise of a horizontal line. What is the slope of a horizontal line?
   The rise is determined by the change in the y-values, which is 0.

   The slope of the horizontal line is 0.

5. Find the run of a vertical line. What is the slope of a vertical line?
   The run is determined by the change in the x-values, which is 0.

   Since division by 0 is undefined, the slope of the vertical line is undefined.

6. **Discussion** If you have a graph of a line, how can you determine whether the slope is positive, negative, zero, or undefined without using points on the line?
   A line that rises from left to right has a positive slope. A line that falls from left to right has a

   negative slope. A horizontal line has a zero slope, and a vertical line has an undefined slope.

COLLABORATIVE LEARNING

Whole Class Activity

Write the coordinates $A\left(9, 2\right)$ and $B\left(5, -1\right)$ on the board. Have half of the class use the slope formula with point A as $\left(x_1, y_1\right)$ and have the other half use point B as $\left(x_1, y_1\right)$. Compare answers. Each method will give a slope of $\frac{3}{4}$. Remind students that it does not matter which point you choose to be, $\left(x_1, y_1\right)$ but once the choice is made, you must subtract the *y*-coordinates and *x*-coordinates in the same order.

Find the slope of each line.

7.

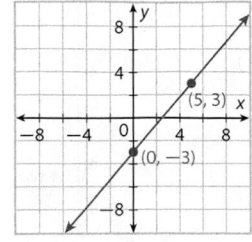

$$\text{slope} = \frac{-3-3}{0-5} = \frac{6}{5}$$

8.

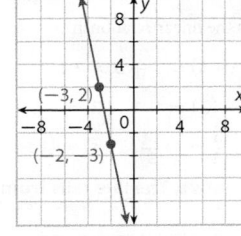

$$\text{slope} = \frac{2-(-3)}{-3-(-2)} = \frac{2+3}{-3+2} = -5$$

🎲 Explain 2   Determining Slope Using the Slope Formula

The **slope formula** for the slope of a line is the ratio of the difference in y-values to the difference in x-values between any two points on the line.

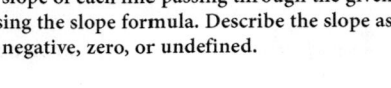

Slope Formula

If (x_1, x_2) and (y_1, y_2) are any two points on a line, the slope of the line is $m = \frac{y_2 - y_1}{x_2 - x_1}$.

Example 2   Find the slope of each line passing through the given points using the slope formula. Describe the slope as positive, negative, zero, or undefined.

Ⓐ   The graph shows the linear relationship.

$$y_2 - y_1 = 3 - (-1) = 3 + 1 = 4$$

$$x_2 - x_1 = 2 - (-2) = 2 + 2 = 4$$

$$m = \frac{y_2 - y_1}{x_2 - x_1} = \frac{4}{4} = 1$$

The slope is positive. The line rises from left to right.

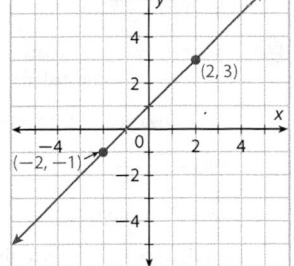

Ⓑ

x	3	3	3	3
y	2	4	6	8

Let $\left(\boxed{3}, 4\right)$ be (x_1, y_1) and $\left(\boxed{3}, 8\right)$ be (x_2, y_2).

$$y_2 - y_1 = 8 - \boxed{4} = \boxed{4}$$

$$x_2 - x_1 = \boxed{3} - \boxed{3} = \boxed{0}$$

$$m = \frac{y_2 - y_1}{x_2 - x_1} = \frac{\boxed{4}}{\boxed{0}}$$

The slope is ___undefined___ and the line is ___vertical___.

DIFFERENTIATE INSTRUCTION

Cognitive Strategies

To help students interpret the meanings of different slopes, emphasize reading the graph from left to right.

- Positive slope → y-values increase from left to right.
- Negative slope → y-values decrease from left to right.
- Zero slope → y-values have zero change from left to right.
- Undefined slope → There is _no_ left to right; the line is vertical.

EXPLAIN 2

Determining Slope Using the Slope Formula

AVOID COMMON ERRORS

When using the slope formula, students may subtract the x-values in a different order from the y-values. Encourage students to label their ordered pairs "point 1" and "point 2" so that they remember to subtract the x- and y-values in the same order.

QUESTIONING STRATEGIES

❓ How do you know which two points to use in the slope formula? It does not matter which points you choose to find the slope of a line. Any two points will work and will give the same answer. Choosing points at the intersections of grid lines makes finding the rise and run easier.

EXPLAIN 3

Interpreting Slope

QUESTIONING STRATEGIES

? How can you use the labels on a graph's axes to help interpret the slope in a real-world context? The labels tell you what two quantities, in what units, are related by the slope. You can say that the dependent variable increases or decreases by a certain amount *per* or *for every* increase of a certain amount in the independent variable.

? How does the slope of a line tell you whether the dependent variable is increasing or decreasing as the independent variable increases? A positive slope indicates that the dependent variable is increasing, and a negative slope indicates that the dependent variable is decreasing.

INTEGRATE MATHEMATICAL PRACTICES
Focus on Modeling

MP.4 Remind students that when time is one of the quantities in a real-world problem, it is usually the independent variable, so it is used to calculate the run in the slope formula.

Your Turn

Find the slope of each line passing through the given points using the slope formula. Describe the slope as positive, negative, zero, or undefined.

9. The graph shows the linear relationship.

$$y_2 - y_1 = 9 - (-5) = 9 + 5 = 14$$

$$x_2 - x_1 = -1 - (2) = -1 - 2 = -3$$

$$m = \frac{y_2 - y_1}{x_2 - x_1} = \frac{14}{-3} = -\frac{14}{3}$$

The slope is negative. The line falls from left to right.

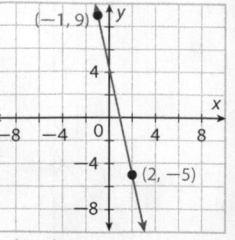

10.

x	1	2	3	4
y	5	5	5	5

Let $(1, 5)$ be (x_1, y_1) and $(3, 5)$ be (x_2, y_2).

$$y_2 - y_1 = 5 - 5 = 0$$

$$x_2 - x_1 = 3 - 1 = 2$$

$$m = \frac{y_2 - y_1}{x_2 - x_1} = \frac{0}{2} = 0$$

The slope is zero and the line is horizontal.

⟳ Explain 3 Interpreting Slope

Given a real-world situation, you can find the slope and then interpret the slope in terms of the context of the situation.

Example 3 Find and interpret the slope for each real-world situation.

Ⓐ The graph shows the relationship between a person's age and his or her estimated maximum heart rate.

Use the two points that are labeled on the graph.

$$\text{slope} = \frac{\text{rise}}{\text{run}} = \frac{180 - 150}{20 - 50} = \frac{30}{-30} = -1$$

Interpret the slope.

The slope being −1 means that for every year a person's age increases, his or her maximum heart rate decreases by 1 beat per minute.

Ⓑ The height of a plant y in centimeters after x days is a linear relationship. The points $(30, 15)$ and $(40, 25)$ are on the line.

Use the two points that are given.

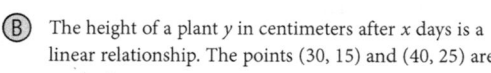

$$\text{slope} = \frac{\text{rise}}{\text{run}} = \frac{\boxed{25} - 15}{\boxed{40} - \boxed{30}} = \frac{\boxed{10}}{\boxed{10}} = \boxed{1}$$

Interpret the slope.

The slope being ___1___ means the plant's height increases by 1 cm each day

---

LANGUAGE SUPPORT **EL**

Connect Vocabulary

Explain to students that the small numbers in the formula $m = \frac{y_2 - y_1}{x_2 - x_1}$ are called *subscripts* because they are written below the base line of the text. Help students connect this word to *submarine*, a ship which goes below the surface of the ocean, or *subway*, an underground train system. Tell students that x_1 is read as "x sub one." Emphasize that a subscript is different from an exponent, which is written above the regular text.

Your Turn

Find and interpret the slope.

11. The graph shows the relationship between the temperature expressed in °F and the temperature expressed in °C.

$$\text{slope} = \frac{\text{rise}}{\text{run}} = \frac{25-10}{77-50} = \frac{15}{27} = \frac{5}{9}$$

The slope is $\frac{5}{9}$ which means that if the

temperature increases by 1 degree

Fahrenheit, the temperature increases

by $\frac{5}{9}$ degree Celsius.

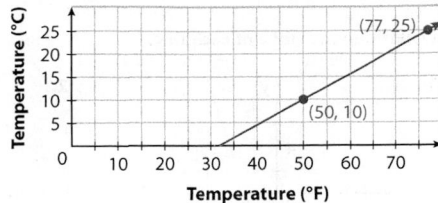

12. The number of cubic feet of water y in a reservoir x hours after the water starts flowing into the reservoir is a linear function. The points (40, 3000) and (60, 4000) are on the line of the function.

$$\text{slope} = \frac{\text{rise}}{\text{run}} = \frac{4000-3000}{60-40} = \frac{1000}{20} = 50$$

Interpret the slope.

The slope is 50, which means that the amount of water in the reservoir is increasing at a

rate of 50 cubic feet each hour.

💬 **Elaborate**

13. How can you relate the rate of change and slope in the linear relationships?
The rate of change for a function can be expressed as a ratio of the change in y-values over

the change in x-values for a specified part of the domain. For a linear function, the rate of

change is the slope of the line.

14. How is the slope formula related to the definition of slope?
The slope formula is $m = \frac{y_2 - y_1}{x_2 - x_1}$ where the numerator is the difference in y-values or the

rise and the denominator is the difference in the x-values or the run. So the slope formula

is the definition of slope stated mathematically.

15. How can you interpret slope in a real-world situation?
The slope can be interpreted as the number of y units change per unit of x.

ELABORATE

INTEGRATE MATHEMATICAL PRACTICES

Focus on Critical Thinking

MP.3 Discuss with students how they can check a slope calculation by looking at the graph. A line that slopes upward from left to right should have a positive slope, and a line that slopes downward should have a negative slope. If they found a slope with the wrong sign, they may have subtracted the x-values in a different order than the y-values, or they may have made an arithmetic error.

QUESTIONING STRATEGIES

❓ In the slope formula, what expression represents the rise, and what expression represents the run? The expression $y_2 - y_1$ represents the rise, and $x_2 - x_1$ represents the run.

SUMMARIZE THE LESSON

❓ How do you find the slope of a line and use it to interpret the rate of change in a real-world situation? To calculate the slope, choose any two points on the line, and find the ratio of the change in y (the rise) to the change in x (the run) between the points. Then use the slope to describe the rate at which the independent variable increases or decreases in the real-world context.

EVALUATE

ASSIGNMENT GUIDE

Concepts and Skills	Practice
Explore Determining Rates of Change	Exercises 17
Example 1 Determining the Slope of a Line	Exercises 1–6, 23
Example 2 Determining Slope Using the Slope Formula	Exercises 7–12, 18, 22
Example 3 Interpreting Slope	Exercises 13–16, 19–21, 24–25

INTEGRATE MATHEMATICAL PRACTICES

Focus on Modeling

MP.4 As students find the slope of a line using the slope formula, make sure they understand that x_1 is the x-value from the first ordered pair, x_2 is the x-value from the second ordered pair, y_1 is the y-value from the first ordered pair, and y_2 is the y-value from the second ordered pair. Remind them that the coordinates have to be subtracted in the same order in the numerator as in the denominator.

Determine the slope of each line.

1.

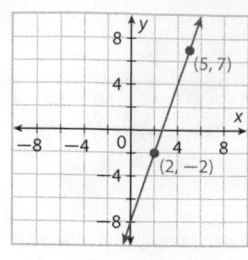

$$\text{slope} = \frac{7 - (-2)}{5 - 2} = \frac{9}{3} = 3$$

2.

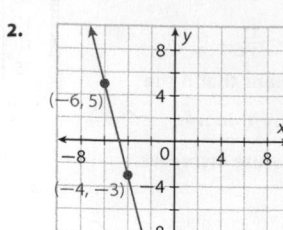

$$\text{slope} = \frac{-3 - 5}{-4 - (-6)} = \frac{-8}{2} = -4$$

3.

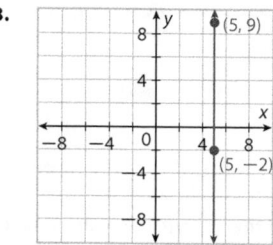

$$\text{slope} = \frac{9 - (-2)}{5 - 5} = \frac{11}{0}.$$
The slope is undefined.

4.

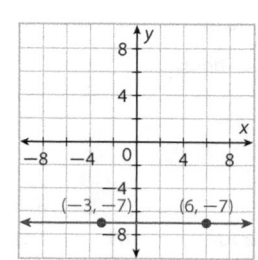

$$\text{slope} = \frac{-7 - (-7)}{6 - (-3)} = \frac{0}{9} = 0$$

5.

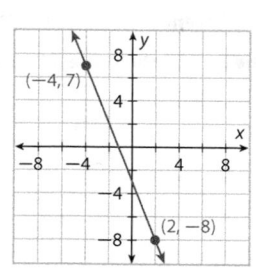

$$\text{slope} = \frac{-8 - 7}{2 - (-4)} = \frac{-15}{6} = -\frac{5}{2}$$

6.

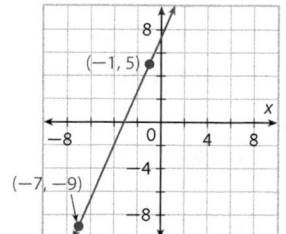

$$\text{slope} = \frac{5 - (-9)}{-1 - (-7)} = \frac{14}{6} = \frac{7}{3}$$

Exercise	Depth of Knowledge (D.O.K.)	COMMON CORE Mathematical Practices
1–12	**1** Recall of Information	**MP.2** Reasoning
13–17	**2** Skills/Concepts	**MP.4** Modeling
18	**1** Recall of Information	**MP.2** Reasoning
19	**2** Skills/Concepts	**MP.4** Modeling
20	**1** Recall of Information	**MP.4** Modeling

Find the slope of each line passing through the given points using the slope formula.
Describe the slope as positive, negative, zero, or undefined.

7. $(5, 3)$ and $(10, 8)$

$y_2 - y_1 = 8 - 3 = 5$

$x_2 - x_1 = 10 - 5 = 5$

slope $= \frac{5}{5} = 1$

The slope is positive.

8. $(-5, 14)$ and $(-1, 2)$

$y_2 - y_1 = 14 - 2 = 12$

$x_2 - x_1 = -5 - (-1) = -4$

slope $= \frac{12}{-4} = -3$

The slope is negative.

9. $(-5, 6)$ and $(8, 6)$

$y_2 - y_1 = 6 - 6 = 0$

$x_2 - x_1 = 8 - (-5) = 13$

slope $= \frac{0}{13} = 0$

The slope is zero.

10. $(-4, -17)$ and $(-4, -3)$

$y_2 - y_1 = -17 - (-3) = -14$

$x_2 - x_1 = -4 - (-4) = 0$

slope $= \frac{-14}{0}$

The slope is undefined.

11. $(12, -7)$ and $(2, -2)$

$y_2 - y_1 = -2 - (-7) = 5$

$x_2 - x_1 = 2 - 12 = -10$

slope $= \frac{5}{-10} = \frac{-1}{2}$

The slope is negative.

12. $(-3, -10)$ and $(-1, -1)$

$y_2 - y_1 = -10 - (-1) = -9$

$x_2 - x_1 = -3 - (-1) = -2$

slope $= \frac{-9}{-2} = \frac{9}{2}$

The slope is positive.

Find and interpret the slope for each real-world situation.

13.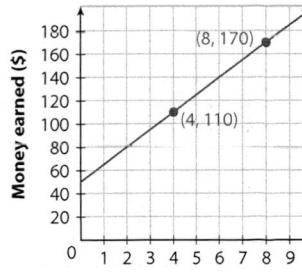

$m = \frac{170 - 110}{8 - 4} = \frac{60}{4} = 15$

The slope is 15. The money earned increases by \$15 for each hour worked.

14.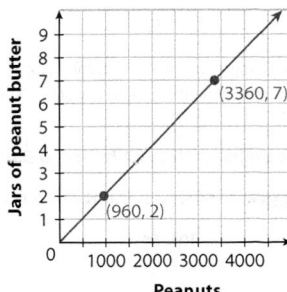

$m = \frac{7 - 2}{3360 - 960} = \frac{5}{2400} = \frac{1}{480}$

The slope is $\frac{1}{480}$. It takes 480 peanuts to make one jar of peanut butter.

To help students remember the slopes of horizontal and vertical lines, have them consider the rise of each line. Just as a flat surface does not rise, a horizontal line has a rise of 0. Since the rise is the numerator of the slope, the slope is also 0.

AVOID COMMON ERRORS

When calculating the slope using ordered pairs with negative coordinates, students will sometimes forget the negative sign when subtracting values. For example, for the points $(-1, 5)$ and $(3, -3)$, $x_2 - x_1$ should be $3 - (-1)$, not $3 - 1$. Remind students that they must retain any negative signs in an ordered pair when using the slope formula.

Exercise	Depth of Knowledge (D.O.K.)	COMMON CORE Mathematical Practices
21	**2** Skills/Concepts	**MP.3** Logic
22	**3** Strategic Thinking H.O.T.	**MP.3** Logic
23	**2** Skills/Concepts H.O.T.	**MP.3** Logic
24–25	**3** Strategic Thinking H.O.T.	**MP.4** Modeling

Interpreting Rate of Change and Slope   **228**

INTEGRATE TECHNOLOGY

 A graphing calculator can be used to find the slope between any two points. Press **STAT**, select **EDIT**, and enter the *x*-coordinates of the points in list **L1** and the *y*-coordinates in list **L2**. Then press **STAT**, select **CALC**, and scroll down to **4:LinReg**. The "a" value that will appear is the slope. If the slope is undefined, the calculator will show an error code.

15.

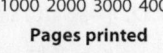

Cost ($) vs Pages printed, with points (1000, 310) and (3500, 460)

$$m = \frac{460 - 310}{3500 - 1000} = \frac{150}{2500} = \frac{3}{50}$$

The slope is $\frac{3}{50}$ or 0.06. The cost to print each page is $0.06 after an initial charge of $250.

16.

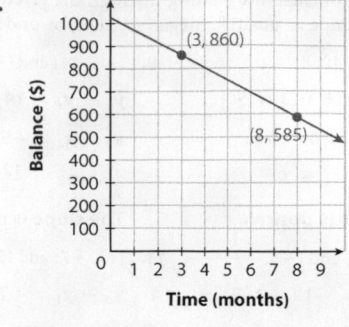

Balance ($) vs Time (months), with points (3, 860) and (8, 585)

$$m = \frac{860 - 585}{3 - 8} = \frac{275}{-5} = -55$$

The slope is −55. The balance decreases by $55 each month.

17. a. The table shows the distance that a group of hikers has traveled from the start of the trail.

Time (hr)	0.5	1	2	3
Distance (km)	3	5	7	13

Use the table to plot the 4 points on the graph and join the points using line segments.

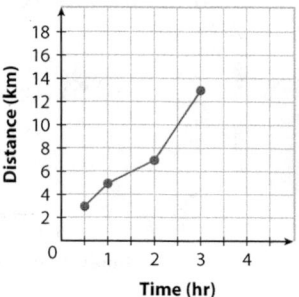

Distance (km) vs Time (hr)

b. Find the slope for each of the three line segments.

0.5 to 1: $\frac{5 - 3}{1 - 0.5} = 4$

1 to 2: $\frac{7 - 5}{2 - 1} = 2$

2 to 3: $\frac{13 - 7}{3 - 2} = 6$

c. Which line segment has the greatest slope? Does this line segment appear to be the steepest on the graph?

The line segment from 2 hours to 3 hours has the greatest slope and it appears to be the steepest line segment.

18. Determine whether each set of points is on a line that has a positive slope, negative slope, zero slope, or undefined slope. Select the correct answer for each part.

a. $(5, 0)$ and $(8, 4)$ ☑ positive ☐ negative ☐ zero ☐ undefined $m = \frac{4-0}{8-5} = \frac{4}{3}$

b. $(-6, 1)$ and $(-6, 9)$ ☐ positive ☐ negative ☐ zero ☑ undefined $m = \frac{9-1}{-6-(-6)} = \frac{8}{0}$

c. $(2, 6)$ and $(11, -3)$ ☐ positive ☑ negative ☐ zero ☐ undefined $m = \frac{-3-6}{11-2} = \frac{-9}{9} = -1$

d. $(3, 4)$ and $(-2, 12)$ ☐ positive ☑ negative ☐ zero ☐ undefined $m = \frac{12-4}{-2-3} = \frac{8}{-5}$

e. $(-3, 5)$ and $(7, 5)$ ☐ positive ☐ negative ☑ zero ☐ undefined $m = \frac{5-5}{7-(-3)} = \frac{0}{10}$

19. What is the slope of the segment shown for a staircase with 10-inch treads and 7.75-inch risers? As you walk up (or down) the stairs, your vertical distance from the floor is a linear function of your horizontal distance from the point on the floor where you started. Is the function discrete or continuous? Explain.

0.775 or $\frac{31}{40}$; discrete; because you make one movement

forward and one up (or down) for each step, the function

is discrete.

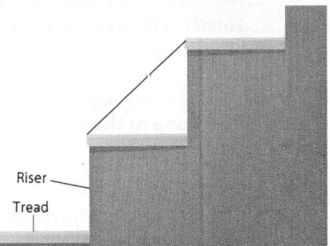

Riser
Tread

20. The Mount Washington Cog Railway in New Hampshire is one of the steepest cog railways in the world. A section of the railway has a slope of approximately 0.37. In this section, a vertical change of 1 unit corresponds to a horizontal change of what length? Round your answer to the nearest hundredth.

$\frac{0.37}{1} = \frac{1}{x};\ 0.37x = 1;\ x \approx 2.70$ **2.70 units**

21. a. Biology The table shows how the number of cricket chirps per minute changes with the air temperature.

Temperature (°F)	40	50	60	70	80	90
Chirps per minute	0	40	80	120	160	200

Find the rates of change.

40 to 50: 4

50 to 60: 4

60 to 70: 4

70 to 80: 4

80 to 90: 4

b. Is the graph of the data a line? If so, what is the slope? If not, explain why not.

Yes, the graph is a line because the slope is constant. The slope is 4.

MULTIPLE REPRESENTATIONS

Show students how to use a "T-Chart" to find slopes.

x	y
1	1
2	4
3	7

$+1$ ... $+3$

$\text{Slope} = \dfrac{\text{change in } y}{\text{change in } x} = \dfrac{+3}{+1} = 3$

This method works whether the x- and y- values are given in a table, shown as a list of ordered pairs, or selected from a graph.

AVOID COMMON ERRORS

Some students may not pay attention to the scale on the x- and y-axes. Emphasize that one grid square does not always equal one unit, so they should be careful to use the scale as a multiplier when calculating the rise and run.

JOURNAL

Have students compare a line with a slope of 3 and a line with a slope of $\frac{1}{3}$. Ask them to explain how they are alike, how they are different, and which line is steeper. Have the students describe a real-world situation in which each slope would be appropriate.

22. Explain the Error A student is asked to find the slope of a line containing the points (4, 3) and (−2, 15) and finds the slope as shown. Explain the error.

$$\text{slope} = \frac{\text{rise}}{\text{run}} = \frac{4 - (-2)}{3 - 15} = \frac{6}{-12} = -\frac{1}{2}$$

The student was supposed to calculate the change in y over the change in x, but calculated the change in x over the change in y.

23. Critical Thinking In this lesson, you learned that the slope of a line is constant. Does this mean that all lines with the same slope are the same line? Explain.

No; when lines have the same slope, the ratio of the rise to the run of those lines is the same but the lines do not necessarily pass through the same points.

24. a. Represent Real-World Problems A ladder is leaned against a building. The bottom of the ladder is 11 feet from the building. The top of the ladder is 19 feet above the ground. What is the slope of the ladder? $\frac{19}{11}$

b. What does the slope of the ladder mean in the real world?
The slope of the ladder is a measure of how steep the ladder is to climb.

c. If the ladder were set closer to the building, would it be harder or easier to climb? Explain in terms of the slope of the ladder.
The slope would be greater because the rise would be greater and the run would be less. It would be harder to climb because the ladder would be steeper.

25. a. The table shows the cost, in dollars, charged by an electric company for various amounts of energy in kilowatt-hours.
Graph the data and show the rates of change.

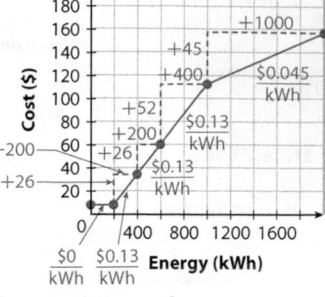

Energy (kWh)	0	200	400	600	1000	2000
Cost ($)	8	8	34	60	112	157

b. Compares the rates of change for each interval. Are they all the same? Explain.

No. The rate of change from 0 to 200 is $0 per kWh and the rate of change from 1000 to 2000 is $0.045 per kWh, while the rate of change from 200 to 400, 400 to 600, and 600 to 1000 are all $0.13 per kWh.

c. What do the rates of change represent?

The cost for 1 kilowatt-hour.

d. Describe in words the electric company's billing plan.

Sample answer: There is a flat fee of $8 for up to the first 200 kilowatt-hours. From 200 to 1000 kilowatt-hours, the cost is $0.13 for each additional kilowatt-hour. For over 1000 kilowatt-hours, the cost is $0.045 for each additional kilowatt-hour.

Lesson Performance Task

A city has three Internet service providers (ISP), each of which charges a usage fee when a subscriber goes over 100 megabytes (MB) per billing cycle. The table below relates the amount of data a subscriber uses with the cost for each ISP.

ISP	100 MB	200 MB	400 MB
A	$54	$74	$94
B	$42	$57	$87
C	$60	$72	$96

Use the table to find the rate of change for each interval of each ISP, and use the rates of change to determine whether the usage fee is constant for each ISP. Interpret the meaning of the rates of change for each ISP. Then determine and explain which ISP would be the least expensive and which ISP would be the most expensive for a subscriber that uses a high amount of data.

ISP A: 100 to 200: $\frac{74-54}{200-100} = \frac{20}{100} = 0.2$ 200 to 400: $\frac{94-74}{400-200} = \frac{20}{200} = 0.1$

The rate of change for ISP A is not constant because the rate of change from 100 MB to 200 MB is 0.2 and the rate of change from 200 to 400 is 0.1. The rates of change mean that it would cost $0.20 for each MB between 100 MB and 200 MB and $0.10 for each MB between 200 MB and 400 MB.

ISP B: 100 to 200: $\frac{57-42}{200-100} = \frac{15}{100} = 0.15$ 200 to 400: $\frac{87-57}{400-200} = \frac{30}{200} = 0.15$

The rate of change for ISP B is constant because the rate of change from 100 MB to 200 MB and from 200 to 400 is 0.15. The rate of change means that it would cost $0.15 for each MB between 100 MB and 400 MB.

ISP C: 100 to 200: $\frac{72-60}{200-100} = \frac{12}{100} = 0.12$ 200 to 400: $\frac{96-72}{400-200} = \frac{24}{200} = 0.12$

The rate of change for ISP C is constant because the rate of change from 100 MB to 200 MB and from 200 to 400 is 0.12. The rate of change means that it would cost $0.12 for each MB between 100 MB and 400 MB.

The least expensive ISP for a high-use subscriber is ISP A, because the cost for each MB seems to be lower as a subscriber uses more data. Even though ISP A costs more than ISP B for 400 MB, the lower rate of change will cause the total amount to be lower for ISP A for a large amount of data.

The most expensive ISP for a high-use subscriber is ISP B. Even though ISP C costs more than ISP A and ISP B for 400 MB, the cost for each MB over 100 MB is higher for ISP B than for ISP C, and the cost for each MB over 200 MB is higher for ISP B than for ISP A.

© Houghton Mifflin Harcourt Publishing Company

EXTENSION ACTIVITY

Have students research the cost of water service in your community. Have them determine if the cost per gallon is constant or if it increases or decreases as customers use more water. Ask students to suggest reasons why the rates might be structured the way they are.

Students may find that the cost per gallon increases with increasing water consumption. The rates may be set that way to encourage water conservation while still making it affordable to meet basic water needs.

Students may not be familiar with some of the terms and phrases used in the Lesson Performance Task. Have student volunteers explain *Internet service provider (ISP)*, *amount of data*, *usage fee*, and *subscriber*.

INTEGRATE MATHEMATICAL PRACTICES
Focus on Modeling

MP.4 Students may have seen the term *megabyte* without understanding what it means. Explain the following units that describe quantities of computer data.

- A *bit* is the smallest unit of data that a computer uses. It represents one digit that can equal either 0 or 1.
- A *byte* (B) is equal to 8 bits.
- A *kilobyte* (kB) is about 1000 bytes.
- A *megabyte* (MB) is about 1000 kilobytes or one million bytes (10^6 B).
- A *gigabyte* (GB) is about 1000 megabytes or one billion bytes (10^9 B).

Note that some of the first personal computers had only 64 kilobytes of memory, while personal computers today may have many gigabytes of memory.

Scoring Rubric

2 points: Student correctly solves the problem and explains his/her reasoning.

1 point: Student shows good understanding of the problem but does not fully solve or explain his/her reasoning.

0 points: Student does not demonstrate understanding of the problem.

Interpreting Rate of Change and Slope   **232**

ASSESSMENT AND INTERVENTION

Assign or customize module reviews.

MODULE PERFORMANCE TASK

COMMON CORE

Mathematical Practices: MP.1, MP.2, MP.4, MP.6
F-LE.A.1b, F-LE.A.2, F-LE.B.5

SUPPORTING STUDENT REASONING

Students should begin this problem by focusing on how they will go about determining the height of several stacked cups. Here are some questions they might have.

- **How tall are you?** Ask students to tell you if they want your height in metric or customary measure. Then give them your height accordingly.

- **How tall is a cup?** Let students measure the height of a cup themselves.

- **How many cups can be used?** Give 3 cups per student or per group. If students protest that this is not enough, explain that they will need to calculate the answer, not simply count the number of cups needed to reach a certain height.

Essential Question: How can you use a linear function to solve real-world problems?

Key Vocabulary

continuous function
(función continua)

discrete function *(función discreta)*

linear function *(función lineal)*

slope *(pendiente)*

KEY EXAMPLE (Lesson 5.1)

Determine whether $4x + y = 7$ is linear. If so, graph the function.

The equation is linear because it is in the standard form of a linear equation: $A = 4$, $B = 1$, and $C = 7$.

To graph the function, first solve the equation for y.

$$4x + y = 7$$
$$\underline{-4x \qquad\qquad -4x}$$
$$y = 7 - 4x$$

Make a table and plot the points. Then connect the points.

x	−1	0	1	2
y	11	7	3	−1

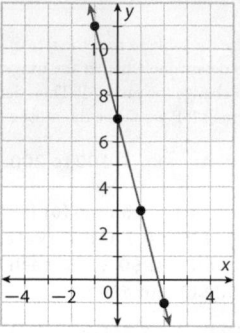

KEY EXAMPLE (Lesson 5.3)

Find the slope of the line passing through the given points using the slope formula. Describe the slope as positive, negative, zero, or undefined.

x	1	2	3	4
y	7	7	7	7

Let $(1, 7)$ be (x_1, y_1) and $(3, 7)$ be (x_2, y_2).

$$y_2 - y_1 = 7 - 7 = 0$$

$$x_2 - x_1 = 3 - 1 = 2$$

$$m = \frac{y_2 - y_1}{x_2 - x_1} = \frac{0}{2} = 0$$

The slope is zero.

SCAFFOLDING SUPPORT

- For students who need more structure, encourage them to record their information in a table that measures the number of cups and their height when stacked. You may want to elicit from some students that stacking the cups creates a "gap height" rather than a full cup height.

- Watch for students who use different units of measure for the cup and for total height.

- Caution students to remember to include the base cup in the number of cups needed.

EXERCISES

Determine whether each equation is linear. *(Lesson 5.1)*

1. $4x^2 + y = 8$

        not linear

2. $7x + y = 3$

        linear

Find the *x*- and *y*-intercepts. *(Lesson 5.2)*

3. $2x - 3y = 12$

      x-int.: 6; *y*-int.: −4

4. $-6x + 8y = 24$

      x-int.: −4; *y*-int.: 3

5. $3x + y = 5$

      x-int.: $\frac{5}{3}$, *y*-int.: 5

6. $5x - 2y = 0$

      x-int.: 0, *y*-int.: 0

Find the slope of the line passing through the given points using the slope formula. *(Lesson 5.3)*

7.

x	0	1	2	3
y	2	5	8	11

$m = 3$

8.

x	0	2	4	6
y	6	5	4	3

$m = -\frac{1}{2}$

MODULE PERFORMANCE TASK

How Many Stacked Cups Do You Need?

You want to stack paper, plastic, or foam cups one inside the next so that the height of the stack is equal to your math teacher's height. How can you determine the number of cups you would need?

Start by listing in the space the questions you will need to answer in order to tackle the problem. Then use your own paper to complete the task. Be sure to write down all your data and assumptions. Then use graphs, numbers, words, or algebra to explain how you reached your conclusion.

SAMPLE SOLUTION

Let *x* represent the "gap height", the distance from the top of each cup to the top of the cup that contains it.

Suppose the teacher is 180 cm tall.

Assume that the height of the base cup is 8 cm and the gap height measures 2 cm.

$180 = 8 + 2x$	Write an equation.
$180 - 8 = 8 - 8 + 2x$	Subtract.
$172 = 2x$	Combine like terms.
$x = 86$	Divide by 2.

The number of gap heights is 86. The number of stacked cups needed for a total height of 180 cm is 87.

DISCUSSION OPPORTUNITIES

- Ask students if they need to cut part of a cup away to reach the correct total height. Ask students why this might be necessary.

- Encourage students to describe how the information gathered for the problem can be used to graph the related equation. What represents the slope? What about the *y*-intercept?

- Ask students how solving strategies would differ if they stacked cups base-to-base and top-to-top.

Assessment Rubric

2 points: Student correctly solves the problem and explains his/her reasoning.

1 point: Student shows good understanding of the problem but does not fully solve or explain.

0 points: Student does not demonstrate understanding of the problem.

Ready to Go On?

ASSESS MASTERY

Use the assessment on this page to determine if students have mastered the concepts and standards covered in this module.

ASSESSMENT AND INTERVENTION

Access Ready to Go On? assessment online, and receive instant scoring, feedback, and customized intervention or enrichment.

ADDITIONAL RESOURCES

Response to Intervention Resources

- Reteach Worksheets

Differentiated Instruction Resources

- Reading Strategies **EL**
- Success for English Learners **EL**
- Challenge Worksheets

Assessment Resources

- Leveled Module Quizzes

235 Module 5

5.1–5.3 Linear Functions

Determine whether each equation is linear. If it is linear, graph the equation, determine the slope, and find the x- and y-intercepts. *(Lessons 5.1, 5.2, 5.3)*

1. $x^3 + y = 8$

not linear

2. $4x + 2y = 6$

linear; $m = -2$; x-int $= 1.5$, y-int $= 3$

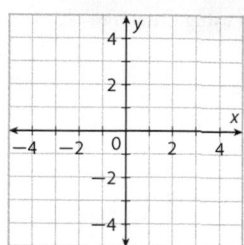

3. $-5x + 4y = 0$

linear; $m = \dfrac{5}{4}$; x-int $= 0$, y-int $= 0$

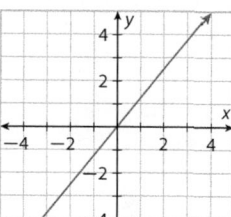

4. $5xy + y = 9$

not linear

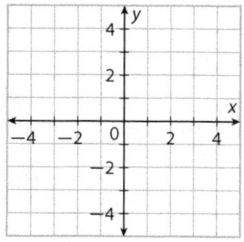

ESSENTIAL QUESTION

5. What do the slope and y-intercept of a real-world linear function represent?

Possible Answer: The slope represents the rate of change in the real-world relationship, and the y-intercept represents the initial value.

© Houghton Mifflin Harcourt Publishing Company

Common Core Standards

Lesson	Items	Content Standards	Mathematical Practices
5.1	1	F-LE.A.1b	MP.6
5.1, 5.2, 5.3	2	A-REI.D.10, F-IF.C.7a, F-IF.B.4, F-IF.B.6	MP.7
5.1, 5.2, 5.3	3	A-REI.D.10, F-IF.C.7a, F-IF.B.4, F-IF.B.6	MP.7
5.1	4	F-LE.A.1b	MP.6

MODULE 5
MIXED REVIEW

Assessment Readiness

1. Look at each equation. Is the equation linear? Select Yes or No.
   A. $\frac{1}{3}x - 2y = 7$ ● Yes   ○ No
   B. $y = x^2 - 8$ ○ Yes   ● No
   C. $3x + \frac{7}{y} = -5$ ○ Yes   ● No

2. Consider the equation $8x - 2y = 24$. Select True or False for each statement.
   A. The x-intercept is 3.   ● True   ○ False
   B. The y-intercept is 12.   ○ True   ● False
   C. It is equivalent to $y = 4x - 12$.   ● True   ○ False

3. Consider the sequence $-8, -4, 0, 4, 8, 12, \ldots$. Select True or False for each statement.
   A. A recursive rule for the sequence is $f(1) = -8; f(n) = -4(n - 1)$ for all $n \geq 2$.   ○ True   ● False
   B. An explicit rule for the sequence is $f(n) = -8 + 4(n - 1)$.   ● True   ○ False
   C. The tenth term is 28.   ● True   ○ False

Use the graph to answer questions 4 and 5.

4. Is the relation represented on the graph a function? Explain.
   Possible answer: Yes, it is a function, because it passes the vertical line test.

5. What is the slope of the line shown on the graph? Explain how you got your answer.
   I picked two points on the line, $(0, -1)$ and $(4, 1)$.
   Then, I used the slope formula: $\frac{1 - (-1)}{4 - 0} = \frac{2}{4} = \frac{1}{2}$.
   The slope is $\frac{1}{2}$.

© Houghton Mifflin Harcourt Publishing Company

ASSESSMENT AND INTERVENTION

Assign ready-made or customized practice tests to prepare students for high-stakes tests.

ADDITIONAL RESOURCES

Assessment Resources

• Leveled Module Quizzes: Modified, B

AVOID COMMON ERRORS

Item 2 Some students have difficulty when the equation of a line is not in slope-intercept form. Encourage students to solve the equation for y so they can put it into the calculator and use the calculator as a visual representation of the function.

COMMON CORE	**Common Core Standards**		

Lesson	*Items*	**Content Standards**	**Mathematical Practices**
5.1	1	**F-LE.A.1b**	**MP.1**
2.3, 5.2	2*	**A-CED.A.4, F-IF.B.4**	**MP.2**
4.2	3*	**F-BF.A.2**	**MP.2**
3.2	4*	**F-IF.A.1**	**MP.1**
5.3	5	**F-IF.B.6**	**MP.2**

* Item integrates mixed review concepts from previous modules or a previous course.

Forms of Linear Equations

ESSENTIAL QUESTION:

Answer: You can use slope-intercept form to model real-world situations when you know the rate of change and an initial value. You can use point-slope form when you know the rate and a non-initial value.

PROFESSIONAL DEVELOPMENT VIDEO

Professional Development Video

Learn effective ways of integrating technology into your classroom to meet a variety of different needs.

Professional
Development
my.hrw.com

MODULE **6**

Forms of Linear Equations

Essential Question: How can you use different forms of linear equations to solve real-world problems?

LESSON 6.1
Slope-Intercept Form

LESSON 6.2
Point-Slope Form

LESSON 6.3
Standard Form

LESSON 6.4
Transforming Linear Functions

LESSON 6.5
Comparing Properties of Linear Functions

© Houghton Mifflin Harcourt Publishing Company • Image Credit: ©Cessna152/Shutterstock

REAL WORLD VIDEO
Periodic comets have orbital periods of less than 200 years. Halley's comet is the only short-period comet that is visible to the naked eye. It returns every 76 years. You can build functions to represent and model predictable occurrences, such as the return of Halley's comet.

MODULE PERFORMANCE TASK PREVIEW

Who Wins the Race

A marathon is a long-distance run that is 26.2 miles long. Marathon events are hosted all over the world, and participants are a mix of athletes with different skill levels. Most runners train for many months to prepare for a marathon. How can linear equations be used to compare the running speeds of two different runners? Stay on track and find out!

Module 6   237

DIGITAL TEACHER EDITION

Access a full suite of teaching resources when and where you need them:

- Access content online or offline
- Customize lessons to share with your class
- Communicate with your students in real-time
- View student grades and data instantly to target your instruction where it is needed most

PERSONAL MATH TRAINER

Assessment and Intervention

Assign automatically graded homework, quizzes, tests, and intervention activities. Prepare your students with updated, Common Core-aligned practice tests.

Are 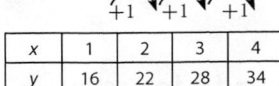 Ready?

Complete these exercises to review skills you will need for this module.

- Online Homework
- Hints and Help
- Extra Practice

Constant Rate of Change

Example 1 Tell if the rate of change is constant.

+1 +1 +1

x	1	2	3	4
y	16	22	28	34

+6 +6 +6

The rate of change, $\frac{6}{1}$, is constant.

For a function defined in terms of x and y, the rate of change of the function is a ratio that compares the change in y to the change in x.

$$\text{rate of change} = \frac{\text{change in } y}{\text{change in } x} = \frac{6}{1}$$

Tell if the rate of change is constant.

1.

x	2	5	8	11
y	6	15	24	33

_____yes_____

2.

x	3	6	9	12
y	2	6	11	17

_____no_____

Two-Step Equations

Example 2 Solve.

$$10 = 3x - 11$$
$$10 + 11 = 3x - 11 + 11 \qquad \text{Add 11 to both sides of the equation.}$$
$$21 = 3x$$
$$\frac{21}{3} = \frac{3x}{3} \qquad \text{Divide both sides of the equation by 3.}$$
$$7 = x$$

Solve each equation.

3. $7n + 17 = 59$ _____$n = 6$_____

4. $24 - 4y = 20$ _____$y = 1$_____

5. $34 = 49 - 3b$ _____$b = 5$_____

Linear Functions

Example 3 Tell whether $y = \frac{4}{x} - 8$ represents a linear function.

$y = \frac{4}{x} - 8$ does not represent a linear function because x appears in the denominator.

When a linear equation is written in standard form, the following are true.

- x and y both have exponents of 1.
- x and y are not multiplied together.
- x and y do not appear in denominators, exponents, or radicands.

Tell whether the equation represents a linear function.

6. $8x^2 + y = 16$ _____no_____

7. $6x + y = 12$ _____yes_____

8. $3y = 2x + 5$ _____yes_____

Are You Ready?

ASSESS READINESS

Use the assessment on this page to determine if students need strategic or intensive intervention for the module's prerequisite skills.

ASSESSMENT AND INTERVENTION

RtI TIER 1, TIER 2, TIER 3 SKILLS

Personal Math Trainer will automatically create a standards-based, personalized intervention assignment for your students, targeting each student's individual needs!

ADDITIONAL RESOURCES

See the table below for a full list of intervention resources available for this module.

Response to Intervention Resources also includes:

- Tier 2 Skill Pre-Tests for each Module
- Tier 2 Skill Post-Tests for each skill

Response to Intervention			Differentiated Instruction
Tier 1 Lesson Intervention Worksheets	**Tier 2** Strategic Intervention Skills Intervention Worksheets	**Tier 3** Intensive Intervention Worksheets available online	
Reteach 6.1 Reteach 6.2 Reteach 6.3 Reteach 6.4 Reteach 6.5	4 Constant Rate... 7 Graphing Linear... 10 Linear Functions 20 Slope 21 Two-Step Equations 23 Unit Rate	Building Block Skills 5, 22, 23, 27, 40, 46, 51, 63, 65, 68, 70, 95, 98	Challenge worksheets Extend the Math Lesson Activities in TE

Slope-Intercept Form

Common Core Math Standards

The student is expected to:

COMMON CORE F-IF.C.7a

Graph linear... functions and show intercepts... Also A-CED.A.2, A-REI.D.10

Mathematical Practices

COMMON CORE MP.6 Precision

Language Objective

Explain to a partner how to write a linear function in slope-intercept form.

ENGAGE

Essential Question: How can you represent a linear function in a way that reveals its slope and y-intercept?

You can determine the slope m of the graph of the function and its y-intercept b and write the equation $y = mx + b$, called the *slope-intercept form* of the equation.

PREVIEW: LESSON PERFORMANCE TASK

View the Engage section online. Discuss the photo and how a gym membership may require a one-time sign-up fee as well as regular monthly fees. Also discuss how a graph of this type of data might look. Then preview the Lesson Performance Task.

6.1 Slope-Intercept Form

Essential Question: How can you represent a linear function in a way that reveals its slope and y-intercept?

Resource Locker

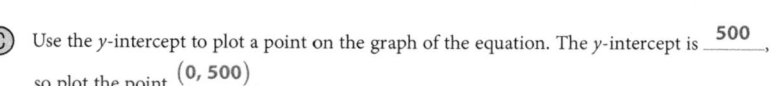

✦ Explore Graphing Lines Given Slope and y-intercept

Graphs of linear equations can be used to model many real-life situations. Given the slope and y-intercept, you can graph the line, and use the graph to answer questions.

Andrew wants to buy a smart phone that costs $500. His parents will pay for the phone, and Andrew will pay them $50 each month until the entire amount is repaid. The loan repayment represents a linear situation in which the amount y that Andrew owes his parents is dependent on the number x of payments he has made.

Ⓐ When $x = 0$, $y = $ <u>$500</u>.

The y-intercept of the graph of the equation that represents

the situation is <u>500</u>

Ⓑ The rate of change in the amount Andrew owes over

time is <u>-50</u> per month.

The slope is <u>-50</u>.

Ⓒ Use the y-intercept to plot a point on the graph of the equation. The y-intercept is <u>500</u>,

so plot the point <u>(0, 500)</u>.

Ⓓ Using the definition of slope, plot a second point.

$$\text{Slope} = \frac{\text{Change in } y}{\text{Change in } x} = \frac{\boxed{-50}}{1} = \boxed{-50}.$$

Start at the point you plotted. Count <u>50</u> units down

and <u>1</u> unit right and plot another point.

Ⓔ Draw a line through the points you plotted.

Amount Andrew Owes

(graph showing a decreasing line from (0, 500) to (9, 0), y-axis: Amount ($) 0–500, x-axis: Time (Months) 0–9)

© Houghton Mifflin Harcourt Publishing Company • Image Credits: ©Echo/Cultura/Getty Images

Module 6 **239** Lesson 1

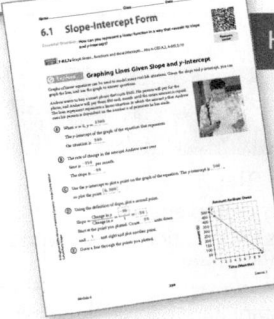

HARDCOVER PAGES 195–202

Turn to these pages to find this lesson in the hardcover student edition.

1. **Discussion** How can you use the same method to find two more points on that same line?
   Possible answer: You can begin at the second point, $(1, 450)$, and move 50 units down and

   1 unit to the right. Then repeat this process beginning at the new point.

2. How many months will it take Andrew to pay off his loan? Explain your answer.
   10 months; the point $(10, 0)$ represents the number of months, 10, for which the amount

   to be repaid is \$0.

🔵 Explain 1 Creating Linear Equations in Slope-Intercept Form

You can use the slope formula to derive the slope-intercept form of a linear equation.

Consider a line with slope m and y-intercept b.

The slope formula is $m = \frac{y_2 - y_1}{x_2 - x_1}$.

Substitute $(0, b)$ for (x_1, y_1) and (x, y) for (x_2, y_2).

$$m = \frac{y - b}{x - 0}$$

$$m = \frac{y - b}{x}$$

$$mx = y - b \qquad \text{Multiply both sides by } x \ (x \neq 0).$$

$$mx + b = y \qquad \text{Add } b \text{ to both sides.}$$

$$y = mx + b$$

Slope-Intercept Form of an Equation

If a line has slope m and y-intercept $(0, b)$, then the line is described by the equation $y = mx + b$.

Example 1 Write the equation of each line in slope-intercept form.

(A) Slope is 3, and $(2, 5)$ is on the line.

Step 1: Find the y-intercept.

$y = mx + b$	Write the slope–intercept form.
$5 = 3(2) + b$	Substitute 3 for m, 2 for x, and 5 for y.
$5 = 6 + b$	Multiply.
$5 - 6 = 6 + b - 6$	Subtract 6 from both sides.
$-1 = b$	Simplify.

Step 2: Write the equation.

$y = mx + b$	Write the slope–intercept form.
$y = 3x + (-1)$	Substitute 3 for m and -1 for b.
$y = 3x - 1$	

© Houghton Mifflin Harcourt Publishing Company

EXPLORE

Graphing Lines Given Slope and y-Intercept

INTEGRATE TECHNOLOGY

Students have the option of completing the activity either in the book or online.

CONNECT VOCABULARY 🔲 EL

Remind students that the word *intercept* means *to come together*. When a player *intercepts* a football, the player and football come together at a certain point. Help students make the connection to the y-intercept on a graph, the place where the line "comes together" with the y-axis.

EXPLAIN 1

Creating Linear Equations in Slope-Intercept Form

AVOID COMMON ERRORS

Some students may not understand how to use the coordinates (x_1, y_1) and (x_2, y_2) to calculate the slope. Explain that the subscripts show which x-value goes with which y-value; for example the x-value of the first point is x_1, the y-value of the second point is y_2.

Remind students that the change in the y-coordinates goes in the numerator and the change in x-coordinates goes in the denominator.

PROFESSIONAL DEVELOPMENT

Learning Progressions

In this lesson, students build on their understanding of linear functions. They focus on the relationships between linear equations and their graphs, including:

- The slope-intercept form of a linear equation is $y = mx + b$, where m represents the slope, and b represents the y-intercept.
- A linear function can be graphed by plotting the y-intercept and using the slope to find other points that lie on the line.
- The slope-intercept form of a linear equation can be used to write functions that model real-world situations.

In future lessons, students compare functions represented in different forms.

EXPLAIN 2

Graphing from Slope-Intercept Form

INTEGRATE MATHEMATICAL PRACTICES
Focus on Reasoning

MP.2 Explain to students that one or both intercepts are often used to calculate the slope of a linear equation because they are easy to determine. However, any two points that satisfy the given equation can be used to determine the slope.

QUESTIONING STRATEGIES

? How does the value of b indicate whether the graph is above or below the origin where it intersects the y-axis? If b is positive, the y-intercept is positive and the graph intersects the y-axis above the origin. If b is negative, the y-intercept is negative and the graph intersects the y-axis below the origin.

? What is the advantage of graphing from slope-intercept form? The intercept is one point on the line and a second point can be found easily by using the slope.

INTEGRATE MATHEMATICAL PRACTICES
Focus on Math Connections

MP.1 Remind students that slope is the ratio of rise over run. Graph a line such as $y = -\frac{1}{2}x + 2$ in two ways, once using a slope of $\frac{-1}{2}$ and once using a slope of $\frac{1}{-2}$, to show that both result in the same line.

B The line passes through $(0, 5)$ and $(2, 13)$.

Step 1: Use the points to find the slope.

$$m = \frac{\boxed{y_2 - y_1}}{\boxed{x_2 - x_1}}$$

Substitute $(0, 5)$ for (x_1, y_1) and $\left(\boxed{2}, \boxed{13}\right)$ for (x_2, y_2).

$$m = \frac{\boxed{13 - 5}}{\boxed{2 - 0}} = \frac{\boxed{8}}{2} = \boxed{4}$$

Step 2: Substitute the slope and x- and y-coordinates of either of the points in the equation $y = mx + b$.

Step 3: Substitute $\underline{\ \ 4\ \ }$ for m and $\underline{\ \ 5\ \ }$ for b in the equation $y = mx + b$.

The equation of the line is $\boxed{y = 4x + 5}$.

$$y = mx + b$$
$$\boxed{13} = \boxed{4}\left(\boxed{2}\right) + b$$
$$\boxed{13} = \boxed{8} + b$$
$$\boxed{13} - \boxed{8} = \boxed{8} + b - \boxed{8}$$
$$\boxed{5} = b$$

Your Turn

Write the equation of each line in slope-intercept form.

3. Slope is -1, and $(3, 2)$ is on the line.

$2 = -1(3) + b; 5 = b$

The equation of the line is $y = -x + 5$.

4. The line passes through $(1, 4)$ and $(3, 18)$.

$m = \frac{18 - 4}{3 - 1} = \frac{14}{2} = 7$

$4 = 7(1) + b; -3 = b$

The equation of the line is $y = 7x - 3$.

⊘ Explain 2 **Graphing from Slope-Intercept Form**

Writing an equation in slope-intercept form can make it easier to graph the equation.

Example 2 Write each equation in slope-intercept form. Then graph the line.

A $y = 5x - 4$

The equation $y = 5x - 4$ is already in slope-intercept form.

Slope: $m = 5 = \frac{5}{1}$

y-intercept: $b = -4$

Step 1: Plot $(0, -4)$

Step 2: Count 5 units up and 1 unit to the right and plot another point.

Step 3: Draw a line through the points.

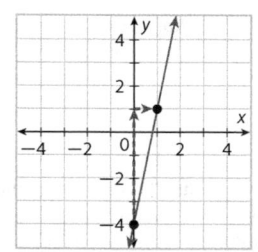

COLLABORATIVE LEARNING

Peer-to-Peer Activity

Group students in pairs. Have each student write slope-intercept equations for four lines: one whose slope is a positive integer, one whose slope is a negative integer, and one whose slope is a fraction. Then have partners trade equations. Partners should first check that the three conditions are met, then graph the lines.

Ⓑ $2x + 6y = 6$

Step 1: Write the equation in slope-intercept form by solving for y.

$2x + 6y - 2x = 6 - \boxed{2x}$ Slope: $\boxed{-\dfrac{1}{3}}$

$6y = \boxed{-2x} + 6$ y-intercept: $\boxed{1}$

$y = \boxed{-\dfrac{1}{3}}x + \boxed{1}$

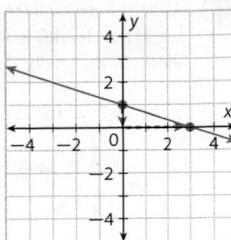

Step 2: Graph the line.

Plot $\left(\boxed{0}, \boxed{1}\right)$. Move $\underline{\quad 1 \quad}$ unit down and $\underline{\quad 3 \quad}$ units to the right to plot a second point. Draw a line through the points.

Your Turn

Write each equation in slope-intercept form. Then graph the line.

5. $2x + y = 4$ $y = -2x + 4$

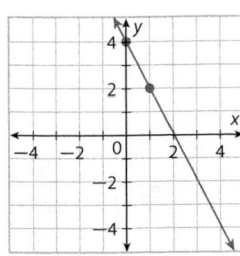

6. $2x + 3y = 6$ $y = -\dfrac{2}{3}x + 2$

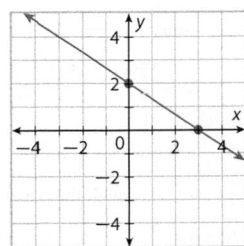

🕐 **Explain 3** **Determining Solutions of Equations in Two Variables**

Given a real-world linear situation described by a table, a graph, or a verbal description, you can write an equation in slope-intercept form. You can use that equation to solve problems.

Example 3 Identify the slope and y-intercept of the graph that represents each linear situation and interpret what they mean. Then write an equation in slope-intercept form and use it to solve the problem.

Ⓐ For one taxi company, the cost y in dollars of a taxi ride is a linear function of the distance x in miles traveled. The initial charge is $2.50, and the charge per mile is $0.35. Find the cost of riding a distance of 10 miles.

The rate of change is $0.35 per mile, so the slope, m, is 0.35.

The initial cost is the cost to travel 0 miles, $2.50, so the y-intercept, b, is 2.50.

Then an equation is $y = 0.35x + 2.50$. $y = 0.35x + 2.50$

To find the cost of riding 10 miles, substitute 10 for x. $= 0.35(10) + 2.50$

$= 6$

$(6, 10)$ is a solution of the equation, and the cost of riding a distance of 10 miles is $6.

© Houghton Mifflin Harcourt Publishing Company

EXPLAIN 3

Determining Solutions of Equations in Two Variables

QUESTIONING STRATEGY

❓ For a real-world problem described by a graph of a linear function in which the value of y indicates the solution for a given value of x, what do you need to do to solve the problem? **Apply the units from the graph to the solution. For example if x is time in hours and y is cost in dollars, then the solution is y dollars for a time of x hours.**

INTEGRATE MATHEMATICAL PRACTICES
Focus on Modeling

MP.4 Remind students that when time is one of the quantities in a real-world problem, it is usually the independent variable.

AVOID COMMON ERRORS

Some students may think that the coefficient of x is the slope of the line of the equation regardless of the form of the equation. Remind them that if the equation is not in the form $y = mx + b$, the coefficient of x may not be the slope.

DIFFERENTIATE INSTRUCTION

Communicating Math

Have students list the steps for writing a linear function from two given points. Sample steps are shown.

1. Use the slope formula to find the slope m.

2. Substitute m and the coordinates of one point into $f(x) = mx + b$.

3. Solve for the y-intercept b.

4. Substitute m and b into $f(x) = mx + b$.

ELABORATE

QUESTIONING STRATEGIES

? How would you graph the equation $c = 35t + 50$? The equation is in slope-intercept form. 35 is the slope and 50 is the y-intercept. Plot the point that corresponds to the y-intercept $(0, 50)$. Then use the slope to locate a second point on the line. Draw a line through the two points.

SUMMARIZE THE LESSON

? How do you write an equation of a line in slope-intercept form when given the slope and y-intercept or when given the slope and a point on the line? Using the form $y = mx + b$, substitute slope for m and the y-intercept for b. If you are given the slope and a point on the line, substitute the slope into $y = mx + b$, substitute the coordinates of the point for x and y, and solve for b.

Ⓑ A chairlift descends from a mountain top to pick up skiers at the bottom. The height in feet of the chairlift is a linear function of the time in minutes since it begins descending as shown in the graph. Find the height of the chairlift 2 minutes after it begins descending.

Height of a Chairlift

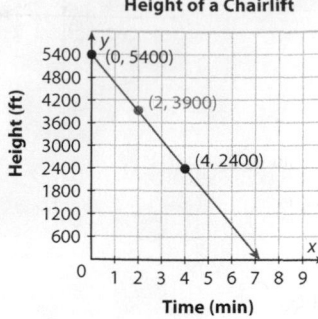

The graph contains the points $(0, \underline{5400})$ and $(\underline{4}, 2400)$.

The slope is $\dfrac{\boxed{2400} - 5400}{\boxed{4} - 0} = \boxed{-750}$.

It represents the rate at which the chairlift __descends__.

The graph passes through the point $(0, \underline{5400})$, so the y-intercept is $\underline{5400}$. It represents the height of the chairlift $\underline{0}$ minutes after it begins descending.

Let x be the time in minutes after the chairlift begins to descend.

Let y be the height of the chairlift in feet.

The equation is $y = \underline{-750x + 5400}$.

To find the height after 2 minutes, substitute 2 for x and simplify.

$$\boxed{y} = \boxed{-750}\left(\boxed{2}\right) + 5400$$

$$= \boxed{-1500} + 5400$$

$$= \boxed{3900}$$

$\underline{(2, 3900)}$ is a solution of the equation, and the height of the chairlift 2 minutes after it begins descending is $\underline{3900}$ feet.

Reflect

7. In the example involving the taxi, how would the equation change if the cost per mile increased or decreased? How would this affect the graph?

Increasing the cost per mile would increase the value of m and make the graph steeper.

Decreasing the cost per mile would decrease the value of m and make the graph less steep.

LANGUAGE SUPPORT EL

Connect Vocabulary

Caution students that a figure called a *graph of a line* should not be confused with a *line graph*. A *line graph* is a graph that uses line segments to connect data points. A *graph of a line* is a graph of a linear equation.

Your Turn

Identify the slope and *y*-intercept of the graph that represents the linear situation and interpret what they mean. Then write an equation in slope-intercept form and use it to solve the problem.

8. A local club charges an initial membership fee as well as a monthly cost. The cost *C* in dollars is a linear function of the number of months of membership. Find the cost of the membership after 4 months.

Membership Cost	
Time (months)	Cost ($)
0	100
3	277
6	454

$m = \frac{277 - 100}{3 - 0} = 59$; and $\frac{454 - 277}{6 - 3} = \frac{177}{3} = 59$,

so the rate of change in the cost is $59 per month.
The initial cost is $100, so the *y*-intercept, *b*, is 100. The equation is $y = 59x + 100$.
$f(4) = 59(4) + 100 = 336$. So, $(4, 336)$ is a solution.

💬 Elaborate

9. What are some advantages to using slope-intercept form?
When graphing, it's easy to recognize the slope and *y*-intercept. It's also easy to find

_y_-values for corresponding _x_-values.

10. What are some disadvantages of slope-intercept form?
The *x*-intercept may not be easily visible, and if a *y*-value is given, the *x*-value may not be

easily obtained.

11. **Essential Question Check-In** When given a real-world situation that can be described by a linear equation, how can you identify the slope and *y*-intercept of the graph of the equation?
To find the slope, identify the rate of change for the situation. To find the *y*-intercept,

identify the initial value for the situation, that is, the value of the dependent variable

when the value of the independent value is 0.

⚙ Evaluate: Homework and Practice

• Online Homework
• Hints and Help
• Extra Practice

For each situation, determine the slope and *y*-intercept of the graph of the equation that describes the situation.

1. John gets a new job and receives a $500 signing bonus. After that, he makes $200 a day.

The rate of change is $200 per day, so the slope is 200. The value of *y*

when *x* is 0 (when John has worked 0 days) is $500, so the *y*-intercept

is 500.

© Houghton Mifflin Harcourt Publishing Company

Exercise	Depth of Knowledge (D.O.K.)	COMMON CORE Mathematical Practices
1–14	**1** Recall of Information	**MP.6** Precision
15–22	**2** Skills/Concepts	**MP.6** Precision
23–24	**2** Skills/Concepts	**MP.4** Modeling
25–26	**3** Strategic Thinking H.O.T.	**MP.2** Reasoning
27	**3** Strategic Thinking H.O.T.	**MP.3** Logic

EVALUATE

ASSIGNMENT GUIDE

Concepts and Skills	Practice
Explore Graphing Lines Given Slope and *y*-Intercept	Exercises 1–4
Example 1 Creating Linear Equations in Slope-Intercept Form	Exercises 5–14
Example 2 Graphing from Slope-Intercept Form	Exercises 15–22, 26
Example 3 Determining Solutions of Equations in Two Variables	Exercise 23–25, 27

INTEGRATE MATHEMATICAL PRACTICES

Focus on Reasoning

MP.2 Remind students that they can quickly check that their graphs are reasonable by looking at the slope. Lines with positive slopes rise from left to right, and lines with negative slopes fall from left to right.

AVOID COMMON ERRORS

Encourage students to use a third point to check a graphed line. They can either choose a point from the graph and check it in the equation, or use the equation to generate a point and check that it is on the graph.

KINESTHETIC EXPERIENCE

Use masking tape to outline a coordinate plane on a floor of square tiles. Then give a pair of students a length of rope. Announce an equation in slope-intercept form, and have the two students move around on the plane so that when they hold the rope taut, it represents the line described by the given equation, with each of them as two points on the line. A third student can check that these two points satisfy the equation.

AVOID COMMON ERRORS

Students may not believe that they have enough information to find the slope of a line. Remind students that, if you know the equation that describes a line, you can find its slope by using any two ordered-pair solutions.

---

2. Jennifer is 20 miles north of her house, and she is driving north on the highway at a rate of 55 miles per hour.

The rate of change is 55 miles per hour, so the slope is 55. The value of y when x is 0 (when Jennifer has driven 0 miles) is 20, so the y-intercept is 20.

Sketch a graph that represents the situation.

3. Morwenna rents a truck. She pays $20 plus $0.25 per mile.

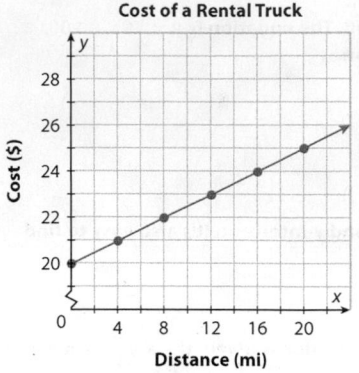

Cost of a Rental Truck

4. An investor invests $500 in a certain stock. After the first six months, the value of the stock has increased at a rate of $20 per month.

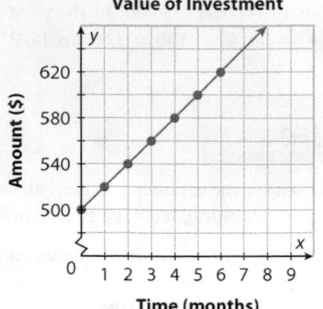

Value of Investment

Write the equation of each line in slope-intercept form.

5. Slope is 3, and $(1, 5)$ is on the line.

$5 = 3(1) + b$, so $2 = b$.

The equation is $y = 3x + 2$.

6. Slope is -2, and $(5, 3)$ is on the line.

$3 = -2(5) + b$, so $13 = b$.

The equation is $y = -2x + 13$.

7. Slope is $\frac{1}{4}$, and $(4, 2)$ is on the line.

$2 = \frac{1}{4}(4) + b$, so $1 = b$.

The equation is $y = \frac{1}{4}x + 1$.

8. Slope is 5, and $(2, 6)$ is on the line.

$6 = 5(2) + b$, so $-4 = b$.

The equation is $y = 5x - 4$.

9. Slope is $-\frac{2}{3}$, and $(-6, -5)$ is on the line.

$-5 = -\frac{2}{3}(-6) + b$, so $-9 = b$.

The equation is $y = -\frac{2}{3}x - 9$.

10. Slope is $-\frac{1}{2}$, and $(-3, 2)$ is on the line.

$2 = -\frac{1}{2}(-3) + b$, so $\frac{1}{2} = b$.

The equation is $y = -\frac{1}{2}x + \frac{1}{2}$.

11. Passes through $(5, 7)$ and $(3, 1)$

$m = \dfrac{7-1}{5-3} = \dfrac{6}{2} = 3$

$1 = 3(3) + b$, so $-8 = b$.

The equation is $y = 3x - 8$.

12. Passes through $(-6, 10)$ and $(-3, -2)$

$m = \dfrac{10 - (-2)}{-6 - (-3)} = \dfrac{12}{-3} = -4$

$-2 = -4(-3) + b$, so $-14 = b$.

The equation is $y = -4x - 14$.

13. Passes through $(6, 6)$ and $(-2, 2)$

$m = \dfrac{6-2}{6-(-2)} = \dfrac{4}{8} = \dfrac{1}{2}$

$2 = \dfrac{1}{2}(-2) + b$, so $3 = b$.

The equation is $y = \dfrac{1}{2}x + 3$.

14. Passes through $(-1, -5)$ and $(2, 6)$

$m = \dfrac{-5-6}{-1-2} = \dfrac{-11}{-3} = \dfrac{11}{3}$

$6 = \dfrac{11}{3}(2) + b$, so $-\dfrac{4}{3} = b$.

The equation is $y = \dfrac{11}{3}x - \dfrac{4}{3}$.

Write each equation in slope-intercept form. Identify the slope and y-intercept. Then graph the line described by the equation.

15. $y = 2x + 3$ $y = 2x + 3; 2; 3$

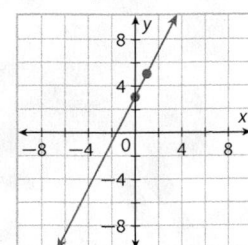

16. $y = -x + 2$ $y = -x + 2; -1; 2$

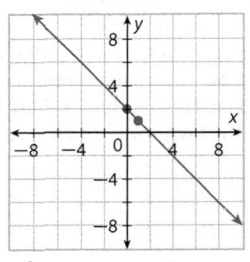

17. $y = \dfrac{2}{3}x - 4$ $y = \dfrac{2}{3}x - 4; -\dfrac{2}{3}; -4$

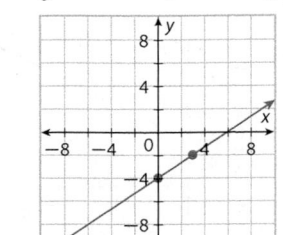

18. $y = -\dfrac{1}{2}x - 1$ $y = -\dfrac{1}{2}x - 1; -\dfrac{1}{2}; -1$

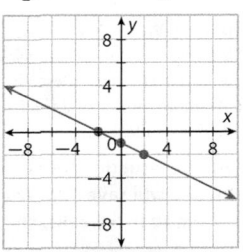

19. $-4x + 2y = 10$ $y = 2x + 5; 2; 5$

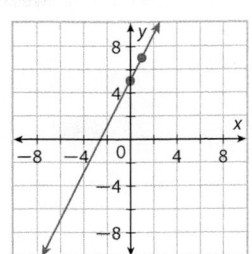

20. $3x - 6y = -12$ $y = \dfrac{1}{2}x + 2; \dfrac{1}{2}; 2$

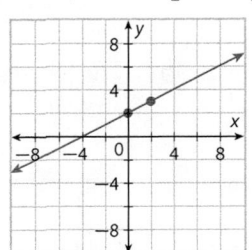

INTEGRATE TECHNOLOGY

Encourage students to use the function graphing capability of a graphing calculator to graph the slope-intercept form and check their answers to the problems. Note that the right side of a function in slope-intercept form can be entered, as the calculator provides **Y** and the equal sign. Students should experiment with the function grapher and window settings as well as consult their calculator manuals to learn more.

AVOID COMMON ERRORS

Students may have difficulty graphing a function that has a fractional rate of change. Remind them that the fraction can be looked at as rise over run, so the rise and run can be used to move from one point to a second point. That is, if the rate of change is expressed as a fraction, use the numerator to move the appropriate number of units up or down (the rise) and use the denominator to move the appropriate number of units rightward (the run) to plot a second point given the first point.

COLLABORATIVE LEARNING

Have students work in groups of three. Give students the following prompt: "Connor is on a 2-day hike. He hiked 10 miles on Day 1. After 4 hours on Day 2, he had hiked a total of 16 miles." Have one student draw a graph representing Connor's progress on Day 2. Have the second student identify the key features (slope and intercept). Have the third student explain what the slope and intercept mean in terms of Connor's hike. **The y-intercept (10) shows how far he hiked on Day 1. The slope (1.5) shows that he hiked an average of 1.5 mi/h on Day 2.**

JOURNAL

Have students show different representations of a linear function: the linear equation, the slope-intercept form of the equation, the graph, and a description of the relationships.

21. $-5x - 2y = 8$ $y = -\frac{5}{2}x - 4; -\frac{5}{2}; -4$

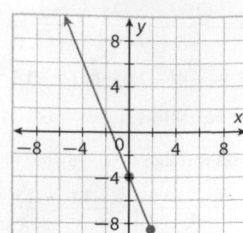

22. $3x + 4y = -12$ $y = -\frac{3}{4}x - 3; -\frac{3}{4}; -3$

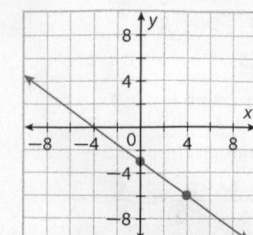

23. Sports A figure skating school offers introductory lessons at $25 per session. There is also a registration fee of $30. Write a linear equation in slope-intercept form that represents the situation. You want to take at least 6 lessons. Can you pay for those lessons using a $200 gift certificate? If so, how much money, if any, will be left on the gift certificate? If not, explain why not.

The cost per lesson is $25, so the slope of the equation that represents the situation is 25. The initial cost of the lessons (that is, before any lessons are paid for), is $30. So the y-intercept is 30. An equation is $y = 25x + 30$. The cost for 6 lessons is $25(6) + 30 = 180$. A $200 gift certificate would pay for the lessons, and $20 would be left.

24. Represent Real World Problems Lorena and Benita are saving money. They began on the same day. Lorena started with $40. Each week she adds $8. The graph describes Benita's savings plan. Which girl will have more money in 6 weeks? How much more will she have? Explain your reasoning.

Lorena; $8; the equation for Lorena is $y = 40 + 8x$, so in 6 weeks, she will save $88. The equation for Benita is $y = 50 + 5x$, so in 6 weeks, she will save $80.

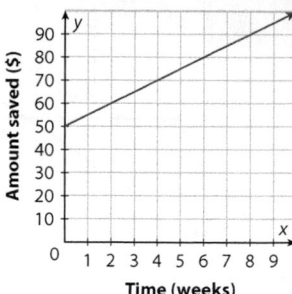

25. Analyze Relationships Julio and Jake start their reading assignments the same day. Jake is reading a 168-page book at a rate of 24 pages per day. Julio's book is 180 pages long and his reading rate is $1\frac{1}{4}$ times Jake's rate. After 5 days, who will have more pages left to read? How many more? Explain your reasoning.

Jake will have 48 more pages left to read. For Jake, the number of pages to read after 0 days is 168, and the rate of change is −24, so the equation is $y = -24x + 168$. Because $-24(5) + 168 = 48$, Jake will have 48 pages left to read after 5 days. Julio's pace is $\frac{5}{4}(24)$, so the equation for Julio is $y = -30x + 180$. Then after 5 days, Julio will have $-30(5) + 180 = 30$ pages left to read, and $48 - 30 = 18$.

So, Jake has $48 - 30 = 18$ more pages to read.

26. Explain the Error John has $2 in his bank account when he gets a job. He begins making $107 dollars a day. A student found that the equation that represents this situation is $y = 2x + 107$. What is wrong with the student's equation? Describe and correct the student's error.

The student switched the slope and the y-intercept. The slope should be 107, and the y-intercept should be 2. So the equation is $y = 107x + 2$.

27. Justify Reasoning Is it possible to write the equation of every line in slope-intercept form? Explain your reasoning.

No; it is not possible to write the equation of a vertical line in slope-intercept form. The equation of a vertical line has form $x = a$, where a is a real number. The slope of a vertical line is undefined.

Lesson Performance Task

The graph shows the cost of a membership in each of two years. What are the values that represent the sign-up fee and the membership monthly fee? How did the values change between the years?

a. Write an equation in slope-intercept form for each of the two lines in the graph.

b. What are the values that represent the sign-up fee and the membership cost? How did the values change between the years?

a. **The equation for Year 1 is $y = 20x + 20$, and the equation for Year 2 is $y = 20x + 60$.**

b. **The y-intercepts of the two graphs are 20 and 60, so each of these represents the cost when the number of months is 0, or the sign-up fee. In year 1, the y-values increase by $20 every month. Since this represents the rate of change in the monthly membership fee, the slope of the line in year 1 is 20. In year 2, the y-values again increase by $20 every month. So the slopes are equal in both years. This means that the monthly membership fees did not change. However, the sign-up fee increased by $40 between years 1 and 2.**

Gym Memberships

EXTENSION ACTIVITY

Have students research the cost of joining two gyms. Have students write an equation to represent the cost of each gym. Then have students graph their equations on the same coordinate grid.

Students will find that some gyms have a higher initial fee, but lower monthly rates than others. Caution students to note whether the fees to attend are weekly or monthly.

QUESTIONING STRATEGIES

? How do the graphs of Year 1 and Year 2 compare? They are parallel lines having the same slope, but different y-intercepts.

? How do the y-values compare for any whole-number x-value? What does this indicate about the costs? y is always 40 more for Year 2 than Year 1; Year 2 costs $40 more for any number of months.

INTEGRATE MATHEMATICAL PRACTICES
Focus on Reasoning

MP.2 Students can check each year's equation for correctness by substituting the values of two ordered pairs from the graph of each line into its equation and verifying that both solutions make the equation true. Remind students that checking their equations requires 2 points to define a line, so at least 2 points must be checked.

Scoring Rubric

2 points: Student correctly solves the problem and explains his/her reasoning.

1 point: Student shows good understanding of the problem but does not fully solve or explain his/her reasoning.

0 points: Student does not demonstrate understanding of the problem.

Point-Slope Form

Common Core Math Standards

The student is expected to:

 A-REI.D.10

Understand that the graph of an equation in two variables is the set of all its solutions plotted in the coordinate plane… Also A-CED.A.2

Mathematical Practices

COMMON CORE **MP.2 Reasoning**

Language Objective

Explain to a partner how to write a linear function in point-slope form.

ENGAGE

Essential Question: How can you represent a linear function in a way that reveals its slope and a point on its graph?

Possible answer: You can determine the slope m of the graph of the function and the coordinates (x_1, y_1) of a point on the graph, then write the equation $y - y_1 = m(x - x_1)$, which is called the point-slope form of the equation.

PREVIEW: LESSON PERFORMANCE TASK

View the Engage section online. Discuss the photo and how the concept of slope applies to snowboarding and can be used to predict the snowboarder's height on the slope at any one specific time. Then preview the Lesson Performance Task.

Name_____ Class_____ Date_____

6.2 Point-Slope Form

Essential Question: How can you represent a linear function in a way that reveals its slope and a point on its graph?

Resource Locker

⊘ Explore   Deriving Point-Slope Form

Suppose you know the slope of a line and the coordinates of one point on the line. How can you write an equation of the line?

Ⓐ A line has a slope m of 4, and the point $(2, 1)$ is on the line. Let (x, y) be any other point on the line. Substitute the information you have in the slope formula.

$$m = \frac{y_2 - y_1}{x_2 - x_1}$$

$$4 = \frac{y - \boxed{1}}{x - \boxed{2}}$$

Ⓑ Use the Multiplication Property of Equality to get rid of the fraction.

$$4\left(x - \boxed{2}\right) = \left(\frac{y - \boxed{1}}{x - \boxed{2}}\right)\left(x - \boxed{2}\right)$$

Ⓒ Simplify.

$$4\left(x - \boxed{2}\right) = \left(y - \boxed{1}\right)$$

Reflect

1. **Discussion** The equation that you derived is written in a form called *point-slope form*. The equation $y = 2x + 1$ is in slope-intercept form. How can you rewrite it in point-slope form?
   The slope is 2. The y-intercept is 1, so the point $(0, 1)$ is on the line. You can use the

   method of the Explore, that is, substitute the known values in the slope formula, write the

   equation without a fraction, and simplify the result. $y - 1 = 2(x - 0)$

🔑 Explain 1   Creating Linear Equations Given Slope and a Point

Point-Slope Form

The line with slope m that contains the point (x_1, y_1) can be described by the equation $y - y_1 = m(x - x_1)$.

Example 1 Write an equation in point-slope form for each line.

Ⓐ Slope is 3.5, and $(-3, 2)$ is on the line.

$y - y_1 = m(x - x_1)$	Point-slope form
$y - 2 = 3.5(x - (-3))$	Substitute.
$y - 2 = 3.5(x + 3)$	Simplify.

Ⓑ Slope is 0, and $(-2, -1)$ is on the line.

$y - y_1 = m(x - x_1)$	Point-slope form
$y - \boxed{(-1)} = \boxed{0}\left(x - \boxed{(-2)}\right)$	Substitute.
$y + \boxed{1} = \boxed{0}$	Simplify.

© Houghton Mifflin Harcourt Publishing Company

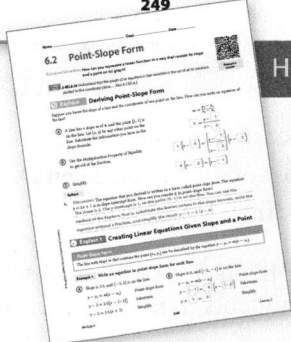

HARDCOVER PAGES 203–212

Turn to these pages to find this lesson in the hardcover student edition.

2. **Communicate Mathematical Ideas** Suppose that you are given that the slope of a line is 0. What is the only additional information you need to write an equation of the line? Explain.

The y-coordinate y_1 of any point on the line. A line with slope 0 is horizontal. Every point

has the same y-coordinate, and the equation of the line is $y = y_1$.

Your Turn

Write an equation in point-slope form for each line.

3. Slope is 6, and $(1, 2)$ is on the line.

$$y - y_1 = m(x - x_1)$$
$$y - 2 = 6(x - 1)$$

4. Slope is $\frac{1}{3}$, and $(-3, 1)$ is on the line.

$$y - y_1 = m(x - x_1)$$
$$y - 1 = \frac{1}{3}(x + 3)$$

Explain 2 **Creating Linear Models Given Slope and a Point**

You can write an equation in point-slope form to describe a real-world linear situation. Then you can use that equation to solve a problem.

Example 2 Solve the problem using an equation in point-slope form.

Ⓐ Paul wants to place an ad in a newspaper. The newspaper charges $10 for the first 2 lines of text and $3 for each additional line of text. Paul's ad is 8 lines long. How much will the ad cost?

Let x represent the number of lines of text. Let y represent the cost in dollars of the ad. Because 2 lines of text cost $10, the point $(2, 10)$ is on the line. The rate of change in the cost is $3 per line, so the slope is 3.

Write an equation in point-slope form.

$y - y_1 = m(x - x_1)$	Point-slope form
$y - 10 = 3(x - 2)$	Substitute 3 for m, 2 for x_1, and 10 for y_1.

To find the cost of 8 lines, substitute 8 for x and solve for y.

$y - 10 = 3(8 - 2)$	Substitute
$y - 10 = 18$	Simplify.
$y = 28$	

The cost of 8 lines is $28.

© Houghton Mifflin Harcourt Publishing Company

Deriving Point-Slope Form

INTEGRATE TECHNOLOGY

Students have the option of completing the activity either in the book or online.

CONNECT VOCABULARY **EL**

Point out that the names *slope-intercept* and *point-slope* tell students what types of information they will use to express a linear relationship.

EXPLAIN 1

Creating Linear Equations Given Slope and a Point

INTEGRATE MATHEMATICAL PRACTICES

Focus on Critical Thinking

MP.3 Show students that they can graph a line starting at *any* point on the line if they know the slope, by counting vertically and horizontally from that point. Show how point-slope form comes from the slope formula, and show how it also simplifies to slope-intercept form.

QUESTIONING STRATEGIES

? Could two different equations in point-slope form represent the same line? Yes; choosing two different points on a line would result in two different equations in point-slope form, although the slope would be the same.

EXPLAIN 2

Creating Linear Models Given Slope and a Point

INTEGRATE MATHEMATICAL PRACTICES
Focus on Reasoning

MP.2 Remind students that once they have the point-slope equation of a line, they can find the value of y if given a value of x, or vice versa, by substituting and solving for the other variable.

QUESTIONING STRATEGIES

? If the independent variable is the number of items and the dependent variable is the weight of the items in pounds, what would the equation in point-slope form represent? **y minus the weight in pounds of a number of items would be equal to the product of the weight in pounds per item and the quantity x minus the number of items.**

EXPLAIN 3

Creating Linear Equations Given Two Points

QUESTIONING STRATEGIES

? Can you write a point-slope equation for a vertical line? Explain. **No; because a vertical line has rise, but no run, it has undefined slope.**

? Can you write a point-slope equation for a horizontal line? Explain. **Yes; the slope would be 0, so the equation would be in the form $y - y_1 = 0$.**

Lesson 6.2

(B) Paul would like to shop for the best price to place the ad. A different newspaper has a base cost of $15 for 3 lines and $2 for every extra line. How much will an 8-line ad cost in this paper?

$$y - y_1 = m(x - x_1) \qquad \text{Point-slope form}$$
$$y - \boxed{15} = 2\left(x - \boxed{3}\right) \qquad \text{Substitute.}$$
$$y - \boxed{15} = 2\left(\boxed{8} - \boxed{3}\right) \qquad \text{Substitute for } x.$$
$$y - \boxed{15} = \boxed{10} \qquad \text{Simplify the right side.}$$
$$y = \boxed{25} \qquad \text{Solve for } y.$$

The cost of 8 lines is $\boxed{25}$.

Reflect

5. **Analyze Relationships** Suppose that you find that the cost of an ad with 8 lines in another publication is $18. How is the ordered pair (8, 18) related to the equation that represents the situation? How is it related to the graph of the equation?
The ordered pair is a solution of the equation. It represents a point on the graph of the equation.

Your Turn

6. Daisy purchases a gym membership. She pays a signup fee and a monthly fee of $11. After 4 months, she has paid a total of $59. Use a linear equation in point-slope form to find the signup fee.
$$y - 59 = 11(x - 4)$$
$$y - 59 = 11(0 - 4)$$
$$y = 15 \text{ The signup fee is } \$15.$$

Explain 3   Creating Linear Equations Given Two Points

You can use two points on a line to create an equation of the line in point-slope form. There is more than one such equation.

Example 3   Write an equation in point-slope form for each line.

(A) (2, 1) and (3, 4) are on the line.

Let $(2, 1) = (x_1, y_1)$ and let $(3, 4) = (x_2, y_2)$.

Find the slope of the line by substituting the given values in the slope formula.

$$m = \frac{y_2 - y_1}{x_2 - x_1}$$
$$= \frac{4 - 1}{3 - 2}$$
$$= 3$$

You can choose either point and substitute the coordinates in the point-slope form.

$$y - y_1 = m(x - x_1) \qquad \text{Point-slope form}$$
$$y - 1 = 3(x - 2) \qquad \text{Substitute 3 for } m, \text{ 2 for } x_1, \text{ and 1 for } y_1.$$

Or:

$$y - y_1 = m(x - x_1) \qquad \text{Point-slope form}$$
$$y - 4 = 3(x - 3) \qquad \text{Substitute 3 for } m, \text{ 3 for } x_1, \text{ and 4 for } y_1.$$

© Houghton Mifflin Harcourt Publishing Company

COLLABORATIVE LEARNING

Small Group Activity

Have students work with in groups of three. Have each student write the coordinates for a point and the slope of a line. Remind students to keep their values reasonable. Students pass their data to the right. The next student writes the point-slope form for the line. When students are finished, pass the papers to the right once more. Now, students match the form to the data; when they are satisfied it is correct, they graph the line.

(B) $(1, 3)$ and $(2, 3)$ are on the line.

Let $(1, 3) = (x_1, y_1)$ and let $(2, 3) = (x_2, y_2)$.

Find the slope of the line by substituting the given values in the slope formula.

$$m = \frac{y_2 - y_1}{x_2 - x_1}$$

$$= \frac{\boxed{3} - \boxed{3}}{\boxed{2} - \boxed{1}}$$

$$= \boxed{0}$$

Choose either point and substitute the coordinates in the point-slope form.

$y - y_1 = m(x - x_1)$ Point-slope form

$y - \boxed{3} = \boxed{0}\left(x - \boxed{1}\right)$ Substitute 0 for m, 1 for x_1, and 3 for y_1.

Or:

$y - y_2 = m(x - x_2)$ Point-slope form

$y - \boxed{3} = \boxed{0}\left(x - \boxed{2}\right)$ Substitute 0 for m, 2 for x_2, and 3 for y_2.

Reflect

7. Given two points on a line, Martin and Minh each found the slope of the line. Then Martin used (x_1, y_1) and Minh used (x_2, y_2) to write the equation in point-slope form. Each student's equation was correct. Explain how they can show both equations are correct.
   Martin can show that (x_2, y_2) is a solution of his equation, and Minh can show that

   (x_1, y_1) is a solution of hers.

Your Turn

Write an equation in point-slope form for each line.

8. $(2, 4)$ and $(3, 1)$ are on the line.

   $(y - 1) = -3(x - 3)$ or $(y - 4) = -3(x - 2)$

9. $(0, 1)$ and $(1, 1)$ are on the line.

   $(y - 1) = 0(x - 0)$ or $(y - 1) = 0(x - 1)$

⊘ Explain 4   Creating a Linear Model Given Two Points

In a real-world linear situation, you may have information that represents two points on the line. You can write an equation in point-slope form that represents the situation and use that equation to solve a problem.

Example 4   Solve the problem using an equation in point-slope form.

An animal shelter asks all volunteers to take a training session and then to volunteer for one shift each week. Each shift is the same number of hours. The table shows the numbers of hours Joan and her friend Miguel worked over several weeks. Another friend, Lili, plans to volunteer for 24 weeks over the next year. How many hours will Lili volunteer?

Volunteer	Weeks worked	Hours worked
Joan	6	15
Miguel	10	23

DIFFERENTIATE INSTRUCTION

Auditory Cues

Students will benefit from saying the point-slope equation aloud when writing it. They might say, for example:

"y minus y one equals m times the quantity x minus x one,"

"y minus y sub one equals m times the quantity x minus x sub one,"

"y minus y one equals the product of m and x minus x one."

Be sure they state it in a way that emphasizes the distribution of m.

🧩 Analyze Information

Identify the important information.

- Joan worked for ___6___ weeks for a total of ___15___ hours.
- Miguel worked for ___10___ weeks for a total of ___23___ hours.
- Lili will work for ___24___ weeks.

🧩 Formulate a Plan

To create the equation, identify the two ordered pairs represented by the situation. Find the ___slope___ of the line that contains the two points. Write the equation in point-slope form. Substitute the ___number of weeks___ that Lili works for x to find y, the ___number of hours that Lili works___

Let x represent the number of weeks worked and y represent the number of hours worked.

The points ___(6, 15)___ and ___(10, 23)___ are on the line. Substitute the coordinates in the slope formula to find the slope.

$$m = \frac{y_2 - y_1}{x_2 - x_1}$$

$$m = \frac{\boxed{23} - \boxed{15}}{\boxed{10} - \boxed{6}}$$

$$m = \boxed{2}$$

Next choose one of the points and find an equation of the line in point-slope form.

$y - y_1 = m(x - x_1)$ Point-slope form

$y - \boxed{15} = \boxed{2}\left(x - \boxed{6}\right)$ Substitute $\boxed{2}$ for m, $\boxed{6}$ for x_1, and $\boxed{15}$ for y_1.

Or:

$y - y_2 = m(x - y_2)$ Point-slope form

$y - \boxed{23} = \boxed{2}\left(x - \boxed{10}\right)$ Substitute $\boxed{2}$ for m, $\boxed{10}$ for x_2, and $\boxed{23}$ for y_2.

Finally, substitute ___24___ in the equation to find y.

$y - \boxed{15} = \boxed{2}\left(x - \boxed{6}\right)$ Substitute $\boxed{2}$ for m, $\boxed{6}$ for x_1, and $\boxed{15}$ for y_1.

$y - \boxed{15} = \boxed{2}\left(\boxed{24} - \boxed{6}\right)$ Substitute $\boxed{24}$ for x.

$y - \boxed{15} = \boxed{2}\left(\boxed{18}\right)$ Simplify.

$y = \boxed{51}$ Simplify.

Or:

$y - \boxed{23} = \boxed{2}\left(x - \boxed{10}\right)$ Substitute $\boxed{2}$ for m, $\boxed{10}$ for x_2, and $\boxed{23}$ for y_2.

$y - \boxed{23} = \boxed{2}\left(\boxed{24} - \boxed{10}\right)$ Substitute $\boxed{24}$ for x.

$y - \boxed{23} = \boxed{2}\left(\boxed{14}\right)$ Simplify.

$y = \boxed{51}$ Simplify.

Lili will work a total of ___51___ hours.

LANGUAGE SUPPORT 🔲 EL

Connect Vocabulary

Explain to students how some English words are formed from two hyphenated words, such as *real-world*, *family-size*, and in this lesson, *point-slope*. The hyphen in these words links the two source words together. Together, *point-slope* is one compound word that describes the form of a linear equation. Contrast this with the *slope-intercept* form of a line, pointing out that each compound adjective describes the information in its equation.

Justify and Evaluate

The ordered pair $\left(\boxed{24}, \boxed{51}\right)$ is a solution of both equations obtained using the given information.

$y - \boxed{15} = \boxed{2}\left(x - \boxed{6}\right)$ Substitute 2 for m, 6 for x_1, and 15 for y_1.

$\boxed{51} - \boxed{15} = \boxed{2}\left(\boxed{24} - \boxed{6}\right)$ Substitute $\boxed{24}$ for x and $\boxed{51}$ for y.

$\boxed{36} = \boxed{36}$ Simplify.

Or:

$y - \boxed{23} = \boxed{2}\left(x - \boxed{10}\right)$ Substitute 2 for m, 10 for x_2, and 23 for y_2.

$\boxed{51} - \boxed{23} = \boxed{2}\left(\boxed{24} - \boxed{10}\right)$ Substitute $\boxed{24}$ for x and $\boxed{51}$ for y.

$\boxed{28} = \boxed{28}$ Simplify.

The answer makes sense because the rate of change in the number of hours is the

slope, $\underline{\quad 2 \quad}$. Because Lili will work $\underline{\quad 14 \quad}$ more weeks than Miguel, she will work

$23 + 2 \underline{\quad (14) \quad}$ hours, or $\underline{\quad 51 \quad}$ hours.

Your Turn

Solve the problem using an equation in point-slope form.

10. A gas station has a customer loyalty program. The graph shows the amount y dollars that two members paid for x gallons of gas. Use an equation in point-slope to find the amount a member would pay for 22 gallons of gas.

$m = \dfrac{49 - 10}{18 - 5} = 3$ $y - 10 = 3(x - 5)$

A member would pay \$61 $y - 10 = 3(22 - 5)$

for 22 gallons of gas. $y = 61$

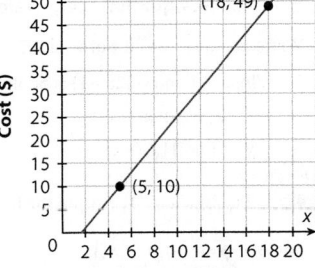

11. A roller skating rink offers a special rate for birthday parties. On the same day, a party for 10 skaters cost \$107 and a party for 15 skaters cost \$137. How much would a party for 12 skaters cost?

$m = \dfrac{137 - 107}{15 - 10} = 6$ $y - 107 = 6(x - 10)$

A party for 12 skaters would cost \$119. $y - 107 = 6(12 - 10)$

$y = 119$

ELABORATE

QUESTIONING STRATEGIES

? How is the point-slope form related to the slope formula? The point-slope form is just the slope formula with the denominator (*x*-values) moved to the other side of the equal sign.

INTEGRATE MATHEMATICAL PRACTICES

Focus on Critical Thinking

MP.3 Ask students to describe the graph of a linear equation with a point-slope form of $y - 3 = 3(x - 1)$ without simplifying the equation. Students should recognize that the slope is 3 and the graph goes through $(1, 3)$, so the graph is the line with slope 3 going through the origin, or $y = 3x$.

SUMMARIZE THE LESSON

? How do you write linear equations in point-slope form if you know a point and the slope, or if you know two points? The point-slope form, $y - y_1 = m(x - x_1)$, uses the *x*- and *y*-coordinates of a point and the slope. If you are given two points, use the slope formula to find the slope. Substitute the slope and the coordinates of a given point into the point-slope form.

💬 **Elaborate**

12. Can you write an equation in point-slope form that passes through any two given points in a coordinate plane?
No; you can't write a linear equation given two points with the same *x*-coordinate. A line through two such points is vertical and has no slope.

13. Compare and contrast the slope-intercept form of a linear equation and the point-slope form.
Possible answers: Both forms of the equation reveal the slope. The point-slope form explicitly reveals a point (x_1, y_1) on the line. The slope-intercept form reveals a point on the line, but not explicitly. It is the point $(0, b)$ where the graph intersects the *y*-axis. Both can be used fairly easily to graph the function. You can plot $(0, b)$ or (x_1, y_1), and then use the slope to plot a second point. The slope-intercept form can be used to graph an equation on a graphing calculator.

14. **Essential Question Check-In** Given a linear graph, how can you write an equation in point-slope form of the line?
Find the slope *m* (if it is defined) by identifying two points on the line and using the slope formula. Then substitute the slope and the coordinates of one of the points in the point-slope form $y - y_1 = m(x - x_1)$.

⭐ **Evaluate: Homework and Practice**

- Online Homework
- Hints and Help
- Extra Practice

1. Is the equation $y + 1 = 7(x + 2)$ in point-slope form? Justify your answer.
Yes; the equation is equivalent to $y - (-1) = 7\big(x - (-2)\big)$.

Write an equation in point-slope form for each line.

2. Slope is 1 and $(-2, -1)$ is on the line.
$$y - y_1 = m(x - x_1)$$
$$y + 1 = 1(x + 2)$$

3. Slope is -2, and $(1, 1)$ is on the line.
$$y - y_1 = m(x - x_1)$$
$$y - 1 = (-2)(x - 1)$$

4. Slope is 0, and $(1, 2)$ is on the line.
$$y - y_1 = m(x - x_1)$$
$$y - 2 = 0(x - 1)$$

5. Slope is $\frac{1}{4}$, and $(1, 2)$ is on the line.
$$y - y_1 = m(x - x_1)$$
$$y - 2 = \left(\frac{1}{4}\right)(x - 1)$$

6. $(1, 6)$ and $(2, 3)$ are on the line.
$$m = \frac{3 - 6}{2 - 1} = -3$$
$$y - y_1 = m(x - x_1)$$
$$y - 6 = (-3)(x - 1) \text{ or } y - 3 = (-3)(x - 2)$$

7. $(-1, 1)$ and $(1, -1)$ are on the line.
$$m = \frac{(-1) - 1}{1 - (-1)} = \frac{-2}{2} = -1$$
$$y - y_1 = m(x - x_1)$$
$$y - 1 = (-1)(x + 1) \text{ or } y + 1 = (-1)(x - 1)$$

8. $(7, 7)$ and $(-3, 7)$ are on the line.

$$m = \frac{7 - 7}{(-3) - 7} = \frac{0}{-10} = 0$$

$$y - y_1 = m(x - x_1)$$

$$y - 7 = 0(x - 7) \text{ or } y - 7 = 0(x + 3)$$

9. $(0, 3)$ and $(2, 4)$ are on the line.

$$m = \frac{4 - 3}{2 - 0} = \frac{1}{2}$$

$$y - y_1 = m(x - x_1)$$

$$y - 3 = \left(\frac{1}{2}\right)(x - 0) \text{ or } y - 4 = \left(\frac{1}{2}\right)(x - 2)$$

Solve the problem using an equation in point-slope form.

10. An oil tank is being filled at a constant rate. The depth of the oil is a function of the number of minutes the tank has been filling, as shown in the table. Find the depth of the oil one-half hour after filling begins.

Time (min)	Depth (ft)
0	3
10	5
15	6

$$m = \frac{5 - 3}{10 - 0} = \frac{1}{5}$$

$$y - y_1 = m(x - x_1)$$

$$y - 3 = \frac{1}{5}(x - 0) \text{ or } y - 5 = \frac{1}{5}(x - 10)$$

$$y - 3 = \frac{1}{5}(30 - 0)$$

$$y - 3 = 6$$

$$y = 9$$

One-half hour after filling begins, the depth of the oil is 9 feet.

11. James is participating in a 5-mile walk to raise money for a charity. He has received $200 in fixed pledges and raises $20 extra for every mile he walks. Use a point-slope equation to find the amount he will raise if he completes the walk.

$$y - 200 = 20(5 - 0)$$

$$y - 200 = 100$$

$$y = 300$$

If he finishes the race, James will raise $300.

12. Keisha is reading a 325-page book at a rate of 25 pages per day. Use a point-slope equation to determine whether she will finish reading the book in 10 days.

$$y - 325 = -25(10 - 0)$$

$$y - 325 = -250$$

$$y = 75$$

No; she will still have 75 pages left to read after 10 days.

Exercise	Depth of Knowledge (D.O.K.)	COMMON CORE Mathematical Practices
1	**3** Strategic Thinking	**MP.3** Logic
2–5	**1** Recall of Information	**MP.5** Using Tools
6–9	**2** Skills/Concepts	**MP.5** Using Tools
10–15	**2** Skills/Concepts	**MP.4** Modeling
16	**3** Strategic Thinking	**MP.4** Modeling
17–18	**2** Skills/Concepts	**MP.4** Modeling

EVALUATE

Personal Math Trainer

ASSIGNMENT GUIDE

Concepts and Skills	Practice
Explore Deriving Point-Slope Form	Exercise 1
Example 1 Creating Linear Equations Given Slope and a Point	Exercises 2–5
Example 2 Creating Linear Models Given Slope and a Point	Exercises 10–12, 16–20
Example 3 Creating Linear Equations Given Two Points	Exercises 6–9, 21–22
Example 4 Creating A Linear Model Given Two Points	Exercises 13–15, 23–24

INTEGRATE MATHEMATICAL PRACTICES
Focus on Reasoning

MP.2 Encourage students to check their answers to make sure they are reasonable. When possible, students should estimate answers before working out the problems.

AUDITORY CUES

To write the equation of a line in point-slope form, students need to know the slope and one point on the line. Students might state the point-slope form as follows: "For a given *point*, *y* minus the *y*-coordinate equals the *slope* times the quantity *x* minus the *x*-coordinate."

AVOID COMMON ERRORS

Remind students to write both the subtraction symbol and negative symbol when they substitute negative values in the point-slope form.

---

13. Lizzy is tiling a kitchen floor for the first time. She had a tough time at first and placed only 5 tiles the first day. She started to go faster, and by the end of day 4, she had placed 35 tiles. She worked at a steady rate after the first day. Use an equation in point-slope form to determine how many days Lizzy took to place all of the 100 tiles needed to finish the floor.

$$m = \frac{35 - 5}{4 - 1} = \frac{30}{3} = 10$$
$$(100 - 5) = 10(x - 1)$$
$$95 = 10x - 10$$
$$95 + 10 = 10x - 10 + 10$$
$$105 = 10x$$
$$10.5 = x$$

Lizzy took 10.5 days to place all the tiles.

14. The amount of fresh water left in the tanks of a nineteenth-century clipper ship is a linear function of the time since the ship left port, as shown in the table. Write an equation in point-slope form that represents the function. Then find the amount of water that will be left in the ship's tanks 50 days after leaving port.

Time (days)	Amount (gal)
1	3555
8	3240
15	2925

$$m = \frac{3555 - 3240}{1 - 8} = \frac{315}{-7} = -45$$
$$y - 3555 = -45(50 - 1)$$
$$y - 3555 = -2205$$
$$y = 1350$$

1350 gallons of water will be left after 50 days.

Exercise	Depth of Knowledge (D.O.K.)		COMMON CORE Mathematical Practices
19–20	**3** Strategic Thinking		**MP.4** Modeling
21	**2** Skills/Concepts		**MP.6** Precision
22–23	**3** Strategic Thinking	H.O.T.	**MP.3** Logic
24	**3** Strategic Thinking	H.O.T.	**MP.6** Precision

15. At higher altitudes, water boils at lower temperatures. This relationship between altitude and boiling point is linear. At an altitude of 1000 feet, water boils at 210 °F. At an altitude of 3000 feet, water boils at 206 °F. Use an equation in point-slope form to find the boiling point of water at an altitude of 6000 feet.

$$m = \frac{206 - 210}{3000 - 1000} = \frac{-4}{2000} = -0.002$$
$$y - 210 = -0.002(6000 - 1000)$$
$$y = 200$$

The boiling point at 6000 feet is 200 °F.

16. In art class, Tico is copying a detail from a painting. He paints slowly for the first few days, but manages to increase his rate after that. The graph shows his progress after he increased his rate. How many square centimeters of his painting will he finish in 5 days after the increase in rate?

$$m = \frac{400 - 175}{8 - 3} = \frac{225}{5} = 45$$
$$y - 175 = 45(5 - 3)$$
$$y = 265$$

He will finish 265 cm² of his painting in 5 days after the increase in rate.

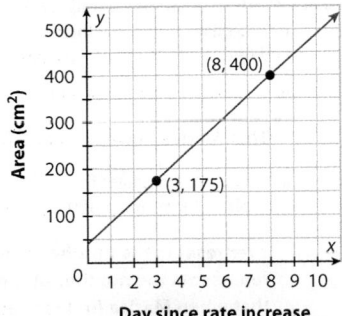

Day since rate increase

17. A hot air balloon in flight begins to ascend at a steady rate of 120 feet per minute. After 1.5 minutes, the balloon is at an altitude of 2150 feet. After 3 minutes, it is at an altitude of 2330 feet. Use an equation in point-slope form to determine whether the balloon will reach an altitude of 2500 feet in 4 minutes.

$$m = \frac{2330 - 2150}{3 - 1.5} = \frac{180}{1.5} = 120$$
$$y - 2150 = 120(4 - 1.5)$$
$$y = 2450$$

The balloon will not reach an altitude of 2500 feet in 4 minutes.

18. A candle burned at a steady rate. After 32 minutes, the candle was 11.2 inches tall. Eighteen minutes later, it was 10.75 inches tall. Use an equation in point-slope form to determine the height of the candle after 2 hours.

$$m = \frac{10.75 - 11.2}{50 - 32} = \frac{-0.45}{18} = -0.025$$
$$y - 11.2 = -0.025(120 - 32)$$
$$y = 9$$

After 2 hours, the candle will be 9 inches tall.

© Houghton Mifflin Harcourt Publishing Company • Image Credits: ©Royalty-Free/Corbis

INTEGRATE MATHEMATICAL PRACTICES
Focus on Math Connections

MP.1 Suggest to students that when they are given two points, they use both points to write equations in point-slope form. They can then check that the equations are equivalent by writing them in slope-intercept form.

COGNITIVE STRATEGIES

Encourage students to look for ways to make problems easier to solve. For example, in some problems, any two points can be used to find the slope, but some pairs may be easier to work with than others.

19. **Volume** A rectangular swimming pool has a volume capacity of 2160 cubic feet. Water is being added to the pool at a rate of about 20 cubic feet per minute. Determine about how long it will take to fill the pool completely if there were already about 1200 gallons of water in the pool. Use the fact that 1 cubic foot of space holds about 7.5 gallons of water.

$$\frac{1200 \text{ gal}}{7.5 \text{ gal/ft}^3} = 160 \text{ ft}^3$$

$$2160 = 160 + 20x$$
$$2000 = 20x$$
$$x = 100$$

It will take about 100 minutes to fill the pool completely.

20. **Multi-Step** Marisa is walking from her home to her friend Sanjay's home. When she is 12 blocks away from Sanjay's home, she looks at her watch. She looks again when she is 8 blocks away from Sanjay's home and finds that 6 minutes have passed.

  a. What do you need to assume in order to treat this as a linear situation?

    That Marisa in walking at a fixed rate.

  b. Identify the variables for the linear situation and identify two points on the line. Explain the meaning of the points in the context of the problem.

    x represents the number of minutes since Marisa first looked at her watch, and y represents the number of blocks she is from Sanjay's home. The point $(0, 12)$ indicates that when Marisa first looked at her watch, she was 12 blocks from Sanjay's home. The point $(6, 8)$ indicates that 6 minutes after she first looked at her watch she was 8 blocks from Sanjay's home.

  c. Find the slope of the line and describe what it means in the context of the problem.

    $m = \dfrac{8 - 12}{6 - 0} = -\dfrac{2}{3}$**; the slope indicates that for every minute Marisa walks, the distance to Sanjay's home decreases by $\frac{2}{3}$ block.**

  d. Write an equation in point-slope form for the situation and use it to find the number of minutes Marisa takes to reach Sanjay's home. Show your work.

    $$0 - 12 = -\frac{2}{3}(x - 0)$$

    $18 = x$ **Marisa takes 18 minutes to reach Sanjay's home.**

21. Match each equation with the pair of points used to create the equation.

  a. $y - 10 = 1(x + 2)$ _____**c**_____ $(0, 0), (-1, 1)$

  b. $y - 0 = 1(x - 0)$ _____**b**_____ $(1, 1), (-1, -1)$

  c. $y - 3 = -1(x + 3)$ _____**a**_____ $(-2, 10), (0, 12)$

  d. $y - 3 = 0(x - 2)$ _____**d**_____ $(1, 3), (-3.5, 3)$

22. Explain the Error Carlota wrote the equation $y + 1 = 2(x - 3)$ for the line passing through the points $(-1, 3)$ and $(2, 9)$. Explain and correct her error.

Carlota replaced x_1 in the point-slope form with y_1 and vice versa. A correct equation using the point $(-1, 3)$ is $y - 3 = 2(x + 1)$. A correct equation using the point $(2, 9)$ is $y - 9 = 2(x - 2)$.

23. Communicate Mathematical Ideas Explain why it is possible for a line to have no equation in point-slope form or to have infinitely many, but it is not possible that there is only one.

If the slope is undefined, there is no equation of the line in point-slope form. Otherwise, there are at least two equations in point-slope form for every pair of points on the line.

24. Persevere in Problem Solving If you know that $A \neq 0$ and $B \neq 0$, how can you write an equation in point-slope form of the equation $Ax + By = C$?

Possible answer: Find the y-intercept.

$$Ax + By = C$$
$$y = \frac{-Ax + C}{B}$$
When $x = 0$, $y = \frac{C}{B}$.

Find the x-intercept.

$$Ax + By = C$$
$$x = \frac{-By + C}{A}$$
When $y = 0$, $x = \frac{C}{A}$.

Then the point $\left(\frac{C}{A}, 0\right)$ is on the line, and an equation in point-slope form

is $y - 0 = \frac{-A}{B}\left(x - \frac{C}{A}\right)$.

Lesson Performance Task

Alberto is snow boarding down a mountain with a constant slope. The slope he is on has an overall length of 1560 feet. The top of the slope has a height of 4600 feet, and the slope has a vertical drop of 600 feet. It takes him 24 seconds to reach the bottom of the slope.

   a. If we assume that Alberto's speed down the slope is constant, what is his height above the bottom of the slope at 10 seconds into the run?

   b. Alberto says that he must have been going 50 miles per hour down the slope. Do you agree? Why or why not?

a. $m = \dfrac{4600 - 4000}{0 - 24} = \dfrac{600}{-24} = -25$

$$(h - h_1) = -25(t - t_1)$$
$$h - 4600 = -25(t - 0)$$
$$h = -25t + 4600$$

Solve for $t = 10$: $h = -25(10) + 4600 = 4350$

So at 10 seconds, Alberto's height is at 4350 feet, which is 350 feet above the bottom of the slope.

b. Alberto's average speed $= \dfrac{1560 \text{ ft}}{24 \text{ sec}} = 65$ ft/sec, which is approximately 44 miles per hour.

© Houghton Mifflin Harcourt Publishing Company

EXTENSION ACTIVITY

Have students research the length (cm) of a snowboard required for a given rider's weight in pounds for several different weights, and then determine if the graph of (weight, length) appears to be linear.

Students should find that the graph of the (weight, length) points is roughly linear, although the points do not all lie on the same line.

CONNECT CONTEXT [EL]

Some students may be confused by what appear to be two different uses of the term *slope*: the mountain has a constant *slope* and Alberto snowboards down the *slope*. Explain that a slope on a graph is a measure of *how steep* the line or hill is. A slope may also mean *a stretch of ground that forms an incline*, as on a hill.

INTEGRATE MATHEMATICAL PRACTICES
Focus on Modeling

MP.4 It may help students to make a sketch of the situation in the Lesson Performance Task. Students should find that the bottom of the slope is not on the horizontal axis; it is along $h = 4000$.

Scoring Rubric

2 points: Student correctly solves the problem and explains his/her reasoning.

1 point: Student shows good understanding of the problem but does not fully solve or explain his/her reasoning.

0 points: Student does not demonstrate understanding of the problem.

Standard Form

Common Core Math Standards

The student is expected to:

 A-CED.A.2

Create equations in two... variables to represent relationships between quantities... Also A-REI.D.10

Mathematical Practices

 MP.2 Reasoning

Language Objective

Work in pairs to complete a table to decide which form of a linear equation to use.

ENGAGE

Essential Question: How can you write a linear equation in standard form given properties of the line including its slope, and points on the line?

You can use the slope and the coordinates of a point to write an equation in slope-intercept form. If two points are given, you can calculate the slope and use either of the given points to write the equation in slope-intercept form. Then you can rewrite it in standard form.

PREVIEW: LESSON PERFORMANCE TASK

View the Engage section online. Discuss how refueling an airplane is not like refueling a car. On large aircraft, the fuel truck must be grounded to the aircraft; and, in order to balance the plane, the wings must be filled first, then the center tank. Then preview the Lesson Performance Task.

6.3 Standard Form

Essential Question: How can you write a linear equation in standard form given properties of the line including its slope and points on the line?

Resource Locker

⊘ Explore   Comparing Forms of Linear Equations

You have seen that the standard form of a linear equation is $Ax + By = C$ where A and B are not both zero. For instance, the equation $2x + 3y = -12$ is in standard form. You can write equivalent equations in slope-intercept form and point-slope form. For instance, the equation in slope-intercept form and an equation in point-slope are shown.

$$\text{Standard form: } 2x + 3y = -12$$

$$\text{Slope-intercept form: } y = -\frac{2}{3}x - 4$$

$$\text{Point-slope from: } y + 8 = -\frac{2}{3}(x - 6)$$

Use the three forms of the equation shown to complete each step.

(A) Circle true or false.

You can read the slope from the equation.

Standard form	True	(False)
Slope-intercept form	(True)	False
Point-slope form	(True)	False

(B) The slope is ___$-\frac{2}{3}$___

(C) Circle true or false.

You can read the y-intercept from the equation.

Standard form	True	(False)
Slope-intercept form	(True)	False
Point-slope form	True	(False)

(D) Identify the y-intercept ___-4___

Reflect

1. Explain how you can find both intercepts using the standard form.
   To find the x-intercept, divide C by A. To find the y-intercept, divide C by B.

2. How can you find a point on the line using the slope-intercept form?
   Because you know that the y-intercept is b, you know the point $(0, b)$ is on the line.

HARDCOVER PAGES 213–220

Turn to these pages to find this lesson in the hardcover student edition.

Given the slope of a line and a point on the line, you can write an equation of the line in standard form.

Example 1 Write an equation in standard form for each line.

 A Slope is 2 and $(-2, 2)$ is on the line.

Method 1: Use the point-slope form. Substitute the given slope and the coordinates of the given point.

$y - 2 = 2(x - (-2))$ Point-slope form   Rewrite in standard form.

$y - 2 = 2x + 4$ Simplify.

$$y - 2 = 2x + 4$$

$$-2x + y = 6$$

Method 2: Use the slope intercept form. Substitute the given slope and the coordinates of the given point. Solve for b.

$y = mx + b$ Slope-intercept form   The slope-intercept form is $y = 2x + 6$.

$2 = 2(-2) + b$ Substitute for x.   Rewrite in standard form as in Method 1: $-2x + y = 6$

$6 = b$ Simplify.

B Slope is 5, and $(-2, 4)$ is on the line.

Method 1: Use the point-slope form. Substitute the given slope and the coordinates of the given point.

$y - \boxed{4} = \boxed{5}\left(x - \left(\boxed{-2}\right)\right)$ Point-slope form

$y - \boxed{4} = \boxed{5}x + \boxed{10}$ Simplify.

Rewrite in standard form.

$y - \boxed{4} = \boxed{5}x + \boxed{10}$

$\boxed{-5}x + y = \boxed{14}$

Method 2: Use the slope-intercept form and substitute the slope and point into the equation to solve for b.

$\boxed{4} = \boxed{5} \cdot \boxed{-2} + b$ This gives the equation $y = \boxed{5}x + \boxed{14}$.

$\boxed{4} = \boxed{-10} + b$ Rewrite in standard form as in Method 1:

$\boxed{14} = b$ $\boxed{-5}x + y = \boxed{14}$

PROFESSIONAL DEVELOPMENT

Learning Progressions

Students have worked with both the slope-intercept and point-slope form of a linear equation. In this lesson, students add to those forms by learning:

- The standard form of a linear equation is $Ax + By = C$ where A, B, and C are real numbers and A and B are not both 0.

- The graph of a linear function is a non-vertical line.

- The equation of a horizontal line is of the form $y = k$. The equation of a vertical line is of the form $x = k$.

EXPLORE

Comparing Forms of Linear Equations

INTEGRATE TECHNOLOGY

Students have the option of completing the activity either in the book or online.

CONNECT VOCABULARY **EL**

Remind students that a *linear function* is a function whose graph forms a line. A *linear equation* is any equation that can be written in the standard form $Ax + By = C$.

EXPLAIN 1

Creating Linear Equations in Standard Form Given Slope and a Point

QUESTIONING STRATEGIES

? In the standard form of a linear equation in two variables, $Ax + By = C$, what are the restrictions on the values of A, B, and C? **A, B, and C represent real numbers where either A and B, but not both, may be zero.**

? How do you find the standard form equation of a line from two points? **Find the slope, substitute the slope and a point into point-slope form, rewrite and simplify the equation.**

EXPLAIN 2

Creating Linear Equations in Standard Form Given Two Points

INTEGRATE MATHEMATICAL PRACTICES
Focus on Critical Thinking

MP.3 Write five ordered pairs in which the change between consecutive x-values is constant. Have half the class select a y-value for each x-value so that the change in y-values is also constant. Have the other half choose y-values so that the change is not constant. Plot some sets of ordered pairs of both types on the board.

Show that the points lie on a straight line only when the change in corresponding y-values is also constant.

QUESTIONING STRATEGIES

? In the standard form of a linear equation, why is it that A and B cannot both be zero? Explain. If A and B were both zero, then for any values of x and y, $Ax + By = 0$, so $C = 0$, which is not an equation of a line.

AVOID COMMON ERRORS

Students may be tempted to write the standard form of a linear equation using all lowercase letters. Remind them that b represents the intercept in the slope-intercept form of a linear equation. Capitalizing the coefficients in standard form avoids confusion, as b and B do not represent the same value.

Reflect

3. **Discussion** Which method do you prefer? Why?
   Possible answers: In general, neither form is considerably more complicated than the other. However, individual preferences may vary. They may depend on particular equations because of the arithmetic involved, for example, or on comfort level with different forms of linear equations.

Your Turn

Write an equation in standard form for each line.

4. Slope is -2, and $(-7, -10)$ is on the line.
$$y - (-10) = -2(x - (-7))$$
$$2x + y = -24$$

5. Slope is 4, and $(-3, 0)$ is on the line.
$$y - 0 = 4(x + 3)$$
$$-4x + y = 12$$

⚙ Explain 2 Creating Linear Equations in Standard Form Given Two Points

You can use two points on a line to create an equation of the line in standard form.

Example 2 Write an equation in standard form for each line.

(A) $(-2, -1)$ and $(0, 4)$ are on the line.

Find the slope using the given points.
$$m = \frac{y_2 - y_1}{x_2 - x_1} = \frac{4 - (-1)}{0 - (-2)} = \frac{5}{2}$$

Substitute the slope and the coordinates of either of the given points in the point-slope form.
$$y - y_1 = m(x - x_1)$$
$$y - 4 = \frac{5}{2}(x - 0)$$
$$y - 4 = \frac{5}{2}x$$

Rewrite in standard form.
$$2y - 8 = 5x$$
$$5x - 2y = -8$$

(B) $(5, 2)$ and $(3, -6)$ are on the line.

Find the slope.
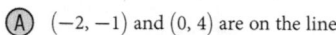
$$m = \frac{y_2 - y_1}{x_2 - x_1} = \frac{\boxed{-6} - \boxed{2}}{\boxed{3} - \boxed{5}} = \frac{\boxed{-8}}{\boxed{-2}} = \boxed{4}$$

Substitute the slope and the coordinates of either of the given points in the point-slope form.
$$y - y_1 = m(x - x_1)$$
$$y - \boxed{2} = \boxed{4}\left(x - \boxed{5}\right)$$
$$y - \boxed{2} = \boxed{4}\,x - \boxed{20}$$

Or:
$$y - \boxed{(-6)} = \boxed{4}\left(x - \boxed{3}\right)$$
$$y + \boxed{6} = \boxed{4}\,x - \boxed{12}$$

Rewrite in standard form.
$$4x - y = 18$$

Reflect

6. Why does it not matter which of the two given points you use in the point-slope form?
   The two equations you get using the two different points are equivalent.

COLLABORATIVE LEARNING

Peer-to-Peer Activity

Have students work with a partner. Each student should draw a graph with a straight line. Partners then exchange the graphs and write an equation for the line in standard form.

Your Turn

Write an equation in standard form for each line.

7. $(4, -7)$ and $(2, -3)$ are on the line.

$$m = \frac{-3 - (-7)}{2 - 4} = \frac{4}{-2} = -2$$

$$y - (-3) = -2(x - 2)$$

$$2x + y = 1$$

8. $(1, 5)$ and $(-10, -6)$ are on the line.

$$m = \frac{-6 - 5}{-10 - 1} = \frac{-11}{-11} = 1$$

$$y - 5 = 1(x - 1)$$

$$x - y = -4$$

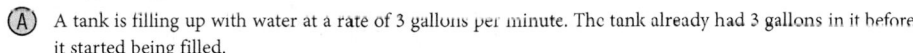 **Explain 3** **Creating Linear Models in Standard Form**

Equations in standard form can be used to model real-world linear situations.

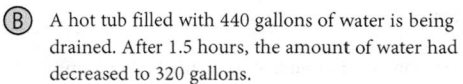 **Example 3** Write an equation in standard form to model the linear situation.

(A) A tank is filling up with water at a rate of 3 gallons per minute. The tank already had 3 gallons in it before it started being filled.

Let x represent the time in minutes since the filling began and y represent the amount of water in gallons. Since 3 gallons were in the tank before filling started, the point $(0, 3)$ is on the line.

The rate is 3 gallons per minute, so $m = 3$.

Substitute the slope and the coordinates of the point in the point-slope form and rewrite in standard form.

$$y - 3 = 3(x - 0)$$

$$y - 3 = 3x$$

$$3x - y = -3$$

(B) A hot tub filled with 440 gallons of water is being drained. After 1.5 hours, the amount of water had decreased to 320 gallons.

The initial amount of water in the hot tub was 440 gallons, so $(0, 440)$ is on the line.

After 1.5 hours, the amount of water had decreased to 320 gallons, so $(1.5, 320)$ is on the line.

Use the given information to find the slope.

$$m = \frac{\boxed{320} - \boxed{440}}{\boxed{1.5} - \boxed{0}} = \frac{\boxed{-120}}{\boxed{1.5}} = \boxed{-80}$$

Substitute the slope and the coordinates of one of the points in the point-slope form, and rewrite in standard form.

$$y - \boxed{440} = \boxed{-80}\left(x - \boxed{0}\right)$$

$$y - \boxed{440} = \boxed{-80}x$$

$$\boxed{80x + y = 440}$$

EXPLAIN 3

Creating Linear Models in Standard Form

QUESTIONING STRATEGIES

? How are the equations $-x + 4y = -20$ and $x - 4y = 20$ related? Explain. They are equivalent. Each equation is in the form $Ax + By = C$, and the second equation can be obtained from the first by multiplying both sides by -1.

INTEGRATE MATHEMATICAL PRACTICES

Focus on Patterns

MP.8 Students should be aware that there is more than one way (in fact, infinitely many ways) to write a linear equation in standard form. This is because for any linear equation $Ax + By = C$, you can multiply or divide both sides of the equation by any nonzero constant and the resulting equation will be equivalent.

AVOID COMMON ERRORS

Students might think that any equation with x and y on the left side is in standard form. Remind them of the other conditions: that x and y are not multiplied together; and that x and y are not in denominators, exponents, or radical signs.

DIFFERENTIATE INSTRUCTION

Critical Thinking

Challenge students to find more than one way to write a linear equation in standard form. There are infinitely many ways to represent a linear equation because for any linear equation $Ax + By = C$, you can multiply or divide both sides of the equation by any nonzero constant and the resulting equation will be equivalent.

ELABORATE

INTEGRATE MATHEMATICAL PRACTICES
Focus on Math Connections

MP.1 In higher math applications, standard form may require that the greatest common factor of the coefficients is 1, and that the leading coefficient be positive. This ensures that everyone uses the same representation of the standard form for a given line.

QUESTIONING STRATEGIES

? When is standard form useful? It is useful for graphing a line or for finding the x- and y-intercepts. It is also useful for vertical lines, which are not functions.

SUMMARIZE THE LESSON

? How can you write a linear equation in standard form given properties of the line, such as slope or points? You can use the slope and the coordinates of a point to write an equation in slope-intercept form. If two points are given, you can calculate the slope and use either of the given points to write the equation in slope-intercept form.

---

9. Your school sells adult and student tickets to a school play. Adult tickets cost \$15 and student tickets cost \$4. The total value of all the tickets sold is \$7000. How could you write an equation in standard form to describe the linear situation?

Let x represent the number of adult tickets and y represent the number of student tickets.

An equation is $15x + 4y = 7000$.

Your Turn

Write an equation in standard form to model the linear situation.

10. A tank is being filled with gasoline at a rate of 4.5 gallons per minute. The gas tank contained 1.5 gallons of gasoline before filling started.

$y - 1.5 = 4.5(x - 0)$

$4.5x - y = -1.5$

11. A pool that is being drained contained 18,000 gallons of water. After 2 hours, 12,500 gallons of water remain.

$m = \dfrac{18{,}000 - 12{,}500}{0 - 2} = \dfrac{5500}{-2} = -2750$

$y - 18{,}000 = -2750(x - 0)$

$2750x + y = 18{,}000$

Elaborate

12. Describe a method other than the one given in the example for writing an equation in standard form given two points on a line.
Find the slope. Substitute the slope and the coordinates of either one of the points in the slope-intercept form and solve for b. Then substitute b into the equation in slope-intercept form and rewrite it in standard form.

13. Why might you choose the standard form of an equation over another form?
Possible answer: To reveal the x-and y-intercepts.

14. Essential Question Check-In When writing a linear equation in standard form, what other forms might you need to use?
Slope-intercept form and point-slope form

⚙ Evaluate: Homework and Practice

- Online Homework
- Hints and Help
- Extra Practice

Identify the form of each equation.

1. **a.** $5x + 4y = 8$ **standard form**   **b.** $y - 3 = 8(x - 2)$ **point-slope form**

c. $y = 3x + 6$ **slope-intercept form** **d.** $2x - 3y = -7$ **standard form**

Rewrite each equation in standard form.

2. $y = 6x - 4$
$-6x + y = -4$

3. $y - 2 = -(x + 7)$
$x + y = -5$

LANGUAGE SUPPORT **EL**

Connect Vocabulary

Have students work in pairs to complete this table.

Given Information	Equation Form to use
Slope and y-intercept	slope-intercept
Two points on the line	point-slope
A horizontal or vertical line and a point on the line	standard
Slope and a point (x, y) on the line, $x \neq 0$	point-slope
Slope and a point (x, y) on the line, $x = 0$	slope-intercept

4. $y = \frac{4}{3}x - \frac{2}{3}$

$3y = 4x - 2$

$-4x + 3y = -2$

5. $y - 4 = \frac{7}{3}(x - 3)$

$3y - 12 = 7x - 21$

$7x - 3y = 9$

Use the information given to write an equation in standard form.

6. Slope is 3, and (1, 4) is on the line.

$y - 4 = 3(x - 1)$

$-3x + y = 1$

7. Slope is −2, and (4, 3) is on the line.

$y - 3 = -2(x - 4)$

$2x + y = 11$

8. Slope is −3, and (0, −4) is on the line.

$y - (-4) = -3(x - 0)$

$3x + y = -4$

9. Slope is 0, and (0, 5) is on the line.

$y - 5 = 0(x - 0)$

$y = 5$

10. Slope is $\frac{4}{7}$, and (1, 3) is on the line.

$y - 3 = \frac{4}{7}(x - 1)$

$-4x + 7y = -17$

11. Slope $= -\frac{3}{2}$, and (2, 3) is on the line.

$y - 3 = -\frac{3}{2}(x - 2)$

$3x + 2y = 12$

12. (−1, 1) and (0, 4) are on the line.

$m = \frac{4 - 1}{0 - (-1)} = 3$

$y - 1 = 3(x + 1)$

$y = 3x + 4$

$3x - y = -4$

13. (6, 11) and (5, 9) are on the line.

$m = \frac{9 - 11}{5 - 6} = \frac{-2}{-1} = 2$

$y - 9 = 2(x - 5)$

$2x - y = 1$

14. (2, −5) and (−1, 1) are on the line.

$m = \frac{-5 - 1}{2 - (-1)} = \frac{-6}{3} = -2$

$y - (-5) = -2(x - 2)$

$2x + y = -1$

15. (25, 34) and (35, 50) are on the line.

$m = \frac{34 - 50}{25 - 35} = \frac{-16}{-10} = \frac{8}{5}$

$y - 34 = \frac{8}{5}(x - 25)$

$-8x + 5y = -30$

16. Use the information on the graph to write an equation in standard form.

(0, −2) and (2, 4) are on the line.

$m = \frac{4 - (-2)}{2 - 0} = \frac{6}{2} = 3$

$y - (-2) = 3(x - 0)$

$3x - y = 2$

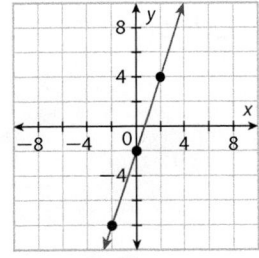

© Houghton Mifflin Harcourt Publishing Company

Exercise	Depth of Knowledge (D.O.K.)	COMMON CORE Mathematical Practices	
1	**1** Recall of Information	**MP.6** Precision	
2–16	**2** Skills/Concepts	**MP.6** Precision	
17–18	**2** Skills/Concepts	**MP.4** Modeling	
19	**2** Skills/Concepts	**MP.2** Reasoning	
20	**2** Skills/Concepts	**MP.6** Precision	
21	**3** Strategic Thinking	H.O.T.	**MP.2** Reasoning
22	**2** Skills/Concepts	H.O.T.	**MP.2** Reasoning

EVALUATE

ASSIGNMENT GUIDE

Concepts and Skills	Practice
Explore Comparing Forms of Linear Equations	Exercises 1–5
Example 1 Creating Linear Equations in Standard Form Given Slope and a Point	Exercises 6–11
Example 2 Creating Linear Equations in Standard Form Given Two Points	Exercises 12–16, 21
Example 3 Creating Linear Models in Standard Form	Exercises 17–20, 22

INTEGRATE MATHEMATICAL PRACTICES

Focus on Technology

 MP.5 Encourage students to use their graphing calculators to check their answers.

AVOID COMMON ERRORS

Students may incorrectly solve for slope when graphing a line from the standard form. Model the process for students.

For example: Graph: $2x + 5y = 10$. First, solve for y by using the formula $y = \frac{-A}{B}x + \frac{C}{B}$. In this form, $m = \frac{-A}{B}$ and the y-intercept $b = \frac{C}{B}$

Plot the y-intercept at $(0, 2)$, then use the slope $\frac{-2}{5}$ to locate a second point. Connect the two points and complete the line.

Standard Form   **266**

For the equations of vertical lines $(x = a)$ and horizontal lines $(y = b)$, show students that the constants a and b are not the same as the A and B in the equation for the standard form of a line. Constants a and b correspond to C in the standard form of a line.

INTEGRATE TECHNOLOGY

Students can use their graphing calculators to graph equations in standard form if A is nonzero. For example, to graph $2x + 5y = 6$, students can solve for y without simplifying to get the equation in $y =$ form:

$$2x + 5y = 6$$

$$5y = 6 - 2x$$

$$y = \frac{6 - 2x}{5}$$

Students can enter $\mathbf{Y} = (6 - 2x)/5$ to graph the equation.

AVOID COMMON ERRORS

Some students may not understand that A, B, and C in the standard form are constants that depend on the equation. Explain that $Ax + By = C$ matches an infinite number of equations where A, B, and C can be any number. A, B, and C are just placeholders for values in an equation, to allow you to recognize the form rather than any one particular equation. Examples of equations in standard form:
$2x + 3y = 4$; $100x - 7y = -45$

JOURNAL

Have students write a journal entry in which they make up a real-world problem that can be expressed in standard form, and then explain how they would graph the line and solve the problem.

Write an equation in standard form to model the linear situation.

17. A bathtub that holds 32 gallons of water contains 12 gallons of water. You begin filling it, and after 5 minutes, the tub is full.

$$m = \frac{32 - 12}{5 - 0} = \frac{20}{5} = 4$$

$$y - 32 = 4(x - 5)$$

$$y - 32 = 4x - 20$$

$$4x - y = -12$$

18. A barrel of oil was filled at a constant rate of 7.5 gal/min. The barrel had 10 gallons before filling began.

$$y - 10 = 7.5(x - 0)$$

$$y - 10 = 7.5x$$

$$-7.5x + y = 10$$

$$7.5x - y = -10$$

19. **Represent Real-World Situations**

A restaurant needs to plan seating for a party of 150 people. Large tables seat 10 people and small tables seat 6. Let x represent the number of large tables and y represent the number of small tables. An expression like the total number of people you can seat using A large tables and B small tables is called a *linear combination*. For instance, 150 people could be seated using 12 large tables and 5 small tables. Use that expression to write an equation in standard form that models all the different combinations of tables the restaurant could use. Then identify at least one possible combination of tables other than $(12, 5)$.

An equation is $10x + 6y = 150$. Other possible combinations are $(15, 0)$, $(9, 10)$, $(6, 15)$, $(3, 20)$, and $(0, 25)$.

20. Match each equation with an equivalent equation in standard form.

a. $y = \frac{2}{3}x + 3$ _**d**_ $7x + 6y = 6$

b. $6 - y = -5x + 8$ _**b**_ $5x - y = 2$

c. $y - 3 = 4(x - 3)$ _**a**_ $2x - 3y = -9$

d. $-\frac{7}{6}x + 1 = y$ _**c**_ $4x - y = 9$

21. Explain the Error Cody was given two points $\left(\frac{1}{2}, 4\right)$ and $\left(\frac{2}{3}, 1\right)$, on a line and asked to create a linear equation in standard form. Cody's work is shown. Identify any errors and correct them.

$m = \frac{1-4}{\frac{2}{3}-\frac{1}{2}} = -\frac{3}{\frac{1}{6}} = -\frac{1}{2}$ **Cody made an error while finding the slope:** $-\frac{3}{\frac{1}{6}} = -3(6) = -18.$

$y - 1 = -\frac{1}{2}\left(x - \frac{2}{3}\right)$ **Cody also should have multiplied both sides of the equation by**

$y - 1 = -\frac{1}{2}x + \frac{1}{3}$ **6, not 3, and should have multiplied all the terms.**

The equation should be $18x + y = 13.$

$2y - 2 = -x + \frac{2}{3}$

$x + 2y = \frac{8}{3}$

22. Communicate Mathematical Ideas In the equation $Ax + By = C$, A and B cannot both be zero. What if only A is zero? What if only B is zero? Explain.

If $A = 0$ **and** $B \neq 0$**, the equation represents a horizontal line through** $y = \frac{C}{B}$**.**

If $A \neq 0$ **and** $B = 0$**, the equation represents a vertical line through** $x = \frac{C}{A}$**.**

Lesson Performance Task

An airplane takes off with a full tank of 40,000 gallons of fuel and flies at an average speed of 550 miles per hour. After 8 hours in flight, there are 14,000 gallons of fuel left. It will take another 3.5 hours for the plane to reach its destination. How much fuel will be left in the tank when the plane lands? What is the total distance of the flight?

(0, 40,000), (8, 14,000)

$\frac{40,000 - 14,000}{0 - 8} = \frac{26,000}{-8} = -3250$ **gallons per hour**

$y - 40,000 = -3250(x - 0)$

$y - 40,000 = -3250x$

$3250x + y = 40,000$

$3250x + y = 40,000$

$3250(11.5) + y = 40,000$

$37,375 + y = 40,000$

$y = 2625$

So the plane lands with 2625 gallons of fuel in the tank.

The total distance flown is 11.5 hours $\times$ **550 miles per hour, or 6325 miles.**

EXTENSION ACTIVITY

Have students research the average cost of jet fuel per gallon for the years since 2000. Then have students graph *(Year – 2000, Cost)* on a coordinate grid to determine whether the cost represents a linear pattern.

Students may find that for the years 2003 through 2007 the pattern appears to be linear.

AVOID COMMON ERRORS

Some students may reverse the independent and dependent variables in the Lesson Performance Task, finding the two points given as $(40,000, 0)$ and $(14,000, 8)$. Remind students that the number of gallons of fuel left, y, depends on the number of hours traveled, x, so the two given points are $(0, 40,000)$ and $(8, 14,000)$.

INTEGRATE MATHEMATICAL PRACTICES

Focus on Communication

MP.3 Have a student who used the point $(0, 40,000)$ write the steps used on the board to find the standard form. Next to these steps, have a student who used the point $(8, 14,000)$ write the steps used on the board to find the standard form. As a class discuss why both methods work.

Scoring Rubric

2 points: Student correctly solves the problem and explains his/her reasoning.

1 point: Student shows good understanding of the problem but does not fully solve or explain his/her reasoning.

0 points: Student does not demonstrate understanding of the problem.

Transforming Linear Functions

Common Core Math Standards

The student is expected to:

 F-BF.B.3

Identify the effect on the graph of replacing $f(x)$ by $f(x) + k$, $kf(x)$,... and $f(x + k)$ for specific values of k (both positive and negative)... Also A. CED.A.2, F-LE.B.5

Mathematical Practices

 MP.5 Using Tools

Language Objective

Be able to explain transformations of linear functions using English words and mathematical language.

ENGAGE

Essential Question: What are the ways in which you can transform the graph of a linear function?

You can transform the graph of a linear function by replacing $f(x)$ in the function with $kf(x)$, $f(x + k)$, $f(x) + k$ and $f(kx)$ for specific values of k. The resulting graph may be a translation, reflection, stretch, or shrink of the original graph.

PREVIEW: LESSON PERFORMANCE TASK

View the Engage section online. Discuss the photo and how a sketch of the graph that represents the depreciation of a car's value over time would look. Then preview the Lesson Performance Task.

6.4 Transforming Linear Functions

Essential Question: What are the ways in which you can transform the graph of a linear function?

Resource Locker

⊘ Explore 1 Building New Linear Functions by Translating

Investigate what happens to the graph of $f(x) = x + b$ when you change the value of b.

Ⓐ Use a graphing calculator. Start with the standard viewing window, which you can obtain by pressing Zoom and selecting ZStandard. Because the distances between consecutive tick marks on the x-axis and on the y-axis are not equal, you can make them equal by pressing Zoom again and selecting ZSquare.

What interval on each axis does the viewing window now show? (Press Window to find out.)

Approximately $-15.16 \leq x \leq 15.16$; $-10 \leq y \leq 10$

Ⓑ Graph the function $f(x) = x$ by pressing Y= and entering the function's rule next to $Y_1 =$. As shown, the graph of the function is a line that makes a 45° angle with each axis.

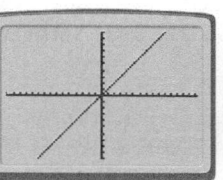

What are the slope and y-intercept of the graph of $f(x) = x$?

Slope: 1; y-intercept: 0

Ⓒ Graph other functions of the form $f(x) = x + b$ by entering their rules next to $Y_2 =$, $Y_3 =$, and so on. Be sure to choose both positive and negative values of b. For instance, graph $f(x) = x + 2$ and $f(x) = x - 3$.

What do the graphs have in common? How are they different?

They all have the same slope, but they have different y-intercepts.

Reflect

1. **Discussion** A *vertical translation* moves all points on a figure the same distance either up or down. Use the idea of a vertical translation to describe what happens to the graph of $f(x) = x + b$ when you increase the value of b and decrease the value of b.
   Increasing the value of b translates the graph up; decreasing the value of b translates the graph down.

2. In this Explore, we replaced the linear function $f(x)$ by $f(x) + k$. Show how replacing $f(x)$ by $f(x + k)$ has exactly the same effect.
   $f(x + k) = x + k = f(x) + k$

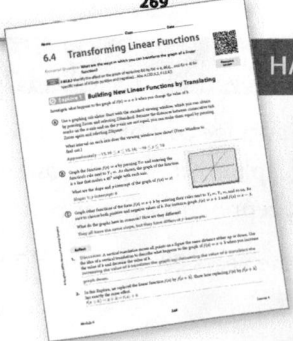

HARDCOVER PAGES 221–228

Turn to these pages to find this lesson in the hardcover student edition.

Explore 2   Building New Linear Functions by Stretching, Shrinking, or Reflecting

Investigate what happens to the graph of $f(x) = mx$ when you change the value of m.

(A) Use a graphing calculator. Press Y= and clear out all but the function $f(x) = x$ from the previous Explore Activity. Then graph other functions of the form $f(x) = mx$ by entering their rules next to $Y_2 =$, $Y_3 =$, and so on. Use only values of m that are greater than 1. For example, graph $f(x) = 2x$ and $f(x) = 6x$.

What do the graphs have in common? How are they different?

As the value of m increases from 1, does the graph become steeper or less steep?

They all have the same y-intercept, but they have different slopes.

The graphs get steeper as m increases.

(B) Again, press Y= and clear out all but the function $f(x) = x$. Then graph other functions of the form $f(x) = mx$ by entering their rules next to $Y_2 =$, $Y_3 =$, and so on. This time use only values of m that are less than 1 but greater than 0. For instance, graph $f(x) = 0.5x$ and $f(x) = 0.2x$.

As the value of m decreases from 1 to 0, does the graph become steeper or less steep?

The graphs get less steep as m decreases.

(C) Again, press Y= and clear out all but the function $f(x) = x$. Then graph the function $f(x) = -x$ by entering its rule next to $Y_2 =$.

What are the slope and y-intercept of the graph of $f(x) = -x$?

How are the graphs of $f(x) = x$ and $f(x) = -x$ geometrically related?

Slope: -1; y-intercept: 0

They are reflections of each other across the x-axis. They are also reflections of each other

across the y-axis.

(D) Again, press Y= and clear out all the functions. Graph $f(x) = -x$ by entering its rule next to $Y_1 =$. Then graph other functions of the form $f(x) = mx$ where $m < 0$ by entering their rules next to $Y_2 =$, $Y_3 =$, and so on. Be sure to choose values of m that are less than -1 as well as values of m between -1 and 0.

Describe what happens to the graph of $f(x) = mx$ as the value of m decreases from -1, and as it increases from -1 to 0.

As the value of m decreases from -1, the graph becomes steeper; as the value of m

increases from -1 to 0, the graph becomes less steep.

© Houghton Mifflin Harcourt Publishing Company

PROFESSIONAL DEVELOPMENT

Math Background

A transformation changes a graph's size, shape, position, or orientation. Although this lesson deals exclusively with transformations of linear functions, most of the results can be extended to polynomial functions in general and to certain other functions, such as absolute value functions. However, linear functions have some unique properties. For instance, a vertical stretch of a linear function is also a horizontal compression, and a vertical compression is also a horizontal stretch.

EXPLORE 1

Building New Linear Functions by Translating

INTEGRATE TECHNOLOGY

Mention to students that a typical graphing calculator screen is 95 pixels wide by 63 pixels high, so using the same scale on each axis stretches the graph horizontally by the quotient of these numbers. Earlier calculators used 96 and 64 pixels, but the lack of a center pixel meant that that the axes could not be perfectly symmetric.

CONNECT VOCABULARY **EL**

In this lesson, the words *transform* and *translate* both start with the prefix *trans-*, which means *across* or *beyond*.

INTEGRATE MATHEMATICAL PRACTICES
Focus on Patterns

MP.8 Point out to students that changing the value of b in $f(x) = mx + b$ causes a change in the y-intercept of the graph of that equation. It translates the graph up or down the y-axis to create parallel lines.

EXPLORE 2

Building New Linear Functions by Stretching, Shrinking, or Reflecting

QUESTIONING STRATEGIES

What happens if you use a value of 0 for m? The function becomes $f(x) = 0$, the x-axis, a horizontal line.

What happens if you use a number for m where $|m|$ is very large? The graph of the function is very close to a vertical line along the y-axis, although it intersects the y-axis at the origin only.

Transforming Linear Functions   **270**

EXPLORE 3

Understanding Function Families

CONNECT VOCABULARY EL

Remind students a *family of functions* is a set of functions whose graphs have basic characteristics in common. The most basic function of a family of functions is called the *parent function*. A *parameter* is one of the constants in a function or equation that determines which variation of the parent function is being considered.

QUESTIONING STRATEGIES

? What can be said about parallel graphs of linear functions? **They all have the same slope but different *y*-intercepts.**

? What happens to the graph of a parent function when it is transformed? **There is a change in either a figure's position or its size.**

? How do parent functions help you visualize the graph of a function? **Once you are familiar with the graphs of the parent functions, you can identify the graphs of many functions that are transformations of these functions.**

Reflect

3. Discussion When $m > 1$, will the graph of $f(x) = mx$ be a *vertical stretch* or a *vertical shrink* of the graph of $f(x) = x$? When $0 < m < 1$, will the graph of $f(x) = mx$ be a *vertical stretch* or a *vertical shrink* of the graph of $f(x) = x$? Explain your answers.

When $m > 1$, the graph of $f(x) = mx$ is a *vertical stretch* of the graph of $f(x) = x$. Imagine holding the top and bottom of the graph and stretching it straight up from the *x*-axis so that the grid squares become long and thin. This is a *vertical stretch*.

When $0 < m < 1$, the graph of $f(x) = mx$ is a *vertical shrink* of the graph of $f(x) = x$. Imagine pinching the graph toward the *x*-axis at both ends so that the grid squares are short and wide. This is a *vertical shrink*.

⊘ Explore 3 Understanding Function Families

Investigate what happens to the graph of $f(x) = mx$ when you change the value of m.

(A) A **family of functions** is a set of functions whose graphs have basic characteristics in common. What do all these variations on the original function $f(x) = x$ have in common?

They are all linear functions.

(B) The most basic function of a family of functions is called the **parent function**. What is the parent function of the family of functions explored in the first two Explore Activities?

$f(x) = x$

(C) A **parameter** is one of the constants in a function or equation that determines which variation of the parent function one is considering. For functions of the form $f(x) = mx + b$, what are the two parameters?

The slope, *m*, and the *y*-intercept, *b*.

© Houghton Mifflin Harcourt Publishing Company

COLLABORATIVE LEARNING

Peer-to-Peer Activity

Have students work in pairs. One student draws a line. The other student then draws another line, in which either the slope or *y*-intercept of the first student's line is changed. The first student then has to determine which parameter was changed and what the new value is. Have students take turns drawing the first line.

4. Discussion For the family of all linear functions, the parent function is $f(x) = x$, where the parameters are $m = 1$ and $b = 0$. Other examples of families of linear functions are shown below. The example on the left shows a family with the same parameter m and differing parameters b. The example on the right shows a family with the same parameter b and differing parameters m.

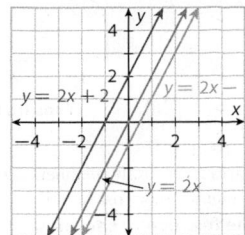 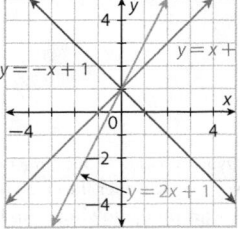

Describe the parameter that is left unchanged in the equations of the lines in the first graph.

All the lines have a slope of 2.

⊘ **Explain 1** **Interpreting Parameter Changes in Linear Models**

Many real-world scenarios can be modeled by linear functions. Changes in a particular scenario can be analyzed by making changes in the corresponding parameter of the linear function.

Example 1 A gym charges a one-time new member fee of $50 and then a monthly membership fee of $25. The total cost C of being a member of the gym is given by the function $C(t) = 25t + 50$, where t is the time (in months) since joining the gym. For each situation described below, sketch a graph using the given graph of $C(t) = 25t + 50$ as a reference.

Ⓐ The gym decreases its one-time fee for new members.

What change did you make to the graph of $C(t) = 25t + 50$ to represent a lower one-time fee?

I decreased the y-intercept but the slope remained the same.

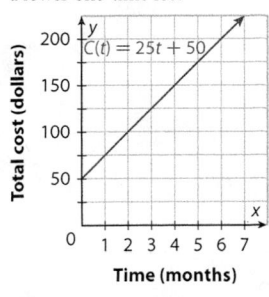

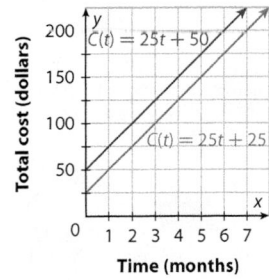

DIFFERENTIATE INSTRUCTION

Manipulatives

Draw a line on a transparency and place it on a grid to show the graph of $y = x$. Explain that $y = x$ is called the parent function because any linear function can be obtained by changing the slope from 1 and moving the y-intercept from 0. Changing m and b in the linear function $f(x) = mx + b$ generates the family of linear functions. Then demonstrate how this can be used to create any line on the coordinate plane by moving the transparency of the line on the grid.

EXPLAIN 1

Interpreting Parameter Changes in Linear Models

QUESTIONING STRATEGIES

? What is the effect on a graph of a line if the y-intercept decreases? **The line is transposed downward.**

? If a graph of a situation shows the height of an object as it slowly falls by the minute, how would the graph of its height change if it were to fall at a faster rate? **The line would have a steeper downward slope.**

AVOID COMMON ERRORS

Students may not pay sufficient attention to units in a problem. Remind students that a change in units is a transformation in itself.

INTEGRATE MATHEMATICAL PRACTICES
Focus on Communication

MP.3 Have students explain in their own words how changing the values of m and b change the graph of the related function. Have them first explain the changes in general, and then use their own choice of values of m and b to explain particular cases.

INTEGRATE TECHNOLOGY

Suggest to students that they not erase graphs in the **Y =** screen before entering another graph with a different b-value. This should help them understand why each graph is a vertical translation of the graph of $f(x) = x$. Using the **TRACE** function with the up and down arrow keys will jump from one function to another.

ELABORATE

Questioning Strategies

? How does a change in *m* affect the graph of $f(x) = 4$? The graph of $f(x) = 4$ is a horizontal line with a slope of 0 and a *y*-intercept of 4. Changing *m* changes the slope so that it is positive or negative, but the *y*-intercept remains 4.

SUMMARIZE THE LESSON

? How is each type of transformation related to the slope and *y*-intercept of the graph of a linear equation?

Translation: same slope, different *y*-intercept

Stretch or shrink: different slope with same sign

Reflection: opposite slope, same *y*-intercept

Ⓑ The gym increases its monthly membership fee.
What change did you make to the graph of $C(t) = 25t + 50$ to represent an increased monthly fee?
I increased the slope but the *y*-intercept remained the same.

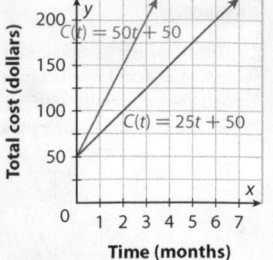

Reflect

5. Suppose the gym increases its one-time new member fee *and* decreases its monthly membership fee. Describe how you would alter the graph of $C(t) = 25t + 50$ to illustrate the new cost function.
Translate the graph up to show the increase in the one-time fee increase for new members,

and make the graph less steep to show the decrease in the monthly membership fee.

Your Turn

Determine what will happen to the graph of the original function when the described changes occur.

6. Once a year the gym offers a special in which the one-time fee for joining is waived for new members. What impact does this special offer have on the graph of the original function $C(t) = 25t + 50$?
The graph will have the same slope, but it has a *y*-intercept of 0.

7. Suppose the gym increases its one-time joining fee *and* decreases its monthly membership fee. Does this have any impact on the domain of the function? Does this have any impact on the range of the function? Explain your reasoning.
No; the domain still starts at 0 and continues for any number of months. Yes; the range has a new minimum value equal to the new joining fee.

LANGUAGE SUPPORT ᴇʟ

Connect Context

A *transformation* changes a graph's size, shape, position, or orientation. Give pairs of students linear functions to explain how transformations of functions from the parent function $f(x) = x$ affect the graphs. Students should use words such as *slide* and *flip,* as well as mathematical language.

8. How do changes to m in the equation $f(x) = mx$ affect the graph of the equation?
As $|m|$ increases, the graph gets steep; as $|m|$ decreases, the graph gets less steep.

9. How do changes to b in the equation $f(x) = x + b$ affect the graph of the equation?
As b increases or decreases, the y-intercept of the graph increases or decreases.

10. Which parameter causes the steepness of the graph of the line to change for the family of linear functions of the form $f(x) = mx + b$?
The parameter m.

11. **Essential Question Check-In** What are the different types of transformations?
There are translations, reflections, stretches, and shrinks.

⭐ **Evaluate: Homework and Practice**

In Exercises 1–4, the graph of $f(x) = x + 2$ is graphed.

• Online Homework
• Hints and Help
• Extra Practice

1. Graph two more functions in the same family for which the parameter being changed is the y-intercept, b.

2. Graph two more functions in the same family for which the parameter being changed is the slope, m, and is greater than 1.

Sample answers are given.

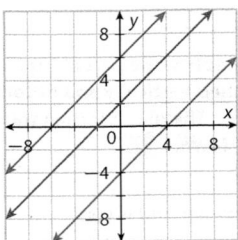

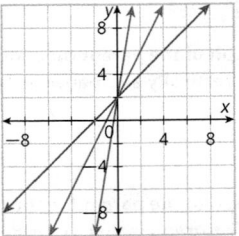

3. Graph two more functions in the same family for which the parameter being changed is the slope, m, and is between 0 and 1.

4. Graph two more functions in the same family for which the parameter being changed is the slope, m, and is less than 0.

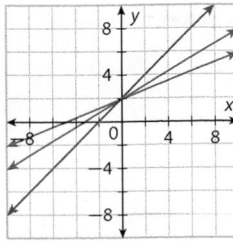

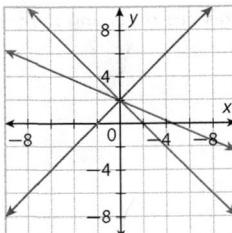

© Houghton Mifflin Harcourt Publishing Company

Exercise	Depth of Knowledge (D.O.K.)	COMMON CORE	Mathematical Practices
1-6	**2** Skills/Concepts		**MP.6** Precision
7–13	**2** Skills/Concepts		**MP.2** Reasoning
14–20	**2** Skills/Concepts		**MP.4** Modeling
21	**3** Strategic Thinking H.O.T.		**MP.2** Reasoning
22	**3** Strategic Thinking H.O.T.		**MP.3** Logic
23	**3** Strategic Thinking H.O.T.		**MP.6** Precision
24–25	**3** Strategic Thinking H.O.T.		**MP.3** Logic

EVALUATE

ASSIGNMENT GUIDE

Concepts and Skills	Practice
Explore 1 Building New Linear Functions by Translating	Exercise 1
Explore 2 Building New Linear Functions by Stretching, Shrinking, or Reflecting	Exercises 2–4
Explore 3 Understanding Function Families	Exercises 5–13, 23–25
Example 1 Interpreting Parameter Changes in Linear Models	Exercises 14–19, 20–22

INTEGRATE MATHEMATICAL PRACTICES

Focus on Technology

 MP.5 Encourage students to use their graphing calculators to check their answers.

PEER-TO-PEER ACTIVITY

Have students work with a partner. Both partners graph the function $f(x) = x - 2$. Then have one partner graph two more functions in the same family for which the parameter being changed is the y-intercept. Have the other partner graph two more functions in the same family for which the parameter being changed is the slope. Have partners compare the results of their graphs.

Transforming Linear Functions   **274**

5. The graph of the parent linear function $f(x) = x$ is shown in black on the coordinate grid. Write the function that represents this function with the indicated parameter changes.

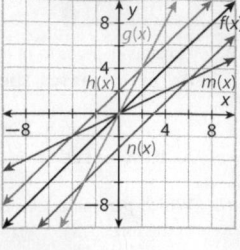

  a. m increased, b unchanged ____$g(x)$____

  b. m decreased, b unchanged ____$m(x)$____

  c. m unchanged, b increased ____$h(x)$____

  d. m unchanged, b decreased, ____$n(x)$____

6. For each linear function graphed on the coordinate grid, state the value of m and the value of b.

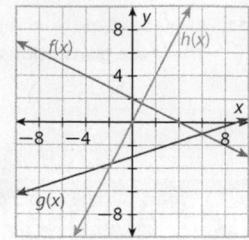

  a. $f(x)$: $m = \underline{-\dfrac{1}{2}}$, $b = \underline{2}$

  b. $g(x)$: $m = \underline{\dfrac{1}{3}}$, $b = \underline{-3}$

  c. $h(x)$: $m = \underline{2}$, $b = \underline{0}$

Describe the transformation(s) on the graph of the parent function $f(x) = x$ that results in the graph of $g(x)$.

7. $g(x) = -x + 9$

   The graph of the parent function is reflected across the y-axis and is translated 9 units up.

8. $g(x) = 3x$

   The graph of the parent function is stretched vertically and becomes steeper.

9. $g(x) = \dfrac{1}{4}x$

   The graph of the parent function is shrunk vertically and becomes less steep.

10. $g(x) = 7x - 8$

   The graph of the parent function is stretched vertically and becomes much steeper. The graph is then translated 8 units down.

11. $g(x) = -\dfrac{3}{4}x + 5$

   The graph of the parent function is reflected across the y-axis and is less steep. The graph is then translated 5 units up.

Use the parent function and the description of the transformation to write the new function.

12. Transform the graph of $f(x) = -x + 2$ in such a way that it has the same steepness in the opposite direction.

   This represents reflecting the graph across the y-axis. Therefore the new function is $g(x) = x + 2$.

© Houghton Mifflin Harcourt Publishing Company

13. Reflect the graph of $f(x) = x - 1$ across the y-axis, and then translate it 4 units down.

The function after reflecting the graph of $f(x) = x - 1$ will be $h(x) = -x - 1$.
Then translating the graph 4 units down will result in the graph of the function
$g(x) = -x - 5$.

Determine how changes in parameters will affect a graph. Write the new function.

14. For large parties, a restaurant charges a reservation fee of $25, plus $15 per person. The total charge for a party of x people is $f(x) = 15x + 25$. How will the graph of this function change if the reservation fee is raised to $50 and if the per-person charge is lowered to $12?

If the reservation fee is raised to $50, then the graph will be translated up so
the value of b is 50. If the per-person charge is lowered to $12, then the line
will become less steep. The new function is $g(x) = 12x + 50$.

15. The number of chaperones on a field trip must include 1 teacher for every 4 students, plus a total of 2 parents. The function describing the number of chaperones for a trip of x students is $f(x) = \frac{1}{4}x + 2$. How will the graph change if the number of parents is reduced to 0? If the number of teachers is raised to 1 for every 3 students?

The graph will be translated 2 units down if the
number of parents is reduced to 0. The graph
becomes steeper than the graph of the parent
function if the number of teachers is raised
to 1 for every 3 students. The new function is
$g(x) = \frac{1}{3}x$.

16. A satellite dish company charges a one-time installation fee of $75 and then a monthly usage charge of $40. The total cost C of using that satellite service is given by the function $C(t) = 40t + 75$, where t is the time (in months) since starting the service. For the situation given below, describe the new function using the graph of $C(t) = 40t + 75$ as a reference.

a. The satellite dish company reduces its one-time installation fee to $60. What change would you make to the graph of $C(t) = 40t + 75$ to obtain the new graph?
I would change the y-intercept to 60, but leave the slope the same.

b. The satellite dish company decreases its monthly fee to $30. What change would you make to the graph of $C(t) = 40t + 75$ to obtain the new graph?
I would change the slope from 40 to 30, but leave the y-intercept the same.

c. What is the new function with both changes?
The new function is $C(t) = 30t + 60$

QUESTIONING STRATEGIES

? The graph of $y = x$ is translated n units up and then n units right. What is the equation of the resulting line? $y = x$

? The graph of $y = f(x)$ is translated p units horizontally and then q units vertically. What is the equation of the resulting line? $y = f(x - p) + q$

AVOID COMMON ERRORS

Students might think that a positive slope will always be steeper than a negative slope because the positive value is greater. To show this is not true, have students graph $f(x) = -6x$ and $g(x) = 2x$. Explain that it is necessary to take the absolute value of each slope before comparing them.

INTEGRATE MATHEMATICAL PRACTICES

Focus on Math Connections

MP.1 It may be difficult for students to identify or distinguish between the effects of some transformations to a linear graph. For example, in many cases, a reflection of a line can also be viewed as a rotation or a translation. Do not let students assume the transformation is a rotation when it is instead a vertical stretch or vertical shrink. These transformations will become clearer when students study nonlinear functions.

17. A salesperson earns a base monthly salary of $2000 plus a 10% commission on sales. The salesperson's monthly income I (in dollars) is given by the function $I(s) = 0.1s + 2000$, where s is the sales (in dollars) that the salesperson makes. Sketch a graph to illustrate each situation using the graph of $I(s) = 0.1s + 2000$ as a reference.

A. The salesperson's base salary is increased.

Sample Answer:

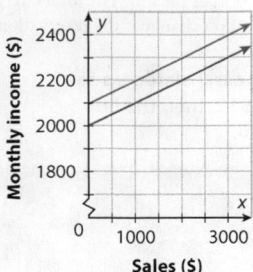

The salesperson's base monthly salary is increased.

B. The salesperson's commission rate is decreased.

Sample Answer:

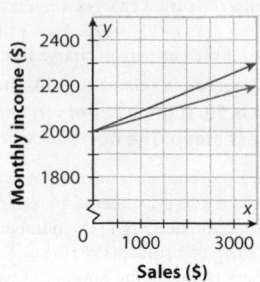

The salesperson's commission percentage rate is decreased.

18. Mr. Resnick is driving at a speed of 40 miles per hour to visit relatives who live 100 miles away from his home. His distance d (in miles) from his destination is given by the function $d(t) = 100 - 40t$, where t is the time (in hours) since his trip began. Sketch a graph to illustrate each situation. The graphs shown already represent the function $d(t)$.

a. He increases his speed to get to the destination sooner. (Hint: His distance from the destination decreases faster.)

Sample Answer:

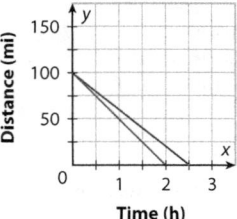

b. His starting distance from the destination is increased because a detour forces him to take a longer route.

Sample Answer:

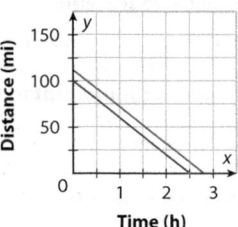

c. Give an example of another linear function within the same family of functions as $d(t) = 100 - 40t$. Explain the meaning of each parameter in your example.

Sample answer: $d(t) = 150 - 40t$, 150 represents the initial distance he has to travel, which is greater; -40 means that the distance from his destination is decreasing at 40 miles per hour.

19. A book club charges a membership fee of $20 and then $12 for each book purchased.

   a. Write a function to represent the cost y of membership in the club based on the number of books purchased x.

      $y = 12x + 20$

   b. Write a second function to represent the cost of membership if the club raises its membership fee to $30.

      $y = 12x + 30$

   c. Describe the relationship between the functions from parts A and B.

      Both functions have the same slope but have a different value for b.

20. Match each effect on a graph with the appropriate change in m. The *steepness* of a line refers to the absolute value of its slope. The greater the absolute value of the slope, the steeper the line. Complete the table to summarize, in terms of steepness, the effect of changing the value of m on the graph of $f(x) = mx$.

How the Value of m Changes	Effect on the Graph of $f(x) = mx$
A. Increase m when $m > 1$.	_A_ Graph becomes steeper.
B. Decrease m when $0 < m < 1$.	_B_ Graph becomes less steep.
C. Decrease m when $m < -1$.	_C_ Graph becomes steeper.
D. Increase m when $0 > m > -1$.	_D_ Graph becomes less steep.

H.O.T. Focus on Higher Order Thinking

21. Explain the Error A student is asked to explain what happens with each of the parameters for the following situation.

It costs a player $20 up front to join a basketball league and then $5 a week to play. If the cost to join the league is reduced to $19 and the weekly fee increases to $6 a week, what will happen to the function of the graph?

The student says that the graph will shift up because the value of b has increased and then the graph will become less steep because the value of m has decreased.

Explain what the student has done incorrectly.

The student has confused the values of b and m. In this situation, the cost to play each week, m, has increased. This will cause the graph to become steeper. The cost to join the league, b, decreases. This will cause the graph to shift down.

© Houghton Mifflin Harcourt Publishing Company

Module 6

278

Lesson 4

VISUAL CUES

Have students graph the function $f(x) = x$ in black on a coordinate grid. Have them write $f(x) = mx + b$ above the grid, writing m in one color and b in another color. Then have them graph several lines for which either the value of m or of b has changed from the given $f(x) = x$. If they change the value of m, have them draw the line in the same color used to write m in the equation. If they change the value of b, have them draw the line in the same color used to write b in the equation.

Transforming Linear Functions **278**

JOURNAL

Have students describe how each of the transformations discussed in this lesson can be represented both graphically and algebraically, and how, given the graph of a function and a transformation of the graph, they can write an equation that describes the transformation.

22. **Critique Reasoning** Geoff says that changing the value of m while leaving b unchanged in $f(x) = mx + b$ has no impact on the intercepts of the graph. Marcus disagrees with this statement. Who is correct? Explain your reasoning.

Marcus is correct. Unless the y-intercept is the same as the x-intercept, which can only happen when both are 0, changing the value of m while leaving b unchanged will cause the x-intercept to change.

23. **Multiple Representations** The graph of $y = x + 3$ is a vertical translation of the graph of $y = x + 1$, 2 units upward. Examine the intercepts of both lines and state another way that the geometric relationship between the two graphs can be described.

The graph of $y = x + 3$ is a horizontal translation of the graph of $y = x + 1$, 2 units to the left.

24. **Critique Reasoning** Stephanie says that the graphs of $y = 3x + 2$ and $y = 3x - 2$ are parallel. Isabella says that the graphs are perpendicular. Who is correct? Explain your reasoning.

Stephanie is correct. The graph of $y = 3x + 2$ is a vertical translation up 4 units of the graph of $y = 3x - 2$, so the two graphs are parallel.

25. **Critical Thinking** It has been shown that the graph of $g(x) = x + 3$ is the result of translating the graph of $f(x) = x$ three units up. However, this can also be thought of as a horizontal translation—that is, a translation left or right. Describe the horizontal translation of $f(x) = x$ to get the graph of $g(x) = x + 3$.

The graph will be translated 3 units to the left.

Lesson Performance Task

High-demand cars that are also in low supply tend to retain their value better than other cars. The data in the table is for a car that won a resale value award.

Year	1	3	5
Value (%)	84	64	44

a. Write a function to represent the change in the percentage of the car's value over time. Assume that the function is linear for the first 5 years.

b. According to the model, by what percent did the car's value drop the day it was purchased and driven off the lot?

c. Would the linear model be useful after 10 years? Explain why or why not.

d. Suppose months were used instead of years to write the function. How would the model change? What is the relationship of the new function to the original function?

a. Slope: $\frac{64-84}{3-1} = \frac{-20}{2} = -10$

 Since the slope is -10, the y-intercept is 94.

 The function is $v(x) = -10x + 94$ where x is the number of years and v is the percent value.

b. The y-intercept is 94, so the car's value dropped by 6%.

c. The model would not be meaningful after 10 years because the model gives a negative percent value.

d. The y-intercept would still be 94. The slope would change since the function is now in months.

 $-10\left(\frac{1}{12}\right) = -\frac{5}{6}$

 So the new function would be $v(x) = -\frac{5}{6}x + 94$, which is not as steep as the original function.

EXTENSION ACTIVITY

Have pairs research the resale of 4 cars, all of the same make, purchased new in the year 2000, and sold in the current year. The only difference in the cars is their mileage: 10,000; 50,000; 100,000; and 200,000 miles. Have students make a table and a graph of the values and then determine whether the relationship between number of miles and sale price is linear.

CONNECT VOCABULARY EL

Some students may not be familiar with the meaning of *depreciate*. When the value of anything becomes less over time, it is said to *depreciate* or *become less valuable*. The depreciation of a car is the difference between what you paid for the car and what it is now worth. The opposite of depreciate is *appreciate*, meaning *to go up in value*.

Explain that there is a theory explaining the interaction between the *supply* of an object and the *demand* for that object. The availability of an object and how much it is desired affect the value. So, a car that is rare and in high demand does not depreciate as quickly as a car that is widely available and in low demand.

The law of supply and demand is the basis of economics.

INTEGRATE MATHEMATICAL PRACTICES
Focus on Technology

MP.5 Have students graph both equations on the same coordinate grid and find their intersection. Have them place a pencil along one line and show how rotating the pencil about the point of intersection places it on the other line.

Scoring Rubric
2 points: Student correctly solves the problem and explains his/her reasoning.
1 point: Student shows good understanding of the problem but does not fully solve or explain his/her reasoning.
0 points: Student does not demonstrate understanding of the problem.

Transforming Linear Functions   **280**

Comparing Properties of Linear Functions

Common Core Math Standards

The student is expected to:

 F-IF.C.9

Compare properties of two functions each represented in a different way...

Mathematical Practices

 MP.4 Modeling

Language Objective

Students will explain how to compare linear functions that are represented in different ways.

ENGAGE

Essential Question: How can you compare linear functions that are represented in different ways?

Possible answer: You can find and compare their slopes, intercepts, domains, and ranges.

PREVIEW: LESSON PERFORMANCE TASK

View the Engage section online. Discuss the photo and different types of jobs that might pay a commission to salespeople. Then preview the Lesson Performance Task.

Name_____ Class_____ Date_____

6.5 Comparing Properties of Linear Functions

Essential Question: How can you compare linear functions that are represented in different ways?

⊘ Explore Comparing Properties of Linear Functions Given Algebra and a Description

Comparing linear relationships can involve comparing relationships that are expressed in different ways.

Dan's Plumbing and Kim's Plumbing have different ways of charging their customers. The function $D(t) = 35t$ represents the total amount in dollars that Dan's Plumbing charges for t hours of work. Kim's Plumbing charges \$35 per hour plus a \$40 flat-rate fee.

(A) Define a function $K(t)$ that represents the total amount Kim's Plumbing charges for t hours of work and then complete the tables.

The function $K(t) = 35t + 40$ represents the total amount in dollars that Kim's Plumbing charges for t hours of work.

Cost for Dan's Plumbing		
t	$D(t) = 35t$	$(t, D(t))$
0	0	$(0, 0)$
1	35	$(1, 35)$
2	70	$(2, 70)$
3	105	$(3, 105)$

Cost for Kim's Plumbing		
t	$K(t) = 35t + 40$	$(t, K(t))$
0	40	$(0, 40)$
1	75	$(1, 75)$
2	110	$(2, 110)$
3	145	$(3, 145)$

(B) What domain and range values for the functions $D(t)$ and for $K(t)$ are reasonable in this context? Explain.

The domain for both functions is nonnegative real numbers. A plumber can work for any fraction of an hour, but not for negative hours. The range for $D(t)$ is nonnegative real numbers because a plumber can earn any fraction of a dollar, but not negative dollars. The range for $K(t)$ is all real numbers greater than or equal to 40. Kim's Plumbing charges a minimum of \$40 for work.

HARDCOVER PAGES 229–238

Turn to these pages to find this lesson in the hardcover student edition.

Ⓒ Graph the two cost functions for the appropriate domain values.

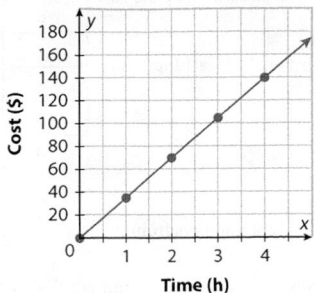
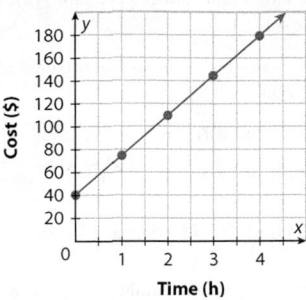

Ⓓ Compare the graphs. How are they alike? How are they different?

Sample answer: The graphs have the same slope, but they have different y-intercepts.

Reflect

1. **Discussion** What information could be found about the two functions without changing their representation?
   the slope, or rate of change

 Explain 1   **Comparing Properties of Linear Functions Given Algebra and a Table**

A table and a rule are two ways that a linear relationship may be expressed. Sometimes it may be helpful to convert one representation to the other when comparing two relationships. There are other times when comparisons are possible without converting either representation.

Example 1   Compare the initial value and the range for each of the linear functions $f(x)$ and $g(x)$.

Ⓐ The domain of each function is the set of all real numbers x such that $5 \le x \le 8$. The table shows some ordered pairs for $f(x)$. The function $g(x)$ is defined by the rule $g(x) = 3x + 7$.

x	f(x)
5	20
6	24
7	28
8	32

The initial value is the output that is paired with the least input. The least input for $f(x)$ and $g(x)$ is 5.

The initial value of $f(x)$ is $f(5) = 20$.

The initial value of $g(x)$ is $g(5) = 3(5) + 7 = 22$.

Since $f(x)$ is a linear function and its domain is the set of all real numbers from 5 to 8, its range will be the set of all real numbers from $f(5)$ to $f(8)$. Since $f(5) = 20$ and $f(8) = 32$, the range of $f(x)$ is the set of all real numbers such that $20 \le f(x) \le 32$.

Since $g(x)$ is a linear function and its domain is the set of all real numbers from 5 to 8, its range will be the set of all real numbers from $g(5)$ to $g(8)$. Since $g(5) = 22$ and $g(8) = 3(8) + 7 = 31$, the range of $g(x)$ is the set of all real numbers such that $22 \le g(x) \le 31$.

PROFESSIONAL DEVELOPMENT

COMMON CORE **Integrate Mathematical Process**

This lesson provides an opportunity to address Mathematical Practice **MP.4,** which calls for students to use "modeling." Students learn how to use various forms of linear functions to solve real-world problems, and to identify which symbolic forms are most useful for which kinds of problems. Students also work with real-world domains that are a subset of the real numbers.

Comparing Properties of Linear Functions Given Algebra and a Description

INTEGRATE TECHNOLOGY

Students have the option of completing the activity either in the book or online.

INTEGRATE MATHEMATICAL PRACTICES
Focus on Patterns

MP.8 Point out to students that when they complete tables, they will use the same values of the independent variable to create their graphs. Then they will compare and contrast the graphs.

AVOID COMMON ERRORS

Some students may forget the meaning of the variables in a function. Remind students that, for a linear function of the forms $f(x) = mx + b$, the slope is m and the y-intercept is b. These values need to be considered in the context and units of the problem's situation.

EXPLAIN 1

Comparing Properties of Linear Functions Given Algebra and a Table

QUESTIONING STRATEGIES

? What does the term *reasonable domain* mean? The set of numbers that make sense for a given situation; a reasonable domain may not include fractions, negative numbers, zero, or large numbers.

AVOID COMMON ERRORS

If students have problems converting linear relationships, remind them that they may or may not be able to compare relationships in the given formats. Sometimes they may need to convert one or both relationships into the same format, such as converting one or both into equations, tables, or graphs.

Ⓑ The domain of each function is the set of all real numbers x such that $6 \leq x \leq 10$. The table shows some ordered pairs for $f(x)$. The function $g(x)$ is defined by the rule $g(x) = 5x + 11$.

x	f(x)
6	36
7	42
8	48
9	54
10	60

The initial value is the output that is paired with the least input. The least input for $f(x)$ and $g(x)$ is ___6___.

The initial value of $f(x)$ is ___$f(6) = 36$___

The initial value of $g(x)$ is ___$g(6) = 5(6) + 11 = 41$___

Since $f(x)$ is a linear function, and its domain is the set of all real numbers from ___6___ to 10, its range will be the set of all real numbers from $f(\boxed{6})$ to $f(10)$. Since $f(\boxed{6}) = \boxed{36}$ and $f(10) = \boxed{60}$, the range of $f(x)$ is the set of all real numbers such that $\boxed{36} \leq f(x) \leq \boxed{60}$.

Since $g(x)$ is a linear function and its domain is the set of all real numbers from ___6___ to 10, its range will be the set of all real numbers from $g(\boxed{6})$ to $g(10)$. Since $g(\boxed{6}) = \boxed{41}$ and $g(10) = 5(\boxed{10}) + 11 = \boxed{61}$, the range of $g(x)$ is the set of all real numbers such that $\boxed{41} \leq g(x) \leq \boxed{61}$.

Reflect

2. **Discussion** How can you use a table of values to find the rate of change for a linear function?
   First, find the difference of the x-values and the difference of the corresponding function values. Then divide the difference of the function values by the difference of the x-values.

Your Turn

3. Find the rate of change for the linear function $f(x)$ that is shown in the table.

x	f(x)
3	22
4	29
5	36
6	43
7	50

Use the ordered pairs $(3, 22)$ and $(5, 36)$.
Difference of x-values: $5 - 3 = 2$
Difference of $f(x)$-values: $36 - 22 = 14$
Divide the difference of the function values by the difference of the x-values: $\frac{14}{2} = 7$
The rate of change is 7.

4. The rule for $f(x)$ in Example 1B is $f(x) = 6x$. If the domains were extended to all real numbers, how would the slopes and y-intercepts of $f(x)$ and $g(x) = 5x + 11$ in Example 1B compare?

   The slope of $f(x)$ is greater than the slope of $g(x)$. The y-intercepts are different because the y-intercept of $f(x)$ is 0 and the y-intercept of $g(x)$ is 11.

© Houghton Mifflin Harcourt Publishing Company

COLLABORATIVE LEARNING

Small Group Activity

Have students work in groups of three. Give students the following prompt: "An employee earns $8.00 an hour. The function $y = 8x$ gives the total pay y the employee will earn for working x hours." Have the first student make a table of ordered pairs. The second student should make a graph for this function. The third student should explain the relationships among the equation, the table, and the graph, and tell how each one describes the situation. Have students change roles so that each student has the opportunity to do each task.

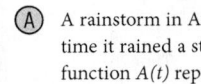 **Comparing Properties of Linear Functions Given a Graph and a Description**

Information about a linear relationship may have to be inferred from the context given in the problem.

Example 2 Write a rule for each function, and then compare their domain, range, slope, and *y*-intercept.

(A) A rainstorm in Austin lasted for 3.5 hours, during which time it rained a steady rate of 4.5 mm per hour. The function $A(t)$ represents the amount of rain that fell in *t* hours.

The graph shows the amount of rain that fell during the same rainstorm in Dallas, $D(t)$ (in millimeters), as a function of time *t* (in hours).

Write a rule for each function. $A(t) = 4.5t$ for $0 \le t \le 3.5$

The line representing $D(t)$ has endpoints at $(0, 0)$ and $(4, 20)$. The slope of $D(t)$ is $\frac{20 - 0}{4 - 0} = 5$. The *y*-intercept is 0, so substituting 5 for *m* and 0 for *b* in $y = mx + b$ produces the equation $y = 5x$. This can be represented by the function $D(t) = 5t$, for $0 \le t \le 4$.

The domains of each function both begin at 0 but end for different values of *t*, because the lengths of time that it rained in Austin and Dallas were not the same.

The range for $A(t)$ is $0 \le A(t) \le 15.75$. The range for $D(t)$ is $0 \le A(t) \le 20$.

The slope for $D(t)$ is 5, which is greater than the slope for $A(t)$, which is 4.5.

The *y*-intercepts of both functions are 0.

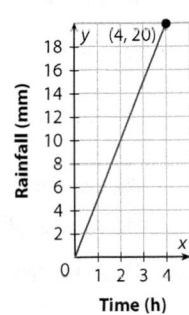

Rainfall (mm) (y-axis)
Time (h) (x-axis)
(4, 20)

EXPLAIN 2

Comparing Properties of Linear Functions Given a Graph and a Description

QUESTIONING STRATEGIES

? Can the graph of a linear function be a segment rather than a line or a ray? Explain. Yes, if the domain is an interval, the graph will be a segment to reflect the situation.

? For a problem involving distance from a location where the *x*-axis represents time, why is the *y*-intercept equal to 0? The initial value for both time and distance is 0, so the initial point is the origin, and both the *x*- and *y*-intercepts are equal to 0.

DIFFERENTIATE INSTRUCTION

Cognitive Strategies

Several characteristics of two linear functions can be compared. Besides the slope and intercepts, there are specific domain and range values such as initial value and maximum and minimum values. Students must recognize that they may need to represent the function in a different way to facilitate comparisons. Guide students with questions such as:

- What are the independent and dependent variables?
- Will the points go upward or downward from left to right?
- How can you find the equation for the relationship?

INTEGRATE MATHEMATICAL PRACTICES

Focus on Critical Thinking

MP.3 Encourage students to think about what characteristics they can determine directly from each different type of representation of a function and what characteristics must be determined through calculation or reasoning. For example, the maximum value of a function over an interval can be read from its graph but must be calculated if the function equation is given.

(B) One group of hikers hiked at a steady rate of 6.5 kilometers per hour for 4 hours. The function $f(t)$ represents the distance this group of hikers hiked in t hours.

The graph shows the distance a second group of hikers hiked, $g(t)$ (in kilometers), as a function of t (in hours).

Write a rule for each function.

$f(t) = \boxed{6.5t}$ for $\boxed{0} \le t \le \boxed{4}$

The line representing $g(t)$ has endpoints at $(0, 0)$

and $\left(\boxed{4.5}, \boxed{36}\right)$. The slope of $g(t)$ is $\dfrac{\boxed{36} - 0}{\boxed{4.5} - 0} = \boxed{8}$.

The y-intercept is $\underline{\ \ 0\ \ }$, so substituting $\underline{\ \ 8\ \ }$ for m and $\underline{\ \ 0\ \ }$ for b in $y = mx + b$ produces the equation

$y = \boxed{8x}$. This can be represented by the function $g(t) = \boxed{8t}$ for $\boxed{0} \le t \le \boxed{4.5}$.

The domains of each function both begin at $\underline{\ \ 0\ \ }$ and end at $\underline{\ \text{different}\ }$ values of t.

The range for $f(t)$ is $\boxed{0} \le f(t) \le \boxed{26}$ and the range for $g(t)$ is $\boxed{0} \le g(t) \le \boxed{36}$.

The slope for $\underline{\ g(t)\ }$ is greater than the slope for $\underline{\ f(t)\ }$.

The y-intercepts are $\underline{\ \text{both 0}\ }$.

LANGUAGE SUPPORT **EL**

Connect Vocabulary

Students acquire academic language through modeling and practice. One particular construction they may not hear in the same context outside of mathematics is the term *given*. Students may have heard expressions such as *he was given a helmet*, but the word *given* by itself may be unfamiliar. Explain to students that, in mathematics, *given* refers to the information that is *provided* to you; the information that you can use to answer the question.

5. What is the meaning of the *y*-intercepts for the functions *A*(*t*) and *D*(*t*) in Example 2A?
The rainfall started at the same time that the rainstorm started. At that time, the total

rainfall was 0 mm in both locations.

Your Turn

6. An experiment compares the heights of two plants over time. A plant was 5 cm tall at the beginning of the experiment and grew 0.3 centimeters each day. The function *f*(*t*) represents the height of the plant (in centimeters) after *t* days. The graph shows the height of the second plant, *g*(*t*) (in centimeters), as a function of time *t* (in days).

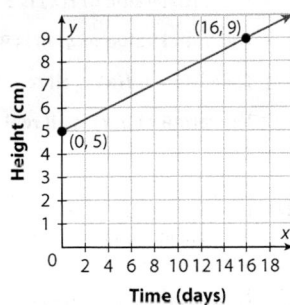

Find the rate of change *g*(*t*) and compare it to the rate of change for *f*(*t*).

Rate of change *g*(*t*): $\frac{9-5}{16-0} = 0.25$

The rate of change for *g*(*t*) is 0.25 centimeters per day,

which is less than the rate of change for *f*(*t*), which is

0.3 centimeters each day.

💬 Elaborate

7. When would representing a linear function by a graph be more helpful than by a table?
Sample answer: A graph would be more helpful than a table when approximating the

value of a function at input values that are not given in a table.

8. When would representing a linear function by a table be more helpful than by a graph?
Sample answer: When the rate of change is not an integer, such as when a function, *f*(*x*),

represents the cost of buying *x* packages of printer paper at a rate of $3.59 per package.

9. Essential Question-Check-In How can you compare a linear function represented in a table to one represented as a graph?
Plot the ordered pairs in the table to convert the representation to a graph. Then compare

the graphs' slopes and intercepts.

ELABORATE

QUESTIONING STRATEGIES

? Do you have to use the standard form of the equation to find the *x*- and *y*-intercepts? Explain. No; however, using standard form will take fewer steps than using point-slope form directly to find the *x*- and *y*-intercepts.

SUMMARIZE THE LESSON

? How do you compare linear functions? It helps to represent each situation in the same way. Sometimes the data can be represented best by function rules. At other times, a graph or a table may be the best way to represent the data.

EVALUATE

ASSIGNMENT GUIDE

Concepts and Skills	Practice
Explore Comparing Properties of Linear Functions Given Algebra and a Description	Exercises 13–15, 17, 20, 22
Example 1 Comparing Properties of Linear Functions Given Algebra and a Table	Exercises 1–6, 16–17, 19
Example 2 Comparing Properties of Linear Functions Given a Graph and a Description	Exercises 7–12, 18, 21, 23–25

CONNECT VOCABULARY EL

Some students may confuse the meaning of *discrete* with the meaning of *discreet*. Both words have the same pronunciation. Point out that *discreet* means *careful*, while *discrete* means *separate or individual*.

Compare the initial value and the range for each of the linear functions $f(x)$ and $g(x)$.

1. The domain of each function is the set of all real numbers x such that $2 \leq x \leq 5$. The table shows some ordered pairs for $f(x)$. The function $g(x)$ is defined by the rule $g(x) = x + 6$.

The initial value of $f(x)$ is **5.**

The initial value of $g(x)$ is **8.**

The range of $f(x)$ is all real numbers such that $5 \leq f(x) \leq 11$.

The range of $g(x)$ is all real numbers such that $8 \leq g(x) \leq 11$.

x	$f(x)$
2	5
3	7
4	9
5	11

2. The domain of each function is the set of all real numbers x such that $8 \leq x \leq 12$. The table shows some ordered pairs for $f(x)$. The function $g(x)$ is defined by the rule $g(x) = 7x - 3$.

The initial value of $f(x)$ is **34.**

The initial value of $g(x)$ is **53.**

The range of $f(x)$ is all real numbers such that $34 \leq f(x) \leq 50$.

The range of $g(x)$ is all real numbers such that $53 \leq g(x) \leq 81$.

x	$f(x)$
8	34
9	38
10	42
11	46
12	50

3. The domain of each function is the set of all real numbers x such that $-4 \leq x \leq -1$. The function $f(x)$ is defined by the rule $f(x) = 2x + 9$. The table shows some ordered pairs for $g(x)$.

The initial value of $f(x)$ is **1.**

The initial value of $g(x)$ is **10.**

The range of $f(x)$ is all real numbers such that $1 \leq f(x) \leq 7$.

The range of $g(x)$ is all real numbers such that $7 \leq g(x) \leq 10$.

x	$g(x)$
−4	10
−3	9
−2	8
−1	7

4. The domain of each function is the set of all real numbers x such that $0 \leq x \leq 4$. The function $f(x)$ is defined by the rule $f(x) = -3x + 15$. The table shows some ordered pairs for $g(x)$.

The initial value of $f(x)$ is **15.**

The initial value of $g(x)$ is **23.**

The range of $f(x)$ is all real numbers such that $3 \leq f(x) \leq 15$.

The range of $g(x)$ is all real numbers such that $7 \leq g(x) \leq 23$.

x	$g(x)$
0	23
1	19
2	15
3	11
4	7

© Houghton Mifflin Harcourt Publishing Company

Exercise	Depth of Knowledge (D.O.K.)	COMMON CORE Mathematical Practices
1–6	**1** Recall of Information	**MP.2** Reasoning
7–8	**2** Skills/Concepts	**MP.2** Reasoning
9–12	**2** Skills/Concepts	**MP.4** Modeling
13–15	**2** Skills/Concepts	**MP.6** Precision
16–17	**2** Skills/Concepts	**MP.2** Reasoning
18	**1** Recall of Information	**MP.6** Precision

5. The domain of each function is the set of all real numbers x such that $10 \leq x \leq 13$. The table shows some ordered pairs for $f(x)$. The function $g(x)$ is defined by the rule $g(x) = \frac{1}{2}x + 12$.

x	f(x)
10	22
11	$\frac{47}{2}$
12	25
13	$\frac{53}{2}$

The initial value of $f(x)$ is 22.

The initial value of $g(x)$ is 17.

The range of $f(x)$ is all real numbers such that $22 \leq f(x) \leq \frac{53}{2}$.

The range of $g(x)$ is of all real numbers such that $17 \leq g(x) \leq \frac{37}{2}$.

6. The domain of each function is the set of all real numbers x such that $2 \leq x \leq 6$. The function $f(x)$ is defined by the rule $f(x) = -\frac{3}{4}x + 10$. The table shows some ordered pairs for $g(x)$.

x	g(x)
2	14
3	$\frac{51}{4}$
4	$\frac{23}{2}$
5	$\frac{41}{4}$
6	9

The initial value of $f(x)$ is $\frac{17}{2}$.

The initial value of $g(x)$ is 14.

The range of $f(x)$ is all real numbers such that $\frac{11}{2} \leq f(x) \leq \frac{17}{2}$.

The range of $g(x)$ is all real numbers such that $9 \leq g(x) \leq 14$.

Write a rule for each function f and g, and then compare their domains, ranges, slopes, and y-intercepts.

7. The function $f(x)$ has a slope of 6 and has a y-intercept of 20. The graph shows the function $g(x)$.

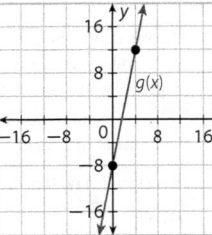

$f(x) = 6x + 20$

$g(x)$ slope: $\frac{12 - (-8)}{4 - 0} = 5$; y-intercept: -8

$g(x) = 5x - 8$

The domain and range of the functions are the same.

The slope of $f(x)$ is greater than $g(x)$.

The y-intercept of $f(x)$ is greater than the y-intercept of $g(x)$.

8. The function $f(x)$ has a slope of -3 and has a y-intercept of 5. The graph shows the function $g(x)$.

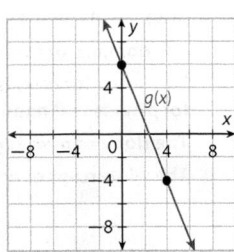

$f(x) = -3x + 5$

$g(x)$ slope: $\frac{-4 - (6)}{4 - 0} = -\frac{5}{2}$; y-intercept: 6

$g(x) = -\frac{5}{2}x + 6$

The domain and range of the functions are the same.

The slope of $f(x)$ is steeper than the slope of $g(x)$.

The y-intercept of $g(x)$ is greater than the y-intercept of $f(x)$.

Exercise	Depth of Knowledge (D.O.K.)	COMMON CORE Mathematical Practices
19–21	**2** Skills/Concepts	**MP.2** Reasoning
22–23	**2** Skills/Concepts H.O.T.	**MP.2** Reasoning
24–25	**3** Strategic Thinking H.O.T.	**MP.2** Reasoning

AVOID COMMON ERRORS

If students have problems converting linear relationships, remind them that they may be able to compare relationships in the given formats. However, sometimes they may need to convert relationships to the same format, such as converting them both into equations, tables, or graphs.

Comparing Properties of Linear Functions **288**

Have students work in pairs to quiz each other
aloud about the various forms of a linear equation.
Have one student state a linear equation, such as
$y - 1 = 3(x - 2)$ or $y = 2x + 2$, and have the other
tell which form the equation is in (slope-intercept,
standard, or point-slope). Then have students reverse
roles so that the first student states a form and the
second student gives an equation in that form.

Write a rule for each function, and then compare their domains, ranges, slopes, and y-intercepts.

9. Jeff, an electrician, had a job that lasted 5.5 hours, during which time he earned $32 per hour and charged a $25 service fee. The function $J(t)$ represents the amount Jeff earns in t hours.

Brendan also works as an electrician. The graph of $B(t)$ shows the amount in dollars that Brendan earns as a function of time t in hours.

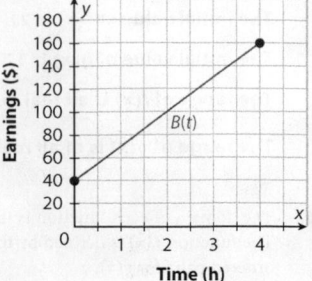

$J(t) = 32t + 25, 0 \leq t \leq 5.5$

$B(t)$

Slope: $\frac{160 - 40}{4 - 0} = 30$

y-intercept: 40

$B(t) = 30t + 40, 0 \leq t \leq 4$

The domain for both functions is real numbers that start at 0, but $B(t)$ ends at 4 and $J(t)$ ends at 5.5.

The range for $B(t)$ is the set of all real numbers $B(t)$, where $40 \leq B(t) \leq 160$. The range for $J(t)$ is the set of all real numbers $J(t)$, where $25 \leq J(t) \leq 201$.

The slope of $J(t)$ is greater than the slope of $B(t)$.

The y-intercept of $B(t)$ is greater than the y-intercept of $J(t)$.

10. Apples can be bought at a farmer's market up to 10 pounds at a time, where each pound costs $1.10. The function $a(w)$ represents the cost of buying w pounds of apples.

The graph of $p(w)$ shows the cost in dollars of buying w pounds of pears.

$a(w) = 1.1w, 0 \leq w \leq 10$

$p(w)$

Slope: $\frac{14 - 0}{10 - 0} = 1.4$

y-intercept: 0

$p(w) = 1.4w, 0 \leq t \leq 10$

The domain for both functions is real numbers from 0 to 10.

The range for $a(w)$ is real numbers $a(w)$, where $0 \leq a(w) \leq 11$. The range for $p(w)$ is real numbers $p(w)$, where $0 \leq p(w) \leq 14$.

The slope of $p(w)$ is greater than the slope of $a(w)$.

The y-intercept of both functions is 0.

11. Biology A gecko travels for 6 minutes at a constant rate of 19 meters per minute. The function $g(t)$ represents the distance the gecko travels after t minutes.

The graph of $m(t)$ shows the distance in meters that a mouse travels after t minutes.

$g(t) = 19t, 0 \leq t \leq 6$

$m(t) = 37.5t, 0 \leq t \leq 8$

The domain for both functions is real numbers that begin at 0, but $g(t)$ ends at 6 and $m(t)$ ends at 8.

The range for $g(t)$ is real numbers $g(t)$, where $0 \leq g(t) \leq 114$. The range for $m(t)$ is real numbers $m(t)$, where $0 \leq m(t) \leq 300$.

The slope of $m(t)$ is greater than the slope of $g(t)$.

The y-intercept of both functions is 0.

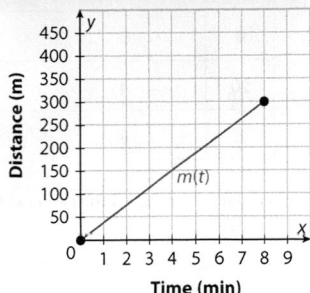

12. Cindy is buying a water pump. The box for Pump A claims that it can move 48 gallons per minute. The function $A(t)$ represents the amount of water (in gallons) Pump A can move after t minutes.

The graph of $B(t)$ shows the amount of water in gallons that Pump B can move after t minutes.

$A(t) = 48t, t \geq 0$

$B(t) = 45t, t \geq 0$

The domain and range for both functions are nonnegative real numbers.

The slope of $A(t)$ is greater than the slope of $B(t)$.

The y-intercept of both functions is 0.

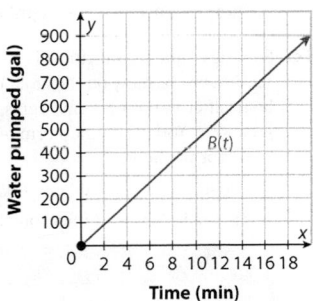

? What is a discrete linear function? A discrete linear function is a linear function whose graph consists of isolated points.

? How are discrete and continuous linear functions alike and how are they different? Discrete and continuous functions are alike in that the points on their graphs lie on a line. They differ in that the graph of a discrete function consists of isolated points, while the graph of a continuous function is an unbroken line or part of a line.

13. Erin is comparing two rental car companies for an upcoming trip. The function $A(d) = 0.20d$ represents the total amount in dollars of driving a car d miles from company A. Company B charges $0.10 per mile and a $10 fee.

a. Define a function $B(d)$ that represents the total amount company B charges for driving d miles and then complete the tables.

Cost for Company A		
d	$A(d) = 0.20d$	$(d, A(d))$
0	0	$(0, 0)$
20	4	$(20, 4)$
40	8	$(40, 8)$

Cost for Company B		
d	$B(d) = 0.10d + 10$	$(d, B(d))$
0	10	$(0, 10)$
20	12	$(20, 12)$
40	14	$(40, 14)$

b. Graph and label the two cost functions for all appropriate domain values.

c. Compare the graphs. How are they alike? How are they different?

Sample answer: the graphs have different slopes and different y-intercepts.

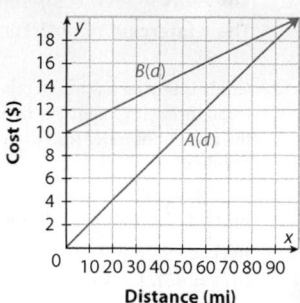

14. Snow is falling in two cities. The function $C(t) = 2t + 8$ represents the amount of snow on the ground, in centimeters, in Carlisle t hours after the snowstorm begins. There was 8 cm of snow on the ground in York when the storm began and the snow accumulates at 1.5 cm per hour.

a. Define a function $Y(t)$ that represents the amount of snow on the ground after t hours in York and then complete the tables.

Carlisle		
t	$C(t) = 2t + 8$	$(t, C(t))$
0	8	$(0, 8)$
1	10	$(1, 10)$
2	12	$(2, 12)$

York		
t	$Y(t) = 1.5t + 8$	$(t, Y(t))$
0	8	$(0, 8)$
1	9.5	$(1, 9.5)$
2	11	$(2, 11)$

b. Graph and label the two cost functions for all appropriate domain values.

c. Compare the graphs. How are they alike? How are they different?

Sample answer: The graphs have the same y-intercepts, but they have different slopes.

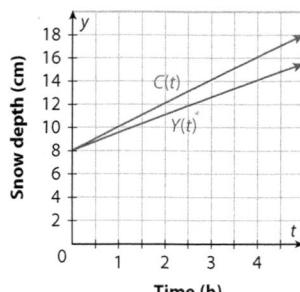

15. Gillian works from 20 to 30 hours per week during the summer. She earns $12.50 per hour. Her friend Emily also has a job. Her pay for t hours each week is given by the function $e(t) = 13t$, where $15 \leq t \leq 25$.

a. Find the domain and range of each function.

The domain of $g(t)$ is the set of real numbers t, where $20 \leq t \leq 30$.

The domain of $e(t)$ is the set of real numbers t, where $15 \leq t \leq 25$.

The range of $g(t)$ is the set of real numbers $g(t)$, where $250 \leq g(t) \leq 375$. The range of $e(t)$ is the set of real numbers $e(t)$, where $195 \leq e(t) \leq 325$.

b. Compare their hourly wages and the amount they earn per week.

Gillian earns less per hour than Emily. Gillian earns from $250 to $375 per week and Emily earns from $195 to $325 per week.

16. The function $A(p)$ defined by the rule $A(p) = 0.13p + 15$ represents the cost in dollars of producing a custom textbook that has p pages for college A, where $0 < p \leq 500$. The table shows some ordered pairs for $B(p)$, where $B(p)$ represents the cost in dollars of producing a custom textbook that has p pages for college B, where $0 < p \leq 500$. For both colleges, only full pages may be printed.

p	B(p)
0	24
50	30
100	36
150	42

Compare the domain, range, slope, and y-intercept of the functions. Interpret the comparisons in context.

The slope for $A(p)$ is 0.13, while the slope for $B(p)$ is $\frac{30-24}{50-0} = 0.12$. The cost per page is higher for college A than for college B.

The y-intercept for $A(p)$ is 15, while the y-intercept for $B(p)$ is 24. The initial cost is greater for college B than for college A.

The domains for each function are the same. Both can produce up to 500 pages.

Ranges: A textbook from college A costs between $15 and $80, and a textbook from college B costs between $24 and $84.

17. Complete the table so that $f(x)$ is a linear function with a slope of 4 and a y-intercept of 7. Assume the domain includes all real numbers between the least and greatest values shown in the table. Compare $f(x)$ to $g(x) = 4x + 7$ if the range of $g(x)$ is $-1 \leq g(x) \leq 11$.

x	f(x)
−2	−1
−1	3
0	7
1	11

The domains, ranges, slopes and y-intercepts are the same for $f(x)$ and $g(x)$. They represent the same function.

18. Which functions have a rate of change that is greater than the one shown in the graph? Select all that apply.

a. $f(x) = \frac{1}{2}x - 5$ $\left|\frac{1}{2}\right| \not> \left|\frac{2}{3}\right|$

b. $g(x) = -x + 6$ $|-1| > \left|\frac{2}{3}\right|$

c. $h(x) = \frac{3}{4}x - 9$ $\left|\frac{3}{4}\right| > \left|\frac{2}{3}\right|$

d. $j(x) = -\frac{1}{4}x + 8$ $\left|-\frac{1}{4}\right| \not> \left|\frac{2}{3}\right|$

e. $k(x) = x$ $|1| > \left|\frac{2}{3}\right|$

The rate of change in the graph is $\frac{2}{3}$.

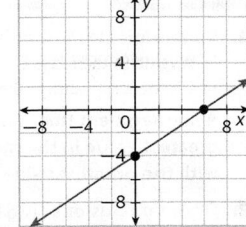

All functions except the ones in choices a and d have a rate of change greater than $\frac{2}{3}$, the one shown in the graph.

INTEGRATE MATHEMATICAL PRACTICES

Focus on Modeling

MP.4 Provide students with a verbal description of a real-world situation that can be modeled by a function. Have them represent the function using a table, a graph, and a rule, and show how each form provides information about the function. Check students' work.

JOURNAL

Have students create a graphic organizer or idea map for the different forms used to represent functions, including tables, graphs, algebra rules, and verbal descriptions. Students should include the advantages of each form in their idea maps.

19. Does the function $f(x) = 5x + 5$ with the domain $6 \leq x \leq 8$ have the same domain as function $g(x)$, whose only function values are shown in the table? Explain.

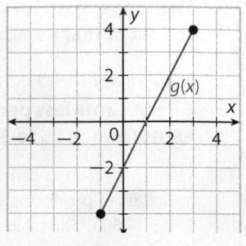

x	g(x)
6	35
7	40
8	45

The functions do not have the same domain. The domain of f(x) includes all real numbers between 6 and 8, while the domain of g(x) is {6, 7, 8}.

20. The linear function $f(x)$ is defined by the table, and the linear function $g(x)$ is shown in the graph. Assume that the domain of $f(x)$ includes all real numbers between the least and greatest values shown in the table.

a. Find the domain and range of each function, and compare them.

x	f(x)
−1	−7
0	−4
1	−1
2	2
3	5

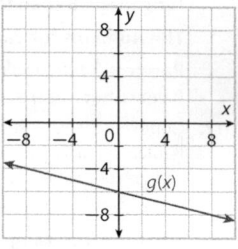

Domain of f(x): $-1 \leq x \leq 3$

Domain of g(x): $-1 \leq x \leq 3$

Range of f(x): $-7 \leq f(x) \leq 5$

Range of g(x): $-4 \leq g(x) \leq 4$

The domains are the same. The ranges are different.

b. What is the slope of the line represented by each function? What is the y-intercept of each function?

The slope is 3 and the y-intercept is −4 for f(x), and the slope is 2 and the y-intercept is −2 for g(x).

21. The linear function $f(x)$ is defined by $f(x) = -\frac{1}{4}x + 6$ for all real numbers, and the linear function $g(x)$ is shown in the graph.

a. Find the domain and range of each function, and compare them.

The domain and range of both f(x) and g(x) is the set of all real numbers.

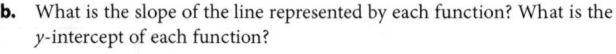

b. What is the slope of the line represented by each function? What is the y-intercept of each function?

The slope is $-\frac{1}{4}$ and the y-intercept is 6 for f(x), and the slope is $-\frac{1}{4}$ and the y-intercept is −6 for g(x).

H.O.T. Focus on Higher Order Thinking

22. Communicate Mathematical Ideas Describe a linear function for which the least value in the range does not occur at the least value of the domain (a function for which the least value in the range is not the initial value.)

A line segment that has a negative slope has an initial value that is the greatest value in the range. The least value in the range will be paired with the greatest value in the domain.

23. Draw Conclusions Two linear functions have the same slope, same x-intercept, and same y-intercept. Must these functions be identical? Explain your reasoning.

The functions do not have to be identical. Each could have a different domain.

24. Draw Conclusions Let $f(x)$ be a line with slope -3 and y-intercept 0 with domain $\{0, 1, 2, 3\}$, and let $g(x) = \{(0, 0), (1, -1), (2, -4), (3, -9)\}$. Compare the two functions.

The domains are the same, but the range of $f(x)$ {0, -2 -4 -6}, while the range of $g(x)$ is {0, -1 -4 -9}. Both have y-intercepts at 0. The slope of $f(x)$ is -3 and the slope of $g(x)$ changes. The function $f(x)$ linear, and the function $g(x)$ is not a line.

25. Draw Conclusions Let $f(x)$ be a line with slope 7 and y-intercept -17 with domain $0 \le x \le 5$, and let $g(x) = \{(0, -17), (1, -10), (2, -3), (3, 4), (4, 11), (5, 18)\}$. Compare the two functions.

The domains are not the same because the domain of $f(x)$ is all real numbers between 0 and 5, while the domain of $g(x)$ is only the integers between 0 and 5. The range of $f(x)$ is $-17 \le f(x) \le 18$ while the range of $g(x)$, {$-17, -10, -3, 4, 11, 18$}. Both have a y-intercept of -17. The function $f(x)$ is linear, but the function $g(x)$ is not linear because it is not a line or a line segment.

Lesson Performance Task

Lindsay found a new job as an insurance salesperson. She has her choice of two different compensation plans. Plan F was described to her as a $450 base weekly salary plus a 10% commission on the amount of sales she made that week. The function $f(x)$ represents the amount Lindsay earns in a week when making sales of x dollars with compensation plan F. Plan G was described to her with the graph shown. The function $g(x)$ represents the amount Lindsay earns in a week when making sales of x dollars with compensation plan G.

Write a rule for the functions $f(x)$ and $g(x)$; then identify and compare their domain, range, slope, and y-intercept. Compare the benefits and drawbacks of each compensation plan. Which compensation plan should Lindsay take? Justify your answer.

Sales ($)

Rule for $f(x)$:

rate of change: 10% = 0.1

$f(x) = 0.1x + 450$

Domain:

$f(x)$: All multiples of 0.01, where $0 \le x < \infty$

$g(x)$: All multiples of 0.01, where $0 \le x < \infty$

Their domains are the same.

Slope:

$f(x)$: 0.1

$g(x)$: 0.15

The slope of $g(x)$ is greater than the slope of $f(x)$.

Rule for $g(x)$:

rate of change: $= \frac{600 - 300}{2000 - 0} = 0.15$

$g(x) = 0.15x + 300$

Range:

$f(x)$: All multiples of 0.01, where $f(x) \ge 450$

$g(x)$: All multiples of 0.01, where $g(x) \ge 300$

The initial value for $f(x)$ is higher than the initial value for $g(x)$, but both can increase without limit.

y-intercept:

$f(x)$: 450

$g(x)$: 300

The y-intercept for $f(x)$ is greater than the y-intercept for $g(x)$.

Plan F has a greater base salary than plan G. If Lindsay doesn't make sales for one week, she would earn more money with plan F than with plan G. Since the slope of $g(x)$ is greater than the slope of $f(x)$, at some point Lindsay would earn more money with plan G. This would actually happen for sales in excess of $3000. Lindsay should take compensation plan G because there is a better potential to earn more money than with compensation plan F.

© Houghton Mifflin Harcourt Publishing Company

EXTENSION ACTIVITY

The Internal Revenue Service considers a commission to be a supplemental wage. Have students research other examples of supplemental wages. Then have them determine the current supplemental wages tax rate and then explain whether they think the tax rate could affect Lindsay's choice in compensation plans.

Students will find that commissions, bonuses, sick leave payments, severance payments, and taxable prizes are a few of the types of supplemental wages. Supplemental wages that total more than $1 million were taxed at a rate of 35% in 2013, while totals less than $1 million could have been taxed at a rate of 25% in 2013.

Some students may not be familiar with the terms *commission* or *incentivize*. Have volunteers use play money to demonstrate earning a commission and then explain how it is calculated. Finally, have another volunteer explain how earning a commission might incentivize someone to work harder to sell more.

INTEGRATE MATHEMATICAL PRACTICES

Focus on Technology

MP.5 Have students graph both equations on the same coordinate grid and find their intersection, $(3000, 750)$. Have students explain what happens to the values to the right of the intersection point and what that means for Lindsay's salary.

Scoring Rubric

2 points: Student correctly solves the problem and explains his/her reasoning.

1 point: Student shows good understanding of the problem but does not fully solve or explain his/her reasoning.

0 points: Student does not demonstrate understanding of the problem.

ASSESSMENT AND INTERVENTION

Assign or customize module reviews.

MODULE PERFORMANCE TASK

COMMON CORE

Mathematical Practices: MP.1, MP.2, MP.4, MP.6
F-IF.C.9, F-LE.B.5, A-CED.A.2

SUPPORTING STUDENT REASONING

Students should begin this problem by organizing the information so they can compare data. Here is some of the information they may ask for.

- **Which of Jamal's different speeds should I use?** Suggest that students find a speed that best represents his overall speed for the entire race.

- **What if I get an unrealistic speed for one of the runners?** Have students check and compare the units as well as the two ratios they used.

Essential Question: How can you use different forms of linear equations to solve real-world problems?

Key Vocabulary

family of functions *(familia de funciones)*

parameter *(parámetro)*

parent function *(función madre)*

KEY EXAMPLE   *(Lesson 6.1)*

For one taxi company, the cost y in dollars of a ride is a linear function of the miles traveled x. The initial charge is $2.00, and the charge per mile is $0.40. Identify the slope and y-intercept of the graph that represents this situation and interpret what they mean. Then write an equation in slope-intercept form and use it to find the cost of riding 15 miles.

The rate of change is $0.40 per mile, so the slope m is 0.4.

The initial cost is the cost to travel 0 miles, $2.00, so the y-intercept b is 2.

So, the equation in slope-intercept form is $y = 0.4x + 2$.

To find the cost of riding 15 miles, substitute 15 for x and simplify.

$$y = 0.4x + 2$$
$$= 0.4(15) + 2$$
$$= 6 + 2$$
$$= 8$$

$(15, 8)$ is a solution of the equation, and the cost of riding 15 miles is $8.

KEY EXAMPLE   *(Lesson 6.3)*

Write an equation in standard form for the line that contains $(-3, 4)$ and $(5, 0)$.

Find the slope using the given points.

$$m = \frac{y_2 - y_1}{x_2 - x_1} = \frac{0 - 4}{5 - (-3)} = \frac{-4}{8} = -\frac{1}{2}$$

Substitute the slope and the coordinates of either of the points in point-slope form.

$$y - y_1 = m(x - x_1)$$
$$y - 0 = -\frac{1}{2}(x - 5)$$
$$y = -\frac{1}{2}x + \frac{5}{2}$$

Rewrite in standard form. $x + 2y = 5$

SCAFFOLDING SUPPORT

- Watch for students who use different measurement units or different ratios.

- For students needing more structure, provide them with the formula $d = rt$. You may also want to provide Jamal's overall average speed of 7.06 miles per hour.

EXERCISES

Write the equation of each line in slope-intercept form. *(Lesson 6.1)*

1. slope is 4 and contains $(3, 6)$

$$y = 4x - 6$$

2. contains $(5, 0)$ and $(9, 4)$

$$y = x - 5$$

Write the equation of each line in point-slope form. *(Lesson 6.2)*

3. slope is -1 and contains $(2, 7)$

$$y - 7 = -(x - 2)$$

4. contains $(-2, 8)$ and $(4, -4)$

$$y - 8 = -2(x + 2)$$

Write the equation of each line in standard form. *(Lesson 6.3)*

5. slope is 3 and contains $(1, 6)$

$$3x - y = -3$$

6. contains $(0, -2)$ and $(10, 2)$

$$2x - 5y = 10$$

7. Describe a series of transformations of the graph of $f(x) = x$ that results in the graph of $g(x) = -x + 6$. *(Lesson 6.4)*

Possible answer: $f(x)$ is reflected across the y-axis and translated 6 units up.

8. Compare the domain and range of $f(x) = -3x + 5$ and $g(x) = 4x - 6$. *(Lesson 6.5)*

Both functions have the same domain and range: all real numbers.

MODULE PERFORMANCE TASK

Who Wins the Race?

Jamal and Kendra are running in a 26.2-mile marathon. Jamal's friend is recording his times in the table as shown, while Kendra's friend uses a scatter plot to show her progress. If both runners continue at the same average pace, who will arrive at the finish line first? How much longer will it take for the other person to finish?

Jamal's Race

Distance (mi)	Time (min)
4	26
8	56
12	90
16	128
20	170

Use your own paper to complete the task. Be sure to write down all your data and assumptions. Then use graphs, numbers, words, or algebra to explain how you reached your conclusion.

Kendra's Distance vs. Time

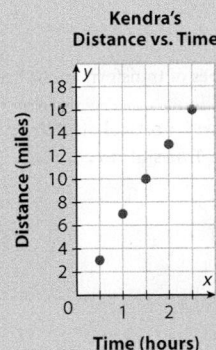

SAMPLE SOLUTION

Assume that Jamal maintains the same average speed that he has established over the first 170 minutes.

Jamal's average speed in miles per hour is $\dfrac{20 \text{ mi}}{170 \text{ min}} \cdot \dfrac{60 \text{ min}}{1 \text{ h}} \approx 7.06$.

Kendra's average speed in miles per hour is $\dfrac{16 \text{ mi}}{2.5 \text{ h}} = 6.4$.

Jamal will win the race.

Use the formula $d = rt$.

For Jamal, $26.2 = 7.06t$, so $t \approx 3.71$ h.

For Kendra, $26.2 = 6.4t$, so $t \approx 4.09$ h.

The difference in times is $4.09 - 3.71$, which is 0.38 hours.

Convert to minutes: $\dfrac{0.38 \text{ h}}{1} \cdot \dfrac{60 \text{ min}}{1 \text{ h}} \approx 23$ min

Jamal will win the race by 23 minutes.

DISCUSSION OPPORTUNITIES

- Ask students to share and compare their different approaches to solving the problem. Elicit from students that neither the method nor the units used has an effect on the final outcome.

- Discuss whether or not it is reasonable to compare two runners' average speeds, knowing that speeds can vary throughout a long race.

Assessment Rubric

2 points: Student correctly solves the problem and explains his/her reasoning.

1 point: Student shows good understanding of the problem but does not fully solve or explain.

0 points: Student does not demonstrate understanding of the problem.

Ready to Go On?

ASSESS MASTERY

Use the assessment on this page to determine if students have mastered the concepts and standards covered in this module.

ASSESSMENT AND INTERVENTION

Access Ready to Go On? assessment online, and receive instant scoring, feedback, and customized intervention or enrichment.

ADDITIONAL RESOURCES

Response to Intervention Resources

- Reteach Worksheets

Differentiated Instruction Resources

- Reading Strategies **EL**
- Success for English Learners **EL**
- Challenge Worksheets

Assessment Resources

- Leveled Module Quizzes

6.1–6.5 Forms of Linear Equations

- Online Homework
- Hints and Help
- Extra Practice

Write an equation for each line in the given form. *(Lessons 6.1, 6.2, 6.3)*

1. slope is -2 and $(1, 7)$ is on the line; standard form

$$2x + y = 9$$

2. contains the points $(3, 4)$ and $(6, 10)$; slope-intercept form

$$y = 2x - 2$$

3. slope is 4 and $(-3, 8)$ is on the line; point-slope form

$$y - 8 = 4(x + 3)$$

4. Describe a transformation of the graph of $f(x) = x$ that results in the graph of $g(x) = 4x$. *(Lesson 6.4)*

Possible answer: The graph of $f(x)$ is stretched vertically, becoming steeper.

5. Jan works from 30 to 40 hours per week during the summer. She earns $12.00 per hour. Her friend Rachel also has a job. Rachel's pay for t hours is given by the function $r(t) = 11t$, where $20 \leq t \leq 30$. Find the domain and range of each function. Compare their hourly wages and the amount they earn per week. *(Lesson 6.5)*

$j(t)$ domain: $30 \leq t \leq 40$, range: $360 \leq j(t) \leq 480$; $r(t)$ domain: $20 \leq t \leq 30$, range: $220 \leq r(t) \leq 330$; Jan earns more per hour than Rachel. Jan earns from $360 to $480 per week and Rachel earns from $220 to $330 per week.

ESSENTIAL QUESTION

6. What type or types of transformations can affect the slope of a linear function? What type or types cannot?

Possible answer: A vertical stretch or shrink or a reflection can change the slope of a linear function. Translation cannot.

© Houghton Mifflin Harcourt Publishing Company

---

297 Module 6

COMMON CORE **Common Core Standards**

Lesson	Items	Content Standards	Mathematical Practices
6.3	1	A-CED.A.2	MP.7
6.1	2	A-CED.A.2	MP.7
6.2	3	A-CED.A.2	MP.7
6.4	4	F-BF.B.3	MP.6
6.5	5	F-LE.B.5, F-IF.C.9, F-IF.A.1	MP.1

Assessment Readiness

1. Look at each equation. Does the equation represent a line with slope $m = 5$, containing the point (3, 8)? Select Yes or No for each equation.

   A. $5x - y = 7$ ● Yes   ○ No

   B. $3x + 8y = 5$ ○ Yes   ● No

   C. $10x - 2y = 14$ ● Yes   ○ No

2. Consider the function $f(x) = 3x - 2$. Select True or False for each statement.

   A. The y-intercept is 2.   ○ True   ● False

   B. The x-intercept is $\frac{2}{3}$.   ● True   ○ False

   C. The slope is 3.   ● True   ○ False

3. Look at each statement. Does the statement describe a transformation of the graph of $f(x) = x$ that would result in the graph of $g(x) = x + 2$? Select Yes or No for each statement.

   A. The graph of the parent function is reflected across the y-axis.   ○ Yes   ● No

   B. The graph of the parent function is translated 2 units up.   ● Yes   ○ No

   C. The graph of the parent function is translated 2 units down.   ○ Yes   ● No

4. What is the x-intercept of $y + 12 = 3(x - 9)$? Explain how you solved this problem.

   13; I substituted 0 for y and solved the equation for x.

5. Write $5x - 3y = -12$ in slope-intercept form. What is the slope? Show your work.

   $5x - 3y = -12$
   $-3y = -5x - 12$
   $y = \frac{5}{3}x + 4$
   The slope is $\frac{5}{3}$.

MIXED REVIEW
Assessment Readiness

ASSESSMENT AND INTERVENTION

Assign ready-made or customized practice tests to prepare students for high-stakes tests.

ADDITIONAL RESOURCES

Assessment Resources

- Leveled Module Quizzes: Modified, B

AVOID COMMON ERRORS

Item 1 Many students will check one parameter of a solution but will forget about additional parameters. Encourage students to put numbers beside what they need to check (i.e., 1 and 2), or to step out what they need to check beside the problem, to make sure they consider every parameter.

COMMON CORE | Common Core Standards

Lesson	Items	Content Standards	Mathematical Practices
6.3	1	A-CED.A.2	MP.2
5.2, 6.1	2*	F-IF.B.4, F-IF.C.7a	MP.2
6.4	3	F-BF.B.3	MP.2
5.2, 6.2	4*	F-IF.B.4, F-IF.C.7a	MP.2
6.1	5	A-CED.A.2	MP.2

* Item integrates mixed review concepts from previous modules or a previous course.

Linear Equations and Inequalities

ESSENTIAL QUESTION:

Answer: You can write and solve an equation or inequality that models any real-world problem that involves a linear relationship.

PROFESSIONAL DEVELOPMENT VIDEO

Professional Development Video

STEM Consultant Michael DiSpezio offers engaging suggestions and activities for integrating science, technology, and engineering into the math classroom.

Professional
Development
my.hrw.com

MODULE **7**

Linear Equations and Inequalities

Essential Question: How can you use linear equations and inequalities to solve real-world problems?

© Houghton Mifflin Harcourt Publishing Company • Image Credit: ©Image Source/Getty Images

REAL WORLD VIDEO
In some sports, such as boxing and wrestling, the athletes and their competitions are categorized by weight. The weight divisions are defined by specific upper and lower weight limits, which can be efficiently described using inequalities.

MODULE PERFORMANCE TASK PREVIEW

Making Weight

Wrestling is a physically demanding contact sport in which two athletes grapple on a mat with the goal of out-maneuvering and gaining control over the opponent. Opponents are matched up based on weight, and there are several weight classes. How can athletes use models to help them meet their weight class goals? Let's hit the mat and find out!

DIGITAL TEACHER EDITION

Access a full suite of teaching resources when and where you need them:

- Access content online or offline
- Customize lessons to share with your class
- Communicate with your students in real-time
- View student grades and data instantly to target your instruction where it is needed most

PERSONAL MATH TRAINER
Assessment and Intervention

Assign automatically graded homework, quizzes, tests, and intervention activities. Prepare your students with updated, Common Core-aligned practice tests.

Are YOU Ready?

Complete these exercises to review skills you will need for this module.

• Online Homework
• Hints and Help
• Extra Practice

Algebraic Expressions

Example 1

Evaluate $5x + 6y$ for $x = -9$ and $y = 7$.

$5x + 6y$

$5(-9) + 6(7)$ Substitute -9 for x and 7 for y.

$-45 + 42$ Multiply.

-3 Add.

Evaluate each expression for the given values of the variables.

1. $7p + 3q$ for $p = 2$ and $q = -6$

   -4

2. $(n + 1)^2$ for $n = -9$

   64

3. $4d - 2e - 13$ for $d = 5$ and $e = -7$

   21

4. $a^2 - b$ for $a = 4$ and $b = 5$

   11

Graphing Linear Proportional Relationships

Example 2

Tell whether the graph represents a linear proportional relationship.

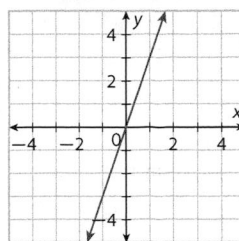

The graph of a proportional relationship is a straight line that passes through the origin.

The graph is a straight line that passes through $(0, 0)$, so it represents a linear proportional relationship.

Tell whether the graph represents a linear proportional relationship.

5.

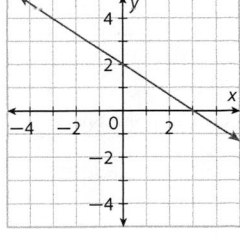

no

6.

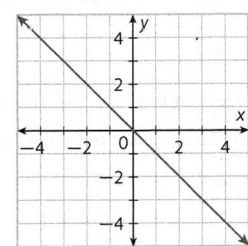

yes

Are You Ready?

ASSESS READINESS

Use the assessment on this page to determine if students need strategic or intensive intervention for the module's prerequisite skills.

ASSESSMENT AND INTERVENTION

TIER 1, TIER 2, TIER 3 SKILLS

Personal Math Trainer will automatically create a standards-based, personalized intervention assignment for your students, targeting each student's individual needs!

ADDITIONAL RESOURCES

See the table below for a full list of intervention resources available for this module.

Response to Intervention Resources also includes:
- Tier 2 Skill Pre-Tests for each Module
- Tier 2 Skill Post-Tests for each skill

	Response to Intervention		Differentiated Instruction
Tier 1 Lesson Intervention Worksheets	**Tier 2** Strategic Intervention Skills Intervention Worksheets	**Tier 3** Intensive Intervention Worksheets available online	
Reteach 7.1 Reteach 7.2 Reteach 7.3	2 Algebraic Expressions 7 Graphing Linear Proportional Relationships 10 Linear Functions 24 Writing Linear Equations	Building Block Skills 19, 22, 23, 24, 27, 40, 46, 52, 59, 70, 81, 111	Challenge worksheets Extend the Math Lesson Activities in TE

Modeling Linear Relationships

Common Core Math Standards

The student is expected to:

 A-CED.A.3

Represent constraints by equations or inequalities, and by systems of equations and/or inequalities, and interpret solutions as viable or non-viable options in a modeling context. Also S-ID.C.7, N-Q.A.1, N-Q.A.2

Mathematical Practices

 MP.4 Modeling

Language Objective

Explain to a partner how to write a linear equation based on a verbal model describing a situation.

ENGAGE

Essential Question: How can you model linear relationships given limited information?

First, determine the units for the problem. Use this information to write a verbal model for the situation. Finally, translate the verbal model into a function.

PREVIEW: LESSON PERFORMANCE TASK

View the Engage section online. Discuss the relative costs of laptops and tablet computers, and consider how a salesperson might persuade a customer to buy one or the other. Then preview the Lesson Performance Task.

7.1 Modeling Linear Relationships

Essential Question: How can you model linear relationships given limited information?

Resource Locker

⊘ Explore Modeling Linear Relationships with Slope-Intercept Form

A department store offers a frequent-buyers card to earn rewards for purchases customers make at the store. Each transaction is worth 12 points, and customers automatically earn 25 points when they sign up.

Write an equation for the function that gives the card value based on the number of transactions that have occurred.

(A) What units would be associated with the variables in this function?

The variables are card value and transactions. The units for card value are points.

(B) Complete the verbal model for the frequent-buyers card function. Include units.

Card Value (points) = Initial Value (points) + Purchase Value (points per transaction) ·

Transactions

(C) Write the function rule for the card-value function C.

$C(t) = \boxed{25} + \boxed{12}\ t$, where t is the number of transactions.

(D) For each 100 points, the customer receives a gift certificate. How many transactions will it take for the customer to earn the first gift certificate?

$100 = 25 + 12t$

$75 = 12t$

$6.25 = t$

It will take the customer more than 6 transactions, so 7 transactions, to earn the first gift certificate.

(E) What is the y-intercept for this linear function, and what does it represent?

The y-intercept is 25, and it represents the beginning value, $C(0)$, in points on a frequent-buyer card.

(F) What is the slope for this linear function, and what does it represent?

The slope is 12, and it represents the rate of change or rate of increase in points per transaction.

© Houghton Mifflin Harcourt Publishing Company

HARDCOVER PAGES 245–250

Turn to these pages to find this lesson in the hardcover student edition.

1. Discussion Use the function rule to show that the units for $C(t)$ are points.

$$\text{points} + \frac{\text{points}}{\text{transaction}} \cdot \text{transactions} = \text{points}$$

2. Critical Thinking What types of number are appropriate for the domain of $C(t)$?
The input for $C(t)$ is transactions, so only whole numbers are appropriate

for the domain.

3. Using inequalities, express the restrictions on the range of $C(t)$.
$C(t)$ are whole numbers such that $C(t) \geq 25$.

✏️ Explain   Creating and Interpreting Linear Models

You can create linear equations and inequalities to model some real-world situations.

Example   Given the real-world situation, solve the problem.

Fundraising The Band Booster Club is selling T-shirts and blanket wraps to raise money for a trip. The band director has asked the club to raise at least $1000.

The booster club president wants to know how many T-shirts and how many blanket wraps the club needs to sell to meet their goal of $1000. The T-shirts cost $10 each, and the blanket wraps cost $25 each. Write a linear equation that describes the problem, and then graph the linear equation. How can the booster club president use the sales price of each item to meet the goal?

🧩 Analyze Information

Identify the important information.

- T-shirts cost $ __10__ each.
- Blanket wraps cost $ __25__ each.
- The booster club needs to raise a total of $ __1000__ .

🧩 Formulate a Plan

The total amount of revenue earned by selling T-shirts is $ __10__ t. The total amount of revenue earned from selling blanket wraps is $ __25__ b. These two results can be added and set equal to the sales goal to find the number of T-shirts and blanket wraps that need to be sold to reach $ __1000__ . Graph this function to find all of the possible combinations of T-shirts and blanket wraps sold to reach $ __1000__ .

🧩 Solve

Write a linear equation for the sales goal.

$$\boxed{25}\ b + \boxed{10}\ t = \boxed{1000}$$

🔵 Integrate Mathematical Practices

This lesson provides an opportunity to address Mathematical Practice **MP.4**, which calls for students to "model with mathematics." Students will model real-world situations using both verbal models and linear equations. Students will then graph their linear equations and use the graphs to answer questions about the real-world situations.

EXPLORE

Modeling Linear Relationships with Slope-Intercept Form

INTEGRATE TECHNOLOGY

Students have the option of completing the Explore activity either in the book or online.

QUESTIONING STRATEGIES

? How can you use a verbal model to help you write a function model for a linear relationship? **Rewrite the verbal model by substituting numbers for known values and variables for unknown values.**

EXPLAIN

Creating and Interpreting Linear Models

AVOID COMMON ERRORS

When writing equations that have two variable terms, each with a different coefficient, students may want to combine the terms so there is only one variable in the equation. Remind students that terms can be combined only when they have the same variable raised to the same power.

QUESTIONING STRATEGIES

? Why is only the first quadrant needed to show a graph modeling the number of items that need to be sold in order to reach a goal? **The number of items sold can never be negative, so all possible values will lie in the first quadrant.**

? In finding points to graph a function, why is it helpful to set x equal to 0 and then set y equal to 0? **Setting y equal to 0 and solving for x gives the x-intercept. Setting x equal to 0 and solving for y gives the y-intercept. These two points are easy to graph.**

Calculate three pairs of values for t and b, and graph a line through those points to find possible solutions. Be sure to label the graph.

t	b
0	40
50	20
100	0

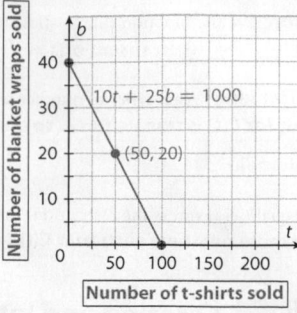

Justify and Evaluate

The x-intercept represents the number of ___T-shirts___ that need to be sold if no ___blanket wraps___ are sold. The y-intercept represents the number of ___blanket wraps___ to be sold if no ___T-shirts___ are sold. The booster club president can use the ___line___ to find the possible combinations of T-shirts and blankets to reach $___1000___.

Reflect

4. **Critical Thinking** Technically, the graph of possible combinations of T-shirts and blanket wraps that reach the goal of $1000 should be discrete, but for convenience the graph is shown as a connected line. Explain why the solutions to this problem would be only the points on the line that have whole-number coordinates.

   They can only sell whole numbers of T-shirts and whole numbers of wraps.

Your Turn

5. **Business** A sandwich shop sell sandwiches for $5 each and bottles of water for $1 each. The owner of this shop needs to earn a total of $100 by the end of the day. Write a linear equation that describes the problem; then graph the linear equation. Make sure to label both axes with appropriate titles. Then use the graph to determine how many sandwiches the shop must sell if no waters are sold.

   An equation for the sales goal is $5s + w = 100$, where s is the number of sandwiches sold, and w is the number of waters sold.

   If no waters are sold, the shop must sell 20 sandwiches.

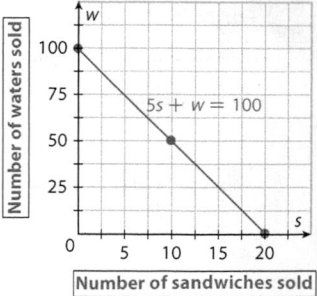

COLLABORATIVE LEARNING

Peer-to-Peer Activity

Have students work in pairs. Have each student write a description of a real-world situation that can be modeled with a linear equation, along with a question that can be solved using a graph of the equation. Have partners solve each other's problems by writing a linear equation and graphing it.

6. How can the graph of a linear function be used to find answers to a real-world problem?
The points along the graph of a linear function are answers to a real-world problem.

7. Essential Question Check-In What is the first step when modeling linear relationships given limited information?
The first step is to determine the units in the relationship.

⭐ Evaluate: Homework and Practice

- Online Homework
- Hints and Help
- Extra Practice

Food A baker sells bread for $3 a loaf and rolls for $1 each. The baker needs to sell $24 worth of baked goods by the end of the day.

1. Write a linear equation that describes the problem.

A linear equation that describes this problem is $3b + r = 24$, where b is the number of loaves of bread sold, and r is the number of rolls sold.

2. Graph the linear equation. Make sure to label both axes with appropriate titles.

3. Use the graph to approximate how many loaves of bread the baker must sell if 12 rolls are sold.

If 12 rolls are sold, the baker must sell 4 loaves of bread.

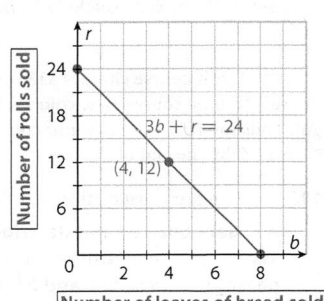

Charity A local charity is selling seats to a baseball game. Seats cost $20 each, and snacks cost an additional $5 each. The charity needs to raise $400 to consider this event a success.

4. Write a linear equation that describes the problem.

A linear equation that describes this problem is $20s + 5y = 400$, where s is the number of seats sold, and y is the number of snacks sold.

5. Graph the linear equation. Make sure to label both axes with appropriate titles.

6. Use the graph to approximate how many snacks the charity must sell if 10 seats are sold.

If 10 seats are sold, the charity must sell 40 snacks.

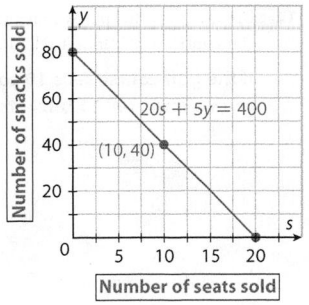

© Houghton Mifflin Harcourt Publishing Company

DIFFERENTIATE INSTRUCTION

Multiple Representations

When modeling real-world situations that involve linear relationships, some students prefer to answer questions about the situation using an equation, while others prefer to use a graph they create. Ask students to discuss how they would answer a question about a real-world situation by substituting values into an equation, and how they would answer the same question by locating points on a graph.

ELABORATE

INTEGRATE MATHEMATICAL PRACTICES
Focus on Communication

MP.3 Discuss with students the importance of labeling the axes on a coordinate graph. In order to accurately answer questions about linear models with more than one variable, students need to know which variable is represented by each axis, as well as the scale for each axis.

SUMMARIZE THE LESSON

? How can you use a linear equation to solve a real-world problem? **Write a linear equation that models the real-world problem, then use the equation to make a graph. The graph can be used to answer questions about the situation.**

EVALUATE

ASSIGNMENT GUIDE

Concepts and Skills	Practice
Explore Modeling Linear Relationships with Slope-Intercept Form	Exercises 19–21
Example 1 Creating and Interpreting Linear Models	Exercises 1–18, 22–25

INTEGRATE MATHEMATICAL PRACTICES

Focus on Math Connections

MP.1 Ask students to explain the relationship between an ordered pair that is a solution to a linear equation, and the graph of the linear equation. Students should understand that the ordered pair represents a point on the graph.

Movies A movie theater sells tickets to a new show for $10 each. The theater also sells small containers of popcorn for $6 each. The theater needs to make $3000 in order to break even on the show.

7. Write a linear equation that describes the problem.

A linear equation that describes this problem is
$10t + 6p = 3000$, where t is the number of tickets sold, and p is the number of containers of popcorn sold.

8. Graph the linear equation. Make sure to label both axes with appropriate titles.

9. Use the graph to approximate how many buckets of popcorn must the movie theater must sell if it sells 210 movie tickets.

If the movie theater sells 210 movie tickets, it must also sell **150 popcorn buckets** to break even.

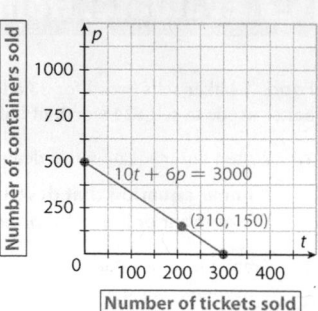

Sports A golf course charges $18 for a package including the full 18-hole course. The course also sells buckets of golf balls for $20 each. The golf course would like to earn $400 by the end of the day.

10. Write a linear equation that describes the problem.

A linear equation that describes the problem is
$18c + 20b = 400$, where c is the number of course packages purchased, and b is the number of buckets of balls purchased.

11. Graph the linear equation. Make sure to label both axes with appropriate titles.

12. Use the graph to approximate how many buckets of balls the golf course must sell if it sells 10 course packages.

If the golf course sells 10 course packages, the golf course must sell **11 buckets of balls.**

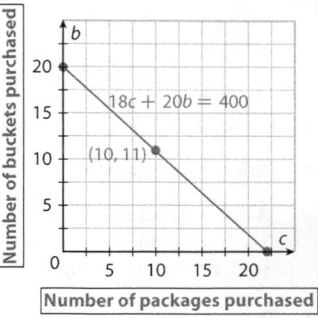

LANGUAGE SUPPORT **EL**

Connect Vocabulary

Ask students to suggest different ways the word *model* can be used. Note that the word can be used as a noun, a verb, or an adjective, all referring to the same concept. Compare the use of *modeling* in a mathematical context with other uses of the word, such as in the expressions *model train* or *fashion model*. Students should understand that just as a model train represents an actual train, and a fashion model shows how an outfit might look on an ordinary person, so do a verbal model, a linear equation, and a graph all show how two quantities are related.

Reading A bookstore sells textbooks for $80 each and notebooks for $4 each. The bookstore would like to sell $800 in merchandise by the end of the week.

13. Write a linear equation that describes the problem.

A linear equation that describes the problem is $80t + 4n = 800$, where t is the number of textbooks sold, and n is the number of notebooks sold.

14. Graph the linear equation. Make sure to label both axes with appropriate titles.

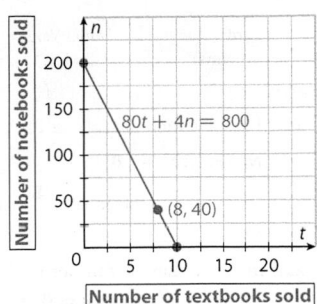

15. Use the graph to approximate how many textbooks the bookstore must sell if it sells 40 notebooks.

If the bookstore sells 40 notebooks, it must also sell 8 textbooks.

Fitness A gym is selling monthly memberships for $30 each and reusable water bottles for $7 each. The gym needs to make $1050 by the end of the month.

16. Write a linear equation that describes the problem.

A linear equation that describes the problem is $30m + 7w = 1050$, where m is the number of monthly memberships sold, and w is the number of reusable water bottles sold.

17. Graph the linear equation. Make sure to label both axes with appropriate titles.

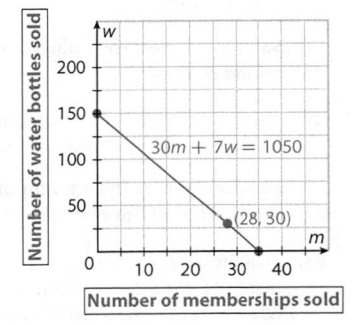

18. Use the graph to approximate the number of water bottles that the gym must sell if it sells 28 gym memberships.

If the gym sells 28 memberships, it must sell 30 water bottles.

Exercise	Depth of Knowledge (D.O.K.)	COMMON CORE Mathematical Practices
1–2	**1** Recall	**MP.2** Reasoning
3	**1** Recall	**MP.7** Using Structure
4–5	**1** Recall	**MP.2** Reasoning
6	**1** Recall	**MP.7** Using Structure
7–8	**1** Recall	**MP.2** Reasoning
9	**1** Recall	**MP.7** Using Structure
10–11	**1** Recall	**MP.2** Reasoning

AVOID COMMON ERRORS

Point out to students that the scales on the x-axis and y-axis are different on many of the coordinate grids provided in this lesson. Students will need to match the appropriate variable with its axis carefully to make sure that each point is plotted correctly.

Modeling Linear Relationships   **306**

TECHNOLOGY

Graphing equations on a calculator can provide an opportunity for students to see how the x- and y-intercepts are related to the linear equations they have written. Remind students that in order to graph a linear equation on a graphing calculator, they first need to rewrite the equation so that y is isolated on one side.

AVOID COMMON ERRORS

Remind students that in writing linear equations, only those terms that have the same variable raised to the same power can be combined. Students who combine terms incorrectly will produce graphs that do not model the original situation.

INTEGRATE MATHEMATICAL PRACTICES
Focus on Critical Thinking

MP.3 Ask students whether it is sufficient to find only the x- and y-intercepts in order to graph a linear equation. Students should understand that when both intercepts are 0, they represent the same point, $(0, 0)$. Since one point is not enough to graph a linear equation, students would need to find another point when graphing a line that passes through the origin.

JOURNAL

Have students explain how making a table of values can be useful when graphing a linear equation. Students should include how to identify the x- and y-intercepts.

307 Lesson 7.1

A shoe store offers a frequent-buyers card. Each transaction is worth 8 points, and customers automatically earn 20 points when they sign up.

19. The value of the card is a function of the number of transactions. What are the units for a card?

The units for a card are points.

20. Complete the verbal model for the transaction function. Include units.

$$\underset{\text{(points)}}{\text{Card Value}} = \underset{\text{(points)}}{\text{Initial Value}} + \boxed{\underset{\text{(points per purchase)}}{\textbf{Purchase Value}}} \cdot \boxed{\underset{\text{(purchases)}}{\textbf{Transactions}}}$$

21. Write the function rule for the transaction function.

$$N(p) = \boxed{20} + \boxed{8}\, p$$

In graphing the function, $\underline{\ 8\ }$ would be the slope and $\underline{\ 20\ }$ would be the y-intercept.

22. In each equation of the form $ax + by = c$, state a, b, and c.

$y = 2$	$a = 0, b = 1, c = 2$
$3x = 0$	$a = 3, b = 0, c = 0$
$3x + 2y = 6$	$a = 3, b = 2, c = 6$
$5x - y = 1$	$a = 5, b = -1, c = 1$
$4y + 2x = 3$	$a = 2, b = 4, c = 3$

H.O.T. Focus on Higher Order Thinking

23. Critical Thinking Suppose that you were given the graph of a monthly revenue function that is a linear relationship and are asked to interpret a point. What would it mean if the point were located on the graph, two units to the right of the origin and slightly above the y-intercept?

Sample answer: The point represents a slight profit after a two-month period of time.

24. Represent Real-World Problems Describe a situation not used in the lesson that is best described by a linear relationship.

Sample answer: The amount of money an employee earns as a function of the number of hours worked

25. Explain the Error Consider the following situation. Lacie pays a babysitter an initial fee of $35 in addition to $6 per hour. When trying to model this situation, Juan created the function $y = 35x + 6$. Explain his error.

Juan assigned the wrong coefficient to x. He should have written the equation $y = 6x + 35$.

Exercise	Depth of Knowledge (D.O.K.)	COMMON CORE Mathematical Practices
12	**1** Recall of Information	**MP.7** Using Structure
13–14	**1** Recall of Information	**MP.2** Reasoning
15	**1** Recall of Information	**MP.7** Using Structure
16–17	**1** Recall of Information	**MP.2** Reasoning
18	**1** Recall of Information	**MP.7** Using Structure
19–21	**1** Recall of Information	**MP.2** Reasoning
22	**1** Recall of Information	**MP.5** Using Tools
23–25	**2** Skills/Concepts H.O.T.	**MP.3** Logic

Lesson Performance Task

A computer store sells both tablets and laptops. One brand of tablet costs $200. That same brand of laptop costs $400. The store manager wants to sell enough of this brand of tablets and laptops to reach the sales goal of $20,000.

a. Write an equation that models the situation. Then graph the equation.

b. Interpret the x- and y-intercepts.

c. Will the store manager meet her goal if the sales team sells 45 tablets and 25 laptops? If so, explain. If not, find how many more tablets need to be sold to meet the goal.

d. Will the store manager meet her goal if the sales team sells 80 tablets and 10 laptops? If so, explain. If not, find how many more tablets need to be sold to meet the goal.

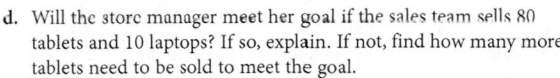

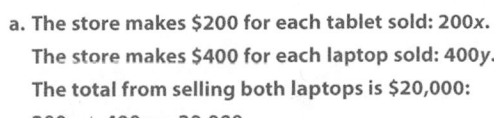

a. The store makes $200 for each tablet sold: 200x.

The store makes $400 for each laptop sold: 400y.

The total from selling both laptops is $20,000:

$$200x + 400y = 20{,}000.$$

b. The x-intercept represents the number of tablets that need to be sold in order to reach the sales goal if no laptops are sold. So, when no laptops are sold, the store must sell 100 tablets.

The y-intercept represents the number of laptops that need to be sold in order to reach the sales goal if no tablets are sold. So, when no tablets are sold, the store must sell 50 laptops.

c. $200(45) + 400(25) \overset{?}{=} 20{,}000$

$\quad\quad 19{,}000 < 20{,}000$

The store will not meet its goal selling 45 tablets and 25 laptops.

$200x + 400(25) = 20{,}000$

$\quad\quad\quad x = 50$

If 25 laptops are sold, then 50 tablets need to be sold in order to meet the goal. So, 5 more tablets need to be sold.

d. $200(80) + 400(10) \overset{?}{=} 20{,}000$

$\quad\quad 20{,}000 = 20{,}000$

The store will meet its goal selling 80 tablets and 10 laptops.

EXTENSION ACTIVITY

Have students investigate how the model for the situation in the Lesson Performance Task would change if the computer store raised its sales goal to $26,000 or lowered it to $8,000.

Students should find that the equations that model these situations are $200x + 400y = 26{,}000$ and $200x + 400y = 8000$. The graphs of these equations are parallel to each other and to the graph of the original equation. The graph for the higher goal has x-intercept 130 and y-intercept 65, and the graph for the lower goal has x-intercept 40 and y-intercept 20.

QUESTIONING STRATEGIES

? After writing a linear equation to model the situation, how can you find pairs of values that represent a number of tablets and a number of laptops sold that will meet the sales goal? **Either choose values for x and solve the equation for y, choose values for y and solve for x, or locate points on the graph whose coordinates are integers.**

? How can you find the amount of money earned by selling a particular number of laptops and tablets? **Evaluate the expression $200x + 400y$ for the number of laptops sold, y, and the number of tablets sold, x.**

INTEGRATE MATHEMATICAL PRACTICES
Focus on Modeling

MP.4 Ask students whether all points on the graph of $200x + 400y = 20{,}000$ are possible solutions in the context of the Lesson Performance Task. Students should understand that although all points on the line are solutions of the linear equation, only the positive integer values are solutions to the real-world Lesson Performance Task, because there cannot be a negative or fractional number of laptops or tablets.

Scoring Rubric
2 points: Student correctly solves the problem and explains his/her reasoning.
1 point: Student shows good understanding of the problem but does not fully solve or explain his/her reasoning.
0 points: Student does not demonstrate understanding of the problem.

Modeling Linear Relationships **308**

Using Functions to Solve One-Variable Equations

Common Core Math Standards

The student is expected to:

 A-REI.D.11

Explain why the x-coordinates of the points where the graphs of the equations $y = f(x)$ and $y = g(x)$ intersect are the solutions of the equation $f(x) = g(x)$ . . .

Mathematical Practices

COMMON CORE **MP.4 Modeling**

Language Objective

Explain to a partner how to use functions to solve one-variable equations.

ENGAGE

Essential Question: How can you use functions to solve one-variable equations?

Possible answer: Write functions related to each side of the equation, use tables or graphs to represent the functions, and find exact or approximate x-values for which the y-values of the functions are equal.

PREVIEW: LESSON PERFORMANCE TASK

View the online Engage. Discuss the photo, why someone might hire a lawyer, and different ways in which a law firm might charge for services, such as a flat rate or an hourly rate. Then preview the Lesson Performance Task.

Name_____ Class_____ Date_____

7.2 Using Functions to Solve One-Variable Equations

Essential Question: How can you use functions to solve one-variable equations?

Resource Locker

⊙ Explore   Creating Functions to Solve One-Variable Equations

Finance Susan wants to hire a babysitter for this weekend for her 3 children. She has two choices. Babysitter A charges $10 per child and $5 per hour. Babysitter B charges $15 per child and $2 per hour. When will they charge the same amount of money?

(A) Write and solve a one-variable equation to find the number of hours for which the two babysitters will charge the same amount of money. Let x represent the number of hours.

$30 + 5x = 45 + 2x$

Subtract $2x$ from both sides.

$30 + 3x = 45$

Subtract 30 from both sides.

$3x = 15$

Divide by 3.

$x = 5$

(B) Write a function for each babysitting service. Enter the two functions in a graphing calculator. Use the graphing calculator to compare their tables and find the intersection point of their graphs.

$y_1 = 30 + 5x$

$y_2 = 45 + 2x$

$f(x) = 30 + 5x$

$g(x) = 45 + 2x$

x	$f(x) = y_1$	$g(x) = y_2$
0	30	45
1	35	47
2	40	49
3	45	51
4	50	53
5	55	55
6	60	57

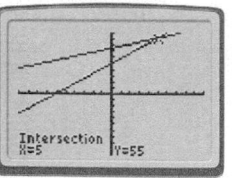

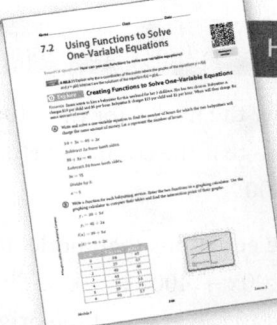

HARDCOVER PAGES 251–258

Turn to these pages to find this lesson in the hardcover student edition.

Reflect

1. **Discussion** Why are the x-coordinates of the points where the graphs of the equations $f(x) = y_1$ and $g(x) = y_2$ intersect the solutions of the equation $f(x) = g(x)$.
The intersection of the equations $f(x)$ and $g(x)$ is the solution to the equation $f(x) = g(x)$ by graphing the equation, the point that the lines have in common is found, which is the same as setting the two equations equal to each other.

2. **Discussion** How should the graph provided by the graphing calculator be changed to make the graph an accurate representation of this situation?
The answer provided by the graphing calculator is misleading because it includes negative results. Only the first quadrant should be displayed. Since this is a real-world problem, negative results are not possible and should not be included in the graph.

⊘ Explain 1   Using Intersections to Determine Approximate Solutions of One-Variable Equations

You can use tables and graphs of the functions $y_1 = f(x)$ and $y_2 = g(x)$ to solve an equation of the form $f(x) = g(x)$.

Example 1 Use a table and a graphing calculator to estimate the solution.

(A) John needs to hire a painter. Painter A is offering his services for an initial 175 in addition to 14.25 per hour. Painter B is offering her services for an initial $200 in addition to $11 per hour. For what number of hours will the two painters charge the same amount of money?

$f(x) = 175 + 14.25x$
$g(x) = 200 + 11x$

x	f(x)	g(x)
0	175	200
1	189.25	211
2	203.5	222
3	217.75	233
4	232	244
5	246.25	255
6	260.5	266
7	274.75	277
8	289	288

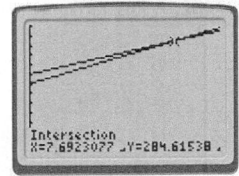

Intersection
X=7.6923077 _Y=284.61538 _

From the table, the solution must be between 7 and 8 hours.

Based on the intersection point in the graph, the solution is approximately 7.7 hours.

© Houghton Mifflin Harcourt Publishing Company • Image Credits: ©PBNJ Productions/Blend Images/Corbis

---

PROFESSIONAL DEVELOPMENT

 Integrate Mathematical Practices

This lesson provides an opportunity to address Mathematical Practice **MP.4**, which calls for students to use "modeling." Students will represent problems with one-variable equations and then with two functions, each function representing one side of the equation. Students then use tables and graphs representing the functions to find or approximate the solution of the one-variable equation and solve the problem.

Creating Functions to Solve One-Variable Equations

INTEGRATE TECHNOLOGY

Have students complete the Explore activity either in the book or online lesson.

INTEGRATE MATHEMATICAL PRACTICES
Focus on Math Connections

MP.1 Point out that each function in the Explore activity represents one side of the one-variable equation.

EXPLAIN 1

Using Intersections to Determine Approximate Solutions of One-Variable Equations

INTEGRATE MATHEMATICAL PRACTICES
Focus on Math Connections

MP.1 Discuss the differences between solving a problem by writing and solving a one-variable equation, and writing two functions and finding the x-value for which the values of the two functions are equal. Point out that it may be easier to solve the one-variable linear equation, but that the method using two functions can be used to solve more complicated equations that are not linear.

QUESTIONING STRATEGIES

? How can you use a graphing calculator to find or approximate the coordinates of the intersection of the graphs of the two functions? Use the Intersect option in the Calculator menu.

Ⓑ Georgia is in need of an electrician. Electrician A is offering his services for an initial fee of $125 in addition to $45 per hour. Electrician B is offering her services for an initial fee of $150 in addition to $38 per hour. For what number of hours will the two electricians charge the same amount of money?

$$f(x) = \frac{125 + 45x}{} \qquad g(x) = \frac{150 + 38x}{}$$

x	f(x)	g(x)
0	125	150
1	170	188
2	215	226
3	260	264
4	305	302
5	350	340
6	395	378

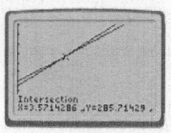

From the table, the solution must be between __3__ and __4__ hours. From the graph, the solution is about 3.6 hours.

Reflect

3. What limitations, if any, exist on the range of the functions?
   The range of the function only exists for real numbers up to the hundredths place,

   representing dollars and cents. {1, 1.01, 1.02, 1.03, . . .}

4. Why is using a graph better than using a table when finding the solution to a one-variable equation?
   If the solution must be approximated, a graphing calculator allows a closer approximation.

Your Turn

5. Sarah would like to hire a clown for her daughter's birthday party. Clown A is offering his services for an initial fee of $100 in addition to $11 per hour. Clown B is offering her services for an initial $150 fee in addition to $8 per hour. When will the two clowns charge the same amount of money? Use a table and a graphing calculator to estimate the solution.

$$f(x) = 100 + 11x \qquad g(x) = 150 + 8x$$

x	f(x)	g(x)
0	100	150
1	111	158
2	122	166
3	133	174
.		
.		
.		
16	276	278
17	287	286

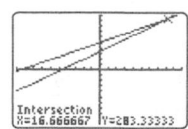

As illustrated in the table above, the solution must be between 16 and 17 hours.

From the graph, the solution to the nearest tenth is 16.7 hours.

COLLABORATIVE LEARNING

Peer-to-Peer Activity

Have students work in groups of two. Each member of the group will solve the same real-world problem about determining when two different rates will have the same value. One student should solve the problem by writing and solving a one-variable equation. The other student should solve the problem by writing two functions and finding the point of intersection of their graphs. Students can verify their work by comparing answers and then discuss the differences between the two methods.

 **Explain 2** **Using Intercepts to Determine Approximate Solutions for One-Variable Equations**

When the amount in a bank account is less than the amount of the payment due, an automatic payment would overdraw the account. That is, the value of the account would be less than zero. In discrete situations like the ones described in the examples, there is no actual point at which the value of the account would be zero, unless the amount in the account is a multiple of the monthly payment. However, you can use the related continuous functions to make an estimation of when the account would theoretically reach zero.

Example 2 Use a table to estimate the solution to the given situation. Then use a graphing calculator to approximate the x-intercept.

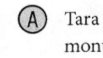 Tara has $800 in a bank account. that she uses to make automatic payments of her $101.51 monthly cable bill. If Tara stops making deposits to that account, when would automatic payments make the value of the account zero?

The function that describes the amount in the account after x automatic payments is $f(x) = 800 - 101.51x$.

The other function that describes the situation is $g(x) = 0$.

x	f(x)	g(x)
0	800	0
1	698.49	0
2	596.98	0
3	495.47	0
4	393.96	0
5	292.45	0
6	190.94	0
7	89.43	0
8	−12.08	0

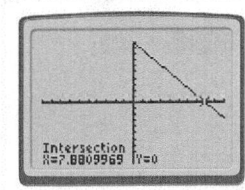

From the table, the value of the account would be 0 between 7 and 8 months. From the graph, the x-intercept is about 7.9.

 Craig has $1850 dollars in a bank account. that he uses to make automatic payments of $400.73 on his car loan. If Craig stops making deposits to that account, when would automatic payments make the value of the account zero?

The function that describes the amount in the account after x automatic payments is

$$f(x) = \underline{1850} - \underline{400.73}\ x.$$

The other function that describes the situation is $g(x) = \underline{0}$.

x	f(x)	g(x)
0	1850	0
1	1449.27	0
2	1048.54	0
3	647.81	0
4	247.08	0
5	−153.65	0

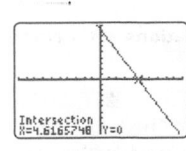

From the table, the value of the account would be 0 between ____4____

and ____5____ months. From the graph, the x-intercept is about ____4.6____.

EXPLAIN 2

Using Intercepts to Determine Approximate Solutions for One-Variable Equations

QUESTIONING STRATEGIES

? How can you use a graphing calculator to find or approximate the x-intercept of the graph of the first function? Use the Intersect option in the Calculator menu.

DIFFERENTIATE INSTRUCTION

Critical Thinking

Discuss with students how they can find closer approximations for the solution of a one-variable equation using tables, when an exact answer is not obtained using integer values for x. Guide students to see that once they have determined the two integers that the solution must be between, they can test decimal values between those numbers to find an even closer approximation.

ELABORATE

INTEGRATE MATHEMATICAL PRACTICES
Focus on Critical Thinking

MP.3 Discuss when the graphs of two linear functions have a point of intersection. Guide students to understand that the graphs have a point of intersection when the slopes of the graphs are not equal or when one is horizontal and one is vertical (If the slopes were equal, the graphs would be parallel.)

SUMMARIZE THE LESSON

? How can you use functions to solve a one-variable equation? Write a function representing each side of the equation; use tables or graphs to represent the functions; then find exact or approximate *x*-values for which the *y*-values of the functions are equal or approximately equal.

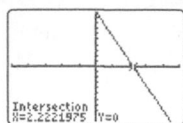

---

6. How are the examples in this section similar to the examples in the previous section?
They are similar to the examples in the first Explain section, except that in this situation one of the equations is $g(x) = 0$ and its graph is a horizontal line

7. Discussion Name one way to better approximate the solution without the use of technology.
Sample Answer: One way to make the solution more accurate without technology is by using smaller intervals for the table.

Your Turn

8. Cassandra has $2000 dollars in a bank account that she uses to make automatic $900.01 mortgage payments each month. If Cassandra stops making deposits to that account, when would automatic payments make the value of the account zero? Use a table to estimate the solution. Then use a graphing calculator to approximate the *x*-intercept.

The functions are $f(x) = 2000 - 900.01x$ and $g(x) = 0$.

x	f(x)	g(x)
0	2000	0
1	1099.99	0
2	199.98	0
3	−700.03	0

From the table, the value of the account would be 0 between 2 and 3 months. From the graph, the *x*-intercept is about 2.2.

💬 Elaborate

9. Throe would like to hire a guitarist for his charity concert. Guitarists A and B are offering their services to Throe but each guitarist charges different initial fees and hourly rates. How can Throe check to see when they will charge the same amount of money? Name three ways to perform this task.
1. Graphing
2. Write two equations, set them equal to each other, and solve.
3. Reasoning

10. Essential Question Check-In What is the first step in using functions to solve one-variable equations?
The first step in using functions to solve a one-variable equation is to write functions related to each side of the equation.

LANGUAGE SUPPORT **EL**

Connect Vocabulary

Discuss how the word *approximate* is used. Make sure that students understand that sometimes the word is being used as an adjective and sometimes as a verb. Point out the difference in pronunciation of the two usages.

Use a table to find the solution to each situation.

1. Bridget needs an actor. Actor A is offering her services for an initial $250 in addition to $50 per day. Actor B is offering her services for an initial $200 in addition to $60 per day. When will the two actors charge the same amount of money?

x	$f(x) = 250 + 50x$	$g(x) = 200 + 60x$
0	250	200
1	300	260
2	350	320
3	400	380
4	450	440
5	500	500

The two actors will charge the same amount of money after 5 days.

2. Yuma needs a singer. Singer A is offering her services for an initial $50 in addition to $20 per hour. Singer B is offering his services for an initial $100 in addition to $10 per hour. When will the two singers charge the same amount of money?

x	$f(x) = 50 + 20x$	$g(x) = 100 + 10x$
0	50	100
1	70	110
2	90	120
3	110	130
4	130	140
5	150	150

The two singers will charge the same amount of money after 5 hours.

EVALUATE

ASSIGNMENT GUIDE

Concepts and Skills	Practice
Explore Creating Functions to Solve One-Variable Equations	Exercises 1–2, 23
Example 1 Using Intersections to Determine Approximate Solutions of One-Variable Equations	Exercises 3–8, 15–18, 26
Example 2 Using Intercepts to Determine Approximate Solutions for One-Variable Equations	Exercises 9–14, 19–22, 24–25

Exercise	Depth of Knowledge (D.O.K.)	COMMON CORE Mathematical Practices
1–22	**2** Skills/Concepts	**MP.4** Modeling
23	**2** Skills/Concepts	**MP.5** Using Tools
24–26	**3** Strategic Thinking H.O.T.	**MP.3** Logic

INTEGRATE MATHEMATICAL PRACTICES

Focus on Math Connections

MP.1 Students have many different ways to solve one-variable equations: algebraically, by using tables representing functions, and by graphing functions. Challenge students to solve some problems using more than one method, and discuss the differences between the different methods.

3. Sam needs a web designer. Designer A is offering her services for an initial $500 in addition to $100 per hour. Designer B is offering her services for an initial $600 in addition to $50 per hour. When will the two designers charge the same amount of money?

x	$f(x) = 500 + 100x$	$g(x) = 600 + 50x$
0	500	600
1	600	650
2	700	700

The two designers will charge the same amount of money after 2 hours.

4. Lindsey needs a jeweler to repair her earrings. Jeweler A is offering her services for an initial $125 in addition to $15 per hour. Jeweler B is offering his services for an initial $140 in addition to $12 per hour. When will the two jewelers charge the same amount of money?

x	$f(x) = 125 + 15x$	$g(x) = 140 + 12x$
0	125	140
1	140	152
2	155	164
3	170	176
4	185	188
5	200	200

The two jewelers will charge the same amount of money after 5 hours.

5. Stan needs a mime. Mime A is offering his services for an initial $75 in addition to $25 per hour. Mime B is offering her services for an initial $30 in addition to $40 per hour. When will the two mimes charge the same amount of money?

x	$f(x) = 75 + 25x$	$g(x) = 30 + 40x$
0	75	30
1	100	70
2	125	110
3	150	150

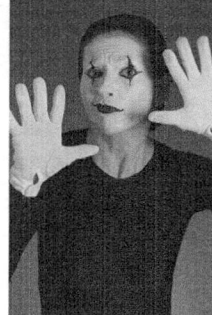

The two mimes will charge the same amount of money after 3 hours.

6. Lottie needs a driver. Driver A is offering his services for an initial $200 in addition to $80 per hour. Driver B is offering his services for an initial $230 in addition to $70 per hour. When will the two drivers charge the same amount of money?

x	$f(x) = 200 + 80x$	$g(x) = 230 + 70x$
0	200	230
1	280	300
2	360	370
3	440	440

The two drivers will charge the same amount of money after 3 hours.

7. Garrett needs a baseball coach. Coach A is offering her services for an initial $5000 in addition to $450 per hour. Coach B is offering her services for an initial $4000 in addition to $700 per hour. When will the two coaches charge the same amount of money?

x	$f(x) = 5000 + 450x$	$g(x) = 4000 + 70x$
0	5000	4000
1	5450	4700
2	5900	5400
3	6350	6100
4	6800	6800

The two coaches will charge the same amount of money after 4 hours.

8. Zena needs a salesperson. Salesperson A is offering his services for an initial $50 in addition to $5 per hour. Salesperson B is offering her services for $15 per hour. When will the two salespeople charge the same amount of money?

x	$f(x) = 50 + 5x$	$g(x) = 15x$
0	50	0
1	55	15
2	60	30
3	65	45
4	70	60
5	75	75

The two salespeople will charge the same amount of money after 5 hours.

AVOID COMMON ERRORS

After finding or approximating the point of intersection of two graphs using a calculator, students may use the y-value instead of x-value as the answer. Have students explain the meanings of the values on the x-axis and the y-axis for each problem so that they realize that they need to use the x-value as the answer.

In Exercises 9–14, each person uses the given bank account to make automatic monthly payments and stops making deposits to the account. Use a table to find when automatic payments would make the value of the account zero.

9. Charles has $1600 dollars in his account and makes automatic $400 monthly payments on a utility bill.

x	f(x) = 1600 − 400x	g(x) = 0
0	1600	0
1	1200	0
2	800	0
3	400	0
4	0	0

in 4 months

10. Lena has $2800 dollars in her account and makes automatic $700 monthly payments on a cell phone bill.

x	f(x) = 2800 − 700x	g(x) = 0
0	2800	0
1	2100	0
2	1400	0
3	700	0
4	0	0

in 4 months

11. Malcolm has $3600 dollars in his account and makes automatic $600 monthly mortgage payments.

x	f(x) = 3600 − 600x	g(x) = 0
0	3600	0
1	3000	0
2	2400	0
3	1800	0
4	1200	0
5	600	0
6	0	0

in 6 months

12. Isabelle has $4900 dollars in her account and makes automatic $700 monthly payments on a home loan.

x	$f(x) = 4900 - 700x$	$g(x) = 0$
0	4900	0
1	4200	0
2	3500	0
3	2800	0
4	2100	0
5	1400	0
6	700	0
7	0	0

in 7 months

13. Larry's small business has $60,000 dollars in its account and makes automatic monthly payments that total $12,000.

x	$f(x) = 60,000 - 12,000x$	$g(x) = 0$
0	60,000	0
1	48,000	0
2	36,000	0
3	24,000	0
4	12,000	0
5	0	0

in 5 months

14. Sharon has $12,000 dollars in her account and makes automatic monthly payments that total $6000.

x	$f(x) = 12,000 - 6000x$	$g(x) = 0$
0	12,000	0
1	6000	0
2	0	0

in 2 months

CRITICAL THINKING

Discuss with students when identifying the x-intercept is useful for finding the intersection of the graphs of two linear functions. Students should understand that finding the x-intercept is useful only when one of the functions is $y = 0$.

Using Functions to Solve One-Variable Equations   **318**

Use a graphing calculator to find the solution to each situation.

15. Aaron needs to hire a waiter. Waiter A is offering his services for an initial $25 in addition to $5.25 per hour. Waitress B is offering her services for an initial $30 in addition to $4.25 per hour. When will the two waiters charge the same amount of money?

Graph Y1 = 25 + 5.25X and Y2 = 30 + 4.25X.

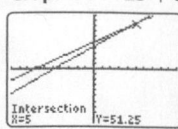

At 5 hours, both waiters will charge the same amount, $51.25.

16. Finance Lucy needs to hire a host. Host A is offering his services for an initial $60 in addition to $13.25 per hour. Hostess B is offering her services for an initial $75 in addition to $11.50 per hour. When will the two hosts charge the same amount of money?

Graph Y1 = 60 + 13.25X and Y2 ≈ 75 + 11.50X.

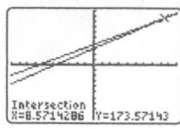

At approximately 8.6 hours, both hosts will charge the about the same amount.

17. Ida needs to hire a singer for her wedding. Singer A is offering his services for an initial $90 in addition to $13.15 per hour. Singer B is offering her services for an initial $100 in addition to $11.85 per hour. When will the two singers charge the same amount of money?

Graph Y1 = 90 + 13.15X and Y2 = 100 + 11.85X.

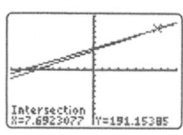

At approximately 7.7 hours, both singers will charge the about the same amount.

18. Emily needs to hire a pilot. Pilot A is offering his services for an initial $32 in addition to $22.18 per hour. Pilot B is offering her services for an initial $46.75 in addition to $18.24 per hour. When will the two pilots charge the same amount of money?

Graph Y1 = 32 + 22.18X and Y2 = 46.75 + 18.24X.

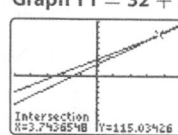

At approximately 3.7 hours, both pilots will charge the about the same amount.

In Exercises 19–22, each person uses the given bank account to make automatic monthly payments and stops making deposits to the account. Use a graphing calculator to approximate the *x*-intercept of the point where the value of the account would be zero.

19. Rafael has $1875 in his account and makes automatic monthly payments of $225.18 for a smartphone service plan.

Graph Y1 = 1875 − 225.18X and Y2 = 0.

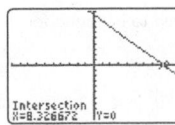

about 8.3

20. Zach has $43,408 dollars in his account and makes automatic monthly rent payments of $4500.

Graph Y1 = 43,408 − 4500X and Y2 = 0.

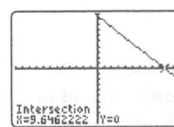

about 9.6

21. Rebecca has $326.74 dollars in her account and makes automatic monthly payments of $113.51 for bike rental.

Graph Y1 = 326.74 − 113.51X and Y2 = 0.

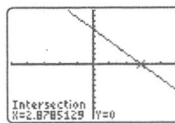

about 2.9

Have students describe the steps needed to find or approximate the point of intersection of the graphs of two linear functions using a graphing calculator. Students should note which buttons to use and in which order.

22. Greg has $1464.54 in his account and makes automatic monthly payments of $321.46 for a car loan.

Graph Y1 = 1464.54 − 321.46X and Y2 = 0.

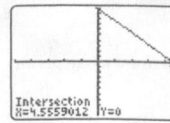

about 4.6

23. Given that $f(x)$ and $g(x)$ are equal, write a one-variable equation. No solutions need to be found for this problem.

   a. $f(x) = 45x + 12$, $g(x) = 244x + 234$ **$45x + 12 = 244x + 234$**

   b. $f(x) = 13x + 48$, $g(x) = 24x + 47$ **$13x + 48 = 24x + 47$**

   c. $f(x) = 71x + 145$, $g(x) = 43x + 17$ **$71x + 145 = 43x + 17$**

   d. $f(x) = 8x + 11$, $g(x) = 55x + 123$ **$8x + 11 = 55x + 123$**

H.O.T. **Focus on Higher Order Thinking**

24. **Critical Thinking** Given a table of values for a one-variable linear equation, how can $f(x)$ be found?

   Given a table of values, $f(x)$ can be found by taking the first term as a constant and taking the difference between any two values, which will be the leading coefficient.

25. **Communicate Mathematical Ideas** In a real-world problem one variable is solved with a graphing calculator. What quadrants of the graph are never used for the problem?

   Quadrants II and III are never used for a real-world problem in one variable.

26. **Explain the Error** A student was trying to solve a problem and came up with this table as a result:

Time (Weeks)	Profit($)
1	200
2	500
3	800
4	1100
5	1400
6	1700
7	2000
8	2300
9	2600

The student stated that the range of this function is all real numbers. What is wrong with the student's answer?

The range is not all real numbers because money cannot be expressed in anything less than cents. The actual range is the set of all positive real numbers up to the hundredths place: {100.01, 100.02 are solutions, but 100.001 is not a solution}.

Lesson Performance Task

Laura wants to hire a lawyer to file deeds for some properties she owns. The graph illustrates costs for her two choices of lawyers. Using the points on the graph, construct a table of results and two equations. Which lawyer is a better choice for her if she has 8 deeds? Which lawyer is a better choice if she has 2 deeds? Why? Over the long run, which lawyer is more cost-effective?

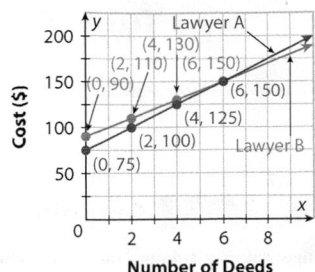

x	Lawyer A f(x)	Lawyer B g(x)
0	75	90
2	100	110
4	125	130
6	150	150
8	175	170

$f(x) = 75 + 12.5x$

$g(x) = 90 + 10x$

If Laura has eight deeds to file, Lawyer B is a better choice. If she has two deeds, Lawyer A is a better choice.

Lawyer B is a better choice when Laura has many deeds because the lawyer charges a much lower hourly rate than Lawyer A. However, Lawyer A is a choice when Laura has only a few deeds because the lawyer's initial cost is lower. Over the long run, Lawyer B is more cost effective.

EXTENSION ACTIVITY

Have students research the deed recorder office for their county to find the cost of getting a copy of a deed versus a certified copy of a deed. Then have students write and graph functions for each type of copy; the functions should associate the number of pages in a deed with the cost of getting a copy of the deed. Students may find that for an uncertified copy there is a rate per page, while for a certified copy there is a flat fee for the first x pages and then another rate for every additional page over x.

AVOID COMMON ERRORS

When the slopes of two lines are very close numerically, their graphs can easily be confused. Have students color code the graphs of Lawyers A and B by highlighting the line for Lawyer A and its label with one color and the line for Lawyer B and its label with another color.

INTEGRATE MATHEMATICAL PRACTICES
Focus on Critical Thinking

MP.3 Typically, people think *more* is better, but for the person paying for something, *less* is better. Have a volunteer tell if it is a better choice for Laura to hire Lawyer A or Lawyer B. Discuss with students when, if ever, the better choice would be to hire the lawyer that charges more.

Scoring Rubric
2 points: Student correctly solves the problem and explains his/her reasoning.
1 point: Student shows good understanding of the problem but does not fully solve or explain his/her reasoning.
0 points: Student does not demonstrate understanding of the problem.

Linear Inequalities in Two Variables

Common Core Math Standards

The student is expected to:

 **A-REI.D.12**

Graph the solutions to a linear inequality in two variables as a halfplane... Also A-CED.A.3

Mathematical Practices

 MP.6 Precision

Language Objective

Explain to a partner how an inequality represents a situation. Explain how to graph a linear inequality in two variables.

ENGAGE

Essential Question: How do you write and graph linear inequalities in two variables?

You write a linear inequality as you would write an equation, using an appropriate inequality symbol instead of an equal sign. To graph a linear inequality in two variables, graph the related linear equation using a solid or dashed boundary line, and shade the appropriate half-plane containing the solutions.

PREVIEW: LESSON PERFORMANCE TASK

View the Engage section online. Discuss the photo and why there is more than one combination of number of candles and number of bars of soap sold that will raise the income to cover the cost of the trip. Then preview the Lesson Performance Task.

7.3 Linear Inequalities in Two Variables

Essential Question: How do you write and graph linear inequalities in two variables?

Resource Locker

⊘ Explore Graphing Linear Inequalities Involving ≤ or ≥

A **linear inequality in two variables** can be written in one of the following forms: $Ax + By < C$, $Ax + By \leq C$, $Ax + By \geq C$, or $Ax + By > C$, where A, B, and C are constants and A and B are not both 0. The **solution of an inequality in two variables** is one or more ordered pairs that make the inequality true.

Some students at a music recital perform 3-minute pieces and some perform 5-minute pieces. The total time of this part of the recital needs to be at least 30 minutes long. An inequality that represents this is $3x + 5y \geq 30$.

(A) Solve the inequality for y.

$$3x + 5y \geq 30$$
$$5y \geq 30 - 3x$$
$$y \geq \frac{30}{5} - \frac{3x}{5}$$
$$y \geq -\frac{3}{5}x + 6$$

(C) Graph the boundary line. The inequality $y \geq -\frac{3}{5}x + 6$ uses the symbol $\geq$, so the line will be solid, to show that the points on the boundary line are part of the solution set.

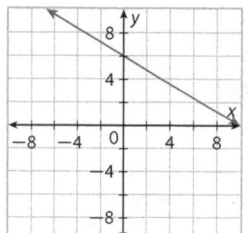

(B) Replace the inequality symbol in the inequality with an equal sign. The inequality is now an equation that will be used to graph a line. The line is called the **boundary line** of the solution set of the inequality. Write the equation of the line.

$$y = -\frac{3}{5}x + 6$$

(D) The part of the coordinate plane containing the solution set to the inequality, which may include the line, is called a **half-plane**. Since the inequality symbol is $\geq$, two conditions must be met. (1) The boundary line is solid, and (2) the half-plane above the boundary line is shaded. Shade the appropriate part of the graph.

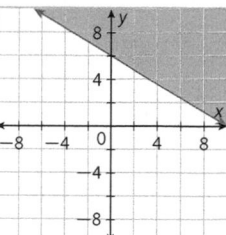

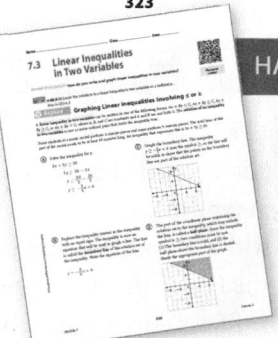

HARDCOVER PAGES 259–264

Turn to these pages to find this lesson in the hardcover student edition.

Ⓔ Check the solution by filling in the table.

Point	Above or Below Line	Inequality	True or False?
$(0, 0)$	Below	$3\left(\boxed{0}\right) + 5\left(\boxed{0}\right) \geq 30$	False
$(8, 8)$	Above	$3\left(\boxed{8}\right) + 5\left(\boxed{8}\right) \geq 30$	True

Reflect

1. **Discussion** How would the graph change if the inequality were $>$ instead of $\geq$?
   The boundary line would be dashed, rather than a solid line.

⊘ **Explain 1** **Graphing Linear Inequalities Involving < or >**

Example 1 Graph the solution set for the given inequality using the method given.

Ⓐ Graph $21 - 3y < 9x$ using a graphing calculator.

Solve the inequality for y.

$21 - 3y < 9x$

$-3y < 9x - 21$

$y > -3x + 7$

Enter the equation into Y_1 in the graphing calculator.

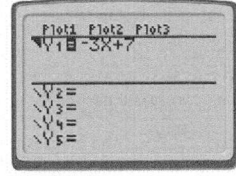

Go to the far left and hit enter two times until it looks like this.

Now view the graph. Note that the calculator will draw a solid line. Determine whether the line should be solid or not.

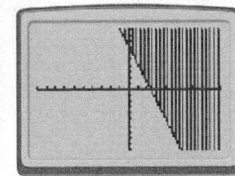

Since the inequality is strictly greater than, the line should be dashed.

© Houghton Mifflin Harcourt Publishing Company

PROFESSIONAL DEVELOPMENT

Math Background

Students may accept that multiplying or dividing by a negative number reverses an inequality's sign but still not understand the reversal at a fundamental level. The idea is to use transformations that produce equivalent inequalities, that is, inequalities with the same solution set. As an illustration, the integers 2 and 3 are in the solution set of $x > 1$. When multiplied by -1, the inequality should be reversed, so the equivalent inequality is $-x < -1$. Notice that the integers 2 and 3 are also in the solution set of this new inequality. If the inequality symbol is not reversed, the inequality becomes $-x > -1$ and 2 and 3 are not in the solution set.

EXPLORE

Graphing Linear Inequalities Involving ≥ or ≤

INTEGRATE TECHNOLOGY

Have students complete the Explore activity either in the book or online lesson.

QUESTIONING STRATEGIES

❓ When is an ordered pair a solution of an inequality? **When the first coordinate is substituted for x and the second coordinate is substituted for y, the resulting inequality is true.**

❓ If an ordered pair is a solution of an inequality, how is that shown on the graph of the inequality? **The point appears in the shaded part of the graph.**

EXPLAIN 1

Graphing Linear Inequalities Involving < or >

QUESTIONING STRATEGIES

❓ Why is the boundary line for an inequality involving < or > dashed rather than solid? **The dashed line indicates that points on the line are *not* part of the graph.**

❓ What is signified by shading an entire half-plane on the graph? Explain. **A shaded half-plane indicates that all points in that half-plane are included in the solution set of the inequality. Every point within this half-plane makes the inequality true.**

AVOID COMMON ERRORS

Because of their work graphing linear equations, some students tend to draw all boundary lines as solid lines. Encourage students to look at the inequality symbol before drawing their boundary lines. If it is < or >, then the boundary line should be dashed.

Linear Inequalities in Two Variables   **324**

Ⓑ Graph $-14 + 2y < -x$ by hand.

Solve the inequality for y.

$$-14 + 2y < -x$$

$$+ 2y < -x + \boxed{14}$$

$$y < \frac{-x + \boxed{14}}{\boxed{2}}$$

$$y < -\boxed{\frac{1}{2}}x + \boxed{7}$$

Graph the boundary line. The inequality uses the symbol ____<____, so use a ___dashed___ line to show that points on the line ___are not___ part of the solution.

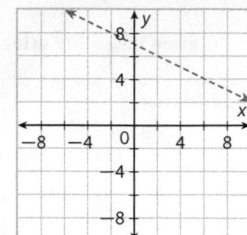

Shade the appropriate part of the graph. The inequality uses the symbol ____<____, so shade ___below___ the boundary line.

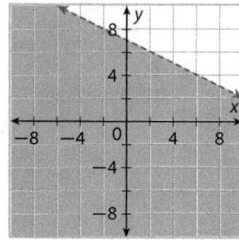

Check the solution by filling in the table.

Point	Above or Below Line	Inequality	True or False?
(0, 0)	Below	$-14 + 2\boxed{0} < -\boxed{0}$	True
(8, 8)	Above	$-14 + 2\boxed{8} < -\boxed{8}$	False

COLLABORATIVE LEARNING

Small Group Activity

Organize students into groups of three or four. Instruct each group to think of a scenario that can be modeled by an inequality in two variables. Have each group create a poster that includes a description of the scenario, the inequality that represents it, a graph of the inequality, and a table showing at least three possible solutions and three ordered pairs that are not solutions. Have each group hang their poster in the classroom.

2. Is $(6, 4)$ part of the solution?
No, because it is on the boundary line, which is not part of the solution set.

Your Turn

Graph the inequality.

3. $3 - y < -5x$

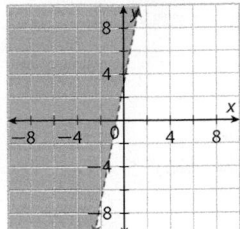

Solve the inequality for y.

$3 - y < -5x$

$-y < -5x - 3$

$y > 5x + 3$

4. $10x + 8y < 64$

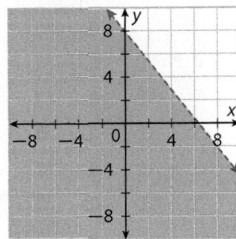

Solve the inequality for y.

$10x + 8y < 64$

$8y < -10x + 64$

$y < -\frac{5}{4}x + 8$

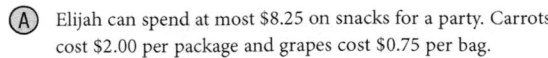 **Explain 2** **Creating Models with Linear Inequalities**

Example 2 Write a linear inequality to represent the information or graph given.

(A) Elijah can spend at most $8.25 on snacks for a party. Carrots cost $2.00 per package and grapes cost $0.75 per bag.

Write a linear inequality to describe the situation.

Let x represent the number of packages of carrots and let y represent the number of bags of grapes.

Use $\leq$ for "at most".

Total cost of carrots	Plus	Total cost of grapes	is at most	$8.25
$2x$	$+$	$0.75y$	$\leq$	8.25

Solve the inequality for y.

$2x + 0.75y \leq 8.25$

$0.75y \leq -2x + 8.25$

$y \leq -\frac{8}{3}x + 11$

EXPLAIN 2

Creating Models with Linear Inequalities

QUESTIONING STRATEGIES

? How can you tell which side of the boundary line should be shaded? Choose a point on one side of the boundary line. Substitute the x- and y-values into the inequality. If the inequality is true, shade the side that the point is on. If the inequality is false, shade the other side.

? Why do you test a point that is not on the boundary line? If the point is on the boundary line, you cannot tell which half-plane should be shaded.

INTEGRATE MATHEMATICAL PRACTICES
Focus on Critical Thinking

MP.3 Discuss with students what kinds of ordered pairs of numbers are reasonable solutions of real-world problems. In many real-world situations, reasonable solutions must be pairs of nonnegative numbers. Sometimes only pairs of whole numbers are reasonable solutions.

DIFFERENTIATE INSTRUCTION

Communicating Math

Many students may benefit from explaining and interpreting an example's solution to one or more other students. Make sure that students explain how they created the inequality, how they graphed the inequality, and how they interpreted the graph.

AVOID COMMON ERRORS

Some students may attempt to determine which half-plane to shade based on the direction of the inequality in relation to one of the variables. While this method works if students understand what they are doing, suggest that they always test one or more points to determine which half-plane to shade. Recommend that students include the point (0, 0) in their tests, provided it is not on the boundary line, because the calculations are usually easy to do.

INTEGRATE TECHNOLOGY

Students can graph their inequalities by using a graphing calculator, entering the corresponding function solved for y, and selecting the appropriate shading (above or below) and boundary line (solid or dashed).

INTEGRATE MATHEMATICAL PRACTICES

Focus on Patterns

MP.8 Emphasize that the simplest way to graph an inequality is to first write the inequality with y isolated on one side of the inequality symbol and with the other side in $mx + b$ form. When inequalities are written in this form, it is easy to see what the boundary line is and whether the shading needs to be above or below it.

Ⓑ

The slope of the line is ___$\frac{4}{3}$___.

The y-intercept of the line is ___3___.

The boundary line is $y = \boxed{\frac{4}{3}x + 3}$.

The boundary line on the graph is ___dashed___ and the shaded region is ___above___ the graph so the symbol will be ___>___.

So the inequality is $\boxed{y > \frac{4}{3}x + 3}$.

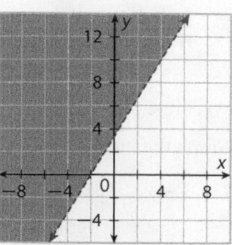

Your Turn

5. Complete the linear inequality that represents the relationship shown in the table: $y \boxed{\leq} 2x$

x	y
−3	−8
−2	−10
−1	−2.5
0	0
1	1
2	4
3	0

6. Ramona has $18 that she can spend on food for her dog. Dry dog food costs $5.50 per small bag and wet dog food costs $2.00 per can. Write a linear inequality that describes how many bags and cans of dog food Ramona can buy.

Let x represent the number of bags of dry food and let y represent the number of cans of wet food. Use $\leq$.

Total cost of dry food	Plus	Total cost of wet food	is at most	$18
5.5x	+	2y	$\leq$	18

Solve the inequality for y.

$5.5x + 2y \leq 18$

$2y \leq 18 - 5.5x$

$y \leq \dfrac{18 - 5.5x}{2}$

$y \leq 9 - \dfrac{11}{4}x$

LANGUAGE SUPPORT EL

Connect Vocabulary

Discuss the structure of the word *inequality*. An inequality represents quantities that are not equal. Remind English learners that the root *equa-* means *equal* and the prefix *in-* added to the root word nullifies it, or means *not*. For example:

Inequality means the condition of being not equal.

Inability means the condition of not being able to do something.

Inappropriate means not appropriate.

7. Describe a real-world problem situation that can be represented by a linear inequality in two variables. Write an inequality and explain what each part means. Are there any solutions of the solution set that are not solutions to the problem?

Answers may vary. Sample answer: Brian is buying new clothes. He knows that jeans cost

$20 and shirts cost $12. Brian can spend at most $120.

Let x represent the number of jeans and y represent the number of shirts.

$20x + 12y \le 120$

Yes, the solution $\left(2, 6\frac{2}{3}\right)$ is part of the solution set but is not a solution to the problem. You

cannot buy $\frac{2}{3}$ of a shirt.

8. How can you tell which side of the boundary line should be shaded?

Choose a point on one side of the boundary line. Substitute the x- and y-values into the

inequality. If the inequality is true, shade the side that the point is on. If the inequality is

false, shade the other side.

9. **Essential Question Check-In** How do you graph a linear inequality in two variables?

Graph the linear inequality as if it were a linear equation to establish the boundary line.

If the inequality symbol used is < or >, the boundary line is dashed. If it is $\le$ or $\ge$, the

boundary line is solid. To determine which side of the boundary line to shade, choose at

least one test point and check whether it is a solution to the inequality. If it is, shade the

side of the boundary line on which the test point lies. If it is not, shade the other side.

ELABORATE

CONNECT VOCABULARY [EL]

Discuss how the words and phrases used to describe a real-world scenario indicate which inequality symbols to use. For example, if a problem uses the expressions *more than* or *less than*, the inequality will use the > or < symbol, while if a problem includes *at least*, *at most*, or *no more than*, the inequality will use the $\ge$ or $\le$ symbol.

SUMMARIZE THE LESSON

Have students complete the graphic organizer by identifying whether the points in each location make the inequality true or false.

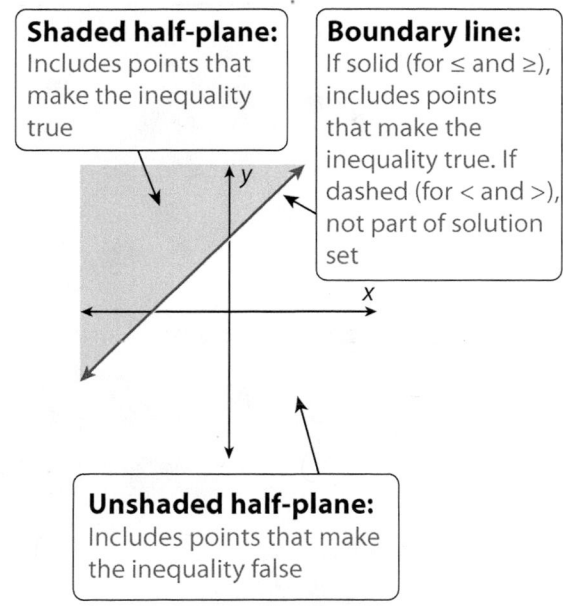

Shaded half-plane: Includes points that make the inequality true

Boundary line: If solid (for $\le$ and $\ge$), includes points that make the inequality true. If dashed (for < and >), not part of solution set

Unshaded half-plane: Includes points that make the inequality false

EVALUATE

ASSIGNMENT GUIDE

Concepts and Skills	Practice
Explore Graphing Linear Inequalities Involving $\geq$ or $\leq$	Exercises 1–8, 10–11, 23
Example 1 Graphing Linear Inequalities Involving $<$ or $>$	Exercises 9, 12–16, 24, 26
Example 2 Creating Models with Linear Inequalities	Exercises 17–22, 25

- Online Homework
- Hints and Help
- Extra Practice

In order to graph the inequality using a graphing calculator, tell what function to enter for the boundary line, whether the graph should be shaded above or below the line, and if the boundary line is included in the solution.

1. $30 + 5y \geq 4x$

Solve the inequality for y.

$30 + 5y \geq 4x$

$5y \geq 4x - 30$

$y \geq \dfrac{4}{5}x - 6$

Boundary line: $y = \dfrac{4}{5}x - 6$

above; boundary included

2. $-\dfrac{1}{2} + y \leq 6x$

Solve the inequality for y.

$-\dfrac{1}{2} + y \leq 6x$

$y \leq 6x + \dfrac{1}{2}$

Boundary line: $y = 6x + \dfrac{1}{2}$

below; boundary included

3. $-\dfrac{1}{2}y \leq -\dfrac{3}{4}x + \dfrac{5}{4}$

Solve the inequality for y.

$-\dfrac{1}{2}y \leq -\dfrac{3}{4}x + \dfrac{5}{4}$

$y \geq \dfrac{3}{2}x - \dfrac{5}{2}$

Boundary line: $y = \dfrac{3}{2}x - \dfrac{5}{2}$

above; boundary included

4. $-\dfrac{8}{3}x \geq y + 9$

Solve the inequality for y.

$-\dfrac{8}{3}x \geq y + 9$

$-\dfrac{8}{3}x - 9 \geq y$

Boundary line: $y = -\dfrac{8}{3}x - 9$

below; boundary included

Graph the inequality.

5. $4x - 4y \geq 28$

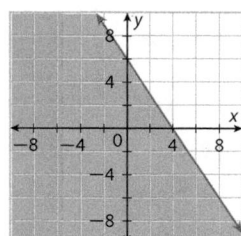

Solve the inequality for y.

$4x - 4y \geq 28$

$-4y \geq 28 - 4x$

$y \leq x - 7$

6. $3x + 2y \leq 12$

Solve the inequality for y.

$3x + 2y \leq 12$

$2y \leq 12 - 3x$

$y \leq -\dfrac{3}{2}x + 6$

© Houghton Mifflin Harcourt Publishing Company

Exercise	Depth of Knowledge (D.O.K.)	COMMON CORE Mathematical Practices
1–16	**2** Skills/Concepts	**MP.4** Modeling
17–18	**2** Skills/Concepts	**MP.4** Modeling
19–20	**2** Skills/Concepts	**MP.4** Modeling
21–22	**2** Skills/Concepts	**MP.2** Reasoning
23	**2** Skills/Concepts	**MP.6** Precision
24	**2** Skills/Concepts	**MP.2** Reasoning

7. $y \le 3$

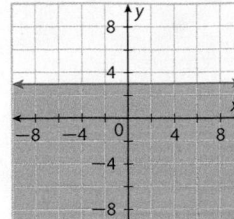

8. $5x - y \ge 4$

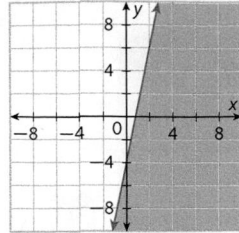

Solve the inequality for y.

$$5x - y \ge 4$$
$$-y \ge 4 - 5x$$
$$y \le 5x - 4$$

In order to graph the inequality using a graphing calculator, tell what function to enter for the boundary line, whether the graph should be shaded above or below the line, and if the boundary line is included in the solution.

9. $x + 5y > 25$

Solve the inequality for y.

$$x + 5y > 25$$
$$5y > -x + 25$$
$$y < -\frac{1}{5}x + 5$$

Boundary line: $y = -\frac{1}{5}x + 5$

below; boundary not included

10. $-x - 7y \ge 0$

Solve the inequality for y.

$$-x - 7y \ge 0$$
$$-7y \ge x$$
$$y \le -\frac{1}{7}x$$

Boundary line: $y = -\frac{1}{7}x$

below; boundary included

11. $-\frac{9}{2}x - y \ge -10y + 3$

Solve the inequality for y.

$$-\frac{9}{2}x - y \ge -10y + 3$$
$$9y \ge \frac{9}{2}x + 3$$
$$y \ge \frac{1}{2}x + \frac{1}{3}$$

Boundary line: $y = \frac{1}{2}x + \frac{1}{3}$

above; boundary included

12. $15x + 20y < 140$

Solve the inequality for y.

$$15x + 20y < 140$$
$$20y < -15x + 140$$
$$y < -\frac{3}{4}x + 7$$

Boundary line: $y = -\frac{3}{4}x + 7$

below; boundary not included

INTEGRATE MATHEMATICAL PRACTICES
Focus on Critical Thinking

MP.3 Students should be aware that testing an inequality for a point does not require the inequality to be simplified or solved algebraically. Instead, students can substitute the values of x and y directly into the original inequality. If the point makes the inequality true, it lies in the shaded half-plane. If the point makes the inequality false, it lies in the unshaded half-plane.

Exercise	Depth of Knowledge (D.O.K.)	COMMON CORE	Mathematical Practices
25	**3** Strategic Thinking **H.O.T.**		**MP.4** Modeling
26	**3** Strategic Thinking **H.O.T.**		**MP.6** Precision

Linear Inequalities in Two Variables   **330**

AVOID COMMON ERRORS

Some students may choose to test whether a point on the boundary line satisfies an inequality. Remind students that a point on the boundary line cannot be used to determine which half-plane to shade.

HOME CONNECTION

Have students search through local advertisements and find two items with different prices under $20 that they would like to purchase several of. Tell students they have a maximum of $150 to buy different combinations of these two items. Have students write a linear inequality to describe the situation. Then have them graph the solutions of their inequalities and give at least two combinations of items they can purchase.

Graph the inequality.

13. $4y + 3x - y > -6x + 12$

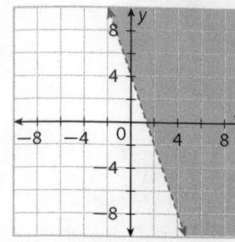

Solve the inequality for y.

$$4y + 3x - y > -6x + 12$$
$$3y > -9x + 12$$
$$y > -3x + 4$$

14. $-15y > 30x - 45$

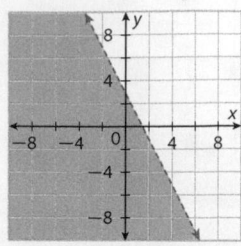

Solve the inequality for y.

$$-15y > 30x - 45$$
$$y < -2x + 3$$

15. $10x - 6y > -36$

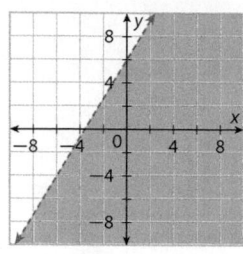

Solve the inequality for y.

$$10x - 6y > -36$$
$$-6y > -36 - 10x$$
$$y < \frac{5}{3}x + 6$$

16. $7x + 2y < 2$

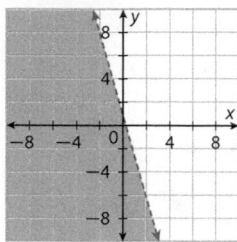

Solve the inequality for y.

$$7x + 2y < 2$$
$$2y < 2 - 7x$$
$$y < -\frac{7}{2}x + 1$$

Write a linear inequality to represent the information or graph given.

17. Shanley would like to give $5 gift cards and $4 teddy bears as party favors. Shanley has $120 to spend on party favors. Write an inequality to find the number of gift cards x and teddy bears y Shanley could purchase. Give one solution to the inequality.

$$5x + 4y \leq 120$$

$$(10, 8)$$

18. The total fees for the high school play are $250. Tickets to the play cost $5 for students and $8 for nonstudents. Write a linear inequality that describes the number of student and nonstudent tickets that need to be sold for the drama class to be able to pay the fees.

$5x + 8y \geq 250$

19.

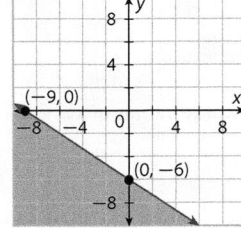

The y-intercept is -6 and the slope is $-\frac{2}{3}$.

The line is solid and the graph is shaded below the line.

$y \leq -\frac{2}{3}x - 6$

20.

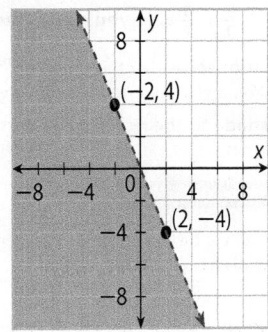

The y-intercept is 0 and the slope is -2.

The line is dashed and the graph is shaded below the line.

$y < -2x$

21. Complete the linear inequality that represents the relationship shown in the table:

$y \boxed{\geq} x + 1$

x	y
−3	0
−2	−1
−1	5
0	1
1	3
2	4
3	4

22. Complete the linear inequality that represents the relationship shown in the table:

$y \boxed{<} 3x - \frac{1}{2}$

x	y
−3	−10.5
−2	−7
−1	−4
0	−1
1	1
2	5
3	7.5

© Houghton Mifflin Harcourt Publishing Company

CRITICAL THINKING

Students should recognize that when modeling certain real-world situations, the variables represent quantities of objects that cannot be divided into parts, so only the whole number solutions make sense. Points within the shaded area whose coordinates are not whole numbers are not solutions to the problem.

AVOID COMMON ERRORS

Some students may have difficulty remembering which inequality symbol to use when the graph includes a solid line, and which to use when the graph includes a dashed line. Have students make the following connection: When the graph includes a solid line, the inequality symbol has a solid line under it ($\leq$ or $\geq$), and when the graph includes a dashed line, the symbol does not include a solid line ($<$ or $>$).

JOURNAL

Have students describe the steps for graphing a simple inequality in two variables, such as $y \leq x + 3$. Have them include how they would decide whether the boundary line is dashed or solid and how they would decide which half-plane to shade.

23. Critique Reasoning Austin thinks that the inequality $6x - 4y \geq 10$ should be shaded above the boundary line because it uses the $\geq$ inequality symbol. Is he correct? Explain.

No; When you solve this equation for y, you must divide both sides

of the equation by a negative number, which reverses the inequality

symbol. $y \leq -\frac{5}{2} + \frac{3}{2}x$, so you must shade below the line.

24. Analyze Relationships For the graph of $x > 10$, the boundary line is the vertical line $x = 10$. Would you shade to the left or right of the boundary? Explain.

You would shade to the right of the vertical line because that is where values of x are greater than 10.

H.O.T. Focus on Higher Order Thinking

25. Multi-step The fare for a taxi cab is $2.50 per passenger and $0.75 for each mile. A group of friends has $22.00 for cab fare.

a. Write a linear inequality to represent how many miles, y, the group can travel if there are x people in the group.

$2.5x + 0.75y \leq 22$

b. If there are 3 people in the group, how far can they travel by taxi? Show all work.

$2.5(3) + 0.75y \leq 22$

$7.5 + 0.75y \leq 22$

$0.75y \leq 14.5$

$y \leq 19\frac{1}{3}$

They can travel $19\frac{1}{3}$ miles.

c. If the group wants to travel 10 miles, what is the greatest number of passengers that can travel by taxi? Explain.

$2.5x + 0.75(10) \leq 22$

$2.5x + 7.5 \leq 22$

$2.5x \leq 14.5$

$x \leq 5.8$

Since the number of passengers has to be a whole number, at most 5 friends can ride in the taxi.

26. Communicate Mathematical Ideas How is graphing a linear inequality on a coordinate plane similar to graphing an inequality on a number line?

On a number line $<$, $>$, $\leq$, and $\geq$ indicate whether or not the boundary point is part of the solution. This is similar to a coordinate plane where these symbols indicate whether or not the boundary line is part of the solution. Also, $>$ and $\geq$ indicate graphing to the right on a number line, while $<$ and $\leq$ indicate graphing to the left. This is similar to a coordinate plane where these symbols indicate whether to graph above or below the boundary line.

Lesson Performance Task

Students are raising money for a field trip by selling candles and soap. The candles cost $0.75 each and will be sold for $2.75, and the soap costs $1.50 per bar and will be sold for $4. The students need to raise at least $300 to cover their trip costs.

a. Write an inequality that relates the number of candles *c* and the number of bars of soap *s* to the needed income.

b. The wholesaler can supply no more than 100 bars of soap and no more than 130 candles. Graph the inequality from part a and the inequalities that represent the constraints. Graph the number of candles on the vertical axis.

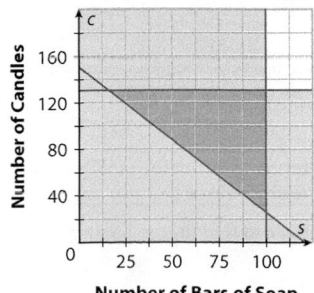

c. What does the shaded area of your graph represent?

a. $2c + 2.5s \geq 300$

b. **Solve the inequality for *c*.**

$2c + 2.5s \geq 300$

$2c \geq -2.5s + 300$

$c \geq -\frac{5}{4}s + 150$

c. **The shaded area represents the points in solution sets of all three inequalities. It shows the possible numbers of candles and bars of soap the students can sell to reach their goal.**

EXTENSION ACTIVITY

Have students research the difference between *gross sales, net sales, gross profit,* and *net profit*.

Students will find that *gross sales* are found by adding all the list prices of items sold; *net sales* equal the gross sales minus any customer discounts, returns, or allowances; *gross profit* equals net sales minus the cost of goods sold, and *net profit* equals the amount of earnings after all costs are accounted for.

AVOID COMMON ERRORS

Some students may not use the correct inequality sign for the inequality written to relate the number of candles and bars of soap to the income needed. Have students write the following on index cards as a reference.

<	**Less than**
	• is fewer
	• is under
	• is no more than
≤	**Less than OR equal to**
	• is not more than
	• is not greater than
	• is at most
	• does not exceed
	• has a maximum value of
>	**Greater than**
	• is more than
	• exceeds
≥	**Greater than OR equal to**
	• is not less than
	• is at least
	• has a minimum value of

QUESTIONING STRATEGIES

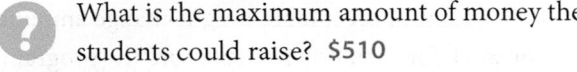 Why must the cost of the candles/soap be subtracted from their sale price when writing the inequality? **The sale price minus the cost results in the profit. Only the profit can be used to cover the trip costs.**

What are the lines of constraints that must be graphed for the situation in the Lesson Performance Task? $2c + 2.5s \leq 300, c \leq 100,$ and $s \leq 130$

What is the maximum amount of money the students could raise? **$510**

Scoring Rubric

2 points: Student correctly solves the problem and explains his/her reasoning.

1 point: Student shows good understanding of the problem but does not fully solve or explain his/her reasoning.

0 points: Student does not demonstrate understanding of the problem.

ASSESSMENT AND INTERVENTION

Assign or customize module reviews.

MODULE PERFORMANCE TASK

COMMON CORE

Mathematical Practices: MP.1, MP.2, MP.4, MP.6
A-CED.A.2, A-CED.A.3, F-LE.B.5

SUPPORTING STUDENT REASONING

Students should begin this problem by considering how to model the weight gain or loss per week goals for the two athletes.

SCAFFOLDING SUPPORT

- Students should write linear equations in one variable to find the amount of weight gain or loss needed per week for each athlete.

- Encourage students to graph their models on the same coordinate grid.

- Because the weight change per week should always be less than or equal to 1.5% body weight, students should write an inequality to determine the maximum acceptable weight change amount per week for each boy to make sure the program is within the limit.

Essential Question: How can you use linear equations and inequalities to solve real-world problems?

Key Vocabulary
linear inequality in two variables *(desigualdad lineal en dos variables)*
solution of an inequality in two variables *(solución de una desigualdad en dos variables)*

KEY EXAMPLE   (Lesson 7.1)

A clothing store offers a rewards program in which customers earn points by making purchases at the store. Every item bought is worth 8 points, and customers earn 20 points when they sign up. Write an equation for the function that gives the number of points based on the number of items bought. How many points will a customer have after making 16 purchases?

Write a verbal model for the situation.

$\quad$ Total points = Initial points + Points Per Item · Number of Items.

Define the variables that you will use for the function.

$\quad n$ = number of items; $P(n)$ = total points

Using the verbal model, variables, and information from the problem, write a function rule.

$\quad P(n) = 20 + 8n$

Substitute $n = 16$ into the function, and solve to find the total points.

$\quad P(16) = 20 + 8(16)$

$\quad P(16) = 148$

The customer will have 148 points after making 16 purchases.

KEY EXAMPLE   (Lesson 7.2)

Sandi is in need of an electrician. Electrician A is offering his services for an initial fee of $50 and $12 per hour. Electrician B is offering her services for an initial fee of $32 and $15 per hour. When will the two electricians charge the same amount of money? Use a table to find the solution.

$f(x) = 12x + 50$

$g(x) = 15x + 32$

x	f(x)	g(x)
0	50	32
1	62	47
2	74	62
3	86	77
4	98	92
5	110	107
6	122	122

The solution is 6 hours.

EXERCISES

Write a linear equation that models the situation. *(Lesson 7.1)*

1. A kiosk sells magazines for $4 each and paperback books for $6 each. The owner would like to make $180 by the end of the day.
$4m + 6b = 180$

2. A theater is selling children's tickets at $8 and adult tickets at $18. The theater would like to sell tickets worth a total of $720 for a performance.
$8c + 18a = 720$

3. Maxine needs a stunt driver. Driver A is offering his services for an initial $150 and $90 per hour. Driver B is offering his services for an initial $210 and $70 per hour. When will the two drivers charge the same amount of money? Fill out the table to find the solution. *(Lesson 7.2)*

x	$f(x) = $ $150 + 90x$	$g(x) = $ $210 + 70x$
0	150	210
1	240	280
2	330	350
3	420	420
4	510	490

Both drivers will charge the same amount of $420 for 3 hours of work.

4. Solve $-9x + 3y \leq 6$ for y and show your work. Graph the solution. *(Lesson 7.3)*

$$-9x + 3y \leq 6$$
$$3y \leq 6 + 9x$$
$$y \leq 3x + 2$$

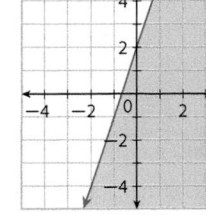

MODULE PERFORMANCE TASK
Making Weight

The National Federation of State High School Associations designates 14 weight classes for wrestlers. Coach Silva has two wrestlers who would like to compete in the 182-pound weight class, Jake and Tawa. Jake weighs 194.6 pounds, Tawa weighs 176 pounds. Coach Silva wants to put each on a diet regimen so that they can meet their weight goal in 6 weeks. For health reasons, neither athlete should lose or gain more than 1.5% of his body weight per week.

If Coach Silva would like for each boy to gain or lose weight at a steady rate over the 6-week time frame, how much does each boy's weight need to change per week? Is this a reasonable goal for each athlete, given the 1.5% per week body weight restriction? Work out your answer on a separate piece of paper.

DISCUSSION OPPORTUNITIES

- Why is it important to match wrestlers with similar weights?

SAMPLE SOLUTION

Assumptions:

Assume a linear model can be used to model the data for each athlete.

First, find the target weight gain or loss per week for each boy by solving equations where m is the change in weight per week:

Jake: $194.6 + 6m = 182 \rightarrow m = -2.1$

Tawa: $176 + 6m = 182 \rightarrow m = 1$

Let $f(x)$ be the boy's weight each week and let $g(x)$ be 0.015 times the boy's weight that week.

Write the functions for each boy.

Jake:

$f(x) = -2.1x + 194.6, g(x) = 0.015(-2.1x + 194.6)$

Tawa:

$f(x) = x + 176, g(x) = 0.015(x + 176)$

Make a table for each boy. Assume that each boy makes his goal each week. Observe from the table that each boy's weight reaches the goal weight at week 6. Then use the table to see if the weight loss each week is less than 1.5% of the boys weight that week.

The tables show that Jake's weekly weight loss of 2.1 lb never exceeds 1.5% of his weight, and Tawa's weekly gain of 1 lb never exceeds 1.5% of his weight.

Assessment Rubric

2 points: Student correctly solves the problem and explains his/her reasoning.

1 point: Student shows good understanding of the problem but does not fully solve or explain.

0 points: Student does not demonstrate understanding of the problem.

Ready to Go On?

ASSESS MASTERY

Use the assessment on this page to determine if students have mastered the concepts and standards covered in this module.

ASSESSMENT AND INTERVENTION

Access Ready to Go On? assessment online, and receive instant scoring, feedback, and customized intervention or enrichment.

ADDITIONAL RESOURCES

Response to Intervention Resources

- Reteach Worksheets

Differentiated Instruction Resources

- Reading Strategies **EL**
- Success for English Learners **EL**
- Challenge Worksheets

Assessment Resources

- Leveled Module Quizzes

Ready to Go On?

7.1–7.3 Linear Equations and Inequalities

· Online Homework
· Hints and Help
· Extra Practice

Write a linear equation that models the situation. *(Lesson 7.1)*

1. A drugstore sells pens for $1.50 each and notebooks for $4 each. The owner would like to sell $35 of these items each day.

   $1.5p + 4n = 35$

2. A movie theater sells tickets to a film for $12 each. The theater also sells beverages for $3. The theater needs to make $1700 in all in order to break even on the film.

   $12t + 3b = 1700$

3. Sylvia has $14,000 dollars in a bank account that she uses to make automatic payments that total $7000 each month. If Sylvia stops making deposits to that account, when would automatic payments make the value of the account zero? *(Lesson 7.2)*

x	$f(x) =$	14,000 − 7000x
0		14,000
1		7000
2		0

in 2 months

4. Solve $10x + 5y \geq 20$ for y and show your work. Graph the solution. *(Lesson 7.3)*

$$10x + 5y \geq 20$$
$$5y \geq 20 - 10x$$
$$y \geq -2x + 4$$

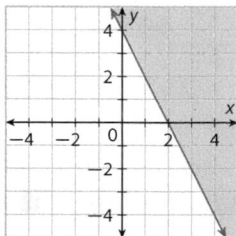

ESSENTIAL QUESTION

5. How can you use the graph of a linear equation to graph an inequality in two variables?

   Possible answer: You can graph the related linear equation as a dashed or solid boundary line, and shade the appropriate half-plane containing the solutions to the inequality.

© Houghton Mifflin Harcourt Publishing Company

COMMON CORE ## Common Core Standards

Lesson	Items	Content Standards	Mathematical Practices
7.1	1	A-CED.A.3, S-ID.C.7, N-Q.A.1, N-Q.A.2	MP.2
7.1	2	A-CED.A.3, S-ID.C.7, N-Q.A.1, N-Q.A.2	MP.2
7.2	3	A-REI.D.11	MP.1
7.3	4	A-REI.D.12	MP.7

Assessment Readiness

1. Look at each equation. Does the graph of the equation include the point $(-6, 3)$? Select Yes or No for each equation.

   A. $y = -2x - 6$ ○ Yes   ● No

   B. $y + 3 = 2(x + 9)$ ● Yes   ○ No

   C. $y - 4 = \frac{1}{2}(x + 4)$ ● Yes   ○ No

2. Consider the inequality represented by the graph. Choose True or False for each statement.

   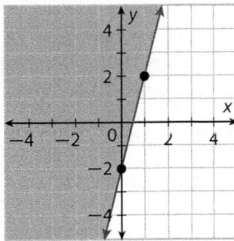

   A. $(1, 4)$ is a solution of the inequality.   ● True   ○ False

   B. $(-3, -2)$ is a solution of the inequality.   ● True   ○ False

   C. The inequality represented is $y < 6x - 2$.   ○ True   ● False

3. Look at each equation. Is the equation linear? Select Yes or No for each equation.

   A. $-3x + y = 8$ ● Yes   ○ No

   B. $3 = xy + 9$ ○ Yes   ● No

   C. $y = x^3 - 3$ ○ Yes   ● No

4. Andre is a small business owner who wants to hire an accountant. Accountant A is offering his services for $50 an hour. Accountant B is offering her services for $35 an hour plus an initial fee of $375. Write a function to represent the cost charged by Accountant A. Write a function to represent the cost charged by Accountant B. For how many hours of work do the two accountants charge the same amount of money? Show your work.

   $f(x) = 50x, g(x) = 35x + 375$

   $50x = 35x + 375$

   $15x = 375$

   $x = 25$

   The accountants charge the same for 25 hours of work.

MIXED REVIEW
Assessment Readiness

ASSESSMENT AND INTERVENTION

Assign ready-made or customized practice tests to prepare students for high-stakes tests.

ADDITIONAL RESOURCES

Assessment Resources

- Leveled Module Quizzes: Modified, B

AVOID COMMON ERRORS

Item 3   Students may mistakenly identify B as a linear equation because neither variable has an exponent. Remind students that the degree of a polynomial is the sum of the exponents, so this does not represent a first-degree equation.

Common Core Standards

Lesson	Items	Content Standards	Mathematical Practices
6.1, 6.2	1*	A-REI.D.10	MP.2
7.3	2	A-REI.D.12	MP.2
5.1	3*	F-LE.A.1b	MP.1
2.2, 7.2	4*	A-CED.A.1, A-REI.D.11	MP.4

* Item integrates mixed review concepts from previous modules or a previous course.

MIXED REVIEW
Assessment Readiness

ASSESSMENT AND INTERVENTION

Assign ready-made or customized practice tests to prepare students for high-stakes tests.

ADDITIONAL RESOURCES

Assessment Resources

- Leveled Unit Tests: Modified, A, B, C

- Performance Assessment

AVOID COMMON ERRORS

Item 1 Some students have difficulty recognizing whether a function is linear when not in slope-intercept form. Encourage students to solve for y to help them recognize whether an equation is linear.

© Houghton Mifflin Harcourt Publishing Company

UNIT 3 MIXED REVIEW

Assessment Readiness

- Online Homework
- Hints and Help
- Extra Practice

1. Is the given equation linear? Select Yes or No.
   A. $-\frac{3}{4}x - \frac{1}{2}y = 2$ ● Yes   ○ No
   B. $y = x^2 - 5$ ○ Yes   ● No
   C. $-\frac{2}{x} = y + 12$ ○ Yes   ● No

2. Consider the equation $2x - \frac{3}{5}y = -6$.
   Determine if the given statement is True or False.
   A. The y-intercept is 10.   ● True   ○ False
   B. It is equivalent to $x = \frac{3}{10}y - 3$.   ● True   ○ False
   C. It is equivalent to $y = \frac{10}{3}x + 10$.   ● True   ○ False

3. A line is represented by the equation $y - 5 = 6\left(x + \frac{1}{2}\right)$.
   Does the given statement describe the line?
   A. The slope of the line is −6.   ○ Yes   ● No
   B. $\left(-\frac{1}{2}, 5\right)$ is a point on the line.   ● Yes   ○ No
   C. The y-intercept of the line is 3.   ○ Yes   ● No

4. Does the given statement describe a step in the transformation of the graph of $f(x) = x$ that would result in the graph of $g(x) = -\frac{1}{3}x - 4$?
   A. The parent function is reflected across the y-axis.   ● Yes   ○ No
   B. The parent function is translated 4 units down.   ● Yes   ○ No
   C. The parent function becomes more steep.   ○ Yes   ● No

5. Consider the graph of the inequality $2y - 10 \leq -\frac{2}{4}x$.
   A. The boundary line is dashed.   ○ Yes   ● No
   B. The boundary line is $y = -\frac{1}{2}x + 5$.   ○ Yes   ● No
   C. The half-plane below the boundary line is shaded.   ● Yes   ○ No

6. Leia and Thaddeus are reading the same 225 page book. Leia starts reading the book and plans to read 25 pages a day. Thaddeus has already read 45 pages and is reading 20 pages a day. Determine if each statement is True or False.
   A. Leia will finish the book in 9 days.   ● True   ○ False
   B. $f(x) = 20x$ represents the number of pages Thaddeus has read after x days.   ○ True   ● False
   C. They will both finish the book in 9 days.   ● True   ○ False

---

COMMON CORE   Common Core Standards

Items	Content Standards	Mathematical Practices
1	F-LE.A.1b	MP.7
2*	A-CED.A.4, F-IF.B.4	MP.2
3	A-CED.A.2	MP.4
4	F-BF.B.3	MP.2
5	A-REI.D.12	MP.4
6*	A-CED.A.1, A-REI.D.11	MP.4

* Item integrates mixed review concepts from previous modules or a previous course.

7. Write $5x = -2y + 6$ in slope-intercept form, and graph the line. Explain how you graphed the line.

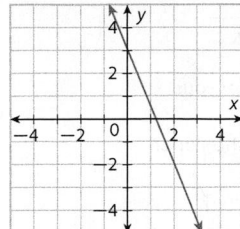

$y = -\frac{5}{2}x + 3$; I plotted a point at the y-intercept, (0, 3). I used the slope, $-\frac{5}{2}$, to find another point on the line. Then, I drew a line through the points.

8. Donnie and Tania are math tutors. The amount Donnie charges for a session h hours long is represented by the function $D(h) = 40h + 10$. Tania charges a flat fee of \$30 plus \$15 an hour. Write a function, $T(h)$, that represents the amount in dollars that Tania charges for h hours of tutoring. Graph both functions on the same coordinate grid, and label each line. Compare the slopes and y-intercepts of the graphs.

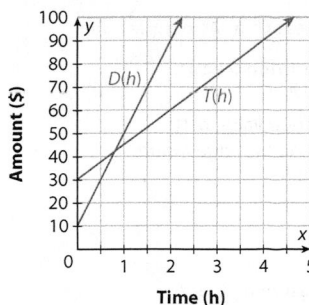

$T(h) = 15h + 30$; The slope of $D(h)$ is greater than the slope of $T(h)$, and the y-intercept of $T(h)$ is greater than the y-intercept of $D(h)$.

Performance Tasks

★ **9.** A bicycle computer or cyclometer uses a magnetic counter that records each wheel rotation to calculate the bike's total distance traveled. To set up the computer, you select a calibration constant for the bike's wheel size. The computer multiplies this constant times the number of tire rotations to find the total distance in miles. Write a function for the distance d in miles if the calibration number is 0.00125. If the function is incorrect and your tire is actually slightly smaller, how should the function change?

$d = 0.00125x$, where x is the number of rotations; if the tire is smaller, the constant should become lower, as the distance covered by one rotation is less.

PERFORMANCE TASKS

There are three different levels of performance tasks:

  * **Novice:** These are short word problems that require students to apply the math they have learned in straightforward, real-world situations.

  ** **Apprentice:** These are more involved problems that guide students step-by-step through more complex tasks. These exercises include more complicated reasoning, writing, and open ended elements.

  *** **Expert:** These are open-ended, nonroutine problems that, instead of stepping the students through, ask them to choose their own methods for solving and justify their answers and reasoning.

SCORING GUIDES

Item 9 (2 points)
1 point for correct function
1 point for explanation

COMMON CORE | Common Core Standards

Items	Content Standards	Mathematical Practices
7*	A-CED.A.4, A-CED.A.2	MP.2
8	F-IF.C.9	MP.4

* Item integrates mixed review concepts from previous modules or a previous course.

SCORING GUIDES

Item 10 (6 points)

A. 1 point for correct equation
   1 point for variable definitions

B. 1 point for identifying intercepts and slope
   1 point for correct interpretations

C. 1 point for correct cost

D. 1 point for giving any plausible reason

Item 11 (6 points)

A. 2 points for correct function

B. 1 point for correct answer

C. 1 point for explanation

D. 2 points for correctly identifying change to model

★★**10.** A marina rents party boats for large social gatherings. They charge the following amounts for a 2-hour rental.

Number of People	10	20	35	50
Cost	$165	$192.50	$233.75	$275

A. Write an equation that represents the data. Include a definition of your variables.

B. What are the intercepts of the graph of your equation? What is the slope? What do they mean in this context?

C. Use your equation to predict the cost of providing a party boat for 75 people.

D. The marina actually charges $460 for 75 people. What might be a reason for the difference?

A. Let $x =$ number of people and $y =$ cost of rental; $y = 2.75x + 137.5$

B. y-intercept: $(0, 137.5)$; x-intercept: $(-50, 0)$; slope: 2.75. The y-intercept means that the cost of the boat with no guests is $137.50; the x-intercept has no meaning in context because it does not make sense to refer to a negative number of people; the slope represents the additional charge per person.

C. $343.75

D. The maximum capacity of one party boat may be less than 75 people. The increased cost might reflect the need to rent an additional boat.

★★★**11.** High demand cars that are also in low supply tend to retain their value better than other cars. The data in the table are for a car that won a resale value award.

Year	1	3	5
Value (%)	84	64	44

A. Write a function to represent the car's value over time, assuming that the car's value is linear for the first 5 years.

B. According to your model, how much did the car's value drop the day it was purchased and driven off the lot?

C. Do you think the linear model would still be useful after 10 years? Explain.

D. Suppose you used months instead of years to write a function. How would your model change?

A. $v(x) = -10x - 94$, where x is the number of years and v is the percent value.

B. 6%

C. The linear model would not be meaningful after 10 years because the model gives a negative percent value.

D. The y-intercept would not change but the slope would change from -10 to $-\frac{5}{6}$.

Wildlife Field Researcher Alexa is a wildlife field researcher who is studying the American black bear. American black bears are the most common bears in the United States. They can be found in 11 of the 21 counties in New Jersey. Most wild male black bears weigh between 125 and 600 pounds, while females generally weigh between 90 and 300 pounds. Their weight depends upon their age, the season of the year, and how much food is available.

a. Write inequalities to show the range of weights for male and female black bears.

b. Black bears hibernate for about 5 months in the winter. They must store 50 to 60 pounds of fat to survive hibernation. During the month before hibernation, a black bear may consume up to 20,000 Calories per day. If a bear consumes an average of 18,500 Calories per day in the month of August, about how many total calories will he consume that month?

c. Use the graph to estimate how much a male bear, weighing $\frac{2}{3}$ pound at birth and 400 pounds at the age of his death, 20 years, weighed when he was 7 years old.

d. A white-tailed deer is running from a black bear at 20 miles per hour. It is $\frac{1}{3}$ mile in front of the bear. The bear is running at 30 miles per hour. How many minutes will it take the bear to catch the deer? Assume both continue running at a constant pace.

e. During the hibernation months, the bear's heart rate slows to about 10 beats per minute. If the bear hibernates for 155 days, how many times will its heart beat?

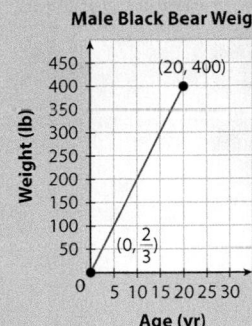

Male Black Bear Weight

a. males: $125 \leq w \leq 600$
   females: $90 \leq w \leq 300$
b. about 573,500 Calories
c. about 140 lb
d. 2 minutes
e. about 2,232,000 times

MATH IN CAREERS

Wildlife Field Researcher In this Unit Performance Task, students can see how a wildlife field researcher uses mathematics on the job.

For more information about careers in mathematics as well as various mathematics appreciation topics, visit the American Mathematical Society at http://www.ams.org.

SCORING GUIDE

Task (6 points)

a. 1 point for correct inequalities

b. 1 point for reasonable estimate

c. 1 point for reasonable estimate

d. 2 points for correct answer

e. 1 point for correct answer

Statistical Models

CONTENTS

Unit Pacing Guide

45-Minute Classes

Module 8

DAY 1	DAY 2	DAY 3	DAY 4	
Lesson 8.1	Lesson 8.2	Lesson 8.2	Module Review and Assessment Readiness	

Module 9

DAY 1	DAY 2	DAY 3	DAY 4	DAY 5
Lesson 9.1	Lesson 9.1	Lesson 9.2	Lesson 9.2	Lesson 9.3

DAY 6	DAY 7	DAY 8		
Lesson 9.3	Lesson 9.4	Module Review and Assessment Readiness		

Module 10

DAY 1	DAY 2	DAY 3	DAY 4	DAY 5
Lesson 10.1	Lesson 10.1	Lesson 10.2	Lesson 10.2	Module Review and Assessment Readiness

DAY 6				
Unit Review and Assessment Readiness				

90-Minute Classes

Module 8

DAY 1	DAY 2	
Lesson 8.1 Lesson 8.2	Lesson 8.2 Module Review and Assessment Readiness	

Module 9

DAY 1	DAY 2	DAY 3	DAY 4
Lesson 9.1	Lesson 9.2	Lesson 9.3	Lesson 9.4 Module Review and Assessment Readiness

Module 10

DAY 1	DAY 2	DAY 3
Lesson 10.1	Lesson 10.2	Module Review and Assessment Readiness Unit Review and Assessment Readiness

Program Resources

HMH Teacher App

Access a full suite of teacher resources online and offline on a variety of devices. Plan present, and manage classes, assignments, and activities.

ePlanner Easily plan your classes, create and view assignments, and access all program resources with your online, customizable planning tool.

Professional Development Videos

Authors Juli Dixon and Matt Larson model successful teaching practices and strategies in actual classroom settings.

QR Codes Scan with your smart phone to jump directly from your print book to online videos and other resources.

Teacher's Edition

Support students with point-of-use Questioning Strategies, teaching tips, resources for differentiated instruction, additional activities, and more.

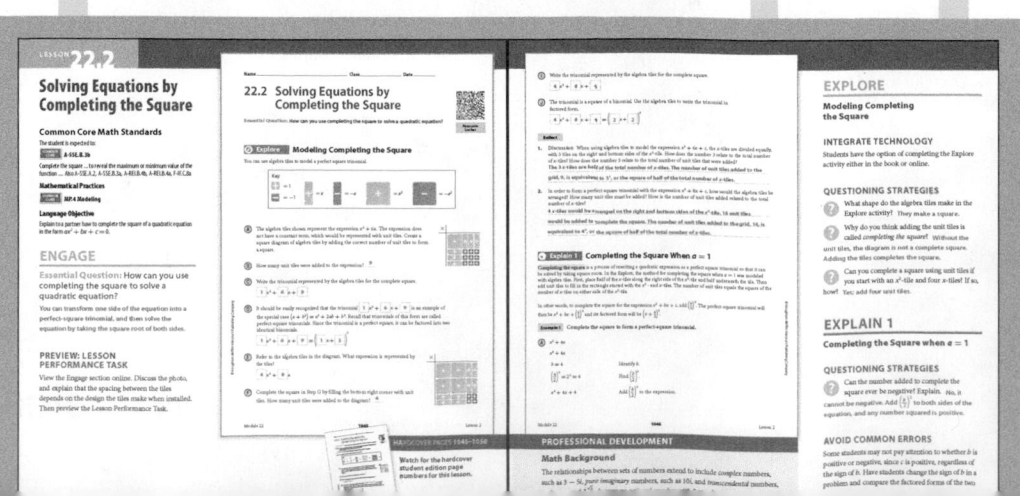

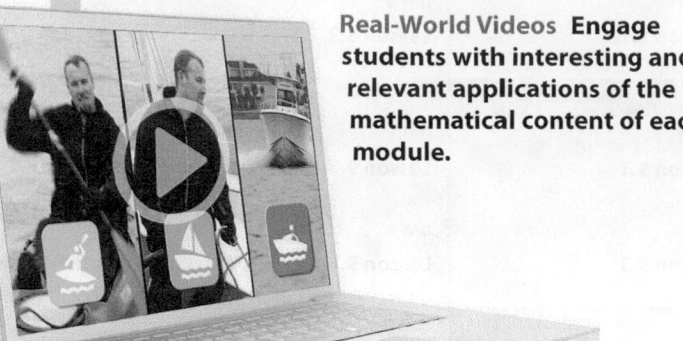

Real-World Videos Engage students with interesting and relevant applications of the mathematical content of each module.

Explore Activities

Students interactively explore new concepts using a variety of tools and approaches.

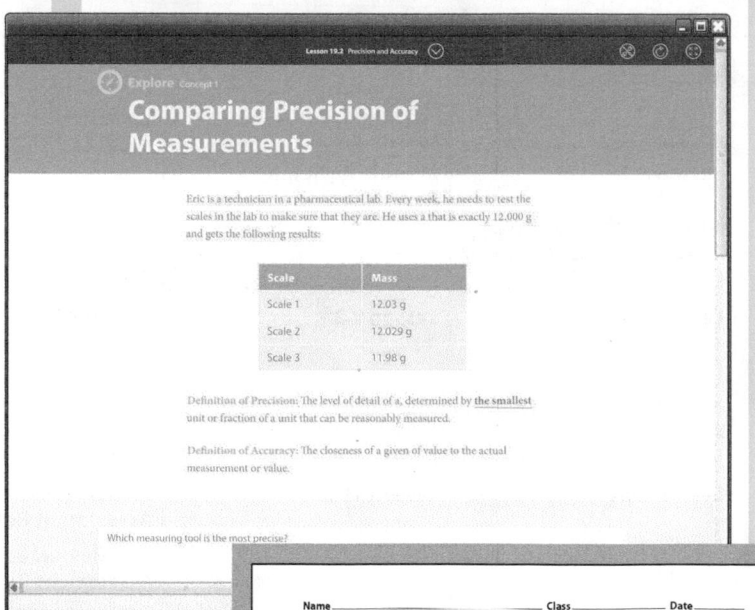

Name _____ Class _____ Date _____

22.2 Solving Equations by Completing the Square

Essential Question: How can you use completing the square to solve a quadratic equation?

A-SSE.B.3b Complete the square ... to reveal the maximum or minimum value of the function ... Also A-SSE.A.2, A-SSE.B.3a, A-REI.B.4b, A-REI.B.4a, F-IF.C.8a

Explore Modeling Completing the Square

You can use algebra tiles to model a perfect square trinomial.

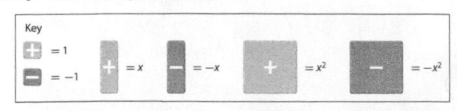

(A) The algebra tiles shown represent the expression $x^2 + 6x$. The expression does not have a constant term, which would be represented with unit tiles. Create a square diagram of algebra tiles by adding the correct number of unit tiles to form a square.

(B) How many unit tiles were added to the expression?

(C) Write the trinomial represented by the algebra tiles for the complete square.

$\boxed{}\,x^2 + \boxed{}\,x + \boxed{}$

(D) It should be easily recognized that the trinomial $\boxed{}\,x^2 + \boxed{}\,x + \boxed{}$ is an example of the special case $(a + b)^2 = a^2 + 2ab + b^2$. Recall that trinomials of this form are called perfect-square trinomials. Since the trinomial is a perfect square, it can be factored into two

TEACH

Math On the Spot video tutorials, featuring program author Dr. Edward Burger, accompany every example in the textbook and give students step-by-step instructions and explanations of key math concepts.

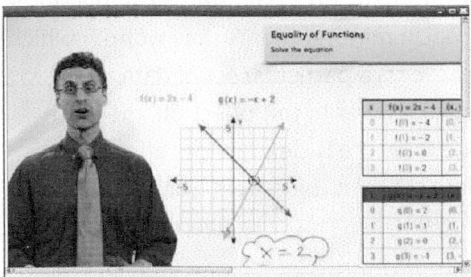

Interactive Teacher Edition

Customize and present course materials with collaborative activities and integrated formative assessment.

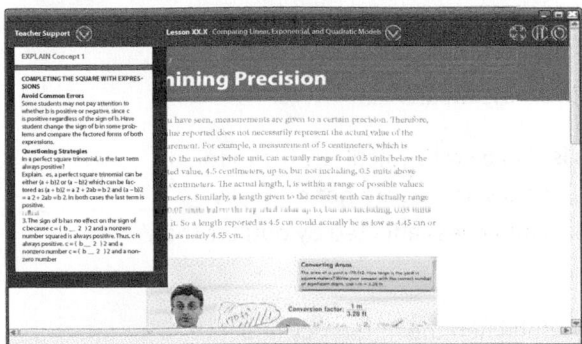

Differentiated Instruction Resources

Support all learners with Differentiated Instruction Resources, including

- **Leveled Practice and Problem Solving**
- **Reading Strategies**
- **Success for English Learners**
- **Challenge**

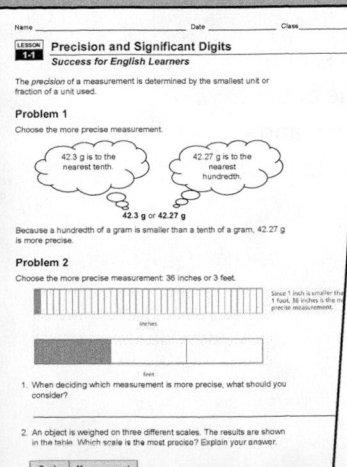
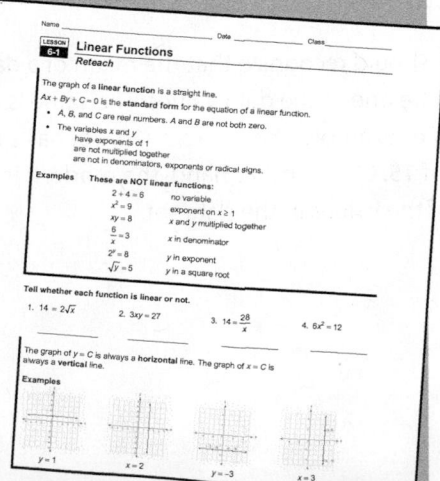

ASSESSMENT AND INTERVENTION

The **Personal Math Trainer** provides online practice, homework, assessments, and intervention. Monitor student progress through reports and alerts. **Create and customize assignments aligned to specific lessons or Common Core standards.**

- **Practice** – With dynamic items and assignments, students get unlimited practice on key concepts supported by guided examples, step-by-step solutions, and video tutorials.

- **Assessments** – Choose from course assignments or customize your own based on course content, Common Core standards, difficulty levels, and more.

- **Homework** – Students can complete online homework with a wide variety of problem types, including the ability to enter expressions, equations, and graphs. Let the system automatically grade homework, so you can focus where your students need help the most!

- **Intervention** – Let the Personal Math Trainer automatically prescribe a targeted, personalized intervention path for your students.

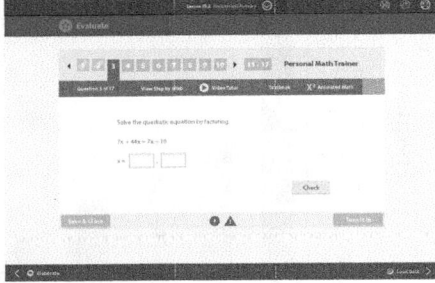

Focus on Higher Order Thinking

Raise the bar with homework and practice that incorporates higher-order thinking and mathematical practices in every lesson.

Assessment Readiness

Prepare students for success on high stakes tests for Algebra 1 with practice at every module and unit

COMMON CORE

Assessment Resources

Tailor assessments and response to intervention to meet the needs of all your classes and students, including

- Leveled Module Quizzes
- Leveled Unit Tests
- Unit Performance Tasks
- Placement, Diagnostic, and Quarterly Benchmark Tests
- Tier 1, Tier 2, and Tier 3 Resources

Math Background

Relative Frequency and Probability   COMMON CORE   S-ID.B.5

LESSON 8.2

Something rather surprising occurs in the frequency distribution of digits in many real-world data sets, including the altitudes of cities, stock prices, baseball statistics, and population figures.

Known as Benford's Law, this principle predicts that in data sets of randomly produced natural numbers, the first nonzero digit in about 30% of the data set will be 1, about 18% will be 2, and the percentages will continue to decrease, with about 4.6% of the data beginning with 9. The results are shown in the graph.

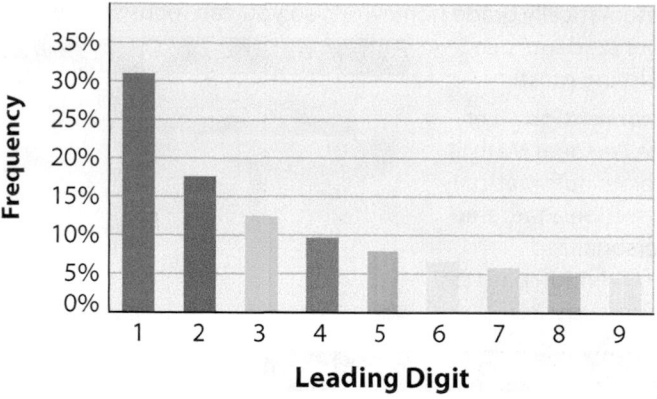

Leading Digit

Although the theory is quite amazing in its own right, Benford's Law can be a powerful tool in fraud detection. People unaware of Benford's Law who create falsified data tend to write numbers that have the initial digit evenly distributed among the nine possible digit choices. Forensic accountants routinely examine financial data, and data which do not follow the predictions of Benford's Law are red-flagged as possibly fraudulent.

Benford's Law does not hold for data sets that typically begin with a limited set of digits, such as IQ scores and the heights of humans.

Measures of Center and Spread   COMMON CORE   S-ID.A.2

LESSON 9.1

The *measures of central tendency*, mean, median, and mode, are three ways of summarizing a data set by using a single value. With this goal in mind, students may wonder which measure best represents a particular set of data. Although there is no definitive answer to this question, there are cases in which one measure is clearly more effective at describing a data set than the others. Some general guidelines for choosing a measure to describe a data set can be established.

Mean: The mean (or average) takes every data value into account, is easy to calculate, and works well for describing data sets that are normally distributed. (In a data set that is normally distributed, the graph of the distribution is a bell-shaped curve with the mean at the center.) The mean is not as useful for sets that contain outliers because the outliers can have a large effect on the mean.

Median: The median is also easy to calculate. The median is useful for describing data sets that are not normally distributed because it is much less affected by outliers than the mean.

Mode: The mode is useful when the frequency of data values is important or when the data cluster around multiple values. Among the mean, median, and mode, only the mode can be used to summarize a set of non-numerical data, such as favorite colors.

Each measure provides a slightly different perspective on a data set. The clearest understanding of a data set is generally obtained when all three measures are considered as a group.

Students should recognize that the mean of a data set need not be one of the data values. The same is true of the median. For example, the data set {10, 20} has a mean and median of 15. On the other hand, the mode, if it exists, must be one of the values in the data set.

Variability  S-ID.A.1

LESSON 9.2

The mean, median, and mode are all ways to describe the "typical" value in a data set. It is also useful to describe the *variability*, or spread, of a data set. The simplest way to quantify variability is with the range.

The *range* of a data set is the difference between the greatest and least values in the set. Consider the two data sets shown below. Both have a mean, median, and mode of 5. However, the values in data set B are more spread out, and this is reflected in the fact that the data set has a greater range. The range of data set B is 6, as compared to a range of 2 for data set A.

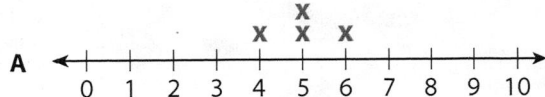

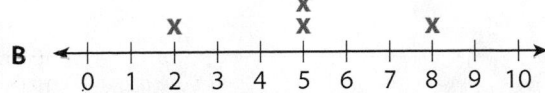

Normal Distributions S-ID.A.2

LESSON 9.4

Students may have heard of normal distributions, but it is not likely that they have experience in using them to make specific estimates. During Instruction, build on their understanding of data distributions to help them see how areas are used in normal distributions to make estimates. Students should learn that not all data are well described by a normal distribution.

The normal distribution, also called a Gaussian distribution or a bell-shaped curve, may well be the most familiar distribution in statistics. Normal distributions can be completely described by giving their mean and standard deviation.

In normal distributions, 68% of all values fall within one standard deviation of the mean. Similarly, 95% of values fall within two standard deviations, and 99.7% of the values fall within three standard deviations of the mean.

The normal distribution can even be used in situations in which the data are not distributed normally. The central limit theorem states that the distribution of the means of random samples has a normal distribution for large sample sizes. So, normal distributions can be used to describe the *averages* of data that do not necessarily have a normal distribution themselves.

Scatter Plots  S-ID.B.5

LESSON 10.1

Scatter plots provide an efficient way to present, analyze, and describe large quantities of data. As such, they are one of the most important applications of relations.

A scatter plot is a graph that shows *bivariate data*; that is, data for which there are two variables. Each point on the scatter plot represents one data pair. The scatter plot below shows the area and the number of counties for the seven smallest U.S. states. Each point represents the data pair for a single state. Rhode Island has an area of approximately 1500 square miles and 5 counties. This is represented by the ordered pair $(1.5, 5)$.

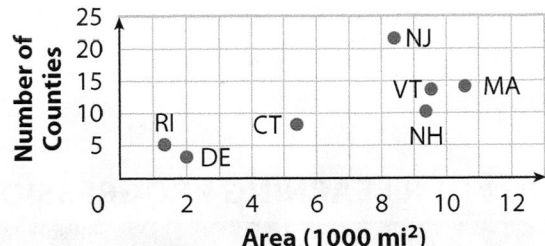

Students should understand that a scatter plot shows all of the collected data and that connecting the points on a scatter plot is meaningless.

Statistical Models

MATH IN CAREERS
Unit Activity Preview

After completing this unit, students will complete a Math in Careers task by examining the data of several U.S. rivers. Critical skills include finding and comparing the mean and median, examining the impact of an outlier on the mean, and finding the range and standard deviation.

For more information about careers in mathematics as well as various mathematics appreciation topics, visit The American Mathematical Society at http://www.ams.org.

Statistical Models

MODULE 8
Multi-Variable Categorical Data

MODULE 9
One-Variable Data Distributions

MODULE 10
Linear Modeling and Regression

MATH IN CAREERS

Geologist A geologist is a scientist who studies Earth—its processes, materials, and history. Geologists investigate earthquakes, floods, landslides, and volcanic eruptions to gain a deeper understanding of these phenomena. They explore ways to extract materials from the earth, such as metals, oil, and groundwater. Geologists devise and use mathematical models and use statistical methods to help them understand Earth's geological processes and history.

If you are interested in a career as a geologist, you should study these mathematical subjects:
- Algebra
- Geometry
- Trigonometry
- Statistics
- Calculus

Research other careers that require using statistical methods to understand natural phenomena. Check out the career activity at the end of the unit to find out how **geologists** use math.

Unit 4   343

TRACKING YOUR LEARNING PROGRESSION

Before	In this Unit	After
Students understand: • graphing ordered pairs • modeling linear relationships • using functions to solve one-variable equations	Students will learn about: • multi-variable data and two-way frequency tables • measures of center and spread • histograms and box plots • normal distributions • fitting a linear model to data	Students will study: • solving systems of linear equations and inequalities • creating systems of linear equations • solving absolute value equations and inequalities

Reading Start-Up

Visualize Vocabulary

Use the ✓ words to complete the graphic.

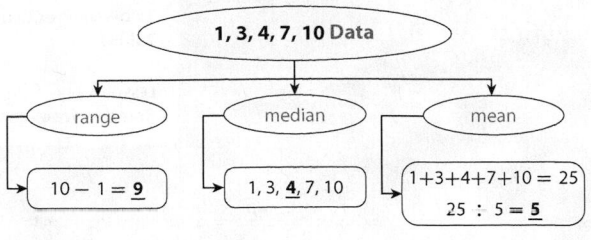

```
                  1, 3, 4, 7, 10 Data

        range          median              mean

     10 − 1 = 9    1, 3, 4, 7, 10    1+3+4+7+10 = 25
                                      25 ∶ 5 = 5
```

Vocabulary

Review Words
- ✔ data *(datos)*
- ✔ mean *(media)*
- ✔ median *(mediana)*
- ✔ range *(rango)*

Preview Words
box plot *(gráfica de caja)*
categorical data *(datos categoricos)*
dot plot *(diagrama de puntos)*
frequency table *(table de frecuencia)*
histogram *(histograma)*
normal distribution *(distribución normal)*
outlier *(valor extremo)*
quartile *(cuartil)*
scatter plot *(diagram de dispersión)*
trend line *(línea de tendencia)*

Understand Vocabulary

To become familiar with some of the vocabulary terms in the module, consider the following. You may refer to the module, the glossary, or a dictionary.

1. A __quartile__ is the median of the upper or lower half of a data set.

2. A graph with points plotted to show a possible relationship between two sets of data is a __scatter plot__.

3. A __histogram__ is a bar graph used to display data grouped in intervals.

4. A data value that is far removed from the rest of the data is an __outlier__.

Active Reading

Booklet Before beginning each module in this unit, create a booklet to help you learn the vocabulary and concepts in the module. Each page of the booklet should contain a main topic from each lesson. As you study each lesson, write details of the main topic, with definitions, diagrams, graphs, and examples, to create an outline that summarizes the main content of the lesson.

Reading Start Up

Have students complete the activities on this page by working alone or with others.

VISUALIZE VOCABULARY

The information graphic helps students review vocabulary associated with three measures of central tendency: mean, median, and mode. If time allows, discuss how each measure differs and how each can sometimes be misleading when used to describe a set of data.

UNDERSTAND VOCABULARY

Use the following explanations to help students learn the preview words.

There are three common measures for the center of a data set: the mean, median, and mode. The **mean** is the average value of a data set. The **mode** is the most common value, and the **median** is the middle data value of the sorted data set, or the average of the two middle values. Some data sets include values that are far away from other values, and these values are called **outliers**. **Quartiles** are values that divide a data set into four equal parts. Data sets can be grouped and presented visually in a **histogram**, which is a special bar graph with all its bars touching.

ACTIVE READING

Students can use these reading and note-taking strategies to help them organize and understand the new concepts and vocabulary in the unit.

ADDITIONAL RESOURCES

Differentiated Instruction

- Reading Strategies

MODULE 8

Multi-Variable Categorical Data

ESSENTIAL QUESTION:

Answer: Gathering data involving more than one variable about a group of subjects allows you to draw conclusions about relationships between the variables.

PROFESSIONAL DEVELOPMENT VIDEO

Professional Development Video

Author Juli Dixon models successful teaching practices in an actual high-school classroom.

Professional Development
my.hrw.com

MODULE 8

Multi-Variable Categorical Data

Essential Question: How can you use multi-variable categorical data to solve real-world problems?

LESSON 8.1
Two-Way Frequency Tables

LESSON 8.2
Relative Frequency

© Houghton Mifflin Harcourt Publishing Company • © Daniel Padavona/Shutterstock

REAL WORLD VIDEO
With emotions riding high, it can be difficult to evaluate popular opinion concerning personal preferences, such as favorite sports teams. Polls and surveys use a methodical, mathematical approach to reduce or eliminate bias.

MODULE PERFORMANCE TASK PREVIEW

Survey Says?

You won't be surprised to learn that the activities people enjoy change with age. Most six-year-olds like climbing on jungle-gyms. Most twenty-year-olds don't, but they do like to attend pop music concerts. In this module, you'll learn ways to analyze surveys of public opinions and preferences. Then you'll look at data relating to the vacation preferences of two different age groups and decide what you can learn from the data.

DIGITAL TEACHER EDITION

Access a full suite of teaching resources when and where you need them:

- Access content online or offline
- Customize lessons to share with your class
- Communicate with your students in real-time
- View student grades and data instantly to target your instruction where it is needed most

PERSONAL MATH TRAINER
Assessment and Intervention

Assign automatically graded homework, quizzes, tests, and intervention activities. Prepare your students with updated, Common Core-aligned practice tests.

Are YOU Ready?

Complete these exercises to review skills you will need for this module.

Percents

Example 1   What percent of 14 is 21?

$$\frac{x}{100} \cdot 14 = 21 \qquad \text{Write an equation.}$$

$$\frac{x}{100} \cdot 14 \cdot \frac{100}{14} = 21 \cdot \frac{100}{14} \qquad \text{Multiply both sides by } \frac{100}{14}.$$

$$x = 150 \qquad \text{Simplify.}$$

21 is 150% of 14.

- Online Homework
- Hints and Help
- Extra Practice

Solve each equation.

1. What percent of 24 is 18?

75%

2. What percent of 400 is 2?

0.5%

3. What percent of 880 is 924?

105%

Two-Way Frequency Tables

Example 2   The table shows the number of adults, teens, and children under 13 who visited the local petting zoo one week. How many people visited it on Friday?

	Su	M	Tu	W	Th	F	Sa
Adult	112	40	33	52	29	8	90
Teen	29	0	6	22	4	2	10
Child	61	32	56	65	38	16	48

Friday is the second to last column. It shows that 8 adults, 2 teens, and 16 children visited that day. The sum is $8 + 2 + 16 = 26$.

The number of people who visited the petting zoo on Friday is 26.

Use the table shown to answer the questions.

4. How many children under 13 visited the petting zoo that week?

316 children

5. How many adults visited the petting zoo on the weekend?

202 adults

6. To the nearest whole percent, what percent of the visitors were teens?

10%

Are You Ready?

ASSESS READINESS

Use the assessment on this page to determine if students need strategic or intensive intervention for the module's prerequisite skills.

ASSESSMENT AND INTERVENTION

RtI Response to Intervention **TIER 1, TIER 2, TIER 3 SKILLS**

Personal Math Trainer will automatically create a standards-based, personalized intervention assignment for your students, targeting each student's individual needs!

ADDITIONAL RESOURCES

See the table below for a full list of intervention resources available for this module.

Response to Intervention Resources also includes:

- Tier 2 Skill Pre-Tests for each Module
- Tier 2 Skill Post-Tests for each skill

Response to Intervention			*Differentiated Instruction*
Tier 1 Lesson Intervention Worksheets	**Tier 2** Strategic Intervention Skills Intervention Worksheets	**Tier 3** Intensive Intervention Worksheets available online	
Reteach 8.1 Reteach 8.2	15 Percents 25 Two-Way Frequency Tables 26 Two-Way Relative Frequency Tables	Building Block Skills 6, 37, 39, 72, 114	Challenge worksheets Extend the Math Lesson Activities in TE

Two-Way Frequency Tables

Common Core Math Standards

The student is expected to:

 S-ID.B.5

Summarize categorical data for two categories in two-way frequency tables. Interpret relative frequencies in the context of the data (including joint, marginal, and conditional relative frequencies). Recognize possible associations and trends in the data.

Mathematical Practices

COMMON CORE **MP.7 Using Structure**

Language Objective

Distinguish between quantitative data and categorical data.

ENGAGE

Essential Question: How can categorical data for two categories be summarized?

You can summarize categorical data for two categories in a two-way frequency table.

PREVIEW: LESSON PERFORMANCE TASK

View the Engage section online, and then take a quick, show-of-hands survey to determine the most popular sports among the students in your class. Discuss whether the survey results might have been different had you surveyed the boys and the girls separately. Then preview the Lesson Performance Task.

Resource Locker

8.1 Two-Way Frequency Tables

Essential Question: How can categorical data for two categories be summarized?

 Explore Categorical Data and Frequencies

Data that can be expressed with numerical measurements are **quantitative data**. In this lesson you will examine qualitative data, or **categorical data**, which cannot be expressed using numbers. Data describing animal type, model of car, or favorite song are examples of categorical data.

(A) Circle the categorical data variable. Justify your choice.

temperature   weight   height   (color)

Temperature, weight, and height are measured on a numerical scale, so they are

quantitative data. Color cannot be expressed numerically.

(B) Identify whether the given data is categorical or quantitative.

large, medium, small ___**categorical**___

120 ft², 130 ft², 140 ft² ___**quantitative**___

(C) A **frequency** table shows how often each item occurs in a set of categorical data. Use the categorical data listed on the left to complete the frequency table.

Ways Students Get to School
bus car walk car car car bus walk walk walk bus bus car bus bus walk bus car bus car

Way	Frequency
bus	8
car	7
walk	5

Reflect

1. How did you determine the numbers for each category in the frequency column?
   You can determine the numbers for each category by counting the number of times each
   category is listed in the data.

2. What must be true about the sum of the frequencies in a frequency table?
   The sum should equal the total number of items in the data set.

© Houghton Mifflin Harcourt Publishing Company

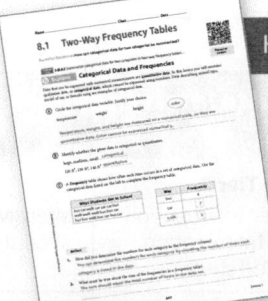

HARDCOVER PAGES 277–288

Turn to these pages to find this lesson in the hardcover student edition.

If a data set has two categorical variables, you can list the frequencies of the paired values in a **two-way frequency table**.

Example 1   Complete the two-way frequency table.

(A) A high school's administration asked 100 randomly selected students in the 9th and 10th grades about what fruit they like best. Complete the table.

Grade	Preferred Fruit			
	Apple	Orange	Banana	Total
9th	19	12	23	
10th	22	9	15	
Total				

Row totals:

9th: $19 + 12 + 23 = 54$

10th: $22 + 9 + 15 = 46$

Column totals:

Apple: $19 + 22 = 41$

Orange: $12 + 9 = 21$

Banana: $23 + 15 = 38$

Grand total:

Sum of row totals: $54 + 46 = 100$

Sum of column totals: $41 + 21 + 38 = 100$

Both sums should equal the grand total.

Grade	Preferred Fruit			
	Apple	Orange	Banana	Total
9th	19	12	23	54
10th	22	9	15	46
Total	41	21	38	100

(B) Jenna asked some randomly selected students whether they preferred dogs, cats, or other pets. She also recorded the gender of each student. The results are shown in the two-way frequency table below. Each entry is the frequency of students who prefer a certain pet and are a certain gender. For instance, 8 girls prefer dogs as pets. Complete the table.

Gender	Preferred Pet			
	Dog	Cat	Other	Total
Girl	8	7	1	16
Boy	10	5	9	24
Total	18	12	10	40

Row totals:

Girl: $8 + 7 + 1 =$ **16**

Boy: $10 + 5 + 9 =$ **24**

Column totals:

Dog: $8 + 10 =$ **18**

Cat: $7 + 5 =$ **12**

Other: $1 + 9 =$ **10**

Grand total:

Sum of row totals: $16 +$ **24** $=$ **40**

Sum of column totals: $18 +$ **12** $+$ **10** $=$ **40**

Both sums should equal the grand total.

PROFESSIONAL DEVELOPMENT

COMMON CORE **Integrate Mathematical Practices**

This lesson provides an opportunity to use Mathematical Practice **MP.7**, which asks students to "look for and make use of structure." In this lesson, students use the structure of two-way frequency tables to analyze data and understand a problem-solving situation.

EXPLORE

Categorical Data and Frequencies

INTEGRATE TECHNOLOGY

Students have the option of completing the Explore Activity online or in the book.

CONNECT VOCABULARY EL

Make sure that students understand the distinction between *quantitative* and *categorical data*. *Quantitative data* can be measured on a numbered scale. *Categorical data* involves either/or choices between two or more descriptive categories. Ask students to provide some examples of quantitative and categorical data.

EXPLAIN 1

Constructing Two-Way Frequency Tables

INTEGRATE MATHEMATICAL PRACTICES
Focus on Communication

MP.3 To check students' understanding of the information presented in a two-way frequency table, have one student ask a question about the data in the table. Have another student answer the question and provide an explanation of how to use the table to arrive at the answer.

QUESTIONING STRATEGIES

? What is the difference between a two-way frequency table and an ordinary frequency table? In a two-way frequency table, each value (other than row and column totals) indicates the number of items that fit two data categories rather than one, such as the number of boys who prefer cats. In an ordinary frequency table, data values correspond to only one data category.

Two-Way Frequency Tables   **348**

EXPLAIN 2

Reading Two-Way Frequency Tables

INTEGRATE MATHEMATICAL PRACTICES
Focus on Reasoning

MP.2 Remind students that there may be more than one process for filling in a particular table. Discuss different ways to fill cells in a table, such as using addition to find the total for a column or row, and working backward to find a missing value that is not a total.

AVOID COMMON ERRORS

Remind students to use the row totals and column totals to check that their work is correct. The sum of the row totals should be the same as the sum of the column totals. If the sums are different, students need to review their work to look for errors.

Reflect

3. Look at the totals for each row. Was Jenna's survey evenly distributed among boys and girls? Explain.
   No, there were 24 boys and 16 girls.

4. Look at the totals for each column. Which pet is preferred by the most students? Justify your answer.
   Dogs; the total for Dog is greater than the total for Cat and the total for Other.

Your Turn

Complete the two-way frequency table.

5. Antonio surveyed 60 of his classmates about their participation in school activities and whether they have a part-time job. The results are shown in the two-way frequency table below. Complete the table.

	Activities				
Job	**Clubs Only**	**Sports Only**	**Both**	**Neither**	**Total**
Yes	12	13	16	4	45
No	3	5	5	2	15
Total	15	18	21	6	60

6. Jen surveyed 100 students about whether they like baseball or basketball. Complete the table.

	Like Basketball		
Like Baseball	**Yes**	**No**	**Total**
Yes	61	13	74
No	16	10	26
Total	77	23	100

✏ Explain 2 Reading Two-Way Frequency Tables

You can extract information about paired categorical variables by reading a two-way frequency table.

Example 2 Read and complete the two-way frequency table.

(A) Suppose you are given the circled information in the table and instructed to complete the table.

	Eat Cereal for Breakfast		
Gender	**Yes**	**No**	**Total**
Girl	(42)	(12)	(54)
Boy	36	(10)	46
Total	78	22	100

Find the total number of boys by subtracting: $100 - 54 = 46$

Find the number of boys who do eat cereal by subtracting: $46 - 10 = 36$

Add to find the total number of students who eat cereal and the total number of students who do not eat cereal.

COLLABORATIVE LEARNING

Peer-to-Peer Activity

Have students work in pairs. Challenge one in each pair to describe a data set for which the partner must create a two-way frequency table. Students should provide as little direct information as possible, while still making it possible to complete the table. For example, instead of saying, "Twenty boys prefer baseball," they might say, "The number of boys who prefer baseball is 15 less than the number of girls who prefer softball." After students complete the frequency tables, have them compare results with their partners. If the students disagree, have them discuss and determine which is correct.

(B) One hundred students were surveyed about which beverage they chose at lunch. Some of the results are shown in the two-way frequency table below. Complete the table.

Gender	Lunch Beverage			
	Juice	Milk	Water	Total
Girl	10	13	17	40
Boy	15	24	21	60
Total	25	37	38	100

Find the total number of girls by subtracting: $100 - 60 = \boxed{40}$

So, the total number of girls is $\boxed{40}$. The number of girls who do not choose milk is $\boxed{17} + \boxed{10} = \boxed{27}$.

Find the number of girls who chose milk by subtracting: $\boxed{40} - \boxed{27} = \boxed{13}$

Reflect

7. Which lunch beverage is the least preferred? How do you know?
   Juice: the total for Juice is less than the total for Milk and the total for Water.

Your Turn

Read and complete the two-way frequency table.

8. 100 students were asked what fruit they chose at lunch. The two-way frequency table shows some of the results of the survey. Complete the table.

Gender	Lunch Fruit			
	Apple	Pear	Banana	Total
Girl	21	17	11	49
Boy	25	10	16	51
Total	46	27	27	100

9. 200 high school teachers were asked whether they prefer to use the chalkboard or projector in class. The two-way frequency table shows some of the results of the survey. Complete the table.

Gender	Preferred Teaching Aid		
	Chalkboard	Projector	Total
Female	43	56	99
Male	44	57	101
Total	87	113	200

? To complete a two-way frequency table that is missing information, is it necessary to know the total of all the values in the table? Explain. **No; if there is enough other information given in the table, the total can be determined using other information.**

DIFFERENTIATE INSTRUCTION

Cognitive Strategies

When students are completing two-way frequency tables that are missing information, discuss how to determine which cells in the table can be completed first. Students should understand that in order for a value to be determined, it must be the only missing value in either its row or its column. By completing a row or column in which only one value is missing, students move one step closer to completing other rows or columns.

ELABORATE

INTEGRATE MATHEMATICAL PRACTICES

Focus on Communication

MP.3 Have students discuss why the order of words is important in identifying a cell in a two-way frequency table. For example, students should understand that "people who watch TV but not movies" refers to a different cell than "people who watch movies but not TV."

SUMMARIZE THE LESSON

? What information is provided by a two-way frequency table, and how is that information organized? A two-way frequency table provides categorical data for two categorical variables, such as color and size or gender and job. Data for one variable is organized in rows, and data for the other variable is organized in columns. The value in each cell of the table identifies the number of items that fit the intersection of the two categories.

⊖ Elaborate

10. You are making a two-way frequency table of 5 fruit preferences among a survey sample of girls and boys. What are the dimensions of the table you would make? How many entries would you need to fill the table with frequencies and totals?

You would make a 2-by-5 table for the frequencies. Adding totals would increase

the dimensions to 3-by-6. You need 3 times 6, or 18, entries to fill the table.

11. A 3 categories-by-3 categories two-way frequency table has a row with 2 numbers, and no row or column totals. Can you fill the row?

This table would be a 4-by-4 table, including the row of totals. You cannot fill the row

because you need 3 numbers to figure out the last one.

12. **Essential Question Check-In** How can you summarize categorical data for 2 categories?
You can use a two-way frequency table.

★ Evaluate: Homework and Practice

- Online Homework
- Hints and Help
- Extra Practice

1. Identify whether the given data is categorical or quantitative.

gold medal, silver medal, bronze medal **categorical**

100 m, 200 m, 400 m **quantitative**

2. A theater company asked its members to bring in canned food for a food drive. Use the categorical data to complete the frequency table.

Cans Donated to Food Drive
peas corn peas soup corn
corn soup soup corn peas
peas corn soup peas corn
peas corn peas corn soup
corn peas soup corn corn

Cans	Frequency
soup	6
peas	8
corn	11

Complete the two-way frequency table.

3. James surveyed some of his classmates about what vegetable they like best. Complete the table.

	Preferred Vegetable			
Grade	Carrots	Green Beans	Celery	Total
9th	30	15	24	69
10th	32	9	20	61
Total	62	24	44	130

LANGUAGE SUPPORT **EL**

Connect Vocabulary

The word *quantitative* in the phrase *quantitative data* shares a root with the word *quantity*, meaning *an amount*. The word *categorical* in the phrase *categorical data* shares a root with the word *category*, meaning *a descriptive grouping*. Categorical data can also be referred to as *qualitative data* because these data describe qualities or characteristics. The word *frequency* in the phrase *frequency table* shares a root with the word *frequent*, meaning *often*. Each value in a frequency table shows how often that value falls into a given category.

4. A high school's extracurricular committee surveyed a randomly selected group of students about whether they like tennis and soccer. Complete the table.

| | Like Tennis | | |
Like Soccer	Yes	No	Total
Yes	37	20	57
No	16	15	31
Total	53	35	88

5. After a school field trip, Ben surveyed some students about which animals they liked from the zoo. Complete the table.

| | Preferred Animal at a Zoo | | | |
Grade	Lion	Zebra	Monkey	Total
11th	9	15	14	38
12th	4	17	15	36
Total	13	32	29	74

6. Jill asked some randomly selected students whether they preferred blue, green, or other colors. She also recorded the gender of each student. The results are shown in the two-way frequency table below. Complete the table.

| | Preferred Color | | | |
Gender	Green	Blue	Other	Total
Girl	15	3	10	28
Boy	3	16	6	25
Total	18	19	16	53

7. Kevin surveyed some students about whether they preferred soccer, baseball, or another sport. He also recorded their gender. Complete the table.

| | Preferred Sport | | | |
Gender	Soccer	Baseball	Other	Total
Girl	33	7	10	50
Boy	15	27	7	49
Total	48	34	17	99

Exercise	Depth of Knowledge (D.O.K.)	COMMON CORE Mathematical Practices
1–12	**1** Recall	**MP.7** Using Structure
13–14	**2** Skills/Concepts	**MP.3** Logic
15–22	**2** Skills/Concepts	**MP.4** Modeling
23	**1** Recall	**MP.7** Using Structure
24	**2** Skills/Concepts	**MP.3** Logic
25–26	**3** Strategic Thinking H.O.T.	**MP.3** Logic

EVALUATE

Personal Math Trainer

ASSIGNMENT GUIDE

Concepts and Skills	Practice
Explore Categorical Data and Frequencies	Exercises 1–2, 23
Example 1 Constructing Two-Way Frequency Tables	Exercises 3–12
Example 2 Reading Two-Way Frequency Tables	Exercises 13–22, 24–26

INTEGRATE MATHEMATICAL PRACTICES
Focus on Patterns

MP.8 Have students try to find the smallest number of filled cells in a two-way frequency table that makes it possible to complete the table. Work backward from a completed frequency table by removing values one at a time, making sure it is possible to do so while leaving a row or column with only one missing value. Students may discover that completing a frequency table requires that the table have at least as many filled cells as the number of interior cells.

MULTIPLE REPRESENTATIONS

Have students create a two-question survey whose results can be summarized in a two-way frequency table. Students should understand that the questions they choose for their surveys should not allow for open-ended answers.

AVOID COMMON ERRORS

Remind students that in a two-way frequency table, the total of the values in each row and the total of the values in each column must add up to the same number. Students can check their work for errors by comparing the sum of the row totals to the sum of the column totals.

8. A school surveyed a group of students about whether they like backgammon and chess. They will use this data to determine whether there is enough interest for the school to compete in these games. Complete the table.

	Like Backgammon		
Like Chess	Yes	No	Total
Yes	10	61	71
No	5	3	8
Total	15	64	79

9. Hugo surveyed some 9th and 10th graders in regard to whether they preferred math, English, or another subject. The results of the survey are in the following table. Complete the table.

	Preferred Subject			
Grade	Math	English	Other	Total
9th	40	35	20	95
10th	41	32	17	90
Total	81	67	37	185

10. Luis surveyed some middle school and high school students about the type of music they prefer. Complete the table.

	Preferred Music			
School Level	Country	Pop	Other	Total
Middle School	18	13	23	54
High School	7	32	15	54
Total	25	45	38	108

11. Natalie surveyed some teenagers and adults on whether they prefer standard cars, vans, or convertibles. Her results are in the following table. Complete the table.

	Preferred Car Type			
Age	Standard	Van	Convertible	Total
Adults	10	25	9	44
Teenagers	11	7	24	42
Total	21	32	33	86

© Houghton Mifflin Harcourt Publishing Company · Image Credits: ©Dragon Images/Shutterstock

12. Eli surveyed some teenagers and adults on whether they prefer apples, oranges, or bananas. His results are in the following table. Complete the table.

Age	Preferred Fruit			
	Apple	Orange	Banana	Total
Adults	22	12	10	44
Teenagers	24	9	9	42
Total	46	21	19	86

200 students were asked to name their favorite science class. The results are shown in the two-way frequency table. Use the table for the following questions.

Gender	Favorite Science Class			
	Biology	Chemistry	Physics	Total
Girl	42	39	23	104
Boy	19	45	32	96
Total	61	84	55	200

13. How many boys were surveyed? Explain how you found your answer.

96 boys: 104 of the 200 students were girls, so 200 − 104 = 96 of them were boys.

14. Complete the table. How many more girls than boys chose biology as their favorite science class? Explain how you found your answer.

42 − 19 = 23, so 23 more girls than boys chose biology.

The results of a survey of 150 students about whether they own an electronic tablet or a laptop are shown in the two-way frequency table.

Gender	Device				
	Electronic tablet	Laptop	Both	Neither	Total
Girl	15	54	10	9	88
Boy	14	35	8	5	62
Total	29	89	18	14	150

15. Complete the table. Do the surveyed students own more laptops or more electronic tablets?

The number of boys is 150 − 88 = 62.

Girls who own both electronic devices: 88 − 9 − 54 − 15 = 10

Boys who own an electronic tablet: 62 − 5 − 8 − 35 = 14; Students own more laptops.

16. Which group had more people answer the survey, boys or students who own an electronic tablet only? Explain.

Boys: 62 boys answered the survey, which is more than the 29 people who own an electronic tablet only.

17. The table shows the results of a survey about students' preferred frozen yogurt flavor. Complete the table, and state the flavors that students preferred the most and the least.

| Gender | Preferred Flavor | | | |
	Vanilla	Mint	Strawberry	Total
Girl	12	15	18	45
Boy	17	25	13	55
Total	29	40	31	100

Students preferred mint the most and vanilla the least.

18. Teresa surveyed 100 students about whether they like pop music or country music. Out of the 100 students surveyed, 42 like only pop, 34 like only country, 15 like both pop and country, and 9 do not like either pop or country. Complete the two-way frequency table.

| Like Country | Like Pop | | |
	Yes	No	Total
Yes	15	34	49
No	42	9	51
Total	57	43	100

19. Forty students in a class at an international high school were surveyed about which non-English language they can speak. Complete the table.

| Gender | Foreign Language | | | |
	Chinese	Spanish	French	Total
Girl	7	8	7	22
Boy	5	6	7	18
Total	12	14	14	40

Luis surveyed 100 students about whether they like soccer. The number of girls and the number of boys completing the survey are equal.

20. Complete the table.

| Gender | Likes Soccer | | |
	Yes	No	Total
Girl	30	20	50
Boy	15	35	50
Total	45	55	100

21. Twice as many girls like soccer as the number that like tennis. The same number of students like soccer as like tennis. Construct a table containing the tennis data.

| Gender | Likes Tennis | | |
	Yes	No	Total
Girl	15	35	50
Boy	30	20	50
Total	45	55	100

© Houghton Mifflin Harcourt Publishing Company

22. A group of 200 high school students were asked about their use of email and text messages. The results are shown in the two-way frequency table. Complete the table.

Email	Text Messages		
	Yes	No	Total
Yes	72	18	90
No	65	45	110
Total	137	63	200

23. Circle the letter of each data set that is categorical. Select all that apply.

A. 75°, 79°, 77°, 85°

(B.) apples, oranges, pears

(C.) male, female

(D.) blue, green, red

E. 2 feet, 5 feet, 12 feet

(F.) classical music, country music

G. 1 centimeter, 3 centimeters, 9 centimeters

24. Explain the Error Find the mistake in completing the two-way frequency table for a survey involving 50 students. Then complete the table correctly.

Gender	Favorite Foreign Language Class			
	Russian	German	Italian	Total
Girl	8	8	8	24
Boy	42	9	7	58
Total	50			

Possible answer: 50 was used as the total whose favorite is Russian instead of as the grand total.

Total boys: 50 − 24 = 26   **Boys who prefer Russian: 26 − 9 − 7 − 10**

Correct table:

Gender	Favorite Foreign Language Class			
	Russian	German	Italian	Total
Girl	8	8	8	24
Boy	10	9	7	26
Total	18	17	15	50

Two-Way Frequency Tables   **356**

JOURNAL

Have students explain the steps they take to complete a two-way frequency table that has missing values. Students should be sure to include descriptions of how to determine column totals and row totals.

25. Justify Reasoning Charles surveyed 100 boys about their favorite color. Of the 100 boys surveyed, 44 preferred blue, 25 preferred green, and 31 preferred red.

a. Explain why it is not possible to make a two-way frequency table from the given data.

Charles only surveyed boys, so there is only one categorical variable: color. You need two categorical variables to make a two-way frequency table.

b. Suppose Charles also surveyed some girls. Of the girls surveyed, 30 preferred blue and 43 preferred green. Can Charles make a two-way frequency table now? Can he complete it?

He can make a table, but he cannot complete it. There are now two categorical variables, color and gender, but there is not enough information about the girls' preferences. In addition to the information provided, you need to know how many girls were surveyed or how many prefer red to complete the table.

26. Persevere in Problem Solving Shown are two different tables about a survey involving students. Each survey had a few questions about musical preferences. All students answered all questions. Complete the tables. What type of music do the students prefer?

Gender	Likes Classical Music		
	Yes	No	Total
Girl	21	28	49
Boy	29	22	51
Total	50	50	100

Gender	Likes Blues Music		
	Yes	No	Total
Girl	34	15	49
Boy	36	15	51
Total	70	30	100

All students answered all the questions, so total girls in both is 49, and the total students in both is 100.

Overall, the students prefer blues music: 70 students like blues, 50 like classical.

Lesson Performance Task

Two hundred students were asked about their favorite sport. Of the 200 students surveyed, 98 were female. Some of the results are shown in the following two-way frequency table.

Gender	Favorite Sport				
	Football	Baseball	Basketball	Soccer	Total
Female	26	24	36	12	98
Male	38	19	21	24	102
Total	64	43	57	36	200

a. Complete the table.

Total number of males: 200 − 98 = 102

Females who chose football: 64 − 38 = 26

Females who chose baseball: 98 − 26 − 36 − 12 = 24

Males who chose soccer: 36 − 12 = 24

Males who chose basketball: 102 − 38 − 19 − 24 = 21

Total baseball: 24 + 19 = 43

Total basketball: 36 + 21 = 57

b. Which sport is the most popular among the students? Which is the least popular? Explain.

Most popular is football; 64 is the greatest total.

Least popular is soccer; 36 is the least total.

c. Which sport is most popular among the females? Which sport is most popular among the males? Explain.

Most popular among females is basketball; 36 is the greatest number of choices.

Most popular among males is football; 38 is the greatest number of choices.

© Houghton Mifflin Harcourt Publishing Company

EXTENSION ACTIVITY

Have students create and conduct a survey of 20 students and then record the results in a two-way frequency table. Students should begin by selecting two categorical variables to record, such as gender and favorite subject, or grade level and music preference. Remind them that quantitative and free-response answers are not appropriate for recording in a frequency table. Encourage students to select a sample of students that is not expected to skew the survey results. Have students share their frequency tables and discuss their findings.

QUESTIONING STRATEGIES

? In what order would you fill in the empty spaces in the table? Explain why. **Possible answer: I would first fill in the numbers given in the text of the problem (200 students in total, and 98 female students). Then I would look for a row or column with only one empty cell, and find the missing number (such as the total number of males, the number of females who chose football, or the number of males who chose soccer). After I fill in those numbers, there would still be other rows and columns with only one empty cell, so I would repeat the process until the table is completed.**

INTEGRATE MATHEMATICAL PRACTICES
Focus on Reasoning

MP.2 Discuss with students how the sample of students chosen for the survey could have influenced the survey results. For example, consider whether age, country of origin, participation in sports, or other characteristics of survey participants might influence the results. Have students describe a target population for which soccer is likely to be the most popular sport among those surveyed.

Scoring Rubric

2 points: Student correctly solves the problem and explains his/her reasoning.

1 point: Student shows good understanding of the problem but does not fully solve or explain his/her reasoning.

0 points: Student does not demonstrate understanding of the problem.

Two-Way Frequency Tables **358**

LESSON 8.2

Relative Frequency

Common Core Math Standards

The student is expected to:

 S-ID.B.5

Summarize categorical data for two categories in two-way frequency tables. Interpret relative frequencies in the context of the data (including joint, marginal, and conditional relative frequencies). Recognize possible associations and trends in the data.

Mathematical Practices

 MP.4 Modeling

Language Objective

In a two-way relative frequency table, identify a joint relative frequency and a marginal relative frequency, and explain what they mean.

ENGAGE

Essential Question: How can you recognize possible associations and trends between two categories of categorical data?

You can use relative frequencies to interpret associations and trends between two categories in two-way frequency tables.

PREVIEW: LESSON PERFORMANCE TASK

View the Engage section online. Discuss whether students believe that boys or girls are more likely to play a musical instrument. Then preview the Lesson Performance Task.

Name_____ Class_____ Date_____

8.2 Relative Frequency

Essential Question: How can you recognize possible associations and trends between two categories of categorical data?

⊘ Explore   Relative Frequencies

To show what portion of a data set each category in a frequency table makes up, you can convert the data to *relative frequencies*. The **relative frequency** of a category is the frequency of the category divided by the total of all frequencies.

The frequency table below shows the results of a survey Kenesha conducted at school. She asked 80 randomly selected students whether they preferred basketball, football, or soccer.

Favorite Sport	Basketball	Football	Soccer	Total
Frequency	20	32	28	80

Ⓐ Use the frequencies to make a relative frequency table expressed with decimals.

Favorite Sport	Basketball	Football	Soccer	Total
Relative Frequency	$\frac{20}{80} = 0.25$	$\frac{32}{80} = 0.4$	$\frac{28}{80} = 0.35$	$\frac{80}{80} =$ 1

Ⓑ Rewrite the relative frequency table using percents instead of decimals.

Favorite Sport	Basketball	Football	Soccer	Total
Relative Frequency	25%	40%	35%	100%

Reflect

1. Explain what the numerator and denominator of the ratio $\frac{20}{80}$ refer to in part A.
   20 refers to the number of students who prefer basketball, and 80 refers to the total number of students surveyed.

2. What types of numbers can you use to write relative frequencies?
   fractions, decimals, and percents

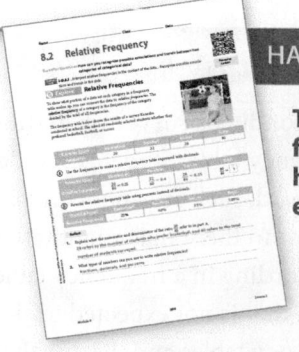

HARDCOVER PAGES 289–298

Turn to these pages to find this lesson in the hardcover student edition.

Explain 1 Two-Way Relative Frequency Tables

Two types of relative frequencies are found in a relative frequency table:

1. A **joint relative frequency** is found by dividing a frequency that is not in the Total row or the Total column by the grand total. It tells what portion of the total has both of the two specified characteristics.

2. A **marginal relative frequency** is found by dividing a row total or a column total by the grand total. It tells what portion of the total has a specified characteristic.

Example 1 Complete a two-way relative frequency table from the data in a two-way frequency table. Identify the joint relative frequencies and the marginal relative frequencies.

Ⓐ For her survey about sports preferences, Kenesha also recorded the gender of each student. The results are shown in the two-way frequency table for Kenesha's data.

Gender	Preferred Sport			
	Basketball	Football	Soccer	Total
Girl	6	12	18	36
Boy	14	20	10	44
Total	20	32	28	80

To find the relative frequencies, divide each frequency by the grand total.

Gender	Preferred Sport			
	Basketball	Football	Soccer	Total
Girl	$\frac{6}{80} = 0.075$	$\frac{12}{80} = 0.15$	$\frac{18}{80} = 0.225$	$\frac{36}{80} = 0.45$
Boy	$\frac{14}{80} = 0.175$	$\frac{20}{80} = 0.25$	$\frac{10}{80} = 0.125$	$\frac{44}{80} = 0.55$
Total	$\frac{20}{80} = 0.25$	$\frac{32}{80} = 0.4$	$\frac{28}{80} = 0.35$	$\frac{80}{80} = 1$

The joint relative frequencies tell what percent of all those surveyed are in each category:

- 7.5% are girls who prefer basketball.
- 15% are girls who prefer football.
- 22.5% are girls who prefer soccer.
- 17.5% are boys who prefer basketball.
- 25% are boys who prefer football.
- 12.5% are boys who prefer soccer.

The marginal relative frequencies tell what percent of totals has a given single characteristic:

- 25% prefer basketball.
- 40% prefer football.
- 35% prefer soccer.
- 45% are girls.
- 55% are boys.

INTEGRATE TECHNOLOGY

Spreadsheet programs can produce tables that automatically make calculations for frequency tables and relative frequency tables. Challenge students to use formulas to program a spreadsheet that computes row totals, column totals, and relative frequencies for a two-way frequency table.

CONNECT VOCABULARY EL

Make sure that students can distinguish between *frequency* and *relative frequency*. *Frequency* is *a measure of the raw data* (for example, 20 students play basketball), while *relative frequency* compares that frequency to the total (for example, 25% of all students play basketball).

EXPLAIN 1

Two-Way Relative Frequency Tables

INTEGRATE MATHEMATICAL PRACTICES
Focus on Math Connections

MP.1 Discuss with students the relationship between two-way frequency tables and two-way relative frequency tables. Make sure they understand that each relative frequency is calculated by dividing the corresponding value in a frequency table by the grand total.

PROFESSIONAL DEVELOPMENT

Math Background

Relative frequencies are often used when determining conditional probability. In the notation of probability, $P(A)$ means *probability of A*. The conditional probability of A being true given that B is true is written as $P(A|B)$, which is read "the probability of A given B." This conditional probability is given by $P(A|B) = \frac{P(A \cap B)}{P(B)}$. In other words, it is found by dividing the number of cases when both A and B are true by the total number of cases when B is true.

QUESTIONING STRATEGIES

? Which values in a frequency table are compared to the total by a joint relative frequency? Which values are compared to the total by a marginal relative frequency? Explain, using examples. A joint relative frequency compares an individual frequency to the grand total. For example, in a table showing gender and sport preference, the percent of the total who are girls who like soccer is a joint relative frequency. A marginal relative frequency compares a category total, either across a row or down a column, to the grand total. For example, in the same table, the percent of the total who are boys is a marginal relative frequency.

(B) Millie performed a survey of students in the lunch line and recorded which type of fruit each student selected along with the gender of each student. The two-variable frequency data she collected is shown in the table.

	Fruit			
	Apple	**Banana**	**Orange**	**Total**
Girl	16	10	14	40
Boy	25	13	14	52
Total	41	23	28	92

	Fruit			
	Apple	**Banana**	**Orange**	**Total**
Girl	17.4%	10.9%	15.2%	43.5%
Boy	27.2%	14.1%	15.2%	56.5%
Total	44.6%	25.0%	30.4%	100.0%

The joint relative frequencies:

- **17.4%** are girls who selected an apple.
- **10.9%** are girls who selected a banana.
- **15.2%** are girls who selected an orange.

- **27.2%** are boys who selected an apple.
- **14.1%** are boys who selected a banana.
- **15.2%** are boys who selected an orange.

The marginal relative frequencies:

- **44.6%** selected an apple.
- **25%** selected a banana.
- **30.4%** selected an orange.

- **43.5%** are girls.
- **56.5%** are boys.

Reflect

3. **Discussion** Explain how you can use joint and marginal relative frequencies to check your relative frequency table.
   You can confirm that the sum of each row and column of joint relative frequencies equals
   the marginal relative frequencies at the end of the same row or column.

COLLABORATIVE LEARNING

Whole Class Activity

Have students conduct their own surveys using left-right handed and a three-category variable of their choice. Then have students organize the data in two-way frequency and relative frequency tables. Finally, have students calculate conditional relative frequencies to analyze the data and investigate any possible association between left-right handed and the other variable.

Use the two-way table of data from another student survey to answer the following questions.

	Like Aerobic Exercise		
Like Weight Lifting	**Yes**	**No**	**Total**
Yes	7	14	21
No	12	7	19
Total	19	21	40

4. Find the joint relative frequency of students surveyed who like aerobics exercise but dislike weight lifting.

   $\dfrac{12}{40} = 0.3$ or 30%

5. What is the marginal relative frequency of students surveyed who like weight lifting?

   $\dfrac{21}{40} = 0.525$ or 52.5%

⊘ Explain 2   Conditional Relative Frequencies

A **conditional relative frequency** describes what portion of a group with a given characteristic also has another characteristic. A conditional relative frequency is found by dividing a frequency that is not in the Total row or the Total column by the total for that row or column.

> **Example 2**   Use the joint relative frequencies to calculate the associated conditional relative frequencies and describe what each one means.

Ⓐ Use the data from Example 1A. Find the conditional relative frequency that a a person in Kenesha's survey prefers soccer, given that the person is a girl.

Divide the number of girls who prefer soccer by the total number of girls.

$\dfrac{\text{Number of girls who prefer soccer}}{\text{Total number of girls}} = \dfrac{18}{36} = 0.5 = 50\%$

Half of the girls in the sample prefer soccer.

Ⓑ Use the data from Example 1B. Find the conditional relative frequency that a student in Millie's survey chose an orange, given that the student is a boy.

$\dfrac{\text{Number of }\boxed{\text{boys}}\text{ who chose an orange}}{\text{Total number of }\boxed{\text{boys}}} = \dfrac{\boxed{14}}{\boxed{52}} \approx 0.269 = \boxed{26.9}\ \%$

Your Turn

Use the data from Your Turn Exercises 4 and 5 after Example 1.

6. What is the conditional relative frequency that a student likes to lift weights, given that the student does not like aerobics?

   $\dfrac{14}{21} = 0.667$ or 66.7%

7. Find the conditional relative frequency that a student likes to lift weights, given that the student likes aerobics.

   $\dfrac{7}{19} = 0.368$ or 36.8%

EXPLAIN 2

Conditional Relative Frequencies

CONNECT VOCABULARY EL

Focus on the term *conditional relative frequency*. A *relative frequency* compares a frequency to the grand total of the data. A *conditional relative frequency* goes one step further and compares this frequency in a conditional sense—that is, under the condition that only a subset of the grand total is considered.

AVOID COMMON ERRORS

When finding conditional relative frequencies, students can avoid errors by remembering that the quantity that is given will be in the denominator of the fraction. For example, to find the conditional relative frequency that a student is a boy, given that the student prefers basketball, the number of boys who prefer basketball must be compared to the total number who prefer basketball, not to the total who are boys.

QUESTIONING STRATEGIES

❓ When determining a conditional relative frequency, how do you know what number to use as the numerator of the fraction? The numerator will be the number of items that satisfy both the given condition and the characteristic for which you are finding the conditional relative frequency.

DIFFERENTIATE INSTRUCTION

Multiple Representations

To help students understand how one characteristic can influence a distribution, use the real-world example of left-handed pitchers in baseball. About 10% of the population is left-handed, so all other things being equal, one would expect 10% of baseball pitchers to be left-handed. In fact, more than 25% of pitchers are left-handed, meaning that there are more than twice as many left-handers as would be expected. This suggests that there are more left-handed pitchers because they enjoy some kind of advantage in being left-handed.

EXPLAIN 3

Finding Possible Associations

INTEGRATE MATHEMATICAL PRACTICES
Focus on Reasoning

MP.2 When looking for possible associations, make sure students understand what kind of data should be expected when no association or influence exists. Remind students to keep this idea in mind as they work through a problem. The actual conditional relative frequencies must always be compared to the conditional relative frequencies that would be expected if there were no association between the variables.

QUESTIONING STRATEGIES

? What numbers in a two-way relative frequency table can be used to determine whether a possible association exists? Explain. Divide the joint relative frequency for a given cell by the marginal relative frequency for that column. Compare the quotient to the marginal relative frequency for the row that includes the given cell. If the two numbers are different, there is a possible association.

⚙ Explain 3 **Finding Possible Associations**

You can analyze two-way frequency tables to locate possible associations or patterns in the data.

Example 3 Analyze the results of the surveys to determine preferences by gender.

Kenesha is interested in the question, "Does gender influence what type of sport students prefer?" If there is no influence, then the distribution of gender within each sport preference will roughly equal the distribution of gender within the whole group. Analyze the results of Kenesha's survey from Example 1. Determine which sport each gender is more likely to prefer.

(A) Analyze the data about girls that were surveyed.

Step 1: Identify the percent of all students surveyed who are girls.

$$\frac{36}{80} = 0.45 = 45\%$$

Step 2: Determine each conditional relative frequency.

Basketball	Football	Soccer
Of the 20 students who prefer basketball, 6 are girls.	Of the 32 students who prefer football, 12 are girls.	Of the 28 students who prefer soccer, 18 are girls.
$\frac{6}{20} = 0.3 = 30\%$	$\frac{12}{32} = 0.375 = 37.5\%$	$\frac{18}{28} \approx 0.643 = 64.3\%$

Step 3: Interpret the results by comparing each conditional relative frequency to the percent of all students surveyed who are girls, 45%.

Basketball	Football	Soccer
30% < 45%	37.5% < 45%	64.3% > 45%
Girls are less likely to prefer basketball.	Girls are less likely to prefer football.	Girls are more likely to prefer soccer.

(B) Analyze the data about boys that were surveyed.

Step 1: Identify the percent of all students surveyed who are boys.

$$\frac{44}{80} = 0.\boxed{55} = \boxed{55}\%$$

Step 2: Determine each conditional relative frequency.

Basketball	Football	Soccer
Of the 20 students who prefer basketball, $\boxed{14}$ are boys.	Of the $\boxed{32}$ students who prefer football, $\boxed{20}$ are boys.	Of the $\boxed{28}$ students who prefer soccer, $\boxed{10}$ are boys.
$\frac{14}{20} = 0.\boxed{7} = \boxed{70}\%$	$\frac{20}{32} = 0.\boxed{625} = \boxed{62.5}\%$	$\frac{10}{28} = 0.\boxed{357} = \boxed{35.7}\%$

© Houghton Mifflin Harcourt Publishing Company

LANGUAGE SUPPORT **EL**

Connect Vocabulary

There are many words in algebra that are borrowed from other languages or have shared Latin roots across languages. English learners who speak Spanish may benefit from looking for words that may already be familiar in their primary language. Many multi-syllabic words that end with *–al* in English (such as *final*, *conditional*, and *visual*) are cognates with words in Spanish that end with *–al* (*final*, *condicional*, and *visual*).

Step 3: Interpret the results by comparing each conditional relative frequency to the percent of all students surveyed who are boys, [55] %.

Basketball	Football	Soccer
70% > 55%	62.5% > 55%	35.7% < 55%
Boys are more likely to prefer basketball.	Boys are more likely to prefer football.	Boys are less likely to prefer soccer.

Reflect

8. **Making Connections** How can the statement "6 out of the 20 students who prefer basketball are girls" be stated as a conditional relative frequency?
Given that a student prefers basketball, 30% are girls.

Your Turn

9. Analyze the data given in the Your Turn after Example 1 to determine if liking aerobic exercise influences whether a person also likes weight lifting. Explain.
Those who like aerobics are less likely than those who do not like aerobics to like weight lifting. Possible answer: 36.8% of respondents who like aerobics like weight lifting, while 52.5% of all respondents like weight lifting.

💬 **Elaborate**

10. What does it mean to say there is an association between characteristics in a two-way frequency table?
It means that there is a pattern between the two variables so that the conditional relative frequencies, or conditional probabilities, are somewhat predictable.

11. **Essential Question Check-In** How can you use two-way frequency data to recognize possible associations between the two categories of categorical data?
You can compare conditional relative frequencies with different givens to each other or to the marginal relative frequencies to see if certain conditions favor a category relative to other conditions or the entire data set.

ELABORATE

INTEGRATE MATHEMATICAL PRACTICES
Focus on Math Connections

MP.1 Discuss the similarities between conditional relative frequencies and conditional probability. Students should understand that for events A and B, the probability of A given B is different from the probability of B given A.

SUMMARIZE THE LESSON

❓ How can you determine whether one category has an influence over the distribution of the data in a two-way frequency table? First, find what percent of the grand total is in the category of interest. Then, find the conditional relative frequencies for the category given each choice of the second categorical variable. Compare each conditional relative frequency to the percent of the entire group made up by the category. If the two percents are roughly equal, the category has little or no influence over the distribution. If the percents are very different, the category does have an influence.

EVALUATE

ASSIGNMENT GUIDE

Concepts and Skills	Practice
Explore Relative Frequencies	Exercises 1–4
Example 1 Two-Way Relative Frequency Tables	Exercises 5–13
Example 2 Conditional Relative Frequencies	Exercises 14–19, 24, 26–27
Example 3 Finding Possible Associations	Exercises 20–23, 25

VISUAL CUES

To visually distinguish between different parts of a two-way relative frequency table, students could use one color to shade the part of the table that represents joint relative frequencies (the cells at the intersection of two categories) and a different color to shade the part of the table that represents marginal relative frequencies (the row and column totals).

AVOID COMMON ERRORS

When finding conditional relative frequencies, some students may divide a frequency by the grand total instead of the frequency's row total or column total. Suggest that students outline or highlight the row or column that is "given" to identify the part of the table that is relevant to the question.

☆ Evaluate: Homework and Practice

• Online Homework
• Hints and Help
• Extra Practice

Use the table of frequency data for Exercises 1–4.

Class Survey of Favorite Colors

Favorite Color	Red	Orange	Yellow	Green	Blue	Purple	Total
Frequency	2	5	1	6	8	2	24

1. Complete the relative frequency table for this data using decimals rounded to the nearest thousandth.

Class Survey of Favorite Colors

Favorite Color	Red	Orange	Yellow	Green	Blue	Purple	Total
Relative Frequency	0.083	0.208	0.042	0.25	0.333	0.083	1

2. Complete the relative frequency table for this data using percents rounded to the nearest tenth.

Class Survey of Favorite Colors

Favorite Color	Red	Orange	Yellow	Green	Blue	Purple	Total
Relative Frequency	8.3%	20.8%	4.2%	25%	33.3%	8.3%	100.0%

3. What is the relative frequency of having blue as a favorite color, expressed as a decimal?

0.333

4. Which color is a favorite color with a relative frequency of 25%?

green

The following frequency data shows the number of states, including the District of Columbia, that favored each party in the presidential popular vote in 1976 and in 2012.

1976 Election	2012 Election		
	Democrat	Republican	Total
Democrat	12 = 23.5%	12 = 23.5%	24 = 47.1%
Republican	15 = 29.4%	12 = 23.5%	27 = 52.9%
Total	27 = 52.9%	24 = 47.1%	51 = 100%

5. Complete the table above with relative frequencies using percents.

6. What percent switched from Democrat in 1976 to Republican in 2012? What type of frequency is this?

23.5%; a joint relative frequency

7. What percent voted Republican in 1976? What type of frequency is this?

52.9%; a marginal relative frequency

Exercise	Depth of Knowledge (D.O.K.)	COMMON CORE Mathematical Practices
1–13	**1** Recall	**MP.4** Modeling
14–24	**2** Skills/Concepts	**MP.4** Modeling
25–27	**3** Strategic Thinking **H.O.T.**	**MP.3** Logic

The results of a survey of 45 students and the foreign language they are studying are shown in the two-way frequency table.

Gender	Language			
	Chinese	French	Spanish	Total
Girl	2	8	15	25
Boy	4	4	12	20
Total	6	12	27	45

8. Fill in the table of two-way relative frequencies using decimals, rounded to the nearest thousandth.

Gender	Language			
	Chinese	French	Spanish	Total
Girl	0.044	0.178	0.333	0.556
Boy	0.089	0.089	0.267	0.444
Total	0.133	0.267	0.6	1

9. What fraction of the surveyed students are boys taking Spanish?

$\frac{4}{15} \approx 0.267$

10. What fraction of the surveyed students are taking Chinese?

$\frac{2}{15} \approx 0.133$

In some states, a driver of a vehicle may not use a handheld cell phone while driving. In one state with this law, 250 randomly selected drivers were surveyed to determine the association between drivers who know the law and drivers who obey the law.
The results are shown in the table below.

11. Complete the table of two-way relative frequencies using percents.

Obeys the Law	Knows the Law		
	Yes	No	Total
Yes	160 = 64%	45 = 18%	82%
No	25 = 10%	20 = 8%	18%
Total	74%	26%	100%

© Houghton Mifflin Harcourt Publishing Company • image credit: ©Leena Robinson/Shutterstock

12. What is the relative frequency of drivers who know and obey the law?

64%

13. What is the relative frequency of drivers who know the law?

74%

COGNITIVE STRATEGIES

Students may want to use the list below to solve conditional relative frequency problems such as this one: *Find the conditional relative frequency that a student is a boy, given that the student prefers soccer.* Students should fill in each item.

Given: _prefers soccer_

Find relative frequency of: _boy_

Frequency of: _boys who play soccer_

Total: _all who prefer soccer_

Percent:
boys who prefer soccer ÷ _all who prefer soccer_

AVOID COMMON ERRORS

Students may select the wrong value to use as the denominator when calculating relative frequencies. Remind students that when finding a joint or marginal relative frequency, the denominator of the fraction is the grand total from the frequency table. When finding a conditional relative frequency, the denominator of the fraction is the quantity that is given as the condition.

Refer to the election data from Exercises 5–7. Answer using percents rounded to the nearest tenth.

14. What is the conditional relative frequency of a state's popular vote being won by the Democrat in 2012, given that it was won by the Democrat in 1976?

$$\frac{12}{24} = 50\%$$

15. What is the conditional relative frequency of a state's popular vote being won by the Democrat in 1976, given that it was won by the Democrat in 2012?

$$\frac{12}{27} \approx 44.4\%$$

Refer to the language data from Exercises 8–10. Answer using decimals rounded to the nearest thousandth.

16. What fraction of girls are studying French?

$$\frac{8}{25} = 0.32$$

17. What fraction of Spanish students are boys?

$$\frac{8}{27} = 0.444$$

Refer to the cell phone law data from Exercises 11–13. Answer using percents rounded to the nearest tenth.

18. What percent of drivers obey the law despite not knowing the law?

$$\frac{45}{65} = 69.2\%$$

19. What is the conditional relative frequency of drivers who obey the law, given that they know the law?

$$\frac{160}{185} = 86.5\%$$

Use the previously described data to determine whether there are associations between the categories surveyed.

20. Refer to the election data from Exercises 5–7. Is there an association between the party that won the popular vote in a state in 1976 and in 2012?

The conditional relative frequency that a state was won by the Democrat in 2012, given that a Democrat won the state in 1976, is $\frac{12}{24} = 50\%$. The conditional relative frequency that a state was won by the Republican in 2012, given that a Republican won the state in 1976, is $\frac{12}{27} \approx 44.4\%$. Since 44.4% < 50%, the 2012 Republican candidate was slightly less likely to win a state that had voted for the party's candidate in 1976 than the Democratic opponent.

21. Refer to the language data from Exercises 8–10. Can you use gender to predict a preference for taking Spanish?

Conditional relative frequency of taking Spanish, given the student is a girl: $\frac{15}{25} = 60\%$ Percent of all students who take Spanish: $\frac{27}{45} = 60\%$ No, both genders are equally likely to be taking Spanish.

© Houghton Mifflin Harcourt Publishing Company

22. Refer to the language data from Exercises 8–10. Is there an association between gender and a preference for French?

Conditional relative frequency of taking French, given the student is a girl:

$\dfrac{8}{25} = 32\%$

Percent of all students who are taking French:

$\dfrac{12}{45} = 26.7\%$

Yes, a girl in the survey is more likely to be taking French than a boy.

23. Refer to the cell phone law data from Exercises 11–13. Most drivers who don't know that it is illegal to operate a cell phone while driving obey the law anyway, presumably out of a general concern for safe driving. Does this mean there is no association between knowledge of the cell phone law and obeying the cell phone law?

The conditional relative frequency of obeying the law, given knowledge of the law, is 86.5% (from Exercise 19), and the percent of all drivers who obey the law is 82%. There is a slight difference, though both frequencies are greater than 50%, so there is a possible association between knowledge of the law and obeying it.

24. Multipart Classification Classify each statement as describing a *joint*, *marginal*, or *conditional* relative frequency.

a. In a study on age and driving safety, 33% of drivers were considered younger and a high accident risk.

joint

b. In a study on age and driving safety, 45% of older drivers were considered a high accident risk.

conditional

c. In a study on age and driving safety, 67% of drivers were classified as younger.

marginal

d. In a pre-election poll, 67% of the respondents who preferred the incumbent were men.

conditional

e. In a pre-election poll, 33% of women preferred the challenger.

conditional

f. In a pre-election poll, 16% of respondents were men who preferred the challenger.

joint

JOURNAL

Have students describe the steps they take when creating a two-way relative frequency table. Students should include instructions for determining both marginal relative frequencies and joint relative frequencies.

25. Explain the Error In the survey on gender and fruit selection (Example 1B), Millicent notices that given a preference for oranges, the conditional relative frequencies of a student being a boy or a girl are the same. She concludes that there is no association between gender and orange preference. Explain her error.

Millie missed the fact that there are more boys than girls in the survey, so a 50% conditional relative frequency of a student who likes an orange being a girl is higher than the 43.5% marginal relative frequency of girls in the whole survey. This means girls in the survey actually had a higher preference for oranges than boys.

26. Communicate Mathematical Ideas Can a joint relative frequency be greater than either of the conditional relative frequencies associated with it? Explain your reasoning.

No. The two conditional frequencies are calculated by dividing the joint frequency by the row total or column total, which is less than the grand total. The joint relative frequency is found by dividing the same joint frequency by the grand total and must therefore be less.

27. Explain the Error Refer to the cell phone data from Exercises 11–13. Cole found the conditional relative frequency that a driver surveyed does not know the law, given that the driver obeys the law, by dividing 45 by 250. Explain Cole's error.

Cole should have divided 45 by the total number of drivers that obey the law, 205.

Lesson Performance Task

Eighty students were surveyed about playing an instrument. The results are shown in the two-way frequency table.

	Play an Instrument		
Gender	Yes	No	Total
Female	28	17	45
Male	20	15	35
Total	48	32	80

a. Complete the two-way relative frequency table for the data.

	Play an Instrument		
Gender	Yes	No	Total
Female	$\frac{28}{80} = 0.35$	$\frac{17}{80} = 0.2125$	$\frac{45}{80} = 0.5625$
Male	$\frac{20}{80} = 0.25$	$\frac{15}{80} = 0.1875$	$\frac{35}{80} = 0.4375$
Total	$\frac{48}{80} = 0.60$	$\frac{32}{80} = 0.40$	$\frac{80}{80} = 1$

b. What percent of the students surveyed play an instrument? What percent of the males surveyed do not play an instrument? Identify what type of frequency each percent is.

60% of the students surveyed play an instrument. This is a marginal relative frequency.

$\frac{20}{35} \approx 0.429 \approx 42.9\%$

42.9% of the males surveyed do not play an instrument. This is a conditional relative frequency.

c. Is there an association between the sex of a student and whether the student plays an instrument? Explain.

Percent of students surveyed who are female: 56.25%

Find the conditional relative frequency that a student surveyed is a female, given that she plays an instrument.

$\frac{28}{48} \approx 0.583 = 58.3\%$

Females make up 58.3% of students who play an instrument, but they only make up 56.25% of the students surveyed. So, females are more likely to play an instrument than males.

© Houghton Mifflin Harcourt Publishing Company

EXTENSION ACTIVITY

Have students conduct a survey to determine whether boys or girls at their school are more likely to play certain kinds of instruments. For example, they might choose to ask whether students play a wind instrument, a string instrument, percussion, or piano. Have students make a two-way relative frequency table from the data. Then have them analyze the data to determine whether there is an association between gender and the type of instrument played.

QUESTIONING STRATEGIES

? How can you check your work to be sure you have calculated the percents correctly in your two-way relative frequency table? Add the joint relative frequencies in each row and each column. The sum should equal the row or column's marginal relative frequency. In addition, the sum of the row totals and the sum of the column totals should both equal 1.

INTEGRATE MATHEMATICAL PRACTICES
Focus on Reasoning

MP.2 To help students approach the question of whether there is an association between gender and playing an instrument, ask what results would be expected if gender does *not* influence whether a person plays an instrument. Students should recognize that if gender has no influence on playing an instrument, one would expect the students who play instruments to have the same percent of males and females as the total group of students surveyed. Alternatively, one would expect the percent of each gender that plays an instrument to be the same as the percent of the whole group that plays an instrument. Urge students to keep these ideas in mind as they analyze the data.

Scoring Rubric
2 points: Student correctly solves the problem and explains his/her reasoning.
1 point: Student shows good understanding of the problem but does not fully solve or explain his/her reasoning.
0 points: Student does not demonstrate understanding of the problem.

Relative Frequency   **370**

Study Guide Review

ASSESSMENT AND INTERVENTION

Assign or customize module reviews.

MODULE PERFORMANCE TASK

COMMON CORE

Mathematical Practices: MP.1, MP.2, MP.3, MP.4, MP.6
S-ID.B.5

SUPPORTING STUDENT REASONING

To help students get started on this project, you may wish to do the following:

- **Review methods for drawing circle graphs, histograms, and bar graphs.** Remind students of the advantages and disadvantages of each type of display.

- **Discuss ways to spot trends in the data.** Ask questions like these: Did students in both groups choose the same activities at the same rates? Why might the activity most chosen by the younger group change as they grew older?

SCAFFOLDING SUPPORT

- Review the method for finding relative frequencies from a two-way frequency table. Example: The two-way table records the results for 200 students. Forty are students in Grades 7–9 and want to attend camp. Relative frequency: $\frac{40}{200} = 0.2$.

Multi-Variable Categorical Data

Essential Question: How can you use multi-variable categorical data to solve real-world problems?

Key Vocabulary
categorical data *(datos categóricos)*
conditional relative frequency *(frecuencia relativa condicional)*
frequency table *(tabla de frecuencia)*
joint relative frequency *(frecuencia relativa conjunta)*
marginal relative frequency *(frecuencia relativa marginal)*
quantitative data *(datos cuantitativos)*
relative frequency *(frecuencia relativa)*

KEY EXAMPLE   *(Lesson 8.1)*

The principal of a high school surveyed 9th and 10th graders as to whether they want to go on a field trip to the museum, zoo, or botanical garden. The results of the survey are in the following table. Complete the table.

	Preferred Field Trip			
Grade	Museum	Zoo	Botanical Garden	Total
9th	42	28	31	
10th		52	62	142
Total	70	80	93	

$42 + 28 + 31 = 101$ Find the 9th grade row total.

$70 - 42 = 28$ Total who prefer the museum — 9th graders who prefer the museum

$70 + 80 + 93 = 243$ and $101 + 142 = 243$ Find the grand total.

	Preferred Field Trip			
Grade	Museum	Zoo	Botanical Garden	Total
9th	42	28	31	101
10th	28	52	62	142
Total	70	80	93	243

KEY EXAMPLE   *(Lesson 8.2)*

The principal wants to know if the percent of 10th graders who prefer the zoo is greater than the percent of total students who prefer the zoo. Find the conditional relative frequency of 10th graders who prefer the zoo and the marginal relative frequency of students who prefer the zoo. Compare the results.

The percent of 10th graders who prefer the zoo is given by the conditional relative frequency:

$$\frac{\text{Number of 10th graders who prefer the zoo}}{\text{Total number of 10th graders}} = \frac{52}{142} \approx 0.37.$$

The percent of total students who prefer the zoo is given by the marginal relative frequency:

$$\frac{\text{Number of students who prefer the zoo}}{\text{Total number of students}} = \frac{80}{243} \approx 0.33.$$

Since 37% > 33%, the percent of 10th graders who prefer the zoo is greater than the percent of total students that prefer the zoo.

SCAFFOLDING SUPPORT (CONTINUED)

- Use the given example ("What is the probability that a student who chose "Attend Camp" is in Grades 7–9?") to review conditional relative probability. To answer the example question, find the ratio of the number of students in grades 7–9 who chose "Attend Camp" (40) to the total number who chose "Attend Camp" (60). Answer: $\frac{40}{60} = \frac{2}{3}$

EXERCISES

1. Complete the two-way frequency table. Interpret the meaning of the number in the starred cell of the table. *(Lesson 8.1)*

Age	Preferred Mode of Transportation			
	Bike	Car	Bus	Total
Adults	25	3	12	40
Teenagers	5	28	12	45
Total	30	*31	24	85

31 is the total number of people surveyed who prefer cars.

2. A middle school student surveyed middle school and high school teachers on whether they preferred to have their students write in pen. *(Lesson 8.2)*

Grade Level	Prefer Students Use Pen		
	Yes	No	Total
Middle School	3	18	21
High School	7	12	19
Total	10	30	40

Are middle school teachers or high school teachers more likely to prefer that their students use pen? Explain.

36.8% is greater than 14.3%, so a greater percent of high school teachers prefer that their students use pen.

MODULE PERFORMANCE TASK

Survey Says?

Students in grades 7–12 were surveyed about which of the following they would most like to do during 2 weeks of a summer vacation: visit a foreign country, attend camp, or visit a national park. The students were divided into two groups, Grades 7–9 and Grades 10–12. Here are the results:

	Visit a Foreign Country	Attend Camp	Visit a National Park
Grades 7–9	25	40	15
Grades 10–12	70	20	30

- Make a table showing the relative frequency of each of the six categories in the table.
- Make a circle graph, histogram, or bar graph showing the frequencies or relative frequencies of each of the six categories in the table.
- Write and answer at least five questions involving conditional relative probability that can be answered by referring to the table.
- Describe any trends you see in the data.

Use your own paper to work on the task. Use numbers, words, or algebra to explain how you reached your conclusion.

SAMPLE SOLUTION

1.

	Visit a Foreign Country	Attend Camp	Visit a National Park
Grades 7–9	0.125	0.2	0.075
Grades 10–12	0.35	0.1	0.15

2.

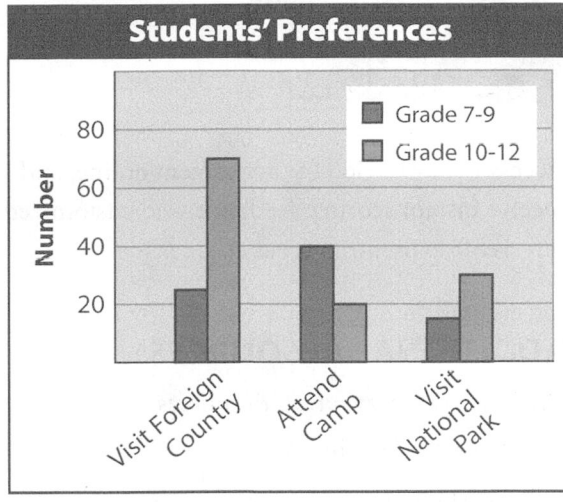

Students' Preferences

3. a. What is the conditional relative probability that a student who chose "Attend Camp" is in Grades 10–12? $\frac{1}{3}$

b. What is the conditional relative probability that a student who chose "Visit a National Park" is in Grades 10–12? $\frac{2}{3}$

c. What is the probability that a student in Grades 10–12 did NOT choose "Visit a Foreign Country"? $\frac{5}{12}$

d. What is the conditional relative probability that if a student is in Grades 7–9, the student chose "Visit a National Park"? $\frac{3}{16}$

e. What is the conditional relative probability that a student who chose "Visit a National Park" is in Grades 7–12? 1

SAMPLE SOLUTION (CONTINUED)

4. Attending camp is the most popular activity in Grades 7–9 and the least popular in Grades 10–12. As students grow older they appear to grow more interested in travel, such as by visiting a foreign country or a national park. In both grade categories, students prefer visiting a foreign country to visiting a national park.

DISCUSSION OPPORTUNITIES

- Ask students to describe and justify the trends in the data that they detected.
- Discuss which of the three given methods is best for displaying the data and why.

Assessment Rubric

2 points: Student correctly solves the problem and explains his/her reasoning.

1 point: Student shows good understanding of the problem but does not fully solve or explain his/her reasoning.

0 points: Student does not demonstrate understanding of the problem.

Study Guide Review   **372**

Ready to Go On?

ASSESS MASTERY

Use the assessment on this page to determine if students have mastered the concepts and standards covered in this module.

ASSESSMENT AND INTERVENTION

Access Ready to Go On? assessment online, and receive instant scoring, feedback, and customized intervention or enrichment.

ADDITIONAL RESOURCES

Response to Intervention Resources

- Reteach Worksheets

Differentiated Instruction Resources

- Reading Strategies **EL**
- Success for English Learners **EL**
- Challenge Worksheets

Assessment Resources

- Leveled Module Quizzes

(Ready) to Go On?

8.1–8.2 Multi-Variable Categorical Data

- Online Homework
- Hints and Help
- Extra Practice

1. A researcher surveyed 135 people, 85 females and 50 males. The researcher asked each person which of the following types of movies they preferred: action, comedy, or drama. Complete the table. *(Lesson 8.1)*

| Gender | Favorite Type of Movie | | | |
	Action	Comedy	Drama	Total
Female	35	32	18	85
Male	12	28	10	50
Total	47	60	28	135

2. Based on the data given in the frequency table below, does a greater percent of 11th or 12th graders surveyed like tennis? Use conditional relative frequencies to support your answer. *(Lesson 8.2)*

| Grade | Like Tennis | | |
	Yes	No	Total
11th	55	55	110
12th	64	32	96
Total	99	97	206

The conditional relative frequency that an 11th grader likes tennis is 0.5.
The conditional relative frequency that a 12th grader likes tennis is about 67%.
Since 50% is less than 67%, a greater percent of 12th graders like tennis.

ESSENTIAL QUESTION

3. How can you compare values in tables of two-variable categorical data?
   Possible Answer: Find and compare the conditional relative frequencies for each two-variable data value.

COMMON CORE Common Core Standards

Lesson	Items	Content Standards	Mathematical Practices
8.1	1	S-ID.B.5	MP.2
8.2	2	S-ID.B.5	MP.6

MODULE 8
MIXED REVIEW

Assessment Readiness

1. Look at each variable. Is the variable best represented by categorical data? Select Yes or No for each variable.

   A. Favorite song — ● Yes ○ No
   B. Car color — ● Yes ○ No
   C. Weight — ○ Yes ● No

2. Mazin asked his classmates whether they like soccer and whether they like running. The table shows the results of his survey.

Like Soccer	Like Running		
	Yes	No	Total
Yes	12	25	37
No	12	6	18
Total	24	31	55

   Complete the table. Choose True or False for each statement.

   A. 12 students like soccer but not running. — ○ True ● False
   B. Mazin surveyed 55 students in all. — ● True ○ False
   C. 25 students like soccer. — ○ True ● False

Use the following information for questions 3 and 4.

Samantha is preparing to do a survey of the language classes taken by ninth and tenth graders at her high school. Each student in ninth and tenth grade takes one language class. From school records, she knows there are 158 students in the ninth grade, as shown in the table.

Grade	Language			
	French	Mandarin	Spanish	Total
9	r	s	t	158
10	x	y	z	
Total				

3. Write an expression to represent the conditional relative frequency that a student takes Mandarin, given that the student is a tenth grader. Explain how you created the expression.

   $\frac{y}{x+y+z}$; the conditional relative frequency is the number of tenth graders taking Mandarin divided by the total number of tenth graders.

4. Based on school records, Samantha finds out that there are 65 students in ninth grade who take Spanish and 35 students in ninth grade that take French. Find the conditional probability that a student takes Mandarin, given that the student is a ninth grader. Show your work.

   $158 = 35 + 65 + s$

   $s = 58$

   $\frac{58}{158} \approx 36.7\%$

ASSESSMENT AND INTERVENTION

Assign ready-made or customized practice tests to prepare students for high-stakes tests.

ADDITIONAL RESOURCES

Assessment Resources

- Leveled Module Quizzes: Modified, B

AVOID COMMON ERRORS

Item 3 Some students may be confused by the use of variables for data. These students may find it easier to temporarily assign invented data values to the variables, and then switch back to variables after writing an expression.

COMMON CORE ## Common Core Standards

Lesson	Items	Content Standards	Mathematical Practices
8.1	1	**S-ID.B.5**	**MP.1**
2.2, 8.1	2*	**A-CED.A.1, S-ID.B.5**	**MP.4**
2.1, 8.2	3*	**S-ID.B.5**	**MP.2**
2.2, 8.2	4*	**A-CED.A.1, S-ID.B.5**	**MP.5**

* Item integrates mixed review concepts from previous modules or a previous course.

ESSENTIAL QUESTION:

Answer: By analyzing data distributions you can compare the typical values and amount of spread in different data sets.

PROFESSIONAL DEVELOPMENT VIDEO

Professional Development Video

Author Juli Dixon models successful teaching practices in an actual high-school classroom.

Professional
Development
my.hrw.com

One-Variable Data Distributions

Essential Question: How can you use one-variable data distributions to solve real-world problems?

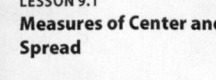

© Houghton Mifflin Harcourt Publishing Company • Shane Osborn/Somos Images/Corbis

REAL WORLD VIDEO
In baseball, there are many options for how a team executes a given play. The use of statistics for in-game decision making sometimes reveals surprising strategies that run counter to the common wisdom.

MODULE PERFORMANCE TASK PREVIEW

Baseball Stats

Most baseball fans keep track of a few statistics relating to their favorite team—the number of home runs their favorite player has hit, for example. An entire field of statistics called sabermetrics goes much farther, keeping track of incredibly detailed data about teams and their players. One website lists 111 such statistics. In this module, you'll study ways to analyze these numbers and then apply what you've learned to some actual baseball stats.

Module 9   **375**

DIGITAL TEACHER EDITION

Access a full suite of teaching resources when and where you need them:

- Access content online or offline
- Customize lessons to share with your class
- Communicate with your students in real-time
- View student grades and data instantly to target your instruction where it is needed most

PERSONAL MATH TRAINER
Assessment and Intervention

Assign automatically graded homework, quizzes, tests, and intervention activities. Prepare your students with updated, Common Core-aligned practice tests.

Are YOU Ready?

Complete these exercises to review skills you will need for this module.

- Online Homework
- Hints and Help
- Extra Practice

Measures of Center

Example 1

Find the mode, median, and mean of these data.

8, 4, 16, 8, 12, 19, 35, 8, 4, 11

4, 4, 8, 8, 8, 11, 12, 16, 19, 35   Order the data.

The mode is 8.

The middle two entries are 8 and 11.

Their mean is $\frac{8 + 11}{2} = 9.5$.

The median is 9.5.

The sum of all the data is 125.

There are 10 entries.

The mean is $\frac{125}{10}$, or 12.5.

Mode: The number with the greatest frequency is the mode.

Median: Find the middle entry or the mean of the two middle entries of the ordered data.

Mean: Find the sum of all the entries and divide it by the number of entries.

Use these data to find the measures of center.
26, 19, 14, 30, 12, 21, 30, 4

1. What is the mean?
19.5

2. What is the mode?
30

3. What is the median?
20

Box Plots

Example 2

The box plot shown represents the ages people of a certain community were when they purchased their first automobile. What is the range of ages?

The box plot extends from 22 to 31, so the range of ages is 31 − 22, or 9 years.

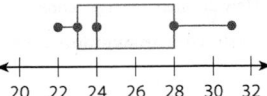

Use the box plot shown to answer the questions.

4. What is the median?
24

5. What is the first quartile?
23

6. What is the third quartile?
28

© Houghton Mifflin Harcourt Publishing Company

Are You Ready?

ASSESS READINESS

Use the assessment on this page to determine if students need strategic or intensive intervention for the module's prerequisite skills.

ASSESSMENT AND INTERVENTION

RtI Response to Intervention **TIER 1, TIER 2, TIER 3 SKILLS**

Personal Math Trainer will automatically create a standards-based, personalized intervention assignment for your students, targeting each student's individual needs!

ADDITIONAL RESOURCES

See the table below for a full list of intervention resources available for this module.

Response to Intervention Resources also includes:

- Tier 2 Skill Pre-Tests for each Module
- Tier 2 Skill Post-Tests for each skill

	Response to Intervention		Differentiated Instruction
Tier 1 Lesson Intervention Worksheets	**Tier 2** Strategic Intervention Skills Intervention Worksheets	**Tier 3** Intensive Intervention Worksheets available online	
Reteach 9.1 Reteach 9.2 Reteach 9.3 Reteach 9.4	28 Measures of Center 29 Box Plots 30 Histograms	Building Block Skills 2, 6, 26, 47, 54, 115, 116, 117, 118	Challenge worksheets Extend the Math Lesson Activities in TE

Measures of Center and Spread

Common Core Math Standards

The student is expected to:

 S-ID.A.2

Use statistics appropriate to the shape of the data distribution to compare center (median, mean) and spread (interquartile range, standard deviation) of two or more different data sets.

Mathematical Practices

COMMON CORE **MP.1 Problem Solving**

Language Objective

Explain the difference between a measure of center and a measure of spread.

ENGAGE

Essential Question: How can you describe and compare data sets?

Use the mean and median to describe and compare the center of data sets. Use the range, interquartile range, or standard deviation to describe and compare the spread of data sets.

PREVIEW: LESSON PERFORMANCE TASK

View the Engage section online. Discuss who might participate in a town choir, and describe the four sections that typically make up a choir: soprano, alto, tenor, and bass. Then preview the Lesson Performance Task.

Name_____ Class_____ Date_____

9.1 Measures of Center and Spread

Essential Question: How can you describe and compare data sets?

⊘ Explore   Exploring Data

Caleb and Kim have bowled three games. Their scores are shown in the chart below.

Name	Game 1	Game 2	Game 3	Average Score
Caleb	151	153	146	**150**
Kim	122	139	189	**150**

Complete the table.

Ⓐ Find Caleb's average score over the three games and enter it in the table.

$$\frac{151 + 153 + 146}{3} = \frac{\boxed{450}}{3} = \boxed{150}$$

Ⓑ Find Kim's average score over the three games and enter it in the table.

$$\frac{122 + 139 + 189}{3} = \frac{\boxed{450}}{3} = \boxed{150}$$

Ⓒ How do their average scores compare?

Both have an average score of 150.

Ⓓ (Caleb's)/ Kim's scores are more consistent.

Ⓔ Caleb's scores are farther from / (closer to) the average than Kim's.

They bowl a fourth game, where Caleb scores 150 and Kim scores a 175. How does this affect their averages?

Ⓕ Caleb's average __stays the same__   Ⓖ Kim's average __increases__

Ⓗ Does the Game 4 score affect the consistency of their scores? Explain.

No, Caleb's scores are still consistent, and Kim's scores are still inconsistent.

HARDCOVER PAGES 305–314

Turn to these pages to find this lesson in the hardcover student edition.

1. **Discussion** Is the average an accurate representation of Caleb's bowling?
   Yes, Caleb is a consistent bowler, and his scores are all very close to his average.

2. **Discussion** Is the average an accurate representation of Kim's bowling?
   No. Kim is an inconsistent bowler and has a fairly wide range of scores.

🖉 Explain 1   Measures of Center: Mean and Median

Two commonly used measures of center for a set of numerical data are the mean and median. Measures of center represent a central or typical value of a data set. The **mean** is the sum of the values in the set divided by the number of values in the set. The **median** is the middle value in a set when the values are arranged in numerical order.

Example 1 Find the mean and median of each data set.

Ⓐ The number of text messages that Isaac received each day for a week is shown.

47, 49, 54, 50, 48, 47, 55

Find the mean. Divide the sum by the numbers of data values.

$\frac{350}{7} = 50$. The mean is 50 text messages a day.

Find the median. Rewrite the values in increasing order.

47, 47, 48, ⑷⑼ 50, 54, 55. The median is 49 text messages a day.

Ⓑ The amount of money Elise earned in tips per day for 6 days is listed below.

$75, $97, $360, $84, $119, $100

Find the mean to the nearest $0.01. Divide the sum by the number of data values.

$\frac{\boxed{835}}{6} = \boxed{\$139.17}$ The mean is $\underline{\$139.17}$.

Find the median. Rewrite the values in increasing order.

75, $\boxed{84}$, $\boxed{97}$, $\boxed{100}$, $\boxed{119}$, 360

Find the mean of the middle two values. $\frac{\boxed{97} + \boxed{100}}{2} = \boxed{98.5}$

The median is $\underline{\$98.50}$.

PROFESSIONAL DEVELOPMENT

 Integrate Mathematical Practices

This lesson provides an opportunity to address Mathematical Practices **MP.1**, which calls for students to "make sense of problems and persevere in solving them." Students learn about statistical measures that describe the center and spread of a set of numerical data. They will perform multi-step calculations to find the mean, median, range, interquartile range, and standard deviation of a data set, and they will use those measures to make sense of data.

EXPLORE

Exploring Data

INTEGRATE MATHEMATICAL PRACTICES

Focus on Modeling

MP.4 Graphing a data set and its mean on a number line can help students visualize how close the values are to the mean value.

QUESTIONING STRATEGIES

? How can you determine the mean value of a data set? **Find the sum of all the numbers, then divide the sum by the number of values in the data set.**

EXPLAIN 1

Measures of Center: Mean and Median

INTEGRATE MATHEMATICAL PRACTICES

Focus on Critical Thinking

MP.3 Ask students what must be true about a data set in order for the median to be one of the values in the data set. Students should understand that when the median is in the data set, either the set has an odd number of values, or the set has an even number of values and the two middle values are the same.

QUESTIONING STRATEGIES

? What is a situation in which the mean would not be the best measure of center? Explain. Possible answer: A set of test scores in which the scores are fairly consistent but there is one very low score; the very low score will lower the mean to below the typical value for the data set.

? If you had test scores that were mostly clustered around a particular value, but one score was a lot higher, would you prefer that your teacher report your class grade using the median or the mean of the scores? Explain. I would prefer the mean, because the higher score would raise the mean, but it would not affect the median much.

EXPLAIN 2

Measures of Spread: Range and IQR

AVOID COMMON ERRORS

Students may include the median in the upper and lower halves of the data set when finding Q_1 and Q_3. Remind them that the median is never included in these halves.

QUESTIONING STRATEGIES

? Why must the median be found before the first and third quartiles? The first and third quartiles are the halfway points of the lower half and upper half of the data, respectively. In order to find these, you must first find the halfway point of the data (the median).

Reflect

3. **Discussion** For the data on tips, which measure of center is more accurate in describing the typical value? Explain.
The median is more accurate. The mean is higher than all but one of the values. That one large value makes the data inconsistent.

Your Turn

Find the mean and median of each data set.

4. Niles scored 70, 74, 72, 71, 73, and 96 on his 6 geography tests.

The mean: $\frac{456}{6} = 76$ The median: $\frac{72 + 73}{2} = 72.5$

The mean is 76, and the median is 72.5.

5. Raul recorded the following golf scores in his last 7 games.

84, 94, 93, 89, 94, 81, 90

The mean: $\frac{625}{7} = 89.3$ The median: 81, 84, 89, (90) 93, 94, 94

The mean is 89.3, and the median is 90.

🔘 Explain 2   Measures of Spread: Range and IQR

Measures of spread are used to describe the consistency of data values. They show the distance between data values and their distance from the center of the data. Two commonly used measures of spread for a set of numerical data are the *range* and *interquartile range (IQR)*. The **range** is the difference between the greatest and the least data values. **Quartiles** are values that divide a data set into four equal parts. The **first quartile** (Q_1) is the median of the lower half of the set, the **second quartile** (Q_2) is the median of the whole set, and the **third quartile** (Q_3) is the median of the upper half of the set. The **interquartile range (IQR)** of a data set is the difference between the third and first quartiles. It represents the range of the middle half of the data.

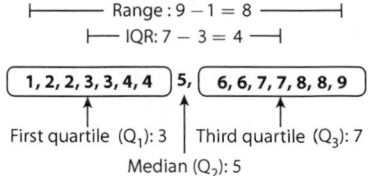

Example 2   Find the median, range, and interquartile range for the given data set.

(A) The April high temperatures for 5 years in Boston are 77 °F, 86 °F, 84 °F, 93 °F, and 90 °F

Order the data values.

Median: 77, 84, 86, 90, 93   Range: $93 - 77 = 16$
                  median
Interquartile range:

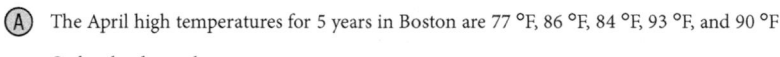

$\underset{\text{lower half}}{} \quad \underset{\text{upper half}}{}$
77, 84, 86, 90, 93 $Q_1 = \frac{77 + 84}{2} = 80.5$ and $Q_3 = \frac{90 + 93}{2} = 91.5$
         median

$IQR = Q_3 - Q_1 = 91.5 - 80.5 = 11$

COLLABORATIVE LEARNING

Peer-to-Peer Activity

Have students work in pairs. Have each pair write 10 different numbers on separate slips of paper, then evenly divide the slips so that each student has 5 numbers to create a data set. Have students determine the standard deviations for their data sets and compare results with their partners. Ask students how they would select a data set so that the standard deviation is as small as possible. Have them discuss strategies.

Ⓑ The numbers of runs scored by a softball team in 20 games are given.

3, 4, 8, 12, 7, 5, 4, 12, 3, 9, 11, 4, 14, 8, 2, 10, 3, 10, 9, 7

Order the data values.

2, 3, 3, 3, 4, 4, 4, $\boxed{5}$, $\boxed{7}$, $\underbrace{\boxed{7} , \boxed{8}}_{\text{median}}$, $\boxed{8}$, $\boxed{9}$, 9, 10, 10, 11, 12, 12, 14

$$\text{Median} = \frac{\boxed{7} + \boxed{8}}{2} = \boxed{7.5}$$

$$\text{Range} = 14 - 2 = \boxed{12}$$

Interquartile range.

$$Q_1 = \frac{\boxed{4} + \boxed{4}}{2} = 4 \text{ and } Q_3 = \frac{\boxed{10} + \boxed{10}}{2} = \boxed{10}$$

$$IQR = Q_3 - Q_1$$

$$= \boxed{10} - \boxed{4}$$

$$= \boxed{6}$$

The median is ____7.5____.

The range is ____12____.

The IQR is ____6____.

Reflect

6. **Discussion** Why is the IQR less than the range?
The IQR is less than the range because the range is the difference of the two extreme values, the largest and smallest data values. The IQR is the difference between numbers within the ordered set, so unless all of the values in the set are the same, Q_1 will be larger than the smallest element of the set, and Q_3 will be smaller than the largest element of the set.

Your Turn

Find the median, range, and interquartile range for the given data set.

7. 21, 31, 26, 24, 28, 26

21, <u>24</u>, <u><u>26</u></u>, <u>26</u>, <u><u>28</u></u>, 31   (median is underlined and quartiles are double underlined)

The median is 26.   Range = 31 − 21 = 10   IQR = 28 − 24 = 4

8. The high temperatures in degrees Fahrenheit on 11 days were 68, 71, 75, 74, 75, 71, 73, 71, 72, 74, and 79.

68, 71, <u>71</u>, 71, 72, <u>73</u>, 74, 74, <u>75</u>, 75, 79

The median is 73.   Range = 79 − 68 = 11   IQR = 75 − 71 = 4

DIFFERENTIATE INSTRUCTION

Critical Thinking

Discuss whether the standard deviation of a data set (the square root of the average squared deviation from the mean) is a better measure of spread than the average unsquared deviation from the mean. Have students calculate and compare the two measures for a few data sets. Students should realize that if deviations are not squared, negative and positive deviations can cancel each other out, so a data set with a large spread could have a very small average deviation. Squaring the deviations makes all the numbers positive, so this does not happen. In addition, squaring gives large deviations more weight than small deviations.

EXPLAIN 3

Measures of Spread: Standard Deviation

INTEGRATE MATHEMATICAL PRACTICES
Focus on Math Connections

MP.1 Discuss the meaning of the standard deviation for a data set. Students should be aware that a low standard deviation means that most data points will be very close to the mean, while a high standard deviation means that the data points are spread out across a large range of values.

QUESTIONING STRATEGIES

❓ How do the three measures of spread—range, interquartile range, and standard deviation—differ? How is each one related to measures of center for a data set? **The range measures the spread of the entire data set, but it is not based on any measure of center. The IQR depends on the median; it measures the spread of the middle half of the data. The standard deviation measures the spread of the data relative to the mean.**

© Houghton Mifflin Harcourt Publishing Company

⚙ **Explain 3** **Measures of Spread: Standard Deviation**

Another measure of spread is the **standard deviation**, which represents the average of the distance between individual data values and the mean.

The formula for finding the standard deviation of the data set $\{x_1, x_2, x_2, x_2 \cdots, x_n\}$, with n elements and mean x, is shown below.

$$\text{standard deviation} = \sqrt{\frac{(x_1 - \bar{x})^2 + (x_2 - \bar{x})^2 + \cdots + (x_n - \bar{x})^2}{n}}$$

Ⓐ Find the standard deviation of 77, 86, 84, 93, 90.

Find the mean.

$$\text{mean} = \frac{77 + 86 + 84 + 93 + 90}{5}$$
$$= \frac{430}{5}$$
$$= 86$$

Complete the table.

Data Value, x	Deviation from Mean, $x - \bar{x}$	Squared Deviation, $(x - \bar{x})^2$
77	$77 - 86 = -9$	$(-9)^2 = 81$
86	$86 - 86 = 0$	$0^2 = 0$
84	$84 - 86 = -2$	$(-2)^2 = 4$
93	$93 - 86 = 7$	$7^2 = 49$
90	$90 - 86 = 4$	$4^2 = 16$

Find the mean of the squared deviations.

$$\text{mean squared deviation} = \frac{81 + 0 + 4 + 49 + 16}{5}$$
$$= \frac{150}{5}$$
$$= 30$$

Find the square root of the mean of the squared deviations, rounding to the nearest tenth. $\sqrt{30} = 5.5$

The standard deviation is approximately 5.5.

Ⓑ Find the standard deviation of 3, 4, 8, 12, 7, 5, 4, 12, 3, 9, 11, 4, 14, 8, 2, 10, 3, 10, 9, 7.

Find the mean.

$$\text{mean} = \frac{2 + 3 + 3 + 3 + 4 + 4 + 4 + 5 + 7 + 7 + 8 + 8 + 9 + 9 + 10 + 10 + 11 + 12 + 12 + 14}{20}$$
$$= \frac{\boxed{145}}{20}$$
$$= \boxed{7.25}$$

LANGUAGE SUPPORT 🇪🇱

Connect Vocabulary

Review the explanations of *measures of center*, *mean*, and *median*. Students may be familiar with the concept of *average*, but not with the academic term *mean*, or they may understand that *mean* is another word for *average*, but may not grasp the concept of *median*. Remind them to ask for additional clarification before moving forward if they don't understand the terms. Remind them that they can also use the glossary as a resource.

Complete the table.

Data Value, x	Deviation from Mean, $x - \bar{x}$	Squared Deviation, $(x - \bar{x})^2$
2	$2 - \boxed{7.25} = \boxed{-5.25}$	$\left(\boxed{-5.25}\right)^2 = \boxed{27.5625}$
3	$3 - \boxed{7.25} = \boxed{-4.25}$	$\left(\boxed{-4.25}\right)^2 = \boxed{18.0625}$
3	-4.25	18.0625
3	-4.25	18.0625
4	$4 - \boxed{7.25} = \boxed{-3.25}$	$\left(\boxed{-3.25}\right)^2 = \boxed{10.5625}$
4	-3.25	10.5625
4	-3.25	10.5625
5	$5 - \boxed{7.25} = \boxed{-2.25}$	$\left(\boxed{-2.25}\right)^2 = \boxed{5.0625}$
7	$7 - \boxed{7.25} = \boxed{-0.25}$	$\left(\boxed{-0.25}\right)^2 = \boxed{0.0625}$
7	-0.25	0.0625
8	$8 - \boxed{7.25} = \boxed{0.75}$	$\left(\boxed{0.75}\right)^2 = \boxed{0.5625}$
8	0.75	0.5625
9	$9 - \boxed{7.25} = \boxed{1.75}$	$\left(\boxed{1.75}\right)^2 = \boxed{3.0625}$
9	1.75	3.0625
10	$10 - \boxed{7.25} = \boxed{2.75}$	$\left(\boxed{2.75}\right)^2 = \boxed{7.5625}$
10	2.75	7.5625
11	$11 - \boxed{7.25} = \boxed{3.75}$	$\left(\boxed{3.75}\right)^2 = \boxed{14.0625}$
12	$12 - \boxed{7.25} = \boxed{4.75}$	$\left(\boxed{4.75}\right)^2 = \boxed{22.5625}$
12	4.75	22.5625
14	$14 - \boxed{7.25} = \boxed{6.75}$	$\left(\boxed{-6.25}\right)^2 = \boxed{45.5625}$

ELABORATE

INTEGRATE MATHEMATICAL PRACTICES
Focus on Technology

MP.5 Explain that measures of center and spread can also be found using a computer spreadsheet. If spreadsheet software is available, demonstrate how to enter the data into cells of a spreadsheet and use the statistical functions available within the software.

You may wish to point out that the standard deviation formula taught in this lesson should be used when a data set includes an entire population. A slightly different formula, with $n - 1$ in the denominator instead of n, is used when the data set is only a sample of a population. The two formulas are available as different functions in spreadsheet software.

SUMMARIZE THE LESSON

? How can you determine the first and third quartile of a data set? First, determine the median. This allows you to determine the lower and upper half of the data set. The first quartile is the median of the lower half of the data set, and the third quartile is the median of the upper half of the data set. Find the median of each half of the data set the same way you find the median of the entire data set.

Find the mean of the squared deviations.

$$\text{mean squared deviation} = \frac{\begin{aligned}&27.5625 + 3(18.0625) + 3(10.5625) + 5.0625 + 2(0.0625) + \\ &2(0.5625) + 2(3.0625) + 2(7.5625) + 14.0625 + 2(22.5625) \\ &+ 45.5625\end{aligned}}{20}$$

$$= \frac{245.75}{20}$$

$$= 12.2875$$

Find the square root of the mean of the squared deviations, rounding to the nearest tenth.

$$\sqrt{12.2875} = 3.5$$

The standard deviation is approximately $\underline{3.5}$.

Reflect

9. In terms of data values used, what makes calculating the standard deviation different from calculating the range?

   The range uses only the largest and smallest values, while the standard deviation

   measures the average distance from each data point to the mean.

Your Turn

10. Find the standard deviation of 21, 31, 26, 24, 28, 26.

$$\text{mean} = \frac{21 + 24 + 2(26) + 28 + 31}{6} = \frac{156}{6} = 26$$

Data Value, x	Deviation from Mean, $x - \bar{x}$	Squared Deviation, $(x - \bar{x})^2$
21	−5	25
24	−2	4
26	0	0
26	0	0
28	2	4
31	5	25

mean of the squared deviations $= \dfrac{25 + 4 + 25 + 4}{6} = \dfrac{58}{6} \approx 9.67$

$\sqrt{9.67} \approx 3.1$ **The standard deviation is approximately 3.1.**

11. Find the standard deviation of 68, 71, 75, 74, 75, 71, 73, 71, 72, 74, and 79.

mean $= \dfrac{68 + 3(71) + 72 + 73 + 2(74) + 2(75) + 79}{11} = 73$

mean of the squared deviations $= \dfrac{25 + 5(4) + 3(1) + 36}{11} \approx 7.64$

$\sqrt{7.64} \approx 2.8$ **The standard deviation is approximately 2.8.**

12. In Your Turn 11, what is the mean of the deviations before squaring? Use your answer to explain why squaring the deviations is helpful.

The mean of the deviations is 0. Squaring the deviations is helpful because it prevents the

positive and negative deviations from averaging to 0.

13. How can you determine the first and third quartiles of a data set?
First, determine the median. This allows you to determine the lower and upper half of the

data set. The first quartile is the median of the lower half of the data set, and the third

quartile is the median of the upper half of the data set. Find the median of each half of the

data set the same way you find the median of the entire data set.

14. How can you determine the standard deviation of a data set?
Find the mean of the data. Then find the square of the distance between each data value

and the mean. Find the mean of the squared values. The standard deviation is the square

root of this mean.

15. Essential Question Check-In What does the measure of center of a data set indicate?
The measure of center identifies either a central or typical value of the data.

☆ Evaluate: Homework and Practice

1. The data set $\{13, 24, 14, 15, 14\}$ gives the times of Tara's one-way ride to school (in minutes) for one week. Is the average (mean) of the times a good description of Tara's ride time? Explain.

- Online Homework
- Hints and Help
- Extra Practice

No. The day the trip took 24 minutes will skew the value of the average to be too high.

Find the mean and median of each data set.

2. The numbers of hours Cheri works each day are 3, 7, 4, 6, and 5.

$\text{mean} = \dfrac{3+7+4+6+5}{5} = \dfrac{25}{5} = 5$

median: 3, 4, <u>5</u>, 6, 7   **The median is 5.**

3. The weights in pounds of 6 members of a basketball team are 125, 136, 150, 119, 150, and 143.

$\text{mean} = \dfrac{125+136+150+119+150+143}{6} = \dfrac{823}{6} \approx 137.2$

median: 119, 125, <u>136, 143</u>, 150, 150   The median is $\dfrac{136+143}{2} = 139.5$.

4. 36, 18, 12, 10, 9

$\text{mean} = \dfrac{36+18+12+10+9}{5} = \dfrac{85}{5} = 17$

median: 9, 10, <u>12</u>, 18, 36   **The median is 12.**

Exercise	Depth of Knowledge (D.O.K.)	COMMON CORE Mathematical Practices
1	**2** Skills/Concepts	**MP.2** Reasoning
2–8	**1** Recall	**MP.2** Reasoning
9–23	**2** Skills/Concepts	**MP.2** Reasoning
24–27	**3** Strategic Thinking **H.O.T.**	**MP.3** Logic

EVALUATE

ASSIGNMENT GUIDE

Concepts and Skills	Practice
Explore Exploring Data	Exercise 1
Example 1 Measures of Center: Mean and Median	Exercises 2–8, 26–27
Example 2 Measures of Spread: Range and IQR	Exercises 9–15, 22, 25
Example 3 Measures of Spread: Standard Deviation	Exercises 16–21, 23–24

INTEGRATE MATHEMATICAL PRACTICES
Focus on Communication

MP.3 Ask students to describe the differences between measures of center and measures of spread. Answers should include information such as the following:

- Measures of center tell how the data clusters around a value, while measures of spread tell how the data is spread out from a central value.

- Measures of center preserve information about the values in a data set, while measures of spread do not.

MULTIPLE REPRESENTATIONS

When finding the standard deviation of a data set, students may benefit from plotting the values on a number line, marking the mean, and identifying the distance of each data value from the mean.

AVOID COMMON ERRORS

Remind students that in order to determine the median of a data set, they must list the values in numerical order. Failing to order the data values before finding the median may result in an incorrect solution.

5. The average yearly gold price for the period from 2000–2009:

$279.11, $271.04, $309.73, $363.38, $409.72, $444.74, $603.46, $695.39, $871.96, $972.35

$$\text{mean} = \frac{279.11 + 271.04 + 309.73 + 363.38 + 409.72 + 444.74 + 603.46 + 659.39 + 871.96 + 972.35}{10}$$

$$= \frac{5220.88}{10} = 522.008, \text{ or } \$522.01$$

median: 271.04, 279.11, 309.73, 363.38, <u>409.72, 444.74</u>, 603.46, 695.39, 871.96, 972.35

The median is $\frac{409.72 + 444.74}{2} = \frac{854.46}{2} = \$427.23.$

6. There are 28, 30, 29, 26, 31, and 30 students in a school's six Algebra 1 classes.

$$\text{mean} = \frac{28 + 30 + 29 + 26 + 31 + 30}{6} = \frac{174}{6} = 29$$

median: 26, 28, <u>29, 30</u>, 30, 31   **The median is** $\frac{29 + 30}{2} = 29.5.$

7. 13, 14, 18, 13, 12, 17, 15, 12

$$\text{mean} = \frac{13 + 14 + 18 + 13 + 12 + 17 + 15 + 12}{8} = \frac{114}{8} = 14.25$$

median: 12, 12, 13, <u>13, 14</u>, 15, 17, 18   **The median is** $\frac{13 + 14}{2} = 13.5.$

8. The numbers of members in five karate classes are 13, 12, 10, 16, and 19.

$$\text{mean} = \frac{13 + 12 + 10 + 16 + 19}{5} = \frac{70}{5} = 14$$

median: 10, 12, <u>13</u>, 16, 19   **The median is 13.**

9. Find the range and interquartile range for 3, 7, 4, 6, and 5.

<u>3, 4</u>, <u>5</u>, <u>6, 7</u>   **Range** $= 7 - 3 = 4$

The interquartile range is IQR $\approx 6.5 - 3.5 = 3.$

10. Find the range and interquartile range for 125, 136, 150, 119, 150, and 143.

119, <u>125</u>, 136, 143, <u>150</u>, 150   **Range** $= 150 - 119 = 31$

The interquartile range is IQR $\approx 150 - 125 = 25.$

11. Find the range and interquartile range for 36, 18, 12, 10, and 9.

<u>9, 10</u>, <u>12</u>, <u>18, 36</u>   **Range** $= 36 - 9 = 27$

The interquartile range is IQR $\approx 27 - 9.5 = 17.5.$

12. Find the range and interquartile range for $279.11, $271.04, $309.73, $363.38, $409.72, $444.74, $603.46, $695.39, $871.96, and $972.35.

271.04, 279.11, <u>309.37</u>, 363.38, 409.72, 444.74, 603.46, <u>695.39</u>, 871.96, 972.35

Range $= 972.35 - 271.04 = 701.31$

The interquartile range is IQR $\approx 695.39 - 309.73 = 385.66.$

13. Find the range and interquartile range for 28, 30, 29, 26, 31, and 30.

26, <u>28</u>, 29, 30, <u>30</u>, 31   **Range** $= 31 - 26 = 5$

The interquartile range is IQR $\approx 30 - 28 = 2.$

14. Find the range and interquartile range for 13, 14, 18, 13, 12, 17, 15, and 12.

12, <u>12</u>, 13, 13, 14, <u>15</u>, 17, 18   Range $= 18 - 12 = 6$

The interquartile range is IQR $= 16 - 12.5 = 3.5$.

15. Find the range and interquartile range for 13, 12, 15, 17, and 9.

9, 12, <u>13</u>, 15, 17   Range $= 17 - 9 = 8$

The interquartile range is IQR $= 16 - 10.5 = 5.5$.

16. Find the standard deviation of 3, 7, 4, 6, and 5.

The mean is 5.

The mean of the squared deviations is $\frac{4 + 1 + 0 + 1 + 4}{5} = 2$.

The standard deviation is $\sqrt{2} \approx 1.4$.

17. Find the standard deviation of 125, 136, 150, 119, 150, and 143.

The mean is 137.17.

The mean of the squared deviations is

$\frac{330.03 + 148.03 + 1.36 + 34.02 + 164.69 + 164.69}{6} \approx \frac{842.83}{6} \approx 140.5$.

The standard deviation is $\sqrt{140.5} \approx 11.9$.

18. Find the standard deviation of 36, 18, 12, 10, and 9.

The mean is 17.

The mean of the squared deviations is $\frac{64 + 49 + 25 + 1 + 361}{5} = 100$.

The standard deviation is $\sqrt{100} = 10$.

19. Find the standard deviation of $279.11, $271.04, $309.73, $363.38, $409.72, $444.74, $603.46, $695.39, $871.96, and $972.35. Round the mean to the nearest $0.01 and the squared deviations to the nearest whole number.

The mean is 522.09.

The mean of the squared deviations is

$\frac{63,025 + 59,038 + 45,096 + 25,188 + 12,627 + 5983 + 6621 + 30,034 + 122,410 + 202,736}{10} = 57,258$.

The standard deviation is $\sqrt{57,258} \approx 239.3$.

20. Find the standard deviation of 28, 30, 29, 26, 31, and 30.

The mean is 29.

The mean of the squared deviations is $\frac{9 + 3(1) + 4}{6} = 2.67$.

The standard deviation is $\sqrt{2.67} \approx 1.6$.

21. Find the standard deviation of 13, 14, 18, 13, 12, 17, 15, and 12.

The mean is 14.25.

The mean of the squared deviations (rounded).

mean $= \frac{2(5.06) + 2(1.56) + 0.06 + 0.56 + 7.56 + 14.06}{8} = 4.44$

$\sqrt{4.44} = 2.1$

The standard deviation is approximately 2.1.

Challenge students to give an example of a data set for which the mean is twice the median. Have students present and explain their answers, then compare the different data sets that students created.

Have students describe the steps to take to find the standard deviation and the interquartile range for a data set. Students should include how to find the mean as a step in finding the standard deviation, as well as how to find the first and third quartiles as a step in finding the interquartile range.

22. Determine whether or not the third quartile has the same value as a member of the data set. Select the correct answer for each lettered part.

A. {79, 91, 90, 99, 91, 80, 80, 90} ☒ Yes ☐ No

B. {98, 96, 96, 95, 91, 81, 87} ☒ Yes ☐ No

C. {88, 95, 89, 93, 88, 93, 84, 93, 85, 92} ☒ Yes ☐ No

D. {97, 84, 96, 82, 93, 88, 82, 91, 94} ☐ Yes ☒ No

E. {94, 85, 95, 80, 97} ☐ Yes ☒ No

F. {85, 89, 81, 89, 85, 84} ☒ Yes ☐ No

Use this data for Exercises 23 and 24. The numbers of members in 6 yoga clubs are 80, 74, 77, 71, 75, and 91.

23. Find the standard deviation of the numbers of members to the nearest tenth.

The mean:

$$\frac{80 + 74 + 77 + 71 + 75 + 91}{6} = \frac{468}{6} = 78$$

The mean of the squared deviations

is $\frac{49 + 16 + 9 + 1 + 4 + 169}{6} = 41.33.$

The standard deviation is $\sqrt{41.33} \approx 6.4.$

H.O.T. Focus on Higher Order Thinking
---

24. Explain the Error Suppose a person in the club with 91 members transfers to the club with 71 members. A student claims that the measures of center and the measures of spread will all change. Correct the student's error.

There are 6 elements in the set, so the IQR is the difference between the 5th element and the 2nd. The only values that are changing are the first and last. This will not affect the IQR. The median is the average of the 3rd and 4th elements and likewise remains unchanged. The mean will also remain unchanged because the sum of all the elements doesn't change. The range will change from 20 to 18. The standard deviation will also decrease because the value of both the first and last elements will be closer to the mean.

25. What If? If all the values in a set are increased by 10, does the range also increase by 10? Explain.

No, the highest and lowest values both increase by 10, so their difference, the range, will stay the same.

26. Communicate Mathematical Ideas Jorge has a data set with the following values: 92, 80, 88, 95, and x. If the median value for this set is 88, what must be true about x? Explain.

$x \le 88$; for 5 ordered values, the median is the 3rd. Since 95 and 92 > 88, they must be 4th and 5th, so x must be $\le$ the median.

27. Critical Thinking If the value for the median of a set is not found in the data set, what must be true about the data set? Explain.

The data set must have an even number of values. When a data set has an odd number of values, the median is always found in the data set.

Lesson Performance Task

The table lists the ages of the soprano and bass singers in a town choir. Find the mean, median, range, interquartile range, and standard deviation for each type of singer in the data set. Interpret each result. What can you conclude about the ages of the different types of singers?

Age of Soprano Singers	63	42	28	45	36	48	32	40	57	49
Age of Bass Singers	32	34	53	35	43	41	29	35	24	34

Soprano Singers

Mean age of sopranos: $\dfrac{63 + 42 + 28 + 45 + 36 + 48 + 32 + 40 + 57 + 49}{10} = \dfrac{440}{10} = 44$

Median age of sopranos: $\dfrac{42 + 45}{2} = \dfrac{87}{2} = 43.5$

Range of ages of sopranos: $63 - 28 = 35$

Interquartile range of ages of sopranos: $IQR = 49 - 36 = 13$

Standard deviation $= \sqrt{\dfrac{361 + 4 + 256 + 1 + 64 + 16 + 44 + 16 + 169 + 25}{10}} = \sqrt{\dfrac{1056}{10}} = \sqrt{105.6} \approx 10.3$

Bass Singers

Mean bass singer age: $\dfrac{32 + 34 + 53 + 35 + 43 + 41 + 29 + 35 + 24 + 34}{10} = \dfrac{360}{10} = 36$

Median bass singer age: $\dfrac{34 + 35}{2} = \dfrac{69}{2} = 34.5$

Range of bass singer ages: $53 - 24 = 29$

Interquartile range of bass singer ages: $IQR = 41 - 32 = 9$

Standard deviation $= \sqrt{\dfrac{16 + 4 + 289 + 1 + 49 + 25 + 49 + 1 + 144 + 4}{10}} = \sqrt{\dfrac{582}{10}} = \sqrt{58.2} = 7.6$

The age of a soprano singer is generally greater than the age of a bass singer.

The ages of the bass singers are more tightly clustered than the ages of the soprano singers.

CONNECT VOCABULARY EL

Some students may not be familiar with the terms *soprano*, *alto*, *tenor*, and *bass*. Explain that they describe types of singing voices, with the soprano section of a choir singing the highest notes and the bass section singing the lowest. Ask for volunteers in the class who sing in a choir to explain or demonstrate these four vocal ranges.

QUESTIONING STRATEGIES

? Which of the statistics that you calculated are measures of center? What does comparing each of these measures for the sopranos to the same measures for the basses tell you about the two groups? **Mean and median; comparing tells you whether the typical age of a soprano is greater or less than the typical age of a bass.**

? Which of the statistics that you calculated are measures of spread? What does comparing each of these measures for the sopranos to the same measures for the basses tell you about the two groups? **Range, interquartile range, and standard deviation; it tells you whether the ages of the sopranos are closer together or farther apart than the ages of the basses.**

EXTENSION ACTIVITY

Have students consider the following scenario. A 17-year-old high school student and his 55-year-old father both join the bass section of the choir. How would adding their ages to the data set given in the Lesson Performance Task affect your conclusions?

Students should find that the mean, median, and interquartile range of the ages in the bass section would remain the same, but the range would increase to 38, and the standard deviation would increase to 10.4. The soprano section would still have the greater typical age, but the ages of the bass singers would be more spread out than the ages of the sopranos.

Scoring Rubric

2 points: Student correctly solves the problem and explains his/her reasoning.

1 point: Student shows good understanding of the problem but does not fully solve or explain his/her reasoning.

0 points: Student does not demonstrate understanding of the problem.

Measures of Center and Spread   **388**

Data Distributions and Outliers

Common Core Math Standards

The student is expected to:

 S-ID.A.1

Represent data with plots on the real number line (dot plots, histograms, and box plots). Also S-ID.A.2, S-ID.A.3, N-Q.A.1

Mathematical Practices

 MP.2 Reasoning

Language Objective

Explain to a partner what an outlier is.

ENGAGE

Essential Question: What statistics are most affected by outliers, and what shapes can data distributions have?

Outliers affect the mean more than the median, and they affect the standard deviation more than the IQR. Data distributions can be described generally as symmetric, skewed to the left, or skewed to the right.

PREVIEW: LESSON PERFORMANCE TASK

View the Engage section online. Discuss why, if you owned a business, you might compare a competitor's sales to your company's sales, and how your findings might lead you to change the way you run your business. Then preview the Lesson Performance Task.

9.2 Data Distributions and Outliers

Essential Question: What statistics are most affected by outliers, and what shapes can data distributions have?

Explore   Using Dot Plots to Display Data

A **dot plot** is a data representation that uses a number line and Xs, dots, or other symbols to show frequency. Dot plots are sometimes called *line plots*.

Finance Twelve employees at a small company make the following annual salaries (in thousands of dollars): 25, 30, 35, 35, 35, 40, 40, 40, 45, 45, 50, and 60.

(A) Choose the number line with the most appropriate scale for this problem. Explain your reasoning.

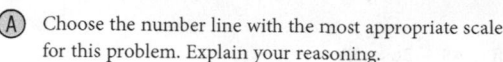

The second number line has the most appropriate scale. The scale of the first number line includes a larger range of numbers than necessary, so dots will be clustered in the middle.

The scale of the third number line does not have convenient tick marks for determining where values between the labels belong.

(B) Create and label a dot plot of the data. Put an X above the number line for each time that value appears in the data set.

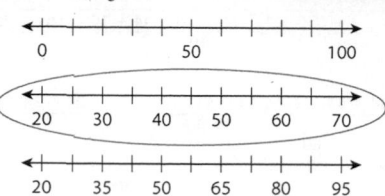

Salary (thousands of dollars)

Reflect

1. **Discussion** Recall that quantitative data can be expressed as a numerical measurement. Categorical, qualitative data is expressed in categories, such as attributes or preferences. Is it appropriate to use a dot plot for displaying quantitative data, qualitative data, or both? Explain.
   A dot plot uses a number line, so it is only appropriate for displaying quantitative data.

© Houghton Mifflin Harcourt Publishing Company ·image credit: ©Blend Images/Alamy

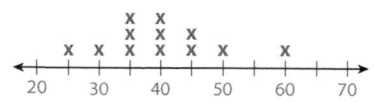

HARDCOVER PAGES 315–324

Turn to these pages to find this lesson in the hardcover student edition.

⏺ Explain 1   The Effects of an Outlier in a Data Set

An **outlier** is a value in a data set that is much greater or much less than most of the other values in the data set. Outliers are determined by using the first or third quartiles and the IQR.

How to Identify an Outlier
A data value x is an outlier if $x < Q_1 - 1.5(\text{IQR})$ or if $x > Q_3 + 1.5(\text{IQR})$.

Example 1   Create a dot plot for the data set using an appropriate scale for the number line. Determine whether the extreme value is an outlier.

Ⓐ Suppose that the list of salaries from the Explore is expanded to include the owner's salary of $150,000. Now the list of salaries is 25, 30, 35, 35, 35, 40, 40, 40, 45, 45, 50, 60, and 150.

To choose an appropriate scale, consider the minimum and maximum values, 25 and 150.

A number line from 20 to 160 will contain all the values. A scale of 5 will be convenient for the data. Label tick marks by 20s.

Plot each data value to see the distribution.

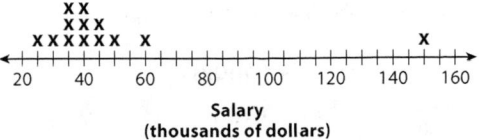

Salary
(thousands of dollars)

Find the quartiles and the IQR to determine whether 150 is an outlier.

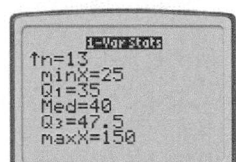

$150 \overset{?}{>} Q_3 + 1.5(\text{IQR})$

$150 \overset{?}{>} 47.5 + 1.5(47.5 - 35)$

$150 > 66.25$ True

150 is an outlier.

Ⓑ Suppose that the salaries from Part A were adjusted so that the owner's salary is $65,000.

Now the list of salaries is 25, 30, 35, 35, 35, 40, 40, 40, 45, 45, 50, 60, and 65.

To choose an appropriate scale, consider the minimum and maximum data values, __25__ and __65__.

A number line from __20__ to __70__ will contain all the data values.

A scale of __5__ will be convenient for the data.

Label tick marks by __10s__.

Plot each data value to see the distribution.

Salary (thousands of dollars)

PROFESSIONAL DEVELOPMENT

[COMMON CORE] Integrate Mathematical Practices

This lesson provides an opportunity to address Mathematical Practice **MP.2**, which calls for students to "reason abstractly and quantitatively." Students solve real-world problems by creating dot plots for data sets. They analyze and describe the shapes of the data distributions, recognizing how the shapes affect the measures of center and spread, and they use both dot plots and statistical measures to compare data sets. Thus, they first take a situation from its real-world context to represent it symbolically, then they interpret the results in the real-world context.

EXPLORE

Using Dot Plots to Display Data

INTEGRATE TECHNOLOGY

To make it easier to create a dot plot for a large data set, students can enter the data values into one column of a spreadsheet, then use the spreadsheet's data-sorting function to arrange them in increasing order.

QUESTIONING STRATEGIES

How can you use a dot plot to find the interquartile range of a data set? First, find the median by counting the same number of marks from each end of the dot plot until the middle value is reached. If there are an even number of marks, find the mean of the two middle values. Then use the same process to find the first quartile (Q_1, the middle value of the lower half) and the third quartile (Q_3, the middle value of the upper half). Finally, subtract Q_1 from Q_3 to find the interquartile range.

EXPLAIN 1

The Effects of an Outlier in a Data Set

AVOID COMMON ERRORS

Students sometimes forget to take the square root of the mean of the squared deviations when calculating standard deviation. Review the steps for calculating the standard deviation.

QUESTIONING STRATEGIES

How does an outlier affect the mean and median of a data set? If a data set includes an outlier, the mean can be increased or decreased significantly. This can make the mean misleading as a measure of center. When there are no outliers, most data values cluster closer to the mean. The median is much less affected by an outlier, because a single outlier shifts the middle of the data set by only a small amount, if at all.

Data Distributions and Outliers   **390**

EXPLAIN 2

Comparing Data Sets

INTEGRATE MATHEMATICAL PRACTICES
Focus on Technology

MP.5 Review the steps generating statistics using a graphing calculator. Students can create a list by pressing **STAT**, then selecting **1:Edit**. A previously entered list can be cleared by highlighting the name of the list, pressing **CLEAR**, then pressing the down arrow.

After entering data in a list, students can find the one-variable statistics by pressing **STAT**, selecting **CALC**, and then selecting **1:1-Var Stats**. For data in lists other than **L1**, they must enter the list number before pressing **ENTER** to generate the statistics.

AVOID COMMON ERRORS

Students may expect their graphing calculators to provide the value of the IQR. Remind them that they must calculate the IQR by finding the difference between the first and third quartiles.

Find the quartiles and the IQR to determine whether 65 is an outlier.

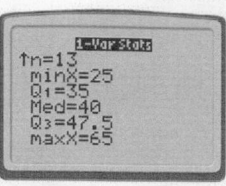

$65 \overset{?}{>} Q_3 + 1.5(IQR)$

$65 \overset{?}{>} \boxed{47.5} + 1.5\left(\boxed{47.5} - \boxed{35}\right)$

$65 > \boxed{66.25}$ True /~~False~~

Therefore, 65 is /~~is not~~ an outlier.

Reflect

2. Explain why the median was NOT affected by changing the max data value from 150 to 65.
The maximum value in the data set changed, but its ordered position did not, so the middle value in the ordered list was not moved or changed.

Your Turn

3. **Sports** Baseball pitchers on a major league team throw at the following speeds (in miles per hour): 72, 84, 89, 81, 93, 100, 90, 88, 80, 84, and 87.

   Create a dot plot using an appropriate scale for the number line. Determine whether the extreme value is an outlier.

   Pitching Speeds (mph)

   $72 \overset{?}{<} Q_1 - 1.5(IQR)$

   $72 \overset{?}{<} 81 - 1.5(9)$

   $72 < 67.5$ False   Therefore, 72 is not an outlier

🖋 Explain 2   Comparing Data Sets

Numbers that characterize a data set, such as measures of center and spread, are called **statistics**. They are useful when comparing large sets of data.

Example 2 Calculate the mean, median, interquartile range (IQR), and standard deviation for each data set, and then compare the data.

Ⓐ **Sports** The tables list the average ages of players on 15 teams randomly selected from the 2010 teams in the National Football League (NFL) and Major League Baseball (MLB). Describe how the average ages of NFL players compare to those of MLB players.

NFL Players' Average Ages, by Team
25.8, 26.0, 26.3, 25.7, 25.1, 25.2, 26.1, 26.4, 25.9, 26.6, 26.3, 26.2, 26.8, 25.6, 25.7

MLB Players' Average Ages, by Team
28.5, 29.0, 28.0, 27.8, 29.5, 29.1, 26.9, 28.9, 28.6, 28.7, 26.9, 30.5, 28.7, 28.9, 29.3

COLLABORATIVE LEARNING

Peer-to-Peer Activity

Have students work in pairs. Have each student create a data set with 10 values, using the definition of outlier to verify that none of the values are outliers. Students then find the mean, median, range, and IQR for their data sets. Have students trade data sets with their partners. Ask each student to add an outlier to the partner's data set, and then calculate the new mean, median, range, and IQR for the set. Students should compare their results and discuss how the outliers affected the statistics.

On a graphing calculator, enter the two sets of data into L_1 and L_2.

Use the "1-Var Stats" feature to find statistics for the data in lists L_1 and L_2. Your calculator may use the following notations: mean $\bar{x}$, standard deviation σ_x.

Scroll down to see the median (Med), Q_1, and Q_3. Complete the table.

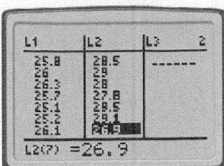

	Mean	Median	IQR ($Q_3 - Q_1$)	Standard deviation
NFL	25.98	26.00	0.60	0.46
MLB	28.62	28.70	1.10	0.91

Compare the corresponding statistics.

The mean age and median age are lower for the NFL than for the MLB, which means that NFL players tend to be younger than MLB players. In addition, the IQR and standard deviation are smaller for the NFL than for the MLB, which means that the ages of NFL players are closer together than those of MLB players.

(B) The tables list the ages of 10 contestants on 2 game shows.

Game Show 1
18, 20, 25, 48, 35, 39, 46, 41, 30, 27

Game Show 2
24, 29, 36, 32, 34, 41, 21, 38, 39, 26

On a graphing calculator, enter the two sets of data into L_1 and L_2.

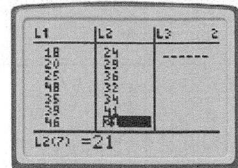

Complete the table. Then circle the correct items to compare the statistics.

	Mean	Median	IQR ($Q_3 - Q_1$)	Standard deviation
Show 1	32.9	32.5	16	10.00
Show 2	32	33	12	6.45

The mean is lower for the 1st /(2nd) game show, which means that contestants in the 1st /(2nd) game show are on average younger than contestants in the (1st)/ 2nd game show. However, the median is lower for the (1st)/ 2nd game show, which means that although contestants are on average younger on the 1st /(2nd) game show, there are more young contestants on the (1st)/ 2nd game show. Finally, the IQR and standard deviation are higher for the (1st)/ 2nd game show, which means that the ages of contestants on the (1st)/ 2nd game show are further apart than the age of contestants on the 1st /(2nd) game show.

? What can you conclude about two data sets by comparing each of the following statistics: mean, median, IQR, and standard deviation?

By comparing the mean and median values, you can conclude whether the typical value for one data set is higher or lower than the typical value for the other set. By comparing the IQR and standard deviation values, you can determine whether the data values in one set are more or less spread out than the values in the other set.

DIFFERENTIATE INSTRUCTION

Multiple Representations

Students may benefit from acting out a real-world example of how adding an outlier to a data set affects measures of center and spread. For example, have five students each begin with 1 to 5 slips of paper (or pennies or markers); each slip represents a dollar. Have the students calculate the mean by equally distributing all the slips of paper among the five students. Then have a sixth student with $25 (25 slips of paper) join the group. Again use the slips of paper to find the mean by distributing them among the six students. Ask whether the new mean is a reasonable measure of center.

EXPLAIN 3

Comparing Data Distributions

AVOID COMMON ERRORS

Students often confuse the terms *skewed to the left* and *skewed to the right*. Encourage students to come up with a mnemonic to help them remember how the direction of a skew should be described. For example, students may easily remember how the "tail" of a data distribution looks on a dot plot. Point out that both *tail* and *skew* have four letters, and that a data distribution is skewed in the direction of its tail.

QUESTIONING STRATEGIES

? Some data distributions are described as *uniform*. What do you think the general shape of a uniform distribution would be? **The general shape of a uniform distribution is fairly even across the plot.**

? What would be true about the mean and median of a data set with a uniform distribution? **The mean and median would be approximately equal.**

---

4. The tables list the age of each member of Congress in two randomly selected states. Complete the table and compare the data.

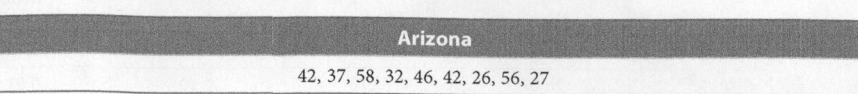

Illinois
26, 24, 28, 46, 39, 59, 31, 26, 64, 40, 69, 62, 31, 28, 26, 76, 57, 71, 58, 35, 32, 49, 51, 22, 33, 56

Arizona
42, 37, 58, 32, 46, 42, 26, 56, 27

	Mean	Median	IQR ($Q_3 - Q_1$)	Standard deviation
Illinois	43.81	39.5	30	16.42
Arizona	40.67	42	21.5	10.84

The mean is lower for Arizona, which means that, on average, members of Congress tend to be younger in Arizona than in Illinois. However, the median is lower in Illinois, which means that there are more young members of Congress in Illinois despite the differences in average age. Finally, the IQR and standard deviation are lower for Arizona, which means that the ages of members of Congress are closer together than they are in Illinois.

⚙ Explain 3 Comparing Data Distributions

A data distribution can be described as **symmetric**, **skewed to the left**, or **skewed to the right**, depending on the general shape of the distribution in a dot plot or other data display.

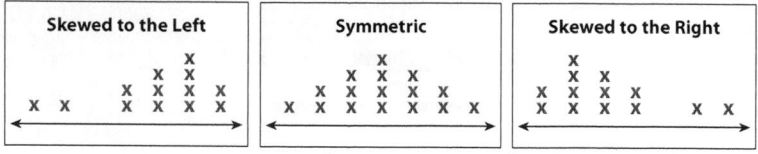

Example 3 For each data set, make a dot plot and determine the type of distribution. Then explain what the distribution means for each data set.

Ⓐ **Sports** The data table shows the number of miles run by members of two track teams during one day.

Miles	3	3.5	4	4.5	5	5.5	6
Members of Team A	2	3	4	4	3	2	0
Members of Team B	1	2	2	3	3	4	3

LANGUAGE SUPPORT **EL**

Connect Vocabulary

English learners who are working on acquiring academic English in algebra may find that some terminology is difficult to pronounce or to differentiate when listening. Words such as *effect* and *affect* may be difficult to distinguish, and words such as *skew* or *interquartile* may be difficult to pronounce. Be sure to enunciate clearly so that students can understand and learn to pronounce the key words correctly.

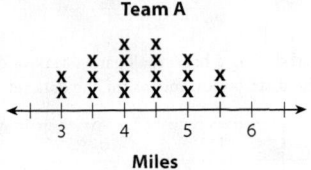

Team A

Miles

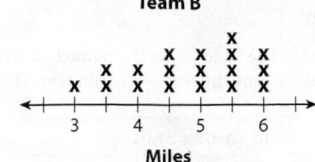

Team B

Miles

The data for team A show a symmetric distribution. This means that the distances run are evenly distributed about the mean.

The data for team B show a distribution skewed to the left. This means that more than half the team members ran a distance greater than the mean.

Ⓑ The table shows the number of days, over the course of a month, that specific numbers of apples were sold by competing grocers.

Number of Apples Sold	0	50	100	150	200	250	300
Grocery Store A	1	4	8	8	4	1	0
Grocery Store B	3	6	8	8	2	2	1

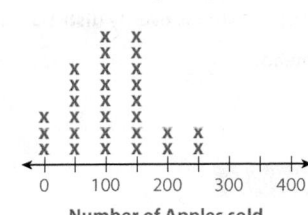

Grocery Store A

Number of Apples sold

Grocery Store B

Number of Apples sold

The distribution for grocery store A is: left-skewed/right-skewed /(symmetric).
This means that the number of apples sold each day is (evenly)/ unevenly distributed about the mean.

The distribution for grocery store B is: left-skewed/(right-skewed)/symmetric.
This means that the number of apples sold each day is evenly/(unevenly) distributed about the mean.

Reflect

7. Will the mean and median in a symmetric distribution always be approximately equal? Explain.
   The mean and median in a symmetric distribution will always be approximately equal

   because the values are equally distributed on either side of the center.

8. Will the mean and median in a skewed distribution always be approximately equal? Explain.
   The mean and median in a skewed distribution will not always be approximately equal

   because the median will sometimes be closer to where the values cluster than the

   mean will be.

ELABORATE

QUESTIONING STRATEGIES

? Can a data set have more than one outlier? Explain. **Yes; More than one value may be less than $Q_1 - 1.5(IQR)$ or greater than $Q_3 + 1.5(IQR)$.**

INTEGRATE MATHEMATICAL PRACTICES
Focus on Critical Thinking

MP.3 Discuss with students whether all the values in a data set could be outliers. Review the definition of *outlier*. Students should understand that because an outlier must be less than Q_1 or greater than Q_3, values between Q_1 and Q_3 will never be outliers for a data set.

SUMMARIZE THE LESSON

? How can you determine whether a value in a data set is an outlier? How does the inclusion of an outlier affect the mean, median, range, and IQR? **An outlier is a value that is less than $Q_1 - 1.5(IQR)$ or greater than $Q_3 + 1.5(IQR)$. Outliers significantly affect the mean and range, but affect the median and IQR very little or not at all.**

---

9. **Sports** The table shows the number of free throws attempted during a basketball game. Make a dot plot and determine the type of distribution. Then explain what the distribution means for the data set.

Free Throws Shot	0	2	4	6	8
Members of Team A	2	2	4	2	2
Members of Team B	3	4	2	2	1

Team A

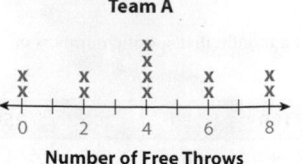

Number of Free Throws

Team B

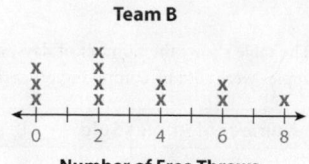

Number of Free Throws

The data for team A show a symmetric distribution. This means that the number of free throws shot is evenly distributed about the mean.

The data for team B show a distribution skewed to the right. This means that fewer than half of the team members shot a number of free throws that were greater than the mean.

💬 Elaborate

10. If the mean increases after a single data point is added to a set of data, what can you tell about this data point?
    If the mean increases after a single data point is added to a set of data, you can tell that the data point added was larger than the mean of the set.

11. How can you use a calculation to decide whether a data point is an outlier in a data set?
    You can decide whether a data point is an outlier in a data set by finding the 1st and 3rd quartile and subtracting them to get the interquartile range. If the data point is larger or smaller than the result found by adding the 3rd quartile to 1.5 times the interquartile range or by subtracting the 1st quartile from 1.5 times the interquartile range, respectively, then the data point is an outlier.

12. **Essential Question Check-In** What three shapes can data distributions have?
    Data distributions can be skewed to the left, skewed to the right, and symmetric.

Exercise	Depth of Knowledge (D.O.K.)	COMMON CORE Mathematical Practices
1–8	**1** Recall	**MP.4** Modeling
9	**1** Recall	**MP.5** Using Tools
10	**2** Skills/Concepts	**MP.7** Using Structure
11	**1** Recall	**MP.5** Using Tools
12	**2** Skills/Concepts	**MP.7** Using Structure

Evaluate: Homework and Practice

• Online Homework
• Hints and Help
• Extra Practice

Fitness The numbers of members in 8 workout clubs are 100, 95, 90, 85, 85, 95, 100, and 90. Use this information for Exercises 1–2.

1. Create a dot plot for the data set using an appropriate scale for the number line.

   Possible plot shown.

   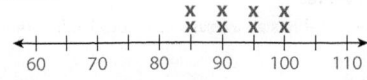

2. Suppose that a new workout club opens and immediately has 150 members. Is the number of members at this new club an outlier?

   $150 > 100 + 1.5(100 - 87.5) = 118.75$ True   **150 members is an outlier.**

Sports The number of feet to the left outfield wall for 10 randomly chosen baseball stadiums is 315, 325, 335, 330, 330, 330, 320, 310, 325, and 335. Use this information for Exercises 3–4.

3. Create a dot plot for the data set using an appropriate scale for the number line.

   Possible plot shown.

   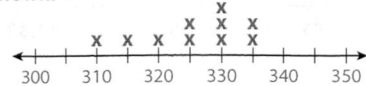

4. The longest distance to the left outfield wall in a baseball stadium is 355 feet. Is this stadium an outlier if it is added to the data set?

   $355 \overset{?}{>} 335 + 1.5(335 - 320) = 357.5$ False   **355 feet is not an outlier.**

Education The numbers of students in 10 randomly chosen classes in a high school are 18, 22, 26, 31, 25, 20, 23, 26, 29, and 30. Use this information for Exercises 5–6.

5. Create a dot plot for the data set using an appropriate scale for the number line. **Possible plot shown.**

   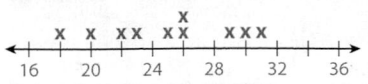

6. Suppose that a new class is opened for enrollment and currently has 7 students. Is this class an outlier if it is added to the data set?

   $7 \overset{?}{<} 20 - 1.5(29 - 20) = 6.5$ False   **7 is not an outlier.**

© Houghton Mifflin Harcourt Publishing Company • Image Credits: ©Blend Images/Alamy

Exercise	Depth of Knowledge (D.O.K.)	COMMON CORE Mathematical Practices	
13–15	**2** Skills/Concepts		**MP.4** Modeling
16	**1** Recall of Information	H.O.T.	**MP.5** Using Tools
17–18	**3** Strategic Thinking	H.O.T.	**MP.3** Logic
19	**2** Skills/Concepts	H.O.T.	**MP.4** Modeling

EVALUATE

ASSIGNMENT GUIDE

Concepts and Skills	Practice
Explore Using Dot Plots to Display Data	Exercises 1, 3, 5, 7
Example 1 The Effects of an Outlier in a Data Set	Exercises 2, 4, 6, 8, 17–18
Example 2 Comparing Data Sets	Exercises 9–12
Example 3 Comparing Data Distributions	Exercises 13–16, 19

INTEGRATE MATHEMATICAL PRACTICES
Focus on Critical Thinking

MP.3 Understanding how outliers can affect the mean and the median of a data set is an important skill, especially for interpreting data. Discuss how statistics can be misleading when outliers that affect the mean value for a data set are included.

MODELING

To help students think about possible causes for outliers in a data set, ask them to consider the distribution of heights of all the people in a kindergarten classroom, in a high school classroom, and on a basketball court. Discuss how many outliers might be expected in each case, and what factors might affect the number of outliers in each situation. Students should recognize that there is often a reason why one value is very different from the others in a data set, such as the fact that a kindergarten teacher may be the only adult in the classroom.

AVOID COMMON ERRORS

Make sure students understand the process for determining the standard deviation for a data set. Encourage them to first create a table to record the deviation and squared deviation for each data value, then add the squared deviations, divide the sum by the number of values, and finally find the square root. Suggest that when they do not record their work, students can easily overlook a step in the process.

Sports The average bowling scores for a group of bowlers are 200, 210, 230, 220, 230, 225, and 240. Use this information for Exercises 7–8.

7. Create a dot plot for the data set using an appropriate scale for the number line.
   Possible plot shown.

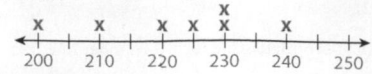

Bowling Scores

8. Suppose that a new bowler joins this group and has an average score of 275. Is this bowler an outlier in the data set?

$275 \overset{?}{>} 235 + 1.5(235 - 215) = 265$ **True** ⟶ **275 is an outlier.**

The tables describe the average ages of employees from two randomly chosen companies. Use this information for Exercises 9–10.

Company A	Company B
23, 29, 35, 46, 51, 50, 42, 37, 30	24, 23, 45, 45, 42, 52, 55, 47, 55

9. Calculate the mean, median, interquartile range (IQR), and standard deviation for each data set.

	Mean	Median	IQR ($Q_3 - Q_1$)	Standard deviation
Company A	38.1	37	18.5	9.27
Company B	43.1	45	20.5	11.33

10. Compare the data sets.
    Employees at company A tend to be younger than employees at company B. The ages of employees at company A are closer together than the ages of employees at company B.

The tables describe the size of microwaves, in cubic feet, chosen randomly from two competing companies. Use this information for Exercises 11–12.

Company A	Company B
1.8, 2.1, 3.1, 2.0, 3.3, 2.9, 3.3, 2.1, 3.2	1.9, 2.6, 1.8, 3.0, 2.5, 2.8, 2.0, 3.6, 3.1

11. Calculate the mean, median, interquartile range (IQR), and standard deviation for each data set.

	Mean	Median	IQR ($Q_3 - Q_1$)	Standard deviation
Company A	2.6	2.9	1.2	0.59
Company B	2.6	2.6	1.1	0.57

12. Compare the data sets.
    Microwaves from company B tend to be smaller than microwaves from company A. The average size of microwaves tend to be closer together at company B than at company A.

© Houghton Mifflin Harcourt Publishing Company

For each data set, make a dot plot and determine the type of distribution. Then explain what the distribution means for each data set.   Possible plot shown.

13. Sports The data table shows the number of miles run by members of two teams running a marathon.

Miles	5	10	15	20	25
Members of Team A	3	5	10	5	3
Members of Team B	6	10	4	1	5

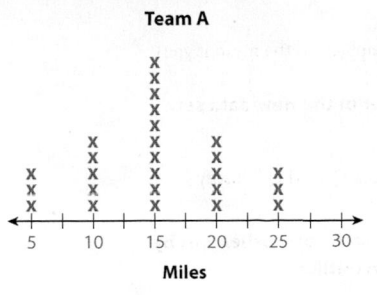

Team A

Miles

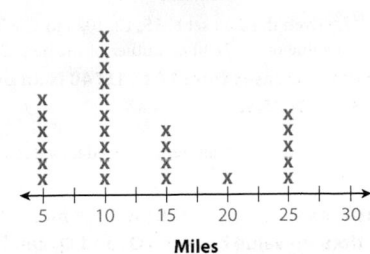

Team B

Miles

The data for team A show a symmetric distribution. The distances run are evenly distributed about the mean.

The data for team B show a right-skewed distribution. This means that fewer than half of the team members ran a distance greater than the mean.

14. Sales The data table shows the number of days that specific numbers of turkeys were sold. These days were in the two weeks before Thanksgiving.

Number of Turkeys	10	20	30	40
Grocery Store A	2	5	5	2
Grocery Store B	5	5	1	3

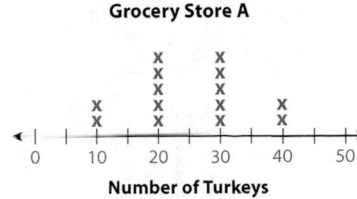

Grocery Store A

Number of Turkeys

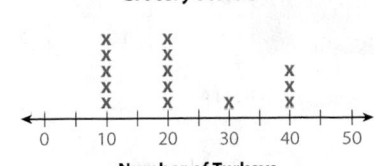

Grocery Store B

Number of Turkeys

The data for grocery store A show a symmetric distribution. This means that the numbers of turkeys sold per day are evenly distributed about the mean.

The data for grocery store B show a right-skewed distribution. This means that the store sold fewer than the average number of turkeys for more than half of the days.

CRITICAL THINKING

Have students analyze and describe the shape of the distribution of a dot plot they created. Ask students how the shape relates to the statistics they would use to characterize the data.

JOURNAL

Have students create their own graphic organizers to share with classmates, outlining the steps for finding mean, median, Q_1, Q_3, IQR, and standard deviation from a dot plot.

15. State whether each set of data is left-skewed, right-skewed, or symmetrically distributed.

A. 3, 5, 5, 3   symmetric

B. 1, 1, 3, 1   right-skewed

C. 7, 9, 9, 11   symmetric

D. 5, 5, 3, 3   symmetric

E. 19, 21, 21, 19   symmetric

H.O.T. Focus on Higher Order Thinking

16. What If? Given the data set 8, 15, 12, 10, and 5, what happens to the mean if you add a data value of 40? Is 40 an outlier of the new data set?

The mean increases from 10 to 15. 40 is an outlier of the new data set because 40 > 25.5.

17. Critical Thinking Can an outlier be a data value between Q_1 and Q_3? Justify your answer.

An extreme value such as the max or min value can be an outlier, but by definition, no value between Q_1 and Q_3 can be an outlier.

18. Justify Reasoning If the distribution has outliers, why will they always have an effect on the range?

When present, outliers will always have an effect on the range since one of the outliers will either be the highest or lowest number in a given data set and the range is found by finding the difference between the highest and lowest numbers.

19. Education The data table describes the average testing scores in 20 randomly selected classes in two randomly selected high schools, rounded to the nearest ten. For each data set, make a dot plot, determine the type of distribution, and explain what the distribution means in context.

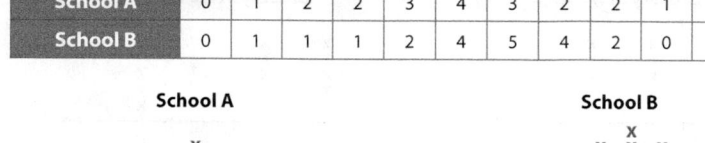

Average Scores	0	10	20	30	40	50	60	70	80	90	100
School A	0	1	2	2	3	4	3	2	2	1	0
School B	0	1	1	1	2	4	5	4	2	0	0

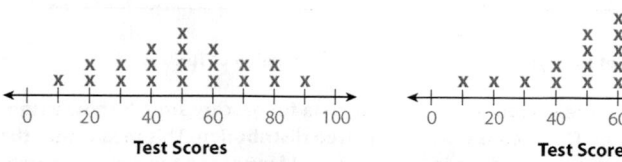

School A

School B

Test Scores   Test Scores

The data for school A show a symmetric distribution. This means that the test scores were evenly distributed about the mean test score.

The data for school B show a left-skewed distribution. This means that more than half of the classes received a test score that was above the mean.

Lesson Performance Task

The tables list the daily car sales of two competing dealerships.

Dealer A			
14	13	15	12
15	16	15	17
17	12	16	14
15	16	14	16
13	14	18	15

Dealer B			
16	17	15	20
18	19	18	17
19	10	19	18
15	17	20	19
18	18	16	17

A. Calculate the mean, median, interquartile range (IQR), and standard deviation for each data set. Compare the measures of center for the two dealers.

	Mean	Median	IQR ($Q_3 - Q_1$)	Standard deviation
Dealer A	14.85	15	2	1.6
Dealer B	17.3	18	2.5	2.2

The number of cars sold by Dealer A tends to be lower than the number of cars sold by Dealer B.

The number of cars sold by Dealer A are more consistent than the number of cars sold by Dealer B.

B. Create a dot plot for each data set. Compare the distributions of the data sets.

Dealer A

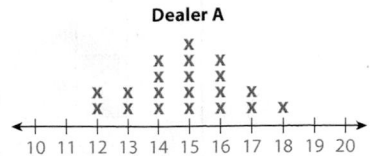

The data for Dealer A show a symmetric distribution, so the number of cars sold daily by Dealer A is evenly distributed about the mean.

Dealer B

The data for Dealer B show a distribution skewed to the left, so during more than half of the days, car sales were greater than the mean.

C. Determine if there are any outliers in the data sets. If there are, remove the outlier and find the statistics for that data set(s). What was affected by the outlier?

Dealer A:

$x < 14 - 1.5\,(2)$ $x > 16 + 1.5\,(2)$

$x < 11$ $x > 19$

There are no values in the data set that satisfy these inequalities for x. So, there are no outliers.

Dealer B:

$x < 16.5 - 1.5\,(2.5)$ $x > 19 + 1.5\,(2.5)$

$x < 12.75$ $x > 22.75$

10 is an outlier in the data set for Dealer B. Removing the outlier increases the mean and decreases the standard deviation. The median is unaffected.

EXTENSION ACTIVITY

Explain to students that a *bimodal* data distribution has two peaks. Have students create a set of 20 daily car-sale values with a bimodal distribution, then create a dot plot and calculate statistics for the data. Ask what situations might produce this distribution. Students may speculate that a sudden change in sales tactics or prices could lead to several days with much higher or lower sales values than preceding days. Point out that neither the mean nor the median accurately represents a bimodal distribution. Explain that in some cases, such as when the data originate from two different sets of conditions, it is appropriate to split it into two data sets and evaluate them separately.

INTEGRATE MATHEMATICAL PRACTICES
Focus on Reasoning

MP.2 Ask students whether the dealer who tended to sell more cars than a competitor would necessarily make the greater profit. Students should recognize that a greater number of car sales leads to a greater profit only when the profit per car is about the same in both cases. If one dealer sold more cars by setting the prices so low that there was a very small profit margin, that dealer could end up with lower profits despite having more sales.

QUESTIONING STRATEGIES

? What might be some reasons for an outlier to occur in a set of daily car sale values? Possible answers: There might have been a day with very bad weather, so no one went car shopping, or a day when the best salespeople were out sick, so they didn't sell any cars.

Histograms and Box Plots

Common Core Math Standards

The student is expected to:

 S-ID.A.2

Use statistics appropriate to the shape of the data distribution to compare center (median, mean) and spread (interquartile range, standard deviation) of two or more different data sets. Also S-ID.A.1, N-Q.A.1

Mathematical Practices

 MP.7 Using Structure

Language Objective

Explain what each part of a histogram represents.

ENGAGE

Essential Question: How can you interpret and compare data sets using data displays?

You can estimate statistics and compare distributions using histograms, and you can compare the centers, spreads, and shapes of the distributions of two data sets by plotting box plots on the same number line.

PREVIEW: LESSON PERFORMANCE TASK

View the Engage section online. Discuss the fact that the batting average of a baseball player is calculated by dividing the number of hits by the number of times at bat. Note that Ty Cobb, the player with the all-time highest career batting average, had a career batting average of .366. Then preview the Lesson Performance Task.

9.3 Histograms and Box Plots

Essential Question: How can you interpret and compare data sets using data displays?

Resource Locker

🧭 Explore   Understanding Histograms

A **histogram** is a bar graph that is used to display the frequency of data divided into equal intervals. The bars must be of equal width and should touch but not overlap. The heights of the bars indicate the frequency of data values within each interval.

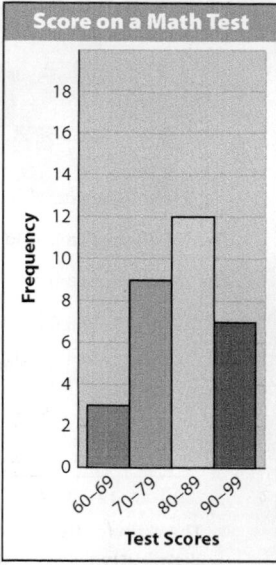

Score on a Math Test

(A) Look at the histogram of "Scores on a Math Test." Which axis indicates the frequency?

The _____vertical_____ axis shows the frequency for each interval.

(B) What does the horizontal axis indicate?

The horizontal axis shows the ___test scores___

(C) How is the horizontal axis organized?

It is organized in groups of ____10____ .

(D) How many had scores in the interval 60–69? **3**

(E) How many had scores in the interval 70–79? **9**

(F) How many had scores in the interval 80–89? **12**

(G) How many had scores in the interval 90–99? **7**

Reflect

1. What statistical information can you tell about a data set by looking at a histogram? What statistical information cannot be determined by looking at a histogram?
Possible answer: It is easy to see the general shape and distribution of the data. It is difficult to know the actual data values.

2. How many test scores were collected? How do you know?
Look at each interval and determine the number of test scores in each.
3 + 9 + 12 + 7 = 31; 31 test scores were collected.

HARDCOVER PAGES 325–336

Turn to these pages to find this lesson in the hardcover student edition.

When creating a histogram, make sure that the bars are of equal width and that they touch without overlapping. Create a frequency table to help organize the data before constructing the histogram. Consider the range of the data values when creating intervals.

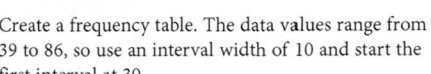 Create a frequency table from the data. Then use the frequency table to create a histogram.

Ⓐ Listed are the ages of the 100 U.S. senators at the start of the 112th Congress on January 3, 2011.

39, 39, 42, 44, 46, 47, 47, 47, 48, 49, **49**, 49, 50, 50, 51, 51,
52, 52, 53, 53, 54, 54, 55, 55, 55, 55, 55, 55, 56, 56, 57, 57,
57, 58, 58, 58, 58, 58, 59, 59, 59, 59, 60, 60, 60, 60, 60, 60,
60, 61, 61, 62, 62, 62, 63, 63, 63, 63, 64, 64, 64, 64, 66, 66,
66, 67, 67, 67, 67, 67, 67, 67, 68, 68, 68, 68, 69, 69, 69, 70,
70, 70, 71, 71, 73, 73, 74, 74, 74, 75, 76, 76, 76, 76, 77, 77,
78, 86, 86, 86

Create a frequency table. The data values range from 39 to 86, so use an interval width of 10 and start the first interval at 30.

Age Interval	Frequency
30–39	2
40–49	10
50–59	30
60–69	37
70–79	18
80–89	3

Check that the sum of the frequencies is 100.

$2 + 10 + 30 + 37 + 18 + 3 = 100$

Use the frequency table to create a histogram.

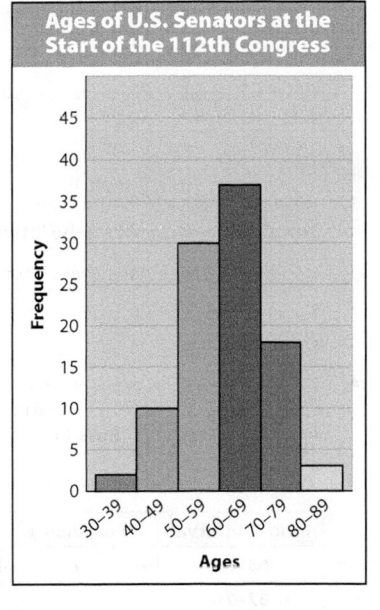

Ages of U.S. Senators at the Start of the 112th Congress

PROFESSIONAL DEVELOPMENT

 Integrate Mathematical Practices

This lesson provides an opportunity to address Mathematical Practice **MP.7**, which calls for students to "look for and make use of structure." By understanding the structure of a histogram, students can estimate the mean value of a data set. When students construct box plots, they understand that the basic structure of a box plot represents the center, spread, and shape of the distribution of a data set; students are then able to compare two different box plots representing two related sets of real-world data.

EXPLORE

Understanding Histograms

INTEGRATE TECHNOLOGY

Point out to students that there are many tools available for creating histograms. These include online tools, spreadsheets, and graphing calculators. An added benefit of using these tools is that they also calculate statistics for the data.

QUESTIONING STRATEGIES

? How is a histogram different from a bar graph? In a histogram, the bars touch, but in a bar graph the bars do not touch. In a histogram, each bar represents a range of values, while in a bar graph, each bar represents a single value or category. Histograms are used for quantitative data, while bar graphs are used to display categorical data.

EXPLAIN 1

Creating Histograms

AVOID COMMON ERRORS

Students may try to draw a histogram with bars representing intervals of different sizes. Point out to students that the bars of a histogram must have the same width, representing the same span of values.

INTEGRATE MATHEMATICAL PRACTICES

Focus on Math Connections

MP.1 Make sure that students understand the connection between number lines, dot plots, and histograms.

? What is a difference between how data are represented on a dot plot and on a histogram? A dot plot gives each individual piece of data, while a histogram combines specific data values to find the frequency of values within intervals.

Ⓑ Listed are the scores from a golf tournament.

68, 78, 76, 71, 69, 73, 72, 74, 76, 70, 77, 74, 75, 76, 71, 74

Create a frequency table. The data values range from 68 to 78 , so use an interval width of 3, and start the first interval at 68 .

Score Interval	Frequency
68– 70	3
71– 73	4
74– 76	7
77– 79	2

Check that the sum of the frequencies is 16 .

$3 + 4 + 7 + 2 =$ 16

Use the frequency table to create a histogram.

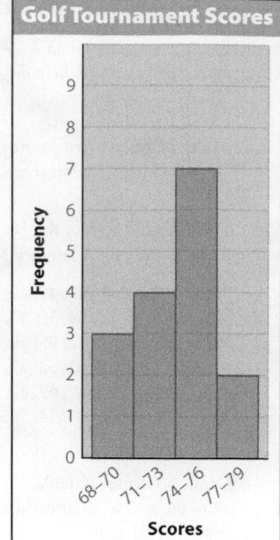

Golf Tournament Scores

Reflect

3. Describe the shape of the distribution of senators' ages. Interpret the meaning.
The data clusters around the intervals 50–59 and 60–69. It appears to be roughly symmetric. This means that about half are older and half are younger than the mean.

Your Turn

4. Listed are the heights of players, in inches, on a basketball team. Create a frequency table from the data. Then use the frequency table to create a histogram. **Possible table and histogram shown.**

79, 75, 74, 68, 63, 76, 74, 73, 69, 65, 71, 68, 74, 73, 70

Height Interval	Frequency
63–66	2
67–70	4
71–74	6
75–78	2
79–82	1

Use the frequency table to create a histogram.

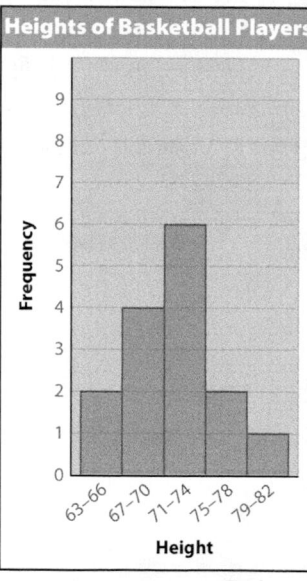

Heights of Basketball Players

© Houghton Mifflin Harcourt Publishing Company

Module 9 **403** Lesson 3

COLLABORATIVE LEARNING

Peer-to-Peer Activity

Have students work in pairs. Have each student create a data set with twenty values, calculate the mean, and create a histogram for the data set. Then have partners trade histograms and estimate the mean value for each other's histograms. After both students have found an estimated value for the mean, have them compare their estimates to the actual values.

You can estimate statistics by studying a histogram.

Example 2 Estimate the mean of the data set displayed in each histogram.

Ⓐ The histogram shows the ages of teachers in a high school.

To estimate the mean, first find the midpoint of each interval, and multiply by the frequency.

1st interval: $\left(\dfrac{20 + 29}{2}\right)(20) = (24.5)(20) = 490$

2nd interval: $\left(\dfrac{30 + 39}{2}\right)(25) = (34.5)(25) = 862.5$

3rd interval: $\left(\dfrac{40 + 49}{2}\right)(30) = (44.5)(30) = 1335$

4th interval: $\left(\dfrac{50 + 59}{2}\right)(15) = (54.5)(15) = 817.5$

5th interval: $\left(\dfrac{60 + 69}{2}\right)(10) = (64.5)(10) = 645$

Add the products and divide by the sum of the frequencies.

Mean: $\dfrac{490 + 862.5 + 1335 + 817.5 + 645}{20 + 25 + 30 + 15 + 10} = \dfrac{4150}{100} = 41.5$

A good estimate for the mean of this data set is an age of 41.5.

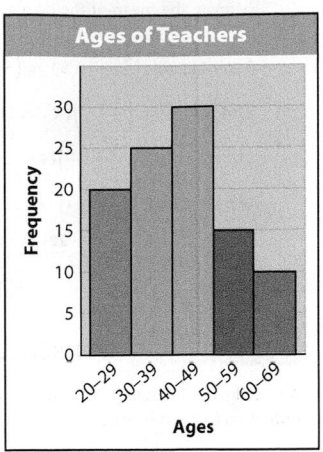

Ages of Teachers

(histogram: Frequency vs Ages; intervals 20-29: 20, 30-39: 25, 40-49: 30, 50-59: 15, 60-69: 10)

Ⓑ The histogram shows the 2012 Olympic results for women's weightlifting.

To estimate the mean, first find the midpoint of each interval, and multiply by the frequency.

1st interval: $\left(\dfrac{160 + 179}{2}\right)$ [1] = [169.5] [1] = [169.5]

2nd interval: $\left(\dfrac{180 + 199}{2}\right)$ [2] = [189.5] [2] = [379]

3rd interval: $\left(\dfrac{200 + 219}{2}\right)$ [4] = [209.5] [4] = [838]

4th interval: $\left(\dfrac{220 + 239}{2}\right)$ [9] = [229.5] [9] = [2065.5]

5th interval: $\left(\dfrac{240 + 259}{2}\right)$ [1] = [249.5] [1] = [249.5]

Add the results and divide by the total number of values in the data set.

Mean: $\dfrac{169.5 + 379 + 838 + 2065.5 + 249.5}{1 + 2 + 4 + 9 + 1} = \dfrac{\boxed{3701.5}}{17} \approx \boxed{217.7}$

A good estimate for the mean of this data set is [217.7] kg.

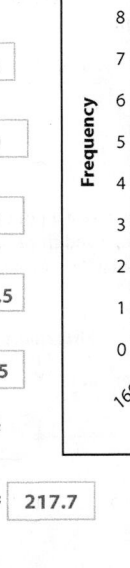

Women's Weightlifting

(histogram: Frequency vs Weight (kg); intervals 160-179: 1, 180-199: 2, 200-219: 4, 220-239: 9, 240-259: 1)

DIFFERENTIATE INSTRUCTION

Multiple Representations

Some students may be troubled by the fact that specific data values are not represented on a histogram. These students may benefit from sketching the histogram on a piece of paper and writing the actual data values into their corresponding intervals. This will help them understand how the estimates are made. For example, by locating the interval that contains the median of the data set and listing all the values in that interval, students can see how the median of the data set is some fraction of the way from the low end to the high end of the interval.

EXPLAIN 2

Estimating from Histograms

AVOID COMMON ERRORS

Students who use mental math to find the midpoint of each interval on a histogram often choose the incorrect midpoint. Remind students that the midpoint of an interval can be found by adding the least and greatest values and dividing the sum by 2.

QUESTIONING STRATEGIES

? Is the median of a data set always represented in one of the middle intervals of a histogram? Explain. No; if the data distribution is skewed to the left or right, the median value may be represented in an interval on either end. For example, if more than half the values are in the rightmost interval, the median would be located in that interval.

? Can you find the exact values of the mean and median of a data set from a histogram? Explain. No; because a histogram does not show individual data values, only an estimate can be determined.

EXPLAIN 3

Constructing Box Plots

INTEGRATE MATHEMATICAL PRACTICES

Focus on Math Connections

MP.1 Help students better understand the connection between dot plots and box plots by drawing a dot plot directly above a box plot for the same set of data. Compare how both data displays show measures of center and spread.

QUESTIONING STRATEGIES

? A box plot combines some of the advantages of a dot plot and of a histogram. What useful characteristics of each does a box plot share? All three diagrams show the shape of a data distribution. Like a dot plot, a box plot displays some specific numbers (the minimum, maximum, median, and first and third quartiles). Like a histogram, a box plot summarizes the data so you can see the shape of the distribution without looking at many individual data points.

? How can you tell that the box in a box plot represents about 50% of the data in a data set? The interval from the first quartile to the median contains about one-fourth of the values in the data set, and the interval from the median to the third quartile also contains about one-fourth of the values. This means the section from the first quartile to the third quartile contains about half the values in the data set.

---

5. The histogram shows the length, in days, of Maria's last vacations. Estimate the mean of the data set displayed in the histogram.

1st interval: $\left(\frac{4+6}{2}\right)(5) = (5)(5) = 25$

2nd interval: $\left(\frac{7+9}{2}\right)(4) = (8)(4) = 32$

3rd interval: $\left(\frac{10+12}{2}\right)(4) = (11)(4) = 44$

4th interval: $\left(\frac{13+15}{2}\right)(2) = (14)(2) = 28$

Mean: $\frac{25+32+44+28}{5+4+4+2} = \frac{129}{15} \approx 8.6$ days

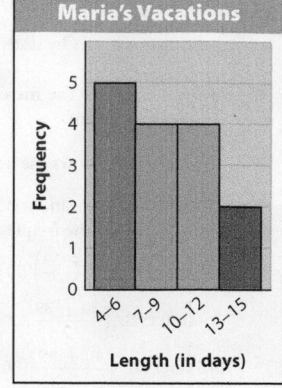

Maria's Vacations

🖊 Explain 3   Constructing Box Plots

A box plot can be used to show how the values in a data set are distributed. You need 5 values to make a box plot: the minimum (or least value), first quartile, median, third quartile, and maximum (or greatest value).

Example 3   Use the data to make a box plot.

(A) The numbers of runs scored by a softball team in 20 games are given.

3, 4, 8, 12, 7, 5, 4, 12, 3, 9, 11, 4, 14, 8, 2, 10, 3, 10, 9, 7

Order the data from least to greatest.

2, 3, 3, 3, 4, 4, 4, 5, 7, 7, 8, 8, 9, 9, 10, 10, 11, 12, 12, 14

Identify the 5 needed values. Those values are the minimum, first quartile, median, third quartile, and maximum.

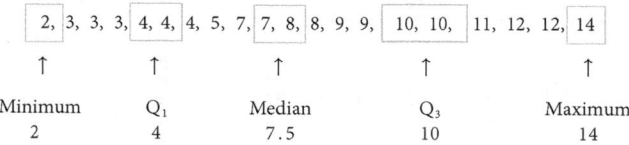

Minimum	Q_1	Median	Q_3	Maximum
2	4	7.5	10	14

Draw a number line and plot a point above each of the 5 needed values. Draw a box whose ends go through the first and third quartiles, and draw a vertical line segment through the median. Draw horizontal line segments from the box to the minimum and maximum.

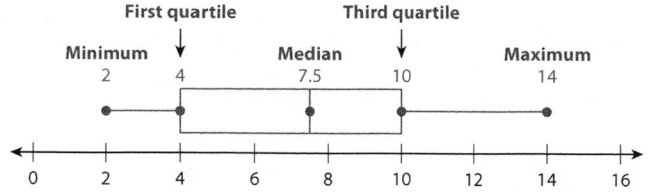

© Houghton Mifflin Harcourt Publishing Company

LANGUAGE SUPPORT 🔵EL

Connect Vocabulary

Students might be familiar with dot plots, measures of center (mean, median), and measures of spread (range) from previous courses, but it is important to make sure that students also know the terms used to describe these measures. When creating box plots and comparing two sets of data, students must find the *first quartile*, *third quartile*, and *interquartile range*. Point out that the English word *quartile* has a Spanish cognate, *cuartil*. Be sure students are aware that first quartile and third quartile refer to specific values, not to the lower and upper quarters of the data set.

Ⓑ 13, 14, 18, 13, 12, 17, 15, 12, 13, 19, 11, 14, 14, 18, 22, 23

Order the data from least to greatest.

[11], 12, 12, [13], [13], 13, 14, [14], [14], 15, 17, [18], [18], 19, 22 [23]

Identify the 5 needed values. Those values are the minimum, first quartile, median, third quartile, and maximum.

[11], 12, 12, [13, 13,] 13, 14, [14, 14,] 15, 17, [18, 18,] 19, 22, [23]

  ↑   ↑   ↑   ↑   ↑

Minimum Q_1 Median Q_3 Maximum

[11]   [13]   [14]   [18]   [23]

Draw a number line and plot a point above each of the 5 needed values. Draw a box whose ends go through the first and third quartiles, and draw a vertical line through the median. Draw horizontal lines from the box to the minimum and maximum.

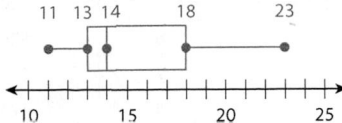

Reflect

6. The lines that extend from the box in a box plot are sometimes called "whiskers." What part (lower, middle, or upper) and about what percent of the data does the box represent? What part and about what percent does each "whisker" represent?

Box: middle 50%; left whisker: lower 25%; right whisker: upper 25%

7. Which measures of spread can be determined from the box plot, and how are they found? Calculate each measure.

The range is the length of the entire box plot: 23 − 11 = 12. The IQR is the length of the box: 18 − 13 = 5.

Your Turn

Use the data to make a box plot.

8. 25, 28, 26, 16, 18, 15, 25, 28, 26, 16

[15,] 16, [16,] 18, [25,] 25, [26,] [26,] 28, [28]

Min Q_1 Median Q_3 Max

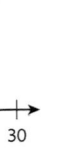

9. The numbers of goals scored by Lisa's soccer team in 13 games are listed below.

2, 3, 4, 1, 1, 3, 4, 2, 6, 2, 2, 3, 2

[1,] 1, [2, 2,] 2, 2, [2,] 3, 3, [3, 4,] 4, 6

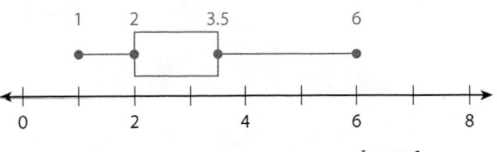

EXPLAIN 4

Comparing Box Plots

AVOID COMMON ERRORS

When comparing box plots, some students may draw each box plot using a number line with a different scale. Remind students that to compare data sets by placing box plots one above the other, both box plots must be drawn using the same number line.

QUESTIONING STRATEGIES

? What effect would outliers have on the center and shape of a box plot? Outliers increase the maximum value or decrease the minimum value of a data set, but they have relatively little effect on the median and the first and third quartiles. Therefore, the length of one or both lines extending from the box would be longer for a data set with outliers, but the box itself would have nearly the same size and position as it would in a box plot for the same data set without the outliers.

⊘ Explain 4 **Comparing Box Plots**

You can plot two box plots above a single number line to compare two data sets.

Example 4 Construct two box plots, one for each data set. Compare the medians and measures of variation for each distribution.

Ⓐ The tables show the total gross earnings, in dollars, for the top 10 movies of 2013 and 2012.

Total Gross Earnings by the Top 25 Movies of 2013 & 2012			
Rank	Total Gross in 2013	Rank	Total Gross in 2012
1	$420,468,544	1	$623,357,910
2	$409,013,994	2	$448,139,099
3	$368,061,265	3	$408,010,692
4	$352,946,000	4	$304,360,277
5	$291,045,518	5	$303,003,568
6	$268,492,764	6	$292,324,737
7	$262,547,000	7	$262,030,663
8	$253,029,814	8	$237,283,207
9	$238,679,850	9	$218,815,487
10	$234,911,825	10	$216,391,482

⊞ Analyze Information

For each set of data, identify the five values you need to make a box plot: the minimum, __first quartile, median, third quartile, and maximum__. In this case, the data is from least to __greatest__ reading from the bottom to the top.

⊞ Formulate a Plan

With the __5__ needed values for each data set, construct 2 __box plots__ on the same number line. The number line for both plots can go from $ __200__ million to $ __650 or 700__ million. Interpret the box plots to compare the gross earnings for the top 10 movies in 2012 and 2013.

© Houghton Mifflin Harcourt Publishing Company

Solve

Using the statistics feature of a graphing calculator, find the five needed values, rounded to the nearest hundred million.

	2013 Top 10 Movies Gross Earnings ($100,000,000s)	2012 Top 10 Movies Gross Earnings ($100,000,000s)
Minimum	235	216
Q_1	253	237
Median	280	298
Q_3	268	408
Maximum	420	623

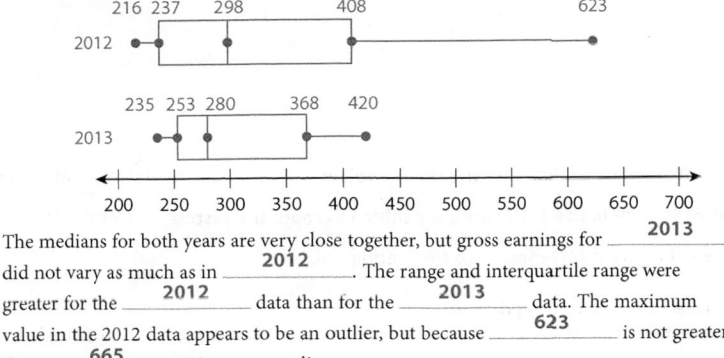

The medians for both years are very close together, but gross earnings for ___**2013**___ did not vary as much as in ___**2012**___. The range and interquartile range were greater for the ___**2012**___ data than for the ___**2013**___ data. The maximum value in the 2012 data appears to be an outlier, but because ___**623**___ is not greater than ___**665**___, it is not an outlier.

Justify and Evaluate

Considering the little difference between minimum values but the great difference between maximum values the data sets, it makes sense that their measures of variation would / (would not) be alike.

Your Turn

Construct two box plots, one for each data set. Compare the medians and measures of variation for each distribution.

10. The net worth of the 10 richest people in the world for 2012 and 2013 (in billions) are:
   2012: 69, 61, 44, 41, 37.5, 36, 30, 26, 25.5, 25.4 **2013:** 73, 67, 57, 53.5, 43, 34, 34, 31, 30, 29

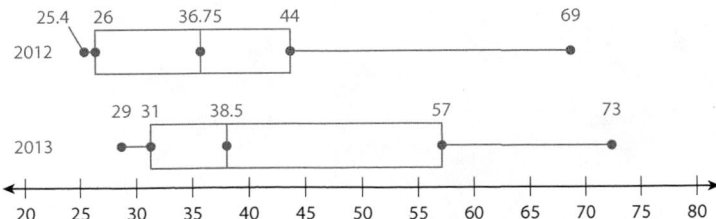

The medians are close, but the median for 2013 is slightly greater than that of 2012. The ranges are close, but the interquartile range for 2013 is much greater than that of 2012.

ELABORATE

QUESTIONING STRATEGIES

? Describe what a box plot representing a symmetric distribution and a box plot representing a skewed distribution would look like. A box plot for a symmetric data distribution would be symmetrical: the median would be in the center of the box, and the lines extending to each side of the box would be about the same length. In a box plot for a skewed distribution, the median would be closer to one end of the box, and the line extending from that end of the box might be shorter than the line at the other end.

INTEGRATE MATHEMATICAL PRACTICES

Focus on Critical Thinking

MP.3 Have students explore how an outlier affects a box plot. Have them first draw a box plot for a data set with no outliers, then add an outlier to the data set and draw a new box plot. Have them compare the two plots. Discuss which changes will occur with any outlier, and which might be different for a different outlier.

SUMMARIZE THE LESSON

? What are the steps for creating a box plot? Order the data. Determine the minimum, median, first quartile, third quartile, and maximum. Draw a number line and plot the values. Draw a vertical line at the median, a box from Q_1 to Q_3, and lines from the box to the minimum and maximum points.

---

11. The ages of the 10 richest people in the world for 2012 and 2013 (in years) are:

2012: 72, 56, 81, 63, 75, 67, 55, 64, 83, 92   **2013:** 72, 57, 76, 82, 68, 77, 72, 84, 90, 63

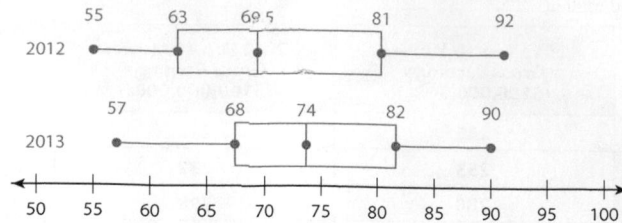

The median for 2013 is much greater than the median for 2012. Both the range and interquartile range for 2013 are less than those of 2012, so the ages were more varied in 2012.

💬 Elaborate

12. How can you create a histogram from a data set?
First, create a frequency table using the data. Look at the range of the data to determine the interval width. Then, use the frequency table to create the histogram, where the bar heights for each interval correspond to the frequency.

13. How can you create a box plot from a data set?
First, order the data from least to greatest. Find the minimum and maximum values, the median, and the first and third quartiles. Draw a box whose ends go through the first and third quartiles, and then draw a vertical line through the median. Draw horizontal lines from the box to the minimum and maximum.

14. **Essential Question Check-In** How can you use histograms and box plots to interpret and compare data sets?
You can use histograms to estimate statistics and compare distributions. You can use box plots to compare the centers, spread, and shape of the distribution.

• Online Homework
• Hints and Help
• Extra Practice

Use the histogram to answer the following questions.

1. What does each axis indicate?
   The vertical axis shows the frequency for each interval, and the horizontal axis shows the bowlers' scores.

2. How is the horizontal axis organized?
   The scores are organized in groups of 20.

3. How many bowlers competed?
   $2 + 4 + 6 + 8 + 9 + 1 = 30$
   30 bowlers competed.

4. Describe the general shape of the distribution.
   The distribution is skewed left .

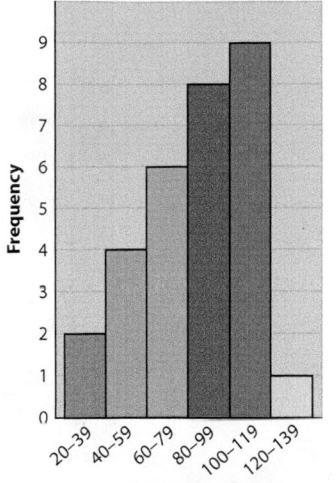

Bowlers' Scores

Create a histogram for the given data. **Possible tables and histograms shown.**

5. Listed are the ages of the first 44 U.S. presidents on the date of their first inauguration.

   57, 61, 57, 57, 58, 57, 61, 54, 68, 51, 49, 64, 50, 48, 65, 52, 56, 46, 54, 49, 51, 47, 55, 55, 54, 42, 51, 56, 55, 51, 54, 51, 60, 62, 43, 55, 56, 61, 52, 69, 64, 46, 54, 47

6. Listed are the breathing intervals, in minutes, of gray whales.

   8, 5, 13, 7 ,16, 9, 15, 11, 8, 6, 10, 9, 9, 11, 14, 12, 13, 15, 16, 11, 14, 9, 15, 6, 14

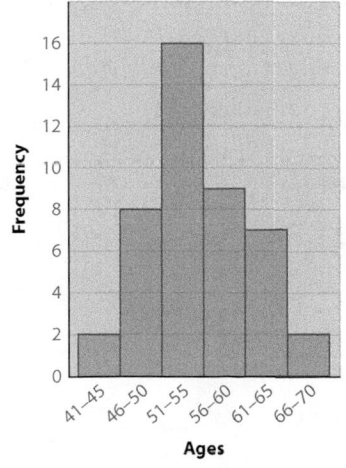

Ages

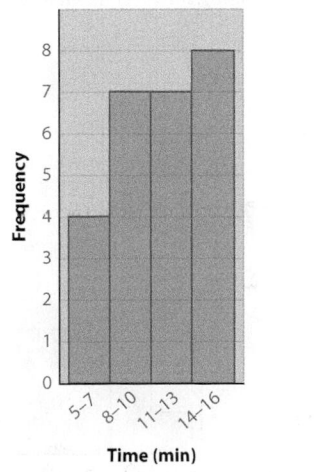

Time (min)

Exercise	Depth of Knowledge (D.O.K.)	COMMON CORE Mathematical Practices
1–4	**1** Recall	**MP.4** Modeling
5–8	**1** Recall	**MP.5** Using Tools
9–18	**2** Skills/Concepts	**MP.4** Modeling
19	**3** Strategic Thinking	**MP.8** Patterns
20–22	**3** Strategic Thinking **H.O.T.**	**MP.3** Logic

EVALUATE

ASSIGNMENT GUIDE

Concepts and Skills	Practice
Explore Understanding Histograms	Exercises 1–4
Example 1 Creating Histograms	Exercises 5–8
Example 2 Estimating from Histograms	Exercises 9–12, 22
Example 3 Constructing Box Plots	Exercises 13–18, 21
Example 4 Comparing Box Plots	Exercises 19–20, 22

INTEGRATE MATHEMATICAL PRACTICES
Focus on Critical Thinking

MP.3 Have students conduct a survey with quantitative results that can be displayed in intervals. Then have them choose at least three different-sized intervals for grouping the data, and make both a frequency table and a histogram for each interval choice. Have students estimate the mean and median from each histogram and compare the estimates to the mean and median calculated from the raw data. Then have students explain which interval they think best displays the survey results.

7. Listed are the heights, in inches, of the students in Marci's karate class.

42, 44, 47, 50, 51, 53, 53, 55,
56, 57, 57, 58, 59, 60, 66

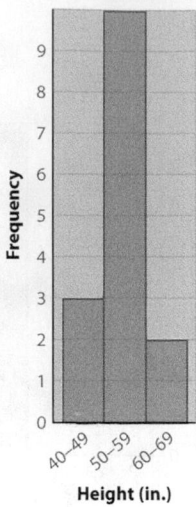

Height (in.)

8. Listed are the starting salaries, in thousands of dollars, for college graduates.

34, 20, 32, 45, 32, 48, 34, 32, 20, 35, 34, 32, 40,
47, 21, 37, 21, 47, 30, 31, 40, 31, 21, 22, 30, 22,
34, 48, 35, 37, 22, 46, 38, 39, 45, 37, 52, 25, 26,
26, 27, 43, 34, 28, 55, 29, 31, 42, 24, 21, 42, 42,
31, 30, 20, 39, 23, 41, 24, 33, 49, 24, 36, 36, 23,
38, 33, 33, 54

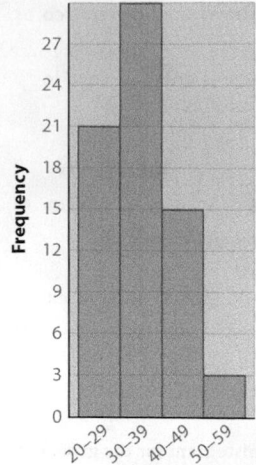

Salary Range (thousands $)

Estimate the mean of the data set displayed in each histogram.

9. The histogram shows the GPAs of the students in George's class.

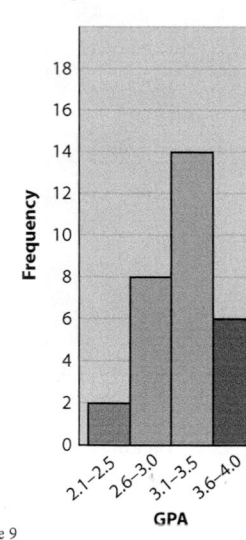

GPA

1st interval: $\left(\dfrac{2.1 + 2.5}{2}\right)(2) = (2.3)(2) = 4.6$

2nd interval: $\left(\dfrac{2.6 + 3.0}{2}\right)(8) = (2.8)(8) = 22.4$

3rd interval: $\left(\dfrac{3.1 + 3.5}{2}\right)(14) = (3.3)(14) = 46.2$

4th interval: $\left(\dfrac{3.6 + 4.0}{2}\right)(6) = (3.8)(6) = 22.8$

Mean: $\dfrac{4.6 + 22.4 + 46.2 + 22.8}{2 + 8 + 14 + 6} = \dfrac{95.7}{30} = 3.19$

The mean GPA is 3.19.

10. The histogram shows long jump distances, in feet, for a track and field team.

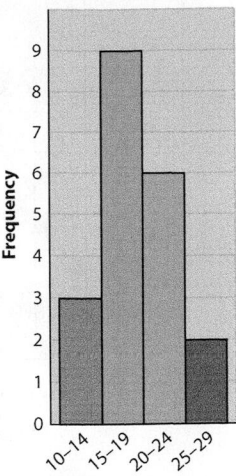

Distance (ft)

1st interval: $\left(\dfrac{10+14}{2}\right)(3) = (12)(3) = 36$

2nd interval: $\left(\dfrac{15+19}{2}\right)(9) = (17)(9) = 153$

3rd interval: $\left(\dfrac{20+24}{2}\right)(6) = (22)(6) = 132$

4th interval: $\left(\dfrac{25+29}{2}\right)(2) = (27)(2) = 54$

Mean: $\dfrac{36+153+132+54}{3+9+6+2} = \dfrac{375}{20} = 18.75$

The mean long jump distance is 18.75 ft.

11. The histogram shows the speeds of downhill skiers, in miles per hour, during a competition.

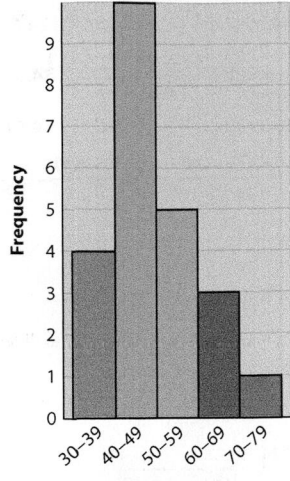

Speed (mi/h)

1st interval: $\left(\dfrac{30+39}{2}\right)(4) = (34.5)(4) = 138$

2nd interval: $\left(\dfrac{40+49}{2}\right)(10) = (44.5)(10) = 445$

3rd interval: $\left(\dfrac{50+59}{2}\right)(5) = (54.5)(5) = 272.5$

4th interval: $\left(\dfrac{60+69}{2}\right)(3) = (64.5)(3) = 193.5$

5th interval: $\left(\dfrac{70+79}{2}\right)(1) = (74.5)(1) = 74.5$

Mean: $\dfrac{138+445+272.5+193.5+74.5}{4+10+5+3+1}$

$= \dfrac{1123.5}{23} \approx 48.8$

The mean speed is about 48.8 mi/h.

MANIPULATIVES

To help students understand how a histogram represents data, allow each student to grab a handful of integer chips or other small objects. Have each student count the number of integer chips he or she holds and write that number on a sticky note. Write intervals of 5 across the board and have students place their numbers above the correct interval. Numbers within the same interval should be lined up vertically. The result will resemble a histogram.

AVOID COMMON ERRORS

Remind students that each interval of a histogram should represent the same span of values, so all the bars must have the same width. Some students may think that each bar of a histogram can represent a range of a different size.

12. The histogram shows the depths a diver has been to, in meters.

1st interval: $\left(\dfrac{10 + 19}{2}\right)(5) = (14.5)(5) = 72.5$

2nd interval: $\left(\dfrac{20 + 29}{2}\right)(6) = (24.5)(6) = 147$

3rd interval: $\left(\dfrac{30 + 39}{2}\right)(7) = (34.5)(7) = 241.5$

4th interval: $\left(\dfrac{40 + 49}{2}\right)(2) = (44.5)(2) = 89$

Mean: $\dfrac{72.5 + 147 + 241.5 + 89}{5 + 6 + 7 + 2} = \dfrac{550}{20} = 27.5$

The mean depth is 27.5 m.

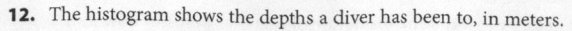

Use the data to make a box plot.

13. The numbers of points Julia's basketball team scored in 11 games are listed below.

50, 62, 37, 36, 34, 44, 44, 36, 37, 42, 36

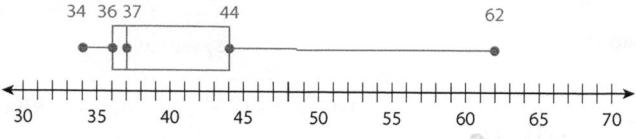

14. The numbers of baskets Kelly's team scored in 9 games are listed below.

14, 24, 29, 15, 16, 20, 24, 15, 15

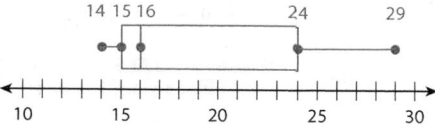

15. The numbers of runs Jane's baseball team scored in 9 games are listed below.

0, 2, 3, 2, 4, 11, 3, 4, 3

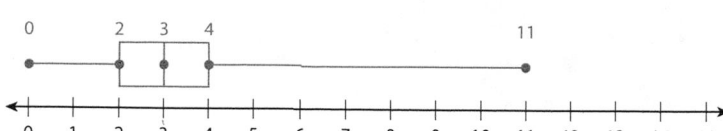

16. The numbers of field goals James' football team scored in 12 games are listed below.

3, 2, 5, 3, 5, 2, 1, 0, 5, 4, 4, 2

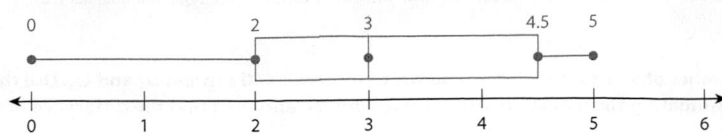

17. The numbers of points scored by Jane in 8 basketball games are listed below.

0, 13, 12, 2, 0, 16, 3, 14

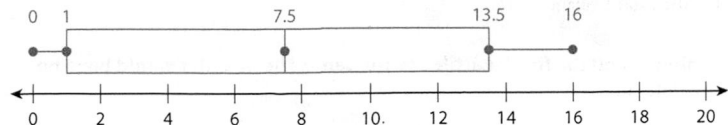

18. The numbers of goals Claudia's soccer team scored in 21 games are shown below.

0, 5, 4, 3, 3, 2, 1, 1, 6, 2, 2, 1, 1, 1, 2, 2, 0, 1, 0, 1, 4

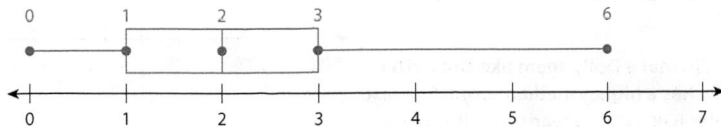

19. Mario and Carlos, two brothers, play for the same basketball team. Here are the points they scored in 10 games:

Game	1	2	3	4	5	6	7	8	9	10
Mario	15	X	X	12	7	11	12	11	10	11
Carlos	10	X	9	12	15	X	19	11	12	12

(Xs mark games each one missed.) Which brother had the highest-scoring game? How many more points did he score in that game than the other brother did in his highest-scoring game?

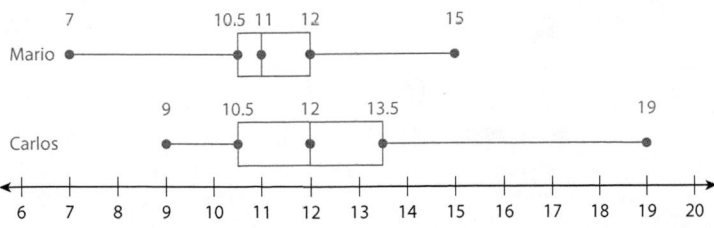

Carlos scored a maximum number of 19 points in a game versus Mario's maximum of 15.

Between these two games, Carlos scored 4 more points than Mario.

JOURNAL

Have students write a paragraph explaining how to compare data sets using box plots. Students should include how to construct a box plot, with instructions on how to find the minimum and maximum values, as well as the first quartile, median, and third quartile.

20. Communicate Mathematical Ideas Describe how you could estimate the IQR of a data set from a histogram.

Count the number of values, and determine which intervals will contain Q_1 and Q_3. Use the method for estimating the median to estimate Q_1 and Q_3, and then find the difference of the two values.

21. Critical Thinking Suppose the minimum in a data set is the same as the first quartile. How would this affect a box plot of the data? Explain.

Because the minimum and the first quartile are the same, the box plot would have no "whisker" on the left side.

22. Draw Conclusions Dolly and Willie's scores are shown. Dolly claims that she is the better student, but Willie claims that he is the better student. What statistics make either Dolly or Willie seem like the better student? Explain.

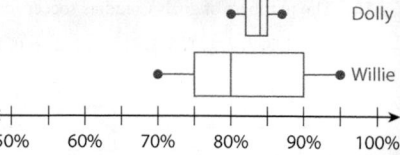

Median and IQR make Dolly seem like the better student. Dolly has a higher median score. She also has the smaller IQR, which means that her scores are more consistent.

Third quartile and maximum make Willie seem like a better student. Willie's set has the higher third quartile and maximum. This means that his greatest 25% of scores are all higher than Dolly's highest score.

© Houghton Mifflin Harcourt Publishing Company

Lesson Performance Task

The batting averages for the starting lineup of two competing baseball teams are given in the table.

Batting Averages for Team A	0.270	0.260	0.300	0.290	0.260	0.280	0.280	0.240	0.270	0.280
Batting Averages for Team B	0.290	0.270	0.240	0.280	0.230	0.280	0.230	0.270	0.250	0.270

a. Create a box plot for each data set on the same number line.

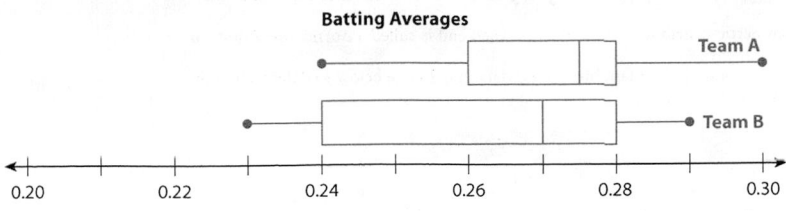

Team A

0.240, 0.260, 0.260, 0.270, 0.270, 0.280, 0.280,

0.280, 0.290, 0.300

Minimum = 0.240

$Q_1 = 0.260$

Median $= \dfrac{0.270 + 0.280}{2} = \dfrac{0.550}{2} = 0.275$

$Q_3 = 0.280$

Maximum = 0.300

Team B

0.230, 0.230, 0.240, 0.250, 0.270, 0.270, 0.270,

0.280, 0.280, 0.290

Minimum = 0.230

$Q_1 = 0.240$

Median $= \dfrac{0.270 + 0.270}{2} = \dfrac{0.540}{2} = 0.270$

$Q_3 = 0.280$

Maximum = 0.290

b. Compare the distributions of the batting averages for each team.

The distribution for Team A is more symmetric and the distribution for Team B is more skewed to the right. Team A has a higher median batting average than Team B. The batting averages are more spread out for Team B than they are for Team A.

c. Which team has a better starting lineup? Explain.

Team A has a higher median and a smaller spread. So, the batting averages of Team A's starting lineup are more consistent. Team A also has a higher maximum, so the highest batting average of Team A's starting lineup is higher than the highest batting average in Team B's starting lineup. So, Team A has a better starting lineup.

EXTENSION ACTIVITY

Have students research the batting averages of the top 10 players on two of their favorite baseball teams. Then have students use the data they collect to create a double box plot of the data and compare the performance of the two sets of players. Students who are not baseball fans may choose to analyze statistics from a different sport or competition, such as basketball, football, or chess.

CONNECT VOCABULARY **EL**

Some students may not know what a *starting lineup* is. Ask students in the class with knowledge of baseball to explain what a starting lineup is—a list of players who will participate in the game when it begins—and the criteria that might be used for including a player on the starting lineup list.

INTEGRATE MATHEMATICAL PRACTICES

Focus on Technology

MP.5 Have students use the one-variable statistics function on a graphing calculator to check the values they calculated for the median and first and third quartile of each data set.

Students can also use graphing calculators to generate the double box plot of the data sets. Have them research the procedure online, apply it to the data from the Lesson Performance Task, and check whether the box plots they drew by hand match the ones shown by the calculator.

Normal Distributions

Common Core Math Standards

The student is expected to:

COMMON CORE S-ID-A.2

Use statistics appropriate to the shape of the data distribution to compare center (median, mean) and spread (interquartile range, standard deviation) of two or more different data sets. Also S-ID.A.1, N-Q.A.1

Mathematical Practices

COMMON CORE MP.7 Using Structure

Language Objective

Describe the characteristics of a normal distribution.

ENGAGE

Essential Question: How can you use characteristics of a normal distribution to make estimates and probability predictions about the population that the data represents?

You can calculate the mean and standard deviation of the data set and then use the fact that 68% of the data is within one standard deviation of the mean, 95% of the data is within two standard deviations, and 99.7% of the data is within three standard deviations, to make estimates and predictions.

PREVIEW: LESSON PERFORMANCE TASK

View the Engage section online. Discuss how fast a runner can complete a 100-meter race, which is equivalent to about 328 feet. Note that the world's fastest sprinters can run that distance in less than 10 seconds. Then preview the Lesson Performance Task.

9.4 Normal Distributions

Essential Question: How can you use characteristics of a normal distribution to make estimates and probability predictions about the population that the data represents?

Resource Locker

⊘ Explore   Investigating Symmetric Distributions

A bell-shaped, symmetric distribution with a tail on each end is called a **normal distribution**.

Use a graphing calculator and the infant birth mass data in the table below to determine if the set represents a normal distribution.

Birth Mass (kg)				
3.3	3.6	3.5	3.4	3.7
3.6	3.5	3.4	3.7	3.5
3.4	3.5	3.2	3.6	3.4
3.8	3.5	3.6	3.3	3.5

Ⓐ Enter the data into a graphing calculator as a list. Calculate the "1-Variable Statistics" for the distribution of data.

Mean, $\bar{x} \approx$ **3.5**   Standard deviation, $\sigma_x \approx$ **0.14**

Median = **3.5** $IQR = Q_3 - Q_1 =$ **0.5**

Ⓑ Sketch the histogram. Always include labels for the axes and the bar intervals.

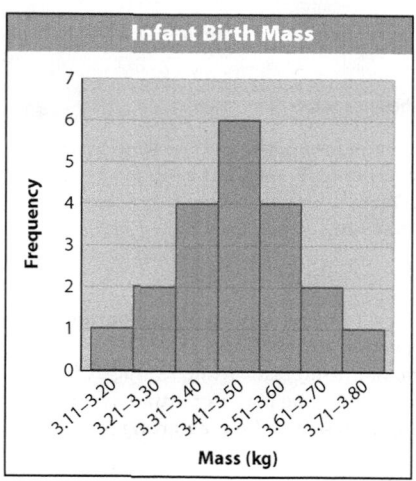

Infant Birth Mass

© Houghton Mifflin Harcourt Publishing Company

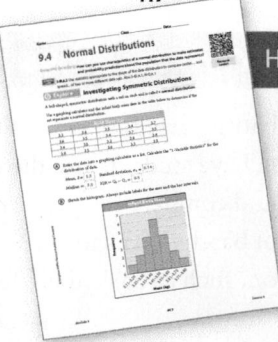

HARDCOVER PAGES 337–344

Turn to these pages to find this lesson in the hardcover student edition.

(C) Could this data be described by a normal distribution? Explain.

Yes; the distribution is bell-shaped and symmetric about the mean and median, with a tail on each end.

Reflect

1. Which intervals on the histogram had the fewest values? Which interval had the greatest number of values?

   The intervals 3.11 — 3.20 and 3.71 — 3.80 had the fewest values, and the interval

   3.41 — 3.50 had the most values.

2. **Make a Conjecture** For the normal distribution, the mean and the median are the same. Is this true for every normal distribution? Explain.

   Yes; the symmetric shape means that the median will be at the exact center of

   the histogram, and it also implies that the mean will equal the central value of

   the distribution.

3. **Counterexamples** Allison thinks that every symmetric distribution must be bell-shaped. Provide a counterexample to show that she is incorrect.

   Possible answer: A histogram where every interval had the same number of values would

   be symmetric but not bell-shaped.

⊘ **Explore 2** **Investigating Symmetric Relative Frequency Histograms**

The table gives the frequency of each mass from the data set used in the first Explore.

Mass (kg)	3.2	3.3	3.4	3.5	3.6	3.7	3.8
Frequency	1	2	4	6	4	2	1

(A) Use the frequency table to make a relative frequency table.
Notice that there are 20 data values.

Mass (kg)	3.2	3.3	3.4	3.5	3.6	3.7	3.8
Relative Frequency	$\frac{1}{20} = 0.05$	0.1	0.2	0.3	0.2	0.1	0.05

What is the sum of the relative frequencies? _____**1**_____

PROFESSIONAL DEVELOPMENT

Math Background

The normal distribution, also called a *Gaussian distribution* or a *bell-shaped curve,* is likely the most well-known distribution in statistics. Normal distributions can be completely described by their mean and standard deviation. Normal distributions will follow the 68–95–99.7 rule (also known as the *three-sigma rule* or *empirical rule),* which states that 68% of all values fall within one standard deviation of the mean, 95% of values fall within two standard deviations, and 99.7% of the values fall within three standard deviations of the mean.

Investigating Symmetric Distributions

INTEGRATE TECHNOLOGY

To make sure all students understand how to use calculators to find the 1-variable statistics, have them work in groups of four and have each person in a group report one of the four statistics.

When creating a histogram, students can use the **SortA** function from the calculator's **STAT** menu to arrange the values in a list in ascending order.

QUESTIONING STRATEGIES

❓ How could you tell whether a data distribution is symmetric by looking only at a frequency table? You could look at the middle interval and check whether it has the greatest frequency. Then look at the intervals on either side of it to see whether they decrease by approximately the same amount. Continue this process out to the first and last intervals. The data is symmetric if the frequencies decrease by about the same amount as you move away from the middle interval.

EXPLORE 2

Investigating Symmetric Relative Frequency Histograms

QUESTIONING STRATEGIES

❓ If you know the frequency of a value in a data set, how do you determine the relative frequency for the value? To find the relative frequency, divide the frequency by the number of values in the data set.

Focus on Math Connections

MP.1 Have students compare their relative frequency histograms to the histograms they created from the original data. Students should see that both have the same shape, but use different scales for the y-axis.

Ⓑ Sketch a relative frequency histogram. The heights of the bars now indicate relative frequencies.

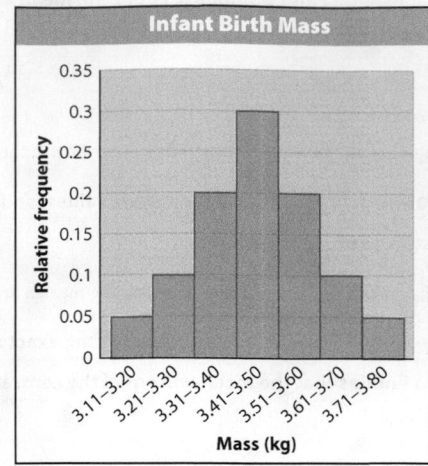

Ⓒ Recall from the first Explore that the mean of this data set is 3.5 and the standard deviation is 0.14. By how many standard deviations does a birth mass of 3.2 kg differ from the mean? Round to one decimal place. Justify your answer.

$3.5 - 3.2 = \boxed{0.3}$ and $\boxed{0.3} \div 0.14 = \boxed{2.1}$, so a birth mass of 3.2 kg is $\underline{\quad 2.1 \quad}$

standard deviations below the mean.

Reflect

4. Identify the interval of values that are within one standard deviation of the mean. Use the frequency table to determine what percent of the values in the set are in this interval.
   The interval is 3.5 − 0.14 to 3.5 + 0.14, or 3.36–3.64. $\frac{14}{20}$ = 70% of the values are in this interval.

5. Identify the interval of values that are within two standard deviations of the mean. Use the frequency table to determine what percent of values in the set are in this interval.
   The interval is 3.5 − 2(0.14) to 3.5 + 2(0.14), or 3.22–3.78. $\frac{18}{20}$ = 90% of the values are in this interval.

© Houghton Mifflin Harcourt Publishing Company

COLLABORATIVE LEARNING

Peer-to-Peer Activity

Have students work in pairs. Provide each pair with a sketch of a normal distribution. Ask one student to sketch a normal distribution with the same mean but a smaller standard deviation. Have the other student sketch a normal distribution with the same mean but a larger standard deviation. Have students compare their results to the original distribution. Students' curves should be centered at the mean and have a symmetric shape. The curve with a small standard deviation should be narrow and tall, while the one with a large standard deviation should be short and wide. Ask pairs to share their results.

⊘ Explain 1   Using Properties of Normal Distributions

The smaller the intervals are in a symmetric, bell-shaped relative frequency histogram, the closer the shape of the histogram is to a curve called a *normal curve*. Let σ represent the standard deviation.

A **normal curve** has the following properties:

- about 68% of the data fall within 1 standard deviation of the mean.
- about 95% of the data fall within 2 standard deviations of the mean.
- about 99.7% of the data fall within 3 standard deviations of the mean.

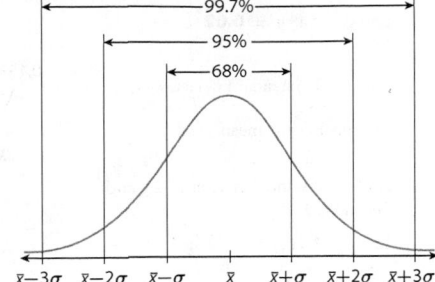

The symmetry of a normal curve allows you to separate the area under the curve into eight parts and know what percent of the data is contained in each part.

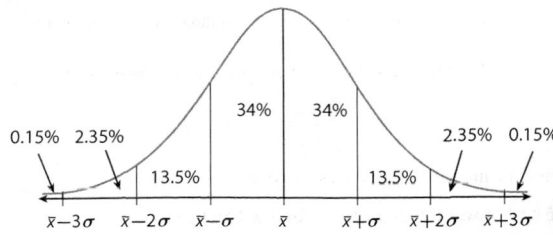

| Example 1 | The masses (in grams) of pennies minted in the United States after 1982 are normally distributed with a mean of 2.50 g and a standard deviation of 0.02 g. |

Ⓐ   Find the percent of these pennies that have a mass between 2.46 g and 2.54 g.

Find the percent between 2.46 g and the mean, 2.50 g.

$2.50\ \text{g} - 2.46\ \text{g} = 0.04\ \text{g}$

This is 2 standard deviations below the mean.

Find the percent between 2.54 g and the mean, 2.50 g.

$2.54\ \text{g} - 2.50\ \text{g} = 0.04\ \text{g}$

This is 2 standard deviations above the mean.

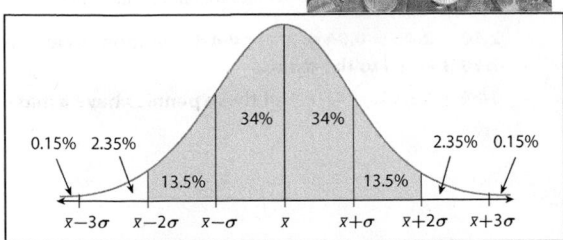

The shaded area represents pennies between 2.46 g and 2.54 g.

95% of the data in a normal distribution fall within 2 standard deviations of the mean.

95% of pennies minted in the United States after 1982 have a mass between 2.46 g and 2.54 g.

© Houghton Mifflin Harcourt Publishing Company • Image Credits: ©trekandshoot/Shutterstock

---

EXPLAIN 1

Using Properties of Normal Distributions

INTEGRATE MATHEMATICAL PRACTICES
Focus on Critical Thinking

MP.3 Students may feel they cannot determine the percent of values in a certain interval without knowing the individual values of the data set. Students should understand that in a normal distribution, a known percent of values fall in each interval defined by the standard deviation of the data. Therefore, if you know that a set of data is normally distributed, and you know the standard deviation and mean, you can determine the percent of values for each interval.

AVOID COMMON ERRORS

When determining the percent of values in a given range, some students will find the percent for just one section of the range. Remind students that when finding the percent (or probability), they must find the sum of all the sections that satisfy the given condition.

DIFFERENTIATE INSTRUCTION

Critical Thinking

Ask students which of the following would be most useful to them when researching colleges. Ask them to explain and defend their answers.

- a list of all of the college entrance exam scores of last year's freshman class
- the average college entrance exam score of last year's freshman class
- a histogram showing the college entrance exam scores and the number of students who received each score

QUESTIONING STRATEGIES

? How is a normal curve similar to a histogram? Both a normal curve and a histogram display the frequency of various data values. A normal curve represents the shape that a histogram for a normally distributed data set would have if each bar represented a very narrow interval.

Ⓑ Find the percent of pennies that have a mass between 2.48 g and 2.52 g.

Find the percent between 2.48 g and the mean, 2.50 g.

$2.50 \text{ g} - 2.48 \text{ g} = \boxed{0.02}$ g

This is $\boxed{1}$ standard deviation(s)

above/⟨below⟩ the mean.

Find the distance between 2.52 g and the mean, 2.50 g.

$2.52 \text{ g} - 2.50 \text{ g} = \boxed{0.02}$ g

This is $\boxed{1}$ standard deviation(s)

⟨above⟩/below the mean.

$\boxed{68}$ % of the data in a normal distribution fall within $\boxed{1}$ standard deviation(s) of the mean.

So, $\boxed{68}$ % of pennies minted in the United States after 1982 have a mass between 2.48 g and 2.52 g.

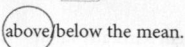

0.15%   2.35%   13.5%   34%   34%   13.5%   2.35%   0.15%

$\bar{x}-3\sigma$ $\bar{x}-2\sigma$ $\bar{x}-\sigma$ $\bar{x}$ $\bar{x}+\sigma$ $\bar{x}+2\sigma$ $\bar{x}+3\sigma$

Shade the area for pennies between 2.48 g and 2.52 g.

YourTurn

6. Find the percent of these pennies that have a mass between 2.44 g and 2.56 g.

2.50 − 2.44 = 0.06 g; 3 standard deviations below the mean
2.56 − 2.50 = 0.06 g; 3 standard deviations above the mean
99.7% of these pennies have a mass between 2.44 g and 2.56 g.

7. Find the percent of these pennies that have a mass between 2.46 g and 2.50 g.

2.50 − 2.46 = 0.04 g; 2 standard deviations below the mean
2.50 is equal to the mean.

34% + 13.5% = 47.5% of these pennies have a mass between 2.46 g and 2.50 g.

LANGUAGE SUPPORT **EL**

Connect Vocabulary

A *normal* distribution is often described as a *bell-shaped*, *symmetric* distribution with a *tail* on each end. Although students may know each of these words in an everyday setting, they may not be familiar with them in an academic setting. To help English learners understand, refer them to the normal curves shown in the lesson to see the shape that is described.

Explain 2 · Estimating Probabilities in Approximately Normal Distributions

You can use the properties of a normal distribution to make estimations about the larger population that the distribution represents.

Example 2   The masses (in grams) of pennies minted in the United States after 1982 are normally distributed with a mean of 2.50 g and a standard deviation of 0.02 g.

Ⓐ Estimate the probability that a randomly chosen penny has a mass greater than 2.52 g.

Find the percent greater than 2.52 g.
2.52 g − 2.50 g = 0.02 g
2.52 g is 1 standard deviation above the mean.

Shade in the percent of data greater than 1 standard deviation above the mean.

13.5% + 2.35% + 0.15% = 16%

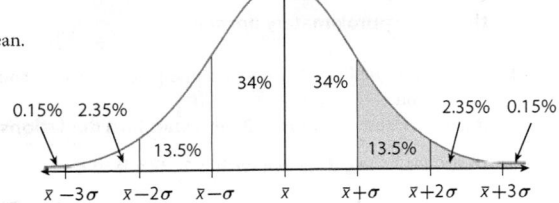

The probability that a randomly chosen penny has a mass greater than 2.52 g is about 16%.

Ⓑ Estimate the probability that a randomly chosen penny has a mass greater than 2.56 g.

Find the percent greater than 2.56 g.

$\boxed{2.56}$ g – $\boxed{2.50}$ g = $\boxed{0.06}$ g

$\boxed{2.56}$ g is $\boxed{3}$ standard deviation(s) (above)/below the mean.

Shade in the percent of data (greater)/less than $\boxed{3}$ standard deviation(s) (above)/below the mean.

$\boxed{0.15}$ %

The probability that a randomly chosen penny has a mass greater than 2.56 g is about $\boxed{0.15}$ %.

Your Turn

8. Find the probability that a randomly chosen penny has a mass less than 2.54 g.

2.54 − 2.5 = 0.04; 2.54 g is 2 standard deviations above the mean.
The probability of randomly choosing a penny with a mass less than 2.54 g is about 13.5% + 34% + 34% + 13.5% + 2.35% + 0.15% = 97.5%

9. Find the probability that a randomly chosen penny has a mass greater than 2.44 g.

2.50 − 2.44 = 0.06; 2.44 g is 3 standard deviations below the mean.
The probability of randomly choosing a penny with a mass greater than 2.44 g is about 2.35% + 13.5% + 34% + 34% + 13.5% + 2.35% + 0.15% = 99.85%.

EXPLAIN 2

Estimating Probabilities in Approximately Normal Distributions

INTEGRATE MATHEMATICAL PRACTICES
Focus on Communication

MP.3 Ask students to explain how they would calculate the probability that a randomly chosen value in a normally distributed data set is between one standard deviation above the mean and two standard deviations below the mean. Have a few students share different methods. Students should recognize that there may be several ways to calculate the same probability. They can add the probabilities for smaller intervals, or they can begin with the probability for a larger interval and subtract to find the probability for the desired interval.

QUESTIONING STRATEGIES

? If you know that the percent of data within one standard deviation of the mean is 68% and the percent of data within two standard deviations of the mean is 95%, how can you explain that 13.5% of the data is between $\overline{x} + 1\sigma$ and $\overline{x} + 2\sigma$? The difference between 95% and 68% is 27%. The symmetry of the curve shows that this difference is split evenly between the interval from $\overline{x} - 2\sigma$ to $\overline{x} - 1\sigma$ and the interval from $\overline{x} + 1\sigma$ to $\overline{x} + 2\sigma$, so each interval represents 13.5% of the data.

? Why are calculations of probability associated with a normal distribution considered estimates? The distribution of a real-world data set may be approximately normal, but it rarely is exactly a normal distribution. Also, probability describes chances, not exact results. Therefore, any prediction of the frequency of a particular value is only an estimate.

ELABORATE

INTEGRATE MATHEMATICAL PRACTICES
Focus on Math Connections

MP.1 Discuss with students why the same procedure can be used to find either the percent of values in a data set that fall in a given interval or the probability that a randomly chosen value will fall in that interval. Students should understand that the greater the fraction of items in a set that meets a condition, the greater the chance is that an item selected at random will meet that condition.

SUMMARIZE THE LESSON

? What pieces of information are needed to find the percent or probability associated with a normal distribution? **the mean and the standard deviation of the data set**

EVALUATE

ASSIGNMENT GUIDE

Concepts and Skills	Practice
Explore 1 Investigating Symmetric Distributions	Exercises 17, 25
Explore 2 Investigating Symmetric Relative Frequency Histograms	
Example 1 Using Properties of Normal Distributions	Exercises 1–4, 9–13, 18–24
Example 2 Estimating Probabilities in Approximately Normal Distributions	Exercises 5–8, 14–16

---

10. For data described by a normal distribution, how do the mean and median compare?
The mean and median of a data set described by a normal distribution are equal.

11. What does the symmetry of the normal distribution tell you about the areas above and below the mean?
These areas are equal; both the area above the mean and the area below the mean are equal to 0.50.

12. How can you tell if data follow a normal distribution by looking at a histogram of the data?
If the histogram is bell-shaped, symmetric about the mean, and has tails on both ends, then it is approximately normal.

13. Essential Question How do you find percents of data and probabilities of events associated with normal distributions?
If a given data value is 1, 2, or 3 standard deviations from the mean, you can use the fact that 68% of the data are within 1 standard deviation of the mean, 95% of the data are within 2 standard deviations of the mean, and 99.7% of the data are within 3 standard deviations of the mean.

⭐ Evaluate: Homework and Practice

• Online Homework
• Hints and Help
• Extra Practice

The scores on a test given to all juniors in a school district are normally distributed with a mean of 74 and a standard deviation of 8.

1. Find the percent of juniors whose score is no more than 90.
90 − 74 = 16; 90 is 2 standard deviations above the mean.
The percent of juniors whose score is 90 or below is
0.15% + 2.35% + 13.5% + 34% + 34% + 13.5% = 97.5%.

2. Find the percent of juniors whose score is between 58 and 74.
74 − 58 = 16; 58 is 2 standard deviations below the mean.
The mean is 74.
The percent of juniors whose score is between 58 and the mean is
13.5% + 34% = 47.5%.

3. Find the percent of juniors whose score is at least 74.
The mean is 74.
The percent of juniors whose score is at or below the mean is 50%.

© Houghton Mifflin Harcourt Publishing Company

Exercise	Depth of Knowledge (D.O.K.)		COMMON CORE Mathematical Practices	
1–8	**2**	Skills/Concepts	**MP.4**	Modeling
9–10	**1**	Recall	**MP.2**	Reasoning
11–16	**2**	Skills/Concepts	**MP.4**	Modeling
17	**1**	Recall	**MP.2**	Reasoning
18	**2**	Skills/Concepts	**MP.2**	Reasoning
19–20	**2**	Skills/Concepts	**MP.4**	Modeling
21–22	**1**	Recall	**MP.4**	Modeling
23–25	**3**	Strategic Thinking **H.O.T.**	**MP.3**	Logic

4. Find the percent of juniors whose score is below 66.

$74 - 66 = 8$; 66 is 1 standard deviation below the mean.

The percent of juniors whose score is at or below the 66 is

$0.15\% + 2.35\% + 13.5\% = 16\%$.

5. Find the probability that a randomly chosen junior has a score above 82.

$82 - 74 = 8$; 82 is 1 standard deviation above the mean.

The probability of randomly choosing a junior whose score is above 82 is

$13.5\% + 2.35\% + 0.15\% = 16\%$.

6. Find the probability that a randomly chosen junior has a score between 66 and 90.

$74 - 66 = 8$; **66 is 1 standard deviation below the mean.**

$90 - 74 = 16$; **90 is 2 standard deviations above the mean.**

The probability of randomly choosing a junior whose score is between 66 and 90 is $34\% + 34\% + 13.5\% = 81.5\%$.

7. Find the probability that a randomly chosen junior has a score below 74.

The mean is 74. The probability of randomly choosing a junior whose score is below the mean is 50%.

8. Find the probability that a randomly chosen junior has a score above 98.

$98 - 74 = 24$; **98 is 3 standard deviations above the mean.**

The probability of randomly choosing a junior whose score is above 98 is 0.15%.

A normal distribution has a mean of 10 and a standard deviation of 1.5.

9. Between which two values do 95% of the data fall?

95% of the data in a normal distribution fall within 2 standard deviations of the mean.

2 standard deviations below the mean is $10 - 3 = 7$.

2 standard deviations above the mean is $10 + 3 = 13$.

95% of the data fall between 7 and 13.

10. Between which two values do 68% of the data fall?

68% of the data in a normal distribution fall within 1 standard deviation of the mean.

1 standard deviation below the mean is $10 - 1.5 = 8.5$.

1 standard deviation above the mean is $10 + 1.5 = 11.5$

68% of the data fall between 8.5 and 11.5.

© Houghton Mifflin Harcourt Publishing Company

INTEGRATE MATHEMATICAL PRACTICES

Focus on Reasoning

MP.2 Discuss with students how to determine what percent of values in a data set are expected to be more than three standard deviations away from the mean. Since 99.7% of values are within three standard deviations, 0.3% must be farther away than three standard deviations. The symmetry of the normal distribution means that about 0.15% will be more than three standard deviations from the mean in each direction.

CRITICAL THINKING

Discuss with students how two normal curves with the same mean but with different standard deviations would differ. Students should understand that for a normal probability distribution, the total area under the curve must equal 1, so a normal curve where the standard deviation is greater will be wider but not as high as a normal curve where the standard deviation is less.

VISUAL CUES

When determining what percent of data values fall between two given values, suggest that students write the given values at the appropriate points along the *x*-axis on a sketch of the normal curve. This will make it easier to see which percents must be added or subtracted to find the percent for the specified interval.

Suppose the heights (in inches) of adult males in the United States are normally distributed with a mean of 72 inches and a standard deviation of 2 inches.

11. Find the percent of men who are no more than 68 inches tall.

$72 - 68 = 4$; 68 is 2 standard deviations below the mean.

The percent of men who are 68 inches tall or less is 0.15% + 2.35% = 2.5%.

12. Find the percent of men who are between 70 and 72 inches tall.

$72 - 70 = 2$; 70 is 1 standard deviation below the mean. The mean is 72.

The percent of men who are between 70 and 72 inches tall is 34%.

13. Find the percent of men who are at least 76 inches tall.

$76 - 72 = 4$; 76 is 2 standard deviations above the mean.

The percent of men who are 76 inches or below is 2.35% + 0.15% = 2.5%

14. Find the probability that a randomly chosen man is more than 72 inches tall.

The mean is 72. The probability of randomly choosing a man who is taller than the mean height of 72 inches is 50%.

15. Find the probability that a randomly chosen man is between 68 and 76 inches tall.

$72 - 68 = 4$; 68 is 2 standard deviations below the mean.

$76 - 72 = 4$; 76 is 2 standard deviations above the mean.

The probability that a randomly chosen man is between 68 and 76 inches tall is 13.5% + 34% + 34% + 13.5% = 95%.

16. Find the probability that a randomly chosen man is less than 76 inches tall.

$76 - 72 = 4$; 76 is 2 standard deviations above the mean.

The probability that a randomly chosen man is less than 76 inches tall is:

0.15% + 2.35% + 13.5% + 34% + 34% + 13.5% = 97.5%

17. Multi-Step Ten customers at Fielden Grocery were surveyed about how long they waited in line to check out. Their wait times, in minutes, are shown.

16	15	10	7	5
5	4	3	3	2

a. What is the mean of the data set?

Mean $= \dfrac{16+15+10+7+5+5+4+3+3+2}{10} = \dfrac{70}{10} = 7$

b. How many data points are below the mean, and how many are above the mean?

6 data points are below, and 3 are above.

c. Does the data appear to be normally distributed? Explain.

No; the data set has 3 values greater than the mean but 6 values less than the mean, so the distribution is not symmetric.

18. Kori is analyzing a normal data distribution, but the data provided is incomplete. Kori knows that the mean of the data is 120 and that 84% of the data values are less than 130. Find the standard deviation for this data set.

84% of the data values in a normal data distribution are less than 1 standard deviation above the mean. So 130 must be equal to 1 standard deviation above the mean. 130 − 120 = 10, so the standard deviation is 10.

19. Suppose compact fluorescent light bulbs last, on average, 10,000 hours. The standard deviation is 500 hours. What percent of light bulbs burn out within 11,000 hours?

11,000 − 10,000 = 1,000; so 11,000 hours is 2 standard deviations above the mean. The percent of light bulbs that burn out at or before 11,000 hours is 0.15% + 2.35% + 13.5% + 34% + 34% + 13.5% = 97.5%.

20. The numbers of raisins per box in a certain brand of cereal are normally distributed with a mean of 339 raisins and a standard deviation of 9 raisins. Find the percent of boxes of this brand of cereal that have fewer than 330 raisins. Explain how you solved this problem.

339 − 330 = 9; 339 is 1 standard deviation below the mean. The percent of boxes that have fewer than 330 raisins is 0.15% + 2.35% + 13.5% = 16%

Suppose the heights of professional basketball players in the United States are distributed normally, with a mean of 79 inches and a standard deviation of 4 inches.

21. How far below the mean is 71 inches and how many standard deviations is this?

71 inches is 8 inches below the mean of 79 inches.

The standard deviation is 4 inches, so 8 inches below the mean is 2 standard deviations below the mean.

22. How far below the mean is 75 inches and how many standard deviations is this?

75 inches is 4 inches below the mean of 79 inches.

The standard deviation is 4 inches, so 4 inches below the mean is 1 standard deviation below the mean.

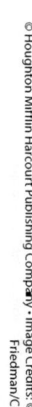

AVOID COMMON ERRORS

Remind students that when determining the percent or probability for a normal distribution, they should include all sections of the normal curve that satisfy the given condition. They may need to add or subtract percents to find the percent of values in a certain range. Some students may look for a percent for only the least or greatest value in a range instead of finding the percent of values that lie between them.

JOURNAL

Have students write a paragraph explaining how to find the percent of values in a normal distribution that lie between two given values.

Suppose the upper-arm length (in centimeters) of adult males in the United States is normally distributed with a mean of 39.4 cm and a standard deviation of 2.3 cm.

23. **Justify Reasoning** What percent of adult males have an upper-arm length between 34.8 cm and 41.7 cm? Explain how you got your answer.

39.4 − 34.8 = 4.6; so 34.8 is 2 standard deviations below the mean.

41.7 − 39.4 = 2.3; so 41.7 is 1 standard deviation above the mean.

The percent of adult males with an upper-arm length between 34.8 cm and 41.7 cm is 13.5% + 34% + 34% = 81.5%.

24. **Communicate Mathematical Ideas** Explain how you can determine whether a set of data is approximately normally distributed.

First, check that the distribution is symmetric. If so, the mean and the median will be about equal. Then examine the distribution to see if it is "bell-shaped." Verify that about 68% of the data values are within 1 standard deviation, about 95% of values are within 2 standard deviations, and about 99.7% of values are within 3 standard deviations.

25. **Critical Thinking** The distribution titled "Heads Up" shows results of many trials of tossing 6 coins and counting the number of "heads" that land facing up. The distribution titled "Number 1s Up" shows results of many trials of tossing 6 number cubes and counting the number of 1s that land facing up. For which distribution is it reasonable to use a normal distribution as an approximation? Justify your answer.

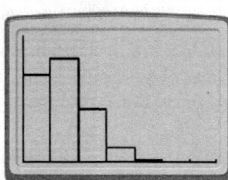

Heads Up   **Number 1s Up**

Use a normal distribution to approximate characteristics for the "Heads Up" experiment because the distribution is symmetric and bell-shaped.

Lesson Performance Task

During a series of 100-meter races, the times of the runners are normally distributed with a mean of 12.5 seconds and a standard deviation of 0.3 seconds.

a. Find the percent of runners that have a time between 11.6 seconds and 12.8 seconds. Explain how you got your answer.

b. Find the probability that a randomly selected runner has a time greater than 12.8 seconds and less than 13.4 seconds.

a. $12.5 - 11.6 = 0.9$; 11.6 is 3 standard deviations below the mean.
   $12.8 - 12.5 = 0.3$; 12.8 is 1 standard deviation above the mean.
   $2.35\% + 13.5\% + 34\% + 34\% = 83.85\%$
   So, 83.85% of the runners have a time between 11.6 seconds and 12.8 seconds.

b. $12.8 - 12.5 = 0.3$; 12.8 is 1 standard deviation above the mean.
   $13.4 - 0.45 = 0.9$; 13.4 is 3 standard deviations above the mean.
   $13.5\% + 2.35\% = 15.85\%$
   So, the probability that a randomly selected runner has a time greater than 12.8 seconds and less than 13.4 seconds is 15.85%.

© Houghton Mifflin Harcourt Publishing Company

EXTENSION ACTIVITY

Ask students to suppose that with extra training, the runners described in the Lesson Performance Task all decreased their running times for the 100-meter race by 0.3 seconds, while the standard deviation of the times stayed the same. Have them explore how the percent of runners with various running times would change.

Students should understand that the mean time would decrease to 12.2 seconds. They may discover that the most dramatic changes in percents occur at the tails of the distribution. For example, the percent of runners with times greater than 12.8 seconds changes from 16% to 2.5%.

CONNECT VOCABULARY EL

The word *normal* in English is a cognate of the word in Spanish. Multisyllabic words that end in –*al* in English often have cognates in Spanish. Have Spanish-speaking students make a list of cognates they know that end in –*al*.

QUESTIONING STRATEGIES

? If you were one of the runners described in the Lesson Performance Task and your time was 11.6 seconds, what percent of the runners would have a time less than yours? Explain 0.15%; 11.6 seconds is 3 standard deviations below the mean, so only 0.15% of runners have a time less than 11.6 seconds.

? If your time was 12.8 seconds, what percent of the runners would have a time greater than yours? Explain. 16%; 12.8 seconds is one standard deviation above the mean. Because 13.5% of runners have times between one and two standard deviations above the mean, 2.35% have times between two and three standard deviations above the mean, and 0.15% have times greater than three standard deviations above the mean, calculate $13.5\% + 2.35\% + 0.15\% = 16\%$.

? How can you use the percents calculated in the two previous questions to check your calculation of the percent of runners with times between 11.6 and 12.8 seconds? Add the percent of runners with times less than 11.6 seconds, the percent with times between 11.6 and 12.8 seconds, and the percent with times greater than 12.8 seconds. The total should be 100%.

Scoring Rubric
2 points: Student correctly solves the problem and explains his/her reasoning.
1 point: Student shows good understanding of the problem but does not fully solve or explain his/her reasoning.
0 points: Student does not demonstrate understanding of the problem.

Normal Distributions   **428**

ASSESSMENT AND INTERVENTION

Assign or customize module reviews.

MODULE PERFORMANCE TASK

COMMON CORE

Mathematical Practices: MP.1, MP.2, MP.4, MP.5
S-ID.A.1, S-ID.A.2, S-ID.A.3

SUPPORTING STUDENT REASONING

Reassure students who are concerned that they don't know much about baseball that they can analyze the numbers in the table without reference to the game. Remind students of some of the ways they can analyze the data. (You may wish to leave it to students to decide which are most useful in completing this Performance Task.)

- **Find and compare measures of central tendency.** The means, medians, and ranges may be useful measures.

- **Draw graphs of the data.** Among methods for illustrating data visually that students know are bar graphs, histograms, circle graphs, scatterplots, box plots, and dot plots.

- **Compare the two leagues.** Students can compare the American and National leagues by displaying relevant data side-by-side or in graphical displays.

Essential Question: How can you use one-variable data distributions to solve real-world problems?

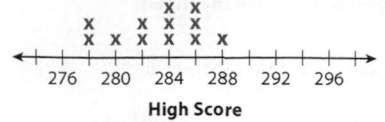 **(Lesson 9.2)**

The dot plot given shows the high score of 12 members of a bowling club. A new member joins whose high score is 294. Determine if the new score is an outlier.

$$\begin{array}{c} \quad\quad\quad x\ x \\ \quad\quad x\ x\ x\ x \\ x\ x\ x\ x\ x\ x \end{array}$$

|—|—|—|—|—|—|—|—|—|—|
276 280 284 288 292 296
High Score

The scores are 278, 278, 280, 282, 282, 284, 284, 284, 286, 286, 286, 288, and 294.

Median = 284 $Q_1 = \dfrac{280 + 282}{2} = 281$ $Q_3 = \dfrac{286 + 286}{2} = 286$ IQR = 286 − 281 = 5

A data value is an outlier if $x < Q_1 - 1.5(\text{IQR})$ or if $x > Q_3 + 1.5(\text{IQR})$.

Since 294 > 286 + 1.5(5), the new score is an outlier.

KEY EXAMPLE   **(Lesson 9.4)**

A machine produces plastic skateboard wheels with diameters that are normally distributed with a mean diameter of 52 mm and a standard deviation of 0.15 mm. Find the percent of wheels made by the machine that have a diameter of less than 51.7 mm.

$52 - 51.7 = 0.3$ $\dfrac{0.3}{0.15} = 2$

51.7 is 2 standard deviations below the mean.

The percent of data that is 2 standard deviations below the mean is 0.15% + 2.35% = 2.5%.

2.5% of the wheels have a diameter less than 51.7 mm.

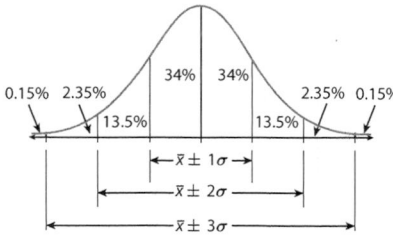

Key Vocabulary

histogram *(histograma)*
interquartile range IQR *(rango entre cuartiles)*
mean *(media)*
median *(mediana)*
normal curve *(curva normal)*
normal distribution *(distribución normal)*
outlier *(valor extremo)*
range *(rango de un conjunto de datos)*

© Houghton Mifflin Harcourt Publishing Company

SCAFFOLDING SUPPORT

- If students wonder what a "run" is, explain that a player scores one run by making a complete circuit of the four bases and crossing home plate.

- To calculate per-game statistics, students will need to know that each team plays 162 games.

EXERCISES

Find the mean, median, range, and interquartile range of each data set. *(Lesson 9.1)*

1. {12, 12, 13, 14, 16, 20, 32,}

Mean: 17

Median: 14

Range: 20

IQR: 8

2. {4, 8, 9, 9, 11, 12, 15, 15}

Mean: 10.375

Median: 10

Range: 11

IQR: 5

3. Make a box plot to represent the data set {28, 30, 32, 32, 34, 35, 36, 38}. *(Lesson 9.3)*

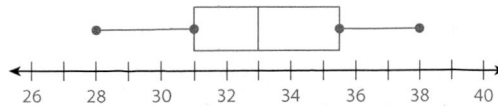

4. The weights of a small box of Healthy Oats are normally distributed with a mean of 8.9 oz and a standard deviation of 0.1 oz. Find the probability that a randomly chosen box of Healthy Oats weighs more than 8.8 oz. Express the probability as a decimal. *(Lesson 9.4)*

0.84

MODULE PERFORMANCE TASK

Baseball Stats

The table below gives the total number of runs scored by each of the 15 teams in each of baseball's two major leagues, the American League and the National League, during the 2013 season.

League								Team							
	1	2	3	4	5	6	7	8	9	10	11	12	13	14	15
American	853	796	767	745	745	733	730	712	700	650	648	624	614	610	598
National	783	706	698	688	685	656	649	640	634	629	619	618	610	602	513

In this module you've learned many ways to analyze a set of data, both numerically and graphically. Which ways might be useful in helping someone to make sense of the statistics in the runs-scored table? Decide on the ones you'll use and apply them, either through numerical calculations or pictorial representations or both. You may also explain why you decided not to calculate certain data measures.

Use your own paper to work on the task. Use numbers, words, or algebra to explain how you reached your conclusion.

© Houghton Mifflin Harcourt Publishing Company

DISCUSSION OPPORTUNITIES

- Ask students to speculate on the results if they were to analyze the combined statistics for the two leagues. **Sample answer: The higher American League numbers would create a combined mean and a combined median greater than those of the National League when measured alone (combined mean: 675.17; combined median: 653). Without graphing, it is unclear whether the data would be roughly symmetric or skewed to the right.**

SAMPLE SOLUTION

American League:

   total number of runs scored: 10,525

   mean: 701.67

   median: 712

   range: 255

National League:

   total number of runs scored: 9,730

   mean: 648.67

   median: 640

   range: 270

The total number of runs scored by the American League, as well as the mean and median number of runs scored by the 15 teams, exceeded the National League figures by a substantial margin. The ranges of both leagues were similar, suggesting that the difference in run production between the top and bottom teams was about the same in both leagues.

One possible graphical representation of the data is a histogram for each league.

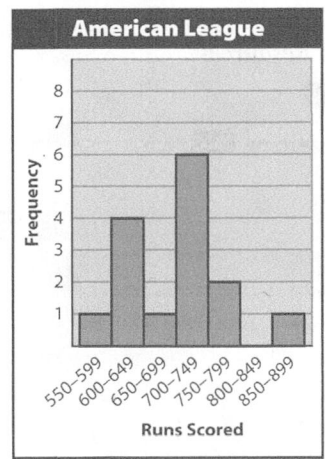
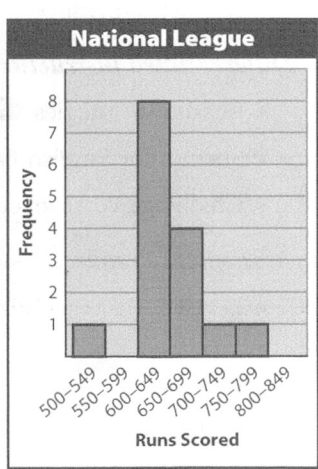

The American League histogram is not quite symmetric but is not strongly skewed in either direction. The National League histogram shows that the data are skewed to the right.

Assessment Rubric

2 points: Student correctly solves the problem and explains his/her reasoning.

1 point: Student shows good understanding of the problem but does not fully solve or explain his/her reasoning.

0 points: Student does not demonstrate understanding of the problem.

Ready to Go On?

ASSESS MASTERY

Use the assessment on this page to determine if students have mastered the concepts and standards covered in this module.

ASSESSMENT AND INTERVENTION

Access Ready to Go On? assessment online, and receive instant scoring, feedback, and customized intervention or enrichment.

ADDITIONAL RESOURCES

Response to Intervention Resources

- Reteach Worksheets

Differentiated Instruction Resources

- Reading Strategies **EL**
- Success for English Learners **EL**
- Challenge Worksheets

Assessment Resources

- Leveled Module Quizzes

(Ready) to Go On?

9.1–9.4 One-Variable Data Distributions

- Online Homework
- Hints and Help
- Extra Practice

1. The dot plot given represents the scores of 10 students on a standardized test. An eleventh student was sick on the test date, took a make-up test, and made a score of 212. Complete the table. If necessary, round to the nearest tenth. *(Lesson 9.1)*

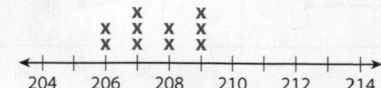

	Mean	Median	Range	IQR	Standard Deviation
Without Make-up Test	207.6	207.5	3	2	1.1
With Make-up Test	208	208	6	2	1.7

2. The ages of students in a tango class are represented by the data set {24, 41, 33, 36, 28, 30, 32, 22, 26, 44}. Complete the frequency table and make a histogram to represent the data. *(Lesson 9.3)*

Age Interval	Frequency
20–24	2
25–29	2
30–34	3
35–39	1
40–44	2

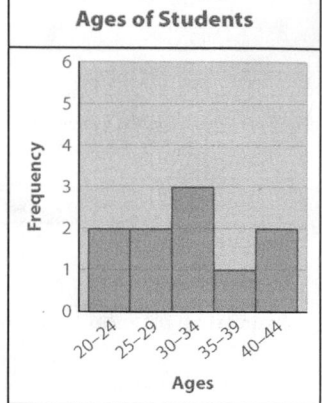

Ages of Students

ESSENTIAL QUESTION

3. When is it better to use a histogram than a dot plot?

    Possible Answer: When individual data values are not repeated often, it may be easier to get a feel for the shape of the data using a histogram instead of a dot plot.

© Houghton Mifflin Harcourt Publishing Company

COMMON CORE   Common Core Standards

Lesson	Items	Content Standards	Mathematical Practices
9.1	1	**S-ID.A.1, S-ID.A.2**	**MP.1**
9.3	2	**S-ID.A.1**	**MP.7**

Assessment Readiness

1. The dot plot shown represents the number of students enrolled in each of the 16 courses at a community college. A new course has started and has 65 enrolled students. Consider the effect of the addition of the new course to the data set. Choose True or False for each statement.

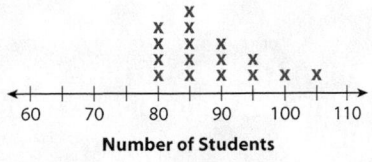

Number of Students

   A. The median class size does not change. ● True ○ False

   B. The new course size is an outlier. ○ True ● False

   C. The range increases by 40. ○ True ● False

2. The histogram shows the number of tomato plants Susan has in each height range. Select True or False for each statement.

   A. Susan has 11 plants. ○ True ● False

   B. Susan has the same number of plants that are 7 to 9 inches high as plants that are 10 to 12 inches high. ● True ○ False

   C. The median height of the plants could be about 11 inches. ○ True ● False

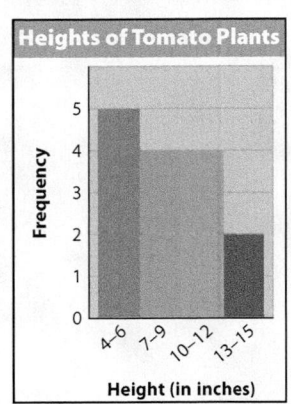

Heights of Tomato Plants

Frequency / Height (in inches)

3. The high temperature, in °F, for the past 4 days was 45, 38, 46, and 35. Carlos knows that the mean high temperature for the past 5 days was 42°F. Write and solve an equation to find the high temperature on the first day. Show your work.

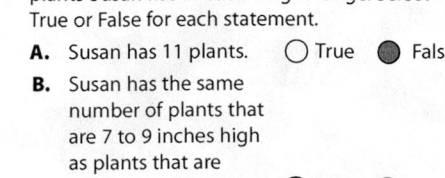

$$\frac{x + 45 + 38 + 46 + 35}{5} = 42$$
$$x + 45 + 38 + 46 + 35 = 210$$
$$x + 164 = 210$$
$$x = 46$$

The high temperature on the first day was 46°F.

4. Write an equation in slope-intercept form to represent a line that includes the points $(3, -4)$ and $(5, 2)$. Explain how you wrote the equation.

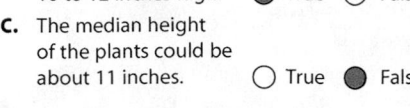

$y = 3x - 13$; **first, I found the slope of the line by using the slope formula,**

$m = \frac{y_2 - y_1}{x_2 - x_1}$. **Then, I found the y-intercept by substituting one point and the**

slope into the general form of the slope-intercept equation and solving for b.

MIXED REVIEW
Assessment Readiness

ASSESSMENT AND INTERVENTION

Personal Math Trainer

Assign ready-made or customized practice tests to prepare students for high-stakes tests.

ADDITIONAL RESOURCES

Assessment Resources

- Leveled Module Quizzes: Modified, B

AVOID COMMON ERRORS

Item 3 Some students may understand how to find a mean, but not how to find a missing data value. Explain that the unknown quantity is the data value, so they should write an expression for mean that includes a variable, and set it equal to the given value of the mean.

![COMMON CORE] **Common Core Standards**

Lesson	Items	Content Standards	Mathematical Practices
9.2	1	**S-ID.A.3**	**MP.4**
9.3	2	**S-ID.A.1**	**MP.4**
2.2, 9.1	3*	**A-CED.A.1, S-ID.A.2**	**MP.4**
5.3, 6.1	4*	**F-IF.B.6, A-CED.A.2**	**MP.2**

* Item integrates mixed review concepts from previous modules or a previous course.

Linear Modeling and Regression

ESSENTIAL QUESTION:

Answer: You can use existing data to create a trend line. Then, you can use that trend line to make a prediction that fits the original data.

PROFESSIONAL DEVELOPMENT VIDEO

Professional Development Video

Author Juli Dixon models successful teaching practices in an actual high-school classroom.

Professional
Development
my.hrw.com

MODULE
10

Linear Modeling and Regression

Essential Question: How can you use linear modeling and regression to solve real-world problems?

© Houghton Mifflin Harcourt Publishing Company • Image Credits ©John Elk III/Alamy

REAL WORLD VIDEO
A fossil is a remnant or trace of an organism from a past geologic age that has been preserved in the earth's crust. Fossils are often dated by using interpolation, a type of calculation that uses an observed pattern to estimate a value between two known values.

MODULE PERFORMANCE TASK PREVIEW

How Does Wingspan Compare with Weight in Birds?

The wingspan of a bird is the distance from one wingtip to the other wingtip. Birds that fly have to support their body weight when in flight. What, if any, relationship exists between the wingspan and body weight for different species of birds? Let's use math to find out!

Module 10   **433**

DIGITAL TEACHER EDITION

Access a full suite of teaching resources when and where you need them:

- Access content online or offline
- Customize lessons to share with your class
- Communicate with your students in real-time
- View student grades and data instantly to target your instruction where it is needed most

PERSONAL MATH TRAINER
Assessment and Intervention

Assign automatically graded homework, quizzes, tests, and intervention activities. Prepare your students with updated, Common Core-aligned practice tests.

Are (YOU) Ready?

Complete these exercises to review skills you will need for this module.

Scatter Plots

Example 1

Tell whether the correlation is positive or negative, or if there is no correlation.

• Online Homework
• Hints and Help
• Extra Practice

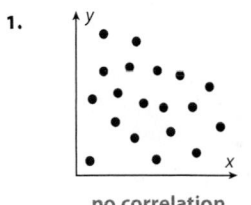

The scatter plot has a negative correlation.

Scatter plots can help you see relationships between two variables.

• In a positive correlation, as the value of one variable increases, the value of the other variable increases.

• In a negative correlation, as the value of one variable decreases, the value of the other variable increases.

• Sometimes there is no correlation, meaning there is no relationship between the variables.

Tell whether the correlation is positive or negative, or if there is no correlation.

1.
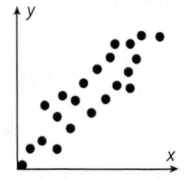
no correlation

2.
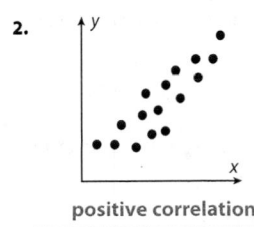
positive correlation

Linear Associations

Example 2

Estimate the correlation coefficient.

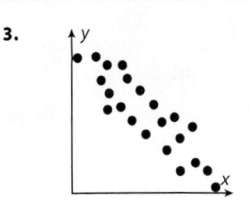

The points lie close to a line with positive slope. r is close to 1.

One measure of the strength and direction of a correlation is the correlation coefficient, denoted by r. The stronger the correlation, the closer the correlation coefficient will be to -1 or 1. The weaker the correlation, the closer r will be to zero.

Estimate the correlation coefficient.

3.
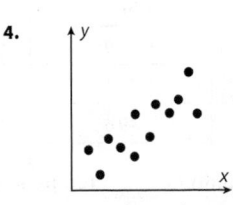
−0.8   any negative coefficient near −1 but not less than −1 is acceptable

4.

0.2   (any positive coefficient near 0 is acceptable)

Are You Ready?

ASSESS READINESS

Use the assessment on this page to determine if students need strategic or intensive intervention for the module's prerequisite skills.

ASSESSMENT AND INTERVENTION

⚠ RtI Response to Intervention **TIER 1, TIER 2, TIER 3 SKILLS**

Personal Math Trainer will automatically create a standards-based, personalized intervention assignment for your students, targeting each student's individual needs!

ADDITIONAL RESOURCES

See the table below for a full list of intervention resources available for this module.

Response to Intervention Resources also includes:

• Tier 2 Skill Pre-Tests for each Module
• Tier 2 Skill Post-Tests for each skill

Response to Intervention			Differentiated Instruction
Tier 1	**Tier 2**	**Tier 3**	
Lesson Intervention Worksheets	Strategic Intervention Skills Intervention Worksheets	Intensive Intervention Worksheets available online	
Reteach 10.1 Reteach 10.2	9 Linear Associations 10 Linear Functions 18 Scatter Plots 24 Writing Linear Equations	Building Block Skills 22, 23, 27, 40, 42, 46, 52, 70, 111	Challenge worksheets Extend the Math Lesson Activities in TE

Module 10   **434**

Scatter Plots and Trend Lines

Common Core Math Standards

The student is expected to:

 S-ID.B.6c

Fit a linear function for a scatter plot that suggests a linear association. Also S-ID.B.6a, S-ID.C.7, S-ID.C.9, F-LE.B.5

Mathematical Practices

COMMON CORE **MP.2 Reasoning**

Language Objective

Explain the difference between correlation and causation.

ENGAGE

Essential Question: How can you describe the relationship between two variables and use it to make predictions?

You can make a scatter plot of the data and observe whether there is a correlation. If there is a strong correlation, you can fit a line to the data and use the equation of the line to make predictions.

PREVIEW: LESSON PERFORMANCE TASK

View the Engage section online. Discuss what types of facts coaches or managers would want to gather about their teams or their opponents' teams. Then preview the Lesson Performance Task.

10.1 Scatter Plots and Trend Lines

Essential Question: How can you describe the relationship between two variables and use it to make predictions?

Resource Locker

⊘ Explore Describing How Variables Are Related in Scatter Plots

Two-variable data is a collection of paired variable values, such as a series of measurements of air temperature at different times of day. One method of visualizing two-variable data is called a **scatter plot**: a graph of points with one variable plotted along each axis. A recognizable pattern in the arrangement of points suggests a mathematical relationship between the variables.

Correlation is a measure of the strength and direction of the relationship between two variables. The correlation is positive if both variables tend to increase together, negative if one decreases while the other increases, and we say there is "no correlation" if the change in the two variables appears to be unrelated.

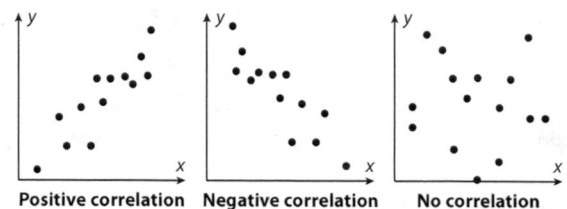

Positive correlation   Negative correlation   No correlation

(A) The table below presents two-variable data for seven different cities in the Northern hemisphere.

City	Latitude (°N)	Average Annual Temperature (°F)
Bangkok	13.7	82.6
Cairo	30.1	71.4
London	51.5	51.8
Moscow	55.8	39.4
New Delhi	28.6	77.0
Tokyo	35.7	58.1
Vancouver	49.2	49.6

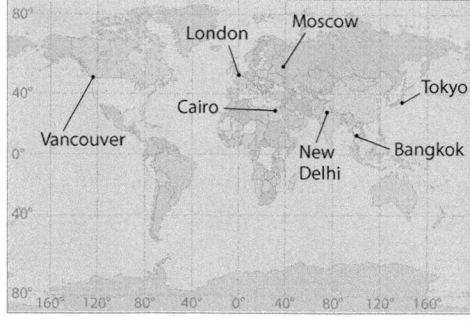

The two variables are __Latitude__ and __Temperature__.

© Houghton Mifflin Harcourt Publishing Company

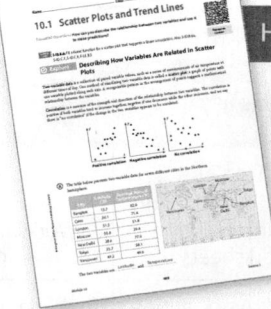

Turn to these pages to find this lesson in the hardcover student edition.

Ⓑ Plot the data on the grid provided.

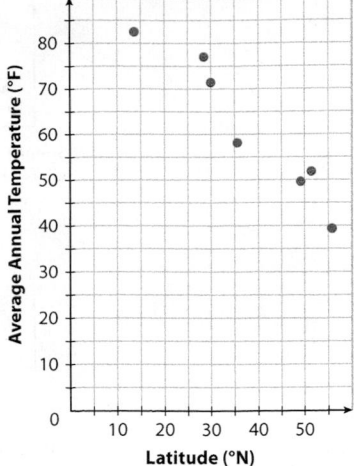

Ⓒ The variables are ___negatively___ correlated.

Reflect

1. **Discussion** Why are the points in a scatter plot not connected in the same way plots of linear equations are?
   A straight line (or any connected trace) on a graph indicates a continuous set of points.

   Solutions to linear equations, for example, can be found anywhere along the line that

   represents the solution. Data in a scatter plot are represented by discrete points. Line

   segments between points would incorrectly imply either data or function along segments

   between the scattered points.

 Explain 1 **Estimating the Correlation Coefficient of a Linear Fit**

One way to quantify the correlation of a data set is with the **correlation coefficient**, denoted by r. The correlation coefficient varies from -1 to 1, with the sign of r corresponding to the type of correlation (positive or negative). Strongly correlated data points look more like points that lie in a straight line, and have values of r closer to 1 or -1. Weakly correlated data will have values closer to 0.

There is a precise mathematical formula that can be used to calculate the correlation coefficient, but it is beyond the scope of this course. It is still useful to learn the qualitative relationship between the appearance of the data and the

---

INTEGRATE TECHNOLOGY

Students have the option of completing the scatter plot activity either in the book or online.

INTEGRATE MATHEMATICAL PRACTICES
Focus on Reasoning

MP.2 Stress that asking whether two variables are correlated is a question about whether or not there is a relationship between them, not about the nature of the relationship. A strong correlation can be positive or negative.

EXPLAIN 1

Estimating the Correlation Coefficient of a Linear Fit

AVOID COMMON ERRORS

Students may confuse the correlation coefficient for a scatter plot with the slope of a linear function. Remind students that the correlation coefficient measures how close the points are to the line of fit, not the steepness of the line.

PROFESSIONAL DEVELOPMENT

🏛 Integrate Mathematical Practices

This lesson provides an opportunity to address Mathematical Practice **MP.2**, which calls for students to "reason abstractly and quantitatively." Students learn to describe and analyze the relationship between two variables in a scatter plot, and they use the line of fit for a scatter plot to make predictions based on the data.

What is the key difference between a scatter plot that shows a strong correlation and one that shows a weak correlation? Explain. In a scatter plot showing a strong correlation, points are close together in what appears to be a linear pattern. With a weak correlation, points are spread out and the pattern is not as clear.

value of r. The chart below shows examples of strong correlations, with r close to -1 and 1, and weak correlations with r close to 0.5. If there is no visible correlation, it means r is closer to 0.

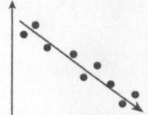

Strong negative correlation; points lie close to a line with negative slope. r is close to -1.

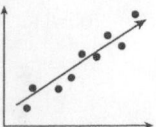

Strong positive correlation; points lie close to a line with positive slope. r is close to 1.

Weak negative correlation; points loosely follow a line with negative slope. r is between 0 and -1.

Weak positive correlation; points loosely follow a line with positive slope. r is between 0 and 1.

Example 1 Use a scatter plot to estimate the value of r. Indicate whether r is closer to $-1, -0.5, 0, 0.5,$ or 1.

(A) Estimate the r-value for the relationship between city latitude and average temperature using the scatter plot you made previously.

This is strongly correlated and has a negative slope, so r is close to -1.

(B)

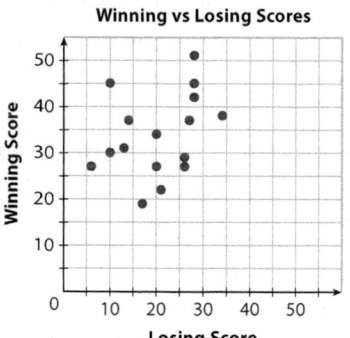

Winning vs Losing Scores

This data represents the football scores from one week with winning score plotted versus losing score.

r is close to $\boxed{0}$.

COLLABORATIVE LEARNING

Small Group Activity

Have students work in groups of three or four. Give each group one set of bivariate data, which each student should display in a scatter plot. Each member of the group will choose a line of fit for the scatter plot. Once each student has chosen a line of fit, have all group members trace their lines of fit onto the same scatter plot and compare their results.

2.

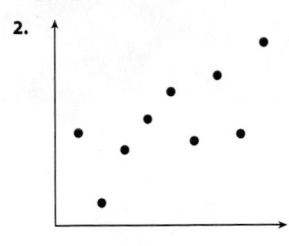

r is close to 0.5.

3.

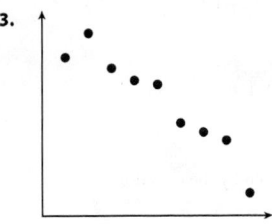

r is close to –1.

⊘ Explain 2 Fitting Linear Functions to Data

A **line of fit** is a line through a set of two-variable data that illustrates the correlation. When there is a strong correlation between the two variables in a set of two-variable data, you can use a line of fit as the basis to construct a linear model for the data.

There are many ways to come up with a line of fit. This lesson addresses a visual method: Using a straight edge, draw the line that the data points appear to be clustered around. It is not important that any of the data points actually touch the line; instead the line should be drawn as straight as possible and should go through the middle of the scattered points.

Once a line of fit has been drawn onto the scatter plot, you can choose two points on the line to write an equation for the line.

Example 2 Determine a line of fit for the data, and write the equation of the line.

Ⓐ Go back to the scatter plot of city temperatures and latitudes and add a line of fit.

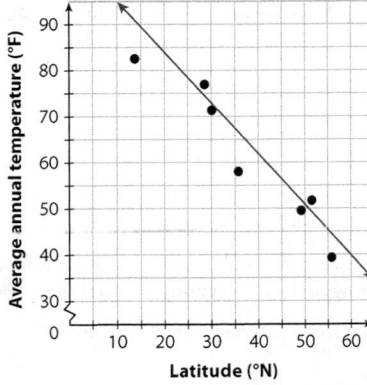

EXPLAIN 2

Fitting Linear Functions to Data

INTEGRATE MATHEMATICAL PRACTICES
Focus on Modeling

MP.4 Emphasize that the line students are drawing is a visual approximation of a line that comes closest to all of the data points, above some of them and below others. At this stage there is no "correct" answer for the perfect line to draw.

AVOID COMMON ERRORS

Remind students that *m*, the slope, is calculated by finding the change in *y* over the change in *x* and not the change in *x* over the change in *y*. Advise students to remember slope as "rise over run."

QUESTIONING STRATEGIES

❓ How is the slope of the line of fit related to the correlation coefficient for a set of data? In what way is it unrelated? **The slope of the line of fit has the same sign (positive or negative) as the correlation coefficient. The magnitude of the slope (the steepness of the line) is not related to the value of the correlation coefficient, which always has a value between –1 and 1.**

❓ What must be true for there to be more than one reasonable line of fit for a data set? **The data points must not be perfectly linear for there to be more than one reasonable line of fit.**

DIFFERENTIATE INSTRUCTION

Critical Thinking

Correlation between two variables can be strong and still fail to indicate causation if a lurking variable is influencing the situation. For example, there is a very strong correlation among young children between shoe size and being able to spell words correctly, but both variables are likely influenced by a third variable, age. Challenge students to determine if a lurking variable exists for problems that do not seem to show causation.

A line of fit has been added to the graph. The points (10, 95) and (60, 40) appear to be on the line.

$$m = \frac{40 - 95}{60 - 10} = -1.1$$

$$y = mx + b$$

$$95 = -1.1(10) + b$$

$$106 = b$$

The model is given by the equation

$$y = -1.1x + 106$$

(B) The boiling point of water is lower at higher elevations because of the lower atmospheric pressure. The boiling point of water in some different cities is given in the table.

City	Altitude (feet)	Boiling Point (°F)
Chicago	597	210
Denver	5300	201
Kathmandu	4600	205
Madrid	2188	207
Miami	6	210

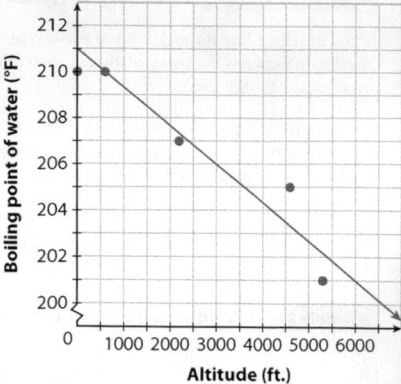

A line of fit may go through points (0 , 211) and (6000 , 201).

$$m = \frac{-10}{6000} \quad b = 211.$$

The equation is of this line of fit is $y = \boxed{\dfrac{-10}{6000}}\, x + \boxed{211}$.

Reflect

4. In the model from Example 2A, what do the slope and y-intercept of the model represent?
   The slope is negative and shows a drop in average annual temperature of ~11°F for

   every 10° increase in latitude. The y-intercept at 0° latitude is the average annual

   temperature at the equator.

LANGUAGE SUPPORT EL

Connect Vocabulary

In this lesson, students use *bivariate* data to describe the correlation between variables. Point out for students that the prefix *bi-* means *two*, as in these words: *bicycle* (two wheels), *bilingual* (two languages), *binomial* (sum of two monomials), and *bisect* (cut in two). The word *correlation* begins with the prefix *co-*, which means *together*, as in these words: *coexist, cooperate*. The variables in a *correlation* are linked and affect each other.

5. Aoiffe plants a tree sapling in her yard and measures its height every year. Her measurements so far are shown. Make a scatter plot and find a line of fit if the variables have a correlation. What is the equation of your line of fit?

Years after Planting	Height (ft)
0	2.1
1	4.3
2	5
3	7.3
4	8.1
5	10.2

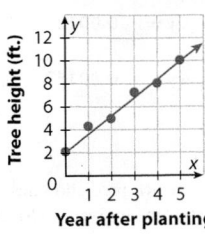

Year after planting

Choosing points: $(0, 2)$ and $(5, 10)$

$m = \dfrac{10 - 2}{5 - 0} = \dfrac{8}{5}$ $b = 2$

The equation is of this line of fit is $y = \frac{8}{5}x + 2$.

⊙ Explain 3   Using Linear Functions Fitted to Data to Solve Problems

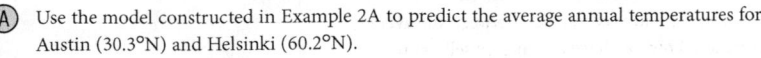**Interpolation** and **extrapolation** are methods of predicting data values for one variable from another based on a line of fit. The domain of the model is determined by the minimum and maximum values of the data set. When the prediction is made for a value within the extremes (minimum and maximum) of the original data set, it is called interpolation. When the prediction is made for a value outside the extremes, it is called extrapolation. Extrapolation is not as reliable as interpolation because the model has not been demonstrated, and it may fail to describe the relationship between the variables outside the domain of the data. Extrapolated predictions will also vary more with different lines of fit.

Example 3   Use the linear fit of the data set to make the required predictions.

(A) Use the model constructed in Example 2A to predict the average annual temperatures for Austin (30.3°N) and Helsinki (60.2°N).

$$y = -1.1x + 106$$

Austin: $y = -1.1 \cdot 30.3 + 106 = 72.67\ °F$

Helsinki: $y = -1.1 \cdot 60.2 + 106 = 39.78\ °F$

EXPLAIN 3

Using Linear Functions Fitted to Data to Solve Problems

QUESTIONING STRATEGIES

? Is it possible to make a prediction based on a scatter plot with no correlation? Explain. **No; no correlation means that there is no relationship between the variables and the points on the graph show no pattern.**

CONNECT VOCABULARY **EL**

Explain that the prefix *inter-* means *between or among,* as in the word *international* (among nations), and the prefix *extra-* means *outside or beyond,* as in the word *extracurricular* (outside of classes). Students can use these meanings to help them remember that *interpolation* is predicting values between data points and *extrapolation* is predicting values outside the range of the data.

EXPLAIN 4

Distinguishing Between Correlation and Causation

INTEGRATE MATHEMATICAL PRACTICES
Focus on Reasoning

MP.2 Distinguishing causation from correlation can be tricky. Stress with students that the key to determining causality is identifying a mechanism for the cause. For example, data might show that dog owners suffer fewer burglaries than people who don't have dogs. A possible mechanism is that a barking dog at a house scares off would-be burglars, so it is reasonable to conclude that owning a dog leads to having fewer burglaries.

QUESTIONING STRATEGIES

? Can a data set be likely to show causation without showing a strong correlation? Explain. **No; a data set must show a strong correlation in order for causation to be likely.**

(B) Use the model of city altitudes and water boiling points to predict the boiling point of water in Mexico City (altitude = 7943 feet) and in Fargo, North Dakota (altitude = 3000 feet)

$$y = -0.00167x + 211$$

Mexico City: $y = \boxed{-0.00167} \cdot 7943 + \boxed{211} = 197.74$

Fargo: $y = \boxed{-0.00167} \cdot 3000 + \boxed{211} = 205.99$

Reflect

6. **Discussion** Which prediction made in Example 3B would you expect to be more reliable? Why? **The boiling point in Fargo, North Dakota is a more reliable prediction because it is an interpolation, while Mexico City is an extrapolation.**

Your Turn

7. Use the model constructed in YourTurn 5 to predict how tall Aoiffe's tree will be 10 years after she planted it.

   $y = 1.6 \cdot 10 + 2 = 18$ft.

🖉 Explain 4 Distinguishing Between Correlation and Causation

A common error when interpreting paired data is to observe a correlation and conclude that causation has been demonstrated. Causation means that a change in the one variable results directly from changing the other variable. In that case, it is reasonable to expect the data to show correlation. However, the reverse is not true: observing a correlation between variables does not necessarily mean that the change to one variable caused the change in the other. They may both have a common cause related to a variable not included in the data set or even observed (sometimes called lurking variables), or the causation may be the reverse of the conclusion.

Example 4 Read the description of the experiments, identify the two variables and describe whether changing either variable is likely, doubtful, or unclear to cause a change in the other variable.

(A) The manager of an ice cream shop studies its monthly sales figures and notices a positive correlation between the average air temperature and how much ice cream they sell on any given day.

The two variables are ice cream sales and average air temperatures.

It is likely that warmer air temperatures cause an increase in ice cream sales.

It is doubtful that increased ice cream sales cause an increase in air temperatures.

(B) A traffic official in a major metropolitan area notices that the more profitable toll bridges into the city are those with the slowest average crossing speeds.

The variables are __profit__ and __crossing speed__.

It is [likely |(doubtful)| unclear] that increased profit causes slower crossing speed.

It is [likely |(doubtful)| unclear] that slower crossing speeds cause an increase in profits.

Reflect

8. Explain your reasoning for your answers in Example 4B and suggest a more likely explanation for the observed correlation.
   Each car pays the same toll regardless of the speed it crosses, so it is doubtful slowing cars down causes an increase in profits.

Your Turn

9. HDL cholesterol is considered the "good" cholesterol as it removes harmful bad cholesterol from where it doesn't belong. A group of researchers are studying the connection between the number of minutes of exercise a person performs weekly and the person's HDL cholesterol count. The researchers surveyed the amount of physical activity each person did each week for 10 weeks and collected a blood sample from 67 adults. After analyzing the data, the researchers found that people who exercised more per week had higher HDL cholesterol counts. Identify the variables in this situation and determine whether it describes a positive or negative correlation. Explain whether the correlation is a result of causation.

   The variables are the number of minutes of exercise per week and the HDL cholesterol count. The greater number of minutes of exercise per week corresponds to a greater HDL cholesterol count, so there is a positive correlation. Causation is possible but it is unknown which variable causes the other. Having a greater HDL cholesterol count may cause a person to exercise more per week. It is also possible that another factor causes a greater number of minutes of exercise per week and a higher HDL cholesterol count.

💬 Elaborate

10. Why is extrapolating from measured data likely to result in a less accurate prediction than interpolating?
    Predictions within the range of data have the same accuracy as the correlation coefficient indicates. What may occur outside of the range of data can be influenced by unknown variables.

11. What will the effect be on the correlation coefficient if additional data is collected that is farther from the line of fit? What will the effect be if the newer data lies along the line of fit? Explain your reasoning.
    Additional data farther from the line of best fit will cause r to get closer to 0; additional data nearer to the line of best fit will cause r to get closer to 1.

12. **Essential Question Check-In** How does a scatter plot help you make predictions from two-variable data?
    The scatter plot is a useful tool to inspect the data visually for correlation. If the data is strongly correlated, then a line of fit can be used to predict values that were not sampled in the original data set.

© Houghton Mifflin Harcourt Publishing Company

ELABORATE

INTEGRATE MATHEMATICAL PRACTICES
Focus on Reasoning

MP.2 When working with real-world problems, make sure that students first identify the two variables in the situation and ask themselves how the two affect one another. Encourage students to think about whether one variable has an effect on the other, and, if so, why it does.

SUMMARIZE THE LESSON

? How do you choose a reasonable line of fit for a set of data? After plotting the points in the set of data, choose a straight line that goes through the middle of the data set, with about as many points above the line as below the line.

EVALUATE

ASSIGNMENT GUIDE

Concepts and Skills	Practice
Explore Describing How Variables are Related in Scatter Plots	Exercises 21–22
Example 1 Estimating the Correlation Coefficient of a Linear Fit	Exercises 1–4, 25
Example 2 Fitting Linear Functions to Data	Exercises 5–8, 20, 24
Example 3 Using Linear Functions Fitted to Data to Solve Problems	Exercises 9–12, 19
Example 4 Distinguishing Between Correlation and Causation	Exercises 13–18, 23

AVOID COMMON ERRORS

Students may think that a positive r-value indicates a stronger correlation than a negative r-value. Explain that the strength of a correlation is determined by the absolute value of r. For example, r-values of -0.8 and 0.8 indicate correlations of equal strength.

⭐ Evaluate: Homework and Practice

- Online Homework
- Hints and Help
- Extra Practice

Estimate the value of r. Indicate whether r is closest to -1, -0.5, 0, 0.5 or 1 for the following data sets.

1.

x	y
1	8
2	4.037522
3	7.200593
4	4.180245
5	4.763788
6	1
7	1.047031
8	2.436249
9	1.844607

The value of r for this data is closest to -0.5.

2. The table below presents exam scores earned by six students and how long they each studied.

Hours of Study	Exam Score
2	63
2	71
2.5	75
3	67
4.5	82
5	95

The value of r for this data is closest to 1.

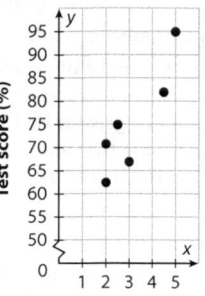

3. Raymond opens a car wash and keeps track of his weekly earnings, as shown in the table

Weeks after Opening	Earnings ($)
0	1050
1	1700
2	2400
3	2000
4	3500
5	3600

The value of r for this data is closest to 1.

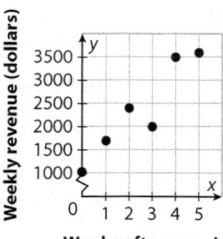

Exercise	Depth of Knowledge (D.O.K.)	COMMON CORE Mathematical Practices
1	**1** Recall of Information	**MP.6** Precision
2–4	**1** Recall of Information	**MP.4** Modeling
5	**1** Recall of Information	**MP.6** Precision
6–8	**1** Recall of Information	**MP.4** Modeling
9	**1** Recall of Information	**MP.6** Precision

4. Rafael is training for a race by running a mile each day. He tracks his progress by timing each trial run.

Trial	Run Time (min)
1	8.2
2	8.1
3	7.5
4	7.8
5	7.4
6	7.5
7	7.1
8	7.1

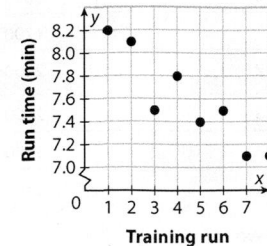

The value of r for this data is closest to -1.

Determine a line of fit for the data, and write the equation of your line.

5.

x	y
1	7.15
2	8.00
3	4.81
4	7.14
5	3.56
6	2.12
7	1.00
8	3.76
9	1.42

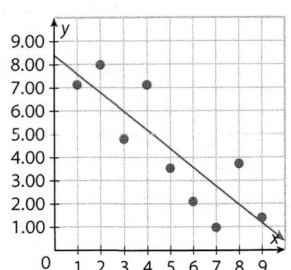

Possible answer:

$$m = \frac{2-6}{8-3} = \frac{-4}{5}$$

$$y = -\frac{4}{5}x + \frac{42}{5} \text{ or } y = -0.8x + 8.4$$

6.

Studying Time (Hours)	Test Score (%)
2	63
2	71
2.5	75
3	67
4.5	82
5	95

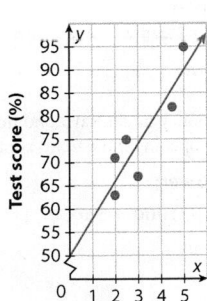

Possible answer:

$$m = \frac{90-50}{5-0} = 8 \quad y = 8x + 50$$

Exercise	Depth of Knowledge (D.O.K.)	COMMON CORE Mathematical Practices
10–12	**1** Recall of Information	**MP.4** Modeling
13–19	**2** Skills/Concepts	**MP.3** Logic
20–21	**2** Skills/Concepts	**MP.6** Precision
22	**2** Skills/Concepts	**MP.4** Modeling
23–25	**2** Skills/Concepts H.O.T.	**MP.3** Logic

AVOID COMMON ERRORS

Students may have difficulty drawing a line of fit on a scatter plot if they are trying to include actual data points on the line. While it is desirable to include points on the line, they should try to balance the number of points above the line with the number of points below the line. Tell students it is more important to locate the line so that the points are evenly distributed above and below the line.

7.

Weeks After Opening	Weekly Revenue (dollars)
0	1050
1	1700
2	2400
3	2000
4	3500
5	3600

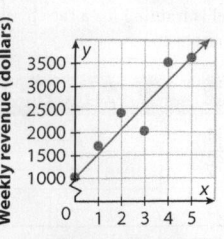

Weeks after opening

Possible answer:

$$m = \frac{3000 - 1000}{4 - 0} = 500 \quad y = 500x + 1000$$

8.

Training Run	Run Time (min)
1	8.2
2	8.1
3	7.5
4	7.8
5	7.4
6	7.5
7	7.1
8	7.1

Possible answer:

$$m \approx \frac{7.2 - 8.3}{7 - 0} = -0.157$$

$$y \approx -0.157x + 8.3$$

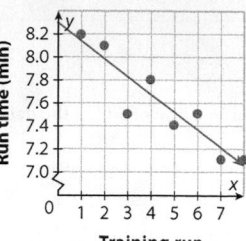

Training run

Use the linear models found in problems 5–8 for 9–12, respectively, to make predictions, and classify each prediction as an interpolation or an extrapolation.

9. Find y when $x = 4.5$.

Possible answer:

$y = -0.8(4.5) + 8.4 = 4.8$

Interpolation

10. What grade might you expect after studying for 4 hours?

Possible answer:

$s = 8 \cdot 4 + 50 = 82\%$

Interpolation

11. How much money might Raymond hope to earn 8 weeks after opening if the trend continues?

Possible answer:

$e = 500 \cdot 8 + 1000 = \$5000$

Extrapolation

12. What mile time does Rafael expect for his next run?

Possible answer:

$t = -0.157 \cdot 9 + 8.3 = 6.887$ minutes

Extrapolation

Read each description. Identify the variables in each situation and determine whether it describes a positive or negative correlation. Explain whether the correlation is a result of causation.

13. A group of biologists is studying the population of wolves and the population of deer in a particular region. The biologists compared the populations each month for 2 years. After analyzing the data, the biologists found that as the population of wolves increases, the population of deer decreases.

The variables are the population of wolves and the population of deer.

The greater population of wolves corresponds to a lower population of deer, so there is a negative correlation.

Causation is possible but it is unknown which variable causes the other.

14. Researchers at an auto insurance company are studying the ages of its policyholders and the number of accidents per 100 policyholders. The researchers compared each year of age from 16 to 65. After analyzing the data, the researchers found that as age increases, the number of accidents per 100 policyholders decreases.

The variables are the age in years and the number of accidents per 100 policyholders. The greater age corresponds to a lower number of accidents per 100 policyholders, so there is a negative correlation. Causation is possible. It is possible that the age of the driver affects safer driving and therefore fewer accidents because of experience and maturity. However it is also possible that other variables affect safe driving.

15. Educational researchers are investigating the relationship between the number of musical instruments a student plays and a student's grade in math. The researchers conducted a survey asking 110 students the number of musical instruments they play and went to the registrar's office to find the same 110 students' grades in math. The researchers found that students who play a greater number of musical instruments tend to have a greater average grade in math.

The variables are the number of musical instruments played and the grade in math. The greater number of musical instruments played corresponds to a higher grade in math, so there is a positive correlation. Causation is possible, but it is unknown which variable causes the other.

16. Researchers are studying the relationship between the median salary of a police officer in a city and the number of violent crimes per 1000 people. The researchers collected the police officers' median salary and the number of violent crimes per 1000 people in 84 cities. After analyzing the data, researchers found that a city with a greater police officers' median salary tends to have a greater number of violent crimes per 1000 people.

The variables are the police officers' median salary and the number of violent crimes per 1000 people. The greater police officers' median salary corresponds to a higher number of violent crimes per 1000 people, so there is a positive correlation. Causation is possible but it is unknown which variable causes the other.

INTEGRATE MATHEMATICAL PRACTICES
Focus on Reasoning

MP.2 Students may believe that for data sets with positive correlations, a line connecting any two points should have a positive slope. Remind students that a positive correlation describes the overall relationship between the two variables, and that any correlation is subject to random deviations.

CRITICAL THINKING

When students identify a data set as an example of correlation but not causation, ask students to think about what third variable might be involved in the situation and explain how that variable could be the cause of the correlation between the two variables.

17. The owner of a ski resort is studying the relationship between the amount of snowfall in centimeters during the season and the number of visitors per season. The owner collected information about the amount of snowfall and the number of visitors for the past 30 seasons. After analyzing the data, the owner determined that seasons that have more snowfall tend to have more visitors.

The variables are the number of centimeters of snowfall and the number of visitors. The greater number of centimeters of snowfall corresponds to a higher number of visitors, so there is a positive correlation. Causation is possible but it is unlikely that the number of visitors affects the amount of snowfall during a season. However, it is also possible that other factors affect both variables.

18. Government researchers are studying the relationship between the price of gasoline and the number of miles driven in a month. The researchers documented the monthly average price of gasoline and the number of miles driven for the last 36 months. The researchers found that the months with a higher average price of gasoline tend to have more miles driven.

The variables are the average price of gasoline and the number of miles driven. The greater average price of gasoline corresponds to a greater number of miles driven, so there is a positive correlation. Causation is possible but it is unknown which variable causes the other.

19. Interpret the Answer Each time Lorelai fills up her gas tank, she writes down the amount of gas it took to refill her tank, and the number of miles she drove between fill-ups. She makes a scatter plot of the data with miles driven on the y-axis and gallons of gas on the x-axis, and observes a very strong correlation. The slope is 35 and the y-intercept is 0.83. Do these numbers make sense, and what do they mean (besides being the slope and intercept of the line)?

The slope is a measure of fuel efficiency in miles per gallon, and a value of 35 is a reasonable value for a car. The intercept is how many miles she can drive with 0 gallons of gas and should be 0. However, fits are not perfect and an intercept of 0.83 is close enough to 0 to be considered reasonable.

20. Multi-Step The owner of a maple syrup farm is studying the average winter temperature in Fahrenheit and the number of gallons of maple syrup produced. The relationship between the temperature and the number of gallons of maple syrup produced for the past 8 years is shown in the table.

a. Make a scatter plot of the data and draw a line of fit that passes as close as possible to the plotted points.

Temperature (°F)	Number of gallons of maple syrup
24	154
26	128
25	141
22	168
28	104
21	170
24	144
22	160

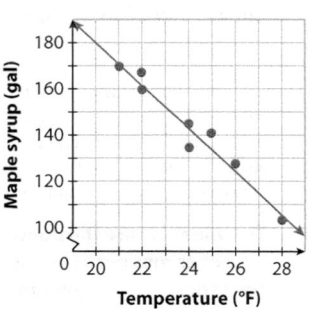

© Houghton Mifflin Harcourt Publishing Company

b. Find the equation of this line of fit.

Using points (20, 180) and (27, 115): $m = \dfrac{180 - 115}{20 - 27} = -\dfrac{65}{7}$

$y = -\dfrac{65}{7}x + 365\dfrac{5}{7}$ or

The equation is of this line of fit is approximately $y = -9.3x + 365.7$.

c. Identify the slope and y-intercept for the line of fit and interpret it in the context of the problem.

The slope is −9.3, so 9.3 fewer gallons of maple syrup are produced per degree F increase. The y-intercept is about 365.7, so about 365.7 gallons of maple syrup are produced at 0 degrees F.

21. The table below shows the number of boats in a marina during the years 2007 to 2014.

Years Since 2000	7	8	9	10	11	12	13	14
Number of Boats	26	25	27	27	39	38	40	39

a. Make a scatterplot by using the data in the table as the coordinates of points on the graph. Use the calendar year as the x-value and the number of boats as the y-value.

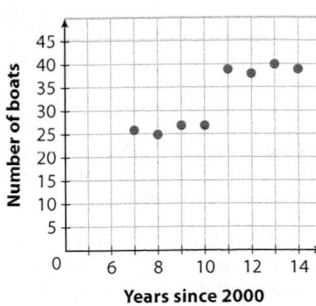

b. Use the pattern of the points to determine whether there is a positive correlation, negative correlation, or no correlation between the number of boats in the marina and the year. What is the trend?

There is no correlation between the variables. The number of boats in the marina is neither increasing nor decreasing over time. The trend since 2011 is for the number of boats to be around 40.

22. Multiple Response Which of the following usually have a positive correlation? Select all that apply.

a. the number of cars on an expressway and the cars' average speed

(b.) the number of dogs in a house and the amount of dog food needed

c. the outside temperature and the amount of heating oil used

d. the weight of a car and the number of miles per gallon

(e.) the amount of time studying and the grade on a science exam

Since coordinates are expressed with the *x*-value first, students may want to determine the slope of a line by finding the change in *x*-values divided by the change in *y*-values. Remind students the slope of a line is the change in *y* divided by the change in *x*.

Have students describe the steps they would follow for making predictions based on a set of bivariate data. Students should include directions for how to graph bivariate data and how to choose a line of fit.

23. Justify Reasoning Does causation always imply linear correlation? Explain.

No, even if one variable affects the second variable, as the first variable increases, the second variable could increase and then decrease.

24. Explain the Error Olivia notices that if she picks a very large scale for her y-axis, her data appear to lie more along a straight line than if she zooms the scale all the way in. She concludes that she can use this to increase her correlation coefficient and make a more convincing case that there is a correlation between the variables she is studying. Is she correct?

No, although this lesson described a method of using a scatter plot to visually estimate r, r is a characteristic of the data, not the plot, and does not change if the data is plotted differently. It is misleading to look at a nearly horizontal (or nearly vertical) set of data and conclude that it appears to be a straight line: estimating r visually requires a plot that is expanded along both axes.

25. What if? If you combined two data sets, each with r values close to 1, into a single data set, would you expect the new data set to have an r value between the original two values?

No, if the two data sets have very different lines of fit, the combined r value could be closer to zero than either of the original sets.

Lesson Performance Task

A 10-team high school hockey league completed its 20-game season. A team in this league earns 2 points for a win, 1 point for a tie, and 0 points for a loss. One of the team's coaches compares the number of goals each team scored with the number of points each team earned during the season as shown in the table.

a. Plot the points on the scatter plot, and use the scatterplot to describe the correlation and estimate the correlation coefficient. If the correlation coefficient is estimated as −1 or 1, draw a line of fit by hand and then find an equation for the line by choosing two points that are close to the line. Identify and interpret the slope and y-intercept of the line in context of the situation.

Goals Scored	Points
46	15
48	11
49	17
51	20
57	18
58	21
59	25
60	23
62	27
64	24

b. Use the line of fit to predict how many points a team would have if it scored 35 goals, 54 goals, and 70 goals during the season.

© Houghton Mifflin Harcourt Publishing Company

c. Use the results to justify whether the coach should only be concerned with the number of goals his or her team scores.

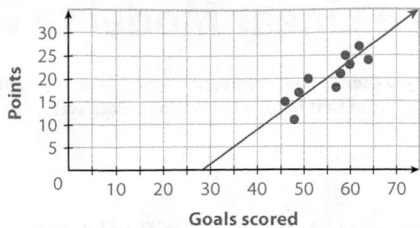

a. As the number of goals increases, the number of points increases. The correlation coefficient is about 1 because the points seem to lie close to a line with positive slope. The correlation coefficient is close to 1 and the line of fit on the graph passes close to the points (46, 15) and (60, 23).

Equation of line:

$$m = \frac{23 - 15}{60 - 46}$$

$$\approx 0.57$$

$$y = mx + b$$

$$15 = 0.57(46) + b$$

$$15 = 26.22 + b$$

$$-11.22 = b$$

The equation of the line of fit is $y = 0.57x - 11.22$. The slope means that a team earns about 0.57 point for each goal that is scored. The y-intercept means that a team with 0 goals would have −11.22 points, which does not make sense because a team cannot have negative points.

b. A team with 35 goals would have about 9 points.

$$0.57(35) - 11.22 = 8.73$$

A team with 54 goals would have about 20 points.

$$0.57(54) - 11.22 = 19.56$$

A team with 70 goals would have about 29 points.

$$0.57(70) - 11.22 = 28.68$$

c. The coach should not be only concerned with the number of goals the team scores as it is a team sport. The team with the most goals this season did not earn the most points. While it is important to score more goals, the coach should also be thinking about how the team can give up fewer goals.

QUESTIONING STRATEGIES

? Did the team with the fewest goals earn the fewest points? No, the team that scored 46 goals earned more points than the team that scored 48 goals.

? Did the team with the most goals earn the most points? No, the team that scored 64 goals earned fewer points than the team that scored 59 goals.

? What could be a reason for the team with the most goals earning fewer points? The team with the most points may have scored most of their goals in fewer games and therefore earned fewer points for winning.

INTEGRATE TECHNOLOGY

Students can use a graphing calculator to make a scatter plot of the data in the Lesson Performance Task. The first step is to press **STAT** and select **1:Edit**, then enter the goals scored in column **L1** and the points in column **L2**. Next, use the **STAT PLOT** menu to select a scatterplot, then adjust the window appropriately. Finally, press **GRAPH** to view the scatter plot.

EXTENSION ACTIVITY

Have students write a letter to a hockey coach. In the letter have students use the data given in the Lesson Performance Task to explain why making the most goals does not necessarily make a team win the most games.

One possible scenario students could describe is that the team that scored 62 goals might have had 13 wins, 1 tie, and 6 losses while the team that scored the most goals, 64, might have had 12 wins, 0 ties, and 8 losses.

Scoring Rubric

2 points: Student correctly solves the problem and explains his/her reasoning.

1 point: Student shows good understanding of the problem but does not fully solve or explain his/her reasoning.

0 points: Student does not demonstrate understanding of the problem.

Scatter Plots and Trend Lines   **450**

Fitting a Linear Model to Data

Common Core Math Standards

The student is expected to:

 S-ID.B.6b

Informally assess the fit of a function by plotting and analyzing residuals.
Also S-ID.B.6c, S-ID.C.8, F-LE.B.5

Mathematical Practices

 MP.5 Using Tools

Language Objective

Demonstrate to a partner how to find and plot the residuals for a line of fit. Explain what the residuals tell you about the quality of fit.

ENGAGE

Essential Question: How can you use the linear regression function on a graphing calculator to find the line of best fit for a two-variable data set?

Using the STAT, STAT PLOT, Y=, and GRAPH keys, you can enter data into the calculator and use it to perform linear regression on a function.

PREVIEW: LESSON PERFORMANCE TASK

View the Engage section online. Discuss why some of the hottest recorded temperatures on Earth were in the deserts nearest the equator and how the angle of the Sun at different latitudes causes temperature differences. Then preview the Lesson Performance Task.

Resource Locker

10.2 Fitting a Linear Model to Data

Essential Question: How can you use the linear regression function on a graphing calculator to find the line of best fit for a two-variable data set?

Explore 1 Plotting and Analyzing Residuals

For any set of data, different lines of fit can be created. Some of these lines will fit the data better than others. One way to determine how well the line fits the data is by using residuals. A **residual** is the signed vertical distance between a data point and a line of fit.

After calculating residuals, a residual plot can be drawn. A **residual plot** is a graph of points whose x-coordinates are the variables of the independent variable and whose y-coordinates are the corresponding residuals.

Looking at the distribution of residuals can help you determine how well a line of fit describes the data. The plots below illustrate how the residuals may be distributed for three different data sets and lines of fit.

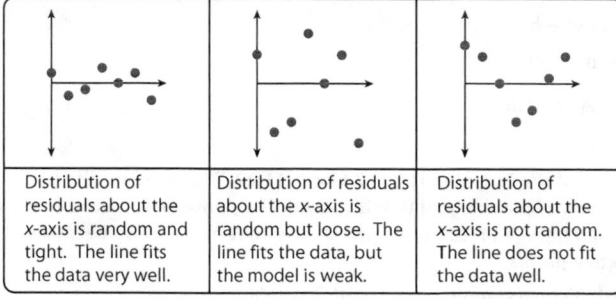

| Distribution of residuals about the x-axis is random and tight. The line fits the data very well. | Distribution of residuals about the x-axis is random but loose. The line fits the data, but the model is weak. | Distribution of residuals about the x-axis is not random. The line does not fit the data well. |

The table lists the median age of females living in the United States, based on the results of the United States Census over the past few decades. Follow the steps listed to complete the task.

 Use the table to create a table of paired values for x and y. Let x represent the time in years after 1970 and y represent the median age of females.

Year	Median Age of Females
1970	29.2
1980	31.3
1990	34.0
2000	36.5
2010	38.2

x	0	10	20	30	40
y	29.2	31.3	34.0	36.5	38.2

Module 10 **451** Lesson 2

© Houghton Mifflin Harcourt Publishing Company • Image Credits: ©bikeriderlondon/Shutterstock

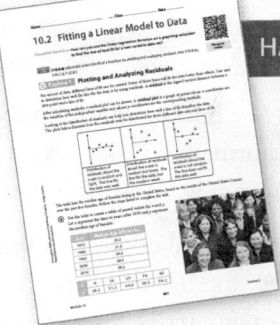

10.2 Fitting a Linear Model to Data

HARDCOVER PAGES 363–374

Turn to these pages to find this lesson in the hardcover student edition.

Ⓑ Use residuals to calculate the quality of fit for the line $y = 0.25x + 29$, where y is median age and x is years since 1970.

x	Actual y	Predicted y based on $y = 0.25x + 29$	Residual Subtract Predicted from Actual to Find the Residual.
0	29.2	29.0	0.2
10	31.3	31.5	−0.2
20	34.0	34.0	0
30	36.5	36.5	0
40	38.2	39.0	−0.8

Ⓒ Plot the residuals.

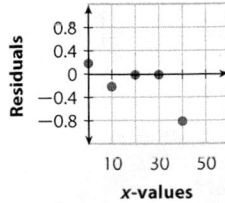

Ⓓ Evaluate the quality of fit to the data for the line $y = 0.25x + 29$.
Since all of the residuals are small and the points on the residual plot are tightly

distributed around the x-axis, the line $y = 0.25x + 29$ is a good model for this situation.

Reflect

1. **Discussion** When comparing two lines of fit for a single data set, how does the residual size show which line is the best model?
   The better model has residuals closer to 0.

2. **Discussion** What would the residual plot look like if a line of fit is not a good model for a data set?
   The residual plot would show points randomly scattered both above and below the x-axis,
   and the distances from the x-axis would be large.

EXPLORE 1

Plotting and Analyzing Residuals

INTEGRATE TECHNOLOGY

Graphing calculators can be used to compute and plot residuals. After students are comfortable doing this work on their own, they can use the graphing calculator to check their work.

QUESTIONING STRATEGIES

? When looking at a plot of the residuals, how do you determine whether your line is a good model for the data? Explain. If the residual values are on or near the x-axis and evenly distributed on both sides of the axis, it means that the residuals are small and therefore the line is close to being ideal for the data. If the residual values are large (not near the x-axis) and/or not evenly distributed on both sides of the axis, it means that the line is not close to being ideal for the data.

PROFESSIONAL DEVELOPMENT

Math Background

Why does linear regression use the sum of the squares of the residuals rather than just the sum? First, adding just the residuals can give misleading results. Large positives and negatives can cancel each other out, allowing a very loose fit of data points to have a very small sum. Summing the absolute values of the residuals might solve this problem but presents other complications. Using squares of residuals solves the positive-negative cancellation problem and also ensures that very large residuals affect the sum more than small residuals.

EXPLORE 2

Analyzing Squared Residuals

AVOID COMMON ERRORS

In squaring decimals, some students may forget to move the decimal point in their answers. Remind students that the square of a decimal should have twice as many decimal places as the original number.

QUESTIONING STRATEGIES

? What must be true for the square of a residual to be less than the residual? **The absolute value of the residual must be less than 1.**

⊘ Explore 2 Analyzing Squared Residuals

When different people fit lines to the same data set, they are likely to choose slightly different lines. Another way to compare the quality of a line of fit is by squaring residuals. In this model, the closer the sum of the squared residuals is to 0, the better the line fits the data.

In the previous section, a line of data was fit for the median age of females over time. After performing this task, two students came up with slightly different results. Student A came up with the equation $y = 0.25x + 29.0$ while Student B came up with the equation $y = 0.25x + 28.8$, where x is the time in years since 1970 and y is the median age of females in both cases.

(A) Complete each table below.

$y = 0.25x + 29.0$			
x	y (Actual)	y (Predicted)	Residual	Square of Residual
0	29.2	29.0	0.2	0.04
10	31.3	31.5	−0.2	0.04
20	34.0	34.0	0	0
30	36.5	36.5	0	0
40	38.2	39.0	−0.8	0.64

$y = 0.25x + 28.8$			
x	y (Actual)	y (Predicted)	Residual	Square of Residual
0	29.2	28.8	0.4	0.16
10	31.3	31.3	0	0
20	34.0	33.8	0.2	0.04
30	36.5	36.3	0.2	0.04
40	38.2	38.8	−0.6	0.36

(B) Find the sum of squared residuals for each line of fit.

$y = 0.25x + 29.0$: **0.72**

$y = 0.25x + 28.8$: **0.60**

(C) Which line has the smaller sum of squared residuals?

$y = 0.25x + 28.8$

Reflect

3. How does squaring a residual affect the residual's value?
If a residual is between 0 and 1, squaring the residual makes the residual smaller. If a residual is negative, squaring the residual makes the residual positive.

4. Are the sums of residuals or the sum of the squares of residuals a better measure of quality of fit?
The sum of the squares of residuals is a better measure of quality of fit.

© Houghton Mifflin Harcourt Publishing Company

COLLABORATIVE LEARNING

Peer-to-Peer Activity

Have students work in pairs. Give each pair a set of bivariate data. Each student will choose a line of fit, find its equation, and calculate the sum of the squares of the residuals. Then the two students should compare their results to determine which line is a better fit for the data. Students can then use a graphing calculator to compare their equations to the equation for the line of best fit.

Explain 1 **Assessing the Fit of Linear Functions from Residuals**

The quality of a line of fit can be evaluated by finding the sum of the squared residuals. The closer the sum of the squared residuals is to 0, the better the line fits the data.

Example 1 The data in the tables are given along with two possible lines of fit. Calculate the residuals for both lines of fit and then find the sum of the squared residuals. Identify the lesser sum and the line with better fit.

(A)

x	2	4	6	8
y	7	8	4	8

$y = x + 2.2$

$y = x + 2.4$

a. Find the residuals of each line.

x	y (Actual)	y Predicted by $y = x + 2.4$	Residual for $y = x + 2.4$	y Predicted by $y = x + 2.2$	Residual for $y = x + 2.2$
2	7	4.4	2.6	4.2	2.8
4	8	6.4	1.6	6.2	1.8
6	4	8.4	−4.4	8.2	−4.2
8	8	10.4	−2.4	10.2	−2.2

b. Square the residuals and find their sum.

$y = x + 2.4 \ (2.6)^2 + (1.6)^2 + (−4.4)^2 + (−2.4)^2 = 6.76 + 2.56 + 19.36 + 5.76 = 34.44$

$y = x + 2.2 \ (2.8)^2 + (1.8)^2 + (−4.2)^2 + (−2.2)^2 = 7.84 + 3.24 + 17.64 + 4.84 = 33.56$

The sum of the squared residuals for $y = x + 2.2$ is smaller, so it provides a better fit for the data.

(B)

x	1	2	3	4
y	5	4	6	10

$y = 2x + 3$

$y = 2x + 2.5$

a. Find the residuals of each line.

x	y (Actual)	y Predicted by $y = 2x + 3$	Residual for $y = 2x + 3$	y Predicted by $y = 2x + 2.5$	Residual for $y = 2x + 2.5$
1	5	5	0	4.5	0.5
2	4	7	−3	6.5	−2.5
3	6	9	−3	8.5	−2.5
4	10	11	−1	10.5	−0.5

b. Square the residuals and find their sum.

$y = 2x + 3 : \boxed{0}^2 + \boxed{-3}^2 + \boxed{-3}^2 + \boxed{-1}^2 = \boxed{0} + \boxed{9} + \boxed{9} + \boxed{1} = \boxed{19}$

$y = 2x + 2.5 : \boxed{0.5}^2 + \boxed{-2.5}^2 + \boxed{-2.5}^2 + \boxed{-0.5}^2 = \boxed{0.25} + \boxed{6.25} + \boxed{6.25} + \boxed{0.25} = \boxed{13}$

The sum of the squared residuals for $y = \boxed{2} x + \boxed{2.5}$ is smaller, so it provides a better fit for the data.

EXPLAIN 1

Assessing the Fit of Linear Functions from Results

INTEGRATE MATHEMATICAL PRACTICES
Focus on Reasoning

MP.2 Explain to students the theoretical underpinning for wanting the sum of squared residuals to be as small as possible. Point out that the residuals are a measure of how far the data points are from the line. Small values for the residuals mean that the data points are closer to the line, which in turn means that the line has a tight fit to the data.

DIFFERENTIATE INSTRUCTION

Technology

Encourage students to try performing regression analysis using an online application. A quick browser search will turn up several online regression calculators. Make sure that students pay attention to the format in which ordered pairs must be entered for the application they choose. Applications typically will plot the data points, show the line of best fit, and provide an equation for the line.

QUESTIONING STRATEGIES

? When comparing different lines of fit, how do you know which line has the best fit? Explain. Find the residuals for each line, square them, and find their sums. The line with the smallest sum for the squares of its residuals is the best fit.

? How can you find the value of a residual by looking at the coordinates of the point on a residual plot? The *y*-coordinate of the point will be the value of the residual.

5. How do negative signs on residuals affect the sum of squared residuals?
Negative residuals do not affect the sum of squared residuals.

6. Why do small values for residuals mean that a line of best fit has a tight fit to the data?
The residuals are a measure of the distance between the data points and the line. The data points are closer to the line if the residuals have small values.

Your Turn

7. The data in the table are given along with two possible lines of fit. Calculate the residuals for both lines of fit and then find the sum of the squared residuals. Identify the lesser sum and the line with better fit.

x	1	2	3	4	$y = x + 4$
y	4	7	8	6	$y = x + 4.2$

x	y (Actual)	y Predicted by $y = x + 4$	Residual for $y = x + 4$	y Predicted by $y = x + 4.2$	Residual for $y = x + 4.2$
1	4	5	−1	5.2	−1.2
2	7	6	1	6.2	0.8
3	8	7	1	7.2	0.8
4	6	8	−2	8.2	−2.2

$y = x + 4 : (-1)^2 + (1)^2 + (1)^2 + (-2)^2 = 7$
$y = x + 4.2 : (-1.2)^2 + (0.8)^2 + (0.8)^2 + (-2.2)^2 = 7.56$
The sum of the squared residuals for $y = x + 4$ is smaller, so it provides a better fit.

LANGUAGE SUPPORT EL

Connect Vocabulary

In this lesson, students work with residuals to find the line of best fit for a data set. Relate the word *residual* to the word *residue*, which students may have used in a science context. Students should be able to make a connection between a small amount that is left over (residue) and the amount that a data value differs from the predicted value (residual). Suggest they think of wanting residuals to be as small as possible as wanting to avoid having a lot of "leftovers."

Explain 2 Performing Linear Regression

The least-squares line for a data set is the line of fit for which the sum of the squared residuals is as small as possible. Therefore the least-squares line is a line of best fit. A **line of best fit** is the line that comes closest to all of the points in the data set, using a given process. **Linear regression** is a method for finding the least-squares line.

Example 2 Given latitudes and average temperatures in degrees Celsius for several cities, use your calculator to find an equation for the line of best fit. Then interpret the correlation coefficient and use the line of best fit to estimate the average temperature of another city using the given latitude.

City	Latitude	Average Temperature (°C)
Barrow, Alaska	71.2°N	−12.7
Yakutsk, Russia	62.1°N	−10.1
London, England	51.3°N	10.4
Chicago, Illinois	41.9°N	10.3
San Francisco, California	37.5°N	13.8
Yuma, Arizona	32.7°N	22.8
Tindouf, Algeria	27.7°N	22.8
Dakar, Senegal	14.0°N	24.5
Mangalore, India	12.5°N	27.1

Estimate the average temperature in Vancouver, Canada at 49.1°N.

Enter the data into data lists on your calculator. Enter the latitudes in column **L1** and the average temperatures in column **L2**.

Create a scatter plot of the data.

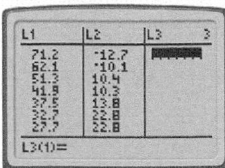

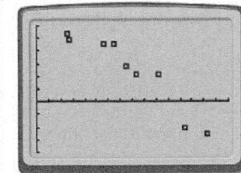

Use the Linear Regression feature to find the equation for the line of best fit using the lists of data you entered. Be sure to have the calculator also display values for the correlation coefficient r and r^2.

The correlation coefficient is about −0.95, which is very strong. This indicates a strong correlation, so we can rely on the line of fit for estimating average temperatures for other locations within the same range of latitudes.

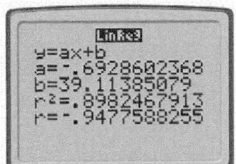

EXPLAIN 2

Performing Linear Regression

INTEGRATE MATHEMATICAL PRACTICES
Focus on Technology

MP.5 Make sure that students understand the purpose of each step when using a calculator to find a line of best fit. They first input the data, then create a scatter plot, then use the linear regression feature to find the equation for the line of best fit. Next they input the equation and graph it. Students should be able to explain what they are doing at each step in the process.

? The calculator's linear regression feature gives you an equation in the form $y = ax + b$. What form of linear equation is that? What do a and b represent? **Slope-intercept form; a is the slope of the line of best fit, and b is the y-intercept.**

? How does the line of fit displayed on the calculator differ from lines of fit found in previous exercises? Explain. **The lines of fit found in previous exercises were estimates; the line of fit found using a calculator is the best possible fit for the data points given.**

The equation for the line of best fit is $y \approx -0.693x + 39.11$.

Graph the line of best fit with the data points in the scatter plot.

Use the TRACE function to find the approximate average temperature in degrees Celsius for a latitude of 49.1°N.

The average temperature in Vancouver should be around 5°C.

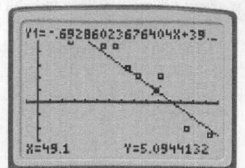

(B)

City	Latitude	Average Temperature (°F)
Fairbanks, Alaska	64.5°N	30
Moscow, Russia	55.5°N	39
Ghent, Belgium	51.0°N	46
Kiev, Ukraine	50.3°N	49
Prague, Czech Republic	50.0°N	50
Winnipeg, Manitobia	49.5°N	52
Luxembourg	49.4°N	53
Vienna, Austria	48.1°N	56
Bern, Switzerland	46.6°N	59

Estimate the average temperature in degrees Fahrenheit in Bath, England, at 51.4°N.

Enter the data into data lists on your calculator.

Use the Linear Regression feature to find the equation for the line of best fit using the lists of data you entered. Be sure to have the calculator also display values for the correlation coefficient r and r^2.

The correlation coefficient is about __−0.95__, which indicates a __very strong__ correlation. The correlation coefficient indicates that the line of best fit [is/ is not] reliable for estimating temperatures of other locations within the same range of latitudes.

The equation for the line of best fit is $y \approx -$ __1.60__ $x +$ __131.05__ .

Use the equation to estimate the average temperature in Bath, England at 51.4°N.

$y \approx -$ __1.60__ $x +$ __131.05__

The average temperature in degrees Fahrenheit in Bath, England, should be around __49__ °F.

Graph the line of best fit with the data points in the scatter plot. Then use the TRACE function to find the approximate average temperature in degrees Fahrenheit for a latitude of 51.4°N.

Reflect

8. Interpret the slope of the line of best fit in terms of the context for Example 2A.
The average temperature in degrees Celsius decreases at a rate of about 0.69 degrees per

degree in latitude.

9. Interpret the y-intercept of the line of best fit in terms of the context for Example 2A.
At 0 degrees in latitude or the equator, the average temperature is 39 degrees Celsius.

Your Turn

10. Use the given data and your calculator to find an equation for the line of best fit. Then interpret the
correlation coefficient and use the line of best fit to estimate the average temperature of another city
using the given latitude.

City	Latitude	Average Temperature (°F)
Anchorage, United States	61.1°N	18
Dublin, Ireland	53.2°N	29
Zurich, Switzerland	47.2°N	34
Florence, Italy	43.5°N	37
Trenton, New Jersey	40.1°N	40
Algiers, Algeria	36.5°N	46
El Paso, Texas	31.5°N	49
Dubai, UAE	25.2°N	56
Manila, Philippines	14.4°N	61

$y \approx -0.93x + 77.7$

$\approx -0.93(40.1) + 77.7$

≈ 40.41

The temperature in Trenton,

New Jersey, should be around

40 degrees Fahrenheit.

**The correlation coefficient is about -0.99, which indicates a very strong correlation. Therefore,
the line of best fit is reliable for estimating temperatures within the same range of latitudes.**

Elaborate

11. What type of line does linear regression analysis make?
A linear regression makes a line of best fit.

12. Why are squared residuals better than residuals?
Squared residuals are better than normal residuals because they provide a more exact

measure of the accuracy of a chosen line of best fit.

13. **Essential Question Check-In** What four keys are needed on a graphing calculator to perform a linear
regression?
STAT, PLOT, Y=, and GRAPH

ELABORATE

CONNECT VOCABULARY EL

Discuss with students the differences and similarities
between a *line of fit* and a *line of best fit*. Students
should realize that while there are many lines of fit
for a data set, there is only one line of best fit.

SUMMARIZE THE LESSON

? How do you use a graphing calculator to
determine a line of best fit for a data set? First,
enter the *x*- and *y*-values into the calculator. Then,
plot the points. Next, find the equation for the line
of best fit. Finally, use the calculator to draw the line
of best fit.

EVALUATE

ASSIGNMENT GUIDE

Concepts and Skills	Practice
Explore Plotting and Analyzing Residuals	Exercise 21
Explore 2 Analyzing Squared Residuals	Exercises 23–24
Example 1 Assessing the Fit of Linear Functions from Residuals	Exercises 1–14, 19–20, 22
Example 2 Performing Linear Regression	Exercises 15–18

The data in the tables below are shown along with two possible lines of fit. Calculate the residuals for both lines of fit and then find the sum of the squared residuals. Identify the lesser sum and the line with better fit.

1.

x	2	4	6	8
y	1	3	5	7

$y = x + 5$
$y = x + 4.9$

$y = x + 5: (-6)^2 + (-6)^2 + (-6)^2 + (-6)^2 = 36 + 36 + 36 + 36 = 144$
$y = x + 4.9: (-5.9)^2 + (-5.9)^2 + (-5.9)^2 + (-5.9)^2 = 139.24$
The sum of the squared residuals for $y = x + 4.9$ is smaller, so it provides a better fit for the data.

2.

x	1	2	3	4
y	1	7	3	5

$y = 2x + 1$
$y = 2x + 1.1$

$y = 2x + 1: 4 + 4 + 16 + 16 = 40$
$y = 2x + 1.1: 4.41 + 4.41 + 16.81 + 16.81 = 42.44$
The sum of the squared residuals for $y = 2x + 1$ is smaller, so it provides a better fit for the data.

3.

x	2	4	6	8
y	2	8	4	6

$y = 3x + 4$
$y = 3x + 4.1$

$y = 3x + 4: (-8)^2 + (-8)^2 + (-18)^2 + (-22)^2 = 936$
$y = 3x + 4.1: (-8.1)^2 + (-8.1)^2 + (-18.1)^2 + (-22.1)^2 = 947.24$
The sum of the squared residuals for $y = 3x + 4$ is smaller, so it provides a better fit.

4.

x	1	2	3	4
y	2	1	4	3

$y = x + 1$
$y = x + 0.9$

$y = x + 1: (0)^2 + (-2)^2 + (0)^2 + (-2)^2 = 8$
$y = x + 0.9: (0.1)^2 + (-1.9)^2 + (0.1)^2 + (-1.9)^2 = 7.24$
The sum of the squared residuals for $y = x + 0.9$ is smaller, so it provides a better fit.

5.

x	2	4	6	8
y	1	5	4	3

$y = 3x + 1.2$
$y = 3x + 1$

$y = 3x + 1.2: (-6.2)^2 + (-8.2)^2 + (-15.2)^2 + (-22.2)^2 = 829.56$
$y = 3x + 1: (-6)^2 + (-8)^2 + (-15)^2 + (-22)^2 = 809$
The sum of the squared residuals for $y = 3x + 1$ is smaller, so it provides a better fit.

Exercise	Depth of Knowledge (D.O.K.)	COMMON CORE Mathematical Practices
1–14	**1** Recall of Information	**MP.2** Reasoning
15–18	**1** Recall of Information	**MP.5** Using Tools
19–20	**1** Recall of Information	**MP.4** Modeling
21	**1** Recall of Information	**MP.2** Reasoning

6.

x	1	2	3	4
y	4	1	3	2

$y = x + 5$
$y = x + 5.3$

$y = x + 5: (-2)^2 + (-6)^2 + (-5)^2 + (-7)^2 = 114$
$y = x + 5.3: (-2.3)^2 + (-6.3)^2 + (-5.3)^2 + (-7.3)^2 = 126.36$
The sum of the squared residuals for $y = x + 5$ is smaller, so it provides a better fit.

7.

x	2	4	6	8
y	3	6	4	5

$y = 2x + 1$
$y = 2x + 1.4$

$y = 2x + 1: (-2)^2 + (-3)^2 + (-9)^2 + (-12)^2 = 238$
$y = 2x + 1.4: (-2.4)^2 + (-3.4)^2 + (-9.4)^2 + (-12.4)^2 = 259.44$
The sum of the squared residuals for $y = 2x + 1$ is smaller, so it provides a better fit.

8.

x	1	2	3	4
y	5	3	6	4

$y = x + 2$
$y = x + 2.2$

$y = x + 2: (2)^2 + (-1)^2 + (1)^2 + (-2)^2 = 10$
$y = x + 2.2: (1.8)^2 + (-1.2)^2 + (0.8)^2 + (-2.2)^2 = 10.16$
The sum of the squared residuals for $y = x + 2$ is smaller, so it provides a better fit.

9.

x	2	4	6	8
y	1	5	7	3

$y = x + 3$
$y = x + 2.6$

$y = x + 3: (-4)^2 + (-2)^2 + (-2)^2 + (-8)^2 = 88$
$y = x + 2.6: (-3.6)^2 + (-1.6)^2 + (-1.6)^2 + (-7.6)^2 = 75.84$
The sum of the squared residuals for $y = x + 2.6$ is smaller, so it provides a better fit.

10.

x	1	2	3	4
y	2	5	4	3

$y = x + 1.5$
$y = x + 1.7$

$y = x + 1.5: (-.5)^2 + (1.5)^2 + (-.5)^2 + (-2.5)^2 = 9$
$y = x + 1.7: (-.7)^2 + (1.3)^2 + (-.7)^2 + (-2.7)^2 = 9.96$
The sum of the squared residuals for $y = x + 1.5$ is smaller, so it provides a better fit.

INTEGRATE MATHEMATICAL PRACTICES
Focus on Critical Thinking

MP.3 Discuss with students the reasons why the squares of the residuals are used to perform a linear regression. Students should understand that using the squares guarantees that the values will be nonnegative and their sum will not be 0 unless the points are perfectly linear.

Exercise	Depth of Knowledge (D.O.K.)	COMMON CORE Mathematical Practices
22	**2** Skills/Concepts H.O.T.	**MP.2** Reasoning
23–24	**2** Skills/Concepts H.O.T.	**MP.2** Reasoning

AVOID COMMON ERRORS

When squaring residuals to find a line of fit, students may forget to move the decimal point in their answers. Remind students to check that their answers have the correct number of decimal places before finding the sum of the squares of the residuals.

11.

x	1	2	3	4
y	2	9	7	12

$y = 2x + 3.1$
$y = 2x + 3.5$

$y = 2x + 3.1: (-3.1)^2 + (1.9)^2 + (-2.1)^2 + (0.9)^2 = 18.44$
$y = 2x + 3.5: (-3.5)^2 + (1.5)^2 + (-2.5)^2 + (0.5)^2 = 21$
The sum of the squared residuals for $y = 2x + 3.1$ is smaller, so it provides a better fit.

12.

x	1	3	5	7
y	2	6	8	13

$y = 1.6x + 4$
$y = 1.8x + 4$

$y = 1.6x + 4: (-3.6)^2 + (-2.8)^2 + (-4.0)^2 + (-2.2)^2 = 41.64$
$y = 1.8x + 4: (-3.8)^2 + (-3.4)^2 + (-5.0)^2 + (-3.6)^2 = 63.96$
The sum of the squared residuals for $y = 1.6x + 4$ is smaller, so it provides a better fit.

13.

x	1	2	3	4
y	7	5	11	8

$y = x + 5$
$y = 1.3x + 5$

$y = x + 5: (1)^2 + (-2)^2 + (3)^2 + (-1)^2 = 15$
$y = 1.3x + 5: (0.7)^2 + (-2.6)^2 + (2.1)^2 + (-2.2)^2 = 16.5$
The sum of the squared residuals for $y = x + 5$ is smaller, so it provides a better fit.

14.

x	1	2	3	4
y	4	11	5	15

$y = 2x + 3$
$y = 2.4x + 3$

$y = 2x + 3: (-1)^2 + (4)^2 + (-4)^2 + (4)^2 = 49$
$y = 2.4x + 3: (-1.4)^2 + (3.2)^2 + (-5.2)^2 + (2.4)^2 = 45$
The sum of the squared residuals for $y = 2.4x + 3$ is smaller, so it provides a better fit.

Use the given data and your calculator to find an equation for the line of best fit. Then interpret the correlation coefficient and use the line of best fit to estimate the average temperature of another city using the given latitude.

15.

City	Latitude	Average Temperature (°F)
Calgary, Alberta	51.0°N	24
Munich, Germany	48.1°N	26
Marseille, France	43.2°N	29
St. Louis, Missouri	38.4°N	34
Seoul, South Korea	37.3°N	36
Tokyo, Japan	35.4°N	38
New Delhi, India	28.4°N	43
Honolulu, Hawaii	21.2°N	52
Bangkok, Thailand	14.2°N	58
Panama City, Panama	8.6°N	63

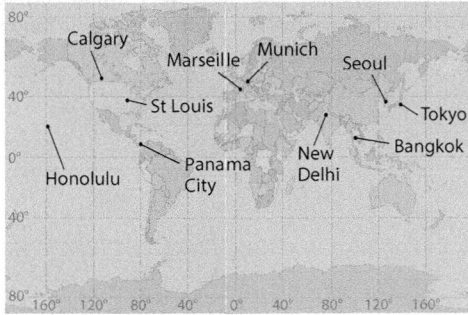

$y \approx -0.95x + 71.14$

$y \approx -0.95(8.6) + 71.14$

$y \approx 63$

The correlation coefficient is about $-0.997 \approx -1$, which indicates a very strong correlation. Therefore, the line of best fit is reliable for estimating temperatures within the same range of latitudes.

The temperature in Panama City should be around 63 degrees Fahrenheit.

GRAPHIC ORGANIZERS

Students can create a flow chart or step-by-step diagram to serve as a visual guide to the process of finding a line of best fit. One chart could describe finding a line of fit by hand, and another could explain how to find a line of best fit using a calculator.

16.

City	Latitude	Average Temperature (°F)
Oslo, Norway	59.6°N	21
Warsaw, Poland	52.1°N	28
Milan, Italy	45.2°N	34
Vatican City, Vatican City	41.5°N	41
Beijing, China	39.5°N	42
Tel Aviv, Israel	32.0°N	48
Kuwait City, Kuwait	29.2°N	48
Key West, Florida	24.3°N	55
Bogota, Columbia	4.4°N	64
Mogadishu, Somalia	2.0°N	66

$y \approx -0.76x + 69.81$

$y \approx -0.76(29.2) + 69.81$

$y \approx 48$

The correlation coefficient is about −0.98, which indicates a very strong correlation. Therefore, the line of best fit is reliable for estimating temperatures within the same range of latitudes.

The temperature in Kuwait City should be around 48 degrees Fahrenheit.

17.

City	Latitude	Average Temperature (°F)
Tornio, Finland	65.5°N	28
Riga, Latvia	56.6°N	36
Minsk, Belarus	53.5°N	39
Quebec City, Quebec	46.5°N	45
Turin, Italy	45.0°N	47
Pittsburgh, Pennsylvania	40.3°N	49
Lisbon, Portugal	38.4°N	52
Jerusalem, Israel	31.5°N	58
New Orleans, Louisiana	29.6°N	60
Port-au-Prince, Haiti	18.3°N	69

$y \approx -0.87x + 85.19$

$y \approx -0.87(31.5) + 85.19$

$y \approx 58$

The correlation coefficient is about −0.999 ≈ −1, which indicates a very strong correlation. Therefore, the line of best fit is reliable for estimating temperatures within the same range of latitudes. The temperature in Jerusalem should be around 58 degrees Fahrenheit.

18.

City	Latitude (°N)	Average Temperature (°F)
Juneau, Alaska	58.2	15
Amsterdam, Netherlands	52.2	24
Salzburg, Austria	47.5	36
Belgrade, Serbia	44.5	38
Philadelphia, Pennsylvania	39.6	41
Tehran, Iran	35.4	44
Nassau, Bahamas	25.0	52
Mecca, Saudi Arabia	21.3	56
Dakar, Senegal	14.4	62
Georgetown, Guyana	6.5	65

$y \approx -0.91x + 74.74$

$y \approx -0.91(14.4) + 74.74$

$y \approx 62$

The correlation coefficient is about -0.97, which indicates a very strong correlation. Therefore, the line of best fit is reliable for estimating temperatures within the same range of latitudes.

The temperature in Dakar should be around 62 degrees Fahrenheit.

Demographics Each table lists the median age of people living in the United States, based on the results of the United States Census over the past few decades. Use residuals to calculate the quality of fit for the line $y = 0.5x + 20$, where y is median age and x is years since 1970.

19.

Year	Median age of men
1970	25.3
1980	26.8
1990	29.1
2000	31.4
2010	35.6

Since the residuals are large, the line $y = 0.5x + 20$ is not a good fit.

INTEGRATE MATHEMATICAL PRACTICES

Focus on Math Connections

MP.1 Students often have the wrong sign for their residuals because they subtract the actual value from the predicted value instead of the other way around. While finding the squares of the residuals will mask this error because the square of a real number is always nonnegative, students should be careful to calculate the residuals correctly if they want to know whether the model's predicted value is an underestimate (positive residual) or an overestimate (negative residual) of the actual value.

JOURNAL

Have students summarize the steps for evaluating a line of best fit by finding the sum of the squares of the residuals.

20.

Year	Median Age of Texans
1970	27.1
1980	29.3
1990	31.1
2000	33.8
2010	37.6

Since the residuals are large, the line $y = 0.5x + 20$ is not a good fit.

21. State the residuals based on the actual y and predicted y values.

  a. Actual: 23, Predicted: 21   **2**

  b. Actual: 25.6, Predicted: 23.3   **2.3**

  c. Actual: 24.8, Predicted: 27.4   **−2.6**

  d. Actual: 34.9, Predicted: 31.3   **3.6**

H.O.T. Focus on Higher Order Thinking

22. Critical Thinking The residual plot of an equation has x-values that are close to the x-axis from $x = 0$ to $x = 10$, but has values that are far from the axis from $x = 10$ to $x = 30$. Is this a strong or weak relationship?

The strength of the relationship is weak because of the weak correlation between $x = 10$ and $x = 30$. A short distance of weak correlation cannot be offset by an otherwise strong correlation.

23. Communicate Mathematical Ideas In a squared residual plot, the residuals form a horizontal line at $y = 6$. What does this mean?

This means that either all of the residuals are either the same as each other or the opposite of each other.

24. Interpret the Answer Explain one situation other than those in this section where squared residuals are useful.

Sample Answer: Squared residuals are useful when the velocity equation of a car is unknown but needs to be approximated as well as possible. Using squared residuals will determine how well the approximated line fits the data.

Lesson Performance Task

The table shows the latitudes and average temperatures for the 10 largest cities in the Southern Hemisphere.

City	Latitude (°S)	Average Temperature (°F)
Sao Paulo, Brazil	23.9	69
Buenos Aires, Argentina	34.8	64
Rio de Janeiro, Brazil	22.8	76
Jakarta, Indonesia	6.3	81
Lodja, DRC	3.5	73
Lima, Peru	12.0	68
Santiago de Chile, Chile	33.2	58
Sydney, Australia	33.4	64
Melbourne, Australia	37.7	58
Johannesburg, South Africa	26.1	61

a. Use a graphing calculator to find a line of best fit for this data set. What is the equation for the best-fit line? Interpret the meaning of the slope of this line.

b. The city of Piggs Peak, Swaziland, is at latitude 26.0°S. Use the equation of your best-fit line to predict the average temperature in Piggs Peak. The actual average temperature for Piggs Peak is 65.3 °F. How might you account for the difference in predicted and actual values?

c. Assume that you graphed the latitude and average temperature for 10 cities in the Northern Hemisphere. Predict how the line of best fit for that data set might compare with the best-fit line for the Southern Hemisphere cities.

a. **The equation of the best-fit line is $y \approx -0.495x + 78.772$. The slope of the line is about -0.5, which indicates that the average temperature decreases about 0.5 °F for every degree of increase in south latitude.**

b. **The predicted average temperature for Piggs Peak is about 107 °F. The correlation coefficient is -0.79, so the correlation is not very strong.**

c. **The line for 10 different cities in the Northern Hemisphere would be similar to this best-fit line. Interested students could research the latitude and average temperature for 10 different cities at a range of latitudes in the Northern Hemisphere and carry out the linear regression.**

EXTENSION ACTIVITY

Have students research the latitude and average temperature for the city in which they live. Then have students use the equation of the line of best fit they found in Part A of the Lesson Performance Task to predict the average temperature in their city and compare it to the known average temperature. Discuss possible reasons why the predicted value is or is not close to the actual average temperature. Students might consider whether altitude, proximity to a large body of water, or other factors influence the temperature in their city.

CONNECT VOCABULARY EL

Some students may not understand the meaning of Earth's *hemispheres*, the *equator*, or *latitude*. Explain that the equator is an imaginary horizontal line that encircles the Earth, dividing it into two equal halves called the Northern and Southern Hemispheres. A series of lines parallel to the equator, called latitude lines, are used to indicate how far north or south of the equator any point on Earth is located. Latitude values are based on a scale that puts the equator at 0° latitude, the north pole at latitude 90° North, and the south pole at latitude 90° South. On a globe of Earth, point out the equator, the lines of latitude and longitude, and the locations of the cities listed in the table.

Scoring Rubric

2 points: Student correctly solves the problem and explains his/her reasoning.

1 point: Student shows good understanding of the problem but does not fully solve or explain his/her reasoning.

0 points: Student does not demonstrate understanding of the problem.

ASSESSMENT AND INTERVENTION

Personal Math Trainer

Assign or customize module reviews.

MODULE PERFORMANCE TASK

COMMON CORE

Mathematical Practices: MP.1, MP.4, MP.5, MP.6
S-ID.B.6a, S-ID.B.6c

SUPPORTING STUDENT REASONING

Students should begin this problem by choosing a model that best reveals a pattern between wingspan and weight. Here are some questions students may have.

- **Which pairs of data should I use for the slope?** Suggest that students use numbers that best represent all the wingspans and all the weights.

- **Which are the independent and dependent variables?** Suggest that students decide for themselves. If all or most other students have decided on one particular relationship, suggest that the student choose the other relationship.

- **Shouldn't the line of best fit pass through (0, 0)?** Remind students to use the given data and not to create any new data to solve this problem.

Essential Question: How can you use linear modeling and regression to solve real-world problems?

Key Vocabulary

correlation *(correlación)*
line of best fit *(línea de mejor ajuste)*
linear regression *(regresión lineal)*
scatter plot *(diagrama de dispersión)*

KEY EXAMPLE (Lesson 10.1)

The boiling point of water is lower at higher elevations because of the lower atmospheric pressure. The boiling point of water at some different elevations is given in the table.

Altitude (feet)	Boiling Point (°F)
500	211
1500	209
5250	202
3650	205.5
2000	207.5

Determine a line of fit for the data, and write the equation of the line. Then use your model to predict the boiling point of water at an altitude of 6400 feet.

Plot the points and sketch a line of fit. One possible line of fit goes through points (0, 212) and (5250, 202).

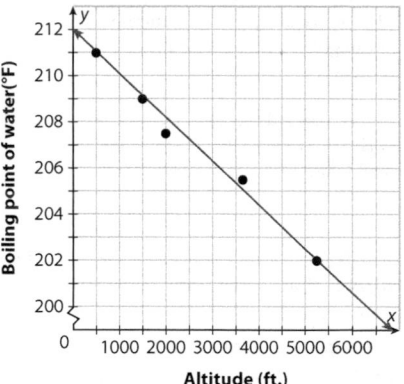

Altitude (ft.)

$m = -\dfrac{10}{5250}$, $b = 212$

The equation of this line of fit is $y = -0.0019x + 212$.

Substituting 6400 feet for x gives you $y = 199.84$. So the boiling point of water at 6400 feet is approximately 199.84°F.

© Houghton Mifflin Harcourt Publishing Company

SCAFFOLDING SUPPORT

- If students are having trouble finding a line of best fit, suggest they draw a line that is *not* a line of best fit. Then have them explain why it is not a good line of best fit and what would need to occur to make it a good line of best fit.

- Students needing more structure may benefit from a discussion about any patterns they notice in the table. Then ask how they might use mathematics to justify their conclusions.

- Interested students may want to find a model that predicts classmates' arm spans given their height or vice versa.

Estimate the correlation coefficient for each data set, indicating whether it is closest to –1, –0.5, 0, 0.5, or 1. *(Lesson 10.1)*

1.

x	y
1	2.569
2	4.236
3	3.49
4	5.62
5	4.3
6	6.1

1

2.

x	y
1	9.6
2	6.3
3	2.8
4	8.73
5	5.9
6	1.2

−0.5

3. Calculate the residuals and give the sum of the squared residuals for the data in the table and the given line of fit. *(Lesson 10.2)*

The sum of the squared residuals is 19.

x	1	3	5	7
y	4	6	9	10

$y = 2x - 1$

How Does Wingspan Compare with Weight in Birds?

How can we use a mathematical model to describe the relationship between wingspan and weight for birds? The table shows the weights and wingspans of several small birds. Use the data to explore a possible mathematical model, and explain how you can use your model to predict weight or wingspan of different birds.

Use your own paper to complete the task. Be sure to write down all your data and assumptions. Then use graphs, numbers, words, or algebra to explain how you reached your conclusion.

Bird	Weight (ounces)	Wingspan (inches)
Blue Jay	3	16
Black-Billed Magpie	6	25
Red-Winged Blackbird	1.8	13
Brown-Headed Cowbird	1.5	12
European Starling	2.9	16
Rusty Blackbird	2.1	14
Brewer's Blackbird	2.2	15.5
Yellow-Headed Blackbird	2.3	15

© Houghton Mifflin Harcourt Publishing Company

SAMPLE SOLUTION

Graph pairs of points (weight, wingspan) for each bird.

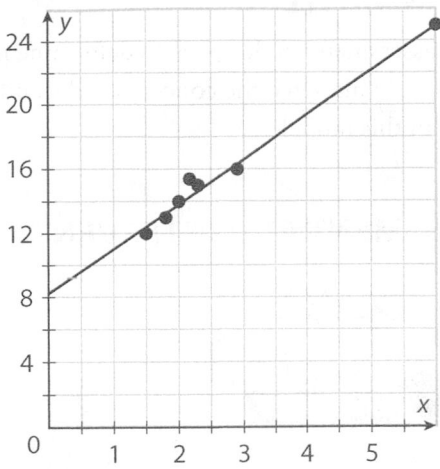

The data appear linear. Using a graphing calculator, the line of best fit for the data is $f(x) \approx 2.785x + 8.223$, where $f(x)$ is the wingspan in inches and x is the weight in ounces.

To use this model to make a prediction about a bird's wingspan, substitute the bird's weight into the function. Multiply the weight by 2.785, and then add 8.223 to the product.

NOTE: If students used the relation (wingspan, weight), the line of best fit would be the graph of the function $f(x) \approx 0.352x - 2.845$.

DISCUSSION OPPORTUNITIES

- If we use the model we came up with to predict a human's weight based on his or her arm span, do you think the predicted weight would be more or less than the average human's weight? Why?

- Discuss with students any reasons why their models might not be identical.

- How can we tell if the weight of flightless birds would be accurately modeled by our equation?

Ready to Go On?

ASSESS MASTERY

Use the assessment on this page to determine if students have mastered the concepts and standards covered in this module.

ASSESSMENT AND INTERVENTION

Access Ready to Go On? assessment online, and receive instant scoring, feedback, and customized intervention or enrichment.

ADDITIONAL RESOURCES

Response to Intervention Resources

- Reteach Worksheets

Differentiated Instruction Resources

- Reading Strategies **EL**
- Success for English Learners **EL**
- Challenge Worksheets

Assessment Resources

- Leveled Module Quizzes

 **(Ready) to Go On?**

10.1–10.2 Linear Modeling and Regression

- Online Homework
- Hints and Help
- Extra Practice

1. The table shows test averages of eight students.

U.S. History Test Average	88	68	73	98	88	83	78	88
Science Test Average	78	73	70	93	90	80	78	90

If $x =$ the U.S. History Test Average, and $y =$ the Science Test Average, the equation of the least-squares line for the data is $y \approx 0.77x + 17.65$ and $r \approx 0.87$. Discuss correlation and causation for the data set. *(Lesson 10.1)*

There is a strong positive correlation between the U.S. history test average and the science test average for these students. There is not a likely cause-and-effect relationship because there is no apparent reason why test scores in one subject would directly affect test scores in the other subject.

2. The table shows numbers of books read by students in an English class over a summer and the students' grades for the following semester.

Books	0	0	0	0	1	1	1	2	2	3	5	8	10	14	20
Grade	64	68	69	72	71	74	76	75	79	85	86	91	94	99	98

Find an equation for the line of best fit. Calculate and interpret the correlation coefficient. Then use your equation to predict the grade of a student who read 7 books. *(Lessons 10.1, 10.2)*

line of best fit: $y \approx 1.707x + 72.44$; correlation coefficient is 0.9 which shows a strong, positive correlation; predicted grade: 84

ESSENTIAL QUESTION

3. How can you use statistical methods to find relationships between sets of data?

Possible Answer: You can plot one set of data against another to calculate r, the correlation coefficient, which tells you how strongly related the data sets are. You can also find linear equations that best fit the data and allow you to make predictions.

© Houghton Mifflin Harcourt Publishing Company

COMMON CORE **Common Core Standards**

Lesson	Items	Content Standards	Mathematical Practices
10.1	1	**S-ID.B.6a, S-ID.C.9**	**MP.6**
10.1, 10.2	2	**S-ID.B.6c, S-ID.B.6a, S-ID.C.7, F-LE.B.5**	**MP.6**

Assessment Readiness

1. Some students were surveyed about how much time they spent playing video games last week and their overall test averages. The equation of the least-squares line for the data is $y \approx -2.82x + 87.50$ and $r \approx -0.89$. Choose True or False for each statement.

   A. The variables are time spent playing games and test averages. ● True ○ False

   B. The variables have a negative correlation. ● True ○ False

   C. The variables have a weak correlation. ○ True ● False

2. Consider $f(x) = -3x - 12$. Choose True or False for each statement.

   A. The slope is -3. ● True ○ False

   B. The y-intercept is -12. ● True ○ False

   C. The x-intercept is 4. ○ True ● False

3. Look at each equation. Does the equation have a solution of $x = 3$? Select Yes or No for each statement.

   A. $2x - 8 = 19 - 7x$ ● Yes ○ No

   B. $-2(3x - 4) = 10$ ○ Yes ● No

   C. $\dfrac{-6x}{2} = -9$ ● Yes ○ No

4. Use your calculator to write an equation for the line of best fit for the following data.

x	12	15	19	31	43	57
y	36	41	44	61	72	94

Calculate and interpret the correlation coefficient. Use your equation to predict the value of y when $x = 25$.

$y \approx 1.25x + 21.08$; the correlation coefficient is approximately 0.997, which is close to 1. Therefore, there is a strong, positive correlation between x and y. $f(25) \approx 52.33$

MIXED REVIEW
Assessment Readiness

ASSESSMENT AND INTERVENTION

Personal **Math Trainer**

Assign ready-made or customized practice tests to prepare students for high-stakes tests.

ADDITIONAL RESOURCES

Assessment Resources

- Leveled Module Quizzes: Modified, B

AVOID COMMON ERRORS

Item 4   Because this item has multiple steps, some students may stop after the first step. Remind students to underline or circle the final question or questions in a problem to make sure they fully answer the problem.

Common Core Standards

Lesson	Items	Content Standards	Mathematical Practices
10.2	1	S-ID.B.6c	MP.4
5.2, 6.1	2*	F-IF.C.7a	MP.2
2.2	3*	A-REI.B.3	MP.2
10.1, 10.2	4	S-ID.B.6c, S-ID.B.8	MP.2

* Item integrates mixed review concepts from previous modules or a previous course.

MIXED REVIEW
Assessment Readiness

ASSESSMENT AND INTERVENTION

Assign ready–made or customized practice tests to prepare students for high–stakes tests.

ADDITIONAL RESOURCES

Assessment Resources

- Leveled Unit Tests: Modified, A, B, C
- Performance Assessment

AVOID COMMON ERRORS

Item 1 Some students may have a hard time finding the median and quartiles from a dot plot. Remind students that, if needed, they can write out the list of numbers and use that to find the median and quartiles.

- Online Homework
- Hints and Help
- Extra Practice

The data plot shown represents the age of the members of a jogging club.

```
                              x  x
                              x  x
                            x x x x x
                    x x x x x x x x x x
  <------|----|----|----|----|----|----|------>
        20   24   28   32   36   40
```

1. Find the median, range, and interquartile range of the data. Is each statement True?

   A. The median age is 36. ● Yes ○ No

   B. The range of ages is 8. ● Yes ○ No

   C. The interquartile range is 4. ○ Yes ● No

2. A new member who is 30 joins the jogging club. Determine if each statement is True or False.

   A. The range increases by 2. ● True ○ False

   B. The median decreases by 1. ○ True ● False

   C. The age of the new member is an outlier. ○ True ● False

3. Is each of the following a linear function?

   A. $y = -\dfrac{4}{5}x$ ● Yes ○ No

   B. $y = 5x^2 - 2$ ○ Yes ● No

   C. $y = -7$ ○ Yes ● No

4. Several hundred people were surveyed about their salary and the length of their commute to work. The equation of the line of best fit for the data is $y \approx 1.14x + 1.45$ and $r \approx 0.45$. Does each phrase accurately describe the data set?

   A. The variables have a strong correlation. ○ Yes ● No

   B. The variables have a positive correlation. ● Yes ○ No

   C. This study shows that there is no correlation between the length of a person's commute and their salary. ○ Yes ● No

5. A student notices that as the town population has gone up steadily over several years, the price of a quart of milk has also gone up steadily. Describe the correlation, if any. Then explain whether you think the situation implies causation.

   Possible answer: There is a positive correlation between the town population and the price of a quart of milk because one increases as the other increases. Neither variable is likely to have caused the other. This situation does not suggest causation.

COMMON CORE Common Core Standards

Items	Content Standards	Mathematical Practices
1	**S-ID.A.1**	**MP.2**
2	**S-ID.A.3**	**MP.1**
3*	**F-IF.A.1, F-LE.A.1b**	**MP.7**
4	**S-ID.B.6c**	**MP.1**
5	**S-ID.C.9**	**MP.3**

* Item integrates mixed review concepts from previous modules or a previous course.

6. Vivian surveyed 10th and 11th graders about whether they like reading comics. Some of the results are shown in the frequency table shown. Complete the table. Find the conditional relative frequency that a student enjoys reading comics given that the student is an 11th grader. Explain how you solved this problem.

| Grade | Enjoy Reading Comics | | |
	Yes	No	Total
10th	45	53	98
11th	72	38	110
Total	117	91	208

$65.\overline{45}\%$; I divided the number of 11th graders who like reading comics by the total number of 11th graders.

7. Thomas drew a line of best fit for the scatter plot as shown. Write an equation for the line of best fit in slope-intercept form. Show your work.

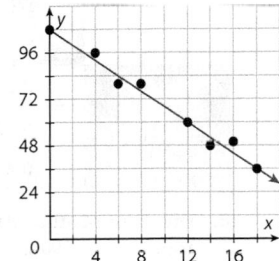

y-intercept $= 108$, slope $= \dfrac{36-60}{18-12} = -\dfrac{24}{6} = -4$

so $y = -4x + 108$

Performance Tasks

★ **8.** Gail counted the number of cars passing a certain store on Tuesday from 4 P.M. to 4:05 P.M. and on Saturday from 4 P.M. to 4:05 P.M. for 6 weeks. Her data sets are shown below.

Week	1	2	3	4	5	6
Cars on Tuesday	10	8	12	3	9	15
Cars on Saturday	24	8	31	36	29	32

A. Use the most appropriate measure of central tendency to compare the centers of these two data sets. Explain your choice.

B. Draw two box plots on the same number line to represent the data.

A. The medians are: 9.5 for Tuesday and 30 for Saturday, so the median for Saturday is more than three times as great. The median is the best choice because the Saturday data contains an outlier.

B.

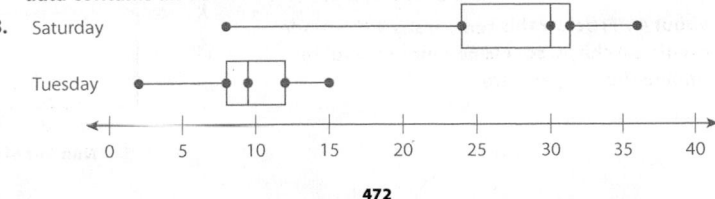

PERFORMANCE TASKS

There are three different levels of performance tasks:

* **Novice:** These are short word problems that require students to apply the math they have learned in straightforward, real-world situations.

** **Apprentice:** These are more involved problems that guide students step-by-step through more complex tasks. These exercises include more complicated reasoning, writing, and open ended elements.

*****Expert:** These are open-ended, nonroutine problems that, instead of stepping the students through, ask them to choose their own methods for solving and justify their answers and reasoning.

SCORING GUIDES

Item 8 (2 points)

A. 1 point for comparing medians and explaining

B. 1 point for correct box plots

Common Core Standards

Items	Content Standards	Mathematical Practices
6	S-ID.B.5	MP.2
7*	A-CED.A.2	MP.4

* Item integrates mixed review concepts from previous modules or a previous course.

Item 9 (6 points)

A. 4 points for complete and correct relative frequency table

B. 1 point for correct percent, and 1 point for correct recommendation

Item 10 (6 points)

A. 1 point for a reasonable answer, 1 point for a reasonable equation, and 2 points for a correct graph

B. 1 point for identifying a reasonable temperature, and 1 point for the explanation.

★★ **9.** A total of 150 students in two grades at Lowell High School were asked whether they usually ate lunch in the cafeteria. If they did not, they were asked if they would or would not eat lunch in the cafeteria if it had a salad bar.

	Now eat in cafeteria	Would eat if salad bar	Would not eat if salad bar
9th graders	36	14	32
10th graders	25	10	28

A. Use the given frequency table to make a new table showing the joint and marginal relative frequencies. Round to the nearest tenth of a percent.

B. The school board has decided that a salad bar should be added to the cafeteria if at least 30% of the students who currently do not eat in the cafeteria would start doing so. Should the salad bar be added?

A.

	Now eat in cafeteria	Would eat if salad bar	Would not eat if salad bar	Total
9th graders	0.248	0.097	0.221	0.566
10th graders	0.172	0.069	0.193	0.434
Total	0.421	0.166	0.414	1

B. There are 84 students who do not now eat in the cafeteria. Of those, 24 students, or about 28.6%, would use a salad bar if it is added. This is less than 30%, so the salad bar should not be added to the cafeteria.

★★★**10.** A scientist theorizes that you can estimate the temperature by counting how often crickets chirp. The scientist gathers the data in the table shown.

Number of chirps in a 14-second interval	37	32	42	37	46	35	34
Temperature (°F)	78	72	81	77	88	75	76

A. How many cricket chirps would you expect to indicate a temperature of 85 degrees? Include a graph and an equation as part of the justification of your answer.

B. What might be the lowest temperature your model could be applied to? Explain your reasoning.

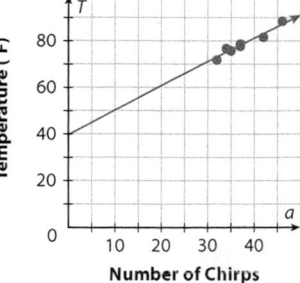

  A. About 46 chirps; $T = c + 39$ where c is the number of chirps and T is the temperature in °F

  B. about 40°F; below this temperature the model predicts 0 chirps, so it is no longer useful for finding the temperature

Geologist A geologist is studying the sediment discharged from several U.S. rivers, as shown in the table.

River	Amount of Sediment Discharged (millions of tons)
Mississippi River	230
Copper River	80
Yukon River	65
Columbia River	40
Susitna River	25
Eel River	15
Brazos River	11

For Parts **a–c**, round your answers to the nearest whole number, if necessary.

a. Find the mean and the median of the data for all seven rivers. Which measure represents the data better? Explain.

b. Find the mean of the data for the six rivers, excluding the Mississippi River. Does this mean represent the data better than the mean you found in part a? Explain.

c. Find the range and standard deviation of the data of all seven rivers. Describe what the measures tell you about the dispersion of the data.

> **a. mean: 67, median: 40;** Sample answer: The median better represents the data because the mean is highly affected by the Mississippi River, which is substantially higher than the other rivers.
>
> **b. mean: 39; Yes.** Sample answer: It is a better representation because the extremely high relative value of the Mississippi River greatly inflated the mean in Part a.
>
> **c. The range is 219 and the standard deviation is 71.** The data lie on a large interval and the deviation from the mean is very high.

MATH IN CAREERS

Geologist In this Unit Performance Task, students can see how a geologist uses mathematics on the job.

For more information about careers in mathematics as well as various mathematics appreciation topics, visit the American Mathematical Society at http://www.ams.org.

SCORING GUIDE

Task (6 points)

a. 1 point for the correct values, and 1 point for a correct explanation

b. 1 point for the correct values, and 1 point for a correct explanation

c. 1 point for the correct values, and 1 point for a correct description

Linear Systems and Piecewise-Defined Functions

CONTENTS

Unit Pacing Guide

45-Minute Classes

Module 11

DAY 1	DAY 2	DAY 3	DAY 4	DAY 5
Lesson 11.1	Lesson 11.1	Lesson 11.2	Lesson 11.3	Lesson 11.4

DAY 6				
Module Review and Assessment Readiness				

Module 12

DAY 1	DAY 2	DAY 3	DAY 4	DAY 5
Lesson 12.1	Lesson 12.2	Lesson 12.2	Lesson 12.3	Lesson 12.3

DAY 6				
Module Review and Assessment Readiness				

Module 13

DAY 1	DAY 2	DAY 3	DAY 4	DAY 5
Lesson 13.1	Lesson 13.1	Lesson 13.2	Lesson 13.2	Lesson 13.3

DAY 6	DAY 7	DAY 8	DAY 9	DAY 10
Lesson 13.3	Lesson 13.4	Lesson 13.4	Module Review and Assessment Readiness	Unit Review and Assessment Readiness

90-Minute Classes

Module 11

DAY 1	DAY 2	DAY 3
Lesson 11.1	Lesson 11.2 Lesson 11.3	Lesson 11.4 Module Review and Assessment Readiness

Module 12

DAY 1	DAY 2	DAY 3
Lesson 12.1 Lesson 12.2	Lesson 12.2 Lesson 12.3	Lesson 12.3 Module Review and Assessment Readiness

Module 13

DAY 1	DAY 2	DAY 3	DAY 4	DAY 5
Lesson 13.1	Lesson 13.2	Lesson 13.3	Lesson 13.4	Module Review and Assessment Readiness Unit Review and Assessment Readiness

Program Resources

PLAN

HMH Teacher App

Access a full suite of teacher resources online and offline on a variety of devices. Plan present, and manage classes, assignments, and activities.

ePlanner Easily plan your classes, create and view assignments, and access all program resources with your online, customizable planning tool.

Professional Development Videos

Authors Juli Dixon and Matt Larson model successful teaching practices and strategies in actual classroom settings.

QR Codes Scan with your smart phone to jump directly from your print book to online videos and other resources.

Teacher's Edition

Support students with point-of-use Questioning Strategies, teaching tips, resources for differentiated instruction, additional activities, and more.

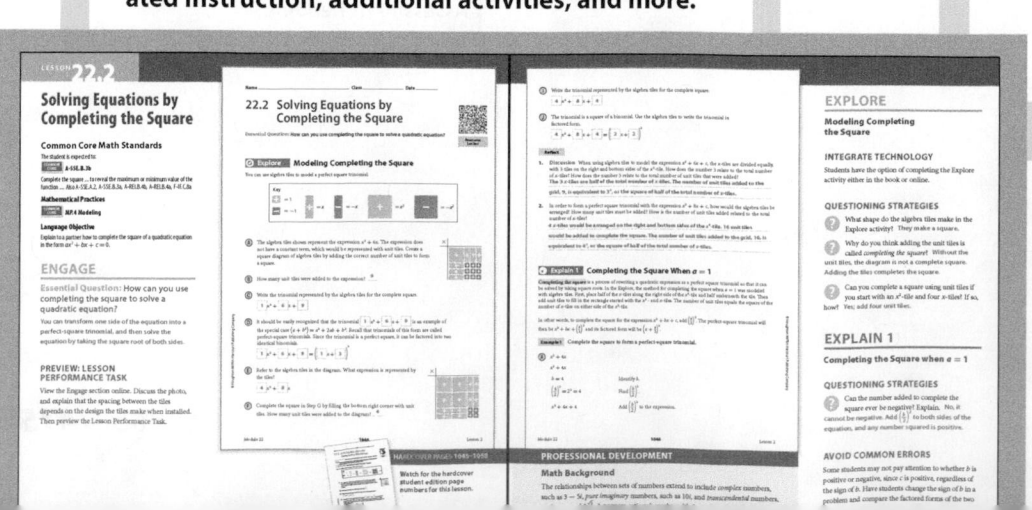

ENGAGE AND EXPLORE

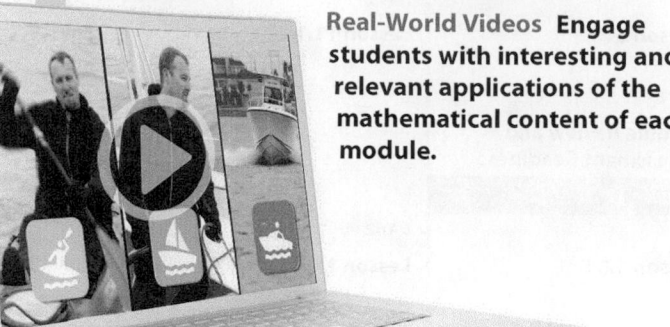

Real-World Videos **Engage students with interesting and relevant applications of the mathematical content of each module.**

Explore Activities

Students interactively explore new concepts using a variety of tools and approaches.

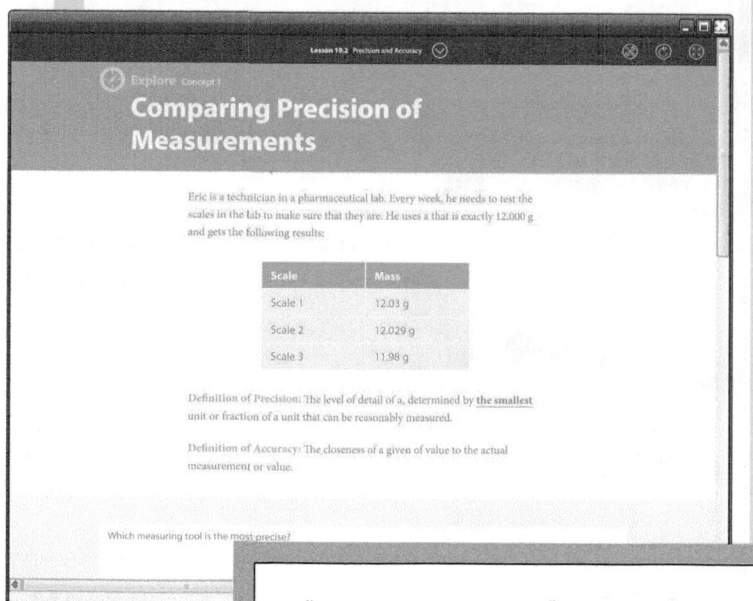

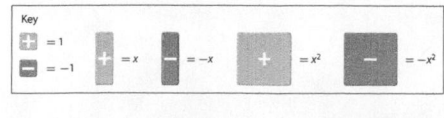

Name_____ Class_____ Date_____

22.2 Solving Equations by Completing the Square

Resource Locker

Essential Question: How can you use completing the square to solve a quadratic equation?

A-SSE.B.3b Complete the square ... to reveal the maximum or minimum value of the function ... Also A-SSE.A.2, A-SSE.B.3a, A-REI.B.4b, A-REI.B.4a, F-IF.C.8a

Explore **Modeling Completing the Square**

You can use algebra tiles to model a perfect square trinomial.

Key

$+$ $= 1$

$-$ $= -1$ $= x$ $= -x$ $= x^2$ $= -x^2$

(A) The algebra tiles shown represent the expression $x^2 + 6x$. The expression does not have a constant term, which would be represented with unit tiles. Create a square diagram of algebra tiles by adding the correct number of unit tiles to form a square.

(B) How many unit tiles were added to the expression? _____

(C) Write the trinomial represented by the algebra tiles for the complete square.

☐ $x^2 +$ ☐ $x +$ ☐

(D) It should be easily recognized that the trinomial ☐ $x^2 +$ ☐ $x +$ ☐ is an example of the special case $(a + b^2) = a^2 + 2ab + b^2$. Recall that trinomials of this form are called

TEACH

Math On the Spot video tutorials, featuring program author Dr. Edward Burger, accompany every example in the textbook and give students step-by-step instructions and explanations of key math concepts.

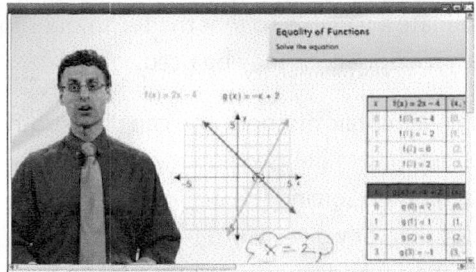

Interactive Teacher Edition

Customize and present course materials with collaborative activities and integrated formative assessment.

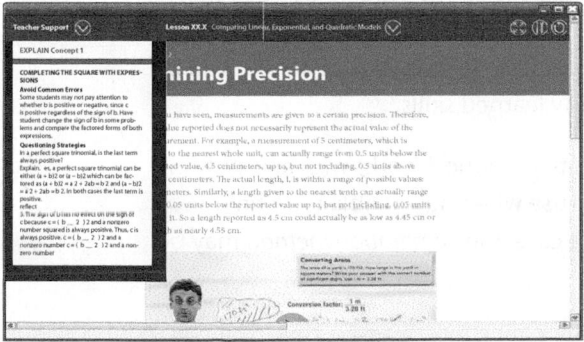

Differentiated Instruction Resources

Support all learners with Differentiated Instruction Resources, including

- **Leveled Practice and Problem Solving**
- **Reading Strategies**
- **Success for English Learners**
- **Challenge**

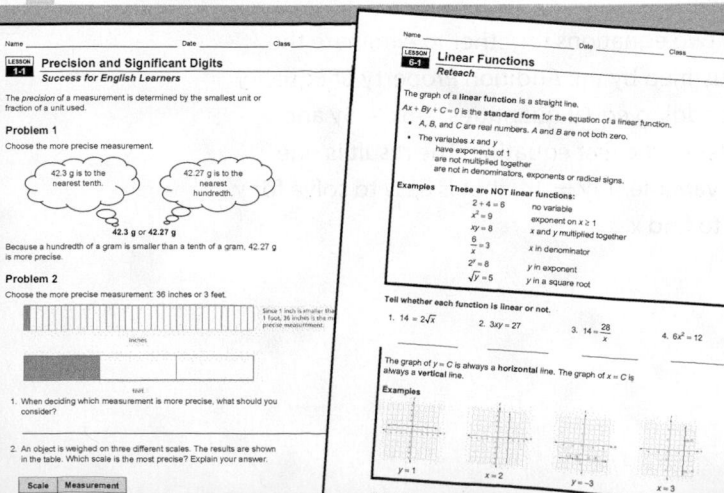

ASSESSMENT AND INTERVENTION

 The Personal Math Trainer **provides online practice, homework, assessments, and intervention. Monitor student progress through reports and alerts. Create and customize assignments aligned to specific lessons or Common Core standards.**

- **Practice** – With dynamic items and assignments, students get unlimited practice on key concepts supported by guided examples, step-by-step solutions, and video tutorials.

- **Assessments** – Choose from course assignments or customize your own based on course content, Common Core standards, difficulty levels, and more.

- **Homework** – Students can complete online homework with a wide variety of problem types, including the ability to enter expressions, equations, and graphs. Let the system automatically grade homework, so you can focus where your students need help the most!

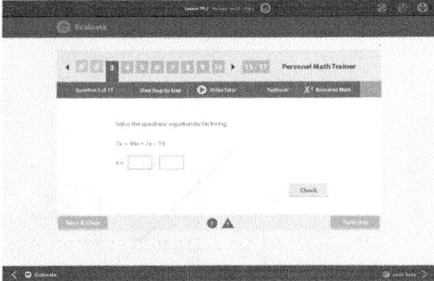

- **Intervention** – Let the Personal Math Trainer automatically prescribe a targeted, personalized intervention path for your students.

Focus on Higher Order Thinking

Raise the bar with homework and practice that incorporates higher-order thinking and mathematical practices in every lesson.

Assessment Readiness

Prepare students for success on high stakes tests for Algebra 1 with practice at every module and unit

COMMON CORE

Assessment Resources

Tailor assessments and response to intervention to meet the needs of all your classes and students, including

- Leveled Module Quizzes
- Leveled Unit Tests
- Unit Performance Tasks
- Placement, Diagnostic, and Quarterly Benchmark Tests
- Tier 1, Tier 2, and Tier 3 Resources

Math Background

Solving Linear Systems  A-REI.C.6

LESSONS 11.1 to 11.4

A *system of linear equations* is a set of two or more linear equations that each contain two or more variables. In this course, the systems consist of two equations that each contain two variables. A *solution* of such a system is an ordered pair that satisfies both equations.

Consider the system $\begin{cases} x + y = 5 \\ y - x = -1 \end{cases}$.

The ordered pair $(3, 2)$ is a solution of the system because it satisfies both equations: $3 + 2 = 5$ and $2 - 3 = -1$. The graph of an equation is the set of all of its solutions. Therefore, if an ordered pair is a solution of two linear equations, it must lie on both graphs. In other words, the solution is the *intersection* of the graphs. The intersection of the graphs of $x + y = 5$ and $y - x = -1$ is $(3, 2)$.

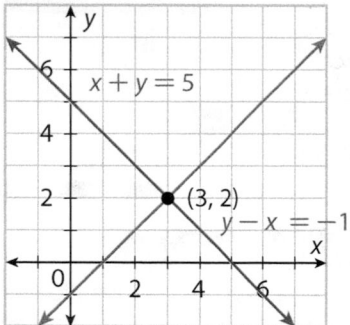

This graphic representation leads naturally to the conclusions that some systems may have no solutions (lines may be parallel), and that some systems may have infinitely many solutions (lines may coincide).

Graphing is an intuitive way to solve systems, and it visually reinforces the meaning of a solution. Graphing also highlights the connection between algebra and geometry; in particular, it shows that you can solve a problem presented in purely algebraic terms by using geometric methods.

Algebraic Methods A-REI.C.5

LESSONS 11.2 to 11.4

The intersection point of two lines may not have integer coordinates, thereby motivating the use of algebraic methods to solve systems. In general, the goal of algebraic methods is to eliminate a variable so that the techniques for solving single-variable equations may be used.

As an example of an algebraic method, one can solve both equations in a system for y to get two equations that can be set equal to each other. Solving the first equation in the system discussed earlier for y gives $y = 5 - x$. Substituting that equation into the second equation gives $(5 - x) - x = -1$. Solving that equation shows that $x = 3$, and substituting that value of x into either of the original equations gives $y = 2$.

This method is called the *substitution method*. In general, solve either equation for either variable and then substitute into the other equation. This yields an equation that can be solved using previously learned skills.

Although the substitution method works with any system, it may be awkward to use when no variable term has a coefficient of 1. In this case, the *elimination method* may be a better choice.

Students should understand that the elimination method is based on the properties of equality. For example,

to solve $\begin{cases} 2x + 3y = 11 \\ -6x + 5y = -19 \end{cases}$, you can multiply both sides of

the first equation by 3 using the Multiplication Property of

Equality. To solve the resulting system, $\begin{cases} 6x + 9y = 33 \\ -6x + 5y = -19 \end{cases}$,

you can add the two equations together to eliminate the x-terms. This is justified by the Addition Property of Equality because you are adding equal quantities, $-6x + 5y$ and -19, to both sides of the first equation. The result is one equation in one variable, $14y = 14$, that is easy to solve for y. Then substitute to find x.

In general, elimination works well for systems of linear equations containing any number of variables, and it is a fundamental process in the study of linear algebra.

Systems of
Linear Inequalities A-REI.D.12

LESSON 12.2

The solution set of a single inequality in two variables can be represented by a half plane. The solution set of a system of two inequalities in two variables is represented by the intersection of two half planes.

For example, the graph below shows the graphs of the two inequalities $y < -x + 5$ and $y \geq 2x - 3$.

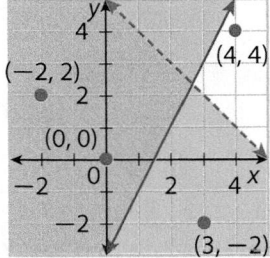

The dashed red line represents the solution set of the equation $y = -x + 5$. The half plane below the dashed line represents the solution set of $y < -x + 5$. The solid blue line represents the solution set of the equation $y = 2x - 3$. The half plane including the blue line and the region above that line represents the solution set of $y \geq 2x - 3$. The purple region is the intersection of those two half planes and represents the solution set of the system of inequalities.

Students should check points inside and outside the solution region in *both* inequalities to verify that the correct solution region has been identified. For example, students should check that $(4, 4)$ does not satisfy either inequality; $(3, -2)$ satisfies the first inequality, but not the second; and $(-2, 2)$ satisfies both inequalities.

Recall that there are three possible solutions of a system of two linear equations:

- a single point (if the two lines intersect)
- no solution (if the two lines are parallel and not collinear)
- infinitely many points (if the equations represent the same line)

In contrast, a system of two linear inequalities has only two solution possibilities. One solution possibility is a region in the coordinate plane where the solutions of the inequalities overlap.

The other solution possibility of a system of two linear inequalities is no solution or the empty set. This can be visualized in the graph below where the two shaded regions do not overlap.

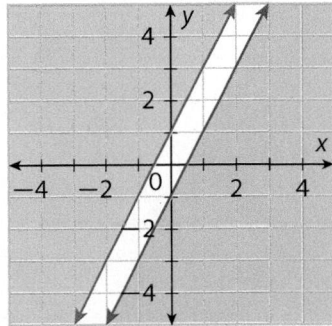

No third possible solution of a system of linear inequalities exists because we cannot create an overlapping region that includes the entire coordinate plane.

Linear Systems and Piecewise-Defined Functions

MATH IN CAREERS

Unit Activity Preview

After completing this unit, students will complete a Math in Careers task by writing and solving a system of linear equations based on a personal shopper's work. Critical skills include representing real-world situations as algebraic equations and solving systems of linear equations.

For more information about careers in mathematics as well as various mathematics appreciation topics, visit The American Mathematical Society at http://www.ams.org.

Linear Systems and Piecewise-Defined Functions

MODULE 11
Solving Systems of Linear Equations

MODULE 12
Modeling with Linear Systems

MODULE 13
Piecewise-Defined Functions

MATH IN CAREERS

Personal Shopper Personal shoppers assist clients in their needs for a variety of merchandise, which can include furniture, clothing, groceries, or gifts. Personal shoppers must have a good understanding of financial math, including percentages. They must be able to stay within the budgetary constraints of their clients. They must also be able to calculate expenses such as transportation costs and reasonable rates for their services.

If you are interested in a career as a personal shopper, you should study these mathematical subjects:
- Algebra
- Business Math

Research other careers that require staying within the constraints of a budget. Check out the career activity at the end of the unit to find out how **personal shoppers** use math.

Unit 5   475

TRACKING YOUR LEARNING PROGRESSION

Before	In this Unit	After
Students understand: • measures of center and spread • frequency tables, histograms, and box plots • normal distributions • scatter plots and trend lines	Students will learn about: • solving systems of linear equations • creating systems of linear equations • graphing systems of linear equalities and inequalities • solving absolute value equations and inequalities	Students will study: • simplifying expressions with rational exponents • simplifying expressions with radicals • geometric sequences • exponential functions

Reading Start-Up

Visualize Vocabulary

Use the ✔ words to complete the chart.

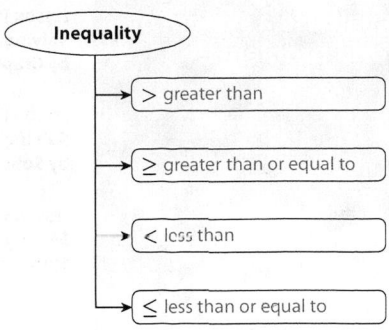

Inequality
- > greater than
- ≥ greater than or equal to
- < less than
- ≤ less than or equal to

Understand Vocabulary

Complete the sentences using the preview words. Match the term on the left to the example on the right.

1. __C__ independent system
2. __B__ consistent system
3. __A__ dependent system

A. a system of equations that has an infinite number of solutions

B. a system of equations or inequalities that has at least one solution

C. a system of equations that has exactly one solution

Active Reading

Three-Panel Flip Chart Create a three-panel flip chart to help you understand the concepts in this unit. Label one flap "Solving Systems of Linear Equations," another "Modeling with Linear Systems," and the last flap "Piecewise-Defined Functions." As you study each module, write important ideas under the appropriate flap. Include any sample equations, inequalities, and functions that will help you remember the concepts later when you look back at your notes.

Vocabulary

Review Words
✔ greater than (*mayor que*)
✔ greater than or equal to (*mayor que o igual a*)
✔ less than (*menor que*)
✔ less than or equal to (*menor que o igual a*)
✔ x-intercept (*intersección con el eje x*)
✔ y-intercept (*intersección con el eje y*)

Preview Words
absolute-value function (*función de valor absoluto*)
consistent system (*sistema consistente*)
dependent system (*sistema dependiente*)
independent system (*sistema independiente*)
piecewise function (*función a trozos*)
system of linear equations (*sistema de ecuaciones lineales*)
system of linear inequalities (*sistema de desigualdades lineales*)

Reading Start Up

Have students complete the activities on this page by working alone or with others.

VISUALIZE VOCABULARY

The definition and example chart graphic helps students review vocabulary associated with an inequality. If time allows, ask students for examples of inequalities and how to interpret them.

UNDERSTAND VOCABULARY

Use the following explanations to help students learn the preview words.

A **system of linear equations** is two (or more) related linear equations for which a common solution is sought. A **system of linear inequalities** is a system in which all of the inequalities are linear. A system of equations or inequalities that has at least one solution is a **consistent system**. A system of equations that has infinitely many solutions is a **dependent system**. A system of equations that has exactly one solution is an **independent system**.

ACTIVE READING

Students can use these reading and note-taking strategies to help them organize and understand the new concepts and vocabulary. Encourage them to ask for help if they become confused with similarities in the vocabulary associated with systems of equations. Have them highlight aspects of their examples that help them distinguish the definitions.

ADDITIONAL RESOURCES

Differentiated Instruction

- Reading Strategies **EL**

Solving Systems of Linear Equations

ESSENTIAL QUESTION:

Answer: Many problem situations are more easily translated into two equations than one equation. You can solve the system of linear equations by graphing, by substitution, by adding or subtracting, or by multiplying first.

PROFESSIONAL DEVELOPMENT VIDEO

Professional Development Video

Author Juli Dixon models successful teaching practices in an actual high-school classroom.

Professional Development
my.hrw.com

MODULE **11**

Solving Systems of Linear Equations

Essential Question: How can you use a system of linear equations to solve real-world problems?

LESSON 11.1
Solving Linear Systems by Graphing

LESSON 11.2
Solving Linear Systems by Substitution

LESSON 11.3
Solving Linear Systems by Adding or Subtracting

LESSON 11.4
Solving Linear Systems by Multiplying First

© Houghton Mifflin Harcourt Publishing Company • Image Credit: ©Handout/Reuters/Corbis

REAL WORLD VIDEO
A Mars rover is sent into space to land on Mars. This feat requires planning the trajectory of the rover to intersect with the orbit of Mars. Systems of equations are used to find the intersection of graphs.

MODULE PERFORMANCE TASK PREVIEW

Do Hybrid Cars Pay for Themselves?

Hybrid cars often get better gas mileage than traditional cars, which can lead to savings on gas money. The longer you drive a hybrid car, the more you are likely to save on gas. In this module, you will explore the question of how many years it would take to save enough money on gas to pay for the extra cost of a hybrid car. Buckle up and let's find out!

Module 11   **477**

DIGITAL TEACHER EDITION

Access a full suite of teaching resources when and where you need them:

- Access content online or offline
- Customize lessons to share with your class
- Communicate with your students in real-time
- View student grades and data instantly to target your instruction where it is needed most

PERSONAL MATH TRAINER
Assessment and Intervention

Assign automatically graded homework, quizzes, tests, and intervention activities. Prepare your students with updated, Common Core-aligned practice tests.

Are(YOU)Ready?

Complete these exercises to review skills you will need for this module.

Graphing Linear Relationships

Example 1

Tell whether the graph represents a linear nonproportional or proportional relationship.

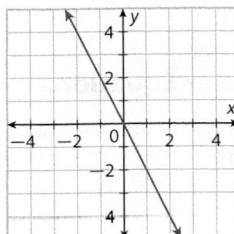

The graph of a linear nonproportional relationship is a straight line that does not pass through the origin.

The graph of a linear proportional relationship is a straight line that passes through the origin.

The graph is a straight line that passes through the origin, so it represents a linear proportional relationship.

Tell whether the graph represents a linear nonproportional or proportional relationship.

1.

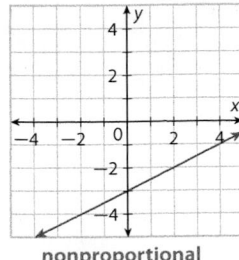

nonproportional

2.

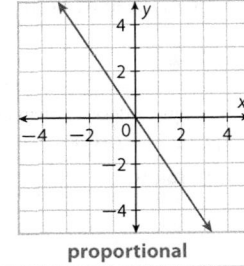

proportional

Algebraic Expressions

Example 2

Evaluate $3x + 4y$ for $x = -2$ and $y = 4$.

$3x + 4y$

$3(-2) + 4(4)$ Substitute -2 for x and 4 for y.

$-6 + 16$ Multiply.

10 Add.

Evaluate each expression for the given values of the variables.

3. $6p - 2q$ for $p = 3$ and $q = -7$

32

4. $5a - 2b$ for $a = -2$ and $b = 5$

-20

5. $8m + 5n$ for $m = 3$ and $n = -5$

-1

6. $7x + 9y$ for $x = -3$ and $y = 2$

-3

Are You Ready?

Are You Ready?

ASSESS READINESS

Use the assessment on this page to determine if students need strategic or intensive intervention for the module's prerequisite skills.

ASSESSMENT AND INTERVENTION

TIER 1, TIER 2, TIER 3 SKILLS

Personal Math Trainer will automatically create a standards-based, personalized intervention assignment for your students, targeting each student's individual needs!

ADDITIONAL RESOURCES

See the table below for a full list of intervention resources available for this module.

Response to Intervention Resources also includes:

- Tier 2 Skill Pre-Tests for each Module
- Tier 2 Skill Post-Tests for each skill

Response to Intervention			Differentiated Instruction
Tier 1 Lesson Intervention Worksheets	**Tier 2** Strategic Intervention Skills Intervention Worksheets	**Tier 3** Intensive Intervention Worksheets available online	
Reteach 11.1 Reteach 11.2 Reteach 11.3 Reteach 11.4	2 Algebraic Expressions 6 Graphing Linear Nonproportional … 7 Graphing Linear Proportional … 10 Linear Functions	Building Block Skills 19, 22, 23, 24, 27, 40, 46, 59, 70, 81	Challenge worksheets Extend the Math Lesson Activities in TE

Solving Linear Systems by Graphing

Common Core Math Standards

The student is expected to:

 A-REI.C.6

Solve systems of linear equations... approximately (e.g., with graphs)...

Mathematical Practices

 MP.5 Using Tools

Language Objective

Use graphs to explain the difference between systems of equations that are inconsistent, consistent and dependent, and consistent and independent.

ENGAGE

Essential Question: How can you find the solution of a system of linear equations by graphing?

Graph the lines. If the graphs intersect in one point (a, b), the system has one solution, (a, b). If the two lines do not intersect, the system has no solution. If the graphs coincide, that is, if they are the same line, the system has infinitely many solutions.

PREVIEW: LESSON PERFORMANCE TASK

View the Engage section online. Discuss how the speed of the current in a river can affect the speed of a boat going upstream or downstream. Then preview the Lesson Performance Task.

11.1 Solving Linear Systems by Graphing

Essential Question: How can you find the solution of a system of linear equations by graphing?

Resource Locker

🧭 Explore   Types of Systems of Linear Equations

A **system of linear equations**, also called a *linear system*, consists of two or more linear equations that have the same variables. A **solution of a system of linear equations** with two variables is any ordered pair that satisfies all of the equations in the system.

Ⓐ Describe the relationship between the two lines in Graph A.

The two lines have different slopes and they intersect at exactly one point.

Graph A

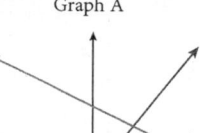

Ⓑ What do you know about every point on the graph on a linear equation?

Every point on the line is a solution of the linear equation.

Ⓒ How many solutions does a system of two equations have if the graphs of the two equations intersect at exactly one point?

exactly one solution

Ⓓ Describe the relationship between the two lines that coincide in Graph B.

The two lines have the same slope and the same *y*-intercept.

They are the same line.

Graph B

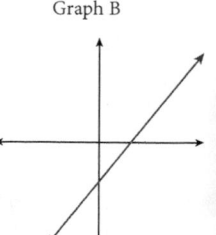

Ⓔ How many solutions does a system of two equations have if the graphs of the two equations intersect at infinitely many points?

infinitely many solutions

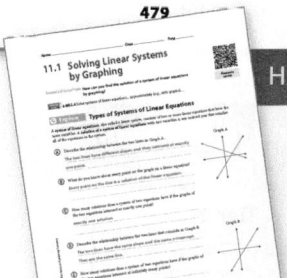

HARDCOVER PAGES 387–394

Turn to these pages to find this lesson in the hardcover student edition.

Ⓕ Describe the relationship between the two lines in Graph C.

Graph C

The two lines have the same slope and different *y*-intercepts.

They are parallel lines.

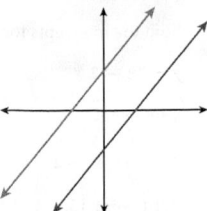

Ⓖ How many solutions does a system of two equations have if the graphs of the two equations do not intersect?

no solutions

Reflect

1. **Discussion** Explain why the solution of a system of two equations is represented by any point where the two graphs intersect.

All points on the graphs of each equation represent the solutions to those equations. If

any point is on both graphs, then it is a solution of both equations.

🔾 **Explain 1** **Solving Consistent, Independent Linear Systems by Graphing**

A **consistent system** is a system with at least one solution. Consistent systems can be either independent or dependent.

An **independent system** has exactly one solution. The graph of an independent system consists of two lines that intersect at exactly one point. A **dependent system** has infinitely many solutions. The graph of a dependent system consists of two coincident lines, or the same line.

A system that has no solution is an **inconsistent system**.

Example 1 Solve the system of linear equations by graphing. Check your answer.

Ⓐ $\begin{cases} 2x + y = 6 \\ -x + y = 3 \end{cases}$

Find the intercepts for each equation, plus a third point for a check. Then graph.

$2x + y = 6$	$-x + y = 3$
x-intercept: 3	*x*-intercept: −3
y-intercept: 6	*y*-intercept: 3
third point: $(-1, 8)$	third point: $(3, 6)$

The two lines appear to intersect at $(1, 4)$. Check.

$2x + y = 6$ $-x + y = 3$

$2(1) + 4 \stackrel{?}{=} 6$ $-(1) + 4 \stackrel{?}{=} 3$

$6 = 6$ $3 = 3$

The point satisfies both equations, so the solution is $(1, 4)$.

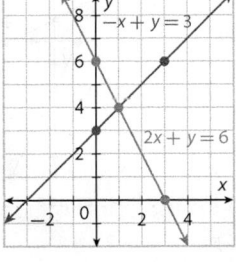

PROFESSIONAL DEVELOPMENT

COMMON CORE **Integrate Mathematical Practices**

This lesson provides an opportunity to address Mathematical Practice **MP.5**, which calls for students to "use tools." To get a correct solution by graphing, students must use graph paper and a straightedge to accurately draw both lines in the system. Using a hand-drawn grid or trying to graph the lines without a guide to make them straight will lead to errors. Students can also use a graphing calculator to solve systems by graphing.

Types of Systems of Linear Equations

INTEGRATE TECHNOLOGY

Students have the option of completing the Explore activity either in the book or online.

QUESTIONING STRATEGIES

❓ What is the difference between the solution of a system of two linear equations and the solution of an equation in one variable? **The solution of a system of equations is an ordered pair that makes both equations true. The solution of an equation in one variable is a single number that makes the equation true.**

EXPLAIN 1

Solving Consistent, Independent Linear Systems by Graphing

CONNECT VOCABULARY 🔲EL

Have students consider the word *consistent*. One definition of *consistent* is *compatible or in agreement*. Systems that are consistent are in agreement somewhere, that is, they have a solution. *Inconsistent* is the opposite of *consistent*; it means *not in agreement*. Systems that are inconsistent are not in agreement and have no solution.

QUESTIONING STRATEGIES

❓ Why is it not sufficient to check your proposed solution in just one of the equations? **There are infinitely many ordered pairs that will satisfy one equation but not the other. Only one ordered pair will satisfy both equations.**

CONNECT VOCABULARY EL

Point out that the terms *dependent* and *independent* have a somewhat different meaning when used to describe systems of equations than when used to describe dependent and independent variables. However, both uses rely on the same underlying meanings of the words. In a dependent system, the two lines are the same, so you could say that each one depends on the other. In an independent system, the two lines go their separate ways and do not depend on one another.

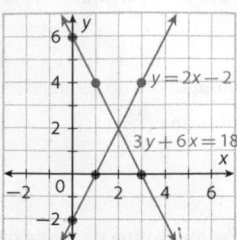

(B) $\begin{cases} y = 2x - 2 \\ 3y + 6x = 18 \end{cases}$

Find the intercepts for each equation, plus a third point for a check. Then graph.

$y = 2x - 2$ $3y + 6x = 18$

x-intercept: **1**   x-intercept: **3**

y-intercept: **−2**   y-intercept: **6**

third point: $\left(3, \boxed{4}\right)$ third point: $\left(1, \boxed{4}\right)$

The two lines appear to intersect at $\boxed{(2, 2)}$. Check.

$y = 2x - 2$ $y + 2x = 6$

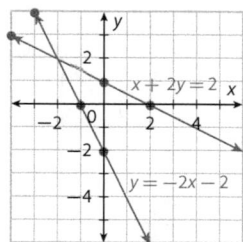

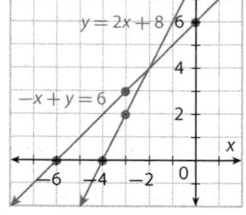

The point satisfies both equations, so the solution is $\boxed{(2, 2)}$.

Reflect

2. How do you know that the systems of equations are consistent? How do you know that they are independent?

I know the systems of equations are consistent because they have at least one solution

and they are independent because they have exactly one solution.

Your Turn

Solve the system of linear equations by graphing. Check your answer.

3. $\begin{cases} y = -2x - 2 \\ x + 2y = 2 \end{cases}$ **4.** $\begin{cases} y = 2x + 8 \\ -x + y = 6 \end{cases}$

The two lines appear to intersect at $(-2, 2)$.   The two lines appear to intersect at $(-2, 4)$.

$y = -2x - 2$ $x + 2y = 2$ $y = 2x + 8$ $-x + y = 6$

$2 \stackrel{?}{=} -2(-2) - 2$ $-2 + 2(2) \stackrel{?}{=} 2$ $4 \stackrel{?}{=} 2(-2) + 8$ $-(-2) + 4 \stackrel{?}{=} 6$

$2 = 2$ $2 = 2$ $4 = 4$ $6 = 6$

The solution is $(-2, 2)$ The solution is $(-2, 4)$.

COLLABORATIVE LEARNING

Peer-to-Peer Activity

Have students work in pairs to find an approximate solution to a system of linear equations whose solution has non-integer coordinates. One should estimate the solution by graphing, and the other should check the reasonableness of the estimate. Have each pair of students solve several systems of equations, taking turns in the two roles.

Solving Special Linear Systems by Graphing

Example 2 Solve the special system of equations by graphing and identify the system.

(A) $\begin{cases} y = 2x - 2 \\ -2x + y = 4 \end{cases}$

Find the intercepts for each equation, plus a third point for a check.

$y = 2x - 2$	$-2x + y = 4$
x-intercept: 1	x-intercept: -2
y-intercept: -2	y-intercept: 4
third point: $(2, 2)$	third point: $(2, 8)$

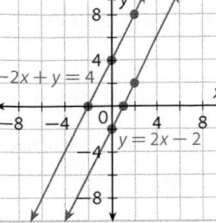

The two lines don't intersect, so there is no solution.
The two lines have the same slope and different y-intercepts so they will never intersect. This is an inconsistent system.

(B) $\begin{cases} y = 3x - 3 \\ -3x + y = -3 \end{cases}$

Find the intercepts for each equation, plus a third point for a check.

$y = 3x - 3$	$-3x + y = -3$
x-intercept: 1	x-intercept: 1
y-intercept: -3	y-intercept: -3
third point: $\left(2, \boxed{3}\right)$	third point: $\left(2, \boxed{3}\right)$

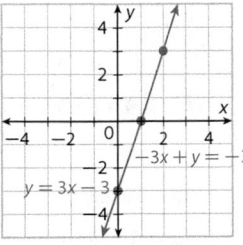

The two lines coincide, so there are __infinitely many__ solutions.

They have the same slope and y-intercept; therefore, they are __the same__ line(s) / equation(s).

This is a __consistent__ and __dependent__ system.

Your Turn

Solve the special system of linear equations by graphing. Check your answer.

5. $\begin{cases} y = -x - 2 \\ x + y + 2 = 0 \end{cases}$

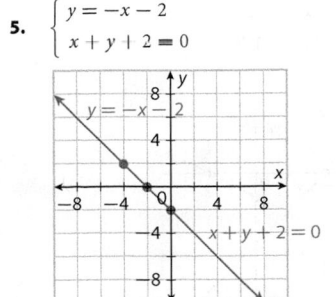

The two lines coincide, so there are infinitely many solutions.

6. $\begin{cases} y = \frac{2}{3}x - 1 \\ -\frac{2}{3}x + y = 1 \end{cases}$

The two lines don't intersect, so there is no solution.

EXPLAIN 2

Solving Special Linear Systems by Graphing

QUESTIONING STRATEGIES

? If you noticed that two lines had the same slope, what conclusion would you reach about the system of equations? Explain. **The lines are either the same or they are parallel. If they have the same y-intercept, they are the same line (forming a consistent and dependent system). If they do not have the same y-intercept, they are parallel (forming an inconsistent system).**

INTEGRATE MATHEMATICAL PRACTICES
Focus on Critical Thinking

MP.3 Have students graph three linear equations on a grid with the following conditions: two of the lines represent an inconsistent system of the equations, and two of the lines represent a consistent and independent system of equations. Students should recognize that two of the lines must be parallel and the third line must intersect the other two.

DIFFERENTIATE INSTRUCTION

Graphic Organizer

Have students complete the graphic organizer that shows the possible solutions to systems of equations.

Graphs of Equations	Number of Solutions	Type of System
Intersecting lines	1	Consistent and independent
Same line	Infinite number	Consistent and dependent
Parallel lines	0	Inconsistent

EXPLAIN 3

Estimating Solutions of Linear Systems by Graphing

AVOID COMMON ERRORS

Make sure students understand that a graph can give only an approximate solution, so they must verify the solution using algebra.

QUESTIONING STRATEGIES

? Why might an estimated solution be very far from the actual solution? Explain. **It could be far from it if the estimations of the x- and y-values were not very precise. That's why it is important to be as precise as possible.**

? If the solution is estimated very precisely, how does this affect your solution check? **The more precisely the solution is estimated, the closer the equations should be to being true.**

AVOID COMMON ERRORS

Some students may reverse the x- and y-coordinates in their solutions. Emphasize that checking their solutions will help correct such errors.

INTEGRATE TECHNOLOGY

Have students use the intersect feature of a graphing calculator to approximate a solution to a system of linear equations.

---

483 Lesson 11.1

You can estimate the solution of a linear system of equations by graphing the system and finding the approximate coordinates of the intersection point.

Example 3 Estimate the solution of the linear system by graphing.

Ⓐ $\begin{cases} x - 3y = 3 \\ -5x + 2y = 10 \end{cases}$

Graph the equations using a graphing calculator.

$Y1 = (3 - X)/(-3)$ and $Y2 = (10 + 5X)/2$

Find the point of intersection.

The two lines appear to intersect at about $(-2.8, -1.9)$.

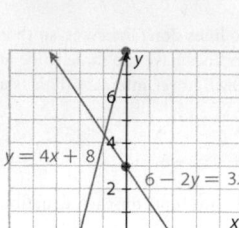

Ⓑ $\begin{cases} 6 - 2y = 3x \\ y = 4x + 8 \end{cases}$

Graph each equation by finding intercepts.

The two lines appear to intersect at about $\boxed{(-1, 4.5)}$.

Check to see if $\boxed{(-1, 4.5)}$ makes both equations true.

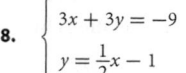

$$6 - 2y = 3x \qquad\qquad y = 4x + 8$$

$$6 - 2\left(\boxed{4.5}\right) \stackrel{?}{=} 3\left(\boxed{-1}\right) \qquad \boxed{4.5} \stackrel{?}{=} 4\left(\boxed{-1}\right) + 8$$

$$\boxed{-3} \approx \boxed{-3} \qquad\qquad \boxed{4.5} \approx \boxed{4}$$

The point does not satisfy both equations, but the results are close.

So, $\boxed{(-1, 4.5)}$ is an approximate solution.

Your Turn

Estimate the solution of the linear system of equations by graphing.

7. $\begin{cases} 2y = -5x + 10 \\ -15 = -3x + 5y \end{cases}$

about $(2.5, -1.5)$

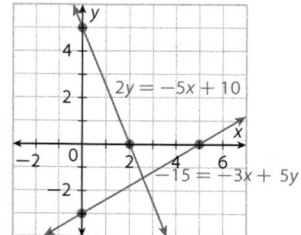

8. $\begin{cases} 3x + 3y = -9 \\ y = \frac{1}{2}x - 1 \end{cases}$

about $(-1.5, -1.5)$

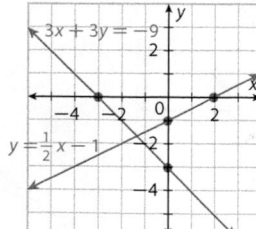

LANGUAGE SUPPORT 🔲EL

Connect Vocabulary

Explain that the prefix *in-* means not, so *independent* is the opposite of *dependent* and *inconsistent* is the opposite of *consistent*. Ask students what other prefixes they have seen turn a word into its opposite. They may think of *un-* as in *unhappy*; *im-* as in *impossible*; and *non-* as in *nonfiction*. Have them list several words and their meanings as examples of how these prefixes function.

Explain 4   Interpreting Graphs of Linear Systems to Solve Problems

You can solve problems with real-world context by graphing the equations that model the problem and finding a common point.

Example 4   Rock and Bowl charges $2.75 per game plus $3 for shoe rental. Super Bowling charges $2.25 per game and $3.50 for shoe rental. For how many games will the cost to bowl be approximately the same at both places? What is that cost?

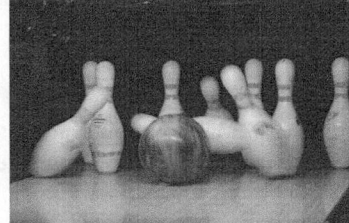

Analyze Information

Identify the important information.

- Rock and Bowl charges $ **2.75** per game plus $ **3** for shoe rental.
- Super Bowling charges $ **2.25** per game and $ **3.50** for shoe rental.
- The answer is the number of games played for which the total cost is approximately the same at both bowling alleys.

Formulate a Plan

Write a system of linear equations, where each equation represents the price at each bowling alley.

$$\begin{cases} y = 2.75x + 3 \\ y = 2.25x + 3.50 \end{cases}$$

Solve

Graph $y = 2.75x + 3$ and $y = 2.25x + 3.50$.

The lines appear to intersect at **(1, 5.75)**. So, the cost at both

places will be the same for **1** game(s) bowled and that

cost will be **$5.75**.

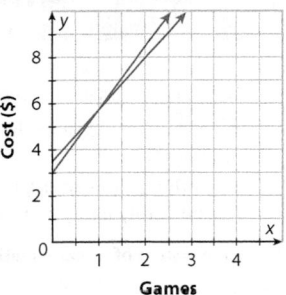

Cost ($) / Games

Justify and Evaluate

Check **(1, 5.75)** using both equations.

$$2.75\left(\boxed{1}\right) + 3 = \boxed{5.75} \qquad 2.25\left(\boxed{1}\right) + 3.5 = \boxed{5.75}$$

Reflect

9. Which bowling alley costs more if you bowl more than 1 game? Explain how you can tell by looking at the graph.

   The Rock and Bowl costs more, because after 1 on the graph, the line that represents the

   Rock and Bowl is higher than the line for Super Bowling.

EXPLAIN 4

Interpreting Graphs of Linear Systems to Solve Problems

INTEGRATE MATHEMATICAL PRACTICES
Focus on Math Connections

MP.1 Point out to students that finding solutions to linear systems of equations is important in the real world. For example, businesses can use systems of equations to model income and expenses and predict profits.

QUESTIONING STRATEGIES

? When you graph a system of linear equations that represents a real-world problem, why does the intersection of the two lines represent the solution to the problem? **Every point on a line satisfies the related linear equation. A point that is on both lines (the intersection point) satisfies both equations, so it represents the solution to the problem.**

AVOID COMMON ERRORS

Students sometimes have difficulty correctly assigning x and y variables in real-world problems. Remind them that the value of y cannot be determined unless the value of x is known. In other words, y is dependent on x.

ELABORATE

INTEGRATE MATHEMATICAL PRACTICES
Focus on Modeling

MP.4 When solving a system of equations by graphing, students should recognize that they can adjust the scale of a graph, setting each grid square to represent a smaller unit, in order to estimate a solution more precisely. The intersection of the lines represents an exact rather than an approximate solution when a solution check reveals that it satisfies both equations.

SUMMARIZE THE LESSON

? How can you use a graph to solve a system of linear equations? First, graph both equations in the system. If the lines are parallel, there is no solution. If the lines are the same, there are infinitely many solutions. If the lines intersect in one point, the coordinates of that point are the solution. If the intersection is on the intersection of grid lines, you can find an exact solution. If not, you can estimate the solution.

Your Turn

10. Video club A charges \$10 for membership and \$4 per movie rental. Video club B charges \$15 for membership and \$3 per movie rental. For how many movie rentals will the cost be the same at both video clubs? What is that cost? Write a system and solve by graphing.

$$\begin{cases} y = 4x + 10 \\ y = 3x + 15 \end{cases}$$

The lines appear to intersect at (5, 30).

The cost will be the same for renting 5 movies, and that cost will be \$30.

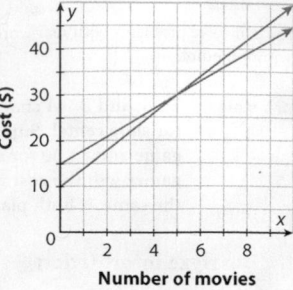

Number of movies

💬 Elaborate

11. When a system of linear equations is graphed, how is the graph of each equation related to the solutions of that equation?
The solution is indicated by the point of intersection.

12. **Essential Question Check-In** How does graphing help you solve a system of linear equations?
If the lines intersect at one point, the solution is the coordinates of the point of intersection. If the lines do not intersect at one point, the system has either infinitely many solutions or no solutions.

⭐ Evaluate: Homework and Practice

- Online Homework
- Hints and Help
- Extra Practice

1. Is the following statement correct? Explain.

A system of two equations has no solution if the graphs of the two equations are coincident lines.

No, if the graphs of the two equations are coincident lines, the system has infinitely many solutions.

Solve the system of linear equations by graphing. Check your answer.

2. $\begin{cases} y = 2x - 4 \\ x + 2y = 12 \end{cases}$ **(4, 4)**

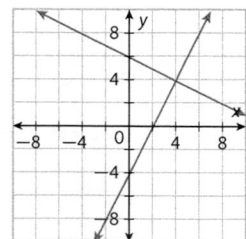

3. $\begin{cases} y = -\frac{1}{3}x + 2 \\ y + 4 = -\frac{4}{3}x \end{cases}$ **(−6, 4)**

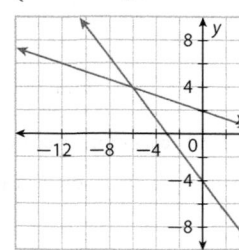

4. $\begin{cases} y = -x - 6 \\ y = x \end{cases}$ $(-3, -3)$

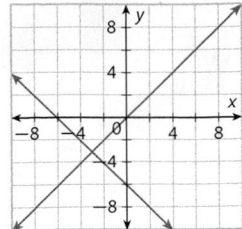

5. $\begin{cases} y = \frac{4}{3}x - 4 \\ y = 4 \end{cases}$ $(6, 4)$

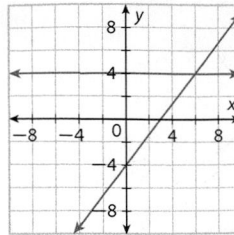

6. $\begin{cases} y = -2x + 2 \\ y + 2 = 2x \end{cases}$ $(1, 0)$

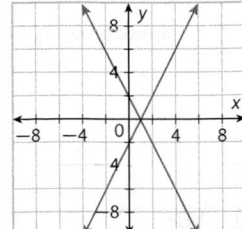

7. $\begin{cases} y = \frac{1}{2}x + 5 \\ \frac{2}{3}x + y = -2 \end{cases}$ $(-6, 2)$

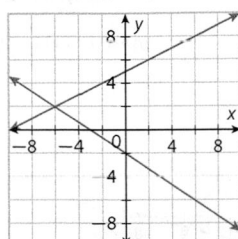

8. $\begin{cases} y = \frac{1}{2}x - 2 \\ -\frac{1}{2}x + y - 3 = 0 \end{cases}$ No solutions

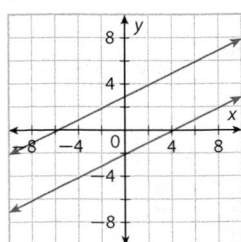

9. $\begin{cases} y = 2x + 4 \\ -4x + 2y = 8 \end{cases}$ Infinitely many solutions

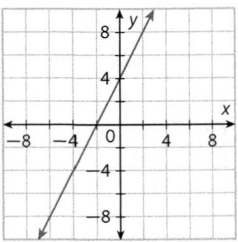

10. $\begin{cases} y = -3x + 1 \\ 12x + 4y = 4 \end{cases}$ Infinitely many solutions

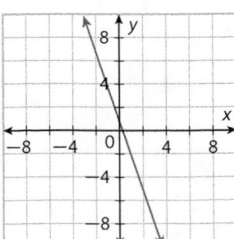

11. $\begin{cases} y = 4x + 4 \\ -4x + y + 4 = 0 \end{cases}$ No solutions

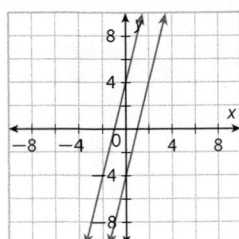

© Houghton Mifflin Harcourt Publishing Company

EVALUATE

ASSIGNMENT GUIDE

Concepts and Skills	Practice
Explore Types of Systems of Linear Equations	Exercises 1, 22
Example 1 Solving Consistent, Independent Linear Systems by Graphing	Exercises 2–7, 24
Example 2 Solving Special Linear Systems by Graphing	Exercises 8–13, 23
Example 3 Estimating Solutions of Linear Systems by Graphing	Exercises 14–17
Example 4 Interpreting Graphs of Linear Systems to Solve Problems	Exercises 18–21, 25

MULTIPLE REPRESENTATIONS

Students can choose one of several methods to graph the linear equations in the systems. They can make a table of values and find ordered pairs; they can find the x- and y-intercepts for each line; or they can find the slope and y-intercept of each line.

Exercise	Depth of Knowledge (D.O.K.)	**COMMON CORE** Mathematical Practices
1	**1** Recall of Information	**MP.2** Reasoning
2–13	**1** Recall of Information	**MP.4** Modeling
14–17	**2** Skills/Concepts	**MP.4** Modeling
18–21	**2** Skills/Concepts	**MP.4** Modeling
22	**2** Skills/Concepts	**MP.2** Reasoning
23–24	**3** Strategic Thinking **H.O.T.**	**MP.2** Reasoning
25	**3** Strategic Thinking **H.O.T.**	**MP.4** Modeling

MULTIPLE REPRESENTATIONS

Some students may need help graphing linear systems. Remind students that they can solve the equation for *y* to give the slope-intercept form of the equation. They can then plot the point for the *y*-intercept, use the slope to find another point, and then draw a line through the points.

12. $\begin{cases} y = -\frac{3}{4}x + \frac{1}{4} \\ \frac{3}{4}x + y - 2 = 0 \end{cases}$ **No solutions**

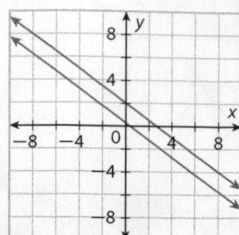

13. $\begin{cases} y = 5x - 1 \\ -5x + y + 4 = 3 \end{cases}$ **Infinitely many solutions**

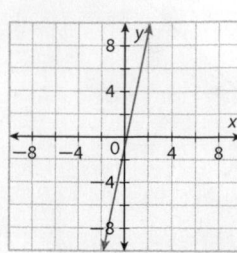

Estimate the solution of the linear system of equations by graphing.

14. $\begin{cases} 3y = -5x + 15 \\ -14 = -2x + 7y \end{cases}$ **approximately** $(4, -1)$

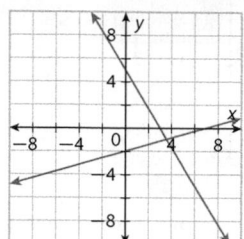

15. $\begin{cases} 2y + 5x = 14 \\ -35 = -5x + 7y \end{cases}$ **approximately** $(4, -2)$

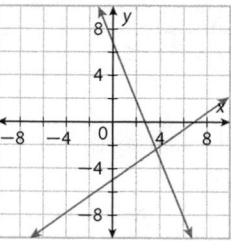

16. $\begin{cases} \frac{4}{7}y = x + 4 \\ 2x - 5y = 10 \end{cases}$ **approximately** $(-7, -5)$

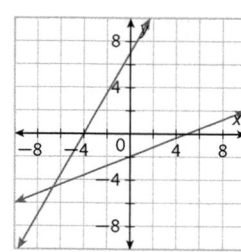

17. $\begin{cases} 6y = 5x + 30 \\ 2 = -\frac{2}{7}x + y \end{cases}$ **approximately** $(-6, 0)$

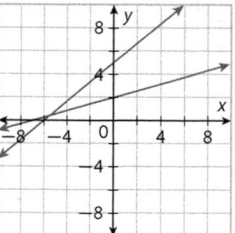

Solve by graphing. Give an approximate solution if necessary.

18. Wren and Jenni are reading the same book. Wren is on page 12 and reads 3 pages every night. Jenni is on page 7 and reads 4 pages every night. After how many nights will they have read the same number of pages? How many pages will that be?

$\begin{cases} y = 3x + 12 \\ y = 4x + 7 \end{cases}$ (5, 27)

Wren and Jenni will each have read 27 pages after 5 nights.

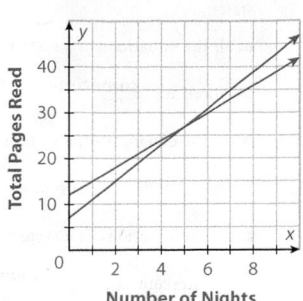

Number of Nights

19. Rusty burns 6 calories per minute swimming and 10 calories per minute jogging. In the morning, Rusty burns 175 calories walking and swims for x minutes. In the afternoon, Rusty will jog for x minutes. How many minutes must he jog to burn at least as many calories y in the afternoon as he did in the morning? Round your answer up to the next whole number of minutes.

$\begin{cases} y = 6x + 175 \\ y = 10x \end{cases}$ approximately (45, 450)

After about 45 minutes, Rusty will have burned about 450 calories each time.

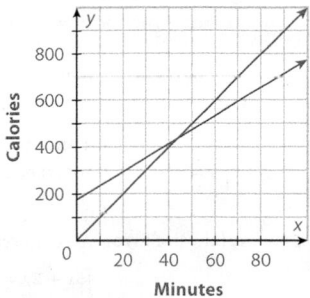

Minutes

20. A gym membership at one gym costs $10 every month plus a one-time membership fee of $15, and a gym membership at another gym costs $4 every month plus a one-time $40 membership fee. After about how many months will the gym memberships cost the same amount?

$\begin{cases} y = 10x + 15 \\ y = 4x + 40 \end{cases}$ approximately (4, 55)

After about 4 months, both gym memberships will cost about $55.

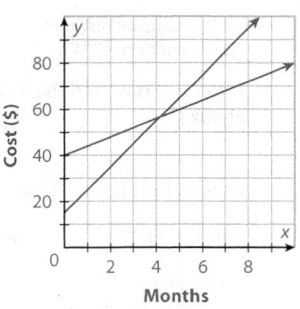

Months

21. Malory is putting money in two savings accounts. Account A started with $150 and Account B started with $300. Malory deposits $16 in Account A and $12 in Account B each month. In how many months will Account A have a balance at least as great as Account B? What will that balance be?

$\begin{cases} y = 16x + 150 \\ y = 12x + 300 \end{cases}$ approximately (37, 750)

Account A have a balance at least as great as Account B in about 37 months. The balance will be about $750.

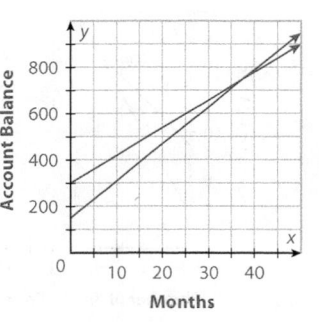

Months

AVOID COMMON ERRORS

Make sure students understand that it is always important to check their solutions. When doing this, they should be sure to substitute the variables into the original equations, not a version of the equation they manipulated while calculating the solution.

PEER-TO-PEER DISCUSSION

Have students discuss with a partner the three types of systems of linear equations (inconsistent; consistent and dependent; and consistent and independent). They should consider the characteristics and number of solutions for each type, then write and graph a system of equations that illustrates each type.

INTEGRATE TECHNOLOGY

Have students use a spreadsheet to model a real-world linear relationship. By changing one or more coefficients, they can easily model variations to a scenario.

JOURNAL

Have students write a journal entry explaining how to solve a system of equations graphically. Students should mention both exact and approximate solutions.

22. Critical Thinking Write *sometimes*, *always*, or *never* to complete the following statements.

a. If the equations in a system of linear equations have the same slope, there are ___**sometimes**___ infinitely many solutions for the system.

b. If the equations in a system of linear equations have different slopes, there is ___**always**___ one solution for the system.

c. If the equations in a system of linear equations have the same slope and a different y-intercept, there is ___**never**___ any solution for the system.

H.O.T. **Focus on Higher Order Thinking**

23. Critique Reasoning Brad classifies the system below as inconsistent because the equations have the same y-intercept. What is his error?

$$\begin{cases} y = 2x - 4 \\ y = x - 4 \end{cases}$$ **Inconsistent systems have the same slope, but different y-intercepts. This system is consistent and independent.**

24. Explain the Error Alexa solved the system

$$\begin{cases} 5x + 2y = 6 \\ x - 3y = -4 \end{cases}$$

by graphing and estimated the solution to be about $(1.5, 0.6)$. What is her error? What is the correct answer?

Alexa has reversed the x- and y-values. The correct answer is about $(0.6, 1.5)$.

25. Represent Real-World Problems Cora ran 3 miles last week and will run 7 miles per week from now on. Hana ran 9 miles last week and will run 4 miles per week from now on. The system of linear equations $\begin{cases} y = 7x + 3 \\ y = 4x + 9 \end{cases}$ can be used to represent this situation. Explain what x and y represent in the equations. After how many weeks will Cora and Hana have run the same number of miles? How many miles? Solve by graphing.

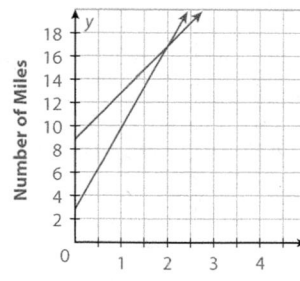

The variable x represents the number of weeks from now, and y represents the total number of miles run by each person.

after 2 weeks; 17 miles

Lesson Performance Task

A boat takes 7.5 hours to make a 60-mile trip upstream and 6 hours on the 60-mile return trip. Let v be the speed of the boat in still water and c be the speed of the current. The upstream speed of the boat is $v - c$ and the downstream boat speed is $v + c$.

a. Use the distance formula to write a system of equations relating boat speed and time to distance, one equation for the upstream part of the trip and one for the downstream part.

b. Graph the system to find the speed of the boat in still water and the speed of the current.

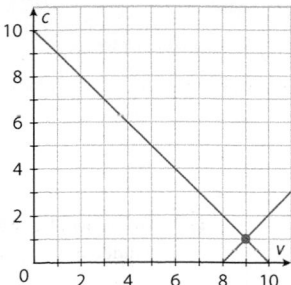

c. How long would it take the boat to travel the 60 miles if there were no current?

a. $\begin{cases} (v - c)7.5 = 60 \\ (v + c)6 = 60 \end{cases}$

b. Find the point of intersection of the graphs. The graphs appear to intersect at (9, 1).

Check using both equations.

$(9 - 1)7.5 = 8(7.5) = 60$

$(9 + 1)6 = 10(6) = 60$

The speed v of the boat in still water is 9 mi/h.

The speed of the current is 1 mi/h.

c. $\dfrac{60 \text{ mi}}{9 \text{ mi/h}} = 6\dfrac{2}{3}$ h or 6 h 40 min

---

INTEGRATE MATHEMATICAL PRACTICES
Focus on Communication

MP.3 Have students explain their reasoning for which variable to put on the horizontal axis and which to put on the vertical axis when graphing the system of equations. Students should discover that whether they put v on the horizontal axis and c on the vertical axis or the other way around, the result will be $v = 9$ when $c = 1$.

INTEGRATE MATHEMATICAL PRACTICES
Focus on Reasoning

MP.2 Before students calculate how long it would take for the boat to travel the 60 miles if there were no current, have them predict whether it will be less than 6 hours, between 6 and 7.5 hours, or more than 7.5 hours, and explain their reasoning. Have them compare their calculated results to their predictions.

EXTENSION ACTIVITY

Have students consider a boat that is traveling from one side of the river to the opposite bank. Have students research how the current affects the speed of this boat differently from the way it affects a boat traveling upstream or downstream.

Students should find that if the boat heads directly toward the opposite shore, the current will cause it to travel at an angle. They may find that the Pythagorean theorem can be used to determine the resulting speed of the boat, because the current is at a right angle to the direction of the boat.

Scoring Rubric

2 points: Student correctly solves the problem and explains his/her reasoning.

1 point: Student shows good understanding of the problem but does not fully solve or explain his/her reasoning.

0 points: Student does not demonstrate understanding of the problem.

Solving Linear Systems by Graphing   **490**

Solving Linear Systems by Substitution

Common Core Math Standards

The student is expected to:

 **A-REI.C.6**

Solve systems of linear equations exactly... focusing on pairs of linear equations in two variables.

Mathematical Practices

 MP.6 Precision

Language Objective

Explain to a partner how to solve a system of linear equations by substitution.

ENGAGE

Essential Question: How can you solve a system of linear equations by using substitution?

Solve one equation for one variable and substitute the resulting expression into the other equation. Solve for the value of the other variable in that equation, and then substitute that value into either equation to find the value of the first variable.

PREVIEW: LESSON PERFORMANCE TASK

View the Engage section online. Discuss why a manufacturer might choose to produce either a cheaper version or a more expensive version of a product. Then preview the Lesson Performance Task.

Name _____ Class _____ Date _____

11.2 Solving Linear Systems by Substitution

Resource Locker

Essential Question: How can you solve a system of linear equations by using substitution?

Explore   Exploring the Substitution Method of Solving Linear Systems

Another method to solve a linear system is by using the substitution method.

In the system of linear equations shown, the value of y is given. Use this value of y to find the value of x and the solution of the system.

$$\begin{cases} y = 2 \\ x + y = 6 \end{cases}$$

(A) Substitute the value of y in the second equation and solve for x.

$$x + y = 6$$
$$x + \boxed{2} = 6$$
$$x = \boxed{4}$$

(B) The values of x and y are known. What is the solution of the system?

Solution: $\left(\boxed{4}, \boxed{2}\right)$

(C) Graph the system of linear equations. How do your solutions compare? **The solutions are the same.**

(D) Use substitution to find the values of x and y in this system of linear equations. Substitute $4x$ for y in the second equation and solve for x. Once you find the value for x, substitute it into either original equation to find the value for y.

$$\begin{cases} y = 4x \\ 5x + 2y = 39 \end{cases}$$

Solution: $\left(\boxed{3}, \boxed{12}\right)$

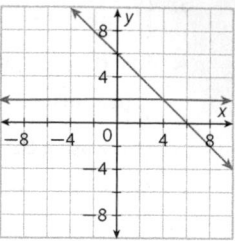

Reflect

1. **Discussion** For the system in Step D, what equation did you get after substituting $4x$ for y in $5x + 2y = 39$ and simplifying?
   $13x = 39$

2. **Discussion** How could you check your solution in part D?
   Graph the system or substitute the values of the variables in both of the original equations.

Module 11　　　　　　　**491**　　　　　　　Lesson 2

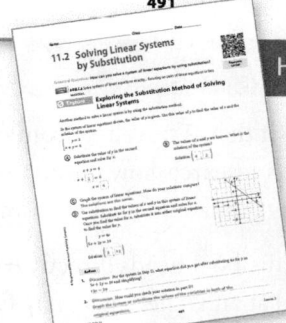

HARDCOVER PAGES 395–404

Turn to these pages to find this lesson in the hardcover student edition.

© Houghton Mifflin Harcourt Publishing Company

The **substitution method** is used to solve a system of equations by solving an equation for one variable and substituting the resulting expression into the other equation. The steps for the substitution method are as shown.

1. Solve one of the equations for one of its variables.
2. Substitute the expression from Step 1 into the other equation and solve for the other variable.
3. Substitute the value from Step 2 into either original equation and solve to find the value of the other variable.

Example 1 Solve each system of linear equations by substitution.

Ⓐ $\begin{cases} 3x + y = -3 \\ -2x + y = 7 \end{cases}$

Solve an equation for one variable.

$3x + y = -3$	Select one of the equations.
$y = -3x - 3$	Solve for y. Isolate y on one side.

Substitute the expression for y in the other equation and solve.

$-2x + (-3x - 3) = 7$	Substitute the expression for y.
$-5x - 3 = 7$	Combine like terms.
$-5x = 10$	Add 3 to both sides.
$x = -2$	Divide each side by -5.

Substitute the value for x into one of the equations and solve for y.

$3(-2) + y = -3$	Substitute the value of x into the first equation.
$-6 + y = -3$	Simplify.
$y = 3$	Add 6 to both sides.

So, $(-2, 3)$ is the solution of the system.

Check the solution by graphing.

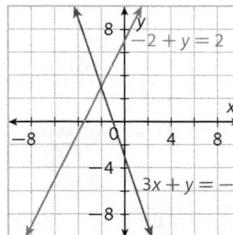

$3x + y = -3$	$-2x + y = 7$
x-intercept: -1	x-intercept: $\dfrac{7}{2}$
y-intercept: -3	y-intercept: 7

The point of intersection is $(-2, 3)$.

EXPLORE

Exploring the Substitution Method of Solving Linear Systems

INTEGRATE TECHNOLOGY

Have students use the graphing tools available in graphing calculators or online to check the solution to a system of linear equations.

INTEGRATE MATHEMATICAL PRACTICES
Focus on Modeling

MP.4 Make sure that students understand the connection between a system of linear equations and its graph. The intersection of the two lines shows the solution of the system of equations.

EXPLAIN 1

Solving Consistent, Independent Linear Systems by Substitution

QUESTIONING STRATEGIES

? How do you choose which equation you solve first and which variable you solve it for? Explain. **Look for an equation that can easily be solved for one variable, such as an equation in which one variable has a coefficient of 1 or −1. The solution will be the same no matter which equation you solve first, but this will make the process easier.**

PROFESSIONAL DEVELOPMENT

Learning Progressions

In this lesson, students continue their work with systems of linear equations. Having learned how to solve a system by graphing, they now learn how to solve a system algebraically by using the substitution method. They learn how to determine whether a system has zero, one, or infinitely many solutions, as well as how to use systems of linear equations to model real-world situations. As they continue, students will learn other algebraic methods for solving systems of linear equations, and will learn how to decide which approach is more efficient for a given system.

AVOID COMMON ERRORS

Make sure students understand that after you find the value of one variable, you must also solve for the other variable. Some students may consider their work done when they have evaluated one variable.

(B) $\begin{cases} x - 3y = 9 \\ x + 4y = 2 \end{cases}$

Solve an equation for one variable.

$x - 3y = 9$	Select one of the equations.
$x = \boxed{3y + 9}$	Solve for x. Isolate x on one side.

Substitute the expression for $\underline{\quad x \quad}$ in the other equation and solve.

$\boxed{\left(3y + 9\right)} + 4y = 2$	Substitute the expression for $\underline{\quad x \quad}$.
$\boxed{7y + 9} = 2$	Combine like terms.
$7y = \boxed{-7}$	Subtract $\boxed{9}$ from both sides.
$y = \boxed{-1}$	Divide each side by $\boxed{7}$.

Substitute the value for y into one of the equations and solve for x.

$x - 3\left(\boxed{-1}\right) = 9$	Substitute the value of y into the first equation.
$\boxed{x + 3} = 9$	Simplify.
$x = \boxed{6}$	Subtract $\boxed{3}$ from both sides.

So, $\left(\boxed{6}, \boxed{-1}\right)$ is the solution by graphing.

Check the solution by graphing.

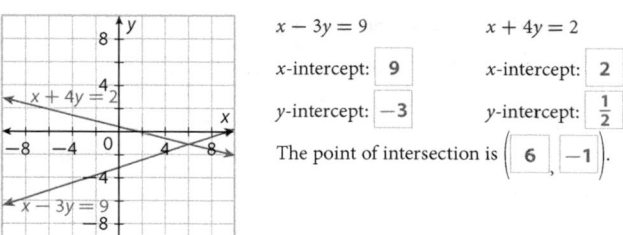

$x - 3y = 9$		$x + 4y = 2$	
x-intercept:	$\boxed{9}$	x-intercept:	$\boxed{2}$
y-intercept:	$\boxed{-3}$	y-intercept:	$\boxed{\frac{1}{2}}$

The point of intersection is $\left(\boxed{6}, \boxed{-1}\right)$.

Reflect

3. Explain how a system in which one of the equations if of the form $y = c$, where c is a constant is a special case of the substitution method.

There is no need to solve for y in terms of x because the value of y is already known.

4. Is it more efficient to solve $-2x + y = 7$ for x than for y? Explain.

No, because more steps are needed and $x = \dfrac{y}{2} - \dfrac{7}{2}$, which is more difficult to substitute than $y = 2x + 7$.

COLLABORATIVE LEARNING

Peer-to-Peer Activity

Group students in pairs, and give each pair a system of linear equations. Have one student solve the first equation for y and the other solve the second equation for y. Then have both students continue to solve independently using substitution. Each should arrive at the same solution. Have partners compare their work and discuss which substitution is more efficient.

5. Solve the system of linear equations by substitution.

$$\begin{cases} 3x + y = 14 \\ 2x - 6y = -24 \end{cases}$$

$y = -3x + 14$

$2x - 6(-3x + 14) = -24$

$x = 3$

$3(3) + y = 14$

$y = 5$

The solution of the system is $(3, 5)$.

Explain 2   Solving Special Linear Systems by Substitution

You can use the substitution method for systems of linear equations that have infinitely many solutions and for systems that have no solutions.

Example 2   Solve each system of linear equations by substitution.

(A) $\begin{cases} x + y = 4 \\ -x - y = 6 \end{cases}$

Solve $x + y = 4$ for x.

$$x = -y + 4$$

Substitute the resulting expression into the other equation and solve.

$-(-y + 4) - y = 6$ Substitute.

$-4 = 6$ Simplify.

The resulting equation is false, so the system has no solutions.

(B) $\begin{cases} x - 3y = 6 \\ 4x - 12y = 24 \end{cases}$

Solve $x - 3y = 6$ for $\underline{x}$.

$$x = \boxed{3y + 6}$$

Substitute the resulting expression into the other equation and solve.

$4\left[\boxed{3y + 6}\right] - 12y = 24$ Substitute.

$\boxed{24} = 24$ Simplify.

The resulting equation is $\underline{\text{true}}$, so the system has $\underline{\text{infinitely many solutions}}$.

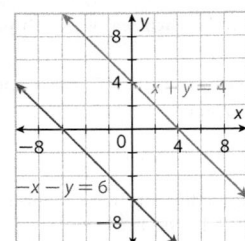

The graph shows that the lines are parallel and do not intersect.

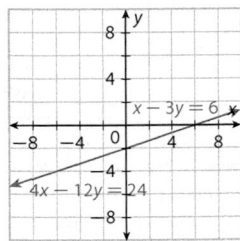

The graphs are $\underline{\text{the same line}}$, so the system has $\underline{\text{infinitely many solutions}}$.

Reflect

6. Provide two possible solutions of the system in Example 2B. How are all the solutions of this system related to one another?

Sample solutions: $(0, -2)$ and $(6, 0)$; all the solutions of this system are points on the line.

EXPLAIN 2

Solving Special Linear Systems by Substitution

QUESTIONING STRATEGIES

? When solving a system of linear equations by substitution, how can you tell if the system has no solution or infinitely many solutions? If it has no solutions, the solution process will result in an equation that is false. If it has infinitely many solutions, the solution process will result in an equation that is always true.

? How does the graph of a system of linear equations tell you it has no solution or infinitely many solutions? When the equations represent two parallel lines, the lines do not intersect, so there is no solution. When both equations represent the same line, the system has infinitely many solutions.

AVOID COMMON ERRORS

Make sure students understand that when you substitute an expression for a variable, the expression should be placed inside parentheses. Remind students to follow the order of operations and to apply the Distributive Property correctly when dealing with expressions inside parentheses.

INTEGRATE MATHEMATICAL PRACTICES
Focus on Critical Thinking

MP.3 You can use algebra tiles to model and solve some systems of linear equations. Solve for one variable using the first equation, then model the second equation.

EXPLAIN 3

Solving Linear System Models by Substitution

AVOID COMMON ERRORS

Some students may struggle with solving by substitution because they automatically start by solving the first equation for y. Encourage them to look at both equations and check whether any of the variables has a coefficient of 1 or -1. Then have students solve for that variable first.

QUESTIONING STRATEGIES

? Is it more accurate to check your solution by graphing or by substituting back into the original equations? Explain. **Substituting, because if the solution does not consist of integers, graphing may not give an accurate check.**

INTEGRATE MATHEMATICAL PRACTICES

Focus on Technology

MP.5 Some real-world problems, especially those involving money, may have systems of equations with decimal coefficients. It is far easier to use a graphing calculator to check the solution than it is to draw the graph by hand.

Solve each system of linear equations by substitution.

7. $\begin{cases} -2x + 14y = -28 \\ x - 7y = 14 \end{cases}$

$x = 7y + 14$
$-2(7y + 14) + 14y = -28$
$-28 = -28$
infinitely many solutions

8. $\begin{cases} -3x + y = 12 \\ 6x - 2y = 18 \end{cases}$

$y = 3x + 12$
$6x - 2(3x + 12) = 18$
$-24 = 18$
no solutions

⊘ Explain 3 Solving Linear System Models by Substitution

You can use a system of linear equations to model real-world situations.

Example 3 Solve each real-world situation by using the substitution method.

(A) Fitness center A has a $60 enrollment fee and costs $35 per month. Fitness center B has no enrollment fee and costs $45 per month. Let t represent the total cost in dollars and m represent the number of months. The system of equations $\begin{cases} t = 60 + 35m \\ t = 45m \end{cases}$ can be used to represent this situation. In how many months will both fitness centers cost the same? What will the cost be?

$60 + 35m = 45m$	Substitute $60 + 35m$ for t in the second equation.
$60 = 10m$	Subtract $35m$ from each side.
$6 = m$	Divide each side by 10.
$t = 45m$	Use one of the original equations.
$= 45(6) = 270$	Substitute 6 for m.
$(6, 270)$	Write the solution as an ordered pair.

Both fitness centers will cost $270 after 6 months.

(B) High-speed Internet provider A has a $100 setup fee and costs $65 per month. High-speed internet provider B has a setup fee of $30 and costs $70 per month. Let t represent the total amount paid in dollars and m represent the number of months. The system of equations $\begin{cases} t = 100 + 65m \\ t = 30 + 70m \end{cases}$ can be used to represent this situation. In how many months will both providers cost the same? What will that cost be?

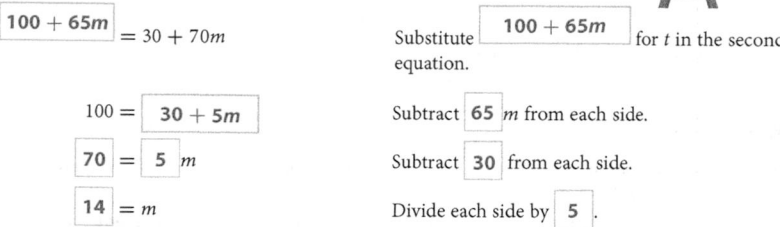

$\boxed{100 + 65m} = 30 + 70m$	Substitute $\boxed{100 + 65m}$ for t in the second equation.
$100 = \boxed{30 + 5m}$	Subtract $\boxed{65}$ m from each side.
$\boxed{70} = \boxed{5}\, m$	Subtract $\boxed{30}$ from each side.
$\boxed{14} = m$	Divide each side by $\boxed{5}$.

DIFFERENTIATE INSTRUCTION

Graphic Organizer

Have students show the steps for solving a system of equations by substitution.

Solving Systems of Equations by Substitution
Step 1 Solve for one variable in one equation.
Step 2 Substitute the resulting expression into the other equation.
Step 3 Solve that equation to get the value of the other variable.
Step 4 Substitute that value into one of the original equations and solve.
Step 5 Write the values from Steps 3 and 4 in an ordered pair (x, y).
Step 6 Check the solution by substituting into both equations or by graphing.

$t = 30 + 70m$ Use one of the original equations.

$t = 30 + 70(\boxed{14})$ Substitute $\boxed{14}$ for m.

$t = \boxed{1010}$

$(\boxed{14}, \boxed{1010})$ Write the sulotion as an ordered pair.

Both Internet providers will cost $\$\underline{1010}$ after $\underline{14}$ months.

Reflect

9. If the variables in a real-world situation represent the number of months and cost, why must the values of the variables be greater than or equal to zero?

The values of the variables must be greater than or equal to zero because the total cost

and the number of months cannot be negative.

Your Turn

10. A boat travels at a rate of 18 kilometers per hour from its port. A second boat is 34 kilometers behind the first boat when it starts traveling in the same direction at a rate of 22 kilometers per hour to the same port. Let d represent the distance the boats are from the port in kilometers and t represent the amount of time in hours. The system of equations $\begin{cases} d = 18t + 34 \\ d = 22t \end{cases}$ can be used to represent this situation. How many hours will it take for the second boat to catch up to the first boat? How far will the boats be from their port? Use the substitution method to solve this real-world application.

$18t + 34 = 22t$ $d = 22t$

$\quad\quad 8.5 = t$ $d = 22(8.5) = 187$

The second boat will catch up in 8.5 hours, and they will be 187 km from their port.

💬 Elaborate

11. When given a system of linear equations, how do you decide which variable to solve for first?

Use a variable that has a coefficient of 1 or −1. If no variables have a coefficient of 1 or −1,

look for a variable that will result in the simplest expression.

12. How can you check a solution for a system of equations without graphing?

Substitute the solution into each equation and determine whether all of the equations in the

system are true.

13. **Essential Question-Check-In** Explain how you can solve a system of linear equations by substitution.

Solve one equation for one variable and use the result to substitute into the other equation.

Solve for the value of the other variable. Then substitute that value into either equation to

find the value of the first variable.

ELABORATE

QUESTIONING STRATEGIES

? Why can you substitute the value of one variable into either of the original equations to find the value of the other variable? **If there is a solution to the system of equations, the values of the variables will satisfy both equations.**

SUMMARIZE THE LESSON

? How do you know if your solution to a system of linear equations is correct? **You can verify your solution by graphing the equations. This allows you to verify that the number of solutions is correct by seeing whether the lines appear to be the same line, two parallel lines, or two lines that intersect at one point. If the lines intersect at one point, you can also substitute the solution back into the original equations to verify your solution.**

LANGUAGE SUPPORT 🔲 EL

Connect Vocabulary

Remind students that the *substitution method* involves *substituting* an expression from one equation into the other equation. Explain that *to substitute* means *to replace*. Note that the word *substitute* can be used as a noun or an adjective: a substitute (noun) in sports replaces the original player, and a substitute (adjective) teacher replaces the regular teacher. Emphasize that expressions used for substitution in math must always be equal in value to the expression they are replacing.

EVALUATE

ASSIGNMENT GUIDE

Concepts and Skills	Practice
Explore Exploring the Substitution Method of Solving Linear Systems	Exercise 1
Example 1 Solving Consistent, Independent Linear Systems by Substitution	Exercises 2–7, 23–25
Example 2 Solving Special Linear Systems by Substitution	Exercises 8–13, 20
Example 3 Solving Linear System Models by Substitution	Exercises 14–19, 21–22

INTEGRATE MATHEMATICAL PRACTICES
Focus on Reasoning

MP.2 Students can check their solutions for correctness by substituting the values into the original equations and verifying that both solutions make both equations true.

☆ Evaluate: Homework and Practice

• Online Homework
• Hints and Help
• Extra Practice

1. In the system of linear equations shown, the value of y is given. Use this value of y to find the value of x and the solution of the system.

$$\begin{cases} y = 12 \\ 2x - y = 4 \end{cases}$$

a. What is the solution of the system?

The solution is $(8, 12)$.

b. Graph the system of linear equations. How do the solutions compare?

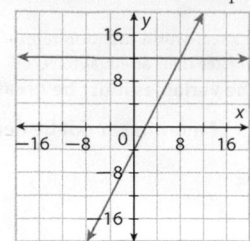

The solutions are the same.

Solve each system of linear equations by substitution.

2. $\begin{cases} 5x + y = 8 \\ 2x + y = 5 \end{cases}$

$y = -5x + 8$
$2x + (-5x + 8) = 5$
$-3x + 8 = 5$
$-3x = -3$
$x = 1$
$5(1) + y = 8$
$5 + y = 8$
$y = 3$
The solution is $(1, 3)$.

3. $\begin{cases} x - 3y = 10 \\ x + 5y = -22 \end{cases}$

$x = 3y + 10$
$(3y + 10) + 5y = -22$
$8y + 10 = -22$
$8y = -32$
$y = -4$
$x - 3(-4) = 10$
$x + 12 = 10$
$x = -2$
The solution is $(-2, -4)$.

4. $\begin{cases} 5x - 3y = 22 \\ -4x + y = -19 \end{cases}$

$y = 4x - 19$
$5x - 3(4x - 19) = 22$
$-7x + 57 = 22$
$-7x = -35$
$x = 5$
$-4(5) + y = -19$
$-20 + y = -19$
$y = 1$
The solution is $(5, 1)$.

5. $\begin{cases} x + 7y = -11 \\ -2x - 5y = 4 \end{cases}$

$x = -7y - 11$
$-2(-7y - 11) - 5y = 4$
$9y + 22 = 4$
$9y = -18$
$y = -2$
$x + 7(-2) = -11$
$x - 14 = -11$
$x = 3$
The solution is $(3, -2)$.

6. $\begin{cases} 2x + 6y = 16 \\ 3x - 5y = -18 \end{cases}$

$2x = -6y + 16$
$x = -3y + 8$
$3(-3y + 8) - 5y = -18$
$-14y + 24 = -18$
$-14y = -42$
$y = 3$
$2x + 6(3) = 16$
$2x + 18 = 16$
$2x = -2$
$x = -1$
The solution is $(-1, 3)$.

7. $\begin{cases} 7x + 2y = 24 \\ -6x + 3y = 3 \end{cases}$

$3y = 6x + 3$
$y = 2x + 1$
$7x + 2(2x + 1) = 24$
$11x + 2 = 24$
$11x = 22$
$x = 2$
$-6(2) + 3y = 3$
$-12 + 3y = 3$
$3y = 15$
$y = 5$
The solution is $(2, 5)$.

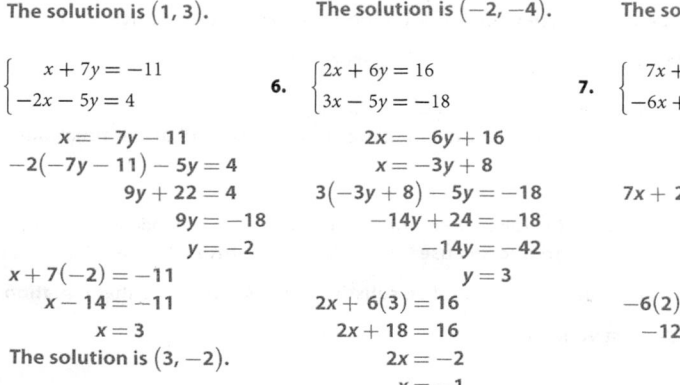

Exercise	Depth of Knowledge (D.O.K.)	**COMMON CORE** Mathematical Practices
1	**2** Skills/Concepts	**MP.4** Modeling
2–13	**1** Recall of Information	**MP.2** Reasoning
14–18	**2** Skills/Concepts	**MP.4** Modeling
19	**3** Strategic Thinking	**MP.4** Modeling
20	**2** Skills/Concepts	**MP.2** Reasoning
21	**2** Skills/Concepts	**MP.4** Modeling

Solve each system of linear equations by substitution.

8. $\begin{cases} x + y = 3 \\ -4x - 4y = 12 \end{cases}$

$x = -y + 3$
$-4(-y + 3) - 4y = 12$
$\qquad -12 = 12$
There is no solution.

9. $\begin{cases} 3x - 3y = -15 \\ -x + y = 5 \end{cases}$

$y = x + 5$
$3x - 3(x + 5) = -15$
$\qquad -15 = -15$
There are infinitely many solutions.

10. $\begin{cases} x - 8y = 17 \\ -3x + 24y = -51 \end{cases}$

$x = 8y + 17$
$-3(8y + 17) + 24y = -51$
$\qquad -51 = -51$
There are infinitely many solutions.

11. $\begin{cases} 5x - y = 18 \\ 10x - 2y = 32 \end{cases}$

$-y = -5x + 18$
$y = 5x - 18$
$10x - 2(5x - 18) = 32$
$\qquad 36 = 32$
There is no solution.

12. $\begin{cases} -2x - 3y = 12 \\ -4x - 6y = 24 \end{cases}$

$x = -\dfrac{3}{2}y - 6$
$-4\left(-\dfrac{3}{2}y - 6\right) - 6y = 24$
$\qquad 24 = 24$
There are infinitely many solutions.

13. $\begin{cases} 3x + 4y = 36 \\ 6x + 8y = 48 \end{cases}$

$3x = -4y + 36$
$x = -\dfrac{4}{3}y + 12$
$6\left(-\dfrac{4}{3}y + 12\right) + 8y = 48$
$\qquad 72 = 48$
There is no solution.

Solve each real-world situation by using the substitution method.

14. The number of DVDs sold at a store in a month was 920 and the number of DVDs sold decreased by 12 per month. The number of Blu-ray discs sold in the same store in the same month was 502 and the number of Blu-ray discs sold increased by 26 per month. Let d represent the number of discs sold and t represent the time in months.

The system of equations $\begin{cases} d = 920 - 12t \\ d = 502 + 26t \end{cases}$ can be

used to represent this situation. If this trend continues, in how many months will the number of DVDs sold equal the number of Blu-ray discs sold? How many of each is sold in that month?

$920 - 12t = 502 + 26t$ 　　　　$d = 502 + 26t$
$\qquad 418 = 38t$ 　　　　　　　$d = 502 + 26(11)$
$\qquad 11 = t$ 　　　　　　　　$d = 788$

There will be 788 DVDs and 788 Blu-Ray discs sold per month in 11 months.

15. One smartphone plan costs \$30 per month for talk and messaging and \$8 per gigabyte of data used each month. A second smartphone plan costs \$60 per month for talk and messaging and \$3 per gigabyte of data used each month. Let c represent the total cost in dollars and d represent the amount of data used in gigabytes. The system of equations $\begin{cases} c = 30 + 8d \\ c = 60 + 3d \end{cases}$ can be used to represent this situation. How many gigabytes would have to be used for the plans to cost the same? What would that cost be?

$30 + 8d = 60 + 3d$ 　　　　$c = 30 + 8(6)$
$\qquad 5d = 30$ 　　　　　　　$c = 78$
$\qquad d = 6$

Both plans would cost \$78 if 6 gigabytes of data are used.

© Houghton Mifflin Harcourt Publishing Company • Image Credits: ©StockPhotosArt/Shutterstock

MODELING

Some students may have difficulty using the substitution method. Suggest to them that they graph the system first, and then use the graph to guide and check their work as they use substitution.

INTEGRATE MATHEMATICAL PRACTICES
Focus on Reasoning

MP.2 Remind students that when using the substitution method to solve a system, it does not matter which variable you solve for first. Demonstrate that whether you solve for x first or y first, you will obtain the same solution. Therefore, you can choose to solve in whichever order is easier. If possible, solve for the variable that has a coefficient of 1 or -1.

Exercise	Depth of Knowledge (D.O.K.)	COMMON CORE Mathematical Practices
22	**3** Strategic Thinking **H.O.T.**	**MP.4** Modeling
23	**3** Strategic Thinking **H.O.T.**	**MP.6** Precision
24–25	**3** Strategic Thinking **H.O.T.**	**MP.3** Logic

16. A movie theater sells popcorn and fountain drinks. Brett buys 1 popcorn bucket and 3 fountain drinks for his family, and pays a total of $9.50. Sarah buys 3 popcorn buckets and 4 fountain drinks for her family, and pays a total of $19.75. If p represents the number of popcorn buckets and d represents the number of drinks, then the system of equations $\begin{cases} 9.50 = p + 3d \\ 19.75 = 3p + 4d \end{cases}$ can be used to represent this situation. Find the cost of a popcorn bucket and the cost of a fountain drink.

$9.50 - 3d = p$ $\qquad\qquad$ $9.50 = p + 3(1.75)$
$19.75 = 3(9.50 - 3d) + 4d$ $\qquad$ $9.50 = p + 5.25$
$\quad 1.75 = d$ $\qquad\qquad\qquad$ $4.25 = p$

The cost of a bucket of popcorn is $4.25 and the cost of a fountain soda is $1.75.

17. Jen is riding her bicycle on a trail at the rate of 0.3 kilometer per minute. Michelle is 11.2 kilometers behind Jen when she starts traveling on the same trail at a rate of 0.44 kilometer per minute. Let d represent the distance in kilometers the bicyclists are from the start of the trail and t represent the time in minutes.

The system of equations $\begin{cases} d = 0.3t + 11.2 \\ d = 0.44t \end{cases}$ can be used to represent this situation. How many minutes will it take Michelle to catch up to Jen? How far will they be from the start of the trail? Use the substitution method to solve this real-world application.

$0.3t + 11.2 = 0.44t$ $\qquad\qquad\qquad$ $d = 0.44t$
$\qquad\quad 80 = t$ $\qquad\qquad\qquad\qquad$ $= 0.44(80) = 35.2$

Michelle will catch up in 80 minutes, and they will be 35.2 km from the start.

18. **Geometry** The length of a rectangular room is 5 feet more than its width. The perimeter of the room is 66 feet. Let L represent the length of the room and W represent the width in feet. The system of equations $\begin{cases} L = W + 5 \\ 66 = 2L + 2W \end{cases}$ can be used to represent this situation. What are the room's dimensions?

$66 = 2(W + 5) + 2W$ $\qquad$ $L = W + 5$
$56 = 4W$ $\qquad\qquad\qquad\quad$ $L = 14 + 5$
$14 = W$ $\qquad\qquad\qquad\quad$ $L = 19$

The room has a width of 14 feet and a length of 19 feet.

19. A cable television provider has a $55 setup fee and charges $82 per month, while a satellite television provider has a $160 setup fee and charges $67 per month. Let c represent the total cost in dollars and t represent the amount of time in months. The system of equations $\begin{cases} c = 55 + 82t \\ c = 160 + 67t \end{cases}$ can be used to represent this situation.

   a. In how many months will both providers cost the same? What will that cost be?

   $55 + 82t = 160 + 67t$ $\qquad$ $c = 55 + 82t$
   $\qquad 15t = 105$ $\qquad\qquad\quad$ $c = 55 + 82(7)$
   $\qquad\quad t = 7$ $\qquad\qquad\qquad\quad$ $= 629$

   Both providers will cost $629 in 7 months.

   b. If you plan to move in 12 months, which provider would be less expensive? Explain.

   Satellite would be less expensive because it costs less per month than cable and 12 months is after 7 months.

20. Determine whether each of the following systems of equations have one solution, infinitely many solutions, or no solution. Select the correct answer for each lettered part.

a. $\begin{cases} x + y = 5 \\ -6y - 6y = 30 \end{cases}$ none

b. $\begin{cases} x + y = 7 \\ 5x + 2y = 23 \end{cases}$ one

c. $\begin{cases} 3x + y = 5 \\ 6x + 2y = 12 \end{cases}$ none

d. $\begin{cases} 2x + 5y = -12 \\ x + 7y = -15 \end{cases}$ one

e. $\begin{cases} 3x + 5y = 17 \\ -6x - 10y = -34 \end{cases}$ infinitely many

21. Finance Adrienne invested a total of $1900 in two simple-interest money market accounts. Account A paid 3% annual interest and account B paid 5% annual interest. The total amount of interest she earned after one year was $83. If a represents the amount invested in dollars in account A and b represents the amount invested in dollars in account B, the system of equations $\begin{cases} a + b = 1900 \\ 0.03a + 0.05b = 83 \end{cases}$ can represent this situation. How much did Adrienne invest in each account?

$$a = -b + 1900 \qquad\qquad a + b = 1900$$
$$0.03(-b + 1900) + 0.05b = 83 \qquad a + (1300) = 1900$$
$$0.02b = 26 \qquad\qquad a = 600$$
$$b = 1300$$

Adrienne invested $600 in account A and $1300 in account B.

H.O.T. **Focus on Higher Order Thinking**

22. Real-World Application The Sullivans are deciding between two landscaping companies. Evergreen charges a $79 startup fee and $39 per month. Eco Solutions charges a $25 startup fee and $45 per month. Let c represent the total cost in dollars and t represent the time in months. The system of equations $\begin{cases} c = 39t + 79 \\ c = 45t + 25 \end{cases}$ can be used to represent this situation.

a. In how many months will both landscaping services cost the same? What will that cost be?

$$39t + 79 = 45t + 25 \qquad\quad c = 45t + 79$$
$$54 = 6t \qquad\qquad c = 39(9) + 79$$
$$9 = t \qquad\qquad\quad = 430$$

Both will cost $430 in 9 months.

b. Which landscaping service will be less expensive in the long term? Explain.

Evergreen will be less expensive than Eco Solutions in the long term. They will cost the same after 9 months but the rate of change for Evergreen is less than the rate of change for Eco Solutions.

VISUAL CUES

After isolating one variable in one equation, some students may find it helpful to highlight the variable with a colored pencil, and then highlight the same variable in the other equation. This will help them remember where in the other equation to substitute the expression for that variable.

JOURNAL

Have students write a journal entry that summarizes how to solve a system of equations by substitution. Students should mention how to decide which equation to use for the substitution.

23. **Multiple Representations** For the first equation in the system of linear equations below, write an equivalent equation without denominators. Then solve the system.

$$\begin{cases} \dfrac{x}{5} + \dfrac{y}{3} = 6 \\ x - 2y = 8 \end{cases}$$

$$15\left(\dfrac{x}{5} + \dfrac{y}{3}\right) = 15(6)$$

$$3x + 5y = 90$$

$$x - 2y = 8$$
$$x = 2y + 8$$

$$3(2y + 8) + 5y = 90$$
$$6y + 24 + 5y = 90$$
$$11y + 24 = 90$$
$$11y = 66$$
$$y = 6$$

$$x - 2(6) = 8$$
$$x - 12 = 8$$
$$x = 20$$

The solution is $(20, 6)$.

24. **Conjecture** Is it possible for a system of three linear equations to have one solution? If so, give an example.

Yes; the solution is an ordered pair that is a solution of each of the equations. For example, the solution of the system containing the equations $3x - y = 5$, $x + y = 3$, and $x = 2y$ is $(2, 1)$.

25. **Conjecture** Is it possible to use substitution to solve a system of linear equations if one equation represents a horizontal line and the other equation represents a vertical line? Explain.

No, the equation of a horizontal line is in the form $y = a$ and the equation of a vertical line is in the form $x = b$. The horizontal line equation has no x-term and the vertical line equation has no y-term.

Lesson Performance Task

A company breaks even from the production and sale of a product if the total revenue equals the total cost. Suppose an electronics company is considering producing two types of smartphones. To produce smartphone A, the initial cost is $20,000 and each phone costs $150 to produce. The company will sell smartphone A at $200. Let $C(a)$ represent the total cost in dollars of producing a units of smartphone A. Let $R(a)$ represent the total revenue, or money the company takes in due to selling a units of smartphone A. The system of equations $\begin{cases} C(a) = 20{,}000 + 150a \\ R(a) = 200a \end{cases}$ can be used to represent the situation for phone A.

To produce smartphone B, the initial cost is $44,000 and each phone costs $200 to produce. The company will sell smartphone B at $280. Let $C(b)$ represent the total cost in dollars of producing b units of smartphone B and $R(b)$ represent the total revenue from

selling b units of smartphone B. The system of equations $\begin{cases} C(b) = 44{,}000 + 200b \\ R(b) = 280b \end{cases}$ can be

used to represent the situation for phone B.

Solve each system of equations and interpret the solutions. Then determine whether the company should invest in producing smartphone A or smartphone B. Justify your answer.

Smartphone A:

$200a = 20{,}000 + 150a$

$50a = 20{,}000$

$a = 400$

$R(a) = 200a$

$= 200(400)$

$= 80{,}000$

The company will break even selling 400 units of smartphone A for a total $80,000.

Smartphone B:

$280b = 44{,}000 + 200b$

$80b = 44{,}000$

$b = 550$

$R(b) = 280b$

$= 280(550)$

$= 154{,}000$

The company will break even selling 550 units of smartphone B for a total of $154,000.

Some students may say that the company should invest in producing smartphone A because the initial cost of producing smartphone A is less than that of producing smartphone B and fewer units of smartphone A would need to be sold for the company to break even. Other students may argue that the company should consider other factors, such as increasing the sale price of smartphone B or looking for ways to cut the initial cost of production.

EXTENSION ACTIVITY

Many companies sell accessories for smartphones. Have students research the different types of accessories sold and make conjectures about how a company might use a system of equations to find the break-even cost in selling these accessories.

QUESTIONING STRATEGIES

? How is profit determined? Profit = total revenue − total cost $= R - C$

? When total revenue equals total cost, what is the profit? What is this situation called? The profit is $0; this is called the break-even point. The break-even points in the Lesson Performance Task are when $C(a) = R(a)$ for smartphone A and $C(b) = R(b)$ for smartphone B.

INTEGRATE MATHEMATICAL PRACTICES

Focus on Technology

MP.8 To check their solutions for smartphone A, have students use graphing calculators to graph $y = 20{,}000 + 150x$ and $y = 200x$ on the same coordinate plane. Then they can go to the **CALC** menu and select the intersect feature to find the coordinates of the point of intersection. Students can use the same procedure with the equations $y = 44{,}000 + 200x$ and $y = 280x$ to check their answers for smartphone B.

Scoring Rubric

2 points: Student correctly solves the problem and explains his/her reasoning.

1 point: Student shows good understanding of the problem but does not fully solve or explain his/her reasoning.

0 points: Student does not demonstrate understanding of the problem.

Solving Linear Systems by Substitution   **502**

Solving Linear Systems by Adding or Subtracting

Common Core Math Standards

The student is expected to:

 A-REI.C.6

Solve systems of linear equations exactly... focusing on pairs of linear equations in two variables.

Mathematical Practices

 MP.2 Reasoning

Language Objective

Explain to a partner what eliminating a variable in a system of linear equations means.

ENGAGE

Essential Question: How can you solve a system of linear equations by adding and subtracting?

If the coefficients of the *x*-terms or *y*-terms are the same or are opposites, you can add or subtract the equations to eliminate a variable. Then you can solve for the remaining variable and substitute that value into either of the original equations to solve for the other variable.

PREVIEW: LESSON PERFORMANCE TASK

View the Engage section online. Discuss how much two runners from the same family save by registering as a family instead of as individuals. Then preview the Lesson Performance Task.

Name_____ Class_____ Date_____

11.3 Solving Linear Systems by Adding or Subtracting

Essential Question: How can you solve a system of linear equations by adding and subtracting?

⊘ Explore Exploring the Effects of Adding Equations

Systems of equations can be solved by graphing, substitution, or by a third method, called **elimination.**

(A) Look at the system of linear equations.
$$\begin{cases} 2x - 4y = -10 \\ 3x + 4y = 5 \end{cases}$$
What do you notice about the coefficients of the *y*-terms?

They are opposites or additive inverses.

(B) What is the sum of $-4y$ and $4y$? How do you know?

0; the sum of opposites is 0.

(C) Find the sum of the two equations by combining like terms.

$2x$	$-4y$	$=$	-10
$+3x$	$+4y$	$=$	$+5$
$\boxed{5x}$ + $\boxed{0}$		$=$	$\boxed{-5}$

(D) Use the equation from Step C to find the value of *x*.

$$x = \boxed{-1}$$

(E) Use the value of *x* to find the value of *y*. What is the solution of the system?

$$y = \boxed{2}$$

Solution: $(-1, 2)$

Reflect

1. **Discussion** How do you know that when both sides of the two equations were added, the resulting sums were equal?
   $2x - 4y = -10$ and $3x + 4y = 5$, so $(2x - 4y) + (3x + 4y) = (-10) + 5$ by the
   Addition Property of Equality.

2. **Discussion** How could you check your solution?
   Solve the system by graphing or substitute the values of the variables into the original
   equations.

Module 11   503   Lesson 3

© Houghton Mifflin Harcourt Publishing Company

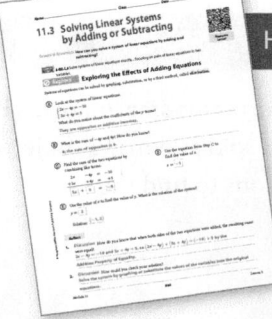

HARDCOVER PAGES 405–412

Turn to these pages to find this lesson in the hardcover student edition.

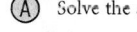

The **elimination method** is a method used to solve systems of equations in which one variable is eliminated by adding or subtracting two equations in the system.

Steps in the Elimination Method
1. Add or subtract the equations to eliminate one variable, and then solve for the other variable.
2. Substitute the value into either original equation to find the value of the eliminated variable.
3. Write the solution as an ordered pair.

Example 1 Solve each system of linear equations using the indicated method. Check your answer by graphing.

(A) Solve the system of linear equations by adding.

$$\begin{cases} 4x - 2y = 12 \\ x + 2y = 8 \end{cases}$$

Add the equations.

$$\begin{array}{r} 4x - 2y = 12 \\ x + 2y = 8 \\ \hline 5x + 0 = 20 \end{array}$$

$$5x = 20$$

$$x = 4$$

Substitute the value of x into one of the equations and solve for y.

$$x + 2y = 8$$
$$4 + 2y = 8$$
$$2y = 4$$
$$y = 2$$

Write the solution as an ordered pair.

$$(4, 2)$$

Check the solution by graphing.

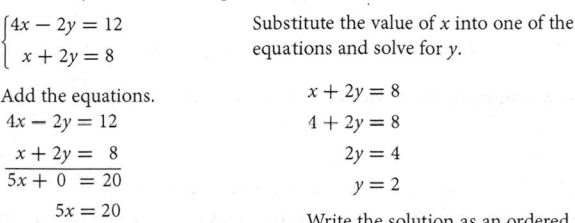

(B) Solve the system of linear equations by subtracting.

$$\begin{cases} 2x + 6y = 6 \\ 2x - y = -8 \end{cases}$$

Subtract the equations.

$$\begin{array}{r} 2x + 6y = 6 \\ -(2x - y = -8) \\ \hline \boxed{0} \quad \boxed{+7y} = \boxed{14} \end{array}$$

$$y = 2$$

Substitute the value of y into one of the equations and solve for x.

$$2x - y = -8$$
$$2x - 2 = -8$$
$$2x = -6$$
$$x = -3$$

© Houghton Mifflin Harcourt Publishing Company

EXPLORE

Exploring the Effects of Adding Equations

INTEGRATE MATHEMATICAL PRACTICES
Focus on Modeling

MP.4 Have students model the linear equations with algebra tiles. They should see that if they add the equations, one of the variables will drop out and they will be able to solve the resulting equation.

QUESTIONING STRATEGIES

? How do you know that the result of adding two equations is a true equation? The left and right sides of an equation are equal to each other. By the Addition Property of Equality, adding one of these equal expressions to each side of a true equation results in a true equation.

EXPLAIN 1

Solving Linear Systems by Adding or Subtracting

QUESTIONING STRATEGIES

? How can you tell if a linear system has a variable that can be eliminated by adding? The equations will have two like terms that are opposites.

? How can you decide whether to add or subtract to eliminate a variable in a linear system? If two of the variable terms are opposites, add to eliminate a variable. If two of the variable terms are the same, subtract to eliminate a variable.

PROFESSIONAL DEVELOPMENT

Integrate Mathematical Practices

This lesson provides an opportunity to address Mathematical Practice **MP.2**, which calls for students to "reason abstractly and quantitatively." Students learn to solve systems of two equations by using elimination. When using this method, students must consider the relationship between the coefficients of the variables to determine whether the equations should be added or subtracted. They connect the results of the algebraic solution method to the graph of the system of equations as they learn to recognize and describe systems that have no solutions or infinitely many solutions.

LANGUAGE SUPPORT **EL**

Connect Vocabulary

Tell students that in the *elimination method*, one variable is eliminated by adding or subtracting. Relate the term *elimination* to what happens in many competitions: teams are eliminated by their opponents. Similarly, a variable is eliminated by its opposite.

Write the solution as an ordered pair.

$$(-3, 2)$$

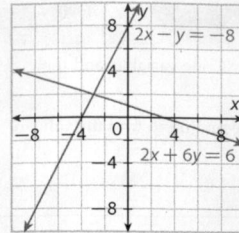

Check the solution by graphing.

Reflect

3. Can the system in part A be solved by subtracting one of the original equations from the other? Why or why not?

No; if either of the original equations in the system is subtracted from the other, neither variable will be eliminated.

4. In part B, what would happen if you added the original equations instead of subtracting?

You would get $4x + 5y = -2$, which would not help to solve the system because neither variable would be eliminated.

Your Turn

Solve each system of linear equations by adding or subtracting.

5. $\begin{cases} 2x + 5y = -24 \\ 3x - 5y = 14 \end{cases}$

$$2x + 5y = -24$$
$$\underline{3x - 5y = 14}$$
$$5x + 0 = -10$$
$$5x = -10$$
$$x = -2$$

$$2(-2) + 5y = -24$$
$$-4 + 5y = -24$$
$$5y = -20$$
$$y = -4$$

Solution: $(-2, -4)$

6. $\begin{cases} 3x + 2y = 5 \\ x + 2y = -1 \end{cases}$

$$3x + 2y = 5$$
$$\underline{-(x + 2y = -1)}$$
$$2x + 0 = 6$$
$$2x = 6$$
$$x = 3$$

$$x + 2y = -1$$
$$3 + 2y = -1$$
$$2y = -4$$
$$y = -2$$

Solution: $(3, -2)$

COLLABORATIVE LEARNING

Peer-to-Peer Activity

Have students work in pairs. Give each pair a system of linear equations to solve. Instruct one student to solve the system of linear equations by elimination. Instruct the other to solve the system by graphing. Have students check that they both got the same solution. Then have students switch roles and repeat the exercise using a different system of linear equations.

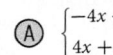

Example 2 Solve each system of linear equations by adding or subtracting.

(A) $\begin{cases} -4x - 2y = 4 \\ 4x + 2y = -4 \end{cases}$

Add the equations.

$$\begin{array}{r} -4x - 2y = 4 \\ +4x + 2y = -4 \\ \hline 0 + 0 = 0 \\ 0 = 0 \end{array}$$

The resulting equation is true, so the system has infinitely many solutions.

Graph the equations to provide more information.

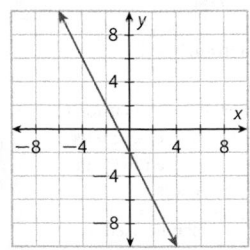

The graphs are the same line, so the system has infinitely many solutions.

(B) $\begin{cases} x + y = -2 \\ x + y = 4 \end{cases}$

 Subtract the equations.

$$\begin{array}{r} x + y = -2 \\ -(x + y = 4) \\ \hline 0 + 0 = -6 \\ 0 = -6 \end{array}$$

The resulting equation is ___false___ ,

so the system has ___no___ solutions.

Graph the equations to provide more information.

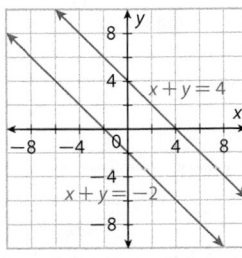

The graph shows that the lines are ___parallel___

and ___do not intersect___ .

EXPLAIN 2

Solving Special Linear Systems by Adding or Subtracting

QUESTIONING STRATEGIES

? How do you know when a system of linear equations has no solution or infinitely many solutions? The solution process will result in a false statement for a system with no solutions and a true statement for a system with infinitely many solutions.

INTEGRATE MATHEMATICAL PRACTICES
Focus on Modeling

MP.4 Remind students that it is possible to model these equations using algebra tiles. Have them predict how the tiles will appear if there are no solutions or infinitely many solutions, then have them try some examples. If there are no solutions, the tiles should be unbalanced after simplifying. If there are infinitely many solutions, there should be zero tiles on both sides after simplifying.

AVOID COMMON ERRORS

Students might think that *infinitely many solutions* means that all ordered pairs are solutions. Remind them that the solutions are the infinite number of ordered pairs that satisfy the equations.

DIFFERENTIATE INSTRUCTION

Graphic Organizers

Have students complete the table to summarize which variable can be eliminated and whether addition or subtraction should be used when solving a system of equations by elimination.

System of Linear Equations Has	Eliminate	By (operation)
x-terms that are opposites	x	adding
y-terms that are opposites	y	adding
x-terms that are the same	x	subtracting
y-terms that are the same	y	subtracting

EXPLAIN 3

Solving Linear System Models by Adding or Subtracting

QUESTIONING STRATEGIES

? After you have found the value of one of the variables, does it matter which equation you substitute the value of that variable into to solve for the other variable? Explain. No; both variables appear in both equations, and since the solution to the system is the ordered pair that satisfies both equations, the result should be the same no matter which equation you choose.

INTEGRATE MATHEMATICAL PRACTICES
Focus on Reasoning

MP.2 Remind students to check that the solution makes sense in the context of the problem.

AVOID COMMON ERRORS

Some students may forget to answer the question in a real-world problem after solving the system of equations. Tell students that the solution to the system may not be the final answer, and remind them to make sure they answer the question in the problem.

Solve each system of linear equations by adding or subtracting.

7. $\begin{cases} 4x - y = 3 \\ 4x - y = -2 \end{cases}$

$$4x - y = 3$$
$$-(4x - y = -2)$$
$$\overline{0 + 0 = 5}$$
$$0 = 5$$

The resulting equation is false, so the system has no solutions.

8. $\begin{cases} x - 6y = 7 \\ -x + 6y = -7 \end{cases}$

$$x - 6y = 7$$
$$-x + 6y = -7$$
$$\overline{0 + 0 = 0}$$
$$0 = 0$$

The resulting equation is true, so the system has infinitely many solutions.

⚙ Explain 3 Solving Linear System Models by Adding or Subtracting

Example 3 Solve by adding or subtracting.

(A) Perfect Patios is building a rectangular deck for a customer. According to the customer's specifications, the perimeter should be 40 meters and the difference between twice the length and twice the width should be 4 meters.

The system of equations $\begin{cases} 2\ell + 2w = 40 \\ 2\ell - 2w = 4 \end{cases}$ can be used to represent this situation, where ℓ is the length and w is the width. What will be the length and width of the deck?

Add the equations.

$$2\ell + 2w = 40$$
$$\underline{2\ell - 2w = 4}$$
$$4\ell + 0 = 44$$
$$4\ell = 44$$
$$\ell = 11$$

Substitute the value of ℓ into one of the equations and solve for w.

$$2\ell + 2w = 40$$
$$2(11) + 2w = 40$$
$$22 + 2w = 40$$
$$2w = 18$$
$$w = 9$$

Write the solution as an ordered pair.

$$(\ell, w) = (11, 9)$$

The length of the deck will be 11 meters and the width will be 9 meters.

LANGUAGE SUPPORT **EL**

Connect Context

Help students eliminate confusion by reminding them of the resources they can use when they are unsure of the meaning of a word. They can consider the context of a problem, use the glossary or a dictionary, think of possible cognates, or ask a friend. Remind them of these synonyms for words in the lesson:
eliminate = remove; opposite = additive inverse; substitute = replace; and false = untrue.

B A video game and movie rental kiosk charges $2 for each video game rented, and $1 for each movie rented. One day last week, a total of 114 video games and movies were rented for a total of $177. The system of equations $\begin{cases} x + y = 114 \\ 2x + y = 177 \end{cases}$ represents this situation, where x represents the number of video games rented and y represents the number of movies rented. Find the numbers of video games and movies that were rented.

Subtract the equations.

$$x + y = 114$$
$$-(2x + y = 177)$$
$$\overline{-x + 0 = -63}$$
$$-x = -63$$
$$x = 63$$

Substitute the value of x into one of the equations and solve for y.

$$x + y = 114$$
$$63 + y = 114$$
$$y = 51$$

Write the solution as an ordered pair.

$$(63, 51)$$

___63___ video games and ___51___ movies were rented.

Your Turn

9. The perimeter of a rectangular picture frame is 62 inches. The difference of the length of the frame and twice its width is 1. The system of equations $\begin{cases} 2\ell + 2w = 62 \\ \ell - 2w = 1 \end{cases}$ represents this situation, where ℓ represents the length in inches and w represents the width in inches. What are the length and the width of the frame?

$$2\ell + 2w = 62$$
$$\underline{\ell - 2w = 1}$$
$$3\ell + 0 = 63$$
$$3\ell = 63$$
$$\ell = 21$$
$$2\ell + 2w = 62$$

$$2(21) + 2w = 62$$
$$42 + 2w = 62$$
$$2w = 20$$
$$w = 10$$

The length is 21 inches and the width is 10 inches.

Elaborate

10. How can you decide whether to add or subtract to eliminate a variable in a linear system? Explain your reasoning.
If two of the variable terms are opposites, then you can add to eliminate a variable. If two of the variable terms are the same, then you can subtract to eliminate a variable.

11. **Discussion** When a linear system has no solution, what happens when you try to solve the system by adding or subtracting?
When the equations are added or subtracted to eliminate a variable, the result is a false statement, such as 0 = 9; this means there is no solution.

12. **Essential Question Check-In** When you solve a system of linear equations by adding or subtracting, what needs to be true about the variable terms in the equations?
The equations must have at least one pair of variable terms that are the same or opposites.

© Houghton Mifflin Harcourt Publishing Company

ELABORATE

QUESTIONING STRATEGIES

? When the equations in a system have like terms with the same coefficient and you want to eliminate a variable by subtracting, does it matter which equation is subtracted from the other equation? Explain. No; since the coefficient of the variable is the same in both equations, the variable will be eliminated whether the second equation is subtracted from the first or the first equation is subtracted from the second.

AVOID COMMON ERRORS

After choosing to use subtraction to solve a linear system of equations, some students may make errors when subtracting negative numbers. Suggest that they use the definition of subtraction to rewrite one of the equations with opposite signs and then add the equations.

SUMMARIZE THE LESSON

? How do you solve a system of linear equations by adding or subtracting? If the equations have like terms whose coefficients are opposites, add the equations to eliminate one variable. If the equations have identical terms, subtract the equations to eliminate one variable. Solve for the value of the remaining variable. Then, substitute that value into either equation and solve for the value of the first variable.

EVALUATE

ASSIGNMENT GUIDE

Concepts and Skills	Practice
Explore Exploring the Effects of Adding Equations	Exercises 1, 22
Example 1 Solving Linear Systems by Adding or Subtracting	Exercises 2–9, 23–24
Example 2 Solving Special Linear Systems by Adding or Subtracting	Exercises 10–15
Example 3 Solving Linear System Models by Adding or Subtracting	Exercises 16–21, 25

 Evaluate: Homework and Practice

1. Which method of elimination would be best to solve the system of linear equations? Explain.

$$\begin{cases} \frac{1}{2}x + \frac{3}{4}y = -10 \\ -x - \frac{3}{4}y = 1 \end{cases}$$ The addition method would be best because the y-values are opposites, or additive inverses.

Solve each system of linear equations by adding or subtracting.

2. $\begin{cases} 3x + 2y = 10 \\ 3x - y = 22 \end{cases}$

$$3x + 2y = 10$$
$$-(3x - y = 22)$$
$$0 + 3y = -12$$
$$y = -4$$
$$3x - (-4) = 22$$
$$x = 6$$
Solution: $(6, -4)$

3. $\begin{cases} -2x + y = 3 \\ 3x - y = -2 \end{cases}$

$$-2x + y = 3$$
$$3x - y = -2$$
$$x + 0 = 1$$
$$x = 1$$
$$3(1) - y = -2$$
$$y = 5$$
Solution: $(1, 5)$

4. $\begin{cases} x + y = 5 \\ x - 3y = 3 \end{cases}$

$$x + y = 5$$
$$-(x - 3y = 3)$$
$$0 + 4y = 2$$
$$y = 0.5$$
$$x + 0.5 = 5$$
$$x = 4.5$$
Solution: $(4.5, 0.5)$

5. $\begin{cases} 7x + y = -4 \\ 2x - y = 1 \end{cases}$

$$7x + y = -4$$
$$2x - y = 1$$
$$9x + 0 = -3$$
$$x = -\frac{1}{3}$$
$$7\left(-\frac{1}{3}\right) + y = -4$$
$$y = -\frac{5}{3}$$
Solution: $\left(-\frac{1}{3}, -\frac{5}{3}\right)$

6. $\begin{cases} -5x + y = -3 \\ 5x - 3y = -1 \end{cases}$

$$-5x + y = -3$$
$$5x - 3y = -1$$
$$0 - 2y = -4$$
$$y = 2$$
$$5x - 3(2) = -1$$
$$x = 1$$
Solution: $(1, 2)$

7. $\begin{cases} 2x + y = -6 \\ -5x + y = 8 \end{cases}$

$$2x + y = -6$$
$$-(-5x + y = 8)$$
$$7x + 0 = -14$$
$$x = -2$$
$$2(-2) + y = -6$$
$$y = -2$$
Solution: $(-2, -2)$

8. $\begin{cases} 6x - 3y = 15 \\ 4x - 3y = -5 \end{cases}$

$$6x - 3y = 15$$
$$-(4x - 3y = -5)$$
$$2x + 0 = 20$$
$$x = 10$$
$$6(10) - 3y = 15$$
$$y = 15$$
Solution: $(10, 15)$

9. $\begin{cases} 8x - 6y = 36 \\ -2x + 6y = 0 \end{cases}$

$$8x - 6y = 36$$
$$-2x + 6y = 0$$
$$6x + 0 = 36$$
$$x = 6$$
$$-2(6) + 6y = 0$$
$$y = 2$$
Solution: $(6, 2)$

Exercise	Depth of Knowledge (D.O.K.)	COMMON CORE Mathematical Practices
1	**1** Recall of Information	**MP.2** Reasoning
2–18	**2** Skills/Concepts	**MP.2** Reasoning
19	**2** Skills/Concepts	**MP.4** Modeling
20	**2** Skills/Concepts	**MP.2** Reasoning
21	**2** Skills/Concepts	**MP.4** Modeling
22	**2** Skills/Concepts	**MP.2** Reasoning

10. $\begin{cases} \frac{1}{2}x - \frac{7}{9}y = -\frac{20}{3} \\ -\frac{1}{2}x + \frac{7}{9}y = 6\frac{2}{3} \end{cases}$

$$\frac{1}{2}x - \frac{7}{9}y = -\frac{20}{3}$$
$$\underline{-\frac{1}{2}x + \frac{7}{9}y = 6\frac{2}{3}}$$
$$0 + 0 = 0$$
$$0 = 0$$

Infinitely many solutions

11. $\begin{cases} -10x + 2y = -7 \\ -10x + 2y = -2 \end{cases}$

$$-10x + 2y = -7$$
$$\underline{-(-10x + 2y = -2)}$$
$$0 + 0 = -5$$
$$0 = -5$$

No solution

12. $\begin{cases} -2x + 5y = 7 \\ 2x - 5y = -7 \end{cases}$

$$-2x + 5y = 7$$
$$\underline{+2x - 5y = -7}$$
$$0 + 0 = 0$$
$$0 = 0$$

Infinitely many solutions

13. $\begin{cases} x + y = 0 \\ -x - y = 0 \end{cases}$

$$x + y = 0$$
$$\underline{-x - y = 0}$$
$$0 + 0 = 0$$
$$0 = 0$$

Infinitely many solutions

14. $\begin{cases} -5x - y = -3 \\ -5x - y = -2 \end{cases}$

$$-5x - y = -3$$
$$\underline{-(-5x - y = -2)}$$
$$0 + 0 = -1$$
$$0 = -1$$

No solution

15. $\begin{cases} ax - by = c \\ ax - by = c \end{cases}$

$$ax - by = c$$
$$\underline{-(ax - by = c)}$$
$$0 + 0 = 0$$
$$0 = 0$$

Infinitely many solutions

16. The sum of two numbers is 65, and the difference of the numbers is 27. The system of linear

equations $\begin{cases} x + y = 65 \\ x - y = 27 \end{cases}$ represents this situation, where x is the larger number and y is the smaller

number. Solve the system to find the two numbers.

$$x + y = 65$$
$$\underline{x - y = 27}$$
$$2x + 0 = 92$$
$$x = 46$$
$$x + y = 65$$
$$46 + y = 65$$
$$y = 19$$

The larger number is 46 and the smaller number is 19.

Suggest that students circle the coefficient of the variable that is to be eliminated in each equation, including the plus or minus sign. This visual cue can help them remember to subtract the equations if the coefficients are the same and to add the equations if the coefficients are opposites.

Exercise	Depth of Knowledge (D.O.K.)	COMMON CORE Mathematical Practices
23	**3** Strategic Thinking **H.O.T.**	**MP.4** Modeling
24	**3** Strategic Thinking **H.O.T.**	**MP.3** Logic
25	**3** Strategic Thinking **H.O.T.**	**MP.6** Precision

AVOID COMMON ERRORS

Point out to students that when they use the elimination method, they must line up both the like terms and the equal signs vertically.

KINESTHETIC EXPERIENCE

To check solutions by graphing, create a coordinate grid on the floor using painter's tape. Have students help you decide where to place a tape line for one of the equations. Then have another student walk the line for the second equation. The student should stop when encountering the tape line for the first equation. The class should help the student identify that position's coordinates and check the solution. If the lines are parallel, the student should note that the paths will never cross.

17. A rectangular garden has a perimeter of 120 feet. The length of the garden is 24 feet greater than twice the width. The system of linear equations $\begin{cases} 2\ell + 2w = 120 \\ \ell - 2w = 24 \end{cases}$ represents this situation, where ℓ is the length of the garden and w is its width. Find the length and width of the garden.

$$2\ell + 2w = 120$$
$$\underline{\ell - 2w = 24}$$
$$3\ell + 0 = 144$$
$$\ell = 48$$
$$2\ell + 2w = 120$$
$$2(48) + 2w = 120$$
$$96 + 2w = 120$$
$$2w = 24$$
$$w = 12$$

The length of the garden is 48 feet and the width is 12 feet.

18. The sum of two angles is 90°. The difference of twice the larger angle and the smaller angle is 105°. The system of linear equations $\begin{cases} x + y = 90 \\ 2x - y = 105 \end{cases}$ represents this situation where x is the larger angle and y is the smaller angle. Find the measures of the two angles.

$$x + y = 90$$
$$\underline{2x - y = 105}$$
$$3x + 0 = 195$$
$$3x = 195$$
$$x = 65$$
$$x + y = 90$$
$$65 + y = 90$$
$$y = 25$$

The larger angle is 65° and the smaller angle is 25°.

19. Max and Sasha exercise a total of 20 hours each week. Max exercises 15 hours less than 4 times the number of hours Sasha exercises. The system of equations $\begin{cases} x + y = 20 \\ x - 4y = -15 \end{cases}$ represents this situation, where x represents the number of hours Max exercises and y represents the number of hours Sasha exercises. How many hours do Max and Sasha exercise per week?

$$x + y = 20$$
$$\underline{-(x - 4y = -15)}$$
$$0 + 5y = 35$$
$$y = 7$$
$$x + y = 20$$
$$x + 7 = 20$$
$$x = 13$$

Max exercises 13 hours a week and Sasha exercises 7 hours a week.

20. The sum of the digits in a two-digit number is 12. The digit in the tens place is 2 more than the digit in the ones place. The system of linear equations $\begin{cases} x + y = 12 \\ x - y = 2 \end{cases}$ represents this situation, where x is the digit in the tens place and y is the digit in the ones place. Solve the system to find the two-digit number.

$$x + y = 12$$
$$\underline{x - y = 2}$$
$$2x + 0 = 14$$
$$x = 7$$
$$x + y = 12$$
$$7 + y = 12$$
$$y = 5$$

The number is 75.

© Houghton Mifflin Harcourt Publishing Company

21. A pool company is installing a rectangular pool for a new house. The perimeter of the pool must be 94 feet, and the length must be 2 feet more than twice the width.

The system of linear equations
$$\begin{cases} 2\ell + 2w = 94 \\ \ell = 2w + 2 \end{cases} \text{represents}$$
this situation, where ℓ is the length and w is the width. What are the dimensions of the pool?

$$2\ell + 2w = 94$$
$$\underline{\ell - 2w = 2}$$
$$3\ell + 0 = 96$$
$$3\ell = 96$$
$$\ell = 32$$

$$2\ell + 2w = 94$$
$$2(32) + 2w = 94$$
$$64 + 2w = 94$$
$$2w = 30$$
$$w = 15$$

The pool is 32 feet long and 15 feet wide.

22. Use one solution, no solutions, or infinitely many solutions to complete each statement.

a. When the solution of a system of linear equations yields the

equation $4 = 4$, the system has __infinitely many solutions__ .

b. When the solution of a system of linear equations yields the

equation $x = 4$, the system has __one solution__ .

c. When the solution of a system of linear equations yields the

equation $0 = 4$, the system has __no solutions__ .

H.O.T. Focus on Higher Order Thinking

23. Multiple Representations You can use subtraction to solve the system of linear equations shown.
$$\begin{cases} 2x + 4y = -4 \\ 2x - 2y = -10 \end{cases}$$

Instead of subtracting $2x - 2y = -10$ from $2x + 4y = -4$, what equation can you add to get the same result? Explain.

You can add $-2x + 2y = 10$ since subtracting is the same as adding the opposite.

COMMUNICATING MATH

Have students discuss when to use each of the methods they have learned for solving systems of equations. Graphing can be used for linear systems that have integer solutions. Substitution can be used when one of the equations has a variable with a coefficient of 1. Adding or subtracting can be used when the coefficient of a variable in one equation is the same as, or the opposite of, the coefficient of the same variable in the other equation.

Have students write a journal entry explaining how to solve a system of linear equations by eliminating a variable. They should include how you know whether to add or subtract the equations.

24. Explain the Error Liang's solution of a system of linear equations is shown. Explain Liang's error and give the correct solution.

$$\begin{cases} 3x - 2y = 12 \\ -x - 2y = -20 \end{cases}$$

Liang added the two equations but subtracted the y-terms. The equations should be subtracted. The solution is $(8, 6)$.

$$3x - 2y = 12$$
$$\underline{-x - 2y = -20}$$
$$2x = -8$$
$$x = -4$$
$$3x - 2y = 12$$
$$3(-4) - 2y = 12$$
$$-12 - 2y = 12$$
$$-2y = 24$$
$$y = -12$$

Solution: $(-4, -12)$

$$3x - 2y = 12$$
$$\underline{-(-x - 2y = -20)}$$
$$4x = 32$$
$$x = 8$$
$$3(8) - 2y = 12$$
$$24 - 2y = 12$$
$$-2y = -12$$
$$y = 6$$

25. Represent Real-World Problems For a school play, Rico bought 3 adult tickets and 5 child tickets for a total of $40. Sasha bought 1 adult ticket and 5 child tickets for a total of $25.

The system of linear equations $\begin{cases} 3x + 5y = 40 \\ x + 5y = 25 \end{cases}$ represents this

situation, where x is the cost of an adult ticket and y is the cost of a child ticket. How much will Julia pay for 5 adult tickets and 3 child tickets?

$$3x + 5y = 40$$
$$\underline{-(x + 5y = 25)}$$
$$2x + 0 = 15$$
$$x = 7.5$$
$$x + 5y = 25$$
$$7.5 + 5y = 25$$
$$5y = 17.5$$
$$y = 3.5$$
$$5(7.5) + 3(3.5) = 48$$

Julia will pay $48.

Lesson Performance Task

A local charity run has a Youth Race for runners under the age of 12. The entry fee is $5 for an individual or $4 each for two runners from the same family. Carter is collecting the registration forms and fees. After everyone has registered, he picks up the cash box and finds a dollar on the ground. He checks the cash box and finds that it contains $200 and the registration slips for 47 runners. Does the dollar belong in the cash box or not? Explain your reasoning. (Hint: You can use the system of equations $i + f = 47$ and $5i + 4f = 200$, where i equals the number of individual tickets and f equals the number of family tickets.)

Solving the system gives the solution $i = 12$ and $f = 35$. However, this result is not possible because f must be an even number since family registrations were sold only as pairs. If we add the $1 to the total cash, we can rewrite the second equation as $5i + 4f = 201$. Solving the new system yields the solution $i = 13$ and $f = 34$, so the dollar does belong in the cash box. (Note that some students may simply reason from the initial solution that they can swap one family registration for one individual registration and get a total of $201.)

© Houghton Mifflin Harcourt Publishing Company

QUESTIONING STRATEGIES

? Family tickets were sold only when two runners from the same family registered at the same time. What does this tell you about the total number of family tickets sold? **It must be an even number.**

AVOID COMMON ERRORS

Some students may try to add the two given equations to solve the system by elimination. Remind them that the elimination method only works when the equations have like terms whose coefficients are the same or opposites. They should recognize that they can solve this system by substitution.

KINESTHETIC EXPERIENCE

Have students use play money, a cash box, and ticket stubs to act out the situation so they can better visualize how different numbers of individual and family tickets sold would result in different amounts of money in the cash box.

EXTENSION ACTIVITY

On an index card, have students write a riddle that can be represented by a system of equations whose solution can be found by elimination. For example: *The sum of one number and another number is 5. The difference between the two numbers is 1.* On the back of the card, have students write the solution and show the system of equations used to find it. Then have students trade cards and solve each other's riddles.

Scoring Rubric
2 points: Student correctly solves the problem and explains his/her reasoning.
1 point: Student shows good understanding of the problem but does not fully solve or explain his/her reasoning.
0 points: Student does not demonstrate understanding of the problem.

Solving Linear Systems by Adding or Subtracting   **514**

Solving Linear Systems by Multiplying First

Common Core Math Standards

The student is expected to:

COMMON CORE A-REI.C.5

Prove that... replacing one equation by the sum of that equation and a multiple of the other produces a system with the same solutions. Also A-REI.C.6

Mathematical Practices

COMMON CORE MP.2 Reasoning

Language Objective

Explain to a partner how you know when to solve a system of linear equations by multiplying first.

ENGAGE

Essential Question: How can you solve a system of linear equations by using multiplication and elimination?

If neither of the like terms in a system of equations has the same or opposite coefficients, multiply one or both equations by a constant so that one variable can be eliminated by adding or subtracting, and then solve the system by elimination.

PREVIEW: LESSON PERFORMANCE TASK

View the Engage section online. Discuss how a chemist can mix solutions with different concentrations to get a solution with a desired concentration. Then preview the Lesson Performance Task.

Name_____ Class_____ Date_____

11.4 Solving Linear Systems by Multiplying First

Resource Locker

Essential Question: How can you solve a system of linear equations by using multiplication and elimination?

⊘ Explore 1 Understanding Linear Systems and Multiplication

A system of linear equations in which one of the like terms in each equation has either the same or opposite coefficients can that be readily solved by elimination.

How do you solve the system if neither of the pairs of like terms in the equations have the same or opposite coefficients?

Ⓐ Graph and label the following system of equations.
$$\begin{cases} 2x - y = 1 \\ x + y = 2 \end{cases}$$

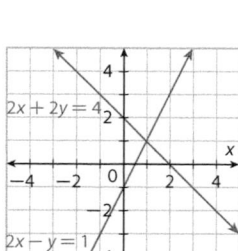

Ⓑ The solution to the system is ___(1, 1)___.

Ⓒ When both sides of an equation are multiplied by the same value, the equation [is/is not] still true.

Ⓓ Multiply both sides of the second equation by 2.
$$\underline{2x + 2y = 4}$$

Ⓔ Write the resulting system of equations.
$$\begin{cases} \boxed{2x + 2y = 4} \\ 2x - y = 1 \end{cases}$$

Ⓕ Graph and label the new system of equations.
Solution: ___(1, 1)___

Ⓖ Can the new system of equations be solved using elimination now that $2x$ appears in each equation?
___Yes___

© Houghton Mifflin Harcourt Publishing Company

Module 11   **515**   Lesson 4

HARDCOVER PAGES 413–422

Turn to these pages to find this lesson in the hardcover student edition.

1. **Discussion** How are the graphs of $x + y = 2$ and $2x + 2y = 4$ related?
   The graphs are the same line.

2. **Discussion** How are the equations $x + y = 2$ and $2x + 2y = 4$ related?
   They are equivalent because the slope-intercept form of both is $y = -x + 2$.

⊘ Explore 2   Proving the Elimination Method with Multiplication

The previous example illustrated that rewriting a system of equations by multiplying a constant term by one of the equations does not change the solutions for the system. What happens if a new system of equations is written by adding this new equation to the untouched equation from the original system?

(A) Original System → New System

$\begin{cases} 2x - y = 1 \\ x + y = 2 \end{cases} \rightarrow \begin{cases} 2x - y = 1 \\ 2x + 2y = 4 \end{cases}$

Add the equations in the new system.

$\begin{array}{r} 2x - y = 1 \\ 2x + 2y = 4 \\ \hline \boxed{4x + y = 5} \end{array}$

(B) Write a new system of equations using this new equation.

$\begin{cases} 2x - y = 1 \\ \boxed{4x + y = 5} \end{cases}$

(C) Graph and label the equations from this new system of equations.

(D) Is the solution to this new system of equations the same as the solution to the original system of equations? Explain.

Yes; the lines intersect at $(1, 1)$, so the solution to the

system of equations is $(1, 1)$, which is the same as the

solution to the original system.

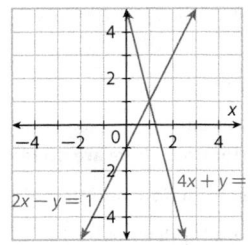

(E) If the original system is $Ax + By = C$ and $Dx + Ey = F$, where $A, B, C, D, E,$ and F are constants, then multiply the second equation by a nonzero constant k to get $kDx + kEy = kF$. Add this new equation to $Ax + By = C$.

$\begin{array}{r} Ax +   Dy = C \\ + \quad kDx + kEy = kF \\ \hline \boxed{(A + kD)}x + \boxed{(B + kE)}y = \boxed{C + kF} \end{array}$

(F) So, the original system is $\begin{cases} Ax + By = C \\ Dx + Ey = F \end{cases}$, and the new system is

$\begin{cases} Ax + By = C \\ \boxed{(A + kD)x + (B + kE)y = C + kF} \end{cases}$.

PROFESSIONAL DEVELOPMENT

Learning Progressions

In this lesson, students extend their work with systems of equations. They learn to solve a system of two linear equations by first multiplying one or both of the equations by a constant, then using elimination. They explore why multiplying both sides of the equations by a constant does not change the solution of the system. Then they apply this method to systems that model real-world situations. Work with linear systems will continue as students learn how to create their own linear systems to model real-world situations and how to solve systems of linear inequalities.

EXPLORE 1

Understanding Linear Systems and Multiplication

INTEGRATE TECHNOLOGY

Have students use a graphing calculator to graph one of the lines in the system of equations. Then have them multiply the equation by a constant and graph the new equation using the graphing calculator. Students should realize that both equations represent the same line.

QUESTIONING STRATEGIES

How is the graph of a linear equation that has been multiplied by a constant related to the graph of the original equation? **The graph is the same line.**

EXPLORE 2

Proving the Elimination Method with Multiplication

INTEGRATE TECHNOLOGY

Have students use a graphing calculator to graph the two lines in the system of equations. Then have them graph the equation for the line formed when the two original equations are added. Students should notice that all three lines intersect at the same point.

INTEGRATE MATHEMATICAL PRACTICES
Focus on Math Connections

MP.1 Encourage students to recall other times they have done proofs in math. Have students talk about the rules they have to follow when creating proofs.

? What does the Addition Property of Equality state? It states that you can add the same thing to both sides of an equation and maintain equality.

? What does the Commutative Property of Addition state? It states that you can change the order of addends and maintain equality.

Ⓖ Let (x_1, y_1) be the solution to the original system. Fill in the missing parts of the following proof to show that (x_1, y_1) is also the solution to the new system.

Ⓗ $Ax_1 + By_1 = \boxed{C}$ Given.

Ⓘ $Dx_1 + Ey_1 = \boxed{F}$ Given.

Ⓙ $\boxed{k}\,(Dx_1 + Ey_1) = kF$ <u>Multiplication</u> Property of Equality

Ⓚ $kDx_1 + kEy_1 = kF$ <u>Distributive Property</u>

Ⓛ $\boxed{C} + kDx_1 + kEy_1 = C + kF$ <u>Addition</u> Property of Equality

Ⓜ $Ax_1 + \boxed{By_1} + kDx_1 + kEy_1 = C + kF$ Substitute $Ax_1 + \boxed{By_1}$ for $\boxed{C}$ on the left.

Ⓝ $Ax_1 + \boxed{kDx_1} + By_1 + kEy_1 = C + kF$ <u>Commutative</u> Property of Addition

Ⓞ $(Ax_1 + kDx_1) + (By_1 + kEy_1) = C + kF$ <u>Associative</u> Property of Addition

Ⓟ $(A + kD)x_1 + \boxed{B + kE}\,y_1 = C + kF$ <u>Distributive Property</u>

Ⓠ Therefore, (x_1, y_1) is the solution to the new system.

Reflect

3. **Discussion** Is a proof required using subtraction? What about division?
   No; since there are no restrictions on k, k could be negative which covers
   subtraction (addition of a negative) or k could be $0 < k < 1$ which covers division
   $\left(\text{multiplication by } \dfrac{1}{k}\right)$**.**

⚙ Explain 1   Solving Linear Systems by Multiplying First

In some systems of linear equations, neither variable can be eliminated by adding or subtracting the equations directly. In these systems, you need to multiply one or both equations by a constant so that adding or subtracting the equations will eliminate one or more of the variables.

Steps for Solving a System of Equations by Multiplying First
1. Decide which variable to eliminate.
2. Multiply one or both equations by a constant so that adding or subtracting the equations will eliminate the variable.
3. Solve the system using the elimination method.

COLLABORATIVE LEARNING

Small Group Activity

Have students work in groups of three to solve a system of linear equations. One student should use elimination to solve for x first. A second student should use elimination to solve for y first. The third student should solve using substitution. Students should compare their methods and decide what advantages, if any, one method has over the others.

Example 1 Solve each system of equations by multiplying. Check the answers by graphing the systems of equations.

(A) $\begin{cases} 3x + 8y = 7 \\ 2x - 2y = -10 \end{cases}$

Multiply the second equation by 4.

$4(2x - 2y = -10) \Rightarrow 8x - 8y = -40$

Add the result to the first equation.

$$\begin{array}{r} 3x + 8y = 7 \\ + \; 8x - 8y = -40 \\ \hline 11x = -33 \end{array}$$

Solve for x.

$11x = -33$

$x = -3$

Substitute -3 for x in one of the original equations, and solve for y.

$3x + 8y = 7$

$3(-3) + 8y = 7$

$-9 + 8y = 7$

$8y = 16$

$y = 2$

The solution to the system is $(-3, 2)$.

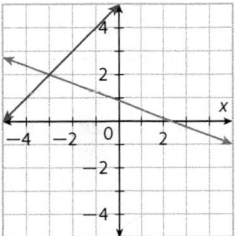

(B) $\begin{cases} -3x + 2y = 4 \\ 4x - 13y = 5 \end{cases}$

Multiply the first equation by $\underline{\;4\;}$ and multiply the second equation by $\underline{\;3\;}$ so the x terms in the system have coefficients of -12 and 12 respectively.

$\boxed{4} \; (-3x + 2y = 4) \qquad \Rightarrow \qquad -12x + \boxed{8} \; y = \boxed{16}$

$\boxed{3} \; (4x - 13y = 5) \qquad\qquad\qquad 12x - \boxed{39} \; y = \boxed{15}$

Add the resulting equations.

$-12x + \boxed{8} \; y - \boxed{16}$

$+12x - \boxed{39} \; y = \boxed{15}$

$\boxed{-31} \; y = \boxed{31}$

Solve for y.

$\boxed{-31} \; y = \boxed{31}$

$y = \boxed{-1}$

EXPLAIN 1

Solving Linear Systems by Multiplying First

QUESTIONING STRATEGIES

? How can you identify a system of linear equations that can be solved by multiplying only one equation by a constant? **Start by looking at the coefficients for the x-terms and ask, "Can either coefficient be multiplied by a constant so that the resulting coefficient is the opposite of, or the same as, the other coefficient?" Repeat the process for the coefficients of the y-term.**

? How can you check that the solution is correct? **Graph the equations or substitute the x- and y-values into both original equations to check the solution.**

Focus on Reasoning

MP.2 Ask students how to determine whether each equation in a system must be multiplied by a different constant in order to solve by elimination. Students should understand that the first step is to check whether the coefficient of a variable in one equation is a multiple of the coefficient of the same variable in the other equation. If not, they must multiply each equation by a different constant. The constants must be chosen so that in the two resulting equations, the coefficients for one variable are opposites or the same.

AVOID COMMON ERRORS

When multiplying an equation of the form $Ax + By = C$ by a constant k, students sometimes multiply the coefficients A and B but forget to multiply the constant C. Remind students that the form of the resulting equation is $kAx + kBy = kC$.

Solve the first equation for x when $y = \boxed{-1}$.

$$-3x + 2y = 4$$

$$-3x + 2\left(\boxed{-1}\right) = 4$$

$$-3x + \boxed{-2} = 4$$

$$-3x = \boxed{6}$$

$$x = \boxed{-2}$$

The solution to the system is $\boxed{(-2, -1)}$.

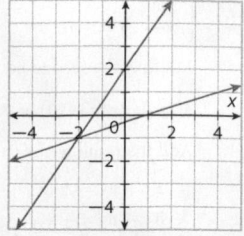

Your Turn

Solve each system of equations by multiplying. Check the answers by graphing the systems of equations.

4. $\begin{cases} -3x + 4y = 12 \\ 2x + y = -8 \end{cases}$

$$\begin{array}{r} -3x + 4y = 12 \\ + \quad -4(2x + y = -8) \end{array} \Rightarrow \begin{array}{r} -3x + 4y = 12 \\ + \quad -8x - 4y = 32 \\ \hline -11x = 44 \\ x = -4 \\ 2(-4) + y = -8 \\ y = 0 \end{array}$$

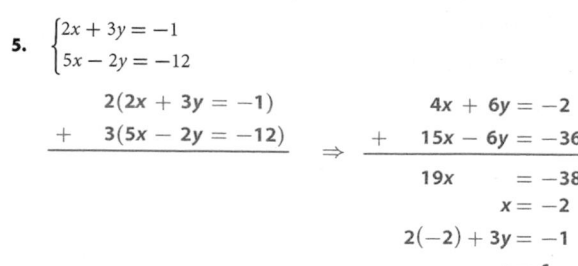

The solution is $(-4, 0)$.

5. $\begin{cases} 2x + 3y = -1 \\ 5x - 2y = -12 \end{cases}$

$$\begin{array}{r} 2(2x + 3y = -1) \\ + \quad 3(5x - 2y = -12) \end{array} \Rightarrow \begin{array}{r} 4x + 6y = -2 \\ + \quad 15x - 6y = -36 \\ \hline 19x = -38 \\ x = -2 \\ 2(-2) + 3y = -1 \\ y = 1 \end{array}$$

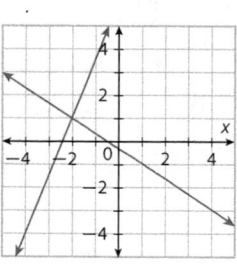

The solution is $(-2, 1)$.

Explain 2 · Solving Linear System Models by Multiplying First

You can solve a linear system of equations that models a real-world example by multiplying first.

Example 2 Solve each problem by multiplying first.

(A) Jessica spent $16.30 to buy 16 flowers. The bouquet contained daisies, which cost $1.75 each, and tulips, which cost $0.85 each. The system of equations $\begin{cases} d + t = 16 \\ 1.75d + 0.85t = 16.30 \end{cases}$ models this situation, where d is the number of daisies and t is the number of tulips. How many of each type of flower did Jessica buy?

Multiply the first equation by -0.85 to eliminate t from each equation. Then, add the equations.

$$\begin{cases} -0.85(d + t) = -0.85(16) \\ 1.75d + 0.85t = 16.30 \end{cases} \Rightarrow \begin{array}{r} -0.85d - 0.85t = -13.60 \\ +1.75d + 0.85t = 16.30 \\ \hline 0.9d = 2.70 \\ d = 3 \end{array}$$

Find t. $\begin{aligned} d + t &= 16 \\ 3 + t &= 16 \\ t &= 13 \end{aligned}$ The solution is $(3, 13)$.

Jessica bought 3 daisies and 13 tulips.

(B) The Tran family is bringing 15 packages of cheese to a group picnic. Cheese slices cost $2.50 per package. Cheese cubes cost $1.75 per package. The Tran family spent a total of $30 on cheese. The system of equations $\begin{cases} s + c = 15 \\ 2.50s + 1.75c = 30 \end{cases}$ represents this situation, where s is the number of packages of cheese slices and c is the number of packages of cheese cubes. How many packages of each type of cheese did the Tran family buy?

Multiply the first equation by a constant so that c can be eliminated from both equations, and then subtract the equations.

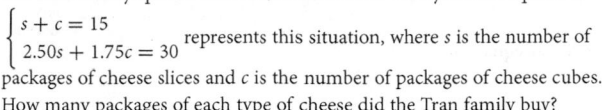

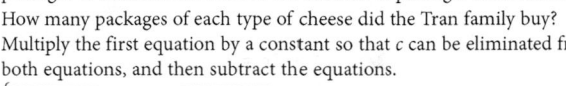

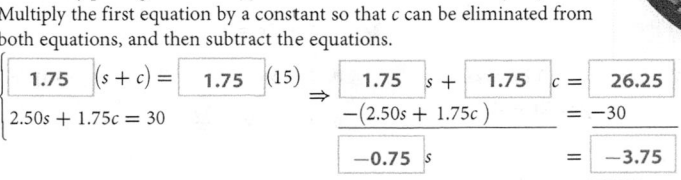

$\begin{cases} \boxed{1.75}\ (s + c) = \boxed{1.75}\ (15) \\ 2.50s + 1.75c = 30 \end{cases} \Rightarrow \begin{array}{r} \boxed{1.75}\ s + \boxed{1.75}\ c = \boxed{26.25} \\ -(2.50s + 1.75c\,) = -30 \\ \hline \boxed{-0.75}\ s = \boxed{-3.75} \\ s = \boxed{5} \end{array}$

Find c. $\begin{aligned} s + c &= 15 \\ \boxed{5} + c &= 15 \\ c &= \boxed{10} \end{aligned}$ The solution is $\boxed{(5, 10)}$.

The Tran family bought ___5___ packages of sliced cheese and ___10___ packages of cheese cubes.

Your Turn

6. Jacob's family bought 4 adult tickets and 2 student tickets to the school play for $64. Tatianna's family bought 3 adult tickets and 3 students tickets for $60. The system of equations $\begin{cases} 4a + 2s = 64 \\ 3a + 3s = 60 \end{cases}$ models this situation, where a is the cost of an adult ticket and s is the cost of a student ticket. How much does each type of ticket cost?

$3(4a + 2s = 64) \Rightarrow 12a + 6s = 192$
$-2(3a + 3s = 60) \Rightarrow -6a - 6s = -120$

$(12, 8)$

Adult tickets cost $12 each and student tickets cost $8 each.

DIFFERENTIATE INSTRUCTION

Critical Thinking

Challenge students to use their understanding of least common multiples to help them solve systems of linear equations. Have them consider the following system: $5x + 9y = 29$ and $7x - 6y = 22$. Students should notice that the coefficients 9 and -6 have a common factor of 3 and that their least common multiple is 18. Therefore, they can multiply the first equation by 2 and the second equation by 3 to transform the coefficients of y to 18 and -18. This approach will make the calculations involved in solving the equation much simpler than multiplying both equations by larger numbers.

EXPLAIN 2

Solving Linear System Models by Multiplying First

QUESTIONING STRATEGIES

? How can you determine what each of the coefficients represents in the system of equations? Read the problem and relate the verbal descriptions to the equations.

INTEGRATE MATHEMATICAL PRACTICES
Focus on Technology

MP.5 Students may want to check their solutions to a word problem by graphing the equations on a graphing calculator. They should enter the equations in the graphing calculator using the **Y=** key, and then select **GRAPH**. They can use the **ZOOM** feature or manually adjust the window if the standard window does not allow them to view the point of intersection of the graphs. The *intersect* feature (in the **CALC** menu) will display the coordinates of the point of intersection.

AVOID COMMON ERRORS

After solving a system of equations that represents a real-world problem, students sometimes forget to go back to the original problem to check what each variable represents and what the problem asks. Make sure students read verbal problems carefully. Suggest that they circle or copy down the definition of each variable so that they can quickly refer to it and correctly answer the question in the problem.

ELABORATE

QUESTIONING STRATEGIES

? Suppose you multiply each equation in a system by a different constant. How will the graphs of the new equations be related to the graphs of the original equations? They will be the same lines as the graphs of the original equations.

? If you then add the two equations to get a third equation, how will its graph be related to the graphs of the two original equations? It will intersect the other two equations at their point of intersection.

AVOID COMMON ERRORS

In systems where students find the value of y first and x second, they may write the ordered pair for the solution in reverse order, listing (y, x) rather than (x, y). Remind students that the solution is always given as an ordered pair (x, y), no matter which variable was evaluated first.

SUMMARIZE THE LESSON

? How do you choose what constant to multiply by when solving a system of linear equations by multiplying and eliminating? Check to see whether any coefficient is a multiple of the coefficient for the same variable in the other equation. If so, multiply one equation by the constant that will make those coefficients opposites or the same. If not, choose two different constants to multiply by the two equations so that the coefficients for one variable will be opposites or the same. Then you can solve by adding or subtracting the equations.

💬 Elaborate

7. When would you solve a system of linear equations by multiplying?
   You would use multiplication when neither variable has coefficients that are either equal or opposites.

8. How can you use multiplication to solve a system of linear equations if none of the coefficients are multiples or factors of any of the other coefficients?
   Multiply both equations by constants so that one of the variables has coefficients that are either equal or opposites.

9. **Essential Question Check-In** How do you solve a system of equations by multiplying?
   Decide which variable you want to eliminate. Then, multiply one or both equations so that the variable has coefficients in the equations that are either equal or opposites. Using the new equation, use elimination to solve the system.

⭐ Evaluate: Homework and Practice

- Online Homework
- Hints and Help
- Extra Practice

For each linear equation,

a. find the product of 3 and the linear equation;

b. solve both equations for y.

1. $2y - 4x = 8$
   a. $3(2y - 4x = 8) \Rightarrow 6y - 12x = 24$
   b. $y = 2x + 4 \qquad\qquad y = 2x + 4$

2. $-5y + 7x = 12$
   a. $3(-5y + 7x = 12) \Rightarrow -15y + 21x = 36$
   b. $y = \frac{7}{5}x - \frac{12}{5} \qquad\qquad y = \frac{7}{5}x - \frac{12}{5}$

3. $4x + 7y = 18$
   a. $3(4x + 7y = 8) \Rightarrow 12x + 21y = 24$
   b. $y = -\frac{4}{7}x + \frac{8}{7} \qquad\qquad y = -\frac{4}{7}x + \frac{8}{7}$

4. $x - 2y = 13$
   a. $3(x - 2y = 13) \Rightarrow 3x - 6y = 39$
   b. $y = \frac{1}{2}x - \frac{13}{2} \qquad\qquad y = \frac{1}{2}x - \frac{13}{2}$

© Houghton Mifflin Harcourt Publishing Company

LANGUAGE SUPPORT 🔲 EL

Connect Context

Some students may recognize the process of combining opposite terms as *cancellation* or *making zero pairs*. Use the word *eliminate* when describing the elimination method, but ask students to think of various names they have used to label this concept. This provides the students with a connection to previous learning.

For each linear system, multiply the first equation by 2 and add the new equation to the second equation. Then, graph this new equation along with both of the original equations.

5. $\begin{cases} 2x + 4y = 24 \\ -12x + 8y = -16 \end{cases}$

$2(2x + 4y = 24) \Rightarrow 4x + 8y = 48$

$\begin{array}{r} 4x + 8y = 48 \\ + -12x + 8y = -16 \\ \hline -8x + 16y = 32 \end{array}$

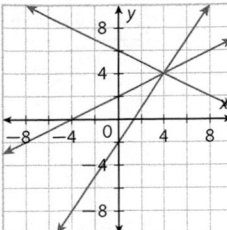

6. $\begin{cases} 2x + 2y = 16 \\ -15x + 3y = -12 \end{cases}$

$2(2x + 2y = 16) \Rightarrow 4x + 4y = 32$

$\begin{array}{r} 4x + 4y = 32 \\ + -15x + 3y = -12 \\ \hline -11x + 7y = 20 \end{array}$

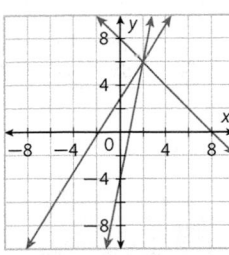

Solve each system of linear equations by multiplying. Verify each answer by graphing the system of equations.

7. $\begin{cases} 5x - 2y = 11 \\ 3x + 5y = 19 \end{cases}$

$\begin{array}{l} 5(5x - 2y = 11) \\ + 2(3x + 5y = 19) \end{array} \Rightarrow$

$\begin{array}{r} 25x - 10y = 55 \\ + 6x + 10y = 38 \\ \hline 31x = 93 \\ x = 3 \\ 5(3) - 2y = 11 \\ y = 2 \end{array}$

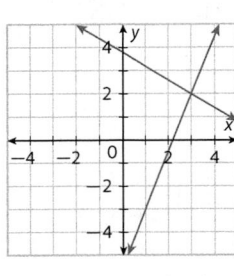

The solution is $(3, 2)$.

8. $\begin{cases} -2x + 2y = 2 \\ -4x + 7y = 16 \end{cases}$

$\begin{array}{l} -2(-2x + 2y = 2) \\ + -4x + 7y = 16 \end{array} \Rightarrow$

$\begin{array}{r} 4x - 4y = -4 \\ + -4x + 7y = 16 \\ \hline 3y = 12 \\ y = 4 \\ -2x + 2(4) = 2 \\ x = 3 \end{array}$

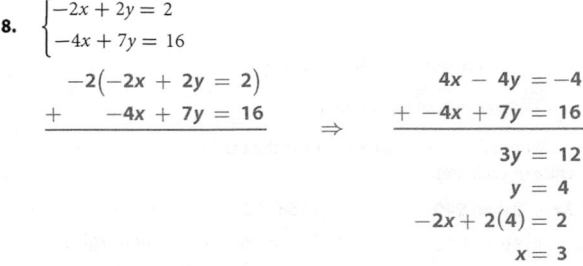
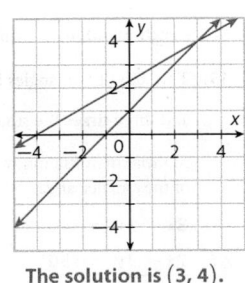

The solution is $(3, 4)$.

ASSIGNMENT GUIDE

Concepts and Skills	Practice
Explore 1 Understanding Linear Systems and Multiplication	Exercises 1–4, 19
Explore 2 Proving the Elimination Method with Multiplication	Exercises 5–6
Example 1 Solving Linear Systems by Multiplying First	Exercises 7–12, 20–22
Example 2 Solving Linear System Models by Multiplying First	Exercises 13–18, 23

AVOID COMMON ERRORS

Students may forget to multiply both sides of the equation by a number when they create an opposite coefficient through multiplication. Remind them that the Multiplication Property of Equality requires both sides of the equation to be multiplied by the same number.

Exercise	Depth of Knowledge (D.O.K.)	COMMON CORE Mathematical Practices
1–12	**1** Recall of Information	**MP.2** Reasoning
13–18	**2** Skills/Concepts	**MP.4** Modeling
19	**2** Skills/Concepts	**MP.2** Reasoning
20	**2** Skills/Concepts	**MP.3** Logic
21	**3** Strategic Thinking	**MP.3** Logic
22	**3** Strategic Thinking H.O.T.	**MP.3** Logic
23	**3** Strategic Thinking H.O.T.	**MP.4** Modeling

Students now know two algebraic methods for solving a system of linear equations: substitution and elimination. Have students underline the coefficients of the variables in both equations in the system and check whether any of the coefficients is 1. Emphasize that substitution works best if one of the variables in the system has a coefficient of 1. Elimination works well in all other cases.

9. $\begin{cases} 3x + 4y = 13 \\ 2x - 2y = -10 \end{cases}$

$$\begin{array}{r} 3x + 4y = 13 \\ + 2(2x - 2y = -10) \\ \hline \end{array} \Rightarrow$$

$$\begin{array}{r} 3x + 4y = 13 \\ + 4x - 4y = -20 \\ \hline 7x = -7 \\ x = -1 \\ 3(-1) + 4y = 13 \\ y = 4 \end{array}$$

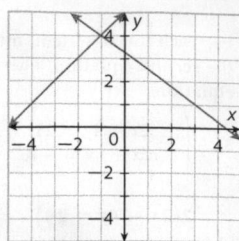

The solution is $(-1, 4)$.

10. $\begin{cases} x - 4y = -1 \\ 5x + 2y = 17 \end{cases}$

$$\begin{array}{r} -5(x - 4y = -1) \\ + 5x + 2y = 17 \\ \hline \end{array} \Rightarrow$$

$$\begin{array}{r} -5x + 20y = 5 \\ + 5x + 2y = 17 \\ \hline 22y = 22 \\ y = 1 \\ 5x + 2(1) = 17 \\ x = 3 \end{array}$$

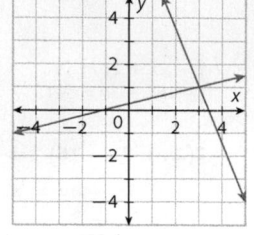

The solution is $(3, 1)$.

Solve each system of linear equations using multiplication.

11. $\begin{cases} -3x + 2y = 4 \\ 5x - 3y = 1 \end{cases}$

$$5(-3x + 2y = 4)$$

$$\begin{array}{r} -15x + 10y = 20 \\ + 15x - 9y = 3 \\ \hline y = 23 \end{array}$$

$$-3x + 2y = 4$$
$$-3x + 2(23) = 4$$
$$x = 14 \quad \text{The solution is } (14, 23).$$

12. $\begin{cases} 3x + 3y = 12 \\ 6x + 11y = 14 \end{cases}$

$$-2(3x + 3y = 12)$$

$$\begin{array}{r} -6x - 6y = -24 \\ + 6x + 11y = 14 \\ \hline 5y = -10 \\ y = -2 \end{array}$$

$$-3x + 3y = 12$$
$$3x + 3(-2) = 12$$
$$x = 6 \quad \text{The solution is } (6, -2).$$

Solve each problem by multiplying first.

13. The sum of two angles is 180°. The difference between twice the larger angle and three times the smaller angle is 150°. The system of equations $\begin{cases} x + y = 180 \\ 2x - 3y = 150 \end{cases}$ models this situation, where x is the measure of the larger angle and y is the measure of the smaller angle. What is the measure of each angle?

$$\begin{array}{r} 3x + 3y = 540 \\ 2x - 3y = 150 \\ \hline 5x = 690 \\ x = 138 \end{array}$$

$$3x + 3y = 540$$
$$3(138) + 3y = 540$$
$$y = 42$$

$(138, 42)$

The measures of the angles are 138° and 42°.

14. The perimeter of a rectangular swimming pool is 126 feet. The difference between the length and the width is 39 feet. The system of equations $\begin{cases} 2x + 2y = 126 \\ x - y = 39 \end{cases}$ models this situation,

where x is the length of the pool and y is the width of the pool. Find the dimensions of the swimming pool.

$2x + 2y = 126$

$2x - 2y = 78$

$\overline{\quad 4x = 204\quad}$

$x = 51$

$2x + 2y = 126$

$2(51) + 2y = 126$

$y = 12$

$(51, 12)$

The swimming pool is 51 feet by 12 feet.

15. Jamian bought a total of 40 bagels and donuts for a morning meeting. He paid a total of $33.50. Each donut cost $0.65 and each bagel cost $1.15. The system of equations $\begin{cases} b + d = 40 \\ 1.15b + 0.65d = 33.50 \end{cases}$ models this situation, where b is the number of bagels and d is the number of donuts. How many of each did Jamian buy?

$0.65b + 0.65d = 26$

$-(1.15b + 0.65d) = -(33.50)$

$\overline{\quad -0.5b = -7.50\quad}$

$b = 15$

$b + d = 40$

$15 + d = 40$

$d = 25$

$(15, 25)$

Jamian bought 15 bagels and 25 donuts.

16. A clothing store is having a sale on shirts and jeans. 4 shirts and 2 pairs of jeans cost $64. 3 shirts and 3 pairs of jeans cost $72. The system of equations $\begin{cases} 4s + 2j = 64 \\ 3s + 3j = 72 \end{cases}$ models this situation, where s is the cost of a shirt and j is the cost of a pair of jeans. How much does one shirt and one pair of jeans cost?

$12s + 6j = 192$

$-(6s + 6j) = -(144)$

$\overline{\quad 6s = 48\quad}$

$s = 8$

$(8, 16)$

$4s + 2j = 64$

$4(8) + 2j = 64$

$j = 16$

One shirt costs $8 and one pair of jeans cost $16.

17. Jayce bought 5 bath towels and returned 2 hand towels. His sister Jayna bought 3 bath towels and returned 4 hand towels. Jayce paid a total of $124 and Jayna paid a total of $24. The system of equations $\begin{cases} 5b - 2h = 124 \\ 3b - 4h = 24 \end{cases}$ models this situation, where b is the price of a bath towel and h is the price of a hand towel. How much does each kind of towel cost?

$10b - 4h = 248$

$-(3b - 4h) = -(24)$

$\overline{\quad 7b = 224\quad}$

$b = 32$

$5b - 2h = 124$

$5(32) - 2h = 124$

$h = 18$

$(32, 18)$

Bath towels cost $32 each and hand towels cost $18 each.

MULTIPLE REPRESENTATIONS

When the two lines in a system of linear equations are parallel, visual learners will benefit by looking at the graphs for both equations first, and then relating the graphs to the algebraic representations.

18. Apples cost $0.95 per pound and bananas cost $1.10 per pound. Leah bought a total of 8 pounds of apples and bananas for $8.05.

The system of equations $\begin{cases} a + b = 8 \\ 0.95a + 1.10b = 8.05 \end{cases}$ models this

situation, where a is the number of pounds of apples and b is the number of pounds of bananas. How many pounds of each did Leah buy?

$$1.10a + 1.10b = 8.80$$
$$-(0.95a + 1.10b) = -(8.05)$$
$$\overline{0.15a = 0.75}$$
$$a = 5$$

$$a + b = 8$$
$$5 + b = 8$$
$$b = 3$$

Leah bought 5 pounds of apples and 3 pounds of bananas.

19. Which of the following are possible ways to eliminate a variable by multiplying first? $\begin{cases} -x + 2y = 3 \\ 4x - 5y = -3 \end{cases}$

a. Multiply the first equation by 4. **Yes**

b. Multiply the first equation by 5 and the second equation by 2. **Yes**

c. Multiply the first equation by 4 and the second equation by 2. **No**

d. Multiply the first equation by 5 and the second equation by 4. **No**

e. Multiply the first equation by 2 and the second equation by 5. **No**

f. Multiply the second equation by 4. **No**

20. Explain the Error A linear system has two equations $Ax + By = C$ and $Dx + Ey = F$. A student begins to solve the equation as shown. What is the error?

$$Ax + By = C$$
$$+ k(Dx + Ey) = F$$
$$\overline{(A + kD)x + (B + kE)y = C + F}$$

The student did not multiply F in the second equation by the constant k before adding it to the first equation. The systems are not equivalent.

21. Critical Thinking Suppose you want to eliminate y in this system: $\begin{cases} 2x + 11y = -3 \\ 3x + 4y = 8 \end{cases}$

By what numbers would you need to multiply the two equations in order to eliminate y? Why might you choose to eliminate x instead?

You could multiply the first equation by 4 and the second equation by -11, and then add the resulting equations to eliminate y. You might choose to eliminate x instead because the numbers you would multiply by are easier to work with.

H.O.T. Focus on Higher Order Thinking

22. Justify Reasoning Solve the following system of equations by multiplying.

$\begin{cases} x + 3y = -14 \\ 2x + y = -3 \end{cases}$ Would it be easier to solve the system by using substitution? Explain your reasoning.

The solution is $(1, -5)$. It may be easier to solve using substitution because in the first equation there is no coefficient for the x-term.

23. Multi-Step The school store is running a promotion on school supplies. Different supplies are placed on two shelves. You can purchase 3 items from shelf A and 2 from shelf B for $16. Or you can purchase 2 items from shelf A and 3 from shelf B for $14. This can be represented by the following system of equations.

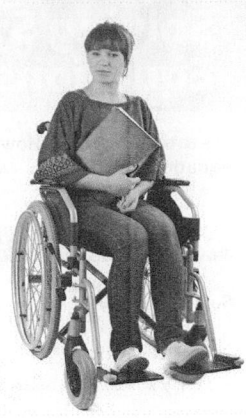

a. Solve the system of equations $\begin{cases} 3A + 2B = 16 \\ 2A + 3B = 14 \end{cases}$ by multiplying first.

$$-2(3A + 2B = 16) \Rightarrow -6A - 4B = -32 \qquad 3A + 2(2) = 16$$
$$\underline{3(2A + 3B = 14)} \Rightarrow \underline{6A + 9B = 42} \qquad\quad 3A + 4 = 16$$
$$\qquad\qquad\qquad\qquad\quad 5B = 10 \qquad\qquad\qquad 3A = 12$$
$$\qquad\qquad\qquad\qquad\quad B = 2 \qquad\qquad\qquad\quad A = 4$$

$4 on shelf A and $2 on shelf B

b. If the supplies on shelf A are normally $6 each and the supplies on shelf B are normally $3 each, how much will you save on each package plan from part A?

$6(3) + 3(2) = 24$ **You save $8 when buying the first package.**

$6(2) + 3(3) = 21$ **You save $7 for buying the second package.**

Lesson Performance Task

A chemist has a bottle of 1% acid solution and a bottle of 5% acid solution. She wants to mix the two solutions to get 100 mL of a 4% acid solution.

a. Complete the table to write the system of equations.

	1% Solution	+	5% Solution	=	4% Solution
Amount of Solution (mL)	x	+	y	=	100
Amount of Acid (mL)	0.01x	+	0.05y	=	0.04(100)

b. Solve the system of equations to find how much she will use from each bottle to get 100 mL of a 4% acid solution.

$$\begin{aligned} x + \quad y &= 100 \\ -100 \quad (0.01x + 0.05y &= 4) \end{aligned}$$

$$\begin{aligned} x + \quad y &= 100 \\ \underline{-x - \quad 5y} &= \underline{-400} \\ - \quad 4y &= -300 \\ y &= 75 \end{aligned}$$

$$\begin{aligned} x + y &= 100 \\ x + 75 &= 100 \\ x &= 25 \end{aligned}$$

Therefore, the chemist will use 25 mL of the 1% solution and 75 mL of the 5% solution.

When multiplying the equation $0.01x + 0.05y = 0.04(100)$ by -100, students might forget to multiply the right-hand side of the equation by -100, since 0.04 is already being multiplied by 100. Suggest that students simplify $0.04(100)$ to 4 before multiplying.

INTEGRATE MATHEMATICAL PRACTICES
Focus on Reasoning

MP.2 Have students suggest various methods they could use to solve the system of equations. Possibilities include: multiplying the second equation by -100 and then adding the equations; multiplying the second equation by 100 and then subtracting; or multiplying the first equation by -1 and the second by 100 and then adding. Students should understand that as long as the multiplication makes the coefficients of a variable opposites or the same, it does not matter which method is used. They may also see that the system could be solved by substitution, resulting in the same solution.

EXTENSION ACTIVITY

Have students research the topics of pharmaceutical compounding and gasoline blending and discuss how systems of equations similar to the one in the Lesson Performance Task might be used in each process. Students may find that in pharmaceutical compounding, a pharmacist needs to figure out how much of each ingredient should be combined to make a medication with exactly the right concentration of the active ingredient. In gasoline blending, engineers need to determine how much of various petroleum products to blend to produce gasoline with the correct octane rating, vapor pressure, and other characteristics.

Scoring Rubric
2 points: Student correctly solves the problem and explains his/her reasoning.
1 point: Student shows good understanding of the problem but does not fully solve or explain his/her reasoning.
0 points: Student does not demonstrate understanding of the problem.

Study Guide Review

ASSESSMENT AND INTERVENTION

Assign or customize module reviews.

MODULE PERFORMANCE TASK

COMMON CORE

Mathematical Practices: MP.1, MP.2, MP.3, MP.4, MP.6
A-REI.C.6, A-CED.A.3

SUPPORTING STUDENT REASONING

Students should begin this problem by focusing on what information they will need. They can then do research, or you can provide them with specific information. Here is some of the information they may ask for.

- **The prices of the cars:** Manufacturer's suggested retail prices (MSRP) are given in the illustration.

- **The distance (in miles) the cars are driven each year:** The US Department of Transportation reports an average of 13,476 miles per year.

- **The miles per gallon each car gets:** The illustration includes the miles per gallon for both city and highway driving. The overall rate would depend on the ratio of city miles driven to highway miles given. A simple approach may be to use the average of the two rates.

- **The cost of gas:** Students can research this or you can give them an estimate of the cost in your area.

Essential Question: How can you use a system of linear equations to solve real-world problems?

Key Vocabulary
elimination method
(eliminación)
substitution method
(sustitución)
system of linear equations
(sistema de ecuaciones lineales)

KEY EXAMPLE (Lesson 11.2)

Solve $\begin{cases} 4x + y = 7 \\ -6x + y = -3 \end{cases}$ by substitution.

Solve an equation for one variable.

$-6x + y = -3$ Select one of the equations.

$y = 6x - 3$ Solve for y. Isolate y on one side.

Substitute the expression for y in the other equation and solve.

$4x + (6x - 3) = 7$ Substitute the expression for y.

$10x - 3 = 7$ Combine like terms.

$10x = 10$ Add 3 to both sides.

$x = 1$ Divide each side by 10.

Substitute the value for x into one of the equations and solve for y.

$4(1) + y = 7$ Substitute the value of x into the first equation.

$4 + y = 7$ Simplify.

$y = 3$ Subtract 4 from both sides.

So, $(1, 3)$ is the solution of the system.

KEY EXAMPLE (Lesson 11.3)

Solve $\begin{cases} -6x + 8y = 19 \\ 6x - 8y = -19 \end{cases}$ by adding.

Add the equations.

$$\begin{array}{r} -6x + 8y = 19 \\ +6x - 8y = -19 \\ \hline 0 + 0 = 0 \\ 0 = 0 \end{array}$$

The resulting equation is always true, so the system has infinitely many solutions.

SCAFFOLDING SUPPORT

- Help students build a linear function to model the cost of each car:

$$total\ cost = purchase\ price + \frac{gas\ used\ (gal)}{year} \cdot \frac{cost(\$)}{gal} \cdot years\ driven$$

- To calculate gallons of gas used per year, students can divide the average number of miles driven in a year by the mpg of each car.

EXERCISES

Solve each system of equations. *(Lessons 11.1, 11.2, 11.3, 11.4)*

1. $\begin{cases} 3x + 7y = -5 \\ 8x + 9y = 6 \end{cases}$

$(3, -2)$

2. $\begin{cases} -5x + 2y = 13 \\ 3x - 2y = -11 \end{cases}$

$(-1, 4)$

3. $\begin{cases} 9x - 2y = -5 \\ -6x + y = -1 \end{cases}$

$\left(\dfrac{7}{3}, 13\right)$

4. $\begin{cases} 7x - 9y = -11 \\ 7x - y = -9 \end{cases}$

$\left(-\dfrac{5}{4}, \dfrac{1}{4}\right)$

5. $\begin{cases} -3x + 5y = 8 \\ 3x - 5y = -8 \end{cases}$

infinitely many solutions

6. $\begin{cases} -2x + 6y = 6 \\ -4x - 8y = 12 \end{cases}$

$(-3, 0)$

MODULE PERFORMANCE TASK

Do Hybrid Cars Pay for Themselves?

Your family wants to buy a specific model of new car and is considering buying the hybrid version. Use the information shown for the two cars to determine how long it will take to save enough money on gas to pay for the extra cost of the hybrid. Then make a recommendation on which car to buy.

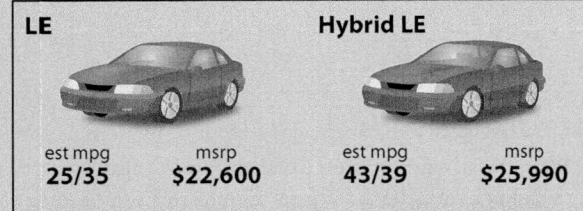

LE		**Hybrid LE**	
est mpg	msrp	est mpg	msrp
25/35	**$22,600**	**43/39**	**$25,990**

Start by listing in the space below the information you will need to solve the problem. Then use your own paper to complete the task. Be sure to write down all your data and assumptions. Then use graphs, numbers, words, or algebra to explain how you reached your conclusion.

DISCUSSION OPPORTUNITIES

- Students may not expect to own the car long enough to reach the point where savings on gas equal the additional cost of the hybrid.

- Students may be willing to accept higher cost as a tradeoff for helping conserve fossil fuels and reduce carbon emissions.

SAMPLE SOLUTION

Assumptions

Purchase price: $22,600 (non-hybrid) and $25,990 (hybrid)

Annual miles driven: 13,476

Average mpg: 30 mpg (non-hybrid) and 41 mpg (hybrid)

Cost of gas: $4 per gallon

Equations

Let x = number of years and y = total cost.

Non-hybrid:

$$y = 22{,}600 + \left(\frac{13{,}476}{30}\right)(4)x$$

Hybrid:

$$y = 25{,}990 + \left(\frac{13{,}476}{41}\right)(4)x$$

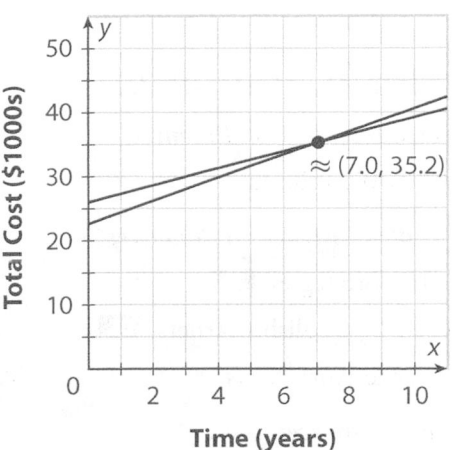

The *y*-intercepts represent the purchase prices of the two cars, and the intersection, about (7.0, 35.2), indicates that it will take about 7 years to save enough on gas to pay for the extra cost of the hybrid. Recommendations may vary. See notes under "Discussion Opportunities."

Assessment Rubric

2 points: Student correctly solves the problem and explains his/her reasoning.

1 point: Student shows good understanding of the problem but does not fully solve or explain.

0 points: Student does not demonstrate understanding of the problem.

Study Guide Review   **528**

Ready to Go On?

ASSESS MASTERY

Use the assessment on this page to determine if students have mastered the concepts and standards covered in this module.

ASSESSMENT AND INTERVENTION

Access Ready to Go On? assessment online, and receive instant scoring, feedback, and customized intervention or enrichment.

ADDITIONAL RESOURCES

Response to Intervention Resources

- Reteach Worksheets

Differentiated Instruction Resources

- Reading Strategies **EL**
- Success for English Learners **EL**
- Challenge Worksheets

Assessment Resources

- Leveled Module Quizzes

11.1–11.4 Solving Systems of Linear Equations

- Online Homework
- Hints and Help
- Extra Practice

Solve each system of equations using the given method. *(Lessons 11.1, 11.2, 11.3, 11.4)*

1. $\begin{cases} -3x + y = 6 \\ 5x + 2y = 23 \end{cases}$; substitution

   $(1, 9)$

2. $\begin{cases} -4x + 9y = 14 \\ 12x - 10y = -8 \end{cases}$; multiplication

   $(1, 2)$

3. $\begin{cases} 7x + 2y = 8 \\ -5x - 2y = -12 \end{cases}$; addition

   $(-2, 11)$

4. $\begin{cases} 6x - 12y = 15 \\ 2x - 4y = 6 \end{cases}$; multiplication

   no solution

5. $\begin{cases} 5x - 3y = 3 \\ 3x - y = 9 \end{cases}$; graphing

   $(6, 9)$

6. $\begin{cases} 9x - 2y = 8 \\ -2x + 2y = 6 \end{cases}$; addition

   $(2, 5)$

ESSENTIAL QUESTION

7. When must a system of linear equations be solved algebraically, not graphically?

   Possible answer: Whenever the solution to a system does not have integer coordinates, it can be difficult or impossible to find the precise answer through graphing.

© Houghton Mifflin Harcourt Publishing Company

COMMON CORE Common Core Standards

Lesson	Items	Content Standards	Mathematical Practices
11.2	1	**A-REI.C.6**	**MP.1**
11.4	2	**A-REI.C.6, A-REI.C.5**	**MP.1**
11.3	3	**A-REI.C.6**	**MP.1**
11.4	4	**A-REI.C.6, A-REI.C.5**	**MP.1**
11.1	5	**A-REI.C.6**	**MP.5**
11.3	6	**A-REI.C.6**	**MP.1**

MODULE 11
MIXED REVIEW

Assessment Readiness

1. A system of equations is represented on the graph. Is each equation part of the system? Select Yes or No for each equation.

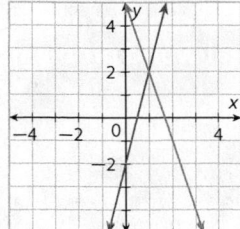

A. $3x + y = 5$	● Yes	○ No
B. $2x + 3y = 8$	○ Yes	● No
C. $-8x + 2y = -4$	● Yes	○ No

2. Consider the lines and solution set of the system of equations $\begin{cases} -8x - 6y = 8 \\ 4x + 3y = 2 \end{cases}$.

   Determine if each of the following statements is True or False.

A. The lines have the same y-intercept.	○ True	● False
B. The lines have the same slope.	● True	○ False
C. The system has no solutions.	● True	○ False

3. Solve the system of equations $\begin{cases} 5x + y = 10 \\ 2x + 3y = -9 \end{cases}$. Explain how you solved this system.

   $(3, -5)$; I substituted $-5x + 10$ for y into $2x + 3y = -9$ and solved for x. Then, I substituted 3 for x in one of the equations and solved for y.

4. The perimeter of a picture frame is 68 inches. The difference between the length of the frame and three times its width is 2. The system of equations $\begin{cases} 2\ell + 2W = 68 \\ 2\ell - 6W = 4 \end{cases}$ represents this situation, where ℓ represents the length in inches and W represents the width in inches. What is the width of the frame? What is the length of the frame?

   The width is 8 inches, and the length is 26 inches.

MIXED REVIEW
Assessment Readiness

ASSESSMENT AND INTERVENTION

Assign ready-made or customized practice tests to prepare students for high-stakes tests.

ADDITIONAL RESOURCES

Assessment Resources

- Leveled Module Quizzes: Modified, B

AVOID COMMON ERRORS

Item 4　Some students will find the opposite of only the first term before eliminating. Remind students that, to make an equivalent equation, they must perform the same action on all terms on both sides of the equation.

COMMON CORE **Common Core Standards**

Lesson	Items	Content Standards	Mathematical Practices
3.3, 6.3	1*	A-CED.A.2	MP.4
6.3, 11.4	2*	A-CED.A.2, A-REI.C.6	MP.1
11.1, 11.2, 11.3, 11.4	3	A-REI.C.6	MP.2
11.3	4	A-REI.C.6	MP.4

* Item integrates mixed review concepts from previous modules or a previous course.

Modeling with Linear Systems

ESSENTIAL QUESTION:

Answer: Once your problem situation is represented by equations, you can graph them and look for the intersection point to find the solution.

PROFESSIONAL DEVELOPMENT VIDEO

Professional Development Video

Learn effective ways of integrating technology into your classroom to meet a variety of different needs.

Professional Development
my.hrw.com

MODULE **12**

Modeling with Linear Systems

Essential Question: How can you model with linear systems to solve real-world problems?

LESSON 12.1
Creating Systems of Linear Equations

LESSON 12.2
Graphing Systems of Linear Inequalities

LESSON 12.3
Modeling with Linear Systems

REAL WORLD VIDEO
When you're playing an arcade game, chances are that you don't have math on your mind. But you might be surprised to find that mathematical reasoning can sometimes help you figure out the best strategy for the winning the game.

© Houghton Mifflin Harcourt Publishing Company · Image Credits: ©Richard Green/Alamy

MODULE PERFORMANCE TASK PREVIEW

How to Win at an Arcade Game

Many arcades have a game that is somewhat like bowling. Players roll a hand-sized ball up an inclined lane so that the ball lands in one of several different holes, each with varying point values. The goal is to collect as many points as possible. How can you use mathematics to help you win at this game? Let's find out!

Module 12   531

DIGITAL TEACHER EDITION

Access a full suite of teaching resources when and where you need them:

- Access content online or offline
- Customize lessons to share with your class
- Communicate with your students in real-time
- View student grades and data instantly to target your instruction where it is needed most

PERSONAL MATH TRAINER
Assessment and Intervention

Assign automatically graded homework, quizzes, tests, and intervention activities. Prepare your students with updated, Common Core-aligned practice tests.

Complete these exercises to review skills you will need for this module.

One-Step Inequalities

· Online Homework
· Hints and Help
· Extra Practice

Example 1   Solve.

$$x + 13 \leq 9$$
$$x + 13 - 13 \leq 9 - 13$$
$$x \leq -4$$

Isolate the variable by subtracting 13 from both sides of the inequality.

Solve each inequality.

1. $k - 12 \geq 5$
$$k \geq 17$$

2. $y + 2 < -9$
$$y < -11$$

3. $\frac{n}{4} > -7$
$$n > -28$$

Two-Step Equations and Inequalities

Example 2   Solve.

$$4b - 19 = 17$$
$$4b - 19 + 19 = 17 + 19$$
$$4b = 36$$
$$\frac{4b}{4} = \frac{36}{4}$$
$$b = 9$$

Add 19 to both sides of the equation.

Divide both sides of the equation by 4.

Solve each equation.

4. $3a + 17 = 38$
$$a = 7$$

5. $27 - 5c = 12$
$$c = 3$$

6. $\frac{3}{4}m - 8 = 10$
$$m = 24$$

Example 3   Solve.

$$11 - 7t < 67$$
$$11 - 11 - 7t < 67 - 11$$
$$-7t < 56$$
$$\frac{-7t}{-7} > \frac{56}{-7}$$
$$t > -8$$

Subtract 11 from both sides of the inequality.

Divide both sides of the inequality by –7.

Reverse the inequality symbol.

Solve each inequality.

7. $9p + 23 < 41$
$$p < 2$$

8. $-6w - 16 \geq 44$
$$w \leq -10$$

9. $\frac{v}{3} + 12 > 7$
$$v > -15$$

ASSESS READINESS

Use the assessment on this page to determine if students need strategic or intensive intervention for the module's prerequisite skills.

ASSESSMENT AND INTERVENTION

RtI Response to Intervention   **TIER 1, TIER 2, TIER 3 SKILLS**

Personal Math Trainer will automatically create a standards-based, personalized intervention assignment for your students, targeting each student's individual needs!

ADDITIONAL RESOURCES

See the table below for a full list of intervention resources available for this module.

Response to Intervention Resources also includes:

- Tier 2 Skill Pre-Tests for each Module
- Tier 2 Skill Post-Tests for each skill

Response to Intervention			Differentiated Instruction
Tier 1	**Tier 2**	**Tier 3**	
Lesson Intervention Worksheets	Strategic Intervention Skills Intervention Worksheets	Intensive Intervention Worksheets available online	
Reteach 12.1 Reteach 12.2 Reteach 12.3	2 Algebraic Expressions 10 Linear Functions 14 One-Step Inequalities 21 Two-Step Equations 22 Two-Step Inequalities	Building Block Skills 19, 22, 23, 24, 27, 40, 52, 54, 59, 81, 88, 98, 110	Challenge worksheets Extend the Math Lesson Activities in TE

Creating Systems of Linear Equations

Common Core Math Standards

The student is expected to:

 A-CED.A.3

Represent constraints by… systems of equations… and interpret solutions as viable or nonviable options in a modeling context. Also F-LE.B.5

Mathematical Practices

MP.2 Reasoning

Language Objective

Describe a real-world situation that can be modeled by a system of two linear equations, and then write the equations.

ENGAGE

Essential Question: How do you use systems of linear equations to model and solve real-world problems?

Translate verbal statements into linear equations that can then be used as a system of equations to solve a problem.

PREVIEW: LESSON PERFORMANCE TASK

View the Engage section online. Discuss the costs and responsibilities of owning a pet and the differences in how the two kennels charge for services. Then preview the Lesson Performance Task.

12.1 Creating Systems of Linear Equations

Essential Question: How do you use systems of linear equations to model and solve real-world problems?

Resource Locker

⊘ Explore   Creating Linear System Models by Changing Parameters

Investigate how a system of equations can help you compare and interpret situations where rates of change affect the outcome.

After leaving her hotel, a student is walking to a café to have breakfast and do some sightseeing. On the way, she passes two stores that rent bicycles. The first shop charges an initial fee of $7.00 and $2.75 for each hour. The second shop charges a flat fee of $3.00 per hour. Over breakfast, the student needs to decide which rental agency to use. How should she start?

(A) Begin by finding functions that represent the cost of each rental. Let $f(t)$ represent the cost of renting a bicycle for t hours from the first shop, and let $g(t)$ represent the cost of renting a bicycle from the second shop.

(B) What is the initial cost of renting a bicycle from the first shop? __$7.00__

(C) This represents the __y-intercept__ of the model for the first business.

(D) The slope of this linear model represents the __rate of change__ of the cost, as a function of time.

(E) The slope of the first model is __2.75__ .

(F) This makes $f(t) =$ __$2.75t + 7$__ .

(G) Similarly, the function modeling the cost for renting a bicycle from the second shop is $g(t) =$ __$3t$__ .

(H) Once the student decides the length of time she plans to spend on her bike ride, she can solve the linear system of the two functions, $\begin{cases} f(t) = 2.75t + 7 \\ g(t) = 3t \end{cases}$, to determine from which company she wants to rent a bicycle.

HARDCOVER PAGES 429–440

Turn to these pages to find this lesson in the hardcover student edition.

1. **Discussion** Under what conditions would this type of real-world situation have no solution?
   There would be no solution if the rental companies had different starting prices but the
   same hourly rate.

2. **Discussion** Under what conditions would this type of real-world situation have infinitely many solutions?
   The system would have infinitely many solutions if the rental companies had
   the same pricing.

✐ Explain 1 — Creating Linear System Models from Verbal Descriptions

Often, a company will charge a start-up fee for its services, followed by a monthly or per unit cost. This can be written as a linear function in slope-intercept form.

When the costs of the same services from two different companies must be compared, the variable amount for each must represent the same thing, and both models should produce values with the same type of unit. For example, if one function models yearly income in terms of thousands of dollars and the other function models monthly income in terms of hundreds of dollars, the comparison will not be accurate.

Example 1 Determine when the cost of the two services will be the same amount, and what the price will be.

Video streaming service Atomic Stream charges $10 for membership and $1.00 for each movie download. Blitz Video charges $15 for a membership and $0.50 per movie download. How many movies would you need to download for the services to have identical costs? What is that cost?

🧩 Analyze Information

Identify the important information.

Atomic Stream has a _____$10_____ membership fee.

Atomic Stream has a _____$1_____ per download fee.

Blitz Video has a _____$15_____ membership fee.

Blitz Video has a _____$0.50_____ per download fee.

🧩 Formulate a Plan

Create two functions to model the cost of each service, $A(x)$ and $B(x)$, where x represents the _number of videos downloaded_.

The solution can be found by setting up an equation so that the function $A(x)$ is _____equal_____ to the function $B(x)$ and then solving for _____x_____.

© Houghton Mifflin Harcourt Publishing Company

PROFESSIONAL DEVELOPMENT

Integrate Mathematical Practices

This lesson provides an opportunity to address Mathematical Practice **MP.2**, which calls for students to "reason abstractly and quantitatively." Students learn to write and solve systems of linear equations for real-world situations represented by verbal descriptions, tables, or graphs. By analyzing the relationships between variables, they are able to translate each of these representations into algebraic equations. After solving the systems of equations, students interpret the solutions by connecting them to the real-world situations they represent.

EXPLORE

Creating Linear System Models by Changing Parameters

INTEGRATE TECHNOLOGY

Students have the option of completing the Explore activity either in the book or online.

QUESTIONING STRATEGIES

? If two companies charge different hourly amounts for a service, does it always cost less to use the company with the lower hourly rate? Explain. No; if the company with the lower hourly rate charges an initial fee, it may cost less to use the other company.

EXPLAIN 1

Creating Linear System Models from Verbal Descriptions

AVOID COMMON ERRORS

Students who have had little experience with paying fees for services may not understand the concept of an initial charge plus a per-unit rate. Discuss with students the nature of the fees used in real-world problems so they can write the appropriate functions.

QUESTIONING STRATEGIES

? When can you set the expressions for the cost of two services equal to each other? You can set expressions equal to each other when both expressions use the same variables and give answers in the same units.

Solve

The model for Atomic Stream is $A(x) = \boxed{10 + x}$.

The model for Blitz Video is $B(x) = \boxed{15 + 0.5x}$.

The two functions are $\begin{cases} A(x) = 10 + x \\ B(x) = 15 + 0.5x \end{cases}$.

Solve using substitution. You can use substitution because you are solving for the value where $A(x) \boxed{=} B(x)$.

$$\boxed{10 + x} = \boxed{15 + 0.5x} \qquad\qquad A\left(\boxed{10}\right) = \boxed{10 + 10}$$

$$0.5x = 5 \qquad\qquad\qquad\qquad\qquad\qquad = \boxed{20}$$

$$x = \boxed{10}$$

$$A(x) = \boxed{10 + x}$$

The cost of each service is _____$20_____ when _____10_____ movies are screened.

Justify and Evaluate

It is reasonable to expect the cost of the services to be the same after a number of uses. The businesses are in the same market but can appeal to different customers.

Atomic Stream is more affordable for customers who stream ___less than 10___ movies a month, while Blitz Video is a better deal for people who stream ___more than 10___ movies a month.

Your Turn

3. One cable television provider has a $60 setup fee and charges $80 per month, and another cable provider has a $160 equipment fee and charges $70 per month.

$$\begin{cases} f(t) = 60 + 780t \\ g(t) = 160 + 70t \end{cases} \quad \begin{aligned} 60 + 80t &\approx 160 + 70t \\ t &\approx 10 \end{aligned} \quad \begin{aligned} f(t) &= 60 + 780t \\ f(10) &= 60 + 780 \cdot 10 = 860 \end{aligned}$$

Both will charge $860 for 10 months.

4. The Strauss family is deciding between two lawn-care services. Green Lawn charges a $49 startup fee plus $29 per month. Yard Guard charges a $25 startup fee plus $37 per month.

$$\begin{cases} G(t) = 49 + 29t \\ Y(t) = 25 + 37t \end{cases} \quad \begin{aligned} 49 + 29t &= 25 + 37t \\ t &= 3 \end{aligned} \quad \begin{aligned} G(t) &= 49 + 29t \\ G(10) &= 49 + 29 \cdot 3 = 136 \end{aligned}$$

Both will charge $136 for 3 months.

COLLABORATIVE LEARNING

Peer-to-Peer Activity

Have students work in pairs. Give each pair a real-world situation represented in both a table and a graph. One student should write a system of linear equations using the table, and the other student should use the graph. Then both should use their systems to find a solution. After student pairs compare solutions, have them review each other's work for accuracy.

⊘ Explain 2   Creating Linear System Models from Tables

Sometimes, there is not enough information to model an equation. Businesses may have a table of rates posted to explain their pricing. To compare the cost of items or services from two or more businesses, table entries can be used to create and solve a linear system.

Example 2 Use the cost tables for two services to create a linear system of equations. Then solve the system to determine when the cost of the two services will be equal.

(A) Two garden supply companies deliver mulch according to the following table.

Mulch (Cubic Yards)	Yard Depot	Lawn & Garden
1	$60	$80
2	$90	$105
3	$120	$130
4	$150	$155

Yard Depot	Lawn & Garden
Use points $(1, 60)$ and $(2, 90)$.	Use points $(1, 80)$ and $(2, 105)$.
$m = \dfrac{90 - 60}{2 - 1} = 30$	$m = \dfrac{105 - 80}{2 - 1} = 25$
Write the equation.	Write the equation.
$y - 60 = 30(x - 1)$	$y - 80 = 25(x - 1)$
$y = 30x + 30$	$y = 25x + 55$

The system of equations is: $\begin{cases} f(x) = 30s + 30 \\ g(x) = 25x + 55 \end{cases}$

Solve for x when $f(x) = g(x)$ to find the amount of cubic yards, x, for which both companies charge the same amount.

$$30s + 30 = 25x + 55$$

$$x = 5 \Rightarrow f(5) = 30(5) + 30 = 180$$

Both companies charge $180 for 5 cubic yards of mulch.

© Houghton Mifflin Harcourt Publishing Company

EXPLAIN 2

Creating Linear System Models from Tables

INTEGRATE MATHEMATICAL PRACTICES
Focus on Reasoning

MP.2 Students who work well with patterns may be tempted to continue the patterns shown in the table in order to find a solution. Discuss with students reasons for writing linear functions based on the table. Students should understand that when the solution is large, extending the patterns in the tables is an inefficient method.

QUESTIONING STRATEGIES

? When using data in a table to write equations, how can you find the slope for each equation? **Divide the difference between consecutive *y*-values by the difference between the corresponding *x*-values.**

? How can you find the *y*-intercept for each equation? **After finding the slope *m*, substitute any pair of corresponding *x*- and *y*-values from the table into the equation $f(x) = mx + b$ and solve for *b*.**

DIFFERENTIATE INSTRUCTION

Multiple Representations

Organizing the same set of data in different ways can help students better visualize how to solve a problem. Challenge students to make a verbal description, table, and graph that all represent the same real-world situation, and discuss how each representation suggests a different strategy for finding a solution.

Focus on Math Connections

MP.1 Solving a linear system by setting the two functions equal to one another may look very different from the solution methods students learned previously. Help students to recognize that setting one function equal to the other is equivalent to substituting an expression that equals y from one equation for the variable into the other equation. The process looks different because the equations are written in function notation, but it is still the substitution method.

Ⓑ The table shows canoe rental prices for two companies.

Time t (in hours)	Canoe Depot	Paddle and Oar
1	$14	$20
2	$19	$23
3	$24	$26

Canoe Depot	Paddle & Oar
Use points $\left(1, \boxed{14}\right)$ and $\left(2, \boxed{19}\right)$.	Use points $\left(1, \boxed{20}\right)$ and $\left(2, \boxed{23}\right)$.
$m = \dfrac{\boxed{19} - \boxed{14}}{2 - 1} = \boxed{5}$	$m = \dfrac{\boxed{23} - \boxed{20}}{2 - 1} = \boxed{3}$
Write the equation.	Write the equation.
$y - \boxed{14} = \boxed{5}\,(x - 1)$	$y - \boxed{20} = \boxed{3}\,(x - 1)$
$y = \boxed{5}\,x + \boxed{9}$	$y = \boxed{3}\,x + \boxed{17}$

The system of equations is
$$\begin{cases} C(x) = \boxed{5}\,x + \boxed{9} \\ P(x) = \boxed{3}\,x + \boxed{17} \end{cases}$$

Solve for x when $C(x) = P(x)$ to find the number of hours, x, for which both canoe rental places charge the same amount.

$$\boxed{5}\,x + \boxed{9} = \boxed{3}\,x + \boxed{17}$$
$$x = \boxed{4} \quad \Rightarrow \quad C\!\left(\boxed{4}\right) = \boxed{29}$$

Both companies charge $ \boxed{29} $ for $ \boxed{4} $ hours of canoe rental.

Your Turn

5. Two garden supply companies deliver pea stone according to the following table.

Pea Stone x (in cubic yards)	Yard Depot	Lawn & Garden
1	$75	$45
2	$110	$85
3	$145	$125

Yard Depot	Lawn & Garden	
$(1, 75)\ (2, 110)$	$(1, 45)\ (2, 85)$	$\begin{cases} f(x) = 35x + 40 \\ g(x) = 40x + 5 \end{cases}$
$m = \dfrac{110 - 75}{2 - 1} = 35$	$m = \dfrac{85 - 45}{2 - 1} = 40$	$35x + 40 = 40x + 5$
$y - 75 = 35(x - 1)$	$y - 40 = 40(x - 1)$	$x = 7$
$y = 35x + 40$	$y = 40x + 5$	$f(7) = 35(7) + 40 = 285$

Both companies charge $285 for 7 cubic yards of pea stone.

© Houghton Mifflin Harcourt Publishing Company

LANGUAGE SUPPORT 🇪🇱

Visual Cues

Real-world problems can be especially challenging for English learners because so many different phrases can represent the same mathematical relationship. Review some of the different ways of expressing fees for services or products. An *initial charge* or starting cost may also be called a *membership fee, joining fee, setup fee, startup fee,* or *delivery charge*. A *per-unit rate* may be a *daily rate, hourly charge,* or *cost per pound* or *per item*. Encourage students to highlight key phrases in problems, using one color for the initial value and another for the per-unit rate.

6. Two beachfront stores rent surfboards according to the following table.

Time t (in hours)	Hang Ten	Waverider
1	$28	$46
2	$48	$63
3	$68	$80
4	$88	$97

Hang Ten	Waverider	
$(1, 28)\ (2, 48)$	$(1, 46)\ (2, 63)$	$\begin{cases} f(x) = 20x + 8 \\ g(x) = 17x + 29 \end{cases}$
$m = \dfrac{48 - 28}{2 - 1} = 20$	$m = \dfrac{63 - 46}{2 - 1} = 40$	$20x + 8 = 17x + 29$
$y - 28 = 20(x - 1)$	$y - 46 = 17(x - 1)$	$x = 7$
$y = 20x + 8$	$y = 17x + 29$	$f(7) = 20(7) + 8 = 148$

Both companies charge $148 for 7 hours of surfboard rental.

⚙ Explain 3 Creating Linear System Models from Graphs

In newspapers and magazines, information is often displayed in the form of a graph. You can use the graph of a linear system to write the function models that are represented.

Example 3 Use the graph to make a linear model of each function. Describe the meaning of the terms in the models. Then create the linear system, and state what the solution represents.

(A)

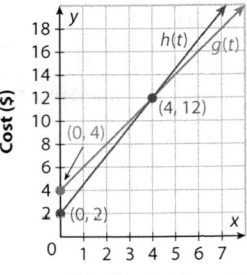

Time Bowled (hours)

$g(x)$	$h(x)$
The y-intercept b is 4.	The y-intercept b is 2.
Initial cost is $4.	Initial cost is $2.
Use $(0, 4)$ and $(4, 12)$:	Use $(0, 2)$ and $(4, 12)$:
$m = \dfrac{12 - 4}{4 - 0} = 2$	$m = \dfrac{12 - 2}{4 - 0} = 2.5$
Charge per hour: $2.00/h	Charge per hour: $2.50/h
$y = 2x + 4$	$y = 2.5x + 2$

The system of equations is: $\begin{cases} g(x) = 2x + 4 \\ h(x) = 2.5x + 2 \end{cases}$

The solution $(4, 12)$ represents the same charge of $12 for 4 hours that both bowling alleys charge.

EXPLAIN 3

Creating Linear System Models from Graphs

INTEGRATE MATHEMATICAL PRACTICES
Focus on Technology

MP.5 After writing functions from a graph, students can verify their work by using a graphing calculator. Students can graph both functions to see if the point of intersection is the same as the point shown in the given graph.

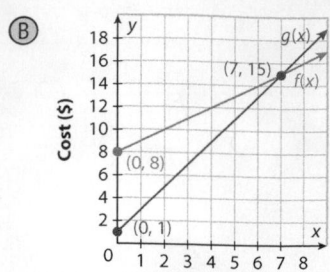

Ⓑ

	$f(x)$	$g(x)$
	The y-intercept b is **8**.	The y-intercept b is **1**.
	Initial cost is $ **8**.	Initial cost is $ **1**.
	Use $\left(0, \boxed{8}\right)$ and $(7, 15)$:	Use $\left(0, \boxed{1}\right)$ and $(7, 15)$:
	$m = \dfrac{15 - \boxed{8}}{\boxed{7} - 0} = \boxed{1}$	$m = \dfrac{15 - \boxed{1}}{\boxed{7} - 0} = \boxed{2}$
	Rate of change: $ **1** /lb	Rate of change: $ **2** /lb
	$y = \boxed{1}\,x + \boxed{8}$	$y = \boxed{2}\,x + \boxed{1}$

The system of equations is
$$\begin{cases} f(x) = \boxed{1}\,x + \boxed{8} \\ g(x) = \boxed{2}\,x + \boxed{1} \end{cases}$$

The solution $(7, 15)$ represents the same charge of $ **15** for **7** pounds of trail mix.

Your Turn

7. Use the graph to make a linear model of each function. Describe the meaning of terms in the models. Then create the linear system and state what the solution represents.

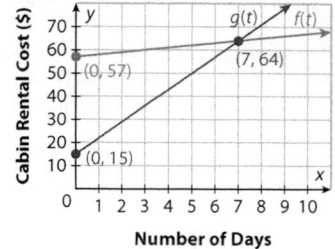

$f(x)$	$g(x)$
y-intercept: 57	y-intercept: 5
initial cost $57	initial cost $15
$m = \dfrac{64 - 57}{7 - 0} = 1$	$m = \dfrac{64 - 15}{7 - 0} = 7$
$y = x + 57$	$y = 7x + 15$

$$\begin{cases} f(x) = x + 57 \\ g(x) = 7x + 15 \end{cases}$$

Solution: $(7, 64)$

The solution represents $64 that both cabins cost to rent for 7 days.

Elaborate

8. When writing a linear model of a situation, what does the slope represent?
The slope represents the rate of change of the dependent variable with respect to the
independent variable.

9. **Discussion** Compare and contrast the system of equations that can be determined from a verbal description of a relationship, a table of values, and a graph.
All three methods will give approximately the same solution, but not always. A table
of prices may have a small degree of rounding to make prices more appealing, either
rounding to the nearest ten or hundred or making the prices end in 9.99 or 9.95. A system
created from a graph may not be as exact if specific points are not identified.

10. **Essential Question Check-In** How do you use systems of linear equations to model and solve real-world problems?
Translate verbal statements or tables of prices into linear equations that can then be used
as a system of equations to solve a problem.

☆ Evaluate: Homework and Practice

- Online Homework
- Hints and Help
- Extra Practice

1. In the graph shown, what do the parameters of each line represent?

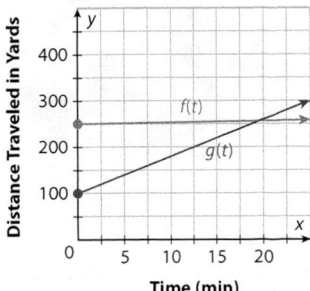

The slope of $f(t)$ represents the speed of the first vehicle and the y-intercept represents the starting distance.

The slope of $g(t)$ represents the speed of the second vehicle and the y-intercept represents the starting distance.

Set up and solve a system of equations to solve the problem.

2. Casey wants to buy a gym membership. One gym has a $150 joining fee and costs $35 per month. Another gym has no joining fee and costs $60 per month. When would Casey pay the same amount to be a member of either gym? How much would he pay?

$\begin{cases} f(t) = 150 + 35t \\ g(t) = 60t \end{cases}$

$150 + 35t = 60t$
$150 = 25t$
$t = 6$

$g(t) = 60t$
$g(6) = 60(6)$
$g(6) = 360$

After 6 months, a member would have paid $360 at either gym.

© Houghton Mifflin Harcourt Publishing Company

Exercise	Depth of Knowledge (D.O.K.)	COMMON CORE Mathematical Practices
1	**1** Recall of Information	**MP.2** Reasoning
2	**2** Skills/Concepts	**MP.4** Modeling
3	**2** Skills/Concepts	**MP.2** Reasoning
4–11	**2** Skills/Concepts	**MP.4** Modeling
11–16	**3** Strategic Thinking	**MP.4** Modeling
17	**3** Strategic Thinking	**MP.3** Logic

ELABORATE

AVOID COMMON ERRORS

Incorrectly calculating the slope will lead to errors in writing functions to model given situations. Make sure students remember that slope is the change in the dependent variable divided by the change in the independent variable.

SUMMARIZE THE LESSON

? How do you use a table or graph to solve a real-world problem that asks when two functions will be equal? First, use the data from the table or graph to find the slope and y-intercept of each function. Write the two functions using the same variables. Then, set the expressions in the functions equal to each other and simplify to solve for the independent variable. Substitute the value of the independent variable into either of the functions to find the value of the dependent variable.

EVALUATE

ASSIGNMENT GUIDE

Concepts and Skills	Practice
Explore Creating Linear System Models by Changing Parameters	Exercises 1, 20
Example 1 Creating Linear System Models from Verbal Descriptions	Exercises 2–6
Example 2 Creating Linear System Models from Tables	Exercises 7–11, 17–19
Example 3 Creating Linear System Models from Graphs	Exercises 12–16

AVOID COMMON ERRORS

After working on several problems that all involve finding the input value for which two functions are equal, students may try to fit every real-world problem into the same pattern. Remind them to read each problem carefully so that they will translate the verbal descriptions to appropriate equations.

INTEGRATE MATHEMATICAL PRACTICES
Focus on Critical Thinking

MP.3 It is not always easiest to solve a system of linear functions by setting the two functions equal to each other. Remind students of other ways to solve systems, such as the elimination method.

---

3. A jar contains n nickels and d dimes. There are 20 coins in the jar, and the total value of the coins is $1.40. How many nickels and how many dimes are in the jar?

$$\begin{cases} n + d = 20 \\ 0.05n + 0.1d = 1.40 \end{cases}$$

There are 12 nickels and 8 dimes in the jar.

4. Helene invested a total of $1000 in two simple-interest bank accounts. One account paid 5% annual interest; the other paid 6% annual interest. The total amount of interest she earned after 1 year was $58. Find the amount invested in each account.

$$\begin{cases} x + y = 1000 \\ 0.05x + 0.06y = 58 \end{cases}$$

Helene invested $200 in the 5% interest account and $800 in the 6% account.

5. A local boys club sold 176 bags of mulch and made a total of $520. It sold two types of mulch: hardwood for $3.50 a bag and pine bark for $2.75 a bag. How many bags of each kind of mulch did it sell?

$$\begin{cases} p + h = 176 \\ 2.75p + 3.5h = 520 \end{cases}$$

The boys club sold 48 bags of hardwood mulch and 128 bags of pine bark mulch.

6. The school band sells carnations on Valentine's Day for $2 each. It buys the carnations from a florist for $0.50 each, plus a $16 delivery charge. When will the cost of the carnations be equal to the revenue from selling them? How many carnations does it need to sell to reach this point?

$$\begin{cases} f(n) = 0.5n + 16 \\ g(n) = 2n \end{cases}$$

The cost of the carnations will be equal to the revenue when it has sold 10.67 carnations. It will reach this point after it sells 11 carnations.

Use the given cost tables for the same product from two different companies to create a linear system. Then solve the system to determine when the cost of the product will be the same and what the price will be.

7. Two online spice retailers sell paprika by the pound using the following pricing chart.

Paprika (lb)	iSpice	Spice Magic
1	$15.75	$26.25
2	$27.50	$36.50
3	$39.25	$46.75
4	$51	$57

$$\begin{cases} i(x) = 11.75x + 4 \\ s(x) = 10.25x + 16 \end{cases}$$

Both iSpice and Spice Magic charge $98 for 8 pounds of paprika.

Exercise	Depth of Knowledge (D.O.K.)	COMMON CORE	Mathematical Practices
18	**3** Strategic Thinking H.O.T.		**MP.2** Reasoning
19	**3** Strategic Thinking H.O.T.		**MP.5** Using Tools
20	**3** Strategic Thinking H.O.T.		**MP.6** Precision

8. Two online retailers sell organic vanilla extract by the ounce using the following pricing chart.

Vanilla Extract (oz)	Chef Mate	Grocery Gourmet
2	$12.50	$17
3	$17.25	$21
4	$22	$25
5	$26.75	$29

$$\begin{cases} c(n) = 4.75n + 3 \\ g(n) = 4n + 9 \end{cases}$$

Both Chef Mate and Grocery Gourmet charge $41 for 8 ounces of vanilla extract.

9. Two dry cleaning companies offer a home pick-up and delivery service. The monthly cost depends on the number of garments laundered, and is shown in the following table.

Number of Garments	Company 1	Company 2
5	$55.25	$31.25
10	$75.50	$57.50
15	$95.75	$83.75

The system is $\begin{cases} f(x) = 4.05x + 35 \\ g(x) = 5.25x + 5 \end{cases}$.

Both Company 1 and Company 2 charge $136.25 for cleaning 25 garments. For cleaning fewer than 25 garments, Company 2 is less expensive.

10. A small town in the mountains needs to buy road salt for the coming winter. It has found two companies that use the following pricing table.

Road Salt (tons)	Company 1	Company 2
5	$1775	$2750
10	$3350	$4000
15	$4925	$5250

The system is $\begin{cases} k(n) = 315n + 200 \\ m(n) = 250n + 1500 \end{cases}$.

Both Company 1 and Company 2 charge $6500 for 20 tons of road salt.

11. A restaurant needs to stock paper towels in its kitchen and bathrooms. It has found two vendors using the following case price chart.

Paper Towels (cases)	Restaurant Warehouse	Supply Side
5	$300.20	$220.20
10	$480.15	$420.15
15	$660.10	$620.10

$$\begin{cases} r(n) = 35.99n + 120.25 \\ s(n) = 39.99n + 20.25 \end{cases}$$

Both Restaurant Warehouse and Supply Side charge $1020 for 25 cases of paper towels.

AVOID COMMON ERRORS

When students find a solution for a real-world problem, some may interpret the solution incorrectly by associating it with the wrong variable. Encourage students to select variables that suggest the value being measured, such as t for time or d for distance.

Use the graph to make a linear model of each function. Describe the meaning of the terms in the models. Then create the linear system, and state what the solution represents.

12.

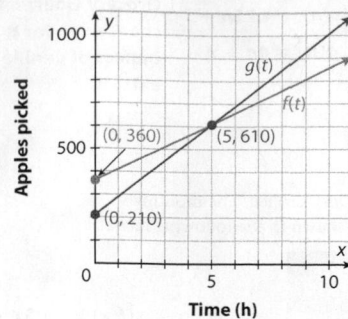

The system is $\begin{cases} f(t) = 50t + 360 \\ g(t) = 80t + 210 \end{cases}$.

The solution $(5, 610)$ represents a total of 610 apples each person has after 5 hours.

13.

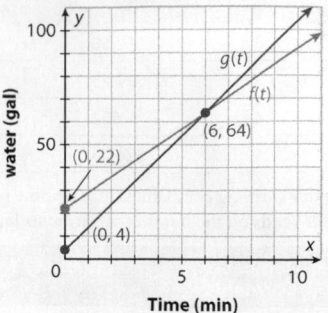

The system is $\begin{cases} f(t) = 7t + 22 \\ g(t) = 10t + 4 \end{cases}$.

The solution $(6, 64)$ represents a total of 64 gallons of water by both functions after 6 minutes.

14.

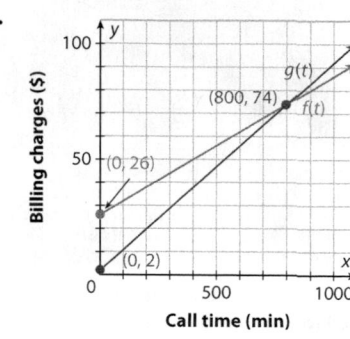

The system is $\begin{cases} f(t) = 0.06t + 26 \\ g(t) = 0.09t + 2 \end{cases}$.

The solution $(800, 74)$ represents total billing charges of $74 from both companies after 800 minutes.

15.

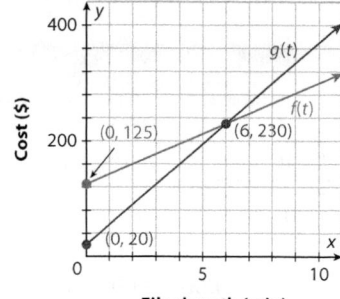

The system is $\begin{cases} f(t) = 17.5t + 125 \\ g(t) = 35t + 20 \end{cases}$.

The solution $(6, 230)$ represents a total cost of $230 from either company for making a film with a running time of 6 minutes.

16. Two office supply stores sell their brand of copy paper by the pound. One company offers a flat rate shipping charge and the other offers free shipping. Use the graph provided to construct a linear system to model this situation. Solve the system to determine the amount of copy paper for which the cost is the same at both stores. Use the graph to verify that your answer is reasonable.

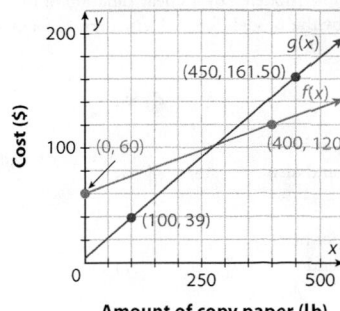

The system is $\begin{cases} f(x) = 0.15x + 60 \\ g(x) = 0.35x + 4 \end{cases}$.

The solution is (280 ,102) so the cost of 280 pounds of copy paper is $102 at both stores.

This solution appears reasonable from the graph because the lines intersect at a point with an x-coordinate between 250 and 300 and a y-coordinate between 100 and 120.

17. Find the Error A student is given the following problem:

A painter can buy 5-gallon containers of paint from two different stores based on the following pricing table.

Containers of Paint	Company A	Company B
2	$512.00	$422.00
4	$904.00	$834.00
6	$1296.00	$1246.00
8	$1688.00	$1658.00

The student's work is shown.

Company A: $m = \dfrac{904 - 512}{4 - 2} = \dfrac{392}{2} = 196$ Company B: $m = \dfrac{1246 - 834}{6 - 2} = \dfrac{412}{4} = 103$

$A(x) = 196x + b$ $B(x) = 103x + b$
$512 = 196(2) + b$ $834 = 103(2) + b$
$120 = b$ $628 = b$

$\begin{cases} A(x) = 196x + 120 \\ B(x) = 103x + 628 \end{cases}$

$196x + 120 = 103x + 628$

$93x = 508$

$x = 5.5$

He concludes that the answer is unreasonable because both of the prices for Company A at $x = 4$ and $x = 6$ are greater than those of Company B. After the two functions intersect, the prices for Company B should be lower than the prices for Company A.

Is the student correct? If not, explain his error and find the correct solution.

The student used a point with incorrect coordinates to calculate the model for Company B. The correct point is either $(2, 422)$ or $(4, 834)$. He used an x-coordinate and y-coordinate from two different points.

The system is $\begin{cases} A(x) = 196x + 120 \\ B(x) = 206x + 10 \end{cases}$.

$196x + 120 = 206x + 10$

$110 = 10x$

$11 = x$

© Houghton Mifflin Harcourt Publishing Company

MODELING

Students can use algebra tiles to model and solve systems of linear equations like the examples in this lesson. After setting two functions equal to one another, use algebra tiles to model the resulting equation. Then manipulate the tiles to solve for the independent variable. Substitute its value into either original equation to find the value for the other variable.

INTEGRATE MATHEMATICAL PRACTICES
Focus on Critical Thinking

MP.3 Most examples of real-world systems of linear equations will have solutions that involve only positive numbers. Students should understand that it is possible in certain situations for the point of intersection to involve negative numbers. Discuss examples of situations in which a solution might be negative, such as falling temperatures.

JOURNAL

Have students write a paragraph that compares the steps used for writing a system of linear equations from a table with the steps used for writing a system of linear equations from a graph.

---

18. Two friends, Jorge and Mark, are taking a trip to the mountains for a camping trip, but they are not leaving together. Both friends separately record the distance they each have traveled from home every hour on the second day. The distance each friend is from his home can be modeled by a linear function of the hours spent traveling. Determine if the linear system created by the models for each situation has a unique solution with a positive value for time.

a. Jorge and Mark each leave at the same time.   Yes   ● No

b. Jorge travels 25 miles on the first day and drives 65 miles per hour on the second day. Mark travels 100 miles on the first day and also drives 65 miles per hour on the second day.   Yes   ● No

c. Jorge travels 25 miles on the first day and drives 65 miles per hour on the second day. Mark travels 100 miles on the first day and drives 45 miles per hour on the second day.   ● Yes   No

d. Jorge traveled 45 miles on the first day and drives 55 miles per hour on the second day. Mark arrived at the campsite on the first day after traveling 300 miles.   ● Yes   No

e. Jorge gets sick before the trip and doesn't get in touch with Mark. Mark travels 40 miles on the first day and drives 67 miles per hour on the second day.   Yes   ● No

19. **Communicate Mathematical Ideas** Given a set of data measuring the distance two planes have traveled after takeoff as a function of when they both passed over the same point, how would you find when they have both traveled the same distance since takeoff?

Sample answer: Plot the data. Then use linear regression to find a function modeling each set of data. Finally, set up and solve a linear system with the two models.

20. **Analyze Relationships** How can you use the slope and the y-intercept of each model in a linear system to determine whether or not there will be a solution?

If the slopes are different, the system will have a solution. If the slopes are the same, then look at the y-intercepts. If the y-intercepts are also the same, then there are infinitely many solutions. If the slopes are the same but the y-intercepts are different, then there is no solution.

Lesson Performance Task

A family is going on vacation and they need to bring their dog to a kennel. Alpha Kennel charges an initial fee of $75 and a daily rate of $30. Beta Kennel charges a flat fee of $34.95 a day. Find linear functions modeling the cost of boarding a dog for n days in each kennel. Set up and solve a system of linear equations. Then interpret the solution.

What if the family has two dogs? Alpha Kennel runs a special where you receive a 10% discount if you board more than one pet. Modify the linear models to give the price of boarding two dogs. Set up, solve, and interpret the linear system covering this case.

Write the functions $C_A(n)$ and $C_B(n)$, where C is the cost of boarding a dog for n days.

The system is $\begin{cases} C_A(n) = 30n + 75 \\ C_B(n) = 34.95n \end{cases}$.

Solve the system.

$30n + 75 = 34.95n$ $C_B(n) = 34.95n$ $C_A(n) = 30n + 75$

     $75 = 4.95n$ $C_B(15.2) = 34.95(15.2)$ $C_A(15.2) = 30(15.2) + 75$

     $n \approx 15.2$ $C_B(15.2) = 531.24$ $C_A(15.2) = 531$

The solution to the linear system is the point where boarding a dog at either kennel costs the same amount. If the family was going away for 15 days, they would want to use Beta Kennel. If they were going away for longer, they would want to use Alpha Kennel.

Let the new functions be $C_{A2}(n)$ and $C_{B2}(n)$. Write the new functions in terms of the old functions and then simplify the new functions.

$C_{A2}(n) = 2(C_A(n)) - 0.1(2(C_A(n)))$ $C_{B2}(n) = 2(C_B(n))$

$= (2 - 0.2)(C_A(n))$ $= 2(34.95n)$

$= 1.8(C_A(n))$ $= 69.90n$

$= 1.8(30n + 75)$

$= 54n + 135$

The new system is $\begin{cases} C_{A2}(n) = 54n + 135 \\ C_{B2}(n) = 69.90n \end{cases}$.

$54n + 135 = 69.9n$ $C_{B2}(n) = 69.90n$ $C_{A2}(n) = 54n + 135$

$135 = 15.9n$ $C_{B2}(8.5) = 69.90(8.5)$ $C_{A2}(8.5) = 54(8.5) + 135$

$n \approx 8.5$ $C_{B2}(8.5) = 594.15$ $C_{A2}(8.5) = 594$

The solution to the new linear system is the point where boarding two dogs at either kennel costs the same amount. If the family was going away for 8 days, they would want to use Beta Kennel. If they were going away for a more extended period of time, they would want to use Alpha Kennel.

© Houghton Mifflin Harcourt Publishing Company • Image Credits: ©taxiphoto/Shutterstock

QUESTIONING STRATEGIES

? What two changes do you need to make to your equation for Alpha Kennel to represent the situation in the Lesson Performance Task when the family boards two dogs? **You need to multiply by 2 to represent the cost of boarding 2 dogs, and you need to apply the 10% discount to the entire cost.**

? If the kennel gives a 10% discount, what percent of the regular price does the customer pay? How can you use this fact when writing an equation for the discounted cost? **90%; multiply the original cost function by 0.9 to find the cost with a 10% discount.**

AVOID COMMON ERRORS

When writing an equation to describe the cost of boarding two dogs at Alpha Kennel, students may fail to adjust all parts of the equation correctly. Point out that both the 10% discount and the doubling due to boarding two dogs must be applied to both the initial fee and the daily rate. Remind students to put the original expression for the cost in parentheses, then apply the Distributive Property when multiplying.

EXTENSION ACTIVITY

Ask students to imagine that they own Beta Kennel. Have them suggest some ways they could entice customers to always use their kennel. Then have them discuss how those changes would affect the equation for the cost of boarding.

Students could suggest, for example, offering a free night for every two nights stayed. The equation for such an offer would not be linear.

Creating Systems of Linear Equations   **546**

Graphing Systems of Linear Inequalities

Common Core Math Standards

The student is expected to:

 A-REI.D.12

...graph the solution set to a system of linear inequalities in two variables as the intersection of the corresponding half-planes. Also A-CED.A.3

Mathematical Practices

 MP.4 Modeling

Language Objective

Explain to a partner how to determine whether a point is a solution to a system of inequalities.

ENGAGE

Essential Question: How do you solve a system of linear inequalities?

Graph each inequality in the system on the same coordinate plane. The solution set will be all points in the area where the solutions of the inequalities overlap.

PREVIEW: LESSON PERFORMANCE TASK

View the Engage section online. Discuss how to graph an inequality on a coordinate grid, and consider what the graph of all points that make two inequalities true at the same time might look like. Then preview the Lesson Performance Task.

12.2 Graphing Systems of Linear Inequalities

Essential Question: How do you solve a system of linear inequalities?

⊘ Explore   Determining Solutions of Systems of Linear Inequalities

A **system of linear inequalities** consists of two or more linear inequalities that have the same variables. The **solutions of a system of linear inequalities** are all the ordered pairs that make all the inequalities in the system true.

Solve the system of equations by graphing.

$$\begin{cases} x + 3y > 3 \\ -x + y \leq 6 \end{cases}$$

(A) First look at $x + 3y > 3$. The equation of the boundary line is $\underline{x + 3y = 3}$.

(B) What are the x- and y-intercepts? x–intercept: 3
   y–intercept: 1

(C) The inequality symbol is $>$ so use a $\underline{dashed}$ line.

(D) Shade $\underline{above}$ the boundary line for solutions that are greater than the inequality.

(E) Graph $x + 3y > 3$.

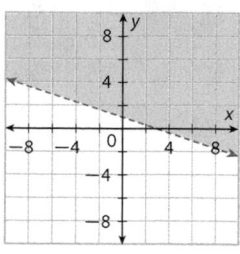

(F) Look at $-x + y \leq 6$. The equation of the boundary line is $\underline{-x + y = 6}$.

(G) What are the x- and y-intercepts? x–intercept: –6
   y–intercept: 6

(H) The inequality symbol is $\leq$ so use a $\underline{solid}$ line.

© Houghton Mifflin Harcourt Publishing Company

Ⓘ Shade __below__ the boundary line for solutions that are less than the inequality.

Ⓙ Graph $-x + y \leq 6$ on the same graph as $x + 3y > 3$.

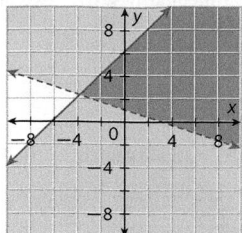

Ⓚ Identify the solutions. They are represented by the __overlapping__ shaded regions.

Ⓛ Check your answer by using a point in each region. Complete the table.

Ordered Pair	Satisfies $x + 3y > 3$?	Satisfies $-x + y \leq 6$?	In the overlapping shaded regions?
(0, 0)	No	Yes	No
(2, 3)	Yes	Yes	Yes
(−8, 2)	No	No	No
(−4, 6)	Yes	No	No

Reflect

1. **Discussion** Why is (0, 0) a good point to use for checking the answer to this system of linear inequalities?
The point (0, 0) does not lie on a boundary line, and it is easy to evaluate each inequality

in the system for $x = 0$ and $y = 0$.

© Houghton Mifflin Harcourt Publishing Company

Determining Solutions of Systems of Linear Inequalities

INTEGRATE TECHNOLOGY

Students can use graphing calculators to help them graph systems of linear inequalities. The calculator will show the boundary line of each graph, and students must specify whether the region above or below each line should be shaded.

QUESTIONING STRATEGIES

 What does the graph of the solutions of a system of two linear inequalities look like?
It is a region on the coordinate plane.

PROFESSIONAL DEVELOPMENT

COMMON CORE Integrate Mathematical Practices

This lesson provides an opportunity to address Mathematical Practice **MP.4**, which calls for students to use "modeling." Students learn to graph systems of linear inequalities, including both systems with intersecting boundary lines and systems with parallel boundary lines. Students also learn to interpret the graphs to determine which points are solutions and which points are not solutions for a system of linear inequalities.

EXPLAIN 1

Solving Systems of Linear Inequalities by Graphing

INTEGRATE MATHEMATICAL PRACTICES
Focus on Communication

MP.3 Discuss with students the differences between finding a solution to a system of linear equations and finding solutions to a system of inequalities. Students should understand that when the lines given by two linear equations intersect, the solution is a single point, but when the boundary lines for the graphs of two inequalities intersect, the system of inequalities has an infinite number of solutions.

QUESTIONING STRATEGIES

? What must be true for a point to be a solution to a system of linear inequalities? The point must make both inequalities true. If the point does not make both inequalities true, it is not a solution.

🧭 **Explain 1** **Solving Systems of Linear Inequalities by Graphing**

You can use a graph of a system of linear inequalities to determine and identify solutions to the system of linear inequalities.

Example 1 Graph the system of linear inequalities. Give two ordered pairs that are solutions and two that are not solutions.

(A) $\begin{cases} -6x + 3y \le 12 \\ y > \frac{1}{2}x - 3 \end{cases}$

Solve the first inequality for y.   Graph the system.

$-6x + 3y \le 12$ $\begin{cases} y \le 2x + 4 \\ y > \frac{1}{2}x - 3 \end{cases}$
$3y \le 6x + 12$
$y \le 2x + 4$

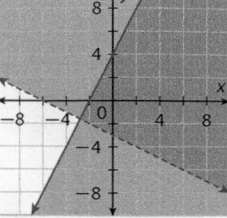

$(0, 0)$ and $(2, 8)$ are solutions. $(-6, -4)$ and $(-4, 4)$ are not solutions.

(B) $\begin{cases} 3x + y \le 1 \\ y > \frac{2}{3}x - 2 \end{cases}$ **Possible answers are given.**

Solve the first inequality for y.   Graph the system.

$3x + y \le 1$ $\begin{cases} y \le \boxed{-3x + 1} \\ y > \frac{2}{3}x - 2 \end{cases}$
$y \le \boxed{-3x + 1}$

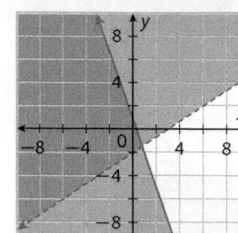

$\underline{(0, 0)}$ and $\underline{(-8, 0)}$ are solutions. $\underline{(0, -8)}$ and $\underline{(4, 4)}$ are not solutions.

Reflect

2. Is $(-6, -6)$ a solution of the system?
No, a solution must satisfy both inequalities.

Your Turn

Graph the system of linear inequalities. Give two ordered pairs that are solutions and two that are not solutions.   **Possible answers are given.**

3. $\begin{cases} y \le x + 3 \\ y < -3 \end{cases}$

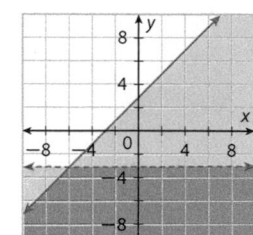

4. $\begin{cases} y > x - 8 \\ 2x + 4y < 16 \end{cases}$

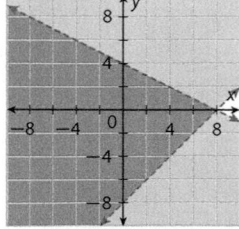

$(2, -4)$ and $(-2, -8)$ **are solutions.** $(0, 0)$ and $(-8, -4)$ **are solutions.**
$(0, 0)$ and $(-8, -4)$ **are not solutions.** $(-2, 8)$ and $(8, -6)$ **are not solutions.**

Module 12   549   Lesson 2

COLLABORATIVE LEARNING

Peer-to-Peer Activity

Have students work in groups of two. Tell each student to write a system of two linear inequalities. Each student should graph the system of linear inequalities written by the partner, and the partner should verify that the graph is correct. Students should either clearly shade their graphs to indicate the region where solutions lie or label each region "contains solution points" or "does not contain solution points".

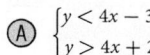

Graphing Systems of Inequalities with Parallel Boundary Lines

If the lines in a system of linear equations are parallel, there are no solutions. However, if the boundary lines in a system of linear inequalities are parallel, the system may or may not have solutions.

Example 2 Graph each system of linear inequalities. Describe the solutions.

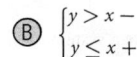 (A) $\begin{cases} y < 4x - 3 \\ y > 4x + 2 \end{cases}$

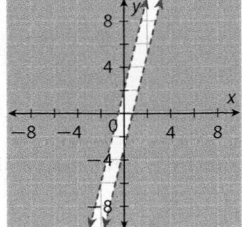

This system has no solution.

(B) $\begin{cases} y > x - 2 \\ y \le x + 4 \end{cases}$

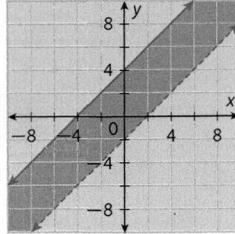

The solutions are all points __between__ the parallel lines and on the __solid__ line.

Your Turn

Graph each system of linear inequalities. Describe the solutions.

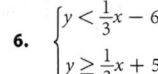 **5.** $\begin{cases} y \le -2x - 3 \\ y \le -2x + 1 \end{cases}$

6. $\begin{cases} y < \frac{1}{3}x - 6 \\ y \ge \frac{1}{3}x + 5 \end{cases}$

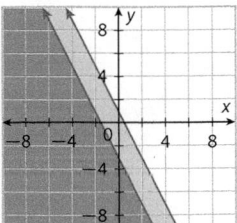

The solutions are the same as the solutions of $y \le -2x - 3$.

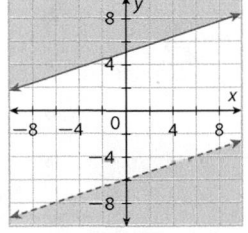

This system has no solution.

DIFFERENTIATE INSTRUCTION

Kinesthetic Experience

Some students may find the different ways of shading the coordinate plane confusing. They may benefit from first graphing one inequality, then folding the coordinate grid along the boundary line so that only the part of the grid with solutions is showing. Students can then graph the second inequality and again fold along the boundary line. The section that remains visible should be the part of the coordinate grid that contains points that are solutions.

EXPLAIN 2

Graphing Systems of Inequalities with Parallel Boundary Lines

AVOID COMMONS ERRORS

When solving systems of inequalities involving parallel boundary lines, it may be easy to assume that the solutions are the points that lie between the lines. Remind students that it is possible for such systems to have no solutions or for the solutions to be the same as the solutions to one of the two inequalities. Students should always check their solutions by making sure they make both original statements true.

QUESTIONING STRATEGIES

? Without graphing, how can you determine whether the functions in a system of inequalities will produce parallel boundary lines? If the slopes of the boundary lines are the same, then the lines will be parallel.

? How do the solutions for a system of inequalities with parallel lines compare to the solutions for a system of equations with parallel lines? For a system of inequalities with parallel boundary lines, either the solution is a region of the coordinate plane or there is no solution. For a system of equations with parallel lines, there is never a solution.

ELABORATE

INTEGRATE MATHEMATICAL PRACTICES
Focus on Math Connections

MP.1 Students should understand that a system of linear inequalities will never have all points in the coordinate plane as solutions. Because the solution set for a system of inequalities is the set of points that satisfy both inequalities, it is always a subset of the solution to each inequality. The graph of the solutions is the area of overlap between two half-planes.

QUESTIONING STRATEGIES

Is it possible for the solutions of a system of two linear inequalities to form a line? If so, give an example. **Yes; possible answer: the solutions of the system of inequalities $y \leq x + 2$ and $y \geq x + 2$ are all the points on the line $y = x + 2$.**

SUMMARIZE THE LESSON

How do you use a graph to find solutions for a system of linear inequalities? **Identify the points on the graph that make both inequalities true. If the boundary lines are parallel, it is possible that the system of linear equalities may have no solutions.**

---

7. Is it possible for a system of two linear inequalities to have every point in the plane as solutions? Why or why not?

No; each boundary line divides the plane into two half-planes, one of each being the solution of each inequality. It is not possible for the two solution half-planes to overlap and completely cover the plane.

8. **Discussion** How would you write a system of linear inequalities from a graph?

To write a system of linear inequalities from a graph, write the linear inequality for each of the graphs that make up the system.

9. **Essential Question Check-In** How does testing specific ordered pairs tell you that the solution you graphed is correct?

Ordered pairs of points from the overlapping shaded region will satisfy both inequalities.

⭐ Evaluate: Homework and Practice

- Online Homework
- Hints and Help
- Extra Practice

1. Match the inequality with the correct boundary line. Answers may be used more than once.

a. $y = 3x$	**b**	$-x + 3y \leq 0$
b. $y = \frac{1}{3}x$	**d**	$y > -x + \frac{1}{2}$
c. $y = x - 0.5$	**b**	$y \leq \frac{1}{3}x$
d. $y = -x + \frac{1}{2}$	**e**	$\frac{2}{3} + \frac{1}{3}y \geq x$
e. $y = 3x - 2$	**d**	$-y > x - 0.5$
f. $y = x$	**a**	$\frac{1}{3}y \geq x$

LANGUAGE SUPPORT 🔲EL

Connect Vocabulary

Discuss with students the meaning of the word *satisfy* as it relates to systems of linear inequalities. Students are probably familiar with many uses for the word outside of the math classroom. Compare these uses to the way the word is used mathematically. Students should understand that an ordered pair *satisfies* a system of linear inequalities when it meets the conditions of the system or, in other words, when it is a solution of the system.

Determine if the given point satisfies either equation and is a solution of the system of inequalities.

2. $\begin{cases} 4y - 20x < 6 \\ \frac{5}{2}y \ge 5x - 10 \end{cases}$; $(0, 0)$

$(0, 0)$ satisfies $\frac{5}{2}y \ge 5x - 10$.

$(0, 0)$ satisfies $4y - 20x < 6$.

The point is a solution of the system.

3. $\begin{cases} x + 5y > -10 \\ x - y \le 4 \end{cases}$; $(2.5, -1.5)$

$(2.5, -1.5)$ satisfies $x - y \le 4$.

$(2.5, -1.5)$ satisfies $x + 5y > -10$.

The point is a solution of the system.

Determine if the given point is a solution of the system of inequalities. If not, find a point that is.

4. $(-9, 4)$

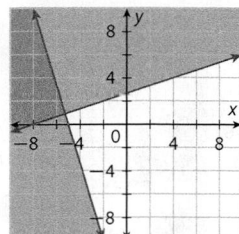

The point $(-9, 4)$ is a solution.

5. $(6, -2)$

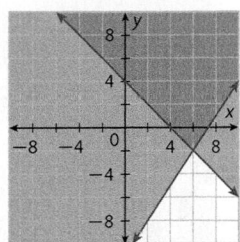

The point $(6, -2)$ is a solution.

6. $(0, -4)$

The point $(0, -4)$ is not a solution.

The point $(-4, 0)$ is a solution.

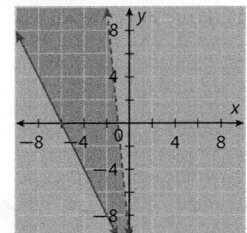

Graph the system of linear inequalities. Give two ordered pairs that are solutions and two that are not solutions. **Possible answers are given.**

7. $\begin{cases} x > 2 \\ y \le -\frac{1}{2}x - 2 \end{cases}$

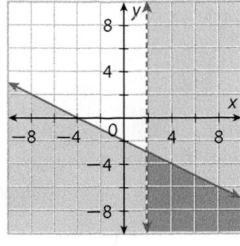

$(4, -4)$ and $(8, -8)$ are solutions.

$(0, 0)$ and $(8, -4)$ are not solutions.

8. $\begin{cases} y > -x \\ y \ge x \end{cases}$

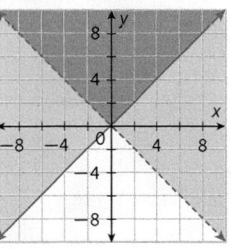

$(4, 4)$ and $(0, 8)$ are solutions.

$(0, 0)$ and $(8, -6)$ are not solutions.

© Houghton Mifflin Harcourt Publishing Company

EVALUATE

ASSIGNMENT GUIDE

Concepts and Skills	Practice
Explore Determining Solutions of Systems of Linear Inequalities	Exercises 1–6
Example 1 Solving Systems of Linear Inequalities by Graphing	Exercises 7–14, 23
Example 2 Graphing Systems of Inequalities with Parallel Boundary Lines	Exercises 15–22, 24–25

INTEGRATE MATHEMATICAL PRACTICES
Focus on Critical Thinking

MP.3 Students may be unsure how to determine which ordered pairs are solutions for a system of linear inequalities if they are not shown on the coordinate grid. Discuss ways to determine whether a point not shown on the grid is a solution, including extending the graph and substituting the coordinates of the point into the inequalities.

Exercise	Depth of Knowledge (D.O.K.)	COMMON CORE Mathematical Practices
1–6	**1** Recall of Information	**MP.2** Reasoning
7–22	**2** Skills/Concepts	**MP.4** Modeling
23	**3** Strategic Thinking **H.O.T.**	**MP.4** Modeling
24	**3** Strategic Thinking **H.O.T.**	**MP.6** Precision
25	**3** Strategic Thinking **H.O.T.**	**MP.3** Logic

Graphing Systems of Linear Inequalities   **552**

When boundary lines are parallel, students may arrive at incorrect solutions by not paying attention to the inequality signs in the inequalities. Remind students to check their solutions by verifying that the points make both original inequalities true.

VISUAL CUES

Remind students that when an inequality is written in the form $y > mx + b$, the inequality sign determines which part of the graph should be shaded. If the sign $>$ or $\geq$ is used, the half-plane above the line should be shaded; if the sign $<$ or $\leq$ is used, it is the half-plane below the line that should be shaded.

9. $\begin{cases} y < -x + 10 \\ y < \frac{1}{10}x + 7 \end{cases}$

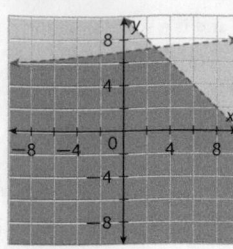

$(0, 0)$ and $(4, 4)$ are solutions.

$(0, 8)$ and $(8, 6)$ are not solutions.

10. $\begin{cases} y \leq \frac{1}{2}x - 5 \\ y \geq -2x + 12 \end{cases}$

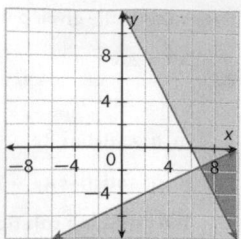

$(8, -2)$ and $(10, -4)$ are solutions.

$(0, 0)$ and $(8, 6)$ are not solutions.

11. $\begin{cases} y \leq -\frac{3}{5}x \\ y > -x - 4 \end{cases}$

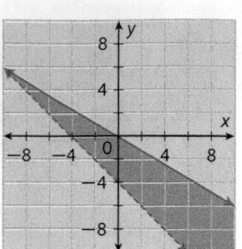

$(0, 0)$ and $(10, -6)$ are solutions.

$(8, -2)$ and $(8, 6)$ are not solutions.

12. $\begin{cases} y \geq 2x + 6 \\ y < -\frac{1}{2}x - 1 \end{cases}$

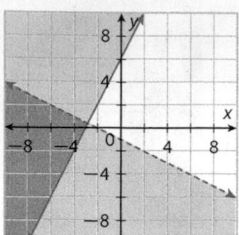

$(-8, -6)$ and $(-6, -6)$ are solutions.

$(0, 0)$ and $(8, 6)$ are not solutions.

13. $\begin{cases} y \leq \frac{4}{5}x - 4 \\ y < 2x - 8 \end{cases}$

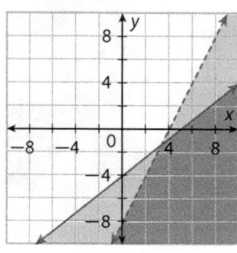

$(4, -6)$ and $(6, -6)$ are solutions.

$(0, 0)$ and $(8, 6)$ are not solutions.

14. $\begin{cases} x \geq -6 \\ y < 3 \end{cases}$

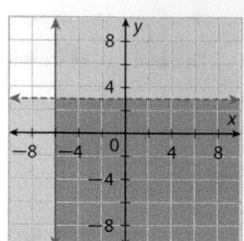

$(0, 0)$ and $(6, -6)$ are solutions.

$(-10, 0)$ and $(8, 6)$ are not solutions.

Graph each system of linear inequalities. Describe the solutions.

15. $\begin{cases} y \le 3x + 6 \\ y < 3x - 8 \end{cases}$

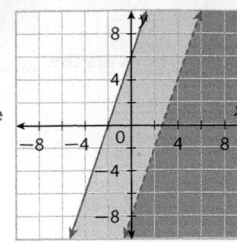

The solutions are the

same as the

solutions of

$y < 3x - 8.$

16. $\begin{cases} y \ge \frac{2}{5}x + 4 \\ y \le \frac{2}{5}x - 6 \end{cases}$

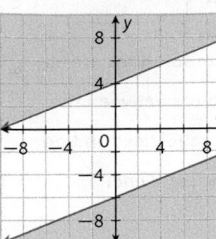

This system has

no solution.

17. $\begin{cases} y \ge \frac{5}{4}x - 6 \\ y \ge \frac{5}{4}x \end{cases}$

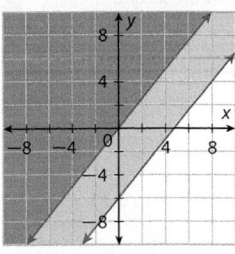

The solutions are the

same as the

solutions of

$y \ge \frac{5}{4}x.$

18. $\begin{cases} y \ge -\frac{3}{2}x - 3 \\ y \le -\frac{3}{2}x + 10 \end{cases}$

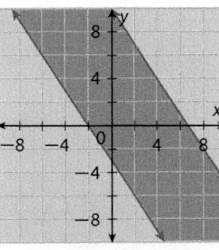

The solutions are all

points between the

parallel lines

and on the solid lines.

19. $\begin{cases} x < 6 \\ x \ge -3 \end{cases}$

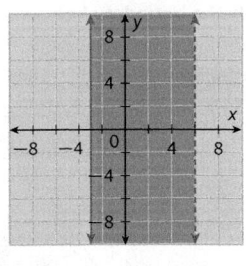

The solutions are all

points between the

parallel lines,

including

points on the

line $x \ge -3.$

20. $\begin{cases} y \ge \frac{9}{4}x - 1 \\ y < \frac{9}{4}x - 9 \end{cases}$

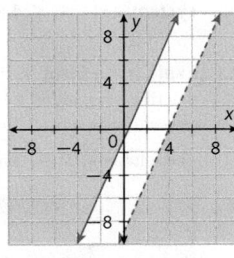

This system has

no solution.

© Houghton Mifflin Harcourt Publishing Company

INTEGRATE MATHEMATICAL PRACTICES
Focus on Critical Thinking

MP.3 Some students will choose points that are not solutions to the system of linear equalities by selecting points that are in the unshaded portion of the graph. Students should understand that while this part of the graph contains points that are not solutions, regions of the graph that contain solutions to only one of the two inequalities also contain non-solution points.

INTEGRATE MATHEMATICAL PRACTICES
Focus on Modeling

MP.4 Warn students that the brace, {, is not always used when writing a system of inequalities. A standardized test might omit the symbol and simply say that the inequalities are a system.

Have students write the steps they use for finding points that are solutions to a system of inequalities. Steps should be written so that they apply to systems that have intersecting boundary lines and to systems that have parallel boundary lines, as well.

21. $\begin{cases} y < -\frac{3}{5}x + 3 \\ y \geq -\frac{3}{5}x - 4 \end{cases}$

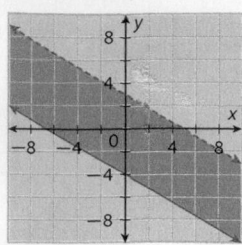

The solutions are all points between the parallel lines and on the solid line.

22. $\begin{cases} y > -\frac{1}{2}x + 5 \\ y > -\frac{1}{2}x - 1 \end{cases}$

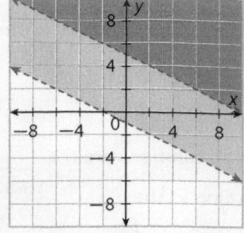

The solutions are the same as the solutions of $y > -\frac{1}{2}x + 5$.

H.O.T. Focus on Higher Order Thinking

23. **Persevere in Problem Solving** Write and graph a system of linear inequalities for which the solutions are all the points in the second quadrant, not including points on the axes.

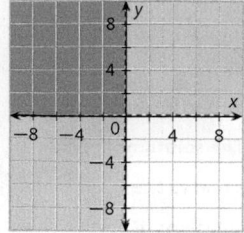

$\begin{cases} y > 0 \\ x < 0 \end{cases}$

24. **Critical Thinking** Can the solutions of a system of linear inequalities be the points on a line? Explain.

Yes; if the inequalities have the same boundary line and one is less than or equal to while the other is greater than or equal to then the solutions are points on the boundary line. The system $-x + 4y \leq 4$ and $-x + 4y \geq 4$ has only the boundary line $-x + 4y = 4$ as its solution.

25. **Explain the Error** A student was asked to graph the system $\begin{cases} y < \frac{3}{2}x - 8 \\ y \leq \frac{3}{2}x + 2 \end{cases}$ and describe the solution set. The student gave the following answer. Explain what the student did wrong, then give the correct answer.

The solutions are the same as the solutions of $y \leq \frac{3}{2}x + 2$.

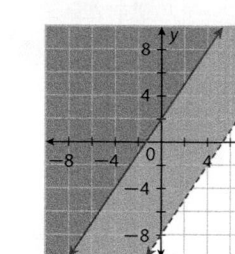

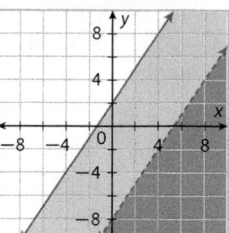

The student switched the inequality signs when graphing them. The correct solution set is the same as the solutions of $y < \frac{3}{2}x - 8$.

Lesson Performance Task

Successful stock market investors know a lot about inequalities. They know up to what point they are willing to accept losses, and at what point they are willing to "lock in" their profits and not subject their investments to additional risk. They often have these inequalities all mapped out at the time they purchase a stock, so they can tell instantly if they are sticking to their investment strategy. Graph the system of linear inequalities. Then describe the solution set and give two ordered pairs that are solutions and two that are not. Is there anything particular to note about the shape of this system?

$$\begin{cases} y < -\frac{3}{5}x + 4 \\ y \leq \frac{3}{2}x + 8 \\ y > -\frac{3}{5}x - 8 \\ y > \frac{3}{2}x - 6 \end{cases}$$

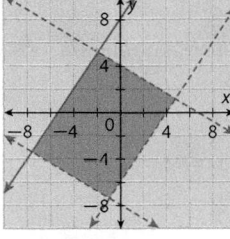

The solution set is a parallelogram. The system is two sets of parallel lines.

Possible answers:

$(0, 0)$ and $(-4, -2)$ are solutions.

$(4, 6)$ and $(6, -6)$ are not solutions.

© Houghton Mifflin Harcourt Publishing Company

? Before graphing the system of inequalities, can you tell whether any of the boundary lines will be parallel? If so, which ones? Explain how you know. **Yes; the boundary line for $y \leq \frac{3}{2}x + 8$ is parallel to the boundary line for $y > \frac{3}{2}x - 6$ since they have the same slope, $\frac{3}{2}$, and the line for $y < -\frac{3}{5}x + 4$ is parallel to the line for $y > -\frac{3}{5}x - 8$ since they have the same slope, $-\frac{3}{5}$.**

? Will any of the boundary lines be perpendicular? Explain how you know. **No; none of the inequalities have slopes that are opposite reciprocals of each other.**

AVOID COMMON ERRORS

Students may incorrectly describe the graph as a square or a rectangle. Remind students that a figure with two pairs of opposite parallel sides is not necessarily a rectangle. For it to be a rectangle, all four interior angles must be right angles. Stress that observing a figure on a graph "looks like" it has right angles is not sufficient. The equations for the sides of the figure must be used to determine whether any sides are perpendicular.

EXTENSION ACTIVITY

Challenge students to sketch a closed figure on a coordinate grid, then write a system of linear inequalities whose solution set is all the points within that figure. Then have each student trade systems of inequalities with a partner and have them graph each other's systems. As a class, discuss what students discovered about the types of regions they can or cannot create with systems of linear inequalities.

Students may find that the solution set of a system of linear inequalities must be a region with straight-line sides and interior angles less than 180°; in other words, all the figures are convex polygons.

Scoring Rubric

2 points: Student correctly solves the problem and explains his/her reasoning.

1 point: Student shows good understanding of the problem but does not fully solve or explain his/her reasoning.

0 points: Student does not demonstrate understanding of the problem.

Graphing Systems of Linear Inequalities   **556**

Modeling with Linear Systems

Common Core Math Standards

The student is expected to:

 A-CED.A.3

Represent constraints... by systems of equations and/or inequalities, and interpret solutions as viable or nonviable options in a modeling context.

Mathematical Practices

 MP.4 Modeling

Apply mathematics to problems arising in everyday life, society, and the workplace.

Language Objective

Describe a real-world situation that can be modeled by a system of two linear inequalities, and then write the inequalities.

ENGAGE

Essential Question: How can you use systems of linear equations or inequalities to model and solve contextual problems?

Write a system of linear equations or inequalities that represent the relationships among quantities in the problem, using the same variables in both equations or both inequalities. Solve the system of equations or graph the system of inequalities to find solutions to the problem.

PREVIEW: LESSON PERFORMANCE TASK

View the Engage section online. Discuss the different ways students in the class determine the maximum number of items they are able to buy when they go shopping. Then preview the Lesson Performance Task.

Name_____ Class_____ Date_____

12.3 Modeling with Linear Systems

Essential Question: How can you use systems of linear equations or inequalities to model and solve contextual problems?

Resource Locker

⊘ Explore Modeling Real-World Constraints with Systems

Real-world situations can often be modeled by systems of equations. Usually, information about prices and the total number of items purchased is given, and the system is solved to find the number of each item purchased.

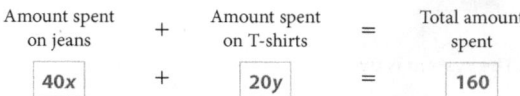

Joe goes to the store to buy jeans and some T-shirts. The jeans cost $40 each and the T-shirts cost $20 each. If Joe spends $160 on 5 items, how many pairs of jeans and how many T-shirts did he buy?

Ⓐ Write an expression to represent the amount that Joe spent on x pairs of jeans. _____$40x$_____

Ⓑ Write an expression to represent the amount that Joe spent on y T-shirts. _____$20y$_____

Ⓒ Now write an equation that represents the total amount spent on jeans and T-shirts.

Amount spent on jeans	+	Amount spent on T-shirts	=	Total amount spent
$40x$	+	$20y$	=	160

Ⓓ What variable represents the number of jeans purchased? _____x_____

Ⓔ What variable represents the number of T-shirts purchased? _____y_____

Ⓕ Write an equation to represent the total number of items purchased. _____$x + y = 5$_____

Ⓖ Write the system that represents the situation.

$$40x + 20y = 160$$
$$x + y = 5$$

Reflect

1. What units are associated with the two expressions that you wrote in steps A and B?
   For 40x and 20y, the number of items bought is multiplied by the cost per item, so each expression represents the total amount spent on that item.

2. When you add the units for the expressions representing the amounts spent on jeans and T-shirts, what units do you get for the total amount spent?
   dollars

© Houghton Mifflin Harcourt Publishing Company · Image Credits: ©Danny Clifford/Alamy

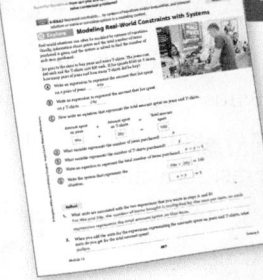

HARDCOVER PAGES 447–454

Turn to these pages to find this lesson in the hardcover student edition.

 **Explain 1** **Modeling Real-World Constraints with Systems of Linear Equations**

You can model real-world constraints, such as the number of items needed and the amount of money one has to spend, with systems of linear equations.

Example 1 Write a system of equations to represent the situation, and then solve the system.

 Bobby will buy coffee and hot chocolate for his co-workers. Each cup of coffee costs $2.25 and each cup of hot chocolate costs $1.50. If he pays a total of $15.75 for 8 cups, how many of each did he buy?

Create a table to organize the information.

	Coffee	Hot Chocolate	Total
Number of Cups	c	h	8
Cost	$\$2.25c$	$\$1.50h$	$\$15.75$

Use the information to write a system of equations.

$2.25c + 1.50h = 15.75$ Total amount spent on c cups of coffee and h cups of hot chocolate

$c + h = 8$ Total number of cups bought

Multiply the second equation by -2.25 to get opposite coefficients for c.

$-2.25(c + h = 8)$

$-2.25c - 2.25h = 18$

Add the new equation to the first equation.

$2.25c + 1.50h = 15.75$
$+(-2.25c - 2.25h = -18)$
$\overline{-0.75h = -2.25}$

Solve for h.

$-0.75h = -2.25$

$h = 3$

Substitute the value found for h back into one of the original equations and solve for c.

$c + h = 8$

$c + 3 = 8$

$c = 5$

So Bobby bought 5 cups of coffee and 3 cups of hot chocolate.

© Houghton Mifflin Harcourt Publishing Company · Image Credits: ©Fotofermer/Shutterstock

PROFESSIONAL DEVELOPMENT

 Integrate Mathematical Practices

This lesson provides an opportunity to address Mathematical Practice **MP.4**, which calls for students to use "modeling." Students will write systems of linear equations and inequalities from verbal descriptions of real-life situations. Students then apply previously learned methods to solve the systems and answer questions about the situations.

EXPLORE

Modeling Real-World Constraints with Systems

INTEGRATE TECHNOLOGY

Students have the option of completing the Explore activity either in the book or online.

INTEGRATE MATHEMATICAL PRACTICES
Focus on Modeling

MP.4 Writing equations from verbal descriptions can be challenging for students. Discuss how to identify the unknown variables in the problem and construct true equations using the numbers in the verbal description. Remind students that when writing a system of two equations, each variable must represent the same quantity, in the same units, in both equations.

EXPLAIN 1

Modeling Real-World Constraints with Systems of Linear Equations

AVOID COMMON ERRORS

When modeling real-world problems with systems of linear equations, students may solve the system correctly but then mix up which value goes with which variable. Discuss with students how to select variable names that relate to the values they are finding, such as c for the number of coffees purchased.

? What are two different methods for solving a system of linear equations? Possible answer: You can isolate a variable in one equation, then substitute the expression for that variable into the other equation, or you can multiply one equation by a constant and add it to the other equation.

Ⓑ A student is buying pens and markers for school. Packs of pens cost $2.75 each and packs of markers cost $3.25 each. If she bought a total of 6 packs and spent $17.50, how many of each did she buy?

Create a table to organize the information.

	Pens	Markers	Total
Number of packs	p	m	6
Cost	$2.75p	$3.25m	$17.50

Use the information to write a system of equations.

$$\boxed{2.75p} + \boxed{3.25m} = 17.50 \qquad \text{Total amount spent on } p \text{ packs of pens and } m \text{ packs of markers}$$

$$p + m = \boxed{6} \qquad \text{Total number of packs bought}$$

Multiply the second equation by $\underline{-2.75}$ to get opposite coefficients for p.

$$\boxed{-2.75}\left(p + m = \boxed{6}\right)$$

$$\boxed{-2.75}\,p + \boxed{-2.75}\,m = \boxed{-16.50}$$

Add the new equation to the first equation.

$$\boxed{2.75}\,p + \boxed{3.25}\,m = 17.50$$
$$+ \boxed{-2.75}\,p + \boxed{-2.75}\,m = \boxed{-16.50}$$
$$\overline{ \boxed{0.5}\,m = \boxed{1}}$$

Solve for m, the number of markers.

$$m = \boxed{2}$$

Substitute the value found for m back into one of the original equations and solve for p.

$$p + m = \boxed{6}$$
$$p + \boxed{2} = \boxed{6}$$
$$p = \boxed{4}$$

So the student bought $\underline{4}$ packs of pens and $\underline{2}$ packs of markers.

Reflect

3. What's another possible way to solve the problem?

One of the equations could be solved for p or m, and the resulting expression could be substituted into the other equation.

COLLABORATIVE LEARNING

Small Group Activity

Have students work in groups of four, and tell each group to divide into two pairs. Have each pair write a real-world problem that can be modeled by a system of two linear equations, then trade problems with the other pair in the group. One student in each pair should solve the system by solving one equation for one variable and substituting into the other equation, while the other student solves by multiplying by a constant and adding or subtracting the equations to eliminate a variable. Then have students compare their results.

Write a system of equations to represent the situation, and then solve the system.

4. A company has to buy computers and printers. Each computer costs $550 and each printer costs $390. If the company spends $8160 and buys a total of 16 machines, how many of each did it buy?

$$550x + 390y = 8160$$
$$x + y = 16$$

Multiply the second equation by -550.

$$550x + 390y = 8160$$
$$-550(x + y = 16)$$

Simplify and then add the two equations.

$$550x + 390y = 8160$$
$$-550x - 550y = -8800$$
$$\overline{\qquad -160y = -640}$$
$$y = 4$$

Substitute 4 for y in the second equation and solve for x.

$$x + 4 = 16$$
$$x = 12$$

So, the company bought 12 computers and 4 printers.

⊘ Explain 2 **Modeling Real-World Constraints with Systems of Linear Inequalities**

You can use a system of linear inequalities and its graph to model many real-world situations.

Example 2 Set up and solve the system of linear equalities.

(A) Sue is buying T-shirts and shorts. T-shirts cost $14 and shorts cost $21. She plans on spending no more than $147 and buy at least 5 items. Show and describe all combinations of the number of T-shirts and shorts she could buy.

First write the system. Let x represent the number of T-shirts, and let y represent the number of shorts.

$x + y \geq 5$ She wants to buy at least 5 items.

$14x + 21y \leq 147$ She wants to spend no more than $147.

Graph the system of inequalities: $\begin{cases} x + y \geq 5 \\ 14x + 21y \leq 147 \end{cases}$

T-shirts and Shorts

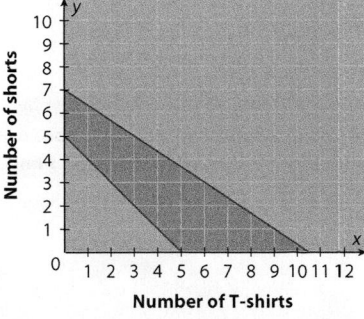

The possible solutions are where the shaded regions overlap. So, a possible solution is 5 T-shirts and 2 shorts. Substitute this value into the inequalities to make sure it is a reasonable solution.

$$\begin{cases} x + y \geq 5 \\ 14x + 21y \leq 147 \end{cases} \rightarrow \begin{cases} 5 + 2 \overset{?}{\geq} 5 \\ 14(5) + 21(2) \overset{?}{\leq} 147 \end{cases} \rightarrow \begin{cases} 7 \geq 5 \\ 112 \leq 147 \end{cases}$$

The result is two inequalities that are true, so this is a reasonable answer.

EXPLAIN 2

Modeling Real-World Constraints with Systems of Linear Inequalities

INTEGRATE MATHEMATICAL PRACTICES
Focus on Critical Thinking

MP.3 When solving real-world systems of inequalities by graphing, students may think that any ordered pair that satisfies both equations is a solution. Remind them to consider how the real-world meaning of each variable may limit its possible values. Students should be able to differentiate between situations that require whole numbers as solutions and situations that could have decimals as answers.

DIFFERENTIATE INSTRUCTION

Cognitive Strategies

Often, systems of linear equations can be solved without algebra. For example, simple arithmetic can be used to determine the number of dogs and the number of birds in a set of 15 animals with 50 legs. If all 15 animals were dogs, there would be $15 \times 4 = 60$ legs. Since that number is too high, figure out how many dogs should be replaced with birds to reduce the total number of legs to 50. Students who find such methods more intuitive than algebra may use them to solve simple problems or to verify their algebraic solutions. However, they should be aware that more complex systems will be difficult to solve without using algebra.

QUESTIONING STRATEGIES

? Why is a graph the best way to show the solution set to a system of a linear inequalities? A system of linear inequalities has a solution set that consists of all ordered pairs that satisfy both inequalities in the system, so you can't write a single solution, as you do for a system of linear equations.

? When graphing a system of inequalities that represents a real-world situation, why might your graph show only the first quadrant of the coordinate plane? If the variables represent quantities that cannot be negative, such as numbers of objects, you should show only the nonnegative solutions to the system.

(B) John has to buy two different kinds of rope. Rope A costs $0.60 per foot and Rope B costs $0.90 per foot. John needs to buy at least 15 feet of rope, but he wants to spend no more than $18. Show and describe all combinations of the number of feet of each type of rope John can buy.

First write the system. Let x represent the amount of Rope A, and let y represent the amount of Rope B.

$$\boxed{x} + \boxed{y} \geq 15$$
$$\boxed{0.6x} + 0.9y \boxed{\leq} 18$$

Graph the system.

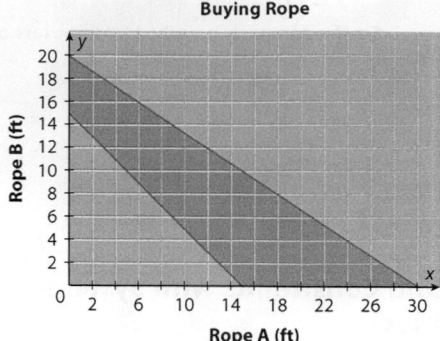

Buying Rope

Describe the solutions to the system.

The possible solutions are ___all of the ordered___ ___pairs that lie in the region shared by___ ___the two inequalities and on the solid___ ___boundary lines.___

Your Turn

Write a system of inequalities for the given situation and graph the system. Then determine if the point (8, 4) is a solution to the system.

5. A student has to buy graph paper and printer paper. The printer paper costs $2 a pack, while the graphing paper costs $3 a pack. She wants to buy at least 6 packs of paper but wants to spend at most $27.

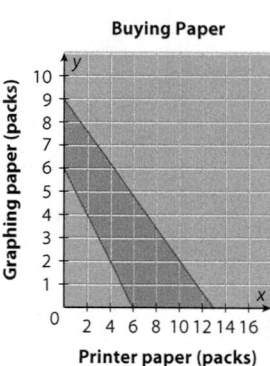

Buying Paper

$$x + y \geq 6$$
$$2x + 3y \leq 27$$

The point (8, 4) is not a solution because it does not lie in the region shared by the two inequalities and it does not satisfy both inequalities.

LANGUAGE SUPPORT EL

Connect Vocabulary

Discuss with students how the word *each* is used in verbal descriptions of real-world problems. In a problem statement, *each* can be a key word that indicates how to write an equation. For example, the phrase "flowers cost $5 each" signals that multiplying 5 by the number of flowers will give the total cost of flowers. In a question such as "How many of each item did he buy?" the word *each* is an important clue about what answer is required. It implies that more than one item is being discussed, so students will need to find the value for more than one variable to have a complete solution.

© Houghton Mifflin Harcourt Publishing Company

6. Now assume that she wants to buy at least 7 packs and will spend at most $30.

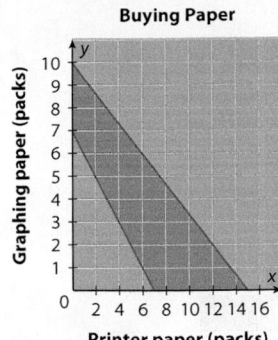

Buying Paper

Graphing paper (packs) vs Printer paper (packs)

$$x + y \geq 7$$
$$2x + 3y \leq 30$$

The point $(8, 4)$ is a solution because it lies in the region shared by the two inequalities, and it does satisfy both inequalities.

💬 Elaborate

7. Is it possible for a system of two linear inequalities to only have one solution?
No, a system of inequalities will always have a region of solutions if it has any solution.

8. Why can't a system of inequalities be solved using the same methods as solving systems of equations?
The solution to a system of two equations can be a single point.

9. **Essential Question Check-In** When writing a system of equations or inequalities from a situation, how do you know that you have possibly written the system correctly?
The system should contain at least two equations with at least two variables.

☆ Evaluate: Homework and Practice

Personal Math Trainer

• Online Homework
• Hints and Help
• Extra Practice

Write a system of equations that corresponds to the situation.
Do not solve.

1. Lisa spends part of her year as a member of a gym. She then finds a better deal at another gym, so she cancels her membership with the first gym and spends the rest of the year with the second gym. The membership to the first gym costs $75 per month, while the membership for the second gym costs $50 per month. She ends up spending a total of $775 over the course of the year.

	First Gym	Second Gym	Total
Number of Months	x	y	12
Cost	$75x$	$50y$	$775

$$x + y = 12$$
$$75x + 50y = 775$$

© Houghton Mifflin Harcourt Publishing Company

ELABORATE

INTEGRATE MATHEMATICAL PRACTICES
Focus on Critical Thinking

MP.3 Discuss with students whether it is possible for a real-world problem involving a system of linear inequalities to have no solution. Challenge students to change the values in one of the examples so that the system has no solution.

SUMMARIZE THE LESSON

? How do you solve a real-world problem using a system of linear equations or inequalities?

Write a system of two equations or inequalities to represent the information in the verbal description. If it is a system of equations, solve the system to find the value of each variable. If it is a system of inequalities, graph the system to find the region of the coordinate plane where the solutions lie.

Modeling with Linear Systems   **562**

EVALUATE

ASSIGNMENT GUIDE

Concepts and Skills	Practice
Explore Modeling Real-World Constraints with Systems	Exercises 1–8
Example 1 Modeling Real-World Constraints with Systems of Linear Equations	Exercises 9–16, 23–24
Example 2 Modeling Real-World Constraints with Systems of Linear Inequalities	Exercises 17–22, 25

INTEGRATE MATHEMATICAL PRACTICES

Focus on Math Connections

MP.1 Remind students that systems of linear equations can be solved by graphing the equations and determining the point of intersection, but algebraic methods (such as solving the system of equations by substitution or elimination) usually are more efficient than graphing.

---

2. Jack is selling tickets to an event. Attendees can either buy a general admission ticket or a VIP ticket. The general adimission tickets are $60 and the VIP tickets are $90. He doesn't know how many of each type he has sold, but he knows he sold a total of 29 tickets and made $2100.

	General Admission	VIP	Total
Number of Tickets	x	y	29
Cost	$60x$	$90y$	$2100

$$x + y = 29$$
$$60x + 90y = 2100$$

3. There are 200 adults and 300 children at a zoo. The zoo makes a total of $7000 from the entrance fees, and the cost for an adult and a child to attend is $30.

	Adult	Child	Total
Price	a	c	$30
Revenue	$200a$	$300c$	$7000

$$a + c = 30$$
$$200a + 300c = 7000$$

4. A local fish market is selling fish and lobsters by the pound. The fish costs $4.50 a pound, while the lobster costs $9.50 a pound. The fish market sells 25.5 pounds and makes $189.75.

	Fish	Lobster	Total
Weight	f	l	25.5
Revenue	$4.50f$	$9.50l$	$189.75

$$f + l = 25.5$$
$$4.50f + 9.50l = 189.75$$

5. Jennifer has 12 nickels and dimes. The value of her coins is $1.

	Nickels	Dimes	Total
Number of Coins	n	d	12
Amount	$0.05n$	$0.10d$	$1

$$n + d = 12$$
$$0.05n + 0.10d = 1$$

6. The sum of 5 times one number and 2 times a second number is 57. The sum of the two numbers is 18.

	First Number	Second Number	Total
Value	x	y	18
Value	$5x$	$2y$	57

$$x + y = 18$$
$$5x + 2y = 57$$

Exercise	Depth of Knowledge (D.O.K.)	COMMON CORE Mathematical Practices
1–5	**1** Recall of Information	**MP.4** Modeling
6	**1** Recall of Information	**MP.2** Reasoning
7–8	**1** Recall of Information	**MP.4** Modeling
9–13	**2** Skills/Concepts	**MP.4** Modeling
14	**2** Skills/Concepts	**MP.2** Reasoning
15	**2** Skills/Concepts	**MP.4** Modeling

7. Gary goes to the grocery store to buy hot dogs and hamburgers for a cookout. He buys a total of 8 packages for a total of $28.52. A package of hot dogs costs $2.29 and a package of hamburgers costs $5.69.

	Hot Dogs	Hamburgers	Total
Value	d	b	8
Amount	2.29d	5.69b	$28.52

$$d + b = 8$$
$$2.29d + 5.69b = 28.52$$

8. The sum of two numbers is 28, and the sum of 6 times the first number and 3 times the second number is 105.

	First Number	Second Number	Total
Value	x	y	28
Value	6x	3y	105

$$x + y = 28$$
$$6x + 3y = 105$$

Find a system of equations that corresponds to the situation and then solve the resulting system.

9. Jan spends part of her year as a member of a gym. She then finds a better deal at another gym, so she cancels her membership with the first gym and spends the rest of the year with the second gym. The membership to the first gym costs $80 per month, while the membership for the second gym costs $45 per month. If she ends up spending a total of $645 over the course of the year, how much time did she spend at each gym?

$$80x + 45y = 645$$
$$x + y = 12$$

$$\begin{array}{r} 80x + 45y = 645 \\ +(-80x - 80y = -960) \\ \hline -35y = -315 \\ y = 9 \end{array}$$

$$x + y = 12$$
$$x + 9 = 12$$
$$x = 3$$

So Jan spent 3 months at the first gym and 9 months at the second gym.

10. John is selling tickets to an event. Attendees can either buy a general admission ticket or a VIP ticket. The general adimission tickets are $70 and the VIP tickets are $105. If he knows he sold a total of 33 tickets and made $2730, how many of each type did he sell?

$$70x + 105y = 2730$$
$$x + y = 33$$

$$\begin{array}{r} 70x + 105y = 2730 \\ +(-70x - 70y = -2310) \\ \hline 35y = 420 \\ y = 12 \end{array}$$

$$x + y = 33$$
$$x + 12 = 33$$
$$x = 21$$

So John sold 21 general admission tickets and 12 VIP tickets.

MULTIPLE REPRESENTATIONS

For systems of linear inequalities that have only whole number solutions, some students may choose to display their answers in a table instead of as a graph. Discuss factors that may make one representation more desirable than the other.

Exercise	Depth of Knowledge (D.O.K.)	COMMON CORE Mathematical Practices
16	**2** Skills/Concepts	**MP.2** Reasoning
17–22	**2** Skills/Concepts	**MP.4** Modeling
23	**2** Skills/Concepts **H.O.T.**	**MP.4** Modeling
24–25	**3** Strategic Thinking **H.O.T.**	**MP.3** Logic

When working with systems of linear equations, remind students that choosing variables that remind them of the value being represented will make it easier to correctly interpret their solutions.

11. There are 150 adults and 225 children at a zoo. If the zoo makes a total of $5100 from the entrance fees, and the cost of an adult and a child to attend is $31, how much does it cost each for a parent and a child?

Write the system.

$$150a + 225c = 5100$$
$$a + c = 31$$

Multiply the second equation by -150 and solve for c.

$$150a + 225c = 5100$$
$$+(-150a - 150c = -4650)$$
$$\overline{75c = 450}$$
$$c = 6$$

Substitute 6 for c into the original second equation.

$$a + 6 = 31$$
$$a = 25$$

So the adult tickets cost $25 and the child tickets cost $6.

12. A local fish market is selling fish and lobsters by the pound. The fish costs $5.25 a pound, while the lobster costs $10.50 a pound. The fish market sells 28.5 pounds and makes $215.25.

Write the system.

$$5.25f + 10.50l = 215.25$$
$$f + l = 28.5$$

Multiply the second equation by -5.25 and solve for l.

$$5.25f + 10.50l = 215.25$$
$$+(-5.25f - 5.25l = -149.625)$$
$$\overline{5.25l = 65.625}$$
$$l = 12.5$$

Substitute 12.5 for l into the original second equation.

$$f + l = 28.5$$
$$f = 16$$

So the market sold 16 pounds of fish and 12.5 pounds of lobster.

13. Nicole has 15 nickels and dimes. If the value of her coins is $1.20, how many of each coin does she have?

Write the system.

$$0.05n + 0.10d = 1.20$$
$$n + d = 15$$

Multiply the second equation by -0.05 and solve for d.

$$0.05n + 0.10d = 1.20$$
$$+(-0.05n - 0.05d = -0.75)$$
$$\overline{0.05d = 0.45}$$
$$d = 9$$

Substitute 9 for d into the original second equation.

$$n + 9 = 15$$
$$n = 6$$

So Nicole has 6 nickels and 9 dimes.

14. The sum of 4 times one number and 3 times a second number is 64. If the sum of the two numbers is 19, find the two numbers.

Write the system.

$4x + 3y = 64$

$x + y = 19$

Multiply the second equation by -4 and solve for y.

$$4x + 3y = 64$$
$$+(-4x - 4y = -76)$$
$$\overline{\qquad -y = -12}$$
$$y = 12$$

Substitute 12 for y into the original second equation.

$x + 12 = 19$

$x = 7$

So the first number is 7 and the second number is 12.

15. Meaghan goes to the grocery store to buy hot dogs and hamburgers for a cookout. She buys a total of 6 packages for a total of $30.46. If a package of hot dogs costs $2.65 and a package of hamburgers costs $6.29, determine how many packs of each she bought.

Write the system.

$2.65d + 6.29b = 30.46$

$d + b = 6$

Multiply the second equation by -2.65 and solve for b.

$$2.65d + 6.29b = 30.46$$
$$+(-2.65d - 2.65b = -15.90)$$
$$\overline{\qquad 3.64b = 14.56}$$
$$b = 4$$

Substitute 4 for b into the original second equation.

$d + 4 = 6$

$d = 2$

So Meaghan bought 2 packages of hot dogs and 4 packages of hamburgers.

16. The sum of two numbers is 33, and the sum of 7 times the first number and 5 times the second number is 197.

Write the system.

$7x + 5y = 197$

$x + y = 33$

Multiply the second equation by -7 and solve for y.

$$7x + 5y = 197$$
$$+(-7x - 7y = -231)$$
$$\overline{\qquad -2y = -34}$$
$$y = 17$$

Substitute 17 for y into the original second equation.

$x + 17 = 33$

$x = 16$

So the first number is 16 and the second number is 17.

AVOID COMMON ERRORS

Graphing calculators can help students find points of intersection after they have written equations for real-world situations. Students should understand, however, that if they write incorrect equations, the graph of the equations will not show the correct answer for the real-world situation. Stress that reading problems carefully and writing equations properly is as important as solving the equations correctly.

© Houghton Mifflin Harcourt Publishing Company

Focus on Math Connections

MP.1 While many students may have a preferred method for solving systems of linear equations, they should understand how to use other methods. Discuss with students how to determine which method would be most efficient for a given system of equations. For example, substitution may be more efficient when equations are written in $y = mx + b$ form, while elimination may be more efficient when the coefficient of one variable in one equation is a multiple of the coefficient of the same variable in the other equation.

Write the system of inequalities that represents the situation. Then graph the system and describe the solutions. Give one possible solution.

17. Angelique is buying towels for her apartment. She finds some green towels that cost \$8 each and blue towels that cost \$10 each. She wants to buy at least 4 towels but doesn't want to spend more than \$70. How many of each towel can she purchase?

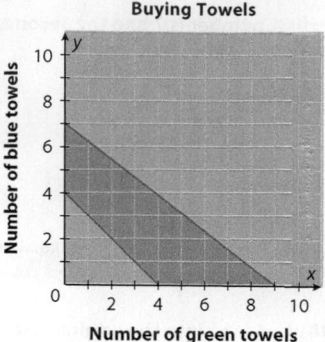

Buying Towels

$8x + 10y \leq 70$
$x + y \geq 4$

The possible solutions are points with integer coordinates that lie in the shaded region shared by the inequalities and on the solid boundary lines. One possible solution is Angelique can buy 4 green towels and 2 blue towels.

18. The sum of two numbers is at least 8, and the sum of one of the numbers and 3 times the second number is no more than 15.

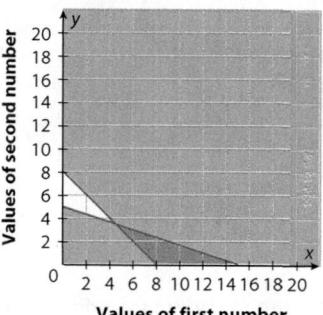

$x + 3y \leq 15$
$x + y \geq 8$

The possible solutions lie in the shaded region shared by the inequalities and on the solid boundary lines. One possible solution is the first number is 8 and the second number is 2.

19. The sum of two numbers is at most 12, and the sum of 3 times the first number and 8 times the second number is at least 48.

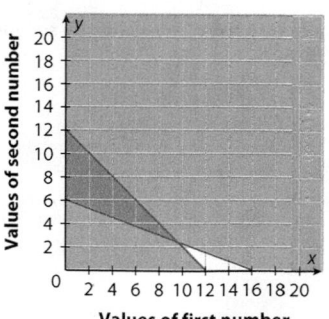

$3x + 8y \geq 48$
$x + y \leq 12$

The possible solutions lie in the shaded region shared by the inequalities and on the solid boundary lines. One possible solution is the first number is 4 and the second number is 6.

20. Katie is purchasing plates and mugs for her house. She would like to buy at least 8 items. Determine the possibilities if the plates cost $8 each and the mugs cost $7 each, and she plans to spend no more than $112.

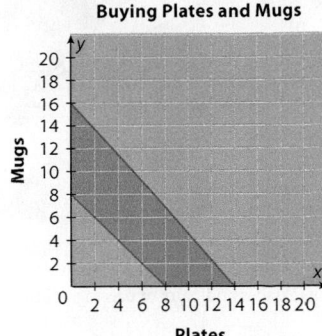

Buying Plates and Mugs

$$8x + 7y \leq 112$$
$$x + y \geq 8$$

The possible solutions are points with integer coordinates that lie in the shaded region shared by the inequalities and on the solid boundary lines. One possible solution is Katie buys 6 plates and 6 mugs.

21. Christine is selling tickets at a museum. She knows that she has sold at least 40 tickets. The adult tickets cost 14 dollars and the children's tickets cost 12 dollars. If she knows she has sold no more than $720 worth of tickets, what are the possible combinations?

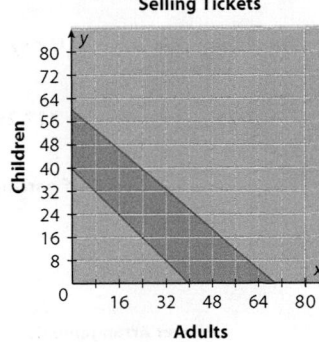

Selling Tickets

$$14x + 12y \leq 720$$
$$x + y \geq 40$$

The possible solutions are points with integer coordinates that lie in the shaded region shared by the inequalities and on the solid boundary lines. One possible solution is 24 adults and 32 children.

22. Mike is bringing cans and bottles to a recycling center. For a type A can or bottle he gets 5 cents, and for a type B can or bottle he gets 10 cents. He knows that he has redeemed at least 11 cans but has no more than 95 cents. What are the possible combinations?

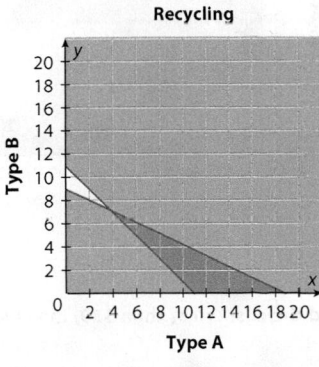

Recycling

$$0.05x + 0.10y \leq 0.95$$
$$x + y \geq 11$$

The possible solutions are points with integer coordinates that lie in the shaded region shared by the inequalities and on the solid boundary lines. One possible solution is 12 Type A cans and bottles and 2 Type B cans and bottles.

© Houghton Mifflin Harcourt Publishing Company

JOURNAL

Have students summarize the steps they follow to solve a real-world problem using a system of linear equations or inequalities. They should note which steps are the same for systems of equations and systems of inequalities, and which steps are different.

23. Explain the Error A student is given the following system. He graphs the system as shown and determines that a solution is $(7, 0)$. Where did the student go wrong? What should the correct answer be?

$$x + y = 6$$
$$x + 2y = 8$$

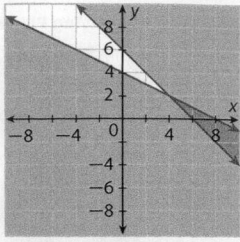

The student graphed the system of equations as a system of inequalities. When graphing a system of equations, the solution is the point of intersection. So the solution should be $(4, 2)$.

24. Justify Reasoning Molly went shopping to buy jewelry. All of the earrings cost $15.25 and the necklaces cost $40.75. If she spends $127.25 and buys 5 items, how many necklaces and pairs of earrings did she buy? Justify your answer.

Write the system.

$$15.25e + 40.75n = 127.25$$
$$e + n = 5$$

Multiply the second equation by −15.25 and solve for n.

$$15.25e + 40.75n = 127.25$$
$$+(-15.25e - 15.25n = -76.25)$$
$$\overline{25.50n = 51}$$
$$n = 2$$

Substitute 2 for n in into the original second equation.

$$e + n = 5$$
$$e + 2 = 5$$
$$e = 3$$

To justify, substitute the obtained values into the system and verify that true statements result.

$$15.25(3) + 40.75(2) \stackrel{?}{=} 127.25 \qquad 127.25 = 127.25$$
$$3 + 2 \stackrel{?}{=} 5 \qquad \rightarrow \qquad 5 = 5$$

The answers check. So Molly bought 3 pairs of earrings and 2 necklaces.

25. Check for Reasonableness Chris is at the florist and has to buy flowers. Arrangements of daisies are $4.25 and arrangements of roses are $6.50. He wants to spend less than $39 and wants to buy more than 4 arrangements. What are possible combinations that Chris can buy? Check to make sure your answer is reasonable.

Write the system.

$$4.25d + 6.50r < 39$$
$$d + r > 4$$

Graph the system.

One possible solution is Chris buys 3 daisy arrangements and 3 rose arrangements. Substitute these values into the inequalities to check for reasonableness.

$$4.25(3) + 6.50(3) \stackrel{?}{<} 39 \qquad \qquad 32.25 < 39$$
$$3 + 3 \stackrel{?}{>} 4 \qquad \rightarrow \qquad 6 > 4$$

Flower Arrangements

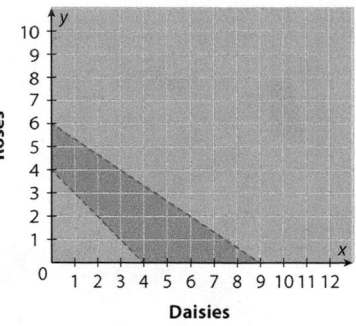

Since the number of arrangement is greater than 4 and the cost is less than $39, the answer is reasonable.

Lesson Performance Task

Amy is at the store to buy shirts and pants. The shirts cost $40 each and the pants cost $50 each. She plans to spend no more than $400 and buy at least 5 items. Find a possible combination of shirts and pants she can buy. How do you know this is a solution? What are two possible ways to show that this is a solution?

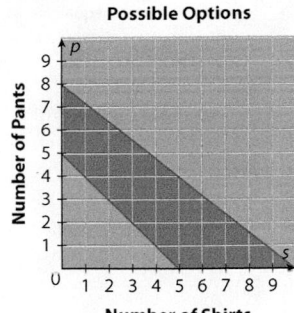

Possible Options

Number of Pants (vertical axis, labeled p, values 1–9)

Number of Shirts (horizontal axis, labeled s, values 1–9)

Write the system of inequalities.

$$s + p \geq 5$$
$$40s + 50p \leq 400$$

Graph the system.

One possible combination is 5 shirts and 2 pairs of pants. This is a known solution because it lies in the shaded region that is shared by the two inequalities.

Finding all ordered pairs in this region is one way to find solutions to the problem. Another way to show that this is a solution is to substitute the ordered pairs into both inequalities and then determine that both resulting inequalities are true.

For example, it can be shown that the ordered pair (5, 2) is a solution as follows:

$$5 + 2 \overset{?}{\geq} 5 \qquad \rightarrow \qquad 7 \geq 5$$
$$40(5) + 50(2) \overset{?}{\leq} 400 \qquad 300 \leq 400$$

EXTENSION ACTIVITY

Tell students to imagine that they have up to $200 to spend. Have students select two types of items they would like to buy and a total number of items to buy. Have them research the cost of the items, either online or in newspaper advertisements. Then have students write and solve a system of inequalities to find possible numbers of the two items they can buy.

INTEGRATE MATHEMATICAL PRACTICES
Focus on Critical Thinking

MP.3 Discuss with students the type(s) of numbers that are reasonable solutions for this Lesson Performance Task. In this scenario, as in many real-world situations, the only reasonable solutions are whole numbers. The total spent, however, does not need to be a whole number.

QUESTIONING STRATEGIES

? Why is the graph of the system shown only in the first quadrant? The number of shirts and pants cannot be negative.

? Are points on the boundary lines of the graphs solutions to the problem? Why or why not? Yes; the problem states that Amy plans to buy *at least* 5 items, which means a number greater than or equal to 5, and that she plans to spend *no more than* $400, which means an amount less than or equal to $400.

Scoring Rubric

2 points: Student correctly solves the problem and explains his/her reasoning.

1 point: Student shows good understanding of the problem but does not fully solve or explain his/her reasoning.

0 points: Student does not demonstrate understanding of the problem.

Study Guide Review

ASSESSMENT AND INTERVENTION

Assign or customize module reviews.

MODULE PERFORMANCE TASK

COMMON CORE

Mathematical Practices: MP.1, MP.2, MP.3, MP.4
A-CED.A.3, A-REI.D.12

SUPPORTING STUDENT REASONING

Students should begin this problem by focusing on what information they will need. They can then do research, or you can provide them with specific information. Here is some of the information they may ask for.

- **What are the possible strategies for playing this game?** Players can either aim for the 100-point hole or for all the other holes valued at 50 points or less.

- **Do point values relate to the difficulty level?** The greater the point value, the more difficult it is to get the ball in the hole.

- **Can a player climb the ramp and drop the ball in the hole?** Students should accept the premise that cheating is not an option. All points must be legitimately earned.

- **Does order have any effect on the total score?** Order doesn't matter. Rolling four 100's followed by five 10's is the same as rolling five 10's and then four 100's.

Modeling with Linear Systems

Essential Question: How can you model with linear systems to solve real-world problems?

Key Vocabulary
system of linear inequalities *(sistema de desigualdades lineales)*
solution of a system of inequalities *(solución de un sistema de desigualdades)*

KEY EXAMPLE (Lesson 12.1)

One cable television provider has a $50 setup fee and charges $90 per month, and another cable provider has a $150 equipment fee and charges $80 per month. Determine when the cost of the two services will be the same amount, and what the price will be.

Let $f(t)$ represent the cost for the first cable company and let $g(t)$ represent the cost of the second cable company, where t is the number of months.

The system of equations is $\begin{cases} f(t) = 50 + 90t \\ g(t) = 150 + 80t \end{cases}$.

Solve the system when $f(t) = g(t)$.

$$50 + 90t = 150 + 80t$$
$$90t - 80t = 150 - 50$$
$$10t = 100$$
$$t = 10$$
$$f(t) = 50 + 90t$$
$$f(10) = 50 + 90(10)$$
$$f(10) = 950$$

A subscriber would have paid either company $950 for 10 months of service.

KEY EXAMPLE (Lesson 12.2)

Graph the system of linear inequalities $\begin{cases} y \le 2x - 2 \\ y > 0.5x + 1 \end{cases}$.

Graph the line $y = 2x - 2$. Use a solid line because the inequality symbol is $\le$. Lightly shade below the line.

Graph the line $y = 0.5x + 1$. Use a dashed line because the inequality symbol is $>$. Lightly shade above the line.

The intersection of the two shaded areas contains the solution set to the system of linear inequalities. For example, (4, 4) is within the intersection and satisfies both inequalities.

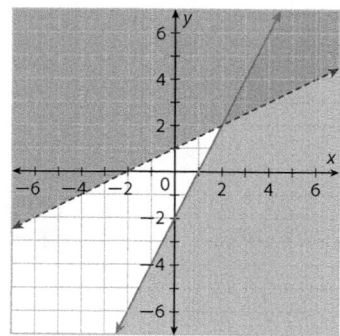

SCAFFOLDING SUPPORT

- If students are unsure of how to get started, suggest that they imagine a person rolling 9 balls, and then make up and write down the 9 scores the person got. Ask if the person would have won the grand prize. If not, ask the student to find other combinations of rolls that do win.

- For students who need more structure, ask whether it's better for the player to always aim for the 100-point hole or for all the other holes.

- If students find a solution without using a graph, encourage them to model the problem using linear systems.

1. Jacob wants to buy a gym membership. The table below shows the total cost of two gyms after several months, including any startup fees.

Month	2	4	6	8
Tony's Gym	$220	$300	$380	$460
Mickey's Gym	$120	$240	$360	$480

Use the data to write a system of equations. Then solve to find out in how many months both memberships will cost the same. What will that cost be? *(Lesson 12.1)*

$$\begin{cases} y = 40x + 140 \\ y = 60x \end{cases}$$; 7 months; $420

2. Graph $\begin{cases} y \leq -2x + 3 \\ 3y \geq 9x - 6 \end{cases}$. Give two ordered pairs that are

solutions and two that are not solutions. *(Lesson 12.2)*

   Possible answers: (0, 0) and (−1, 1) are

   solutions; (1, 4) and (1, −4) are not solutions.

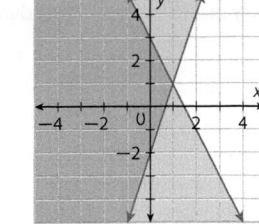

3. A local fish market is selling fish and lobster by the pound. The fish costs $5.00 a pound, while the lobster costs $10.50 a pound. The fish market sells 30 total pounds and makes $194. Represent this situation with a system of equations and solve it to find how many pounds of fish and lobster were sold. *(Lesson 12.3)*

$$\begin{cases} 5x + 10.5y = 194 \\ x + y = 30 \end{cases}$$; 22 pounds of fish, 8 pounds of lobster

MODULE PERFORMANCE TASK

How to Win at an Arcade Game

You are playing an arcade game that involves rolling a ball up a ramp. If you earn at least 450 points, you win the grand prize. You want to figure out a winning strategy. Here is some background information that will help you to formulate your plan.

- One round of the game uses 9 balls.
- Earning 100, 50, 40, 30, and 20 points is fairly obvious as the ball has to go down the corresponding hole. However, if you miss all of those holes, a big curve catches the balls and empties into the 10-points hole So, you will almost always earn at least 10 points.

Use your own paper to complete the task. Be sure to write down all your data and assumptions. Then use graphs, numbers, words, or algebra to explain how you reached your conclusion.

DISCUSSION OPPORTUNITIES

- What is the highest total possible score?
- How many total combinations of 10-point rolls and 100-point rolls are there that result in winning the grand prize? How can you find this information using your graph?

SAMPLE SOLUTION

Aiming for holes other than 100 requires getting all 9 balls into the 50-point hole. This gives only one possible chance to score 450 points.

Always aiming for the 100-point hole means getting either 100 points or 10 points with each ball. You need only 4 of the 9 balls to go into the 100-point hole to get 450 points. Since you can win by getting 4, 5, 6, 7, 8, or 9 balls in the 100-point hole, you have a better chance of winning the grand prize with this strategy.

To show this, let x = number of 10-point rolls and y = number of 100-point rolls. The number of rolls is given by $x + y \leq 9$. The total score needed to win the grand prize is given by $10x + 100y \geq 450$.

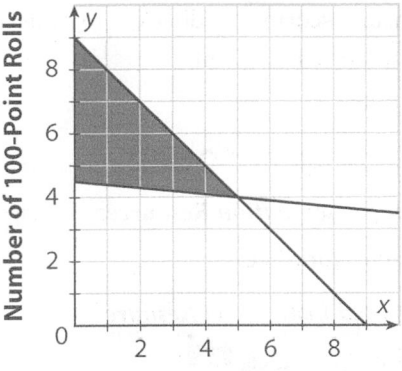

Grid intersections within the shaded region and on the boundary lines represent the combinations of 10-point and 100-point rolls with point totals greater than or equal to 450: (0, 5), (0, 6), (0, 7), (0, 8), (0, 9), (1, 5), (1, 6), (1, 7), (1, 8), (2, 5), (2, 6), (2, 7), (3, 5), (3, 6), (4, 5), and (5, 4).

Assessment Rubric

2 points: Student correctly solves the problem and explains his/her reasoning.

1 point: Student shows good understanding of the problem but does not fully solve or explain his/her reasoning.

0 points: Student does not demonstrate understanding of the problem.

Ready to Go On?

ASSESS MASTERY

Use the assessment on this page to determine if students have mastered the concepts and standards covered in this module.

ASSESSMENT AND INTERVENTION

Access Ready to Go On? assessment online, and receive instant scoring, feedback, and customized intervention or enrichment.

ADDITIONAL RESOURCES

Response to Intervention Resources

- Reteach Worksheets

Differentiated Instruction Resources

- Reading Strategies **EL**
- Success for English Learners **EL**
- Challenge Worksheets

Assessment Resources

- Leveled Module Quizzes

573 Module 12

1. A jar contains n nickels and d dimes. There are 30 coins in the jar, and the total value of the coins is $2.10. Set up and solve a system of equations to find how many nickels and how many dimes are in the jar. *(Lesson 12.1)*

$$\begin{cases} 5n + 10d = 210 \\ n + d = 30 \end{cases} ; \text{18 nickels and 12 dimes}$$

Tell whether each ordered pair is a solution of $\begin{cases} y < 2x + 5 \\ 4y > -4x - 8 \end{cases}$ *(Lesson 12.2)*

2. $(1, 2)$

   yes

3. $(0, 6)$

   no

4. $(-1, -2)$

   no

5. $(-1, 2)$

   yes

6. Nathan buys coffee and hot chocolate for his co-workers. Each cup of coffee costs $1.75 and each cup of hot chocolate costs $1.20. If he pays a total of $11.15 for 7 cups, how many of each does he buy? *(Lesson 12.3)*

   5 cups of coffee and 2 cups of hot chocolate

ESSENTIAL QUESTION

7. How can the graph of a system of linear equations help you find the solution to a real-world problem?

   Possible Answer: Translate the real-world situation into two equations, and graph them both. If the lines are parallel, there is no solution. If the lines are the same, there are infinitely many solutions. If the lines intersect in one point, that point is the solution.

COMMON CORE Common Core Standards

Lesson	Items	Content Standards	Mathematical Practices
12.1	1	**A-CED.A.3, F-LE.B.5**	**MP.1**
12.2	2	**A-REI.D.12**	**MP.2**
12.2	3	**A-REI.D.12**	**MP.2**
12.2	4	**A-REI.D.12**	**MP.2**
12.2	5	**A-REI.D.12**	**MP.2**
12.3	6	**A-CED.A.3**	**MP.2**

Assessment Readiness

1. Consider each ordered pair. Is the ordered pair a solution of $\begin{cases} y \le 3x + 5 \\ y \ge -\frac{2}{3}x + 5 \end{cases}$?

   A. $(-1, 4)$ ○ Yes ● No
   B. $(0, 5)$ ● Yes ○ No
   C. $(2, 9)$ ● Yes ○ No

2. Consider the graph of $y - 5 = \frac{1}{5}(x + 2)$.
   Determine whether each statement is True or False.
   A. The slope of the graph is $\frac{1}{5}$.   ● True   ○ False
   B. The graph includes the point $(0, 2)$.   ○ True   ● False
   C. The graph includes the point $(2, -5)$.   ○ True   ● False

3. The sum of 4 times one number and 3 times a second number is 65. The sum of the two numbers is 18. Write and solve a system of equations to find the two numbers. Show your work.

   $$\begin{cases} 4x + 3y = 65 \\ x + y = 18 \end{cases}$$

   $$4x + 3(18 - x) = 65$$
   $$4x + 54 - 3x = 65$$
   $$x = 11$$
   $$x + y = 18$$
   $$y = 18 - 11$$
   $$y = 7$$

   The numbers are 11 and 7.

4. Steven wants to buy a couch that costs $475. He has already saved $120. He plans to save $25 a week. Write a function to represent the amount Steven will have saved in x weeks. Will he have enough to buy the couch in 10 weeks? Explain your answer.

   $f(x) = 25x + 120$; In 10 weeks, he will not have saved enough to buy the couch. I found $f(10)$, which is 370. This means that he will have saved $370 in 10 weeks. The couch costs $475, which is more than $370.

MIXED REVIEW
Assessment Readiness

ASSESSMENT AND INTERVENTION

Assign ready-made or customized practice tests to prepare students for high-stakes tests.

ADDITIONAL RESOURCES

Assessment Resources

- Leveled Module Quizzes: Modified, B

AVOID COMMON ERRORS

Item 3   Some students may try to use the same variable for both numbers rather than realizing that two different variables are needed. Encourage students to look for key words to figure out how many variables they should use.

Common Core Standards

Lesson	Items	Content Standards	Mathematical Practices
12.2	1	A-REI.D.12	MP.2
6.2	2*	A-CED.A.2	MP.4
12.3	3	A-CED.A.3	MP.4
3.3	4*	F-LE.A.2	MP.3

* Item integrates mixed review concepts from previous modules or a previous course.

Piecewise-Defined Functions

ESSENTIAL QUESTION:

Answer: Piecewise-defined functions can be used to determine total cost for situations where rates change, such as with a cable service that has a special introductory rate and then a higher rate.

PROFESSIONAL DEVELOPMENT VIDEO

Professional Development Video

Author Juli Dixon models successful teaching practices in an actual high-school classroom.

Professional Development

my.hrw.com

MODULE **13**

Piecewise-Defined Functions

Essential Question: How can you use piecewise-defined functions to solve real-world problems?

REAL WORLD VIDEO
Optimizing sales prices is key to running a successful retail business. Cost and pricing structures are rarely linear, instead taking "jumps" at certain price points.

MODULE PERFORMANCE TASK PREVIEW

A Taxing Situation

United States citizens pay sales taxes on items they buy, gasoline taxes when they fill up their cars at the pump, and property taxes if they own a home. Everyone who earns more than a certain minimum amount also pays the federal government a tax on their income. The amount paid is defined not as a percent of income but by a "piecewise" function. You'll learn about these functions in this module and then use them to analyze the income tax system.

Module 13   575

© Houghton Mifflin Harcourt Publishing Company • Sfuse/Getty Images

---

DIGITAL TEACHER EDITION

Access a full suite of teaching resources when and where you need them:

- Access content online or offline
- Customize lessons to share with your class
- Communicate with your students in real-time
- View student grades and data instantly to target your instruction where it is needed most

PERSONAL MATH TRAINER
Assessment and Intervention

Assign automatically graded homework, quizzes, tests, and intervention activities. Prepare your students with updated, Common Core-aligned practice tests.

Are YOU Ready?

Complete these exercises to review skills you will need for this module.

Multi-Step Equations

Example 1 Solve. $\frac{3}{4}b + 2 = 38$

$\quad\quad\quad \frac{3}{4}b = 36$ Subtract 2 from both sides.

$\quad\quad\quad b = 48$ Multiply both sides by $\frac{4}{3}$.

• Online Homework
• Hints and Help
• Extra Practice

Solve each equation.

1. $10x - 15 = -4$
    $\underline{\quad x = 1.1 \quad}$

2. $5x - 7 = 2(3x + 1)$
    $\underline{\quad x = -9 \quad}$

3. $5(8v - 4) = -2$
    $\underline{\quad v = 0.45 \quad}$

Two-Step Inequalities

Example 2 Solve. $-2w + 3 \le 4$

$\quad\quad\quad -2w \le 1$ Subtract 3 from both sides.

$\quad\quad\quad w \ge -0.5$ Divide both sides by –2 and flip the sign.

Solve.

4. $n - 7 \ge -4$
    $\underline{\quad n \ge 3 \quad}$

5. $\frac{3x}{2} < -6$
    $\underline{\quad x < -4 \quad}$

6. $5 - 9a \le 32$
    $\underline{\quad a \ge -3 \quad}$

Absolute Value

Example 3 Use the definition of absolute value to write two equations that represent the equation $|3x - 11| = 1$.

If $3x - 11 > 0$, then $3x - 11 = 1$.

If $3x - 11 < 0$, then $3x - 11 = -1$.

The two equations are $3x - 11 = 1$ and $3x - 11 = -1$.

Write two equations that represent the given function.

7. $\left|\frac{k}{9} + \frac{1}{3}\right| = 12$
    $\underline{\frac{k}{9} + \frac{1}{3} = 12, \frac{k}{9} + \frac{1}{3} = -12}$

8. $|6(r - 4)| = 4.8$
    $\underline{6(r - 4) = 4.8, 6(r - 4) = -4.8}$

9. $\left|\frac{n}{22}\right| = 16$
    $\underline{\frac{n}{22} = 16, \frac{n}{22} = -16}$

Are You Ready?

ASSESS READINESS

Use the assessment on this page to determine if students need strategic or intensive intervention for the module's prerequisite skills.

ASSESSMENT AND INTERVENTION

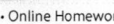

RtI Response to Intervention TIER 1, TIER 2, TIER 3 SKILLS

Personal Math Trainer will automatically create a standards-based, personalized intervention assignment for your students, targeting each student's individual needs!

ADDITIONAL RESOURCES

See the table below for a full list of intervention resources available for this module.

Response to Intervention Resources also includes:

• Tier 2 Skill Pre-Tests for each Module
• Tier 2 Skill Post-Tests for each skill

Response to Intervention			Differentiated Instruction
Tier 1	**Tier 2**	**Tier 3**	
Lesson Intervention Worksheets	Strategic Intervention Skills Intervention Worksheets	Intensive Intervention Worksheets available online	
Reteach 13.1 Reteach 13.2 Reteach 13.3 Reteach 13.4	10 Linear Functions 11 Multi-Step Equations 22 Two-Step Inequalities 27 Absolute Value	Building Block Skills 1, 4, 22, 23, 27, 40, 52, 54, 59, 88, 98, 110	Challenge worksheets Extend the Math Lesson Activities in TE

Understanding Piecewise-Defined Functions

Common Core Math Standards

The student is expected to:

 F-IF.C.7b

Graph square root, cube root, and piecewise-defined functions, including step functions and absolute value functions. Also F-BF.A.1b

Mathematical Practices

 MP.6 Precision

Language Objective

Describe a real-world situation that can be modeled by a piecewise function.

ENGAGE

Essential Question: How are piecewise-defined functions different from other functions?

A piecewise-defined function has different rules for different parts of its domain. Functions that are not piecewise-defined have only one function rule.

PREVIEW: LESSON PERFORMANCE TASK

View the Engage section online. Discuss why one's speed would vary on a long car trip. Then preview the Lesson Performance Task.

13.1 Understanding Piecewise-Defined Functions

Essential Question: How are piecewise-defined functions different from other functions?

Resource Locker

🧭 Explore   Exploring Piecewise-Defined Function Models

A **piecewise function** has different rules for different parts of its domain. The following situation can be modeled by a piecewise function.

Armando drives from his home to the grocery store at a speed of 0.9 mile per minute for 4 minutes, stops for 2 minutes to buy snacks, and then drives to the soccer field at a speed of 0.7 mile per minute for 3 minutes. The graph shows Armando's distance from home.

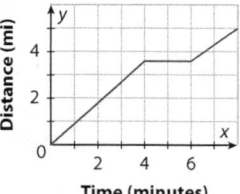

Time (minutes)

The three different sections in the graph show that there are three different parts to the function. The function for this graph will have three function rules, each for a different range of values for x.

The following steps can be used to build the piecewise function to model this situation.

Ⓐ Determine the function rule for the first 4 minutes for the domain, $0 \leq x \leq 4$. The rate of change is Armando's speed in miles per minute.

$$m = \frac{\boxed{0.9} \text{ mi}}{\boxed{1} \text{ min}} = \boxed{0.9}$$

The y-intercept is $\boxed{0}$.

The function for the first 4 minutes is $y = \boxed{0.9x}$.

Ⓑ Determine the function rule for the next 2 minutes for the domain, $4 < x \leq 6$.

Because the distance is not changing, the rate of change is $m = \dfrac{\boxed{0} \text{ mi}}{\boxed{2} \text{ min}} = \boxed{0}$.

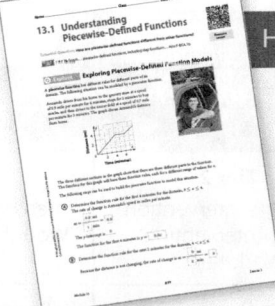

HARDCOVER PAGES 461–470

Turn to these pages to find this lesson in the hardcover student edition.

The function for the next 2 minutes is a constant function. The constant y-value is Armando's distance from home at the end of the first 4 minutes.

$y = 0.9x$

$y = 0.9(4) = \boxed{3.6}$

Ⓒ Determine the function rule for the last 3 minutes.
The rate of change is Armando's speed in miles per minute.

$m = \dfrac{\boxed{0.7}\ \text{mi}}{\boxed{1}\ \text{min}} = \boxed{0.7}$

The point at which the function begins is $\left(\boxed{6}\,,\boxed{3.6}\right)$.

Use the point and slope to construct the function rule for the last 3 minutes.

$y - \boxed{3.6} = \boxed{0.7}\left(x - \boxed{6}\right)$

$y - \boxed{3.6} = \boxed{0.7}\,x - \boxed{4.2}$

$y = \boxed{0.7}\,x - \boxed{0.6}$

Ⓓ Use all three parts to build the piecewise function that represents this situation.

$$f(x) = \begin{cases} \boxed{0.9x} & \text{if } 0 \le x \le 4 \\ \boxed{3.6} & \text{if } 4 < x \le 6 \\ \boxed{0.7x - 0.6} & \text{if } 6 < x \le 9 \end{cases}$$

Reflect

1. **Discussion** Describe how the domain is constructed so that the piecewise function is a function with no more than one dependent variable for any independent variable.
   The domain is described by inequalities. At a boundary domain value, one of the function
   rules will include the boundary value and the other will not. For example, the x-value of
   4 is included in the domain for the first function rule, but not in the domain for the next
   function rule.

⚙ Explain 1   Evaluating Piecewise-Defined Functions

The **greatest integer function** is a piecewise function whose rule is denoted by $\lfloor x \rfloor$, which represents the greatest integer less than or equal to x. The greatest integer function is an example of a **step function**, a piecewise function in which each function rule is a constant function. To evaluate a piecewise function for a given value of x, substitute the value of x into the rule for the part of the domain that includes x.

PROFESSIONAL DEVELOPMENT

Integrate Mathematical Practices

This lesson provides an opportunity to use Mathematical Practice **MP.6**, which asks students to "attend to precision." In this lesson, students need to pay close attention to the domains used for piecewise functions in order to graph the functions accurately. In addition, students must construct graphs carefully to make sure the graphs accurately represent the data.

EXPLORE

Exploring Piecewise-Defined Function Models

INTEGRATE TECHNOLOGY

Piecewise functions can be modeled on a graphing calculator. First, be sure that Dot is selected on the **MODE** screen to allow for discontinuous functions. Enter the function in the form *(first piece)(first condition)* + *(second piece)* *(second condition)* + ... Use the **TEST** menu to enter inequality symbols. Compound inequalities must be entered using the word *and*, which can be found by selecting **LOGIC** on the **TEST** menu.

INTEGRATE MATHEMATICAL PRACTICES
Focus on Modeling

MP.4 Explain that in real-world contexts, functions are often defined by different rules for different parts of their domain. Ask students to think of some situations in which price, speed, or another quantity is defined in different ways for different input values.

EXPLAIN 1

Evaluating Piecewise-Defined Functions

AVOID COMMON ERRORS

When evaluating the greatest integer function, students may be confused about how to round a number. Help students remember to always round down by telling them that the greatest integer function is also referred to as the "floor" function.

QUESTIONING STRATEGIES

❓ What are the domain and range of the greatest integer function? **domain: all real numbers; range: all integers**

Understanding Piecewise-Defined Functions   **578**

EXPLAIN 2

Graphing Piecewise-Defined Functions

AVOID COMMON ERRORS

Students may confuse the symbol for the absolute value function with the symbol for the greatest integer function. Remind students that the absolute value function notation shows x between bars, $|x|$, while the greatest integer function notation is $\lfloor x \rfloor$.

QUESTIONING STRATEGIES

? What effect would multiplying a positive constant by the greatest integer function have on its graph? What if the positive constant were multiplied by the term inside the brackets? In either case, the graph would be stretched vertically by a factor equal to the constant, so the vertical spaces between the line segments would be larger for a constant greater than 1 and smaller for a constant less than 1.

Example 1 Evaluate each piecewise function for the given values.

(A) Find $f(-3)$, $f(-2.9)$, $f(0.7)$, and $f(1.06)$ for $f(x) = \lfloor x \rfloor$.

The greatest integer function $f(x) = \lfloor x \rfloor$ can also be written in the form below.

$$f(x) = \begin{cases} \vdots \\ -3 & \text{if } -3 \leq x < -2 \\ -2 & \text{if } -2 \leq x < -1 \\ -1 & \text{if } -1 \leq x < 0 \\ 0 & \text{if } 0 \leq x < 1 \\ 1 & \text{if } 1 \leq x < 2 \\ 2 & \text{if } 2 \leq x < 3 \\ \vdots \end{cases}$$

-3 is in the interval $-3 \leq x < -2$, so $f(-3) = -3$.

-2.9 is in the interval $-3 \leq x < -2$, so $f(-2.9) = -3$.

0.7 is in the interval $0 \leq x < 1$, so $f(0.7) = 0$.

1.06 is in the interval $1 \leq x < 2$, so $f(1.06) = 1$.

(B) Find $f(-3)$, $f(-0.2)$, $f(0)$, and $f(2)$ for $f(x) = \begin{cases} -x & \text{if } x < 0 \\ x + 1 & \text{if } x \geq 0 \end{cases}$

$-3 < 0$, so $f(-3) = -(-3) = \boxed{3}$

$-0.2 < 0$, so $f(-0.2) = \boxed{-(-0.2)} = \boxed{0.2}$

$0 \geq 0$, so $f(0) = \boxed{0} + 1 = \boxed{1}$

$2 \geq 0$, so $f(2) = \boxed{2} + \boxed{1} = \boxed{3}$

Reflect

2. For positive numbers, how is applying the greatest integer function different from the method of rounding to the nearest whole number?
For the greatest integer function, you always round down.

Your Turn

3. Find $f(-2)$, $f(-0.4)$, $f(3.7)$, and $f(5)$ for $f(x) = \begin{cases} -x & \text{if } x < 2 \\ 2x + 3 & \text{if } 2 \leq x < 4. \\ x^2 & \text{if } x \geq 4 \end{cases}$
$f(-2) = 2$; $f(-0.4) = 0.4$; $f(3.7) = 10.4$; $f(5) = 25$

⚙ Explain 2   Graphing Piecewise-Defined Functions

You can graph piecewise-defined functions to illustrate their behavior.

Example 2 Graph each function.

(A) $f(x) = \begin{cases} -x & \text{if } x < 0 \\ x + 1 & \text{if } x \geq 0 \end{cases}$

Make a table of values.

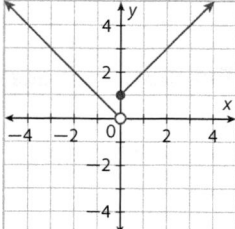

x	−3	−2	−1	0	1	2
f(x)	3	2	1	1	2	3

© Houghton Mifflin Harcourt Publishing Company

COLLBORATIVE LEARNING

Whole Class Activity

As a class, have students research electricity rates and design a pricing program that reflects actual household electrical usage but also encourages conservation. Ask students to find the average amount of energy (in kilowatt-hours) a household uses per day. Then have them set up variable rate levels depending on how much energy is used. The lowest usage should be rewarded with the lowest rate. Usage above a "reasonable" level should cost more in order to discourage energy waste. Have students create and graph a piecewise function that represents their selected rates.

Ⓑ $f(x) = \lfloor x \rfloor$

Make a table of values.

x	−3	−2.9	−2.1	−2	−1.5	−1	0	1	1.5	2
f(x)	−3	−3	−3	−2	−2	−1	0	1	1	2

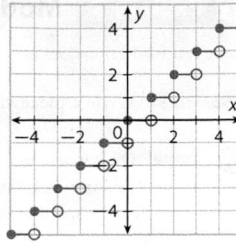

Reflect

4. Why does the graph in Example 2A use rays and not lines?
   Each rule has a separate domain. If the graph contained lines, the domains would overlap.

   Since each rule is an inequality with one endpoint, the graph contains rays.

5. Use the graph of the greatest integer function from Example 2B to explain why this function is called a step function.
   This function is called a step function because the sections of the graph are horizontal

   segments and look like a set of stairs.

Your Turn

6. $f(x) = \begin{cases} x & \text{if} & x < 2 \\ 2x + 3 & \text{if} & 2 \le x < 4 \\ x^2 & \text{if} & x \ge 4 \end{cases}$

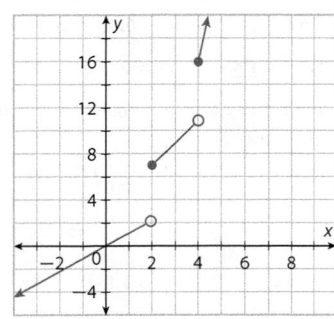

© Houghton Mifflin Harcourt Publishing Company

INTEGRATE MATHEMATICAL PRACTICES

Focus on Reasoning

MP.2 Explain to students the difference between a continuous function, whose graph is an unbroken line or curve, and a discontinuous function, whose graph contains a break or "jump" between sections. Then challenge students to define a continuous piecewise function that has a different rule for the domain $x < 3$ than for the domain $x \ge 3$. Students should recognize that in order for the function to be continuous, both pieces of the function must have the same y value when $x = 3$.

DIFFERENTIATE INSTRUCTION

Modeling

When finding an equation in $y = mx + b$ form from a graph, students can use "rise over run" to quickly compute slopes. To do this, students should draw a right triangle connecting any two points on the graph. The rise over run ratio will be the height of the triangle (in units) divided by the base of the triangle (in units).

EXPLAIN 3

Modeling with Piecewise-Defined Functions

INTEGRATE MATHEMATICAL PRACTICES
Focus on Reasoning

MP.2 Discuss with students whether the function modeling distance over a period of time is a piecewise function. Some students may feel that the function should not be described as piecewise because it is continuous. Remind students that any function that has different rules for different parts of its domain is a piecewise function, whether it is continuous or not.

AVOID COMMON ERRORS

When writing rules for piecewise functions, some students may define overlapping domains for two pieces of a function. Remind students that a function should have exactly one output value for each input value, so each value of x should be included in only one portion of the domain. For example, if one function rule applies to the domain $0 < x \le 3$, the next rule should apply to the domain $3 < x$, not $3 \le x$.

QUESTIONING STRATEGIES

? Why are all sections of the piecewise function called by the same function name, $d(t)$, rather than, for example, $d(t)$, $g(t)$, and $h(t)$? All three sections are part of a single function that has three different rules. They are not three different functions.

Some real-world situations can be described by piecewise functions.

Example 3 Write a piecewise function for each situation. Then graph the function.

Ⓐ **Travel** On her way to a concert, Maisee walks at a speed of 0.03 mile per minute from her car for 5 minutes, waits in line for a ticket for 3 minutes, and then walks to her seat for 4 minutes at a speed of 0.01 mile per minute.

Express the Maisee's distance traveled d (in miles) as a function of time t (in minutes).

For $0 \le t \le 5$, $m = 0.03$ and $b = 0$, so $d(t) = 0.03t$.

For $5 < t \le 8$, $m = 0$ and $b = 0.15$, so $d(t) = 0.15$.

For $8 < t \le 12$, $m = 0.01$ beginning at $(8, 0.15)$, so $d(t) = 0.01t + 0.07$.

$$d(t) = \begin{cases} 0.03t & \text{if } 0 \le t \le 5 \\ 0.15 & \text{if } 5 < t \le 8 \\ 0.01t + 0.07 & \text{if } 8 < t \le 12 \end{cases}$$

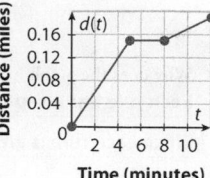

Ⓑ **Travel** On his way to class from his dorm room, a college student walks at a speed of 0.05 mile per minute for 3 minutes, stops and talks to a friend for 1 minute, and then to avoid being late for class, runs at a speed of 0.10 mile per minute for 2 minutes.

Express the student's distance traveled d (in miles) as a function of time t (in minutes).

For $0 \le t \le 3$, $m = \boxed{0.05}$ and $b = 0$, so $d(t) = \boxed{0.05}\,t$.

For $3 < t \le \boxed{4}$, $m = 0$ and $b = 0.15$, so $d(t) = 0.15$.

For $4 < t \le 6$, $m = \boxed{0.1}$ beginning at $\boxed{(4, 0.15)}$, so $y = \boxed{0.1}\,x - \boxed{0.25}$.

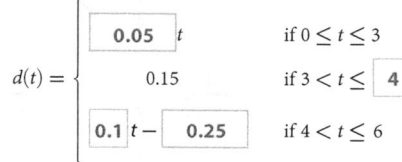

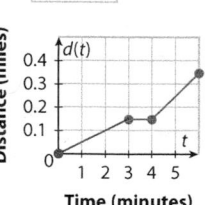

Your Turn

7. **Finance** A savings account earns 1.4% simple interest annually for balances of $100 or less, 2.4% simple interest for balances greater than $100 and up to $500, and 3.4% simple interest for balances greater than $500. Write a function rule for the interest paid by the account and graph the function.

$$p(d) = \begin{cases} 0.014d & \text{if } 0 \le d \le 100 \\ 0.024d - 1 & \text{if } 100 < d \le 500 \\ 0.034d - 6 & \text{if } 500 < d \end{cases}$$

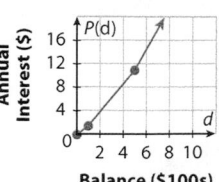

LANGUAGE SUPPORT **EL**

Connect Vocabulary

This lesson introduces the new term *piecewise function*. Explain that a piecewise function is *a function that is defined by different formulas for different parts of its domain.* Have students underline the word *piece* in *piecewise* to indicate that the term refers to defining a function piece by piece, or one piece at a time. Point out that the suffix *-wise* indicates a direction or manner of doing something, as in the words *clockwise* and *lengthwise*.

You can find the function rules for a piecewise function when you are given the graph of the function.

Example 4 Write an equation for each graph.

Ⓐ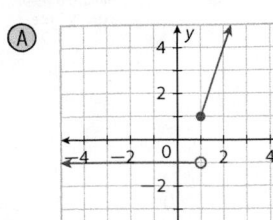

Find the equation of the ray on the right.

$m = \dfrac{1-4}{1-2} = \dfrac{-3}{-1} = 3$

Because the point (1, 1) is on the ray, $y - 1 = 3(x - 1)$, so $y = 3x - 2$

The equation of the line that contains the horizontal ray is $y = -1$.

The equation for the function is $y = \begin{cases} -1 & \text{if } x < 1. \\ 3x - 2 & \text{if } x \geq 1 \end{cases}$

Ⓑ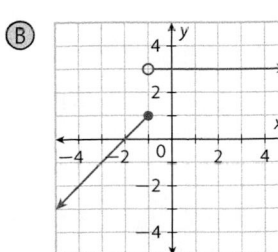

Find the equation for the ray on the left.

$m = \dfrac{1 - \boxed{-2}}{-1 - \boxed{-4}} = \dfrac{\boxed{3}}{\boxed{3}} = \boxed{1}$

Because the point $(-1, 1)$ is on the ray, $y \boxed{-1} = \boxed{1}\left(x \boxed{+1}\right)$,

so $y = \boxed{x + 2}$

The equation of the horizontal ray is $y = \boxed{3}$.

The equation for the function is $y = \begin{cases} \boxed{1}\,x + \boxed{2} & \text{if } x \leq -1 \\ \boxed{3} & \text{if } x > -1 \end{cases}$

Your Turn

8.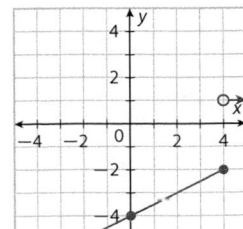

$y = \begin{cases} \frac{1}{2}x - 4 & \text{if } x \leq 4 \\ 1 & \text{if } x > 4 \end{cases}$

💬 Elaborate

9. How are the greatest integer function and $f(x) = 2\lfloor x \rfloor$ related?
   The range values of $f(x)$ are twice those of the corresponding range value of the greatest integer function.

10. **Essential Question Check-In** How many function rules do functions that are not piecewise-defined have?
    Functions that are not piecewise-defined only have 1 function rule.

EXPLAIN 4

Building Piecewise-Defined Functions from Graphs

INTEGRATE MATHEMATICAL PRACTICES
Focus on Modeling

MP.4 Review using points on a line to find the equation of the line. Substitute the coordinates of two points into the slope formula, $m = \dfrac{y_2 - y_1}{x_2 - x_1}$, then substitute the value of m and the coordinates of one point into $y = mx + b$ and solve for b.

QUESTIONING STRATEGIES

? If the graph of a piecewise function is discontinuous at $x = 5$, what must be true about the equation for the function? **The equation for the function must include a different rule for the domain $x > 5$ than for the domain $x < 5$.**

ELABORATE

INTEGRATE MATHEMATICAL PRACTICES
Focus on Critical Thinking

MP.3 Discuss whether it is possible for a piecewise function to include a non-linear function as one of the rules. Students should understand that the definition for a piecewise function still applies when one rule is non-linear.

SUMMARIZE THE LESSON

? How do you determine whether a function is a piecewise function or a step function? **A piecewise function's rule has two or more parts; each part is applied to a different subset of the domain. A step function is a special piecewise function whose graph consists of horizontal line segments.**

EVALUATE

ASSIGNMENT GUIDE

Concepts and Skills	Practice
Explore Exploring Piecewise-Defined Function Models	
Example 1 Evaluating Piecewise-Defined Functions	Exercises 1–8, 22
Example 2 Graphing Piecewise-Defined Functions	Exercises 9–12, 21, 25
Example 3 Modeling with Piecewise-Defined Functions	Exercises 17–20, 23
Example 4 Building Piecewise-Defined Functions from Graphs	Exercises 13–16, 24

INTEGRATE MATHEMATICAL PRACTICES

Focus on Reasoning

MP.2 When working with a piecewise function whose domain uses the symbol $>$, discuss with students how the function would be different if you changed the symbol to $\geq$. Students should understand that if you change one part of the domain, you will also need to change another part of the domain so that no two parts overlap. In addition, the graph of the function will change, with a filled dot representing the endpoint indicated by $\geq$, instead of an open dot for $>$.

⭐ Evaluate: Homework and Practice

• Online Homework
• Hints and Help
• Extra Practice

Evaluate each piecewise function for the given values.

1. Find $f(-4)$, $f(-3.1)$, $f(1.2)$, and $f(2.8)$ for $f(x) = \lfloor x \rfloor$.

   $f(-4) = -4$ and $f(-3.1) = -4$; $f(1.2) = 1$; $f(2.8) = 2$

2. Find $f(-3)$, $f(-2.1)$, $f(0.6)$, and $f(3.3)$ for $f(x) = \begin{cases} -1 & \text{if } x \leq 0 \\ 3x & \text{if } 0 < x < 1 \\ x+3 & \text{if } x \geq 1 \end{cases}$.

   $f(-2.1) = -1$ and $f(-3) = -1$; $f(0.6) = 1.8$; $f(3.3) = 6.3$

3. Find $f(-4)$, $f(-2.9)$, and $f(1.9)$ for $f(x) = \begin{cases} -5 & \text{if } x \leq -3 \\ x+2 & \text{if } -3 < x \leq 0 \\ x^2 + 7 & \text{if } x \geq 0 \end{cases}$.

   $f(-4) = -5$; $f(-2.9) = -0.9$; $f(1.9) = 10.61$

4. Find $f(-6)$, $f(-2.2)$, $f(1.4)$ and $f(3.6)$ for $f(x) = -2\lfloor x \rfloor$.

   $f(-6) = 12$; $f(-2.2) = 6$; $f(1.4) = -2$; $f(3.6) = -6$

5. Find $f(-3)$, $f(-1)$, and $f(1)$ for $f(x) = \begin{cases} \frac{2}{x} & \text{if } x \leq -2 \\ x & \text{if } -2 < x \leq 0 \\ 1 & \text{if } x \geq 0 \end{cases}$

   $f(-3) = -\frac{2}{3}$; $f(-1) = -1$; $f(1) = 1$

6. Find $f(-2)$, $f(-1)$, $f(0)$, $f(4)$, and $f(9)$ for $f(x) = \begin{cases} -x^2 & \text{if } x \leq -2 \\ 2x & \text{if } -2 < x < 2 \\ x+6 & \text{if } 2 \leq x \leq 4 \\ \sqrt{x} + 8 & \text{if } x > 4 \end{cases}$.

   $f(-2) = -4$; $f(-1) = -2$ and $f(0) = 0$; $f(4) = 10$; $f(9) = 11$

7. Find $f(-2.8)$, $f(-1.2)$, $f(0.4)$, and $f(1.6)$ for $f(x) = \lfloor x \rfloor^2$

   $f(-2.8) = 9$; $f(-1.2) = 4$; $f(0.4) = 0$; $f(1.6) = 1$

8. Find $f(0)$, $f(2)$, and $f(4)$ for $f(x) = \begin{cases} 8 & \text{if } x \leq 0 \\ 0 & \text{if } x > 0 \end{cases}$.

   $f(0) = 8$; $f(2) = 0$ and $f(4) = (0)$

Graph each piecewise function.

9. $f(x) = \begin{cases} -x + 1 & \text{if } x < 0 \\ x & \text{if } x \geq 0 \end{cases}$

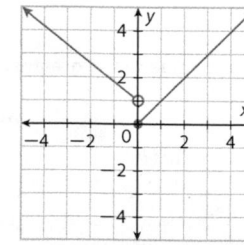

10. $f(x) = \begin{cases} -1 & \text{if } x < 1 \\ 2x - 2 & \text{if } x \geq 1 \end{cases}$

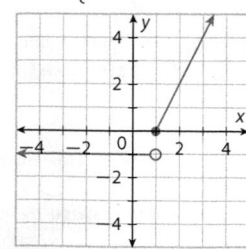

Exercise	Depth of Knowledge (D.O.K.)	**COMMON CORE** Mathematical Practices
1–6	**1** Recall	**MP.5** Using Tools
7–8	**2** Skills/Concepts	**MP.5** Using Tools
9–12	**1** Recall	**MP.2** Reasoning
13–16	**1** Recall	**MP.7** Using Structure
17–19	**1** Recall	**MP.4** Modeling
20	**2** Skills/Concepts	**MP.4** Modeling

11. $f(x) = \lfloor x \rfloor + 1$

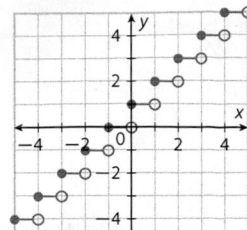

12. $f(x) = 2\lfloor x \rfloor - 2$

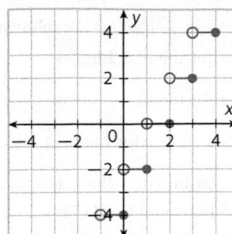

Write an equation for each graph.

13.

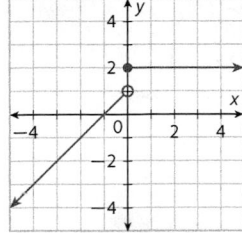

$$y = \begin{cases} x + 1 & \text{if } x < 0 \\ 2 & \text{if } x \geq 0 \end{cases}.$$

14.

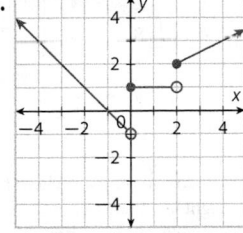

$$y = \begin{cases} -x - 1 & \text{if } x < 0 \\ 1 & \text{if } 0 \leq x < 2. \\ \frac{1}{2}x + 1 & \text{if } x \geq 2 \end{cases}$$

15.

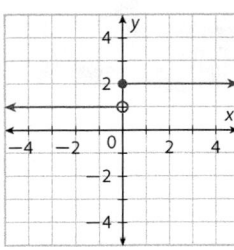

$$y = \begin{cases} 1 & \text{if } x < 0 \\ 2 & \text{if } x \geq 0 \end{cases}$$

16.

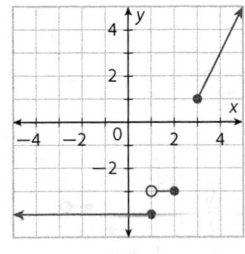

$$y = \begin{cases} -4 & \text{if } x \leq 1 \\ -3 & \text{if } 1 < x \leq 2 \\ 2x - 5 & \text{if } x \geq 3 \end{cases}$$

INTEGRATE MATHEMATICAL PRACTICES

Focus on Patterns

MP.8 When writing equations from given graphs, students should recognize that any linear graph that is a horizontal line will have a slope of 0. A horizontal line function has the same y-value for every x-value, so it will have the form $y = c$, where c is a constant.

Exercise	Depth of Knowledge (D.O.K.)	COMMON CORE Mathematical Practices
21	**1** Recall	**MP.6** Precision
22	**2** Skills/Concepts H.O.T.	**MP.3** Logic
23	**3** Strategic Thinking H.O.T.	**MP.3** Logic
24	**2** Skills/Concepts H.O.T.	**MP.3** Logic
25	**3** Strategic Thinking H.O.T.	**MP.3** Logic

Understanding Piecewise-Defined Functions   **584**

AVOID COMMON ERRORS

Review the definition of function to remind students that each input in a piecewise function should have exactly one output. Students should keep this definition in mind when writing piecewise functions, so that each *x*-value is included in only one domain.

Write a piecewise function for each situation. Then complete the table and the graph.

17. Finance A garage charges the following rates for parking (with an 8 hour limit):

$4 per hour for the first 2 hours

$2 per hour for the next 4 hours

No additional charge for the next 2 hours

Express the cost *C* (in dollars) as a function of the time *t* (in hours) that a car is parked in the garage.

$$C(t) = \begin{cases} 4t & \text{if } 0 < t \le 2 \\ 2t + 4 & \text{if } 2 < t \le 6 \\ 16 & \text{if } 6 < t \le 8 \end{cases}$$

t	0	1	2	3	4
C(t)	0	4	8	10	12

t	5	6	7	8
C(t)	14	16	16	16

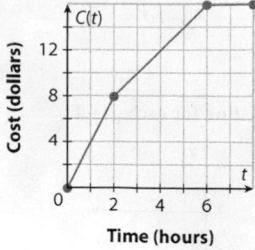

18. Cost Analysis The cost to send a package between two cities is $8.00 for any weight less than 1 pound. The cost increases by $4.00 when the weight reaches 1 pound and again each time the weight reaches a whole number of pounds after that.

Express the shipping cost *C* (in dollars) as a function of the weight (in pounds). Express your answer in terms of the greatest integer function $\lfloor w \rfloor$.

$$C(w) = 8 + 4\lfloor w \rfloor$$

w	0.5	1	1.5	2	2.5
C(w)	8	12	12	16	16

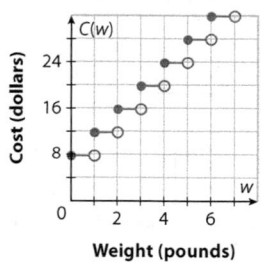

19. Golfing A local golf course charges members \$30 an hour for the first three hours, \$35 an hour for the next five hours, and nothing for the last 2 hours, for a maximum of 10 hours.

Express the cost C (in dollars) as a function of the time t (in hours) that a member plays golf at this golf course.

$$C(t) = \begin{cases} 30t & \text{if } 0 < t \le 3 \\ 35t - 15 & \text{if } 3 < t \le 8 \\ 265 & \text{if } 8 < t \le 10 \end{cases}$$

t	2	4	6	8	10
$C(t)$	60	125	195	265	265

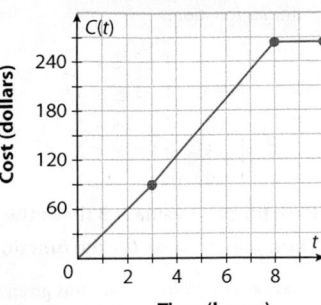

20. Construction A construction company is building a new parking garage and is charging the following rates: \$5000 a month for the first 2 months; \$8000 a month for the next 4 months; \$6000 in total for the last 4 months, when the garage will be completed. This amount will be paid in a lump sum at the end of the 6th month.

Express the cost C (in thousands of dollars) as a function of the time t (in months) that the construction company works on the parking garage.

$$C(t) = \begin{cases} 5t & \text{if } 0 < t \le 2 \\ 8t - 6 & \text{if } 2 < t \le 6 \\ 48 & \text{if } 6 < t \le 10 \end{cases}$$

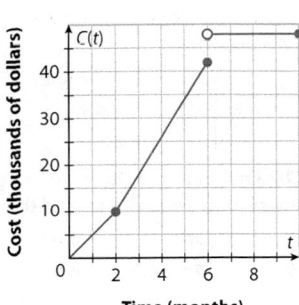

t	2	4	6	8	10
$C(t)$	10	26	42	48	48

21. State the domain and range of each piecewise function.

A. $y = \begin{cases} 5 & \text{if } 0 < x \le 1 \\ 0 & \text{if } x > 1 \end{cases}$

D: all real numbers $x > 0$,
R: $y = 0$ and $y = 5$

B. $y = \begin{cases} -x & \text{if } x \le 0 \\ x & \text{if } x > 0 \end{cases}$

D: all real numbers x, R: all
real numbers $y \ge 0$

C. $y = \begin{cases} x^2 & \text{if } x \le 4 \\ x^3 & \text{if } x > 4 \end{cases}$

D: all real numbers x, R:
all real numbers $y \ge 0$

D. $y = \begin{cases} x^2 + 1 & \text{if } x \le -2 \\ x^3 & \text{if } -2 < x < 4 \\ x^x & \text{if } x \ge 4 \end{cases}$

D: all real numbers x, R:
all real numbers $y \ge -8$

E. $y = \begin{cases} 1 & \text{if } x \le -3 \\ 1 & \text{if } -3 < x < 8 \\ 1 & \text{if } x \ge 8 \end{cases}$

D: all real numbers x, R:
$y = 1$

COGNITIVE STRATEGIES

When evaluating greatest integer functions, advise students to envision a number line. The location of any point on the number line automatically shifts to the next integer point to its left. Thus, for example, 1.7 shifts left to 1, while −1.6 shifts left to −2.

JOURNAL

Have students write a journal entry describing what a step function is, why it is called a step function, and how to graph it.

22. Critical Thinking Rewrite the piecewise function into a function of the greatest integer function.

$$f(x) = \begin{cases} -6 & \text{if } -2 \le x < -1 \\ -3 & \text{if } -1 \le x < 0 \\ 0 & \text{if } 0 \le x < 1 \\ 3 & \text{if } 1 \le x < 2 \\ 6 & \text{if } 2 \le x < 3 \end{cases}$$

Each function value is 3 times the corresponding value of the greatest integer function. Thus, the equation for the function is $f(x) = 3\lfloor x \rfloor$.

23. Explain the Error Clara was given the following situation and told to write a piecewise function to describe it.

While exercising, a person loses weight in the following manner:
0.5 pound per hour for the first hour
0.7 pound per hour for the next three hours
0.1 pound per hour until the workout is finished

Clara produced the following result. What did she do wrong and what is the correct answer?

$$W(t) = \begin{cases} 0.5t & \text{if } 0 \le t \le 1 \\ 0.7t & \text{if } 1 \le t < 4 \\ 0.1t & \text{if } t \ge 4 \end{cases}$$

Clara needed to include the weight already lost when writing an equation for the second and third rays of the piecewise function. The correct answer is

$$W(t) = \begin{cases} 0.5t & \text{if } 0 \le t \le 1 \\ 0.7t - 0.2 & \text{if } 1 \le t < 4 \\ 0.1t + 2.2 & \text{if } t \ge 4 \end{cases}$$

24. Critical Thinking Write an equation for the shown graph. Express the answer in terms of $\lfloor x \rfloor$.

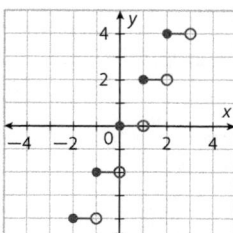

This graph illustrates a greatest integer function. Since each function value is twice the corresponding value of the greatest integer function, $f(x) = 2\lfloor x \rfloor$.

25. Communicate Mathematical Ideas Is a piecewise function still a function if it contains a vertical line? Explain why or why not.

A piecewise function is not a function if it contains a vertical line because a vertical line contains more than one x-value for a single y-value, which goes against the definition of a function.

Lesson Performance Task

Suppose someone is traveling from New York City to Miami, Florida. The following table describes the average speeds at various intervals on this 1200-mile trip.

Distance Traveled (hundreds of miles)	Average Speed (mi/h)
$0 < d \leq 2$	37.7
$2 < d \leq 4$	46.6
$4 < d \leq 6$	63.3
$6 < d \leq 8$	45.5
$8 < d \leq 10$	64.4
$10 < d \leq 12$	49.9

A. Graph the distance function. Make sure to use appropriate labels.

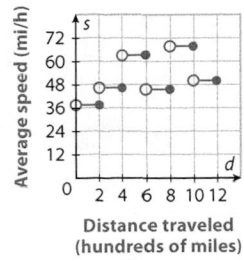

Distance traveled (hundreds of miles)

B. Write the piecewise function that is given by the table.

$$s = \begin{cases} 37.7 \text{ if } 0 < d \leq 2 \\ 46.6 \text{ if } 2 < d \leq 4 \\ 63.3 \text{ if } 4 < d \leq 6 \\ 45.5 \text{ if } 6 < d \leq 8 \\ 64.4 \text{ if } 8 < d \leq 10 \\ 49.9 \text{ if } 10 < d \leq 12 \\ 28.8 \text{ if } d > 12 \end{cases}$$

where d is the distance traveled in hundreds of miles and s is the speed in miles per hour.

C. Suppose the destination was changed from Miami, Florida to Minneapolis, Minnesota instead. Explain why it is not okay to use the piecewise function created for the trip from New York to Miami when traveling to Minneapolis, even though the distance is comparable.

Although the distance from New York to Minneapolis is comparable to the distance from New York to Miami, a variety of conditions such as weather, road speeds, and traffic make it difficult to obtain an accurate time estimate for the trip from New York to Minneapolis by using the piecewise function created for the trip from New York to Miami.

EXTENSION ACTIVITY

Have students create a table of speed limits and distances traveled along their routes to or from school. Each student should begin by creating a map of the route, and labeling the speed limit on each road and the approximate distance traveled on that road. Then have students write and graph the piecewise functions that are given by their tables.

AVOID COMMON ERRORS

Students may use incorrect inequality signs when writing a piecewise function. Be sure they understand that an open circle on the graph corresponds to a $<$ or $>$ sign in the inequality describing a part of the domain, while a filled circle on the graph corresponds to a $\leq$ or $\geq$ sign.

INTEGRATE MATHEMATICAL PRACTICES
Focus on Modeling

MP.4 Discuss with students how you could use the piecewise function created in the Lesson Performance Task to calculate the total amount of time it would take to drive from New York to Miami. Students should recognize that you can divide the distance traveled in each segment by the average speed for that segment to find the time it would take to drive that distance.

Scoring Rubric
2 points: Student correctly solves the problem and explains his/her reasoning.
1 point: Student shows good understanding of the problem but does not fully solve or explain his/her reasoning.
0 points: Student does not demonstrate understanding of the problem.

Absolute Value Functions and Transformations

Common Core Math Standards

The student is expected to:

COMMON CORE **F-IF.C.7b**

Graph square root, cube root, and piecewise-defined functions, including step functions and absolute value functions. Also F-BF.B.3

Mathematical Practices

COMMON CORE **MP.8 Patterns**

Language Objective

Describe transformations of graphs, including translations, vertical stretches, and vertical compressions or shrinks.

ENGAGE

Essential Question: What are the effects of parameter changes on the graph of $y = a|x - h| + k$?

Changes to h result in a horizontal shift in the graph; changes to k result in a vertical shift in the graph; and changes to a result in a vertical stretch, or shrink, of the graph.

PREVIEW: LESSON PERFORMANCE TASK

View the Engage section online. Discuss the photo and how you could represent the flight pattern of a flock of birds by a graph on the coordinate plane. Then preview the Lesson Performance Task.

13.2 Absolute Value Functions and Transformations

Essential Question: What are the effects of parameter changes on the graph of $y = a|x - h| + k$?

Resource Locker

⊘ Explore   Understanding the Parent Absolute Value Function

The most basic **absolute value function** is a piecewise function given by the following rule.

$$f(x) = |x| = \begin{cases} x & \text{if } x \geq 0 \\ -x & \text{if } x < 0 \end{cases}$$

This function is sometimes called the parent absolute value function. Complete each step to graph this function.

Ⓐ Complete the table of values.

x	$f(x) = |x|$
−3	3
−2	2
−1	1
0	0
1	1
2	2
3	3

Ⓑ Plot these points on a graph and using two rays, connect them to display the absolute value function.

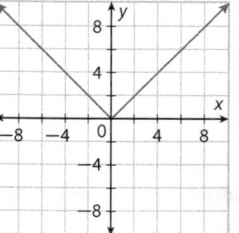

Ⓒ The vertex of an absolute value function is the single point that both rays have in common. Identify the vertex of the parent absolute value function.

The vertex of the parent absolute value function is $(0, 0)$.

HARDCOVER PAGES 471–478

Turn to these pages to find this lesson in the hardcover student edition.

Reflect

1. What is the domain of $f(x) = |x|$? What is the range?

Domain: all real numbers; Range: $y \geq 0$

2. For what values of x is the function $f(x) = |x|$ increasing? decreasing?

Increasing for $x \geq 0$; decreasing for $x \leq 0$

🖊 Explain 1   Graphing Translations of Absolute Value Functions

You can compare the graphs of absolute value functions in the form $g(x) = |x - h| + k$, where h and k are real numbers, with the graph of the parent function $f(x) = |x|$ to see how h and k affect the parent function.

Example 1   Graph each absolute value function with respect to the parent function $f(x) = |x|$.

Ⓐ $g(x) = |x + 3| - 5$

First, create a table of values for x and $g(x)$.

x	$g(x) = |x + 3| - 5$
−6	−2
−3	−5
−1	−3
0	−2
1	−1
3	1
6	4

Now graph the function along with the parent function.

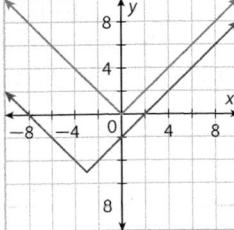

Understanding the Parent Absolute Value Function

INTEGRATE TECHNOLOGY

 Students can use graphing calculators to check their graphs of absolute value functions. The absolute value function can be accessed by going to the MATH menu, selecting NUM, and then selecting 1:abs(.

QUESTIONING STRATEGIES

? Is the parent absolute value function defined for all x-values or just certain x-values? What is the domain of the function? **It is defined for all x-values. The domain is all real numbers**

? Does the parent absolute value function output all y-values or just certain y-values? What is the range of the function? **The function outputs only non-negative y-values. The range is all non-negative numbers.**

EXPLAIN 1

Graphing Translations of Absolute Value Functions

INTEGRATE MATHEMATICAL PRACTICES
Focus on Critical Thinking

MP.3 Students may wonder why the graph of an absolute value function shows negative values in the range. Students should understand that a translated absolute value function will have negative values in the range when k is negative.

PROFESSIONAL DEVELOPMENT

🔲 Integrate Mathematical Practices

This lesson provides an opportunity to use Mathematical Practice **MP.8**, which asks students to "look for and express regularity in repeated reasoning." In this lesson, students observe how changing the parameters of absolute value functions results in predictable changes in the graphs of those functions.

How do the domain and range for the parent absolute value function compare to the domain and range for an absolute value function in the form $g(x) = |x - h| + k$? The domain for both functions is all real numbers, but the range for a function in the form $g(x) = |x - h| + k$ is all numbers greater than or equal to k.

Ⓑ $g(x) = |x - 4| + 2$

First, create a table of values for x and $g(x)$.

x	$g(x) = |x - 4| + 2$
−5	11
−3	9
−1	7
0	6
1	5
3	3
5	3

Now graph the function along with the parent function.

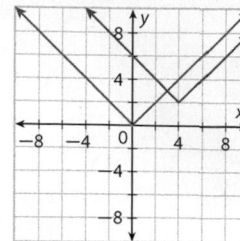

Reflect

3. How is the graph of $g(x) = |x - 4| + 2$ related to the graph of the parent function $f(x) = |x|$?
   The graph of $g(x) = |x - 4| + 2$ is a horizontal translation of 4 units to the right and a vertical translation of 2 units up of the parent function $f(x) = |x|$.

4. In general, how is the graph of $g(x) = |x - h| + k$ related to the graph of $f(x) = |x|$?
   The graph of $g(x) = |x - h| + k$ is a translation of h units horizontally (to the right if $h > 0$, to the left if $h < 0$) and k units vertically (up if $k > 0$, down if $k < 0$) of the graph of $f(x) = x$.

YourTurn

5. Graph the absolute value function $g(x) = |x + 1| + 2$ along with the parent function $f(x) = |x|$.

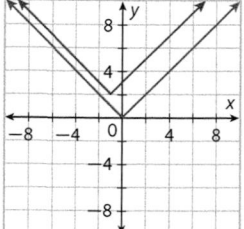

COLLABORATIVE LEARNING

Peer-to-Peer Activity

Have students work in pairs and take turns describing a transformation of $f(x) = |x|$. While one student describes a transformation, the other student should write the function rule for the transformed function. Have students compare their functions and discuss any differences until they agree on the correct function rule.

Constructing Functions for Given Graphs of Absolute Value Functions

You can write an absolute value function from a graph of the function.

Example 2 Write an equation for each absolute value function whose graph is shown.

Ⓐ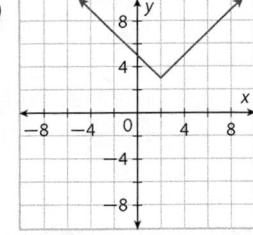

- h is the number of units that the parent function is translated horizontally. For a translation to the right, h is positive; for a translation to the left, h is negative. In this situation, $h = 2$.

- k is the number of units that the parent function is translated vertically. For a translation up, k is positive; for a translation down, k is negative. In this situation, $k = 3$.

The function is $g(x) = |x - 2| + 3$.

Ⓑ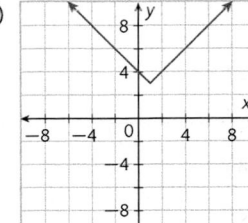

- h is the number of units that the parent function is translated horizontally. For a translation to the right, h is positive; for a translation to the left, h is negative. In this situation, $h = \boxed{1}$.

- k is the number of units that the parent function is translated vertically. For a translation up, k is positive; for a translation down, k is negative. In this situation, $k = \boxed{3}$.

The function is $g(x) = \left| x - \boxed{1} \right| + \boxed{3}$.

Reflect

6. If the graph of an absolute value function is a translation of the graph of the parent function, explain how you can use the vertex of the translated graph to help you determine the equation for the function.

If the vertex has coordinates (h, k), then the function has the equation $g(x) = |x - h| + k$.

© Houghton Mifflin Harcourt Publishing Company

EXPLAIN 2

Constructing Functions for Given Graphs of Absolute Value Functions

AVOID COMMON ERRORS

Students may write an incorrect function if they transpose the values for h and k. Students can use the fact that *horizontal* starts with the letter h to help them remember that for functions in the form $f(x) = |x - h| + k$, the value of h represents the horizontal change.

QUESTIONING STRATEGIES

? What point on the graph of an absolute value function can you use to determine how the graph of the parent function has been translated? Explain. **The vertex; by comparing the position of the vertex to the point (0, 0), which is the vertex of the graph of $f(x) = |x|$, you can easily see how many units the graph has been translated in each direction. Other points on the graph, because they lie on infinite rays, are not as easily compared.**

? What does the direction in which a graph has been translated tell you about the parameters of the equation $g(x) = |x - h| + k$? **The horizontal direction (left or right) determines the sign of h, and the vertical direction (up or down) determines the sign of k.**

DIFFERENTIATE INSTRUCTION

Graphic Organizers

Have students complete the graphic organizer to summarize how each parameter in an equation for an absolute value function affects its graph.

Transforming the Graph of $f(x) = |x|$ to $g(x) = a|x - h| + k$		
$a > 1$: stretch vertically	$h > 0$: translate right	$k > 0$: translate up
$0 \leq a < 1$: shrink vertically		
$-1 < a < 0$: shrink and flip vertically	$h < 0$: translate left	$k < 0$: translate down
$a = -1$: flip vertically		
$a < -1$: stretch and flip vertically		

EXPLAIN 3

Graphing Stretches and Compressions of Absolute Value Functions

INTEGRATE MATHEMATICAL PRACTICES

Focus on Patterns

MP.8 Relate the graphs of compressed or stretched absolute value functions to the graphs of linear functions. For example, the graph of $f(x) = 5|x|$ is similar to the graph of $f(x) = 5x$ except that the portion of the line to the left of the y-axis is reflected across the x-axis to create a V-shape. The portion of each graph to the right of the y-axis has slope 5, so it is steeper than the graphs of $f(x) = x$ and $f(x) = |x|$, which have slope 1. Similarly, the graph of $f(x) = \frac{1}{2}|x|$ is less steep than the graph of $f(x) = |x|$ because its slope (to the right of the y-axis) is less than 1.

QUESTIONING STRATEGIES

Given a real number a other than 0 or 1, for what value(s) of x will $f(x) = |x|$ and $g(x) = a|x|$ have the same y-value? Use the relationship between the graphs of the two functions to explain your answer. $x = 0$; multiplying the parent absolute value function by a will either stretch or compress the graph, so the two graphs will coincide at only one point. That point is the vertex of both functions, $(0, 0)$.

7.

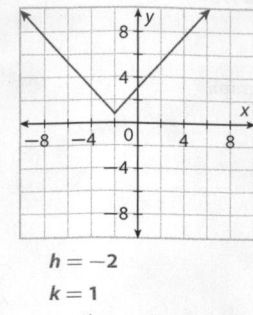

$h = -2$

$k = 1$

$g(x) = |x + 2| + 1$

⟳ Explain 3 **Graphing Stretches and Compressions of Absolute Value Functions**

You can compare the graphs of absolute value functions in the form $g(x) = a|x|$, where a is a real number, with the graph of the parent function $f(x) = |x|$ to see how a affects the absolute value function.

Example 3 Graph each absolute value function.

Ⓐ $g(x) = -2|x|$

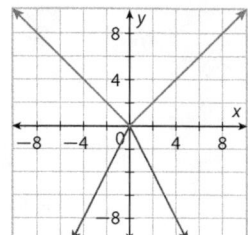

Ⓑ $g(x) = \frac{1}{4}|x|$

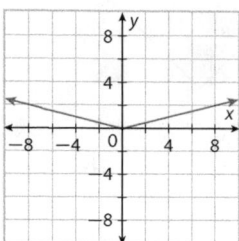

Reflect

8. Describe how the graphs of $g(x) = \frac{1}{4}|x|$ and $h(x) = -2|x|$ compare with the graph of $f(x) = |x|$. Use either the word *stretch* or *shrink*, and include the directions of movement.
   The graph of $g(x) = \frac{1}{4}|x|$ is a vertical shrink of the graph of $f(x) = |x|$. The graph of $h(x) = -2|x|$ is a vertical stretch of the graph of $f(x) = |x|$.

9. What other transformation occurs when the value of a in $g(x) = a|x|$ is negative?
   When the value of a in $g(x) = a|x|$ is negative, a reflection across the x-axis occurs.

© Houghton Mifflin Harcourt Publishing Company

LANGUAGE SUPPORT ㉈

Connect Vocabulary

The word *absolute* has different meanings outside of mathematics. For example, students may know that it can mean *complete or total,* as in "an absolute ruler" or "I'm absolutely sure." Point out that the term *absolute value* has a specialized meaning in mathematics. It refers to the distance a number is from zero (in either direction) and, in practice, the absolute value can be found by removing any negative sign that is in front of a number.

Graph each absolute value function.

10. $g(x) = -\frac{1}{2}|x|$

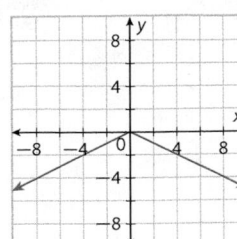

11. $g(x) = 4|x|$

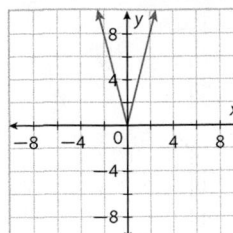

💬 **Elaborate**

12. Why is it important to note both the direction and the distance that a point has been translated either vertically or horizontally?
It is important to note both the direction and the distance that a point has been translated either vertically or horizontally because the horizontal and vertical directions determine the signs of h and k, respectively, while the distance determines their magnitude.

13. How does knowing a point in the graph other than the vertex help you find the value of a?
If you have a point other than $(0, 0)$, you can substitute the coordinates into $g(x) = a|x|$ and solve for a.

14. When graphing an absolute value function, how are $g(x) = a|x|$ and $h(x) = -a|x|$ related?
$h(x) = -a|x|$ is the reflection of $g(x) = a|x|$ across the x-axis. This means that the y-coordinates are opposites of each other.

15. **Essential Question Check-In** How would the graph of the parent function $f(x) = |x|$ be affected if $h > 0, k < 0$ and $a > 1$?
The graph of the parent function $f(x) = |x|$ would be shifted right h unit and down k units, and stretched vertically by a factor of a.

INTEGRATE MATHEMATICAL PRACTICES
Focus on Reasoning

MP.2 When multiplying absolute value functions by a constant, point out the difference between placing the coefficient inside or outside of the absolute value bars. When working with positive coefficients, students may see that there is no difference between the graphs of, for example, $f(x) = |2x|$ and $f(x) = 2|x|$. However, placing a negative coefficient outside of the absolute value bars, as in $f(x) = -2|x|$, does result in a different function from the one that results from placing the same coefficient inside the bars, as in $f(x) = |-2x|$. Discuss with students the differences between the functions.

ELABORATE

INTEGRATE MATHEMATICAL PRACTICES
Focus on Critical Thinking

MP.3 Ask students what the values of a, h, and k are if you write the parent absolute value function in the form $y = a|x - h| + k$. Students should understand that $h = 0$, $k = 0$, and $a = 1$.

SUMMARIZE THE LESSON

? How do you write a function for a given graph of an absolute value function? Find the slope of the graph to determine the amount the function is stretched or compressed. Find the location of the vertex to determine the direction and distance the parent function has been translated. Use these values to write the function in the form $y = a|x - h| + k$.

ASSIGNMENT GUIDE

Concepts and Skills	Practice
Explore Understanding the Parent Absolute Value Function	
Example 1 Graphing Translations of Absolute Value Functions	Exercises 1–6, 13–16, 22–24
Example 2 Constructing Functions for Given Graphs of Absolute Value Functions	Exercises 7–12
Example 3 Graphing Stretches and Compressions of Absolute Value Functions	Exercises 17–21, 24–27

INTEGRATE MATHEMATICAL PRACTICES
Focus on Critical Thinking

MP.3 When working with stretches and compressions of absolute value functions, discuss with students the difference between the slopes of the two rays that make up the graph. Students should understand that the slopes will always be opposites.

⚝ Evaluate: Homework and Practice

• Online Homework
• Hints and Help
• Extra Practice

Graph each absolute value function.

1. $g(x) = |x + 1| + 1$

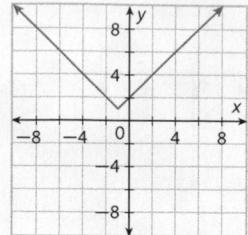

2. $g(x) = |x - 4| + 2$

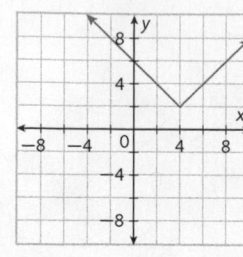

3. $g(x) = |x - 3| - 5$

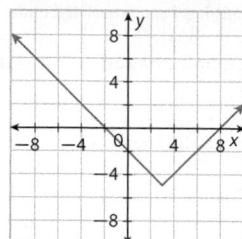

4. $g(x) = |x + 7| - 1$

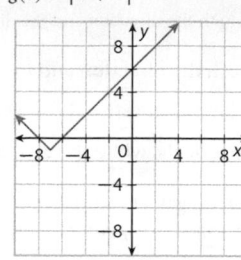

5. $g(x) = |x + 3| - 1$

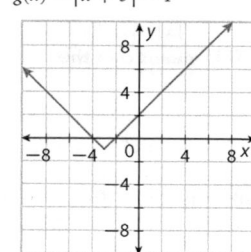

6. $g(x) = |x + 5| - 3$

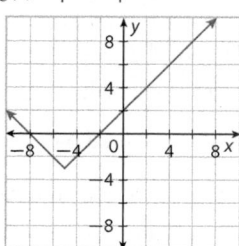

Write an equation for each absolute value function whose graph is shown.

7.

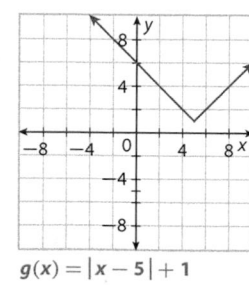

$g(x) = |x - 5| + 1$

8.

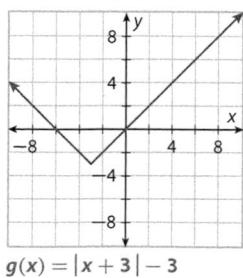

$g(x) = |x + 3| - 3$

© Houghton Mifflin Harcourt Publishing Company

Exercise	Depth of Knowledge (D.O.K.)	**COMMON CORE** Mathematical Practices
1–12	**1** Recall of Information	**MP.7** Using Structure
13–16	**1** Recall of Information	**MP.6** Precision
17–20	**1** Recall of Information	**MP.7** Using Structure
21	**1** Recall of Information	**MP.5** Using Tools
22–23	**1** Recall of Information	**MP.2** Reasoning
24	**2** Skills/Concepts **H.O.T.**	**MP.6** Precision

9.

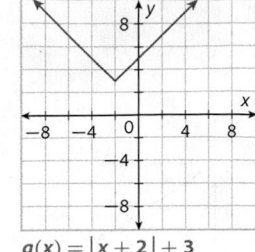

$g(x) = |x + 2| + 3$

10.

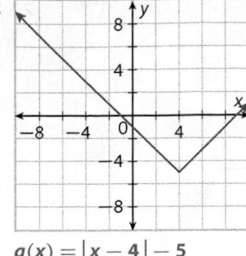

$g(x) = |x - 4| - 5$

11.

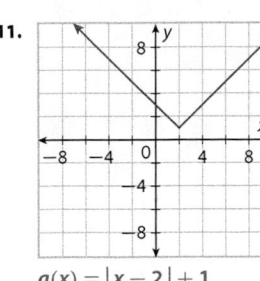

$g(x) = |x - 2| + 1$

12.

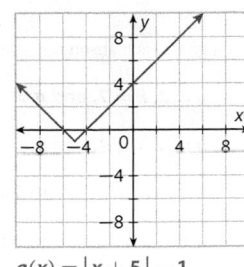

$g(x) = |x + 5| - 1$

Determine the domain and range of each function.

13. $g(x) = |x + 3| - 1$

Domain $= \{$real numbers$\}$

Range $= \{y | y \geq -1\}$

14. $g(x) = |x + 2| + 2$

Domain $= \{$real numbers$\}$

Range $= \{y | y \geq 2\}$

15. $g(x) = |x| + 1$

Domain $= \{$real numbers$\}$

Range $= \{y | y \geq 1\}$

16. $g(x) = |x - 9| + 6$

Domain $= \{$real numbers$\}$

Range $= \{y | y \geq 6\}$

Graph each absolute value function.

17. $g(x) = 3|x|$

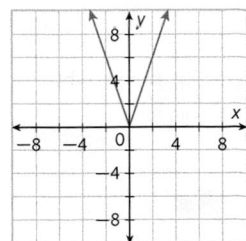

18. $g(x) = -2.5|x|$

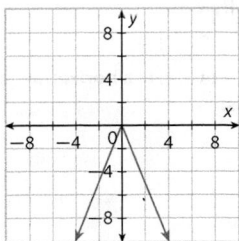

© Houghton Mifflin Harcourt Publishing Company

Exercise	Depth of Knowledge (D.O.K.)	COMMON CORE Mathematical Practices	
25–26	**2** Skills/Concepts **H.O.T.**	**MP.7** Using Structure
27	**3** Strategic Thinking **H.O.T.**	**MP.2** Reasoning

MODELING

When graphing stretches and compressions of absolute value functions, analytic thinkers may reason that doubling the coefficient of $|x|$ will double the y-value of the function and therefore stretch it. Remind visual learners that they can construct a table of coordinates, and then use the points to graph the function.

AVOID COMMON ERRORS

Remind students that absolute value bars act as grouping symbols. To evaluate an expression containing an absolute value, follow this sequence of steps: First, perform operations inside the absolute value bars; then take the absolute value; and, finally, perform operations outside the absolute value bars. For example, when evaluating $f(x) = |x - 4| + 2$ for $x = -3$, first subtract 4, then take the absolute value of the result, and, finally, add 2, which gives $f(-3) = |-3 - 4| + 2 = |-7| + 2 = 7 + 2 = 9$. Students who do not follow the correct order of operations will arrive at incorrect results.

19. $g(x) = \frac{1}{2}|x|$

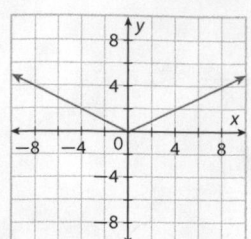

20. $g(x) = -\frac{2}{3}|x|$

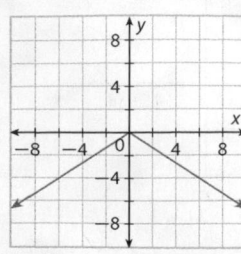

21. Identify the values of h, k, and a given each absolute value function.

A. $f(x) = 3|x - 2| + 2$ $h = 2$, $k = 2$, and $a = 3$

B. $f(x) = -0.2|x - 3| + 4$ $h = 3$, $k = 4$, and $a = -0.2$

C. $f(x) = -5|x + 6| - 1$ $h = -6$, $k = -1$, and $a = -5$

D. $f(x) = 0.5|x + 2| - 7$ $h = -2$, $k = -7$, and $a = 0.5$

E. $f(x) = 0.8|x| + 3$ $h = 0$, $k = 3$, and $a = 0.8$

22. Body Temperature The average body temperature of a human is generally accepted to be 98.6 °F. Complete the absolute value function below describing the difference $d(x)$ in degrees Fahrenheit of the temperature x of an individual human and the average temperature of a human. How is the graph of $d(x)$ related to the graph of the parent function $f(x) = |x|$?

$d(x) = |x - \boxed{98.6}|$

The graph of $d(x)$ is a horizontal translation of the graph of $f(x) = |x|$ to the right 98.6 units.

23. Population Statistics The average height of an American man is 69.3 inches. Complete the absolute value function below describing the difference $d(x)$ in inches of the height x of an individual American man and the average height of an American man. How is the graph of $d(x)$ related to the graph of the parent function.

$f(x) = |x|$?

$d(x) = |x - \boxed{69.3}|$

The graph of $d(x)$ is a horizontal translation of the graph of $f(x) = |x|$ to the right 69.3 units.

24. Make a Prediction Complete the table and graph all the functions on the same coordinate plane. How do the graphs of $f(x) = a|x|$ and $g(x) = |ax|$ compare?

x	−6	−3	0	3	6
$g(x) = \frac{1}{3}|x|$	2	1	0	1	2
$g(x) = \left|\frac{1}{3}x\right|$	2	1	0	1	2
$g(x) = -\frac{1}{3}|x|$	−2	−1	0	−1	−2
$g(x) = \left|-\frac{1}{3}x\right|$	2	1	0	1	2

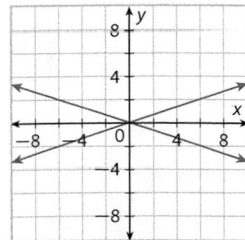

If $a > 0$, the graphs are the same and if $a < 0$, then the graphs are a reflection across the x-axis.

Multiple Representations Write an equation for each absolute value function whose graph is shown.

25.

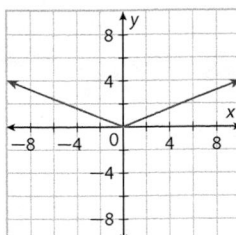

Note: One point on this graph is $(10, 4)$.

$g(x) = a|x|$

$g(10) = a|10| = 4$

$a(10) = 4$

$a = \frac{4}{10} = \frac{2}{5}$

$g(x) = \frac{2}{5}|x|$

26.

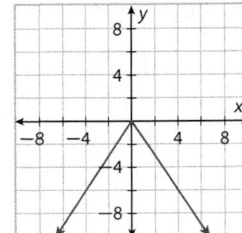

Note: One point on this graph is $(6, -9)$.

$g(x) = a|x|$

$g(6) = a|6| = -9$

$a(6) = -9$

$a = \frac{-9}{6} = -\frac{3}{2}$

$g(x) = -\frac{3}{2}|x|$

CRITICAL THINKING

Discuss with students what the graphs of all absolute value functions have in common. Students should understand that all absolute value functions that can be written in the form $y = a|x - h| + k$ will have a line of symmetry at $x = h$.

INTEGRATE MATHEMATICAL PRACTICES

Focus on Reasoning

MP.2 Have students explain how they would write an equation from the graph of a stretched or compressed absolute value function of the form $g(x) = a|x|$. One approach is to substitute the coordinate of a point on the graph into $g(x) = a|x|$ and solve for a. Another approach is to recognize that a is equal to the slope of the graph when $x \geq 0$, which can be found by calculating rise over run for that part of the graph.

Have students make a graphic organizer to show how horizontal and vertical translations of the graph of $f(x) = |x|$ are related to changes in the equation. Have students write "Start with the graph of $f(x) = |x|$" in the center of the graphic organizer and use arrows pointing up, down, right, and left to record how the equation changes when the graph is translated in each direction.

27. **Represent Real-World Problems** From his driveway at point $(4, 6)$, Kerry is adjusting his rearview mirror before backing out onto the street. The farthest object behind him to the left he can see is a neighbor's mailbox at $(-4, 12)$. The farthest object behind him to the right he can see is a telephone pole at $(20, 18)$. Create an absolute value function in the form $f(x) = a|x - h| + k$, with Kerry at the vertex, to represent the boundaries of Kerry's visual field in the rearview mirror. Graph the function, and label Kerry, the mailbox, and the telephone pole.

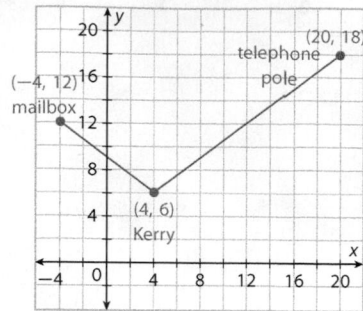

$$f(x) = \frac{3}{4}|x - 4| + 6 \text{ or } f(x) = 0.75|x - 4| + 6$$

Lesson Performance Task

Geese are initially flying south in a V-shaped pattern that can be modeled by the absolute value function $f(x) = a|x - h| + k$, where a represents the growth or shrinkage of the distance between geese, k represents the height change of the flock, and h represents a left or right shift in the flock.

A. Graph the original flock function, $g(x) = |x|$. State the function's domain and range in words.

 > **Domain: all real numbers;**
 >
 > **Range: all nonnegative real numbers**

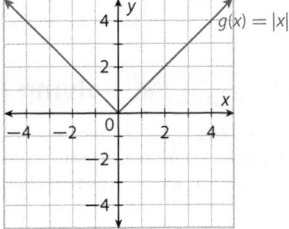

B. While flying south, the flock encounters a jet stream and is forced to drop 2 feet. Write the new equation and graph this function along with the original. State the new function's domain and range in words.

 > $h(x) - |x| - 2$
 >
 > **Domain: all real numbers;**
 >
 > **Range: all real numbers greater than or equal to −2.**

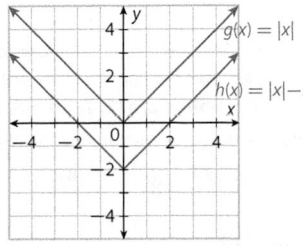

C. A short while after passing through the jet stream, the flock of geese encounters a rain storm and is forced to double the distance between each of its members in order to avoid colliding with one another. Write the new equation and graph all three functions. State the new function's domain and range in words.

 > $q(x) = 2|x|$
 >
 > **Domain: all real numbers;**
 >
 > **Range: all nonnegative real numbers**

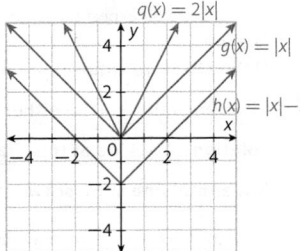

QUESTIONING STRATEGIES

? Recall that an absolute value function is an example of a piecewise function; it has different characteristics for different parts of its domain. What is the slope of each part of the function $g(x) = |x|$? The slope is −1 when $x < 0$ and 1 when $x \geq 0$.

? What is the slope of each part of the function $q(x) = a|x|$? The slope is $-a$ when $x < 0$ and a when $x \geq 0$.

INTEGRATE MATHEMATICAL PRACTICES
Focus on Patterns

MP.8 When working with the general form $y = |x - h| + k$, students may wonder why h is subtracted while k is added. They are looking for a symmetry in the structure of the function's rule that is not evident unless they rewrite the equation as $y - k = |x - h|$. In this form, both h (which produces a horizontal translation and is therefore associated with x) and k (which produces a vertical translation and is therefore associated with y) are subtracted from their associated variables.

EXTENSION ACTIVITY

Have students investigate why migrating birds fly in a V-shaped formation. Have them explain what they find most interesting about their findings.

Students may discover that when birds fly in formation, they are able to conserve energy while maintaining visual contact with one another. Researchers have found that birds flying in a V formation arrange themselves in the optimum position for each bird to take advantage of the rising air created by the flapping wings of the bird in front of it. In addition, the birds regulate the pace at which they flap their wings to best take advantage of the airflow.

Scoring Rubric
2 points: Student correctly solves the problem and explains his/her reasoning.
1 point: Student shows good understanding of the problem but does not fully solve or explain his/her reasoning.
0 points: Student does not demonstrate understanding of the problem.

Absolute Value Functions and Transformations   **600**

Solving Absolute Value Equations

Common Core Math Standards

The student is expected to:

COMMON CORE **A.REI.B.3**

Solve linear equations… in one variable… Also A.REI.D.11, A-CED.A.1

Mathematical Practices

COMMON CORE **MP.6 Precision**

Language Objective

Explain to a partner why solutions to a variety of absolute value equations make sense and contain more than one solution, one solution, or no solution.

ENGAGE

Essential Question: How can you solve an absolute value equation?

Possible answer: Isolate the absolute value expression, then write two related equations with a disjunction, also known as an "or" statement.

PREVIEW: LESSON PERFORMANCE TASK

View the Engage section online. Discuss the photo and why this situation can be represented by a V-shaped path and an absolute value equation. Then preview the Lesson Performance Task.

13.3 Solving Absolute Value Equations

Essential Question: How can you solve an absolute value equation?

Resource Locker

⊘ Explore   Solving Absolute Value Equations Graphically

Absolute value equations differ from linear equations in that they may have two solutions. This is indicated with a **disjunction**, a mathematical statement created by a connecting two other statements with the word "or." To see why there can be two solutions, you can solve an absolute value equation using graphs.

(A) Solve the equation $2|x - 5| - 4 = 2$.

Plot the function $f(x) = 2|x - 5| - 4$ on the grid. Then plot the function $g(x) = 2$ as a horizontal line on the same grid, and mark the points where the graphs intersect.

The points are (2, 2) and (8, 2).

(B) Write the solution to this equation as a disjunction:

$x = \underline{\quad 2 \quad}$ or $x = \underline{\quad 8 \quad}$

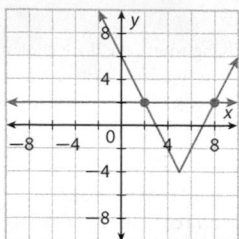

Reflect

1. Why might you expect most absolute value equations to have two solutions? Why not three or four?

   If the absolute value expression is not equal to zero, the expression inside an

   absolute value can be either positive or negative. So, there can be at most two

   solutions. Looking at this graphically, an absolute value graph can intersect a

   horizontal line at most two times.

2. Is it possible for an absolute value equation to have no solutions? one solution? If so, what would each look like graphically?

   Yes; yes; A graph with the horizontal line entirely below an upward-opening

   absolute value function, or above a downward-opening absolute value function,

   will not have points of intersection and the equation will have no solutions. A graph

   with the horizontal line passing through the vertex will have exactly 1 solution.

HARDCOVER PAGES 479–484

Turn to these pages to find this lesson in the hardcover student edition.

To solve absolute value equations algebraically, first isolate the absolute value expression on one side of the equation the same way you would isolate a variable. Then use the rule:

If $|x| = a$ (where a is a positive number), then $x = a$ OR $x = -a$.

Notice the use of a **disjunction** here in the rule for values of x. You cannot know from the original equation whether the expression inside the absolute value bars is positive or negative, so you must work through both possibilities to finish isolating x.

Example 1 Solve each absolute value equation algebraically. Graph the solutions on a number line.

Ⓐ $|3x| + 2 = 8$

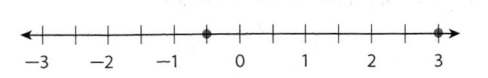

Subtract 2 from both sides. $\qquad |3x| = 6$

Rewrite as two equations. $\qquad 3x = 6 \quad$ or $\quad 3x = -6$

Solve for x. $\qquad x = 2 \quad$ or $\quad x = -2$

Ⓑ $3|4x - 5| - 2 = 19$

Add 2 to both sides. $\qquad 3|4x - 5| = \boxed{21}$

Divide both sides by 3. $\qquad |4x - 5| = \boxed{7}$

Rewrite as two equations. $\qquad 4x - 5 = \boxed{7} \quad$ or $\quad 4x - 5 = \boxed{-7}$

Add 5 to all four sides. $\qquad 4x = \boxed{12} \quad$ or $\quad 4x = \boxed{-2}$

Solve for x. $\qquad x = \boxed{3} \quad$ or $\quad x = -\boxed{\dfrac{1}{2}}$

Your Turn

Solve each absolute value equation algebraically. Graph the solutions on a number line.

3. $\frac{1}{2}|x + 2| = 10$

$|x + 2| = 20$

$x + 2 = 20 \quad$ or $\quad x + 2 = -20$

$x = 18 \quad$ or $\quad x = -22$

4. $-2|3x - 6| + 5 = 1$

$-2|3x - 6| = -4$

$|3x - 6| = 2$

$3x - 6 = 2 \quad$ or $\quad 3x - 6 = -2$

$x = \frac{8}{3} \quad$ or $\quad x = \frac{4}{3}$

© Houghton Mifflin Harcourt Publishing Company

PROFESSIONAL DEVELOPMENT

 Integrate Mathematical Practices

This lesson provides an opportunity to address Mathematical Practice **MP.6**, which calls for students to "attend to precision" and communicate precisely. Students find the solutions to absolute value equations both by graphing them, with and without technology, and through algebra. Students learn that a *disjunction* is often used to express the solutions to absolute value equations, and they use the properties of algebra to accurately and efficiently find the solutions to various types of absolute value equations.

EXPLORE

Solving Absolute Value Equations Graphically

INTEGRATE TECHNOLOGY

Students have the option of completing the graphing activity either in the book or online.

QUESTIONING STRATEGIES

? How do you solve an absolute value equation graphically? Plot each side as if it were a separate function of x, and find the x-coordinates of the intersection points.

? Why do you write the solutions to the absolute value equation as a disjunction? If two values of the variable both satisfy an equation, then one *or* the other can be correct.

EXPLAIN 1

Solving Absolute Value Equations Algebraically

AVOID COMMON ERRORS

Some students may not isolate the absolute value expression on one side of the equation as a first step when solving the equation. Stress the importance of this step so that the equation is in the form $|x| = a$, which has the solution $x = a$ or $x = -a$.

QUESTIONING STRATEGIES

? How do you interpret the solutions to an absolute value equation like $|x| = a$ on a number line? Sample answer: The solutions are the same distance from 0 on either side of the number line.

? Why is it important to isolate the absolute value expression when solving an absolute value equation? So you can remove the absolute value bars and rewrite the expression as a disjunction.

Solving Absolute Value Equations   **602**

EXPLAIN 2

Absolute Value Equations with Fewer than Two Solutions

QUESTIONING STRATEGIES

? When does an absolute value equation have fewer than two solutions? **when the absolute value expression is equal to zero or equal to a negative number**

? In the absolute value expression $d|ax + b| - c = -c$ for nonzero variables, how does d affect the solution? **It does not affect it. The first step is to add c to both sides to get $d|ax + b| = 0$. Because the product of a number and 0 is 0, you can divide both sides by d to get $|ax + b| = 0$.**

INTEGRATE TECHNOLOGY

A graphing calculator can be used to check the number of solutions to an absolute value equation. Graph each side of the equation as a function and then count the number of intersection points.

AVOID COMMON ERRORS

Some students may think that if an absolute value equation does not have two solutions, then there must be no solution. Explain to students that when the absolute value expression equals zero, there will be one solution. For example, $|3x + 6| = 0$ has one solution, $x = -2$, because 0 is neither positive nor negative.

⚙ Explain 2 **Absolute Value Equations with Fewer than Two Solutions**

You have seen that absolute value equations have two solutions when the isolated absolute value expression is equal to a positive number. When the absolute value is equal to zero, there is a single solution because zero is its own opposite. When the absolute value expression is equal to a negative number, there is no solution because absolute value is never negative.

Example 2 Isolate the absolute value expression in each equation to determine if the equation can be solved. If so, finish the solution. If not, write "no solution."

Ⓐ $-5|x + 1| + 2 = 12$

Subtract 2 from both sides.	$-5	x + 1	= 10$
Divide both sides by -5.	$	x + 1	= -2$
Absolute values are never negative.	No Solution

Ⓑ $\frac{3}{5}|2x - 4| - 3 = -3$

Add 3 to both sides.	$\frac{3}{5}	2x - 4	= \boxed{0}$
Multiply both sides by $\frac{5}{3}$.	$	2x - 4	= \boxed{0}$
Rewrite as one equation.	$2x - 4 = \boxed{0}$
Add 4 to both sides.	$2x = \boxed{4}$
Divide both sides by 2.	$x = \boxed{2}$

Your Turn

Isolate the absolute value expression in each equation to determine if the equation can be solved. If so, finish the solution. If not, write "no solution."

5. $3\left|\frac{1}{2}x + 5\right| + 7 = 5$

$3\left|\frac{1}{2}x + 5\right| = -2$

$\left|\frac{1}{2}x + 5\right| = -\frac{2}{3}$

No solution

6. $9\left|\frac{4}{3}x - 2\right| + 7 = 7$

$9\left|\frac{4}{3}x - 2\right| = 0$

$\left|\frac{4}{3}x - 2\right| = 0$

$x = \frac{3}{2}$

COLLABORATIVE LEARNING

Peer-to-Peer Activity

Have students work in pairs to brainstorm types of absolute value equations that have two solutions, one solution, or no solution. For example, instruct one student to write a conjecture about what type of absolute value equation has no solutions, and give an example. Then have the other student solve the example and write an explanation about whether the conjecture is correct or incorrect. Have students switch roles and repeat the exercise using an equation that has a different number of solutions.

7. Why is important to solve both equations in the disjunction arising from an absolute value equation? Why not just pick one and solve it, knowing the solution for the variable will work when plugged backed into the equation?

The solution to a mathematical equation is not simply any value of the variable

that makes the equation true. Supplying only one value that works in the equation

implies that it is the only value that works, which is incorrect.

8. Discussion Discuss how the range of the absolute value function differs from the range of a linear function. Graphically, how does this explain why a linear equation always has exactly one solution while an absolute value equation can have one, two, or no solutions?

The range of a non-constant linear function is all real numbers. The range of an

absolute value function is $y \geq k$ if the function opens upward and $y \leq k$ if the

function opens downward. Because the graph of a linear function is a line, a

horizontal line will intersect it only once. Because the graph of an absolute value

function is a V, a horizontal line can intersect it once, twice, or not at all.

9. Essential Question Check-In Describe, in your own words, the basic steps to solving absolute value equations and how many solutions to expect.

Isolate the absolute value expression. If the absolute value expression is equal to

a positive number, solve for both the positive and negative case. If the absolute

value expression is equal to zero, then remove the absolute value bars and solve

the equation. There is one solution. If the absolute value expression is equal to a

negative number, then there is no solution.

DIFFERENTIATE INSTRUCTION

Critical Thinking

Some students may need help in deciding whether absolute value equations have no solutions, one solution, or two solutions. You may want to suggest that they *always* follow this solving plan: (1) Write the original equation; then (2) isolate the absolute value expression on one side of the equal sign. It will have the form $|ax + b| = c$. (3) Rewrite the equation as two equations of the form $ax + b = c$ and $ax + b = -c$; and (4) solve each equation for x. There may be 0, 1, or 2 solutions. (5) If there are two solutions, write the answer using "or." (6) Check the solution(s) in the original problem.

ELABORATE

INTEGRATE MATHEMATICAL PRACTICES
Focus on Patterns

MP.8 Discuss with students how to solve an absolute value equation of the form $|ax + b| = c$. Students should routinely rewrite the next step as a disjunction, or a compound equation of the form $ax + b = c$ or $ax + b = -c$ and then solve each part of the equation.

QUESTIONING STRATEGIES

? How is the process of solving a linear absolute value equation like the process of solving a regular linear equation? Both processes are similar initially, except that you isolate the absolute value in one case, but isolate the variable in the case of the linear equation. From there, the process is the same for each part of the disjunction of the two linear equations for the absolute value equation.

PEER-TO-PEER ACTIVITY

Have students work in pairs. Have one student write an absolute value equation and have the partner solve it. The partner then explains why the solution(s) makes sense. Students switch roles and repeat the process. Encourage students to use the phrase "distance from zero" and the statement "This negative/positive integer makes the equation true."

SUMMARIZE THE LESSON

? How do you solve a linear absolute value equation? Isolate the absolute value; write the resulting equation as the disjunction of two linear equations; and solve each equation.

EVALUATE

ASSIGNMENT GUIDE

Concepts and Skills	Practice
Explore Solving Absolute Value Equations Graphically	Exercise 1–4
Example 1 Solving Absolute Value Equations Algebraically	Exercises 5–8, 17–20, 22, 23
Example 2 Absolute Value Equations with Fewer than Two Solutions	Exercises 9–16, 21, 24

INTEGRATE MATHEMATICAL PRACTICES

Focus on Reasoning

MP.2 Remind students to check their solutions by substituting the values into the original equation and verifying that both solutions make the equation true. When solving equations graphically, remind students that the *x*-value of an intersection point is a solution to the original equation.

Solve the following absolute value equations by graphing.

1. $|x - 3| + 2 = 5$

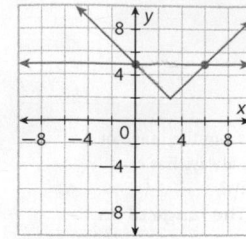

$x = 0$ or $x = 6$

2. $2|x + 1| + 5 = 9$

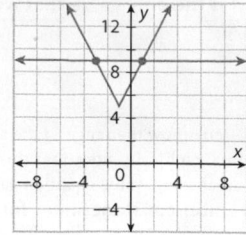

$x = -3$ or $x = 1$

3. $-2|x + 5| + 4 = 2$

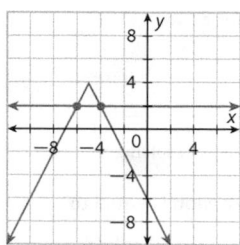

$x = -4$ or $x = -6$

4. $\left|\dfrac{3}{2}(x - 2)\right| + 3 = 2$

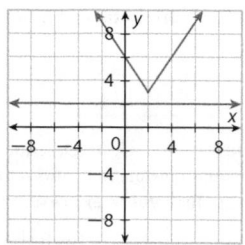

No solution

Solve each absolute value equation algebraically. Graph the solutions on a number line.

5. $|2x| = 3$

$2x = 3$ or $2x = -3$

$x = \dfrac{3}{2}$ or $x = -\dfrac{3}{2}$

6. $\left|\dfrac{1}{3}x + 4\right| = 3$

$\left(\dfrac{1}{3}\right)x + 4 = 3$ or $\left(\dfrac{1}{3}\right)x + 4 = -3$

$\left(\dfrac{1}{3}\right)x = -1$ or $\left(\dfrac{1}{3}\right)x = -7$

$x = -3$ or $x = -21$

Exercise	Depth of Knowledge (D.O.K.)	COMMON CORE Mathematical Practices
1–4	**2** Skills/Concepts	**MP.5** Using Tools
5–16	**2** Skills/Concepts	**MP.6** Precision
17	**3** Strategic Thinking	**MP.4** Modeling
18, 21	**3** Strategic Thinking	**MP.4** Modeling
19	**3** Strategic Thinking	**MP.6** Precision
20	**2** Skills/Concepts	**MP.6** Precision
22	**3** Strategic Thinking H.O.T.	**MP.3** Logic
23–25	**3** Strategic Thinking H.O.T.	**MP.6** Precision

7. $3|2x - 3| + 2 = 3$

$$2x - 3 = \frac{1}{3}$$
$$2x - 3 = \frac{1}{3} \quad \text{or} \quad 2x - 3 = \frac{-1}{3}$$
$$2x = \frac{10}{3} \quad \text{or} \quad 2x = \frac{8}{3}$$
$$x = \frac{5}{3} \quad \text{or} \quad x = \frac{4}{3}$$

8. $-8|-x - 6| + 10 = 2$

$$-8|-x - 6| = -8$$
$$|-x - 6| = 1$$
$$-x - 6 = 1 \quad \text{or} \quad -x - 6 = -1$$
$$x = -7 \quad \text{or} \quad x = -5$$

Isolate the absolute value expressions in the following equations to determine if they can be solved. If so, find and graph the solution(s). If not, write "no solution".

9. $\frac{1}{4}|x + 2| + 7 = 5$

$$\frac{1}{4}|x + 2| = -2$$
No solution

10. $-3|x - 3| + 3 = 6$

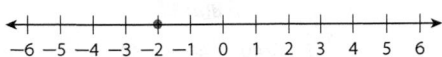

$$-3|x - 3| = 3$$
$$|x - 3| = -1$$
No solution

11. $2(|x + 4| + 3) = 6$

$$2|x + 4| + 6 = 6$$
$$2|x + 4| = 0$$
$$|x + 4| = 0$$
$$x = -4$$

12. $5|2x + 4| - 3 = -3$

$$5|2x + 4| = 0$$
$$|2x + 4| = 0$$
$$2x + 4 = 0$$
$$x = -2$$

Solve the absolute value equations.

13. $|3x - 4| + 2 = 1$

$$|3x - 4| = -1$$
No solution

14. $7|\frac{1}{2}x + 3\frac{1}{2}| - 2 = 5$

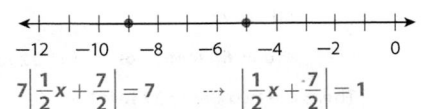

$$7|\frac{1}{2}x + \frac{7}{2}| = 7 \quad \longrightarrow \quad |\frac{1}{2}x + \frac{7}{2}| = 1$$
$$\frac{1}{2}x + \frac{7}{2} = 1 \quad \text{or} \quad \frac{1}{2}x + \frac{7}{2} = -1$$
$$\frac{1}{2}x = -\frac{5}{2} \quad \text{or} \quad \frac{1}{2}x = -\frac{9}{2}$$
$$x = -5 \quad \text{or} \quad x = -9$$

Students may erroneously include points on the graph *between* the solution points when they graph solutions. Remind students that the solution process gives 0, 1, or 2 solutions to an absolute value equation, not infinitely many solutions.

INTEGRATE MATHEMATICAL PRACTICES

Focus on Critical Thinking

MP.3 Ask students to give examples of absolute value equations that have no solutions. Suggest that they think about how a graph of an equation with no solution will look. This graph should not show any points, so it is an empty graph.

INTEGRATE MATHEMATICAL PRACTICES

Focus on Modeling

MP.4 When modeling a problem in which an absolute value equation applies, have students start with a V-shaped diagram. This will help them remember that this type of function may have 0, 1, or 2 solutions to the associated equation, depending on the original real-world problem.

AVOID COMMON ERRORS

When solving absolute equations algebraically, watch for students who do not solve these equations by first rewriting them in the form $|ax + b| = c$. Remind them that the absolute value expression should be nonnegative before they proceed with the solution steps.

---

15. $|2(x + 5) - 3| + 2 = 6$

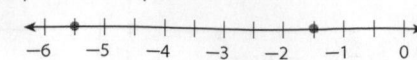

$|2x + 7| = 4$

$2x + 7 = 4 \quad$ or $\quad 2x + 7 = -4$

$2x = -3 \quad$ or $\quad 2x = -11$

$x = -\dfrac{3}{2} \quad$ or $\quad x = -\dfrac{11}{2}$

16. $-5|-3x + 2| - 2 = -2$

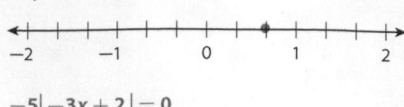

$-5|-3x + 2| = 0$

$|-3x + 2| = 0$

$-3x + 2 = 0$

$-3x = -2$

$x = \dfrac{2}{3}$

17. The bottom of a river makes a V-shape that can be modeled with the absolute value function, $d(h) = \frac{1}{5}|h - 240| - 48$, where d is the depth of the river bottom (in feet) and h is the horizontal distance to the left-hand shore (in feet).

A ship risks running aground if the bottom of its keel (its lowest point under the water) reaches down to the river bottom. Suppose you are the harbormaster and you want to place buoys where the river bottom is 30 feet below the surface. How far from the left-hand shore should you place the buoys?

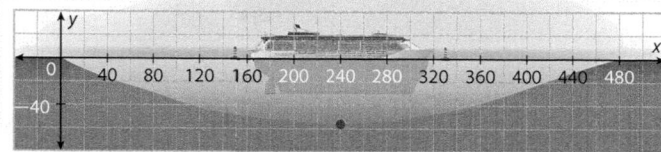

$d(h) = -30$

$\frac{1}{5}|h - 240| - 48 = -30$

$h = 330 \quad$ or $\quad h = 150$

The buoys should be placed at 150 ft and 330 ft from the left-hand shore.

18. A flock of geese is flying past a photographer in a V-formation that can be described using the absolute value function $b(d) = \frac{3}{2}|d - 50|$, where $b(d)$ is the distance (in feet) of a goose behind the leader, and d is the distance from the photographer. If the flock reaches 27 feet behind the leader on both sides, find the distance of the nearest goose to the photographer.

$\frac{3}{2}|d - 50| = 27$

$d = 68 \text{ feet} \quad$ or $\quad d \doteq 32 \text{ feet}$

There are two geese 27 feet behind the leader, but only the one 32 feet from the photographer is the closest.

$d = 32 \text{ feet}$

19. Geometry Find the points where a circle centered at (3, 0) with a radius of 5 crosses the x-axis. Use an absolute value equation and the fact that all points on a circle are the same distance (the radius) from the center.

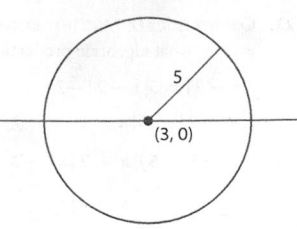

The points on the x-axis that are a distance of 5 from

the center of the circle at $x = 3$ are given by $|x - 3| = 5$.

Solving $|x - 3| = 5$ gives $x = 8$ or $x = -2$.

The points are $(-2, 0)$ and $(8, 0)$.

20. Select the value or values of x that satisfy the equation $-\frac{1}{2}|3x - 3| + 2 = 1$.

Ⓐ $x = \frac{5}{3}$ B. $x = -\frac{5}{3}$ $-\frac{1}{2}|3x - 3| = -1$

Ⓒ $x = \frac{1}{3}$ D. $x = -\frac{1}{3}$ $|3x - 3| = 2$

E. $x = 3$ F. $x = -3$ $3x - 3 = 2$ or $3x - 3 = -2$

                                   $3x = 5$ or $3x = 1$

G. $x = 1$ H. $x = -1$ $x = \frac{5}{3}$ or $x = \frac{1}{3}$

21. Terry is trying to place a satellite dish on the roof of his house at the recommended height of 30 feet. His house is 32 feet wide, and the height of the roof can be described by the function $h(x) = -\frac{3}{2}|x - 16| + 24$, where x is the distance along the width of the house. Where should Terry place the dish?

Use the model function to solve for x when $h(x) = 30$ feet.

$-\frac{3}{2}|x - 16| + 24 = 30$

$|x - 16| = -4$

No Solution. Terry does not have a spot on his roof that is 30 feet

high.

H.O.T. Focus on Higher Order Thinking

22. Explain the Error While attempting to solve the equation $-3|x - 4| - 4 = 3$, a student came up with the following results. Explain the error and find the correct solution:

$-3|x - 4| - 4 = 3$

$-3|x - 4| = 7$

$|x - 4| = -\frac{7}{3}$

$x - 4 = -\frac{7}{3}$ or $x - 4 = \frac{7}{3}$

$x = \frac{5}{3}$ or $x = \frac{19}{3}$

The student tried to replace the absolute value equation with two equations using the positive and negative values of the number on the other side of the equal sign. However, this number was negative and cannot be treated like a positive number. The isolated absolute value expression is equal to a negative number and therefore this equation has no solution.

SMALL GROUP ACTIVITY

Have students work in small groups to make a poster showing how to apply the steps for solving an absolute value equation. Give each group a different equation to solve. Then have each group present its poster to the rest of the class, and ask for a volunteer from the group to explain each step.

INTEGRATE MATHEMATICAL PRACTICES

Focus on Reasoning

MP.2 When solving absolute value equations of the form $-|ax + b| = c$, where $c > 0$, students should recognize that the equation states that a negative absolute value is equal to a positive number. This is not possible because of the definition of absolute value, so while "solving the equation" gives numerical answers, these answers are not solutions to the original equation. You may want students to verify this by graphing. There will be no intersection points.

AVOID COMMON ERRORS

Watch for students who are confused by nested absolute value equations. Remind students to carefully write disjunctions for each part of the solution, as appropriate, using the same solution process they use for a single absolute value equation.

PEER-TO-PEER DISCUSSION

Ask students to discuss with a partner what the solution to $|ax + b| = c$ means in terms of the graph of the related functions $f(x) = |ax + b|$ and $g(x) = c$. Then ask students to make conjectures about the solutions to $|ax + b| = c$ and the graphs of their related functions. Conjectures should include the possible number of intersection points and how the graph of the function looks. The solutions to $|ax + b| = c$ are the x-coordinates of the intersection points of the related functions. Based on this, conjectures should include that the graphs of $f(x) = |ax + b|$ and $g(x) = c$ can have two, one, or no intersection points, and that the graph of $f(x)$ is V-shaped and this graph can intersect a line in two or fewer places.

JOURNAL

Have students compare and contrast the methods they have learned for solving absolute value equations.

23. **Communicate Mathematical Ideas** Solve this absolute value equation and explain what algebraic properties make it possible to do so.

$$3|x - 2| = 5|x - 2| - 7$$

$3|x - 2| - 5|x - 2| = -7$	Subtraction Property of Equality
$(3 - 5)|x - 2| = -7$	Distributive Property
$|x - 2| = \dfrac{7}{2}$	Division Property of Equality
$x - 2 = \dfrac{7}{2}$ or $x - 2 = -\dfrac{7}{2}$	Definition of absolute value
$x = \dfrac{11}{2}$ or $x = -\dfrac{3}{2}$	Addition Property of Equality

24. **Justify Your Reasoning** This absolute value equation has nested absolute values. Use your knowledge of solving absolute value equations to solve this equation. Justify the number of possible solutions.

$$\left| |2x + 5| - 3 \right| = 10$$

Follow each possible solution path and use more disjunctions if needed.

$\left| |2x + 5| - 3 \right| = 10$

$|2x + 5| - 3 = 10$ or $|2x + 5| - 3 = -10$

$|2x + 5| = 13$ or $|2x + 5| = -7$

$|2x + 5| = 13$ or No solution

$|2x + 5| = 13$

$2x + 5 = 13$ or $2x + 5 = -13$

$2x = 8$ or $2x = -18$

$x = 4$ or $x = -9$

There are two possible solutions because only one path produced solutions.

25. **Check for Reasonableness** For what type of real-world quantities would the negative answer for an absolute value equation not make sense?

Answers will vary. Sample answer: time, distance, height, length, speed

Lesson Performance Task

A snowball comes apart as a child throws it north, resulting in two halves traveling away from the child. The child is standing 12 feet south and 6 feet east of the school door, along an east-west wall. One fragment flies off to the northeast, moving 2 feet east for every 5 feet north of travel, and the other moves 2 feet west for every 5 feet north of travel. Write an absolute value function that describes the northward position, $n(e)$, of both fragments as a function of how far east of the school door they are. How far apart are the fragments when they strike the wall?

The fragments can be described as two lines originating at the child's coordinates, and then be replaced by a single absolute value function.

$$n(e) = \frac{5}{2}(e - 6) \quad \text{or} \quad n(e) = -\frac{5}{2}(e - 6)$$

$$n(e) = \frac{5}{2}|e - 6|$$

To find where the fragments strike the school wall, solve for the eastward position when the fragments are 12 feet north of the child.

$$n(e) = \frac{5}{2}|e - 6| = 12$$

$$|e - 6| = \frac{24}{5}$$

$$e - 6 = \frac{24}{5} \quad \text{or} \quad e - 6 = -\frac{24}{5}$$

$$e = \frac{54}{5} \quad \text{or} \quad e = \frac{6}{5}$$

The fragments are $\left| \frac{54}{5} - \frac{6}{5} \right| = \left| \frac{48}{5} \right| = 9\frac{3}{5}$ feet apart.

© Houghton Mifflin Harcourt Publishing Company

Some students may use the ratio $\frac{2}{5}$ in their equation instead of $\frac{5}{2}$. Explain that the snowball *rises* 5 feet north for every 2 feet west it *runs*. Thus, the ratio is $\frac{5}{2}$.

INTEGRATE MATHEMATICAL PRACTICES
Focus on Communication

MP.3 Discuss with students how solving for the eastward position solves for the distance of the snowball on the right, $e - 6 = \frac{24}{5}$, and the snowball on the left, $e - 6 = -\frac{24}{5}$. Then discuss how solving for e does not answer the problem. The difference between the two distances is equal to the distance the two are apart.

EXTENSION ACTIVITY

Have students try to find an alternate solution method using the formula for the slope of a line. Student should find the coordinates for the snowball on the right to be $\left(10\frac{4}{5}, 12 \right)$. Subtracting 6 from the value of x gives the distance from $(6, 12)$ to $(x, 12)$. That distance is $4\frac{4}{5}$ ft. The distance from the y-axis to the snowball on the left is $6 - 4\frac{4}{5} = 1\frac{1}{5}$ ft. So the fragments are $10\frac{4}{5} - 1\frac{1}{5} = 9\frac{3}{5}$ feet apart.

Scoring Rubric
2 points: Student correctly solves the problem and explains his/her reasoning.
1 point: Student shows good understanding of the problem but does not fully solve or explain his/her reasoning.
0 points: Student does not demonstrate understanding of the problem.

Solving Absolute Value Inequalities

Common Core Math Standards

The student is expected to:

 **A.REI.B.3**

Solve linear... inequalities in one variable... Also A.REI.D.11, A-CED.A.1

Mathematical Practices

COMMON CORE **MP.4 Modeling**

Language Objective

Match absolute value equations and inequalities with their graphs, explaining and justifying reasoning.

ENGAGE

Essential Question: What are two ways to solve an absolute value inequality?

Possible answer: You can solve an absolute value inequality graphically or algebraically. For a graphical solution, treat each side of the inequality as a function and graph the two functions. Use the inequality symbol to determine the intervals on the x-axis where one graph lies above or below the other. For an algebraic solution, isolate the absolute value expression and rewrite the inequality as a compound inequality that doesn't involve absolute value so that you can finish solving the inequality.

PREVIEW: LESSON PERFORMANCE TASK

View the Engage section online. Discuss the names of the planets, the elliptical path the planets follow, and why the distance a planet is from the sun might relate to absolute value inequalities. Then preview the Lesson Performance Task.

Name_____ Class_____ Date_____

13.4 Solving Absolute Value Inequalities

Essential Question: What are two ways to solve an absolute value inequality?

Resource Locker

🧭 Explore Visualizing the Solution Set of an Absolute Value Inequality

You know that when solving an absolute value equation, it's possible to get two solutions. Here, you will explore what happens when you solve absolute value inequalities.

(A) Determine whether each of the integers from -5 to 5 is a solution of the inequality $|x| + 2 < 5$. Write *yes* or *no* for each number in the table. If a number is a solution, plot it on the number line.

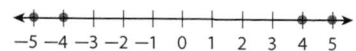

Number	Solution?
$x = -5$	no
$x = -4$	no
$x = -3$	no
$x = -2$	yes
$x = -1$	yes
$x = 0$	yes
$x = 1$	yes
$x = 2$	yes
$x = 3$	no
$x = 4$	no
$x = 5$	no

(B) Determine whether each of the integers from -5 to 5 is a solution of the inequality $|x| + 2 > 5$. Write *yes* or *no* for each number in the table. If a number is a solution, plot it on the number line.

Number	Solution?
$x = -5$	yes
$x = -4$	yes
$x = -3$	no
$x = -2$	no
$x = -1$	no
$x = 0$	no
$x = 1$	no
$x = 2$	no
$x = 3$	no
$x = 4$	yes
$x = 5$	yes

© Houghton Mifflin Harcourt Publishing Company

Module 13 611 Lesson 4

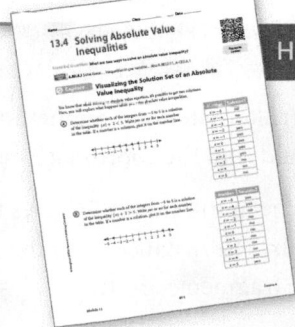

HARDCOVER PAGES 485–492

Turn to these pages to find this lesson in the hardcover student edition.

Ⓒ State the solutions of the equation $|x| + 2 = 5$ and relate them to the solutions you found for the inequalities in Steps A and B.

> The solutions are —3 and 3. These are the only numbers that are not solutions of the
>
> inequalities $|x| + 2 < 5$ and $|x| + 2 > 5$.

Ⓓ If x is any real number and not just an integer, graph the solutions of $|x| + 2 < 5$ and $|x| + 2 > 5$.

Graph of all real solutions of $|x| + 2 < 5$:

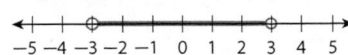

Graph of all real solutions of $|x| + 2 > 5$:

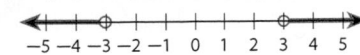

Reflect

1. It's possible to describe the solutions of $|x| + 2 < 5$ and $|x| + 2 > 5$ using inequalities that don't involve absolute value. For instance, you can write the solutions of $|x| + 2 < 5$ as $x > -3$ and $x < 3$. Notice that the word *and* is used because x must be both greater than —3 and less than 3. How would you write the solutions of $|x| + 2 > 5$? Explain.

   > Write the solutions of $|x| + 2 > 5$ as $x < -3$ or $x > 3$. Use the word *or* because x must be
   >
   > either less than —3 or greater than 3; it can't be both.

2. Describe the solutions of $|x| + 2 \le 5$ and $|x| + 2 \ge 5$ using inequalities that don't involve absolute value.

   > The solutions of $|x| + 2 \le 5$ are the values of x for which $x \ge -3$ and $x \le 3$. The solutions
   >
   > of $|x| + 2 \ge 5$ are the values of x for which $x \le -3$ or $x \ge 3$.

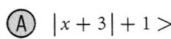 **Explain 1** **Solving Absolute Value Inequalities Graphically**

You can use a graph to solve an absolute value inequality of the form $f(x) > g(x)$ or $f(x) < g(x)$, where $f(x)$ is an absolute value function and $g(x)$ is a constant function. Graph each function separately on the same coordinate plane and determine the intervals on the x-axis where one graph lies above or below the other. For $f(x) > g(x)$, you want to find the x-values for which the graph $f(x)$ is above the graph of $g(x)$. For $f(x) < g(x)$, you want to find the x-values for which the graph of $f(x)$ is below the graph of $g(x)$.

Example 1 Solve the inequality graphically.

Ⓐ $|x + 3| + 1 > 4$

The inequality is of the form $f(x) > g(x)$, so determine the intervals on the x-axis where the graph of $f(x) = |x + 3| + 1$ lies above the graph of $g(x) = 4$.

The graph of $f(x) = |x + 3| + 1$ lies above the graph of $g(x) = 4$ to the left of $x = -6$ and to the right of $x = 0$, so the solution of $|x + 3| + 1 > 4$ is $x < -6$ or $x > 0$.

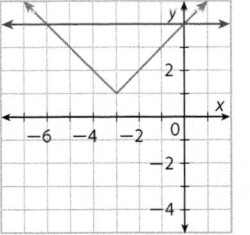

Visualizing the Solution Set of an Absolute Value Inequality

QUESTIONING STRATEGIES

? How would you characterize the solutions to an absolute value inequality? **Sample answer:** They lie either between two values or everywhere else except between the two values, depending on the inequality.

? Why do you write the solution to the absolute value inequality as a compound inequality statement? **Sample answer: because the solution** consists of the union or intersection of the solutions of the two related linear inequalities.

EXPLAIN 1

Solving Absolute Value Inequalities Graphically

QUESTIONING STRATEGIES

? How do you interpret which points are solutions of the inequality? **Sample answer:** If $f(x) > g(x)$, the graph of $f(x)$ must be "above" the graph of $g(x)$. The solutions are the x-values in the interval along the x-axis where $f(x)$ has y-values greater than $g(x)$. If $f(x) < g(x)$, the graph of $f(x)$ must be "below" the graph of $g(x)$. The solutions are the x-values in the interval along the x-axis where $f(x)$ has y-values less than $g(x)$.

? How do you know when the endpoints of the solution interval on the x-axis are not included in the solution? **The original inequality is** $<$ or $>$.

PROFESSIONAL DEVELOPMENT

Math Background

An absolute value inequality is often in the form $|ax + b| < c$ or $|ax + b| > c$. If the inequality is in the form $|ax + b| < c$, then it can be rewritten as the compound inequality $-c < ax + b < c$, and solved for x. The solution will be of the form $\frac{-c-b}{a} < x$ and $x < \frac{c-b}{a}$. If the inequality is in the form $|ax + b| > c$, it can be rewritten as the compound inequality $c < ax + b$ or $ax + b < -c$, and solved for x. The solution will be of the form $\frac{c-b}{a} < x$ or $x < \frac{-c-b}{a}$. The solutions are easily adjusted for $\le$ and $\ge$.

Ⓑ $|x - 2| - 3 < 1$

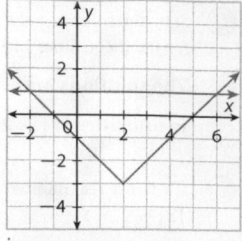

The inequality is of the form $f(x) < g(x)$, so determine the intervals

on the x-axis where the graph of $f(x) = |x - 2| - 3$ lies ___below___ the graph of $g(x) = 1$.

The graph of $f(x) = |x - 2| - 3$ lies ___below___ the graph of

$g(x) = 1$ between $x =$ ⎡−2⎤ and $x =$ ⎡6⎤ , so the solution of

$|x - 2| - 3 < 1$ is $x >$ ⎡−2⎤ $and\ x <$ ⎡6⎤ .

Reflect

3. Suppose the inequality in Part A is $|x + 3| + 1 \geq 4$ instead of $|x + 3| + 1 > 4$. How does the solution change?

The solution now includes the endpoints of the interval: $x \leq -6$ or $x \geq 0$.

4. In Part B, what is another way to write the solution $x > -2$ and $x < 6$?

$-2 < x < 6$

5. **Discussion** Suppose the graph of an absolute value function $f(x)$ lies entirely above the graph of the constant function $g(x)$. What is the solution of the inequality $f(x) > g(x)$? What is the solution of the inequality $f(x) < g(x)$?

The solution of $f(x) > g(x)$ is all real numbers, because every point on the graph of $f(x)$ is

above the corresponding point on the graph of $g(x)$. The solution of $f(x) < g(x)$ is no real

number, because no point on the graph of $f(x)$ is below the corresponding point on the

graph of $g(x)$.

Your Turn

6. Solve $|x + 1| - 4 \leq -2$ graphically.

The inequality is of the form $f(x) \leq g(x)$, so determine the intervals on the x-axis
where the graph of $f(x) = |x + 1| - 4$ intersects or lies below the graph of $g(x) = -2$.
The graph of $f(x) = |x + 1| - 4$ intersects the graph of $g(x) = -2$ at $x = -3$ and $x = 1$
and lies below the graph of $g(x) = -2$ between those x-values, so the solution of
$|x + 1| - 4 \leq -2$ is $x \geq -3$ and $x \leq 1$.

COLLABORATIVE LEARNING

Small Group Activity

Have students work in groups to make a flowchart that explains how to solve each

of the four types of an absolute value inequality of the form $|ax + b| \,\square\, c$ or

$|ax - b| \,\square\, c$, where the box represents the inequality symbol. For example:

$|2x + 3| \leq 6$ $|2x + 3| < 6$ $|2x + 3| > 6$ $|2x + 3| \geq 6$

Ask each student in a group to finish one branch of the flowchart. Then have the

group collate the branches to make the entire flowchart.

Explain 2 Solving Absolute Value Inequalities Algebraically

To solve an absolute value inequality algebraically, start by isolating the absolute value expression. When the absolute value expression is by itself on one side of the inequality, apply one of the following rules to finish solving the inequality for the variable.

Solving Absolute Value Inequalities Algebraically

1. If $|x| > a$ where a is a positive number, then $x < -a$ or $x > a$.

2. If $|x| < a$ where a is a positive number, then $-a < x < a$.

Example 2 Solve the inequality algebraically. Graph the solution on a number line.

Ⓐ $|4 - x| + 15 > 21$

$|4 - x| > 6$

$4 - x < -6$ or $4 - x > 6$

$-x < -10$ or $-x > 2$

$x > 10$ or $x < -2$

The solution is $x > 10$ or $x < -2$.

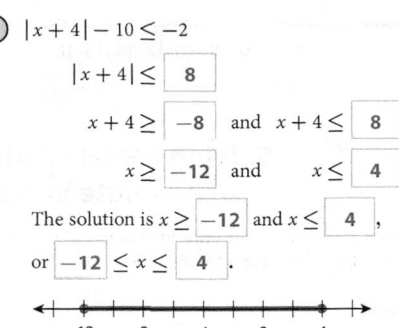

Ⓑ $|x + 4| - 10 \le -2$

$|x + 4| \le \boxed{8}$

$x + 4 \ge \boxed{-8}$ and $x + 4 \le \boxed{8}$

$x \ge \boxed{-12}$ and $x \le \boxed{4}$

The solution is $x \ge \boxed{-12}$ and $x \le \boxed{4}$,

or $\boxed{-12} \le x \le \boxed{4}$.

Reflect

7. In Part A, suppose the inequality were $|4 - x| + 15 > 14$ instead of $|4 - x| + 15 > 21$. How would the solution change? Explain.
   The first step in solving would be to subtract 15 from both sides and get $|4 - x| > -1$.

   At this point, the solving process can stop, because the absolute value of every number is

   greater than -1. So, the solution is all real numbers.

8. In Part B, suppose the inequality were $|x + 4| - 10 \le -11$ instead of $|x + 4| - 10 \le -2$. How would the solution change? Explain.
   The first step in solving would be to add 10 to both sides and get $|x + 4| \le -1$. At this

   point, the solving process can stop, because there are no real numbers whose absolute

   value is less than or equal to -1. So, there is no solution.

DIFFERENTIATE INSTRUCTION

Visual Cues

You may want students to use visual models to help them understand some simple inequalities as well as some real-world inequalities. For simple inequalities of the form $|x| < a$ or $|x| > a$, constructing a graph of possible solutions on a number line as a first step may be helpful. For a real-world problem, drawing a number line with all points graphed between the starting value and the tolerance amounts may be most helpful. This should help students visualize how to construct an inequality based on the graph.

EXPLAIN 2

Solving Absolute Value Inequalities Algebraically

QUESTIONING STRATEGIES

? When does the graph of the solution to an inequality include the endpoints? **when the original inequality is $\le$ or $\ge$**

? When does the graph of the solution include the points between the endpoints found in the solution? **When the original inequality is $<$ or $\le$, the compound inequality is an "and" statement, so its graph includes the intersection of two graphs. These graphs intersect between the endpoints.**

INTEGRATE TECHNOLOGY

A graphing calculator can be used to check the solution graph for an inequality. For example, you would graph $y = |4 - x| + 15 > 21$ to check the solution for $|4 - x| + 15 > 21$. The graph will be a broken horizontal line above the x-axis with endpoints at -2 and 10. You must interpret the graph to be open at the endpoints. So, the solution graph is $x < -2$ or $x > 10$.

AVOID COMMON ERRORS

Some students confuse when to use *or* and *and* when rewriting an absolute value inequality. Remind students that when the inequality is $|ax + b| < c$ or $|ax + b| \le c$, they should rewrite the inequality using *and*. When the inequality is $|ax + b| > c$ or $|ax + b| \ge c$, they should rewrite the inequality using *or*. Emphasize the importance of checking some of the solutions in the original inequality to help avoid this error.

EXPLAIN 3

Solving a Real-World Problem with Absolute Value Inequalities

QUESTIONING STRATEGIES

? When does an absolute value inequality apply to a real-world situation? **Sample answer:** When a model for the real-world situation includes a range of values where the sign of the difference between the values doesn't matter, you can write an absolute value model that will apply. For example, if the model is $|\ell - 3.25| \le 0.02$, solving the inequality gives $3.23 \le \ell \le 3.27$, which gives possible values on either side of ℓ.

INTEGRATE MATHEMATICAL PRACTICES
Focus on Reasoning

MP.2 Encourage students to solve the absolute value inequality for a real-world problem in the standard way: (1) Write a compound inequality using *and* or *or*, depending on the original problem; (2) solve each inequality; (3) rewrite the solution as a compound inequality using *and* or *or*; (4) graph the compound inequality if needed; and (5) check some values from the solution in the original problem to see if they make sense.

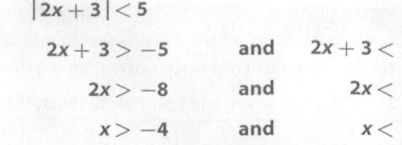

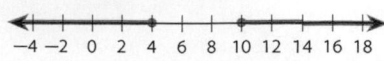
Your Turn

Solve the inequality algebraically. Graph the solution on a number line.

9. $3|x - 7| \ge 9$

$3|x - 7| \ge 9$

$|x - 7| \ge 3$

$x - 7 \le -3$ or $x - 7 \ge 3$

$x \le 4$ or $x \ge 10$

The solution is $x \le 4$ or $x \ge 10$.

(number line from −4 to 18)

10. $|2x + 3| < 5$

$|2x + 3| < 5$

$2x + 3 > -5$ and $2x + 3 < 5$

$2x > -8$ and $2x < 2$

$x > -4$ and $x < 1$

The solution is $-4 < x < 1$.

(number line from −5 to 5)

⚙ Explain 3 **Solving a Real-World Problem with Absolute Value Inequalities**

Absolute value inequalities are often used to model real-world situations involving a margin of error or *tolerance*. Tolerance is the allowable amount of variation in a quantity.

Example 3

A machine at a lumber mill cuts boards that are 3.25 meters long. It is acceptable for the length to differ from this value by at most 0.02 meters. Write and solve an absolute value inequality to find the range of acceptable lengths.

⚏ Analyze Information

Identify the important information.

- The boards being cut are **3.25** meters long.
- The length can differ by at most 0.02 meters.

⚏ Formulate a Plan

Let the length of a board be ℓ. Since the sign of the difference between ℓ and 3.25 doesn't matter, take the absolute value of the difference. Since the absolute value of the difference can be at most 0.02, the inequality that models the situation is

$\left| \ell - \boxed{3.25} \right| \le \boxed{0.02}$.

⚏ Solve

$|\ell - 3.25| \le 0.02$

$\ell - 3.25 \ge -0.02$ and $\ell - 3.25 \le 0.02$

$\ell \ge \boxed{3.23}$ and $\ell \le \boxed{3.27}$

So, the range of acceptable lengths is $\boxed{3.23} \le \ell \le \boxed{3.27}$.

© Houghton Mifflin Harcourt Publishing Company

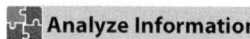

LANGUAGE SUPPORT **EL**

Connect Vocabulary

Help students understand the term *compound inequality* as it is used to solve an absolute value inequality. Have them recall that a *disjunction* is a compound statement joined by the word *or*. A disjunction applies to all inequalities of the form $|x| > a$ or $|x| \ge a$. Since inequalities can also be of the form $|x| < a$ or $|x| \le a$, students also need to learn a compound statement joined by the word *and*. Have students use note cards to write examples of all four types of inequalities they may see in the lesson, and ask them to write the associated compound inequality with a graph of the solution set for each example.

Justify and Evaluate

The bounds of the range are positive and close to 3.25, so this is a reasonable answer.

The answer is correct since $3.23 + 0.02 = 3.25$ and $3.27 - 0.02 = 3.25$.

Your Turn

11. A box of cereal is supposed to weigh 13.8 oz, but it's acceptable for the weight to vary as much as 0.1 oz. Write and solve an absolute value inequality to find the range of acceptable weights.

   Let the weight of the cereal be w. The sign of the difference between w and 13.8 doesn't matter, so take the absolute value of the difference. Since the absolute value of the difference can be as much as 0.1, the inequality that models the situation is $|w - 13.8| \leq 0.1$.

   Solve:

   $|w - 13.8| \leq 0.1$

   $w - 13.8 \geq -0.1$ and $w - 13.8 \leq 0.1$

   $w \geq 13.7$ and $w \leq 13.9$

   So, the range of acceptable weights of the cereal (in ounces) is $13.7 \leq w \leq 13.9$.

💬 Elaborate

12. Describe the values of x that satisfy the inequalities $|x| < a$ and $|x| > a$ where a is a positive constant.
   For $|x| < a$, the solutions are values of x between $-a$ and a. For $|x| > a$, the solutions are the values of x beyond $-a$ and a (that is, the values of x less than $-a$ or the values of x greater than a).

13. How do you algebraically solve an absolute value inequality?
   Isolate the absolute value expression. Then rewrite the inequality as a compound inequality that uses either and or or and that doesn't involve absolute value. Finish solving for the variable.

14. Explain why the solution of $|x| > a$ is all real numbers if a is a negative number.
   Since the absolute value of any number is always nonnegative, it is always greater than any negative number. So, all real numbers satisfy the inequality.

15. **Essential Question Check-In** How do you solve an absolute value inequality graphically?
   Treat each side of the inequality as a function and graph the two functions. Use the inequality symbol to determine the intervals on the x-axis where one graph lies above or below the other.

ELABORATE

INTEGRATE MATHEMATICAL PRACTICES
Focus on Patterns

MP.8 Discuss with students how to solve an absolute value inequality of the form $|ax + b| < c$ and $|ax + b| > c$. Students should routinely rewrite the next step as a compound inequality using *and* or *or*, and then solve each part of the inequality.

QUESTIONING STRATEGIES

? How is solving an absolute value inequality like and different from solving an absolute value equation? They are alike in that some of the solution steps are the same once a compound statement is written for the absolute value equation or inequality. They are different in that an absolute value inequality may be an *and* statement with infinitely many solutions as well as an *or* statement with infinitely many solutions, but an absolute value equation is only an *or* statement with two, one, or zero solutions.

CONNECT VOCABULARY 🔲EL

Relate the word *conjunction* to its opposite, *disjunction* (discussed in the previous lesson). Explain that the prefix *con* means *to join*. For a conjunction to be true, all of its parts (*joined*) must be true.

SUMMARIZE THE LESSON

? How do you solve a linear absolute value inequality? Isolate the absolute value expression; write the absolute value inequality as a compound statement of two linear inequalities; solve each inequality; and rewrite the solution as a compound statement.

EVALUATE

ASSIGNMENT GUIDE

Concepts and Skills	Practice
Explore Visualizing the Solution Set of an Absolute Value Inequality	Exercises 1–2
Example 1 Solving Absolute Value Inequalities Graphically	Exercises 3–10, 23
Example 2 Solving Absolute Value Inequalities Algebraically	Exercises 11–16, 24
Example 3 Solving a Real-World Problem with Absolute Value Inequalities	Exercises 17–22

INTEGRATE MATHEMATICAL PRACTICES

Focus on Reasoning

MP.2 Remind students to check their solutions by substituting some values into the original inequality and verifying that they make the inequality true. When solving inequalities graphically, remind students that the interval or intervals on the x-axis where $f(x) > g(x)$ or $f(x) < g(x)$ comprise the solution set.

- Online Homework
- Hints and Help
- Extra Practice

1. Determine whether each of the integers from -5 to 5 is a solution of the inequality $|x - 1| + 3 \geq 5$. If a number is a solution, plot it on the number line.

The integers from -5 to 5 that satisfy the inequality are $-5, -4, -3, -2, -1, 3, 4,$ and 5.

2. Determine whether each of the integers from -5 to 5 is a solution of the inequality $|x + 1| - 2 \leq 1$. If a number is a solution, plot it on the number line.

The integers from -5 to 5 that satisfy the inequality are $-4, -3, -2, -1, 0, 1,$ and 2.

Solve each inequality graphically.

3. $2|x| \leq 6$

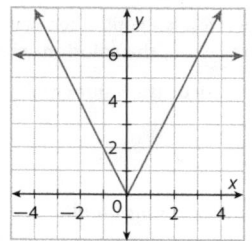

The solution is $-3 \leq x \leq 3$.

4. $|x - 3| - 2 > -1$

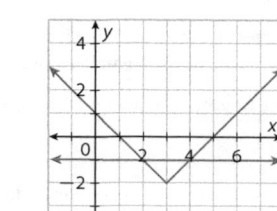

The solution is $x < 2$ or $x > 4$.

5. $\frac{1}{2}|x| + 2 < 3$

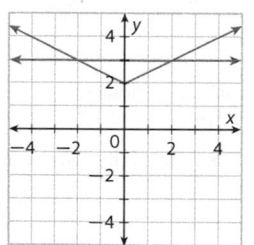

The solution is $-2 < x < 2$.

6. $|x + 2| - 4 \geq -2$

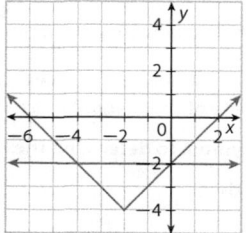

The solution is $x \leq -4$ or $x \geq 0$.

Exercise	Depth of Knowledge (D.O.K.)		COMMON CORE Mathematical Practices	
1–2	**1**	Recall of Information	**MP.6**	Precision
3–6	**1**	Recall of Information	**MP.4**	Modeling
7–16	**2**	Skills/Concepts	**MP.2**	Reasoning
17–21	**2**	Skills/Concepts	**MP.1**	Problem Solving
22	**2**	Skills/Concepts H.O.T.	**MP.4**	Modeling
23	**3**	Strategic Thinking H.O.T.	**MP.6**	Precision
24	**3**	Strategic Thinking H.O.T.	**MP.2**	Reasoning

Match each graph with the corresponding absolute value inequality. Then give the solution of the inequality.

A. $2|x| + 1 > 3$ **B.** $2|x + 1| < 3$ **C.** $2|x| - 1 > 3$ **D.** $2|x - 1| < 3$

7.

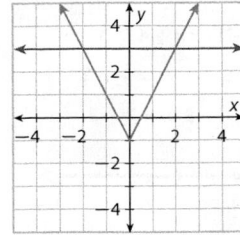

C. The solution is $x < -2$ or $x > 2$.

8.

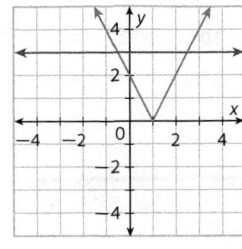

D. The solution is $-\frac{1}{2} < x < \frac{5}{2}$.

9.

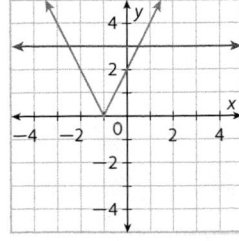

B. The solution is $-\frac{5}{2} < x < \frac{1}{2}$.

10.

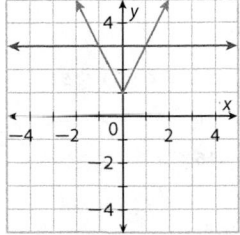

A. The solution is $x < -1$ or $x > 1$.

Solve each absolute value inequality algebraically. Graph the solution on a number line.

11. $2\left|x - \frac{7}{2}\right| + 3 > 4$

$2\left|x - \frac{7}{2}\right| + 3 > 4$

$2\left|x - \frac{7}{2}\right| > 1$

$\left|x - \frac{7}{2}\right| > \frac{1}{2}$

$x - \frac{7}{2} < -\frac{1}{2}$ or $x - \frac{7}{2} > \frac{1}{2}$

$x < 3$ $\qquad$ $x > 4$

The solution is $x < 3$ or $x > 4$.

(number line graph: points at 3 and 4 open circles, from −2 to 9)

SMALL GROUP ACTIVITY

Have students work in small groups to make a poster showing how to apply the steps for solving an absolute value inequality. Give each group a different inequality to solve. Then have each group present its poster to the rest of the class, and ask for a volunteer from the group to explain each step.

Focus on Math Connections

MP.1 Point out that the concept *margin of error* is used in surveys to describe how many percentage points higher or lower a poll result can be and still be considered a "true" figure, meaning a result that is representative of the population.

12. $|2x + 1| - 4 < 5$

$|2x + 1| - 4 < 5$

$|2x + 1| < 9$

$2x + 1 > -9$ and $2x + 1 < 9$

$2x > -10 \qquad 2x < 8$

$x > -5 \qquad x < 4$

The solution is $-5 < x < 4$.

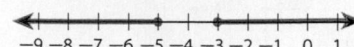

13. $3|x + 4| + 2 \geq 5$

$3|x + 4| + 2 \geq 5$

$3|x + 4| \geq 3$

$|x + 4| \geq 1$

$x + 4 \leq -1$ or $x + 4 \geq 1$

$x \leq -5 \qquad x \geq -3$

The solution is $x \leq -5$ or $x \geq -3$.

14. $|x + 11| - 8 \leq -3$

$|x + 11| - 8 \leq -3$

$|x + 11| \leq 5$

$x + 11 \geq -5$ and $x + 11 \leq 5$

$x \geq -16 \qquad x \leq -6$

The solution is $-16 \leq x \leq -6$.

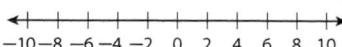

15. $-5|x - 3| - 5 < 15$

$-5|x - 3| < 20$

$|x - 3| > -4$

all real numbers

16. $8|x + 4| + 10 < 2$

$8|x + 4| < -8$

$|x + 4| < -1$

no solution

Solve each problem using an absolute value inequality.

17. The thermostat for a house is set to 68 °F, but the actual temperature may vary by as much as 2 °F. What is the range of possible temperatures?

Let the temperature in the house be *T*. The sign of the difference between *T* and 68 doesn't matter, so take the absolute value of the difference. Since the absolute value of the difference can be as much as 2, the inequality that models the situation is $|T - 68| \leq 2$.

$|T - 68| \leq 2$

$|T - 68| \geq -2$ and $|T - 68| \leq 2$

$T \geq 66$ $T \leq 70$

The range of house temperatures (in degrees Fahrenheit) is $66 \leq T \leq 70$.

18. The balance of Jason's checking account is $320. The balance varies by as much as $80 each week. What are the possible balances of Jason's account?

Let the balance of Jason's account be *B*. The sign of the difference between *B* and 320 doesn't matter, so take the absolute value of the difference. Since the absolute value of the difference can be as much as 80, the inequality that models the situation is $|B - 320| \leq 80$.

$|B - 320| \leq 80$

$B - 320 \geq -80$ and $B - 320 \leq 80$

$B \geq 240$ $B \leq 400$

The range of possible balances (in dollars) is $240 \leq B \leq 400$.

19. On average, a squirrel lives to be 6.5 years old. The lifespan of a squirrel may vary by as much as 1.5 years. What is the range of ages that a squirrel lives?

Let the age of a squirrel be *a*. The sign of the difference between *a* and 6.5 doesn't matter, so take the absolute value of the difference. Since the absolute value of the difference can be as much as 1.5, the inequality that models the situation is $|a - 6.5| \leq 1.5$.

$|a - 6.5| \leq 1.5$

$a - 6.5 \geq -1.5$ and $a - 6.5 \leq 1.5$

$a \geq 5$ $a \leq 8$

The range of ages (in years) that a squirrel lives is $5 \leq a \leq 8$.

Ask students to discuss with a partner what the solution to an inequality of the form $|ax + b| < c$ means in terms of the graph of the related functions $f(x) = |ax + b|$ and $g(x) = c$. Then ask students to make conjectures about the solutions to $|ax + b| < c$ based on the graphs of their related functions. Conjectures should include the interval along the *x*-axis that represents the solutions and how the graphs of these functions look. The solutions to $|ax + b| < c$ are points in the interval along the *x*-axis for which $f(x) < g(x)$. Based on this, conjectures should include that the graphs of $f(x) = |ax + b|$ and $g(x) = c$ show the interval of points that satisfy the compound statement $-c < ax + b < c$.

Watch for students who confuse which type of compound statement to use, *and* or *or*. Remind students that the solution process gives infinitely many solutions to the inequality, and that the type of compound statement determines whether the solution points are between the endpoints or everywhere but between the endpoints.

20. You are playing a history quiz game where you must give the years of historical events. In order to score any points at all for a question about the year in which a man first stepped on the moon, your answer must be no more than 3 years away from the correct answer, 1969. What is the range of answers that allow you to score points?

Let your answer be *a*. The sign of the difference between *a* and 1969 doesn't matter, so take the absolute value of the difference. Since the absolute value of the difference can be no more than 3, the inequality that models the situation is
$|a - 1969| \leq 3.$

$|a - 1969| \leq 3$

$a - 1969 \geq -3$ and $a - 1969 \leq 3$

$a \geq 1966 \qquad a \leq 1972$

The range of answers that allows you to score points is $1966 \leq a \leq 1972$.

21. The speed limit on a road is 30 miles per hour. Drivers on this road typically vary their speed around the limit by as much as 5 miles per hour. What is the range of typical speeds on this road?

Let the speed of a car be *s*. The sign of the difference between *s* and 30 doesn't matter, so take the absolute value of the difference. Since the absolute value of the difference can be as much as 5, the inequality that models the situation is $|s - 30| \leq 5$.

$|s - 30| \leq 5$

$s - 30 \geq -5$ and $s - 30 \leq 5$

$s \geq 25 \qquad s \leq 35$

The range of typical speeds (in miles per hour) is $25 \leq s \leq 35$.

22. **Represent Real-World Problems** A poll of likely voters shows that the incumbent will get 51% of the vote in an upcoming election. Based on the number of voters polled, the results of the poll could be off by as much as 3 percentage points. What does this mean for the incumbent?

Let the incumbent's percentage of votes among all likely voters (not just

those polled) be v. The sign of the difference between v and 51 doesn't

matter, so take the absolute value of the difference. Since the absolute

value of the difference can be as much as 3, the inequality that models

the situation is $|v - 51| \leq 3$.

$|v - 51| \leq 3$

$v - 51 \geq -3$ and $v - 51 \leq 3$

$v \geq 48$ and $v \leq 54$

The range for the incumbent's percentage of votes among all likely

voters is $48 \leq v \leq 54$, which means that the incumbent could still lose the

election if the incumbent's percentage of votes among all likely voters

(not just those polled) is less than 50%.

23. **Explain the Error** A student solved the inequality $|x - 1| - 3 > 1$ graphically. Identify and correct the student's error.

I graphed the functions $f(x) = |x - 1| - 3$ and $g(x) = 1$. Because the graph of $g(x)$ lies above the graph of $f(x)$ between $x = -3$ and $x = 5$, the solution of the inequality is $-3 < x < 5$.

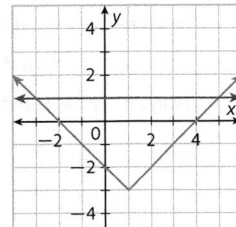

The student identified where the graph of $g(x)$ lies above the

graph of $f(x)$, but the student should have identified where the

graph of $f(x)$ lies above the graph of $g(x)$ because the inequality

has the form $f(x) > g(x)$. So, the solution of the inequality is

$x < -3$ or $x > 5$.

INTEGRATE MATHEMATICAL PRACTICES

Focus on Modeling

MP.4 When modeling a problem in which an absolute value inequality involving tolerance applies, have students start with a number line diagram. Have them plot the starting value and then all points within the tolerance range greater than and less than the starting value. This will provide a visual connection to the inequality that applies, depending on the original real-world problem.

24. **Multi-Step** Recall that a literal equation or inequality is one in which the constants have been replaced by letters.

a. Solve $|ax + b| > c$ for x. Write the solution in terms of a, b, and c. Assume that $a > 0$ and $c \geq 0$.

$|ax + b| > c$

$ax + b < -c$	or	$ax + b > c$
$ax < -c - b$		$ax > c - b$
$x < \dfrac{-c - b}{a}$		$x > \dfrac{c - b}{a}$

The solution is $x < \dfrac{-c - b}{a}$ or $x > \dfrac{c - b}{a}$.

b. Use the solution of the literal inequality to find the solution of $|10x + 21| > 14$.

Substitute 10 for a, 21 for b, and 14 for c in the solution of the literal

inequality and simplify.

The solution is $x < \dfrac{-14 - 21}{10}$ or $x > \dfrac{14 - 21}{10}$, which simplifies to $x < -3.5$

or $x > -0.7$.

c. Explain why you must assume that $a > 0$ and $c \geq 0$ before you begin solving the literal inequality.

If $a = 0$, you would not be able to divide by a. If $a < 0$, you would need

to reverse the direction of the inequality and get a different solution. If

$c < 0$, solution would consist of all real numbers because $|ax + b|$ will

always be greater than c.

Lesson Performance Task

The distance between the Sun and each planet in our solar system varies because the planets travel in elliptical orbits around the Sun. Here is a table of the average distance and the variation in the distance for the five innermost planets in our solar system.

	Average Distance	Variation
Mercury	36 million miles	7.5 million miles
Venus	67.2 million miles	0.5 million miles
Earth	92.75 million miles	1.75 million miles
Mars	141 million miles	13 million miles
Jupiter	484 million miles	24 million miles

a. Write and solve an inequality to represent the range of distances that can occur between the Sun and each planet.

b. Calculate the percentage variation (variation divided by average distance) in the orbit of each of the planets. Based on these percentages, which planet has the most elliptical orbit?

a. (Measurements are in millions of miles.)

Mercury $|x - 36| \leq 7.5$

$x - 36 \leq 7.5$ AND $x - 36 \geq -7.5$

$x \leq 43.5$ $x \geq 28.5$

Range for Mercury is $28.5 \leq x \leq 43.5$.

Venus $|x - 67.2| \leq 0.5$

$x - 67.2 \leq 0.5$ AND $x - 67.2 \geq -0.5$

$x \leq 67.7$ $x \geq 66.7$

Range for Venus is $66.7 \leq x \leq 67.7$.

Earth $|x - 92.75| \leq 1.75$

$x - 92.75 \leq 1.75$ AND $x - 92.75 \geq -1.75$

$x \leq 94.5$ $x \geq 91$

Range for Earth is $91 \leq x \leq 94.5$.

Mars $|x - 141| \leq 13$

$x - 141 \leq 13$ AND $x - 141 \geq -13$

$x \leq 154$ $x \geq 128$

Range for Mars is $128 \leq x \leq 154$.

Jupiter $|x - 484| \leq 24$

$x - 484 \leq 24$ AND $x - 484 \geq -24$

$x \leq 508$ $x \geq 460$

Range for Jupiter is $460 \leq x \leq 508$.

b. Mercury 21%, Venus 1%, Earth 2%, Mars 9%, Jupiter 5%; Mercury has the most elliptical orbit.

EXTENSION ACTIVITY

Have students research the dwarf planet Pluto to find its average distance and its range of distance from the sun. Students will find that Pluto is approximately 39.5 AU (astronomical units) from the sun. Pluto's closest point to the sun is 29.7 AU. Pluto's farthest point away from the sun is 49.7 AU. 1 AU is equal to Earth's distance from the sun, or 1 AU is about 93 million miles.

CONNECT CONTEXT EL

Some students may not be familiar with the meanings of *average distance* and *variation*. Draw a horizontal line segment on the board. To the left of the line segment, some distance away, draw the sun. At the middle point of the line segment write "average distance". To the right and left of the middle point write "variation". Explain that the planet's location is at some point on the line segment. Its exact location varies, but the average of all of its possible locations is the middle point.

AVOID COMMON ERRORS

Some students may subtract from the average distance. For example, for Mercury they may write $|36 - x| \leq 7.5$ instead of $|x - 36| \leq 7.5$. Because they are finding the absolute value of the expression, they will still get the correct values of x.

Scoring Rubric

2 points: Student correctly solves the problem and explains his/her reasoning.

1 point: Student shows good understanding of the problem but does not fully solve or explain his/her reasoning.

0 points: Student does not demonstrate understanding of the problem.

Solving Absolute Value Inequalities   **624**

Study Guide Review

ASSESSMENT AND INTERVENTION

Assign or customize module reviews.

MODULE PERFORMANCE TASK

 COMMON CORE

Mathematical Practices: MP.1, MP.2, MP.4, MP.6, MP.7
F-IF.C.7b, F-BF.A.1b

SUPPORTING STUDENT REASONING

Here are some questions students might ask:

- **What is "taxable" income?** Some types of income are not taxed. Also, all taxpayers get to deduct a certain amount from their income. Taxable income is the amount left over after the deduction and the exclusion of non-taxable income.

- **How do you calculate something like "$892.50 plus 15% of the amount over $8,925"?** Suppose your taxable income is $20,000. Amount over $8,925 = $20,000 − $8,925 = $11,075; 15% of $11,075 = 0.15 × $11,075 = $1,661.25; $892.50 + $1,661.25 = $2,553.75

- **How can I write a single equation that covers all taxable incomes less than or equal to $100,000?** You can't. The tax table defines a piecewise function, each section of which has a different equation. You'll need to write four equations, one for each of the four income intervals from $0 to $100,000.

Piecewise-Defined Functions

Essential Question: How can you use piecewise-defined functions to solve real-world problems?

Key Vocabulary
absolute-value equation *(ecuación de valor absoluto)*
absolute-value function *(función de valor absoluto)*
mean *(media)*
greatest integer function *(función de entero mayor)*
piecewise function *(función a trozos)*
step function *(función escalón)*

KEY EXAMPLE   *(Lesson 13.1)*

Graph the piecewise function $f(x) = \begin{cases} -2x & \text{if } x \leq 2 \\ \frac{1}{2}x + 1 & \text{if } x > 2 \end{cases}$.

x	−4	−2	0	2	4	6
$f(x)$	$-2(-4) = 8$	$-2(-2) = 4$	$-2(0) = 0$	$-2(2) = -4$	$\frac{1}{2}(4) + 1 = 3$	$\frac{1}{2}(6) + 1 = 4$

The transition from one rule to the other occurs at $x = 2$. Show a closed dot at $(2, -4)$, since this point is part of the graph. Show an open dot at $(2, 2)$, since this is not part of the graph.

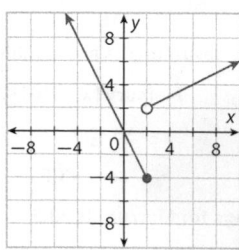

KEY EXAMPLE   *(Lesson 13.3)*

Solve $-4|x + 5| = -2$.

$|x + 5| = \frac{1}{2}$ Divide both sides by −4.

$x + 5 = \frac{1}{2}$ or $x + 5 = -\frac{1}{2}$ Write as two equations.

$x = -4\frac{1}{2}$ or $x = -5\frac{1}{2}$ Subtract 5 from both sides.

KEY EXAMPLE   *(Lesson 13.4)*

Solve $\frac{1}{2}|x| - 3 \leq 1$ graphically.

Let $f(x) = \frac{1}{2}|x| - 3$ and $g(x) = 1$.

Graph $f(x)$ and $g(x)$.

Determine when $f(x) \leq g(x)$.

The solution is $x \geq -8$ and $x \leq 8$.

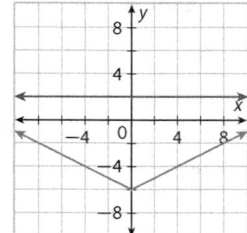

SCAFFOLDING SUPPORT

- Students may need help writing the equations for the four parts of their graphs. Use Bracket 3 of the table as an example. For taxable income of x dollars, the amount over $36,250 is $x - 36,250$; 25% of the amount over $36,250 is $0.25(x - 36,250)$; $4,991.25 plus that amount is $0.25(x - 36,250) + 4,991.25$. That equation can be simplified to $y = 0.25x - 4,071.25$.

EXERCISES

1. Complete the table of values for $f(x) = \begin{cases} x - 3 & \text{if } x < -1 \\ -2x + 4 & \text{if } x \geq -1 \end{cases}$. Graph the function. *(Lesson 13.1)*

x	f(x)
−3	−6
−2	−5
−1	6
0	4
1	2
2	0
3	−2

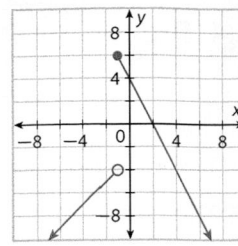

Solve each equation and inequality. *(Lesson 13.3)*

2. $6|x| + 4 = -2$

No solution

3. $2|4x - 1| = 6$

$x = -0.5 \text{ and } x = 1$

4. $|2x + 3| + 7 = 7$

$x = -1.5$

5. $|x + 4| - 12 \leq 20$

$x \geq -36 \text{ and } x \leq 28$

MODULE PERFORMANCE TASK

A Taxing Situation

The table below defines the amount of income tax a single U.S. taxpayer must pay to the federal government for income earned in 2013.

If taxable income is over	but not over	the tax is
$0	$8,925	10% of the amount over $0
$8,926	$36,250	$892.50 plus 15% of the amount over $8,925
$36,251	$87,850	$4,991.25 plus 25% of the amount over $36,250
$87,851	$183,250	$17,891.25 plus 28% of the amount over $87,850
$183,251	$398,350	$44,603.25 plus 33% of the amount over $183,250
$398,351	$400,000	$115,586.25 plus 35% of the amount over $398,350
$400,001	no limit	$116,163.75 plus 39.6% of the amount over $400,000

So, if your taxable income is $30,000, you owe $892.50 plus 15% of the amount by which your earnings exceed $8,925.

- Write the equations for the piecewise-defined function that gives the income tax y on taxable income of x (where $x \leq \$100,000$).
- Graph the function.
- Find the percent of total taxable income that a person making $50,000 and a person making $100,000 pay in income tax.

Use your own paper to work on the task. Then use numbers, words, or algebra to explain how you reached your conclusion.

SAMPLE SOLUTION

The four equations that define the piecewise function for $x \leq \$100,000$ are:

$y = 0.1x$ $(x \leq 8{,}925)$

$y = 0.15x - 446.25$ $(8{,}925 < x \leq 36{,}250)$

$y = 0.25x - 4{,}071.25$ $(36{,}250 < x \leq 87{,}850)$

$y = 0.28x - 6{,}706.75$ $(87{,}850 < x \leq 100{,}000)$

The starting and ending points for the four sections of the graph are $(0, 0)$, $(8{,}925, 892.5)$, $(36{,}250, 4{,}991.25)$, $(87{,}850, 17{,}891.25)$, and $(100{,}000, 21{,}293.25)$.

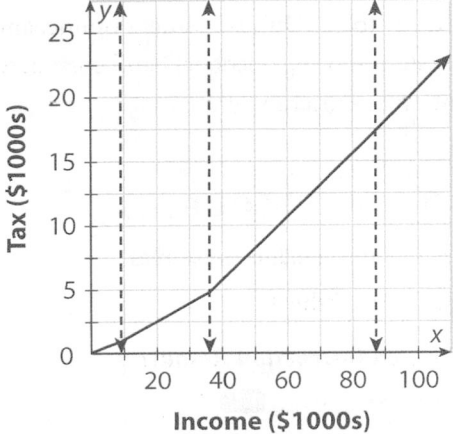

A person with $50,000 in taxable income pays $\frac{8{,}428.75}{50{,}000} \approx 16.9\%$ of that amount in income tax. A person with $100,000 in taxable income pays $\frac{21{,}293.25}{100{,}000} \approx 21.3\%$ of that amount in income tax.

DISCUSSION OPPORTUNITIES

- Suppose everyone with taxable income under $100,000 paid a fixed percent of their income as income tax. How would the graph of income tax as a function of taxable income differ from the graph under the current system? **It would be a line rather than a four-part piecewise graph. The line would start at $(0, 0)$ and have a slope equal to the fixed percent.**

Assessment Rubric

2 points: Student correctly solves the problem and explains his/her reasoning.

1 point: Student shows good understanding of the problem but does not fully solve or explain his/her reasoning.

0 points: Student does not demonstrate understanding of the problem.

Ready to Go On?

ASSESS MASTERY

Use the assessment on this page to determine if students have mastered the concepts and standards covered in this module.

ASSESSMENT AND INTERVENTION

Access Ready to Go On? assessment online, and receive instant scoring, feedback, and customized intervention or enrichment.

ADDITIONAL RESOURCES

Response to Intervention Resources
- Reteach Worksheets

Differentiated Instruction Resources
- Reading Strategies **EL**
- Success for English Learners **EL**
- Challenge Worksheets

Assessment Resources
- Leveled Module Quizzes

(Ready) to Go On?

13.1–13.4 Piecewise-Defined Functions

- Online Homework
- Hints and Help
- Extra Practice

Write a function to represent each graph shown. *(Lesson 13.1)*

1.

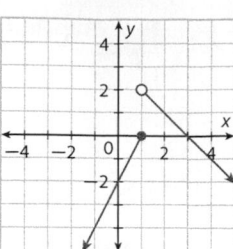

$$f(x) = \begin{cases} 2x - 2 & \text{if } x \leq 1 \\ -x + 3 & \text{if } x > 1 \end{cases}$$

2.

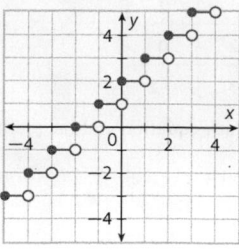

$$f(x) = \lfloor x \rfloor + 2$$

3. $g(x)$ is a transformation of $f(x) = |x|$ left 2 units and reflected across the x-axis. Write a function for $g(x)$, and graph $g(x)$. *(Lesson 13.2)*

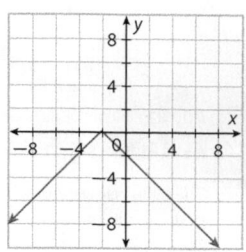

$$g(x) = -|x + 2|$$

Solve each equation and inequality. *(Lessons 13.3, 13.4)*

4. $|5x| + 4 = 19$

$x = -3$ and $x = 3$

5. $|2x| + 3 \geq 11$

$x \leq -4$ or $x \geq 4$

6. $|4x + 2| - 2 = -18$

No solution

7. $|x + 8| - 5 < 2$

$x < -1$ and $x > -15$

ESSENTIAL QUESTION

8. Write a real-world situation that could be modeled by $|x - 14| \leq 3$.

Possible Answer: There are supposed to be 14 biscuits in a package, but there could be as many as 3 extra or 3 fewer in each bag, depending on the weight of the biscuits.

COMMON CORE ## Common Core Standards

Lesson	Items	Content Standards	Mathematical Practices
13.1	1	F-IF.C.7b	MP.7
13.1	2	F-IF.C.7b	MP.7
13.2	3	F-IF.C.7b, F-BF.B.3	MP.7
13.3	4	A.REI.B.3	MP.1
13.4	5	A.REI.B.3	MP.1
13.3	6	A.REI.B.3	MP.1
13.4	7	A.REI.B.3	MP.1

MODULE 13
MIXED REVIEW

Assessment Readiness

1. Consider the function $f(x) = \begin{cases} 3 & \text{if } x < 2 \\ -x + 1 & \text{if } 2 \leq x < 6 \\ x & \text{if } x \geq 6 \end{cases}$. Determine if each of the following is a solution of $f(x)$. Select Yes or No for each possible solution.

   A. $(-5, 3)$ ● Yes   ○ No
   B. $(2, -1)$ ● Yes   ○ No
   C. $(8, -7)$ ○ Yes   ● No

2. Consider the relation represented by the mapping diagram. Determine if the statement is True or False.

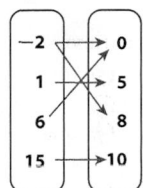

   A. The domain is $\{-2, 1, 6, 15\}$.   ● True   ○ False
   B. The range is $\{0, 5, 8, 10\}$.   ● True   ○ False
   C. The relation is a function.   ○ True   ● False

3. Find the intercepts and slope of $8x - \frac{1}{2}y = 12$. Is the given statement True or False?

   A. The x-intercept is 4.   ○ True   ● False
   B. The y-intercept is -24.   ● True   ○ False
   C. The slope is 8.   ○ True   ● False

4. How many solutions does the equation $|x + 6| - 4 = c$ have if $c = 5$? If $c = -10$? Justify your answers.

   The equation has 2 solutions when $c = 5$, because $|x + 6| = 9$ has 2 solutions. The equation has no solutions when $c = -10$, because when $c = -10$, $|x + 6| = -6$. The absolute value of a number cannot be negative.

© Houghton Mifflin Harcourt Publishing Company

MIXED REVIEW
Assessment Readiness

ASSESSMENT AND INTERVENTION

Assign ready-made or customized practice tests to prepare students for high-stakes tests.

ADDITIONAL RESOURCES

Assessment Resources

- Leveled Module Quizzes: Modified, B

AVOID COMMON ERRORS

Item 4 Some students will continue to perform solution steps after finding an equation where the absolute value is equal to a negative number, eventually finding incorrect answers. Point out that checking answers by substituting them into the original equation will identify any such mistakes.

COMMON CORE **Common Core Standards**

Lesson	Items	Content Standards	Mathematical Practices
13.1	1	**F-IF.C.7b**	**MP.2**
3.2	2*	**F-IF.A.1**	**MP.1**
5.2, 5.3	3*	**F-IF.B.4, F-IF.B.6**	**MP.1**
13.3	4	**A-REI.B.3**	**MP.3**

* Item integrates mixed review concepts from previous modules or a previous course.

MIXED REVIEW
Assessment Readiness

ASSESSMENT AND INTERVENTION

Assign ready-made or customized practice tests to prepare students for high-stakes tests.

ADDITIONAL RESOURCES

Assessment Resources

- Leveled Unit Tests: Modified, A, B, C
- Performance Assessment

AVOID COMMON ERRORS

Item 5 If students have difficulty setting up and solving the absolute value inequality, remind them that substituting the possible answers into the inequality is also a valid way to solve the problem.

UNIT 5 MIXED REVIEW
Assessment Readiness

- Online Homework
- Hints and Help
- Extra Practice

1. One equation of a system of two equations is $y = \frac{2}{5}x - 3$. If the second equation is one of the following, is the given number of solutions correct? Select Yes or No for each pair.

   A. $y = \frac{2}{5}x + 1$; no solutions — ● Yes ○ No
   B. $y = -2x - 3$; 1 solution — ● Yes ○ No
   C. $y = -\frac{2}{5}x - 3$; infinite number of solutions — ○ Yes ● No

2. Solve the system of equations $\begin{cases} 2x + 3y = 18 \\ x + y = 6 \end{cases}$
   Determine if the given statement below is True or False.

   A. $x = 0$. — ● True ○ False
   B. $y = 6$. — ● True ○ False
   C. The only solution is $(0, 6)$. — ● True ○ False

3. Is the following a solution of the system $\begin{cases} y < 2x + 5 \\ y \geq -\frac{1}{2}x - 2 \end{cases}$?
   Select Yes or No for each possible solution.

   A. $(-1, 3)$ — ○ Yes ● No
   B. $(5, 2)$ — ● Yes ○ No
   C. $(0, 8)$ — ○ Yes ● No

4. Asif spent $745.10 on 13 new file cabinets for his office. Small file cabinets cost $43.50 and large file cabinets cost $65.95. Write and solve a system of equations to find the number of small cabinets and large cabinets he purchased.
   Determine if each statement is True or False.

   A. He purchased 5 small cabinets. — ● Yes ○ No
   B. He purchased 7 large cabinets. — ○ Yes ● No
   C. He spent $527.60 on large cabinets. — ● Yes ○ No

5. Solve $\frac{2}{3}|x - 6| \leq 8$. Is each of the following a solution of the inequality? Select Yes or No for each possible solution.

   A. $x = -6$ — ● Yes ○ No
   B. $x = 0$ — ● Yes ○ No
   C. $x = 20$ — ○ Yes ● No

COMMON CORE ## Common Core Standards

Items	Content Standards	Mathematical Practices
1	**A-REI.C.6**	**MP.1**
2*	**A-CED.A.2, A-REI.C.6**	**MP.1**
3	**A-REI.D.12**	**MP.2**
4	**A-CED.A.3**	**MP.4**
5	**A-REI.B.3**	**MP.2**
6*	**F-IF.A.1, F-BF.B.3**	**MP.1**
7	**A-REI.C.6**	**MP.7**

* Item integrates mixed review concepts from previous modules or a previous course.

6. Graph $y = \frac{1}{2}|x - 2| - 6$. Is the relation a function? Explain why or why not.

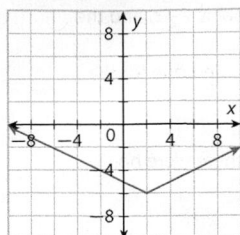

It is a function, because it passes the vertical line test. In other words, there is exactly one output value for each input value.

7. Write the system represented on the graph below. Find and explain the meaning of the point of intersection of the lines.

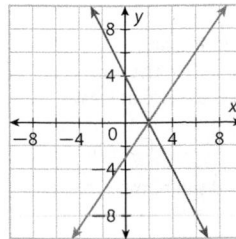

The system is $\begin{cases} y = -2x + 4 \\ y = \frac{3}{2}x - 3 \end{cases}$. The point of intersection is $(2, 0)$. This point represents the solution of the system, $x = 2$ and $y = 0$.

Performance Tasks

★ 8. A coffee shop purchased 60 pounds of Guatemalan coffee beans and 90 pounds of Nicaraguan coffee beans. The total purchase price was $180. The next week it purchased 80 pounds of Guatemalan coffee and 20 pounds of Nicaraguan coffee, and the cost was $100. Write and solve a system of equations to find the cost per pound for both the Guatemalan and Nicaraguan coffee beans.

System of equations:

$60x + 90y = 180$

$80x + 20y = 100$

Here x is the price per pound of Guatemalan coffee beans and y is the price per pound of Nicaraguan coffee beans.

Solution to the system of equations: $(0.9, 1.4)$.

Guatemalan coffee beans cost $0.90 per pound and Nicaraguan coffee beans cost $1.40 per pound.

PERFORMANCE TASKS

There are three different levels of performance tasks:

* **Novice:** These are short word problems that require students to apply the math they have learned in straightforward, real-world situations.

** **Apprentice:** These are more involved problems that guide students step-by-step through more complex tasks. These exercises include more complicated reasoning, writing, and open ended elements.

***Expert:** These are open-ended, nonroutine problems that, instead of stepping the students through, ask them to choose their own methods for solving and justify their answers and reasoning.

SCORING GUIDES

Item 8 (2 points)

1 point for correctly writing the system

1 point for correctly solving the system

Item 9 (6 points)

A. 2 points for correctly writing the system
(1 point per equation)

B. 2 points for correctly solving the system

C. 1 point for correct time
1 point for explanation

Item 10 (6 points)

A. 1 point for correct profits

B. 1 point for correct inequality

C. 3 points for graph correctly showing all three
constraint lines

D. 1 point for explanation

★★ **9.** A boat takes 6.5 hours to make a 70-mile trip upstream and 5 hours on the 70-mile return trip. Let v be the speed of the boat in still water and c be the speed of the current. Therefore, the upstream speed of the boat is $v - c$, and the downstream boat speed is $v + c$.

A. Write two equations, one for the upstream part of the trip and one for the downstream part, relating boat speed, distance, and time.

B. Solve the equations in part **A** for the speed of the current.

C. How long would it take the boat to travel the 70 miles if there were no current? How did you determine your answer?

A. Generally: distance = velocity × time

upstream: $70 = (v - c)6.5$

downstream: $70 = (v + c)5$

B. c is approximately 1.6 mi/hr.

C. v is approximately 12.4 mi/hr. Divide 70 miles by 12.4 miles per hour to find that it would take approximately 5.6 hours to travel 70 miles with no current.

★★★**10.** Students are raising money for a field trip by selling scented candles and specialty soap. The candles cost $0.75 each and will be sold for $1.75. The soap costs $1.25 per bar and will be sold for $3.25. The students need to raise at least $200 to cover their trip costs.

A. What is the profit per item for the candles and soap?

B. Write an inequality that relates the number of candles c and the number of bars of soap s to the needed income.

C. The wholesaler can supply no more than 80 bars of soap and no more than 140 candles. Graph the inequality from part **B** and these constraints, using number of candles for the vertical axis.

D. What does the shaded area of your graph represent?

A. $1 per candle; $2 per bar of soap

B. $c + 2s \geq 200$

C. $s \leq 80; c \leq 140$

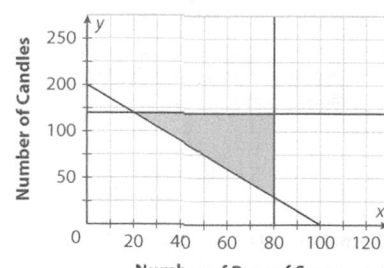

D. The shaded region and filled in boundary lines around it represent solutions to the three constraints. The whole number values within this region represent the numbers of candles and bars of soap the students must sell to cover the costs of their trip.

Personal Shopper Delia is a personal shopper and is tasked with purchasing jeans and T-shirts for her client. Jeans cost $35 and T-shirts cost $15.

a. Write an equation to represent the total amount Delia will pay for x pairs of jeans and y T-shirts if her client wants to spend $115.

b. Delia's client wants a total of 5 items. Write an equation in x and y representing the total number of items Delia will purchase.

c. Solve the system of equations found in parts **a** and **b** algebraically. Show your work.

d. Graph the system, and state the point of intersection.

e. Was it easier to solve the system algebraically or by graphing? Explain your reasoning.

a. $35x + 15y = 115$

b. $x + y = 5$

c. $x + y = 5$

$y = -x + 5$

$35x + 15(-x + 5) = 115$

$35x - 15x + 75 = 115$

$20x + 75 = 115$

$20x = 40$

$x = 2$

$2 + y = 5$

$y = 3$

$x = 2, y = 3$

d.

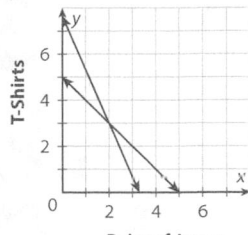

$(2, 3)$

e. Possible answer: Algebraically; the x- and the y-intercepts for the equation $35x + 15y = 115$ are both mixed numbers, so the lines were difficult to graph accurately.

MATH IN CAREERS

Personal Shopper In this Unit Performance Task, students can see how a personal shopper uses mathematics on the job.

For more information about careers in mathematics as well as various mathematics appreciation topics, visit the American Mathematical Society http://www.ams.org

SCORING GUIDE

Task (6 points)

a. 1 point for correct equation

b. 1 point for correct equation

c. 1 point for correct answer, with work

d. 1 point for correct graph and coordinates of point

e. 2 points for reasonable explanation

CONTENTS

Unit Pacing Guide

45-Minute Classes

Module 14

DAY 1	DAY 2	DAY 3	DAY 4	
Lesson 14.1	Lesson 14.2	Lesson 14.2	Module Review and Assessment Readiness	

Module 15

DAY 1	DAY 2	DAY 3	DAY 4	DAY 5
Lesson 15.1	Lesson 15.2	Lesson 15.2	Lesson 15.3	Lesson 15.3
DAY 6	DAY 7	DAY 8	DAY 9	DAY 10
Lesson 15.4	Lesson 15.4	Lesson 15.5	Lesson 15.5	Module Review and Assessment Readiness

Module 16

DAY 1	DAY 2	DAY 3	DAY 4	DAY 5
Lesson 16.1	Lesson 16.1	Lesson 16.2	Lesson 16.3	Lesson 16.3
DAY 6	DAY 7	DAY 8		
Lesson 16.4	Module Review and Assessment Readiness	Unit Review and Assessment Readiness		

90-Minute Classes

Module 14

DAY 1	DAY 2			
Lesson 14.1 Lesson 14.2	Lesson 14.2 Module Review and Assessment Readiness			

Module 15

DAY 1	DAY 2	DAY 3	DAY 4	DAY 5
Lesson 15.1 Lesson 15.2	Lesson 15.2 Lesson 15.3	Lesson 15.3 Lesson 15.4	Lesson 15.4 Lesson 15.5	Lesson 15.5 Module Review and Assessment Readiness

Module 16

DAY 1	DAY 2	DAY 3	DAY 4	
Lesson 16.1	Lesson 16.2 Lesson 16.3	Lesson 16.3 Lesson 16.4	Module Review and Assessment Readiness Unit Review and Assessment Readiness	

Program Resources

PLAN

HMH Teacher App

Access a full suite of teacher resources online and offline on a variety of devices. Plan present, and manage classes, assignments, and activities.

ePlanner Easily plan your classes, create and view assignments, and access all program resources with your online, customizable planning tool.

Professional Development Videos

Authors Juli Dixon and Matt Larson model successful teaching practices and strategies in actual classroom settings.

QR Codes Scan with your smart phone to jump directly from your print book to online videos and other resources.

Teacher's Edition

Support students with point-of-use Questioning Strategies, teaching tips, resources for differentiated instruction, additional activities, and more.

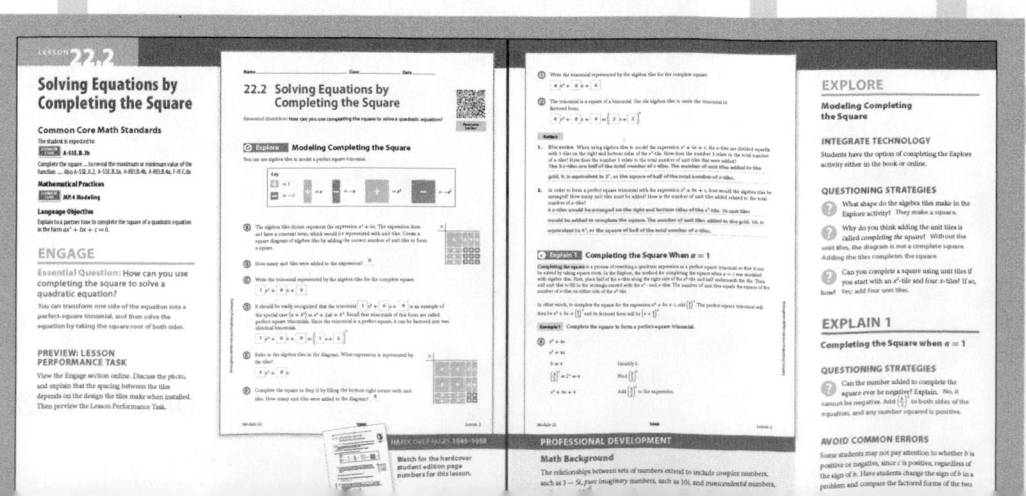

ENGAGE AND EXPLORE

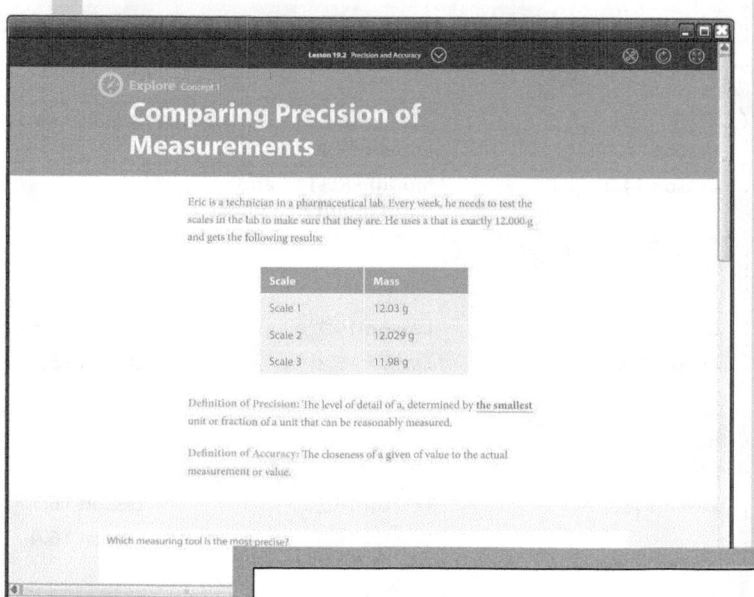

Real-World Videos Engage students with interesting and relevant applications of the mathematical content of each module.

Explore Activities

Students interactively explore new concepts using a variety of tools and approaches.

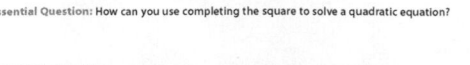

Comparing Precision of Measurements

Eric is a technician in a pharmaceutical lab. Every week, he needs to test the scales in the lab to make sure that they are. He uses a that is exactly 12.000 g and gets the following results:

Scale	Mass
Scale 1	12.03 g
Scale 2	12.029 g
Scale 3	11.98 g

Definition of Precision: The level of detail of a, determined by **the smallest** unit or fraction of a unit that can be reasonably measured.

Definition of Accuracy: The closeness of a given of value to the actual measurement or value.

Which measuring tool is the most precise?

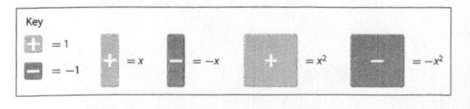

Name _____ Class _____ Date _____

22.2 Solving Equations by Completing the Square

Essential Question: How can you use completing the square to solve a quadratic equation?

Resource Locker

Explore Modeling Completing the Square

You can use algebra tiles to model a perfect square trinomial.

Key

$+$ = 1 $-$ = -1   = x = $-x$ $+$ = x^2 = $-x^2$

(A) The algebra tiles shown represent the expression $x^2 + 6x$. The expression does not have a constant term, which would be represented with unit tiles. Create a square diagram of algebra tiles by adding the correct number of unit tiles to form a square.

(B) How many unit tiles were added to the expression? __9__

(C) Write the trinomial represented by the algebra tiles for the complete square.
1 $x^2 +$ 6 $x +$ 9

(D) It should be easily recognized that the trinomial 1 $x^2 +$ 6 $x +$ 9 is an example of the special case $(a + b^2) = a^2 + 2ab + b^2$. Recall that trinomials of this form are called

TEACH

Math On the Spot video tutorials, featuring program author Dr. Edward Burger accompany every example in the textbook and give students step-by-step instructions and explanations of key math concepts.

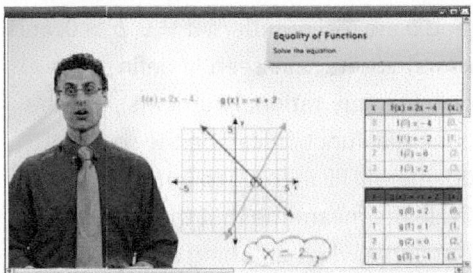

Interactive Teacher Edition

Customize and present course materials with collaborative activities and integrated formative assessment.

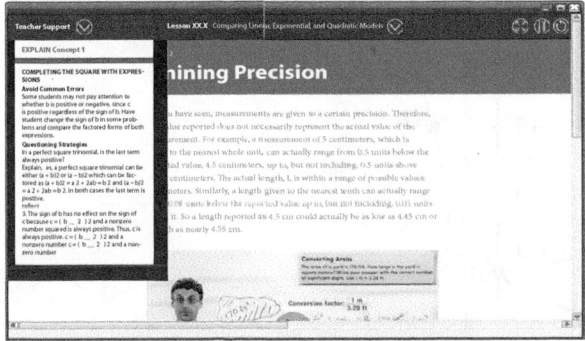

Differentiated Instruction Resources

Support all learners with Differentiated Instruction Resources, including

- **Leveled Practice and Problem Solving**
- **Reading Strategies**
- **Success for English Learners**
- **Challenge**

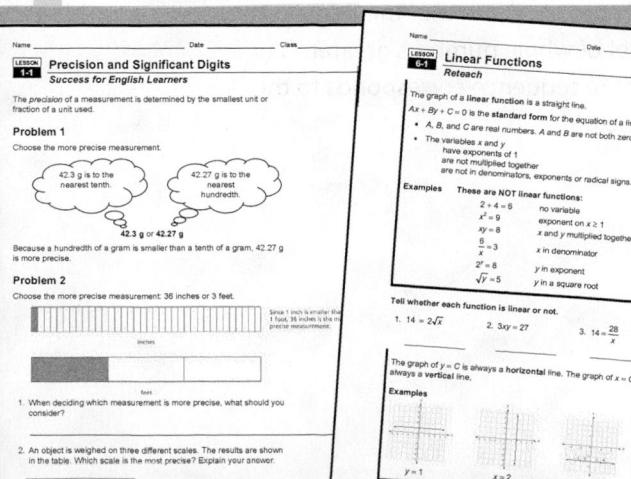
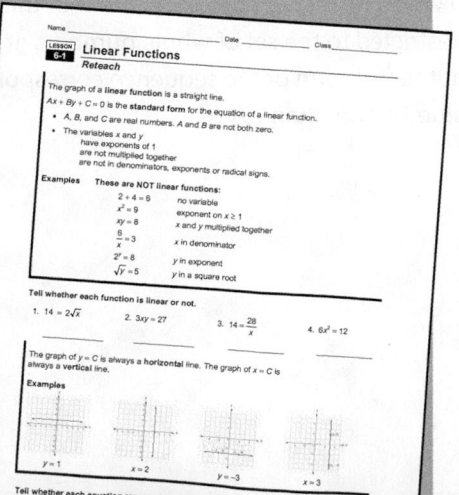

ASSESSMENT AND INTERVENTION

 The **Personal Math Trainer** provides online practice, homework, assessments, and intervention. Monitor student progress through reports and alerts. **Create and customize assignments aligned to specific lessons or Common Core standards.**

- **Practice** – With dynamic items and assignments, students get unlimited practice on key concepts supported by guided examples, step-by-step solutions, and video tutorials.

- **Assessments** – Choose from course assignments or customize your own based on course content, Common Core standards, difficulty levels, and more.

- **Homework** – Students can complete online homework with a wide variety of problem types, including the ability to enter expressions, equations, and graphs. Let the system automatically grade homework, so you can focus where your students need help the most!

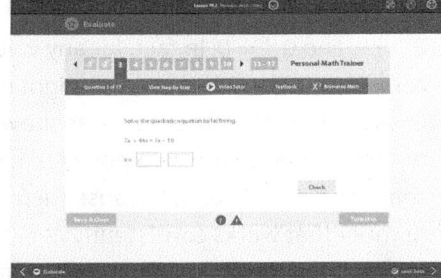

- **Intervention** – Let the Personal Math Trainer automatically prescribe a targeted, personalized intervention path for your students.

Focus on Higher Order Thinking

Raise the bar with homework and practice that incorporates higher-order thinking and mathematical practices in every lesson.

Assessment Readiness

Prepare students for success on high stakes tests for Algebra 1 with practice at every module and unit

COMMON CORE

Assessment Resources

Tailor assessments and response to intervention to meet the needs of all your classes and students, including

- Leveled Module Quizzes
- Leveled Unit Tests
- Unit Performance Tasks
- Placement, Diagnostic, and Quarterly Benchmark Tests
- Tier 1, Tier 2, and Tier 3 Resources

Math Background

Exponents  N-RN.A.1

LESSON 14.1

One common difficulty students have with exponents is the use of zero. For example, students are often puzzled by the fact that any nonzero number raised to the power 0 is 1. It makes sense to think of 2^4 as a product where 2 is a factor 4 times $(2^4 = 2 \cdot 2 \cdot 2 \cdot 2)$, but when it comes to evaluating 2^0, how does one write a product with 2 as a factor zero times? Students should understand that 2^0 is *defined* to be 1 in order to make it consistent with the rules of exponent arithmetic. For example, in order for the Quotient of Powers Property to work in as many situations as possible, it must be true that $\frac{2^4}{2^4} = 2^{4-4} = 2^0$, but $\frac{2^4}{2^4} = 1$. Thus, $2^0 = 1$.

This idea of defining certain powers in order to create a system that is as consistent as possible also explains why the expression 0^0 is undefined. First, it is clear that $0^1 = 0$, $0^2 = 0$, and $0^{13} = 0$. In fact, for any value of n greater than zero, $0^n = 0$. For this reason, it might make sense to define 0^0 as zero. On the other hand, as shown above, any nonzero number raised to the zero power is 1, so it might also make sense to define 0^0 as 1. Because there is no single real number that works consistently as a definition of 0^0, this expression is considered *indeterminate* and is left undefined.

An exponent can be any rational number. Thus, terms can have whole number exponents, as in $5^3 = 5 \cdot 5 \cdot 5$, rational exponents as in $5^{\frac{4}{3}} = \sqrt[3]{5^4}$, negative exponents as in $5^{-2} = \frac{1}{5^2}$, and negative rational exponents as in $5^{-\frac{4}{3}} = \frac{1}{5^{\frac{4}{3}}} = \frac{1}{\sqrt[3]{5^4}}$.

Geometric Sequences F-LE.A.2

LESSON 15.1

Informally, we move from one term of an arithmetic sequence to the next by addition. In a geometric sequence, we move from one term to the next by multiplication. More precisely, in a geometric sequence, the ratio of each term to the preceding term is constant. This constant is called *the common ratio*. The sequence 1, 3, 9, 27, 81, . . . is an example of a geometric sequence. The common ratio is 3. Each term of the sequence is multiplied by 3 to get the next term.

Exponential Functions  F-IF.C.7e

LESSONS 15.3 and 15.4

To understand the connection between geometric sequences and exponential functions, we begin with the definition of *exponential function*: a function of the form $y = ab^x$, where a and b are real numbers, $a \neq 0$, $b > 0$, and $b \neq 1$. In this course, students have seen b^x defined for limited x-values only (namely, rational numbers), but the domain of an exponential function can be the set of all real numbers. Students will fill in this gap in future courses and can be assured in the meantime that they may draw a smooth, continuous curve when graphing an exponential function.

For $a > 0$, the range of an exponential function is the set of all positive real numbers, as illustrated in the graph of $y = 3(2)^x$.

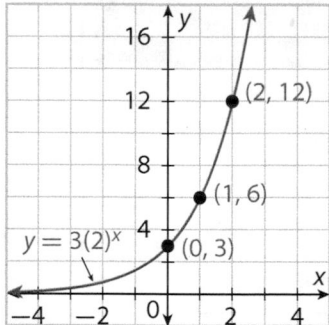

When the domain is restricted to whole numbers, the graph becomes a set of discrete points, the first few of which are shown above. The points' y-values are 3, 6, 12, . . . ; this is precisely the *geometric sequence* defined by $a_n = 3(2)^{n-1}$. In other words, a geometric sequence is simply an exponential function with a restricted domain. (Note that the domain is usually restricted to the set of whole numbers greater than 0, so that the first term of the sequence corresponds to the input value 1 rather than to 0.)

Exponential Growth and Decay **COMMON CORE** F-LE.A.1c

LESSON 16.2

Exponential growth and decay are important applications of exponential functions.

Exponential growth occurs when a quantity increases by the same rate in each time period. Thus, exponential growth can be understood as an extension of percent change in which a percent increase is repeatedly applied. *Exponential decay* occurs when a quantity decreases by the same rate in each time period and, like exponential growth, can be understood as an extension of percent change in which a percent decrease is repeatedly applied.

In an exponential growth situation with initial amount a $(a > 0)$ and rate of growth after one time period, r, expressed as a decimal, the new amount is $a + ar$, or $a(1 + r)$. After the second time period, the new amount is $a(1 + r)(1 + r)$, or $a(1 + r)^2$. Continuing in this way shows that after t time periods, the final amount y is given by $y = a(1 + r)^t$. For exponential decay, a similar argument shows that the final amount y after t time periods is given by $y = a(1 - r)^t$. An important attribute of exponential growth and decay is the fact that the amount added or subtracted in each time period is proportional to the amount already present. For exponential growth, this means that as the amount becomes greater, the amount of increase in each time period also becomes greater. Contrast this to linear growth, in which the amount of increase remains constant.

Exponential Regression **COMMON CORE** S-ID.B.6a

LESSON 16.3

Exponential regression is the process of finding an exponential function that approximates the relationship between two variables in a data set. The original data, along with the best-fit curve given by the exponential regression process, can be represented on an scatter plot. The correlation coefficient (r) indicates how well the regression model fits the data. The exponential function $y = f(x) = ab^x$ can be used to model the data set. An exponential regression is used when a straight line does not

fit the data, but an exponential function might. A residual is the difference between the observed y-value in the data set and the predicted y-value $(y_d - y_m)$. Residuals can be used to assess how well a model fits a data set with the following guidelines:

- The numbers of positive and negative residuals are roughly equal.
- The residuals are randomly distributed about the x-axis, not in a pattern.
- The absolute value of the residuals is small relative to the data.

Linear and Exponential Models **COMMON CORE** S-ID.B.6a

LESSON 16.4

A linear model should be used when the amount of increase or decrease in each interval is constant, such as a fixed dollar increase. An exponential model is appropriate when the increase or decrease per interval grows, such as a fixed percent increase. Consider the following situation. Two students each have $20 in savings. Student 1 increases how much he has saved by $4 per month by saving $4 per month. Student 2 increases how much he has saved by 15% per month. Graphing the above scenario shows the number of months it takes for Student 2 to have more money saved.

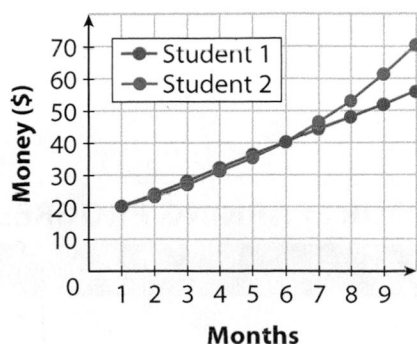

Students' Savings

Exponential Relationships

MATH IN CAREERS

Unit Activity Preview

After completing this unit, students will complete a Math in Careers task by writing and interpreting exponential functions based on a graph. Critical skills include modeling real-world situations and interpreting functional relationships.

For more information about careers in mathematics as well as various mathematics appreciation topics, visit The American Mathematical Society at http://www.ams.org.

UNIT 6

Exponential Relationships

© Houghton Mifflin Harcourt Publishing Company • Image Credits: ©Dragon Images/Shutterstock

Unit 6   633

MATH IN CAREERS

Financial Research Analyst Financial research analysts perform quantitative analysis of market conditions. They use statistics and mathematical models to determine investment strategies and communicate findings.

If you are interested in a career as a financial research analyst, you should study these mathematical subjects:
- Algebra
- Business math
- Statistics
- Calculus
- Differential equations

Research other careers that require understanding how to calculate interest rates. Check out the career activity at the end of the unit to find out how **financial research analysts** use math.

TRACKING YOUR LEARNING PROGRESSION

Before	In this Unit	After
Students understand: • systems of linear equations and inequalities • absolute value equations and inequalities	Students will learn about: • simplifying expressions with rational exponents • simplifying expressions with radicals • geometric sequences • exponential functions	Students will study: • adding polynomial expressions • subtracting polynomial expressions • multiplying polynomial expressions • special products of binomials

Reading Start-Up

Visualize Vocabulary

Use the ✔ words to complete the Summary Triangle.

Write one word in each box.

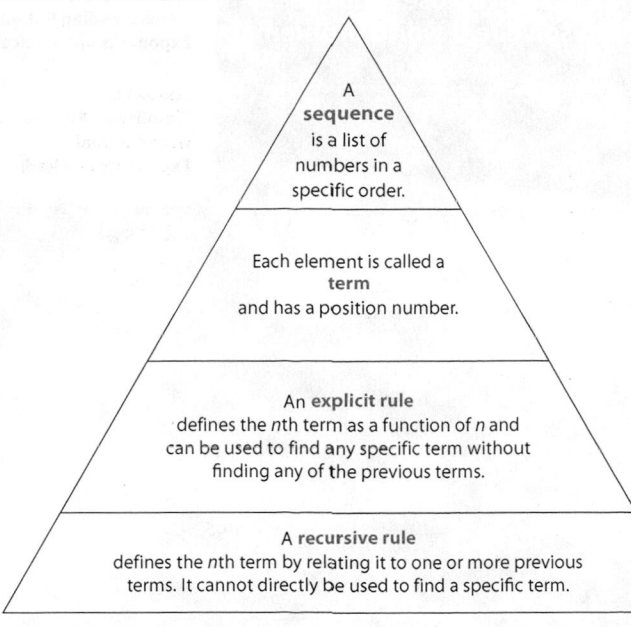

A
sequence
is a list of
numbers in a
specific order.

Each element is called a
term
and has a position number.

An **explicit rule**
defines the *n*th term as a function of *n* and
can be used to find any specific term without
finding any of the previous terms.

A **recursive rule**
defines the *n*th term by relating it to one or more previous
terms. It cannot directly be used to find a specific term.

Vocabulary

Review Words

✔ explicit rule (*fórmula explícita*)
exponent (*exponente*)
irrational number (*número irracional*)
✔ linear function (*función lineal*)
rational number (*número racional*)
✔ recursive rule (*fórmula recurrente*)
✔ sequence (*sucesión*)
✔ term (*término*)

Preview Words

exponential function (*función exponencial*)
index (*índice*)
radical expression (*expresión radical*)
radicand (*radicando*)
rational exponent (*exponente racional*)

Understand Vocabulary

To become familiar with some of the vocabulary terms in this unit, consider the following. You may refer to the module, the glossary, or a dictionary.

1. A __rational exponent__ can be expressed as $\frac{m}{n}$ such that if *m* and *n* are integers, then $b^{\frac{m}{n}} = \sqrt[n]{b^m} = \left(\sqrt[n]{b}\right)^m$.

2. The __index__ item in the __radical expression__ indicates which root to take of the __radicand__.

Active Reading

Key-Term Fold Before beginning the unit, create a key-term fold note to help you organize what you learn. Write a vocabulary term on each tab of the key-term fold. Under each tab, write the definition of the term and an example of the term.

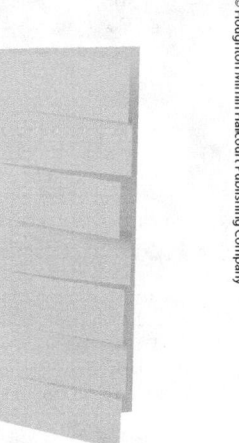

Reading Start Up

Have students complete the activities on this page by working alone or with others.

VISUALIZE VOCABULARY

The summary triangle graphic helps students review vocabulary associated with sequences. If time allows, brainstorm other mathematical relationships among the words.

UNDERSTAND VOCABULARY

Use the following explanations to help students learn the preview words.

> In an **exponential function** the independent variable is an exponent. An expression that contains a radical sign is a **radical expression** and has a fractional exponent. The expression under a radical sign is the **radicand**. In a radical expression, the **index** represents the root of the radical.

ACTIVE READING

Students can use these reading and note-taking strategies to help them organize and understand the new concepts and vocabulary. Encourage them to use mathematical vocabulary precisely and to question terminology that is unclear or misleading. Have students include any additional vocabulary words that they feel will be helpful in their key-term fold.

ADDITIONAL RESOURCES

Differentiated Instruction

- Reading Strategies **EL**

Rational Exponents and Radicals

ESSENTIAL QUESTION:

Answer: You can change rational exponents into radicals when solving problems that have a rational exponent in a formula.

PROFESSIONAL DEVELOPMENT VIDEO

Professional Development Video

STEM Consultant Michael DiSpezio offers engaging suggestions and activities for integrating science, technology, and engineering into the math classroom.

Professional
Development
my.hrw.com

MODULE 14

Rational Exponents and Radicals

Essential Question: How can you use rational exponents and radicals to solve real-world problems?

© Houghton Mifflin Harcourt Publishing Company•Image Credits:
©Photodisc/Getty Images

REAL WORLD VIDEO
Zoo managers must determine the amount of food needed for a healthy diet for the animals.

MODULE PERFORMANCE TASK PREVIEW

How Much Should We Feed the Animals?

You have been selected to be the next reptile chef at the local zoo. This means you are in charge of feeding the reptiles. Reptiles get much of their moisture from the foods they eat, so they need food to stay hydrated as well as to keep from starving. Of course, if they don't get enough food, they starve. If they get too much food, however, they can develop serious health issues that may cause death. So, how much food is enough? How much is too much? Let's find out!

DIGITAL TEACHER EDITION

Access a full suite of teaching resources when and where you need them:

- Access content online or offline
- Customize lessons to share with your class
- Communicate with your students in real-time
- View student grades and data instantly to target your instruction where it is needed most

PERSONAL MATH TRAINER
Assessment and Intervention

Assign automatically graded homework, quizzes, tests, and intervention activities. Prepare your students with updated, Common Core-aligned practice tests.

Are **YOU** Ready?

Complete these exercises to review skills you will need for this module.

• Online Homework
• Hints and Help
• Extra Practice

Exponents

Example 1

Write $(-4)^3$ as a multiplication of factors. Then find its value.

$(-4)^3 = (-4)(-4)(-4)$ Write the base -4 multiplied by itself 3 times.

$(-4)(-4)(-4) = -64$ Multiply.

Write each expression as a multiplication of factors. Then find its value.

1. 13^2
     $13 \cdot 13; 169$

2. $(-5)^4$
     $(-5)(-5)(-5)(-5); 625$

3. 9^3
     $9 \cdot 9 \cdot 9; 729$

4. 2^5
     $2 \cdot 2 \cdot 2 \cdot 2 \cdot 2; 32$

Algebraic Expressions

Example 2

Evaluate $x^2 + 4$ for $x = -2$.

$x^2 + 4$

$(-2)^2 + 4$ Substitute -2 for x.

$4 + 4$ Evaluate the exponent.

8 Add.

Evaluate each expression for the given value of the variables.

5. $p^3 - 2$ for $p = 3$
     25

6. $5a + b^2$ for $a = -3$ and $b = 4$
     1

7. $6m - n^2$ for $m = 5$ and $n = -7$
     -19

8. $x^2 - y^3$ for $x = 6$ and $y = -2$
     44

Real Numbers

Example 3

Tell if 13 is a rational number or an irrational number.

13 can be written as $\frac{13}{1}$,   A rational number can be expressed in the form $\frac{p}{q}$,

so 13 is a rational number.   where p and q are integers and $q \neq 0$.

An irrational number cannot be written as the quotient of two integers.

Tell if the number is a rational number or irrational number.

9. -23
     rational

10. $\sqrt{8}$
     irrational

11. $\frac{3}{8}$
     rational

Are You Ready?

ASSESS READINESS

Use the assessment on this page to determine if students need strategic or intensive intervention for the module's prerequisite skills.

ASSESSMENT AND INTERVENTION

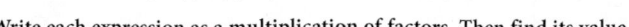

RtI Response to Intervention **TIER 1, TIER 2, TIER 3 SKILLS**

Personal Math Trainer will automatically create a standards-based, personalized intervention assignment for your students, targeting each student's individual needs!

ADDITIONAL RESOURCES

See the table below for a full list of intervention resources available for this module.

Response to Intervention Resources also includes:

• Tier 2 Skill Pre-Tests for each Module

• Tier 2 Skill Post-Tests for each skill

Response to Intervention			Differentiated Instruction
Tier 1	**Tier 2**	**Tier 3**	
Lesson Intervention Worksheets	Strategic Intervention Skills Intervention Worksheets	Intensive Intervention Worksheets available online	
Reteach 14.1 Reteach 14.2	2 Algebraic Expressions 5 Exponents 16 Real Numbers	Building Block Skills 19, 22, 23, 24, 27, 29, 30, 38, 40, 59, 69, 76, 81, 100, 109	Challenge worksheets Extend the Math Lesson Activities in TE

Understanding Rational Exponents and Radicals

Common Core Math Standards

The student is expected to:

 N-RN.A.1

Explain how ...rational exponents follows from extending the properties of integer exponents ... allowing for a notation for radicals... Also N-RN.A.2

Mathematical Practices

MP.2 Reasoning

Language Objective

Students will explain how radicals and rational exponents are related.

ENGAGE

Essential Question: How are radicals and rational exponents related?

Radicals and rational exponents can be converted back and forth into one another, showing that they are two different forms of notation for the same mathematical idea.

PREVIEW: LESSON PERFORMANCE TASK

View the Engage section online. Discuss the photo, and the fact that carbon-14, a radioactive isotope of carbon, occurs in trace amounts, making up about 1 part per trillion of the carbon in the atmosphere. Then preview the Lesson Performance Task.

14.1 Understanding Rational Exponents and Radicals

Essential Question: How are radicals and rational exponents related?

Resource Locker

⊘ Explore 1 Understanding Integer Exponents

Recall that powers like 3^2 are evaluated by repeating the base (3) as a factor a number of times equal to the exponent (2). So $3^2 = 3 \cdot 3 = 9$. What about a negative exponent, or an exponent of 0? You cannot write a product with a negative number of factors, but a pattern emerges if you start from a positive exponent and divide repeatedly by the base.

(A) Starting with powers of 3:

$3^3 = \boxed{27}$

$3^2 = \boxed{9}$

$3^1 = \boxed{3}$

(B) Dividing a power of 3 by 3 is equivalent to $\underline{\text{reducing}}$ the exponent by $\underline{1}$.

(C) Complete the pattern:

$$3^3 \xrightarrow{\div 3} 3^2 \xrightarrow{\div 3} 3^1 \xrightarrow{\div 3} 3^0 \xrightarrow{\div 3} 3^{-1} \xrightarrow{\div 3} 3^{-2}$$

$$27 \xrightarrow{\div 3} 9 \xrightarrow{\div 3} 3 \xrightarrow{\div 3} \boxed{1} \xrightarrow{\div 3} \boxed{\frac{1}{3}} \xrightarrow{\div 3} \boxed{\frac{1}{9}}$$

(D) $3^{-1} = \frac{1}{3}$, $3^{-2} = \frac{1}{9} = \frac{1}{3^2}$

Integer exponents less than 1 can be summarized as follows:

Words	Numbers	Variables
Any non-zero number raised to the power of 0 is 1; 0^0 is undefined	$3^0 = 1$ $(2.4)^0 = 1$	$x^0 = 1$ for $x \neq 0$
Any non-zero number raised to a negative power is equal to 1 divided by the same number raised to the opposite, positive power.	$3^{-2} = \frac{1}{3^2} = \frac{1}{9}$	$x^{-n} = \frac{1}{x^n}$ for $x \neq 0$, and integer n.

Reflect

1. **Discussion** Why does there need to be an exception in the second rule for the case of $x = 0$?
   For a negative exponent, using $x = 0$ would put a 0 in the denominator and division by zero is not defined.

© Houghton Mifflin Harcourt Publishing Company

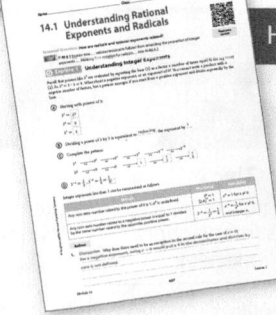

HARDCOVER PAGES 505–510

Turn to these pages to find this lesson in the hardcover student edition.

A radical expression is an expression that contains the radical symbol, $\sqrt{}$.

For $\sqrt[n]{a}$, n is called the **index** and a is called the **radicand.** n must be an integer greater than 1. a can be any real number when n is odd, but must be non-negative when n is even. When $n = 2$, the radical is a square root and the index 2 is usually not shown.

You can write a radical expression as a power. First, note what happens when you raise a power to a power.

$$\left(2^3\right)^2 = (2\cdot2\cdot2)^2 = (2\cdot2\cdot2)(2\cdot2\cdot2) = 2^6, \text{ so } \left(2^3\right)^2 = 2^{3\cdot2}.$$

In fact, for all real numbers a and all rational numbers m and n, $\left(a^m\right)^n = a^{m\cdot n}$. This is called the **Power of a Power Property.**

A radical expression can be written as an exponential expression: $\sqrt[n]{a} = a^k$. Find the value for k when $n = 2$.

Ⓐ Start with the equation. $\sqrt{a} = a^k$

Square both sides. $\left(\sqrt{a}\right)^{\boxed{2}} = \left(a^k\right)^{\boxed{2}}$

Ⓑ Definition of square root $\boxed{a} = (a^k)^2$

Ⓒ Power of a power property $a^1 = a^{\boxed{2k}}$

Ⓓ Equate exponents. $1 = \boxed{2k}$

Ⓔ Solve for k. $k = \boxed{\frac{1}{2}}$

Reflect

2. What do you think will be the rule for other values of the radical index n?
Other radicals can be written as $a^{\frac{1}{n}}$.

🛠 **Explain 1** **Simplifying Numerical Expressions with nth Roots**

For any integer $n > 1$, the nth root of a is a number that, when multiplied by itself n times, is equal to a.
$$x = \sqrt[n]{a} \Rightarrow x^n = a$$
The nth root can be written as a radical with an index of n, or as a power with an exponent of $\frac{1}{n}$. An exponent in the form of a fraction is a **rational exponent**.
$$\sqrt[n]{a} = a^{\frac{1}{n}}$$
The expressions are interchangeable, and to evaluate the nth root, it is necessary to find the number, x, that satisfies the equation $x^n = a$.

Example 1 Find the root and simplify the expression.

Ⓐ $64^{\frac{1}{3}}$

Convert to radical. $64^{\frac{1}{3}} = \sqrt[3]{64}$

Rewrite radicand as a power. $= \sqrt[3]{4^3}$

Definition of nth root. $= 4$

Ⓑ $81^{\frac{1}{4}} + 9^{\frac{1}{2}}$

Convert to radicals. $81^{\frac{1}{4}} + 9^{\frac{1}{2}} = \sqrt[4]{\boxed{81}} + \sqrt{\boxed{9}}$

Rewrite radicands as powers. $= \sqrt[4]{\boxed{3}^{\boxed{4}}} + \sqrt{\boxed{3}^{\boxed{2}}}$

Apply definition of nth root. $= \boxed{3} + \boxed{3}$

Simplify. $= \boxed{6}$

© Houghton Mifflin Harcourt Publishing Company

PROFESSIONAL DEVELOPMENT

Learning Progressions

In this lesson, students extend their knowledge of exponents to the properties of integer and rational exponents while allowing for a notation for radicals in terms of rational exponents. Some key understandings for students are as follows:

- The definition $b^{\frac{1}{n}} = \sqrt[n]{b}$, where $b > 1$ and n is a positive integer, is used to simplify expressions with rational exponents.

- The square root and cube root of a number can be written with rational exponents.

EXPLORE 1

Understanding Integer Exponents

INTEGRATE TECHNOLOGY

Students have the option of completing the activity either in the book or online.

QUESTIONING STRATEGIES

❓ What pattern can you use to evaluate negative exponents? As the value of the exponent decreases by 1, the value of the power is divided by the base.

❓ How can you evaluate a number written with a negative exponent? A number with a negative exponent can be written as the reciprocal of the number written with a positive exponent.

EXPLORE 2

Exploring Rational Exponents

QUESTIONING STRATEGIES

❓ When you convert between radical form and rational exponent form, what are the restrictions on the radicand and index? Conversions are done for all real numbers for which the radical is defined. The index must be a positive integer and the power of the radicand must be an integer.

EXPLAIN 1

Simplifying Numerical Expressions with nth Roots

QUESTIONING STRATEGIES

❓ When you write $\left(\sqrt{25}\right)^3$ with a fractional exponent, what is the denominator of the fractional exponent? Why? 2; the square root indicates a power of $\frac{1}{2}$.

Focus on Modeling

MP.4 Review powers and roots by reviewing $5^3 = 5 \cdot 5 \cdot 5 = 125$ and $\sqrt[3]{125} = 5$ with students. Have students practice writing several similar examples. Then present the definition of $b^{\frac{1}{n}}$ and discuss the Example. Show students two special cases: $1^{\frac{1}{n}} = 1$ and $0^{\frac{1}{n}} = 0$ for all natural-number values of n.

AVOID COMMON ERRORS

With fractional exponents with a numerator other than 1, students may confuse the index with the power. Write base $\frac{\text{exponent}}{\text{index}}$ on the board for students to use as a reference.

EXPLAIN 2

Simplifying Numerical Expressions with Rational Exponents

QUESTIONING STRATEGY

? How do you simplify $81^{\frac{1}{4}}$? **Determine the 4th root of 81, or 3.**

? When you simplify the rational exponent, what does it mean if the simplified form is an integer? If it is a fraction? **If the exponent is an integer, the final form will not contain a radical sign. If the exponent is a fraction, the final form will contain a radical sign.**

---

3. $8^{\frac{1}{3}}$

$8^{\frac{1}{3}} = \sqrt[3]{8}$

$\qquad = \sqrt[3]{2^3}$

$\qquad = 2$

4. $16^{\frac{1}{2}} + 27^{\frac{1}{3}}$

$16^{\frac{1}{2}} + 27^{\frac{1}{3}} = \sqrt{16} + \sqrt[3]{27}$

$\qquad = \sqrt{4^2} + \sqrt[3]{3^3}$

$\qquad = 4 + 3$

$\qquad = 7$

🔘 Explain 2   Simplifying Numerical Expressions with Rational Exponents

Given that for an integer n greater than 1, $\sqrt[n]{b} = b^{\frac{1}{n}}$, you can use the Power of a Power Property to define $b^{\frac{m}{n}}$ for any positive integer m.

$$b^{\frac{m}{n}} = b^{\frac{1}{n} \cdot m} \qquad\qquad b^{\frac{m}{n}} = b^{m \cdot \frac{1}{n}}$$

$$= \left(b^{\frac{1}{n}}\right)^m \quad \text{Power of a Power Property} \quad = (b^m)^{\frac{1}{n}}$$

$$= \left(\sqrt[n]{b}\right)^m \quad \text{Definition of } b^{\frac{1}{n}} \quad = \sqrt[n]{b^m}$$

The definition of a number raised to the power of $\frac{m}{n}$ is the nth root of the number raised to the mth power. The power of m and the nth root can be evaluated in either order to obtain the same answer, although it is generally easier to find the nth root first when working without a calculator.

Example 2   Simplify expressions with fractional exponents.

(A) $27^{\frac{2}{3}}$

Definition of $b^{\frac{m}{n}}$ $\qquad\qquad 27^{\frac{2}{3}} = \left(\sqrt[3]{27}\right)^2$

Rewrite radicand as a power. $\qquad = \left(\sqrt[3]{3^3}\right)^2$

Definition of cube root $\qquad\qquad = 3^2$

$\qquad\qquad = 9$

(B) $25^{\frac{3}{2}}$

Definition of $b^{\frac{m}{n}}$ $\qquad\qquad 25^{\frac{3}{2}} = \left(\sqrt{25}\right)^3$

Rewrite radicand as a power. $\qquad = \left(\sqrt{\boxed{5}^{\boxed{2}}}\right)^3$

Definition of $\boxed{\text{square}}$ root $\qquad = 5^3$

$\qquad\qquad = \boxed{125}$

COLLABORATIVE LEARNING

Peer-to-Peer Activity

Have students work in pairs. Students take turns rolling both a red (r) and a blue (b) number cube. After each roll, the student uses the numbers shown on the cubes to complete the expression $64^{\frac{r}{b}}$. Then the student simplifies the expression or states that it cannot be simplified. The other student checks the answer and then rolls the number cubes to decide the next expression.

5. $32^{\frac{3}{5}}$

$$32^{\frac{3}{5}} = \left(\sqrt[5]{32}\right)^3$$
$$= \left(\sqrt[5]{2^5}\right)^3$$
$$= 2^3$$
$$= 8$$

6. $4^{\frac{5}{2}} - 4^{\frac{3}{2}}$

$$4^{\frac{5}{2}} - 4^{\frac{3}{2}} = \left(\sqrt{4}\right)^5 - \left(\sqrt{4}\right)^3$$
$$= \left(\sqrt{2^2}\right)^5 - \left(\sqrt{2^2}\right)^3$$
$$= 2^5 - 2^3$$
$$= 32 - 8$$
$$= 24$$

💬 Elaborate

7. Why can you evaluate an odd root for any radicand, but even roots require non-negative radicands?
Multiplying a number by a negative number changes the sign, so that in a product with multiple factors, an odd number of negative factors results in a negative product, while an even number of negative factors results in a positive product. Positive factors do not change the sign of a product. There is no way to make a negative product with an even number of identical factors. For odd roots, a negative number simply has a negative root since an odd number of negative factors results in a negative product, while a positive number has a positive root.

8. In evaluating powers with rational exponents with values like $\frac{2}{3}$, why is it usually better to find the root before the power? Would it change the answer to switch the order?
The nth root is a smaller number than the base, while evaluating the power of m first requires finding the nth root of a larger number than the base. Roots of large numbers can be found by guessing, but smaller numbers are more familiar (you are more likely to simply recognize the root or pick it on the first guess) and even if a few guesses are required, it is easier to check with small numbers.
No, switching the order would not change the answer.

9. **Essential Question Check-In** How can radicals and rational exponents be used to simplify expressions involving one or the other?
Radical expressions are interchangeable with exponents of the form $\frac{1}{n}$. Powers with rational exponents can be evaluated by converting them into radical expressions with index n. Radical expressions with powers can sometimes be simplified by switching to rational exponents and using the properties of powers.

INTEGRATE TECHNOLOGY

Encourage the use of graphing calculators to check the results of simplifying numerical radical expressions and numerical expressions with rational exponents. Ask students to use the following sample problems to practice entering expressions correctly into their calculators:

Enter $\sqrt[3]{6^2}$ as 6^(2/3); enter $32^{\frac{3}{2}}$ as 32^(3/2); enter $25^{-\frac{1}{2}}$ as 25^(−1/2). Make sure students understand the importance of including parentheses due to the order of operations.

ELABORATE

QUESTIONING STRATEGIES

? When simplifying a fractional exponent with the form $\frac{m}{n}$, will you get a different answer if you find the root first and then raise the answer to the power, or raise to a power first and then take the root? Explain. **No, the order doesn't matter. You get the same answer either way, although it is often easier to take the root first.**

SUMMARIZE THE LESSON

? How do you simplify an equation with a rational exponent? **If the exponent has the form $\frac{1}{n}$, find the nth root of the base. If the exponent has the form $\frac{m}{n}$, find the nth root of the base raised to the mth power.**

DIFFERENTIATED INSTRUCTION

Kinesthetic Experience

As students work on a problem, suggest that kinesthetic learners write the base, index, and power on separate small pieces of paper. Have students arrange the pieces of paper to form the original expression. Then have students draw a radical on a sheet of paper and move pieces of paper into their correct positions in the radical.

Evaluate the expressions.

1. 10^{-2}

$$10^{-2} = \frac{1}{10^2}$$
$$= \frac{1}{100}$$

2. 56^{-1}

$$56^{-1} = \frac{1}{56^1}$$
$$= \frac{1}{56}$$

• Online Homework
• Hints and Help
• Extra Practice

3. 2^{-4}

$$2^{-4} = \frac{1}{2^4}$$
$$= \frac{1}{16}$$

4. $\left(\frac{1}{3}\right)^{-2}$

$$\left(\frac{1}{3}\right)^{-2} = \frac{1}{\left(\frac{1}{3}\right)^2}$$
$$= \frac{1}{\left(\frac{1}{9}\right)}$$
$$= 9$$

5. $(-2)^{\circ}$

$$(-2^{\circ}) = 1$$

6. $3 \cdot 6^{-2}$

$$3 \cdot 6^{-2} = 3 \cdot \left(\frac{1}{6^2}\right)$$
$$= 3 \cdot \left(\frac{1}{36}\right)$$
$$= \frac{3}{36}$$
$$= \frac{1}{12}$$

Find the root(s) and simplify the expression.

7. $81^{\frac{1}{2}}$

$$81^{\frac{1}{2}} = \sqrt{81}$$
$$= \sqrt{9^2}$$
$$= 9$$

8. $125^{\frac{1}{3}}$

$$125^{\frac{1}{3}} = \sqrt[3]{125}$$
$$= \sqrt[3]{5^3}$$
$$= 5$$

9. $49^{\frac{1}{2}} - 4^{\frac{1}{2}}$

$$49^{\frac{1}{2}} - 4^{\frac{1}{2}} = \sqrt{49} - \sqrt{4}$$
$$= \sqrt{7^2} - \sqrt{2^2}$$
$$= 7 - 2$$
$$= 5$$

10. $16^{\frac{1}{4}} + 32^{\frac{1}{5}}$

$$16^{\frac{1}{4}} + 32^{\frac{1}{5}} = \sqrt[4]{16} + \sqrt[5]{32}$$
$$= \sqrt[4]{2^4} + \sqrt[5]{2^5}$$
$$= 2 + 2$$
$$= 4$$

LANGUAGE SUPPORT **EL**

Connect Vocabulary

Write the terms $\sqrt{5}$ and $\sqrt[3]{n^5}$ on the board. Point out that the first term, $\sqrt{5}$, is known as *the square root* or the *second root* of 5.

Explain that, in more complicated radical expressions, such as $\sqrt[3]{n^5}$, the "inside" expression, n^5, is called the *radicand*, while the "root" term (3, in the upper left of the radical symbol) is called the *index*. $\sqrt[3]{n^5}$ means *the third root*, or *cube root*, of n to the fifth power.

Simplify the expressions with rational exponents.

11. $49^{\frac{3}{2}}$

$$49^{\frac{3}{2}} = \left(\sqrt{49}\right)^3$$
$$= \left(\sqrt{7^2}\right)^3$$
$$= 7^3$$
$$= 343$$

12. $8^{\frac{5}{3}}$

$$8^{\frac{5}{3}} = \left(\sqrt[3]{8}\right)^5$$
$$= \left(\sqrt[3]{2^3}\right)^5$$
$$= 2^5$$
$$= 32$$

13. $27^{\frac{4}{3}} + 4^{\frac{3}{2}}$

$$27^{\frac{4}{3}} + 4^{\frac{3}{2}} = \left(\sqrt[3]{27}\right)^4 + \left(\sqrt{4}\right)^3$$
$$= \left(\sqrt[3]{3^3}\right)^4 + \left(\sqrt{2^2}\right)^3$$
$$= 3^4 + 2^3$$
$$= 81 + 8$$
$$= 89$$

14. $25^{\frac{3}{2}} + 16^{\frac{3}{2}}$

$$25^{\frac{3}{2}} + 16^{\frac{3}{2}} = \left(\sqrt{25}\right)^3 + \left(\sqrt{16}\right)^3$$
$$= \left(\sqrt{5^2}\right)^3 + \left(\sqrt{4^2}\right)^3$$
$$= 5^3 + 4^3$$
$$= 125 + 64$$
$$= 189$$

Simplify the expressions.

15. $25^{-\frac{1}{2}}$

$$25^{-\frac{1}{2}} = \frac{1}{25^{\frac{1}{2}}}$$
$$= \frac{1}{\sqrt{25}}$$
$$= \frac{1}{\sqrt{5^2}}$$
$$= \frac{1}{5}$$

16. $8^{-\frac{1}{3}}$

$$8^{-\frac{1}{3}} = \frac{1}{8^{\frac{1}{3}}}$$
$$= \frac{1}{\sqrt[3]{8}}$$
$$= \frac{1}{\sqrt[3]{2^3}}$$
$$= \frac{1}{2}$$

17. $1^{-\frac{2}{3}}$

$$1^{-\frac{2}{3}} = 1$$

18. $8^{\frac{2}{3}} + 8^{-\frac{2}{3}}$

$$8^{\frac{2}{3}} + 8^{-\frac{2}{3}} = 8^{\frac{2}{3}} + \frac{1}{8^{\frac{2}{3}}}$$
$$= \left(\sqrt[3]{8}\right)^2 + \frac{1}{\left(\sqrt[3]{8}\right)^2}$$
$$= \left(\sqrt[3]{2^3}\right)^2 + \frac{1}{\left(\sqrt[3]{2^3}\right)^2}$$
$$= 2^2 + \frac{1}{2^2}$$
$$= 4 + \frac{1}{4}$$
$$= 4\frac{1}{4}$$

EVALUATE

Personal Math Trainer

ASSIGNMENT GUIDE

Concepts and Skills	Practice
Explore 1 Understanding Integer Exponents	Exercises 1–6
Explore 2 Exploring Rational Exponents	Exercise 26
Example 1 Simplifying Numerical Expressions with nth Roots	Exercises 7–10, 27
Example 2 Simplifying Numerical Expressions with Rational Exponents	Exercises 11–28

INTEGRATE MATHEMATICAL PRACTICES

Focus on Communication

MP.3 Circulate as students solve the problems. Invite students to explain their reasoning as they begin a new problem.

Exercise	Depth of Knowledge (D.O.K.)		COMMON CORE Mathematical Practices
1–23	**2** Skills/Concepts		**MP.4** Modeling
24–25	**2** Skills/Concepts		**MP.4** Modeling
26	**2** Skills/Concepts		**MP.3** Logic
27	**3** Strategic Thinking	H.O.T.	**MP.3** Logic
28	**3** Strategic Thinking	H.O.T.	**MP.2** Reasoning

Understanding Rational Exponents and Radicals   **642**

Focus on Math Connections

MP.1 Explain that, when writing an expression with a rational exponent as a radical, the power can also be placed under the radical sign.

For example, $216^{\frac{2}{3}}$ can be written as

$\left(\sqrt[3]{216}\right)^2$ or $\sqrt[3]{216^2}$. However, it is usually more convenient to evaluate the root and then evaluate the power.

AVOID COMMON ERRORS

Students will sometimes multiply the base by the negative exponent. Have these students re-read the definition of a negative exponent. Point out that 10^{-3} means a number less than one, not a number less than zero.

19. $\dfrac{25^{\frac{1}{2}}}{27^{\frac{1}{3}}}$

$\dfrac{25^{\frac{1}{2}}}{27^{\frac{1}{3}}} = \dfrac{\sqrt{25}}{\sqrt[3]{27}}$

$= \dfrac{\sqrt{5^2}}{\sqrt[3]{3^3}}$

$= \dfrac{5}{3} = 1\dfrac{2}{3}$

20. $7 \cdot 10^{-3}$

$7 \cdot 10^{-3} = 7 \cdot \dfrac{1}{10^3}$

$= 7 \cdot \dfrac{1}{1000}$

$= \dfrac{7}{1000}$

21. $\left(\dfrac{1}{4}\right)^{-\frac{3}{2}}$

$\left(\dfrac{1}{4}\right)^{-\frac{3}{2}} = \dfrac{1}{\left(\dfrac{1}{4}\right)^{\frac{3}{2}}}$

$= \dfrac{1}{\left(\sqrt{\dfrac{1}{4}}\right)^3}$

$= \dfrac{1}{\left(\dfrac{1}{\sqrt{4}}\right)^3}$

$= \dfrac{1}{\left(\dfrac{1}{\sqrt{2^2}}\right)^3}$

$= \dfrac{1}{\left(\dfrac{1}{2}\right)^3}$

$= \dfrac{1}{\left(\dfrac{1}{8}\right)}$

$= 8$

22. $2 \cdot 36^{-\frac{1}{2}} + 6^{-1}$

$2 \cdot 36^{-\frac{1}{2}} + 6^{-1} = \dfrac{2}{36^{\frac{1}{2}}} + \dfrac{1}{6^1}$

$= \dfrac{2}{\sqrt{36}} + \dfrac{1}{6}$

$= \dfrac{2}{\sqrt{6^2}} + \dfrac{1}{6}$

$= \dfrac{2}{6} + \dfrac{1}{6}$

$= \dfrac{1}{2}$

23. **Geometry** The volume of a cube is related to the area of a face by the formula $V = A^{\frac{3}{2}}$.

What is the volume of a cube whose face has an area of 100 cm²?

$v = 100^{\frac{3}{2}}$

$= \left(\sqrt{100}\right)^3$

$= \left(\sqrt{10^2}\right)^3$

$= 10^3$

$= 1000 \text{ cm}^3$

24. Biology The approximate number of Calories, C, that an animal needs each day is given by $C = 72m^{\frac{3}{4}}$, where m is the animal's mass in kilograms. Find the number of Calories that a 16 kilogram dog needs each day.

$$C = 72(16)^{\frac{3}{4}}$$
$$= 72\left(\sqrt[4]{16}\right)^3$$
$$= 72\left(\sqrt[4]{2^4}\right)^3$$
$$= 72 \cdot 2^3$$
$$= 72 \cdot 8$$
$$= 576 \text{ Calories}$$

25. Rocket Science Escape velocity is a measure of how fast an object must be moving to escape the gravitational pull of a planet or moon with no further thrust. The escape velocity for the moon is given approximately by the equation

$V = 5600 \cdot \left(\dfrac{d}{1000}\right)^{-\frac{1}{2}}$, where v is the escape velocity in miles per hour and d is the

distance from the center of the moon (in miles). If a lunar lander thrusts upwards until it reaches a distance of 16,000 miles from the center of the moon, about how fast must it be going to escape the moon's gravity?

$$v \approx 5600 \cdot \left(\frac{16{,}000}{1000}\right)^{-\frac{1}{2}}$$
$$= 5600 \cdot 16^{-\frac{1}{2}}$$
$$= 5600 \cdot \frac{1}{16^{\frac{1}{2}}}$$
$$= 5600 \cdot \frac{1}{\sqrt{16}}$$
$$= 5600 \cdot \frac{1}{4}$$
$$= 1400$$

It needs to be moving at about 1400 miles per hour.

26. Multiple Response Which of the following expressions cannot be evaluated? **b, e and f are undefined.**

a. $4^{\frac{1}{2}}$

b. $(-4)^{-\frac{1}{2}}$

c. 4^{-2}

d. $(-4)^{-2}$

e. $0^{-\frac{1}{2}}$

f. 0^{-2}

? What generalization can you make when the radicand's exponent and the index are equal, as in $\sqrt[4]{3^4}$? When the exponent in the radicand and the index are the same, the expression simplifies to the base of the radicand. Thus, $\sqrt[4]{3^4}$ simplifies to 3.

INTEGRATE MATHEMATICAL PRACTICES
Focus on Modeling

MP.4 Make sure students understand that the denominator in the exponent determines the index in the radical equivalent. For example, in $16^{\frac{1}{4}}$, the 4 in the exponent indicates the 4th root of 16.

COLLABORATIVE LEARNING

Small Group Activity

Have students work in groups of three or four. To help students master the concepts in the lesson, have members of a small group create problems involving rational exponents or radicals, then have them solve each other's problems. Encourage students to make their problems as elaborate as they like, but they must be able to supply the correct answer for any problem that they submit.

JOURNAL

In their journals, have students write the steps they would use to simplify $729^{\frac{5}{6}}$.

27. Explain the Error Yuan is asked to evaluate the expression $(-8)^{\frac{2}{3}}$ on his exam, and writes that it is unsolvable because you cannot evaluate a negative number to an even fractional power. Is he correct, and if so, why? If he is not correct, what is the correct answer?

No, he is not correct. It is only even numbers in the denominator of an exponent that cannot be evaluated with a negative base. With an odd denominator and an even numerator in the exponent, there is no problem. The correct answer is:

$$(-8)^{\frac{2}{3}} = \left(\sqrt[3]{-8}\right)^2$$
$$= \left(\sqrt[3]{(-2)^3}\right)^2$$
$$= (-2)^2$$
$$= 4$$

28. Communicate Mathematical Ideas Show that the nth root of a number, a, can be expressed with an exponent of $\frac{1}{n}$ for any positive integer, n.

$$\sqrt[n]{a} = a^k$$

Raise both sides to the nth power. $\quad \left(\sqrt[n]{a}\right)^n = \left(a^k\right)^n$

Definition of nth root $\quad a = \left(a^k\right)^n$

Power of a Power Property $\quad a^1 = a^{kn}$

Equate Exponents. $\quad 1 = kn$

Solve for k. $\quad k = \frac{1}{n}$

29. Explain the Error Gretchen thinks she has figured out how to evaluate the square root of a negative number. Explain why her solution is flawed.

$$(-1)^2 (-1)^{\frac{1}{2}} = (-1)^{2\frac{1}{2}}$$
$$= (-1)^0$$
$$= 1$$

Then she solves for $(-1)^{\frac{1}{2}}$ which is the same thing as $\sqrt{-1}$.

$$(-1)^2 \cdot (-1)^{\frac{1}{2}} = 1$$
$$(-1)^{\frac{1}{2}} = \frac{1}{(-1)^2}$$
$$= \frac{1}{1}$$
$$= 1$$

But the square root of -1 cannot be 1, since $1 \cdot 1 = 1$, not -1. What mistake did she make?

Gretchen's method has no validity because it is based on calculations involving the square root of a negative number, which is not defined.

It is also riddled with errors.

Lesson Performance Task

Carbon-14 dating is used to determine the age of archeological artifacts of biological (plant or animal) origin. Items that are dated using carbon-14 include objects made from bone, wood, or plant fibers. This method works by measuring the fraction of carbon-14 remaining in an object. The fraction of the original carbon-14 remaining can be expressed by the function, $f = 2^{\left(-\frac{t}{5700}\right)}$,

where t is the length of time since the organism died.

a. Fill in the following table to see what fraction of the original carbon-14 still remains after the passage of time.

t	$\dfrac{t}{5700}$	Fraction of Carbon-14 Remaining
0	0	1
5700	1	$\dfrac{1}{2}$
11,400	2	$\dfrac{1}{4}$
17,100	3	$\dfrac{1}{8}$

b. The duration of 5700 years is referred to as the "half-life" of carbon-14 because the amount of carbon-14 drops in half 5700 years after any starting point (not just $t = 0$ years). Verify this property by comparing the amount of remaining carbon-14 after 11,400 years and 17,100 years.

c. Write the corresponding expression for the remaining fraction of uranium-234, which has a half-life of about 80,000 years.

a. $f = 2^{\left(-\frac{5700}{5700}\right)},\ f = 2^{\left(-\frac{11,400}{5700}\right)},\ f = 2^{\left(-\frac{17,100}{5700}\right)}$

$\quad = 2^{-1} \qquad\quad = 2^{-2} \qquad\quad = 2^{-3}$

$\quad = \dfrac{1}{2} \qquad\quad = \dfrac{1}{2^2} \qquad\quad = \dfrac{1}{2^3}$

$\qquad\qquad\qquad\quad = \dfrac{1}{4} \qquad\quad = \dfrac{1}{8}$

b. From the table, $f(17,100) = \dfrac{1}{8}$ and $f(11,400) = \dfrac{1}{4}$.

$\dfrac{1}{8} \div \dfrac{1}{4} = \dfrac{1}{2}$

Therefore, 5700 years after 11,400, half of the carbon-14 is remaining.

c. $f = 2^{\left(-\frac{t}{80,000}\right)}$

EXTENSION ACTIVITY

Have students make a table of values for uranium-234, similar to the table they made in Part A of the Lesson Performance Task for carbon-14. Then have students describe any patterns they see in the tables as they substitute values for t.

Students will find that the values in the last two columns are exactly like the values in the last two columns of the table for carbon-14.

CONNECT VOCABULARY EL

Some students may not be familiar with the term *half-life* $\left(t_{\frac{1}{2}}\right)$ used in this Lesson Performance Task. Explain that the half-life of any substance is the time it takes for the amount of the substance to decrease to half of what it originally was. To illustrate, draw a long line on the board, then draw successively shorter lines: half as long as the original line; then $\dfrac{1}{4}$ as long; then $\dfrac{1}{8}$ as long; and so on. The lines represent the shrinking by half at equal time intervals.

INTEGRATE MATHEMATICAL PRACTICES
Focus on Modeling

MP.4 Have students begin with the number 40 and take half of it, then half of that result, then half of that, and so on. Discuss with students when there might no longer be anything to take half of. Students should continue taking half until it is apparent to them that they will never reach 0, although they will come close. Discuss how a graph of ordered pairs (number of times halved, result) would look.

Scoring Rubric

2 points: Student correctly solves the problem and explains his/her reasoning.

1 point: Student shows good understanding of the problem but does not fully solve or explain his/her reasoning.

0 points: Student does not demonstrate understanding of the problem.

Simplifying Expressions with Rational Exponents and Radicals

Common Core Math Standards

The student is expected to:

 N-RN.A.2

Rewrite expressions involving radicals and rational exponents using the properties of exponents. Also N-RN.B.3, A-SSE.A.1b

Mathematical Practices

 MP.7 Using Structure

Language Objective

Students will explain to a partner what the subsets and properties of real numbers are.

ENGAGE

Essential Question: How can you write a radical expression as an expression with a rational exponent?

You can write a radical expression as an expression with a rational exponent by using the properties of rational exponents.

PREVIEW: LESSON PERFORMANCE TASK

View the Engage section online. Discuss the photo and how a net for a ball (sphere) might look. Then preview the Lesson Performance Task.

Name_____ Class_____ Date_____

14.2 Simplifying Expressions with Rational Exponents and Radicals

Resource Locker

Essential Question: How can you write a radical expression as an expression with a rational exponent?

⊘ Explore   Exploring Operations with Rational and Irrational Numbers

What happens when you add two rational numbers? Is the result always another rational number or can it be irrational? Will the sum of two irrational numbers always be rational, always be irrational, or can it be either? What about the product of two irrational numbers?

These questions are all used to determine whether a set of numbers is closed under an operation. If the sum of two rational numbers is always rational, the set of rational numbers would be said to be closed under addition. The following tables will combine rational and irrational numbers in various ways. The various sums and products should provide a general idea of which sets are closed under the different operations.

Ⓐ Define rational and irrational numbers.

A rational number is any number that can be written as the ratio of two numbers, $\frac{a}{b}$, where a and b are integers and $b \neq 0$. An irrational number is a real number that is not rational.

Ⓑ Complete the following addition table. Note that there are both rational and irrational addends.

+	$-\pi$	7	$\frac{1}{4}$	0	$\sqrt{3}$	$-\sqrt{3}$
$-\pi$	-2π	$7-\pi$	$\frac{1}{4}-\pi$	$-\pi$	$\sqrt{3}-\pi$	$-\sqrt{3}-\pi$
7	$7-\pi$	14	$7\frac{1}{4}$	7	$7+\sqrt{3}$	$7-\sqrt{3}$
$\frac{1}{4}$	$\frac{1}{4}-\pi$	$7\frac{1}{4}$	$\frac{1}{2}$	$\frac{1}{4}$	$\frac{1}{4}+\sqrt{3}$	$\frac{1}{4}-\sqrt{3}$
0	$-\pi$	7	$\frac{1}{4}$	0	$\sqrt{3}$	$-\sqrt{3}$
$\sqrt{3}$	$\sqrt{3}-\pi$	$7+\sqrt{3}$	$\frac{1}{4}+\sqrt{3}$	$\sqrt{3}$	$2\sqrt{3}$	0
$-\sqrt{3}$	$-\sqrt{3}-\pi$	$7-\sqrt{3}$	$\frac{1}{4}-\sqrt{3}$	$-\sqrt{3}$	0	$-2\sqrt{3}$

Ⓒ Based on the results in the table, will the sum of two rational numbers sometimes, always, or never be a rational number?

The sum of two rational numbers will always be a rational number.

Module 14   **647**   Lesson 2

© Houghton Mifflin Harcourt Publishing Company

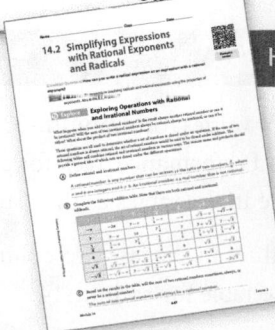

HARDCOVER PAGES 511–520

Turn to these pages to find this lesson in the hardcover student edition.

(D) What about the sum of two irrational numbers?

The sum of two irrational numbers will sometimes be a rational number.

(E) And finally, the sum of a rational number and an irrational number?

The sum of a rational number and an irrational number will never be a rational number.

(F) Now complete the following multiplication table. Similarly, it has both rational and irrational factors.

×	$-\pi$	7	$\frac{1}{4}$	0	$\sqrt{3}$	$\frac{1}{\sqrt{3}}$
$-\pi$	π^2	-7π	$\frac{-\pi}{4}$	0	$-\pi\sqrt{3}$	$-\frac{\pi}{\sqrt{3}}$
7	-7π	49	$\frac{7}{4}$	0	$7\sqrt{3}$	$\frac{7}{\sqrt{3}}$
$\frac{1}{4}$	$\frac{-\pi}{4}$	$\frac{7}{4}$	$\frac{1}{16}$	0	$\frac{\sqrt{3}}{4}$	$\frac{1}{4\sqrt{3}}$
0	0	0	0	0	0	0
$\sqrt{3}$	$-\pi\sqrt{3}$	$7\sqrt{3}$	$\frac{\sqrt{3}}{4}$	0	3	1
$\frac{1}{\sqrt{3}}$	$-\frac{\pi}{\sqrt{3}}$	$\frac{7}{\sqrt{3}}$	$\frac{1}{4\sqrt{3}}$	0	1	$\frac{1}{3}$

(G) Based on the results in the table, will the product of two rational numbers sometimes, always, or never be a rational number?

The product of two rational numbers will always be rational.

(H) What about the product of two irrational numbers?

The product of two irrational numbers will sometimes be a rational number.

(I) And finally, the product of a rational number and an irrational number?

The product of a rational number and an irrational number will never be a rational number.

EXPLORE

Exploring Operations with Rational and Irrational Numbers

INTEGRATE TECHNOLOGY

Students have the option of completing the activity either in the book or online.

CONNECT VOCABULARY EL

Students may be confused about the subsets of real numbers. Draw a diagram in which you divide real numbers into rational and irrational numbers. Then, further subdivide the rational numbers into integers and whole numbers. Write several examples of each type and invite students to add more examples to each category.

PROFESSIONAL DEVELOPMENT

Math Background

A set of numbers is closed under an operation if the result of the operation on any two numbers in the set is another number in the set. For example, the set $\{0, 1\}$ is closed under multiplication because $0 \times 0 = 0$, $1 \times 0 = 0$, $0 \times 1 = 0$, and $1 \times 1 = 1$. The products 0 and 1 are both in the original set, and they represent all possible products of the original numbers in the set. The set $\{0, 1\}$ is not closed under addition, however, because $1 + 1 = 2$, and the sum 2 is a number that is not in the original set. Finding one counterexample (the sum 2) is sufficient to prove that a set is not closed under an operation (addition in this case).

Simplifying Expressions with Rational Exponents and Radicals   **648**

EXPLAIN 1

Simplifying Multivariable Expressions Containing Radicals

QUESTIONING STRATEGIES

? Why do you sometimes simplify an expression containing a radical by changing it to an expression with a rational exponent and then back to a radical? Changing it to an expression with a rational exponent allows you to simplify the exponent. If the simplified exponent is a fraction, convert back to the radical. This makes it easier to evaluate.

AVOID COMMON ERRORS

Students may assume that there is an addition of powers property. Emphasize that the property that involves addition of exponents is the Product of Powers Property. Remind them that $3^2 + 3^3 = 9 + 27 = 36$, but $3^5 = 243$.

Reflect

1. Prove that the product of two rational numbers is a rational number by confirming the general case.
   Let p, q, r, and s be integers with $q \neq 0$ and $s \neq 0$. Then $\frac{p}{q}$ and $\frac{r}{s}$ are rational numbers by definition.

   $$\frac{p}{q} \cdot \frac{r}{s} = \frac{pr}{qs}$$

   We know that pr and qs are integers because the product of integer factors is an integer and $qs \neq 0$ because $q \neq 0$ and $s \neq 0$.

   Thus, $\frac{pr}{qs}$ is a rational number and therefore, the product of two rational numbers is also a rational number.

2. **Discussion** Consider the following statement: The product of two rational numbers is an irrational number. Is it a true statement? Justify your answer.
   The statement is false. An irrational number is defined as a number that is not rational.

   In the previous proof, we demonstrated that the product of two rational numbers is always rational. Since a number can only be irrational if it is not rational, the statement must be false.

⚙ Explain 1 Simplifying Multivariable Expressions Containing Radicals

As you have seen, to simplify expressions containing radicals, you can rewrite the expressions as powers with rational exponents. You can use properties of exponents. You have already seen the Power of a Power Property of exponents. There are additional properties of exponents that are suggested by the following examples.

$$2^2 \cdot 2^3 = (2 \cdot 2)(2 \cdot 2 \cdot 2) = 2^5 = 2^{2+3}$$

$$\frac{2^3}{2^2} = \frac{2 \cdot 2 \cdot 2}{2 \cdot 2} = 2^1 = 2^{3-2}$$

$$(2 \cdot 3)^2 = (2 \cdot 3)(2 \cdot 3) = (2 \cdot 2)(3 \cdot 3) = 2^2 \cdot 3^2$$

$$\left(\frac{2}{3}\right)^2 = \frac{2}{3} \cdot \frac{2}{3} = \frac{2 \cdot 2}{3 \cdot 3} = \frac{2^2}{3^2}$$

$$(2^3)^2 = (2 \cdot 2 \cdot 2)^2 = (2 \cdot 2 \cdot 2)(2 \cdot 2 \cdot 2) = 2^6 = 2^{2 \cdot 3}$$

These relationships are formalized in the table on the following page.

COLLABORATIVE LEARNING

Small Group Activity

Have students work in small groups. Give students a problem such as $\left(\sqrt[10]{25}\right)^5$. Have one student do the first simplification step and explain the property used, then pass the paper to the next student, who carries out and explains the second step. Continue this process until students have solved the problem. Continue with a new problem and new beginning student. Solution:

$$\left(\sqrt[10]{25}\right)^5 = \left(25^{\frac{1}{10}}\right)^5 = 25^{\frac{1}{10} \cdot \frac{5}{1}} = 25^{\frac{1}{2}} = \sqrt{25} = 5$$

Previous lessons have covered the properties of integer exponents. A natural extension of this is to ask if a number can be raised to an exponent that is a rational number. The answer is yes. If we define $a^{\frac{1}{n}} = \sqrt[n]{a}$ where n is an integer and $n \neq 0$, we can demonstrate that $a^{\frac{m}{n}} = (\sqrt[n]{a})^m$ when m and n are integers and $n \neq 0$.

$$a^{\frac{m}{n}} = a^{\frac{1}{n} \cdot m} = \left(a^{\frac{1}{n}}\right)^m = (\sqrt[n]{a})^m$$

Notice that $\sqrt[n]{a}$ is not defined if n is even and $a < 0$.

Properties of Exponents	
Let a and b be real numbers and m and n be rational numbers.	
Product of Powers Property	$a^m \cdot a^n = a^{m+n}$
Quotient of Powers Property	$\dfrac{a^m}{a^n} = a^{m-n}, a \neq 0$
Power of a Product Property	$(a \cdot b)^n = a^n \cdot b^n$
Power of a Quotient Property	$\left(\dfrac{a}{b}\right)^n = \dfrac{a^n}{b^n}, b \neq 0$
Power of a Power Property	$(a^m)^n = a^{mn}$

Example 1 Simplify each expression. Assume all variables are positive.

(A) $\sqrt[3]{(xy)^9}$

$\sqrt[3]{(xy)^9} = (xy)^{\frac{9}{3}}$ Rewrite using rational exponent.

$= (xy)^3$ Simplify the fraction in the exponent.

$= x^3 y^3$ Power of a Product Property

(B) $\sqrt[5]{x} \sqrt{x}$

$\sqrt[5]{x} \sqrt{x} = x^{\boxed{\frac{1}{5}}} x^{\frac{1}{2}}$ Rewrite using rational exponents.

$= x^{\boxed{\frac{1}{5} + \frac{1}{2}}}$ Product of Powers Property

$= x^{\boxed{\frac{7}{10}}}$ Simplify the exponent.

$= \sqrt[\boxed{10}]{x^{\boxed{7}}}$ Rewrite the expression in radical form.

Reflect

3. **Discussion** Why is $\sqrt[n]{a}$ not defined when n is even and $a < 0$?
By the definition of an nth root, $(\sqrt[n]{a})^n = a$. If n is even, this expression must be nonnegative, because any number raised to an even power is nonnegative. Therefore, a cannot be negative.

4. Rewrite the expression $\sqrt[-n]{a}$ so that n has a coefficient of 1. Then state the conditions under which the expression is undefined.
$\sqrt[-n]{a} = a^{\left(\frac{1}{-n}\right)} = a^{-\left(\frac{1}{n}\right)} = \dfrac{1}{a^{\left(\frac{1}{n}\right)}} = \dfrac{1}{\sqrt[n]{a}}$. The expression is undefined when $n = 0$ or when $a < 0$ and n is even.

DIFFERENTIATE INSTRUCTION

Kinesthetic Experience

Have students write each property of rational exponents on a separate index card. Distribute problems written on index cards to each student. Have students arrange the properties that they use in the order in which they used them to solve the problem.

EXPLAIN 2

Simplifying Multivariable Expressions Containing Rational Exponents

INTEGRATE MATHEMATICAL PRACTICES
Focus on Patterns

MP.8 Help students recognize that all problems with radicals and rational exponents can be related to a pattern that is shown in the basic equivalence $b^{\frac{m}{n}} = \sqrt[n]{b^m}$. Students can use this basic pattern to convert back and forth through different forms of expressions, making problem solving quick and efficient.

QUESTIONING STRATEGIES

? What property are you using when you change $(xy)^2$ to $x^2 y^2$? the Power of a Product Property

? What property allows you to write $x^{\frac{1}{2}} \cdot x^{\frac{1}{3}}$ as $x^{\frac{1}{2}+\frac{1}{3}}$? the Product of Powers Property

AVOID COMMON ERRORS

When evaluating an expression such as $12x^{\frac{3}{5}}$, students may multiply by 12 before evaluating the fifth root of x. Remind students of the order of operations: grouping symbols, exponents, multiply/divide, add/subtract. Remind them that radical signs are grouping symbols.

Simplify each expression. Assume all variables are positive.

5. $\left(x^2 y\right)^2 \sqrt[4]{y^4}$

$$x^2 y^2 \ \sqrt[4]{y^4} = x^4 \cdot y^2 \cdot y^{\frac{4}{4}}$$
$$= x^4 \cdot y^{2+1}$$
$$= x^4 y^3$$

6. $\dfrac{\sqrt[4]{x^8}}{\sqrt[4]{x^6}}$

$$\frac{\sqrt[4]{x^8}}{\sqrt[4]{x^6}} = \frac{x^{\frac{8}{4}}}{x^{\frac{6}{4}}}$$
$$= \frac{x^2}{x^{\frac{3}{2}}}$$
$$= x^{2-\frac{3}{2}}$$
$$= x^{\frac{1}{2}}$$
$$= \sqrt{x}$$

Explain 2   Simplifying Multivariable Expressions Containing Rational Exponents

Use Properties of Rational Exponents to simplify expressions.

Example 2   Simplify each expression. Assume all variables are positive.

Ⓐ $\left(8x^9\right)^{\frac{2}{3}}$

$$\left(8x^9\right)^{\frac{2}{3}} = \left(2^3\right)^{\frac{2}{3}}\left(x^9\right)^{\frac{2}{3}} \qquad \text{Power of a Product Property}$$
$$= 2^{\left(3\cdot\frac{2}{3}\right)} x^{\left(9\cdot\frac{2}{3}\right)} \qquad \text{Power of a Power Property}$$
$$= 2^2 x^6 \qquad \text{Simplify within the parentheses.}$$
$$= 4x^6 \qquad \text{Simplify.}$$

Ⓑ $\left(64x^{12}\right)^{\frac{1}{6}}$

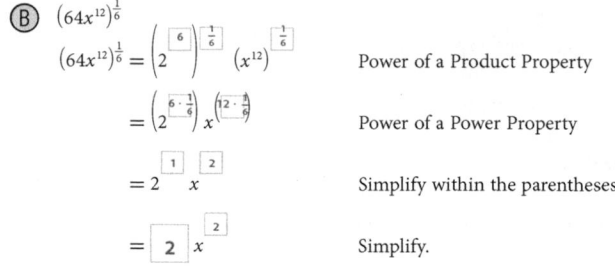

$$\left(64x^{12}\right)^{\frac{1}{6}} = \left(2^{\boxed{6}}\right)^{\boxed{\frac{1}{6}}}\left(x^{12}\right)^{\boxed{\frac{1}{6}}} \qquad \text{Power of a Product Property}$$
$$= \left(2^{\boxed{6\cdot\frac{1}{6}}}\right) x^{\boxed{12\cdot\frac{1}{6}}} \qquad \text{Power of a Power Property}$$
$$= 2^{\boxed{1}} x^{\boxed{2}} \qquad \text{Simplify within the parentheses.}$$
$$= \boxed{2}\, x^{\boxed{2}} \qquad \text{Simplify.}$$

Reflect

7. Simplify $\left(8x^9\right)^{-\frac{2}{3}}$. How is it related to the simplified form of $\left(8x^9\right)^{\frac{2}{3}}$ found in example 2A? Verify the relationship if one exists.

$$\left(8x^9\right)^{-\frac{2}{3}} = \left(2^3\right)^{\frac{-2}{3}}\left(x^9\right)^{-\frac{2}{3}} \qquad \frac{1}{4x^6} \text{ and } 4x^6 \text{ are reciprocals so } \left(8x^9\right)^{-\frac{2}{3}} \text{ and } \left(8x^9\right)^{\frac{2}{3}} \text{ are reciprocals.}$$
$$= 2^{-2} x^{-6} \qquad\qquad \left(8x^9\right)^{-\frac{2}{3}}\left(8x^9\right)^{\frac{2}{3}} = \left(8x^9\right)^{\left(-\frac{2}{3}+\frac{2}{3}\right)}$$
$$= \frac{1}{4x^6} \qquad\qquad\qquad\qquad = \left(8x^9\right)^0$$
$$\qquad\qquad\qquad\qquad\qquad\qquad = 1$$

Your Turn

Simplify each expression. Assume all variables are positive.

8. $\left(\dfrac{1}{4x^4} \cdot x^{12}\right)^{-\frac{1}{2}}$

$$\left(\dfrac{1}{4x^4} \cdot x^{12}\right)^{-\frac{1}{2}} = \left(2^{-2}\,x^{-4}\,x^{12}\right)^{-\frac{1}{2}}$$
$$= \left(2^{-2}\,x^{8}\right)^{-\frac{1}{2}}$$
$$= \left(2^{-2}\right)^{-\frac{1}{2}} \left(x^{8}\right)^{-\frac{1}{2}}$$
$$= 2^{-2\left(-\frac{1}{2}\right)}\,x^{\,8\left(-\frac{1}{2}\right)}$$
$$= 2^{1}\,x^{-4}$$
$$= \dfrac{2}{x^4}$$

9. $\left(\dfrac{1}{9x^{12}} \cdot x^{4}\right)^{\frac{1}{2}}$

$$\left(\dfrac{1}{9x^{12}} \cdot x^{4}\right)^{\frac{1}{2}} = \left(3^{-2}\,x^{-12}\,x^{4}\right)^{\frac{1}{2}}$$
$$= \left(3^{-2}\,x^{-8}\right)^{\frac{1}{2}}$$
$$= \left[\left(3^{1}\,x^{4}\right)^{-2}\right]^{\frac{1}{2}}$$
$$= \left(3x^{4}\right)^{-1}$$
$$= \dfrac{1}{3x^4}$$

⚙ Explain 3 · Simplifying Real-World Expressions with Rational Exponents

The relationship between some real-world quantities can be more complicated than a linear or quadratic model can accurately represent. Sometimes, in the most accurate model, the dependent variable is a function of the independent variable raised to a rational exponent. Use the properties of rational exponents to solve the following real world scenarios.

Example 3 Biology Application The approximate number of Calories C that an animal needs each day is given by $C = 72m^{\frac{3}{4}}$, where m is the animal's mass in kilograms.

(A) Find the number of Calories that a 625 kg bear needs each day.
To solve this, evaluate the equation when $m = 625$.

$$C = 72m^{\frac{3}{4}}$$
$$= 72(625)^{\frac{3}{4}} \qquad \text{Substitute 625 for } m.$$
$$= 72\left(\sqrt[4]{625}\right)^{3}$$
$$= 72\left(\sqrt[4]{5^4}\right)^{3} \qquad \text{Definition of } b^{\frac{m}{n}}$$
$$= 72(5)^{3}$$
$$= 72(125) = 9000$$

A 625 kilogram bear needs 9000 Calories each day.

© Houghton Mifflin Harcourt Publishing Company

EXPLAIN 3

Simplifying Real-World Expressions with Rational Exponents

QUESTIONING STRATEGY

? When you convert between radical form and rational exponent form, what are the restrictions on the radicand and index? Conversions are done for all real numbers for which the radical is defined. The index must be a positive integer and the power of the radicand must be an integer.

? What do you need to do if the units in your equation do not match the units in the real-world quantity you need to substitute into the equation? Use a conversion factor, such as 1 foot $=$ 12 inches, before substituting.

LANGUAGE SUPPORT EL

Connect Vocabulary

English learners may know the common meaning of some of the key vocabulary in this lesson. Words such as *power, expression, real, rational,* and *property* have common meanings in everyday use. When learning vocabulary in a new language, students benefit from many repetitions and some supporting context to help them sort out and remember the math meanings. You may wish to have students draw pictures or diagrams that represent the everyday meaning and math meaning of each term.

(B) A particular panda consumes 1944 Calories each day. How much does this panda weigh?

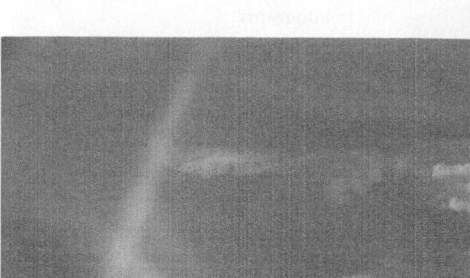

Substitute $\boxed{1944}$ for C in the original equation and solve for m.

$$C = 72m^{\frac{3}{4}} \qquad \text{Original equation}$$

$$\boxed{1944} = 72m^{\frac{3}{4}} \qquad \text{Substitute for } C.$$

$$\frac{\boxed{1944}}{72} = m^{\frac{3}{4}} \qquad \text{Divide each side by 72.}$$

$$\boxed{27} = m^{\frac{3}{4}} \qquad \text{Simplify.}$$

$$3^3 = m^{\frac{3}{4}} \qquad \text{Rewrite the left side as a power.}$$

$$\left(3^3\right)^{\boxed{\frac{4}{3}}} = \left(m^{\frac{3}{4}}\right)^{\boxed{\frac{4}{3}}} \qquad \text{Raise both sides to the } \boxed{\frac{4}{3}} \text{ power.}$$

$$3^{\left(3 \cdot \boxed{\frac{4}{3}}\right)} = m^{\left(\frac{3}{4} \cdot \boxed{\frac{4}{3}}\right)} \qquad \text{Power of a Power Property}$$

$$3^4 = m \qquad \text{Simplify inside the parentheses.}$$

$$m = \boxed{81} \qquad \text{Simplify.}$$

The panda weighs $\boxed{81}$ kilograms.

Your Turn

Solve each real-world scenario.

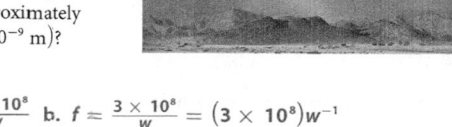

10. The speed of light is the product of its frequency f and its wavelength w. In air, the speed of light is 3×10^8 m/s.

   a. Write an equation for the relationship described above, and then solve this equation for frequency.

   b. Rewrite this equation with w raised to a negative exponent.

   c. What is the frequency of violet light when its wavelength is approximately 400 nanometers $(1 \text{ nm} = 10^{-9} \text{ m})$?

a. $3 \times 10^8 = fw \Rightarrow f = \frac{3 \times 10^8}{w}$ **b.** $f = \frac{3 \times 10^8}{w} = \left(3 \times 10^8\right)w^{-1}$

c. $w = 400 \text{ nm}\left(\frac{1 \text{ m}}{10^9 \text{ nm}}\right) = \frac{400}{10^9}\text{m} = \frac{4 \times 10^2}{10^9}\text{ m} = 4 \times 10^{-7}\text{ m}$

$f = \left(3 \times 10^8\right)w^{-1} = \left(3 \times 10^8\right)\left(4 \times 10^{-7}\right)^{-1} = \frac{3 \times 10^8}{4 \times 10^{-7}} = 0.75 \times 10^{15} = 7.5 \times 10^{14}$

The frequency of violet light with a wavelength of 400 nanometers is 7.5×10^{14} cycles per second.

11. Geometry The formula for the surface area of a sphere S in terms of its volume V is $S = (4\pi)^{\frac{1}{3}}(3V)^{\frac{2}{3}}$. What is the surface area of a sphere that has a volume of 36π cm cubed? Leave the answer in terms of π. What do you notice?

$$S = (4\pi)^{\frac{1}{3}}(3V)^{\frac{2}{3}}$$

$$= (4\pi)^{\frac{1}{3}}\left[3(36\pi)\right]^{\frac{2}{3}}$$

$$= (4\pi)^{\frac{1}{3}}\left[3(3 \cdot 3 \cdot 4 \cdot \pi)\right]^{\frac{2}{3}}$$

$$= (4\pi)^{\frac{1}{3}} \cdot 3^{3 \cdot \frac{2}{3}} \cdot (4\pi)^{\frac{2}{3}}$$

$$= (4\pi)^{\frac{1}{3}} \cdot 3^{2} \cdot (4\pi)^{\frac{2}{3}}$$

$$= 9 \cdot 4\pi$$

$$= 36\pi$$

The sphere has surface area of 36π cm squared. While the units are different, the number is the same.

💬 Elaborate

12. A set of elements is said to be closed under some operation if performance of that operation on elements of the set always produces an element of the set. Examine the set of integers and the set of rational numbers. Is each set closed under each of the following operations: addition, multiplication, division, and subtraction? Provide a counterexample if the set is not closed under an operation.

Addition, multiplication, and subtraction are closed over both the integers and the

rational numbers. Division is not closed over the integers or the rational numbers. Zero is

an element of each set, and for each set, division by zero is undefined. A second counter

example for integers is $\frac{1}{2}$. Both 1 and 2 are integers but $\frac{1}{2}$ is not.

13. Why are integers closed under multiplication?

For integers, multiplication is defined as a sum. For integers a and b, $ab = \dfrac{\overbrace{a + \cdots + a}}{b}$. If

integers are closed under addition, they will be closed under multiplication.

14. Is the set of all numbers of the form a^x, where a is a positive constant and x is a rational number, closed under multiplication? Justify your answer.

Yes. By the Product of Powers Property, $a^{x_1} \cdot a^{x_2} = a^{(x_1 + x_2)}$. $x_1 + x_2$ is rational because the

rational numbers are closed under addition. Therefore, $a^{(x_1 + x_2)}$ belongs to the given set by

the definition of the set.

15. Essential Question Check-In How can you write a radical expression as a power with a rational exponent?

You can write a radical expression as an expression with a rational exponent by extending

the properties of integer exponents. Rational exponents and radicals are related by the

formula $a^{\frac{m}{n}} = \sqrt[n]{a^m} = \left(\sqrt[n]{a}\right)^m$, $n \neq 0$, $a > 0$ for even n.

© Houghton Mifflin Harcourt Publishing Company

ELABORATE

QUESTIONING STRATEGIES

? Is the following equation correct? $\sqrt[3]{b^3} = 1$. Explain. **No, cubing a number and taking the cube root are inverse operations that undo each other, so $\sqrt[3]{b^3} = b$. The equation is true when $b = 1$.**

SUMMARIZE THE LESSON

? What properties can you use to write a radical expression as an expression with a rational exponent? **the Product of Powers, Quotient of Powers, Power of a Product, Power of a Quotient, Power of a Power, and Negative Exponent properties**

EVALUATE

ASSIGNMENT GUIDE

Concept and Skills	Practice
Explore Exploring Operations with Rational and Irrational Numbers	Exercises 1–2, 27–30
Example 1 Simplifying Multivariable Expressions Containing Radicals	Exercises 3–8
Example 2 Simplifying Multivariable Expressions Containing Rational Exponents	Exercises 9–22, 31
Example 3 Simplifying Real-World Expressions with Rational Exponents	Exercises 23–26

INTEGRATE MATHEMATICAL PRACTICES

Focus on Reasoning

MP.2 Encourage students to estimate answers for each problem. For example, if a rational exponent is less than 1, the answer will be less than the base. If the rational exponent is greater than 1, the answer will be greater than the base.

INTEGRATE MATHEMATICAL PRACTICES

Focus on Technology

MP.5 Remind students that they can enter fractional exponents on their calculators for evaluation, but they must use parentheses. For example, if they are trying to evaluate $15^{\frac{4}{5}}$, they must put parentheses around the $\frac{4}{5}$. Without the parentheses, the calculator will evaluate $\left(15^4\right) \div 5$.

⭐ Evaluate: Homework and Practice

• Online Homework
• Hints and Help
• Extra Practice

1. Why are the addition and multiplication tables in the Explore activity symmetric about the diagonal from the upper-left corner to the lower-right? For example, why is the entry in the third row of the second column equal to the entry in the second row of the third column? Would a subtraction table be symmetric about the same diagonal?

   Addition and multiplication are commutative. A subtraction table would not be symmetric because subtraction is not commutative.

2. Prove that the rational numbers are closed under addition.

   Let p, q, r, and s be integers with $q \neq 0$ and $s \neq 0$. Then $\frac{p}{q}$ and $\frac{r}{s}$ are rational numbers by definition.

   $$\frac{p}{q} + \frac{r}{s} = \frac{p \cdot s + q \cdot r}{q \cdot s}$$

   We know that ps, qr, and qs are integers because the product of integer factors is an integer, $p \cdot s + q \cdot r$ is also an integer because integers are closed under addition, and $qs \neq 0$ because $q \neq 0$ and $s \neq 0$.

   Thus, $\frac{p \cdot s + q \cdot r}{q \cdot s}$ is a rational number and therefore, the sum of two rational numbers is a rational number.

Simplify the given expression.

3. $\sqrt[3]{\left(27x^3\right)^4}$
   $= \left(27x^3\right)^{\frac{4}{3}}$
   $= \left(3^3 x^3\right)^{\frac{4}{3}}$
   $= \left(\left(3x\right)^3\right)^{\frac{4}{3}}$
   $= \left(3x\right)^{\left(3 \cdot \frac{4}{3}\right)}$
   $= \left(3x\right)^4$
   $= 81x^4$

4. $\sqrt[3]{\left(8x^3\right)^2}$
   $= \left(8x^3\right)^{\frac{2}{3}}$
   $= \left(2^3 x^3\right)^{\frac{2}{3}}$
   $= \left(\left(2x\right)^3\right)^{\frac{2}{3}}$
   $= \left(2x\right)^{\left(3 \cdot \frac{2}{3}\right)}$
   $= \left(2x\right)^2$
   $= 4x^2$

5. $\sqrt[3]{\left(8y^3\right)^4} \sqrt[6]{\left(8y^3\right)^4}$
   $= \left(8y^3\right)^{\frac{4}{3}} \left(8y^3\right)^{\frac{4}{6}}$
   $= \left(2^3 y^3\right)^{\frac{4}{3}} \left(2^3 y^3\right)^{\frac{2}{3}}$
   $= \left(\left(2y\right)^3\right)^{\frac{4}{3}} \left(\left(2y\right)^3\right)^{\frac{2}{3}}$
   $= \left(\left(2y\right)^3\right)^{\frac{4}{3} + \frac{2}{3}}$
   $= \left(\left(2y\right)^3\right)^2$
   $= \left(2y\right)^6$
   $= 64y^6$

6. $\sqrt[10]{0x}$
   $= 0$

7. $\sqrt{\left(2x\right)^2 \sqrt{2y}}$
   $= \left(\left(2x\right)^2 \left(2y\right)^{\frac{1}{2}}\right)^{\frac{1}{2}}$
   $= \left(\left(2x\right)^2\right)^{\frac{1}{2}} \left(\left(2y\right)^{\frac{1}{2}}\right)^{\frac{1}{2}}$
   $= \left(2x\right)^1 \left(2y\right)^{\frac{1}{4}}$
   $= 2x \sqrt[4]{2y}$

8. $\dfrac{\sqrt{8x}}{\sqrt[3]{16x^2}}$
   $= \dfrac{\left(4 \cdot 2x\right)^{\frac{1}{2}}}{\left(8 \cdot 2x\right)^{\frac{1}{3}}}$
   $= \dfrac{4^{\frac{1}{2}} \cdot \left(2x\right)^{\frac{1}{2}}}{8^{\frac{1}{3}} \cdot \left(2x\right)^{\frac{1}{3}}}$
   $= \dfrac{2}{2} \cdot \left(2x\right)^{\frac{1}{2} - \frac{1}{3}}$
   $= \left(2x\right)^{\frac{1}{6}}$
   $= \sqrt[6]{2x}$

Exercise	Depth of Knowledge (D.O.K.)	COMMON CORE Mathematical Practices
1	**1** Recall of Information	**MP.3** Logic
2	**2** Skills/Concepts	**MP.3** Logic
3–6	**1** Recall of Information	**MP.2** Reasoning
7–22	**2** Skills/Concepts	**MP.2** Reasoning
23–26	**2** Skills/Concepts	**MP.4** Modeling
27	**2** Skills/Concepts	**MP.2** Reasoning
28–31	**3** Strategic Thinking H.O.T.	**MP.3** Logic

9. $(0x)^{\frac{1}{3}}$

$= 0$

10. $10,000^{\frac{1}{4}} \cdot z + 10,000^{\frac{1}{2}} \cdot z$

$= \left(10,000^{\frac{1}{4}} + 10,000^{\frac{1}{2}}\right) z$

$= \left((10^4)^{\frac{1}{4}} + (10^4)^{\frac{1}{2}}\right) z$

$= \left(10^{\frac{4}{4}} + 10^{\frac{4}{2}}\right) z$

$= (10 + 10^2) z$

$= (10 + 100) z$

$= 110 z$

11. $\left(\frac{1}{25x} \cdot x^9\right)^{-\frac{1}{2}}$

$= (5^{-2} x^{-1} x^9)^{-\frac{1}{2}}$

$= (5^{-2} x^8)^{-\frac{1}{2}}$

$= (5^{-2})^{-\frac{1}{2}} (x^8)^{-\frac{1}{2}}$

$= 5^{\left(-2\left(-\frac{1}{2}\right)\right)} x^{\left(8\left(-\frac{1}{2}\right)\right)}$

$= 5x^{-4}$

$= \frac{5}{x^4}$

12. $\left(\frac{1}{125x^3}\right)^{-\frac{1}{3}}$

$= \left(\frac{1}{5^3 x^3}\right)^{-\frac{1}{3}}$

$= \left((5x)^{-3}\right)^{-\frac{1}{3}}$

$= (5x)^{-3\left(-\frac{1}{3}\right)}$

$= (5x)^1$

$= 5x$

13. $\left[(2x)^x (2x)^{2x}\right]^{\frac{1}{x}}$

$= \left[(2x)^{x+2x}\right]^{\frac{1}{x}}$

$= \left[(2x)^{3x}\right]^{\frac{1}{x}}$

$= (2x)^3$

$= 8x^3$

14. $\left[(1,000,000x^6)^{-\frac{1}{3}}\right]^{-\frac{1}{2}}$

$= (10^6 x^6)^{\left(-\frac{1}{3} \cdot -\frac{1}{2}\right)}$

$= 10x^{\left(6 \cdot \frac{1}{3} \cdot \frac{1}{2}\right)} = 10x$

15. $(x^2 y)^3 \sqrt[2]{y^4}$

$= x^6 \cdot y^3 \cdot y^{\frac{4}{2}}$

$= x^6 \cdot y^3 \cdot y^2$

$= x^6 y^5$

16. $\dfrac{\left[(x^2 y)^4\right]^{\frac{1}{2}}}{\left[(x^2 y)^{\frac{1}{2}}\right]^4}$

$= \dfrac{(x^2 y)^{\left(4 \cdot \frac{1}{2}\right)}}{(x^2 y)^{\left(\frac{1}{2} \cdot 4\right)}}$

$= \dfrac{(x^2 y)^2}{(x^2 y)^2}$

$= 1$

17. $\left(x^{\frac{1}{8}} y^{\frac{1}{4}} z^{\frac{1}{2}}\right)^8$

$= x^{8 \cdot \frac{1}{8}} y^{8 \cdot \frac{1}{4}} z^{8 \cdot \frac{1}{2}} = xy^2 z^4$

18. $\left(\sqrt{z\sqrt{y\sqrt{x}}}\right)^8$

$= \left(\left(z\sqrt{y\sqrt{x}}\right)^{\frac{1}{2}}\right)^8$

$= \left(z\sqrt{y\sqrt{x}}\right)^4$

$= z^4 \left(\sqrt{y\sqrt{x}}\right)^4$

$= z^4 \left(\left(y\sqrt{x}\right)^{\frac{1}{2}}\right)^4$

$= z^4 \left(y\sqrt{x}\right)^2$

$= z^4 y^2 \left(\sqrt{x}\right)^2$

$= z^4 y^2 x$

19. $\dfrac{(x^{10})^{\frac{1}{5}}}{\sqrt[2]{x^8}}$

$= \dfrac{x^{10 \cdot \frac{1}{5}}}{x^{\frac{8}{2}}}$

$= \dfrac{x^2}{x^4}$

$= x^{2-4}$

$= x^{-2}$

$= \dfrac{1}{x^2}$

20. $\dfrac{\left[(x^{-8})^{\frac{1}{4}}\right]^{-1} \sqrt[3]{x^2}}{\sqrt[6]{x^4}}$

$= \dfrac{(x^{-8})^{-\frac{1}{4}} x^{\frac{2}{3}}}{x^{\frac{4}{6}}}$

$= x^{-8\left(-\frac{1}{4}\right)} x^{\frac{2}{3}} x^{-\frac{4}{6}}$

$= x^2 x^{\frac{2}{3}} x^{-\frac{2}{3}}$

$= x^{2 + \frac{2}{3} - \frac{2}{3}}$

$= x^2$

© Houghton Mifflin Harcourt Publishing Company

AVOID COMMON ERRORS

Students may think that an expression such as $72m^{\frac{3}{4}}$ is equivalent to $72^{\frac{3}{4}} \cdot m^{\frac{3}{4}}$. Point out that the exponent does not distribute over both m and 72 unless there are parentheses, such as $(72m)^{\frac{3}{4}}$. In the original example, only the variable m is raised to the $\frac{3}{4}$ power.

GRAPHIC ORGANIZER

To help students learn the properties of rational exponents, you may want to have students make a graphic organizer by copying the table and adding a column that includes examples of each property. Students can then quickly refer to the table as they begin each problem.

21. $\left(x^2y\right)^4\left(\sqrt{y^{\frac{1}{2}}}\right)$

$= x^8y^4\left(y^{\frac{1}{2}}\right)^{\frac{1}{2}}$

$= x^8y^4y^{\frac{1}{4}}$

$= x^8y^4\sqrt[4]{y}$

22. $\left(\sqrt{y^{\frac{1}{4}}}\right)^8$

$= \left(\left(y^{\frac{1}{4}}\right)^{\frac{1}{2}}\right)^8$

$= y^{\frac{1}{4}\cdot\frac{1}{2}\cdot 8}$

$= y$

23. Biology Biologists use a formula to estimate the mass of a mammal's brain. For a mammal with a mass of m grams, the approximate mass B of the brain, also in grams, is given by $B = \frac{1}{8}m^{\frac{2}{3}}$. Find the approximate mass of the brain of a mouse that has a mass of 64 grams.

$B = \frac{1}{8}m^{\frac{2}{3}}$

$= \frac{1}{8}(64)^{\frac{2}{3}}$

$= \frac{1}{2^3}(2^6)^{\frac{2}{3}}$

$= 2^{-3}2^{6\cdot\left(\frac{2}{3}\right)}$

$= 2^{-3}2^4$

$= 2$

The brain of the mouse has an approximate mass of 2 grams.

24. Multi-Step Scientists have found that the life span of a mammal living in captivity is related to the mammal's mass. The life span in years L can be approximated by the formula $L = 12m^{\frac{1}{5}}$, where m is the mammal's mass in kilograms. How much longer is the life span of a lion compared with that of a wolf?

Typical Mass of Mammals	
Mammal	**Mass (kg)**
Koala	8
Wolf	32
Lion	243
Giraffe	1024

Let L_L represent the life span of a lion and L_W represent the lifespan of a wolf. In captivity, the lifespan of a lion is 12 years longer than that of a wolf.

Find $L_L - L_W$.

$L_L - L_W = 12m_L^{\frac{1}{5}} - 12m_W^{\frac{1}{5}}$

$= 12\left(m_L^{\frac{1}{5}} - m_W^{\frac{1}{5}}\right)$

$= 12\left(243^{\frac{1}{5}} - 32^{\frac{1}{5}}\right)$

$= 12\left(\left(3^5\right)^{\frac{1}{5}} - \left(2^5\right)^{\frac{1}{5}}\right)$

$= 12\left(3^{5\cdot\frac{1}{5}} - 2^{5\cdot\frac{1}{5}}\right)$

$= 12(3-2)$

$= 12$

Tim and Tom are painters. Use the given information to provide the desired estimate.

25. Tim and Tom use a liters of paint on a large shipping crate. If the next crate they need to paint is similar but has twice the volume, how much paint should they plan on buying?

The amount of paint used is directly proportional to the surface area of the crate. The larger crate has twice the volume of the smaller crate which means that the length scale is $\sqrt[3]{2}:1$. The ratio of the surface areas of the crates is the square of the length scale: $\left(\sqrt[3]{2}\right)^2:1$.

Simplifying, we get the ratio $\sqrt[3]{4}:1 \approx 1.59$.

They should plan on buying approximately 1.59a liters of paint.

26. Tim and Tom are painting a crate. Tom paints 10 square feet per minute. They painted a particular crate in 1 day. Tim uses a sprayer and is 4.7 times as fast as Tom. How long would it take them to paint a crate with twice the volume and of similar shape?

The product of the rate of work and the time it takes for them to do a job is the amount of work: $r_1t + r_2t = (r_1 + r_2)t = W$, where r_1 and r_2 are their rates of work. The W is in units of surface area painted. If you increase the work by a factor of 1.59, the time would increase by that factor. It will take them 1.59 days to paint the bigger crate. The rest of the given information is not important.

27. Determine whether each of the following are rational or irrational. Select the correct answer for each lettered part.

a. The product of $\sqrt{2}$ and $\sqrt{50}$ ● Rational   ○ Irrational

b. The product of $\sqrt{2}$ and $\sqrt{25}$ ○ Rational   ● Irrational

c. $C = 2\pi r$ evaluated for $r = \pi^{-1}$ ● Rational   ○ Irrational

d. $C = 2\pi r$ evaluated for $r = 1$ ○ Rational   ● Irrational

e. $A = 2\pi r^2$ evaluated for $r = \pi^{\frac{1}{2}}$ ○ Rational   ● Irrational

f. The product of $\sqrt{\frac{2}{\pi}}$ and $\sqrt{50\pi}$ ● Rational   ○ Irrational

g. The product of $\sqrt{2}$ and $\sqrt{\frac{9}{2}}$ ● Rational   ○ Irrational

QUESTIONING STRATEGIES

? How would you simplify the expression $27\left(x^9\right)^{\frac{2}{3}}$? Explain. The rational exponent would apply only to the variable part, x^9. Multiply the exponents and simplify. The final answer would be $27x^6$.

AVOID COMMON ERRORS

Students may confuse the Product Rule of Exponents, $a^m \cdot a^n$, with the Power Rule of Exponents, $\left(a^m\right)^n$. Remind them to add exponents for $a^m \cdot a^n$, and multiply exponents for $\left(a^m\right)^n$. If they forget, suggest they write both rules again, as a reference.

JOURNAL

Give each student a cut-up, scrambled copy of the tables of properties of real numbers and of rational exponents. Have students reassemble each table correctly without looking at the tables in the lesson.

28. Explain the Error Jim tried to show how to write a radical expression as a power with a rational exponent.

Suppose that $-\sqrt[n]{a} = a^k$.

$\left(-\sqrt[n]{a}\right)^n = \left(a^k\right)^n$	Raise each side to the nth power.
$a = \left(a^k\right)^n$	Definition of nth root
$a = a^{kn}$	Power of a Power Property
$a^1 = a^{kn}$	
$1 = kn$	Equate exponents.
$k = \dfrac{1}{n}$	Solve for k.

Jim claimed to have shown that $\sqrt[n]{a} = a^{\frac{1}{n}}$. Explain and correct his error.

Jim started with $-\sqrt[n]{a}$, and $\left(-\sqrt[n]{a}\right)^n = a$ only when n is even. When n is odd, $\left(-\sqrt[n]{a}\right)^n$ $= -a$. To correct the error, change $-\sqrt[n]{a}$ in each of Jim's first two steps to $\sqrt[n]{a}$.

29. What If? Assume the integers are not closed under addition.

a. Are the rational numbers closed under multiplication?

No. The proof of closure under multiplication relies on the integers being closed under addition. If the integers are not closed under addition, they cannot be closed under multiplication. If the integers are not closed under multiplication then there exist integers p, q, r, and s such that pr and qs in the equation $\dfrac{p}{q} \cdot \dfrac{r}{s} = \dfrac{pr}{qs}$ are not integers and as a result $\dfrac{pr}{qs}$ is not rational.

b. Are the rational numbers closed under addition?

No. The proof of this relies on the integers being closed under addition (and multiplication, but that is a consequence of being closed under addition). If the integers are not closed under addition, then there exists integers p, q, r, and s such that $p \cdot s + q \cdot r$ is not an integer, and as a result, $\dfrac{p \cdot s + q \cdot r}{q \cdot s}$ is not rational.

30. Communicate Mathematical Ideas Prove by contradiction that a rational number plus an irrational number is irrational. To do this assume the negation of what you are trying to prove and show how it will logically lead to something contradicting the given. Assume that a rational number plus an irrational number is rational.

$r_1 + i_1 = r_2$	Given
$r_1 + i_1 - r_1 = r_2 - r_1$	Subtract r_1 from both sides.
$i_1 = r_2 - r_1$	Simplify left side.

Provide the contradiction statement to finish the proof.

$r_2 - r_1$ is rational but i_1 is irrational. This contradicts the given so a rational number plus an irrational number is irrational.

31. Critical Thinking Show that a number raised to the $\frac{1}{3}$ power is the same as the cube root of that number.

$\left(\sqrt[3]{x}\right)^3 = x$	Definition of cube root
$\left(x^k\right)^3 = x$	Substitute x^k for $\sqrt[3]{x}$.
$x^{3k} = x^1$	Power of a Power Property
$3k = 1$	Equate the exponents.
$k = \frac{1}{3}$	Solve for k.

Lesson Performance Task

The balls used in soccer, baseball, basketball, and golf are spheres. How much material is needed to make each of the balls in the table?

The formula for the surface area of a sphere is $S_A = 4\pi r^2$ and the formula for the volume of a sphere is $V = \frac{4}{3}\pi r^3$. Use algebra to find the formula for the surface area of a sphere given its volume.

Complete the table with the surface area of each ball.

Ball	Volume (in cubic inches)	Surface Area (in square inches)
soccer ball	356.8	243.3
baseball	12.8	26.5
basketball	455.9	286.5
golf ball	2.48	8.86

$$V = \frac{4}{3}\pi r^3$$
$$\frac{3V}{4\pi} = r^3$$
$$r = \left(\frac{3V}{4\pi}\right)^{\frac{1}{3}}$$

$$S_A = 4\pi r^2$$
$$= 4\pi\left(\left(\frac{3V}{4\pi}\right)^{\frac{1}{3}}\right)^2$$
$$= 4\pi\left(\frac{3V}{4\pi}\right)^{\frac{2}{3}}$$
$$= 4\pi\frac{(3V)^{\frac{2}{3}}}{(4\pi)^{\frac{2}{3}}}$$

$$= 4\pi(4\pi)^{-\frac{2}{3}}(3V)^{\frac{2}{3}}$$
$$= (4\pi)^{\frac{1}{3}}(3V)^{\frac{2}{3}}$$
$$= \pi^{\frac{1}{3}}(6V)^{\frac{2}{3}}$$
$$= \left(36\pi V^2\right)^{\frac{1}{3}}$$

AVOID COMMON ERRORS

Some students may try simplifying the expression $4\pi\left(\left(\frac{3v}{4\pi}\right)^{\frac{1}{3}}\right)^2$ by canceling both 4π terms, thus ignoring the parentheses. Review the order of operations with students. The term 4π on the outside of the parentheses has a power of 1. The term 4π in the denominator, within the parentheses, has a power of $\frac{2}{3}$. Students should look at this as simplifying $\frac{(4\pi)^1}{(4\pi)^{\frac{2}{3}}} \cdot (3v)^{\frac{2}{3}}$

INTEGRATE MATHEMATICAL PRACTICES

Focus on Technology

MP.2 Students can use a calculator to check their solutions for correctness by substituting the values for surface area into the formula $S_A = 4\pi r^2$ to get the value of r^2, take the square root of r^2, and then substitute that value of r into the formula for volume, $V = \frac{4}{3}\pi r^3$. The value found for the volume should come very close to the value for volume given in the table.

EXTENSION ACTIVITY

Have students measure the circumference of a ball, one not used in the Lesson Performance Task. Then have students use $C = 2\pi r$ to calculate that ball's radius, and use the radius to calculate the volume. Finally, have students trade with each other and find the surface area of the other ball, using only the calculated volume.

If students chose a regulation tennis ball, they might discover that it has a radius of about 1.25 inches and a circumference of about 7.9 inches. The surface area would then be about 19.6 square inches and the volume would be about 8.2 cubic inches.

Scoring Rubric

2 points: Student correctly solves the problem and explains his/her reasoning.

1 point: Student shows good understanding of the problem but does not fully solve or explain his/her reasoning.

0 points: Student does not demonstrate understanding of the problem.

Simplifying Expressions with Rational Exponents and Radicals   **660**

Study Guide Review

ASSESSMENT AND INTERVENTION

Assign or customize module reviews.

MODULE PERFORMANCE TASK

COMMON CORE

Mathematical Practices: MP.1, MP.2, MP.4, MP.6, MP.7
N-RN.A.2, S-ID.B.6a

SUPPORTING STUDENT REASONING

Students should begin this problem by checking to see if the formula for reptiles is the same as for mammals. Here are some question they might have.

- **Is the exponent with the variable m the same as for mammals?** Some scientists question this as well. However, they tend to agree that the exponent should be the same for all species. Since $\frac{3}{4}$ was used for mammals, use it for the reptiles, too.

- **What does y stand for?** The variable y stands for the number of Calories required to sustain the animal.

Rational Exponents and Radicals

Essential Question: How can you use rational exponents and radicals to solve real-world problems?

Key Vocabulary
index *(índice)*
radical expression *(expresión radical)*
radicand *(radicando)*
rational exponent *(exponente racional)*

KEY EXAMPLE   (Lesson 14.1)

Evaluate the expression 3^{-4}.

$3^{-4} = \dfrac{1}{3^4}$ Definition of negative exponent

$\quad\ = \dfrac{1}{81}$ Evaluate.

KEY EXAMPLE   (Lesson 14.1)

Simplify $64^{\frac{2}{3}}$.

$64^{\frac{2}{3}} = \left(\sqrt[3]{64}\right)^2$ Definition of $b^{\frac{m}{n}}$

$\quad\ = \left(\sqrt[3]{4^3}\right)^2$ Rewrite radicand as a power.

$\quad\ = 4^2$ Definition of cube root

$\quad\ = 16$

Simplify $128^{-\frac{8}{7}}$.

$128^{-\frac{8}{7}} = \dfrac{1}{\left(\sqrt[7]{128}\right)^8}$ Definition of negative exponent and $b^{\frac{m}{n}}$

$\quad\ = \dfrac{1}{\left(\sqrt[7]{2^7}\right)^8}$ Rewrite radicand as a power.

$\quad\ = \dfrac{1}{2^8}$ Definition of nth root

$\quad\ = \dfrac{1}{256}$

KEY EXAMPLE   (Lesson 14.2)

Simplify $\dfrac{\sqrt[3]{x^8}}{\sqrt[3]{x^6}}$. Assume x is positive.

$\dfrac{\sqrt[3]{x^8}}{\sqrt[3]{x^6}} = \dfrac{x^{\frac{8}{3}}}{x^{\frac{6}{3}}}$

$\qquad = x^{\frac{8}{3} - \frac{6}{3}}$

$\qquad = x^{\frac{2}{3}}$

$\qquad = \sqrt[3]{x^2}$

© Houghton Mifflin Harcourt Publishing Company

SCAFFOLDING SUPPORT

- Some students will stop working once they derive the formula for reptiles. Have them reread the problem to ensure that they have completely answered the question.

- This task could be made more challenging by having students use the mean of all of the reptile types for the constant in the formula.

EXERCISES

Simplify each expression. *(Lesson 14.1)*

1. $25^{\frac{3}{2}}$

   125

2. $81^{\frac{1}{2}} - 16^{\frac{1}{2}}$

   5

3. $27^{\frac{4}{3}}$

   81

4. $8^{\frac{5}{3}} + 4^{\frac{5}{2}}$

   64

Simplify each expression. *(Lesson 14.2)*

5. $1{,}000{,}000^{\frac{1}{3}} \cdot d + 1{,}000{,}000^{\frac{1}{2}} \cdot d$

   $1100d$

6. $\sqrt[3]{(64x^3)^4}$

   $256x^4$

7. $\sqrt[3]{(27x^3)^2}$

   $9x^2$

8. $\left(\dfrac{1}{216x^3}\right)^{-\frac{1}{3}}$

   $6x$

MODULE PERFORMANCE TASK

How Much Should We Feed the Reptiles?

The zoo is expecting a new alligator to arrive in a few days. The previous Reptile Chef fed other species of reptiles currently at the zoo according to the information in the table. You speak with the Mammal Chef, who uses the formula $y = 72m^{\frac{3}{4}}$ to determine the daily Calorie intake for mammals, where y is the number of Calories eaten and m is the mammal's mass in kilograms. You wonder if a similar formula might help determine the number of Calories for the new alligator. Substitute data pairs from the table into the formula to find a number a so that the expression $y = am^{\left(\frac{3}{4}\right)}$ gives the daily number of Calories required by a reptile with a mass of m kilograms.

Reptile Type	Mass	Daily Calories
Bearded Dragon	0.4 kg	5.0
Spur-thighed Tortoise	4.2 kg	29.3
Spectacled Caiman	34 kg	142
Rhinoceros Iguana	7.4 kg	44.9
Giant Tortoise	250 kg	629

If the alligator has a mass of 400 kilograms, how many Calories will it require per day?

Complete the task on your own paper. Use graphs, numbers, words, or algebra to support your conclusion.

DISCUSSION OPPORTUNITIES

- Have students graph the function on their graphing calculators. Is it straight or curved? If the mass of a reptile doubles, does its Caloric intake also double?

- Compare the a-values that students got and discuss why they might be slightly different from each other.

SAMPLE SOLUTION

Substitute values into the formula $y = am^{\frac{3}{4}}$ and solve for a for at least two of the reptile species from the table.

For the bearded dragon:

$5.0 = a(0.4)^{\frac{3}{4}} \longrightarrow a = \dfrac{5.0}{0.4^{\frac{3}{4}}} \approx 9.94.$

For the caiman:

$142 = a(34)^{\frac{3}{4}} \longrightarrow a = \dfrac{142}{34^{\frac{3}{4}}} \approx 10.09.$

Both values are quite close to 10, so the formula for reptiles is approximately $y = 10m^{\frac{3}{4}}$.

The mass of the new alligator is 400 kg. So its Caloric needs are $10 \cdot 400^{\frac{3}{4}} \approx 894.4$, or 894.4, Calories per day.

Assessment Rubric

2 points: Student correctly solves the problem and explains his/her reasoning.

1 point: Student shows good understanding of the problem but does not fully solve or explain.

0 points: Student does not demonstrate understanding of the problem.

Ready to Go On?

ASSESS MASTERY

Use the assessment on this page to determine if students have mastered the concepts and standards covered in this module.

ASSESSMENT AND INTERVENTION

Access Ready to Go On? assessment online, and receive instant scoring, feedback, and customized intervention or enrichment.

ADDITIONAL RESOURCES

Response to Intervention Resources
- Reteach Worksheets

Differentiated Instruction Resources
- Reading Strategies **EL**
- Success for English Learners **EL**
- Challenge Worksheets

Assessment Resources
- Leveled Module Quizzes

663 Module 14

(Ready) to Go On?

14.1–14.2 Rational Exponents and Radicals

- Online Homework
- Hints and Help
- Extra Practice

Simplify each expression. *(Lesson 14.1)*

1. $216^{\frac{1}{3}} - 125^{\frac{1}{3}}$

1

2. $3 \cdot 49^{-\frac{1}{2}} + 7^{-1}$

$\frac{4}{7}$

Simplify each expression. *(Lesson 14.2)*

3. $\left(\frac{1}{16x} \cdot x^7\right)^{-\frac{1}{2}}$

$\frac{4}{x^3}$

4. $\left(xy^2\right)^2 \sqrt[2]{y^8}$

x^2y^8

5. The volume of a cube is related to the area of a face by the formula $V = A^{\frac{3}{2}}$. What is the volume of a cube whose face has an area of 25 mm²? *(Lesson 14.1)*

125 mm^3

6. Biologists use a formula to estimate the mass of a mammal's brain. For a mammal with a mass of m grams, the approximate mass B of the brain, also in grams, is given by $B = \frac{1}{8}m^{\frac{2}{3}}$. Find the approximate mass of the brain of a squirrel that has a mass of 27 grams. *(Lesson 14.2)*

1.125 g

ESSENTIAL QUESTION

7. How are rational exponents and radicals related?

Possible Answer: Rational exponents and radicals can be converted back and forth into one another, showing that they are two different forms of notation for the same mathematical idea.

COMMON CORE ## Common Core Standards

Lesson	Items	Content Standards	Mathematical Practices
14.1	1	N-RN.A.1, N-RN.A.2	MP.7
14.1	2	N-RN.A.1, N-RN.A.2	MP.7
14.2	3	N-RN.A.1, N-RN.A.2, A-SSE.A.1b	MP.7
14.2	4	N-RN.A.1, N-RN.A.2, A-SSE.A.1b	MP.7
14.1	5	N-RN.A.1, N-RN.A.2	MP.2
14.2	6	N-RN.A.1, N-RN.A.2	MP.2

Assessment Readiness

1. Consider each expression. Is the expression equivalent to $\frac{512^{\frac{1}{3}}}{64^{\frac{2}{3}}}$? Select Yes or No for each.

   A. $\left(\dfrac{64^{\frac{2}{3}}}{512^{\frac{1}{3}}}\right)^{-1}$ ● Yes   ○ No

   B. $\left(64^{\frac{2}{3}} \times 512^{-\frac{1}{3}}\right)^{-1}$ ● Yes   ○ No

   C. $\dfrac{64^{-\frac{2}{3}}}{512^{-\frac{1}{3}}}$ ● Yes   ○ No

2. Consider each set. Does the set represent a function? Select Yes or No for each.

   A. $\{(5, -2), (5, 0), (5, 2), (5, 4)\}$ ○ Yes   ● No

   B. $\{(3, 4), (4, 4), (5, 2), (6, 4)\}$ ● Yes   ○ No

   C. $\{(-4, 1), (-2, 3), (0, 4), (2, 3)\}$ ● Yes   ○ No

3. Consider the graph of $y = \left(\sqrt[3]{8x^3}\right) + 8$. Determine if each of the following statements is True or False.

   A. The slope is 8.   ○ Yes   ● No

   B. The y-intercept is 8.   ● Yes   ○ No

   C. The x-intercept is −4.   ● Yes   ○ No

4. Simplify $216^{\frac{2}{3}}$.

   36

5. Jasmine believes that the sum of two positive irrational numbers can be a rational number. She gives the following example: $\sqrt{2} + \sqrt{2}$. Do you agree with Jasmine? Explain why or why not.

   I do not agree with Jasmine. The sum of $\sqrt{2}$ and $\sqrt{2}$ is $2\sqrt{2}$ which is not a rational number. The sum of two positive irrational numbers is irrational.

MIXED REVIEW
Assessment Readiness

ASSESSMENT AND INTERVENTION

Assign ready-made or customized practice tests to prepare students for high-stakes tests.

ADDITIONAL RESOURCES

Assessment Resources

- Leveled Module Quizzes: Modified, B

AVOID COMMON ERRORS

Item 1 Some students may be thrown off when they find that all answers are "Yes" and may change a correct answer to an incorrect one after second-guessing themselves. Remind students to check their answers but not to change them unless they find mathematical evidence that their first answer was incorrect.

Common Core Standards

Lesson	Items	Content Standards	Mathematical Practices
14.1	1	**N-RN.A.2**	**MP.7**
3.2	2*	**F-IF.A.1**	**MP.1**
6.1, 14.2	3*	**F-IF.C.7a, N-RN.A.1**	**MP.4**
14.1	4	**N-RN.A.2**	**MP.2**
14.2	5	**N-RN.B.3**	**MP.3**

* Item integrates mixed review concepts from previous modules or a previous course.

Geometric Sequences and Exponential Functions

ESSENTIAL QUESTION:

Answer: Geometric sequences and exponential functions have a wide range of applications in fields including economics and biology.

PROFESSIONAL DEVELOPMENT VIDEO

Professional Development Video

Author Juli Dixon models successful teaching practices in an actual high-school classroom.

Professional Development

my.hrw.com

MODULE 15

Geometric Sequences and Exponential Functions

Essential Question: How can you use geometric sequences and exponential functions to solve real-world problems?

© Houghton Mifflin Harcourt Publishing Company • Image Credits: ©RLHambley/Shutterstock

REAL WORLD VIDEO
Pythons originally kept as pets but later released into the Florida ecosystem find themselves in an environment with no natural predators and prey ill-equipped to evade or defend itself. As a result, the python population can grow exponentially, causing havoc among local wildlife and pets.

MODULE PERFORMANCE TASK PREVIEW
What Does It Take to Go Viral?

You have just created a great video, and you share it with some of your friends. Then each of them shares it with the same number of their own friends. If this pattern continues, to how many friends should you show your video to make it go viral within a few days? Let's find out!

Module 15   **665**

DIGITAL TEACHER EDITION

Access a full suite of teaching resources when and where you need them:

- Access content online or offline
- Customize lessons to share with your class
- Communicate with your students in real-time
- View student grades and data instantly to target your instruction where it is needed most

PERSONAL MATH TRAINER
Assessment and Intervention

Assign automatically graded homework, quizzes, tests, and intervention activities. Prepare your students with updated, Common Core-aligned practice tests.

Are **YOU** Ready?

Complete these exercises to review skills you will need for this module.

Exponents

Example 1

Evaluate $(-6)^3$.

$(-6)^3 = (-6)(-6)(-6)$ Write the base -6 multiplied by itself 3 times.

$(-6)(-6)(-6) = -216$ Multiply.

- Online Homework
- Hints and Help
- Extra Practice

Evaluate each power.

1. 2^4

16

2. $(-3)^5$

-243

3. 5^0

1

Example 2

Simplify $x^3 \cdot x^5$.

$x^3 \cdot x^5 = x^{3+5} = x^8$ When multiplying numbers with the same base, add the exponents.

Simplify.

4. $x \cdot x^6$

x^7

5. $x^3y^2 \cdot y^4$

x^3y^6

6. $3a^2b \cdot 5a^2b^4$

$15a^4b^5$

7. $4mno \cdot 7n^2o^2 \cdot mn$

$28m^2n^4o^3$

Algebraic Expressions

Example 3

Evaluate $\frac{2}{3}x^2$ for $x = 6$.

$\frac{2}{3}(6)^2$ Substitute 6 for x.

$\frac{2}{3}(36)$ Evaluate the power.

24 Multiply.

Evaluate each expression for the given value of the variables.

8. $\frac{1}{2}x^3$ for $x = 4$

32

9. $\frac{3}{4}x^4$ for $x = -2$

12

10. $8x^2$ for $x = \frac{1}{2}$

2

11. $18x^3$ for $x = -\frac{1}{3}$

$-\frac{2}{3}$

© Houghton Mifflin Harcourt Publishing Company

Are You Ready?

ASSESS READINESS

Use the assessment on this page to determine if students need strategic or intensive intervention for the module's prerequisite skills.

ASSESSMENT AND INTERVENTION

R∞I Response to Intervention **TIER 1, TIER 2, TIER 3 SKILLS**

Personal Math Trainer will automatically create a standards-based, personalized intervention assignment for your students, targeting each student's individual needs!

ADDITIONAL RESOURCES

See the table below for a full list of intervention resources available for this module.

Response to Intervention Resources also includes:

- Tier 2 Skill Pre-Tests for each Module
- Tier 2 Skill Post-Tests for each skill

Response to Intervention			Differentiated Instruction
Tier 1 Lesson Intervention Worksheets	**Tier 2** Strategic Intervention Skills Intervention Worksheets	**Tier 3** Intensive Intervention Worksheets available online	
Reteach 15.1 Reteach 15.2 Reteach 15.3 Reteach 15.4 Reteach 15.5	2 Algebraic Expressions 5 Exponents 11 Multi-Step Equations	Building Block Skills 19, 22, 23, 24, 27, 29, 30, 40, 59, 69, 76, 81, 98, 100	Challenge worksheets Extend the Math Lesson Activities in TE

Understanding Geometric Sequences

Common Core Math Standards

The student is expected to:

 F-LE.A.2

Construct… geometric… sequences, given a graph, a description of a relationship, or two input-output pairs… Also F-LE.A.3

Mathematical Practices

 MP.7 Using Structure

Language Objective

Explain to a partner how to tell whether a sequence is a geometric sequence.

ENGAGE

Essential Question: How area the terms of a geometric sequence related?

The terms of a geometric sequence are related by a common ratio, often represented by r.

PREVIEW: LESSON PERFORMANCE TASK

View the Engage section online. Discuss the photo and examples of payment plans students might use when charging for odd jobs. Then preview the Lesson Performance Task.

Name_____ Class_____ Date_____

15.1 Understanding Geometric Sequences

Essential Question: How are the terms of a geometric sequence related?

Resource Locker

Explore 1 Exploring Growth Patterns of Geometric Sequences

The sequence 3, 6, 12, 24, 48, … is a *geometric sequence*. In a **geometric sequence**, the ratio of successive terms is constant. The constant ratio is called the **common ratio**, often represented by r.

(A) Complete each division.

$$\frac{6}{3} = \boxed{2} \qquad \frac{12}{6} = \boxed{2} \qquad \frac{24}{12} = \boxed{2} \qquad \frac{48}{24} = \boxed{2}$$

(B) The common ratio r for the sequence is ___2___.

(C) Use the common ratio you found to identify the next term in the geometric sequence.

The next term is $48 \cdot \boxed{2} = \boxed{96}$.

Reflect

1. Suppose you know the twelfth term in a geometric sequence. What do you need to know to find the thirteenth term? How would you use that information to find the thirteenth term?
You need to know the common ratio, r. You can multiply the twelfth term by r.

2. **Discussion** Suppose you know only that 8 and 128 are terms of a geometric sequence. Can you find the term that follows 128? If so, what is it?
Only if you know that 8 and128 are successive terms. In that case, the common ratio is 16, and the next term is 2048. However, 8 and 128 could be terms of a different geometric sequence. For example, in the geometric sequence 8, 16, 32, 64, 128, …, the next term is 256.

Explore 2 Comparing Growth Patterns of Arithmetic and Geometric Sequences

Recall that in arithmetic sequences, successive (or consecutive) terms differ by the same nonzero number d, called the common difference. In geometric sequences, the ratio r of successive terms is constant. In this Explore, you will examine how the growth patterns in arithmetic and geometric sequences compare. In particular, you will look at the arithmetic sequence 3, 5, 7, … and the geometric sequence 3, 6, 12, … .

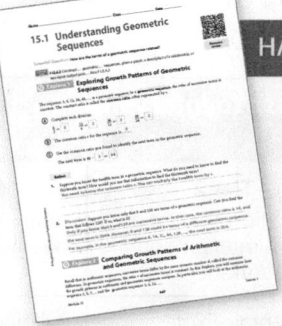

HARDCOVER PAGES 527–534

Turn to these pages to find this lesson in the hardcover student edition.

The tables shows the two sequences.

3, 5, 7, ...	
Term Number	**Term**
1	3
2	5
3	7
4	9
5	11

3, 6, 12, ...	
Term Number	**Term**
1	3
2	6
3	12
4	24
5	48

(A) The common difference d of the arithmetic sequence is $5 - 3 = 2$. The common ratio r of the geometric sequence is $\dfrac{6}{3} = \boxed{2}$.

(B) Complete the table. Find the differences of successive terms.

Arithmetic: 3, 5, 7, ...		
Term Number	**Term**	**Difference**
1	3	—
2	5	$5 - 3 = \boxed{2}$
3	7	$7 - 5 = \boxed{2}$
4	9	$9 - 7 = \boxed{2}$
5	11	$11 - 9 = \boxed{2}$

Geometric: 3, 6, 12, ...		
Term Number	**Term**	**Difference**
1	3	—
2	6	$6 - 3 = \boxed{3}$
3	12	$12 - 6 = \boxed{6}$
4	24	$24 - 12 = \boxed{12}$
5	48	$48 - 24 = \boxed{24}$

EXPLORE 1

Exploring Growth Patterns of Geometric Sequences

INTEGRATE TECHNOLOGY

Have students complete the Explore activity in either the book or online lesson.

CONNECT VOCABULARY EL

Make sure that students understand the meanings of *successive terms* and *ratio of successive terms*. You can explain that two successive terms are two terms that are next to each other in the sequence. Have students give examples of pairs of successive terms. Explain that successive terms can also be called *consecutive terms*.

EXPLORE 2

Comparing Growth Patterns of Arithmetic and Geometric Sequences

QUESTIONING STRATEGIES

? How are the graphs of geometric sequences and arithmetic sequences alike? How are they different? Possible answer: They can both be represented by a function with a domain that is the set of positive integers, or a subset of consecutive positive integers beginning with 1. The graph of a geometric sequence follows a curve, while the graph of an arithmetic sequence is linear.

PROFESSIONAL DEVELOPMENT

Learning Progressions

In an earlier module, students studied arithmetic sequences and wrote general recursive and explicit rules for them. Students used these rules to solve real-world problems involving arithmetic sequences. In this module, students will learn about geometric sequences and exponential functions. In the next module, students will learn more about exponential functions, including exponential growth and decay functions.

Focus on Modeling

MP.4 Show students a graph of the first 4 terms of $f(n) = 2 + 2(n - 1)$ and $f(n) = 2 \cdot 2^{n-1}$. Point out that the shape formed by the points indicates whether the graph represents an arithmetic or geometric sequence. Look at three or more points before determining whether the graph is linear or exponential, since arithmetic and geometric sequences can have the same first two terms.

EXPLAIN 1

Extending Geometric Sequences

AVOID COMMON ERRORS

When finding a common ratio, students might divide in the wrong order. Tell them they are really finding what each term is being multiplied by to get the next term, so the inverse operation (division), will produce r. For example, when finding the common ratio of the geometric sequence $16, 4, 1, \frac{1}{4}, \ldots$, divide 4 by 16.

Ⓒ Compare the growth patterns of the sequences based on the tables.

For the arithmetic sequence, the differences are equal. The terms of the arithmetic sequence increase by a fixed amount. For the geometric sequence, the differences increase. The terms of the geometric sequence increase by an increasing amount.

Ⓓ Graph both sequences in the same coordinate plane. Compare the growth patterns based on the graphs.

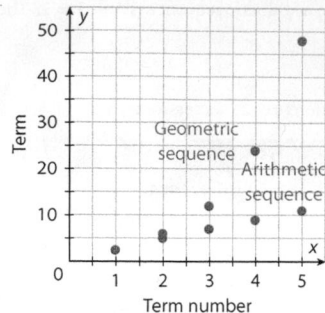

For the arithmetic sequence, the slope is constant, so the vertical distances between successive points are the same. For the geometric sequence, the vertical distances between the points increase by increasing amounts.

Reflect

3. Which grows more quickly, the arithmetic sequence or the geometric sequence?
The geometric sequence

© Houghton Mifflin Harcourt Publishing Company

🔎 **Explain 1** **Extending Geometric Sequences**

In Explore 1, you saw that each term of a geometric sequence is the product of the preceding term and the common ratio. Given terms of a geometric sequence, you can use this relationship to write additional terms of the sequence.

Finding a Term of a Geometric Sequence
For $n \geq 2$, the nth term, $f(n)$, of a geometric sequence with common ratio r is $$f(n) = f(n-1)r.$$

COLLABORATIVE LEARNING

Peer-to-Peer Activity

Have students work in pairs. Have one student write and graph a geometric sequence for which the common ratio r is greater than 1. Have the other student write and graph a geometric sequence for which the common ratio r is $0 < r < 1$. Have the students compare the graphs. Have the students switch roles and repeat the exercise.

Example 1 Find the common ratio r for each geometric sequence and use r to find the next three terms.

Ⓐ 6, 12, 24, 48, …

$\frac{12}{6} = 2$, so the common ratio r is 2.

For this sequence, $f(1) = 6$, $f(2) = 12$, $f(3) = 24$, and $f(4) = 48$.

$f(4) = 48$, so $f(5) = 48(2) = 96$.

$f(5) = 96$, so $f(6) = 96(2) = 192$.

$f(6) = 192$, so $f(7) = 192(2) = 384$.

The next three terms of the sequence are 96, 192, and 384.

Ⓑ 100, 50, 25, 12.5, …

$\frac{50}{\boxed{100}} = \boxed{0.5}$, so the common ratio r is $\underline{\ \ 0.5\ \ }$.

For this sequence, $f(1) = 100$, $f(2) = 50$, $f(3) = 25$, and $f(4) = 12.5$.

$f(4) = 12.5$, so $f(5) = \boxed{12.5}(0.5) = \boxed{6.25}$.

$f(5) = \boxed{6.25}$, so $f(6) = \boxed{6.25}(0.5) = \boxed{3.125}$.

$f(6) = \boxed{3.125}$, so $f(7) = \boxed{3.125}(0.5) = \boxed{1.5625}$.

The next three terms of the sequence are $\boxed{6.25}$, $\boxed{3.125}$, and $\boxed{1.5625}$.

Reflect

4. **Communicate Mathematical Ideas** A geometric sequence has a common ratio of 3. The 4th term is 54. What is the 5th term? What is the 3rd term?
   The 5th term is 3 times the 4th, or 162. The 4th term, 54, is 3 times the 3rd term, so the 3rd term is 18.

Your Turn

Find the common ratio r for each geometric sequence and use r to find the next three terms.

5. 5, 20, 80, 320, …

$\frac{20}{5} = 4 = r$

$f(4) = 320$, so $f(5) = 320(4) = 1280$.

$f(5) = 1280$, so $f(6) = 1280(4) = 5120$.

$f(6) = 5120$, so $f(7) = 5120(4) = 20{,}480$.

The next three terms are 1280, 5120, and 20,480.

6. $9, -3, 1 -\frac{1}{3}, \ldots$

$\frac{-3}{9} = -\frac{1}{3} = r$

$f(4) = -\frac{1}{3}$, so $f(5) = -\frac{1}{3}\left(-\frac{1}{3}\right) = \frac{1}{9}$.

$f(5) = \frac{1}{9}$, so $f(6) = \frac{1}{9}\left(-\frac{1}{3}\right) = -\frac{1}{27}$.

$f(6) = -\frac{1}{27}$, so $f(7) = -\frac{1}{27}\left(-\frac{1}{3}\right) = \frac{1}{81}$.

The next three terms are $\frac{1}{9}, -\frac{1}{27}$, and $\frac{1}{81}$.

❓ In giving the formula for the nth term of a geometric sequence, why does the book say "For $n \geq 2$"? It is understood that n is an integer. The first term of the sequence is $f(1)$. For $n = 0$ and 1, $f(n - 1)$ is not defined.

DIFFERENTIATE INSTRUCTION

Multiple Representations

Help students making connections between a table representing an arithmetic sequence and a graph of the sequence. For example, start with the table and have students make the graph. Then start with the graph and have students make the table. Do the same for a geometric sequence. Have students compare the graphs of the two sequences.

EXPLAIN 2

Recognizing Growth Patterns of Geometric Sequences in Context

QUESTIONING STRATEGIES

 If you know that a sequence is a geometric sequence, how can you find the common ratio? Choose any term after the first term and divide it by the preceding term. The result is the common ratio.

Explain 2 **Recognizing Growth Patterns of Geometric Sequences in Context**

You can find a term of a sequence by repeatedly multiplying the first term by the common ratio.

Example 2

(A) A bungee jumper jumps from a bridge. The table shows the bungee jumper's height above the ground at the top of each bounce. The heights form a geometric sequence. What is the bungee jumper's height at the top of the 5th bounce?

Bounce	Height (feet)
1	200
2	80
3	32

Find r.

$$\frac{80}{200} = 0.4 = r$$

$$f(1) = 200$$

$$f(2) = 80$$
$$\quad = 200(0.4) \text{ or } 200(0.4)^1$$

$$f(3) = 32$$
$$\quad = 80(0.4)$$
$$\quad = 200(0.4)(0.4)$$
$$\quad = 200(0.4)^2$$

In each case, to get $f(n)$, you multiply 200 by the common ratio, 0.4, $n-1$ times. That is, you multiply 200 by $(0.4)^{n-1}$.

The jumper's height on the 5th bounce is $f(5)$.

Multiply 200 by $(0.4)^{5-1} = (0.4)^4$.

$$200(0.4)^4 = 200(0.0256)$$
$$\quad\quad = 5.12$$

The height of the jumper at the top of the 5th bounce is 5.12 feet.

LANGUAGE SUPPORT EL

Connect Vocabulary

Remind students that in a geometric sequence, the ratio of successive terms is constant. This constant ratio is called the *common ratio,* often written as r. Point out that it is called a *common* ratio because it is *shared by* all the pairs of successive terms. Discuss other uses of this meaning of the word *common*; for example, a *common* boys' name.

Example 2

(B) A ball is dropped from a height of 144 inches. Its height on the 1st bounce is 72 inches. On the 2nd and 3rd bounces, the height of the ball is 36 inches and 18 inches, respectively. The heights form a geometric sequence. What is the height of the ball on the 6th bounce to the nearest tenth of an inch?

Find r.

$$\frac{36}{72} = \frac{1}{2} = r$$

$f(1) = \boxed{72}$

$f(2) = \boxed{36}$

$\qquad = 72\left(\boxed{\frac{1}{2}}\right) \text{ or } 72\left(\boxed{\frac{1}{2}}\right)^1$

$f(3) = \boxed{18}$

$\qquad = 36\left(\boxed{\frac{1}{2}}\right)$

$\qquad = 72\left(\boxed{\frac{1}{2}}\right)\left(\boxed{\frac{1}{2}}\right)$

$\qquad = 72\left(\boxed{\frac{1}{2}}\right)^2$

In each case, to get $f(n)$, you multiply 72 by the common ratio, $\underline{\frac{1}{2}}$, $\underline{n-1}$ times. That is, you

multiply 72 by $\underline{\left(\frac{1}{2}\right)^{n-1}}$.

The height of the ball on the 6th bounce is $f\left(\boxed{6}\right)$.

Multiply 72 by $\underline{\left(\frac{1}{2}\right)^{6-1}} = \underline{\left(\frac{1}{2}\right)^5}$.

$$72\left(\frac{1}{2}\right)^5 = 72\left(\frac{1}{32}\right)$$

$$\qquad = 72(0.3125)$$

$$\qquad = 2.25$$

The height of the ball at the top of the 6th bounce is about $\underline{2.3}$ inches.

Reflect

7. Is it possible for a sequence that describes the bounce height of a ball to have a common ratio greater than 1?

   No; if the common ratio were greater than 1, the bounce height would increase, which

   could not happen in the real world.

HOME CONNECTION

Have students think of a real-world situation that can be represented by a geometric sequence.

ELABORATE

INTEGRATE MATHEMATICAL PRACTICES

Focus on Critical Thinking

MP.3 Use examples to help students make generalizations about geometric sequences of positive numbers for which the common ratio r is greater than 1 and geometric sequences of positive numbers for which the common ratio r is between 0 and 1, that is, $0 < r < 1$.

SUMMARIZE THE LESSON

Complete the graphic organizer with students to discuss and summarize lesson concepts. In each box, write a way to represent the geometric sequence.

<table>
<tr><td colspan="2">Ways to Represent the Geometric Sequence 1, 2, 4, 8, …</td></tr>
<tr><td>Table</td><td>

Term Number	1	2	3	4
Term	1	2	4	8

</td></tr>
<tr><td>Formula</td><td>$f(n) = 1(2)^{n-1}$</td></tr>
<tr><td>Words</td><td>Start with 1 and multiply each term by 2 to get the next term.</td></tr>
</table>

Your Turn

8. **Physical Science** A ball is dropped from a height of 8 meters. The table shows the height of each bounce. The heights form a geometric sequence. How high does the ball bounce on the 4th bounce? Round your answer to the nearest tenth of a meter.

Bounce	Height (m)
1	6
2	4.5
3	3.375

$$\frac{4.5}{6} = 0.75 = r$$

$$f(4) = 6(0.75)^{4-1}$$

$$f(4) = 6(0.75)^3$$

$$= 2.53125$$

The ball bounces about 2.5 meters on the 4th bounce.

Elaborate

9. Suppose all the terms of a geometric sequence are positive, and the common ratio r is between 0 and 1. Is the sequence increasing or decreasing? Explain.
   If r is between 0 and 1 and all the terms are positive, then each term is less than the

   preceding term. So, the sequence is decreasing.

10. **Essential Question Check-In** If the common ratio of a geometric sequence is less than 0, what do you know about the signs of the terms of the sequence? Explain.
    The signs of the terms alternate. If $r < 0$ and the first term is negative, the second is

    positive. Then the third must be negative. The signs of the terms continue to alternate.

    If the first term is positive, the results are similar.

© Houghton Mifflin Harcourt Publishing Company

673 Lesson 15.1

• Online Homework
• Hints and Help
• Extra Practice

Find the common ratio *r* for each geometric sequence and use *r* to find the next three terms.

1. 5, 15, 45, 135 …

$$\frac{15}{5} = 3 = r$$

$f(4) = 135$, so $f(5) = 135(3) = 405$.

$f(6) = 405(3) = 1215$

$f(7) = 1215(3) = 3645$

The next three terms of the sequence are 405, 1215, and 3645.

2. −2, 6, −18, 54 …

$$\frac{6}{-2} = -3 = r$$

$f(4) = 54$, so $f(5) = 54(-3) = -162$.

$f(6) = -162(-3) = 486$

$f(7) = 486(-3) = -1458$

The next three terms of the sequence are −162, 486, and −1458.

3. 4, 20, 100, 500, …

$$\frac{20}{4} = 5 = r$$

$f(4) = 500$, so $f(5) = 500(5) = 2500$.

$f(6) = 2500(5) = 12,500$

$f(7) = 12,500(5) = 62,500$

The next three terms of the sequence are 2500, 12,500, and 62,500.

4. 8, 4, 2, 1, …

$$\frac{4}{8} = \frac{1}{2} = r$$

$f(4) = 1$, so $f(5) = 1\left(\frac{1}{2}\right) = \frac{1}{2}$.

$f(6) = \frac{1}{2}\left(\frac{1}{2}\right) = \frac{1}{4}$

$f(7) = \frac{1}{4}\left(\frac{1}{2}\right) = \frac{1}{8}$

The next three terms of the sequence are

$\frac{1}{2}, \frac{1}{4},$ and $\frac{1}{8}$.

5. 72, −36, 18, −9, …

$$\frac{-36}{72} = -\frac{1}{2} = r$$

$f(4) = -9$, so $f(5) = -9\left(-\frac{1}{2}\right) = 4.5$.

$f(6) = 4.5\left(-\frac{1}{2}\right) = -2.25$

$f(7) = -2.25\left(-\frac{1}{2}\right) = 1.125$

The next three terms of the sequence are

4.5, −2.25, and 1.125.

6. 200, −80, 32, −12.8, …

$$\frac{-80}{200} = -0.4 = r$$

$f(4) = -12.8$, so $f(5) = -12.8(-0.4) = 5.12$.

$f(6) = 5.12(-0.4) = -2.048$

$f(7) = -2.048(-0.4) = 0.8192$

The next three terms of the sequence are 5.12, −2.048, and 0.8192.

7. 10, 30, 90, 270, …

$$\frac{30}{10} = 3 = r$$

$f(4) = 270$, so $f(5) = 270(3) = 810$.

$f(6) = 810(3) = 2430$

$f(7) = 2430(3) = 7290$

The next three terms of the sequence are 810, 2430, and 7290.

8. 5, 3, 1.8, 1.08, …

$$\frac{3}{5} = 0.6 = r$$

$f(4) = 1.08$, so $f(5) = 1.08(0.6) = 0.648$.

$f(6) = 0.648(0.6) = 0.3888$

$f(7) = 0.3888(0.6) = 0.23328$

The next three terms of the sequence are 0.648, 0.3888, and 0.23328.

EVALUATE

ASSIGNMENT GUIDE

Concepts and Skills	Practice
Explore 1 Exploring Growth Patterns of Geometric Sequences	Exercise 22
Explore 2 Comparing Growth Patterns of Arithmetic and Geometric Sequences	Exercise 23
Example 1 Extending Geometric Sequences	Exercises 1–14, 21
Example 2 Recognizing Growth Patterns of Geometric Sequences in Context	Exercises 15–20

Exercise	Depth of Knowledge (D.O.K.)	COMMON CORE Mathematical Practices
1–10	**1** Recall of Information	**MP.6** Precision
11–14	**2** Skills/Concepts	**MP.5** Using Tools
15–20	**1** Recall of Information	**MP.5** Using Tools
21	**2** Skills/Concepts	**MP.2** Reasoning
22	**3** Strategic Thinking H.O.T.	**MP.5** Using Tools
23	**3** Strategic Thinking H.O.T.	**MP.3** Logic

Understanding Geometric Sequences   **674**

AVOID COMMON ERRORS

When finding a common ratio, students might divide in the wrong order. Make sure that students divide each term after the first term by the preceding term to find the common ratio.

9. 18, 36, 72, 144

$$\frac{36}{18} = 2 = r$$

$f(4) = 144$, so $f(5) = 144(2) = 288$

$f(6) = 288(2) = 576$

$f(7) = 576(2) = 1152$

The next three terms of the sequence are 288, 576, and 1152.

10. 243, 162, 108, 72, …

$$\frac{162}{243} = \frac{2}{3} = r$$

$f(4) = 72$, so $f(5) = 72\left(\frac{2}{3}\right) = 48$.

$f(6) = 48\left(\frac{2}{3}\right) = 32$

$f(7) = 32\left(\frac{2}{3}\right) = 21\frac{1}{3}$

The next three terms of the sequence are 48, 32, and $21\frac{1}{3}$.

Find the indicated term of each sequence by repeatedly multiplying the first term by the common ratio. Use a calculator.

11. 1, 8, 64, …; 5th term

$$\frac{8}{1} = 8 = r$$

$f(5) = 1(8)^{5-1}$

$\quad = 1(8)^4$

$\quad = 4096$

12. 16, −3.2, 0.64, …; 7th term

$$\frac{-3.2}{16} = -0.2 = r$$

$f(7) = 16(-0.2)^{7-1}$

$\quad = 16(-0.2)^6$

$\quad = 0.001024$

13. −50, 15, −4.5, …; 5th term

$$\frac{15}{-50} = -0.3 = r$$

$f(5) = -50(-0.3)^{5-1}$

$\quad = -50(-0.3)^4$

$\quad = -0.405$

14. 3, −12, 48, …; 6th term

$$\frac{-12}{3} = -4 = r$$

$f(n) = f(1)r^{n-1}$

$f(6) = 3(-4)^{6-1}$

$\quad = 3(-4)^5$

$\quad = -3072$

Solve. You may use a calculator and round your answer to the nearest tenth of a unit if necessary.

15. Physical Science A ball is dropped from a height of 900 centimeters. The table shows the height of each bounce. The heights form a geometric sequence. How high does the ball bounce on the 5th bounce?

Bounce	Height (cm)
1	800
2	560
3	392

$$\frac{560}{800} = 0.7 = r$$

Find the 5th term of the sequence.

$f(5) = 800(0.7)^{5-1}$

$\quad = 800(0.7)^4$

$\quad = 192.08$ **centimeters**

16. Leo's bank balances at the end of months 1, 2, and 3 are $1500, $1530, and $1560.60, respectively. The balances form a geometric sequence. What will Leo's balance be after 9 months?

The first two terms of the sequence are 1500 and 1530.

$$\frac{1530}{1500} = 1.02 = r$$

Find the 9th term of the sequence.

$$f(9) = 1500(1.02)^{9-1}$$

$$= 1500(1.02)^{8}$$

$$= \$1757.49$$

17. Biology A biologist studying ants started on day 1 with a population of 1500 ants. On day 2, there were 3000 ants, and on day 3, there were 6000 ants. The increase in an ant population can be represented using a geometric sequence. What is the ant population on day 5?

$$\frac{3000}{1500} = 2 = r$$

Find the 5th term of the sequence.

$$f(5) = 1500 \cdot 2^{5-1}$$

$$= 1500 \cdot 2^{4}$$

$$= 24{,}000 \text{ ants}$$

18. Physical Science A ball is dropped from a height of 625 centimeters. The table shows the height of each bounce. The heights form a geometric sequence. How high does the ball bounce on the 8th bounce?

Bounce	Height (cm)
1	500
2	400
3	320

$$\frac{400}{500} = 0.8 = r$$

Find the 8th term of the sequence.

$$f(8) = 500(0.8)^{8-1}$$

$$= 500(0.8)^{7}$$

$$= 104.8576 \text{ centimeters.}$$

19. Finance The table shows the balance in an investment account after each month. The balances form a geometric sequence. What is the amount in the account after month 6?

Month	Amount ($)
1	1700
2	2040
3	2448

$$\frac{2040}{1700} = 1.2 = r$$

Find the 6th term of the sequence.

$$f(6) = 1700(1.2)^{6-1}$$

$$= 1700(1.2)^{5}$$

$$= \$4230.14$$

CRITICAL THINKING

Have students explain why some sequences alternate signs and some do not. (When the common ratio, *r*, is negative, the terms in a geometric sequence alternate signs. When the common ratio is positive, the terms are all positive or all negative.)

JOURNAL

Have students explain the difference between the rules used to create the following sequences, and determine whether each sequence is arithmetic, geometric, or neither:

3, 6, 9, 12, 15, … **arithmetic**

3, 6, 10, 15, 21, … **neither**

3, 6, 12, 24, 48, … **geometric**

20. **Biology** A turtle population grows in a manner that can be represented by a geometric sequence. Given the table of values, determine the turtle population after 6 years.

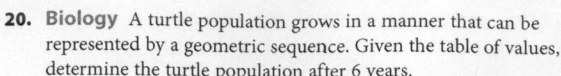

Year	Number of Turtles
1	5
2	15
3	45

$\frac{15}{5} = 3 = r$

Find the 6th term of the sequence.

$f(6) = 5 \cdot 3^{6-1}$

$= 5 \cdot 3^5$

$= 1215$ **turtles**

21. Consider the geometric sequence −8, 16, −32, … Select all that apply.

   a. The common ratio is 2.

   $\frac{16}{-8} = -2$, **so the common ratio is −2.**

   b. The 5th term of the sequence is −128.

   The common ratio is −2, and the 1st term is −8, $f(n) = -8(-2)^{n-1}$, and

   $f(5) = -8(-2)^4 = -128$, **and the 5th term of the sequence is −128.**

   c. The 7th term is 4 times the 5th term.

   The 7th term is −2 times the 6th term, which is −2 times the 5th term, so the 7th term is 4 times the 5th term.

   d. The 8th term is 1024.

   The 8th term is $-8(-2)^7 = 1024$.

   e. The 10th term is greater than the 9th term.

   $-8(-2)^9$ **is positive and $-8(-2)^8$ is negative, so the 10th term is greater than the 9th term. So, B, C, D, and E all apply.**

H.O.T.   Focus on Higher Order Thinking

22. **Justify Reasoning** Suppose you are given a sequence with $r < 0$. What do you know about the signs of the terms of the sequence? Explain.
Because $r < 0$, if the first term is negative, the second is positive. Then the third must be negative. The signs of the terms continue to alternate.

23. **Critique Reasoning** Miguel writes the following: 8, x, 8, x, … He tells Alicia that he has written a geometric sequence and asks her to identify the value of x. Alicia says the value of x must be 8. Miguel says that Alicia is incorrect. Who is right? Explain.
The value that Alicia gave is correct, but it is not the only correct value. x could also be −8. 8, −8, 8, −8, … is also a geometric sequence, so Miguel is correct.

Lesson Performance Task

Multi-Step Gifford earns money by shoveling snow for the winter. He offers two payment plans: either pay $400 per week for the entire winter or pay $5 for the first week, $10 for the second week, $20 for the third week, and so on. Explain why each plan does or does not form a geometric sequence. Then determine the number of weeks after which the total cost of the second plan will exceed the total cost of the first plan.

The two plans form a geometric sequence. In the first plan, the geometric sequence is $a_n = 400 \cdot 1^{n-1}$. In the second plan, the geometric sequence is $a_n = 5 \cdot 2^{n-1}$.

Create a table of values listing the weekly cost for each plan along with a column to accumulate the payments. In week 9, the second plan's payment will be $1280, and the total payments for weeks 1–9 will be $2555, which is less than the $3600 of total payments for the first plan. In week 10, the second plan's payment will be $2560, and the total payments for weeks 1–10 will be $5115, which is more than the $4000 of total payments for the first plan. The total payments will equalize between weeks 9 and 10.

INTEGRATE MATHEMATICAL PRACTICES
Focus on Modeling

MP.4 Guide students who need help in representing the geometric sequence 5, 10, 20, … by giving them an explicit function.

INTEGRATE MATHEMATICAL PRACTICES
Focus on Reasoning

MP.2 Have students explain how they could use reasoning to check their answers for the approximate number of weeks when the plans cost about the same amount of money. For example, some students may say they wrote out the geometric sequence until they could see that $400 would occur between weeks 7 and 8.

EXTENSION ACTIVITY

Have students explain which of the following two options they would prefer. Have students explain their reasoning.

Option 1: They receive 1¢ on the first day, 2¢ on the second day, 4¢ on the third day, 8¢ on the fourth day, and so on, doubling each day, for a total of 20 days.

Option 2: They receive $5000 on the first day and $0 after that.

Students will find that with Option 1, on the 20th day, without including the amounts from the previous 19 days, the amount received would be $5242.88, which is more than $5000. So, the total amount received in Option 1 would be much more than the total amount, $5000, received in Option 2.

Scoring Rubric
2 points: Student correctly solves the problem and explains his/her reasoning.
1 point: Student shows good understanding of the problem but does not fully solve or explain his/her reasoning.
0 points: Student does not demonstrate understanding of the problem.

Understanding Geometric Sequences   **678**

Constructing Geometric Sequences

Common Core Math Standards

The student is expected to:

 F-BF.A.1a

...Determine an explicit expression, a recursive process, or steps for calculation from a context. Also F-LE.A.2, F-BF.A.2

Mathematical Practices

 MP.4 Modeling

Language Objective

Explain to a partner the difference between a recursive and an explicit rule for a geometric sequence.

ENGAGE

Essential Question: How do you write a geometric sequence?

You write down an initial term and then multiply each term by a common factor to get the next term.

PREVIEW: LESSON PERFORMANCE TASK

View the Engage section online. Discuss the photo and reasons why a rabbit population might change rapidly; for example, gestation is 31 days, litter size is 4 to 12, and rabbits mate as early as age 3 months. Then preview the Lesson Performance Task.

Name_____ Class_____ Date_____

15.2 Constructing Geometric Sequences

Essential Question: How do you write a geometric sequence?

⊘ Explore   Understanding Recursive and Explicit Rules for Sequences

You learned previously that an explicit rule for a sequence defines the nth term as a function of n. A recursive rule defines the nth term of a sequence in terms of one or more previous terms.

You can use what you know to identify recursive and explicit rules for sequences, and identify whether the sequences are arithmetic, geometric, or neither.

A rule for the sequence 6, 9, 13.5,... is $f(n) = 6\left(\frac{3}{2}\right)^{n-1}$.

(A) The given rule is a(n) ____explicit____ rule because you do not need to know the value of ____$f(n-1)$____.

(B) The only unknown in the expression is ____n____, which represents ____the term number____.

(C) The sequence is a(n) ____geometric____ sequence because each term is the ____product____ of the previous term and $\frac{3}{2}$.

Reflect

1. **Discussion** How can you differentiate between a geometric sequence and an arithmetic sequence?
   An arithmetic sequence involves addition (or subtraction) and a geometric sequence involves multiplication (or division).

2. How can you tell by looking at a function rule for a sequence whether it is a recursive rule?
   If a given rule is recursive, the first term $f(1)$ appears in the rule.

HARDCOVER PAGES 535–544

Turn to these pages to find this lesson in the hardcover student edition.

 **Explain 1** **Constructing Recursive and Explicit Rules for Given Geometric Sequences**

To write a recursive rule for a sequence, you need to know the first term, and a rule for successive terms.

Example 1 Write a recursive rule and an explicit rule for each geometric sequence.

 (A) Makers of Japanese swords in the 1400s repeatedly folded and hammered the metal to form layers. The folding process increased the strength of the sword.

The table shows how the number of layers depends on the number of folds.

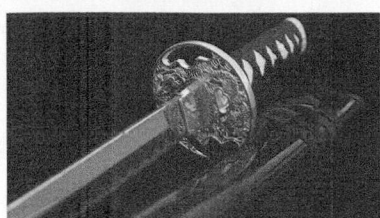

Number of Folds	n	1	2	3	4	5
Number of Layers	$f(n)$	2	4	8	16	32

To write a recursive rule, find the common ratio by calculating the ratio of consecutive terms.

$\frac{4}{2} = 2$

The common ratio r is 2.

The first term is 2, so $f(1) = 2$.

All terms after the first term are the product of the previous term and the common ratio:

$f(2) = f(1) \cdot 2, f(3) = f(2) \cdot 2, f(4) = f(3) \cdot 2, \ldots$

State the recursive rule by providing the first term and the rule for successive terms.

$f(1) = 2$

$f(n) = f(n-1) \cdot 2$ for $n \geq 2$

Write an explicit rule for the sequence by writing each term as the product of the first term and a power of the common ratio.

n	$f(n)$
1	$2(2)^0 = 2$
2	$2(2)^1 = 4$
3	$2(2)^2 = 8$
4	$2(2)^3 = 16$
5	$2(2)^4 = 32$

Generalize the results from the table: $f(n) = 2 \cdot 2^{n-1}$.

© Houghton Mifflin Harcourt Publishing Company • Image Credits: ©kazenouta/Shutterstock

Understanding Recursive and Explicit Rules for Sequences

INTEGRATE TECHNOLOGY

Have students complete the Explore activity in either the book or online lesson.

INTEGRATE MATHEMATICAL PRACTICES

Focus on Math Connections

MP.1 Ask students to explain the difference between a recursive rule and an explicit rule for a sequence, and tell how each one is written.

EXPLAIN 1

Constructing Recursive and Explicit Rules for Given Geometric Sequences

INTEGRATE MATHEMATICAL PRACTICES

Focus on Communication

MP.3 Ask students to explain what each of the values in the explicit rule in this Example represents. Ask them how the rule would change if various changes were made to the sequence.

PROFESSIONAL DEVELOPMENT

 Integrate Mathematical Practices

This lesson provides an opportunity to address Mathematical Practice **MP.4**, which calls for students to use "modeling." Students use a specific geometric sequence to help them obtain general rules, both recursive and explicit, for representing geometric sequences. They then use those general rules to represent other geometric sequences.

Which rule, the recursive rule or the explicit rule, would be more useful in determining the 20th term of a given sequence? Explain your reasoning. **The explicit rule is more useful because you can easily evaluate $f(20)$ to find the 20th term. To use the recursive rule, you would have to calculate each successive term until you get to the 20th term.**

AVOID COMMON ERRORS

Some students may confuse the recursive and explicit rules. Remind students that the recursive rule for a geometric sequence is stated by providing the first term, $f(1)$, and the rule for terms after the first term, so $f(n-1)$, should appear in this rule. An explicit rule for a geometric sequence is stated by writing each term as the product of the first term and a power of the common ratio.

(B)

n	1	2	3	4	5
$f(n)$	5	15	45	135	405

To write a recursive rule, find the common ratio by calculating the ratio of consecutive terms.

$$\frac{15}{5} = \boxed{3}$$

The common ratio r is $\underline{\quad 3 \quad}$.

The first term is $\underline{\quad 5 \quad}$. So, the recursive rule is:

$$f(n) = f(n-1) \boxed{3} \text{ for } n \geq 2$$

Write an explicit rule for the sequence by writing each term as the product of the first term and a power of the common ratio.

n	$f(n)$
1	$5(3)^0 = \boxed{5}$
2	$5(3)^1 = \boxed{15}$
3	$5(3)^2 = \boxed{45}$
4	$5(3)^3 = \boxed{135}$
5	$5(3)^4 = \boxed{405}$

Generalize the results from the table: $f(n) = \boxed{5 \cdot 3}^{\,n-1}$.

Reflect

3. Explain why the sequence 5, 10, 20, 40, 80, ... appears to be a geometric sequence.
   The quotient of successive terms is always 2.

4. **Draw Conclusions** How can you use properties of exponents to simplify the explicit rule $f(n) = 2 \cdot 2^{n-1}$?
   Use the product of powers rule: $2 \cdot 2^{n-1} = 2^1 \cdot 2^{n-1} = 2^{1+n-1} = 2^n$. Therefore, the explicit rule can be simplified to $f(n) = 2^n$.

COLLABORATIVE LEARNING

Peer-to-Peer Activity

Have students work in pairs. Have one student write an explicit rule for a geometric sequence and the other write a recursive rule for a different geometric sequence. Have students trade papers and write the first five terms of the sequence as well as the rule that is not already written, either explicit or recursive. Have students do this two or three times.

Your Turn

Write a recursive rule and an explicit rule for each geometric sequence.

5.

n	1	2	3	4	5
$f(n)$	7	14	28	56	112

$\dfrac{14}{7} = 2 = r$ and the first term is 7.

Recursive rule: $f(1) = 7$ and $f(n) = f(n-1) \cdot 2$ for $n \geq 2$

Explicit rule: $f(n) = 7 \cdot 2^{n-1}$

6. Write a recursive rule and an explicit rule for the geometric sequence 128, 32, 8, 2, 0.5, ...

$\dfrac{32}{128} = 0.25 = r$ and the first term is 128.

Recursive rule: $f(1) = 128$ and $f(n) = f(n-1) \cdot 0.25$ for $n \geq 2$

Explicit rule: $f(n) = 128 \cdot (0.25)^{(n-1)}$

⚙ Explain 2 Deriving the General Forms of Geometric Sequence Rules

Example 2 Use each geometric sequence to help write a recursive rule and an explicit rule for any geometric sequence. For the general rules, the values of n are consecutive integers starting with 1.

Ⓐ   6, 24, 96, 384, 1536, ...

Find the common ratio.

Numbers

6, 24, 96, 384, 1536,...

Common ratio = 4

Algebra

$f(1), f(2), f(3), f(4), f(5),...$

Common ratio = r

Write a recursive rule.

Numbers

$f(1) = 6$ and

$f(n) = f(n-1) \cdot 4$ for $n \geq 2$

Algebra

Given $f(1)$,

$f(n) = f(n-1) \cdot r$ for $n \geq 2$

Write an explicit rule.

Numbers

$f(n) = 6 \cdot 4^{n-1}$

Algebra

$f(n) = f(1) \cdot r^{n-1}$

EXPLAIN 2

Deriving the General Forms of Geometric Sequence Rules

QUESTIONING STRATEGIES

? If you know the second term and the common ratio of a geometric sequence, can you write an explicit rule for the sequence? If so, explain how. Yes; you can divide the second term by the common ratio to get the first term. Then, you can substitute the first term and the common ratio into the general explicit rule to get the explicit rule for the sequence.

DIFFERENTIATE INSTRUCTION

Kinesthetic Experience

Students may benefit from acting out a situation that can be represented by a geometric sequence, such as folding a piece of paper in half repeatedly. The number of folds is the term number, n, and the number of layers is the term, $f(n)$. Have students write a recursive rule and an explicit rule for the sequence.

VISUAL CUES

Have students color code the matching information found in the recursive rule and explicit rule of a geometric sequence as shown:

Explicit Rule:

$$f(n) = f(1) \cdot r^{n-1}$$

Recursive Rule:

Given $f(1)$, $f(n) = f(n-1) \cdot r$.

(B) 4, 12, 36, 108, 324,...

Find the common ratio.

Numbers	Algebra
4, 12, 36, 108, 324,...	$f(1), f(2), f(3), f(4), f(5),...$
Common ratio = 3	Common ratio = r

Write a recursive rule.

Numbers	Algebra
$f(1) =$ 4 and	Given $f(1)$,
$f(n) = f(n-1) \cdot$ 3 for $n \geq$ 2	$f(n) = f(n-1) \cdot$ r for $n \geq$ 2

Write an explicit rule.

Numbers	Algebra
$f(n) =$ 4 $\cdot$ 3^{n-1}	$f(n) = f\left(1 \right) \cdot r^{n-1}$

Reflect

7. **Discussion** The first term of a geometric sequence is 81 and the common ratio is $\frac{1}{3}$. Explain how the 4th term of the sequence can be determined.

   The 4th term of the sequence can be determined by raising $\frac{1}{3}$ to the 3rd power and multiplying this result by 81.

8. What is the recursive rule for the sequence $f(n) = 5(4)^{n-1}$?

   The first term is 5 and the common ratio is 4. So a recursive rule is $f(1) = 5$, $f(n) = f(n-1) \cdot 4$

Your Turn

Use each geometric sequence to help write a recursive rule and an explicit rule for any geometric sequence.

9. 6, 12, 24, 48, 96,...

   Find the common ratio.

Numbers	Algebra
6, 12, 24, 48, 96, ...	$f(1), f(2), f(3), f(4), f(5), ...$
Common ratio $=$ 2	Common ratio $= r$

   Write a recursive rule.

Numbers	Algebra
$f(1) = 6$ and	Given $f(1)$,
$f(n) = f(n-1) \cdot 2$ for $n \geq 2$	$f(n) = f(n-1) \cdot r$ for $n \geq 2$

   Write an explicit rule.

Numbers	Algebra
$f(n) = 6 \cdot 2^{n-1}$	$f(n) = f(1) \cdot r^{n-1}$

LANGUAGE SUPPORT 🔲EL

Connect Vocabulary

In this lesson, students learn about general rules, recursive rules, and explicit rules. Using the text, review with them and help them differentiate the meaning of each of these terms. Point out that the word *recursive* begins with the prefix *re-*, which means *again*. Tell them to think about the word *repeat*. *Recursive* refers to a procedure that can be repeated over and over. Speakers of Spanish will likely connect this with the prefix *re-* in Spanish, which has the same meaning. Words such as *repetir* (repeat) and *reforzar* (reinforce) are examples of Spanish words with the *re-* prefix.

Explain 3 **Constructing a Geometric Sequence Given Two Terms**

The explicit and recursive rules for a geometric sequence can also be written in subscript notation. In subscript notation, the subscript indicates the position of the term in the sequence. a_1, a_2, and a_3 are the first, second, and third terms of a sequence respectively. In general, a_n is the nth term of a sequence.

 Example 3 Write an explicit rule for each sequence using subscript notation.

(A) **Photography** The shutter speed settings on a camera form a geometric sequence where a_n is the shutter speed in seconds and n is the setting number. The fifth setting on the camera is $\frac{1}{60}$ second and the seventh setting on the camera is $\frac{1}{15}$ second.

Identify the given terms in the sequence.

The fifth setting is $\frac{1}{60}$ second, so the 5th term of the sequence is $\frac{1}{60}$.

$$a_5 = \frac{1}{60}$$

The seventh setting is $\frac{1}{15}$ second, so the 7th term of the sequence is $\frac{1}{15}$.

$$a_7 = \frac{1}{15}$$

Find the common ratio.

$a_7 = a_6 \cdot r$	Write the recursive rule for a_7.
$a_6 = a_5 \cdot r$	Write the recursive rule for a_6.
$a_7 = a_5 \cdot r \cdot r$	Substitute the expression for a_6 into the rule for a_7.
$\frac{1}{15} = \frac{1}{60} \cdot r^2$	Substitute $\frac{1}{15}$ for a_7 and $\frac{1}{60}$ for a_5.
$4 = r^2$	Multiply both sides by 60.
$2 = r$	Definition of positive square root.

Find the first term of the sequence.

$a_n = a_1 \cdot r^{n-1}$	Write the explicit rule.
$\frac{1}{60} = a_1 \cdot 2^{5-1}$	Substitute $\frac{1}{60}$ for a_n, 2 for r, and 5 for n.
$\frac{1}{60} = a_1 \cdot 16$	Simplify.
$\frac{1}{960} = a_1$	Divide both sides by 16.

Write the explicit rule.

$a_n = a_1 \cdot r^{n-1}$	Write the general rule.
$a_n = \frac{1}{960} \cdot (2)^{n-1}$	Substitute $\frac{1}{960}$ for a_1 and 2 for r.

EXPLAIN 3

Constructing a Geometric Sequence Given Two Terms

QUESTIONING STRATEGIES

? How is an explicit rule for a geometric sequence, written using function notation, related to an explicit rule for a geometric sequence, written using subscript notation? When the position numbers start with 1, the variable n is used in both notations to represent the nth term of the sequence. In both cases, the nth term is found by multiplying the first term by the common ratio raised to the power of $(n - 1)$.

Focus on Patterns

MP.8 Show students the relationship between the terms of a geometric sequence using the following pattern:

$$a_1 = a_1$$
$$a_2 = a_1 \cdot r$$
$$a_3 = a_1 \cdot r \cdot r$$
$$a_4 = a_1 \cdot r \cdot r \cdot r$$

Ask students to find other patterns that may be helpful when constructing a geometric sequence given two terms. For example:

$$a_1 = a_1$$
$$a_2 = a_1 \cdot r$$
$$a_3 = a_2 \cdot r$$
$$a_4 = a_3 \cdot r$$

Ⓑ **Viral Video** You tell a number of friends about an interesting video you saw online. Each of those friends tells the same number of friends about it. This pattern continues, and there are no repeats in the people told. The numbers of people who hear about this video through you form a geometric sequence. There are 256 people at the fourth round and 4096 people at the sixth round.

Identify the given terms in the sequence.

The 4th term of the sequence is ⟨256⟩.

$a_4 = $ ⟨256⟩

The 6th term of the sequence is ⟨4096⟩.

$a_6 = $ ⟨4096⟩

Find the common ratio.

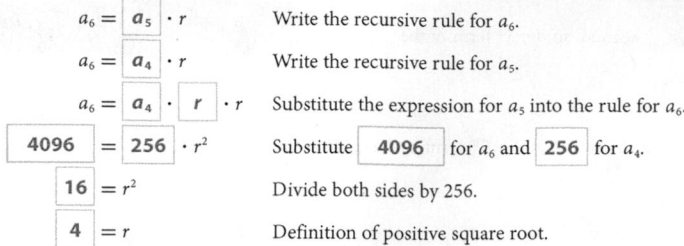

$a_6 = $ ⟨a_5⟩ $\cdot r$	Write the recursive rule for a_6.
$a_6 = $ ⟨a_4⟩ $\cdot r$	Write the recursive rule for a_5.
$a_6 = $ ⟨a_4⟩ $\cdot$ ⟨r⟩ $\cdot r$	Substitute the expression for a_5 into the rule for a_6.
⟨4096⟩ $= $ ⟨256⟩ $\cdot r^2$	Substitute ⟨4096⟩ for a_6 and ⟨256⟩ for a_4.
⟨16⟩ $= r^2$	Divide both sides by 256.
⟨4⟩ $= r$	Definition of positive square root.

Find the first term of the sequence.

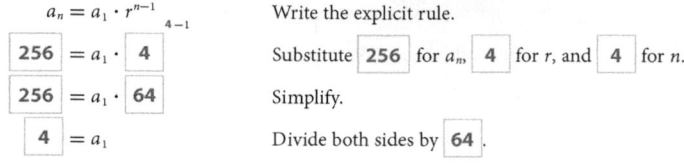

$a_n = a_1 \cdot r^{n-1}$	Write the explicit rule.
⟨256⟩ $= a_1 \cdot$ ⟨4⟩$^{4-1}$	Substitute ⟨256⟩ for a_n, ⟨4⟩ for r, and ⟨4⟩ for n.
⟨256⟩ $= a_1 \cdot$ ⟨64⟩	Simplify.
⟨4⟩ $= a_1$	Divide both sides by ⟨64⟩.

Write the explicit rule.

$$a_n = a_1 \cdot r^{n-1} \qquad \text{Write the general rule.}$$
$$a_n = ⟨4⟩ \cdot \left(⟨4⟩ \right)^{n-1} \qquad \text{Substitute ⟨4⟩ for } a_1 \text{ and ⟨4⟩ for } r.$$

Reflect

10. Finding the common ratio in the shutter speed example involved finding a square root. Why was the negative square root not considered?

The common ratio must be positive. The sequence represents shutter speeds, which must

be positive.

Write an explicit rule for the sequence using subscript notation.

11. The third term of a geometric sequence is $\frac{1}{27}$ and the fifth term is $\frac{1}{243}$. All the terms of the sequence are positive.

Common ratio:	First term:	Write the explicit rule:
$a_5 = a_3 \cdot r^2$	$\frac{1}{27} = a_1\left(\frac{1}{3}\right)^{3-1}$	$a_n = \frac{1}{3}\left(\frac{1}{3}\right)^{n-1}$
$\frac{1}{243} = \frac{1}{27} \cdot r^2$	$\frac{1}{27} = a_1\left(\frac{1}{3}\right)^2$	
$r = \frac{1}{3}$	$\frac{1}{3} = a_1$	

💬 Elaborate

12. **What If** Suppose you are given the terms a_3 and a_6 of a geometric sequence. How can you find the common ratio r?
Use the fact that $a_6 = a_3 \cdot r \cdot r \cdot r = a_3 \cdot r^3$ and find the cube root of $\frac{a_6}{a_3}$.

13. If you know the second term and the common ratio of a geometric sequence, can you write an explicit rule for the sequence? If so, explain how.
Yes; you can divide the second term by the common ratio to get the first term. Then, you can substitute the first term and the common ratio into the general explicit rule to get the explicit rule for the sequence.

14. **Essential Question Check-In** How can you write the explicit rule for a geometric sequence if you know the recursive rule for the sequence?
Use the first term of the sequence and the common ratio as given in the recursive rule. Use these values in the form $f(n) = f(1) \cdot r^{n-1}$.

ELABORATE

INTEGRATE MATHEMATICAL PRACTICES
Focus on Modeling
MP.4 In this lesson, students write a recursive rule and an explicit rule for a geometric sequence. Ensure that students understand what each value in the rules represents.

SUMMARIZE THE LESSON

? How can you write a recursive and an explicit rule for a geometric sequence? To write a recursive rule, assume $f(1)$ is given and use the general rule $f(n) = f(n-1) \cdot r$ for each whole number $n \geq 2$, where r is the common ratio. To write an explicit rule, use the general rule $f(n) = f(1) \cdot r^{n-1}$, where $f(1)$ is the first term in the sequence, r is the common ratio, and the domain of the function is the set of positive integers or a subset of consecutive positive integers beginning with 1.

EVALUATE

ASSIGNMENT GUIDE

Concepts and Skills	Practice
Explore Understanding Recursive and Explicit Rules for Sequences	Exercise 24
Example 1 Constructing Recursive and Explicit Rules for Given Geometric Sequences	Exercises 1–11
Example 2 Deriving the General Forms of Geometric Sequence Rules	Exercises 12–15, 25
Example 3 Constructing a Geometric Sequence Given Two Terms	Exercises 16–23, 26–28

⭐ Evaluate: Homework and Practice

• Online Homework
• Hints and Help
• Extra Practice

For each geometric sequence, write a recursive rule by finding the common ratio by calculating the ratio of consecutive terms. Write an explicit rule for the sequence by writing each term as the product of the first term and a power of the common ratio.

1.

n	1	2	3	4	5
a_n	2	6	18	54	162

$\frac{6}{2} = 3 = r$ and $a_1 = 2$

Recursive rule: $a_1 = 2$ and $a_n = 3a_{n-1}$ for $n \geq 2$; Explicit rule: $a_n = 2(3)^{n-1}$

2.

n	1	2	3	4	5
a_n	10	3	0.9	0.27	0.081

$\frac{3}{10} = 0.3 = r$ and $a_1 = 10$

Recursive rule: $a_1 = 10$ and $a_n = 0.3a_{n-1}$ for $n \geq 2$; Explicit rule: $a_n = 10(0.3)^{n-1}$

3.

n	1	2	3	4	5
a_n	5	20	80	320	1280

$\frac{20}{5} = 4 = r$ and $a_1 = 5$

Recursive rule: $a_1 = 5$ and $a_n = 4a_{n-1}$ for $n \geq 2$; Explicit rule: $a_n = 5(4)^{n-1}$

4.

n	1	2	3	4	5
a_n	6	−3	1.5	−0.75	0.375

$\frac{-3}{6} = -\frac{1}{2} = r$ and $a_1 = 6$

Recursive rule: $a_1 = 6$ and $a_n = -\frac{1}{2}a_{n-1}$ for $n \geq 2$; Explicit rule: $a_n = 6\left(-\frac{1}{2}\right)^{n-1}$

5.

n	1	2	3	4	5
a_n	9	6	4	$2\frac{2}{3}$	$1\frac{7}{9}$

$\frac{6}{9} = \frac{2}{3} = r$ and $a_1 = 9$

Recursive rule: $a_1 = 9$ and $a_n = \frac{2}{3}a_{n-1}$ for $n \geq 2$; Explicit rule: $a_n = 9\left(\frac{2}{3}\right)^{n-1}$

Exercise	Depth of Knowledge (D.O.K.)		**COMMON CORE** Mathematical Practices
1–15	**2** Recall of Information		**MP.2** Reasoning
16–24	**2** Skills/Concepts		**MP.4** Modeling
25–26	**3** Strategic Thinking	H.O.T.	**MP.4** Modeling
27	**3** Strategic Thinking	H.O.T.	**MP.3** Logic
28	**3** Strategic Thinking	H.O.T.	**MP.5** Using Tools

6.

n	1	2	3	4	5
a_n	-12	6	-3	1.5	-0.75

$\dfrac{6}{-12} = -0.5 = r$ and $a_1 = -12$

Recursive rule: $a_1 = -12$ and $a_n = -0.5a_{n-1}$ for $n \geq 2$; Explicit rule: $a_n = -12(-0.5)^{n-1}$

7.

n	1	2	3	4	5
a_n	4	24	144	864	5184

$\dfrac{24}{4} = 6 = r$ and $a_1 = 4$

Recursive rule: $a_1 = 4$ and $a_n = 6a_{n-1}$ for $n \geq 2$; Explicit rule: $a_n = 4(6)^{n-1}$

8.

n	1	2	3	4	5
a_n	10	5	2.5	1.25	0.625

$\dfrac{5}{10} = 0.5 = r$ and $a_1 = 10$

Recursive rule: $a_1 = 10$ and $a_n = 0.5a_{n-1}$ for $n \geq 2$; Explicit rule: $a_n = 10(0.5)^{n-1}$

9.

n	1	2	3	4	5
a_n	3	21	147	1029	7203

$\dfrac{21}{3} = 7 = r$ and $a_1 = 3$

Recursive rule: $a_1 = 3$ and $a_n = 7a_{n-1}$ for $n \geq 2$; Explicit rule: $a_n = 3(7)^{n-1}$

$a_n = 3(7)^{n-1}$

10.

n	1	2	3	4	5
a_n	8	72	648	5832	52,488

$\dfrac{72}{8} = 9 = r$ and $a_1 = 8$

Recursive rule: $a_1 = 8$ and $a_n = 9a_{n-1}$ for $n \geq 2$; Explicit rule: $a_n = 8(9)^{n-1}$

11.

n	1	2	3	4	5
a_n	6	30	150	750	3750

$\dfrac{30}{6} = 5 = r$ and $a_1 = 6$

Recursive rule: $a_1 = 6$ and $a_n = 5a_{n-1}$ for $n \geq 2$; Explicit rule: $a_n = 6(5)^{n-1}$

INTEGRATE MATHEMATICAL PRACTICES
Focus on Math Connections

MP.1 After students have written the general algebraic formulas for recursive and explicit rules for geometric sequences, compare the process for substituting values for the variables in the formulas for geometric sequences with the process for arithmetic sequences. Point out the similarities such as the use of a common difference in arithmetic sequences and the use of a common ratio in geometric sequences. Also, point out the differences such as how the common difference is added in a recursive rule for an arithmetic sequence, while the common ratio is multiplied in a recursive rule for a geometric sequence.

Constructing Geometric Sequences **688**

AVOID COMMON ERRORS

Some students may confuse the recursive and explicit rules for geometric sequences. Remind students that the recursive rule for a geometric sequence is stated by providing the first term, $f(1)$, and a rule for terms after the first term in terms of the previous term. Such a rule has the general form $f(n) = f(n-1) \cdot r$, where r is the common ratio. An explicit rule for a geometric sequence is stated by indicating the domain of the sequence and giving a rule for the nth term, with the general form $f(n) = f(1) \cdot r^{n-1}$, where r is the common ratio. Show students examples.

COMMUNICATING MATH

Tell students that they have learned about two kinds of sequences in this course: arithmetic and geometric. Arithmetic sequences have common differences and geometric sequences have common ratios. Common ratios are found by dividing each term after the first term by the term before it. Have students state in their own words how to find any term in a geometric sequence.

Use the geometric sequence to help write a recursive rule and an explicit rule for any geometric sequence. For the general rules, the values of n are consecutive integers starting with 1.

12. 5, 15, 45, 135, 405,…

	Numbers	Algebra
Common ratio:	5, 15, 45, 135, 405,… Common ratio = 3	$f(1), f(2), f(3), f(4), f(5),…$ Common ratio = r
Recursive rule:	$f(1) = 5$ and $f(n) = f(n-1) \cdot 3$ for $n \geq 2$	Given $f(1)$, $f(n) = f(n-1) \cdot r$ for $n \geq 2$
Explicit rule:	$f(n) = 5 \cdot 3^{n-1}$	$f(n) = f(1) \cdot r^{n-1}$

13. 10, 40, 160, 640, 2,560,…

	Numbers	Algebra
Common ratio:	10, 40, 160, 640, 2560,… Common ratio = 4	$f(1), f(2), f(3), f(4), f(5),…$ Common ratio = r
Recursive rule:	$f(1) = 10$ and $f(n) = f(n-1) \cdot 4$ for $n \geq 2$	Given $f(1)$, $f(n) = f(n-1) \cdot r$ for $n \geq 2$
Write an explicit rule:	$f(n) = 10 \cdot 4^{n-1}$	$f(n) = f(1) \cdot r^{n-1}$

14. 5, 10, 20, 40, 80,…

	Numbers	Algebra
Common ratio:	5, 10, 20, 40, 80, 160,… Common ratio = 2	$f(1), f(2), f(3), f(4), f(5),…$ Common ratio = r
Recursive rule:	$f(1) = 5$ and $f(n) = f(n-1) \cdot 2$ for $n \geq 2$	Given $f(1)$, $f(n) = f(n-1) \cdot r$ for $n \geq 2$
Explicit rule:	$f(n) = 5 \cdot 2^{n-1}$	$f(n) = f(1) \cdot r^{n-1}$

15. 18, 90, 450, 2250, 11,250,…

	Numbers	Algebra
Common ratio:	18, 90, 450, 2250, 11,250,… Common ratio = 5	$f(1), f(2), f(3), f(4), f(5),…$ Common ratio = r
Recursive rule:	$f(1) = 18$ and $f(n) = f(n-1) \cdot 5$ for $n \geq 2$	Given $f(1)$, $f(n) = f(n-1) \cdot r$ for $n \geq 2$
Explicit rule:	$f(n) = 18 \cdot 5^{n-1}$	$f(n) = f(1) \cdot r^{n-1}$

Write an explicit rule for each geometric sequence using subscript notation. Use a calculator and round your answer to the nearest tenth if necessary.

16. The fifth term of the sequence is 5. The sixth term is 2.5.

Common ratio: $a_6 = a_5 \cdot r$

$$2.5 = 5 \cdot r$$
$$r = 0.5$$

First term: $2.5 = a_1(0.5)^5$

$$2.5 = a_1(0.03125)$$
$$80 = a_1$$

Equation: $a_n = 80(0.5)^{n-1}$

17. The third term of the sequence is 120. The fifth term is 76.8.

Common ratio: $a_5 = a_3 \cdot r^2$

$$76.8 = 120 \cdot r^2$$
$$\frac{76.8}{120} = r^2$$
$$0.64 = r^2$$
$$r = 0.8$$

First term: $76.8 = a_1(0.8)^4$

$$76.8 = a_1(0.4096)$$
$$187.5 = a_1$$

Equation: $a_n = 187.5(0.8)^{n-1}$

18. The fourth term of the sequence is 216. The sixth term is 96.

Common ratio: $a_6 = a_4 \cdot r^2$

$$96 = 216 \cdot r^2$$
$$\frac{4}{9} = r^2$$
$$r = \frac{2}{3}$$

First term: $96 = a_1\left(\frac{2}{3}\right)^5$

$$96 = a_1\left(\frac{32}{243}\right)$$
$$729 = a_1$$

Equation: $a_n = 729\left(\frac{2}{3}\right)^{n-1}$

19. **Sports** The numbers of teams remaining in each round of a single-elimination tennis tournament represent a geometric sequence where a_n is the number of teams competing and n is the round. There are 32 teams remaining in round 4 and 8 teams in round 6.

Common ratio: $a_6 = a_4 \cdot r^2$

$$8 = 32 \cdot r^2$$
$$\frac{8}{32} = r^2$$
$$r = \frac{1}{2}$$

First term: $8 = a_1\left(\frac{1}{2}\right)^5$

$$8 = a_1\left(\frac{1}{32}\right)$$
$$256 = a_1$$

Equation: $a_n = 256\left(\frac{1}{2}\right)^{n-1}$

20. **Video Games** The numbers of points that a player must accumulate to reach each next level of a video game form a geometric sequence where a_n is the number of points needed to complete level n. You need 20,000 points to complete level 3 and 8,000,000 points to complete level 5.

Common ratio:

$$a_5 = a_3 \cdot r^2$$
$$8{,}000{,}000 = 20{,}000 \cdot r^2$$
$$400 = r^2$$
$$r = 20$$

First term:

$$8{,}000{,}000 = a_1(20)^4$$
$$8{,}000{,}000 = a_1(160{,}000)$$
$$50 = a_1$$

Write the equation:

$$a_n = 50(20)^{n-1}$$

QUESTIONING STRATEGIES

? In the explicit rule of a function, can you substitute any term in the sequence for a_1? No; the correct terms would not be generated if a term other than a_1 were substituted.

Constructing Geometric Sequences   **690**

Have students write the first five terms of a geometric sequence for which r is greater than 1. Then have them write the first five terms of a geometric sequence for which r is less than 1. Have the students explain how to write the explicit and recursive rules for each sequence.

21. **Conservation** A state began an effort to increase the deer population. In year 2 of the effort, the deer population in a state forest was 1200. In year 4, the population was 1728.

Common ratio:

$$a_4 = a_2 \cdot r^2$$
$$1728 = 1200 \cdot r^2$$
$$\frac{1728}{1200} = r^2$$
$$r = \frac{6}{5}$$

First term:

$$1728 = a_1\left(\frac{6}{5}\right)^3$$
$$1728 = a_1\left(\frac{216}{125}\right)$$
$$1000 = a_1$$

Equation: $a_n = 1000\left(\frac{6}{5}\right)^{n-1}$

22. **Biology** The growth of a local raccoon population approximates a geometric sequence where a_n is the number of raccoons in a given year and n is the year. After 6 years there are 45 raccoons and after 8 years there are 71 raccoons.

Common ratio:

$$a_8 = a_7 \cdot r$$
$$a_7 = a_6 \cdot r$$
$$a_8 = a_6 \cdot r^2$$
$$71 = 45 \cdot r^2$$
$$1.58 \approx r^2$$
$$r \approx 1.26$$

First term:

$$45 = a_1(1.26)^{6-1}$$
$$45 = 3.18a_1$$
$$14 = a_1$$

Write the equation:

$$a_n = 14(1.26)^{n-1}$$

23. **Chemistry** A chemist measures the temperature in degrees Fahrenheit of a chemical compound every hour. The temperatures approximate a geometric sequence where a_n is the temperature at a given hour, and n is the hour. At hour 4, the temperature is $70\,°F$ and at hour 6 the temperature is $80\,°F$.

Common ratio:

$$a_6 = a_4 \cdot r^2$$
$$80 = 70 \cdot r^2$$
$$\frac{80}{70} = r^2$$
$$1.14 \approx r^2$$
$$r \approx 1.07$$

First term:

$$80 = a_1(1.07)^5$$
$$80 = a_1(1.40255)$$
$$57 \approx a_1$$

Write the equation:

$$a_n = 57(1.07)$$

24. Yusuf was asked to write a recursive rule for a sequence. Which of the following is an appropriate answer? Select all that apply.

a. $f(n) = 11(5)^{n-1}$ b. $f(n) = 11f(n-1), f(1) = 555$ c. $f(n) = f(n-1) + 15, f(1) = 36$

d. $f(n) = 12 + 19 \cdot f(n-1)$ e. $f(n) = -4\left(\frac{2}{3}\right)^{n-1}$ **So only b and c are recursive.**

25. Multi-Step An economist predicts that the cost of food will increase by 4% per year for the next several years.

    a. Write an explicit rule for the sequence that gives the cost $f(n)$ in dollars of a box of cereal in year n that costs \$3.20 in year 1. Justify your answer.

       $f(n) = 3.2 \cdot 1.04^{n-1}$; the cost in year 1, $f(1)$, is \$3.20. An increase of 4% means the cost is multiplied by 1.04, that is, $f(n) = f(n-1) \cdot 1.04$

    b. What is the fourth term of the sequence? What does it represent in this situation? Justify your answer.

       \$3.60; it represents the cost of the box of cereal in year 4. $f(4) = 3.2 \cdot 1.04^3 \approx 3.60$

26. Analyze Relationships Suppose you know the 8th term of a geometric sequence and the common ratio r. How can you find the 3rd term of the sequence without writing a rule for the sequence? Explain.

    Divide the 8th term by the common ratio 5 times. If you were given the 3rd term, you would multiply it by the common ratio 5 times to get the 8th term, so perform the inverse operation.

27. Explain the Error Given that the second term of a sequence is 64 and the fourth term is 16, Francis wrote the explicit rule $a_n = 128 \cdot \left(\frac{1}{4}\right)^{n-1}$ for the sequence. Explain his error.

    Francis used the square of the common ratio. For the given sequence, $a_2 = 64$, and $a_4 = 16$, so $16 = 64 \cdot r^2$. Then $r^2 = \frac{1}{4}$ and $r = \frac{1}{2}$.

28. Communicate Mathematical Ideas Suppose you are given two terms of a geometric sequence like the ones in Example 3, except that both terms are negative. Explain how writing the explicit rule for the sequence would differ from the examples in this lesson.

    When you find the common ratio r, you have to consider both the positive and negative values. The term between the given terms might be negative or it might be positive. If it is positive, then the common ratio r is negative. If it is negative, then r is positive. You would have to consider both possibilities. If $r > 0$, then the first term must be negative. If $r < 0$, then the first term must be positive.

Lesson Performance Task

The table shows how a population of rabbits has changed over time. Write an explicit rule for the geometric sequence described in the table. In what year will there be more than 5000 rabbits?

Time (years), n	Population, a_n
1	800
2	1200
3	1800
4	2700

$\dfrac{1200}{800} = 1.5 = r$ $a_n = 800 \cdot 1.5^{n-1}$

Problem can be solved by extending the table:

In year 5 there will be 4050 rabbits and in year 6 there will be 6075 rabbits.

There will be more than 5000 rabbits in year 6.

QUESTIONING STRATEGIES

? Is there a common difference in the sequence of population values? If so, what is it? no

? Is there a common ratio in the sequence of population values? If so, what is it? yes; 1.5

INTEGRATED MATHEMATICAL PRACTICES

Focus on Technology

MP.5 Students can use a computer spreadsheet to extend the geometric sequence for this situation by following these instructions. Enter 800 in cell A1. Then click on cell A2 and input the formula, =A1*1.5, into the formula window and touch Enter. The value 1200 will appear in cell A2. Place your cursor on the bottom right hand corner of cell A2 so that a plus sign appears. Click the plus sign and drag the cursor down 10 or more cells below A2. The successive terms of the sequence will appear.

EXTENSION ACTIVITY

Have students investigate the Fibonacci sequence, a sequence that is neither arithmetic or geometric. The first two terms of the sequence are 1 and 1. Each term after that is generated by adding the previous two terms. The sequence is 1, 1, 2, 3, 5, 8, 13, …. Have students write a recursive rule for this sequence and extend the sequence for at least 4 more terms.

A recursive rule is $a_1 = 1$, $a_2 = 1$, $a_n = a_{n-2} + a_{n-1}$ for $n \geq 3$. The next 4 terms are 21, 34, 55, 89.

Scoring Rubric

2 points: Student correctly solves the problem and explains his/her reasoning.

1 point: Student shows good understanding of the problem but does not fully solve or explain his/her reasoning.

0 points: Student does not demonstrate understanding of the problem.

Constructing Exponential Functions

Common Core Math Standards

The student is expected to:

 COMMON CORE F-LE.A.2

Construct… geometric… sequences, given a graph, a description of a relationship, or two input-output pairs… Also F-IF.A.2, F-IF.C.7e

Mathematical Practices

 COMMON CORE MP.6 Precision

Language Objective

Explain to a partner what the graph of a discrete exponential function looks like.

ENGAGE

Essential Question: What are discrete exponential functions and how do you represent them?

Possible answer: Discrete exponential functions are exponential functions whose domains are limited, such as the set of integers, making the graph appear as isolated points instead of a continuous curve.

PREVIEW: LESSON PERFORMANCE TASK

View the Engage section online. Discuss the photo and why the population of invasive species might grow exponentially. Then preview the Lesson Performance Task.

Name_____ Class_____ Date_____

15.3 Constructing Exponential Functions

Essential Question: What are discrete exponential functions and how do you represent them?

Resource Locker

⊘ Explore Understanding Discrete Exponential Functions

Recall that a discrete function has a graph consisting of isolated points.

(A) The table represents the cost of tickets to an annual event as a function of the number t of tickets purchased. Complete the table by *adding* 10 to each successive cost. Plot each ordered pair from the table.

Tickets t	Cost ($)	$(t, f(t))$
1	10	(1, 10)
2	20	(2, 20)
3	30	(3, 30)
4	40	(4, 40)
5	50	(5, 50)

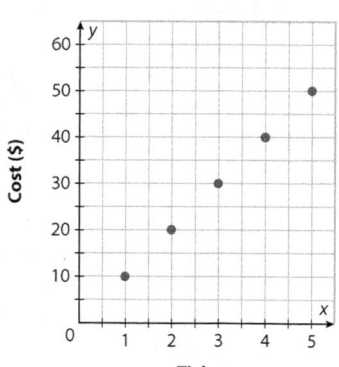

© Houghton Mifflin Harcourt Publishing Company

693

HARDCOVER PAGES 545–554

Turn to these pages to find this lesson in the hardcover student edition.

Ⓑ The number of people attending an event doubles each year. The table represents the total attendance at each annual event as a function of the event number n. Complete the table by *multiplying* each successive attendance by 2. Plot each ordered pair from the table.

Event Number n	Attendance	$(n, g(n))$
1	20	(1, 20)
2	40	(2, 40)
3	80	(3, 80)
4	160	(4, 160)
5	320	(5, 320)

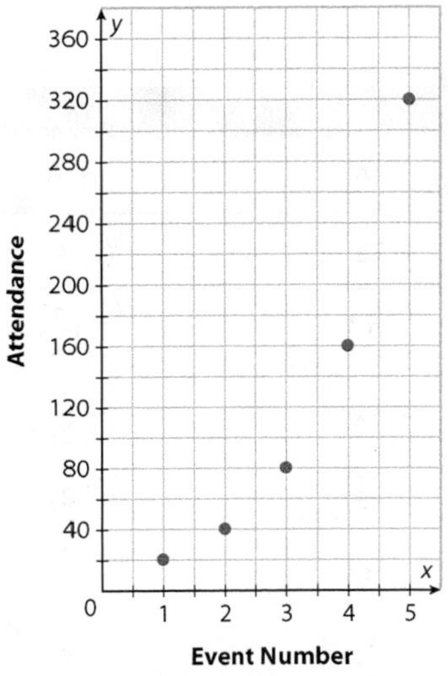

Ⓒ Complete the table.

Function	Linear?	Discrete?
$f(t)$	Yes	Yes
$g(n)$	No	Yes

Reflect

1. **Communicate Mathematical Ideas** What are the limitations on the domains of these functions? Why? **The domains include only whole numbers. You cannot buy a fraction of a ticket to an event, nor stage a fraction of an event.**

PROFESSIONAL DEVELOPMENT

Learning Progressions

In this lesson, students learn how to identify and represent exponential functions. Some key understandings for students are as follows:

- An exponential function can be represented by an equation of the form $f(x) = ab^x$, where a, b, and x are real numbers, $a \neq 0$, $b > 0$, and $b \neq 1$.
- For an exponential function $f(x)$, if x is in the domain of the function, then the ratio of $f(x+1)$ to $f(x)$ is a constant ratio.

In the next module, students will learn more about exponential functions, including exponential growth and decay functions.

EXPLORE

Understanding Discrete Exponential Functions

INTEGRATE TECHNOLOGY

Have students complete the Explore activity in either the book or online lesson.

QUESTIONING STRATEGIES

How are the tables for the functions different? **They are different because successive output values of the first function have a common difference, while successive output values of the second function have a common ratio.**

EXPLAIN 1

Representing Discrete Exponential Functions

INTEGRATE MATHEMATICAL PRACTICES

Focus on Math Connections

MP.1 Point out that the constant b in a function of the form $f(x) = ab^x$, where a and b are real numbers, $a \neq 0$, $b > 0$, and $b \neq 1$, corresponds to the common ratio, r, in a geometric sequence. Explain to students that if the domain of the function is the set of positive integers, the points of the graph of a discrete exponential function represent a geometric sequence. The x-values are the term numbers of the sequence and the y-values are the corresponding terms.

QUESTIONING STRATEGIES

? How do you evaluate a complex fraction, such as $\dfrac{1}{\frac{1}{2}}$? Multiply the numerator by the reciprocal of the denominator: $1 \cdot \dfrac{2}{1} = \dfrac{2}{1} = 2$.

Explain 1 **Representing Discrete Exponential Functions**

An **exponential function** is a function whose successive output values are related by a constant ratio. An exponential function can be represented by an equation of the form $f(x) = ab^x$, where a, b, and x are real numbers, $a \neq 0$, $b > 0$, and $b \neq 1$. The constant ratio is the base b.

When evaluating exponential functions, you will need to use the properties of exponents, including zero and negative exponents.

Recall that, for any nonzero number c:

$$c^0 = 1,\ c \neq 0$$
$$c^{-n} = \frac{1}{c^n},\ c \neq 0.$$

Example 1 Complete the table for each function using the given domain. Then graph the function using the ordered pairs from the table.

(A) $f(x) = 3 \cdot \left(\frac{1}{2}\right)^x$ with a domain of $\left\{-1, 0, 1, 2, 3, 4\right\}$

$f(-1) = 3 \cdot \left(\frac{1}{2}\right)^{-1} = 3 \cdot \frac{1}{\left(\frac{1}{2}\right)} = 3 \cdot 2 = 6$

x	$f(x)$	$(x, f(x))$
-1	6	$(-1, 6)$
0	3	$(0, 3)$
1	$1\frac{1}{2}$	$\left(1, 1\frac{1}{2}\right)$
2	$\frac{3}{4}$	$\left(2, \frac{3}{4}\right)$
3	$\frac{3}{8}$	$\left(3, \frac{3}{8}\right)$
4	$\frac{3}{16}$	$\left(4, \frac{3}{16}\right)$

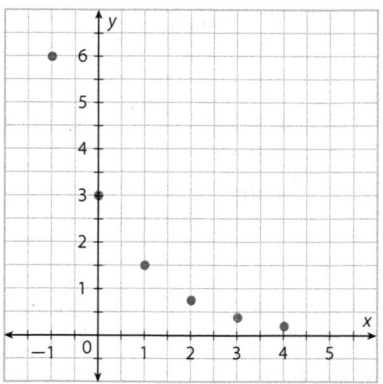

COLLABORATIVE LEARNING

Peer-to-Peer Activity

Have students work in pairs. Instruct one student in each pair to construct a table of values and graph for the function defined by $h(x) = 3x$ with the domain $\left\{-2, -1, 0, 2\right\}$. Instruct the other student to do the same for the function defined by $g(x) = 3^x$ with the same domain. Have the students compare and contrast the tables of values and the graphs.

Ⓑ $f(x) = 3\left(\frac{4}{3}\right)^x$; domain $= \left\{-2, -1, 0, 1, 2, 3\right\}$

$$f(-2) = 3\left(\frac{4}{3}\right)^{-2} = 3 \cdot \frac{1}{\left(\frac{4}{3}\right)^2} = 3 \cdot \frac{\boxed{3}^{2}}{\boxed{4}^{2}} = 3 \cdot \frac{\boxed{9}}{\boxed{16}} = \frac{\boxed{27}}{16} = 1\frac{\boxed{11}}{16}$$

x	f(x)	(x, f(x))
−2	$1\frac{11}{16}$	$\left(-2, \boxed{1\frac{11}{16}}\right)$
−1	$2\frac{1}{4}$	$\left(-1, \boxed{2\frac{1}{4}}\right)$
0	3	$\left(0, \boxed{3}\right)$
1	4	$\left(1, \boxed{4}\right)$
2	$5\frac{1}{3}$	$\left(2, \boxed{5\frac{1}{3}}\right)$
3	$7\frac{1}{9}$	$\left(3, 7\frac{1}{9}\right)$

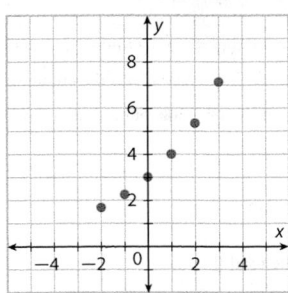

Reflect

2. **What If** What would happen to the function $f(x) = ab^x$ if a were 0? What if b were 1?
   If $a = 0$ then $f(x) = 0$ for all x, and if $b = 1$, then $f(x) = a$ for all x. Neither of these
   constant functions are exponential functions.

3. **Discussion** Why is a geometric sequence a discrete exponential function?
   A sequence is a function. When the input values increase by 1, the successive output
   values are related by a constant ratio, the common ratio. The general recursive rule for a
   geometric sequence is the form of an exponential function.

DIFFERENTIATE INSTRUCTION

Cognitive Strategies

Encourage students to isolate the necessary information from any problem
scenario they are given. It may help to circle or underline values or to write the
important information on a separate sheet of paper.

EXPLAIN 2

Constructing Exponential Functions from Verbal Descriptions

MODELING

Have students fold a piece of paper in half repeatedly. Have them make a table representing the number of layers of paper after 0 folds, 1 fold, 2 folds, and so on.

QUESTIONING STRATEGIES

? How do you find the value of b in order to write an exponential function in the form $f(x) = ab^x$? Choose a number x in the domain of the function. Then divide $f(x + 1)$ by $f(x)$ to get b.

Make a table for the function using the given domain. Then graph the function using the ordered pairs from the table.

4. $f(x) = 4\left(\dfrac{3}{2}\right)^x$; domain $= \left\{-3, -2, -1, 0, 1, 2\right\}$

x	f(x)	(x, f(x))
-3	$\left(\dfrac{32}{27}\right) = 1\dfrac{5}{27}$	$\left(-3, 1\dfrac{5}{27}\right)$
-2	$\left(\dfrac{16}{9}\right) = 1\dfrac{7}{9}$	$\left(-2, 1\dfrac{7}{9}\right)$
-1	$\left(\dfrac{8}{3}\right) = 2\dfrac{2}{3}$	$\left(-1, 2\dfrac{2}{3}\right)$
0	4	$(0, 4)$
1	6	$(1, 6)$
2	9	$(2, 9)$

Explain 2 **Constructing Exponential Functions from Verbal Descriptions**

You can write an equation for an exponential function $f(x) = ab^x$ by finding or calculating the values of a and b. The value of a is the value of the function when $x = 0$. The value of b is the common ratio of successive function values, $b = \dfrac{f(x + 1)}{f(x)}$. For discrete functions with integer or whole number domains, these will be successive values of the function.

Example 2 Write an equation for the function.

(A) When a piece of paper is folded in half, the total thickness doubles. Suppose an unfolded piece of paper is 0.1 millimeter thick. The total thickness $t(n)$ of the paper is an exponential function of the number of folds n.

The value of a is the original thickness of the paper before any folds are made, or 0.1 millimeter.

Because the thickness doubles with each fold, the value of b (the constant ratio) is 2.

The equation for the function is $t(n) = 0.1(2)^n$.

© Houghton Mifflin Harcourt Publishing Company · Image Credits: ©Digital Vision/Getty Images

---

LANGUAGE SUPPORT **EL**

Connect Vocabulary

In this lesson there are several key words that begin with the prefix *in-*. Learning the meaning of prefixes helps all students of math and science, since many key terms in both disciplines originated in Latin or have Latin prefixes. In this lesson, the words *increase* and *input* both start with the prefix *in-*, which means *in, into, on, near,* or *towards*. The prefix *in-* can also mean *not*, as in the word *inverse*. Another key prefix in this lesson is *non-*, which means *not*. The term *nonzero*, for example, means *not zero*.

(B) A savings account with an initial balance of $1000 earns 1% interest per month. That means that the account balance grows by a factor of 1.01 each month if no deposits or withdrawals are made. The account balance in dollars $B(t)$ is an exponential function of the time t in months after the initial deposit.

Let B represent the balance in dollars as a function of time t in months.

The value of a is the original balance, __1000__.

The value of b is the factor by which the balance changes every month, __1.01__.

The equation for the function is $B(t) = $ __$1000(1.01)^t$__.

Reflect

5. Why is the exponential function in the paper-folding example discrete?
   The paper can only be folded a whole number of times.

Your Turn

6. A piece of paper that is 0.2 millimeters thick is folded. Write an equation for the thickness t of the paper in millimeters as a function of the number n of folds.

   Initial thickness $(n = 0)$ $a = 0.2$

   Change per fold: double $b = 2$

   Equation: $t(n) = 0.2 \cdot 2^n$

Explain 3   **Constructing Exponential Functions from Input-Output Pairs**

You can use given two successive values of a discrete exponential function to write an equation for the function.

Example 3   Write an equation for the function that includes the points.

(A) $(3, 12)$ and $(4, 24)$

Find b by dividing the function value of the second pair by the function value of the first: $b = \frac{24}{12} = 2$.

Evaluate the function for $x = 3$ and solve for a.

Write the general form.	$f(x) = ab^x$
Substitute the value for b.	$f(x) = a \cdot 2^x$
Substitute a pair of input-output values.	$12 = a \cdot 2^3$
Simplify.	$12 = a \cdot 8$
Solve for a.	$a = \frac{3}{2}$
Use a and b to write an equation for the function.	$f(x) = \frac{3}{2} \cdot 2^x$

EXPLAIN 3

Constructing Exponential Functions from Input-Output Pairs

AVOID COMMON ERRORS

When calculating the value of b, students may divide in the wrong order. Remind them that they should always divide an output value by the preceding output value. For example, if they are using $(4, 27)$ and $(5, 9)$, they should divide the function value of the second pair by the function value of the first pair:

$$b = \frac{9}{27} = \frac{1}{3}.$$

INTEGRATE MATHEMATICAL PRACTICES
Focus on Critical Thinking

MP.3 After students have found an equation for an exponential function, have them check both pairs in the equation to verify that the equation is correct.

? If an exponential function includes the points (4, 64) and (5, 32), what is the common ratio? Explain how you found it. **The common ratio is 0.5. I found it by dividing 32 by 64:** $\frac{64}{32} = \frac{1}{2} = 0.5$.

ELABORATE

CRITICAL THINKING

Have students give an example of an increasing exponential function and of a decreasing exponential function.

SUMMARIZE THE LESSON

? What are discrete exponential functions and how can you represent them? **A discrete exponential function is a function of the form $f(x) = ab^x$, with $a \neq 0$, $b > 1$, and $b \neq 1$, such that the graph of the function is a set of isolated points. For example, the domain of the function could be the set of whole numbers. Such a function can be represented by a set of input and output values in a table or by a graph of ordered pairs.**

Ⓑ (1, 3) and $\left(2, \frac{9}{4}\right)$

Find b by dividing the function value of the second pair by the first: $b = \frac{9}{4} \div 3 = \boxed{\frac{3}{4}}$.

Write the general form. $f(x) = \boxed{ab^x}$

Substitute the value for b. $f(x) = a \cdot \boxed{\left(\frac{3}{4}\right)}^x$

Substitute a pair of input-output values. $\boxed{3} = a \cdot \left(\frac{3}{4}\right)^{\boxed{1}}$

Simplify. $3 = a \cdot \boxed{\frac{3}{4}}$

Solve for a. $a = \boxed{4}$

Use a and b to write an equation for the function. $f(x) = \boxed{4\left(\frac{3}{4}\right)}^x$

Your Turn

Write an equation for the function that includes the points.

7. $\left(-2, \frac{2}{5}\right)$ and $(-1, 2)$

$b = 2 \div \frac{2}{5} = 5$

$2 = a \cdot 5^{-1}; 2 = \frac{a}{5}; a = 10$

$f(x) = 10 \cdot 5^x$

💬 Elaborate

8. Explain why the following statement is true: For $0 < b < 1$ and $a > 0$, the function $f(x) = ab^x$ decreases as x increases.
   When you multiply a number a by a fraction b between 0 and 1, the product is less than the original number a. When you multiply by this fraction b repeatedly, the results decrease further.

9. Explain why the following statement is true: For $b > 1$ and $a > 0$, the function $f(x) = ab^x$ increases as x increases.
   When you multiply a number a by a number b greater than 1, the product is greater than the original number a. When you multiply by this number b repeatedly, the results increase further.

10. **Essential Question Check-In** What property do all pairs of adjacent points of a discrete exponential function share?
    The ratio of function values is the same for any two pairs.

• Online Homework
• Hints and Help
• Extra Practice

Complete the table for each function using the given domain.
Then graph the function using the ordered pairs from the table.

1. $f(x) = \frac{1}{2} \cdot 4^x$; domain $= \{-2, -1, 0, 1, 2\}$.

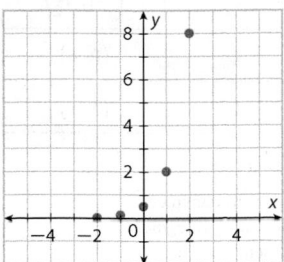

x	$f(x)$	$(x, f(x))$
-2	$\frac{1}{32}$	$\left(-2, \frac{1}{32}\right)$
-1	$\frac{1}{8}$	$\left(-1, \frac{1}{8}\right)$
0	$\frac{1}{2}$	$\left(0, \frac{1}{2}\right)$
1	2	$(1, 2)$
2	8	$(2, 8)$

2. $f(x) = 9\left(\frac{1}{3}\right)^x$; domain $= \{0, 1, 2, 3, 4, 5\}$.

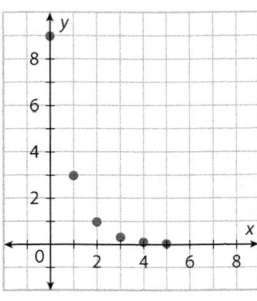

x	$f(x)$	$(x, f(x))$
0	9	$(0, 9)$
1	3	$(1, 3)$
2	1	$(2, 1)$
3	$\frac{1}{3}$	$\left(3, \frac{1}{3}\right)$
4	$\frac{1}{9}$	$\left(4, \frac{1}{9}\right)$
5	$\frac{1}{27}$	$\left(5, \frac{1}{27}\right)$

3. $f(x) = 6\left(\frac{2}{3}\right)^x$; domain $= \{-1, 0, 1, 2, 3, 4\}$.

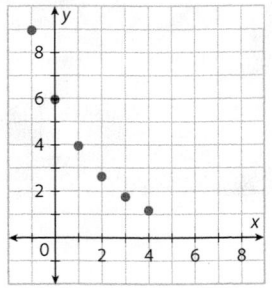

x	$f(x)$	$(x, f(x))$
-1	9	$(-1, 9)$
0	6	$(0, 6)$
1	4	$(1, 4)$
2	$2\frac{2}{3}$	$\left(2, 2\frac{2}{3}\right)$
3	$1\frac{7}{9}$	$\left(3, 1\frac{7}{9}\right)$
4	$1\frac{5}{27}$	$\left(4, 1\frac{5}{27}\right)$

EVALUATE

ASSIGNMENT GUIDE

Concepts and Skills	Practice
Explore Understanding Discrete Exponential Functions	Exercise 19
Example 1 Representing Discrete Exponential Functions	Exercises 1–4, 22–23
Example 2 Constructing Exponential Functions from Verbal Descriptions	Exercises 5–8, 20–21
Example 3 Constructing Exponential Functions from Input-Output Pairs	Exercises 9–18, 24

Exercise	Depth of Knowledge (D.O.K.)	COMMON CORE Mathematical Practices
1–4	**1** Recall of Information	**MP.6** Precision
5–8	**2** Skills/Concepts	**MP.4** Modeling
9–21	**2** Skills/Concepts	**MP.2** Reasoning
22	**1** Recall of Information	**MP.2** Reasoning
23–24	**3** Strategic Thinking **H.O.T.**	**MP.3** Logic

Constructing Exponential Functions   **700**

4. $f(x) = 6\left(\frac{4}{3}\right)^x$; domain $= \left\{-3, -2, -1, 0, 1\right\}$

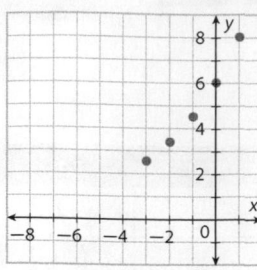

x	f(x)	(x, f(x))
−3	$2\frac{17}{32}$	$\left(-3, 2\frac{17}{32}\right)$
−2	$3\frac{3}{8}$	$\left(-2, 3\frac{3}{8}\right)$
−1	$4\frac{1}{2}$	$\left(-1, 4\frac{1}{2}\right)$
0	6	(0, 6)
1	8	(1, 8)

Write an equation for each function.

5. **Business** A recent trend in advertising is viral marketing. The goal is to convince viewers to share an amusing advertisement by e-mail or social networking. Imagine that the video is sent to 100 people on day 1. Each person agrees to send the video to 5 people the next day, and to request that each of those people send it to 5 people the day after they receive it. The number of viewers $v(n)$ is an exponential function of the number n of days since the video was first shown.

$a = 100$

$b = 5$

$v(n) = 100 \cdot 5^n$

6. A pharmaceutical company is testing a new antibiotic. The number of bacteria present in a sample when the antibiotic is applied is 100,000. Each hour, the number of bacteria present decreases by half. The number of bacteria remaining $r(n)$ is an exponential function of the number n of hours since the antibiotic was applied.

$a = 100{,}000$

$b = \frac{1}{2}$

$r(n) = 100{,}000\left(\frac{1}{2}\right)^n$

7. **Optics** A laser beam with an output of 5 milliwatts is directed into a series of mirrors. The laser beam loses 1% of its power every time it reflects off of a mirror. The power $p(n)$ is a function of the number n of reflections.

$a = 5$

$b = 0.99,$ (power remaining after 1% lost)

$p(n) = 5(0.99)^n$

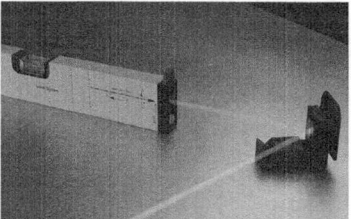

8. The NCAA basketball tournament begins with 64 teams, and after each round, half the teams are eliminated. The number of remaining teams $t(n)$ is an exponential function of the number n of rounds already played.

$a = 64$

$b = \frac{1}{2}$

$t(n) = 64\left(\frac{1}{2}\right)^n$

Write an equation for the function that includes the points.

9. $(2, 100)$ and $(3, 1000)$

$b = \frac{1000}{100}$

$= 10$

$100 = a \cdot 10^2$

$100 = 100a$

$a = 1$

$f(x) = 10^x$

10. $(-2, 4)$ and $(-1, 8)$

$b = \frac{8}{4}$

$= 2$

$8 = a \cdot 2^{-1}$

$8 = \frac{a}{2}$

$a = 16$

$f(x) = 16 \cdot 2^x$

11. $\left(1, \frac{4}{5}\right)$ and $\left(2, \frac{2}{3}\right)$

$b = \frac{\left(\frac{2}{3}\right)}{\left(\frac{4}{5}\right)}$

$= \frac{2}{3} \cdot \frac{5}{4}$

$= \frac{5}{6}$

$\frac{4}{5} = a \cdot \left(\frac{5}{6}\right)^1$

$\frac{4}{5} = a \cdot \frac{5}{6}$

$a = \frac{4}{5} \cdot \frac{6}{5}$

$= \frac{24}{25}$

$f(x) = \frac{24}{25} \cdot \left(\frac{5}{6}\right)^x$

12. $\left(-3, \frac{1}{16}\right)$ and $\left(-2, \frac{3}{8}\right)$

$b = \frac{\left(\frac{3}{8}\right)}{\left(\frac{1}{16}\right)}$

$= \frac{3}{8} \cdot \frac{16}{1}$

$= 6$

$\frac{1}{16} = a \cdot 6^{-3}$

$\frac{1}{16} = a \cdot \frac{1}{216}$

$a = \frac{1}{16} \cdot 216$

$= 13.5$

$f(x) = 13.5 \cdot 6^x$

Use two points to write an equation for the function.

13.

x	f(x)
1	2
2	$\frac{2}{7}$
3	$\frac{2}{49}$
4	$\frac{2}{343}$

$b = \frac{\left(\frac{2}{7}\right)}{2}$

$= \frac{1}{7}$

$2 = a \cdot \left(\frac{1}{7}\right)^1$

$2 = a \cdot \frac{1}{7}$

$a = 14$

$f(x) = 14 \cdot \left(\frac{1}{7}\right)^x$

AVOID COMMON ERRORS

Students may forget to find the value of both a and b when writing a function rule for an exponential function of the form $f(x) = ab^x$. Remind students that they need to determine the common ratio and the initial value of an exponential function in order to write the function rule.

14.

x	$f(x)$
-4	0.53
-3	5.3
-2	53
-1	530

Use points $(-2, 53)$ and $(-1, 530)$

$$b = \frac{530}{53}$$
$$= 10$$
$$530 = a \cdot (10)^{-1}$$
$$530 = a \cdot \frac{1}{10}$$
$$a = 5300$$
$$f(x) = 5300 \cdot (10)^x$$

15.

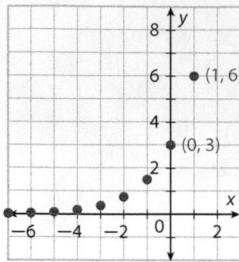

Use points $(0, 3)$ and $(1, 6)$

$$b = \frac{6}{3}$$
$$= 2$$
$$a = 3$$
$$f(x) = 3 \cdot 2^x$$

16.

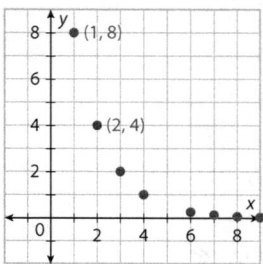

Use points $(1, 8)$ and $(2, 4)$

$$b = \frac{4}{8}$$
$$= \frac{1}{2}$$
$$8 = a\left(\frac{1}{2}\right)^1$$
$$8 = \frac{a}{2}$$
$$a = 16$$
$$f(x) = 16 \cdot \left(\frac{1}{2}\right)^x$$

17. The height $h(n)$ of a bouncing ball is an exponential function of the number n of bounces. One ball is dropped and on the first bounce reaches a height of 6 feet. On the second bounce it reaches a height of 4 feet.

$$b = \frac{4}{6}$$
$$= \frac{2}{3}$$
$$6 = a\left(\frac{2}{3}\right)^1$$
$$6 = a \cdot \frac{2}{3}$$
$$a = 6 \cdot \frac{3}{2}$$
$$= 9$$
$$h(n) = 9 \cdot \left(\frac{2}{3}\right)^n$$

18. A child starts a playground swing from standing and doesn't use her legs to keep swinging. On the first swing she swings forward by 18 degrees, and on the second swing she only comes 13.5 degrees forward. The measure in degrees of the angle $m(n)$ is an exponential function of the number n of swings.

$$b = \frac{13.5}{18}$$

$$= \frac{3}{4}$$

$$18 = a\left(\frac{3}{4}\right)^1$$

$$18 = a \cdot \frac{3}{4}$$

$$a = 18 \cdot \frac{4}{3}$$

$$= 24$$

$$m(n) = 24\left(\frac{3}{4}\right)^n$$

19. Make a Prediction A town's population has been declining in recent years. The table shows the population since 1980. Is this data consistent with an exponential function? Explain. If so, predict the population for 2010 assuming the trend holds.

Year	Population
1980	5000
1990	4000
2000	3200
2010	2560

To check for exponential behavior, find the ratios between successive values of the function.

$$\frac{4000}{5000} = \frac{4}{5}, \frac{3200}{4000} = \frac{4}{5}$$

The ratio between successive function values is $\frac{4}{5}$, so this is consistent with an exponential function.

$$3200 \cdot \frac{4}{5} = 2560$$

20. A piece of paper has a thickness of 0.15 millimeters. Write an equation to describe the thickness $t(n)$ of the paper when it is repeatedly folded in thirds, where n is the number of foldings.

$$b = 3$$

$$a = 0.15$$

$$t(n) = 0.15 \cdot 3^n$$

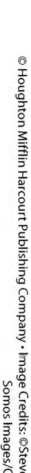

INTEGRATE MATHEMATICAL PRACTICES
Focus on Patterns

MP.8 Point out to students that, unlike linear functions, the letter b in an exponential function of the form $f(x) = ab^x$ does not represent the y-intercept.

Have students describe a specific discrete exponential function in at least two different ways. They can describe it with words, a function rule, a table, and/or a graph.

21. **Probability** The probability of getting heads on a single coin flip is $\frac{1}{2}$. The probability of getting nothing but heads on a series of coin flips decreases by $\frac{1}{2}$ for each additional coin flip. Write an exponential function for the probability $p(n)$ of getting all heads in a series of n coin flips.

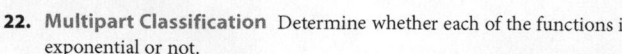

$$b = \frac{1}{2}$$
$$\frac{1}{2} = a\left(\frac{1}{2}\right)^1$$
$$\frac{1}{2} = a \cdot \frac{1}{2}$$
$$a = 1$$
$$p(n) = \left(\frac{1}{2}\right)^n$$

22. **Multipart Classification** Determine whether each of the functions is exponential or not.

a. $f(x) = x^2$ — ◯ Exponential ⬤ Not exponential

b. $f(x) = 3 \cdot 2^x$ — ⬤ Exponential ◯ Not exponential

c. $f(x) = 3 \cdot \frac{1}{2} x$ — ◯ Exponential ⬤ Not exponential

d. $f(x) = 1.001^x$ — ⬤ Exponential ◯ Not exponential

e. $f(x) = 2 \cdot x^3$ — ◯ Exponential ⬤ Not exponential

f. $f(x) = \frac{1}{10} \cdot 5^x$ — ⬤ Exponential ◯ Not exponential

H.O.T. Focus on Higher Order Thinking

23. **Explain the Error** Biff observes that in every math test he has taken this year, he has scored 2 points higher than the previous test. His score on the first test was 56. He models his test scores with the exponential function $s(n) = 28 \cdot 2^n$ where $s(n)$ is the score on his nth test. Is this a reasonable model? Explain.

No; Biff's test scores do not increase by a constant ratio. Instead they go up by 2 points each test. His scores are not consistent with an exponential function.

24. **Find the Error** Kaylee needed to write the equation of an exponential function from points on the graph of the function. To determine the value of b, Kaylee chose the ordered pairs $(1, 6)$ and $(3, 54)$ and divided 54 by 6. She determined that the value of b was 9. What error did Kaylee make?

She should use ordered pairs with x-values that differ by 1. The value Kaylee found is not the constant ratio of successive values.

Lesson Performance Task

In ecology, an invasive species is a plant or animal species newly introduced to an ecosystem, often by human activity. Because invasive species often lack predators in their new habitat, their populations typically experience exponential growth. A small initial population grows to a large population that drastically alters an ecosystem. Feral rabbits that populate Australia and zebra mussels in the Great Lakes are two examples of problematic invasive species that grew exponentially from a small initial population.

An ecologist monitoring a local stream has been collecting samples of an unfamiliar fish species over the past four years and has summarized the data in the table.

Here are the results so far:

Year	Average Population Per Mile
2009	32
2010	48
2011	72
2012	108
2013	
2014	

a. Look at the data in the table and confirm that the growth pattern is exponential.

$$\frac{48}{32} = 1.5 \qquad \frac{72}{48} = 1.5 \qquad \frac{108}{72} = 1.5$$

Since there is a common ratio, $r = 1.5$, the growth pattern is exponential.

b. Write the equation that represents the average population per square meter as a function of years since 2009.

The function is $f(t) = 32\left(\frac{3}{2}\right)^t$.

c. Predict the average populations expected for 2013 and 2014.

2013: 162 individuals per mile

2014: 243 individuals per mile

d. Graph the population versus time since 2009 and include the predicted values.

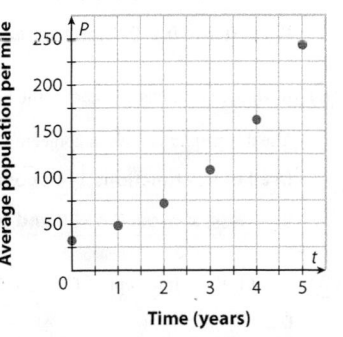

EXTENSION ACTIVITY

Have students research the feral rabbit population in Australia or the zebra mussel population in the Great Lakes. Have students find out how the population was introduced into the new habitat and describe efforts to control the population.

INTEGRATE MATHEMATICAL PRACTICES

Focus on Communication

MP.3 Have students explain why they would choose to use the fraction $\frac{3}{2}$ or its decimal equivalent, 1.5, when solving Part C of the Lesson Performance Task.

INTEGRATE MATHEMATICAL PRACTICES

Focus on Math Connections

MP.1 After students have completed the graph of the populations versus time, discuss how the value of b, when a is positive, causes the graph to increase over time. Then discuss what happens to the graph when students let $b = \frac{2}{3}$ in $f(t) = 32\left(\frac{2}{3}\right)^t$.

Scoring Rubric

2 points: Student correctly solves the problem and explains his/her reasoning.

1 point: Student shows good understanding of the problem but does not fully solve or explain his/her reasoning.

0 points: Student does not demonstrate understanding of the problem.

Constructing Exponential Functions   **706**

Graphing Exponential Functions

Common Core Math Standards

The student is expected to:

 F-IF.C.7e

Graph exponential... functions, showing intercepts and end behavior...
Also F-IF.C.8b

Mathematical Practices

MP.4 Modeling

Language Objective

Explain the domain, range, and end behavior of the graphs of exponential functions of the form $f(x) = ab^x$ with $a < 0$ and $0 < b < 1$.

ENGAGE

Essential Question: How do you graph an exponential function of the form $f(x) = ab^x$?

Use the value of a to find the y-intercept. Choose several values of x other than 0 to plot a few more ordered pairs and connect them with a smooth curve. Use the values of a and b to determine the end behavior of the function.

PREVIEW: LESSON PERFORMANCE TASK

View the Engage section online. Discuss the photo and the fact that the weight of a pumpkin might grow exponentially. Then preview the Lesson Performance Task.

Name_____ Class_____ Date_____

15.4 Graphing Exponential Functions

Essential Question: How do you graph an exponential function of the form $f(x) = ab^x$?

Resource Locker

⊘ Explore **Exploring Graphs of Exponential Functions**

Exponential functions follow the general shape $y = ab^x$.

Ⓐ Graph the exponential functions on a graphing calculator, and match the graph to the correct function rule.

1. $y = 3(2)^x$ a
2. $y = 0.5(2)^x$ c
3. $y = 3(0.5)^x$ b
4. $y = -3(2)^x$ d

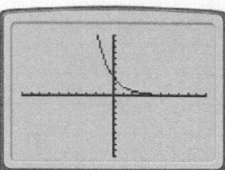

a.

b.

c.

d.

Ⓑ In all the functions 1–4 above, the base $b > 0$.

Use the graphs to make a conjecture: State the domain and range of $y = ab^x$ if $a > 0$.

In all of the functions 1–4 above, the domain values are all real numbers, or $-\infty < x < \infty$.

If $a > 0$ and $b > 0$, then the range values are all positive, or $y > 0$.

Ⓒ In all the functions 1–4 above, the base $b > 0$.

Use the graphs to make a conjecture: State the domain and range of $y = ab^x$ if $a < 0$.

In all of the functions 1–4 above, the domain values are all real numbers,

or $-\infty < x < \infty$. If $a < 0$ and $b > 0$, then the range values are all negative, or $y < 0$.

Ⓓ What is the y-intercept of $f(x) = 0.5(2)^x$?

0.5

© Houghton Mifflin Harcourt Publishing Company

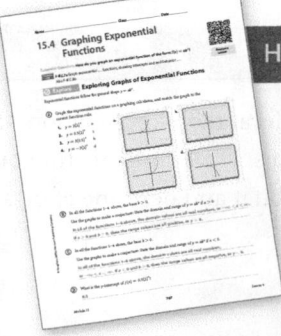

HARDCOVER PAGES 555–562

Turn to these pages to find this lesson in the hardcover student edition.

(E) Note the similarities between the *y*-intercept and *a*. What is their relationship?

The value of *a* in $y = ab^x$ is the *y*-intercept.

Reflect

1. **Discussion** What is the domain for any exponential function $y = ab^x$?
   all real numbers, or $-\infty < x < \infty$.

2. **Discussion** Describe the values of *b* for all functions $y = ab^x$.
   The base *b* is positive, or $b > 0$, in functions of the form $y = ab^x$

⚙️ **Explain 1** **Graphing Increasing Positive Exponential Functions**

The symbol ∞ represents *infinity*. We can describe the *end behavior* of a function by describing what happens to the function values as *x* approaches positive infinity ($x \rightarrow \infty$) and as *x* approaches negative infinity ($x \rightarrow -\infty$).

Example 1 Graph each exponential function. After graphing, identify *a* and *b*, the *y*-intercept, and the end behavior of the graph.

(A) $f(x) = 2^x$

Choose several values of *x* and generate ordered pairs.

x	$f(x) = 2^x$
−1	0.5
0	1
1	2
2	4

Graph the ordered pairs and connect them with a smooth curve.

$a = 1$

$b = 2$

y-intercept: $(0, 1)$

End Behavior: As *x*-values approach positive infinity ($x \rightarrow \infty$), *y*-values approach positive infinity ($y \rightarrow \infty$). As *x*-values approach negative infinity ($x \rightarrow -\infty$), *y*-values approach zero ($y \rightarrow 0$).

Using symbols only, we say: As $x \rightarrow \infty, y \rightarrow \infty$, and as $x \rightarrow -\infty, y \rightarrow 0$.

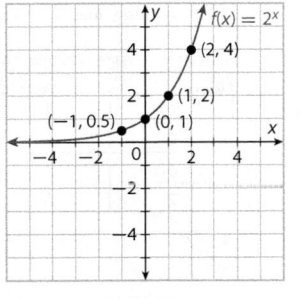

PROFESSIONAL DEVELOPMENT

 Integrate Mathematical Practices

This lesson provides an opportunity to address Mathematical Practice **MP.4**, which calls for students to use "modeling." Students use tables and graphs to represent exponential functions. They can use the graphs to determine the end behavior of the functions, and make generalizations about the effect of parameters *a* and *b* on the end behavior of an exponential function of the form $f(x) = ab^x$.

EXPLORE

Exploring Graphs of Exponential Functions

INTEGRATE TECHNOLOGY

Have students complete the Explore activity in either the book or online lesson.

QUESTIONING STRATEGIES

❓ What is the relationship between the value of *a* and the *y*-intercept of the graph of $f(x) = ab^x$? The *y*-intercept is equal to *a*.

EXPLAIN 1

Graphing Increasing Positive Exponential Functions

AVOID COMMON ERRORS

When generating ordered pairs for exponential functions of the form $f(x) = ab^x$, students may multiply *a* by *b* and then raise that product to *x*. Remind students to use the correct order of operations.

QUESTIONING STRATEGIES

? If an exponential function is of the form $f(x) = ab^x$, both a and b are positive real numbers, and the domain is the set of all real numbers, what is the range of the function? **The range is set of all positive real numbers.**

B $f(x) = 3(4)^x$

Choose several values of x and generate ordered pairs.

x	$f(x) = 3(4)^x$
−1	0.75
0	3
1	12
2	48

Graph the ordered pairs and connect them with a smooth curve.

$a = \boxed{3}$

$b = \boxed{4}$

y-intercept: $\left(\boxed{0}, \boxed{3}\right)$

End Behavior: As $x \to \infty$, $y \to \boxed{\infty}$ and as $x \to -\infty$, $y \to \boxed{0}$.

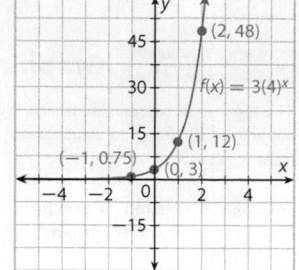

Reflect

3. If $a > 0$ and $b > 1$, what is the end behavior of the graph?
   If $a > 0$ and $b > 1$, as x approaches infinity y approaches infinity, and as x approaches negative infinity y approaches 0.

4. Describe the y-intercept of the exponential function $f(x) = ab^x$ in terms of a and b.
   A graph of the exponential $f(x) = ab^x$ will have a y-intercept at $(0, a)$.

Your Turn

5. Graph the exponential function $f(x) = 2(2)^x$
   After graphing, identify a and b, the y-intercept, and the end behavior of the graph.

x	$f(x) = 2(2)^x$
−1	1
0	2
1	4
2	8

$a = 2$

$b = 2$

y-intercept: $(0, 2)$

End Behavior: As $x \to \infty$, $y \to \infty$ and as $x \to -\infty$, $y \to 0$.

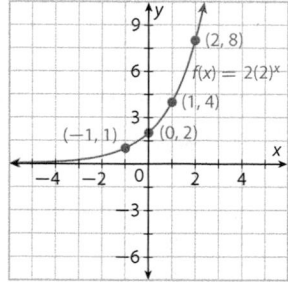

COLLABORATIVE LEARNING

Peer-to-Peer Activity

In pairs, have students develop and record their own rules for determining whether a graph represents one of the four main types of exponential functions: increasing positive, decreasing negative, decreasing positive, and increasing negative. For example, the rules might be $a > 0$ and $b > 1$, $a < 0$ and $0 < b < 1$, $a > 0$ and $0 < b < 1$, and $a < 0$ and $b > 1$. Then, give each pair one of each type of function and its graph. Have the students use their rules to determine which type of exponential function each graph represents. As a class, discuss the rules that worked.

Graphing Decreasing Negative Exponential Functions

You can use end behavior to discuss the behavior of a graph.

Example 2 Graph each exponential function. After graphing, identify a and b, the y-intercept, and the end behavior of the graph. Use end behavior to discuss the behavior of the graph.

Ⓐ $f(x) = -2(3)^x$

Choose several values of x and generate ordered pairs.

x	$f(x) = -2(3)^x$
−1	−0.7
0	−2
1	−6
2	−18

Graph the ordered pairs and connect them with a smooth curve.

$a = -2$

$b = 3$

y-intercept: $(0, -2)$

End Behavior: As $x \to \infty$, $y \to -\infty$ and as $x \to -\infty$, $y \to 0$.

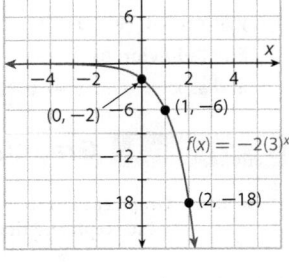

Ⓑ $f(x) = -3(4)^x$

Choose several values of x and generate ordered pairs.

x	$f(x) = -3(4)^x$
−1	−0.75
0	−3
1	−12
2	−48

Graph the ordered pairs and connect them with a smooth curve.

$a = \boxed{-3}$

$b = \boxed{4}$

y-intercept: $\left(\boxed{0}, \boxed{-3} \right)$

End Behavior: As $x \to \infty$, $y \to \boxed{-\infty}$ and as $x \to -\infty$, $y \to \boxed{0}$.

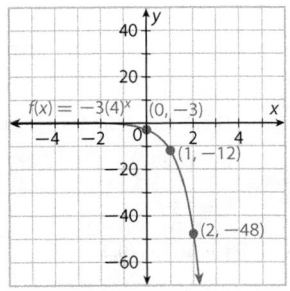

EXPLAIN 2

Graphing Decreasing Negative Exponential Functions

QUESTIONING STRATEGIES

❓ How can the value of a tell you in which quadrants the graph of an exponential function in the form $f(x) = ab^x$ is located? If a is greater than 0, the graph is located in quadrants I and II. If a is less than 0, the graph is located in quadrants III and IV.

AVOID COMMON ERRORS

Students may forget that by the order of operations rules, $f(x) = -2^x$ means that $f(x) = -1(2^x)$, and therefore the negative sign is not raised to the power. Tell students that the base of an exponential function cannot be negative.

DIFFERENTIATE INSTRUCTION

Cognitive Strategies

Guide students to see that for exponential functions of the form $f(x) = ab^x$, $b > 1$ represents growth (the graph is increasing), and $b < 1$ represents decline (the graph is decreasing). Remind students that if $b = 1$, the function is linear and not exponential; the function represents no change: no growth or decline.

EXPLAIN 3

Graphing Decreasing Positive Exponential Functions

QUESTIONING STRATEGIES

? If $0 < b < 1$ and a is a positive constant, how can you alter b to make the graph of $y = ab^x$ decrease more gradually? **Increase the value of b.**

Reflect

6. If $a < 0$ and $b > 1$, what is the end behavior of the graph?
   If $a < 0$ and $b > 1$, as x approaches infinity y approaches negative infinity, and as x approaches negative infinity y approaches 0.

Your Turn

7. Graph the exponential function. $f(x) = -3(3)^x$
   After graphing, identify a and b, the y-intercept, and the end behavior of the graph.

x	$f(x) = -3(3)^x$
−1	−1
0	−3
1	−9
2	−27

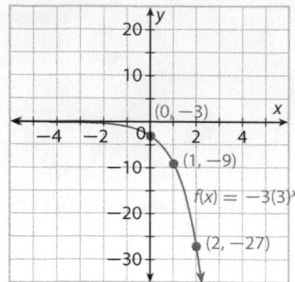

$a = -3$

$b = 3$

y-intercept: $(0, -3)$

End Behavior: As $x \to \infty$, $y \to -\infty$

and as $x \to -\infty$, $y \to 0$.

🖈 Explain 3 Graphing Decreasing Positive Exponential Functions

Example 3 Graph each exponential function. After graphing, identify a and b, the y-intercept, and the end behavior of the graph.

A $f(x) = (0.5)^x$

Choose several values of x and generate ordered pairs.

x	$f(x) = (0.5)^x$
−1	2
0	1
1	0.5
2	0.25

Graph the ordered pairs and connect them with a smooth curve.

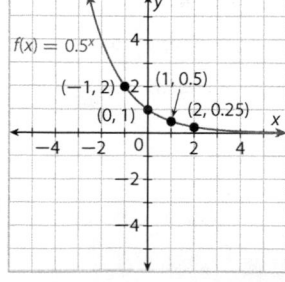

$a = 1$

$b = 0.5$

y-intercept: $(0, 1)$

End Behavior: As $x \to \infty$, $y \to 0$ and as $x \to -\infty$, $y \to \infty$.

LANGUAGE SUPPORT **EL**

Connect Vocabulary

Make sure that students understand what is meant by the *end behavior* of a function. The end behavior of a function describes what happens to the function values as x gets larger and larger (for example, as x becomes 100, 1000, and 1,000,000) and what happens to the function values as the values of x get smaller and smaller (for example, as x becomes –100, –1000, and –1,000,000). So, *end behavior* describes what happens to $f(x)$ when x is farther and farther to the right and what happens to $f(x)$ when x is farther and farther to the left.

B $f(x) = 2(0.4)^x$

Choose several values of x and generate ordered pairs.

x	$f(x) = 2(0.4)^x$
−1	5
0	2
1	0.8
2	0.32

Graph the ordered pairs and connect them with a smooth curve.

$a = \boxed{2}$

$b = \boxed{.4}$

y-intercept: $\left(\boxed{0}, \boxed{2}\right)$

End Behavior: As $x \to \infty$, $y \to \boxed{0}$ and as $x \to -\infty$, $y \to \boxed{\infty}$.

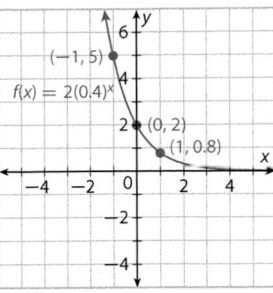

Reflect

8. If $a > 0$ and $0 < b < 1$, what is the end behavior of the graph?

   If $a > 0$ and $0 < b < 1$, as x approaches infinity y approaches zero, and as x approaches

   negative infinity y approaches infinity.

Your Turn

9. Graph the exponential function. After graphing, identify a and b, the y-intercept, and the end behavior of the graph.

   $f(x) = 3(0.5)^x$

x	$f(x) = 3(0.5)^x$
−1	6
0	3
1	1.5
2	0.75

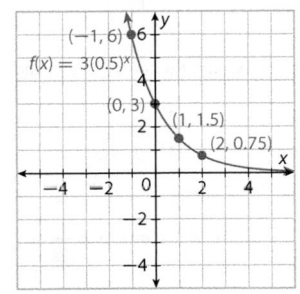

   $a = 3$

   $b = 0.5$

   y-intercept: $(0, 3)$

   End Behavior: As $x \to \infty$, $y \to 0$

   and as $x \to -\infty$, $y \to \infty$.

COGNITIVE STRATEGIES

Show students that the graph of $y = a\left(\dfrac{1}{b}\right)^x$ is the reflection of $y = ab^x$ over the y-axis by graphing $y = 3\left(\dfrac{1}{2}\right)^x$ and $y = 3(2)^x$.

EXPLAIN 4

Graphing Increasing Negative Exponential Functions

QUESTIONING STRATEGIES

? Why does it make sense for the graph of $f(x) = ab^x$ to stretch when $a > 1$, and for the graph to shrink when $0 < a < 1$, compared to the graph of $f(x) = b^x$? Multiplying by a factor a greater than 1 increases the outputs, compared with the function $f(x) = b^x$, and multiplying by a factor a between 0 and 1 decreases the outputs, compared with the function $f(x) = b^x$.

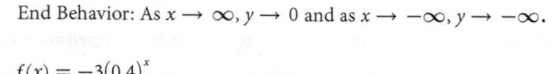

Explain 4 **Graphing Increasing Negative Exponential Functions**

Example 4 Graph each exponential function. After graphing, identify a and b, the y-intercept, and the end behavior of the graph.

(A) $f(x) = -0.5^x$

Choose several values of x and generate ordered pairs.

x	$f(x) = -0.5^x$
−1	−2
0	−1
1	−0.5
2	−0.25

Graph the ordered pairs and connect them with a smooth curve.

$a = -1$

$b = 0.5$

y-intercept: $(0, -1)$

End Behavior: As $x \to \infty, y \to 0$ and as $x \to -\infty, y \to -\infty$.

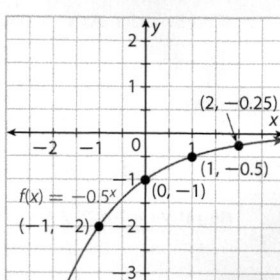

(B) $f(x) = -3(0.4)^x$

Choose several values of x and generate ordered pairs.

x	$f(x) = -3(0.4)^x$
−1	−7.5
0	−3
1	−1.2
2	−0.48

Graph the ordered pairs and connect them with a smooth curve.

$a = \boxed{-3}$

$b = \boxed{0.4}$

y-intercept: $\left(\boxed{0}, \boxed{-3} \right)$

End Behavior: As $x \to \infty, y \to \boxed{0}$ and as $x \to -\infty, y \to \boxed{-\infty}$.

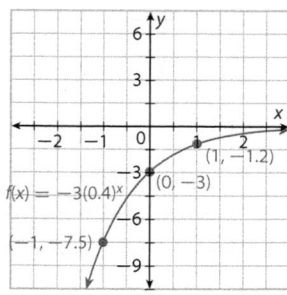

Reflect

10. If $a < 0$ and $0 < b < 1$, what is the end behavior of the graph?

If $a < 0$ and $0 < b < 1$, as x approaches infinity y approaches zero, and as x approaches

negative infinity y approaches negative infinity.

Your Turn

11. Graph the exponential function. After graphing, identify a and b, the y-intercept, and the end behavior of the graph.

$$f(x) = -2(0.5)^x$$

x	$f(x) = -2(0.5)^x$
-1	-4
0	-2
1	-1
2	-0.5

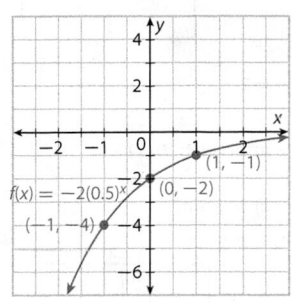

$a = -2$

$b = 0.5$

y-intercept: $(0, -2)$

End Behavior: As $x \to \infty$, $y \to 0$

and as $x \to -\infty$, $y \to -\infty$.

Elaborate

12. Why is $f(x) = 3(-0.5)^x$ not an exponential function?

$f(x) = 3(-0.5)^x$ is not an exponential function because its values alternate between

negative and positive, creating a line that jumps between increasingly smaller positive

and negative values as x approaches infinity. An exponential function has a smooth curve

that takes on increasingly smaller positive or negative values as x approaches infinity.

13. Essential Question Check-In When an exponential function of the form $f(x) = ab^x$ is graphed, what does a represent?

a represents the y-intercept of the function.

INTEGRATE TECHNOLOGY

Using graphing calculators can allow students to compare the graphs of exponential functions quickly, but they must enter the functions correctly. Show students that $y = -3 \cdot \left(\dfrac{2}{3}\right)^x$ is not the same as $y = -\left(3 \cdot \dfrac{2}{3}\right)^x$ by graphing both functions on a calculator.

ELABORATE

QUESTIONING STRATEGIES

Which of the following functions has the greatest y-intercept and which has the least y-intercept: $y = 2.5^x$, $y = \dfrac{1}{2}(2.5)^x$, $y = 2(2.5)^x$, or $y = 4(2.5)^x$? Explain. $y = 4(2.5)^x$ has the greatest y-intercept (4), and $y = \dfrac{1}{2}(2.5)^x$ has the least y-intercept $\left(\dfrac{1}{2}\right)$.

SUMMARIZE THE LESSON

Copy and complete the graphic organizer with your students. In each box, give an example of an appropriate exponential function and sketch its graph.

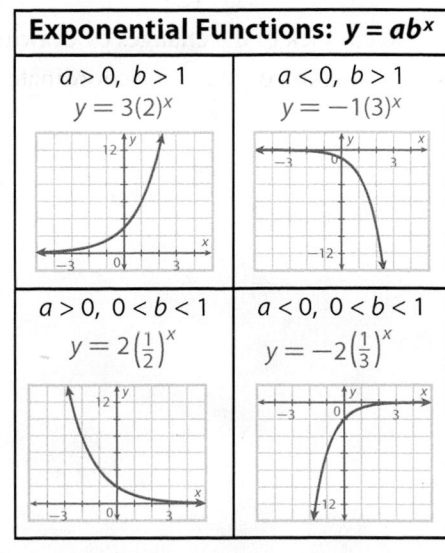

Exponential Functions: $y = ab^x$

$a > 0,\ b > 1$	$a < 0,\ b > 1$
$y = 3(2)^x$	$y = -1(3)^x$
$a > 0,\ 0 < b < 1$	$a < 0,\ 0 < b < 1$
$y = 2\left(\dfrac{1}{2}\right)^x$	$y = -2\left(\dfrac{1}{3}\right)^x$

EVALUATE

ASSIGNMENT GUIDE

Concepts and Skills	Practice
Explore Exploring Graphs of Exponential Functions	Exercises 1–2, 19
Example 1 Graphing Increasing Positive Exponential Functions	Exercises 5, 9, 13, 15, 18, 20–22
Example 2 Graphing Decreasing Negative Exponential Functions	Exercises 8, 12, 16, 23
Example 3 Graphing Decreasing Positive Exponential Functions	Exercises 4, 7, 10, 17, 25
Example 4 Graphing Increasing Negative Exponential Functions	Exercises 3, 6, 11, 14, 24

INTEGRATE TECHNOLOGY

On a graphing calculator, have students graph $y = 3(2)^x$, $y = -3(2)^x$, $y = 3\left(\frac{1}{2}\right)^x$, and $y = -3\left(\frac{1}{2}\right)^x$.

Have them keep track of the changes by drawing sketches of each graph on the same coordinate grid.

• Online Homework
• Hints and Help
• Extra Practice

State a, b, and the y-intercept then graph the function on a graphing calculator.

1. $f(x) = 2(3)^x$

Graph:

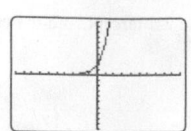

$a = 2$
$b = 3$
y-intercept: $(0, 2)$

2. $f(x) = -6(2)^x$

Graph:

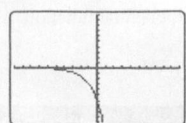

$a = -6$
$b = 2$
y-intercept: $(0, -6)$

3. $f(x) = -5(0.5)^x$

Graph:

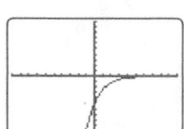

$a = -5$
$b = 0.5$
y-intercept: $(0, -5)$

4. $f(x) = 3(0.8)^x$

Graph:

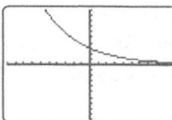

$a = 3$
$b = 0.8$
y-intercept: $(0, 3)$

5. $f(x) = 6(3)^x$

Graph:

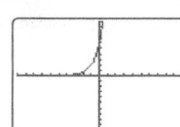

$a = 6$
$b = 3$
y-intercept: $(0, 6)$

6. $f(x) = -4(0.2)^x$

Graph:

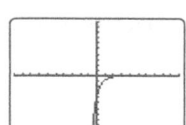

$a = -4$
$b = 0.2$
y-intercept: $(0, -4)$

Exercise	Depth of Knowledge (D.O.K.)	COMMON CORE Mathematical Practices
1–8	**1** Recall of Information	**MP.2** Reasoning
9–18	**2** Skills/Concepts	**MP.2** Reasoning
19	**2** Recall of Information	**MP.5** Using Tools
20–21	**1** Skills/Concepts	**MP.4** Modeling
22–25	**3** Strategic Thinking H.O.T.	**MP.3** Logic

7. $f(x) = 7(0.9)^x$

Graph:

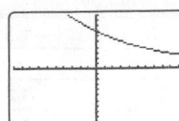

$a = 7$

$b = 0.9$

y-intercept: (0, 7)

8. $f(x) = -3(2)^x$

Graph:

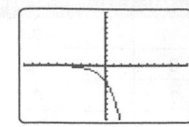

$a = -3$

$b = 2$

y-intercept: (0, −3)

State a, b, and the y-intercept then graph the function and describe the end behavior of the graphs.

9. $f(x) = 3(3)^x$

Ordered pairs:

x	$f(x) = 3(3)^x$
−1	1
0	3
1	9
2	27

Graph the ordered pairs and connect them with a smooth curve.

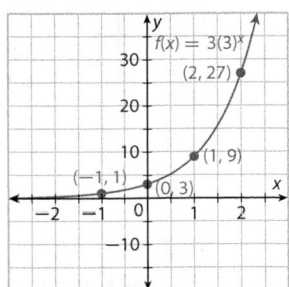

$a = 3$

$b = 3$

y-intercept: (0, 3)

End Behavior: As $x \to \infty$, $y \to \infty$ and as $x \to -\infty$, $y \to 0$.

10. $f(x) = 5(0.6)^x$

Ordered pairs:

x	$f(x) = 5(0.6)^x$
−1	8.3
0	5
1	3
2	1.8

Graph the ordered pairs and connect them with a smooth curve.

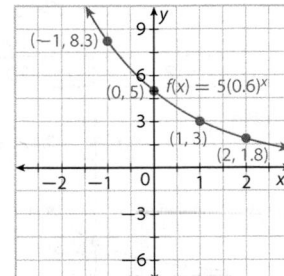

$a = 5$

$b = 0.6$

y-intercept: (0, 5)

End Behavior: As $x \to \infty$, $y \to 0$ and as $x \to -\infty$, $y \to \infty$.

? How do you know the exponent in ab^x applies to b and not ab? By the order of operations, bases are raised to exponents before multiplying.

AVOID COMMON ERRORS

Students may have trouble raising a number to a negative power. Remind them that a number raised to a negative power is the reciprocal of the number raised to the opposite power. For example,

$$4^{-2} = \left(\frac{1}{4}\right)^2 = \frac{1}{16}.$$

11. $f(x) = -6(0.7)^x$

x	$f(x) = -6(0.7)^x$
−1	−8.6
0	−6
1	−4.2
2	−2.9

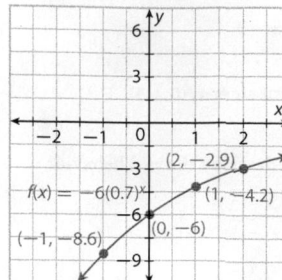

$a = -6; b = 0.7$

y-intercept: $(0, -6)$

End Behavior: As $x \to \infty$, $y \to 0$ and as $x \to -\infty$, $y \to -\infty$.

12. $f(x) = -4(3)^x$

x	$f(x) = -4(3)^x$
−1	−1.3
0	−4
1	−12
2	−36

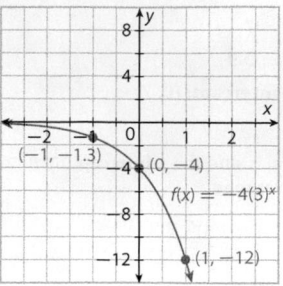

$a = -4; b = 3$

y-intercept: $(0, -4)$

End Behavior: As $x \to \infty$, $y \to -\infty$ and as $x \to -\infty$, $y \to 0$.

13. $f(x) = 5(2)^x$

x	$f(x) = 5(2)^x$
−1	2.5
0	5
1	10
2	20

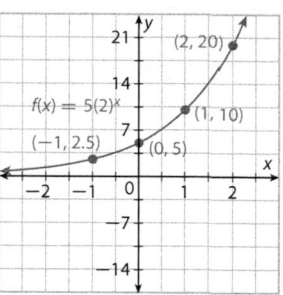

$a = 5; b = 2$

y-intercept: $(0, 5)$

End Behavior: As $x \to \infty$, $y \to \infty$ and as $x \to -\infty$, $y \to 0$.

14. $f(x) = -2(0.8)^x$

x	$f(x) = -2(0.8)^x$
−1	−2.5
0	−2
1	−1.6
2	−1.3

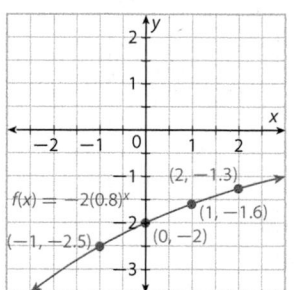

$a = -2; b = 0.8$

y-intercept: $(0, -2)$

End Behavior: As $x \to \infty$, $y \to 0$ and as $x \to -\infty$, $y \to -\infty$.

15. $f(x) = 9(3)^x$

x	$f(x) = 9(3)^x$
−1	3
0	9
1	27
2	81

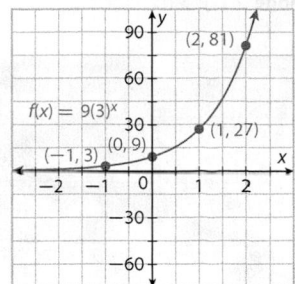

$a = 9; b = 3$

y-intercept: $(0, 9)$

End Behavior: As $x \to \infty, y \to \infty$ and as $x \to -\infty, y \to 0$.

16. $f(x) = -5(2)^x$

x	$f(x) = -5(2)^x$
−1	−2.5
0	−5
1	−10
2	−20

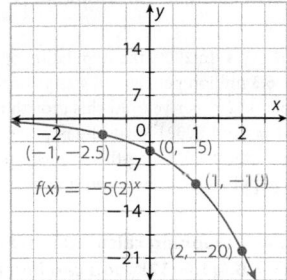

$a = -5; b = 2$

y-intercept: $(0, -5)$

End Behavior: As $x \to \infty, y \to -\infty$ and as $x \to -\infty, y \to 0$.

17. $f(x) = 7(0.4)^x$

x	$f(x) = 7(0.4)^x$
−1	17.5
0	7
1	2.8
2	1.1

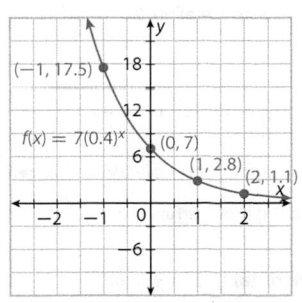

$a = 7; b = 0.4$

y-intercept: $(0, 7)$

End Behavior: As $x \to \infty, y \to 0$ and as $x \to -\infty, y \to \infty$.

18. $f(x) = 6(2)^x$

x	$f(x) = 6(2)^x$
−1	3
0	6
1	12
2	24

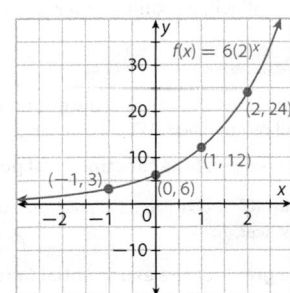

$a = 6; b = 2$

y-intercept: $(0, 6)$

End Behavior: As $x \to \infty, y \to \infty$ and as $x \to -\infty, y \to 0$.

COGNITIVE STRATEGIES

Show students that the graph of $y = -ab^x$ is the reflection of $y = ab^x$ over the x-axis.

INTEGRATE MATHEMATICAL PRACTICES

Focus on Math Connections

MP.1 Introduce students to the term *horizontal asymptote*. A horizontal asymptote is a line that the graph gets closer and closer to, but never reaches. The line $y = 0$ is the horizontal asymptote of the graphs in this lesson.

JOURNAL

Have students describe the four basic shapes of the graphs of exponential functions, including the quadrants each graph occupies and the end behavior of each graph. Also have them write an exponential function of each type.

19. Identify the domain and range of each function. Make sure to provide these answers using inequalities.

a. $f(x) = 3(2)^x$ Domain: $\{x \mid -\infty < x < \infty\}$, Range: $\{y \mid y > 0\}$

b. $f(x) = 7(0.4)^x$ Domain: $\{x \mid -\infty < x < \infty\}$, Range: $\{y \mid y > 0\}$

c. $f(x) = -2(0.6)^x$ Domain: $\{x \mid -\infty < x < \infty\}$, Range: $\{y \mid y < 0\}$

d. $f(x) = -3(4)^x$ Domain: $\{x \mid -\infty < x < \infty\}$, Range: $\{y \mid y < 0\}$

e. $f(x) = 2(22)^x$ Domain: $\{x \mid -\infty < x < \infty\}$, Range: $\{y \mid y > 0\}$

20. **Statistics** In 2000, the population of Massachusetts was 6.3 million people and was growing at a rate of about 0.32% per year. At this growth rate, the function $f(x) = 6.3(1.0032)^x$ gives the population, in millions x years after 2000. Using this model, find the year when the population reaches 7 million people.

Using a graphing calculator and the graph of $f(x) = 6.3(1.0032)^x$, you can find that when the graph reaches a y-value of 7, x is approximately 33, and the year is $2000 + 33 = 2033$.

The population will reach approximately 7 million people during the year 2033.

21. **Physics** A ball is rolling down a slope and continuously picks up speed. Suppose the function $f(x) = 1.2(1.11)^x$ describes the speed of the ball in inches per minute. How fast will the ball be rolling in 20 minutes? Round the answer to the nearest whole number.

$f(x) = 1.2(1.11)^x$

$f(x) = 1.2(1.11)^{20}$

$f(x) \approx 1.2(8.06)$

$f(x) \approx 9.67$

The ball will be rolling at a rate of about 10 inches per minute after 20 minutes.

H.O.T. Focus on Higher Order Thinking

22. **Draw Conclusions** Assume that the domain of the function $f(x) = 3(2)^x$ is the set of all real numbers. What is the range of the function?

The range of the function is all positive real numbers since $f(x)$ is always positive.

23. **What If?** If $b = 1$ in an exponential function, what will the graph of the function look like?

The graph of the exponential function will be a horizontal line at $y = a$.

24. **Critical Thinking** Using the graph of an exponential function, how can b be found?

Identify two points (x_1, y_1) and (x_2, y_2) on the graph of the exponential function with $x_1 < x_2$. If $x_2 - x_1 = 1$, then $b = \frac{y_2}{y_1}$, otherwise $b = \sqrt[x_2 - x_1]{\frac{y_2}{y_1}}$.

25. Critical Thinking Use the table to write the equation for the exponential function.

x	f(x)
−1	$\frac{4}{5}$
0	4
1	20
2	100

The y-intercept of the function is located at $(0, 4)$, so $a = 4$. To find b, divide the y-coordinate of $(1, 20)$ by the y-coordinate of $(0, 4)$.

$$b = \frac{20}{4} = 5$$

$$f(x) = 4(5)^x$$

Lesson Performance Task

A pumpkin is being grown for a contest at the state fair. Its growth can be modeled by the equation $P = 25(1.56)^n$, where P is the weight of the pumpkin in pounds and n is the number of weeks the pumpkin has been growing. By what percentage does the pumpkin grow every week? After how many weeks will the pumpkin be 80 pounds?

After the pumpkin grows to 80 pounds, it grows more slowly. From then on, its growth can be modeled by $P = 25(1.23)^n$, where n is the number of weeks since the pumpkin reached 80 pounds. Estimate when the pumpkin will reach 150 pounds.

The pumpkin grows by 56% every week until it reaches 80 pounds, then it grows by 23%.

Using a graphing calculator and the graph of $f(x) = 25(1.56)^x$, you can find that when the graph reaches a y-value of 80, x is approximately 2.6, so $x \approx 2.6$.

The pumpkin will be 80 pounds after 2.6 weeks.

It only needs to grow $150 - 80 = 70$ more pounds. Let $P = 70$ and solve the new equation. Add the solution to this equation to the original estimate to find the total time it will take to grow to 150 pounds.

$$70 = 25(1.23)^n$$

Using a graphing calculator and the graph of $f(x) = 25(1.23)^x$, you can find that when the graph reaches a y-value of 70, x is approximately 4.9, so $x \approx 4.9$.

$4.9 + 2.6 = 7.5$

It will take the pumpkin about 7.5 weeks to grow to 150 pounds.

INTEGRATE TECHNOLOGY

Have students use a graphing calculator to graph both equations on the same graph. Compare the two graphs.

INTEGRATE MATHEMATICAL PRACTICES
Focus on Reasoning

MP.2 Have students describe how the pumpkin grew over the period of time until it reached 150 pounds. They could say that the pumpkin grew to a weight of 80 pounds in about 2.6 weeks, while it took about 4.9 weeks to gain another 70 pounds. They could also say that the rate provided in the first equation is 156% per week, while the second equation shows the rate declined to 123%.

EXTENSION ACTIVITY

Have students research how the weight of a giant pumpkin can be estimated before it is picked. Have students do an Internet search for "over the top (OTT) weight tables." There are three measurements that must be found and added together to get the over-the-top measurement. Have students use the data they find to determine what the relationship appears to be between the over-the-top measurement in inches and the weight of a giant pumpkin in pounds. A graph of these values is a scatter plot that could be represented by an exponential function.

Scoring Rubric
2 points: Student correctly solves the problem and explains his/her reasoning.
1 point: Student shows good understanding of the problem but does not fully solve or explain his/her reasoning.
0 points: Student does not demonstrate understanding of the problem.

Graphing Exponential Functions   **720**

Transforming Exponential Functions

Common Core Math Standards

The student is expected to:

COMMON CORE F-BF.B.3

Identify the effect on the graph of replacing $f(x)$ by $f(x) + k$, $kf(x)$, $f(kx)$, and $f(x + k)$ for specific values of k (both positive and negative); find the value of k given the graphs. Experiment with cases and illustrate an explanation of the effects on the graph using technology. Also F-IF.C.9, F-BF.A.1b

Mathematical Practices

COMMON CORE MP.7 Using Structure

Language Objective

Describe how the graph of an exponential function changes when you add a constant to the function.

ENGAGE

Essential Question: How does the graph of $f(x) = ab^x$ change when a and b are changed?

If $a > 0$ and $b > 1$, increasing the value of b makes the graph rise more quickly as x increases. For $a > 0$ and $0 < b < 1$, increasing the value of b makes the graph fall more gradually as x increases. Increasing the absolute value of a stretches the graph vertically, and changing the sign of a reflects the graph across the x-axis.

PREVIEW: LESSON PERFORMANCE TASK

View the Engage section online. Discuss how heat flows from a hotter object to a colder object until both are the same temperature. Then preview the Lesson Performance Task.

15.5 Transforming Exponential Functions

Essential Question: How does the graph of $f(x) = ab^x$ change when a and b are changed?

Resource Locker

Explore Changing the Value of b in $f(x) = b^x$

Investigate the effect of b on the function $f(x) = b^x$.

(A) Complete the table of values for the functions $f_1(x) = 1.2^x$ and $f_2(x) = 1.5^x$. Use a calculator to find the values and round to the nearest thousandth if necessary.

x	$f_1(x) = 1.2^x$	$f_2(x) = 1.5^x$
−2	0.694	0.444
−1	0.833	0.667
0	1	1
1	1.2	1.5
2	1.44	2.25

(B) Select the option that makes the statement true.

$(f_1(x)/\boxed{f_2(x)})$ increases more quickly as x increases.

$(f_1(x)/\boxed{f_2(x)})$ approaches 0 more quickly as x decreases.

(C) The y-intercept of $f_1(x)$ is $\boxed{1}$. The y-intercept of $f_2(x)$ is $\boxed{1}$.

(D) Fill in the table of values for the functions $f_3(x) = 0.6^x$ and $f_4(x) = 0.9^x$. Round to the nearest thousandth again.

x	$f_3(x) = 0.6^x$	$f_4(x) = 0.9^x$
−2	2.778	1.235
−1	1.667	1.111
0	1	1
1	0.6	0.9
2	0.36	0.81

(E) $(\boxed{f_3(x)}/f_4(x))$ increases more quickly as x decreases.

$(\boxed{f_3(x)}/f_4(x))$ approaches 0 more quickly as x increases.

(F) The y-intercept of $f_3(x)$ is $\boxed{1}$. The y-intercept of $f_4(x)$ is $\boxed{1}$.

HARDCOVER PAGES 563–572

Turn to these pages to find this lesson in the hardcover student edition.

1. Consider the function, $y = 1.3^x$. How will its graph compare with the graphs of $f_1(x)$ and $f_2(x)$? Discuss end behavior and the y-intercept.

All three graphs have the same y-intercept of 1. The graph of $y = 1.3^x$ falls between

the other two graphs and increases more quickly than $f_1(x)$ but less quickly than $f_2(x)$ as

x increases to the right of 0. The graph falls more quickly than that of $f_1(x)$ but less

quickly than that of $f_2(x)$ as x decreases to the left of 0.

✏ Explain 1   Changing the Value of a in $f(x) = ab^x$ with $b > 1$

Multiplying a growing exponential function $(b > 1)$ by a constant a does not change the growth rate, but it does stretch or compress the graph vertically, and reflects the graph across the x-axis if $a < 0$.

A **vertical stretch** of a graph is a transformation that pulls the graph away from the x-axis. By multiplying the y-value of each (x, y) pair by a, where $|a| > 1$, the graph is stretched by a factor of $|a|$.

A **vertical compression** of a graph is a transformation that pushes the graph toward the x-axis. By multiplying the y-value of each (x, y) pair by a, where $|a| < 1$, the graph is compressed by a factor of $|a|$.

Example 1   Make a table of values for the function given. Then graph it on the same coordinate plane with the graph of $y = 1.5^x$. Describe the end behavior and find the y-intercept of each graph.

Ⓐ $f(x) = 0.3(1.5)^x$

x	$f(x) = 0.3(1.5)^x$
−2	0.133
−1	0.2
0	0.3
1	0.45
2	0.675
3	1.013
4	1.519

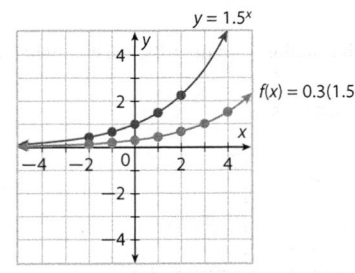

End Behavior:

$f(x) \to \infty$ as $x \to \infty$

$f(x) \to 0$ as $x \to -\infty$

y-intercept: 0.3

PROFESSIONAL DEVELOPMENT

 Integrate Mathematical Practices

This lesson provides an opportunity to address Mathematical Practice **MP.7**, which calls for students to "look for and make use of structure." Students will compare exponential functions. They will explore how changing the parameters of the functions affects the shapes of their graphs, including how quickly the graphs rise or fall, end behavior, and y-intercepts. They will identify patterns that will allow them to predict how increasing, decreasing, or changing the sign of a parameter will affect the graph of an exponential function.

EXPLORE

Changing the Value of b in $f(x) = b^x$

INTEGRATE TECHNOLOGY

After students have used tables to explore the effects of changing the value of b in the function $f(x) = b^x$, have students use calculators to graph functions with different values of b on the same grid.

QUESTIONING STRATEGIES

? For two values of b that are both greater than 1, why is the graph of $y = b^x$ steeper for the larger value of b? **The value of b determines by what factor the function grows for each unit increase in the value of x. A larger value of b means more growth per unit and a steeper graph.**

EXPLAIN 1

Changing the Value of a in $f(x) = ab^x$ with $b > 1$

INTEGRATE MATHEMATICAL PRACTICES
Focus on Patterns

MP.8 Select a value for a and b, then graph both $f(x) = ab^x$ and $f(x) = -ab^x$. Discuss with students why the graph of $f(x) = ab^x$ is a reflection of $f(x) = -ab^x$ over the x-axis.

QUESTIONING STRATEGIES

? What are the domain and range of an exponential function $f(x) = ab^x$ when a is positive? **The domain will be all real numbers, and the range will be all numbers greater than 0.**

? What are the domain and range of an exponential function $f(x) = ab^x$ when a is negative? **The domain will be all real numbers, and the range will be all numbers less than 0.**

Transforming Exponential Functions   **722**

Ⓑ $f(x) = -2(1.5)^x$

x	$f(x) = -2(1.5)^x$
-4	-0.395
-3	-0.593
-2	-0.889
-1	-1.333
0	-2
1	-3
2	-4.5

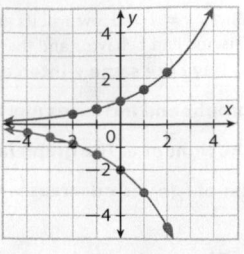

End Behavior:

$f(x) \rightarrow \boxed{-\infty}$ as $x \rightarrow \infty$

$f(x) \rightarrow \boxed{0}$ as $x \rightarrow -\infty$

y-intercept: $\boxed{-2}$

Reflect

2. **Discussion** What can you say about the common behavior of graphs of the form $f(x) = ab^x$ with $b > 1$? What is different when a changes sign?

All graphs of the form $f(x) = ab^x$ with $b > 1$ approach 0 as x approaches $-\infty$ and have a

y-intercept at $(0, a)$. The sign of a determines the end behavior as x approaches ∞; for $a > 0$,

$f(x)$ increases toward infinity, and for $a < 0$, $f(x)$ decreases toward negative infinity.

Your Turn

Graph each function, and describe the end behavior and find the y-intercept of each graph.

3. $f(x) = -0.5(1.5)^x$

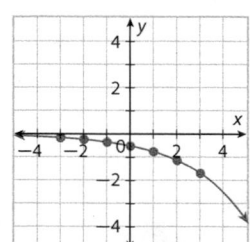

End behavior:

$f(x) \rightarrow -\infty$ as $x \rightarrow \infty$

$f(x) \rightarrow 0$ as $x \rightarrow -\infty$

y-intercept: -0.5

4. $f(x) = 4(1.5)^x$

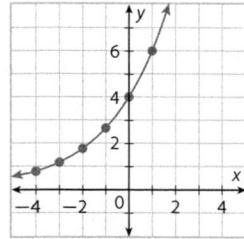

End behavior:

$f(x) \rightarrow \infty$ as $x \rightarrow \infty$

$f(x) \rightarrow 0$ as $x \rightarrow -\infty$

y-intercept: 4

© Houghton Mifflin Harcourt Publishing Company

COLLABORATIVE LEARNING

Whole Class Activity

As a class, work together to determine what occurs when a constant h is introduced in the exponential function $f(x) = b^{x-h}$. Have students select a value for b and three values for h, then write three functions in the form $f(x) = b^{x-h}$ using their chosen values. Create a table that shows the output of each function for several x-values. Graph all three functions on the same coordinate grid. Discuss how h affects the parent function $f(x) = b^x$. Students should realize that positive values of h translate the graph to the right, while negative values of h translate the graph to the left.

Explain 2 Changing the Value of a in $f(x) = ab^x$ with $0 < b < 1$

Multiplying a decaying exponential function $(b < 1)$ by a constant a does not change the growth rate, but it does stretch or compress the graph vertically.

Example 2 Make a table of values for the function given. Then graph it on the same coordinate plane with the graph of $y = 0.6^x$. Describe the end behavior and find the y-intercept of each graph.

Ⓐ $f(x) = -3(0.6)^x$

x	$f(x) = -3(0.6)^x$
−1	−5
0	−3
1	−1.8
2	−1.08
3	−0.648

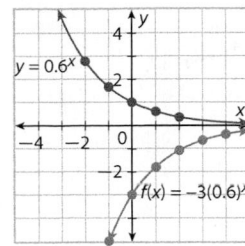

End behavior:

$f(x) \rightarrow 0$ as $x \rightarrow \infty$

$f(x) \rightarrow -\infty$ as $x \rightarrow -\infty$

y-intercept: -3

Ⓑ $f(x) = 0.5\,(0.6)^x$

x	$f(x) = 0.5(0.6)^x$
−4	3.858
−3	2.315
−2	1.389
−1	0.833
0	0.5
1	0.3
2	0.18

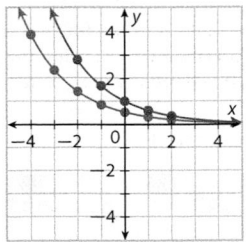

End Behavior:

$f(x) \rightarrow \boxed{0}$ as $x \rightarrow \infty$

$f(x) \rightarrow \boxed{\infty}$ as $x \rightarrow -\infty$

y-intercept: $\boxed{0.5}$

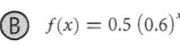

Reflect

5. **Discussion** What can you say about the common behavior of graphs of the form $f(x) = ab^x$ with $0 < b < 1$? What is different when a changes sign?

All graphs of the form $f(x) = ab^x$ with $0 < b < 1$ approach 0 as x approaches ∞ and have a

y-intercept at $(0, a)$. The sign of a determines the end behavior as x approaches $-\infty$;

for $a > 0$, $f(x)$ approaches ∞ as x approaches $-\infty$, and for $a < 0$, $f(x)$ approaches $-\infty$ as

x approaches $-\infty$.

DIFFERENTIATE INSTRUCTION

Visual Cues

Have students graph, on the same grid, a parent exponential function and exponential functions in which the value of a or b has been changed or to which a constant has been added. Students can draw each graph in a different color and write the equation for each function in the same color as its graph. Then have them circle the value that was changed in each equation. Students may wish to keep this graph as a visual reference to use when working with transformations of other exponential functions.

EXPLAIN 2

Changing the Value of a in $f(x) = ab^x$ with $0 < b < 1$

AVOID COMMON ERRORS

Remind students that variables can have different meanings when they are used in different functions. Students should understand that while b in a linear function $y = mx + b$ represents the y-intercept, b in an exponential function $y = ab^x$ does not represent the y-intercept.

QUESTIONING STRATEGIES

? For a function $f(x) = ab^x$, what can the values of a and b tell you about the shape of the graph and in which quadrants the graph is located? When $b > 1$, the graph becomes farther away from the x-axis as x increases. When $0 < b < 1$, the graph approaches the x-axis as x increases. When $a > 0$, the graph is in quadrants 1 and 2 (above the x-axis). When $a < 0$, the graph is in quadrants 3 and 4 (below the x-axis).

? How is the y-intercept of a function $f(x) = ab^x$ related to the value of a? Explain. Since the y-intercept of a function is its value when $x = 0$, and $b^0 = 1$ for any value of b, the y-intercept of $f(x) = ab^x$ is always equal to a.

? How is the effect of changing a when $0 < b < 1$ similar to the effect of changing a when $b > 1$? In both cases, increasing the absolute value of a creates a vertical stretch of the graph and decreasing the absolute value of a creates a vertical compression of the graph. Changing the sign of a reflects the graph across the x-axis.

EXPLAIN 3

Adding a Constant to an Exponential Function

INTEGRATE MATHEMATICAL PRACTICES

Focus on Critical Thinking

MP.3 Make sure students understand that adding a constant to a parent exponential function shifts the graph up or down but does not change the shape of the graph. Contrast this to the effect of either changing the base b in the function or multiplying the function by a constant a, both of which do change the shape of the graph.

QUESTIONING STRATEGIES

? Can the graph of an exponential function be translated in any desired direction by adding a constant to the function? Explain. No; adding a constant to an exponential function can only translate the graph vertically, either up or down. It cannot translate the graph horizontally.

Graph each function, and describe its end behavior and y-intercept.

6. $f(x) = 2(0.6)^x$

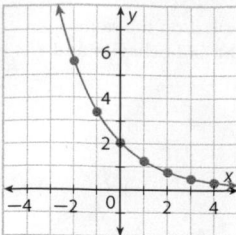

End behavior:

$f(x) \to 0$ as $x \to \infty$

$f(x) \to \infty$ as $x \to -\infty$

y-intercept: 2

7. $f(x) = -0.25(0.6)^x$

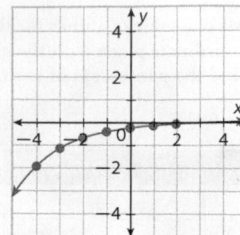

End behavior:

$f(x) \to 0$ as $x \to \infty$

$f(x) \to -\infty$ as $x \to -\infty$

y-intercept: -0.25

🖉 Explain 3   Adding a Constant to an Exponential Function

Adding a constant to an exponential function causes the graph of the function to translate up or down, depending on the sign of the constant.

Example 3   Make a table of values for each function and graph them together on the same coordinate plane. Find the y-intercepts, and explain how they relate to the translation of the graph.

(A) $f(x) = 2^x$ and $g(x) = 2^x + 2$

x	$f(x) = 2^x$	$g(x) = 2^x + 2$
−2	0.25	2.25
−1	0.5	2.5
0	1	3
1	2	4
2	4	6

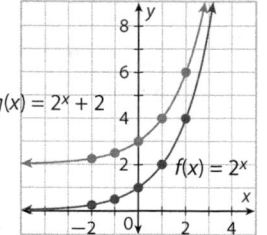

The y-intercept of $f(x)$ is 1.

The y-intercept of $g(x)$ is 3.

The y-intercept of $g(x)$ is 2 more than that of $f(x)$ because $g(x)$ is a vertical translation of $f(x)$ up by 2 units.

LANGUAGE SUPPORT EL

Communicate Math

To accurately describe the transformations of functions explored in this lesson, students must be careful to use precise language. Provide sentence starters to help English learners frame explanations of changes in the behavior of a function. For example:

- If [$b > 1$ / $b < 1$], increasing the value of b causes the function to [approach infinity / approach zero] more [quickly / slowly] as x increases.

- [Increasing / Decreasing] the absolute value of a causes a [vertical stretch / vertical compression / translation / reflection] of the graph.

Ⓑ $f(x) = 0.7^x$ and $g(x) = 0.7^x - 3$

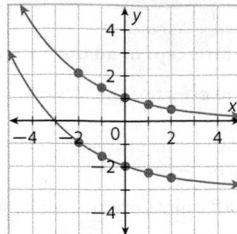

x	$f(x) = 0.7^x$	$g(x) = 0.7^x - 3$
−2	2.041	−0.959
−1	1.429	−1.571
0	1.0	−2
1	0.7	−2.3
2	0.49	−2.51

The y-intercept of $f(x)$ is ⬚ 1 .

The y-intercept of $g(x)$ is ⬚ −2 .

The y-intercept of $g(x)$ is 3 (more/less) than that of $f(x)$ because $g(x)$ is a vertical translation of $f(x)$ (up/down) by 3 units.

Reflect

8. What do you think will happen to the y-intercept of an exponential function with both a stretch and a translation, such as $f(x) = 3(0.7)^x + 2$?

   The y-intercept is stretched up from 1 to 3 by the vertical stretch and then translated up

   from 3 to 5 by the translation.

YourTurn

Graph the functions together on the same coordinate plane. Find the y-intercepts, and explain how they relate to the translation of the graph.

9. $f(x) = 0.4^x$ and $g(x) = 0.4^x + 4$

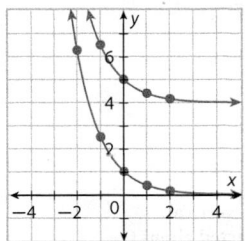

The y-intercept of $f(x)$ is 1.

The y-intercept of $g(x)$ is 5.

The y-intercept of $g(x)$ is 4 more than that of $f(x)$ because $g(x)$ is a vertical translation of $f(x)$ up by 4 units.

10. $f(x) = 2(1.5)^x$ and $g(x) = 2(1.5)^x - 3$

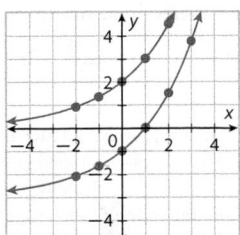

The y-intercept of $f(x)$ is 2.

The y-intercept of $g(x)$ is −1.

The y-intercept of $g(x)$ is 3 less than that of $f(x)$ because $g(x)$ is a vertical translation of $f(x)$ down by 3 units.

Transforming Exponential Functions   **726**

ELABORATE

INTEGRATE MATHEMATICAL PRACTICES
Focus on Reasoning

MP.2 Some students may feel that the change that results from adding a constant to an exponential function is not a translation of the graph, because the curves can appear to be closer to each other on one side of the grid than on the other side. To illustrate that the transformation represents a translation, have students determine the vertical distance between the transformed graph and the graph of its parent function for any *x*-value. They should find that the distance is the same for all values of *x*, verifying that both graphs are increasing or decreasing at the same rate.

SUMMARIZE THE LESSON

? How does changing *a*, *b*, or *k* change the graph of an exponential function in the form $f(x) = ab^x + k$? Increasing the absolute value of *a* stretches the graph vertically; decreasing the absolute value of *a* compresses the graph vertically. If $b > 1$, increasing the value of *b* makes the graph move away from the *x*-axis more quickly as *x* increases. If $0 < b < 1$, increasing the value of *b* makes the graph approach the *x*-axis more slowly as *x* increases. Adding a constant *k* translates the graph of the parent function upward if $k > 0$, and translates the graph downward if $k < 0$.

---

11. How do you determine the *y*-intercept of an exponential function $f(x) = ab^x + k$ that has been both stretched and translated?

The *y*-intercept of all the parent exponential functions $f(x) = b^x$ is 1. First multiply 1 by *a* to find the effect of the stretch, and then add *k* to find the effect of the translation.

12. Describe the end behavior of a translated exponential function $f(x) = b^x + k$ with $b > 1$ as *x* approaches $-\infty$.

Since all points are shifted by *k*, the function approaches *k* as *x* approaches $-\infty$.

13. **Essential Question Check-in** If *a* and *b* are positive real numbers and $b \neq 1$, how does the graph of $f(x) = ab^x$ change when *b* is changed?

If $b > 1$, increasing *b* makes the graph rise more quickly as *x* increases. If $0 < b < 1$, increasing *b* makes the graph fall more gradually as *x* increases.

⭐ Evaluate: Homework and Practice

- Online Homework
- Hints and Help
- Extra Practice

Exercises 1 and 2 refer to the functions $f_1(x) = 2.5^x$ and $f_2(x) = 3^x$.

1. Which function grows faster as *x* increases toward ∞?

$f_2(x)$

2. Which function approaches 0 faster as *x* decreases toward $-\infty$?

$f_2(x)$

Exercises 3 and 4 refer to the functions $f_1(x) = 0.5^x$ and $f_2(x) = 0.7^x$.

3. Which function grows faster as *x* decreases toward $-\infty$?

$f_1(x)$

4. Which function approaches 0 faster as *x* increases toward ∞?

$f_1(x)$

Label each of the following functions, $g(x)$, as a vertical stretch or a vertical compression of the parent function, $f(x)$, and tell whether it is reflected about the *x*-axis.

5. $g(x) = 0.7(0.5)^x$, $f(x) = 0.5^x$

vertical compression, no reflection

6. $g(x) = -1.2(5)^x$, $f(x) = 5^x$

vertical stretch and reflection

© Houghton Mifflin Harcourt Publishing Company

Exercise	Depth of Knowledge (D.O.K.)	COMMON CORE Mathematical Practices
1–8	**1** Recall	**MP.7** Using Structure
9–12	**1** Recall of Information	**MP.6** Precision
13–16	**1** Recall of Information	**MP.7** Using Structure
17	**2** Skills/Concepts	**MP.4** Modeling
18	**2** Skills/Concepts	**MP.7** Using Structure
19–20	**2** Skills/Concepts	**MP.4** Modeling

Label each of the following functions, $g(x)$, as a vertical stretch or a vertical compression of the parent function, $f(x)$, and tell whether it is reflected about the x-axis.

7.

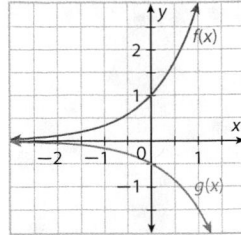

vertical compression and reflection

8.

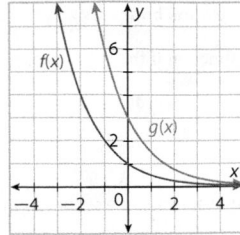

vertical stretch, no reflection

Find the y-intercept for each of the functions, $g(x)$, from Exercises 5–8.

9. $g(x) = 0.7(0.5)^x$

0.7

10. $g(x) = -1.2(5)^x$

−1.2

11. Use $g(x)$ from Exercise 7.

−0.5

12. Use $g(x)$ from Exercise 8.

3

Describe the translation of each of the functions, $g(x)$, compared to the parent function, $f(x)$.

13. $f(x) = 0.4^x, g(x) = 0.4^x + 5$

$g(x)$ is translated up by 5 units from $f(x)$.

14. $f(x) = -2(1.5)^x, g(x) = -2(1.5)^x - 2$

$g(x)$ is translated down by 2 units from $f(x)$.

15.

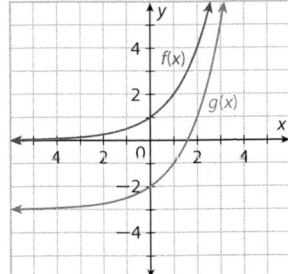

$g(x)$ is translated down by 3 units from $f(x)$.

16.

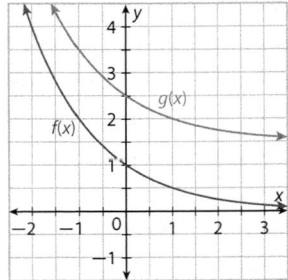

$g(x)$ is translated up by 3 units from $f(x)$.

Exercise	Depth of Knowledge (D.O.K.)		COMMON CORE Mathematical Practices	
21–22	**1**	Recall of Information	**MP.6**	Precision
23	**2**	Skills/Concepts	**MP.6**	Precision
24	**1**	Recall of Information	**MP.6**	Precision
25–26	**2**	Skills/Concepts	**MP.6**	Precision
27–29	**3**	Strategic Thinking **H.O.T.**	**MP.3**	Logic

EVALUATE

ASSIGNMENT GUIDE

Concepts and Skills	Practice
Explore Changing the Value of b in $f(x) = b^x$	Exercises 1–4, 27–29
Example 1 Changing the Value of a in $f(x) = ab^x$ with $b > 1$	Exercises 6–7, 10–11, 20–25
Example 2 Changing the Value of a in $f(x) = ab^x$ with $0 < b < 1$	Exercises 5, 8–9, 12, 17–18, 26
Example 3 Adding a Constant to an Exponential Function	Exercises 13–16, 19

INTEGRATE MATHEMATICAL PRACTICES

Focus on Communication

MP.3 When working with exponential functions, students might use the word *slope* to describe either the parameter a or b. Remind students that *slope* refers to a rate of change. A linear function has a constant rate of change, so the slope for a linear function $f(x) = mx + b$ is represented by a constant, m. An exponential function does not have a constant rate of change, so its slope cannot be represented by a constant parameter.

TECHNOLOGY

When using calculators to graph exponential functions, remind students that a calculator will read numbers separated by parentheses as implied multiplication, so a function such as $f(x) = 3(4)^x$ can be entered either as $y = 3*4^x$ or as $y = 3(4)^x$.

AVOID COMMON ERRORS

Students may have trouble differentiating between a vertical stretch or compression and a vertical translation. Remind them that changing the value of a in $f(x) = ab^x$ causes a vertical stretch or compression, which is a change in the shape of the graph. Adding a constant k produces a vertical translation, which slides the graph up or down without changing its shape.

The height h above the floor of the nth bounce of a bouncy ball dropped from a height of 10 feet above the floor can be characterized by a decaying exponential function, $h(n) = 10(0.8)^n$, where each bounce reaches 80% of the height of the previous bounce.

17. Write the new function if the ball is dropped from 5 feet.

$h(n) = 5(0.8)^n$

18. What kind of transformation was that from the original function, $h(n) = 10(0.8)^n$?

a vertical compression

19. Write the function that describes what happens if the ball is dropped from 10 feet above a table top that is at a height of 3 feet.

The function is translated up by 3 feet.

$k = 3 \quad h(n) = 10(0.8)^n + 3$

20. Biology Unrestrained growth of cells in a petri dish can be extremely rapid, with a single cell growing into a number of cells, N, given by the formula, $N(t) = 8^t$, after t hours.

a. Write the formula for the number of cells in the petri dish when a culture is started with 50 isolated cells.

$N(t) = 50(8)^t$

b. How many cells do you expect after 3 hours?

$N(3) = 50(8)^3 = 50 \cdot 512 = 25,600$ **cells**

A bank account with an initial deposit of $1000 and an interest rate of 5% increases by 5% each year. The balance (B) as a function of time in years (t) can be described by an exponential function: $B(t) = 1000(1.05)^t$

21. What parameter of the exponential form $f(x) = ab^x + k$ represents the initial balance of $1000?

 a

22. What is the *y*-intercept of $B(t)$?

 1000

23. What parameter would change if the interest rate were changed to 7%?

 b

24. Which bank account balance grows faster, the one with 5% interest or the one with 7% interest?

 the one with the 7% interest rate

25. What kind of transformation is represented by changing the initial balance to $500?

 a vertical compression

26. Match the graph to the characteristics of the function $f(x) = ab^x$.

 1. $a < 0, b > 1$ **b** **2.** $a > 0, 0 < b < 1$ **c** **3.** $a > 0, b > 1$ **a** **4.** $a < 0, 0 < b < 1$ **d**

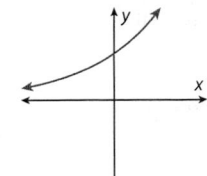

a.

b.

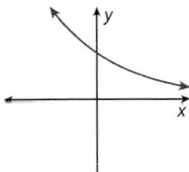

c.

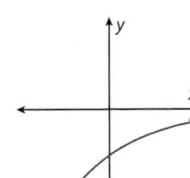

d.

MODELING

When working with exponential functions that have an added constant, draw the graph of a parent exponential function on a grid on a clear transparency sheet. On another clear transparency sheet, trace the graph only. Slide the second sheet over the first sheet to show a translation. Visual learners may wish to make and use their own pairs of transparency sheets to help with translations.

Transforming Exponential Functions **730**

JOURNAL

Have students create a graphic organizer like the one shown to explain each type of transformation studied in this lesson. Students may include either verbal explanations or graphs to show the effect of each change.

$f(x) = ab^x$		
Changing the absolute value of a:	Changing the value of b when $b > 1$:	Adding a positive constant k:
Changing the sign of a:	Changing the value of b when $0 < b < 1$:	Adding a negative constant k:

27. Critical Thinking Describe how the graph of $f(x) = ab^x$ changes for a given positive value of a as you increase the value of b when $b > 1$. Discuss the rise and fall of the graph and the y-intercept.

The y-intercept equals a for all values of $b > 1$ because $ab^0 = a$. As the value of b increases, the graph rises more quickly as x increases to the right of 0, and it falls more quickly as x decreases to the left of 0.

28. Communicate Mathematical Ideas Consider the functions $f_1(x) = (1.02)^x$ and $f_2(x) = (1.03)^x$. Which function increases more quickly as x increases to the right of 0? How do the growth factors support your answer?

$f_2(x)$ grows more quickly. $f_2(x)$ has the greater growth rate (3% rather than 2%), so you would expect $f_2(x)$ to increase more quickly as x increases to the right of 0.

29. Communicate Mathematical Ideas Consider the function $f_1(x) = (0.94)^x$ and $f_2(x) = (0.98)^x$. Which function decreases more quickly as x increases to the right of 0? How do the growth factors support your answer?

$f_1(x)$ decreases more quickly. $f_1(x)$ has the greater decay rate (6% rather than 2%), so you would expect $f_1(x)$ to decrease more quickly as x increases to the right of 0.

Lesson Performance Task

A coffee shop serves two patrons cups of coffee. The initial temperature of the coffee is 170 °F. As the coffee sits in the 70 °F room, the temperature follows the pattern of a transformed exponential function. One patron leaves her coffee untouched, resulting in a slow cooling toward room temperature. The other patron is in a hurry and stirs her coffee, resulting in a faster cooling rate.

Both cups of coffee can be modeled with transformed exponential functions of the form $T(t) = ab^t + k$.

Each minute, the unstirred coffee gets 10% closer to room temperature, and the stirred coffee gets 20% closer. Find the functions $T_s(t)$ and $T_u(t)$ for the stirred and unstirred cups of coffee, fill in the table of values, and graph the functions. Determine how long it takes each cup to drop below 130 °F (don't try to solve the equations exactly, just use the table to answer to the nearest minute).

Time (minutes)	Temperature (°F, unstirred)	Temperature (°F, stirred)
0	170.0	170.0
1	160.0	150.0
2	151.0	134.0
3	142.9	121.2
4	135.6	111.0
5	129.0	102.8

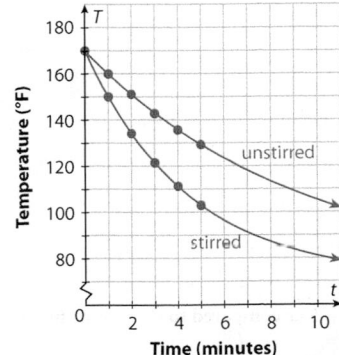

First, recognize that the end behavior as described is for $T_s(t)$ and $T_u(t)$ to approach 70 °F as time increases, so $k = 70$ for both functions.

You can also determine that $b < 1$ and $a > 0$ for both cups of coffee since they are both decreasing functions that approach a constant value as time increases.

To find a, use the y-intercept. In this case, the y-intercept is the temperature of the coffee at $t = 0$, or 170 °F:

y-intercept $= a + k$, so $170 = a + 70$ and $100 = a$ for both functions.

A 10% drop each minute for the unstirred coffee means $b = (100\% - 10\%) = 90\% = 0.9$. For the stirred coffee, $b = (100\% - 20\%) = 80\% = 0.8$.

$T_u(t) = 100(0.9)^t + 70$ for the unstirred coffee
$T_s(t) = 100(0.8)^t + 70$ for the stirred coffee

The unstirred cup takes 5 minutes to drop below 130 °F, and the stirred cup takes 3 minutes to drop below 130 °F.

© Houghton Mifflin Harcourt Publishing Company

EXTENSION ACTIVITY

Have students research Newton's law of cooling and use it to explain why an exponential function may be used to model the cooling of a cup of coffee.

Newton's law of cooling states that the rate of heat loss of an object, or its temperature change per unit time, is proportional to the difference in temperature between the object and its surroundings. As the coffee cools, the temperature difference between the coffee and its surroundings decreases, so the temperature change per minute also decreases. In other words, the temperature decreases at a steadily decreasing rate, as described by an exponential function.

QUESTIONING STRATEGIES

? In the Lesson Performance Task, is the temperature of the coffee described by an increasing or decreasing exponential function? What can you conclude about the value of b?
decreasing; $b < 1$

? What value does the temperature of the coffee approach as t approaches infinity? In the general exponential function $T(t) = ab^t + k$ with $b < 1$, what value does ab^t approach as t approaches infinity? How can you use this information to find one of the parameters of the temperature functions? As t approaches infinity, the temperature of the coffee approaches room temperature, 70°F, and ab^t approaches 0. Therefore, as t approaches infinity, the equation $T(t) = ab^t + k$ becomes $70 = 0 + k$, so $k = 70$ for both functions.

INTEGRATE MATHEMATICAL PRACTICES
Focus on Technology

MP.5 Have students graph the two temperature functions on a graphing calculator to explore the temperature change over a longer period of time. Have them adjust the viewing window so that the maximum and minimum values of y represent the initial and final temperatures (170°F and 70°F), respectively. Then have them use the **TRACE** feature to determine how long it takes for the coffee temperature to drop below 71°F. Students may find that the stirred cup takes about 21 minutes and the unstirred cup takes about 44 minutes.

Scoring Rubric
2 points: Student correctly solves the problem and explains his/her reasoning.
1 point: Student shows good understanding of the problem but does not fully solve or explain his/her reasoning.
0 points: Student does not demonstrate understanding of the problem.

Transforming Exponential Functions   **732**

Study Guide Review

ASSESSMENT AND INTERVENTION

Assign or customize module reviews.

MODULE PERFORMANCE TASK

 COMMON CORE

Mathematical Practices: MP.1, MP.2, MP.4, MP.6, MP.8
F-LE.A.2, F-BF.A.1a

SUPPORTING STUDENT REASONING

Students should begin this problem by listing appropriate strategies and choosing one. Here are some questions they might have.

- **What is the maximum number of days that can be used?** Students should assume that the required time is no more than 6 or 7 days.

- **How long does a round of sharing take?** Students can assume that each round of sharing takes a full day.

Geometric Sequences and Exponential Functions

Essential Question: How can you use geometric sequences and exponential functions to solve real-world problems?

© Houghton Mifflin Harcourt Publishing Company

Key Vocabulary
common ratio
  (razón común)
explicit rule
  (fórmula explícita)
exponential function
  (función exponencial)
geometric sequence
  (sucesión geométrica)
recursive rule
  (fórmula recurrente)

KEY EXAMPLE   (Lesson 15.1)

Find the common ratio r for the geometric sequence 2, 6, 18, 54, … and use r to find the next three terms.

$\frac{6}{2} = 3$, so the common ratio r is 3.

For this sequence, $f(1) = 2$, $f(2) = 6$, $f(3) = 18$, and $f(4) = 54$.

$f(4) = 54$, so $f(5) = 54(3) = 162$.

$f(5) = 162$, so $f(6) = 162(3) = 486$.

$f(6) = 486$, so $f(7) = 486(3) = 1458$.

The next three terms of the sequence are 162, 486, and 1458.

KEY EXAMPLE   (Lesson 15.3)

Write an equation for the exponential function that includes the points $(2, 8)$ and $(3, 16)$.

Find b by dividing the function value of the second pair by the function value of the first: $b = \frac{16}{8} = 2$.

Evaluate the function for $x = 2$ and solve for a.

$f(x) = ab^x$	Write the general form.
$f(x) = a \cdot 2^x$	Substitute the value for b.
$8 = a \cdot 2^2$	Substitute a pair of input-output values.
$8 = a \cdot 4$	Simplify.
$a = 2$	Solve for a.
$f(x) = 2 \cdot 2^x$	Use a and b to write an equation for the function.

KEY EXAMPLE   (Lesson 15.5)

Describe the transformations of the function $g(x) = 2(3)^x + 5$ as compared to the parent function $f(x) = 3^x$.

a has changed from 1 to 2.

This corresponds to a vertical stretch by a factor of 2.

The constant has changed from 0 to 5.

This corresponds to a translation of 5 units up.

$g(x)$ has been stretched by a factor of 2 and translated 5 units up.

SCAFFOLDING SUPPORT

- Elicit from students that fewer friends require more time and more friends require less time to meet the goal.

- For students who need more structure, provide a range of 9 to 15 friends in 6 to 7 days.

- This task could be made more challenging by suggesting that only a certain percentage of friends will share the video within the time frame. Ask how this changes the number of original contacts.

Find the common ratio r for each geometric sequence and use r to find the next three terms. *(Lesson 15.1)*

1. 1701, 567, 189,…

$r = \frac{1}{3}$; **63, 21, 7**

2. 5, 20, 80,…

$r = 4$; **320, 1280, 5120**

Write a recursive rule and an explicit rule for each geometric sequence. *(Lesson 15.2)*

3. 4, 12, 36, 108, 324,…

$f(1) = 4$ and $f(n) = f(n-1) \cdot 3$;

$f(n) = 4 \cdot 3^{n-1}$

4. 6, 30, 150, 750, 3750,…

$f(1) = 6$ and $f(n) = f(n-1) \cdot 5$;

$f(n) = 6 \cdot 5^{n-1}$

Write an equation for the exponential function that includes the pair of given points. *(Lesson 15.3)*

5. $(2, 16)$ and $(3, 32)$

$f(x) = 4 \cdot 2^x$

6. $(2, 4)$ and $(3, 2)$

$f(x) = 16 \cdot \left(\frac{1}{2}\right)^x$

7. Find a, b, and the y-intercept for $f(x) = 5(2)^x$, and then describe its end behavior. *(Lesson 15.4)*

$a = 5$; $b = 2$; y-intercept $= 5$; end behavior: As $x \to \infty$, $y \to \infty$ and as $x \to -\infty$, $y \to 0$.

MODULE PERFORMANCE TASK

What Does It Take to Go Viral?

You want your newest video to be so popular that it gets more than 750,000 daily views within a week after you post it. You share it with friends and assume that each friend will share the video with the same number of people that you do, and so on. How can you determine the smallest number of friends you need to show your video to? What answer do you think would be too big? Too small?

Start by listing in the space below how you plan to tackle the problem. Then use your own paper to complete the task. Be sure to write down all your data and assumptions. Then use numbers, tables, or algebra to explain how you reached your conclusion.

© Houghton Mifflin Harcourt Publishing Company

DISCUSSION OPPORTUNITIES

- Which, if any, parameters can change without affecting the number of friends you first share with?
- Have students compare and evaluate different strategies and assumptions that classmates used to solve the problem.

SAMPLE SOLUTION

Assumptions:

- The video takes a full week to reach 750,000 views.

First, find the relationship between friends, days, and number of views. If you show the video to n friends on Day 1 and they each show it to n people, then on Day 2, $n \cdot n = n^2$ people will see it for the first time. On Day 3, $n^2 \cdot n = n^3$ people will see it, and so on. So the relationship is:

$$\text{views} = (\text{friends})^{\text{days}}$$

Now use a guess and check strategy to see how many friends are needed for the video to hit the goal on Day 7. Make a table with the help of a calculator to find the least value of n that satisfies the inequality $n^7 \geq 750{,}000$.

10^7	10,000,000	Too high
9^7	4,782,969	Too high
8^7	2,097,152	Acceptable
7^7	823,543	Best
6^7	279,936	Too low

So, you would need to show the video to 7 friends on the first day.

Ready to Go On?

ASSESS MASTERY

Use the assessment on this page to determine if students have mastered the concepts and standards covered in this module.

ASSESSMENT AND INTERVENTION

Access Ready to Go On? assessment online, and receive instant scoring, feedback, and customized intervention or enrichment.

ADDITIONAL RESOURCES

Response to Intervention Resources

- Reteach Worksheets

Differentiated Instruction Resources

- Reading Strategies **EL**
- Success for English Learners **EL**
- Challenge Worksheets

Assessment Resources

- Leveled Module Quizzes

735 Module 15

15.1–15.5 Geometric Sequences and Exponential Functions

- Online Homework
- Hints and Help
- Extra Practice

Write a recursive rule and an explicit rule for each geometric sequence, and then find the next three terms. *(Lessons 15.1, 15.2)*

1. 2, 8, 32,...

$f(1) = 2$ and $f(n) = f(n-1) \cdot 4$

$f(n) = 2 \cdot 4^{n-1}$

128, 512, 2048

2. 1024, 512, 256,...

$f(1) = 1024$ and $f(n) = f(n-1) \cdot \frac{1}{2}$

$f(n) = 1024 \cdot \left(\frac{1}{2}\right)^{n-1}$

128, 64, 32

Write an equation for the exponential function that includes the pair of given points. Find a, b, and the y-intercept, and then graph the function and describe its end behavior. *(Lessons 15.3, 15.4)*

3. $(1, 12)$ and $(-1, 0.75)$

$f(x) = 3 \cdot 4^x$; $a = 3$; $b = 4$; y-int $= (0, 3)$;

As $x \to \infty$, $y \to \infty$ and as $x \to -\infty$, $y \to 0$.

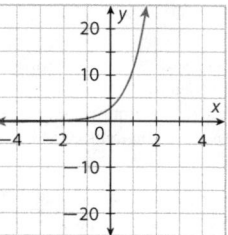

4. $(-1, -8)$ and $(1, -2)$

$f(x) = -4\left(\frac{1}{2}\right)^x$; $a = -4$; $b = \frac{1}{2}$;

y-int $= (0, -4)$; As $x \to \infty$, $y \to 0$

and as $x \to -\infty$, $y \to -\infty$.

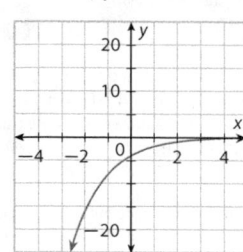

5. Describe the transformations of the function $g(x) = 0.25(5)^x - 2$ as compared to the parent function $f(x) = 5^x$. *(Lesson 15.5)*

$g(x)$ **has been vertically compressed by a factor of 0.25 and translated 2 units down.**

ESSENTIAL QUESTION

6. How does the rate of change of an exponential function behave as the value of x increases?

Possible Answer: As x increases, the rate of change of an exponential function is either consistently increasing or consistently decreasing.

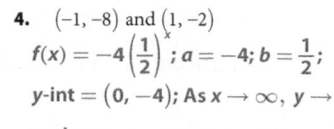 Common Core Standards

Lesson	Items	Content Standards	Mathematical Practices
15.1, 15.2	1	F-LE.A.2, F-BF.A.1a	MP.7
15.1, 15.2	2	F-LE.A.2, F-BF.A.1a	MP.7
15.3, 15.4	3	F-LE.A.2, F-IF.A.2, F-IF.C.7	MP.7
15.3, 15.4	4	F-LE.A.2, F-IF.A.2, F-IF.C.7	MP.7

MODULE 15
MIXED REVIEW

Assessment Readiness

1. Consider the geometric sequence 6, 24, 96, 384, ...
   Choose True or False for each statement.

   A. The sixth term is 1536. ○ True ● False
   B. The explicit rule is $f(n) = 6(4)^{n-1}$. ● True ○ False
   C. The recursive rule is $f(1) = 4; f(n) = f(n-1) \cdot 6$. ○ True ● False

2. Does the given system of equations have exactly one solution? Select Yes or No for each system.

   A. $\begin{cases} 3x - 2y = 6 \\ 2x + 2y = 14 \end{cases}$ ● Yes ○ No

   B. $\begin{cases} y = -4x - 5 \\ y = -4x + 2 \end{cases}$ ○ Yes ● No

   C. $\begin{cases} 5x - 3y = 15 \\ 5x + 3y = 15 \end{cases}$ ● Yes ○ No

3. Is the given number a term in both the sequence $f(n) = f(n-1) + 5$ and the sequence $f(n) = 3(2)^{n-1}$, if $f(1) = 3$? Select Yes or No for each number.

   A. 8 ○ Yes ● No
   B. 18 ○ Yes ● No
   C. 24 ○ Yes ● No
   D. 48 ● Yes ○ No

4. A laser beam with an output of 6 milliwatts is focused at a series of mirrors. The laser beam loses 2% of its power every time it reflects off of a mirror. The power $p(n)$ is an exponential function of the number of reflections in the form of $p(n) = ab^n$. Write the equation $p(n)$ for this laser beam. Explain how you determined the values of a and b.

   $p(n) = 6(0.98)^n$; a is the original output of the beam, and b is $1 - 0.02$, or the percent of power retained after each reflection.

ASSESSMENT AND INTERVENTION

Assign ready-made or customized practice tests to prepare students for high-stakes tests.

ADDITIONAL RESOURCES

Assessment Resources

- Leveled Module Quizzes: Modified, B

AVOID COMMON ERRORS

Item 2 Some students will attempt to solve each system the same way, even though each system is set up such that they are solved most easily using different methods. Remind students to consider each system individually when choosing a solution method.

Common Core Standards

Lesson	Items	Content Standards	Mathematical Practices
15.1, 15.2	1	F-LE.A.2	MP.4
11.1	2*	A-REI.C.6	MP.1
4.1, 15.1	3*	F-LE.A.2	MP.1
15.3	4	F-IF.A.2	MP.4

* Item integrates mixed review concepts from previous modules or a previous course.

Exponential Equations and Models

ESSENTIAL QUESTION:

Answer: Many real-world situations cannot be represented by linear functions. Exponential equations can be used to represent situations in which the output values increase or decrease by a constant ratio for each unit increase in the input value.

PROFESSIONAL DEVELOPMENT VIDEO

Professional Development Video

Author Juli Dixon models successful teaching practices in an actual high-school classroom.

Professional Development
my.hrw.com

MODULE **16**

Exponential Equations and Models

Essential Question: How can you use exponential equations to represent real-world situations?

LESSON 16.1
Using Graphs and Properties to Solve Equations with Exponents

LESSON 16.2
Modeling Exponential Growth and Decay

LESSON 16.3
Using Exponential Regression Models

LESSON 16.4
Comparing Linear and Exponential Models

© Houghton Mifflin Harcourt Publishing Company • Image Credits: ©Everett Collection Inc./Alamy

REAL WORLD VIDEO
Scientists have found many ways to use radioactive elements that decay exponentially over time. Uranium-235 is used to power nuclear reactors, and scientists use Carbon-14 dating to calculate how long ago an organism lived.

MODULE PERFORMANCE TASK PREVIEW

Half-Life

Accidents at nuclear reactors like the one in Fukushima, Japan, in 2011 commonly release the radioactive isotopes iodine-131 and cesium-137. Iodine-131 often causes thyroid problems, whereas cesium-137 permeates the entire body and can cause death. Each isotope decays over time but at very different rates. How can you figure out the concentration of isotopes at a nuclear accident? Let's find out!

Module 16

737

DIGITAL TEACHER EDITION

Access a full suite of teaching resources when and where you need them:

- Access content online or offline
- Customize lessons to share with your class
- Communicate with your students in real-time
- View student grades and data instantly to target your instruction where it is needed most

PERSONAL MATH TRAINER
Assessment and Intervention

Assign automatically graded homework, quizzes, tests, and intervention activities. Prepare your students with updated, Common Core-aligned practice tests.

Are (YOU) Ready?

Complete these exercises to review skills you will need for this module.

Constant Rate of Change

Example 1

Tell if the rate of change is constant.

	+1	+1	+1	
Time (hr)	1	2	3	4
Distance (mi)	45	90	135	180

+45 +45 +45

$$\text{rate of change} = \frac{\text{change in miles}}{\text{change in hours}}$$
$$= \frac{45}{1}$$

The rate of change is constant.

• Online Homework
• Hints and Help
• Extra Practice

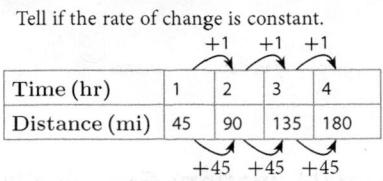

Tell if the rate of change is constant.

1.

Age (mo)	3	6	9	12
Weight (lb)	12	16	18	20

no

2.

Hours	2	4	6	8
Pay ($)	16	32	48	64

yes

Percent

Example 2

Write 7% as a decimal.

$$7\% = \frac{7}{100} = 0.07$$

Write the percent in the form $\frac{r}{100}$ and then write the decimal.

Write the percent as a decimal.

3. 21%
0.21

4. 3.5%
0.035

5. 108%
1.08

6. 0.25%
0.0025

Exponents

Example 3

Find the value of $2(3)^4$.

$$2(3)^4 = 2(3 \cdot 3 \cdot 3 \cdot 3)$$
$$= 162$$

Write the power as a multiplication expression. Multiply.

Find the value.

7. $3(4)^2$
48

8. $24(0.5)^3$
3

9. $5(2)^5$
160

10. $350(0.1)^3$
0.35

Are You Ready?

ASSESS READINESS

Use the assessment on this page to determine if students need strategic or intensive intervention for the module's prerequisite skills.

ASSESSMENT AND INTERVENTION

Response to Intervention **TIER 1, TIER 2, TIER 3 SKILLS**

Personal Math Trainer will automatically create a standards-based, personalized intervention assignment for your students, targeting each student's individual needs!

ADDITIONAL RESOURCES

See the table below for a full list of intervention resources available for this module.

Response to Intervention Resources also includes:

• Tier 2 Skill Pre-Tests for each Module
• Tier 2 Skill Post-Tests for each skill

Response to Intervention			*Differentiated Instruction*
Tier 1 Lesson Intervention Worksheets	**Tier 2** Strategic Intervention Skills Intervention Worksheets	**Tier 3** Intensive Intervention Worksheets available online	
Reteach 16.1 Reteach 16.2 Reteach 16.3 Reteach 16.4	4 Constant Rate of Change 5 Exponents 15 Percent 18 Scatter Plots	Building Block Skills 5, 24, 27, 29, 30, 37, 39, 46, 59, 63, 65, 68, 69, 70, 72, 76, 100	Challenge worksheets Extend the Math Lesson Activities in TE

Using Graphs and Properties to Solve Equations with Exponents

Common Core Math Standards

The student is expected to:

 A-CED.A.1

Create equations ...and use them to solve problems... arising from... exponential functions. Also A-SSE.B.3c, A-REI.D.11, F-BF.A.1, F-LE.A.2

Mathematical Practices

 MP.5 Using Tools

Language Objective

Explain to a partner how to use a graph to find the solution to an equation with a variable exponent.

ENGAGE

Essential Question: How can you solve equations involving variable exponents?

When the bases are equal, use the Equality of Bases Property. When the bases are not equal, graph each side of the equation as its own function and find the intersection.

PREVIEW: LESSON PERFORMANCE TASK

View the Engage section online. Discuss why a town government might need to know the rate at which the town's population is growing. Then preview the Lesson Performance Task.

Name_____ Class_____ Date_____

16.1 Using Graphs and Properties to Solve Equations with Exponents

Resource Locker

Essential Question: How can you solve equations involving variable exponents?

🧭 Explore 1 Solving Exponential Equations Graphically

In previous lessons, variables have been raised to rational exponents and you have seen how to simplify and solve equations containing these expressions. How do you solve an equation with a rational number raised to a variable? In certain cases, this is not a difficult task. If $2^x = 4$ it is easy to see that $x = 2$ since $2^2 = 4$. In other cases, like $3(2)^x = 96$, where would you begin? Let's find out.

Ⓐ Solve for $3(2)^x = 96$ for x.

Ⓑ Let $f(x) = 3(2)^x$. Complete the table for $f(x)$.

x	f(x)
1	6
2	12
3	24
4	48
5	96
6	192
7	384

Ⓒ Using the table of values, graph $f(x)$ on the axes provided.

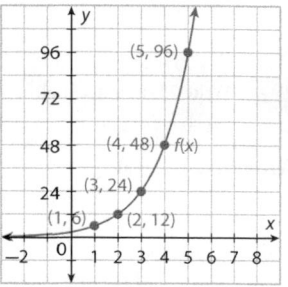

Ⓓ Let $g(x) = 96$. Complete the table for $g(x)$.

x	g(x)
1	96
2	96
3	96
4	96
5	96
6	96
7	96

Ⓔ Using the table, graph $g(x)$ on the same axes as $f(x)$.

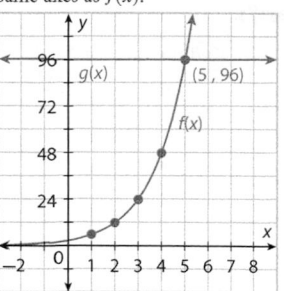

Ⓕ The graphs intersect at point(s): $(5, 96)$ This means that $f(x) = g(x)$ when $x = 5$.

© Houghton Mifflin Harcourt Publishing Company

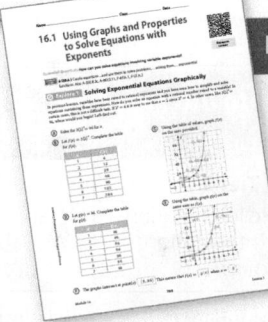

HARDCOVER PAGES 579–586

Turn to these pages to find this lesson in the hardcover student edition.

1. **Discussion** Consider the function $h(x) = -96$. Where do $f(x)$ and $h(x)$ intersect?
   The graphs would not intersect as $f(x)$ is always greater than 0. Raising any positive

   number to a positive exponent yields a positive number.

2. Divide the equation $3(2)^x = 96$ by 3 on both sides (an Algebraic Step) and utilize the same method as

   in Explore 1 to graph each side of the equation as a function. The point of intersection would be: $(5, 32)$.

   Is this the same point of intersection? Is this the same answer? Can this be done? Elaborate as to why or why not.

   It is not the same point of intersection. The y-values of the points are different. They

   do represent the same solution because the equations are equivalent by the Division

   Property of Equality.

Explore 2   Solving Exponential Equations Algebraically

Recall the example $2^x = 4$, with the solution $x = 2$. What about a slightly more complicated equation? Can an equation like $5(2)^x = 160$ be solved using algebra?

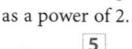 Solve $5(2)^x = 160$ for x. The first step in isolating the term containing the variable

on one side of the equation is to ___**divide each side of the equation by 5**___ .

$$\frac{5(2)^x}{5} = \frac{160}{5}$$

(B) Simplify.   (C) Rewrite the right hand side   (D) Solve.

as a power of 2.

$(2)^x = \boxed{32}$ $(2)^x = (2)^{\boxed{5}}$ $x = \boxed{5}$

3. **Discussion** The last step of the solution process seems to imply that if $b^x = b^y$ then $x = y$. Is this true for all values of b? Justify your answer.
   No, it is not true. For example, $0^5 = 0^8$ but $5 \neq 8$, or $1^7 = 1^{958}$ but $7 \neq 958$.

4. In Reflect 2, we started to solve $3(2)^x = 96$ algebraically. Finish solving for x.
   $3(2)^x = 96$

   $2^x = 32$

   $2^x = 2^5$

   $x = 5$

PROFESSIONAL DEVELOPMENT

Learning Progressions

In this lesson, students continue to build on their understanding of geometric sequences and exponential functions. They learn the Equality of Bases Property, which states that If $b > 0$ and $b \neq 1$, then $b^x = b^y$ if and only if $x = y$. They learn to solve equations involving variable exponents either by using the Equality of Bases Property or by graphing. They also begin to model real-world situations using exponential equations, which can then be solved by either method. Work with exponential functions will continue as students learn about exponential growth and decay models and exponential regression.

EXPLORE 1

Solving Exponential Equations Graphically

INTEGRATE TECHNOLOGY

Students can use graphing calculators to solve an exponential equation by the method shown in the Explore activity. Students should enter the appropriate exponential function and constant function, graph both functions, and use the calculator's *intersect* feature to find their point of intersection.

QUESTIONING STRATEGIES

? When solving an exponential equation of the form $ab^x = c$ graphically, what two functions do you graph? **the exponential function $f(x) = ab^x$ and the horizontal line $g(x) = c$**

? How does graphing these two functions on the same grid help you determine the value of the exponent? **The value of the exponent is the x-value of the point of intersection.**

EXPLORE 2

Solving Exponential Equations Algebraically

QUESTIONING STRATEGIES

? In the equation $4^x = 64$, how can you evaluate x? **Write 64 as a power of 4.** $64 = 4^3$, so $x = 3$.

? Assuming that x is an integer in the equation $b^x = c$, what must be true for this method to work? **The value of c must be a power of b.**

EXPLAIN 1

Solving Equations by Equating Exponents

QUESTIONING STRATEGIES

? In an equation such as $36(2)^x = 576$, what property of equality can you use to isolate 2^x? Explain how. **Division Property of Equality; divide both sides by 36.**

? How does this step compare to isolating a variable on one side of a linear equation? **It is done for the same reason. By isolating the power, you have isolated the variable as well. Then you can compare the exponents in the final equivalent expression.**

INTEGRATE MATHEMATICAL PRACTICES
Focus on Reasoning

MP.2 Discuss with students the limitations on the Equality of Bases Property. Have students give examples to show why the property does not apply when the base is 0, 1, or −1. For example: $0^5 = 0^8 = 0$ but $5 \neq 8$; $1^{20} = 1^{99} = 1$ but $20 \neq 99$; and $(-1)^4 = (-1)^6 = 1$ but $4 \neq 6$.

AVOID COMMON ERRORS

Some students may misread the base b in an expression b^x as a coefficient of x and try to divide both sides of the equation by b to isolate the variable. Remind them that when a number is raised to a power, it cannot be treated as a single factor. They must use the properties of equality to isolate b^x, then use the Equality of Bases Property to solve for the variable.

Solving the previous exponential equation for x used the idea that if $2^x = 2^5$, then $x = 5$. This will be a powerful tool for solving exponential equations if it can be generalized to if $b^x = b^y$ then $x = y$. However, there are values for which this is clearly not true. For example, $0^7 = 0^3$ but $7 \neq 3$. If the values of b are restricted, we get the following property.

> **Equality of Bases Property**
>
> Two powers with the same positive base other than 1 are equal if and only if the exponents are equal.
>
> Algebraically, if $b > 0$ and, $b \neq 1$, then $b^x = b^y$ if and only if $x = y$.

Example 1 Solve by equating exponents and using the Equality of Bases Property.

Ⓐ $\frac{2}{5}(5)^x = 250$

$\frac{5}{2} \cdot \frac{2}{5}(5)^x = 250 \cdot \frac{5}{2}$ Multiply both sides by $\frac{5}{2}$.

$5^x = 625$ Simplify.

$5^x = 5^4$ Rewrite the right side as a power of 5.

$x = 4$ Equality of Bases Property.

Ⓑ $2\left(\frac{5}{3}\right)^x = \frac{250}{27}$

$\dfrac{2\left(\frac{5}{3}\right)^x}{\boxed{2}} = \dfrac{\frac{250}{27}}{\boxed{2}}$ Divide both sides by $\boxed{2}$.

$\left(\frac{5}{3}\right)^x = \dfrac{\boxed{125}}{27}$ Simplify.

$\left(\frac{5}{3}\right)^x = \left[\left(\frac{5}{3}\right)\right]^{\boxed{3}}$ Rewrite the right side as a power of $\boxed{\frac{5}{3}}$.

$x = \boxed{3}$ Equality of $\underline{\text{Bases}}$ Property.

Reflect

5. Suppose while solving an equation algebraically you are confronted with:

$5^x = 15$

$5^x = 5^{\square}$

Can you find x using the method in the examples above?

No, you cannot. It is not possible because 15 is not a whole number power of 5.

COLLABORATIVE LEARNING

Peer-to-Peer Activity

Have students work in pairs. Have each student write an equation involving a variable exponent in the form $b^x = c$. After students exchange equations, each partner should first decide whether c can be expressed as a whole number power of b. If so, the student should rewrite c as a power of b and solve for x. If not, the student should use a graphing calculator to graph each side of the equation as a separate function and use the *intersect* feature to find the x-coordinate of the intersection point, which is the solution to the original equation. Have students check each other's work.

Solve by equating exponents and using the Equality of Bases Property.

6. $\frac{2}{3}(3)^x = 18$

$$\frac{2}{3}(3)^x = 18$$
$$\frac{3}{2} \cdot \frac{2}{3}(3)^x = 18 \cdot \frac{3}{2}$$
$$3^x = 27$$
$$3^x = 3^3$$
$$x = 3$$

7. $\frac{3}{2}\left(\frac{4}{3}\right)^x = \frac{8}{3}$

$$\frac{3}{2}\left(\frac{4}{3}\right)^x = \frac{8}{3}$$
$$\frac{2}{3} \cdot \frac{3}{2}\left(\frac{4}{3}\right)^x = \frac{2}{3} \cdot \frac{8}{3}$$
$$\left(\frac{4}{3}\right)^x = \frac{16}{9}$$
$$\left(\frac{4}{3}\right)^x = \left(\frac{4}{3}\right)^2$$
$$x = 2$$

◯ Explain 2 **Solving a Real-World Exponential Equation by Graphing**

Some equations cannot be solved using the method in the previous example because it isn't possible to write both sides of the equation as a whole number power of the same base. Instead, you can consider the expressions on either side of the equation as the rules for two different functions. You can then solve the original equation in one variable by graphing the two functions. The solution is the input value for the point where the two graphs intersect.

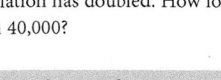

Example 2 Solve by graphing two functions.

An animal reserve has 20,000 elk. The population is increasing at a rate of 8% per year. There is concern that food will be scarce when the population has doubled. How long will it take for the population to reach 40,000?

 Analyze Information

Identify the important information.
- The starting population is   20,000.
- The ending population is   <u>40,000</u>.
- The growth rate is   <u>8% or 0.08</u>.

Formulate a Plan

With the given situation and data there is enough information to write and solve an exponential model of the population as a function of time. Write the exponential equation and then solve it using a graphing calculator.

Set $f(x) = $ <u>the target population</u> and $g(x) = $ <u>the exponential model</u>.

Input $Y_1 = f(x)$ and $Y_2 = g(x)$ into a graphing calculator, graph the functions, and <u>find their intersection</u>

EXPLAIN 2

Solving a Real-World Exponential Equation by Graphing

QUESTIONING STRATEGIES

? If a population grows by 5% each year, by what factor is the population multiplied each year? Explain. **1.05; if the population is p one year, it will be $p + 0.05p = 1.05p$ the next year.**

? Why is it appropriate to round a prediction involving time to the nearest year?

A prediction is usually just an estimate, so rounding is appropriate.

DIFFERENTIATE INSTRUCTION

Graphic Organizers

Have students complete a graphic organizer that shows when to solve an equation involving a variable exponent algebraically and when to solve it graphically.

Solving $b^x = c$ (where $b > 0$, $b \neq 1$, and $c > 0$)	
Value of c	Solution Method
$c = b^d$ for some whole number d.	Algebraic: $b^x = b^d$, so $x = d$.
c is not a whole number power of b.	Graph: intersection of $f(x) = b^x$ and $g(x) = c$

INTEGRATE TECHNOLOGY

When solving exponential equations graphically, have a student demonstrate how to identify the two functions to be graphed, enter them into a graphing calculator, and find the solution by finding the point of intersection. Discuss how to adjust the viewing window so that the graph and the point of intersection are clearly visible.

Solve

Write a function $P(t) = ab^t$, where $P(t)$ is the population and t is the number of years since the population was initially measured.

a represents __the initial population of elk__

$a = \boxed{20,000}$

b represents __the yearly growth rate of the elk population__

$b = \boxed{1.08}$

The function is $P(t) = \boxed{20,000}\left(\boxed{1.08}\right)^t$.

To find the time when the population is 40,000, set __the function__ or __$P(t)$__ equal to 40,000 and __solve for t__

$40,000 = \boxed{20,000}\left(\boxed{1.08}\right)^t$.

Write functions for the expressions on either side of the equation.

$f(x) = \dfrac{\boxed{40,000}}{}$

$g(x) = \underline{\boxed{20,000}\,(1.08)^x}$

Using a graphing calculator, set $Y_1 = f(x)$ and $Y_2 = g(x)$. View the graph.
Use the intersect feature on the CALC menu to find the intersection of the two graphs.
The approximate x-value where the graphs intersect is $\boxed{9.006468}$.
Therefore, the population will double in just a little over $\boxed{9}$ years.

Justify and Evaluate

Check the solution by evaluating the function at $t = \boxed{9}$.

$P\left(\boxed{9}\right) = 20,000 \cdot \boxed{(1.08)^9}$

$= 20,000 \cdot \boxed{1.9990}$

$= \boxed{39,980}$

Since $\boxed{39,980} \approx 40,000$, it __is__ accurate to say the population will double in $\underline{9}$ years.

This prediction __is__ reasonable because $1.08^{\boxed{9}} \approx \boxed{2}$.

LANGUAGE SUPPORT EL

Connect Context

Support students in interpreting the language used in problem statements. Explain that the word *suppose* at the beginning of a problem signals that what follows is a hypothetical example, meaning that readers should use their imaginations to consider a possible scenario.

Often, a problem will be followed by the question, *Why or why not?* Explain that the question is phrased this way so as not to give away the answer. Students should understand that they need to explain either why a result is true or why it is not true, depending on the situation.

Solve using a graphing calculator.

8. There are 225 wolves in a state park. The population is increasing at the rate of 15% per year. You want to make a prediction for how long it will take the population to reach 500.

Graph $\begin{aligned} Y_1 &= 500 \\ Y_2 &= 225(1.15)^x \end{aligned}$ **The intersection point is $(5.713341, 500)$. The wolf population will reach 500 in approximately 5.7 years.**

9. There are 175 deer in a state park. The population is increasing at the rate of 12% per year. You want to make a prediction for how long it will take the population to reach 300.

Graph $\begin{aligned} Y_1 &= 300 \\ Y_2 &= 175(1.12)^x \end{aligned}$ **The intersection point is $(4.756046, 300)$. The deer population will reach 300 in approximately 4.8 years.**

💬 Elaborate

10. Explain how you would solve $0.25 = 0.5^x$. Which method can always be used to solve an exponential equation?
Possible answer: Algebraically.

$0.25 = 0.5^x$

$(0.5)^2 = (0.5)^x \rightarrow x = 2$

Exponential equations can always be solved graphically.

11. What would you do first to solve the equation $\frac{1}{4}(6)^x = 54$?
Multiply each side of the equation by 4 to isolate the power.

12. How does isolating the power in an exponential equation like $\frac{1}{4}(6)^x = 54$ compare to isolating the variable in a linear equation?
Both are done for the same reason. By isolating the power, you have isolated the variable as well. Then you can compare the exponents in the final equivalent expressions.

13. Given a population decreasing by 1% per year, when will the population double? What will this type of situation look like when graphed on a calculator?
It will never double as the population is decreasing. The equation representing this

situation, $2 = 0.99^x$, has no solution for $x > 0$. The graphing calculator will show a

horizontal line at 2 and an exponential function with a y-intercept of 1 decreasing towards

the positive x axis.

14. Solve $0.5 = 1.01^x$ graphically. Suppose this equation models the point where a population increasing at a rate of 1% per year is halved. When will the population be halved?
Since $x = -69.66072$, you would have to go back in time, which is not possible. Seventy

years or so ago the population was half of what it is now.

15. **Essential Question Check-In** How can you solve equations involving variable exponents?
When the bases are equal, use the Equality of Bases Property. When there are not equal

bases on both sides of the equation, graph each side of the equation as its own function

and find the intersection.

ELABORATE

QUESTIONING STRATEGIES

? What is the shape of the graph of an exponential function of the form $f(x) = b^x$ when $b > 1$? It is a curve that rises in greater and greater amounts as x increases.

? What is the shape of the graph of a function $f(x) = b^x$ when $0 < b < 1$? It is a curve that falls more and more gradually as x increases.

SUMMARIZE THE LESSON

? How can you solve an equation where the variable is an exponent? First, use the properties of equality to isolate the number raised to a variable power. Then check whether the constant on the other side of the equation can be written as a whole number power of the same base. If it can, use the Equality of Bases Property to solve. If not, graph each side of the equation as its own function and find the x-value of the point of intersection.

EVALUATE

ASSIGNMENT GUIDE

Concepts and Skills	Practice
Explore 1 Solving Exponential Equations Graphically	Exercises 2–3
Explore 2 Solving Exponential Equations Algebraically	Exercises 1, 3
Example 1 Solving Equations by Equating Exponents	Exercises 4–16, 24 –25
Example 2 Solving a Real-World Exponential Equation by Graphing	Exercises 17–23

INTEGRATE MATHEMATICAL PRACTICES

Focus on Communication

MP.3 Circulate as students solve the practice exercises. Invite students to explain their reasoning as they begin a new problem.

⭐ Evaluate: Homework and Practice

• Online Homework
• Hints and Help
• Extra Practice

1. Would it have been easier to find the solution to the equation in Explore 1, $3(2)^x = 96$, algebraically? Justify your answer. In general, if you can solve an exponential equation graphing by hand, why can you solve it algebraically?

   Yes, $3(2)^x = 96$ becomes $(2)^x = 32$ after dividing both sides of the equation by 3 and 32 is an integer power of 2.

   In general, the input-output tables for $f(x)$ and $g(x)$ have integers in the domain and the values in the range are easy to calculate.

2. The equation $2 = (1.01)^x$ models a population that has doubled. What is the rate of increase? What does x represent?

   The rate of increase is 1% per unit time. x is number of units of time.

3. Can we solve equations using both algebraic and graphical methods?

   Yes. We can simplify the equation algebraically and then use graphing.

Solve the given equation.

4. $4(2)^x = 64$

   $\dfrac{4(2)^x}{4} = \dfrac{64}{4}$

   $2^x = 16$

   $2^x = 2^4$

   $x = 4$

5. $7(3)^x = 63$

   $\dfrac{7(3)^x}{7} = \dfrac{63}{7}$

   $3^x = 9$

   $3^x = 3^2$

   $x = 2$

6. $\dfrac{6^x}{4} = 54$

   $4 \cdot \dfrac{6^x}{4} = 4 \cdot 54$

   $6^x = 216$

   $6^x = 6^3$

   $x = 3$

7. $\left(\dfrac{1}{4}\right)\left(\dfrac{5}{6}\right)^x = \dfrac{75}{432}$

   $4 \cdot \left(\dfrac{1}{4}\right)\left(\dfrac{5}{6}\right)^x = 4 \cdot \dfrac{75}{432}$

   $\left(\dfrac{5}{6}\right)^x = \dfrac{25}{36}$

   $\left(\dfrac{5}{6}\right)^x = \left(\dfrac{5}{6}\right)^2$

   $x = 2$

8. $2\left(\dfrac{7}{2}\right)^x = \dfrac{49}{2}$

   $\dfrac{2\left(\dfrac{7}{2}\right)^x}{2} = \dfrac{\frac{49}{2}}{2}$

   $\left(\dfrac{7}{2}\right)^x = \dfrac{49}{4}$

   $\left(\dfrac{7}{2}\right)^x = \left(\dfrac{7}{2}\right)^2$

   $x = 2$

9. $3(11)^x = 3993$

   $\dfrac{3(11)^x}{3} = \dfrac{3993}{3}$

   $11^x = 1331$

   $11^x = 11^3$

   $x = 3$

Exercise	Depth of Knowledge (D.O.K.)	COMMON CORE Mathematical Practices
1	**2** Skills/Concepts	**MP.6** Precision
2	**2** Skills/Concepts	**MP.4** Modeling
3	**2** Skills/Concepts	**MP.6** Precision
4–12	**1** Recall of Information	**MP.2** Reasoning
13–16	**2** Skills/Concepts	**MP.2** Reasoning
17–22	**2** Skills/Concepts	**MP.4** Modeling

10. $2(9)^x = 162$

$9^x = 81$

$9^x = 9^2$

$x = 2$

11. $2\left(\frac{1}{9}\right)^x = \frac{2}{81}$

$\dfrac{2\left(\frac{1}{9}\right)^x}{2} = \dfrac{\frac{2}{81}}{2}$

$\left(\frac{1}{9}\right)^x = \frac{1}{81}$

$\left(\frac{1}{9}\right)^x = \left(\frac{1}{9}\right)^2$

$x = 2$

12. $2\left(\frac{4}{13}\right)^x = \frac{32}{169}$

$\dfrac{2\left(\frac{4}{13}\right)^x}{2} = \dfrac{\frac{32}{169}}{2}$

$\left(\frac{4}{13}\right)^x = \frac{16}{169}$

$\left(\frac{4}{13}\right)^x = \left(\frac{4}{13}\right)^2$

$x = 2$

13. $\left(\frac{1}{2}\right)\left(\frac{2}{3}\right)^x = \left(\frac{1}{4}\right)\left(\frac{16}{27}\right)$

$2\left(\frac{1}{2}\right)\left(\frac{2}{3}\right)^x = 2\left(\frac{1}{4}\right)\left(\frac{16}{27}\right)$

$\left(\frac{2}{3}\right)^x = \frac{8}{27}$

$\left(\frac{2}{3}\right)^x = \left(\frac{2}{3}\right)^3$

$x = 3$

14. $(8)\left(\frac{2}{3}\right)^x = (4)\left(\frac{16}{27}\right)$

$\dfrac{8\left(\frac{2}{3}\right)^x}{8} = \dfrac{4\left(\frac{16}{27}\right)}{8}$

$\left(\frac{2}{3}\right)^x = \left(\frac{8}{27}\right)$

$\left(\frac{2}{3}\right)^x = \left(\frac{2}{3}\right)^3$

$x = 3$

15. $\left(\frac{2}{5}\right)\left(\frac{2}{5}\right)^x = \frac{8}{125}$

$\left(\frac{5}{2}\right)\left(\frac{2}{5}\right)\left(\frac{2}{5}\right)^x = \left(\frac{5}{2}\right)\frac{8}{125}$

$\left(\frac{2}{5}\right)^x = \frac{4}{25}$

$\left(\frac{2}{5}\right)^x = \left(\frac{2}{5}\right)^2$

$x = 2$

16. $\left(\frac{2}{5}\right)^x\left(\frac{2}{5}\right)^x = \left(\frac{8}{125}\right)\left(\frac{8}{125}\right)$

$\left(\frac{2}{5}\right)^{2x} = \left(\frac{8}{125}\right)^2$

$\left(\frac{2}{5}\right)^{2x} = \left(\left(\frac{2}{5}\right)^3\right)^2$

$\left(\frac{2}{5}\right)^{2x} = \left(\frac{2}{5}\right)^6$

$2x = 6$

$\frac{2x}{2} = \frac{6}{2}$

$x = 3$

17. There is a drought and the oak tree population is decreasing at the rate of 7% per year. If the population continues to decrease at the same rate, how long will it take for the population to be half of what it is?

The model for the oak tree population is $P(t) = P_i(0.93)^t$, where t is the time in years, P_i is the initial population, and $P(t)$ is the population in year t. To find when the population is half of its initial value, solve $P(t) = \frac{P_i}{2}$ for t.

$\frac{P_i}{2} = P_i(0.93)^t$ Using a calculator graph each side of the equation

$\dfrac{\frac{P_i}{2}}{P_i} = \dfrac{P_i(0.93)^t}{P_i}$ as a function and find their intersection.

$\frac{1}{2} = (0.93)^t$ **The population will reach half of its original value in approximately 9.6 years.**

$t \approx 9.55$

INTEGRATE MATHEMATICAL PRACTICES

Focus on Patterns

MP.8 When solving an equation involving a variable exponent, suggest that students try to structure the solution so that they are solving an equation of the form $b^x = c^y$. If $c = b$, then $x = y$; if $c \neq b$, then they should solve by graphing.

Exercise	Depth of Knowledge (D.O.K.)	COMMON CORE Mathematical Practices
23	**3** Strategic Thinking	**MP.4** Modeling
24–25	**3** Strategic Thinking H.O.T.	**MP.3** Logic

Using Graphs and Properties to Solve Equations with Exponents   **746**

AVOID COMMON ERRORS

Students may be confused by complicated equations that involve variable exponents as well as additional factors. Remind them to first apply the properties of equality to isolate the number with the variable exponent, then use the Equality of Bases Property to solve.

18. An animal reserve has 40,000 elk. The population is increasing at a rate of 11% per year. How long will it take for the population to reach 80,000?

The model for population is $P(t) = 40{,}000(1.11)^t$, where t is the time in years and $P(t)$ is the population in year t. To find when the population is 80,000, solve $P(t) = 80{,}000$ for t.

Using a calculator graph each side of the equation as a function and find their intersection.

$t \approx 6.64$

The population will reach 80,000 in approximately 6.6 years.

19. A lake has a small population of a rare endangered fish. The lake currently has a population of 10 fish. The number of fish is increasing at a rate of 4% per year. When will the population double? How long will it take the population to be 80 fish?

The model for population is $P(t) = 10(1.04)^t$, where t is the time in years and $P(t)$ is the population in year t.

Solve $P(t) = 20$ for t.

Using a calculator graph each side of the equation as a function and find their intersection.

$t \approx 17.67$

The population of the fish will double in 18 years.

To find when the population will be 80, you can solve $P(t) = 80$ for t.

Alternatively, note that $80 = 10 \cdot 8 = 10 \cdot 2^3$. This corresponds to the population doubling three times, from 10 to 20, from 20 to 40, and from 40 to 80. The population will be 80 in 54 years $(3 \cdot 18)$.

20. Tim has a savings account with the bank. The bank pays him 1% per year. He has $5000 and wonders when it will reach $5200. When will his savings reach $5200?

The model is $S(t) = 5000(1.01)^t$. Solve $S(t) = 5200$ for t.

$5200 = 5000(1.01)^t$

Using a calculator graph each side of the equation as a function and find their intersection.

Graphing $f(x)$ and $g(x)$, we get the point of intersection $(3.941648, 1.04)$.

Rounding up and considering interest is calculated yearly, it will take Tim 4 years.

21. Tim is considering a different savings account that pays 1%, but this time it is compounded monthly.

(When interest is compounded monthly, the bank pays interest every month instead of every year. The function representing compounded interest is $S(t) = P\left(1 + \frac{r}{n}\right)^{nt}$, where P is the principal, or initial deposit in the account, r is the interest rate, n is the number of times the interest is compounded per year, t is the year, and $S(t)$ is the savings after t years.)

How many years will it take Tim to earn $200 at this bank? Should he switch?

The model is $S(t) = 5000\left(1 + \frac{0.01}{12}\right)^{12t}$ or $S(t) = 5000(1.00083)^{12t}$. Solve $S(t) = 5200$ for t.

$$5200 \approx 5000(1.00083)^{12t}$$

Using a calculator, graph each side of the equation as a function and find their intersection.

$t \approx 3.92$

Graphing $f(x)$ and $g(x)$, we get the point of intersection (3.923705, 1.04). x is approximately 4 years. Both accounts will reach $5200 in about 4 years.

Switching won't make much difference.

22. Lisa has a credit card that charges 3% interest on a monthly balance. She buys a $200 bike and plans to pay for it by making monthly payments of $100. How many months will it take her to pay it off? Assume the first payment she makes is charged no interest because she paid it before the first bill.
Her first payment is $100. At that time she owes $100 plus interest or $103. The second month she pays $100 and the third month she pays the rest. It takes her three months to pay it off. You do not have to solve an exponential because 3% is not a very high interest.

23. **Analyze Relationships** A city has 175,000 residents. The population is increasing at the rate of 10% per year.

a. You want to make a prediction for how long it will take for the population to reach 300,000. Round your answer to the nearest tenth of a year.

b. Suppose there are 350,000 residents of another city. The population of this city is decreasing at a rate of 3% per year. Which city's population will reach 300,000 sooner? Explain.

On parts a. and b. using a calculator graph each side of the equation as a function and find their intersection.

a. $300{,}000 = 175{,}000(1.1)^x$

$x \approx 5.7$

The population will reach 300,000 in approximately 5.7 years.

b. $300{,}000 = 350{,}000(.97)^x$

$x \approx 5.1$

$5.1 < 5.7$

The second city's population will reach 300,000 sooner.

AVOID COMMON ERRORS

Some students may be unsure how to raise a fraction to a power. Remind them that both the numerator and the denominator must be raised to the same power.

CURRICULUM INTEGRATION

Encourage students to research applications of exponential functions. They should consider applications in science and business as well as uses in other math courses.

INTEGRATE MATHEMATICAL PRACTICES
Focus on Reasoning

MP.2 As students solve real-world problems involving time, have them make predictions before calculating their results. Write the predictions on the board, then compare them to the solutions found algebraically or graphically. Encourage students to improve their predictions by analyzing whether their predictions tend to be too high or too low and by considering how they can change their estimation methods.

VISUAL CUES

Have students create posters as visual reminders of how to solve equations involving exponents. Remind students to include examples as well as step-by-step procedures.

JOURNAL

In their journals, have students explain how to use the Equality of Bases Property to solve an equation with a variable exponent.

24. Explain the Error Jean and Marco each solved the equation $9(3)^x = 729$. Whose solution is incorrect? Explain your reasoning. How could the person who is incorrect fix the work?

Jean	Marco
$9(3)^x = 729$	$9(3)^x = 729$
$\left(\frac{1}{9}\right) \cdot 9(3)^x = \left(\frac{1}{9}\right) \cdot 729$	$3^2 \cdot (3)^x = 729$
$3^x = 81 = 3^4$	$3^{2+x} = 729 = 3^6$
$x = 4$	$x = 6$

Jean is completely correct and Marco could correct his work as follows:

$$Marco$$
$$9(3)^x = 729$$
$$3^2 \cdot (3)^x = 729$$
$$3^{2+x} = 729 = 3^6$$
$$x + 2 = 6$$
$$x = 4$$

He substituted for $x = 6$ instead of $x + 2 = 6$, which yields $x = 4$.

25. Critical Thinking Without solving, state the column containing the equation with the greater solution for each pair of equations. Explain your reasoning.

$$\left(\frac{1}{3}\right)(3)^x = 243 \qquad\qquad \left(\frac{1}{3}\right)(9)^x = 243$$

The equation $\frac{1}{3}(3)^x = 243$ has a greater solution. Since the values of the powers of 3 increase less quickly than the values of the powers of 9, the value of x in $\frac{1}{3}(3)^x = 243$ will be greater than the value of x in $\frac{1}{3}(9)^x = 243$.

Lesson Performance Task

A town has a population of 78,918 residents. The town council is offering a prize for the best prediction of how long it will take the population to reach 100,000. The population rate is increasing 6% per year. Find the best prediction in order to win the prize. Write an exponential equation in the form $y = ab^x$ and explain what a and b represent.

Write an exponential equation.

Let y represent the population and x represent time in years.

a **represents the initial population 78,918**

b **represents the rate of increase in the population per year**

$y = 78{,}918(1 + 0.06)^x$

Substitute the target population for y: $100{,}000 = 78{,}918(1 + 0.06)^x$

Write the functions.

Substitute the target population for y: $100{,}000 = 78{,}918(1 + 0.06)^x$

$f(x) = 100{,}000$

$g(x) = 78{,}918(1 + 0.06)^x$

Use the intersect feature on a graphing calculator to find the point of intersection.

The point of intersection is $(4.063245, 100{,}000)$.

The population will reach 100,000 in just over 4 years.

EXTENSION ACTIVITY

Have students research the current population of their community or state and the rate at which it is growing or decreasing. Then have students write an exponential equation in which y represents the population and x represents time in years. Finally, have students choose a future population size and predict when the population will reach that size.

INTEGRATE MATHEMATICAL PRACTICES
Focus on Modeling

MP.4 Before students write an equation for the situation in the Lesson Performance Task, discuss how they know that the base to be raised to a power in the exponential equation is 1.06 and not 0.06. Have them consider "What factor multiplied by the population makes the number 6% greater?" Then ask what the base would be if the population were decreasing by 6% per year. Students should recognize that it would be $1 - 0.06 = 0.94$. Discuss what a graph showing each growth rate would look like.

INTEGRATE MATHEMATICAL PRACTICES
Focus on Technology

MP.5 As students use their graphing calculators to graph the two functions and find their intersection, remind them to adjust the viewing window so that the intersection is shown clearly.

INTEGRATE MATHEMATICAL PRACTICES
Focus on Communication

MP.3 Have students share their reasons for why the point where the graphs of the right- and left-hand sides of the equation intersect is the solution.

Scoring Rubric

2 points: Student correctly solves the problem and explains his/her reasoning.

1 point: Student shows good understanding of the problem but does not fully solve or explain his/her reasoning.

0 points: Student does not demonstrate understanding of the problem.

Using Graphs and Properties to Solve Equations with Exponents   **750**

Modeling Exponential Growth and Decay

Common Core Math Standards

The student is expected to:

 F-IF.C.7e

Graph exponential... functions, showing intercepts and end behavior...
Also F-IF.B.5, F-BF.A.1a, F-LE.A.1c, F-LE.A.2

Mathematical Practices

 MP.4 Modeling

Apply mathematics to problems arising in everyday life, society, and
Language Objective

Compare and contrast exponential growth and exponential
decay functions.

ENGAGE

Essential Question: How can you use exponential functions to model the increase or decrease of a quantity over time?

An exponential function represents growth when
$b > 1$ and decay when $0 < b < 1$. You can use
$y = a(1 + r)^t$ where $a > 0$ to represent exponential
growth and $y = a(1 - r)^t$ where $a > 0$ to represent
exponential decay.

PREVIEW: LESSON PERFORMANCE TASK

View the Engage section online. Discuss what an
archeologist might learn from studying the bones,
tools, weapons, and other objects left by prehistoric
people. Then preview the Lesson Performance Task.

16.2 Modeling Exponential Growth and Decay

Essential Question: How can you use exponential functions to model the increase or
decrease of a quantity over time?

◎ Explore 1   Describing End Behavior of a Growth Function

When you graph a function $f(x)$ in a coordinate plane, the x-axis represents the independent variable and
the y-axis represents the dependent variable. Therefore, the graph of $f(x)$ is the same as the graph of the
equation $y = f(x)$. You will use this form when you use a calculator to graph functions.

Ⓐ   Use a graphing calculator to graph the exponential growth
function $f(x) = 200(1.10)^x$, using Y_1 for $f(x)$. Use a viewing
window from -20 to 20 for x, with a scale of 2, and
from -100 to 1000 for y, with a scale of 50. Sketch the curve on the axes provided.

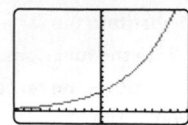

Ⓑ   To describe the end behavior of the function, you describe the function values as
x increases or decreases without bound. Using the TRACE feature, move the cursor to the
right along the curve. Describe the end behavior as x increases without bound.

As x increases without bound, the graph grows larger at an exponentially increasing rate.

Ⓒ   Using the TRACE feature, move the cursor to the left along the curve. Describe the end
behavior as x decreases without bound.

As x decreases without bound, the graph approaches, but never hits, 0.

Reflect

1.   Describe the domain and range of the function using inequalities.
   Domain: $\{x \mid -\infty < x < \infty\}$ Range: $\{y \mid y > 0\}$

2.   Identify the y-intercept of the graph of the function.
   The y-intercept of the graph of the function is $(0, 200)$.

3.   An asymptote of a graph is a line the graph approaches more and more closely. Identify an asymptote of
   this graph.
   The line $y = 0$ is an asymptote of this graph.

4.   **Discussion** Why is the value of the function always greater than 0?
   Since a positive number is being multiplied by another positive number, it is impossible

   for the growth function to go below the x-axis.

© Houghton Mifflin Harcourt Publishing Company

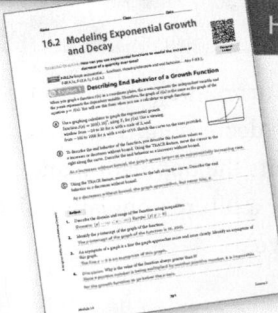

HARDCOVER PAGES 587–596

**Turn to these pages to
find this lesson in the
hardcover student
edition.**

Use the form from the first Explore exercise to graph another function on your calculator.

(A) Use a graphing calculator to graph the exponential decay function $f(x) = 500(0.8)^x$, using Y_1 for $f(x)$. Use a viewing window from -10 to 10 for x, with a scale of 1, and from -500 to 5000 for y, with a scale of 500. Sketch the curve on the axes provided.

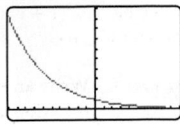

(B) Using the TRACE feature, move the cursor to the right along the curve. Describe the end behavior as x increases without bound.

As x increases without bound, the graph approaches, but never hits, 0.

(C) Using the TRACE feature, move the cursor to the left along the curve. Describe the end behavior as x decreases without bound.

As x decreases without bound, the graph grows larger at an exponentially increasing rate.

Reflect

5. **Discussion** Describe the domain and range of the function using inequalities.
   Domain: $\{x| -\infty < x < \infty\}$

   Range: $\{y| y > 0\}$

6. Identify the y-intercept of the graph of the function.
   The y-intercept of the graph of the function is (0, 500).

7. Identify an asymptote of this graph. Why is this line an asymptote?
   An asymptote of this graph is the line $y = 0$. It is an asymptote of the graph because the line approaches, but never hits, $y = 0$.

EXPLORE 1

Describing End Behavior of a Growth Function

INTEGRATE TECHNOLOGY

Students will use graphing calculators to complete the Explore activities that investigate the end behavior of exponential functions.

CONNECT VOCABULARY [EL]

Connect the word *bound* in the phrase "as x increases without bound" to the more familiar word *boundary*. To increase without bound means to increase without reaching an end point or boundary. Another way to state the same idea is "as x approaches infinity."

QUESTIONING STRATEGIES

? Describe the x-intercepts of the exponential growth function. **There are no x-intercepts for this function because there are no values of x for which $f(x) = 0$.**

? Are there any asymptotes for this function other than the line $y = 0$? Explain. **No; the graph gets closer and closer to $y = 0$ as x decreases without bound, and it is ever-increasing as x increases without bound.**

EXPLORE 2

Describing End Behavior of a Decay Function

QUESTIONING STRATEGIES

? Before you graph it, how can you tell that the function $f(x) = 500(0.8)^x$ will decrease as x increases? **A positive number is being multiplied x times by a number between 0 and 1, so it will get smaller as x increases.**

Math Background

The end behavior of a function $f(x)$ is a description of what happens to a function $f(x)$ as x increases or decreases without bound. The value of an exponential growth function $f(x) = ab^x$, where $b > 1$ and $a > 0$, increases without bound as x increases without bound, and approaches 0 as x decreases without bound. The value of an exponential decay function $f(x) = ab^x$, where $0 < b < 1$ and $a > 0$, approaches 0 as x increases without bound, and increases without bound as x decreases without bound. Such end behavior can also be described using the notation $f(x) \to \infty$ as $x \to -\infty$ and $f(x) \to 0$ as $x \to \infty$, where the symbol ∞ represents infinity.

EXPLAIN 1

Modeling Exponential Growth

QUESTIONING STRATEGIES

? How do you use a percent increase amount when writing an exponential growth equation? Give an example. Convert the percent increase to a decimal and add it to 1 to find the number that is raised to a power. Possible answer: For a 4% increase, the decimal 1.04 will be raised to a power.

? Why doesn't the graph of an exponential growth model intersect the y-axis at the origin? When $x = 0$, y is the initial value of the increasing quantity.

© Houghton Mifflin Harcourt Publishing Company • Image Credits: ©Tetra Images/Corbis

---

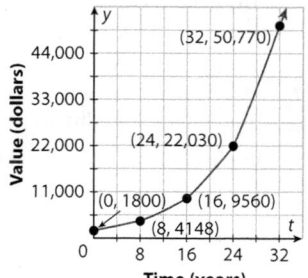

⚡ **Explain 1** Modeling Exponential Growth

Recall that a function of the form $y = ab^x$ represents exponential growth when $a > 0$ and $b > 1$. If b is replaced by $1 + r$ and x is replaced by t, then the function is the **exponential growth model** $y = a(1 + r)^t$, where a is the initial amount, the base $(1 + r)$ is the growth factor, r is the growth rate, and t is the time interval. The value of the model increases with time.

Example 1 Write an exponential growth function for each situation. Graph each function and state its domain, range and an asymptote. What does the y-intercept represent in the context of the problem?

(A) A painting is sold for $1800, and its value increases by 11% each year after it is sold. Find the value of the painting in 30 years.

Write the exponential growth function for this situation.

$$y = a(1 + r)^t$$
$$= 1800(1 + 0.11)^t$$
$$= 1800(1.11)^t$$

Find the value in 30 years.

$$y = 1800(1.11)^t$$
$$= 1800(1.11)^{30}$$
$$\approx 41{,}206.13$$

After 30 years, the painting will be worth approximately $41,206.

Create a table of values to graph the function.

t	y	(t, y)
0	1800	(0, 1800)
8	4148	(8, 4148)
16	9560	(16, 9560)
24	22,030	(24, 22,030)
32	50,770	(32, 50,770)

Determine the domain, range and an asymptote of the function.

The domain is the set of real numbers t such that $t \geq 0$.

The range is the set of real numbers y such that $y \geq 1800$.

An asymptote for the function is $y = 0$.

The y-intercept is the value of y when $t = 0$, which is the value of the painting when it was sold.

COLLABORATIVE LEARNING

Small Group Activity

Divide students into groups of three or four. Have students research several banks, either locally or online, for interest rates on savings accounts, money market accounts, and CDs. Have them work as a group to develop exponential growth models for each type of account at each bank on an initial deposit of $500. Ask students to make a chart comparing the rates and potential earnings after 5 years for the different types of accounts at each bank.

Ⓑ A baseball trading card is sold for $2, and its value increases by 8% each year after it is sold. Find the value of the baseball trading card in 10 years.

Write the exponential growth function for this situation.

$y = a(1 + r)^t$

$= \boxed{2}\left(1 + \boxed{0.08}\right)^t$

$= \boxed{2}\left(\boxed{1.08}\right)^t$

Find the value in 10 years.

$y = a(1 + r)^t$

$= \boxed{2}\left(\boxed{1.08}\right)^t$

$= \boxed{2}\left(\boxed{1.08}\right)^{\boxed{10}}$

$\approx \boxed{4.32}$

After 10 years, the baseball trading card will be worth approximately $_____4.32_____.

Create a table of values to graph the function.

t	y	(t, y)
0	2	(0, 2)
3	2.52	(3, 2.52)
6	3.17	(6, 3.17)
9	4.00	(9, 4.00)
12	5.04	(12, 5.04)

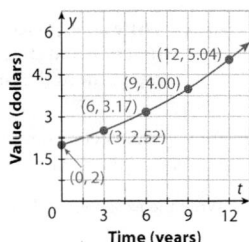

Determine the domain, range, and an asymptote of the function.

The domain is the set of real numbers t such that $t \geq \boxed{0}$.

The range is the set of real numbers y such that $y \geq \boxed{2}$.

An asymptote for the function is ____$y = 0$____.

The y-intercept is the value of y when $t = 0$, which is the ___value of the card when it was sold___.

Reflect

8. Find a recursive rule that models the exponential growth of $y = 1800(1.11)^t$.

   $a_1 = 1800, a_n = 1.11a_{n-1}$

9. Find a recursive rule that models the exponential growth of $y = 2(1.08)^t$.

   $a_1 = 2, a_n = 1.08a_{n-1}$

DIFFERENTIATE INSTRUCTION

Critical Thinking

To help students understand the difference between exponential growth and linear growth, point out that in exponential growth or decay, the amount added or subtracted in each time period is proportional to the amount already present. For exponential growth, this means that as the amount becomes greater, the amount of increase in each time period also becomes greater. Contrast this to linear growth, in which the amount of increase remains constant.

EXPLAIN 2

Modeling Exponential Decay

QUESTIONING STRATEGIES

? What is the domain for a function that represents the exponential growth or decay of a population? Explain. The domain is all non-negative real numbers, because the model applies to all future times (positive values of t) but not past times (negative values of t).

? What is the range for a function describing the exponential growth or decay of a population? For a growth function, the range consists of all numbers greater than or equal to the starting value of the population. For a decay function, the range includes all numbers between the starting value and 0.

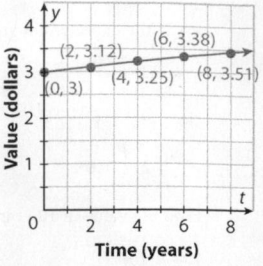

Your Turn

10. Write and graph an exponential growth function, and state the domain and range. Tell what the y-intercept represents. Sara sold a coin for \$3, and its value increases by 2% each year after it is sold. Find the value of the coin in 8 years.

$$y = a(1 + r)^t \qquad\qquad y = 3(1.02)^8$$
$$= 3(1.02)^t \qquad\qquad \approx 3.51$$

After 8 years, the coin will be worth approximately \$3.51.

The domain is the set of real numbers t such that $t \geq 0$.
The range is the set of real numbers y such that $y \geq 3$.
The y-intercept is the value of y when $t = 0$, which is the value of the coin when it was sold.

⊘ Explain 2 Modeling Exponential Decay

Recall that a function of the form $y = ab^x$ represents exponential decay when $a > 0$ and $0 < b < 1$. If b is replaced by $1 - r$ and x is replaced by t, then the function is the **exponential decay model** $y = a(1 - r)^t$, where a is the initial amount, the base $(1 - r)$ is the decay factor, r is the decay rate, and t is the time interval.

Example 2 Write an exponential decay function for each situation. Graph each function and state its domain and range. What does the y-intercept represent in the context of the problem?

Ⓐ The population of a town is decreasing at a rate of 3% per year. In 2005, there were 1600 people. Find the population in 2013.

Write the exponential decay function for this situation.

$$y = a(1 - r)^t$$
$$= 1600(1 - 0.03)^t$$
$$= 1600(0.97)^t$$

Find the value in 8 years.

$$y = 1600(0.97)^t$$
$$= 1600(0.97)^8$$
$$\approx 1254$$

After 8 years, the town's population will be about 1254 people.

LANGUAGE SUPPORT **EL**

Connect Vocabulary

Remind students that *exponential growth* refers to an increasing function and *exponential decay* refers to a decreasing function. While students are probably familiar with the word *growth*, they may be less familiar with *decay*. Explain that, in everyday use, it can mean *rot*, or *loss of strength and health*. Have students list key words that can indicate growth or decay in descriptions of real-world situations. Examples of key words for *growth* include *increases, goes up, rises, gains*. Examples of key words for *decay* include *decreases, goes down, falls, loses value, declines, depreciates*.

Create a table of values to graph the function.

t	y	(t, y)
0	1600	(0, 1600)
8	1254	(8, 1254)
16	983	(16, 983)
24	770	(24, 770)
32	604	(32, 604)

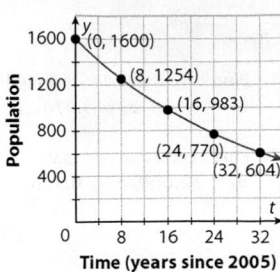

Determine the domain and range of the function.

The domain is the set of real numbers t such that $t \geq 0$. The range is the set of real numbers y such that $0 \leq y \leq 1600$.

The y-intercept is the value of y when $t = 0$, the number of people before it started to lose population.

Ⓑ The value of a car is depreciating at a rate of 5% per year. In 2010, the car was worth $32,000. Find the value of the car in 2013.

Write the exponential decay function for this situation.

$y = a(1 - r)^t$

$= \boxed{32{,}000}\left(1 - \boxed{0.05}\right)^t$

$= \boxed{32{,}000}\left(\boxed{0.95}\right)^t$

Find the value in 3 years.

$y = a(1 - r)^t$

$= \boxed{32{,}000}\left(\boxed{0.95}\right)^t = \boxed{32{,}000}\left(\boxed{0.95}\right)^3 \approx \boxed{27{,}436}$

After 3 years, the car's value will be $ \boxed{27{,}436} .

Create a table of values to graph the function.

t	y	(t, y)
0	32,000	(0, 32,000)
1	30,400	(1, 30,400)
2	28,880	(2, 28,880)
3	27,436	(3, 27,436)

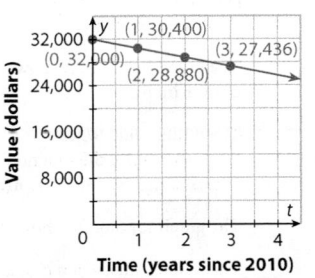

Determine the domain and range of the function.

The domain is the set of real numbers t such that $t \geq \boxed{0}$. The range is the set of real numbers y such that $\boxed{0} \leq y \leq \boxed{32{,}000}$.

The y-intercept, 32,000, is the value of y when $t = 0$, the $\underline{\text{original}}$ value of the car.

EXPLAIN 3

Comparing Exponential Growth and Decay

AVOID COMMON ERRORS

Some students may forget to convert the percent growth rate to decimal form. Remind them that growth rate must be written as a decimal because the percent sign means "parts out of 100."

QUESTIONING STRATEGIES

? When you graph two functions on the same coordinate grid, what does the intersection point of the graphs represent? the time when the two functions are equal in value

---

11. Find a recursive rule that models the exponential decay of $y = 1600(0.97)^t$.
$a_1 = 1,600, a_n = 0.97a_{n-1}$

12. Find a recursive rule that models the exponential decay of $y = 32,000(0.95)^t$.
$a_1 = 32,000, a_n = 0.95a_{n-1}$

Your Turn

13. The value of a boat is depreciating at a rate of 9% per year. In 2006, the boat was worth $17,800. Find the worth of the boat in 2013. Write an exponential decay function for this situation. Graph the function and state its domain and range. What does the y-intercept represent in the context of the problem?

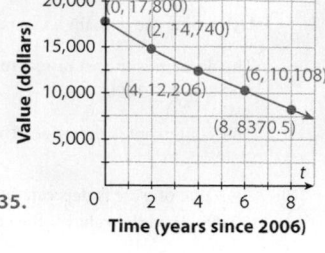

$$y = a(1-r)^t = 17,800(0.91)^t$$

$$y = 17,800(0.91)^7 \approx 9198.35$$

After 7 years, the boat will be worth approximately $9,198.35. The domain is the set of real numbers t such that $t \geq 0$. The range is the set of real numbers y such that $0 \leq y \leq 17,800$.

The y-intercept is 17,800, the value of y when $t = 0$, which is the original value of the boat.

✪ Explain 3 Comparing Exponential Growth and Decay

Graphs can be used to describe and compare exponential growth and exponential decay models over time.

Example 3 Use the graphs provided to write the equations of the functions. Then describe and compare the behaviors of both functions.

Ⓐ The graph shows the value of two different shares of stock over the period of 4 years since they were purchased. The values have been changing exponentially.

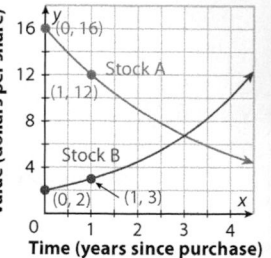

The graph for Stock A shows that the value of the stock is decreasing as time increases.

The initial value, when $t = 0$, is 16. The value when $t = 1$ is 12. Since $12 \div 16 = 0.75$, the function that represents the value of Stock A after t years is $A(t) = 16(0.75)^t$. $A(t)$ is an exponential decay function.

The graph for Stock B shows that the value of the stock is increasing as time increases.

The initial value, when $t = 0$, is 2. The value when $t = 1$ is 3. Since $3 \div 2 = 1.5$, the function that represents the value of Stock B after t years is $B(t) = 2(1.5)^t$. $B(t)$ is an exponential growth function.

The value of Stock A is going down over time. The value of Stock B is going up over time. The initial value of Stock A is greater than the initial value of Stock B. However, after about 3 years, the value of Stock B becomes greater than the value of Stock A.

B The graph shows the value of two different shares of stocks over the period of 4 years since they were purchased. The values have been changing exponentially.

The graph for Stock A shows that the value of the stock is __decreasing__ as time increases.

The initial value, when $t = 0$, is $\boxed{100}$. The value when $t = 1$ is $\boxed{50}$. Since $\boxed{50} \div \boxed{100} = \boxed{0.5}$, the function that represents the value of Stock A after t years is $A(t) = \boxed{100}\left(\boxed{0.5}\right)^t$.

$A(t)$ is an exponential __decay__ function.

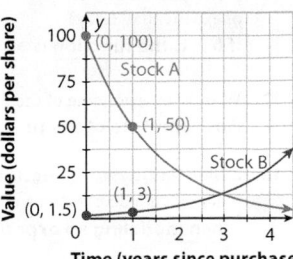

The graph for Stock B shows that the value of the stock is __increasing__ as time increases.

The initial value, when $t = 0$, is $\boxed{1.5}$. The value when $t = 1$ is $\boxed{3}$. Since $\boxed{3} \div \boxed{1.5} = \boxed{2}$, the function that represents the value of Stock B after t years is $B(t) = \boxed{1.5}\left(\boxed{2}\right)^t$. $B(t)$ is an exponential __growth__ function.

The value of Stock A is going __down__ over time. The value of Stock B is going __up__ over time.

The initial value of Stock A is __greater__ than the initial value of Stock B. However, after about $\boxed{3}$ years, the value of Stock B becomes __greater__ than the value of Stock A.

Reflect

14. Discussion In the function $B(t) = 1.5(2)^t$, is it likely that the value of B can be accurately predicted in 50 years?

The exponential function grows much more quickly than any stock can reasonably grow, it is unlikely that the value of B can be accurately predicted in 50 years by using the function.

Your Turn

15. The graph shows the value of two different shares of stocks over the period of 4 years since they were purchased. The values have been changing exponentially. Use the graphs provided to write the equations of the functions. Then describe and compare the behaviors of both functions.

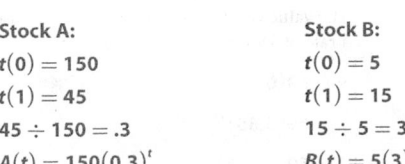

Stock A:
$t(0) = 150$
$t(1) = 45$
$45 \div 150 = .3$
$A(t) = 150(0.3)^t$

Stock B:
$t(0) = 5$
$t(1) = 15$
$15 \div 5 = 3$
$B(t) = 5(3)^t$

The value of Stock A is going down over time. The value of Stock B is going up over time. The initial value of Stock A is greater than the initial value of Stock B. However, after about 1.5 years, the value of Stock B becomes greater than the value of Stock A.

© Houghton Mifflin Harcourt Publishing Company

INTEGRATE MATHEMATICAL PRACTICES

Focus on Math Connections

MP.1 When modeling real-world examples of exponential growth and decay, ensure that students understand the meaning of the real-world values on the graph. Point out that the independent variable represents time, while the meaning of the dependent variable can vary with the situation. Remind students to label the axes of their graphs with the correct quantities and units. Students should also recognize that the y-intercept is the value of the independent variable at time $t = 0$, which may be called its initial value or starting value.

AVOID COMMON ERRORS

Make sure that students understand that Exercises 13–20 are asking for the domain and range of the exponential function and not for the restricted values that have meaning in the given context.

ELABORATE

QUESTIONING STRATEGIES

? Describe three real-world situations that can be described by exponential growth or exponential decay functions. **Possible answers: interest earned on an investment, population growth or decline, radioactive decay**

SUMMARIZE

? How do you write an exponential growth or decay function? **The formula for growth is $y = a(1 + r)^t$, and the formula for decay is $y = a(1 - r)^t$, where y represents the final amount, a represents the original amount, r represents the rate of growth expressed as a decimal, and t represents time.**

 **Elaborate**

16. If $b > 1$ in a function of the form $y = ab^x$, is the function an example of exponential growth or an example of exponential decay?

If $b > 1$, the function is an example of exponential growth.

17. What is an asymptote of the function $y = 35(1.1)^x$?

An asymptote of the function $y = 35(1.1)^x$ is $y = 0$.

18. Essential Question Check-In What equation should be used when modeling an exponential function that models a decrease in a quantity over time?

When modeling an exponential function that models a decrease in a quantity over time, the equation $y = a(1 - r)^t$ should be used.

⭐ Evaluate: Homework and Practice

- Online Homework
- Hints and Help
- Extra Practice

Graph the function on a graphing calculator, and state its domain, range, end behavior, and an asymptote.

1. $f(x) = 300(1.16)^x$

Domain: $\{x \mid -\infty < x < \infty\}$ **Range:** $\{y \mid y > 0\}$
End behavior: As $x \to -\infty$, $y \to 0$ and as $x \to \infty$, $y \to \infty$ Asymptote: $y = 0$

2. $f(x) = 800(0.85)^x$

Domain: $\{x \mid -\infty < x < \infty\}$ **Range:** $\{y \mid y > 0\}$
End behavior: As $x \to -\infty$, $y \to \infty$ and as $x \to \infty$, $y \to 0$ Asymptote: $y = 0$

3. $f(x) = 65(1.64)^x$

Domain: $\{x \mid -\infty < x < \infty\}$ **Range:** $\{y \mid y > 0\}$
End behavior: As $x \to -\infty$, $y \to 0$ and as $x \to \infty$, $y \to \infty$ Asymptote: $y = 0$

4. $f(x) = 57(0.77)^x$

Domain: $\{x \mid -\infty < x < \infty\}$ **Range:** $\{y \mid y > 0$
End behavior: As $x \to -\infty$, $y \to \infty$ and as $x \to \infty$, $y \to 0$ Asymptote: $y = 0$

Write an exponential function to model each situation. Then find the value of the function after the given amount of time.

5. Annual sales for a company are $155,000 and increases at a rate of 8% per year for 9 years.

$y = 155{,}000(1.08)^t$

$y = 155{,}000(1.08)^9$

$= 155{,}000(1.999)$

$= \$309{,}845.72$

6. The value of a textbook is $69 and decreases at a rate of 15% per year for 11 years.

$y = 69(0.85)^t$

$= 69(0.85)^{11}$

$= 69(0.167)$

$= \$11.52$

7. A new savings account is opened with $300 and gains 3.1% yearly for 5 years.

$y = 300(1.031)^t$
$= 300(1.031)^5$
$= 300(1.16)$
$= \$349.47$

8. The value of a car is $7800 and decreases at a rate of 8% yearly for 6 years.

$y = 7800(0.92)^t$
$= 7800(0.92)^6$
$= 7800(0.61)$
$= \$4729.57$

9. The starting salary at a construction company is fixed at $55,000 and increases at a rate of 1.8% yearly for 4 years.

$y = 55,000(1.018)^t$
$= 55,000(1.018)^4$
$= 55,000(1.074)$
$= \$59,068.21$

10. The value of a piece of fine jewelry is $280 and decreases at a rate of 3% yearly for 7 years.

$y = 280(0.97)^t$
$= 280(0.97)^7$
$= 280(0.808)$
$= \$226.24$

11. The population of a town is 24,000 and is increasing at a rate of 6% per year for 3 years.

$y = 24,000(1.06)^t$
$= 24,000(1.06)^3$
$= 24,000(1.191)$
$= 28,584$

12. The value of a new stadium is $3.4 million and decreases at a rate of 2.39% yearly for 10 years.

$y = 3.4(0.9761)^t$
$= 3.4(0.9761)^{10}$
$= 3.4(0.785)$
$= \$2.67 \text{ million}$

Write an exponential function for each situation. Graph each function and state its domain and range. Determine what the y-intercept represents in the context of the problem.

13. The value of a boat is depreciating at a rate of 7% per year. In 2004, the boat was worth $192,000. Find the value of the boat in 2013.

$y = a(1 - r)^t = 192,000(0.93)^t$
$y = 192,000(0.93)^9 \approx 99,918,93$

After 9 years, the boat will be worth approximately $99,918.93.

Domain: $\{x \mid 0 < x < \infty\}$ **Range:** $\{y \mid y > 0\}$

The y-intercept is 192,000, the original value of the boat in 2004.

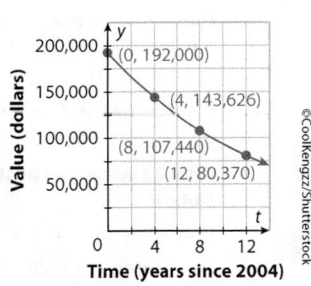

Value (dollars) vs Time (years since 2004)

(0, 192,000)
(4, 143,626)
(8, 107,440)
(12, 80,370)

© Houghton Mifflin Harcourt Publishing Company • Image Credits: ©CoolKengzz/Shutterstock

Exercise	Depth of Knowledge (D.O.K.)	COMMON CORE Mathematical Practices
1–4	**1** Recall of Information	**MP.5** Using Tools
5–12	**1** Recall of Information	**MP.4** Modeling
13–20	**2** Skills/Concepts	**MP.6** Precision
21–24	**2** Skills/Concepts	**MP.5** Using Tools
25	**1** Recall of Information	**MP.5** Using Tools
26–28	**3** Strategic Thinking H.O.T.	**MP.3** Logic

EVALUATE

ASSIGNMENT GUIDE

Concepts and Skills	Practice
Explore 1 Describing End Behavior of a Growth Function	Exercises 1, 3
Explore 2 Describing End Behavior of a Decay Function	Exercises 2, 4
Example 1 Modeling Exponential Growth	Exercises 5, 7, 9, 11, 14, 16, 18, 20, 25
Example 2 Modeling Exponential Decay	Exercises 6, 8, 10, 12–13, 15, 17, 19, 26–28
Example 3 Comparing Exponential Growth and Decay	Exercises 21–24

INTEGRATE MATHEMATICAL PRACTICES

Focus on Technology

MP.5 Students may want to check their results on a graphing calculator. They can enter the function in the **Y =** menu and then press **GRAPH**. Then they can press the **TABLE** key to get a list of x- and y-values, and can scroll up or down to see more values. This method is especially convenient when seeking the value of the function for more than one input value, because it is an alternative to repeatedly typing the expression into the calculator.

Modeling Exponential Growth and Decay   **760**

Focus on visual cues as you discuss how to recognize exponential growth and decay from a graph. Students should recognize that a rising line represents growth and a falling line represents decay. The steeper the line, the greater the rate of growth or decay.

AVOID COMMON ERRORS

Some students may forget to add 1 to the rate of growth in the exponential growth model. Remind students that $1 + r$ is the growth factor in the model.

CONNECT VOCABULARY **EL**

Students may not be familiar with the word *depreciate*. Explain that to *depreciate* is to *decrease in value*. One meaning of the word *appreciate* is the opposite of depreciate: *to increase in value*.

14. The value of a collectible baseball card is increasing at a rate of 0.5% per year. In 2000, the card was worth $1350. Find the value of the card in 2013.

$y = a(1 + r)^t = 1350(1.005)^t$

$y = 1350(1.005)^{13} \approx 1440.43$

After 13 years, the card will be worth approximately $1440.43.

Domain: $\{x | 0 < x < \infty\}$ **Range:** $\{y | y > 0\}$

The y-intercept is 1350.00, the original value of the card in 2000.

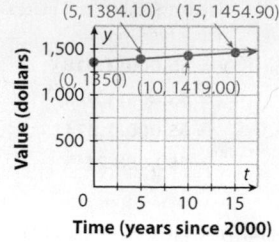

15. The value of an airplane is depreciating at a rate of 7% per year. In 2004, the airplane was worth $51.5 million. Find the value of the airplane in 2013.

$y = a(1 - r)^t = 51.5(0.93)^t$

$y = 51.5(0.93)^9 \approx 26.8$

After 9 years, the airplane will be worth approximately $26.8 million.

Domain: $\{x | 0 < x < \infty\}$ **Range:** $\{y | y > 0\}$

The y-intercept is 51.5, the original value of the airplane in 2004.

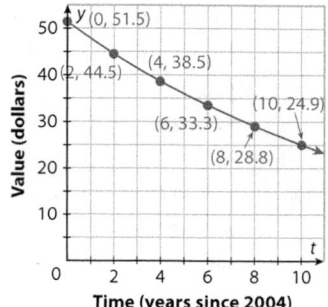

16. The value of a movie poster is increasing at a rate of 3.5% per year. In 1990, the poster was worth $20.25. Find the value of the poster in 2013.

$y = a(1 + r)^t = 20.25(1.035)^t$

$y = 20.25(1.035)^{23} \approx 44.67$

After 23 years, the poster will be worth approximately $44.67.

Domain: $\{x | 0 < x < \infty\}$ **Range:** $\{y | y > 0\}$

The y-intercept is 20.25, the original value of the poster in 1990.

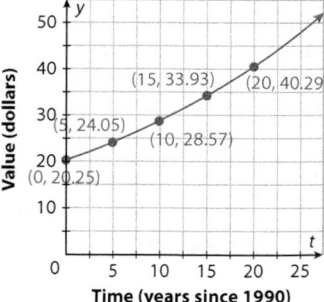

17. The value of a couch is decreasing at a rate of 6.2% per year. In 2007, the couch was worth $1232. Find the value of the couch in 2014.

$y = a(1 - r)^t = 1232(0.938)^t$

$y = 1232(0.938)^7 \approx 787.10$

After 7 years, the couch will be worth approximately $787.10.

Domain: $\{x \mid 0 < x < \infty\}$ **Range:** $\{y \mid y > 0\}$

The y-intercept is 1232, the original value of the couch in 2007.

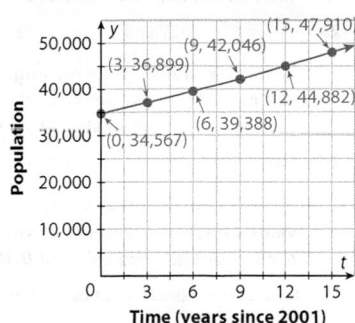

18. The population of a town is increasing at a rate of 2.2% per year. In 2001, the town had a population of 34,567. Find the population of the town in 2018.

$y = a(1 + r)^t = 34,567(1.022)^t$

$y = 34,567(1.022)^{17} \approx 50,041$

After 17 years, the town will have about 50,041 people.

Domain: $\{x \mid 0 < x < \infty\}$ **Range:** $\{y \mid y > 0\}$

The y-intercept is 34,567, the original population of the town in 2001.

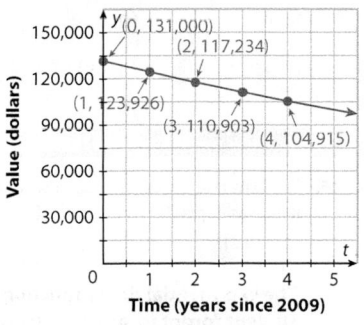

19. A house is losing value at a rate of 5.4% per year. In 2009, the house was worth $131,000. Find the worth of the house in 2019.

$y = a(1 - r)^t = 131,000(0.946)^t$

$y = 131,000(0.946)^{10} \approx 75,194$

After 10 years, the house will be worth about $75,194.

Domain: $\{x \mid 0 < x < \infty\}$ **Range:** $\{y \mid y > 0\}$

The y-intercept is 131,000, the original value of the house in 2009.

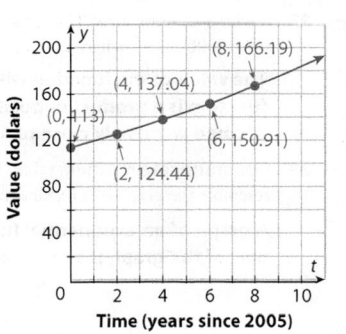

20. An account is gaining value at a rate of 4.94% per year. The account held $113 in 2005. What will the bank account hold in 2017?

$y = a(1 + r)^t = 113(1.0494)^t$

$y = 113(1.0494)^{12} \approx 201.54$

After 12 years, the bank account will hold about $201.54.

Domain: $\{x \mid 0 < x < \infty\}$ **Range:** $\{y \mid y > 0\}$

The y-intercept is 113, the original amount in the account in 2005.

QUESTIONING STRATEGIES

The population of a town is decreasing at the rate of 1% a year. You are asked to find the population after four years. Solving the exponential growth function, you get an answer of 1248.77. What answer will you record? Explain. **Round the answer to 1249 because there cannot be a fraction of a person.**

AVOID COMMON ERRORS

Some students may fail to write percents as decimals before applying the exponential growth model. Encourage them to write out the decimal equivalent of a growth or decay rate before adding it to 1 or subtracting it from 1 in the exponential equation.

JOURNAL

Have students write a journal entry in which they describe how to graph an exponential growth or decay function, and how to find the equation for a real-world situation involving exponential growth or decay.

Use a calculator to graph the functions. Describe and compare each pair of functions.

21. $A(t) = 13(0.6)^t$ and $B(t) = 4(3.2)^t$

The value of $A(t)$ is decreasing. The value of $B(t)$ is increasing. The initial value of $A(t)$ is greater than the initial value of $B(t)$. However, for t greater than about 0.7, the value of $B(t)$ becomes greater than the value of $A(t)$.

22. $A(t) = 9(0.4)^t$ and $B(t) = 0.6(1.4)^t$

The value of $A(t)$ is decreasing. The value of $B(t)$ is increasing. The initial value of $A(t)$ is greater than the initial value of $B(t)$. However, for t greater than about 2.2, the value of $B(t)$ becomes greater than the value of $A(t)$.

23. $A(t) = 547(0.32)^t$ and $B(t) = 324(3)^t$

The value of $A(t)$ is decreasing. The value of $B(t)$ is increasing. The initial value of $A(t)$ is greater than the initial value of $B(t)$. However, for t greater than about 0.2, the value of $B(t)$ becomes greater than the value of $A(t)$.

24. $A(t) = 2(0.6)^t$ and $B(t) = 0.2(1.4)^t$

The value of $A(t)$ is decreasing. The value of $B(t)$ is increasing. The initial value of $A(t)$ is greater than the initial value of $B(t)$. However, for t greater than about 2.7, the value of $B(t)$ becomes greater than the value of $A(t)$.

25. Identify the y-intercept of each of the exponential functions.

a. $3123(432{,}543)^x$ **(0, 3123)**   d. $76(89{,}047{,}832)^x$ **(0, 76)**

b. 0 **(0, 0)**   e. 1 **(0, 1)**

c. $45(54)^x$ **(0, 45)**

H.O.T. Focus on Higher Order Thinking

26. Explain the Error A student was asked to find the value of a $2500 item after 4 years. The item was depreciating at a rate of 20% per year. What is wrong with the student's work?

$2500(0.2)^4$

$4

The exponential decay function is $y = 2500(1 - 0.2)^t$, or $y = 2500(0.8)^t$. The student forgot to subtract the rate of depreciation from 1 before solving.

27. Make a Conjecture The value of a certain car can be modeled by the function $y = 18000(0.76)^t$, where t is time in years. Will the value of the function ever be 0?

The value of the function will never be 0 because the right side of the function is a product of positive numbers. Although the value can become extremely close to 0, it can never equal 0.

28. Communicate Mathematical Ideas Explain how a graph of an exponential function may resemble the graph of a linear function.

A graph of an exponential function may appear to be a linear function if only a small part of the graph is shown and the values in that part are changing slowly.

Lesson Performance Task

Archeologists have several methods of determining the age of recovered artifacts. One method is radioactive dating.

All matter is made of atoms. Atoms, in turn, are made of protons, neutrons, and electrons. An "element" is defined as an atom with a given number of protons. Carbon, for example, has exactly 6 protons. Carbon atoms can, however, have different numbers of neutrons. These are known as "isotopes" of carbon. Carbon-12 has 6 neutrons, carbon-13 has 7 neutrons, and carbon-14 has 8 neutrons. All carbon-based life forms contain these different isotopes of carbon.

Carbon-12 and carbon-13 account for over 99% of all the carbon in living things. Carbon-14, however, accounts for approximately 1 part per trillion or 0.0000000001% of the total carbon in living things. More importantly, carbon-14 is unstable and has a half-life of approximately 5700 years. This means that, within the span of 5700 years, one-half of any amount of carbon will "decay" into another atom. In other words, if you had 10 g of carbon-14 today, only 5 g would remain after 5700 years.

But, as long as an organism is living, it keeps taking in and releasing carbon-14, so the level of it in the organism, as small as it is, remains constant. Once an organism dies, however, it no longer ingests carbon-14, so the level of carbon-14 in it drops due to radioactive decay. Because we know how much carbon-14 an organism had when it was alive, as well as how long it takes for that amount to become half of what it was, you can determine the age of the organism by comparing these two values.

Use the information presented to create a function that will model the amount of carbon-14 in a sample as a function of its age. Create the model $C(n)$ where C is the amount of carbon-14 in parts per quadrillion (1 part per trillion is 1000 parts per quadrillion) and n is the age of the sample in half-lives. Graph the model.

$$C(n) = 1000(0.5)^n$$

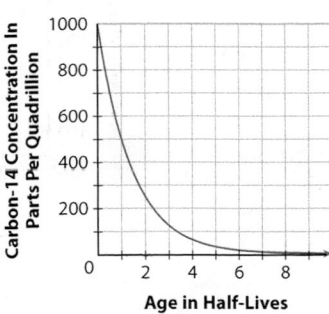

CONNECT VOCABULARY [EL]

Some students may not be familiar with the terms *archeologist*, *artifacts*, or *radiometric dating*. Explain that an *archeologist* studies prehistoric people and cultures by analyzing items that remain for us to find, such as their bones, weapons, artifacts, and tools. *Artifacts* are objects that the people made, such as pottery. *Radiometric dating*, also called *radioactive dating*, is a method of determining the age of an object based on the rate of decay of an element in the object.

QUESTIONING STRATEGIES

? What is the growth factor (the base raised to a power) in the exponential model? Explain. It is $1 - 0.5 = 0.5$, because the amount of carbon-14 decreases by half during every time period.

EXTENSION ACTIVITY

Have students research how very large numbers such as million, billion, trillion, and quadrillion compare to each other. Then have students rewrite the model $C(n)$ in different units and tell how the graph would change.

Students may find that since 1 trillion, or 10^{12}, is equal to 1000 billion, or $10^3 \cdot 10^9$, 1 part per trillion is the same as 0.001 parts per billion. Therefore, the model could be $C(n) = 0.001(0.5)^n$. The graph would differ only in that the scale of the vertical axis would be in parts per billion rather than parts per quadrillion.

Scoring Rubric

2 points: Student correctly solves the problem and explains his/her reasoning.

1 point: Student shows good understanding of the problem but does not fully solve or explain his/her reasoning.

0 points: Student does not demonstrate understanding of the problem.

Modeling Exponential Growth and Decay   **764**

Using Exponential Regression Models

Common Core Math Standards

The student is expected to:

 S-ID.B.6a

Fit a function to the data ... to solve problems in the context of the data. Also S-ID.B.6b, A-CED.A.2, A-REI.D.11, F-LE.A.1c

Mathematical Practices

MP.5 Using Tools

Language Objective

Demonstrate how to use residuals to evaluate how well an exponential regression equation fits a set of data.

ENGAGE

Essential Question: How can you use exponential regression to model data?

You can enter the data into a graphing calculator and use the exponential regression program to generate an equation for the data. Plot and analyze the residuals to determine how well the model fits the data and whether it can be used to make predictions.

PREVIEW: LESSON PERFORMANCE TASK

View the Engage section online. Discuss why it would be better to save money in an interest-bearing savings account than to store it in a shoebox. Then preview the Lesson Performance Task.

16.3 Using Exponential Regression Models

Essential Question: How can you use exponential regression to model data?

Resource Locker

⊘ Explore 1 Fitting an Exponential Function to Data

One of the reasons data is valuable is that it allows us to make predictions for values that fall outside of the data set. In order to do this, the data needs to be synthesized into a function. An **exponential regression** is a graphing calculator tool used to generate an exponential equation that fits data exhibiting exponential growth or decay. The statistical tools on a graphing calculator offer several possible methods for finding a regression model for a set of data. Use a graphing calculator to find the exponential regression equation that models the data provided.

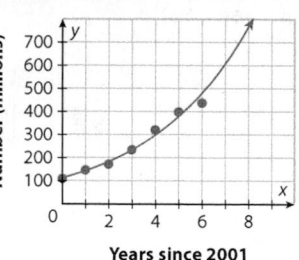

Number of Internet Hosts							
Years since 2001	0	1	2	3	4	5	6
Number (millions)	110	147	172	233	318	395	433

(A) Enter the data from the table on a graphing calculator, with years since 2001 in L1. Input the number of Internet hosts in L2. Create a scatter plot of the data on the calculator. Plot the data points on the given grid.

(B) Use the statistical calculation features of a graphing calculator to calculate the exponential regression equation for the data you entered into L1 and L2.

The exponential regression function is
$f(x) = 113(1.27)^x$ or $y = 113(1.27)^x$
(Round to three significant digits.)

(C) Graph the exponential regression equation with the data points on the calculator. Sketch a graph of the exponential regression equation on the grid with the data points that you plotted.

Reflect

1. **Discussion** Which parameter, a or b, represents the initial value of the function? Explain how you know. **The initial value of the function is represented by a. The initial value of the function**

corresponds to $f(x)$ when $x = 0$, and any number raised to the zero power is 1.

$f(x) = a(b)^x$ and $f(0) = a(b)^0 = a(1) = a$

So the initial value of the function is 113, which is also close to the first data point, $(0, 110)$.

© Houghton Mifflin Harcourt Publishing Company • Image Credits: Chad Baker/ Getty Images

HARDCOVER PAGES 597–608

Turn to these pages to find this lesson in the hardcover student edition.

2. What is the growth rate of this exponential model?
The growth rate is 0.27 which corresponds to a 27% yearly increase.

⊘ Explore 2   Plotting and Analyzing Residuals of Exponential Models

Recall that a residual is the difference between the actual y-value in the data set and the predicted y-value. Residuals can be used to assess how well a model fits a data set. If a model fits the data well, then the following are true.

- The numbers of positive and negative residuals are roughly equal.
- The residuals are randomly distributed about the x-axis on a residual plot.
- The absolute value of the residuals is small relative to the data values.

Ⓐ According to the data, in 2002 there were 147,000,000 Internet hosts. Find the y-value predicted by the model.

$y = ub^r$ $y = 113(1.27)^1$ $y = \boxed{143}$
The actual y-value from the data is $\underline{147}$.

Ⓑ Find the difference between the data y-value and the model's predicted y-value.

data $-$ model $= 147 - 143 = \boxed{4}$

Ⓒ On your calculator, enter the regression equation as the rule for equation Y_1. Then view the table to find the y-values predicted by model (y_m). Complete the table.

Number of Internet Hosts

x	Actual y-value, y_d	Predicted y-value, y_m	Residual $y_d - y_m$
0	110	113	−3
1	147	143	4
2	172	182	−10
3	233	231	2
4	318	294	24
5	395	373	22
6	433	474	−41

Ⓓ Create a residual scatter plot by plotting the x-values and the residuals in the last column as the second coordinate.

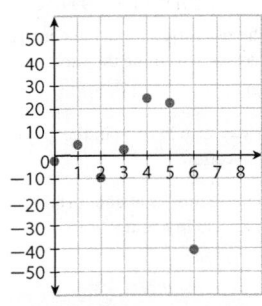

© Houghton Mifflin Harcourt Publishing Company

Math Background

A simple example of an exponential function is $y = 2^x$, in which values for y increase as follows: $f(1) = 2^1 = 2$; $f(2) = 2^2 = 4$; $f(x) = 2^3 = 8$; $f(4) = 2^4 = 16$; and so on. This creates a rapidly increasing pattern. A classic real-world application of an exponential function is the doubling problem. Give a person a penny on day 1 and double the amount each day. How much will the person have after one month? $(\$0.01)(2)^{30}$ is more than $10 million!

EXPLORE 1

Fitting an Exponential Function to Data

INTEGRATE TECHNOLOGY

Students will use a graphing calculator to find an exponential regression equation in the Explore activity.

AVOID COMMON ERRORS

Students may incorrectly substitute values for a, b, and r into the basic exponential equation. Explain that the variable a is the coefficient while b is the base that is being taken to the x power. Thus, if $a = 3$ and $b = 5$, the exponential equation should be $y = 3(5)^x$. Values given by the calculator should be rounded to the same number of significant digits as the input data. Point out that r is the correlation coefficient, which gives a measure of how well the equation fits the data. It is not a value to be substituted into the equation.

EXPLORE 2

Plotting and Analyzing Residuals of Exponential Models

QUESTIONING STRATEGIES

How do you find the residual for each data value? First find the predicted y-values by substituting each x-value into the exponential regression model. To find the residuals, subtract each predicted y-value from the corresponding observed y-value.

AVOID COMMON ERRORS

Students may mistakenly compute residuals by subtracting y_d from y_m rather than y_m from y_d. This will not change the absolute value of the residuals, but it will change the sign of the residuals. Stress that it is important to calculate all residuals in the same way so that you can determine whether the number of positive and negative residuals is about equal.

INTEGRATE MATHEMATICAL PRACTICES

Focus on Reasoning

MP.2 Students may think that the points on a residual plot should follow an exponential curve because they come from an exponential function. Explain that the purpose of subtracting the predicted y-values from the actual y-values is to find how much the data deviate from the prediction. You could say that the curve is subtracted out from the data. If the model fits the data well, the residuals will be relatively small and randomly distributed about the x-axis. They will not follow a sloped line or a curve.

EXPLAIN 1

Modeling with Exponential Functions

AVOID COMMON ERRORS

Students may be confused by the many steps involved in making a prediction based on a set of data. Encourage them to start by listing the sequence of tasks they need to accomplish, such as the following:

1. Make a scatter plot of the data.

2. Find an exponential regression model.

3. Graph the regression function.

4. Find the input value for which the function will reach the value given in the problem.

Then, students can learn the specific steps needed to complete each task.

Reflect

3. **Multiple Representations** What does the residual plot reveal about the fit of the model? Does this agree with the correlation coefficient?
   In the residual plot, there are roughly equal numbers of positive and negative values, which are randomly distributed about the x-axis and are small relative to the data. This suggests the model is a good fit, as does the correlation coefficient.

4. **Look for Patterns** What can you infer about the accuracy of the model as it moves further away from the initial value? Explain.
   The residuals get larger as x increases, indicating a growing disparity between the data and the model. This suggests the model is becoming less accurate for later years.

⚙ Explain 1   Modeling with Exponential Functions

Exponential regression functions can be used to make predictions.

Example 1   Find an exponential regression function for the given data, and use the model to make predictions.

(A) The table shows the population y of Middleton, where x is the number of years since the end of 2000.

Suppose Middleton's town council decides to build a new high school when its population exceeds 25,000.

When will the population likely exceed 25,000?

Years since 2000, x	Population, y
0	5,005
1	6,010
2	7,203
3	8,700
4	10,521
5	12,420
6	14,982
7	18,010

Enter the x-values into L1 and the y-values into L2 in a graphing calculator and view a scatter plot of the data.

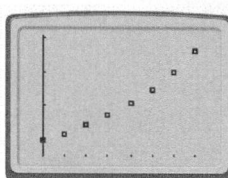

Find the exponential regression model and the regression coefficient for the data. Plot the regression function on the scatter plot.
$$y = 5011(1.201)^x \quad r = 0.999$$

Use the regression model to construct an equation in one variable to solve in order to determine the time x when the population will reach 25,000.
$$25,000 = 5011(1.201)^x$$

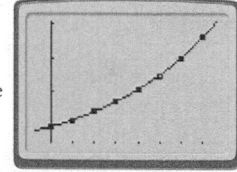

Enter $y = 25,000$ as Y_2 in the graphing calculator, and find the point of intersection.

The intersection is at about (8.792, 25,000). The population will reach 25,000 in about 9 years.

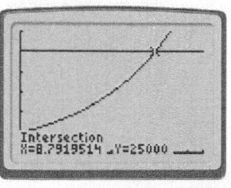

COLLABORATIVE LEARNING

Peer-to-Peer Activity

Have students work in pairs. Give each pair a data set for a real-world situation that can be modeled by an exponential function, and instruct them to take turns using a graphing calculator to complete the following steps:

1. Input the data and make a scatter plot.

2. Perform an exponential regression on the data.

3. Input the exponential regression function and graph it.

4. Make a prediction about a future value of the dependent variable.

Then have students reverse roles and solve a different problem.

B The table shows the value of a car every year since it was purchased.

The owner plans to sell the car when it reaches 10% of its original value. How long will she have owned the car when she sells it?

Find the exponential regression model and the regression coefficient for the data. Round to four significant digits.

$y =$ ┃ $25{,}100(0.8493)^x$ ┃ $r =$ ┃ 0.9998 ┃

Use the regression model to construct an equation in one variable to solve in order to determine the time x when the value will reach 10% of the original value.

$2500 = 25{,}100(0.8493)^x$

The intersection is at ___(14.12, 2500)___. The car will have dropped to a value of $2500

after ___15___ years.

Age of Car, x	Value, y
0	$25,000.00
1	$21,462.50
2	$17,881.88
3	$15,506.66
4	$12,919.65
5	$11,203.56
6	$9,523.03
7	$7,934.28
8	$6,880.39
9	$5,732.52
10	$4,872.64

Reflect

5. Use the regression model to predict the population at the end of 2015 and at the end of 2030. Round to four significant digits. Which prediction is likely to be more accurate? Explain your reasoning.
78,180 people; 1,220,000 people; The 2015 prediction is likely to be more accurate

because the trend of the data is more likely to continue for a short time than for a

long time.

6. During what year does the population reach 25,000? Explain your reasoning.
2009; The graphs intersect when $x \approx 8.792$. Since 8 years from the end of 2000 is the end

of 2008, 8.792 years from the end of 2000 is in the latter half of 2009.

7. Suppose the town will need a new high school already in place when the population reaches 25,000. How will the prediction above help the town make plans?
The town can use the prediction to work backward and decide when plans for funding,

design, and construction of the school must begin.

? Why is it useful to plot the regression function on the same grid as the scatter plot? **It allows you to see how closely the model fits the data.**

? How do you use the graph of a regression function to predict when a variable will reach a given value? **On the same grid where you graphed the regression function, graph a constant function equal to the given value. The point where the two graphs intersect shows the x-value at which the regression function reaches that value.**

DIFFERENTIATE INSTRUCTION

Modeling

Students may have difficulty performing an exponential regression. Encourage them to practice the steps by first solving a simpler problem. For example, have them find an exponential regression for the values in the table:

x	0	1	2	3
y	10	20	40	80

Students should obtain the regression equation $y = 10(2)^x$.

ELABORATE

INTEGRATE MATHEMATICAL PRACTICES

Focus on Reasoning

MP.2 Draw students' attention to the way in which they interpret a regression model to make predictions. Stress the importance of comparing the model with actual values instead of assuming that the model is a good fit for the data. Explain that a model may be more accurate for years closer to the given data than for years farther out.

SUMMARIZE

? How do you model changes in population using an exponential function? Graph the data on a graphing calculator and perform exponential regression to generate an exponential function, then compute residuals to check whether the model is a good fit. If it is, you can use the exponential regression model to make predictions about the population.

Your Turn

Create a model from the table of values and answer the questions.

8. The table shows the population of Arizona (in thousands) in each census from 1900–2000.

   Use the model to predict the census results from 2010 and compare the estimate to 6,392,017, the actual population according to the 2010 national census.

   $f(x) = 135.9(1.037)^x$
   $f(110) = 7,394$

   The model is significantly off from the actual value.

Years Since 1900 (x)	Population, (y)
0	123
10	204
20	334
30	436
40	499
50	750
60	1302
70	1771
80	2718
90	3665
100	5131

9. The table shows the population of box turtles in a Tennessee wildlife park over a period of 5 years.

   Use the model to predict the number of box turtles in the sixth year.

   $f(x) = 17.51(1.230)^x$
   $f(6) = 61$

Year, (x)	Population, (y)
1	21
2	27
3	33
4	41
5	48

💬 Elaborate

10. What does a pattern in the plot of the regression data indicate?
    A pattern indicates that the model is not a good one. The relationship between the

    dependent and independent variables is probably not exponential.

11. **Discussion** While it is typically the best model for population growth, what are some factors that cause population growth to deviate from the exponential format?
    The model does not take into account factors that might cause surges or large drops

    in population.

    Essential Question Check-In What do the variables a and b represent in the regression equation $f(x) = ab^x$?
    The variable a represents the initial quantity, or the quantity at $x = 0$, and b represents the

    growth rate of the item being modeled.

LANGUAGE SUPPORT **EL**

Connect Vocabulary

In the guidelines for how to evaluate residuals to determine how well a model fits the data, we see the phrase *roughly equal*, which means *almost equal*. Explain to students that when we say there are *roughly equal* numbers of positive values and negative values, we mean that there are *close to the same number* of positive values and negative values. The numbers are close to equal, but are not equal.

• Online Homework
• Hints and Help
• Extra Practice

1. The concentration of ibuprofen in a person's blood was plotted each hour. An exponential model fit the data with $a = 400$ and $b = 0.71$. Interpret these parameters.

   The initial amount of ibuprofen was approximately 400 units. 71% of the previous hour's amount of ibuprofen remains after each hour.

2. The table shows the temperature of a pizza over three-minute intervals after it is removed from the oven.

   a. Find an exponential regression function for the data.

   $f(t) = 433(0.935)^x$

Time	Temperature
0	450
3	350
6	290
9	230
12	190
15	150
18	130
21	110

   b. Complete the table to calculate the residuals. Plot the residuals on the scatter plot.

Time	Temperature	Predicted Temperature	Residual
0	450	433	17
3	350	354	−4
6	290	289	1
9	230	236	−6
12	190	193	−3
15	150	158	−8
18	130	129	1
21	110	106	4

   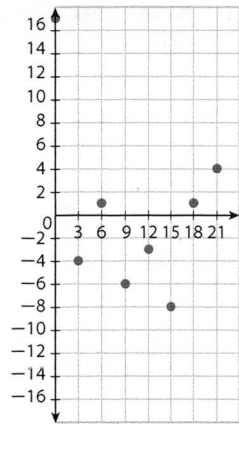

   © Houghton Mifflin Harcourt Publishing Company

   c. Graph y = 70 and the exponential regression function together with the graphing calculator, and find the intersection to predict how long it will take the pizza to cool down to 70° F.

   It will take a little over 27 minutes for the pizza to cool to 70° F.

Exercise	Depth of Knowledge (D.O.K.)	COMMON CORE Mathematical Practices
1	**1** Recall of Information	**MP.2** Reasoning
2–13	**2** Skills/Concepts	**MP.5** Using Tools
14	**3** Strategic Thinking	**MP.5** Using Tools
15	**2** Skills/Concepts	**MP.2** Reasoning
16–18	**3** Strategic Thinking H.O.T.	**MP.3** Logic

ASSIGNMENT GUIDE

Concepts and Skills	Practice
Explore 1 Fitting an Exponential Function to Data	Exercise 1
Explore 2 Plotting and Analyzing Residuals of Exponential Models	Exercise 2
Example 1 Modeling with Exponential Functions	Exercises 3–18

INTEGRATE MATHEMATICAL PRACTICES
Focus on Technology

MP.5 Spend time going over the steps for entering given data in a graphing calculator, finding an exponential function that models the data, and making a prediction based on the model. Ask students to explain the purpose of each step.

For Exercises 3 and 4, use a graphing calculator to calculate the exponential regression equation, and use it to solve the problem.

3. The table shows the monthly membership in an online gaming club. When will there be more than 3000 members?

Month	Membership
0	2100
1	2163
2	2199
3	2249
4	2285
5	2329
6	2376
7	2415
8	2464
9	2514
10	2576

The club will have 3000 members in about 18 months.

4. The table below shows a set of data that can be modeled with an exponential function. When will y be 6000?

x	y
0	15
1	22
2	34
3	50
4	75
5	113
6	170
7	258
8	388
9	575
10	857

When x is about 14.77, y will be 6000.

5. A researcher is conducting an experiment on the rate that caffeine is eliminated from the body. Three volunteers are given four 8-ounce servings of coffee and asked to consume it as quickly as possible. The researchers then tested the caffeine remaining in each volunteer's blood every 20 minutes for 4 hours to determine the rate of elimination. The table gives the results in milligrams for the three volunteers.

Time (hr)	Student A (mg)	Student B (mg)	Student C (mg)
0	400	400	400
0.33	383	374	387
0.67	365	357	370
1.00	349	341	353
1.33	333	326	337
1.67	318	311	322
2.00	304	297	308
2.33	290	284	294
2.67	277	271	281
3.00	264	259	269
3.33	252	247	257
3.67	241	236	246
4.00	230	225	235

Find the hourly rate at which each student metabolizes caffeine and the time when each student will have 10 mg of caffeine in the blood.

$C_A(t) = 400.7(0.8705)^t$

$C_B(t) = 394.0(0.8691)^t$

$C_C(t) = 403.2(0.8738)^t$

Student A metabolizes caffeine at a rate of 12.95% per hour and will have 10 mg of caffeine in the blood after approximately 26.6 hours.

Student B metabolizes caffeine at a rate of 13.09% per hour and will have 10 mg of caffeine in the blood after approximately 26.2 hours.

Student C metabolizes caffeine at a rate of 12.62% per hour and will have 10 mg of caffeine in the blood after approximately 27.4 hours.

Focus on Math Connections

MP.1 Ask students to think of applications of exponential functions they may have seen in their reading or studied in another course. Point out that some real-world situations can be modeled by linear functions, some can be modeled by exponential functions, and others can be modeled by more complicated functions that they have not yet studied.

6. The population of Boston, MA in thousands of people is given in the table below.

1990	572	2001	602
1991	561	2002	608
1992	552	2003	608
1993	552	2004	607
1994	551	2005	610
1995	558	2006	612
1996	556	2007	623
1997	556	2008	637
1998	555	2009	645
1999	555	2010	618
2000	590	2011	625

Find a model for the population of Boston as a function of years since 1990 using the even years and a model using the odd years. Compare the models.

$$P_e(t) = 546.67(1.007)^t$$

$$p_o(t) = 539.61(1.008)^t$$

Both functions are increasing, have approximately the same rate of increase, and a similar P-intercept. They differ in exact value.

Find an exponential model for the radioactive decay of the given isotope.

7. Nobelium-253

Minutes	Mass (grams)
0	10,000.00
1	6651.56
2	4424.33
3	2942.87
4	1957.47
5	1302.02
6	866.05
7	576.06
8	383.17
9	254.87
10	169.53

$$y = 10,000(0.665)^x$$

8. Manganese-52

Weeks	Mass (ounces)
0	200.00
1	83.97
2	35.26
3	14.80
4	6.22
5	2.61
6	1.10
7	.0.46
8	0.19
9	0.08
10	0.03

$$y = 203.9(0.4171)^x$$

Find an exponential model for the data in the given table.

9.

x	y
0	7
1	10.86
2	16.86
3	26.16
4	40.60
5	63
6	97.77
7	151.72
8	235.44
9	365.37
10	567

$y = 7(1.552)^x$

10.

x	y
0	2.6
1	3.91
2	5.88
3	8.85
4	13.31
5	20.01
6	30.1
7	45.27
8	68.10
9	102.42
10	154.05

$y = 2.6(1.504)^x$

11.

x	y
0	11
1	11.1
2	11.21
3	11.32
4	11.43
5	11.53
6	11.64
7	11.76
8	11.87
9	11.98
10	12.09

$y = 11(1.010)^x$

12.

x	y
0	4
1	7.36
2	13.54
3	24.92
4	45.85
5	84.36
6	155.23
7	285.62
8	525.54
9	966.99
10	1779.26

$y = 4(1.840)^x$

COGNITIVE STRATEGIES

Students often confuse the parameters in an exponential function. Suggest this way of thinking about them: *a* is the *first* letter of the alphabet, so it is the *first* y-value, and *b* stands for *base*, so it is the *base* for the exponent.

MULTIPLE REPRESENTATIONS

Some students may see an exponential equation such as $f(x) = (135.9)(1.037)^x$ as exceedingly abstract. To bring the calculation down to a concrete level, do it "by hand" for $f(10)$.

$f(10) = (135.9)(1.037)^{10} = 135.9 \times 1.037 \times 1.037 \times 1.037 \times 1.037 \times 1.037 \times 1.037 \times 1.037 \times 1.037 \times 1.037 \times 1.037 = 195.437$. Students can use a graphing calculator to confirm that the answer is the same either way.

13. The yearly profits of Company A are shown in the table. Use the information given to find a function P(t) that models the yearly profits P of the company as a function of t, the number of years since 1995.

Year	Profit (millions)
1995	5.00
1996	5.15
1997	5.30
1998	5.47
1999	5.63
2000	5.79
2001	5.97
2002	6.15
2003	6.33
2004	6.52
2005	6.71

$P(t) = 5.00(1.03)^t$

14. Find the Error A student is doing homework and comes to the following question.

The table shows the balance in a student's savings account for 10 years. The student hasn't deposited or withdrawn any money over the time period. Find the exponential model for the student's balance as a function of time.

The student performs exponential regression on the data and compares the result with the answer in the back of the text.

The text gives the solution as $b(t) = 200(1.05)^t$, but the student's model is $b(t) = 190.48(1.05)^t$. Find the error in the student's calculations or explain why the student's model is correct.

Year	Balance
2001	$200.00
2002	$210.00
2003	$220.50
2004	$231.53
2005	$243.10
2006	$255.26
2007	$268.02
2008	$281.42
2009	$295.49
2010	$310.27

Both the student's model and the model in the text are correct. The student's model gives the balance b in the account as a function of the number of years since 2000 and the text gives the model as a function of years since 2001.

15. Determine whether each of the following represents an increasing exponential function, a decreasing exponential function, or a non-exponential function. Select the correct answer for each part.

a. $f(t) = \frac{1}{2}t^5$

   ○ Increasing exponential   ○ Decreasing exponential   ● Non-exponential

b.

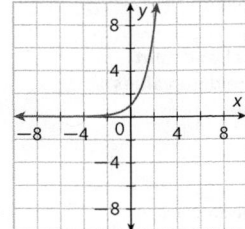

   ● Increasing exponential   ○ Decreasing exponential   ○ Non-exponential

c.

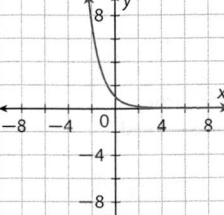

   ○ Increasing exponential   ● Decreasing exponential   ○ Non-exponential

d. $f(x) = 20(0.85)^x$

   ○ Increasing exponential   ● Decreasing exponential   ○ Non-exponential

e. $f(x) = 7(1.16)^x$

   ● Increasing exponential   ○ Decreasing exponential   ○ Non-exponential

f.

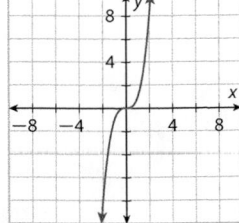

   ○ Increasing exponential   ○ Decreasing exponential   ● Non-exponential

INTEGRATE MATHEMATICAL PRACTICES

Focus on Math Connections

MP.1 Explain that businesses use exponential equations to compute mortgages. Typically a monthly mortgage payment is calculated using the formula

$$L\frac{c(1 + c)^n}{(1 + c)^n - 1},$$ where L is the amount borrowed,

c is the monthly interest charge (for example, $6\% \div 12$ months $= 0.005$), and n is the number of months. Have students work together to calculate the monthly payment on a loan of $\$100,000$ for a 30-year term ($n = 360$ months), using the monthly interest above. They should find that the monthly payment is $\$599.55$.

VISUAL CUES

When discussing how to calculate residuals, provide a visual connection by displaying the data table on an overhead projector and drawing arrows from each predicted y-value to the corresponding actual y-value. Then show the differences under the arrows.

JOURNAL

Have students list the steps for making a prediction based on population data. They should include using a calculator to fit a function to the data, graphing the function, checking whether it is a good fit for the data, and using the function to make predictions.

16. Critique Reasoning The absolute values of the residuals in Mark's regression model are less than 20. Working on a different data set, Sandy obtained residuals in the hundreds. This led Mark to conclude his data is a better fit than Sandy's. Explain why Mark is wrong to base his assessment of their regression models on the values of the residuals.

It is the size of the residual relative to that of the data that is important. Sandy's data values may have been quite large relative to the data values Mark was using.

17. Make a Conjecture When Chris used exponential regression on the Arizona population data, he obtained the following results: $a = 186$, $b = 1.026$, $r = 0.813$, which differed from the given exponential regression function of $f(x) = 135.9(1.037)^x$. When he reviewed the data in his lists, he found he had entered a number incorrectly. Is it more likely that his error was in entering the last population value too high or too low? Justify your reasoning.

too low; The growth rate is too small and the initial value is too large. Entering a lower value for the last population value would have caused the modeled curve to shift "down" at the end and thus "up" at the beginning.

18. Draw Conclusions Madelyn has recorded the number of bacteria on her growth plate every hour for 3 hours. She finds that a linear model fits her data better than the expected exponential model. What should she do to improve her model?

She needs to gather data for longer than 3 hours. Exponential functions can appear linear, especially in the beginning.

Lesson Performance Task

A student with an interest-bearing savings account reports the yearly balance in her account in the following table.

Years Since Opening the Account	Balance
1	$6152.42
2	$6305.22
3	$6459.59
4	$6626.83
5	$6793.00
6	$6965.05
7	$7148.27
8	$7322.20
9	$7505.25
10	$7710.33
11	$7906.32
12	$8092.77

Perform an exponential regression on the data. Then estimate the amount of money the student placed in the account initially and the yearly interest rate.

Using a graphing calculator, the exponential regression formula is

$f_r(x) = 5995.64(1.0253)^x$

The student probably opened her account with $6000 and is earning about

2.53% interest every year.

QUESTIONING STRATEGIES

? How can you find the initial amount in the savings account from the exponential regression equation? The initial amount is approximately the value of a in the equation $y = ab^x$.

? How can you find the interest rate from the exponential regression equation $y = ab^x$? Explain. Since this is an exponential growth model, we know that the base b for the exponent is equal to $1 + r$, where r is the interest rate expressed as a decimal. So, to express the interest rate as a percent, find $100(b - 1)$.

TECHNOLOGY

When students graph the data from the table, depending on the settings used, they may notice that the points appear to be nearly linear. If the window settings are changed so that the x-axis includes a greater range of values, it will become more evident that that the points follow an increasing curve. Graphing a horizontal line on the same grid for comparison will also make the curve more evident.

EXTENSION ACTIVITY

Have students investigate how many years it would take the student in the Lesson Performance Task to double the money in her account. Have students use the equation $y = 6000(1.0253)^x$. Then ask students to estimate what interest rate would cause the money to double in just 18 years. Have them check their estimates and adjust them as needed.

Students will find that the graphs of $y = 6000(1.0253)^x$ and $y = 12,000$ intersect at about $(27.8, 12,000)$, so the amount in the student's account will have doubled after 27.8 years. They should find that an interest rate of 3.9% will cause the money to double in 18 years.

Scoring Rubric
2 points: Student correctly solves the problem and explains his/her reasoning.
1 point: Student shows good understanding of the problem but does not fully solve or explain his/her reasoning.
0 points: Student does not demonstrate understanding of the problem.

Using Exponential Regression Models   **778**

Comparing Linear and Exponential Models

Common Core Math Standards

The student is expected to:

COMMON CORE **F-LE.A.1c**

Recognize situations in which a quantity grows or decays by a constant percent rate ... relative to another. Also F-LE.A.1a, F-LE.A.1b, F-LE.A.3

Mathematical Practices

COMMON CORE **MP.6 Precision**

Language Objective

Describe the difference between a salary that changes by the same amount each year and a salary that changes by the same percent each year.

ENGAGE

Essential Question: How can you recognize when to use a linear model or an exponential model?

A linear model should be used when the amount of increase or decrease in each successive interval is a constant. An exponential model is appropriate when the increase or decrease per successive interval grows.

PREVIEW: LESSON PERFORMANCE TASK

View the Engage section online. Discuss why city officials might need to monitor population growth in their community. Then preview the Lesson Performance Task.

Name_____ Class_____ Date_____

16.4 Comparing Linear and Exponential Models

Essential Question: How can you recognize when to use a linear model or an exponential model?

Resource Locker

Explore 1 Comparing Constant Change and Constant Percent Change

Suppose that you are offered a job that pays you $1000 the first month with a raise every month after that. You can choose a $100 raise or a 10% raise. Which option would you choose? What if the raise were 8%, 6%, or 4%?

Ⓐ Find the monthly salaries for the first three months. Record the results in the table, rounded to the nearest dollar.

- For the $100 raise, enter 1000 into your graphing calculator, press ENTER, enter +100, press ENTER, and then press ENTER repeatedly.
- For the 10% raise, enter 1000, press ENTER, enter ·1.10, press ENTER, and then press ENTER repeatedly.
- For the other raises, multiply by 1.08, 1.06, or 1.04.

Monthly Salary after Indicated Monthly Raise					
Month	$100	10%	8%	6%	4%
0	$1000	$1000	$1000	$1000	$1000
1	$1100	$1100	$1080	$1060	$1040
2	$1200	$1210	$1166	$1124	$1082
3	$1300	$1331	$1260	$1191	$1125

Ⓑ For each option, find how much the salary changes each month, both in dollars and as a percent of the previous month's salary. Round the each percent to the nearest whole number. Record the values in the table.

Change in Salary per Month for Indicated Monthly Raise										
Interval	$100		10%		8%		6%		4%	
	$	%	$	%	$	%	$	%	$	%
0 – 1	100	10	100	10	80	8	60	6	40	4
1 – 2	100	9	110	10	86	8	64	6	42	4
2 – 3	100	8	121	10	94	8	67	6	43	4

HARDCOVER PAGES 609–618

Turn to these pages to find this lesson in the hardcover student edition.

C Continue the calculations you did in Part A until you find the number of months it takes for each salary with a percent raise to exceed the salary with the $100 raise. Record the number of months in the table below.

Number of Months until Salary with Percent Raise Exceeds Salary with $100 Raise			
10%	8%	6%	4%
2	7	18	43

Reflect

1. **Discussion** Compare and contrast the salary changes per month for the raise options. Explain the source of any differences.
   A fixed raise increases by a constant amount monthly. A percent raise increases by an

   increasing amount monthly. A smaller percentage results in a slower increase.

2. **Discussion** Would you choose a constant change per month or a percent increase per month? What would you consider when deciding? Explain your reasoning.
   Sample answer: A final decision should depend on which percent increase is offered and

   how long a person expects to keep the job.

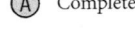 **Explore 2** **Exploring How Linear and Exponential Functions Grow**

Linear functions change by equal differences, while exponential functions change by equal factors. Now you will explore the proofs of these statements. $x_2 - x_1$ and $x_4 - x_3$ represent two intervals in the x-values of a function.

A Complete the proof that linear functions grow by equal differences over equal intervals.

Given: $x_2 - x_1 = x_4 - x_3$

f is linear function of the form $f(x) = mx + b$.

Prove: $f(x_2) - f(x_1) = f(x_4) - f(x_3)$

Proof:
1. $x_2 - x_1 = x_4 - x_3$ Given

2. $m(x_2 - x_1) = \boxed{m}(x_4 - x_3)$ Multiplication Property of Equality

3. $mx_2 - \boxed{mx_1} = mx_4 - \boxed{mx_3}$ Distributive Property

4. $mx_2 + b - mx_1 - b =$ Addition & Subtraction Properties of Equality
   $mx_4 + \boxed{b} - mx_3 - \boxed{b}$

5. $mx_2 + b - (mx_1 + b) =$ Distributive property
   $mx_4 + b - \boxed{(mx_3 + b)}$

6. $f(x_2) - f(x_1) = \boxed{f(x_4) - f(x_3)}$ Definition of $f(x)$

Module 16   780   Lesson 4

© Houghton Mifflin Harcourt Publishing Company

PROFESSIONAL DEVELOPMENT

Learning Progressions

In this lesson, students bring together their understanding of linear and exponential functions. They learn how to determine whether a given situation is best modeled by a linear or exponential function. A key concept is that if the dependent variable changes by equal differences over equal intervals a linear model is more appropriate, while if it changes by equal factors over equal intervals, an exponential model is more appropriate. Work with functions will continue when students learn about quadratic functions.

Comparing Constant Change and Constant Percent Change

INTEGRATE TECHNOLOGY

 Students can use graphing calculators to do repeated calculations for the Explore activity.

AVOID COMMON ERRORS

When calculating percent increases, remind students to take a percentage of the total from the previous interval, not from the original amount. For example, for a $1000 salary with a 10% raise each month, the increase in month 1 is 10% of $1000, but to find the increase in month 2, students need to take 10% of $1100, not 10% of the original $1000.

EXPLORE 2

Exploring How Linear and Exponential Functions Grow

INTEGRATE MATHEMATICAL PRACTICES
Focus on Reasoning

MP.2 Go over the goal of each proof. Students should recognize that the first proof seeks to prove that in a linear function, the change in function values over equal intervals will be constant. The second proof shows that in an exponential function, the ratio of the function values over equal intervals will be constant.

QUESTIONING STRATEGIES

? In the proof for linear functions, why were b and $-b$ added to both sides of the equation? What purpose did this step serve? The goal was to get each term of the equation, mx_1, mx_2, mx_3, and mx_4, in the form of $mx + b$. In that form, those quantities are equivalent to the functions $f(x_1)$, $f(x_2)$, $f(x_4)$, and $f(x_4)$, so they can be replaced by those functions in $f(x)$ form.

EXPLAIN 1

Comparing Linear and Exponential Functions

QUESTIONING STRATEGIES

? How do you know that you should write a linear equation to describe a salary that increases by $100 a month and an exponential equation to describe a salary that increases by 10% a month? An increase of $100 a month is an equal change over equal intervals, so it is a linear increase. An increase of the same percent each month is a change by equal factors over equal intervals, so it is an exponential function.

? What does the intersection point of the graphs of the linear and exponential functions tell you? The intersection point tells how long it will take until both functions have the same value.

(B) Complete the proof that exponential functions grow by equal factors over equal intervals.

Given: $x_2 - x_1 = x_4 - x_3$

g is an exponential function of the form $g(x) = ab^x$.

Prove: $\dfrac{g(x_2)}{g(x_1)} = \dfrac{g(x_4)}{g(x_3)}$

Proof:

1. $x_2 - x_1 = x_4 - x_3$		Given
2. $b^{(x_2 - x_1)} = b^{(x_4 - x_3)}$		If $x = y$, then $b^x = b^y$.
3. $\dfrac{b^{x_2}}{b^{x_1}} = \dfrac{b^{x_4}}{\boxed{b^{x_3}}}$		Quotient of Powers Property
4. $\dfrac{ab^{x_2}}{ab^{x_1}} = \dfrac{ab^{x_4}}{\boxed{ab^{x_3}}}$		Multiplication Property of Equality
5. $\dfrac{g(x_2)}{g(x_1)} = \dfrac{g(x_4)}{\boxed{g(x_3)}}$		Definition of $g(x)$

3. In the previous proofs, what do $x_2 - x_1$ and $x_4 - x_3$ represent?
$x_2 - x_1$ and $x_4 - x_3$ **represent two intervals in the x-values of a function.**

Explain 1 **Comparing Linear and Exponential Functions**

When comparing raises, a fixed dollar increase can be modeled by a linear function and a fixed percent increase can be modeled by an exponential function.

Example 1 Compare the two salary plans listed by using a graphing calculator. Will Job B ever have a higher monthly salary than Job A? If so, after how many months will this occur?

(A) • Job A: $1000 for the first month with a $100 raise every month thereafter

• Job B: $1000 for the first month with a 1% raise every month thereafter

Write the functions that represent the monthly salaries. Let t represent the number of elapsed months.

Job A: $S_A(t) = 1000 + 100t$ Job B: $S_B(t) = 1000(1.01)^t$

Graph the functions on a calculator using Y_1 for Job A and Y_2 for Job B. Estimate the number of months it takes for the salaries to become equal using the intersect feature of the calculator. At $x \approx 364$ months, the salaries are equal.

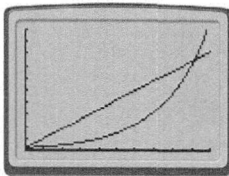 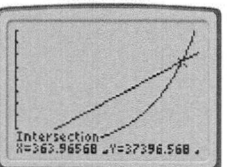

COLLABORATIVE LEARNING

Peer-to-Peer Activity

Have students work with a partner. Provide them with the following problem: Job C provides a starting salary of $150 per day and a 0.5% increase each day. Job D provides a starting salary of $150 per day and a $1 increase each day. Will Job C ever have a higher daily salary than Job D? If so, after how many days will this occur? Have students predict the answers and then work out the problem independently. Students should compare their answers, discuss any differences, and discuss ways to make their predictions more accurate. **On day 112, Job C will have a higher salary.**

Go to the estimated intersection point in the table feature. Find the first x-value at which Y_2 exceeds Y_1. Job B will have a higher monthly salary than Job A after 364 months.

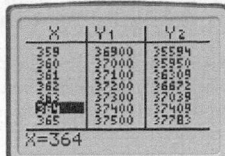

(B) • Job A: $1000 for the first month with a $200 raise every month thereafter
   • Job B: $1000 for the first month with a 4% raise every month thereafter

Write the functions that represent the monthly salaries. Let t represent the number of elapsed months.

Job A: $S_A(t) =$ | 1000 | $+$ | 200 | t Job B: $S_B(t) =$ | 1000 | (| 1.04 |)^t

Graph the functions on a calculator and use this graph to estimate the number of months it takes for the salaries to become equal.

At $x \approx$ | 69 | months, the salaries are equal.

Job B will have a higher salary than Job A after | 69 | months.

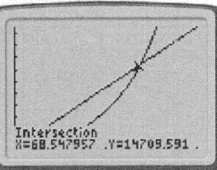

Reflect

4. In Example 1A, which job offers a monthly salary that reflects a constant change, and which offers a monthly salary that reflects a constant percent change?

   Job A's salary reflects a constant change. Job B's salary represents a constant percent

   change.

5. Describe an exponential increase in terms of multiplication.

   An exponential increase can be obtained by repeatedly multiplying by the same factor

   greater than 1.

Your Turn

6. • Job A: $2000 for the first month with a $300 raise every month thereafter
   • Job B: $1500 for the first month with a 5% raise every month thereafter

   Job A: $S_A(t) = 2000 + 300t$
   Job B: $S_B(t) = 1500(1.05)^t$
   At $x \approx 50$ months, the salaries are equal.
   Job B will have a higher salary than Job A after 50 months.

INTEGRATE MATHEMATICAL PRACTICES
Focus on Critical Thinking

MP.3 Ask students to explain how they know that the graphs for the linear and exponential function will eventually intersect. Students should recognize that an ever-increasing exponential function will eventually overtake a function that increases by a constant amount. Even with a small percent increase, sooner or later the total value of the exponential function will be sufficiently large to make the increase per unit time greater than the constant increase per unit time in the linear function. That said, there is no guarantee that the two quantities will be equal within a reasonable and practical amount of time.

DIFFERENTIATE INSTRUCTION

Visual Cues

It will be helpful for visual learners to study a graph that shows two functions representing job salaries, one starting at a low value and increasing exponentially, and the other starting at a higher value and increasing linearly. They can see that the exponential graph starts off below the linear graph; thus, the salary it represents is less. They can also see that at some point the exponential graph crosses the linear graph and goes above it, thus indicating that the salary represented by the exponential graph eventually will exceed the salary represented by the linear graph.

EXPLAIN 2

Choosing Between Linear and Exponential Models

QUESTIONING STRATEGIES

? How do you decide whether to use a linear or exponential regression model for a data set? First calculate the difference in *y*-values over each equal interval and the ratio of *y*-values over each equal interval. If the differences are roughly equal, use a linear model. If the ratios are roughly equal, use an exponential model.

⚙ Explain 2 **Choosing between Linear and Exponential Models**

Both linear equations and exponential equations and their graphs can model real-world situations. Determine whether the dependent variable appears to change by a common difference or a common ratio to select the correct model. A model may not fit real-world data exactly, so differences or factors between successive intervals may not be constant, but may be nearly so.

Example 2 Determine whether each situation is better described by an increasing or decreasing function, and whether a linear or exponential regression should be used. Then find a regression equation for each situation by using a graphing calculator. Evaluate the fit.

Ⓐ The size of an elk population is studied each year during a period in which there is an increase in its predator population.

Population over Time		Change per Interval	
Year	Population, *P*	Difference $P(t_n) - P(t_{n-1})$	Factor $\dfrac{P(t_n)}{P(t_{n-1})}$
0	9739	_____	_____
1	4637	−5102	≈0.48
2	2007	−2630	≈0.43
3	997	−1010	≈0.50
4	458	−539	≈0.46
5	226	−232	≈0.49

The dependent variable is population, and it is decreasing while the number of years is increasing. This means that the function is decreasing.

Note that because the factor changes are relatively close to equal while the difference changes are not, an exponential regression model should be used.

Perform the exponential regression analysis and evaluate the fit.

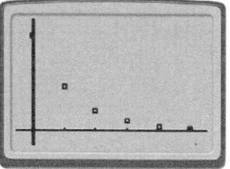 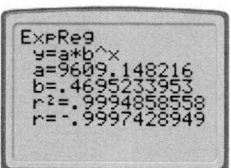

To draw a residual plot, you can calculate the residuals, enter them in column L3, and make a scatter plot using L1 as the XList and L3 as the YList.

The analysis of residuals suggests a good fit.

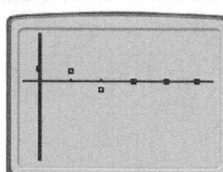

LANGUAGE SUPPORT **EL**

Connect Context

Discuss the various ways that a change per unit of time may be expressed in verbal descriptions. For example, the phrases *yearly*, *each year*, and *annually* are all ways of saying *per year*. In statements about changing salaries such as "employees receive a $0.75 per hour raise each year," remind students to read carefully to distinguish the rate of pay from the rate at which the pay is changing.

Ⓑ The size of a raccoon population is studied each year during a period in which there is a decrease in its predator population.

Population over Time		Change per Interval	
Year	Population, P	Difference $P(t_n) - P(t_{n-1})$	Factor $\dfrac{P(t_n)}{P(t_{n-1})}$
0	190		
2	256	66	≈1.35
4	338	82	≈1.32
6	451	113	≈1.33
8	611	160	≈1.35
10	801	190	≈1.31

Is the function increasing or decreasing? Explain. **Population, which is the dependent variable, is increasing as time increases. This means that the function is increasing.**

Which changes are closer to being equal, the differences or the factors? **factors**

Which type of regressions should be used? **exponential**

Perform the regression analysis and evaluate the fit.

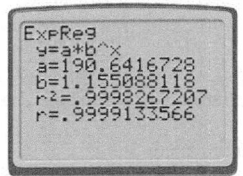 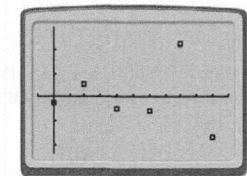

Note that the r-value suggests a **good** fit. The analysis of residuals suggests a **good** fit.

Reflect

7. What would the residual plot look like if an exponential regression was not a good fit for a function?
   The numbers of positive and negative residuals would not be roughly equal, the residuals would not be randomly distributed about the x-axis but would show a pattern, and the absolute values of the residuals would not be small relative to the data values.

© Houghton Mifflin Harcourt Publishing Company

AVOID COMMON ERRORS

ELABORATE

INTEGRATE MATHEMATICAL PRACTICES

Focus on Math Connections

MP.1 As students work with functions modeling real-world examples of increase and decrease, review what the parameters of the equations mean in this context. In a linear equation of the form $y = mx + b$, the coefficient m is the rate of change, and the constant b is the initial value, or the value of y when x is 0. In an exponential equation of the form $y = ab^x$, the coefficient a is the initial value, and the base b is the growth factor.

SUMMARIZE THE LESSON

? How can you recognize when to use a linear model or an exponential model? **A linear model should be used when consecutive function values appear to be changing by a constant amount. An exponential model is appropriate when consecutive function values appear to be changing by a constant factor.**

Your Turn

Determine whether this situation is better described by an increasing or decreasing function, and whether a linear or exponential regression should be used. Then find a regression equation. Evaluate the fit.

8. The price of a barrel of oil is recorded each month.

	Price over Time	Change per Interval	
Year	Price, P (dollars)	Difference $P(t_n) - P(t_{n-1})$	Factor $\dfrac{P(t_n)}{P(t_{n-1})}$
0	42.00		
1	50.40	8.40	$=1.20$
2	60.41	10.01	≈ 1.20
3	72.58	12.17	≈ 1.20
4	87.16	14.58	≈ 1.20
5	105.25	18.09	≈ 1.21

Increasing function; factor changes are relatively close to equal, difference changes are not, so an exponential model should be used.

Regression equation: $y \approx 41.93(1.20)^x$; $r \approx 1$, and analysis of the residual plot would also suggest a good fit.

💬 Elaborate

9. In the long term, which type of raise will guarantee a larger paycheck: a fixed raise or a percentage raise? **In the long term, a percentage raise will always guarantee a larger paycheck.**

10. What type of function is typically represented by a linear function? **A function with a constant increase or decrease is typically represented by a linear function.**

11. **Essential Question Check-In** An exponential growth model is appropriate when consecutive function values appear to be changing by a constant **factor**

Evaluate: Homework and Practice

State whether each situation is best represented by an exponential or linear function. Then write an exponential or linear function for the model and state whether the model is increasing or decreasing.

1. Enrollment at a school is initially 454 students and grows by 3% per year.

exponential; $E(t) = 454(1.03)^t$; increasing

2. A salesperson initially earns $50,434 dollars per year and receives a yearly raise of $675.

linear; $S(t) = 50,434 + 675t$; increasing

3. A customer borrows $450 at 5% interest compounded annually.

exponential; $C(t) = 450(1.05)^t$; increasing

4. A wildlife park has 35 zebras and sends 1 zebra to another wildlife park each year.

linear; $Z(t) = 35 - t$; decreasing

5. The value of a house is $546,768 and decreases by 3% each year.

exponential; $H(t) = 546,768(.97)^t$; decreasing

6. The population of a town is 66,666 people and decreases by 160 people each year.

linear; $P(t) = 66,666 - 160t$; decreasing

7. A business has a total income of $236,000 and revenues go up by 6.4% per year.

exponential; $I(t) = 236,000(1.064)^t$; increasing

Use a graphing calculator to answer each question.

8. Statistics Companies A and B each have 100 employees. If Company A increases its workforce by 31 employees each month and Company B increases its workforce by an average of 10% each month, when will Company B have more employees than Company A?

Company B will have more employees than Company A after about 21 months.

9. Finance Employees A and B each initially earn $18.00 per hour. If Employee A receives a $1.50 per hour raise each year and Employee B receives a 4% raise each year, when will Employee B make more per hour than Employee A?

Employee B will make more than Employee A after about 35 years.

10. Finance Account A and B each start out with $400. If Account A earns $45 each year and Account B earns 5% of its value each year, when will Account B have more money than Account A?

Account B will have more money than Account A after about 31 years.

11. Finance Stock A starts out with $900 and gains $50 each month. Stock B starts out with $800 and gains 11% each month. When will Stock B be worth more money than Stock A?

Stock B will be worth more than Stock A after about 80 months.

Exercise	Depth of Knowledge (D.O.K.)	COMMON CORE Mathematical Practices	
1–7	**1** Recall of Information	**MP.2** Reasoning	
8–15	**2** Skills/Concepts	**MP.4** Modeling	
16–19	**2** Skills/Concepts	**MP.6** Precision	
20	**1** Recall of Information	**MP.2** Reasoning	
21	**2** Skills/Concepts	**MP.4** Modeling	
22	**2** Skills/Concepts H.O.T.	**MP.4** Modeling	
23	**2** Skills/Concepts H.O.T.	**MP.2** Reasoning	

EVALUATE

ASSIGNMENT GUIDE

Concept and Skills	Practice
Explore 1 Comparing Constant Change and Constant Percent Change	Exercise 21
Explore 2 Exploring How Linear and Exponential Functions Grow	Exercises 1–7, 20
Example 1 Comparing Linear and Exponential Functions	Exercises 8–15, 22–23
Example 2 Choosing Between Linear and Exponential Models	Exercises 16–19, 24

INTEGRATE MATHEMATICAL PRACTICES

Focus on Technology

MP.5 Remind students how to find an appropriate viewing window for the graphs they generate to solve problems. They can either manually input minimum and maximum x- and y-values appropriate to the range of the data, or they can use the various options on the calculator's **ZOOM** menu. They may need to adjust the window a few times until they can see the intersection point of the graphs.

MODELING

When graphs have enormous scales, they may seem abstract. Students may fail to grasp the idea that the intersection of two graphs identifies where they are equal in value. To help students see this, have them graph $y = 2x + 2$ and $y = 2^x$ by hand. Students can readily see that both functions have the same value at $x = 3$.

12. **Finance** Accounts A and B both start out with $800. If Account A earns $110 per year and Account B earns 3% of its value each year, when will Account B have more money than Account A?

Account B will have more money than Account A after about 87 years.

13. **Finance** Two factory workers, A and B, each earn $24.00 per hour. If Employee A receives a $0.75 per hour raise each year and Employee B receives 1.9% raise each year, when will Employee B make more per hour than Employee A?

Employee B will make more than Employee A after about 50 years.

14. **Statistics** Two car manufacturers, A and B, each have 500 employees. If Manufacturer A increases its workforce by 15 employees each month and Manufacturer B increases its workforce by 1% each month, when will Manufacturer B have more employees?

Manufacturer B will have a larger workforce after about 192 months.

15. **Finance** Stock A is initially worth $1300 and loses $80 each month. Stock B is initially worth $400 and gains 9.5% each month. When will Stock B be worth more than Stock A?

Stock B will be worth more than Stock A after about 7 months.

Exercise	Depth of Knowledge (D.O.K.)	COMMON CORE Mathematical Practices
24	3 Strategic Thinking H.O.T.	MP.3 Logic

Biology Each table shows an animal population's change over time. Determine whether each situation is best described by an increasing or decreasing function and whether a linear or exponential regression should be used. Then find a regression equation for each situation. Evaluate the fit.

16.

x	y	difference $y_2 - y_1$	factor $\frac{y_2}{y_1}$
1	49		
2	58	9	1.18
3	70	12	1.21
4	83	13	1.19
5	101	18	1.22

Since the values of y are increasing over time, the function is increasing. Since the factor changes are relatively close together while the difference changes are relatively far apart, an exponential regression should be used.

regression equation: $y \approx 40.7\,(1.20)^x$; $r \approx 1$ and analysis of the residual plot would also suggest a good fit.

17.

x	y	difference $y_2 - y_1$	factor $\frac{y_2}{y_1}$
1	31	1	1.03
2	32	2	1.06
3	34	1	1.03
4	35	2	1.06
5	37		

Since the values of y are increasing over time, the function is increasing. Since both the factor changes and the difference changes are close together , neither choice is clearly better than the other.

Linear regression equation is $y \approx 1.5x + 29.3$, with $r \approx 0.993$; exponential regression equation is $y \approx 29.53(1.05)^x$, with $r \approx 0.994$. Although both residual plots would also show a good fit, it is likely that neither function is a good model over a wider domain.

© Houghton Mifflin Harcourt Publishing Company

INTEGRATE MATHEMATICAL PRACTICES
Focus on Patterns

MP.8 Before students begin manipulating data from a table, have them observe the pattern of the raw data. Discuss how the difference between successive values of the function changes from one interval to the next. Students should recognize that if the differences are the same, a linear model may fit the data. If differences increase or decrease in successive intervals, an exponential model may fit the data. Then have students explain what the change means in terms of the real-world situation.

AVOID COMMON ERRORS

After using a calculator to perform a regression, some students may write the function incorrectly. Remind them that, for a linear regression, the parameter a represents the slope and b represents the y-intercept, so the function is $y = ax + b$. For an exponential regression, a is the coefficient and b is the base of the exponent, so the function is $y = ab^x$.

18.

x	y	difference $y_2 - y_1$	factor $\frac{y_2}{y_1}$
1	46		
2	61	15	1.33
3	83	22	1.36
4	107	24	1.29
5	143	36	1.34

Since the values of y are increasing over time, the function is increasing. Since the factor changes are relatively close together while the difference changes are relatively far apart, an exponential regression should be used.

regression equation: $y \approx 34.8(1.33)^x$; $r \approx 1$ and analysis of the residual plot would also suggest a good fit.

19.

x	y	difference $y_2 - y_1$	factor $\frac{y_2}{y_1}$
1	22		
2	35	13	1.59
3	60	25	1.71
4	104	44	1.73
5	189	85	1.82

Since the values of y are increasing over time, the function is increasing. Since the factor changes are relatively close together and the difference changes are not, an exponential regression should be used regression equation: $y \approx 12.3(1.71)^x$; $y \approx 1$ and analysis of the residual plot would also suggest a good fit.

20. Using the given exponential functions, state a and b.

a. $y = 3(4)^x$
$a = 3, b = 4$

b. $y = -5(8)^x$
$a = -5, b = 8$

c. $y = 4(0.6)^x$
$a = 4, b = 0.6$

d. $y = -5(0.9)^x$
$a = -5, b = 0.9$

e. $y = 2^x$
$a = 1, b = 2$

21. Suppose that you are offered a job that pays you $2000 the first month with a raise every month after that. You can choose a $400 raise or a 15% raise. Which option would you choose? What if the raise were 10%, 8%, or 5%?

	Monthly Salary after Indicated Monthly Raise				
Month	$400	15%	10%	8%	5%
0	$2000	$2000	$2000	$2000	$2000
1	$2400	$2300	$2200	$2160	$2100
2	$2800	$2645	$2420	$2333	$2205
3	$3200	$3042	$2662	$2519	$2315

	Change in Salary per Month for Indicated Monthly Raise									
	$400		15%		10%		8%		5%	
Interval	$	%	$	%	$	%	$	%	$	%
0–1	400	20	300	15	200	10	160	8	100	5
1–2	400	17	345	15	220	10	173	8	105	5
2–3	400	14	397	15	242	10	186	8	110	5

Number of Months until Salary with Percent Raise Exceeds Salary with $400 Raise			
15%	10%	8%	5%
5	15	22	49

The salary chosen would depend on the length of the job and the percentage change in salary offered.

MULTIPLE REPRESENTATIONS

Students may benefit from using simple numbers and number sense to justify algebraic steps in proofs. For example, to justify

$$x_2 - x_1 = x_4 - x_3$$

$$m(x_2 - x_1) = m(x_4 - x_3)$$

$$mx_2 - mx_1 = mx_4 - mx_3$$

write

$$5 - 2 = 7 - 4$$

$$3(5 - 2) = 3(7 - 4)$$

$$3(5) - 3(2) = 3(7) - 3(4)$$

$$15 - 6 = 21 - 12$$

$$9 = 9$$

Students can readily see that the algebraic steps are "legal" because the original equation, which started out as true, remained true even though it was manipulated.

© Houghton Mifflin Harcourt Publishing Company

JOURNAL

Ask students to draw a table in their journals comparing a linear function with a positive slope to an exponential function with a positive coefficient.

	Linear Function	Exponential Function
Change per equal interval	constant	increasing
Ratio over equal intervals $\dfrac{f(x_n)}{f(x_{n-1})}$	decreasing	constant
Equation	$f(x) = a + bx$	$f(x) = ab^x$

22. Draw Conclusions Liam would like to put $6000 in savings for a 5-year period. Should he choose a simple interest account that pays an interest rate of 5% of the principal (initial amount) each year or a compounded interest account that pays an interest rate of 1.5% of the total account value each month?

Yearly:

$y = 6000(1.05)^x$

$= 6000(1.05)^5$

$= 6000(1.276)$

$= \$7657.69$

Monthly:

$y = 6000(1.015)^x$

$= 6000(1.015)^{60}$

$= 6000(2.44)$

$= \$14,659.32$

$\$14,659.32 - \$7657.69 = \$7001.63$

Liam should choose a monthly account as it will earn roughly $7001.63 more dollars in a 5-year period.

23. Critical Thinking Why will an exponential growth function always eventually exceed a linear growth function?

Since the exponential growth function eventually curves upward while a linear growth function continues in a straight line with a positive slope, the exponential growth function will eventually exceed the linear growth function.

24. Explain the Error JoAnn analyzed the following data showing the number of cells in a bacteria culture over time.

Time (min)	0	6.9	10.8	13.5	15.7	17.4
Cells	8	16	24	32	40	48

She concluded that since the number of cells showed a constant change and the time did not, neither a linear function nor an exponential function modeled the number of cells over time well. Was she correct?

JoAnn was incorrect. Because the time intervals are not uniform, she cannot make a determination by just looking at the data. An exponential function is a good model as exponential regression gives an equation with $r = 0.9999$.

Lesson Performance Task

Two major cities each have a population of 25,000 people.
The population of City A increases by about 150 people per year.
The population of City B increases by about 0.5% per year.

a. Find the population increase for each city for the first
5 years. Round to the nearest whole number, if necessary.
Then compare the changes in the populations of each city
per year.

b. Will City B ever have a larger population than City A? If
so, what year will this occur?

a. First, find the yearly population
of each city for the first 5 years.

Yearly Population		
Year	City A	City B
0	25,000	25,000
1	25,150	25,125
2	25,300	25,251
3	25,450	25,377
4	25,600	25,504
5	25,750	25,632

Next, find the population increase
for each city for the first 5 years.

Yearly Population Increase		
Year	City A	City B
0–1	150	125
1–2	150	126
2–3	150	126
3–4	150	127
4–5	150	128

The population of City A is increasing
at a constant 150 people per year. The
population of City B is increasing at small
intervals and not at a constant rate.

b. Let t represent the number of elapsed years.

City A: $P_A(t) = 25,000 + 150t$

City B: $P_B(t) = 25,000(1.005)^t$

The estimated intersection point is (72, 35,794).

City B will have a larger population after about 72 years.

AVOID COMMON ERRORS

Some students may use the growth factor 1.05 for
City B because they incorrectly converted 0.5% to
the decimal 0.05 instead of 0.005. Remind students
that percent means *per hundred* and hundredths have
two decimal places. Therefore, when converting a
percent to a decimal, move the decimal point two
places to the left.

QUESTIONING STRATEGIES

? What type of function describes each city's
growth? Explain. The growth of City A is
described by a linear function, because it increases
by a constant amount per year. The growth of City B
is described by an exponential function because it
increases by a constant percent per year.

? How do you use the initial population value in
the equation for each function? In the linear
function for City A, the initial population is the
y-intercept. In the exponential function for City B,
the initial population is the coefficient.

EXTENSION ACTIVITY

Have students research factors that affect the growth rate of any city. Then have
students tell which factors may cause a decrease in population and which may
cause an increase.

Students should find that births, deaths, immigration, and emigration affect
growth rate. Deaths and emigration cause a decrease in population, while births
and immigration cause an increase in population. The growth rate is determined
using this equation:

growth rate = birth rate − death rate + immigration rate − emigration rate

Scoring Rubric
2 points: Student correctly solves the problem and explains his/her reasoning.
1 point: Student shows good understanding of the problem but does not fully
solve or explain his/her reasoning.
0 points: Student does not demonstrate understanding of the problem.

Comparing Linear and Exponential Models   **792**

Study Guide Review

ASSESSMENT AND INTERVENTION

Assign or customize module reviews.

MODULE PERFORMANCE TASK

COMMON CORE

Mathematical Practices: MP.1, MP.2, MP.4, MP.5, MP.6
A-CED.A.2, F-BF.A.1, F-LE.A.1c, F-LE.A.2

SUPPORTING STUDENT REASONING

Students should begin this problem by figuring out what information they need before they find the amount of iodine-131 released. Here are some questions they might ask.

- **What is a half-life?** Nuclear isotopes decay into stable molecules at a predictable rate. A half-life is the amount of time it takes for half of an isotope to decay.

- **How can you calculate nuclear decay?** You can use the formula $y = a\left(\frac{1}{2}\right)^x$, where a is the original amount of the substance, x is the number of half-lives, and y is the remaining amount of the substance.

- **Should I use 365 days per year or 365.25 days per year?** The difference is negligible in this case, so either can be used.

Exponential Equations and Models

Essential Question: How can you use exponential equations to represent real-world situations?

Key Vocabulary
exponential decay
  (decremento exponencial)
exponential growth
  (crecimiento exponencial)
exponential regression
  (regresión exponencial)

KEY EXAMPLE   (Lesson 16.2)

A comic book is sold for $3, and its value increases by 6% each year after it is sold. Write an exponential growth function to find the value of the comic book in 25 years. Then graph it and state its domain and range. What does the y-intercept represent?

Write the exponential growth function for this situation.

$$y = a(1 + r)^t$$
$$= 3(1 + 0.06)^t$$
$$= 3(1.06)^t$$

Find the value in 25 years.

$$y = 3(1.06)^t$$
$$= 3(1.06)^{25}$$
$$\approx 12.88$$

After 25 years, the comic book will be worth approximately $12.88.

Create a table of values to graph the function.

t	y	(t, y)
0	3	(0, 3)
5	4.01	(5, 4.01)
10	5.37	(10, 5.37)
15	7.19	(15, 7.19)
20	9.62	(20, 9.62)
25	12.88	(25, 12.88)
30	17.23	(30, 17.23)

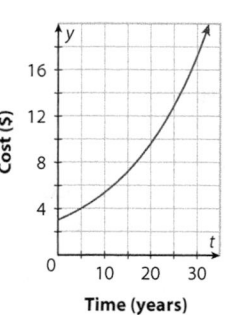

The domain is the set of real numbers t such that $t \geq 0$.

The range is the set of real numbers y such that $y \geq 3$.

The y-intercept is the value of y when $t = 0$, which is the time when the comic book was sold.

SCAFFOLDING SUPPORT

- Students who assume the decay for cesium-137 over 40 days is negligible and solve for a mass of 100 g of iodine-131 will get an initial mass of 3200 g for cesium-137. This is a difference of less than 0.3% and is acceptable.

- Watch for students who neglect to convert years to units of days.

EXERCISES

Solve each equation for *x*. (Lesson 16.1)

1. $3(2)^x = 96$

$x = 5$

2. $\frac{5^x}{25} = 25$

$x = 4$

3. The value of a textbook is $120 and decreases at a rate of 12% per year. Write a function to model the situation, and then find the value of the textbook after 9 years. (Lesson 16.2)

$f(t) = 120(0.88)^t$; $37.98

Find an exponential model for the data in the given table. (Lesson 16.3)

4.

x	0	1	2	3	4	5	6	7	8	9	10
y	9	12.85	16.89	28.15	42.58	65.1	99.34	153	237.6	339.2	478.61

$f(x) = 8.37(1.51)^x$

State whether each situation is best represented by an exponential or linear function. Then write an exponential or linear function for the model and state whether the model is increasing or decreasing. (Lesson 16.4)

5. A customer borrows $950 at 6% interest compounded annually.
exponential; $C(t) = 950(1.06)^t$; increasing

6. The population of a town is 8548 people and decreases by 90 people each year.
linear; $P(t) = 8548 - 90t$; decreasing

MODULE PERFORMANCE TASK

Half-Life

The half-life of iodine-131 is 8 days, and the half-life of cesium-137 is 30 years. Both of these isotopes can be released into the environment during a nuclear accident.

Suppose that a nuclear reactor accident released 100 grams of cesium-137 and an unknown amount of iodine-131. After 40 days the amount of iodine-131 is equal to the amount of cesium-137. About how much iodine-131 was released by the accident?

Start by listing in the space below how you plan to tackle the problem. Then use your own paper to complete the task. Be sure to write down all your data and assumptions. Then use numbers, graphs, tables, or algebra to explain how you reached your conclusion.

DISCUSSION OPPORTUNITIES

- Ask students why knowing the initial mass of radioisotopes released can be useful.

- Have students share techniques and strategies. Discuss and evaluate different approaches that classmates used to solve the problem.

SAMPLE SOLUTION

First, find the amount of cesium-137 that remains after 40 days. The proportion that relates 40 days to 30 years is $\frac{40}{365.25 \cdot 30}$, so 40 days is about 0.00365 of a half-life. Substitute and solve:

$$y = 100\left(\frac{1}{2}\right)^{0.00365} \approx 99.75$$

After 40 days, there are about 99.75 g of cesium-137 and the same amount of iodine-131.

For iodine-131, 40 days is equivalent to $\frac{40}{8} = 5$ half-lives.

$99.75 = a\left(\frac{1}{2}\right)^5$ Substitute.

$99.75 = a\left(\frac{1}{32}\right)$ Simplify.

$a = 3192$ Solve.

There were 3192 g of iodine-131 released in the accident.

Assessment Rubric

2 points: Student correctly solves the problem and explains his/her reasoning.

1 point: Student shows good understanding of the problem but does not fully solve or explain.

0 points: Student does not demonstrate understanding of the problem.

Ready to Go On?

ASSESS MASTERY

Use the assessment on this page to determine if students have mastered the concepts and standards covered in this module.

ASSESSMENT AND INTERVENTION

Access Ready to Go On? assessment online, and receive instant scoring, feedback, and customized intervention or enrichment.

ADDITIONAL RESOURCES

Response to Intervention Resources

- Reteach Worksheets

Differentiated Instruction Resources

- Reading Strategies **EL**
- Success for English Learners **EL**
- Challenge Worksheets

Assessment Resources

- Leveled Module Quizzes

16.1–16.4 Exponential Equations and Models

- Online Homework
- Hints and Help
- Extra Practice

1. Mike has a savings account with the bank. The bank pays him annual interest of 1.5%. He has $4000 and wonders how much he will have in the account in 5 years. Write an exponential function to model the situation and then find how much he will have. *(Lesson 16.1)*

$S(t) = 4000(1.015)^t$; about $4309.14

State each function's domain, range, and end behavior. *(Lesson 16.2)*

2. $f(x) = 900(0.65)^x$

Domain: $\left\{x \mid -\infty < x < \infty\right\}$

Range: $\left\{y \mid y > 0\right\}$

End behavior: As $x \to -\infty, y \to \infty$

and as $x \to \infty, y \to 0$.

3. $f(x) = 400(1.23)^x$

Domain: $\left\{x \mid -\infty < x < \infty\right\}$

Range: $\left\{y \mid y > 0\right\}$

End behavior: As $x \to -\infty, y \to 0$

and as $x \to \infty, y \to \infty$.

4. The table shows the temperature of a pizza over three-minute intervals after it is removed from the oven.

Time, (x)	0	4	8	12	16
Temperature, (y)	450	340	240	190	145

Create a model describing the data and use it to predict the temperature after 20 minutes. *(Lesson 16.3)*

$f(x) = 445(0.931)^x$; 106.5 degrees

5. Account A and B each start out with $600. If Account A earns $50 each year and Account B earns 6% of its value each year, after how many years will Account B have more money than Account A? *(Lesson 16.4)*

after about 12 years

ESSENTIAL QUESTION

6. How can you identify an exponential equation?

Possible Answer: An exponential equation has the form $f(x) = ab^x$, for real numbers a, b, and x where $a \neq 0$, $b > 0$, and $b \neq 1$. In an exponential equation, as the input values increase by 1, the successive output values are related by a constant ratio.

Common Core Standards

Lesson	Items	Content Standards	Mathematical Practices
16.1	1	A-CED.A.1, A-SSE.B.3c, F-BF.A.1, F-LE.A.2	MP.4
16.2	2–3	F-IF.C.7e, F-IF.B.5	MP.2
16.3	4	A-SSE.B.3c, F-BF.A.1, F-LE.A.2, F-LE.A.1c, S-ID.B.6a, F-LE.A.1b	MP.4
16.4	5	A-SSE.B.3c, F-LE.A.2, F-LE.A.1c, S-ID.B.6a, F-LE.A.1b	MP.4

Assessment Readiness

1. Consider the end behavior of $f(x) = 75(1.25)^x$. Select True or False for each statement.

A. As $x \to -\infty, y \to -\infty$. ○ True ● False

B. As $x \to -\infty, y \to 0$. ● True ○ False

C. As $x \to \infty, y \to \infty$. ● True ○ False

2. Is the given expression equivalent to $\sqrt{16^{-\frac{1}{2}}}$? Select Yes or No for each expression.

A. $\sqrt[4]{\dfrac{1}{16}}$ ● Yes ○ No

B. $16^{\frac{1}{4}}$ ○ Yes ● No

C. $\sqrt{\dfrac{1}{4}}$ ● Yes ○ No

3. Solve $36(3)^x = 4$. What is the value of x? Explain how you got your answer.

-2; I divided both sides by 36 and got $3^x = \frac{1}{9}$. Then I rewrote $\frac{1}{9}$ as a power of 3 to get $3^x = 3^{-2}$ Applying the equality of bases property, I found that x equals -2.

4. Consider the following situation: enrollment at a school is initially 322 students and grows by 4% per year. Write an equation to represent this situation, and use it to predict the number of students at the school in 5 years.

$E(t) = 322(1.04)^t$; In 5 years, the school will have approximately 392 students.

MIXED REVIEW
Assessment Readiness

ASSESSMENT AND INTERVENTION

Assign ready-made or customized practice tests to prepare students for high-stakes tests.

ADDITIONAL RESOURCES

Assessment Resources

- Leveled Module Quizzes: Modified, B

COMMON CORE Common Core Standards

Lesson	Items	Content Standards	Mathematical Practices
16.2	1	F-IF.B.4	MP.1
14.2	2*	N-RN.A.2	MP.2
14.1, 16.1	3*	N-RN.A.2	MP.2
16.2	4	F-BF.A.1a	MP.4

* Item integrates mixed review concepts from previous modules or a previous course.

ASSESSMENT AND INTERVENTION

Assign ready-made or customized practice tests to prepare students for high-stakes tests.

ADDITIONAL RESOURCES

Assessment Resources

- Leveled Unit Tests: Modified, A, B, C
- Performance Assessment

AVOID COMMON ERRORS

Item 7 Some students will only test whether the set is closed under one operation rather than testing both listed. Encourage students to underline each step in the question to be sure they complete it fully.

- Online Homework
- Hints and Help
- Extra Practice

1. Is the given expression equivalent to $\dfrac{x^{\frac{1}{2}}}{16^{-\frac{1}{2}}}$?

   A. $(4x)^{\frac{1}{2}}$ — ○ Yes ● No

   B. $4x^{\frac{1}{2}}$ — ● Yes ○ No

   C. $\dfrac{16^{\frac{1}{2}}}{x^{-\frac{1}{2}}}$ — ● Yes ○ No

2. Consider the graph of $y = \sqrt{4^3 x^2} - 24$. Select True or False for each statement.

   A. The x-intercept is -3. — ● True ○ False

   B. The y-intercept is 4. — ○ True ● False

   C. The x-intercept is 3. — ● True ○ False

3. Consider the sequence 8, 4, 0, -4,…. Determine if each statement is True or False.

   A. It is a geometric sequence. — ○ True ● False

   B. The fifth term is -8. — ● True ○ False

   C. $f(10) = -28$. — ● True ○ False

4. Write an explicit and recursive rule for the geometric sequence -5, 10, -20, 40,… and use it to find the 12th term of the sequence. Is each statement correct?

   A. The recursive rule is $f(1) = -2$; $f(n) = 5 \cdot f(n-1)$. — ○ Yes ● No

   B. The explicit rule is $f(n) = -5(-2)^{n-1}$. — ● Yes ○ No

   C. The 12th term is $-20{,}480$. — ○ Yes ● No

5. Consider the end behavior of $f(x) = -6\left(\dfrac{1}{2}\right)^x$. Is each statement True or False?

   A. As $x \to -\infty$, $y \to -\infty$ — ● True ○ False

   B. As $x \to \infty$, $y \to 0$ — ● True ○ False

   C. As $x \to \infty$, $y \to -\infty$ — ○ True ● False

Common Core Standards

Items	Content Standards	Mathematical Practices
1	**N-RN.A.2**	**MP.2**
2*	**F-IF.C.7a, N-RN.A.1**	**MP.7**
3*	**F-LE.A.2**	**MP.1**
4	**F-BF.A.1a**	**MP.4**
5	**F-IF.C.7e**	**MP.4**
6*	**A-REI.B.3**	**MP.2**
7	**N-RN.B.3**	**MP.3**

* Item integrates mixed review concepts from previous modules or a previous course.

6. Solve each equation. Is the given solution correct?

A. $5(2x - 7) = -6x - 27; x = \frac{1}{2}$ ● Yes   ○ No

B. $6 - \frac{2}{3}x = -2x - 2; x = -3$ ○ Yes   ● No

C. $9p = 3(4 - p) + 12; p = 12$ ○ Yes   ● No

7. Is the set $\{-1, 0, 1\}$ closed under addition? Is it closed under multiplication? Justify your answers.

A set is closed under an operation if performing the operation always produces an element of the set. The set is not closed under addition: $1 + 1 = 2$, and 2 is not an element of the set. The set is closed under multiplication because all possible products are included in the set: $-1(-1) = 1$, $0(0) = 0$, $1(1) = 1$, $-1(0) = 0$, $0(1) = 0$, $-1(1) = -1$.

8. Graph $f(x) = 4\left(\frac{1}{2}\right)^x$. What are the domain and range of the function?

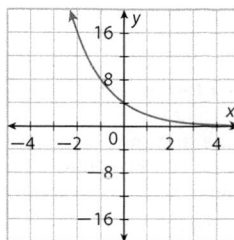

Domain: $\{x \mid -\infty < x < \infty\}$; Range: $\{y \mid y > 0\}$

9. Solve $3(16)^{\frac{x}{4}} = 192$ for x. Show your work.

$3(16)^{\frac{x}{4}} = 192$

$(16)^{\frac{x}{4}} = 64$

$2^{4\left(\frac{x}{4}\right)} = 2^6$

$2^x = 2^6$

$x = 6$

Performance Tasks

★**10.** Scientists have found that the life span of a mammal living in captivity is related to the mammal's mass. The life span in years can be approximated by the formula $L = 12m^{\frac{1}{5}}$, where m is the mammal's mass in kilograms. Which animal's life span is about twice the life span of a wolf? **giraffe**

Typical Mass of Mammals	
Mammal	**Mass (kg)**
Koala	8
Wolf	32
Lion	243
Giraffe	1024

© Houghton Mifflin Harcourt Publishing Company

PERFORMANCE TASKS

There are three different levels of performance tasks:

   * **Novice:** These are short word problems that require students to apply the math they have learned in straightforward, real-world situations.

   ** **Apprentice:** These are more involved problems that guide students step-by-step through more complex tasks. These exercises include more complicated reasoning, writing, and open-ended elements.

   ***Expert:** These are open-ended, nonroutine problems that, instead of stepping the students through, ask them to choose their own methods for solving and justify their answers and reasoning.

SCORING GUIDES

Item 10 (2 points)   2 points for correct answer

COMMON CORE **Common Core Standards**

Items	Content Standards	Mathematical Practices
8	F-IF.C.7e	MP.4
9	A-CED.A.1	MP.2

* Item integrates mixed review concepts from previous modules or a previous course.

SCORING GUIDES

Item 11 (6 points)

A. 1 point for stating that the payments form a geometric sequence
   2 points for explanation

B. 1 point for correctly choosing Plan 1
   2 points for explanation

Item 12 (6 points)

A. 1 point for correct amount

B. 1 point for correct answer

C. 1 point for correct amount

D. 1 point for correct percent

E. 2 points for answer and explanation

★★11. Billy earns money by mowing lawns for the summer. He offers two payment plans.

> **Plan 1:** Pay $250 for the entire summer.
> **Plan 2:** Pay $1 the first week, $2 the second week, $4 the third week, and so on.

A. Do the payments for Plan 2 form a geometric sequence? Explain.

B. If you were one of Billy's customers, which plan would you choose? (Assume that the summer is 10 weeks long.) Explain your choice.

A. Yes, it is a geometric sequence with $r = 2$.

B. Possible answer: Plan 1; under Plan 2, the cost for the 10th week alone is $512, which is more than the cost for the entire summer under Plan 1.

★★★12. As a promotion, a clothing store draws the name of one of its customers each week. The prize is a coupon for the store. If the winner is not present at the drawing, he or she cannot claim the prize, and the amount of the coupon increases for the following week's drawing. The function $f(x) = 20(1.2)^x$ gives the amount of the coupon in dollars after x weeks of the prize going unclaimed.

A. What is the amount of the coupon after 2 weeks of the prize going unclaimed?

B. After how many weeks of the prize going unclaimed will the amount of the coupon be greater than $100?

C. What is the original amount of the coupon?

D. Find the percent increase each week.

E. Do you think it would be wise for the owner of the store to set a limit on the number of weeks a prize can go unclaimed? Why or why not?

A. $28.80

B. 9 whole weeks

C. $20

D. 20%

E. Yes; If the prize is claimed then the total cost through several weeks grows linearly. When the prize is not claimed it grows exponentially. After several weeks the exponential curve is more expensive.

Financial Research Analyst The graph shows the value of two different shares of stock over the period of four years since they were purchased. The values have been changing exponentially.

a. For Stock A, which model fits the graph, exponential growth or exponential decay? Find the initial value and the growth or decay factor.

b. For Stock B, which model fits the graph, exponential growth or exponential decay? Find the initial value and the growth or decay factor.

c. According to the graph, after how many years was the value of Stock A about equal to the value of Stock B? What was that value?

d. After how many years was the value of Stock A about twice the value of Stock B? Explain how you found your answer.

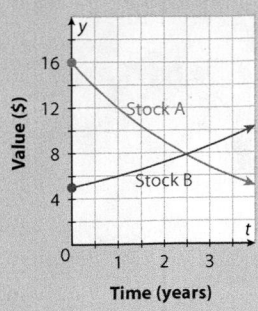

a. exponential decay; initial value: $16, decay factor: 0.75

b. exponential growth; initial value : $5, growth factor: 1.2

c. About 2.5 years; in 2.5 years, the value of both stocks was about $8 per share.

d. About 1 year; in 1 year, the value of Stock B was about $6 and the value of Stock A was about $12, which was twice the value of Stock B.

MATH IN CAREERS

Financial Research Analyst In this Unit Performance Task, students can see how a financial research analyst uses mathematics on the job.

For more information about careers in mathematics as well as various mathematics appreciation topics, visit the American Mathematical Society at http://www.ams.org.

SCORING GUIDE

Task (6 points)

a. 1 point for correct model and initial value
   1 point for correct decay factor

b. 1 point for correct model and initial value
   1 point for correct growth factor

c. 1 point for correct number of years and value

d. 1 point for correct number of years and explanation

Polynomial Operations

CONTENTS

Unit Pacing Guide

45-Minute Classes

Module 17

DAY 1	DAY 2	DAY 3	DAY 4	
Lesson 17.1	**Lesson 17.2**	**Lesson 17.3**	Module Review and Assessment Readiness	

Module 18

DAY 1	DAY 2	DAY 3	DAY 4	DAY 5
Lesson 18.1	**Lesson 18.2**	**Lesson 18.3**	**Lesson 18.3**	Module Review and Assessment Readiness

DAY 6
Unit Review and Assessment Readiness

90-Minute Classes

Module 17

DAY 1	DAY 2
Lesson 17.1 **Lesson 17.2**	**Lesson 17.3** Module Review and Assessment Readiness

Module 18

DAY 1	DAY 2	DAY 3
Lesson 18.1 **Lesson 18.2**	**Lesson 18.3**	Module Review and Assessment Readiness Unit Review and Assessment Readiness

Program Resources

PLAN

HMH Teacher App

Access a full suite of teacher resources online and offline on a variety of devices. Plan present, and manage classes, assignments, and activities.

ePlanner
Easily plan your classes, create and view assignments, and access all program resources with your online, customizable planning tool.

Professional Development Videos

Authors Juli Dixon and Matt Larson model successful teaching practices and strategies in actual classroom settings.

QR Codes **Scan with your smart phone to jump directly from your print book to online videos and other resources.**

Teacher's Edition

Support students with point-of-use Questioning Strategies, teaching tips, resources for differentiated instruction, additional activities, and more.

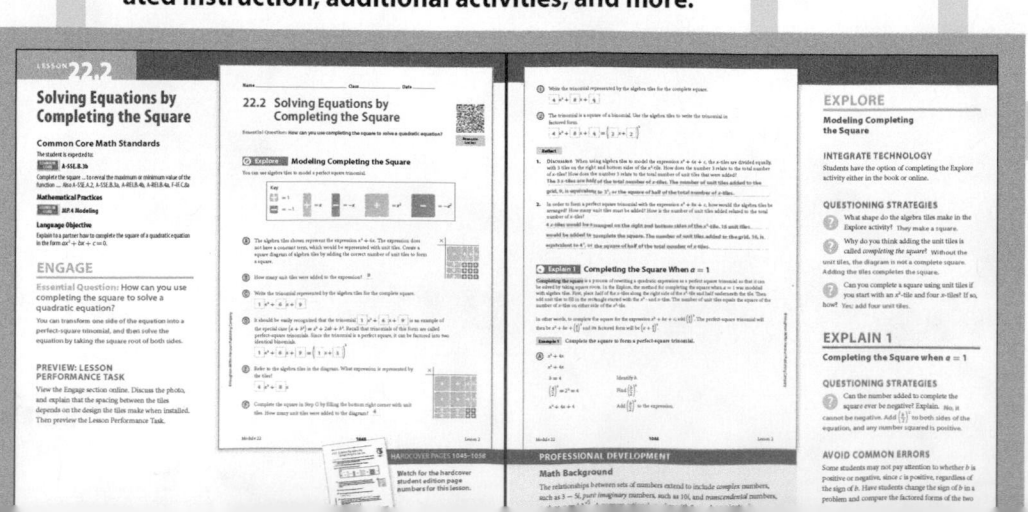

ENGAGE AND EXPLORE

Real-World Videos **Engage students with interesting and relevant applications of the mathematical content of each module.**

Explore Activities

Students interactively explore new concepts using a variety of tools and approaches.

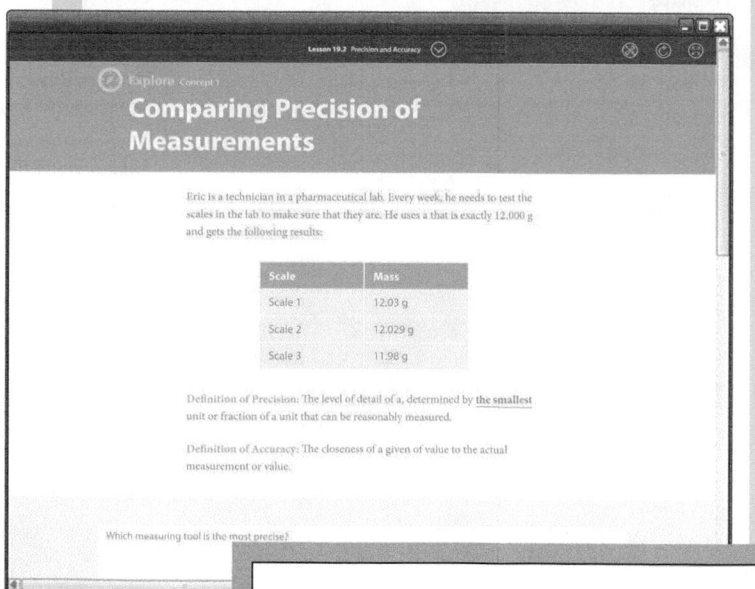

Comparing Precision of Measurements

Eric is a technician in a pharmaceutical lab. Every week, he needs to test the scales in the lab to make sure that they are. He uses a that is exactly 12.000 g and gets the following results:

Scale	Mass
Scale 1	12.03 g
Scale 2	12.029 g
Scale 3	11.98 g

Definition of Precision: The level of detail of a, determined by __the smallest__ unit or fraction of a unit that can be reasonably measured.

Definition of Accuracy: The closeness of a given of value to the actual measurement or value.

Which measuring tool is the most precise?

Name _____ Class _____ Date _____

22.2 Solving Equations by Completing the Square

Essential Question: How can you use completing the square to solve a quadratic equation?

COMMON CORE **A-SSE.B.3b** Complete the square ... to reveal the maximum or minimum value of the function ... Also A-SSE.A.2, A-SSE.B.3a, A-REI.B.4b, A-REI.B.4a, F-IF.C.8a

Explore **Modeling Completing the Square**

You can use algebra tiles to model a perfect square trinomial.

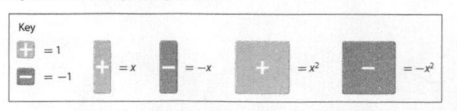

(A) The algebra tiles shown represent the expression $x^2 + 6x$. The expression does not have a constant term, which would be represented with unit tiles. Create a square diagram of algebra tiles by adding the correct number of unit tiles to form a square.

(B) How many unit tiles were added to the expression? _____

(C) Write the trinomial represented by the algebra tiles for the complete square.

$\boxed{}x^2 + \boxed{}x + \boxed{}$

(D) It should be easily recognized that the trinomial $\boxed{}x^2 + \boxed{}x + \boxed{}$ is an example of the special case $(a + b)^2 = a^2 + 2ab + b^2$. Recall that trinomials of this form are called

TEACH

Math On the Spot video tutorials, featuring program author Dr. Edward Burger, accompany every example in the textbook and give students step-by-step instructions and explanations of key math concepts.

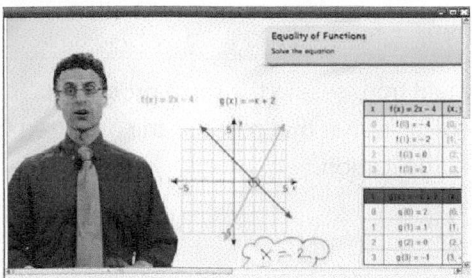

Interactive Teacher Edition

Customize and present course materials with collaborative activities and integrated formative assessment.

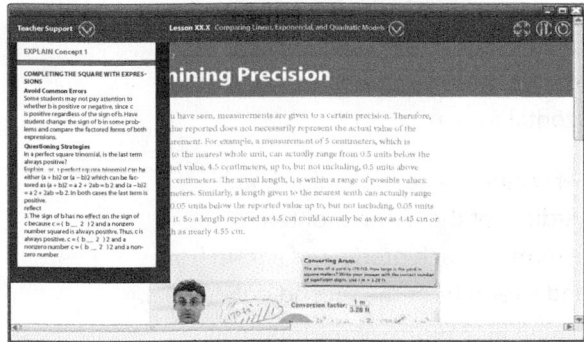

Differentiated Instruction Resources

Support all learners with Differentiated Instruction Resources, including

- **Leveled Practice and Problem Solving**
- **Reading Strategies**
- **Success for English Learners**
- **Challenge**

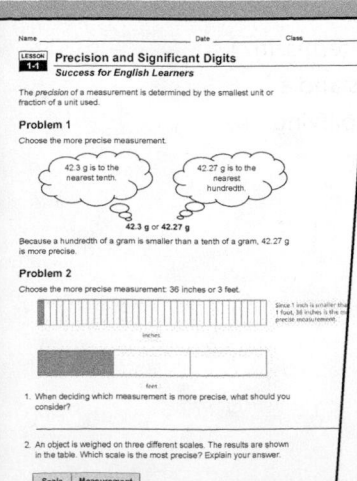

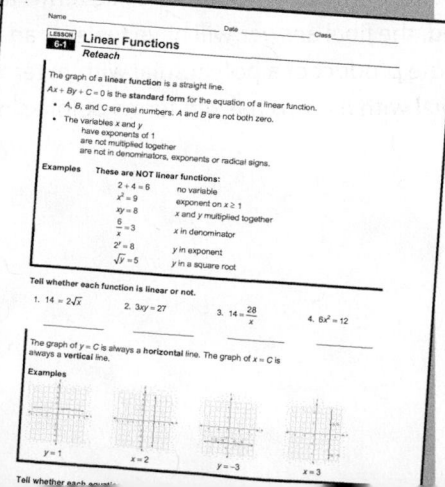

ASSESSMENT AND INTERVENTION

The **Personal Math Trainer** provides online practice, homework, assessments, and intervention. Monitor student progress through reports and alerts. **Create and customize assignments aligned to specific lessons or Common Core standards.**

- **Practice** – With dynamic items and assignments, students get unlimited practice on key concepts supported by guided examples, step-by-step solutions, and video tutorials.

- **Assessments** – Choose from course assignments or customize your own based on course content, Common Core standards, difficulty levels, and more.

- **Homework** – Students can complete online homework with a wide variety of problem types, including the ability to enter expressions, equations, and graphs. Let the system automatically grade homework, so you can focus where your students need help the most!

- **Intervention** – Let the Personal Math Trainer automatically prescribe a targeted, personalized intervention path for your students.

Focus on Higher Order Thinking

Raise the bar with homework and practice that incorporates higher-order thinking and mathematical practices in every lesson.

Assessment Readiness

Prepare students for success on high stakes tests for Algebra 1 with practice at every module and unit

Assessment Resources

Tailor assessments and response to intervention to meet the needs of all your classes and students, including

- Leveled Module Quizzes
- Leveled Unit Tests
- Unit Performance Tasks
- Placement, Diagnostic, and Quarterly Benchmark Tests
- Tier 1, Tier 2, and Tier 3 Resources

Math Background

Understanding Polynomial Expressions   COMMON CORE   A-SSE.A.1a
LESSON 17.1

In order to discuss polynomials, we must agree on terminology. The basic unit is the monomial. A *monomial is a product of a real number and one or more variables with whole-number exponents*. (The real number is usually rational, particularly within the scope of Algebra 1, but this is not a requirement.) A *polynomial is a sum of monomials*. For example, the polynomial $8x^4 - 3x - 1$ may be written as $8x^4 + (-3x) + (-1)$, which is the sum of the monomials $8x^4$, $-3x$, and -1.

There are special terms for polynomials with two or three terms. *A polynomial with two terms is a binomial,* and a *polynomial with three terms is a trinomial.*

Adding and Subtracting Polynomials   COMMON CORE   A-APR.A.1
LESSONS 17.2 and 17.3

Adding and subtracting polynomials is fairly straightforward because the process is nothing more than combining like terms.

$$\left(3x^2 + 7x + 5\right) + \left(2x + 6\right) = 3x^2 + 7x + 2x + 6 + 5$$
$$= 3x^2 + 9x + 11$$

Polynomial Multiplication   COMMON CORE   A-APR.A.1
LESSONS 18.1 and 18.2

Polynomial multiplication can present greater difficulty for students, so it is essential to build gradually. Multiplication of two monomials is a natural starting point. You can use the Commutative and Associative Properties to show that $(4x)(2x) = 8x^2$.

The Distributive Property is used when multiplying a monomial and a binomial:

$$5x(2x + 3) = (5x)(2x) + (5x)(3) = 10x^2 + 15x$$

The Distributive Property is used repeatedly when multiplying a binomial by a binomial:

$$(3x + 2)(7x + 4) = (3x)(7x + 4) + (2)(7x + 4)$$
$$= (3x)(7x) + (3x)(4) + (2)(7x) + (2)(4)$$
$$= 21x^2 + 12x + 14x + 8$$
$$= 21x^2 + 26x + 8$$

Students may benefit from seeing the same product calculated in a vertical format that parallels the one used for whole-number multiplication.

$$
\begin{array}{r}
7x + 4 \\
\times \quad 3x + 2 \\
\hline
14x + 8 \leftarrow 2(7x + 4) \\
21x^2 + 12x \qquad \leftarrow 3x(7x + 4) \\
\hline
21x^2 + 26x + 8
\end{array}
$$

Notice the similarities in the two methods. As shown in the vertical format, the expressions in the intermediate rows come from the products $2(7x + 4)$ and $3x(7x + 4)$, which are precisely the two intermediate products that are calculated in the horizontal format.

The Distributive Property can be used to multiply any two polynomials, regardless of the number of terms. The product will have one term for each product of a term from the first polynomial and a term from the second polynomial. So, the product of a binomial (2 terms) and a trinomial (3 terms) will have $2 \cdot 3 = 6$ terms before simplifying:

$$(x + 2)(x^2 + 6x + 8)$$
$$= (x + 2)(x^2) + (x + 2)(6x) + (x + 2)(8)$$
$$= (x)(x^2) + 2(x^2) + x(6x) + 2(6x) + x(8) + 2(8)$$

It is important to remember that this rule about the number of terms is true before the product is simplified. Clearly, some of the terms above are like terms and will be combined; the final answer will have fewer than 6 terms. In general, the product of a polynomial with m terms and a polynomial with n terms has mn terms before simplifying.

Special Products of Binomials COMMON CORE A-APR.A.1

LESSON 18.3

Two binomials with the same two terms but opposite signs separating the terms are called *conjugates* of each other. For example, $3x + 1$ and $3x - 1$ are conjugates. When conjugates are multiplied together, the answer is the difference of the squares of the terms in the original binomials.

$$(3x + 1)(3x - 1) = 9x^2 - 3x + 3x - 1 = 9x^2 - 1$$

In general, $(x + y)(x - y) = x^2 - y^2$. The product of conjugates is the difference of two squares.

The squaring of a binomial also produces a special pattern.

$$(x + 1)(x + 1) = x^2 + 1x + 1x + 1 = x^2 + 2x + 1$$

First, notice that the answer is a trinomial. Second, notice that there is a pattern in the terms. The first and last terms are the squares of the first and last terms of the binomial. The middle term is twice the product of the two terms in the binomial. In general, $(x + y)^2 = x^2 + 2xy + y^2$ and $(x - y)^2 = x^2 - 2xy + y^2$.

Polynomial Operations

MATH IN CAREERS
Unit Activity Preview

After completing this unit, students will complete a Math in Careers task by writing and performing operations on several functions based on camp enrollment and expenses. Critical skills include modeling real-world situations and polynomial addition, subtraction, and multiplication.

For more information about careers in mathematics as well as various mathematics appreciation topics, visit The American Mathematical Society at http://www.ams.org.

UNIT 7

Polynomial Operations

MODULE 17
Adding and Subtracting Polynomials

MODULE 18
Multiplying Polynomials

MATH IN CAREERS

Camp Director A camp director is in charge of organizing activities, hiring and supervising staff, and overseeing maintenance of the camp facilities. Camp directors use math for bookkeeping, creating budgets, negotiating vendor contracts, and planning new construction of camp buildings and outdoor spaces.

If you are interested in a career as a camp director, you should study these mathematical subjects:
- Algebra
- Geometry
- Business math

Research other careers that require keeping financial books. Check out the career activity at the end of the unit to find out how **camp directors** use math.

Unit 7   801

TRACKING YOUR LEARNING PROGRESSION

Before	In this Unit	After
Students understand: • expressions with rational exponents • expressions with radicals • geometric sequences • exponential functions	Students will learn about: • adding polynomial expressions • subtracting polynomial expressions • multiplying polynomial expressions • special products of binomials • dividing polynomial expressions	Students will study: • graphing quadratic functions • interpreting vertex and standard form of quadratic functions • connecting intercepts and zeros • solving quadratic equations using the Zero Product Property

Reading Start-Up

Visualize Vocabulary

Use the ✔ words to complete the chart.

Closure The property that states that the sum or product of any two real numbers will equal another real number	**Associative Property** The property that states that for all real numbers, the sum is always the same, regardless of their grouping
Commutative Property The property that states that for all real numbers, the sum is always the same, regardless of their ordering	**Distributive Property** The property that states that if you multiply a sum by a number, you will get the same result if you multiply each addend by that number and then add the products

Properties (center oval)

Understand Vocabulary

To become familiar with some of the vocabulary terms in this unit, consider the following. You may refer to the module, the glossary, or a dictionary.

1. The prefix *tri-* is used to identify an item that has three parts, such as a *triangle*. What do you think a **trinomial** might be?
    an algebraic expression with three terms

2. The prefix *poly-* is used to identify an item with many elements, such as a *polygon*. What do you think a **polynomial** might be?
    an algebraic expression with many terms

Active Reading

Four-Corner Fold Before beginning the unit, create a four-corner fold to help you organize what you learn. Label the flaps "Adding Polynomials," "Subtracting Polynomials," "Multiplying Polynomials," and "Special Products of Binomials." As you study this unit note important ideas and concepts used when performing operations with polynomials under the appropriate flap. You can use your FoldNote later to study for tests and complete assignments.

Reading Start Up

Have students complete the activities on this page by working alone or with others.

VISUALIZE VOCABULARY

The four-square graphic helps students review vocabulary associated with properties of real numbers. If time allows, ask students for examples of expressions that can be used to demonstrate each property using variables and numbers.

UNDERSTAND VOCABULARY

Use the following explanations to help students learn the preview words.

A **monomial** is a number or product of numbers and variables with whole-number exponents. A **polynomial** is a monomial or sum or difference of monomials. A polynomial with two terms is a **binomial.** A polynomial with three terms is a **trinomial.** A **perfect-square trinomial** has a factored form that is the square of a binominal. **FOIL** is a memory device for a method of multiplying two binomials.

ACTIVE READING

Students can use these reading and note-taking strategies to help them organize and understand the new concepts and vocabulary. Encourage them to ask questions about related words that cause any confusion. Suggest that students use different colors to highlight the prefixes of related words. They can use the highlight colors in the corresponding examples as they fill in the four-corner fold.

ADDITIONAL RESOURCES

Differentiated Instruction

- Reading Strategies

Adding and Subtracting Polynomials

ESSENTIAL QUESTION:

Answer: You can use polynomials to model real-world quantities such as profit or loss.

PROFESSIONAL DEVELOPMENT VIDEO

Professional Development Video

Learn effective ways of integrating technology into your classroom to meet a variety of different needs.

Professional
Development
my.hrw.com

MODULE 17

Adding and Subtracting Polynomials

Essential Question: How can you use adding and subtracting polynomials to solve real-world problems?

LESSON 17.1
Understanding Polynomial Expressions

LESSON 17.2
Adding Polynomial Expressions

LESSON 17.3
Subtracting Polynomial Expressions

© Houghton Mifflin Harcourt Publishing Company·Image Credits: © Joseph McNally/Photonica World/Getty Images

REAL WORLD VIDEO
Vehicles, such as planes and cars, are aerodynamically tested in a wind tunnel. The complex factors involved in wind tunnel testing can be modeled with polynomial functions.

MODULE PERFORMANCE TASK PREVIEW

Ozone Levels in the Los Angeles Basin

Ozone in the upper atmosphere helps protect living things from the harmful effects of ultraviolet radiation. However, ozone near the ground is harmful and a major component of air pollution. Suppose you have some data on ozone levels in a community for an entire year. How would you find out the trend in ozone levels for that community? Let's find out!

Module 17　　　803

DIGITAL TEACHER EDITION

Access a full suite of teaching resources when and where you need them:

- Access content online or offline
- Customize lessons to share with your class
- Communicate with your students in real-time
- View student grades and data instantly to target your instruction where it is needed most

PERSONAL MATH TRAINER
Assessment and Intervention

Assign automatically graded homework, quizzes, tests, and intervention activities. Prepare your students with updated, Common Core-aligned practice tests.

Are **YOU** Ready?

Complete these exercises to review skills you will need for this module.

• Online Homework
• Hints and Help
• Extra Practice

Add and Subtract Integers

Example 1   Add or subtract.

$-9 + (-6)$	Think: Find the sum of 9 and 6.
-15	Same sign, so use the sign of the integers.
$14 + (-17)$	Think: Find the difference of 14 and
-3	17. $17 > 14$, so use the sign of 17.
$3 - (-11)$	Think: Add the opposite of –11.
$3 + 11$	Same sign, so use the sign of the integers.
14	

Add or subtract.

1. $-16 + 21$
5

2. $-13 - 12$
-25

3. $-23 - (-8)$
-15

Algebraic Expressions

Example 2   Simplify $15 + 9x - 6 - 5x$ by combining like terms.

$15 + 9x - 6 - 5x$	
$9x - 5x + 15 - 6$	Reorder, grouping like terms together.
$9x - 5x + 9$	Subtract the integers.
$4x + 9$	Combine the like terms.

Simplify by combining like terms.

4. $8a + 5 - 10a - 11$
$-2a - 6$

5. $-7 + d - 6 + 2d$
$3d - 13$

6. $19z + 14y - y - 3z$
$13y + 16z$

7. $21 - 13p + 12q - 5 + 2p - 15q$
$-11p - 3q + 16$

Exponents

Example 3   Find the value of $x^3 + x^2$ when $x = 2$.

$x^3 + x^2$	
$2^3 + 2^2$	Substitute 2 for x.
$8 + 4$	Evaluate the exponents.
12	Add.

Find the value.

8. $x^3 + x^2$ when $x = -2$
-4

9. $x^3 - 4$ when $x = 3$
23

10. $x^3 - 4$ when $x = -3$
-31

© Houghton Mifflin Harcourt Publishing Company

Are You Ready?

ASSESS READINESS

Use the assessment on this page to determine if students need strategic or intensive intervention for the module's prerequisite skills.

ASSESSMENT AND INTERVENTION

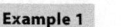

RtI Response to Intervention **TIER 1, TIER 2, TIER 3 SKILLS**

Personal Math Trainer will automatically create a standards-based, personalized intervention assignment for your students, targeting each student's individual needs!

ADDITIONAL RESOURCES

See the table below for a full list of intervention resources available for this module.

Response to Intervention Resources also includes:

• Tier 2 Skill Pre-Tests for each Module
• Tier 2 Skill Post-Tests for each skill

	Response to Intervention		Differentiated Instruction
Tier 1 Lesson Intervention Worksheets	**Tier 2** Strategic Intervention Skills Intervention Worksheets	**Tier 3** Intensive Intervention Worksheets available online	
Reteach 17.1 Reteach 17.2 Reteach 17.3	1 Add and Subtract Integers 2 Algebraic Expressions 5 Exponents	Building Block Skills 19, 22, 23, 24, 27, 29, 30, 40, 59, 69, 76, 81, 100, 105, 107	Challenge worksheets Extend the Math Lesson Activities in TE

Understanding Polynomial Expressions

Common Core Math Standards

The student is expected to:

 **A-SSE.A.1a**

Interpret parts of an expression, such as terms, factors, and coefficients. Also A-SSE.A.1b, A-SSE.A.2, A-APR.A.1, A-CED.A.1

Mathematical Practices

 **MP.2 Reasoning**

Language Objective

Explain to a partner how to find the degree of a polynomial.

ENGAGE

Essential Question: What are polynomial expressions, and how do you simplify them?

A polynomial expression is a monomial or a sum of monomials. You simplify them by combining like terms.

PREVIEW: LESSON PERFORMANCE TASK

View the Engage section online. Discuss the designs left in the sky by aerial fireworks and the paths the fireworks follow before they explode. Then preview the Lesson Performance Task.

Name _____ Class _____ Date _____

17.1 Understanding Polynomial Expressions

Essential Question: What are polynomial expressions, and how do you simplify them?

Resource Locker

🔍 Explore   Identifying Monomials

A **monomial** is an expression consisting of a number, variable, or product of numbers and variables that have whole number exponents. *Terms* of an expression are parts of the expression separated by plus signs. (Remember that $x - y$ can be written as $x + (-y)$.) A monomial cannot have more than one term, and it cannot have a variable in its denominator. Here are some examples of monomials and expressions that are not monomials.

Monomials					Not Monomials				
4	x	$-4xy$	$0.25x^3$	$\frac{xy}{4}$	$4 + x$	$x - 1$	$0.7x^{-2}$	$0.25x^{-1}$	$\frac{y}{x^3}$

Use the following process to determine if $5ab^2$ is a monomial.

(A) $5ab^2$ has __one__ term(s), so it __could__ be a monomial.

(B) Does $5ab^2$ have a denominator?

__No__

(C) If possible, split it into a product of numbers and variables.

$5ab^2 = 5 \cdot \boxed{a} \cdot \boxed{b^2}$

(D) List the numbers and variables in the product.

Numbers: __5__   Variables: __a, b__

(E) Check the exponent of each variable. Complete the following table.

Variable	Exponent
a	1
b	2

(F) The exponents of the variables in $5ab^2$ are all __whole numbers__. Therefore, $5ab^2$ __is__ a monomial.

(G) Is $\frac{5}{k^2}$ a monomial?

__No, a monomial cannot have a variable in the denominator.__

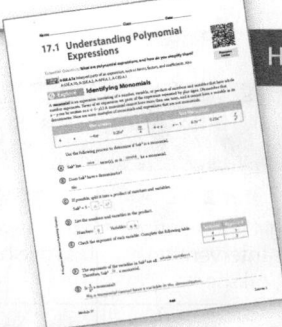

HARDCOVER PAGES 631–640

Turn to these pages to find this lesson in the hardcover student edition.

Term	Is this a monomial?	Explain your reasoning.
$5ab^2$	yes	$5ab^2$ is the product of a number, 5, and the variables a and b.
x^2	yes	x^2 is the product of the variable x, two times.
$\sqrt{y}$	no	$\sqrt{y}$ can be written as $y^{\frac{1}{2}}$. Variables must have whole number exponents.
2^2	yes	2^2 is equal to the number 4. It is the product of 2, two times.
$\dfrac{5}{k^2}$	no	A monomial cannot have a variable in the denominator.
$5x + 7$	no	A monomial cannot have more than one term.
$x^2 + 4ab$	no	A monomial cannot have more than one term.
$\dfrac{k^2}{4}$	yes	$\dfrac{k^2}{4}$ the product of the variable k, two times, times $\dfrac{1}{4}$.

Reflect

1. **Discussion** Explain why $16^{\frac{1}{3}}$ is a monomial but $x^{\frac{1}{3}}$ is not a monomial.

   $16^{\frac{1}{3}}$ is a monomial because it is a number, and numbers are monomials. $x^{\frac{1}{3}}$ is not a

   monomial because monomials can only have variables with whole number exponents.

2. **Discussion** Is x^0 a monomial? Justify your answer in two ways.

   Yes. x^0 and 1 is a number. Also, a variable with a whole number exponent is a monomial

   and 0 is a whole number.

🔧 **Explain 1** **Classifying Polynomials**

A **polynomial** can be a monomial or the sum of monomials. Polynomials are classified by the number of terms they contain. A monomial has one term, a **binomial** has two terms, and a **trinomial** has three terms. $8xy^2 - 5x^3y^3z$, for example, is a binomial.

Polynomials are also classified by their degree. The **degree of a polynomial** is the greatest value among the sums of the exponents on the variables in each term.

The binomial $8xy^2 - 5x^3y^3z$ has two terms. The variables in the first term are x and y. The exponent on x is 1, and the exponent on y is 2. The number 8 is not a variable, so it has a degree of 0. The first term has a degree of $0 + 1 + 2 = 3$. The degree of the second term is $0 + 3 + 3 + 1 = 7$. Therefore, $8xy^2 - 5x^3y^3z$ is a 7th degree binomial.

EXPLORE

Identifying Monomials

QUESTIONING STRATEGIES

❓ Why is $0.3x^{-2}$ not considered to be a monomial? In a monomial, a variable must have whole number exponents.

❓ Why is $\dfrac{1}{2x}$ not considered to be a monomial? Explain. A monomial cannot have a variable in the denominator. Also, $\dfrac{1}{2x} = \dfrac{x^{-1}}{2}$; the exponent in a monomial must be a whole number.

INTEGRATE MATHEMATICAL PRACTICES
Focus on Communication

MP.3 Make sure that students are clear on the definition of a monomial before they begin work on the problems. A *monomial* is *a number, a variable, or a product of numbers and variables that have whole number exponents.*

EXPLAIN 1

Classifying Polynomials

AVOID COMMON ERRORS

Students often confuse the degree of a polynomial with the number of terms. Students may be less likely to confuse the two if they equate the word *degree* with a phrase related to exponents such as *maximum power.*

QUESTIONING STRATEGIES

❓ Why is the degree of a constant always zero? Think of the constant term attached to a variable with degree 0, which is really 1. For example, think of the constant 5 as $5x^0$ which is really 5×1, or 5. This shows that the degree of a constant is 0.

PROFESSIONAL DEVELOPMENT

Math Background

Polynomials are in many ways analogous to counting numbers. Because our number system is base 10, all counting numbers can be written in terms of powers of 10. For example: $653 = 6 \cdot 100 + 5 \cdot 10 + 3 \cdot 1 = 6 \cdot 10^2 + 5 \cdot 10^1 + 3 \cdot 1$. Replacing each of the 10s with a variable creates a polynomial: $6 \cdot 10^2 + 5 \cdot 10^1 + 3 \cdot 10^0 \rightarrow 6 \cdot x^2 + 5 \cdot x^1 + 3 \cdot x^0 = 6x^2 + 5x + 3$. In counting numbers, the only permissible multipliers of the powers of 10 are the digits 0 through 9. For polynomials, any real number can be a multiplier of the variable terms. This analogy demonstrates how diverse mathematical concepts can share underlying structures.

CONNECT VOCABULARY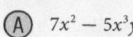

Prefixes such as *mono-*, *bi-*, *tri-*, and *poly-* occur often in English. For example, the word *monotonous* means *having one tone* and the word *bisect* means *cut into two*. In the native languages of some English learners, these prefixes do not occur, so the meanings of *monomial*, *binomial*, *trinomial*, and *polynomial* may not be familiar. Try using language that may be more familiar, such as saying *one term* instead of *monomial* when classifying various polynomials.

EXPLAIN 2

Writing Polynomials in Standard Form

QUESTIONING STRATEGIES

? Why is the coefficient of the term with the greatest degree also the leading coefficient of the polynomial? When a polynomial is written in standard form, the first term has the greatest degree. Its coefficient is the leading coefficient.

INTEGRATE MATHEMATICAL PRACTICES
Focus on Patterns

MP.8 Discuss with students what pattern to look for to determine whether a polynomial is written in standard form. A polynomial is in standard form when written so that the exponents of a variable decrease from left to right. Thus, the coefficient of the first term is called the *leading coefficient* because it leads the polynomial. Point out that the leading coefficient is not the largest coefficient and that it can be positive or negative.

AVOID COMMON ERRORS

Some students may arrange a polynomial using the values of the coefficients instead of the degrees of the terms. Remind them to arrange the terms in order from greatest degree to least degree.

Example 1 Classify each polynomial by its degree and the number of terms.

(A) $7x^2 - 5x^3y^3$

Find the degree of each term by adding the exponents of the variables in that term. The greatest degree is the degree of the polynomial. The degree of the term $-5x^3y^3$ is 6, which you obtain by adding the exponents of x and y: $6 = 3 + 3$. Numbers have degree 0.

$7x^2 - 5x^3y^3$

Degree : 6 $7x^2$ has degree 2, and $-5x^3y^3$ has degree $6 = 3 + 3$.

Binomial   There are two terms.

(B) $3^2 + 2n^3 + 8n$

$3^2 + 2n^3 + 8n$

Degree: 3 3^2 has degree 0 , $2n^3$ has degree 3 , and $8n$ has degree 1 .

Trinomial   There are 3 terms.

Reflect

3. What is the degree of $5x^0y^0 + 5$?
$5x^0 y^0 + 5 = 5 \cdot 1 \cdot 1 + 5 = 10$, a number with a degree of 0.

4. Is $5x^0y^{0.5} + 5$ a polynomial? Justify your answer.
No, the variable y has an exponent of 0.5, which is a decimal number, not a whole number.

Your Turn

Classify each polynomial by its degree and the number of terms.

5. $3x^2y^2 + 3xy^2 + 5xy$

4th degree trinomial

6. $8ab^2 - 3a^2b$

3rd degree binomial

🔵 Explain 2   Writing Polynomials in Standard Form

The terms of a polynomial may be written in any order, but when a polynomial contains only one variable there is a standard form in which it can be written.

The **standard form of a polynomial** containing only one variable is written with the terms in order of decreasing degree. The first term will have the greatest degree, the next term will have the next greatest degree, and so on, until the final term, which will have the lowest degree.

When written in this form, the coefficient of the first term is called **the leading coefficient**.

$5x^4 + 4x^2 + x - 2$ is a 4th degree polynomial written in standard form. It consists of one variable, and its first term is $5x^4$. The leading coefficient is 5 because it is in front of the highest-degree term.

© Houghton Mifflin Harcourt Publishing Company

COLLABORATIVE LEARNING

Peer-to-Peer Activity

Have each student work with a partner to write examples of 1st degree through 6th degree monomials, binomials, and trinomials. Suggest that they create a table to organize their work. Encourage students to write some polynomials with more than one variable per term. Have partners exchange their polynomials so that each one can check that the other's polynomials fit the descriptions.

Example 2 Write each polynomial in standard form. Then give the leading coefficient.

(A) $20x - 4x^3 + 1 - 2x^2$

Find the degree of each term and then arrange them in descending order of their degree.

$$20x - 4x^3 + 1 - 2x^2 = -4x^3 - 2x^2 + 20x + 1$$
Degree: $\underbrace{}_{1}\ \underbrace{}_{3}\ \underbrace{}_{0}\ \underbrace{}_{2}\quad \underbrace{}_{3}\ \underbrace{}_{2}\ \underbrace{}_{1}\ \underbrace{}_{0}$

The standard form is $-4x^3 - 2x^2 + 20x + 1$. The leading coefficient is -4.

(B) $z^3 - z^6 + 4z$

Find the degree of each term and then arrange them in descending order of their degree.

$$z^3 - z^6 + 4z = \boxed{-z^6} \boxed{+z^3} \boxed{+4z}$$
Degree: $\boxed{3}\ \boxed{6}\ \boxed{1}\qquad \boxed{6}\ \boxed{3}\ \boxed{1}$

The standard form is $\underline{-z^6 + z^3 + 4z}$. The leading coefficient is $\boxed{-1}$.

Your Turn

Write each polynomial in standard form. Then give the leading coefficient.

7. $10 - 3x^2 + x^5 + 4x^3$
$x^5 + 4x^3 - 3x^2 + 10,\ 1$

8. $18y^5 - 3y^8 + 10y$
$-3y^8 + 18y^5 + 10y,\ -3$

9. $10x + 13 - 15x^2$
$-15x^2 + 10x + 13,\ -15$

10. $-3b^2 + 2b - 7 + 6b^3 + 12b^4 + 7$
$12b^4 + 6b^3 - 3b^2 + 2b,\ 12$

⊘ Explain 3   Simplifying Polynomials

Polynomials are simplified by combining like terms. Like terms are monomials that have the same variables raised to the same powers. Unlike terms have different powers.

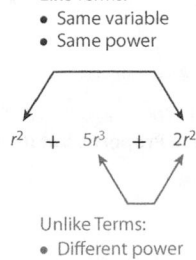

Like Terms:
• Same variable
• Same power

$r^2\ +\ 5r^3\ +\ 2r^2$

Unlike Terms:
• Different power

© Houghton Mifflin Harcourt Publishing Company

DIFFERENTIATE INSTRUCTION

Kinesthetic Experience

Divide students into groups of four, and have each group member write a monomial on an index card in large print. Students may write a constant or a monomial with a variable. Tell them the variable must be x, but it can be raised to any power between 1 and 4, and it can have any coefficient. Then have the students in each group stand and arrange themselves to form a polynomial written in standard form. If two students use the same power of x, the student who has the larger coefficient should stand first. Have students identify the leading coefficient of the polynomial.

EXPLAIN 3

Simplifying Polynomials

CONNECT VOCABULARY EL

English learners may know the word *like* when referring to a preference, but may be unfamiliar with the phrases *like terms* and *unlike terms*. Have students demonstrate their understanding of like and unlike terms by using items that belong to the same category.

2 apples + 3 oranges (unlike)

2 cats + 3 dogs (unlike)

2 apples + 3 apples (like)

2 cats + 4 cats (like)

QUESTIONING STRATEGIES

? What mathematical property allows you to rearrange the terms of a polynomial? **The Commutative Property of Addition allows you to switch the order of two addends.**

? What does rearrangement of the terms accomplish? **The rearrangement groups like terms with one another so they can be combined.**

? What mathematical property allows you to combine the like terms of a polynomial? **The Distributive Property of Addition allows you to factor out a common factor of like terms so that you can simplify the polynomial.**

Focus on Reasoning

MP.2 Make sure that students understand how the Distributive Property is used to simplify polynomials. Give an example using simple numbers to demonstrate, such as $5(4) + 3(4) = 4(5 + 3)$. Students should recognize that the common factor, 4, can be "taken out" and distributed over the sum of the other two factors.

AVOID COMMON ERRORS

In determining the degree of a polynomial, some students forget to count 1 for the exponent of a variable that has no visible exponent. Remind them that $x = x^1$, so, it has degree 1.

Identify like terms and combine them using the Distributive Property. Simplify.

$r^2 + 5r^3 + 2r^2$

$(r^2 + 2r^2) + 5r^3$ Identify like terms by grouping them together in parentheses.

$r^2(1 + 2) + 5r^3$ Combine using the Distributive Property.

$3r^2 + 5r^3$ Simplify.

Example 3   Combine like terms to simplify each polynomial.

(A) $-2y^3 - 8y^2 + y^2 + 2y^3$

$-2y^3 + 2y^3 - 8y^2 + y^2$ Rearrange in descending order of exponents.

$(-2y^3 + 2y^3) + (-8y^2 + y^2)$ Group like terms.

$y^3(-2 + 2) + y^2(-8 + 1)$ Combine using the Distributive Property.

$y^3(0) + y^2(-7)$ Simplify.

$-7y^2$

(B) $p^2q^3 - 4p^5q^4 - 4p^2q^3 + 3p^5q^4$

$-4p^5q^4 + 3p^5q^4 + p^2q^3 - 4p^2q^3$ Rearrange in descending order of exponents.

$(-4p^5q^4 + 3p^5q^4) + (p^2q^3 - 4p^2q^3)$ Group like terms.

$p^5q^4 \boxed{-4 + 3} + p^2q^3 \boxed{1 - 4}$ Combine using the Distributive Property.

$p^5q^4 \boxed{-1} + p^2q^3 \boxed{-3}$ Simplify.

$-p^5q^4 - 3p^2q^3$

Reflect

11. Can you combine like terms without formally showing the Distributive Property? Explain.
You do not have to show the Distributive Property to use it. In the initial example, you could have simplified with either of these methods, where you place the polynomial in standard form and add coefficients or just identify like terms and add coefficients.

$r^2 + 5r^3 + 2r^2$

$5r^3 + r^2 + 2r^2$ or $r^2 + 5r^3 + 2r^2$

$5r^3 + 3r^2$ $5r^3 + 3r^2$

Both methods depend on the Distributive Property, but its use is not obvious.

Simplify.

12. $3p^2q^2 - 3p^2q^3 + 4p^2q^3 - 3p^2q^2 + pq$
$3p^2q^2 - 3p^2q^3 + 4p^2q^3 - 3p^2q^2 + pq$
$-3q^3p^2 + 4q^3p^2 + 3p^2q^2 - 3p^2q^2 + pq$
$(-3q^3p^2 + 4q^3p^2) + (pq)$
$q^3p^2(-3 + 4) + pq$
$-q^3p^2 + pq$

13. $3(a + b) - 6(b + c) + 8(a - c)$
$3(a + b) - 6(b + c) + 8(a - c)$
$3a + 3b - 6b - 6c + 8a - 8c$
$3a + 8a + 3b - 6b - 6c - 8c$
$11a - 3b - 14c$

14. $ab - a^2 + 4^2 - 5ab + 3a^2 + 10$
$ab - a^2 + 4^2 - 5ab + 3a^2 + 10$
$(-a^2 + 3a^2) + (ab - 5ab) + (16 + 10)$
$2a^2 - 4ab + 26$

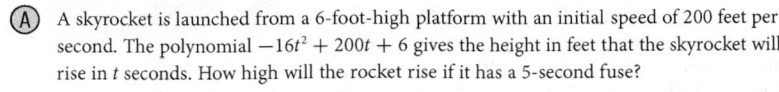 **Explain 4** **Evaluating Polynomials**

Given a polynomial expression describing a real-world situation and a specific value for the variable(s), evaluate the polynomial by substituting for the variable(s). Then interpret the result.

Example 4 Evaluate the given polynomial to find the solution in each real-world scenario.

(A) A skyrocket is launched from a 6-foot-high platform with an initial speed of 200 feet per second. The polynomial $-16t^2 + 200t + 6$ gives the height in feet that the skyrocket will rise in t seconds. How high will the rocket rise if it has a 5-second fuse?

$-16t^2 + 200t + 6$ Write the expression.

$-16(5)^2 + 200(5) + 6$ Substitute 5 for t.

$-16(25) + 200(5) + 6$ Simplify using the order of operations.

$-400 + 1000 + 6$

606

The rocket will rise 606 feet.

(B) Lisa wants to measure the depth of an empty well. She drops a ball from a height of 3 feet into the well and measures how long it takes the ball to hit the bottom of the well. She uses a stopwatch, starting when she lets go of the ball and ending when she hears the ball hit the bottom of the well. The polynomial $-16t^2 + 0t + 3$ gives the height of the ball after t seconds where 0 is the initial speed of the ball and 3 is the initial height the ball was dropped from. Her stopwatch measured a time of 2.2 seconds. How deep is the well? (Neglect the speed of sound and air resistance).

$\underline{-16t^2 + 0t + 3}$ Write the expression.

$\underline{-16(2.2)^2 + 3}$ Substitute $\underline{2.2}$ for t.

$\underline{-16(4.84) + 3}$ Simplify using order of operations.

$\underline{-74.44}$

The ball goes $\boxed{74.44}$ feet below the ground. The well is $\boxed{74.44}$ feet deep.

EXPLAIN 4

Evaluating Polynomials

INTEGRATE TECHNOLOGY

 Students can use a calculator to check that they have evaluated each expression correctly.

QUESTIONING STRATEGIES

When evaluating an expression, what steps do you follow? Explain why. Use the order of operations. First, perform operations in parentheses or other grouping symbols. Second, simplify powers. Third, perform all multiplication and division from left to right. Fourth, perform all addition and subtraction from left to right. If you don't do the steps in order, you may end up with an answer that is incorrect.

LANGUAGE SUPPORT **EL**

Connect Vocabulary

To help students remember the new terminology for this lesson, remind them of other words they know that share these Greek and Latin prefixes:

polynomial – (*poly-* means many) can be one monomial, or the sum or difference of more than one monomial

monomial – (*mono-* means one) has only one term

binomial – (*bi-* means two) has two terms

trinomial – (*tri-* means three) has three terms

Understanding Polynomial Expressions   **810**

ELABORATE

INTEGRATE MATHEMATICAL PRACTICES

Focus on Critical Thinking

MP.3 Discuss the fact that the lowest degree a polynomial can have is 0. Be sure to explain that a polynomial can be a monomial, and a monomial can be a number. A polynomial that is a number has no variables or exponents, so its degree is 0.

SUMMARIZE THE LESSON

? How do you simplify a polynomial? First, rearrange it in descending order of exponents. Then, identify like terms and group them together. Next, use the Distributive Property to factor out a term that is common to each like term. Add or subtract the numbers that are left over. Finally, write the simplified expression.

Solve each real-world scenario.

15. Nate's client said she wanted the width w of every room in her house increased by 2 feet and the length $2w$ decreased by 5 feet. The polynomial $(2w - 5)(w + 2)$ or $2w^2 - w - 10$ gives the new area of any room in the house. The current width of the kitchen is 16 feet. What is the area of the new kitchen?

$2w^2 - w - 10$

$2(16)^2 - (16) - 10 = 486$

The area of the new kitchen is 486 square feet.

16. A skyrocket is launched from a 20-foot-high platform, with an initial speed of 200 feet per second. If the polynomial $-16t^2 + 200t + 20$ gives the height that the rocket will rise in t seconds, how high will a rocket with a 4-second fuse rise?

$-16t^2 + 200t + 20$

$-16(4)^2 + 200(4) + 20 = 564$

The rocket will rise 564 feet.

💬 Elaborate

17. What is the degree of the expression $-16t^2 + 200t + 20$, where t is a variable? What is the degree of the expression if $t = 1$? Are the expressions monomials, binomials, or trinomials?
    When t is a variable, the expression is a 2nd degree trinomial. When $t = 1$, the polynomial is

    evaluated at 1 and it is a constant. A constant is a monomial of degree 0.

18. Two cars drive toward each other along a straight road at a constant speed. The distance between the cars is $\ell - (r_1 + r_2)t$, where r_1 and r_2 are their speeds, t is a variable representing time and ℓ is the length of their original separation. Write the expression in standard form. What is its degree? What is its leading coefficient?
    $-(r_1 + r_2)t + \ell$; **Degree 1;** $-(r_1 + r_2)$ **is its leading coefficient.**

19. The polynomial $-16t^2 + 200t + 20$ gives the height of a projectile launched with an initial speed of 200 feet per second t seconds after launch. A second projectile is launched at the same time but with an initial speed of 300 feet per second, with its height given by the polynomial $-16t^2 + 300t + 20$. How much higher will the second projectile be than the first after 10 seconds?
    Evaluating each expression for $t = 10$ yields a difference of 1000, so the second projectile

    will be 1000 feet higher than the first after 10 seconds.

20. **Essential Question Check-In** What do you have to do to simplify sums of polynomials? What property do you use to accomplish this?
    You simplify sums of polynomials (which are also polynomials) by combining like terms.

    You combine like terms using the Distributive Property.

⭐ Evaluate: Homework and Practice

- Online Homework
- Hints and Help
- Extra Practice

1. Is $(5 + 4x^0)2x$ a monomial? What about $(5 + 4x^2)2x$?

$(5 + 4x^0)2x$ ⠀⠀⠀ $(5 + 4x^2)2x$

$(5 + 4)2x$ ⠀⠀⠀⠀⠀ $2x(5) + 2x(4x^2)$

$(9)2x$ ⠀⠀⠀⠀⠀⠀⠀ $10x + 8x^3$

$18x$

$(5 + 4x^0)2x$ is a monomial,

but $(5 + 4x^2)2x$ is a binomial.

2. Is the sum of two monomials always a monomial? Is their product always a monomial?

Their sum is not always a monomial. For example $x + y$ is not a monomial. The product of two monomials will always be a monomial.

Classify each polynomial by its degree and the number of terms.

3. $x^2 - 5x^3$

3rd degree binomial

4. $x^2 - x^4 + y^2x^3$

5th degree trinomial

5. $a^4b^3 - a^3b^2 + a^2b$

7th degree trinomial

6. $15 + x\sqrt{2}$

1st degree binomial

7. $x + y + z$

1st degree trinomial

8. $a^5 + b^2 + a^2b^2$

5th degree trinomial

Write each polynomial in standard form. Then give the leading coefficient.

9. $2x - 40x^3 - 2x^2$

$-40x^3 - 2x^2 + 2x; -40$

10. $3 + c - c^2$

$-c^2 + c + 3; -1$

11. $3b^2 - 2b + b^2$

$4b^2 - 2b; 4$

12. $4a - 3a + 21 + 6$

$a + 27; 1$

Simplify each polynomial.

13. $-2y^3 - y^2 + y^2 + y^3$

$-2y^3 - y^2 + y^2 + y^3$

$(y^3 - 2y^3) + (-y^2 + y^2)$

$y^3(1 - 2) + y^2(-1 + 1)$

$y^3(-1) + y^2(0)$

$-y^3$

14. $-y^3x - y^2x + y^2 + y^3x + y^2$

$-y^3x - y^2x + y^2 + y^3x + y^2$

$(-y^3x + y^3x) - y^2x + (y^2 + y^2)$

$y^3x(-1 + 1) - y^2x + y^2(1 + 1)$

$y^3x(0) - y^2x + y^2(2)$

$-y^2x + 2y^2$

EVALUATE

ASSIGNMENT GUIDE

Concepts and Skills	Practice
Explore Identifying Monomials	Exercises 1–2, 23
Example 1 Classifying Polynomials	Exercises 3–8
Example 2 Writing Polynomials in Standard Form	Exercises 9–12, 21
Example 3 Simplifying Polynomials	Exercises 13–16, 24
Example 4 Evaluating Polynomials	Exercises 17–20, 22, 25

COLLABORATIVE LEARNING

Have students work in small groups. Give each group a set of cards that each show a monomial, binomial, trinomial, or polynomial with more than three terms. Include some like terms and do not write them in standard form. Also give the group cards with the words *monomial, binomial, trinomial,* and *polynomial.* Have students match each polynomial to the correct word. Then have the students in each group simplify the polynomials by combining like terms and writing them in standard form.

Exercise	Depth of Knowledge (D.O.K.)	COMMON CORE Mathematical Practices
1	**1** Recall of Information	**MP.2** Reasoning
2	**2** Skills/Concepts	**MP.3** Logic
3–16	**1** Recall of Information	**MP.2** Reasoning
17–19	**2** Skills/Concepts	**MP.4** Modeling
20	**3** Strategic Thinking	**MP.4** Modeling
21	**2** Skills/Concepts **H.O.T.**	**MP.3** Logic

Understanding Polynomial Expressions　**812**

When determining the degree of a polynomial, some students tally all of the exponents in all of the terms rather than choosing the single term with the greatest sum of exponents. Remind students that the degree of a polynomial is equal to the highest degree of any monomial in the polynomial.

15. $xyz\sqrt[3]{2} + 2^5xyz + 2^{10}xy$

$xyz\sqrt[3]{2} + 2^5xyz + 2^{10}xy$

$xyz\left(\sqrt[3]{2} + 2^5\right) + 2^{10}xy$

or

$\left(32 + \sqrt[3]{2}\right)xyz + 1024xy$

16. $a^3 + a^2 + ab$

$a^3 + a^2 + ab$

It is already simplified.

Use the information to solve the problem.

17. Persevere in Problem Solving Lisa is measuring the depth of a well. She drops a ball from a height of h feet into the well and measures how long it takes the ball to hit the bottom of the well. The polynomial $-16t^2 + 0t + h$ models this situation, where 0 is the initial speed of the ball and h is the height it was dropped from. (This is a different well from the problem you solved before.) She raises her arm very high and drops the ball from a height of 6.0 feet. Her stopwatch measured a time of 3.5 seconds. How deep is the well?

$-16t^2 + 0t + h$

$-16(3.5)^2 + 6$

$-16(12.25) + 6$

$-196 + 6$

-190

The well is 190 feet deep.

18. Multi-Step Claire and Richard are both artists who use square canvases. Claire uses the polynomial $50x^2 + 250$ to decide how much to charge for her paintings, and Richard uses the polynomial $40x^2 + 350$ to decide how much to charge for his paintings. In each polynomial, x is the height of the painting in feet.

a. How much does Claire charge for a 6-foot painting?

$50(6)^2 + 250 = 1800 + 250 = \$2050$

b. How much does Richard charge for a 5-foot painting?

$40(5)^2 + 350 = 40 \cdot 25 + 350 = \$1350$

c. To the nearest tenth, for what height will both Claire and Richard charge the same amount for a painting? Explain how to find the answer.

You set the expressions equal and solve.

$50x^2 + 250 = 40x^2 + 350$

$10x^2 = 100$

$x^2 = 10$

$x = \sqrt{10} \approx 3.2 \text{ feet}$

d. When both Claire and Richard charge the same amount for a painting, how much does each charge?

$40(10) + 350 = 400 + 350 = \$750$

Exercise	Depth of Knowledge (D.O.K.)	COMMON CORE Mathematical Practices
22	**3** Strategic Thinking H.O.T.	**MP.3** Logic
23	**2** Skills/Concepts H.O.T.	**MP.3** Logic
24	**3** Strategic Thinking H.O.T.	**MP.3** Logic
25	**2** Skills/Concepts H.O.T.	**MP.2** Reasoning

19. Make a Prediction The number of cells in a bacteria colony increases according to a polynomial expression that depends on the temperature. The expression for the number of bacteria is $t^2 + 4t + 4$ when the temperature of the colony is 20°C and $t^2 + 3t + 4$ when the colony grows at 30°C. t represents the time in seconds that the colony grows at the given temperature.

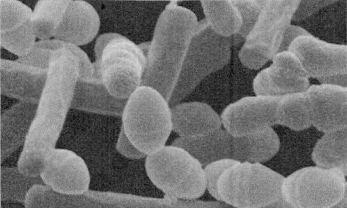

a. After 1 minute, will the population be greater in a colony at 20°C or 30°C? Explain.

$t^2 + 4t + 4$	$t^2 + 3t + 4$
$(60)^2 + 4(60) + 4$	$(60)^2 + 3(60) + 4$
$3600 + 240 + 4$	$3600 + 180 + 4$
3844	3784

When t is 60 seconds, the colony at 20°C will have 60 more bacteria.

b. After 10 minutes, how will the colonies compare in size? Explain.

The colony at 20°C will have 600 more bacteria after 10 minutes.

c. After 1000 minutes, how will the colonies compare in size? Will one colony always have more bacteria? Explain.

The colony at 20°C will have 60,000 more bacteria after 1000 minutes.

After $t = 0$, the 20°C colony will always have t more bacteria.

20. Two cars are driving toward each other along a straight road. Their separation distance is $\ell - (r_1 + r_2)t$, where ℓ is their original separation distance and r_1 and r_2 are their speeds. Will the cars meet? When? What if they are going in the same direction and not driving toward one another? Will they meet then?

$$\ell - (r_1 + r_2)t = 0 \Rightarrow \ell = (r_1 + r_2)t \Rightarrow \frac{\ell}{r_1 + r_2} = t$$

If they are going in the same direction, you can change the sign of one of

the rates $t = \frac{\ell}{r_1 - r_2} \rightarrow r_1 - r_2 > 0 \rightarrow r_1 > r_2$. If both cars are going to the

right, the one on the left has to go faster and they will meet at $t = \frac{\ell}{r_1 - r_2}$.

If they are going the same speed, however, t will be undefined or negative

and they will never meet.

GRAPHIC ORGANIZERS

Divide students into groups of three or four and have them create posters to reinforce their understanding of polynomials. Have half the groups make posters titled *Polynomials* and the other half make posters titled *Not Polynomials*. Each poster should include the definition of a polynomial and give three examples of polynomials or non-polynomials. Have the group that writes polynomials write each one in standard form and identify its degree. Have the group that writes non-polynomials explain why each example is not a polynomial.

For many students it is easier to identify the degree of each term in a polynomial when every term is written with the variables and their exponents. Encourage students to look at each term of a polynomial. If a variable does not have an exponent, have them write a 1 as the exponent. Then have them circle each exponent and add the exponents of the variables in a term to find the degree of the term. Repeat the procedure for each term in a polynomial. The greatest degree among the terms is the degree of the polynomial.

JOURNAL

Have students explain how to classify a polynomial according to its degree and number of terms.

© Houghton Mifflin Harcourt Publishing Company

21. Explain the Error Enrique thinks that the polynomial $2^2x^2 + 2^3x + 2^4$ has a degree of 4 since $2 + 2 = 3 + 1 = 4$. Explain his error and determine the correct degree.
Enrique treated the numbers like variables, but their degree is 0.

The degree of the polynomial is 2 from the exponent of 2 over the x in the term 2^2x^2.

22. Analyze Relationships Sewell is doing a problem regarding the area of pairs of squares. Sewell says that the expression $(x + 1)^2$ will be greater than $(x - 1)^2$ for all values of x because $x + 1$ will always be greater than $x - 1$. Why is he correct when the expressions are areas of squares? Is he correct for any real x outside this model?

If $x = 0$, they are equal.
$$(0 + 1)^2 = (1)^2 = 1 \qquad (0 - 1)^2 = (-1)^2 = 1$$
If $x < 0$, then $(x + 1)^2 < (x - 1)^2$.

The expressions are areas of squares, which are strictly positive. The lengths of the sides are $x + 1$ and $x - 1$, which are also strictly positive. Thus, $x - 1 > 0 \rightarrow x > 1$. For these values of x, the expression $(x + 1)^2 > (x - 1)^2$ will always be true. He is correct in this model but not correct for all real values of x.

23. Counterexamples Prove by counterexample that the sum of monomials is not necessarily a monomial.

By counterexample, $x + y$ is not a monomial, although it is a sum of monomials.

24. Communicate Mathematical Ideas Polynomials are simplified by combining like terms. When combining like terms, you use the Distributive Property. Prove that the Distributive Property, $a \cdot (b + c) = a \cdot b + a \cdot c$, holds over the positive integers $a, b, c > 0$ from the definition of multiplication: $a \cdot b = \underbrace{a + a + \ldots + a}_{b \text{ times}}$.

$$a \cdot b + a \cdot c = \underbrace{a + a + \ldots + a}_{b \text{ times}} + \underbrace{a + a + \ldots + a}_{c \text{ times}} = \underbrace{a + a + \ldots + a}_{b + c \text{ times}} = a \cdot (b + c)$$

The a variables can be "shuffled" around using the Associative and Commutative Properties of the integers. Induction should be used to be very rigorous.

25. Analyze Relationships A right triangle has height h and base $h + 8$. Write an expression that represents the area of the triangle. Then calculate the area of a triangle with a height of 16 cm.

$\frac{1}{2}h(h + 8)$; **area = 192 cm²**

Lesson Performance Task

A pyrotechnics specialist is designing a firework spectacular for a company's 75th anniversary celebration. She can vary the launch speed to 200, 250, 300, or 400 feet per second, and can set the fuse on each firework for 3, 4, 5, or 6 seconds. Create a table of the various heights the fireworks can explode at if the height of the firework is modeled by the function $h(t) = -16t^2 + v_0 t$, where t is the time in seconds and v_0 is the initial speed of the firework.

Design a fireworks show using 3 firing heights and at least 30 fireworks. Have some fireworks go off simultaneously at different heights. Describe your display so you will know what needs to be launched and when they will go off.

The polynomials are as follows:

$h_A(t) = -16t^2 + 200t$

$h_B(t) = -16t^2 + 250t$

$h_C(t) = -16t^2 + 300t$

$h_D(t) = -16t^2 + 400t$

The table shows the value of each polynomial

evaluated at 3, 4, 5, and 6 seconds. The method

of evaluation is shown below.

$h_A(3) = -16(3)^2 + 200(3)$

$\qquad = -16(9) + 600$

$\qquad = -144 + 600$

$\qquad = 456$

Launch Speed	3 Second Fuse	4 Second Fuse	5 Second Fuse	6 Second Fuse
200	456	544	600	624
250	606	744	850	924
300	756	944	1100	1224
400	1056	1344	1600	1824

The remainder of the answers will vary, but all answers should involve a list

of when the fireworks will go off, the speeds fired, and the fuse settings.

Answers should also include a second list showing which fireworks are

exploding every second and their heights.

EXTENSION ACTIVITY

Ask students to consider the path of a firework that goes up and comes back down without exploding. Have them use graphing calculators, trial and error, or equation solving to find the maximum height that a firework reaches with each launch speed.

Students can analyze each firework's height after t seconds by entering the functions on a graphing calculator. They can use the **TRACE** or **TABLE** features to find the maximum height. The fireworks launched at 200, 250, 300, and 400 feet per second reach maximum heights of 625, 976, 1406, and 2500 feet, respectively.

CONNECT VOCABULARY [EL]

Some students may not be familiar with the terms in this Lesson Performance Task. Have a student volunteer describe *pyrotechnics*, *launch speed*, and *fuse*. Pyrotechnics is *the art of making fireworks.* Launch speed is *the speed of each firework at the moment it is fired.* A *fuse* is *a flammable cord that is lit in order to set off an explosive.*

INTEGRATE TECHNOLOGY

Students can use a calculator to check that they have evaluated the polynomials correctly.

Scoring Rubric

2 points: Student correctly solves the problem and explains his/her reasoning.

1 point: Student shows good understanding of the problem but does not fully solve or explain his/her reasoning.

0 points: Student does not demonstrate understanding of the problem.

Understanding Polynomial Expressions   **816**

Adding Polynomial Expressions

Common Core Math Standards

The student is expected to:

 A-APR.A.1

Understand that polynomials form a system analogous to the integers, namely, they are closed under the operations of addition... Also A-SSE.A.1, A-CED.A.1

Mathematical Practices

COMMON CORE **MP.7 Using Structure**

Language Objective

Explain to a partner how to add two polynomial expressions.

ENGAGE

Essential Question: How do you add polynomials?

Combine the like terms of the polynomials.

PREVIEW: LESSON PERFORMANCE TASK

View the Engage section online. Discuss why a lap pool is likely to have a rectangular prism shape while other pools may have different shapes. Then preview the Lesson Performance Task.

Name _____ Class _____ Date _____

17.2 Adding Polynomial Expressions

Essential Question: How do you add polynomials?

Resource Locker

⊘ Explore **Modeling Polynomial Addition Using Algebra Tiles**

You have added numbers and variables, which is the same as adding polynomials of degree 0 and degree 1. Adding polynomials of higher degree is similar, but there are more possible like terms to consider.

You can use algebra tiles to model polynomial addition.

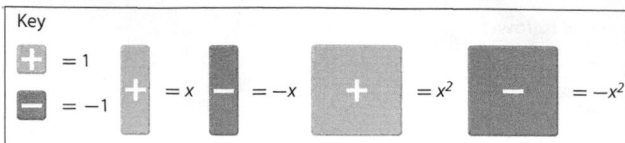

Key
$+$ = 1
$-$ = -1
$+$ = x
$-$ = -x
$+$ = x^2
$-$ = $-x^2$

As the Key shows, a different-sized tile represents each monomial. Like terms have the same shape and size, but if they are positive, they have a + (plus) sign. If they are negative, they have a − (minus) sign. Use these visual aids to add polynomials.

To add polynomials, start by representing each addend with tiles. Add them by placing the tiles for each polynomial next to each other. Cancel out opposite tiles that are of the same size but have a different symbol. Count the remaining tiles of each size and note the symbol. Translate the tiles to a polynomial. This polynomial represents the simplified sum.

Use algebra tiles to find $(2x^2 - x) + (x^2 + 3x - 1)$.

Ⓐ Which of the two polynomials in the addition expression do these algebra tiles represent?

Model	Algebra
+ + −	$2x^2 - x$

Ⓑ Which polynomial do these algebra tiles represent?

Model	Algebra
+ + + + −	$x^2 + 3x - 1$

Module 17 **817** Lesson 2

© Houghton Mifflin Harcourt Publishing Company

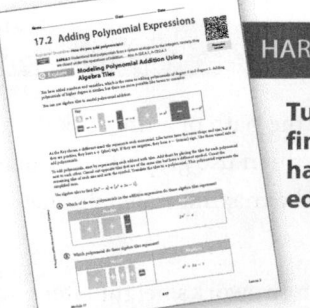

HARDCOVER PAGES 641–648

Turn to these pages to find this lesson in the hardcover student edition.

C Place the algebra tiles representing each expression next to each other. This represents (addition)/subtraction.

Model	Algebra
	$(2x^2 - x) + (x^2 + 3x - 1)$

D Rearrange tiles so that like tiles are together. *Like tiles* are the same size and shape.

Model	Algebra
	$2x^2 + x^2 - x + 3x - 1$

E *Zero pairs* are like tiles with opposite signs. Together they equal zero. Simplify the sum by __removing__ zero pairs.

Model	Algebra
	$3x^2 + 2x - 1$

Reflect

1. **Discussion** What properties of addition allow you to rearrange the tiles?
The Associative and Commutative Properties allow you to rearrange the tiles.

⚙ Explain 1 Adding Polynomials Using a Vertical Format

To add polynomials vertically, add like terms in columns. Write the first polynomial in standard form; then write the second polynomial below the first, aligning like terms. Use a monomial with a zero coefficient as a placeholder for missing terms. Add the coefficients of each group and write the sum aligned with the like terms above. Simplify if necessary.

EXPLORE

Modeling Polynomial Addition Using Algebra Tiles

INTEGRATE TECHNOLOGY

Students may either complete the algebra tiles activity online or use physical tiles and record their work in the book.

INTEGRATE MATHEMATICAL PRACTICES

Focus on Modeling

MP.4 Compare like terms and like tiles. In like terms, the same variables are raised to the same powers, but the coefficients may differ. In like tiles, the size and shape are the same, but the number of tiles and the color of the tiles (whether they are positive or negative) may differ.

EXPLAIN 1

Adding Polynomials Using a Vertical Format

QUESTIONING STRATEGIES

? How can you add two polynomials using a vertical format if a particular power of the variable appears in one polynomial but not the other? Leave a space in that column, or write the term with a coefficient of 0.

INTEGRATE MATHEMATICAL PRACTICES

Focus on Reasoning

MP.2 Point out that the number of terms in the sum of two polynomials may be the same as or less than the sum of the number of terms in the two polynomials. Ask students to give examples of both cases and justify their examples.

PROFESSIONAL DEVELOPMENT

Learning Progressions

In this lesson, students begin to work with polynomial expressions that can model real-world situations. They learn to use the Commutative and Associative Properties of addition and the Distributive Property to add polynomials. Adding polynomial expressions produces polynomial expressions, so the set of polynomial expressions is closed under addition. Students will see that operations with polynomials abide by the same properties as those of real numbers. As students progress into higher mathematics, they will apply many of the real number properties and operational algorithms to polynomial expressions.

AVOID COMMON ERRORS

Students may forget to follow the rules for adding positive and negative integers. Remind them that if the signs of two integers are not the same, they must subtract the integers and use the sign of the integer that is farther from 0.

Example 1 Use the vertical format to find the sum.

(A) $5x^2 + 2x - 1$ and $4x^2 - x + 2$

$(5x^2 + 2x - 1) + (4x^2 - x + 2)$

Rewrite the problem, vertically aligning the terms.

$$\begin{array}{r} 5x^2 + 2x - 1 \\ +4x^2 - 1x + 2 \\ \hline 9x^2 + 1x + 1 \end{array}$$

Simplify.

$9x^2 + x + 1$

(B) $3y^3 + 2y + 1$ and $y^2 - 1$

$(3y^3 + 2y + 1) + (y^2 - 1)$

Rewrite the problem, vertically aligning the terms.

$$\begin{array}{r} 3y^3 + \boxed{0}\,y^2 + \quad 2y + \boxed{1} \\ +0y^3 + \quad 1y^2 + \boxed{0}\,y + \boxed{-1} \\ \hline 3y^3 + \boxed{1y^2} + \quad 2y + \boxed{0} \end{array}$$

Simplify.

$3y^3 + y^2 + 2y$

Reflect

2. Is the sum of two polynomials always another polynomial? Explain.
    Yes; the two addends consist of a sum of monomials that can be rearranged using

    the Associative and Commutative Properties to make a sum of monomials with more

    elements: another polynomial.

Your Turn

Add the given polynomials using the vertical format.

3. $-x^2 - 1$ and $4x^2 - x$
$$\begin{array}{r} -x^2 + 0x - 1 \\ +4x^2 - 1x + 0 \\ \hline 3x^2 - \ x - 1 \end{array}$$

4. $-z^3 - 2z - 1$ and $2z^3 - z^2 + 2z$
$$\begin{array}{r} -z^3 + 0z^2 - 2z - 1 \\ +2z^3 - 1z^2 + 2z + 0 \\ \hline z^3 - \ z^2 + 0z - 1 = z^3 - z^2 - 1 \end{array}$$

5. $x - 1$ and $4x - 6$
$$\begin{array}{r} x - 1 \\ +4x - 6 \\ \hline 5x - 7 \end{array}$$

COLLABORATIVE LEARNING

Peer-to-Peer Activity

Have students work in pairs. Prepare a bag with small slips of paper (at least four times as many slips as there are students), each with one of the following written on it: 7, −3, 8, −5, x, $2x$, −3x, 4x, −6x, 5x^2, x^2, −2x^2, and 8x^2. Have each student randomly select three slips of paper, then combine the terms, simplify if possible, and write the resulting polynomial. Then have each pair of students find the sum of their polynomials.

⊘ Explain 2 Adding Polynomials Using a Horizontal Format

To add polynomials horizontally, combine like terms. Use the Associative and Commutative Properties to regroup. Place all like terms within the same parentheses. Combine like terms by adding their coefficients, simplifying if necessary.

Example 2 Add the polynomials using the horizontal format.

(A) $5x^2 + 2x + 1$ and $-4x^2 - x - 2$

$(5x^2 + 2x + 1) + (-4x^2 - x - 2)$ Add.

$= (5x^2 - 4x^2) + (2x - x) + (1 - 2)$ Group like terms by using the Commutative and Associative Properties.

$= x^2 + x - 1$ Combine like terms.

(B) $-ab + b$ and $ab - a$

$(-ab + b) + (ab - a)$ Add.

$= \left(-ab + \boxed{ab}\right) + b + \left(\boxed{-a}\right)$ Group like terms together.

$= \boxed{b - a}$ Combine like terms.

Your Turn

Use the horizontal format to find the sum.

6. $(-6x^2 + 2)$ and $(-4x^2)$

$(-6x^2 + 2) + (-4x^2)$
$= (-6x^2 - 4x^2) + 2$
$= -10x^2 + 2$

7. $(-x^3 + 2)$ and $(-4x^3 + y + x)$

$(-x^3 + 2) + (-4x^3 + y + x)$
$= (-x^3 - 4x^3) + x + y + 2$
$= -5x^3 + x + y + 2$

8. $(y - 7)$ and $(3y + 18)$

$(y - 7) + (3y + 18)$
$= (y + 3y) + (-7 + 18)$
$= 4y + 11$

DIFFERENTIATE INSTRUCTION

Curriculum Integration

Connect the lesson to creative writing by having students create a narrative scenario that involves addition of polynomials. Urge students to be creative in working the math concepts into a story format. Examples might include two builders comparing buildings to see which holds more material; private detectives trying to solve a mystery; NASA engineers planning to send rockets to another planet; or businesspeople finding ways to maximize their profits. Have students present their creations to the class, and challenge classmates to solve the problems that are presented.

EXPLAIN 2

Adding Polynomials Using a Horizontal Format

QUESTIONING STRATEGIES

? Why is it important to write the terms in each polynomial in order of degree before adding the polynomials? It is easier to see whether there are like terms in the two polynomials and it is easier to group the like terms.

CONNECT VOCABULARY EL

The Commutative Property is sometimes referred to as the *order property* because the order of the addends does not affect the sum. Point out that the word *commutative* sounds like *commute*, which means *to go back and forth*. In the Commutative Property, the terms can go back and forth, changing places, just as a commuter goes between home and work.

The Associative Property is sometimes called the *grouping property* because the grouping of the addends doesn't affect the sum. Point out that the word *associative* is related to *associate*. Explain to students that their *associates* are those they join together with, in pairs or groups. In the Associative Property, the terms can be grouped together.

AVOID COMMON ERRORS

Remind students that when they add like terms, the variable part never changes.

Adding Polynomial Expressions **820**

EXPLAIN 3

Modeling with Polynomials

QUESTIONING STRATEGIES

? Do you get the same result whether you add the polynomials in the problem vertically or horizontally? Why or why not? **Yes; in either case you find the sum by combining like terms, so the results of the two methods are the same.**

AVOID COMMON ERRORS

Point out that the best way to avoid errors when adding complicated polynomials is to rewrite them with like terms grouped before combining them. Students who try to combine terms in their heads often get confused or make arithmetic mistakes. Encourage students to rewrite the terms in each step of the process to avoid errors.

INTEGRATE TECHNOLOGY

When solving a real-world problem by modeling with a polynomial, students may need to evaluate the polynomial. Students can use a graphing calculator to evaluate the polynomial for a particular value.

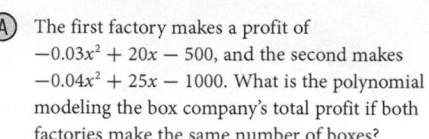

You can model many situations using polynomials. Sometimes you can model a new situation by adding two or more polynomials.

For example, a company offers two services. The number of people using each service at a given time can be modeled by polynomials that use the same variable. The total number of people using both services can be modeled by adding the two polynomials.

Example 3 A box company owns two factories in different parts of the country. The profit for each factory is modeled by a polynomial with x representing the number of boxes each produces. Solve by adding the polynomials. The models needed in each situation are provided.

(A) The first factory makes a profit of $-0.03x^2 + 20x - 500$, and the second makes $-0.04x^2 + 25x - 1000$. What is the polynomial modeling the box company's total profit if both factories make the same number of boxes?

$$\left(-0.03x^2 + 20x - 500\right) + \left(-0.04x^2 + 25x - 1000\right) \qquad \text{Add.}$$

$$= \left(-0.03x^2 - 0.04x^2\right) + \left(20x + 25x\right) + \left(-500 - 1000\right) \qquad \text{Group like terms together.}$$

$$= -0.07x^2 + 45x - 1,500 \qquad \text{Simplify.}$$

The factories make a total profit of $-0.07x^2 + 45x - 1500$.

(B) The company plans to open a third factory with a projected profit of $-0.03x^2 + 50x - 100$. What will be the total profit of the box company, written as a polynomial, if the projected profit is correct?

The total profit from the first two factories mentioned is $-0.07x^2 + 45x - 1500$. The projected profit from the new factory is $-0.03x^2 + 50x - 100$. Add to solve.

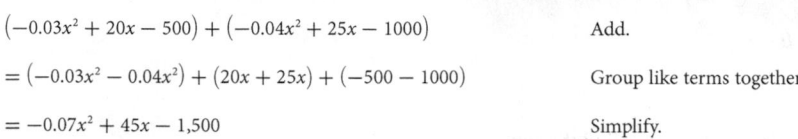

$$\left(-0.07x^2 + 45x - 1,500\right) + \left(-0.03x^2 + 50x - 100\right) \qquad \text{Add.}$$

$$= \left(-0.07x^2 - 0.03x^2\right) + \left(45x + 50x\right) + \left(-1,500 - 100\right) \qquad \text{Group like terms together.}$$

$$= -0.10x^2 + 95x - 1600 \qquad \text{Simplify.}$$

The total projected profit is 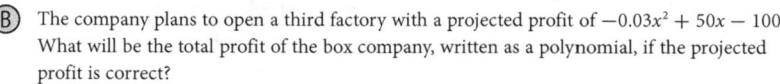 $\underline{-0.10x^2 + 95x - 1600}$.

LANGUAGE SUPPORT EL

Connect Vocabulary

Students who speak Latin-based languages, such as Spanish, French, or Portuguese, may recognize many math words and concepts that are shared as cognates. Students who have an academic language background in Spanish may recognize these terms:

English	Spanish
properties of addition	propiedades de la adición
commutative	conmutativa
associative	asociativa

9. **Discussion** How could the polynomials be added if the first factory produced x boxes, the second factory produce y boxes, and the third company z boxes? What kind of polynomial would it be?

The polynomial would be

$-0.03x^2 + 20x - 500 - 0.04y^2 + 25y - 1000 - 0.03z^2 + 50z - 100$

$= -0.03x^2 - 0.04y^2 - 0.03z^2 + 20x + 25y + 50z - 1600$

Here x, y, and z are the different number of boxes each factory produced. The only like

terms that can be combined are the constants. It is a 2nd degree polynomial with 7 terms.

Model various situations with the sum of polynomials. Simplify their sum.

10. A scientist is growing cell cultures and examining the effects of various substances on them as part of his research. The culture in one petri dish increases according to the expression $t^2 + 4t + 4$ for time t in minutes. Another increases according to $t^2 + 2t + 4$. He needs to feed all the cells equally, so he needs to know the expression for the total number of cells in both dishes because the food is proportional to the total number of cells. Find the expression.

$\left(t^2 + 4t + 4\right) + \left(t^2 + 2t + 4\right)$

$= \left(t^2 + t^2\right) + \left(4t + 2t\right) + \left(4 + 4\right)$

$= 2t^2 + 6t + 8$ The total number of cells is $2t^2 + 6t + 8$ for time t.

11. A farmer must add the areas of two plots of land to determine the amount of seed to plant. The area of Plot A can be represented by $3x^2 + 7x - 5$, and the area of Plot B can be represented by $5x^2 - 4x + 11$. Write a polynomial that represents the total area of both plots of land.

$\left(3x^2 + 7x - 5\right) + \left(5x^2 - 4x + 11\right)$

$= \left(3x^2 + 5x^2\right) + \left(7x - 4x\right) + \left(-5 + 11\right)$

$= 8x^2 + 3x + 6$

Elaborate

12. Is adding polynomials horizontally or vertically equivalent? Explain, describing how the steps are similar or different.

Adding polynomials horizontally and vertically is equivalent. In both, you identify like terms

and group them together.

13. A car company is analyzing the profits of two car manufacturing plants. The profit of each plant is modeled by a polynomial. What operation would it use to compute the total profit of both plants? The amount of success of one plant versus the other? The total profit of both plants if the polynomials modeling each plant's profits are the same? Will the results be polynomials?

Sum; difference; sum; the results will all be polynomials.

14. **Essential Question Check-In** What do you have to do to simplify sums of polynomials? What property do you use to accomplish this?

You simplify sums of polynomials (which are also polynomials) by combining like terms.

You combine like terms using the Distributive Property.

© Houghton Mifflin Harcourt Publishing Company

ELABORATE

QUESTIONING STRATEGIES

? Is the sum of two polynomials always another polynomial? Explain. Yes; the two addends consist of a sum of monomials. After adding, the result also consists of a sum of monomials, so it is a polynomial.

? Emma says that the sum of two polynomials of degree 2 is always a polynomial of degree 2. Do you agree? Give an example to explain your answer. No; possible answer:

$\left(x^2 + 3x\right) + \left(-x^2 + 6x + 5\right) = 9x + 5$

SUMMARIZE THE LESSON

? How do you add polynomials? Use a vertical or horizontal format to add polynomials. To use a vertical format, align like terms in columns. To use a horizontal format, group like terms and simplify. Then add the like terms.

EVALUATE

ASSIGNMENT GUIDE

Concepts and Skills	Practice
Explore Modeling Polynomial Addition Using Algebra Tiles	Exercise 2
Example 1 Adding Polynomials Using a Vertical Format	Exercises 3–8
Example 2 Adding Polynomials Using a Horizontal Format	Exercises 1, 9–14, 20–25
Example 3 Modeling with Polynomials	Exercises 15–19

⭐ **Evaluate: Homework and Practice**

• Online Homework
• Hints and Help
• Extra Practice

1. In adding with tiles, one step corresponds to grouping like terms. Do you think this is more similar to the horizontal or vertical method? Explain your reasoning.

This is a lot like the horizontal method, but you can make an argument for either. The algebra in the Explore is written using the horizontal method.

2. Show how to add $(x^2 + x)$ and $(-x^2 - 2x)$ with tiles.

Model	Algebra
	$(x^2 + x) + (-x^2 - 2x)$
	$(x^2 - x^2) + (x - 2x) \quad = \quad -x$

Find each sum vertically.

3. $(x^2 - x^4) + (x^4 - x^2)$

$$\begin{array}{r} -x^4 + x^2 \\ + \quad x^4 - x^2 \\ \hline 0x^4 + 0x^2 \end{array}$$

$$0$$

4. $(y^2 - x^4) + (x^4 - x^2)$

$$\begin{array}{r} y^2 - x^4 + 0x^2 \\ + \quad 0y^2 + x^4 - x^2 \\ \hline y^2 + 0x^4 - x^2 \end{array}$$

$$y^2 - x^2$$

5. Add $0.5x + 2$ and $x^2 + 1.5x$.

$$\begin{array}{r} 0x^2 + 0.5x + 2 \\ + \quad x^2 + 1.5x + 0 \\ \hline x^2 + 2x + 2 \end{array}$$

6. $(2x + y + z) + (-x + y - z)$

$$\begin{array}{r} 2x + y + z \\ + \quad -x + y - z \\ \hline x + 2y + 0z \end{array}$$

$$x + 2y$$

© Houghton Mifflin Harcourt Publishing Company

Exercise	Depth of Knowledge (D.O.K.)	COMMON CORE Mathematical Practices
1	**2** Skills/Concepts	**MP.3** Logic
2–14	**1** Recall of Information	**MP.2** Reasoning
15–16	**1** Recall of Information	**MP.4** Modeling
17	**2** Skills/Concepts	**MP.2** Reasoning
18	**3** Strategic Thinking	**MP.4** Modeling
19	**2** Skills/Concepts H.O.T.	**MP.3** Logic

7. $(x^2 + y + z) + (-x + y - z) + x - y$

$$\begin{array}{r} x^2 + 0x + y + z \\ + 0x^2 - x + y - z \\ \underline{0x^2 + x - y + 0z} \\ x^2 + 0x + y + 0z \\ x^2 + y \end{array}$$

8. $-a^5 + (b^2 + a^2b^2) + (a^5 + b^2 - a^2b^2)$

$$\begin{array}{r} -a^5 + 0b^2 + 0a^2b^2 \\ 0a^5 + b^2 + a^2b^2 \\ \underline{+ a^5 + b^2 - a^2b^2} \\ 0a^5 + 2b^2 + 0a^2b^2 \\ 2b^2 \end{array}$$

Find each sum horizontally.

9. $(-x^2 + x) + (x^2 - x - 1)$

$(-x^2 + x) + (x^2 - x - 1)$

$= (-x^2 + x^2) + (x - x) - 1$

$= -1$

10. $(a + b - c^2) + (a + b)$

$(a + b - c^2) + (a + b)$

$= (a + a) + (b + b) - c^2$

$= 2a + 2b - c^2$

11. $(ab^2 + b^2) + (-2cab^2 + b^2)$

$(ab^2 + b^2) + (-2cab^2 + b^2)$

$= -2cab^2 + ab^2 + (b^2 + b^2)$

$= -2cab^2 + ab^2 + 2b^2$

12. $(2x - x^3 - 2x^2) + (-x^3 - 2x)$

$(2x - x^3 - 2x^2) + (-x^3 - 2x)$

$= (-x^3 - x^3) + (-2x^2) + (2x - 2x)$

$= -2x^3 - 2x^2$

13. $(2^{10}a + ab) + (ab\sqrt[3]{2} + ab - 2^{10}a)$

$(2^{10}a + ab) + (ab\sqrt[3]{2} + ab - 2^{10}a)$

$= (2 + \sqrt[3]{2})ab$

14. $(7q^3r^2 + 6qr^2 + 21q) + (-6qr^2 - qr^2 - 11q - 3q^3r^2)$

$(7q^3r^2 + 6qr^2 + 21q) + (-6qr^2 - qr^2 - 11q - 3q^3r^2)$

$= (7q^3r^2 - 3q^3r^2) - qr^2 + (21q - 11q)$

$= 4q^3r^2 - qr^2 + 10q$

Model various situations using the sum of polynomials. Simplify their sum.

15. A pool is being filled with a large water hose. The height of the water in a pool is determined by $8g^2 + 3g - 4$. Previously, the pool had been filled with a different hose. Then, the height was determined by $6g^2 + 2g - 1$. Write an expression that determines the height of the water in the pool if both hoses are on at the same time. Simplify the expression.

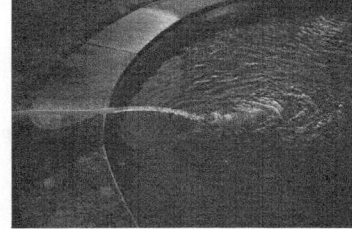

$(8g^2 + 3g - 4) + (6g^2 + 2g - 1)$

$= (8g^2 + 6g^2) + (2g + 3g) + (-4 - 1)$

$= 14g^2 + 5g - 5$

16. The polynomial $-2x^2 + 500x$ represents the budget surplus of the town of Alphaville. Betaville's surplus is represented by $x^2 - 100x + 10,000$. If x represents the tax revenue in thousands from both towns, which expression represents the total surplus of both towns together?

$-2x^2 + 500x + x^2 - 100x + 10,000$

$= -2x^2 + x^2 + 500x - 100x + 10,000$

$= -x^2 + 400x + 10,000$

Exercise	Depth of Knowledge (D.O.K.)	COMMON CORE Mathematical Practices
20	2 Skills/Concepts H.O.T.	MP.3 Logic
21–22	2 Skills/Concepts H.O.T.	MP.3 Logic
23	3 Strategic Thinking H.O.T.	MP.3 Logic
24–25	2 Skills/Concepts H.O.T.	MP.2 Reasoning

AUDITORY CUES

Suggest to students that they say each term aloud as they do the exercises in order to hear the difference between like and unlike terms.

Adding Polynomial Expressions　**824**

AVOID COMMON ERRORS

Remind students to line up the like terms when adding vertically. If a particular power of the variable appears in one polynomial but not in the other, leave a space in that column, or write the term with a coefficient of 0.

VISUAL CUES

Have students highlight like terms in different colors to make it easier to see how to group them.

---

17. Geometry The length of a rectangle is represented by $4a + 3b$, and its width is represented by $3a - 2b$. Write a polynomial for the perimeter of the rectangle. What is the minimum perimeter of the rectangle if $a = 12$ and b is a non-zero whole number?

$2(4a + 3b) + 2(3a - 2b)$

$= 8a + 6b + 6a - 4b$

$= (8a + 6a) + (6b - 4b)$

$= 14a + 2b$

For $a = 12$:

$14a + 2b = 14(12) + 2b$

$\qquad = 168 + 2b$

$\qquad = 168 + 2(1)$

$\qquad = 170$

18. Multi-Step Tara plans to put wallpaper on the walls of her room. She will not put the wallpaper across the doorway, which is 3 feet wide and 7 feet tall.

a. Write an expression that represents the number of square feet of wallpaper she will need if the height of her room is x feet, with a length and width that are each 3 times the height of the room. Assume that the walls are four rectangles.

$A = 2h\ell + 2hw - 21$

$A = 2(x)(3x) + 2(x)(3x) - 21$

$A = 6x^2 + 6x^2 - 21$

$A = 12x^2 - 21$

Tara will need $12x^2 - 21$ square feet of wallpaper for her bedroom.

b. Write the expression for the amount of wallpaper in square feet Tara needs for the living room, which is the same height and width as her bedroom, but has a length that is 5 times the height of the room. The living room has 2 doors that are the same size as the door in her bedroom.

$2h\ell + 2hw - 2(3)(7)$

$= 2(x)(5x) + 2(x)(3x) - 42$

$= 10x^2 + 6x^2 - 42$

$= 16x^2 - 42$

c. Tara decides to get the same wallpaper for both rooms. Write the expression for the total amount of wallpaper she needs.

$(12x^2 - 21) + (16x^2 - 42)$

$= (12x^2 + 16x^2 - 21 - 42)$

$= (28x^2 - 63)$

Tara will need $28x^2 - 63$ square feet of wallpaper.

d. If $x = 8$, how much more wallpaper will Tara need for the living room than for the bedroom?

Living room: $16x^2 - 42 = (16)(64) - 42 = 982$

Bedroom: $12x^2 - 21 = (12)(64) - 21 = 747$

$982 - 747 = 235$

Tara will need 235 more square feet of wallpaper for the living room.

19. Critical Thinking Subtracting one polynomial from another is the same as adding the opposite of the polynomial by distributing a -1.

Substitute $n = -1$ in $(x^2 + x) + n(x^2 + 2x)$ and simplify.

$(x^2 + x) + n(x^2 + 2x)$

$= (x^2 + x) + (-1)(x^2 + 2x)$

$= x^2 + x - x^2 - 2x$

$= (x^2 - x^2) + (x - 2x)$

$= (0) + x(1 - 2)$

$= x(-1)$

$= -x$

20. Multiple Representations Two polynomials model different financial information for a company. The first polynomial, $40,000 + 3x^2$ represents the gross monthly income from selling x units, while the second one, $0.05x + 100$ represents the monthly production cost of x units.

Which of the following expressions models gross income less production costs?

a. $40,000 + 3x^2 - 0.05x + 100$

b. $(40,000 - 100) + 3x^2 - 0.05x$

c. $3x^2 - 0.05x + 39,900$

d. $3x^2 - 0.05x + 40,100$

e. a and b

f. b and c

f. Both b and c are different forms of the answer. c is in simplified form.

21. Explain the Error Jane and Jill were simplifying the expression $(2x^2 + x) + 2(-x^2 + x)$ and obtained different answers. Who is correct and why?

Jane	Jill
$= (2x^2 + x) + 2(-x^2 + x)$	$= (2x^2 + x) + 2(-x^2 + x)$
$= (2x^2 + x) + (-x^2 + x) + (-x^2 + x)$	$= (2x^2 + x) - 2x^2 + x$
$= (2x^2 - x^2 - x^2) + (x + x + x)$	$= 2x$
$= 3x$	

Jane is correct. Jill distributed the 2 incorrectly. She should have written

$= (2x^2 + x) + 2(-x^2 + x)$

$= 2x^2 + x - 2x^2 + 2x$

$= 3x$

COLLABORATIVE LEARNING

Have students work in small groups to make posters showing how to add the same two polynomials vertically and horizontally. Give each group two different polynomials to add. Then have each group present its poster to the rest of the class, explaining each step.

22. Critical Thinking A set is **closed** under an operation if performing that operation on two members of the set results in another member of the set. Is the set of polynomials closed under addition? Is the set of polynomials closed under multiplication by a constant? Explain.

Polynomials are closed under addition by the Associative and Commutative properties. They are closed under multiplication by a constant because the Distributive Property can be used to multiply the constant through the terms of the polynomial. Since this is still the addition of monomials, and the addition of monomials is closed, then the multiplication of polynomials by a constant is closed.

23. Counterexamples You can prove that a statement isn't true by finding a single example that contradicts the statement, which is called a *counterexample*. Show that the set of polynomials is not closed under division by finding a counterexample of division of a polynomial by a polynomial that does not result in a polynomial.

Sample answer: $\frac{1}{x}$ is the quotient of two monomials but is not a monomial.

24. Communicate Mathematical Ideas Simplify $(x^2 + x) + n(x^2 + 2x)$ by distributing the n. Show that it is equivalent for $n = 2$ to $(x^2 + x) + (x^2 + 2x) + (x^2 + 2x)$.

$(x^2 + x) + n(x^2 + 2x)$
$= x^2 + x + nx^2 + 2nx$
$= (x^2 + nx^2) + (x + 2nx)$
$= (1 + n)x^2 + (1 + 2n)x$

Substitute $n = 2$ into the above polynomial and simplify.

$(1 + n)x^2 + (1 + 2n)x$
$= (1 + 2)x^2 + (1 + 2(2))x$
$= 3x^2 + 5x$

Now simplify the expression $(x^2 + x) + (x^2 + 2x) + (x^2 + 2x)$.

$(x^2 + x) + (x^2 + 2x) + (x^2 + 2x)$
$= (x^2 + x^2 + x^2) + (x + 2x + 2x)$
$= 3x^2 + 5x$

25. Multiple Representations Write two polynomials whose sum is $4m^2 + 2m$. Write two polynomials whose difference is $4m^2 + 2m$.

Sample answers:

$(3m^2 + m) + (m^2 + m) = 4m^2 + 2m$

$5(m^2 + m) - (m^2 + 3m)$
$= (5m^2 - m^2) + (5m - 3m) = 4m^2 + 2m$

Lesson Performance Task

Swimming pools offer a wide range of activities for both health and leisure. They typically service everyone in the community, from the very young to the elderly. In community pools, the water temperature is often a much debated topic. If the water is too cold, children and older individuals may not be able to use the pool for the length of time they wish. On the other hand, if the pool is too warm, people swimming laps can get overheated.

An architect is working with a health club to design a multi-use aquatics facility that will have two pools. One pool will be primarily used by lap swimmers and local school swim teams. A second pool will be more of a mixed usage pool and have regions of various depths to service the remainder of the community.

Design two swimming pools for the aquatics center and calculate the volume of each pool. The lap pool should be 25 yards long, between 4 and 6 feet deep, and should consist of x lanes, with the width of each lane between 6 and 8 feet. The multi-use pool should have 3 sections. The first section should be a shallow end, where the depth begins between 2.5 and 3.5 feet, and slopes down to a depth equal to one-sixth the width of the pool over about one-third of the pool's length. The last section should slope down to the maximum depth of the pool which should be between 9 and 12 feet. Both pools should have approximately the same width and the multi-use pool should be between 2 and 3 times as long as it is wide.

Produce polynomials representing the volume of each pool and the total volume of water needed by the facility.

Lap pool:

$V_L(x) = \ell \cdot w \cdot d$ **Note that 25 Is multiplied by 3 because 25**
$ = 25 \cdot 3(6x)(5)$ **yards needs to be converted into feet.**
$ = 2250x$

The volume is broken up into 3 sections: shallow end, intermediate zone, and deep end.

length $= \frac{2x \cdot 6}{3}$; Width $= 6x$

$V_m(x) = V_s(x) + V_i(x) + V_d(x)$

$V_s(x) = \ell_s \cdot w \cdot d_{avg}$ $V_i(x) = \ell_i \cdot w \cdot d_{avg}$ $V_d(x) = \ell_d \cdot w \cdot d$

$ = \ell_s \cdot w \cdot \frac{d_1 + d_2}{2}$ $ = \ell_i \cdot w \cdot \frac{d_1 + d_2}{2}$ $ = \frac{2x \cdot 6}{3} \cdot 6x \cdot 12$

$ = \frac{2x \cdot 6}{3} \cdot 6x \cdot \frac{2.5 + x}{2}$ $ = \frac{2x \cdot 6}{3} \cdot 6x \cdot \frac{x + 11}{2}$ $ = 4x \cdot 6x \cdot 12$

$ = 30x^2 + 12x^3$ $ = 12x^3 + 132x^2$ $ = 288x^2$

$V_m(x) = 30x^2 + 12x^3 + 12x^3 + 132x^2 + 288x^2$ $V_A(x) = V_L(x) + V_m(x)$

$ = 24x^3 + 450x^2$ $ = 2250x + 24x^3 + 450x^2$

$ = 24x^3 + 450x^2 + 2250x$

The total amount of water needed by the facility is given by the polynomial
$24x^3 + 450x^2 + 2250x.$

© Houghton Mifflin Harcourt Publishing Company

EXTENSION ACTIVITY

Have students research the number of gallons per cubic foot and the weight of 1 gallon of water. Then have students calculate the volume of the pools in gallons and the weight of the water in the pools if the lap pool has 8 lanes.

Students will find that there are 7.48 gallons per cubic foot and that 1 gallon of water weighs about 8.33 pounds. They can substitute 8 for x in the polynomial representing the pools' volume to find the volume in cubic feet. Then they can multiply the result by 7.48 to find the volume in gallons, then multiply that result by 8.33 to find the weight in pounds.

AVOID COMMON ERRORS

Some students may forget to convert the length of the pool (25 yards) to feet. Suggest that students draw a diagram of the pool, including labels for all dimensions given in the Lesson Performance Task. They should note that only the length of the pool is given in yards. Remind students that 3 ft = 1 yd, so 25 yd = 25 yd × 3 ft/yd = 75 ft.

QUESTIONING STRATEGIES

? The volume of the multi-use pool is the sum of the volumes of its three sections. Why might its total volume be represented by a polynomial with only two terms? When the polynomials representing the volume of each section are added together, some of the terms may be like terms that can be combined, reducing the total number of terms.

Scoring Rubric
2 points: Student correctly solves the problem and explains his/her reasoning.
1 point: Student shows good understanding of the problem but does not fully solve or explain his/her reasoning.
0 points: Student does not demonstrate understanding of the problem.

Adding Polynomial Expressions   **828**

Subtracting Polynomial Expressions

Common Core Math Standards

The student is expected to:

 A-APR.A.1

Understand that polynomials form a system analogous to the integers, namely, they are closed under the operations of ... subtraction... Also A-SSE.A.1, A-CED.A.1

Mathematical Practices

COMMON CORE **MP.3 Logic**

Language Objective

Explain to a partner how to subtract two polynomial expressions.

ENGAGE

Essential Question: How do you subtract polynomials?

Subtract polynomials by adding the opposite of the polynomial that is being subtracted.

PREVIEW: LESSON PERFORMANCE TASK

View the Engage section online. Discuss the factors that may affect the profits of a manufacturing plant. Then preview the Lesson Performance Task.

Name_____ Class_____ Date_____

17.3 Subtracting Polynomial Expressions

Essential Question: How do you subtract polynomials?

Resource Locker

Explore **Modeling Polynomial Subtraction Using Algebra Tiles**

You can also use algebra tiles to model polynomial subtraction.

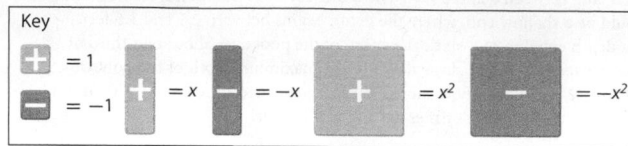

To subtract polynomials, recall that subtraction is equivalent to addition of the opposite.

$5 - 6 = 5 + (-6)$

Polynomial subtraction is the same. To subtract polynomial B from polynomial A, create a new polynomial C that consists of the opposite of each monomial in polynomial B. Add polynomial A and polynomial C.

When using tiles, switch every tile in the polynomial being subtracted for its opposite, the tile of the same size but the opposite sign. Once this is done, place the tiles representing the first polynomial and the new set of tiles next to each other and add like you have done previously. (The opposite of a polynomial is the negative of it. When you add a polynomial to its opposite you get 0.)

(A) Use algebra tiles to find $(2x^2 + 4) - (4x^2)$. Write the polynomial expression for each set of algebra tiles.

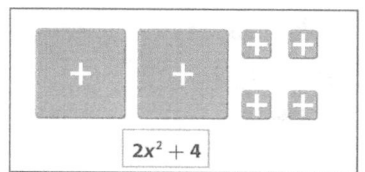 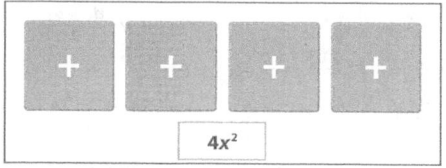

(B) Write the opposite of $4x^2$.

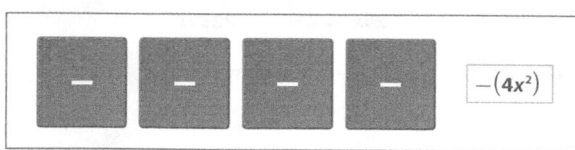

© Houghton Mifflin Harcourt Publishing Company

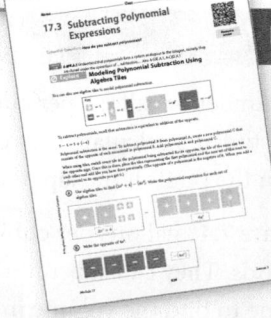

HARDCOVER PAGES 649–656

Turn to these pages to find this lesson in the hardcover student edition.

Ⓒ Write the subtraction as addition of the opposite.

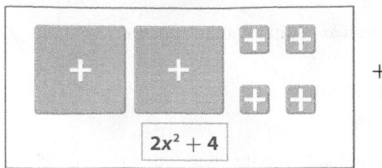 +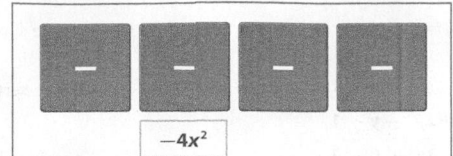

Ⓓ Group like terms and remove zero pairs. Write the resulting expression.

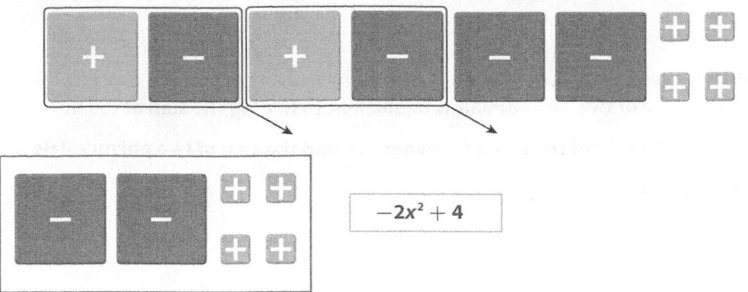

$-2x^2 + 4$

Reflect

1. **Discussion** Explain how removing zero pairs is an application of the additive inverse and the Identity Property of Addition.

Zero pairs represent opposites, which have a sum of 0. According to the Identity Property of Addition, removing zero results in the same quantity.

 Explain 1 **Subtracting Polynomials Using a Vertical Format**

To subtract polynomials, rewrite the subtraction as addition of the opposite.

Example 1 Subtract using the vertical method.

Ⓐ $(5x + 2) - (-2x^2 - 3x + 4)$

$(5x + 2) + (2x^2 + 3x - 4)$ Rewrite subtraction as addition of the opposite.

$\begin{aligned} 0x^2 + 5x + 2 \\ + 2x^2 + 3x - 4 \\ \hline 2x^2 + 8x - 2 \end{aligned}$

Use the vertical method. Write $0x^2$ as a placeholder.

Combine like terms.

© Houghton Mifflin Harcourt Publishing Company

PROFESSIONAL DEVELOPMENT

COMMON CORE Integrate Mathematical Practices

This lesson provides an opportunity to address Mathematical Practice **MP.3**, which calls for students to "construct logical arguments." In this lesson, as students learn procedures for subtracting polynomials, they use properties to justify why each step of the procedure is valid. For example, the Distributive Property allows them to multiply a polynomial by −1 to change each term to its opposite, and the Commutative and Associative Properties of Addition allow them to rearrange and regroup terms.

EXPLORE

Modeling Polynomial Subtraction Using Algebra Tiles

INTEGRATE TECHNOLOGY

Students may complete the algebra tiles activity online or use physical tiles and record their work in the book.

QUESTIONING STRATEGIES

? What is the effect of multiplying a polynomial by −1? The operation signs are changed to their opposites: + becomes − and − becomes +.

EXPLAIN 1

Subtracting Polynomials Using a Vertical Format

QUESTIONING STRATEGIES

? Why do you need to find the opposite of a polynomial when doing polynomial subtraction? Subtraction is defined as addition of the opposite. You find the opposite of a polynomial that is being subtracted so that you can add that opposite to the first polynomial.

? How can you use a vertical format to subtract two polynomials if a particular power of the variable appears in one polynomial but not in the other? Leave a space in that column, or write the term with a coefficient of 0.

INTEGRATE MATHEMATICAL PRACTICES
Focus on Reasoning

MP.2 Ask students to consider how polynomial subtraction is like subtraction with numbers. Just as subtracting an integer is the same as adding its opposite, subtracting a polynomial is equivalent to adding the opposite of the polynomial.

Subtracting Polynomial Expressions   **830**

EXPLAIN 2

Subtracting Polynomials Using a Horizontal Format

QUESTIONING STRATEGIES

? Does the order in which you subtract polynomials affect the difference? Explain. Yes; in subtracting two polynomials, the subtraction sign is distributed among all terms in the second polynomial, changing all the signs to their opposites.

INTEGRATE MATHEMATICAL PRACTICES

Focus on Patterns

MP.8 Remind students that the Distributive Property works in two directions. The parentheses form, $a(b + c)$, expands to $ab + ac$. Students use this form to distribute -1. When combining like terms, however, it is necessary to start with the expanded form, $de + df$, and work back to the parentheses form $d(e + f)$.

AVOID COMMON ERRORS

The most common error in subtracting polynomials is failing to reverse the sign of all terms in the polynomial that is being subtracted. To avoid this mistake, students should check that each sign in a polynomial has been changed to its opposite before they start subtracting or regrouping.

Ⓑ $(y^2 + y - 1) - (-2y^2 + y + 1)$

$(y^2 + y - 1) + (\boxed{+}\ 2y^2\ \boxed{-}\ y\ \boxed{-}\ 1)$ Rewrite subtraction as addition of the opposite.

$$\begin{array}{r} y^2 + y - 1 \\ +\ 2y^2 - y - 1 \\ \hline 3y^2 + 0 - 2 \end{array}$$ Use the vertical method.

Combine like terms and simplify.

$3y^2 - 2$ Simplify.

Reflect

2. Is the difference of two polynomials always another polynomial? Explain. Yes; finding a difference of two polynomials is equivalent to finding the sum of the first polynomial and the opposite of the second polynomial, and the sum of two polynomials is always another polynomial.

Your Turn

Find the difference using a vertical format.

3. $(4x^2 - x) - (-x^2 - 1)$
$$\begin{array}{r} 4x^2 - 1x + 0 \\ +\quad x^2 + 0x + 1 \\ \hline 5x^2 - x + 1 \end{array}$$

4. $(-z^3 - 2z - 1) - (-z^3 + 2z + 1)$
$$\begin{array}{r} -z^3 + 0z^2 - 2z - 1 \\ +\quad z^3 + 0z^2 - 2z - 1 \\ \hline 0z^3 + 0z^2 - 4z - 2 = -4z - 2 \end{array}$$

5. $(8y - 7) - (1 - 3y)$
$$\begin{array}{r} 8y - 7 \\ +\quad 3y - 1 \\ \hline 11y - 8 \end{array}$$

⊘ Explain 2 **Subtracting Polynomials Using a Horizontal Format**

Once the subtraction problem has been rewritten as a sum, the polynomials can be added using the horizontal method. Recall that this method uses the Associative, Commutative, and Distributive properties to group and combine like terms.

Example 2 Find the difference of the polynomials horizontally.

Ⓐ $(2q^2 - q - 8) - (2q^2 + q - 4)$

$= (2q^2 - q - 8) + (-2q^2 - q + 4)$ Rewrite subtraction as addition of the opposite.

$= (2q^2 - 2q^2) + (-q - q) + (-8 + 4)$ Group like terms together.

$= -2q - 4$ Simplify.

COLLABORATIVE LEARNING

Peer-to-Peer Activity

Have students work in pairs. In each pair, have one student use the vertical method to find the difference between two polynomials and the other student use the horizontal method. Then, have partners switch methods to find the difference between two other polynomials. Ask students whether they prefer one method over the other and, if so, to explain why to their partners.

Ⓑ $(2ab - b + a) - (2b^2 + b + a + 4)$

$= (2ab - b + a) + \dfrac{(-2b^2 - b - a - 4)}{\rule{4cm}{0.4pt}}$ Rewrite subtraction as addition of the opposite.

$= \dfrac{-2b^2 + 2ab + (-b - b) + (a - a) + (-4)}{\rule{5cm}{0.4pt}}$ Group like terms together.

$= \dfrac{-2b^2 + 2ab - 2b - 4}{\rule{4cm}{0.4pt}}$ Simplify.

Your Turn

Find each difference.

6. $(-x^3 + y^2 + y - x) - (-x^3 + y + x)$

$= (-x^3 + y^2 + y - x) + (x^3 - y - x)$

$= (-x^3 + x^3) + y^2 + (y - y) + (-x - x)$

$= y^2 - 2x$

7. $(18z + 12) - (11z - 5)$

$= (18z + 12) + (-11z + 5)$

$= (18z - 11z) + (12 + 5)$

$= 7z + 17$

⌖ **Explain 3**   **Modeling with Polynomials**

Some scenarios can be modeled by the difference of two polynomials.

Example 3   Find the difference between two polynomials to solve a real-world problem.

Ⓐ The cost in dollars of producing x toothbrushes is given by the polynomial $400{,}000 + 3x$, and the revenue generated from sales is given by the polynomial $20x - 0.00004x^2$. Write a polynomial expression for the profit from making and selling x toothbrushes. Then find the profit for selling 200,000 toothbrushes.

Use the formula: Profit = revenue − cost

$(20x - 0.00004x^2) - (400{,}000 + 3x)$

$= (20x - 0.00004x^2) + (-400{,}000 - 3x)$ Add the opposite.

$= -0.00004x^2 + 17x - 400{,}000$ Combine like terms.

To find the profit for selling 200,000 toothbrushes, evaluate the polynomial when $x = 200{,}000$.

$-0.00004x^2 + 17x - 400{,}000$

$= -0.00004(200{,}000)^2 + 17(200{,}000) - 400{,}000 = 1{,}400{,}000$

The company will make $1.4 million from the sale of 200,000 toothbrushes.

© Houghton Mifflin Harcourt Publishing Company · Image Credits: ©Emilio Ereza/Alamy

---

QUESTIONING STRATEGIES

? Does it matter whether you subtract the polynomials in the problem vertically or horizontally? Why or why not? **No; in either case you are adding the opposite of the second polynomial to the first one, so the results of the two methods are the same.**

DIFFERENTIATE INSTRUCTION

Modeling

Modeling using symbols can bring greater understanding of subtraction. For example, model the subtraction of two polynomials $(5n^2 + 4n + 7) - (-3n^2 - 5n + 7)$ by replacing n^2 with a square and n with a triangle. Remind students to write the opposite of the second polynomial directly under the first polynomial.

$$-5\,\square + 4\,\triangle + 7$$
$$\underline{+3\,\square + 5\,\triangle - 7}$$
$$-2\,\square + 9\,\triangle + 0$$

AVOID COMMON ERRORS

Students may get the wrong answer to a real-world problem involving polynomial subtraction if they subtract the polynomials in the wrong order. Remind them to read each problem carefully to determine which polynomial is to be subtracted from the other. Suggest that they look for key phrases such as "find the profit" or "how many more" to determine the correct relationship.

INTEGRATE TECHNOLOGY

When solving problems by modeling, students may need to substitute a given value for a variable in the polynomial. Students can use a graphing calculator to evaluate the polynomial.

Ⓑ The revenue made by a car company from the sale of y cars is given by $0.005y^2 + 10y$. The cost to produce y cars is given by the polynomial $20y + 1,000,000$. Write a polynomial expression for the profit from making and selling y cars. Find the profit the company will make if it sells 30,000 cars.

$\left(0.005y^2 + 10y\right) - \boxed{\left(20y + 1,000,000\right)}$ Profit = revenue − cost

$= \left(0.005y^2 + 10y\right) + \boxed{\left(-20y - 1,000,000\right)}$ Add the opposite.

$= 0.005y^2 \boxed{-} \underline{10y} - 1,000,000$ Combine like terms.

To find the profit for selling 30,000 cars, evaluate the polynomial when $x = 30,000$.

$0.005y^2 - \boxed{10y} - 1,000,000$

$= 0.005(30,000)^2 - \boxed{10(30,000)} - 1,000,000 = \boxed{3,200,000}$

The company will make _____$3.2_____ million from the sale of 30,000 cars.

Reflect

8. What is the addition problem corresponding to profit = revenue − cost? How do you find revenue if you know profit and cost?

The addition problem is revenue = profit + cost.

Your Turn

Find the difference between two polynomials to solve a real-world problem.

9. Jen, a biologist, is growing bacterial cultures at different temperatures as part of her research. The number of cells in the culture growing at 25 °C is given by the polynomial $t^2 + 4t + 4$, where t is the time elapsed in minutes. The number of cells in the second culture growing at 35 °C is modeled by the polynomial $t^2 + 4$. She needs to measure the success of the 25 °C culture over the 35 °C culture. Find the polynomial representing how many more cells are in the 25 °C culture for time t. How many more cells are there after 15 minutes?

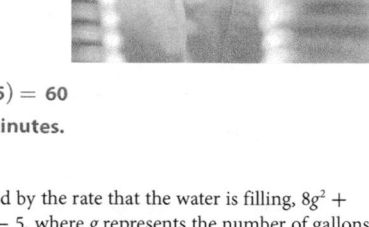

$\left(t^2 + 4t + 4\right) - \left(t^2 + 4\right)$

$= \left(t^2 + 4t + 4\right) + \left(-t^2 - 4\right) = \mathbf{4t}$

The 25 °C culture has 4t more cells at time t. $4t = 4(15) = $ 60

There are 60 more cells in the 25 °C culture after 15 minutes.

10. The number of gallons of water in a leaking pool is determined by the rate that the water is filling, $8g^2 + 3g - 4$, and the rate that water leaks from the pool, $9g^2 - 2g - 5$, where g represents the number of gallons entering or leaving the pool per minute. Write an expression for the net change in gallons per minute of the water in the pool. Find the change in the amount when the rate, g, is 5 gallons per minute.

$\left(8g^2 + 3g - 4\right) - \left(9g^2 - 2g - 5\right)$ $-g^2 + 5g + 1$

$= \left(8g^2 + 3g - 4\right) + \left(-9g^2 + 2g + 5\right)$ $= -(5)^2 + 5(5) + 1$

$= -g^2 + 5g + 1$ $= 1$

At a rate of 5 gallons per minute, the change of the volume will be 1 gallon per minute.

LANGUAGE SUPPORT 🔲EL

Connect Context

Review words that students may encounter when modeling financial situations. Explain that *revenue* is the amount of money received, and *cost* is money spent. The difference between these amounts (*revenue − cost*) is a company's *profit* or a government's *budget surplus*. If costs are greater than revenues, the result is a negative number, which is referred to as a company's *loss* or a government's *budget deficit*. It may be helpful for students to create a chart summarizing the meaning of these terms.

11. You can turn a polynomial subtraction problem into an addition problem. Can you turn a polynomial addition problem into a subtraction problem?

Yes, you can. Addition is subtraction of the opposite: $P_1 + P_2 = P_1 - (-P_2)$ for polynomials

P_1 **and** P_2**. (This was done in horizontal format.)**

12. Discussion Write a pair of polynomials whose sum is $3m^2 + 1$. Write a pair of polynomials whose difference is $3m^2 + 1$. Write a pair of polynomials whose sum and difference are both $3m^2 + 1$.

P_1 **and** P_2 **are polynomials.** $P_1 + P_2 = (3m^2) + (1) = 3m + 1$ **or** $(2m^2 + m) + (m^2 - m + 1)$

$= 3m^2 + 1$ **works.** $P_1 - P_2 = (4m^2 + 2) - (m^2 + 1)$ **works.**

For both sum and difference, choose $(3m^2 + 1) \pm (0) = 3m^2 + 1$**.**

13. Essential Question Check-In What do you have to do to simplify differences of polynomials? What properties do you use to accomplish this?

You simplify differences of polynomials by turning the subtraction problem into an

addition problem. To subtract, you add the opposite. Change the operation from

subtraction to addition and use the Distributive Property to multiply the polynomial being

subtracted by -1**.**

☆ Evaluate: Homework and Practice

- Online Homework
- Hints and Help
- Extra Practice

1. Use algebra tiles to model the difference: $(x^2 + x - 3) - (x^2 + 2x + 1)$.

Model	Algebra
	$(x^2 + x - 3) + (-x^2 - 2x - 1)$
	$x^2 + (-x^2) + x + (-2x) - 3 + (-1)$
	$-x - 4$

Exercise	Depth of Knowledge (D.O.K.)	COMMON CORE Mathematical Practices	
1–2	**2** Skills/Concepts	**MP.3** Logic	
3–14	**1** Recall of Information	**MP.2** Reasoning	
15–16	**1** Recall of Information	**MP.4** Modeling	
17–18	**2** Skills/Concepts	**MP.4** Modeling	
19	**2** Skills/Concepts	**MP.2** Reasoning	
20	**3** Strategic Thinking	**MP.2** Reasoning	

ELABORATE

INTEGRATE MATHEMATICAL PRACTICES
Focus on Reasoning

MP.2 Ask students to consider the number of terms in the polynomial that results from subtracting two polynomials. Does it equal the sum of the number of terms in the two polynomials? Can it be more than that sum? Can it be less than the number of terms in either one? Have them give examples to support their conclusions. They should recognize that the number of terms in the difference can vary. It can be no more than the total number in the two original polynomials, but it could be less than the number in either polynomial if like terms cancel out.

SUMMARIZE THE LESSON

? How do you subtract two polynomials? You can use a vertical or horizontal format to subtract polynomials. First, rewrite subtraction as addition. Identify the like terms and rearrange terms so that like terms are together. Combine like terms and simplify if necessary.

EVALUATE

ASSIGNMENT GUIDE

Concepts and Skills	Practice
Explore Modeling Polynomial Subtraction Using Algebra Tiles	Exercises 1–2
Example 1 Subtracting Polynomials Using a Vertical Format	Exercises 3–8
Example 2 Subtracting Polynomials Using a Horizontal Format	Exercises 9–14, 21–25
Example 3 Modeling with Polynomials	Exercises 15–20

Subtracting Polynomial Expressions **834**

To remind students to change the sign to the opposite for all terms in the polynomial being subtracted, have students mark the terms (for example, by circling the whole polynomial) as a reminder.

AVOID COMMON ERRORS

Point out that the best way to avoid errors when subtracting complicated polynomials is to make sure to rewrite terms before combining them. Students who try to combine terms in their heads may miss a term or fail to change signs when subtracting. Encourage students to rewrite each term as its opposite to avoid making mistakes.

2. James was solving a subtraction problem using algebra tiles, and he ended with 1 x^2-tile, 2 $-x^2$-tiles, 3 1-tiles, and 1 -1-tile. Model these results with algebra tiles. Assuming James' steps were correct up to that point, explain his mistake. Write the algebraic expression and draw the tiles that should be his result.

James has not finished simplifying. The tiles of the same size with opposite signs are zero pairs and cancel each other out. The completely simplified expression is $-x^2 + 2$. The algebra tiles model is shown.

Model	Algebra
	$x^2 + (-2x^2) + 3 + (-1)$ $= -x^2 + 2$

Find each difference vertically.

3. $(2x^2 - 2x^4) - (x^4 - x^2)$

$(2x^2 - 2x^4) + (-x^4 + x^2)$

$\; -2x^4 + 2x^2$
$\underline{+\; -x^4 \;+\; x^2}$
$\; -3x^4 + 3x^2$

4. $(y^2 - x^4) - (-x^4 - x^2)$

$(y^2 - x^4) + (x^4 + x^2)$

$\; y^2 \;-\; x^4 + 0x^2$
$\underline{+\; 0y^2 + x^4 \;+\;\; x^2}$
$\; y^2 + 0x^4 + \;\; x^2 \; = x^2 + y^2$

5. $(0.75x + 2) - (2.75x + x^2)$

$(0.75x + 2) + (-2.75x - x^2)$

$\; 0x^2 + 0.75x + 2$
$\underline{+\; -x^2 - 2.75x + 0}$
$\; -x^2 -\;\; 2x \;+ 2$

6. $(x^2 + y^2x + z) - (-x + xy^2 - z)$

$(x^2 + y^2x + z) + (x - xy^2 + z)$

$\; y^2x \;+\;\; x^2 + 0x + z$
$\underline{+\; -y^2x + 0x^2 +\;\; x + z}$
$\; x^2 +\;\; x + 2z$

7. $(m + x + 2z) - (x - y)$

$(m + x + 2z) + (-x + y)$

$\; m + x + 2z + 0y$
$\underline{+\; 0m - x + 0z + y}$
$\; m + 0x + 2z + y \;\; = m + 2z + y$

8. $-a^5 - (b^2 + a^2b^2) - (-a^5 - a^2b^2)$

$-a^5 + (-b^2 - a^2b^2) + (a^5 + a^2b^2)$

$\; -a^5 + 0b^2 + 0a^2b^2$
$\; 0a^5 -\;\; b^2 -\;\; a^2b^2$
$\underline{+\; a^5 + 0b^2 +\;\; a^2b^2}$
$\; 0a^5 -\;\; b^2 + 0a^2b^2 \;\; = -b^2$

Find each difference horizontally.

9. $(-2x^2 + x + 1) - (2x^2 - x - 1)$

$= (-2x^2 + x + 1) + (-2x^2 + x + 1)$

$= (-2x^2 - 2x^2) + (x + x) + (1 + 1)$

$= -4x^2 + 2x + 2$

10. $(a + b - 2c) - (a + b + 2c)$

$= (a + b - 2c) + (-a - b - 2c)$

$= (a - a) + (b - b) + (-2c - 2c)$

$= -4c$

© Houghton Mifflin Harcourt Publishing Company

Exercise	Depth of Knowledge (D.O.K.)		COMMON CORE Mathematical Practices
21	**2** Skills/Concepts		**MP.4** Modeling
22	**2** Skills/Concepts	H.O.T.	**MP.3** Logic
23–24	**3** Strategic Thinking	H.O.T.	**MP.3** Logic
25	**2** Skills/Concepts	H.O.T.	**MP.3** Logic

11. $\left(-2cab^2 + ab^2 + b^2\right) - \left(-b^2\right)$

$= \left(-2cab^2 + ab^2 + b^2\right) + \left(b^2\right)$

$= -2cab^2 + ab^2 + 2b^2$

12. $\left(-2cab^2 + ab^2 + b^2\right) - \left[-\left(-b^2\right)\right]$

$= \left(-2cab^2 + ab^2 + b^2\right) + \left(-b^2\right)$

$= -2cab^2 + ab^2$

13. $\left(4^{10}a + ab\sqrt[3]{2}\right) - \left(ab\sqrt[3]{2} + ab + 4^{10}a\right)$

$= \left(4^{10}a + ab\sqrt[3]{2}\right) + \left(-ab\sqrt[3]{2} - ab - 4^{10}a\right)$

$= \left(ab\sqrt[3]{2} - ab\sqrt[3]{2} - ab\right) + \left(4^{10}a - 4^{10}a\right)$

$= -ab$

14. $\left(q^3r^2 - 6qr^2 - 21q\right) - \left(-qr^2 - 6qr^2 - 11q - 3q^3r^2\right)$

$= \left(q^3r^2 - 6qr^2 - 21q\right) + \left(7qr^2 + 11q + 3q^3r^2\right)$

$= q^3r^2 - 6qr^2 - 21q + 7qr^2 + 11q + 3q^3r^2$

$= \left(q^3r^2 + 3q^3r^2\right) + \left(-6qr^2 + 7qr^2\right) + \left(-21q + 11q\right)$

$= 4q^3r^2 + qr^2 - 10q$

Model various situations with the difference of polynomials.
Simplify.

15. A bicycle company produces y bicycles at a cost represented by the polynomial $y^2 + 10y + 100,000$. The revenue for y bicycles is represented by $2y^2 + 10y + 500$. Find a polynomial that represents the company's profit. If the company only has enough materials to make 300 bicycles, should it make the bicycles?

$\left(2y^2 + 10y + 500\right) - \left(y^2 + 10y + 100,000\right)$

$= \left(2y^2 + 10y + 500\right) + \left(-y^2 - 10y - 100,000\right)$

$= \left(2y^2 - y^2\right) + \left(10y - 10y\right) + \left(500 - 100,000\right)$

$= y^2 - 99,500$

$y^2 - 99,500$

$= (300)^2 - 99,500 = -9500$

If the company can only make 300

bicycles, they will lose money.

16. The polynomial $-2x^2 + 500x$ represents the budget surplus of the town of Alphaville for the year 2010. Alphaville's surplus in 2011 can be modeled by $-1.5x^2 + 400x$. If x represents the yearly tax revenue in thousands, by how much did Alphaville's budget surplus increase from 2010 to 2011? If Alphaville took in \$750,000 in tax revenue in 2011, what was the budget surplus that year?

$\left(-1.5x^2 + 400x\right) - \left(-2x^2 + 500x\right)$

$= \left(-1.5x^2 + 400x\right) + \left(2x^2 - 500x\right)$

$= \left(-1.5x^2 + 2x^2\right) + \left(400x - 500x\right)$

$= 0.5x^2 - 100x$

$0.5x^2 - 100x$

$= 0.5(750)^2 - 100(750) = 206,250$

Alphaville's budget surplus was

\$206,250 thousand or \$206.25 million.

COLLABORATIVE LEARNING

Have students work with a partner. Have each student write two different polynomials, using any of the following as the variable part of the terms: x, y, x^2, y^2. Then have partners share papers and find the difference between the polynomials. Have students repeat the activity with two different polynomials.

MULTIPLE REPRESENTATIONS

The following demonstration of multiplying a simple polynomial by -1 may help students understand the concept of finding opposites.

$$-1(4 + 5) = -1(4) + -1(5)$$
$$= -4 + -5$$
$$= -9$$
$$-1(4 + 5) = -(9)$$
$$= -9$$

Students can readily see that distributing produces a valid equation.

QUESTIONING STRATEGIES

? Harper made an error when finding $(8xy - 3x^2 + 6y - 7) - (4x^2 + 5xy + 6x + 3)$. She says the difference is $3xy - 7x^2 - 10$. Identify Harper's error and give the correct difference. **Harper thought that $6y - 6x$ is equal to 0. The correct answer is $3xy - 7x^2 + 6y - 6x - 10$.**

VISUAL CUES

Have students pay careful attention to signs when subtracting polynomials. When they change each term of the subtrahend to its opposite, have them write the new sign in red to indicate this change.

Geometry Mrs. Isabelle is making paper and plastic foam animals for her first-grade class. She is calculating the amount of wasted materials for environmental and financial reasons.

17. Mrs. Isabelle is cutting circles out of square pieces of paper to make paper animals in her class. Write a polynomial that represents the amount of paper wasted if the class cuts out the biggest circles possible in squares of length ℓ.

The biggest radius possible of a circle in the square is half the square's length, or $\frac{\ell}{2}$. The area of the waste is the difference between the area of the square and the area of the circle:

$$\ell^2 - \pi\left(\frac{\ell}{2}\right)^2 = \ell^2 + \left[-\pi\frac{\ell^2}{4}\right] = \ell^2\left(1 - \frac{\pi}{4}\right).$$

18. Mrs. Isabelle's class is making plastic foam spheres out of plastic foam cubes. Write a polynomial that represents the amount of plastic foam wasted if the class cuts out the biggest spheres possible from cubes with side lengths of l. The volume of a sphere of radius r is $\frac{4}{3}\pi r^3$.

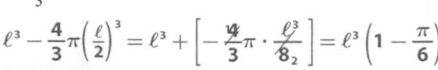

$$\ell^3 - \frac{4}{3}\pi\left(\frac{\ell}{2}\right)^3 = \ell^3 + \left[-\frac{\cancel{4}}{3}\pi \cdot \frac{\ell^3}{\cancel{8}_2}\right] = \ell^3\left(1 - \frac{\pi}{6}\right)$$

Persevere in Problem Solving John has yellow, green, and red cubes, each with side length c. Eight yellow cubes are glued together to make a larger cube. An even larger cube is made by gluing on green cubes until no yellow cubes can be seen. After that, John covers the green cubes with red ones so that green also cannot be seen, making an even larger cube. The minimum number of green and red cubes were used to cover previous colors. Use this information for Exercises 19 and 20.

19. What is the volume of the final big red cube?

The green cube has to cover every yellow face of the big yellow cube.

Without counting the yellow faces, visualize covering the big yellow cube.

Place green cubes at the corners and get a big green cube one layer thicker.

The length is now $4c$, adding c to both sides of the length. Similarly, you get a big red cube by adding one layer and get a length of $6c$.

The volume of the cube is $(6c)^3 = 216c^3$.

20. Write an expression for the volume of the final cube after performing this procedure with n colors of cubes.

For n colors the volume is $(2n)^3 c^3 = 8n^3 c^3$. At each stage the side length increases by $2c$.

21. Suppose you have two polynomials regarding the financial situation of a bicycle company. The first polynomial, $20,000 + x^2$, represents revenue from selling x units, and the second, $0.05x + 300$, represents the cost to produce x units.

Which of the following can be the net profit for the company?

a. $20,000 + x^2 - (0.05x + 300)$
b. $(20,000 + x^2) - (0.05x + 300)$
c. $(20,000 + x^2) - 0.05x + 300$
d. $(20,000 + x^2) - 0.05x - 300$
e. $(20,000 + x^2) - 0.05y - 300$

C is incorrect because the -1 was distributed incorrectly. E is correct in the case that the number of units sold, x, is not the same number of units produced, y. A, b and d are also correct and are algebraiically equivalent.

---

22. Explain the Error Kate performed the following subtraction problem. Explain her error and correct it.

$(5x^2 + x) - (x^3 + 2x)$

$= 5x^2 + x - x^3 + 2x$

$= 5x^2 - x^3 + (1 + 2)x$

$= -x^3 + 5x^2 + 3x$

Kate needs to distribute the -1 so she can drop the parentheses.

This is her corrected work.

$(5x^2 + x) - (x^3 + 2x)$	**Subtraction Problem**
$= (5x^2 + x) + (-x^3 - 2x)$	**Rewrite subtraction as addition of the opposite.**
$= 5x^2 + x - x^3 - 2x$	**Drop parentheses to get a single polynomial.**
$= 5x^2 - x^3 + (1 - 2)x$	**Combine like terms using the Distributive Property.**
$= -x^3 + 5x^2 - x$	**Simplify.**

INTEGRATE MATHEMATICAL PRACTICES
Focus on Math Connections

MP.1 When faced with complex-looking expressions in a real-world problem, students should recognize that the solution might still be found by following the same procedure for subtracting two polynomials that they used in simpler exercises.

AVOID COMMON ERRORS

Students should be aware that there is no Commutative Property for subtraction. The difference $a - b$ does not equal $b - a$ when $a \neq b$. Therefore, they should be careful to note which polynomial should be subtracted from the other when finding the solution to a real-world problem.

Have students write a journal entry comparing the addition and subtraction of polynomials and identifying key similarities and differences between the two operations.

23. **Communicate Mathematical Ideas** Hallie subtracted a quantity from the polynomial $3y^2 + 8y - 16$ and produced the expression $y^2 - 4$. What quantity did Hallie subtract? Explain how you got your answer.

You can write $\left(3y^2 + 8y - 16\right) - P_1 = y^2 - 4$ for some polynomial P_1.

Just rewrite the equation and solve for P_1. By the Subtraction Property of Equality, $\left(3y^2 + 8y - 16\right) - P_1 = y^2 - 4$ is equivalent to $\left(3y^2 + 8y - 16\right) - \left(y^2 - 4\right) = P_1$.

Simplify the left side.

$$\left(3y^2 + 8y - 16\right) - \left(y^2 - 4\right) = P_1$$
$$\left(3y^2 + 8y - 16\right) + \left(-y^2 + 4\right) = P_1$$
$$\left(3y^2 - y^2\right) + 8y + \left(-16 + 4\right) = P_1$$
$$2y^2 + 8y - 12 = P_1$$

Hallie subtracted the quantity $2y^2 + 8y - 12$.

24. **Counterexamples** The Associative Property works for polynomial addition. Does it work for polynomial subtraction? If not, provide a counterexample. Remember, the Associative Property for addition is $(a + b) + c = a + (b + c)$.

No, it does not:

$(5x - 3x) - 2x = 2x - 2x = 0$

$5x - (3x - 2x) = 5x - 1x = 4x$

$0 \neq 4x$

This is a counterexample.

25. **Draw Conclusions** Finish a standard proof that the Associative Property does not work for polynomial subtraction.

To show $(a - b) - c \neq a - (b - c)$, take the right side of the Associative Property and simplify it:

$a - (b - c) = a + \left(\boxed{-b} + \boxed{c} \right) = a - \boxed{b} + \boxed{c}$, which is not generally the same as $a - b - c$ unless $c = 0$.

Lesson Performance Task

The profits of two different manufacturing plants can be modeled as shown, where x is the number of units produced at each plant.

Plant 1: $P_1(x) = -0.03x^2 + 25x - 1500$

Plant 2: $P_2(x) = -0.02x^2 + 21x - 1700$

Find polynomials representing the difference in profits between the companies. Find $P_1(x) - P_2(x)$ and $P_2(x) - P_1(x)$. Compare the two differences and draw conclusions.

$P_1(x) - P_2(x)$
$\left(-0.03x^2 + 25x - 1500\right)$

$-\left(-0.02x^2 + 21x - 1700\right)$

$P_1(x) - P_2(x) = -0.01x^2 + 4x + 200$

$$\Rightarrow \quad \begin{array}{r} -0.03x^2 + 25x - 1500 \\ + \ 0.02x^2 - 21x + 1700 \\ \hline -0.01x^2 + 4x + 200 \end{array}$$

$P_2(x) - P_1(x)$
$\left(-0.02x^2 + 21x - 1700\right)$

$-\left(-0.03x^2 + 25x - 1500\right)$

$$\Rightarrow \quad \begin{array}{r} -0.02x^2 + 21x - 1700 \\ + \ 0.03x^2 - 25x + 1500 \\ \hline 0.01x^2 - 4x - 200 \end{array}$$

The like terms of the two polynomials are the additive inverses of each other. In subtraction, order matters.

INTEGRATE MATHEMATICAL PRACTICES

Focus on Critical Thinking

MP.3 Students may notice that the x^2 term in each polynomial has a negative coefficient, while the x term has a positive coefficient. Ask students to describe how each of these terms affects the total profit as the number of units produced increases. They should recognize that the x term represents an increase in profits with increasing production, while the x^2 term represents a decrease in profits with increasing production. Since the absolute value of the x term is greater for small values of x, and the absolute value of the x^2 term is greater for large values of x, profits will first increase, then decrease, as the number of units produced increases.

QUESTIONING STRATEGIES

? What property do you use when subtracting the polynomial for Plant 2 from the polynomial for Plant 1? Explain. **Distributive Property; you distribute −1 to each term of Plant 2's polynomial.**

? What property are you testing by comparing $P_1(x) - P_2(x)$ to $P_2(x) - P_1(x)$? What conclusion can you draw? **Commutative Property; the Commutative Property does not hold for subtraction.**

EXTENSION ACTIVITY

Ask students which company in the Lesson Performance Task makes a greater profit if both produce 100 units, and which makes a greater profit if both produce 600 units. Then have students use a graphing calculator to determine at what level of production the two companies will have equal profits.

By substituting the given numbers for x, students will find that Plant 1 makes a greater profit for 100 units and Plant 2 makes a greater profit for 600 units. By graphing both functions and finding the point of intersection, students should find that profits are about equal when both plants produce 445 units.

Scoring Rubric
2 points: Student correctly solves the problem and explains his/her reasoning.
1 point: Student shows good understanding of the problem but does not fully solve or explain his/her reasoning.
0 points: Student does not demonstrate understanding of the problem.

Subtracting Polynomial Expressions   **840**

Study Guide Review

ASSESSMENT AND INTERVENTION

Assign or customize module reviews.

MODULE PERFORMANCE TASK

 COMMON CORE

Mathematical Practices: MP.1, MP.4, MP.5, MP.6
A-CED.A.2, S-ID.B.6a

SUPPORTING STUDENT REASONING

Students should begin this problem by calculating the mean for each month and plotting the points on a coordinate grid. Here are some questions they might have.

- **Where do I find numbers for the *x*-values?**
  Remind students that January = 1, February = 2, and so on.

- **How can I graph the points to show their differences?** Point out to students that the scale for the ozone level can use increments less than one.

Essential Question: How can you use adding and subtracting polynomials to solve real-world problems?

> ### Key Vocabulary
> binomial *(binomio)*
> degree of a polynomial *(grado de un polinomio)*
> leading coefficient *(coeficiente principal)*
> monomial *(monomio)*
> polynomial *(polinomio)*
> standard form of a polynomial *(forma estándar de un polinomio)*
> trinomial *(trinomio)*

KEY EXAMPLE   (Lesson 17.1)

Combine like terms to simplify the polynomial.

$5y^2 + 12xy + 10 - y^2 + 6xy - 20$	*Rearrange in descending order of exponents.*
$5y^2 - y^2 + 12xy + 6xy + 10 - 20$	
$\left(5y^2 - y^2\right) + (12xy + 6xy) + (10 - 20)$	*Group like terms.*
$y^2(5 - 1) + xy(12 + 6) + (10 - 20)$	*Distributive Property*
$y^2(4) + xy(18) + (-10)$	*Simplify.*
$4y^2 + 18xy - 10$	

KEY EXAMPLE   (Lesson 17.2)

A city planner must add the area of 2 lots to determine the total area of a new park. The area of lot A can be represented by $\left(2x^2 + 6x + 4\right)$ ft². The area of lot B can be represented by $\left(5x^2 - 5x + 10\right)$ ft². Write an expression that represents the total area of the park.

$\left(2x^2 + 6x + 4\right) + \left(5x^2 - 5x + 10\right)$	*Add.*
$= \left(2x^2 + 5x^2\right) + (6x - 5x) + (4 + 10)$	*Group like terms.*
$= 7x^2 + x + 14$	*Simplify.*

The area of the park is $\left(7x^2 + x + 14\right)$ ft².

KEY EXAMPLE   (Lesson 17.3)

Find the difference.

$\left(b^2 + 9ab + 15a\right) - \left(3b^2 - 25ab + 1\right)$	
$= \left(b^2 + 9ab + 15a\right) + \left(-3b^2 + 25ab - 1\right)$	*Rewrite subtraction as addition of the opposite.*
$= \left(b^2 - 3b^2\right) + (9ab + 25ab) + 15a - 1$	*Group like terms.*
$= -2b^2 + 34ab + 15a - 1$	*Simplify.*

SCAFFOLDING SUPPORT

- Help students realize that the scales for the *x*- and *y*-axes need not be identical.

- Watch for students who number the months in the table consecutively.

- This task could be simplified for some students by numbering the months in the table rather than naming them.

- Students may be reluctant to make more than one model to describe a single set of data. They may need explicit permission to do so.

EXERCISES

Classify each polynomial by degree and number of terms. *(Lesson 17.1)*

1. $z^2 - 12$

      2nd degree binomial

2. $r^2 + 8 - 7r^3s$

      4th degree trinomial

Combine like terms. *(Lesson 17.1)*

3. $5y - 7y^2 + 10 - 10y^2 + y$

      $-17y^2 + 6y + 10$

4. $4b(a + b) - 8b^2 + 9ab$

      $-4b^2 + 13ab$

Add or subtract. *(Lessons 17.2, 17.3)*

5. $(7p^2 - 5p + 10) + (p^2 - 8)$

      $8p^2 - 5p + 2$

6. $(4r^2 + 9r - 4) - (-2r^2 + 7r + 6)$

      $6r^2 + 2r - 10$

7. A student is cutting a square out of a piece of poster board. The area of the poster board can be represented as $(4x^2 + 14x - 8)$ in². The area of the square can be represented as $(x^2 + 8x + 16)$ in². Write an expression to represent the area of the poster board left after the student cuts out the square. *(Lesson 17.3)*

      $(3x^2 + 6x - 24)$ in²

MODULE PERFORMANCE TASK

Ozone Levels in the Los Angeles Basin

You probably know that ozone in the upper atmosphere protects Earth from ultraviolet radiation, but ozone near the ground is harmful and a major component of air pollution. The table below provides maximum and minimum surface-level ozone concentrations in parts per million (ppm) in the Los Angeles Basin area for several months during 2012.

	Jan	Mar	May	June	Aug	Oct	Dec
Max	0.049	0.078	0.097	0.123	0.098	0.076	0.049
Min	0.020	0.040	0.048	0.054	0.053	0.041	0.038

Use the data to find an equation that models the average ozone level by month and use it to predict the average level for the months of February, April, September, and November of 2012.

Use your own paper to complete the task. Be sure to write down all your data and assumptions. Then use numbers, tables, graphs, or algebra to explain how you reached your conclusion.

DISCUSSION OPPORTUNITIES

- What possible trends do the data show?
- What would happen if you attempted to find a single linear function that describes all of the data?
- Ask students to share and compare their solutions, especially if they differ. Discuss the validity of the various strategies and solutions.

SAMPLE SOLUTION

First, find the mean values for each of the given months and record them in a table.

Month	1	3	5	6
Mean	0.0345	0.059	0.0725	0.0885

Month	8	10	12
Mean	0.0755	0.0585	0.0435

Then plot points (month number, ozone level) on a coordinate plane.

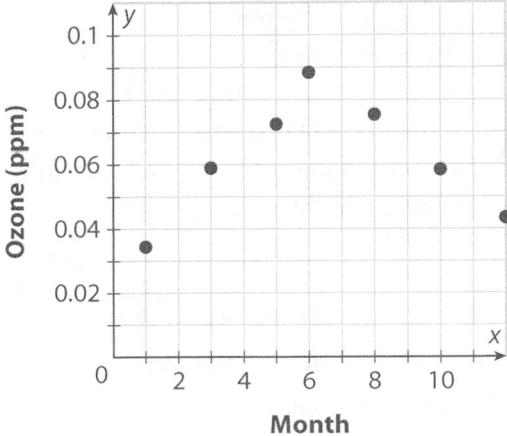

The points clearly follow one line from 0 to 6, and a different line from 6 to 12. Use linear regression on each set of data separately:

When $0 < x \le 6$, $y = 0.0102x + 0.0253$.

When $6 \le x \le 12$, $y = -0.0076x + 0.1349$.

Then, be sure to use the appropriate function to make predictions. Use the first function for February (2) and April (4), the second function for September (9) and November (11):

Feb: 0.0457 ppm   April: 0.0661 ppm

Sep: 0.0665 ppm   Nov: 0.0513 ppm

Assessment Rubric

2 points: Student correctly solves the problem and explains his/her reasoning.

1 point: Student shows good understanding of the problem but does not fully solve or explain.

0 points: Student does not demonstrate understanding of the problem.

Ready to Go On?

ASSESS MASTERY

Use the assessment on this page to determine if students have mastered the concepts and standards covered in this module.

ASSESSMENT AND INTERVENTION

Access Ready to Go On? assessment online, and receive instant scoring, feedback, and customized intervention or enrichment.

ADDITIONAL RESOURCES

Response to Intervention Resources

• Reteach Worksheets

Differentiated Instruction Resources

• Reading Strategies **EL**
• Success for English Learners **EL**
• Challenge Worksheets

Assessment Resources

• Leveled Module Quizzes

(Ready) to Go On?

17.1–17.3 Adding and Subtracting Polynomials

• Online Homework
• Hints and Help
• Extra Practice

Simplify each expression by combining like terms. Classify the simplified expression by degree and number of terms. *(Lesson 17.1)*

1. $16 - 5x^2 + 6x - 2x^2 + 10$

$-7x^2 + 6x + 26$; **2nd degree trinomial**

2. $p^4 - 5p + 3p(p^3 + 4)$

$4p^4 + 7p$; **4th degree binomial**

Add or subtract. Write the expression in standard form. *(Lessons 17.1, 17.2, 17.3)*

3. $(9z^2 + 28) - (z^2 + 8z - 8)$

$8z^2 - 8z + 36$

4. $(12y - 8 + 6y^2) + (9 - 4y)$

$6y^2 + 8y + 1$

5. A community swimming pool has a deep end and a shallow end. The volume of water in the deep end can be represented by $(2x^3 + 12x^2 + 10x)$ ft³, and the volume of water in the shallow end can be represented by $(4x^3 - 100x)$ ft³. Write an expression that represents the total volume of water in the pool in ft³. *(Lesson 17.2)*

$(6x^3 + 12x^2 - 90x)$ **ft³**

ESSENTIAL QUESTION

6. What is one way that adding and subtracting polynomials is similar to adding and subtracting whole numbers and integers?

Possible Answer: Polynomials are a closed system under addition and subtraction, as are whole numbers and integers. When you add or subtract polynomials, you end up with other polynomials.

COMMON CORE Common Core Standards

Lesson	Items	Content Standards	Mathematical Practices
17.1	1–2	A-SSE.A.1a, A-SSE.A.1b, A-SSE.A.2, A-APR.A.1	MP.7
17.1, 17.3	3	A-SSE.A.1a, A-SSE.A.1b, A-SSE.A.2, A-APR.A.1	MP.7
17.1, 17.2	4	A-SSE.A.1a, A-SSE.A.1b, A-SSE.A.2, A-APR.A.1	MP.7
17.2	5	A-APR.A.1, A-SSE.A.1a, A-SSE.A.1b, A-CED.A.1	MP.4

Assessment Readiness

1. Is the given polynomial in standard form? Select Yes or No for each polynomial.

   A. $-10r^3 + 3r - 18$ ● Yes   ○ No

   B. $-35t^3 - 13t + t^2$ ○ Yes   ● No

   C. $12x^4 - 12x^2 - 5$ ● Yes   ○ No

2. Consider the sum of $6m^2n + mn - 15$ and $-10mn^2 + mn + 12$.
   Choose True or False for each statement.

   A. The constant term of the sum is -3.   ● True   ○ False

   B. $6m^2n$ and $-10mn^2$ are like terms.   ○ True   ● False

   C. In simplest form, the sum has 4 terms.   ● True   ○ False

3. A clothing store sells t-shirts and jeans. The store charges customers $15 per t-shirt and $35 per pair of jeans. The store pays $4.50 per t-shirt and $5.00 per pair of jeans, plus a flat fee of $150 per order. Write an expression that represents the store's profit for an order if they sell t t-shirts and j pairs of jeans. Show your work.

   Revenue: $15t + 35j$

   Cost: $4.5t + 5j + 150$

   Profit = Revenue − Cost

   $$= \left(15t + 35j\right) - \left(4.5t + 5j + 150\right)$$

   $$= 15t + 35j - 4.5t - 5j - 150$$

   $$= 10.5t + 30j - 150$$

4. The value of a company, in millions of dollars, during its first 10 years increased by 2% each year. The original valuation of the company was 2.1 million dollars. Write a function to represent the value of the company x years after being founded. How much more was the company worth, in millions of dollars, after 6 years than after 2 years? Explain how you solved this problem.

   $V(x) = 2.1(1.02)^x$; The company is worth about $0.18 million more after 6 years than after 2 years. I found $V(6) - V(2)$.

MIXED REVIEW
Assessment Readiness

ASSESSMENT AND INTERVENTION

Assign ready-made or customized practice tests to prepare students for high-stakes tests.

ADDITIONAL RESOURCES

Assessment Resources

- Leveled Module Quizzes: Modified, B

AVOID COMMON ERRORS

Item 4 The multiple steps required in this question might cause some students to stop before the problem is completely done. Encourage students to number each step as it is mentioned within the problem, which will help them remember to complete every step.

Common Core Standards

Lesson	Items	Content Standards	Mathematical Practices
17.1	1	**A-SSE.A.2**	**MP.1**
17.2	2	**A-APR.A.1**	**MP.2**
2.1, 17.3	3*	**A-APR.A.1**	**MP.4**
16.2	4*	**F-LE.A.2**	**MP.4**

* Item integrates mixed review concepts from previous modules or a previous course.

Multiplying Polynomials

ESSENTIAL QUESTION:

Answer: You can use multiplying polynomials in applications in fields such as business, engineering, and science.

PROFESSIONAL DEVELOPMENT VIDEO

Professional Development Video

Author Juli Dixon models successful teaching practices in an actual high-school classroom.

Professional Development
my.hrw.com

Multiplying Polynomials

★

Essential Question: How can you use multiplying polynomials to solve real-world problems?

LESSON 18.1
Multiplying Polynomial Expressions by Monomials

LESSON 18.2
Multiplying Polynomial Expressions

LESSON 18.3
Special Products of Binomials

© Houghton Mifflin Harcourt Publishing Company • Image Credits: ©Will Chesser/Alamy

REAL WORLD VIDEO
The production of agricultural crops is affected by factors such as weather, pests, and disease. Orange growers can use polynomial expressions to estimate costs, profits, and yield available for consumers.

MODULE PERFORMANCE TASK PREVIEW

Orange Consumption

Do you eat oranges? You probably already know they are high in vitamin C, but they are also good for your skin, eyes, heart, and immune system. Each year the price of oranges increases while the amount consumed varies. In this module, you will explore polynomial operations that will help you model the per capita spending on oranges. So, about how much do Americans spend on oranges each year? Let's find out!

DIGITAL TEACHER EDITION

Access a full suite of teaching resources when and where you need them:

- Access content online or offline
- Customize lessons to share with your class
- Communicate with your students in real-time
- View student grades and data instantly to target your instruction where it is needed most

PERSONAL MATH TRAINER
Assessment and Intervention

Assign automatically graded homework, quizzes, tests, and intervention activities. Prepare your students with updated, Common Core-aligned practice tests.

Are YOU Ready?

Complete these exercises to review skills you will need for this module.

Multiply and Divide Integers

Example 1

Multiply or divide.

$-7 \cdot (-3)$ Think: Multiply 7 and 3.

21   Same signs, so the product is positive.

$18 \div (-9)$ Think: Divide 18 by 9.

-2 Different signs, so the quotient is negative.

- Online Homework
- Hints and Help
- Extra Practice

Multiply or divide.

1. $-36 \div 4$
-9

2. $13 \cdot (-5)$
-65

3. $-56 \div -8$
7

Algebraic Expressions

Example 2

Multiply $3(2x - 5)$.

$3(2x - 5)$

$3(2x) - 3(5)$ Distributive Property

$6x - 15$ Multiply.

Multiply.

4. $8(3a + 5)$
$24a + 40$

5. $4(6 - 2d)$
$24 - 8d$

6. $9(2x - 7y)$
$18x - 63y$

Exponents

Example 3

Simplify.

$x^4 \cdot x^2 = x^{4+2} = x^6$ The bases are the same. Add the exponents.

$\dfrac{x^7}{x^3} = x^{7-3} = x^4$ The bases are the same. Subtract the exponents.

Simplify.

7. $y^3 \cdot y^6$
y^9

8. $\dfrac{n^{10}}{n^2}$
n^8

9. $\dfrac{a^3 \cdot a^9}{a^4}$
a^8

10. $m^2 \cdot m^5 \cdot m^3$
m^{10}

Are You Ready?

ASSESS READINESS

Use the assessment on this page to determine if students need strategic or intensive intervention for the module's prerequisite skills.

ASSESSMENT AND INTERVENTION

RtI Response to Intervention **TIER 1, TIER 2, TIER 3 SKILLS**

Personal Math Trainer will automatically create a standards-based, personalized intervention assignment for your students, targeting each student's individual needs!

ADDITIONAL RESOURCES

See the table below for a full list of intervention resources available for this module.

Response to Intervention Resources also includes:

- Tier 2 Skill Pre-Tests for each Module
- Tier 2 Skill Post-Tests for each skill

Response to Intervention			Differentiated Instruction
Tier 1	**Tier 2**	**Tier 3**	
Lesson Intervention Worksheets	Strategic Intervention Skills Intervention Worksheets	Intensive Intervention Worksheets available online	
Reteach 18.1 Reteach 18.2 Reteach 18.3	2 Algebraic Expressions 5 Exponents 12 Multiply and Divide Integers	Building Block Skills 19, 22, 23, 24, 26, 27, 29, 30, 40, 58, 59, 69, 76, 81, 100	Challenge worksheets Extend the Math Lesson Activities in TE

Multiplying Polynomial Expressions by Monomials

Common Core Math Standards

The student is expected to:

 A-APR.A.1

Understand that polynomials form a system analogous to the integers, namely, they are closed under the operations of ... multiplication... Also A-SSE.A.1, A-CED.A.1

Mathematical Practices

 MP.5 Using Tools

Language Objective

Explain to a partner how to use the Product of Powers Property when multiplying monomials.

ENGAGE

Essential Question: How can you multiply polynomials by monomials?

Multiply coefficients and add exponents to multiply monomials. Use the Distributive Property to multiply a polynomial by a monomial.

PREVIEW: LESSON PERFORMANCE TASK

View the Engage section online. Discuss the variety of shapes of musical instruments and their corresponding unique sounds. Then preview the Lesson Performance Task.

18.1 Multiplying Polynomial Expressions by Monomials

Essential Question: How can you multiply polynomials by monomials?

Resource Locker

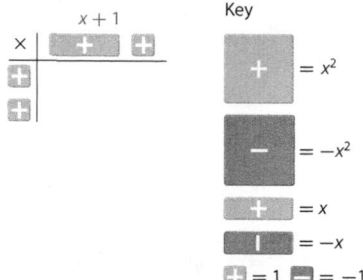 **Explore**   Modeling Polynomial Multiplication

Algebra tiles can be used to model the multiplication of a polynomial by a monomial.

Rules
1. The first factor goes on the left side of the grid, the second factor on the top.
2. Fill in the grid with tiles that have the same height as tiles on the left and the same length as tiles on the top.
3. Follow the key. The product of two tiles of the same color is positive; the product of two tiles of different colors is negative.

(A) Use algebra tiles to find $2(x + 1)$. Then recount the tiles in the grid and write the expression.

First, fill in the factors.

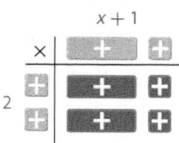

Now fill in the table.

The simplified expression for $2(x + 1) =$ ⬚2⬚ $x +$ ⬚2⬚ .

HARDCOVER PAGES 669–676

Turn to these pages to find this lesson in the hardcover student edition.

Ⓑ Use algebra tiles to model $2x(x - 3)$. Then write the expression.

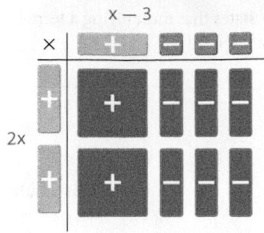

The simplified expression for
$2x(x - 3) = \underline{2}\,x^2 - \underline{6}\,x.$

Reflect

1. **Discussion** How do the tiles illustrate the idea of x^2 geometrically?
   Each side of the square tile measures x. Therefore, the area of the square tile is its side
   length squared, or x^2.

2. **Discussion** How does the grid illustrate the Distributive Property?
   Each item in the left column combines with each item in the top column. In Step B above,
   each positive x tile on the left combines with another x tile to give x^2 and three -1 tiles to
   give $-3x$.

🖉 Explain 1 Multiplying Monomials

When multiplying monomials, variables with exponents may need to be multiplied. Recall the Product of Powers Property, which states that $a^m \cdot a^n = a^{(m+n)}$.

Example 1 Find each product.

Ⓐ $(6x^3)(-4x^4)$

$(6x^3)(-4x^4)$

$= (6 \cdot -4)(x^3 \cdot x^4)$

$= (6 \cdot -4)(x^{3+4})$

$= -24x^7$

Ⓑ $(5xy^2)(7xy)$

$(5xy^2)(7xy)$

$= \left(5 \cdot \boxed{7}\right)\left(x \cdot \boxed{x}\right)\left(\boxed{y^2} \cdot y\right)$

$= \left(5 \cdot \boxed{7}\right)\left(x^{1 + \boxed{1}}\right)\left(y^{\boxed{2} + 1}\right)$

$= \boxed{35}\,x^{\boxed{2}}y^{\boxed{3}}$

Reflect

3. In the Product of Powers Property, do the bases need to be the same or can they be different?
   In the Product of Powers Property, the bases have to be the same.

Your Turn

4. $\left(18y^2x^3z\right)\left(3x^8y^6z^4\right)$
   $(18 \cdot 3)\left(x^3 \cdot x^8\right)\left(y^2 \cdot y^6\right)\left(z \cdot z^4\right)$
   $= 54x^{11}y^8z^5$

PROFESSIONAL DEVELOPMENT

Learning Progressions

In this lesson, students make connections between multiplication of polynomials and the real number properties of multiplication and exponents. They learn to use the Distributive Property, the Commutative and Associative Properties of Multiplication, and the Product of Powers Property when multiplying polynomials and writing expressions in equivalent forms. As students progress, they will see that polynomial expressions form a system that is closed under addition, subtraction and multiplication.

EXPLORE

Modeling Polynomial Multiplication

INTEGRATE TECHNOLOGY

Students have the option of completing the algebra tiles activity either in the book or online.

QUESTIONING STRATEGIES

❓ How do you know which algebra tiles you should use to fill in the table? The length and width of each tile should match the tiles above and at the left of the table.

INTEGRATE MATHEMATICAL PRACTICES
Focus on Modeling

MP.4 When multiplication is modeled with algebra tiles, the factors are put at the left and top of the table, and the algebra tiles in the table represent the product. When modeling the factors, point out that the small square represents a constant and the rectangle represents a variable. The large square in the product represents the variable squared.

EXPLAIN 1

Multiplying Monomials

QUESTIONING STRATEGIES

❓ How are exponents combined when two exponential numbers with the same base are multiplied? When the numbers are multiplied, the exponents are added.

❓ When you multiply any two monomials, what kind of polynomial will the product be? The product of two monomials will also be a monomial.

INTEGRATE MATHEMATICAL PRACTICES

Focus on Reasoning

MP.2 Remind students that the Commutative Property of Multiplication allows them to reorder any factors that are being multiplied. Reordering factors so that constants are grouped together and all factors with the same variable are grouped together can make multiplication of monomials easier.

EXPLAIN 2

Multiplying a Polynomial by a Monomial

AVOID COMMON ERRORS

Students may be tempted to find the sum of exponents when multiplying factors with different bases. Remind them that exponents can be added only when they have the same base. Thus $m^3 \cdot m^2$ can be rewritten as m^5, but $n^2 \cdot m^2$ cannot be rewritten because n^2 and m^2 have different bases.

QUESTIONING STRATEGIES

? When multiplying a polynomial by the monomial $3x$, why might you write $3x$ with an exponent, $3x^1$? Including the exponent highlights the fact that when $3x$ is multiplied by another x term, the exponent 1 is added to the exponent of the other x term. For example, $(3x)(x^2) = 3x^3$.

INTEGRATE MATHEMATICAL PRACTICES

Focus on Patterns

MP.8 Point out that by definition, a monomial always has one term and a polynomial has more than one term. Therefore, multiplication of a monomial by a polynomial will always show the same pattern: the single-term monomial will be distributed over the multi-term polynomial.

⚙ Explain 2 **Multiplying a Polynomial by a Monomial**

Remember that the Distributive Property states that multiplying a term by a sum is the same thing as multiplying the term by each part of the sum then adding the results.

Example 2 Find each product.

Ⓐ $3x(3x^2 + 6x - 5)$

$3x(3x^2 + 6x - 5)$ Distribute and simplify.

$= 3x(3x^2) + 3x(6x) + 3x(-5)$

$= 9x^{1+2} + 18x^{1+1} - 15x^1$

$= 9x^3 + 18x^2 - 15x$

Ⓑ $2xy(5x^2y + 3xy^2 + 7xy)$

$2xy(5x^2y + 3xy^2 + 7xy)$ Distribute and simplify.

$= 2xy(5x^2y) + 2xy\left(\boxed{3xy^2}\right) + 2xy\left(\boxed{7xy}\right)$

$= 10x^{1+2}y^{1+1} + \boxed{6}\,x^{1+\boxed{1}}y^{1+\boxed{2}} + \boxed{14}\,x^{1+\boxed{1}}y^{1+\boxed{1}}$

$= 10x^3y^2 + \boxed{6}\,x^{\boxed{2}}y^{\boxed{3}} + \boxed{14}\,x^{\boxed{2}}y^{\boxed{2}}$

Reflect

5. Is the product of a monomial and a polynomial always a polynomial? Explain. If so, how many terms does it have?
   Yes, after using the Distributive Property and multiplying monomials, the product consists of a sum of monomials, so it is a polynomial. It has the same number of terms as the polynomial factor.

Your Turn

6. $2a^2(5b^2 + 3ab + 6a + 1)$
   $10a^2b^2 + 6a^{2+1}b + 12a^{2+1} + 2a^2$
   $= 10a^2b^2 + 6a^3b + 12a^3 + 2a^2$

COLLABORATIVE LEARNING

Small Group Activity

Have students work in groups of three. Have one student in each group write a monomial, another student write a binomial, and the third student write a trinomial. The expressions should be of degrees one and two only. Have the students in each group multiply the monomial by the binomial and the trinomial. They should check that they all have the same answers, and help each other find errors, if necessary.

Explain 3 · Multiplying a Polynomial by a Monomial to Solve a Real-World Problem

Knowing how to multiply polynomials and monomials is useful when solving real-world problems.

Example 3 Write a polynomial equation and solve the problem.

Design Harry is building a fish tank that is a square prism. He wants the height of the tank to be 6 inches longer than the length and width. If he needs the volume to be as close as possible to 3500 in³, what should be the length of the tank? Round to the nearest inch.

 Analyze Information

Identify the important information
- Since the bases are squares, the length and width are ___equal___.
- The height of the tank is ___6___ more inches than the length.
- The total volume of the model should be as close as possible to ___3500___ in³.

 Formulate a Plan

Since the desired volume of the model is given, the volume formula should be used to find the answer. The volume formula for a square prism is

$V =$ ⊡ length · width · height ⊡. Use this formula and the given information to write and solve an equation.

Solve

Build the equation.
Since the length and width are equal, let s represent these measurements. The volume will be $V = (s \cdot s)\left(\boxed{s+6}\right) = s^{\boxed{2}}\left(\boxed{s+6}\right) = s^{\boxed{3}} + \boxed{6}\,s^{\boxed{2}}$.

s	$s^{\boxed{3}} + \boxed{6}\,s^{\boxed{2}}$
11	2057
12	2592
13	3211
14	3920

 Justify and Evaluate

___3211___ is closer to ___3500___ than any of the other results, so the length of the fish tank to the nearest whole inch should be ___13___ inches.

EXPLAIN 3

Multiplying a Polynomial by a Monomial to Solve a Real-World Problem

QUESTIONING STRATEGIES

? Why is it helpful to make a table listing possible solutions to a real-world problem? You can find the solution by substituting each possible value for the variable in the polynomial expression until you find the one that gives the desired result.

INTEGRATE TECHNOLOGY

When solving real-world problems by using polynomial multiplication, students may need to substitute a particular value for the variable in the product polynomial. Students can then use a graphing calculator to evaluate the polynomial.

DIFFERENTIATE INSTRUCTION

Visual Cues

Encourage students to add visual cues by following this procedure to find products of monomials and polynomials:

1. Circle the plus and minus operation signs in the factors. If there are no such signs, as in $5x(3x^2)$, multiplication can proceed directly.

2. If there are operation signs, as in $4(2x^2 + 3)$, draw large arcs connecting the factor outside the parentheses to each term within the parentheses to show that it needs to be multiplied by each of them.

3. Multiply and simplify to finish the problem.

ELABORATE

QUESTIONING STRATEGIES

? How many terms does the product of two monomials have? How many terms does the product of a monomial and a polynomial with n terms have? Explain. **The product of two monomials always has one term. The product of a monomial and an n-term polynomial has n terms, because the monomial is multiplied by each term of the polynomial to create a term in the product.**

SUMMARIZE THE LESSON

? How do you multiply a monomial by another monomial or by a polynomial? **When multiplying two monomials, you group factors that contain the same variable and apply the Product of Powers Property. When multiplying a monomial by a polynomial, you first use the Distributive Property and then multiply each pair of monomials to find the terms of the product.**

EVALUATE

ASSIGNMENT GUIDE

Concepts and Skills	Practice
Explore Modeling Polynomial Multiplication	Exercise 21
Example 1 Multiplying Monomials	Exercises 1–8, 20, 24
Example 2 Multiplying a Polynomial by a Monomial	Exercises 9–16, 22–23
Example 3 Multiplying a Polynomial by a Monomial to Solve a Real-World Problem	Exercises 17–19

---

7. Engineering Diane needs a piece of paper whose length is 4 more inches than the width, and the area is as close as possible to 50 in². To the nearest whole inch, what should the dimensions of the paper be?

Let x represent the width of the paper and y represent the total area.
$y = x(x + 4) = x^2 + 4x$.
x = 5 inches is the closest possible answer.
$x + 4 = 5 + 4 = 9$

The width should be 5 inches and the length should be 9 inches.

x	$x^2 + 4x$
4	32
5	45
6	60

💬 Elaborate

8. What is the power if a monomial is multiplied by a constant?
If a monomial is multiplied by a constant, the degree of the monomial will be the highest power.

9. Essential Question Check-In What properties and rules are used to multiply a multi-term polynomial by a monomial?
The Distributive Property and Product of Powers Property are used when multiplying a polynomial by a monomial.

⭐ Evaluate: Homework and Practice

- Online Homework
- Hints and Help
- Extra Practice

Find each product.

1. $(3x)(2x^2)$
$6x^3$

2. $(19x^5)(8x^3)$
$152x^8$

3. $(6x^7)(3x^3)$
$18x^{10}$

4. $(3x^2)(2x^3)$
$6x^5$

5. $7xy(3x^2y^3)$
$21x^3y^4$

6. $(6xyz^4)(5xy^3)$
$30x^{1+1}y^{1+3}z^4$
$= 30x^2y^4z^4$

7. $(8xy^3)(4y^4z^2)$
$32x^1y^{3+4}z^2$
$= 32xy^7z^2$

8. $(11xy)(x^3y^2)$
$11x^{1+3}y^{1+2}$
$= 11x^4y^3$

9. $(x^2 + x)(x^3)$
$x^{2+3} + x^{1+3}$
$= x^5 + x^4$

LANGUAGE SUPPORT **EL**

Connect Vocabulary

In English, words that end with *-tive* are cognates with Spanish words ending in *-tivo* or *-tiva*.

English *-tive*	Spanish *-tivo*
positive	positivo
negative	negativo
additive	aditivo
distributive	distributivo

10. $(x^3 + 2x^2)(x^4)$

$x^{3+4} + 2x^{2+4}$

$= x^7 + 2x^6$

11. $(x^2 + 2x + 5)(x^3)$

$x^{2+3} + 2x^{1+3} + 5x^3$

$= x^5 + 2x^4 + 5x^3$

12. $(x^4 + 3x^3 + 2x^2 + 11x + 4)(x^2)$

$x^{4+2} + 3x^{3+2} + 2x^{2+2} + 11x^{1+2} + 4x^2$

$= x^6 + 3x^5 + 2x^4 + 11x^3 + 4x^2$

13. $(x^3 + 2y^2 + 3xy)(4x^2y)$

$4x^{3+2}y + 8x^2y^{2+1} + 12x^{1+2}y^{1+1}$

$= 4x^5y + 8x^2y^3 + 12x^3y^2$

14. $(2x^3 + 5y)(3xy)$

$6x^{3+1}y + 15x^1y^{1+1}$

$= 6x^4y + 15xy^2$

15. $(x^4 + 3x^3y + 3xy^3)(6xy^2)$

$6x^{4+1}y^2 + 18x^{3+1}y^{1+2} + 18x^{1+1}y^{3+2}$

$= 6x^5y^2 + 18x^4y^3 + 18x^2y^5$

16. $(x^4 + 3x^3y^2 + 4x^2y + 8xy + 12x)(11x^2y^3)$

$11x^{4+2}y^3 + 33x^{3+2}y^{2+3} + 44x^{2+2}y^{1+3} + 88x^{1+2}y^{1+3} + 132x^{1+2}y^3$

$= 11x^6y^3 + 33x^5y^5 + 44x^4y^4 + 88x^3y^4 + 132x^3y^3$

Write a polynomial equation for each situation and then solve the problem.

17. Design A bedroom has a length of $x + 3$ feet and a width of x feet. Find the area when $x = 10$.

$y = x(x + 3) = x^2 + 3x.$

When $x = 10$, the area is 130 square feet.

$y = 10^2 + 3(10)$

$y = 100 + 30$

$y = 130$

18. Engineering A flat-screen television has a length that is 1 more inch than its width. The area of the television's screen is $1500\ \text{in}^2$. To the nearest whole inch, what are the dimensions of the television?

$y = x(x + 1) = x^2 + x.\ 1500 = x^2 + x$

x	$x^2 + x$
37	1406
38	1482
39	1560

$x = 38$ inches is the closest possible answer. So the television would have approximate dimensions of length 39 inches and width 38 inches.

© Houghton Mifflin Harcourt Publishing Company • Image Credits: ©Peter Cade/Getty Images

---

INTEGRATE MATHEMATICAL PRACTICES
Focus on Math Connections

MP.1 Review with students how to apply the Product of Powers Property. Give students examples in which the bases are whole numbers, such as $3^4 \cdot 3^2 = 3^6$, and examples in which the bases are variables, such as $4x^2 \cdot x^3y = 4x^5y$. Remind students that the bases of two factors must be the same in order to apply the Product of Powers Property.

NUMBER SENSE

Students can check their polynomial products by substituting numerical values for the variables in the factors and the product. They should choose small numbers, but not 0 or 1, to simplify the calculation. If the product is correct, multiplying the values of the two factors will give the value of the product. Note that it is possible to get a correct answer even if the polynomial is wrong, but a wrong answer clearly signals that an error was made.

MODELING

Students who are having difficulty multiplying polynomials may wish to continue to use algebra tiles to help them visualize the factors and the product. However, it should be pointed out to these students that at some point they will need to internalize how to perform the multiplication without using the tiles. They should transition from using tiles to do the multiplication to using tiles to check their multiplication.

Exercise	Depth of Knowledge (D.O.K.)	COMMON CORE Mathematical Practices
1–16	**1** Recall of Information	**MP.5** Using Tools
17–19	**1** Recall of Information	**MP.4** Modeling
20	**1** Recall of Information	**MP.2** Reasoning
21	**1** Recall of Information	**MP.5** Using Tools
22	**2** Skills/Concepts H.O.T.	**MP.4** Modeling
23–24	**2** Skills/Concepts H.O.T.	**MP.3** Logic

Focus on Math Connections

MP.1 Remind students that when they approach a real-world problem involving complex-looking expressions, they should first read the problem carefully to determine what they need to do with those expressions. A problem that looks complicated may require only a straightforward multiplication of monomials and polynomials.

AVOID COMMON ERRORS

Some students may multiply the exponents of two factors instead of adding them. Suggest that when they are unsure what to do, they recall a simple illustration of why the Product of Powers Property is true, such as $x^2 \cdot x^3 = (x \cdot x) \cdot (x \cdot x \cdot x) = x^5$. Based on this model, they should recognize that the product of two exponential terms with the same base is the base raised to the sum of the exponents.

JOURNAL

Have students write a journal entry explaining how to multiply a polynomial by a monomial.

---

19. **Construction** Zach is building a new shed shaped like a square prism. He wants the height of the shed to be 2 feet less than the length and width. If he needs the volume to be as close as possible to 3174 ft³, what should the length be? Round to the nearest foot.

$y = (x)(x)(x - 2) = x^2(x - 2) = x^3 - 2x^2$

$y = x^3 - 2x^2$

$3174 = x^3 - 2x^2$

$x = 15$ feet is the closest possible answer.

x^3	$x^2 - 2x^2$
14	2352
15	2925
16	3584

20. State whether each polynomial is also a monomial.

a. x^3 ● Yes   ○ No

b. $a^2 + 2a^b + b^c$ ○ Yes   ● No

c. $x^3 + 4x^3$ ● Yes   ○ No

d. y^{2^x} ● Yes   ○ No

e. $xyz + txy + tyz + txz$ ○ Yes   ● No

21. Draw the algebra tiles that model the factors in the multiplication shown. Then determine the simplified product.

$(-x + 1)(x - 2) = -x^2 + 3x - 2$

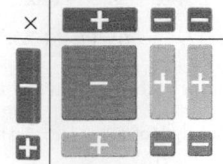

H.O.T. Focus on Higher Order Thinking

22. **Critical Thinking** When finding the product of a monomial and a binomial, how is the degree of the product related to the degree of the monomial and the degree of the binomial?

The degree of the product is the sum of the degrees of the monomial and the binomial.

23. **Explain the Error** Sandy says that the product of x^2 and $x^3 + 5x^2 + 1$ is $x^6 + 5x^4 + x^2$. Explain the error that Sandy made.

Sandy multiplied the exponents for x^2 and x^3 instead of adding them.

24. **Communicate Mathematical Ideas** What is the lowest degree that a polynomial can have? Explain.

The lowest degree that a polynomial can have is 0, which would occur with any constant.

© Houghton Mifflin Harcourt Publishing Company

Lesson Performance Task

A craftsman is making a dulcimer with the same dimensions as the one shown. The surface shown requires a special, more durable type of finish. Write a polynomial that represents the area to be finished on the dulcimer shown.

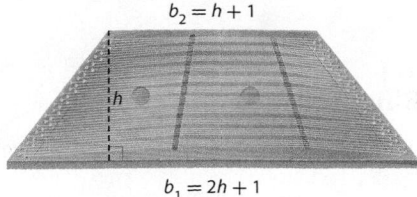

$$A = \frac{1}{2}h(b_1 + b_2)$$
$$= \frac{1}{2}h\left[(2h + 1) + (h + 1)\right]$$
$$= \frac{1}{2}h(3h + 2)$$
$$= \frac{3}{2}h^2 + h$$

QUESTIONING STRATEGIES

? How does knowing the shape of a flat surface help you write a polynomial to represent its area? Knowing the shape helps you choose an appropriate formula for area. You can substitute the expressions for the dimensions of the shape into the area formula to write the polynomial expression for the area.

? What shape is the top face of the dulcimer? trapezoid

? What formula can you use to find the area of a trapezoid? If you don't remember a formula for a trapezoid, how else can you find the area? $A = \frac{1}{2}h(b_1 + b_2)$; divide the shape into a rectangle and two triangles and find the area of each piece.

INTEGRATE MATHEMATICAL PRACTICES
Focus on Math Connections

MP.1 Ask students to compare the lengths of the two bases of the trapezoid. Students should notice that the top base, b_2, is shorter than the bottom base, b_1. The difference between the two lengths, $b_1 - b_2$, is equal to $(2h + 1) - (h + 1) = h$, the height of the trapezoid.

EXTENSION ACTIVITY

Have students determine the volume of the dulcimer described in the Lesson Performance Task if it is a trapezoidal prism with thickness $\frac{h}{4}$.

Students should find the volume by multiplying the area of the trapezoid by $\frac{h}{4}$ to get $\frac{3}{8}h^3 + \frac{1}{4}h^2$.

Scoring Rubric

2 points: Student correctly solves the problem and explains his/her reasoning.
1 point: Student shows good understanding of the problem but does not fully solve or explain his/her reasoning.
0 points: Student does not demonstrate understanding of the problem.

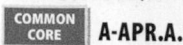
Multiplying Polynomial Expressions

Common Core Math Standards

The student is expected to:

 A-APR.A.1

Understand that polynomials form a system analogous to the integers, namely, they are closed under the operations of ... multiplication... Also A-SSE.A.1, A-CED.A.1

Mathematical Practices

MP.4 Modeling

Language Objective

Explain to a partner what FOIL means and how you use the FOIL method to multiply two binomials.

ENGAGE

Essential Question: How do you multiply binomials and polynomials?

Use the Distributive Property to multiply binomials and polynomials. Use the FOIL method to multiply binomials.

PREVIEW: LESSON PERFORMANCE TASK

View the Engage section online. Discuss what types of herbs and vegetables one might plant in a backyard garden. Then preview the Lesson Performance Task.

Name_____ Class_____ Date_____

18.2 Multiplying Polynomial Expressions

Essential Question: How do you multiply binomials and polynomials?

Resource Locker

Explore   Modeling Binomial Multiplication

Using algebra tiles to model the product of two binomials is very similar to using algebra tiles to model the product of a monomial and a polynomial.

Rules
1. The first factor goes on the left side of the grid, and the second factor goes on the top.
2. Fill in the grid with tiles that have the same height as tiles on the left and the same length as tiles on the top.
3. Follow the key. The product of two tiles of the same color is positive; the product of two tiles of different colors is negative.

Use algebra tiles to model $(x + 1)(x - 2)$. Then write the product. First fill in the factors and mat.

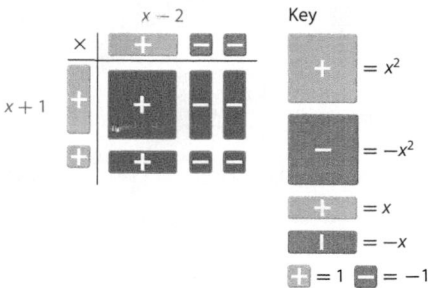

Now remove any zero pairs.

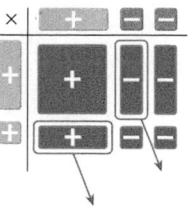

The product $(x + 1)(x - 2)$ in simplest form is $\boxed{1}\ x^2 - \boxed{1}\ x - \boxed{2}$.

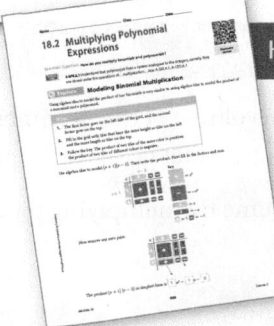

HARDCOVER PAGES 669–676

Turn to these pages to find this lesson in the hardcover student edition.

© Houghton Mifflin Harcourt Publishing Company

PROFESSIONAL DEVELOPMENT

Learning Progressions

In this lesson, students use what they have learned about adding and subtracting polynomials and multiplying polynomials by monomials to find products of larger polynomials. Some key understandings for students are that the FOIL method can be used to multiply any two binomials, and the Distributive Property can be used to multiply any size or degree of polynomial. Students make connections between operations with numbers and operations with polynomials. As students progress, they will extend this understanding to multiplying and dividing a variety of polynomial expressions.

EXPLORE

Modeling Binomial Multiplication

INTEGRATE TECHNOLOGY

Students have the option of completing the algebra tiles activity either in the book or online.

QUESTIONING STRATEGIES

? What do the algebra tiles in the grid represent? The tiles in the grid represent the product of the factors shown above and to the left of the grid.

? Why can you remove pairs of like tiles? A positive (yellow) shape matched with a negative (red) shape of equal size will result in a zero pair, so a total of 0 is being erased.

EXPLAIN 1

Multiplying Binomials Using the Distributive Property

QUESTIONING STRATEGIES

? Is the Commutative Property of Multiplication true for the multiplication of two binomials? Explain. Yes, the product will be the same regardless of the order in which the binomials are multiplied and regardless which binomial is distributed across the other.

AVOID COMMON ERRORS

Students sometimes overlook the subtraction sign in binomials of the form $ax - b$. It may be helpful to have students rewrite the binomial as $ax + (-b)$ so that it is clear to them that the constant in the binomial is negative. Highlighting or circling negative constants and coefficients is also a good idea so that students pay attention to them as they multiply binomials.

INTEGRATE MATHEMATICAL PRACTICES

Focus on Technology

MP.5 Have students use graphing to check their products. For example, use a graphing calculator to display the graphs of $y_1 = (x + 3)(x + 2)$ and $y_2 = x^2 + 5x + 6$ in the same viewing window. Because the graphs coincide, they confirm that the product of $x + 3$ and $x + 2$ is $x^2 + 5x + 6$.

EXPLAIN 2

Multiplying Binomials Using FOIL

QUESTIONING STRATEGIES

What terms from FOIL can often be combined? Explain. **The product of the inner terms and the product of the outer terms can often be combined because they are like terms.**

INTEGRATE MATHEMATICAL PRACTICES

Focus on Patterns

MP.8 Point out that the sign of the last term in the product will be determined by the signs from the last term in each binomial. It will be positive if the signs of the last terms are the same, and it will be negative if the signs are different.

AVOID COMMON ERRORS

Students need to remember that any like terms that result from a FOIL expansion need to be combined.

⚙ Explain 2   Multiplying Binomials Using FOIL

Another way to use the Distributive Property is the *FOIL* method. The **FOIL** method uses the Distributive Property to multiply terms of binomials in this order: First terms, Outer terms, Inner terms, and Last terms.

Example 2   Multiply by using the FOIL method.

Ⓐ $(x^2 + 3)(x + 2)$

Use the FOIL method.

$(x^2 + 3)(x + 2) = (x^2 + 3)(x + 2)$	F	Multiply the first terms. Result: x^3
$= (x^2 + 3)(x + 2)$	O	Multiply the outer terms. Result: $2x^2$
$= (x^2 + 3)(x + 2)$	I	Multiply the inner terms. Result: $3x$
$= (x^2 + 3)(x + 2)$	L	Multiply the last terms. Result: 6

Add the result.

$(x^2 + 3)(x + 2) = x^3 + 2x^2 + 3x + 6$

Ⓑ $(3x^2 - 2x)(x + 5)$

Use the FOIL method.

$(3x^2 - 2x)(x + 5) = (3x^2 - 2x)(x + 5)$	F	Multiply the first terms. Result: $\boxed{3x^3}$
$= (3x^2 - 2x)(x + 5)$	O	Multiply the outer terms. Result: $\boxed{15x^2}$
$= (3x^2 - 2x)(x + 5)$	I	Multiply the inner terms. Result: $\boxed{-2x^2}$
$= (3x^2 - 2x)(x + 5)$	L	Multiply the last terms. Result: $\boxed{-10x}$

Add the result.

$(3x^2 - 2x)(x + 5) = \boxed{3}\,x^3 + \boxed{13}\,x^2 - \boxed{10}\,x$

Reflect

4. The FOIL method finds the sum of four partial products. Why does the result from part B only have three terms?
When there are like terms to combine, the result will have fewer than four terms.

5. Can the FOIL method be used for numeric expressions? Give an example.
Sample answer: The FOIL method can be used for numeric expressions. For example, when multiplying 55 × 47, you can rewrite as $(50 + 5)(40 + 7)$ and use FOIL:

$(50 \times 40) + (50 \times 7) + (5 \times 40) + (5 + 7) = 2000 + 350 + 200 + 35$

$= 2585$

Your Turn

6. $(x^2 + 3)(x + 6)$
$(x^2 + 3)(x + 6)$
$= x^3 + 6x^2 + 3x + 18$

COLLABORATIVE LEARNING

Small Group Activity

Show students that they can also multiply two polynomials vertically or by using a table. Then have students work in small groups to multiply two polynomials, such as $(x + 3)(x^2 - 5x + 2)$. Each student in the group should choose a different method, such as multiplying horizontally, multiplying vertically, or using a table. Have students discuss the ways in which the methods are alike and the ways in which they differ.

To multiply polynomials with more than two terms, the Distributive Property must be used several times.

Example 3 Multiply the polynomials.

(A) $(x + 2)(x^2 - 5x + 4)$

$$(x + 2)(x^2 - 5x + 4) = x(x^2 - 5x + 4) + 2(x^2 - 5x + 4)$$ Distribute.

$$= x(x^2 - 5x + 4) + 2(x^2 - 5x + 4)$$ Redistribute.

$$= x(x^2) + x(-5x) + x(4) + 2(x^2) + 2(-5x) + 2(4)$$ Simplify.

$$= x^3 - 5x^2 + 4x + 2x^2 - 10x + 8$$

$$= x^3 - 3x^2 - 6x + 8$$

(B) $(3x - 4)(-2x^2 + 5x - 6)$

$$(3x - 4)(-2x^2 + 5x - 6) = 3x(-2x^2 + 5x - 6) - \boxed{4}(-2x^2 + 5x - 6)$$ Distribute.

$$= 3x(-2x^2 + 5x - 6) - \boxed{4}(-2x^2 + 5x - 6)$$ Redistribute.

$$= 3x(-2x^2) + 3x\boxed{5x} + 3x\boxed{-6} - 4\boxed{-2x^2} - 4\boxed{5x} - 4\boxed{-6}$$

Simplify.

$$= \boxed{-6}x^{\boxed{3}} + \boxed{15}x^{\boxed{2}} - \boxed{18}x + \boxed{8}x^{\boxed{2}} - \boxed{20}x + \boxed{24}$$

$$= \boxed{-6}x^{\boxed{3}} + \boxed{23}x^{\boxed{2}} - \boxed{38}x + \boxed{24}$$

Reflect

7. **Discussion** Is the product of two polynomials always another polynomial?
Yes. The product, after using the Distributive Property and multiplying monomials,

consists of a monomial or a sum or difference of monomials.

8. Can the Distributive Property be used to multiply two trinomials?
Yes. Multiply each term in the first trinomial by each term in the second trinomial.

9. $(3x + 1)(x^3 + 4x^2 - 7)$

$$= 3x(x^3 + 4x^2 - 7) + 1(x^3 + 4x^2 - 7)$$

$$= 3x(x^3) + 3x(4x^2) + 3x(-7) + x^3 + 4x^2 - 7$$

$$= 3x^4 + 12x^3 - 21x + x^3 + 4x^2 - 7$$

$$= 3x^4 + 13x^3 + 4x^2 - 21x - 7$$

EXPLAIN 3

Multiplying Polynomials

QUESTIONING STRATEGIES

? Why can't you use the FOIL method for multiplying a binomial by a trinomial or a larger polynomial? Since one of the factors has more than two terms, you would miss some terms if you used the FOIL method. Terms between the first and last term of the polynomial would not be included in the multiplication.

AVOID COMMON ERRORS

It may be helpful for students to insert placeholders where there is no term for a given power of the variable. Advise students to use $0x^2$, $0x$, or 0 when necessary to make sure that all places contain a term.

INTEGRATE MATHEMATICAL PRACTICES
Focus on Reasoning

MP.2 Explain that polynomials can also be multiplied using a vertical format. Multiplying vertically is similar to multiplying multi-digit whole numbers. Multiply the top polynomial by each term of the bottom polynomial in turn, then add the results.

DIFFERENTIATE INSTRUCTION

Graphic Organizers

Students may find it easier to do polynomial multiplication in a table, as shown here for $(4x - 7)(x^2 + 2x + 3)$. Each cell in the table is the product of one term from the factor written at the top and one term from the factor written at the left.

	x^2	$+2x$	$+3$
4x	$4x^3$	$8x^2$	$12x$
−7	$-7x^2$	$-14x$	-21

$$(4x - 7)(x^2 + 2x + 3) = 4x^3 + 8x^2 - 7x^2 + 12x - 14x - 21 = 4x^3 + x^2 - 2x - 21$$

Multiplying Polynomial Expressions   **858**

EXPLAIN 4

Modeling with Polynomial Multiplication

QUESTIONING STRATEGIES

? How could drawing a diagram help you to solve a real-world problem? You can label the diagram with the information that you know, and then write an expression to model the situation.

INTEGRATE MATHEMATICAL PRACTICES
Focus on Technology

MP.5 After substituting a value for the variable in a polynomial that models a real-world situation, students can use a graphing calculator to evaluate the result.

Explain 4 **Modeling with Polynomial Multiplication**

Polynomial multiplication is sometimes necessary in problem solving.

(A) **Gardening** Trina is building a garden. She designs a rectangular garden with length $(x + 4)$ feet and width $(x + 1)$ feet. When $x = 4$, what is the area of the garden?

Let y represent the area of Trina's garden. Then the equation for this situation is $y = (x + 4)(x + 1)$.

$y = (x + 4)(x + 1)$

Use FOIL.

$y = x^2 + x + 4x + 4$

$y = x^2 + 5x + 4$

Now substitute 4 for x to finish the problem.

$y = x^2 + 5x + 4$

$y = (4)^2 + 5(4) + 4$

$y = 16 + 20 + 4$

$y = 40$

The area of Trina's garden is 40 ft².

(B) **Design** Orik has designed a rectangular mural that measures 20 feet in width and 30 feet in length. Laura has also designed a rectangular mural, but it measures x feet shorter on each side. When $x = 6$, what is the area of Laura's mural?

Let y represent the area of Laura's mural. Then the equation for this situation is

$y = (20 - x)(30 - x)$.

$y = (20 - x)(30 - x)$

Use FOIL.

$y = \boxed{600} - \boxed{20}\,x - \boxed{30}\,x + \boxed{1}\,x^2$

$y = \boxed{1}\,x^2 - \boxed{50}\,x + \boxed{600}$

Now substitute $\boxed{6}$ for x to finish the problem.

$y = \boxed{6}^2 - \boxed{50} \cdot \boxed{6} + \boxed{600}$

$y = \boxed{36} - \boxed{300} + \boxed{600}$

$y = \boxed{336}$

The area of Laura's mural is $\boxed{336}$ ft².

LANGUAGE SUPPORT **EL**

Cognitive Strategies

The English language often uses acronyms. Explain to students that an *acronym* is a word formed from the initial letters of other words. The acronym FOIL represents the order of the steps used in multiplying binomials: First terms, Outer terms, Inner terms, Last terms.

FOIL = First, Outer, Inner, Last

Have students discuss other acronyms they have encountered at school or in their community.

10. **Landscaping** A landscape architect is designing a rectangular garden in a local park. The garden will be 20 feet long and 15 feet wide. The architect wants to place a walkway with a uniform width all the way around the garden. What will be the area of the garden, including the walkway?

Let x be the width of the walkway. The length of the garden, including the walkway, is $(20 + 2x)$ feet. The width of the garden, including the walkway, is $(15 + 2x)$ feet.

$$(20 + 2x)(15 + 2x) = 300 + 40x + 30x + 4x^2$$

$$= 300 + 70x + 4x^2$$

$$= 4x^2 + 70x + 300$$

So the area, including the walkway, is $(4x^2 + 70x + 300)\text{ft}^2$.

💬 Elaborate

11. How is the FOIL method different from the Distributive Property? Explain.
    There is no difference. FOIL simply gives an order in which to use the Distributive Property.

12. Why can FOIL not be used for polynomials with three or more terms?
    FOIL refers to four partial products within a product: first, outer, inner, and last.

    When polynomials with three or more terms are multiplied, there are more than

    four partial products.

13. **Essential Question Check–In** How do you multiply two binomials?
    Use the FOIL method to find the partial products of the first terms, the outer terms, the

    inner terms, and the last terms in the binomials. Then, add the partial products to find the

    product of the binomials.

ELABORATE

INTEGRATE MATHEMATICAL PRACTICES
Focus on Communication

MP.3 Tell students that the product of a polynomial with m terms and a polynomial with n terms has mn terms before you simplify it. Have students offer explanations for why this is true.

SUMMARIZE THE LESSON

? How is the FOIL method similar to using the Distributive Property to multiply larger polynomials? The FOIL method is a double use of the Distributive Property. The first term of the first binomial is distributed across the second binomial (F and O), and then the second term of the first binomial is distributed across the second binomial (I and L).

EVALUATE

ASSIGNMENT GUIDE

Concepts and Skills	Practice
Explore Modeling Binomial Multiplication	Exercise 24
Example 1 Multiplying Binomials Using the Distributive Property	Exercises 1–6, 27
Example 2 Multiplying Binomials Using FOIL	Exercises 7–12, 25
Example 3 Multiplying Polynomials	Exercises 13–18, 23
Example 4 Modeling with Polynomial Multiplication	Exercises 19–22, 26

VISUAL CUES

Show students the "FOIL face" to help them keep track of which terms to multiply when finding a product of binomials.

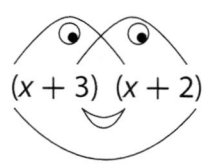

☆ Evaluate: Homework and Practice

- Online Homework
- Hints and Help
- Extra Practice

Multiply by using the Distributive Property.

1. $(x + 6)(x - 4)$

$$(x + 6)(x - 4) = x(x - 4) + 6(x - 4)$$
$$= x(x) + x(-4) + 6(x) + 6(-4)$$
$$= x^2 - 4x + 6x - 24$$
$$= x^2 + 2x - 24$$

2. $(2x + 5)(x - 3)$

$$(2x + 5)(x - 3) = 2x(x - 3) + 5(x - 3)$$
$$= 2x(x) + 2x(-3) + 5(x) + 5(-3)$$
$$= 2x^2 - 6x + 5x - 15$$
$$= 2x^2 - x - 15$$

3. $(x - 6)(x + 1)$

$$(x - 6)(x + 1) = x(x + 1) - 6(x + 1)$$
$$= x(x) + x(1) - 6(x) - 6(1)$$
$$= x^2 + x - 6x - 6$$
$$= x^2 - 5x - 6$$

4. $(x^2 + 3)(x - 4)$

$$(x^2 + 3)(x - 4) = x^2(x - 4) + 3(x - 4)$$
$$= x^2(x) + x^2(-4) + 3(x) + 3(-4)$$
$$= x^3 - 4x^2 + 3x - 12$$

5. $(x^2 + 11)(x + 6)$

$$(x^2 + 11)(x + 6) = x^2(x + 6) + 11(x + 6)$$
$$= x^2(x) + x^2(6) + 11(x) + 11(6)$$
$$= x^3 + 6x^2 + 11x + 66$$

6. $(x^2 + 8)(x - 5)$

$$(x^2 + 8)(x - 5) = x^2(x - 5) + 8(x - 5)$$
$$= x^2(x) + x^2(-5) + 8(x) + 8(-5)$$
$$= x^3 - 5x^2 + 8x - 40$$

Multiply by using the FOIL method.

7. $(x + 3)(x + 7)$

$$(x + 3)(x + 7) = x^2 + 7x + 3x + 21$$
$$= x^2 + 10x + 21$$

8. $(4x + 2)(x - 2)$

$$(4x + 7)(x - 2) = 4x^2 - 8x + 7x - 14$$
$$= 4x^2 - x - 14$$

9. $(3x + 2)(2x + 5)$

$$(3x + 2)(2x + 5) = 6x^2 + 15x + 4x + 10$$
$$= 6x^2 + 19x + 10$$

10. $(x^2 - 6)(x - 4)$

$$(x^2 - 6)(x - 4) = x^3 - 4x^2 - 6x + 24$$

11. $(x^2 + 9)(x - 3)$

$$(x^2 + 9)(x - 3) = x^3 - 3x^2 + 9x - 27$$

12. $(4x^2 - 4)(2x + 1)$

$$(4x^2 - 4)(2x + 1) = 8x^3 + 4x^2 - 8x - 4$$

Exercise	Depth of Knowledge (D.O.K.)	COMMON CORE Mathematical Practices
1–16	**1** Recall of Information	**MP.5** Using Tools
17–18	**2** Skills/Concepts	**MP.5** Using Tools
19–22	**1** Recall of Information	**MP.4** Modeling
23	**1** Recall of Information	**MP.5** Using Tools
24	**1** Recall of Information	**MP.4** Modeling
25–26	**2** Skills/Concepts H.O.T.	**MP.2** Reasoning
27	**2** Skills/Concepts H.O.T.	**MP.3** Logic

Multiply the polynomials.

13. $(x-3)(x^2+2x+1)$

$$(x-3)(x^2+2x+1) = x(x^2+2x+1)-3(x^2+2x+1)$$
$$= x(x^2)+x(2x)+x(1)-3(x^2)-3(2x)-3(1)$$
$$= x^3+2x^2+x-3x^2-6x-3$$
$$= x^3-x^2-5x-3$$

14. $(x+5)(x^3+6x^2+18x)$

$$(x+5)(x^3+6x^2+18x) = x(x^3+6x^2+18x)+5(x^3+6x^2+18x)$$
$$= x(x^3)+x(6x^2)+x(18x)+5(x^3)+5(6x^2)+5(18x)$$
$$= x^4+6x^3+18x^2+5x^3+30x^2+90x$$
$$= x^4+11x^3+48x^2+90x$$

15. $(x+4)(x^4+x^2+1)$

$$(x+4)(x^4+x^2+1) = x(x^4+x^2+1)+4(x^4+x^2+1)$$
$$= x(x^4)+x(x^2)+x(1)+4(x^4)+4(x^2)+4(1)$$
$$= x^5+x^3+x+4x^4+4x^2+4$$
$$= x^5+4x^4+x^3+4x^2+x+4$$

16. $(x-6)(x^5+4x^3+6x^2+2x)$

$$(x-6)(x^5+4x^3+6x^2+2x) = x(x^5+4x^3+6x^2+2x)-6(x^5+4x^3+6x^2+2x)$$
$$= x(x^5)+x(4x^3)+x(6x^2)+x(2x)-6(x^5)-6(4x^3)-6(6x^2)-6(2x)$$
$$= x^6+4x^4+6x^3+2x^2-6x^5-24x^3-36x^2-12x$$
$$= x^6-6x^5+4x^4-18x^3-34x^2-12x$$

17. $(x^2+x+3)(x^3-x^2+4)$

$$(x^2+x+3)(x^3-x^2+4) = x^2(x^3-x^2+4)+x(x^3-x^2+4)+3(x^3-x^2+4)$$
$$= x^2(x^3)+x^2(-x^2)+x^2(4)+x(x^3)+x(-x^2)+x(4)+3(x^3)$$
$$\quad +3(-x^2)+3(4)$$
$$= x^5-x^4+4x^2+x^4-x^3+4x+3x^3-3x^2+12$$
$$= x^5+2x^3+x^2+4x+12$$

18. $(x^3+x^2+2x)(x^4-x^3+x^2)$

$$(x^3+x^2+2x)(x^4-x^3+x^2) = x^3(x^4-x^3+x^2)+x^2(x^4-x^3+x^2)+2x(x^4-x^3+x^2)$$
$$= x^3(x^4)+x^3(-x^3)+x^3(x^2)+x^2(x^4)+x^2(-x^3)+x^2(x^2)+2x(x^4)$$
$$\quad +2x(-x^3)+2x(x^2)$$
$$= x^7-x^6+x^5+x^6-x^5+x^4+2x^5-2x^4+2x^3$$
$$= x^7+2x^5-x^4+2x^3$$

© Houghton Mifflin Harcourt Publishing Company

CURRICULUM INTEGRATION

In biology, a Punnett square is used to show possible ways that genes can combine at fertilization. Discuss how filling out a Punnett square is similar to multiplying binomials using a table or algebra tiles.

Multiplying Polynomial Expressions   **862**

When using the FOIL method, students may forget to combine like terms. Remind them that the terms that result from multiplying the inner and outer terms of two binomials need to be combined.

Write a polynomial equation for each situation.

19. **Gardening** Cameron is creating a garden. He designs a rectangular garden with a length of $(x + 6)$ feet and a width of $(x + 2)$ feet. When $x = 5$, what is the area of the garden?

Let y represent the area of Cameron's garden. Then the equation for this situation is $y = (x + 6)(x + 2)$. Use FOIL.

$y = x^2 + 2x + 6x + 12$

$y = x^2 + 8x + 12$

Now substitute 5 for x to finish the problem.

$y = x^2 + 8x + 12$

$y = 5^2 + 8 \cdot 5 + 12$

$y = 25 + 40 + 12$

$y = 77$

The area of Cameron's garden is 77 ft².

20. **Design** Sabrina has designed a rectangular painting that measures 50 feet in length and 40 feet in width. Alfred has also designed a rectangular painting, but it measures x feet shorter on each side. When $x = 3$, what is the area of Alfred's painting?

Let y represent the area of Alfred's painting. Then the equation for this situation is $y = (50 - x)(40 - x)$.

$y = (50 - x)(40 - x)$

Use FOIL.

$y = 2000 - 50x - 40x + x^2$

$y = x^2 - 90x + 2000$

Now substitute 3 for x to finish the problem.

$y = x^2 - 90 + 2000$

$y = 3^2 - 90 \cdot 3 + 2000$

$y = 9 - 270 + 2000$

$y = 1739$

The area of Alfred's painting is 1739 ft².

21. **Photography** Karl is putting a frame around a rectangular photograph. The photograph is 12 inches long and 10 inches wide, and the frame is the same width all the way around. What will be the area of the framed photograph?

Let x be the width of the frame. The length of the framed photograph is $(12 + 2x)$ inches and the width is $(10 + 2x)$ inches.

$(12 + 2x)(10 + 2x) = 120 + 24x + 20x + 4x^2$

$= 120 + 44x + 4x^2$

$= 4x^2 + 44x + 120$

The area of the framed photograph is $\left(4x^2 + 44x + 120\right)$ in².

22. Sports A tennis court is surrounded by a fence so that the distance from each boundary of the tennis court to the fence is the same. If the tennis court is 78 feet long and 36 feet wide, what is the area of the entire surface inside the fence?

Let x be the distance between each side of the court and the fence.

The length of the fenced area is $(78 + 2x)$ feet, and the width is $(36 + 2x)$ feet.

$(78 + 2x)(36 + 2x) = 2808 + 156x + 72x + 4x^2$

$= 2808 + 228x + 4x^2$

$= 4x^2 + 228x + 2808$

The area of fenced surface is $(4x^2 + 228x + 2808)\text{ft}^2$.

23. State the first term of each product.

a. $(2x + 1)(3x + 4)$

b. $(x^4 + x^2)(3x^8 + x^{11})$

c. $x(x + 9)$

d. $(x^2 + 9)(3x + 4)(2x + 6)$

e. $(x^3 + 4)(x^2 + 6)(x + 5)$

a. $6x^2$

b. $3x^{12}$

c. x^2

d. $6x^4$

e. x^6

24. Draw algebra tiles to model the factors in the polynomial multiplication modeled on the mat. Then write the factors and the product in simplest form.

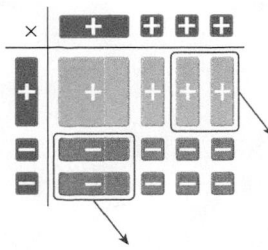

$(x - 2)(x + 3) = x^2 + x - 6$

© Houghton Mifflin Harcourt Publishing Company · Image Credits: ©Berna Namoglu/Shutterstock

GRAPHIC ORGANIZERS

Have students refer to the following patterned graphic organizer, in which each column represents one term of a binomial, as a model for the FOIL method of multiplying binomials.

First				
Outer				
Inner				
Last				

AVOID COMMON ERRORS

When finding the product of polynomials with many terms, students may miss some terms. Remind students that the product of a polynomial with m terms and a polynomial with n terms has mn terms before you simplify it. Encourage them to count the number of terms in the product to make sure they have enough.

JOURNAL

Have students make a table summarizing methods for multiplying polynomials. They should include examples for multiplying monomials, binomials, and trinomials.

25. Critical Thinking The product of 3 consecutive odd numbers is 2145. Write an expression for finding the numbers.

$$n(n + 2)(n + 4) = n^3 + 6n^2 + 8n$$

26. Represent Real-World Problems The town swimming pool is d feet deep. The width of the pool is 10 feet greater than 5 times its depth. The length of the pool is 35 feet greater than 5 times its depth. Write and simplify an expression to represent the volume of the pool.

$$(d)(5d + 10)(5d + 35)$$
$$= (5d^2 + 10d)(5d + 35)$$
$$= 25d^3 + 175d^2 + 50d^2 + 350d$$
$$= 25d^3 + 225d^2 + 350d$$

27. Explain the Error Bill argues that $(x + 1)(x + 19)$ simplifies to $x^2 + 20x + 20$. Explain his error.

Bill added the constants in the binomials. He should have multiplied the constant of each binomial together instead.

Lesson Performance Task

Roan is planning a large vegetable garden in her yard. She plans to have at least six x by x regions for rotating crops and some 2 or 3 feet by x strips for fruit bushes like blueberries and raspberries.

Design a rectangular garden for Roan and write a polynomial that will give its area.

The answers will vary widely but the method for finding the polynomial will be multiplying the length of the garden by its width. The dimensions will just be the sum of the defined regions along the horizontal edge and the vertical edge.

If each shaded region is one of the x by x plots and the others are 2 by x regions, then the dimensions are represented as follows:

$w = 3x + 4$

$\ell = 2x + 2$

The area will be represented by the following:

$A = \ell \cdot w$

$\quad = (2x + 2)(3x + 4)$

$\quad = 2x \cdot 3x + 2x \cdot 4 + 2 \cdot 3x + 2 \cdot 4$

$\quad = 6x^2 + 8x + 6x + 8$

$\quad = 6x^2 + 14x + 8$

If the regions for fruit bushes are 3 feet by x feet, the width is $3x + 6$, the length is $2x + 3$, and the area is $6x^2 + 21x + 18$.

INTEGRATE MATHEMATICAL PRACTICES
Focus on Modeling

MP.4 Encourage students to draw and label a diagram of the garden, and then use the labels to find the polynomials that represent the length and width of the garden.

INTEGRATE MATHEMATICAL PRACTICES
Focus on Communication

MP.3 Have students create a drawing or diagram to explain the method they used to multiply the polynomials representing the length and width of their gardens. Have students share their drawings with the class.

EXTENSION ACTIVITY

Have students select a value of x, find the perimeter and area of their garden designs, and then revise their designs to maximize the area without increasing the perimeter of their gardens.

Students may find that designing a square garden allows them to increase the area while keeping the same perimeter.

Scoring Rubric

2 points: Student correctly solves the problem and explains his/her reasoning.

1 point: Student shows good understanding of the problem but does not fully solve or explain his/her reasoning.

0 points: Student does not demonstrate understanding of the problem.

Multiplying Polynomial Expressions   **866**

Special Products of Binomials

Common Core Math Standards

The student is expected to:

COMMON CORE A-APR.A.1

Understand that polynomials form a system analogous to the integers, namely, they are closed under the operations of ... multiplication... Also A-SSE.A.1, A-CED.A.1

Mathematical Practices

COMMON CORE MP.7 Using Structure

Language Objective

Explain to a partner what a perfect square trinomial is.

ENGAGE

Essential Question: How can you find special products of binomials?

Use the special products rules for squaring a binomial or for finding the product of a sum and a difference.

PREVIEW: LESSON PERFORMANCE TASK

View the Engage section online. Discuss what safety precautions one would need to keep in mind when designing a fireplace. Then preview the Lesson Performance Task.

Resource Locker

18.3 Special Products of Binomials

Essential Question: How can you find special products of binomials?

⊘ Explore Modeling Special Products

Use algebra tiles to model the special products of binomials.

(A) Use algebra tiles to model $(2x + 3)^2$. Then write the product in simplest form.

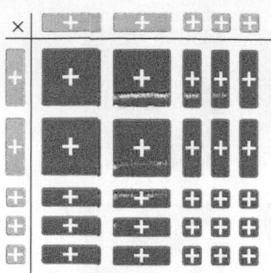

$(2x + 3)^2 = \boxed{4}\, x^2 + \boxed{12}\, x + \boxed{9}$.

(B) Use algebra tiles to model $(2x - 3)^2$. Then write the product in simplest form.

(C) Use algebra tiles to model $(2x + 3)(2x - 3)$. Then recount the tiles in the grid and write the expression.

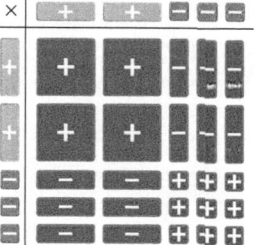

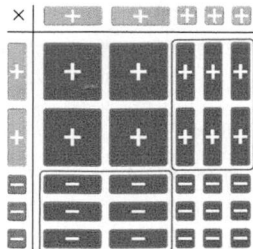

$(2x - 3)^2 = \boxed{4}\, x^2 - \boxed{12}\, x + \boxed{9}$.

$(2x + 3)(2x - 3) = \boxed{4}\, x^2 + \boxed{0}\, x - \boxed{9}$.

HARDCOVER PAGES 677–684

Turn to these pages to find this lesson in the hardcover student edition.

1. **Discussion** In Step A, which terms of the trinomial are perfect squares? What is the coefficient of x in the product? How can you use the values of a and b in the expression $(2x + 3)^2$ to produce the coefficient of each term in the trinomial? How can you generalize these results to write a rule for the product $(a + b)^2$?
   $4x^2$ and 9; 12; $4 = 2^2$, $9 = 3^2$, and $12 = 2(3) + 2(3) = 2(2)(3)$; $(a + b)^2 = a^2 + 2ab + b^2$.

2. **Discussion** In Step B, which terms of the trinomial are perfect squares? What is the coefficient of x in the trinomial? How can you use the values of a and b in the expression $(2x - 3)^2$ to produce the coefficient of each term in the trinomial? How can you generalize these results to write a rule for the product $(a - b)^2$?
   $4x^2$ and 9; -12; $4 = 2^2$, $9 = 3^2$, and $-12 = 2(-3) + 2(-3) = -2(2)(3)$; $(a - b)^2 = a^2 - 2ab + b^2$.

3. **Discussion** In Step C, which terms of the product are perfect squares? What is the coefficient of x in the product? How can you use the values of a and b in the expression $(2x + 3)(2x - 3)$ to produce the coefficient of each term in the product? How can you generalize these results to write a rule for the product $(a + b)(a - b)$?
   $4x^2$ and 9; 0; $4 = 2^2$, $9 = 3^2$, and $0 = 2(3) + 2(-3)$; $(a - b)(a + b) = a^2 - b^2$.

Explain 1   Multiplying $(a + b)^2$

In the Explore, you determined a formula for the square of a binomial sum, $(a + b)^2 = a^2 + 2ab + b^2$. A trinomial of the form $a^2 + 2ab + b^2$ is called a *perfect-square trinomial*. A **perfect-square trinomial** is a trinomial that is the result of squaring a binomial.

Example 1   Multiply.

(A) $(x + 4)^2$

$$a + b = a^2 + 2ab + b^2$$
$$(x + 4)^2 = x^2 + 2(x)(4) + 4^2$$
$$= x^2 + 8x + 16$$

(B) $(3x + 2y)^2$

$$(a + b)^2 = a^2 + 2ab + b^2$$
$$(3x + 2y)^2 = (3x)^2 + 2\left(\boxed{3}\ x\right)\left(\boxed{2}\ y\right) + \left(\boxed{2}\ y\right)^2$$
$$= 9x^2 + \boxed{12}\ xy + \boxed{4}\ y^2$$

4. In the perfect square trinomial $x^2 + bx + c$, what is the relationship between b and c? Explain.
   $c = \left(\dfrac{b}{2}\right)^2$; $(a + b)^2 = a^2 + 2ab + b^2$, and in this case, $a^2 = 1$, $2ab = b$, and $b^2 = c$

Your Turn

Multiply.

5. $(4 + x^2)^2$
   $$(4 + x^2)^2 = 4^2 + 2(4)(x^2) + (x^2)^2$$
   $$= 16 + 8x^2 + x^4$$

6. $(-x + 3)^2$
   $$(-x + 3)^2 = (-x)^2 + 2(-x)(3) + (3)^2$$
   $$= x^2 - 6x + 9$$

PROFESSIONAL DEVELOPMENT

Math Background

Special products of binomials are predictable patterns that can be applied as rules to save time and effort when multiplying binomials. They are also useful in a variety of situations that students will encounter as they progress in math. For example, the binomials $(a + b)$ and $(a - b)$ are called *conjugates*. Their product is always a difference of squares, $a^2 - b^2$. One use of conjugates is to rewrite an expression to eliminate a square root in the denominator, as follows:

$$\frac{1}{5 - \sqrt{3}} = \frac{1}{5 - \sqrt{3}} \cdot \frac{5 + \sqrt{3}}{5 + \sqrt{3}} = \frac{5 + \sqrt{3}}{5^2 - (\sqrt{3})^2} = \frac{5 + \sqrt{3}}{22}$$

EXPLORE

Modeling Special Products

INTEGRATE TECHNOLOGY

Students have the option of completing the algebra tiles activity either in the book or online.

INTEGRATE MATHEMATICAL PRACTICES
Focus on Modeling

MP.4 Remind students that when modeling multiplication with algebra tiles, the product of a yellow (positive) tile and a red (negative) tile is a red tile, while the product of two yellow tiles or two red tiles is a yellow tile.

EXPLAIN 1

Multiplying $(a + b)^2$

QUESTIONING STRATEGIES

? When squaring binomials, how many terms do you expect in the answer? Explain. Three terms; using the FOIL method, you will get four terms, but the outer and inner products will be like terms that can be combined, so the simplified result will have three terms.

? Why is the middle term of $(a + b)^2$ equal to $2ab$? If you use the Distributive Property to multiply the binomials, the result is $a^2 + ab + ab + b^2$ before simplifying. Combining the two middle terms gives $2ab$.

AVOID COMMON ERRORS

When students see a square of a binomial such as $(3x + 2)^2$, they sometimes square only the two terms, losing the x-term of the trinomial. To avoid this error, have students rewrite the expression in the form of the special products rule for $(a + b)^2$:

$$(3x + 2)^2 = (3x)^2 + (2)(3x)(2) + (2)^2.$$

EXPLAIN 2

Multiplying $(a-b)^2$

QUESTIONING STRATEGIES

? How is the product of $(a-b)^2$ similar to and different from the product of $(a+b)^2$? Both products are trinomials. The first and last terms are the same in both products, but the sign of the middle term is negative for $(a-b)^2$ and positive for $(a+b)^2$.

INTEGRATE MATHEMATICAL PRACTICES

Focus on Critical Thinking

MP.3 When finding the product of $(a-b)^2$, some students might believe that the middle term and the last term will both be negative numbers. Remind them that the last term comes from a number being squared, and thus will never be negative.

AVOID COMMON ERRORS

Students may forget to square all factors of each term when squaring a binomial. Suggest that they circle the coefficient and any exponents in each term so that they do not overlook them as they apply the special product rule.

⊘ Explain 2 Multiplying $(a-b)^2$

In the Explore, you determined the square of a binomial difference, $(a-b)^2 = a^2 - 2ab + b^2$. Because $a^2 - 2ab + b^2$ is the result of squaring the binomial $(a-b)$, $a^2 - 2ab + b^2$ is also a perfect-square trinomial.

Example 2 Multiply.

Ⓐ $(x-5)^2$

$(a-b)^2 = a^2 - 2ab + b^2$

$(x-5)^2 = x^2 - 2(x)(5) + 5^2$

$\qquad = x^2 - 10x + 25$

Ⓑ $(6x-1)^2$

$(a-b)^2 = a^2 - 2ab + b^2$

$(6x-1)^2 = \boxed{6x}^2 - 2\boxed{6x}\boxed{1} + \boxed{1}^2$

$\qquad = \boxed{36}x^2 - \boxed{12}x + \boxed{1}$

Reflect

7. Why is the last term of a perfect square trinomial always positive?
Because it is either the product of two positive numbers or the product of two negative numbers. In either case, the product is positive.

Your Turn

Multiply.

8. $(4x-3y)^2$
$(4x-3y)^2 = (4x)^2 - 2(4x)(3y) + (3y)^2$
$\qquad\qquad = 16x^2 - 24xy + 9y^2$

9. $(3-x^2)^2$
$(3-x^2)^2 = (3)^2 - 2(3)(x^2) + (x^2)^2$
$\qquad\qquad = 9 - 6x^2 + x^4$

⊘ Explain 3 Multiplying $(a+b)(a-b)$

In the Explore, you determined the formula $(a+b)(a-b) = a^2 - b^2$. A binomial of the form $a^2 - b^2$ is called a **difference of two squares**.

Example 3 Multiply.

Ⓐ $(x+6)(x-6)$

$(a+b)(a-b) = a^2 - b^2$

$(x+6)(x-6) = x^2 - 6^2$

$\qquad = x^2 - 36$

Ⓑ $(x^2+2y)(x^2-2y)$

$(a+b)(a-b) = a^2 - b^2$

$(x^2+2y)(x^2-2y) = \boxed{x^2}^2 - \boxed{2y}^2$

$\qquad = \boxed{1}x^{\boxed{4}} - \boxed{4}y^{\boxed{2}}$

Reflect

10. Why does the product of $a+b$ and $a-b$ always include a minus sign?
Because b and $-b$ have opposite signs, their product is negative.

Your Turn

11. $(7+x)(7-x)$

$(a+b)(a-b) = a^2 - b^2$
$(7+x)(7-x) = 7^2 - x^2$
$\qquad = 49 - x^2$

COLLABORATIVE LEARNING

Peer-to-Peer Activity

Have students work in pairs. Instruct each student to write two binomial multiplication problems: a square of a binomial and a product of a sum and difference with the same terms. Have partners switch papers and find the products, showing their work. Then have them check each other's results. Have students repeat with additional problems.

Explain 4   Modeling with Special Products

Example 4   Write and simplify an expression to represent the situation.

Design   A designer adds a border with a uniform width to a square rug. The original side length of the rug is $(x-5)$ feet. The side length of the entire rug including the original rug and the border is $(x+5)$ feet. What is the area of the border? Evaluate the area of the border if $x=10$ feet.

Analyze Information

Identify the important information.
The answer will be an expression that represents the area of the border.
List the important information:
- The rug is a square with a side length of $\boxed{x-5}$ feet.
- The side length of the entire square area including the original rug and the border
  is $\boxed{x+5}$ feet.

Formulate a Plan

The area of the rug in square feet is $\boxed{x-5}^2$. The total area of the rug plus the border in square feet
is $\boxed{x+5}^2$. The area of the rug can be subtracted from the total area to find the area of the border.

Solve

Find the total area:

$(x+5)^2 = \boxed{1}\,x^2 + 2\boxed{x}\boxed{5} + \boxed{5}^2$

$= \boxed{1}\,x^2 + \boxed{10}\,x + \boxed{25}$

Find the area of the rug:

$(x-5)^2 = \boxed{1}\,x^2 - 2\boxed{x}\boxed{5} + \boxed{5}^2$

$= \boxed{1}\,x^2 - \boxed{10}\,x + \boxed{25}$

Find the area of the border:

Area of border = total area − area of rug

$\text{Area} = \boxed{1}\,x^2 + \boxed{10}\,x + \boxed{25} - \left(\boxed{1}\,x^2 - \boxed{10}\,x + \boxed{25} \right)$

$= \boxed{1}\,x^2 + \boxed{10}\,x + \boxed{25} - \boxed{1}\,x^2 + \boxed{10}\,x - \boxed{25}$

$= \left(\boxed{1}\,x^2 - \boxed{1}\,x^2 \right) + \left(\boxed{10}\,x + \boxed{10}\,x \right) + \left(\boxed{25} - \boxed{25} \right)$

$= \boxed{0}\,x^2 + \boxed{20}\,x + \boxed{0}$

$= \boxed{20}\,x$

The area of the border is $\boxed{0}\,x^2 + \boxed{20}\,x + \boxed{0} = \boxed{20x}$ square feet.

Justify and Evaluate

Suppose that $x=10$. The rug is $\boxed{5}$ feet by $\boxed{5}$ feet, so its area is $\boxed{25}$ square feet. The total area is

$\left(\boxed{10} + \boxed{5} \right)^2 = \boxed{225}$ square feet, so the area of the border is $\boxed{225} - \boxed{25} = \boxed{200}$ square feet,

which is $\boxed{20}$ (10) when $x=10$. So the answer makes sense.

© Houghton Mifflin Harcourt Publishing Company

DIFFERENTIATE INSTRUCTION

Visual Cues

When students use the special product patterns, encourage them to (1) write the general pattern, (2) list which terms are represented by a and b in the general pattern, (3) substitute the terms into the pattern, and (4) simplify.

For example, to find $\left(3x^2+4\right)^2$, they would write:

Find $(a+b)^2 = a^2 + 2ab + b^2$ for $a=3x^2$ and $b=4$.

$$\left(3x^2+4\right)^2 = \left(3x^2\right)^2 + 2\left(3x^2\right)(4) + (4)^2$$

$$= 9x^4 + 24x^2 + 16$$

EXPLAIN 3

Multiplying $(a+b)(a-b)$

QUESTIONING STRATEGIES

?   What can you say about the sign of the last term in the product of a sum and a difference? Explain. **The sign of the last term is always negative because you are multiplying a positive term and a negative term.**

?   In a product of the form $(a+b)(a-b)$, how many terms do you expect in the answer? Explain. **There are only two terms because the product of the inner terms and the product of the outer terms are opposites, so their sum is zero.**

?   Is the product $(9-x)(9+x)$ a perfect square trinomial? Explain. **No; the two binomials are not the same, so it is not a perfect square. The product is $81-x^2$, which is the difference of two squares.**

EXPLAIN 4

Modeling with Special Products

QUESTIONING STRATEGIES

?   Why is it helpful to draw a diagram when solving a real-world problem involving length, area, or volume? **Labeling the dimensions in the diagram with the expressions that you know can help you see how to use those expressions to find the solution.**

INTEGRATE MATHEMATICAL PRACTICES
Focus on Technology

MP.5   When a real-world problem calls for evaluating a polynomial for a particular value of the variable, students can use a graphing calculator to check their calculations.

ELABORATE

INTEGRATE MATHEMATICAL PRACTICES

Focus on Patterns

MP.8 Point out that when you use special product patterns, a and b can be numbers, variables, or variable expressions.

SUMMARIZE THE LESSON

Complete the graphic organizer with students to summarize the rules for special products of binomials. Add a third column for students to provide examples of each type of product.

Special Products	
$(a+b)^2$	perfect square trinomial $a^2 + 2ab + b^2$
$(a-b)^2$	perfect square trinomial $a^2 - 2ab + b^2$
$(a+b)(a-b)$	difference of two squares $a^2 - b^2$

Reflect

12. **Critique Reasoning** Estelle solved a problem just like the example, except that the value of b in the two expressions was 8. Her expression for the area of the border was $-32x$. How do you know that she made an error? What do you think her error might have been?

   Because x is a length, x is positive, so $-32x$ represents a negative number. Area cannot be negative. She probably subtracted the total area from the area of the rug instead of the other way around.

Your Turn

Write and simplify an expression.

13. A square patio has a side length of $(x-3)$ feet. It is surrounded by a flower garden with a uniform width. The side length of the entire square area including the patio and the flower garden is $(x+3)$ feet. Write an expression for the area of the flower garden.

   Total area
   $$(x+3)^2 = x^2 + 2(x)(3) + 3^2 = x^2 + 6(x) + 9$$
   Area of patio
   $$(x-3)^2 = x^2 - 2(x)(3) + 3^2 = x^2 - 6(x) + 9$$
   Area of flower garden = total area − area of patio
   $$= x^2 + 6x + 9 - (x^2 - 6x + 9)$$
   $$= 12x$$

💬 Elaborate

14. How can you use the formula for the square of a binomial sum to write a formula for the square of a binomial difference?
   $$(a-b)^2 = \left(a + (-b)\right)^2 = a^2 + 2a(-b) + (-b)^2 = a^2 - 2ab + b^2$$

15. Can you use the formula for the square of a binomial sum to write a formula for a difference of squares?
   No; there is no way to rewrite a binomial squared as a difference of squares.

16. **Essential Question Check-In** Use one of the special product rules to describe in words how to find the coefficient of xy in the product $(5x - 3y)^2$.
   Multiply the coefficient of x in the binomial and the coefficient of y in the binomial. Then multiply the product by -2. The coefficient of xy in the product is $-2(5)(3) = -30$.

LANGUAGE SUPPORT 🔲EL

Connect Vocabulary

Discuss with students the various ways that the word *square* is used in this lesson. To *square* a number or expression is to raise it to a power of 2, or multiply it by itself. A *perfect square* is a number that results from squaring a number. A binomial raised to the second power, such as $(x+3)^2$ or $(x-3)^2$, equals a trinomial whose first and third terms are perfect squares. The trinomial as a whole is called a *perfect square trinomial*. The product of a binomial and a similar binomial with the opposite sign in the middle, such as $(x+2)(x-2)$, is a *difference of two squares*, $x^2 - 2^2$ or $x^2 - 4$.

⭐ Evaluate: Homework and Practice

- Online Homework
- Hints and Help
- Extra Practice

Multiply.

1. $(x + 8)^2$

$(a + b)^2 = a^2 + 2ab + b^2$
$(x + 8)^2 = x^2 + 2(x)(8) + 8^2$
$= x^2 + 16x + 64$

2. $(4x + 6y)^2$

$(a + b)^2 = a^2 + 2ab + b^2$
$(4x + 6y)^2 = (4x)^2 + 2(4x)(6y) + (6y)^2$
$= (16x)^2 + 48xy + 36y^2$

3. $(6 + x^2)^2$

$(a + b)^2 = a^2 + 2ab + b^2$
$(6 + x^2)^2 - 6^2 + 2(6)(x^2) + (x^2)^2$
$= 36 + 12x^2 + x^4$

4. $(-x + 5)^2$

$(a + b)^2 = a^2 + 2ab + b^2$
$(-x + 5)^2 = (-x)^2 + 2(-x)(5) + 5^2$
$= x^2 - 10x + 25$

5. $(x + 11)^2$

$(a + b)^2 = a^2 + 2ab + b^2$
$(x + 11)^2 = x^2 + 2(x)(11) + 11^2$
$= x^2 + 22x + 121$

6. $(8x + 9y)^2$

$(a + b)^2 = a^2 + 2ab + b^2$
$(8x + 9y)^2 = (8x)^2 + 2(8x)(9y) + (9y)^2$
$= 64x^2 + 144xy + 81y^2$

7. $(x - 3)^2$

$(a - b)^2 = a^2 - 2ab + b^2$
$(x - 3)^2 = x^2 - 2(x)(3) + 3^2$
$= x^2 - 6x + 9$

8. $(5x - 2)^2$

$(a - b)^2 = a^2 - 2ab + b^2$
$(5x - 2)^2 = (5x)^2 - 2(5x)(2) + 2^2$
$= 25x^2 - 20x + 4$

9. $(6x - 7y)^2$

$(a - b)^2 = a^2 - 2ab + b^2$
$(6x - 7y)^2 = (6x)^2 - 2(6x)(7y) + (7y)^2$
$= (36x^2) - 84xy + 49y^2$

10. $(5 - x^2)^2$

$(a - b)^2 = a^2 - 2ab + b^2$
$(5 - x^2)^2 = 5^2 - 2(5)(x^2) + (x^2)^2$
$= 25 - 10x^2 + x^4$

11. $(5x - 4y)^2$

$(a + b)^2 = a^2 + 2ab + b^2$
$(5x - 4y)^2 = (5x)^2 - 2(5x)(4y) + (4y)^2$
$= 25x^2 - 40xy + 16y^2$

12. $(7 - 2x^2)^2$

$(a + b)^2 = a^2 + 2ab + b^2$
$(7 - 2x^2)^2 = (7)^2 - 2(7)(2x^2) + (2x^2)^2$
$= 49 - 28x^2 + 4x^4$

EVALUATE

Personal Math Trainer

ASSIGNMENT GUIDE

Concepts and Skills	Practice
Explore Modeling Special Products	Exercise 25
Example 1 Multiplying $(a + b)^2$	Exercises 1–6
Example 2 Multiplying $(a - b)^2$	Exercises 7–12, 24, 26
Example 3 Multiplying $(a + b)(a - b)$	Exercises 13–18
Example 4 Modeling with Special Products	Exercises 19–23

COGNITIVE STRATEGIES

Remind students that if they forget the formulas for special product patterns, they can always use the Distributive Property to find the product.

Exercise	Depth of Knowledge (D.O.K.)	COMMON CORE Mathematical Practices	
1–18	**1** Recall of Information	**MP.5**	Using Tools
19–20	**1** Recall of Information	**MP.4**	Modeling
21	**2** Skills/Concepts	**MP.4**	Modeling
22–23	**2** Skills/Concepts	**MP.5**	Using Tools
24	**2** Skills/Concepts	**MP.3**	Logic
25–26	**2** Skills/Concepts **H.O.T.**	**MP.3**	Logic

When using the rules for special products, students often forget to square the coefficients of terms in the binomial. Suggest that students first write the coefficient and variable with the exponent applied to each one, and then simplify. For example, to find $(3y - 5x^2)^2$, they would write $3^2y^2 - 2(3y)(5x^2) + 5^2(x^2)^2$, then simplify to $9y^2 - 30x^2y + 25x^4$.

13. $(x + 4)(x - 4)$

$$(a + b)(a - b) = a^2 - b^2$$
$$(x + 4)(x - 4) = x^2 - 4^2$$
$$= x^2 - 16$$

14. $(x^2 + 6y)(x^2 - 6y)$

$$(a + b)(a - b) = a^2 - b^2$$
$$(x^2 + 6y)(x^2 - 6y) = (x^2)^2 - (6y)^2$$
$$= x^4 - 36y^2$$

15. $(9 + x)(9 - x)$

$$(a + b)(a - b) = a^2 - b^2$$
$$(9 + x)(9 - x) = 9^2 - x^2$$
$$= 81 - x^2$$

16. $(2x + 5)(2x - 5)$

$$(a + b)(a - b) = a^2 - b^2$$
$$(2x + 5)(2x - 5) = (2x)^2 - 5^2$$
$$= 4x^2 - 25$$

17. $(3x^2 + 8y)(3x^2 - 8y)$

$$(a + b)(a - b) = a^2 - b^2$$
$$(3x^2 + 8y)(3x^2 - 8y) = (3x^2)^2 - (8y)^2$$
$$= 9x^4 - 64y^2$$

18. $(7 + 3x)(7 - 3x)$

$$(a + b)(a - b) = a^2 - b^2$$
$$(7 + 3x)(7 - 3x) = 7^2 - (3x)^2$$
$$= 49 - 9x^2$$

Write and simplify an expression to represent the situation.

19. Design A square swimming pool is surrounded by a cement walkway with a uniform width. The swimming pool has a side length of $(x - 2)$ feet. The side length of the entire square area including the pool and the walkway is $(x + 1)$ feet. Write an expression for the area of the walkway. Then find the area of the cement walkway when $x = 7$ feet.

Area of walkway = Total area − area of pool
$$= (x + 1)^2 - (x - 2)^2$$
$$= x^2 + 2x + 1 - (x^2 - 4x + 4)$$
$$= x^2 + 2x + 1 - x^2 + 4x - 4$$
$$= 6x - 3$$

When $x = 7$ feet, the area of the walkway is $6(7) - 3 = 39$ square feet.

20. This week Leo worked $(x + 4)$ hours at a pizzeria. He is paid $(x - 4)$ dollars per hour. Leo's friend Frankie worked the same number of hours, but he is paid $(x - 2)$ dollars per hour. Write an expression for the total amount paid to the two workers. Then find the total amount if $x = 12$ dollars.

Total amount paid = Leo's pay + Frankie's pay
$$= (x + 4)(x - 4) + (x + 4)(x - 2)$$
$$= x^2 - 16 + (x^2 + 2x - 8)$$
$$= 2x^2 + 2x - 24$$

When $x = 12$, $2x^2 + 2x - 24 = 2(144) + 2(12) - 24 = 288$.

The total amount paid to the two workers was $288.

21. Kyra is framing a square painting with side lengths of $(x + 8)$ inches. The total area of the painting and the frame has a side length of $(2x - 6)$ inches. The material for the frame will cost $0.08 per square inch. Write an expression for the area of the frame. Then find the cost of the material for the frame if $x = 16$.

Area of frame = Total Area − Area of painting
$$= (2x - 6)^2 - (x + 8)^2$$
$$= 4x^2 - 24x + 36 - (x^2 + 16x + 64)$$
$$= 4x^2 - 24x + 36 - x^2 - 16x - 64$$
$$= 3x^2 - 40x - 28$$

When $x = 16$, $3x^2 - 40x - 28 = 3(256) - 640 - 28 = 100$.

The area of the frame is 100 square inches, so the cost is $0.08(100) = $8.

22. Geometry Circle A has a radius of $(x + 4)$ units. A larger circle, B, has a radius of $(x + 5)$ units. Use the formula $A = \pi r^2$ to write an expression for the difference in the areas of the circles. Leave your answer in terms of π. Then use 3.14 for π to approximate to the nearest whole number the difference in the areas when $x = 10$.

Differece = Area of circle B − area of circle A
$$= \pi(x + 5)(x + 5) - \pi(x + 4)(x + 4)$$
$$= \pi(x^2 + 10x + 25) - \pi(x^2 + 8x + 16)$$
$$= \pi x^2 + 10\pi x + 25\pi - \pi x^2 - 8\pi x - 16\pi$$
$$= 2\pi x + 9\pi$$

When $x - 10$, $2\pi x + 9\pi = 29\pi \approx 91$ square units.

23. A square has sides with lengths of $(x - 1)$ units. A rectangle has a length of x units and a width of $(x - 2)$ units. Which statements about the situation are true? Select all that apply.

a. The area of the square is $(x^2 - 1)$ square units.
Area of square = $(x - 1)^2 = x^2 - 2x + 1$, not $(x^2 - 1)$ square units.

b. The area of the rectangle is $x^2 - 2x$ square units.
Area of rectangle = $x(x - 2) = (x^2 - 2x)$ square units.

c. The area of the square is greater than the area of the rectangle.
For all values of x, $x^2 - 2x + 1 > x^2 - 2x$.

d. The value of x must be greater than 2.
If $x \leq 2$, the length of the rectangle is less than or equal to 0, which is not possible.

e. The difference in the areas is $2x - 1$.

The difference in the areas is $x^2 - 2x + 1 - (x^2 - 2x) = 1$.

So, b, c, and d are true.

AUDITORY CUES

Have students learn "verbal rules" for special products and repeat them aloud to help remember them. For example, the square of a binomial $(a + b)^2$ or $(a - b)^2$ is:

- first term squared
- plus (or minus) two times the product of the terms
- plus last term squared.

Have students create a similar verbal rule for $(a + b)(a - b) = a^2 - b^2$.

AVOID COMMON ERRORS

Students may confuse the square of a difference, $(p - q)^2$, with the difference of two squares, $p^2 - q^2$. Remind them that the square of a binomial is always a trinomial. The product of two binomials can be a binomial only if one term "drops out" because like terms cancel, as it does when a sum is multiplied by a difference.

24. **Explain the Error** Marco wrote the expression $(2x - 7y)^2 = 4x^2 - 49y^2$. Explain and correct his error.

Marco may have confused a difference of squares and the square of a binomial difference. He wrote the difference of the squares of the terms instead of square of a binomial difference. The correct product is $4x^2 - 28xy + 49y^2$.

H.O.T. Focus on Higher Order Thinking

25. **Critical Thinking** Use the FOIL method to justify each special product rule.

a. $(a + b)^2$

$$(a + b)^2 = a^2 + ab + ab + b^2$$
$$= a^2 + 2ab + b^2$$

b. $(a - b)^2$

$$(a - b)^2 = a^2 - ab - ab - b^2$$
$$= a^2 - 2ab + b^2$$

c. $(a + b)(a - b)$

$$(a + b)(a - b) = a^2 + ab - ab - b^2$$
$$= a^2 - b^2$$

26. **Communicate Mathematical Ideas** Explain how you can use the special product rules and the Distributive Property to write a general rule for $(a - b)^3$. Then write the rule.

First write $(a - b)^3$ as $(a - b)(a - b)(a - b)$, then use the Distributive Property to write the product.

$$(a - b)^3 = (a - b)(a - b)(a - b)$$
$$= (a^2 - 2ab + b^2)(a - b)$$
$$= a^3 - a^2b - 2a^2b + 2ab^2 + ab^2 - b^3$$
$$= a^3 - 3a^2b + 3ab^2 - b^3$$

Lesson Performance Task

When building a square-shaped outdoor fireplace, the ground needs to be replaced with stone for an additional two feet on each side. Write a polynomial for the area that needs to be excavated to create an x by x fireplace.

Design your ideal space for sitting around a fire pit and relaxing. Add furniture, flowerbeds, rock gardens, and any other desired features.

Evaluate the polynomial for the size fireplace you are including.

The length and width of the area to be excavated are both $2 + x + 2$ or $x + 4$ feet.

Therefore, the area that needs to be excavated is the following:

$A(x) = \ell \cdot w$

$= (x + 4)(x + 4)$

$= (x + 4)^2$

$= x^2 + 2 \cdot 4 \cdot x + 16$

$= x^2 + 8x + 16$

The plans for the outdoor space and excavated area will vary with the individual, but the excavated area will be $A(x)$ evaluated for x, where x is the length/width of the fire pit.

INTEGRATE MATHEMATICAL PRACTICES

Focus on Modeling

MP.4 Encourage students to draw and label a diagram for the situation in the Lesson Performance Task.

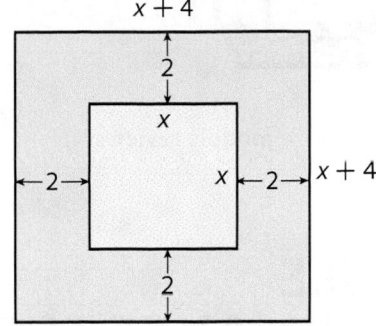

QUESTIONING STRATEGIES

? What type of special product represents the area of the outdoor fireplace? It is a perfect-square trinomial, the result of squaring a binomial.

EXTENSION ACTIVITY

Have students investigate how Pascal's triangle, which was developed by 17th–century mathematician Blaise Pascal, is related to products of binomials. Students should find that the coefficients of a binomial raised to the nth power match the nth row in the triangle. For example, the fourth row of the triangle corresponds to $(a + b)^4 = 1a^4 + 4a^3b + 6a^2b^2 + 4ab^3 + 1b^4$.

```
            1
          1 2 1
        1 3 3 1
      1 4 6 4 1
    1 5 10 10 5 1
```

Scoring Rubric

2 points: Student correctly solves the problem and explains his/her reasoning.

1 point: Student shows good understanding of the problem but does not fully solve or explain his/her reasoning.

0 points: Student does not demonstrate understanding of the problem.

Special Products of Binomials   **876**

ASSESSMENT AND INTERVENTION

Assign or customize module reviews.

MODULE PERFORMANCE TASK

COMMON CORE

Mathematical Practices: MP.1, MP.2, MP.4, MP.5, MP.6
A-APR.A.1, A-CED.A.2, S-ID.B.6a

SUPPORTING STUDENT REASONING

Students should begin this problem by deciding how to represent the trends in pounds consumed and in price. Here are some questions they might have.

- **The regression line for the average annual cost does not seem linear. How can I fix this?** Point out that the student plotted the product of pounds and prices per year. Encourage the student to find a model that predicts the average number of pounds and another that represents the average price for each year.

- **What is an easy way to represent each year to find a linear regression line on my calculator?** Suggest that students use 0 for 2004, 1 for 2005, and so on.

- **I have an expression for the price per pound and another one for the pounds. What do I do with them?** Elicit from students that they are trying to find the total cost for a future year, and that to find the total cost for any year is a product of the price per pound and the number of pounds.

Essential Question: How can you use multiplying polynomials to solve real-world problems?

© Houghton Mifflin Harcourt Publishing Company

Key Vocabulary
difference of two squares
  (*diferencia de dos cuadrados*)
FOIL (*FOIL*)
perfect-square trinomial
  (*trinomio cuadrado perfecto*)

KEY EXAMPLE   (Lesson 18.1)

Multiply.

$(-3x^2y^4)(-6x^3y)$

$(-3 \cdot -6)(x^2 \cdot x^3)(y^4 \cdot y)$ *Group terms with the same base.*

$(-3 \cdot -6)(x^{2+3})(y^{4+1})$ *Apply the Product of Powers Property:* $a^m \cdot a^n = a^{m+n}$.

$18x^5y^5$

KEY EXAMPLE   (Lesson 18.2)

Multiply.

$(3x + 7)(x - 1)$ *Multiply using FOIL.*

$= 3x^2 - 3x + 7x - 7$ *First terms* $(3x \cdot x)$ *Outer terms* $(3x \cdot -1)$ *Inner terms* $(7 \cdot x)$ *and Last terms* $(7 \cdot -1)$

$= 3x^2 + 4x - 7$

$(4x - 2)(-2x - 9)$

$= (4x)(-2x) + (4x)(-9) + (-2)(-2x) + (-2)(-9)$

$= -8x^2 - 36x + 4x + 18$

$= -8x^2 - 32x + 18$

KEY EXAMPLE   (Lesson 18.3)

Multiply

$(x - 7)(x + 7)$ *The product will be the difference of two squares.*

$= x^2 - 7^2$ $(a + b)(a - b) = a^2 - b^2$

$= x^2 - 49$

$(2x + 5)^2$ *The product will be a perfect-square trinomial.*

$= (2x)^2 + 2(2x)(5) + 5^2$ $(a + b)^2 = a^2 + 2ab + b^2$

$= 4x^2 + 20x + 25$

SCAFFOLDING SUPPORT

- For students who don't know how to start, suggest that they find a way to model the year and price and another one to model the year and the pounds.

- Watch for students who forget to consider the average price of oranges for each year.

- Students are expected to write different expressions for the price and the pounds. They may need to be reminded that their goal is to predict how much the average person will spend in 2014.

EXERCISES

Multiply. *(Lessons 18.1, 18.2)*

1. $(7y^5)(-4y^2)$

$-28y^7$

2. $(3p^4q)(12p^3q^2)$

$36p^7q^3$

3. $(x-4)(x+8)$

$x^2 + 4x - 32$

4. $(4x-1)(2x+6)$

$8x^2 + 22x - 6$

Multiply. Identify each product as a perfect-square trinomial or a difference of squares. *(Lesson 18.3)*

5. $(3x+9)(3x-9)$

$9x^2 - 81$; difference of squares

6. $(x-8)^2$

$x^2 - 16x + 64$, perfect-square trinomial

MODULE PERFORMANCE TASK

Orange Consumption

About how much do Americans spend per capita on oranges each year? The average price of oranges was $0.57 per pound in 2004 and has been increasing at a rate of $0.02 per year. The table below shows the per capita orange consumption (in pounds) in the United States from 2004–2012.

Year	2004	2005	2006	2007	2008	2009	2010	2011	2012
Pounds Consumed	83.6	80.3	72.8	65.2	62.3	62.7	61.8	62.3	54.9

How can you use this data to find a model and use it to predict how much money the average American spent on oranges in 2014?

Use your own paper to complete the task. Be sure to write down all your data and assumptions. Then use graphs, numbers, words, or algebra to explain how you reached your conclusion.

SAMPLE SOLUTION

Assumptions

The data in the table can be represented by a linear model. The price of oranges can also be represented by a linear model. The product of the two linear expressions models the average amount spent per capita per year.

Let the years go from 0 for 2004 through 8 for 2012. The price per pound for oranges can be modeled by $y = 0.57 + 0.02x$, where x is the year and y is the price. For the data in the table, linear regression from a calculator gives the equation $y = -3.22x + 80.2$.

Multiply the expressions:

$(-3.22x + 80.2)(0.02x + 0.57)$
$= -0.0644x^2 - 0.2314x + 45.714$

So, a model for the average amount spent per capita for oranges during the years 2004–2012 is $y = -0.0644x^2 - 0.2314x + 45.714$, where x is the number of years since 2004.

If the pattern continues, the amount spent in 2014 (year 10) is $-0.0644(10)^2 - 0.2314(10) + 45.714$ $= 36.96$. Therefore, the amount the average American will spend on oranges in 2014 is $36.96.

DISCUSSION OPPORTUNITIES

- In what ways can you check to see if the model you created is reasonable?

- Under what circumstances might the model we found today not work in future decades?

Ready to Go On?

ASSESS MASTERY

Use the assessment on this page to determine if students have mastered the concepts and standards covered in this module.

ASSESSMENT AND INTERVENTION

Access Ready to Go On? assessment online, and receive instant scoring, feedback, and customized intervention or enrichment.

ADDITIONAL RESOURCES

Response to Intervention Resources

- Reteach Worksheets

Differentiated Instruction Resources

- Reading Strategies **EL**
- Success for English Learners **EL**
- Challenge Worksheets

Assessment Resources

- Leveled Module Quizzes

879 Module 18

(Ready) to Go On?

18.1–18.3 Multiplying Polynomials

- Online Homework
- Hints and Help
- Extra Practice

Multiply. Identify each product as a perfect-square trinomial, a difference of squares, or neither. *(Lessons 18.1, 18.2, 18.3)*

1. $(2y - 5)(2y + 5)$

$4y^2 - 25$; difference of squares

2. $(9r^3s^3)(10r^3s^2)$

$90r^6s^5$; neither

3. $(4x + 1)^2$

$16x^2 + 8x + 1$; perfect-square trinomial

4. $(3x - 4)(x + 8)$

$3x^2 + 20x - 32$; neither

Use the model of the rectangular prism to answer Exercises 5 and 6. The width of the prism is $(2x - 2)$ ft, and its height is $(x + 6)$ ft. The area of the base of the prism is $(3x^2 + 2x - 4)$ ft².

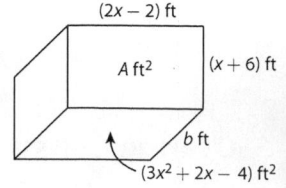

5. Write an expression to represent the area of side A. *(Lesson 18.3)*

$2x^2 + 10x - 12$

6. Could the length of b be $(3x - 1)$ ft? Explain why or why not. *(Lesson 18.3)*

No. The area of the bottom face of the prism is $(3x^2 + 2x - 4)$ ft², but the product of $(3x - 1)$ ft and $(2x - 2)$ ft is $(6x^2 - 8x + 2)$ ft².

ESSENTIAL QUESTION

7. Is it necessary to use the formulas for special products of binomials to multiply these binomials? Explain.

Possible Answer: No, it is not necessary. Special products of binomials can be found by using FOIL instead of their formulas. However, the formulas are likely to be faster to use.

© Houghton Mifflin Harcourt Publishing Company

COMMON CORE **Common Core Standards**

Lesson	Items	Content Standards	Mathematical Practices
18.2	1	**A-APR.A.1**	**MP.7**
18.1	2	**A-APR.A.1**	**MP.7**
18.3	3	**A-APR.A.1**	**MP.7**
18.2	4	**A-APR.A.1**	**MP.7**
18.3	5	**A-APR.A.1, A-SSE.A.1, A-CED.A.1**	**MP.4**
18.3	6	**A-APR.A.1, A-SSE.A.1, A-CED.A.1**	**MP.6**

Assessment Readiness

1. Find the standard form for the product of $(x^2 + 8)$ and $(x^2 - 2)$. Choose True or False for each statement about the product.
   - **A.** It is a 4th degree polynomial.   ● True   ○ False
   - **B.** The constant term is -16.   ● True   ○ False
   - **C.** It has 3 terms.   ● True   ○ False

2. Multiply $(5x - 9)^2$. Choose True or False for each statement about the product.
   - **A.** The coefficient of the x-term is -45.   ○ True   ● False
   - **B.** The leading term is $25x^2$.   ● True   ○ False
   - **C.** The constant term is 81.   ● True   ○ False

3. Find the product $(3x + 6)(3x - 6)$. Show your work.

   $9x^2 - 36;$

   $$(3x + 6)(3x - 6) = (3x)^2 - (6)^2$$
   $$= 9x^2 - 36$$

4. Find the product $(x + 10)(4x + 5)$. Show your work.

   $4x^2 + 45x + 50\,;$

   $$(x + 10)(4x + 5) = x(4x) + 5(x) + 10(4x) + 5(10)$$
   $$= 4x^2 + 5x + 40x + 50$$
   $$= 4x^2 + 45x + 50$$

5. A rectangle has a length $(x + 6)$ m and a width of 7 m. Write expressions to represent the perimeter and area of the rectangle. Explain how you determined your answers.

   The perimeter is $(2x + 26)$ m, and the area is $(7x + 42)$ m². Possible

   answer: I added the length and width together and doubled the sum to

   find the perimeter. I multiplied the length by the width to find the area.

© Houghton Mifflin Harcourt Publishing Company

MIXED REVIEW
Assessment Readiness

ASSESSMENT AND INTERVENTION

Assign ready-made or customized practice tests to prepare students for high-stakes tests.

ADDITIONAL RESOURCES

Assessment Resources

- Leveled Module Quizzes: Modified, B

AVOID COMMON ERRORS

Item 5 When completing an expression for the perimeter, some students may forget that there are two instances of each side, and instead just add $(x + 6)$ and 7 to get $x + 13$. Remind students to double-check their formulas.

COMMON CORE Common Core Standards

Lesson	Items	Content Standards	Mathematical Practices
17.1, 18.2	1*	A-SSE.A.1a, A-APR.A.1	MP.1
17.1, 18.3	2*	A-SSE.A.1a, A-APR.A.1	MP.1
18.3	3	A-APR.A.1	MP.2
18.2	4	A-APR.A.1	MP.2
17.2, 18.1	5*	A-CED.A.1, A-APR.A.1	MP.4

* Item integrates mixed review concepts from previous modules or a previous course.

MIXED REVIEW
Assessment Readiness

ASSESSMENT AND INTERVENTION

Assign ready-made or customized practice tests to prepare students for high-stakes tests.

ADDITIONAL RESOURCES

Assessment Resources

- Leveled Unit Tests: Modified, A, B, C
- Performance Assessment

AVOID COMMON ERRORS

Item 7   Some students may graph the two equations after finding them, but they may only look at a small window that does not include the intersection. Remind students to use a larger window or use the table function whenever it seems necessary.

Assessment Readiness

- Online Homework
- Hints and Help
- Extra Practice

1. Solve each equation. Is the correct solution given?
   - **A.** $-4(p + 3) = -3p - 7; p = -5$ ● Yes   ○ No
   - **B.** $8r - 18 = -14; r = \frac{1}{2}$ ● Yes   ○ No
   - **C.** $\frac{t}{5} - 2 = -5; t = 15$ ○ Yes   ● No

2. Simplify $5x^2\left(\frac{2}{5} - x\right)$. Determine if each statement is True or False.
   - **A.** The expression is a trinomial.   ○ True   ● False
   - **B.** The expression has a degree of 3.   ● True   ○ False
   - **C.** The expression has a constant term of -2.   ○ True   ● False

3. Is the given polynomial in standard form?
   - **A.** $-5y^2 + 5y + 24$ ● Yes   ○ No
   - **B.** $7x^5 - 19 + x$ ○ Yes   ● No
   - **C.** $15z - 3$ ● Yes   ○ No

4. Simplify $(3x - 8)(x + 2)$. Is the given statement True or False?
   - **A.** The coefficient of the x-term is -2.   ● Yes   ○ No
   - **B.** The leading term is $3x^2$.   ● Yes   ○ No
   - **C.** The constant term is -16.   ● Yes   ○ No

5. Is the product of each of the following pairs of factors a difference of squares?
   - **A.** $3(x - 3)$ ○ Yes   ● No
   - **B.** $4(4x^2 - 1)$ ● Yes   ○ No
   - **C.** $(5x - 2)(5x + 2)$ ● Yes   ○ No

6. Write the difference of the following polynomials in standard form: $(11 - 8y + 2y^2) - (y^2 - 15)$. Classify the difference by its degree and number of terms.

   $y^2 - 8y + 26;$ 2nd degree trinomial

COMMON CORE Common Core Standards

Items	Content Standards	Mathematical Practices
1*	A-REI.B.3	MP.2
2	A-SSE.A.1a	MP.1
3	A-SSE.A.2	MP.7
4	A-APR.A.1	MP.2
5	A-APR.A.1	MP.2
6	F-LE.A.3	MP.5

* Item integrates mixed review concepts from previous modules or a previous course.

7. Sandra has been offered two jobs. Job A pays $25,000 a year with an 8% raise each year. Job B pays $28,000 a year with a $2,500 raise each year. Write a function to represent each salary t years after being hired. Use a graphing calculator to compare the two salary plans. Will Job A ever have a higher salary than Job B? If so, after how many years will this occur? Explain how you solved this problem.

$A(t) = 25,000(1.08)^t$ and $B(t) = 2500t + 28,000$; Yes, after 10 years; I graphed

both functions on my graphing calculator and found the x-value of the point

of intersection of the graphs, which is about 9.4 and rounded up.

8.

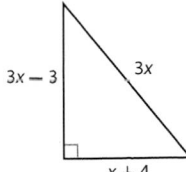

$3x - 3$ $3x$

$x + 4$

Write an expression that represents the perimeter of the triangle in terms of x and an expression that represents the area of the triangle in terms of x. If the perimeter is 36 cm, what is the area of the triangle? Explain how you solved this problem.

Perimeter $= x + 4 + 3x - 3 + 3x = 7x + 1$ cm,

Area: $\frac{1}{2}(x + 4)(3x - 3) = 1.5x^2 + 4.5x - 6$. I solved $7x + 1 = 36$ and found $x = 5$,

so the base length is $5 + 4 = 9$ cm and the height is $3(5) - 3 = 12$ cm.

The area of the triangle is $\frac{1}{2}(9)(12) = 54$ cm^2.

Performance Tasks

★ **9.** The profits of two different manufacturing plants can be modeled as shown.

Eastern: $-0.03x^2 + 25x - 1500$

Southern: $-0.02x^2 + 21x - 1700$

A. Write a polynomial that represents the difference of the profits at the Eastern plant and the profits at the Southern plant.

B. Write a polynomial that represents the total profits from both plants.

A. $-0.01x^2 + 4x + 200$

B. $-0.05x^2 + 46x - 3200$

PERFORMANCE TASKS

There are three different levels of performance tasks:

   * **Novice:** These are short word problems that require students to apply the math they have learned in straightforward, real-world situations.

   ** **Apprentice:** These are more involved problems that guide students step-by-step through more complex tasks. These exercises include more complicated reasoning, writing, and open-ended elements.

   *****Expert:** These are open-ended, nonroutine problems that, instead of stepping the students through, ask them to choose their own methods for solving and justify their answers and reasoning.

SCORING GUIDES

Item 9 (2 points)

A. 1 point for correct polynomial difference

B. 1 point for correct polynomial sum

Common Core Standards

Items	Content Standards	Mathematical Practices
7	A-APR.A.1	MP.2
8*	A-CED.A.1	MP.4

* Item integrates mixed review concepts from previous modules or a previous course.

Item 10 (6 points)

a. 3 points for a correct diagram

b. 1 point for correct length expression
   1 point for correct width expression
   1 point for correct area expressions

Item 11 (6 points)

a. 2 points for correct polynomial

b. 1 point for correct answer
   2 points for explanation

c. 1 point for correct dimensions

★★**10.** A rectangular swimming pool is 25 feet long and 10 feet wide. It is surrounded by a fence that is x feet from each side of the pool.

  A. Draw a diagram of the situation.

  B. Write expressions for the length, width, and area of the fenced region.

  A.

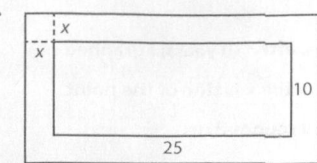

  B. $L: 2x + 25$

   $W: 2x + 10$

   $A: 4x^2 + 70x + 250$

★★★**11.** Tammy plans to put a wallpaper border around the perimeter of her room. She will not put the border across the doorway, which is 3 feet wide.

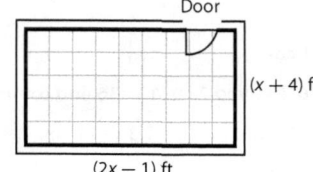

  A. Write a polynomial that represents the number of feet of wallpaper border that Tammy will need.

  B. A local store has 50 feet of the border that Tammy has chosen. What is the greatest whole-number value of x for which this amount would be enough for Tammy's room? Justify your answer.

  C. Determine the dimensions of Tammy's room for the value of x that you found in part **B**.

  A. $6x + 3$

  B. 7; if $x = 7$, Tammy will need $6(7) + 3 = 45$ feet of wallpaper border.

   However, if $x = 8$, Tammy will need $6(8) + 3 = 51$ feet of wallpaper

   border, which is more than the store has.

  C. 13 ft by 11 ft

Camp Director For the initial year of a summer camp, 44 girls and 56 boys enrolled. Each year thereafter, 5 more girls and 8 more boys enrolled in the camp.

a. Let t be the time (in years) since the camp opened. Write a rule for each of the following functions:

- $g(t)$, the number of girls enrolled as a function of time t
- $b(t)$, the number of boys enrolled as a function of time t
- $T(t)$, the total enrollment as a function of time t

b. The cost per child each year was $200. Write a rule for each of the following functions:

- $C(t)$, the cost per child as a function of time t
- $R(t)$, the revenue generated by the total enrollment as a function of time t

c. Explain why $C(t)$ is a constant function.

d. What was the initial revenue for the camp? What was the annual rate of change in the revenue?

e. The camp director had initial expenses of $18,000, which increased each year by $2,500. Write a rule for the expenses function $E(t)$. Then write a rule for the profit function $P(t)$ based on the fact that profit is the difference between revenue and expenses.

---

a. $g(t) = 5t + 44$

$b(t) = 8t + 56$

$T(t) = 13t + 100$

b. $C(t) = 200$

$R(t) = 200 \times (13t + 100) = 2600t + 20,000$

c. There is no change in the cost of the camp from year to year.

d. $20,000; $2,600 per year

e. $E(t) = 2,500t + 18,000$; $P(t) = R(t) - E(t) = 100t + 2000$

MATH IN CAREERS

Camp Director In this Unit Performance Task, students can see how a camp director uses mathematics on the job.

For more information about careers in mathematics as well as various mathematics appreciation topics, visit the American Mathematical Society at http://www.ams.org.

SCORING GUIDE

Task (6 points)

a. 1 point for correct functions

b. 1 point for correct functions

c. 1 point for correct explanation

d. 1 point for correct initial revenue
1 point for correct rate of change

e. 1 point for correct functions

Quadratic Functions

CONTENTS

Unit Pacing Guide

45-Minute Classes

Module 19

DAY 1	DAY 2	DAY 3	DAY 4	
Lesson 19.1	Lesson 19.2	Lesson 19.3	Module Review and Assessment Readiness	

Module 20

DAY 1	DAY 2	DAY 3	DAY 4	DAY 5
Lesson 20.1	Lesson 20.2	Lesson 20.3	Lesson 20.3	Module Review and Assessment Readiness

DAY 6
Unit Review and Assessment Readiness

90-Minute Classes

Module 19

DAY 1	DAY 2
Lesson 19.1	Lesson 19.3
Lesson 19.2	Module Review and Assessment Readiness

Module 20

DAY 1	DAY 2	DAY 3
Lesson 20.1	Lesson 20.3	Module Review and Assessment Readiness
Lesson 20.2		Unit Review and Assessment Readiness

Program Resources

PLAN

HMH Teacher App

Access a full suite of teacher resources online and offline on a variety of devices. Plan present, and manage classes, assignments, and activities.

ePlanner
Easily plan your classes, create and view assignments, and access all program resources with your online, customizable planning tool.

Professional Development Videos
Authors Juli Dixon and Matt Larson model successful teaching practices and strategies in actual classroom settings.

QR Codes
Scan with your smart phone to jump directly from your print book to online videos and other resources.

Teacher's Edition

Support students with point-of-use Questioning Strategies, teaching tips, resources for differentiated instruction, additional activities, and more.

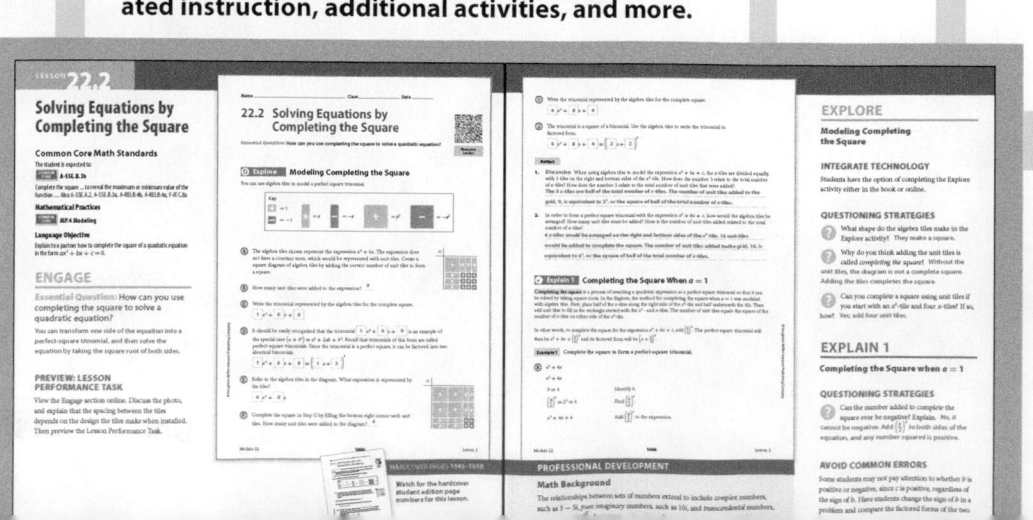

ENGAGE AND EXPLORE

Real-World Videos
Engage students with interesting and relevant applications of the mathematical content of each module.

Explore Activities
Students interactively explore new concepts using a variety of tools and approaches.

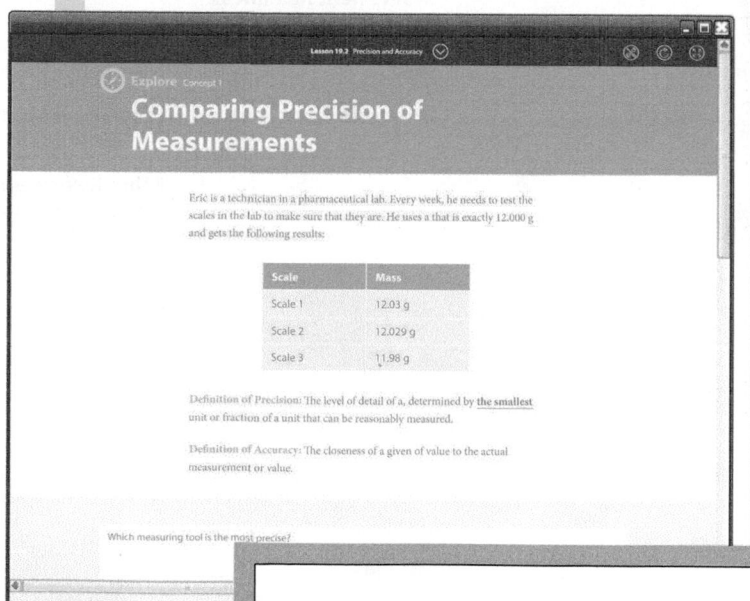

Comparing Precision of Measurements

Eric is a technician in a pharmaceutical lab. Every week, he needs to test the scales in the lab to make sure that they are. He uses a that is exactly 12.000 g and gets the following results:

Scale	Mass
Scale 1	12.03 g
Scale 2	12.029 g
Scale 3	11.98 g

Definition of Precision: The level of detail of a, determined by the smallest unit or fraction of a unit that can be reasonably measured.

Definition of Accuracy: The closeness of a given of value to the actual measurement or value.

Which measuring tool is the most precise?

Name_____ Class_____ Date_____

22.2 Solving Equations by Completing the Square

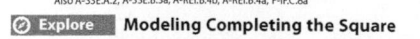

Essential Question: How can you use completing the square to solve a quadratic equation?

COMMON CORE A-SSE.B.3b Complete the square ... to reveal the maximum or minimum value of the function ... Also A-SSE.A.2, A-SSE.B.3a, A-REI.B.4b, A-REI.B.4a, F-IF.C.8a

Resource Locker

Explore Modeling Completing the Square

You can use algebra tiles to model a perfect square trinomial.

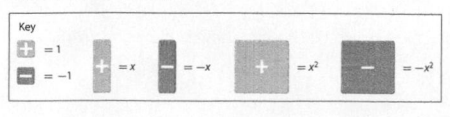

Key

$+$ = 1

$-$ = -1 = x   = -x $+$ = x^2 $-$ = $-x^2$

(A) The algebra tiles shown represent the expression $x^2 + 6x$. The expression does not have a constant term, which would be represented with unit tiles. Create a square diagram of algebra tiles by adding the correct number of unit tiles to form a square.

(B) How many unit tiles were added to the expression? _____

(C) Write the trinomial represented by the algebra tiles for the complete square.

$\boxed{}x^2 + \boxed{}x + \boxed{}$

(D) It should be easily recognized that the trinomial $\boxed{}x^2 + \boxed{}x + \boxed{}$ is an example of the special case $(a + b)^2 = a^2 + 2ab + b^2$. Recall that trinomials of this form are called

TEACH

Math On the Spot video tutorials, featuring program author Dr. Edward Burger, accompany every example in the textbook and give students step-by-step instructions and explanations of key math concepts.

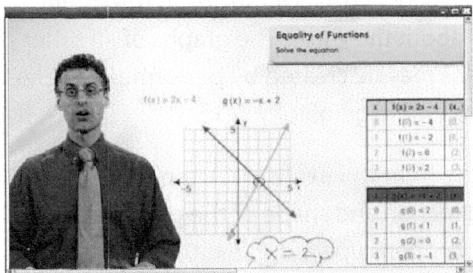

Interactive Teacher Edition

Customize and present course materials with collaborative activities and integrated formative assessment.

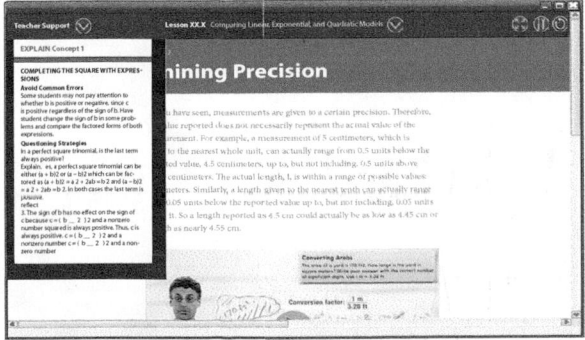

Differentiated Instruction Resources

Support all learners with Differentiated Instruction Resources, including

- **Leveled Practice and Problem Solving**
- **Reading Strategies**
- **Success for English Learners**
- **Challenge**

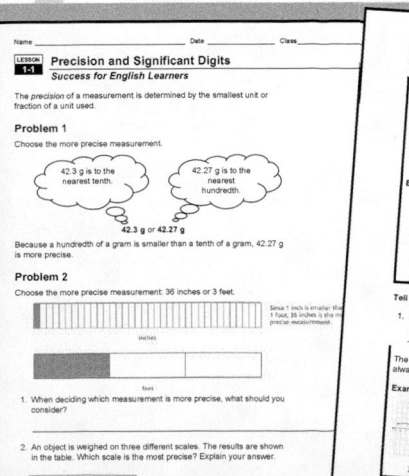

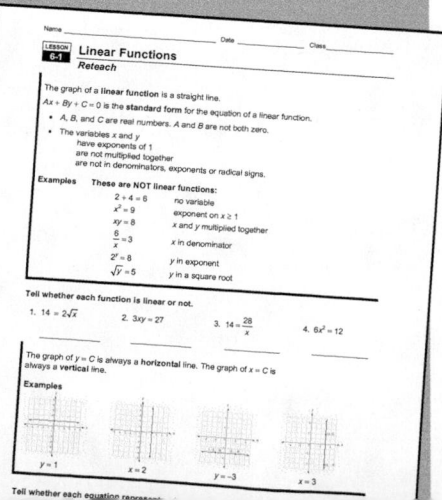

ASSESSMENT AND INTERVENTION

The **Personal Math Trainer** provides online practice, homework, assessments, and intervention. Monitor student progress through reports and alerts. **Create and customize assignments aligned to specific lessons or Common Core standards.**

- **Practice** – With dynamic items and assignments, students get unlimited practice on key concepts supported by guided examples, step-by-step solutions, and video tutorials.

- **Assessments** – Choose from course assignments or customize your own based on course content, Common Core standards, difficulty levels, and more.

- **Homework** – Students can complete online homework with a wide variety of problem types, including the ability to enter expressions, equations, and graphs. Let the system automatically grade homework, so you can focus where your students need help the most!

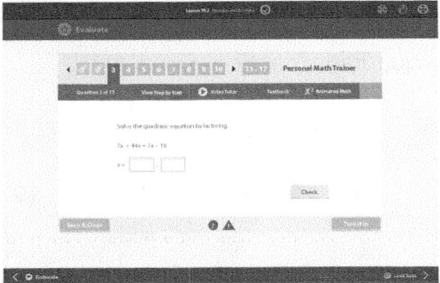

- **Intervention** – Let the Personal Math Trainer automatically prescribe a targeted, personalized intervention path for your students.

Focus on Higher Order Thinking

Raise the bar with homework and practice that incorporates higher-order thinking and mathematical practices in every lesson.

Assessment Readiness

Prepare students for success on high stakes tests for Algebra 1 with practice at every module and unit

COMMON CORE

Assessment Resources

Tailor assessments and response to intervention to meet the needs of all your classes and students, including

- Leveled Module Quizzes
- Leveled Unit Tests
- Unit Performance Tasks
- Placement, Diagnostic, and Quarterly Benchmark Tests
- Tier 1, Tier 2, and Tier 3 Resources

Math Background

Understanding Quadratic Functions   `COMMON CORE` F-BF.B.3

LESSON 19.1

A *quadratic function* is any function that can be written in the form $y = ax^2 + bx + c$, where a, b, and c are real numbers and $a \neq 0$. This is called the *standard form* of a quadratic function.

There are several ways to identify a quadratic function. One way is to use a table of values. Recall that linear functions have a constant rate of change. Therefore, in a table of values for a linear function, a constant change in the x-values corresponds to a constant change in the y-values. For quadratic functions, it is the rate of change itself that has a constant rate of change. In other words, when there is a constant change in x-values, a quadratic function has *constant second differences*. The table illustrates this for the quadratic function $y = x^2 + 3$.

x	2	3	4	5	6
y	7	12	19	28	39

First differences: + 5   + 7   + 9   + 11

Second differences: + 2   + 2   + 2

Developing Quadratic Functions   `COMMON CORE` F-BF.B.3

LESSONS 19.2 and 19.3

The simplest quadratic function is $y = x^2$. Its graph is a *parabola* that opens upward, has its vertex at the origin, and is symmetric about the y-axis. The graphs of all other quadratic functions may be created by performing a series of transformations on the graph of $y = x^2$.

For functions in the form $y = ax^2$ $(a \neq 0)$, the value of a determines the direction and shape of the parabola. If $a > 0$, the parabola opens upward; if $a < 0$, the parabola opens downward. If $|a| > 1$, the parabola is narrower than the graph of $y = x^2$; if $|a| < 1$, the parabola is wider than the graph of $y = x^2$.

The graph of a function in the form $y = a(x - h)^2$ is a horizontal translation of the graph of $y = ax^2$. For example, the graph of $y = 2(x - 3)^2$ is identical to the graph of $y = 2x^2$, but shifted 3 units to the right.

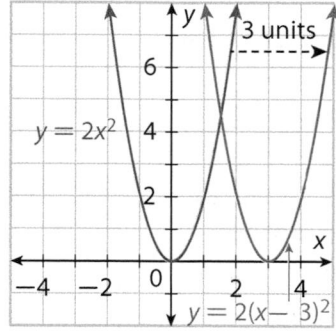

Finally, the constant k in $y = a(x - h)^2 + k$ represents a vertical translation of the graph of $y = a(x - h)^2$. The translation is k units upward if $k > 0$ and $|k|$ units downward if $k < 0$.

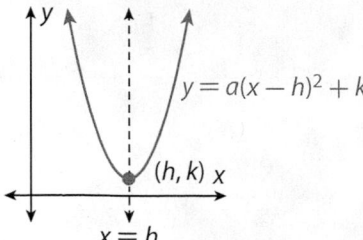

The equation $y = a(x - h)^2 + k$ is called the *vertex form* of a quadratic function. This form makes it easy to identify the vertex of the parabola, (h, k), and the axis of symmetry, $x = h$.

One way to find the formula for the axis of symmetry of a parabola is by using vertex form. As shown below, the basic idea is to transform vertex form into standard form and then write the equation of the axis of symmetry, $x = h$, in terms of a, b, and c.

$$y = a(x - h)^2 + k$$

$$y = a(x^2 - 2hx + h^2) + k$$

$$y = ax^2 - 2ahx + ah^2 + k$$

In standard form, the value of b is the coefficient of x, so $b = -2ah$. Solving for h gives $h = -\dfrac{b}{2a}$. Thus, the

axis of symmetry is the vertical line $x = -\dfrac{b}{2a}$.

Connecting Intercepts and Zeros `COMMON CORE` **F-IF.C.7a**

LESSON 20.1

A *quadratic equation* is an equation that can be written in the form $ax^2 + bx + c = 0$, where a, b, and c are real numbers and $a \neq 0$. This is the *standard form* of a quadratic equation. Every quadratic equation written in this form has a related quadratic function, $y = ax^2 + bx + c$.

As with other equations, a solution of a quadratic equation is a value of the variable that makes the equation true. One way to solve a quadratic equation in standard form is to graph the related quadratic function and find its x-intercepts.

For example, for the quadratic equation $x^2 + x - 6 = 0$, the graph of the related function $y = x^2 + x - 6$ is the set of all ordered pairs of the form $(x, x^2 + x - 6)$. It must be true that at any point where the graph intersects the x-axis, the y-coordinate is 0; that is, $x^2 + x - 6 = 0$. In other words, the x-intercepts of the graph are precisely the solutions of the quadratic equation.

Students should understand that this is a general method that works for any equation with one side equal to 0, if the related function can be graphed. For example, the linear equation $\frac{1}{2}x - 2 = 0$ may be solved by graphing the related linear function $y = \frac{1}{2}x - 2$ and noticing that the graph intersects the x-axis at $x = 4$.

Quadratic Functions

MATH IN CAREERS
Unit Activity Preview

After completing this unit, students will complete a Math in Careers task by graphing and writing an equation for a function that fits a data set comparing gas mileage to speed. Critical skills include modeling real-world situations and fitting a function to a set of data.

For more information about careers in mathematics as well as various mathematics appreciation topics, visit The American Mathematical Society at http://www.ams.org.

Quadratic Functions

MODULE **19**
Graphing Quadratic Functions

MODULE **20**
Connecting Intercepts, Zeros, and Factors

MATH IN CAREERS

Transportation Engineer
Transportation engineers design and modify plans for transportation systems including airports, trains, highways, and bridges. They use math when preparing budgets and project costs. They also use mathematical models to simulate traffic flow and analyze engineering data.
If you are interested in a career as a transportation engineer, you should study these mathematical subjects:
- Algebra
- Geometry
- Trigonometry
- Calculus
- Differential Equations

Research other careers that require developing and analyzing mathematical models. Check out the career activity at the end of the unit to find out how **transportation engineers** use math.

Unit 8   885

TRACKING YOUR LEARNING PROGRESSION

Before	In this Unit	After
Students understand: • adding and subtracting polynomial expressions • multiplying polynomial expressions • special products of binomials	Students will learn about: • graphing quadratic functions • interpreting vertex and standard form of quadratic functions • connecting intercepts and zeros • solving quadratic equations using the Zero Product Property	Students will study: • solving quadratic equations by factoring • solving quadratic equations by completing the square • using the quadratic formula to solve equations • comparing linear, quadratic, and exponential models

Reading Start-Up

Visualize Vocabulary

Use the ✔ words to complete the graphic. Write the name of a form of linear equation that best fits each equation.

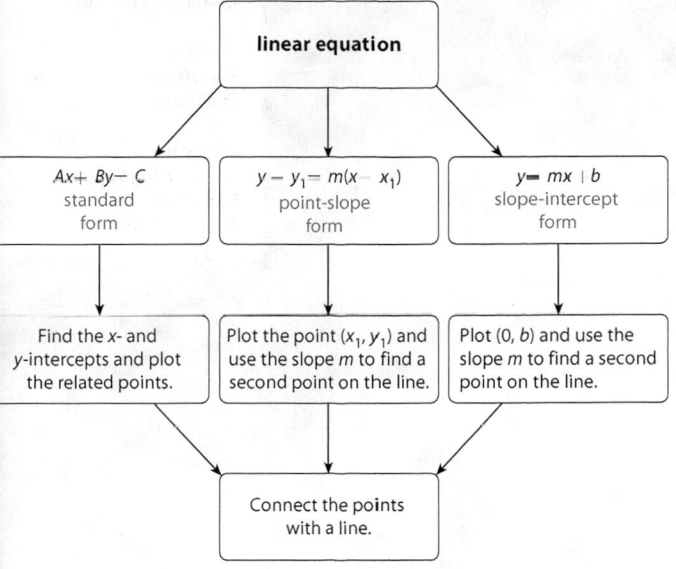

linear equation

| $Ax + By = C$ standard form | $y - y_1 = m(x - x_1)$ point-slope form | $y = mx + b$ slope-intercept form |

Find the x- and y-intercepts and plot the related points.

Plot the point (x_1, y_1) and use the slope m to find a second point on the line.

Plot $(0, b)$ and use the slope m to find a second point on the line.

Connect the points with a line.

Vocabulary

Review Words

✔ point-slope form
(forma de punto y pendiente)

✔ slope-intercept form
(forma de pendiente-intersección)

✔ standard form
(forma estándar)

x-intercept
(intersección con el eje x)

y-intercept
(intersección con el eje y)

Preview Words

intercept form of a quadratic equation
(forma en intersección de una función cuadrática)

standard form of a quadratic equation
(forma estándar de una ecuación cuadrática)

vertex form of a quadratic function
(forma en vértice de una función cuadrática)

Understand Vocabulary

Match the term on the left to the example on the right.

1. __C__ standard form of a quadratic equation A. $y = -(x - 2)^2 + 9$

2. __B__ intercept form of a quadratic equation B. $y = -(x + 1)(x - 5)$

3. __A__ vertex form of a quadratic function C. $y = -x^2 + 4x + 5$

Active Reading

Tri-Fold Before beginning the unit, create a tri-fold to help you learn the concepts and vocabulary in this unit. Fold the paper into three sections. Label the columns "What I Know," "What I Need to Know," and "What I Learned." Complete the first two columns before you read. After studying the unit, complete the third column.

Reading Start Up

Have students complete the activities on this page by working alone or with others.

VISUALIZE VOCABULARY

The decision tree graphic helps students review vocabulary associated with linear equations. If time allows, discuss the advantages of each form of a linear equation.

UNDERSTAND VOCABULARY

Use the following explanations to help students learn the preview words.

The **intercept form of a quadratic equation** shows the zeros, or x-intercepts, on the graph of the function. The **vertex form of a quadratic equation** shows the coordinates of the vertex on the graph of the parabola. The **standard form of a quadratic equation** lists the terms in decreasing order of the exponents.

ACTIVE READING

Students can use these reading and note-taking strategies to help them organize and understand the new concepts and vocabulary. Encourage them to be confident in their use of familiar vocabulary and question any terms that are unfamiliar.

ADDITIONAL RESOURCES

Differentiated Instruction

- Reading Strategies **EL**

Graphing Quadratic Functions

ESSENTIAL QUESTION:

Answer: If you throw a ball, shoot an arrow, or fire a missile, it will go up into the air, slowing down as it goes, then come down again. If you graph the path of the ball, arrow, or missile, you will find that it is the graph of a quadratic function.

PROFESSIONAL DEVELOPMENT VIDEO

Professional Development Video

Author Juli Dixon models successful teaching practices in an actual high-school classroom.

Professional Development

my.hrw.com

Graphing Quadratic Functions

MODULE **19**

Essential Question: How can you use the graph of a quadratic function to solve real-world problems?

© Houghton Mifflin Harcourt Publishing Company • Image Credits: ©Image Source/Getty Images

REAL WORLD VIDEO
Projectile motion describes the height of an object thrown or fired into the air. The height of a football, volleyball, or any projectile can be modeled by a quadratic equation.

MODULE PERFORMANCE TASK PREVIEW

Throwing for a Completion

Do you wonder how fast a football leaves the hands of a quarterback or how high up it goes? Some professionals can throw approximately 45 miles per hour or faster. The height the ball reaches depends on the initial velocity as well as the angle at which it was thrown. You can use a mathematical model to see how high a football is at different times.

DIGITAL TEACHER EDITION

Access a full suite of teaching resources when and where you need them:

- Access content online or offline
- Customize lessons to share with your class
- Communicate with your students in real-time
- View student grades and data instantly to target your instruction where it is needed most

PERSONAL MATH TRAINER
Assessment and Intervention

Assign automatically graded homework, quizzes, tests, and intervention activities. Prepare your students with updated, Common Core-aligned practice tests.

Are YOU Ready?

Complete these exercises to review skills you will need for this module.

• Online Homework
• Hints and Help
• Extra Practice

Linear Functions

Example 1　Tell whether $6x - 2y = 9$ represents a linear function.

When a linear equation is written in standard form, the following are true.

- x and y both have exponents of 1.
- x and y are not multiplied together.
- x and y do not appear in denominators, exponents, or radicands.

$6x - 2y = 9$ represents a linear function.

Tell whether the equation represents a linear function.

1. $y = 3x^2 + 4x + 1$ ___no___　　**2.** $3y = 12 - \frac{1}{2}x$ ___yes___　　**3.** $y = 2x + 5$ ___yes___

Algebraic Representations of Transformations

Example 2　The vertices of a triangle are $A(-3, 1)$, $B(0, -2)$, and $C(-4, 2)$. Find the vertices if the figure is translated by the rule $(x, y) \rightarrow (x + 4, y - 3)$.

A　$(-3, 1) \rightarrow A'(-3 + 4, 1 - 3)$, so $A'(1, -2)$　　Add 4 to each x-coordinate and subtract 3 from each y-coordinate.

B　$(0, -2) \rightarrow B'(0 + 4, -2 - 3)$, so $B'(4, -5)$

C　$(-4, 2) \rightarrow C'(-4 + 4, 2 - 3)$, so $C'(0, -1)$

The vertices of a triangle are $A(0, 3)$, $B(-2, -4)$, and $C(1, 5)$. Find the new vertices.

4. Use the rule $(x, y) \rightarrow (x - 2, y + 4)$ to translate each vertex.

$A'(-2, 7), B'(-4, 0), C'(-1, 9)$

5. Use the rule $(x, y) \rightarrow (x + 1, y - 2)$ to translate each vertex.

$A'(1, 1), B'(-1, -6), C'(2, 3)$

Algebraic Expressions

Example 3　Find the value of $x^2 + 5x - 3$ when $x = 2$.

$x^2 + 5x - 3$

$(2)^2 + 5(2) - 3$　　Substitute 2 for x.

$4 + 10 - 3$　　Follow the order of operations.

11

Find the value.

6. $x^2 - 7x + 9$ when $x = 6$ ___3___　　**7.** $2x^2 + 4x - 7$ when $x = -3$ ___−1___

Are You Ready?

ASSESS READINESS

Use the assessment on this page to determine if students need strategic or intensive intervention for the module's prerequisite skills.

ASSESSMENT AND INTERVENTION

RtI Response to Intervention **TIER 1, TIER 2, TIER 3 SKILLS**

Personal Math Trainer will automatically create a standards-based, personalized intervention assignment for your students, targeting each student's individual needs!

ADDITIONAL RESOURCES

See the table below for a full list of intervention resources available for this module.

Response to Intervention Resources also includes:

- Tier 2 Skill Pre-Tests for each Module
- Tier 2 Skill Post-Tests for each skill

Response to Intervention			Differentiated Instruction
Tier 1 Lesson Intervention Worksheets	**Tier 2** Strategic Intervention Skills Intervention Worksheets	**Tier 3** Intensive Intervention Worksheets available online	
Reteach 19.1 Reteach 19.2 Reteach 19.3	2 Algebraic Expressions 3 Algebraic Representations of Transformations 5 Exponents 10 Linear Functions	Building Block Skills 19, 22, 23, 24, 27, 29, 30, 40, 46, 51, 59, 69, 76, 81, 100	Challenge worksheets Extend the Math Lesson Activities in TE

Understanding Quadratic Functions

Common Core Math Standards

The student is expected to:

COMMON CORE F-BF.B.3

Identify the effect on the graph of replacing $f(x)$ by... $f(kx)$... for specific values of k (both positive and negative)... Also F-IF.A.2, F-IF.B.4, F-IF.C.7a

Mathematical Practices

COMMON CORE MP.2 Reasoning

Language Objective

Describe terms associated with quadratic functions.

ENGAGE

Essential Question: What is the effect of the constant a on the graph of $f(x) = ax^2$?

Possible answer: The effect of the constant a is to either vertically stretch or vertically shrink the graph relative to the graph of the parent quadratic function. A negative value of a reflects the graph across the x-axis.

PREVIEW: LESSON PERFORMANCE TASK

View the Engage section online. Discuss the photo and how the path of a real helicopter landing would be different from the path of a paper helicopter being dropped. Then preview the Lesson Performance Task.

Name_____ Class_____ Date_____

19.1 Understanding Quadratic Functions

Resource Locker

Essential Question: What is the effect of the constant a on the graph of $f(x) = ax^2$?

⊘ Explore Understanding the Parent Quadratic Function

A function that can be represented in the form of $f(x) = ax^2 + bx + c$ is called a **quadratic function**. The terms a, b, and c, are constants where $a \neq 0$. The greatest exponent of the variable x is 2. The most basic quadratic function is $f(x) = x^2$, which is the parent quadratic function.

(A) Here is an incomplete table of values for the parent quadratic function. Complete it.

x	$f(x) = x^2$
-3	$f(x) = x^2 = (-3)^2 = 9$
-2	4
-1	1
0	0
1	1
2	4
3	9

(B) Plot the ordered pairs as points on the graph, and connect the points to sketch a curve.

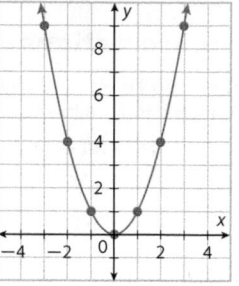

The curve is called a **parabola**. The point through which the parabola turns direction is called its **vertex**. The vertex occurs at $(0, 0)$ for this function. A vertical line that passes through the vertex and divides the parabola into two symmetrical halves is called the **axis of symmetry**. For this function, the axis of symmetry is the y-axis.

Reflect

1. **Discussion** What is the domain of $f(x) = x^2$?
   The domain is the set of all real numbers.

2. **Discussion** What is the range of $f(x) = x^2$?
   The range is the set $y \geq 0$.

© Houghton Mifflin Harcourt Publishing Company

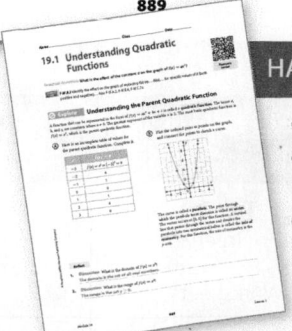

HARDCOVER PAGES 697–708

Turn to these pages to find this lesson in the hardcover student edition.

The graph $g(x) = ax^2$, is a vertical stretch or compression of its parent function $f(x) = x^2$. The graph opens upward when $a > 0$.

Vertical Stretch

$g(x) = ax^2$ with $|a| > 1$.

The graph of $g(x)$ is narrower than the parent function $f(x)$.

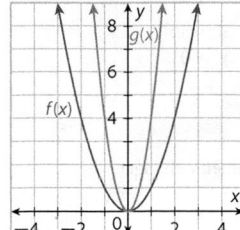

Vertical Compression

$g(x) = ax^2$ with $0 < |a| < 1$.

The graph of $g(x)$ is wider than the parent function $f(x)$.

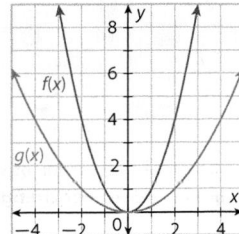

The domain of a quadratic function is all real numbers. When $a > 0$, the graph of $g(x) = ax^2$ opens upward, and the function has a **minimum value** that occurs at the vertex of the parabola. So, the range of $g(x) = ax^2$, where $a > 0$, is the set of real numbers greater than or equal to the minimum value.

Example 1   Graph each quadratic function by plotting points and sketching the curve. State the domain and range.

   $g(x) = 2x^2$

x	$g(x) = 2x^2$
−3	18
−2	8
−1	2
0	0
1	2
2	8
3	18

Domain: all real numbers x

Range: $y \geq 0$

© Houghton Mifflin Harcourt Publishing Company

PROFESSIONAL DEVELOPMENT

 Integrate Mathematical Practices

This lesson provides an opportunity to address Mathematical Practice **MP.2,** which calls for students to "reason abstractly and quantitatively." Students learn to recognize the parent function of a quadratic equation and then to analyze the relationship between the value of a and the graph of the quadratic function.

EXPLORE

Understanding the Parent Quadratic Function

INTEGRATE TECHNOLOGY

Students have the option of completing the activity either in the book or online.

CONNECT VOCABULARY   **EL**

This lesson tells students that if a is positive, the graph opens *upward*, and if a is negative, the graph opens *downward*. The suffix *-ward* means *in the direction of*. Students may know the word *toward*; point out also the words *outward* and *inward,* used in the FOIL method.

EXPLAIN 1

Graphing $g(x) = ax^2$ when $a > 0$

QUESTIONING STRATEGIES

?   How are the graphs of $g(x) = 2x^2$ and $g(x) = \frac{1}{2} x^2$ similar? How are they different? The graphs are similar because both have the same parent graph, $f(x) = x^2$; both are symmetric in the y-axis; and both have the same vertex, $(0, 0)$. They are different in that the graph of $g(x) = 2x^2$ is a vertical stretch of the graph of $f(x) = x^2$, while the graph of $g(x) = \frac{1}{2} x^2$ is a vertical compression of the graph of $f(x) = x^2$.

?   If $(0, 0)$ and $(3, 7)$ are two points on the graph of $g(x)$, where $(0, 0)$ is the vertex, what is another point on the graph? $(-3, 7)$, because the graph is symmetrical about the y-axis

EXPLAIN 2

Graphing $g(x) = ax^2$ when $a < 0$

AVOID COMMON ERRORS

Students may think that increasing $|a|$ increases the width of the graph. Make sure that students understand that the value of a tells how the parent function $f(x) = x^2$ is stretched or compressed vertically. When the absolute value of a is greater than 1, the graph is stretched, away from the x-axis. When the absolute value of a is greater than 0 but less than 1, the graph is compressed toward the x-axis. When a graph is stretched vertically, it appears to shrink horizontally.

QUESTIONING STRATEGIES

? How would the graph of the function $g(x) = -15x^2$ differ from the graph of $f(x) = x^2$? **It would reflect the curve across the x-axis and stretch it downward by a factor of 15.**

Ⓑ $g(x) = \frac{1}{2}x^2$

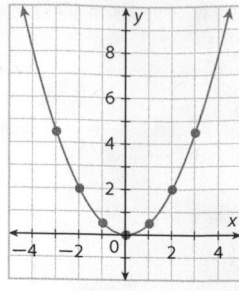

x	$g(x) = \frac{1}{2}x^2$
-3	$4\frac{1}{2}$
-2	2
0	0
2	2
3	$4\frac{1}{2}$

Domain:
all real numbers

Range:
$y \geq 0$

Reflect

3. For a graph that has a vertical compression or stretch, does the axis of symmetry change?
No, the axis of symmetry does not change.

Your Turn

Graph each quadratic function. State the domain and range.

4. $g(x) = 3x^2$ **D: all real; R: $y \geq 0$**

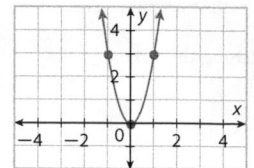

5. $g(x) = \frac{1}{3}x^2$ **D: all real; R: $y \geq 0$**

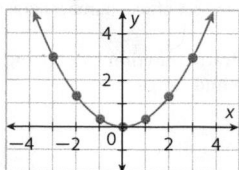

⊘ Explain 2 **Graphing $g(x) = ax^2$ when $a < 0$**

The graph of $y = -x^2$ opens downward. It is a reflection of the graph of $y = x^2$ across the x-axis. So, When $a < 0$, the graph of $g(x) = ax^2$ opens downward, and the function has a **maximum value** that occurs at the vertex of the parabola. In this case, the range is the set of real numbers less than or equal to the maximum value.

Vertical Stretch

$g(x) = ax^2$ with $|a| > 1$.

The graph of $g(x)$ is narrower than the parent function $f(x)$.

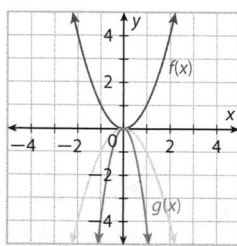

Vertical Compression

$g(x) = ax^2$ with $0 < |a| < 1$.

The graph of $g(x)$ is wider than the parent function $f(x)$.

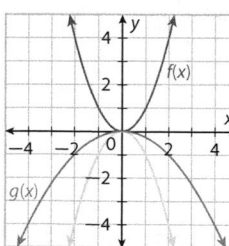

Module 19

891

Lesson 1

COLLABORATIVE LEARNING

Peer to Peer Activity

Have students work in pairs. Ask one student to draw a graph of $y = ax^2$ for some value of a. The second student then writes the equation for the graph. Finally, the pairs determine whether the equation is correct for the given graph. Students then switch roles and repeat.

Example 2 Graph each quadratic function by plotting points and sketching the curve. State the domain and range.

Ⓐ $g(x) = -2x^2$

x	$g(x) = 2x^2$
−3	−18
−2	−8
−1	−2
0	0
1	−2
2	−8
3	−18

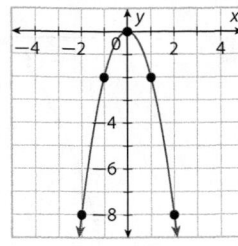

Domain: __all real numbers__

Range: __$y \leq 0$__

Ⓑ $g(x) = -\frac{1}{2}x^2$

x	$g(x) = -\frac{1}{2}x^2$
−3	$-4\frac{1}{2}$
−2	−2
−1	$-\frac{1}{2}$
0	0
1	$-\frac{1}{2}$
2	−2
3	$-4\frac{1}{2}$

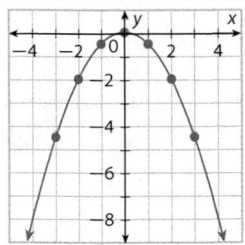

Domain: __all real numbers__

Range: __$y \leq 0$__

Reflect

6. Does reflecting the parabola across the x-axis ($a < 0$) change the axis of symmetry?
No, the axis of symmetry is a line that extends both up and down and does not change

upon reflection.

INTEGRATE MATHEMATICAL PRACTICES

Focus on Modeling

MP.4 As students reflect a function across the x-axis and stretch or compress the function vertically, make sure they understand that making the function negative reflects it across the x-axis and changing the value of *a* affects its width.

CONNECT VOCABULARY EL

You may wish to have English language learners express terms from the lesson in their own words. For example, tell students: "An *axis* is an imaginary line. Use this information and your understanding of symmetry to define the term *axis of symmetry.*" an imaginary line that splits a figure so that one side of the figure is a mirror image of the other.

DIFFERENTIATE INSTRUCTION

Visual Cues

Have students draw the graph of a function that is wider than the graph of $f(x) = x^2$ and one for which the graph is narrower. Have them use a different color for each graph. Then have them write the function above each graph in black, except for the value of *a*, which should be the same color as the corresponding graph. This may help students to remember which values of *a* lead to wider graphs and which lead to narrower graphs.

EXPLAIN 3

Writing a Quadratic Function Given a Graph

QUESTIONING STRATEGIES

? How can you immediately tell from the graph that the value of a in the quadratic function is negative? The graph opens downward.

? How does having a point of the parabola other than the vertex help you find the value of a? If you have a point other than $(0, 0)$, you can substitute the x- and y-values into $y = ax^2$ and solve for a.

AVOID COMMON ERRORS

Students may forget that the square of a negative number is positive. Remind students to check whether their calculated values of a are reasonable for the graph. A positive value of a for a graph that opens downward indicates a sign error.

Your Turn

Graph each function. State the domain and range.

7. $g(x) = -3x^2$ D: all real; R: $y \leq 0$

8. $g(x) = -\frac{1}{3}x^2$ D: all real; R: $y \leq 0$

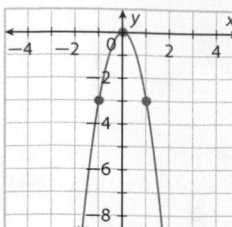 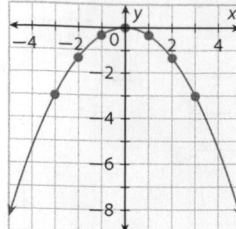

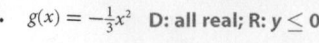

Explain 3 **Writing a Quadratic Function Given a Graph**

You can determine a function rule for a parabola with its vertex at the origin by substituting x and y values for any other point on the parabola into $g(x) = ax^2$ and solving for a.

Example 3 Write the rule for the quadratic functions shown on the graph.

(A)

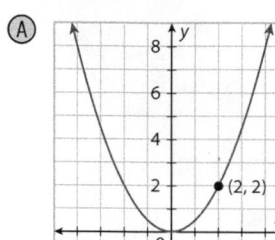

Use the point $(2, 2)$.

Start with the functional form.	$g(x) = ax^2$
Replace x and $g(x)$ with point values.	$2 = a(2)^2$
Evaluate x^2.	$2 = 4a$
Divide both sides by 4 to isolate a.	$\frac{1}{2} = a$
Write the function rule.	$g(x) = \frac{1}{2}x^2$

(B)

$(-2, -8)$

Use the point $\left(-2, \boxed{-8}\right)$.

Start with the functional form.	$g(x) = ax^2$
Replace x and $g(x)$ with point values.	$\boxed{-8} = a\left(\boxed{-2}\right)^2$
Evaluate x^2.	$-8 = \boxed{4}\,a$
Divide both sides by $\boxed{4}$ to isolate a.	$\boxed{-2} = a$
Write the function rule.	$g(x) = \boxed{-2x^2}$

LANGUAGE SUPPORT **EL**

Communicate Math

English learners may find the spelling patterns in English somewhat puzzling, especially if they are literate in a language that has a very consistent set of spelling and pronunciation rules. Some words they need to understand and use for algebra may require additional support and review; for example, focusing on the final sounds of: graph /-f/, stretch /-ch/, vertex /-x/, and intercept /-pt/

Have students work in small, mixed language-proficiency groups to generate a word bank of English and mathematical terms students can use to describe quadratic function graphs (such as *upward*, *downward*, *symmetry*, *vertex*).

9.

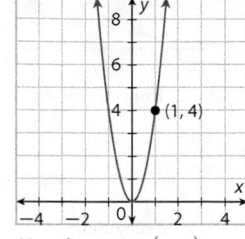

Use the point $(1, 4)$.

$g(x) = ax^2$

$4 = a\,(1)^2$

$4 = a$

$g(x) = 4x^2$

10.

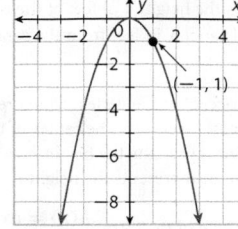

Use the point $(1, -1)$.

$g(x) = ax^2$

$-1 = a\,(1)^2$

$-1 = a$

$g(x) = -x^2$

⌀ Explain 4 Modeling with a Quadratic Function

Real-world situations can be modeled by parabolas.

Example 4 For each model, describe what the vertex, y-intercept, and endpoint(s) represent in the situation it models, and then determine the equation of the function.

(A) This graph models the depth in yards below the water's surface of a dolphin before and after it rises to take a breath and descends again. The depth d is relative to time t, in seconds, and $t = 0$ is when dolphin reaches a depth of 0 yards at the surface.

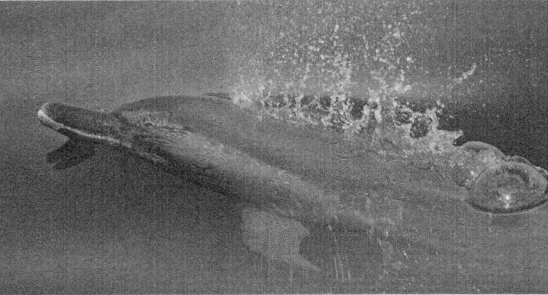

The y-intercept occurs at the vertex of the parabola at $(0, 0)$, where the dolphin is at the surface to breathe.

The endpoint $(-4, -32)$ represents a depth of 32 yards below the surface at 4 seconds before the dolphin reaches the surface to breathe.

The endpoint $(4, -32)$ represents a depth of 32 yards below the surface at 4 seconds after the dolphin reaches the surface to breathe. The graph is symmetric about the y-axis with the vertex at the origin, so the function will be of the form $y = ax^2$, or $d(t) = at^2$. Use a point to determine the equation.

$d(t) = at^2$

$-32 = a(4)^2$

$-32 = a \cdot 16$

$-2 = a$

The function is $d(t) = -2t^2$.

EXPLAIN 4

Modeling with a Quadratic Function

QUESTIONING STRATEGIES

? What would happen to the graph if the dolphin ascends at the same rate, but starts at a shallower depth? **The starting and ending points would be closer to the x-axis.**

? What would happen to the graph if the dolphin ascends and descends at a slower speed? **The graph would be wider.**

INTEGRATE MATHEMATICAL PRACTICES

Focus on Modeling

MP.4 When students have to write an equation for the quadratic function shown in a graph, make sure they understand that they need to pick a point on the graph to substitute in the equation $y = ax^2$ to find a.

ELABORATE

INTEGRATE MATHEMATICAL PRACTICES

Focus on Technology

MP.5 Have students use graphing calculators to graph $g(x) = ax^2$ for several different values of a on the same screen by using the graphing functions Y_1, Y_2, and so on. This will allow them to create many graphs in a short period of time and to compare the effects of different values of a.

SUMMARIZE

? How does the value of a affect the graph of $f(x) = ax^2$ in relation to the graph of the quadratic parent function?

Use the whiteboard and have students complete the table below.

Value of a	Type of transformation	Graph opens
$a > 1$	stretch	up
$0 < a < 1$	compression	up
$-1 < a < 0$	compression	down
$a = -1$	reflection	down
$a < -1$	stretch	down

B Satellite dishes reflect radio waves onto a collector by using a reflector (the dish) shaped like a parabola. The graph shows the height h in feet of the reflector relative to the distance x in feet from the center of the satellite dish.

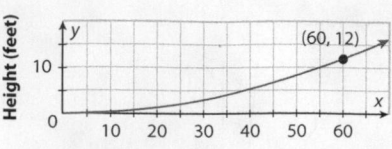

The y-intercept occurs at the vertex, which represents the distance $x = \underline{0}$ feet from the center of the dish.

The left end-point represents the height $h = \underline{0}$ feet at the center of the dish.

The right end-point represents the height $h = \underline{12}$ feet at the distance $x = \underline{60}$ feet from the center of the dish.

The function will be of the form $\underline{h(x) = ax^2}$. Use $\boxed{60}$, $\boxed{12}$ to determine the equation.

$h(x) = ax^2$

$\boxed{12} = a\left(\boxed{60}\right)^2$

$12 = \boxed{3600}\ a$

$a = \dfrac{1}{300}$

$h(x) = \boxed{\dfrac{1}{300}}\ x^2$

Your Turn

11. The graph shows the height h in feet of a rock dropped down a deep well as a function of time t in seconds.

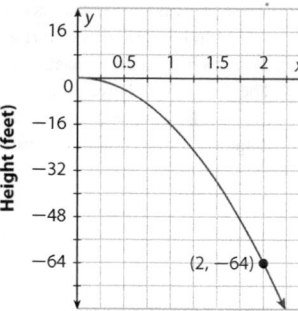

The y-intercept occurs at the left end-point, which is also the vertex, and represents the height $h = 0$ at which the rock was released at ground level.

The right end point represents the height $h = \underline{-64}$ feet at which the rock hits the bottom of the well $t = \underline{2}$ seconds after it was released.

Using the point $(2, -64)$ to determine the equation:

$h(t) = at^2$

$-64 = a(2)^2$

$-64 = 4a$

$a = -16$

$d(t) = -16t^2$

12. Discussion In example 1A the points $(3, 18)$ and $(-3, 18)$ did not fit on the grid. Describe some strategies for selecting points used to guide the shape of the curve.
Sample Answers:

1. Start with point $(0, 0)$ and work outwards.

2. Skip x values that don't place the y values on the grid (if you can spot the pattern).

3. Change the grid limits so that more calculated points fit in the plot.

13. Describe how the axis of symmetry of the parabola sitting on the y-axis can be used to help plot the graph of $f(x) = ax^2$.
The graph should look the same on either side of the axis, so once the positive x portion of

the parabola has been drawn, points on the parabola can be duplicated across the y axis.

If the point $(2, 5)$ is on the plot, for example, then so is the point $(-2, 5)$.

14. Essential Question Check-In How can you use the value of a to predict the shape of $f(x) = ax^2$ without plotting points?
The effect of the constant a is to either vertically stretch $\left(\text{if } |a| > 1\right)$ or shrink $\left(\text{if } 0 < |a| < 1\right)$

the graph compared to the parent function. A negative value of a causes the graph to open

downwards.

☆ **Evaluate: Homework and Practice**

• Online Homework
• Hints and Help
• Extra Practice

1. Plot the function $f(x) = x^2$ and $g(x) = -x^2$ on the grid.

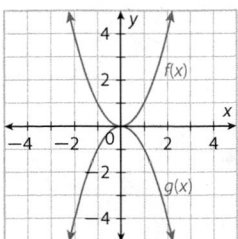

Which of the following features are the same and which are different for the two functions?

a. Domain

b. Range

c. Vertex

d. Axis of symmetry

e. Minimum

f. Maximum

Domain, vertex, and axis of symmetry are the same. Range, maximum, and minimum are different. $\left(f(x)\text{ doesn't have a maximum, and }g(x)\text{ doesn't have a minimum.}\right)$

Exercise	Depth of Knowledge (D.O.K.)	COMMON CORE Mathematical Practices
1	**1** Recall of Information	**MP.4** Modeling
2–9	**2** Skills/Concepts	**MP.4** Modeling
10–13	**2** Skills/Concepts	**MP.2** Reasoning
14–17	**2** Skills/Concepts	**MP.4** Modeling
18–19	**2** Skills/Concepts	**MP.2** Reasoning
20–21	**2** Skills/Concepts	**MP.2** Reasoning

EVALUATE

ASSIGNMENT GUIDE

Concepts and Skills	Practice
Explore Understanding the Parent Quadratic Function	Exercises 1, 25
Example 1 Graphing $g(x) = ax^2$ when $a > 0$	Exercises 2–5, 23–24
Example 2 Graphing $g(x) = ax^2$ when $a < 0$	Exercises 6–9, 22
Example 3 Writing a Quadratic Function Given a Graph	Exercises 10–13
Example 4 Modeling with a Quadratic Function	Exercises 14–21

INTEGRATE MATHEMATICAL PRACTICES
Focus on Modeling

MP.4 Review the characteristics of a parabola with students. Show students how to use these characteristics to graph a parabola. Then show them how to interpret the graph of a quadratic function when it models a real-world relationship such as height over time.

Watch for students who do not graph points on both sides of the vertex of the parabola. Remind these students that a parabola is U-shaped and symmetric, and they can use that symmetry to locate points on both sides of the vertex.

Graph each quadratic function. State the domain and range.

2. $g(x) = 4x^2$

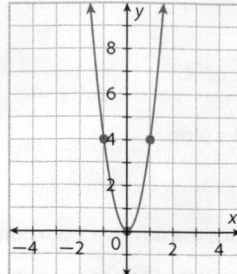

D: all real; R: $y \geq 0$

3. $g(x) = \frac{1}{4}x^2$

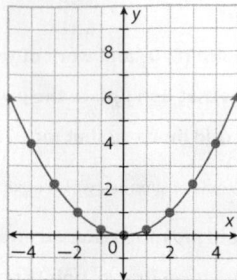

D: all real; R: $y \geq 0$

4. $g(x) = \frac{3}{2}x^2$

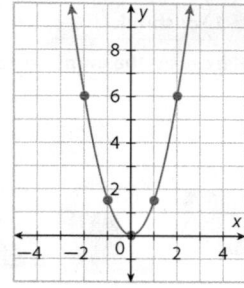

D: all real; R: $y \geq 0$

5. $g(x) = 5x^2$

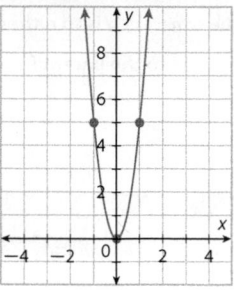

D: all real; R: $y \geq 0$

6. $g(x) = -\frac{1}{4}x^2$

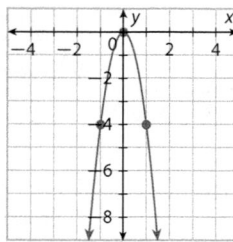

D: all real; R: $y \leq 0$

7. $g(x) = -4x^2$

D: all real; R: $y \leq 0$

© Houghton Mifflin Harcourt Publishing Company

Exercise	Depth of Knowledge (D.O.K.)		COMMON CORE Mathematical Practices
22–23	**3** Strategic Thinking	H.O.T.	**MP.3** Logic
24–25	**3** Strategic Thinking	H.O.T.	**MP.2** Reasoning

8. $g(x) = -\frac{3}{2}x^2$ D: all real; R: $y \leq 0$

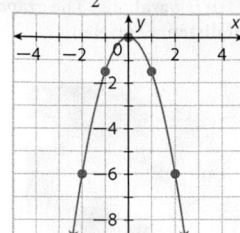

9. $g(x) = -5x^2$ D: all real; R: $y \leq 0$

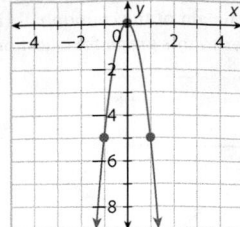

Determine the equation of the parabola graphed.

10.

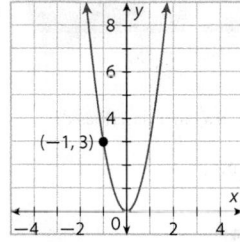

Use the point $(-1, 3)$.

$g(x) = ax^2$

$3 = a(-1)^2$

$3 = a$

$g(x) = 3x^2$

11.

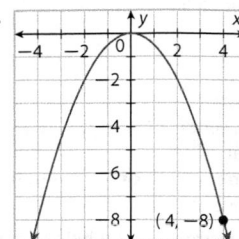

Use the point $(4, -8)$.

$g(x) = ax^2$

$-8 = a(4)^2$

$-8 = 16a$

$-\frac{1}{2} = a$

$g(x) = -\frac{1}{2}x^2$

12.

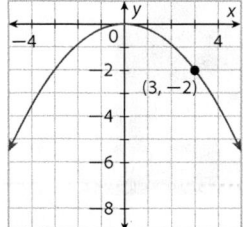

Use the point $(3, -2)$.

$g(x) = ax^2$

$-2 = a(3)^2$

$-2 = 9a$

$-\frac{2}{9} = a$

$g(x) = -\frac{2}{9}x^2$

13.

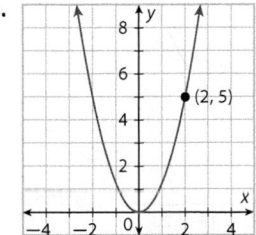

Use the point $(2, 5)$.

$g(x) = ax^2$

$5 = a(2)^2$

$5 = 4a$

$\frac{5}{4} = a$

$g(x) = \frac{5}{4}x^2$

MULTIPLE REPRESENTATIONS

Show students the graph of the function $g(x) = -1.5x^2$, and instruct them to make a table showing several x- and y-values for both the given graph and the parent function $f(x) = x^2$. Have them compare the values in the table and describe how the values of $g(x)$ are related to the values of $f(x)$ for any value of x. Then have them write the equation for $g(x)$. They should find that for a given value of x, the value of $g(x)$ is -1.5 times the value of the parent function, so they can conclude that $g(x) = -1.5x^2$.

INTEGRATE MATHEMATICAL PRACTICES

Focus on Critical Thinking

MP.3 Give students the graphs of two parabolas, $f(x) = ax^2$ and $g(x) = -ax^2$, that are symmetric about the x-axis. Have them consider the sum of their a-values. Students should see that the values of a are opposites, so the sum of these values is 0. Have them verify that for any value of x the sum of the function values is 0.

A cannonball fired horizontally appears to travel in a straight line, but drops to earth due to gravity, just like any other object in freefall. The height of the cannonball in freefall is parabolic. The graph shows the change in height of the cannonball (in meters) as a function of distance traveled (in kilometers). Refer to this graph for questions 14 and 15.

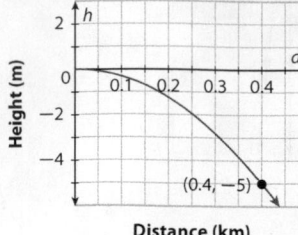

14. Describe what the vertex, y-intercept, and endpoint represent.

The vertex is the position of the cannon that fired the cannonball.

The y-intercept represents the height of the cannonball relative to the cannon at $d = 0$.

The endpoint is the end of the cannonball's trajectory.

15. Find the function $h(d)$ that describes these coordinates.

Use the point $(0.4, -5)$.

$$h(d) = ad^2$$
$$-5 = a(0.4)^2$$
$$-5 = 0.16a$$
$$-31.25 = a$$
$$h(d) = -31.25d^2$$

A slingshot stores energy in the stretched elastic band when it is pulled back. The amount of stored energy versus the pull length is approximately parabolic. Questions 16 and 17 refer to this graph of the stored energy in millijoules versus pull length in centimeters.

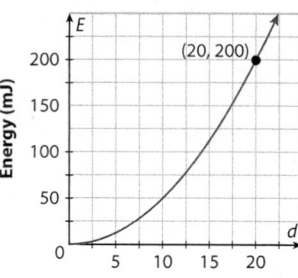

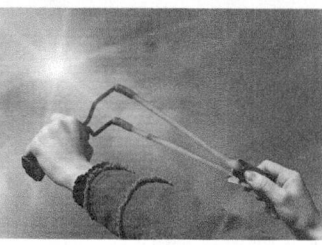

16. Describe what the vertex, y-intercept, and endpoint represent.

The vertex is the point at which the slingshot is relaxed and stores no energy.

The y-intercept is the energy, 0 mJ, when the pull length is 0 cm at the beginning.

The endpoint is at the maximum extent the slingshot is pulled back and the maximum stored energy.

17. Determine the function, $E(d)$, that describes this plot.

Use the point $(20, 200)$.

$$E(d) = ad^2$$
$$200 = a(20)^2$$
$$200 = 400a$$
$$\frac{1}{2} = a$$
$$E(d) = \frac{1}{2}d^2$$

Newer clean energy sources like solar and wind suffer from unsteady availability of energy. This makes it impractical to eliminate more traditional nuclear and fossil fuel plants without finding a way to store extra energy when it is not available.

One solution being investigated is storing energy in mechanical flywheels. Mechanical flywheels are heavy disks that store energy by spinning rapidly. The graph shows how much energy is in a flywheel, as a function of revolution speed.

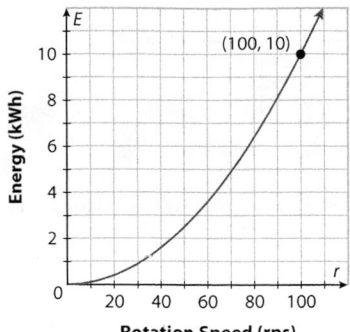

Rotation Speed (rps)

18. Describe what the vertex, y-intercept, and endpoint represent.

The vertex represents the flywheel at rest with no rotation and no stored energy.

The y-intercept is the energy, 0 kWh, when the rotation speed is 0 rps at the beginning.

The endpoint represents the maximum rotation speed and energy storage.

19. Determine the function, $E(r)$, that describes this plot.
Use the point $(100, 10)$.

$E(r) = ar^2$

$10 = a(100)^2$

$10 = 10,000a$

$0.001 = a$.

$E(r) = 0.001r^2$

Phineas is building a homemade skate ramp and wants to model the shape as a parabola. He sketches out a cross section shown in the graph.

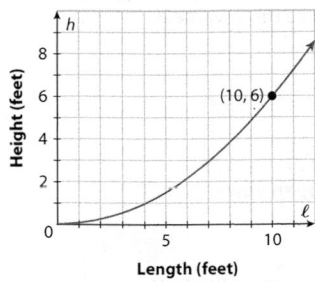

Length (feet)

20. Describe what the vertex y-intercept, and endpoint represent.

The vertex is the bottom of the ramp.

The y-intercept represents the height of the ramp relative to the length at $\ell = 0$.

The endpoint is the highest point on the curved portion.

21. Determine the function, $h(\ell)$, that describes this plot.
Use the point $(10, 6)$.

$h(\ell) = a\ell^2$

$6 = a(10)^2$

$0.06 = a$

$E(\ell) = 0.06\ell^2$

For a function in the form $y = ax^2$, where $a \neq 0$, what is the relationship between the value of a and the graph of the function? The value of a determines the direction and shape of the parabola. If $a > 0$, the parabola opens upward; if $a < 0$, the parabola opens downward. If $|a| > 1$, the parabola is narrower than the graph of $y = x^2$; if $|a| < 1$, the parabola is wider than the graph of $y = x^2$.

JOURNAL

In their journals, have students explain how the graphs of $y = 5x^2$ and $\frac{1}{5}x^2$ compare to the graph of $y = x^2$.

22. Multipart Classification

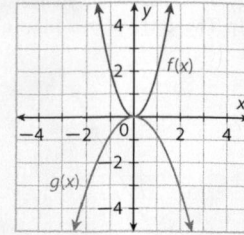

Mark the following statements about $f(x) = x^2$ and $g(x) = ax^2$ as true or false.

a. $a > 1$ **false**

b. $a < 0$ **true**

c. $a > 0$ **false**

d. $|a| < 0$ **false**

e. $|a| < 1$ **true**

f. The graphs of $f(x)$ and $g(x)$ share a vertex.   **true**

g. The graphs share an axis of symmetry.   **true**

h. The graphs share a minimum.   **false**

i. The graphs share a maximum.   **false**

23. Check for Reasonableness The graph of $g(x) = ax^2$ is a parabola that passes through the point $(-2, 2)$. Kyle says the value of a must be $-\frac{1}{2}$. Explain why this value of a is not reasonable.

When a is negative, the y values cannot be positive. Since the y-value is positive, a must be positive.

24. Communicate Mathematical Ideas Explain how you know, without graphing, what the graph of $g(x) = \frac{1}{10}x^2$ looks like.

Compared to the graph of the parent function, $f(x) = x^2$, the graph of $g(x)$ would be wider (vertically compressed). It will open upwards because a is positive.

25. Critical Thinking A quadratic function has a minimum value when the function's graph opens upward, and it has a maximum value when the function's graph opens downward. In each case, the minimum or maximum value is the y-coordinate of the vertex of the function's graph. What can you say about a when the function $f(x) = ax^2$ has a minimum value? A maximum value? What is the minimum or maximum value in each case?

When $f(x)$ has a minimum value, it means $a > 0$. When it has a maximum value, $a < 0$. In either case, the minimum or the maximum value will be 0.

Lesson Performance Task

Kylie made a paper helicopter and is testing its flight time from two different heights. The graph compares the height of the helicopter during the two drops. The graph of the first drop is labeled $g(x)$ and the graph of the second drop is labeled $h(x)$.

a. At what heights did Kylie drop the helicopter? What is the helicopter's flight time during each drop?

The y–intercepts are 16 and 36 so Kylie dropped the helicopter from 16 feet and 36 feet.

The x–intercepts are 1 and 1.5 so the flight times of the helicopter are 1 second and 1.5 seconds, respectively.

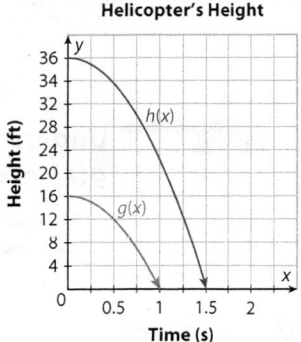

Helicopter's Height

Height (ft) vs *Time (s)*

b. If each graph is represented by a function of the form $f(x) = ax^2$, are the coefficients positive or negative? Explain.

Both graphs open downward, so the coefficients are both negative.

c. Estimate the functions for each graph.

The graph of $g(x)$ is the graph of $f(x) = x^2$ translated up 16 units. The parabola opens downward, so the coefficient a is negative. The x–intercept of the graph is 1. Solve for a.

$g(x) = ax^2 + b$

$0 = a(1)^2 + 16$

$0 = a + 16$

$-16 = a$

The function for the first drop is $g(x) = -16x^2 + 16$.

The graph of $h(x)$ is the graph of $f(x) = x^2$ translated up 36 units. The parabola opens downward, so the coefficient a is negative. The x–intercept of the graph is 1.5. Solve for a.

$h(x) = ax^2 + b$

$0 = a(1.5)^2 + 36$

$0 = 2.25a + 36$

$-36 = 2.25a$

$-16 = a$

The function for the second drop is $h(x) = -16x^2 + 36$.

EXTENSION ACTIVITY

Have small groups of students investigate how to make a paper helicopter and then make their own. Then have students set up their own helicopter flight test to test two different height drops and their flight times. Finally, have students graph the results of their helicopter drops and write functions to represent each graph.

QUESTIONING STRATEGIES

? What information to help you write the functions do you get when you look at the graph? The graphs give the x- and y-intercepts of both curves and, because both curves open downward, a will have a negative value.

INTEGRATED MATHEMATICAL PRACTICES
Focus on Modeling

MP.4 Discuss the difference between the two models shown.

$$h = -4.9t^2 + h_0$$

$$h = -16t^2 + h_0$$

The first equation is given in metric units (h in meters) while the second is in customary units (h in feet). Students should recognize that time in seconds is the only unit of measure that is the same for both models.

INTEGRATE MATHEMATICAL PRACTICES
Focus on Technology

MP.5 Have students use graphing calculators to graph their two equations, $f(x) = -16x^2 + 16$ and $h(x) = -16x^2 + 36$, as a way to check that the functions are good representations of the situation described.

Scoring Rubric

2 points: Student correctly solves the problem and explains his/her reasoning.

1 point: Student shows good understanding of the problem but does not fully solve or explain his/her reasoning.

0 points: Student does not demonstrate understanding of the problem.

Transforming Quadratic Functions

Common Core Math Standards

The student is expected to:

 **F-BF.B.3**

Identify the effect on the graph of replacing $f(x)$ by $f(x) + k$, $kf(x)$, $f(kx)$, and $f(x + k)$ for specific values of k (both positive and negative)... Also F-BF.A.1, F-BF.B.4, F-IF.B.4, F-IF.A.2

Mathematical Practices

 MP.8 Patterns

Language Objective

Students work in pairs or small groups to both give and listen to oral clues about graphs of quadratic functions.

ENGAGE

Essential Question: How can you obtain the graph of $g(x) = a(x - h)^2 + k$ from the graph of $f(x) = x^2$?

Possible answer: Identify the vertex (h, k) and use the sign of a to determine whether the graph opens up or down. Generate a few points on one side of the vertex and sketch the graph using those points and symmetry.

PREVIEW: LESSON PERFORMANCE TASK

View the Engage section online. Discuss the photo and how the path of a ball used in sports can be modeled by a quadratic function. Then preview the Lesson Performance Task.

19.2 Transforming Quadratic Functions

Essential Question: How can you obtain the graph of $g(x) = a(x - h)^2 + k$ from the graph of $f(x) = x^2$?

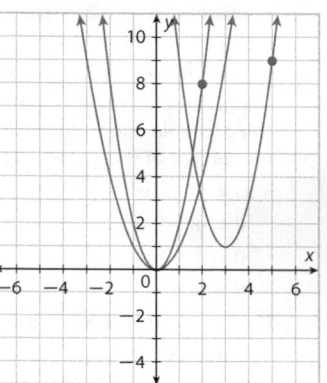
Resource Locker

⊘ Explore   Understanding Quadratic Functions of the Form $g(x) = a(x - h)^2 + k$

Every quadratic function can be represented by an equation of the form $g(x) = a(x - h)^2 + k$. The values of the parameters a, h, and k determine how the graph of the function compares to the graph of the parent function, $y = x^2$. Use the method shown to graph $g(x) = 2(x - 3)^2 + 1$ by transforming the graph of $f(x) = x^2$.

Ⓐ Graph $f(x) = x^2$.

Ⓑ Stretch the graph vertically by a factor of __2__ to obtain the graph of $y = 2x^2$. Graph $y = 2x^2$.

Notice that point $(2, 4)$ moves to point $\boxed{(2, 8)}$.

Ⓒ Translate the graph of $y = 2x^2$ right 3 units and up 1 unit to obtain the graph of $g(x) = 2(x - 3)^2 + 1$. Graph $g(x) = 2(x - 3)^2 + 1$.

Notice that point $(2, 8)$ moves to point $\boxed{(5, 9)}$.

Ⓓ The vertex of the graph of $f(x) = x^2$ is $\underline{(0, 0)}$ while the vertex of the graph of $g(x) = 2(x - 3)^2 + 1$ is $\underline{(3, 1)}$.

© Houghton Mifflin Harcourt Publishing Company

HARDCOVER PAGES 709–716

Turn to these pages to find this lesson in the hardcover student edition.

1. **Discussion** Compare the minimum values of $f(x) = x^2$ and $g(x) = 2(x - 3)^2 + 1$. How is the minimum value related to the vertex?

   The minimum value of $f(x) = x^2$ is 0 and the minimum value $g(x) = 2(x - 3)^2 + 1$ is 1. The minimum value is the y-coordinate of the vertex.

2. **Discussion** What is the axis of symmetry of the function $g(x) = 2(x - 3)^2 + 1$? How is the axis of symmetry related to the vertex?

   The axis of symmetry of $g(x) = 2(x - 3)^2 + 1$ is $x = 3$. The axis of symmetry always passes through the vertex of the parabola. The x-coordinate of the vertex gives the equation of the axis of symmetry of the parabola.

⊘ Explain 1   Understanding Vertical Translations

A **vertical translation** of a parabola is a shift of the parabola up or down, with no change in the shape of the parabola.

Vertical Translations of a Parabola

The graph of the function $f(x) = x^2 + k$ is the graph of $f(x) = x^2$ translated vertically.

If $k > 0$, the graph $f(x) = x^2$ is translated k units up.

If $k < 0$, the graph $f(x) = x^2$ is translated $|k|$ units down.

Example 1   Graph each quadratic function. Give the minimum or maximum value and the axis of symmetry.

Ⓐ $g(x) = x^2 + 2$

Make a table of values for the parent function $f(x) = x^2$ and for $g(x) = x^2 + 2$. Graph the functions together.

x	$f(x) = x^2$	$g(x) = x^2 + 2$
−3	9	11
−2	4	6
−1	1	3
0	0	2
1	1	3
2	4	6
3	9	11

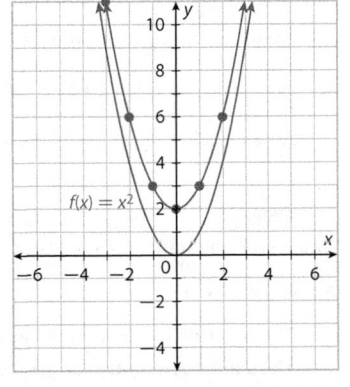

The function $g(x) = x^2 + 2$ has a minimum value of 2.

The axis of symmetry of $g(x) = x^2 + 2$ is $x = 0$.

PROFESSIONAL DEVELOPMENT

Math Background

In this lesson, students graph the family of quadratic functions of the form $g(x) = a(x - h)^2 + k$ and compare those graphs to the graph of the parent function $f(x) = x^2$. Some key understandings are:

- The function $f(x) = x^2$ is the parent of the family of all quadratic functions.

- To graph a quadratic function of the form $g(x) = a(x - h)^2 + k$, identify the vertex (h, k). Then determine whether the graph opens upward or downward. Then generate points on either side of the vertex and sketch the graph of the function.

EXPLORE

Understanding Quadratic Functions of the Form $g(x) = a(x - h)^2 + k$

INTEGRATE TECHNOLOGY

Students have the option of completing the activity either in the book or online.

CONNECT VOCABULARY   🔲 **EL**

This lesson discusses *translation* in terms of a transformation of a function graph. English learners may know about language *translation*. Discuss with students how the two meanings of *translate* are different.

EXPLAIN 1

Understanding Vertical Translations

QUESTIONING STRATEGIES

? How is the graph of $g(x) = x^2 + 2$ related to the graph of $g(x) = x^2 - 5$? Both are translated graphs of the same parent function, $f(x) = x^2$, but $g(x) = x^2 + 2$ is translated 2 units up and $g(x) = x^2 - 5$ is translated 5 units down. So, the graph of $g(x) = x^2 + 2$ is 7 units higher than the graph of $g(x) = x^2 - 5$.

? Is the vertex of the graph of $g(x) = x^2 + 2$ the same as the vertex of the graph of $g(x) = x^2 - 5$? No; $g(x) = x^2 + 2$ has vertex $(0, 2)$, and $g(x) = x^2 - 5$ has vertex $(0, -5)$.

Ⓑ $g(x) = x^2 - 5$

Make a table of values for the parent function $f(x) = x^2$
and for $g(x) = x^2 - 5$. Graph the functions together.

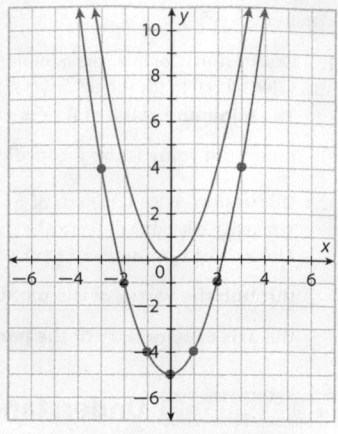

x	$f(x) = x^2$	$g(x) = x^2 - 5$
−3	9	4
−2	4	−1
−1	1	−4
0	0	−5
1	1	−4
2	4	−1
3	9	4

The function $g(x) = x^2 - 5$ has a minimum value of $\underline{-5}$.

The axis of symmetry of $g(x) = x^2 - 5$ is $\underline{x = 0}$.

Reflect

3. How do the values in the table for $g(x) = x^2 + 2$ compare with the values in the table for the parent
   function $f(x) = x^2$?
   For each x in the table, g(x) is 2 greater than f(x).

4. How do the values in the table for $g(x) = x^2 - 5$ compare with the values in the table for the parent
   function $f(x) = x^2$?
   For each x in the table, g(x) is 5 less than f(x).

Your Turn

Graph each quadratic function. Give the minimum or maximum value and the axis of symmetry.

5. $g(x) = x^2 + 4$

   The function $g(x) = x^2 + 4$ has a minimum value of 4.
   The axis of symmetry for $g(x) = x^2 + 4$ is $x = 0$.

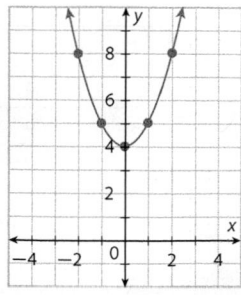

COLLABORATIVE LEARNING

Peer-to-Peer Activity

Have students work in pairs. Have one student draw a graph of $y = x^2 + k$ for
some value of k. The second student then writes the equation for the graph.
Students then compare their results and determine whether the equation is correct
for the given graph. Have students take turns in the two roles.

6. $g(x) = x^2 - 7$

The function $g(x) = x^2 - 7$ has a minimum value of -7.

The axis of symmetry for $g(x) = x^2 - 7$ is $x = 0$.

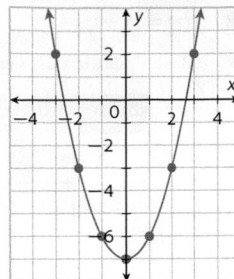

⊘ **Explain 2** **Understanding Horizontal Translations**

A **horizontal translation** of a parabola is a shift of the parabola left or right, with no change in the shape of the parabola.

> **Horizontal Translations of a Parabola**
>
> The graph of the function $f(x) = (x - h)^2$ is the graph of $f(x) = x^2$ translated horizontally.
>
> If $h > 0$, the graph $f(x) = x^2$ is translated h units right.
>
> If $h < 0$, the graph $f(x) = x^2$ is translated $|h|$ units left.

Example 2 Graph each quadratic function. Give the minimum or maximum value and the axis of symmetry.

Ⓐ $g(x) = (x - 1)^2$

Make a table of values for the parent function $f(x) = x^2$ and for $g(x) = (x - 1)^2$. Graph the functions together.

x	$f(x) = x^2$	$g(x) = (x-1)^2$
−3	9	16
−2	4	9
−1	1	4
0	0	1
1	1	0
2	4	1
3	9	4

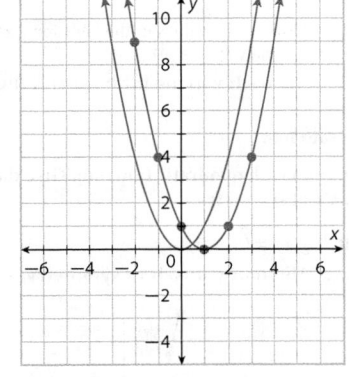

The function $g(x) = (x - 1)^2$ has a minimum value of 0.

The axis of symmetry of $g(x) = (x - 1)^2$ is $x = 1$.

EXPLAIN 2

Understanding Horizontal Translations

QUESTIONING STRATEGIES

? How is the graph of $g(x) = (x - 1)^2$ related to the graph of $g(x) = (x + 2)^2$? Both are translated graphs of the same parent function, $f(x) - x^2$, but the graph of $g(x) = (x - 1)^2$ is translated 1 unit to the right and has vertex $(1, 0)$, while the graph of $g(x) = (x + 2)^2$ is translated 2 units to the left and has vertex $(-2, 0)$. So, the graph of $g(x) = (x - 1)^2$ is 3 units to the right of the graph of $g(x) = (x + 2)^2$.

? What is the vertex of the graph of $g(x) = (x - h)^2$? $(h, 0)$

DIFFERENTIATE INSTRUCTION

Visual Cues

Have students take a coordinate grid and label it "Vertex of $g(x) = (x - h)^2 + k$."
Have them place these points, labels, and functions into the four quadrants.

$(2, 3)$	$h = 2, k = 3$	$g(x) = (x - 2)^2 + 3$
$(-2, 3)$	$h = -2, k = 3$	$g(x) = (x + 2)^2 + 3$
$(-2, -3)$	$h = -2, k = -3$	$g(x) = (x + 2)^2 - 3$
$(2, -3)$	$h = 2, k = -3$	$g(x) = (x - 2)^2 - 3$

Students can use this graph as a reminder of how the location of the vertex and the function are related.

Students may forget that they can use a pattern to write equations from graphs. Remind students that adding k to x^2 moves the graph up for $k > 0$ or down for $k < 0$ and that *subtracting h from x* moves the graph left for $h < 0$ or right for $h > 0$. This is true for all nonzero values of k and h.

Ⓑ $g(x) = (x + 1)^2$

Make a table of values and graph the functions together.

x	$f(x) = x^2$	$g(x) = (x + 1)^2$
−3	9	4
−2	4	1
−1	1	0
0	0	1
1	1	4
2	4	9
3	9	16

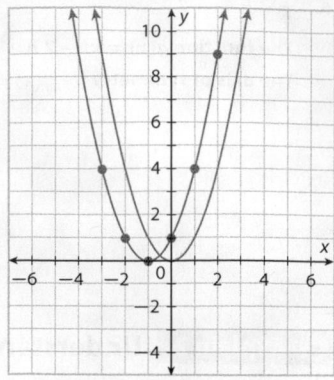

The function $g(x) = (x + 1)^2$ has a minimum value of __0__.

The axis of symmetry of $g(x) = (x + 1)^2$ is __$x = -1$__.

Reflect

7. How do the values in the table for $g(x) = (x - 1)^2$ compare with the values in the table for the parent function $f(x) = x^2$?

   For each x in the table, g(x) is the same as f(x − 1).

8. How do the values in the table for $g(x) = (x + 1)^2$ compare with the values in the table for the parent function $f(x) = x^2$?

   For each x in the table, g(x) is the same as f(x + 1).

Your Turn

Graph each quadratic function. Give the minimum or maximum value and the axis of symmetry.

9. $g(x) = (x - 2)^2$
   Minimum: 0; axis of symmetry: $x = 2$

   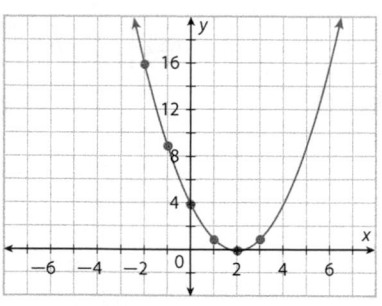

10. $g(x) = (x + 3)^2$
    Minimum: 0; axis of symmetry: $x = -3$

    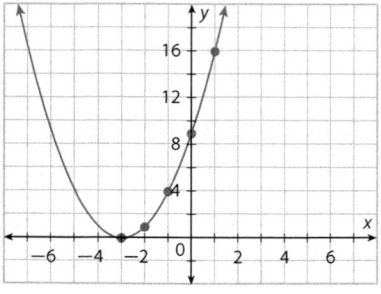

Module 19

907

Lesson 2

© Houghton Mifflin Harcourt Publishing Company

LANGUAGE SUPPORT EL

Communicate Math

Have each student sketch a graph of a parabola on a card, and write a quadratic function in any form on another card. Then have them write clues about the graph and about the function. For example, "The parabola opens upward/downward. Its axis of symmetry is _____; the vertex is at the point _____. The function's graph will open downward/upward." Provide sentence stems if needed to help students begin their clues. Collect the graph and function cards in one pile, and the clue cards in another. Have other students match graph and function cards to fit the clues.

Explain 3   Graphing $g(x) = a(x - h)^2 + k$

The **vertex form of a quadratic function** is $g(x) = a(x - h)^2 + k$, where the point (h, k) is the vertex. The *axis of symmetry* of a quadratic function in this form is the vertical line $x = h$.

To graph a quadratic function in the form $g(x) = a(x - h)^2 + k$, first identify the vertex (h, k). Next, consider the sign of a to determine whether the graph opens upward or downward. If a is positive, the graph opens upward. If a is negative, the graph opens downward. Then generate two points on each side of the vertex. Using those points, sketch the graph of the function.

Example 3   Graph each quadratic function.

(A) $g(x) = -3(x + 1)^2 - 2$

Identify the vertex.

The vertex is at $(-1, -2)$.

Make a table for the function. Find two points on each side of the vertex.

x	−3	−2	−1	0	1
g(x)	−14	−5	−2	−5	−14

Plot the points and draw a parabola through them.

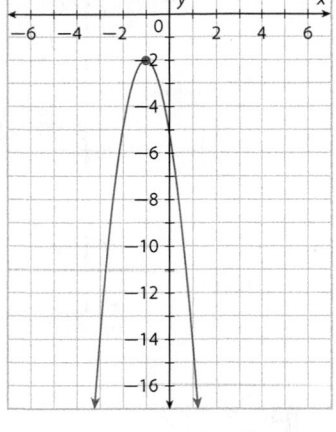

(B) $g(x) = 2(x - 1)^2 - 7$

Identify the vertex.

The vertex is at $(1, -7)$.

Make a table for the function. Find two points on each side of the vertex.

x	−2	0	1	2	4
g(x)	11	−5	−7	−5	11

Plot the points and draw a parabola through them.

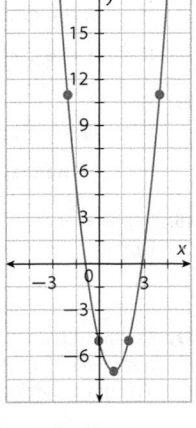

Reflect

11. How do you tell from the equation whether the vertex is a maximum value or a minimum value?

If the value of *a* is positive, the vertex is a minimum value. If the value of *a* is negative, the vertex is a maximum value.

EXPLAIN 3

Graphing $g(x) = a(x - h)^2 + k$

QUESTIONING STRATEGIES

? What can you tell about the graph of a function from its equation in the form $g(x) = a(x - h)^2 + k$? **the location of the vertex and whether the graph opens upward or downward**

? What are the domain and range for a quadratic function whose graph opens downward? **The domain is all real numbers, and the range is the set of all values less than or equal to the maximum value.**

AVOID COMMON ERRORS

Students may try to graph a quadratic function of the form $g(x) = a(x - h)^2 + k$ by using a value other than $x = h$. Remind them that they need to first identify and plot the vertex. Then they should identify and plot other points and use the plotted points to draw a parabola.

INTEGRATE MATHEMATICAL PRACTICES
Focus on Modeling

MP.4 Tell students that a transformed quadratic function models the height of an object dropped from a given height, based upon the time since it was dropped. Sketch a quadratic function that models the situation, and draw students' attention to the vertex $(0, k)$ being the maximum point of the graph. Ask about the sign of a in the function $g(x) = ax^2 + k$, and note that the values to the left of the y-axis are not considered.

ELABORATE

INTEGRATE MATHEMATICAL PRACTICES
Focus on Technology

MP.5 Give students a function in the form $g(x) = a(x - h)^2 + k$. Have students use the whiteboard to identify and plot the vertex and then identify and plot other points on the graph before drawing the graph of the function.

SUMMARIZE

? How do you graph a quadratic function of the form $g(x) = a(x - h)^2 + k$? First, identify and plot the vertex. Then, identify and plot other points on the graph. Finally, draw the graph.

Graph each quadratic function.

12. $g(x) = -(x - 2)^2 + 4$

x	−1	0	2	4	5
g(x)	−5	0	4	0	−5

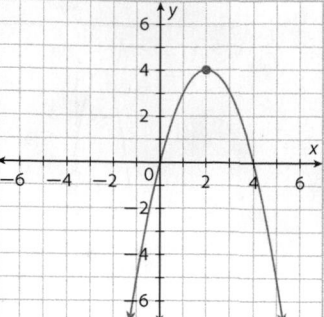

13. $g(x) = 2(x + 3)^2 - 1$

x	−5	−4	−3	−2	−1
g(x)	7	1	−1	1	7

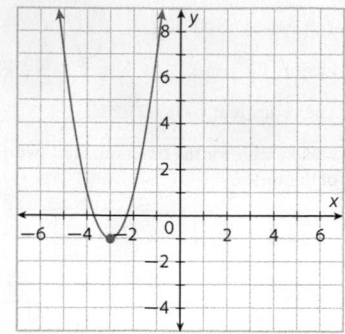

💬 Elaborate

14. How does the value of k in $g(x) = x^2 + k$ affect the translation of $f(x) = x^2$?
If $k > 0$, the graph $f(x) = x^2$ is translated k units up.

If $k < 0$, the graph $f(x) = x^2$ is translated k units down.

15. How does the value of h in $g(x) = (x - h)^2$ affect the translation of $f(x) = x^2$?
If $h > 0$, the graph $f(x) = x^2$ is translated h units right.

If $h < 0$, the graph $f(x) = x^2$ is translated h units left.

16. In $g(x) = a(x - h)^2 + k$, what are the coordinates of the vertex?
(h, k)

17. Essential Question Check-In How can you use the values of a, h, and k, to obtain the graph of $g(x) = a(x - h)^2 + k$ from the graph $f(x) = x^2$?
The graph of $f(x) = x^2$ is stretched or compressed by a factor of $|a|$, and reflected across the

x-axis if a is negative; it is translated h units horizontally and k units vertically.

Graph each quadratic function by transforming the graph of $f(x) = x^2$. Describe the transformations.

1. $g(x) = 2(x-2)^2 + 5$

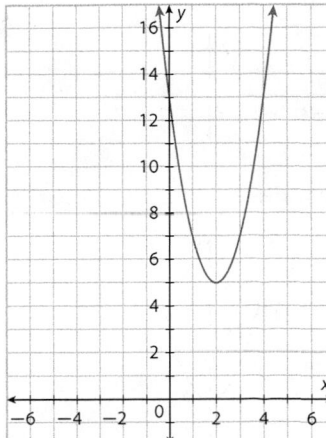

The parent function has been translated 2 units right and 5 units up. It has been stretched vertically by a factor of 2.

2. $g(x) = 2(x+3)^2 - 6$

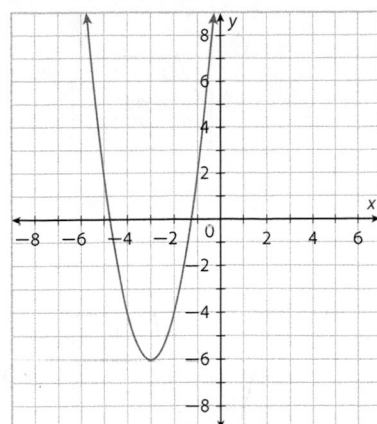

The parent function has been translated 3 units left and 6 units down. It has been stretched vertically by a factor of 2.

3. $g(x) = \frac{1}{2}(x-3)^2 - 4$

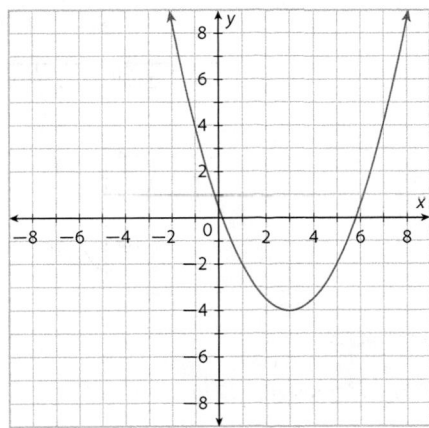

The parent function has been translated 3 units right and 4 units down. It has been vertically compressed by a factor of $\frac{1}{2}$.

4. $g(x) = 3(x-4)^2 - 2$

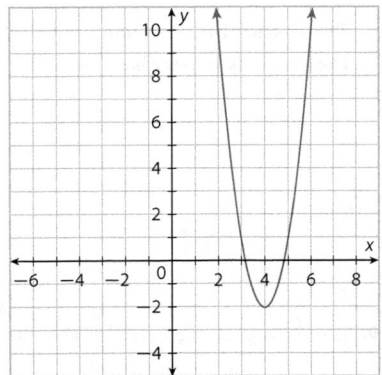

The parent function has been translated 4 units right and 2 units down. It has been stretched vertically by a factor of 3.

© Houghton Mifflin Harcourt Publishing Company

Exercise	Depth of Knowledge (D.O.K.)	COMMON CORE Mathematical Practices
1–8	**1** Recall of Information	**MP.6** Precision
9–12	**2** Skills/Concepts	**MP.5** Using Tools
13–16	**2** Skills/Concepts	**MP.2** Reasoning
17–20	**2** Skills/Concepts	**MP.6** Precision
21–22	**2** Skills/Concepts	**MP.2** Reasoning
23–25	**3** Strategic Thinking H.O.T.	**MP.3** Logic
26–27	**3** Strategic Thinking H.O.T.	**MP.2** Reasoning

EVALUATE

Personal Math Trainer

ASSIGNMENT GUIDE

Concepts and Skills	Practice
Explore Understanding Quadratic Functions of the Form $g(x) = a(x-h)^2 + k$	Exercises 1–4
Example 1 Understanding Vertical Translations	Exercises 5–10
Example 2 Understanding Horizontal Translations	Exercises 11–16
Example 3 Graphing $g(x) = a(x-h)^2 + k$	Exercises 17–27

INTEGRATE MATHEMATICAL PRACTICES

Focus on Modeling

MP.4 Make sure that students understand where h, k, and a come from. Give coordinates for a vertex and have students substitute the x- and y-values of the vertex into the equation of h and k, determine the value of a, and then write the equation of the function.

Transforming Quadratic Functions　**910**

Graph each quadratic function.

5. $g(x) = x^2 - 2$

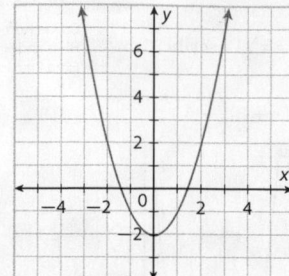

6. $g(x) = x^2 + 5$

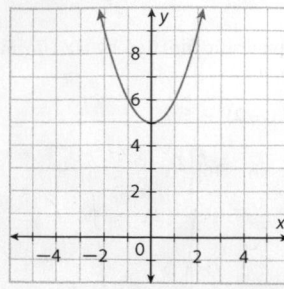

7. $g(x) = x^2 - 6$

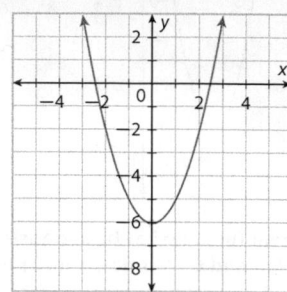

8. $g(x) = x^2 + 3$

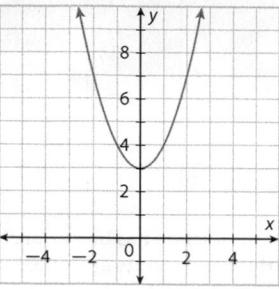

9. Graph $g(x) = x^2 - 9$. Give the minimum or maximum value and the axis of symmetry.

The function has a minimum value of −9.

The axis of symmetry is $x = 0$.

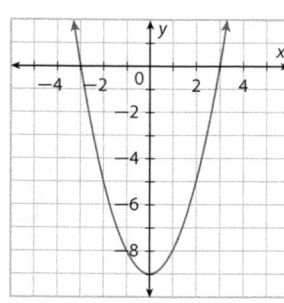

10. How is the graph of $g(x) = x^2 + 12$ related to the graph of $f(x) = x^2$?

The graph of $g(x) = x^2 + 12$ is the graph of $f(x) = x^2$ translated 12 units up.

© Houghton Mifflin Harcourt Publishing Company

Graph each quadratic function. Give the minimum or maximum value and the axis of symmetry.

11. $g(x) = (x - 3)^2$

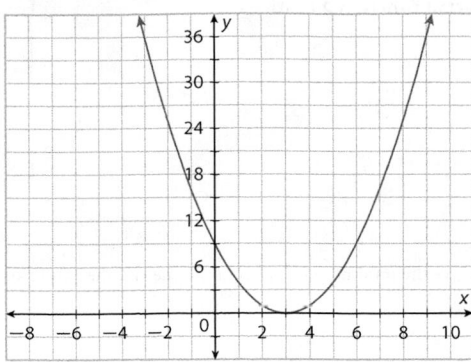

The function has a minimum value of 0.

The axis of symmetry is $x = 3$.

12. $g(x) = (x + 2)^2$

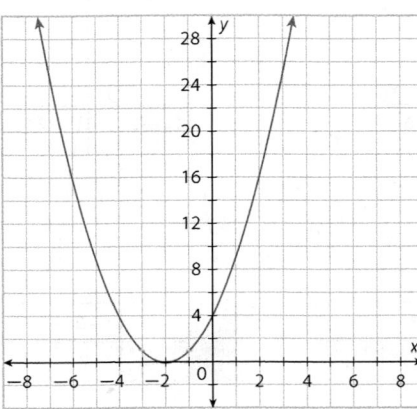

The function has a minimum value of 0.

The axis of symmetry is $x = -2$.

13. How is the graph of $g(x) = (x + 12)^2$ related to the graph of $f(x) = x^2$?

The graph of $g(x) = (x + 12)^2$ is the graph of $f(x) = x^2$ translated 12 units left.

14. How is the graph of $g(x) = (x - 10)^2$ related to the graph of $f(x) = x^2$?

The graph of $g(x) = (x - 10)^2$ is the graph of $f(x) = x^2$ translated 10 units right.

AVOID COMMON ERRORS

Some students may automatically say that the function has a minimum when a parabola opens downward, and a maximum when a parabola opens upward, because of word association. Tell students to visualize the graph before determining whether it has a minimum or maximum.

KINESTHETIC EXPERIENCE

Display each function below, one at a time. Have students discuss, in pairs, whether to lift their arms up in the shape of a U to signal the graph opens upward, or move them downward in the shape of an upside-down U, to signal that the graph opens downward. Then have students demonstrate their decisions.

$y = -3x^2 + 18$ down

$y = 5x + 8 - \frac{1}{5}x^2$ down

$-2x^2 + y = -5$ up

$3x - y = -x^2$ up

---

15. Compare the given graph to the graph of the parent function $f(x) = x^2$. Describe how the parent function must be translated to get the graph shown here.

Translate the graph of the parent function 2 units to the right.

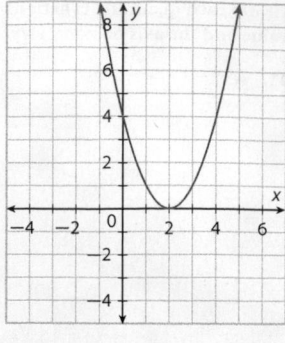

16. For the function $g(x) = (x - 9)^2$ give the minimum or maximum value and the axis of symmetry.

The minimum value is 0.

The axis of symmetry is $x = 9$.

Graph each quadratic function. Give the minimum or maximum value and the axis of symmetry.

17. $g(x) = (x - 1)^2 - 5$

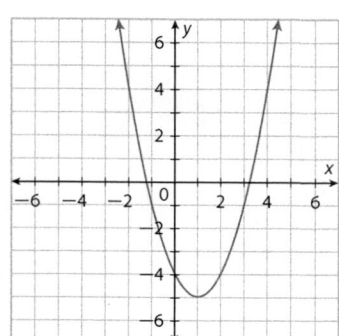

x	−2	0	1	3	4
g(x)	4	−4	−5	−1	4

The function has a minimum value of −5.

The axis of symmetry is $x = 1$.

18. $g(x) = -(x + 2)^2 + 5$

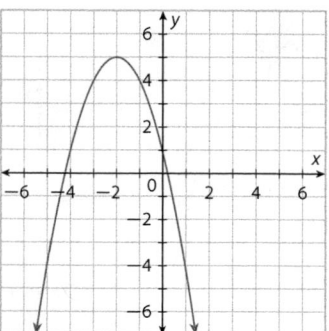

x	−5	−3	−2	0	1
g(x)	−4	4	5	1	−4

The function has a maximum value of 5.

The axis of symmetry is $x = -2$.

19. $g(x) = \frac{1}{4}(x + 1)^2 - 7$

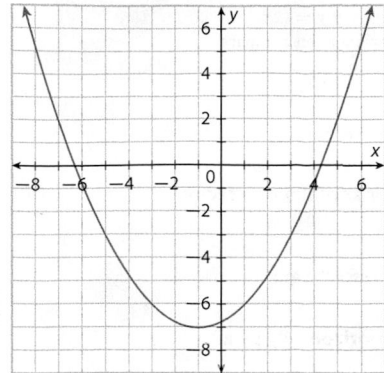

x	−8	−5	−1	3	5
g(x)	5.25	−3	−7	−3	2

The function has a minimum value of −7.

The axis of symmetry is $x = -1$.

20. $g(x) = -\frac{1}{3}(x + 3)^2 + 8$

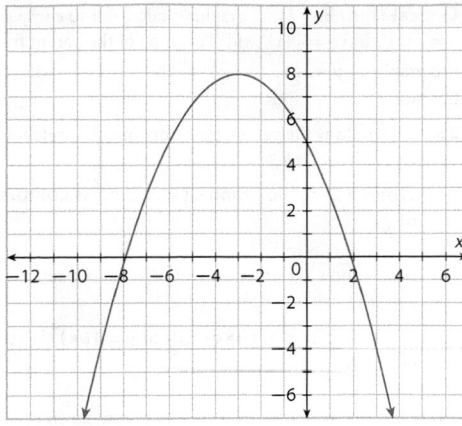

x	−7	−6	−3	0	3
g(x)	2.67	5	8	5	2.67

The function has a maximum value of 8.

The axis of symmetry is $x = -3$.

21. Compare the given graph to the graph of the parent function $f(x) = x^2$. Describe how the parent function must be translated to get the graph shown here.

Translate the graph of the parent function 3 units to the right and 2 units up.

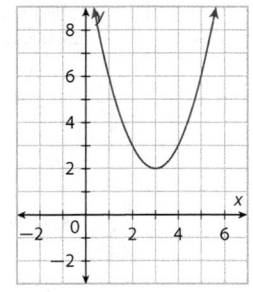

22. Multiple Representations Write an equation for the function represented by the graph of a parabola that is a translation of $f(x) = x^2$. The graph has been translated 11 units to the left and 5 units down.

a. $g(x) = (x - 11)^2 - 5$

b. $g(x) = (x + 11)^2 - 5$

c. $g(x) = (x + 11)^2 + 5$

d. $g(x) = (x - 11)^2 + 5$

e. $g(x) = (x - 5)^2 - 11$

f. $g(x) = (x - 5)^2 + 11$

g. $g(x) = (x + 5)^2 - 11$

h. $g(x) = (x + 5)^2 + 11$

PEER-TO-PEER ACTIVITY

Have students work in pairs. Have each student change one or more of the parameters in $f(x) = a(x - h)^2 + k$ and graph the function. Then have students trade graphs and try to write the function equation for the other student's graph. Have each student justify the function equation and discuss it with the partner.

JOURNAL

In their journals, have students explain how to use the values of a, h, and k to obtain the graph of $g(x) = a(x - h)^2 + k$ from the graph of $f(x) = x^2$.

Critical Thinking Use a graphing calculator to compare the graphs of $y = (2x)^2$, $y = (3x)^2$, and $y = (4x)^2$ with the graph of the parent function $y = x^2$. Then compare the graphs of $y = \left(\frac{1}{2}x\right)^2$, $y = \left(\frac{1}{3}x\right)^2$, and $y = \left(\frac{1}{4}x\right)^2$ with the graph of the parent function $y = x^2$.

23. Explain how the parameter b horizontally stretches or compresses the graph of $y = (bx)^2$ when $b > 1$.

    When $b > 1$, the graph of $y = (bx)^2$ is compressed horizontally by a factor of $\frac{1}{b}$.

24. Explain how the parameter b horizontally stretches or compresses the graph of $y = (bx)^2$ when $0 < b < 1$.

    When $0 < b < 1$, the graph of $y = (bx)^2$ is stretched horizontally by a factor of $\frac{1}{b}$.

25. **Explain the Error** Nina is trying to write an equation for the function represented by the graph of a parabola that is a translation of $f(x) = x^2$. The graph has been translated 4 units to the right and 2 units up. She writes the function as $g(x) = (x + 4)^2 + 2$. Explain the error.

    Nina should have subtracted 4 from x in the equation instead of adding it.

26. **Multiple Representations** A group of engineers drop an experimental tennis ball from a catwalk and let it fall to the ground. The tennis ball's height above the ground (in feet) is given by a function of the form $f(t) = a(t - h)^2 + k$ where t is the time (in seconds) after the tennis ball was dropped. Use the graph to find the equation for $f(t)$.

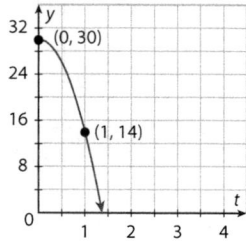 

$f(t) = a(t - 0)^2 + 30$, **or** $f(t) = at^2 + 30$

$14 = a(1)^2 + 30$

$-16 = a$

The equation for the function is $f(t) = -16t^2 + 30$.

27. **Make a Prediction** For what values of a and c will the graph of $f(x) = ax^2 + c$ have one x-intercept?

    For any real value of a with $a \neq 0$, the function will have one x-intercept when $c = 0$.

Lesson Performance Task

The path a baseball takes after it has been hit is modeled by the graph. The baseball's height above the ground is given by a function of the form $f(t) = a(t - h)^2 + k$, where t is the time in seconds since the baseball was hit.

a. What is the baseball's maximum height? At what time was the baseball at its maximum height?

b. When does the baseball hit the ground?

c. Find an equation for $f(t)$.

d. A player hits a second baseball. The second baseball's path is modeled by the function $g(t) = -16(t - 4)^2 + 256$. Which baseball has a greater maximum height? Which baseball is in the air for the longest?

Baseball's Height

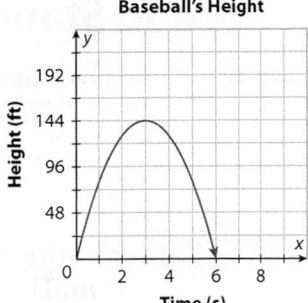

a. The vertex of the parabola is $(3, 144)$. So, the baseball is at its maximum height of 144 feet after 3 seconds.

b. The second x-intercept of the graph is $(6, 0)$. So, the baseball hits the ground after 6 seconds.

c. The vertex of the parabola is $(3, 144)$ and one intercept of the graph is $(6, 0)$. Solve for a.

$$f(t) = a(t - h)^2 + k$$
$$0 = a(6 - 3)^2 + 144$$
$$-144 = 9a$$
$$-16 = a$$

So, $f(t) = -16(t - 3)^2 + 144$.

d. The vertex is $(4, 256)$ so the baseball was at its maximum height of 256 feet after 4 seconds.

$$g(t) = -16(t-4)^2 + 256$$
$$0 = -16(t-4)^2 + 256$$
$$-256 = -16(t-4)^2$$
$$16 = (t-4)^2$$
$$\sqrt{16} = t-4$$
$$\pm 4 + 4 = t$$
$$0, 8 = t$$

The ball hits the ground after 8 seconds.

So, the second baseball has a greater maximum height and it traveled longer in the air than the first.

© Houghton Mifflin Harcourt Publishing Company

EXTENSION ACTIVITY

Have groups of students draw or tape a large, first-quadrant coordinate grid on the chalkboard. Have one student toss a tennis ball in front of the grid, making sure that the path of the ball stays within the grid's borders, while another student videotapes the toss at a rate of about 15 frames per second. Then have students play back the video, marking points on the grid to show the path of the ball. Finally, have students use the model $f(t) = a(t - h)^2 + k$ to write a function that models the path of the tennis ball. Students may discover that the angle at which the ball is tossed affects the height and width of the curved path the ball follows. Have students save their data for Part 2 of the Extension Activity in the following lesson.

INTEGRATE MATHEMATICAL PRACTICES
Focus on Patterns

MP.8 Discuss with students which type of hit—a ground ball, a pop-up, or a line drive—would likely make a baseball have the path shown in the graph. Ask how knowing the maximum height of the ball and the time it takes the ball to hit the ground help you write an equation to represent the path of the baseball.

The highest height of the ball, the vertex of the path, is the ordered pair (h, k), and the time it takes the ball to hit the ground is the ordered pair $(t, f(t))$, so the h, k, t, and $f(t)$ values can be substituted into the standard form $f(t) = a(t - h)^2 + k$ to find the value of a.

INTEGRATE MATHEMATICAL PRACTICES
Focus on Critical Thinking

MP.3 Point out that the model students write in the form $f(t) = a(t - h)^2 + k$ to represent the path the baseball takes can be used to approximate the height h in feet above the ground after t seconds because it does not account for air resistance, wind, or other real-world factors.

Scoring Rubric

2 points: Student correctly solves the problem and explains his/her reasoning.

1 point: Student shows good understanding of the problem but does not fully solve or explain his/her reasoning.

0 points: Student does not demonstrate understanding of the problem.

Interpreting Vertex Form and Standard Form

Common Core Math Standards

The student is expected to:

 F-IF.B.4

For a function that models a relationship between two quantities, interpret key features of graphs... Also F-IF.C.8, F-IF.A.2, F-IF.B.4, F-BF.A.1

Mathematical Practices

 MP.2 Reasoning

Language Objective

Work with a partner to describe how to write quadratic functions in vertex form and standard form.

ENGAGE

Essential Question: How can you change the vertex form of a quadratic function to standard form?

Sample answer: You can rewrite the quadratic expression in the vertex form by multiplying and then combining like terms so that the function rule is written in descending order of the exponents.

PREVIEW: LESSON PERFORMANCE TASK

View the Engage section online. Discuss the photo and the type of data that is needed in order to represent the path of the tennis ball as a function. Then preview the Lesson Performance Task.

Name _____ Class _____ Date _____

19.3 Interpreting Vertex Form and Standard Form

Essential Question: How can you change the vertex form of a quadratic function to standard form?

Resource Locker

⊘ Explore Identifying Quadratic Functions from Their Graphs

Determine whether a function is a quadratic function by looking at its graph. If the graph of a function is a parabola, then the function is a quadratic function. If the graph of a function is not a parabola, then the function is not a quadratic function.

Use a graphing calculator to graph each of the functions. Set the viewing window to show −10 to 10 on both axes. Determine whether each function is a quadratic function.

Ⓐ Use a graphing calculator to graph $f(x) = x + 1$.

Ⓑ Determine whether the function $f(x) = x + 1$ is a quadratic function.

The function $f(x) = x + 1$ __is not__ a quadratic function.

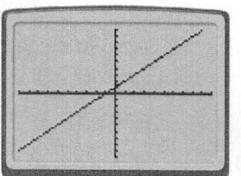

Ⓒ Use a graphing calculator to graph $f(x) = x^2 + 2x - 6$.

Ⓓ Determine whether the function $f(x) = x^2 + 2x - 6$ is a quadratic function.

The function $f(x) = x^2 + 2x - 6$ __is__ a quadratic function.

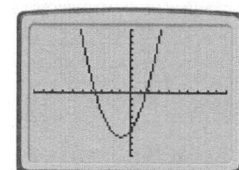

Ⓔ Use a graphing calculator to graph $f(x) = 2^x$.

Ⓕ Determine whether the function $f(x) = 2^x$ is a quadratic function.

The function $f(x) = 2^x$ __is not__ a quadratic function.

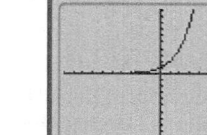

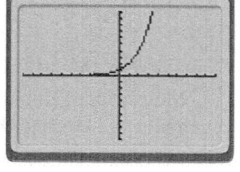

HARDCOVER PAGES 717–728

Turn to these pages to find this lesson in the hardcover student edition.

Ⓖ Use a graphing calculator to graph $f(x) = 2x^2 - 3$.

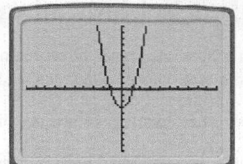

Ⓗ Determine whether the function $f(x) = 2x^2 - 3$ is a quadratic function.

The function $f(x) = 2x^2 - 3$ __is__ a quadratic function.

Ⓘ Use a graphing calculator to graph $f(x) = -(x - 3)^2 + 7$.

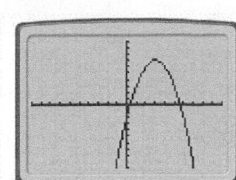

Ⓙ Determine whether the function $f(x) = -(x - 3)^2 + 7$ is a quadratic function.

The function $f(x) = -(x - 3)^2 + 7$ __is__ a quadratic function.

Ⓚ Use a graphing calculator to graph $f(x) = \sqrt{x}$.

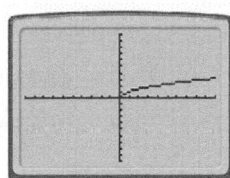

Ⓛ Determine whether the function $f(x) = \sqrt{x}$ is a quadratic function.

The function $f(x) = \sqrt{x}$ __is not__ a quadratic function.

Reflect

1. How can you determine whether a function is quadratic or not by looking at its graph?
Sample answer: All quadratic functions have graphs that are parabolas, opening either upward or downward. If the graph of a function does not have this shape, then the function is not quadratic.

2. **Discussion** How can you tell if a function is a quadratic function by looking at the equation?
Sample answer: If the highest power of the variable is x^2, then the function is quadratic.

EXPLORE

Identifying Quadratic Functions from Their Graphs

INTEGRATE TECHNOLOGY

Students have the option of completing the activity either in the book or online.

INTEGRATE MATHEMATICAL PRACTICES
Focus on Patterns

MP.8 Point out to students that the graph of a parabola is symmetric about a vertical line through its vertex.

PROFESSIONAL DEVELOPMENT

 Integrate Mathematical Practices

This lesson provides an opportunity to address Mathematical Practice **MP.2,** which calls for students to "reason abstractly and quantitatively." Students analyze the relationship between quadratic functions in standard and vertex forms and convert between vertex form and standard form.

EXPLAIN 1

Identifying Quadratic Functions in Standard Form

QUESTIONING STRATEGIES

? How can you tell by looking at an equation whether the value of a in $y = ax^2 + bx + c$ is 0? If there is no squared term, $a = 0$.

? If the values of a, b, and c in $y = ax^2 + bx + c$ are all positive, what do you know about the graph? The graph opens up because a is positive; and the vertex is to the left of the y-axis because $-\frac{b}{2a}$ is negative.

INTEGRATE MATHEMATICAL PRACTICES

Focus on Reasoning

MP.2 Point out to students that an equation must be solved for y in terms of x before they determine whether the equation represents a quadratic function. For example $y + x^2 = x^2 + 4x + 1$ does not represent a quadratic function. Even though there is an x^2 term in the equation, when the equation is solved for y and simplified, there is no x^2 term.

If a function is quadratic, it can be represented by an equation of the form $y = ax^2 + bx + c$, where a, b, and c are real numbers and $a \neq 0$. This is called the **standard form of a quadratic equation**.

The axis of symmetry for a quadratic equation in standard form is given by the equation $x = -\frac{b}{2a}$. The vertex of a quadratic equation in standard form is given by the coordinates $\left(-\frac{b}{2a}, f\left(-\frac{b}{2a}\right)\right)$.

Example 1 Determine whether the function represented by each equation is quadratic. If so, give the axis of symmetry and the coordinates of the vertex.

(A) $y = -2x + 20$

$y = -2x + 20$ Compare to $y = ax^2 + bx + c$.

This is not a quadratic function because $a = 0$.

(B) $y + 3x^2 = -4$

Rewrite the function in the form $y = ax^2 + bx + c$.

$y = \underline{-3x^2 - 4}$

Compare to $y = ax^2 + bx + c$.

This __is__ a quadratic function.

If $y + 3x^2 = -4$ is a quadratic function, give the axis of symmetry. $\underline{x = 0}$

If $y + 3x^2 = -4$ is a quadratic function, give the coordinates of the vertex. $\underline{(0, -4)}$

Reflect

3. Explain why the function represented by the equation $y = ax^2 + bx + c$ is quadratic only when $a \neq 0$.
   If $a = 0$, there is no x-squared term and all quadratic equations include an __x-squared term.__

4. Why might it be easier to determine whether a function is quadratic when it is expressed in function notation?
   All the terms are already on one side of the equal sign; they only need to be arranged in __standard form.__

5. How is the axis of symmetry related to standard form?
   The axis of symmetry for a quadratic equation in standard form is given by the equation __$x = -\frac{b}{2a}$, where a and b are constants in $y = ax^2 + bx + c$.__

Your Turn

Determine whether the function represented by each equation is quadratic.

6. $y - 4x + x^2 = 0$
   $y = -x^2 + 4x$
   $y - 4x + x^2 = 0$ is
   a quadratic function.

7. $x + 2y = 14x + 6$
   $y = \frac{13}{2}x + 3$
   Compare $y = \frac{13}{2}x + 3$ to $y = ax^2 + bx + c$.
   This is not a quadratic function because $a = 0$.

COLLABORATIVE LEARNING

Peer to Peer Activity

Have students work with a partner. Have each partner make up a quadratic function in vertex form. Then have students exchange papers and convert the vertex form to standard form, showing each step in the solution. Encourage students to repeat this several times, using different signs and reorganizing the equation to make it more difficult. For example, "Convert $y - 3 = (x - 5)^2$ to standard form." $y = (x - 5)^2 + 3$; $y = x^2 - 10x + 25 + 3$; $y = x^2 - 10x + 28$

Changing from Vertex Form to Standard Form

It is possible to write quadratic equations in various forms.

Example 2 Rewrite a quadratic function from vertex form, $y = a(x - h)^2 + k$, to standard form, $y = ax^2 + bx + c$.

Ⓐ $y = 4(x - 6)^2 + 3$

$y = 4(x^2 - 12x + 36) + 3$ Expand $(x - 6)^2$.

$y = 4x^2 - 48x + 144 + 3$ Multiply.

$y = 4x^2 - 48x + 147$ Simplify.

The standard form of $y = 4(x - 6)^2 + 3$ is $y = 4x^2 - 48x + 147$.

Ⓑ $y = -3(x + 2)^2 - 1$

$y = -3\left(\boxed{x^2 + 4x + 4}\right) - 1$ Expand $(x + 2)^2$.

$y = \boxed{-3x^2 - 12x - 12} - 1$ Multiply.

$y = \boxed{-3x^2 - 12x - 13}$ Simplify.

The standard form of $y = -3(x + 2)^2 - 1$ is $y = \boxed{-3x^2 - 12x - 13}$.

Reflect

8. If in $y = a(x - h)^2 + k$, $a = 1$, what is the simplified form of the standard form, $y = ax^2 + bx + c$?

$y = x^2 + bx + c$

Your Turn

Rewrite a quadratic function from vertex form, $y = a(x - h)^2 + k$, to standard form, $y = ax^2 + bx + c$.

9. $y = 2(x + 5)^2 + 3$

$y = 2(x^2 + 10x + 25) + 3$
$y = 2x^2 + 20x + 50 + 3$
$y = 2x^2 + 20x + 53$

The standard form of
$y = 2(x + 5)^2 + 3$ is $y = 2x^2 + 20x + 53$.

10. $y = -3(x - 7)^2 + 2$

$y = -3(x^2 - 14x + 49) + 2$
$y = -3x^2 + 42x - 147 + 2$
$y = -3x^2 + 42x - 145$

The standard form of
$y = -3(x - 7)^2 + 2$ is $y = -3x^2 + 42x - 145$.

EXPLAIN 2

Changing from Vertex Form to Standard Form

QUESTIONING STRATEGIES

? When is the vertex form of a quadratic function useful? When is standard form useful? **Vertex form makes it easy to identify the vertex, (h, k), and the axis of symmetry, $x = h$. Standard form makes it easy to identify the y-intercept, c.**

? How do you change the vertex form to standard form? **Use the FOIL method to expand and simplify the binomial square.**

? What value is the same in vertex form as in standard form? Why? **The value of a. If you expand $a(x - h)^2 + k$, the coefficient of x^2 is a.**

MODELING

Have students consider what value is the same in vertex form as in standard form. Students comfortable with manipulating variables and constants might try to expand $a(x - h)^2 + k$ to determine the values of a, b, and c in terms of a, h, and k. They should find:

$a(x - h)^2 + k$

$a(x^2 - 2hx + h^2) + k$

$ax^2 - 2ahx + ah^2 + k$

So, $a = a$, $b = -2ah$, and $c = ah^2 + k$.

DIFFERENTIATE INSTRUCTION

Technology

Have students set **Xmin** = 0 and **Ymin** = 0 when graphing the example on a graphing calculator. **Ymax** should be set to slightly above the maximum height. To generate a table from the function, set **TblStart** to 0.

EXPLAIN 3

Writing a Quadratic Function Given a Table of Values

QUESTIONING STRATEGIES

? What do you look for in a table of values in order to decide that it is quadratic?

A minimum or maximum value of *y*, indicating the vertex and axis of symmetry, and values of *y* that are equal for *x*-values that are the same distance from the vertex.

AVOID COMMON ERRORS

Some students may overlook the negative sign in $-\frac{b}{2a}$ when calculating the axis of symmetry. Suggest that students double check that they included the negative sign before finding the vertex of the graph.

You can write a quadratic function from a table of values.

Example 3 Use each table to write a quadratic function in vertex form, $y = a(x - h)^2 + k$. Then rewrite the function in standard form, $y = ax^2 + bx + c$.

Ⓐ The minimum value of the function occurs at $x = -3$.

The vertex of the parabola is $(-3, 0)$.

x	y
−6	9
−4	1
−3	0
−2	1
0	9

Substitute the values for *h* and *k* into $y = a(x - h)^2 + k$.

$y = a(x - (-3))^2 + 0$, or $y = a(x + 3)^2$

Use any point from the table to find *a*.

$y = a(x + 3)^2$

$1 = a(-2 + 3)^2 = a$

The vertex form of the function is $y = 1(x - (-3))^2 + 0$ or $y = (x + 3)^2$.

Rewrite the function $y = (x + 3)^2$ in standard form, $y = ax^2 + bx + c$.

$y = (x + 3)^2 = x^2 + 6x + 9$

The standard form of the function is $y = x^2 + 6x + 9$.

Ⓑ The minimum value of the function occurs at $x = -2$.

The vertex of the parabola is is $(-2, -3)$.

x	y
0	13
−1	1
−2	−3
−3	1
−4	13

Substitute the values for *h* and *k* into $y = a(x - h)^2 + k$.

$y = \boxed{a(x + 2)^2 - 3}$

Use any point from the table to find *a*. $a = \boxed{4}$

The vertex form of the function is $y = \boxed{4(x + 2)^2 - 3}$.

Rewrite the resulting function in standard form, $y = ax^2 + bx + c$.

$y = \boxed{4x^2 + 16x + 13}$

Reflect

11. How many points are needed to find an equation of a quadratic function?
two points, the vertex and one other point

LANGUAGE SUPPORT EL

Communicate Math

Hand out cards to pairs of students with three numbers between −5 and 5 for *a*, *h*, and *k*; for example $a = 2$, $h = -4$, and $k = 1$. Have one student describe to the other how to write the function in vertex form, and then convert it to standard form. Then have them reverse roles and use the opposites of the numbers (in this example, $a = -2$, $h = 4$, and $k = -1$) to write a new function in vertex form, and convert that to standard form. Then have students describe how the graphs of these functions would be related to each other.

Use each table to write a quadratic function in vertex form, $y = a(x - h)^2 + k$.
Then rewrite the function in standard form, $y = ax^2 + bx + c$.

12. The vertex of the function is (2, 5).

x	y
−1	59
1	11
2	5
3	11
5	59

$y = a(x - 2)^2 + 5$

$11 = a(1 - 2)^2 + 5$

$6 = a(-1)^2$

$6 = a$

vertex form $y = 6(x - 2)^2 + 5$.

$y = 6(x^2 - 4x + 4) + 5$

$y = 6x^2 \quad 24x + 24 + 5$

$y = 6x^2 - 24x + 29$

standard form $y = 6x^2 - 24x + 29$.

13. The vertex of the function is (−2, −7).

x	y
0	−27
−1	−12
−2	−7
−3	−12
−4	−27

$y = a(x + 2)^2 - 7$

$-12 = a(-3 + 2)^2 - 7$

$5 = a(-1)^2$

$-5 = a$

vertex form $y = -5(x + 2)^2 - 7$.

$y = -5(x^2 + 4x + 4) - 7$

$y = -5x^2 - 20x - 20 - 7$

$y = -5x^2 - 20x - 27$

standard form $y = -5x^2 - 20x - 27$.

 Explain 4 **Writing a Quadratic Function Given a Graph**

The graph of a parabola can be used to determine the corresponding function.

Example 4 Use each graph to find an equation for $f(t)$.

(A) A house painter standing on a ladder drops a paintbrush, which falls to the ground. The paintbrush's height above the ground (in feet) is given by a function of the form $f(t) = a(t - h)^2$ where t is the time (in seconds) after the paintbrush is dropped.

The vertex of the parabola is $(h, k) = (0, 25)$.

$f(t) = a(x - h)^2 + k$

$f(t) = a(t - 0)^2 + 25$

$f(t) = at^2 + 25$

Use the point (1, 9) to find a.

$f(t) = at^2 + 25$

$9 = a(1)^2 + 25$

$-16 = a$

The equation for the function is $f(t) = -16t^2 + 25$.

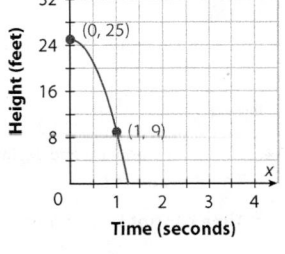

EXPLAIN 4

Writing a Quadratic Function Given a Graph

QUESTIONING STRATEGIES

? In order to find the equation of the graph of an object that is dropped and falls from a height over time, what values can you use? **the y-coordinate of the vertex, and the coordinates of another point on the curve**

Remind students that, when graphing a curve of an object in free fall, the graph represents the distance the object is above the surface and not the path of the object.

Ⓑ A rock is knocked off a cliff into the water far below. The falling rock's height above the water (in feet) is given by a function of the form $f(t) = a(t - h)^2 + k$ where t is the time (in seconds) after the rock begins to fall.

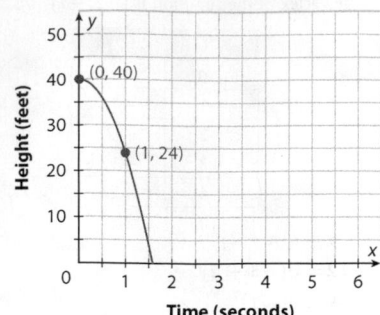

The vertex of the parabola is $(h, k) = \boxed{(0, 40)}$.

$$f(t) = a(t - h)^2 + k$$

$$f(t) = a\left(t - \boxed{0}\right)^2 + \boxed{40}$$

$$f(t) = \boxed{at^2 + 40}$$

Use the point $(1, 24)$ to find a.

$$f(t) = at^2 + \boxed{40}$$

$$\boxed{24} = a\boxed{1}^2 + \boxed{40}$$

$$a = \boxed{-16}$$

The equation for the function is $f(t) = \boxed{-16t^2 + 40}$.

Reflect

14. Identify the domain and explain why it makes sense for this problem.
    The domain is $t \geq 0$.

    Time cannot be negative.

15. Identify the range and explain why it makes sense for this problem.
    The range is $f(t) \geq 0$.

    Height cannot be negative.

16. The graph of a function in the form $f(x) = a(x - h)^2 + k$, is shown. Use the graph to find an equation for $f(x)$.

The vertex of the parabola is $(h, k) = (1, 1)$.

$$f(x) = a(x - 1)^2 + 1$$

From the graph $f(3) = -3$ Substitute 3 for x and -3 for $f(x)$ and solve for a.

$$-3 = a(3 - 1)^2 + 1$$

$$-4 = a(2)^2$$

$$-4 = 4a$$

$$-1 = a$$

The equation for the function is

$$f(x) = -(x - 1)^2 + 1.$$

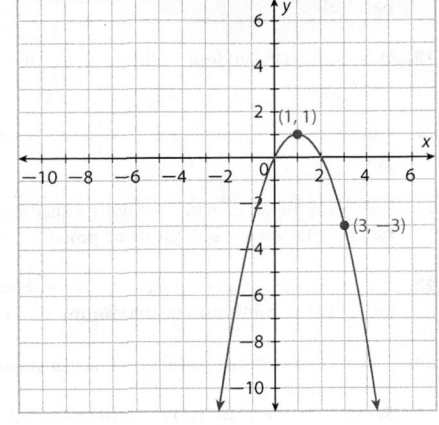

17. A roofer accidentally drops a nail, which falls to the ground. The nail's height above the ground (in feet) is given by a function of the form $f(t) = a(t - h)^2 + k$, where t is the time (in seconds) after the nail drops. Use the graph to find an equation for $f(t)$.

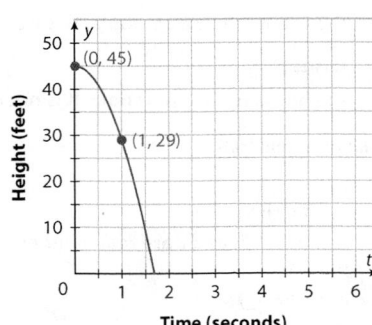

The vertex of the parabola is $(h, k) = (0, 45)$.

$$f(t) = a(t - 0)^2 + 45, \quad \text{or} \quad f(t) = at^2 + 45$$

From the graph $f(1) = 29$. Substitute 1 for t and 29 for $f(t)$ and solve for a.

$$29 = a(1)^2 + 45$$

$$-16 = a$$

The equation for the function is $f(t) = -16t^2 + 45$.

ELABORATE

INTEGRATE MATHEMATICAL PRACTICES
Focus on Modeling

MP.4 Have two students hold the ends of a jump rope at the same height from the ground. Use a measuring tape to place the students 4 feet, 6 feet, and 8 feet apart. Have the students verify whether the lowest point of the jump rope is always halfway between the students holding the rope. Students can graph the height of the rope based on the distance from either end and determine appropriate quadratic functions to describe it. Mention that the curve is called a *catenary*, but that because the shape of a catenary is similar to the shape of a parabola, a quadratic model is appropriate.

SUMMARIZE THE LESSON

? How can you change the vertex form of a quadratic function to standard form? You can rewrite the quadratic expression in the vertex form by multiplying and then combining like terms so that the function rule is written in descending order of the exponents.

 **Elaborate**

18. Describe the graph of a quadratic function.
parabola

19. What is the standard form of the quadratic function?
$y = ax^2 + bx + c$

20. Can any quadratic function in vertex form be written in standard form?
yes

21. How many points are needed to write a quadratic function in vertex form, given the table of values?
two points; vertex and another point

22. If a graph of the quadratic function is given, how do you find the vertex?
Look for the minimum or maximum value on the graph.

23. Essential Question Check-In What can you do to change the vertex form of a quadratic function to standard form?
Sample answer: You can rewrite the quadratic expression in the vertex form by

multiplying and then combine like terms so that the function rule is written in

descending order of the exponents.

☆ Evaluate: Homework and Practice

- Online Homework
- Hints and Help
- Extra Practice

Determine whether each function is a quadratic function by graphing.

1. $f(x) = 0.01 - 0.2x + x^2$
The graph is a parabola. It is quadratic.

2. $f(x) = \frac{1}{2}x - 4$
The graph is not a parabola. It is not quadratic.

3. $f(x) = -4x^2 - 2$
The graph is a parabola. It is quadratic.

4. $f(x) = 2^{x-3}$
The graph is not a parabola. It is not quadratic.

Determine whether the function represented by each equation is quadratic.

5. $y = -3x + 15$
No, $a = 0$

6. $y - 6 = 2x^2$
$y = 2x^2 + 6$
Yes, $a \neq 0$, b, and c are real numbers.

7. $3 + y + 5x^2 = 6x$
$y = -5x^2 + 6x - 3$
Yes, $a \neq 0$, b, and c are real numbers.

8. $y + 6x = 14$
$y = -6x + 14$
No, $a = 0$

9. Which of the following functions is a quadratic function? Select all that apply.

   a. $2x = y + 3$

   (b.) $2x^2 + y = 3x - 1$

   c. $5 = -6x + y$

   (d.) $6x^2 + y = 0$

   e. $y - x = 4$

10. For $f(x) = x^2 + 8x - 14$, give the axis of symmetry and the coordinates of the vertex.

$$-\frac{b}{2a} = -\frac{8}{2(1)} = -4$$

$$f(-4) = -30$$

The vertex is at $(-4, -30)$.

The axis of symmetry is $x = -4$.

11. Describe the axis of symmetry of the graph of the quadratic function represented by the equation $y = ax^2 + bx + c$. when $b = 0$.

The axis of symmetry is the y-axis, or $x = 0$.

Rewrite each quadratic function from vertex form, $y = a(x - h)^2 + k$, to standard form, $y = ax^2 + bx + c$.

12. $y = 5(x - 2)^2 + 7$

$y = 5(x^2 - 4x + 4) + 7$
$y = 5x^2 - 20x + 20 + 7$
$y = 5x^2 - 20x + 27$
The standard form of
$y = 5(x - 2)^2 + 7$ is $y = 5x^2 - 20x + 27$.

13. $y = -2(x + 4)^2 - 11$

$y = -2(x^2 + 8x + 16) - 11$
$y = -2x^2 - 16x - 32 - 11$
$y = -2x^2 - 16x - 43$
The standard form of
$y = -2(x + 4)^2 - 11$ is $y = -2x^2 - 16x - 43$.

14. $y = 3(x + 1)^2 + 12$

$y = 3(x^2 + 2x + 1) + 12$
$y = 3x^2 + 6x + 3 + 12$
$y = 3x^2 + 6x + 15$
The standard form of
$y = 3(x + 1)^2 + 12$ is $y = 3x^2 + 6x + 15$.

15. $y = -4(x - 3)^2 - 9$

$y = -4(x^2 - 6x + 9) - 9$
$y = -4x^2 + 24x - 36 - 9$
$y = -4x^2 + 24x - 45$
The standard form of
$y = -4(x - 3)^2 - 9$ is $y = -4x^2 + 24x - 45$.

16. Explain the Error Tim wrote $y = -6(x + 2)^2 - 10$ in standard form as $y = 6x^2 + 24x + 14$. Find his error.

$y = -6(x^2 + 4x + 4) - 10$
$y = -6x^2 - 24x - 24 - 10$
$y = -6x^2 - 24x - 34$
The standard form of $y = -6(x + 2)^2 - 10$ is $y = -6x^2 - 24x - 34$.
Tim multiplied by 6 instead of -6.

17. How do you change from vertex form, $f(x) = a(x - h)^2 + k$, to standard form, $y = ax^2 + bx + c$?

Sample answer: Expand the squared term. Then distribute the a-value.
Finally, combine like terms.

EVALUATE

Personal Math Trainer

ASSIGNMENT GUIDE

Concepts and Skills	Practice
Explore Identifying Quadratic Functions from Their Graphs	Exercises 1–4
Example 1 Identifying Quadratic Functions in Standard Form	Exercises 5–11
Example 2 Changing from Vertex Form to Standard Form	Exercises 12–17
Example 3 Writing a Quadratic Function Given a Table of Values	Exercises 18–22
Example 4 Writing a Quadratic Function Given a Graph	Exercises 23–25

QUESTIONING STRATEGIES

? When you graph the points of a quadratic function, why are the points connected by a curve rather than straight line segments? The values of a quadratic function change constantly and smoothly, but the rate of change is not constant. A quadratic function results in a U-shaped graph.

Exercise	Depth of Knowledge (D.O.K.)	COMMON CORE Mathematical Practices
1–4	**2** Skills/Concepts	**MP.5** Using Tools
5–11	**2** Skills/Concepts	**MP.6** Precision
12–21	**2** Skills/Concepts	**MP.2** Reasoning
22	**3** Strategic Thinking H.O.T.	**MP.4** Modeling
23	**3** Strategic Thinking H.O.T.	**MP.6** Precision
24	**2** Skills/Concepts H.O.T.	**MP.4** Modeling
25	**3** Strategic Thinking H.O.T.	**MP.2** Reasoning

Interpreting Vertex Form and Standard Form   **926**

? Is the function represented by the equation $y - 10x^2 = 9$ quadratic? Explain. **Yes, because the equation can be written in the form $y = ax^2 + bx + c$, where $a = 10$, $b = 0$, and $c = 9$.**

INTEGRATE MATHEMATICAL PRACTICES

Focus on Patterns

MP.8 Remind students that in a table of values for a quadratic function, the vertex can be identified by looking for the single least or greatest function value. If function values appear more than once, they represent points that are symmetric about the vertex; the vertex will be halfway between them.

AVOID COMMON ERRORS

Students may make a sign error in converting from vertex form when the value of a is negative and the squared value is in the form $x - h$ where h is positive. Remind students that when squaring a term like $x - 3$, the result has a negative coefficient of x and a positive constant term, so multiplying by a negative value for a reverses those signs.

Use each table to write a quadratic function in vertex form, $y = a(x - h)^2 + k$. Then rewrite the function in standard form, $y = ax^2 + bx + c$.

18. The vertex of the function is $(6, -8)$.

x	y
10	24
8	0
6	-8
4	0
2	24

$y = a(x - 6)^2 - 8$
$0 = a(4 - 6)^2 - 8$
$8 = a(4)$
$2 = a$
vertex form $y = 2(x - 6)^2 - 8$.
$y = 2(x^2 - 12x + 36) - 8$
$y = 2x^2 - 24x + 72 - 8$
$y = 2x^2 - 24x + 64$
standard form $y = 2x^2 - 24x + 64$.

19. The vertex of the function is $(4, 7)$.

x	y
0	-1
2	5
4	7
6	5
8	-1

$y = a(x - 4)^2 + 7$
$-1 = a(0 - 4)^2 + 7$
$-8 = a(16)$
$-\frac{1}{2} = a$
vertex form $y = -\frac{1}{2}(x - 4)^2 + 7$.
$y = -\frac{1}{2}(x^2 - 8x + 16) + 7$
$y = -\frac{1}{2}x^2 + 4x - 8 + 7$
$y = -\frac{1}{2}x^2 + 4x - 1$
standard form $y = -\frac{1}{2}x^2 + 4x - 1$.

20. The vertex of the function is $(-2, -12)$.

x	y
2	52
0	4
-2	-11
-4	4
-6	52

$y = a(x - (-2))^2 + (-12)$,
or $y = a(x + 2)^2 - 12$
$4 = a(0 + 2)^2 - 12$
$16 = a(4)$
$4 = a$
vertex form $y = 4(x + 2)^2 - 12$.
$y = 4(x^2 + 4x + 4) - 12$
$y = 4x^2 + 16x + 16 - 12$
$y = 4x^2 + 16x + 4$
standard form $y = 4x^2 + 16x + 4$.

21. The vertex of the function is $(-3, 10)$.

x	y
-1	-6
-2	6
-3	10
-4	6
-5	-6

$y = a(x - (-3))^2 + 10$, or $y = a(x + 3)^2 + 1$
$-6 = a(-1 + 3)^2 + 10$
$-16 = a(4)$
$-4 = a$
vertex form $y = -4(x + 3)^2 + 10$.
$y = -4(x^2 + 6x + 9) + 10$
$y = -4x^2 - 24x - 36 + 10$
$y = -4x^2 - 24x - 26$
standard form $y = -4x^2 - 24x - 26$.

22. Make a Prediction A ball was thrown off a bridge. The table relates the height of the ball above the ground in feet to the time in seconds after it was thrown. Use the data to write a quadratic model in vertex form and convert it to standard form. Use the model to find the height of the ball at 1.5 seconds.

Time (seconds)	Height (feet)
0	128
1	144
2	128
3	80
4	0

The vertex is at $(1, 144)$.

$$y = a(x - 1)^2 + 144$$
$$128 = a(0 - 1)^2 + 144$$
$$-16 = a(1)$$
$$-16 = a$$

vertex form $y = -16(x - 1)^2 + 144$.
$$y = -16(x^2 - 2x + 1) + 144.$$
$$y = -16x^2 + 32x - 16 + 144.$$
$$y = -16x^2 + 32x + 128$$

standard form $y = -16x^2 + 32x + 128$.
$$y = -16(1.5)^2 + 32(1.5) + 128$$
$$y = -16(2.25) + 48 + 128$$
$$y = -36 + 176$$
$$y = 140$$

The height of the ball is 140 feet after 1.5 seconds.

23. Multiple Representations A performer slips and falls into a safety net below. The function $f(t) = a(t - h)^2 + k$, where t represents time (in seconds), gives the performer's height above the ground (in feet) as he falls. Use the graph to find an equation for $f(t)$.

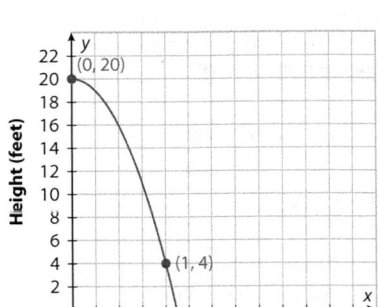

$$f(t) = a(t - 0)^2 + 20 \quad \text{or} \quad f(t) = at^2 + 20$$
$$4 = a(1)^2 + 20$$
$$-16 = a(1)$$
$$-16 = a$$

The equation for the function is $f(t) = -16t^2 + 20$.

MULTIPLE REPRESENTATIONS

Give students the graph of a quadratic function. Have students give the vertex of the graph, identify the vertex as a maximum or minimum value of the graph, find the equation of the axis of symmetry, and find an equation of the parabola.

INTEGRATE MATHEMATICAL PRACTICES

Focus on Communication

MP.3 Ask whether a quadratic function in the form $f(x) = 2(x - h)^2 + k$ could be the same function as one in the form $f(x) = 4x^2 + bx + c$ in standard form. Students should recognize that the values of a are not equal, and that the 2 is not squared in the first function.

JOURNAL

In their journals, have students explain where the letters a, b, c, h, and k come from in the standard and vertex forms of a quadratic function.

24. Represent Real-World Problems After a heavy snowfall, Ken and Karin made an igloo. The dome of the igloo is in the shape of a parabola, and the height of the igloo in inches is given by the function $f(x) = a(x - h)^2 + k$. Use the graph to find an equation for $f(x)$.

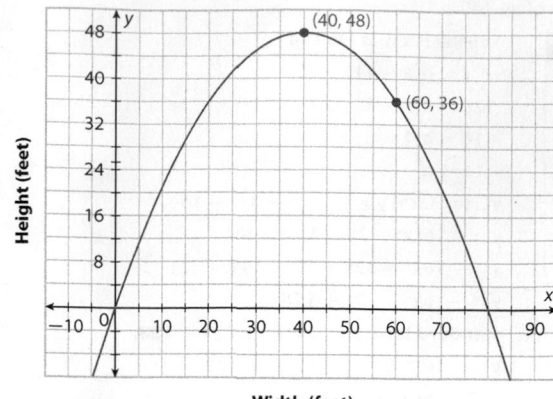

Width (feet)

$$f(x) = a(x - 40)^2 + 48$$
$$36 = a(60 - 40)^2 + 48$$
$$-12 = a(400)$$
$$-0.03 = a$$

The equation for the function is $f(t) = -0.03x^2 + 2.4x$.

25. Check for Reasonableness Tim hits a softball. The function $f(t) = a(t - h)^2 + k$ describes the height (in feet) of the softball, and t is the time (in seconds). Use the graph to find an equation for $f(t)$. Estimate how much time elapses before the ball hits the ground. Use the equation for the function and your estimate to explain whether the equation is reasonable.

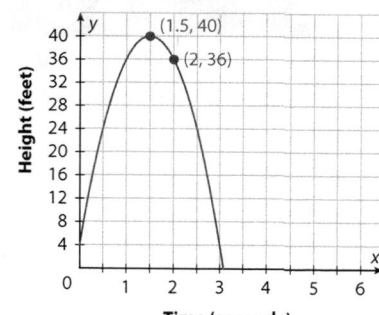

Time (seconds)

$$f(t) = a(t - 1.5)^2 + 40$$
$$36 = a(2 - 1.5)^2 + 40$$
$$-4 = a(0.25)$$
$$-16 = a$$

The equation for the function is $f(t) = -16(t - 1.5)^2 - 40$.

The curve appears to intersect the x-axis at 3.1. So, evaluate the function $f(t)$ at 3.1; $f(3.1) = -16(3.1 - 1.5)^2 + 40 = -0.96$ -0.96 is close to the expected value of 0, so the equation is reasonable.

Lesson Performance Task

The table gives the height of a tennis ball t seconds after it has been hit, where the maximum height is 4 feet.

Time (s)	Height (ft)
0.125	3.75
0.25	4
0.375	3.75
0.5	3
0.625	1.75
0.75	0

a. Use the data in the table to write the quadratic function $f(t)$ in vertex form, where t is the time in seconds and $f(t)$ is the height of the tennis ball in feet.

b. Rewrite the function found in part a in standard form.

c. At what height was the ball originally hit? Explain.

a. The maximum height is 4 feet, so the vertex of the parabola is $(0.25, 4)$. Using a second point from the table, $(0.75, 0)$, solve for a in the function $f(t) = a(t - h)^2 + k$.

$f(t) = a(t - h)^2 + k$

$0 = a(0.75 - 0.25)^2 + 4$

$-4 = a(0.5)^2$

$-4 = 0.25a$

$-16 = a$

The function for the height of the tennis ball is $f(t) = -16(t - 0.25)^2 + 4$.

b. $f(t) = -16(t - 0.25)^2 + 4$

$\quad = -16(t^2 - 0.5t + 0.0625) + 4$

$\quad = -16t^2 + 8t - 1 + 4$

$\quad = -16t^2 + 8t + 3$

c. The ball was originally hit at a height corresponding to $t = 0$, or the y-intercept. In a function of the form $f(x) = ax^2 + bx + c$, the y-intercept is c. In $f(t) = -16t^2 + 8t + 3$, the value of c is 3. So, the ball was originally hit 3 feet above the ground.

© Houghton Mifflin Harcourt Publishing Company

INTEGRATE MATHEMATICAL PRACTICES

Focus on Critical Thinking

MP.3 When distributing the value of a, -16, to the binomial square, $(t - 0.25)^2$ in $-16(t - 0.25)^2 + 4$, some students may err by distributing -16 to 4. Have students analyze their results. If they distributed -16 incorrectly, they may have gotten $-16t^2 + 8t - 65$, in which case the original height of the ball (when hit) would have been 65 feet above the ground. This is not a likely scenario, so it is an indication that an error was made in calculation.

INTEGRATE MATHEMATICAL PRACTICES

Focus on Reasoning

MP.2 Have students suppose that they are told that $a = 16$. Have students justify how they know why it makes sense that the given value of a is incorrect and that this situation makes sense only if it is modeled with a downward opening parabola with a as a negative number.

EXTENSION ACTIVITY

For students who completed the Extension Activity in the previous lesson, videotaping the path of a tennis ball against a grid and writing a quadratic function for the path of the ball, ask them to rewrite the function they wrote in standard form, determine the height of the ball using each function after it has gone a distance of 2 feet, and compare these distances to the actual height. Students should discuss the two functions and tell what information each gives about the situation.

Scoring Rubric

2 points: Student correctly solves the problem and explains his/her reasoning.

1 point: Student shows good understanding of the problem but does not fully solve or explain his/her reasoning.

0 points: Student does not demonstrate understanding of the problem.

Interpreting Vertex Form and Standard Form **930**

ASSESSMENT AND INTERVENTION

Personal Math Trainer

Assign or customize module reviews.

MODULE PERFORMANCE TASK

COMMON CORE

Mathematical Practices: MP.1, MP.4, MP.5
F-IF.B.4, F-IF.C.7a, A-CED.A.2

SUPPORTING STUDENT REASONING

Students should begin this problem by focusing on what information they will need. They can then do research, or you can provide them with specific information. Here is some of the information they may ask for.

- **What units are being used in the formula?** feet for distance, and seconds for time.

- **What do the variables stand for?** The h represents the height of the ball, t represents the time the ball is in the air, v represents the initial vertical velocity of the ball, and h_0 represents the initial height of the ball at the time it is thrown.

- **What is the initial height of the throw?** Give students a reasonable initial height of 5 ft or a range of heights from 4 ft to 5.5 ft.

- **What is the height of the receiver?** Have students choose a receiving height anywhere from 2 ft to 4 ft.

Essential Question: How can you use the graph of a quadratic function to solve real-world problems?

Key Vocabulary

axis of symmetry *(eje de simetría)*

parabola *(parábola)*

quadratic function *(función cuadrática)*

standard form of a quadratic equation *(forma estándar de una ecuación cuadrática)*

vertex *(vértex)*

KEY EXAMPLE   *(Lesson 19.3)*

The graph of a function in the form $f(x) = a(x - h)^2 + k$ is shown. Use the graph to find an equation for $f(x)$.

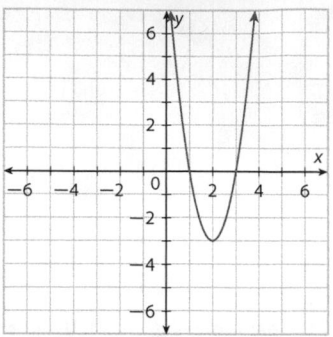

The vertex of the parabola is $(h, k) = (2, -3)$.

$f(x) = a(x - 2)^2 - 3$

From the graph, $f(3) = 0$. Substitute 3 for x and 0 for $f(x)$ and solve for a.

$0 = a(3 - 2)^2 - 3$

$3 = a$

The equation for the function is $f(x) = 3(x - 2)^2 - 3$.

KEY EXAMPLE   *(Lesson 19.2)*

Graph $g(x) = -2(x + 2)^2 + 2$.

The vertex is at $(-2, 2)$.

Make a table for the function. Find two points on each side of the vertex.

x	-4	-3	-2	-1	0
$g(x)$	-6	0	2	0	-6

Plot the points and draw a parabola through them.

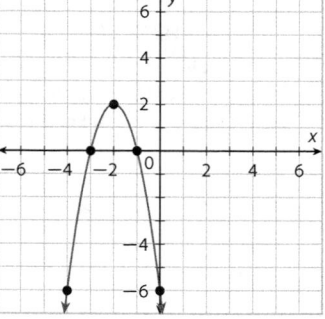

© Houghton Mifflin Harcourt Publishing Company

SCAFFOLDING SUPPORT

- Watch for students who use the initial velocity of 66 feet per second in their formulas. Have them carefully reread the problem to verify that velocity.

- Once students find the maximum height of the ball, they may think they've answered the question. Remind them to reread the problem to ensure that they've done all necessary work.

- Watch for students who graph the ball's height over time thinking they are graphing the ball's horizontal and vertical positions.

- For students who need more structure, name an initial and end height.

- Challenge students by having them compare results of two different velocities or two different initial heights.

EXERCISES

Graph each quadratic function. Give the minimum or maximum value and the axis of symmetry. *(Lessons 19.1, 19.2)*

1. $f(x) = 2x^2$

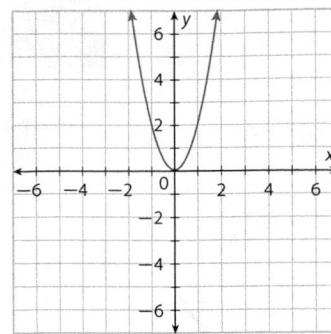

minimum $= 0$; $x = 0$

2. $g(x) = -(x + 2)^2 + 4$

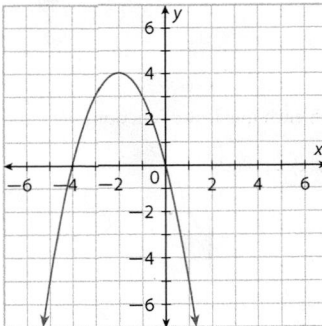

maximum $= 4$; $x = -2$

Write the equation for the function in each graph, in vertex form. *(Lesson 19.3)*

3.

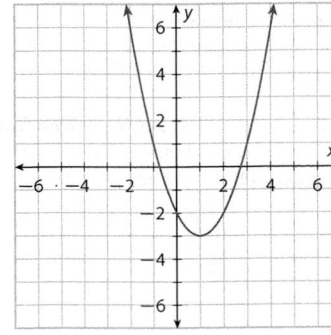

$f(x) = (x - 1)^2 - 3$

4.

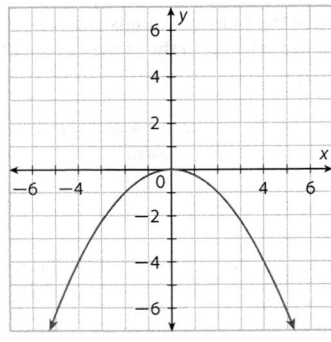

$f(x) = -\dfrac{1}{4}x^2$

MODULE PERFORMANCE TASK
Throwing for a Completion

Professional quarterbacks can throw a football to a receiver with a velocity of 66 feet per second or greater. If a quarterback throws a pass with that velocity at a 30° angle with the ground, then the initial vertical velocity is 33 feet per second. How can you use the formula $h = -16t^2 + vt + h_0$ to describe the quarterback's pass? Find the maximum height that the football reaches, and then find the total amount of time that the pass is in the air.

DISCUSSION OPPORTUNITIES

- Have students compare their answers. Ask them why their graphs and answer might be similar but not exactly the same.

- Have students discuss any obstacles they needed to overcome to answer the question.

SAMPLE SOLUTION

Assume that the initial height is 5 ft and that the receiver catches the ball at a height of 3 ft. Substitute 5 ft for h_0 and 33 for the initial vertical velocity v into the formula, creating the equation. $h = -16t^2 + 33t + 5$. Then graph it.

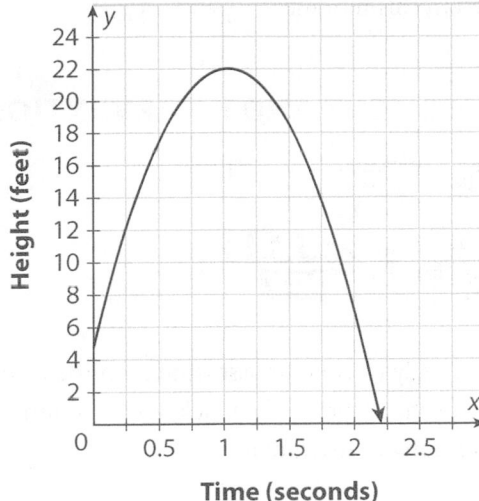

The graph shows the maximum height is about 22 ft. It also shows that the total time the ball is in the air is about 2.2 seconds if the ball is allowed to hit the ground. If the ball were caught by a receiver at a height of 3 ft, the ball would be in the air about 2.1 seconds.

Assessment Rubric

2 points: Student correctly solves the problem and explains his/her reasoning.

1 point: Student shows good understanding of the problem but does not fully solve or explain.

0 points: Student does not demonstrate understanding of the problem.

Ready to Go On?

ASSESS MASTERY

Use the assessment on this page to determine if students have mastered the concepts and standards covered in this module.

ASSESSMENT AND INTERVENTION

Access Ready to Go On? assessment online, and receive instant scoring, feedback, and customized intervention or enrichment.

ADDITIONAL RESOURCES

Response to Intervention Resources

• Reteach Worksheets

Differentiated Instruction Resources

• Reading Strategies **EL**

• Success for English Learners **EL**

• Challenge Worksheets

Assessment Resources

• Leveled Module Quizzes

Ready to Go On?

19.1–19.3 Graphing Quadratic Functions

• Online Homework
• Hints and Help
• Extra Practice

Graph each quadratic function. *(Lesson 19.1)*

1. $f(x) = -4x^2$

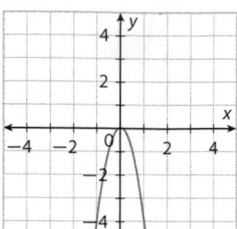

2. $g(x) = \frac{1}{2}x^2$

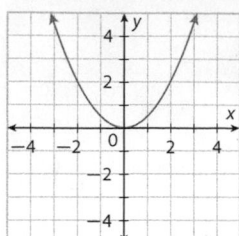

Describe the transformations necessary to get from the graph of the parent function $f(x) = x^2$ to the graph of each of the given functions. *(Lesson 19.2)*

3. $g(x) = (x + 4)^2 - 7$

Translate the graph 4 units to the left and 7 units down.

4. $g(x) = 5(x - 6)^2 + 9$

Stretch the graph vertically by a factor of 5, and then translate the graph 6 units to the right and 9 units up.

Rewrite each function in standard form. *(Lesson 19.3)*

5. $f(x) = 2(x + 3)^2 - 6$

$$f(x) = 2x^2 + 12x + 12$$

6. $f(x) = 3(x - 2)^2 + 3$

$$f(x) = 3x^2 - 12x + 15$$

ESSENTIAL QUESTION

7. If the only information you have about a parabola is the location of its vertex, what other characteristics of the graph do you know?

Possible Answer: You know the axis of symmetry, which goes through the x-coordinate of the vertex. You also know that the y-coordinate of the vertex is either the maximum or minimum of the parabola, though you don't know which.

COMMON CORE Common Core Standards

Lesson	Items	Content Standards	Mathematical Practices
19.1	1–2	F-BF.B.3, F-IF.A.2, F-IF.C.7a	MP.1
19.2	3	F-BF.B.3, F-IF.B.4	MP.6
19.2	4	F-BF.B.3, F-IF.B.4	MP.6
19.3	5	F-IF.B.4, F-IF.C.8, F-IF.B.4	MP.7
19.3	6	F-IF.B.4, F-IF.C.8, F-IF.B.4	MP.7

MODULE 19
MIXED REVIEW

Assessment Readiness

1. Consider the graph of $f(x) = \frac{2}{3}(x-3)^2$.
   Choose True or False for each statement about the graph.
   - **A.** The vertex is $(3, 0)$. ● True ○ False
   - **B.** The minimum value is 0. ● True ○ False
   - **C.** The axis of symmetry is $x = \frac{2}{3}$. ○ True ● False

2. Is the given expression equivalent to $16^{\frac{3}{4}} + 32^{\frac{2}{5}}$? Select Yes or No for each expression.
   - **A.** $\left(16^{\frac{1}{4}}\right)^3 + \left(32^{\frac{1}{5}}\right)^2$ ● Yes ○ No
   - **B.** $\sqrt[4]{16^3} + \sqrt[5]{32^2}$ ● Yes ○ No
   - **C.** $2^3 + 2^2$ ● Yes ○ No

3. Write the slope-intercept equation of the line that has the same slope as $y - 3 = \frac{1}{2}(x + 3)$ and contains the point $(8, 4)$. Explain how you wrote the equation.

   $y = \frac{1}{2}x$; I transformed the given equation into slope-intercept form, $y = mx + b$, to get $y = \frac{1}{2}x + \frac{9}{2}$. The slope, m, is $\frac{1}{2}$. Then, I substituted 8 for x and 4 for y in $y = \frac{1}{2}x + b$ and solved for b, which is 0.

4. Write $f(x) = -2(x - 5)^2 + 3$ in standard form. In which form is it easier to determine the maximum value of the graph? Explain.

   $f(x) = -2x^2 + 20x - 47$; It is easier to find the maximum value when the equation is written as $f(x) = -2(x - 5)^2 + 3$. The vertex is $(5, 3)$, so the maximum value is 3.

MIXED REVIEW
Assessment Readiness

ASSESSMENT AND INTERVENTION

Assign ready-made or customized practice tests to prepare students for high-stakes tests.

ADDITIONAL RESOURCES

Assessment Resources

- Leveled Module Quizzes: Modified, B

AVOID COMMON ERRORS

Item 3 Some students may not notice that they are looking for a line parallel to the given line, and they will instead stop after finding the slope-intercept form of the given equation. Remind students to highlight or underline important parts of the problem to help them focus on all the necessary information.

COMMON CORE **Common Core Standards**

Lesson	Items	Content Standards	Mathematical Practices
19.1	1	F-IF.B.4	MP.4
14.1	2*	N-RN.A.1	MP.2
6.1, 6.2	3*	A-CED.A.2	MP.4
19.3	4	F-IF.C.8	MP.3

* Item integrates mixed review concepts from previous modules or a previous course.

Connecting Intercepts, Zeros, and Factors

ESSENTIAL QUESTION:

Answer: You can use quadratic functions to solve real-world area problems. Each dimension can represent a linear factor of the quadratic function. The intercepts may represent the solution to the problem.

PROFESSIONAL DEVELOPMENT VIDEO

Professional Development Video

STEM Consultant Michael DiSpezio offers engaging suggestions and activities for integrating science, technology, and engineering into the math classroom.

Professional
Development
my.hrw.com

MODULE **20**

Connecting Intercepts, Zeros, and Factors

Essential Question: How can you use intercepts of a quadratic function to solve real-world problems?

LESSON 20.1
Connecting Intercepts and Zeros

LESSON 20.2
Connecting Intercepts and Linear Factors

LESSON 20.3
Applying the Zero Product Property to Solve Equations

© Houghton Mifflin Harcourt Publishing Company • Image Credits: ©Vladimir Ivanovich Danilov/Shutterstock

REAL WORLD VIDEO
Skateboard ramps come in many shapes and sizes. The iconic half-pipe ramp has a flat section in the middle and curved, raised sides. Skateboarders can use a half-pipe ramp to perform tricks, turns, and flips.

MODULE PERFORMANCE TASK PREVIEW

Skateboard Ramp

Skateboard riders often use curved ramps to perform difficult tricks and have fun. In this module, you will imagine that you are a design engineer hired by the local government to help construct a new skateboard ramp for the skateboard riders in the area. How do you model the curve of the ramp? Let's find out!

DIGITAL TEACHER EDITION

Access a full suite of teaching resources when and where you need them:

- Access content online or offline
- Customize lessons to share with your class
- Communicate with your students in real-time
- View student grades and data instantly to target your instruction where it is needed most

PERSONAL MATH TRAINER
Assessment and Intervention

Assign automatically graded homework, quizzes, tests, and intervention activities. Prepare your students with updated, Common Core-aligned practice tests.

Are YOU Ready?

Complete these exercises to review skills you will need for this module.

- Online Homework
- Hints and Help
- Extra Practice

Exponents

Example 1

Simplify.

$x^5 \cdot x^3 = x^{5+3} = x^8$ The bases are the same. Add the exponents.

$\dfrac{x^9}{x^4} = x^{9-4} = x^5$ The bases are the same. Subtract the exponents.

Simplify.

1. $b^2 \cdot b^6$

   b^8

2. $\dfrac{a^{12}}{a^7}$

   a^5

3. $\dfrac{n^4 \cdot n^7}{n^5 n^6}$

Algebraic Expressions

Example 2

Find the value of $3x - 6$ when $x = 2$.

$3x - 6$

$3(2) - 6$ Substitute 2 for x.

$6 - 6$ Follow the order of operations.

0

Find the value.

4. $6x + 3$ when $x = -\dfrac{1}{2}$

   0

5. $2x - 5$ when $x = \dfrac{5}{2}$

   0

6. $9x + 6$ when $x = -\dfrac{2}{3}$

   0

Linear Functions

Example 3

Tell whether $y = x^2 - 7$ represents a linear function.

$y = x^2 - 7$ does not represent a linear function because x has an exponent of 2.

When a linear equation is written in standard form, the following are true.

- x and y both have exponents of 1.
- x and y are not multiplied together.
- x and y do not appear in denominators, exponents, or radicands.

Tell whether the equation represents a linear function.

7. $y = 3^x + 1$

   no

8. $3x - 2y = 6$

   yes

9. $xy + 5 = 8$

   no

Are You Ready?

ASSESS READINESS

Use the assessment on this page to determine if students need strategic or intensive intervention for the module's prerequisite skills.

ASSESSMENT AND INTERVENTION

Rtl Response to Intervention **TIER 1, TIER 2, TIER 3 SKILLS**

Personal Math Trainer will automatically create a standards-based, personalized intervention assignment for your students, targeting each student's individual needs!

ADDITIONAL RESOURCES

See the table below for a full list of intervention resources available for this module.

Response to Intervention Resources also includes:

- Tier 2 Skill Pre-Tests for each Module
- Tier 2 Skill Post-Tests for each skill

Response to Intervention			Differentiated Instruction
Tier 1	**Tier 2**	**Tier 3**	
Lesson Intervention Worksheets	Strategic Intervention Skills Intervention Worksheets	Intensive Intervention Worksheets available online	
Reteach 20.1 Reteach 20.2 Reteach 20.3	2 Algebraic Expressions 5 Exponents 10 Linear Functions	Building Block Skills 19, 22, 23, 24, 27, 29, 30, 40, 59, 69, 76, 81, 100	Challenge worksheets Extend the Math Lesson Activities in TE

Connecting Intercepts and Zeros

Common Core Math Standards

The student is expected to:

 **F-IF.C.7a**

Graph ...quadratic functions and show intercepts, maxima, and minima.
Also A-REI.B.4, A-APR.B.3, A-REI.D.11

Mathematical Practices

 MP.5 Using Tools

Language Objective

Given a quadratic function modeling a real-world situation, explain to a partner what the zeros of the function represent.

ENGAGE

Essential Question: How can you use the graph of a quadratic function to solve its related quadratic equation?

You can write the equation with one side equal to 0, graph the related function, and find the zeros of the function.

PREVIEW: LESSON PERFORMANCE TASK

View the Engage section online. Discuss what type of path is made by a diver diving into the water when her initial height is the height of the diving platform. Then preview the Lesson Performance Task.

20.1 Connecting Intercepts and Zeros

Essential Question: How can you use the graph of a quadratic function to solve its related quadratic equation?

⊘ Explore   Graphing Quadratic Functions in Standard Form

A parabola can be graphed using its vertex and axis of symmetry. Use these characteristics, the y-intercept, and symmetry to graph a quadratic function.

Graph $y = x^2 - 4x - 5$ by completing the steps.

(A) Find the axis of symmetry.

$$x = -\frac{b}{2a}$$

$$= -\frac{\boxed{-4}}{2 \cdot \boxed{1}}$$

$$= \boxed{2}$$

The axis of symmetry is $x = \boxed{2}$.

(B) Find the vertex.

$$y = x^2 - 4x - 5$$

$$= \boxed{2}^2 - 4 \cdot \boxed{2} - 5$$

$$= \boxed{4} - \boxed{8} - 5$$

$$= \boxed{-9}$$

The vertex is $\left(\boxed{2}, \boxed{-9}\right)$.

(C) Find the y-intercept.

$$y = x^2 - 4x - 5$$

$$y = \boxed{0}^2 - 4\boxed{0} + \left(\boxed{-5}\right)$$

The y-intercept is $\boxed{-5}$; the graph passes through $\left(0, \boxed{-5}\right)$.

(D) Find two more points on the same side of the axis of symmetry as the y-intercept.

a. Find y when $x = 1$.

$$y = x^2 - 4x - 5$$

$$= \boxed{1}^2 - 4 \cdot \boxed{1} - 5$$

$$= \boxed{1} - \boxed{4} - 5$$

$$= \boxed{-8}$$

The first point is $\left(\boxed{1}, \boxed{-8}\right)$.

b. Find y when $x = -1$.

$$y = x^2 - 4x - 5$$

$$= \boxed{-1}^2 - 4 \cdot \left(\boxed{-1}\right) - 5$$

$$= \boxed{1} - \left(\boxed{-4}\right) - 5$$

$$= \boxed{0}$$

The second point is $\left(\boxed{-1}, \boxed{0}\right)$.

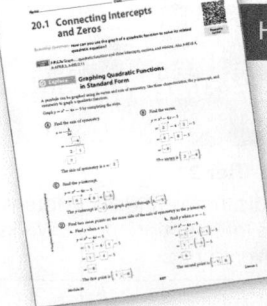

HARDCOVER PAGES 735–744

Turn to these pages to find this lesson in the hardcover student edition.

(E) Graph the axis of symmetry, the vertex, the y-intercept, and the two extra points on the same coordinate plane. Then reflect the graphed points over the axis of symmetry to create three more points, and sketch the graph.

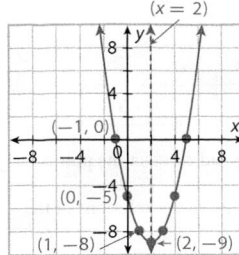

Reflect

1. **Discussion** Why is it important to find additional points before graphing a quadratic function? **Additional points provide more information about the shape of the parabola, and the**

sketch of the quadratic function will be more accurate.

⚙ Explain 1 Using Zeros to Solve Quadratic Equations Graphically

A **zero of a function** is an x-value that makes the value of the function 0. The zeros of a function are the x-intercepts of the graph of the function. A quadratic function may have one, two, or no zeros.

Quadratic equations can be solved by graphing the related function of the equation. To write the related function, rewrite the quadratic equation so that it equals zero on one side. Replace the zero with y.

Graph the related function. Find the x-intercepts of the graph, which are the zeros of the function. The zeros of the function are the solutions to the original equation.

Example 1 Solve by graphing the related function.

(A) $2x^2 - 5 = -3$

a. Write the related function. Add 3 to both sides to get $2x^2 - 2 = 0$. The related function is $y = 2x^2 - 2$.

b. Make a table of values for the related function.

x	−2	−1	0	1	2
y	6	0	−2	0	6

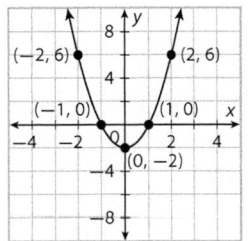

c. Graph the points represented by the table and connect the points.

d. The zeros of the function are −1 and 1, so the solutions of the equation $2x^2 - 5 = -3$ are $x = -1$ and $x = 1$.

© Houghton Mifflin Harcourt Publishing Company

PROFESSIONAL DEVELOPMENT

Math Background

Quadratic equations are often used to model the motion of falling objects. The general formula for this motion is $h = -16t^2 + v_0t + h_0$, where h represents the height of the object in feet, t is the number of seconds the object has been falling, v_0 is the initial vertical velocity of the object in feet per second, and h_0 is the initial height of the object in feet. The coefficient −16 is equal to half of the constant acceleration due to gravity, -32 ft/s². Students can compare the quadratic equations given for falling objects in this lesson to the general formula to determine the values of v_0 and h_0 in each case.

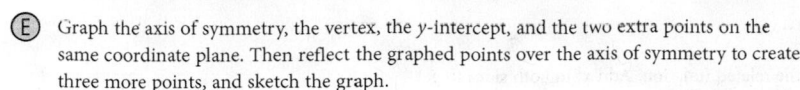

EXPLORE

Graphing Quadratic Functions in Standard Form

QUESTIONING STRATEGIES

? How many points on the graph of a quadratic function are on the axis of symmetry? Explain. One; the only point on the graph of a quadratic function that is on the axis of symmetry is the vertex of the function.

? Why is it helpful to find the axis of symmetry when graphing a quadratic function? After you find the axis of symmetry and a few points on one side of it, you can use symmetry to quickly and easily find an equal number of points on the other side.

EXPLAIN 1

Using Zeros to Solve Quadratic Equations Graphically

AVOID COMMON ERRORS

Students may think that the zeros of a quadratic function can be found by substituting 0 for x in the function. Make sure students understand that the zeros of a function are the values of x when $y = 0$, not the values of y when $x = 0$.

INTEGRATE MATHEMATICAL PRACTICES
Focus on Critical Thinking

MP.3 For cases in which a quadratic function has two zeros, discuss with students how to use the zeros to determine the function's axis of symmetry. Students should realize that the axis of symmetry will be the x-value of the point that is midway between the two zeros.

When a quadratic function has two zeros that are opposites, what must be true about the function? **The axis of symmetry must be $x = 0$, and the vertex must not be $(0, 0)$.**

Ⓑ $6x + 8 = -x^2$

a. Write the related function. Add x^2 to both sides to get $x^2 + 6x + 8 = \boxed{0}$. The related function is $\boxed{y} = \boxed{x^2} + 6x + 8$.

b. Make a table of values for the related function.

x	-5	-4	-3	-2	-1
y	3	0	-1	0	3

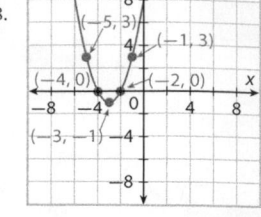

c. Graph the points represented by the table and connect the points.

d. The zeros of the function are $\boxed{-4}$ and $\boxed{-2}$, so the solutions of the equation

$6x + 8 = -x^2$ are $x = \boxed{-4}$ and $x = \boxed{-2}$.

Reflect

2. How would the graph of a quadratic equation look if the equation has one zero?
If the quadratic equation has one zero, the graph will intersect the x-axis at its vertex.

Your Turn

3. $x^2 - 4 = -3$

$x^2 - 4 = -3$

$x^2 - 1 = 0$

The related function is $y = x^2 - 1$.

Graph:

The zeros of the function are 1 and -1, so the solutions of the equation are $x = -1$ and $x = 1$.

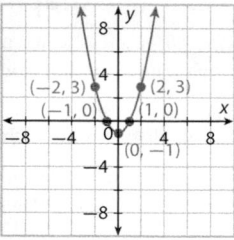

COLLABORATIVE LEARNING

Peer-to-Peer Activity

Have students work in pairs. Have each student find the solution to the same quadratic equation by graphing. One student in each pair then solves the equation by finding the zeros of the function, and the other student uses points of intersection to find the solution. Students compare their answers; while the graphs may be different, the solution should be the same regardless of the method used.

 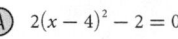

Explain 2 **Using Points of Intersection to Solve Quadratic Equations Graphically**

You can solve a quadratic equation by rewriting the equation in the form $ax^2 + bx = c$ or $a(x - h)^2 = k$ and then using the expressions on each side of the equal sign to define a function.

Graph both functions and find the points of intersection. The x-coordinates are the points of intersection on the graph. As with using zeros, there may be two, one, or no points of intersection.

Example 2 Solve each equation by finding points of intersection of two related functions.

(A) $2(x - 4)^2 - 2 = 0$ Write in vertex form.

    $2(x - 4)^2 = 2$ Write as $a(x - h)^2 = k$.

  a. Let $f(x) = 2(x - 4)^2$. Let $g(x) = 2$.

  b. Graph $f(x)$ and $g(x)$ on the same graph.

  c. Determine the points at which the graphs of $f(x)$ and $g(x)$ intersect.

    The graphs intersect at two locations: $(3, 2)$ and $(5, 2)$.

    This means $f(x) = g(x)$ when $x = 3$ and $x = 5$.

    So the solutions of $2(x - 4)^2 - 2 = 0$ are $x = 3$ and $x = 5$.

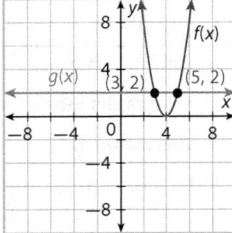

(B) $3(x - 5)^2 - 12 = 0$

    $3(x - 5)^2 = \boxed{12}$

  a. Let $f(x) = \boxed{3}\ (x - 5)^2$. Let $g(x) = \boxed{12}$.

  b. Graph $f(x)$ and $g(x)$ on the same graph.

  c. Determine the points at which the graphs of $f(x)$ and $g(x)$ intersect.

    The graphs intersect at two locations:

    $\left(\boxed{3}, \boxed{12}\right)$ and $\left(\boxed{7}, \boxed{12}\right)$.

    This means $f(x) = g(x)$ when $x = \boxed{3}$ and $x = \boxed{7}$.

    Therefore, the solutions of the equation $f(x) = g(x)$ are $\boxed{3}$ and $\boxed{7}$.

    So the solutions of $3(x - 5)^2 - 12 = 0$ are $x = \boxed{3}$ and $x = \boxed{7}$.

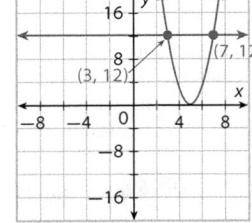

EXPLAIN 2

Using Points of Intersection to Solve Quadratic Equations Graphically

INTEGRATE MATHEMATICAL PRACTICES
Focus on Math Connections

MP.1 Remind students that quadratic equations in the form $a(x - h)^2 + k$ will have the vertex at (h, k). After identifying the vertex, students can use substitution to find enough points to graph the quadratic function.

INTEGRATE MATHEMATICAL PRACTICES
Focus on Modeling

MP.4 When using points of intersection to find solutions to quadratic equations, make sure that students understand that only the x-values of the points of intersection are solutions to the equation. The y-values come from the function that was created to find the solutions; they are not part of the solution.

QUESTIONING STRATEGIES

? How can you use graphing to determine that a quadratic equation has no solutions? After rewriting the equation in the form $ax^2 + bx = c$, if the graphs of the functions $f(x) = ax^2 + bx$ and $g(x) = c$ do not intersect, then the quadratic function has no solutions.

DIFFERENTIATE INSTRUCTION

Communicating Math

Review the parameters of a parabola that students can use when graphing a function. Students should understand that being able to identify the vertex of a parabola will make it easier to graph the function, but they may have different ideas about how to find enough other points in order to make an accurate graph. Discuss how students can be sure that they have plotted enough points to sketch the function on a coordinate grid.

EXPLAIN 3

Modeling a Real-World Problem

INTEGRATE TECHNOLOGY

Before students are familiar with using the quadratic formula, graphing calculators offer the most accessible way to find the solutions to quadratic equations that do not have simple whole-number solutions.

INTEGRATE MATHEMATICAL PRACTICES

Focus on Modeling

MP.4 The functions used to determine the height of a thrown object can be difficult to understand. Discuss different ways to rewrite the functions used to determine height. Students may wish to rewrite a function like $h(t) = -16t^2 + 100$ as $h(t) = 100 - 16t^2$ to make it more evident that the object loses height for each second of time.

© Houghton Mifflin Harcourt Publishing Company • Image Credits: ©USBFCO/ Shutterstock

Reflect

4. In Part B above, why is the x-coordinates the answer to the equation and not the y-coordinates?
   The x-coordinates are the solution because the x-values are the unknown amount being solved for in the original equation. The y-values are used to create a related function to find the x values, but since they are not part of the original equation, the y values are not part of the solution.

Your Turn

5. $3(x - 2)^2 - 3 = 0$

   $3(x - 2)^2 - 3 = 0$

   $3(x - 2)^2 = 3$

   Let $f(x) = 3(x - 2)^2$ and let $g(x) \approx 3$.

   The graphs intersect at two locations: $(1, 3)$ and $(3, 3)$.

   This means $f(x) = g(x)$ when $x \approx 1$ and $x = 3$.

   So the solutions of $3(x - 2)^2 - 3 = 0$ are 1 and 3.

🞕 Explain 3 　Modeling a Real-World Problem

Many real-world problems can be modeled by quadratic functions.

Example 3　Create a quadratic function for each problem and then solve it by using a graphing calculator.

Nature　A squirrel is in a tree holding a chestnut at a height of 46 feet above the ground. It drops the chestnut, which lands on top of a bush that is 36 feet below the squirrel. The function $h(t) = -16t^2 + 46$ gives the height in feet of the chestnut as it falls, where t represents time. When will the chestnut reach the top of the bush?

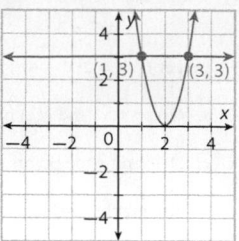

🧩 Analyze Information

Identify the important information.

- The chestnut is 　46　 feet above the ground, and the top of the bush is 　36　 feet below the chestnut.

- The chestnut's height as a function of time can be represented by
  $h(t) = \boxed{-16}\, t^2 + \boxed{46}$, where $(h)t$ is the height of the chestnut in feet as it is falling.

🧩 Formulate a Plan

Create a related quadratic equation to find the height of the chestnut in relation to time. Use $h(t) = -16t^2 + 46$ and insert the known value for h.

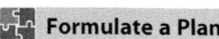

LANGUAGE SUPPORT 🔤

Connect Vocabulary

Students may expect that problems involving points of intersection will always have solutions. Relate the word *intersection* to its uses outside the math classroom. Just as two streets in a town may or may not intersect, the graphs of two functions may or may not intersect. When dealing with the intersection of a quadratic function and a linear function, remind students that there may be 0, 1, or 2 points of intersection.

Write the equation that needs to be solved. Since the top of the bush is 36 feet below the squirrel, it is 10 feet above the ground.

$-16t^2 + 46 = 10$

Separate the function into $y = f(t)$ and $y = g(t)$. $f(t) = \boxed{-16}\,t^{\boxed{2}} + \boxed{46}$ and

$g(t) = \boxed{10}$.

To graph each function on a graphing calculator, rewrite them in terms of x and y.

$y = \boxed{-16}\,x^{\boxed{2}} + \boxed{46}$ and $y = \boxed{10}$

Graph both functions. Use the intersect feature to find the amount of time it takes for the chestnut to hit the top of the bush.

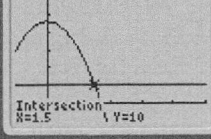
Intersection
X=1.5   Y=10

The chestnut will reach the top of the bush in $\boxed{1.5}$ seconds.

Justify and Evaluate

$-16\left(\boxed{1.5}\right)^2 + 46 = 10$

$\boxed{-36} + 46 = 10$

$\boxed{10} = \boxed{10}$

When t is replaced by $\underline{1.5}$ in the original equation, $-16t^2 + 46 = 10$ is true.

Reflect

6. In Example 3 above, the graphs also intersect to the left of the y-axis. Why is that point irrelevant to the problem?

That point is irrelevant to the problem since negative time has no meaning in this problem.

Your Turn

7. **Nature** An egg falls from a nest in a tree 25 feet off the ground and lands on a potted plant that is 20 feet below the nest. The function $h(t) = -16t^2 + 25$ gives the height in feet of the egg as it drops, where t represents time. When will the egg land on the plant?

$-16x^2 + 25 = 5$

$y = -16x^2 + 25$ and $y = 5$.

The egg will hit the plant after about 1.12 seconds.

QUESTIONING STRATEGIES

? When finding the time it takes for an object to fall to the ground, why is only the positive zero of the function used as an answer? Since the value for time will always be a positive number, the negative zero of the function can be ignored as a solution.

INTEGRATE MATHEMATICAL PRACTICES

Focus on Technology

MP.5 Students who have the minimum and maximum x- and y-values set incorrectly on their graphing calculators may not be able to see the point of intersection when they graph two functions. Discuss how to change the dimensions of the graph by accessing the **WINDOW** menu.

EXPLAIN 4

Interpreting a Quadratic Model

AVOID COMMON ERRORS

When viewing graphs of quadratic functions modeling height, students may believe that the shape of the graph represents the path an object takes while in the air. Remind students that while the y-axis represents the height of the object, the x-axis does not show distance, but rather time.

QUESTIONING STRATEGIES

? For quadratic functions that model the height of a thrown object, how can you use the zeros of the function to determine when the object is at its maximum height? Explain. **Since the axis of symmetry for a quadratic function lies midway between the two zeros of the function, the maximum height is reached at a time halfway between the two zeros.**

? For a quadratic function modeling the height of a thrown object, when one of the zeros of the function is 0, what must be true about the object? **The object must have been thrown from ground level, so that the height of the object equals 0 at time 0.**

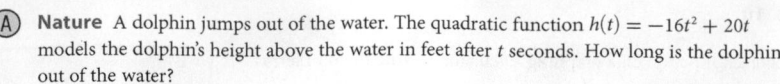

The solutions of a quadratic equation can be used to find other information about the situation modeled by the related function.

Example 4 Use the given quadratic function model to answer questions about the situation it models.

(A) **Nature** A dolphin jumps out of the water. The quadratic function $h(t) = -16t^2 + 20t$ models the dolphin's height above the water in feet after t seconds. How long is the dolphin out of the water?

Use the level of the water as a height of 0 feet. When the dolphin leaves and then reenters the water again, its height is 0 feet.

Solve $0 = -16t^2 + 20t$ to find the times when the dolphin both leaves the water and then reenters. The difference between the times is the amount of time the dolphin is out of the water.

a. Write the related function for $0 = -16x^2 + 20x$.

$y = -16x^2 + 20x$

b. Graph the function on a graphing calculator. Use the trace feature to estimate the zeros.

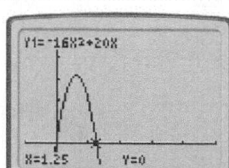

The zeros appear to be 0 and 1.25.

When $x = 0$, the equation reduces to $0 = 0$, which is true. So $x = 0$ is a solution.

Check $x = 1.25$.

$-16(1.25)^2 + 20(1.25) = -16(1.5625) + 25 = -25 + 25 = 0$
so 1.25 is a solution.

Since $1.25 - 0 = 1.25$, the dolphin is out of the water for 1.25 seconds.

(B) **Sports** A baseball coach uses a pitching machine to simulate pop flies during practice. The quadratic function $y = -16t^2 + 80t + 5$ models the height in feet of the baseball after x seconds. The ball leaves the pitching machine and is caught at a height of 5 feet. How long is the baseball in the air?

Solve $0 = -16t^2 + 80t + 5$ to find the times when the baseball enters the air and when it is caught.

a. Write the related function for $0 = -16t^2 + 80t + 5$.

$y = -16x^2 + 80x + 5$

b. Graph the function on a graphing calculator. Use the trace feature to find the zeros.

The zeros appear to be $\boxed{0}$ and $\boxed{5}$.

Since $x = \boxed{0}$ makes the right side of the equation equal to 5, which is the height of the baseball when it is released by the pitching machine, it is a solution. Check to

see if 5 is a solution.

$-16x^2 + 80x + 5 = -16\left(\boxed{5}\right)^2 + 80\left(\boxed{5}\right) + 5 = -\boxed{400} + \boxed{400} + 5 = \boxed{5}$,

so 5 is a solution.

The ball is in the air for 5 seconds.

Your Turn

8. **Nature** The quadratic function $y = -16x^2 + 5x$ models the height, in feet, of a flying fish above the water after x seconds. How long is the flying fish out of the water?
The graph of $y = -16x^2 + 5x$ shows a zero at about 0.3125.

The fish is out of the water for 0.3125 second.

💬 Elaborate

9. How is graphing quadratic functions in standard form similar to using zeros to solve quadratic equations graphically?
If there are two solutions for a quadratic function, the reflection of the point representing

one solution across the axis of symmetry will be the other point, which represents the

other solution. Both methods use the value of the function at 0 to find the second point.

10. How can graphing calculators be used to solve real-world problems represented by quadratic equations?
Graphing calculators can be used to solve real-world quadratic equations by writing the

equation and then finding either an intersection or the zeros of the equation's graph.

11. **Essential Question Check-In** How can you use the graph of a quadratic function to solve a related quadratic equation by way of intersection?
You can graph the two sides of the equation as two functions and find their points of

intersection. The x-coordinate or coordinates of the intersection(s) will be the solution to

the quadratic equation.

ELABORATE

INTEGRATE MATHEMATICAL PRACTICES
Focus on Communication

MP.3 Discuss with students what kinds of real-world problems can be solved by identifying the zeros of a quadratic function. Students should understand that the zeros of a quadratic function will not be the solution for every real-world problem.

SUMMARIZE THE LESSON

? How do you solve equations graphically using zeros and points of intersection? To solve quadratic equations graphically using zeros, rewrite the equation so one side is equal to zero, then graph the other side of the equation and identify the zeros. To solve quadratic equations graphically using points of intersection, rewrite the equation in the form $ax^2 + bx = c$, graph both sides of the equation, then find the x-values of the points of intersection.

EVALUATE

ASSIGNMENT GUIDE

Concepts and Skills	Practice
Explore 1 Graphing Quadratic Functions in Standard Form	Exercises 21–22
Example 1 Using Zeros to Solve Quadratic Equations Graphically	Exercises 1–6, 25
Example 2 Using Points of Intersection to Solve Quadratic Equations Graphically	Exercises 7–12, 23
Example 3 Modeling a Real-World Problem	Exercises 13–16, 24
Example 4 Interpreting a Quadratic Model	Exercises 17–20

• Online Homework
• Hints and Help
• Extra Practice

Solve each equation by graphing the related function and finding its zeros.

1. $3x^2 - 9 = -6$

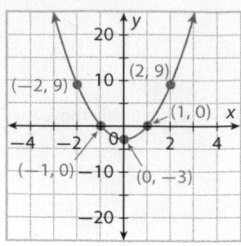

The zeros of $y = 3x^2 - 3$ are 1 and -1, so $x = -1$ or $x = 1$.

2. $2x^2 - 9 = -1$

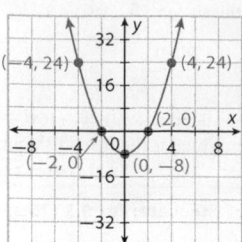

The zeros $y = 2x^2 - 8$ are 2 and -2, so $x = -2$ or $x = 2$.

3. $4x^2 - 7 = -3$

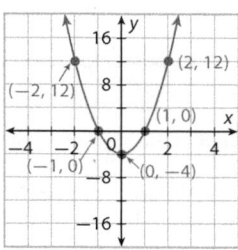

The zeros of $y = 4x^2 - 4$ are 1 and -1, so $x = -1$ or $x = 1$.

4. $7x + 10 = -x^2$

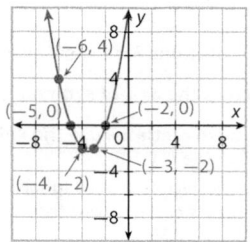

The zeros of $y = x^2 + 7x + 10$ are -5 and -2, so $x = -5$ or $x = -2$.

5. $2x - 3 = -x^2$

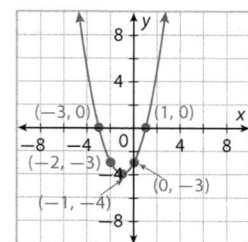

The zeros of $y = x^2 + 2x - 3$ are -3 and -1, so $x = -3$ or $x = 1$.

6. $-1 = -x^2$

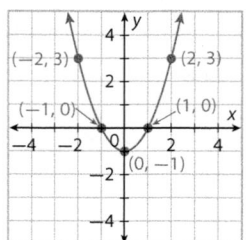

The zeros of $y = x^2 - 1$ are -1 and 1, $x = -1$ or $x = 1$.

© Houghton Mifflin Harcourt Publishing Company

Exercise	Depth of Knowledge (D.O.K.)	COMMON CORE Mathematical Practices
1–12	**1** Recall of Information	**MP.4** Modeling
13–20	**1** Recall of Information	**MP.4** Modeling
21	**1** Recall of Information	**MP.5** Using Tools
22	**1** Recall of Information	**MP.4** Modeling
23–25	**2** Skills/Concepts H.O.T.	**MP.3** Logic

Solve each equation by finding points of intersection of two functions.

7. $2(x-3)^2 - 4 = 0$

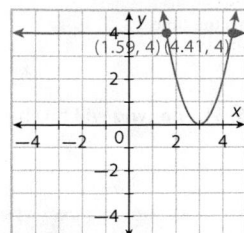

The graphs of $f(x) = 2(x-3)^2$ and $g(x) = 4$ intersect at $(1.59, 4)$ and $(4.41, 4)$. So $x = 1.59$ or $x = 4.41$.

8. $(x+2)^2 - 4 = 0$

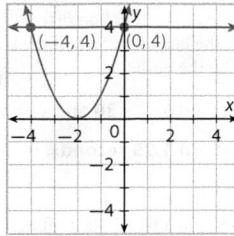

The graphs of $f(x) = (x+2)^2$ and $g(x) = 4$ intersect at $(-4, 4)$ and $(0, 4)$. So $x = 0$ or $x = -4$.

9. $-(x-3)^2 + 4 = 0$

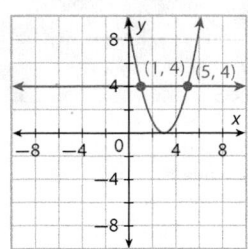

The graphs of $f(x) = (x-3)^2$ and $g(x) = 4$ intersect at $(5, 4)$ and $(1, 4)$. So $x = 5$ or $x = 1$.

10. $-(x+2)^2 - 2 = 0$

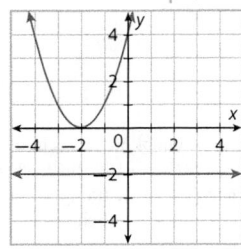

The graphs of $f(x) = (x+2)^2$ and $g(x) = -2$ do not intersect. So there is no solution.

11. $(x+1)^2 - 1 = 0$

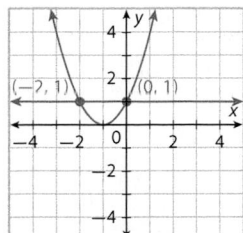

The graphs of $f(x) = (x+1)^2$ and $g(x) = 1$ intersect at $(-2, 1)$ and $(0, 1)$. So $x = -2$ or $x = 0$.

12. $(x+2)^2 - 2 = 0$

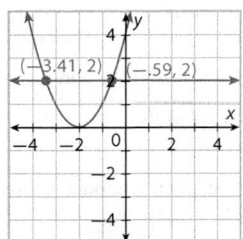

The graphs of $f(x) = (x+2)^2$ and $g(x) = 2$ intersect at $(-3.41, 2)$ and $(-0.59, 2)$. So $x \approx -3.4$ or $x \approx -0.6$.

INTEGRATE MATHEMATICAL PRACTICES

Focus on Communication

MP.3 Students may feel that certain equations must be solved using certain methods. Discuss the fact that most problems can be solved using more than one of the methods outlined in this lesson, and that they will learn additional methods as they continue in algebra.

Connecting Intercepts and Zeros   **946**

When solving quadratic equations graphically, students may mistake the zeros of a quadratic function for the places where the function intersects the *y*-axis. Remind students that the zeros of a function are the *x*-values at the points where the function intersects the *x*-axis.

Create a quadratic equation for each problem and then solve the equation with a related function using a graphing calculator.

13. **Nature** A bird is in a tree 30 feet off the ground and drops a twig that lands on a rosebush 25 feet below. The function $h(t) = -16t^2 + 30$, where *t* represents the time in seconds, *h* gives the height, in feet, of the twig above the ground as it falls. When will the twig land on the bush?

    The graphs of $y = -16x^2 + 30$ and $y = 5$ intersect at about $(1.25, 5)$. The twig will hit the

    rosebush after about 1.25 seconds.

14. **Nature** A monkey is in a tree 50 feet off the ground and drops a banana, which lands on a shrub 30 feet below. The function $h(t) = -16t^2 + 50$, where *t* represents the time in seconds, *h* gives the height, in feet, of the banana above the ground as it falls. When will the banana land on the shrub?

    The graphs of $y = -16x^2 + 50$ and $y = 20$ intersect at

    about $(1.4, 20)$. The banana will hit the shrub after

    about 1.4 seconds.

15. **Sports** A trampolinist jumps 60 inches in the air off a trampoline 2 inches off the ground. The function $h(t) = -16t^2 + 60$, where *t* represents the time in seconds, *h* gives the height, in inches, of the trampolinist above the ground as he falls. When will the trampolinist land on the trampoline?

    The graphs of $y = -16x^2 + 60$ and $y = 58$ intersect at about $(0.4, 58)$. The

    trampolinist will land back on the trampoline after about 0.4 seconds.

16. **Physics** A ball is dropped from 10 feet above the ground. The function $h(t) = -16t^2 + 10$, where *t* represents the time in seconds, *h* gives the height, in feet, of the ball above the ground. When will the ball be 4 feet above the ground?

    The graphs of $y = -16x^2 + 10$ and $y = 4$ intersect at about $(0.6, 4)$. The ball

    will land on the roof of the trash shed in about 0.6 seconds.

Use the given quadratic function model to answer questions about the situation it models.

17. **Nature** A shark jumps out of the water. The quadratic function $f(x) = -16x^2 + 18x$ models the shark's height, in feet, above the water after *x* seconds. How long is the shark out of the water?

    The graph of $f(x) = -16x^2 + 18x$ shows a zero of 1.125. The shark is out

    of the water for 1.125 seconds.

18. Sports A baseball coach uses a pitching machine to simulate pop flies during practice. The quadratic function $f(x) = -16x^2 + 70x + 10$ models the height in feet of the baseball after x seconds. How long is the baseball in the air?

The graph of $f(x) = -16x^2 + 70x + 10$ shows a zero of about 4.5. The ball is in the air for 4.5 seconds.

19. The quadratic function $f(x) = -16x^2 + 11x$ models the height, in feet, of a fish above the water after x seconds. How long is the fish out of the water?

The graph of $f(x) = -16x^2 + 11x$ shows a zero of about 0.7.

The fish is in the air for about 0.7 seconds.

20. A football coach uses a passing machine to simulate 50-yard passes during practice. The quadratic function $f(x) = -16x^2 + 60x + 5$ models the height in feet of the football after x seconds. How long is the football in the air?

The graph of $f(x) = -16x^2 + 60x + 5$ shows a zero of about 3.8. The football is in the air for about 3.8 seconds.

Challenge students to solve a quadratic equation graphically using two different methods: by finding the zeros of the function and by finding points of intersection. They should find that the graphs look similar, but that one is translated vertically relative to the other. Students should understand that when solving one problem using two different methods, the graphs may look different, but the final solutions will be the same.

JOURNAL

Have students write a paragraph outlining the steps they take when graphing a quadratic function by hand. Students should be sure to describe how to find enough points so that the function can be accurately graphed on a coordinate grid.

21. In each polynomial function in standard form, identify a, b, and c.

a. $y = 3x^2 + 2x + 4$ a. $a = 3, b = 2, c = 4$

b. $y = 2x + 1$ b. $a = 0, b = 2, c = 1$

c. $y = x^2$ c. $a = 1, b = 0, c = 0$

d. $y = 5$ d. $a = 0, b = 0, c = 5$

e. $y = 3x^2 + 8x + 11$ e. $a = 3, b = 8, c = 11$

22. Identify the axis of symmetry, y-intercept, and vertex of the quadratic function $y = x^2 + x - 6$ and then graph the function on a graphing calculator to confirm.

Axis of symmetry: $x = -\dfrac{b}{2a} = -\dfrac{1}{2}$

y-Intercept: $y = 0^2 + 0 - 6 = -6$

Vertex: $\left(-\dfrac{1}{2}, -6\dfrac{1}{4}\right)$ because $y = \left(-\dfrac{1}{2}\right)^2 - \dfrac{1}{2} - 6 = -6\dfrac{1}{4}$

H.O.T.   **Focus on Higher Order Thinking**

23. **Counterexamples** Pamela says that if the graph of a function opens upward, then the related quadratic equation has two solutions. Provide a counterexample to refute Pamela's claim.

Sample answer: The graph of $f(x) = x^2$ opens upward, but the related equation, $x^2 = 0$, has only one solution.

24. **Explain the Error** Rodney was given the function $h(t) = -16t^2 + 50$ representing the height above the ground (in feet) of a water balloon t seconds after being dropped from a roof 50 feet above the ground. He was asked to find how long it took the balloon to fall 20 feet. Rodney used the equation $-16t^2 + 50 = 20$ to solve the problem. What was his error?

Falling 20 feet means that the balloon would have been $50 - 20 = 30$ feet above the ground, so Rodney should have solved the equation $-16t^2 + 50 = 30$ instead.

25. **Critical Thinking** If Jamie is given the graph of a quadratic function with only the x-intercepts and a random point labeled, can she determine an equation for the function? Explain.

Yes; Jamie can find the zeros of the function using the x-intercepts, and write the equation in the factored form $f(x) = k(x - a)(x - b)$, where a and b are the zeros. She can then substitute the coordinates of the given point to find the value of k.

Lesson Performance Task

Stella is competing in a diving competition. Her height in feet above the water is modeled by the function $f(x) = -16x^2 + 8x + 48$, where x is the time in seconds after she jumps from the diving board. Graph the function and solve the related equation $0 = -16x^2 + 8x + 48$. What do the solutions mean in the context of the problem? Are there solutions that do not make sense? Explain.

The graph crosses the x-axis at about $(2, 0)$ so the x-intercept is about 2. So, one solution of the equation $0 = -16x^2 + 8x + 48$ is about 2. This solution means that Stella reaches the surface of the water almost 2 seconds after she starts the dive.

If the graph is extended on the left, it will cross the x-axis once more. Since time cannot be negative, this solution does not make sense.

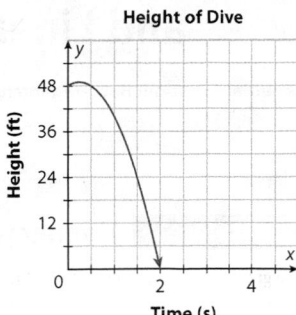

Height of Dive

EXTENSION ACTIVITY

Give students the functions $g(t) = -16t^2 + 8t + 24$ and $h(t) = -16t^2 + 16$ and explain that they represent the height in feet of two different divers, where t is time in seconds from the start of each dive. Have students compare the initial height, maximum height, and time to reach the water for the two divers.

Students should find that $g(t)$ represents a dive starting at 24 feet, reaching a maximum of 25 feet, and hitting the water after 1.5 seconds, and $h(t)$ represents a dive starting at 16 feet, which is also its maximum height, and hitting the water after 1 second.

QUESTIONING STRATEGIES

? How can you find the height at which the diver starts her dive? **Find the value of the function when $t = 0$.**

? How can you find the maximum height that the diver reaches? **Use the graph to find the y-value of the vertex of the parabola, or find the x-value halfway between the two zeros and calculate the corresponding y-value.**

INTEGRATE MATHEMATICAL PRACTICES
Focus on Reasoning

MP.2 Have students examine how the zeros, intercepts, function, and graph modeling the dive would be different if the diver had started the dive at the level of the water, that is, at height 0.

Scoring Rubric

2 points: Student correctly solves the problem and explains his/her reasoning.

1 point: Student shows good understanding of the problem but does not fully solve or explain his/her reasoning.

0 points: Student does not demonstrate understanding of the problem.

Connecting Intercepts and Zeros   **950**

Connecting Intercepts and Linear Factors

Common Core Math Standards

The student is expected to:

 A-APR.B.3

Identify zeros of polynomials … and use the zeros to construct a rough graph of the function defined by the polynomial. Also F-IF.C.7c, A-APR.A.1, A-SSE.A.2

Mathematical Practices

 MP.2 Reasoning

Language Objective

Explain to a partner how to determine the zeros of a quadratic function from an equation written in factored form.

ENGAGE

Essential Question: How are x-intercepts of a quadratic function and its linear factors related?

The x-intercepts of a quadratic function are the same as the x-intercepts of its linear factors.

PREVIEW: LESSON HPERFORMANCE TASK

View the Engage section online. Discuss how engineers might be able to use a quadratic function to model the shape of an arched underpass. Then preview the Lesson Performance Task.

Name_____ Class_____ Date_____

20.2 Connecting Intercepts and Linear Factors

Essential Question: How are x-intercepts of a quadratic function and its linear factors related?

Resource Locker

⊙ Explore   Connecting Factors and x–Intercepts

Use graphs and linear factors to find the x–intercepts of a parabola.

(A) Graph $y = x + 4$ and $y = x - 2$ using a graphing calculator. Then sketch the graphs on the grid.

(B) Identify the x-intercept of each line.

The x-intercepts are $\underline{-4}$ and $\underline{2}$.

(C) The quadratic function $y = (x + 4)(x - 2)$ is the product of the two linear factors that have been graphed. Use a graphing calculator to graph the function $y = (x + 4)(x - 2)$. Then sketch a graph of the quadratic function on the same grid with the linear factors that have been graphed.

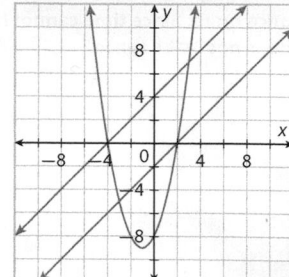

(D) Identify the x-intercepts of the parabola.

The x-intercepts are $\underline{-4}$ and $\underline{2}$.

(E) What do you notice about the x–intercepts of the parabola?

The x–intercepts of the parabola are the same as those of the two linear factors.

Reflect

1. Use a graph to determine whether $2x^2 + 5x - 12$ is the product of the linear factors $2x - 3$ and $x + 4$.

   Yes. The x-intercepts of $y = 2x^2 + 5x - 12$ are the same as those of $y = 2x - 3$ and $y = x + 4$.

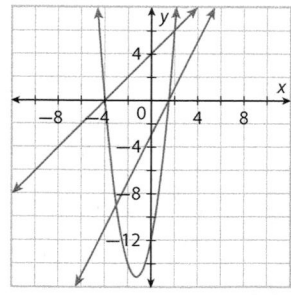

2. **Discussion** Make a conjecture about the linear factors and x-intercepts of a quadratic function.

   The x-intercepts of the parabola are the same as those of the two linear factors.

© Houghton Mifflin Harcourt Publishing Company

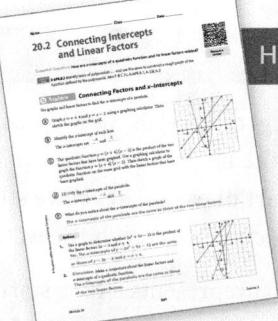

HARDCOVER PAGES 745–750

Turn to these pages to find this lesson in the hardcover student edition.

A quadratic function is in **factored form** when it is written as $y = k(x - a)(x - b)$ where $k \neq 0$.

Example 1 Write each function in standard form.

(A) $y = 2(x + 1)(x - 4)$

Multiply the two linear factors.

$y = 2(x^2 - 4x + x - 4)$

$y = 2(x^2 - 3x - 4)$

Multiply the resulting trinomial by 2.

$y = 2x^2 - 6x - 8$

The standard form of $y = 2(x + 1)(x - 4)$ is
$y = 2x^2 - 6x - 8$.

(B) $y = 3(x - 5)(x - 2)$

Multiply the two linear factors.

$y = 3\left(\boxed{x - 5}\right)\left(\boxed{x - 2}\right)$

$y = 3\left(\boxed{x^2 - 7x + 10}\right)$

Multiply the resulting trinomial by 3.

$y = \boxed{3x^2 - 21x + 30}$

The standard form of $y = 3(x - 5)(x - 2)$ is
$y = \mathbf{3x^2 - 21x + 30}$.

Reflect

3. How do the signs in the factors affect the sign of the x–term in the resulting trinomial?
If both signs in the factors are negative, then the x-term will be negative. If both signs in
the factors are positive, then the x-term will be positive.

4. How do the signs in the factors affect the sign of the constant term in the resulting trinomial?
If both signs in the factors are different, then the constant term will be negative. If both
signs in the factors are the same, then the constant term will be positive.

Your Turn

Write each function in standard form.

5. $y = (x - 7)(x - 1)$

$y = x^2 - x - 7x + 7$

$y = x^2 - 8x + 7$

$y = x^2 - 8x + 7$

6. $y = 4(x - 1)(x + 3)$

$y = 4(x^2 + 3x - x - 3)$

$y = 4(x^2 + 2x - 3)$

$y = 4x^2 + 8x - 12$

PROFESSIONAL DEVELOPMENT

Integrate Mathematical Practices

This lesson provides an opportunity to address Mathematical Practice **MP.2**,
which calls for students to "reason abstractly and quantitatively." Students will
expand quadratic functions in factored form so that they are in standard form.
Students will then graph the standard form of the function and analyze the graph
to determine the relationship between the function in factored form and the
x-intercepts of the function.

EXPLORE

Connecting Factors and x-Intercepts

INTEGRATE TECHNOLOGY

Students will use graphing calculators to graph
quadratic functions on the same grid as the
linear functions representing their factors. By
comparing the graphs, they can discover relationships
between a quadratic function and the x-intercepts of
its factors.

QUESTIONING STRATEGIES

If a quadratic function and a linear function
share the same x-intercept, must the
expression in the linear function be a factor of the
quadratic function? Explain. No; the expression
could be a factor of the quadratic equation, but
since many linear functions have the same
x-intercept, the expression does not have to be a
factor of the quadratic equation.

EXPLAIN 1

Rewriting from Factored Form to Standard Form

AVOID COMMON ERRORS

When multiplying two binomials, it can be easy to
forget to multiply both parts of one binomial by both
parts of the other binomial. Review the FOIL method
with students so they can remember to multiply the
First, Outer, Inner, and Last terms together.

QUESTIONING STRATEGIES

When the coefficient of the x^2 term is negative
for a quadratic function in standard form,
what must be true about the function in factored
form? When factored as, $y = k(x - a)(x - b)$, k will
be negative.

INTEGRATE MATHEMATICAL PRACTICES

Focus on Reasoning

MP.2 Remind students that the Commutative and Associative Properties of Multiplication state that factors can be rearranged and regrouped without changing the product. Therefore, when rewriting an equation from factored form into standard form, the factors can be multiplied in any order.

EXPLAIN 2

Connecting Factors and Zeros

INTEGRATE MATHEMATICAL PRACTICES

Focus on Modeling

MP.4 Review the formula for finding the axis of symmetry for a quadratic function written in standard form. Emphasize the importance of using the correct sign for each number in the equation $x = -\left(\frac{b}{2a}\right)$.

AVOID COMMON ERRORS

When expanding a quadratic function written in factored form, students may forget to combine like terms after multiplying factors. To help students check their work, remind them that a quadratic equation can have at most three terms.

QUESTIONING STRATEGIES

? When a quadratic function has two zeros, how do the zeros relate to the factored form of the function? When the function is in the form, $y = k(x - a)(x - b)$ the zeros will be a and b.

? How can you find the axis of symmetry for a function in factored form without rewriting it in standard form? First find the x-intercepts, then average them. The axis of symmetry is at the x-value that is halfway between the x-intercepts.

⚙ Explain 2 **Connecting Factors and Zeros**

In the Explore you learned that the factors in factored form indicate the x-intercepts of a function. In a previous lesson you learned that the x-intercepts of a graph are the zeros of the function.

Example 2 Write each function in standard form. Determine x-intercepts and zeros of each function.

Ⓐ $y = 2(x - 1)(x - 3)$

Write the function in standard form.

The factors indicate the x-intercepts.

* Factor $(x - 1)$ indicates an x-intercept of 1.

* Factor $(x - 3)$ indicates an x-intercept of 3.

$y = 2(x^2 - 3x - x + 3)$
$y = 2(x^2 - 4x + 3)$
$y = 2x^2 - 8x + 6$

The x-intercepts of a graph are the zeros of the function.

* An x-intercept of 1 indicates that the function has a zero of 1.

* An x-intercept of 3 indicates that the function has a zero of 3.

Ⓑ $y = 2(x + 4)(x + 2)$

Write the function in standard form.

The factors indicate the x-intercepts.

* Factor $(x + 4)$ indicates an x-intercept of $\underline{-4}$.

* Factor $(x + 2)$ indicates an x-intercept of -2.

$y = 2\boxed{\;x+4\;}\boxed{\;x+2\;}$

$y = 2\boxed{\;x^2 + 6x + 8\;}$

$y = \boxed{\;2x^2 + 12x + 16\;}$

The x-intercepts of a graph are the zeros of the function.

* An x-intercept of -4 indicates that the function has a zero of $\underline{-4}$.

* An x-intercept of $\underline{-2}$ indicates that the function has a zero of -2.

Reflect

7. **Discussion** What are the zeros of a function?
A zero of a function is an x–value that makes the y-value equal to zero. The zeros of a function are the x–intercepts.

8. How many x-intercepts can quadratic functions have?
0, 1, or 2

COLLABORATIVE LEARNING

Peer-to-Peer Activity

Have students work in pairs. Have each student write, then graph, a quadratic equation in factored form, $y = k(x-a)(x-b)$. Each student then rewrites the equation in standard form. Students trade the equations in standard form and graph the partners' equations. After completing both graphs, students compare their work and discuss whether standard form or factored form was easier to graph.

Write each function in standard form. Determine x–intercepts and zeros of each function.

9. $y = -2(x + 5)(x + 1)$

$y = -2(x + 5)(x + 1)$

$y = -2(x^2 + 6x + 5)$

$y = -2x^2 - 12x - 10$

The factored form shows that x–intercepts are -5 and -1.; the zeros are -5 and -1.

10. $y = 5(x - 3)(x - 1)$

$y = 5(x - 3)(x - 1)$

$y = 5(x^2 - 4x + 3)$

$y = 5x^2 - 20x + 15$

The factored form shows that x–intercepts are 1 and 3; the zeros are 1 and 3.

⚙ Explain 3   Writing Quadratic Functions Given x-Intercepts

Given two quadratic functions $f(x) = (x - a)(x - b)$ and $g(x) = k(x - a)(x - b)$, where k is any non-zero real constant, examine the x–intercepts for each quadratic function.

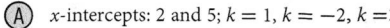

$f(x) = (x - a)(x - b)$	$g(x) = k(x - a)(x - b)$
$0 = (x - a)(x - b)$	$0 = k(x - a)(x - b)$
$x - a = 0$ or $x - b = 0$	$0 = (x - a)(x - b)$
$x = a$ $\qquad$ $x = b$	$x - a = 0$ or $x - b = 0$
	$x = a$ $\qquad$ $x = b$

Notice that $f(x) = (x - a)(x - b)$ and $g(x) = k(x - a)(x - b)$ have the same x-intercepts. You can use the factored form to construct a quadratic function given the x-intercepts and the value of k.

Example 3   For the two given intercepts, use the factored form to generate a quadratic function for each given constant k. Write the function in standard form.

(A) x-intercepts: 2 and 5; $k = 1$, $k = -2$, $k = 3$

Write the quadratic function with $k = 1$ using $f(x) = k(x - a)(x - b)$.

$f(x) = 1(x - 2)(x - 5)$

$f(x) = (x - 2)(x - 5)$

$f(x) = x^2 - 7x + 10$

Write the quadratic function with $k = -2$.

$f(x) = -2(x - 2)(x - 5)$

$f(x) = -2(x^2 - 7x + 10)$

$f(x) = -2x^2 + 14x - 20$

Write the quadratic function with $k = 3$.

$f(x) = 3(x - 2)(x - 5)$

$f(x) = 3(x^2 - 7x + 10)$

$f(x) = 3x^2 - 21x + 30$

EXPLAIN 3

Writing Quadratic Functions Given x-Intercepts

INTEGRATE MATHEMATICAL PRACTICES
Focus on Modeling

MP.4 When writing multiple quadratic functions that have the same x-intercepts but different values for k, students may have trouble visualizing how the functions are alike and how they are different. Graphing the functions on the same coordinate grid can make it easier to identify the functions' similarities and differences.

DIFFERENTIATE INSTRUCTION

Critical Thinking

When working with a function in factored form, students can identify the x-intercepts by finding x-values that will make $y = 0$. For a function such as $y = 5(x - 2)(x + 4)$, challenge students to find a value for x that will make $x - 2 = 0$, and a value for x that will make $x + 4 = 0$. Review the Zero Property of Multiplication so students understand that when one factor equals 0, the entire function will be equal to 0.

QUESTIONING STRATEGIES

? If you know the two **x**-intercepts for a quadratic function and want to write the function in factored form, does it matter which value is assigned to *a* and which is assigned to *b*? Explain. No; it does not matter because the factors are being multiplied by each other, and by the Commutative Property of Multiplication, they can be multiplied in either order and give the same result.

Ⓑ *x*-intercepts: −3 and 4; $k = 1, k = -3, k = 2$

Write the quadratic function with $k = 1$.

$f(x) = \boxed{(x+3)(x-4)}$

$f(x) = \boxed{x^2 - x - 12}$

Write the quadratic function with $k = -3$.

$f(x) = \boxed{-3(x+3)(x-4)}$

$f(x) = \boxed{-3x^2 + 3x + 36}$

Write the quadratic function with $k = 2$.

$f(x) = \boxed{2(x+3)(x-4)}$

$f(x) = 2x^2 - 2x - 24$

Reflect

11. How are the functions with same intercepts but different constant factors the same? How are they different?
Same intercepts and zeros, same axis of symmetry; They have different vertices.

Your Turn

For the given two intercepts and three values of *k* generate three quadratic functions. Write the functions in factored form and standard form.

12. *x*-intercepts: 1 and 8; $k = 1, k = -4, k = 5$

$k = 1:$

$f(x) = 1(x-1)(x-8)$

$f(x) = (x-1)(x-8)$

$f(x) = x^2 - 9x + 8$

$k = -4:$

$f(x) = -4(x-1)(x-8)$

$f(x) = -4(x^2 - 9x + 8)$

$f(x) = -4x^2 + 36x - 32$

$k = 5:$

$f(x)\ 5(x-1)(x-8)$

$f(x) = 5(x^2 - 9x + 8)$

$f(x) = 5x^2 - 45x + 40$

13. *x*-intercepts: −7 and 3; $k = 1, k = -5, k = 7$

$k = 1:$

$f(x) = 1(x+7)(x-3)$

$f(x) = (x+7)(x-3)$

$f(x) = x^2 + 4x - 21$

$k = -5:$

$f(x) = -5(x+7)(x-3)$

$f(x) = -5(x^2 + 4x - 21)$

$f(x) = -5x^2 - 20x + 105$

$k = 7:$

$f(x) = 7(x+7)(x-3)$

$f(x) = 7(x^2 + 4x - 21)$

$f(x) = 7x^2 + 28x - 147$

LANGUAGE SUPPORT EL

Graphic Organizers

Help students to complete the following table. Caution students that *a*, *b*, and *k* do not represent the same values in the different forms.

Standard Form	Vertex Form	Factored Form or Intercept Form
$y = ax^2 + bx + c$	$y = a(x-h)^2 + k$	$y = k(x-a)(x-b)$
axis of **symmetry** $x = \dfrac{-b}{2a}$	**vertex** (h, k) axis of symmetry $x = h$	**factors** $(x-a)$ and $(x-b)$ **x-intercepts** *a* and *b* axis of symmetry $x = \dfrac{a+b}{2}$

14. If the x-intercepts of a quadratic function are 3 and 8, what can be said about the x-intercepts of its linear factors?

The x-intercepts of its linear factors are 3 and 8.

15. If a quadratic function has only one zero, it has to occur at the vertex of the parabola. Using the graph of a quadratic function, explain why.

If there is only one zero, then the graph of the function has only one x-intercept.

This can only occur when the vertex of the parabola lies on the x-axis because a

parabola is symmetric.

16. How are x-intercepts and zeros related?

The x-intercepts of a quadratic function are the same as the zeros of a quadratic function.

17. What would the factored form look like if there were only one x-intercept?

$f(x) = k(x - a)^2$ **where a is the x-intercept.**

18. Essential Question Check-In How can you find x-intercepts of a quadratic function if its linear factors are known?

The x-intercepts of a quadratic function are the same as the x-intercepts of its

linear factors.

ELABORATE

INTEGRATE MATHEMATICAL PRACTICES
Focus on Math Connections

MP.1 Compare the factored form for a quadratic function with one x-intercept, $f(x) = k(x - a)^2$, with the vertex form of a quadratic function, $f(x) = a(x - h)^2 + k$. Students should realize that when the vertex form has $k = 0$, both forms will look the same.

SUMMARIZE THE LESSON

? How do you identify the x-intercepts of a quadratic function in factored form? For a function in the form, $y = k(x - a)(x - b)$ the x-intercepts will be a and b.

EVALUATE

ASSIGNMENT GUIDE

Concepts and Skills	Practice
Explore Connecting Factors and x-Intercepts	Exercises 1–4
Example 1 Rewriting from Factored Form to Standard Form	Exercises 5–10
Example 2 Connecting Factors and Zeros	Exercises 11–16
Example 3 Writing Quadratic Functions Given x-Intercepts	Exercises 17–21

INTEGRATE MATHEMATICAL PRACTICES

Focus on Technology

MP.5 Students may want to expand a quadratic equation in factored form before entering it into a graphing calculator. Remind students that quadratic equations can be entered into a calculator in either standard or factored form.

• Online Homework
• Hints and Help
• Extra Practice

Graph each quadratic function and each of its linear factors. Then identify the x-intercepts and the axis of symmetry of each parabola.

1. $y = (x - 2)(x - 6)$

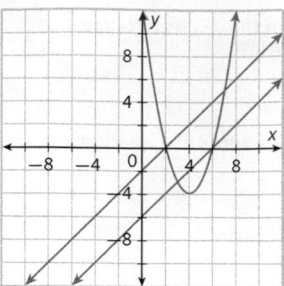

The x-intercepts are 2 and 6.

The axis of symmetry is $x = 4$.

2. $y = (x + 3)(x - 1)$

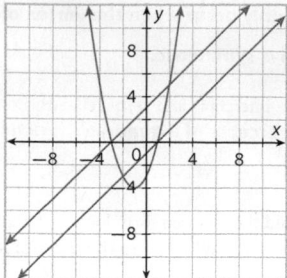

The x-intercepts are –3 and 1.

The axis of symmetry is $x = -1$.

3. $y = (x - 5)(x + 2)$

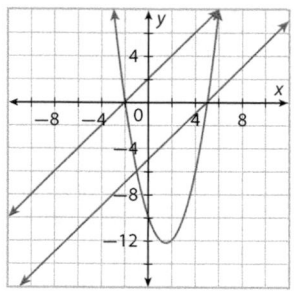

The x-intercepts are –2 and 5.

The axis of symmetry is $x = 1.5$.

4. $y = (x - 5)(x - 5)$

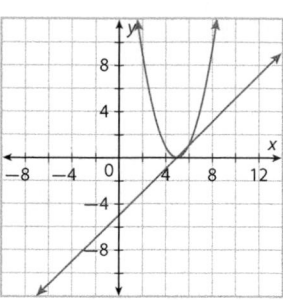

The x–intercept is 5.

The axis of symmetry is $x = 5$.

Exercise	Depth of Knowledge (D.O.K.)	COMMON CORE Mathematical Practices
1–4	**2** Skills/Concepts	**MP.6** Precision
5–10	**1** Recall of Information	**MP.6** Precision
11–14	**2** Skills/Concepts	**MP.2** Reasoning
15–16	**2** Skills/Concepts	**MP.1** Problem Solving
17–18	**2** Skills/Concepts	**MP.6** Precision
19–21	**3** Strategic Thinking H.O.T.	**MP.2** Reasoning

Write each function in standard form.

5. $y = 5(x - 2)(x + 1)$

$y = 5(x^2 - x - 2)$

$y = 5x^2 - 5x - 10$

6. $y = 2(x + 6)(x + 3)$

$y = 2(x^2 + 9x + 18)$

$y = 2x^2 + 18x + 36$

7. $y = -2(x + 4)(x - 5)$

$y = -2(x^2 - x - 20)$

$y = -2x^2 + 2x + 40$

8. $y = -4(x + 2)(x + 3)$

$y = -4(x^2 - 5x + 6)$

$y = -4x^2 + 20x - 24$

9. Which of the following is the correct standard form of $y = 3(x - 8)(x - 5)$?

a. $y = 3x^2 + 39x - 120$ $y = 3(x^2 - 13x + 40)$

b. $y = x^2 - 13x + 40$ $y = 3x^2 - 39x + 120$

(c.) $y = 3x^2 - 39x + 120$

d. $y = x^2 - 39x + 40$

e. $y = 3x^2 + 13x + 120$

10. The area of a Japanese rock garden is $y = 7(x - 3)(x + 1)$. Write $y = 7(x - 3)(x + 1)$ in standard form.

$y = 7(x^2 - 2x - 3)$

$y = 7x^2 - 14x - 21$

Write each function in standard form. Determine x–intercepts and zeros of each function.

11. $y = -(2x - 4)(x - 2)$

$y = -(2x^2 - 6x + 8) = -2x^2 + 12x - 16$

The factored form shows that x-intercepts are 2 and 4. The zeros are 2 and 4.

12. $y = 2(x + 4)(x - 2)$

$y = 2(x^2 + 2x - 8) = 2x^2 + 4x - 16$

The factored form shows that x–intercepts are −4 and 2. The zeros are −4 and 2.

13. $y = -3(x + 1)(x - 3)$

$y = -3(x^2 - 2x - 3) = -3x^2 + 6x + 9$

The factored form shows that x-intercepts are −1 and 3. The zeros are −1 and 3.

14. $y = 2(x + 2)(x - 1)$

$y = 2(x^2 + x - 2) = 2x^2 + 2x - 4$

The factored form shows that x-intercepts are −2 and 1. The zeros are −2 and 1.

CRITICAL THINKING

Discuss with students why the graphs of the factors of a quadratic equation in factored form are always parallel. Note that when a function is in the form $y = k(x - a)(x - b)$, the graphs for the factors are the lines $y = x - a$ and $y = x - b$. Students should realize that these lines have the same slope, so they must be parallel.

AVOID COMMON ERRORS

When expanding a quadratic function written in factored form, students may forget to combine the results from multiplying the inner and outer terms of the factors. Remind students that a quadratic equation in standard form should have at most one x^2 term, one x term, and one constant.

INTEGRATE MATHEMATICAL PRACTICES

Focus on Math Connections

MP.1 Relate the factored form of a quadratic function to the factors of an integer. Students should understand that just as an integer can have many factor pairs, a quadratic function can be factored in many different ways. The factored form is presented as $y = k(x - a)(x - b)$ where $k \neq 0$ so that the x-intercepts will be easy to identify as a and b.

When a quadratic equation is written so that the x terms in the factors have coefficients other than 1, the x-intercepts are not as readily apparent. For example, in the equation $y = (3x - 6)(2x + 8)$, the x-intercepts are not 6 and −8. Discuss with students how to divide each factor by a constant so that the x-intercepts can be determined more easily.

Have students explain how a quadratic equation looks when written in factored form, and how they can use the information in the factored form of a quadratic equation to find the zeros, x-intercepts, and axis of symmetry of a function.

15. A soccer ball is kicked from ground level. The function $y = -16x(x - 2)$ gives the height (in feet) of the ball, where x is time (in seconds). After how many seconds will the ball hit the ground? Use a graphing calculator to verify your answer.

The x-intercepts are 0 and 2. The ball will hit the ground in 2 seconds.

16. A tennis ball is tossed upward from a balcony. The height of the ball in feet can be modeled by the function $y = -4(2x + 1)(2x - 3)$ where x is the time in seconds after the ball is released. Find the maximum height of the ball and the time it takes the ball to reach this height. Graph the function to determine approximately how long it takes the ball to hit the ground.

The x-intercepts are −0.5 and 1.5. It will take 1.5 seconds to hit the ground. The axis

of symmetry is $x = 0.5$. So it takes 0.5 second to reach a maximum height of 16 feet.

For the two given intercepts, use the factored form to generate a quadratic function for each given constant k. Write the function in standard form.

17. x-intercepts: −5 and 3; $k = 1, k = -2, k = 5$

$k = 1: f(x) = 1(x + 5)(x - 3)$

$f(x) = x^2 + 2x - 15$

$k = -2: f(x) = -2(x + 5)(x - 3)$

$f(x) = -2x^2 - 4x + 30$

$k = 5: f(x) = 5(x + 5)(x - 3)$

$f(x) = 5x^2 + 10x - 75$

18. x-intercepts: 4 and 7; $k = 1, k = -3, k = 5$

$k = 1: f(x) = 1(x - 4)(x - 7)$

$f(x) = x^2 - 11x + 28$

$k = -3: f(x) = -3(x - 4)(x - 7)$

$f(x) = -3x^2 + 33x - 84$

$k = 5: f(x) = 5(x - 4)(x - 7)$

$f(x) = 5x^2 - 55x + 140$

H.O.T. Focus on Higher Order Thinking

19. Explain the Error For the given two intercepts, 3 and 9, $k = 4$, Kelly wrote a quadratic function in factored form, $f(x) = 4(x + 3)(x + 9)$, and in standard form, $f(x) = 4x^2 + 48x + 108$. What error did she make?

The factored form is $f(x) = 4(x - 3)(x - 9)$ and the standard form is

$f(x) = 4x^2 - 48x + 108$. Kelly substituted negative values for the x–intercepts.

20. Critical Thinking How is the graph of $f(x) = 7(x + 3)(x - 2)$ similar to and different from the graph of $f(x) = -7x^2 - 7x + 42$?

The graph of $f(x) = 7(x + 3)(x - 2)$ opens upward, and the graph

of $f(x) = -7x^2 - 7x + 42$ opens downward. The two graphs have the same

x-intercepts, and they are reflections of one another across the x-axis.

21. Make a Prediction How could you find an equation of a quadratic function with zeros at −3 and at 1?

Find the product $(x - (-3))(x - 1)$, or $(x + 3)(x - 1)$. Then write a quadratic function

using this product. So a possible quadratic function is $y = x^2 + 2x - 3$.

Lesson Performance Task

The cross-sectional shape of the archway of a bridge (measured in feet) is modeled by the function $f(x) = -0.5x^2 + 6x$ where $f(x)$ is the height of the arch and x is the horizontal distance from one side of the base. How wide is the arch at its base? Will a box truck that is 8 feet wide and 13.5 feet tall fit under the arch? If not, what is the maximum height a truck that is 8 feet wide and is passing under the bridge can be?

Write the function in intercept form, and then identify the x–intercepts of the graph.

$$f(x) = -0.5x^2 + 6x$$
$$= -0.5(x^2 - 12x)$$
$$= -0.5x(x - 12)$$
$$= -0.5(x - 0)(x - 12)$$

The x–intercepts are 0 and 12.

The width of the arch at its base is the horizontal distance between the two x-intercepts. The horizontal distance between 0 and 12 is 12 units. So, the arch is 12 units wide at its base.

Find the vertex.

The x-coordinate of the vertex is halfway between 0 and 12, or 6.

$$f(6) = -0.5(6 - 0)(6 - 12)$$
$$= -0.5(6)(-6)$$
$$= 18$$

The y–coordinate of the vertex is 18.

So, the vertex is $(6, 18)$

Graph the function and sketch the box truck centered on the graph to determine if it fits under the arch.

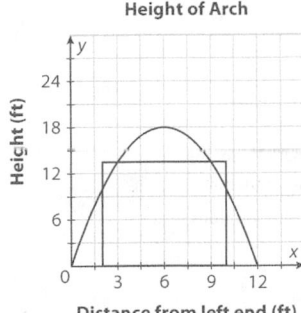

Height of Arch

Distance from left end (ft)

The upper corners of the box truck are higher than the arch, so the box truck does not fit under the arch.

The box truck is 8 feet wide. Since it is centered on the arch, the corners are an equal distance from the axis of symmetry, $x = 6$. So, the corners are located at $x = 2$ and $x = 10$.

The maximum height a truck that is 8 feet wide can be to fit under the arch is equal to the value of the function evaluated at one of these two x values.

$$f(2) = -0.5(x - 0)(x - 12)$$
$$= -0.5(2 - 0)(2 - 12)$$
$$= -0.5(2)(-10)$$
$$= 10$$

So, the maximum height a truck that is 8 feet wide can be to fit under the arch is 10 feet.

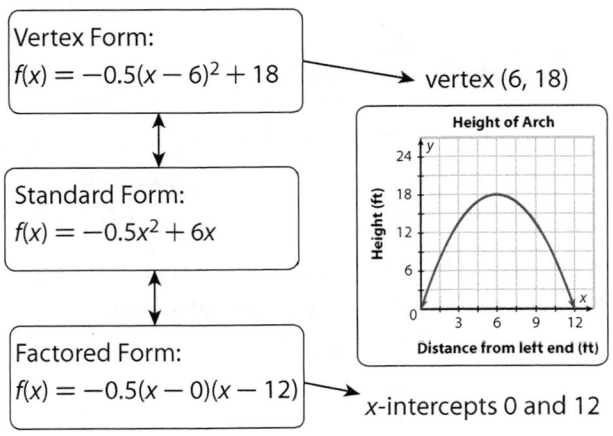

Vertex Form:
$$f(x) = -0.5(x - 6)^2 + 18$$
→ vertex $(6, 18)$

Standard Form:
$$f(x) = -0.5x^2 + 6x$$

Factored Form:
$$f(x) = -0.5(x - 0)(x - 12)$$
→ x-intercepts 0 and 12

Height of Arch

Distance from left end (ft)

EXTENSION ACTIVITY

Have students use a coordinate grid to design an arched entranceway tall enough and wide enough so that they can walk through the archway with their heads just touching the top and their arms extended straight out from side to side. Have students model the arched entrance by a quadratic function.

Students may find that they can use three points representing the top of the head and the tips of the fingers to define a parabola, then translate the parabola vertically to make it the correct total height.

Applying the Zero Product Property to Solve Equations

Common Core Math Standards

The student is expected to:

 A-REI.B.4

Solve quadratic equations in one variable. Also A-APR.B.3, A-SSE.A.2, A-SSE.B.3

Mathematical Practices

 MP.2 Reasoning

Language Objective

Explain what the Zero Product Property says, and give an example.

ENGAGE

Essential Question: How can you use the Zero Product Property to solve quadratic equations in factored form?

You can use the Zero Product Property to set each linear factor equal to 0 and then solve each resulting linear equation.

PREVIEW: LESSON PERFORMANCE TASK

View the Engage section online. Discuss why it might be a good idea for a pole vaulter to understand the shape of her path as she sails over the bar. Then preview the Lesson Performance Task.

20.3 Applying the Zero Product Property to Solve Equations

Essential Question: How can you use the Zero Product Property to solve quadratic equations in factored form?

Resource Locker

🧭 Explore   Understanding the Zero Product Property

For all real numbers a and b, if the product of the two quantities equals zero, then at least one of the quantities equals zero.

Zero Product Property		
For all real numbers a and b, the following is true.		
Words	**Sample Numbers**	**Algebra**
If the product of two quantities equals zero, at least one of the quantities equals zero.	$9\left(\boxed{0}\right) = 0$ $0(4) = \boxed{0}$	If $ab = 0$, then $\boxed{a} = 0$ or $b = \boxed{0}$.

(A) Consider the equation $(x - 3)(x + 8) = 0$. Let $a = x - 3$ and $b = \boxed{x + 8}$.

(B) Since $ab = 0$, you know that $a = 0$ or $b = 0$. $\boxed{x - 3} = 0$ or $x + 8 = 0$

(C) Solve for x.

$x - 3 = 0$ or $x + 8 = 0$

$x = \boxed{3}$ $x = \boxed{-8}$

(D) So, the solutions of the equation $(x - 3)(x + 8) = 0$ are $x = \boxed{3}$ and $x = \boxed{-8}$.

(E) Recall that the solutions of an equation are the zeros of the related function. So, the solutions of the equation $(x - 3)(x + 8) = 0$ are the zeros of the related function $f(x) = \dfrac{(x - 3)(x + 8)}{}$ because they satisfy the equation $f(x) = 0$. The solutions of the related function $f(x) = \dfrac{(x - 3)(x + 8)}{}$ are $\underline{\quad 3 \quad}$ and $\underline{\quad -8 \quad}$.

Reflect

1. Describe how you can find the solutions of the equation $(x - a)(x - b) = 0$ using the Zero Product Property.

Let $x - a = 0$ and $x - b = 0$, and then solve each equation for x. The solutions are a and b.

© Houghton Mifflin Harcourt Publishing Company

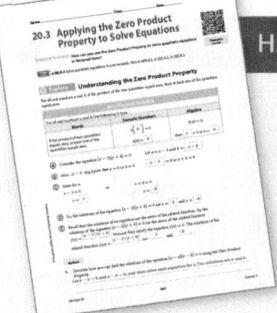

HARDCOVER PAGES 751–758

Turn to these pages to find this lesson in the hardcover student edition.

✏️ Explain 1 Applying the Zero Product Property to Functions

When given a function of the form $f(x) = (x + a)(x + b)$, you can use the Zero Product Property to find the zeros of the function.

Example 1 Find the zeros of each function.

Ⓐ $f(x) = (x - 15)(x + 7)$

Set $f(x)$ equal to zero.	$(x - 15)(x + 7) = 0$
Apply the Zero Product Property.	$x - 15 = 0$ or $x + 7 = 0$
Solve each equation for x.	$x = 15$ $x = -7$

The zeros are 15 and −7.

Ⓑ $f(x) = (x + 1)(x + 23)$

Set $f(x)$ equal to zero. $(x + 1)(x + 23) = \boxed{0}$

Apply the Zero Product Property. $x + \boxed{1} = 0$ or $x + 23 = \boxed{0}$

Solve for x. $x = \boxed{-1}$ $x = \boxed{-23}$

The zeros are $\boxed{-1}$ and $\boxed{-23}$.

Reflect

2. Discussion Jordie was asked to identify the zeros of the function $f(x) = (x - 5)(x + 3)$. Her answers were $x = -5$ and $x = 3$. Do you agree or disagree? Explain.
Disagree; If $(x - 5)(x + 3) = 0$, then $x - 5 = 0$ or $x + 3 = 0$; so $x = 5$ or $x = -3$

3. How would you find the zeros of the function $f(x) = -4(x - 8)$?
The x-values that make $f(x) = 0$ are zeros of the function, so solve $-4(x - 8) = 0$. The only solution is 8.

4. What are the zeros of the function $f(x) = x(x - 12)$? Explain.
0 and 12 because they are the solutions of $x(x - 12) = 0$.

Your Turn

Find the zeros of each function.

5. $f(x) = (x - 10)(x - 6)$
$(x - 10)(x - 6) = 0$
$x - 10 = 0$, so $x = 10$, or
$x - 6 = 0$, so $x = 6$.
The zeros are 10 and 6.

6. $f(x) = 7(x - 13)(x + 12)$
$7(x - 13)(x + 12) = 0$
Since $7 \neq 0$, set only the factors $(x - 13)$
and $(x + 12)$ equal to 0 and solve.
$x - 13 = 0$, so $x = 13$, or $x + 12 = 0$, so $x = -12$.
The zeros are 13 and −12.

PROFESSIONAL DEVELOPMENT

🔲 COMMON CORE Integrate Mathematical Practices

This lesson provides an opportunity to address Mathematical Practice **MP.2**, which calls for students to "reason abstractly and quantitatively." Students will rewrite quadratic equations so that they can apply the Zero Product Property to find the solutions. They build on their previous understanding of the connection between zeros, x-intercepts, and factors of quadratic functions, as well as the relationship between different forms of quadratic equations. In working with real-world problems, students interpret the solutions of equations to connect them to the real-world context.

EXPLORE

Understanding the Zero Product Property

INTEGRATE TECHNOLOGY

🔲 To check their answers for the zeros of a function, students can enter the equation into a graphing calculator and use the **TABLE** function to find the x-values for which $y = 0$.

QUESTIONING STRATEGIES

❓ If an equation has two factors, a and b, and $ab = 0$, can both a and b equal 0? Explain.
Yes; the Zero Product Property states that at least one of the factors a and b must equal zero. It is possible that both factors are equal to zero.

EXPLAIN 1

Applying the Zero Product Property to Functions

AVOID COMMON ERRORS

When finding the zeros of a quadratic function, students sometimes choose the constants in the binomial factors as the solutions. For example, students might say that the zeros of $f(x) = (x - 2)(x - 9)$ are −2 and −9. Remind students to find the value of x that would make each factor equal 0. For this example, the zeros are 2 and 9.

QUESTIONING STRATEGIES

❓ When using the Zero Product Property to find the zeros of a function, why do you set each factor equal to zero? You set each factor equal to zero because when at least one of the factors is zero, the product is equal to zero.

EXPLAIN 2

Solving Quadratic Equations Using the Distributive Property and the Zero Product Property

AVOID COMMON ERRORS

When instructed to use the Distributive Property to rewrite an equation, students may think that they should expand the equation. Remind students that if they want to use the Zero Product Property to find the solutions to the equation, they should use the Distributive Property in the other direction, that is, to rewrite the equation as the product of factors.

QUESTIONING STRATEGIES

? What must be true about an equation for it to be possible to use the Distributive Property to rewrite that equation as the product of factors? The same factor must appear in more than one term of the equation.

? How can you verify that the solutions to an equation are correct? You can substitute the values into the original equation to check that they make the equation true.

INTEGRATE MATHEMATICAL PRACTICES
Focus on Math Connections

MP.1 For some equations, it is necessary to factor part of the equation before using the Distributive Property to rewrite the equation in factored form. Remind students to look for terms with a common factor.

The Distributive Property states that, for real numbers a, b, and c, $a(b + c) = ab + ac$ and $ab + ac = a(b + c)$. The Distributive Property applies to polynomials, as well. For instance, $3x(x − 4) + 5(x − 4) = (3x + 5)(x − 4)$. You can use the Distributive Property along with the Zero Product Property to solve certain equations.

Example 2 Solve each equation using the Distributive Property and the Zero Product Property.

Ⓐ $3x(x − 4) + 5(x − 4) = 0$

Use the Distributive Property to rewrite the expression $3x(x − 4) + 5(x − 4)$ as a product.	$3x(x − 4) + 5(x − 4) = (3x + 5)(x − 4)$
Rewrite the equation.	$(3x + 5)(x − 4) = 0$
Apply the Zero Product Property.	$3x + 5 = 0$ or $x − 4 = 0$
Solve each equation for x.	$3x = −5$ $x = 4$
	$x = −\dfrac{5}{3}$

The solutions are $x = −\dfrac{5}{3}$ and $x = 4$.

Ⓑ $−9(x + 2) + 3x(x + 2) = 0$

Use the Distributive Property to rewrite the expression $−9(x + 2) + 3x(x + 2)$ as a product.	$−9(x + 2) + 3x(x + 2) = \left(\boxed{−9} + 3x\right)\left(x + \boxed{2}\right)$
Rewrite the equation.	$\left(\boxed{−9} + 3x\right)\left(x + \boxed{2}\right) = 0$
Apply the Zero Product Property.	$\boxed{−9} + 3x = 0$ or $x + \boxed{2} = 0$
Solve each equation for x.	$3x = \boxed{9}$ $x = \boxed{−2}$
	$x = \boxed{3}$

The solutions are $x = \boxed{3}$ and $x = \boxed{−2}$.

Reflect

7. How can you solve the equation $5x(x − 3) + 4x − 12 = 0$ using the Distributive Property?
   Factor $4x − 12$ as $4(x − 3)$ first. Then $5x(x − 3) + 4(x − 3) = 0$ becomes
   $(5x + 4)(x − 3) = 0.$

Your Turn

Solve each equation using the Distributive Property and the Zero Product Property.

8. $7x(x − 11) − 2(x − 11) = 0$

   $(7x − 2)(x − 11) = 0$

   $7x − 2 = 0$ or $x − 11 = 0$

   $x = \dfrac{2}{7}$ $x = 11$

9. $−8x(x + 6) + 3x + 18 = 0$

   $−8x(x + 6) + 3(x + 6) = 0$

   $(−8x + 3)(x + 6) = 0$

   $−8x + 3 = 0$ or $x + 6 = 0$

   $x = \dfrac{3}{8}$ $x = −6$

COLLABORATIVE LEARNING

Peer-to-Peer Activity

Have students work in pairs. Have each student write two factored equations: one in the form $y = k(x − a)(x − b)$, and one that is factored so that the x terms have coefficients other than 1. Students solve their equations, then trade equations and solve both equations written by their partners. Have partners discuss how they solved each equation and tell which equations they found easiest to solve.

Explain 3 Solving Real-World Problems Using the Zero Product Property

Example 3

The height of one diver above the water during a dive can be modeled by the equation $h = -4(4t + 5)(t - 3)$, where h is height in feet and t is time in seconds. Find the time it takes for the diver to reach the water.

Analyze Information

Identify the important information.
- The height of the diver is given by the equation
  $h = -4(4t + 5)(t - 3)$.
- The diver reaches the water when $h = \boxed{0}$.

Formulate a Plan

To find the time it takes for the diver to reach the water, set the equation equal to $\boxed{0}$ and use the $\underline{\text{Zero Product}}$ Property to solve for t.

Solve

Set the equation equal to zero. $\qquad -4(4t + 5)(t - 3) = 0$

Apply the Zero Product Property. $\qquad 4t + 5 = 0 \quad$ or $\quad t - 3 = 0$

Since $-4 \neq 0$, set the other factors equal to 0.

Solve each equation for x. $\qquad 4t + 5 = 0 \quad$ or $\quad t - 3 = 0$

$$4t = \boxed{-5} \qquad\qquad t = \boxed{3}$$

$$t = \boxed{-\tfrac{5}{4}}$$

The zeros are $t = \boxed{-\tfrac{5}{4}}$ and $t = \boxed{3}$. Since time cannot be negative, the time it takes for the diver to reach the the water is $\boxed{3}$ seconds.

Justify and Evaluate

Check to see that the answer is reasonable by substituting 3 for t in the equation $-4(4t + 5)(t - 3) = 0$.

$$-4(4(3) + 5)((3) - 3) = -4\left(\boxed{12} + 5\right)\left(\boxed{3} - 3\right)$$

$$= -4\left(\boxed{17}\right)\left(\boxed{0}\right)$$

$$= \boxed{0}$$

Since the equation is equal to $\boxed{0}$ for $t = 3$, the solution is reasonable. The diver will reach the water after $\boxed{3}$ seconds.

EXPLAIN 3

Solving Real-World Problems Using the Zero Product Property

INTEGRATE MATHEMATICAL PRACTICES
Focus on Math Connections

MP.1 When working with real-world problems that give the factored form of a quadratic function modeling the height of a falling object, have students multiply the factors and write the function in standard form. They should find that all the functions fit the same standard form: $f(t) = -16t^2 + v_0 t + h_0$, where $f(t)$ is the height in feet at time t, t is the time in seconds, v_0 is the initial vertical velocity, and h_0 is the initial height. (The coefficient of t^2 will differ if the units are different.) Explain that this general form is found in all problems modeling falling objects because the force of gravity affects the motion of all objects in the same way.

DIFFERENTIATE INSTRUCTION

Multiple Representations

For problems involving quadratic functions that model the height of a falling object, have students create a table of values for the height of the object. Continue the table until the object reaches a height of 0. Point out to students that the time when $h = 0$ represents the time it takes for the object to reach the ground. Discuss the differences between using this method and using the Zero Product Property to find the solution to a falling object problem.

QUESTIONING STRATEGIES

Not all quadratic functions can be written in a factored form. Can quadratic functions that model the height of a falling object always be written in factored form? Explain. **Yes; a function modeling the height of a falling object will have a value of 0 when the object reaches the ground, so it will have x-intercepts. Any quadratic function that has x-intercepts can be written in factored form.**

ELABORATE

INTEGRATE MATHEMATICAL PRACTICES

Focus on Communication

MP.3 Discuss with students whether the Zero Product Property can be applied only to quadratic functions. Students should realize that the Zero Product Property can be used to find the x-intercept of any factorable function.

SUMMARIZE THE LESSON

How do you solve a quadratic equation using the Zero Product Property? **If the function is in the form $f(x) = (x + a)(x + b)$, you can use the Zero Product Property by setting both $x + a = 0$ and $x + b = 0$, and finding both solutions for x.**

Reflect

10. If you were to graph the function $f(t) = -4(4t + 5)(t - 3)$, what points would be associated with the zeros of the function?
the points associated with the x-intercepts of the graph of the function, $\left(-\frac{5}{4}, 0\right)$ and $(3, 0)$

Your Turn

11. The height of a golf ball after it has been hit from the top of a hill can be modeled by the equation $h = -8(2t - 4)(t + 1)$, where h is height in feet and t is time in seconds. How long is the ball in the air?

The ball is in the air from the time it leaves the ground to the time it returns to the ground.

The height of the ball when it returns to the ground is $h = 0$.

Set the equation equal to 0.

$-8(2t - 4)(t + 1) = 0$

Since $-8 \neq 0$, set the factors $(2t - 4)$ and $(t + 1)$ equal to 0 and solve each equation.

$2t - 4 = 0$, so $t = 2$, or $t + 1 = 0$, so $t = -1$.

The zeros are $t = 2$ and $t = -1$. Since time cannot be negative, the ball is in the air for 2 seconds.

Elaborate

12. Can you use the Zero Product Property to find the zeros of the function $f(x) = (x - 1) + (2 - 9x)$? Explain.
No; the expression $(x - 1) + (2 - 9x)$ is not a product of factors, so the Zero Product Property cannot be used.

13. Suppose a and b are the zeros of a function. Name two points on the graph of the function and explain how you know they are on the graph. What are the x-coordinates of the points called?
$(a, 0)$ and $(b, 0)$; zeros of a function are values of x that make the function value 0; the x-intercepts of the graph of the function.

14. Essential Question Check-In Suppose you are given a quadratic function in factored form that is set equal to 0. Why can you solve it by setting each factor equal to 0?
The Zero Product Property states that if the product of two numbers is 0, then at least one of the numbers must be 0. A quadratic function in factored form is the product of two linear factors, so at least one of the factors must be 0.

LANGUAGE SUPPORT EL

Connect Vocabulary

When encountering the Zero Product Property for the first time, the formal construction of the sentences in the property may be difficult for English learners to understand. Point out that the phrase *the following is true* directs the reader's attention to the information that follows and emphasizes that it is true.

Find the solutions of each equation.

1. $(x - 15)(x - 22) = 0$

$x - 15 = 0$ or $x - 22 = 0$

$x = 15$ $x = 22$

2. $(x + 2)(x - 18) = 0$

$x + 2 = 0$ or $x - 18 = 0$

$x = -2$ $x = 18$

Find the zeros of each function.

3. $f(x) = (x + 15)(x + 17)$

$(x + 15)(x + 17) = 0$

$x + 15 = 0$ or $x + 17 = 0$

$x = -15$ $x = -17$

4. $f(x) = \left(x - \frac{2}{9}\right)\left(x + \frac{1}{2}\right)$

$\left(x - \frac{2}{9}\right)\left(x + \frac{1}{2}\right) = 0$

$x - \frac{2}{9} = 0$ or $x + \frac{1}{2} = 0$

$x = \frac{2}{9}$ $x = -\frac{1}{2}$

5. $f(x) = -0.2(x - 1.9)(x - 3.5)$

$-0.2(x - 1.9)(x - 3.5) = 0$

$x - 1.9 = 0$ or $x - 3.5 = 0$

$x = 1.9$ $x = 3.5$

6. $f(x) = x(x + 20)$

$(x - 0)(x + 20) = 0$

$x - 0 = 0$ or $x - 20 = 0$

$x = 0$ $x = 20$

7. $f(x) = \frac{3}{4}\left(x - \frac{3}{4}\right)$

$\frac{3}{4}\left(x - \frac{3}{4}\right) = 0$

$x - \frac{3}{4} = 0$

$x = \frac{3}{4}$

8. $f(x) = (x + 24)(x + 24)$

$(x + 24)(x + 24) = 0$

$x + 24 = 0$ or $x + 24 = 0$

$x = -24$ $x = -24$

EVALUATE

ASSIGNMENT GUIDE

Concepts and Skills	Practice
Explore Understanding the Zero Product Property	Exercises 1–2
Example 1 Applying the Zero Product Property to Functions	Exercises 3–8, 24
Example 2 Solving Quadratic Equations Using the Distributive Property and the Zero Product Property	Exercises 9–14, 21–22, 25
Example 3 Solving Real-World Problems Using the Zero Product Property	Exercises 15–20, 23

Exercise	Depth of Knowledge (D.O.K.)	COMMON CORE Mathematical Practices
1–13	**1** Recall of Information	**MP.2** Reasoning
14	**2** Skills/Concepts	**MP.2** Reasoning
15–20	**2** Skills/Concepts	**MP.4** Modeling
21	**2** Skills/Concepts	**MP.2** Reasoning
22	**3** Strategic Thinking H.O.T.	**MP.3** Logic
23	**3** Strategic Thinking H.O.T.	**MP.4** Modeling

INTEGRATE MATHEMATICAL PRACTICES

Focus on Communication

MP.3 Discuss with students whether the Zero Product Property can be used to find the zero of a function that has only one zero. Students should understand that a function with only one zero will have the form $f(x) = (x + a)(x + a)$ or $f(x) = (x + a)^2$.

Solve each equation using the Distributive Property and the Zero Product Property.

9. $-6x(x + 12) - 15(x + 12) = 0$

$(-6x - 15)(x + 12) = 0$

$-6x = 15$ or $x = -12$.

$x = -\dfrac{15}{6}$

10. $10(x - 3) - x(x - 3) = 0$

$(10 - x)(x - 3) = 0$

$x = 10$ or $x = 3$.

11. $5x\left(x + \dfrac{2}{3}\right) + \left(x + \dfrac{2}{3}\right) = 0$

$(5x + 1)\left(x + \dfrac{2}{3}\right) = 0$

$5x = -1$ or $x = -\dfrac{2}{3}$

$x = -\dfrac{1}{5}$

12. $-(x + 4) + x(x + 4) = 0$

$(-1 + x)(x + 4) = 0$

$-1 = -x$ or $x = -4$

$1 = x$

13. $7x(9 - x) + \dfrac{1}{3}(9 - x) = 0$

$\left(7x + \dfrac{1}{3}\right)(9 - x) = 0$

$7x = -\dfrac{1}{3}$ or $9 = x$

$x = -\dfrac{1}{21}$

14. $-x(x - 3) + 6x - 18 = 0$

$-x(x - 3) + 6(x - 3) = 0$

$(-x + 6)(x - 3) = 0$

$-x = -6$ or $x = 3$

$x = 6$

Solve using the Zero Product Property.

15. The height of a football after it has been kicked from the top of a hill can be modeled by the equation $h = 2(-2 - 4t)(2t - 5)$, where h is the height of the football in feet and t is the time in seconds. How long is the football in the air?

$2(-2 - 4t)(2t - 5) = 0$

$-2 = 4t$ or $2t = 5$

$-\dfrac{1}{2} = t \qquad t = \dfrac{5}{2}$

Exercise	Depth of Knowledge (D.O.K.)		COMMON CORE Mathematical Practices
24	**3** Strategic Thinking	H.O.T.	**MP.3** Logic
25	**3** Strategic Thinking	H.O.T.	**MP.1** Problem Solving

16. **Football** During football practice, a football player kicks a football. The height h in feet of the ball t seconds after it is kicked can be modeled by the function $h = -4t(-4t - 11)$. How long is the football in the air?

$-4t(4t - 11) = 0$

$-4t = 0$ or $4t - 11 = 0$

$t = 0 \qquad\qquad 4t = 11$

$\qquad\qquad\qquad t = 2.75$

The solutions are $t = 0$ and $t = 2.75$. Since the starting time is 0, the

football in the air for 2.75 seconds.

17. **Physics** The height of a flare fired from a platform can be modeled by the equation $h = 8t(-2t + 10) + 4(-2t + 10)$, where h is the height of the flare in feet and t is the time in seconds. Find the time it takes for the flare to reach the ground.

$-8t(2t + 10) + 4(-2t + 10) = 0$

$(-8t + 4)(-2t + 10) = 0$

$8t + 4 = 0 \qquad$ or $\qquad -2t + 10 = 0$

$8t = -4 \qquad\qquad\qquad -2t = -10$

$t = -0.5 \qquad\qquad\qquad\quad t = 5$

The solutions are $t = -0.5$ and $t = 5$. Since time cannot be negative, the

flare is in the air for 5 seconds.

18. **Diving** The depth of a scuba diver can be modeled by the equation $d = 0.5t(3.5t - 28.25)$, where d is the depth in meters of the diver and t is the time in minutes. Find the time it takes for the diver to reach the surface. Give your answer to the nearest minute.

$0.5t(3.5t - 28.25) = 0$

$0.5t = 0$ or $3.5t - 28.25 = 0$

$t = 0 \qquad\qquad 3.5t = 28.25$

$\qquad\qquad\qquad t \approx 8$

The solutions are $t = 0$ and $t \approx 8$. Since the starting time is 0, the time it takes for the diver to reach the surface is about 8 minutes.

CRITICAL THINKING

Not all quadratic equations are shown in the factored form $y = k(x - a)(x - b)$, where a and b are the zeros of the function. After finding the zeros of a function not in this form, discuss with students ways to rewrite the function so that the zeros will be more evident.

In a factored quadratic equation, it is easy to mistake the constants for the zeros. Remind students that finding the zeros of the function requires finding the values of x that make each factor equal to 0.

19. A group of friends tries to keep a small beanbag from touching the ground by kicking it. On one kick, the beanbag's height can be modeled by the equation $h = -2(t - 1) - 16t(t - 1)$, where h is the height of the beanbag in feet and t is the time in seconds. Find the time it takes the beanbag to reach the ground.

$2(t - 1) - 16t(t - 1) = 0$

$(2 - 16t)(t - 1) = 0$

$2 = 16t$ or $\quad t = 0$

$\dfrac{1}{8} = t = 0.125$

The solutions are $t = -0.125$ and $t = 1$. Since time cannot be negative, the time it takes for the beanbag to reach the ground is 1 second.

20. Elizabeth and Markus are playing catch. Elizabeth throws the ball first. The height of the ball can be modeled by the equation $h = -16t(t - 5)$, where h is the height of the ball in feet and t is the time in seconds. Markus is distracted at the last minute and looks away. The ball lands at his feet. If the ball travels horizontally at an average rate of 3.5 feet per second, how far is Markus standing from Elizabeth when the ball hits the ground?

$-16t(t - 5) = 0$

$-16t = 0$ or $t - 5 = 0$

$t = 0 \qquad\quad t = 5$

The solutions are $t = 0$ and $t = 5$. Since the starting time is 0, the ball is in the air for 5 seconds.

Find the distance the ball travels in that time.

$d = rt = (3.5)(5) = 17.5$

Markus is standing 17.5 feet away from Elizabeth when the ball hits the ground.

21. Match the function on the left with its zeros on the right. Indicate a match by writing the letter for a function on the line in front of the corresponding values of x and y.

A. $f(x) = 11(x - 9) + x(x - 9)$

$(11 + x)(x - 9) = 0$

$\underline{\quad E \quad}$ **a.** $x = -11$ and $x = -9$

B. $f(x) = (x + 9)(x - 11)$

$(x + 9)(x - 11) = 0$

$\underline{\quad A, D \quad}$ **b.** $x = 9$ and $x = -11$

C. $f(x) = 11(x - 9) - x(x - 9)$

$(11 - x)(x - 9) = 0$

$\underline{\quad C \quad}$ **c.** $x = 9$ and $x = 11$

D. $f(x) = (x - 9)(x + 11)$

$(x - 9)(x + 11) = 0$

$\underline{\quad B \quad}$ **d.** $x = -9$ and $x = 11$

E. $f(x) = -x(x + 9) - 11(x + 9)$

$(-x - 11)(x + 9) =$

22. **Explain the Error** A student found the zeros of the function
$f(x) = 2x(x - 5) + 6(x - 5)$. Explain what the student did wrong. Then give the
correct answer.

$2x(x - 5) + 6(x - 5) = 0$

$2x(x - 5) = 0$, so $2x = 0$, and $x = 0$, or

$x - 5 = 0$, so $x = 5$, or

$6(x - 5) = 0$, so $x = 5$

Zeros: 0, 5 and 5

The student should have used the Distributive Property to rewrite the

equation as $(2x + 6)(x - 5) = 0$.

Then $2x + 6 = 0$, so $x = -3$, or $x - 5 = 0$, so $x = 5$

Zeros: -3 and 5

23. **Draw Conclusions** A ball is kicked into the air from ground level. The height h
in meters that the ball reaches at a distance d in meters from the point where it was
kicked is given by $h = -2d(d - 4)$. The graph of the equation is a parabola.

a. At what distance from the point where it is kicked does the ball reach its
maximum height? Explain.

The ball is on the ground when $h = 0$.

$-2d(d - 4) = 0$

$-2d = 0$, so $d = 0$, or $d - 4 = 0$, so $d = 4$.

The solutions are $d = 0$ and $d = 4$. Since the ball starts at $d = 0$, it will hit

the ground at $d = 4$. Since the curve is symmetric, the ball will be at its

maximum height at half this distance, or 2 meters.

b. Find the maximum height. What is the point $(2, h)$ on the graph of the function
called?

The ball is at its maximum height when $d = 2$. Substitute 2 for d in the

equation and solve for h.

$h = -2(2)(2 - 4) = -4(-2) = 8$

The maximum height is 8 meters. The point $(2, h)$, or $(2, 8)$, is the vertex

of the graph of the function.

24. Justify Reasoning Can you solve $(x - 2)(x + 3) = 5$ by solving $x - 2 = 5$ and $x + 3 = 5$? Explain.

No. You can't use the Zero Product Property because the product is not equal to 0. If $x - 2 = 5$ then $x = 7$, and if $x + 3 = 5$, then $x = 2$. Neither 7 nor 2 is a solution of $(x - 2)(x + 3) = 5$. Instead, $(7 - 2)(7 + 3) = 50$ and $(2 - 2)(2 + 3) = 0$.

25. Persevere in Problem Solving Write an equation to find three numbers with the following properties. Let x be the first number. The second number is 3 more than the first number. The third number is 4 times the second number. The sum of the third number and the product of the first and second numbers is 0. Solve the equation and give the three numbers.

First number: x

Second number: $x + 3$

Third number: $4(x + 3)$

The sum of the third number and the product of the first and second numbers is 0.

$$4(x + 3) + x(x + 3) = 0$$

$$(4 + x)(x + 3) = 0$$

$4 + x = 0$, so $x = -4$, or $x + 3 = 0$, so $x = -3$

Suppose $x = -4$

First number: -4

Second number: $-4 + 3 = -1$

Third number: $4(-4 + 3) = 4(-1) = -4$

Suppose $x = -3$

First number: -3

Second number: $-3 + 3 = 0$

Third number: $4(-3 + 3) = 4(0) = 0$

So, the three numbers are either -4, -1, and -4, or -3, 0, and 0.

© Houghton Mifflin Harcourt Publishing Company

Lesson Performance Task

The height of a pole vaulter as she jumps over the bar is modeled by the function $f(t) = -1.75(t - 0)(t - 3.5)$, where t is the time at which the pole vaulter leaves the ground.

   a. Find the solutions of the function when $t = 0$ using the Zero Product Property. What do these solutions mean in the context of the problem?

   b. If the bar is 6 feet high, will the pole vaulter make it over?

   a. $f(t) = -1.75(t - 0)(t - 3.5)$

     $t - 0 = 0 \quad t - 3.5 = 0$

     $t = 0 \qquad t = 3.5$

     The solutions are $t = 0$ and $t = 3.5$

     This means that the pole vaulter left the ground at 0 seconds and

     returned to the ground after 3.5 seconds. So, the pole vaulter was in

     the air for 3.5 seconds.

   b. Find the vertex of the parabola. First, rewrite the function in

     standard form.

$$f(t) = -1.75(t - 0)(t - 3.5)$$
$$= -1.75(t^2 - 3.5t)$$
$$= -1.75t^2 + 6.125t$$

     The vertex is $\left(-\dfrac{b}{2a}, f\left(-\dfrac{b}{2a}\right)\right)$.

$$-\frac{b}{2a} = -\frac{6.125}{2(-1.75)} = 1.75$$

$$f\left(-\frac{b}{2a}\right) = f(1.75) = -1.75(1.75)^2 + 6.125(1.75) \approx 5.36$$

     The pole vaulter's maximum height is 5.36 feet, so she will not make

     it over the 6-foot high bar.

© Houghton Mifflin Harcourt Publishing Company

INTEGRATE MATHEMATICAL PRACTICES

Focus on Technology

MP.5 To check their results, have students graph the function using a graphing calculator, then use the **TRACE** feature or the **TABLE** feature to check the maximum height and the x-intercepts that they calculated.

INTEGRATE MATHEMATICAL PRACTICES

Focus on Communication

MP.3 Have students explain why one zero of the function is 0. They should understand that a pole vaulter is at height 0 both when starting to jump and when landing.

EXTENSION ACTIVITY

Have students research the "Fosbury Flop" and investigate how a high jumper tries to control the location of his or her center of gravity in order to reach the maximum height possible.

Students may find that an athlete's center of mass is about two-thirds of the way up the body when standing or running. However, by curling themselves into an inverted U-shape as they sail over the bar, high jumpers cause their centers of gravity to drop below the bar. In this way they are able to minimize the energy needed to jump over the bar.

Scoring Rubric

2 points: Student correctly solves the problem and explains his/her reasoning.
1 point: Student shows good understanding of the problem but does not fully solve or explain his/her reasoning.
0 points: Student does not demonstrate understanding of the problem.

Study Guide Review

ASSESSMENT AND INTERVENTION

Assign or customize module reviews.

MODULE PERFORMANCE TASK

COMMON CORE

Mathematical Practices: MP.1, MP.2, MP.4
A-CED.A.2, F-BF.A.1

SUPPORTING STUDENT REASONING

Students should begin this problem by focusing on what information they will need. Here is some of the information they may ask for.

- **The horizontal distance between point _A_ and point _B_:** This information is not given but is up to the student. Students must choose a value between 3 meters and 6 meters.

- **The coordinates of the points on the diagram:** The coordinates of point A can be seen on the diagram. The _x_-coordinates of points _B_ and _C_ will depend on the width chosen.

- **The location of the vertex:** From the given information and the diagram, students should be able to deduce the location of the vertex themselves.

Connecting Intercepts, Zeros, and Factors

Essential Question: How can you use intercepts of a quadratic function to solve real-world problems?

Key Vocabulary
Zero Product Property
(Propiedad del producto cero)
zero of a function
(cero de una función)

KEY EXAMPLE   (Lesson 20.2)

Generate the quadratic function with _x_-intercepts 3 and −2 and $k = 3$. Write the function in factored form and standard form.

Write the quadratic function with $k = 3$. Substitute the given values of the _x_-intercepts and _k_ into $f(x) = k(x − a)(x − b)$ and simplify.

$f(x) = 3(x + 2)(x − 3)$

Write $f(x) = 3(x + 2)(x − 3)$ in standard form.

$$f(x) = 3(x + 2)(x − 3)$$
$$= 3x^2 − 3x − 18$$

KEY EXAMPLE   (Lesson 20.3)

Solve $2x(x − 2) + 4(x − 2) = 0$ by using the Distributive Property and the Zero Product Property.

Use the Distributive Property to rewrite the expression $2x(x − 2) + 4(x − 2)$ as a product of binomials.

$$2x(x − 2) + 4(x − 2) = (2x + 4)(x − 2)$$

Rewrite the equation. $(2x + 4)(x − 2) = 0$

Apply the Zero Product Property. $2x + 4 = 0$ and $x − 2 = 0$

Solve each equation for _x_. $2x = −4$ $x = 2$

$x = −2$

The solutions are $x = −2$ and $x = 2$.

SCAFFOLDING SUPPORT

- Although it is not strictly necessary to solve the problem, you may wish to remind students of the vertex form of a quadratic equation, $y = (x − h)^2 + k$.

- Solution methods may include using the vertex form of a quadratic equation, using quadratic regression, or other methods. Any method that leads to a correct equation is acceptable.

EXERCISES

Solve each equation by graphing. *(Lesson 20.1)*

1. $x^2 - 2x - 1 = 2$

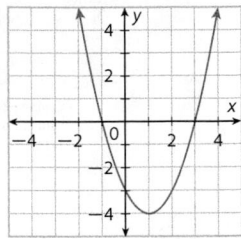

$x = -1$ and 3

2. $(x + 2)^2 - 4 = 0$

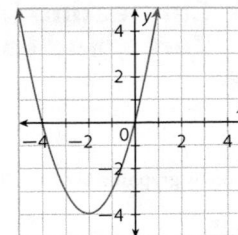

$x = -4$ and 0

Write a function in factored and standard form for each k and set of x-intercepts. *(Lesson 20.2)*

3. x-intercepts: -3 and 4; $k = -2$

$f(x) = -2(x + 3)(x - 4)$

$f(x) = -2x^2 + 2x + 24$

4. x-intercepts: 7 and 2; $k = 3$

$f(x) = 3(x - 2)(x - 7)$

$f(x) = 3x^2 - 27x + 42$

Find the zeros of each function. *(Lesson 20.3)*

5. $f(x) = x(x + 17)$

$x = -17$ or 0

6. $f(x) = -4(x - 2.3)(x - 4.6)$

$x = 2.3$ or 4.6

MODULE PERFORMANCE TASK

Designing a Skateboard Ramp

The local government has made partial plans for the construction of a skateboard ramp, which are shown here. Your task is to complete the plans by modeling the parabolic curve of the ramp itself.

First, choose the total width of the parabola from point A to point C, which should be between 3 meters and 6 meters. Then, create an equation that models the parabola that starts at point A, reaches a minimum at point B, and ends at point C. Note that the x- and y-axes are marked in the diagram. Express your equation in standard form.

Use your own paper to complete the task, using graphs, numbers, or algebra to explain how you reached your conclusion.

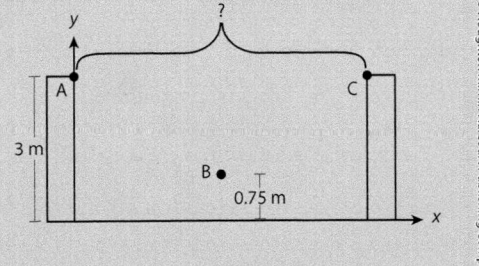

DISCUSSION OPPORTUNITIES

- Some ramps use semicircular curves, or have a flat portion at the bottom of the ramp. Discuss how closely the curve of a parabola matches any actual half-pipe ramps students have seen.

- Students may be interested in making additional recommendations to the local government about the construction of future half-pipe skateboard ramps.

SAMPLE SOLUTION

Assumptions

The width of the skateboard ramp is 5 m.

The vertex (point B) is half the ramp width, or 2.5 m. The diagram shows the vertex is 0.75 m above the ground. Substitute $(2.5, 0.75)$ for (h, k) into the vertex form of a quadratic equation.

$$y = a(x - h)^2 + k$$

$$y = a(x - 2.5)^2 + 0.75$$

The diagram shows that one point on the parabola is $(0, 3)$. Substitute $(0, 3)$ for (x, y) and solve for a.

$$3 = a(0 - 2.5)^2 + 0.75$$

$$2.25 = a(6.25)$$

$$0.36 = a$$

In vertex form, the equation that models the parabola is $y = 0.36(x - 2.5)^2 + 0.75$. The standard form of this equation that models the ramp curve is $y = 0.36x^2 - 1.8x + 3$.

Assessment Rubric

2 points: Student correctly solves the problem and explains his/her reasoning.

1 point: Student shows good understanding of the problem but does not fully solve or explain.

0 points: Student does not demonstrate understanding of the problem.

Ready to Go On?

ASSESS MASTERY

Use the assessment on this page to determine if students have mastered the concepts and standards covered in this module.

ASSESSMENT AND INTERVENTION

Access Ready to Go On? assessment online, and receive instant scoring, feedback, and customized intervention or enrichment.

ADDITIONAL RESOURCES

Response to Intervention Resources

- Reteach Worksheets

Differentiated Instruction Resources

- Reading Strategies **EL**
- Success for English Learners **EL**
- Challenge Worksheets

Assessment Resources

- Leveled Module Quizzes

(Ready) to Go On?

20.1–20.3 Connecting Intercepts, Zeros, and Factors

- Online Homework
- Hints and Help
- Extra Practice

Solve each equation by graphing. (Lesson 20.1)

1. $-4x + 4 = -x^2$

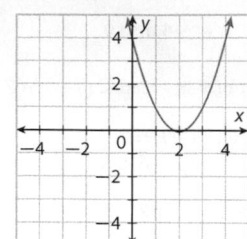

$x = 2$

2. $-x^2 + 1 = 0$

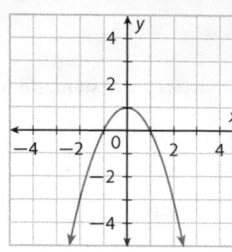

$x = -1$ or 1

Write a function in factored and standard form for each k and set of x-intercepts. (Lesson 20.2)

3. x-intercepts: 5 and -7; $k = -3$

$f(x) = -3(x - 5)(x + 7)$

$f(x) = -3x^2 - 6x + 105$

4. x-intercepts: -1 and -8; $k = 4$

$f(x) = 4(x + 1)(x + 8)$

$f(x) = 4x^2 + 36x + 32$

Find the zeros of each function. (Lesson 20.3)

5. $f(x) = -8(x + 7)(x - 8.6)$

$x = -7$ or 8.6

6. $f(x) = x(x - 42)$

$x = 0$ or 42

7. $f(x) = 9x(x - 4) + 3(x - 4)$

$x = -\dfrac{1}{3}$ or 4

8. $f(x) = -2x(x + 4) + 6x + 24$

$x = -4$ or 3

ESSENTIAL QUESTION

9. How can you use factoring to solve quadratic equations in standard form?

Factor the right side of the equation. Set each linear factor equal to 0, and then solve each linear equation. These are the solutions of the original quadratic equation.

COMMON CORE Common Core Standards

Lesson	Items	Content Standards	Mathematical Practices
20.1	1–2	F-IF.C.7a, A-APR.B.3	MP.7
20.2	3–4	A-APR.B.3, A-APR.A.1, A-SSE.A.2	MP.2
20.3	5	A-REI.B.4, A-APR.B.3	MP.2
20.3	6	A-REI.B.4, A-APR.B.3	MP.2
20.3	7	A-REI.B.4, A-APR.B.3	MP.2
20.3	8	A-REI.B.4, A-APR.B.3	MP.2

MODULE 20
MIXED REVIEW

Assessment Readiness

1. Solve $8x(7 - x) + \frac{1}{5}(7 - x) = 0$.

   A. $x = -7$ ○ Yes   ● No

   B. $x = -\frac{8}{5}$ ○ Yes   ● No

   C. $x = -\frac{1}{40}$ ● Yes   ○ No

2. For each statement, determine if it is True or False for the graph of $6x - 3y = 21$.

   A. The x-intercept is $3\frac{1}{2}$.   ● Yes   ○ No

   B. The y-intercept is -7.   ● Yes   ○ No

   C. The slope is 3.   ○ Yes   ● No

3. Is the sequence 6, 3, 0, −3, −6, −9, … arithmetic, geometric, or neither? Explain your answer. Write a recursive rule for the sequence.

   The sequence is arithmetic because it has a common difference of −3.
   $f(1) = 6; f(n) = f(n - 1) - 3$

4. Graph $f(x) = (x - 2)^2 - 4$. Describe the relationship between the x-intercepts of the graph and the solutions of $(x - 2)^2 - 4 = 0$.

   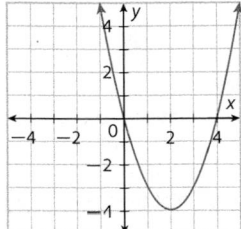

   The x-intercepts are the solution of the equation.

© Houghton Mifflin Harcourt Publishing Company

Assessment Readiness

ASSESSMENT AND INTERVENTION

Assign ready-made or customized practice tests to prepare students for high-stakes tests.

ADDITIONAL RESOURCES

Assessment Resources

- Leveled Module Quizzes: Modified, B

AVOID COMMON ERRORS

Item 2 Some students may have a hard time finding the slope of an equation that is not in slope-intercept form. Remind students that they can rewrite equations in new forms whenever needed, and they can also find the slope using the intercepts.

Common Core Standards

Lesson	Items	Content Standards	Mathematical Practices
20.3	1	A-REI.B.4	MP.2
5.2	2*	F-IF.B.4	MP.2
4.2	3*	F-BF.A.2	MP.3
20.1	4	A-REI.D.11	MP.7

* Item integrates mixed review concepts from previous modules or a previous course.

MIXED REVIEW
Assessment Readiness

ASSESSMENT AND INTERVENTION

Assign ready-made or customized practice tests to prepare students for high-stakes tests.

ADDITIONAL RESOURCES

Assessment Resources

- Leveled Unit Tests: Modified, A, B, C
- Performance Assessment

AVOID COMMON ERRORS

Item 7   Some students may attempt to distribute the fraction to both of the other factors of the function. Remind them to fully multiply polynomials before distributing monomial factors.

UNIT 8 MIXED REVIEW
Assessment Readiness

- Online Homework
- Hints and Help
- Extra Practice

1. Consider the graph of $f(x) = -2x^2 - \frac{1}{2}$.
Determine if each statement is True or False.

A. The vertex is $\left(-2, \frac{1}{2}\right)$. ○ True ● False

B. The maximum value is $-\frac{1}{2}$. ● True ○ False

C. The axis of symmetry is $x = -2$. ○ True ● False

2. Does the given statement describe a step in the transformation of the graph of $f(x) = x^2$ that would result in the graph of $g(x) = -5(x + 2)^2$?

A. The parent function is reflected across the x-axis. ● Yes ○ No

B. The parent function is stretched by a factor of 5. ● Yes ○ No

C. The parent function is translated 2 units up. ○ Yes ● No

3. Use the graph of $f(x)$ to determine if each statement is True or False.

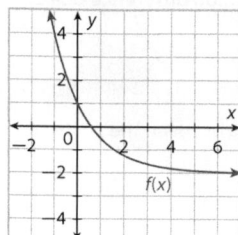

A. As $x \to \infty, y \to -2$. ● True ○ False

B. The graph represents a quadratic function. ○ True ● False

C. When $f(x) = 1, x = 0$. ● True ○ False

4. Solve $\left(2x + \frac{2}{3}\right)(x + 5) = 0$. Is each of the following a solution of the equation?

A. $x = -\frac{1}{3}$ ● Yes ○ No

B. $x = -5$ ● Yes ○ No

C. $x = \frac{2}{3}$ ○ Yes ● No

COMMON CORE | ## Common Core Standards

Items	Content Standards	Mathematical Practices
1	**F-IF.B.4**	**MP.7**
2	**F-BF.B.3**	**MP.7**
3*	**F-LE.A.1.b, F-IF.A.2**	**MP.1**
4	**A-APR.B.3**	**MP.2**
5	**A-REI.D.11**	**MP.4**
6	**F-IF.B.4, F-IF.C.8**	**MP.4**
7*	**A-APR.A.1, F-IF.C.7c**	**MP.4**

* Item integrates mixed review concepts from previous modules or a previous course.

5. Use the table of values for $h(x)$ to determine if each statement is True or False.

x	−4	−2	0	2	4
h(x)	3	0	−3	0	3

A. A zero of the function is −3.   ○ True   ● False

B. A zero of the function is −2.   ● True   ○ False

C. A solution of the equation $h(x) = 0$ is $x = 2$.   ● True   ○ False

6. Graph $y = -2x^2 + 16x - 31$. What is the axis of symmetry of the graph? What is its vertex?

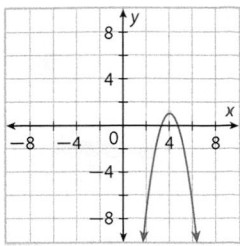

The axis of symmetry is $x = 4$; the vertex is $(4, 1)$.

7. Graph $t(x) = \frac{1}{2}(x + 2)(x - 4)$, and write the function in standard form.

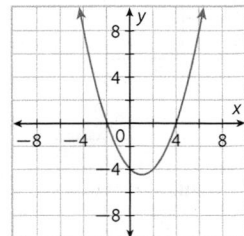

$t(x) = \frac{1}{2}x^2 - x - 4$

Performance Tasks

★ **8.** A rectangular picture measuring 6 in. by 10 in. is surrounded by a frame with uniform width x.

A. Write a quadratic function to show the combined area of the picture and frame.

B. Write a quadratic function for the area of the frame.

A. $f(x) = 4x^2 + 32x + 60$

B. $A(x) = 4x^2 + 32x$

PERFORMANCE TASKS

There are three different levels of performance tasks:

* Novice: These are short word problems that require students to apply the math they have learned in straightforward, real-world situations.

** Apprentice: These are more involved problems that guide students step-by-step through more complex tasks. These exercises include more complicated reasoning, writing, and open-ended elements.

***Expert: These are open-ended, nonroutine problems that, instead of stepping the students through, ask them to choose their own methods for solving and justify their answers and reasoning.

SCORING GUIDES

Item 8 (2 points)

A. 1 point for correct function for combined area

B. 1 point for correct function for frame area

Item 9 (6 points)

A. 2 points for reasonable estimate

B. 2 points for reasonable estimate

C. 2 points for explanation

Item 10 (6 points)

A. 3 points for correct demonstration

B. 2 points for correct graph

C. 1 point for correct answer

★★ **9. Estimation** The graph shows the approximate height y in meters of a volleyball x seconds after it is served.

    A. Estimate the time it takes for the volleyball to reach its greatest height.

    B. Estimate the greatest height that the volleyball reaches.

    C. If the domain of a quadratic function is all real numbers, why is the domain of this function limited to nonnegative numbers?

    A. about 0.375 s

    B. about 2.25 m

    C. The independent variable x represents the time since the volleyball is served, so this makes sense only for nonnegative numbers.

★★★**10.** A rocket team is using simulation software to create and study water bottle rockets. The team begins by simulating the launch of a rocket without a parachute. The table gives data for one rocket design.

    A. Show that the data represent a quadratic function.

    B. Graph the function.

    C. The acceleration due to gravity is 9.8 m/s². How is this number related to the data for this water bottle rocket?

Time (s)	Height (m)
0	0
1	34.3
2	58.8
3	73.5
4	78.4
5	73.5
6	58.8
7	34.3
8	0

A.

Time (s)	Height (m)
0	0
1	34.3
2	58.8
3	73.5
4	78.4
5	73.5
6	58.8
7	34.3
8	0

+34.3   −9.8
+24.5   −9.8
+14.7   −9.8
+4.9   −9.8
−4.9   −9.8
−14.7   −9.8
−24.5   −9.8
−34.3

B.

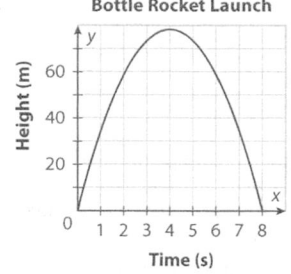

Bottle Rocket Launch

C. The acceleration is the absolute value of the second differences.

Transportation Engineer The Center for Transportation Analysis in the Oak Ridge National Laboratory publishes data about the transportation industry. One study relates gas mileage and a car's speed. The mileage (in miles per gallon) for a particular year, make, and model of car is shown in the table.

a. Identify the independent and dependent variables in this situation. State the units associated with each variable.

b. Make a scatter plot of the data, and sketch a parabola that you think best fits the plotted points. (You will not be able to make the parabola pass through all the points. Instead, you should try to draw the parabola so that some points fall above it and some below it.) Explain why a parabola is a reasonable curve to fit to the data.

c. Write the equation for a function of the form $m(s) = a(s - h)^2 + k$, where s is the speed and m is the gas mileage. Use the coordinates of the vertex of your parabola to determine h and k, and a point on your parabola other than the vertex to solve for the unknown a.

d. Suppose that when the car was driven at a steady speed, its gas mileage was 25 miles per gallon. Describe how you can use your model to find the car's speed. Is only one speed or more than one speed possible? Explain, and then find the speed(s).

Speed (miles per hour)	Gas Mileage (miles per gallon)
40	23.0
50	27.3
55	29.1
60	28.2
70	22.9

a. **Independent variable: speed (in miles per hour); dependent variable: gas mileage (in miles per gallon)**

b. **As speed increases, the gas mileage increases and then decreases, so a parabola that opens down is a reasonable fit. Possible answer:**

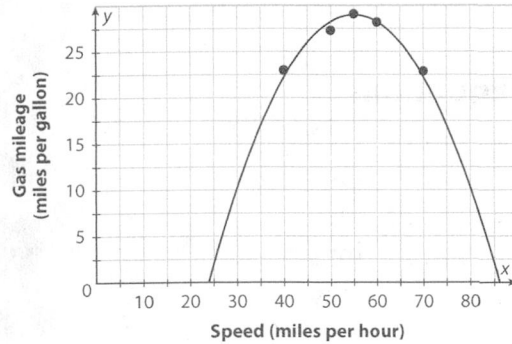

c. **Possible answer: $m(s) = -0.03(s - 55)^2 + 29$**

d. **Possible answer based on the model $m(s) = -0.03(s - 55)^2 + 29$:**

Let $m(s) = 25$ and solve for s; two speeds, because 25 mpg is less than the maximum value of 29.1 mpg; $s \approx 43.5$ mph or $s \approx 66.5$ mph.

Transportation Engineer In this Unit Performance Task, students can see how a transportation engineer uses mathematics on the job.

For more information about careers in mathematics as well as various mathematics appreciation topics, visit the American Mathematical Society at http://www.ams.org.

SCORING GUIDE

Task (6 points)

a. 1 point for correct answer

b. 1 point for reasonable graph
   1 point for explanation

c. 1 point for reasonable function

d. 1 point for correct explanation
   1 point for correct speeds

Quadratic Equations and Modeling

CONTENTS

Unit Pacing Guide

45-Minute Classes

Module 21

DAY 1	DAY 2	DAY 3	DAY 4	
Lesson 21.1	Lesson 21.2	Lesson 21.3	Module Review and Assessment Readiness	

Module 22

DAY 1	DAY 2	DAY 3	DAY 4	DAY 5
Lesson 22.1	Lesson 22.1	Lesson 22.2	Lesson 22.2	Lesson 22.3

DAY 6	DAY 7	DAY 8		
Lesson 22.4	Lesson 22.5	Module Review and Assessment Readiness		

Module 23

DAY 1	DAY 2	DAY 3	DAY 4	DAY 5
Lesson 23.1	Lesson 23.1	Lesson 23.2	Lesson 23.2	Module Review and Assessment Readiness

DAY 6				
Unit Review and Assessment Readiness				

90-Minute Classes

Module 21

DAY 1	DAY 2
Lesson 21.1 Lesson 21.2	Lesson 21.3 Module Review and Assessment Readiness

Module 22

DAY 1	DAY 2	DAY 3	DAY 4
Lesson 22.1	Lesson 22.2	Lesson 22.3 Lesson 22.4	Lesson 22.5 Module Review and Assessment Readiness

Module 23

DAY 1	DAY 2	DAY 3
Lesson 23.1	Lesson 23.2	Module Review and Assessment Readiness Unit Review and Assessment Readiness

Program Resources

PLAN

HMH Teacher App

Access a full suite of teacher resources online and offline on a variety of devices. Plan present, and manage classes, assignments, and activities.

ePlanner Easily plan your classes, create and view assignments, and access all program resources with your online, customizable planning tool.

Professional Development Videos

Authors Juli Dixon and Matt Larson model successful teaching practices and strategies in actual classroom settings.

QR Codes Scan with your smart phone to jump directly from your print book to online videos and other resources.

Teacher's Edition

Support students with point-of-use Questioning Strategies, teaching tips, resources for differentiated instruction, additional activities, and more.

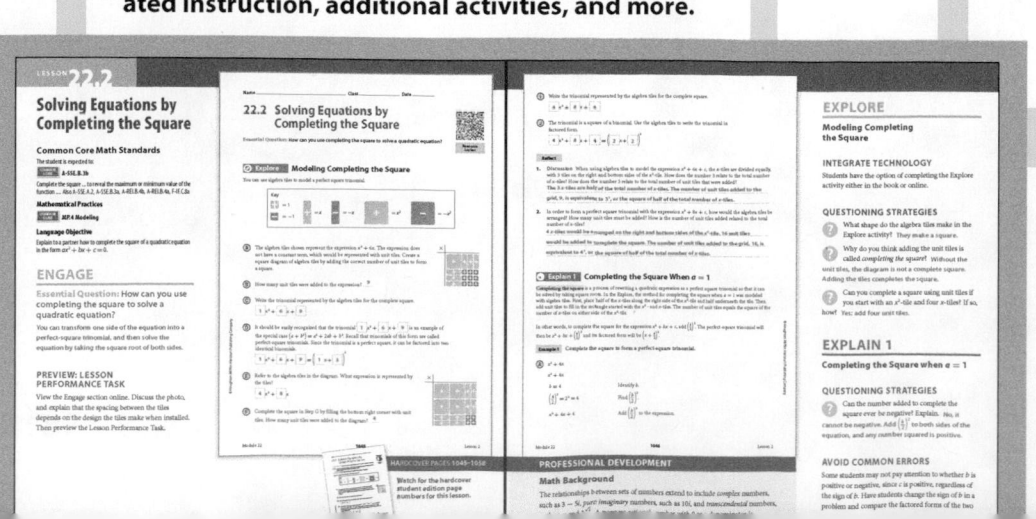

ENGAGE AND EXPLORE

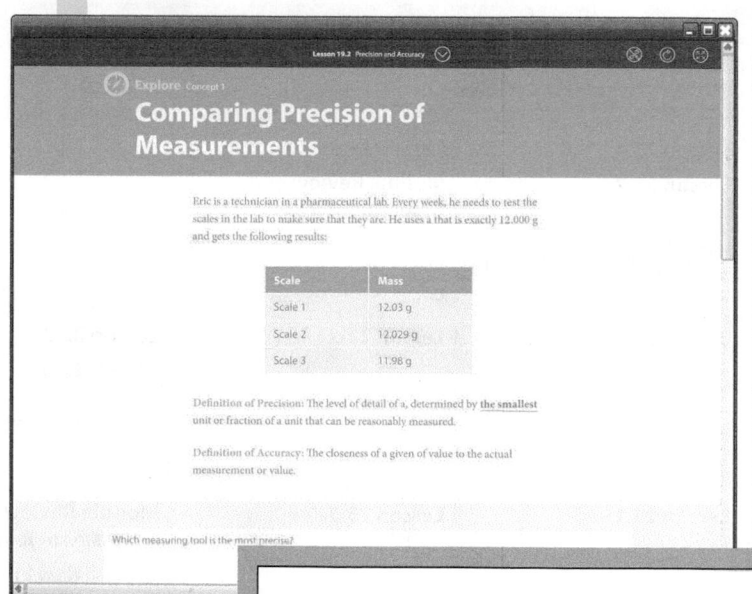

Real-World Videos Engage students with interesting and relevant applications of the mathematical content of each module.

Explore Activities

Students interactively explore new concepts using a variety of tools and approaches.

Comparing Precision of Measurements

Eric is a technician in a pharmaceutical lab. Every week, he needs to test the scales in the lab to make sure that they are. He uses a that is exactly 12.000 g and gets the following results:

Scale	Mass
Scale 1	12.03 g
Scale 2	12.029 g
Scale 3	11.98 g

Definition of Precision: The level of detail of a, determined by <u>the smallest</u> unit or fraction of a unit that can be reasonably measured.

Definition of Accuracy: The closeness of a given of value to the actual measurement or value.

Which measuring tool is the most precise?

Name _____ Class _____ Date _____

22.2 Solving Equations by Completing the Square

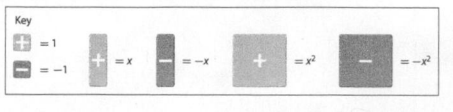

Resource Locker

Essential Question: How can you use completing the square to solve a quadratic equation?

COMMON CORE **A-SSE.B.3b** Complete the square ... to reveal the maximum or minimum value of the function ... Also A-SSE.A.2, A-SSE.B.3a, A-REI.B.4b, A-REI.B.4a, F-IF.C.8a

Explore   Modeling Completing the Square

You can use algebra tiles to model a perfect square trinomial.

Key

| $+$ = 1 | | $+$ = x | $-$ = $-x$ | $+$ = x^2 | $-$ = $-x^2$ |

| $-$ = -1 | | | | | |

(A) The algebra tiles shown represent the expression $x^2 + 6x$. The expression does not have a constant term, which would be represented with unit tiles. Create a square diagram of algebra tiles by adding the correct number of unit tiles to form a square.

(B) How many unit tiles were added to the expression? _____

(C) Write the trinomial represented by the algebra tiles for the complete square.

$\boxed{}\,x^2 + \boxed{}\,x + \boxed{}$

(D) It should be easily recognized that the trinomial $\boxed{}\,x^2 + \boxed{}\,x + \boxed{}$ is an example of the special case $(a + b^2) = a^2 + 2ab + b^2$. Recall that trinomials of this form are called

TEACH

Math On the Spot video tutorials, featuring program author Dr. Edward Burger, accompany every example in the textbook and give students step-by-step instructions and explanations of key math concepts.

Interactive Teacher Edition

Customize and present course materials with collaborative activities and integrated formative assessment.

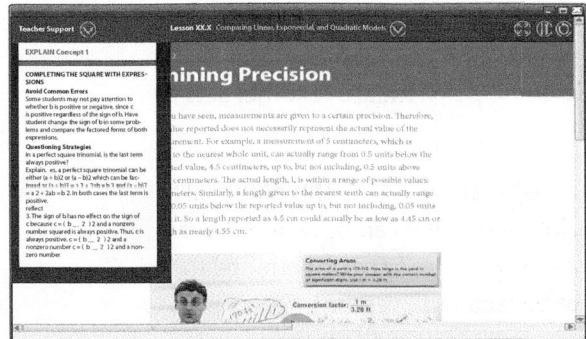

Differentiated Instruction Resources

Support all learners with Differentiated Instruction Resources, including

- **Leveled Practice and Problem Solving**
- **Reading Strategies**
- **Success for English Learners**
- **Challenge**

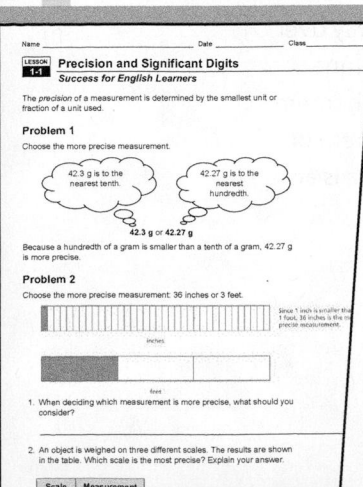

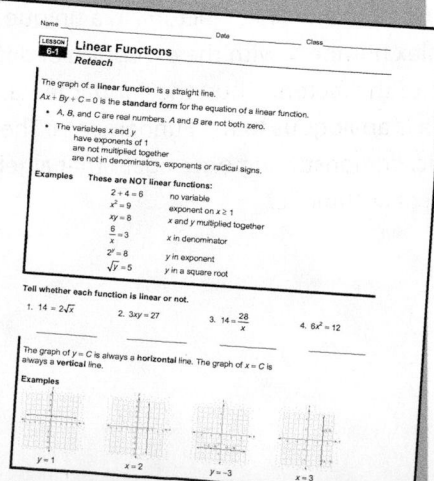

ASSESSMENT AND INTERVENTION

The **Personal Math Trainer** provides online practice, homework, assessments, and intervention. Monitor student progress through reports and alerts. **Create and customize assignments aligned to specific lessons or Common Core standards.**

- **Practice** – With dynamic items and assignments, students get unlimited practice on key concepts supported by guided examples, step-by-step solutions, and video tutorials.

- **Assessments** – Choose from course assignments or customize your own based on course content, Common Core standards, difficulty levels, and more.

- **Homework** – Students can complete online homework with a wide variety of problem types, including the ability to enter expressions, equations, and graphs. Let the system automatically grade homework, so you can focus where your students need help the most!

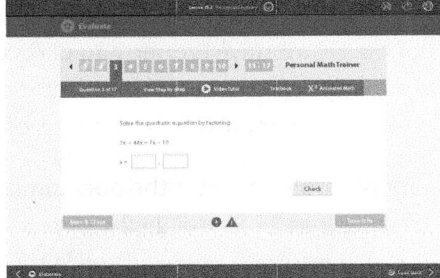

- **Intervention** – Let the Personal Math Trainer automatically prescribe a targeted, personalized intervention path for your students.

Focus on Higher Order Thinking

Raise the bar with homework and practice that incorporates higher-order thinking and mathematical practices in every lesson.

Assessment Readiness

Prepare students for success on high stakes tests for Algebra 1 with practice at every module and unit

COMMON CORE

Assessment Resources

Tailor assessments and response to intervention to meet the needs of all your classes and students, including

- Leveled Module Quizzes
- Leveled Unit Tests
- Unit Performance Tasks
- Placement, Diagnostic, and Quarterly Benchmark Tests
- Tier 1, Tier 2, and Tier 3 Resources

Math Background

Factoring Polynomials A-SSE.B.3a

LESSON 21.1

Algebra is an extension of arithmetic. As such, there are many parallels between the two. For example, the arithmetic idea of factoring a number can be extended into the realm of algebra by considering factorizations of polynomials.

Factoring polynomials is an essential algebraic skill. As students will see, it provides a powerful method for solving quadratic equations. However, students must first develop an arsenal of techniques for factoring.

Factoring Methods A-REI.B.4b

LESSON 21.2

The simplest factoring methods are direct applications of the Distributive Property. In particular, the Distributive Property makes it possible to factor out the greatest common factor (GCF) of the terms of a polynomial.

For example, to factor the polynomial $3x^2 + 12x^3$, we may rewrite it as $3 \cdot x \cdot x + 2 \cdot 2 \cdot 3 \cdot x \cdot x \cdot x$, where the integer coefficients have been written in their prime factorizations. This form of the polynomial makes it easy to see that the GCF of the terms is $3x^2$, and by the Distributive Property, $3x^2 + 12x^3 = 3x^2(1 + 4x)$.

The Distributive Property is also at work when students use more general methods to factor binomials. To factor the polynomial $x^2 + 7x + 12$, students will look for two factors of 12 whose sum is 7. This leads to the factorization $(x + 4)(x + 3)$. However, it is instructive to look at the intermediate steps. Once the correct factors of 12 have been identified, we can write

1. $x^2 + 7x + 12 = x^2 + 3x + 4x + 12$

2. $ = x(x + 3) + 4(2x + 3)$

3. $ = (x + 4)(x + 3)$

The Distributive Property has been used twice to go from Step 1 to Step 2 and has been applied again to go from Step 2 to Step 3. It is also useful to recognize that the polynomial on the right side of the equation in

Step 1 consists precisely of the set of terms that result from multiplying $(x + 4)(x + 3)$ by using the FOIL method. In other words, multiplying polynomials and factoring polynomials are inverse processes based on the Distributive Property.

Unfactorable Polynomials A-SSE.B.3b

LESSON 22.2

Students should understand that some polynomials cannot be factored. For example, the trinomials $x^2 + x + 1$ and $2x^2 + 5x + 4$ are unfactorable. We call these polynomials *prime polynomials*.

Note that when we say a polynomial is unfactorable in an Algebra 1 course, this generally means that it cannot be factored *over the integers*. In other words, the polynomial cannot be written as a product of polynomials of lesser degree whose terms have integer coefficients. However, it may be possible to factor the polynomial over other sets of numbers.

For example, consider the binomial $x^2 - 2$. This binomial is unfactorable over the integers, but it can be factored over the real numbers as $(x + \sqrt{2})(x - \sqrt{2})$. Furthermore, the binomial $x^2 + 4$ cannot be factored over the integers or over the real numbers, but it can be factored over the complex numbers as $(x + 2i)(x - 2i)$, where $i = \sqrt{-1}$. (Students will be introduced to the set of complex numbers in Algebra 2.)

To take this a step further, the Fundamental Theorem of Algebra asserts that every polynomial with complex coefficients of degree $n \geq 1$ has n complex roots, counted with multiplicity. As a result, every polynomial can be completely factored (that is, written as a product of a complex number and linear factors) in a unique way over the complex numbers, with the exception of different orderings of the factors. Thus, the Fundamental Theorem of Algebra is analogous to the Fundamental Theorem of Arithmetic, demonstrating once again that algebra is an extension of arithmetic.

Solution Methods  A-REI.B.4b

LESSONS 21.1, 21.2, 22.1 to 22.4

Although graphing has the advantage of being a fairly intuitive solution method, it is often inefficient and imprecise. These drawbacks motivate the choice of other solution techniques.

The method of solving a quadratic equation by factoring springs from the Zero Product Property: If the product of two real numbers is zero, then at least one of the numbers is zero. This property justifies solving quadratic equations by factoring. For example, to solve $x^2 + x - 6 = 0$, note that $x^2 + x - 6 = (x - 2)(x + 3)$. By the Zero Product Property, it must be true that $x - 2 = 0$ or $x + 3 = 0$, which gives the solutions 2 and -3.

Some quadratic equations do not lend themselves to factoring, so still more methods are needed. The techniques of completing the square and using the Quadratic Formula work for *any* quadratic equation. It is essential for students to realize that graphing, factoring, and the Quadratic Formula can be used to solve quadratic equations only when one side of the quadratic equation is equal to zero (that is, the equation is written in standard form).

Comparing Linear, Quadratic, and Exponential Models  F-LE.A.3

LESSON 23.2

Understanding types of functions helps to decide which type to use when modeling. Some key understandings are as follows:

- Examining the end behavior of a function requires looking at the corresponding y-values of the graph of the function as x gets very large or very small.
- To examine the rate of growth of a function, look at the successive differences.
- For linear, quadratic, and exponential functions, certain patterns emerge indicating when and where the functions increase or decrease on specific intervals.

Linear functions grow by equal differences over equal intervals, while for quadratic functions, the second differences are equal over equal intervals, but not the first differences. Notice that graphs that grow exponentially eventually exceed both linear and quadratic graphs over the same interval. Using the proper tools to find an appropriate model is a necessary and continually practiced skill.

Quadratic Equations and Modeling

MATH IN CAREERS
Unit Activity Preview

After completing this unit, students will complete a Math in Careers task by modeling the heights of two divers with equations for projectile motion. Critical skills include modeling real-world situations and interpreting the graphs of quadratic functions.

For more information about careers in mathematics as well as various mathematics appreciation topics, visit The American Mathematical Society at http://www.ams.org.

Quadratic Equations and Modeling

MODULE 21
Using Factors to Solve Quadratic Equations

MODULE 22
Using Square Roots to Solve Quadratic Equations

MODULE 23
Linear, Exponential, and Quadratic Models

MATH IN CAREERS

Competitive Diver Diving is the sport of jumping into the water from a springboard or platform. Competitive divers should have a strong understanding of the mathematics of projectile motion, including the time spent in the air, the speed at which they hit the water, and the maximum height of a jump.

If you are interested in a career as a competitive diver, you should study these mathematical subjects:
- Algebra
- Business math

Research other careers that require understanding of the mathematics of projectile motion. Check out the career activity at the end of the unit to find out how **competitive divers** use math.

Unit 9   981

TRACKING YOUR LEARNING PROGRESSION

Before	In this Unit	After
Students understand: • graphing quadratic functions • the vertex and standard form of quadratic functions • intercepts and zeros • the Zero Product Property	Students will learn about: • solving quadratic equations by factoring • solving quadratic equations by completing the square • using the quadratic formula to solve equations • comparing linear, quadratic, and exponential models	Students will study: • inverse functions • graphs of polynomial, square root, and cube root functions

Reading Start-Up

Visualize Vocabulary

Use the ✔ words to complete the chart.

perfect square	a square of a whole number
square root	one of two equal factors of a number
greatest common factor	the largest common factor of two or more given numbers
irrational number	a real number that cannot be expressed as the ratio of two integers
coefficient	a number that is multiplied by a variable

Understand Vocabulary

To become familiar with some of the vocabulary terms in this unit, consider the following. You may refer to the module, the glossary, or a dictionary.

1. The **quadratic formula** gives the solutions of a quadratic equation.
2. **Completing the square** is a process that forms a perfect square trinomial.
3. By the **Quotient Property of Square Roots**, $\pm\sqrt{\frac{16}{9}} = \pm\frac{\sqrt{16}}{\sqrt{9}} = \pm\frac{4}{3}$.

Active Reading

Pyramid Before beginning this unit create a pyramid to help you organize what you learn. Label each side with one of the module titles from this unit: "Using Factors to Solve Quadratic Equations," "Using Square Roots to Solve Quadratic Equations," and "Linear, Exponential, and Quadratic Models." As you study each module, write important ideas like vocabulary, properties, and formulas on the appropriate side.

Have students complete the activities on this page by working alone or with others.

VISUALIZE VOCABULARY

The definition chart graphic helps students review vocabulary associated with quadratic equations. If time allows, ask students to provide several examples to add to each definition.

UNDERSTAND VOCABULARY

Use the following explanations to help students learn the preview words.

To solve a quadratic equation means to find its roots. Factoring, **completing the square**, and the **quadratic formula** are different methods that can be used to solve quadratic equations. The **quadratic formula** uses the coefficients of the terms to find the roots. **Completing the square** is a process used to form a perfect-square trinomial that is factorable. The **difference of two squares** can be factored into a product in which the factors are the sum and difference of the square roots of the squares.

ACTIVE READING

Students can use these reading and note-taking strategies to help them organize and understand the new concepts and vocabulary. Encourage students to ask for additional help in understanding increasingly specific vocabulary.

ADDITIONAL RESOURCES

Differentiated Instruction

- Reading Strategies **EL**

Vocabulary

Review Words

✔ coefficient *(coeficiente)*

✔ greatest common factor *(máximo común divisor (MCD))*

✔ irrational number *(número irracional)*

✔ perfect square *(cuadrado perfecto)*

✔ square root *(raíz cuadrada)*

Preview Words

completing the square *(completar el cuadrado)*

difference of two squares *(diferencia de dos cuadrados)*

Product Property of Square Roots *(Propiedad del producto de raíces cuadradas)*

quadratic formula *(fórmula cuadrática)*

Quotient Property of Square Roots *(Propiedad del cociente de raíces cuadradas)*

Using Factors to Solve Quadratic Equations

ESSENTIAL QUESTION:

Answer: Real-world situations involving topics such as height of an object thrown, velocity, and profit, can sometimes be modeled by factorable quadratic equations in standard form.

PROFESSIONAL DEVELOPMENT VIDEO

Professional Development Video

Author Juli Dixon models successful teaching practices in an actual high-school classroom.

Professional Development

my.hrw.com

Using Factors to Solve Quadratic Equations

MODULE **21**

Essential Question: How can you use factoring a quadratic equation to solve real-world problems?

LESSON 21.1
Solving Equations by Factoring $x^2 + bx + c$

LESSON 21.2
Solving Equations by Factoring $ax^2 + bx + c$

LESSON 21.3
Using Special Factors to Solve Equations

REAL WORLD VIDEO
Ruling out common elements in a scientific experiment is similar to removing common factors in an equation; logically, whatever is common to two samples can't be the cause of differences between them.

MODULE PERFORMANCE TASK PREVIEW

Fitting Through the Arch

An arched doorway is a strong structure that can usually support more weight than a rectangular doorway. An arched opening is also far less likely than a rectangular opening to topple from vibrations of a train passing through it. However, many man-made objects are rectangular, not curved as an arch is curved. So, how big can a rectangular object be and still pass through an arched door? Let's find out!

Module 21   **983**

DIGITAL TEACHER EDITION

Access a full suite of teaching resources when and where you need them:

- Access content online or offline
- Customize lessons to share with your class
- Communicate with your students in real-time
- View student grades and data instantly to target your instruction where it is needed most

PERSONAL MATH TRAINER

Assessment and Intervention

Assign automatically graded homework, quizzes, tests, and intervention activities. Prepare your students with updated, Common Core-aligned practice tests.

Are Ready?

Complete these exercises to review skills you will need for this module.

Exponents

Example 1   Simplify $8^5 \cdot 8^{-2}$.

$8^5 \cdot 8^{-2} = 8^{5 + (-2)}$ The bases are the same. Add the exponents.

$= 8^3$

$= 512$ Multiply.

• Online Homework
• Hints and Help
• Extra Practice

Simplify.

1. $3^7 \cdot 3^{-3}$

81

2. $7^7 \cdot 7^{-5}$

49

3. $6^9 \cdot 6^{-4} \cdot 6^{-5}$

1

Algebraic Expressions

Example 2   Simplify $13x + 5 - 9x^2 - 8$.

$13x + 5 - 9x^2 - 8$

$-9x^2 + 13x + 5 - 8$ Reorder in descending order of exponents.

$-9x^2 + 13x - 3$ Combine like terms.

Simplify.

4. $12x + 4x^2 - 3 - 7x$

$4x^2 + 5x - 3$

5. $7x^2 - 6 + 8x - 2x^2$

$5x^2 + 8x - 6$

6. $5 + 7x - 2x^2 - 6$

$-2x^2 + 7x - 1$

7. $-4x + 6x^2 - 8 + 9x - 3x^2$

$3x^2 + 5x - 8$

Example 3   Multiply $(x + 7)(x - 3)$.

$(x + 7)(x - 3)$

$x(x) - 3(x) + 7(x) + 7(-3)$ Use FOIL.

$x^2 - 3x + 7x - 21$ Simplify.

$x^2 + 4x - 21$ Combine like terms.

Multiply.

8. $(x - 4)(x + 5)$

$x^2 + x - 20$

9. $(x - 9)(x - 6)$

$x^2 - 15x + 54$

10. $(2x - 3)(2x + 3)$

$4x^2 - 9$

11. $(3x - 2)(2x + 5)$

$6x^2 + 11x - 10$

Are You Ready?

ASSESS READINESS

Use the assessment on this page to determine if students need strategic or intensive intervention for the module's prerequisite skills.

ASSESSMENT AND INTERVENTION

RtI Response to Intervention **TIER 1, TIER 2, TIER 3 SKILLS**

Personal Math Trainer will automatically create a standards-based, personalized intervention assignment for your students, targeting each student's individual needs!

ADDITIONAL RESOURCES

See the table below for a full list of intervention resources available for this module.

Response to Intervention Resources also includes:

• Tier 2 Skill Pre-Tests for each Module
• Tier 2 Skill Post-Tests for each skill

Response to Intervention			Differentiated Instruction
Tier 1 Lesson Intervention Worksheets	**Tier 2** Strategic Intervention Skills Intervention Worksheets	**Tier 3** Intensive Intervention Worksheets available online	
Reteach 21.1 Reteach 21.2 Reteach 21.3	2 Algebraic Expressions 5 Exponents 21 Two-Step Equations	Building Block Skills 19, 22, 23, 24, 27, 29, 30, 40, 59, 69, 76, 81, 98, 100	Challenge worksheets Extend the Math Lesson Activities in TE

Module 21   **984**

Solving Equations by Factoring $x^2 + bx + c$

Common Core Math Standards

The student is expected to:

 **A-SSE.B.3a**

Factor a quadratic expression to reveal the zeros of the function it defines. Also A-SSE.A.2, A-REI.B.4b

Mathematical Practices

 **MP.7 Using Structure**

Language Objective

Explain to a partner how to solve $x^2 - 6x - 16 = 0$.

ENGAGE

Essential Question: How can you use factoring to solve quadratic equations in standard form for which $a = 1$?

Factor the quadratic equation. Set each linear factor equal to 0. Solve each linear equation. The solutions are the solutions of the original quadratic equation.

PREVIEW: LESSON PERFORMANCE TASK

View the Engage section online. Discuss how green roofs can help control storm-water runoff and reduce stress on sewer systems. Then preview the Lesson Performance Task.

Name_____ Class_____ Date_____

21.1 Solving Equations by Factoring $x^2 + bx + c$

Essential Question: How can you use factoring to solve quadratic equations in standard form for which $a = 1$?

⊘ Explore 1   Using Algebra Tiles to Factor $x^2 + bx + c$

In this lesson, multiplying binomials using the FOIL process will be reversed and trinomials will be factored into two binomials. To learn how to factor, let's start with the expression $x^2 + 7x + 6$.

(A) Identify and draw the tiles needed to model the expression $x^2 + 7x + 6$.

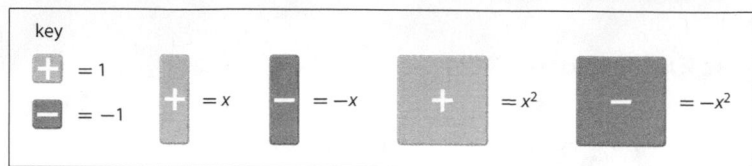

The tiles needed to model the expression $x^2 + 7x + 6$ are:

____1____ x^2-tiles(s), ____7____ x-tile(s), and ____6____ unit tile(s).

(B) Arrange and draw the algebra tiles on the grid. Place the ____1____ x^2-tile(s) in the upper left

corner and arrange the ____6____ unit tiles in two rows and three columns in the lower right corner.

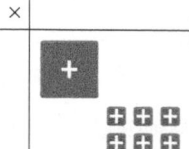

(C) Try to complete the rectangle with the x-tiles. Notice that only ____5____ x-tiles fit on the grid,

which leaves out ____2____ tile(s), so this arrangement is not correct.

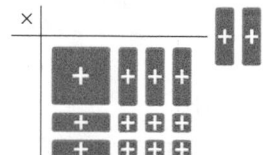

(D) Rearrange the unit tiles so that all of the ____7____ x-tiles fit on the mat.

© Houghton Mifflin Harcourt Publishing Company

HARDCOVER PAGES 771–780

Turn to these pages to find this lesson in the hardcover student edition.

(E) Complete the multiplication grid by placing the factor tiles on the sides. Then write the factors modeled in this product.

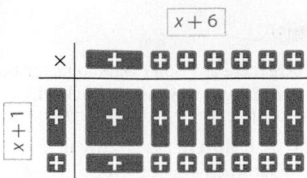

$$x^2 + 7x + 6 = \left(x + \boxed{1}\right)\left(x + \boxed{6}\right)$$

(F) Now let's look at how to factor a quadratic expression with a negative constant term. Use algebra tiles to factor $x^2 + x - 2$. Identify the tiles needed to model the expression.

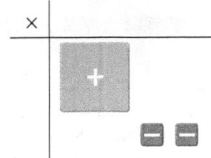

__1__ positive x^2-tile(s), __1__ positive x-tile(s), and __2__ negative unit tile(s)

(G) Arrange the algebra tiles on the grid. Place the __1__ positive x^2-tile(s) in the upper left

corner and arrange the __2__ negative unit tiles in the lower right corner.

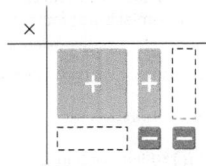

(H) Try to fill in the empty spaces on the grid with x tiles. There is/are __1__ positive x-tile(s) to

place on the grid, so there will be __2__ empty places for x-tiles.

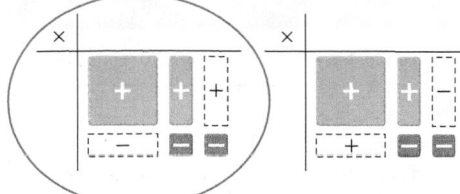

(I) Complete the rectangle on the mat by using *zero pairs*. Add __1__ positive x-tile(s) and __1__ negative x-tile(s) to the grid in such a way that the factors work with all the tiles on the mat. Circle the mat showing the correct position of zero pairs.

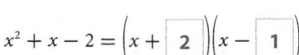

(J) Complete the multiplication grid by placing the factor tiles on the sides. Then write the factors modeled in this product.

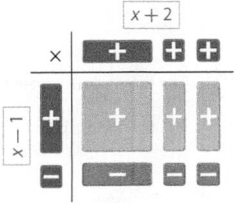

$$x^2 + x - 2 = \left(x + \boxed{2}\right)\left(x - \boxed{1}\right)$$

EXPLORE 1

Using Algebra Tiles to Factor $x^2 + bx + c$

INTEGRATE TECHNOLOGY

Students have the option of completing the algebra tiles activity either in the book or online.

QUESTIONING STRATEGIES

? When using algebra tiles to factor a polynomial, when do you need to add a zero pair of x-tiles? You need to add a zero pair when there are empty spaces in the grid but there is no way to rearrange the tiles that are already there to fill those spaces. By adding one positive x-tile and one negative x-tile, you fill in the grid without changing the value of the original polynomial.

PROFESSIONAL DEVELOPMENT

Learning Progressions

In this lesson, students learn to reverse the process of multiplying two binomials with FOIL to find two binomials whose product is a given trinomial. Some key understandings for students are as follows:

- To factor a trinomial $x^2 + bx + c$, list factor pairs of c, then use the factor pair whose sum is equal to b to factor the trinomial.

- To solve an equation of the form $x^2 + bx + c = 0$, factor the trinomial, then set each factor equal to 0 and solve for x.

Solving Equations by Factoring $x^2 + bx + c$ **986**

EXPLORE 2

Factoring $x^2 + bx + c$

QUESTIONING STRATEGIES

? How are the terms in a trinomial of the form $x^2 + bx + c$ related to the four products in the FOIL method (First, Outer, Inner, Last)? The x^2-term is the product of the two First terms in the binomial. The term bx is the sum of the products of the Outer terms and the Inner terms. The constant c is the product of the two Last terms in the two binomials.

VISUAL CUES

When factoring a trinomial of the form $x^2 + bx + c$, suggest that students start by writing down what the product and sum of the two constants in the binomials should be. They can write P for product and S for sum next to the trinomial as a reminder to complete this step. Remind students to include the sign for each product or sum as they write it.

© Houghton Mifflin Harcourt Publishing Company

Reflect

1. Are there any other ways to factor the polynomial $x^2 + 7x + 6$ besides $(x + 6)(x + 1)$? Explain.
   No, 2-by-3 was also checked.

2. **Discussion** If c is positive in $x^2 + bx + c$, what sign can the constant terms of the factors have? What about when c is negative?
   If c is positive, then both factors are positive or both factors are negative.

   If c is negative, the factors have opposite signs.

⊘ Explore 2   Factoring $x^2 + bx + c$

To factor $x^2 + bx + c$, you need to find two factors of c whose sum is b.

Factoring $x^2 + bx + c$	
WORDS	**EXAMPLE**
To factor a quadratic trinomial of the form $x^2 + bx + c$, find two factors of c whose sum is b. If no such Integers exist, the trinomial is not factorable.	To factor $x^2 + 9x + 18$, look for factors of 18 whose sum is 9. Factors of 18 Sum 1 and 18 19 x 2 and 9 11 x 3 and 6 9 ✓ $x^2 + 9x + 18 = (x + 3)(x + 6)$

If c is positive, the constant terms of the factors have the same sign.

If c is negative, then one constant term of the factors is positive and one is negative.

(A) First, look at $x^2 + 11x + 30$. Find the values of b and c. $b = \boxed{11}$ $c = \boxed{30}$

(B) c is ⊙positive / negative. The sign of the factors will be ⊙the same / different.

(C) List the factor pairs of c, 30, and find the sum of each pair.

Factors of 30	Sum of Factors
1 and $\boxed{30}$	$1 + \boxed{30} = \boxed{31}$
2 and $\boxed{15}$	$2 + \boxed{15} = \boxed{17}$
3 and $\boxed{10}$	$3 + \boxed{10} = \boxed{13}$
5 and $\boxed{6}$	$5 + \boxed{6} = \boxed{11}$

(D) The factor pair whose sum equals b is ___5 and 6___.

Use this factor pair to factor the polynomial. $x^2 + 11x + 30 = \left(x + \boxed{5}\right)\left(x + \boxed{6}\right)$

COLLABORATIVE LEARNING

Peer-to-Peer Activity

Have students work in pairs. Each student should write two binomial factors of the form $(x + a)$ or $(x - a)$ and multiply them together to form a trinomial. Then have partners factor each other's trinomials. Have students check each other's work and discuss what makes some trinomials easier or harder to factor than others.

(E) Now, look at $x^2 + 13x - 30$. Find the values of b and c.

$b = \boxed{13}$ $c = \boxed{-30}$

(F) c is positive / (negative). The sign of the factors will be the same / (different).

(G) List the factor pairs of c, –30, and find the sum of each pair.

Factors of −30	Sum of Factors
1 and $\boxed{-30}$	$1 + \boxed{-30} = \boxed{-29}$
2 and $\boxed{-15}$	$2 + \boxed{-15} = \boxed{-13}$
3 and $\boxed{-10}$	$3 + \boxed{-10} = \boxed{-7}$
5 and $\boxed{-6}$	$5 + \boxed{-6} = \boxed{-1}$
−1 and $\boxed{30}$	$-1 + \boxed{30} = \boxed{29}$
−2 and $\boxed{15}$	$-2 + \boxed{15} = \boxed{13}$
−3 and $\boxed{10}$	$-3 + \boxed{10} = \boxed{7}$
−5 and $\boxed{6}$	$-5 + \boxed{6} = \boxed{1}$

(H) The factor pair whose sum equals b is $\underline{\text{15 and }-2}$.

Use this factor pair to factor the polynomial.

$x^2 + 13x - 30 = \left(x + \boxed{15}\right)\left(x - \boxed{2}\right)$

Reflect

3. **Discussion** When factoring a trinomial of the form $x^2 + bx + c$, where c is negative, one binomial factor contains a positive factor of c and one contains a negative factor of c. How do you know which factor of c should be positive and which should be negative?

If b is positive, the factor of c with the greater absolute value must be positive. If b is

negative, the factor of c with the greater absolute value is negative.

© Houghton Mifflin Harcourt Publishing Company

Focus on Math Connections

MP.1 Discuss with students how they can use the signs of b and c in $x^2 + bx + c$ to determine whether to use positive or negative factors of c to factor the trinomial. Work together to complete a table like the following:

	Sign of Constant Terms in Binomial Factors of $x^2 + bx + c$
$c > 0$, $b > 0$	both constants positive
$c > 0$, $b < 0$	both constants negative
$c < 0$	one constant positive, one constant negative

DIFFERENTIATE INSTRUCTION

Critical Thinking

Show students how to create quadratic equations with given solutions by working backward. For example, if the solutions are −2 and 5, then $x = -2$ or $x = 5$. The factors can be written as $(x + 2)(x - 5)$, which is equivalent to $x^2 - 3x - 10$. Therefore, the quadratic equation is $x^2 - 3x - 10 = 0$. Explain that an infinite number of equivalent equations can be generated by performing the same operation on both sides of this equation.

EXPLAIN 1

Solving Equations of the Form $x^2 + bx + c = 0$ by Factoring

AVOID COMMON ERRORS

When solving quadratic equations by factoring, students sometimes make the mistake of naming the constants in the binomial factors as the solutions. Remind students that they need to find the value of x that would make each factor equal to 0. For example, the solutions of $(x - 6)(x - 4) = 0$ are 6 and 4, not -6 and -4.

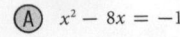 **Explain 1** **Solving Equations of the Form $x^2 + bx + c = 0$ by Factoring**

As you have learned, the Zero Product Property can be used to solve quadratic equations in factored form.

Example 1 Solve each equation by factoring. Check your answer by graphing.

Ⓐ $x^2 - 8x = -12$

First, write the equation in the form $x^2 - bx + c = 0$.

$$x^2 - 8x = -12 \qquad \text{Original equation}$$

$$x^2 - 8x + 12 = 0 \qquad \text{Add 12 to both sides.}$$

The expression $x^2 - 8x + 12$ is in the form $ax^2 + bx + c$, with $b < 0$ and $c > 0$, so the factors will have the same sign and they both will be negative.

Factors of 12	Sum of Factors
-1 and -12	$-1 + (-12) = -13$
-2 and -6	$-1 + (-12) = -8$
-3 and -4	$-1 + (-12) = -7$

The factor pair whose sum equals -8 is -2 and -6. Factor the equation, and use the Zero Product Property.

$$x^2 - 8x + 12 = 0$$

$$(x - 2)(x - 6) = 0$$

$$x - 2 = 0 \qquad \text{or} \qquad x - 6 = 0$$

$$x = 2 \qquad\qquad\qquad x = 6$$

The zeros of the equation are 2 and 6. Check this by graphing the related function, $f(x) = x^2 - 8x + 12$.

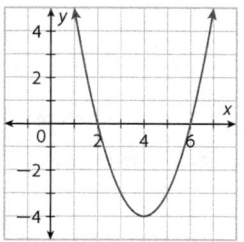

The x-intercepts of the graph are 2 and 6, which are the same as the zeros of the equation. The solutions of the equation are 2 and 6.

LANGUAGE SUPPORT **EL**

Auditory Cues

Have students explain how to factor $x^2 + bx + c$ when c is positive. Write out and model sentence frames for students to structure their answers. For example:

First find two numbers whose _____ is c and whose _____ is b. If c is positive, then both numbers are _____ or both are _____. If b is positive, then I choose the _____ factors of c. If b is negative, then I choose the _____ factors of c.

Ⓑ $x^2 - 2x = 15$

First, rewrite the expression in the form $x^2 + bx + c = 0$.

$x^2 - 2x = 15$ Original equation

$x^2 - 2x - \boxed{15} = 0$ Subtract 15 from both sides.

To find the zeros of the equation, start by factoring. List the factor pairs of c and find the sum of each pair. Since $c < 0$, the factors will have opposite signs. Since $c < 0$ and $b < 0$, the factor with the greater absolute value will be negative.

Factors of −15	Sum of Factors
1 and $\boxed{-15}$	$1 + \boxed{-15} = \boxed{-14}$
3 and $\boxed{-5}$	$3 + \boxed{-5} = \boxed{-2}$
-1 and $\boxed{15}$	$-1 + \boxed{15} - \boxed{14}$
-3 and $\boxed{5}$	$-3 + \boxed{5} = \boxed{2}$

The factor pair whose sum equals −2 is $\underline{3 \text{ and } -5}$. Factor the equation, and use the Zero Product Property.

$$x^2 - 2x - 15 = 0$$

$$\left(x + \boxed{3}\right)\left(x - \boxed{5}\right) = 0$$

$x + 3 = 0$ or $x - 5 = 0$

$x = \boxed{-3}$ $x = \boxed{5}$

The zeros of the equation are $\boxed{-3}$ and $\boxed{5}$. Check this by graphing the related function, $f(x) = x^2 - 2x = 15$.

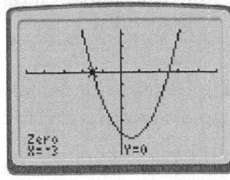 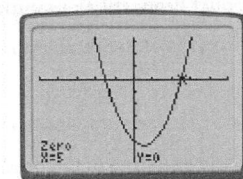

Your Turn

Solve each equation.

4. $x^2 + 15x = -54$

$x^2 + 15x + 54 = 0$
$(x + 6)(x + 9) = 0$
$x + 6 = 0$ or $x + 9 = 0$
$x = -6$ $x = -9$

5. $x^2 - 13x = -12$

$x^2 - 13x + 12 = 0$
$(x - 12)(x - 1) = 0$
$x - 12 = 0$ or $x - 1 = 0$
$x = 12$ $x = 1$

6. $x^2 - x = 56$

$x^2 - x - 56 = 0$
$(x + 7)(x - 8) = 0$
$x + 7 = 0$ or $x - 8 = 0$
$x = -7$ $x = 8$

QUESTIONING STRATEGIES

? After factoring a polynomial to solve an equation, why do you set each factor equal to zero? You set each factor equal to zero because, by the Zero Product Property, at least one of the factors must be zero if the product is equal to zero.

EXPLAIN 2

Solving Equation Models of the Form $x^2 + bx + c = 0$ by Factoring

QUESTIONING STRATEGIES

? A frame has dimensions $(x + 4)$ inches and $(x + 7)$ inches and a total area of 108 square inches. What polynomial do you need to factor in order to find the dimensions of the frame? Explain. $x^2 + 11x - 80$; you need to solve the equation $(x + 4)(x + 7) = 108$. To solve, rewrite it as $x^2 + 11x + 28 = 108$.

AVOID COMMON ERRORS

Students may forget to interpret the solutions using the context of the problem. Remind students that values that do not make sense in the context of the problem should not be listed as solutions.

ELABORATE

QUESTIONING STRATEGIES

? Alonso says the product of two binomials is always a trinomial. Max says that it is possible to multiply two binomials and get a product that is still a binomial. Who is correct? Max is correct. If you multiply two binomials with the same values but the opposite sign, the result is a binomial, for example $(x + 4)(x - 4) = x^2 - 16$.

SUMMARIZE THE LESSON

Have students copy the graphic organizer and then complete it by writing a step used to solve a quadratic equation in each box.

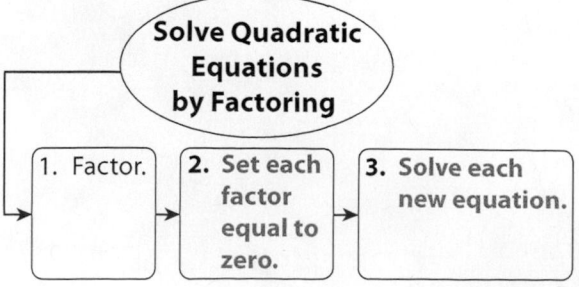

Explain 2 **Solving Equation Models of the Form $x^2 + bx + c = 0$ by Factoring**

Some real-world problems can be solved by factoring a quadratic equation.

Example 2 Solve each model by factoring.

Architecture A rectangular porch has dimensions of $(x + 12)$ and $(x + 5)$ feet. If the area of the porch floor is 120 square feet, what are its length and width?

Write an equation for the problem. Substitute 120 for A for the area of the porch.

$$(x + 12)(x + 5) = A$$

$$x^2 + 17x + 60 = A$$

$$x^2 + 17 + 60 = 120$$

$$x^2 + 17x - 60 = 0$$

The factors are of -60 that have a sum of 17 are 20 and -3. Use Zero Product Property to find x.

$$(x + 20)(x - 3) = 0$$

$$x + 20 = 0 \quad \text{or} \quad x - 3 = 0$$

$$x = -20 \qquad x = 3$$

Since the area cannot be negative, $x = 3$ feet.

Therefore, the dimensions of the porch are $3 + 12 = 15$ feet long and $3 + 5 = 8$ feet wide.

💬 Elaborate

7. How are the solutions of a quadratic equation related to the zeros of the related function?
By the Zero Product Property, the solutions found from the factored form of a quadratic equation are the zeros of the related function.

8. **Essential Question Check-In** How can you solve a quadratic equation by factoring?
Write the equation in standard form and find the factors of c that add to b. Use those factors to write the equation in factored form. Use the Zero Product Property to solve each linear equation.

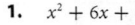

Use algebra tiles to model the factors of each expression.

1. $x^2 + 6x + 8$

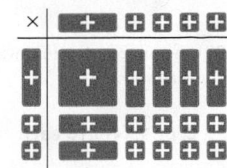

$x^2 + 6x + 8 = \left(x + \boxed{4}\right)\left(x + \boxed{2}\right)$

2. $x^2 + 2x - 3$

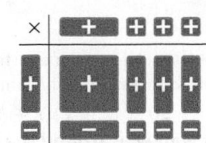

$x^2 + 2x - 3 = \left(x + \boxed{3}\right)\left(x - \boxed{1}\right)$

Factor the expressions.

3. $x^2 - 15x + 44$

$(x - 4)(x - 11)$

4. $x^2 + 22x + 120$

$(x + 10)(x + 12)$

5. $x^2 + 14x - 32$

$(x - 2)(x + 16)$

6. $x^2 - 12x - 45$

$(x + 3)(x - 15)$

7. $x^2 + 10x + 24$

$(x + 4)(x + 6)$

8. $x^2 + 7x - 8$

$(x - 1)(x + 8)$

Solve each equation.

9. $x^2 + 19x = -84$

$x^2 + 19x + 84 = 0$

$(x + 7)(x + 12) = 0$

$x + 7 = 0$ or $x + 12 = 0$

$x = -7$ $x = -12$

10. $x^2 - 18x = -56$

$x^2 - 18x + 56 = 0$

$(x - 4)(x - 14) = 0$

$x - 4 = 0$ or $x - 14 = 0$

$x = 4$ $x = 14$

11. $x^2 - 12x + 27 = 0$

$(x - 3)(x - 9) = 0$

$x - 3 = 0$ or $x - 9 = 0$

$x = 3$ $x = 9$

12. $x^2 - 9x - 10 = 0$

$(x + 1)(x - 10) = 0$

$x + 1 = 0$ or $x - 10 = 0$

$x = -1$ $x = 10$

13. $x^2 + 6x = 135$

$x^2 + 6x - 135 = 0$

$(x - 9)(x + 15) = 0$

$x - 9 = 0$ or $x + 15 = 0$

$x = 9$ $x = -15$

14. $x^2 + 13x = -40$

$x^2 + 13x + 40 = 0$

$(x + 5)(x + 8) = 0$

$x + 5 = 0$ or $x + 8 = 0$

$x = -5$ $x = -8$

Exercise	Depth of Knowledge (D.O.K.)	COMMON CORE Mathematical Practices
1–2	**1** Recall of Information	**MP.5** Using Tools
3–16	**1** Recall of Information	**MP.2** Reasoning
17–20	**2** Skills/Concepts	**MP.4** Modeling
21	**2** Skills/Concepts	**MP.2** Reasoning
22–23	**3** Strategic Thinking **H.O.T.**	**MP.3** Logic
24	**3** Strategic Thinking **H.O.T.**	**MP.4** Modeling
25	**3** Strategic Thinking **H.O.T.**	**MP.2** Reasoning

EVALUATE

ASSIGNMENT GUIDE

Concepts and Skills	Practice
Explore 1 Using Algebra Tiles to Factor $x^2 + bx + c$	Exercises 1–2
Explore 2 Factoring $x^2 + bx + c$	Exercises 3–8, 23, 25
Example 1 Solving Equations of the form $x^2 + bx + c = 0$ by Factoring	Exercises 9–16, 21–22
Example 2 Solving Equation Models of the Form $x^2 + bx + c = 0$ by Factoring	Exercises 17–20, 24

AVOID COMMON ERRORS

Students may think they have made an error if both factors of a trinomial are the same. Remind them of the perfect square trinomial patterns:

$(a + b)^2 = a^2 + 2ab + b^2$ and

$(a - b)^2 = a^2 - 2ab + b^2$.

AVOID COMMON ERRORS

When factoring a trinomial with a negative value of c, students may write a minus sign in the wrong binomial factor. Remind students that the binomial factor with the greater constant term should have the same sign as b.

15. $x^2 + x - 132 = 0$

$(x - 11)(x + 12) = 0$

$x - 11 = 0$ or $x + 12 = 0$

$x = 11$ $x = -12$

16. $x^2 - 14x = 32$

$x^2 - 14x - 32 = 0$

$(x + 2)(x - 16) = 0$

$x + 2 = 0$ or $x - 16 = 0$

$x = -2$ $x = 16$

17. Construction The area of a rectangular fountain is $(x^2 + 12x + 20)$ square feet. A 2-foot walkway is built around the fountain. Find the dimensions of the outside border of the walkway.

$x^2 + 12x + 20 = (x + 2)(x + 10)$

A 2-foot walkway around the fountain will add an extra 2 + 2, or 4, feet to each dimension.

$(x + 2) + 4 = x + 6;$ $(x + 10) + 4 = x + 14$
So, the dimensions of the outside border of the walkway are $(x + 6)$ feet and $(x + 14)$ feet.

18. The area of a room is 396 square feet. The length is $(x + 3)$, and the width is $(x + 7)$ feet. Find the dimensions of the room.

$(x + 3)(x + 7) = 396$

$x^2 + 10x + 21 = 396$

$x^2 + 10x - 375 = 0$

$(x - 15)(x + 25) = 0$

$x - 15 = 0$ or $x + 25 = 0$

$x = 15$ $x = -25$

Since length and width cannot be negative, the solution is $x = 15$.

Length: 15 + 3 = 18 feet

Width: 15 + 7 = 22 feet

19. A rectangular Persian carpet has an area of $(x^2 + x - 20)$ square feet and a length of $(x + 5)$ feet. The Persian carpet is displayed on a wall. The wall has a width of $(x + 2)$ feet and an area of $(x^2 + 17x + 30)$ square feet. Find the dimensions of the rug and the wall if $x = 20$ feet.

Rug: $x^2 + x - 20 = (x + 5)(x - 4)$

Let $x = 20$.

Length: 20 + 5 = 25 feet

Width: 20 − 4 = 16 feet

Wall: $x^2 + 17x + 30 = (x + 2)(x + 15)$

Let $x = 20$.

Width: 20 + 2 = 22 ft

Length: 20 + 15 = 35 ft

20. The area of a poster board is $x^2 + 3x - 10$ square inches. Find the dimensions of the poster board if $x = 14$.

$x^2 + 3x - 10 = (x - 2)(x + 5)$

Let $x = 14$: $14 - 2 = 12$ $14 + 5 = 19$

The dimensions of the poster board are 12 inches by 19 inches.

21. Match the equation to its solutions.

a. $x^2 - 3x - 18 = 0$ $\underline{\ b\ }$ 3 and 6
    $(x + 3)(x - 6) = 0$

b. $x^2 - 9x + 18 = 0$ $\underline{\ d\ }$ −3 and −6
    $(x - 3)(x - 6) = 0$

c. $x^2 + 3x - 18 = 0$ $\underline{\ c\ }$ 3 and −6
    $(x - 3)(x + 6) = 0$

d. $x^2 + 9x + 18 = 0$ $\underline{\ a\ }$ −3 and 6
    $(x + 3)(x + 6) = 0$

H.O.T. Focus on Higher Order Thinking

22. Explain the Error Amelie found the solutions of the equation $x^2 - x = 42$ to be 6 and −7. Explain why this answer is incorrect. Then, find the correct solutions.

Amelie factored the expression $x^2 - x - 42$ correctly and found the factor pair whose sum equals −1. However, she did not continue and find the solutions of the equation.

$x^2 - x - 42 = 0$

$(x + 6)(x - 7) = 0$

$x + 6 = 0$ or $x - 7 = 0$

$x = -6$ $x = 7$

23. Communicate Mathematical Ideas Rico says the expression $x^2 + bx + c$ is factorable when $b = c = 4$. Are there any other values where $b = c$ that make the expression factorable? Explain.

There are no other values where $b = c$ that make the expression factorable. The expression $x^2 + 4x + 4$ is factorable because $2 + 2 = 4$ and $2 \cdot 2 = 4$. The only number that has equal factors which sum to the number itself is 4, so no other factorable expressions exist where $b = c$.

MODELING

If students have difficulty factoring by listing factor pairs in a table, have them use algebra tiles as demonstrated in the Explore activity. To factor a trinomial of the form $x^2 + bx + c$, they should arrange the algebra tiles in a rectangular grid so that the x^2-tile is in the upper left, the unit tiles form a rectangle in the lower right, and x-tiles fill in the remaining spaces. The dimensions of the grid are the factors. Help students make the connection between the ways the unit tiles can be arranged in a rectangle and the factor pairs of the constant term.

?

How can you check the solutions to a quadratic equation? Give an algebraic method and a method using a graph. You can substitute the values into the original equation and verify that they make the equation true. If you write the equation so that one side is 0, you can use a graphing calculator to graph the related function and check that the solutions are the x-intercepts of the graph.

JOURNAL

Have students compare factoring a trinomial of the form $x^2 + bx + c$ when c is negative and b is positive to factoring a trinomial when c is negative and b is negative.

---

24. Multi-Step A homeowner wants to enlarge a rectangular closet that has an area of $(x^2 + 3x + 2)$ square feet. The length of the closet is greater than the width. After construction, the area will be $(x^2 + 8x + 15)$ square feet.

a. Find the dimensions of the closet before construction.

$x^2 + 3x + 2 = (x + 1)(x + 2)$

$x + 1 < x + 2$ because $1 < 2$. So, the length is $x + 2$ and the width is $x + 1$ before construction.

b. Find the dimensions of the closet after construction.

$x^2 + 8x + 15 = (x + 3)(x + 5)$

$x + 3 < x + 5$ because $3 < 5$. So, the length is $x + 5$ and the width is $x + 3$ after construction.

c. By how many feet will the length and width increase after construction?

Length: $(x + 5) - (x + 2) = 3$

Width: $(x + 3) - (x + 1) = 2$

The length will increase by 3 feet and the width will increase by 2 feet.

25. Critical Thinking Given $x^2 + bx + 64$, find all the values of b for which the quadratic expression has factors $(x + p)$ and $(x + q)$, where p and q are integers.

List the factor pairs of 64 and find the sum of each pair. Since $c > 0$, the factors will have the same sign.

Factors of 64	Sum of Factors
1 and 64	$1 + 64 = 65$
2 and 32	$2 + 32 = 34$
4 and 16	$4 + 16 = 20$
8 and 8	$8 + 8 = 16$
−1 and −64	$-1 + (-64) = -65$
−2 and −32	$-2 + (-32) = -34$
−4 and −16	$-4 + (-16) = -20$
−8 and −8	$-8 + (-8) = -16$

The possible values of b are the sums of the factors of 64: $\pm 65, \pm 34, \pm 20,$ and ± 16.

Lesson Performance Task

Part of the roof of a factory is devoted to mechanical support and part to green space. The area R of the roof can be modeled by the polynomial $2x^2 - 251x + 80{,}000$ and the area M devoted to mechanical support $x^2 + 224x + 31{,}250$. Given that the area G of the green space is 123,750 square feet, write and solve quadratic equations to find the dimensions of the green space.

$R = M + G$

$G = R - M$

$G = 2x^2 - 251x + 80{,}000 - \left(x^2 + 224x + 31{,}250\right)$

$\quad = 2x^2 - 251x + 80{,}000 - x^2 - 224x - 31{,}250$

$\quad = 2x^2 - x^2 - 251x - 224x + 80{,}000 - 31{,}250$

$\quad = x^2 - 475x + 48{,}750$

$G = 123{,}750$, so substitute and solve for x.

$123{,}750 = x^2 - 475x + 48{,}750$

$\quad\quad 0 = x^2 - 475x - 75{,}000$

$\quad\quad 0 = (x - 600)(x + 125)$

$\quad\quad x = 600 \text{ or } x = -125$

Since negative numbers do not apply in the context of this problem, use $x = 600$.

Now, factor $G = x^2 - 475x + 48{,}750$.

$G = x^2 - 475x + 48{,}750$

$\quad = (x - 150)(x - 325)$

Substitute $x = 600$ from the previous step.

$G = (600 - 150)(600 - 325)$

$\quad = (450)(275)$

Therefore, the area of the green space is 450 feet by 275 feet.

© Houghton Mifflin Harcourt Publishing Company

QUESTIONING STRATEGIES

? How can you find a polynomial that represents the area of the green space? Subtract the polynomial representing the area devoted to mechanical support from the polynomial representing the total area of the roof.

? Using that polynomial, how can you find the values of x that give the correct area for the green space? Set the polynomial equal to 123,750, then subtract 123,750 from both sides of the equation so that one side is 0. Next, factor the other side, set each factor equal to 0, and solve.

? After finding the values of x, how can you find the dimensions of the green space? Since the area of a rectangle is equal to the product of the length and the width, factor the polynomial representing the area of the green space, then substitute the values for x in each factor and evaluate. Discard any negative solutions.

EXTENSION ACTIVITY

Have students research historical examples of green roofs, such as the Hanging Gardens of Babylon or the sod roofs used by Native Americans and American pioneers. Have them describe how the construction of modern green roofs is different from the construction of their ancient counterparts.

Scoring Rubric

2 points: Student correctly solves the problem and explains his/her reasoning.

1 point: Student shows good understanding of the problem but does not fully solve or explain his/her reasoning.

0 points: Student does not demonstrate understanding of the problem.

Solving Equations by Factoring $ax^2 + bx + c$

Common Core Math Standards

The student is expected to:

 A-REI.B.4b

Solve quadratic equations by ... factoring, as appropriate to the initial form of the equation ... Also A-SSE.A.2, A-SSE.B.3a

Mathematical Practices

 MP.5 Using Tools

Language Objective

Explain to a partner how to factor a trinomial in the form $ax^2 + bx + c$.

ENGAGE

Essential Question: How can you use factoring to solve quadratic equations in standard form for which a ≠ 1?

Factor the quadratic equation. Set each linear factor equal to 0. Solve each linear equation. The solutions are the solutions of the original quadratic equation.

PREVIEW: LESSON PERFORMANCE TASK

View the Engage section online. Have students demonstrate how a car accelerating from a stopped position could first be passed by a bus traveling at a constant speed, then overtake and pass the bus. Then preview the Lesson Performance Task.

Name_____ Class_____ Date_____

21.2 Solving Equations by Factoring $ax^2 + bx + c$

Essential Question: How can you use factoring to solve quadratic equations in standard form for which $a \neq 1$?

Resource Locker

Explore   Factoring $ax^2 + bx + c$ When $c > 0$

When you factor a quadratic expression in standard form $(ax^2 + bx + c)$, you are looking for two binomials, and possibly a constant numerical factor whose product is the original quadratic expression.

Recall that the product of two binomials is found by applying the Distributive Property, abbreviated sometimes as FOIL:

$$(2x + 5)(3x + 2) = 6x^2 + 4x + 15x + 10 = 6x^2 + 19x + 10$$
$$\underbrace{\quad}_{F} \underbrace{\quad}_{O} \underbrace{\quad}_{I} \underbrace{\quad}_{L}$$

F   The product of the coefficients of the first terms is a.

O⎫
 ⎬   The sum of the coefficients of the outer and inner products is b.
I⎭

L   The product of the last terms is c.

Because the a and c coefficients result from a single product of terms from the binomials, the coefficients in the binomial factors will be a combination of the factors of a and c. The trick is to find the combination of factors that results in the correct value of b.

Follow the steps to factor the quadratic $4x^2 + 26x + 42$.

Ⓐ First, factor out the largest common factor of 4, 26, and 42 if it is anything other than 1.

$$4x^2 + 26x + 42 = \boxed{2}\,(2x^2 + 13x + 21)$$

Ⓑ Next, list the factor pairs of 2:

1 and 2

Ⓒ List the factor pairs of 21:

1 and 21, 3 and 7

Ⓓ Make a table listing the combinations of the factors of a and c, and find the value of b that results from summing the outer and inner products of the factors.

Factors of 2	Factors of 21	Outer + inner
1 and 2	1 and 21	$(1)(21) + (2)(1) = 23$
1 and 2	_3_ and 7	$(1)(7) + (2)(3) = 13$
1 and 2	7 and 3	$(1)(3) + (2)(7) = 17$
1 and 2	_21_ and 1	$(1)(1) + (2)(21) = 43$

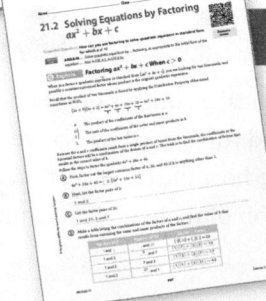

HARDCOVER PAGES 781–790

Turn to these pages to find this lesson in the hardcover student edition.

(E) Copy the pair of factors that resulted in an outer + inner sum of 13 into the binomial factors. Be careful to keep the inner and outer factors from the table as inner and outer coefficients in the binomials.

$$2x^2 + 13x + 21 = (\boxed{1}\,x + \boxed{3})(\boxed{2}\,x + \boxed{7})$$

(F) Replace the common factor of the original coefficients to complete the factorization of the original quadratic.

$$4x^2 + 26x + 42 = \boxed{2}\,(x + 3)(2x + 7)$$

Reflect

1. **Critical Thinking** Explain why you should use negative factors of c when factoring a quadratic with $c > 0$ and $b < 0$.
   A negative value of b tells you at least one of the factors of c must be negative, but since $c > 0$, in fact both must be negative.

2. **What If?** If none of the factor pairs for a and c result in the correct value for b, what do you know about the quadratic?
   The quadratic cannot be factored into the product of two binomials.

3. **Discussion** Why did you have to check each factor pair twice for the factors of c (3 and 7 versus 7 and 3) but only once for the factors of a (1 and 2, but not 2 and 1)? Hint: Compare the outer and inner sums of rows two and three in the table, and also check the outer and inner sums by switching the order of both pairs from row 2 (check 2 and 1 for a with 7 and 3 for c).
   It would be redundant to switch the order of both sets of factor pairs. Switching one set represents a different set of possible binomial factors, while switching both pairs corresponds to exchanging the order of the two binomial factors, which is not a different answer. The second and third rows of the table (switching the factor order of c only) have different outer plus inner sums (17 versus 13). Switching both pairs results in a sum of $(2)(3) + (1)(7) = 13$, which is the correct value. The corresponding factored equation would be written as $4x^2 + 26x + 42 = 2(2x + 7)(x + 3)$, which is the same set of binomial factors as the original answer, just written in a different order.

🖊 Explain 1   Factoring $ax^2 + bx + c$ When $c < 0$

Factoring $x^2 + bx + c$ when $c < 0$ requires one negative and one positive factor of c. The same applies for expressions of the form $ax^2 + bx + c$ as long as $a > 0$. When checking factor pairs, remember to consider factors of c in both orders, **and** consider factor pairs with the negative sign on either member of the pair of c factors.

When you find a combination of factors whose outer and inner product sum is equal to b, you have found the solution. Make sure you fill in the factor table systematically so that you do not skip any combinations.

If $a < 0$, factor out -1 from all three coefficients, or use a negative common factor, so that the factors of a can be left as positive numbers.

© Houghton Mifflin Harcourt Publishing Company

PROFESSIONAL DEVELOPMENT

Math Background

Quadratic equations were probably first examined in Babylonia about 4000 years ago. Around 800 BCE in India, geometric methods were used to solve quadratic equations. These methods were similar to the method of completing the square, which was developed between 300 and 200 BCE. Both Euclid and Pythagoras grappled with finding a formula or procedure for solving quadratic equations. It was not until around 600 CE that the first explicit solution to the standard form of the equation was given, although it was not completely general. The practical notation using the symbols and methods currently in use was developed during the 15th century.

EXPLORE

Factoring $ax^2 + bx + c$ When $c > 0$

INTEGRATE TECHNOLOGY

Students have the option of completing the factoring activity either in the book or online.

QUESTIONING STRATEGIES

? If there are three factor pairs for a and one factor pair for c, how many possible arrangements of factor pairs are there? Explain. **6; the factor pair for c can be paired with each factor pair for a in either order.**

? After finding the combination of factors of a and c that give the correct value of b, how do you know which factor to put in each position in the binomial factors? **The factors of a are the coefficients of x, and the factors of c are the constant terms. The factors you used to find the inner product should be the two inner values, and the factors you used to find the outer product should be the two outer values.**

EXPLAIN 1

Factoring $ax^2 + bx + c$ When $c < 0$

AVOID COMMON ERRORS

Make sure students understand that the order of the coefficients in the binomials matters. Encourage students to check for errors by making sure that the product of the x-coefficients is a, the product of the constant terms is c, and the sum of the products of the inner and outer terms is b.

? How many possible arrangements of factor pairs are there when $a = 3$ and $c = -2$? What are they? 4;

Factors of a	Factors of c
1 and 3	1 and -2
1 and 3	2 and -1
1 and 3	-1 and 2
1 and 3	-2 and 1

? What pairs of binomial factors result from these arrangements of factor pairs?

$(x + 1)(3x - 2)$, $(x + 2)(3x - 1)$, $(x - 1)(3x + 2)$, and $(x - 2)(3x + 1)$

Example 1 Factor the quadratic by checking factor pairs.

(A) $6x^2 - 21x - 45$

Find the largest common factor of 6, 21, and 45, and factor it out, keeping the coefficient of x^2 positive.

$6x^2 - 21x - 45 = 3(2x^2 - 7x - 15)$

Factors of a	Factors of c	Outer Product + Inner Product
1 and 2	1 and -15	$(1)(-15) + (2)(1) = -13$
1 and 2	3 and -5	$(1)(-5) + (2)(3) = 1$
1 and 2	5 and -3	$(1)(-3) + (2)(5) = 7$
1 and 2	15 and -1	$(1)(-1) + (2)(15) = 29$
1 and 2	-1 and 15	$(1)(15) + (2)(-1) = 13$
1 and 2	-3 and 5	$(1)(5) + (2)(-3) = -1$
1 and 2	-5 and 3	$(1)(3) + (2)(-5) = -7$
1 and 2	-15 and 1	$(1)(1) + (2)(-15) = -29$

Use the combination of factor pairs that results in a value of -7 for b.
$2x^2 - 7x - 15 = (x - 5)(2x + 3)$

Replace the common factor of the original coefficients to factor the original quadratic.

$6x^2 - 21x - 45 = 3(x - 5)(2x + 3)$

(B) $20x^2 - 40x - 25$

Factor out common factors of the terms.

$20x^2 - 40x - 25 = \boxed{5}\,(4x^2 - 8x - 5)$

Factors of a	Factors of c	Outer Product + Inner Product
1 and 4	1 and -5	$(1)(-5) + (4)(1) = \boxed{-1}$
1 and 4	5 and -1	$\boxed{(1)(-1)} + \boxed{(4)(5)} = \boxed{19}$
1 and 4	-1 and 5	$\boxed{(1)(5)} + \boxed{(4)(-1)} = \boxed{1}$
1 and 4	-5 and 1	$\boxed{(1)(1)} + \boxed{(4)(-5)} = \boxed{-19}$
2 and 2	1 and -5	$\boxed{(2)(-5)} + \boxed{(2)(1)} = \boxed{-8}$
2 and 2	-1 and 5	$\boxed{(2)(-1)} + \boxed{(2)(5)} = \boxed{8}$

Use the combination of factor pairs that results in a value of $\boxed{-8}$ for b.

$4x^2 - 8x - 5 = \left(\boxed{2}\,x + \boxed{1}\right)\left(\boxed{2}\,x + \boxed{-5}\right)$

Replace the common factor of the original coefficients to factor the original quadratic.

$20x^2 - 40x - 25 = \boxed{5}\,(2x + 1)(2x - 5)$

COLLABORATIVE LEARNING

Peer-to-Peer Activity

Have student pairs discuss how to use the signs of b and c to decide whether binomial factors should contain $+$ or $-$ signs and then complete this chart:

b	c	Example	Sign in Factors	Factors
$+$	$+$	$2x^2 + 9x + 4$	both $+$	$(2x + 1)(x + 4)$
$-$	$+$	$3n^2 - 11n + 6$	both $-$	$(3n - 2)(n - 3)$
$-$	$-$	$4t^2 - t - 10$	product with greater absolute value has $-$	$(2t - 5)(t + 2)$
$+$	$-$	$6q^2 + q - 7$	product with greater absolute value has $+$	$(6q + 7)(q - 1)$

4. **What If?** Suppose a is a negative number. What would be the first step in factoring $ax^2 + bx + c$?

Factor out a negative common factor from all of the coefficients, even if the common

factor is -1. This will result in a new quadratic to factor with a positive value of a to which

the previous methods can be applied.

Your Turn

5. Factor. $-5x^2 + 8x + 4$

$-1(5x^2 - 8x - 4) = -1(x - 2)(5x + 2)$

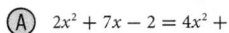 **Explain 2** **Solving Equations of the Form $ax^2 + bx + c = 0$ by Factoring**

For a quadratic equation in standard form, $ax^2 + bx + c = 0$, factoring the quadratic expression into binomials lets you use the Zero Product Property to solve the equation, as you have done previously. If the equation is not in standard form, convert it to standard form by moving all terms to one side of the equation and combining like terms.

Example 2 Change the quadratic equation to standard form if necessary and then solve by factoring.

(A) $2x^2 + 7x - 2 = 4x^2 + 4$

Convert the equation to standard form:

Subtract $4x^2$ and 4 from both sides. $-2x^2 + 7x - 6 = 0$

Multiply both sides by -1. $2x^2 - 7x + 6 = 0$

Consider factor pairs for 2 and 6. Use negative factors of 6 to get a negative value for b.

Use the combination pair that results in a sum of -7 and write the equation in factored form. Then solve it using the Zero Product Property.

$$(x - 2)(2x - 3) = 0$$

$$x - 2 = 0 \quad \text{or} \quad 2x - 3 = 0$$

$$x = 2 \qquad\qquad 2x = 3$$

$$x = \frac{3}{2} = 1.5$$

The solutions are 2 and $\frac{3}{2}$, or 1.5.

The solution can be checked by graphing the related function, $f(x) = 2x^2 - 7x + 6$, and finding the x-intercepts.

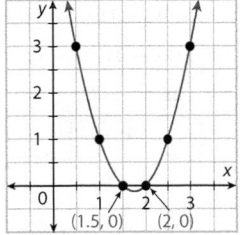

© Houghton Mifflin Harcourt Publishing Company

EXPLAIN 2

Solving Equations of the Form $ax^2 + bx + c = 0$ by Factoring

INTEGRATE MATHEMATICAL PRACTICES
Focus on Communication

MP.3 Ask students to describe the general form of solutions to a factored quadratic equation of the form $(ax + b)(cx + d) = 0$. Students should find that the solutions are $x = -\frac{b}{a}$ and $x = -\frac{d}{c}$. Therefore, when the coefficients of x in the factored form are not 1, the solutions are likely to be proper or improper fractions.

DIFFERENTIATE INSTRUCTION

Multiple Representations

Show students this alternate factoring method. Any trinomial can be written as a polynomial with four terms and then factored by grouping. To factor $6x^2 + 19x + 15$, first find ac: $6 \cdot 15 = 90$. Then find factors of ac that sum to b: 9 and 10 are factors of 90 whose sum is 19. Rewrite the trinomial using those factors: $6x^2 + 10x + 9x + 15$. Finally, factor by grouping:

$(6x^2 + 10x) + (9x + 15) = 2x(3x + 5) + 3(3x + 5) = (3x + 5)(2x + 3)$

? What is the first step for solving
$7x^2 + 20x = x + 6$? **Convert the equation to
standard form by subtracting $x + 6$ from both sides
of the equation, which results in $7x^2 + 19x - 6 = 0$.**

? Why is this step necessary for solving the
equation by factoring? **In order to use the
Zero Product Property to solve the equation, the
expression that you factor must be equal to zero.**

Ⓑ $3(x^2 - 1) = -3x^2 + 2x + 5$

Write the equation in standard form and factor so you can apply the Zero Product Property.

$$\boxed{3}\,x^2 - \boxed{3} = -3x^2 + 2x + 5$$

$$\boxed{6}\,x^2 - 2x - \boxed{8} = 0$$

$$\boxed{3}\,x^2 - x - 4 = 0$$

Use the combination pair that results in a sum of $\underline{-1}$.

$$(x + 1)\left(\boxed{3}\,x + \boxed{-4}\right) = 0$$

$$x + 1 = \boxed{0} \qquad \text{or} \qquad 3x - 4 = 0$$

$$x = \boxed{-1} \qquad\qquad \boxed{3}\,x = 4$$

$$x = \boxed{\dfrac{4}{3}}$$

The solutions are -1 and $\dfrac{4}{3}$.

Use a graphing calculator to check the solutions.

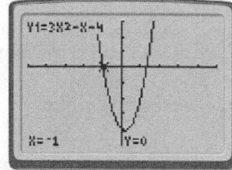 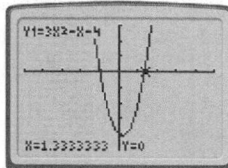

Reflect

6. In the two examples, a common factor was divided out at the beginning of the solution, and it was not used again. Why didn't you include the common term again when solving x for the original quadratic equation? **Solutions are arrived at by applying the Zero Product Property to the factors of the quadratic expression. Although the common factor is a factor of the quadratic expression, it cannot equal 0.**

Your Turn

7. $12x^2 + 48x + 45 = 0$

$$3\left(4x^2 + 16x + 15\right) = 0$$

$$(2x + 3)(2x + 5) = 0$$

$$2x + 3 = 0 \qquad \text{or} \qquad 2x + 5 = 0$$

$$x = -\frac{3}{2} \qquad \text{and} \qquad x = -\frac{5}{2}$$

LANGUAGE SUPPORT 🔲EL

Connect Vocabulary

English learners may need numerous exposures and structured practice with new vocabulary to truly acquire it for their own use. Before describing the new terminology for this lesson, review more basic terms such as *sum*, *product*, and *factor*. Students will need to rely on their understanding of these words to grasp phrases such as *outer products*, *inner products*, *sum of inner and outer products*, and *common factors*. It may be helpful for students to use diagrams and examples to record the meaning of new terminology.

Explain 3 ## Solving Equation Models of the Form $ax^2 + bx + c = 0$ by Factoring

A projectile is an object moving through the air without any forces other than gravity acting on it. The height of a projectile at a time in seconds can be found by using the formula $h = -16t^2 + vt + s$, where v is in the initial upwards velocity in feet per second (and can be a negative number if the projectile is launched downwards) and s is starting height in feet. The a term of -16 accounts for the effect of gravity accelerating the projectile downwards and is the only appropriate value when measuring distance with feet and time in seconds.

To use the model to make predictions about the behavior of a projectile, you need to read the description of the situation carefully and identify the initial velocity, the initial height, and the height at time t.

Example 3 Read the real-world situation and substitute in values for the projectile motion formula. Then solve the resulting quadratic equation by factoring to answer the question.

(A) When a baseball player hits a baseball into the air, the height of the ball at t seconds after the ball is hit can be modeled with the projectile motion formula. If the ball is hit at 3 feet off the ground with an upward velocity of 47 feet per second, how long will it take for the ball to hit the ground, assuming it is not caught?

Use the equation $h = -16t^2 + vt + s$. Find the parameters v and s from the description of the problem.

$v = 47$ $s = 3$ $h = 0$

Substitute parameter values. $-16t^2 + 47t + 3 = 0$

Divide both sides by -1. $16t^2 - 47t - 3 = 0$

Use the combination pair that results in a sum of -47.

$$(t - 3)(16t + 1) = 0$$

$$t - 3 = 0 \quad \text{or} \quad 16t + 1 = 0$$

$$t = 3 \qquad\qquad 16t = -1$$

$$t = -\frac{1}{16}$$

The solutions are 3 and $-\frac{1}{16}$.

The negative time answer can be rejected because it is not a reasonable value for time in this situation. The correct answer is 3 seconds.

EXPLAIN 3

Solving Equation Models of the Form $ax^2 + bx + c = 0$ by Factoring

QUESTIONING STRATEGIES

(?) To model the motion of a projectile when distance is measured in meters instead of feet, you use the formula $h = -4.9t^2 + vt + s$ instead of $h = -16t^2 + vt + s$. By what factor does the coefficient of t^2 change? Why does that factor make sense? **The coefficient is reduced by a factor of 3.3, because there are 3.3 feet in a meter.**

INTEGRATE MATHEMATICAL PRACTICES

Focus on Modeling

MP.4 When using an equation of the form $h = -16t^2 + vt + s$ to determine how many seconds it takes for an object to reach the ground, remind students that v represents the initial *upward* velocity. If a problem states that an object is thrown downward, students must use a negative value for v.

INTEGRATE MATHEMATICAL PRACTICES

Focus on Technology

MP.5 Have students use a graphing calculator to graph an equation that represents the height of an object that is thrown upward, then falls. Discuss the shape of the graph, and ask students at what time the projectile reaches its maximum height. Students should recognize that the time of the object's maximum height is the x-value for the vertex of the parabola. Because the graph is symmetric, they can also find this value by determining the x-value that is half way between the x-intercepts, or zeros, of the function.

ELABORATE

QUESTIONING STRATEGIES

? How is factoring a trinomial in the form $ax^2 + bx + c$ similar to factoring a trinomial in the form $x^2 + bx + c$? How is it different? For both forms, you find factors of the coefficient of x^2 and of c such that the sum of products of factors is equal to b. When the trinomial is in the form $x^2 + bx + c$, the coefficient of x^2 is 1, so the products of the factors are simply the factors of c.

(B) A child standing on a river bank ten feet above the river throws a rock toward the river at a speed of 12 feet per second. How long does it take before the rock splashes into the river?

Find the parameters v and s from the description of the problem.

$v = \boxed{-12}$ $s = \boxed{10}$ $h = \boxed{0}$

Substitute parameter values. $\boxed{-16}\,t^2 + \boxed{-12}\,t + \boxed{10} = 0$

Divide both sides by $\boxed{-2}$. $8t^2 + \boxed{6}\,t + \boxed{-5} = 0$

Use the combination pair that results in a sum of 6.

$$\left(\boxed{2}\,t - 1\right)\left(\boxed{4}\,t + 5\right) = 0$$

$2t - 1 = 0$ or $4t + 5 = 0$

$2t = \boxed{1}$ $4t = \boxed{-5}$

$t = \boxed{\dfrac{1}{2}}$ $t = \boxed{-\dfrac{5}{4}}$

The solutions are $\boxed{\dfrac{1}{2}}$ and $\boxed{-\dfrac{5}{4}}$.

The only correct solution to the time it takes the rock to hit the water is $\boxed{\dfrac{1}{2}}$ second.

Your Turn

8. How long does it take a rock to hit the ground if thrown off the edge of a 72-foot tall building roof with an upward velocity of 24 feet per second?

$v = 24;\ s = 72;\ h = 0$

$-16t^2 + 24t + 72 = 0$

$-8(2t^2 - 3t - 9) = 0$

$(t - 3)(2t + 3) = 0$

$t - 3 = 0$ or $2t + 3 = 0$

$t = 3$ $t = -\dfrac{3}{2}$

The rock lands 3 seconds after it is thrown.

9. **Discussion** What happens if you do not remove the common factor from the coefficients before trying to factor the quadratic equation?
If you do not remove the common factor from the coefficients, you can still find binomial

factors, but you may need to check many more factor pairs before you find the correct

answer. Additionally, when you do find a set of factor pairs that work, one of the binomial

factors will not be fully factored, such as $(2x + 4)$, which should be written as $2(x + 2)$ if

you are asked to find the factors of a quadratic expression.

10. Explain how you can know there are never more than two solutions to a quadratic equation, based on what you know about the graph of a quadratic function.
The graph of a quadratic equation is shaped like a parabola and can only cross the x-axis

twice. The solutions of a quadratic equation in standard form are the x-intercepts of the

corresponding quadratic function, and it can have up to two.

11. **Essential Question Check-In** Describe the steps it takes to solve a quadratic equation by factoring.
Change the quadratic equation to standard form if it is not there already, and then find the

factors of the quadratic expression by checking factor pairs of a and c. When the quadratic

is factored, set each binomial equal to zero to find a possible solution.

☆ Evaluate: Homework and Practice

Factor the following quadratic expressions.

1. $6x^2 + 5x + 1$

   $(3x + 1)(2x + 1)$

2. $9x^2 + 33x + 30$

   $3(3x^2 + 11x + 10) = 3(x + 2)(3x + 5)$

3. $4x^2 - 8x + 3$

   $(2x - 1)(2x - 3)$

4. $24x^2 - 44x + 12$

   $4(6x^2 - 11x + 3) = 4(2x - 3)(3x - 1)$

5. $3x^2 - 2x - 5$

   $(x + 1)(3x - 5)$

6. $-10x^2 + 3x + 4$

   $-1(10x^2 - 3x - 4) = -1(2x + 1)(5x - 4)$

7. $12x^2 + 22x - 14$

   $2(6x^2 + 11x - 7) = 2(2x - 1)(3x + 7)$

8. $-15x^2 + 21x + 18$

   $-3(5x^2 - 7x - 6) = -3(x - 2)(5x + 3)$

© Houghton Mifflin Harcourt Publishing Company

Exercise	Depth of Knowledge (D.O.K.)	COMMON CORE Mathematical Practices
1–16	**2** Skills/Concepts	**MP.4** Modeling
17–20	**2** Skills/Concepts	**MP.4** Modeling
21–22	**2** Skills/Concepts	**MP.4** Modeling
23	**1** Recall of Information	**MP.2** Reasoning
24	**2** Skills/Concepts H.O.T.	**MP.4** Modeling
25–26	**3** Strategic Thinking H.O.T.	**MP.4** Modeling

SUMMARIZE THE LESSON

Create a flowchart like the one below for factoring trinomials in the form $ax^2 + bx + c$.

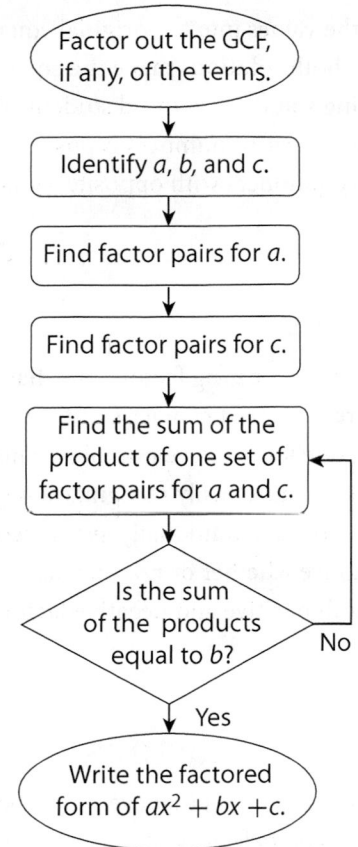

Factor out the GCF, if any, of the terms.

↓

Identify a, b, and c.

↓

Find factor pairs for a.

↓

Find factor pairs for c.

↓

Find the sum of the product of one set of factor pairs for a and c.

↓

Is the sum of the products equal to b? → No

↓ Yes

Write the factored form of $ax^2 + bx + c$.

EVALUATE

ASSIGNMENT GUIDE

Concepts and Skills	Practice
Explore Factoring $ax^2 + bx + c$ When $c > 0$	Exercises 1–4, 22
Example 1 Factoring $ax^2 + bx + c$ When $c < 0$	Exercises 5–8, 21, 23, 25–26
Example 2 Solving Equations of the Form $ax^2 + bx + c = 0$ by Factoring	Exercises 9–16
Example 3 Solving Equation Models of the Form $ax^2 + bx + c = 0$ by Factoring	Exercises 17–20, 24

INTEGRATE MATHEMATICAL PRACTICES

Focus on Reasoning

MP.2 Students can check their solutions by substituting the values into the original equations and verifying that both solutions make the equation true. When checking solutions, remind students that the product of two negative numbers is positive and the product of two numbers with opposite signs is negative.

VISUAL CUES

When students are creating factor pairs, have them use two different colored pencils, one for positive numbers and one for negative numbers. This will allow students to more easily recognize a negative as they are multiplying. Additionally, using two colors helps them notice whether or not they have considered both positive and negative factor pairs, as needed.

AVOID COMMON ERRORS

Students sometimes forget that every number has 1 and itself as two of its factors. When students are making their lists of factors, remind them to try all possible factors.

Solve the following quadratic equations.

9. $5x^2 + 18x + 9 = 0$

$(x + 3)(5x + 3) = 0$

$x + 3 = 0$ or $5x + 3 = 0$

$x = -3$ or $x = -\dfrac{3}{5}$

10. $12x^2 - 36x + 15 = 0$

$12x^2 - 36x + 15 = 0$

$4x^2 - 12x + 5 = 0$

$(2x - 1)(2x - 5) = 0$

$2x - 1 = 0$ or $2x - 5 = 0$

$x = \dfrac{1}{2}$ or $x = \dfrac{5}{2}$

11. $6x^2 + 28x - 2 = 2x - 10$

$6x^2 + 28x - 2 = 2x - 10$

$6x^2 + 26x + 8 = 0$

$3x^2 + 13x + 4 = 0$

$(x + 4)(3x + 1) = 0$

$x + 4 = 0$ or $3x + 1 = 0$

$x = -4$ or $x = -\dfrac{1}{3}$

12. $-100x^2 + 55x + 3 = 50x^2 - 55x + 23$

$-100x^2 + 55x + 3 = 50x^2 - 55x + 23$

$-150x^2 + 110x - 20 = 0$

$15x^2 - 11x + 2 = 0$

$(3x - 1)(5x - 2) = 0$

$3x - 1 = 0$ or $5x - 2 = 0$

$x = \dfrac{1}{3}$ or $x = \dfrac{2}{5}$

13. $8x^2 - 10x - 3 = 0$

$(2x - 3)(4x + 1) = 0$

$2x - 3 = 0$ or $4x + 1 = 0$

$x = \dfrac{3}{2}$ or $x = -\dfrac{1}{4}$

14. $-12x^2 = 34x - 28$

$-12x^2 = 34x - 28$

$-12x^2 - 34x + 28 = 0$

$6x^2 + 17x - 14 = 0$

$(2x + 7)(3x - 2) = 0$

$2x + 7 = 0$ or $3x - 2 = 0$

$x = -\dfrac{7}{2}$ or $x = \dfrac{2}{3}$

15. $(8x + 7)(x + 1) = 9$

$(8x + 7)(x + 1) = 9$

$8x^2 + 8x + 7x + 7 = 9$

$8x^2 + 15x - 2 = 0$

$(x + 2)(8x - 1) = 0$

$x + 2 = 0$ or $8x - 1 = 0$

$x = -2$ or $x = \dfrac{1}{8}$

16. $3(4x - 1)(4x + 3) = 48x$

$3(4x - 1)(4x + 3) = 48x$

$3(16x^2 + 8x - 3) = 48x$

$48x^2 + 24x - 9 = 48x$

$48x^2 - 24x - 9 = 0$

$16x^2 - 8x - 3 = 0$

$(4x + 1)(4x - 3) = 0$

$4x + 1 = 0$ or $4x - 3 = 0$

$x = -\dfrac{1}{4}$ or $x = \dfrac{3}{4}$

Read the real-world situation and substitute in values for the projectile motion formula. Then solve the resulting quadratic equation by factoring to answer the question.

17. A golfer takes a swing from a hill twenty feet above the cup with an initial upwards velocity of 32 feet per second. How long does it take the ball to land on the ground near the cup?

$v = 32$

$s = 20$

$h = 0$

$-16t^2 + 32t + 20 = 0$

$4t^2 - 8t - 5 = 0$

$(2t + 1)(2t - 5) = 0$

$2t + 1 = 0$ or $2t - 5 = 0$

$t = -\dfrac{1}{2}$ or $t = \dfrac{5}{2}$

It takes the ball $2\frac{1}{2}$ seconds to land.

18. An airplane pilot jumps out of an airplane and has an initial velocity of 60 feet per second downwards. How long does it take to fall from 1000 feet to 900 feet before the parachute opens?

$v = -60$

$s = 1000$

$h = 900$

$-16t^2 - 60t + 1000 = 900$

$-16t^2 - 60t + 100 = 0$

$4t^2 + 15t - 25 = 0$

$(t + 5)(4t - 5) = 0$

$t + 5 = 0$ or $4t - 5 = 0$

$t = -5$ or $t = \dfrac{5}{4}$

The pilot falls for $1\frac{1}{4}$ seconds before the parachute opens.

A race car driving under the caution flag at 80 feet per second begins to accelerate at a constant rate after the warning flag. The distance traveled since the warning flag in feet is characterized by $30t^2 + 80t$, where t is the time in seconds after the car starts accelerating again.

19. How long does it take the car to travel 30 feet after it begins accelerating?

$30t^2 + 80t = 30$

$30t^2 + 80t - 30 = 0$

$3t^2 + 8t - 3 = 0$

$(t + 3)(3t - 1) = 0$

$t + 3 = 0$ or $3t - 1 = 0$

$t = -3$ or $t = \dfrac{1}{3}$

It takes $\frac{1}{3}$ second to travel 30 more feet.

20. How long will the car take to travel 160 feet?

$30t^2 + 80t = 160$

$30t^2 + 80t - 160 = 0$

$3t^2 + 8t - 16 = 0$

$(t + 4)(3t - 4) = 0$

$t + 4 = 0$ or $3t - 4 = 0$

$t = -4$ or $t = \dfrac{4}{3}$

It will take $1\frac{1}{3}$ seconds.

AVOID COMMON ERRORS

Students may forget how to determine the signs of the constant terms in the binomial factors. Remind students that the sign of c in a trinomial determines the signs of the constant terms in its binomial factors. If $c > 0$, then the signs of the constants must be the same. If $c < 0$, then the signs must be opposites.

Solving Equations by Factoring $ax^2 + bx + c$ **1006**

Focus on Reasoning

MP.2 When solving equations to determine how many seconds it takes for an object to reach the ground, discuss with students what the x- and y- intercepts of a graph of the equation represent. If time is represented on the x-axis and height is represented on the y-axis, the x-intercept represents the time it takes the object to reach the ground, and the y-intercept represents the original height of the object.

JOURNAL

Have students explain how to factor a trinomial of the form $ax^2 + bx + c$ when a and b are positive and c is negative.

Geometry For each rectangle with area given, determine the binomial factors that describe the dimensions.

21.

area $= 6x^2 + 17x - 3$

$6x^2 + 17x - 3 = (x + 3)(6x - 1)$

length $= (6x - 1)$, **width** $= (x + 3)$

22.

area $= 21x^2 + 13x + 2$

$21x^2 + 13x + 2 = (3x + 1)(7x + 2)$

length $= (7x + 2)$, **width** $= (3x + 1)$

23. **Multiple Response** Which of the following expressions in the list describes the complete factorization of the quadratic expression $15x^2 - 25x - 10$? Circle all that apply.

  a. $(3x + 1)(5x - 10)$ **b.** $5(3x + 1)(x - 2)$ **c.** $5(x + 2)(3x - 1)$

  d. $5(x - 2)(3x + 1)$ **e.** $5(3x - 1)(x + 2)$ **f.** $(5x - 10)(3x + 1)$

H.O.T. Focus on Higher Order Thinking

24. **Multi-Part Response** A basketball player shoots at the basket from a starting height of 6 feet and an upwards velocity of 20 feet per second. Determine how long it takes for the shot to drop through the basket, which is mounted at a height of 10 feet.

  a. Set up the equation for projectile motion to solve for time and convert it to standard form.

    $v = 20$ $s = 6$ $h = 10$ $-16t^2 + 20t + 6 = 10$

                                              $-16t^2 + 20t - 4 = 0$

  b. Solve the equation by factoring.

    $-16t^2 + 20t - 4 = 0$ $t - 1 = 0$ or $4t - 1 = 0$

    $4t^2 - 5t + 1 = 0$ $t = 1$ $t = \dfrac{1}{4}$

    $(t - 1)(4t - 1) = 0$

  c. Explain why you got two positive solutions to the equation, and determine how you can rule one of them out to find the answer to the question. Hint: Solving the equation graphically may give you a hint.

    The solutions to the equation are the times at which the basketball is at the same height as the basket. The basketball must go up past the height of the basket before coming back down, and both times are positive (after the player shoots). The earlier time is when the ball passes the basket's height traveling upward, and the later time is when it drops through the hoop. Therefore the correct answer is 1 second.

25. **Critical Thinking** Find the binomial factors of $4x^2 - 25$.

  Rewrite the expression as $4x^2 + 0x - 25$. The factor combination will have a sum of 0.

    $4x^2 + 0x - 25 = (2x + 5)(2x - 5) = (2x + 5)^2$

26. **Communicate Mathematical Ideas** Find all the values of b that make the expression $3x^2 + bx - 4$ factorable.

  $-1, 4, 11, 1, -4,$ and -11 can be used for the value of b.

Lesson Performance Task

The equation for the motion of an object with constant acceleration is $d = d_0 + vt + \frac{1}{2}at^2$, where d is distance from a given point in meters, d_0 is the initial distance from the starting point in meters, v is the starting velocity in meters per second, a is acceleration in meters per second squared, and t is time in seconds.

A car is stopped at a traffic light. When the light turns green, the driver begins to drive, accelerating at a constant rate of 4 meters per second squared. A bus is traveling at a speed of 15 meters per second in another lane. The bus is 7 meters behind the car as it begins to accelerate.

Find when the bus passes the car, when the car passes the bus, and how far each has traveled each time they pass one another.

The distance traveled from the intersection by the car is the following:

$$d_c(t) = (0)t + \frac{1}{2}(4)t^2 = 2t^2$$

The distance traveled from the intersection by the bus is the following:

$$d_b(t) = -7 + 15t + \frac{1}{2}(0)t^2 = -7 + 15t$$

Set $d_c(t)$ equal to $d_b(t)$ to find the time when the bus passes the car and the

time when the car passes the bus.

$d_c(t) = d_b(t)$	$2t - 1 = 0$	$t - 7 = 0$
$2t^2 = -7 + 15t$	$2t = 1$ or	$t = 7$
$0 = 2t^2 - 15t + 7$	$t = \frac{1}{2}$	
$0 = (2t - 1)(t - 7)$		

The bus passes the car at $t = \frac{1}{2}$ and the car passes the bus at $t = 7$.

The bus passes the car at $t = \frac{1}{2}$ seconds. Substitute $t = \frac{1}{2}$ into the

equation for $d_c(t)$.

$$d_c(t) = 2t^2 = 2\left(\frac{1}{2}\right)^2 = 0.5$$

Recall that the bus is 7 meters behind the car as it begins to accelerate. So, $7 + 0.5 = 7.5$. Therefore, the bus travels a total of 7.5 meters before it passes the car, while the car travels 0.5 meter.

The car passes the bus at $t = 7$ seconds. Substitute $t = 7$ into the equation for $d_c(t)$.

$$d_c(t) = 2t^2 = 2(7)^2 = 98$$

Recall that the bus is 7 meters behind the car as it begins to accelerate. So, $7 + 98 = 105$. Therefore, the car travels a total of 98 meters before it passes the bus, while the bus travels 105 meters.

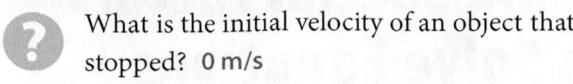
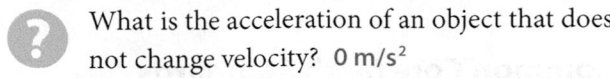
? What is the initial velocity of an object that is stopped? 0 m/s

? What is the acceleration of an object that does not change velocity? 0 m/s²

? If the car's initial position is $d_0 = 0$, what value of d_0 describes the initial position of the bus? Explain. −7; since the bus is 7 meters behind the car's starting point, the value for its position must be negative.

INTEGRATE MATHEMATICAL PRACTICES
Focus on Math Connections

MP.1 Because the bus is moving at a constant speed, its motion is represented by a linear equation. Discuss with students why the car's motion is described by a quadratic equation. At the start, the car is stopped, so its initial velocity is 0 m/s. As the car accelerates, its speed increases steadily, so the distance traveled increases at an increasing rate. The increasing curve of a parabola models this type of motion.

EXTENSION ACTIVITY

Have students use graphing calculators to display the graphs of $y = 2t^2$ and $y = -7 + 15t$ in the same window. Have them explain what information the graphs provide, and compare it to the information provided by the graph of $y = 2t^2 - 15t + 7$.

Students should recognize that the intersection points of the two graphs represent the times and locations at which the vehicles pass each other. The x-intercepts of the graph of $y = 2t^2 - 15t + 7$ indicate the times when the vehicles pass, but this graph does not provide any direct information about the distance traveled.

Scoring Rubric

2 points: Student correctly solves the problem and explains his/her reasoning.

1 point: Student shows good understanding of the problem but does not fully solve or explain his/her reasoning.

0 points: Student does not demonstrate understanding of the problem.

Solving Equations by Factoring $ax^2 + bx + c$ **1008**

Using Special Factors to Solve Equations

Common Core Math Standards

The student is expected to:

COMMON CORE **A-SSE.B.3a**

Factor a quadratic expression to reveal the zeros of the function it defines. Also A-SSE.A.2, A-REI.B.4b

Mathematical Practices

COMMON CORE **MP.1 Problem Solving**

Language Objective

Explain to a partner what a perfect-square trinomial is and how you can recognize one.

ENGAGE

Essential Question: How can you use special products to aid in solving quadratic equations by factoring?

By recognizing that a polynomial is a perfect-square trinomial or a difference of squares, you can use the appropriate special product rule to factor the polynomial, and then use the zero product property to solve the equation.

PREVIEW: LESSON PERFORMANCE TASK

View the Engage section online. Discuss how the shape of the base of a fountain could affect the possible patterns made by the falling water. Then preview the Lesson Performance Task.

Name _____ Class _____ Date _____

21.3 Using Special Factors to Solve Equations

Essential Question: How can you use special products to aid in solving quadratic equations by factoring?

Resource Locker

Explore **Exploring Factors of Perfect Square Trinomials**

When you use algebra tiles to factor a polynomial, you must arrange the unit tiles on the grid in a rectangle. Sometimes, you can arrange the unit tiles to form a square. Trinomials of this type are called perfect-square trinomials.

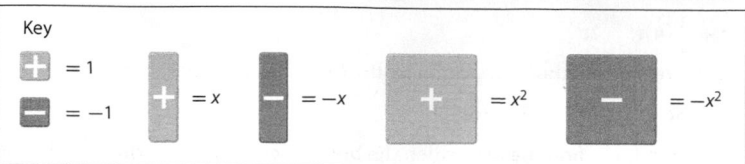

Key
$\boxed{+} = 1$
$\boxed{-} = -1$
$\boxed{+} = x$
$\boxed{-} = -x$
$\boxed{+} = x^2$
$\boxed{-} = -x^2$

(A) Use algebra tiles to factor $x^2 + 6x + 9$.

Identify the number of tiles you need to model the expression. You need $\boxed{1}$ x^2-tiles, $\boxed{6}$ x-tiles, and $\boxed{9}$ unit tiles.

(B) Arrange the algebra tiles on the grid. Place the $\boxed{1}$ x^2-tile in the upper left corner, and arrange the $\boxed{9}$ unit tiles in the lower right corner.

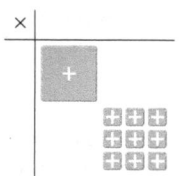

(C) Fill in the empty spaces on the grid with x-tiles.

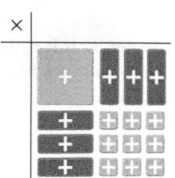

Module 21 1009 Lesson 3

© Houghton Mifflin Harcourt Publishing Company

HARDCOVER PAGES 791–800

Turn to these pages to find this lesson in the hardcover student edition.

(D) All ⬚6⬚ x-tiles were used, so all the tiles are accounted for and fit in the square with sides of length __$x + 3$__. Read the length and width of the square to get the factors of the trinomial $x^2 + 6x + 9 = \left(x + \boxed{3}\right)\left(x + \boxed{3}\right)$.

(E) Now, use algebra tiles to factor $x^2 - 8x + 16$.

You need ⬚1⬚ x^2-tiles, ⬚8⬚ $-x$-tiles, and ⬚16⬚ unit tiles to model the expression.

(F) Arrange the algebra tiles on the grid. Place the ⬚1⬚ x^2-tile in the upper left corner, and arrange the ⬚16⬚ unit tiles in the lower right corner.

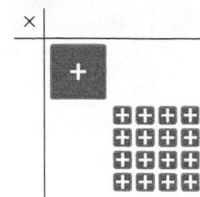

(G) Fill in the empty spaces on the grid with $-x$-tiles.

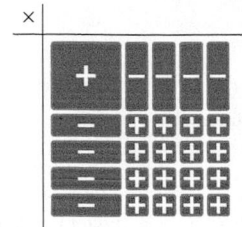

(H) All ⬚8⬚ $-x$-tiles were used, so all the tiles are accounted for and fit in a square with sides of length __$x - 4$__. Read the length and width of the square to get the factors of the trinomial $x^2 - 8x + 16 = \left(\boxed{x - 4}\right)\left(\boxed{x - 4}\right)$.

Reflect

1. **What If?** Suppose that the middle term in $x^2 + 6x + 9$ was changed from $6x$ to $10x$. How would this affect the way you factor the polynomial?
   The arrangement of unit tiles would have to be in a rectangle, not a square. The factored form $x^2 + 10x + 9$ is $(x + 1)(x + 9)$.

© Houghton Mifflin Harcourt Publishing Company

Exploring Factors of Perfect-Square Trinomials

INTEGRATE TECHNOLOGY

Students have the option of completing the algebra tiles activity either in the book or online.

INTEGRATE MATHEMATICAL PRACTICES
Focus on Modeling

MP.4 Remind students that modeling the factors of trinomials with algebra tiles means the tiles must be arranged in a rectangle. When the factors of a perfect-square trinomial are modeled with algebra tiles, the tiles will be arranged in a square.

PROFESSIONAL DEVELOPMENT

Learning Progressions

In this lesson, students expand their understanding of factoring trinomials of the form $ax^2 + bx + c$ by learning to recognize and factor perfect-square trinomials, the difference of two squares, and polynomials that consist of one of these special products multiplied by a monomial factor. They also solve equations and real-world problems that involve these polynomials. As they work with polynomial expressions that follow certain patterns, students learn to recognize the patterns and apply them when appropriate. The ability to factor special products efficiently will be valuable in algebra as well as in future courses that require repeated reasoning with polynomials.

EXPLAIN 1

Factoring $a^2x^2 + 2abx + b^2$ and $a^2x^2 - 2abx + b^2$

QUESTIONING STRATEGIES

? How can you tell whether a trinomial of the form $ax^2 + bx + c$ is a perfect-square trinomial? If it is a perfect-square trinomial, both a and c will be perfect squares, and b will be equal to twice the product of the square roots of a and c, or twice the opposite of that product.

AVOID COMMON ERRORS

When asked to factor a trinomial that has a common monomial factor, such as $18x^2 - 60x + 50$, students may see that the first and last terms are not perfect squares and therefore assume that they cannot use the rule for factoring perfect squares. Remind students to always begin by factoring out any common factors, and then examine the trinomial that remains to decide whether they can use a special product rule.

---

2. If the positive unit squares are arranged in a square of unit tiles when factoring with algebra tiles, what will be true about the binomial factors? (The coefficient of the x^2 term is 1 as in the previous problems.) **Both factors will be the same, as in $(x + 3)(x + 3)$.**

⊘ Explain 1 **Factoring $a^2x^2 + 2abx + b^2$ and $a^2x^2 - 2abx + b^2$**

Recall that a perfect-square trinomial can be represented algebraically in either the form $a^2 + 2ab + b^2$ or the form $a^2 - 2ab + b^2$.

Perfect-Square Trinomials

Perfect-Square Trinomials	
Perfect-Square Trinomial	**Examples**
$a^2 + 2ab + b^2 = (a + b)(a + b)$ $= (a + b)^2$	$x^2 + 6x + 9 = (x + 3)(x + 3)$ $= (x + 3)^2$
	$c^2x^2 + 2cdx + d^2 = (cx)^2 + 2cdx + d^2$ $= (cx + d)(cx + d)$ $= (cx + d)^2$
$a^2 - 2ab + b^2 = (a - b)(a - b)$ $= (a - b)^2$	$x^2 - 10x + 25 = (x - 5)(x - 5)$ $= (x - 5)^2$
	$c^2x^2 - 2cdx + d^2 = (cx)^2 - 2cdx + d^2$ $= (cx - d)(cx - d)$ $= (cx - d)^2$

Example 1 Factor perfect-square trinomials.

(A) $4x^3 - 24x^2 + 36x$

$4x^3 - 24x^2 + 36x = 4x(x^2 - 6x + 9)$ Factor out the common monomial factor $4x$.

$= 4x[x^2 - 2(1 \cdot 3)x + 3^2]$ Rewrite the perfect square trinomial in the form $a^2x^2 - 2abx + b^2$.

$= 4x(x - 3)(x - 3)$ Rewrite the perfect square trinomial in the form $(ax - b)(ax - b)$ to obtain factors.

The factored form of $4x^3 - 24x^2 + 36x$ is $4x(x - 3)(x - 3)$, or $4x(x - 3)^2$.

(B) $x^2 + 16x + 64$

$x^2 + 16x + 64 = x^2 + 2\left(\boxed{1} \cdot \boxed{8}\right)x + \boxed{8}^2$ Rewrite in the form $a^2x^2 + 2abx + b^2$.

$= \left(x + \boxed{8}\right)\left(x + \boxed{8}\right)$ Rewrite in the form $(ax + b)(ax + b)$.

The factored form of $x^2 + 16x + 64$ is $\left(x + \boxed{8}\right)\left(x + \boxed{8}\right)$, or $\left(x + \boxed{8}\right)^2$.

© Houghton Mifflin Harcourt Publishing Company

COLLABORATIVE LEARNING

Peer-to-Peer Activity

Have students work in pairs. Ask each student to write five polynomials, each of which is a perfect-square trinomial or the difference of two squares. Students then trade polynomials and factor the ones they receive. Finally, ask students to explain to each other what steps they used to factor each polynomial.

Factor perfect-square trinomials.

3. $2y^3 + 12y^2 + 18y$

$2y^3 + 12y^2 + 18y = 2y(y^2 + 6y + 9)$

$= 2y[y^2 + 2(1 \cdot 3)y + 3^2]$

$= 2y(y + 3)(y + 3)$

$= 2y(y + 3)^2$

4. $100z^2 - 20z + 1$

$100z^2 - 20z + 1 = 10^2z^2 - 2(10 \cdot 1)z + 1^2$

$= (10z - 1)(10z - 1)$

$= (10z - 1)^2$

⚙ Explain 2 **Factoring $a^2x^2 - b^2 = 0$**

Recall that a difference of squares can be written algebraically as $a^2 - b^2$ and factored as $(a + b)(a - b)$.

Difference of Squares

Difference of Two Squares	
Perfect-Square Trinomial	**Examples**
$a^2 - b^2 = (a + b)(a - b)$	$x^2 - 9 = (x + 3)(x - 3)$
	$4x^2 - 9 = (2x + 3)(2x - 3)$
	$9x^2 - 1 = (3x + 1)(3x - 1)$
	$c^2x^2 - d^2 = (cx)^2 - d^2$
	$= (cx + d)(cx - d)$

Example 2 Factor each difference of squares.

Ⓐ $x^2 - 49$

$x^2 - 49 = x^2 - 7^2$ Rewrite in the form $a^2x^2 - b^2$.

$= (x + 7)(x - 7)$ Rewrite in the form $(ax + b)(ax - b)$.

The factored form of $x^2 - 49$ is $(x + 7)(x - 7)$.

Ⓑ $49q^2 - 4p^2$

$49q^2 - 4p^2 = \left(\boxed{7}\ \boxed{q}\right)^2 - \left(\boxed{2p}\right)^2$ Rewrite in the form $a^2x^2 - b^2$.

$= \left(\boxed{7q + 2p}\right)\left(\boxed{7q - 2p}\right)$ Rewrite in the form $(ax + b)(ax - b)$.

The factored form of $49q^2 - 4p^2$ is $\left(\boxed{7q + 2p}\right)\left(\boxed{7q - 2p}\right)$.

DIFFERENTIATE INSTRUCTION

Number Sense

Show students a quick way to rule out the possibility that a trinomial is a perfect-square trinomial. Remind them that if $ax^2 + bx + c$ is a perfect-square trinomial, then b must be an even number. This is because, in a perfect-square trinomial, $b = 2 \cdot \sqrt{a} \cdot \sqrt{b}$. If b is odd, then the trinomial is not a perfect square.

EXPLAIN 2

Factoring $a^2x^2 - b^2 = 0$

AVOID COMMON ERRORS

Students might think that y^6 is not a perfect square because the number 6 is not a perfect square. Remind them of the Product of Powers Property, which states that $a^m \cdot a^n = a^{m+n}$. Thus, y^6 is a perfect square because it can be written as $y^3 \cdot y^3$. The Power of a Power Property can also be used to show this as $y^6 = \left(y^3\right)^2$.

QUESTIONING STRATEGIES

? Can you factor $x^2 + 25$ as a difference of two squares? Explain. No; it is a sum of two squares, not a difference. The operation sign for the difference of two squares must be $-$.

? What are the values of a and b in the difference of squares $9 - x^4$? $a = 3$ and $b = x^2$

INTEGRATE MATHEMATICAL PRACTICES

Focus on Reasoning

MP.2 Discuss with students what happens if you forget to factor out a common factor of the terms in a difference of two squares. For example, to factor $4x^2 - 16y^4$, you could first factor out a common factor of 4 to get $4\left(x^2 - 4y^4\right)$, then factor the difference of squares to get $4\left(x + 2y^2\right)\left(x - 2y^2\right)$. If you do not notice the common factor, you can still factor the expression as a difference of squares, to get $\left(2x + 4y^2\right)\left(2x - 4y^2\right)$. Help students to see that this would be an equivalent expression, but it would not be a complete factorization. You would still need to factor a 2 out of each binomial to get the same final result as before.

EXPLAIN 3

Solving Equations with Special Factors

INTEGRATE MATHEMATICAL PRACTICES
Focus on Patterns

MP.8 When students factor a perfect-square trinomial, they should first look at the sign of the x-term, as this will tell them which pattern to use. If it is $+$, they should use $(a + b)^2$; if it is $-$, they should use $(a - b)^2$.

QUESTIONING STRATEGIES

? How are the equations $25x^2 + 20x + 4 = 0$ and $75x^2 + 60x + 12 = 0$ related? How do their solutions compare? Explain. The second equation is equal to the first one multiplied by 3. Both equations have the same solution, $x = -\frac{2}{5}$. The common factor of 3 in the second equation has no effect on the solution, because when you divide both sides of the equation by 3, it is identical to the first equation.

Reflect

5. **Discussion** James was factoring a difference of squares but did not finish his work. What steps is he missing?

$$16x^4 - 1 = (4x^2)^2 - 1$$
$$= (4x^2 + 1)(4x^2 - 1)$$

James factored the first difference of squares, $16x^4 - 1$, but forgot to factor the second one that came up, $4x^2 - 1$. This is his completed work:

$$16x^4 - 1 = (4x^2)^2 - 1$$
$$= (4x^2 + 1)(4x^2 - 1)$$
$$= (4x^2 + 1)\left[(2x)^2 - 1\right]$$
$$= (4x^2 + 1)(2x + 1)(2x - 1)$$

Your Turn

Factor each difference of squares.

6. $x^2 - 144$

$x^2 - 144 = x^2 - 12^2$
$= (x + 12)(x - 12)$

7. $81y^4 - 9y^2$

$81y^4 - 9y^2 = 9y^2(9y^2 - 1)$
$= 9y^2(3^2y^2 - 1)$
$= 9y^2(3y + 1)(3y - 1)$

⊘ Explain 3 Solving Equations with Special Factors

Equations with special factors can be solved using the Zero Product Property. Remember, the Zero Product Property states that if the product of two factors is zero, then at least one of the factors must be zero. For example, if $(x + 1)(x + 9) = 0$ then $x + 1 = 0$ or $x + 9 = 0$. Consequently, the solutions for the equation are $x = -1$ or $x = -9$.

Example 3 Solve the following equations with special factors.

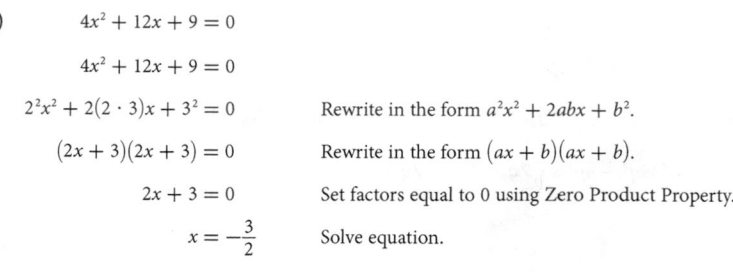

(A)

$$4x^2 + 12x + 9 = 0$$

$4x^2 + 12x + 9 = 0$	
$2^2x^2 + 2(2 \cdot 3)x + 3^2 = 0$	Rewrite in the form $a^2x^2 + 2abx + b^2$.
$(2x + 3)(2x + 3) = 0$	Rewrite in the form $(ax + b)(ax + b)$.
$2x + 3 = 0$	Set factors equal to 0 using Zero Product Property.
$x = -\dfrac{3}{2}$	Solve equation.

LANGUAGE SUPPORT EL

Modeling

Students may know and use the word *perfect* to mean flawless, but in mathematics the term *perfect square* has a specific meaning. A number that is a perfect square is *the square of a whole number,* and a *perfect-square trinomial* is *the square of a binomial.*

Demonstrate how to model the factors of trinomials with algebra tiles. Point out that if a trinomial can be factored, the tiles form a rectangle. For a perfect-square trinomial, the tiles will be arranged in a square. Be sure to use and repeat the terminology as you work together so that students hear the words in context, which helps clarify their meaning.

Ⓑ $25x^2 - 1 = 0$

$25x^2 - 1 = 0$

$\boxed{5}^2 x^2 - \boxed{1}^2 = 0$ Rewrite in the form $a^2x^2 - b^2$.

$\left(\boxed{5x + 1}\right)\left(\boxed{5x - 1}\right) = 0$ Rewrite in the form $(ax + b)(ax - b)$.

$\boxed{5x - 1} = 0$ or $\boxed{5x + 1} = 0$ Set factors equal to 0 using Zero Product Property.

$x = \boxed{\frac{1}{5}}$ or $x = \boxed{-\frac{1}{5}}$ Solve equation.

Your Turn

Solve the following equations with special factors.

8. $25x^2 - 10x + 1 = 0$

$25x^2 - 10x + 1 = 0$

$5^2x^2 - 2(5 \cdot 1)x + 1^2 = 0$

$(5x - 1)(5x - 1) = 0$

$5x - 1 - 0$

$5x = 1$

$x = \dfrac{1}{5}$

9. $8x^4 - 2x^2 = 0$

$8x^4 - 2x^2 = 0$

$2x^2(4x^2 - 1) = 0$

$2x^2(2^2x^2 - 1) = 0$

$2x^2(2x + 1)(2x - 1) = 0$

$x^2 = 0$ or $2x + 1 = 0$ or $2x - 1 = 0$

$x = 0$ $2x = -1$ $2x = 1$

$x = 0$ or $x = -\dfrac{1}{2}$ or $x = \dfrac{1}{2}$

 Explain 4   **Solving Equation Models with Special Factors**

For each real-world scenario, solve the model which involves an equation with special factors.

Example 4   Write the given information and manipulate into a familiar form. Solve the equation to answer a question about the situation.

As a satellite falls from outer space onto Mars, its distance in miles from the planet is given by the formula $d = -9t^2 + 776$, where t is the number of hours it has fallen. Find when the satellite will be 200 miles away from Mars.

🧩 Analyze Information

Identify the important information
- The satellite's distance in miles is given by the formula $\underline{d = -9t^2 + 776}$.
- The satellite distance at some time t is $d = \boxed{200}$.

EXPLAIN 4

Solving Equation Models with Special Factors

AVOID COMMON ERRORS

Remind students that the Zero Product Property can be applied only to quadratic equations in standard form, because it applies only to equations for which one side is zero. Students often try to apply it before setting one side equal to zero.

QUESTIONING STRATEGIES

? If the equation that models a real-world problem has the form $x^2 - b^2 = 0$ for some constant b, why might you need to discard one solution for x? Factoring $x^2 - b^2$ gives $(x + b)(x - b)$, so the solutions to the equation are $x = b$ and $x = -b$. One of these values is positive and one is negative. If x represents a quantity such as time or distance, a negative value may not make sense in the context of the problem.

Formulate a Plan

Substituting the value of the constant $d = \boxed{200}$ into the equation $\underline{d = -9t^2 + 776}$ you get the equation $\underline{200 = -9t^2 + 776}$. Simplify the new equation into a familiar form and solve it.

Solve

Rewrite the equation to be equal to 0.

$\boxed{200} = -9t^2 + 776$ Subtract 200 from both sides.

$0 = -9t^2 + \boxed{576}$ Divide both sides by -1.

$0 = 9t^2 - \boxed{576}$ Factor out 9.

$0 = \boxed{9}\left(t^2 - \boxed{64}\right)$

The equation contains a $\underline{\text{difference of squares}}$ that you can factor.

$0 = 9\left(\boxed{t + 8}\right)\left(\boxed{t - 8}\right)$

Use the $\underline{\text{Zero Product}}$ Property to solve.

$0 = 9\left(t + \boxed{8}\right)\left(t - \boxed{8}\right)$

$\boxed{t + 8} = 0 \text{ or } t - 8 = \boxed{0}$

$t = \boxed{\pm 8}$

The answer is $t = \boxed{8}$ because time must be $\underline{\text{positive}}$. So, the satellite has fallen for $\boxed{8}$ hours.

Justify and Evaluate

$t = \boxed{8}$ makes sense because time must be $\underline{\text{positive}}$. Check by substituting this value of t into the original equation.

$-9 \cdot \boxed{8}^2 + 776 = -9 \cdot \boxed{64} + 776$

$= 776 - \boxed{576}$

$= \boxed{200}$

This is what is expected from the given information.

Write the given information and manipulate it into a familiar form. Solve the equation to answer a question about the situation.

10. A volleyball player sets the ball in the air, and the height of the ball after t seconds is given in feet by $h = -16t^2 + 12t + 6$. A teammate wants to wait until the ball is 8 feet in the air before she spikes it. When should the teammate spike the ball? How many reasonable solutions are there to this problem? Explain.

$$-16t^2 + 12t + 6 = 8$$

$$-16t^2 + 12t - 2 = 0$$

$$8t^2 - 6t + 1 = 0$$

$$(4t - 1)(2t - 1) = 0$$

$$4t - 1 = 0 \quad \text{or} \quad 2t - 1 = 0$$

$$t = \frac{1}{4} \qquad\qquad t - \frac{1}{2}$$

At 0.25 second or 0.5 second the ball will be 8 ft high. There are two solutions because both occur after $t = 0$, when the ball is set.

11. The height of a model rocket is given (in centimeters) by the formula $h = -490t^2$, where t is measured in seconds and $h = 0$ refers to its original height at the top of a mountain. It begins to fly down from the mountain-top at time $t = 0$. When has the rocket descended 490 centimeters?

$$-490 = -490t^2$$

$$490t^2 - 490 = 0$$

$$490(t^2 - 1) = 0$$

$$490(t + 1)(t - 1) = 0$$

$$t = \pm 1$$

After one second, the rocket will have descended a distance of 490 centimeters. The negative time cannot be used in this context.

Elaborate

12. Are the perfect square trinomials $a^2 + 2ab + b^2$ and $a^2 - 2ab + b^2$ very different? How can you get one from the other?

Start with the first form $a^2 + 2ab + b^2$. Let $b = -b_{new}$ and simplify.

$$a^2 + 2ab + b^2 = a^2 + 2a(-b_{new}) + (-b_{new})^2$$

$$= a^2 - 2ab_{new} + \left[(-1)(b_{new})\right]^2$$

$$= a^2 - 2ab_{new} + (-1)^2(b_{new})^2$$

$$= a^2 - 2ab_{new} + b_{new}^2$$

$a^2 - 2ab_{new} + b_{new}^2$ **is the other form. They are not very different.**

ELABORATE

QUESTIONING STRATEGIES

? What types of quadratic equations have only one real solution? Quadratic equations that can be factored as perfect squares have only one real solution. For example, $4x^2 - 16x + 16 = 0$, which can be factored as $4(x - 2)^2 = 0$, has one real solution, $x = 2$.

SUMMARIZE THE LESSON

? What are two characteristics of a perfect-square trinomial of the form $ax^2 + bx + c$? *a* and *c* are perfect squares, and $b = 2\sqrt{ac}$.

? What are two characteristics of a difference of squares? **Both terms are perfect squares, and one term is subtracted from the other.**

---

13. How would you go about factoring $a^2 - 2ab + b^2 - 1$?
There is a perfect-square trinomial inside the expression that you can factor. There is also a difference of squares.

$$a^2 - 2ab + b^2 - 1 = (a - b)^2 - 1^2$$
$$= (a - b + 1)(a - b - 1)$$

14. Setting a perfect-square trinomial equal to zero, $a^2x^2 + 2abx + b^2 = 0$, produces how many solutions? How many solutions are produced setting a difference of squares equal to zero, $a^2x^2 - b^2 = 0$?

$a^2x^2 + 2abx + b^2 = 0$	$a^2x^2 - b^2 = 0$
$(ax + b)^2 = 0$	$(ax + b)(ax - b) = 0$
$ax = -b$	$ax = \pm b$
$x = -\frac{b}{a}$	$x = \pm\frac{b}{a}$

$a^2x^2 + 2abx + b^2 = 0$ **produces one solution for x.**

$a^2x^2 - b^2 = 0$ **produces two solutions for x.**

15. Physical problems involving projectile motion can be modeled using the general equation $h = -16t^2 + v_0t$. Here, *h* refers to the relative height of the projectile from its initial position, v_0 is its initial vertical velocity, and *t* is time elapsed from launch. If you are measuring the height of the projectile as it descends from a high place, and it was launched with $v_0 = 0$ (which means it was thrown horizontally or dropped), how would you use special products to find the time at which it reaches a given height? (Assume that the height the projectile has descended is a square number in this question, although this is not a requirement in real life).

Set $v_0 = 0$ and $h = -s^2$ for some value of s. h is negative because the projectile is descending from its original position. Substitute these values into the equation and simplify.

$$h = -16t^2 + v_0t$$
$$h = -16t^2$$
$$-s^2 = -16t^2$$
$$16t^2 - s^2 = 0$$

At this point you can use the difference of squares to solve.

$$(4t + s)(4t - s) = 0$$
$$4t = \pm s$$
$$t = \pm\frac{s}{4} = \pm\frac{\sqrt{-h}}{4}$$

Only the positive answer applies to the model, so the solution is $t = \frac{\sqrt{-h}}{4}$. The difference of squares was used to find this.

16. Essential Question Check-In How can you use special products to solve quadratic equations?
Once you recognize that a polynomial is a perfect-square trinomial or a difference of squares, you can factor the polynomial. Then, use the Zero Product Property to solve the equation.

☆ Evaluate: Homework and Practice

• Online Homework
• Hints and Help
• Extra Practice

For each trinomial, draw algebra tiles to show the factored form. Then, write the factored form.

1. $x^2 - 10x + 25$

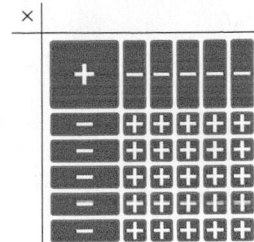

$x^2 - 10x + 25 = (x - 5)(x - 5)$

2. $x^2 + 8x + 16$

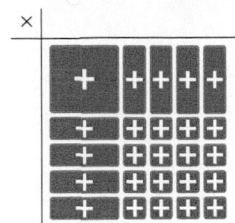

$x^2 + 8x + 16 = (x + 4)(x + 4)$

Factor.

3. $4x^2 + 4x + 1$

$4x^2 + 4x + 1 = 2^2x^2 + 2(2 \cdot 1)x + 1$

$= (2x + 1)(2x + 1)$

$= (2x + 1)^2$

4. $9x^2 - 18x + 9$

$9x^2 - 18x + 9 = 9(x^2 - 2x + 1)$

$= 9(x - 1)(x - 1)$

$= 9(x - 1)^2$

5. $16x^3 + 8x^2 + x$

$16x^3 + 8x^2 + x = x(16x^2 + 8x + 1)$

$= x(4x + 1)(4x + 1)$

$= x(4x + 1)^2$

6. $32x^3 - 16x^2 + 2x$

$32x^3 - 16x^2 + 2x = 2x(16x^2 - 8x + 1)$

$= 2x(4x - 1)(4x - 1)$

$= 2x(4x - 1)^2$

7. $x^2 - 169$

$x^2 - 169 = x^2 - 13^2$

$= (x + 13)(x - 13)$

8. $4p^2 - 9q^4$

$4p^2 - 9q^4 = (2p)^2 - (3q^2)^2$

$= (2p + 3q^2)(2p - 3q^2)$

9. $32x^4 - 8x^2$

$32x^4 - 8x^2 = 8x^2(4x^2 - 1)$

$= 8x^2(2^2x^2 - 1)$

$= 8x^2(2x + 1)(2x - 1)$

10. $2y^5 - 32z^4y$

$2y^5 - 32z^4 y = 2y(y^4 - 16z^4)$

$= 2y[(y^2)^2 - (4z^2)^2]$

$= 2y(y^2 + 4z^2)(y^2 - 4z^2)$

$= 2y(y^2 + 4z^2)[y^2 - (2z)^2]$

$= 2y(y^2 + 4z^2)(y + 2z)(y - 2z)$

EVALUATE

ASSIGNMENT GUIDE

Concepts and Skills	Practice
Explore Exploring Factors of Perfect-Square Trinomials	Exercises 1–2
Example 1 Factoring $a^2x^2 + 2abx + b^2$ and $a^2x^2 - 2abx + b^2$	Exercises 3–6
Example 2 Factoring $a^2x^2 - b^2 = 0$	Exercises 7–10, 25, 28, 30
Example 3 Solving Equations with Special Factors	Exercises 11–18, 26, 29
Example 4 Solving Equation Models with Special Factors	Exercises 19–24, 27

Exercise	Depth of Knowledge (D.O.K.)	COMMON CORE Mathematical Practices
1–10	**1** Recall of Information	**MP.2** Reasoning
11–18	**2** Skills/Concepts	**MP.2** Reasoning
19–24	**2** Skills/Concepts	**MP.4** Modeling
25	**3** Strategic Thinking	**MP.3** Logic
26	**2** Skills/Concepts	**MP.2** Reasoning
27	**2** Skills/Concepts H.O.T.	**MP.4** Modeling
28–30	**3** Strategic Thinking H.O.T.	**MP.3** Logic

Using Special Factors to Solve Equations   **1018**

QUESTIONING STRATEGIES

? If the values of a and c in a trinomial in the form $ax^2 + bx + c$ are both perfect squares, is the trinomial always a perfect-square trinomial? Explain. Provide an example to defend your answer. No; if the first and last terms are both perfect squares, the coefficient of the middle term must be two times the square root of the first coefficient, a, times the square root of the constant, c. Possible example: $16x^2 + 90x + 36$; both 16 and 36 are perfect squares, but the middle term would need to be $48x$ for this to be a perfect-square trinomial.

Solve the following equations with special factors.

11. $25x^2 + 20x + 4 = 0$

$$25x^2 + 20x + 4 = 0$$
$$5^2 x^2 + 2(5 \cdot 2)x + 2^2 = 0$$
$$(5x + 2)(5x + 2) = 0$$
$$(5x + 2)^2 = 0$$
$$5x + 2 = 0$$
$$5x = -2$$
$$x = -\frac{2}{5}$$

12. $x^3 - 10x^2 + 25x = 0$

$$x^3 - 10x^2 + 25x = 0$$
$$x(x^2 - 10x + 25) = 0$$
$$x\left[x^2 - 2(1 \cdot 5)x + 5^2\right] = 0$$
$$x(x - 5)(x - 5) = 0$$
$$x(x - 5)^2 = 0$$
$$x = 0 \text{ or } x - 5 = 0$$
$$x = 5$$

13. $4x^4 + 8x^3 + 4x^2 = 0$

$$4x^4 + 8x^3 + 4x^2 = 0$$
$$4x^2(x^2 + 2x + 1) = 0$$
$$4x^2\left[x^2 + 2(1 \cdot 1)x + 1^2\right] = 0$$
$$4x^2(x + 1)(x + 1) = 0$$
$$4x^2(x + 1)^2 = 0$$
$$4x^2 = 0 \text{ or } x + 1 = 0$$
$$x = 0 \qquad x = -1$$

14. $4x^2 - 8x + 4 = 0$

$$4x^2 - 8x + 4 = 0$$
$$4(x^2 - 2x + 1) = 0$$
$$4\left[x^2 - 2(1 \cdot 1) + 1^2\right] = 0$$
$$4(x - 1)(x - 1) = 0$$
$$4(x - 1)^2 = 0$$
$$x - 1 = 0$$
$$x = 1$$

15. $x^2 - 81 = 0$

$$x^2 - 81 = 0$$
$$x^2 - 9^2 = 0$$
$$(x + 9)(x - 9) = 0$$
$$x + 9 = 0 \text{ or } x - 9 = 0$$
$$x = -9 \qquad x = 9$$

16. $2x^3 - 2x = 0$

$$2x^3 - 2x = 0$$
$$2x^2(x^2 - 1) = 0$$
$$2x(x + 1)(x - 1) = 0$$
$$2x = 0 \quad \text{or} \quad x + 1 = 0 \quad \text{or} \quad x - 1 = 0$$
$$x = 0 \qquad x = -1 \qquad x = 1$$

17. $16q^2 - 81 = 0$

$$16q^2 - 81 = 0$$
$$(4q)^2 - (9)^2 = 0$$
$$(4q + 9)(4q - 9) = 0$$
$$4q + 9 = 0 \quad \text{or} \quad 4q - 9 = 0$$
$$4q = -9 \qquad 4q = 9$$
$$q = -\frac{9}{4} \qquad q = \frac{9}{4}$$

18. $4p^4 - 25p^2 = -16p^2$

$$4p^4 - 25p^2 + 16p^2 = 0$$
$$4p^4 - 9p^2 = 0$$
$$p^2(4p^2 - 9) = 0$$
$$p^2\left[(2p)^2 - 3^2\right] = 0$$
$$p^2(2p + 3)(2p - 3) = 0$$
$$p^2 = 0 \quad \text{or} \quad 2p + 3 = 0 \quad \text{or} \quad 2p - 3 = 0$$
$$p = 0 \qquad 2p = -3 \qquad 2p = 3$$
$$\qquad p = -\frac{3}{2} \qquad p = \frac{3}{2}$$

Jivesh is analyzing the flight of a few of his model rockets with various equations. In each equation, h is the height of the rocket in centimeters, and the rocket was fired from the ground at time $t = 0$, where t is measured in seconds.

19. For Jivesh's Model A rocket, he uses the equation $h = -490t^2 + 1120t$. When is the height of the Model A rocket 640 centimeters?

$$h = -490t^2 + 1120t$$

$$640 = -490t^2 + 1120t$$

$$490t^2 - 1120t + 640 = 0$$

$$49t^2 - 112t + 64 = 0$$

$$(7t - 8)(7t - 8) = 0$$

$$(7t - 8)^2 = 0$$

$$7t = 8$$

$$t = \frac{8}{7}$$

After $t = \frac{8}{7} \approx 1.14$ seconds, the rocket will have reached a height of 640 centimeters.

20. Jivesh also has a more powerful Model B rocket. For this rocket, he uses the equation $h = -490t^2 + 1260t$. When is the height of the Model B rocket 810 centimeters?

$$h = -490t^2 + 1260t$$

$$810 = -490t^2 + 1260t$$

$$490t^2 - 1260t + 810 = 0$$

$$49t^2 - 126t + 81 = 0$$

$$(7t - 9)(7t - 9) = 0$$

$$(7t - 9)^2 = 0$$

$$7t = 9$$

$$t = \frac{9}{7}$$

After $t = \frac{9}{7} \approx 1.29$ seconds, the rocket will have reached a height of 810 centimeters.

21. Jivesh brought his Model B rocket on a camping trip near the top of a mountain. He wants to model how it descends down the mountain. Here, he uses the equation $h = -490t^2$. When has the rocket descended 1000 centimeters?

$$h = -490t^2$$

$$-1000 = -490t^2$$

$$490t^2 - 1000 = 0$$

$$49t^2 - 100 = 0$$

$$(7t + 10)(7t - 10) = 0$$

$$7t = \pm 10$$

$$t = \pm\frac{10}{7}$$

After $t = \frac{10}{7} \approx 1.43$ seconds, the rocket will have descended a distance of 1000 centimeters. The negative value of t cannot be used in this context.

MODELING

Students may wish to check their answers to factoring problems by using algebra tiles. Remind them that the algebra tiles that model a perfect-square trinomial will form a square.

AVOID COMMON ERRORS

When checking the answer for a perfect-square trinomial, such as $(x + 6)^2$, students might write the product as $x^2 + 6^2 = x^2 + 36$. Encourage students to write $(x + 6)^2$ as $(x + 6)(x + 6)$ and then use the FOIL method.

QUESTIONING STRATEGIES

? Explain why the product of binomials $(r + s)(r - s)$ is not a trinomial. When you multiply these binomials together by FOIL, the inner and outer products cancel each other out, so the result is a difference of two squares: $(r + s)(r - s) = r^2 - s^2$.

---

22. **Geometry** Claire is cutting a square out of a bigger square for an art project. She cuts out a square with an area of 9 cm². The leftover area is 16 cm². What is the length of one of the sides of the bigger square? The area of a square is $A = l^2$ where l is the length of one of its sides.

    Solve for l.

    $l^2 - 9 = 16$

    $l^2 - 9 - 16 = 0$

    $l^2 - 25 = 0$

    $(l + 5)(l - 5) = 0$

    $l = \pm 5$

    Disregard the negative value of l because squares cannot have negative lengths.

    The square has side lengths of 5 centimeters.

23. The height of a diver during a dive can be modeled by $h = -16t^2$, where h is height in feet relative to the diving platform and t is time in seconds. Find the time it takes for the diver to reach the water if the platform is 49 feet high.

    $-49 = -16t^2$

    $16t^2 - 49 = 0$

    $(4t + 7)(4t - 7) = 0$

    $4t = \pm 7$

    $t = \pm \frac{7}{4}$

    After $t = \frac{7}{4} = 1.75$ seconds, the diver will have reached the water. The negative value of t cannot be used in this context.

24. **Physics** Consider a particular baseball player at bat. The height of the ball at time t can be modeled by $h = -16t^2 + v_0 t + h_0$. Here, v_0 is the initial upward velocity of the ball, and h_0 is the height at which the ball is hit. If a ball is 4 feet off the ground when it is hit with a negligible upward velocity close to 0 feet per second, when will the ball hit the ground?

    $h = -16t^2 + v_0 t + h_0$

    $0 = -16t^2 + 0t + 4$

    $0 = 16t^2 - 4$

    $0 = 4(4t^2 - 1)$

    $0 = 4(2t + 1)(2t - 1)$

    $t = \pm \frac{1}{2}$

    The answer should be positive, so $t = \frac{1}{2}$ second.

25. Explain the Error Jeremy factored $144x^2 - 100$ as follows:

$$144x^2 - 100 = (12x + 10)(12x - 10)$$
$$= 2(6x + 5)(6x - 5)$$

What was his error? Correct his work.

He factored out a 2 from both $(12x + 10)$ and $(12x + 10)$, which is the same as

factoring out a 4 from the whole expression. It should be $4(6x + 5)(6x - 5)$.

$$144x^2 - 100 = (12x + 10)(12x - 10)$$
$$= 2(6x + 5) \cdot 2(6x - 5)$$
$$= 4(6x + 5)(6x - 5)$$

26. Which of the following are solutions to the equation $x^5 - 2x^3 + x = 0$? Select all that apply.

a. $x = -1$	$x^5 - 2x^3 + x = 0$
b. $x - 2$	$x(x^4 - 2x^2 + 1) = 0$
c. $x = 1$	$x(x^2 - 1)(x^2 - 1) = 0$
d. $x = 0.5$	$x(x^2 - 1)^2 = 0$
e. $x = 0$	$x[(x + 1)(x - 1)]^2 = 0$

$$x(x + 1)^2(x - 1)^2 = 0$$
$$x = 0 \quad \text{or} \quad x + 1 = 0 \quad \text{or} \quad x - 1 = 0$$
$$x = -1 \qquad\qquad x = 1$$

The letters a, c, and e correspond to solutions of

the equation $x^5 - 2x^3 + x = 0$.

H.O.T. Focus on Higher Order Thinking

27. Multi-Step An artist framed a picture. The picture is a square with a side length of 2y. It is surrounded by a square frame with a side length of 4x.

a. Find and completely factor the expression for the area of the frame.

The area of the frame only is the difference of

the large square number and the small square

number.

$$16x^2 - 4y^2 = 4(4x^2 - y^2)$$
$$= 4(2x + y)(2x - y)$$

The area of the frame is $4(2x + y)(2x - y)$.

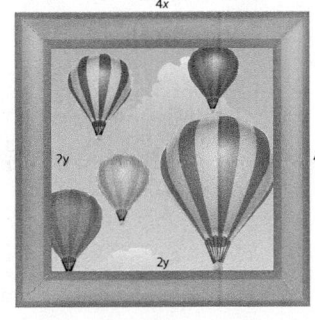

4x

?y

4x

2y

QUESTIONING STRATEGIES

? Is $4x^2 + 20x - 25$ a perfect-square trinomial? How can you tell? No; the last term is negative. This means that the operation sign in one binomial factor is $+$ and in the other is $-$. In a perfect-square trinomial, the constant term is always positive.

? Is $16x^4 - 1$ the difference of two squares? Explain. Yes; $16x^4 - 1$ is equivalent to $(4x^2)^2 - 1^2$.

AVOID COMMON ERRORS

When the constant term of the difference of two squares is even, such as in $x^2 - 16$, some students may divide by 2 rather than taking the square root, producing an answer of $(x + 8)(x - 8)$. Emphasize to students that they are taking the square root of each term, so the correct factorization is $(x + 4)(x - 4)$.

INTEGRATE MATHEMATICAL PRACTICES

Focus on Math Connections

MP.1 Some students may speculate that because a difference of squares in the form $a^2 - b^2$ can be factored as $(a+b)(a-b)$, a difference of cubes can be factored similarly. Inform students that there are different patterns for the factors of the sum and difference of cubes:

$$a^3 + b^3 = (a+b)(a^2 - ab + b^2)$$
$$a^3 - b^3 = (a-b)(a^2 + ab + b^2).$$

Have them multiply each pair of factors together to confirm these patterns.

QUESTIONING STRATEGIES

? When factoring a trinomial, do you think it is easier to first list all the factor pairs or to first check whether it fits the pattern for a perfect-square trinomial? Explain your reasoning. **Possible answer: It is easier to check for the pattern, because once you see that *a* and *c* are perfect squares, you have only to check one product of factors to confirm whether it gives the correct value of *b* for a perfect-square trinomial. If it does, you can write the answer, and if it does not, you can list more factor pairs to determine how to factor the trinomial.**

---

b. The frame has an area of 11 square inches and the picture has an area of 25 square inches. Find the width of the frame.

Solve for the width of the frame, which is the width of the frame minus the width of the square picture, divided by two:

$$\frac{4x - 2y}{2} = 2x - y$$

Set the area of the picture, $4y^2$, to 25 and solve.

$$25 = 4y^2$$
$$0 = 4y^2 - 25$$
$$0 = (2y + 5)(2y - 5)$$
$$\pm 5 = 2y$$
$$\pm \frac{5}{2} = y$$

In the context of lengths and area, you can only take the positive y as a possible solution, so $y = \frac{5}{2}$.

Next, solve for x. The area of the frame is $4(4x^2 - y^2) = 11$. Substitute $y = \frac{5}{2}$ into this equation and solve for x.

$$4(4x^2 - y^2) = 11$$
$$4\left[4x^2 - \left(\frac{5}{2}\right)^2\right] = 11$$
$$4\left[4x^2 - \left(\frac{25}{4}\right)\right] = 11$$
$$16x^2 - 25 = 11$$
$$16x^2 - 25 - 11 = 0$$
$$16x^2 - 36 = 0$$
$$(4x + 6)(4x - 6) = 0$$
$$4x = \pm 6$$
$$x = \pm \frac{3}{2}$$

Use the positive value of $x \approx \frac{3}{2}$. Solve for the width of the frame using the values for x and y.

$$2x - y = 2 \cdot \frac{3}{2} - \frac{5}{2} = 3 - \frac{5}{2} \approx \frac{1}{2}$$

The frame is $\frac{1}{2}$ inch wide.

28. Critical Thinking Sinea thinks that the fully factored form of the expression $x^4 - 1$ is $(x^2 - 1)(x^2 + 1)$. Is she correct? Explain.

No, the binomial $(x^2 - 1)$ is also a difference of squares, so the fully factored form is $(x + 1)(x - 1)(x^2 + 1)$.

29. Persevere in Problem Solving Samantha has the equation $x^3 + 2x^2 + x = x^3 - x$. Explain how she can find the solutions of the equation. Then solve the equation.

She can factor each side of the equation, and then subtract the right side from both

sides so one side of the equation is 0. She can then simplify the equation and set the

factors equal to 0 to solve for x. .

$$x^3 + 2x^2 + x = x^3 - x$$
$$x(x^2 + 2x + 1) = x(x^2 - 1)$$
$$x(x + 1)(x + 1) - x(x + 1)(x \quad 1)$$
$$x(x + 1)(x + 1) - x(x + 1)(x - 1) = 0$$
$$x(x + 1)\big[(x + 1) - (x - 1)\big] = 0$$
$$x(x + 1)[2] = 0$$
$$2x(x + 1) = 0$$

$2x = 0$ or $x + 1 = 0$

$x = 0$ $x = -1$

The solutions are 0 and -1.

30. Communicate Mathematical Ideas Explain how to fully factor the expression $x^4 - 2x^2y^2 + y^4$.

Use the rule for perfect square trinomials to factor $x^4 - 2x^2y^2 + y^4$ as $\left(x^2 - y^2\right)^2$. The

binomial $\left(x^2 - y^2\right)$ is a difference of squares that can be factored as $(x + y)(x - y)$, so

the fully factored form is $(x + y)^2(x - y)^2$.

JOURNAL

Have students write a journal entry explaining how a perfect-square trinomial and a difference of squares are alike and how they are different.

AVOID COMMON ERRORS

Students may see that the first two fountain equations are the difference of squares and surmise that they each have a square shape. Remind students that a square's area is the product of two equal lengths. The difference of squares does not factor into the product of two identical expressions.

Lesson Performance Task

A designer is planning to place a fountain in the lobby of an art museum. Four artists have each designed a fountain to fit the space. Some have designed rectangular fountains and the others designed square fountains. Given a quadratic equation representing the area of the fountain and the actual area of the fountain, find the dimensions of each fountain.

Artist	Artemis	Beatrice	Geoffrey	Daniel
Area equation	$A_A = 9x^2 - 25$	$A_B = 4x^2 - 25$	$A_G = 25x^2 + 80x + 64$	$A_D = 81x^2 + 198x + 121$
Fountain area	39 square feet	$28x - 74$ square feet	$160x$ square feet	$198x + 242$ square feet

Artemis:

$$A_A = 9x^2 - 25$$
$$= (3x + 5)(3x - 5)$$
$$39 = 9x^2 - 25$$
$$0 = 9x^2 - 64$$
$$0 = (3x - 8)(3x + 8)$$
$$x = \frac{8}{3} \quad \text{or} \quad x = -\frac{8}{3}$$

Since a dimension cannot be a negative and the solution $x = -\frac{8}{3}$ would give negative values for $3x + 5$ and $3x - 5$, disregard $x = -\frac{8}{3}$.

$$A_A = (3x + 5)(3x - 5)$$
$$= \left(3\left(\frac{8}{3}\right) + 5\right)\left(3\left(\frac{8}{3}\right) - 5\right)$$
$$= (8 + 5)(8 - 5)$$
$$= (13)(3)$$

The fountain by Artemis is a rectangle measuring 13 feet by 3 feet.

Beatrice:

$$A_B = 4x^2 - 25$$
$$= (2x + 5)(2x - 5)$$
$$28x - 74 = 4x^2 - 25$$
$$0 = 4x^2 - 28x + 49$$
$$0 = (2x - 7)^2$$
$$2x - 7 = 0$$
$$2x = 7$$
$$x = \frac{7}{2}$$
$$A_B = (2x + 5)(2x - 5)$$
$$= \left(2\left(\frac{7}{2}\right) + 5\right)\left(2\left(\frac{7}{2}\right) - 5\right)$$
$$= (7 + 5)(7 - 5)$$
$$= (12)(2)$$

The fountain by Beatrice is a rectangle measuring 12 feet by 2 feet.

EXTENSION ACTIVITY

Have students consider a square fountain with side length x feet. Ask them to explore how the area of the fountain changes if they make each side d feet longer. Have them draw a diagram to show the area of each fountain and explain how the diagram corresponds to the algebraic expressions representing the area.

Students should find that while the original fountain has area x^2, the enlarged fountain has area $x^2 + 2dx + d^2$. A diagram may show that the area of the enlarged fountain can be divided into a square with area x^2, a square with area d^2, and two rectangles with area dx.

Geoffrey:

$$A_G = 25x^2 + 80x + 64$$
$$= (5x + 8)^2$$
$$160x = 25x^2 + 80x + 64$$
$$0 = 25x^2 - 80x + 64$$
$$0 = (5x - 8)^2$$
$$5x - 8 = 0$$
$$5x = 8$$
$$x = \frac{8}{5}$$

$$A_G = (5x + 8)^2$$
$$= \left(5\left(\frac{8}{5}\right) + 8\right)^2$$
$$= (8 + 8)^2$$
$$= 16^2$$

The fountain by Geoffrey is a square with 16-foot sides.

Daniel:

$$A_D = 81x^2 + 198x + 121$$
$$= (9x + 11)^2$$
$$198x + 242 = 81x^2 + 198x + 121$$
$$0 = 81x^2 - 121$$
$$0 = (9x - 11)(9x + 11)$$
$$9x - 11 = 0 \qquad 9x + 11 = 0$$
$$9x = 11 \quad \text{or} \quad 9x = -11$$
$$x = \frac{11}{9} \qquad\qquad x = -\frac{11}{9}$$

Disregard $x = -\dfrac{11}{9}$.

$$A_D = (9x + 11)^2$$
$$= \left(9\left(\frac{11}{9}\right) + 11\right)^2$$
$$= (11 + 11)^2$$
$$= 22^2$$

The fountain by Daniel is a square with 22-foot sides.

QUESTIONING STRATEGIES

? How many possible values of x are there for the fountains designed by Beatrice and Geoffrey? Explain. For each of these fountains, there is only one solution for x, because when the appropriate equation is written in standard form, the expression set equal to zero is a perfect-square trinomial. Both factors are the same, so setting each factor equal to zero yields the same solution.

Scoring Rubric

2 points: Student correctly solves the problem and explains his/her reasoning.

1 point: Student shows good understanding of the problem but does not fully solve or explain his/her reasoning.

0 points: Student does not demonstrate understanding of the problem.

Using Special Factors to Solve Equations   **1026**

Study Guide Review

ASSESSMENT AND INTERVENTION

Assign or customize module reviews.

MODULE PERFORMANCE TASK

Mathematical Practices: MP.1, MP.2, MP.4, MP.6
A-SSE.A.2, A-SSE.B.3a, F-IF.B.4

SUPPORTING STUDENT REASONING

Students should begin this problem by first finding the width of the arched doorway. Then they should focus on what additional information they will need. Here is some of the information they may ask for.

- **How much clearance should I allow?** The crate is sliding and will not need much "wiggle room". However, the crate should not scrape against the archway.

- **Can the crate be turned on its side?** Students should assume that the crate has a top and bottom and that turning the crate might damage its contents.

- **Can I decide on a crate that has less depth than width and can therefore be turned?** Students should assume that the crate's depth is greater than its width.

Using Factors to Solve Quadratic Equations

Essential Question: How can you use factoring a quadratic equation to solve real-world problems?

Key Vocabulary
difference of two squares
(*diferencia de dos cuadrados*)
perfect-square trinomial
(*trinomio cuadrado perfecto*)

KEY EXAMPLE (Lesson 21.1)

Factor $x^2 - 2x - 8$.

Find the factor pair of -8 whose sum is -2.
The factor pair is -4 and 2.
$x^2 - 2x - 8 = (x - 4)(x + 2)$

Factors of −8	Sum of Factors
−1 and 8	7
1 and −8	−7
−2 and 4	2
2 and −4	−2

KEY EXAMPLE (Lesson 21.2)

Solve $4x^2 + 8x + 3 = 0$.

Find the factor pairs of 4 and 3 that result in a sum of 8.
The factor pairs are 2 and 2 and 1 and 3.

$$4x^2 + 8x + 3 = 0$$
$$(2x + 1)(2x + 3) = 0$$
$$2x + 1 = 0 \quad \text{or} \quad 2x + 3 = 0$$
$$x = -\frac{1}{2} \quad \text{or} \quad x = -\frac{3}{2}$$

Factors of 4	Factors of 3	Outer Product + Inner Product
1 and 4	1 and 3	$(1)(3) + (4)(1) = 7$
1 and 4	3 and 1	$(1)(1) + (4)(3) = 13$
2 and 2	1 and 3	$(2)(3) + (2)(1) = 8$

KEY EXAMPLE (Lesson 21.3)

Solve $16x^2 - 25 = 0$.

$4^2 \cdot x^2 - 5^2 = 0$	*Rewrite in the form $a^2 x^2 - b^2$.*
$(4x + 5)(4x - 5) = 0$	*Rewrite in the form $(ax + b)(ax - b)$.*
$4x + 5 = 0 \quad \text{or} \quad 4x - 5 = 0$	*Set factors equal to 0 using Zero Product Property.*
$x = -\frac{5}{4} \quad \text{or} \quad x = \frac{5}{4}$	

SCAFFOLDING SUPPORT

- Students may initially find that the arch is 4 feet wide. Point out that 4 feet is only half the width of the base of the arch, since the width includes 4 feet on both sides of the origin.

- Some students may need help in understanding that the taller the crate is, the narrower the base needs to be.

- Students who need more structure will benefit from being given a specific height, such as 5 feet.

- Challenge students by asking them in how many different ways a crate having dimensions of 5 ft × 6 ft × 7 ft could fit through the archway, assuming it is packed well enough that it can be turned on any of its faces.

Solve each equation. *(Lessons 21.1, 21.2, 21.3)*

1. $x^2 - 81 = 0$

    −9 and 9

2. $2x^2 - 8x - 10 = 0$

    −1 and 5

3. $x^2 + 7x + 12 = 0$

    −4 and −3

4. $x^2 - 14x = -49$

    7

5. $16 - 4x^2 = 0$

    −2 and 2

6. $6x^2 + 5x + 1 = 0$

    $-\frac{1}{2}$ and $-\frac{1}{3}$

7. The area of a rectangular pool is $(x^2 + 17x + 72)$ square meters. The dimensions of the pool are the factors of this polynomial. There is a 3-meter-wide concrete walkway around the pool. Write expressions to represent the dimensions of the outside border of the walkway. *(Lesson 21.1)*

    $(x + 15)$ **meters and** $(x + 14)$ **meters**

MODULE PERFORMANCE TASK

Fitting Through the Arch

The Ship-Shape Shipping Company ships items in rectangular crates. At one shipping destination, each crate must be able to fit through an arched doorway. The shape of this arched doorway can be modeled by the quadratic equation $y = -x^2 + 16$, where x is the distance in feet from the center of the arch and y is the height of the arch. Find the width of the archway at its base.

The Ship-Shape Shipping Company just unloaded several crates outside the arch ranging in height from 2 feet to 6 feet. Choose a particular crate height. Then, find the maximum width the crate could have and still fit through the arched doorway.

Start by listing in the space below how you will tackle this problem. Then use your own paper to complete the task. Be sure to write down all your data and assumptions. Then use graphs, tables, or algebra to explain how you reached your conclusion.

DISCUSSION OPPORTUNITIES

- What happens if the crate is light enough to be tilted up on one of its edges? Would a larger crate then be able to fit through the arch? (Students will not be able to model this mathematically, but if they are interested, encourage them to explore the issue by manipulating various rectangular cutouts on a graph of the parabola.)

SAMPLE SOLUTION

The width of the arched doorway at its base $(y = 0)$ is found by solving $-x^2 + 16 = 0$. Factor to solve: $(4 + x)(4 - x) = 0$.

Therefore, $x = 4, -4$. The width of the doorway at its base is $4 - (-4) = 8$, or 8 ft.

If the height of the crate is 5 ft, its maximum width can be found by solving $5 = -x^2 + 16$. Students may wish to sketch the parabola and draw a box of height 5 to better visualize the situation:

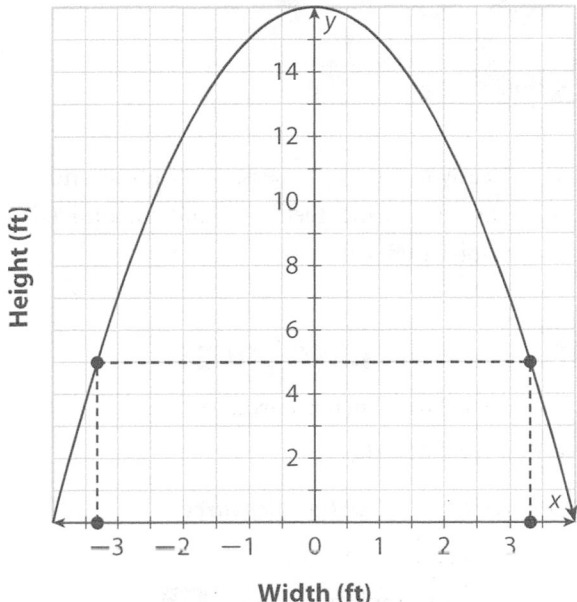

Use a graphing calculator to find the points of intersection of $y = -x^2 + 16$ and $y = 5$.

So, $x \approx \pm 3.3$ and the maximum width is about 6.6 feet.

Assessment Rubric

2 points: Student correctly solves the problem and explains his/her reasoning.

1 point: Student shows good understanding of the problem but does not fully solve or explain.

0 points: Student does not demonstrate understanding of the problem.

Ready to Go On?

ASSESS MASTERY

Use the assessment on this page to determine if students have mastered the concepts and standards covered in this module.

ASSESSMENT AND INTERVENTION

Access Ready to Go On? assessment online, and receive instant scoring, feedback, and customized intervention or enrichment.

ADDITIONAL RESOURCES

Response to Intervention Resources

- Reteach Worksheets

Differentiated Instruction Resources

- Reading Strategies **EL**
- Success for English Learners **EL**
- Challenge Worksheets

Assessment Resources

- Leveled Module Quizzes

1029 Module 21

21.1–21.3 Using Factors to Solve Quadratic Equations

- Online Homework
- Hints and Help
- Extra Practice

Identify each expression as a perfect-square trinomial, a difference of squares, or neither. Factor each expression. *(Lessons 21.1, 21.2, 21.3)*

1. $4p^2 + 12p + 9$

perfect-square trinomial; $(2p + 3)^2$

2. $a^2 - 9a - 36$

neither; $(a - 12)(a + 3)$

Solve each equation. *(Lessons 21.1, 21.2, 21.3)*

3. $x^2 - 4x - 21 = 0$

−3 and 7

4. $49x^2 - 100 = 0$

$-\frac{10}{7}$ and $\frac{10}{7}$

5. $5x^2 - 33x - 14 = 0$

$-\frac{2}{5}$ and 7

6. $x^2 + 16x + 64 = 0$

−8

7. A golfer hits a ball from a starting elevation of 4 feet with a vertical velocity of 70 feet per second down to a green with an elevation of −5 feet. The number of seconds t it takes the ball to hit the green can be represented by the equation $-16t^2 + 70t + 4 = -5$. How long does it take the ball to land on the green? *(Lesson 21.2)*

4.5 seconds

ESSENTIAL QUESTION

8. How can you use factoring to solve quadratic equations in standard form?

Possible Answer: You can factor the right side of the quadratic equation. Then set each linear factor equal to 0. Solve each linear equation. These are the solutions of the original quadratic equation.

©Houghton Mifflin Harcourt Publishing Company

COMMON CORE Common Core Standards

Lesson	Items	Content Standards	Mathematical Practices
21.2	1–2	A-SSE.B.3a, A-SSE.A.2	MP.2
21.1	3, 6	A-SSE.B.3a, A-SSE.A.2, A-REI.B.4	MP.2
21.3	4	A-SSE.B.3a, A-SSE.A.2, A-REI.B.4	MP.2
21.2	5	A-SSE.B.3a, A-SSE.A.2, A-REI.B.4	MP.2
21.2	7	A-SSE.B.3a, A-SSE.A.2, A-REI.B.4	MP.1

Assessment Readiness

1. Consider the equation $5x(2x + 1) - 3(2x + 1) = 0$.
   Choose True or False for each statement about the equation.

   A. It is equivalent to $(5x - 3)(2x + 1) = 0$.   ● True   ○ False

   B. A solution of the equation is $x = \frac{1}{2}$.   ○ True   ● False

   C. A zero of the equation is $\frac{3}{5}$.   ● True   ○ False

2. Factor to solve each equation. Does the equation have a solution of $x = 2$?
   Select Yes or No for each.

   A. $4x^2 - 16 = 0$ ● Yes   ○ No

   B. $x^2 - 4x + 4 = 0$ ● Yes   ○ No

   C. $4x^2 + 16x + 16 = 0$ ○ Yes   ● No

3. Larry thinks the quotient of $\frac{4x^2 + 7x - 15}{x + 3}$ is $4x - 5$. Explain how you can check his answer using multiplication. Then, check his answer. Is Larry correct?

   Possible answer: You can check the quotient by multiplying the quotient by the

   divisor, or $(4x - 5)(x + 3)$. The product is $4x^2 + 7x - 15$, so Larry is correct.

4. Marcello is replacing a rectangular sliding glass door with dimensions of $(x + 7)$ and $(x + 3)$ feet. The area of the glass door is 45 square feet. What are the length and width of the door? Explain how you got your answer.

   I found the area of the glass door by multiplying the length by the width, which is

   $x^2 + 10x + 21$. I set this product, which represents the area in terms of x, equal to

   45. Then, I rewrote the equation so one side was 0 and solved for x or got $x = -12$

   or $x = 2$. A dimension of the door cannot be negative, so $x = 2$. The length of the

   door is $2 + 7$, or 9 feet, and the width is $2 + 3$, or 5 feet.

MIXED REVIEW
Assessment Readiness

ASSESSMENT AND INTERVENTION

Assign ready-made or customized practice tests to prepare students for high-stakes tests.

ADDITIONAL RESOURCES

Assessment Resources

- Leveled Module Quizzes: Modified, B

AVOID COMMON ERRORS

Item 2 If students have trouble factoring the expressions quickly, point out that an alternate solution method would be to substitute the value into each equation and directly check whether it is a solution.

COMMON CORE Common Core Standards

Lesson	Items	Content Standards	Mathematical Practices
20.3	1*	A-APR.B.3	MP.1
21.3	2	A-SSE.A.2	MP.2
18.2	3*	A-SSE.A.1	MP.3
18.2, 21.1	4*	A-SSE.A.1, A-REI.B.4a	MP.4

* Item integrates mixed review concepts from previous modules or a previous course.

Using Square Roots to Solve Quadratic Equations

ESSENTIAL QUESTION:

Answer: You can choose a method depending on the form of the quadratic equation that is written from the real-world problem. If you can't solve it using square roots, factoring, or completing the square, then you can use the quadratic formula to solve the equation.

PROFESSIONAL DEVELOPMENT VIDEO

Professional Development Video

Author Juli Dixon models successful teaching practices in an actual high-school classroom.

Professional Development
my.hrw.com

Using Square Roots to Solve Quadratic Equations

MODULE 22

Essential Question: How can you use quadratic equations to solve real-world problems?

LESSON 22.1
Solving Equations by Taking Square Roots

LESSON 22.2
Solving Equations by Completing the Square

LESSON 22.3
Using the Quadratic Formula to Solve Equations

LESSON 22.4
Choosing a Method for Solving Quadratic Equations

LESSON 22.5
Solving Nonlinear Systems

© Houghton Mifflin Harcourt Publishing Company • Image Credits: ©Getty Images/PhotoDisc

REAL WORLD VIDEO
The designers of a fireworks display need to make precise timing calculations. An explosion too soon or too late could spell disaster!

MODULE PERFORMANCE TASK PREVIEW

Fireworks Display

As with any other projectile, the relationship between the time since a firework was launched and its height is quadratic. Fireworks must be carefully timed in order to ignite at the most impressive height. In this task, you will figure out how you can use math to launch fireworks that are safe and achieve the maximum possible effect.

Module 22   **1031**

DIGITAL TEACHER EDITION

Access a full suite of teaching resources when and where you need them:

- Access content online or offline
- Customize lessons to share with your class
- Communicate with your students in real-time
- View student grades and data instantly to target your instruction where it is needed most

PERSONAL MATH TRAINER
Assessment and Intervention

Assign automatically graded homework, quizzes, tests, and intervention activities. Prepare your students with updated, Common Core-aligned practice tests.

Are (YOU) Ready?

Complete these exercises to review skills you will need for this module.

Exponents

Example 1	Simplify $25^{\frac{1}{2}}$.

$$25^{\frac{1}{2}} = \sqrt{25} = 5$$

A number raised to the $\frac{1}{2}$ power is equal to the square root of the number.

- Online Homework
- Hints and Help
- Extra Practice

Simplify.

1. $100^{\frac{1}{2}}$

   10

2. $50^{\frac{1}{2}}$

   $5\sqrt{2}$

3. $\left(\frac{36}{81}\right)^{\frac{1}{2}}$

   $\frac{2}{3}$

Algebraic Expressions

Example 2	Evaluate $\left(\frac{b}{2}\right)^2$ when $b = 18$.

$$\left(\frac{b}{2}\right)^2$$

$$\left(\frac{18}{2}\right)^2 = 9^2 = 81$$

Substitute 18 for b and evaluate the expression.

Evaluate $\left(\frac{b}{2}\right)^2$ for the given value of b.

4. $b = 24$

   144

5. $b = -10$

   25

6. $b = 3$

   $\frac{9}{4}$

Example 3	Factor $x^2 + 14x + 49$.

$x^2 + 14x + 49$ $x^2 + 14x + 49$ is a perfect square.

$x^2 + 2(x)(7) + 7^2$ Rewrite in the form $a^2 + 2ab + b^2$.

$(x + 7)(x + 7)$ Rewrite in the form $(a + b)(a + b)$.

$(x + 7)^2$

Factor each perfect square trinomial.

7. $x^2 - 12x + 36$

   $(x - 6)^2$

8. $x^2 + 22x + 121$

   $(x + 11)^2$

9. $4x^2 + 12x + 9$

   $(2x + 3)^2$

10. $16x^2 - 40x + 25$

    $(4x - 5)^2$

Are You Ready?

ASSESS READINESS

Use the assessment on this page to determine if students need strategic or intensive intervention for the module's prerequisite skills.

ASSESSMENT AND INTERVENTION

RtI Response to Intervention **TIER 1, TIER 2, TIER 3 SKILLS**

Personal Math Trainer will automatically create a standards-based, personalized intervention assignment for your students, targeting each student's individual needs!

ADDITIONAL RESOURCES

See the table below for a full list of intervention resources available for this module.

Response to Intervention Resources also includes:

- Tier 2 Skill Pre-Tests for each Module
- Tier 2 Skill Post-Tests for each skill

Response to Intervention			Differentiated Instruction
Tier 1	**Tier 2**	**Tier 3**	
Lesson Intervention Worksheets	Strategic Intervention Skills Intervention Worksheets	Intensive Intervention Worksheets available online	
Reteach 22.1 Reteach 22.2 Reteach 22.3 Reteach 22.4 Reteach 22.5	2 Algebraic Expressions 5 Exponents 11 Multi-Step Equations	Building Block Skills 19, 22, 23, 24, 27, 29, 30, 40, 59, 69, 76, 81, 98, 100	Challenge worksheets Extend the Math Lesson Activities in TE

Solving Equations by Taking Square Roots

Common Core Math Standards

The student is expected to:

COMMON CORE **A-REI.B.4b**

Solve quadratic equations by... taking square roots . . .

Mathematical Practices

COMMON CORE **MP.8 Patterns**

Language Objective

Explain to a partner how to solve $ax^2 = c$ by taking square roots, and how to tell if there are one, two, or no real solutions.

ENGAGE

Essential Question: How can you solve quadratic equations using square roots?

Isolate the square root on one side of the equation by adding, subtracting, multiplying, or dividing. Then take the square root. Finally, solve for both the positive and negative square root.

PREVIEW: LESSON PERFORMANCE TASK

View the Engage section online. Discuss the photo, explaining that the motion of a clock's pendulum is accelerated by gravity. The pendulum swings back and forth with a period that is proportional to the square root of its length. Then preview the Lesson Performance Task.

Name_____ Class_____ Date_____

22.1 Solving Equations by Taking Square Roots

Essential Question: How can you solve quadratic equations using square roots?

Resource Locker

⊙ Explore   Exploring Square Roots

Recall that the **square root** of a nonnegative number a is the real number b such that $b^2 = a$. Since $4^2 = 16$ and $(-4)^2 = 16$, the square roots of 16 are 4 and −4. Thus, every positive real number has two square roots, one positive and one negative. The positive square root is given by $\sqrt{a}$ and the negative square root by $-\sqrt{a}$. These can be combined as $\pm\sqrt{a}$.

Properties of Radicals		
Property	**Symbols**	**Example**
Product Property of Radicals	For $a \geq 0$ and $b \geq 0$, $\sqrt{ab} = \sqrt{a} \cdot \sqrt{b}$.	$\sqrt{36} = \sqrt{9 \cdot 4}$ $= \sqrt{9} \cdot \sqrt{4}$ $= 3 \cdot 2$ $= 6$
Quotient Property of Radicals	For $a \geq 0$ and $b > 0$, $\sqrt{\dfrac{a}{b}} = \dfrac{\sqrt{a}}{\sqrt{b}}$.	$-\sqrt{0.16} = -\sqrt{\dfrac{16}{100}}$ $= -\dfrac{\sqrt{16}}{\sqrt{100}}$ $= -\dfrac{4}{10}$ $= -0.4$

Find each square root.

(A) $\pm\sqrt{49} = +\boxed{7}$ and $-\boxed{7}$

(B) $\pm\sqrt{25} = +\boxed{5}$ and $-\boxed{5}$

(C) $\pm\sqrt{12} = \pm\sqrt{\boxed{4} \cdot 3} = \pm\sqrt{\boxed{4}} \cdot \sqrt{\boxed{3}}$
$= \pm\boxed{2} \cdot \sqrt{\boxed{3}}$

(D) $\pm\sqrt{\dfrac{16}{9}} = \pm\dfrac{\sqrt{\boxed{16}}}{\sqrt{\boxed{9}}}$
$= \pm\dfrac{\boxed{4}}{\boxed{3}}$

(E) $\pm\sqrt{0.27} = \pm\sqrt{\dfrac{27}{100}} = \pm\dfrac{\sqrt{\boxed{27}}}{\sqrt{100}} = \pm\dfrac{\sqrt{\boxed{9} \cdot 3}}{\boxed{10}} = \pm\dfrac{\sqrt{\boxed{9}} \cdot \sqrt{3}}{\boxed{10}} = \pm\dfrac{\boxed{3} \cdot \sqrt{\boxed{3}}}{\boxed{10}}$

Module 22   **1033**   Lesson 1

© Houghton Mifflin Harcourt Publishing Company

22.1 Solving Equations by Taking Square Roots

HARDCOVER PAGES 807–814

Turn to these pages to find this lesson in the hardcover student edition.

Reflect

1. **Discussion** Explain why $\sqrt{6^2}$ and $\sqrt{(-6)^2}$ have the same value.
   $6^2 = (-6)^2 = 36$ and the symbol $\sqrt{\ }$ represents the positive square root of 36, or 6.

2. **Discussion** Explain why a must be nonnegative when you find $\sqrt{a}$.
   By the definition of a square root of a, $a = b^2$ for some b, so a is equal to the square
   of a real number, and the square of a real number is always nonnegative.

3. Does 0 have any square roots? Why or why not?
   Yes, because $0^2 = 0$, 0 is its own (and only) square root.

⊘ Explain 1 Solving $ax^2 - c = 0$ by Using Square Roots

Solving a quadratic equation by using square roots may involve either finding square roots of perfect squares or finding square roots of numbers that are not perfect squares. In the latter case, the solution is irrational and can be approximated.

Example 1 Solve the equation. Give the answer in radical form, and then use a calculator to approximate the solution to two decimal places, if necessary. Use a graphing calculator to graph the related function and compare the roots of the equation to the zeros of the related function.

(A) $4x^2 - 5 = 2$

Solve the equation for x.

$4x^2 - 5 = 2$	Original equation
$4x^2 - 5 + 5 = 2 + 5$	Add 5 to both sides.
$4x^2 = 7$	Simplify.
$\dfrac{4x^2}{4} = \dfrac{7}{4}$	Divide both sides by 4.
$x^2 = 1.75$	Simplify.
$x = \pm\sqrt{1.75}$	Definition of a square root.
$x \approx \pm 1.32$	Use a calculator to approximate the square roots.

The approximate solutions of the equation are $x \approx 1.32$ and $x \approx -1.32$.

Use a graphing calculator to graph the related function, $f(x) = 4x^2 - 7$, and find the zeros of the function.

The graph intersects the x-axis at approximately $(1.32, 0)$ and $(-1.32, 0)$. So, the roots of the equation are the zeros of the related function.

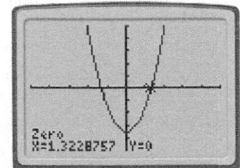
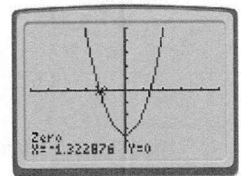

EXPLORE

Exploring Square Roots

INTEGRATE TECHNOLOGY

Students have the option of completing the Engage activity either in the book or online.

INTEGRATE MATHEMATICAL PRACTICES
Focus on Math Connections

MP.1 Make certain that students understand the difference between $\sqrt{a}$, $-\sqrt{a}$, and the phrase *take the square roots of a*. The first is the positive square root of a. The second is the negative square root of a. The third is both the positive and negative square roots of a and can be represented by $\pm\sqrt{a}$.

EXPLAIN 1

Solving $ax^2 - c = 0$ by Using Square Roots

AVOID COMMON ERRORS

Remind students to first add or subtract to isolate the x^2 term before taking square roots.

PROFESSIONAL DEVELOPMENT

Math Background

For a positive number a, we write the positive square root of a as $\sqrt{a}$. Likewise, for a positive number b, we write the positive square root of b as $\sqrt{b}$. By the definition of square root, $(\sqrt{a})^2 = a$ and $(\sqrt{b})^2 = b$. Therefore, $ab = (\sqrt{a})^2(\sqrt{b})^2 = (\sqrt{a} \cdot \sqrt{b})^2$ by the Power of a Product Property. This means, again by the definition of square root, that $\sqrt{a} \cdot \sqrt{b} = \sqrt{ab}$. A similar argument can be made for the Quotient Property of Radicals.

? When does a quadratic equation of the form $x^2 = c$ have one solution? When $c = 0$ the equation has one solution, because $\sqrt{0} = 0$.

Ⓑ $2x^2 - 8 = 0$

Solve the equation for x.

$2x^2 - 8 = 0$	Original equation
$2x^2 - 8 + \boxed{8} = 0 + \boxed{8}$	Add $\boxed{8}$ to both sides.
$2x^2 = \boxed{8}$	Simplify.
$\dfrac{2x^2}{\boxed{2}} = \dfrac{\boxed{8}}{\boxed{2}}$	Divide both sides by $\boxed{2}$.
$x^2 = \boxed{4}$	Simplify.
$x = \pm\sqrt{\boxed{4}}$	Definition of a square root
$x = \pm\,\boxed{2}$	Evaluate the square roots.

The solutions of the equation are $x = \boxed{2}$ and $x = \boxed{-2}$.

Use a graphing calculator to graph the related function, $f(x) = 2x^2 - 8$, and find the zeros of the function.

The graph intersects the x-axis at $\left(\boxed{2},\boxed{0}\right)$ and $\left(\boxed{-2},\boxed{0}\right)$. So,

the _____roots_____ of the equation are

the _____zeros_____ of the related function.

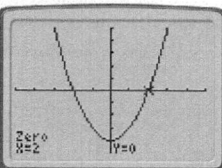
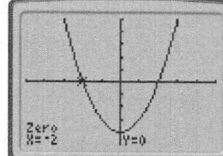

Your Turn

Solve the equation. Give the answer in radical form, and then use a calculator to approximate the solution to two decimal places, if necessary. Use a graphing calculator to graph the related function to check your answer.

4. $3x^2 + 6 = 33$

$3x^2 + 6 = 33$
$3x^2 = 27$
$x^2 = 9$
$x = \pm\sqrt{9}$
$x = \pm 3$

The solutions are 3 and −3.
The graph intersects the x-axis at $(3, 0)$ and $(-3, 0)$.

5. $5x^2 - 9 = 2$

$5x^2 - 9 = 2$
$5x^2 = 11$
$x^2 = 2.2$
$x = \pm\sqrt{2.2}$
$x \approx \pm 1.48$

The approximate solutions are 1.48 and −1.48.
The graph intersects the x-axis at approximately $(1.48, 0)$ and $(-1.48, 0)$.

COLLABORATIVE LEARNING

Peer-to-Peer Activity

Have students work in pairs to write a real-world problem and solution that can be solved by using square roots. Some common themes in real-world problems are finding the area of a rectangle, square, or triangle. Encourage students to draw a model to go along with the problem. Have each pair share their problem with the class. Discuss any extraneous solutions.

Solving a quadratic equation may involve isolating the squared part of a quadratic expression on one side of the equation first.

Example 2 Solve the equation. Give the answer in radical form, and then use a calculator to approximate the solution to two decimal places, if necessary.

Ⓐ $(x+5)^2 = 36$

$(x+5)^2 = 36$	Original equation
$x + 5 = \pm\sqrt{36}$	Take the square root of both sides.
$x + 5 = \pm 6$	Simplify the square root.
$x = \pm 6 - 5$	Subtract 5 from both sides.
$x = -6 - 5$ or $x = 6 - 5$	Solve for both cases.
$x = -11$ $\qquad$ $x = 1$	

The solutions are $x = -11$ and $x = 1$.

Ⓑ $3(x-5)^2 = 18$

$3(x-5)^2 = 18$	Original equation
$(x-5)^2 = \boxed{6}$	Divide both sides by $\boxed{3}$.
$x - 5 = \pm\sqrt{\boxed{6}}$	Take the square roots of both sides.
$x = \pm\sqrt{\boxed{6}} + \boxed{5}$	Add $\boxed{5}$ to both sides.
$x = \sqrt{\boxed{6}} + 5$ or $x = -\sqrt{6} + \boxed{5}$	Solve for both cases.
$x \approx \boxed{7.45}$ or $x \approx \boxed{2.55}$	

The approximate solutions are $x \approx \boxed{7.45}$ and $x \approx \boxed{2.55}$.

Reflect

6. Find the solution(s), if any, of $2(x-3)^2 = -32$. Explain your reasoning.

$2(x-3)^2 = -32$

$(x-3)^2 = -16$

The square of a number is never negative, so this equation does not have any real-number solutions.

EXPLAIN 2

Solving $a(x+b)^2 = c$ by Using Square Roots

INTEGRATE MATHEMATICAL PRACTICES
Focus on Reasoning

MP.2 When students come across equations with no real solution, explain that although it is possible to create a square root of a negative number, it is not a real number. No real number squared is equal to a negative number since a negative times a negative is a positive, and a positive times a positive is a positive.

DIFFERENTIATE INSTRUCTION

Critical Thinking

Introduce the idea that squaring and finding square roots are inverse operations. This means that squaring undoes the effect of taking the square root, and taking the square root undoes the effect of squaring. Other examples of inverse operations are addition and subtraction, and multiplication and division. Stress to students that before taking a square root of a squared term, they must isolate the squared term on one side of the equation.

QUESTIONING STRATEGIES

? When are there two solutions to an equation in the form $ax^2 - c = 0$? When you apply the definition of a square root, you get two square roots, a positive and a negative. For this to be true, $\frac{c}{a}$ must be greater than or equal to 0.

EXPLAIN 3

Solving Equation Models by Using Square Roots

AVOID COMMON ERRORS

Some students may incorrectly interpret the solution to a real-world problem and include an extraneous solution. Remind students to use the context of the word problem to interpret the solution. Often, the negative solution will not make sense, so it should be disregarded.

Your Turn

Solve the equation. Give the answer in radical form, and then use a calculator to approximate the solution to two decimal places, if necessary.

7. $4(x + 10)^2 = 24$

$$(x + 10)^2 = 6$$
$$x + 10 = \pm \sqrt{6}$$
$$x = \pm \sqrt{6} - 10$$
$$x = -\sqrt{6} - 10 \quad \text{or} \quad x = \sqrt{6} - 10$$
$$x \approx -12.45 \qquad\qquad x \approx -7.55$$

8. $(x - 9)^2 = 64$

$$x - 9 = \pm \sqrt{64}$$
$$x - 9 = \pm 8$$
$$x = \pm 8 + 9$$
$$x = -8 + 9 \quad \text{or} \quad x = 8 + 9$$
$$x = 1 \qquad\qquad x = 17$$

🔧 Explain 3 Solving Equation Models by Using Square Roots

Real-world situations can sometimes be analyzed by solving a quadratic equation using square roots.

Example 3 Solve the problem.

(A) A contractor is building a fenced-in playground at a daycare. The playground will be rectangular with its width equal to half its length. The total area will be 5000 square feet. Determine how many feet of fencing the contractor will use.

First, find the dimensions.
Let $A = 5000$, $\ell = x$, and $w = \frac{1}{2}x$.

$$A = \ell w$$
$$5000 = x \cdot \frac{1}{2}x$$
$$5000 = \frac{1}{2}x^2$$
$$10{,}000 = x^2$$
$$\pm\sqrt{10{,}000} = x \qquad\qquad \text{Take the square root of both sides.}$$
$$\pm 100 = x \qquad\qquad \text{Evaluate the square root.}$$

Since the width of a rectangle cannot be negative, the length of the playground is 100 feet. The width is half the length, or 50 feet.

Find the amount of fencing.

$$P = 2\ell + 2w$$
$$= 2(100) + 2(50)$$
$$= 200 + 100 \qquad\qquad \text{Multiply.}$$
$$= 300 \qquad\qquad \text{Add.}$$

So, the contractor will use 300 feet of fencing.

LANGUAGE SUPPORT **EL**

Connect Vocabulary

Preview this lesson with English learners to review new terms such as *square root*, *real number*, *non-negative*, and *property*. Students need to review and revisit this key vocabulary in order to understand and acquire its use. After explaining the vocabulary, have students try to rephrase it in their own words to a partner. Listen for students who may need support.

Ⓑ A person standing on a second-floor balcony drops keys to a friend standing below the balcony. The keys are dropped from a height of 10 feet. The height in feet of the keys as they fall is given by the function $h(t) = -16t^2 + 10$, where t is the time in seconds since the keys were dropped. The friend catches the keys at a height of 4 feet. Find the elapsed time before the keys are caught.

Let $h(t) = \boxed{4}$. Substitute the value into the equation and solve for t.

$$h(t) = -16t^2 + 10 \qquad \text{Original equation}$$

$$\boxed{4} = -16t^2 + 10 \qquad \text{Substitute.}$$

$$4 - \boxed{10} = -16t^2 + 10 - \boxed{10} \qquad \text{Subtract 10 from both sides.}$$

$$\boxed{-6} = -16t^2 \qquad \text{Simplify.}$$

$$\frac{-6}{\boxed{-16}} = \frac{-16t^2}{\boxed{-16}} \qquad \text{Divide both sides by } -16.$$

$$\boxed{0.375} = t^2 \qquad \text{Simplify.}$$

$$\pm\sqrt{\boxed{0.375}} = t \qquad \text{Take the square root of both sides.}$$

$$\pm\boxed{0.61} \approx t \qquad \text{Use a calculator to approximate the square roots.}$$

Since time cannot be negative, the elapsed time before the keys are caught is approximately $\boxed{0.61}$ second(s).

Your Turn

9. A zookeeper is buying fencing to enclose a pen at the zoo. The pen is an isosceles right triangle. There is already a fence along the hypotenuse, which borders a path. The area of the pen will be 4500 square feet. The zookeeper can buy the fencing in whole feet only. How many feet of fencing should he buy?

The equation for the area of a triangle is $A = \frac{1}{2}bh$. The length of the base and the height of an isosceles triangle are equal, so let $b = h = x$. Let $A = 4500$.

Substitute the values into the equation for the area and solve for x.

$$A = \frac{1}{2}bh$$

$$4500 = \frac{1}{2}x \cdot x$$

$$4500 = \frac{1}{2}x^2$$

$$9000 = x^2$$

$$\pm\sqrt{9000} = x$$

$$\pm 94.87 \approx x$$

Since the length of the base and the height of a triangle cannot be negative, the length of the base and height of the pen is approximately 94.87.

Since the zookeeper can only buy fencing in whole feet, use 95 as the length. There are two sides of the same length that need fencing, so the zookeeper should buy 95 + 95, or 190, feet of fencing.

© Houghton Mifflin Harcourt Publishing Company

INTEGRATE MATHEMATICAL PRACTICES
Focus on Modeling

MP.4 Make sure that students understand the connections between the real-world situation and the equations they create. They should always make a note of what the variables and solutions represent.

QUESTIONING STRATEGIES

? When solving a quadratic equation using square roots, what must you do before you can take the square root of both sides of the equation? isolate the square of the variable on one side of the equation

ELABORATE

QUESTIONING STRATEGIES

? When solving equations of the form $(x + b)^2 = c$, is it possible to get two positive or two negative answers? If so, give an example of each. **It is possible to get two positive answers; for example, solving $(x - 8)^2 = 25$ gives solutions of 13 and 3. It is also possible to get two negative answers. For example, solving $(x + 5)^2 = 4$ gives solutions of -7 and -3.**

SUMMARIZE THE LESSON

Copy and complete the graphic organizer to review the lesson. In each box, write an example of a quadratic equation with the given number of solutions. Solve each equation.

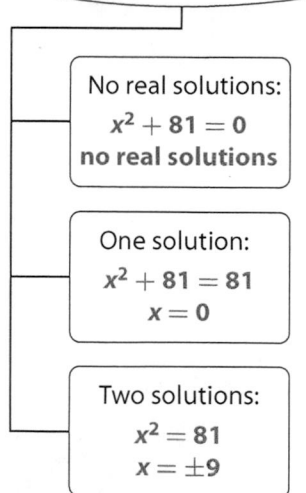

Solving Quadratic Equations by Using Square Roots When the Equation Has ...

No real solutions:
$x^2 + 81 = 0$
no real solutions

One solution:
$x^2 + 81 = 81$
$x = 0$

Two solutions:
$x^2 = 81$
$x = \pm 9$

---

10. How many real solutions does $x^2 = -25$ have? Explain.
$x^2 = -25$ has no real solutions, because the square of a real number is always nonnegative.

11. Suppose the function $h(t) = -16t^2 + 20$ models the height in feet of an object after t seconds. If the final height is given as 2 feet, explain why there is only one reasonable solution for the time it takes the object to fall.
The equation $2 = -16t^2 + 20$ has two real solutions for t. One solution is positive, and the other is negative. Since time cannot be negative, the negative solution is rejected. So, the positive solution is the only reasonable solution for the time it takes the object to fall.

12. **Essential Question Check-In** What steps would you take to solve $6x^2 - 54 = 42$?
Isolate the squared term by adding 54 to both sides, and then divide both sides by 6. Finally, take the square root of both sides and solve for both the negative and positive square root.

⭐ Evaluate: Homework and Practice

- Online Homework
- Hints and Help
- Extra Practice

Use the Product Property of Radicals, the Quotient Property of Radicals, or both to simplify each expression.

1. $\pm\sqrt{0.0081}$

$\pm\sqrt{\dfrac{81}{10,000}}$

$= \pm\dfrac{\sqrt{81}}{\sqrt{10,000}}$

$= \pm\dfrac{9}{100}$

$= \pm 0.09$

2. $\pm\sqrt{\dfrac{8}{25}}$

$\pm\dfrac{\sqrt{8}}{\sqrt{25}}$

$= \pm\dfrac{\sqrt{4 \cdot 2}}{5}$

$= \pm\dfrac{\sqrt{4} \cdot \sqrt{2}}{5}$

$= \pm\dfrac{2\sqrt{2}}{5}$

3. $\pm\sqrt{96}$

$\pm\sqrt{16 \cdot 6}$

$= \pm\sqrt{16} \cdot \sqrt{6}$

$= \pm 4\sqrt{6}$

Solve each equation. Give the answer in radical form, and then use a calculator to approximate the solution to two decimal places, if necessary. Use a graphing calculator to graph the related function to check your answer.

4. $5x^2 - 21 = 39$

$5x^2 = 60$

$x^2 = 12$

$x = \pm\sqrt{12}$

$x \approx \pm 3.46$

The graph intersects the x-axis at approximately $(3.46, 0)$ and $(-3.46, 0)$.

5. $0.1x^2 - 1.2 = 8.8$

$0.1x^2 = 10$

$x^2 = 100$

$x = \pm\sqrt{100}$

$x = \pm 10$

The graph intersects the x-axis at $(10, 0)$ and $(-10, 0)$.

© Houghton Mifflin Harcourt Publishing Company

Exercise	Depth of Knowledge (D.O.K.)	COMMON CORE Mathematical Practices
1–3	**1** Recall of Information	**MP.2** Reasoning
4–9	**1** Recall of Information	**MP.5** Using Tools
10–15	**1** Recall of Information	**MP.2** Reasoning
16–21	**2** Skills/Concepts	**MP.4** Modeling
22	**2** Skills/Concepts	**MP.2** Reasoning
23	**3** Strategic Thinking **H.O.T.**	**MP.3** Logic
24	**3** Strategic Thinking **H.O.T.**	**MP.4** Modeling

6. $6x^2 - 21 = 33$
$$6x^2 = 54$$
$$x^2 = 9$$
$$x = \pm\sqrt{9}$$
$$x = \pm 3$$

The graph intersects the x-axis at $(3, 0)$ and $(-3, 0)$.

7. $6 - \frac{1}{3}x^2 = -20$
$$-\frac{1}{3}x^2 = -26$$
$$x^2 = 78$$
$$x = \pm\sqrt{78}$$
$$x \approx \pm 8.83$$

The graph intersects the x-axis at approximately $(8.83, 0)$ and $(-8.83, 0)$.

8. $5 - 2x^2 = -3$
$$-2x^2 = -8$$
$$x^2 = 4$$
$$x = \pm\sqrt{4}$$
$$x = \pm 2$$

The graph intersects the x-axis at $(2, 0)$ and $(-2, 0)$.

9. $7x^2 + 10 = 18$
$$7x^2 = 8$$
$$x^2 = \frac{8}{7}$$
$$x = \pm\sqrt{\frac{8}{7}}$$
$$x \approx \pm 1.07$$

The graph intersects the x-axis at approximately $(1.07, 0)$ and $(-1.07, 0)$.

Solve each equation. Give the answer in radical form, and then use a calculator to approximate the solution to two decimal places, if necessary.

10. $5(x - 9)^2 = 15$
$$(x - 9)^2 = 3$$
$$x - 9 = \pm\sqrt{3}$$
$$x = \pm\sqrt{3} + 9$$
$$x = -\sqrt{3} + 9 \quad \text{or} \quad x = \sqrt{3} + 9$$
$$x \approx 7.27 \qquad\qquad x \approx 10.73$$

11. $(x + 15)^2 = 81$
$$x + 15 = \pm\sqrt{81}$$
$$x + 15 = \pm 9$$
$$x = \pm 9 - 15$$
$$x = -9 - 15 \quad \text{or} \quad x = 9 - 15$$
$$x = -24 \qquad\qquad x = -6$$

12. $3(x + 1)^2 = 27$
$$(x + 1)^2 = 9$$
$$x + 1 = \pm\sqrt{9}$$
$$x + 1 = \pm 3$$
$$x = \pm 3 - 1$$
$$x = -3 - 1 \quad \text{or} \quad x = 3 - 1$$
$$x = -4 \qquad\qquad x = 2$$

13. $\frac{2}{3}(x - 40)^2 = 24$
$$(x - 40)^2 = 36$$
$$x - 40 = \pm\sqrt{36}$$
$$x - 40 = \pm 6$$
$$x = \pm 6 + 40$$
$$x = -6 + 40 \quad \text{or} \quad x = 6 + 40$$
$$x = 34 \qquad\qquad x = 46$$

14. $(x - 12)^2 = 54$
$$x - 12 = \pm\sqrt{54}$$
$$x - 12 = \pm\sqrt{9 \cdot 6}$$
$$x - 12 = \pm\sqrt{9} \cdot \sqrt{6}$$
$$x - 12 = \pm 3\sqrt{6}$$
$$x = \pm 3\sqrt{6} + 12$$
$$x = -3\sqrt{6} + 12 \quad \text{or} \quad x = 3\sqrt{6} + 12$$
$$x \approx 4.65 \qquad\qquad x \approx 19.35$$

15. $(x + 5.4)^2 = 1.75$
$$x + 5.4 = \pm\sqrt{1.75}$$
$$x + 5.4 = \pm\sqrt{\frac{7}{4}}$$
$$x + 5.4 = \pm\frac{\sqrt{7}}{\sqrt{4}}$$
$$x + 5.4 = \pm\frac{\sqrt{7}}{2}$$
$$x = \pm\frac{\sqrt{7}}{2} - 5.4$$
$$x = -\frac{\sqrt{7}}{2} - 5.4 \quad \text{or} \quad x = \frac{\sqrt{7}}{2} - 5.4$$
$$x \approx -6.72 \qquad\qquad x \approx -4.08$$

© Houghton Mifflin Harcourt Publishing Company

EVALUATE

Personal Math Trainer

ASSIGNMENT GUIDE

Concepts and Skills	Practice
Explore Exploring Square Roots	Exercises 1–3
Example 1 Solving $ax^2 - c = 0$ by Using Square Roots	Exercises 4–9, 22
Example 2 Solving $a(x + b)^2 = c$ by Using Square Roots	Exercises 10–15, 22
Example 3 Solving Equation Models by Using Square Roots	Exercises 16–21, 23–26

INTEGRATE TECHNOLOGY

A graphing calculator can be used to check irrational solutions to an equation. Write the equation solved for 0, for example, in the form $0 = a(x + b)^2 - c$. Graph $y = a(x + b)^2 - c$. Compare the graph's zeros, or x-intercepts, to the approximate decimal equivalent of the solutions.

Exercise	Depth of Knowledge (D.O.K.)	COMMON CORE Mathematical Practices
25	**3** Strategic Thinking H.O.T.	**MP.3** Logic
26	**3** Strategic Thinking H.O.T.	**MP.3** Logic

Solving Equations by Taking Square Roots   **1040**

QUESTIONING STRATEGIES

? How do you take the square root of a fraction? Take the square root of the numerator and denominator separately. For example, $\sqrt{\frac{4}{9}} = \frac{\sqrt{4}}{\sqrt{9}} = \pm\frac{2}{3}$.

? What is wrong with solving the equation $x^2 = 3x$ by dividing both sides by x? When you divide by x, you lose the solution $x = 0$. If $x = 0$, division of both sides by x is undefined.

VISUAL CUES

Encourage students to circle on their papers what is to be isolated in each step of solving the equations in this lesson.

1. Circle the entire x^2–term and think of how it can be isolated.

2. Circle only x^2 and think of how it can be isolated.

3. Circle the x in x^2, showing that the last operation to be undone is the square.

---

16. The area on a wall covered by a rectangular poster is 320 square inches. The length of the poster is 1.25 times longer than the width of the poster. What are the dimensions of the poster?

$A = \ell w$

$320 = 1.25x \cdot x$

$320 = 1.25x^2$

$256 = x^2$

$\pm\sqrt{256} = x$

$\pm 16 = x$

Since the width of a rectangle cannot be negative, the width of the poster is 16 inches. So, the length of the poster is $1.25 \cdot 16$, or 20, inches.

17. A circle is graphed with its center on the origin. The area of the circle is 144 square units. What are the coordinates of the x-intercepts of the graph? Round to the nearest tenth.

$A = \pi r^2$

$144 = \pi r^2$

$\frac{144}{\pi} = r^2$

$\pm\sqrt{\frac{144}{\pi}} = r$

$\pm\frac{12}{\sqrt{\pi}} = r$

$\pm 6.8 \approx r$

Since the radius of a circle cannot be negative, the radius of the graphed circle is approximately 6.8 units. The x-intercepts are 6.8 units from the origin. So, they are located at $(-6.8, 0)$ and $(6.8, 0)$.

18. The equation $d = 16t^2$ gives the distance d in feet that a golf ball falls in t seconds. How many seconds will it take a golf ball to drop to the ground from a height of 4 feet? 64 feet?

$4 = 16t^2$

$\frac{1}{4} = t^2$

$\pm\sqrt{\frac{1}{4}} = t$

$\pm\frac{1}{2} = t$

Since time cannot be negative, it will take a golf ball $\frac{1}{2}$ second to drop to the ground from a height of 4 feet.

$64 = 16t^2$

$4 = t^2$

$\pm\sqrt{4} = t$

$\pm 2 = t$

Since time cannot be negative, it will take a golf ball 2 seconds to drop to the ground from a height of 64 feet.

19. Entertainment For a scene in a movie, a sack of money is dropped from the roof of a 600-foot skyscraper. The height of the sack above the ground in feet is given by $h = -16t^2 + 600$, where t is the time in seconds. How long will it take the sack to reach the ground? Round to the nearest tenth of a second.

$0 = -16t^2 + 600$

$-600 = -16t^2$

$37.5 = t^2$

$\pm\sqrt{37.5} = t$

$\pm 6.12 \approx t$

Since time cannot be negative, the solution is $t = 6.12$. So, it will take the sack approximately 6.12 seconds to reach the ground.

20. A lot for sale is shaped like a trapezoid. The bases of the trapezoid represent the widths of the front and back yards. The width of the back yard is twice the width of the front yard. The distance from the front yard to the backyard, or the height of the trapezoid, is equal to the width of the back yard. Find the width of the front and back yards, given that the area is 6000 square feet. Round to the nearest foot.

$$A = \tfrac{1}{2}h(b_1 + b_2).$$
$$6000 = \tfrac{1}{2}(2x)(x + 2x)$$
$$6000 = \tfrac{1}{2}(2x)(3x)$$
$$6000 = 3x^2$$
$$2000 = x^2$$
$$\pm\sqrt{2000} = x$$
$$\pm 45 \approx x$$

Since the length of the base of a trapezoid cannot be negative, the width of the front yard is approximately 45 feet. So, the width of the back yard is 2 · 45, or 90, feet.

21. To study how high a ball bounces, students drop the ball from various heights. The function $h(t) = -16t^2 + h$ gives the height (in feet) of the ball at time t measured in seconds since the ball was dropped from a height of h. If the ball is dropped from a height of 8 feet, find the elapsed time until the ball hits the floor. Round to the nearest tenth.

$$0 = -16t^2 + 8$$
$$-8 = -16t^2$$
$$\tfrac{1}{2} = t^2$$
$$\pm\sqrt{\tfrac{1}{2}} = t$$
$$\pm 0.7 \approx t$$

Since time cannot be negative, the ball will hit the ground after approximately 0.7 second.

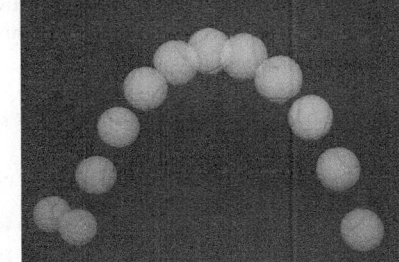

22. Match each equation with its solutions.

a. $2x^2 - 2 = 16$
   $x^2 = 9$

b. $2(x - 2)^2 = 16$
   $(x - 2)^2 = 8$

c. $3x^2 + 4 = 48$
   $x^2 = \frac{44}{3}$

d. $3(x + 4)^2 = 48$
   $(x + 4)^2 = 16$

   ___C___ $= \pm\frac{2\sqrt{33}}{3}$

   ___A___ $x = \pm 3$

   ___B___ $x = 2 \pm 2\sqrt{2}$

   ___D___ $x = -8$ and $x = 0$

When solving equations in which the number isolated on one side is the opposite of a perfect square, students may take the square root as if the number were positive. Remind students that you cannot take the square root of the opposite of a perfect square, such as -25. It has no square roots; 5 and -5 are the square roots of 25, not -25.

JOURNAL

Have students explain how to solve an equation of the form $ax^2 - c = 0$ by using square roots.

23. Explain the Error Trent and Lisa solve the same equation, but they disagree on the solution of the equation. Their work is shown. Which solution is correct? Explain.

Trent:

$$5x^2 + 1000 = -125$$

$$5x^2 = -1125$$

$$x^2 = -225$$

$$x = \pm\sqrt{-225}$$

$$x = \pm 15$$

Lisa:

$$5x^2 + 1000 = -125$$

$$5x^2 = -1125$$

$$x^2 = -225$$

no real solutions

Lisa's solution is correct. By the definition of a square root of a $x^2 = a$, so the square of a real number is always nonnegative. So, a must be nonnegative. In the equation $x^2 = -225$, a is negative. So, there are no real solutions of the equation.

24. Multi-Step Construction workers are installing a rectangular, in-ground pool. To start, they dig a rectangular hole in the ground where the pool will be. The area of the ground that they will be digging up is 252 square feet. The length of the pool is twice the width of the pool.

a. What are the dimensions of the pool? Round to the nearest tenth.

$$A = \ell w$$

$$252 = 2x \cdot x$$

$$126 = x^2$$

$$\pm 11.2 \approx x$$

The width is approximately 11.2 feet. So, the length is approximately 2 · 11.2, or 22.4, feet. The pool is approximately 11.2 feet by 22.4 feet.

b. Once the pool is installed, the workers will build a fence, that encloses a rectangular region, around the perimeter of it. The fence will be 10 feet from the edges of the pool, except at the corners. How many feet of fencing will the workers need?

$11.2 + 20 = 31.2$ $22.4 + 20 = 42.4$ $31.2 + 31.2 + 42.4 + 42.4 = 147.2$

So, the workers will need approximately 147.2 feet of fencing.

25. Communicate Mathematical Ideas Explain why the quadratic equation $x^2 + b = 0$ where $b > 0$, has no real solutions, but the quadratic equation $x^2 - b = 0$ where $b > 0$, has two real solutions.

When $b > 0$, the solution of $x^2 + b = 0$ is the square root of a negative number, which is not real; but the solution of $x^2 - b = 0$ is the square root of a positive number, which has 2 possible values.

26. Justify Reasoning For the equation $x^2 = a$, describe the values of a that will result in two real solutions, one real solution, and no real solution. Explain your reasoning.

Two real solutions: If a is positive, x will have the values $\sqrt{a}$ and $-\sqrt{a}$.

One real solution: If a is equal to 0, x will have the value $\sqrt{0} = 0$.

If a is negative, there are no real values of x because no real number squared is negative.

© Houghton Mifflin Harcourt Publishing Company

Lesson Performance Task

You have been asked to create a pendulum clock for your classroom. The clock will be placed on one wall of the classroom and go the entire height of the wall. Choose how large you want the face and hands on your clock to be and provide measurements for the body of the clock. The pendulum will start halfway between the center of the clock face and its bottom edge and will initially end 1 foot above the floor. Calculate the period of the pendulum using the formula $L = 9.78t^2$, where L is the length of the pendulum in inches and t is the length of the period in seconds.

Now, adjust the length of your pendulum so the number of periods in 1 minute or 60 seconds is an integer value. How long is your pendulum and how many periods equal one minute?

Possible answer: If the ceiling height is 10 feet and the clock face has a radius of 2, the pendulum goes from about 7 feet off the ground to 1 foot off the ground, so it has a length of 6 feet or 72 inches.

$$L = 9.78t^2$$
$$\frac{L}{9.78} = t^2$$
$$t = \sqrt{\frac{L}{9.78}}$$

When $L = 72$,
$$t = \sqrt{\frac{72}{9.78}}$$
$$\approx 2.71 \text{ seconds}$$

There are 60 seconds in one minute. Divide 60 by 2.71 to find the number of periods in 1 minute.

$$\frac{60}{2.71} \approx 22.14$$

The number of periods is not an integer value, so try a period of 2.5 seconds since 60 divided by 2.5 is 24, which is an integer value.

$$L = 9.78(2.5)^2$$
$$= 9.78(6.25)$$
$$= 61.125$$

So, make the pendulum 61.125 inches or 5 feet $1\frac{1}{8}$ inches long.

EXTENSION ACTIVITY

Have students look at the first eleven perfect squares, and ask them to look for patterns. Some patterns students may find include the following.

- The difference between two consecutive perfect squares goes up by consecutive odd integers (0, 1, 4, 9, 16, …, the difference is 1, 3, 5, 7, …).

- All perfect squares end in 0, 1, 4, 5, 6, or 9.

- The ones digits of the first eleven perfect squares form a symmetrical pattern (**0**, **1**, **4**, **9**, 16, 25, 36, 49, 64, 81, 100).

CONNECT VOCABULARY EL

Some students may not understand some of the terms used in this Lesson Performance Task. Have a volunteer draw a pendulum clock on the board and locate the *pendulum* and *clock face*. Explain that the *period* of a pendulum's motion is how long it takes to swing back (the tick) and forward (the tock), in seconds. The longer the pendulum, the longer the period.

AVOID COMMON ERRORS

Some students may fail to convert the length of the pendulum to inches. Have students begin writing their solutions by rewriting the formula, then stating what each variable stands for.

Scoring Rubric

2 points: Student correctly solves the problem and explains his/her reasoning.

1 point: Student shows good understanding of the problem but does not fully solve or explain his/her reasoning.

0 points: Student does not demonstrate understanding of the problem.

Solving Equations by Completing the Square

Common Core Math Standards

The student is expected to:

COMMON CORE **A-SSE.B.3b**

Complete the square ... to reveal the maximum or minimum value of the function .... Also A-SSE.A.2, A-SSE.B.3a, A-REI.B.4b, A-REI.B.4a, F-IF.C.8a

Mathematical Practices

COMMON CORE **MP.4 Modeling**

Language Objective

Explain to a partner how to complete the square of a quadratic equation in the form $ax^2 + bx + c = 0$.

ENGAGE

Essential Question: How can you use completing the square to solve a quadratic equation?

You can transform one side of the equation into a perfect-square trinomial, and then solve the equation by taking the square root of both sides.

PREVIEW: LESSON PERFORMANCE TASK

View the Engage section online. Discuss how different sizes and colors of tiles can be used to make designs on the floor of a room. Then preview the Lesson Performance Task.

22.2 Solving Equations by Completing the Square

Essential Question: How can you use completing the square to solve a quadratic equation?

Resource Locker

Explore **Modeling Completing the Square**

You can use algebra tiles to model a perfect square trinomial.

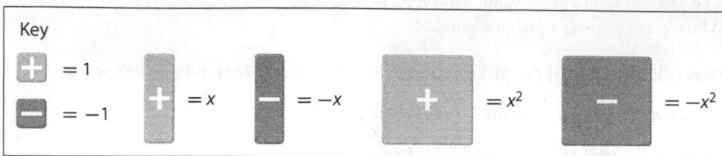

(A) The algebra tiles shown represent the expression $x^2 + 6x$. The expression does not have a constant term, which would be represented with unit tiles. Create a square diagram of algebra tiles by adding the correct number of unit tiles to form a square.

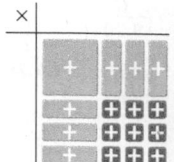

(B) How many unit tiles were added to the expression? __9__

(C) Write the trinomial represented by the algebra tiles for the complete square.

| 1 | $x^2 +$ | 6 | $x +$ | 9 |

(D) It should be easily recognized that the trinomial | 1 | $x^2 +$ | 6 | $x +$ | 9 | is an example of the special case $(a + b)^2 = a^2 + 2ab + b^2$. Recall that trinomials of this form are called perfect-square trinomials. Since the trinomial is a perfect square, it can be factored into two identical binomials.

| 1 | $x^2 +$ | 6 | $x +$ | 9 | $= \left(\boxed{1} x + \boxed{3}\right)^2$

(E) Refer to the algebra tiles in the diagram. What expression is represented by the tiles?

| 4 | $x^2 +$ | 8 | x |

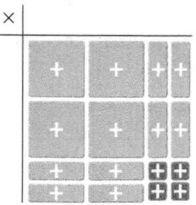

(F) Complete the square in Step E by filling the bottom right corner with unit tiles. How many unit tiles were added to the diagram? __4__

© Houghton Mifflin Harcourt Publishing Company

HARDCOVER PAGES 815–826

Turn to these pages to find this lesson in the hardcover student edition.

Ⓖ Write the trinomial represented by the algebra tiles for the complete square.

$\boxed{4}\ x^2 +\ \boxed{8}\ x +\ \boxed{4}$

Ⓗ The trinomial is a square of a binomial. Use the algebra tiles to write the trinomial in factored form.

$\boxed{4}\ x^2 +\ \boxed{8}\ x +\ \boxed{4} = \left(\boxed{2}\ x +\ \boxed{2}\right)^2$

Reflect

1. **Discussion** When using algebra tiles to model the expression $x^2 + 6x + c$, the x-tiles are divided equally, with 3 tiles on the right and bottom sides of the x^2-tile. How does the number 3 relate to the total number of x-tiles? How does the number 3 relate to the total number of unit tiles that were added?
   The 3 x-tiles are half of the total number of x-tiles. The number of unit tiles added to the grid, 9, is equivalent to 3^2, or the square of half of the total number of x-tiles.

2. In order to form a perfect square trinomial with the expression $x^2 + 8x + c$, how would the algebra tiles be arranged? How many unit tiles must be added? How is the number of unit tiles added related to the total number of x-tiles?
   4 x-tiles would be arranged on the right and bottom sides of the x^2-tile. 16 unit tiles would be added to complete the square. The number of unit tiles added to the grid, 16, is equivalent to 4^2, or the square of half of the total number of x-tiles.

⊘ **Explain 1** **Completing the Square When $a = 1$**

Completing the square is a process of rewriting a quadratic expression as a perfect square trinomial so that it can be solved by taking square roots. In the Explore, the method for completing the square when $a = 1$ was modeled with algebra tiles. First, place half of the x-tiles along the right side of the x^2-tile and half underneath the tile. Then add unit tiles to fill in the rectangle started with the x^2- and x-tiles. The number of unit tiles equals the square of the number of x-tiles on either side of the x^2-tile.

In other words, to complete the square for the expression $x^2 + bx + c$, add $\left(\frac{b}{2}\right)^2$. The perfect-square trinomial will then be $x^2 + bx + \left(\frac{b}{2}\right)^2$ and its factored form will be $\left(x + \frac{b}{2}\right)^2$.

Example 1 Complete the square to form a perfect-square trinomial.

Ⓐ $x^2 + 4x$

$x^2 + 4x$

$b = 4$ Identify b.

$\left(\frac{4}{2}\right)^2 = 2^2 = 4$ Find $\left(\frac{b}{2}\right)^2$.

$x^2 + 4x + 4$ Add $\left(\frac{b}{2}\right)^2$ to the expression.

© Houghton Mifflin Harcourt Publishing Company

PROFESSIONAL DEVELOPMENT

Math Background

The relationships between sets of numbers extend to include *complex* numbers, such as $3 - 5i$, *pure imaginary* numbers, such as $10i$, and *transcendental* numbers, such as π and $3^{\sqrt{2}}$. A nonzero rational number with 0 as a denominator is undefined and thus not a real number. However, 0 divided by 0 is *indeterminate* because any number multiplied by 0 is 0, so the quotient can be any number.

EXPLORE

Modeling Completing the Square

INTEGRATE TECHNOLOGY

Students have the option of completing the Explore activity either in the book or online.

QUESTIONING STRATEGIES

? What shape do the algebra tiles make in the Explore activity? They make a square.

? Why do you think adding the unit tiles is called *completing the square*? Without the unit tiles, the diagram is not a complete square. Adding the tiles completes the square.

? Can you complete a square using unit tiles if you start with an x^2-tile and four x-tiles? If so, how? Yes; add four unit tiles.

EXPLAIN 1

Completing the Square when $a = 1$

QUESTIONING STRATEGIES

? Can the number added to complete the square ever be negative? Explain. No, it cannot be negative. Add $\left(\frac{b}{2}\right)^2$ to both sides of the equation, and any number squared is positive.

AVOID COMMON ERRORS

Some students may not pay attention to whether b is positive or negative, since c is positive, regardless of the sign of b. Have students change the sign of b in a problem and compare the factored forms of the two expressions.

EXPLAIN 2

Solving $x^2 + bx + c = 0$ by Completing the Square

QUESTIONING STRATEGIES

? In what form should the equation be before you add $\left(\frac{b}{2}\right)^2$ to each side? The equation should be in the form $x^2 + bx = c$.

? When will solutions be irrational? Give an example. Solutions will be irrational when $c + \left(\frac{b}{2}\right)^2$ is not a perfect square. For example, the solutions of $x^2 + 6x + 3 = 0$ will be irrational, since, $-3 + \left(\frac{6}{2}\right)^2 = 6$ which is not a perfect square.

(B) $x^2 - 8x$

$x^2 - 8x$

$b = \boxed{-8}$ Identify b.

$\left(\dfrac{\boxed{-8}}{2}\right)^2 = \left(\boxed{-4}\right)^2 = \boxed{16}$ Find $\left(\frac{b}{2}\right)^2$.

$x^2 - 8x + \boxed{16}$ Add $\left(\frac{b}{2}\right)^2$ to the expression.

Reflect

3. When b is negative, why is the result added to the expression still positive?
   When b is negative, the result added to the expression is still positive because the squared numbers are always positive.

Your Turn

4. Complete the square: $x^2 + 12x$

   $\left(\dfrac{12}{2}\right)^2 = 6^2 = 36$ $x^2 + 12x + 36$

⚙ Explain 2 Solving $x^2 + bx + c = 0$ by Completing the Square

Completing the square can also be used to solve equations in the forms $x^2 + bx + c = 0$ or $x^2 + bx = c$.

Example 2 Solve each equation by completing the square. Check the answers.

(A) $x^2 - 4x = 3$

$\quad x^2 - 4x = 3$

$\quad x^2 - 4x + 4 = 3 + 4$ Add $\left(\frac{b}{2}\right)^2 = \left(\frac{-4}{2}\right)^2 = 4$ to both sides.

$\quad (x - 2)^2 = 7$ Factor and simplify.

$\quad x - 2 = \pm\sqrt{7}$ Take the square root of both sides.

$\quad x - 2 = \sqrt{7} \quad$ or $\quad x - 2 = -\sqrt{7}$ Write and solve two equations.

$\quad x = 2 + \sqrt{7} \qquad x = 2 - \sqrt{7}$ Add 2 to both sides.

Check the answers.

$\left(2 + \sqrt{7}\right)^2 - 4\left(2 + \sqrt{7}\right)$ $\qquad$ $\left(2 - \sqrt{7}\right)^2 - 4\left(2 - \sqrt{7}\right)$

$= 4 + 4\sqrt{7} + 7 - 8 - 4\sqrt{7}$ $\qquad$ $= 4 - 4\sqrt{7} + 7 - 8 + 4\sqrt{7}$

$= 4 + 7 - 8 + 4\sqrt{7} - 4\sqrt{7}$ $\qquad$ $= 4 + 7 - 8 - 4\sqrt{7} + 4\sqrt{7}$

$= 3$ $\qquad\qquad\qquad\qquad$ $= 3$

$2 + \sqrt{7}$ and $2 - \sqrt{7}$ are both solutions of the equation $x^2 - 4x = 3$.

© Houghton Mifflin Harcourt Publishing Company

COLLABORATIVE LEARNING

Peer-to-Peer Activity

Have pairs of students create a content table to show the number of unit tiles needed to complete the square for trinomials in the form $x^2 + bx + c$ and $ax^2 + bx + c$. Have students use algebra tiles, if necessary, to write trinomials and complete the table. **Sample:**

Expression	Number of Unit Tiles Needed to Complete Square	Square Form of Expression
$x^2 - 4x$	4	$(x - 2)^2$

Ⓑ $x^2 + 16x = 36$

$$x^2 + 16x = 36$$

$\boxed{1}\,x^2 + \boxed{16}\,x + \boxed{64} = \boxed{36} + \boxed{64}$ Add $\left(\dfrac{b}{2}\right)^2 = \boxed{64}$ to both sides.

$\left(\boxed{1}\,x + \boxed{8}\right)^2 = \boxed{100}$ Factor and simplify.

$\boxed{1}\,x + \boxed{8} = \pm\,\boxed{10}$ Take the square root of both sides.

$\boxed{1}\,x + \boxed{8} = \boxed{10}$ or $\boxed{1}\,x + \boxed{8} = -\,\boxed{10}$

$x = \boxed{2}$ $x = \boxed{-18}$

Check the answers.

$$x^2 + 16x = 36$$

$(-18)^2 + 16 \cdot \boxed{-18} = 36$

$\boxed{324} - \boxed{288} = 36$

$\boxed{36} = 36$

$x = -18$ ⓘⓢ/is not a solution to the equation $x^2 + 16x = 36$.

$$x^2 + 16x = 36$$

$2^2 + 16 \cdot \boxed{2} = 36$

$\boxed{4} + \boxed{32} = 36$

$\boxed{36} = 36$

$x = 2$ ⓘⓢ/is not a solution to the equation $x^2 + 16x = 36$

Your Turn

Solve each equation by completing the square. Check the answers.

5. $x^2 - 10x = 11$

$x^2 - 10x + 25 = 36$
$(x - 5)^2 = 36$
$x - 5 = \pm\sqrt{36} = \pm 6$

     $x - 5 = 6$ or $x - 5 = -6$
        $x = 11$ $x = -1$

6. $x^2 + 6x = 2$

$x^2 + 6x + 9 = 11$
$(x + 3)^2 = 11$
$x + 3 = \pm\sqrt{11}$

   $x + 3 = \sqrt{11}$ or $x + 3 = -\sqrt{11}$
     $x = -3 + \sqrt{11}$ $x = -3 - \sqrt{11}$

© Houghton Mifflin Harcourt Publishing Company

INTEGRATE TECHNOLOGY

A graphing calculator can be used to check if an equation of the form $x^2 + bx + c = 0$ has one, two, or no real solutions. Students can graph the equation as $y = x^2 + bx + c$ and see if the graph of the resulting parabola crosses the x-axis once, twice, or never.

DIFFERENTIATE INSTRUCTION

Modeling

When solving an equation such as $x^2 + 4x = 5$, students can use algebra tiles to complete the square on $x^2 + 4x$. If they need further visualization, they can use a large $=$ and construct the entire equation using algebra tiles. When they add 4 to one side of the equation to complete the square, remind them to add 4 to the other side to maintain the equality. Have them form a square with nine unit tiles so that they can compare the side lengths of the two squares. On the left, the side length is $x + 2$, while on the right, the side length is 3, so $x + 2 = 3$. Because length is not negative, $x + 2 = -3$ is discarded.

EXPLAIN 3

Solving $ax^2 + bx + c = 0$ by Completing the Square When a is a Perfect Square

AVOID COMMON ERRORS

Students may have difficulty finding $\left(\frac{b}{2}\right)^2$ when b is a fraction. Remind them that dividing by 2 is the same as multiplying by $\frac{1}{2}$. For example, if $b = -\frac{3}{4}$, $\left(\frac{b}{2}\right)^2$ becomes $-\frac{3}{4} \cdot \frac{1}{2}$, or $-\frac{3}{8}$. Let students practice with a few examples and lead them to see that dividing a fraction by 2 is the same as doubling the denominator.

QUESTIONING STRATEGIES

 What are the first ten perfect squares, starting with 1? 1, 4, 9, 16, 25, 36, 49, 64, 81, 100

When a is a perfect square, completing the square is easier than in other cases. Recall that the number of unit tiles needed is equal to the square of b divided by four times a, or $\frac{b^2}{4a}$. This is always the case when a is a perfect square.

Example 3 Solve each equation by completing the square.

Ⓐ $4x^2 - 8x = 21$

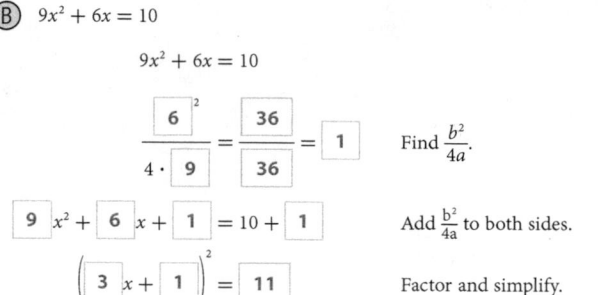

$4x^2 - 8x = 21$	
$\frac{(-8)^2}{4 \cdot 4} = \frac{64}{16} = 4$	Find $\frac{b^2}{4a}$.
$4x^2 - 8x + 4 = 21 + 4$	Add $\frac{b^2}{4a}$ to both sides.
$2x - 2 = 25$	Factor and simplify.
$(2x - 2)^2 = \pm\sqrt{25}$	Take the square root of the both sides.
$2x - 2 = \pm 5$	Simplify.
$2x - 2 = 5$ or $2x - 2 = -5$	Write and solve 2 equations.
$2x = 7$ or $2x = -3$	Add to both sides.
$x = \frac{7}{2}$ or $x = -\frac{3}{2}$	Divide both sides by 2.

Ⓑ $9x^2 + 6x = 10$

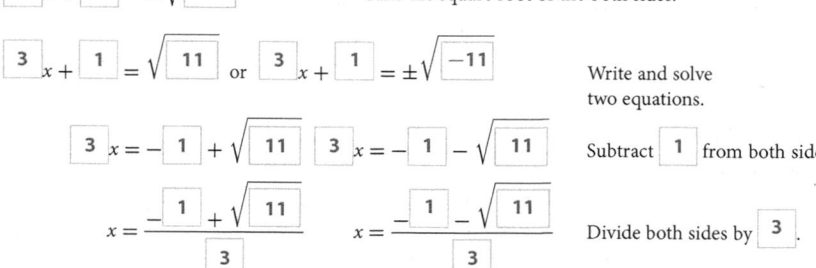

$9x^2 + 6x = 10$

$\dfrac{\boxed{6}^2}{4 \cdot \boxed{9}} = \dfrac{\boxed{36}}{\boxed{36}} = \boxed{1}$ ⟶ Find $\frac{b^2}{4a}$.

$\boxed{9}\,x^2 + \boxed{6}\,x + \boxed{1} = 10 + \boxed{1}$ ⟶ Add $\frac{b^2}{4a}$ to both sides.

$\left(\boxed{3}\,x + \boxed{1}\right)^2 = \boxed{11}$ ⟶ Factor and simplify.

$\boxed{3}\,x + \boxed{1} = \pm\sqrt{\boxed{11}}$ ⟶ Take the square root of the both sides.

$\boxed{3}\,x + \boxed{1} = \sqrt{\boxed{11}}$ or $\boxed{3}\,x + \boxed{1} = \pm\sqrt{\boxed{-11}}$ ⟶ Write and solve two equations.

$\boxed{3}\,x = -\boxed{1} + \sqrt{\boxed{11}}$ $\boxed{3}\,x = -\boxed{1} - \sqrt{\boxed{11}}$ ⟶ Subtract $\boxed{1}$ from both sides.

$x = \dfrac{-\boxed{1} + \sqrt{\boxed{11}}}{\boxed{3}}$ $x = \dfrac{-\boxed{1} - \sqrt{\boxed{11}}}{\boxed{3}}$ ⟶ Divide both sides by $\boxed{3}$.

LANGUAGE SUPPORT 🔲EL

Connect Vocabulary

Help students to understand how the phrase *completing the square* is used in the visual representation of the concept (using algebra tiles) and how the phrase is used in the symbolic representation (the algebraic solution). Point out the geometric and algebraic uses of the word *square* and explain how they are related in this context.

7. In order for the procedure used in this section to work, why does a have to be a perfect square?
If a binomial is squared, by definition, the leading coefficient will always be a perfect square.

Your Turn

Solve each equation by completing the square.

8. $16x^2 - 16x = 5$

$\dfrac{(-16)^2}{4 \cdot 16} = \dfrac{256}{64} = 4$

$16x^2 - 16x + 4 = 9$

$(4x - 2)^2 = 9$

$4x - 2 = \pm\sqrt{9} = \pm 3$

$4x - 2 = 3$	or	$4x - 2 = -3$
$4x = 5$		$4x = -1$
$x = \frac{5}{4}$		$x = -\frac{1}{4}$

9. $4x^2 + 12x = 5$

$\dfrac{12^2}{4 \cdot 16} = \dfrac{144}{16} = 9$

$4x^2 + 12x + 9 = 14$

$(2x + 3)^2 = 14$

$2x + 3 = \pm\sqrt{14}$

$2x + 3 = \sqrt{14}$	or	$2x + 3 = -\sqrt{14}$
$2x = -3 + \sqrt{14}$		$2x = -3 - \sqrt{14}$
$x = \frac{-3 + \sqrt{14}}{2}$		$x = \frac{-3 - \sqrt{14}}{2}$

 Explain 4 ## Solving $ax^2 + bx + c = 0$ by Completing the Square When a Is Not a Perfect Square

When the leading coefficient a is not a perfect square, the equation can be transformed by multiplying both sides by a value such that a becomes a perfect square.

Example 4 Solve each equation by completing the square.

(A) $2x^2 - 6x = 5$

Since the coefficient of x^2 is 2, which is not a perfect square, multiply both sides by a value so the coefficient will have a perfect square. In this case, use 2.

$2x^2 - 6x = 5$	
$2(2x^2 - 6x) = 2(5)$	Multiply both sides by 2.
$4x^2 - 12x = 10$	Simplify.
$\dfrac{(-12)^2}{4 \cdot 4} = \dfrac{144}{16} = 9$	Find $\dfrac{b^2}{4a}$.
$4x^2 - 12x + 9 = 10 + 9$	Add $\dfrac{b^2}{4a}$ to both sides.
$(2x - 3)^2 = 19$	Factor and simplify.
$2x - 3 = \pm\sqrt{19}$	Take the square root of the both sides.
$2x - 3 = \sqrt{19}$ or $2x - 3 = -\sqrt{19}$	Write and solve 2 equations.
$2x = 3 + \sqrt{19}$ $2x = 3 - \sqrt{19}$	Add to both sides.
$x = \dfrac{3 + \sqrt{19}}{2}$ $x = \dfrac{3 - \sqrt{19}}{2}$	Divide both sides by 2.

EXPLAIN 4

Solving $ax^2 + bx + c = 0$ by Completing the Square When a is Not a Perfect Square

QUESTIONING STRATEGIES

? Is the process of completing the square the same for quadratic equations with leading coefficients of 1 and those with leading coefficients that are perfect squares not equal to 1? Explain. **Mostly; the only difference is that the constant added to each side changes from $\left(\dfrac{b}{2}\right)^2$ to $\dfrac{b^2}{4a}$ when a is a perfect square that is not equal to 1.**

AVOID COMMON ERRORS

Emphasize that when multiplying both sides of an equation so that the coefficient of x^2 is a perfect square, and then adding $\frac{b^2}{4a}$ to both sides, b and a are the new coefficients that result from the multiplication. Some students will mistakenly revert to the original equation to find the coefficients.

(B) $3x^2 + 3x = 16$

Since the coefficient of x^2 is ___3___, which is not a perfect square, multiply both sides by a value so the coefficient will have a perfect square. In this case, use ___3___.

$$3x^2 + 3x = 16$$

$\boxed{3}\,(3x^2 + 2x) = \boxed{3}\,(16)$ Multiply both sides by $\boxed{3}$.

$\boxed{9}\,x^2 + \boxed{6}\,x = \boxed{48}$ Simplify.

$\dfrac{\boxed{6}^{\,2}}{4\cdot\boxed{9}} = \dfrac{36}{\boxed{36}} = \boxed{1}$ Find $\frac{b^2}{4a}$.

$\boxed{9}\,x^2 + \boxed{6}\,x + \boxed{1} = \boxed{48} + \boxed{1}$ Add $\frac{b^2}{4a}$ to both sides.

$\left(\boxed{3}\,x + \boxed{1}\right)^{2} = \boxed{49}$ Factor and simplify.

$\boxed{3}\,x + \boxed{1} = \pm\sqrt{\boxed{49}} = \pm\boxed{7}$ Take the square root of the both sides.

$\boxed{3}\,x + \boxed{1} = \boxed{7}$ or $\boxed{3}\,x + \boxed{1} = -\boxed{7}$ Write and solve two equations.

$\boxed{3}\,x = \boxed{6}$ $\boxed{3}\,x = -\boxed{8}$ Subtract $\boxed{1}$ from both sides.

$x = \boxed{2}$ $x = -\frac{8}{3}$ Divide both sides by $\boxed{3}$.

Reflect

10. Consider the equation $2x^2 + 11x = 12$. Why is 2 the best value by which to multiply both sides of the equation before completing the square?

Since 2 is the least value by which to multiply so that a will be a perfect square, it is the best value by which to multiply both sides of the equation.

Your Turn

Solve each equation by completing the square.

11. $\frac{1}{2}x^2 + 3x = 14$

$x^2 + 6x = 28$ $\frac{6^2}{4\cdot 1} = \frac{36}{4} = 9$

$x^2 + 6x + 9 = 37$

$(x + 3)^2 = 37$

$x + 3 = \sqrt{37}$ or $x + 3 = -\sqrt{37}$

$x = -3 + \sqrt{37}$ $x = -3 - \sqrt{37}$

12. $2x^2 - 4x = 16$

$4x^2 - 8x = 32$ $\frac{(-8)^2}{4\cdot 4} = \frac{64}{16} = 4$

$4x^2 - 8x + 4 = 36$

$(2x - 2)^2 = 36$

$2x - 2 = 6$ or $2x - 2 = -6$

$x = 4$ $x = -2$

© Houghton Mifflin Harcourt Publishing Company

Completing the square can be useful when solving problems involving quadratic functions, especially if the function cannot be factored. In these cases, complete the square to rewrite the function in vertex form: $f(x) = a(x - h)^2 + k$. Completing the square in this situation is similar to solving equations by completing the square, but instead of adding a term to both sides of the equation, you will both add and subtract it from the function's rule.

Recall that the height of an object moving under the force of gravity, with no other forces acting on it, can be modeled by the quadratic function $h = -16t^2 + vt + s$, where t is the time in seconds, v is the initial vertical velocity, and s is the initial height in feet.

Example 5   Write a function in standard form for each model. Then, rewrite the equation in vertex form and solve the problem. Graph the function on a graphing calculator and find the *x*-intercepts and maximum value of the graph.

Ⓐ   **Sports**   A baseball is thrown from a height of 5 feet. If the person throws the baseball at a velocity of 30 feet per second, what will be the maximum height of the baseball? How long will it take the baseball to hit the ground?

The function for this situation is $h = -16t^2 + 30t + 5$.

Complete the square to find the vertex of the function's graph.

$$h = -16\left(t^2 - \frac{30}{16}t\right) + 5 \qquad \text{Factor out } -16.$$

$$\frac{\left(-\frac{30}{16}\right)^2}{4} = \frac{\frac{900}{256}}{4} = \frac{900}{256} \cdot \frac{1}{4} = \frac{225}{256} \qquad \text{Find } \frac{b^2}{4}.$$

$$h = -16\left(t^2 - \frac{30}{16}t + \frac{225}{256} - \frac{225}{256}\right) + 5 \qquad \text{Complete the square.}$$

$$h = -16\left(\left(t - \frac{15}{16}\right)^2 - \frac{225}{256}\right) + 5 \qquad \text{Factor the perfect-square trinomial.}$$

$$h = -16\left(t - \frac{15}{16}\right)^2 + \frac{225}{16} + 5 \qquad \text{Distribute the } -16.$$

$$h = -16\left(t - \frac{15}{16}\right)^2 + \frac{305}{16} \qquad \text{Combine the last two terms.}$$

The coordinates of the vertex are $\left(\frac{15}{4}, \frac{305}{16}\right)$, or about (3.75, 19.06). The maximum height will be about 19 feet.

The graph of the function confirms the vertex at about (3.75, 19.06). The *t*-intercept at about 2.03 indicates that the baseball will hit the ground after about 2 seconds.

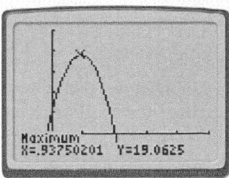

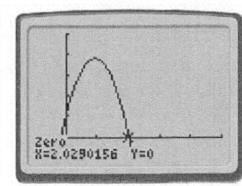

EXPLAIN 5

Modeling Completing the Square for Quadratic Functions

QUESTIONING STRATEGIES

❓ Describe in words what happens to an object thrown upward. **The object moves upward until it reaches its maximum height; then, it falls to the ground.**

❓ Describe in words how the vertex of the graph relating time and height of an object thrown upwards relates to the motion of the object. **The value of $h(t)$ at the vertex is the object's greatest height. The value of t at the vertex is the amount of time it takes the object to reach its greatest height.**

❓ You know that the graph of a quadratic function is a parabola. Why isn't the complete parabola drawn when graphing $h(t)$? **Time and distance are both non-negative, and this restricts the graph to first-quadrant values.**

AVOID COMMON ERRORS

Some students may be less comfortable working with functions than with equations, or may not know the difference. As a result, they may try to solve a function as they would an equation, dividing both sides or adding to both sides. Explain that $f(x)$ is read *f of x*, and that it is not treated the same way as a variable like *y*. Tell students that to complete the square given a function, they must add and subtract the same thing to the same side to preserve equality. So that the addition does not undo the subtraction, keep terms separate using parentheses.

AVOID COMMON ERRORS

Make sure students understand that they must keep the equation balanced by adding $\frac{b^2}{4a}$ to both sides of the equation, not to one side only.

SUMMARIZE THE LESSON

Copy and complete the graphic organizer shown below. In each box, write and solve an example of the given type of quadratic equation.

Solving Quadratic Equations by Completing the Square

$$x^2 + bx = c$$
$$x^2 - 4x = 5$$
$$x^2 - 4x + 4 = 5 + 4$$
$$(x - 2)^2 = 9$$
$$x - 2 = \pm 3$$
$$x = -1 \text{ or } x = 5$$

$$x^2 + bx + c = 0$$
$$x^2 - \frac{3}{2}x - 1 = 0$$
$$x^2 - \frac{3}{2}x = 1$$
$$x^2 - \frac{3}{2}x + \frac{9}{16} = 1 + \frac{9}{16}$$
$$\left(x - \frac{3}{4}\right)^2 = \frac{25}{16}$$
$$x - \frac{3}{4} = \pm \frac{5}{4}$$
$$x = -\frac{1}{2} \text{ or } x = 2$$

$$ax^2 + bx + c = 0$$
$$2(2x^2 + 4x - 20) = 0$$
$$4x^2 + 8x - 40 = 0$$
$$4x^2 + 8x = 40$$
$$4x^2 + 8x + 4 = 40 + 4$$
$$(2x + 2)^2 = 44$$
$$2x + 2 = \pm\sqrt{44}$$
$$2x + 2 = \pm 2\sqrt{11}$$
$$2x + 2 = 2\sqrt{11} \text{ or } 2x + 2 = -2\sqrt{11}$$
$$2x = -2 + 2\sqrt{11} \text{ or } 2x = -2 - 2\sqrt{11}$$
$$x = -1 + \sqrt{11} \text{ or } x = -1 - \sqrt{11}$$

(B) **Sports** A person kicks a soccer ball with an initial upward velocity of 16 feet per second. What is the maximum height of the soccer ball? When will the soccer ball hit the ground?

An equation for this situation is $h = -16t^2 + \boxed{16}\,t + \boxed{0}$.

Complete the square to find the vertex of the function's graph.

$$h = -16t^2 + \boxed{16}\,t + \boxed{0}$$

$$h = \boxed{-16}\left(\boxed{1}\,t^2 - \boxed{1}\,t\right) + \boxed{0} \qquad \text{Factor out } \boxed{-16}.$$

$$h = \boxed{-16}\left(\boxed{1}\,t^2 - \boxed{1}\,t + \frac{1}{\boxed{4}} - \frac{1}{\boxed{4}}\right) + 0 \qquad \text{Complete the square.}$$

$$h = \boxed{-16}\left(\left(\boxed{1}\,t - \frac{1}{\boxed{2}}\right)^2 - \frac{1}{\boxed{4}}\right) + 0 \qquad \text{Factor the perfect-square trinomial.}$$

$$h = \boxed{-16}\left(\boxed{1}\,t - \frac{1}{\boxed{2}}\right)^2 + \frac{16}{\boxed{4}} + 0 \qquad \text{Distribute the } -16.$$

$$h = \boxed{-16}\left(\boxed{1}\,t - \frac{1}{\boxed{2}}\right)^2 + \boxed{4} \qquad \text{Combine the last two terms.}$$

The coordinates of the vertex are $\left(\dfrac{1}{\boxed{2}},\ \boxed{4}\right)$.

The soccer ball will be at its highest when it is at its vertex, or at $\boxed{4}$ feet.

The graph of the function confirms the vertex at (0.5, 4). The x-intercept at 1 indicates that the ball will hit the ground after 1 second.

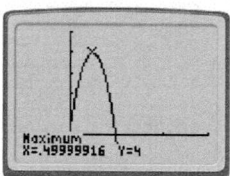 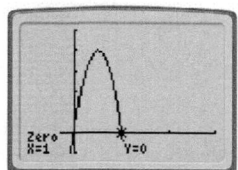

Your Turn

13. **Physics** A person standing at the edge of a cliff 48 feet tall throws a ball up and just off the cliff with an initial upward velocity of 8 feet per second. What is the maximum height of the ball? When will the ball hit the ground? **49 feet; after 2 seconds**

💬 Elaborate

14. When $b > 0$, the perfect square-trinomial of the expression $x^2 + bx$ is $x^2 + bx + \left(\frac{b}{2}\right)^2$. What is the perfect-square trinomial when $b < 0$? Does the sign of the constant change? Why or why not?

When $b < 0$, the perfect-square trinomial is $x^2 + bx + \left(\frac{b}{2}\right)^2$. The sign of the constant

does not change since the squaring function will get rid of the negative value.

15. Essential Question Check-In What is the first step in completing the square to solve a quadratic equation of the form $ax^2 + bx = c$?

The first step in completing the square to solve a quadratic equation in the form

$ax^2 + bx = c$ is to transform the left side of the equation into a perfect-square trinomial.

⭐ Evaluate: Homework and Practice

- Online Homework
- Hints and Help
- Extra Practice

Complete the square to form a perfect-square trinomial.

1. $x^2 + 26x$
$x^2 + 26x + 169$

2. $x^2 - 18x$
$x^2 - 18x + 81$

3. $x^2 - 2x$
$x^2 - 2x + 1$

4. $x^2 - 24x$
$x^2 - 24x + 144$

Solve each equation by completing the square. Check the answers.

5. $x^2 + 8x = 33$
$x^2 + 8x + 16 = 49$
$(x + 4)^2 = 49$
$x + 4 = \pm\sqrt{49} = \pm 7$
$x + 4 = 7$ or $x + 4 = -7$
$x = 3$ $x = -11$

6. $x^2 - 6x = 8$
$x^2 - 6x + 9 = 17$
$(x - 3)^2 = 17$
$x - 3 = \pm\sqrt{17}$
$x - 3 = \sqrt{17}$ or $x - 3 = -\sqrt{17}$
$x = 3 + \sqrt{17}$ $x = 3 - \sqrt{17}$

7. $x^2 + 12x = 5$
$x^2 + 12x + 36 = 41$
$(x + 6)^2 = 41$
$x + 6 = \pm\sqrt{41}$
$x + 6 = \sqrt{41}$ or $x + 6 = -\sqrt{41}$
$x = -6 + \sqrt{41}$ $x = -6 - \sqrt{41}$

8. $x^2 - 14x = 95$
$x^2 - 14x + 49 = 144$
$(x - 7)^2 = 144$
$x - 7 = \pm\sqrt{144} = \pm 12$
$x - 7 = 12$ or $x - 7 = -12$
$x = 19$ $x = -5$

Solve each equation by completing the square.

9. $9x^2 + 12x = 32$
$9x^2 + 12x + 4 = 36$
$(3x + 2)^2 = 36$
$3x + 2 = 6$ or $3x + 2 = -6$
$x = \frac{4}{3}$ $x = -\frac{8}{3}$

10. $4x^2 + 20x = 2$
$4x^2 + 20x + 25 = 27$
$(2x + 5)^2 = 27$
$2x + 5 = 3\sqrt{3}$ or $2x + 5 = -3\sqrt{3}$
$x = \frac{-5 + 3\sqrt{3}}{2}$ $x = \frac{-5 - 3\sqrt{3}}{2}$

© Houghton Mifflin Harcourt Publishing Company

EVALUATE

ASSIGNMENT GUIDE

Concepts and Skills	Practice
Explore Modeling Completing the Square	Exercise 22
Example 1 Completing the Square when $a = 1$	Exercises 1–4
Example 2 Solving $x^2 + bx + c = 0$ by Completing the Square	Exercises 5–8, 23–24
Example 3 Solving $ax^2 + bx + c = 0$ by Completing the Square when a Is a Perfect Square	Exercises 9–12, 21
Example 4 Solving $ax^2 + bx + c = 0$ by Completing the Square when a Is Not a Perfect Square	Exercises 13–16, 21
Example 5 Modeling Completing the Square for Quadratic Functions	Exercises 17–20, 25

Exercise	Depth of Knowledge (D.O.K.)	COMMON CORE Mathematical Practices
1–16	**1** Recall of Information	**MP.5** Using Tools
17–20	**2** Skills/Concepts	**MP.4** Modeling
21	**2** Skills/Concepts	**MP.5** Using Tools
22	**2** Skills/Concepts	**MP.4** Modeling
23	**3** Strategic Thinking H.O.T.	**MP.3** Logic
24	**3** Strategic Thinking H.O.T.	**MP.3** Logic
25	**3** Strategic Thinking H.O.T.	**MP.3** Logic

Solving Equations by Completing the Square   **1054**

CONNECT VOCABULARY EL

Relate *completing the square* to arranging algebra tiles in a shape that is part of a square, and then adding 1-tiles to *complete the square*.

QUESTIONING STRATEGIES

? In a perfect square trinomial, is the last term always positive? Explain. Yes; a perfect square trinomial can take either the form $(a + b)^2 = a^2 + 2ab + b^2$ or the form $(a - b)^2 = a^2 - 2ab + b^2$. In both forms, the last term is positive.

---

11. $16x^2 - 32x = 65$

$16x^2 - 32x + 16 = 81$

$(4x - 4)^2 = 81$

$4x = 4 + 9$ or $4x = 4 - 9$

$x = \dfrac{13}{4}$ $\qquad x = -\dfrac{5}{4}$

12. $9x^2 - 24x = 1$

$9x^2 - 24x + 16 = 17$

$(3x - 4)^2 = 17$

$3x - 4 = \sqrt{17}$ or $3x - 4 = -\sqrt{17}$

$x = \dfrac{4 + \sqrt{17}}{3}$ $\qquad x = \dfrac{4 - \sqrt{17}}{3}$

13. $\dfrac{1}{2}x^2 + 4x = 10$

$x^2 + 8x = 20$

$x^2 + 8x + 16 = 36$

$(x + 4)^2 = 36$

$x + 4 = 6$ or $x + 4 \approx -6$

$x = 2$ $\qquad x \approx -10$

14. $3x^2 - 4x = 20$

$9x^2 - 12x = 60$

$(3x - 2)^2 = 64$

$3x - 2 = 8$ or $3x - 2 = -8$

$x = \dfrac{10}{3}$ $\qquad x = -2$

15. $2x^2 + 14x = 4$

$4x^2 + 28x = 8$

$4x^2 + 28x + 49 = 57$

$(2x + 7)^2 = 57$

$2x + 7 = \sqrt{57}$ or $2x + 7 = -\sqrt{57}$

$x = \dfrac{-7 + \sqrt{57}}{2}$ $\qquad x = \dfrac{-7 - \sqrt{57}}{2}$

16. $\dfrac{1}{2}x^2 - 5x = 18$

$x^2 - 10x = 36$

$x^2 - 10x + 25 = 61$

$(x - 5)^2 = 61$

$x - 5 = \sqrt{61}$ or $x - 5 = -\sqrt{61}$

$x = 5 + \sqrt{61}$ $\qquad x = 5 - \sqrt{61}$

Projectile Motion Write an equation for each model, rewrite the equation into vertex form, and solve the problem. Then graph the function on a graphing calculator and state the *x*-intercepts of the graph.

17. **Sports** A person kicks a ball into the air with an initial upward velocity of 8 feet per second. What is the maximum height of the ball? When will the ball hit the ground?

model: $h = -16t^2 + 8t$

$h = -16t^2 + 8t$

$h = -16\left(t^2 - \dfrac{1}{2}t\right)$

$h = -16\left(t^2 - \dfrac{1}{2}t + \dfrac{1}{16} - \dfrac{1}{16}\right)$

$h = -16\left(t^2 - \dfrac{1}{2}t + \dfrac{1}{16}\right) + (-16)\left(-\dfrac{1}{16}\right)$

$h = -16\left(t - \dfrac{1}{4}\right)^2 + 1$

The ball will be at its highest when it is at its vertex, or at 1 foot.

The graph of the function confirms the vertex at (0.25, 1). The *x*-intercept at 0.5 indicates that the ball will hit the ground after 0.5 second.

18. Physics A person reaching out to the edge of a building ledge 85 feet off the ground flicks a twig up and off the ledge with an initial upward velocity of 11 feet per second. What is the maximum height of the twig? When will the twig hit the ground?

$$h = -16t^2 + 11t + 85$$

$$h = -16\left(t^2 - \frac{11}{16}t\right) + 85$$

$$h = -16\left[t^2 - \frac{11}{16}t + \left(\frac{11}{32}\right)^2 - \left(\frac{11}{32}\right)^2\right] + 85$$

$$h = -16\left[t^2 - \frac{11}{16}t + \left(\frac{11}{32}\right)^2\right] + (-16)\left(-\frac{11^2}{32^2}\right) + 85$$

$$h = -16\left(t - \frac{11}{32}\right)^2 + \frac{5561}{64}$$

The vertex is $\left(\frac{11}{32}, \frac{5561}{64}\right)$.

The twig will be at its highest when it is at its vertex, or at $\frac{5561}{64} \approx 86.89$ **feet.**

The graph of the function confirms the vertex at about (0.34, 86.89). The x-intercept at about 2.7 indicates that the twig will hit the ground after about 2.7 seconds.

19. Volleyball A volleyball player hits a ball from a height of 5 feet with an initial vertical velocity of 16 feet per second. What is the maximum height of the volleyball? Assuming it is not hit by another player, when will the volleyball hit the ground?
The equation is $h = -16t^2 + 16t + 5$.

$$h = -16(t^2 - t) + 5; \frac{b^2}{4} = \frac{(-1)^2}{4} = \frac{1}{4}$$

$$h = -16\left[t^2 - t + \frac{1}{4} - \frac{1}{4}\right] + 5; = -16\left(t - \frac{1}{2}\right)^2 + 9$$

The vertex is $\left(\frac{1}{2}, 9\right)$, so the maximum height is 9 feet.

$$0 = -16\left(t - \frac{1}{2}\right)^2 + 9; -9 = -16\left(t - \frac{1}{2}\right)^2; \pm\sqrt{\frac{9}{16}} = t - \frac{1}{2}; t = -0.25 \text{ or } t = 1.25$$

Since t cannot be negative, the volleyball will hit the ground after 1.25 seconds.

20. Lacrosse A lacrosse player throws a ball into the air from a height of 8 feet with an initial vertical velocity of 32 feet per second. What is the maximum height of the ball? When will the ball hit the ground?

The equation is $h = -16t^2 + 32t + 8$.

$$h = -16(t^2 - 2t) + 8; \frac{b^2}{4} = \frac{(-2)^2}{4} = 1$$

$$h = -16(t^2 - 2t + 1 - 1) + 8; -16(t - 1)^2 + 24$$

The vertex is $(1, 24)$, so the maximum height is 24 feet.

$$0 = -16(t - 1)^2 + 24; -24 = -16(t - 1)^2$$

$$\pm\sqrt{\frac{24}{16}} = t - 1; t \approx \pm 1.22 \pm 1$$

$t \approx -0.22$ or $t \approx 2.22$. Since t cannot be negative, the ball will hit the ground after about

2.22 seconds.

VISUAL CUES

Suggest that students circle the leading coefficient in each step of the solution process. This visual cue can help them to remember to take this coefficient into account when completing the square.

COLLABORATIVE LEARNING

Have students work in small groups to make a poster showing how to apply the steps for solving quadratic equations by completing the square. Give each group a different equation to solve. Then have each group present its poster to the rest of the class, explaining each step.

? How can you confirm that you have factored a perfect square trinomial correctly? Use FOIL to square the binomial to make sure that the result is equal to the trinomial being factored.

INTEGRATE MATHEMATICAL PRACTICES
Focus on Math Connections

MP.1 A perfect square trinomial can be used to show that a quadratic equation can have only one solution, even when the leading coefficient is not 1. For example, $4x^2 - 12x + 9$ can be factored as $(2x - 3)^2$, so the equation $4x^2 - 12x + 9 = 0$ has a single solution, $x = \frac{3}{2}$.

JOURNAL

Have students explain what it means to complete the square.

---

21. Identify the value of a in each equation of the form $ax^2 + bx + c = 0$.

   a. $11x^2 + 2x = 4$ $a = 11$

   b. $4x^2 + 5 = 0$ $a = 4$

   c. $3x^3 = 7$ $a = 0$

   d. $5x^2 + 11x = 1$ $a = 5$

   e. $3x^2 = 5$ $a = 3$

22. The diagram represents the expression $x^2 + 8x$. Use algebra tiles to model completing the square. Then write the perfect square trinomial expression.

$x^2 + 8x + 16$

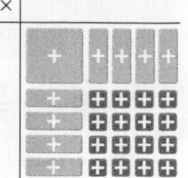

H.O.T. Focus on Higher Order Thinking

23. **Explain the Error** A student was instructed to solve the equation $x^2 + 4x = 77$ and produced the following work. Explain the student's error. What is the correct solution?

$$x^2 + 4x = 77$$
$$x^2 + 4x + 4 = 77 + 4$$
$$(x + 2)^2 = 81$$
$$x + 2 = 9$$
$$x = 7$$

The student forgot that the square root of 81 has two solutions: -9 and 9. The correct solution is $x + 2 = \pm 9$, or $x = 7$ and $x = -11$.

24. **Justify Reasoning** Will the equation $x^2 + 6x = -10$ produce an answer that is a real number after the square is completed? Explain.

The equation $x^2 + 6x = -10$ will not produce an answer that is a real number after the square is completed, since completing the square will produce the equation $x^2 + 6x + 9 = -1$, and there are no real solutions whose square is -1.

25. **Draw Conclusions** When solving a quadratic model, why are some solutions considered extraneous? Is this always the case, or can some quadratic models have two solutions?

When solving a quadratic model, some solutions are considered extraneous because they have a negative value, which is not useful in a real-world context. However, this is not always the case, as some quadratic models will have two valid solutions.

Lesson Performance Task

An architect is designing the lobby of a new office building. The company that hired her has reclaimed a large quantity of stone floor tiles from the building previously on the site and wishes to use them to tile the lobby. The tiled area needs to be a rectangle 18 feet longer than it is wide to incorporate an information desk. The table below shows the types of tile available, the general color of the tile, and the area that can be covered by the tile.

Stone	Color	Area in Square Feet
Marble	Cream	175
Marble	Cream with gold flecks	115
Marble	Black	648
Marble	White with black flecks	360
Slate	Gray	280
Slate	Gray with blue gray regions	243
Travertine	Caramel	208
Travertine	Latte	760
Adoquin	Dark gray with black regions	319
Adoquin	Light gray with darker gray regions	403
Limestone	Pewter	448
Limestone	Beige	544

Design the lobby using at least all of one type of tile. You can add additional types of tiles to create patterns in the floor. For this exercise, you can decide on the dimensions of the tiles in order to make any pattern you wish. What are the dimensions of the tiled area for your design?

Answers will vary but the procedure will be as follows.

Use the marble tiles that are white with black flecks.

length · width = area

$$(x + 18)x = 360$$
$$x^2 + 18x = 360$$

Find $\left(\frac{b}{2}\right)^2$.

$$\left(\frac{b}{2}\right)^2 = \left(\frac{18}{2}\right)^2$$
$$= 9^2$$
$$= 81$$

Complete the square and solve.

$$x^2 + 18x + 81 = 360 + 81$$
$$(x + 9)^2 = 441$$
$$x + 9 = \pm 21$$
$$x + 9 = 21 \quad x + 9 = -21$$

or

$$x = 12 \quad x = -30$$

In the context of this problem, a negative dimension does not make sense. So, use $x = 12$.

length = $x + 18$
$$= 12 + 18$$
$$= 30$$

The tiled area will be 30 feet long by 12 feet wide.

INTEGRATE MATHEMATICAL PRACTICES
Focus on Modeling

MP.4 Regardless of the types of tiles used, students should recognize that they should all begin their solutions with a length of $(x + 18)$, a width of x, and an area of $x^2 + 18x$. Discuss with students why everyone will find that $\left(\frac{b}{2}\right)^2 = \left(\frac{18}{2}\right)^2 = 81$ when they complete the square.

INTEGRATE MATHEMATICAL PRACTICES
Focus on Communication

MP.3 Have students explain how they would use algebra tiles to represent the situation in this task. Students should report that there is 1 x^2-tile with 9 x-tiles to its right and 9 x-tiles below it. It takes 81 unit tiles to complete the diagram.

EXTENSION ACTIVITY

Have students investigate "tiling" a floor with pennies. Have students choose how much money they will spend in pennies; determine how many square inches their pennies will cover; and then create and solve a real-world problem similar to the Lesson Performance Task.

Students may determine that, for example, an 18" by 16" penny tiling requires an array of 22 by 20 pennies or 440 pennies ($4.40). If the area to be covered, in square inches, is 1152 and the length is 4 inches longer than the width, then $(x + 4)x = 1152$ and $(x + 2)^2 = 1156$, so $x = 32$ and $(x + 4) = 36$. This would describe a floor covered with four of the 18" by 16" penny tiles at a cost of $17.60.

Using the Quadratic Formula to Solve Equations

Common Core Math Standards

The student is expected to:

COMMON CORE A-REI.B.4a

Use ... completing the square to ... Derive the quadratic formula ... Also A-REI.B.4b

Mathematical Practices

COMMON CORE MP.5 Using Tools

Language Objective

Explain to a partner how to solve an equation in the form $ax^2 + bx + c = 0$ using the quadratic formula.

ENGAGE

Essential Question: What is the quadratic formula, and how can you use it to solve quadratic equations?

The quadratic formula is a formula derived from the general quadratic equation by completing the square. It gives the real solutions (zero, one, or two) of any quadratic equation.

PREVIEW: LESSON PERFORMANCE TASK

View the Engage section online. Discuss the photo, asking students to speculate on how math could be used to place an outfielder in exactly the right spot to make a catch. Then preview the Lesson Performance Task.

22.3 Using the Quadratic Formula to Solve Equations

Essential Question: What is the quadratic formula, and how can you use it to solve quadratic equations?

Resource Locker

Explore   Deriving the Quadratic Formula

You can complete the square on the general form of a quadratic equation to derive a formula that can be used to solve any quadratic equation.

(A) Write the standard form of a quadratic equation.

$$ax^2 + bx + c = \boxed{0}$$

(B) Subtract c from both sides.

$$ax^2 + bx = \boxed{-c}$$

(C) Multiply both sides by $4a$ to make the coefficient of x^2 a perfect square.

$$4a^2x^2 + \boxed{4abx} = \boxed{-4ac}$$

(D) Add b^2 to both sides of the equation to complete the square.

$$4a^2x^2 + 4abx + b^2 = -4ac + \boxed{b^2}$$

(E) Factor the left side to write the trinomial as the square of a binomial.

$$\left(\boxed{2ax + b} \right)^2 = b^2 - 4ac$$

(F) Take the square roots of both sides.

$$\boxed{2ax + b} = \pm\sqrt{\boxed{b^2 - 4ac}}$$

(G) Subtract b from both sides.

$$2ax = \boxed{-b} \pm \sqrt{\boxed{b^2 - 4ac}}$$

(H) Divide both sides by $2a$ to solve for x.

$$x = \frac{\boxed{-b} \pm \sqrt{\boxed{b^2 - 4ac}}}{\boxed{2a}}$$

© Houghton Mifflin Harcourt Publishing Company

HARDCOVER PAGES 827–834

Turn to these pages to find this lesson in the hardcover student edition.

Ⓘ The formula you just derived, $x = \dfrac{-b \pm \sqrt{b^2 - 4ac}}{2a}$, is called the **quadratic formula**. It gives you the values of x that solve any quadratic equation where $a \neq 0$.

Reflect

1. **What If?** If the derivation had begun by dividing each term by a, what would the resulting binomial of x have been after completing the square? Does one derivation method appear to be simpler than the other? Explain.

$$ax^2 + bx + c = 0$$
$$x^2 + \frac{b}{a}x + \frac{c}{a} = 0$$
$$x^2 + \frac{b}{a}x = -\frac{c}{a}$$
$$x^2 + \frac{b}{a}x + \left(\frac{b}{2a}\right)^2 = -\frac{c}{a} + \left(\frac{b}{2a}\right)^2$$
$$\left(x + \frac{b}{2a}\right)^2 = -\frac{c}{a} + \left(\frac{b}{2a}\right)^2$$

The resulting binomial is $x + \left(\dfrac{b}{2a}\right)$. The previous derivation appears simpler because no fractions are involved in the derivation.

⊘ Explain 1 **Using the Discriminant to Determine the Number of Real Solutions**

Recall that a quadratic equation, $ax^2 + bx + c = 0$, can have two, one, or no real solutions. By evaluating the part of the quadratic formula under the radical sign, $b^2 - 4ac$, called the **discriminant**, you can determine the number of real solutions.

Example 1 Determine how many real solutions each quadratic equation has.

Ⓐ $x^2 - 4x + 3 = 0$

$a = 1, b = -4, c = 3$	Identify a, b, and c.
$b^2 - 4ac$	Use the discriminant.
$(-4)^2 - 4(1)(3)$	Substitute the identified values into the discriminant.
$16 - 12 = 4$	Simplify.

Since $b^2 - 4ac > 0$, the equation has two real solutions.

Ⓑ $x^2 - 2x + 2 = 0$

$a = \boxed{1}, b = \boxed{-2}, c = \boxed{2}$	Identify a, b, and c.
$b^2 - 4ac$	Use the discriminant.
$\left(\boxed{-2}\right)^2 - 4\left(\boxed{1}\right)\left(\boxed{2}\right)$	Substitute the identified values into the discriminant.
$\boxed{4} - \boxed{8} = \boxed{-4}$	Simplify.

Since $b^2 - 4ac \boxed{<} 0$, the equation has $\underline{\text{no}}$ real solution(s).

PROFESSIONAL DEVELOPMENT

Learning Progressions

In this lesson, students derive the quadratic formula and use it to solve equations. They also learn to recognize when the quadratic formula gives complex-number solutions. The quadratic formula is a generalization of the method of completing the square. Students should choose the method that best fits the situation at hand when solving quadratic equations. Students can use the quadratic formula to find the zeros of and to graph non-factorable quadratic equations, an important skill for college readiness.

EXPLORE

Deriving the Quadratic Formula

INTEGRATE TECHNOLOGY

Students have the option of completing the Explore activity either in the book or online.

QUESTIONING STRATEGIES

? What is it called when you add b^2 to both sides of the equation? What does this step allow you to do? Completing the square; it allows you to rewrite the left side of the equation as the square of a binomial, so that you can then take the square roots of both sides.

EXPLAIN 1

Using the Discriminant to Determine the Number of Real Solutions

QUESTIONING STRATEGIES

? Does the discriminant include the radical sign? No, the discriminant is $b^2 - 4ac$, the expression under the radical sign.

INTEGRATE MATHEMATICAL PRACTICES
Focus on Reasoning

MP.2 Point out the benefit of finding the discriminant first, so that students will be aware of the number of real solutions. Knowing this will help students later verify whether their solutions are correct.

EXPLAIN 2

Solving Equations by Using the Quadratic Formula

AVOID COMMON ERRORS

Students might make sign errors in finding $-b$ or $b^2 - 4ac$ when any of a, b, or c are negative. Encourage students to use parentheses and to write down every step.

© Houghton Mifflin Harcourt Publishing Company

Reflect

2. When the discriminant is positive, the quadratic equation has two real solutions. When the discriminant is negative, there are no real solutions. How many real solutions does a quadratic equation have if its discriminant equals 0? Explain.

One real solution; if the discriminant is 0, then you are adding or subtracting the square

root of 0 in the quadratic formula. Since the only square root of 0 is 0, the answer will be

the same whether it is added or subtracted.

Your Turn

Use the discriminant to determine the number of real solutions for each quadratic equation.

3. $x^2 + 4x + 1 = 0$

$a = 1, b = 4, c = 1$

$b^2 - 4ac$

$(4)^2 - 4(1)(1)$

$16 - 4 = 12$

two real solutions

4. $2x^2 - 6x + 15 = 0$

$a = 2, b = -6, c = 15$

$b^2 - 4ac$

$(-6)^2 - 4(2)(15)$

$36 - 120 = -84$

no real solutions

5. $x^2 + 6x + 9 = 0$

$a = 1, b = 6, c = 9$

$b^2 - 4ac$

$(6)^2 - 4(1)(9)$

$36 - 36 = 0$

one real solution

⚙ Explain 2   Solving Equations by Using the Quadratic Formula

To use the quadratic formula to solve a quadratic equation, check that the equation is in standard form. If not, rewrite it in standard form. Then substitute the values of a, b, and c into the formula.

Example 2   Solve using the quadratic formula.

(A) $2x^2 + 3x - 5 = 0$

$a = 2, b = 3, c = -5$ Identify a, b, and c.

$x = \dfrac{-b \pm \sqrt{b^2 - 4ac}}{2a}$ Use the quadratic formula.

$x = \dfrac{-3 \pm \sqrt{(3)^2 - 4(2)(-5)}}{2(2)}$ Substitute the identified values into the quadratic formula.

$x = \dfrac{-3 \pm \sqrt{49}}{4}$ Simplify the radicand and the denominator.

$x = \dfrac{-3 \pm 7}{4}$ Evaluate the square root.

$x = \dfrac{-3 + 7}{4}$ or $x = \dfrac{-3 - 7}{4}$ Write as two equations.

$x = 1$ or $x = -\dfrac{5}{2}$ Simplify both equations.

The solutions are 1 and $-\dfrac{5}{2}$.

COLLABORATIVE LEARNING

Peer-to-Peer Activity

Have students work in pairs to make a poster showing how to apply the steps for solving quadratic equations by using the quadratic formula. Give each pair a different equation to solve. Then have each pair of students present its poster to another pair, explaining each step.

Graph $y = 2x^2 + 3x - 5$ to verify your answers.

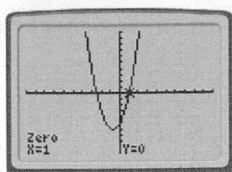 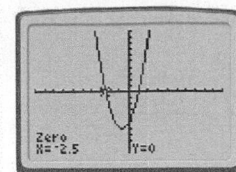

The graph does verify the solutions.

 $2x = x^2 - 4$

$x^2 - \boxed{2x} - 4 = 0$ Write in standard form.

$a = \boxed{1}, b = \boxed{-2}, c = \boxed{-4}$ Identify a, b, and c.

$x = \dfrac{-b \pm \sqrt{b^2 - 4ac}}{2a}$ Use the quadratic formula.

$x = \dfrac{-\left(\boxed{-2}\right) \pm \sqrt{\left(\boxed{-2}\right)^2 - 4\left(\boxed{1}\right)\left(\boxed{-4}\right)}}{2\left(\boxed{1}\right)}$ Substitute the identified values into the quadratic formula.

$x = \dfrac{2 \pm \sqrt{\boxed{20}}}{2}$ Simplify the radicand and the denominator.

$x = \dfrac{2 \pm \sqrt{\boxed{4} \cdot 5}}{2} = \dfrac{2 \pm 2\boxed{\sqrt{5}}}{2} = 1 \pm \boxed{\sqrt{5}}$ Simplify.

$x = \boxed{1 + \sqrt{5}}$ or $x = \boxed{1 - \sqrt{5}}$ Write as two equations.

$x \approx \boxed{3.236}$ or $x \approx \boxed{-1.236}$ Use a calculator to find approximate solutions to three decimal places.

The exact solutions are $\boxed{1 + \sqrt{5}}$ and $\boxed{1 - \sqrt{5}}$. The approximate solutions are $\boxed{3.236}$ and $\boxed{-1.236}$.

Graph $y = x^2 - \boxed{2x} - 4$ and find the zeros using the graphing calculator. The calculator will give approximate values.

The graph __does__ confirm the solutions.

Reflect

6. **Discussion** How can you use substitution to check your solutions?
Substitute each value into the given quadratic equation to see if it leads to a true equality.

Using the Quadratic Formula to Solve Equations   **1062**

QUESTIONING STRATEGIES

? Why is the symbol $\pm$ in the quadratic formula? The definition of square root is the positive or negative number that, when multiplied by itself, equals the number inside the radical.

? Where does the Quadratic Formula come from? The quadratic formula comes from completing the square and simplifying the general form of a quadratic equation.

DIFFERENTIATE INSTRUCTION

Visual Cues

To help prevent computational errors, some students may find it helpful to circle everything after b^2, calculate that, and then add the answer to b^2. For example:

$$\sqrt{7^2 \boxed{- 4(2)(-3)}} = \sqrt{49 + 24}$$
$$= \sqrt{73}$$

EXPLAIN 3

Using the Discriminant with Real-World Models

QUESTIONING STRATEGIES

? How can you use the discriminant to determine the number of real solutions of a quadratic equation? How is the process different when using a quadratic equation to model situations in the real world? Evaluate the discriminant. If it is negative, there are no real solutions; if it is positive, there are two real solutions; if it is zero, there is one real solution. In some cases, when using a quadratic equation to model a real-world situation, negative solutions will not make sense; in that case, even if real solutions exist they may be disregarded.

Solve using the quadratic formula.

7. $x^2 - 6x - 7 = 0$

$$x = \frac{-(-6) \pm \sqrt{(-6)^2 - 4(1)(-7)}}{2(1)}$$

$$x = \frac{6 \pm \sqrt{64}}{2}$$

$$x = \frac{6 \pm 8}{2}$$

$$x = \frac{6 + 8}{2} \text{ or } x = \frac{6 - 8}{2}$$

$$x = 7 \quad \text{or} \quad x = -1$$

The solutions are 7 and −1.

8. $2x^2 = 8x - 7$

$$x = \frac{-(-8) \pm \sqrt{(-8)^2 - 4(2)(7)}}{2(2)}$$

$$x = \frac{8 \pm \sqrt{8}}{4}$$

$$x = \frac{8 \pm 2\sqrt{2}}{4}$$

$$x = \frac{8 + 2\sqrt{2}}{4} \text{ or } x = \frac{8 - 2\sqrt{2}}{4}$$

$$x = 2 + \frac{\sqrt{2}}{2} \text{ or } x = 2 - \frac{\sqrt{2}}{2}$$

The solutions are $2 + \frac{\sqrt{2}}{2}$ and $2 - \frac{\sqrt{2}}{2}$.

⚙ Explain 3 Using the Discriminant with Real-World Models

Given a real-world situation that can be modeled by a quadratic equation, you can find the number of real solutions to the problem using the discriminant, and then apply the quadratic formula to obtain the solutions. After finding the solutions, check to see if they make sense in the context of the problem.

In projectile motion problems the projectile height h is modeled by the equation $h = -16t^2 + vt + s$, where t is the time in seconds the object has been in the air, v is the initial vertical velocity in feet per second, and s is the initial height in feet. The -16 coefficient in front of the t^2 term refers to the effect of gravity on the object. This equation can be written using metric units as $h = -4.9t^2 + vt + s$, where the units are converted from feet to meters. Time remains in units of seconds.

Example 3 For each problem, use the discriminant to determine the number of real solutions for the equation. Then, find the solutions and check to see if they make sense in the context of the problem.

(A) A diver jumps from a platform 10 meters above the surface of the water. The diver's height is given by the equation $h = -4.9t^2 + 3.5t + 10$, where t is the time in seconds after the diver jumps. For what time t is the diver's height 1 meter?

Substitute $h = 1$ into the height equation. Then, write the resulting quadratic equation in standard form to solve for t.

$$1 = -4.9t^2 + 3.5t + 10 \qquad 0 = -4.9t^2 + 3.5t + 9$$

First, use the discriminant to find the number of real solutions of the equation.

$$b^2 - 4ac \qquad\qquad\qquad \text{Use the discriminant.}$$

$$(3.5)^2 - 4(-4.9)(9) = 188.65$$

Since $b^2 - 4ac > 0$, the equation has two real solutions.

© Houghton Mifflin Harcourt Publishing Company

LANGUAGE SUPPORT [EL]

Connect Vocabulary

In the introduction, students learn about the *discriminant* of the quadratic formula. Students may know the word *discriminate*, which means to *differentiate* or *make a distinction*. A *discriminant* is something used to help make a distinction.

Next, use the quadratic formula to find the real number solutions.

$a = -4.9, b = 3.5, c = 9$ — Identify a, b, and c.

$t = \dfrac{-b \pm \sqrt{b^2 - 4ac}}{2a}$ — Use the quadratic formula.

$t = \dfrac{-3.5 \pm \sqrt{188.65}}{2(-4.9)}$ — Substitute the identified values into the quadratic formula and the value of the discriminant.

$t \approx \dfrac{-3.5 \pm 13.73}{-9.8}$ — Simplify.

$t \approx \dfrac{-3.5 + 13.73}{-9.8}$ or $t \approx \dfrac{-3.5 - 13.73}{-9.8}$ — Write as two equations.

$t \approx -1.04$ or $t \approx 1.76$ — Solutions

Disregard the negative solution because t represents the seconds after the diver jumps and a negative value has no meaning in this context. So, the diver is at height 1 meter after a time of $t \approx 1.76$ seconds.

(B) The height in meters of a model rocket on a particular launch can be modeled by the equation $h = -4.9t^2 + 102t + 100$, where t is the time in seconds after its engine burns out 100 meters above the ground. When will the rocket reach a height of 600 meters?

Substitute $h = \boxed{600}$ into the height equation. Then, write the resulting quadratic equation in standard form to solve for t.

$h = -4.9t^2 + 102t + 100$

$\boxed{600} = -4.9t^2 + 102t + 100$

$0 = -4.9t^2 + 102t - \boxed{500}$

First, use the discriminant to find the number of real solutions of the equation.

$a = -4.9, b = \boxed{102}, c = \boxed{-500}$ — Identify a, b, and c.

$b^2 - 4ac$ — Use the discriminant.

$\left(\boxed{102}\right)^2 - 4(-4.9)\left(\boxed{-500}\right)$ — Substitute the identified values into the discriminant.

$\boxed{10404} - \boxed{9800} = \boxed{604}$ — Simplify.

Since $b^2 - 4ac \boxed{>} 0$, the equation has $\boxed{2}$ real solutions.

© Houghton Mifflin Harcourt Publishing Company

AVOID COMMON ERRORS

Students may forget to write the equation in standard form before finding the values of a, b, and c. Remind them that the quadratic equation must be in the form $ax^2 + b + c = 0$ before they can begin to use the Quadratic Formula.

Next, use the quadratic formula to find the real number solutions.

$$t = \dfrac{-\boxed{102} \pm \sqrt{\boxed{604}}}{2(-4.9)}$$

Substitute the identified values into the quadratic formula and the value of the discriminant.

$$t = \dfrac{\boxed{-102} \pm \boxed{24.58}}{-9.8}$$

Simplify.

$$t \approx \dfrac{-102 + \boxed{24.58}}{-9.8} \text{ or } t \approx \dfrac{-102 - \boxed{24.58}}{-9.8}$$

Write as two equations.

$$t \approx \boxed{-7.90} \quad \text{or} \quad t \approx \boxed{12.92}$$

Solutions

Disregard the ___**negative**___ solution because t represents the seconds after the rocket has launched and a ___**negative**___ value has no meaning in this context. So, the rocket is at height 600 meters after a time of $t \approx \boxed{12.92}$ seconds.

Your Turn

For each problem, use the discriminant to determine the number of real solutions for the equation. Then, find the solutions and check to see if they make sense in the context of the problem.

9. A soccer player uses her head to hit a ball up in the air from a height of 2 meters with an initial vertical velocity of 5 meters per second. The height h in meters of the ball is given by $h = -4.9t^2 + 5t + 2$, where t is the time elapsed in seconds. How long will it take the ball to hit the ground if no other players touch it?

$h = -4.9t^2 + 5t + 2$

$0 = -4.9t^2 + 5t + 2$

Find the discriminant.

$(5)^2 - 4(-4.9)(2) = 64.2$

Since $b^2 - 4ac > 0$, the equation has two real solutions.

Use the quadratic formula to find the solutions of the quadratic equation.

$$t = \dfrac{-5 \pm \sqrt{64.2}}{-9.8}$$

$$t \approx \dfrac{-5 \pm 8.01}{-9.8}$$

$t \approx -0.31$ or $t \approx 1.33$

Disregard the negative solution because there is no negative time in this problem context.

The soccer ball reached the ground after about $t \approx 1.33$ seconds.

© Houghton Mifflin Harcourt Publishing Company

10. The quarterback of a football team throws a pass to the team's receiver. The height h in meters of the football can be modeled by $h = -4.9t^2 + 3t + 1.75$, where t is the time elapsed in seconds. The receiver catches the football at a height of 0.25 meters. How long does the ball remain in the air until it is caught by the receiver?

The ball is caught by the receiver when $h = 0.25$.

$h = -4.9t^2 + 3t + 1.75$

$0.25 = -4.9t^2 + 3t + 1.75$

$0 = -4.9t^2 + 3t + 1.5$

$(3)^2 - 4(-4.9)(1.5) = 38.4$

Since $b^2 - 4ac > 0$, the equation has two real solutions.

Use the quadratic formula to find the solutions of the quadratic equation.

$t = \dfrac{-3 \pm \sqrt{38.4}}{-9.8}$

$t \approx \dfrac{-3 \pm 6.20}{-9.8}$

$t \approx -0.33$ or $t \approx 0.94$

Disregard the negative solution because there is no negative time In this problem

context.The ball was in the air for $t \approx 0.94$ second.

💬 Elaborate

11. How can the discriminant of a quadratic equation be used to determine the number of zeros (x-intercepts) that the graph of the equation will have?

If the discriminant is zero, the equation will have one solution: it will intersect the x-axis

at one point. If the discriminant is positive, the equation will have two solutions: it will

intersect the x-axis at two points. If the discriminant is negative, the equation will have no

solutions: the graph will not intersect the x-axis at all.

12. What advantage does using the quadratic formula have over other methods of solving quadratic equations?

The quadratic formula works for all quadratic equations. Other methods only work in

certain situations.

13. Essential Question Check-In How can you derive the quadratic formula?

The quadratic formula is derived by completing the square for the standard form of a

quadratic equation.

ELABORATE

QUESTIONING STRATEGIES

? Explain why the value of the discriminant indicates the number of solutions. When the number inside the radical sign is positive, there are two solutions, because you can take the positive and negative square root of a positive number. When the number is negative, there are no real solutions because you cannot take the square root of a negative number. When the number inside the radical sign is 0, there is one solution, because the square root of 0 is 0 and adding and subtracting 0 will not change the value of $-b$.

SUMMARIZE THE LESSON

Copy and complete the graphic organizer shown below with students to summarize lesson concepts. In each box, write the number of real solutions.

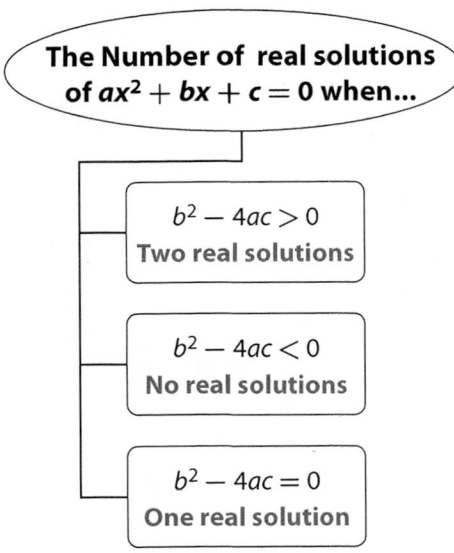

The Number of real solutions of $ax^2 + bx + c = 0$ when...

$b^2 - 4ac > 0$
Two real solutions

$b^2 - 4ac < 0$
No real solutions

$b^2 - 4ac = 0$
One real solution

EVALUATE

ASSIGNMENT GUIDE

Concepts and Skills	Practice
Explore Deriving the Quadratic Formula	
Explore 1 Using the Discriminant to Determine the Number of Real Solutions	Exercises 1–8, 20, 22
Explore 2 Solving Equation by Using the Quadratic Formula	Exercises 9–14
Explore 3 Using the Discriminant with Real-World Models	Exercises 15–19

 Evaluate: Homework and Practice

• Online Homework
• Hints and Help
• Extra Practice

Determine how many real solutions each quadratic equation has.

1. $4x^2 + 4x + 1 = 0$

$a = 4, b = 4, c = 1$
$b^2 - 4ac$
$(4)^2 - 4(4)(1)$
$16 - 16 = 0$
Since $b^2 - 4ac = 0$, the equation has one real solution.

2. $x^2 - x + 3 = 0$

$a = 1, b = -1, c = 3$
$b^2 - 4ac$
$(-1)^2 - 4(1)(3)$
$1 - 12 = -11$
Since $b^2 - 4ac < 0$, the equation has no real solutions.

3. $x^2 - 8x^2 - 9 = 0$

$a = 1, b = -8, c = -9$
$b^2 - 4ac$
$(-8)^2 - 4(1)(-9)$
$64 + 36 = 100$
Since $b^2 - 4ac > 0$, the equation has two real solutions.

4. $2x^2 - x\sqrt{5} + 2 = 0$

$a = 2, b = -\sqrt{5}, c = 2$
$b^2 - 4ac$
$\left(-\sqrt{5}\right)^2 - 4(2)(2)$
$5 - 16 = -11$
Since $b^2 - 4ac < 0$, the equation has no real solutions.

5. $\frac{x^2}{2} - x + \frac{1}{4} = 0$

$a = \frac{1}{2}, b = -1, c = \frac{1}{4}$
$b^2 - 4ac$
$(-1)^2 - 4\left(\frac{1}{2}\right)\left(\frac{1}{4}\right)$
$1 - \frac{1}{2} = \frac{1}{2}$
Since $b^2 - 4ac > 0$, the equation has two real solutions.

6. $\frac{x^2}{4} - x\sqrt{7} + 7 = 0$

$a = \frac{1}{4}, b = -\sqrt{7}, c = 7$
$b^2 - 4ac$
$\left(-\sqrt{7}\right)^2 - 4\left(\frac{1}{4}\right)(7)$
$7 - 7 = 0$
Since $b^2 - 4ac = 0$, the equation has one real solution.

7. $\frac{x^2}{2} - x\sqrt{2} + 1 = 0$

$a = \frac{1}{2}, b = -\sqrt{2}, c = 1$
$b^2 - 4ac$
$\left(-\sqrt{2}\right)^2 - 4\left(\frac{1}{2}\right)(1)$
$2 - 2 = 0$
Since $b^2 - 4ac = 0$, the equation has one real solution.

8. $x^2\sqrt{2} - x + \frac{1}{2} = 0$

$a = \sqrt{2}, b = -1, c = \frac{1}{2}$
$b^2 - 4ac$
$(-1)^2 - 4\left(\sqrt{2}\right)\left(\frac{1}{2}\right)$
$1 - 2\sqrt{2} < 0$
Since $b^2 - 4ac < 0$, the equation has no real solutions.

© Houghton Mifflin Harcourt Publishing Company

Exercise	Depth of Knowledge (D.O.K.)	COMMON CORE Mathematical Practices	
1–16	2 Skills/Concepts		**MP.2** Reasoning
17	2 Skills/Concepts		**MP.4** Modeling
18–19	3 Strategic Thinking		**MP.4** Modeling
20	3 Strategic Thinking		**MP.3** Logic
21	3 Strategic Thinking	H.O.T.	**MP.3** Logic
22	3 Strategic Thinking	H.O.T.	**MP.4** Modeling

Solve using the quadratic formula. Leave answers that are not perfect squares in radical form.

9. $10x + 4 = 6x^2$

$10x + 4 = 6x^2$

$5x + 2 = 3x^2$

$0 = 3x^2 - 5x - 2$

$x = \dfrac{-(-5) \pm \sqrt{(-5)^2 - 4(3)(-2)}}{2(3)}$

$x = \dfrac{5 \pm \sqrt{25 + 24}}{6}$

$x = \dfrac{5 \pm \sqrt{49}}{6}$

$x = \dfrac{5 \pm 7}{6}$

$x = \dfrac{5 + 7}{6}$ or $x = \dfrac{5 - 7}{6}$

$x = 2$ or $\qquad x = -\dfrac{1}{3}$

The solutions are 2 and $-\dfrac{1}{3}$.

10. $x^2 + x - 20 = 0$

$x = \dfrac{-1 \pm \sqrt{1^2 - 4(1)(-20)}}{2}$

$x = \dfrac{-1 \pm \sqrt{1 + 80}}{2}$

$x = \dfrac{-1 \pm \sqrt{81}}{2}$

$x = \dfrac{-1 \pm 9}{2}$

$x = \dfrac{-1 + 9}{2}$ or $x = \dfrac{-1 - 9}{2}$

$x = 4$ or $\qquad x = -5$

The solutions are 4 and −5.

11. $4x^2 = 4 - x$

$4x^2 + x - 4 = 0$

$x = \dfrac{-1 \pm \sqrt{1^2 - 4(4)(-4)}}{2(4)}$

$x = \dfrac{-1 \pm \sqrt{1 + 64}}{8}$

$x = \dfrac{-1 \pm \sqrt{65}}{8}$

$x = \dfrac{-1 + \sqrt{65}}{8}$ or $x = \dfrac{-1 - \sqrt{65}}{8}$

The solutions are $\dfrac{-1 + \sqrt{65}}{8}$ and $\dfrac{-1 - \sqrt{65}}{8}$.

12. $9x^2 + 3x - 2 = 0$

$x = \dfrac{-3 \pm \sqrt{3^2 - 4(9)(-2)}}{2(9)}$

$x = \dfrac{-3 \pm \sqrt{9 + 72}}{18}$

$x = \dfrac{-3 \pm \sqrt{81}}{18}$

$x = \dfrac{-3 \pm 9}{18}$

$x = \dfrac{-3 + 9}{18}$ or $x = \dfrac{-3 - 9}{18}$

$x = \dfrac{1}{3}$ or $\qquad x = -\dfrac{2}{3}$

The solutions are $\dfrac{1}{3}$ and $-\dfrac{2}{3}$.

INTEGRATE MATHEMATICAL PRACTICES

Focus on Reasoning

MP.2 Students can check their solutions for correctness by substituting the values into the original equations and verifying that both solutions make the equation true. When checking solutions, remind students that the square of a negative number is a positive number.

INTEGRATE MATHEMATICAL PRACTICES

Focus on Modeling

MP.4 To help students follow the derivation of the quadratic formula, you may want to have them assign specific values to a, b, and c and show what each step of the derivation looks like in terms of those values in order to check the reasonableness of the steps.

AVOID COMMON ERRORS

Students may not write solutions involving radicals in simplest form. Show them examples, such as

$\dfrac{3 \pm \sqrt{63}}{3}$, which can be simplified to $1 \pm \sqrt{7}$.

---

13. $14x + 3 = -8x^2$

$14x + 3 = -8x^2$

$8x^2 + 14x + 3 = 0$

$a = 8, b = 14, c = 3$

$x = \dfrac{-14 \pm \sqrt{14^2 - 4(8)(3)}}{2(8)}$

$x = \dfrac{-14 \pm \sqrt{196 - 96}}{16}$

$x = \dfrac{-14 \pm \sqrt{100}}{16}$

$x = \dfrac{-14 \pm 10}{16}$

$x = \dfrac{-14 + 10}{16}$ or $x = \dfrac{-14 - 10}{16}$

$x = -\dfrac{1}{4}$ or $x = -\dfrac{3}{2}$

The solutions are $-\dfrac{1}{4}$ and $-\dfrac{3}{2}$.

14. $x^2 + 3x^2 + 1 = 0$

$a = 1, b = 3, c = 1$

$x = \dfrac{-3 \pm \sqrt{3^2 - 4(1)(1)}}{2(1)}$

$x = \dfrac{-3 \pm \sqrt{9 - 4}}{2}$

$x = \dfrac{-3 \pm \sqrt{5}}{2}$

$x = \dfrac{-3 + \sqrt{5}}{2}$ or $x = \dfrac{-3 - \sqrt{5}}{2}$

The solutions are $\dfrac{-3 + \sqrt{5}}{2}$ and $\dfrac{-3 - \sqrt{5}}{2}$.

For each problem, use the discriminant to determine the number of real solutions for the equation. Then, find the solutions and check to see if they make sense in the context of the problem.

15. Sports A soccer player kicks the ball to a height of 1 meter inside the goal. The equation for the height h of the ball at time t is $h = -4.9t^2 - 5t + 2$. Find the time the ball reached the goal.

The ball is 1 meter off the ground when

$h = 1$. Substitute for h in the equation.

$h = -4.9t^2 - 5t + 2$

$1 = -4.9t^2 - 5t + 2$

$0 = -4.9t^2 - 5t + 1$

Find the discriminant.

$(-5)^2 - 4(-4.9)(1) = 44.6$

Since $b^2 - 4ac > 0$, the equation has two real solutions.

Use the quadratic formula to find the solutions of the quadratic equation.

$t = \dfrac{5 \pm \sqrt{44.6}}{-9.8}$

$t \approx \dfrac{5 \pm 6.68}{-9.8}$

$t \approx -1.19$ or $t \approx 0.17$

Disregard the negative solution because there is no negative time in this

context. The soccer ball reached the goal after about $t \approx 0.17$ seconds.

16. The length and width of a rectangular patio are, $(x + 8)$ feet and $(x + 6)$ feet, respectively. If the area of the patio is 160 square feet, what are the dimensions of the patio?

$$A = (x + 6)(x + 8)$$
$$A = (x + 6)(x + 8)$$
$$160 = (x + 6)(x + 8)$$
$$160 = x^2 + 14x + 48$$
$$0 = x^2 + 14x - 112$$
$$x = \frac{-14 \pm \sqrt{644}}{2}$$
$$x \approx \frac{-14 \pm 25.38}{2}$$
$$x \approx 5.69 \text{ or } x \approx -19.69$$

Disregard the negative solution because it yields a negative length.

Length: $5.69 + 8 = 13.69$ feet

Width: $5.69 + 6 = 11.69$ feet

17. Chemistry A scientist is growing bacteria in a lab for study. One particular type of bacteria grows at a rate of $y = 2t^2 + 3t + 500$. A different bacteria grows at a rate of $y = 3t^2 + t + 300$. In both of these equations, y is the number of bacteria after t minutes. When is there an equal number of both types of bacteria?

$$3t^2 + t + 300 = 2t^2 + 3t + 500$$
$$3t^2 + t + 300 - 2t^2 - 3t - 500 = 0$$
$$t^2 - 2t - 200 = 0$$
$$t = \frac{2 \pm \sqrt{804}}{2}$$
$$t \approx \frac{2 \pm 28.35}{2}$$
$$t \approx 15.18 \text{ or } t \approx -13.18$$

Disregard the negative solution because there is no negative time in

this context. There is an equal number of both types of bacteria at

$t \approx 15.18$ minutes.

Use this information for Exercises 18 and 19. A gymnast, who can stretch her arms up to reach 6 feet, jumps straight up on a trampoline. The height of her feet above the trampoline can be modeled by the equation $h = -16x^2 + 12x$, where x is the time in seconds after her jump.

18. Do the gymnast's hands reach a height of 10 feet above the trampoline? Use the discriminant to explain. (Hint: Since $h =$ height of feet, you must use the difference between the heights of the hands and feet.)

Evaluating the discriminant for $h = 10 - 6 = 4$ gives $d = -112 < 0$, so there are no real solutions for this height. Thus, her feet never reach 4 feet, so her hands never reach 10 feet.

QUESTIONING STRATEGIES

? If the discriminant of a quadratic equation that models a real-world situation is greater than 0, will the problem have two solutions? Only when both solutions make sense in the context; for example, if there is a positive and a negative solution to a problem that asks for a length, the negative solution does not make sense, because length cannot be negative.

Focus on Math Connections

MP.1 Let students know that any quadratic equation can be solved by using the quadratic formula and that it will always give exact solutions—but that this may not always be the quickest method. Encourage students to recall earlier lessons and try the other methods, as needed.

MULTIPLE REPRESENTATIONS

Remind students that the solutions to a quadratic equation are also the zeros of its related function.

JOURNAL

Have students write a quadratic equation and use the discriminant to find the number of real solutions. Have them use the Quadratic Formula to find the real solution(s), if any exist. If there are no real solutions, have them explain what this means.

---

19. Which of the following are possible heights she achieved? Select all that apply.

   a. $h = \dfrac{9}{4}$
   b. $h = 4$
   c. $h = 3$
   d. $h = 0.5$
   e. $h = \dfrac{1}{4}$

   Use the discriminant to determine the maximum height h_m the gymnast reaches. When the discriminant equals 0, there is one real solution, which will be when the maximum height occurs. Write the equation in standard form and set the discriminant equal to zero. Solve for $-c = h_m$.

   $$h_m = -16x^2 + 12x$$
   $$0 = -16x^2 + 12x - h_m$$
   $$b^2 - 4ac = 12^2 - 4(-16)(-h_m)$$
   $$0 = 12^2 - 4(-16)(-h_m)$$
   $$-144 = -64(h_m)$$
   $$\frac{9}{4} = h_m$$

   The letters A, D, and E are possible heights of the gymnast since they are all less or equal to $h_m = \dfrac{9}{4}$.

20. **Explain the Error** Dan said that if a quadratic equation does not have any real solutions, then it does not represent a function. Explain Dan's error.

   Having no real solutions means that the value of the function can never be zero. That is, the function has no zeros (or x-intercepts). The quadratic expression is a function as it is a polynomial.

   H.O.T. Focus on Higher Order Thinking

21. **Communicate Mathematical Ideas** Explain why a positive discriminant results in two real solutions.

   Because every positive number has two square roots, a positive discriminant results in two solutions to a quadratic equation.

22. **Multi-Step** A model rocket is launched from the top of a hill 10 meters above ground level. The rocket's initial speed is 10 meters per second. Its height h can be modeled by the equation $h = -4.9t^2 + 10t + 10$, where t is the time in seconds.

   a. When does the rocket achieve a height of 100 meters?
   $$h = -4.9t^2 + 10t + 10$$
   $$100 = -4.9t^2 + 10t + 10$$
   $$0 = -4.9t^2 + 10t - 90$$
   $$(10)^2 - 4(-4.9)(-90) = -1664 < 0$$

   Since $b^2 - 4ac < 0$, the equation has no real solutions. The rocket never reaches a height of 100 meters.

   b. How long does it take the rocket to reach ground level?
   $$t = \frac{-10 \pm \sqrt{296}}{-9.8}$$
   $$t \approx \frac{-10 \pm 17.20}{-9.8}$$
   $$t \approx -0.74 \text{ or } t \approx 2.78$$

   Taking only the positive solution, the rocket will reach ground level after $t \approx 2.78$ seconds.

Lesson Performance Task

A baseball field is next to a building that is 130 feet tall. A series of batters hit pitched balls into the air with the given initial vertical velocities. (Assume each ball is hit from a height of 3 feet.) After the game, a fan reports that several hits resulted in the ball hitting the roof of the building. How can you use the discriminant to determine whether any of the hits described below could be among them? Explain. If any of the balls hit could have hit the roof, identify them. Can you tell if the ball actually did hit the roof?

Player	Initial Vertical Velocity (ft/s)
Janok	99
Jimenez	91
Serrano	88
Sei	89

Write the equation. Then substitute the height of the building, 130, for h and set the equation equal to zero. Check the discriminant to see if the equation has any solutions. If an equation has no solution it means the ball never achieved a height of 130 feet, and could not have hit the roof.

The equation for each player is of the form $h = -16t^2 + v_0t + 3$ and you need to find the discriminant of the equation $0 = -16t^2 + v_0t - 127$.

Janok: $99^2 - 4(-16)(127) = 1673$

The discriminant is positive so there are two solutions.

Jimenez: $91^2 - 4(-16)(127) = 153$

The discriminant is positive so there are two solutions.

Serrano: $88^2 - 4(-16)(127) = -384$

The discriminant is negative so there is no solution.

Sei: $89^2 - 4(-16)(127) = -207$

The discriminant is negative so there is no solution.

So the balls hit by Janok and Jimenez could have hit the roof. There is not enough information to determine whether either ball actually did. You would have to know how far the building is from home plate and whether the path of the ball intersected with the building.

AVOID COMMON ERRORS

Some students may assume that a parabola modeling the height of a ball as a function of time describes the path of the ball through space. Encourage students to graph the parabola, and point out the units of the axes. The x-axis measures time and does not represent the horizontal distance the ball has travelled.

QUESTIONING STRATEGIES

? How many real values for t are possible when using the formula for height? two

? Do you think both values for t will make sense for the problem in the Lesson Performance Task? No; the path the ball takes is a parabola; one value for t will be right after the ball is hit, before it reaches its highest point, and the other will be in the outfield, after the ball reaches its highest point.

? How many real values for d are possible when using the formula for distance? 1

EXTENSION ACTIVITY

Have students investigate the longest home run ever recorded in regular season major-league baseball, hit by Mickey Mantle on September 10, 1960. Ask them to find its maximum height and greatest horizontal distance from home plate, and then ask them what other information they would need to model the height of the ball using a quadratic equation. Students may find that the ball reached a height of about 145 feet and traveled about 643 feet from home plate. They should recognize that in order to model the height, they could use the height at which the ball was hit, and the time it took the ball to hit the ground.

Scoring Rubric

2 points: Student correctly solves the problem and explains his/her reasoning.

1 point: Student shows good understanding of the problem but does not fully solve or explain his/her reasoning.

0 points: Student does not demonstrate understanding of the problem.

Using the Quadratic Formula to Solve Equations   **1072**

Choosing a Method for Solving Quadratic Equations

Common Core Math Standards

The student is expected to:

COMMON CORE A-REI.B.4b

Solve quadratic equations ... as appropriate to the initial form of the equation ...

Mathematical Practices

COMMON CORE MP.5 Using Tools

Language Objective

Explain to a partner how you decide whether to use square roots, completing the square, or the quadratic formula to solve a quadratic equation.

ENGAGE

Essential Question: How can you choose a method for solving a given quadratic equation?

The choice of method usually depends on the form of the equation, the coefficient values, or personal preference. For example, you can solve $ax^2 - c = 0$ or $a(x^2 + b) = c$ by taking square roots. You can solve any quadratic equation $ax^2 + bx + c = 0$ by completing the square or by using the quadratic equation, but one or the other may be preferable depending on the values of a, b, and c.

PREVIEW: LESSON PERFORMANCE TASK

View the Engage section online. Discuss the photo, asking how a quadratic equation could be used to help a landscaper design a stone patio. Then preview the Lesson Performance Task.

22.4 Choosing a Method for Solving Quadratic Equations

Essential Question: How can you choose a method for solving a given quadratic equation?

⊘ Explore   **Comparing Solution Methods for Quadratic Equations**

$7x^2 - 3x - 5 = 0$

Try to solve the equation by factoring.

(A) Find the factors of 7 and −5 to complete the table:

Factors of 7	Factors of −5	Outer Product + Inner Product
1, 7	1, −5	2
1, 7	5, −1	34
1, 7	−1, 5	−2
1, 7	−5, 1	−34

(B) None of the sums of the inner and outer products of the factor pairs of 7 and −5 equal −3.

Does this mean the equation cannot be solved? **No** .

Now, try to solve the equation by completing the square.

(C) The leading coefficient is not a perfect square. Multiply both sides by a value that makes the coefficient a perfect square.

$$\boxed{7}\,(7x^2 - 3x - 5) = (0)\,\boxed{7}$$

$$\boxed{49}\,x^2 - \boxed{21}\,x - \boxed{35} = \boxed{0}$$

(D) Add or subtract to move the constant term to the other side of the equation.

$$\boxed{49}\,x^2 - \boxed{21}\,x = \boxed{35}$$

(E) Find $\dfrac{b^2}{4a}$ and reduce to simplest form.

$$\frac{b^2}{4a} = \frac{\boxed{21}^{\,2}}{4\left(\boxed{49}\right)} = \frac{\boxed{441}}{\boxed{196}} = \frac{\boxed{9}}{\boxed{4}}$$

© Houghton Mifflin Harcourt Publishing Company

Ⓕ Add $\frac{b^2}{4a}$ to both sides of the equation,

$$\boxed{49}\,x^2 - \boxed{21}\,x + \frac{\boxed{9}}{4} = \boxed{35} + \frac{\boxed{9}}{4}$$

$$\boxed{49}\,x^2 - \boxed{21}\,x + \frac{\boxed{9}}{4} = \frac{\boxed{149}}{4}$$

Ⓖ Factor the perfect-square trinomial on the left side of the equation.

$$\left(\boxed{7}\,x - \frac{\boxed{3}}{\boxed{2}}\right)^2 = \frac{\boxed{149}}{\boxed{4}}$$

Ⓗ Take the square root of both sides. $\boxed{7}\,x - \frac{\boxed{3}}{2} = \pm\sqrt{\frac{\boxed{149}}{\boxed{4}}}$

Ⓘ Add the constant to both sides, and then divide by a. Find both solutions for x.

$$\boxed{7}\,x - \frac{\boxed{3}}{2} + \frac{\boxed{3}}{2} = \pm\sqrt{\frac{\boxed{149}}{4}} + \frac{\boxed{3}}{2}$$

$$\frac{\boxed{7}\,x}{\boxed{7}} = \frac{\pm\sqrt{\frac{\boxed{149}}{4}} + \frac{\boxed{3}}{2}}{\boxed{7}}$$

$$x = \frac{\pm\sqrt{\frac{\boxed{149}}{4}} + \frac{\boxed{3}}{2}}{\boxed{7}}$$

$$x = \frac{\sqrt{\frac{\boxed{149}}{4}} + \frac{\boxed{3}}{2}}{\boxed{7}} \quad \text{or} \quad x = -\frac{\sqrt{\frac{\boxed{149}}{4}} + \frac{\boxed{3}}{2}}{\boxed{7}}$$

Ⓙ Solve both equations to three decimal places using your calculator.

$x = \boxed{1.086}$ or $x = \boxed{-0.658}$

Now use the quadratic formula to solve the same equation.

Ⓚ Identify the values of a, b, and c. $a = \boxed{7}$, $b = \boxed{-3}$, $c = \boxed{-5}$

Ⓛ Substitute values into the quadratic formula.

$$x = \frac{-\boxed{-3} \pm \sqrt{\boxed{-3}^2 - 4(7)\left(\boxed{-5}\right)}}{2\left(\boxed{7}\right)}$$

Module 22   1074   Lesson 4

© Houghton Mifflin Harcourt Publishing Company

EXPLORE

Comparing Solution Methods for Quadratic Equations

INTEGRATE TECHNOLOGY

Students have the option of completing the Explore activity either in the book or online.

QUESTIONING STRATEGIES

? Which solution method works best when there is no x-term? Taking square roots is quickest when there is no x-term. Isolate x^2, then take the square root of both sides of the equation.

PROFESSIONAL DEVELOPMENT

Learning Progressions

In this lesson, students use different solution methods to solve quadratic equations, including taking the square root, completing the square, using the quadratic formula, and factoring. It is important that students understand that the different solution methods result in the same solution. Students should choose the method that best fits the situation at hand when solving quadratic equations. This is an important skill for college readiness.

EXPLAIN 1

Solving Quadratic Equations Using Different Methods

QUESTIONING STRATEGIES

How is the first step in solving a quadratic equation by completing the square different from solving one by using the quadratic formula? The first step in completing the square is to place the variable terms on one side of the equation and the constant on the other. The first step in using the quadratic formula is to write the equation in standard form, $ax^2 + bx + c = 0$.

Ⓜ Simplify the discriminant and the denominator.

$$x = \frac{3 \pm \sqrt{\boxed{149}}}{\boxed{14}}$$

Ⓝ Use your calculator to finish simplifying the expression for x.

$x = \boxed{1.086}$ or $x = \boxed{-0.658}$

Reflect

1. **Discussion** Another method you learned for solving quadratics is taking square roots. Why would that not work in this case?
   Taking square roots only works when there are is no x term in the standard form $\big($as in $4x^2 - 9 = 0\big)$**, or when the quadratic is already expressed as a perfect square of a binomial plus constant terms** $\big($as in $(x + 4)^2 - 5 = 10\big)$**.**

⊘ **Explain 1**   **Solving Quadratic Equations Using Different Methods**

You have seen several ways to solve a quadratic equation, but there are reasons why you might choose one method over another.

Factoring is usually the fastest and easiest method. Try factoring first if it seems likely that the equation is factorable.

Both completing the square and using the quadratic formula are more general. Quadratic equations that are solvable can be solved using either method.

Example 1   Speculate which method is the most appropriate for each equation and explain your answer. Then solve the equation using factoring (if possible), completing the square, and the quadratic formula.

Ⓐ $x^2 + 7x + 6 = 0$

Factor the quadratic.

Set up a factor table adding factors of c.

Factors of c	Sum of Factors
1, 6	7
2, 3	5

Substitute in factors. $(x + 1)(x + 6) = 0$

Use the Zero Product Property $x + 1 = 0$ or $x + 6 = 0$

Solve both equations for x. $x = -1$ or $x = -6$

© Houghton Mifflin Harcourt Publishing Company

COLLABORATIVE LEARNING

Peer-to-Peer Activity

Have students work in pairs. Instruct each student to write three different equations, each one as an example of an equation that is best solved using one of the solution methods learned in this module: using square roots, completing the square, and using the quadratic formula. Have the students switch problems and solve each equation. Have them discuss why they did or did not use the methods preferred by their partners.

Complete the square.

Move the constant term to the right side.
$$x^2 + 7x = -6$$

Add $\frac{b^2}{4a}$ to both sides.
$$x^2 + 7x + \frac{49}{4} = -6 + \frac{49}{4}$$

Simplify.
$$x^2 + 7x + \frac{49}{4} = \frac{25}{4}$$

Factor the perfect-square trimonial on the left.
$$\left(x + \frac{7}{2}\right)^2 = \frac{25}{4}$$

Take the square root of both sides.
$$x + \frac{7}{2} = \pm\frac{5}{2}$$

Write two equations.
$$x + \frac{7}{2} = \frac{5}{2} \quad \text{or} \quad x + \frac{7}{2} = -\frac{5}{2}$$

Solve both equations.
$$x = -1 \quad \text{or} \quad x = -6$$

Apply the quadratic formula.

Identify the values of a, b, and c.
$$a = 1, b = 7, c = 6$$

Substitute values into the quadratic formula.
$$x = \frac{-7 + \sqrt{7^2 - 4(1)(6)}}{2(1)}$$

Simplify the discriminant and denominator.
$$x = \frac{-7 \pm \sqrt{25}}{2}$$

Evaluate the square root and write as two equations.
$$x = \frac{-7 + 5}{2} \quad \text{or} \quad x = \frac{-7 - 5}{2}$$

Simplify.
$$x = -1 \quad \text{or} \quad x = -6$$

Because the list of possible factors that needed to be checked was short, it makes sense to try factoring $x^2 + 7x + 6$ first, even if you don't know if you will be able to factor it. Once factored, the remaining steps are fewer and simpler than either completing the square or using the quadratic formula.

(B) $2x^2 + 8x + 3 = 0$

Factor the quadratic.

Factors of c	Factors of c	Sum of Inner and Outer Products
1, 2	1, 3	5
1, 2	3, 1	7

Can the quadratic be factored? __No__.

Complete the square.

Move the constant term to the right side.
$$2x^2 + 8x = -3$$

Multiply both sides by 2 to make a perfect square. 4 $x^2 + 16x =$ -6

Add $\frac{b^2}{4a}$ to both sides.
$$4x^2 + 16x + \boxed{16} = 10$$

Factor the left side.
$$\left(\boxed{2}\,x + \boxed{4}\right)^2 = 10$$

Students often forget how to apply the quadratic formula to an equation that does not have an x-term or constant. Remind students that the missing term has a coefficient of 0, so they can substitute 0 for the value of b or c.

DIFFERENTIATE INSTRUCTION

Multiple Representations

Students should realize that no matter what method they use to solve a quadratic equation, the solutions are always the same. They should, therefore, choose the easiest method or the one they feel most comfortable with. Students should keep in mind, however, that not all quadratic equations can be solved by taking the square root.

Take the square root of both sides.	$2x + 4 = \boxed{\pm} \sqrt{\boxed{10}}$
Write two equations.	$2x + 4 = \sqrt{\boxed{10}}$ or $2x + 4 = -\sqrt{10}$
Solve both equations.	$x = -2 \boxed{+} \dfrac{\sqrt{\boxed{10}}}{2}$ or $x = -2 \boxed{-} \dfrac{\sqrt{10}}{2}$

Apply the quadratic formula.

Identify the values of a, b, and c.	$a = \boxed{2}$, $b = \boxed{8}$, $c = \boxed{3}$
Substitute values into the quadratic formula.	$x = \dfrac{\boxed{-8} \pm \sqrt{\boxed{8}^{\boxed{2}} - 4\left(\boxed{2}\right)\left(\boxed{3}\right)}}{2\left(\boxed{2}\right)}$
Simplify the discriminant and denominator.	$x = \dfrac{-8 \pm \sqrt{\boxed{40}}}{4}$
Evaluate the square root and write as two equations.	$x = \dfrac{-8 \pm \boxed{2}\sqrt{\boxed{10}}}{4}$
Simplify.	$x = \boxed{-2} \pm \dfrac{\sqrt{10}}{\boxed{2}}$

Reflect

2. What are the advantages and disadvantages of solving a quadratic equation by taking square roots?
Taking square roots is the easiest approach and least likely to result in an error due to

the minimal number of computations, but it is also the most restrictive, only working for

values of $b = 0$ in the standard form.

3. What are the advantages and disadvantages of solving a quadratic equation by factoring?
Sample answer: If the equation is not difficult to factor, factoring will usually be easier

than completing the square or applying the quadratic formula. It usually requires fewer

calculations, allowing for fewer opportunities to make a mistake. However, many quadratic

equations that can be solved for two real solutions are not solvable by factoring.

4. What are the advantages and disadvantages of solving a quadratic equation by completing the square?
Sample answer: The method can be used on any solvable quadratic equation, but is

usually more time consuming than either factoring or the quadratic formula. If $\frac{b}{2a}$ is a

small integer, it will involve fewer computations and simpler numbers than the quadratic

formula. It may be easier to remember than the quadratic formula, because the process

can be checked along the way.

© Houghton Mifflin Harcourt Publishing Company

LANGUAGE SUPPORT **EL**

Connect Vocabulary

The disregarded solution of a problem is called an *extraneous* solution. Help students understand what this means. Analyze the words *disregard* (*not give regard to*) and *extraneous* (its root word is *extra*).

5. What are the advantages and disadvantages of solving a quadratic equation by using the quadratic formula?
Sample answer: The quadratic formula works for all solvable equations and is usually

less work than completing the square. It will be more work and more likely to result in an

error from an incorrect computation than factoring or taking square roots. It is also more

likely to result in errors than any other technique due to misremembering the formula or

copying it incorrectly (the negative signs often lead to sign errors).

Your Turn

Solve the quadratic equations by any method you chose. Identify the method and explain why you chose it. **Sample explanations given.**

6. $9x^2 - 100 = 0$
Take the square roots because $b = 0$.
$9x^2 = 100$
$3x = \pm 10$
$x = \pm \dfrac{10}{3}$

7. $x^2 + 4x - 7 = 0$
Complete the square, because it is not factorable, but the coefficients are small and will not lead to a lot of fractional terms.
$$x^2 + 4x = 7$$
$$x^2 + 4x + 4 = 11$$
$$(x + 2)^2 = 11$$
$$x + 2 = \pm \sqrt{11}$$
$$x = -2 \pm \sqrt{11}$$

⚙ **Explain 2** **Choosing Solution Methods for Quadratic Equation Models**

Recall that the formula for height, in feet, of a projectile under the influence of gravity is given by $h = -16t^2 + vt + s$, where t is the time in seconds, v is the upward initial velocity (at $t = 0$), and s is the starting height.

Example 2 Marco is throwing a tennis ball at a kite that is stuck 42 feet up in a tree, trying to knock it loose. He can throw the ball at a velocity of 45 feet per second upward at a height of 4 feet. Will his throw reach the kite? How hard does Marco need to throw the ball to reach the kite?

🧩 **Analyze Information**

The initial velocity is: __45__

The starting height is: __4__

The height of the kite is: __42__

EXPLAIN 2

Choosing Solution Methods for Quadratic Equation Models

AVOID COMMON ERRORS

When using the quadratic formula, some students may forget to first write the equation in standard form. Remind students that the form in which they should write the equation depends on the method they plan to use to solve it.

QUESTIONING STRATEGIES

? How can you use completing the square to solve a quadratic equation? Write the equation in the form $x^2 + bx = c$, and add $\left(\dfrac{b}{2}\right)^2$ to both sides. Then, factor the perfect square trinomial, and find the square root of both sides of the equation.

? How can you use the quadratic formula to solve a quadratic equation? What is one advantage of using it? Possible answer: Write the equation in standard form. Then, substitute a, b, and c into the quadratic formula, $\dfrac{-b \pm \sqrt{b^2 - 4ac}}{2a}$, and simplify. One advantage of using the quadratic formula is that you can quickly evaluate the discriminant, $b^2 - 4ac$, to determine the number of real solutions.

Formulate a Plan

Use the projectile motion formula to write an equation for the height of the ball t seconds after Marco throws it.

$$h = \boxed{-16}\,t^2 + \boxed{45}\,t + \boxed{4}$$

To determine if the ball can reach the height of the kite, set up the equation to find the time it takes the ball to reach the height of the kite.

$$-16t^2 + 45t + 4 = \boxed{42}$$

Convert the equation to standard form.

$$-16t^2 + 45t + \boxed{-38} = 0$$

This problem will be easiest to solve by <u>using the quadratic formula.</u> To check if the ball reaches the kite, begin by calculating the <u>discriminant</u>. To determine the velocity that Marco must throw the ball to reach the kite, we should find the velocity where the <u>discriminant</u> is equal to <u>0</u>, which is the exact moment at which the ball changes direction and falls back to earth.

Solve

Identify values of a, b, and c. $\qquad a = \boxed{-16}$, $b = \boxed{45}$, $c = \boxed{-38}$

Evaluate the discriminant first. $\qquad b^2 - 4ac = \boxed{45}^2 - 4\left(\boxed{-16}\right)\left(\boxed{-38}\right)$

$$= \boxed{-407}$$

A negative discriminant means that there are $\underline{\ \ 0\ \ }$ solutions to the equation. Marco's throw will/(will not) reach as high as the kite.

The velocity with which Marco needs to throw the ball to reach the kite is the coefficient b of the x-term of the quadratic equation.

$$b = \boxed{v}$$

Substitute v into the discriminant and solve for a discriminant equal to 0 to find the velocity at which Marco needs to throw the ball.

Identify values of a, b, and c. $\qquad a = \boxed{-16}$, $b = \boxed{v}$, $c = \boxed{-38}$

Evaluate the discriminant first. $\qquad \boxed{v}^2 - 4\left(\boxed{-16}\right)\left(\boxed{-38}\right) = 0$

Simplify. $\qquad\qquad\qquad\qquad\qquad v^2 - \boxed{2432} = 0$

This quadratic equation should be solved by <u>taking square roots</u> because it has no x-term.

Move the constant term to the right. $\qquad v^2 = \boxed{2432}$

Take square roots of both sides. Use your calculator. $\qquad v \approx \pm\ \boxed{49.3}$

The negative velocity represents a downward throw and will not result in the ball hitting the kite. The tennis ball must have a velocity of at about $\underline{\ 49.3\ }$ feet per second to reach the kite.

© Houghton Mifflin Harcourt Publishing Company

Justify and Evaluate

Plot the graph of Marco's throw on your graphing calculator to see that the conclusion you reached (no solution) makes sense because the graphs do not intersect. Sketch the graph.

Then plot the height of the ball when the discriminant is equal to zero. The graphs intersect in one point. Sketch the graph.

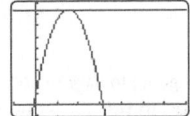

Your Turn

8. The wheel of a remote controlled airplane falls off while the airplane is climbing at 40 feet in the air. The wheel starts with an initial upward velocity of 24 feet per second. How long does it take to fall to the ground? Set up the equation to determine the time and pick one method to solve it. Explain why you chose that method.

$$h = -16t^2 + vt + s$$
$$0 = -16t^2 + 24t + 40$$
$$0 = -8(2t^2 - 3t - 5)$$
$$0 = -8(t + 1)(2t - 5)$$
$$t + 1 = 0 \quad \text{or} \quad 2t - 5 = 0$$
$$t = -1 \quad \text{or} \quad t = \frac{5}{2} \text{ or } 2.5$$

The wheel will not hit the ground before it falls off, so the answer must be the positive, and the time is 2.5 seconds. I chose to solve by factoring because after 8 was factored out, the quadratic was easy to factor.

ELABORATE

INTEGRATE MATHEMATICAL PROCESSES
Focus on Communication

Have students tell which method of solving a quadratic equation they like best, explaining their reasons for choosing it.

SUMMARIZE THE LESSON

Complete the graphic organizer with students to discuss and summarize lesson concepts. Write one equation that would be best solved using each solution method and explain why.

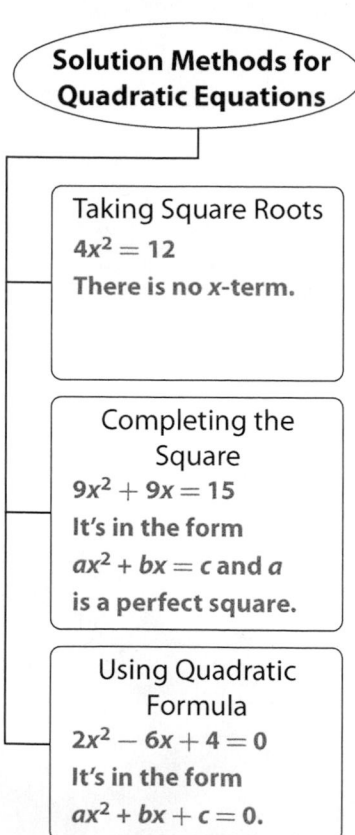

Solution Methods for Quadratic Equations

Taking Square Roots
$4x^2 = 12$
There is no x-term.

Completing the Square
$9x^2 + 9x = 15$
It's in the form
$ax^2 + bx = c$ and a
is a perfect square.

Using Quadratic Formula
$2x^2 - 6x + 4 = 0$
It's in the form
$ax^2 + bx + c = 0$.

---

9. Marco's brother, Jessie, is helping Marco knock a kite from the tree. He can throw the ball 50 feet per second upwards, from a height of 5 feet. Is he throwing the ball hard enough to reach the kite, and if so, how long does it take the ball to reach the kite?

$$-16t^2 + 50t + 5 = 42$$

$$-16t^2 + 50t - 37 = 0$$

$$b^2 - 4ac = 50^2 - 4(-16)(-37) = 132$$

$$t = \frac{-50 \pm \sqrt{132}}{2(-16)}$$

$$t = \frac{-50 + \sqrt{132}}{-32} \quad \text{or} \quad t = \frac{-50 - \sqrt{132}}{-32}$$

$$t \approx 1.20 \text{ s} \qquad\qquad t \approx 1.92 \text{ s}$$

The ball reaches the same height as the kite at about 1.20 seconds, and then again on the way back down at 1.92 seconds.

💬 Elaborate

10. Which method do you think is best if you are going to have to use a calculator?
If a calculator is needed, the best method in this situation is probably to either use the quadratic formula or to solve graphically.

11. Some factorable quadratic expressions are still quite difficult to solve by factoring rather than using another method. What makes an equation difficult to factor?
Sample answer: When the a and c terms have many factors, the number of combinations of factor pairs to try can be very large. If either a or c is a negative number, this also increases the number of combinations of factor pairs to try.

12. You are taking a test on quadratic equations and you can't decide which method would be the fastest way to solve a particular problem. How could looking at a graph of the equation on a calculator help you decide which method to use?
By graphing the related function on a calculator, I can estimate where the zeros are. If the zeros are integers, then the equation would probably be easy to factor. If there are no zeros, I know that there is no solution.

13. **Essential Question Check-In** How should you determine a method for solving a quadratic equation?
The choice of method depends on the equation. If taking square roots or factoring can be used, those should be the first choices. Convert to standard form first (unless the equation starts with squares on both sides of the equation) and then determine which method to use based on the coefficients.

• Online Homework
• Hints and Help
• Extra Practice

1. Look at this quadratic equation and explain what you think will be the best approach to solving it. Do not solve the equation.

$3.38x^2 + 2.72x - 9.31 = 0$

This formula is expressed with two digit decimal coefficients. Factoring and completing the squares could be attempted by multiplying the equation by 100 to get to integer coefficients, but the amount of work in either method would be unreasonable. The quadratic formula, on the other hand, can be used easily with a calculator to evaluate the coefficients without any further manipulation.

Solve the quadratic equation by any means. Identify the method and explain why you chose it. Irrational answers may be left in radical form or approximated with a calculator (round to two decimal places).

2. $x^2 - 7x + 12 = 0$

Factoring, because there are not many factors to check.

$x^2 - 7x + 12 = 0$

$(x - 3)(x - 4) = 0$

$x - 3 = 0$ or $x - 4 = 0$

$x = 3$ or $x = 4$

3. $36x^2 - 64 = 0$

Taking square roots, because $b = 0$.

$36x^2 = 64$

$6x = \pm 8$

$x = \pm \dfrac{4}{3}$

4. $4x^2 - 4x - 3 = 2$

Completing the square, because it is not factorable, but the coefficients are small and will not lead to a lot of fractional terms.

$4x^2 \quad 4x = 5$

$4x^2 - 4x + 1 = 6$

$(2x - 1)^2 = 6$

$2x - 1 = \pm \sqrt{6}$

$2x = 1 \pm \sqrt{6}$

$x = \dfrac{1}{2} \pm \dfrac{\sqrt{6}}{2}$

5. $8x^2 + 9x + 2 = 1$

Factoring, because there are not many factors to check, and in this case, it works.

$8x^2 + 9x + 1 = 0$

$(8x + 1)(x + 1) = 0$

$8x + 1 = 0$ or $x + 1 = 0$

$x = -\dfrac{1}{8}$ or $x = -1$

EVALUATE

ASSIGNMENT GUIDE

Concepts and Skills	Practice
Explore Comparing Solution Methods for Quadratic Equations	Exercise 1
Example 1 Solving Quadratic Equations Using Different Methods	Exercises 2–17, 22–25
Example 2 Choosing Solution Methods for Quadratic Equation Models	Exercises 18–21

QUESTIONING STRATEGIES

? Which of the methods for solving a quadratic equation give an answer every time? Using the quadratic formula and completing the square give an answer every time. Using square roots is not always possible.

Exercise	Depth of Knowledge (D.O.K.)	**COMMON CORE** Mathematical Practices	
1–17	**2** Skills/Concepts		**MP.2** Reasoning
18–21	**2** Skills/Concepts		**MP.1** Problem Solving
22	**2** Skills/Concepts		**MP.2** Reasoning
23	**3** Strategic Thinking	H.O.T.	**MP.3** Logic
24	**3** Strategic Thinking	H.O.T.	**MP.3** Logic
25	**3** Strategic Thinking	H.O.T.	**MP.3** Logic

Have students write the general quadratic equation in standard form and then write the quadratic formula. Have them indicate how the coefficients and constants move from the equation to the formula. They can use colors, highlighting, arrows, or whatever appeals to them as long as the process is clear. A sample is shown below.

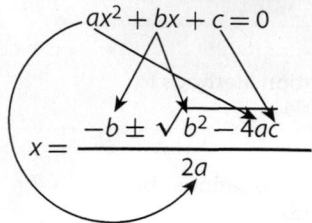

$$ax^2 + bx + c = 0$$

$$x = \frac{-b \pm \sqrt{b^2 - 4ac}}{2a}$$

---

6. $5x^2 + 0x - 13 = 0$

Taking square roots, because $b = 0$.

$$5x^2 = 13$$
$$\sqrt{5x^2} = \pm\sqrt{13}$$
$$x = \pm\frac{\sqrt{13}}{\sqrt{5}}$$
$$x = \pm\frac{\sqrt{65}}{5}$$

7. $7x^2 - 5x - 5 = 0$

The quadratic formula, because the equation cannot be factored and completing the square will be complicated.

$$a = 7, b = -5, c = -5$$
$$x = \frac{-(-5) \pm \sqrt{(-5)^2 - 4(7)(-5)}}{2(7)}$$
$$x = \frac{5 \pm \sqrt{165}}{14}$$
$$x = 1.27 \quad \text{or} \quad x = -0.56$$

8. $3x^2 - 6x = 0$

Factoring, because it is easy to factor a quadratic expression with no constant term.

$$3x(x - 2) = 0$$
$$3x = 0 \quad \text{or} \quad x - 2 = 0$$
$$x = 0 \quad \text{or} \quad x = 2$$

9. $2x^2 + 4x - 3 = 0$

Completing the square, because it is not factorable, but the coefficients are small and will not lead to a lot of fractional terms.

$$2x^2 + 4x = 3$$
$$4x^2 + 8x = 6$$
$$4x^2 + 8x + 4 = 10$$
$$(2x + 2)^2 = 10$$
$$2x + 2 = \pm\sqrt{10}$$
$$2x = -2 \pm \sqrt{10}$$
$$x = -1 \pm \frac{\sqrt{10}}{2}$$

10. $(x - 5)^2 = 16$

Taking square roots, because the equation is already expressed as a squared binomial and a constant.

$$(x - 5)^2 = 16$$
$$x - 5 = \pm4$$
$$x - 5 = 4 \quad \text{or} \quad x - 5 = -4$$
$$x = 9 \quad \text{or} \quad x = 1$$

11. $(2x - 1)^2 = x$

$$4x^2 - 4x + 1 = x$$
$$4x^2 - 5x + 1 = 0$$

Factoring, because there are not too many factors to check, and in this case, it works.

$$(x - 1)(4x - 1) = 0$$
$$x - 1 = 0 \quad \text{or} \quad 4x - 1 = 0$$
$$x = 1 \quad \text{or} \quad x = \frac{1}{4}$$

12. $2(x+2)^2 - 5 = 3$

Taking square roots, because the equation can be easily converted to a squared binomial and a constant.

$$2(x+2)^2 = 8$$
$$(x+2)^2 = 4$$
$$x+2 = \pm 2$$
$$x+2 = 2 \quad \text{or} \quad x+2 = -2$$
$$x = 0 \quad \text{or} \quad x = -4$$

13. $(2x-3)^2 = 4x$

$$(2x-3)^2 = 4x$$
$$4x^2 - 12x + 9 = 4x$$
$$4x^2 - 16x + 9 = 0$$

Completing the square, because it is not factorable, but the coefficients are small and will not lead to a lot of fractional terms.

$$4x^2 - 16x = -9$$
$$4x^2 - 16x + 16 = -9 + 16$$
$$(2x-4)^2 = 7$$
$$2x - 4 = \pm\sqrt{7}$$
$$x = 2 \pm \frac{\sqrt{7}}{2}$$

14. $6x^2 - 5x + 12 = 0$

The quadratic formula, because the equation cannot be factored and completing the square will be complicated.

$a = 6, b = -5, c = 12$

$$x = \frac{-(-5) \pm \sqrt{(-5)^2 - 4(6)(12)}}{2(6)}$$
$$x = \frac{5 \pm \sqrt{-263}}{12}$$

The discriminant is negative, so there is no real solution.

15. $3x^2 + 6x + 2 = 0$

Completing the square, because it is not factorable, but the coefficients are small and will not lead to a lot of fractional terms.

$$3x^2 + 6x = -2$$
$$9x^2 + 18x = -6$$
$$9x^2 + 18x + 9 = -6 + 9$$
$$(3x+3)^2 = 3$$
$$3x + 3 = \pm\sqrt{3}$$
$$x = -1 \pm \frac{\sqrt{3}}{3}$$

16. $\frac{1}{2}x^2 + 3x + \frac{5}{2} = 0$

Factoring, because after multiplying by 2 to eliminate the fractional coefficients, it is apparent that will be easy to factor.

$$x^2 + 6x + 5 = 0$$
$$(x+1)(x+5) = 0$$
$$x + 1 = 0 \quad \text{or} \quad x + 5 = 0$$
$$x = -1 \quad \text{or} \quad x = -5$$

17. $(6x+7)(x+1) = 26$

$$6x^2 + 13x + 7 = 26$$
$$6x^2 + 13x - 19 = 0$$

The quadratic formula, because factoring and completing the square may be time-comsuming.

$a = 6, b = 13, c = -19$

$$x = \frac{-(13) \pm \sqrt{(13)^2 - 4(6)(-19)}}{2(6)}$$
$$x = \frac{-13 \pm \sqrt{625}}{12}$$
$$x = \frac{-13 + 25}{12} \quad \text{or} \quad x = \frac{-13 - 25}{12}$$
$$x = 1 \quad \text{or} \quad x = -\frac{19}{6}$$

Use the projectile motion formula and solve the quadratic equation by any means. Identify the method and explain why you chose it. Irrational answers and fractions should be converted to decimal form and rounded to two places.

18. Gary drops a pair of gloves off of a balcony that is 64 feet high down to his friend on the ground. How long does it take the pair of gloves to hit the ground?

$v = 0 \quad s = 64 \quad h = 0$

$-16t^2 + 64 = 0$

Because there is no initial velocity, there is no t term and the solution can be solved by finding square roots.

$-16t^2 = -64$

$16t^2 = 64$

$4t = \pm 8$

$4t = 8 \qquad \text{or} \qquad 4t = -8$

$t = 2 \qquad \text{or} \qquad t = -2$

The pair of gloves hits the ground after it is dropped, not before, so the answer must be the positive time: 2 seconds after it is dropped.

19. A soccer player jumps up and heads the ball while it is 7 feet above the ground. It bounces up at a velocity of 20 feet per second. How long will it take the ball to hit the ground?

$v = 20 \quad s = 7 \quad h = 0$

$-16t^2 + 20t + 7 = 0$

The quadratic formula, because the equation cannot be factored and completing the square will be complicated.

$a = -16, b = 20, c = 7$

$t = \dfrac{-(20) \pm \sqrt{(20)^2 - 4(-16)(7)}}{2(-16)}$

$t = \dfrac{-20 \pm \sqrt{848}}{-32}$

$t = \dfrac{-20 + \sqrt{848}}{-32} \qquad \text{or} \qquad t = \dfrac{-20 - \sqrt{848}}{-32}$

$t = -0.29 \qquad\qquad\qquad \text{or} \qquad\quad t = 1.54$

The ball hits the ground after it is headed, not before, so the answer must be the positive time: 1.54 seconds after it is headed.

20. A stomp rocket is a toy that is launched into the air from the ground by a sudden burst of pressure exerted by stomping on a pedal. If the rocket is launched at 24 feet per second, how long will it be in the air?

$v = 24$

$s = 0$

$h = 0$

$-16t^2 + 24t = 0$

Factoring, because the quadratic expression does not have a constant term.

$-8t(2t - 3) = 0$

$-8t = 0$ or $2t - 3 = 0$

$t = 0$ or $t = 1.5$

The rocket goes up at first, so the answer cannot be 0. It is in the air for 1.5 seconds.

21. A dog leaps off of the patio from 2 feet off of the ground with an upward velocity of 15 feet per second. How long will the dog be in the air?

$v = 15$

$s = 2$

$h = 0$

$-16t^2 + 15t + 2 = 0$

The quadratic formula, because the equation cannot be factored and completing the square will be complicated.

$a = -16, b = 15, c = 2$

$t = \dfrac{-(15) \pm \sqrt{(15)^2 - 4(-16)(2)}}{2(-16)}$

$t = \dfrac{-15 \pm \sqrt{353}}{-32}$

$t = \dfrac{-15 + \sqrt{353}}{-32}$ or $t = \dfrac{-15 - \sqrt{353}}{-32}$

$t = -0.12$ or $t = 1.06$

The dog will be in the air for a positive amount of time, so the answer is 1.06 seconds.

22. Multipart Classification Indicate whether the following statements about finding solutions to quadratic equations with integer coefficients are true or false.

a. Any quadratic equation with a real solution can be solved by using the quadratic formula.   ● True   ○ False

b. Any quadratic equation with a real solution can be solved by completing the square.   ● True   ○ False

c. Any quadratic equation with a real solution can be solved by factoring.   ○ True   ● False

d. Any quadratic equation with a real solution can be solved by taking the square root of both sides of the equation.   ○ True   ● False

e. If the equation can be factored, it has rational solutions.   ● True   ○ False

f. If the equation has only one real solution, it cannot be factored.   ○ True   ● False

INTEGRATE MATHEMATICAL PRACTICES

Focus on Math Connections

MP.1 Point out to students that completing the square and using the quadratic formula to solve a quadratic equation should produce the same solutions. Remind them that using multiple solution methods is a good way to check their answers.

JOURNAL

Have students write about their preferred methods of solving quadratic equations. Have them describe the method's advantages and disadvantages.

23. **Justify Reasoning** Any quadratic equation with a real solution can be solved with the quadratic formula. Describe the kinds of equations where that would not be the best choice, and explain your reasoning.

   Equations that can be solved by taking square roots or by factoring are usually solved that way because there is less computation involved in both of those methods. The answer will usually be found in less time and with fewer errors. If an equation cannot be factored, but can be solved by completing the square without large or fractional terms, it will probably be easier to solve by completing the square rather than using the quadratic formula.

24. **Critique Reasoning** Marisol decides to solve the quadratic equation by factoring $21x^2 + 47x - 24 = 0$. Do you think she chose the best method? How would you solve this equation?

   Answers will vary: Some students will say to factor because it can be factored, others will notice that it requires checking a lot of factor pairs and point out that it may be better to go straight to the quadratic equation.

25. **Communicate Mathematical Ideas** Explain the difference between the statements "The quadratic formula can be used to solve any quadratic equation with a real solution" and "Every quadratic equation has a real solution."

   The second statement is false. Some quadratic equations cannot be solved for a real value of x. If there are real solutions, then the quadratic formula can be used to find them. Either way, the first statement is true.

Lesson Performance Task

A landscaper is designing a patio for a customer who has several different ideas about what to make.

Use the given information to set up a quadratic equation modeling the situation and solve it using the quadratic formula. Then determine if another method for solving quadratic equations would have been easier to use and explain why.

a. One of the customer's ideas is to buy bluestone tiles from a home improvement store using several gift cards he has received as presents over the past few years. If the total value of the gift cards is $6500 and the bluestone costs $9 per square foot, what are the dimensions of the largest patio that can be made that is 12 feet longer than it is wide?

b. Another of the customer's ideas is simply a quadratic equation scrawled on a napkin.

$x^2 - 54x + 720 = 0$

c. The third idea is also a somewhat random quadratic polynomial.

$x^2 - 40x + 397 = 0$

a. The amount of bluestone is $\dfrac{6500}{9} = 722.\overline{2}$ square feet.

The area of the patio is $x^2 + 12x = 722$, so $x^2 + 12x - 722 = 0$.

Solve by completing the square:

$x^2 + 12x + 36 = 722 + 36$
$(x + 6)^2 = 758$

$x + 6 = \pm\sqrt{758}$
$x \approx -6 + 27.53 \qquad\qquad x \approx -6 - 27.53$
$\qquad \approx 21.53 \qquad\quad \text{or} \qquad\quad \approx -33.53$

Disregard the negative solution. The length is 12 feet greater than the width, so length $\approx 21.53 + 12 \approx 33.53$. Therefore, the patio will be approximately 21.5 feet by 33.5 feet.

b. Assume that the solutions to the equation represent the dimensions of the patio. Solve by factoring:

$x^2 - 54x + 720 = 0$
$(x - 24)(x - 30) = 0$

$x = 24$ or $x = 30$

Therefore, the patio will be 30 feet by 24 feet.

c. $x = \dfrac{-(-40) \pm \sqrt{(-40)^2 - 4(1)(397)}}{2(1)}$

$= \dfrac{40 \pm \sqrt{1600 - 1588}}{2}$

$= \dfrac{40 \pm \sqrt{12}}{2} \qquad\qquad x = 20 + \sqrt{3} \qquad\qquad x = 20 - \sqrt{3}$

$= \dfrac{40 \pm 2\sqrt{3}}{2} \qquad\qquad\quad \approx 20 + 1.73 \quad \text{or} \quad \approx 20 - 1.73$

$= 20 \pm \sqrt{3} \qquad\qquad\qquad \approx 21.73 \qquad\qquad\qquad \approx 18.27$

If the solutions to the equation represent the dimensions of the patio, the patio will be 21.7 feet by 18.3 feet.

AVOID COMMON ERRORS

Students may make computational errors under the radical in the quadratic formula. Some students may find it helpful to circle everything after b^2, and evaluate it separately before adding.

INTEGRATE MATHEMATICAL PRACTICES
Focus on Technology

MP.5 Have students check their answers for reasonableness by graphing the equations. The x-intercepts should appear to be close to their calculated answers.

EXTENSION ACTIVITY

Have students design their own problems that involve solving a quadratic equation to find the dimensions of a patio. The problem statement should include a description of how the length and width of the patio are related, as well as information about the total area of the patio.

Solving Nonlinear Systems

Common Core Math Standards

The student is expected to:

 A-REI.C.7

Solve a simple system consisting of a linear equation and a quadratic equation in two variables algebraically and graphically.

Mathematical Practices

 MP.1 Problem Solving

Language Objective

Explain to a partner how to solve a system consisting of a quadratic equation and a linear equation by graphing.

ENGAGE

Essential Question: How can you solve a system of equations when one equation is linear and the other is quadratic?

You can graph both equations and find the points of intersection, if there are any. Create a graph by hand and read approximate solutions from it, or use a graphing calculator to find precise intersection points. You can also find the solution algebraically by setting the two functions equal and solving the resulting quadratic equation.

PREVIEW: LESSON PERFORMANCE TASK

View the Engage section online. Discuss students' experiences of having another driver enter traffic in front of them while they are driving or riding in a car. Then preview the Lesson Performance Task.

Name _____ Class _____ Date _____

22.5 Solving Nonlinear Systems

Essential Question: How can you solve a system of equations when one equation is linear and the other is quadratic?

Resource Locker

⊘ Explore   **Determining the Possible Number of Solutions of a System of Linear and Quadratic Equations**

A system of one linear and one quadratic equation may have zero, one, or two solutions.

Ⓐ The graph of the quadratic function $f(x) = x^2 - 2x - 2$ is shown. On the same coordinate plane, graph the following linear functions:

$$g(x) = -x - 2, h(x) = 2x - 6, j(x) = 0.5x - 5$$

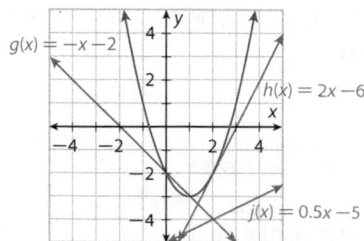

Ⓑ Look at the graph of the system consisting of the quadratic function, $f(x)$, and the linear function, $g(x)$. Based on the intersections of these two graphs, how many solutions exist in a system consisting of these two functions? ___2___

Ⓒ Look at the graph of the system consisting of the quadratic function, $f(x)$, and the linear function, $h(x)$. Based on the intersections of these two graphs, how many solutions exist in a system consisting of these two functions? ___1___

Ⓓ Look at the graph of the system consisting of the quadratic function, $f(x)$, and the linear function, $j(x)$. Based on the intersections of these two graphs, how many solutions exist in a system consisting of these two functions? ___0___

Reflect

1. A system consisting of a quadratic equation and a linear equation can have ___0___, ___1___, or ___2___ solutions.

© Houghton Mifflin Harcourt Publishing Company

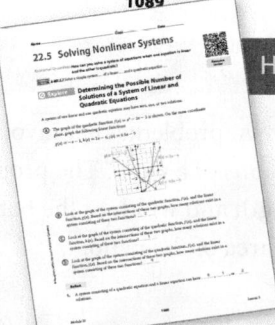

HARDCOVER PAGES 845–852

Turn to these pages to find this lesson in the hardcover student edition.

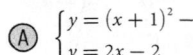

A system of equations consisting of a linear and quadratic equation can be solved graphically by finding the points where the graphs intersect.

Example 1 Solve the system of equations graphically.

Ⓐ $\begin{cases} y = (x + 1)^2 - 4 \\ y = 2x - 2 \end{cases}$

Graph the quadratic function. The vertex is the point $(-1, -4)$.
The x-intercepts are the points where $y = 0$.

$(x + 1)^2 - 4 = 0$

$(x + 1)^2 = 4$

$x + 1 = \pm 2$

$x = 1$ or $x = -3$

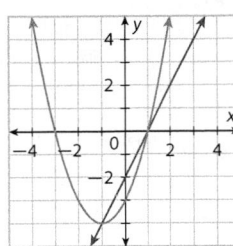

Graph the linear function on the same coordinate plane.

The solutions of the system are the points where the graphs intersect. The solutions are $(\ 1, -4)$ and $(1, 0)$.

Ⓑ $\begin{cases} y = 2(x - 2)^2 - 2 \\ y = -x - 1 \end{cases}$

Graph the quadratic function. The vertex is the point $\left(2, \boxed{-2}\right)$.

The x-intercepts are the points where $y = 0$.

$2(x - 2)^2 - 2 = 0$

$2(x - 2)^2 = \boxed{2}$

$(x - 2)^2 = \boxed{1}$

$\boxed{x - 2} = \pm 1$

$x = \boxed{3}$ or $x = \boxed{1}$

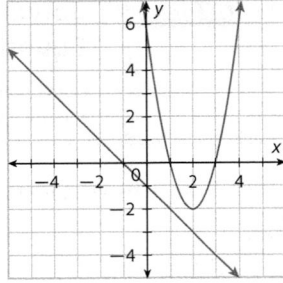

Graph the linear function on the same coordinate plane.

There are $\underline{\quad 0 \quad}$ intersection points. This system has $\underline{\quad 0 \quad}$ solution(s).

PROFESSIONAL DEVELOPMENT

 Integrate Mathematical Practices

This lesson provides an opportunity to address Mathematical Practice **MP.1**, which calls for students to "make sense of problems and persevere in solving them." Students consider the meaning of a problem while planning how to find a solution. Students use graphs to determine the number of solutions for a system of equations. They solve systems by graphing manually or with a calculator, and they also solve systems algebraically. Finally, students interpret the solutions in the context of real-world situations.

EXPLORE

Determining the Possible Number of Solutions of a System of Linear and Quadratic Equations

INTEGRATE TECHNOLOGY

Introduce students to solving systems of equations by using a graphing calculator to graph the systems and find the intersection points. To verify each point of intersection, students can substitute its x-value into both equations and check that the y-value is the same for both equations.

QUESTIONING STRATEGIES

How does graphing a system of equations help you find the number of solutions of the system? **The number of points at which the graphs intersect is the number of solutions.**

If the graph of a quadratic function intersects a horizontal line at exactly one point, what must be true about that point? **It must be the vertex of the parabola.**

EXPLAIN 1

Solving a System of Linear and Quadratic Equations Graphically

INTEGRATE MATHEMATICAL PRACTICES
Focus on Patterns

MP.8 Discuss with students how symmetry can be useful in graphing a quadratic function in vertex form. Students should understand that chosen points can be reflected across the axis of symmetry.

? Why do the points where the graphs of two functions intersect represent the solutions to the system of equations? The coordinates of the intersection points are the pairs of values that satisfy both equations.

EXPLAIN 2

Solving a System of Linear and Quadratic Equations Algebraically

INTEGRATE MATHEMATICAL PRACTICES
Focus on Modeling

MP.4 Students who are comfortable with solving systems of linear and quadratic equations by graphing may not see the value in using algebra to find solutions. Discuss reasons for solving algebraically: solutions that are not on grid lines can be hard to read, and the intersection may be located outside of the portion of the coordinate grid shown.

AVOID COMMON ERRORS

When solving a system, students sometimes stop after finding the value(s) of one of the variables. Remind them that solutions of a system are ordered pairs. They need to substitute the value(s) they find into one of the original equations and solve for the other variable.

QUESTIONING STRATEGIES

? When finding solutions algebraically, how can you check your answers? Substitute the x-values of the solutions into both original equations and verify that the resulting y-values are the same for both equations.

Your Turn

Solve the system of equations graphically.

2. $\begin{cases} y = -2(x+2)^2 + 8 \\ y = 4x + 16 \end{cases}$

Solution: $(-4, 0)$ or $(-2, 8)$

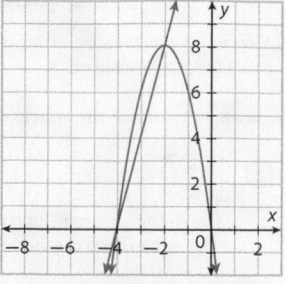

3. $\begin{cases} y = (x+1)^2 - 9 \\ y = 6x - 12 \end{cases}$

Solution: $(2, 0)$

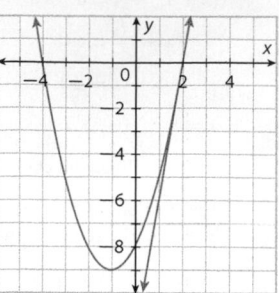

⊘ Explain 2 **Solving a System of Linear and Quadratic Equations Algebraically**

Systems of equations can also be solved algebraically by using the substitution method to eliminate a variable. If the system is one linear and one quadratic equation, the equation resulting after substitution will also be quadratic and can be solved by selecting an appropriate method.

Example 2 Solve the system of equations algebraically.

Ⓐ $\begin{cases} y = (x+1)^2 - 4 \\ y = 2x - 2 \end{cases}$

Set the two the expressions for y equal to each other, and solve for x.

$(x+1)^2 - 4 = 2x - 2$

$x^2 + 2x - 3 = 2x - 2$

$x^2 - 1 = 0$

$x^2 = 1$

$x = \pm 1$

Substitute 1 and −1 for x to find the corresponding y-values.

$y = 2x - 2$	$y = 2x - 2$
$y = 2(1) - 2 = 0$	$y = 2(-1) - 2 = -4$

The solutions are $(1, 0)$ and $(-1, -4)$.

COLLABORATIVE LEARNING

Peer-to-Peer Activity

Have students work in pairs. Ask each student to write a quadratic function, and have partners graph each other's functions. Next, have students draw three parallel lines on the graphs they created: one that does not intersect the graph of the quadratic function, one that intersects it at one point, and one that intersects it at two points. Have students write an equation for each line and identify the coordinates of each point of intersection.

Ⓑ $\begin{cases} y = (x+4)(x+1) \\ y = -x-5 \end{cases}$

Set the two the expressions for y equal to each other, and solve for x.

$$(x+4)(x+1) = \boxed{-x-5}$$

$$x^2 + \boxed{5}x + \boxed{4} = -x - 5$$

$$x^2 + \boxed{6}x + \boxed{9} = 0$$

$$\left(x + \boxed{3}\right)(x+3) = 0$$

$$x = \boxed{-3}$$

Substitute -3 for x to find the corresponding y-value.

$$y = -x - 5$$

$$y = -\left(\boxed{-3}\right) - 5 = \boxed{-2}$$

The solution is $\boxed{(-3, -2)}$.

Reflect

4. **Discussion** After finding the x-values of the intersection points, why use the linear equation to find the y-values rather than the quadratic? What if the quadratic equation is used instead?
   The linear equation will usually be easier to evaluate, having fewer operations. Both

   equations give the same y-values.

Your Turn

Solve the system of equations algebraically.

5. $\begin{cases} y = 2x^2 + 9x + 5 \\ y = 3x - 3 \end{cases}$

$$2x^2 + 9x + 5 = 3x - 3$$

$$2x^2 + 6x + 8 = 0$$

$$x^2 + 3x + 4 = 0$$

$$x = \frac{-(3) \pm \sqrt{(3)^2 - 4(1)(4)}}{2(1)}$$

$$x = \frac{-(3) \pm \sqrt{-7}}{2}$$

The discriminant is negative, so there are no real solutions.

DIFFERENTIATE INSTRUCTION

Critical Thinking

Initiate a discussion about how many points of intersection are possible when a system consists of two quadratic equations. Have students sketch graphs representing all of the possibilities. Students should find that the graphs of two quadratic functions can intersect at 0, 1, or 2 points. Discuss what similarities exist among systems that have the same number of solutions.

EXPLAIN 3

Solving a Real-World Problem with a System of Linear and Quadratic Equations

AVOID COMMON ERRORS

 When using a graphing calculator to graph a linear-quadratic system, students may find that the graph shows no intersection points and conclude that the system has no solutions. It is possible that the two graphs actually do intersect but that the domain or range of the graphs needs to be extended to include the intersection point. Caution students that they need to use a suitable viewing window to look for intersections before they come to a conclusion.

INTEGRATE MATHEMATICAL PRACTICES
Focus on Modeling

MP.4 When solving real-world problems, remind students that solutions involving negative numbers can often be discarded, but not always. Give students examples in which negative solutions are valid, such as distance above or below sea level or time before or after an event. Remind students that it is important to look at each context to check whether or not a solution is valid.

QUESTIONING STRATEGIES

? How can you determine in which direction a parabola will open? If the coefficient of the x^2 term of the equation is positive, the parabola will open upward. If the coefficient of the x^2 term is negative, the parabola will open downward.

Systems of equations can be solved by graphing both equations on a graphing calculator and using the Intersect feature.

Example 3 Create and solve a system of equations to solve the problem.

(A) A rock climber is pulling his pack up the side of a cliff that is 175.5 feet tall at a rate of 2 feet per second. The height of the pack in feet after t seconds is given by $h = 2t$. The climber drops a coil of rope from directly above the pack. The height of the coil in feet after t seconds is given by $h = -16t^2 + 175.5$. At what time does the coil of rope hit the pack?

Create the system of equations to solve.
$$\begin{cases} h = -16t^2 + 175.5 \\ h = 2t \end{cases}$$
Graph the functions together and find any points of intersection.

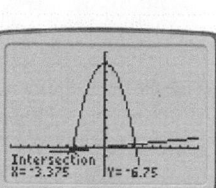 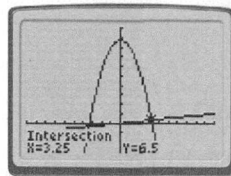

The intersection is at $(-3.375, -6.75)$.

The x-value represents time, so this solution is not reasonable.

The intersection is at $(3.25, 6.5)$.

This solution indicates that the coil hits the pack after 3.25 seconds.

(B) A window washer is ascending the side of a building that is 520 feet tall at a rate of 3 feet per second. The elevation of the window washer after t seconds is given by $h = 3t$. The supplies are lowered to the window washer from the top of the building at the same time that he begins to ascend the building. The height of the supplies in feet after t seconds is given by $h = -2t^2 + 520$. At what time do the supplies reach the window washer?

Create the system of equations to solve.

$$\begin{cases} h = \boxed{-2}\, t^2 + \boxed{520} \\ h = \boxed{3}\, t \end{cases}$$

LANGUAGE SUPPORT **EL**

Connect Vocabulary

When solving real-world problems, students may encounter words describing occupations or pastimes. Point out to English learners that in English, nouns that name an occupation often end with *-er*. Have them think of occupation words that could be used in a word problem, such as *teacher*, *bus driver*, and *football player*.

Graph the functions together and find any points of intersection.

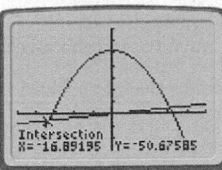 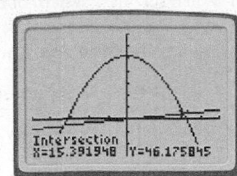

The intersection is at about (-16.9, -50.7).

The x-value represents **time**, so this solution is **not reasonable**

The intersection is at about (15.4, 46.2).

This solution indicates that **the supplies** reach the window washer about

15 seconds later

Reflect

6. How did you know which intersection to use in the example problems?

In both cases, the other intersection has a negative value of t, so it represents a time before the moving objects in each problem begin to move. The equations describing the object heights only apply after $t = 0$.

Your Turn

Create and solve a system of equations to solve the problem.

7. A billboard painter is using a pulley system to hoist a can of paint up to a scaffold at a rate of half a meter per second. The height of the can of paint as a function of time is given by $h(t) = 0.5t$. Five seconds after he starts raising the can of paint, his partner accidentally kicks a paint brush off of the scaffolding, which falls to the ground. The height of the falling paint brush can be represented by $h(t) = -4.9(t - 5)^2 + 30$. When does the brush pass the paint can?

$$\begin{cases} h(t) = -4.9(t - 5)^2 + 30 \\ h(t) = 0.5t \end{cases}$$

The paint brush passes by the can about 7.3 seconds after the painter starts hoisting it up or about 2.3 seconds after the paintbrush starts to fall.

ELABORATE

INTEGRATE MATHEMATICAL PRACTICES

Focus on Patterns

MP.8 Review the standard form and vertex form of a quadratic function. Understanding how to quickly find the vertex and axis of symmetry from the vertex form of the equation can make it easier for students to solve nonlinear systems by graphing.

SUMMARIZE THE LESSON

? How can you solve a system of a quadratic and a linear equation algebraically? Rewrite each equation so that y is given in terms of x, then set the two expressions for y equal to each other. Simplify the resulting quadratic equation, then solve it for x by factoring, taking a square root, completing the square, or using the quadratic formula. Substitute each x-value into one of the original equations to find the corresponding y-value.

Elaborate

8. Discussion When solving a system of equations consisting of a quadratic equation and a linear equation by graphing, why is it difficult to be sure there is one solution as opposed to zero or two?
For the system to have one solution, the line must just touch the parabola without crossing it. A slight translation closer and they will cross twice, while a slight translation away means they will miss entirely.

9. How can you use the discriminant to determine how many solutions a linear-quadratic system has?
After using substitution, you will have one quadratic equation to solve. The number of solutions of the system is equal to the number of solutions of that resulting quadratic equation.

10. Essential Question Check-in How can the graphs of two functions be used to solve a system of a quadratic and a linear equation?
The x and y coordinates of the points of intersection of the two curves are solutions to the system of equations.

⭐ Evaluate: Homework and Practice

- Online Homework
- Hints and Help
- Extra Practice

1. The graph of the function $f(x) = -\frac{1}{4}(x-3)^2 + 4$ is shown. Graph the functions $g(x) = x + 1$, $h(x) = x + 2$, and $j(x) = x + 3$ with the graph of $f(x)$, and determine how many solutions each system has.

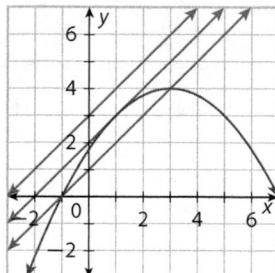

$f(x)$ and $g(x)$: __2__

$f(x)$ and $h(x)$: __1__

$f(x)$ and $j(x)$: __0__

Solve each system of equations graphically.

2. $\begin{cases} y = (x+3)^2 - 4 \\ y = 2x + 2 \end{cases}$

$(-3, -4), (-1, 0)$

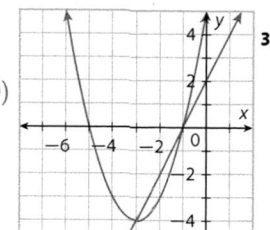

3. $\begin{cases} y = x^2 - 1 \\ y = x - 2 \end{cases}$

No Solutions

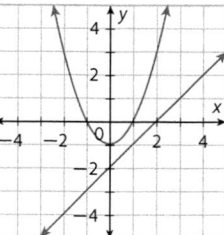

4. $\begin{cases} y = (x - 4)^2 - 2 \\ y = -2 \end{cases}$

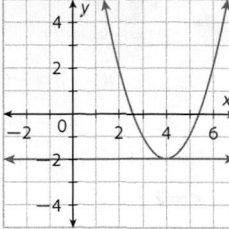

$(4, -2)$

5. $\begin{cases} y = -x^2 + 4 \\ y = -3x + 6 \end{cases}$

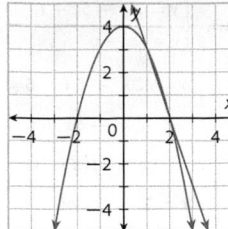

$(2, 0) \ (1, 3)$

6. $\begin{cases} y = -(x - 2)^2 + 9 \\ y = 3x + 3 \end{cases}$

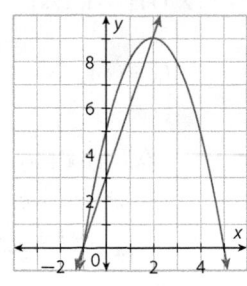

$(-1, 0) \ (2, 9)$

7. $\begin{cases} y = 3(x + 1)^2 - 1 \\ y = x - 4 \end{cases}$

No Solutions

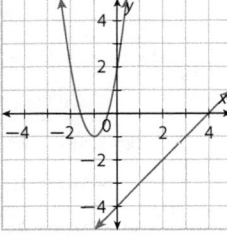

Solve the system of equations algebraically.

8. $\begin{cases} y = x^2 + 1 \\ y = 5 \end{cases}$

$x^2 + 1 = 5$

$x^2 = 4$

$x = \pm 2$

$y = 5$

$(2, 5) \ (-2, 5)$

9. $\begin{cases} y = x^2 - 3x + 2 \\ y = 4x - 8 \end{cases}$

$x^2 - 3x + 2 = 4x - 8$

$x^2 - 7x + 10 = 0$

$(x - 2)(x - 5) = 0$

$x = 2 \qquad$ or $\qquad x = 5$

$y = 4(2) - 8 = 0 \qquad y = 4(5) - 8 = 12$

$(2, 0) \ (5, 12)$

10. $\begin{cases} y = (x - 3)^2 \\ y = 4 \end{cases}$

$(x - 3)^2 = 4$

$x - 3 = \pm 2$

$x = 5 \qquad$ or $\qquad x = 1$

$(1, 4) \ (5, 4)$

11. $\begin{cases} y = -x^2 + 4x \\ y = x + 2 \end{cases}$

$-x^2 + 4x = x + 2$

$x^2 - 3x + 2 = 0$

$(x - 2)(x - 1) = 0$

$x = 2 \qquad$ or $\qquad x = 1$

$y = 2 + 2 = 4 \qquad y = 1 + 2 = 3$

$(2, 4) \ (1, 3)$

Exercise	Depth of Knowledge (D.O.K.)	COMMON CORE Mathematical Practices
1–7	**2** Skills/Concepts	**MP.7** Using Structure
8–15	**2** Skills/Concepts	**MP.6** Precision
16–19	**2** Skills/Concepts	**MP.4** Modeling
20	**2** Skills/Concepts	**MP.6** Precision
21	**2** Skills/Concepts	**MP.3** Logic
22	**2** Skills/Concepts	**MP.7** Using Structure

EVALUATE

ASSIGNMENT GUIDE

Concepts and Skills	Practice
Explore Determining the Possible Number of Solutions of a System of Linear and Quadratic Equations	Exercises 1, 22, 26
Example 1 Solving a System of Linear and Quadratic Equations Graphically	Exercises 2–7
Example 2 Solving a System of Linear and Quadratic Equations Algebraically	Exercises 8–15, 20, 25
Example 3 Solving a Real-World Problem with a System of Linear and Quadratic Equations	Exercises 16–19, 21, 23–24

INTEGRATE MATHEMATICAL PRACTICES

Focus on Communication

MP.5 Have students share how they decide which method to use for solving a system of equations. For example, they may prefer to solve algebraically when the equations involve small, easily factored numbers, and to graph with a calculator when the problem involves decimals or very large numbers. The choice of whether to solve a quadratic equation by factoring or by using the quadratic formula may also depend on the coefficients in the equations, but approaches will vary from one student to another.

MODELING

Review the different forms of a linear equation. Students should understand that linear equations presented in slope-intercept form and in point-slope form will provide them with information that can be helpful in graphing the function.

AVOID COMMON ERRORS

When students are solving a system of equations algebraically, remind them that the solutions will be ordered pairs. Students may feel they have found the solution after finding the value of one variable, but they must substitute the value(s) they find into one of the original equations in order to find the other value of the ordered pair.

12. $\begin{cases} y = 2x^2 - 5x + 6 \\ y = 5x - 6 \end{cases}$

$2x^2 - 5x + 6 = 5x - 6$

$x^2 - 5x + 6 = 0$

$(x - 2)(x - 3) = 0$

$x = 2$ or $x = 3$

$y = 5(2) - 6 = 4$ $y = 5(3) - 6 = 9$

$(2, 4)\ (3, 9)$

13. $\begin{cases} y = x^2 + 7 \\ y = -9x + 29 \end{cases}$

$x^2 + 7 = -9x + 29$

$x^2 + 9x - 22 = 0$

$(x - 2)(x + 11) = 0$

$x = 2$ or $x = -11$

$y = -9(2) + 29 = 11$ $y = -9(-11) + 29 = 128$

$(2, 11)\ (-11, 128)$

14. $\begin{cases} y = 4x^2 + 45x + 83 \\ y = 5x - 17 \end{cases}$

$4x^2 + 45x + 83 = 5x - 17$

$x^2 + 10x + 25 = 0$

$(x + 5)(x + 5) = 0$

$x = -5$

$y = 5(-5) - 17 = -42$

$(-5, -42)$

15. $\begin{cases} y = (x + 2)(x + 4) \\ y = 3x + 2 \end{cases}$

$(x + 2)(x + 4) = 3x + 2$

$x^2 + 3x + 6 = 0$

$x = \dfrac{-3 \pm \sqrt{-15}}{2}$

There are no real solutions.

Create and solve a linear quadratic system to solve the problem.

16. The height in feet of a skydiver t seconds after deploying her parachute is given by $h(t) = -300t + 1000$. A ball is thrown up toward the skydiver, and after t seconds, the height of the ball in feet is given by $h(t) = -16t^2 + 100t$. When does the ball reach the skydiver?

$\begin{cases} h(t) = -16t^2 + 100t \\ h(t) = -300t + 1000 \end{cases}$

Two intersections: $(2.82, 154.74)$ and $(22.18, -5654.74)$
The ball reaches the skydiver at 2.82 seconds.

17. A wildebeest fails to notice a lion that is charging from behind at 65 feet per second until the lion is 40 feet away. The lion's position as a function of time is given by $p(t) = 65t - 40$. The wildebeest has to begin accelerating from a standstill until it is captured or reaches a top speed fast enough to stay ahead of the lion. The wildebeest's position as a function of time is given by $d(t) = 35t^2$. Does the wildebeest escape?

$\begin{cases} p(t) = 65t - 40 \\ d(t) = 35t^2 \end{cases}$

The lion will catch the wildebeest if their positions are ever the same, which is indicated by an intersection.
The graphs to do not intersect, so the wildebeest escapes.

Module 22   **1097**   Lesson 5

Exercise	Depth of Knowledge (D.O.K.)	COMMON CORE Mathematical Practices
23–24	**3** Strategic Thinking H.O.T.\	**MP.4** Modeling
25	**3** Strategic Thinking H.O.T.\	**MP.6** Precision
26	**3** Strategic Thinking H.O.T.\	**MP.3** Logic

18. An elevator in a hotel moves at 20 feet per second. Leaving from the ground floor, its height in feet after t seconds is given by the formula $h(t) = 20t$. A bolt comes loose in the elevator shaft above, and its height in feet after falling for t seconds is given by $h(t) = -16t^2 + 200$. At what time and at what height does the bolt hit the elevator?

$$\begin{cases} h(t) = -16t^2 + 200 \\ h(t) = 20t \end{cases}$$

2 intersections: $(2.97, 59.31)$ and $(-4.22, -84.31)$

The bolt hits the elevator 2.97 seconds later, at a height of 59.31 feet.

19. A bungee jumper leaps from a bridge 100 meters over a gorge. Before the 40-meter-long bungee begins to slow him down, his height is characterized by $h(t) = -4.9t^2 + 100$. Two seconds after he jumps, a car on the bridge blows out a tire. The sound of the tire blow-out moves down from the top of the bridge at the speed of sound and has a height given by $h(t) = -340(t - 2) + 100$. How high will the bungee jumper be when he hears the sound of the blowout?

$$\begin{cases} h(t) = -4.9t^2 + 100 \\ h(t) = -340t + 780 \end{cases}$$

The graphs intersect at about $(2.1, 79.2)$, so the jumper hears the tire blow-out at a height of about 79.2 meters. (There is another intersection at a negative height, so it is unreasonable).

20. Explain the Error A student is asked to solve the system of equations $y = x^2 + 2x - 7$ and $y - 2 = x + 1$. For the first step, the student sets the right hand sides equal to each other to get the equation $x^2 + 2x - 7 = x + 1$. Why does this not give the correct solution?

Before equating the two right sides, both equations must be solved for y.

21. Explain the Error After solving the system of equations in Exercise 18 (the elevator and the bolt), a student concludes that there are two different times that the bolt hits the elevator. What is the error in the student's reasoning?

One solution has a negative value of t, which would mean the bolt hit the elevator before it began to fall.

22. Multi-part Classification

The functions listed are graphed here.

$f_1(x) = 2(x + 3)^2 + 1$ and $f_2(x) = -\dfrac{3}{4}(x - 2)^2 + 3$

$g_1(x) = x + 3$ and $g_2(x) = 3$ and $g_3(x) = -\dfrac{1}{2}x + 1$

Use the graph to classify each system as having 0, 1, or 2 solutions.

a. $\begin{cases} y = f_1(x) \\ y = g_1(x) \end{cases}$ 0   **b.** $\begin{cases} y = f_1(x) \\ y = g_2(x) \end{cases}$ 2   **c.** $\begin{cases} y = f_1(x) \\ y = g_3(x) \end{cases}$ 2

d. $\begin{cases} y = f_2(x) \\ y = g_1(x) \end{cases}$ 0   **e.** $\begin{cases} y = f_2(x) \\ y = g_2(x) \end{cases}$ 1   **f.** $\begin{cases} y = f_2(x) \\ y = g_3(x) \end{cases}$ 2

KINESTHETIC EXPERIENCE

After they create graphs for a system of equations, have students trace the paths of both graphs using their index fingers or colored pencils. They should note the shape of each graph and how the parabola turns toward and away from the line at different points. This process may help students recognize situations in which the graphs are likely to intersect if they are extended beyond the grid.

CRITICAL THINKING

When students are working with real-world situations, remind them that they have to read the problem carefully and analyze the given information to determine whether the x-values or the y-values represent the solution to the problem.

In their journals, have students sketch graphs of linear-quadratic systems with no solutions, with one solution, and with two solutions. Then have them describe how to solve the systems algebraically as well as by graphing.

23. Explain the Error After solving the system of equations in Exercise 16 (the skydiver and the ball), a student concludes there are two valid solutions because they both have positive times. The ball must pass by the skydiver twice. What is the error in the student's reasoning?

The second intersection point at 22.18 seconds corresponds to a height −5654.74 feet, or under the ground. The second intersection point is outside the range of the model even though it has a positive time, and it cannot be a valid solution.

24. Multi-Part Problem The path of a baseball hit for a home run can be modeled by $y = -\dfrac{x^2}{484} + x + 3$, where x and y are in feet and home plate is at the origin.

The ball lands in the stands, which are modeled by $4y - x = -352$ for $x \geq 400$. Use a graphing calculator to graph the system.

a. What do the variables x and y represent?

x is the horizontal distance from home plate. y is the height above the ground.

b. About how far is the baseball from home plate when it lands?

The only intersection point with non-negative coordinates is $(458.96, 26.74)$.

So the baseball is about 459 feet from the plate when it lands.

c. About how high up in the stands does the baseball land?

26.7 feet

25. Draw Conclusions A certain system of a linear and a quadratic equation has two solutions, $(2, 7)$ and $(5, 10)$. The quadratic equation is $y = x^2 - 6x + 15$. What is the linear equation? Justify your answer.

The two solutions are points on the line and can be used to solve for the line.

$$y = mx + b$$

$$m = \frac{10 - 7}{5 - 2} = 1 \qquad 10 = 1(5) + b$$
$$b = 5$$

The line is $y = x + 5$. Two points define a line, so there is no need to use the quadratic equation.

26. Justify Reasoning It is possible for a system of two linear equations to have infinitely many solutions. Explain why this is not possible for a system with one linear and one quadratic equation.

Two linear equations can have infinite solutions if the related linear functions represent the same line, which will overlap itself at every point on the line. A parabola and a line are different shapes and can intersect only at certain points. Since the parabola can only change direction once, it cannot cross the line more than twice.

Lesson Performance Task

A race car leaves pit row at a speed of 40 feet per second and accelerates at a constant rate of 44 feet per second squared. Its distance from the pit exit is given by the function $d_r(t) = 22t^2 + 40t$. The race car leaves ahead of an approaching pace car traveling at a constant speed of 120 feet per second. In each case, find out if the pace car will catch up to the race car, and if so, how far down the track it will catch up. If there is more than one solution, explain how you know which one to select.

a. The pace car passes by the exit to pit row 1 second after the race car exits.

The race car is traveling at a constant speed, so its position is a linear function of time, $d_p(t) = mt + b$.

The slope of the line is the speed of the pace car, $m = 120$. To find b, use the time and position when the pace car passes the pit row exit.

$d_p(1) = 0$

$120(1) + b = 0$

$120 + b = 0$

$b = -120$

The position of the pace car is given by $d_p(t) = 120t - 120$.

To find out if the pace car catches up to the race car, plot both functions on a graphing calculator, with x for time and y for distance. The line does not intersect the parabola, so the pace car never catches up to the race car.

b. The pace car passes the exit half a second after the race car exits.

To solve part b, find the function for the pace car again: $m = 120$.

$d_p\left(\dfrac{1}{2}\right) = 0$

$120\left(\dfrac{1}{2}\right) + b = 0$

$60 + b = 0$

$b = -60$

The position of the pace car is given by $d_p(t) = 120t - 60$.

Plot both functions on the graphing calculator. Two intersections are found, one at $(1.06, 66.9)$ and the other at $(2.58, 249.5)$. There are two solutions because the pace car first passes the race car at 1.06 seconds, and then the race car passes in front again at 2.58 seconds. The pace car initially catches up to the race car at the first intersection, or 66.9 feet down the track.

EXTENSION ACTIVITY

Have students find and graph an equation for the position of a pace car that catches up to the race car exactly once, but does not pass it. Students need to find a line with slope 120 that is tangent to the parabola. They can sketch a line that appears to be tangent, then adjust the y-intercept until they find a line with only one intersection point. Alternatively, they can set the equation $d_p(t) = 120t + b$ equal to $d_r(t) = 22t^2 + 40t$, put the resulting quadratic equation in standard form, and find the value of b that will make the discriminant equal to zero. When the equation is $d_p(t) = 120t - 72.7$, the pace car will catch up to the race car at about $t = 1.82$ seconds, 145.7 feet from the pit exit.

CONNECT VOCABULARY EL

Some students may not be familiar with the terms *pit row* and *pace car*. Ask volunteers familiar with motor racing to help define these terms. The *pit row* is *the area where teams set up garages during races*. Each team may have one pit per car. The *pace car* is *a car that leads the racing cars at a safe speed either at the start of the race or during a caution period*, such as when debris is on the track. The pace car enters the track ahead of the leading car in the race, and race cars are not allowed to pass the pace car during a caution period.

INTEGRATE MATHEMATICAL PRACTICES
Focus on Modeling

MP.4 Have students compare the y-intercepts for the two cars and explain what they represent. Students should recognize that they represent the positions of the two cars at time $t = 0$. The starting position of the race car is 0. The pace car does not reach the pit exit until after the race car leaves, so its starting position is represented by a negative number.

INTEGRATE MATHEMATICAL PRACTICES
Focus on Communication

MP.3 Show students a graph of the two equations for part **a** that shows x ranging from 0 to 5 and y ranging from 0 to 500. Have students explain how they know that the graphs will never intersect, even though they see only a small section of the graph. Students should recognize that the distance between the two graphs increases as you extend the curves in either direction.

Scoring Rubric
2 points: Student correctly solves the problem and explains his/her reasoning.
1 point: Student shows good understanding of the problem but does not fully solve or explain his/her reasoning.
0 points: Student does not demonstrate understanding of the problem.

Study Guide Review

ASSESSMENT AND INTERVENTION

Assign or customize module reviews.

MODULE PERFORMANCE TASK

 COMMON CORE

Mathematical Practices: MP.1, MP.2, MP.4, MP.6
A-CED.A.2, F-BF.A.1, F-IF.B.4

SUPPORTING STUDENT REASONING

Students should begin this problem by focusing on what information they will need. Here is some of the information they may ask for.

- **What equation should I use for the parabola?** Students can use $h = -4.9t^2 + vt + h_0$. The values for v and h_0 are provided in the problem.

- **How fast does the firework need to go to reach a height above 70 m?** Students should choose a velocity and then check to see whether it works. Some will not.

- **How do I find the maximum height of a firework?** The maximum height of the firework is at the vertex of the parabola.

Essential Question: How can you use quadratic equations to solve real-world problems?

© Houghton Mifflin Harcourt Publishing Company

KEY EXAMPLE — (Lesson 22.1)

Solve $(x - 8)^2 = 49$ by taking the square root.

$(x - 8)^2 = 49$	*Equations in the form $a(x + b)^2 = c$ can be solved by taking square roots.*
$x - 8 = \pm 7$	*Take the square root of both sides.*
$x = \pm 7 + 8$	
$x = 7 + 8 \text{ or } x = -7 + 8$	*Solve both cases.*
$x = 15 \text{ or } x = 1$	

KEY EXAMPLE — (Lesson 22.2)

Solve $9x^2 - 6x = 20$ by completing the square.

$\dfrac{(-6)^2}{4(9)} = 1$	*Find $\dfrac{b^2}{4a}$.*
	Complete the square.
$9x^2 - 6x + 1 = 20 + 1$	
$(3x - 1)^2 = 21$	
$3x - 1 = \pm\sqrt{21}$	
$x = \dfrac{\sqrt{21} + 1}{3} \text{ or } x = \dfrac{-\sqrt{21} + 1}{3}$	

KEY EXAMPLE — (Lesson 22.3)

Solve $8x^2 - 8x + 2 = 0$ using the quadratic formula.

$a = 8, b = -8, c = 2$	*Identify a, b, and c.*
$x = \dfrac{-b \pm \sqrt{b^2 - 4ac}}{2a}$	*Use the quadratic formula.*
$x = \dfrac{8 \pm \sqrt{(-8)^2 - (4)(8)(2)}}{2(8)}$	
$x = \dfrac{8 \pm \sqrt{0}}{16}$	*Since $b^2 - 4ac = 0$, the equation has one real solution.*
$x = \dfrac{1}{2}$	

Key Vocabulary

completing the square
(*completar el cuadrado*)

discriminant (*discriminante*)

quadratic formula
(*fórmula cuadrática*)

square root (*raíz cuadrada*)

SCAFFOLDING SUPPORT

- For students needing more guidance, provide the formula $h = -4.9t^2 + vt + h_0$ with the problem context.

- If students have trouble finding the maximum heights of different parabolas, remind them that $-\dfrac{b}{2a}$ is the x-coordinate of the vertex.

- Encourage students to find the maximum height of the firework at a particular velocity before working on the firing delay. (If the fire officials won't approve a particular velocity, then they can't use it in the show.)

- For the part of the problem dealing with firing delays, you may wish to remind them that the t-coordinate of the vertex represents the time from the firing until the time of the explosion.

Solve each equation. *(Lessons 22.1, 22.2, 22.3, 22.4)*

1. $x^2 + 12x = -17$

   $x = \sqrt{19} - 6$ or $x = -\sqrt{19} - 6$

2. $(4x - 11)^2 = 100$

   $x = \frac{1}{4}$ or $x = \frac{21}{4}$

3. $4x^2 + 8x = 10$

   $x = \frac{\sqrt{14} - 2}{2}$ or $x = \frac{-\sqrt{14} - 2}{2}$

4. $3x^2 + 17x + 10 = 0$

   $x = -5$ or $x = -\frac{2}{3}$

5. A diver jumps off a high diving board that is 33 feet above the surface of the pool with an initial upward velocity of 6 feet per second. The height of the diver above the surface of the pool can be represented by the equation $-16t^2 + 6t + 33 = 0$. How long will the diver be in the air, to the nearest hundredth of a second? Identify the method you used to solve the quadratic equation, and explain why you chose it. *(Lesson 22.4)*

   1.64 seconds; Possible answer: I used the quadratic formula because the equation cannot be factored and completing the square would be time-consuming with these numbers.

MODULE PERFORMANCE TASK

Fireworks Display

You are planning a fireworks show for a local Fourth of July celebration. Fire officials require that all fireworks explode at a height greater than 70 meters so that debris has a chance to cool off as it falls.

The firing platform for the fireworks is 1.9 meters off the ground. You have the option of firing your fireworks at an initial vertical velocity of anywhere between 35 and 42 meters/second. If every firework is timed to explode when it reaches its maximum height, find two different initial velocities that are acceptable to the local fire officials. Then, figure out how long to delay the firing of the slower firework so that it will explode at the same time as the faster firework.

Use your own paper to complete the task. Be sure to write down all your data and assumptions. Then use graphs, tables, or algebra to explain how you reached your conclusion.

SAMPLE SOLUTION

Assume the initial velocity 37 m/s. The equation describing this velocity is $y = -4.9x^2 + 37x + 1.9$. The vertex of the graph has an x-value of:

$$-\frac{b}{2a} = -\frac{37}{2(-4.9)}$$
$$\approx 3.776$$

and the height at the vertex is about:

$$y = -4.9x^2 + 37x + 1.9$$
$$= -4.9(3.776)^2 + 37(3.776) + 1.9$$
$$\approx -69.865 + 139.712 + 1.9$$
$$\approx 71.75 \text{ meters}$$

So, this initial velocity is acceptable to the fire officials. Similarly, at an initial velocity of 40 m/s, the equation of the parabola is $y = -4.9x^2 + 40x + 1.9$, the x-coordinate of the vertex is at $-\frac{40}{2(-4.9)} \approx 4.082$, and the maximum height is:

$$y = -4.9(4.082)^2 + 40(4.082) + 1.9$$
$$\approx 83.53 \text{ meters}$$

This is also high enough for the fire officials.

The slower firework explodes about 3.776 seconds after firing, and the faster firework explodes about 4.082 seconds after firing. For both fireworks to explode at the same time, the slower firework should be delayed by $4.082 - 3.776$, or 0.306 second.

DISCUSSION OPPORTUNITIES

Students may wish to combine their findings into a plan for a fireworks show, in which fireworks explode at different heights and different times.

Assessment Rubric

2 points: Student correctly solves the problem and explains his/her reasoning.

1 point: Student shows good understanding of the problem but does not fully solve or explain.

0 points: Student does not demonstrate understanding of the problem.

Ready to Go On?

ASSESS MASTERY

Use the assessment on this page to determine if students have mastered the concepts and standards covered in this module.

ASSESSMENT AND INTERVENTION

Access Ready to Go On? assessment online, and receive instant scoring, feedback, and customized intervention or enrichment.

ADDITIONAL RESOURCES

Response to Intervention Resources

- Reteach Worksheets

Differentiated Instruction Resources

- Reading Strategies **EL**
- Success for English Learners **EL**
- Challenge Worksheets

Assessment Resources

- Leveled Module Quizzes

1103 Module 22

 **Ready to Go On?**

22.1–22.5 Using Square Roots to Solve Quadratic Equations

- Online Homework
- Hints and Help
- Extra Practice

Find the discriminant of each quadratic equation, and determine the number of real solutions of each equation. *(Lesson 22.4)*

1. $3x^2 + 2x + 6 = 0$

-68; no real solutions

2. $4x^2 + 6x = 8$

164; two real solutions

Solve each equation using the given method. *(Lessons 22.1, 22.2, 22.3, 22.4)*

3. $8x^2 - 72 = 0$; square root

-3 and 3

4. $25x^2 + 20x = 6$; completing the square

$\dfrac{-\sqrt{10} - 2}{5}$ and $\dfrac{\sqrt{10} - 2}{5}$

5. $2x^2 + 14x + 12 = 0$; factoring

-6 and -1

6. $3x^2 + 7x + 8 = 0$; quadratic formula

no real solution

7. Find the solution or solutions of the system of equations $\begin{cases} y = x^2 + 2 \\ y = x + 4 \end{cases}$. *(Lesson 22.5)*

$(-1, 3)$ and $(2, 6)$

ESSENTIAL QUESTION

8. What are the methods of solving a quadratic equation without factoring? When can you use each method?

Possible Answer: You can use square roots, completing the square, or the quadratic formula. You can use square roots only when the equation is of the form $a(x + b)^2 = c$, but you can use the other two methods with any quadratic equation.

© Houghton Mifflin Harcourt Publishing Company

COMMON CORE **Common Core Standards**

Lesson	Items	Content Standards	Mathematical Practices
22.4	1	**A-REI.B.4b**	**MP.2**
22.4	2	**A-REI.B.4b**	**MP.2**
22.1	3	**A-REI.B.4b**	**MP.1**
22.2	4	**A-REI.B.4b**	**MP.1**
22.4	5	**A-REI.B.4b**	**MP.1**
22.3	6	**A-REI.B.4b**	**MP.1**
22.5	7	**A-REI.C.7**	**MP.2**

Assessment Readiness

1. Is the given expression a perfect-square trinomial? Select Yes or No for each expression.

   A. $x^2 + 24x + 144$ ● Yes   ○ No

   B. $4x^2 + 36x + 9$ ○ Yes   ● No

   C. $9x^2 - 6x + 1$ ● Yes   ○ No

2. Consider the following statements. Choose True or False for each.

   A. $4x^2 - 64 = 0$ has 2 real solutions.   ● True   ○ False

   B. $x^2 - 5x - 9 = 0$ has only 1 real solution.   ○ True   ● False

   C. $3x^2 + 4x + 2 = 0$ has no real solutions.   ● True   ○ False

3. Solve $-2x^2 - 9x = -4$. What are the solutions? Explain how you solved the problem.

   $x = \dfrac{9 - \sqrt{113}}{-4}$ or $x = \dfrac{9 + \sqrt{113}}{-4}$; I used the quadratic formula and set a equal to -2, b equal to -9, and c equal to 4.

4. A landscaper is making a garden bed in the shape of a rectangle. The length of the garden bed is 2.5 feet longer than twice the width of the bed. The area of the garden bed is 62.5 square feet. Find the perimeter of the bed. Show your work.

   $$x(2x + 2.5) = 62.5$$
   $$2x^2 + 2.5x - 62.5 = 0$$
   $$x = \frac{-2.5 \pm \sqrt{2.5^2 - 4(2)(-62.5)}}{2(2)}$$
   $$x = \frac{-2.5 \pm \sqrt{506.25}}{4}$$
   $$x = \frac{-2.5 \pm 22.5}{4}$$
   $$x = 5 \text{ or } x = -6.25$$

   The width cannot be negative. The perimeter of the bed is $2(5 + 12.5) = 35$ feet.

MIXED REVIEW
Assessment Readiness

ASSESSMENT AND INTERVENTION

Assign ready-made or customized practice tests to prepare students for high-stakes tests.

ADDITIONAL RESOURCES

Assessment Resources

- Leveled Module Quizzes: Modified, B

AVOID COMMON ERRORS

Item 2 Some students may use the quadratic formula for each equation, which is more time-consuming than necessary. Remind students that they could use the determinant or graph the equations on their calculators and look for the x-intercepts.

COMMON CORE   Common Core Standards

Lesson	Items	Content Standards	Mathematical Practices
21.3	1*	A-SSE.A.2	MP.1
22.3	2	A-REI.B.4b	MP.1
22.4	3	A-REI.B.4b	MP.2
18.1, 22.4	4*	A-CED.A.1, A-APR.A.1, A-REI.B.4b	MP.4

* Item integrates mixed review concepts from previous modules or a previous course.

Linear, Exponential, and Quadratic Models

ESSENTIAL QUESTION:

Answer: You can make a table of values or you can graph a model for the real-world problem to see how the values change as the *x*-values of the function increase.

PROFESSIONAL DEVELOPMENT VIDEO

Professional Development Video

Learn effective ways of integrating technology into your classroom to meet a variety of different needs.

Professional Development
my.hrw.com

Linear, Exponential, and Quadratic Models

MODULE 23

Essential Question: How can you use linear, exponential, and quadratic models to solve real-world problems?

LESSON 23.1
Modeling with Quadratic Functions

LESSON 23.2
Comparing Linear, Exponential, and Quadratic Models

REAL WORLD VIDEO
The Kemp's Ridley sea turtle is an endangered species of turtle that nests along the Texas coast. Functions can be used to model the survivorship curve of the Kemp's Ridley sea turtle.

© Houghton Mifflin Harcourt Publishing Company · Image Credits: ·Kip Evans/Alamy

MODULE PERFORMANCE TASK PREVIEW
What Model Fits a Survivorship Curve?

Survivorship curves are graphs that show the number or proportion of individuals in a particular population that survive over time. Survivorship curves are used in diverse fields such as actuarial science, demography, biology, and epidemiology. How can you determine what mathematical model best fits a certain type of survivorship curve? Let's find out!

DIGITAL TEACHER EDITION

Access a full suite of teaching resources when and where you need them:

- Access content online or offline
- Customize lessons to share with your class
- Communicate with your students in real-time
- View student grades and data instantly to target your instruction where it is needed most

PERSONAL MATH TRAINER
Assessment and Intervention

Assign automatically graded homework, quizzes, tests, and intervention activities. Prepare your students with updated, Common Core-aligned practice tests.

Are YOU Ready?

Complete these exercises to review skills you will need for this module.

Exponents

Example 1 Find the value of 2^{-5}.

$2^{-5} = \dfrac{1}{2^5} = \dfrac{1}{32}$

Any nonzero number raised to a negative power is equal to 1 divided by the number raised to the opposite power.

• Online Homework
• Hints and Help
• Extra Practice

Find the value.

1. 3^{-4}

$\dfrac{1}{81}$

2. 4^{-3}

$\dfrac{1}{64}$

3. $\left(\dfrac{2}{3}\right)^{-2}$

$\dfrac{9}{4}$

Algebraic Expressions

Example 2 Find the value of $y = -2x^2 + 7$ when $x = -3$.

$y = -2x^2 + 7$

$y = -2(-3)^2 + 7$ Substitute -3 for x.

$y = -2(9) + 7$ Evaluate the power.

$y = -18 + 7$ Multiply.

$y = -11$ Add.

Find the value of y for $x = -2$.

4. 4. $y = 5x + 6$

-4

5. 5. $y = 2x^2 - 10$

-2

6. 6. $y = \dfrac{1}{4} 2^x$

$\dfrac{1}{4}$

Example 3 Find the product of $(2x^3)(-3x^4)$.

$(2x^3)(-3x^4)$

$(2 \cdot (-3))(x^3 \cdot x^4)$ Group factors that use the same variable.

$-6x^7$ The bases are the same, so add the exponents.

Find each product.

7. $(-5y^2)(3y^6)$

$-15y^8$

8. $(-6x^6y^2)(-4x^4y)$

$24x^{10}y^3$

9. $(7x^4y)(-5xy)$

$-35x^5y^2$

10. $(14ab^3)(5b^2c^2)$

$70ab^5c^2$

© Houghton Mifflin Harcourt Publishing Company

Are You Ready?

ASSESS READINESS

Use the assessment on this page to determine if students need strategic or intensive intervention for the module's prerequisite skills.

ASSESSMENT AND INTERVENTION

RtI Response to Intervention **TIER 1, TIER 2, TIER 3 SKILLS**

Personal Math Trainer will automatically create a standards-based, personalized intervention assignment for your students, targeting each student's individual needs!

ADDITIONAL RESOURCES

See the table below for a full list of intervention resources available for this module.

Response to Intervention Resources also includes:

• Tier 2 Skill Pre-Tests for each Module
• Tier 2 Skill Post-Tests for each skill

Response to Intervention			Differentiated Instruction
Tier 1 Lesson Intervention Worksheets	**Tier 2** Strategic Intervention Skills Intervention Worksheets	**Tier 3** Intensive Intervention Worksheets available online	
Reteach 23.1 Reteach 23.2	4 Constant Rate of Change 6 Graphing Linear Nonproportional... 7 Graphing Linear Proportional... 10 Linear Functions	Building Block Skills 5, 22, 23, 27, 40, 46, 63, 65, 68, 70	Challenge worksheets Extend the Math Lesson Activities in TE

Modeling with Quadratic Functions

Common Core Math Standards

The student is expected to:

 **A-CED.A.2**

Create equations in two... variables to represent relationships between quantities... Also F-IF.B.4, F-IF.B.5

Mathematical Practices

 **MP.5 Using Tools**

Language Objective

Explain to a partner how to create a quadratic function to fit data.

ENGAGE

Essential Question: How can you use tables to recognize quadratic functions and use technology to create them?

You can compare second differences from the table to determine if a relationship is quadratic. Then you can perform a quadratic regression using the values in the table to create a function.

PREVIEW: LESSON PERFORMANCE TASK

View the Engage section online. Discuss the photo and how knowing the times that it takes for an object to reach various heights above the ground might help determine a function that models the data. Then preview the Lesson Performance Task.

Name_____ Class_____ Date_____

23.1 Modeling with Quadratic Functions

Essential Question: How can you use tables to recognize quadratic functions and use technology to create them?

Resource Locker

⊘ Explore Using Second Differences to Identify Quadratic Functions

A linear function is a straight line, a quadratic function is a parabola, and an exponential function is a curve that approaches a horizontal asymptote in one direction and curves upward to infinity in the other direction.

You can determine if a function is linear or exponential when the values of x and y are presented in a table. For a constant change in x-values, if the difference between the associated y-values is constant, then the function is linear. If the ratio of the associated y-values is constant, then the function is exponential.

What if neither the ratio of successive terms nor the first differences are roughly constant? There is a clue in the method for recognizing a linear function. Find the second difference. The second difference is the value obtained by subtracting consecutive first differences. If this number is a non-zero constant, then the function will be quadratic. Examine the graph of the given quadratic function; then construct a table with values for x, y, and the first and second differences.

(A) Graph the function $f(x) = x^2$ on the given axes.

Use the table to complete Steps B, D, and F.

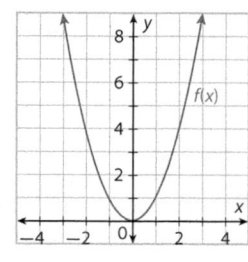

x	$y = f(x)$	First Difference	Second Difference
1	1	_____	_____
2	$2^2 =$ __4__	$4 - 1 =$ __3__	_____
3	$3^2 =$ __9__	$9 - 4 =$ __5__	$5 - 3 =$ __2__
4	$4^2 =$ __16__	$16 - 9 = 7$	$7 - 5 =$ __2__
5	$5^2 =$ __25__	$25 - 16 = 9$	$9 - 7 = 2$

(B) Complete the $y = f(x)$ column of the table with indicated values of $f(x) = x^2$.

(C) Is there a constant difference between x-values? ⟨yes⟩ no

(D) Recall that the differences between y-values are called the *first differences*. Complete the First Difference column of the table with the indicated first differences.

© Houghton Mifflin Harcourt Publishing Company

HARDCOVER PAGES 859–870

Turn to these pages to find this lesson in the hardcover student edition.

(E) Are the first differences constant (the same)? yes/no

(F) The differences between the first differences are called the **second differences**. Complete the Second Difference column of the table with the indicated second differences.

(G) Are the second differences constant (the same)? yes/no

(H) Complete the table for another quadratic function: $f(x) = -3x^2$.

x	y = f(x)	First Difference	Second Difference
1	$-3 \cdot 1 = $ __−3__		
2	$-3 \cdot 2^2 = $ __−12__	$-12 - (-3) = $ __−9__	
3	$-3 \cdot 3^2 = $ __−27__	$-27 - (-12) = $ __−15__	$-15 - (-9) = $ __−6__
4	$-3 \cdot 4^2 = $ __−48__	$-48 - (-27) = $ __−21__	$-21 - (-15) = $ __−6__
5	$-3 \cdot 5^2 = $ __−75__	$-75 - (-48) = $ __−27__	$-27 - (-21) = $ __−6__

(I) Is there a constant difference between x-values? yes/no

Are the first differences constant (the same)? yes/no

Are the second differences constant (the same)? yes/no

Reflect

1. **Discussion** When a table of values with constant x-values leads to constant y-values (*first* differences), what kind of function does that indicate? (linear/quadratic)

2. When a table of values with constant x-values leads to constant *second* differences, what kind of function does that indicate? (linear/quadratic)

 Explain 1 **Verify Quadratic Relationships Using Quadratic Regression**

The second differences for $f(x) = x^2$, the parent quadratic function, are constant for values of y when the corresponding differences between x-values are constant. Now, do the reverse. For a given set of data, verify that the second differences are constant and then use a graphing calculator to find a quadratic model for the data. Enter the independent variable into List 1 and the dependent variable into List 2, and perform a **quadratic regression** on the data. When your calculator performs a quadratic regression, it uses a specific statistical method to fit a quadratic model to the data.

As with linear regression, the data will not be perfect. When finding a model, if the first differences are close but not exactly equal, a linear model will still be a good fit. Likewise, if the second differences aren't exactly the same, a quadratic model will be a good fit if the second differences are close to being the same.

EXPLORE

Using Second Differences to Identify Quadratic Functions

INTEGRATE TECHNOLOGY

Have students complete the Explore activity in either the book or online lesson.

QUESTIONING STRATEGIES

? How do you determine the second differences for a function? Second differences are found by finding the difference between consecutive first differences, which are the differences between y-values for a constant change in x-values.

EXPLAIN 1

Verifying Quadratic Relationships Using Quadratic Regression

AVOID COMMON ERRORS

Make sure students can correctly substitute values for a, b, and c into the standard form of a quadratic equation, $y = ax^2 + bx + c$. For example, if $a = 3$, $b = 5$, and $c = -6$, the quadratic equation should be $y = 3x^2 + 5x - 6$.

PROFESSIONAL DEVELOPMENT

◼ **COMMON CORE** Integrate Mathematical Practices

This lesson provides an opportunity to address Mathematical Practice **MP.5**, which calls for students to "use tools." Students use paper and pencil to find the first differences and second differences in order to determine whether a quadratic function can fit given data. Students also use graphing calculators to find a quadratic function that fits a data set, and use that function to solve real-world problems.

INTEGRATE MATHEMATICAL PRACTICES

Focus on Technology

MP.5 Tell students that to enter values for plotting on a graphing calculator, they must enter values in **L1** and **L2** by using **STAT1:Edit**. To find the equation for the quadratic regression, select **STAT:CALC:5:QuadReg**.

Example 1 Find a quadratic model for the given situation. Begin by creating a scatter plot of the given data on your graphing calculator, and then find the second differences to verify the data is quadratic. Finally, use a graphing calculator to perform a quadratic regression on the data and graph the regression equation on the scatter plot.

(A) A student is measuring the kinetic energy of a pickup truck as it is travels at various speeds. The speed is given in meters per second, and the kinetic energy is given in kilojoules. Use the given data to find a quadratic model for the data.

Speed x	Kinetic Energy y = K(x)	First Difference	Second Difference
20	410		
25	640	230	
30	922	282	52
35	1256	334	52
40	1640	384	50
45	2076	436	52
50	2563	487	51

Enter the data into a graphing calculator, placing the x-values into List 1 and the y-values into List 2.

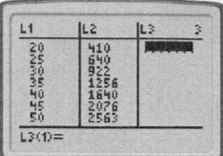

Next view a scatter plot of the data points. The calculator window shown is $15 < x < 55$ with an x-scale of 5 and $0 < y < 3000$ with a y-scale of 500.

Next find the first and second differences and fill in the table.

The first difference of the first and second y-value is found by evaluating the expression below.

$K(25) - K(20)$

$640 - 410$

230

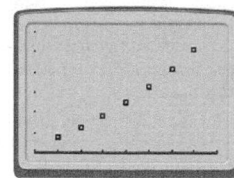

Find the next first difference in the same manner.

$K(30) - K(25)$

$922 - 640$

282

Find the rest of the first differences and fill in the table.

COLLABORATIVE LEARNING

Peer-to-Peer Activity

Have students work in groups of two. Have each student create a data set by roughly sketching a parabola, then selecting 10 points that are close to the parabola to create a data set. Students trade data sets, and use quadratic regression to find and graph a quadratic equation that fits the data. Each student sketches a graph of the function, and compares it to the original sketch made by the partner.

The first of the second differences is the difference between the values in the third and fourth rows of the first difference column.

$282 - 230 = 52$

Find the rest of the second differences and fill in the rest of the table.

Notice that the second differences are very close to being constant.

Use a graphing calculator to find the equation for the quadratic regression. $y \approx 1.026x^2 - 0.0548x + 0.3571$

Note that the correlation coefficient is very close to 1, so the model is a good fit.

Plot the regression equation over the scatter plot.

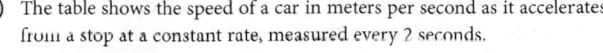

B The table shows the speed of a car in meters per second as it accelerates from a stop at a constant rate, measured every 2 seconds.

Time	2	4	6	8	10
Speed	5.1	20.4	45.8	81.2	126.1

Create a scatter plot of the data using a graphing calculator.

Find the first and second differences and fill out the table.

Time x	Speed y	First Difference	Second Difference
2	5.1	_____	_____
4	20.4	15.3	_____
6	45.8	25.4	10.1
8	81.2	35.4	10
10	126.1	44.9	9.5

Find the regression equation using a graphing calculator. Report the results to 4 significant digits.

  $y \approx 1.236x^2 + 0.3114x - 0.52$

Based on the correlation coefficient, the model __is__ a good fit.

Plot the regression equation over the scatter plot.

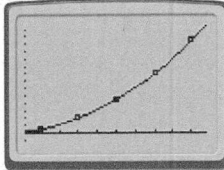

QUESTIONING STRATEGIES

? How is performing a quadratic regression on a data set similar to performing a linear regression on a data set? **Performing a quadratic regression produces a quadratic equation that fits the data. Performing a linear regression produces an equation of a line that fits the data.**

DIFFERENTIATE INSTRUCTION

Critical Thinking

After finding first differences and second differences for a data set, students may be interested in extending the concept to third differences. Point out that a data set with similar first differences can be modeled with a function in the form $y = ax + b$, and a data set with similar second differences can be modeled with a function in the form $y = ax^2 + bx + c$. Discuss with students what kind of function would model a data set with similar third differences. For example, have students find the third differences of the data sets generated by $y = x^3$ and $y = x^3 + 4x^2 - 6x + 7$.

3. **Discussion** Give examples of reasons why the second differences in real-world data won't necessarily be equal.

Sample answer: The second differences will not be exactly equal because of human error,

inexactness of measurements, minor differences between theoretical and real-world

conditions, and using multiple measuring devices that are not calibrated to the same

degree of accuracy.

Your Turn

Find a quadratic model for the given situation. Begin by creating a scatter plot of the given data on your graphing calculator, and then find the second differences to verify the data is quadratic. Finally, use a graphing calculator to perform a quadratic regression on the data and graph the regression equation on the scatter plot.

4. The table shows the height of a soccer ball in feet for every half-second after a goalie dropkicks it.

Time	0.5	1.0	1.5	2.0	2.5	3.0	3.5
Height	54	104	142	173	195	208	216

Time	Height	First Difference	Second Difference
0.5	54		
1.0	104	50	
1.5	142	38	−12
2.0	173	31	−7
2.5	195	22	−9
3.0	208	13	−9
3.5	216	8	−5

$a = -16.8 \quad b = 120.6 \quad c = -1.143 \quad R^2 = 0.9997$

$y \approx -16.8x^2 + 120.6x - 1.143$

LANGUAGE SUPPORT **EL**

Connect Vocabulary

Students may not be familiar with the word *regression* beyond a mathematical context. Explain that the word *regress* means *to move in reverse* and that this describes what happens in the mathematical process. One step is to find data points that are on the graph of a quadratic equation. The reverse action is to find a quadratic equation that fits given data points.

5. A company that makes flying discs to use as promotional materials will produce a flying disc of any size. The table shows the cost of 100 flying discs based on the desired size.

Size	4	4.5	5	5.5	6	6.5	7
Cost	34.99	44.99	54.99	66.99	79.99	92.99	107.99

Size	Cost	First Difference	Second Difference
4	34.99	_____	_____
4.5	44.99	10	_____
5	54.99	10	0
5.5	66.99	12	2
6	79.99	13	1
6.5	92.99	13	0
7	107.99	15	2

$a = 2$ $b = 2.286$ $c = -6.081$ $R^2 = 0.9999$

$y \approx 2x^2 + 2.286x - 6.081$

⊘ Explain 2   Using Quadratic Regression to Solve a Real-World Problem

After performing quadratic regression on a given data set, the regression equation can be used to answer questions about the scenario represented by the data.

Example 2   Use a graphing calculator to perform quadratic regression on the data given. Then solve the problem and identify and interpret the domain and range of the function.

(A) The height of a model rocket in feet t seconds after it is launched vertically is shown in the following table. Determine the maximum height the rocket attains.

Time	1	2	3	4	5	6	7	8
Height	342	667	902	1163	1335	1459	1584	1864

Enter the data into List 1 and List 2 of a graphing calculator and perform the quadratic regression.

```
QuadReg
y=ax²+bx+c
a=-11.19047619
b=304.0714286
c=81.53571429
R²=.990929803
```

EXPLAIN 2

Using Quadratic Relationships to Solve a Real-World Problem

INTEGRATE MATHEMATICAL PRACTICES
Focus on Modeling

MP.4 When students use calculators to perform quadratic regressions, help them understand how to interpret the value of R^2. It is a measure of how closely data, on average, fit a regression line. Explain to students that the closer R^2 is to 1, the better the function fits the data.

? How do you use a calculator to find the intersection of two functions? To find the point of intersection, select the **Calculate** menu and then choose the **Intersect** option.

Then plot the regression function over a scatter plot of the data.

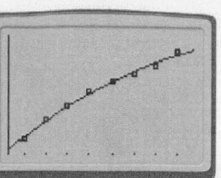

Increase the values of Xmax and Ymax until you can see the maximum value of the function. Then use the maximum function on your graphing calculator to find the maximum height of the rocket.

The model rocket attains a maximum height of approximately 2150 feet 13.5 seconds after launch.

The domain of the function will be $0 \le t \le +\infty$. Because the independent variable is time, it doesn't make sense to consider negative time.

The range of the function is $0 \le y \le 2150$ because the height of the rocket should never be negative and it will not go higher than its maximum height.

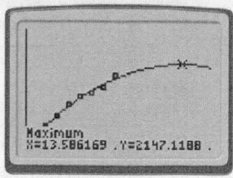

Ⓑ When a rock is thrown into a pond, it makes a series of circular waves. The area enclosed by the first wave is recorded every second and is shown in the table below. If the rock lands 15 meters from shore, when will the first wave reach the shoreline?

Time	1	2	3	4	5	6
Area	9.0	35.8	79.8	145.2	225.1	319.1

Enter the values into List 1 and List 2 of a graphing calculator and use __quadratic regression__ or __QuadReg__ to find the model.

$y \approx \boxed{8.564} \; x^2 + \boxed{2.444} \; x + \boxed{-2.78}$ $R^2 \approx \boxed{0.9999}$

$y \approx \boxed{8.564x^2 + 2.444x - 2.78}$

Based on the value of R^2, this function __will be__ a close fit for the data.

The area enclosed by the wave is a circle, so the wave will reach the shore when the __radius__ of the wave is __15__ meters.

The area of a circle is given by $A = \pi r^2$.

$A = \pi r^2$

$= \pi \boxed{15}^2 = \boxed{225} \pi \approx \boxed{706.858}$

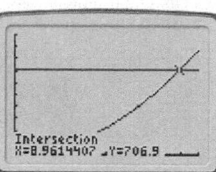

Plot the regression equation as Y_2 and let $Y_2 = \boxed{706.9}$.

Find the __intersection__ of the two lines.

The model intersects the line $y = 706.9$ at $x =$ ⟨8.9614⟩. The first wave will reach the shoreline in __9 seconds__.

The function only makes sense while the wave is still __circular__. Once it reaches __the shore__, the wave will no longer increase in size in the same way. Therefore, the domain of the function is __$0 \leq x < 9.0$__ and the range is __$0 \leq y \leq 706.9$__.

Your Turn

Use a graphing calculator to perform quadratic regression on the data given. Then solve the problem and identify and interpret the domain and range of the function.

6. A company needs boxes to package the goods it produces. One product has a standard shape and thickness but comes in a variety of sizes. The sizes are given as integers. The costs of the various sizes in cents are shown in the table. When the packaging cost reaches $2.00, the company will need to add a surcharge. What is the first size that will have the surcharge added?

Size	1	2	3	4	5	6	7
Cost	7.1	13.8	20.1	29.3	50.1	62.3	86.9

$y \approx 1.693x^2 - 0.457x + 6.486$ $R^2 \approx 0.9946$

The intersection of $y = 1.693x^2 - 0.457x + 6.486$ and $y = 200$ is $(10.83, 200)$. So the first size with the surcharge will be size 11.

The function represents the cost of specific sizes so the domain will be integer values of x with $x > 0$ and the range will be $y > 0$.

7. A company sells simple circular wall clocks in a variety of sizes. The production cost of each clock is dependent on the diameter of the clock in inches. The costs of making several sizes of clocks in dollars are given in the table. How big would a clock be that costs $4.00 to make? (Round to the nearest eighth.)

Size	8	$8\frac{1}{2}$	9	$9\frac{3}{8}$	$9\frac{1}{2}$	10	12
Cost	1.07	1.16	1.30	1.32	1.36	1.53	2.23

$y \approx 0.0344x^2 - 0.3996x + 2.071$ $R^2 \approx 0.9967$

The intersection of $y = 0.0344x^2 - 0.3996x + 2.071$ and $y = 4$ is $(15.28, 4)$. A clock with diameter of $15\frac{1}{4}$ inches can be made for $4.00.

The function represents the cost of different sizes of clocks, so the domain will be $x > 0$ and the range will be $y > 0$.

ELABORATE

INTEGRATE MATHEMATICAL PRACTICES

Focus on Communication

MP.3 Explain to students that for a quadratic equation to have a value of $R^2 = 1$, all the points in the data set must lie exactly on the graph of the quadratic function.

SUMMARIZE THE LESSON

? How do you know when to use quadratic regression instead of linear regression?

The shape of the scatter plot tells you which kind of regression to perform. Linear regression is appropriate if the data appear to fall along a line. Quadratic regression is appropriate if the data appear to fall along a curve that resembles a quadratic function.

EVALUATE

ASSIGNMENT GUIDE

Concepts and Skills	Practice
Explore 1 Using Second Differences to Identify Quadratic Functions	Exercises 1-4
Example 1 Verifying Quadratic Relationships Using Quadratic Regression	Exercises 5-11
Example 2 Using Quadratic Regression to Solve a Real-World Problem	Exercises 12-20

---

8. Are there any limitations to identifying data that can be modeled by a quadratic function using the method of second differences?
   Yes, the method of second differences can only be used if there is fairly uniform separation between the x-values of the data points.

9. A function modeling a situation can be represented as both a function and a graph. Identify some situations where one representation is more helpful than the other.
   Possible answers: A graph of a model allows for estimation of the value of the function for given values of the independent variable while an equation will give an exact value; a graph can be used to find the independent variable associated with a specific value of the dependent variable.

10. **Essential Question Check-In** When using technology to create a regression model, name two methods for judging the fit of the regression equation.
    Technology produces the square of the correlation coefficient. The closer that value is to 1, the better the fit is. Using technology, it is also possible to plot the regression equation over a scatter plot of the data and gauge the fit by eye.

⭐ Evaluate: Homework and Practice

• Online Homework
• Hints and Help
• Extra Practice

Determine if the function represented in the table is quadratic by finding the second differences.

1.

x	f(x)	First Difference	Second Difference
1	2		
2	4	2	
3	8	4	2
4	16	8	4
5	32	16	8
6	64	32	16

The function __is not__ quadratic.

© Houghton Mifflin Harcourt Publishing Company

Exercise	Depth of Knowledge (D.O.K.)	COMMON CORE Mathematical Practices
1–4	**1** Recall of Information	**MP.2** Reasoning
5	**2** Skills/Concepts	**MP.2** Reasoning
6–7	**2** Skills/Concepts	**MP.5** Using Tools
8	**2** Skills/Concepts	**MP.2** Reasoning
9	**2** Skills/Concepts	**MP.5** Using Tools
10	**2** Skills/Concepts	**MP.2** Reasoning
11–14	**2** Skills/Concepts	**MP.5** Using Tools

2.

x	f(x)	First Difference	Second Difference
1	3	_____	_____
2	12	9	_____
3	27	15	6
4	48	21	6
5	75	27	6
6	108	33	6

The function __is__ quadratic.

3.

x	f(x)	First Difference	Second Difference
1	9	_____	_____
2	13	4	_____
3	17	4	0
4	21	4	0
5	25	4	0
6	29	4	0

The function __is not__ quadratic.

4.

x	f(x)	First Difference	Second Difference
1	2	_____	_____
2	18	16	_____
3	48	30	14
4	92	44	14
5	150	58	14
6	222	72	14

The function __is__ quadratic.

INTEGRATE MATHEMATICAL PRACTICES

Focus on Critical Thinking

MP.3 Review the standard form for quadratic equations, $y = ax^2 + bx + c$. Students should understand that if $a > 0$, the function will have no maximum value, and if $a < 0$, the function will have no minimum value.

Exercise	Depth of Knowledge (D.O.K.)	COMMON CORE Mathematical Practices
15–17	**3** Strategic Thinking	**MP.4** Modeling
18–19	**3** Strategic Thinking H.O.T.	**MP.5** Using Tools
20	**3** Strategic Thinking H.O.T.	**MP.2** Reasoning

Modeling with Quadratic Functions   **1116**

MODELING

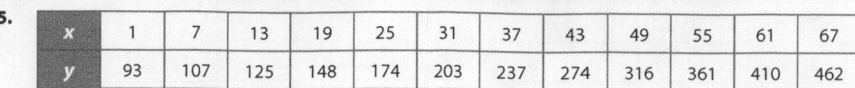

When graphing the quadratic function that fits a data set, show the points of the data set as well as the graph of the function to help students see how well the function fits the data. To show the points of the data set, go to the **STAT PLOT** menu and select **Plot1**; select **On**, then select the first option under **Type**, which is the scatter plot option. Then select **GRAPH** to view the scatter plot. To graph the function, select **Y=**, enter the function rule in Y1, and press **GRAPH** again.

Find the second differences of the given data to verify that the relationship will be quadratic. Then use a graphing calculator to find the quadratic regression equation.

5.

x	1	7	13	19	25	31	37	43	49	55	61	67
y	93	107	125	148	174	203	237	274	316	361	410	462

Second Difference: 4, 5, 3, 3, 5, 3, 5, 3, 4, 3

$y \approx 0.0531x^2 + 1.990x + 90.67$

6.

x	8	11.4	14.8	18.2	21.6	25	28.4	31.8	35.2	38.6	42	45.4
y	24	60	106	161	227	302	387	483	588	703	827	962

Second Difference: 10, 9, 11, 9, 10, 11, 9, 10, 9, 11

$y \approx 0.4273x^2 + 2.265x - 21.41$

7.

x	3.6	17.9	32.2	46.5	60.8	75.1	89.4	103.7	118	132.3	146.6	160.9
y	1946	1684	1442	1219	1012	821	648	494	357	237	133	44

Second Difference: 20, 19, 16, 16, 18, 19, 17, 17, 16, 15

$y \approx 0.0423x^2 - 19.03x + 2012$

8.

x	9	9.2	9.4	9.6	9.8	10	10.2	10.4	10.6	10.8	11	11.2
y	44	465	844	1180	1475	1728	1941	2117	2255	2355	2409	2416

Second Difference: −42, −43, −41, −42, −40, −37, −38, −38, −46, −47

$y \approx -503.4x^2 + 11250x - 60400$

9.

x	17	20.1	23.2	26.4	29.5	32.7	35.8	38.9	42.1	45.2	48.4	51.5
y	1000	995	974	936	882	814	729	627	510	376	225	58

Second Difference: −16, −17, −16, −14, −17, −17, −15, −17, −17, −16

$y \approx -0.8172x^2 - 28.73x - 747.5$

Find a quadratic model for the given situation. Begin by creating a scatter plot of the given data on your graphing calculator, and then find the second differences to verify the data is quadratic. Finally, use a graphing calculator to perform a quadratic regression on the data.

10. The table shows the height of an arrow in feet x seconds after being released toward a target down range by an archery student.

Time	0.25	0.5	0.75	1.0	1.25	1.5	1.75
Height	17	28.7	37.5	44.3	49.6	52.5	52.8

Second Difference: $-2.9, -2, -1.5, -2.4, -2.6$

$y \approx -17.05x^2 + 57.97x + 3.686$

11. The table shows the cost of cleaning a lap pool based on the number of lanes it has.

Number of Lanes	6	8	10	12	14	16
Cleaning Cost	30	95	263	518	875	1299

Second Difference: 103, 87, 102, 67

$y \approx 11.39x^2 - 122.8x + 353.6$

Use a graphing calculator to find a quadratic model for the given data.

12.

x	2.9	3.9	4.7	5.6	6.9	7.7	8.5
y	8	14	23	29	40	53	70

$y \approx 1.189x^2 - 3.132x + 8.335$

AVOID COMMON ERRORS

Students may incorrectly assume that quadratic regression will produce a function that passes through most of the points in the data set. Remind students that the quadratic function that fits the data set should be close to the points in the data set, but probably will not pass through all the points.

13.

x	4.7	6.7	8.5	10.1	12.8	14.3	15.9
y	32	17	−27	−94	−193	−321	−499

$y \approx -4.645x^2 + 50.89x - 113.4$

14.

x	−2.7	−1.9	−0.9	0	0.9	1.9	2.7
y	−13	−8	−6	−4	−5	−8	−13

$y \approx -1.184x^2 + 0.0384x - 4.180$

Use a graphing calculator to perform quadratic regression on the given data. Then solve the problem and identify and interpret the domain and range of the function.

15. The revenue of a company based on the price of its product is in the table below. How much should the company sell the product for to maximize revenue?

Price ($)	1.00	2.00	2.75	4.00	4.50	6.00	8.00	8.40	9.00
Revenue	90	228	303	384	406	396	282	229	135

$y \approx -18.43x^2 + 191.4x - 83.36$

The maximum value of the function is about 413.57.

If the company sells its product for $5.19, it will maximize its revenue.

The model is for selling price and revenue, so the domain will be x > 0 and the range will be 0 < y ≤ 413.57.

16. A scuba diver brought an air-filled balloon 150 feet underwater to the bottom of a lake. The diver conducts an experiment to measure the surface area of the balloon while ascending back to the surface. The results of the measurements are shown in the table. How far will the balloon have risen when it has doubled in surface area?

Distance from Bottom	0	20	40	60	80	100	120
Surface Area	28.6	32.2	35.4	39.5	45.0	52.8	65.4

$y \approx 0.0021x^2 + 0.035x + 29.64$

Find the intersection of the graphs of the regression equation and $y = 57.2$.

The surface area of the balloon will have doubled when it has risen about 106.5 feet from the bottom.

The function models the surface area of a real-world object based on its distance from the bottom of a lake and it applies only when the balloon is under water, so the domain is 0 < x ≤ 150 and the range is 0 < y ≤ 82.1.

17. The height of a ski jumper with respect to the low point of the ramp in meters is measured every 0.3 seconds. The results are given in the table. If the skier lands at a point 30 meters below the reference point, how long was the skier in the air?

Time	0.3	0.6	0.9	1.2	1.5	1.8	2.1	2.4
Height	11.2	14.06	16.32	18.47	19.48	20.52	21.01	21.01

$y \approx -2.627x^2 + 11.74x + 7.942$

Find the intersection of the regression equation and $y = -30$.

The skier was in the air for 6.6 seconds.

The function models height based on a reference point after an event begins, the jump height has a maximum and a minimum (the landing point) so the domain will be $0 < x \leq 6.6$ and the range is $-30 \leq y \leq 21.06$.

© Houghton Mifflin Harcourt Publishing Company • Image Credits: ©Tetra Images/Alamy

---

H.O.T. Focus on Higher Order Thinking

Use the table for Exercises 18 and 19.

x	1	1.25	1.5	1.75	2	3	4	5	6	7	8	9
y	2	2.378	2.828	3.364	4	8	16	32	64	128	256	512

18. What If? If you perform a quadratic regression on the data, will the value of R^2 be close to 1? Justify your answer.

No. The second differences between y-values are not constant, but the ratios of consecutive y-values are constant, so an exponential model is better than a quadratic model for this data set. The value of R^2 for a quadratic regression model is about 0.95, but the value of R^2 for an exponential regression is nearly 1.

19. Communicate Mathematical Ideas Perform a quadratic regression on the data; then perform a quadratic regression using only the first four data points. Explain the difference in R^2 values between the two models.

Full Set: $y \approx 13.84x^2 - 86.13x + 104.6$ $R^2 = 0.9493$
Four points: $y \approx 0.632x^2 + 0.0788x + 1.290$ $R^2 = 1$

The value of R^2 reflects how well the equation models the data. When only a few data points are used, the equation may model those few data points well, but may not do so for the entire data set.

JOURNAL

Have students write the steps for using quadratic regression to find a quadratic equation that models a data set. Students should include which calculator options to use in order to identify and graph a quadratic equation that fits the data.

---

20. **Multi-Part** A trebuchet is a catapult that was used in the Middle Ages to hurl projectiles during a siege. It is now used in various regions of the United States to throw pumpkins. Teams build trebuchets to compete to see who can throw a pumpkin the farthest. On the practice field, one team has measured the height of its pumpkin after it is launched at 1-second intervals. The results are displayed in the table below.

Time	1	2	3	4	5	6	7	8
Height	152	265	377	441	470	450	396	342

a. Find a quadratic function that models the data.

$y \approx -17.36x^2 + 182.9x - 18.45$ $R^2 = 0.9925$

b. Determine the flight time of the pumpkin.

The pumpkin will travel until its height is 0. This occurs 10.43 seconds after launch.

c. If the pumpkin travels horizontally at a speed of 120 feet per second, how far does it travel before it hits the ground?

$10.43 \cdot 120 = 1251.6$ feet.

d. At the official competition, the trebuchet is situated on a slight rise 10 feet above the targeting area. How far will the pumpkin travel in the competition, assuming the height relative to the base of the trebuchet is modeled by the same function and it moves with the same horizontal speed?

Add 10 to the regression function, find the zero of the new function to find the time, and then multiply by the horizontal speed.

The new zero is 10.49 seconds after launch. So the pumpkin will travel $10.49 \cdot 120 = 1258.8$ feet.

© Houghton Mifflin Harcourt Publishing Company

Lesson Performance Task

A student stands at the top of a lighthouse that is 200 feet tall. The base of the lighthouse is an additional 300 feet above the ocean below, and the student has a clear shot to the water below to examine the claims made by Galileo. But, this being the 21st century, the student also has a sophisticated laser tracker that continually tracks the exact height of the dropped object from the ground as well as the length of time elapsed from the drop. At the end of the trial, the student gets sample data in the form of a table.

Time	Height above Ground
0	200
0.5	196
1	184
1.5	164
2	136
2.5	100
3	56
3.5	4
4	−56
4.5	−124
5	−200

Examine the data and determine the relationship between time and height. Then find the function that models the data. (Hint: Negative values represent when the object passes the base of the lighthouse.)

The common ratio and first difference are not constant. The second difference is constant so the data is quadratic.

The formula modeling the height of the ball above ground at time t is $h(t) = -16t^2 + 200$.

MODELING

Relate the negative values in the data table to the distances below the base of the lighthouse. Draw a sketch of the lighthouse with its base at point 0 and its top at point 200. The water level should be at −300. **Ask:** After 5 seconds have elapsed, has the object fallen into the water? No, it has not; it is at −200, which is 100 feet above the water.

AVOID COMMON ERRORS

Some students may subtract in the wrong order when finding the first differences or the second differences. Remind students that to find a first difference, they need to pick a height and then subtract the previous height. A second difference is a first difference minus the difference before it.

EXTENSION ACTIVITY

Have students find out more about Galileo's experiment, dropping two cannonballs of different weights from the Leaning Tower of Pisa. Students may discover that Galileo's experiment may actually have been a thought experiment, and that someone else later dropped the cannonballs from the tower. Have students research how air resistance affects the rate of fall of, for example, a hammer and a feather. Then have students investigate how astronauts on the moon showed that a hammer and a feather dropped together from the same height above the surface struck the ground at the same time. There was no air resistance because the moon has no atmosphere.

Scoring Rubric
2 points: Student correctly solves the problem and explains his/her reasoning.
1 point: Student shows good understanding of the problem but does not fully solve or explain his/her reasoning.
0 points: Student does not demonstrate understanding of the problem.

Modeling with Quadratic Functions   **1122**

Comparing Linear, Exponential, and Quadratic Models

Common Core Math Standards

The student is expected to:

 F-LE.A.1b

Recognize ... changes at a constant rate per unit interval relative to another. Also F-IF.B.6, F-LE.A.1, F-LE.A.3

Mathematical Practices

 MP.5 Using Tools

Language Objective

Explain to a partner how to determine whether a data set is best modeled by a linear, quadratic, or exponential function.

ENGAGE

Essential Question: How can you determine whether a given data set is best modeled by a linear, quadratic, or exponential function?

You can (a) look at the graph of the function and consider its shape and its end behavior; (b) use a table of data and determine first differences, second differences, and ratios of consecutive function values; or (c) perform regressions on the data and compare the fit of the data.

PREVIEW: LESSON PERFORMANCE TASK

View the Engage section online. Discuss the photo and what type of function might model the weight of a Great Dane in the first 10 months of its life. Then preview the Lesson Performance Task.

23.2 Comparing Linear, Exponential, and Quadratic Models

Essential Question: How can you determine whether a given data set is best modeled by a linear, quadratic, or exponential function?

Resource Locker

⊘ Explore Exploring End Behavior of Linear, Quadratic, and Exponential Functions

Recall that you learned to characterize the end behavior of a function by recognizing what the behavior of the function is as x approaches positive or negative infinity. Look at the three graphs to see what the function does as x approaches infinity or negative infinity.

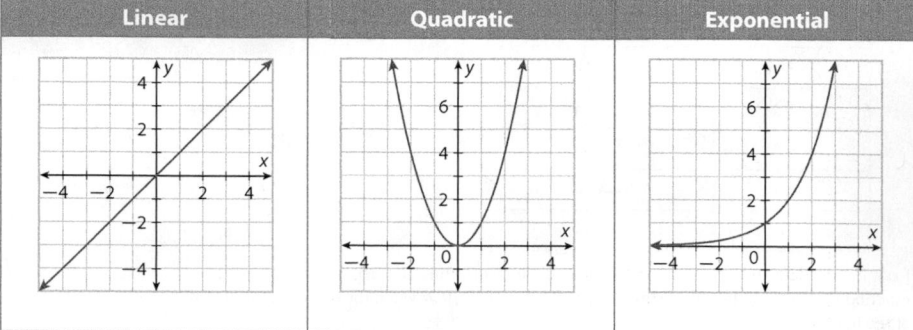

| Linear | Quadratic | Exponential |

(A) For the linear function, $f(x)$, as x approaches infinity, $f(x)$ __approaches infinity__, and as x approaches negative infinity, $f(x)$ __approaches negative infinity__

(B) For the quadratic function, $g(x)$, as x approaches infinity, $g(x)$ __approaches infinity__, and as x approaches negative infinity, $g(x)$ __approaches infinity__

(C) For the exponential function, $h(x)$, as x approaches infinity, $h(x)$ __approaches infinity__, and as x approaches negative infinity, $h(x)$ __approaches zero__

23.2 Comparing Linear, Exponential, and Quadratic Models

HARDCOVER PAGES 871–886

Turn to these pages to find this lesson in the hardcover student edition.

Examine the end behavior and the rate of the change of the three function types by filling in the values of the table.

(D) Fill in the missing values of the table

	Linear	Quadratic	Exponential
x	$L(x) = 5x - 2$	$Q(x) = 5x^2 - 2$	$E(x) = 5^x - 2$
1	3	3	3
2	8	18	23
3	13	43	123
4	18	78	623
5	23	123	3123
6	28	178	15,623
7	33	243	78,123
8	38	318	390,623

(E) Use first differences to find the growth rate over each interval and determine which function ultimately grows fastest.

	Linear	Quadratic	Exponential
x	$L(x+1) - L(x)$	$Q(x+1) - Q(x)$	$E(x+1) - E(x)$
1	5	15	20
2	5	25	100
3	5	35	500
4	5	45	2500
5	5	55	12,500

(F) The fastest growing function of the three is the __exponential__.

Reflect

1. What is the end behavior of $y = 7x + 12$?
As x approaches infinity, y approaches infinity. As x approaches negative infinity, y approaches negative infinity.

2. What is the end behavior of $y = 5x^2 + x + 2$?
As x approaches infinity, y approaches infinity. As x approaches negative infinity, y approaches infinity.

3. What is the end behavior of $y = 3^x - 5$?
As x approaches infinity, y approaches infinity. As x approaches negative infinity, y approaches -5.

Module 23   **1124**   Lesson 2

INTEGRATE TECHNOLOGY

Have students complete the Explore activity in either the book or online lesson.

QUESTIONING STRATEGIES

 How can you tell what happens to a function as x approaches infinity? As x approaches negative infinity? Evaluate the function for larger and larger values of x. Evaluate the function for smaller and smaller values of x, such as -10, -100, -1000.

PROFESSIONAL DEVELOPMENT

COMMON CORE Integrate Mathematical Practices

This lesson provides an opportunity to address Mathematical Practice **MP.5**, which calls for students to "use tools." Students compare the end behavior of the graphs of linear, quadratic, and exponential equations. Students construct tables to identify the best model for a particular data set, and use calculators to perform regressions to identify a function that best fits a data set.

EXPLAIN 1

Justifying a Quadratic Model as More Appropriate Than a Linear Model

AVOID COMMON ERRORS

Some students may think that a quadratic function will not model a data set if, as x increases, y always increases, or if, as x increases, y always decreases. Use sketches to show that a quadratic function can model such a data set. For example, $y = -x^2$ might model the data set that begins $(1, -1)$, $(2, -4)$, $(3, -9)$.

4. Make a Conjecture Does an increasing exponential function always grow faster than an increasing quadratic function? Will the growth rate of an increasing exponential function eventually exceed that of an increasing quadratic function?

The exponential will not always grow faster initially, because the average growth in an interval depends on the parameters $\left(\text{for example } Q(x) = 5x^2 \text{ grows faster than } E(x) = 2^x \text{ from 0 to 1}\right)$. However, the exponential will always catch up and grow faster than the quadratic.

 Explain 1   **Justifying a Quadratic Model as More Appropriate Than a Linear Model**

The first step in modeling data is selecting an appropriate functional form. If you are trying to decide between a quadratic and a linear model, for example, you may compare interval rates of change or the end behavior. First and second differences are useful for identifying linear and quadratic functions if the data points have equally spaced x-values.

Example 1   Examine the data sets provided and determine whether a quadratic or linear model is more appropriate by examining the graph, the end behavior, and the first and second differences.

(A)

x	f(x)
0	3
1	1.5
2	1
3	1.5
4	3
5	5.5
6	9

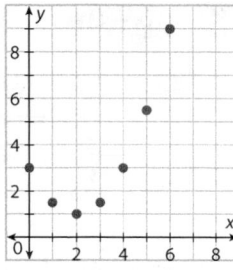

Shape:

The graph of the data appears to follow a curved path that starts downward and turns back upward.

End Behavior:

The path appears to increase without end as x approaches infinity and to increase without end as x approaches negative infinity.

Based on the apparent curvature and end behavior, the function is quadratic.

COLLABORATIVE LEARNING

Small Group Activity

Have students work in groups of four. Have each student write the equation of a linear function, a quadratic function, or an exponential function, then create a data set of points that are close to the graph of the function. Then, each student graphs a data set selected by another in the group, decides which type of function is modeled by the graph, and uses a regression to identify the function. Finally, students check with the student who wrote the original function to see whether they chose the right kind of function.

Interval Behavior:

x	f(x)	First Difference	Second Difference
0	3		
1	1.5	−1.5	
2	1	−0.5	1
3	1.5	0.5	1
4	3	1.5	1
5	5.5	2.5	1
6	9	3.5	1

The first differences increase as x increases, while the second differences are constant, which is characteristic of a quadratic function.

Ⓑ

x	f(x)
0	8
1	6.75
2	5
3	2.75
4	0
5	−3.25
6	−7

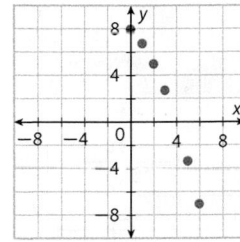

Plot the data on the graph.

Shape:

The graph of the data appears to follow a (curved) | straight, (downward) | upward path.

End Behavior:

The path appears to __decrease__ as x increases and to __increase__ as x decreases.

The curvature is more consistent with a quadratic than a line, but the apparent end behavior is not. Fill in the first and second differences to discuss interval behavior.

Interval Behavior:

x	f(x)	First Difference	Second Difference
0	8		
1	6.75	−1.25	
2	5	−1.75	−0.5
3	2.75	−2.25	−0.5
4	0	−2.75	−0.5
5	−3.25	−3.25	−0.5
6	−7	−3.75	−0.5

The absolute values of the first differences __increase__ as x increases, while the second differences are constant, which is characteristic of a quadratic function.

QUESTIONING STRATEGIES

❓ What are two things that differentiate a data set that is better modeled by a quadratic function from a data set that is better modeled by a linear function? The graph of the quadratic data set appears to follow a curve, while the graph of the linear set appears to follow a line. The quadratic set does not have constant first differences but does have constant second differences, while the linear set has constant first differences.

DIFFERENTIATE INSTRUCTION

Curriculum Integration

Discuss why having a function that models a data set can be useful. For example, having such a model can help people make projections into the future, which may help them plan and make policy decisions. Have students brainstorm issues for which data might be useful in making such decisions.

Comparing Linear, Exponential, and Quadratic Models   **1126**

Reflect

5. Was the end behavior helpful in determining that the function in Example 1B was a quadratic? Explain.
No, it would have been misleading to assume the small range of data supplied

demonstrated the same behavior as the overall function. All quadratic functions change

vertical direction at the vertex of the parabola and have the same end behavior for

increasing and decreasing x. However, a data set corresponding to a quadratic function

need not include the vertex, and the apparent end behavior can be misleading.

6. **Discussion** Can you always tell that a function is quadratic by looking at a graph of it?
No, it depends on how much of the function is plotted. A quadratic function can appear

linear or exponential depending on how many data points are shown on the graph.

Your Turn

7.

x	f(x)
0	−4
1	−3.8
2	−3.2
3	−2.2
4	−0.8
5	1
6	3.2

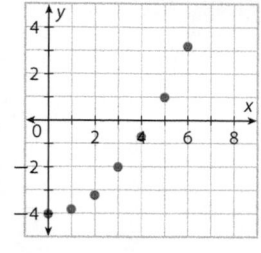

Examine the data set and determine whether a quadratic or linear model is more appropriate by examining the graph, the end behavior, and the first and second differences.
The shape appears curved upward.

$f(x)$ appears to increase without end as x approaches infinity and to flatten out as x approaches negative infinity.

The function appears to be quadratic based on the curvature, although the apparent end behavior is not consistent with either a linear or a quadratic function.

Interval behavior:

x	f(x)	First Difference	Second Difference
0	−4	_____	_____
1	−3.8	0.2	_____
2	−3.2	0.6	0.4
3	−2.2	1	0.4
4	−0.8	1.4	0.4
5	1	1.8	0.4
6	3.2	2.2	0.4

The function has increasing first differences and constant second differences so it is a quadratic function.

LANGUAGE SUPPORT **EL**

Connect Vocabulary

Make sure that students understand what it means for a variable to *approach infinity* and to *approach negative infinity*. For example, to say that as x approaches infinity, f(x) approaches infinity means that as x gets larger and larger, f(x) gets larger and larger without any limit. If you pick a number N, no matter how large, you can find a number x so that $f(x) > N$. In other words, there is no limit to how large f(x) gets as x increases.

Explain 2 · Justifying a Quadratic Model as More Appropriate Than an Exponential Model

Previously, you learned to model data with an exponential function. How do you choose between a quadratic and an exponential function to model a given set of data? Graph the given data points and compare the trend of the data with the general shape and end behavior of the parent quadratic and exponential functions. Use the results to decide if the function appears to be quadratic or exponential. Then examine the first and second differences and the ratios of the function using the function values corresponding to x-values separated by a constant amount.

Properties of $f(x) = x^2$ and $g(x) = b^x$		
	$f(x) = x^2$	$g(x) = b^x$ with $b > 1$
End behavior as:		
x approaches infinity	$f(x)$ approaches infinity	$g(x)$ approaches infinity
x approaches negative infinity	$f(x)$ approaches infinity	$g(x)$ approaches zero

Example 2 Determine if the function represented in the given table is quadratic or exponential. Plot the given points and analyze the graph. Draw a conclusion if possible. Then find the first and second differences and ratios and either verify your conclusion or determine the family of the function.

Ⓐ

x	$f(x)$
−3	3
−2	1.5
−1	1
0	1.5
1	3
2	5.5
3	9

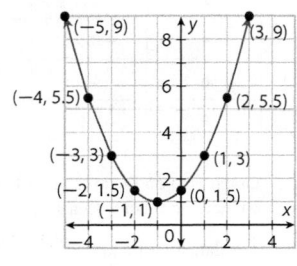

Graph $f(x)$ on the axes provided by plotting the given points and connecting them with a smooth curve.

The data appears to be parabolic.

Also, as x approaches infinity, $f(x)$ appears to increase without end, and as x approaches negative infinity, $f(x)$ appears to increase without end.

It appears that $f(x)$ is a quadratic function.

Now find the first and second differences and the ratio of the values of $f(x)$.

EXPLAIN 2

Justifying a Quadratic Model as More Appropriate Than an Exponential Model

AVOID COMMON ERRORS

Sometimes students confuse quadratic functions with exponential functions because both have exponents. Remind students that in order for a function to be an exponential function, it must be of the form, $f(x) = ab^x$, with the variable x as an exponent.

Suppose that you are trying to determine whether a quadratic function or an exponential function is a more appropriate model for a data set. If the difference between successive x values of the data set is a constant c, how do you find the ratios? Find the ratio of consecutive function values, that is, the ratio of $f(x + c)$ to $f(x)$ for each x in the data set (except the last one).

x	$f(x)$	First Difference	Second Difference	Ratio
−3	3	_____	_____	_____
−2	1.5	−1.5	_____	0.5
−1	1	−0.5	1	0.67
0	1.5	0.5	1	1.5
1	3	1.5	1	2
2	5.5	2.5	1	1.83
3	9	3.5	1	1.64

The second differences are constant so the function is quadratic as predicted.

Ⓑ

x	$f(x)$	First Difference	Second Difference	Ratio
−2	4	_____	_____	_____
0	3.5	−0.5	_____	0.875
2	2	−1.5	−1	0.571
4	−0.5	−2.5	−1	−0.25
6	−4	−3.5	−1	8
8	−8.5	−4.5	−1	2.125

Graph $f(x)$ on the axes provided by plotting the given points and connecting them with a smooth curve.

The data appears to be __either quadratic or exponential__

As x approaches infinity, $f(x)$ __appears to decrease without end__

What appears to happen to $f(x)$ as x approaches negative infinity? __it cannot be determined__

It appears that $f(x)$ could be __either quadratic or exponential__

Now find the first and second differences and the ratio of the values of $f(x)$.

The __second differences__ are constant so the function is __quadratic__

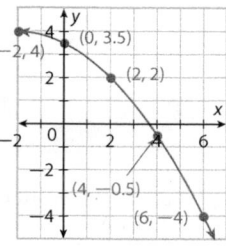

(−2, 4) (0, 3.5) (2, 2) (4, −0.5) (6, −4)

© Houghton Mifflin Harcourt Publishing Company

Determine if the function represented in the given table is quadratic or exponential. Plot the given points and analyze the graph. Draw a conclusion if possible. Then find the first and second differences and ratios and either verify your conclusion or determine the family of the function.

8.

x	f(x)	First Difference	Second Difference	Ratio
−3	−5			
−2	−3.11	1.89		0.62
−1	−1.44	1.67	−0.22	0.46
0	0	1.44	−0.23	0
1	1.22	1.22	−0.22	Undefined
2	2.22	1	−0.22	1.82
3	3	0.78	−0.22	1.35
4	3.56	0.56	−0.22	1.19
5	3.89	0.33	−0.23	1.09
6	4	0.11	−0.22	1.03

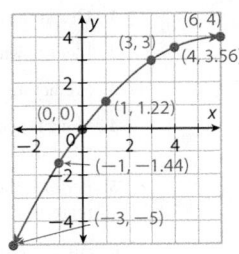

The end behavior of the function as x approaches infinity cannot be determined. As x approaches negative infinity, f(x) appears to decrease without end. Based on the graph, the data could be either quadratic or exponential.

The second differences are nearly constant. Therefore, the function is quadratic.

9.

x	f(x)	First Difference	Second Difference	Ratio
−2	8.25			
0	6	−2.25		0.73
2	4.25	−1.75	0.5	0.71
4	3	−1.25	0.5	0.71
6	2.25	−0.75	0.5	0.75
8	2	−0.25	0.5	0.89

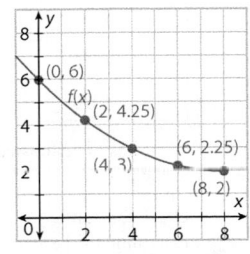

Based on the graph, the data could be either quadratic or exponential. Since f(x) has not been defined for x > 8, the end behavior of the function as x approaches infinity cannot be determined. As x approaches negative infinity, f(x) appears to increase without end.

No conclusions can be drawn about f(x) from the graph. The second differences are constant. Therefore, the function is quadratic.

EXPLAIN 3

Selecting an Appropriate Model Given Linear, Exponential, or Quadratic Data

INTEGRATE MATHEMATICAL PRACTICES

Focus on Technology

MP.5 As students work with finding a model that fits the data, discuss why it is important to identify the type of function before performing a regression using a graphing calculator. Students should understand that the calculator will perform different calculations depending on the type of regression.

Explain 3 **Selecting an Appropriate Model Given Linear, Exponential, or Quadratic Data**

It is important to be able to choose among a variety of models when solving real-world problems.

Example 3 Decide which type of function is best represented by each of the following data sets. Perform the following steps:

1. Graph the data on a scatter plot and draw a fit curve.

2. Identify which function the data appear to represent.

3. Predict the function's end behavior as x approaches infinity.

4. Use a function table to calculate the first differences, second differences, and ratios.

5. Perform the appropriate regression on a graphing calculator. Plot the regression equation and data together to evaluate the fit of regression.

6. Answer any additional questions.

Ⓐ **Demographics** The data table describes the average lifespan in the United States over time.

Year	Average Lifespan (years)
1900	47.3
1910	50.0
1920	54.1
1930	59.7
1940	62.9
1950	68.2
1960	69.7
1970	70.8
1980	73.1
1990	75.4

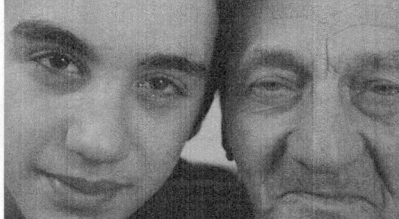

What was the estimated average lifespan in 2000 according to the model?

Graph the scatter plot and an approximate line of fit to determine the best function to use for this data set.

The data set appears to best fit a linear function.

The end behavior of the data is that as x approaches infinity, $f(x)$ approaches infinity.

Complete the function table for first differences, second differences, and ratios.

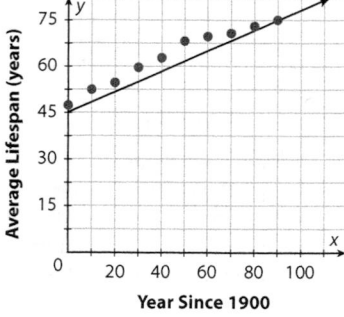

Year	Average Lifespan (years)	First Difference	Second Difference	Ratio
1900	47.3	_____	_____	_____
1910	50.0	2.7	_____	$\frac{50.0}{47.3} = 1.06$
1920	54.1	4.1	1.4	$\frac{54.1}{50.0} = 1.08$
1930	59.7	5.6	1.5	$\frac{59.7}{54.1} = 1.10$
1940	62.9	3.2	−2.4	$\frac{62.9}{59.7} = 1.05$
1950	68.2	5.3	2.1	$\frac{68.2}{62.9} = 1.08$
1960	69.7	1.5	−3.8	$\frac{69.7}{68.2} = 1.02$
1970	70.8	1.1	−0.4	$\frac{70.8}{69.7} = 1.02$
1980	73.1	2.3	1.2	$\frac{73.1}{70.8} = 1.03$
1990	75.4	2.3	0	$\frac{75.4}{73.1} = 1.03$

Since the ratios are dropping, it is possible that the data set can be modeled by an exponential regression. Since the average of the second differences is around 0, however, it is most likely that the data set should be modeled by a linear regression.

Perform the linear regression by first creating a data table by using the STAT function on a calculator. Use the numbers 0 through 9 to represent the 10-year intervals since 1900, starting with 0 for 1900.

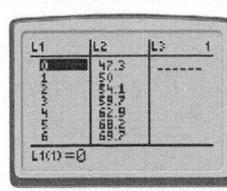

Go to STAT, move over to CALC, type 4, and press ENTER to perform the regression.

Press ZOOM and 9 to fit the data. Plot the line from the regression to test its fit.

The linear regression is a good fit for the data set.

To find the estimated average lifespan in 2000, use the equation $y = 3.23x + 48.57$ and substitute 10 for x.

$y = 3.23x + 48.57$

$y = 3.23(10) + 48.57$

$\quad = 32.3 + 48.57$

$\quad = 80.87$

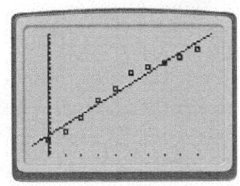

According to the model, the average lifespan in the year 2000 was 80.87 years.

AVOID COMMON ERRORS

Remind students that the value for r, the correlation coefficient, will be close to 1 if the function is a good fit for the data set. Students who select an inappropriate model for the data should notice that r is low and conclude that the model is incorrect.

When determining the first differences, second differences, and the ratio between x-values, what must be true about the x-values in the data set in order to select an appropriate model? To select an appropriate model, the differences between successive x-values must be the same.

(B) **Biology** The data table lists the whooping crane population in one habitat over time.

Whooping Crane	
Year	Population
1940	22
1950	34
1960	33
1970	56
1980	76
1990	146
2000	177
2010	281

What is the expected whooping crane population for 2020?

Graph the scatter plot and an approximate line of fit to determine the best function to use for this data set. Use the numbers 0 through 7 to represent the 10-year intervals since 1940, starting with 0 for 1940.

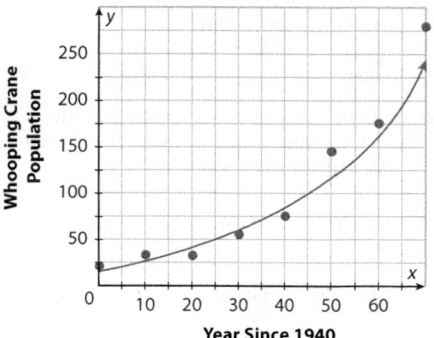

The data set appears to best fit an linear/quadratic/exponential function.

The end behavior of this data is that as x approaches infinity, $f(x)$ approaches infinity.

Complete the function table for first differences, second differences, and ratios.

Year	Population	First Difference	Second Difference	Ratio
1940	22	_____	_____	_____
1950	34	12	_____	$\frac{34}{22} = 1.55$
1960	33	−1	−13	$\frac{33}{34} = 0.97$
1970	56	23	24	$\frac{56}{33} = 1.70$
1980	76	20	−3	$\frac{76}{56} = 1.36$
1990	146	70	50	$\frac{146}{76} = 1.92$
2000	177	31	−39	$\frac{177}{146} = 1.21$
2010	281	104	73	$\frac{281}{177} = 1.59$

Since the ratios are (changing)/not changing and the second difference does/(does not) have an average that is close to 0, linear/quadratic/(exponential) regression should be used.

Perform the exponential regression by first creating a data table by using the STAT function on a calculator. Use the numbers 0 through 7 to represent the 10-year intervals since 1940, starting with 0 for 1940.

Go to STAT, move over to CALC, type 0, and press ENTER to perform the regression.

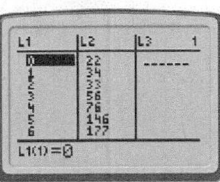

Press ZOOM and 9 to fit the data. Plot the line from the regression to test its fit.

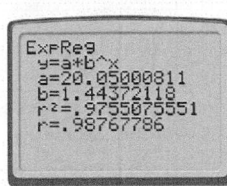

The linear/quadratic/(exponential) regression is (a good)/poor fit for the data set.

To find the estimated number of whooping cranes in 2020, use the equation $y = \boxed{20.05(1.44)^x}$ and substitute ___8___ for x.

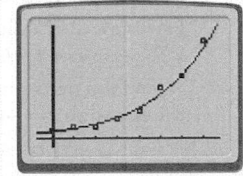

$y = \boxed{20.05(1.44)^x}$

$y = \boxed{20.05(1.44)^8}$

$= \boxed{20.05(18.49)}$

$= \boxed{370.7}$

Since it is unrealistic to round up in this situation, the predicted whooping crane population in this habitat in 2020 is ___370___.

Decide which type of function is best represented by each of the following data sets. Perform the following steps:

1. Graph the data on a scatter plot and draw a fit curve.

2. Identify which function the data appear to represent.

3. Predict the function's end behavior as x approaches infinity.

4. Use a function table to calculate the first differences, second differences, and ratios.

5. Perform the appropriate regression on a graphing calculator. Plot the regression equation and data together to evaluate the fit of regression.

6. Answer any additional questions.

10. **Population** The data table describes the percentage of people living in central cities in the United States over time. According to the model, what percentage of people were living in central cities in the United States in 2000?

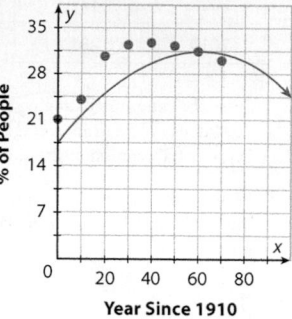

Year	% of People
1910	21.2
1920	24.2
1930	30.8
1940	32.5
1950	32.8
1960	32.3
1970	31.4
1980	30.0

Graph the scatter plot and an approximate line of fit to determine the best function to use for this data set.

The function appears to best fit a quadratic function.

The end behavior of the data is as x approaches infinity, $f(x)$ approaches negative infinity.

Since the ratios increase quickly and then decrease quickly, a quadratic function should probably be used for this data set.

Perform a quadratic regression, using the numbers 0 through 7 to represent the 10-year intervals since 1910. The quadratic regression is a good fit for the data set.

To find the percentage of people living in central cities in the United States in 2000, use the equation $y = -0.61x^2 + 5.46x + 20.89$ and substitute 9 for x.

$$y = -0.61x^2 + 5.46x + 20.89$$
$$= -0.61(9)^2 + 5.46(9) + 20.89$$
$$= -49.41 + 49.14 + 20.89$$
$$= 20.62$$

By the year 2000, 20.62% of people were living in central cities in the United States.

11. **Automobiles** The data table describes the car weight versus horsepower for automobiles produced in 2012. If a car weighed 6500 pounds in 2012, how much horsepower should the car have had?

Car Weight (pounds)	Horsepower in 2012
2000	70
2500	105
3000	145
3500	179
4000	259
4500	338
5000	400
5500	557
6000	556

Graph the scatter plot and an approximate line of fit to determine the best function to use for this data set.

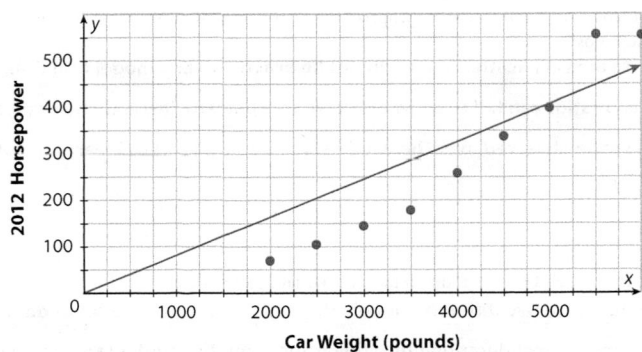

The data set appears to best fit a linear function.

The end behavior of the data is that as x approaches infinity, $f(x)$ approaches infinity.

The changing ratios suggest that the data set is best described by a quadratic or linear function. However, the average of the second differences is close to 0, so a linear regression should be used.

The linear regression is a good fit for the data set.

To find the horsepower a car weighing 6500 pounds should have in 2012, use the equation $y = 0.13x - 239.31$ and substitute 6500 for x.

$y = 0.13x - 239.31$

$\quad = 0.13(6500) - 239.31$

$\quad = 845.00 - 239.31$

$\quad = 605.69$

It makes sense to round in this problem since horsepower is typically expressed in terms of whole numbers, so a car weighing 6500 pounds in 2012 should have had 606 horsepower.

ELABORATE

INTEGRATE MATHEMATICAL PRACTICES

Focus on Critical Thinking

MP.3 Discuss with students the information that can be determined about a model to fit a data set based solely upon the shape of the graph. Guide students to see that the shape of the graph is useful but that making a function table and finding first differences, second differences, and ratios can also provide important information when selecting the model to fit a data set.

SUMMARIZE THE LESSON

> **?** How do you select an appropriate model to fit a data set? Use the shape of the graph to determine whether the function seems to be a linear, quadratic, or exponential equation. If more than one model may fit, use first differences, second differences, and the ratio of consecutive function values to select a model.

💬 **Elaborate**

12. In general, what are three possible end behaviors of exponential, linear, and quadratic graphs as x increases without bound? When do these end behaviors occur?

$f(x)$ can increase without bound, which occurs when $a > 0$ in growing exponential or quadratic function and when $m > 0$ in a linear function.

$f(x)$ can decrease without bound, which occurs when $a < 0$ in a quadratic function, when $a < 0$ and $b > 1$ in an exponential and when $m < 0$ in a linear function.

$f(x)$ can approach a constant value, which occurs when $0 < b < 1$ in an exponential function.

13. What do function tables tell you that graphs don't ? How can this information be used to help you select a model?

Function tables can be used to find first and second differences as well as the ratio between terms to help you distinguish linear, quadratic, and exponential models when the data do not show the end behavior.

14. When does a graph help determine an appropriate model better than examining first and second differences and ratios?

When the data are very scattered and do not lie exactly on any model function, the differences and ratios can fail to show a discernable pattern. Instead, the end behavior and general shape observed over the whole set of data will offer a clearer picture of the preferred model.

15. Can two different models be created that represent the same set of data?

It is possible to create two different models that represent the same set of data. For example, in a model best described by a linear function, the model can also be described by an exponential model with a very small growth rate.

16. **Essential Question Check-In** How can a graph be used to determine whether a given data set is best modeled by a linear, quadratic, or exponential function?

A graph can be used to determine whether a given data set is best modeled by a linear, quadratic, or exponential function by identifying its general shape and end behavior.

© Houghton Mifflin Harcourt Publishing Company

• Online Homework
• Hints and Help
• Extra Practice

1. For the two functions $f(x) = 2x + 1$ and $g(x) = 2^x + 1$, which function has the greatest average rate of change over the interval from 0 to 1? What about the interval from 2 to 3?

$$\frac{f(1) - f(0)}{1 - 0} = \frac{2 + 1 - 1}{1} = 2 \qquad \frac{f(3) - f(2)}{3 - 2} = \frac{6 + 1 - (4 + 1)}{1} = 2$$

$$\frac{g(1) - g(0)}{1 - 0} = \frac{2 + 1 - (1 + 1)}{1} = 1 \qquad \frac{g(3) - g(2)}{3 - 2} = \frac{8 + 1 - (4 + 1)}{1} = 4$$

$f(x)$ **increases faster from 0 to 1.** $g(x)$ **increases faster from 2 to 3.**

2. Plot the data and describe the observed shape and end behavior. Does it appear linear or quadratic? Calculate first and second differences and identify the type of function.

x	f(x)	First Difference	Second Difference
0	−0.79	————	————
1	2.81	3.6	————
2	4.41	1.6	−2
3	4.01	−0.4	−2
4	1.61	−2.4	−2
5	−2.79	−4.4	−2

The shape appears curved downward.

$f(x)$ **appears to decrease without end as x approaches infinity and to decrease without end as x approaches negative infinity.**

The function appears to be quadratic.

The function has constant second differences and decreasing first differences, so it is quadratic.

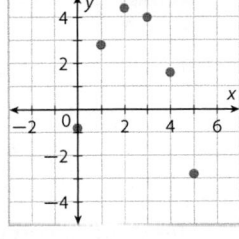

Exercise	Depth of Knowledge (D.O.K.)	COMMON CORE Mathematical Practices
1	**2** Skills/Concepts	**MP.2** Reasoning
2-8	**2** Skills/Concepts	**MP.4** Modeling
9	**3** Strategic Thinking H.O.T.	**MP.5** Using Tools
10	**3** Strategic Thinking H.O.T.	**MP.5** Using Tools
11	**3** Strategic Thinking H.O.T.	**MP.3** Logic

EVALUATE

ASSIGNMENT GUIDE

Concepts and Skills	Practice
Explore Exploring End Behavior of Linear, Quadratic, and Exponential Functions	Exercises 1, 10
Example 1 Justifying a Quadratic Model as More Appropriate Than a Linear Model	Exercises 2–5
Example 2 Justifying a Quadratic Model as More Appropriate Than an Exponential Model	Exercises 6–8
Example 3 Selecting an Appropriate Model Given Linear, Exponential, or Quadratic Data	Exercises 9, 11

INTEGRATE MATHEMATICAL PRACTICES
Focus on Reasoning

MP.2 Discuss with students whether it is possible for a data set to have constant values for the first differences and the second differences. Guide students to understand that a linear function will have constant values for first differences and second differences. (The second differences will all be 0.)

Comparing Linear, Exponential, and Quadratic Models   **1138**

KINESTHETIC EXPERIENCE

Have students sketch the graphs of a linear function, a quadratic function, and an exponential function. Have students trace the paths of the functions using their index fingers or colored pencils. Have them focus on the shape of each graph and on how the linear function changes compared to the quadratic function or the exponential function.

3. Plot the data that fits on the grid and describe the observed shape and end behavior. Does it appear to be linear or quadratic? Calculate first and second differences and identify the type of function.

x	f(x)	First Difference	Second Difference
−2	−4	_____	_____
−1	−3.3	0.7	_____
0	−1.2	2.1	1.4
1	2.3	3.5	1.4
2	7.2	4.9	1.4
3	13.5	6.3	1.4

The shape appears slightly curved upward.

$f(x)$ appears to increase without end as x approaches infinity and to decrease without end as x approaches negative infinity.

The function appears to be quadratic because of the curvature, but the apparent end behavior is not consistent with a quadratic function.

The function has constant second differences and decreasing first differences, so it is quadratic.

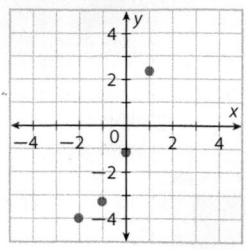

4. Plot the data on the grid and describe the observed shape and end behavior. Does it appear linear or quadratic? Calculate first and second differences and identify the type of function.

x	f(x)	First Difference	Second Difference
0	7.6	_____	_____
1	6.25	−1.35	_____
2	4.6	−1.65	−0.3
3	2.65	−1.95	−0.3
4	0.4	−2.25	−0.3

The shape appears curved.

$f(x)$ appears to decrease without end as x approaches infinity and to increase without end as x approaches negative infinity.

The function appears to be quadratic because of the curvature, but the apparent end behavior is not consistent with a quadratic function.

The function has constant second differences so it is quadratic.

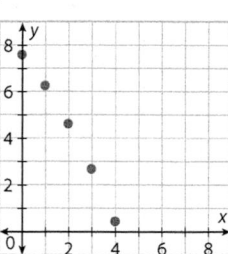

5. Plot the data and describe the observed shape and end behavior. Does it appear linear or quadratic? Calculate first and second differences and identify the type of function.

x	f(x)	First Difference	Second Difference
1	−7.2	_____	_____
2	−3.8	3.4	_____
3	0	3.8	0.4
4	4.2	4.2	0.4
5	8.8	4.6	0.4

The shape appears straight.

f(x) appears to increase without end as x increases and to decrease as x decreases.

The function appears to be linear.

The function has constant second differences, so it is quadratic.

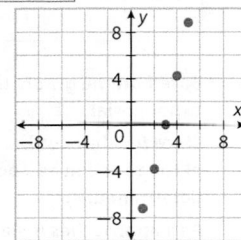

6. Plot the given points. Describe the general shape and end behavior of the graph. Draw a conclusion about the function, if possible. Then complete the table and use the differences to to verify your conclusions.

x	f(x)	First Difference	Second Difference	Ratio
−2	−5.75	_____	_____	_____
0	1	6.75	_____	−0.17
2	6.25	5.25	−1.5	6.25
4	10	3.75	−1.5	1.6
6	12.25	2.25	−1.5	1.23
8	13	0.75	−1.5	1.06
10	12.25	−0.75	−1.5	0.94
12	10	−2.25	−1.5	0.82
14	6.25	−3.75	−1.5	0.63

The data appear to be parabolic.

Also, as x approaches infinity, f(x) appears to decrease without end, and as x approaches negative infinity, f(x) appears to decrease without end.

It appears that f(x) is a quadratic function.

The second differences are constant. Therefore, the function is quadratic.

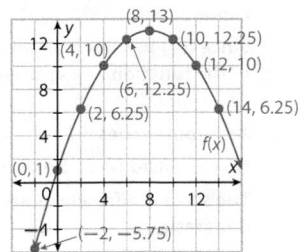

AVOID COMMON ERRORS

Sometimes students confuse quadratic functions with exponential functions because both have exponents. Emphasize to students that, when they perform regressions using a calculator, it is important to differentiate between quadratic and exponential functions. Remind students that in order for a function to be an exponential function, it must be of the form $f(x) = ab^x$, with the variable x as an exponent.

JOURNAL

Have students compare and contrast the clues they can use to identify a function as linear, quadratic, or exponential. Students should include information about the shape of the graph and its end behavior, as well as first differences, second differences, and the ratio of consecutive function values.

7. Plot the given points. Describe the general shape and end behavior of the graph. Draw a conclusion about the function, if possible. Then complete the table and use the differences to to verify your conclusions.

x	f(x)	First Difference	Second Difference	Ratio
−2	9	————	————	————
0	5.5	−3.5	————	0.61
2	3	−2.5	1	0.55
4	1.5	−1.5	1	0.5
6	1	−0.5	1	0.67

Based on the graph, the data could be either quadratic or exponential.

Since f(x) has not been defined for x > 6, the end behavior of the function as x approaches infinity cannot be determined.

As x approaches negative infinity, f(x) appears to increase without end.

No conclusions can be drawn about f(x) from the graph.

The second differences are constant. Therefore, the function is quadratic.

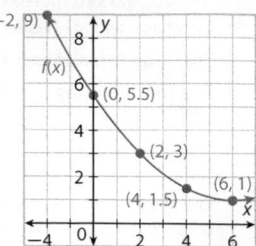

8. Plot the given points. Describe the general shape and end behavior of the graph. Draw a conclusion about the function, if possible. Then complete the table and use the differences to to verify your conclusions.

x	f(x)	First Difference	Second Difference	Ratio
−5	−3	————	————	————
−2	−2	1	————	0.67
1	1	3	2	−0.5
4	6	5	2	6
7	13	7	2	2.17

Based on the graph, the data could be either quadratic or exponential.

Since f(x) has not been defined for x < −5, the end behavior of the function as x approaches negative infinity cannot be determined.

As x approaches infinity, f(x) appears to increase without end.

No conclusions can be drawn about f(x) from the graph.

The second differences are constant. Therefore, the function is quadratic.

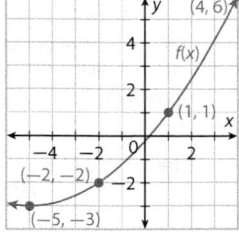

9. **Critical Thinking** A set of real-world data was modeled by using the quadratic, linear, and exponential forms of regression. The calculator showed that all three regression equations were close fits for the data provided. Which regression model do you think you should use? Explain.

Possible answer: Consider the data. For example, quadratic models are not the best choice for cost data, because costs don't usually increase as the number of items increases, then reach a maximum and decrease as the number of items continues to increase.

10. **Explain the Error** To determine if the data represents a linear model, Louise looked at the difference in y-values: 110, 110, 110, 110, 110.

x	7	9	12	14	18
y	150	260	370	480	590

She decided that since the differences between the y-values are all the same, a linear model would be appropriate. Explain her mistake.

Although the y-values are separated by the same difference, this difference does not correspond to an equal change in x-values. Louise should have checked that the x-values changed by a constant interval before finding the difference between y-values.

11. **Critical Thinking** Suppose that the following r-values were produced from regressions performed on the same set of data.

r-values	
Linear	**Exponential**
0.15	0.13

What type of regression model should be chosen for this data set? Explain.

Since both regression model have extremely low r-values, neither should be chosen for this data set.

Lesson Performance Task

The table shows general guidelines for the weight of a Great Dane at various ages. Create a function modeling the ideal weight for a Great Dane at any age. Justify your choice of models. How well do you think your model will do when the puppy is one or two years old?

Age (months)	Weight (kg)
2	12
4	23
6	33
8	40
10	45

The first differences are very different and the ratios are decreasing. Use quadratic regression to find a model, even though the second differences are not very similar. $w(t) = -0.268t^2 + 7.364t - 1.8$, where w is the weight of the puppy and t is the age of the puppy. The model should be fairly accurate when $t = 12$ because it is fairly close to the domain of the data set. At $t = 24$ and most likely for any ages much greater than 10, the model will probably not be very accurate because for a quadratic function with a negative leading term, as t increases without end, $w(t)$ decreases without end. The weight of a dog will usually increase with age but then level off.

INTEGRATE TECHNOLOGY

Have students plot the data values and the quadratic function on the same coordinate plane to see how the function fits the data.

INTEGRATE MATHEMATICAL PRACTICES
Focus on Modeling

MP.4 Have students create a scatter plot of the data and perform a linear regression, then a quadratic regression of the data. Ask questions such as: Which model best describes the data set? Explain why. The quadratic model best describes the data set because the points appear to lie on a parabola rather than on a straight line. Why does neither model represent the data very accurately? The weight of a dog does not increase endlessly over time as indicated by the linear function, nor does it decrease endlessly over time as indicated by the quadratic function.

EXTENSION ACTIVITY

Have students research a table of typical weights for Great Danes. Have students use data from their research to extend or modify the data table given in the Lesson Performance Task. Ask students to evaluate how the new data would change their answers to the Task.

Students may find that most weight charts are given in pounds, so they will need to convert to kilograms in order to extend the data in the table. Students will also find that the weight of a Great Dane reaches its maximum and then remains there throughout the dog's maturity.

Scoring Rubric
2 points: Student correctly solves the problem and explains his/her reasoning.
1 point: Student shows good understanding of the problem but does not fully solve or explain his/her reasoning.
0 points: Student does not demonstrate understanding of the problem.

Comparing Linear, Exponential, and Quadratic Models   **1142**

ASSESSMENT AND INTERVENTION

Assign or customize module reviews.

MODULE PERFORMANCE TASK

COMMON CORE

Mathematical Practices: MP.1, MP.2, MP.4, MP.5, MP.6, MP.7
A-CED.A.2, S-ID.B.6a, F-LE.A.1b, F-BF.A.1

SUPPORTING STUDENT REASONING

Students should begin by focusing on how to find the number of survivors for each year. They can then do research, or you can provide them with specific information. Here is some of the information they may ask for.

- **How can more than one function be used to model data?** Students can research piecewise-defined functions, in which a different function is given for particular domain intervals.

Essential Question: How can you use linear, exponential, and quadratic models to solve real-world problems?

Key Vocabulary
quadratic regression
(*regresión cuadrática*)

KEY EXAMPLE   *(Lesson 23.1)*

Find the second differences of the given data to verify that the relationship will be quadratic. Use a graphing calculator to find the quadratic regression equation for the data and R^2 to 4 significant digits.

The table below shows the cost of shipping a box that has a volume of x cubic feet.

Volume	Cost ($)	First Difference	Second Difference
1	$6.15	_____	_____
2	$8.00	$8 - 6.15 = 1.85$	_____
3	$13.90	$13.9 - 8 = 5.9$	$5.9 - 1.85 = 4.05$
4	$23.75	$23.75 - 13.9 = 9.85$	$9.85 - 5.9 = 3.95$
5	$38.25	$38.25 - 23.75 = 14.5$	$14.5 - 9.85 = 4.65$

$a \approx 2.09$
$b \approx -4.54$
$c \approx 8.65$
$R^2 \approx 0.9999$

Enter the volumes, as the x-values, and the costs, as the y-values, into the graphing calculator and perform a quadratic regression.

The quadratic regression equation is $y \approx 2.09x^2 - 4.54x + 8.65$.

KEY EXAMPLE   *(Lesson 23.2)*

Determine which type of function appears to best represents the data shown on the scatter plot: linear, exponential, or quadratic.

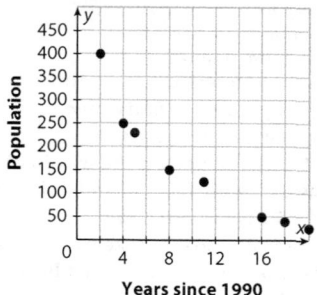

Based on the curvature of the shape formed by the points, this function appears to be exponential or quadratic.

As x increases, the function that best fits the points appears to decrease to zero. As x decreases, the function appears to increase without end.

Based on the scatter plot, an exponential function appears to are best represent this data.

SCAFFOLDING SUPPORT

- Students should understand that to find the number of survivors, they will need to subtract the number of deaths from the previous year's survivors. For the first year, they will need to subtract from the initial population of 1000 goats.

- If students are having trouble identifying the function that fits the goat data, encourage them to consider the scatter plot in two parts, one for the domain $0 \leq x \leq 10$ and one for the domain $10 < x \leq 20$.

EXERCISES

1. The table below shows the height of a baseball in inches x seconds after it was thrown. Fill in the table with the first differences and second differences. Then, use a graphing calculator to find the quadratic regression equation for the data. *(Lesson 23.1)*

Time	Height	First Difference	Second Difference
0	60	_____	_____
0.25	59	$59 - 60 = -1$	_____
0.5	57	$57 - 59 = -2$	$-2 + 1 = -1$
0.75	52	$52 - 57 = -5$	$-5 + 2 = -3$
1	44	$44 - 52 = -8$	$-8 + 5 = -3$
1.25	35	$35 - 44 = -9$	$-9 + 8 = -1$

$$y \approx -18.29x^2 + 2.86x + 59.86$$

2. The scatter plot shown represents a company's profit over 10 years. Which type of function best represents the data? *(Lesson 23.2)*

   A quadratic function appears to best fit the data. The curvature of the function traces a "U" shape, approximating the shape of a parabola.

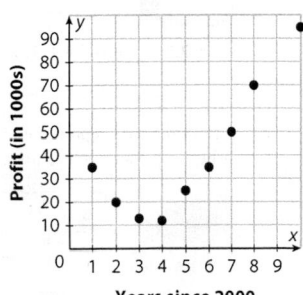

Years since 2000

MODULE PERFORMANCE TASK

What Model Fits a Survivorship Curve?

A survivorship curve shows the number of surviving members of a population over time from a given set of births. The graph shows the three types of survivorship curves that commonly occur.

The data table presents the results of a survivorship study for a population of 1000 goats. What type of survivorship curve most closely matches the goat data? Can you find a good mathematical model for these data, using either a linear, quadratic, or exponential function, or a combination of different functions over different parts of the data set?

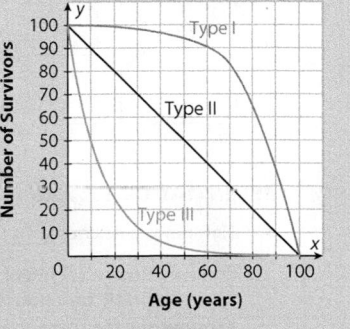

Age (years)

Age (years)	1	2	3	4	5	6	7	8	9	10
Number of Deaths During Year	12	13	9	11	12	11	9	11	11	11
Age (years)	11	12	13	14	15	16	17	18	19	20
Number of Deaths During Year	28	14	46	62	52	92	101	133	159	203

1144

Study Guide Review

DISCUSSION OPPORTUNITIES

What species could be modeled by each of the survival curve types and why?

SAMPLE SOLUTION (CONTINUED)

Calculate the number of survivors from the goat data:

Age	Survivors	Age	Survivors
1	988	11	862
2	975	12	848
3	966	13	802
4	955	14	740
5	943	15	688
6	932	16	596
7	923	17	495
8	912	18	362
9	901	19	203
10	890	20	0

Make a scatter plot of the data:

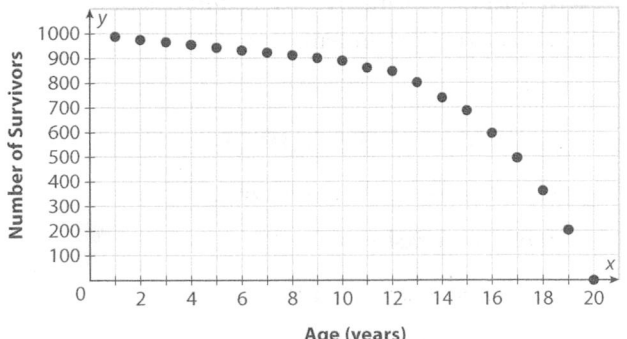

Age (years)

The data look like a Type I curve.

Looking at the first ten years, the data appear linear. Regression gives the model:

$$y = -10.77x + 997.7$$

For the second ten years, the data appear quadratic. Regression gives the model:

$$y = -10.34x^2 + 228.0x - 403.1$$

So the model is:

$$y = \begin{cases} -10.77x + 997.7, & 0 \le x \le 10 \\ -10.34x^2 + 228.0x - 403.1, & 10 < x \le 20 \end{cases}$$

Assessment Rubric

2 points: Student correctly solves the problem and explains his/her reasoning.

1 point: Student shows good understanding of the problem but does not fully solve or explain.

0 points: Student does not demonstrate understanding of the problem.

Study Guide Review **1144**

Ready to Go On?

ASSESS MASTERY

Use the assessment on this page to determine if students have mastered the concepts and standards covered in this module.

ASSESSMENT AND INTERVENTION

Access Ready to Go On? assessment online, and receive instant scoring, feedback, and customized intervention or enrichment.

ADDITIONAL RESOURCES

Response to Intervention Resources

- Reteach Worksheets

Differentiated Instruction Resources

- Reading Strategies **EL**
- Success for English Learners **EL**
- Challenge Worksheets

Assessment Resources

- Leveled Module Quizzes

(Ready) to Go On?

23.1–23.2 Linear, Exponential, and Quadratic Models

- Online Homework
- Hints and Help
- Extra Practice

1. The height of a plant, in inches, x weeks after it was planted is given in the table below. Use a graphing calculator to write a quadratic regression equation for the data set given. About how many weeks did it take the plant to reach a height of 40 inches? *(Lesson 23.1)*

Weeks	5	10	15	20	25
Height	15	31	55	87	127

$y = 0.16x^2 + 0.8x + 7$; about 12 weeks

2. Graph the data represented in the given table. Determine if the function represented in the given table is best represented by a linear, exponential, or quadratic function. Explain your answer. *(Lesson 23.2)*

x	−3	−2	−1	0	1	2	3
$f(x)$	5.5	3.5	1.5	1	0.6	0.3	0.1

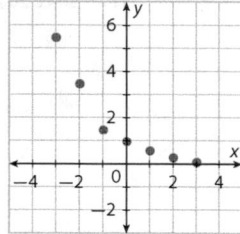

The data are best represented by an exponential function. The curvature of the function that best fits the data shows that it is either exponential or quadratic. The end behavior, which approaches 0 as x increases, indicates that the data are better represented by an exponential function.

ESSENTIAL QUESTION

3. How can you determine if a function is linear, quadratic, or exponential?

Possible Answer: A linear function grows by equal first differences over equal intervals; for a quadratic function, the second differences are equal over equal intervals. An exponential function changes by equal factors over equal intervals.

COMMON CORE Common Core Standards

Lesson	Exercise	Math Standards	Mathematical Practices
23.1	1	A-CED.A.2, F-IF.B.4, F-IF.B.5	MP.7
23.2	2	F-LE.A.1b	MP.6

Assessment Readiness

1. Consider each data set and if it is best represented by a linear, exponential, or quadratic model. Choose True or False for each statement.

   A. $\{(-5, 2), (-3, 6), (-1, 10), (1, 14), (3, 18)\}$
   is best represented by a linear model. ● True ○ False

   B. $\{(-2, 12), (-1, 6), (0, 3), (1, 1.5), (2, 0.75)\}$
   is best represented by a quadratic model. ○ True ● False

   C. $\{(-5, 4), (-4, 1), (-3, 0), (-2, 1), (-1, 4)\}$
   is best represented by an exponential
   model. ○ True ● False

2. Does the given equation have two real solutions? Select Yes or No for each equation.

   A. $6x^2 + 15 = 0$ ○ Yes ● No

   B. $8x^2 - 50 = 0$ ● Yes ○ No

   C. $3x^2 + 4x - 10 = 0$ ● Yes ○ No

3. Consider data represented by the following points:
   $\{(-2, 0.25), (-1, 1.5), (0, 4), (1, 15), (2, 60)\}$. Determine if the data are best represented by a linear, exponential, or quadratic function. Explain your answer.

   The data are best represented by an exponential model. The first differences are not constant, so the data should not be represented by a linear model. As x increases, the function appears to increase without end. As x decreases, the function appears to approach 0.

4. The equation $2x^2 + 8x + c = 0$ has one real solution. What is the value of c? Explain how you found the value of c.

   Possible answer: The value of c is 8. For the equation to have 1 real solution, the discriminant must equal zero, so $b^2 - 4ac = 8^2 - 4(2)c = 0$, so $8c = 64$ and $c = 8$.

MIXED REVIEW
Assessment Readiness

ASSESSMENT AND INTERVENTION

Assign ready-made or customized practice tests to prepare students for high-stakes tests.

ADDITIONAL RESOURCES

Assessment Resources

- Leveled Module Quizzes: Modified, B

AVOID COMMON ERRORS

Item 3   Some students have a hard time deciding between quadratic and exponential representations because they seem to have similar shapes when using only a few data points. Remind students to look for second differences. When the second differences are the same, the function must be quadratic. When the second differences are increasing or decreasing, the function may be exponential.

Common Core Standards

Lesson	Exercise	Math Standards	Mathematical Practices
23.1, 23.2	1	F-LE.A.1, F-LE.A.3	MP.4
22.3	2*	A-REI.B.4	MP.2
23.1, 23.2	3	F-LE.A.1, F-LE.A.3	MP.3
21.2	4*	A-SSE.A.2	MP.3

* Item integrates mixed review concepts from previous modules or a previous course.

MIXED REVIEW
Assessment Readiness

ASSESSMENT AND INTERVENTION

Assign ready-made or customized practice tests to prepare students for high-stakes tests.

ADDITIONAL RESOURCES

Assessment Resources

- Leveled Unit Tests: Modified, A, B, C
- Performance Assessment

AVOID COMMON ERRORS

Item 6 Since the first differences are the same, and the second differences are also shown and the same, some students will have a hard time choosing between linear and quadratic. Remind students that if a difference is consistently zero, the previous difference should be considered the correct difference.

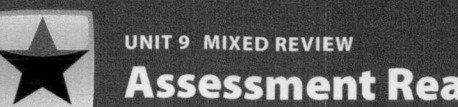

- Online Homework
- Hints and Help
- Extra Practice

1. A quadratic equation has the zeros −3 and 6. Can the quadratic equation be the given equation?

   A. $(2x + 6)(x - 6) = 0$ — ● Yes ○ No

   B. $(6x - 1)(x + 3) = 0$ — ○ Yes ● No

   C. $-3x(x - 6) = 0$ — ○ Yes ● No

2. Factor and solve each equation. Does the equation have a solution of $x = -5$?

   A. $3x^2 + 14x - 5 = 0$ — ● Yes ○ No

   B. $x^2 + 3x - 40 = 0$ — ○ Yes ● No

   C. $x^2 - 3x - 40 = 0$ — ● Yes ○ No

3. Consider the equation $4x^2 - 20 = 0$. Is the given statement True or False?

   A. The equation has 2 solutions. — ● True ○ False

   B. A zero of the related function is $-\sqrt{20}$. — ○ True ● False

   C. A solution of the equation is $\sqrt{5}$. — ● True ○ False

4. Solve $\left(2x + \frac{2}{3}\right)(x + 5) = 0$. Is the given value a solution of the equation?

   A. $x = -\frac{1}{3}$ — ● Yes ○ No

   B. $x = -5$ — ● Yes ○ No

   C. $x = \frac{2}{3}$ — ○ Yes ● No

5. The equation $ax^2 + 12x + c = 0$ has one solution. Can a and c equal each of the following values?

   A. $a = 4, c = 9$ — ● Yes ○ No

   B. $a = 9, c = 16$ — ○ Yes ● No

   C. $a = 36, c = 1$ — ● Yes ○ No

Unit 9   **1147**

Common Core Standards

Items	Content Standards	Mathematical Practices
1*	A-APR.B.3	MP.7
2	A-SSE.B.3a	MP.2
3	A-REI.A.2	MP.1
4*	A-APR.B.3	MP.2
5	A-SSE.A.2	MP.2
6	F-LE.A.3	MP.5

* Item integrates mixed review concepts from previous modules or a previous course.

6. The table given has been filled out for the function $g(x)$. The values of $g(x)$ are not shown. Is $g(x)$ a linear or quadratic function? Justify your answer.

x	$g(x)$	First Difference	Second Difference
−2	_____	_____	_____
0	_____	−4	_____
2	_____	−4	0
4	_____	−4	0
6	_____	−4	0

It's a linear function because the first difference is constant.

7. The area of a square table top can be represented by $(9x^2 − 30x + 25)$ square feet. The perimeter of the table top is 34 feet. What is the value of x? Explain how you solved this problem.

4.5; Each side of the table is 8.5 ft long. I factored $(9x^2 − 30x + 25)$ which is a perfect square trinomial. Each side of the table is also $(3x − 5)$ ft long. I solved $3x − 5 = 8.5$ and found that $x = 4.5$.

8. Solve $4x^2 + 8x = −3$. Which of the following solution methods did you use: factoring, completing the square, or the quadratic formula? Why? Show your work.

Possible answer: I completed the square because 4 is a perfect square.

$4x^2 + 8x = −3$

$4x^2 + 8x + 4 = −3 + 4$

$(2x + 2)^2 = 1$

$2x + 2 = 1$ or $2x + 2 = −1$

$2x = −1$ or $2x = −3$

$x = −0.5$ or $x = −1.5$

Performance Tasks

★ **9.** Abigail has a rectangular quilt with dimensions 36 inches by 48 inches. She decides to sew a border on the quilt, so that the total area of the quilt is 1900 square inches. What will be the width of the border?

1 inch

Dimensions of quilt with border should be $36 + 2x$ and $48 + 2x$, so $(36 + 2x)(48 + 2x) = 1900$. Solve to get $x = 1$ or $x = −43$. Use the positive value for x. Finished dimensions are 38 inches by 50 inches.

PERFORMANCE TASKS

There are three different levels of performance tasks:

   * **Novice:** These are short word problems that require students to apply the math they have learned in straightforward, real-world situations.

   ** **Apprentice:** These are more involved problems that guide students step-by-step through more complex tasks. These exercises include more complicated reasoning, writing, and open-ended elements.

   *****Expert:** These are open-ended, nonroutine problems that, instead of stepping the students through, ask them to choose their own methods for solving and justify their answers and reasoning.

SCORING GUIDES

Item 9 (2 points)   2 points for correct answer

COMMON CORE **Common Core Standards**

Items	Content Standards	Mathematical Practices
7*	A-CED.A.1	MP.4
8	A-REI.B.4b	MP.3

* Item integrates mixed review concepts from previous modules or a previous course.

SCORING GUIDES

Item 10 (6 points)

A. 1 point for reasonable choice

   1 point for explanation

B. 1 point for reasonable prediction

C. 1 point for correct answer

   2 points for explanation

Item 11 (6 points)

A. 1 point for correct models

B. 1 point for correct function for College 1

   1 point for correct function for College 2

C. 1 point for correct explanation

D. 2 points for correct explanation

★★**10.** The table shows the average weight of a particular variety of sheep of various ages.

Sheep	
Age (mo)	Weight (lb)
2	36
4	69
6	99
8	120
10	135

A. None of the three models—linear, quadratic, or exponential—fits the data exactly. Which of these is the best model for the data? Explain your choice.

B. What would you predict for the weight of a sheep that is 1 year old?

C. Do you think you could use your model to find the weight of a sheep any age? Why or why not?

Possible answers:

A. quadratic: the second differences are approximately constant, while first differences and ratios are decreasing.

B. about 144 lbs

C. No; this quadratic model will begin to decrease although the sheep's weight will continue to grow at a decreasing rate until it eventually remains constant.

★★★**11.** Examine the two models that represent annual tuition for two colleges.

A. Describe each model as linear, quadratic, or exponential.

B. Write a function rule for each model.

C. Both models have the same value for year 0. What does this mean?

D. Why do both models have the same value for year 1?

Years After 2004	Tuition at College 1 ($)	Tuition at College 2 ($)
0	2000.00	2000.00
1	2200.00	2200.00
2	2400.00	2420.00
3	2600.00	2662.00
4	2800.00	2928.20

A. College 1: linear; College 2: exponential

B. College 1: $y = 200x + 2000$

   College 2: $y = 2000(1.1)^x$

C. Both have the same tuition ($2000) in 2004.

D. For College 1, $200 is added each year. For College 2, 10% is added each year, so $(0.1)(2000) = \$200$ is added in the first year. So tuition for each college in year 1 is $2000 + 200 = \$2200$.

Competitive Diver Franco and Grace are competitive divers. Grace dives from a 20-meter cliff into the water, with an initial upward speed of 3.2 m/s. Franco dives from a springboard that is 10 meters above the water surface with an initial upward speed of 4.2 m/s.

The height in meters of an object projected into the air with an initial vertical velocity of v meters per second and initial height of h_0 can be modeled by $h(t) = -4.9t^2 + vt + h_0$.

a. Write a function $h_{Grace}(t)$ that models the height of Grace's dive.

b. Write a function $h_{Franco}(t)$ that models the height of Franco's dive.

c. Use a graphing calculator to graph both functions on the same screen. Label each function.

d. What are the domain and range of each function in terms of the situation? Explain. Round values to the nearest tenth.

e. Compare the maximum heights and the time that elapses before each diver hits the water.

---

a. $h_{Grace}(t) = -4.9t^2 + 3.2t + 20$

b. $h_{Franco}(t) = -4.9t 2 + 4.2t + 10$

c.

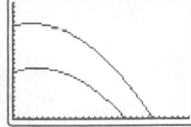

d. **Grace: domain, approximately $0 \le t \le 2.4$; range approximately $0 \le h \le 20.5$.**

Franco: domain, approximately $0 \le t \le 1.9$; range, $0 \le h \le 10.9$.

The domain represents the times t for the duration of the dive, the range represents heights h at or above the surface of the water during the dive.

e. **Grace: maximum height, about 20.5 m; time for dive, about 2.4 s**

Franco: maximum height, 10.9 m; time for dive, about 1.9 s

Grace achieves a greater height and stays in the air longer than Franco.

MATH IN CAREERS

Competitive Diver In this Unit Performance Task, students can see how a competitive diver uses mathematics on the job.

For more information about careers in mathematics as well as various mathematics appreciation topics, visit the American Mathematical Society at http://www.ams.org.

SCORING GUIDE

Task (6 points)

a. 1 point for correct function

b. 1 point for correct function

c. 1 point for correct graph

d. 1 point for correct ranges and domains
   1 point for explanation

e. 1 point for correct values and comparisons

UNIT 10

Inverse Relationships

CONTENTS

Unit Pacing Guide

45-Minute Classes

Module 24

DAY 1	DAY 2	DAY 3	DAY 4	DAY 5
Lesson 24.1	**Lesson 24.1**	**Lesson 24.2**	**Lesson 24.2**	**Lesson 24.3**

DAY 6	DAY 7	DAY 8		
Lesson 24.4	**Module Review and Assessment Readiness**	**Unit Review and Assessment Readiness**		

90-Minute Classes

Module 24

DAY 1	DAY 2	DAY 3	DAY 4
Lesson 24.1	**Lesson 24.2**	**Lesson 24.3**	**Module Review and Assessment Readiness**
		Lesson 24.4	**Unit Review and Assessment Readiness**

Program Resources

PLAN

HMH Teacher App

Access a full suite of teacher resources online and offline on a variety of devices. Plan present, and manage classes, assignments, and activities.

ePlanner Easily plan your classes, create and view assignments, and access all program resources with your online, customizable planning tool.

Professional Development Videos

Authors Juli Dixon and Matt Larson model successful teaching practices and strategies in actual classroom settings.

QR Codes Scan with your smart phone to jump directly from your print book to online videos and other resources.

Teacher's Edition

Support students with point-of-use Questioning Strategies, teaching tips, resources for differentiated instruction, additional activities, and more.

ENGAGE AND EXPLORE

Real-World Videos Engage students with interesting and relevant applications of the mathematical content of each module.

Explore Activities

Students interactively explore new concepts using a variety of tools and approaches.

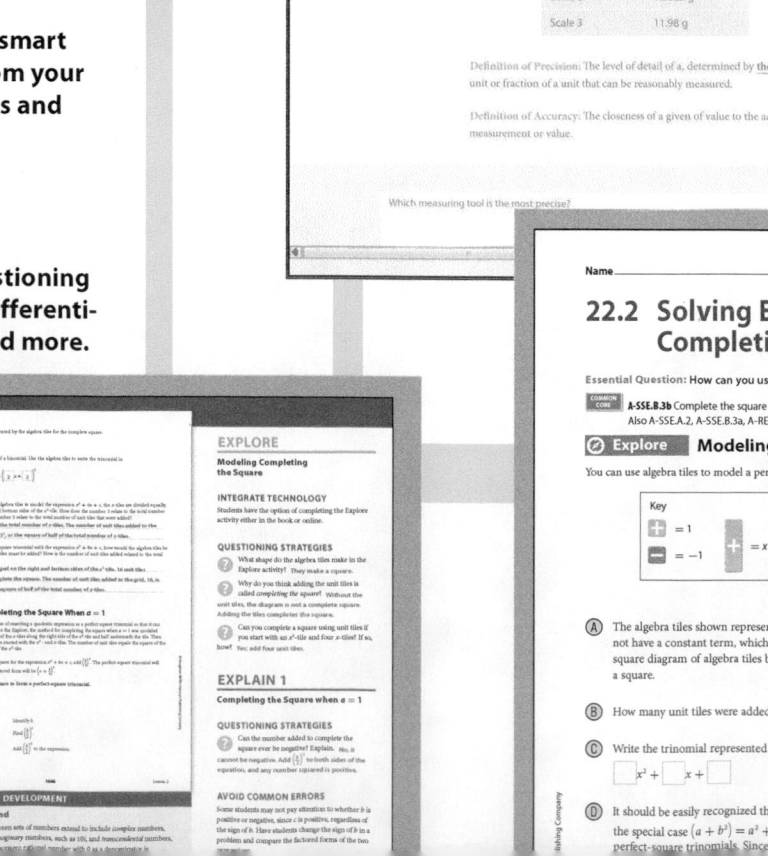

Name _____ Class _____ Date _____

22.2 Solving Equations by Completing the Square

Essential Question: How can you use completing the square to solve a quadratic equation?

COMMON CORE **A-SSE.B.3b** Complete the square ... to reveal the maximum or minimum value of the function ... Also A-SSE.A.2, A-SSE.B.3a, A-REI.B.4b, A-REI.B.4a, F-IF.C.8a

Resource Locker

Explore Modeling Completing the Square

You can use algebra tiles to model a perfect square trinomial.

Key

$+$ = 1 $-$ = −1 $+$ = x $-$ = −x $+$ = x^2 $-$ = $-x^2$

(A) The algebra tiles shown represent the expression $x^2 + 6x$. The expression does not have a constant term, which would be represented with unit tiles. Create a square diagram of algebra tiles by adding the correct number of unit tiles to form a square.

(B) How many unit tiles were added to the expression? _____

(C) Write the trinomial represented by the algebra tiles for the complete square.

☐x^2 + ☐x + ☐

(D) It should be easily recognized that the trinomial ☐x^2 + ☐x + ☐ is an example of the special case $(a + b)^2 = a^2 + 2ab + b^2$. Recall that trinomials of this form are called perfect-square trinomials. Since the trinomial is a perfect square, it can be factored into two

TEACH

Math On the Spot video tutorials, featuring program author Dr. Edward Burger, accompany every example in the textbook and give students step-by-step instructions and explanations of key math concepts.

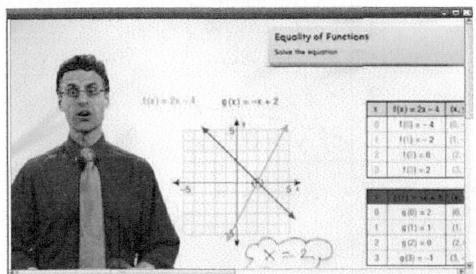

Interactive Teacher Edition

Customize and present course materials with collaborative activities and integrated formative assessment.

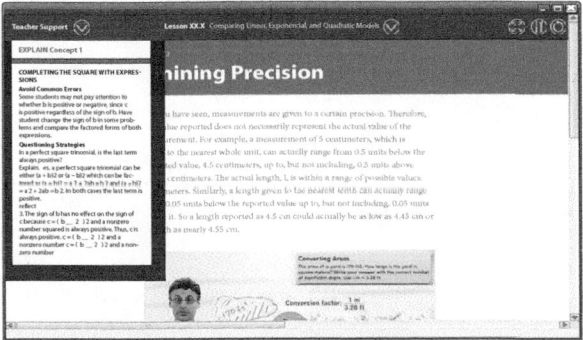

Differentiated Instruction Resources

Support all learners with Differentiated Instruction Resources, including

- **Leveled Practice and Problem Solving**
- **Reading Strategies**
- **Success for English Learners**
- **Challenge**

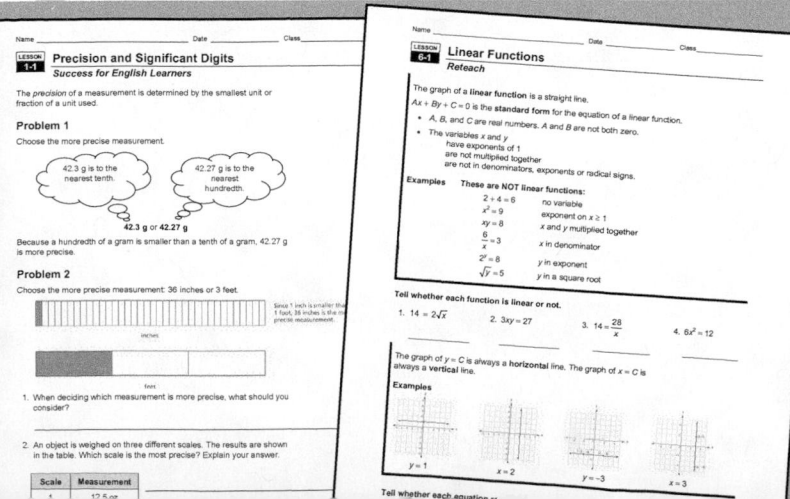

ASSESSMENT AND INTERVENTION

 The **Personal Math Trainer** provides online practice, homework, assessments, and intervention. Monitor student progress through reports and alerts. **Create and customize assignments aligned to specific lessons or Common Core standards.**

- **Practice** – With dynamic items and assignments, students get unlimited practice on key concepts supported by guided examples, step-by-step solutions, and video tutorials.

- **Assessments** – Choose from course assignments or customize your own based on course content, Common Core standards, difficulty levels, and more.

- **Homework** – Students can complete online homework with a wide variety of problem types, including the ability to enter expressions, equations, and graphs. Let the system automatically grade homework, so you can focus where your students need help the most!

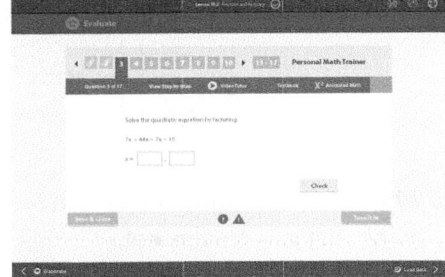

- **Intervention** – Let the Personal Math Trainer automatically prescribe a targeted, personalized intervention path for your students.

Focus on Higher Order Thinking

Raise the bar with homework and practice that incorporates higher-order thinking and mathematical practices in every lesson.

Assessment Readiness

Prepare students for success on high stakes tests for Algebra 1 with practice at every module and unit

COMMON CORE

Assessment Resources

Tailor assessments and response to intervention to meet the needs of all your classes and students, including

- Leveled Module Quizzes
- Leveled Unit Tests
- Unit Performance Tasks
- Placement, Diagnostic, and Quarterly Benchmark Tests
- Tier 1, Tier 2, and Tier 3 Resources

Math Background

Functions and Inverses [COMMON CORE] F-BF.B.4a

LESSONS 24.2 to 24.4

Given a relation defined by a set of ordered pairs (x, y), the inverse relation is the set of ordered pairs (y, x).

This means that the graph of an inverse relation is the *reflection* of the graph of the original relation across the line $y = x$.

The graph below shows that $y = \pm\sqrt{x}$ is the inverse relation of $y = x^2$.

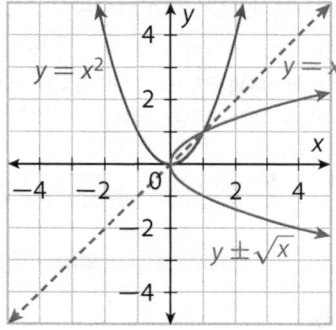

While $y = x^2$ is a function, we can see immediately from the graph that $y = \pm\sqrt{x}$ is not.

The relation becomes a function when the domain of $y = x^2$ is restricted to nonnegative values of x. In this case, the inverse function is the principal square root of x; that is, $y = \sqrt{x}$. This corresponds to the portion of the graph of $y = \pm\sqrt{x}$ that lies on or above the x-axis.

Note that for $y = x^3$ no restrictions are necessary to ensure that the inverse relation is a function. The inverse function is simply $y = \sqrt[3]{x}$. In this case, both the original function and its inverse have all real numbers as the domain and all real numbers as the range.

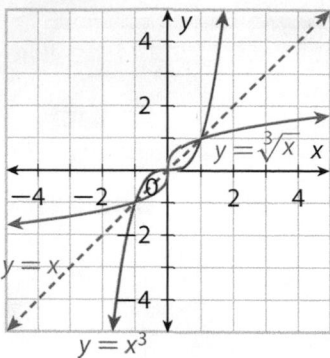

Square Roots and Cube Roots $\;$ COMMON CORE $\;$ F-IF.C.7b

LESSONS 24.3 and 24.4

In Algebra 1, students have learned that $\sqrt{x^2} = |x|$. This is because the symbol $\sqrt{}$ indicates the principal, or nonnegative, square root. The absolute-value symbol is important since x may be negative.

When simplifying other combinations of radicals and powers, the situation becomes more complicated. Absolute value is not needed for $\sqrt[3]{x^3}$ because a cube root may be positive or negative. On the other hand, $\sqrt{x^6} = |x^3|$ since x^3 may be negative but the symbol indicates that the square root must be nonnegative. To simplify matters, students may assume that all variables are nonnegative unless otherwise specified.

Rational exponents are defined to be consistent with definitions and properties for integer exponents. For example, given a real number a, we want to define $a^{\frac{1}{3}}$ so that it is consistent with the Power of a Power Property; it must be true that $\left(a^{\frac{1}{3}}\right)^3 = a^{\frac{1}{3} \cdot 3} = a^1 = a$.

This shows that $a^{\frac{1}{3}}$ must be the cube root of a: $a^{\frac{1}{3}} = \sqrt[3]{a}$. In general, for any natural number n, $a^{\frac{1}{n}} = \sqrt[n]{a}$.

Similarly, in defining $a^{\frac{m}{n}}$ where m is an integer and n is a natural number, the Power of a Power Property should be true:

$$a^{\frac{m}{n}} = \left(a^{\frac{1}{n}}\right)^m = (a^m)^{\frac{1}{n}}.$$

Using $a^{\frac{1}{n}} = \sqrt[n]{a}$ shows that the required definition is $a^{\frac{m}{n}} = \left(\sqrt[n]{a}\right)^m = \sqrt[n]{a^m}$.

Inverse Relationships

MATH IN CAREERS
Unit Activity Preview

After completing this unit, students will complete a Math in Careers task by examining a model for the length and weight of a freshwater fish. Critical skills include writing an inverse function, describing what the inverse function means for the given situation, and finding a reasonable domain and range for the inverse function model.

For more information about careers in mathematics as well as various mathematics appreciation topics, visit The American Mathematical Society at http://www.ams.org.

UNIT 10

MODULE 24
Functions and Inverses

Inverse Relationships

MATH IN CAREERS

Ichthyologist An ichthyologist is a biologist who specializes in the study of fish. Ichthyologists work in a variety of disciplines relating to fish and their environment, including ecology, taxonomy, behavior, and conservation. Ichthyologists might perform tasks such as monitoring water quality, designing and conducting experiments, evaluating data using statistics, and publishing results in scientific journals. Ichthyologists utilize mathematical models and collect and analyze experimental and observational data to help them understand fish and their environment.

If you are interested in a career as an ichthyologist, you should study these mathematical subjects:
- Geometry
- Algebra
- Statistics
- Calculus

Research other careers that require using mathematical models to understand an organism and its environment. Check out the career activity at the end of the unit to find out how **ichthyologists** use math.

Unit 10   1151

TRACKING YOUR LEARNING PROGRESSION

Before	In this Unit	After
Students understand: • fitting linear models to data • solving systems of equations • adding, subtracting, and multiplying polynomials	Students will learn about: • graphing polynomial functions • understanding inverse functions • graphing square root functions • graphing cube root functions	Students will study: • transforming functions graphically and algebraically • working with absolute value functions, rational functions, and logarithmic functions

Reading Start-Up

Visualize Vocabulary

Use the ✔ words to complete the graphic.

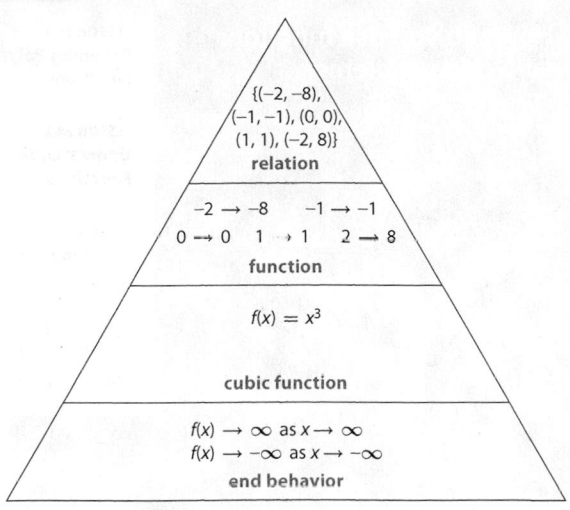

{(−2, −8), (−1, −1), (0, 0), (1, 1), (−2, 8)}
relation

−2 → −8   −1 → −1
0 → 0   1 → 1   2 → 8
function

$f(x) = x^3$

cubic function

$f(x) \to \infty$ as $x \to \infty$
$f(x) \to -\infty$ as $x \to -\infty$
end behavior

Vocabulary

Review Words
✔ cubic function *(función cúbica)*
✔ end behavior *(comportamiento extremo)*
✔ function *(función)*
✔ relation *(relación)*

Preview Words
cube root function *(función raíz cúbica)*
inverse function *(función inversa)*
inverse relation *(relación inversa)*
radical function *(función radical)*
square root function *(function de raíz cuadrada)*
turning point *(punto de inflexión)*

Understand Vocabulary

To become familiar with some of the vocabulary terms in the module, consider the following. You may refer to the module, the glossary, or a dictionary.

1. An **inverse function** results from exchanging the input and output values of a one-to-one function.

2. A **radical function** has a rule that contains a variable within a radical.

3. A **turning point** occurs on the graph of a function where the graph changes from increasing to decreasing (or vice versa).

Active Reading

Tri-Fold As you complete each lesson in this unit, create a tri-fold to help you track your progress with the material in the lesson. Organize the lesson topic into what you know, what you want to know, and what you learn. Label the three sections "Know," "Want," and "Learn" and record notes to see how much you have learned after completing the lesson. Be sure to use exact vocabulary and to include specific examples, with corresponding graphs, in your notes.

Reading Start Up

Have students complete the activities on this page by working alone or with others.

VISUALIZE VOCABULARY

The information graphic helps students review vocabulary for a function and its relationship with relations, specific functions, and characteristics of functions. If time allows, discuss how the review words are related.

UNDERSTAND VOCABULARY

Use the following explanations to help students learn the preview words.

All functions have an **inverse relation** that may or may not be an **inverse function**. The **square root function** is an example of the inverse of a quadratic function (with a domain restricted to positive values). Similarly, the **cube root function** is the inverse of a cubic function. Both the square root and cube root functions are examples of **radical functions**, which are functions with a variable under a radical symbol.

ACTIVE READING

Students can use these reading and note-taking strategies to help them organize and understand the new concepts and vocabulary in the unit.

ADDITIONAL RESOURCES

Differentiated Instruction

• Reading Strategies

Functions and Inverses

ESSENTIAL QUESTION:

Answer: If you have a formula that represents a relationship between two variables in any real-world situation, you can use the inverse to find the independent variable given the dependent variable.

PROFESSIONAL DEVELOPMENT VIDEO

Professional Development Video

Author Juli Dixon models successful teaching practices in an actual high-school classroom.

Professional Development
my.hrw.com

MODULE

24

Functions and Inverses

Essential Question: How can you use functions and inverses to solve real-world problems?

© Houghton Mifflin Harcourt Publishing Company • ©Mandy Godbehear/ Alamy

REAL WORLD VIDEO
Balls of different diameters and volumes can present a variety of packaging challenges for sports equipment manufacturers. Check out how inverse functions can help lead to efficient solutions.

MODULE PERFORMANCE TASK PREVIEW

The Smallest Cube

If you know the dimensions of a box that is shaped like a rectangular prism, you can easily find the volume of the box using the formula $v = l \times w \times h$. But what if you know the volume and want to know the dimensions? That's the problem package designers face when they know the size of a new product and must find the dimensions of the package it will be sold in. You'll do just that after you learn to "unpack" functions in this module—that is, find their inverses.

Module 24

DIGITAL TEACHER EDITION

Access a full suite of teaching resources when and where you need them:

- Access content online or offline
- Customize lessons to share with your class
- Communicate with your students in real-time
- View student grades and data instantly to target your instruction where it is needed most

PERSONAL MATH TRAINER
Assessment and Intervention

Assign automatically graded homework, quizzes, tests, and intervention activities. Prepare your students with updated, Common Core-aligned practice tests.

Are YOU Ready?

Complete these exercises to review skills you will need for this module.

Squares and Square Roots

Example 1   Evaluate $\sqrt{225}$.

Since $15^2 = 15 \cdot 15 = 225$,
the square root of 225 is 15.

- Online Homework
- Hints and Help
- Extra Practice

Evaluate.

1. $\sqrt{144}$
$\underline{12}$

2. $\sqrt{256}$
$\underline{16}$

3. $\sqrt{\frac{4}{9}}$
$\underline{\frac{2}{3}}$

Cubes and Cube Roots

Example 2   Evaluate $\sqrt[3]{-27}$.

Since $(-3)^3 = (-3) \cdot (-3) \cdot (-3) = -27$,
the cube root of –27 is –3.

Evaluate.

4. $\sqrt[3]{1000}$
$\underline{10}$

5. $\sqrt[3]{-125}$
$\underline{-5}$

6. $\sqrt[3]{-64}$
$\underline{-4}$

Linear Functions

Example 3   Write $8x - 2y = 20$ in slope-intercept form.

$-2y = -8x + 20$ Isolate the y-term.

$y = 4x - 10$ Divide both sides by –2.

Write each equation in slope-intercept form.

7. $2x + 3y = 24$
$y = -\frac{2}{3}x + 8$

8. $3(2y - x) = -15$
$y = 0.5x - 2.5$

9. $3x + 0.4y = -1$
$y = -7.5x - 2.5$

Are You Ready?

ASSESS READINESS

Use the assessment on this page to determine if students need strategic or intensive intervention for the module's prerequisite skills.

ASSESSMENT AND INTERVENTION

Personal Math Trainer

RtI Response to Intervention **TIER 1, TIER 2, TIER 3 SKILLS**

Personal Math Trainer will automatically create a standards-based, personalized intervention assignment for your students, targeting each student's individual needs!

ADDITIONAL RESOURCES

See the table below for a full list of intervention resources available for this module.

Response to Intervention Resources also includes:

- Tier 2 Skill Pre-Tests for each Module
- Tier 2 Skill Post-Tests for each skill

Response to Intervention			Differentiated Instruction
Tier 1	**Tier 2**	**Tier 3**	
Lesson Intervention Worksheets	Strategic Intervention Skills Intervention Worksheets	Intensive Intervention Worksheets available online	
Reteach 24.1 Reteach 24.2 Reteach 24.3 Reteach 24.4	6 Graphing Linear Nonproportional ... 10 Linear Functions 31 Squares and ... 32 Cubes and Cube Roots	Building Block Skills 22, 23, 27, 29, 30, 38, 40, 46, 70, 100	Challenge worksheets Extend the Math Lesson Activities in TE

Graphing Polynomial Functions

Common Core Math Standards

The student is expected to:

 F-IF.C.7c

Graph polynomial functions, identifying zeros when suitable factorizations are available, and showing end behavior. Also F-BF.B.3

Mathematical Practices

 MP.6 Precision

Language Objective

Explain to a partner how to recognize the graph of a polynomial function of odd degree.

ENGAGE

Essential Question: How does the value of *n* affect the end behavior of the function $f(x) = x^n$?

For all values of n, $f(x)$ approaches $+\infty$ as x approaches $+\infty$. If n is even, then $f(x)$ approaches $+\infty$ as x approaches $-\infty$. If n is odd, then $f(x)$ approaches $-\infty$ as x approaches $-\infty$.

PREVIEW: LESSON PERFORMANCE TASK

View the Engage section online. Discuss how you could use a polynomial to model the volume of a package of a given shape. Then preview the Lesson Performance Task.

24.1 Graphing Polynomial Functions

Essential Question: How does the value of *n* affect the behavior of the function $f(x) = x^n$?

Explore **Exploring Graphs of Cubic and Quartic Functions**

Resource Locker

The **end behavior** of a function is a description of the values of the function as x approaches positive infinity ($x \rightarrow +\infty$) or negative infinity ($x \rightarrow -\infty$). The degree and leading coefficient of a polynomial function determine its end behavior.

(A) Use your graphing calculator to plot each of the cubic functions in the table, and complete the table to describe each function's general shape and end behavior.

Function	Number of Direction Changes	End Behavior as $x \rightarrow +\infty$	End Behavior as $x \rightarrow -\infty$
$f(x) = x^3 - 5x$	2	$f(x) \rightarrow \boxed{+\infty}$	$f(x) \rightarrow \boxed{-\infty}$
$f(x) = -2x^3$	0	$f(x) \rightarrow \boxed{-\infty}$	$f(x) \rightarrow \boxed{+\infty}$
$f(x) = \frac{3}{2}x^3 + x + 1$	0	$f(x) \rightarrow \boxed{+\infty}$	$f(x) \rightarrow \boxed{-\infty}$

(B) All three of these functions are cubic, which means that they have degree ___3___. Their shapes vary, but one feature they all share is that the end behavior is the (same/opposite) on the two ends.

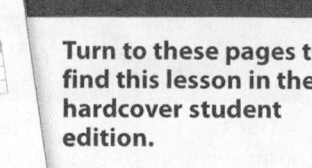

HARDCOVER PAGES 899–908

Turn to these pages to find this lesson in the hardcover student edition.

Ⓒ The graphs show quartic functions. Fill in the blanks to describe each function's general shape and end behavior.

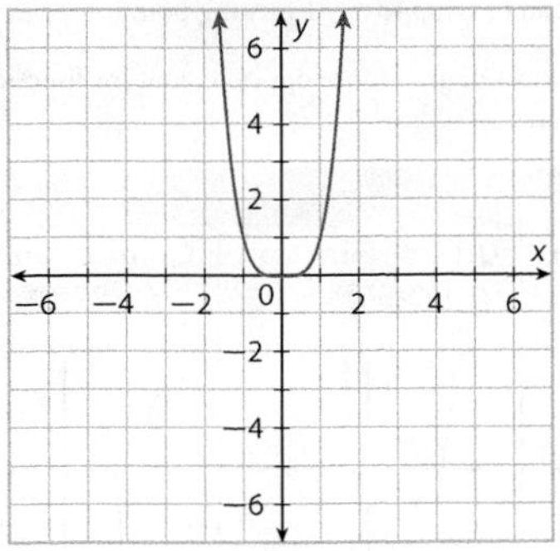

$f(x) = x^4$

1 direction change(s)

As $x \to +\infty$, $f(x) \to$ $+\infty$.

As $x \to -\infty$, $f(x) \to$ $+\infty$.

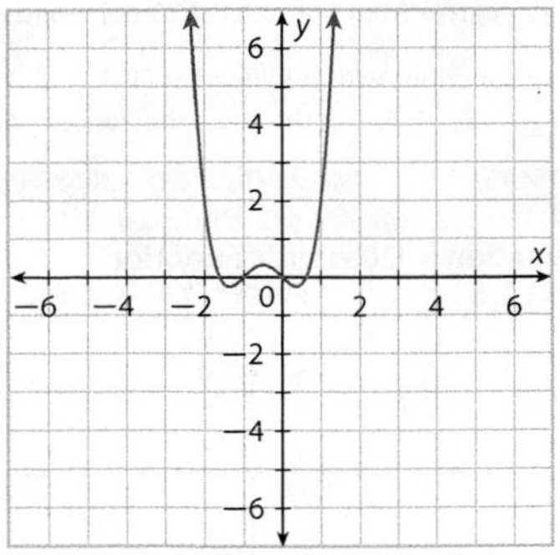

$f(x) = x^4 + 2x^3 - x$

3 direction change(s)

As $x \to +\infty$, $f(x) \to$ $+\infty$.

As $x \to -\infty$, $f(x) \to$ $+\infty$.

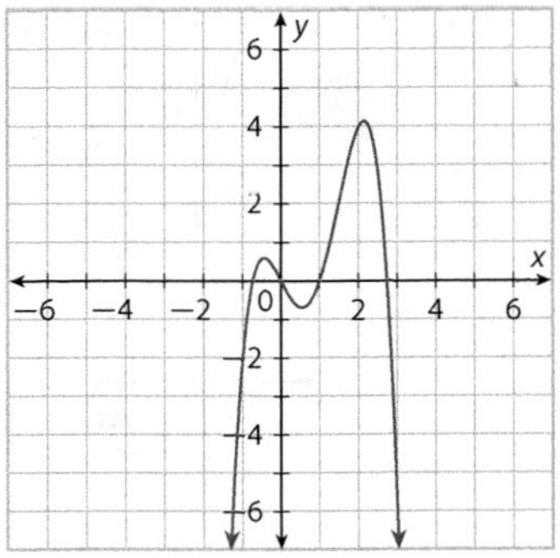

$f(x) = -x^4 + 3x^3 - 2x$

3 direction change(s)

As $x \to +\infty$, $f(x) \to$ $-\infty$.

As $x \to -\infty$, $f(x) \to$ $-\infty$.

Ⓓ All three of these functions are quartic, which means that they have degree 4. Their shapes vary, but one feature they all share is that the end behavior is the (same / opposite) on the two ends.

Each of the graphs of the functions in Steps A and C change directions at least once. These direction changes are called **turning points**.

Reflect

1. **Discussion** How many turning points did the cubic functions have? the quartic functions? Do you notice a pattern?
The cubic functions had 0 or 2 turning points. The quartic functions had 1 or 3 turning points. The numbers of turning points for cubic functions are even, while the numbers of turning points for quartic functions are odd.

EXPLORE

Exploring Graphs of Cubic and Quartic Functions

INTEGRATE TECHNOLOGY

Students will use graphing calculators to explore the shapes and end behaviors of the graphs of cubic and quartic functions.

QUESTIONING STRATEGIES

Can you distinguish between a cubic and quartic function by examining the end behavior for one end of the graph? Explain. **No; you must examine end behaviors for both $x \to -\infty$ and $x \to +\infty$ to distinguish between cubic and quartic functions. Both types of functions may approach either positive or negative infinity at either end, but the end behavior is opposite at the two ends for cubic functions, while it is the same at both ends for quartic functions.**

PROFESSIONAL DEVELOPMENT

Integrate Mathematical Practices

This lesson provides an opportunity to use Mathematical Practice **MP.6**, which asks students to "attend to precision." In this lesson, students must use precise language to accurately identify the differences between polynomial functions of even and odd degree, including symmetry, number of turning points, and end behavior at each end of the domain and range.

EXPLAIN 1

Even and Odd Degree Polynomial Functions

INTEGRATE MATHEMATICAL PRACTICES

Focus on Reasoning

MP.2 Ask students to list the possible numbers of turning points for polynomial functions of various degrees. Students should understand that a polynomial function of degree n has at most $n - 1$ turning points. They should also see that in order to have the correct end behavior, a function of even degree must have an odd number of turning points, while a function of odd degree must have an even number of turning points. Therefore, a linear function has 0 turning points, a quadratic function has 1, a cubic function has 0 or 2, and a quartic function has 1 or 3 turning points.

The degree of a polynomial affects the shape of its graph. The table shows representative graphs for polynomial functions with degrees from 1 through 5. A polynomial of degree n can have up to $n - 1$ turning points.

Notice that for functions with odd degrees (1, 3, 5, …), the end behaviors of graphs are opposite, and for functions with even degrees (2, 4, 6, …), the end behaviors of graphs are the same.

Graphs of Polynomial Functions				
Linear Function Degree 1	Quadratic Function Degree 2	Cubic Function Degree 3	Quartic Function Degree 4	Quintic Function Degree 5

The sign of the leading coefficient determines the end behavior. The table summarizes the end behavior rules for polynomials.

$f(x)$ is a polynomial with...	Odd Degree	Even Degree
Leading coefficient $a > 0$	As $x \to +\infty$, $f(x) \to +\infty$ As $x \to -\infty$, $f(x) \to -\infty$	As $x \to -\infty$, $f(x) \to +\infty$ As $x \to +\infty$, $f(x) \to +\infty$
Leading coefficient $a < 0$	As $x \to -\infty$, $f(x) \to +\infty$ As $x \to +\infty$, $f(x) \to -\infty$	As $x \to -\infty$, $f(x) \to -\infty$ As $x \to +\infty$, $f(x) \to -\infty$

Example 1 For each graph, identify whether the polynomial $f(x)$ is of odd or even degree, and whether the leading coefficient is positive or negative.

Ⓐ

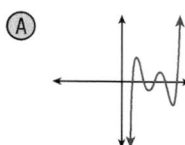

End behavior:

As $x \to +\infty$, $f(x) \to +\infty$.

The leading coefficient is positive.

As $x \to -\infty$, $f(x) \to -\infty$

⇒ Opposite end behaviors

⇒ The polynomial's degree is odd.

COLLABORATIVE LEARNING

Small Group Activity

Have students work in groups of three or four. Have each student roll a number cube four times, use the results as the coordinates of two points, and graph those points on a coordinate grid. Then have each student roll the number cube again and sketch the graph of a polynomial function of that degree so that it passes through the two graphed points. Finally, ask students to explain to others in their group whether the function is even, odd, or neither.

Ⓑ

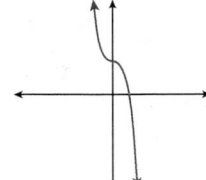

As $x \to +\infty$, $f(x) \to \boxed{-\infty}$.

$\Rightarrow$ The leading coefficient is negative.

As of $x \to -\infty$, $f(x) \to \boxed{-\infty}$.

$\Rightarrow$ $\boxed{\text{Same}}$ end behaviors

$\Rightarrow$ The polynomial's degree is $\boxed{\text{even}}$.

Reflect

2. **Discussion** Explain why the leading coefficient is the only polynomial coefficient that determines end-behavior.

As *x* moves away from 0, the highest-degree term increases or decreases the fastest. Far

enough from 0, the highest-degree term will be greater (or less) than all of the other

terms and the function will not turn again.

Your Turn

For each graph, identify whether the polynomial is of odd or even degree, and whether the leading coefficient is positive or negative.

3.

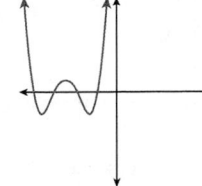

Odd degree, negative leading coefficient

4.

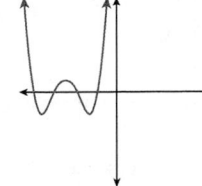

Even degree, positive leading coefficient

❓ If the graph of a polynomial function decreases as *x* approaches both negative and positive infinity, what can you conclude about the leading term of the polynomial? **The leading term has a negative coefficient and an even degree.**

DIFFERENTIATE INSTRUCTION

Cognitive Strategies

Have students create cards showing the general shapes of graphs of polynomial functions of degree 2 through degree 5. They may choose to sketch two graphs on each card, one for a function with a positive leading coefficient, and the other for a function with a negative leading coefficient. On the back of each card, suggest students add additional information about each function, such as the possible numbers of turning points, the end behavior in each direction, and whether the function can be even or odd. Students can use the cards as a reference when interpreting the graphs of polynomial functions.

EXPLAIN 2

Classifying Even and Odd Functions

AVOID COMMON ERRORS

Students may believe that any polynomial function of even degree is even and any function of odd degree is odd. Remind them that for a function to be even, its graph must be symmetric about the y-axis, and for a function to be odd, its graph must be rotationally symmetric around the origin. While some even-degree polynomials are even functions and some odd-degree polynomials are odd functions, some polynomials are neither even nor odd.

INTEGRATE MATHEMATICAL PRACTICES

Focus on Reasoning

MP.2 Have students compare the graphs of the parent functions $f(x) = x^2$ and $f(x) = x^4$ with related functions such as $f(x) = x^2 - 5x$, $f(x) = x^2 - 5$, $f(x) = x^4 - 3x^3$, and $f(x) = x^4 - 3x^2$, and determine which are even functions and which are not. Students should understand that if a parent function is even, other functions in the same "family" may or may not be even. They may discover that adding two even functions produces an even function, while adding an even function and an odd function does not.

⊘ Explain 2 Classifying Even and Odd Functions

A function is an **even function** if $f(-x) = f(x)$ for all values of x. This means that if the point (x, y) is on the graph, then the point $(-x, y)$ is also on the graph.

A function is an **odd function** if $f(-x) = -f(x)$ for all values of x. This means that if the point (x, y) is on the graph, then the point $(-x, -y)$ is also on the graph.

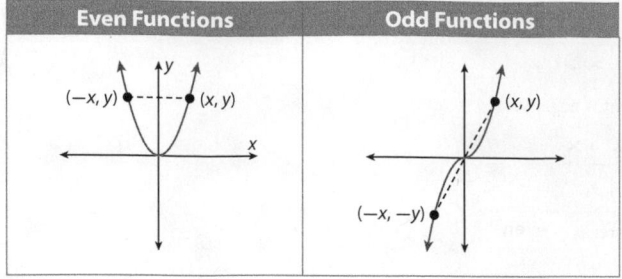

Example 2 Classify each graphed polynomial as an odd or even function, and identify whether the leading coefficient is positive or negative.

(A)

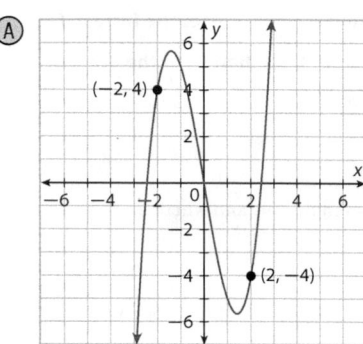

The points $(-2, 4)$ and $(2, -4)$ are on the graph, so the polynomial is an odd function.

End Behavior:

As $x \to +\infty$, $f(x) \to +\infty$, so the leading coefficient is positive.

LANGUAGE SUPPORT **EL**

Connect Vocabulary

The words *quartic* and *quintic* are used in this lesson to describe polynomial functions of degree 4 and degree 5. Point out that the roots *quart-* and *quint-* refer to the numbers four and five, respectively. Challenge students to identify other words that start with *quart-* (such as *quarter* and *quartet)* and words that start with *quint-* (such as *quintet* and *quintuplets*).

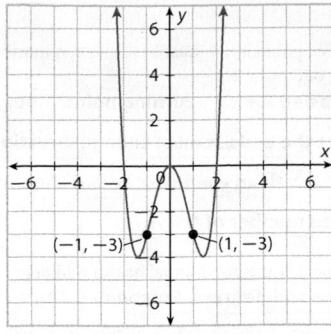

Ⓑ

The points __(−1, −3)__ and __(1, −3)__ are on the graph, so the polynomial is

a(n) __even__ function.

End Behavior:

As $x \to +\infty$, $f(x) \to$ $\boxed{+\infty}$, so the leading coefficient is __positive__.

Your Turn

Classify each graphed polynomial as an odd or even function, and identify whether the leading coefficient is positive or negative.

5.

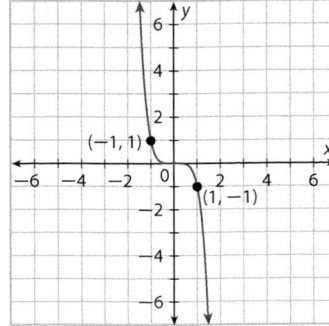

odd function; the leading coefficient is negative

6.

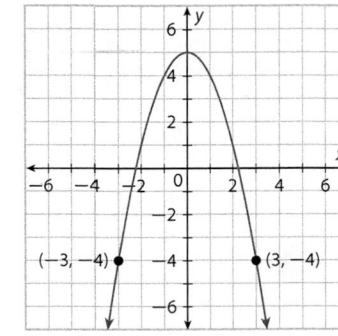

even function; the leading coefficient is negative

QUESTIONING STRATEGIES

? If an odd function increases as x approaches infinity, what is its end behavior as x approaches negative infinity? Explain. It decreases as x approaches negative infinity. For an odd function, $f(-x) = -f(x)$, so the function's behavior as x decreases below zero is the opposite of its behavior as x increases above zero.

ELABORATE

QUESTIONING STRATEGIES

? How can you determine the end behavior of a polynomial function by looking at only one term of the polynomial? Look at the leading term of the polynomial. Its sign indicates whether the graph increases or decreases as x approaches positive infinity. Its degree tells whether the end behavior as x approaches negative infinity is the same as or the opposite of the behavior as x approaches positive infinity.

INTEGRATE MATHEMATICAL PRACTICES

Focus on Critical Thinking

MP.3 After working with examples of polynomial functions with degrees one through five, students may question whether there is a function of degree zero. Discuss with students what a function of degree zero would look like. Since $x^0 = 1$, a function whose highest degree term contains x^0 is a constant function. It has the form $f(x) = b$, where b is a constant. Its graph is a horizontal line.

SUMMARIZE THE LESSON

? How can you determine the shape of a polynomial function if you know its degree and the leading coefficient? Functions of odd degree will have opposite end behavior as x approaches positive and negative infinity, while functions of even degree will have the same end behavior in both directions. As x approaches positive infinity, $f(x)$ approaches positive infinity for functions with a positive leading coefficient, but $f(x)$ approaches negative infinity for functions with a negative leading coefficient.

💬 Elaborate

7. How can you tell based on the end behavior that an odd degree polynomial must have an even number of turning points, and an even degree polynomial must have an odd number?
   The function switches between increasing and decreasing for each turning point. Since a function with an odd degree has opposite behavior at the ends, it must change direction an even number of times, or not at all. Since a function with an even degree has the same behavior at the ends, it must change directions an odd number of times.

8. If $f(x)$ is a polynomial and $f(-x) = -f(x)$, how do you know that the polynomial has an odd degree?
   All polynomials that are odd functions must also have odd degrees. Polynomial degree can only be even or odd, and you know from the end behavior of polynomials with even degrees that they cannot be odd functions.

9. **Essential Question Check-In** How does the degree of a polynomial affect its end behavior?
   If the degree is odd, the end behavior will be opposite at opposite ends, and if the degree is even, the end behavior will be the same at the opposite ends.

• Online Homework
• Hints and Help
• Extra Practice

1. Use a graphing calculator to plot the function $f(x) = x^3 + 2x^2 - 3x - 4$ and determine how many turning points there are and what the end behavior is.

There are two turning points.

As $x \to -\infty$, $f(x) \to -\infty$.

As $x \to +\infty$, $f(x) \to +\infty$.

For each graph, identify whether the polynomial $f(x)$ is of odd or even degree, and whether the leading coefficient is positive or negative.

2.

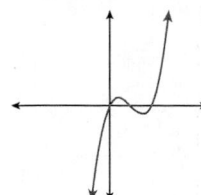

odd degree, positive leading coefficient

3.

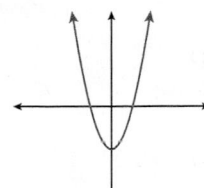

even degree, positive leading coefficient

4.

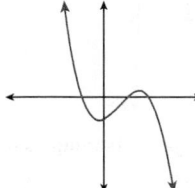

odd degree, negative leading coefficient

5.

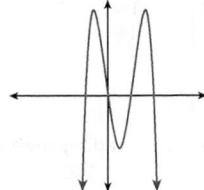

even degree, negative leading coefficient

6.

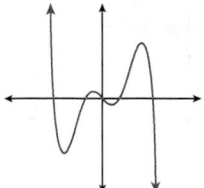

odd degree, negative leading coefficient

7.

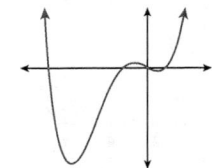

even degree, positive leading coefficient

8.

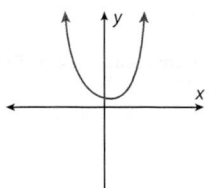

even degree, positive leading coefficient

9.

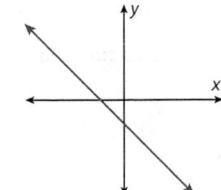

odd degree, negative leading coefficient

ASSIGNMENT GUIDE

Concepts and Skills	Practice
Explore Exploring Graphs of Cubic and Quartic Functions	Exercise 1
Example 1 Even and Odd Degree Polynomial Functions	Exercises 2–11, 18–19, 21
Example 2 Classifying Even and Odd Functions	Exercises 12–17, 20

INTEGRATE MATHEMATICAL PRACTICES
Focus on Modeling

MP.4 The rotational symmetry of an odd function can be illustrated using a transparency. Have students trace the graph of the function $y = x^3$ on a transparency. Students can rotate the transparency 180° to illustrate that an odd function has rotational symmetry about the origin.

Exercise	Depth of Knowledge (D.O.K.)	COMMON CORE Mathematical Practices
1	**2** Skills/Concepts	**MP.5** Using Tools
2-17	**1** Recall	**MP.7** Using Structure
18	**2** Skills/Concepts	**MP.7** Using Structure
19-20	**2** Skills/Concepts H.O.T.	**MP.3** Logic
21	**3** Strategic Thinking H.O.T.	**MP.5** Using Tools

VISUAL CUES

Have students verify that even functions have symmetry with respect to the *y*-axis by folding the graph of an even function on the line *x* = 0. Students should see that the two halves of the graph will line up when the graph is folded.

AVOID COMMON ERRORS

Students may try to determine whether a graph represents a polynomial function of odd or even degree based only on the end behavior in one direction. Remind them that they must compare the end behavior as *x* approaches positive infinity to the behavior as *x* approaches negative infinity. If both are the same, the polynomial has even degree; if they are opposites, the polynomial has odd degree.

10.

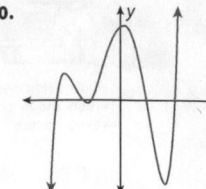

odd degree, positive leading coefficient

11.

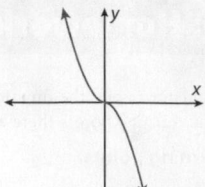

odd degree, negative leading coefficient

Label each function as an odd or even function, and identify the sign of the leading coefficient.

12.

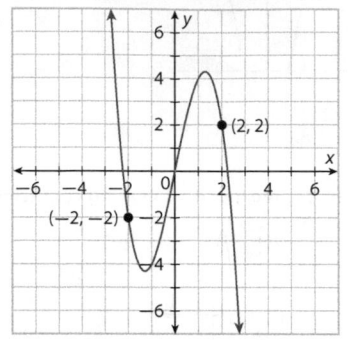

odd function, negative leading coefficient

13.

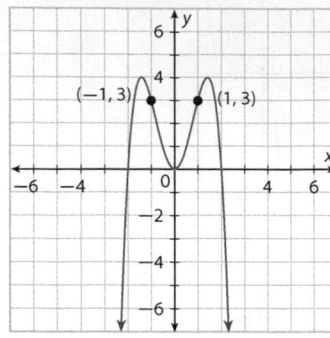

even function; negative leading coefficient

14.

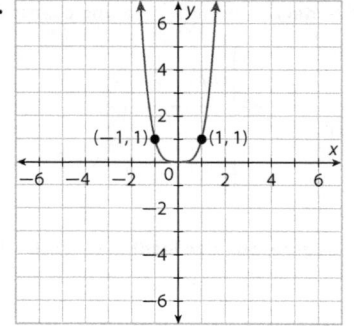

even function, positive leading coefficient

15.

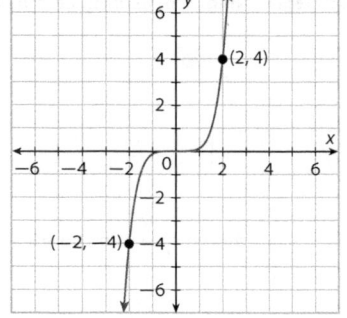

odd function, positive leading coefficient

16.

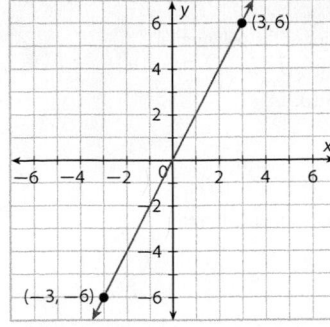

odd function, positive leading coefficient

17.

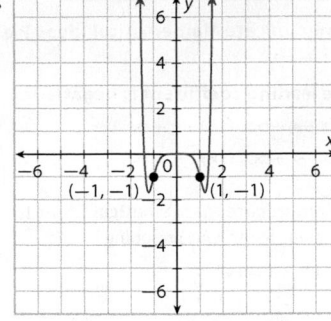

even function, positive leading coefficient

18. **Matching** Use the end behavior to match each polynomial function to its graph.

a.

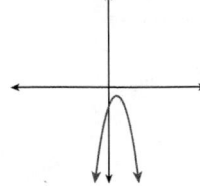

b.

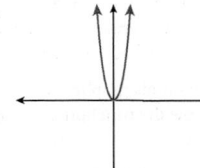

c.

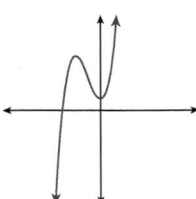

d.

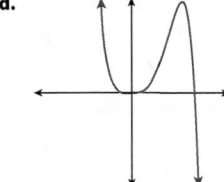

1. $f(x) = 5x^3 + 9x^2 + 1$ **c**

2. $f(x) = 2x^6 + 3x^4 + 5x^2$ **b**

3. $f(x) = -x^5 + 3x^4 + x$ **d**

4. $f(x) = -4x^2 + 3x - 1$ **a**

Students may confuse the terms *even* and *odd function* with *even* and *odd degree*. Remind them that the *degree* of a polynomial function is the highest power to which the variable in the function is raised. Even and odd *functions* are defined based on the value of $f(-x)$. For even functions, $f(-x) = f(x)$ for all values of x, while for odd functions, $f(-x) = -f(x)$ for all values of x.

JOURNAL

Have students create a graphic organizer identifying all the ways in which polynomial functions of even degree are different from polynomial functions of odd degree. Students should include sketches that illustrate the differences between the shapes of the two groups of functions.

19. Communicate Mathematical Ideas Predict the end behavior of the polynomial $f(x) = -x^9$.

The leading coefficient is negative and the degree is odd.

As $x \rightarrow -\infty, f(x) \rightarrow +\infty$.

As $x \rightarrow +\infty, f(x) \rightarrow -\infty$.

20. Communicate Mathematical Ideas Is the function $f(x) = x^3$ an odd or even function? Show your reasoning.

$$f(-x) = (-1x)^3$$
$$= (-1)^3 x^3$$
$$= -x^3$$

The function is odd.

21. Explain the Error Carlos and Rhonda are disagreeing over the answer to a math problem. Rhonda claims that the polynomial $f(x) = \frac{1}{3}x^3 + 6x^2 + 21x + 16$ should approach negative infinity as x approaches negative infinity, because the leading term has a positive coefficient and is of odd degree.

Carlos entered the function on his graphing calculator and produced the following graph, which appears to show the function approaching positive infinity as x approaches negative infinity.

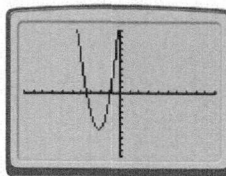

Who is right? Can you figure out what the mistake is?

Rhonda is correct. The end behavior of a polynomial is entirely determined by the term with the highest degree. Carlos missed a turning point because he did not adjust the graph window from the default settings. (To see all of the important features of the graph, adjust Ymax to 80 and Xmin to −20).

Lesson Performance Task

A company that specializes in gift baskets is making a pyramid-shaped package with a rectangular base. The base must have a perimeter of 54 centimeters, and the height of the package must be equal to the length of its base.

A. Write a polynomial function, $V(x)$, for the volume of the package, where x is the length of the base. What are the constraints on x for this situation?

B. Use a graphing calculator to find the maximum volume of the package. What value of x corresponds to the maximum volume?

C. What dimensions result in a package with the maximum volume?

A. Volume of pyramid: $V = \frac{1}{3}Bh$, where $B = \ell w$ and $x = \ell$.

$$54 = 2x + 2w$$
$$w = \frac{54 - 2x}{2}$$
$$= 27 - x$$
$$V(x) = \frac{1}{3}\big[x(27 - x)\big]x$$
$$= \frac{1}{3}\big[27x - x^2\big]x$$
$$= 9x^2 - \frac{x^3}{3}$$

Because the volume must be positive, $9x^2 > \frac{x^3}{3}$. The constraints on x are $0 < x < 27$ for this situation.

B. The maximum volume is 972 cm³, where $x = 18$.

C. $w = 27 - x$
$$= 27 - (18)$$
$$= 9$$

The package has a length of 18 centimeters, a width of 9 centimeters, and a height of 18 centimeters.

EXTENSION ACTIVITY

Have students consider how the solutions to the Lesson Performance Task would differ if the height of the package is required to equal twice the length of its base.

Students should find that the constraints on x are unchanged, the maximum volume is doubled to 1944 cm³, the dimensions of the base are unchanged, and the height is doubled to 36 cm.

INTEGRATE MATHEMATICAL PRACTICES
Focus on Modeling

MP.4 Explain that the phrase "the constraints on x" refers to the range of x-values that makes sense in the context of the problem. Students should recognize that length and volume measurements cannot be negative. They can use this fact to determine upper and lower bounds on the value of x.

QUESTIONING STRATEGIES

? How can you use a graphing calculator to find the maximum possible value of a function? Graph the function, and locate the point with the greatest y-value that corresponds to an x-value in the domain of the function. Use the **TRACE** or **TABLE** feature, or select **4:maximum** from the **CALC** menu, to find the coordinates of that point.

? What is another way to find the maximum of a function? Possible answer: Make a table of input and output values, trying additional values as needed until you find the x-value (input) that results in the greatest y-value (output).

AVOID COMMON ERRORS

Students may have trouble locating the maximum value of the function if they do not enlarge the viewing window on their calculators. Encourage them to think about the expected shape of the graph of a cubic function and to adjust the window until they can see both turning points of the graph.

Scoring Rubric
2 points: Student correctly solves the problem and explains his/her reasoning.
1 point: Student shows good understanding of the problem but does not fully solve or explain his/her reasoning.
0 points: Student does not demonstrate understanding of the problem.

Graphing Polynomial Functions   **1166**

Understanding Inverse Functions

Common Core Math Standards

The student is expected to:

 F-BF.B.4a

Solve an equation of the form $f(x) = c$ for a simple function f that has an inverse and write an expression for the inverse. Also F-BF.B.4c, A-CED.A.4, F-IF.B.5

Mathematical Practices

 MP.1 Problem Solving

Language Objective

Explain what the inverse of a function is and how its graph compares to the graph of the original function.

ENGAGE

Essential Question: How can you recognize inverses of functions from their graphs and how can you find inverses of functions?

You can recognize that inverses of functions are reflections across the line $y = x$, and you can find inverses of functions by using inverse operations.

PREVIEW: LESSON PERFORMANCE TASK

View the Engage section online. Discuss why planners and government officials might want to predict when the population of a city or state will reach a particular value. Then preview the Lesson Performance Task.

24.2 Understanding Inverse Functions

Essential Question: How can you recognize inverses of functions from their graphs and how can you find inverses of functions?

Resource Locker

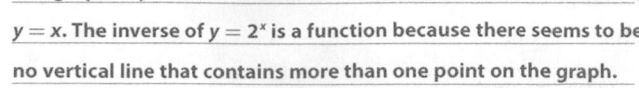 **Explore** **Exploring Inverses of Functions**

You can use a graphing calculator to explore inverse functions and their relationships to the linear parent function $f(x) = x$.

(A) Using a standard viewing window, graph the function $y = 2^x$ and the linear function $y = x$ on a graphing calculator. Describe the end behavior of $y = 2^x$ as $x \to +\infty$.

As $x \to +\infty$, $y \to +\infty$.

(B) Use the DrawInv feature on the calculator to draw the graph of the inverse of $y = 2^x$ along with $y = 2^x$ and $y = x$. How are the graphs of $y = 2^x$ and its inverse related? Is the inverse of $y = 2^x$ a function? Explain your answer.

The graph of $y = 2^x$ is the reflection of its inverse across the line $y = x$. The inverse of $y = 2^x$ is a function because there seems to be no vertical line that contains more than one point on the graph.

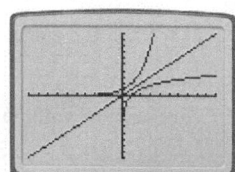

(C) Now graph the function $y = x^2$ and the linear function $y = x$ on a graphing calculator. Use the DrawInv feature to draw the graph of the inverse $y = x^2$ along with $y = x^2$ and $y = x$. How are the graphs of $y = x^2$ and its inverse related? Is the inverse of $y = x^2$ a function? Explain your answer.

The graph of $y = x^2$ is the reflection of its inverse across the line $y = x$. The inverse of $y = x^2$ is not a function because there is at least one vertical line that contains more than one point on the graph.

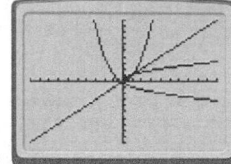

Reflect

1. **Make a Conjecture** Functions and their inverses appear to be reflections across which line?
In general, inverses of functions tend to be reflections of the original equation across the line $y = x$.

2. Do you think all inverses of functions are functions? Why or why not?
No. For example, $y = x^2$ is a function but its inverse is not.

© Houghton Mifflin Harcourt Publishing Company

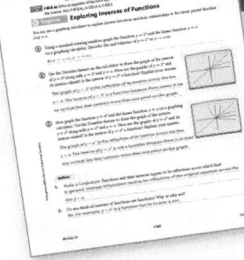

HARDCOVER PAGES 909–916

Turn to these pages to find this lesson in the hardcover student edition.

Explain 1 **Graphing Inverse Relations**

You have seen the word *inverse* used in various ways.

The additive inverse of 3 is −3.

The multiplicative inverse of 5 is $\frac{1}{5}$.

You can also find and apply inverses to relations, which are sets of ordered pairs, and functions. To graph the **inverse relation**, you can reflect each point across the line $y = x$. This is equivalent to switching the x- and y-values in each ordered pair of the relation.

Example 1 Graph the relation and connect the points. Then graph the inverse. Identify the domain and range of each relation.

Ⓐ

x	0	1	2	4	8
y	2	4	5	6	7

Graph each ordered pair and connect the points.

Switch the x- and y-values in each ordered pair.

x	2	4	5	6	7
y	0	1	2	4	8

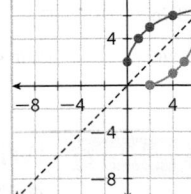

Reflect each point across $y = x$, and connect the new points. Make sure the points match those in the table.

Original relation: Domain: $0 \leq x \leq 8$ Range: $2 \leq y \leq 7$

Inverse relation: Domain: $2 \leq x \leq 7$ Range: $0 \leq y \leq 8$

Ⓑ

x	1	3	4	5	6
y	0	1	2	3	5

Graph each ordered pair and connect the points.

Switch the x- and y-values in each ordered pair.

x	0	1	2	3	5
y	1	3	4	5	6

Reflect each point across $y = x$, and connect the new points. Make sure the points match those in the table.

Original relation: Domain: $\boxed{1} \leq x \leq \boxed{6}$ Range: $\boxed{0} \leq y \leq \boxed{5}$

Inverse relation: Domain: $\boxed{0} \leq x \leq \boxed{5}$ Range: $\boxed{1} \leq y \leq \boxed{6}$

PROFESSIONAL DEVELOPMENT

 Integrate Mathematical Practices

This lesson provides an opportunity to use Mathematical Practice **MP.1**, which asks students to "make sense of problems and persevere in solving them." To solve a real-world problem by finding an inverse function, students must realize that they are looking for a function that undoes what the original function does. They write a function to model a given situation, then follow a solution process that involves exchanging the variables x and y and using inverse operations to solve for the desired quantity.

EXPLORE

Exploring Inverses of Functions

INTEGRATE TECHNOLOGY

Students will use calculators to graph a function and its inverse. By comparing the exact shapes of the graphs, they will discover how the two graphs are related.

INTEGRATE MATHEMATICAL PRACTICES
Focus on Reasoning

MP.2 Discuss with students whether a point can lie both on the graph of a function and on the graph of its inverse. Students should understand that since the inverse is the reflection of the original graph across the line $y = x$, a point must be on the line $y = x$ in order to lie on both graphs.

EXPLAIN 1

Graphing Inverse Relations

INTEGRATE MATHEMATICAL PRACTICES
Focus on Modeling

MP.4 To illustrate that the graph of an inverse is a reflection of the graph of the original relation, have students draw the graphs of a relation and its inverse on the same grid, then fold the grid along the line $y = x$. The original graph should align with the graph of the inverse when the paper is folded.

QUESTIONING STRATEGIES

? How is the y-intercept of the graph of a relation related to the x-intercept of the graph of its inverse? Explain. They are equal. The y-intercept is the y-coordinate of the point where $x = 0$. When you switch the coordinates of each point to graph the inverse, the corresponding point on the inverse will have $y = 0$. The x-coordinate of this point is the x-intercept.

Understanding Inverse Functions **1168**

Point out that the word *inverse* refers to something that is *reversed or the opposite of the original or usual situation*. In an *inverse relation*, the roles of x and y are reversed.

EXPLAIN 2

Writing Inverse Functions by Using Inverse Operations

INTEGRATE MATHEMATICAL PRACTICES

Focus on Math Connections

MP.1 Remind students that to write inverse functions correctly, they must be aware of the order of operations. When they evaluate an algebraic expression, students should perform operations in this order: (1) operations within parentheses, (2) exponents, (3) multiplication and division, and (4) addition and subtraction. Remind students that when they apply inverse operations to an expression to find the inverse of a function, they should perform the operations in the opposite order.

AVOID COMMON ERRORS

Students often misinterpret $f^{-1}(x)$ as a function raised to the -1 power. Stress that, in this context, -1 is not an exponent, even though it is written as a superscript. The notation $f^{-1}(x)$ can be read as "f inverse of x."

QUESTIONING STRATEGIES

? If $f(10) = 16$, what do you know about $f^{-1}(16)$? Explain. $f^{-1}(16) = 10$; because an inverse function undoes the original function, using 16 (the output of the original function) as the input in the inverse function should yield an output of 10 (the input for the original function).

Reflect

3. **Discussion** How are the domain and range of a relation related to the domain and range of its inverse? **The domain of a relation is the range of its inverse, while the range of a relation is the domain of its inverse.**

Your Turn

Graph the relation and connect the points. Then graph the inverse. Identify the domain and range of each relation.

4.

x	1	2	3	5	7
y	2	4	6	8	9

x	2	4	6	8	9
y	1	2	3	5	7

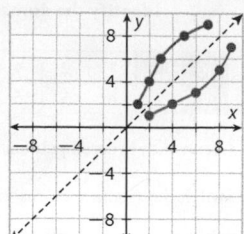

Original: Domain: $1 \le x \le 7$ Range: $2 \le y \le 9$

Inverse: Domain: $2 \le x \le 9$ Range: $1 \le y \le 7$

⊘ Explain 2 **Writing Inverse Functions by Using Inverse Operations**

When a relation is also a function, you can write the inverse of the function $f(x)$ as $f^{-1}(x)$. This notation does *not* indicate a reciprocal.

Functions that undo each other are called **inverse functions**.

You can find the inverse function by writing the original function with x and y switched and solving for y.

Example 2 Use inverse operations to find each inverse. Then check your solution.

(A) $f(x) = 2x$

$$y = 2x \qquad \text{Write } y \text{ for } f(x).$$
$$x = 2y \qquad \text{Switch } x \text{ and } y.$$
$$y = \frac{x}{2} \qquad \text{Solve for } y.$$

The inverse is $f^{-1}(x) = \frac{x}{2}$.

Check:

1. Use the input $x = 7$ in $f(x)$.
$$f(x) = 2x$$
$$f(7) = 2(7) = 14$$
The output is 14.

2. Verify that the output, 14, gives the input, 7.
$$f^{-1}(x) = \frac{x}{2}$$
$$f^{-1}(14) = \frac{14}{2} = 7$$

Since the inverse function *does* undo the original function, $f^{-1}(x) = \frac{x}{2}$ is correct.

COLLABORATIVE LEARNING

Peer-to-Peer Activity

Have students work in pairs. Each student will need two coordinate grids whose x- and y-axes have the same scale. Have each student write a function and graph it on one grid. Then have students tell their partners the function rules. Have each partner find the inverse of the function and graph the inverse on the second coordinate grid. Finally, have the pairs compare the graphs of the original functions to the graphs of their inverses and discuss how they are related.

(B) $f(x) = \frac{x}{4} - 5$

$y = \frac{x}{4} - 5$ Write y for $\boxed{f(x)}$.

$\boxed{x} = \frac{\boxed{y}}{4} - 5$ Switch $\boxed{x}$ and y.

$y = \boxed{4}\left(x + \boxed{5}\right)$ Solve for $\boxed{y}$.

Check:

1. Use the input $x = 40$ in $f(x)$.

$f(40) = \frac{\boxed{40}}{4} - 5 = \boxed{10} - 5 = \boxed{5}$

The output is $\boxed{5}$.

2. Verify that the output, $\boxed{5}$, gives the input, $\boxed{40}$.

$f^{-1}\left(\boxed{5}\right) = 4\left(\boxed{5} + 5\right) = 4\left(\boxed{10}\right) = \boxed{40}$

Since the inverse function (ⓓⓞⓔⓢ/does not) undo the original function, it (ⓘⓢ/is not) correct.

Your Turn

Use inverse operations to find the inverse. Then check your solution.

5. $f(x) = 5x - 7$

$f^{-1}(x) = \frac{x+7}{5}$ Sample check: $f(5) = 5(5) - 7 = 25 - 7 = 18$ $f^{-1}(18) = \frac{18+7}{5} = \frac{25}{5} = 5$

🔘 **Explain 3**   **Graphing Inverse Functions**

A function and its inverse are reflections across the line $y = x$.

Example 3   Write the inverse of each function. Then graph the function together with its inverse.

Ⓐ $f(x) = 3x + 6$

$y = 3x + 6$ Write y for $f(x)$.

$x = 3y + 6$ Switch x and y.

$y = \frac{x - 6}{3}$ Solve for y.

$y = \frac{1}{3}x - 2$ Simplify.

The inverse is $f^{-1}(x) = \frac{1}{3}x - 2$.

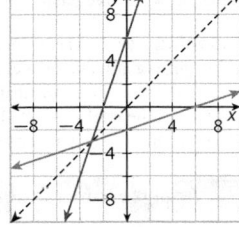

EXPLAIN 3

Graphing Inverse Functions

INTEGRATE MATHEMATICAL PRACTICES

Focus on Reasoning

MP.2 Discuss with students why they can find the inverse for a function by exchanging x and y in the function, then solving for y. Students should understand that exchanging x and y is the same as switching the domain and range for the function. Outputs become inputs, and inputs become outputs, so the new function undoes the original function.

QUESTIONING STRATEGIES

? When graphing a function, how can you tell if the graph of a function and its inverse will cross each other? If the graph crosses the line $y = x$, then the graphs of the function and its inverse will cross each other.

DIFFERENTIATE INSTRUCTION

Critical Thinking

Challenge students to find a function that is its own inverse. The easiest example is most likely $y = x$, but there are other linear functions that are their own inverses. Students may choose to fold a coordinate grid along the line $y = x$ and think about where a line would have to be positioned in order to line up with itself when folded. Students should realize that in addition to the line $y = x$, any linear function in the form $y = -x + b$ (where b is any real number) will be its own inverse. Students can check this result algebraically by reversing x and y in the equation: $y = -x + b$ is equivalent to $x = -y + b$.

EXPLAIN 4

Using Inverse Functions to Solve Real-World Problems

INTEGRATE MATHEMATICAL PRACTICES
Focus on Modeling

MP.4 When working with real-world situations, students may benefit from thinking of an inverse as a function that switches the roles of the quantities involved in the original function. For example, for a function that yields the cost of a bag of oranges given the weight, the inverse yields the weight if given the cost of the bag of oranges.

QUESTIONING STRATEGIES

? When writing an inverse function to solve a real-world problem, which variable should be isolated? **The variable representing the quantity you want to find should be isolated on one side of the equation.**

(B) $f(x) = \frac{2}{3}x + 2$

$\boxed{y} = \frac{2}{3}x + 2$ Write y for $f(x)$.

$\boxed{x} = \frac{2}{3}\boxed{y} + 2$ Switch x and y.

$y = \dfrac{\boxed{3}}{\boxed{2}}\left(x - \boxed{2}\right)$ Solve for $\boxed{y}$.

$y = \dfrac{\boxed{3}}{\boxed{2}}x - \boxed{3}$ Simplify.

The inverse is $f^{-1}(x) = \dfrac{\boxed{3}}{\boxed{2}}x - \boxed{3}$.

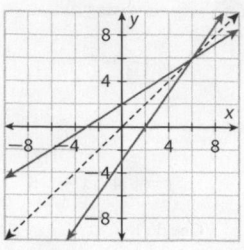

Your Turn

Write the inverse of each function. Then graph the function together with its inverse.

6. $f(x) = 2x - 4$

$y = 2x - 4$

$x = 2y - 4$

$y = \frac{1}{2}x + 2$

$f^{-1}(x) = \frac{1}{2}x + 2$

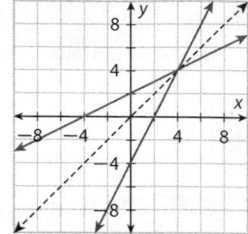

 Explain 4 **Using Inverse Functions to Solve Real-World Problems**

Any time you need to work backward from a result to the original input, you can apply inverse functions.

Example 4 Solve each problem by finding and evaluating the inverse function.

Shopping Lloyd is trying to find the original price of a camera he bought as a gift, but he does not have the store receipt. From the bank transaction, he knows that including a $3 gift-wrap charge and 8% tax, the total was $103.14. What was the original price of the camera? Justify your answer.

🧩 **Analyze Information**

Identify the important information.

- Lloyd paid a total of $ $\boxed{103.14}$ for the camera.

- The total includes a gift-wrapping charge of $ $\boxed{3}$ and a sales tax of $\boxed{8}$ % of the original price.

🧩 **Formulate a Plan**

Build a function for the total cost t of the camera. Then determine the inverse of the function, and use it to find the original price p.

LANGUAGE SUPPORT **EL**

Connect Vocabulary

An inverse function is often described as a function that undoes the original function. Ask students to discuss with a partner the meaning of the word *undo*. Demonstrate tying a knot, then undoing it. Discuss what kinds of actions can be undone, and compare the concept to mathematical operations that can be undone.

Solve

total cost = original price + tax + gift-wrapping charge

$$t = p + p \cdot \boxed{8}\% + \boxed{3}$$

$$t = p + \boxed{0.08}\,p + \boxed{3}$$

$$t = \boxed{1.08}\,p + \boxed{3}$$

Find the inverse function.

$$t = \boxed{1.08}\,p + \boxed{3}$$

$$t - \boxed{3} = \boxed{1.08}\,p$$

$$\frac{t - \boxed{3}}{\boxed{1.08}} = p$$

Use the inverse function to find the original price p for a total price of $ \boxed{103.14}$.

$$p = \frac{\boxed{103.14} - \boxed{3}}{\boxed{1.08}} \approx \boxed{92.72}$$

The original price of the camera was $ \boxed{92.72}$.

Justify and Evaluate

Use the original function to check your answer.

$$t = \boxed{1.08}\,p + \boxed{3}$$

$$t = \boxed{1.08} \cdot \left(\boxed{92.72}\right) + \boxed{3} \approx \boxed{103.14}$$

Since the inverse function (does/does not) undo the original function, it (is/is not) correct.

Reflect

7. What are the domain and range of the function for the total cost and its inverse in Example 4?

   Total cost function:

   Domain: all non-negative real numbers   **Range: all real numbers greater than 3**

   Inverse:

   Domain: all real numbers greater than 3   **Range: all non-negative real numbers**

Your Turn

8. To make tea, use $\frac{1}{6}$ teaspoon of tea per ounce of water plus a teaspoon for the pot. Use the inverse to find the number of ounces of water needed if 7 teaspoons of tea are used. Check your answer.

   $t = \frac{1}{6}w + 1$, **where t is the number of teaspoons of tea and w is the number of ounces of water**

   Inverse: $w = 6(t - 1)$

   For 7 teaspoons,

   $w = 6(7 - 1) = 36$, **so 36 ounces of water are needed.**

   Check: $t = \frac{1}{6}(36) + 1 = 7$

ELABORATE

INTEGRATE MATHEMATICAL PRACTICES

Focus on Math Connections

MP.1 When students find the inverse of a function by exchanging x and y, then solving for y, discuss a similar method: first solve the original function for x, then exchange x and y. Compare the steps used in the two methods to demonstrate that both methods use the same operations to find the inverse of the original function.

SUMMARIZE THE LESSON

? How can you write the inverse for a function? You can write an inverse for a function by applying inverse operations to the function rule, in the reverse of the order of operations. You can also exchange x and y in the function, then solve for y.

---

9. Explain the result of interchanging x and y to find the inverse function of $f(x) = x$. How could you have predicted this from the graph of $f(x)$?

When x and y are interchanged, the inverse function is the same as the original function.

You could have predicted this from the graph of $f(x)$ since the graph of an inverse is the

reflection across $y = x$, but the original function is $y = x$.

10. Give an example of a function whose inverse is a function. Give an example of a function whose inverse is not a function.

Possible answers: $y = x$; $y = x^2$

11. Describe what happens when you take the inverse of the inverse of a function. Is the result necessarily a function? Explain.

Taking the inverse of the inverse of a function will give you back the original function,

which is a function.

12. **Essential Question Check-In** Inverses are reflections of functions across which line?

Inverses are reflections of functions across the line $y = x$.

⭐ Evaluate: Homework and Practice

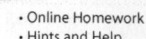

Graph the relation and connect the points. Then graph the inverse. Identify the domain and range of each relation.

- Online Homework
- Hints and Help
- Extra Practice

1.

x	1	2	3	4
y	1	2	4	8

2.

x	3	4	1	−1
y	−1	−2	−4	−4

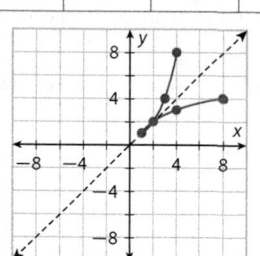
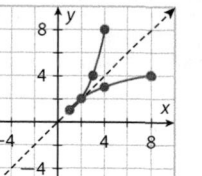

Original:

Domain: $1 \leq x \leq 4$ Range: $1 \leq y \leq 8$

Inverse:

Domain: $1 \leq x \leq 8$ Range: $1 \leq y \leq 4$

Original:

Domain: $-1 \leq x \leq 4$ Range: $-4 \leq y \leq -1$

Inverse:

Domain: $-4 \leq x \leq -1$ Range: $-1 \leq y \leq 4$

3.

x	1	3	5	7
y	0	3	6	9

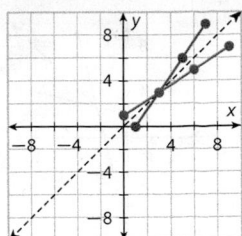

Original:

Domain: $1 \leq x \leq 7$ Range: $0 \leq y \leq 9$

Inverse:

Domain: $0 \leq x \leq 9$ Range: $1 < y \leq 7$

4.

x	−2	0	3	7
y	0	−1	−4	−9

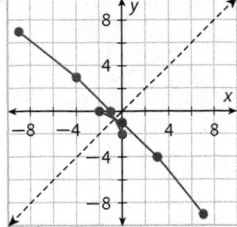

Original:

Domain: $-2 \leq x \leq 7$ Range: $-9 \leq y \leq 0$

Inverse:

Domain: $9 \leq x \leq 0$ Range: $-2 \leq y \leq 7$

Use inverse operations to find each inverse. Then check your solution.

5. $f(x) = 5x - 1$

$f^{-1}(x) = \dfrac{x+1}{5}$

Sample check:

$f(4) = 5(4) - 1 = 19$ and $f^{-1}(19) = \dfrac{19+1}{5} = 4$

6. $f(x) = \dfrac{x}{2} + 3$

$f^{-1}(x) = 2(x - 3)$

Sample check:

$f(2) = \dfrac{2}{2} + 3 = 4$ and $f^{-1}(4) = 2(4 - 3) = 2$

7. $f(x) = 3 - \dfrac{1}{2}x$

$f^{-1}(x) = -2(x - 3)$

Sample check:

$f(8) = 3 - \dfrac{1}{2}(8) = -1$ and

$f^{-1}(-1) = -2(-1 - 3) = 8$

8. $f(x) = \dfrac{1}{2}(3 - 3x)$

$f^{-1}(x) = \dfrac{-2x + 3}{3}$

Sample check: $f(5) = \dfrac{1}{2}(3 - 3(5)) = \dfrac{1}{2}(-12) = -6$

and $f^{-1}(-6) = \dfrac{-2(-6) + 3}{3} = \dfrac{12 + 3}{3} = \dfrac{15}{3} = 5$

9. $f(x) = 4(x + 1)$

$f^{-1}(x) = \dfrac{x - 4}{4}$

Sample check: $f(3) = 4(3 + 1) = 4 \cdot 4 = 16$

and $f^{-1}(16) = \dfrac{16 - 4}{4} = \dfrac{12}{4} = 3$

10. $f(x) = \dfrac{3x - 5}{2}$

$f^{-1}(x) = \dfrac{2x + 5}{3}$

Sample check: $f(5) = \dfrac{3(5) - 5}{2} = \dfrac{10}{2} = 5$

and $f^{-1}(5) = \dfrac{2(5) + 5}{3} = \dfrac{15}{3} = 5$

Exercise	Depth of Knowledge (D.O.K.)	COMMON CORE Mathematical Practices	
1–4	**1** Recall	**MP.7** Using Structure	
5–10	**1** Recall	**MP.6** Precision	
11–14	**1** Recall	**MP.7** Using Structure	
15–20	**1** Recall	**MP.4** Modeling	
21	**1** Recall	**MP.6** Precision	
22	**1** Recall	**MP.5** Using Tools	
23–24	**2** Skills/Concepts **H.O.T.**	**MP.3** Logic	

EVALUATE

ASSIGNMENT GUIDE

Concepts and Skills	Practice
Explore Exploring Inverses of Functions	Exercise 22
Example 1 Graphing Inverse Relations	Exercises 1–4
Example 2 Writing Inverse Functions by Using Inverse Operations	Exercises 5–10, 21, 23–24
Example 3 Graphing Inverse Functions	Exercises 11–14
Example 4 Using Inverse Functions to Solve Real-World Problems	Exercises 15–20

COGNITIVE STRATEGIES

When writing inverse functions for real-world situations, students may benefit from viewing the situation as a problem with an unknown that they can work backward to find. The operations students use when working backward can be used to write the inverse function.

Write the inverse of each function. Then graph the function together with its inverse.

11. $f(x) = 5 - 2x$

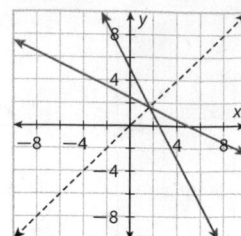

$y = 5 - 2x$

$x = 5 - 2y$

$y = -\frac{1}{2}x + \frac{5}{2}$

$f^{-1}(x) = -\frac{1}{2}x + \frac{5}{2}$

12. $f(x) = \frac{x}{4} + 2$

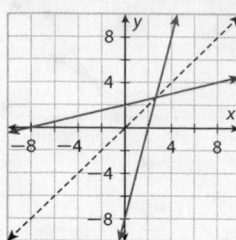

$y = \frac{x}{4} + 2$

$x = \frac{y}{4} + 2$

$y = 4x - 8$

$f^{-1}(x) = 4x - 8$

13. $f(x) = 10 + 0.6x$

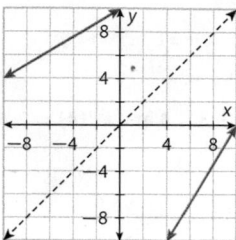

$y = 10 + 0.6x$

$x = 10 + 0.6y$

$y = \frac{x - 10}{0.6}$

$f^{-1}(x) = \frac{x - 10}{0.6}$ or $\frac{5}{3}x - \frac{50}{3}$

14. $f(x) = 2 + 3x$

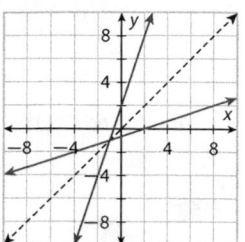

$y = 2 + 3x$

$x = 2 + 3y$

$y = \frac{1}{3}x - \frac{2}{3}$

$f^{-1}(x) = \frac{1}{3}x - \frac{2}{3}$

Solve each problem using an inverse function.

15. Meteorology The formula $C = \frac{5}{9}(F - 32)$ gives degrees Celsius as a function of degrees Fahrenheit. Find the inverse of this function to convert degrees Celsius to degrees Fahrenheit, and use it to find 16 °C in degrees Fahrenheit.

$C = \frac{5}{9}(F - 32)$ $F = \frac{9}{5}(16) + 32 = 60.8$; 16 °C is equal to 60.8 °F.

$\frac{9}{5}C = F - 32$ Check

$\frac{9}{5}C + 32 = F$ $C = \frac{5}{9}(60.8 - 32) = 16$

16. To make coffee using a home drip coffee maker, use $\frac{1}{4}$ tablespoon of coffee grounds per ounce of water plus 2 tablespoons for the coffee pot. Use the inverse to find the number of ounces of water needed if 11 tablespoons of coffee grounds are used.

$c = \frac{1}{4}w + 2$, where c is the number of tablespoons of coffee grounds and w is the number of ounces of water

$$C = \frac{1}{4}w + 2 \qquad w = 4(11 - 2) = 36$$

36 ounces of water are needed.

$$C - 2 = \frac{1}{4}w \qquad \text{Check}$$

$$4(c - 2) = w \qquad C = \frac{1}{4}(36) + 2 = 11$$

17. Shopping A shopping attendant needs to price a large jigsaw puzzle returned by a customer. The customer paid a total of $33.14, including a convenience charge of $1.50 and 11% sales tax on the subtotal. Use the inverse to find the original price of the puzzle.

$t = 1.11(p + 1.5)$, where t is the total cost of the jigsaw puzzle and p is the price of the puzzle

$$t = 1.11(p + 1.5) \qquad p = \frac{33.14}{1.11} - 1.5 \approx 28.36; \text{ the price was } \$28.36.$$

$$\frac{t}{1.11} = p + 1.5 \qquad \text{Check}$$

$$\frac{t}{1.11} - 1.5 = p \qquad t = 1.11(28.36 + 1.5) \approx 33.14$$

18. Education A student wants to figure out her raw score on a test she recently took. Including a 5-point bonus and a 2% increase after the bonus, the student scored a 94. Use the inverse to find the raw score.

$s = 1.02(r + 5)$, where s is the score and r is the raw score

$$s = 1.02(r + 5) \qquad r = 94/1.02 - 5 \approx 87.16; \text{ the raw score was } 87.$$

$$\frac{s}{1.02} = r + 5 \qquad \text{Check}$$

$$\frac{s}{1.02} - 5 = r \qquad s = 1.02(87 + 5) \approx 94$$

19. Currency At one point, the currency exchange rate between the U.S. dollar and the British pound sterling was 0.600 pound per dollar after a 3-dollar exchange fee. Use the inverse to determine how many U.S. dollars 100 British pounds would be worth.

$p = 0.600(d - 3)$, where d is the number of U.S. dollars and p is the number of British pounds

$$p = 0.600(d - 3) \qquad d = \frac{100}{0.600} + 3 \approx 169.67; \text{ 100 pounds was worth } \$169.67.$$

$$\frac{p}{0.600} = d - 3 \qquad \text{Check}$$

$$\frac{p}{0.600} + 3 = d \qquad p = 0.600(169.67 - 3) \approx 100$$

AVOID COMMON ERRORS

When writing inverse functions, remind students that undoing operations in the reverse order of the order of operations is a separate method from exchanging x and y in a function, then solving for y. Using both methods together will yield the original function.

20. **Travel** A taxi driver charges $2 for service plus 65¢ per mile. Use the inverse to determine the number of miles driven if the total charge is $11.75.

$t = 0.65m + 2$, where m is the number of miles driven and t is the total that the taxi charges for a ride

$$t = 0.65m + 2 \qquad m = \frac{11.75 - 2}{0.65} = 15; \text{ the taxi drove 15 miles.}$$

$$t - 2 = 0.65m$$

$$\frac{t - 2}{0.65} = m \qquad\qquad \textbf{Check}$$

$$t = 0.65(15) + 2 = 11.75$$

21. Identify whether you need to use an additive inverse, multiplicative inverse, or both to find the inverse of the given function. Select the correct answer for each lettered part.

A. $f(x) = 3x$ ○ Additive Inverse ● Multiplicative Inverse ○ Both

B. $f(x) = 3x + 4$ ○ Additive Inverse ○ Multiplicative Inverse ● Both

C. $f(x) = \frac{x}{6}$ ○ Additive Inverse ● Multiplicative Inverse ○ Both

D. $f(x) = 5x + 6$ ○ Additive Inverse ○ Multiplicative Inverse ● Both

E. $f(x) = \frac{x + 6}{x + 2}$ ○ Additive Inverse ○ Multiplicative Inverse ● Both

22. Use a graphing calculator to graph the function $y = 3^x$ on a standard viewing window along with its inverse and the line $y = x$. Is the function's inverse a function? Explain your answer.

The inverse is a function because there is no element of the domain that pairs with more than one element of the range, so it passes the vertical line test.

H.O.T. Focus on Higher Order Thinking

23. **Critical Thinking** Find the inverse of $f(x) = \frac{x - 3}{x + 4}$. Then use a sample input and output to check your answer.

$$y = \frac{x - 3}{x + 4} \qquad\qquad \textbf{Sample check:}$$

$$x = \frac{y - 3}{y + 4} \qquad\qquad f(6) = \frac{6 - 3}{6 + 4} = \frac{3}{10}$$

$$x(y + 4) = y - 3$$

$$xy + 4x = y - 3 \qquad f^{-1}\left(\frac{3}{10}\right) = \frac{-4\left(\frac{3}{10}\right) - 3}{\left(\frac{3}{10}\right) - 1} = \frac{-\frac{12}{10} - \frac{30}{10}}{\frac{-7}{10}} = \frac{\frac{-42}{10}}{\frac{-7}{10}} = \frac{-42}{-7} = 6$$

$$xy - y = -4x - 3$$

$$y(x - 1) = -4x - 3$$

$$y = \frac{-4x - 3}{x - 1}$$

24. **Explain the Error** A student produced the following result when attempting to find the inverse of $f(x) = \frac{x}{6} + 5$. Explain the student's error and state the correct answer.

$$y = \frac{x}{6} + 5 \qquad\qquad \text{\textbf{The student did not distribute 6 over the entire}}$$

$$x = \frac{y}{6} + 5 \qquad\qquad \text{\textbf{expression }} (x - 5) \text{ \textbf{when multiplying both sides by 6.}}$$

$$x - 5 = \frac{y}{6} \qquad\qquad \text{\textbf{The correct answer is }} 6x - 30 = y.$$

$$6x - 5 = y$$

Lesson Performance Task

The population p in thousands for the state of Oregon can be modeled by the linear function $p = 39.016t + 1039.614$, where t is the time in years since 1940.

A. Find an equation for the inverse function, rounding the constants and coefficients to three decimal places. What is the meaning of the slope and y-intercept of the inverse function?

B. Use the inverse function to estimate when the population of Oregon was 3,000,000.

C. The population of Oregon was estimated as 3,930,065 in 2013. Use the model to predict when the population of Oregon will be 4,800,000. What would have to be assumed for your answer to be valid?

A. $p = 39.016t + 1039.614$

$p - 1039.614 = 39.016t$

$\dfrac{p - 1039.614}{39.016} = t$

$0.026p - 26.646 \approx t$

The inverse is $t = 0.026p - 26.646$.

The slope of the inverse function means that the population increases by 1000 people every 0.026 year. The y-intercept of the inverse function means that the population was zero 26.646 years before 1940, or around

B. A population of 3,000,000 corresponds to $p = 3000$.

$t = 0.026(3000) - 26.646$

$= 51.354$

$1940 + 51.354 \approx 1991$

The population of Oregon was 3,000,000 around the year 1991.

C. A population of 4,800,000 corresponds to $p = 4800$.

$t - 0.026(4800) - 26.646$

$= 98.154$

$1940 + 98.154 \approx 2038$

The population of Oregon will be 4,800,000 around the year 2038. It is assumed that the population would continue to grow at the same rate.

EXTENSION ACTIVITY

Have students consider a city whose population can be modeled by $p = 280t^2 + 18,900$, where t is the time in years since 1990. Ask students to find the inverse function for this model and use it to estimate the year when the population is expected to exceed 250,000.

Students should find that the inverse function is $t = \sqrt{\dfrac{p - 18,900}{280}}$, and that the population will exceed 250,000 in 2019.

QUESTIONING STRATEGIES

? Which estimate is likely to be more accurate, the year in which the population of Oregon was 3,000,000, or the year in which the population will reach 4,800,000? Explain. the year in which the population was 3,000,000; the model for population growth was most likely based on past population data, so it can be expected to model past population growth reasonably well. But, extrapolation to predict future growth will not be accurate if the rate of population growth changes.

INTEGRATE MATHEMATICAL PRACTICES
Focus on Modeling

MP.4 Discuss with students what factors affect the growth of a state's population, and what combination of factors could lead to the population remaining constant. Students should recognize that population will be increased by births and immigration to the state and decreased by deaths and people moving out of the state. For the population to remain constant, total births and immigration would have to equal total deaths and emigration.

Scoring Rubric
2 points: Student correctly solves the problem and explains his/her reasoning.
1 point: Student shows good understanding of the problem but does not fully solve or explain his/her reasoning.
0 points: Student does not demonstrate understanding of the problem.

Understanding Inverse Functions   **1178**

Graphing Square Root Functions

Common Core Math Standards

The student is expected to:

 F-IF.C.7b

Graph square root, cube root, and piecewise-defined functions, including step functions and absolute value functions. Also F-BF.B.3, F-BF.B.4a, F-BF.B.4c, F-BF.B.4d

Mathematical Practices

 MP.8 Patterns

Language Objective

Describe how the graph of the function $f(x) = \sqrt{x}$ changes when the function is multiplied by a constant a.

ENGAGE

Essential Question: How can you use transformations of the parent square root function to graph functions of the form $f(x) = a\sqrt{x-h} + k$?

You can graph $f(x) = a\sqrt{x-h} + k$ by starting with, $f(x) = \sqrt{x}$, translating it h units to the right, vertically stretching or compressing it by the factor of a, and translating it k units up.

PREVIEW: LESSON PERFORMANCE TASK

View the Engage section online. Discuss how the height of a building above ground level affects the distance from which you can see it, taking into account the curvature of the Earth. Then preview the Lesson Performance Task.

24.3 Graphing Square Root Functions

Essential Question: How can you use transformations of the parent square root function to graph functions of the form $f(x) = a\sqrt{x-h} + k$?

Resource Locker

⊘ Explore 1   Exploring the Inverse of $y = x^2$

Use the steps that follow to explore the inverse of $y = x^2$.

Ⓐ Use a graphing calculator to graph $y = x^2$ and $y = x$. Describe the graph.

There is a line with a slope of 1 that passes through the origin. There is also a vertical parabola that opens up with a vertex located at the origin. The graphs of the functions intersect at $(0, 0)$ and $(1, 1)$.

Ⓑ Use the DrawInv feature to graph the inverse of $y = x^2$ along with $y = x^2$ and $y = x$. Describe the new graph.

There is a horizontal parabola that opens to the right with a vertex located at the origin. The new parabola intersects the other graphs at $(0, 0)$ and $(1, 1)$.

Ⓒ State whether the inverse is a function. Explain your reasoning.

The inverse is not a function because its graph fails the vertical line test. There is at least one vertical line that would contain more than one point on the graph.

Ⓓ Use inverse operations to write the inverse of $y = x^2$.

Switch x and y in the equation. $x = y^2$

Take the square root of both sides of the equation. $\pm\sqrt{x} = y$

Reflect

1. **Discussion** Explain why the inverse of $y = x^2$ is not a function.
   When taking the square root, you need to consider both positive and negative cases, which usually yields two values of the range for a single domain value: $y = \pm\sqrt{x}$.

© Houghton Mifflin Harcourt Publishing Company

HARDCOVER PAGES 917–926

Turn to these pages to find this lesson in the hardcover student edition.

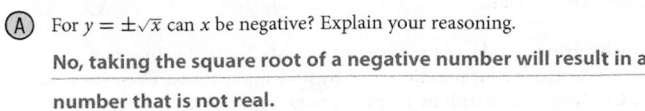 **Explore 2** Graphing the Parent Square Root Function

The graph shows $y = \pm\sqrt{x}$, $y = x^2$, and $y = x$. You have discovered that $y = \pm\sqrt{x}$ is not a function. You will find out how to alter $y = \pm\sqrt{x}$ so that it becomes a function.

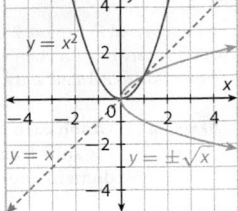

Ⓐ For $y = \pm\sqrt{x}$ can x be negative? Explain your reasoning.

No, taking the square root of a negative number will result in a

number that is not real.

Ⓑ If the domain of $y = x^2$ was restricted to $x \leq 0$, would the inverse be a function? Explain your reasoning.

With this restriction, the inverse would be a function because its graph passes

the vertical line test.

Ⓒ If the domain of $y = x^2$ was restricted to $x \geq 0$, would the inverse be a function? Explain your reasoning.

With this restriction, the inverse would be a function because its graph passes

the vertical line test.

Ⓓ Typically the domain of $y = x^2$ is restricted to $x \geq 0$ before finding its inverse to create the parent square root function. What is the equation of the parent square root function?

$y = \sqrt{x}$

Ⓔ A **radical function** is a function whose rule is a radical expression. A **square root function** is a radical function involving $\sqrt{x}$.

Graph the parent square root function $y = \sqrt{x}$ by first making a table of values.

x	$y = \sqrt{x}$	(x, y)
0	$\sqrt{0}$	$(0, 0)$
1	$\sqrt{1}$	$(1, \underline{1})$
4	$\sqrt{4}$	$(4, \underline{2})$
9	$\sqrt{9}$	$(9, \underline{3})$

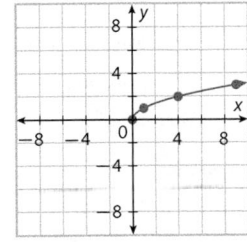

Ⓕ Plot the points on the graph and draw a smooth curve through them.

Reflect

2. What are the domain and range of the parent square root function?
   Domain: $x \geq 0$

   Range: $y \geq 0$

© Houghton Mifflin Harcourt Publishing Company

PROFESSIONAL DEVELOPMENT

 Integrate Mathematical Practices

This lesson provides an opportunity to address Mathematical Practice **MP.8**, which calls for students to "look for and express regularity in repeated reasoning." When transforming square root functions, students make use of patterns they have seen when transforming other functions. Students first explore how subtracting a constant from x or adding a constant to the parent function causes a translation of its graph. Then students explore how multiplying the parent function by a constant causes a vertical stretch or compression of the graph. Finally, students use transformed square root functions to solve real-world problems.

EXPLORE 1

Exploring the Inverse of $y = x^2$

INTEGRATE TECHNOLOGY

Students will use calculators to graph the inverse of the function $y = x^2$. By recognizing that the inverse is not a function, students are prepared for the idea that the domain of $y = x^2$ must be restricted before it is inverted to create the square root function.

INTEGRATE MATHEMATICAL PRACTICES
Focus on Reasoning

MP.2 Review the vertical line test for functions. Students should understand that if a vertical line passes through the graph of an equation at more than one point, then the equation will have two y-values for a single x-value and, therefore, is not a function.

EXPLORE 2

Graphing the Parent Square Root Function

INTEGRATE MATHEMATICAL PRACTICES
Focus on Communication

MP.3 Make sure students understand that the expression $\sqrt{x}$ always refers to a positive number. For that reason, the parent square root function, $f(x) = \sqrt{x}$, always has a positive output. In order to denote both the positive and negative values whose square is x, you must write $\pm\sqrt{x}$.

QUESTIONING STRATEGIES

What is the difference between the domain and range for the equation $y = \pm\sqrt{x}$ and the domain and range for the function $f(x) = \sqrt{x}$? For the equation $y = \pm\sqrt{x}$, the domain is all non-negative numbers and the range is all real numbers. The function $f(x) = \sqrt{x}$ has the same domain, but the range is all non-negative numbers.

Graphing Square Root Functions   **1180**

EXPLAIN 1

Graphing Translations of the Parent Square Root Function

AVOID COMMON ERRORS

When writing radical expressions, students sometimes draw the radical symbol too far or not far enough to the right. For example, they may write $f(x) = \sqrt{x} - 2 + 1$ or $f(x) = \sqrt{x - 2 + 1}$ instead of $f(x) = \sqrt{x - 2} + 1$. Remind students to be careful to extend the radical symbol over the appropriate part of each expression, so that they can evaluate it correctly.

QUESTIONING STRATEGIES

? When $h = k$, is a square root function in the form $f(x) = \sqrt{x - h} + k$ equivalent to the parent square root function? Explain. No; the entire expression $x - h$ is under the radical symbol, so $-h$ and k do not cancel. The function $f(x) = \sqrt{x - h} + k$ is equivalent to the parent function only when both h and k equal 0.

? How are the domain and range of the parent square root function affected by the parameters h and k in functions of the form $f(x) = \sqrt{x - h} + k$? Adding the parameter k, which causes a vertical translation, has no effect on the domain, but it shifts the minimum value of the range by an amount equal to k. Subtracting the parameter h from x, which causes a horizontal translation, shifts the minimum value of the domain by an amount equal to h, but it has no effect on the range.

1181   Lesson 24.3

You discovered in Explore 2 that the parent square root function is $y = \sqrt{x}$. The equation $y = \sqrt{x - h} + k$ is the parent square root function with horizontal and vertical translations, where h and k are constants. The constant h will cause a horizontal shift and k will cause a vertical shift.

Example 1   Graph each function by using a table and plotting the points. State the direction of the shift from the parent square root function, and by how many units. Then state the domain and range. Confirm your graph by graphing with a graphing calculator.

Ⓐ $y = \sqrt{x - 1} + 2$

x	$y = \sqrt{x - 1} + 2$	(x, y)
1	$\sqrt{1 - 1} + 2$	$(1, 2)$
2	$\sqrt{2 - 1} + 2$	$(2, 3)$
5	$\sqrt{5 - 1} + 2$	$(5, 4)$
10	$\sqrt{10 - 1} + 2$	$(10, 5)$

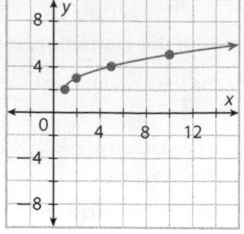

The graph is translated 2 units up and 1 unit right.

Domain: $x \geq 1$ Range: $y \geq 2$

Ⓑ $y = \sqrt{x + 3} - 2$

x	$y = \sqrt{x + 3} - 2$	(x, y)
-3	$\sqrt{-3 + 3} - 2$	$(-3, -2)$
-2	$\sqrt{-2 + 3} - 2$	$(-2, -1)$
1	$\sqrt{1 + 3} - 2$	$(1, 0)$
6	$\sqrt{6 + 3} - 2$	$(6, 1)$
13	$\sqrt{13 + 3} - 2$	$(13, 2)$

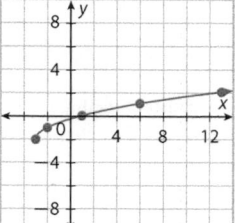

The graph is translated __2__ unit(s) (up/~~down~~) and

__3__ unit(s) to the (~~left~~/right).

Domain: __$x \geq -3$__ Range: __$y \geq -2$__

Your Turn

3. $y = \sqrt{x + 1}$

x	$y = \sqrt{x + 1}$	(x, y)
-1	$\sqrt{-1 + 1}$	$(-1, 0)$
0	$\sqrt{0 + 1}$	$(0, 1)$
3	$\sqrt{3 + 1}$	$(3, 2)$
8	$\sqrt{8 + 1}$	$(8, 3)$

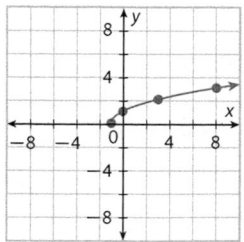

There is a horizontal translation 1 unit to the left.

Domain: $x \geq -1$ Range: $y \geq 0$

© Houghton Mifflin Harcourt Publishing Company

COLLABORATIVE LEARNING

Peer-to-Peer Activity

Have students work in pairs. Have each student write a square root function in the form $f(x) = a\sqrt{x - h} + k$ and graph the function. Then have partners look at each other's graphs and use what they know about the effect of the parameters a, h, and k to write the function represented by the graph. Have students compare the functions they write to the functions that their partners used to make the graphs.

4. $y = \sqrt{x} - 4$

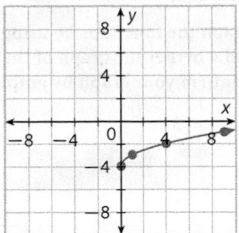

x	$y = \sqrt{x} - 4$	(x, y)
0	$\sqrt{0} - 4$	$(0, -4)$
1	$\sqrt{1} - 4$	$(1, -3)$
4	$\sqrt{4} - 4$	$(4, -2)$
9	$\sqrt{9} - 4$	$(9, -1)$

There is a vertical translation 4 units down.

Domain: $x \geq 0$ Range: $y \geq -4$

⊘ Explain 2 Graphing Stretches/Compressions and Reflections of the Parent Square Root Function

The equation $y = a\sqrt{x}$, where a is a constant, is the parent square root function with a vertical stretch or compression. If the absolute value of a is less than 1 the graph will be compressed by a factor of $|a|$, and if the absolute value of a is greater than 1 the graph will be stretched by a factor of $|a|$. If a is negative, the graph will be reflected across the x-axis.

Example 2 Graph the functions by using a table and plotting the points. State the stretch/compression factor and whether the graph of the parent function was reflected or not. Then state the domain and range. Confirm your graph by graphing with a graphing calculator.

Ⓐ $y = -2\sqrt{x}$

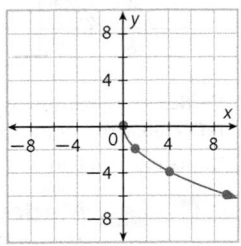

x	$y = -2\sqrt{x}$	(x, y)
0	$-2\sqrt{0}$	$(0, 0)$
1	$-2\sqrt{1}$	$(1, -2)$
4	$-2\sqrt{4}$	$(4, -4)$
9	$-2\sqrt{9}$	$(9, -6)$

There is a vertical stretch by a factor of 2, and the graph is reflected across the x-axis.

Domain: $x \geq 0$ Range: $y \leq 0$

Ⓑ $y = \frac{1}{2}\sqrt{x}$

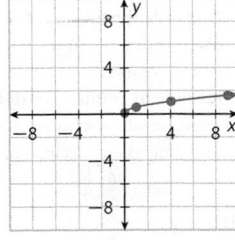

x	$y = \frac{1}{2}\sqrt{x}$	(x, y)
0	$\frac{1}{2}\sqrt{0}$	$(0, 0)$
1	$\frac{1}{2}\sqrt{1}$	$(1, \frac{1}{2})$
4	$\frac{1}{2}\sqrt{4}$	$(4, 1)$
9	$\frac{1}{2}\sqrt{9}$	$(9, \frac{3}{2})$

There is a vertical (stretch/⟨compression⟩) by a factor of $\frac{1}{2}$, and the graph (is/⟨is not⟩) reflected across the x-axis.

Domain: $\underline{x \geq 0}$ Range: $\underline{y \geq 0}$

EXPLAIN 2

Graphing Stretches/Compressions and Reflections of the Parent Square Root Function

INTEGRATE MATHEMATICAL PRACTICES
Focus on Modeling

MP.4 When working with stretches and compressions of the parent square root function, students may benefit from graphing both the parent function and the transformation on the same grid. Students can then compare the distance between the x-axis and the transformed function to the distance between the x-axis and the parent function. The ratio of the two distances should be the stretch factor.

QUESTIONING STRATEGIES

? What is the value of a for the parent square root function? Because the parent function is neither stretched nor compressed, the value of a is 1.

? How are the domain and range of the parent square root function affected by the parameter a in functions of the form $f(x) = a\sqrt{x}$? Multiplying $\sqrt{x}$ by a constant a does not change the domain or range of the function.

DIFFERENTIATE INSTRUCTION

Visual Cues

As students work with translations and stretches/compressions of the parent square root function, have them use pencils of different colors to create a graphic organizer illustrating how each of the parameters affects the graph of the function. Ask them to use a different color for each parameter: a, h, and k. The colors will then illustrate how each parameter's value can be determined by looking at the graph.

EXPLAIN 3

Modeling Real-World Situations with Square Root Functions

INTEGRATE MATHEMATICAL PRACTICES
Focus on Critical Thinking

MP.3 Often a function modeling a real-world situation needs to have a restricted domain because negative numbers do not make sense in the context of the problem. Discuss with students whether the domains of the square root functions modeling real-world situations should be further restricted because of their context. Students should understand that since the domain of the square root function is already restricted to non-negative numbers, a function of the form $f(x) = a\sqrt{x}$ needs no further restriction of its domain.

QUESTIONING STRATEGIES

? How do you find the value of a function for a given value of the independent variable? Substitute the given value for the independent variable in the function. Use the order of operations to evaluate the resulting expression.

Your Turn

Graph the functions by using a table and plotting the points. State the stretch/compression factor and whether the graph of the parent function was reflected or not. Then state the domain and range. Confirm your graph by graphing with a graphing calculator.

5. $y = 3\sqrt{x}$

x	$y = 3\sqrt{x}$	(x, y)
0	$3\sqrt{0}$	$(0, 0)$
1	$3\sqrt{1}$	$(1, 3)$
4	$3\sqrt{4}$	$(4, 6)$
9	$3\sqrt{9}$	$(9, 9)$

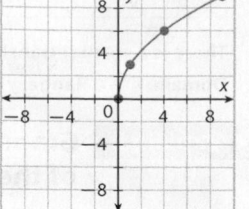

There is a vertical stretch by a factor of 3, and there is no reflection across the x-axis.

Domain: $x \geq 0$ **Range:** $y \geq 0$

6. $y = -\frac{1}{4}\sqrt{x}$

x	$y = -\frac{1}{4}\sqrt{x}$	(x, y)
0	$-\frac{1}{4}\sqrt{0}$	$(0, 0)$
1	$-\frac{1}{4}\sqrt{1}$	$\left(1, -\frac{1}{4}\right)$
4	$-\frac{1}{4}\sqrt{4}$	$\left(4, -\frac{1}{2}\right)$
9	$-\frac{1}{4}\sqrt{9}$	$\left(9, -\frac{3}{4}\right)$

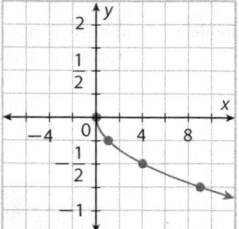

Vertical compression by a factor of $\frac{1}{4}$, and the graph is reflected across the x-axis.

Domain: $x \geq 0$ **Range:** $y \leq 0$

🔧 Explain 3 Modeling Real-World Situations with Square Root Functions

You can use transformations of square root functions to model real-world situations.

Example 3 Construct a square root function to solve each problem.

(A) On Earth, the function $f(x) = \frac{6}{5}\sqrt{x}$ approximates the distance in miles to the horizon observed by a person whose eye level is x feet above the ground. Use the function to estimate the distance to the horizon for someone whose eyes are 6.5 ft above Earth's surface, rounding to one decimal place.

$f(x) = \frac{6}{5}\sqrt{x}$

$f(6.5) = \frac{6}{5}\sqrt{6.5}$ Substitute 6.5 for x.

$f(6.5) \approx 3.1$ miles   Simplify.

LANGUAGE SUPPORT **EL**

Connect Vocabulary

When discussing transformations of functions, review the directional words *horizontal* and *vertical*. Point out that the word *horizontal* is derived from *horizon*, the flat line that we see between Earth and the sky, and it means *flat, level,* or *in a side-to-side direction*. The word *vertical*, derived from a Latin word meaning *high point*, means *upright* or *in an up-and-down direction*. The words *horizontal* and *vertical* are cognates in Spanish, so some students may know their meanings in their primary language.

(B) Using the function from Example 3A, estimate the distance to the horizon for someone whose eyes are 5.8 ft above Earth's surface, rounding to one decimal place.

$$f(x) = \frac{6}{5}\sqrt{x}$$

$$f(\underline{5.8}) = \frac{6}{5}\sqrt{\underline{5.8}} \qquad \text{Substitute} \underline{\quad 5.8 \quad} \text{ for } x.$$

$$f(\underline{5.8}) \approx \underline{2.9} \text{ miles} \qquad \text{Simplify.}$$

Your Turn

7. On Earth, the function $f(x) = \frac{6}{5}\sqrt{x}$ approximates the distance in miles to the horizon observed by a person whose eye level is x feet above the ground. The graph of the corresponding function for Mars has a vertical stretch relative to $f(x)$ of $\frac{\sqrt{5}}{3}$. Write the corresponding function $g(x)$ for Mars and use it to estimate the distance to the horizon for an astronaut whose eyes are 6.2 ft above Mars's surface, rounding to one decimal place.

$$g(x) = \frac{\sqrt{5}}{3}\left(\frac{6}{5}\sqrt{x}\right) = \frac{6\sqrt{5}}{15}\sqrt{x} = \frac{2\sqrt{5}}{5}\sqrt{x}$$

$$g(6.2) = \frac{2\sqrt{5}}{5}\sqrt{6.2} \approx \textbf{2.2 miles}$$

8. Using the function from the previous question, estimate the distance to the horizon for an astronaut whose eyes are 5.5 ft above Mars's surface, rounding to one decimal place.

$$g(x) = \frac{2\sqrt{5}}{5}\sqrt{x} \qquad g(5.5) = \frac{2\sqrt{5}}{5}\sqrt{5.5} \approx \textbf{2.1 miles}$$

💬 Elaborate

9. What can be said about the inverse of $y = x^2$ when the domain isn't restricted?
The inverse is $y = \pm\sqrt{x}$, which is a horizontal parabola. The inverse is not a function because it fails the vertical line test.

10. Are there any square root functions that do not have a restricted domain? Explain.
No, the domain must be restricted. There cannot be a negative number under the square root symbol.

11. **Essential Question Check-In** What is the domain and range of the function $f(x) = \sqrt{x - h} + k$?
The domain is $x \geq h$. The range is $y \geq k$.

© Houghton Mifflin Harcourt Publishing Company

ELABORATE

INTEGRATE MATHEMATICAL PRACTICES
Focus on Math Connections

MP.1 Have students compare the general form for a square root function, $f(x) = a\sqrt{x - h} + k$, to the vertex form for a quadratic function, $f(x) = a(x - h)^2 + k$, and to similar forms they have learned for transformations of absolute value functions and exponential functions. Discuss whether the parameters a, h, and k have the same effect in different types of functions. Students should recognize that in each case, subtracting h from x translates the graph of the parent function horizontally, adding a constant k to the parent function translates it vertically, and multiplying by a constant a causes a vertical stretch or compression of the graph.

SUMMARIZE THE LESSON

? How do graphs of functions of the form $f(x) = a\sqrt{x - h} + k$ compare to the graph of the parent square root function? When $|a| > 1$, there is a vertical stretch of the graph of the parent function. When $|a| < 1$, there is a vertical compression of the graph of the parent function. If a is negative, the graph is also reflected across the x-axis. The graph is translated h units to the right if h is positive and $|h|$ units to the left if h is negative. The graph is translated k units up if k is positive and $|k|$ units down if k is negative.

EVALUATE

ASSIGNMENT GUIDE

Concepts and Skills	Practice
Explore 1 Exploring the Inverse of $y = x^2$	Exercise 1
Explore 2 Graphing the Parent Square Root Function	Exercise 2
Example 1 Graphing Translations of the Parent Square Root Function	Exercises 3–8, 23
Example 2 Graphing Stretches/Compressions and Reflections of the Parent Square Root Function	Exercises 9–14, 18–22
Example 3 Modeling Real-World Situations with Square Root Functions	Exercises 15–17, 24

INTEGRATE MATHEMATICAL PRACTICES

Focus on Modeling

MP.4 To reinforce understanding of vertical and horizontal translations, have students graph the parent function $f(x) = \sqrt{x}$ on a transparency, then slide the transparency vertically and horizontally on top of a blank coordinate grid to represent the function $f(x) = \sqrt{x - h} + k$ for various values of h and k. Have them write the function rule for each transformation.

⭐ Evaluate: Homework and Practice

- Online Homework
- Hints and Help
- Extra Practice

1. What is the inverse of $y = x^2$? Select the correct answer.

    A. $y = \sqrt{x}$ **(B.)** $y = \pm\sqrt{x}$ **C.** $y = -\sqrt{x}$ **D.** $y = x$

2. What is the parent square root function? What is its domain and range?

The parent square root function is $y = \sqrt{x}$.
The domain is $x \geq 0$. The range is $y \geq 0$.

For Exercises 3–14, graph each function, describe any transformation from the parent function, and state the domain and range.

3. $y = \sqrt{x + 1} - 4$

x	$y = \sqrt{x + 1} - 4$	(x, y)
-1	$\sqrt{-1 + 1} - 4$	$(-1, -4)$
0	$\sqrt{0 + 1} - 4$	$(0, -3)$
3	$\sqrt{3 + 1} - 4$	$(3, -2)$
8	$\sqrt{8 + 1} - 4$	$(8, -1)$

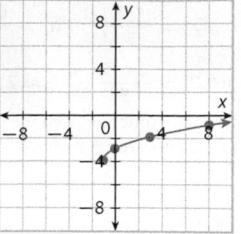

The graph is translated 4 units down and 1 unit to the left.
Domain: $x \geq -1$ Range: $y \geq -4$

4. $y = \sqrt{x} + 6$

x	$y = \sqrt{x} + 6$	(x, y)
0	$\sqrt{0} + 6$	$(0, 6)$
1	$\sqrt{1} + 6$	$(1, 7)$
4	$\sqrt{4} + 6$	$(4, 8)$
9	$\sqrt{9} + 6$	$(9, 9)$

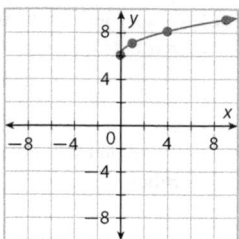

The graph is translated 6 units up. Domain: $x \geq 0$ Range: $y \geq 6$

5. $y = \sqrt{x + 8}$

x	$y = \sqrt{x + 8}$	(x, y)
-8	$\sqrt{-8 + 8}$	$(-8, 0)$
-7	$\sqrt{-7 + 8}$	$(-7, 1)$
-4	$\sqrt{-4 + 8}$	$(-4, 2)$
1	$\sqrt{1 + 8}$	$(1, 3)$
8	$\sqrt{8 + 8}$	$(8, 4)$

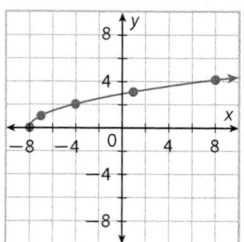

The graph is translated to the left 8 units. Domain: $x \geq -8$ Range: $y \geq 0$

Exercise	Depth of Knowledge (D.O.K.)	COMMON CORE Mathematical Practices
1	**1** Recall of Information	**MP.6** Precision
2	**2** Skills/Concepts	**MP.6** Precision
3–14	**1** Recall of Information	**MP.7** Using Structure
15–17	**2** Skills/Concepts	**MP.4** Modeling
18–21	**2** Skills/Concepts	**MP.7** Using Structure
22	**3** Strategic Thinking H.O.T.	**MP.6** Precision

6. $y = \sqrt{x-4} + 3$

x	$y = \sqrt{x-4}+3$	(x, y)
4	$\sqrt{4-4}+3$	$(4, 3)$
5	$\sqrt{5-4}+3$	$(5, 4)$
8	$\sqrt{8-4}+3$	$(8, 5)$

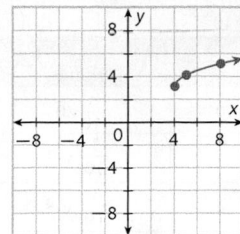

The graph is translated 3 units up and 4 units to the right. Domain: $x \geq 4$ Range: $y \geq 3$

7. $y = \sqrt{x+5} - 7$

x	$y = \sqrt{x+5}-7$	(x, y)
-5	$\sqrt{-5+5}-7$	$(-5, -7)$
-4	$\sqrt{-4+5}-7$	$(-4, -6)$
-1	$\sqrt{-1+5}-7$	$(-1, -5)$
4	$\sqrt{4+5}-7$	$(4, -4)$

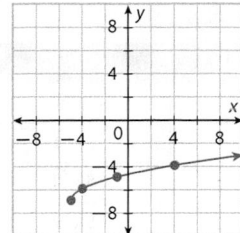

The graph is translated 7 units down and 5 units to the left. Domain: $x \geq -5$ Range: $y \geq -7$

8. $y = \sqrt{x+4} + 7$

x	$y = \sqrt{x+4}+7$	(x, y)
-4	$\sqrt{-4+4}+7$	$(-4, 7)$
-3	$\sqrt{-3+4}+7$	$(-3, 8)$
0	$\sqrt{0+4}+7$	$(0, 9)$
5	$\sqrt{5+4}+7$	$(5, 10)$

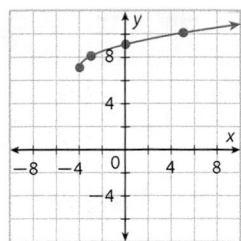

The graph is translated 7 units up and 4 units to the left. Domain: $x \geq -4$ Range: $y \geq 7$

9. $y = -\sqrt{x}$

x	$y = -\sqrt{x}$	(x, y)
0	$-\sqrt{0}$	$(0, 0)$
1	$-\sqrt{1}$	$(1, -1)$
4	$-\sqrt{4}$	$(4, -2)$
9	$-\sqrt{9}$	$(9, -3)$

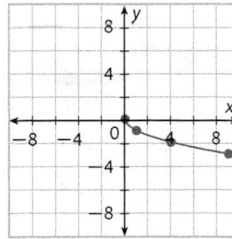

The graph is reflected across the x-axis. Domain: $x \geq 0$ Range: $y \leq 0$

CRITICAL THINKING

Have students make a conjecture about the effect on the graph of a square root function when the variable under the radical symbol is multiplied by a constant. For example, what does the graph of $f(x) = \sqrt{4x - 8}$ look like, compared to $f(x) = \sqrt{x - 8}$? Challenge students to explain or prove their conjectures.

AVOID COMMON ERRORS

When using the general form $f(x) = \sqrt{x - h}$, students may be confused by the minus sign in front of h and translate the graph in the wrong direction. Remind students that h is always subtracted from x in this form of the equation. When h is positive, for example, the function will look like $f(x) = \sqrt{x - 2}$ and the graph of the parent function will be translated to the right. When h is negative, the function will look like $f(x) = \sqrt{x + 2}$ and the graph will be translated to the left.

Exercise	Depth of Knowledge (D.O.K.)	COMMON CORE Mathematical Practices
23	**3** Strategic Thinking **H.O.T.**	**MP.3** Logic
24	**2** Skills/Concepts **H.O.T.**	**MP.4** Modeling

10. $y = \frac{1}{10}\sqrt{x}$

x	$y = \frac{1}{10}\sqrt{x}$	(x, y)
0	$\frac{1}{10}\sqrt{0}$	(0, 0)
1	$\frac{1}{10}\sqrt{1}$	(1, 0.1)
4	$\frac{1}{10}\sqrt{4}$	(4, 0.2)
9	$\frac{1}{10}\sqrt{9}$	(9, 0.3)

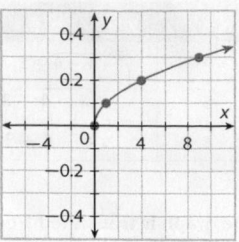

The graph is compressed by a factor of $\frac{1}{10}$. Domain: $x \geq 0$ Range: $y \geq 0$

11. $y = -5\sqrt{x}$

x	$y = -5\sqrt{x}$	(x, y)
0	$-5\sqrt{0}$	(0, 0)
1	$-5\sqrt{1}$	(1, -5)
4	$-5\sqrt{4}$	(4, -10)
9	$-5\sqrt{9}$	(9, -15)

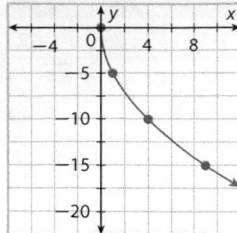

The graph is stretched by a factor of 5 and is reflected across the x-axis. Domain: $x \geq 0$ Range: $y \leq 0$

12. $y = \frac{1}{3}\sqrt{x}$

x	$y = \frac{1}{3}\sqrt{x}$	(x, y)
0	$\frac{1}{3}\sqrt{0}$	(0, 0)
1	$\frac{1}{3}\sqrt{1}$	$\left(1, \frac{1}{3}\right)$
4	$\frac{1}{3}\sqrt{4}$	$\left(4, \frac{2}{3}\right)$
9	$\frac{1}{3}\sqrt{9}$	(9, 1)

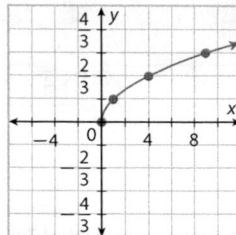

The graph is compressed by a factor of $\frac{1}{3}$. Domain: $x \geq 0$ Range: $y \geq 0$.

13. $y = 6\sqrt{x}$

x	$y = 6\sqrt{x}$	(x, y)
0	$6\sqrt{0}$	(0, 0)
1	$6\sqrt{1}$	(1, 6)
4	$6\sqrt{4}$	(4, 12)
9	$6\sqrt{9}$	(9, 18)
16	$6\sqrt{16}$	(16, 24)

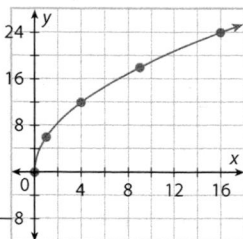

The graph is stretched by a factor of 6. Domain: $x \geq 0$ Range: $y \geq 0$

14. $y = -\frac{1}{2}\sqrt{x}$

x	$y = -\frac{1}{2}\sqrt{x}$	(x, y)
0	$-\frac{1}{2}\sqrt{0}$	$(0, 0)$
1	$-\frac{1}{2}\sqrt{1}$	$\left(1, -\frac{1}{2}\right)$
4	$-\frac{1}{2}\sqrt{4}$	$(4, -1)$
9	$-\frac{1}{2}\sqrt{9}$	$\left(9, -\frac{3}{2}\right)$

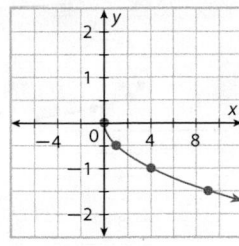

The graph is compressed by a factor of $\frac{1}{2}$, and there is reflection across the *x*-axis.
Domain: $x \geq 0$ Range: $y \leq 0$

Construct a square root function to solve the problem.

15. The speed in miles per hour of a tsunami can be modeled by the function $s(d) = 3.86\sqrt{d}$, where *d* is the average depth in feet of the water over which the tsunami travels. Predict the speed of a tsunami over water with a depth of 1500 feet, rounding to the nearest tenth.

$s(1500) = 3.86\sqrt{1500} \approx 149.5$
The speed of the tsunami is about 149.5 mph.

16. Pilots use the function $D(A) = 3.56\sqrt{A}$ to approximate the distance *D* in kilometers to the horizon from an altitude *A* in meters. What is the approximate distance to the horizon observed by a pilot flying at an altitude of 11,000 meters? (Round to the nearest tenth of a kilometer.)
$D(11,000) = 3.56\sqrt{11,000} \approx 373.4$
The distance to the horizon is approximately 373.4 kilometers.

17. A pharmaceutical company samples the raw materials it receives before they are used in the manufacture of drugs. For inactive ingredients, the company uses the function $s(x) = \sqrt{x} + 1$ to determine the number of samples *s* that should be taken from a shipment of *x* containers. How many samples should be taken from a shipment of 45 containers of an inactive ingredient? (Round to the nearest whole number.)
$s(45) = \sqrt{45} + 1 \approx 8$ **samples**

18. Graph the equation $y = 2\sqrt{x + 2} + 2$. Then state the domain and range.

x	$y = 2\sqrt{x+2}+2$	(x, y)
−2	$2\sqrt{-2+2}+2$	$(-2, 2)$
−1	$2\sqrt{-1+2}+2$	$(-1, 4)$
2	$2\sqrt{2+2}+2$	$(2, 6)$
7	$2\sqrt{7+2}+2$	$(7, 8)$

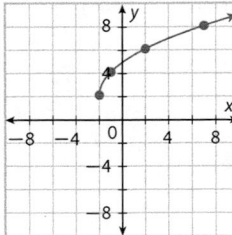

Domain: $x \geq -2$ **Range:** $y \geq 2$

JOURNAL

In their journals, have students copy and complete the graphic organizer shown below to summarize transformations of the square root function $f(x) = \sqrt{x}$. In each box, ask students to write an equation and sketch a graph showing an example of the given transformation.

Transformation	Example
Vertical translation	
Horizontal translation	
Reflection	
Vertical stretch	
Vertical compression	

Write an equation for each graph. Explain your reasoning.

19.

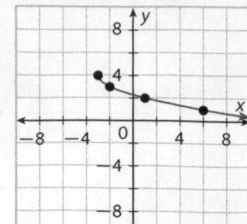

$y \approx -\sqrt{x+3} + 4$

Since the graph is translated 3 units to the left, reflected across the x-axis, and translated 4 units up.

20.

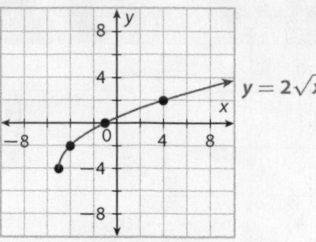

$y = 2\sqrt{x+5} - 4$

The graph is translated 5 units to the left, stretched vertically by a factor of 2, and translated 4 units down.

H.O.T. Focus on Higher Order Thinking

21. Explain the Error A student said the domain and range for the equation $y = \frac{1}{2}\sqrt{x + 10} - 7$ was $x \leq -10$ and $y \geq 7$. Is the student correct? If not, give the mistake and the correct answer.

Both the domain and range are incorrect. The correct domain is $x \geq -10$ and the correct range is $y \geq -7$.

22. Multi-Step The time t in seconds required for an object to fall from a certain height can be modeled by the function $t(h) = \frac{1}{4}\sqrt{h}$, where h is the initial height of the object in feet. How much longer will it take for a piece of an iceberg to fall into the ocean from a height of 240 ft than from a height of 100 ft? (Round to the nearest hundredth of a second.)

$$t(240) - t(100) = \frac{1}{4}\sqrt{240} - \frac{1}{4}\sqrt{100} \approx 1.37$$

It will take about 1.37 seconds longer.

23. Analyze Relationships Describe how a horizontal translation and a vertical translation of the function $f(x) = \sqrt{x}$ each affect the function's domain and range.

Possible Answer: A horizontal translation affects the domain, but not the range. The domain of the translated function is $x \geq h$, where h is the number of units the function is translated horizontally. A vertical translation affects the range, but not the domain. The range of the translated function is $f(x) \geq k$, where k is the number of units the function is translated vertically.

© Houghton Mifflin Harcourt Publishing Company

Module 24

1189

Lesson 3

1189 Lesson 24.3

24. Represent Real-World Problems Pilots use the function $D(A) = 3.56\sqrt{A}$ to approximate the distance D in kilometers to the horizon from an altitude A in meters on a clear day.

a. A vertical compression of $D(A)$ by a factor of $\frac{1}{4}$ can be used to model the distance to the horizon on a partly cloudy day. Write the new function and approximate the distance to the horizon observed by a pilot flying at an altitude of 5000 m. (Round to the nearest whole kilometer.)

$$D(A) = \left(\frac{1}{4}\right)3.56\sqrt{A} = 0.89\sqrt{A}$$

$$D(5000) = 0.89\sqrt{5000} \approx 63$$

The distance to the horizon is about 63 kilometers.

b. How will the distance to the horizon on a partly cloudy day change if the pilot descends by 1500 m?

5000 m − 1500 m = 3500m

$$D(3500) = 0.89\sqrt{3500} \approx 53$$

$$D(5000) - D(3500) \approx 63 - 53 = 10$$

The distance to the horizon will decrease by about 10 kilometers.

Lesson Performance Task

On a clear day, the ability to see a faraway unobstructed object on flat land is limited by the curvature of Earth. For an object with a height H in meters being observed by a person at height h in meters above the ground, the approximate distance d, in kilometers, at which the object falls below the horizon is given by the function $d(H) = 3.57\sqrt{H} + 3.57\sqrt{h}$.

A. What is the effect of the observer's height h on the graph of $d(H)$?

The graph is translated up by 3.57 $\sqrt{h}$ meters.

B. An observational tower has two levels, one at 100 meters and the second at 200 meters, so more visitors are able to visit the tower and the visitors have two different perspectives. Several tall buildings are in different directions and are all unobstructed from the observational tower. Plot two functions for the distance required to see a building over the horizon versus the height of the building, one for each level on the observational tower.

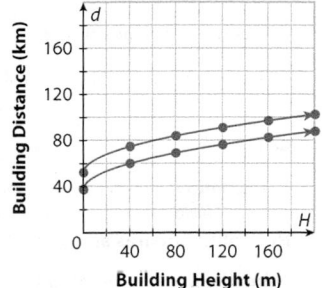

C. Building A is 40 meters tall and 60 kilometers away, building B is 80 meters tall and 62 kilometers away, building C is 110 meters tall and is 68 kilometers away, and building D is 150 meters tall and is 80 kilometers away. Which buildings can be seen from both levels on a clear day? Which buildings can be seen from the top level on a clear day? Explain.

Since $d_{100}(40) \approx 58.3$ which is less than 60, and $d_{200}(40) \approx 73.1$ which is greater than 60, building A can only be seen from the top level. Since $d_{100}(80) \approx 67.6$ and $d_{200}(80) \approx 82.4$ are both greater than 62, building B can be seen from both levels. Since $d_{100}(110) \approx 73.1$ and $d_{200}(110) \approx 87.9$ are both greater than 68, building C can be seen from both levels. Since $d_{100}(150) \approx 79.4$ which is less than 80, and $d_{200}(150) \approx 94.2$ which is greater than 80, building D can only be seen from the top level.

INTEGRATE MATHEMATICAL PRACTICES
Focus on Math Connections

MP.1 Before working with the equation given in the Lesson Performance Task, discuss with students how the distance you can see to the horizon is affected by both your height and the height of the object you are looking at. In addition to drawing on personal experiences of distant views from high points, it may help students to sketch a diagram showing the round Earth and the straight line of sight between two vertical objects on Earth's surface. Students should recognize that the higher the objects, the farther you can see them without having your view blocked by the curving surface of Earth.

QUESTIONING STRATEGIES

? In the equation $d(H) = 3.57\sqrt{H} + 3.57\sqrt{h}$, how does the factor 3.57 affect the graph? **It causes the graph of $d(H) = \sqrt{H}$ to be vertically stretched by a factor of 3.57.**

EXTENSION ACTIVITY

Have students derive the formula $d(H) = 3.57\sqrt{H} + 3.57\sqrt{h}$ using the figure shown, where R is the Earth's radius, 6378 km, by applying the Pythagorean Theorem to both right triangles: $(R + H)^2 = R^2 + y^2$, so $y = \sqrt{2RH + H^2}$. Similarly, $x = \sqrt{2Rh + h^2}$. Since R is much greater than both H and h, write these expressions as $x \approx \sqrt{2Rh}$ and $y \approx \sqrt{2RH}$. Substitute 6378 for R, divide h and H by 1000 to convert from meters to kilometers, and add the two expressions to get the final equation.

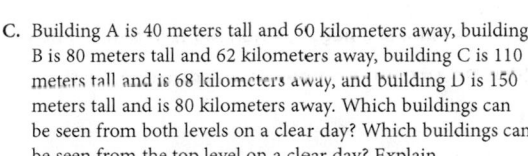

Scoring Rubric

2 points: Student correctly solves the problem and explains his/her reasoning.

1 point: Student shows good understanding of the problem but does not fully solve or explain his/her reasoning.

0 points: Student does not demonstrate understanding of the problem.

Graphing Square Root Functions   **1190**

Graphing Cube Root Functions

Common Core Math Standards

The student is expected to:

COMMON CORE **F-IF.C.7b**

Graph square root, cube root, and piecewise-defined functions, including step functions and absolute value functions. Also F-BF.B.3, F-BF.B.4a

Mathematical Practices

COMMON CORE **MP.2 Reasoning**

Language Objective

Describe what changes to the parent cube root function cause horizontal and vertical translations of its graph.

ENGAGE

Essential Question: How can you use transformations of the parent cube root function to graph functions of the form $f(x) = a\sqrt[3]{x-h} + k$?

You can graph $f(x) = a\sqrt[3]{x-h} + k$ by starting with $f(x) = \sqrt[3]{x}$, translating it h units to the right, vertically stretching or compressing it by the factor of a, and translating it k units up.

PREVIEW: LESSON PERFORMANCE TASK

View the Engage section online. Discuss what properties of metals, such as hardness, flexibility, and density, might be considered by an engineer designing a part for a machine. Then preview the Lesson Performance Task.

Name _____ Class _____ Date _____

24.4 Graphing Cube Root Functions

Essential Question: How can you use transformations of the parent cube root function to graph functions of the form $f(x) = a\sqrt[3]{x-h} + k$?

Resource Locker

⊘ Explore 1 Exploring the Inverse of $y = x^3$

The inverse of a function can be found both algebraically and graphically. Explore the graph of the inverse of $y = x^3$ first and then find the functional form.

(A) Use your graphing calculator to plot the functions $y = x^3$ and $y = x$, with the standard window settings. The graph of $\underline{y = x}$ produces a diagonal line across the screen.

(B) Use the DrawInv feature to draw the graph of the inverse of $y = x^3$ along with $y = x^3$ and $y = x$.

The newly drawn inverse should look like a $\underline{\text{reflection}}$ of the graph of $y = x^3$ across the line, $y = x$.

(C) The inverse graph drawn by the calculator passes the $\underline{\text{vertical}}$ line test, indicating that it is a function.

(D) Cube roots are the inverse operation of cubing. Use inverse operations to write the inverse of $y = x^3$.

Switch x and y in the equation. $\qquad x = y^3$

Take the cube root of both sides of the equation. $\qquad \underline{\sqrt[3]{x}} = y$

Reflect

1. **Discussion** When you take the cube root of a number or variable, do you have to consider both positive and negative cases? Explain why or why not.

No. Unlike squares and square roots, the cube of a negative number is negative, and the cube of a positive number is positive. Because cubing does not ever change the sign, neither does taking the cube root.

© Houghton Mifflin Harcourt Publishing Company

Module 24 **1191** Lesson 4

HARDCOVER PAGES 927–934

Turn to these pages to find this lesson in the hardcover student edition.

⊘ Explore 2 Graphing the Parent Cube Root Function

The graph shows and $y = x^3$ and $y = \sqrt[3]{x}$.

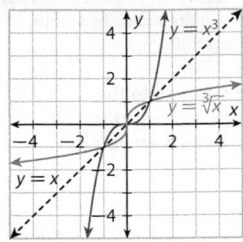

(A) What is the range of $y = x^3$?

$\boxed{-\infty} < y < \boxed{\infty}$

(B) What values of y cannot result from evaluating the cubic function, $y = x^3$? __none__

(C) If any value of y can result from evaluating the cubic function, $y = x^3$, then __any__ value of x can be used to evaluate the function $y = \sqrt[3]{x}$.

(D) The domain of $y = \sqrt[3]{x}$ is $\boxed{-\infty} < x < \boxed{\infty}$.

(E) Is there any need to restrict the domain of $y = \sqrt[3]{x}$? __no__

(F) A **cube root function** is a function whose rule is a cube root expression. $y = \sqrt[3]{x}$ is the parent cube root function. Plot the function for yourself by completing the table of values, and plotting the points.

x	$y = \sqrt[3]{x}$
−8	−2
−1	−1
0	0
1	1
8	2

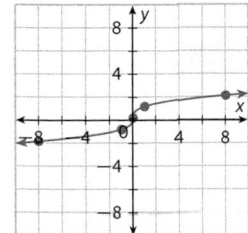

Reflect

2. Why is it that x can be a negative number in the cube root function, but not the square root function?
The square root function is different than the cube root function. Because squared

numbers are always positive, there is no number that can be squared to produce a

negative number. Thus, the square root of a negative number is not a real number.

There is no such restriction on cubes and cube roots.

Module 24   1192   Lesson 4

© Houghton Mifflin Harcourt Publishing Company

PROFESSIONAL DEVELOPMENT

COMMON CORE Integrate Mathematical Practices

This lesson provides an opportunity to address Mathematical Practice **MP.2**, which calls for students to "reason abstractly and quantitatively." As students work with transformations of cube root functions, they express the relationship between two quantities in equations, tables, and graphs. Students explore how changes to the equation affect the graph of the cube root function, and they are then able to write an equation from a given graph.

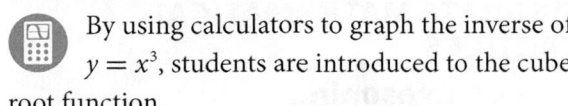

EXPLORE 1

Exploring the Inverse of $y = x^3$

INTEGRATE TECHNOLOGY

By using calculators to graph the inverse of $y = x^3$, students are introduced to the cube root function.

INTEGRATE MATHEMATICAL PRACTICES
Focus on Math Connections

MP.1 When graphing the equation $y = x^3$, review the shapes of graphs of polynomial functions. Students should understand that because x^3 is an odd degree polynomial, the function will have opposite end behavior at its two ends.

EXPLORE 2

Graphing the Parent Cube Root Function

INTEGRATE MATHEMATICAL PRACTICES
Focus on Modeling

MP.4 Because the graphs of $f(x) = \sqrt{x}$ and $f(x) = \sqrt[3]{x}$ have a similar shape, students may think they are the same function for non-negative values of x. Construct a table of values for both functions to show that the functions do not have identical values.

QUESTIONING STRATEGIES

? Because the graphs of $y = x^3$ and $y = \sqrt[3]{x}$ are reflections of each other across the line $y = x$, what must be true about the points of intersection of the two graphs? What are the points of intersection?
The graphs intersect when $y = x$, at the points $(-1, -1)$, $(0, 0)$, and $(1, 1)$.

Graphing Cube Root Functions   **1192**

EXPLAIN 1

Graphing Translations of the Parent Cube Root Function

INTEGRATE MATHEMATICAL PRACTICES

Focus on Reasoning

MP.2 Students may have difficulty remembering which of the parameters h and k represents a horizontal translation and which represents a vertical translation. Remind students that the x-value represents a horizontal position, so the horizontal change is determined by the constant that is more closely associated with x.

AVOID COMMON ERRORS

Remind students to draw the radical symbol so that it covers the entire expression to which it applies. Drawing the radical symbol over too many or too few terms may cause students to identify and graph incorrect points for a translated function.

QUESTIONING STRATEGIES

? Do the parameters h and k in the cube root function $f(x) = \sqrt[3]{x - h} + k$ have the same effect as in the square root function $f(x) = \sqrt{x - h} + k$? Explain. **Yes; in both functions, subtracting h from x causes a horizontal translation of the graph of the parent function, and adding k to the parent function causes a vertical translation.**

⊘ Explain 1 **Graphing Translations of the Parent Cube Root Function**

Functions of the form $y = \sqrt[3]{x - h} + k$ are translations of the cube root parent function $y = \sqrt[3]{x}$. For example, the graph of $y = \sqrt[3]{x - h} + k$ looks like the graph of $y = \sqrt[3]{x}$ shifted to the right by h units and up by k units. Negative values of h result in a shift to the left, and negative values of k result in a downward shift.

> **Example 1** Use a table of values to add the graph of the transformed function to the parent function provided. Describe how the graph of the parent function was shifted. State the domain and range. Check your graphs on a graphing calculator.

(A) $y = \sqrt[3]{x - 3} - 4$

x	y
−5	−6
2	−5
3	−4
4	−3
11	−2

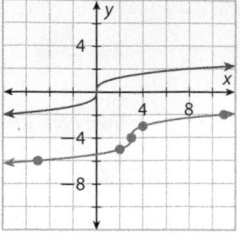

The graph was shifted right by 3 units and down by 4 units.

Domain: $-\infty < x < \infty$

Range: $-\infty < y < \infty$

(B) $y = \sqrt[3]{x + 2} + 8$

x	y
−10	6
−3	7
−2	8
−1	9
6	10

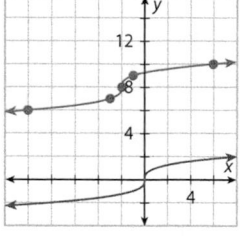

The graph was shifted ___**left**___ by 2 units and ___**up**___ by 8 units.

Domain: ___−∞___ $< x <$ ___∞___

Range: ___−∞___ $< y <$ ___∞___

COLLABORATIVE LEARNING

Peer-to-Peer Activity

Have students work in pairs. Ask students to write and graph a cube root function in the form $f(x) = a\sqrt[3]{x - h} + k$ and then exchange graphs with their partners. By examining the shape of the graph and comparing it to the parent cube root function, students can determine the values of the parameters a, h, and k. Have students use these parameters to write the functions for each other's graphs. Then have them check whether their functions match the functions that were used to make the graphs.

Graph the function and compare it to the graph of the parent cube root function. State the shift in direction and by how many units. Then state the domain and range.

3. $y = \sqrt[3]{x + 3} - 6$

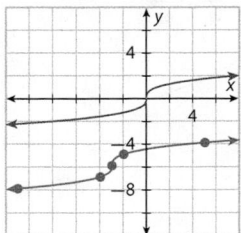

The graph was shifted left by 3 units and down by 6 units.

Domain: $-\infty < x < \infty$

Range: $-\infty < y < \infty$

⊘ Explain 2 · Graphing Stretches/Compressions and Reflections of the Parent Cube Root Function

Functions of the form $y = a\sqrt[3]{x}$ with $a \neq 0$ are vertical stretches and compressions of the cube root parent function. The graph of $y = a\sqrt[3]{x}$ looks like the graph of $y = \sqrt[3]{x}$ but will be stretched vertically by a factor of $|a|$ if $|a| > 1$ or compressed vertically by a factor of $|a|$ if $|a| < 1$. If $a < 0$, the graph will also be reflected across the x-axis.

Example 2 Use a table of values to add the graph of the transformed function to the graph of the parent function provided. Describe how the graph was stretched, compressed, and/or reflected. State the domain and range. Check your graphs on a graphing calculator.

Ⓐ $y = \frac{1}{2}\sqrt[3]{x}$

x	y
−1	−0.5
0	0
1	0.5

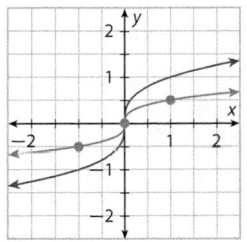

The graph was compressed by a factor of $\frac{1}{2}$ and is not reflected across the x-axis.

Domain: $-\infty < x < \infty$

Range: $-\infty < y < \infty$

EXPLAIN 2

Graphing Stretches/Compressions and Reflections of the Parent Cube Root Function

AVOID COMMON ERRORS

Because a negative value for the parameter a in a square root function makes all output values negative, students may assume that the same is true for cube root functions. Remind students that when a is negative, multiplying it by the parent function will reverse the sign of all the output values.

QUESTIONING STRATEGIES

? How do the output values for the function $f(x) = a\sqrt[3]{x}$ compare to the output values for the parent function $f(x) = \sqrt[3]{x}$? For each input, the output is a times the output of the parent function.

? How do the domain and range of transformed cube root functions compare to the domain and range of the parent cube root function? They are the same. Both the domain and the range of the transformed functions, like the domain and range of the parent function, include all real numbers.

DIFFERENTIATE INSTRUCTION

Multiple Representations

When working with translations of the parent cube root function, suggest that students create a table in which they first identify points on the parent function, then subtract h from each x-value and add k to each y-value to find points on the transformed function. By first finding points on the graph of the parent function, then translating each point, students may be more likely to remember the meanings of the parameters h and k.

INTEGRATE MATHEMATICAL PRACTICES

Focus on Modeling

MP.4 Discuss with students how the end behavior of functions of the form $f(x) = a\sqrt[3]{x}$ is affected by the value of a. Students should recognize that for positive values of a, $f(x)$ increases as x increases, and for negative values of a, $f(x)$ decreases as x increases.

Ⓑ $y = -4\sqrt[3]{x}$

x	y
−8	8
−1	4
0	0
1	−4
8	−8

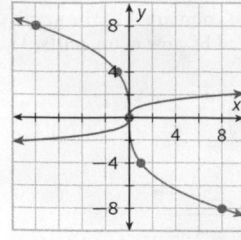

The graph was stretched by a factor of __4__ and __reflected__ across the x-axis.

Domain: $-\infty < x < \infty$

Range: $-\infty < y < \infty$

YourTurn

Graph the function and compare it to the parent cube root function. State the stretch/compression factor and whether the graph was reflected or not. Then state the domain and range.

4. $y = 2\sqrt[3]{x}$

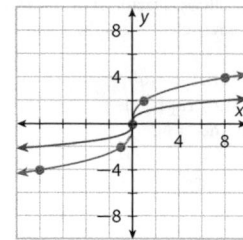

The graph was stretched by a factor of 2 and is not reflected across the x-axis.

Domain: $-\infty < x < \infty$

Range: $-\infty < y < \infty$

LANGUAGE SUPPORT **EL**

Connect Vocabulary

Many examples in this lesson involve *translating* graphs. English learners are probably familiar with translating between languages. Discuss with students how the two meanings of *translate* are different. Have them make a list of words they encounter whose specialized meanings in math differ from their everyday meanings. For example, *parent* is an everyday word that also has a special meaning in this lesson.

5. Does the domain of $y = x^3$ need to be restricted in order for its inverse to be a function? Explain why or why not.

No. Because $y = x^3$ is already a one-to-one function, even if the domain is all real numbers, its inverse will only have one output value for each input value without restricting the domain.

6. How do the transformation parameters a, h, and k affect the domain and range of $y = a\sqrt[3]{x - h} + k$?

They do not. For all values of a, h, and k except $a = 0$, the domain and range are all real numbers.

7. **Essential Question Check-In** Describe how the parameters a, h, and k affect the graph of $y = a\sqrt[3]{x - h} + k$ as they are changed.

The parameter a controls the vertical stretch or compression. As a is increased, the graph stretches up and down. As a is decreased, the graph compresses up and down. If a changes signs, the graph is reflected across the x-axis. The parameter h moves the graph to the right if it is positive and to the left if it is negative. The parameter k moves the graph up if it is positive and down if it is negative.

ELABORATE

INTEGRATE MATHEMATICAL PRACTICES
Focus on Modeling

MP.4 When using tables of values to graph cube root functions, remind students that the graph and the equation of a function are representations of the same relationship. They should be consistent at every point. Have students work in groups to verify that the estimated coordinates of a few points on their sketched graphs satisfy their equations.

SUMMARIZE THE LESSON

? How does each of the parameters a, h, and k in functions of the form $f(x) = a\sqrt[3]{x - h} + k$ affect the graph of the cube function? The graph is a vertical stretch of the graph of the parent function when $|a| > 1$ and a vertical compression when $|a| < 1$. When a is negative, the graph is also reflected across the x–axis. The graph of the parent function is translated to the right if h is positive and to the left if h is negative, and it is translated up if k is positive and down if k is negative.

EVALUATE

ASSIGNMENT GUIDE

Concepts and Skills	Practice
Explore 1 Exploring the Inverse of $y = x^3$	Exercise 1
Explore 2 Graphing the Parent Cube Root Function	Exercise 2
Example 1 Graphing Translations of the Parent Cube Root Function	Exercises 3–14, 25
Example 2 Graphing Stretches/Compressions and Reflections of the Parent Cube Root Function	Exercises 15–24

INTEGRATE MATHEMATICAL PRACTICES

Focus on Math Connections

MP.1 Have students work together to create a list of perfect cubes from 0 to 125. Having a familiarity with perfect cubes is useful when creating a table of values to graph a cube root function. For example, when working with horizontal translations of cube root functions, it is helpful to choose x-values so that $x - h$ is a perfect cube.

INTEGRATE MATHEMATICAL PRACTICES

Focus on Critical Thinking

MP.3 Remind students that although all the problems in this lesson involve cube root functions, it is always important to pay attention to what root is denoted by the radical symbol. When encountering problems involving radicals, students should not assume that the root is the type with which they are most familiar.

1197 Lesson 24.4

• Online Homework
• Hints and Help
• Extra Practice

1. Use inverse operations to find the inverse of $y = 8x^3$.

$x = 8y^3$

$\sqrt[3]{\dfrac{x}{8}} = y$

$\dfrac{\sqrt[3]{x}}{2} = y$

The inverse of $y = 8x^3$ is $y = \dfrac{\sqrt[3]{x}}{2}$ or $y = \dfrac{1}{2}\sqrt[3]{x}$.

2. Graph $y = \sqrt[3]{x}$ together with $y = \sqrt{x}$ shown from 0 to 10. For what positive values of x is the cube root of x greater than the square root of x? For what positive values of x is the square root of x greater than the cube root of x?

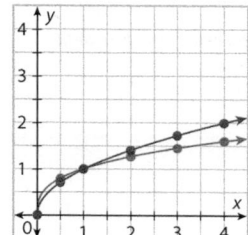

Cube root greater: $0 < x < 1$

Square root greater: $1 < x$

Graph each function.

3. $y = \sqrt[3]{x} - 4$

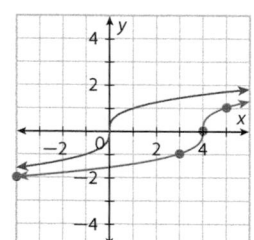

4. $y = \sqrt[3]{x} - 5$

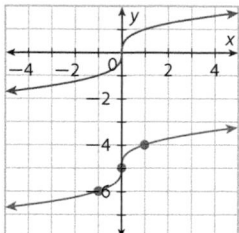

Exercise	Depth of Knowledge (D.O.K.)	COMMON CORE Mathematical Practices
1	**2** Skills/Concepts	**MP.2** Reasoning
2	**2** Skills/Concepts	**MP.6** Precision
3–18	**1** Recall	**MP.7** Using Structure
19–21	**2** Skills/Concepts	**MP.4** Modeling
22	**2** Skills/Concepts	**MP.7** Using Structure
23	**3** Strategic Thinking H.O.T.	**MP.7** Using Structure

© Houghton Mifflin Harcourt Publishing Company

5. $y = \sqrt[3]{x - 2} - 2$

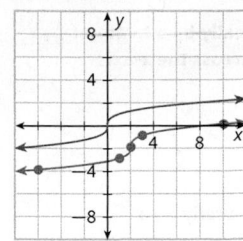

6. $y = \sqrt[3]{x + 3} + 7$

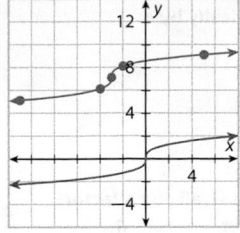

7. $y = -2\sqrt[3]{x}$

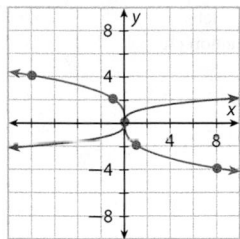

8. $y = \frac{1}{4}\sqrt[3]{x}$

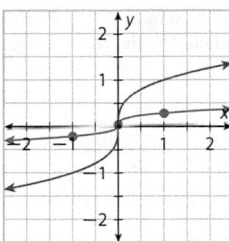

9. $y = 5\sqrt[3]{x}$

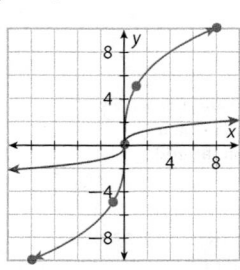

10. $y = -\frac{1}{2}\sqrt[3]{x}$

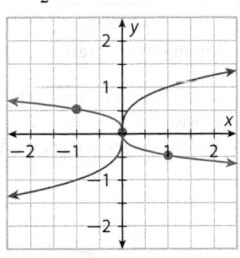

Describe the transformation or transformations of each function from the parent cube root function, $y = \sqrt[3]{x}$.

11. $y = \sqrt[3]{x - 1} + 5$

translated right by 1 unit and up by 5 units

12. $y = \sqrt[3]{x + 5} + 7$

translated left by 5 units and up by 7 units

13. $y = \sqrt[3]{x - 3} - 3$

translated right by 3 units and down by 3 units

14. $y = \sqrt[3]{x + 7} - 2\frac{1}{2}$

translated left by 7 unit and down by $2\frac{1}{2}$ units

TECHNOLOGY

Discuss with students how to access the cube root function on a graphing calculator by selecting option **4:** $\sqrt[3]{\;}($ under the **MATH** menu. Students should be aware that they will have to close the parentheses after entering the value whose cube root they are calculating.

Exercise	Depth of Knowledge (D.O.K.)		COMMON CORE Mathematical Practices	
24	**3** Strategic Thinking	H.O.T.	**MP.3**	Logic
25	**2** Skills/Concepts	H.O.T.	**MP.4**	Modeling

Graphing Cube Root Functions   **1198**

15. $y = 3\sqrt[3]{x}$

stretched vertically by a factor of 3

16. $y = -\frac{3}{2}\sqrt[3]{x}$

stretched vertically by a factor of $\frac{3}{2}$, and reflected across the x-axis

17. $y = -\frac{1}{5}\sqrt[3]{x}$

compressed vertically by a factor of $\frac{1}{5}$, and reflected across the x-axis

18. $y = \frac{1}{10}\sqrt[3]{x}$

compressed vertically by a factor of $\frac{1}{10}$

19. A cylindrical water holding tank with a height equal to its diameter has a height of $h = \sqrt[3]{\frac{4}{\pi}}\sqrt[3]{V}$, where V is the volume of the tank. Graph the height function on the grid provided.

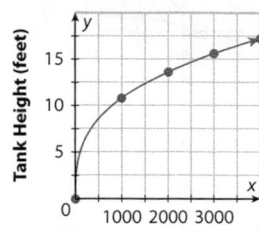

20. **Geometry** The Louvre Palace in Paris has a large glass pyramid in the main court. For a square pyramid with height equal to length, the height is related to the volume by $h = \sqrt[3]{3}\sqrt[3]{V}$. Graph the height of a pyramid as a function of volume on the grid provided.

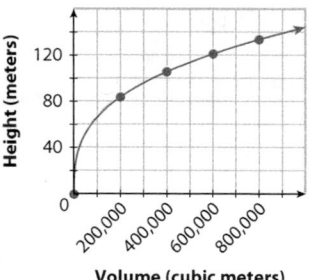

21. Geometry The diameter of a ball as a function of its volume is given by $d = 2\sqrt[3]{\frac{3}{4\pi}}\sqrt[3]{V} \approx 1.24\sqrt[3]{V}$. Describe the transformations of a graph of the diameter of a sphere compared to the parent cube root function, $r = \sqrt[3]{V}$, and graph the function on the grid provided.

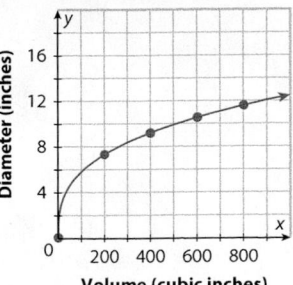

It is a vertical stretch by a factor of 1.24.

22. The function $y = \frac{1}{3}\sqrt[3]{x + 2} - 5$ has been transformed from the parent function, $y = \sqrt[3]{x}$, by which of the following transformations? Select all that apply.

A. vertical stretch by $\frac{1}{3}$

B. vertical compression by $\frac{1}{3}$

C. reflection across the y-axis

D. reflection across the x-axis

E. shifted up by 5

F. shifted down by 5

G. shifted right by 2

H. shifted left by 2

H.O.T. **Focus on Higher Order Thinking**

23. Critical Thinking If the graph of $y = \frac{1}{2}\sqrt[3]{x}$ is shifted left 2 units, what is the equation of the translated graph?

$$y = \frac{1}{2}\sqrt[3]{x + 2}$$

24. Communicate Mathematical Ideas Mitchio says that cube root functions of the form $y = a\sqrt[3]{x}$ should be considered to have a limited domain, because a cannot equal 0. Explain why you do or do not agree with Mitchio.

Mitchio is correct that a cannot be equal to 0, but restrictions on transformation parameters are not the same as restrictions on the input of a function. The domain of the function only refers to limits on the input variables. If y is considered a function of a rather than a function of x, then y would be a linear function of a, not a cube root function.

JOURNAL

Have students write a paragraph explaining how the values of the parameters a, h, and k affect transformations of the parent cube root function. Students should provide sample equations and graphs to illustrate each type of transformation.

25. **Multi-step** The length of a cube as a function of total volume is given by $\ell = \sqrt[3]{V_t}$.

   a. Write the function for the length of a cubic box needed to hold a cube-shaped glass vase that has a volume of 125 cubic inches and the packing material that surrounds the vase, which has a volume of V_p.

   $$V_t = V_p + 125$$
   $$\ell = \sqrt[3]{V_p + 125}$$

   b. What are the domain and range of this function?

   Domain: $V_p \geq 0$

   Range: $\ell \geq 5$ inches

   c. Graph the function on the grid.

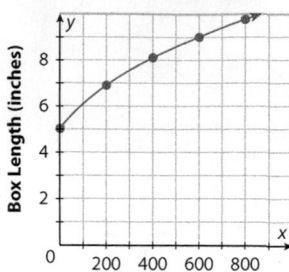

Volume of Packing Material
(cubic inches)

Lesson Performance Task

A manufacturer wants to make a ball bearing that is made of a mixture of zinc, iron, and copper and has come down to a choice of two alloys. Alloy A has a density of 7.5 grams per cubic centimeter and alloy B has a density of 8.5 grams per cubic centimeter.

A. Use the formula for the volume of a sphere, $V = \frac{4}{3}\pi r^3$, and the formula for density, $D = \frac{m}{V}$, to write an equation for m as a function of r for each alloy.

$$D = \frac{m}{V}$$

$$m = DV$$

$$m_A = \left(\frac{15}{2}\right)\frac{4}{3}\pi r_A{}^3 \qquad m_B = \left(\frac{17}{2}\right)\frac{4}{3}\pi r_B{}^3$$

$$= 10\pi r_A{}^3 \qquad\qquad = \frac{34}{3}\pi r_B{}^3$$

B. Find the inverse of each function. Write the function in the form $r = a\sqrt{m}$, where a is rounded to three decimal places.

$$m_A = 10\pi r_A{}^3 \qquad\qquad m_B = \frac{34}{3}\pi r_B{}^3$$

$$\frac{m_A}{10\pi} = r_A{}^3 \qquad\qquad \frac{3m_B}{34\pi} = r_B{}^3$$

$$\sqrt[3]{\frac{m_A}{10\pi}} = r_A \qquad\qquad \sqrt[3]{\frac{3m_B}{34\pi}} = r_B$$

$$\frac{\sqrt[3]{m_A}}{\sqrt[3]{10\pi}} = r_A \qquad\qquad \sqrt[3]{\frac{3}{34\pi}} \cdot \sqrt[3]{m_B} = r_B$$

$$0.317\sqrt[3]{m_A} \approx r_A \qquad\qquad 0.304\sqrt[3]{m_B} \approx r_B$$

C. How does the graph of each inverse function compare to the parent cube root function? For a given mass, which alloy would have a greater radius?

The inverse function for alloy A is the parent cube root function compressed by a factor of approximately 0.317. The inverse function for alloy B is the parent cube root function compressed by a factor of approximately 0.304. For a given mass, alloy A would have a greater radius because the value of a is greater.

D. The manufacturer wants the ball bearings to have a mass of 12 grams and to have a radius as close to 0.7 centimeter as possible. Which alloy would be closer to the manufacturer's desired specifications? Explain.

Alloy B would be closer to the manufacturer's desired specifications.

Substitute 12 for m_A.	Substitute 12 for m_B.
$r_A = 0.317\sqrt[3]{12}$	$r_B = 0.304\sqrt[3]{12}$
≈ 0.726	≈ 0.696

$|0.726 - 0.7| = 0.026; |0.696 - 0.7| = 0.004$

Since 0.004 is less than 0.026, a ball bearing made from alloy B would have a radius that is closer to 0.7 cm than a ball bearing made from alloy A.

CONNECT VOCABULARY EL

Some students may not be familiar with the terms *alloy* and *density*. Have student volunteers explain these terms. An *alloy* is *a uniform mixture of two or more metals or of a metal and a nonmetal*. The *density* of a substance is a measure of its *mass per unit volume*.

INTEGRATE TECHNOLOGY

As an alternative to using a graphing calculator, students can use an online graphing program or a spreadsheet program to graph multiple functions on the same coordinate plane.

QUESTIONING STRATEGIES

? After finding an equation for mass, m, as a function of radius, r, in the form $m = cr^3$ where c is a constant, how can you find the inverse of the function? **Divide both sides by c, then take the cube root of both sides.**

? How can you calculate the cube root of a number on a calculator if it does not have a cube root key? **Raise the number to the exponent 1/3. Use parentheses around the fraction when entering it into the calculator.**

EXTENSION ACTIVITY

Have students research the densities of three different metals and find the radius of a 12-gram sphere of each metal.

Students may find, for example, that aluminum has a density of 2.70 g/cm³, copper has a density of 8.96 g/cm³, and gold has a density of 19.3 g/cm³. The aluminum sphere would have a radius of 1.02 cm, the copper sphere would have a radius of 0.684 cm, and the gold sphere would have a radius of 0.529 cm.

Scoring Rubric

2 points: Student correctly solves the problem and explains his/her reasoning.

1 point: Student shows good understanding of the problem but does not fully solve or explain his/her reasoning.

0 points: Student does not demonstrate understanding of the problem.

Graphing Cube Root Functions   **1202**

Study Guide Review

ASSESSMENT AND INTERVENTION

Assign or customize module reviews.

MODULE PERFORMANCE TASK

COMMON CORE

Mathematical Practices: MP.1, MP.2, MP.4, MP.5, MP.6, MP.7, MP.8
F-BF.B.4a, A-CED.A.4

SUPPORTING STUDENT REASONING

Students should begin this problem by focusing on what information they will need. Here are some issues they might bring up.

- **How big does the box need to be?** If a ball has a diameter of 10 inches, the smallest box that can contain the ball would be a cubical box measuring 10 inches on a side.

- **Can I measure the balls' dimensions directly?** The dimensions of all three ball types can easily be found on the Internet or measured directly. The objective here, however, is to show how those dimensions can be derived from the volumes of the balls, so encourage students to use mathematical methods.

Functions and Inverses

Essential Question: How can you use functions and inverses to solve real-world problems?

KEY EXAMPLE *(Lessons 24.1, 24.2, 24.3)*

Graph $f(x) = x^2 + 1$ and its inverse.

$$y = x^2 + 1$$
$$x = y^2 + 1$$
$$x - 1 = y^2$$
$$\pm\sqrt{x - 1} = y$$

To find the inverse of $f(x)$, or $f^{-1}(x)$, switch x and y, and solve for y.

For the inverse to be a function, restrict it to nonnegative numbers, $f^{-1}(x) = \sqrt{x - 1}$.

Fill in a table of values for $f(x)$ and $f^{-1}(x)$.

x	$f(x)$	$f^{-1}(x)$
-2	$(-2)^2 + 1 = 5$	not a real number
-1	$(-1)^2 + 1 = 2$	not a real number
0	$(0)^2 + 1 = 1$	not a real number
1	$(1)^2 + 1 = 2$	$\sqrt{1 - 1} = 0$
2	$(2)^2 + 1 = 5$	$\sqrt{2 - 1} = 1$
3	$(3)^2 + 1 = 10$	$\sqrt{3 - 1} \approx 1.41$
4	$(4)^2 + 1 = 17$	$\sqrt{4 - 1} \approx 1.73$

Graph the ordered pairs.

$f^{-1}(x)$ is a reflection of $f(x)$ over $y = x$ for nonnegative values of x.

The domain of $f(x)$ is all real numbers, and the range of $f(x)$ is $y \geq 1$.

The domain of $f^{-1}(x)$ is $x \geq 1$, and the range of $f^{-1}(x)$ is $y \geq 0$.

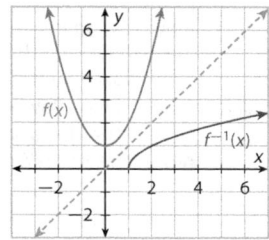

Key Vocabulary
cube root function
(función de raíz cubo)
inverse function
(inverso de una function)
radical function
(radical de una function)
square root function
(función de raíz cuadrada)

SCAFFOLDING SUPPORT

- The function giving the diameter of a sphere as a function of the volume can be derived from the formula for the volume of a sphere. Let x represent the volume of a sphere and let y represent its diameter. Then:

$$x = \left(\frac{4}{3}\right)\pi r^3$$

$$x = \left(\frac{4}{3}\right)\pi \left(\frac{1}{2}y\right)^3 \text{ because radius} = \frac{1}{2}\text{ diameter}$$

$$x = \left(\frac{4}{3}\right)\pi \left(\frac{1}{8}y^3\right)$$

$$x = \left(\frac{1}{6}\right)\pi y^3$$

$$\sqrt[3]{6x/\pi} = y$$

EXERCISES

1. Graph $f(x) = \frac{1}{2}(x + 2)^3$. *(Lesson 24.1)*

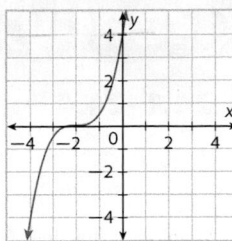

Write the inverse of each function. *(Lesson 24.2)*

2. $g(x) = 4x^2 + 7$

$g^{-1}(x) = \frac{\pm\sqrt{x - 7}}{2}$

3. $t(x) = (x + 15)^3 - 4$

$t^{-1}(x) = (x + 4)^{\frac{1}{3}} - 15$

4. Graph $h(x) = \sqrt[3]{x} - 2$. Find the domain and range of $h(x)$. *(Lesson 24.4)*

Domain: all real numbers; Range: all real numbers

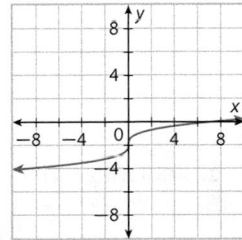

MODULE PERFORMANCE TASK

The Smallest Cube

Foolish Sports makes sporting equipment for people who play unusual sports like lawnmower racing, pie eating, and cheese rolling. For some reason, companies that make footballs, roller skates, and hockey sticks make a lot more money.

So, Foolish is going into the ordinary-sports business. Its first project is to make and sell baseballs, basketballs, and golf balls. The company's package designer found the typical volumes of the three products and now must determine the dimensions of the boxes they will be sold in. Each box must be cubical and must be the smallest box that can contain the ball.

Basketball	448 in³
Baseball	14.1 in³
Golf ball	2.48 in³

What are the dimensions of the three boxes? Explain how you found the dimensions.

Start by listing in the space below the information you will need to solve the problem. Then use your own paper to work on the task. Use numbers, words, or algebra to explain how you reached your conclusion.

© Houghton Mifflin Harcourt Publishing Company

Module 24   **1204**   Study Guide Review

DISCUSSION OPPORTUNITIES

How could you check to see whether your expression for the diameter is correct? **Sample answer: You could substitute one-half of the expression (which equals the radius) for *r* in the formula** $x = \frac{4}{3}\pi r^3$ **and see if, after simplification, a true statement such as** $x = x$ **results.**

SAMPLE SOLUTION

basketball: $x = 448$ in³

$$y = \sqrt[3]{\frac{6x}{\pi}}$$

$$\approx \sqrt[3]{\frac{6(448)}{3.14}}$$

$$\approx \sqrt[3]{856}$$

$$\approx 9.5$$

The box for a basketball measures about 9.5 in. by 9.5 in. by 9.5 in.

baseball: $x = 14.1$ in³

$$y = \sqrt[3]{\frac{6x}{\pi}}$$

$$\approx \sqrt[3]{\frac{6(14.1)}{3.14}}$$

$$\approx \sqrt[3]{26.9}$$

$$= 3.0$$

The box for a baseball measures about 3 in. by 3 in. by 3 in.

golf ball: $x = 2.48$ in³

$$y = \sqrt[3]{\frac{6x}{\pi}}$$

$$\approx \sqrt[3]{\frac{6(2.48)}{3.14}}$$

$$\approx \sqrt[3]{4.74}$$

$$\approx 1.68$$

The box for a golf ball measures about 1.68 in. by 1.68 in. by 1.68 in.

Assessment Rubric

2 points: Student correctly solves the problem and explains his/her reasoning.

1 point: Student shows good understanding of the problem but does not fully solve or explain.

0 points: Student does not demonstrate understanding of the problem.

Study Guide Review   **1204**

Ready to Go On?

ASSESS MASTERY

Use the assessment on this page to determine if students have mastered the concepts and standards covered in this module.

ASSESSMENT AND INTERVENTION

Access Ready to Go On? assessment online, and receive instant scoring, feedback, and customized intervention or enrichment.

ADDITIONAL RESOURCES

Response to Intervention Resources

- Reteach Worksheets

Differentiated Instruction Resources

- Reading Strategies **EL**
- Success for English Learners **EL**
- Challenge Worksheets

Assessment Resources

- Leveled Module Quizzes

(Ready) to Go On?

24.1–24.4 Functions and Inverses

- Online Homework
- Hints and Help
- Extra Practice

Graph each function. *(Lesson 24.1)*

1. Graph $g(x) = \frac{1}{4}(x + 1)^3 - 4$.

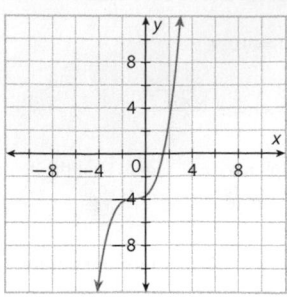

2. Find and graph the inverse of $f(x) = 2x^2 - 4$. *(Lessons 24.2, 24.3)*

$$f^{-1}(x) = \pm\sqrt{\frac{(x + 4)}{2}}$$

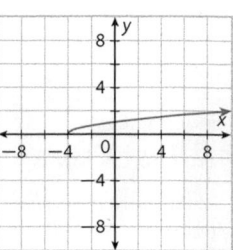

3. Graph $h(x) = 2\sqrt[3]{x + 6} + 2$. *(Lesson 24.4)*

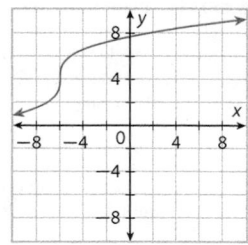

ESSENTIAL QUESTION

4. How could you sketch the inverse of an exponential function?

Possible Answer: As with other types of functions, I could graph the exponential function and then reflect it over the line $y = x$ to graph the inverse.

COMMON CORE Common Core Standards

Lesson	Items	Content Standards	Mathematical Practices
24.1	1	**F-IF.C.7c, F-BF.B.3**	**MP.7**
24.2, 24.3	2	**F-BF.B.4a**	**MP.7**
24.4	3	**F-IF.C.7b**	**MP.7**

MODULE 24
MIXED REVIEW

Assessment Readiness

1. Find the solutions of $-2x(x + 1)(3x + 5) = 0$. Is the given value of x a solution? Select Yes or No for each possible solution.

   A. $x = -\frac{5}{3}$ ● Yes   ○ No

   B. $x = 0$ ● Yes   ○ No

   C. $x = 1$ ○ Yes   ● No

2. Find the inverse of $f(x) = \frac{1}{3}x - 2$.

   Use the inverse to determine if each of the following equations is True or False.

   A. $f^{-1}(-2) = 0$ ● True   ○ False

   B. $f^{-1}(0) = 2$ ○ True   ● False

   C. $f^{-1}(3) = 15$ ● True   ○ False

3. Factor $8x^2 - 50$ completely. Is the following expression a factor of this expression? Select Yes or No for each possible factor.

   A. $(x - 10)$ ○ Yes   ● No

   B. $(2x + 5)$ ● Yes   ○ No

   C. 2 ● Yes   ○ No

4. Graph $f(x) = \frac{1}{2}x^3 + 2$. Describe the end behavior of the graph.

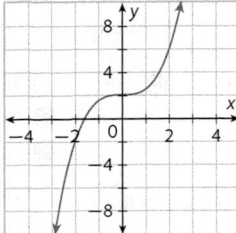

As x approaches infinity, y approaches infinity. As x approaches negative infinity, y approaches negative infinity.

MIXED REVIEW
Assessment Readiness

ASSESSMENT AND INTERVENTION

Assign ready-made or customized practice tests to prepare students for high-stakes tests.

ADDITIONAL RESOURCES

Assessment Resources

- Leveled Module Quizzes: Modified, B

AVOID COMMON ERRORS

Item 3 Some students may factor out the initial coefficient of 8, and then run into difficulty when attempting to factor a fractional term. Remind students to look for the greatest common factor of all terms in the expression.

COMMON CORE	**Common Core Standards**			
Lesson	**Items**	**Content Standards**	**Mathematical Practices**	
20.3	1*	A-APR.B.3	MP.1	
24.2	2	F-BF.B.4a	MP.2	
21.3	3*	A-SSE.A.2	MP.3	
24.1	4	F-IF.C.7c	MP.7	

* Item integrates mixed review concepts from previous modules or a previous course.

MIXED REVIEW
Assessment Readiness

ASSESSMENT AND INTERVENTION

Assign ready-made or customized practice tests to prepare students for high-stakes tests.

ADDITIONAL RESOURCES

Assessment Resources

• Leveled Unit Tests: Modified, A, B, C

• Performance Assessment

AVOID COMMON ERRORS

Item 7 Some students will notice that the y-intercept is 8 and give the answer $x = 0$. Remind them to pay close attention to the details, including negative signs.

Assessment Readiness

• Online Homework
• Hints and Help
• Extra Practice

1. Consider the system $\begin{cases} y \le \frac{1}{2}x + 3 \\ y \ge 2x \end{cases}$. Is each of the following a solution of the system?

Select Yes or No for each possible solution.

A. $(-2, -5)$ ⚪ Yes ⚫ No

B. $(2, 4)$ ⚫ Yes ⚪ No

C. $(3, -1)$ ⚪ Yes ⚫ No

2. Is −4 a solution of the equation?

Select Yes or No for each equation.

A. $x^2 + 4x + 16 = 0$ ⚪ Yes ⚫ No

B. $2x^2 - 8x + 32 = 0$ ⚪ Yes ⚫ No

C. $5x^2 - 80 = 0$ ⚫ Yes ⚪ No

3. Find the inverse of $f(x) = x^2 - 2$. Determine if the given statement is True of False.

A. $f^{-1}(x)$ is a square root function. ⚫ True ⚪ False

B. The domain of is $f^{-1}(x)$ is $x \ge -2$. ⚫ True ⚪ False

C. The range of $f^{-1}(x)$ is all real numbers. ⚪ True ⚫ False

4. Does the given statement describe a step in the transformation of the graph of $f(x) = \sqrt[3]{x}$ that would result in the graph of $g(x) = -4\sqrt[3]{x-1}$?

A. The graph is reflected across the x-axis ⚫ Yes ⚪ No

B. The graph is translated 1 unit down. ⚪ Yes ⚫ No

C. The graph is compressed. ⚪ Yes ⚫ No

5. The graph of $f(x) = \frac{1}{3}x + 1$ is shown. Find and graph the inverse of $f(x)$.

$f^{-1}(x) = 3x - 3$

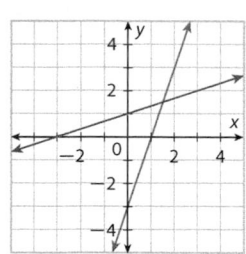

© Houghton Mifflin Harcourt Publishing Company

COMMON CORE ## Common Core Standards

Items	Content Standards	Mathematical Practices
1*	**A-REI.D.12**	**MP.2**
2*	**A-SSE.A.2**	**MP.2**
3	**F-BF.B.4a**	**MP.7**
4	**F-BF.B.3**	**MP.4**
5*	**F-IF.A.2**	**MP.4**
6	**F-BF.B.3**	**MP.4**
7*	**A-REI.D.11**	**MP.4**

* Item integrates mixed review concepts from previous modules or a previous course.

6. The equation that is represented on the graph is a transformation of one of the following parent functions: $y = x^2$, $y = x^3$, $y = \sqrt{x}$, $y = \sqrt[3]{x}$. Write an equation to represent the graph. Explain how you determined which parent function to use.

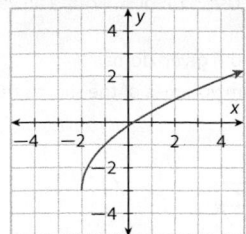

$y = 2\sqrt{x + 2} - 3$; Due to the shape of the graph, I knew it was a transformation of either $y = \sqrt{x}$ or $y = \sqrt[3]{x}$. The domain is limited to $x \geq -2$, while the domain of a cube root function is all real numbers, so it must be a square root function.

7. Graph $f(x) = (x + 2)^3$. Use the graph to solve $-8 = (x + 2)^3$.

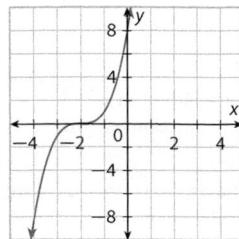

$x = -4$

Performance Tasks

★ **8.** The relationship between the radius r, in centimeters, of a solid gold sphere and its mass m, in grams, is given by $r = 0.23\sqrt[3]{m}$. Graph this relationship for the interval $0 \leq m \leq 10$.

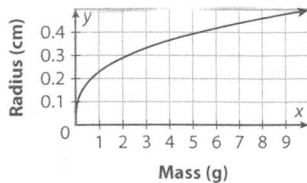

© Houghton Mifflin Harcourt Publishing Company

PERFORMANCE TASKS

There are three different levels of performance tasks:

   * **Novice:** These are short word problems that require students to apply the math they have learned in straightforward, real-world situations.

   ** **Apprentice:** These are more involved problems that guide students step-by-step through more complex tasks. These exercises include more complicated reasoning, writing, and open-ended elements.

   *** **Expert:** These are open-ended, nonroutine problems that, instead of stepping the students through, ask them to choose their own methods for solving and justify their answers and reasoning.

SCORING GUIDES

Item 8 (2 points)

2 points for a correct graph

Item 9 (6 points)

A. 2 points for writing the correct function

B. 2 points for a correct graph

C. 1 point for correct minimum
   1 point for correct maximum

Item 10 (6 points)

A. 1 point for correct function

B. 1 point for correct answer

C. 1 point for correct function

D. 3 points for correct answer and explanation

★★ **9.** A grain silo is in the shape of a cylinder with a hemisphere dome on top. The volume of the silo is given by $V = \frac{2}{3}\pi r^3 + \pi r^2 h$. A farmer decides to build a grain silo with a height of 15 feet, and radius between 3 feet and 6 feet.

   A. Write the function $V(r)$ for $h = 15$ ft. Use 3.14 for π. Round all values to two decimal places.

   B. Graph your function from part **A** for the given domain.

   C. What are the minimum and maximum volumes of the silo, to the nearest cubic foot?

   a. $V = 2.09r^3 + 47.1r^2$

   b.

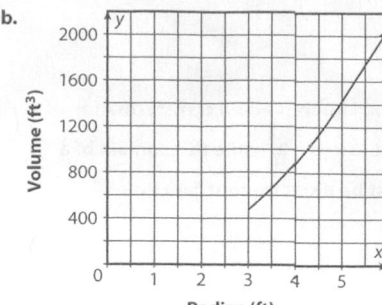

   c. minimum: 480 ft³; maximum: 2148 ft³

★★★ **10.** The distance, d, in meters, an object falls after time t, in seconds, is given by $d = 4.9t^2$. Assume that the domain of the function is $t \geq 0$.

   A. Find the inverse of this function.

   B. How much time does it take for a stone dropped from the edge of a cliff to hit the ground 80 meters below? Round your answer to the nearest tenth of a second.

   C. The relationship between the temperature in degrees Fahrenheit and kelvins is given by $F = \frac{9}{5}(K - 273) + 32$. Find the inverse of this function.

   D. If the speed of sound in air is given by $s = 20.1\sqrt{K}$, where s is in meters per second and K is the temperature in kelvins, how long after dropping the stone can the sound of the stone striking the ground be heard at the edge of the cliff, if the temperature is 77°F? Explain how you got your answer.

   A. $t = \sqrt{\frac{d}{4.9}}$

   B. 4.0 s

   C. $K = \frac{5}{9}(F - 32) + 273$

   D. $K = \frac{5}{9}(F - 32) + 273$

   $= \frac{5}{9}(77 - 32) + 273$

   $= 298$

   $s = 20.1\sqrt{K}$

   $= 20.1\sqrt{298}$

   ≈ 347.0 m/s

   The time for the sound to travel from the base of the cliff to the top is $\frac{1\,s}{347\,m} \cdot 80\,m = 0.23$ s, so the total time is 4.0 s + 0.23 s = 4.23 s.

Ichthyologist A pike is a type of freshwater fish. A ichthyologist uses the function $W(L) = \dfrac{L^3}{3500}$ to find the approximate weight W in pounds of a pike with length L inches.

a. Write the inverse function $L(W)$.

b. Graph the inverse function.

c. What is the significance in the context of the problem of the point at approximately $(6, 28)$ on the graph of $L(W)$?

d. What are the reasonable domain and range of the function $L(W)$?

a. $L(W) = \sqrt[3]{3500W}$

b.

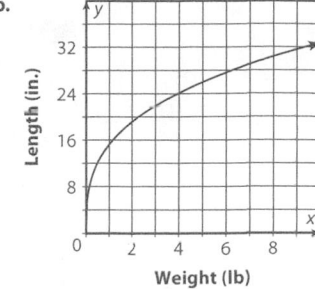

Weight (lb)

c. A pike that weighs 6 pounds is about 28 inches long.

d. Both the domain and the range are all nonnegative real numbers. Because L represents length and W represents weight, neither quantity can be negative.

CAREERS IN MATH

Ichthyologist In this Unit Performance Task, students can see how an ichthyologist uses mathematics on the job.

For more information about careers in mathematics as well as various mathematics appreciation topics, visit the American Mathematical Society at http://www.ams.org.

SCORING GUIDE

Task (6 points)

a. 1 point for a correct function

b. 1 point for a correct graph

c. 2 points for a correct explanation

d. 2 points for a correct response

Glossary/Glosario

A

ENGLISH	SPANISH	EXAMPLES
absolute value The absolute value of x is the distance from zero to x on a number line, denoted $\lvert x \rvert$. $$\lvert x \rvert = \begin{cases} x & \text{if } x \geq 0 \\ -x & \text{if } x < 0 \end{cases}$$	**valor absoluto** El valor absoluto de x es la distancia de cero a x en una recta numérica, y se expresa $\lvert x \rvert$. $$\lvert x \rvert = \begin{cases} x & \text{si } x \geq 0 \\ -x & \text{si } x < 0 \end{cases}$$	$\lvert 3 \rvert = 3$ $\lvert -3 \rvert = 3$
absolute-value equation An equation that contains absolute-value expressions.	**ecuación de valor absoluto** Ecuación que contiene expresiones de valor absoluto.	$\lvert x + 4 \rvert = 7$
absolute-value function A function whose rule contains absolute-value expressions.	**función de valor absoluto** Función cuya regla contiene expresiones de valor absoluto.	$y = \lvert x + 4 \rvert$
absolute-value inequality An inequality that contains absolute-value expressions.	**desigualdad de valor absoluto** Desigualdad que contiene expresiones de valor absoluto.	$\lvert x + 4 \rvert > 7$
accuracy The closeness of a given measurement or value to the actual measurement or value.	**exactitud** Cercanía de una medida o un valor a la medida o el valor real.	
Addition Property of Equality For real numbers a, b, and c, if $a = b$, then $a + c = b + c$.	**Propiedad de igualdad de la suma** Dados los números reales a, b y c, si $a = b$, entonces $a + c = b + c$.	$\begin{aligned} x - 6 &= 8 \\ +6 \quad &+6 \\ x \quad\ &= 14 \end{aligned}$
Addition Property of Inequality For real numbers a, b, and c, if $a < b$, then $a + c < b + c$. Also holds true for $>$, $\leq$, $\geq$, and $\neq$.	**Propiedad de desigualdad de la suma** Dados los números reales a, b y c, si $a < b$, entonces $a + c < b + c$. Es válido también para $>$, $\leq$, $\geq$ y $\neq$.	$\begin{aligned} x - 6 &< 8 \\ +6 \quad &+6 \\ x \quad\ &< 14 \end{aligned}$
additive inverse The opposite of a number. Two numbers are additive inverses if their sum is zero.	**inverso aditivo** El opuesto de un número. Dos números son inversos aditivos si su suma es cero.	The additive inverse of 5 is -5. The additive inverse of -5 is 5.
algebraic expression An expression that contains at least one variable.	**expresión algebraica** Expresión que contiene por lo menos una variable.	
AND A logical operator representing the intersection of two sets.	**Y** Operador lógico que representa la intersección de dos conjuntos.	$A = \{2, 3, 4, 5\}$ $B = \{1, 3, 5, 7\}$ The set of values that are in A AND B is $A \cap B = \{3, 5\}$.

ENGLISH	SPANISH	EXAMPLES
arithmetic sequence A sequence whose successive terms differ by the same nonzero number d, called the common difference.	**sucesión aritmética** Sucesión cuyos términos sucesivos difieren en el mismo número distinto de cero d, denominado *diferencia común*.	4, 7, 10, 13, 16, ... $+3 +3 +3 +3$ $d = 3$
Associative Property of Addition For all numbers a, b, and c, $(a + b) + c = a + (b + c)$.	**Propiedad asociativa de la suma** Dados tres números cualesquiera a, b y c, (a + b) + c = a + (b + c).	$(5 + 3) + 7 = 5 + (3 + 7)$
Associative Property of Multiplication For all numbers a, b, and c, $(a \cdot b) \cdot c = a \cdot (b \cdot c)$.	**Propiedad asociativa de la multiplicación** Dados tres números cualesquiera a, b y c, $(a \cdot b) \cdot c = a \cdot (b \cdot c)$.	$(5 \cdot 3) \cdot 7 = 5 \cdot (3 \cdot 7)$
asymptote A line that a graph gets closer to as the value of a variable becomes extremely large or small.	**asíntota** Línea recta a la cual se aproxima una gráfica a medida que el valor de una variable se hace sumamente grande o pequeño.	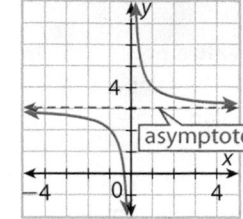
axis of symmetry A line that divides a plane figure or a graph into two congruent reflected halves.	**eje de simetría** Línea que divide una figura plana o una gráfica en dos mitades reflejadas congruentes.	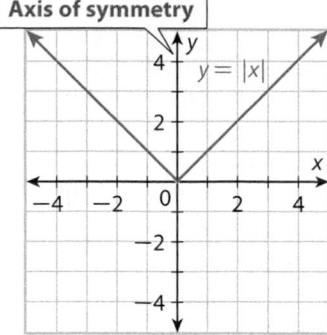

B

base of a power The number in a power that is used as a factor.	**base de una potencia** Número de una potencia que se utiliza como factor.	$3^4 = 3 \cdot 3 \cdot 3 \cdot 3 = 81$ 3 is the base.
base of an exponential function The value of b in a function of the form $f(x) = ab^x$, where a and b are real numbers with $a \neq 0$, $b > 0$, and $b \neq 1$.	**base de una función exponencial** Valor de b en una función del tipo $f(x) = ab^x$, donde a y b son números reales con $a \neq 0$, $b > 0$ y $b \neq 1$.	In the function $f(x) = 5(2)^x$, the base is 2.
binomial A polynomial with two terms.	**binomio** Polinomio con dos términos.	$x + y$ $2a^2 + 3$ $4m^3n^2 + 6mn^4$

boundary line A line that divides a coordinate plane into two half-planes.

línea de límite Línea que divide un plano cartesiano en dos semiplanos.

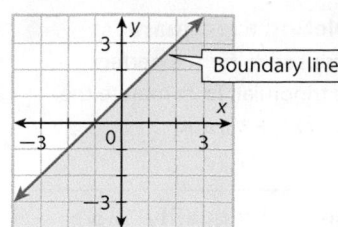

Boundary line

C

categorical data Data that are qualitative in nature, such as "liberal," "moderate," and "conservative."	**datos categóricos** Datos de índole cualitativa, como "liberal", "moderado" y "conservador".	
closure A set of numbers is said to be closed, or to have closure, under a given operation if the result of the operation on any two numbers in the set is also in the set.	**cerradura** Se dice que un conjunto de números es cerrado, o tiene cerradura, respecto de una operación determinada, si el resultado de la operación entre dos números cualesquiera del conjunto también está en el conjunto.	The natural numbers are closed under addition because the sum of two natural numbers is always a natural number.
coefficient A number that is multiplied by a variable.	**coeficiente** Número que se multiplica por una variable.	In the expression $2x + 3y$, 2 is the coefficient of x and 3 is the coefficient of y.
common difference In an arithmetic sequence, the nonzero constant difference of any term and the previous term.	**diferencia común** En una sucesión aritmética, diferencia constante distinta de cero entre cualquier término y el término anterior.	In the arithmetic sequence 3, 5, 7, 9, 11, …, the common difference is 2.
common factor A factor that is common to all terms of an expression or to two or more expressions.	**factor común** Factor que es común a todos los términos de una expresión o a dos o más expresiones.	Expression: $4x^2 + 16x^3 - 8x$ Common factor: $4x$ Expressions: 12 and 18 Common factors: 2, 3, and 6
common ratio In a geometric sequence, the constant ratio of any term and the previous term.	**razón común** En una sucesión geométrica, la razón constante entre cualquier término y el término anterior.	In the geometric sequence 32, 16, 8, 4, 2, …, the common ratio is $\frac{1}{2}$.
Commutative Property of Addition For any two numbers a and b, $a + b = b + a$.	**Propiedad conmutativa de la suma** Dados dos números cualesquiera a y b, $a \cdot b = b \cdot a$.	$3 + 4 = 4 + 3 = 7$
Commutative Property of Multiplication For any two numbers a and b, $a \cdot b = b \cdot a$.	**Propiedad conmutativa de la multiplicación** Dados dos números cualesquiera a y b, $a \cdot b = b \cdot a$	$3 \cdot 4 = 4 \cdot 3 = 12$

completing the square A process used to form a perfect-square trinomial. To complete the square of $x^2 + bx$, add $\left(\frac{b}{2}\right)^2$.

completar el cuadrado Proceso utilizado para formar un trinomio cuadrado perfecto. Para completar el cuadrado de $x^2 + bx$, hay que sumar $\left(\frac{b}{2}\right)^2$.

$x^2 + 6x + \rule{1cm}{0.3cm}$

Add $\left(\frac{6}{2}\right)^2 = 9$.

$x^2 + 6x + 9$

---

compound inequality Two inequalities that are combined into one statement by the word *and* or *or*.

desigualdad compuesta Dos desigualdades unidas en un enunciado por la palabra *y* u *o*.

$x \geq 2$ AND $x < 7$ (also written $2 \leq x < 7$)

0 2 4 6 8

$x < 2$ OR $x > 6$

0 2 4 6 8

---

compound interest Interest earned or paid on both the principal and previously earned interest. The formula for compound interest is $A = P\left(1 + \frac{r}{n}\right)^{nt}$, where A is the final amount, P is the principal, r is the interest rate expressed as a decimal, n is the number of times interest is compounded, and t is the time.

interés compuesto Intereses ganados o pagados sobre el capital y los intereses ya devengados. La fórmula de interés compuesto es $A = P\left(1 + \frac{r}{n}\right)^{nt}$, donde A es la cantidad final, P es el capital, r es la tasa de interés expresada como un decimal, n es la cantidad de veces que se capitaliza el interés y t es el tiempo.

If \$100 is put into an account with an interest rate of 5% compounded monthly, then after 2 years, the account will have $100\left(1 + \frac{0.05}{12}\right)^{12 \cdot 2} = \$110.49$.

---

compound statement Two statements that are connected by the word *and* or *or*.

enunciado compuesto Dos enunciados unidos por la palabra *y* u *o*.

The sky is blue and the grass is green. I will drive to school or I will take the bus.

---

conditional relative frequency The ratio of a joint relative frequency to a related marginal relative frequency in a two-way table.

frecuencia relativa condicional Razón de una frecuencia relativa conjunta a una frecuencia relativa marginal en una tabla de doble entrada.

---

consistent system A system of equations or inequalities that has at least one solution.

sistema consistente Sistema de ecuaciones o desigualdades que tiene por lo menos una solución.

$\begin{cases} x + y = 6 \\ x - y = 4 \end{cases}$

solution: $(5, 1)$

---

constant A value that does not change.

constante Valor que no cambia.

$3, 0, \pi$

---

constant of variation The constant k in direct and inverse variation equations.

constante de variación La constante k en ecuaciones de variación directa e inversa.

$y = 5x$

constant of variation

---

continuous function A function whose graph is an unbroken line or curve with no gaps or breaks.

función continua Función cuya gráfica es una línea recta o curva continua, sin espacios ni interrupciones.

$f(x) = 2^x$

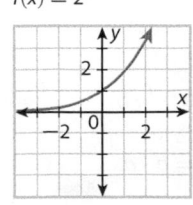

ENGLISH	SPANISH	EXAMPLES
continuous graph A graph made up of connected lines or curves.	**gráfica continua** Gráfica compuesta por líneas rectas o curvas conectadas.	**Angelique's Heart Rate** 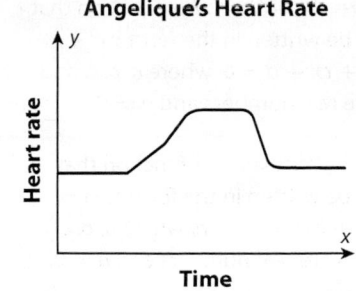
conversion factor The ratio of two equal quantities, each measured in different units.	**factor de conversión** Razón entre dos cantidades iguales, cada una medida en unidades diferentes.	$\dfrac{12 \text{ inches}}{1 \text{ foot}}$
correlation A measure of the strength and direction of the relationship between two variables or data sets.	**correlación** Medida de la fuerza y dirección de la relación entre dos variables o conjuntos de datos.	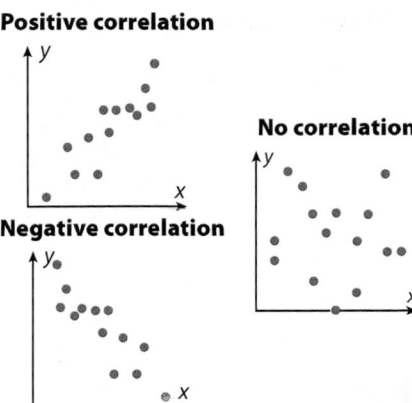
correlation coefficient A number r, where $-1 \le r \le 1$, that describes how closely the points in a scatter plot cluster around the least-squares line.	**coeficiente de correlación** Número r, donde $-1 \le r \le 1$, que describe a qué distancia de la recta de mínimos cuadrados se agrupan los puntos de un diagrama de dispersión.	An r-value close to 1 describes a strong positive correlation. An r-value close to 0 describes a weak correlation or no correlation. An r-value close to -1 describes a strong negative correlation.
cross products In the statement $\frac{a}{b} = \frac{c}{d}$, bc and ad are the cross products.	**productos cruzados** En el enunciado $\frac{a}{b} = \frac{c}{d}$, bc y ad son productos cruzados.	$\frac{1}{2} = \frac{3}{6}$ Cross products: $2 \cdot 3 = 6$ and $1 \cdot 6 = 6$
Cross Product Property For any real numbers a, b, c, and d, where $b \ne 0$ and $d \ne 0$, if $\frac{a}{b} = \frac{c}{d}$, then $ad = bc$.	**Propiedad de productos cruzados** Dados los números reales a, b, c y d, donde $b \ne 0$ y $d \ne 0$, si $\frac{a}{b} = \frac{c}{d}$, entonces $ad = bc$.	If $\frac{4}{6} = \frac{10}{x}$, then $4x = 60$, so $x = 15$.
cube root A number, written as $\sqrt[3]{x}$, whose cube is x.	**raíz cúbica** Número, expresado como $\sqrt[3]{x}$, cuyo cubo es x.	$\sqrt[3]{64} = 4$, because $4^3 = 64$; 4 is the cube root of 64.
cube-root function The function $f(x) = \sqrt[3]{x}$.	**función de raíz cúbica** La función $f(x) = \sqrt[3]{x}$.	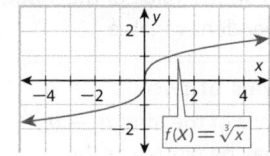

Glossary/Glosario

cubic equation An equation that can be written in the form $ax^3 + bx^2 + cx + d = 0$, where a, b, c, and d are real numbers and $a \neq 0$. | **ecuación cúbica** Ecuación que se puede expresar como $ax^3 + bx^2 + cx + d = 0$, donde a, b, c, y d son números reales y $a \neq 0$. | $4x^3 + x^2 - 3x - 1 = 0$

cubic function A function that can be written in the form $f(x) = ax^3 + bx^2 + cx + d$, where a, b, c, and d are real numbers and $a \neq 0$. | **función cúbica** Función que se puede expresar como $f(x) = ax^3 + bx^2 + cx + d$, donde a, b, c, y d son números reales y $a \neq 0$. | $f(x) = x^3 + 2x^2 - 6x + 8$

cubic polynomial A polynomial of degree 3. | **polinomio cúbico** Polinomio de grado 3. | $x^3 + 4x^2 - 6x + 2$

cumulative frequency The frequency of all data values that are less than or equal to a given value. | **frecuencia acumulativa** Frecuencia de todos los valores de los datos que son menores que o iguales a un valor dado. | For the data set 2, 2, 3, 5, 5, 6, 7, 7, 8, 8, 8, 9, the cumulative frequency table is shown below.

Data	Frequency	Cumulative Frequency
2	2	2
3	1	3
5	2	5
6	1	6
7	2	8
8	3	11
9	1	12

D

data Information gathered from a survey or experiment. | **datos** Información reunida en una encuesta o experimento. |

degree of a monomial The sum of the exponents of the variables in the monomial. | **grado de un monomio** Suma de los exponentes de las variables del monomio. | $4x^2y^5z^3$ Degree: $2 + 5 + 3 = 10$
 $5 = 5x^0$ Degree: 0

degree of a polynomial The degree of the term of the polynomial with the greatest degree. | **grado de un polinomio** Grado del término del polinomio con el grado máximo. | $3x^2y^2 \quad + \quad 4xy^5 \quad - \quad 12x^3y^2 \qquad$ Degree 6
 Degree 4 $\quad$ Degree 6 $\quad$ Degree 5

dependent system A system of equations that has infinitely many solutions. | **sistema dependiente** Sistema de ecuaciones que tiene infinitamente muchas soluciones. | $\begin{cases} x + y = 2 \\ 2x + 2y = 4 \end{cases}$

dependent variable The output of a function; a variable whose value depends on the value of the input, or independent variable. | **variable dependiente** Salida de una función; variable cuyo valor depende del valor de la entrada, o variable independiente. | For $y = 2x + 1$, y is the dependent variable.
 input: x $\quad$ output: y

difference of two cubes A polynomial of the form $a^3 - b^3$, which may be written as the product $(a - b)(a^2 + ab + b^2)$. | **diferencia de dos cubos** Polinomio del tipo $a^3 - b^3$, que se puede expresar como el producto $(a - b)(a^2 + ab + b^2)$. | $x^3 - 8 = (x - 2)(x^2 + 2x + 4)$

ENGLISH	SPANISH	EXAMPLES
difference of two squares A polynomial of the form $a^2 - b^2$, which may be written as the product $(a + b)(a - b)$.	**diferencia de dos cuadrados** Polinomio del tipo $a^2 - b^2$, que se puede expresar como el producto $(a + b)(a - b)$.	$x^2 - 4 = (x + 2)(x - 2)$
dimensional analysis A process that uses rates to convert measurements from one unit to another.	**análisis dimensional** Un proceso que utiliza tasas para convertir medidas de unidad a otra.	$12 \text{ pt} \cdot \dfrac{1 \text{ qt}}{2 \text{ pt}} = 6 \text{ qt}$
direct variation A linear relationship between two variables, x and y, that can be written in the form $y = kx$, where k is a nonzero constant.	**variación directa** Relación lineal entre dos variables, x e y, que puede expresarse en la forma $y = kx$, donde k es una constante distinta de cero.	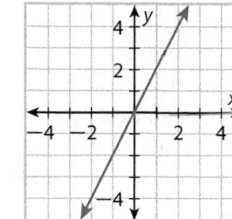
discrete function A function whose graph is made up of unconnected points.	**función discreta** Función cuya gráfica compuesta de puntos no conectados.	
discrete graph A graph made up of unconnected points.	**gráfica discreta** Gráfica compuesta de puntos no conectados.	**Theme Park Attendance** 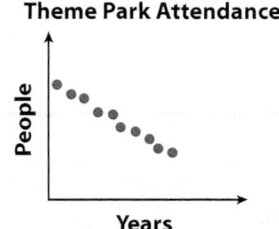
discriminant The discriminant of the quadratic equation $ax^2 + bx + c = 0$ is $b^2 - 4ac$.	**discriminante** El discriminante de la ecuación cuadrática $ax^2 + bx + c = 0$ es $b^2 - 4ac$.	The discriminant of $2x^2 - 5x - 3 = 0$ is $(-5)^2 - 4(2)(-3)$ or 49.
Distance Formula In a coordinate plane, the distance from (x_1, y_1) to (x_2, y_2) is $$d = \sqrt{(x_2 - x_1)^2 + (y_2 - y_1)^2}.$$	**Fórmula de distancia** En un plano cartesiano, la distancia desde (x_1, y_1) hasta (x_2, y_2) es $$d = \sqrt{(x_2 - x_1)^2 + (y_2 - y_1)^2}.$$	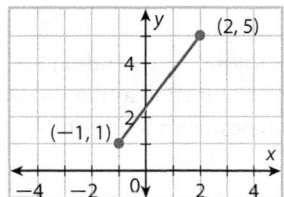 The distance from $(2, 5)$ to $(-1, 1)$ is $d = \sqrt{(-1 - 2)^2 + (1 - 5)^2}$ $= \sqrt{(-3)^2 + (-4)^2}$ $= \sqrt{9 + 16} = \sqrt{25} = 5.$
Distributive Property For all real numbers a, b, and c, $a(b + c) = ab + ac$, and $(b + c)a = ba + ca$.	**Propiedad distributiva** Dados los números reales a, b y c, $a(b + c) = ab + ac$, y $(b + c)a = ba + ca$.	$3(4 + 5) = 3 \cdot 4 + 3 \cdot 5$ $(4 + 5)3 = 4 \cdot 3 + 5 \cdot 3$
Division Property of Equality For real numbers a, b, and c, where $c \neq 0$, if $a = b$, then $\frac{a}{c} = \frac{b}{c}$.	**Propiedad de igualdad de la división** Dados los números reales a, b y c, donde $c \neq 0$, si $a = b$, entonces $\frac{a}{c} = \frac{b}{c}$.	$4x = 12$ $\dfrac{4x}{4} = \dfrac{12}{4}$ $x = 3$

Glossary/Glosario

ENGLISH	SPANISH	EXAMPLES
Division Property of Inequality If both sides of an inequality are divided by the same positive quantity, the new inequality will have the same solution set. If both sides of an inequality are divided by the same negative quantity, the new inequality will have the same solution set if the inequality symbol is reversed.	**Propiedad de desigualdad de la división** Cuando ambos lados de una desigualdad se dividen entre el mismo número positivo, la nueva desigualdad tiene el mismo conjunto solución. Cuando ambos lados de una desigualdad se dividen entra el mismo número negativo, la nueva desigualdad tiene el mismo conjunto solución si se invierte el símbolo de desigualdad.	$4x \geq 12$ $\frac{4x}{4} \geq \frac{12}{4}$ $x \geq 3$ $-4x \geq 12$ $\frac{-4x}{-4} \leq \frac{12}{-4}$ $x \leq -3$
domain The set of all first coordinates (or x-values) of a relation or function.	**dominio** Conjunto de todos los valores de la primera coordenada (o valores de x) de una función o relación.	The domain of the function $\{(-5, 3), (-3, -2), (-1, -1), (1, 0)\}$ is $\{-5, -3, -1, 1\}$.
dot plot A number line with marks or dots that show frequency.	**diagrama de puntos** Recta numérica con marcas o puntos que indican la frecuencia.	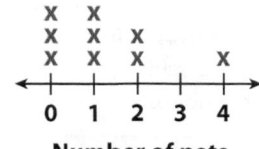

E

ENGLISH	SPANISH	EXAMPLES
elimination method A method used to solve systems of equations in which one variable is eliminated by adding or subtracting two equations of the system.	**eliminación** Método utilizado para resolver sistemas de ecuaciones por el cual se elimina una variable sumando o restando dos ecuaciones del sistema.	
empty set A set with no elements.	**conjunto vacío** Conjunto sin elementos.	The solution set of $\lvert x \rvert < 0$ is the empty set, $\{\ \}$, or $\varnothing$.
end behavior The trends in the y-values of a function as the x-values approach positive and negative infinity.	**comportamiento extremo** Tendencia de los valores de y de una función a medida que los valores de x se aproximan al infinito positivo y negativo.	
Equality of Bases Property Two powers with the same positive base other than 1 are equal if and only if the exponents are equal.	**Propiedad de igualdad de las bases** Dos potencias con la misma base positiva distinta de 1 son iguales si y solo si los exponentes son iguales.	If $b > 0$ and, $b \neq 1$, then $b^x = b^y$ if and only if $x = y$.
equation A mathematical statement that two expressions are equivalent.	**ecuación** Enunciado matemático que indica que dos expresiones son equivalentes.	$x + 4 = 7$ $2 + 3 = 6 - 1$ $(x - 1)^2 + (y + 2)^2 = 4$
equivalent ratios Ratios that name the same comparison.	**razones equivalentes** Razones que expresan la misma comparación.	$\frac{1}{2}$ and $\frac{2}{4}$ are equivalent ratios.

ENGLISH	SPANISH	EXAMPLES
evaluate To find the value of an algebraic expression by substituting a number for each variable and simplifying by using the order of operations.	**evaluar** Calcular el valor de una expresión algebraica sustituyendo cada variable por un número y simplificando mediante el orden de las operaciones.	Evaluate $2x + 7$ for $x = 3$. $2x + 7$ $2(3) + 7$ $6 + 7$ 13
even function A function in which $f(-x) = f(x)$ for all x in the domain of the function.	**función par** Función en la que para todos los valores de x dentro del dominio de la función.	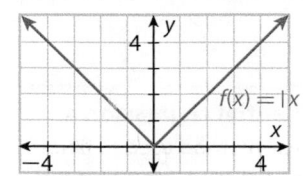 $f(x) = |x|$ is an even function.
explicit rule for nth term of a sequence A rule that defines the nth term a_n, or a general term, of a sequence as a function of n.	**fórmula explícita** Fórmula que define el enésimo término a_n, o término general, de una sucesión como una función de n.	
exponent The number that indicates how many times the base in a power is used as a factor.	**exponente** Número que indica la cantidad de veces que la base de una potencia se utiliza como factor.	$3^4 = 3 \cdot 3 \cdot 3 \cdot 3 = 81$ 4 is the exponent.
exponential decay An exponential function of the form $f(x) = ab^x$ in which $0 < b < 1$. If r is the rate of decay, then the function can be written $y = a(1 - r)^t$, where a is the initial amount and t is the time.	**decremento exponencial** Función exponencial del tipo $f(x) = ab^x$ en la cual $0 < b < 1$. Si r es la tasa decremental, entonces la función se puede expresar como $y = a(1 - r)^t$, donde a es la cantidad inicial y t es el tiempo.	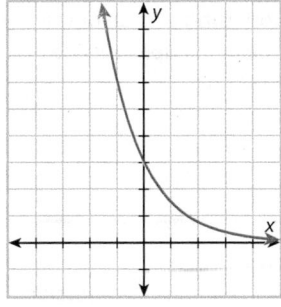
exponential expression An algebraic expression in which the variable is in an exponent with a fixed number as the base.	**expresión exponencial** Expresión algebraica en la que la variable está en un exponente y que tiene un número fijo como base.	2^{x+1}
exponential function A function of the form $f(x) = ab^x$, where a and b are real numbers with $a \neq 0$, $b > 0$, and $b \neq 1$.	**función exponencial** Función del tipo $f(x) = ab^x$, donde a y b son números reales con $a \neq 0$, $b > 0$ y $b \neq 1$.	$f(x) = 3 \cdot 4^x$ 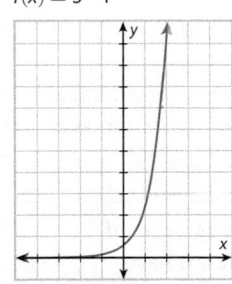

exponential growth An exponential function of the form $f(x) = ab^x$ in which $b > 1$. If r is the rate of growth, then the function can be written $y = a(1 + r)^t$, where a is the initial amount and t is the time.

crecimiento exponencial Función exponencial del tipo $f(x) = ab^x$ en la que $b > 1$. Si r es la tasa de crecimiento, entonces la función se puede expresar como $y = a(1 + r)^t$, donde a es la cantidad inicial y t es el tiempo.

$f(x) = 2^x$

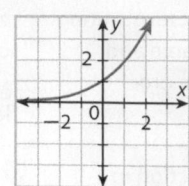

---

exponential regression A statistical method used to fit an exponential model to a given data set.

regresión exponencial Método estadístico utilizado para ajustar un modelo exponencial a un conjunto de datos determinado.

---

expression A mathematical phrase that contains operations, numbers, and/or variables.

expresión Frase matemática que contiene operaciones, números y/o variables.

$6x + 1$

---

extraneous solution A solution of a derived equation that is not a solution of the original equation.

solución extraña Solución de una ecuación derivada que no es una solución de la ecuación original.

To solve $\sqrt{x} = -2$, square both sides; $x = 4$.
Check $\sqrt{4} = -2$ is false; so 4 is an extraneous solution.

---

extrapolation Making a prediction using a value of the independent variable outside of a model's domain.

extrapolación Hacer una predicción con un valor de la variable independiente que esté fuera del dominio de un modelo.

F

---

factor A number or expression that is multiplied by another number or expression to get a product. *See also factoring.*

factor Número o expresión que se multiplica por otro número o expresión para obtener un producto. *Ver también* factoreo.

$12 = 3 \cdot 4$
3 and 4 are factors of 12.
$x^2 - 1 = (x - 1)(x + 1)$
$(x - 1)$ and $(x + 1)$ are factors of $x^2 - 1$.

---

factored form A quadratic function written as $y = k(x - a)(x - b)$ where $k \neq 0$.

forma factorizada Función cuadrática expresada en la forma $y = k(x - a)(x - b)$ donde $k \neq 0$.

$f(x) = x^2 + 2x - 8$
$ = (x + 4)(x - 2)$

---

factoring The process of writing a number or algebraic expression as a product.

factorización Proceso por el que se expresa un número o expresión algebraica como un producto.

$x^2 - 4x - 21 = (x - 7)(x + 3)$

---

family of functions A set of functions whose graphs have basic characteristics in common. Functions in the same family are transformations of their parent function.

familia de funciones Conjunto de funciones cuyas gráficas tienen características básicas en común. Las funciones de la misma familia son transformaciones de su función madre.

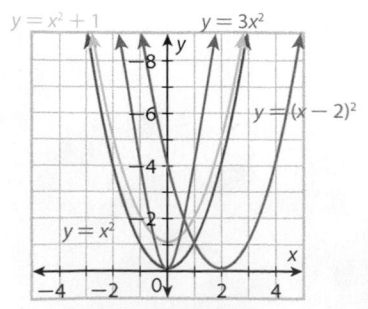

ENGLISH	SPANISH	EXAMPLES

first differences The differences between y-values of a function for evenly spaced x-values.

primeras diferencias Diferencias entre los valores de y de una función para valores de x espaciados uniformemente.

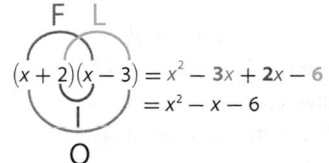

---

first quartile The median of the lower half of a data set, denoted Q_1. Also called *lower quartile*.

primer cuartil Mediana de la mitad inferior de un conjunto de datos, expresada como Q_1. También se llama *cuartil inferior*.

Lower half   Upper half

18, ⃝23 28,   29,   36,   42

First quartile

FOIL A mnemonic (memory) device for a method of multiplying two binomials:
Multiply the **First** terms.
Multiply the **Outer** terms.
Multiply the **Inner** terms.
Multiply the **Last** terms.

FOIL Regla mnemotécnica para recordar el método de multiplicación de dos binomios:
Multiplicar los términos **Primeros** (*First*).
Multiplicar los términos **Externos** (*Outer*).
Multiplicar los términos **Internos** (*Inner*).
Multiplicar los términos **Últimos** (*Last*).

$(x + 2)(x - 3) = x^2 - 3x + 2x - 6$
$= x^2 - x - 6$

---

formula A literal equation that states a rule for a relationship among quantities.

fórmula Ecuación literal que establece una regla para una relación entre cantidades.

$A = \pi r^2$

---

fractional exponent *See* rational exponent.

exponente fraccionario *Ver* exponente racional.

---

frequency The number of times the value appears in the data set.

frecuencia Cantidad de veces que aparece el valor en un conjunto de datos.

In the data set 5, 6, 6, 7, 8, 9, the data value 6 has a frequency of 2.

---

frequency table A table that lists the number of times, or frequency, that each data value occurs.

tabla de frecuencia Tabla que enumera la cantidad de veces que ocurre cada valor de datos, o la frecuencia.

Data set: 1, 1, 2, 2, 3, 4, 5, 5, 5, 6, 6, 6, 6

Frequency table:

Data	Frequency
1	2
2	2
3	1
4	1
5	3
6	4

---

function A relation in which every domain value is paired with exactly one range value.

función Relación en la que a cada valor de dominio corresponde exactamente un valor de rango.

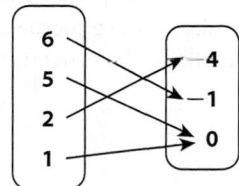

function notation If x is the independent variable and y is the dependent variable, then the function notation for y is $f(x)$, read "f of x," where f names the function.

notación de función Si x es la variable independiente e y es la variable dependiente, entonces la notación de función para y es $f(x)$, que se lee "f de x," donde f nombra la función.

equation: $y = 2x$
function notation: $f(x) = 2x$

---

function rule An algebraic expression that defines a function.

regla de función Expresión algebraica que define una función.

$$f(x) = 2x^2 + 3x - 7$$

↑
function rule

G

geometric sequence A sequence in which the ratio of successive terms is a constant r, called the common ratio, where $r \neq 0$ and $r \neq 1$.

sucesión geométrica Sucesión en la que la razón de los términos sucesivos es una constante r, denominada razón común, donde $r \neq 0$ y $r \neq 1$.

1, 2, 4, 8, 16, …
·2 ·2 ·2 ·2 $r = 2$

---

graph of a function The set of points in a coordinate plane with coordinates (x, y), where x is in the domain of the function f and $y = f(x)$.

gráfica de una función Conjunto de los puntos de un plano cartesiano con coordenadas (x, y), donde x está en el dominio de la función f e $y = f(x)$.

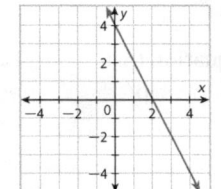 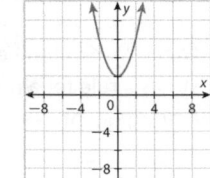

---

graph of a system of linear inequalities The region in a coordinate plane consisting of points whose coordinates are solutions to all of the inequalities in the system.

gráfica de un sistema de desigualdades lineales Región de un plano cartesiano que consta de puntos cuyas coordenadas son soluciones de todas las desigualdades del sistema.

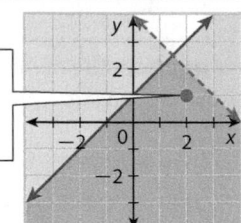

(2, 1) is in the overlapping shaded regions, so it is a solution.

---

graph of an inequality in one variable The set of points on a number line that are solutions of the inequality.

gráfica de una desigualdad en una variable Conjunto de los puntos de una recta numérica que representan soluciones de la desigualdad.

$x \geq 2$

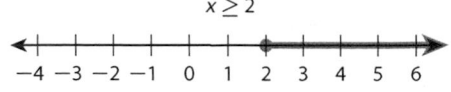

---

graph of an inequality in two variables The set of points in a coordinate plane whose coordinates (x, y) are solutions of the inequality.

gráfica de una desigualdad en dos variables Conjunto de los puntos de un plano cartesiano cuyas coordenadas (x, y) son soluciones de la desigualdad.

$y \leq x + 1$

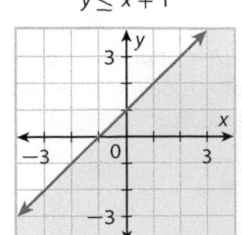

Glossary/Glosario

greatest common factor (monomials) (GCF) The product of the greatest integer and the greatest power of each variable that divide evenly into each monomial.

máximo común divisor (monomios) (MCD) Producto del entero mayor y la potencia mayor de cada variable que divide exactamente cada monomio.

The GCF of $4x^3y$ and $6x^2y$ is $2x^2y$.

---

greatest common factor (numbers) (GCF) The largest common factor of two or more given numbers.

máximo común divisor (números) (MCD) El mayor de los factores comunes compartidos por dos o más números dados.

The GCF of 27 and 45 is 9.

---

greatest integer function A function denoted by $f(x) = [x]$ in which the number x is rounded down to the greatest integer that is less than or equal to x.

función de entero mayor Función expresada como $f(x) = [x]$ en la cual el número x se redondea hacia abajo hasta el entero mayor que sea menor o igual a x.

---

grouping symbols Symbols such as parentheses ( ), brackets [ ], and braces { } that separate part of an expression. A fraction bar, absolute-value symbols, and radical symbols may also be used as grouping symbols.

símbolos de agrupación Símbolos tales como paréntesis ( ), corchetes [ ] y llaves { } que separan parte de una expresión. La barra de fracciones, los símbolos de valor absoluto y los símbolos de radical también se pueden utilizar como símbolos de agrupación.

$6 + \{3 - [(4 - 3) + 2] + 1\} - 5$
$6 + \{3 - [1 + 2] + 1\} - 5$
$6 + \{3 - 3 + 1\} - 5$
$6 + 1 - 5$
2

H

---

half-plane The part of the coordinate plane on one side of a line, which may include the line.

semiplano La parte del plano cartesiano de un lado de una línea, que puede incluir la línea.

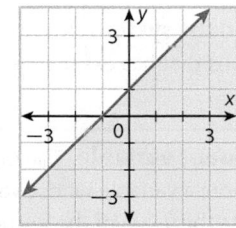

Heron's Formula A triangle with side lengths a, b, and c has area $A = \sqrt{s(s - a)(s - b)(s - c)}$, where s is one-half the perimeter, or $s = \frac{1}{2}(a + b + c)$.

fórmula de Herón Un triángulo con longitudes de lado a, b y c tiene un área $A = \sqrt{s(s - a)(s - b)(s - c)}$, donde s es la mitad del perímetro ó $s = \frac{1}{2}(a + b + c)$.

---

histogram A bar graph used to display data grouped in intervals.

histograma Gráfica de barras utilizada para mostrar datos agrupados en intervalos de clases.

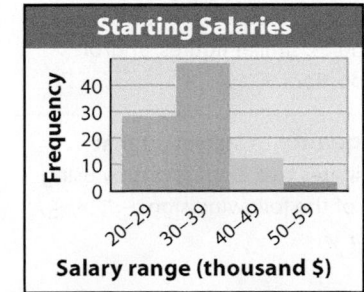

horizontal line A line described by the equation $y = b$, where b is the y-intercept.

línea horizontal Línea descrita por la ecuación $y = b$, donde b es la intersección con el eje y.

$y = 4$

horizontal translation (of a parabola) is a shift of the parabola left or right, with no change in the shape of the parabola.

traslación horizontal (de una parábola) Desplazamiento de la parábola hacia la izquierda o hacia la derecha, sin producir cambios en la forma de la parábola.

hypotenuse The side opposite the right angle in a right triangle.

hipotenusa Lado opuesto al ángulo recto de un triángulo rectángulo.

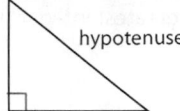
hypotenuse

I

identity An equation that is true for all values of the variables.

identidad Ecuación verdadera para todos los valores de las variables.

$3 = 3$
$2(x - 1) = 2x - 2$

inconsistent system A system of equations or inequalities that has no solution.

sistema inconsistente Sistema de ecuaciones o desigualdades que no tiene solución.

$\begin{cases} x + y = 0 \\ x + y = 1 \end{cases}$

independent system A system of equations that has exactly one solution.

sistema independiente Sistema de ecuaciones que tiene sólo una solución.

$\begin{cases} x + y = 7 \\ x - y = 1 \end{cases}$
Solution: $(4, 3)$

independent variable The input of a function; a variable whose value determines the value of the output, or dependent variable.

variable independiente Entrada de una función; variable cuyo valor determina el valor de la salida, o variable dependiente.

For $y = 2x + 1$, x is the independent variable.

index In the radical $\sqrt[n]{x}$, which represents the nth root of x, n is the index. In the radical $\sqrt{x}$, the index is understood to be 2.

índice En el radical $\sqrt[n]{x}$, que representa la enésima raíz de x, n es el índice. En el radical $\sqrt{x}$, se da por sentado que el índice es 2.

The radical $\sqrt[3]{8}$ has an index of 3.

indirect measurement A method of measurement that uses formulas, similar figures, and/or proportions.

medición indirecta Método de medición en el que se usan fórmulas, figuras semejantes y/o proporciones.

inequality A statement that compares two expressions by using one of the following signs: $<$, $>$, $\leq$, $\geq$, or $\neq$.

desigualdad Enunciado que compara dos expresiones utilizando uno de los siguientes signos: $<$, $>$, $\leq$, $\geq$, o $\neq$.

$x \geq 2$

$-4 \;\; -3 \;\; -2 \;\; -1 \;\; 0 \;\; 1 \;\; 2 \;\; 3 \;\; 4 \;\; 5 \;\; 6$

Glossary/Glosario

ENGLISH	SPANISH	EXAMPLES
input A value that is substituted for the independent variable in a relation or function.	**entrada** Valor que sustituye a la variable independiente en una relación o función.	For the function $f(x) = x + 5$, the input 3 produces an output of 8.
input-output table A table that displays input values of a function or expression together with the corresponding outputs.	**tabla de entrada y salida** Tabla que muestra los valores de entrada de una función o expresión junto con las correspondientes salidas.	Input x 1 2 3 4 / Output y 4 7 10 13
intercept *See x*-intercept and *y*-intercept.	**intersección** *Ver* intersección con el eje *x* e intersección con el eje *y*.	
interest The amount of money charged for borrowing money or the amount of money earned when saving or investing money. *See also* compound interest, simple interest.	**interés** Cantidad de dinero que se cobra por prestar dinero o cantidad de dinero que se gana cuando se ahorra o invierte dinero. *Ver también* interés compuesto, interés simple.	
interpolation Making a prediction using a value of the independent variable from within a model's domain.	**interpolación** Hacer una predicción con un valor de la variable independiente a partir del dominio de un modelo.	
interquartile range (IQR) The difference of the third (upper) and first (lower) quartiles in a data set, representing the middle half of the data.	**rango entre cuartiles** Diferencia entre el tercer cuartil (superior) y el primer cuartil (inferior) de un conjunto de datos, que representa la mitad central de los datos.	Lower half Upper half 18, (23,) 28, 29, (36,) 42 First quartile Third quartile Interquartile range: $36 - 23 = 13$
intersection The intersection of two sets is the set of all elements that are common to both sets, denoted by ∩.	**intersección de conjuntos** La intersección de dos conjuntos es el conjunto de todos los elementos que son comunes a ambos conjuntos, expresado por ∩.	$A = \{1, 2, 3, 4\}$ $B = \{1, 3, 5, 7, 9\}$ $A \cap B = \{1, 3\}$
inverse of a function The relation that results from exchanging the input and output values of a function.	**inverso de una función** La relación que se genera al intercambiar los valores de entrada y de salida de una función.	
inverse operations Operations that undo each other.	**operaciones inversas** Operaciones que se anulan entre sí.	Addition and subtraction of the same quantity are inverse operations: $5 + 3 = 8, 8 - 3 = 5$ Multiplication and division by the same quantity are inverse operations: $2 \cdot 3 = 6$, $6 \div 3 = 2$
inverse relation The relation that results from exchanging the input and output values of a relation.	**relación inversa** La relación que se genera al intercambiar los valores de entrada y de salida de una relación.	

Glossary/Glosario

Glossary/Glosario

inverse variation A relationship between two variables, x and y, that can be written in the form $y = \frac{k}{x}$, where k is a nonzero constant and $x \neq 0$.

variación inversa Relación entre dos variables, x e y, que puede expresarse en la forma $y = \frac{k}{x}$, donde k es una constante distinta de cero y $x \neq 0$.

$y = \frac{8}{x}$

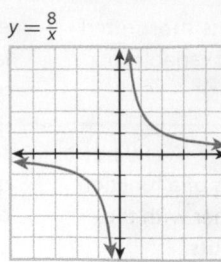

irrational number A real number that cannot be expressed as the ratio of two integers.

número irracional Número real que no se puede expresar como una razón de enteros.

$\sqrt{2}, \pi, e$

isosceles triangle A triangle with at least two congruent sides.

triángulo isósceles Triángulo que tiene al menos dos lados congruentes.

J

joint relative frequency The ratio of the frequency in a particular category divided by the total number of data values.

frecuencia relativa conjunta La línea de ajuste en que la suma de cuadrados de los residuos es la menor.

L

leading coefficient The coefficient of the first term of a polynomial in standard form.

coeficiente principal Coeficiente del primer término de un polinomio en forma estándar.

$3x^2 + 7x - 2$
Leading coefficient: 3

least common denominator (LCD) The least common multiple of the denominators of two or more given fractions or rational expressions.

mínimo común denominador (MCD) Mínimo común múltiplo de los denominadores de dos o más fracciones dadas o expresionnes racionales.

The LCD of $\frac{3}{4}$ and $\frac{5}{6}$ is 12.

least common multiple (monomials) (LCM) The product of the smallest positive number and the lowest power of each variable that divide evenly into each monomial.

mínimo común múltiplo (monomios) (MCM) El producto del número positivo más pequeño y la menor potencia de cada variable que divide exactamente cada monomio.

The LCM of $6x^2$ and $4x$ is $12x^2$.

least common multiple (numbers) (LCM) The smallest whole number, other than zero, that is a multiple of two or more given numbers.

mínimo común múltiplo (números) (MCM) El menor de los números cabales, distinto de cero, que es múltiplo de dos o más números dados.

The LCM of 10 and 18 is 90.

least-squares line The line of fit for which the sum of the squares of the residuals is as small as possible

línea de mínimos cuadrados La línea de ajuste en que la suma de cuadrados de los residuos es la menor.

Glossary/Glosario

ENGLISH	SPANISH	EXAMPLES
like terms Terms with the same variables raised to the same exponents.	**términos semejantes** Términos con las mismas variables elevadas a los mismos exponentes.	
line graph A graph that uses line segments to show how data changes.	**gráfica lineal** Gráfica que se vale de segmentos de recta para mostrar cambios en los datos.	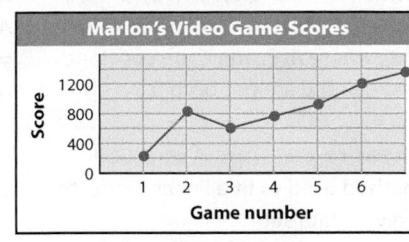
line plot A number line with marks or dots that show frequency.	**diagrama de acumulación** Recta numérica con marcas o puntos que indican la frecuencia.	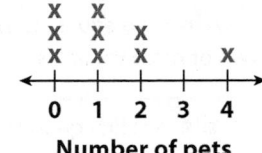
line of best fit The line that comes closest to all of the points in a data set.	**línea de mejor ajuste** Línea que más se acerca a todos los puntos de un conjunto de datos.	
line of fit *See trend line.*	**línea de ajuste** *Ver línea de tendencia.*	
linear equation in one variable An equation that can be written in the form $ax = b$ where a and b are constants and $a \neq 0$.	**ecuación lineal en una variable** Ecuación que puede expresarse en la forma $ax = b$ donde a y b son constantes y $a \neq 0$.	$x + 1 = 7$
linear equation in two variables An equation that can be written in the form $Ax + By = C$ where A, B, and C are constants and A and B are not both 0.	**ecuación lineal en dos variables** Ecuación que puede expresarse en la forma $Ax + By = C$ donde A, B y C son constantes y A y B no son ambas 0.	$2x + 3y = 6$
linear function A function that can be written in the form $y = mx + b$, where x is the independent variable and m and b are real numbers. Its graph is a line.	**función lineal** Función que puede expresarse en la forma $y = mx + b$, donde x es la variable independiente y m y b son números reales. Su gráfica es una línea.	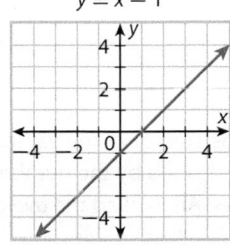
linear inequality in one variable An inequality that can be written in one of the following forms: $ax < b$, $ax > b$, $ax \leq b$, $ax \geq b$, or b, where a and b are constants and $a \neq 0$.	**desigualdad lineal en una variable** Desigualdad que puede expresarse de una de las siguientes formas: $ax < b$, $ax > b$, $ax \leq b$, $ax \geq b$ o $ax \neq b$, donde a y b son constantes y $a \neq 0$.	$3x - 5 \leq 2(x + 4)$

ENGLISH	SPANISH	EXAMPLES
linear inequality in two variables An inequality that can be written in one of the following forms: $Ax + By < C$, $Ax + By > C$, $Ax + By \leq C$, $Ax + By \geq C$, or $Ax + By \neq C$, where A, B, and C are constants and A and B are not both 0.	**desigualdad lineal en dos variables** Desigualdad que puede expresarse de una de las siguientes formas: $Ax + By < C$, $Ax + By > C$, $Ax + By \leq C$, $Ax + By \geq C$ o $Ax + By \neq C$, donde A, B y C son constantes y A y B no son ambas 0.	$2x + 3y > 6$
linear regression A statistical method used to fit a linear model to a given data set.	**regresión lineal** Método estadístico utilizado para ajustar un modelo lineal a un conjunto de datos determinado.	
literal equation An equation that contains two or more variables.	**ecuación literal** Ecuación que contiene dos o más variables.	$d = rt$ $A = \frac{1}{2}h(b_1 + b_2)$
lower quartile *See* first quartile.	**cuartil inferior** *Ver* primer cuartil.	

M

ENGLISH	SPANISH	EXAMPLES
mapping diagram A diagram that shows the relationship of elements in the domain to elements in the range of a relation or function.	**diagrama de correspondencia** Diagrama que muestra la relación entre los elementos del dominio y los elementos del rango de una función.	**Mapping Diagram**
marginal relative frequency The sum of the joint relative frequencies in a row or column of a two-way table.	**frecuencia relativa marginal** La suma de las frecuencias relativas conjuntas en una fila o columna de una tabla de doble entrada.	
maximum value of a function The y-value of the highest point on the graph of the function.	**máximo de una función** Valor de y del punto más alto en la gráfica de la función.	The maximum of the function is 2.
mean The sum of all the values in a data set divided by the number of data values. Also called the *average*.	**media** Suma de todos los valores de un conjunto de datos dividida entre el número de valores de datos. También llamada *promedio*.	Data set: 4, 6, 7, 8, 10 Mean: $\frac{4+6+7+8+10}{5} = \frac{35}{5} = 7$
measure of central tendency A measure that describes the center of a data set.	**medida de tendencia dominante** Medida que describe el centro de un conjunto de datos.	mean, median, or mode

Glossary/Glosario

median For an ordered data set with an odd number of values, the median is the middle value. For an ordered data set with an even number of values, the median is the average of the two middle values.

mediana Dado un conjunto de datos ordenado con un número impar de valores, la mediana es el valor medio. Dado un conjunto de datos con un número par de valores, la mediana es el promedio de los dos valores medios.

8, 9, (9,) 12, 15   Median: 9

4, 6, (7, 10,) 10, 12

Median: $\frac{7+10}{2} = 8.5$

---

midpoint The point that divides a segment into two congruent segments.

punto medio Punto que divide un segmento en dos segmentos congruentes.

Point B is the midpoint of $\overline{AC}$.

---

minimum value of a function The y-value of the lowest point on the graph of the function.

mínimo de una función Valor de y del punto más bajo en la gráfica de la función.

$(0, -2)$

The minimum of the function is -2.

---

mode The value or values that occur most frequently in a data set; if all values occur with the same frequency, the data set is said to have no mode.

moda El valor o los valores que se presentan con mayor frecuencia en un conjunto de datos. Si todos los valores se presentan con la misma frecuencia, se dice que el conjunto de datos no tiene moda.

Data set: 3, 6, 8, 8, 10 Mode: 8

Data set: 2, 5, 5, 7, 7   Modes: 5 and 7

Data set: 2, 3, 6, 9, 11 No mode

---

monomial A number or a product of numbers and variables with whole-number exponents, or a polynomial with one term.

monomio Número o producto de números y variables con exponentes de números cabales, o polinomio con un término.

$3x^2y^4$

Multiplication Property of Equality If a, b, and c are real numbers and $a = b$, then $ac = bc$.

Propiedad de igualdad de la multiplicación Si a, b y c son números reales y $a = b$, entonces $ac = bc$.

$$\frac{1}{3}x = 7$$
$$(3)\left(\frac{1}{3}x\right) = (3)(7)$$
$$x = 21$$

Multiplication Property of Inequality If both sides of an inequality are multiplied by the same positive quantity, the new inequality will have the same solution set. If both sides of an inequality are multiplied by the same negative quantity, the new inequality will have the same solution set if the inequality symbol is reversed.

Propiedad de desigualdad de la multiplicación Si ambos lados de una desigualdad se multiplican por el mismo número positivo, la nueva desigualdad tendrá el mismo conjunto solución. Si ambos lados de una desigualdad se multiplican por el mismo número negativo, la nueva desigualdad tendrá el mismo conjunto solución si se invierte el símbolo de desigualdad.

$$\frac{1}{3}x > 7$$
$$(3)\left(\frac{1}{3}x\right) > (3)(7)$$
$$x > 21$$
$$-x \leq 2$$
$$(-1)(-x) \geq (-1)(2)$$
$$x \geq -2$$

---

multiplicative inverse The reciprocal of the number.

inverso multiplicativo Recíproco de un número.

The multiplicative inverse of 5 is $\frac{1}{5}$.

N

negative correlation Two data sets have a negative correlation if one set of data values increases as the other set decreases.

correlación negativa Dos conjuntos de datos tienen una correlación negativa si un conjunto de valores de datos aumenta a medida que el otro conjunto disminuye.

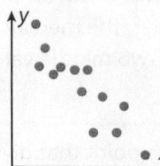

negative exponent For any nonzero real number x and any integer n, $x^{-n} = \frac{1}{x^n}$.

exponente negativo Para cualquier número real distinto de cero x y cualquier entero n, $x^{-n} = \frac{1}{x^n}$.

$$x^{-2} = \frac{1}{x^2}; \; 3^{-2} = \frac{1}{3^2}$$

negative number A number that is less than zero. Negative numbers lie to the left of zero on a number line.

número negativo Número menor que cero. Los números negativos se ubican a la izquierda del cero en una recta numérica.

−2 is a negative number.

−4 −3 −2 −1   0   1   2   3   4

net A diagram of the faces of a three-dimensional figure arranged in such a way that the diagram can be folded to form the three-dimensional figure.

plantilla Diagrama de las caras de una figura tridimensional que se puede plegar para formar la figura tridimensional.

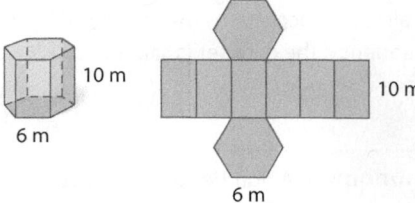

10 m   10 m

6 m   6 m

no correlation Two data sets have no correlation if there is no relationship between the sets of values.

sin correlación Dos conjuntos de datos no tienen correlación si no existe una relación entre los conjuntos de valores.

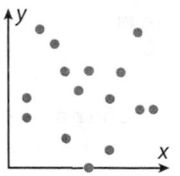

nonlinear system of equations A system in which at least one of the equations is not linear.

sistema no lineal de ecuaciones Sistema en el cual por lo menos una de las ecuaciones no es lineal.

A system that contains one quadratic equation and one linear equation is a nonlinear system.

normal curve The graph of a probability density function that corresponds to a normal distribution; bell-shaped and symmetric about the mean, with the x-axis as a horizontal asymptote.

curva normal La gráfica de una función de densidad de probabilidad que corresponde a la distribución normal; con forma de campana y simétrica con relación a la media, el eje x es una asíntota horizontal.

normal distribution A distribution of data that varies about the mean in such a way that the graph of its probability density function is a normal curve.

distribución normal Distribución de datos que varía respecto de la media de tal manera que la gráfica de su función de densidad de probabilidad es una curva normal.

Glossary/Glosario

nth root The *n*th root of a number *a*, written as $\sqrt[n]{a}$ or $a^{\frac{1}{n}}$, is a number that is equal to *a* when it is raised to the *n*th power.

enésima raíz La enésima raíz de un número *a*, que se escribe $\sqrt[n]{a}$ o $a^{\frac{1}{n}}$, es un número igual a *a* cuando se eleva a la enésima potencia.

$\sqrt[5]{32} = 2$, because $2^5 = 32$.

---

numerical expression An expression that contains only numbers and operations.

expresión numérica Expresión que contiene únicamente números y operaciones.

O

---

obtuse triangle A triangle with one obtuse angle.

triángulo obtusángulo Triángulo con un ángulo obtuso.

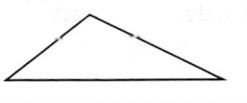

---

odd function A function in which $f(-x) = -f(x)$ for all *x* in the domain of the function.

función impar Función en la que $f(-x) = -f(x)$ para todos los valores de *x* dentro del dominio de la función

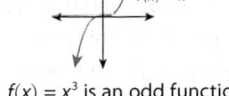

$f(x) = x^3$ is an odd function.

---

opposite The opposite of a number *a*, denoted $-a$, is the number that is the same distance from zero as *a*, on the opposite side of the number line. The sum of opposites is 0.

opuesto El opuesto de un número *a*, expresado $-a$, es el número que se encuentra a la misma distancia de cero que *a*, del lado opuesto de la recta numérica. La suma de los opuestos es 0.

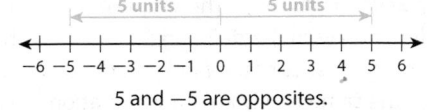

5 and -5 are opposites.

---

opposite reciprocal The opposite of the reciprocal of a number. The opposite reciprocal of any nonzero number *a* is $-\frac{1}{a}$.

recíproco opuesto Opuesto del recíproco de un número. El recíproco opuesto de *a* es $-\frac{1}{a}$.

The opposite reciprocal of $\frac{2}{3}$ is $-\frac{3}{2}$.

OR A logical operator representing the union of two sets.

O Operador lógico que representa la unión de dos conjuntos.

$A = \{2, 3, 4, 5\}$ $B = \{1, 3, 5, 7\}$
The set of values that are in *A* OR *B* is $A \cup B = \{1, 2, 3, 4, 5, 7\}$.

---

outlier A data value that is far removed from the rest of the data.

valor extremo Valor de datos que está muy alejado del resto de los datos.

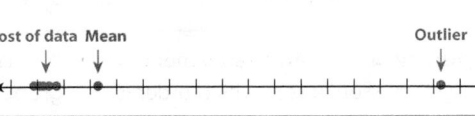

---

output The result of substituting a value for a variable in a function.

salida Resultado de la sustitución de una variable por un valor en una función.

For the function $f(x) = x^2 + 1$, the input 3 produces an output of 10.

Glossary/Glosario

P

Glossary/Glosario

ENGLISH	SPANISH	EXAMPLES
parabola The shape of the graph of a quadratic function.	**parábola** Forma de la gráfica de una función cuadrática.	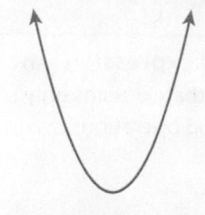
parallel lines Lines in the same plane that do not intersect.	**líneas paralelas** Líneas en el mismo plano que no se cruzan.	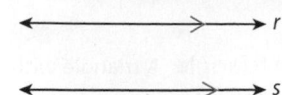
parameter One of the constants in a function or equation that may be changed. Also the third variable in a set of parametric equations.	**parámetro** Una de las constantes en una función o ecuación que se puede cambiar. También es la tercera variable en un conjunto de ecuaciones paramétricas.	
parent function The simplest function with the defining characteristics of the family. Functions in the same family are transformations of their parent function.	**función madre** La función más básica que tiene las características distintivas de una familia. Las funciones de la misma familia son transformaciones de su función madre.	$f(x) = x^2$ is the parent function for $g(x) = x^2 + 4$ and $h(x) = (5x + 2)^2 - 3$.
perfect square A number whose positive square root is a whole number.	**cuadrado perfecto** Número cuya raíz cuadrada positiva es un número cabal.	36 is a perfect square because $\sqrt{36} = 6$.
perfect-square trinomial A trinomial whose factored form is the square of a binomial. A perfect-square trinomial has the form $a^2 - 2ab + b^2 = (a - b)^2$ or $a^2 + 2ab + b^2 = (a + b)^2$.	**trinomio cuadrado perfecto** Trinomio cuya forma factorizada es el cuadrado de un binomio. Un trinomio cuadrado perfecto tiene la forma $a^2 - 2ab + b^2 = (a - b)^2$ o $a^2 + 2ab + b^2 = (a + b)^2$.	$x^2 + 6x + 9$ is a perfect-square trinomial, because $x^2 + 6x + 9 = (x + 3)^2$.
permutation An arrangement of a group of objects in which order is important.	**permutación** Arreglo de un grupo de objetos en el cual el orden es importante.	For objects *A, B, C,* and *D,* there are 12 different permutations of 2 objects. *AB, AC, AD, BC, BD, CD* *BA, CA, DA, CB, DB, DC*
perpendicular Intersecting to form 90° angles.	**perpendicular** Que se cruza para formar ángulos de 90°.	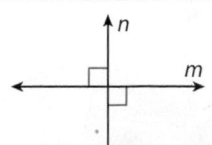
perpendicular lines Lines that intersect at 90° angles.	**líneas perpendiculares** Líneas que se cruzan en ángulos de 90°.	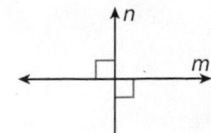

ENGLISH	SPANISH	EXAMPLES
piecewise function A function that is a combination of one or more functions.	**función a trozos** Función que es una combinación de una o más funciones.	
plane A flat surface that has no thickness and extends forever.	**plano** Una superficie plana que no tiene grosor y se extiende infinitamente.	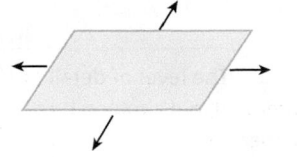
point A location that has no size.	**punto** Ubicación exacta que no tiene ningún tamaño.	$P \bullet$ point P
point-slope form The point-slope form of a linear equation is $y - y_1 = m(x - x_1)$, where m is the slope and (x_1, y_1) is a point on the line.	**forma de punto y pendiente** La forma de punto y pendiente de una ecuación lineal es $y - y_1 = m(x - x_1)$, donde m es la pendiente y (x_1, y_1) es un punto en la línea.	$y - 3 = 2(x - 3)$
polynomial A monomial or a sum or difference of monomials.	**polinomio** Monomio o suma o diferencia de monomios.	$2x^2 + 3xy - 7y^2$
polynomial long division A method of dividing one polynomial by another.	**división larga polinomial** Método por el que se divide un polinomio entre otro.	$\begin{array}{r} x+1 \\ x+2{\overline{\smash{\big)}\,x^2+3x+5}} \\ \underline{-(x^2+2x)} \\ x+5 \\ \underline{-(x+2)} \\ 3 \end{array}$ $\frac{x^2+3x+5}{x+2} = x + 1 + \frac{3}{x+2}$
population The entire group of objects or individuals considered for a survey.	**población** Grupo completo de objetos o individuos que se desea estudiar.	In a survey about the study habits of high school students, the population is all high school students.
positive correlation Two data sets have a positive correlation if both sets of data values increase.	**correlación positiva** Dos conjuntos de datos tienen correlación positiva si los valores de ambos conjuntos de datos aumentan.	
Power of a Power Property If a is any nonzero real number and m and n are integers, then $(a^m)^n = a^{mn}$.	**Propiedad de la potencia de una potencia** Dado un número real a distinto de cero y los números enteros m y n, entonces $(a^m)^n = a^{mn}$.	$(6^7)^4 = 6^{7 \cdot 4}$ $= 6^{28}$
Power of a Product Property If a and b are any nonzero real numbers and n is any integer, then $(ab)^n = a^n b^n$.	**Propiedad de la potencia de un producto** Dados los números reales a y b distintos de cero y un número entero n, entonces $(ab)^n = a^n b^n$.	$(2 \cdot 4)^3 = 2^3 \cdot 4^3$ $= 8 \cdot 64$ $= 512$

Glossary/Glosario

Glossary/Glosario

ENGLISH	SPANISH	EXAMPLES
Power of a Quotient Property If a and b are any nonzero real numbers and n is an integer, then $\left(\frac{a}{b}\right)^n = \frac{a^n}{b^n}$.	**Propiedad de la potencia de un cociente** Dados los números reales a y b distintos de cero y un número entero n, entonces $\left(\frac{a}{b}\right)^n = \frac{a^n}{b^n}$.	$\left(\frac{3}{5}\right)^4 = \frac{3}{5} \cdot \frac{3}{5} \cdot \frac{3}{5} \cdot \frac{3}{5}$ $= \frac{3 \cdot 3 \cdot 3 \cdot 3}{5 \cdot 5 \cdot 5 \cdot 5}$ $= \frac{3^4}{5^4}$
precision The level of detail of a measurement, determined by the unit of measure.	**precisión** Detalle de una medición, determinado por la unidad de medida.	A ruler marked in millimeters has a greater level of precision than a ruler marked in centimeters.
prediction An estimate or guess about something that has not yet happened.	**predicción** Estimación o suposición sobre algo que todavía no ha sucedido.	
prime factorization A representation of a number or a polynomial as a product of primes.	**factorización prima** Representación de un número o de un polinomio como producto de números primos.	The prime factorization of 60 is $2 \cdot 2 \cdot 3 \cdot 5$.
prime number A whole number greater than 1 that has exactly two positive factors, itself and 1.	**número primo** Número cabal mayor que 1 que es divisible únicamente entre sí mismo y entre 1.	5 is prime because its only positive factors are 5 and 1.
principal An amount of money borrowed or invested.	**capital** Cantidad de dinero que se pide prestado o se invierte.	
Product of Powers Property If a is any nonzero real number and m and n are integers, then $a^m \cdot a^n = a^{m+n}$.	**Propiedad del producto de potencias** Dado un número real a distinto de cero y los números enteros m y n, entonces $a^m \cdot a^n = a^{m+n}$.	$6^7 \cdot 6^4 = 6^{7+4}$ $= 6^{11}$
Product Property of Radicals For $a \geq 0$ and $b \geq 0$, $\sqrt{ab} = \sqrt{a} \cdot \sqrt{b}$.	**Propiedad del producto de radicales** Dados $a \geq 0$ y $b \geq 0$, $\sqrt{ab} = \sqrt{a} \cdot \sqrt{b}$.	$\sqrt{9 \cdot 25} = \sqrt{9} \cdot \sqrt{25}$ $= 3 \cdot 5 = 15$
proportion A statement that two ratios are equal; $\frac{a}{b} = \frac{c}{d}$.	**proporción** Ecuación que establece que dos razones son iguales; $\frac{a}{b} = \frac{c}{d}$.	$\frac{2}{3} = \frac{4}{6}$
Pythagorean Theorem If a right triangle has legs of lengths a and b and a hypotenuse of length c, then $a^2 + b^2 = c^2$.	**Teorema de Pitágoras** Dado un triángulo rectángulo con catetos de longitudes a y b y una hipotenusa de longitud c, entonces $a^2 + b^2 = c^2$.	13 cm, 5 cm, 12 cm $5^2 + 12^2 = 13^2$ $25 + 144 = 169$
Pythagorean triple A set of three positive integers a, b, and c such that $a^2 + b^2 = c^2$.	**Tripleta de Pitágoras** Conjunto de tres enteros positivos a, b y c tal que $a^2 + b^2 = c^2$.	The numbers 3, 4, and 5 form a Pythagorean triple because $3^2 + 4^2 = 5^2$.

Q

quadrant One of the four regions into which the *x*- and *y*-axes divide the coordinate plane.

cuadrante Una de las cuatro regiones en las que los ejes *x* e *y* dividen el plano cartesiano.

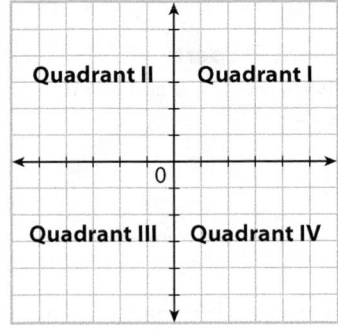

quadratic equation An equation that can be written in the form $ax^2 + bx + c = 0$, where *a*, *b*, and *c* are real numbers and $a \neq 0$.

ecuación cuadrática Ecuación que se puede expresar como $ax^2 + bx + c = 0$, donde *a*, *b* y *c* son números reales y $a \neq 0$.

$x^2 + 3x - 4 = 0$
$x^2 - 9 = 0$

Quadratic Formula The formula $x = \frac{-b \pm \sqrt{b^2 - 4ac}}{2a}$, which gives solutions, or roots, of equations in the form $ax^2 + bx + c = 0$, where $a \neq 0$.

fórmula cuadrática La fórmula $x = \frac{-b \pm \sqrt{b^2 - 4ac}}{2a}$, que da soluciones, o raíces, para las ecuaciones del tipo $ax^2 + bx + c = 0$, donde $a \neq 0$.

The solutions of $2x^2 - 5x - 3 = 0$ are given by
$$x = \frac{-(-5) \pm \sqrt{(-5)^2 - 4(2)(-3)}}{2(2)}$$
$$= \frac{5 \pm \sqrt{25 + 24}}{4} = \frac{5 \pm 7}{4}$$
$x = 3$ or $x = -\frac{1}{2}$

quadratic function A function that can be written in the form $f(x) = ax^2 + bx + c$, where *a*, *b*, and *c* are real numbers and $a \neq 0$.

función cuadrática Función que se puede expresar como $f(x) = ax^2 + bx + c$, donde *a*, *b* y *c* son números reales y $a \neq 0$.

$f(x) = x^2 - 6x + 8$

quadratic polynomial A polynomial of degree 2.

polinomio cuadrático Polinomio de grado 2.

$x^2 - 6x + 8$

quadratic regression A statistical method used to fit a quadratic model to a given data set.

regresión cuadrática Método estadístico utilizado para ajustar un modelo cuadrático a un conjunto de datos determinado.

quantitative data Numerical data.

datos cuantitativos Datos numéricos.

quartile The median of the upper or lower half of a data set. *See also* first quartile, third quartile.

cuartil La mediana de la mitad superior o inferior de un conjunto de datos. *Ver también* primer cuartil, tercer cuartil.

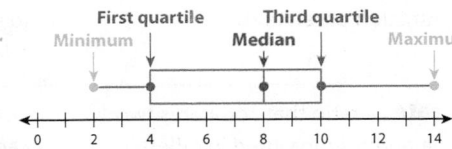

Glossary/Glosario

ENGLISH	SPANISH	EXAMPLES
Quotient of Powers Property If a is a nonzero real number and m and n are integers, then $\frac{a^m}{a^n} = a^{m-n}$.	**Propiedad del cociente de potencias** Dado un número real a distinto de cero y los números enteros m y n, entonces $\frac{a^m}{a^n} = a^{m-n}$.	$\frac{6^7}{6^4} = 6^{7-4} = 6^3$
Quotient Property of Radicals For $a \geq 0$ and $b > 0$, $\sqrt{\frac{a}{b}} = \frac{\sqrt{a}}{\sqrt{b}}$.	**Propiedad del cociente de radicales** Dados $a \geq 0$ y $b > 0$, $\sqrt{\frac{a}{b}} = \frac{\sqrt{a}}{\sqrt{b}}$.	$\sqrt{\frac{9}{25}} = \frac{\sqrt{9}}{\sqrt{25}} = \frac{3}{5}$

R

ENGLISH	SPANISH	EXAMPLES
radical equation An equation that contains a variable within a radical.	**ecuación radical** Ecuación que contiene una variable dentro de un radical.	$\sqrt{x+3} + 4 = 7$
radical expression An expression that contains a radical sign.	**expresión radical** Expresión que contiene un signo de radical.	$\sqrt{x+3} + 4$
radical function A function whose rule contains a variable within a radical.	**función radical** Función cuya regla contiene una variable dentro de un radical.	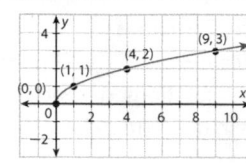 $f(x) = \sqrt{x}$
radical symbol The symbol $\sqrt{\ }$ used to denote a root. The symbol is used alone to indicate a square root or with an index, $\sqrt[n]{\ }$, to indicate the nth root.	**símbolo de radical** Símbolo $\sqrt{\ }$ que se utiliza para expresar una raíz. Puede utilizarse solo para indicar una raíz cuadrada, o con un índice, $\sqrt[n]{\ }$, para indicar la enésima raíz.	$\sqrt{36} = 6$ $\sqrt[3]{27} = 3$
radicand The expression under a radical sign.	**radicando** Número o expresión debajo del signo de radical.	Expression: $\sqrt{x+3}$ Radicand: $x + 3$
range of a data set The difference of the greatest and least values in the data set.	**rango de un conjunto de datos** La diferencia del mayor y menor valor en un conjunto de datos.	The data set {3, 3, 5, 7, 8, 10, 11, 11, 12} has a range of $12 - 3 = 9$.
range of a function or relation The set of all second coordinates (or y-values) of a function or relation.	**rango de una función o relación** Conjunto de todos los valores de la segunda coordenada (o valores de y) de una función o relación.	The range of the function $\{(-5, 3), (-3, -2), (-1, -1), (1, 0)\}$ is $\{-2, -1, 0, 3\}$.
rate A ratio that compares two quantities measured in different units.	**tasa** Razón que compara dos cantidades medidas en diferentes unidades.	$\frac{55 \text{ miles}}{1 \text{ hour}} = 55 \text{ mi/h}$
rate of change A ratio that compares the amount of change in a dependent variable to the amount of change in an independent variable.	**tasa de cambio** Razón que compara la cantidad de cambio de la variable dependiente con la cantidad de cambio de la variable independiente.	The cost of mailing a letter increased from 22 cents in 1985 to 25 cents in 1988. During this period, the rate of change was $\frac{\text{change in cost}}{\text{change in year}} = \frac{25 - 22}{1988 - 1985} = \frac{3}{3}$ $= 1$ cent per year.

ratio A comparison of two quantities by division.	**razón** Comparación de dos cantidades mediante una división.	$\frac{1}{2}$ or $1:2$
rational exponent An exponent that can be expressed as $\frac{m}{n}$ such that if m and n are integers, then $b^{\frac{m}{n}} = \sqrt[n]{b^m} = \left(\sqrt[n]{b}\right)^m$.	**exponente racional** Exponente que se puede expresar como $\frac{m}{n}$ tal que si m y n son números enteros, entonces $b^{\frac{m}{n}} = \sqrt[n]{b^m} = \left(\sqrt[n]{b}\right)^m$.	$64^{\frac{1}{6}} = \sqrt[6]{64}$
rational expression An algebraic expression whose numerator and denominator are polynomials and whose denominator has a degree ≥ 1.	**expresión racional** Expresión algebraica cuyo numerador y denominador son polinomios y cuyo denominador tiene un grado ≥ 1.	$\frac{x+2}{x^2+3x-1}$
rational number A number that can be written in the form $\frac{a}{b}$, where a and b are integers and $b \neq 0$.	**número racional** Número que se puede expresar como $\frac{a}{b}$, donde a y b son números enteros y $b \neq 0$.	$3, 1.75, 0.\overline{3}, -\frac{2}{3}, 0$
rationalizing the denominator A method of rewriting a fraction by multiplying by another fraction that is equivalent to 1 in order to remove radical terms from the denominator.	**racionalizar el denominador** Método que consiste en escribir nuevamente una fracción multiplicándola por otra fracción equivalente a 1 a fin de eliminar los términos radicales del denominador.	$\frac{1}{\sqrt{2}} \cdot \frac{\sqrt{2}}{\sqrt{2}} = \frac{\sqrt{2}}{2}$
real number A rational or irrational number. Every point on the number line represents a real number.	**número real** Número racional o irracional. Cada punto de la recta numérica representa un número real.	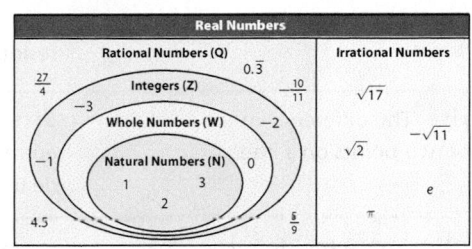
reciprocal For a real number $a \neq 0$, the reciprocal of a is $\frac{1}{a}$. The product of reciprocals is 1.	**recíproco** Dado el número real $a \neq 0$, el recíproco de a es $\frac{1}{a}$. El producto de los recíprocos es 1.	Number Reciprocal table below
recursive rule for nth term of a sequence A rule for a sequence in which one or more previous terms are used to generate the next term.	**fórmula recurrente para hallar el enésimo término de una sucesión** Fórmula para una sucesión en la cual uno o más términos anteriores se usan para generar el término siguiente.	
reflection A transformation that reflects, or "flips," a graph or figure across a line, called the line of reflection.	**reflexión** Transformación en la que una gráfica o figura se refleja o se invierte sobre una línea, denominada la línea de reflexión.	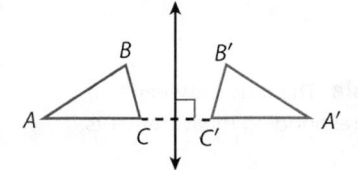

Number	Reciprocal
2	$\frac{1}{2}$
1	1
-1	-1
0	No reciprocal

Glossary/Glosario

ENGLISH	SPANISH	EXAMPLES
relation A set of ordered pairs.	**relación** Conjunto de pares ordenados.	$\{(0, 5), (0, 4), (2, 3), (4, 0)\}$
relative frequency The relative frequency of a category is the frequency of the category divided by the total of all frequencies.	**frecuencia relativa** La frecuencia relativa de una categoría es la frecuencia de la categoría dividido por el total de todas las frecuencias.	
repeating decimal A rational number in decimal form that has a nonzero block of one or more digits that repeat continuously.	**decimal periódico** Número racional en forma decimal que tiene un bloque de uno o más dígitos que se repite continuamente.	$1.\overline{3}, 0.\overline{6}, 2.\overline{14}, 6.77\overline{3}$
replacement set A set of numbers that can be substituted for a variable.	**conjunto de reemplazo** Conjunto de números que pueden sustituir una variable.	
residual The signed vertical distance between a data point and a line of fit.	**residuo** La diferencia vertical entre un dato y una línea de ajuste.	
residual plot A scatter plot of points whose x-coordinates are the values of the independent variable and whose y-coordinates are the corresponding residuals.	**diagrama de residuos** Diagrama de dispersión de puntos en el que la coordenada x representa los valores de la variable independiente y la coordenada y representa los residuos correspondientes.	
rise The difference in the y-values of two points on a line.	**distancia vertical** Diferencia entre los valores de y de dos puntos de una línea.	For the points $(3, -1)$ and $(6, 5)$, the rise is $5 - (-1) = 6$.
rotation A transformation that rotates or turns a figure about a point called the center of rotation.	**rotación** Transformación que rota o gira una figura sobre un punto llamado centro de rotación.	
run The difference in the x-values of two points on a line.	**distancia horizontal** Diferencia entre los valores de x de dos puntos de una línea.	For the points $(3, -1)$ and $(6, 5)$, the run is $6 - 3 = 3$.

S

ENGLISH	SPANISH	EXAMPLES
sample A part of the population.	**muestra** Una parte de la población.	In a survey about the study habits of high school students, a sample is a survey of 100 students.
scale The ratio between two corresponding measurements.	**escala** Razón entre dos medidas correspondientes.	1 cm : 5 mi

ENGLISH	SPANISH	EXAMPLES
scale drawing A drawing that uses a scale to represent an object as smaller or larger than the actual object.	**dibujo a escala** Dibujo que utiliza una escala para representar un objeto como más pequeño o más grande que el objeto original.	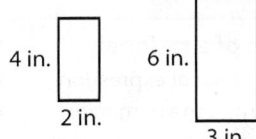 A blueprint is an example of a scale drawing.
scale factor The multiplier used on each dimension to change one figure into a similar figure.	**factor de escala** El multiplicador utilizado en cada dimensión para transformar una figura en una figura semejante.	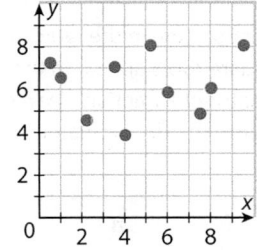 4 in. 6 in. 2 in. 3 in. Scale factor: $\frac{3}{2} = 1.5$
scale model A three-dimensional model that uses a scale to represent an object as smaller or larger than the actual object.	**modelo a escala** Modelo tridimensional que utiliza una escala para representar un objeto como más pequeño o más grande que el objeto real.	
scatter plot A graph with points plotted to show a possible relationship between two sets of data.	**diagrama de dispersión** Gráfica con puntos que se usa para demostrar una relación posible entre dos conjuntos de datos.	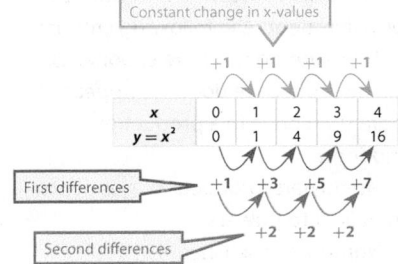
second differences Differences between first differences of a function.	**segundas diferencias** Diferencias entre las primeras diferencias de una función.	Constant change in x-values +1 +1 +1 +1 | x | 0 | 1 | 2 | 3 | 4 | | $y = x^2$ | 0 | 1 | 4 | 9 | 16 | First differences +1 +3 +5 +7 Second differences +2 +2 +2
second quartile The median of an entire data set, denoted Q_2.	**segundo cuartil** Mediana de un conjunto de datos completo, expresada como Q_2.	8, 9, ⑨, 12, 15 Q_2: 9 4, 6, ⑦, ⑩, 10, 12 $Q_2: \frac{7 + 10}{2} = 8.5$
sequence A list of numbers that often form a pattern.	**sucesión** Lista de números que generalmente forman un patrón.	1, 2, 4, 8, 16, …
set A collection of items called elements.	**conjunto** Grupo de componentes denominados elementos.	$\{1, 2, 3\}$
set-builder notation A notation for a set that uses a rule to describe the properties of the elements of the set.	**notación de conjuntos** Notación para un conjunto que se vale de una regla para describir las propiedades de los elementos del conjunto.	$\{x \mid x > 3\}$ is read "The set of all x such that x is greater than 3."

Glossary/Glosario

Glossary/Glosario

significant digits The digits used to express the precision of a measurement.

dígitos significativos Dígitos usados para expresar la precisión de una medida.

---

simple interest A fixed percent of the principal. For principal P, interest rate r, and time t in years, the simple interest is $I = Prt$.

interés simple Porcentaje fijo del capital. Dado el capital P, la tasa de interés r y el tiempo t expresado en años, el interés simple es $I = Prt$.

---

simplest form of a rational expression A rational expression is in simplest form if the numerator and denominator have no common factors.

forma simplificada de una expresión racional Una expresión racional está en forma simplificada cuando el numerador y el denominador no tienen factores comunes.

$$\frac{x^2 - 1}{x^2 + x - 2} = \frac{(x-1)(x+1)}{(x-1)(x+2)}$$
$$= \frac{x+1}{x+2}$$

↑ Simplest form

---

simplest form of a square root expression A square root expression is in simplest form if it meets the following criteria:
1. No perfect squares are in the radicand.
2. No fractions are in the radicand.
3. No square roots appear in the denominator of a fraction. *See also* rationalizing the denominator.

forma simplificada de una expresión de raíz cuadrada Una expresión de raíz cuadrada está en forma simplificada si reúne los siguientes requisitos:
1. No hay cuadrados perfectos en el radicando.
2. No hay fracciones en el radicando.
3. No aparecen raíces cuadradas en el denominador de una fracción. *Ver también* racionalizar el denominador.

Not Simplest Form	Simplest Form
$\sqrt{180}$	$6\sqrt{5}$
$\sqrt{216a^2b^2}$	$6ab\sqrt{6}$
$\frac{\sqrt{7}}{\sqrt{2}}$	$\frac{\sqrt{14}}{2}$

---

simplest form of an exponential expression An exponential expression is in simplest form if it meets the following criteria:
1. There are no negative exponents.
2. The same base does not appear more than once in a product or quotient.
3. No powers, products, or quotients are raised to powers.
4. Numerical coefficients in a quotient do not have any common factor other than 1.

forma simplificada de una expresión exponencial Una expresión exponencial está en forma simplificada si reúne los siguientes requisitos:
1. No hay exponentes negativos.
2. La misma base no aparece más de una vez en un producto o cociente.
3. No se elevan a potencias productos, cocientes ni potencias.
4. Los coeficientes numéricos en un cociente no tienen ningún factor común que no sea 1.

Not Simplest Form	Simplest Form
$7^8 \cdot 7^4$	7^{12}
$(x^2)^{-4} \cdot x^5$	$\frac{1}{x^3}$
$\frac{a^5b^9}{(ab)^4}$	ab^5

---

skewed distribution A type of distribution in which the right or left side of its display indicates frequencies that are much greater than those of the other side. In a distribution skewed to the left, more than half the data are greater than the mean. In a distribution skewed to the right, more than half the data are less than the mean.

distribución sesgada Tipo de distribución en la que el lado derecho o izquierdo muestra frecuencias mucho mayores que las del otro lado. En una distribución sesgada a la izquierda, más de la mitad de los datos son menores que la media. En una distribución sesgada a la derecha, más de la mitad de los datos son menores que la media.

ENGLISH	SPANISH	EXAMPLES
slope A measure of the steepness of a line. If (x_1, y_1) and (x_2, y_2) are any two points on the line, the slope of the line, known as m, is represented by the equation $m = \frac{y_2 - y_1}{x_2 - x_1}$.	**pendiente** Medida de la inclinación de una línea. Dados dos puntos (x_1, y_1) y (x_2, y_2) en una línea, la pendiente de la línea, denominada m, se representa con la ecuación $m = \frac{y_2 - y_1}{x_2 - x_1}$.	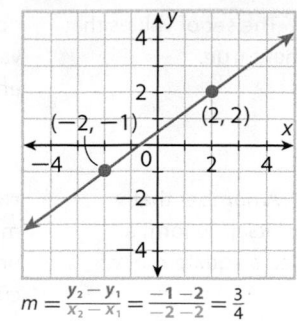 $m = \frac{y_2 - y_1}{x_2 - x_1} = \frac{-1 - 2}{-2 - 2} = \frac{3}{4}$
slope formula If (x_1, y_1) and (x_2, y_2) are any two points on a line, the slope of the line is $m = \frac{y_2 - y_1}{x_2 - x_1}$.	**fórmula de la pendiente** Dados dos puntos (x_1, y_1) y (x_2, y_2) en una línea, la pendiente de la línea es $m = \frac{y_2 - y_1}{x_2 - x_1}$.	
slope-intercept form The slope-intercept form of a linear equation is $y = mx + b$, where m is the slope and b is the y-intercept.	**forma de pendiente-intersección** La forma de pendiente-intersección de una ecuación lineal es $y = mx + b$, donde m es la pendiente y b es la intersección con el eje y.	$y = -2x + 4$ The slope is -2. The y-intercept is 4.
solution of a linear inequality in one variable A value or values that make the inequality true.	**solución de una desigualdad lineal en una variable** Valor o valores que hacen que la desigualdad sea verdadera.	Inequality: $x + 2 < 6$ Solution: $x < 4$
solution of a linear equation in two variables An ordered pair or ordered pairs that make the equation true.	**solución de una ecuación lineal en dos variables** Un par ordenado o pares ordenados que hacen que la ecuación sea verdadera.	$(4, 2)$ is a solution of $x + y = 6$.
solution of a system of linear equations Any ordered pair that satisfies all the equations in a linear system.	**solución de un sistema de ecuaciones lineales** Cualquier par ordenado que resuelva todas las ecuaciones de un sistema lineal.	$\begin{cases} x + y = -1 \\ -x + y = -3 \end{cases}$ The solution of the system is the ordered pair $(1, -2)$.
solution of a system of linear inequalities Any ordered pair that satisfies all the inequalities in a linear system.	**solución de un sistema de desigualdades lineales** Cualquier par ordenado que resuelva todas las desigualdades de un sistema lineal.	$\begin{cases} y \leq x + 1 \\ y < -x + 4 \end{cases}$ $(2, 1)$ is in the overlapping shaded regions, so it is a solution. 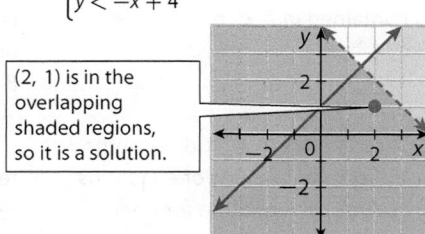
solution of an inequality in two variables An ordered pair or ordered pairs that make the inequality true.	**solución de una desigualdad en dos variables** Un par ordenado o pares ordenados que hacen que la desigualdad sea verdadera.	$(3, 1)$ is a solution of $x + y < 6$.

Glossary/Glosario

ENGLISH	SPANISH	EXAMPLES
solution set The set of values that make a statement true.	**conjunto solución** Conjunto de valores que hacen verdadero un enunciado.	Inequality: $x + 3 \geq 5$ Solution set: $\{x \mid x \geq 2\}$
square root A number that is multiplied by itself to form a product is called a square root of that product.	**raíz cuadrada** El número que se multiplica por sí mismo para formar un producto se denomina la raíz cuadrada de ese producto.	A square root of 16 is 4, because $4^2 = 4 \cdot 4 = 16$. Another square root of 16 is -4 because $(-4)^2 = (-4)(-4) = 16$.
standard form of a linear equation $Ax + By = C$, where A, B, and C are real numbers and A and B are not both 0.	**forma estándar de una ecuación lineal** $Ax + By = C$, donde A, B y C son números reales y A y B no son ambos cero.	$2x + 3y = 6$
standard form of a polynomial A polynomial in one variable is written in standard form when the terms are in order from greatest degree to least degree.	**forma estándar de un polinomio** Un polinomio de una variable se expresa en forma estándar cuando los términos se ordenan de mayor a menor grado.	$4x^5 - 2x^4 + x^2 - x + 1$
standard form of a quadratic equation $ax^2 + bx + c = 0$, where a, b, and c are real numbers and $a \neq 0$.	**forma estándar de una ecuación cuadrática** $ax^2 + bx + c = 0$, donde a, b y c son números reales y $a \neq 0$.	$2x^2 + 3x - 1 = 0$
standard deviation A measure of dispersion of a data set. The standard deviation σ is the square root of the variance	**desviación estándar** Medida de dispersión de un conjunto de datos. La desviación estándar σ es la raíz cuadrada de la varianza	Data set: $\{6, 7, 7, 9, 11\}$ Mean: $\frac{6 + 7 + 7 + 9 + 11}{5} = 8$ Variance: $\frac{1}{5}(4 + 1 + 1 + 1 + 9) = 3.2$ Standard deviation: $\sigma = \sqrt{3.2} \approx 1.8$
statistics Numbers that describe a sample or samples.	**estadísticas** Números que describen una o varias muestras.	
step function A piecewise function that is constant over each interval in its domain.	**función escalón** Función a trozos que es constante en cada intervalo en su dominio.	
subset A set that is contained entirely within another set. Set B is a subset of set A if every element of B is contained in A, denoted $B \subset A$.	**subconjunto** Conjunto que se encuentra dentro de otro conjunto. El conjunto B es un subconjunto del conjunto A si todos los elementos de B son elementos de A; se expresa $B \subset A$.	
substitution method A method used to solve systems of equations by solving an equation for one variable and substituting the resulting expression into the other equation(s).	**sustitución** Método utilizado para resolver sistemas de ecuaciones resolviendo una ecuación para una variable y sustituyendo la expresión resultante en las demás ecuaciones.	

ENGLISH	SPANISH	EXAMPLES
Subtraction Property of Equality If a, b, and c are real numbers and $a = b$, then $a - c = b - c$.	**Propiedad de igualdad de la resta** Si a, b y c son números reales y $a = b$, entonces $a - c = b - c$.	$\begin{aligned} x + 6 &= 8 \\ -6 \quad &-6 \\ \hline x \quad\;\; &= 2 \end{aligned}$
Subtraction Property of Inequality For real numbers a, b, and c, if $a < b$, then $a - c < b - c$. Also holds true for $>$, $\leq$, $\geq$, and $\neq$.	**Propiedad de desigualdad de la resta** Dados los números reales a, b y c, si $a < b$, entonces $a - c < b - c$. Es válido también para $>$, $\leq$, $\geq$ y $\neq$.	$\begin{aligned} x + 6 &< 8 \\ -6 \quad &-6 \\ \hline x \quad\;\; &< 2 \end{aligned}$
symmetric distribution A type of distribution in which the right and left sides of its display indicate frequencies that are mirror images of each other.	**distribución simétrica** Tipo de distribución en la que los lados derecho e izquierdo muestran frecuencias que son idénticas.	
system of linear equations A system of equations in which all of the equations are linear.	**sistema de ecuaciones lineales** Sistema de ecuaciones en el que todas las ecuaciones son lineales.	$\begin{cases} 2x + 3y = -1 \\ x - 3y = 4 \end{cases}$
system of linear inequalities A system of inequalities in which all of the inequalities are linear.	**sistema de desigualdades lineales** Sistema de desigualdades en el que todas las desigualdades son lineales.	$\begin{cases} 2x + 3y > -1 \\ x - 3y \leq 4 \end{cases}$

T

term of a sequence An element or number in the sequence.	**término de una sucesión** Elemento o número de una sucesión.	5 is the third term in the sequence 1, 3, 5, 7, …
term of an expression The parts of the expression that are added or subtracted.	**término de una expresión** Parte de una expresión que debe sumarse o restarse.	$3x^2 + 6x - 8$ Term Term Term
third quartile The median of the upper half of a data set. Also called *upper quartile*.	**tercer cuartil** La mediana de la mitad superior de un conjunto de datos. También se llama *cuartil superior*.	Lower half Upper half 18, 23, 28, 29, (36,) 42 Third quartile
tolerance The amount by which a measurement is permitted to vary from a specified value.	**tolerancia** La cantidad por que una medida se permite variar de un valor especificado.	
transformation A change in the position, size, or shape of a figure or graph.	**transformación** Cambio en la posición, tamaño o forma de una figura o gráfica.	Preimage Image $\triangle ABC \rightarrow \triangle A'B'C'$

translation A transformation that shifts or slides every point of a figure or graph the same distance in the same direction.

traslación Transformación en la que todos los puntos de una figura o gráfica se mueven la misma distancia en la misma dirección.

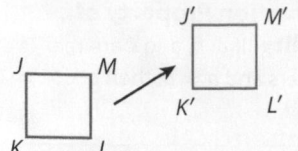

trend line A line on a scatter plot that helps show the correlation between data sets more clearly.

línea de tendencia Línea en un diagrama de dispersión que sirve para mostrar la correlación entre conjuntos de datos más claramente.

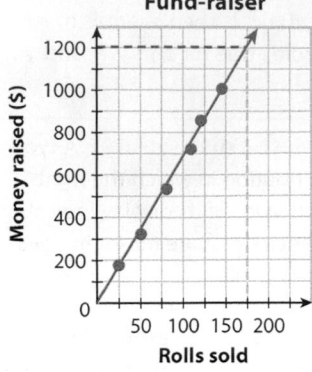

trinomial A polynomial with three terms.

trinomio Polinomio con tres términos.

$4x^2 + 3xy - 5y^2$

turning point A point on the graph of a function that corresponds to a local maximum (or minimum) where the graph changes from increasing to decreasing (or vice versa).

punto de inflexión Punto de la gráfica de una función que corresponde a un máximo (o mínimo) local donde la gráfica pasa de ser creciente a decreciente (o viceversa).

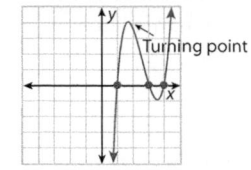

two-variable data A collection of paired variable values, such as a series of measurements of air temperature at different times of day.

datos de dos variables Conjunto de valores variables agrupados en pares, como una serie de mediciones de la temperatura del aire en diferentes momentos del día.

Time	Temperature (°F)
8 A.M.	65
9 A.M.	69
10 A.M.	72

two-way frequency table A frequency table that displays two-variable data in rows and columns.

table de frecuencia de doble entrada Una tabla de frecuencia que muestra los datos de dos variables organizados en filas y columnas.

		Preference		
		inside	Outside	Total
Pet	Cats	35	15	50
	Dogs	20	30	50
	Total	55	45	100

U

union The union of two sets is the set of all elements that are in either set, denoted by ∪.

unión La unión de dos conjuntos es el conjunto de todos los elementos que se encuentran en ambos conjuntos, expresado por ∪.

$A = \{1, 2, 3, 4\}$
$B = \{1, 3, 5, 7, 9\}$
$A \cup B = \{1, 2, 3, 4, 5, 7, 9\}$

unit rate A rate in which the second quantity in the comparison is one unit.

tasa unitaria Tasa en la que la segunda cantidad de la comparación es una unidad.

$\frac{30 \text{ mi}}{1 \text{ h}} = 30 \text{ mi/h}$

Glossary/Glosario

unlike radicals Radicals with a different quantity under the radical.

radicales distintos Radicales con cantidades diferentes debajo del signo de radical.

$2\sqrt{2}$ and $2\sqrt{3}$

---

unlike terms Terms with different variables or the same variables raised to different powers.

términos distintos Términos con variables diferentes o las mismas variables elevadas a potencias diferentes.

$4xy^2$ and $6x^2y$

---

upper quartile *See* third quartile.

cuartil superior *Ver* tercer cuartil.

V

value of a function The result of replacing the independent variable with a number and simplifying.

valor de una función Resultado de reemplazar la variable independiente por un número y luego simplificar.

The value of the function $f(x) = x + 1$ for $x = 3$ is 4.

---

value of a variable A number used to replace a variable to make an equation true.

valor de una variable Número utilizado para reemplazar una variable y hacer que una ecuación sea verdadera.

In the equation $x + 1 = 4$, the value of x is 3.

---

value of an expression The result of replacing the variables in an expression with numbers and simplifying.

valor de una expresión Resultado de reemplazar las variables de una expresión por un número y luego simplificar.

The value of the expression $x + 1$ for $x = 3$ is 4.

---

variable A symbol used to represent a quantity that can change.

variable Símbolo utilizado para representar una cantidad que puede cambiar.

In the expression $2x + 3$, x is the variable.

---

vertex form of a quadratic function A quadratic function written in the form $f(x) = a(x - h)^2 + k$, where a, h, and k are constants and (h, k) is the vertex.

forma en vértice de una función cuadrática Una function cuadrática expresada en la forma $f(x) = a(x - h)^2 + k$, donde a, h y k son constantes y (h, k) es el vértice.

---

vertex of a parabola The highest or lowest point on the parabola.

vértice de una parábola Punto más alto o más bajo de una parábola.

The vertex is $(0, -2)$.

---

vertex of an absolute-value graph The point on the axis of symmetry of the graph.

vértice de una gráfica de valor absoluto Punto en el eje de simetría de la gráfica.

$y = |x|$

ENGLISH	SPANISH	EXAMPLES
vertical compression A transformation that pushes the points of a graph toward the x-axis.	**vertical compresión** Transformación que desplaza los puntos de una gráfica hacia el eje x.	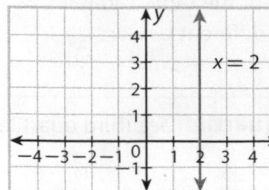
vertical line A line whose equation is $x = a$, where a is the x-intercept.	**línea vertical** Línea cuya ecuación es $x = a$, donde a es la intersección con el eje x.	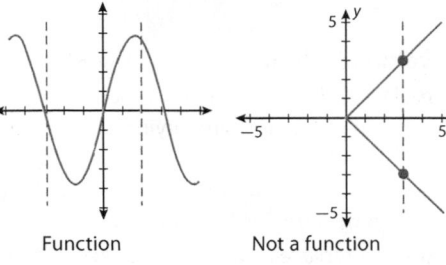
vertical-line test A test used to determine whether a relation is a function. If any vertical line crosses the graph of a relation more than once, the relation is not a function.	**prueba de la línea vertical** Prueba utilizada para determinar si una relación es una función. Si una línea vertical corta la gráfica de una relación más de una vez, la relación no es una función.	Function Not a function
vertical stretch A transformation that pulls the points of a graph away from the x–axis.	**vertical estiramiento** Transformación que desplaza los puntos de una gráfica en forma vertical alejándolos del eje x.	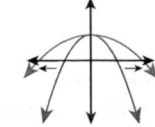
vertical translation (of a parabola) is a shift of the parabola up or down, with no change in the shape of the parabola.	**traslación vertical (de una parábola)** Desplazamiento de la parábola hacia arriba o hacia abajo, sin producir cambios en la forma de la parábola.	

X

x-intercept The x-coordinate(s) of the point(s) where a graph intersects the x-axis.	**intersección con el eje x** Coordenada(s) x de uno o más puntos donde una gráfica corta el eje x.	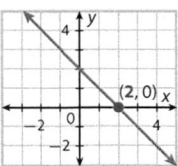 The x-intercept is 2.

Y

y-intercept The y-coordinate(s) of the point(s) where a graph intersects the y-axis.	**intersección con el eje y** Coordenada(s) y de uno o más puntos donde una gráfica corta el eje y.	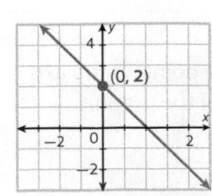 The y-intercept is 2.

Z

zero exponent For any nonzero real number x, $x^0 = 1$.

exponente cero Dado un número real distinto de cero x, $x^0 = 1$.

$5^0 = 1$

---

zero of a function For the function f, any number x such that $f(x) = 0$.

cero de una función Dada la función f, todo número x tal que $f(x) = 0$.

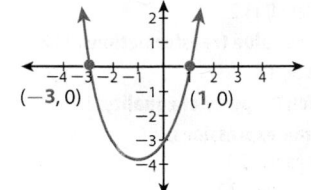

The zeros are -3 and 1.

Zero Product Property For real numbers p and q, if $pq = 0$, then $p = 0$ or $q = 0$.

Propiedad del producto cero Dados los números reales p y q, si $pq = 0$, entonces $p = 0$ o $q = 0$.

If $(x - 1)(x + 2) = 0$, then $x - 1 = 0$ or $x + 2 = 0$, so $x = 1$ or $x = -2$.

Glossary/Glosario

Index

Index locator numbers are in Module. Lesson form. For example, 2.1 indicates Module 2, Lesson 1 as listed in the Table of Contents.

Index

Index

Table of Measures

LENGTH

1 inch = 2.54 centimeters

1 meter = 39.37 inches

1 mile = 5,280 feet

1 mile = 1760 yards

1 mile = 1.609 kilometers

1 kilometer = 0.62 mile

CAPACITY

1 cup = 8 fluid ounces

1 pint = 2 cups

1 quart = 2 pints

1 gallon = 4 quarts

1 gallon = 3.785 liters

1 liter = 0.264 gallons

1 liter = 1000 cubic centimeters

MASS/WEIGHT

1 pound = 16 ounces

1 pound = 0.454 kilograms

1 kilogram = 2.2 pounds

1 ton = 2000 pounds

Symbols

$\neq$	is not equal to	π	pi: (about 3.14)
$\approx$	is approximately equal to	$\perp$	is perpendicular to
10^2	ten squared; ten to the second power	$\parallel$	is parallel to
		$\overleftrightarrow{AB}$	line AB
$2.\overline{6}$	repeating decimal 2.66666...	$\overrightarrow{AB}$	ray AB
$\lvert-4\rvert$	the absolute value of negative 4	$\overline{AB}$	line segment AB
$\sqrt{}$	square root	$m\angle A$	measure of $\angle A$

Formulas

Triangle	$A = \frac{1}{2} bh$	Pythagorean Theorem	$a^2 + b^2 = c^2$
Parallelogram	$A = bh$	Quadratic Formula	$x = \dfrac{-b \pm \sqrt{b^2 - 4ac}}{2a}$
Circle	$A = \pi r^2$	Arithmetic Sequence	$a_n = a_1 + (n-1)d$
Circle	$C = \pi d$ or $C = 2\pi r$	Geometric Sequence	$a_n = a_1 r^{n-1}$
General Prisms	$V = Bh$	Geometric Series	$S_n = \dfrac{a_1 - a_1 r^n}{1 - r}$ where $r \neq 1$
Cylinder	$V = \pi r^2 h$	Radians	$1\ radian = \frac{180}{\pi}\ degrees$
Sphere	$V = \frac{4}{3} \pi r^3$	Degrees	$1\ degree = \frac{\pi}{180}\ radians$
Cone	$V = \frac{1}{3} \pi r^2 h$	Exponential Growth/Decay	$A = A_0\, e^{k(t - t_0)} + B_0$
Pyramid	$V = \frac{1}{3} Bh$		